KT-385-750

The **Rough Guide** to

India

written and researched by

**David Abram, Nick Edwards, Mike Ford,
Daniel Jacobs, Devdan Sen, Gavin Thomas
and Beth Wooldridge**

with additional contributions from

**Shafik Meghji, David Lepeska
and Richard Wignell**

NEW YORK · LONDON · DELHI

www.roughguides.com

Contents

Crafts to go colour section following p.264

Bollywood and beyond colour section following p.712

Sacred spaces colour section following p.1016

◄◄ Releasing flower candles on the River Ganges ◄ Pilgims bathing in the Tungabhadra River

CHINA
AFGHANISTAN
PAKISTAN
TIBET AUTONOMOUS REGION
NEPAL
BHUTAN
BANGLADESH
N
Metres
6000
5000
4000
3000
2000
1000
500
200
0
JAMMU & KASHMIR
Srinagar
Leh
Jammu Tawi
Dharamsala
Manali
Pathankot
Kullu
Amritsar
HIMACHAL PRADESH
Shimla
Chandigarh
PUNJAB
Mussoorie
Rishikesh
Haridwar
UTTARAKHAND
Naini Tal
HARYANA
CORBETT NATIONAL PARK
DELHI
Bikaner
UTTAR PRADESH
Mathura
Agra
Jaisalmer
RAJASTHAN
Bharatpur
Jaipur
Jodhpur
Ganges
Yamuna
Gwalior
Kota
Mount Abu
Udaipur
Gorakhpur
Kushinagar
Lucknow
Kanpur
Sarnath
Allahabad
Varanasi
Orchha
Khajuraho
BIHAR
Patna
Gaya
JHARKHAND
BANDHAVGARH NATIONAL PARK
Jabalpur
Sanchi
Ujjain
Bhopal
Indore
Mandu
MADHYA PRADESH
KANHA NATIONAL PARK
Bhuj
Gandhidham
Ahmedabad
GUJARAT
Dwarka
Vadodara
WEST BENGAL
KOLKATA (CALCUTTA)
SIKKIM
Gangtok
Kalimpong
Darjeeling
ARUNACHAL PRADESH
Itanagar
ASSAM
Guwahati
NAGALAND
Kohima
Shillong
MEGHALAYA
Imphal
MANIPUR
TRIPURA
Agartala
MIZORAM
Aizawl

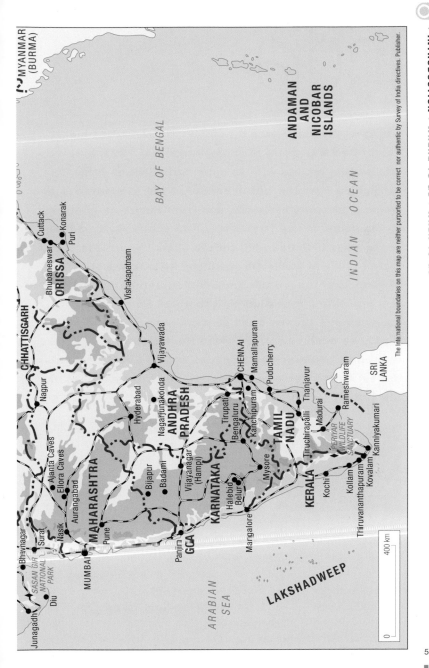

MYANMAR (BURMA)

CHHATTISGARH

Cuttack
Konarak
Bhubaneswar
ORISSA
Puri

Nagpur

Vishakapatnam

BAY OF BENGAL

ANDAMAN
AND
NICOBAR
ISLANDS

INDIAN OCEAN

Ajanta Caves
Ellora Caves
Aurangabad
Nasik
MAHARASHTRA
Pune
MUMBAI

Bhavnagar
Surat
Diu
SASAN GIR
NATIONAL
PARK
Junagadh

Hyderabad
Nagarjunakonda
ANDHRA
PRADESH
Vijayawada

CHENNAI
Mamallapuram
Puducherry

Bijapur
Badami
Vijayanagar (Hampi)
KARNATAKA
Halebid
Belur
Mysore
Mangalore

Panjim
GOA

Tirupati
Bengaluru
Kanchipuram
TAMIL
NADU
Tiruchirapalli
Thanjavur
Madurai
Rameshwaram

PERIYAR
WILDLIFE
SANCTUARY
KERALA
Kochi
Kollam
Kovalam
Thiruvananthapuram
Kanniyakumari

SRI
LANKA

ARABIAN
SEA

LAKSHADWEEP

0   400 Km

90°E

The International boundaries on this map are neither purported to be correct nor authentic by Survey of India directives. Publisher.

5

Introduction to
India

"Unity in Diversity" was the slogan chosen when India celebrated fifty years of Independence in 1997, a declaration replete with as much optimism as pride. Stretching from the frozen barrier of the Himalayas to the tropical greenery of Kerala, and from the sacred Ganges to the sands of the Thar desert, the country's boundaries encompass incomparable variety. Walk the streets of any Indian city and you'll rub shoulders with representatives of several of the world's great faiths, a multitude of castes and outcastes, fair-skinned, turbanned Punjabis and dark-skinned Tamils. You'll also encounter temple rituals that have been performed since the time of the Egyptian Pharaohs, onion-domed mosques erected centuries before the Taj Mahal was ever dreamt of, and quirky echoes of the British Raj on virtually every corner.

That so much of India's past remains discernible today is all the more astonishing given the pace of change since **Independence** in 1947. Spurred by the free-market reforms of the early 1990s, the economic revolution started by Rajiv Gandhi has transformed the country with new consumer goods, technologies and ways of life. Today the land where the Buddha lived and taught, and whose **religious festivals** are as old as the rivers that sustain them, is the second-largest producer of computer software in the world, with its own satellites and nuclear weapons.

However, the presence in even the most far-flung market towns of Internet cafés and Japanese hatchbacks has thrown into sharp relief the problems that have bedevilled the Subcontinent since long before it became the world's **largest secular democracy**. Poverty remains a harsh fact of life for around a quarter of India's inhabitants; no other nation on earth has slum settlements on the scale of those in Delhi, Mumbai and Kolkata (Calcutta), nor so many malnourished children, uneducated women and homes without access to clean water and waste disposal.

Many first-time visitors find themselves unable to see past such glaring disparities. Others come expecting a timeless ascetic wonderland and are surprised to encounter one of the most materialistic societies on the planet. Still more find themselves intimidated by what may seem, initially, an incomprehensible and bewildering continent. But for all its jarring juxtapositions, intractable paradoxes and frustrations, India remains an utterly compelling destination. Intricate and worn, its distinctive patina – the stream of life in its crowded bazaars, the ubiquitous *filmi* music, the pungent melange of beedi smoke, cooking spices, dust and cow dung – casts a spell that few forget from the moment they step off a plane. Love it or hate it – and most travellers oscillate between the two – India will shift the way you see the world.

Fact file

• The Republic of India, whose capital is New Delhi, borders Afghanistan, China, Nepal and Bhutan to the north, Bangladesh and Myanmar (formerly Burma) to the east and Pakistan to the west.

• The world's seventh-largest country, covering more than 3 million square kilometres, it is second only to China in terms of population, which stands at over 1.1 billion. Hindus comprise eighty percent of the population, Muslims thirteen percent, and there are millions of Christians, Sikhs, Buddhists and Jains. Twenty-three major languages and more than a thousand minor languages and dialects are spoken; Hindi is the language of forty percent of the population, but English is widely spoken.

• The caste system is all-pervasive and, although integral to Hindu belief, it also encompasses non-Hindus. A system of social hierarchy that holds especial sway in rural areas, it may dictate where a person lives and what their occupation is.

• Literacy extends to 73 percent of males and 48 percent of females: 61 percent of the total population.

▲ Baha'i Temple, Delhi

Where to go

The best Indian itineraries are the simplest. It just isn't possible to see everything in a single expedition, even if you spent a year trying. Far better, then, to concentrate on one or two specific regions and, above all, to be flexible. While Indian cities are undoubtedly adrenalin-fuelled, upbeat places, it is possible – and certainly less stressful – to travel for months around the Subcontinent and rarely have to set foot in one.

The most-travelled circuit in the country, combining spectacular monuments with the flat, fertile landscape that for many people is archetypally Indian, is the so-called "**Golden Triangle**" in the north: Delhi itself, the colonial capital; Agra, home of the Taj Mahal; and the Pink City of Jaipur in **Rajasthan**. Rajasthan is probably the single most popular state with travellers, who are drawn by its desert scenery and its imposing medieval forts and palaces.

> **Glimpse the continuing practice of India's most ancient religious traditions**

East of Delhi, the River Ganges meanders through some of India's most densely populated regions to reach the extraordinary holy Hindu city of **Varanasi** (also known as Benares). Here you can witness the daily rituals of life and death focused around the waterfront *ghats* (bathing places). Further east still is the great city of **Kolkata** (Calcutta), the capital until early last century of the British Raj, and now a teeming metropolis that epitomizes contemporary India's most pressing problems.

The majority of travellers follow the well-trodden Ganges route to reach Nepal, perhaps unaware that the Indian Himalayas offer superlative trekking and mountain scenery to rival any in the range. With Kashmir effectively off the tourist map since the escalation of its civil war, **Himachal Pradesh** – where Dharamsala is the home of a Tibetan community that includes the Dalai Lama himself – and the remote province of **Ladakh**, with its myste-rious lunar landscape and cloud-swept monasteries, have become the major targets for journeys into the mountains. Less visited, but possessing some of Asia's highest peaks, is the niche of **Uttarakhand** bordering Nepal, where the glacial source of the sacred

▼ Banana leaf meal, Kerala

India's sacred geography

It's hard to think of a more visibly religious country than India. The very landscape of the Subcontinent – its rivers, waterfalls, trees, hilltops, mountains and rocks – comprises a vast sacred geography for adherents of the dozen or more faiths rooted here. Connecting the country's countless holy places is a network of pilgrimage routes along which tens of thousands of worshippers may be moving at any one time – on regular trains, specially decorated buses, tinsel-covered bicycles, barefoot, alone or in noisy family groups. For the visitor, joining devotees in the teeming temple precincts of the south, on the *ghats* at

Varanasi, at the Sufi shrines of Ajmer and Delhi, before the naked Jain colossi of Sravanabelagola, or at any one of the innumerable religious festivals that punctuate the astrological calendar is to experience India at its most intense.

River Ganges has attracted pilgrims for over a thousand years. At the opposite end of the chain, **Sikkim**, north of Bengal, is another low-key trekking destination, harbouring scenery and a Buddhist culture similar to that of neighbouring Bhutan. The **Northeast Hill States** boast remarkably diverse landscapes and an incredible fifty percent of India's biodiversity.

Heading south from Kolkata (Calcutta) along the coast, your first likely stop is **Konarak** in Orissa, site of the famous Sun Temple, a giant carved pyramid of stone that lay submerged under sand until its rediscovery at the start of the twentieth century. Although it bore the brunt of the 2004 Asian tsunamis, **Tamil Nadu**, further south, has retained its own tradition of magnificent architecture, with towering *gopura* gateways dominating towns whose vast temple complexes are still the focus of everyday life. You could spend months wandering between the sacred sites of the Kaveri Delta and the fragrant Nilgiri Hills, draped in the **tea terraces** that have become the hallmark of South Indian landscapes. **Kerala**, near the southernmost tip of the Subcontinent on the western coast, is India at its most tropical and relaxed, its lush backwaters teeming with simple wooden craft of all shapes and sizes, and red-roofed towns and villages all but invisible beneath a canopy of palm trees. Further up the coast is **Goa**, the former Portuguese colony, whose hundred-kilometre coastline is fringed with beaches to suit all tastes and budgets.

▲ Lush tea plantations, Munnar, Kerala

North of here sits **Mumbai**, an ungainly beast that has been the major focus of the nationwide drift to the big cities. Centre of the country's formidable popular movie industry, it reels along on an undeniable energy that, after a few days of acclimatization, can prove addictive. Beyond Mumbai is the state of **Gujarat**, renowned for the unique culture and crafts of the barren Kutch region.

Some of India's most memorable monuments lie far inland, on long-forgotten trading routes across the heart of the Subcontinent – the abandoned city of **Vijayanagar** (or Hampi) in Karnataka; the painted and sculpted Buddhist caves of **Ajanta** and **Ellora** in Maharashtra; the erotic temples of **Khajuraho** in Madhya Pradesh.

On a long trip, it makes sense to pause and rest every few weeks. Certain places have fulfilled that function for generations including the many former

▲ Decorating hands with henna, Agra

colonial hill stations that dot the country, from **Ootacamund** (Ooty), in the far south, to that archetypal British retreat, **Shimla**. Elsewhere, the combination of sand and sea, and a picturesque rural or religious backdrop are usually enough to loosen even the tightest itineraries.

When to go

India's weather is extremely varied, something you must take into account when planning your trip. The most influential feature of the Subcontinent's climate is the wet season, or **monsoon**. This breaks on the Keralan coast at the end of May, working its way northeast across the country over

> **For all its jarring juxtapositions, India remains an utterly compelling destination**

the following month and a half. While it lasts, regular and prolonged downpours are interspersed with bursts of hot sunshine, and the pervasive humidity can be intense. At the height of the monsoon – especially in the jungle regions of the northwest and the low-lying delta lands of Bengal – flooding can severely disrupt communications, causing widespread destruction. In the Himalayan foothills, landslides are common, and entire valley systems can be cut off for weeks.

By September, the monsoon has largely receded from the north. The east coast of Andhra Pradesh and Tamil Nadu, and the south of Kerala, get a second drenching between October and December, when the "northwest" or "retreating" monsoon sweeps in from the Bay of Bengal. By December, however, most of the Subcontinent enjoys clear skies and relatively cool temperatures.

Indian railways

India's railways, which daily transport millions of commuters, pilgrims, animals and hessian-wrapped packages between the four corners of the Subcontinent, are often cited as the best thing the British Raj bequeathed to its former colony. And yet, with its hierarchical legion of clerks, cooks, coolies, bearers, ticket inspectors, station managers and ministers, the network has become a quintessentially Indian institution.

Travelling across India by rail – whether you rough it in dirt-cheap second-class, or pamper yourself with starched cotton sheets and hot meals in an air-conditioned carriage – is likely to yield some of the most memorable moments of your trip. Open around the clock, the stations in themselves are often great places to watch the world go by, with hundreds of people from all walks of life eating, sleeping, buying and selling, regardless of the hour. This is also where you'll grow familiar with one of the unforgettable sounds of the Subcontinent: the robotic drone of the chai-wallah, dispensing cups of hot, sweet tea. For the practical low-down on train travel see p.43.

Kashmir

Few civil wars on earth can have been fought against a more idyllic backdrop than the current troubles in Kashmir. During the run-up to Partition in 1947, when the local Hindu maharaja threw the lot of this Muslim-majority valley in with India instead of neighbouring Pakistan, he sowed the seeds of a conflict that would erupt into a full-scale uprising forty years later, between various factions of Islamic, Pakistani-backed militants and the Indian state.

Since 1989, around 68,000 Kashmiri separatists, Indian troops and civilians have died in a campaign of appalling violence that has, on several occasions, brought south Asia's two nuclear powers to the brink of all-out war. Peace talks over the past few years (see p.1355) have dramatically improved the situation, and a few tourists are now venturing back to Srinagar, although the situation remains volatile and liable to change at short notice. If you are planning on visiting Kashmir, check the latest security situation carefully first. For more background, see p.1354.

Mid-winter sees the most marked contrasts between the climates of north and south India. While Delhi, may be ravaged by chill winds blowing off the snowfields of the Himalayas, the Tamil plains and coastal Kerala, more than 1000km south, still stew under fierce post-monsoon sunshine. As spring gathers pace, the centre of the Subcontinent heats up again, and by late March thermometers nudge 33°C across most of the Gangetic Plains and Deccan plateau. Temperatures peak in May and early June, when anyone who can retreats to the hill stations. Above the baking Subcontinental land mass, hot air builds up and sucks in humidity from the southwest, causing the onset of the monsoon, and bringing relief to millions of overheated Indians.

The best time to visit most of the country, therefore, is during the cool, dry season, between November and March. Delhi, Agra, Varanasi, Rajasthan and Madhya Pradesh are ideal at this time, and temperatures in Goa and central India also remain comfortable. The heat of the south is never less than intense but it becomes stifling in May and June, so a good time to be in Tamil Nadu and Kerala between January and March. From this time onwards, the Himalayas grow increasingly accessible, and the trekking season reaches its peak in August and September while the rest of the Subcontinent is being soaked by the rains.

The international boundaries on this map are neither purported to be correct nor authentic by Survey of India directives. Publisher.

N

Shimla
DELHI
Jaisalmer
Darjeeling
Varanasi
Ahmedabad
KOLKATA (CALCUTTA)
MUMBAI
Puri
Hyderabad
Panjim
BAY OF BENGAL
ARABIAN SEA
Bengaluru
CHENNAI
Kochi
INDIAN OCEAN
0   800 km

Average daily temperatures in degrees Celsius, and monthly rainfall in millimetres.

	Jan	Feb	Mar	Apr	May	June	July	Aug	Sept	Oct	Nov	Dec
Ahmedabad (Guj)												
Temp Max	29	31	36	40	41	38	33	32	33	36	33	30
Rainfall	4	0	1	2	5	100	316	213	163	13	5	1
Bangalore (Kar)												
Temp Max	28	31	33	34	33	30	28	29	28	28	27	27
Rainfall	4	14	6	37	119	65	93	95	129	195	46	16
Chennai (TN)												
Temp Max	29	31	33	35	38	37	35	35	34	32	29	28
Rainfall	24	7	15	25	52	53	83	124	118	267	309	139
Darjeeling (WB)												
Temp Max	9	11	15	18	19	19	20	20	20	19	15	12
Rainfall	22	27	52	109	187	522	713	573	419	116	14	5
Delhi												
Temp Max	21	24	30	36	41	40	35	34	34	35	29	23
Rainfall	25	22	17	7	8	65	211	173	150	31	1	5
Hyderabad (AP)												
Temp Max	29	31	35	37	39	34	30	29	30	30	29	28
Rainfall	2	11	13	24	30	107	165	147	163	71	25	5
Jaisalmer (Raj)												
Temp Max	24	28	33	38	42	41	38	36	36	36	31	26
Rainfall	2	1	3	1	5	7	89	86	14	1	5	2
Kochi (Ker)												
Temp Max	31	31	31	31	31	29	28	28	28	29	30	30
Rainfall	9	34	50	139	364	756	572	386	235	333	184	37
Kolkata (Calcutta) (WB)												
Temp Max	26	29	34	36	36	34	32	32	32	31	26	27
Rainfall	13	22	30	50	135	263	320	318	253	134	29	4
Mumbai (M)												
Temp Max	31	32	33	33	33	32	30	29	30	32	33	32
Rainfall	0	1	0	0	20	647	945	660	309	17	7	1
Panjim (Goa)												
Temp Max	31	32	32	33	33	31	29	29	29	31	33	33
Rainfall	2	0	4	17	18	580	892	341	277	122	20	37
Puri (Ori)												
Temp Max	27	28	30	31	32	31	31	31	31	31	29	27
Rainfall	9	20	14	12	63	187	296	256	258	242	75	8
Shimla (HP)												
Temp Max	9	10	14	19	23	24	21	20	20	18	15	11
Rainfall	65	48	58	38	54	147	415	385	195	45	7	24
Varanasi (UP)												
Temp Max	23	27	33	39	41	39	33	32	32	32	29	25
Rainfall	23	8	14	1	8	102	346	240	261	38	15	2

41

things not to miss

It's not possible to see everything India has to offer in one trip, and we don't suggest you try. What follows is a selective taste of the country's highlights: outstanding buildings, natural wonders, spectacular festivals and unforgettable journeys. They're arranged in five colour-coded categories, which you can browse through to find the very best things to see and experience. All highlights have a page reference to take you straight to the Guide, where you can find out more.

01 Hampi/Vijayanagar Page **1303** • Deserted capital of the last great Hindu empire, scattered over a bizarre landscape of giant golden-brown boulders.

02 **Taj Mahal** Page **279** • Simply the world's greatest building: Shah Jahan's monument to love fully lives up to all expectations.

04 **Bandhavgarh National Park** Page **450** • Deep in the eastern tracts of Madhya Pradesh, this park is rich in animal and birdlife, including tigers and leopards.

03 **Palolem** Page **829** • Exquisite crescent-shaped beach in Goa's relaxed south, famous for its dolphins and local alcoholic spirit, feni.

05 **Meherangarh Fort, Jodhpur** Page **213** • The epitome of Rajput power and extravagance, its ramparts towering above a labyrinthine, blue-painted old city.

07 **Varanasi** Page **318** • City of Light, founded by Shiva, where the bathing *ghats* beside the Ganges teem with pilgrims.

08 **Kathakali** Page **1230** • Kerala is the place to experience Kathakali and other esoteric ritual theatre forms.

06 **Kaziranga National Park** Page **969** • Take a dawn elephant ride as the mists slowly lift: sightings of the one-horned rhino, symbol of Assam, are virtually guaranteed.

09 Classical music Page 1380
• Winter is the season for classical music in India, when recitals can last all night. Cities renowned for their music styles, or *gharanas*, include Delhi, Kolkata (Calcutta), Gwalior, Varanasi and Chennai.

10 Amritsar Page 602
• Site of the fabled Golden Temple, the Sikhs' holiest shrine.

12 Ashrams Page 362
• Brush up on your yoga and meditation in the holy town of Rishikesh on the Ganges, where the Beatles came to meet Maharishi Yogi.

11 Mysore market Page 1271
• Jaggery, incense and garlands are made and veggies and kitsch paraphernalia are sold in Mysore's covered market.

13 Dharamsala Page 502
• Perched on the edge of the Himalayas, this is the home of the Dalai Lama and Tibetan Buddhism in exile.

14 **Keoladeo National Park, Bharatpur** Page 191 • Asia's most famous bird reserve, where millions of migrants nest each winter. The perfect antidote to the frenzy and pollution of nearby Agra and Jaipur.

15 **Rajasthani handicrafts** Page 165 • The teeming bazaars of the Pink City in Jaipur burst with vibrant cloth, jewellery, Persian-style pottery and semi-precious stones. Simply the best place to shop in the Subcontinent.

16 **Gokarna** Page 1296 • The beautiful beaches on the edge of this temple town are popular with budget travellers fleeing the commercialism of nearby Goa.

17 **Madurai** Page 1151 • The definitive South Indian city, centred on a spectacular medieval temple.

19 **Scuba diving** in the Andamans Page **1080** • Plunge into some of the most unspoilt waters on earth, with abundant marine life and magnificent coral.

18 **Thrissur Puram** Page **1239** • More than one hundred sumptuously caparisoned elephants march in Kerala's biggest temple festival, accompanied by ear-shattering South Indian drum orchestras.

20 **Khajuraho** Page **430** • Immaculately preserved temples renowned for their uncompromisingly erotic carvings.

21 **Durga Puja** Page **847** • An exuberant festival held in September or October, when every street and village erects a shrine to the goddess Durga. Kolkata (Calcutta) has the most lavish festivities.

26 **Jaisalmer** Page **219** • A honey-coloured citadel, emerging from the sands of the Thar Desert.

27 **Rath Yatra, Puri** Page **1026** • Three colossal chariots with brightly coloured canopies are pulled by crowds of devotees through the streets of eastern India's holiest town.

28 **Tikse** Page **568** • One of many dramatic monasteries within striking distance of Leh.

29 **Kochi** Page **1223** • Kochi's atmospheric harbourside is strung with elegant Chinese fishing nets.

30 **Fatehpur Sikri** Page **291** • The Moghul emperor Akbar's elegant palace complex now lies deserted on a ridge near Agra, but remains one of India's architectural masterpieces.

31 **Pushkar camel mela** Page **208** • November sees the largest livestock market on earth, where 200,000 Rajasthani herders in traditional costume converge on the desert oasis of Pushkar to trade and bathe in the sacred lake.

32 **Orchha** Page **426** • This semi-ruined former capital of the Bundela Rajas is an architectural gem, rising up through the surrounding jungle.

33 **Manali-Leh Highway** Page **543** • India's epic Himalayan road trip, along the second-highest road in the world.

34 **Konark** Page **1031** • A colossal thirteenth-century temple, buried under sand until its rediscovery by the British.

36 **Movies** Page **708** • Take in the latest Bollywood blockbuster at one of Mumbai's mega movie houses, which feature huge screens, wrap-around sound and rowdy audiences.

35 **Mamallapuram** Page **1112** • A fishing and stone-carving village, with magnificent boulder friezes, shrines and the sea-battered Shore Temple.

37 Boating on the backwaters of Kerala

Page **1208** • Lazy boat trips wind through the lush tropical waterways of India's deep south.

39 Varkala Page **1197** • This
pleasantly low-key Keralan resort boasts sheer red cliffs, amazing sea views and a legion of Ayurvedic masseurs.

38 Udaipur Page **239** • Arguably
the most romantic city in India, with ornate Rajput palaces floating in the middle of two shimmering lakes.

40 Ellora caves Page **732** •
Buddhist, Hindu and Jain caves, and the colossal Hindu Kailash temple, carved from a spectacular volcanic ridge at the heart of the Deccan plateau.

41 Gangotri
Page **366**
• An atmospheric village on the Ganges that serves as a base for the trek into the heart of the Hindu faith – Gomukh, the source of the Ganges.

Basics

Basics

Getting there

With most overland routes into India (except from Nepal) effectively blocked by closed or trouble-prone borders, the most practicable way of getting to India is by plane. There are numerous nonstop services from the UK, plus a few from North America and one from Australia. Most of these arrive at either Delhi or Mumbai, although there are also nonstop flights from the UK into Kolkata (Calcutta), Chennai and Bengaluru (Bangalore).

Fares worldwide always depend on the season, with the highest being roughly November to March, when the weather in India is best; fares drop during the shoulder seasons – April to May and August to early October – and you'll get the best prices during the low season, June and July. The most expensive fares of all are those coinciding with **Diwali** in November, when demand peaks as Indian emigrants travel home for holidays with their families.

For beach destinations like Goa and Kerala, you may find it cheaper to pick up a bargain **package deal** from one of the tour operators listed on pp.31–32. Indian law prohibits the sale of flight-only tickets by charter companies, but operators sometimes get around this by tacking budget "bunkhouse" accommodation to their tickets, which (if it exists at all) travellers ditch on arrival. Note also that the Indian government places restriction of 28 days on the period of time a charter ticket can cover. If you wish to stay in the country for longer than that, you technically have to take a scheduled flight. Nor is it possible to fly in on a charter and out on a scheduled flight, or vice versa.

Packages

Lots of operators run **package holidays** to India, covering activities ranging from trekking and wildlife-watching through to general sightseeing or just lying on the beach, not to mention more specialist-interest tours focusing on anything from steam locomotives to food. In addition, many companies can also arrange **tailor-made tours** where you plan your own itinerary. Of course, any package holiday is a lot easier than going under your own steam, particularly if you only have a short time and don't want to use it up on making your own travel bookings. On the other hand, a typical sightseeing tour can rather isolate you from the country, shutting you off in air-conditioned hotels and buses. Specialist trips such as trekking and tailor-made tours will work out quite expensive, compared to what you'd pay if you organized everything independently, but they do cut out a lot of hassle.

Flights from the UK and Ireland

It takes between around eight and eleven hours to fly from the UK direct to India. A number of carriers fly nonstop from London Heathrow to Delhi and Mumbai; these currently include Air India, Jet Airways, Virgin Atlantic and British Airways (who also fly nonstop to Kolkata, Chennai and Bengaluru). Numerous other European and Middle Eastern carriers offer one-stop services via their home city in Europe or the Gulf. From elsewhere in the UK and Ireland you'll have to take an indirect flight, changing planes at either Heathrow or somewhere else in Europe, the Middle East or Asia. Scheduled fares usually start from around £400, although flight-only deals with charters (see above) go for as little as £250 low season (and sometimes even less).

Flights from the US and Canada

India is on the other side of the planet from the US and Canada. If you live on the East Coast it's quicker to travel via Europe, while from the West Coast it's roughly the same distance (and price) whether you travel via Europe or the Pacific. There are currently

Fly less – stay longer! Travel and Climate Change

Climate change is perhaps the single biggest issue facing our planet. It is caused by a build-up in the atmosphere of carbon dioxide and other greenhouse gases, which are emitted by many sources – including planes. Already, **flights** account for three to four percent of human-induced global warming: that figure may sound small, but it is rising year on year and threatens to counteract the progress made by reducing greenhouse emissions in other areas.

Rough Guides regard travel as a **global benefit**, and feel strongly that the advantages to developing economies are important, as are the opportunities for greater contact and awareness among peoples. But we also believe in travelling responsibly, which includes giving thought to how often we fly and what we can do to redress any harm that our trips may create.

We can travel less or simply reduce the amount we travel by air (taking fewer trips and staying longer, or taking the train if there is one); we can avoid night flights (which are more damaging); and we can make the trips we do take "climate neutral" via a carbon offset scheme. **Offset schemes** run by climatecare.org, carbonneutral .com and others allow you to "neutralize" the greenhouse gases that you are responsible for releasing. Their websites have simple calculators that let you work out the impact of any flight – as does our own. Once that's done, you can pay to fund projects that will reduce future emissions by an equivalent amount. Please take the time to visit our website and make your trip climate neutral, or get a copy of the *Rough Guide to Climate Change* for more detail on the subject.

www.roughguides.com/climatechange

nonstop flights from **New York** to Delhi and Mumbai on Air India and Continental (and also to Mumbai on Delta), and from **Chicago** to Delhi on American Airlines. Otherwise, you'll probably stop over somewhere in Europe (most often London), the Gulf, or both. Nonstop flights take around 15–16hr, with fares from New York to Mumbai/Delhi starting at around $1000. There are currently no nonstop flights from the **West Coast**; count on a minimum 22 hours' travel time. Fares start at around $1400.

There are also no nonstop flights from **Canada** to India – you'll have to travel via a connecting city in the US, Europe or Asia with a minimum travel time of around 20hr. Fares start at around CDN$1600 from Toronto and CDN$1800 from Vancouver.

Flights from Australia and New Zealand

The only nonstop flight to India from either **Australia** or **New Zealand** at present is Qantas's service from Sydney to Mumbai (with a flying time of around 13hr); otherwise, you'll have to make at least one change of plane in a southeast Asian hub city (usually Kuala Lumpur, Singapore or Bangkok). Fares

start from around A$1000. Flying from New Zealand, the cheapest fares to India start at around NZ$2000 from Auckland; add on approximately NZ$150 for flights from Wellington or Christchurch.

Round-the-world tickets

If India is only one stop on a longer journey, you might want to consider buying a **Round-the-World (RTW) ticket**. Some travel agents can sell you an "off-the-shelf" RTW ticket that will have you touching down in about half a dozen cities (Delhi and Mumbai feature on many itineraries); others will have to assemble one for you, which can be tailored to your needs but is apt to be more expensive. Figure on between £1000/$1500 and £1500/$2500 for an RTW ticket including India, valid for one year.

Airlines, agents and operators

Online booking

ⓦ www.cheapflights.co.uk (in UK)
ⓦ www.ebookers.com (in UK), ⓦ www .ebookers.ie (in Republic of Ireland)

himalayankingdoms.com

TREKS
TREKKING PEAKS
CULTURAL TOURS

Worldwide Treks & Tours

0845 330 8579

ATOL Protected 2973 AiTO

W www.expedia.co.uk (in UK), W www.expedia
.com (in US), W www.expedia.ca (in Canada)
W www.lastminute.com (in UK)
W www.opodo.co.uk (in UK)
W www.orbitz.com (in US)
W www.travel.com.au (Australia)
W www.travelocity.co.uk (in UK), W www
.travelocity.com (in US), W www.travelocity
.ca (in Canada)
W www.travelonline.co.za (in South Africa)
W www.zuji.com.au (in Australia), W www.zuji
.co.nz (in New Zealand)

Airlines

Air Canada Canada ☏ 1-888/247-2262,
W www.aircanada.com.
Air France UK ☏ 0870/142 4343, US
☏ 1-800/237-2747, Canada ☏ 1-800/667-
2747, Australia ☏ 1300/390 190, South Africa
☏ 0861/340 340; W www.airfrance.com.
Air India UK ☏ 020/8560 9996 or 8745 1000, US
☏ 1-800/223-7776, Canada ☏ 1800/625 6424,
Australia ☏ 02/9283 4020, New Zealand ☏ 09/631
5651; W www.airindia.com.
Air New Zealand New Zealand ☏ 0800/737 000,
Australia ☏ 0800/132 476; W www.airnz.co.nz.
American Airlines US & Canada
☏ 1-800/433 7300.
Biman Bangladesh Airlines UK ☏ 020/7629
0252 or 020/7629 0161, US ☏ 1-212/808-4477 or
1-212/808-4523; W www.bimanair.com.
British Airways UK ☏ 0870/850 9850, Republic
of Ireland ☏ 1890/626 747, US & Canada
☏ 1-800/AIRWAYS, South Africa ☏ 114/418 600;
W www.ba.com.
Cathay Pacific Australia ☏ 13 17 47, New Zealand
☏ 09/379 0861; W www.cathaypacific.com.
Continental Airlines US & Canada ☏ 1-800/523-
3273, W www.continental.com.
Delta US & Canada ☏ 1-800/221-1212,
W www.delta.com.
Emirates UK ☏ 0870/243 2222, US & Canada
☏ 1-800/777-3999, South Africa ☏ 0861/363 728;
W www.emirates.com.
Gulf Air UK ☏ 0870/777 1717, Republic of Ireland
☏ 0818/272 828, South Africa ☏ 11/268 8909;
W www.gulfairco.com.
Jet Airways UK ☏ 0808/1011 199, US
☏ 201/653-8001; W www.jetairways.com.
KLM (Royal Dutch Airlines) UK ☏ 0870/507
4074, Republic of Ireland ☏ 1850/747 400, US &
Canada ☏ 1-800/225-2525, South Africa ☏ 11/961
6727; W www.klm.com.
Lufthansa UK ☏ 0870/837 7747,
Republic of Ireland ☏ 01/844 5544,

US ☏ 1-800/3995-838, Canada ☏ 1-800/563-
5954, South Africa ☏ 0861/842 538; W www
.lufthansa.com.
Malaysia Airlines Australia ☏ 13 26 27, New
Zealand ☏ 0800/777 747; W www.malaysia
-airlines.com.
PIA (Pakistan International Airlines) UK
☏ 0800/587 1023, US & Canada ☏ 1-800/578-
6786; W www.piac.com.pk.
Qantas Airways Australia ☏ 13 13 13, New
Zealand ☏ 0800/808 767 or 09/357 8900;
W www.qantas.com.
Qatar Airways UK ☏ 0870/770 4215,
US ☏ 1-877/777-2827, Canada ☏ 1-888/366-
5666, South Africa ☏ 11/523 2928; W www
.qatarairways.com
Royal Jordanian UK ☏ 020/7878 6300, US
☏ 1-800/223-0470, Canada ☏ 1-800/363-0711 or
514/288-1647; W www.rja.com.jo.
Royal Nepal Airlines ☏ 1-800/266-3725,
W www.royalnepal.com.
Singapore Airlines Australia ☏ 13 10 11, New
Zealand ☏ 0800/808 909; W www.singaporeair.com.
South African Airways South Africa ☏ 11/978
1111, W www.flysaa.com.
SriLankan Airlines UK ☏ 020/8538 2001,
Republic of Ireland ☏ 1/241 8000; W www
.srilankan.aero.

B

BASICS

60,900 km of unforgettable experience

Indrail Pass: Unlimited rail travel on entire rail network.

Rail/ Hotel Itineraries: covering Rajasthan, Kerala & wildlife.

Luxury Train travel in India.
Palace on Wheels, Heritage on Wheels, Deccan Odyssey & The Royal Chariot

SD Enterprises Ltd.
GSA for Indrail passes in UK

Ph: 0208 9033411
info@indiarail.co.uk
www.indiarail.co.uk

Incredible !ndia

 **india**

the first thing you'll discover is that we love travel as much as you do

taj express

£429 8 days · A classic short tour of north India that takes in Delhi both old and new, the breathtaking Taj Mahal and the riotously coloured Pink City of Jaipur.

deserts, palaces & ganges

£749 13 days · Our definitive two-week tour that takes in Jaipur, the Taj Mahal, temples of Khajuraho & the city of Varanasi on the banks of holy Ganges.

triple **AAA** bonded!

onthegotours.com
68 North End Road, West Kensington, London W14 9EP
020 7371 1113
Phone for our FREE colour brochure

ESSENTIAL INDIA TRAVEL LTD

Essential India Travel offers tailormade and special interest holidays that include photography, trekking and cookery workshops to the Indian Subcontinent.

Email: info@essential-india.co.uk
Tel: 01225 868544. Web: www. essential-india.co.uk

For *authentic* Indian holidays...

Boutique India
LOCAL KNOWLEDGE AT YOUR FINGERTIPS

www.boutiqueindia.com
+44 (0)845 1238381

Thai Airways Australia ☎1300/651 960, New Zealand ☎09/377 3886; ⊛www.thaiair.com.

United Airlines US ☎1-800/UNITED-1, ⊛www.united.com.

Virgin Atlantic UK ☎0870/380 2007, US ☎1-800/821-5438; ⊛www.virgin-atlantic.com.

Agents and operators

Andrew Brock/Coromandel ☎01572/821330, ⊛www.coromandelabt.com. Small but unusual selection of itineraries, including Hooghly and Brahmaputra cruises and driving tours of the south and centre.

Audley Travel UK ☎01869/276218, ⊛www.audleytravel.com. Tailor-made and small-group tours that use interesting accommodation (homestays, tented camps and heritage properties); they're also strong on wildlife.

Bales UK ☎0870/241 3208, ⊛www.balesworldwide.com. Wide range of group and tailor-made tours covering most of India.

Blazing Trails UK ☎01293/533338, ⊛www.blazingtrailstours.com. Escorted motorcycle tours (on Enfields) in Goa, Kerala, Rajasthan and the Himalayas.

Culture Aangan ⊛www.cultureaangan.com. Homestays in southern coastal Maharashtra. Profits go to support local communities and help preserve the area's traditional culture.

Discovery Initiatives UK ☎01285/643333, ⊛www.discoveryinitiatives.co.uk. Nature-tour specialist offering small groups or tailor-made trips with an accent on conservation and ecology.

Essential India UK ☎01225/868544, ⊛www.essential-india.co.uk. Inventive themed holidays and courses focusing on subjects ranging from photography and cooking to wildlife and trekking, for individuals or groups. They favour low-impact travel and use local companies wherever possible.

Exodus UK ☎020/8675 5550, ⊛www.exodustravels.co.uk. Experienced specialists in small-group itineraries, treks and overland tours.

Geographic Expeditions US ☎1-800/777-8183, ⊛www.geoex.com. Unusual tours, ranging from Tamil Nadu temple trips to Sikkim village walks.

High Places ☎0114/275 7500, ⊛www.highplaces.co.uk. Sheffield-based trekking and mountaineering specialists; they also run an interesting 16-day tour through Kerala.

Himalayan Kingdoms UK ☎01453/844400, ⊛www.himalayankingdoms.com. Quality treks in Sikkim, Garhwal, Himachal Pradesh, Ladakh and Arunachal Pradesh.

Insider Tours UK ☎01233/811771, ⊛www.insider-tours.com. Some of the most original,

"hands-on" and ethical itineraries on the market, taking visitors to wonderful off-track corners of Kerala, Goa, the Northeast and elsewhere.

Jewel in the Crown UK ☎01293/533338, ⊛www.jewelholidays.com. Established Goa and Kerala specialist, offering a wide range of holidays across the state, as well as cheap flights.

Kerala Connections UK ☎01892/722440, ⊛www.keralaconnect.co.uk. South India specialists, offering numerous itineraries in Kerala, as well as Tamil Nadu and Karnataka, for a wide range of budgets.

Lakshmi Tours UK ☎01985/844183, ⊛www.lakshmi.com. Special-interest tours (drawing, textiles, Ayurveda) for small groups, mostly focusing on Rajasthan and Kerala.

Mountain Travel/Sobek US ☎1-888/687-6235 or 510/527-8100, ⊛www.mtsobek.com. Small range of challenging Himalayan treks, plus wildlife and sightseeing tours in Rajasthan and the south.

Myths and Mountains US ☎1-800/670-6984 or 775/832-5454, ⊛www.mythsandmountains.com. Special-interest trips (tailor-made or group) to some very unusual places, ranging from tribal Chhattisgarh to deepest Gujarat, with the emphasis on culture, crafts and religion.

North South Travel UK ☎01245/608 291, ⊛www.northsouthtravel.co.uk. Friendly, competitive travel agency, offering discounted fares worldwide. Profits are used to support projects in the developing world, especially the promotion of sustainable tourism.

Out There Biking UK ⊛www.out-there-biking.com. Small, UK-based bicycle-adventure company specialising in the Indian Himalayas. The tours are either self- or Jeep-supported, with a low-impact travel philosophy and excellent local knowledge.

Peregrine Adventures Australia ☎03/9663 8611, ⊛www.peregrine.net.au. Small-group wildlife and culture tours in Rajasthan and South India, plus trekking in Ladakh.

Pettitts India ☎01892/515966, ⊛www.pettitts.co.uk. Tailor-made holidays off the beaten track.

SD Enterprises ☎0208/903 0392, ⊛www.indiarail.co.uk. Run by Indian rail experts, SD Enterprises put together itineraries for independent travellers wanting to explore India by train, plus a range of other cheap countrywide packages and charter flights to Kerala and Goa.

Soul of India ☎020/8901 7320, ⊛www.soulofindia.com. Guided tours (set or tailor-made, and for individuals or groups) of sacred India, including the source of the Ganges, Sikh shrines, the Hindu and Christian south, and landmarks associated with the Buddha and Gandhi.

US: 001 - 213 - 9853430

Your trip to India starts here...

Ladakh, Rajasthan, South India, East and North East India.

www.shantitravel.com

Tailor Made Tour

shanti travel

Tel India.: 0091 11 46077800
contact@shantitravel.com

STA Travel US ☎ 1-800/781-4040, UK ☎ 0871/2300 040, Australia ☎ 134 STA, New Zealand ☎ 0800/474 400, SA ☎ 0861/781 781; ⓦ www.statravel.com. Worldwide specialists in independent travel; also student IDs, travel insurance, car rental, rail passes, and more. Good discounts for students and under-26s.

Trailfinders UK ☎ 0845/058 5858, Republic of Ireland ☎ 01/677 7888, Australia ☎ 1300/780 212; ⓦ www.trailfinders.com. One of the best-informed and most efficient agents for independent travellers.

Trans Indus Travel UK ☎ 020/8566 2729, ⓦ www.transindus.co.uk. Fixed and tailor-made packages from various Indian cities, including wildlife, fishing and trekking tours.

Voyages Jules Verne UK ☎ 020/7616 1000, ⓦ www.vjv.co.uk. Classic heritage tours, including some by rail.

Western & Oriental Travel UK ☎ 0870/499 1111, ⓦ www.westernoriental.com. Award-winning, upmarket agency with tailor-made itineraries covering all of India but favouring Goa and Rajasthan.

Wilderness Travel US ☎ 1-800/368-2794, ⓦ www.wildernesstravel.com. Varied tours ranging from Himalayan treks to southern temple tours, with the emphasis on culture, history and wildlife.

Entry requirements

Gone are the days when Commonwealth nationals could stroll visa-less into India and stay for as long as they pleased: today, everyone except citizens of Nepal and Bhutan needs a visa.

If you're going to India on business or to study, you'll need to apply for a special student or business visa; otherwise, a **standard tourist visa** will suffice. These are valid for six months from the date of issue (not of departure from your home country or entry into India) and cost £30/US$60/CDN$62/A$75/NZ$90. As you're asked to specify whether you need a single-entry or a multiple-entry visa, and the same rates apply to both, it makes sense to ask for the latter, just in case you decide to make a side trip to Nepal or another neighbouring country.

Much the best place to get a visa is in your country of residence (see the list of embassies and high commissions on pp.33–34); you should be able to download forms from the embassy and consulate websites. In Britain and North America, you'll need a passport valid for at least six months, two passport photographs and an **application form**, obtainable in advance by post or on the day; address applications to the Postal Visa Section of the consulate in question. In Australia and New Zealand, one passport-sized photo and your flight/travel itinerary are required, together with the visa application form. As a rule, visas are issued in a matter of hours, although embassies in India's neighbouring countries often drag their feet, demand letters of recommendation from your embassy (expensive if you are, for example, British), or make you wait and pay for them to send your application to Delhi. In the US, postal applications take a month as opposed to a same-day service if you do it in person – check with your nearest embassy, high commission or consulate. Make sure that your visa is signed by someone at the embassy, as you may be refused entry into the country otherwise.

In many countries it's also possible to pay a **visa agency** (or "visa expediter") to process the visa on your behalf. This is an option worth considering if you're not able to get to your nearest Indian High Commission, embassy or consulate yourself, or simply can't be bothered to deal with the frequently long queues. Prices vary a little from company to company, as do turn-around times. In the UK, expediters charge from as little as £15 up to £50, plus the price of the visa; prices in the US run from around $45 up to more than $180. Two working weeks is about standard, but you can get a visa in as little as 24 hours if you're prepared to pay premium rates. For a full rundown of services, check the company websites below, from where you can usually download visa application forms and confirm requirements. In Britain, try The Visa Service (☎0844/800 4650, ⓦwww.visaservice.co.uk), the India Visa Office (☎0844/800 4018, ⓦwww.indiavisa headoffice.co.uk), or the India Visa Company (☎020/8582 1117, ⓦwww .skylorduk.com/gle_visa.htm). Alternatively, check out the links to other visa expediters at ⓦwww.visaexpress.com. In North America, where you can expect to pay anywhere between US$140–260 to obtain a visa within two weeks, reliable expediters include Travel Document Systems (ⓦwww .traveldocs.com), with offices in New York, Washington and San Francisco, and Visa Connection (ⓦwww.visaconnection.com), who have offices in Vancouver, Calgary, Ottawa and Surrey.

Visa extensions

It is no longer possible to **extend a visa**, though exceptions may be made in special circumstances. Most people whose standard six-month tourist visas are about to expire head for Bangkok or neighbouring capitals such as Colombo in Sri Lanka or Kathmandu in Nepal, and apply for a new one. However, in recent years this has been something of a hit-and-miss business, with some tourists having their requests turned down for no apparent reason. The Indian High Commission in Kathmandu is particularly notorious for this; you can telephone them or visit their website (ⓦwww.south -asia.com/Embassy-India) to check their current policy, but the online advice is confused and you shouldn't, in any case, expect the story to be the same when you arrive. Try to find out from other travellers what the visa situation is, and always allow enough time on your current permit to re-enter India and catch a flight out of the country in case your request is refused.

If you do stay more than 180 days, you are supposed to get a **tax clearance certificate** before you leave the country, available at the foreigners' section of the income-tax department in every major city. They are free, but you should take bank receipts to show you have changed your money legally. In practice, tax clearance certificates are rarely demanded, but you never know.

For details of **other kinds of visas** – five-year visas can be obtained by foreigners of Indian origin, business travellers and even students of yoga – contact your nearest Indian embassy.

Indian embassies

Australia High Commission: 3–5 Moonah Place, Yarralumla, Canberra, ACT 2600 ☎02/6273 3999, ⓦwww.hcindia-au.org. Consulates: Level 27, 25 Bligh St, Sydney, NSW 2000 ☎02/9223 9500, ⓦwww.indianconsulatesydney.org; 15 Munro St, Coburg, Melbourne, Vic 3058 ☎03/9384 0141, ⓦwww.cgimelb.org. Honorary Consulates: Suite 21, 2nd Floor, Lincoln House, 4 Ventnor Ave, West Perth, WA 6005 ☎08/9486 9011, ⓔconsul@wa1.quik .com.au; 175A Swann Rd, Taringa, Brisbane, QLD 4068 ☎07/3871 3362, ⓔindcon@optusnet.com.au. **Bangladesh** High Commission: House no. 2, Rd no. 142, Gulshan-1, Dhaka ☎02/988 9339,

Indian public holidays: a warning

Wherever you intend to get your visa from, bear in mind that your nearest High Commission, Embassy or Consulate will observe **Indian public holidays** (as well as most of the local ones), and that it might therefore be closed. Always check opening hours in advance by phone, or via the website, beforehand.

ⓦwww.hcidhaka.org. Consulate: House no. 2, B-@, Rd no. 1, Kulshi, Chittagong ☏031/654148.
Bhutan Embassy of India, India House Estate, Thimpu ☏0975/22162, ✉loplg@druknet.net.bt.
Canada High Commission: 10 Springfield Rd, Ottawa, ON K1M 1C9 ☏613/744-3751, ⓦwww .hciottawa.ca. Consulates: 365 Bloor St (East), Suite #500, Toronto, ON M4W 3L4 ☏416/960-0751, ⓦwww.cgitoronto.ca; #201–325 Howe St, Vancouver, BC V6C 1Z7 ☏604/662-8811, ⓦwww .cgivancouver.com.
China Embassy: Ri Tan Dong Lu, Beijing ☏01/6532 1908, ⓦwww.indianembassy.org.cn. Consulate: 1008, Shanghai International Trade Centre, 2201 Yan An Xi Lu (West) Rd, Shanghai ☏021/6275 8885, ⓦwww.indianembassy.org.cn.
Ireland Embassy: 6 Leeson Park, Dublin 6 ☏01/497 0843, ⓦwww.indianembassy.ie.
Nepal Embassy: 336 Kapurdhara Marg, Kathmandu ☏01/441 0900, ⓦwww.south-asia.com /embassy-india.
New Zealand High Commission: 180 Molesworth St, PO Box 4045, Wellington ☏04/473 6390, ⓦwww.hicomind.org.nz.
Pakistan High Commission: G-5, Diplomatic Enclave, Islamabad ☏051/814371. Consulate: India House, 3 Fatima Jinnah Rd, PO Box 8542, Karachi ☏021/522275.
Singapore Embassy: India House, 31 Grange Rd, Singapore 239702 ☏6737 6777, ⓦwww .embassyofindia.com.
Sri Lanka High Commission: 36–38 Galle Rd, Colombo 3 ☏011/232 7587, ⓦwww.hcicolombo .org. Consulate: 31 Rajapihilla Mawatha, PO Box 47, Kandy ☏081/222 4563.
Thailand Embassy: 46 Prasarnmitr, Sukhumvit Rd 23, Bangkok 10110 ☏02/258 0300, ⓦwww .indianembassy.gov.in/bangkok. Consulate: 113 Bumruangrat Rd, Chiang Mai 50000 ☏053/243066, ⓕ247879.
UK High Commission: India House, Aldwych, London WC2B 4NA ☏020/7632 3149, ⓦwww.hcilondon .net. Consulates: 20 Augusta St, Jewellery Quarter,

Hockley, Birmingham B18 6GL ☏0121/ 212 2782, ⓦwww.cgibirmingham.org; 17 Rutland Square, Edinburgh EH1 2BB ☏0131/229 2144, ⓦwww .cgiedinburgh.org.
USA Embassy of India (Consular Services): 2536 Massachusetts Ave NW, Washington DC 20008 ☏202/939-7000, ⓦwww.indianembassy .org. Consulates: 3 E 64th St, New York, NY 10021 ☏212/774-0600, ⓦwww.indiacgny .org; 540 Arguello Blvd, San Francisco, CA 94118 ☏415/668-0683, ⓦwww.cgisf.org; 455 N Cityfront Plaza Drive, NBC Tower Building, Suite 850, Chicago IL 60611 ☏312/595-0405, ⓦchicago .indianconsulate.com.

Special permits

In addition to a visa, **special permits** may be required for travel to certain areas of India – notably Sikkim, parts of Ladakh, the Andaman Islands, Lakshadweep, the far west of the Thar desert beyond Jaisalmer, the fringes of Kutch in Gujarat near the Pakistani border and the northeastern hill states of Meghalaya and Manipur. Details of all the various permits are given in the relevant Guide chapters. Some areas (parts of Sikkim, and the border region between India, Pakistan and China in Jammu–Kashmir for example) remain **completely out of bounds** to tourists. If you have some special reason for going to any of these latter areas, apply for a permit to the Ministry for Home Affairs Foreigners' Section, Lok Nayak Bhawan, Khan Market, New Delhi 110003, at least three months in advance.

Should you get your hands on a **visa for Bhutan**, you'll also need a transit permit for the border area from the Ministry of External Affairs.

Health

There are plenty of scare stories about the health risks of travelling in India, but in fact cases of serious illness are very much the exception rather than the rule. Standards of hygiene and sanitation have increased greatly over the past decade or so and, if you're careful, there's no reason you can't stay healthy throughout your trip – indeed many travellers now visit in the Subcontinent without even experiencing the traditional dose of "Delhi belly". Having said that, it's still important to keep your resistance high and to be aware of the dangers of untreated water, mosquito bites and undressed open cuts.

What you **eat and drink** is crucial: a poor diet lowers your resistance. Ensure you eat a balance of protein and carbohydrates, as well as making sure you get enough vitamins and minerals. Meat and fish are obvious sources of protein for non-vegetarians in the West, but not necessarily in India: eggs, *paneer*, pulses, rice, curd and nuts are all good sources of protein. Overcooked vegetables lose a lot of their vitamin content; eating plenty of peeled fresh fruit helps keep up your vitamin and mineral intake. With all that sweating, too, make sure you get enough salt (put extra on your food) and drink enough water. It's also worth taking daily multi-vitamin and mineral tablets with you. Above all, make sure you eat enough – unfamiliar food may mean you eat less – and get enough sleep and rest: it's easy to get run down if you're on the move a lot, especially in a hot climate.

It's worth knowing, if you are ill and can't get to a doctor, that almost any medicine can be bought over the counter without a prescription.

Precautions

The lack of **sanitation** in India can be exaggerated. It's not worth getting too worked up about it or you'll never enjoy anything, but a few common-sense precautions are in order, bearing in mind that things such as bacteria multiply far more quickly in a tropical climate, and that your body will have little immunity to Indian germs.

For details on the **water**, see the box on p.36. When it comes to **food**, be particularly wary of prepared dishes that have to be reheated – they may have been on display in the heat and covered with flies for some time. Anything that is boiled or fried (and thus sterilized) in your presence is usually all right, though meat can sometimes be dodgy, especially in towns or cities where the electricity supply (and thus refrigerators) frequently fails; anything that has been left out for any length of time is definitely suspect. Raw unpeeled fruit and vegetables should always be viewed with suspicion, and you should avoid salads unless you know they have been soaked in an iodine or potassium permanganate solution. Wiping down a plate before eating is sensible, and avoid straws as they are usually dusty or secondhand. As a rule of thumb, stick to cafés and restaurants that are doing a brisk trade and where the food is thus freshly cooked, and you should be fine.

Be vigilant about **personal hygiene**. Wash your hands often, especially before eating, keep all cuts clean, treat them with iodine or antiseptic, and cover them to prevent infection. Be fussier than usual about sharing things like drinks and cigarettes. Going around barefoot is also best avoided – and it's best to wear flip-flops even in the shower.

Advice on avoiding **mosquito bites** is given under "Malaria" below. If you do get bites or itches try not to scratch them: it's hard, but infection and tropical ulcers can result if you do. Tiger balm and even dried soap may relieve the itching.

Finally, especially if you are going on a long trip, have a **dental check-up** before you leave home – you don't want to go down with unexpected tooth trouble in India. If you do, and it feels serious, head for Delhi, Mumbai or Kolkata (Calcutta), and ask a foreign consulate to recommend a dentist.

Vaccinations

No **vaccinations** are legally required for entry into India unless you're arriving from a country infected with yellow fever, in which case you'll be asked for an inoculation certificate. All the same, meningitis, typhoid and hepatitis A jabs are recommended, and it's worth ensuring that you are up to date with tetanus, polio and other boosters. All vaccinations can be obtained in Delhi, Mumbai and other major cities if necessary; just make sure the needle is new.

Hepatitis A is not the worst disease you can catch in India, but the frequency with which it strikes travellers makes a strong case for immunization. Transmitted through contaminated food and water, or through saliva, it can lay a victim low for several months with exhaustion, fever and diarrhoea, and may cause liver damage. The Havrix vaccine has been shown to be extremely effective; though expensive, it lasts for up to ten years. The protection given by gamma-globulin, the traditional serum of hepatitis antibodies, wears off quickly and the injection should therefore be given as late as possible before departure: the longer your planned stay, the larger the dose. Symptoms of hepatitis include a yellowing of the whites of the eyes, nausea, general flu-like malaise, orange urine (though dehydration could also cause that) and light-coloured stools. If you think you have it, avoid alcohol and get lots of rest. More serious is **hepatitis B**, passed on like HIV through blood or sexual contact. There is a vaccine, but it is only recommended for those planning to work in a medical environment.

Typhoid, also spread through contaminated food or water, is endemic in India, but rare outside the monsoon. It produces a persistent high fever with malaise, headaches and abdominal pains, followed by diarrhoea. Vaccination is by injection (two shots are required, or one for a booster), giving three years' cover.

What about the water?

In general, it's best to avoid drinking Indian **tap water**. This isn't because tap water is particularly virulent (and in big cities it's usually chlorinated), but the unfamiliar microorganisms it contains are likely to precipitate mild stomach upsets, especially if you've got a delicate stomach. Having said that, you'll find it almost impossible to avoid untreated tap water completely, since it's used to make ice, which may appear in drinks without being asked for, to wash utensils, and so on.

Bottled water, available in all but the most remote places these days, may seem like the simplest and most cost-effective solution, but it has some major drawbacks. The first is that the water itself might not always be as safe as it seems. Independent tests carried out in 2003 on major Indian brands revealed levels of **pesticide** concentration up to 104 times higher than EU norms. Top sellers Kinley, Bisleri and Aquaplus were named as the worst offenders.

The second downside of bottled water is the **plastic pollution** it causes. Visualize the size of the pile you'd leave behind you after getting through a couple of bottles per day, and imagine that multiplied by millions, which is the amount of non-biodegradable land-fill waste generated each year by tourists alone.

The best solution from the point of view of your health and the environment is to purify your own water. **Chemical sterilisation** is the cheapest method. **Iodine** isn't recommended for long trips, but **chlorine** is completely effective, fast and inexpensive, and you can remove the nasty taste it leaves with neutralizing tablets or lemon juice.

Alternatively, invest in some kind of **purifying filter** incorporating chemical sterilization to kill even the smallest viruses. An ever-increasing range of compact, lightweight products are available these days through outdoor shops and large pharmacies, but anyone who's pregnant or suffers from thyroid problems should check that iodine isn't used as the chemical sterilizer.

Cholera, spread the same way as hepatitis A and typhoid, causes sudden attacks of watery diarrhoea with cramps and debilitation. It is endemic in the Ganges basin, but only during periodic epidemics. If you get it, take copious amounts of water with rehydration salts and seek medical treatment. There is currently no effective vaccination against cholera.

Most medical authorities now recommend vaccination against meningitis too. Spread by airborne bacteria (through coughs and sneezes for example), it attacks the lining of the brain and can be fatal. Symptoms include fever, a severe headache, stiffness in the neck and a rash on the stomach and back.

You should have a tetanus booster every ten years whether you travel or not. Tetanus (or lockjaw) is picked up through contaminated open wounds and causes severe muscular spasms; if you cut yourself on something dirty and are not covered, get a booster as soon as you can.

Assuming that you were vaccinated against polio in childhood, only one (oral) booster is needed during your adult life. Immunizations against mumps, measles, TB and rubella are a good idea for anyone who wasn't vaccinated as a child and hasn't had the diseases.

Rabies is a problem in India. The best advice is to give dogs and monkeys a wide berth, and not to play with animals at all, no matter how cute they might look. A bite, a scratch or even a lick from an infected animal could spread the disease; wash any such wound immediately but gently with soap or detergent, and apply alcohol or iodine if possible. Find out what you can about the animal and swap addresses with the owner (if there is one) just in case. If the animal might be infected or the wound begins to tingle and fester, act immediately to get treatment – rabies is invariably fatal once symptoms appear. There is an (expensive) vaccine, which serves only to shorten the course of treatment you need, and is effective for a maximum of three months.

Medical resources for travellers

For up-to-the-minute information, make an appointment at a travel clinic. These clinics also sell travel accessories, including mosquito nets and first-aid kits. Information about specific diseases and conditions, drugs and herbal remedies is provided by the websites below; you could also consult the *Rough Guide to Travel Health* by Dr Nick Jones.

Health-related websites

ⓦ wwwn.cdc.gov/travel US Department of Health and Human Services travel health and disease control department, listing precautions, diseases and preventive measures by region.
ⓦ www.fitfortravel.scot.nhs.uk UK NHS website carrying information about travel-related diseases and how to avoid them.
ⓦ www.istm.org The website of the International Society for Travel Medicine, with a full list of clinics worldwide specializing in travel health.
ⓦ www.tripprep.com Travel Health Online provides a comprehensive database of necessary vaccinations for most countries, as well as destination and medical service provider information.

Medical resources for travellers

UK and Ireland

British Airways Travel Clinics ☎0845/600 2236, ⓦ www.britishairways.com/travel /healthclinintro/public/en_gb for nearest clinic.
Hospital for Tropical Diseases Travel Clinic ☎0845/155 5000 or 020/7387 4411, ⓦ www .thehtd.org.
MASTA (Medical Advisory Service for Travellers Abroad) ⓦ www.masta.org or ☎0870/606 2782 for the nearest clinic.
Travel Medicine Services ☎028/9031 5220.
Tropical Medical Bureau Republic of Ireland ☎1850/487 674, ⓦ www.tmb.ie.

US and Canada

CDC ☎1-877/394-8747, ⓦ www.cdc.gov/travel. Official US government travel health site.
International Society for Travel Medicine ☎1-770/736-7060, ⓦ www.istm.org. Has a full list of travel health clinics.
Canadian Society for International Health ⓦ www.csih.org. Extensive list of travel health centres.

Australia, New Zealand and South Africa

Travellers' Medical and Vaccination Centre ⓦ www.tmvc.com.au, ☎1300/658 844. Lists travel clinics in Australia, New Zealand and South Africa.

Malaria

Malaria is one of the Subcontinent's big killers, and it's essential that you check with your doctor whether you'll need to take anti-malarial medication for your visit. The disease, caused by a parasite carried in the saliva of female Anopheles mosquitoes, can be found in many parts of India, and is especially prevalent in the northeast, although non-existent in the high Himalayan regions (there's a useful malaria map of the country at ⓦ www.fitfortravel.scot.nhs.uk/destinations /malariamaps/india.htm, showing varying levels of risk across the country). Malaria has a variable incubation period of a few days to several weeks, so you can become ill long after being bitten – which is why it's important to carry on taking the tablets even after you've returned home.

Ideas about appropriate **antimalarial medication** tend to vary from country to country, and prophylaxis remains a controversial subject; it's important that you get expert medical advice on which treatment is right for you. In addition, resistance to established antimalarial drugs is growing alarmingly – none of the following provide complete protection, so avoiding being bitten in the first place remains important. Chloroquine- and proguanil-resistant strains of malaria are particularly prevalent in **Assam and the northeast**; travellers to this region might consider taking a course of malarone, doxycycline or mefloquine instead.

The most established regime – widely prescribed in Europe, but not in North America – is a combination of **chloroquine** (trade names Nivaquin or Avloclor) taken weekly either on its own or in conjunction with a daily dose of **proguanil** (Paludrine). You need to start this regime a week before arriving in a malarial area and continue it for four weeks after leaving. In India chloroquine is easy to come by but proguanil isn't, so stock up before you arrive. **Mefloquine** (Lariam) is a newer and stronger treatment. As a prophylactic, you need take just one tablet weekly, starting two weeks before entering a risk area and continuing for four weeks after leaving. Mefloquine is a very powerful and effective antimalarial, though there have been widely reported concerns about its side effects, including psychological problems.

Doxycycline is often prescribed in Australasia. One tablet is taken daily, starting a day or two before entering a malarial zone and continuing for four weeks after leaving. It's not suitable for children under ten and it can cause thrush in women, while three percent of users develop a sensitivity to light, causing a rash, so it's not ideal for beach holidays. It also interferes with the effectiveness of the contraceptive pill. **Malarone** (a combination of atovaquone and proguanil) is the most recent drug to come on the market. The bonus is that you only have to start taking it on the day you enter a malarial zone and

A travellers' first-aid kit

Below are items you might want to take, especially if you're planning to go trekking – all are available in India itself, at a fraction of what you might pay at home:

- Antiseptic cream
- Insect repellent and cream such as Anthisan for soothing bites
- Plasters/Band-Aids
- A course of Flagyl antibiotics
- Water sterilization tablets or water purifier
- Lint and sealed bandages
- Knee supports
- Imodium (Lomotil) for emergency diarrhoea treatment
- A mild oral anesthetic such as Bonjela for soothing ulcers or mild toothache
- Paracetamol/aspirin
- Multi-vitamin and mineral tablets
- Rehydration sachets
- Hypodermic needles and sterilized skin wipes

continue for just a week after leaving, meaning that, although it's expensive, it can prove economical for short trips.

Malarial symptoms

The first signs of malaria are remarkably similar to a severe flu, and may take months to appear: if you suspect anything go to a hospital or clinic for a blood test immediately. The shivering, burning fever and headaches come in waves, usually in the early evening. Malaria is not infectious, but some strains are dangerous and occasionally even fatal when not treated promptly, in particular, the chloroquine-resistant cerebral malaria. This virulent and lethal strain of the disease, which affects the brain, is treatable, but has to be diagnosed early. Erratic body temperature, lack of energy and aches are the first key signs.

Preventing mosquito bites

The best way of combating malaria is of course to avoid getting bitten: malarial mosquitoes are active from dusk until dawn and during this time you should use mosquito repellent and take all necessary precautions. Sleep under a mosquito net if possible, burn mosquito coils (widely available in India, but easy to break in transit) or electrically heated repellents such as All Out. An Indian brand of repellent called Odomos is widely available and very effective, though most travellers bring their own from home, usually one containing the noxious but effective compound DEET. DEET can cause rashes and a strength of more than thirty percent is not advised for those with sensitive skin. A natural alternative is citronella or, in the UK, Mosi-guard Natural, made from a blend of eucalyptus oils; those with sensitive skin should still use DEET on clothes and nets. Mosquito "buzzers" – plug-in contraptions that smoulder tablets of DEET compounds slowly overnight – are pretty useless, but wrist and ankle bands are as effective as spray and a good alternative for sensitive skin. Though active from dusk till dawn, female Anopheles mosquitoes prefer to bite in the evening, so be especially careful at that time. Wear long sleeves, skirts and trousers, avoid dark colours, which attract mosquitoes, and put repellent on all exposed skin.

Dengue fever and Japanese encephalitis

Another illness spread by mosquito bites is dengue fever, whose symptoms are similar to those of malaria, plus aching bones. There is no vaccine available and the only treatment is complete rest, with drugs to assuage the fever. Japanese encephalitis, a mosquito-borne viral infection causing fever, muscle pains and headaches, is most prevalent in wet, rural rice-growing areas. However, it only rarely affects travellers, and the vaccine isn't usually recommended unless you plan to spend much time around paddy fields during and immediately after the monsoons.

Intestinal troubles

Diarrhoea is the most common bane of travellers. When mild and not accompanied by other major symptoms, it may just be your stomach reacting to unfamiliar food. Accompanied by cramps and vomiting, it could well be food poisoning. In either case, it will probably pass of its own accord in 24–48 hours without treatment. In the meantime, it is essential to replace the fluids and salts you're losing, so take lots of water with oral rehydration salts (commonly referred to as ORS, or called Electrolyte in India). If you can't get ORS, use half a teaspoon of salt and eight of sugar in a litre of water, and if you are too ill to drink, seek medical help immediately. Travel clinics and pharmacies sell double-ended moulded plastic spoons with the exact ratio of sugar to salt.

While you are suffering, it's a good idea to avoid greasy food, heavy spices, caffeine and most fruit and dairy products. Some say bananas and pawpaws are good, as are *kitchri* (a simple dhal and rice preparation) and rice soup and coconut water, while curd or a soup made from Marmite or Vegemite (if you happen to have some with you) are forms of protein that can be easily absorbed by your body when you have the runs. **Drugs** like Lomotil or Imodium simply plug you up – undermining the body's efforts to rid itself of infection – though they can be useful if you have to travel. If symptoms persist for more than a few days, a course of antibiotics may be necessary; this should be seen as a last resort, following medical advice.

Sordid though it may seem, it's a good idea to look at what comes out when you go to the toilet. If your diarrhoea contains blood or mucus and if you are suffering other symptoms including rotten-egg belches and farts, the cause may be dysentery or giardia. With a fever, it could well be caused by **bacillic dysentery**, and may clear up without treatment. If you're sure you need it, a course of antibiotics such as tetracycline should sort you out, but they also destroy gut flora in your intestines (which help protect you – curd can replenish them to some extent). If you start a course, be sure to finish it, even after the symptoms have gone. Similar symptoms, without fever, indicate **amoebic dysentery**, which is much more serious, and can damage your gut if untreated. The usual cure is a course of Metronidazole (Flagyl) or Fasigyn, both antibiotics which may themselves make you feel ill, and must not be taken with alcohol. Symptoms of **giardia** are similar – including frothy stools, nausea and constant fatigue – for which the treatment is again Metronidazole. If you suspect that you have either of these, seek medical help, and only start on the Metronidazole (750mg three times daily for a week for adults) if there is definitely blood in your diarrhoea and it is impossible to see a doctor.

Finally, bear in mind that oral drugs, such as malaria pills and the Pill, are likely to be largely ineffective if taken while suffering from diarrhoea.

Bites and creepy crawlies

Worms may enter your body through skin (especially the soles of your feet) or food. An itchy anus is a common symptom, and you may even see them in your stools. They are easy to treat: if you suspect you have them, get some worming tablets such as Mebendazole (Vermox) from any pharmacy.

Biting insects and similar animals other than mosquitoes may also aggravate you. The obvious suspects are **bed bugs** – look for signs of squashed ones around beds in cheap hotels. An infested mattress can be left in the hot sun all day to get rid of them, but they often live in the frame or even in

walls or floors. **Head** and **body lice** can also be a nuisance, but medicated soap and shampoo (preferably brought with you from home) usually see them off. Avoid **scratching bites**, which can lead to infection. Bites from ticks and lice can spread **typhus**, characterized by fever, muscle aches, headaches, and, later, red eyes and a measles-like rash. If you think you have it, seek treatment (tetracycline is usually prescribed).

Snakes are unlikely to bite unless accidentally disturbed, and most are harmless in any case. To see one at all, you need to search stealthily – walk heavily and they usually oblige by disappearing. If you do get bitten, remember what the snake looked like (kill it if you can), try not to move the affected part, and seek medical help: antivenins are available in most hospitals. A few **spiders** have poisonous bites too. Remove **leeches**, which may attach themselves to you in jungle areas, with salt or a lit cigarette: never just pull them off.

Heat trouble

The sun and the heat can cause a few unexpected problems. Before they've acclimatized, many people get a bout of **prickly heat rash**, an infection of the sweat ducts caused by excessive perspiration that doesn't dry off. A cool shower, zinc oxide powder (sold in India) and loose cotton clothes should help. **Dehydration** is another possible problem, so make sure you're drinking enough liquid, and drink rehydration salts frequently, especially when hot and/or tired. The main danger sign is irregular urination (only once a day for instance); dark urine definitely means you should drink more (although it could also indicate hepatitis).

The **sun** can burn, or even cause sunstroke; a high-factor sun block is vital on exposed skin, especially when you first arrive. A light hat is also a very good idea, especially if you're doing a lot of walking around in the sun.

Finally, be aware that overheating can cause **heatstroke**, which is potentially fatal. Signs are a very high body temperature, without a feeling of fever but accompanied by headaches and disorientation. Lowering body temperature (taking a tepid shower for example) and resting in an air-conditioned room is the first step in treatment; also take in plenty of fluids, and seek medical advice if the condition doesn't improve after 24 hours.

Altitude sickness

At high altitudes, you may develop symptoms of **acute mountain sickness** (AMS). Just about everyone who ascends to around 4000m or more experiences mild symptoms, but serious cases are rare. The simple cure – descent – almost always brings immediate recovery.

AMS is caused by the fact that at high elevations there is not only less oxygen, but also lower atmospheric pressure. This can have all sorts of weird effects on the body: it can cause the brain to swell and the lungs to fill with fluid, and even bring on uncontrollable farting. The syndrome varies from one person to the next, but symptoms include breathlessness, headaches and dizziness, nausea, difficulty sleeping and appetite loss. More extreme cases may involve disorientation and loss of balance, and the coughing up of pink frothy phlegm.

AMS strikes without regard for fitness – in fact, young people seem to be more susceptible, possibly because they're more reluctant to admit they feel sick and they dart about more energetically. Most people are capable of acclimatizing to very high altitudes but the process takes time and must be done in stages. The golden rule is not to go too high, too fast; or if you do, spend the night at a lower height ("Climb High, Sleep Low"). Above 3000m, you should not ascend more than 500m per day; take mandatory acclimatization days at 3500m and 4000m – more if you feel unwell – and try to spend these days day-hiking higher.

The general symptoms of AMS can be treated with the drug acetazolamide (Diamox) but this is not advised as it will block the early signs of severe AMS, which can be fatal. It is better to stay put for a day or two, eat a high-carbohydrate diet, drink plenty of water (three litres a day is recommended), take paracetamol or aspirin for the headaches, and descend if the AMS persists or worsens. If you fly direct to a high-altitude

Ayurvedic medicine

Ayurveda, a Sanskrit word meaning the "knowledge for prolonging life", is a 5000 year-old holistic medical system that is widely practised in India. Ayurvedic doctors and clinics in large towns deal with foreigners as well as their usual patients, and some **pharmacies** specialize in Ayurvedic preparations, including toiletries such as soaps, shampoos and toothpastes.

Ayurveda assumes the fundamental sameness of self and nature. Unlike the allopathic medicines of the West, which depend on finding out what's ailing you and then killing it, Ayurveda looks at the whole patient: disease is regarded as a symptom of **imbalance**, so it's the imbalance that's treated, not the disease. Ayurvedic theory holds that the body is controlled by three forces, which reflect the forces within the self: *pitta*, the force of the sun, is hot, and rules the digestive processes and metabolism; *kapha*, likened to the moon, the creator of tides and rhythms, has a cooling effect and governs the body's organs; and *vata*, wind, relates to movement and the nervous system. The healthy body is one that has the three forces in balance. To diagnose an imbalance, the Ayurvedic **vaid** (doctor) responds not only to the physical complaint but also to family background, daily habits and emotional traits.

Imbalances are typically treated with herbal remedies designed to alter whichever of the three forces is out of whack. Made according to traditional formulae, using indigenous plants, Ayurvedic medicines are cheaper than branded or imported drugs. In addition, the doctor may prescribe various forms of yogic cleansing to rid the body of waste substances. To the uninitiated, these techniques will sound rather off-putting – for instance, swallowing a long strip of cloth, a short section at a time, and then pulling it back up again to remove mucus from the stomach. Ayurvedic **massage** with herbal oils is especially popular in Kerala where courses of treatments are available to combat a wide array of ailments.

destination such as Leh, be especially careful to acclimatize (plan for three days of initial rest); you'll certainly want to avoid doing anything strenuous at first.

Other precautions to take at high altitudes include avoiding alcohol and sleeping pills, drinking more liquid, and protecting your skin against UV solar glare.

HIV and AIDS

The rapidly increasing presence of **HIV/AIDS** has only recently been acknowledged by the Indian government as a national problem. The reluctance to address the issue is partly due to the disease's association with sex, a traditionally closed subject in India. As yet only NGOs and foreign agencies such as the WHO have embarked on awareness and prevention campaigns. As elsewhere in the world, high-risk groups include prostitutes and intravenous drug users. It is extremely unwise to contemplate casual sex without a condom – carry some with you (preferably brought from home as Indian ones may be less reliable; also, be aware that heat affects the durability of condoms), and insist upon using them.

Should you need an **injection** or a **transfusion** in India, make sure that new, sterile equipment is used; any blood you receive should be from voluntary rather than commercial donor banks. If you have a shave from a barber, make sure he uses a clean blade, and don't undergo processes such as ear-piercing, acupuncture or tattooing unless you can be sure that the equipment is sterile.

Getting medical help

Pharmacies can usually advise on minor medical problems, and most doctors in India speak English. Also, many hotels keep a

doctor on call; if you do get ill and need medical assistance, take advice as to the best facilities around. Basic medicaments are made to Indian Pharmacopoea (IP) standards, and most medicines are available without prescription (always check the sell-by date). **Hospitals** vary in standard: private clinics and mission hospitals are often better than state-run ones, but may not have the same facilities. Hospitals in big cities, including university or medical-school hospitals, are generally pretty good, and cities such as Delhi, Mumbai and Bengaluru (Bangalore) boast state-of-the-art medical facilities, but at a price. Many hospitals require patients (even emergency cases) to buy necessities such as medicines, plaster casts and vaccines, and to pay for X-rays, before procedures are carried out. Remember to keep receipts for insurance reimbursements.

However, **government hospitals** provide all surgical and after-care services free of charge and in most other state medical institutions charges are usually so low that for minor treatment the expense may well be lower than the initial "excess" on your insurance. You will, however, need a companion to stay, or you'll have to come to an arrangement with one of the hospital cleaners, to help you out in hospital – relatives are expected to wash, feed and generally take care of the patient. Beware of scams by private clinics in tourist towns such as Agra where there have been reports of overcharging and misdiagnosis by doctors to claim insurance money. Addresses of foreign consulates (who will advise in an emergency), and of clinics and hospitals, can be found in the Listings sections in the accounts of major towns in this book.

Getting around

Inter-city transport in India may not be the fastest or the most comfortable in the world, but it's cheap, goes more or less everywhere, and generally gives you the option of train or bus, sometimes plane, and occasionally even boat. Transport around town comes in even more permutations, ranging in Kolkata (Calcutta), for example, from human-pulled rickshaws to a spanking new metro system.

Whether you're on road or rail, public transport or your own vehicle, India offers the chance to try out some classics: narrow-gauge railways, steam locomotives, the Ambassador car and the Enfield Bullet motorbike – indeed some people come to India for these alone.

By train

Travelling by train is one of India's classic experiences. The national rail network covers almost the entire country; only a few places (such as the mountainous regions of Sikkim, Ladakh, Uttarakhand (Uttaranchal) and most of Himachal Pradesh) are inaccessible by train. Although the railway system might look like chaos, it does work, and generally better than you might expect. Trains are often late of course, sometimes by hours rather than minutes, but they do run, and when the train you've been waiting for rolls into the station, the reservation you made halfway across the country several weeks ago will be on a list pasted to the side of your carriage.

It's worth bearing in mind, with journeys frequently lasting twelve hours or more, that an **overnight train** can save you a day's travelling and a night's hotel bill, assuming you sleep well on trains. When travelling overnight, always padlock your bag to your bunk; an attached chain is usually provided beneath the seat of the lower bunk.

Indian Railway's website at Ⓦwww .indianrail.gov.in is an extremely useful source of information about latest fares, timetables and availability of berths.

Types of train

There are three basic types of passenger train in India. You're most likely to use long-distance **inter-city trains** (called "express" or "mail") along with the speedier "**super-fast**" air-conditioned trains – these include the various "Rajdhani" expresses, which link Delhi with cities nationwide, and "Shatabdi" expresses, daytime trains that connect major cities within an eight-hour travelling distance. There are also painfully slow local "**passenger**" trains, which stop everywhere, and which you'll only use if you want to get right off the beaten track. In addition to these three basic types of train, there are also a few dedicated **tourist trains** and other special services, such as the famous Palace on Wheels and the toy train to Darjeeling – see p.47 for more on these.

Classes of train travel

Indian Railways distinguishes between no fewer than seven **classes** of travel. Different types of train carry different classes of carriage, though you'll seldom have more than four to choose from any one service. The simplest and cheapest class, used by

Travel details

At the end of each chapter in this book, you'll find a **Travel details** section summarizing major transport connections in the relevant state. In addition, boxes at the end of each major city detail **moving on** from that city.

the majority of Indians, is **second-class unreserved** (or "second seating"). These basic carriages have hard wooden seats and often become incredibly packed during the day – bearable for shortish daytime journeys, but best avoided for longer trips and (especially) overnight travel, unless you're exceptionally hardy or unusually poor. On the plus side, fares in second-class unreserved are so cheap as to be virtually free. It also represents a way of getting on a train at the last minute if you haven't been able to secure a reserved seat.

Far more civilized, and only around fifty percent more expensive, is **second-class sleeper** ("sleeper class"), consisting of carriages of three-tiered padded bunks that convert to seats during the day. All seats in these carriages must be booked in advance even for daytime journeys, meaning that they don't get horrendously overcrowded like second-class unreserved, although there's usually still plenty going on, with itinerant chai- and coffee-sellers, travelling musicians, beggars and sweepers passing through the carriages. Overnight trips in second-class sleeper compartments are reasonably comfy. **First class** consists of non-a/c seating in comfortable if ageing compartments of two to four berths, though this class is being phased out and is now found on relatively few trains.

The other four classes are all air-conditioned (available only on inter-city and super-fast trains). **A/c chair car** (often denoted as "CC") is found almost exclusively on superfast services and consists of comfortable reclining seats; they're really designed for daytime travel, since they don't convert to bunks, and aren't generally found on overnight services. Shatabdi expresses are made up entirely of chair-car carriages (ordinary a/c chair car and, for double the price, an executive a/c chair car).

There are three classes of air-conditioned sleepers. The cheapest, **third-class a/c**, has open carriages with three-tier bunks – basically the same as second-class sleeper, except with a/c. Less crowded (and found on more services) is **second-class a/c**, which has two-tier berths. Most comfortable of all is **first-class a/c**, which consists of two-tier bunks in two- or four-person private compartments, complete with carpeting and relatively presentable bathrooms – although fares can work out only slightly cheaper than taking a plane.

Note that bed linen is provided free on most a/c services, while bottled water, snacks and simple meals are included in the ticket price of Rajdhani and Shatabdi services.

Ladies' compartments exist on all overnight trains for women travelling on their own or with other women; they are usually small and can be full of noisy kids, but can give untold relief to women travellers who otherwise have to endure incessant staring in the open section of the carriage. They can be a good place to meet Indian women, particularly if you like (or are with) children. Some stations also have ladies-only waiting rooms.

Timetables and fares

Easily the most convenient place to check timetables, fares and availability is online at

Rail records

Comprising 42,000 miles (over 60,000km) of track and 14,000 locomotives, which transport an average of 12 million passengers every day, India's **rail network** is the second largest in the world. It's also the biggest employer on the planet, with a workforce of around 1.6 million.

One record the country's transport ministers are somewhat less proud of, however, is the Indian Railways' **accident rate**. Four to five hundred crashes occur annually in India, causing between seven and eight hundred fatalities, which makes this the most dangerous rail network in the world, by a long chalk. Having said that, travelling by rail is considerably safer than using the buses. According to official statistics, an average of 233 people die on the country's roads every day – that's 85,000 annually.

@ www.indianrail.gov.in. Alternatively, Indian Railways' *Trains at a Glance* (Rs30; updated twice a year) contains timetables of all intercity and superfast trains and is available from information counters and newsstands at all main stations.

All rail **fares** are calculated according to the exact distance travelled. *Trains at a Glance* prints a chart of fares by kilometres, and also gives the distance in kilometres of stations along each route in the timetables, making it possible to calculate what the basic fare will be for any given journey. You can also check fares online. For the purposes of illustration, fares from Delhi to Agra (195km) are currently Rs79 (second-class unreserved), Rs121 (second-class sleeper), Rs266 (chair car), Rs311 (third-class a/c), Rs427 (second-class a/c) and Rs756 (first-class a/c).

Reserving tickets

It's important to plan your train journeys in advance, as demand often makes it impossible to buy a long-distance ticket on the same day that you want to travel (although the new Tatkal quota system – see below – has made life a little easier). Travellers following tight itineraries tend to buy their departure tickets from particular towns the moment they arrive, to avoid having to trek out to the station again. At most large stations, it's possible to reserve tickets for journeys starting elsewhere in the country. You can even book tickets for specific journeys before you leave home, with Indian Railways representatives abroad (see p.47). They accept bookings up to six months in advance, with a minimum of one month for first class, and three months for second.

When **reserving a ticket**, the first thing you'll have to do is fill in a little form at the booking office stating your name, age and sex, your proposed date of travel, and the train you wish to catch (giving the train's **name and number**, which should be displayed on a timetable in the booking hall). Most stations have computerized booking counters and you'll be told immediately whether or not seats are available. **Reservation offices** in the main stations are generally open from Monday to Saturday from 8am to 8pm, and on Sunday to 2pm. In larger cities, major stations have special tourist sections to cut queues for foreigners, with helpful English-speaking staff. Elsewhere, buying a ticket can often involve a longish wait, though women can often bypass this by simply walking to the head of the queue and forming their own "ladies' queue" (men may often find ladies pushing in front of them on the same principle). Some stations also operate a number system of queuing, allowing you to repair to the chai stall or check the timetable until your number is called. A good alternative to queuing yourself is to get someone else to buy your ticket for you. Many **travel agents** will do this for a small fee (typically around Rs30–50); alternatively, ask at your guesthouses if they can sort it out.

It's now also possible to **book train tickets online** at @ www.irctc.co.in. The site is good, albeit slow, and only works during Indian opening hours. You can book up to sixty days in advance. Having booked your travel, you can then print out your own e-tickets, taking this along with some photo ID, such as a passport, when you board the train.

If there are no places available on the train you want, you have a number of choices. First, some seats and berths are set aside as a "**tourist quota**" – ask at the tourist counter if you can get in on this, or else try the stationmaster. This quota is available in advance but usually only at major or originating stations. Failing that, other special quotas such as one for "emergencies", only released on the day of travel, may remain unused – however, if you get a booking on the emergency quota and a pukka emergency or VIP turns up, you lose the reservation. Alternatively, you can stump up extra cash for a Tatkal ticket (see p.46), which guarantees you access to a special ten-percent quota on most trains, though certain catches and conditions apply.

RAC – or "Reservation Against Cancellation" – tickets are another option, giving you priority if sleepers do become available – the ticket clerk should be able to tell you your chances. With an RAC ticket you are allowed onto the train and can sit until the conductor can find you a berth. The worst sort of ticket to have is a wait-listed one – identifiable by the letter "W" prefixing your passenger number – which will allow you onto the train but not in a reserved compartment; in this case go and see the ticket inspector as soon as possible to persuade him to find you a place if one is free: something usually is, but you'll be stuck in unreserved if it isn't. Wait-listed ticket holders are not allowed onto Shatabdi and Rajdhani trains. Finally, and as a last resort if you get on where the train starts its journey, baksheesh may persuade a ticket controller to "reserve" you an unreserved seat. You could even fight your way on and grab one yourself, although your chances are slim.

Another possibility is to try to get a **Tatkal** ticket. A quota of ten percent of places on the more important intercity services is reserved under this scheme, bookable at any computerized office. Tickets are released from 8am five days before the train departs, and there's an extra charge of Rs150 in sleeper or chair car, and Rs300 in first or a/c sleepers. The real catch, however, is that you also have to pay for the entire length of the journey from originating to terminating station, however much or little of the ride you do, meaning that Tatkal obviously isn't worth it if, for instance, you want to get on the Guwahati–Kanniyakumari Express between Trichy and Madurai. If you're covering most of the route, though, you're pretty well guaranteed to find a place, especially if you get in the day before, as a lot of resident Indians have been put off by the price hike. One of the routes on which Tatkal is most likely to assist foreign travellers is **Mumbai–Goa**, on the Konkan Railway, where standard tickets sell out weeks in advance and are thus not available to tourists newly arrived in the country (unless they've booked at premium rates via Indian Railways agents abroad).

The only other alternative to reserving a ticket through these channels is to simply buy an unreserved second-class ticket, then board the train and ask the ticket collector if there are any reserved seats available. Obviously this is very much a question of pot luck, and not recommended for long journeys, although potentially useful for short trips. Note that you must have some form of valid ticket

Indrail passes

Indrail passes, sold to foreigners and Indians resident abroad, cover all fares and reservation fees for periods ranging from half a day to ninety days. Even if you travel a lot, this works out considerably more expensive than buying your tickets individually (especially in second class), but it will save you queuing for tickets, allow you to make and cancel reservations with impunity (and without charge), and generally smooth your way in, for example, finding a seat or berth on a "full" train: passholders get priority for tourist quota places. Indrail passes are available, for sterling or US dollars, at main station tourist counters in India, and outside the country at IR agents (see opposite). If you're travelling **from the UK**, Dr Dandapani of SD Enterprises Ltd (see opposite) is an excellent contact, providing information on all aspects of travel on Indian Railways.

	a/c First-Class Sleeper, or a/c Chair car		First-Class or a/c		Second-Class	
	Adult	Child	Adult	Child	Adult	Child
4 days*	$220	$110	$110	$55	$50	$25
7 days	$270	$135	$135	$68	$80	$40
15 days	$370	$185	$185	$95	$90	$45
21 days	$396	$198	$198	$100	$100	$50
30 days	$495	$248	$248	$125	$125	$63
60 days	$800	$400	$400	$200	$185	$95
90 days	$1060	$530	$530	$265	$235	$120

Children under 5 travel free
*For sale outside India only

before you board the train or you'll face a fine. In addition, if you have an unreserved ticket and travel in a sleeper carriage, even if it isn't full, you'll be charged a Rs60 fine as well as the difference in fare.

Tourist trains and other special services

Inspired by the Orient Express, Indian Railways runs two packaged holidays on luxury tourist trains, with exorbitant prices charged in dollars. The flagship of the scheme is the **Palace on Wheels**, with luxurious ex-maharajas' carriages updated into modern air-conditioned coaches, still decorated with the original designs. The all-inclusive, one-week whistle-stop tour (Sept–April weekly) starts from Delhi and tours through Jaipur and Jodhpur to the sands of Jaisalmer before turning south to Udaipur and returning via Agra; prices start from around £2400/US$4680 per person for the full trip, with discounts off season (Sept & April). The similar *Heritage on Wheels* makes a four-day trip through Jaipur, Shekhawati and Bikaner (Sept–April; from £450/US$880).

Other alternatives include the *Fairy Queen*, driven by the oldest working steam engine in the world, which makes a two-day trip through eastern Rajasthan to Alwar and the Sariska Tiger Reserve (Oct–Feb twice monthly; around £850/US$1660); and the *Royal Orient*, with thirteen lavishly decorated saloon cars, which travels from Delhi through southern Rajasthan to Gujarat (Oct–March; around £850/US$1660).

The *Palace on Wheels* and *Heritage on Wheels* can be booked through RTDC, Bikaner House, Pandara Road, New Delhi (☏011/2338 1884); the *Fairy Queen* through the Tourism Directorate, Rail Bhawan, New Delhi (☏011/2338 3000); and the *Royal Orient* through the Tourism Corporation of Gujarat, II Floor, A–6, State Emporia Complex, Baba Kharak Singh Marg, New Delhi (☏011/2336 4724). Alternatively, book online at ⓦwww.indiarailtours.com.

There are also a few **narrow-gauge** lines (often referred to as "toy trains"), notably to the hill stations of Darjeeling (now a World Heritage line), Shimla, Matheran and Ootacamund. Although being phased out, steam locomotives are still used on the first and last (the latter on Sun only) of these, and you may well see some in use in shunting yards, but they are fast disappearing. Almost all trains nowadays are diesel-hauled, although some main and suburban lines are electric.

Indian Railways sales agents abroad

Australia Adventure World, 73 Walker St (PO Box 480), N Sydney, NSW 2059 ☏02/9956 7766, ⓦwww.adventureworld.com.au.
UK SD Enterprises Ltd, 103 Wembley Park Drive, Wembley, Middx HA9 8HG ☏020/8903 3411, ⓦwww.indiarail.co.uk.

By air

Considering the huge distances involved in getting around the country, and the time it takes to get from A to B, **flying** is an attractive option, despite the cost – the journey from Delhi to Chennai, for example, takes a mere 2hr 30min by plane compared to 36 hours on the train. Delays and cancellations can whittle away the time advantage, especially over small distances, but if you're short of time and plan to cover a lot of ground, flying can be a godsend. There's also been a massive proliferation of privately run domestic airlines in India in recent years, with more planes covering more routes than ever before.

As with train tickets, making an airline **booking** can be a time-consuming business – it's much easier to book through your hotel or a travel agent – we've listed useful agents throughout the Guide. If you haven't got a confirmed seat, be sure to get to the airport early; even if you have got a confirmed seat, always reconfirm 72 hours before your flight. Airlines have **offices** or accredited agents in all the places they fly to, listed in this book in the relevant Guide chapters. Children under twelve pay half fare and under-twos (one per adult) pay ten percent.

With so many competing airlines, it's virtually impossible to generalize about **fares**. Flights on popular routes can be extremely cheap, with no-frills carriers like Air Deccan offering flights from Delhi to Mumbai, for example from around £25/$50. The best advice is to shop around.

The whole Indian aviation market is currently in a state of massive flux, so don't be surprised if new companies have entered the market by the time you read this (or some of the ones listed below have disappeared). The situation is further complicated by the ongoing merger of the two huge state-owned carriers, **Air India** and **Indian Airlines** (along with their respective subsidiaries, Air-India Express and Alliance Airways). The two airlines formally merged in August 2007, though it's expected to take at least two years for the two airlines to fully integrate their various operations. In addition, leading private carriers Kingfisher and Air Deccan also announced merger proposals in late 2007.

Domestic airlines in India

Air Deccan ⓦ www.airdeccan.net. India's original low-cost airline, which has slashed fares across the board by adopting the "no-frills" approach. They fly to 35 destinations in India, often at rock-bottom prices.

Air India ⓦ www.airindia.com. The nation's flagship international carrier also runs a few services between Mumbai and Delhi, Kolkata, Bengaluru (Bangalore), Chennai and Thiruvananthapuram.

Air-India Express ⓦ www.airindiaexpress.in. Low-cost subsidiary of Air India, offering a limited number of domestic flights.

Go Air ⓦ www.goair.in. Low-cost airline, with good connections across the south.

Indian Airlines ⓦ www.indian-airlines.nic.in. The leading domestic carrier, with flights nationwide serving over 140 routes.

IndiGo ⓦ book.goindigo.in. One of the newer and smaller private airlines, with services to fourteen destinations countrywide.

Jet Airways ⓦ www.jetairways.com. India's biggest private airline, flying many of the major routes covered by Indian Airlines, generally providing a more efficient, dynamic and slicker service than the national airline.

JetLite (formerly Air Sahara) ⓦ www.jetlite.com. Recently acquired by Jet Airways (hence the new name). Based in Delhi, but with services nationwide.

Kingfisher Airlines ⓦ www.flykingfisher .com. India's answer to Virgin Atlantic, launched in May 2005 by flamboyant beer tycoon Vijay Mallya. Kingfisher offers a flashier experience than the competition, calling its planes "funliners" and kitting them out with designer white-and-red upholstery and exclusively female cabin crews of so-called "flying models".

Spicejet ⓦ www.spicejet.com. Based in Delhi, prioritizing low prices over frills.

By bus

Although trains are generally the most characterful and comfortable way to travel in India, there are some places, particularly in the Himalayas, not covered by the rail network, or where trains are inconvenient. By contrast, **buses** go almost everywhere, usually more frequently than trains (though mostly in daylight hours), and are also sometimes faster (including in parts of Rajasthan and other places without broad-gauge track). Going by bus also usually saves you the bother of reserving a ticket in advance.

Services vary enormously in terms of price and standard. Ramshackle **government-run buses**, packed with people, livestock and luggage, cover most routes, both short- and long-distance. In addition, popular routes between larger cities, towns and resorts are usually covered by **private buses**. These tend to be more comfortable, with extra legroom, tinted windows and padded reclining seats. Note, however, that smaller private bus companies may be only semi-legal and have little backup in case of breakdown.

The description of the service usually gives some clue about the level of comfort. "Ordinary" buses usually have minimally padded, bench-like seats with upright backs. "Deluxe" or "luxury" are more or less interchangeable terms but sometimes the term deluxe signifies a luxury bus past its sell-by date; occasionally a bus will be described as a "2 by 2" which means a deluxe bus with just two seats on either side of the aisle. When applied to government services, these may hardly differ from "ordinary" buses, but with private companies, they should guarantee a softer, individual seat. It's worth asking when booking if your bus will have a video or music system (a "video bus"), as their deafening noise ruins any chances of sleep. Always try to avoid the back seats – they accentuate bumpy roads.

Luggage travels in the hatch of private buses – for which you will have to part with about Rs5–10 as "security" for the safekeeping of your bags. On state-run buses, you can usually squeeze it into an unobtrusive corner, although you may sometimes be requested to have it travel on the roof (you may be able to travel up there yourself if the bus is too crowded, though it's dangerous and illegal); check that it's well secured (ideally, lock it there) and not liable to get squashed. Baksheesh is in order for whoever puts it up there for you.

Buying a bus ticket is usually less of an ordeal than buying a train ticket, although at large city bus stations there may be twenty or so counters, each assigned to a different route. When you buy your ticket you'll be given the registration number of the bus and, sometimes, a seat number. As at railway stations, women can form a separate, quicker, "ladies' queue". You can usually only pay on board on most ordinary state buses, and at bus stands outside major cities. Prior booking is usually available and preferable for express and private services, and it's a good idea to check with the agent exactly where the bus will depart from. You can usually pay on board private buses too, though doing so reduces your chances of a seat.

By boat

Apart from river ferries, few **boat services** run in India. The Andaman Islands are connected to Kolkata (Calcutta) and Chennai by boat – as well as to each other. Kerala has a regular passenger service with a number of services operating out of Alappuzha and Kollam, including the popular "backwater trip" between the two. The Sunderbans in the delta region to the south of Kolkata (Calcutta) is only accessible by boat.

By car

It is much more usual for tourists to be driven in India than it is for them to drive themselves; **car rental** firms operate on the basis of supplying **chauffeur-driven vehicles**, and taxis are available at cheap daily rates. Arranged through tourist offices, local car rental firms, or branches of Hertz, Budget or Europcar, a chauffeur-driven car will run to about £25/$40 per day. On longer trips, the driver sleeps in the car. The big international chains are the best bet for **self-drive car rental**; in India they charge around thirty percent less than chauffeur-driven, with a Rs1000 deposit against damage, though if

you pay in your home country it can cost a whole lot more.

Driving in India is not for beginners. If you do drive yourself, expect the unexpected, and expect other drivers to take whatever liberties they can get away with. Traffic circulates on the left, but don't expect road regulations to be obeyed; generally the vehicle in front seems to have right of way, so at busy intersections or roundabouts (rotaries) drivers try and get out in front as soon as possible. Another unstated law of the road is that might is right.

Traffic in the cities is heavy and undisciplined; vehicles cut in and out without warning, and pedestrians, cyclists and cows wander nonchalantly down the middle of the road. In the country the roads are narrow, in terrible repair, and hogged by overloaded Tata trucks that move aside for nobody, while something slow-moving like a bullock cart or a herd of goats can take up the whole road. To overtake, sound your horn (an essential item on Indian roads) – the driver in front will signal if it is safe to do so; if not, he will wave his hand, palm downwards, up and down. A huge number of potholes don't make for a smooth ride either. Furthermore, during the monsoon roads can become flooded; rivers burst their banks and bridges get washed away. Ask local people before you set off, and proceed with caution, sticking to main highways if possible.

You should have an **international driving licence** to drive in India, but this is often overlooked if you have your licence from home. Insurance is compulsory, but not expensive. Car seat belts are not compulsory in most cities (though they are now mandatory in Delhi, Mumbai and a few other places) but are very strongly recommended. Accident rates are high, and you should be on your guard at all times. It is particularly dangerous to drive at night – not everyone uses lights, and bullock carts don't have any. If you have an **accident**, it might be an idea to leave the scene quickly and go straight to the police to report it; mobs can assemble fast, especially if pedestrians or cows are involved.

Fuel is reasonably cheap compared to home, but the state of the roads will take its toll, and mechanics are not always very reliable, so a knowledge of vehicle maintenance is a help, as is a checkup every so often. Luckily, if you get a flat tyre, puncture-wallahs can be easily found almost everywhere.

To **import a car or motorbike** into India, you'll have to show a carnet de passage, a document intended to ensure that you don't sell the vehicle illegally. These are available from foreign motoring organizations such as the AA. It's also worth bringing a few basic spares, as parts for foreign makes can be hard to find in India, although low-quality imitations are more widely available. All in all, the route is arduous, and bringing a vehicle to India is something of a commitment.

The classic Indian automobile is the **Hindustan Ambassador** (basically a Morris Oxford), nowadays largely superseded by more modern vehicles such as the Maruti Suzuki. Renting a car, you'll probably have a choice of these two or others such as the Land Rover-like Tata Sumo, popular in hill regions. Worth knowing if you're interested in buying one is that the Ambassador is not famed for its mod cons or low mpg, but has a certain style and historical interest; later models make little sense as prices are higher and quality lower than in the West.

By motorbike

Riding a **motorbike** around India has become increasingly popular but is not without its hazards. Beside the appalling road conditions (see p.49) and the ensuing fatigue, renting a bike, unless you are well versed in maintenance, can be a bit of a nightmare, with breakdowns often in the most inconvenient places. If you do break down in the middle of nowhere, you may need to flag down an empty truck to transport the bike to the nearest town for repairs. Motorbike rental is available in some tourist towns and useful for local use, but the quality of the bikes is never assured. You could bring your own, but then you'll need to consider spares. Helmets are best brought from home.

Buying a motorbike in India is a much more reasonable proposition, and again, if it's an old British classic you're after, the Enfield Bullet (350 model), sold cheapest in Puducherry, on the Tamil Nadu coast, leads the field (check one of several motoring magazines for details and reviews). If low price and practicality are your priorities, however, a smaller model, perhaps even a moped or a scooter, might better fit the bill. Many Japanese bikes are now made in India, as are Vespas and Lambrettas, and various types of motorcycles can easily be bought new or **secondhand**. Garages and repair shops are a good place to start; Delhi's Karol Bagh area is renowned for its motorcycle shops (see p.141). Obviously, you'll have to haggle over the price, but you can expect to pay half to two-thirds the original price for a bike in reasonable condition. Given the right bargaining skills, you can sell it again later for a similar price – perhaps to another foreign traveller – by advertising it in hotels and restaurants. A certain amount of bureaucracy is involved in transferring vehicle ownership, but a garage should be able to put you on to a broker ("auto consultant") who, for a modest commission (around Rs500), will help you find a seller or a buyer, and do the necessary paperwork. A motorbike can be taken in the luggage car of a train for the same price as a second-class passenger fare (get a form and pay a small fee at the station luggage office).

Some knowledge of **mechanics** is necessary to ensure that you're not being sold a pup, so if you aren't too savvy yourself, make sure you take someone who is able to give the once-over to important parts like the engine, forks, brakes and suspension. Experienced overlanders often claim that making sure the seat is comfy is the crucial element to an enjoyable trip.

If you are unsure of negotiating your own bike or travelling around on your own you may consider joining one of several motorbike tours offered by the following companies:

Blazing Trails Blazing Trails UK ☎01293/533338, ⊛www.blazingtrailstours.com.
Classic Bike Adventure India Goa ☎0832/226 8467, ⊛www.classic-bike-india.de.
Ferris Wheels Motorcycle Safaris Australia ☎02/9970 6370, ⊛www.ferriswheels.com.au.
H-C Travel UK ☎01256/770775, ⊛www .hctravel.com.
Himalayan Roadrunners US ☎802/738 6500, ⊛www.ridehigh.com.

By bicycle

In many ways a **bicycle** is the ideal form of transport in India, offering total independence without loss of contact with local people. You can camp out, though there are cheap lodgings in almost every village – take the bike into your room with you – and, if you get tired of pedalling, you can put it on top of a bus as luggage, or transport it by train.

Bringing a bike from abroad requires no carnet or special paperwork, but spare parts and accessories may be of different sizes and standards in India, and you may have to improvise. Bring basic spares and tools, and a pump. **Buying a bike** in India couldn't be easier, since most towns have cycle shops and even entire markets devoted to bikes. The advantages of a local bike are that spare parts are easy to get, locally produced tools and parts will fit, and your bike will not draw a crowd every time you park it. Disadvantages are that Indian bikes tend to be heavier and less state-of-the-art than ones from abroad; mountain bikes are beginning to appear in cities and bigger towns, but with insufficient gears and a low level of equipment, they're not worth buying. Selling should be quite easy: you won't get a tremendously good deal at a cycle market, but you may well be able to sell privately, or even to a rental shop.

Bicycles can be **rented** in most towns, usually for local use only: this is a good way to find out if your legs and bum can survive an Indian bike before buying one. Rates can be anything from Rs10 to Rs50 per day, and you may have to leave a deposit or your passport as security. Several adventure-tour operators such as Exodus (see p.31) offer bicycle tours of the country, with most customers bringing their own cycles.

As for contacts, International Bicycle Fund in the US (☏206/767-0848, ⦿www.ibike .org) publishes information and offers advice on bicycle travel around the world and maintains a useful website. In India, the Cycle Federation of India, C-5A/262, DDA Flats, Janak Puri, New Delhi 110058 (☏011/2255 3006), is the main cycle-sports organization.

City transport

Transport around towns takes various forms. City **buses** can get unbelievably crowded, so beware of pickpockets, razor-armed pocket-slitters and "Eve-teasers" (see p.77); the same applies to **suburban trains** in Mumbai (Chennai is about the only other place where you might want to use trains for local city transport). Any visitor to Delhi or Kolkata (Calcutta) will be amazed by the clean efficiency of India's two **metro** systems.

You can also take **taxis**, usually rather battered Ambassadors (painted black and yellow in the large cities) and Maruti omnivans. With luck, the driver will agree to use the meter; in theory you're within your rights to call the police if he doesn't, but the usual compromise is to agree a fare for the journey before you get in. Naturally, it helps to have an idea in advance what the fare should be, though any figures quoted in this or any other book should be treated as being the broadest of guidelines only. From places such as main stations, you may be able to find other passengers to share a taxi to the town centre. Many stations, and certainly most airports, operate **pre-paid taxi schemes** with set fares that you pay before departure; more expensive pre-paid limousines are also available.

The **auto-rickshaw**, that most Indian of vehicles, is the front half of a motor scooter with a couple of seats mounted on the back. Cheaper than taxis, better at nipping in and out of traffic, and usually metered (although again very few drivers are willing to use theirs and you should agree a fare before setting off), auto-rickshaws are a little unstable and their drivers often rather reckless, but that's all part of the fun. In major tourist centres rickshaw-wallahs can, however, hassle you endlessly on the street, often shoving themselves right in your path to prevent you from ignoring them, and once you're inside they may take you to several shops before reaching your destination. Moreover, agreeing a price before the journey will not necessarily stop your rickshaw-wallah reopening discussion when the trip is under way or at its end. In general it is better to hail a rickshaw than to take one that's been following you, and to avoid those that hang around outside posh hotels.

Some towns also have larger versions of auto-rickshaws known as **tempos** (or Vikrams), with six or eight seats behind, which usually ply fixed routes at flat fares. Here and there, you'll also come across horse-drawn carriages, or **tongas**. Tugged by underfed and often lame horses, these are the least popular with tourists.

Slower and cheaper still is the **cycle rickshaw** – basically a glorified tricycle. Foreign visitors often feel uncomfortable about travelling this way; except in the major tourist cities, cycle rickshaw-wallahs are invariably emaciated pavement-dwellers who earn only a pittance for their pains. In the

end, though, to deny them your custom on those grounds is spurious logic; they will earn even less if you don't use them. Also you will invariably pay a bit more than a local would. Only in Kolkata (Calcutta) do the rickshaw-wallahs continue to haul the city's pukka rickshaws on foot.

If you want to see a variety of places around town, consider hiring a taxi, rickshaw or auto-rickshaw for the day. Find a driver who speaks English reasonably well, and agree a price beforehand. You will probably find it a lot cheaper than you imagine: the driver will invariably act as a guide and source of local knowledge, and tipping is usually in order.

Accommodation

There are far more Indians travelling around their own country at any one time – whether for holidays, on pilgrimages, or for business – than there are foreign tourists, and a vast infrastructure of hotels and guesthouses caters for their needs. On the whole, accommodation, like so many other things in India, provides good value for money, though in the major cities, especially, expect to pay international prices for luxury establishments that provide Western-style comforts and service.

Budget accommodation

While accommodation prices in India are generally on the up, there's still an abundance of inexpensive **hotels** and **hostels**, catering for foreign backpackers, tourists and less well-off Indians. Most charge Rs200–300 for a double room, although rates outside big cities and tourist centres may fall below Rs150 (roughly £2/$4). The rock-bottom option is usually in a dormitory of a hostel or hotel, where you may pay as little as Rs50. Even cheaper still are **dharamshalas**, hostels run by religious establishments and pilgrim guesthouses (see p.55).

Budget accommodation varies from filthy fleapits to homely guesthouses and, naturally, tends to be cheaper the further you

get off the beaten track. It's most expensive in Delhi and Mumbai, where prices are at least double those for equivalent accommodation in most other cities.

The cheapest rooms usually have shared showers and toilets and cold water only, although increasing numbers of places are offering en-suite bathrooms (or "attached" rooms, as they're known locally) and hot water, either on tap or in a bucket. Even so, it's always wise to check out the state of the bathrooms and toilets before taking a room. Bed bugs and mosquitoes are other things to check for – splotches of blood around the bed and on the walls where people have squashed them are tell-tale signs.

If a **taxi driver** or **rickshaw-wallah** tells you that the place you ask for is full, closed

Accommodation price codes

All **accommodation prices** in this book are **coded** using the symbols below. The prices given are for a double room; in the case of dorms, we give the per-person price in rupees. Most mid-range and all expensive and luxury hotels charge a luxury tax of around ten to fifteen percent, and a local tax of around five percent. All taxes are included in the prices we quote.

India doesn't have a **tourist season** as such, and most accommodation keeps the same prices throughout the year. Certain resorts however, and some spots on established tourist trails, do experience some variation and will be more expensive, or less negotiable, when demand is at its peak. For the hill stations, this will be in the summer (April–July); for Rajasthan, Goa and other beach resorts in the south, it'll be the winter, especially around Christmas and New Year. We've mentioned regional price fluctuations in the accommodation listings throughout the guide chapters.

①	Under Rs200	④	Rs501–1000	⑦	Rs2001–3000
②	Rs201–300	⑤	Rs1001–1500	⑧	Rs3001–5000
③	Rs301–500	⑥	Rs1501–2000	⑨	Over Rs5001

or has moved, it's more than likely that it's because he wants to take you to a hotel that pays him commission – added, in some cases, to your bill. Hotel touts operate in many popular tourist spots, working for commission from the hotels they take you to; this can become annoying, but sometimes paying the little extra can be well worth it, especially if you arrive alone in a new place at night.

Mid-range hotels

Even if you value your creature comforts, you don't need to pay through the nose for them. A large clean room, freshly made bed, your own spotless bathroom and hot and cold running water can still cost as little as Rs400 (£5/$10). Extras that bump up the price include local taxes, a TV, mosquito nets, a balcony and, above all, **air-conditioning**. Abbreviated in this book (and in India itself) as a/c, air-conditioning is not necessarily the advantage you might expect – in some hotels you can find yourself paying double for a system that is so dust-choked and noisy as to be more of a drawback than an advantage. Some offer **air-coolers** instead of a/c – these can be noisy and are less effective than full-blown a/c, but much better than just a fan. They're only found in drier climes as they don't work in areas of extreme humidity such as along the coasts of South India and the Bay of Bengal. Many medium-priced hotels also have attached restaurants, and also offer room service.

Most state governments run their own hotels sometime known as **"tourist bungalows"**, similar to mid-range hotels, but sometimes also offering cheaper dorms. They are usually good value, though they vary a lot from state to state. We've indicated such places throughout this guide by including the state acronym in the name – eg *MPTDC Palace* (standing for Madhya Pradesh Tourist Development Corporation). Bookings for state-run hotels can be made in advance through the state tourist offices throughout the country.

Upmarket hotels

Most luxury hotels in India fall into one of two categories. Most popular with foreign tourists are the country's **heritage hotels**, typically occupying old forts, palaces, hunting lodges, havelis, Raj-era bungalows and the like, brimming with old-world atmosphere and offering a quintessentially Indian "experience", complete with turbaned bellboys and antique automobiles. Heritage properties can be found countrywide, although by far the greatest concentration is in **Rajasthan**, which positively overflows with venerable old properties, ranging from ultra-luxurious and world-famous establishments like the *Rambagh Palace* in Jaipur and the *Umaid Bhawan Palace* in Jaipur to rickety old ancestral forts which retain their original decor, paint and plumbing from a hundred years past. Prices vary accordingly, from as

Accommodation practicalities

Check-out time is often noon, but confirm this when you arrive: some expect you out by 9am, but many others operate a 24-hour system, under which you are simply obliged to leave by the same time as you arrived. Some places let you use their facilities after the official check-out time, sometimes for a small charge, others won't even let you leave your baggage after check-out unless you pay for another night.

Unfortunately, not all hotels offer **single rooms**, so it can often work out more expensive to travel alone; in hotels that don't, you may be able to negotiate a slight discount. It's not unusual to find rooms with three or four beds, however – great value for families and small groups.

In cheap hotels and hostels, you needn't expect any additions to your basic bill, but as you go up the scale, you'll find **taxes** and **service charges** creeping in, sometimes adding as much as a third on top of the original tariff. Service is generally ten percent, but taxes are a matter for local governments and vary from state to state.

Like most other things in India, the price of a room may well be open to **negotiation**. If you think the price is too high, or if all the hotels in town are empty, try haggling. You may get nowhere – but nothing ventured, nothing gained.

little as $40 per night up to $500 or more: relatively expensive by Indian standards, although still excellent value compared to what you'd pay back home.

There are also plenty of modern **chain hotels** in the larger cities and tourist resorts, run by familiar international names like Sheraton and Hilton, as well as the Indian Taj and Oberoi groups. These tend to be slick and functional rather than memorable, although the Oberoi and Aman chains both boast a clutch of marvellously atmospheric modern properties built in traditional style, which show contemporary India at its most sumptuously hedonistic – as they should do, with room rates of up to $1000 per night.

Note that many top-end hotels offer significant **discounts** if you book through their website. You may also find discounts

through travel agencies such as the Travel Corporation of India, who offer up to sixty percent off certain luxury hotels, depending on the season.

Other options

Many railway stations have **"retiring rooms"**: basic private rooms with a bed and bathroom (some stations also have dorms too). They can be handy if you're catching an early morning train and are usually amongst the cheapest accommodation available anywhere, but can be noisy. Retiring rooms cannot be booked in advance and are allocated on a first-come-first-serve basis; just turn up and ask if there's a vacancy.

In one or two places, it's possible to rent rooms in people's homes. In Rajasthan, Mumbai and Kerala the local tourist offices run **"paying guest"** or "homestay schemes" to place tourists with families offering lodging. Servas (ⓦwww.indiaservas.org), established in 1949 as a peace organization, is now devoted to providing homestays, representing some over six hundred hosts in India; you have to join before travelling by applying to the local Servas secretary (located via the website) – you then get a list of hosts to contact in the place you are visiting. Some people provide free accommodation, others are just day-hosts. There is no guarantee a bed will be provided – it's up to the individual.

Camping is possible too, although in most of the country it's hard to see why you'd want to be cooped up in a tent overnight when you could be sleeping on a cool *charpoi* (a sort of basic bed) on a roof terrace for a handful of rupees – let alone

why you'd choose to carry a tent around India in the first place. Except possibly on treks, it's not usual simply to pitch a tent in the countryside, though many hotels allow camping in their grounds. The YMCA runs a few sites, as do state governments (Maharashtra in particular), and the Scouts and Guides.

YMCAs and **YWCAs**, confined to big cities, are plusher and pricier than mid-range hotels. They are usually good value, but are often full, and some are exclusively single-sex. Official and nonofficial **youth hostels**, some run by state governments, are spread haphazardly across the country. They give HI cardholders a discount, but rarely exclude nonmembers, nor do they usually impose daytime closing. Prices match the cheapest hotels; where there is a youth hostel, it usually has a dormitory and may well be the best budget accommodation available – which goes especially for the Salvation Army ones.

Finally, **religious institutions**, particularly Sikh *gurudwaras*, offer accommodation for pilgrims and visitors, and may put up tourists; a donation is often expected, and certainly appreciated, but some of the bigger ones charge a fixed, nominal fee. Pilgrimage sites, especially those far from other accommodation, also have **dharamshalas** where visitors can stay – very cheap and very simple, usually with basic, communal washing facilities; some charitable institutions even have rooms with simple attached bathrooms. *Dharamshalas*, like *gurudwaras*, offer accommodation either on a donations system or charge a nominal fee, which can be as low as Rs20.

Food and drink

Indian food has a richly deserved reputation as one of the world's great cuisines. Stereotyped abroad as the ubiquitous "curry", the cooking of the Subcontinent covers a wealth of different culinary styles, with myriad regional variations and specialities, from the classic creamy meat and fruit Mughal dishes of the north through to the banana-leaf vegetarian thalis of the south.

The basic distinction in Indian food is between the cuisines of the north and south. **north Indian food** (which is the style generally found in Indian restaurants abroad) is characterized by its rich meat and vegetable dishes in thick tomato, onion and yoghurt-based sauces, accompanied by thick breads. **South Indian food**, by contrast, is almost exclusively vegetarian, with spicy chilli and coconut flavours and lots of rice, either served in its natural state or made into one of the south's distinctive range of pancakes, such as the *dosa*, *iddli* and *uttapam*.

For **vegetarians**, in particular, Indian food is a complete delight. Some of the Subcontinent's best food is meat-free, and even confirmed carnivores will find themselves tucking into delicious dhals and vegetable curries with relish. Most religious Hindus, and the majority of people in the south, don't eat meat or fish, while some orthodox Brahmins and Jains also avoid onions and garlic, which are thought to inflame the baser instincts. **Veganism** is not common, however; if you're vegan, you'll have to keep your eyes open for eggs and dairy products. Many eating places state whether they are vegetarian or non-vegetarian either on signs outside or at the top of the menu. The terms used in India (and throughout our eating listings) are "veg" and "non-veg". You'll also see "pure veg", which means that no eggs or alcohol are served. As a rule, **meat-eaters** should exercise caution in India: even when meat is available, especially in the larger towns, its quality can be poor, except in the best restaurants, and you won't get much in a dish anyway – especially in cheaper canteens where it's mainly there for flavouring. Hindus, of course, do not eat beef

and Muslims shun pork, so you'll only find those in a few Christian enclaves such as the beach areas of Goa, and Tibetan areas. Note that what is called "mutton" on menus is in fact goat.

Where to eat

Broadly speaking, eating establishments divide into three main types: cheap and unpretentious local cafés (known variously as *dhabas*, *bhojanalayas* and *udipis*); Indian restaurants aimed at more affluent locals; and tourist restaurants. **Dhabas** and **bhojanalayas** are cheap cafés, where food is basic but often good, consisting of vegetable curry, dhal (a kind of lentil broth), rice or Indian bread (the latter more standard in the north) and sometimes meat. Often found along the sides of highways, *dhabas* traditionally cater to truck drivers – one way of telling a good *dhaba* is to judge from the number of trucks parked outside. *Bhojanalayas* are basic eating places, usually found in towns (especially around bus stands and train stations) in the north and centre of the country; they tend to be vegetarian, especially those signed as "Vaishno". Both *dhabas* and *bhojanalayas* can be grubby – look them over before you commit yourself. The same is rarely true of their southern equivalent, **udipi** canteens, which serve cheap, delicious snacks such as masala dosa, *iddli*, *vadai* and rice-based dishes, all freshly cooked to order and dished up by uniformed waiters.

There are all sorts of **Indian restaurants**, veg and non-veg and typically catering to Indian businessmen and middle-class families. These are the places to go for reliably good Indian food at bargain prices. The more expensive Indian restaurants, such

For advice on **drinking water** in India, see p.36.
For a **glossary** of food terms, see pp.1405–1408.

as those in five-star hotels, can be very expensive by local standards, but offer a rare chance to try top-notch classic Indian cooking, and still at significantly cheaper prices than you'd pay back home – assuming you could find Indian food that good.

Tourist restaurants, found across India wherever there are significant numbers of western visitors, cater specifically for foreign travellers with unadventurous tastebuds, serving up a stereotypical array of pancakes, omelettes, chips, muesli and fruit salad, along with a basic range of curries. The downside is that they tend to be relatively pricey, while the food can be very hit and miss – Indian spaghetti bolognaise, enchiladas and chicken chow mein can be every bit as weird as you might expect. International-style **fast food**, including burgers (without beef – usually chicken or mutton) and pizzas, is also available in major cities.

Indian food

What Westerners call a "curry" covers a huge variety of dishes, each made with a different masala, or mix of **spices**. Curry powder does not exist in India, the nearest equivalent being garam masala ("hot mix"), a combination of spices added to a dish at the last stage of cooking to spice it up. Commonly used spices include chilli, turmeric, garlic, ginger, cinnamon, cardamom, cloves, coriander – both leaf and seed – cumin and saffron. These are not all added at the same time, and some (particularly cardamom and cloves) are used whole, so beware of chewing on them.

Chilli is another key element in the Indian spice cabinet, but the idea that all Indian food is fiery hot is a complete myth. north Indian food, in particular, tends to be quite mildly spiced, often more so than Indian food in restaurants abroad. South Indian food can be hotter, but not invariably so. If you don't like hot food, there are mild dishes such as korma and biriyani where meat or vegetables are cooked with rice. Indians tend to assuage the effects of chilli with chutney, *dahi* (curd) or raita (curd with mint and

cucumber, or other herbs and vegetables). Otherwise, beer is one of the best things for washing chilli out of your mouth; the essential oils that cause the burning sensation dissolve in alcohol, but not in water.

Vegetarian curries are usually identified (even on menus in English) by the Hindi names of their main ingredients, such as *paneer* (cheese), *alu* (potatoes), *chana* (chickpeas) or *muttar* (peas). **Meat curries** are more often given specific names such as *korma* or *dopiaza*, to indicate the kind of masala used or the method of cooking.

North Indian food

North Indian cooking has been heavily influenced by the various Muslim invaders who arrived in the Subcontinent from Central Asia and Persia and who gave Indian cooking many of its most popular dishes and accompaniments, such as the biriyani and the naan bread, as well as its relatively greater emphasis on meat compared to the south. The classic north Indian fusion of native and Central Asian influences (although it can be found as far south as Hyderabad) is so-called **Mughlai cooking**, the creation of the Mughal dynasty. Mostly non-veg, the food is mildly spiced but extremely rich, using ingredients such as cream, almonds, sultanas and saffron – the classic korma sauce is the best-known example.

The other big northern style is **tandoori**. The name refers to the deep clay oven (tandoor) in which the food is cooked. Tandoori chicken is marinated in yoghurt, herbs and spices before cooking. Boneless pieces of meat, marinated and cooked in the same way are known as tikka; they may be served in a medium-strength masala (tikka masala). one thickened with almonds (*pasanda*), or in a rich butter sauce (*murg makhan*, or butter chicken). Breads such as naan and roti are also baked in the tandoor.

A main dish – which may be a curry, but could also be a dry dish such as a kebab, or a tandoori dish without a masala – is usually served with a dhal (lentils) and bread such as chapatis or naan. Rice is usually an optional extra in North India, and has to be ordered separately. Many restaurants also offer set meals, or **thalis**. This is a stainless-steel tray with a number of little dishes in it, containing a selection of curries, a chutney and a sweet. In the middle you'll get bread and usually rice. In many places, waiters will keep coming round with refills until you've had enough.

In North India, food is usually served with **bread**, which comes in a number of varieties, all of them flatbreads rather than loaves. **Chapati** is a generic term for breads, but tends to refer to the simplest, unleavened type. It's usually made from wheat flour. The term **roti** is likewise generic, and a roti can be exactly the same as a chapati, but the term tends to refer more to a thicker bread baked in a tandoor. **Naan** is a leavened bread, thick and chewy, and invariably baked in a tandoor; it's a favourite in non-veg restaurants as it best accompanies rich meaty dishes. You may also come across fried breads, of which **paratha** (or *parantha*) is rolled out, basted with ghee, folded over and rolled out again several times before cooking, and often stuffed with ingredients such as potato (*alu paratha*); it's popular for breakfast. **Puris** are little fried puffballs. **Poppadum** (papad) is a crisp wafer made from lentil flour and is typically served as an appetizer.

There's an enormous variety of regional cuisines across the north. **Bengalis** love fish and cook a mean *mangsho* (meat) curry as well as exotic vegetable dishes such as *mocha* – cooked banana flower. They also like to include fish bones for added flavour in their vegetable curries – a nasty surprise for vegetarians. **Tibetans** and **Bhotias** from the Himalayas have a simple diet of *thukpa* (meat soup) and *momo* (meat dumplings), as well as a salty tea made with either rancid yak butter (where available) or with ordinary butter. In **Punjab** and much of northern India, home cooking consists of dhal and vegetables along with roti and less rice than the Bengalis. Food in **Gujarat**, predominantly veg, is often cooked with a bit of sugar. Certain combinations are traditional and seasonally repeated, such as *makki ki roti* (fried corn bread) with *sarson ka sag* (mustard-leaf greens) around Punjab and other parts of North India. *Baingan bharta*

(puréed roast aubergine) is commonly eaten with plain yoghurt and roti. In good Muslim cooking from the north, delicately thin *rumali roti* ("handkerchief" bread) often accompanies rich meat and chicken dishes.

South Indian food

The food of South India is a world away from that of the north. Southern cooking also tends to use a significantly different repertoire of spices, with sharper, simpler flavours featuring coconut, tamarind, curry leaves and plenty of dried red and fresh green chillies. **Rice** is king, not only eaten in its natural form, but also made into regional staples such as *iddlis* (steamed rice cakes) and *dosas* (rice pancakes), such as the ubiquitous masala dosa, a potato curry wrapped in a crispy rice pancake. The lavish naans, *parathas*, rotis and other breads that are such a feature of north Indian cooking aren't usually available, apart from the fluffy little *puri*, while meat is comparatively uncommon.

Set meals are another common feature in the south, where they are generally referred to simply as "meals". They generally consist of a mound of rice surrounded by various vegetable curries, *sambar* dhal, chutney and curd, and usually accompanied by *puris* and *rasam*, a thin, hot, peppery soup. Traditionally served on a round metal tray or thali (also found in North India), with each side dish in a separate metal bowl, set meals are sometimes served up on a rectangle of banana leaf instead. In most traditional restaurants, you can eat as much as you want, and staff circulate with refills of everything. In the south even more than elsewhere, eating with your fingers is *de rigueur* (you want to feel the food as well as taste it) and cutlery may be unavailable.

Wherever you eat, remember to use only your **right hand**, and wash your hands before you start. Try and avoid getting food on the palm of your hand by eating with the tips of your fingers.

Snacks and street food

India abounds in **snacks** and **street food**. *Chana puri*, a chickpea curry with a *puri* (or sometimes other type of bread) to dunk, is a great favourite in the north; *iddli sambar* – lentil

Paan

You may be relieved to know that the red stuff people spit all over the streets isn't blood, but juice produced by chewing **paan** – a digestive, commonly taken after meals, and also a mild stimulant, found especially in the northeast, where it is fresh and much stronger.

Paan consists of chopped or shredded nut (always referred to as betel nut, though in fact it comes from the areca palm), wrapped in a leaf (which *does* come from the betel vine) that is first prepared with ingredients such as *katha* (a red paste), *chuna* (slaked white lime), *mitha masala* (a mix of sweet spices, which can be ingested) and *zarda* (chewing tobacco, not to be swallowed on any account, especially if made with *chuna*). The triangular package thus formed is wedged inside your cheek and chewed slowly, and, in the case of *chuna* and *zarda* paans, spitting out the juice as you go.

Paan, and paan masala, a mix of betel nut, fennel seeds, sweets and flavourings, are sold by paan-wallahs, often from tiny stalls squeezed between shops. Paan-wallahs develop big reputations; those in the tiny roads of Varanasi are the most renowned, asking astronomical prices for paan made to elaborate specifications including silver and even gold foil. Paan is an acquired taste; novices should start off, and preferably stick with, the sweet and harmless *mitha* variety, which is perfectly alright to ingest.

and vegetable sauce with rice cakes to dunk – is the southern equivalent. Street finger-food includes *bhel puris* (a Mumbai speciality consisting of a mix of puffed rice, deep fried vermicelli, potato and crunchy *puri* with tamarind sauce), *pani puris* (the same *puris* dunked in peppery and spicy water – only for the seasoned), *bhajis* (deep-fried cakes of vegetables in chickpea flour), samosas (meat or vegetables in a pastry triangle, fried), and pakoras (vegetables or potato dipped in chickpea flour batter and deep-fried). In the south, you'll also come across the ever-popular vada, a spicy deep-fried lentil cake which looks rather like a doughnut.

Kebabs are common in the north, most frequently seekh kebab, minced lamb grilled on a skewer, but also shami kebab, small minced-lamb cutlets. Kebabs rolled into griddle-fried bread, known as *kathi* rolls, originated in Kolkata (Calcutta) but are now available in other cities as well. With all street snacks, though, remember that food left lying around attracts germs – make sure it's freshly cooked. Be especially careful with snacks involving water, such as *pani puris*, and cooking oil, which is often recycled. Generally, it's a good idea to acclimatize to Indian conditions before you start eating street snacks.

You won't find anything called "**Bombay mix**" in India, but there's no shortage of dry spicy snack mixes, often referred to as

channa chur. Jackfruit chips are sometimes sold as a savoury snack – though they are rather bland – and cashew nuts are a real bargain. Peanuts, also known as "monkey nuts" or *mumfuli*, usually come roasted and unshelled.

Non-Indian food

Chinese food is widely available in large towns. It's generally cooked by Indian chefs and isn't exactly authentic, except in the few Indian cities, most notably Kolkata (Calcutta), that have large Chinese communities where you can get very good Chinese cuisine.

Tourist restaurants and backpacker cafés nationwide offer a fair choice of **Western food**, from unpretentious little bakeries serving cakes and sandwiches to smart tourist restaurants dishing up fine Italian cooking on candle-lit terraces. However, quality is very hit and miss. Some places offer surprisingly good versions of Western standards, but many are dire, and Western food is also often relatively pricey compared to Indian dishes. Delhi and Mumbai are also home to a range of specialist non-Indian restaurants featuring Tex-Mex, Thai, Japanese, Italian and French cuisines – usually in the restaurants of luxury hotels.

In addition to these places, international **fast-food** chains serve the same standard fare as elsewhere in the world at much cheaper prices. Branches of *Pizza Hut*, *Domino's*, *KFC* and *McDonald's* can be found in ever-increasing numbers of Indian cities. *Wimpy*, home-grown chains such as *Nirula's* and *Kwality*, and independently owned fast-food cafés can also be found in many towns.

Sweets

Most Indians have rather a sweet tooth and **Indian sweets**, usually made of milk, can be very sweet indeed. Of the more solid type, *barfi*, a kind of fudge made from milk which has been boiled down and condensed, varies from moist and delicious to dry and powdery. It comes in various flavours from plain creamy white to *pista* (pistachio) in livid green and is often sold covered with silver leaf (which you eat). Smoother-textured, round *penda* and thin diamonds of *kaju katri*, plus moist *sandesh* and the harder *paira*, both popular in Bengal, are among many other sweets made from *chhana* or boiled-down milk. Crunchier *mesur* is made with chickpeas; numerous types of gelatinous halwa, not the Middle Eastern variety, include the rich *gajar ka halwa* made from carrots and cream.

Jalebis, circular orange tubes made of deep-fried treacle and dripping with syrup, are as sickly as they look. *Gulab jamuns*, deep-fried spongy dough balls soaked in syrup, are just as unhealthy. Common in both the north and the south, *ladoo* consists of balls made from semolina flour with raisins and sugar and sometimes made of other grains and flour, while among Bengali sweets, widely considered to be the best are *rasgullas*, rosewater-flavoured cream-cheese balls floating in syrup. *Ras malai*, found throughout North India, is similar, but soaked in cream instead of syrup.

Chocolate is improving rapidly in India and you'll find various Cadbury's and Amul bars. None of the various indigenous brands of imitation Swiss and Belgian chocolates appearing on the cosmopolitan markets are worth eating.

Among the large **ice-cream** vendors, Kwality (now owned and branded as Walls), Vadilal's, Gaylord and Dollops stand out. Uniformed men push carts of ice cream around and the bigger companies have many imitators, usually quite obvious. Some have no scruples – stay away from water ices unless you have a seasoned constitution. Ice-cream parlours selling elaborate concoctions including sundaes have really taken off; Connaught Circus in Delhi has several. Be sure to try **kulfi**, a pistachio- and cardamom-flavoured frozen sweet which is India's answer to ice cream; bhang kulfi (popular during the festival of Holi) is laced with cannabis and has an interesting kick to it, but should be approached with caution.

Fruit

What **fruit** is available varies with region and season, but there's always a fine choice. Ideally, you should peel all fruit including apples (*sev*), or soak them in strong iodine or potassium permanganate solution for half an hour. Roadside vendors sell fruit which they often cut up and serve sprinkled with salt and even masala – don't buy anything that looks like it's been hanging around for a while.

Mangoes (*aam*) of various kinds are usually on offer, but not all are sweet enough to eat fresh – some are used for pickles or curries. Indians are very picky about their mangoes, which they feel and smell before buying; if you don't know the art of choosing the fruit, you could be sold the leftovers. Among the species appearing at different times in the season, which lasts from spring to summer, look out for Alphonso and Langra. Bananas (*kela*) of one sort or another are also on sale all year round, and oranges and tangerines are generally easy to come by, as are sweet melons and thirst-quenching watermelons.

Tropical fruits such as coconuts, papayas (pawpaws) and pineapples are more common in the south, while things such as lychees and pomegranates are very seasonal. In the north, temperate fruit from the mountains can be much like that in Europe and North America, with strawberries, apricots and even rather soft apples available in season.

Among less familiar fruit, the *chiku*, which looks like a kiwi and tastes a bit like a pear, is worth a mention, as is the watermelon-sized jackfruit, whose spiny green exterior encloses sweet, slightly rubbery yellow segments, each containing a seed. Individual segments are sold at roadside stalls.

Nonalcoholic drinks

India sometimes seems to run on **tea**, or chai, grown in Darjeeling, Assam and the Nilgiri Hills, and sold by chai-wallahs on just about every street corner. Tea is usually made by putting tea, milk and water in a pan, boiling it all up, straining it into a cup or glass with lots of sugar and pouring back and forth from one cup to another to stir. Ginger and/or cardamoms are often added. If you're quick off the mark, you can get them to hold the sugar. English tea it isn't, but most travellers get used to it. Sometimes, especially in tourist spots, you might get a pot of European-style "tray" tea, generally consisting of a tea bag in lukewarm water – you'd do better to stick to the pukka Indian variety, unless, that is, you are in a traditional tea-growing area.

Instant **coffee** (*kofi*) is becoming increasingly common, and in some cases is more popular than tea, especially in the south. In the north, most coffee is instant, although increasing numbers of cafés and restaurants are now investing in proper coffee machines, especially in tourist centres. Café society has finally arrived in the major cities, and Delhi and Mumbai now have a fair share of trendy coffee shops serving real cappuccino and espresso. In the south, coffee is just as common as tea, and far better than it is in the north. One of the best places to get it is in outlets of the *India Coffee House* chain, found in every southern town, and occasionally in the north. A whole ritual is attached to the drinking of milky Keralan coffee in particular, poured in flamboyant sweeping motions between tall glasses to cool it down.

Soft drinks are ubiquitous. Coca-Cola and Pepsi returned to India in the early 1990s after being banned from the country for seventeen years and have now largely replaced their old Indian equivalents such as Campa Cola and Thums Up, although you'll still find the pleasantly lemony Limca (rumoured to have dubious connections to Italian companies, and to contain additives banned there). All contain a lot of sugar but little else: adverts for Indian soft drinks have been known to boast "Absolutely no natural ingredients!" None will quench your thirst for long.

More recommendable is **water**, either treated or boiled tap water (see box, p.36) or bottled water (though quality may be suspect – see p.36). You'll also find cartons of Frooti, Jumpin, Réal and similar brands of **fruit juice** drinks, which come in mango, guava, apple and lemon varieties. If the carton looks at all mangled, it is best not to touch it as it may have been recycled. At larger stations, there will be a stall on the platform selling Himachali apple juice. Better still, green **coconuts**, common around coastal areas especially in the south, are cheaper than any of these, and sold on the street by vendors who will hack off the top for you with a machete and give you a straw to suck up the coconut water (you then scoop out the flesh and eat it). You will also find street stalls selling freshly made sugar-cane juice: delicious, and not in fact too sweet, but not always as safe healthwise as you might like.

India's greatest cold drink, **lassi**, is made with beaten curd and drunk either sweetened with sugar, salted, or mixed with fruit. It varies widely from smooth and delicious to insipid and watery, and is sold at virtually every café, restaurant and canteen in the country. Freshly made milkshakes are also commonly available at establishments with blenders. They'll also sell you what they call a fruit juice, but which is usually fruit, water and sugar (or salt) liquidized and strained; also, street vendors selling fresh fruit juice in less than hygienic conditions are apt to add salt and garam masala. With all such drinks, however appetizing they may seem, you should exercise great caution in deciding where to drink them: find out where the water is likely to have come from.

Alcohol

Prohibition, once widespread in India, is now only fully enforced in Gujarat and some of the northeastern hill states, although Tamil Nadu, Andhra Pradesh and some other states retain partial prohibition in the form of "dry" days, high taxes, restrictive licences, and health warnings on labels ("Liquor – ruins country, family and life," runs Tamil Nadu's).

Most Indians drink to get drunk as quickly as possible, and this trend has had a terrible toll on family life especially among the working classes and peasantry. Because of this, politicians searching for votes have from time to time played the prohibition card. The government in Haryana introduced prohibition in 1996 which, in a state that produces huge amounts of liquor, led to lost revenue and, as is common in all prohibition areas, the rapid growth of a highly organized illicit trade, but no evidence of less drinking. Haryana is no longer dry, but in states like Tamil Nadu, which persist with these policies, every now and then papers report cases of mass contamination from illicit stills that have tragically led to an extraordinary number of deaths.

Alcoholic enclaves in prohibition states can become major drinking centres: Daman and Diu in Gujarat, and Puducherry and Karaikal in Tamil Nadu are the main ones. Goa, Sikkim and Mahé (Kerala) join them as places where the booze flows especially freely and cheaply. Interestingly, all were outside the British Raj. Liquor permits – free, and available from Indian embassies, high commissions and tourist offices abroad, and from tourist offices in Delhi, Mumbai, Kolkata (Calcutta) and Chennai, and even at airports on arrival – allow those travellers who bother to apply for one to evade certain restrictions in Gujarat.

Beer is widely available, if rather expensive by local standards. Price varies from state to state, but you can usually expect to pay around Rs60–100 for a 650ml bottle. A pub culture, not dissimilar to that of the West, has taken root amongst the wealthier classes in cities like Bengaluru (Bangalore) and Mumbai and also in Delhi. Kingfisher, King's Black Label and Fosters are the leading brands, but there are plenty of others. All lagers, which tend to contain chemical additives including glycerine, are usually pretty palatable if you can get them cold. In certain places, notably unlicensed restaurants in Tamil Nadu, beer comes in the form of "special tea" – a teapot of beer, which you pour into and drink from a teacup to disguise what it really is.

A cheaper, and often delicious, alternative to beer in Kerala and one or two other places is **toddy** (palm wine). In Bengal it is made from the date palm, and is known as *taddy*.

Sweet and nonalcoholic when first tapped, it ferments within twelve hours. In the Himalayas, the Bhotia people, of Tibetan stock, drink *chang*, a beer made from millet, and one of the nicest drinks of all – *tumba*, where fermented millet is placed in a bamboo flask and topped with hot water, then sipped through a bamboo pipe.

Spirits usually take the form of "Indian Made Foreign Liquor" (IMFL), although the recently legitimized foreign liquor industry is expanding rapidly. Some Scotch, such as Seagram's Hundred Pipers, is now being bottled in India and sold at a premium, as is Smirnoff vodka, amongst other known brands. Some of the brands of Indian whisky are not too bad and are affordable in comparison; gin and brandy can be pretty rough, while Indian rum is sweet and distinctive. In Goa, *feni* is a spirit distilled from coconut or cashew fruit. Steer well clear of illegally distilled *arak* however, which often contains methanol (wood alcohol) and other poisons. A look through the press, especially at festival times, will soon reveal numerous cases of blindness and death as a result of drinking bad hooch (or "spurious liquor" as it's called). Licensed country liquor, sold in several states under such names as *bangla*, is an acquired taste. Unfortunately, Indian **wine** – despite the efforts of a few pioneering vineyards such as Grovers (near Bengaluru) – is still generally of a poor quality, and also expensive, while foreign wine available in upmarket restaurants and luxury hotels comes with an exorbitant price-tag.

Smoking

One of the great smells of India is the *beedi*, the cheapest smoke, made of low-grade tobacco wrapped in a single *tendu* leaf and fastened with a tiny piece of coloured thread. Though free from chemical additives, it's worth knowing that *beedis* produce three times more carbon monoxide and nicotine than regular cigarettes, and five times more tar. *Beedis* are available at shops and from roadside kiosks – basically, anywhere which sells cigarettes. Paan-wallahs sometimes have a supply, too.

The media

With well over a billion people and a literacy rate of more than sixty percent, India produces a staggering 4700 daily papers in over three hundred languages, and another 39,000 journals and weeklies. There are a large number of English-language daily newspapers, both national and regional. The most prominent of the nationals are The Hindu, The Statesman, the Times of India, The Independent, the Economic Times and the Indian Express (usually the most critical of the government). All are pretty dry and sober, and concentrate on Indian news; The Independent and Kolkata's Telegraph tend to have better coverage of world news than the rest. Asian Age, published simultaneously in India, London and New York, is a conservative tabloid that sports a motley collection of the world's more colourful stories. All the major Indian newspapers have websites (see p.64), with the Times of India, The Hindu and the Hindustan Times providing the most up-to-date and detailed news services.

India's press is the freest in Asia and attacks on the government are often quite outspoken. However, as in the West, most papers can be seen as part of the political establishment, and are unlikely to print anything that might upset the "national consensus".

There are also a number of *Time/Newsweek*–style **news magazines**, with a strong emphasis on politics. The best of these are *India Today* and *Frontline*, published by *The Hindu*. Others include *Outlook*, which presents the most readable, broadly themed analysis, *Sunday* and *The Week*. As they give more of an overview of stories and issues than the daily papers, you will probably get a better insight into Indian politics, and most tend to have a higher proportion of international news too. *Business India* is more financially oriented and *The India Magazine* more cultural. Film **fanzines** and gossip mags are very popular (*Screen* and *Filmfare* are the best, though you'd have to be reasonably *au fait* with Indian movies to follow a lot of it), but magazines and periodicals in English cover all sorts of popular and minority interests, so it's worth having a look through what's available.

Foreign publications such as the *International Herald Tribune*, *Time*, *Newsweek*, *The Economist* and the international edition of the British *Guardian* are all available in the main cities, though it's easier (and cheaper) to read the day's edition for free online. For a read through the British press, try the British Council in Delhi, Mumbai, Kolkata (Calcutta) and Chennai; the USIS is the American equivalent. Expat-oriented bookstalls, such as those in New Delhi's Khan Market, stock slightly out-of-date and expensive copies of magazines like *Vogue* and *NME*.

BBC World Service radio can be picked up on short wave on 15.31MHz (19.6m) between about 8.30am and 10.30pm (Indian time). Alternative frequencies if reception is poor include 17.79MHz (16.9m), 15.56MHz (19.3m) and 11.96MHz (25.1m).

The government-run **TV company**, Doordarshan, which broadcasts a sober diet of edifying programmes, has tried to compete with the onslaught of mass access to **satellite TV**. The main broadcaster in English is Rupert Murdoch's Star TV network, which incorporates the BBC World Service and Zee TV (with Z News), a progressive blend of Hindi-oriented chat, film, news and music programmes. Star Sports and ESPN churn out a mind-boggling amount of cricket with an occasional sprinkling of other sports. Others include CNN, some sports channels, the Discovery Channel, the immensely popular Channel V, hosted by scantily clad Mumbai models and DJs, and a couple of American soap and chat stations. There are now several local-language channels as well.

News and media online

ⓦ **www.guardian.co.uk/india** High-quality news features are the meat of this "Special Report" section of the *Guardian*'s award-winning website, which also has links to its archived India articles and an excellent dossier on Kashmir. Access is free.

ⓦ **indiatoday.digitaltoday.in** Homepage of India's best-selling news magazine.

ⓦ **www.samachar.com** One of the best news gateway sites, featuring headlines and links to leading Indian newspapers.

ⓦ **www.tehelka.com** Alternative news webzine, famous for exposing corruption scandals in government.

ⓦ **timesofindia.indiatimes.com**; ⓦ **www.hinduonline.com**; ⓦ **www.hindustantimes.com**; ⓦ **www.deccanherald.com** Websites of some of India's leading daily papers, with detailed national coverage.

Festivals and holidays

Virtually every temple in every town or village across the country has its own festival. The biggest and most spectacular include Puri's Rath Yatra festival in June or July, the Hemis festival in Ladakh, also held in June or July, Pushkar's camel fair in November, Kullu's Dussehra, Madurai's three annual festivals, and, of course, the Kumbh Mela, held at Allahabad, Haridwar, Nasik and Ujjain. While mostly religious in nature, merrymaking rather than solemnity are generally the order of the day, and onlookers are usually welcome. Indeed, if you're lucky enough to coincide with a local festival, it may well prove to be the highlight of your trip.

There isn't space to list every festival in every village across India here, but local festivals are listed throughout the body of the Guide. The following pages include details of the main national and regional celebrations. Hindu, Sikh, Buddhist and Jain festivals follow the Indian **lunar calendar** and their dates therefore vary from year to year – we've given the lunar month (Magha, Phalguna, Chaitra, and so on), where relevant, in the listings below. The lunar calendar adds a leap month every two or three years to keep it in line with the seasons. Muslim festivals follow the **Islamic calendar**, whose year is shorter and which thus loses about eleven days per annum against the Gregorian.

You may, while in India, be lucky enough to be invited to a **wedding**. These are jubilant affairs, always scheduled on auspicious days. A Hindu bride dresses in red for the ceremony, and marks the parting of her hair with red *sindur* and her forehead with a *bindi*. She wears gold or bone bangles, which she keeps on for the rest of her married life. Although the practice is officially illegal, large dowries often change hands. These are usually paid by the bride's family to the groom, and can be contentious; poor families feel obliged to save for years to get their daughters married.

Principal Indian holidays

India has only four **national public holidays** as such: Jan 26 (Republic Day); Aug 15 (Independence Day); Oct 2 (Gandhi's birthday); and Dec 25 (Christmas Day). Each state, however, has its own calendar of public holidays; you can expect most businesses to close on the major holidays of their own religion. The Hindu lunar calendar months are given in brackets below.

Key: B=Buddhist; C=Christian; H=Hindu; J=Jain; M=Muslim; N=nonreligious; P=Parsi; S=Sikh.

Jan–Feb (Magha–Phalguna)

H Pongal (1 Magha): Tamil harvest festival celebrated with decorated cows, processions and rangolis (chalk designs on the doorsteps of houses).

Pongal is a sweet porridge made from newly harvested rice and eaten by all, including the cows. The festival is also known as Makar Sankranti, and celebrated in Karnataka, Andhra Pradesh and the east of India.

H Ganga Sagar: Pilgrims come from all over the country to Sagar Dwip, on the mouth of the Hooghly 150km south of Kolkata (Calcutta), to bathe during Makar Sankranti.

H Vasant Panchami (5 Magha): One-day spring festival in honour of Saraswati, the goddess of learning, celebrated with kite-flying, the wearing of yellow saris and the blessing of schoolchildren's books and pens by the goddess.

N Republic Day (Jan 26): A military parade in Delhi typifies this state celebration of India's republic-hood, followed on Jan 29 by the "Beating the Retreat" ceremony outside the presidential palace in Delhi.

N Goa Carnival: Goa's own Mardi Gras features float processions and feni-induced mayhem in the state capital, Panjim.

N International Kite Festival at Aurangabad (Maharashtra).

H Teppa Floating Festival (16 Magha) at Madurai (Tamil Nadu). Meenakshi and Shiva are towed around the temple tank in boats lit with fairy lights – a prelude to the Tamil marriage season.

N Elephanta Music and Dance Festival (Mumbai). Feb–March (Phalguna). Classical Indian dance performed with the famous rock-cut caves in Mumbai harbour as a backdrop.

B Losar (1 Phalguna): Tibetan New Year celebrations among Tibetan and Himalayan Buddhist communities, especially at Dharamsala (HP).

H Shivratri (10 Phalguna): Anniversary of Shiva's tandav (creation) dance, and his wedding anniversary. Popular family festival but also a sadhu festival of pilgrimage and fasting, especially at important Shiva temples.

H Holi (15 Phalguna): Water festival held during Dol Purnima (full moon) to celebrate the beginning of spring, most popular in the north. Expect to be bombarded with water, paint, coloured powder and other mixtures; they can permanently stain clothing, so don't go out in your Sunday best.

N Khajuraho (Madhya Pradesh) Dance Festival: The country's finest dancers perform in front of the famous erotic sculpture-carved shrines.

C Carnival (Mardi Gras): The last day before Lent, forty days before Easter, is celebrated in Goa, as in the rest of the Catholic world.

March–April (Chaitra)

H Gangaur (3 Chaitra): Rajasthani festival (also celebrated in Bengal and Orissa) in honour of Parvati, marked with singing and dancing.

H Ramanavami (9 Chaitra): Birthday of Rama, the hero of the Ramayana, celebrated with readings of the epic and discourses on Rama's life and teachings.

C Easter (movable feast): Celebration of the resurrection of Christ. Good Friday in particular is a day of festivity.

P Pateti: Parsi new year, also known as Nav Roz, celebrating the creation of fire. Feasting, services and present-giving.

P Khorvad Sal (a week after Pateti): Birthday of Zarathustra (aka Zoroaster). Celebrated in the Parsis' Fire Temples, and with feasting at home.

H Chittirai, Madurai (Tamil Nadu): Elephant-led procession.

April–May (Vaisakha)

HS Baisakhi (1 Vaisakha): To the Hindus, it's the solar new year, celebrated with music and dancing; to the Sikhs, it's the anniversary of the foundation of the Khalsa (Sikh brotherhood) by Guru Gobind Singh. Processions and feasting follow readings of the Granth Sahib scriptures.

J Mahavir Jayanti (13 Vaisakha): Birthday of Mahavir, the founder of Jainism. The main Jain festival of the year, observed by visits to sacred Jain sites, especially in Rajasthan and Gujarat, and with present-giving.

H Puram Festival, Thrissur (Kerala): Frenzied drumming and elephant parades.

B Buddha Jayanti (16 Vaisakha): Buddha's birthday. He achieved enlightenment and nirvana on the same date. Sarnath (UP) and Bodh Gaya (Bihar) are the main centres of celebration.

May–June (Jyaishtha)

H Ganga Dussehra (10 Jyaishtha): Bathing festival to celebrate the descent to earth of the goddess of the Ganges.

June–July (Ashadha)

H Rath Yatra (2 Ashadha): Festival held in Puri (and other places, especially in the south) to commemorate Krishna's (Lord Jagannath's) journey to Mathura.

H Teej (3 Ashadha): Festival in honour of Parvati to welcome the monsoon. Particularly celebrated in Rajasthan.

B Hemis Festival, Leh (Ladakh): Held sometime between late June and mid-July, this spectacular festival features chaam (lama dances) to signify the victory of Buddhism over evil.

July–Aug (Shravana)

H Naag Panchami (3 Shravana): Snake festival in honour of the naga snake deities. Mainly celebrated in Rajasthan and Maharashtra.

H Raksha Bandhan/Narial Purnima (16 Shravana): Festival to honour the sea god Varuna. Brothers and sisters exchange gifts, the sister tying a thread known as a rakhi to her brother's wrist. Brahmins, after a day's fasting, change the sacred thread they wear.

N Independence Day (15 Aug): India's biggest secular celebration, on the anniversary of independence from Britain.

Aug–Sept (Bhadraparda)

H Ganesh Chaturthi (4 Bhadraparda): Festival dedicated to Ganesh, especially celebrated in Maharashtra. In Mumbai, huge processions carry images of the god to immerse in the sea.

H Onam: Keralan harvest festival, celebrated with snake-boat races. The Nehru Trophy snake-boat race at Alappuzha (held on the second Sat of Aug) is the most spectacular, with long boats crewed by 150 rowers.

H Janmashtami (23 Bhadraparda): Krishna's birthday, an occasion for fasting and celebration, especially in Agra, Mumbai, Mathura (UP) and Vrindaban (UP).

H Avani Mula festival, Madurai (Tamil Nadu): Celebration of the coronation of Shiva.

Sept–Oct (Ashvina)

H Dussehra (1–10 Ashvina): Ten-day festival (usually two days' public holiday) associated with vanquishing demons, in particular Rama's victory over Ravana in the Ramayana, and Durga's over the buffalo-headed Mahishasura (particularly in West Bengal, where it is called Durga Puja). Dussehra celebrations include performances of the Ram Lila (life of Rama). Best in Mysore (Karnataka), Ahmedabad (Gujarat) and Kullu (Himachal Pradesh). Durga Puja is best seen in Kolkata (Calcutta) where it is an occasion for exchanging gifts, and every locality has its own competing street-side image.

N Mahatma Gandhi's Birthday (2 Oct): Solemn commemoration of Independent India's founding father.

Oct–Nov (Kartika)

H Diwali (Deepavali) (15 Kartika): Festival of lights, and India's biggest, to celebrate Rama's and Sita's homecoming in the Ramayana. Festivities include the lighting of oil lamps and firecrackers, and the giving and receiving of sweets and gifts. Diwali coincides with Kali Puja, celebrated in temples dedicated to the wrathful goddess, especially in Bengal, and often accompanied by the ritual sacrifice of goats.

J Jain New Year (15 Kartika): Coincides with Diwali, so Jains celebrate alongside Hindus.

S Nanak Jayanti (16 Kartika): Guru Nanak's birthday marked by prayer readings and processions, especially in Amritsar and in the rest of the Punjab, and at Patna (Bihar).

Nov–Dec (Margashirsha, or Agrahayana)

H Sonepur Mela: World's largest cattle fair at Sonepur (Bihar).

N Pushkar (Rajasthan) Camel Fair. Camel herders don their finest attire for this massive livestock market on the fringes of the Thar Desert.

N Hampi Festival (Karnataka): Government-sponsored music and dance festival.

Dec–Jan (Pausa)

CN Christmas (Dec 25): Christian festival celebrated throughout the world, popular in Christian areas of Goa and Kerala, and in big cities.

N Posh Mela (Dec 27): Held in Shantiniketan near Kolkata (Calcutta), a festival renowned for baul music.

Moveable

H Kumbh Mela: Major three-yearly festival held at one of four holy cities: Nasik (Maharashtra), Ujjain (MP), Haridwar (UP), or Prayag (Maharashtra) as well as at Allahabad (UP). The Maha Kumbh Mela or "Great" Kumbh Mela, the largest religious fair in India, is held every twelve years in Allahabad (UP); the next festival is due to take place in 2013 (Jan 27 to Feb 25; main bathing day Feb 10).

M Ramadan: The start of a month during which Muslims may not eat, drink or smoke from sunrise to sunset, and should abstain from sex. Future estimated dates are: Sept 1–29, 2008; Aug 21 to Sept 19, 2009; Aug 11 to Sept 8, 2010; Ramadan: Aug 1–29, 2011.

M Id ul-Fitr: Feast to celebrate the end of Ramadan. The precise date of the festival depends on exactly when the new moon is sighted, and so cannot be predicted with complete accuracy. Estimated dates (though these may vary by a day or two) are: Sept 30, 2008; Sept 20, 2009; Sept 9, 2010; and Aug 30, 2011.

M Id ul-Zuha: Pilgrimage festival to commemorate Abraham's preparedness to sacrifice his son Ismail. Celebrated with slaughtering and consumption of sheep. Estimated future dates are: Dec 10, 2008; Dec 1, 2009; Nov 20, 2010; and Nov 9, 2011.

M Muharram: The Islamic month of Muharram is the second holiest in the Muslim calendar (after Ramadan). Festivals are held to commemorate the martyrdom of the (Shi'ite) Imam, the Prophet's grandson and popular saint, Hussain, culminating on Ashura, the tenth day of the month. Estimated future dates for Muharram are: Dec 18 to Jan 15, 2009; Dec 7 to Jan 4, 2010; and Nov 26 to Dec 24, 2011.

Sports

India is not perhaps a place that most people associate with sports (the country won only one medal at the Athens Olympics in 2004), but cricket, hockey and football (soccer, that is) all have their place.

Cricket is by far the most popular of these, and a fine example of how something quintessentially British (well, English) has become something quintessentially Indian. Travellers to India will find it hard to get away from the game – it's everywhere, especially on television. Cricketing heroes such as the legendary batting maestro Sachin Tendulkar and new wicket-keeping superstar Mahendra Dhoni live under the constant scrutiny of the media and public; expectations are high and disappointments acute. India versus Pakistan matches are especially emotive – the entire country received a fillip when India beat their arch rivals in the final of the inaugural Twenty20 World Cup in 2007. Besides spectator cricket, you'll see games being played on open spaces all around the country.

Test matches are rare, but interstate cricket is easy to catch – the most prestigious competition is the Ranji Trophy. Occasionally, in cities like Kolkata (Calcutta), you may even come across a match blocking a road, and will have to be patient as the players begrudgingly let your vehicle continue.

Horse racing can be a good day out, especially if you enjoy a flutter. The racecourse at Kolkata (Calcutta) is the most popular, often attracting crowds of over fifty thousand, especially on New Year's Day. There are several other racecourses around the country, mostly in larger cities such as Mumbai, Delhi, Pune, Hyderabad, Mysore, Bengaluru (Bangalore) and Ooty. Other (mainly) spectator sports include **polo**, originally from upper Kashmir, but taken up by the British to become one of the symbols of the Raj. Certain Rajasthani princes, such as the late Hanut Singh of Jodhpur were considered to be the best polo players in the world between the 1930s and 1950s, but since the 1960s, when the privy purses were abolished, they have been unable to maintain their stables, and the tradition of polo has declined. Today, it's mainly the army who plays the game; the best place to catch a match is at the Delhi Gymkhana during the winter season. Polo, in more or less its original form, is still played on tiny mountain ponies

India's Twenty20 vision

The whole global cricket scene has recently been massively shaken up by the creation of two new Indian Twenty20 leagues showcasing a mix of local talent and overseas cricketing stars. The unofficial **Indian Cricket League (ICL)** was first held in December 2007 in Chandigarh, with fifteen games featuring a mix of Indian players and foreign stars like Brian Lara and Inzamam ul-Haq, and is due to be repeated in October 2008. Despite its undoubted success, however, the ICL has since been completely eclipsed by the razzmatazz surrounding the India Cricket Board's new **Indian Premier League**, due to be held for the first time in April 2008, with 59 matches featuring a mix of young up-and-coming locals, established Indian test-match players and international cricketing megastars like Shane Warne, Ricky Ponting, Muttiah Muralitharan and Shoaib Malik. Each of the league's eight regional teams has been allowed to supplement their home-grown playing staff by signing up star Indian and international players, whose services were auctioned off via a series of sealed bids in January 2008 – the most expensive player, Mahendra Dhoni, went for a cool $1.5 million.

in Ladakh; a good place to see a game played in traditional style is in Leh during the Ladakh Festival in early September.

After years in the doldrums, **Indian hockey**, which used to regularly furnish the country with Olympic medals, is making a strong comeback. The haul of medals dried up in the 1960s when international hockey introduced astro-turf – which was, and still is, a rare surface in India. However, hockey remains very popular, especially in schools and colleges and, interestingly, amongst the tribal girls of Orissa, who supply the Indian national team with a regular clutch of players.

Football (soccer) is similarly popular with a keenly contested national championship. The best teams are based in Kolkata (Calcutta) and include three legendary clubs – Mohan Bagan, East Bengal and Mohamadan Sporting – who all command fanatical support. Unlike most of the league, these teams employ professional players and even include some minor internationals, mostly from Africa. International soccer tournaments are becoming increasingly common.

Tennis in India has always been a sport for the middle and upper classes. The country has produced a number of world-class players, such as the men's duo of Mahesh Bhupati and Leander Paes, who briefly achieved a world number-one ranking in the men's doubles in 1999, while the glamorous young Sania Mirza, currently ranked around 30th in the world in singles (the highest ranking ever achieved by an Indian woman), is beginning to rival the nation's cricket players in popularity.

Volleyball is very popular throughout India, and you may even see army men playing at extraordinary altitudes on the road to Leh. Standards aren't particularly high and joining a game should be quite easy. **Motorsport** is also popular in the south and there is a race-track on the outskirts of Chennai. Golf is extremely popular and relatively inexpensive in India, again amongst the middle classes; the second-oldest golf course in the world is in Kolkata (Calcutta), and one of the highest in the world is at Shimla.

One indigenous sport you're likely to see in North India is **kabadi**, played on a small (badminton-sized) court, and informally on any suitable open area. The game, with seven players in each team, consists of a player from each team alternately attempting to "tag" as many members of the opposing team as possible in the space of a single breath (cheating is impossible; the player has to maintain a continuous chant of kabadikabadikabadikabadi etc), and getting back to his/her own side of the court without being caught. The game can get quite rough, with slaps and kicks in tagging allowed, and the defending team must try to tackle and pin the attacker so as not to allow him or her to even touch the dividing line. Tagged victims are required to leave the court. Although still an amateur sport, kabadi is taken very seriously with state and national championships, and now features in the Asian Games.

Popular with devotees of the monkey god, Hanuman, **Indian wrestling**, or kushti, has a small but dedicated following. Wrestlers are known as *pahalwaans* or "strong men" and can be seen exercising early in the morning with clubs and weights along river *ghats* such as those in Varanasi or Kolkata (Calcutta).

Trekking and outdoor activities

Trekking and outdoor activities

India offers plenty of opportunities for adventure sports, including trekking, mountaineering, whitewater rafting, caving and diving – just make sure you've got comprehensive insurance (see p.83) before getting stuck in.

Trekking

Though trekking in India is not nearly as commercialized as in neighbouring Nepal, the country can claim some of the world's most spectacular routes, especially in the Ladakh and Zanskar Himalayas, where the mountain passes frequently top 5000m. Himalayan routes are not all extreme, with relatively gentle short trails exploring the Singalila range around Darjeeling, low-level forest walks through the rhododendron-clad hillsides of Sikkim and the well-beaten pilgrim trails of Garhwal.

Hiring a **guide-cum-cook** is recommended whenever possible, especially on more difficult and less frequented routes, where the consequences of getting lost or running out of supplies could be serious. Porters (with or without ponies) can also make your trip a lot less arduous, and on longer routes where a week or more's worth of provisions have to be carried, they may be essential. You'll usually be approached in towns and villages leading to the trailhead by men touting for work. Finding out what the going day rate is can be difficult, and you should expect to have to haggle.

If the prospect of organizing a trek yourself seems too daunting, consider employing a **trekking company** to do it for you. Agencies at places like Manali, Leh, Darjeeling and Gangtok are detailed in the Guide, while specialist tour operators offering trips based around trekking are listed on pp.31–32.

Himachal Pradesh is the easiest state in which to plan a trek. Uttarakhand (Uttaranchal) sees fewer trekkers, and there are plenty of opportunities to wander off the beaten track and either escape the hordes of pilgrims or, alternatively, to join them on their way to the sacred sites of Badrinath, Gangotri, Joshimath and Kedarnath. There are also exciting and exotic high-mountain

trekking opportunities in the ancient Buddhist kingdoms of Ladakh and Zanskar, where trails can vary in length from relatively short four-day excursions to epics of ten days or more. At the eastern end of the Himalayas, Darjeeling makes a good base from which to explore the surrounding mountains. Neighbouring Sikkim has the greatest variations in altitude, from steamy river valleys to the third highest massif in the world. Shorter and less strenuous treks are available in the Ghats and the Nilgiri hills of southern India.

Having the right **equipment** for a trek is important, but hi-tech gear isn't essential – bring what you need to be comfortable but keep weight to a minimum. You can rent equipment in places such as Leh and Darjeeling, but otherwise, you'll have to buy what you need or bring it with you. Make sure everything (zips for example) is in working order before you set off. Clothes should be lightweight and versatile, especially considering the range of temperatures you might encounter: dress in layers for maximum flexibility.

Mountaineering

Mountaineering is a more serious venture, requiring planning and organization; if you've never climbed, don't start in the Himalayas. Mountaineering institutes at Darjeeling, Uttarkashi and Dharamsala run training courses. The one at Uttarkashi in Uttarakhand (@uttarkashi.nic.in/nim/courses.htm) is popular with foreigners: you can learn rock- and ice-climbing skills and expedition techniques for a fraction of what you'd pay in the West, but the 28-day basic mountaineering course run by Siachen Glacier veterans of the Indian army is extremely gruelling. Permission for mountaineering expeditions should be sought at least six months in advance from the Indian

Mountaineering Federation, Anand Niketan, Benito Juarez Road, New Delhi 110021 (℡011/2411 1211, ⓦwww.indmount.org). Peak fees range from $1500 to $4000, according to height, and expeditions must be accompanied by an IMF liaison officer equipped to the same standard as the rest of the party. The IMF can also supply lists of local mountaineering clubs; climbing with such clubs enables you to get to know local climbers, and obtain permits for otherwise restricted peaks.

Skiing

Despite the mammoth spread of the Himalayas, skiing in India remains relatively undeveloped. The only option for organized skiing is the western Himalayas, in particular Uttarakhand (Uttaranchal) and Himachal Pradesh; the eastern Himalayas have unreliable snowfall at skiing altitudes.

The ski area at **Auli** (see p.371), near Joshimath in Uttarakhand, has had money poured into it but suffers from a short season, limited (though cheap) skiing and nonexistent après-ski activity. In **Himachal Pradesh**, the skiing in the vicinity of Shimla is far too underdeveloped to warrant a detour, but the possibilities around Manali are more enticing because of the prospect of virgin powder: two or three surface tows operate in the Solang Nala for three months every winter.

There are two options for **back-country skiing** – the first is to plan your own ski-tour and bring your own equipment, but you should never go alone. The other way to float down trackless slopes is to go heliskiing but, at around US$500 a day, you'd have to be pretty well off to explore what aficionados describe as some of the best powder in the world.

Whitewater rafting

Though not as well known as some of the mighty rivers of Nepal, the rivers Chenab and Beas in Himachal Pradesh, the Rangit and Teesta in Sikkim, the Zanskar and Indus in Ladakh, and the Ganges in Uttarakhand all combine exciting waters with magnificent scenery. Kullu, Manali, Leh, Gangtok and Rishikesh are among the main rafting centres. Prices start at around Rs500 per day including food, but it's worth sounding

out a few agents to find the best deals. For more details see the relevant accounts in the Guide.

Caving

Meghalaya has the best caving potential of all the Indian states. The three main areas are the East Khasi hills, the South Garo hills and the Jainta hills (home to the 21.4km-long Krem Kotsati–Umlawan cave, the longest system in mainland Asia). For potholing contacts in Meghalaya, see p.975.

Diving and snorkelling

Because of the number of rivers draining into the sea around the Subcontinent, India's **coastal waters** are generally silt-laden and too murky for decent diving or snorkelling. However, in many areas abundant hard coral and colourful fish make up for the relatively poor visibility. India also counts two beautiful tropical-island archipelagos in its territory, both surrounded by exceptionally clear seas. Served by well-equipped and reputable diving centres, the Andaman Islands and Lakshadweep offer world-class diving on a par with just about anything in Asia. Don't come here expecting rock-bottom prices though. Compared to Thailand, India's dive schools are pricey, typically charging around Rs15,000 ($350) for a four-day PADI-approved open-water course.

For independent travellers, the most promising destination for both scuba-diving and snorkelling is the **Andaman Islands** in the Bay of Bengal, around 1000km east of the mainland. Part of a chain of submerged mountains that stretch north from Sumatra to the coast of Burma (Myanmar), this isolated archipelago is ringed by gigantic coral reefs whose crystal-clear waters are teeming with tropical fish and other marine life. Given the high cost of diving courses, most visitors stick to snorkelling, but if you already have your PADI permit, it's well worth renting equipment from one of the two dive schools in the capital, Port Blair, and joining an excursion to an offshore dive-site such as Cinque Island or the Mahatma Gandhi Marine Reserve. If you want to do an open-water course, book ahead as places tend to be in short supply especially during the peak season, between December and February.

Lakshadweep (see pp.1232–1233) is a classic coconut palm-covered atoll, some 400km west of Kerala in the Arabian Sea. The shallow lagoons, extensive coral reefs and exceptionally good visibility make this a perfect option for both first-timers and more experienced divers.

As with other countries, qualified divers should take their current certification card and/or logbook; if you haven't used it for one year or more, expect to have to take a short test costing around Rs300 ($7).

Yoga, meditation and ashrams

The birthplace of yoga and the spiritual home of the world's most famous meditation traditions, India offers unrivalled opportunities for spiritual nourishment, ranging from basic yoga and pranayama classes to extended residential meditation retreats.

Yoga is taught virtually everywhere in India and there are several internationally known centres where you can train to become a teacher. **Meditation** is similarly practised all over the country and specific courses are available in temples, meditation centres, monasteries and ashrams. **Ashrams** are communities where people work, live and study together, drawn by a common, usually spiritual, goal.

Details of yoga and meditation courses and ashrams are provided throughout the Guide chapters of this book. Most centres offer courses that you can enrol on at short notice, but many of the more popular ones, listed on p.73, need to be booked well in advance.

Yoga

Yoga (meaning "to unite") aims to help the practitioner unite his or her individual consciousness with the divine. This is achieved by raising awareness of one's self through spiritual, mental and physical exercises and discipline. **Hatha yoga**, the most popular form of yoga in the West, is based on physical postures called *asanas*, which stretch, relax and tone the muscular system of the body and also massage the internal organs. Each *asana* has a beneficial effect on a particular muscle group or organ,

and although they vary widely in difficulty, consistent practice will lead to improved suppleness and health benefits. For serious practitioners, however, hatha yoga is seen simply as the first step leading to more subtle stages of meditation which commence when the energies of the body have been awakened and sensitized by stretching and relaxing. Other forms of yoga include *raja* yoga, which includes moral discipline, and *bhakti* yoga, the yoga of devotion, which entails a commitment to one's guru or teacher. *Jnana* yoga (the yoga of knowledge) is centred around the deep philosophies that underlie Hindu spiritual thinking.

Rishikesh, in Uttarakhand, is India's yoga capital, with a bumper crop of ashrams offering all kinds of courses (see p.362 for more details). The country's most famous teachers, however, work from institutes further south. **Iyengar** yoga is one of the most famous approaches studied today, named after its founder, BKS Iyengar (a student of the great yoga teacher Sri Tirumalai Krishnamacharya), with its main centre, the Ramamani Iyengar Memorial Yoga Institute, in Pune, Maharashtra. Iyengar's style is based upon precise physical alignment during each posture. With much practice, and the aid of props such as blocks, straps and chairs, the student can attain perfect physical balance and, the theory goes, perfect balance of mind will follow. Iyengar yoga has a strong therapeutic element and has been used successfully for treating a wide variety of structural and internal problems.

Ashtanga yoga is an approach developed by Pattabhi Jois, who also studied under Krishnamacharya. Unlike Iyengar yoga, which centres around a collection of separate *asanas*, Ashtanga links various postures into a series of flowing moves called *vinyasa*, with the aim of developing strength and agility. The perfect synchronization of movement with breath is a key objective throughout these sequences. Although a powerful form it can be frustrating for beginners as each move has to be perfected before moving on to the next one.

The son of Krishnamacharya, TKV Desikachar, established a third major branch in modern yoga, emphasizing a more versatile and adaptive approach to teaching, focused on the situation of the individual practitioner. This style became known as Viniyoga, although Desikachar has long tried to distance himself from the term. In the mid-1970s, he co-founded the Krishnamacharya Yoga Mandiram (KYM), now a flagship institute in Chennai, in neighbouring Tamil Nadu and, in 2006, an off-shoot now steered by his son Kausthub, called the Krishnamacharya Healing and Yoga Foundation (KHYF).

The other most influential Indian yoga teacher of the modern era has been Swami Vishnu Devananda, an acolyte of the famous sage Swami Sivanda, who established the International Sivananda Yoga Vedanta Center, with more than twenty branches in India and abroad. **Sivananda**-style yoga tends to introduce elements in a different order from its counterparts – teaching practices regarded by others as advanced to relative beginners. This fast-forward approach has proved particularly popular with Westerners, who flock in their thousands to intensive introductory courses staged at centres all over India – the most renowned of them at Neyyar Dam, in the hills east of the Keralan capital, Thiruvananthapuram.

Meditation

Meditation is often practised after a session of yoga, when the energy of the body has been awakened, and is an essential part of both Hindu and Buddhist practice. In both religions, meditation is considered the most powerful tool for understanding the true nature of mind and self, an essential step on the path to **enlightenment**. In Vedanta, meditation's aim is to realize the true self as non-dual Brahman or godhead – the foundation of all consciousness and life. *Moksha* (or liberation – the Nirvana of the Buddhists), achieved through disciplines of yoga and meditation, eventually helps believers release the soul from endless cycles of birth and rebirth.

Vipassana meditation is a technique, originally taught by the Buddha, whereby practitioners learn to become more aware of physical sensations and mental processes. Courses last for a minimum of ten days and are austere – involving 4am kick-offs, around ten hours of meditation a day, no solid food after noon, segregation of the sexes, and no talking for the duration (except with the leaders of the course). Courses are free for all first-time students, to allow everyone an opportunity to learn and benefit from the technique. Vipassana is taught in more than 25 centres throughout India including in Bodhgaya, Bengaluru (Bangalore), Chennai, Hyderabad and Jaipur.

Tibetan Buddhist meditation is attracting more and more followers around the world. With its four distinct schools, Tibetan Buddhism incorporates a huge variety of meditation practices, including Vipassana, known as *shiné* in Tibetan, and various visualization techniques involving the numerous deities that make up the complex and colourful Tibetan pantheon. India, with its large Tibetan diaspora, has become a major centre for those wanting to study Tibetan Buddhism and medicine. Dharamsala in Himachal Pradesh, home to the Dalai Lama and Tibetan government-in-exile, is the main centre for Tibetan studies, offering numerous opportunities for one-on-one study with the Tibetan monks and nuns who live there. Other major Tibetan diaspora centres in India include Darjeeling in West Bengal and Bylakuppe near Mysore in Karnataka. For further details of courses available locally, see the relevant Guide chapters.

Ashrams

Ashrams can range in size from just a handful of people to several thousand, and their rules, regulations and restrictions vary enormously. Some offer on-site accommodation, others will require you to stay in the nearest town or village. Some charge Western prices, others local prices, and some operate on a donation basis. Many ashrams have set programmes each day, while others are less structured, teaching as and when requested.

Courses and ashrams

Astanga Yoga Nilayam 235 8th Cross, 3rd stage, Gokulam, Mysore 570002, Karnataka ⓦwww.ayri.org. Run by Pattabhi Jois, one of the great innovators of yoga in India, and offering tuition in dynamic yoga, affiliated with martial arts. Courses last between one and six months and need to be booked in advance.

Divine Life Society PO Shivanandanagar, Muni ki Reti, Rishikesh, District Tehri Garhwal, Uttarakhand ☏0135/430040, ⓦwww.sivanandadlishq.org. The original Sivananda ashram – well organized if institutional, with several retreats and courses on all aspects and forms of yoga.

International Society for Krishna Consciousness (ISKCON) 3c Albert Rd, Kolkata (Calcutta) ☏033/247 3757; Bhaktivedanta Swami Marg, Raman Reti, Vrindavan ☏0565/442478, ⓦwww.iskcon.com. Large and well-run international organization with major ashrams and temples in Mayapur, north of Kolkata (Calcutta) in West Bengal, Vrindavan in west UP and centres in several major Indian cities and abroad. Promotes bhakti yoga (the yoga of devotion) through good deeds, right living and chanting – a way of life rather than a short course.

Mata Amritanandamayi Math Amritapuri, Vallikkavu, Kerala ⓦwww.amritapuri.org. The ashram of the famous "Hugging Saint", Amma, visited annually by hundreds of thousands, who pass through for darshan and a hug from the smiley guru, whose charitable works have earned for her near-divine status in the south.

Osho Commune International 17 Koregaon Park, Pune, Maharashtra 411001 ☏020/612 6655, ⓦwww.osho.com. Established by the enigmatic Osho, who generated a huge following of both Western and Indian devotees, this centre is set in 31 acres of beautifully landscaped gardens and offers a variety of courses in personal therapy, healing

and meditation. For full details see p.767. There are numerous other Indian and international centres.

Prasanthi Nilayam Puttaparthi, Andhra Pradesh ☏08555/87236, ⓦwww.saionline.org. The ashram of Satya Sai Baba, one of India's most revered and popular gurus, who has a worldwide following of millions despite the deaths of four followers in mysterious circumstances in 2000. The ashram is four or five hours by bus from Bangalore. Visitors sometimes comment on the strict security staffing and rigid rules and regulations. Cheap accommodation is available in dormitories or "flats" for four people. There is no need to book in advance though you should phone to check availability; see p.1060 for more details. Sai Baba also has a smaller ashram in Bangalore and one in Kodaikanal.

Root Institute for Wisdom Culture Bodhgaya, Bihar ☏0631/400714, ⓦwww.rootinstitute.com. Regular seven- to ten-day courses on Tibetan Buddhism and meditation are held here from Oct to March, and there are facilities for individual retreats. Accommodation for longer stays should be booked well in advance. See p.920 for further details.

Saccidananda Ashram Thanneepalli, Kullithalai, near Tiruchirapelli Tamil Nadu ☏04323/22260, ⓦwww.bedegriffiths.com. Also known as Shantivanam (meaning Peace Forest in Sanskrit), it is situated on the banks of the sacred river Cauvery. Founded by Father Bede Griffiths, a visionary Benedictine monk, it presents a curious but sympathetic fusion of Christianity and Hinduism. Visitors can join in the services and rituals or just relax here. Accommodation is in simple huts dotted around the grounds and meals are communal. Very busy during the major Christian festivals.

Sivananda Yoga Vedanta Dhanwantari Ashram Thiruvananthapuram, Kerala ☏0471/227 3093, ⓦwww.sivananda.org. An offshoot of the original Divine Life Society, this yoga-based ashram focuses on *asanas*, breathing techniques (*pranayama*) and meditation. They also run month-long yoga teacher-training programmes, but book well in advance. There are further branches in Madurai, Chennai, Delhi and Uttarkashi – see the website for details.

Tushita Meditation Centre McLeod Ganj, Dharamsala 176219, Himachal Pradesh ☏01892/21866, ⓦwww.tushita.info. Offers a range of Tibetan meditation courses. A ten-day course costs in the region of Rs3500; book well in advance.

Vipassana International Academy Runs a wide variety of 3- to 45-day courses in Vipassana meditation at around 25 centres across India. See the website, ⓦwww.dhamma.org, for details.

Culture and etiquette

Cultural differences extend to all sorts of little things. While allowances will usually be made for foreigners, visitors unacquainted with Indian customs may need a little preparation to avoid causing offence or making fools of themselves. The list of do's and don'ts here is hardly exhaustive: when in doubt, watch what the Indian people around you are doing.

Eating and the right-hand rule

The biggest minefield of potential faux pas has to do with **eating**. This is usually done with the fingers, and requires practice to get absolutely right. Rule one is: **eat with your right hand only**. In India, as right across Asia, the left hand is for wiping your bottom, cleaning your feet and other unsavoury functions (you also put on and take off your shoes with your left hand), while the right hand is for eating, shaking hands, and so on.

Quite how rigid individuals are about this tends to vary, with brahmins (who, at the top of the hierarchical ladder, are one of the two "right-handed castes") and southerners likely to be the strictest. While you can hold a cup or utensil in your left hand, and you can usually get away with using it to help tear your chapati, you should not eat, pass food or wipe your mouth with your left hand. Best is to keep it out of sight below the table.

This rule extends beyond food. In general, do not pass anything to anyone with your left hand, or point at anyone with it either; and Indians won't be impressed if you put it in your mouth. In general, you should accept things given to you with your right hand – though using both hands is a sign of respect.

The other rule to beware of when eating or drinking is that your lips should not touch other people's food – *jhutha*, or sullied food, is strictly taboo. Don't, for example, take a bite out of a chapati and pass it on. When drinking out of a cup or bottle to be shared with others, don't let it touch your lips, but rather pour it directly into your mouth. This custom also protects you from things like hepatitis. It is customary to wash your hands before and after eating.

Temples and religion

Religion is taken very seriously in India; it's important always to show due respect to religious buildings, shrines, images, and people at prayer. When entering a **temple or mosque**, remove your shoes and leave them at the door (socks are acceptable and protect your feet from burning-hot stone ground). Some temples – Jain ones in particular – do not allow you to enter wearing or carrying leather articles, and forbid entry to menstruating women. When entering a religious establishment, dress conservatively (see below), and try not to be obtrusive.

In a mosque, you'll not normally be allowed in at prayer time and women are sometimes not let in at all. In a Hindu temple, you are not often allowed into the inner sanctum; and at a Buddhist stupa or monument, you should always walk round clockwise (ie, with the stupa on your right). Hindus are very superstitious about taking photographs of images of deities and inside temples; if in doubt, desist. Do not take photos of funerals or cremations.

Funeral processions are private affairs, and should be left in peace. In Hindu funerals, the body is normally carried to the cremation site within hours of death by white-shrouded relatives (white is the colour of mourning). The eldest son is expected to shave his head and wear white following the death of a parent. At Varanasi and other places, you may see cremations; such occasions should be treated with respect, and photographs should not be taken.

Dress

Indian people are very conservative about dress. **Women** are expected to dress modestly, with legs and shoulders covered. Trousers are acceptable, but shorts and short skirts are offensive to many. **Men** should always wear a shirt in public, and avoid shorts (a sign of low caste) away from beach areas. These rules go double in temples and mosques. Cover your head with a cap or cloth when entering a *dargah* (Sufi shrine) or Sikh *gurudwara*; women in particular are also required to cover their limbs. Men are similarly expected to dress appropriately with their legs and head covered. Caps are usually available on loan, often free, for visitors, and sometimes cloth is available to cover up your arms and legs.

Never mind sky-clad Jains (see p.1369) or *naga sadhus*, **nudity** is not acceptable in India. The mild-mannered people of Goa may not say anything about nude bathing (though it is in theory prohibited), but you can be sure they don't like it.

In general, Indians find it hard to understand why rich Westerners should wander round in ragged clothes or imitate the lowest ranks of Indian society, who would love to have something more decent to wear. Staying well groomed and dressing "respectably" vastly improves the impression you make on local people, and reduces sexual harassment for women too.

Other possible gaffes

Kissing and **embracing** are regarded in India as part of sex: do not do them in public. In more conservative areas (ie outside westernized parts of big cities), it is not even a good idea for couples to hold hands, though Indian men can sometimes be seen holding hands as a sign of "brotherliness". Be aware of your **feet**. When entering a private home, you should normally remove your shoes (follow your host's example); when sitting, avoid pointing the soles of your feet at anyone. Accidental contact with one's foot is always followed by an apology.

Indian English can be very formal and even ceremonious. Indian people may well call you "sir" or "madam", even "good lady" or "kind sir". At the same time, you should be aware that your English may seem rude to them. In particular, swearing is taken rather seriously, and casual use of the F-word is likely to shock.

Meeting people

Westerners have an ambiguous status in Indian eyes. In one way, you represent the rich sahib, whose culture dominates the world, and the old colonial mentality has not completely disappeared. On the other hand, as a non-Hindu, you are an outcaste, your presence in theory polluting to an orthodox or high-caste Hindu, while to members of all religions, your morals and your standards of spiritual and physical cleanliness are suspect.

As a traveller, you will constantly come across people who want to strike up a **conversation**. English not being their first language, they may not be familiar with the conventional ways of doing this, and thus their opening line may seem abrupt if at the same time very formal. "Excuse me good gentleman, what is your mother country?" is a typical one. It is also the first in a series of questions that Indian men seem sometimes to have learnt from a single book in order to ask Western tourists. Some of the questions may baffle at first ("What is your qualification?" "Are you in service?"), some may be queries about the ways of the West or the purpose of your trip, but mostly they will be about your family and your job.

You may find it odd or even intrusive that complete strangers should want to know that sort of thing, but these subjects are considered polite conversation between strangers in India, and help people place one another in terms of social position. Your family, job, even income, are not considered "personal" subjects, and it is completely normal to ask people about them. Asking the same questions back will not be taken amiss – far from it. Being curious does not have the "nosey" stigma in India that it has in the West.

Things that Indian people are likely to find strange about you are lack of religion (you could adopt one), travelling alone, leaving your family to come to India, being an unmarried couple (letting people think you are married can make life easier), and travelling second class or staying in cheap hotels when, as a tourist, you are relatively rich. You will probably end up having to explain the same things many times to many different people; on the other hand, you can ask questions too, so you could take it as an opportunity to ask things you want to know about India. English-speaking Indians and members of the large and growing middle class in particular are usually extremely well informed and well educated.

 # Shopping

So many beautiful and exotic souvenirs are on sale in India, at such low prices, that it's sometimes hard to know what to buy first. On top of that, all sorts of things (such as made-to-measure clothes) that would be vastly expensive at home are much more reasonably priced in India. Even if you lose weight during your trip, your baggage might well put on quite a bit – unless of course you post some of it home. For details on what to buy while in India, see the "Crafts to go" colour section.

Where to shop

Quite a few items sold in tourist areas are made elsewhere and, needless to say, it's more fun (and cheaper) to pick them up at source. Best buys are noted in the relevant sections of the Guide, along with a few specialities that can't be found outside their regions. India is awash with **street hawkers**, often very young kids. Although they can be annoying and should be dealt with firmly if you are not interested, do not write them off completely as they sometimes have decent souvenirs at lower than shop prices and are open to hard bargaining.

Virtually all the state governments in India run handicraft **"emporia"**, most with branches in the major cities such as Delhi, Mumbai, Chennai and Kolkata. Those four cities also have **Central Cottage Industries Emporiums**. Goods in these emporiums are generally of a high quality, even if their fixed prices are a little expensive, and they are worth a visit to get an idea of what crafts are available and how much they should cost.

Bargaining

Whatever you **buy** (except food and cigarettes), you will almost always be expected to **haggle** over the price.

Bargaining is very much a matter of personal style, but should always be lighthearted, never acrimonious. There are no hard and fast rules – it's really a question of how much something is worth to you. It's a good plan, therefore, to have an idea of how much you want to pay. Bid low and let the shopkeeper argue you up. If they'll settle for your price or less, you have a deal. If not, you don't, but you've had a pleasant conversation and no harm is done.

Don't worry too much about the first quoted prices. Some people suggest paying a third of the opening price, but it really depends on the shop, the goods and the shopkeeper's impression of you. You may not be able to get the seller much below the first quote; on the other hand, you may end up paying as little as a tenth of it. If you bid too low, you may be hustled out of the shop for offering an "insulting" price, but this is all part of the game, and you'll no doubt be welcomed as an old friend if you return the next day.

"Green" tourists are easily spotted, so try and look like you know what you are up to, even on your first day, or leave it till later; you could wait and see what the going rate is first.

Haggling is a little bit like bidding in an auction, and similar rules apply. Don't start haggling for something if you know you don't want it, and never let any figure pass your lips that you are not prepared to pay – having mentioned a price, you are obliged to pay it. If the seller asks you how much you would pay for something, and you don't want it, say so.

Sometimes rickshaw-wallahs and taxi drivers stop unasked at shops where they get a small **commission** simply for bringing customers. In places like Jaipur and Agra where this is common practice, tourists sometimes even strike a deal with their drivers – agreeing to stop at five shops and splitting the commission for the time wasted. If you're taken to a shop by a tout or driver and you buy something, you pay around fifty percent extra. Stand firm about not entering shops and getting to your destination if you have no appetite for such shenanigans. If you want a bargain, shop alone, and never let anybody on the street take you to a shop – if you do, they'll be getting a commission, and you'll be paying it.

Women travellers

India is not a country that provides huge obstacles to women travellers, petty annoyances being more the order of the day. In the days of the Raj, upper-class eccentrics started a tradition of lone women travellers, taken up enthusiastically by the flower children of the hippy era. Women today still do it, but few get through their trip without any hassle, and it's good to prepare yourself to be a little thick-skinned.

Indian streets are almost without exception male-dominated – something that may take a bit of getting used to, particularly when you find yourself subjected to incessant staring, whistling and name calling. This can usually be stopped by ignoring the offender(s) and quickly moving on, or by firmly telling them to stop looking at you. Most of your fellow travellers on trains and buses will be men who may start up most unwelcome conversations about sex, divorce and the freedom of relationships in the West. These cannot often be avoided, but demonstrating too much enthusiasm about discussing such topics can lure men into thinking that you are easy about sex, and the situation could become threatening. At its worst in larger cities, all this can become very tiring. You can get round it to a certain extent by joining women in public places, and you'll notice an immense difference if you join up with a male travelling companion. In this case, expect Indian men to approach him (assumed, of course, to be your husband – an assumption it is sometimes advantageous to go along with) and talk to him about you quite happily as if you were not there. Beware, however, if you are (or look) Indian with a non-Indian male companion: this may well cause you harassment, as you might be seen to have brought shame on your family by adopting the loose morals of the West.

In addition to staring and suggestive comments and looks, sexual harassment, or **"Eve teasing"**, as it's quaintly known in India, is likely to be a nuisance, but not generally a threat. north Indian men are particularly renowned for their disregard of women's rights, and it is on the plains of Uttar Pradesh and Bihar that you are most likely to experience physical hassle. Expect to get groped in crowds, and to have men "accidentally" squeeze past you at any opportunity. It tends to be worse in cities than in small towns and villages, but being followed can be a real problem pretty much anywhere.

In time you'll learn to gauge a situation – sometimes wandering around on your own may attract so much unwanted attention that you may prefer to go back to your hotel room or disappear into a café until you've recharged your batteries or your male fan club has moved on. It's always best to dress modestly – a *salwar kameez* is perfect, as is any baggy clothing – and refrain from smoking and drinking in public, which only reinforces prejudices that Western women are "loose" and "easy".

Returning an unwanted touch with a punch or slap is perfectly in order (Indian women often become aggressive when offended), and does serve to vent a little frustration. It should also attract attention and urge someone to help you, or at least deal with the offending man – a man transgressing social norms is always out of line, and any passer-by will want to let him know it. If you feel someone getting too close in a crowd or on a bus, brandishing your left shoe in his face can be very effective.

Violent sexual assaults on tourists are extremely rare, but the number of reported cases of rape is rising. Though no assault can be predicted, you can take precautions: avoid quiet, dimly lit streets and alleys at night; if you find a trustworthy rickshaw/taxi driver in the day keep him for the night journey; and try to get someone to accompany you to your hotel whenever possible. While Indian women are still quite timid about reporting rape – it is considered as much a disgrace to the victim as to the perpetrator – Western victims should always report it to the police, and before leaving the area try to let other tourists, or locals, know, in the hope that pressure from the community may uncover the offender and see him brought to justice. At present there's nowhere for tourists who've suffered sexual violence to go for sanctuary; most victims seek support from other travellers, or go home.

The **practicalities of travel** take on a new dimension for lone women travellers. Often you can turn your gender to your advantage. For example, on buses the driver and conductor will often take you under their wing, watch out for you and buy you chai at each stop, and there will be countless other instances of kindness wherever you travel. You'll also be more welcome in some private houses than a group of Western males, and may find yourself learning the finer points of Indian cooking round the family's clay stove. Women frequently get preference at bus and railway stations where they can form a separate "ladies' queue", effectively queue-jumping past any waiting men, and use ladies' waiting rooms. On overnight trains the enclosed ladies' compartments are peaceful havens (unless filled with noisy children); you could also try to share a berth section with a family where you are usually drawn into the security of the group and are less exposed to lusty gazes. In hotels watch out for "peep-holes" in your door (and in shared bathrooms), be sure to cover your window when changing and when sleeping, and avoid the sleazy permit-room hotels of the southern cities.

Lastly, bring your own supply of tampons, which are not widely available outside Indian cities.

Travel essentials

Costs

For Western visitors, India is still one of the world's less expensive countries. A little foreign currency can go a long way, and you can be confident of getting good value for your money, whether you're setting out to keep your budget to a minimum or to enjoy the opportunities that spending a bit more will make possible.

What you spend obviously depends on where you go, where you stay, how you get around, what you eat and what you buy. You could just about survive on a **budget** of as little as Rs500 (£6/$12) per day, if you eat in local *dhabas*, stay in the cheapest hotels and don't travel too much. In reality, most backpackers nowadays tend to spend at least double that. For Rs1000 per day you'll be able to afford comfortable mid-range hotels, and meals in smarter restaurants, regular rickshaw or taxi rides and entrance fees to monuments. Spend around Rs2000 (£36/$72) per day and you can stay in swish hotels, eat in the top restaurants, travel first class on trains. Although it is possible to travel very comfortably in India, it's also

possible to spend a great deal of money, if you want to experience the very best the country has to offer, and there are plenty of hotels now charging $500 per night, sometimes a lot more.

Budget **accommodation** is still very good value, however. Cheap double rooms usually start from around Rs250 (£3/$6) per night, while a no-frills vegetarian **meal** in an ordinary restaurant will typically cost no more than Rs100. Long-distance **transport** can work out to be phenomenally good value if you stick to state buses and standard second-class non-a/c trains, but soon starts to add up if you opt for air-conditioned carriages on the superfast intercity services. The 200km trip from Delhi to Agra, for example, can cost anywhere from Rs79 (£1/$2) in second class unreserved up to Rs756 (£10/$20) in first-class a/c.

Where you are also makes a difference: Mumbai is notoriously pricey, especially for accommodation, and Delhi is also substantially more expensive than most parts of the country. Fierce competition tends to keep accommodation prices down in popular

---

Things to take

Most things are easy to find in India and cheaper than at home, but here is a list of **useful** items worth bringing with you bearing in mind that your bags should not get too heavy:

- A padlock and chain
- A universal sink plug (few sinks or bathtubs have them)
- A mosquito net
- A pillowcase
- A small flashlight and spare bulbs
- Earplugs (for street noise in hotel rooms and music on buses)
- High-factor sunblock (difficult to find in India)
- A multipurpose penknife
- A needle and some thread (but dental floss is better than cotton for holding baggage together)
- Plastic bags (to sort your baggage, make it easier to pack and unpack, and keep out damp and dust)
- Tampons
- Condoms
- Multi-vitamin and mineral tablets

ASI entrance fees

The Archeological Survey of India (ASI), who manage many of India's most popular monuments, such as the Taj Mahal, currently operates a **two-tier entry system** at all its sites, whereby foreign visitors, including nonresident Indians, pay more (sometimes a lot more) than Indian residents; we've listed entrance fees for both foreigners and Indian residents throughout the Guide. At the time of writing it was still technically possible to pay in either dollars or rupees, although there have been suggestions that the ASI will soon be accepting payment in rupees only.

destinations like the Goa beaches and the more touristy towns in Rajasthan, although what you save on your guesthouse you might spend on food, which is usually pricier in travellers' cafés than in local *dhabas*. Out in the sticks, on the other hand, and particularly away from your fellow tourists, you will often find things incredibly cheap, though your choice will obviously be more limited.

Don't make any rigid assumptions at the outset of a long trip that your money will last for a certain number of weeks or months. On any one day it may be possible to spend very little, but cumulatively you won't be doing yourself any favours if you don't make sure you keep yourself well rested and properly fed. As a foreigner in India, you will find yourself penalized by double-tier entry prices to museums and historic sites (see box above) as well as in upmarket hotels and air fares, both of which are levied at a higher rate and in dollars.

Some independent travellers tend to indulge in wild and highly competitive **penny-pinching**, which Indian people find rather pathetic – they know how much an air ticket to Delhi or Mumbai costs, and they have a fair idea of what you can earn at home. Bargain where appropriate, but don't begrudge a few rupees to someone who's worked hard for them: consider what their services would cost at home, and how much more valuable the money is to them than it is

to you. Even if you get a bad deal on every rickshaw journey you make, it will only add a minuscule fraction to the cost of your trip. Remember too, that every pound or dollar you spend in India goes that much further, and luxuries you can't afford at home become possible here: sometimes it's worth spending more simply because you get more for it. At the same time, don't pay well over the odds for something if you know what the going rate is. Thoughtless extravagance can, particularly in remote areas that see a disproportionate number of tourists, contribute to inflation, putting even basic goods and services beyond the reach of local people.

Crime and personal safety

In spite of the crushing poverty and the yawning gulf between rich and poor, India is, on the whole, a safe country in which to travel. As a tourist, however, you are an obvious target for the tiny number of thieves (who may include some of your fellow travellers), and stand to face serious problems if you do lose your passport, money and ticket home. Common sense, therefore, suggests a few precautions.

Beware of crowded locations, such as packed buses or trains, in which it is easy for pickpockets to operate – slashing pockets or bags with razor blades is not unheard of in certain locations, and itching powder is sometimes used to distract the unwary. Don't leave valuables unattended on the beach when you go for a swim; backpacks in dormitory accommodation are also obvious targets, as is luggage on the roof of buses. Even monkeys rate a mention here, since it's not unknown for them to steal things from hotel rooms with open windows, or even to snatch bags from unsuspecting shoulders.

Budget travellers would do well to carry a **padlock**, as these are usually used to secure the doors of cheap hotel rooms and it's reassuring to know you have the only key. You can also use them to lock your bag to seats or racks in trains, for which a length of chain also comes in handy. Don't put valuables in your luggage for bus or plane journeys: keep them with you at all times. If your baggage is on the roof of a bus, make sure it is well secured. On trains and buses,

Drugs

Future is black if sugar is brown

Indian anti-drugs poster

India is a centre for the production of **cannabis** and to a lesser extent **opium**, and derivatives of these drugs are widely available. **Charas** (hashish) is produced all along the Himalayas. The use of cannabis is frowned upon by respectable Indians – if you see anyone in a movie smoking a chillum, you can be sure it's the baddie. Sadhus, on the other hand, are allowed to smoke **ganja** (marijuana) legally as part of their religious devotion to Shiva, who is said to have originally discovered its narcotic properties.

Bhang (a preparation made from marijuana leaves, which it is claimed sometimes contains added hallucinogenic ingredients such as datura) is legal and widely available in bhang shops: it is used to make sweets and drinks such as the notoriously potent bhang lassis which have waylaid many an unwary traveller. Bhang shops also frequently sell ganja, low-quality *charas* and opium (*chandu*), mainly from Rajasthan and Madhya Pradesh. Opium derivatives morphine and heroin are widespread too, with addiction an increasing problem among the urban poor. "Brown sugar" that you may be offered on the street is number-three heroin; Varanasi is becoming notorious for its heroin problem. Use of other illegal drugs such as LSD, ecstasy and cocaine is largely confined to tourists in party locations such as Goa.

All of these drugs except bhang are strictly controlled under Indian **law**. Anyone arrested with less than five grams of cannabis, which they are able to prove is for their own use, is liable to a six-month maximum, but cases can take years to come to trial (two is normal, and eight not unheard of). Police raids and searches are particularly common at the following places: Manali, the Kullu valley and Almora, and on buses from those places to Delhi, especially at harvest time; buses and trains crossing certain state lines, notably between Gujarat and Maharastra; budget hotels in Delhi's Paharganj; the beach areas of Goa; and around Idukki and Kumily in Kerala. "Paying a fine now" may be possible on arrest (though it will probably mean all the money you have), but once you are booked in at the station, your chances are slim; a minority of the population languishing in Indian jails are foreigners on drugs charges.

the prime time for theft is just before you leave, so keep a particular eye on your gear then, beware of deliberate diversions, and don't put your belongings next to open windows. Remember that routes popular with tourists tend to be popular with thieves too; knifepoint muggings are on the increase in Goa. Druggings leading to theft and worse are rare but not unheard of and so you are best advised to politely refuse food and drink from fellow passengers or passing strangers, unless you are completely confident it's the family picnic you are sharing or have seen the food purchased from a vendor.

However, **don't get paranoid**; the best way of enjoying the country is to stay relaxed but with your wits about you. Crime levels in India are a long way below those of Western countries, and violent crime against tourists is extremely rare. Virtually none of the people who approach you on the street intend any

harm: most want to sell you something (though this is not always made apparent immediately), some want to practise their English, others (if you're a woman) to chat you up, while more than a few just want to add your address to their book or have a snap taken with you. Anyone offering wonderful-sounding moneymaking schemes, however, is almost certain to be a con artist.

If you do feel threatened, it's worth looking for help. **Tourism police** are found sitting in clearly marked booths in the main railway stations, especially in big tourist centres, where they will also have a booth in the main bus station. They may also have a marked booth outside major tourist sites.

Be wary of **credit card fraud**; a credit card can be used to make duplicate forms to which your account is then billed for fictitious transactions, so don't let shops or restaurants take your card away to process – insist they do it in front of you or follow them to the point of transaction.

It's not a bad idea to keep $100 or so separately from the rest of your money, along with your traveller's cheque receipts, insurance policy number and phone number for claims, and a photocopy of the pages in your passport containing personal data and your Indian visa. This will cover you in case you do lose all your valuables.

If the worst happens and you get **robbed**, the first thing to do is report the theft as soon as possible to the local police. They are very unlikely to recover your belongings, but you need a report from them in order to claim on your travel insurance. Dress smartly and expect an uphill battle – city cops in particular tend to be jaded from too many insurance and traveller's cheque scams.

Losing your passport is a real hassle, but does not necessarily mean the end of your trip. First, report the loss immediately to the police, who will issue you with the all-important "complaint form" that you need to be able to travel around and check into hotels, as well as claim back any expenses incurred in replacing your passport from your insurer. A complaint form, however, will not allow you to change money or traveller's cheques. If you've run out of cash, your best bet is to ask your hotel manager to help you out (staff will have seen your passport when you checked in, and the number will be in the register). The next thing to do is telephone your nearest embassy or consulate in India. Normally, passports have to be applied for and collected in person, but if you are stranded, it is usually possible to arrange to receive the necessary forms in the post. However, you still have to go to the embassy or consulate to pick up your new passport. "Emergency passports" are the cheapest form of replacement, but are normally only valid for the few days of your return flight. If you're not sure when you're leaving India, you'll have to obtain a more costly "full passport"; these can only be issued by embassies and larger consulates in Delhi or Mumbai, and not those in Chennai, Kolkata (Calcutta) or Panjim.

Duty free allowance

Anyone over 17 can bring in one US quart (0.95 litre – but nobody's going to quibble about the other 5ml) of spirits, or a bottle of wine and 250ml spirits; plus 200 cigarettes, or 50 cigars, or 250g tobacco. You may be required to register anything valuable on a tourist baggage re-export form to make sure you can take it home with you, and to fill in a currency declaration form if carrying more than $10,000 or the equivalent.

Electricity

Generally 220V 50Hz AC, though direct current supplies also exist, so check before plugging in. Most sockets are triple round-pin (accepting European-size double round-pin plugs). British, Irish and Australasian plugs will need an adaptor, preferably universal; American and Canadian appliances will need a transformer too, unless multi-voltage. Power cuts and voltage variations are very common; voltage stabilizers should be used to run sensitive appliances such as laptops.

Gay and lesbian travellers

Homosexuality is not generally open or accepted in India. "Carnal intercourse against the order of nature" (anal intercourse) is a ten-year offence under article 377 of the penal code, while laws against "obscene behaviour" can be used to arrest gay men for cruising or liaising anywhere that could be considered a public place. The same law could in theory be used against lesbians.

The homosexual scene in India was brought into the spotlight in 1998 with the nationwide screening of the highly controversial film *Fire* by Deepa Mehta, about two sisters-in-law living together under the same roof who become lesbian lovers. Flying in the face of the traditional emphasis on heterosexual family life, the film created a storm and was banned in some states. Right-wing extremists attacked cinemas that showed it, and in the wake of the attacks, many gay men and lesbians came out into the open for the first time to hold candle-lit protest vigils in Delhi, Mumbai, Kolkata (Calcutta), Chennai and Bengaluru (Bangalore) – all cities known for their more open-minded younger generations.

For **lesbians**, making contacts is rather difficult; even the Indian women's movement does not readily promote lesbianism as an issue that needs confronting. The only public faces of a hidden scene are the organizations listed below and a few of the nationwide women's organizations.

For gay men, homosexuality is no longer solely the preserve of the alternative scene of actors and artists, and is increasingly accepted by the middle-line urban middle and upper classes. If you keep your finger on the social pulse of the larger cities, especially Bengaluru (Bangalore) and Mumbai, you will soon discover which nightclubs and bars have a gay scene. Also, the organizations listed below can tell you about gay events and parties.

Lesbian–Gay contacts and resources

Bombay Dost @www.bombaydost.com. Has contacts nationwide and also publishes *Bombay Dost* (Rs50), a quarterly with news, views and useful information on gay and lesbian issues.
Gay Bombay @www.gaybombay.org. Informal support, chat, background and guides to gay Mumbai.
Good As You @www.geocities.com /goodasyoubangalore. Gay support group in Bengaluru (Bangalore). They also run a helpline on ☎080/2223 0950 (Tues & Fri 7–9pm).
Humrahi @www.geocities.com/WestHollywood /Heights/7258. Forum for gay men in New Delhi.
Humsafar Trust @www.humsafar.org. Set up to promote safe sex among gay men, but the website has lots of links and up-to-date information.
Indian Dost @www.indiandost.com. India-wide gay contacts and info.
Queer India @queerindia.blogspot.com. Interesting blog on gay issues in India.
Sangini @members.tripod.com/~dating_service /sangini.html. New Delhi-based lesbian support group offering information and support, as well as a helpline (☎011/2685 1970; Tues 6–8pm).
Sappho ☎033/2441 9995, @sappho.shoe.org. Lesbian support group in Kolkata.

Timeless India Delhi ☎011/2617 4205, @www .timelessexcursions.com. Delhi-based tour operator offering a gay-friendly tour of Rajasthan and trips through the Kerala backwaters.

Insurance

It's imperative that you take out proper **travel insurance** before setting off for India. In addition to covering medical expenses and emergency flights, travel insurance also insures your money and belongings against loss or theft. Before paying for a new policy, however, it's worth checking whether you are already covered: some all-risks home insurance policies may cover your possessions when overseas, and many private medical schemes include cover when abroad. In Canada, provincial health plans usually provide partial medical cover for mishaps overseas, while holders of official student/teacher/youth cards in Canada and the US are entitled to meagre accident coverage and hospital in-patient benefits. Students will often find that their student health coverage extends during the vacations and for one term beyond the date of last enrolment.

After exhausting the possibilities above, you might want to contact a specialist travel insurance company, or consider the travel insurance deal offered by Rough Guides (see box below). A typical travel insurance policy usually provides cover for the loss of baggage, tickets and – up to a certain limit – cash or cheques, as well as cancellation or curtailment of your journey. Most of them exclude so-called dangerous sports unless an extra premium is paid: in India this can mean scuba diving, whitewater rafting, windsurfing and trekking with ropes, though probably not Jeep

---

Rough Guides travel insurance

Rough Guides has teamed up with Columbus Direct to offer you **travel insurance** that can be tailored to suit your needs. Products include a low-cost **backpacker** option for long stays; a **short break** option for city getaways; a typical **holiday package** option; and others. There are also annual **multi-trip** policies for those who travel regularly. Different sports and activities (trekking, skiing etc) can usually be covered if required.

See our website (@www.roughguides.com/website/shop) for eligibility and purchasing options. Alternatively, UK residents should call ☎0870/033 9988; Australians should call ☎1300/669 999 and New Zealanders should call ☎0800/55 9911. All other nationalities should call ☎+44 870/890 2843.

safaris. Many policies can be chopped and changed to exclude coverage you don't need – for example, sickness and accident benefits can often be excluded or included at will. If you do take medical coverage, ascertain whether benefits will be paid as treatment proceeds or only after return home, and whether there is a 24-hour medical emergency number. When securing baggage cover, make sure that the per-article limit – typically under £500 – will cover your most valuable possession. If you need to make a claim, you should keep receipts for medicines and medical treatment, and in the event you have anything stolen, you must obtain an official statement from the police.

Internet

All large cities and tourist towns now have at least a few (usually dozens) of places where you can get online, either at cyber cafés or your hotel or guesthouse. Prices typically range from around Rs20 to Rs60 per hour. Unfortunately, connections are still poor in many places, with antiquated computers and maddeningly slow and unreliable dial-up connections, making it difficult to load complex websites or to perform online transactions (like booking a train ticket).

Laundry

In India, no one goes to the laundry: if they don't do their own, they send it out to a dhobi. Wherever you are staying, there will either be an in-house dhobi, or one very close by to call on. The dhobi will take your dirty washing to a *dhobi ghat*, a public clothes-washing area (the bank of a river for example), where it is shown some old-fashioned discipline: separated, soaped and given a damn good thrashing to beat the dirt out of it. Then it is hung out to dry in the sun and, once dried, taken to the ironing sheds where every garment is endowed with razor-sharp creases and then matched to its rightful owner by hidden cryptic markings. Your clothes will come back from the dhobi absolutely spotless, though this kind of violent treatment does take it out of them: buttons get lost and eventually the cloth starts to fray. If you'd rather not entrust your Savile Row made-to-measure to their tender mercies, there are dry-cleaners in large towns.

Left luggage

Most stations in India have "cloakrooms" (sometimes called parcel offices) for passengers to leave their baggage. These can be extremely handy if you want to go sightseeing in a town and move on the same day. In theory, you need a train ticket or Indrail pass to deposit luggage, but staff don't always ask; they may, however, refuse to take your bag if you can't lock it. Losing your reclaim ticket causes problems; the clerk will be assumed to have stolen the bag if he can't produce it, so there'll be untold running around to obtain clearance before you can get your bag without it. Make sure, when checking baggage in, that the cloakroom will be open when you need to pick it up. The standard charge is currently Rs10 per 24 hours.

Mail

Mail can take anything from three days to four weeks to get to or from India, depending largely on where you are; ten days is about the norm. Stamps are not expensive, and aerogrammes and postcards cost the same to anywhere in the world. Ideally, you should have mail franked in front of you. Most post offices keep the same opening hours (Mon–Fri 10am–5pm & Sat 10am–noon), but big city GPOs, where the poste restante is usually located, are open longer (Mon–Fri 9.30am–6pm, Sat 9.30am–1pm). You can also buy stamps at big hotels.

Poste restante (general delivery) services throughout the country are pretty reliable, though exactly how long individual offices hang on to letters is more or less at their own discretion; for periods of longer than a month, it makes sense to mark mail with your expected date of arrival. Letters are filed alphabetically; in larger offices, you sort through them yourself. To avoid misfiling, your name should be printed clearly, with the surname in large capitals and underlined, but it is still a good idea to check under your first name too, just in case. Have letters addressed to you c/o Poste Restante, GPO (if it's the main post office you want), and the name of the town and state. In Delhi, you will probably want to specify "GPO, New Delhi", since "GPO, Delhi" means Old Delhi GPO, a lot less convenient for most tourists. Sometimes too, as in Kolkata (Calcutta) and Chennai, local tourist offices might be more convenient than the GPO. Don't forget to take ID with you to claim your mail. American Express offices also keep mail for holders of their charge card or traveller's cheques. Having parcels sent out to you in India is not such a good idea – chances are they'll go astray. If you do have a parcel sent, have it registered.

Sending a parcel out of India can be quite a performance. First you have to get it cleared by customs at the post office (they often don't bother, but check), then you take it to a tailor and agree a price to have it wrapped in cheap cotton cloth (which you may have to go and buy yourself), stitched up and sealed with wax. In big city GPOs, there will often be someone outside the main entrance offering this service. Next, take it to the post office, fill in and attach the relevant customs forms (it's best to tick the box marked "gift" and give its value as less than Rs1000 or "no commercial value", to avoid bureaucratic entanglements), buy your stamps, see them franked, and dispatch it. Parcels should not be more than 1m long, nor weigh more than 20kg. Surface mail is

incredibly cheap, and takes an average of six months to arrive – it may take half, or four times that, however. It's a good way to dump excess baggage and souvenirs, but don't send anything fragile this way.

As in Britain, North America, Australia and New Zealand, books and magazines can be sent more cheaply, unsealed or wrapped around the middle, as printed papers ("book post"). Alternatively, there are numerous **courier** services. These are not as reliable as they should be and there have been complaints of packages going astray; it's safest to stick to known international companies such as DHL. Remember that all packages from India are likely to be suspect at home, and therefore searched or X-rayed: don't send anything dodgy.

Maps

Getting good maps of India, in India, can be difficult: the government – in an archaic suspicion of cartography – forbids the sale of detailed maps of border areas, which includes the entire coastline. In theory, certain maps, especially detailed ones of border areas skirting Tibet and Pakistan, are

41 Years! 17 Awards!

6 Office Locations in INDIA & NEPAL.
More than a million clients serviced.

Custom made, to ready made Tours for your family, friends or groups and even weddings in Palaces of RAJASTHAN or the Beaches of GOA

Our Budget to Luxury Tours are resold by hundreds of agents worldwide, visit us at www.tourism-india.com www.aumtours.com

Price vs Service guaranteed!
Budget Tours starting from **USD 999** for 15 days for 2 people with Accomodation* Transport* Private Driver* Sight Seeing

Capital City Travels and Tours
Hotel Ajanta

Contact Us :
Tel : +91-11-29562097 / 41764563
Mobile No: +91-9990001122
Fax : +91-11-29561338/41764538
E mail : ccity@nda.vsnl.net.in, info@tourism-rajasthan.com

illegal, so use them very discreetly. These maps are available outside India, and useful if you are going to be trekking in places like Ladakh, Spiti, Sikkim and Garhwal.

It makes sense to bring a basic **country map** of India with you, such as Bartholomew's 1:4,000,000 map of South Asia, which has coloured contours and serves as a reliable route map of the whole country; a handful of other publishers, including the Daily Telegraph World Series, produce a similar map, while the Lascelles map on the same scale is also good. Geocentre produces an excellent three-set map of India at a scale of 1:2,500,000, showing good road detail.

Rough Guides, in conjunction with the World Mapping Project, publishes a regional map of South India (1:1,200,000) printed on untearable, water-resistant plastic paper and road-tested by the authors of this book. Nelles also covers parts of the country with 1:1,500,000 regional maps. These are generally excellent, with colour contours, road distances, inset city plans and even the tiniest places marked, but cost a fortune if you buy the complete set. Their double-sided map of the Himalayas is useful for roads and planning and has some detail but is not sufficient as a trekking map. Ttk, a Chennai-based company, publishes basic state maps which are widely available in India, and in some specialized travel and map shops in the UK such as Stanfords; these are poorly drawn but useful for road distances. The Indian Railways map at the back of the publication *Trains at a Glance* (see p.45) is useful for planning railway journeys.

If you need larger-scale **city maps** than the ones we provide in this book – which are keyed to show recommended hotels and restaurants – you can sometimes get them from tourist offices. Both Ttk and the official Indian mapping organization, the Survey of India (Janpath Barracks A, New Delhi 110001; ☎011/2332 2288), have town plans at scales of 1:10,000 and 1:50,000, but they're on the whole far less accurate and up to date than the excellent Eicher series of glossy, A–Z-style books (Delhi, Mumbai, Kolkota, Chennai and Bengaluru {Bangalore} only), produced in India and available at all good bookstores.

As for **trekking maps**, the US Army Map Service produced maps in the 1960s which, with a scale of 1:250,000, remain sufficiently accurate on topography, but are of course outdated on the latest road developments. Most other maps you can buy are based on their work. Their maps of Kanchenjunga, Leh, Palampur (including Bara Bangal, Manali and Lahaul), Tso Moriri (including Tabo, Kaza and Kibber) and Chini (including Kinnaur and the Baspa valley) are some of the best you can get. One exception is the superb Swiss Stiftung für Alpine Forschunger map of the Sikkim Himalayas at a scale of 1:150,000. The Survey of India, recognizing the competition, has come out with a version of the Sikkim map that is not particularly accurate. Leomann Maps (1:200,000) cover Srinagar, Zanskar, West Ladakh, Leh and around, Dharamsala, Kulu with Lahaul and Spiti, Garhwal and Kumaon. These are not contour maps and are therefore better for planning and basic reference than as reliable trekking maps. The Survey of India publishes a rather poor 1:250,000 series for trekkers in the Uttarakhand Himalayas; they are simplified versions of their own infinitely more reliable maps, produced for the military, which are absolutely impossible for an outsider to get hold of.

Money

India's unit of currency is the **rupee**, usually abbreviated "Rs" and divided into a hundred paise. Almost all money is paper, with notes of 5, 10, 20, 50, 100, 500 and 1000 rupees. Coins start at 10 paise and range up to 20, 25 and 50 paise, and 1, 2 and 5 rupees. Note that it's technically illegal to take rupees in or out of India (although they are widely available at overseas forexes), so you might want to wait until you arrive before changing money.

Banknotes, especially lower denominations, can get into a terrible state. Don't accept torn banknotes, since no one else will be prepared to take them and you'll be left saddled with the things, though you can change them at the Reserve Bank of India and large branches of other big banks. Don't pass them on to beggars; they can't use them either, so it amounts to an insult.

Large denominations can also be a problem, as change is usually in short supply. Many Indian people cannot afford to keep much lying around, and you shouldn't necessarily expect shopkeepers or rickshaw-wallahs to have it (and they may – as may you – try to hold onto it if they do). Paying for your groceries with a Rs100 note will probably entail waiting for the grocer's errand boy to go off on a quest to try and change it. Larger notes – like the Rs500 note – are good for travelling with and can be changed for smaller denominations at hotels and other suitable establishments. A word of warning – the Rs500 note looks remarkably similar to the Rs100 note.

At the time of writing (Feb 2008), the **exchange rate** was approximately Rs80 to £1, or Rs40 to $1, and Rs60 to €1. You can check latest exchange rates online at Ⓦwww.xe.com.

Credit cards and traveller's cheques

The easiest way to access your money is with **plastic**, though it's a good idea to also have some back-up in the form of cash or traveller's cheques. You will find ATMs at main banks in all major towns and tourist resorts, though your card issuer may well add a foreign transaction fee, and the Indian bank will also charge a small fee, generally around Rs25. The daily limit on ATM cash withdrawals is usually Rs15,000.

Credit cards are accepted for payment at major hotels, top restaurants, some shops and airline offices, but virtually nowhere else. American Express, MasterCard and Visa are the likeliest to be accepted. Beware of people making extra copies of the receipt, to fraudulently bill you later; insist that the transaction is done before your eyes.

One big downside of relying on plastic as your main access to cash, of course, is that cards can easily get lost or stolen, so take along a couple of alternative ones if you can, keep an emergency stash of cash just in case, and make a note of your home bank's telephone number and website addresses for emergencies.

US dollars are the easiest **currency** to convert, with euros and pounds sterling not far behind. Major hard currencies can be changed easily in tourist areas and big cities,

less so elsewhere. If you enter the country with more than $10,000 or the equivalent, you are supposed to fill in a currency declaration form.

In addition to cash and plastic (or as a generally less convenient alternative to the latter), consider carrying some **traveller's cheques**. You pay a small commission (usually 1%) to buy these with cash in the same currency, a little more to convert from a different currency, but they have the advantage over cash that, if lost or stolen, they can be replaced. Not all banks, however, accept them. Well-known brands such as Thomas Cook and American Express are your best bet, but in some places even American Express is only accepted in US dollars and not as pounds sterling.

Banks and forex bureaux

Changing money in regular banks, especially government-run banks such as the State Bank of India (SBI), can be a time-consuming business, involving lots of form-filling and queuing at different counters, so it's best to change substantial amounts at any one time. In larger towns and tourist centres you'll also find **forex bureaux**, which are a lot less hassle than banks, though their rates may not be as good. Rates of commission vary – most banks charge a percentage, many forex bureaux charge none, and some charge a flat rate, so it's always worth asking before you change.

Outside banking hours (Mon–Fri 10am till 2–4pm, Sat 10am–noon), large hotels may change money, usually at a lower rate, and exchange bureaux have longer opening hours. In Delhi, Thomas Cook at New Delhi station is open 24 hours.

Hold on to exchange receipts ("encashment certificates"); they will be required if you want to change back any excess rupees when you leave the country, and to buy air tickets and reserve train berths with rupees.

If you are having money wired, many larger post offices act as agencies for Western Union (Ⓦwww.westernunion.com), while Moneygram (Ⓦwww.moneygram.com) are represented by Trade Wings, Indusind Bank and Thomas Cook. American Express (Ⓦwww.americanexpress.com/india) and Thomas Cook (Ⓦwww.thomascook.co.in)

International dialling

To call India from abroad, dial the international access code, followed by 91 for India, the local code minus the initial zero, then the number you want.

	From India	To India
UK	☏ 00 44	☏ 00 91
Irish Republic	☏ 00 353	☏ 00 91
US and Canada	☏ 001	☏ 011 91
Australia	☏ 00 61	☏ 0011 91
New Zealand	☏ 00 64	☏ 00 91
South Africa	☏ 00 27	☏ 00 91

both have offices in Delhi and agents in Agra and Jaipur.

Lost and stolen cards/cheques

American Express ☏ 011/2614 5920 or 2687 5050 (24hr), ⊛ www.americanexpress.com. **Thomas Cook** ☏ 0044-1733/318949, ⊛ www .thomascook.co.in.

Baksheesh

As a presumed-rich sahib or memsahib, you will, like wealthy Indians, be expected to be liberal with the baksheesh, which takes three main forms.

The most common is **tipping**: a small reward for a small service, which can encompass anyone from a waiter or porter to someone who lifts your bags onto the roof of a bus or keeps an eye on your vehicle for you. Large amounts are not expected – ten rupees should satisfy all the aforementioned. Taxi drivers and staff at cheaper hotels and restaurants do not necessarily expect tips, but always appreciate them, of course, and they can keep people sweet for the next time you call.

More expensive than plain tipping is paying people to **bend the rules**, many of which seem to have been invented precisely in order to elicit baksheesh. Examples might include letting you into a historical site after hours, finding you a seat or a sleeper on a train that is "full", or speeding up some bureaucratic process. This should not be confused with bribery, a more serious business with its own risks and etiquette, which is best not entered into.

The last kind of baksheesh is **alms giving**. In a country without a welfare system, this is an important social custom. People with disabilities and mutilations are the traditional recipients, and it seems right to join local people in giving out small change to them. Kids demanding money, pens, sweets or the like are a different case, pressing their demands only on tourists. In return for a service it is fair enough, but to yield to any request encourages them to go and pester others.

Opening hours

Standard shop opening hours in India are Monday to Saturday 9.30am to 6pm. Most big stores, at any rate, keep those hours, while smaller shops vary from town to town, religion to religion, and one to another, but usually keep longer hours. Government tourist offices are open Monday to Friday 9.30am to 5pm, Saturday 9.30am to 1pm, closed on the third Saturday of the month, and occasionally also the second Saturday of the month; state-run tourist offices are likely to be open Monday to Friday 10am to 5pm.

Net2Phone

A few Internet cafés in India's larger cities are now starting to offer **Net2Phone** services, which allow you to make international telephone calls over the Web for very low rates (as little as Rs3 per minute for calls to the UK/US). We've listed where you can access Net2Phone in the Guide, but more providers are popping up each month, so keep you eyes peeled for the logo.

Phones

You can make national and international phone calls easily and quickly from any of the innumerable privately owned **phone offices** that can be found in even the smallest towns. These places advertise themselves with the acronyms STD/ISD (standard trunk dialling/ international subscriber dialling), and many have fax machines and email facilities too; some stay open 24 hours.

Both national and international calls are dialled direct. To **call abroad**, dial the international access code (00), the code for the country you want – 44 for the UK, for example – the appropriate area code (leaving out the initial zero), and the number you want; then you speak and pay your bill, which is calculated in seconds. **Prices** vary: private places are usually slightly more expensive than official telecommunications offices, while calling from hotels is usually even more expensive. Direct dialling rates are very expensive during the day – Monday to Saturday 8am to 7pm – but fall by half on Sundays, national holidays, and daily from 7am to 8am and 7pm to 8.30pm, after which the charge is reduced further.

Home country direct services are now available from any phone in India to the UK, the USA, Canada, Ireland, Australia, New Zealand, and a growing number of other countries. These allow you to make a collect or telephone credit card call to that country via an operator there. If you can't find a phone with home country direct buttons, you can use any phone toll-free, by dialling ☎000, your country code, and 17 (except Canada which is ☎000-127).

"**Call back**" (or "back call", as it is often known) is possible at most phone booths and hotels, although check before you call and be aware that, in the case of booths, this facility rarely comes without a charge of Rs3–10 per minute.

Mobile phones

Call charges to and from **mobile phones** are far lower in India than Western countries, which is why lots of foreign tourists opt to sign up to a local network while they're travelling. To do this you'll need to buy an Indian SIM card from a mobile-phone shop; these cost around Rs150, plus the price of a top-up card (varying from Rs150–500). Your retailer will help you get connected. They'll also advise you on which company to use. Different states tend to be dominated by one or other of the main firms – Airtel, BPL or Idea (formerly AT&T). If you intend to stay inside their designated coverage area, charges for texts and calls are cheap. However, to use your phone outside your company's coverage you'll need to shell out extra for a roaming facility – otherwise, you'll have to buy a new SIM card each time you change states. Note that when roaming, both you and your caller pay for incoming calls.

Indian **mobile numbers** are ten-digit, starting with a 9. However, if you are calling from outside the state where the mobile is based (but not from abroad), you will need to add a zero in front of that.

Photography

Beware of pointing your camera at anything that might be considered "strategic", including airports and anything military, but even at bridges, railway stations and main roads. Remember too that some people prefer not to be photographed, so it's a good idea to ask before you take a snapshot of them. More likely, you'll get people, especially kids, volunteering to pose.

You'll find facilities for downloading digital photos and burning them to disc in all larger cities and tourist centres, either in dedicated photography shops or, increasingly, in Internet cafés. Memory cards are also quite widely available. Camera film, sold at average Western prices, is widely available in India (but check the date on the box, and note that false boxes containing outdated film are often sold – Konica have started painting holograms on their boxes to prevent this). It's fairly easy to get films developed, though they don't always come out as well as they might at home; Konica and Kodak film laboratories are usually of a good standard. If you're after slide film, slow film or fast film, buy it in the big cities, and don't expect to find specialist brands such as Velvia; it is rare to find a dealer who keeps film refrigerated. Also, remember to guard your equipment from dust – reliable repair is extremely hard to come by in India.

Time

India is all in one time zone: GMT+5hr 30min. This makes it 5hr 30min ahead of London, 10hr 30min ahead of New York, 13hr 30min ahead of LA, 4hr 30min behind Sydney and 6hr 30min behind NZ; however, summertime in those places will change the difference by an hour. Indian time is referred to as IST (Indian Standard Time, which cynics refer to as "Indian stretchable time").

Toilets

Western toilets are becoming much more common in India now, though you'll probably still come across a few traditional "squat" toilets – basically a hole in the ground. Paper, if used, often goes in a bucket next to the loo rather than down it. Instead, Indians use a jug of water and their left hand, a method you may also come to prefer, but if you do use paper, keep some handy. Some guesthouses and hotels do supply it, but don't count on it, and it's a good idea to stock up before going too far off the beaten track as it's not available everywhere. Travelling is especially difficult for women as facilities are limited or nonexistent, especially when travelling by road rather than by rail. However, toilets in the a/c carriages of trains are usually kept clean, as are those in mid-range and a/c restaurants. In the touristy areas, most hotels offer Western-style loos, even in budget lodges. The latest development is tourist toilets at every major historical site. They cost Rs2 and you get water, mirrors, toilet paper and a clean sit-down loo.

Tourist information

The Indian government maintains a number of **tourist offices abroad**, whose staff are usually helpful and knowledgeable. Other sources of information include the websites of Indian embassies and tourist offices, travel agents (who are in business for themselves, so their advice may not always be totally unbiased), and the Indian Railways representatives listed on p.47.

Inside India, both national and local governments run tourist information offices, providing general travel advice and handing out an array of printed material, from city maps to glossy leaflets on specific destinations. The Indian government's tourist department, whose main offices are on Janpath in New Delhi and opposite Churchgate railway station in Mumbai (see p.104 & p.685), has branches in most regional capitals. These, however, operate independently of the state government information counters and their commercial bureaux run by the state tourism development corporations, usually referred to by their initials (e.g. MPTDC in Madhya Pradesh, RTDC in Rajasthan, and so on), which offer a wide range of travel facilities, including guided tours, car rental and their own hotels. A list of state tourist office websites is given on pp.141–142.

Just to confuse things further, the Indian government's tourist office has a corporate wing too. The Indian Tourism Development Corporation (ITDC) is responsible for the Ashok chain of hotels and operates tour and travel services, frequently competing with its state counterparts.

There's all sorts of information available about India **online** – we've listed the best websites in relevant places throughout the book. One particularly good general site is ⓦwww.indiamike.com, a popular travel forum run out of a bedroom in New Jersey by inveterate India-phile Mike Szewczyk and featuring lively chat rooms, bulletin boards, photo archives and banks of members' travel articles.

Indian government tourist offices

International website ⓦwww.incredibleindia.org
Australia Level 5, 135 King St, Glasshouse Shopping Complex, Sydney ☎02/9221 9555, ⓔindiatourism@com.au.
Canada 60 Bloor St (West), #1003, Toronto, ON M4W 3B8 ☎416/ 962-3787, ⓔindiatourism @bellnet.ca.
South Africa PO Box 412 542, Craighall 2024, Hyde Lane, Lancaster Gate, Johannesburg 2000 ☎011/325 0880, ⓔgoito@global.co.za.
UK 7 Cork St, London W1S 3LH ☎020/7437 3677, ⓔinfo@indiatouristoffice.org.
USA 3550 Wilshire Blvd, Suite #204, Los Angeles, CA 90010 ☎213/380-8855, ⓔindiatourismindla @aol.com; Suite 1808, 1270 Ave of the Americas, New York NY 10020 ☎212/586 4901, ⓔrd@itonyc.com.

Travel warnings and advice

Australian Department of Foreign Affairs
Ⓦ www.dfat.gov.au, Ⓦ www.smartraveller.gov.au.
British Foreign & Commonwealth Office
Ⓦ www.fco.gov.uk.
Canadian Department of Foreign Affairs
Ⓦ www.dfait-maeci.gc.ca.
Irish Department of Foreign Affairs Ⓦ www
.foreignaffairs.gov.ie.
New Zealand Ministry of Foreign Affairs
Ⓦ www.mft.govt.nz.
US State Department Ⓦ www.travel.state.gov.

Travellers with disabilities

Disability is common in India; many conditions that would be curable in the West, such as cataracts, are permanent disabilities in the Subcontinent because people can't afford the treatment. Disabled people are unlikely to get jobs (though there is a famous blind barber in Delhi), and the choice is usually between staying at home being looked after by your family, and going out on the street to beg for alms.

For the disabled traveller, this has its advantages: disability doesn't get the same embarrassed reaction from Indian people that it does from some able-bodied Westerners. On the other hand, you'll be lucky to see a state-of-the-art wheelchair or a disabled loo (major airports usually have both, though the loo may not be in a useable state), and the streets are full of all sorts of obstacles that would be hard for a blind or wheelchair-bound tourist to negotiate independently. Kerbs are often high, pavements uneven and littered, and ramps nonexistent. There are potholes all over the place and open sewers. Some of the more expensive hotels have ramps for the movement of luggage and equipment, but if that makes them accessible to wheelchairs, it is by accident rather than design.

If you walk with difficulty, you will find India's many street obstacles and steep stairs hard going. Another factor that can be a problem is the constant barrage of people proffering things (hard to wave aside if you are, for instance, on crutches), and all that queuing, not to mention heat, will take it out of you if you have a condition that makes you tire quickly. A light, folding camp-stool is one thing that could be invaluable if you have limited walking or standing power.

Then again, Indian people are likely to be very helpful if, for example, you need their help getting on and off buses or up stairs. Taxis and rickshaws are easily affordable and very adaptable; if you rent one for a day, the driver is certain to help you on and off, and perhaps even around the sites you visit. If you employ a guide, they may also be prepared to help you with steps and obstacles.

If complete independence is out of the question, going with an able-bodied companion might be on the cards. Contact one of the specialist organizations listed below for further advice on planning your trip. Otherwise, some package tour operators try to cater for travellers with disabilities, but you should always contact any operator and discuss your exact needs with them before making a booking. You should also make sure you are covered by any insurance policy you take out.

Travelling with children

Travelling with kids can be both challenging and rewarding. Indians are very tolerant of children so you can take them almost anywhere without restriction, and they always help break the ice with strangers.

However the main problem with children, especially small children, is their extra vulnerability. Even more than their parents they need protection from the sun, unsafe drinking water, heat and unfamiliar food. All that chilli in particular may be a problem, even with older kids, if they're not used to it. Remember too, that diarrhoea, perhaps just a nuisance to you, could be dangerous for a child: rehydration salts (see p.39) are vital if your child goes down with it. Make sure too, if possible, that your child is aware of the dangers of rabies; keep children away from animals, and consider a rabies jab.

For babies, nappies (diapers) are available in most large towns at similar prices to the West, but it's worth taking an additional pack in case of emergencies, and bringing sachets of Calpol or similar, which aren't readily available in India. And if your baby is on powdered milk, it might be an idea to bring some of that: you can certainly get it in India, but it may not taste the same. Dried baby food could also be worth taking – any café or chai-wallah should be able to supply you with boiled water.

For touring, hiking or walking, child-carrier backpacks are ideal; some even come with mosquito nets these days. When it comes to luggage, bring as little as possible so you can manage the kids more easily. If your child is small enough, a fold-up buggy is also well worth packing, even if you no longer use a buggy at home, as kids tire so easily in the heat. If you want to cut down on long train or bus journeys by flying, remember that children under 2 travel for ten percent of the adult fare, and under-12s for half price.

Voluntary organizations

While in India, you may consider doing some voluntary charitable work. Several charities welcome volunteers on a medium-term commitment, say over two months. If you do want to spend your time working for an NGO (Non-Government [voluntary] Organization), you should make arrangements well before you arrive by contacting the body in question, rather than on spec. Special visas are not generally required unless you intend to work for longer than six months.

Voluntary work resources

The following organizations provide useful resources:

Charities Aid Foundation (CAF) UK ☎01732/520000, ⊛www.cafonline.org/cafindia/i _search.cfm. CAF is a gateway to the contact details and objectives of 2350 voluntary organizations in India.

India Development Information Network The British Council, 17 Kasturba Gandhi Marg, New Delhi 110 001 ☎011/2371 1401, ⊛www.indev .org. INDEV is another huge databank, accessed through their website, with over 1000 Indian NGOs.

Peace Corps of America US ☎1-800/424-8580, ⊛www.peacecorps.gov. The US-government sponsored aid and voluntary organization, with projects all over the world.

Voluntary Service Overseas (VSO) UK ☎020/8780 7200, ⊛www.vso.org.uk. A British

government-funded organization that places volunteers on various projects around the world and in India.

Voluntary Service Overseas (VSO) Canada ⊛www.vsocanada.org, ☎1-888-VSO-2911 (1-888/876-2911). Canadian-based organization affiliated to the British VSO.

Charities

Here are just some of the charities that accept voluntary workers:

Denjong Padma Choeling Academy c/o Sonam Yongda, Pemayengtse Gompa, West Sikkim 737113 ☎03595/50760 or 50141. The academy, with around two hundred orphans and destitute children, relies on donations and welcomes voluntary teachers. Sikkim is a restricted area, so you will have to make arrangements with the academy to get a special permit.

The Farm Project International Society for Ecology and Culture (ISEC) UK ☎01803/868650, ⊛www .isec.org.uk. Part of the Ladakhi Women's Alliance, set up by ISEC to help promote the rehabilitation of traditional Ladakhi agriculture. The project uses volunteers on two- to three-month agricultural projects; experience helps but is not a prerequisite.

The Missionaries of Charity UK ☎020/8574 1892, ⊛www.mcpriests.com, or Ishu Bhavan, 88 Dr Sundari Mohan Ave, Kolkata (Calcutta) 14 ☎033/2286 5600. Mother Teresa's Missionaries of Charity has numerous charitable institutions throughout India, some of which use casual volunteers. Contact the International Committee of Co-Workers to find out more.

SECMOL (Students' Educational and Cultural Movement of Ladakh), Leh, Ladakh ☎01982/52421, ⊛www.secmol.org. SECMOL was set up to protect Ladakh's culture against the detrimental effects of modernization and strives to increase awareness of developmental issues amongst the young. Qualified English teachers are welcome, especially during their summer schools.

SOS Children's Villages of India A-7 Nizamuddin (West), New Delhi 110 013 ☎011/2435 9450, ⊛www.soscvindia.org. SOS has 32 villages and numerous allied projects in different parts of India, including Karnataka and Rajasthan, giving shelter to distressed children by providing a healthy environment and education including vocational training. Volunteers are welcomed at some of their centres – contact them first.

Guide

Guide

Delhi

CHAPTER 1 # Highlights

✴ **Rajpath** The centrepiece of Lutyens' imperial New Delhi, this wide boulevard epitomizes the spirit of the British Raj. See p.114

✴ **Paharganj Bazaars** Frenetic market and hotel district opposite New Delhi railway station. See p.117

✴ **National Museum** The country's finest museum, with exhibits from over 5000 years of Indian culture. See p.118

✴ **Red Fort** Delhi's most famous monument, this imposing sandstone fort is a ghostly vestige of Mughal splendour. See p.119

✴ **Jama Masjid** Shah Jahan's great mosque, with huge minarets offering birds'-eye views over the old city. See p.121

✴ **Humayun's Tomb** An elegant red-brick forerunner of the Taj Mahal, whose lovely gardens offer an escape from the heat. See p.124

✴ **Hazrat Nizamuddin** A Sufi shrine in a deeply traditional Muslim quarter, where hypnotic *qawwali* music is performed every Thursday. See p.125

✴ **Qutb Minar** The ruins of this twelfth-century city are dominated by the Qutb Minar or Victory Tower. See p.129

▲ Paan-wallah in Old Delhi

1

Delhi

Delhi is the symbol of old India and new... even the stones here whisper to our ears of the ages of long ago and the air we breathe is full of the dust and fragrances of the past, as also of the fresh and piercing winds of the present.

Jawaharlal Nehru

Site of no fewer than eight successive cities, India's capital **DELHI** is the hub of the country, a buzzing international metropolis which draws people from across India and the globe. Home to 1.3 crore (thirteen million) people, it's big and it's growing. Yet tucked away inside Delhi's modern suburbs and developments are tombs, temples and ruins that date back centuries; in some places, the remains of whole cities from the dim and distant past nestle among homes and highways built in just the last decade or two. The result is a city full of fascinating nooks and crannies that you could happily spend weeks or even months exploring.

From a tourist's point of, Delhi is divided into two main parts. **Old Delhi** is the city of the Mughals, created by Shah Jahan and dating back to the seventeenth century. It's the capital's most frenetic quarter, and its most Islamic, a reminder that for over seven hundred years Delhi was a Muslim city, ruled by sultans. While many of the buildings that enclose Old Delhi's teeming bazaars have a tale to tell, its greatest monuments are undoubtedly the magnificent constructions of the Mughals, most notably the mighty **Red Fort**, and the **Jama Masjid**, India's largest and most impressive mosque.

To the south, encompassing the modern city centre, is **New Delhi**, built by the British to be the capital of their empire's key possession. A spacious city of tree-lined boulevards, New Delhi is impressive in its own way. The **Rajpath**, stretching from **India Gate** to the Presidential Palace, is at least as mighty a statement of imperial power as the Red Fort, and it's among the broad avenues of New Delhi that you'll find most of the city's museums, not to mention its prime shopping area, centred around the colonnaded facades of **Connaught Place**, the heart of downtown Delhi.

As the city expands, however – which it is doing at quite a pace – the centre of New Delhi is becoming too small to house the shops, clubs, bars and restaurants needed to cater to the city's affluent and growing middle class. Many businesses are moving into **South Delhi**, the vast area beyond the colonial city. Here, among the modern developments and new business and shopping areas, is where you'll find some of Delhi's most ancient and fascinating attractions. Facing each other at either end of Lodi Road, for example, lie the constructions marking two ends of the great tradition of Mughal garden tombs: **Humayun's Tomb**, its genesis, and **Safdarjang's Tomb**, its last gasp. Here too, you'll find the remains of six cities which

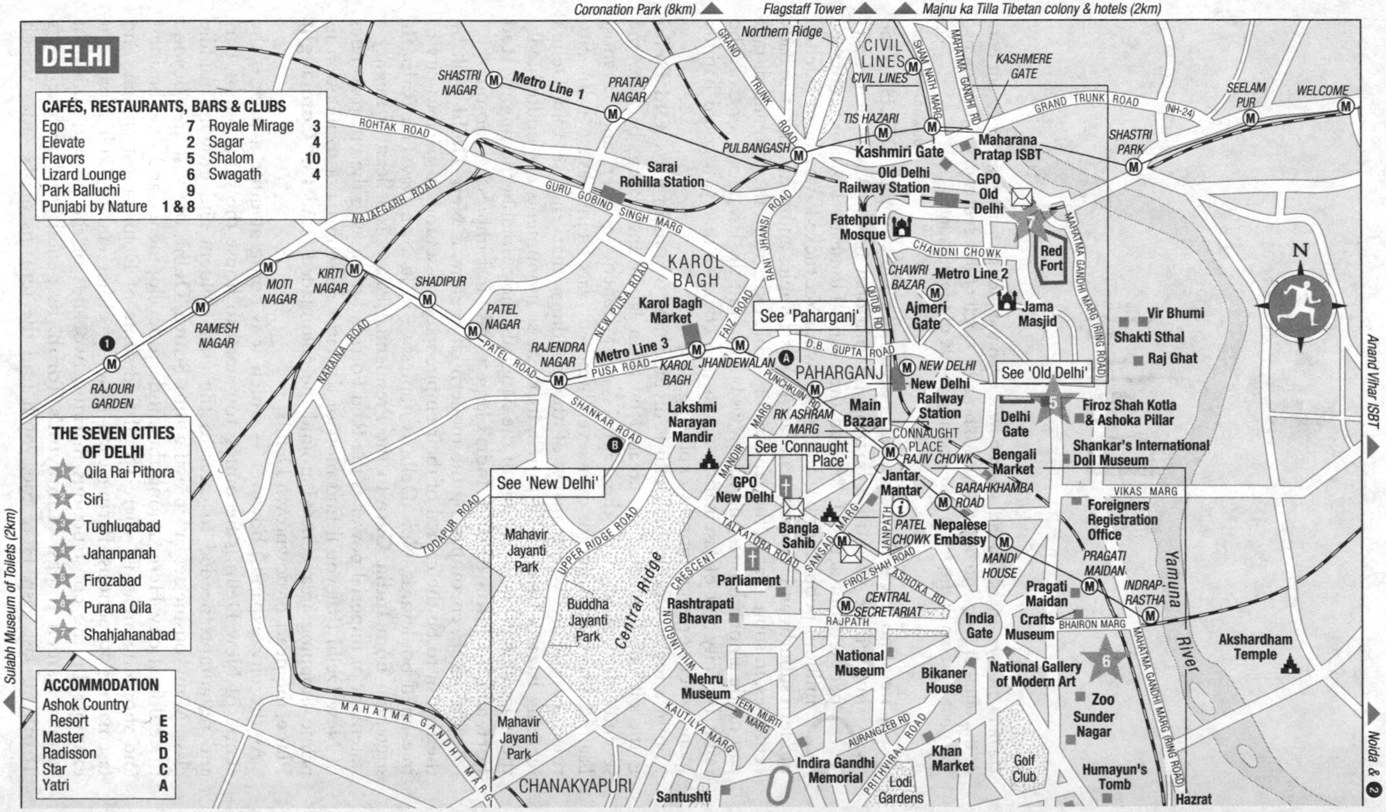
DELHI
CAFÉS, RESTAURANTS, BARS & CLUBS
Ego 7
Elevate 2
Flavors 5
Lizard Lounge 6
Park Balluchi 9
Punjabi by Nature 1 & 8
Royale Mirage 3
Sagar 4
Shalom 10
Swagath 4
THE SEVEN CITIES OF DELHI
1 Qila Rai Pithora
2 Siri
3 Tughluqabad
4 Jahanpanah
5 Firozabad
6 Purana Qila
7 Shahjahanabad
ACCOMMODATION
Ashok Country Resort E
Master B
Radisson D
Star C
Yatri A
Coronation Park (8km)
Flagstaff Tower
Majnu ka Tilla Tibetan colony & hotels (2km)
Anand Vihar ISBT
Noida & 2
Sulabh Museum of Toilets (2km)
N
Northern Ridge
CIVIL LINES
CIVIL LINES
SHAM NATH MARG
MAHATMA GANDHI RD
KASHMERE GATE
GRAND TRUNK ROAD
(NH-24)
SEELAM PUR
WELCOME
SHASTRI PARK
SHASTRI NAGAR
Metro Line 1
PRATAP NAGAR
ROHTAK ROAD
TIS HAZARI
Kashmiri Gate
Maharana Pratap ISBT
PULBANGASH
Sarai Rohilla Station
Old Delhi Railway Station
GPO Old Delhi
GURU GOBIND SINGH MARG
NAJAFGARH ROAD
Fatehpuri Mosque
CHANDNI CHOWK
Red Fort
MAHATMA GANDHI MARG (RING ROAD)
KAROL BAGH
RANI JHANSI ROAD
CHAWRI BAZAR
Metro Line 2
Jama Masjid
KIRTI NAGAR
MOTI NAGAR
SHADIPUR
NEW PUSA ROAD
Karol Bagh Market
FAIZ ROAD
See 'Paharganj'
QUTUB RD
Ajmeri Gate
Vir Bhumi
Shakti Sthal
Raj Ghat
PATEL NAGAR
RAMESH NAGAR
NARAINA ROAD
RAJENDRA NAGAR
Metro Line 3
KAROL BAGH
JHANDEWALAN
D.B. GUPTA ROAD
NEW DELHI
PAHARGANJ
New Delhi Railway Station
See 'Old Delhi'
PATEL ROAD
PUSA ROAD
PUNCHKUIN RD
RAJOURI GARDEN
SHANKAR ROAD
Lakshmi Narayan Mandir
RK ASHRAM MARG
Main Bazaar
CONNAUGHT PLACE
RAJIV CHOWK
Delhi Gate
Firoz Shah Kotla & Ashoka Pillar
Shankar's International Doll Museum
Bengali Market
See 'Connaught Place'
MANDIR MARG
GPO New Delhi
Jantar Mantar
BARAKHAMBA ROAD
VIKAS MARG
Foreigners Registration Office
See 'New Delhi'
TODAPUR ROAD
Mahavir Jayanti Park
UPPER RIDGE ROAD
Bangla Sahib
SANSAD MARG
JANPATH
PATEL CHOWK
Nepalese Embassy
MANDI HOUSE
PRAGATI MAIDAN
Yamuna River
TALKATORA ROAD
CRESCENT
Central Ridge
Parliament
FIROZ SHAH ROAD
ASHOKA RD
Pragati Maidan
INDRAPRASTHA
Buddha Jayanti Park
Rashtrapati Bhavan
CENTRAL SECRETARIAT
RAJPATH
India Gate
Crafts Museum
BHAIRON MARG
Akshardham Temple
WILLINGDON
National Museum
Nehru Museum
Bikaner House
National Gallery of Modern Art
TEEN MURTI MARG
Zoo
Sunder Nagar
MAHATMA GANDHI MARG
KAUTILYA MARG
AURANGZEB RD
PRITHVIRAJ ROAD
Mahavir Jayanti Park
Khan Market
Golf Club
Humayun's Tomb
CHANAKYAPURI
Indira Gandhi Memorial
Lodi Gardens
Santushti
Hazrat

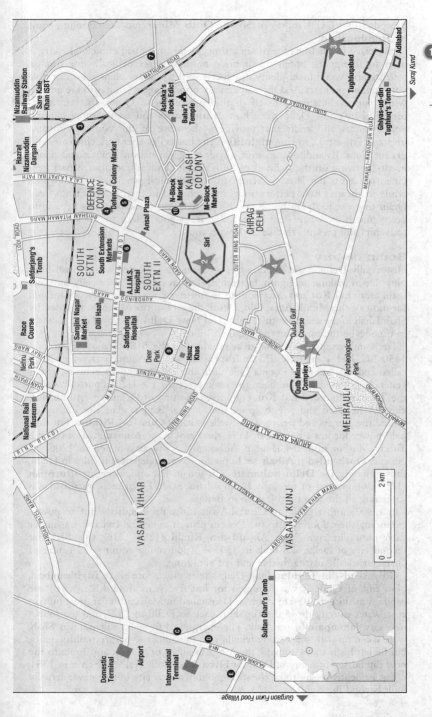

▶ Suraj Kund

▲ Gurgaon Fun Food Village

Nizamuddin Railway Station
Sare Kale Khan ISBT
⑦
MATHURA ROAD
Hazrat Nizamuddin Dargah
③
Ashoka's Rock Edict
Baha'i Temple
GURU RAVIDAS MARG
Tughluqabad ③
Ghiyas-ud-din Tughluq's Tomb
□ Adilabad
LALA LAJPAT RAI PATH
Defence Colony Market
DEFENCE COLONY
④
Ansal Plaza
BHISHAM PITAMAH MARG
⑤
N-Block Market
KAILASH COLONY
⑩
M-Block Market
CHIRAG DELHI
MEHRAULI-BADARPUR ROAD
LODI ROAD
Safdarjang's Tomb
SOUTH EXTN I
South Extension Markets
Siri ②
⑥
OUTER RING ROAD
④
A.I.I.M.S. Hospital
AUROBINDO MARG
SOUTH EXTN II
KHEL GAON MARG
Race Course
VINAY MARG
Sarojni Nagar Market
MAHATMA GANDHI MARG RING ROAD
Dilli Haat
Safdarjung Hospital
Qutab Golf Course
AUROBINDO MARG
⭐
Nehru Park
SHANTIPATH
Deer Park
⑨
Hauz Khas
AFRICA AVENUE
Qutb Minar Complex
MEHRAULI-GURGAON RD
National Rail Museum
RING ROAD
OUTER RING ROAD
ARUNA ASAF ALI MARG
MEHRAULI
Archeological Park
⑧
VASANT VIHAR
VASANT KUNJ
NELSON MANDELA MARG
ABDUL GAFFAR KHAN MARG
Sultan Ghari's Tomb
SARDAR PATEL MARG
Domestic Terminal
Airport
Ⓒ
International Terminal
Ⓓ
NH-8
PALWARI ROAD
Ⓔ

0   2 km

preceded Old Delhi, most notably the **Qutb Minar** and the rambling ruins of **Tughluqabad**.

As a place to hit India for the first time, Delhi isn't a bad choice. The city is used to foreigners: hotels in all price ranges cater specifically for foreign tourists, and you'll meet plenty of experienced fellow travellers who can give you tips and pointers. And there's certainly no shortage of things to see and do while you acclimatize yourself to the Subcontinent. Quite apart from its historical treasures, Delhi has a host of **museums** and art treasures, cultural performances and crafts that provide a showcase of the country's diverse heritage. The city's growing **nightlife** scene boasts designer bars, chic cafés and decent clubs. Its auditoriums host a wide range of national music and dance events, drawing on the richness of India's great classical traditions. Smart new cinemas screen the latest offerings from both Hollywood and Bollywood, while its theatres hold performances in Hindi and in English. And if it's from Delhi that you're flying home, you'll find that you can buy goods here from pretty much anywhere else in India, so it's a good place to stock up with souvenirs and presents to take back with you.

Some history

Historically, Delhi is said to consist of seven successive cities, with British-built New Delhi making an eighth. In truth, Delhi has centred historically on three main areas: **Lal Kot** and extensions to its northeast, where the city was located for most of the Middle Ages; **Old Delhi**, the city of the Mughals, founded by Shah Jahan in the seventeenth century; and **New Delhi**, built by the British just in time to be the capital of independent India.

The Pandavas, heroes of the great Hindu epic the Mahabharata, set around 1450 BC, had a capital called **Indraprastha** on the Yamuna river; a village called Indrapat stood at Purana Qila until the early twentieth century, and is generally assumed to have been the same place. In 1060, a Rajput clan called the **Tomars** founded **Lal Kot**, considered the first of Delhi's seven historical cities. A hundred and twenty years later, a rival Rajput clan, the Chauhans, ousted the Tomars and renamed the walled citadel **Qila Rai Pithora**, but they held power for just a decade. In 1191, their city fell to Muhammad of Ghor, a Turkic Muslim from Afghanistan. Although he was assassinated in 1206, his general, **Qutb-ud-din Aibak**, set himself up as an independent ruler in Delhi, thus founding the **Delhi Sultanate**. His son-in-law and successor **Iltutmish** (1211–36), greatest of the early Delhi sultans, made Delhi the capital of lands stretching all the way from Punjab to Bengal.

In 1290, another group of Central Asian Turks, the **Khaljis**, came to power, extending their dominion to the Deccan plateau of central India. It was under their most illustrious king, **Ala-ud-din Khalji** (1296–1316), that **Siri**, the second city of Delhi, was built in 1303 – a flourishing commercial centre of characteristically ornate marble and red sandstone.

Ghiyas-ud-din Tughluq built Delhi's third city, a fortress at **Tughluqabad**, 8km east of Qutb. It was occupied for just five years from 1321, when the capital was shifted 1100km south to Daulatabad in Maharashtra at great human cost. Water scarcity drove the Tughluqs back to Delhi in 1327, and the fourth new city, **Jahanpanah**, was built. The energies of the next sultan, Firoz Shah, were taken up with suppressing rebellion, as the Sultanate began to disintegrate, but he left his mark by moving the Ashokan pillars of Meerut and Topra to the new capital, the fifth city of Delhi, at **Firozabad**. Built beside the river in 1354, it was evidently meant to be the stronghold of a new city, but he never actually built beyond the citadel.

The Tughluq line came to an end in 1398, when Timur the Lame (Tamerlaine), a Central Asian Turk, invaded Delhi. His successors, the **Sayyids** (1414–44), were in turn ousted by **Buhlul Lodi** who established a dynasty that left behind the fine tombs and mosques still to be seen in the beautiful Lodi Gardens. The Lodi dynasty ended when Sultan Ibrahim Lodi died in battle, fighting the brilliant and enigmatic **Babur**, founder of the Mughal Empire. Babur's son **Humayun** lost Delhi, along with most of his father's conquests, to the Afghan king **Sher Shah Suri**, who is credited with building the "sixth city of Delhi" at **Purana Qila**. Humayun retook Delhi in 1555, but died the following year. His son **Akbar** shifted the capital to Agra, but Akbar's grandson **Shah Jahan** shifted it back in 1638, creating Delhi's "seventh city", Shahjahanabad, now known as **Old Delhi**.

Following the death of Shah Jahan's son, Aurangzeb, in 1707, the city fell victim to successive invasions. In 1739, Nadir Shah, the emperor of Persia, sacked the city and slaughtered an estimated 15,000 of its inhabitants. The massacre hastened the demise of Mughals, who by the end of the eighteenth century had been reduced by successive marauders – Jats, Hindu Marathas and Afghans – to puppet kings presiding over decaying palaces. By the time the **British** (who had already established toe-holds in Calcutta, Madras and Bombay) appeared on the scene in 1803, Delhi was a remote outpost of a spent empire, at the mercy of lawless tribes. The British swiftly took control, leaving the Mughal ruler, **Bahadur Shah II**, with his palace and his pension, but no power. British forces fended off a number of Maratha attacks in the next decade, and faced determined opposition during 1857 when the city strongly supported the **uprising** (or First War of Independence – see p.1344), forcibly evicting the British, killing many of them, and proclaiming Bahadur Shah Hindustani emperor in the Red Fort. When the British finally recaptured the city, after a long siege, they went on a rampage of destruction, desecrating mosques and executing some three thousand people in bloody **reprisals**. Bahadur Shah was sent off to exile in Burma, his family shot, and the city's entire population turfed out, the Muslims not allowed to return for two years.

After abolishing "John Company" (as the East India Company was known), following the uprising, the British, in their new incarnation as the **Raj**, at first kept their administration in Calcutta, but when George V came to India for his coronation as emperor in 1911, they decided to make Delhi India's new **capital**. Fervent construction of bungalows, parliamentary buildings and public offices followed, and in 1931 Delhi was officially inaugurated as the capital of Britain's most important colonial possession, with British-built New Delhi as the city's eighth incarnation.

When **Independence** finally came in 1947, it was in Delhi that the British handed over power to India's first democratically elected government under **Jawaharlal Nehru**. In the wake of **Partition**, however, Hindu mobs turned on Delhi's Muslim population, nearly half of whom fled to Pakistan, ending centuries of Muslim dominance in the city. They were replaced by an influx of Hindu and Sikh refugees from the Pakistani sectors of Punjab and Bengal, to the extent that whole new districts had to be created to house them (Chittaranjan Park in South Delhi, for example, was originally EBDPC – East Bengal Displaced Persons' Colony).

Indira Gandhi's **Emergency** in 1975–77 saw violent evictions of Old Delhi's predominantly Muslim slum-dwellers, who were sent to live in disease-ridden jerry-built housing out of town, an event recalled by Salman Rushdie at the end of his novel *Midnight's Children*. Following Indira's 1984 assassination by her Sikh bodyguards, it was the turn of the city's Sikh population to fall victim to **sectarian riots** (Khushwant Singh, in his novel *Delhi*, records that evil episode in fiction).

In 1992, having previously been a **Union Territory**, administered directly by the federal government, Delhi gained a status similar to that of Washington DC or Canberra ACT, with its own government, but lesser powers than those of a state. The Hindu sectarian BJP won power that year in the first **Capital Territory** election, but lost in 1998 to Congress, who have controlled the administration ever since. The biggest change in recent years has been the phenomenal growth of Delhi's **middle class**, with increasing numbers of relatively prosperous professionals, particularly in South Delhi.

Arrival

Delhi is India's main point of arrival for overseas visitors, and the major transport hub for destinations in the states of Rajasthan, the Punjab, Himachal Pradesh and Ladakh as well as central north India. The **airport**, 15km southwest of the centre, has two separate terminals – one handling international flights, the other domestic services; although adjacent, they're 6km apart by road, but are connected by half-hourly free shuttle buses (or you could use a pre-paid taxi). The capital is served by four long-distance **railway stations**; the vast majority of services used by tourists arrive and depart from either Old Delhi or New Delhi stations, although a few useful services use Hazrat Nizamuddin in the southeast and Sarai Rohilla in the northwest. State **buses** from all over the country pull into the Maharana Pratap Inter-state Bus Terminal (ISBT) in Old Delhi, while a few destinations in Uttar Pradesh and Uttarakhand are served by the Anand Vihar ISBT in the east of the city.

By air

International flights land at **Indira Gandhi International (IGI) Airport** Terminal 2, while domestic services land at Terminal 1. There are no ATMs at the airport (though this may change), but Punjab National Bank and Thomas Cook in the arrivals lounge offer 24hr money-changing facilities; be sure to get some small change for taxis and rickshaws. For those seeking accommodation, 24hr desks here, including Indian Tourism (ITDC) and Delhi Tourism (DTTDC), have a list of approved hotels and will secure reservations by phone. A free AAI **shuttle** bus runs half-hourly between the two terminals.

From the international airport the easiest way to get into Delhi is by **taxi**, and are particularly advisable if you arrive late at night. There are several official pre-paid taxi kiosks in the restricted area outside the arrival hall; the fare will be around Rs250 to the city centre, with a 25 percent surcharge between 11pm and 5am; prices vary from kiosk to kiosk, so you might check a few before plumping. It's worth noting, however, that even these pre-paid taxi drivers may try to take you to hotels not of your choice (see box opposite).

Alternatively there's the **bus** (Rs50; 40min), leaving hourly for Maharana Pratap ISBT in Old Delhi (which is only really handy if you're staying in the Tibetan colony Majnu Ka Tilla, though the EATS services may agree to drop you in Connaught Place); tickets are available from the DTC and EATS counters in the arrival hall, and the buses travel via the domestic terminal too. The **auto-rickshaws** that wait in line at the departure gate constitute the most precarious and least reliable form of transport from the airport, especially at night, though they're cheaper than a taxi; fares are around Rs100–150. Many hotels, including some of the Paharganj budget options, now offer **pick-up services** from the airport, where you will be met with a driver bearing your name on a placard. This presents the smoothest and most reliable method of getting to your hotel from the airport, though prices vary considerably, starting from around Rs250, but often twice as much or more.

An **Airport Express Link** metro line is now under construction, scheduled for completion in 2010. When finished, it should speed travellers into central New Delhi in as little as sixteen minutes.

By train

Delhi has two major **railway stations**. **New Delhi Station** is at the eastern end of Paharganj Main Bazaar, within easy walking distance of many of the area's budget hotels. The station has two exits: take the Paharganj exit for Connaught Place and most points south, and the Ajmeri Gate exit for Old Delhi. Cycle rickshaws ply the congested main bazaar toward Connaught Place

Delhi scams

Delhi can be a headache for the first-time visitor because of **scams** to entrap the unwary – one dodge is to dump dung onto visitors' shoes, then charge to clean it off. The most common wheeze, though, is for taxi drivers or touts to convince you that the hotel you've chosen is full, closed or has just burned to the ground so as to take you to one that pays them commission. More sophisticated scammers will pretend to phone your hotel to check for yourself, or will take you to a travel agent (often claiming to be a "tourist office") who will do it, dialling for you (a different number); the "receptionist" on the line will corroborate the story, or deny all knowledge of your reservation. The driver or tout will then take you to a "very good hotel" – usually in Karol Bagh – where you'll be charged well over the odds for a night's accommodation. To **reduce the risk of being caught out**, write down your taxi's registration number (make sure the driver sees you doing it), and insist on going to your hotel with no stops en route. Heading for Paharganj, your driver may try to take you to a hotel of his choice rather than yours. To avoid this, you could ask to be dropped at New Delhi railway station and walk from there. You may even encounter fake "doormen" outside hotels who'll tell you the place is full; check at reception first, and even if the claim is true, never follow the tout to anywhere he recommends. These problems can be avoided by **reserving in advance**; many hotels will arrange for a car and driver to meet you at your point of arrival.

New Delhi railway station is the worst place for touts; assume that anyone who approaches you here – even in uniform – with offers of help, or to direct you to the foreigners' booking hall, is up to no good. Most are trying to lure travellers to the fake "official" tourist offices opposite the Paharganj entrance, where you'll end up paying way over the odds, often for unconfirmed tickets. And don't believe stories that the foreigners' booking hall has closed. On **Connaught Place** and along **Janpath**, steer clear of phoney "tourist information offices" or travel agents that falsely claim to be "government authorized" – some are even decorated with GOI tourist posters. For the record, India Tourism is at 88 Janpath and the DTTDC is in Block N, Middle Circle.

Finally, be aware that taxi, auto and rental-car drivers get a hefty commission for taking you to certain shops, and that commission will be added to your bill should you buy anything. You can assume that auto-wallahs who accost you on the street do so with the intention of overcharging you, or of taking you to shops which pay them commission rather than straight to where you want to go. Always hail a taxi or auto-rickshaw yourself, rather than taking one whose driver approaches you, and don't let them take you to places where you haven't asked to go.

– which is just 800m down the road – but cannot enter Connaught Place itself. Auto-rickshaws start at Rs20 for Connaught Place, or Rs35 to Old Delhi – agree a price before getting in. **Old Delhi Station** (officially **Delhi Junction**), west of the Red Fort, is also well connected to the city by taxis, auto-rickshaws and cycle rickshaws; for autos there's a booth selling fixed-price pre-paid tickets – Connaught Place is Rs45, plus Rs5 per piece of baggage. Both rail stations are notorious for **theft**: don't take your eyes off your luggage for a moment. They are also on the metro, but travelling on it with heavy baggage is prohibited. The other long-distance stations are **Hazrat Nizamuddin**, southeast of the centre, for trains from Agra (except the Shatabdi Express); and **Sarai Rohilla**, west of Old Delhi station, for some services from Rajasthan. Hazrat Nizamuddin has a pre-paid auto booth; Connaught Place is Rs50, and around the same from Sarai Rohilla. If you're lucky you may connect with a local train into New Delhi, but these tend to be sardine-can packed, and buying a ticket can be a real scrum.

By bus

State buses pull in at the **Maharana Pratap Inter-state Bus Terminal (ISBT)**, north of Old Delhi railway station. Auto-rickshaws to New Delhi or Paharganj take about fifteen minutes (Rs50, plus Rs5 per piece of baggage), cycle rickshaws take twice that (and cost around Rs30). There's a pre-paid auto-rickshaw booth at the terminal, and also a metro station (Kashmiri Gate). **Private buses** from all over India pull up in the street outside New Delhi railway station; some also drop passengers in Connaught Place. Some services from UP and Uttarakhand leave you at **Anand Vihar ISBT**, across the Yamuna towards Ghaziabad in east Delhi, which also has a pre-paid auto-rickshaw booth (Rs75 to Connaught Place, plus Rs5 per piece of baggage), and is served by bus #70 or #85 to Connaught Place. Buses from Agra and some from Rajasthan may leave you at **Sarai Kale Khan ISBT** by Hazrat Nizamuddin train station (cross over by the footbridge for pre-paid autos). Buses from Jaipur, Ajmer, Jodhpur and Udaipur may drop you at **Bikaner House** near India Gate, Rs30 from Connaught Place by auto.

Information

There are reasonably helpful tourist offices at the international and domestic airports, railway stations and bus terminals, and **India Tourism** at 88 Janpath, just south of Connaught Place (Mon–Fri 9am–6pm, Sat 9am–2pm; ☎011/2332 0005 or 8), is a good place to pick up information on historical sites, city tours, shopping and cultural events, as well as free city maps. **DTTDC** (Delhi Tourism and Transport Development Corporation) have an office at *Coffee House*, 1 Annexe, Emporium Complex, Baba Kharak Singh Marg, opposite Hanuman Mandir (daily 7am–9pm; ☎011/2336 5358, ⓦdelhitourism.nic.in). They also have a kiosk a little further along the same street, and others in New Delhi rail station (Mon–Sat 9.30am–5.30pm; ☎011/2374 2374), Hazrat Nizamuddin station (Mon–Sat 9.30am–5.30pm; ☎011/6547 0605), and at the airport. Beware of any other firms that look like or claim to be tourist offices (see box, p.103).

Exhibitions and cultural events are listed in local **magazines** such as the weekly *Delhi Diary*, fortnightly *Delhi City*, and monthly *First City*, all available from bookshops and street stalls; *Delhi Diary* can sometimes be found for free at big hotels or at the GOI tourist office. **Online**, apart from the DTTDC's website, it's worth checking the Delhi pages of India for You at ⓦ www.indfy .com/delhi.html for sightseeing information, the Delhi city government's tourism pages at ⓦ delhigovt.nic.in/page.asp for general information, and for current listings ⓦ www.delhi-india.net or ⓦ www.delhilive.com.

City transport

Despite a spanking new metro system, **public transport** in Delhi is still inadequate for the city's population and size, and increased car ownership is adding to the general chaos. **Cows** have been banned from much of central Delhi, but not the city's more traditional districts. In an effort to reduce pollution, the city's buses, taxis and auto-rickshaws have all now been converted from petrol and diesel to run on **compressed natural gas** (CNG), but most inner-city thoroughfares are still choked with exhaust fumes and congested.

The metro

New Delhi's brand-new **metro system** opened in December 2002, with the capacity to carry 200,000 passengers daily. It's being built in several phases, with work projected to continue until at least 2021. There are three lines: the **red line** (line 1) runs from Barwala in the northwest to Shahdara across the Yamuna river in the northeast; the **yellow line** (line 2) runs from Vishwa Vidyalaya in the north to the Central Secretariat, interchanging with the red line at Kashmere Gate (by the main Inter-state Bus Terminal), and continuing to Old Delhi (Chandni Chowk) and New Delhi rail stations and Connaught Place (Rajiv Chowk). The **blue line** (line 3) starts at Dwarka in the southwest and terminates at Indrapastha near Purana Qila, interchanging with the yellow line at Rajiv Chowk. All three lines are due to be extended at both ends in the near future. For progress updates, ask at the tourist offices (see opposite) or visit ⓦ www.delhimetrorail.com. The minimum fare is currently Rs6, while the highest fare from the centre Rs15. The metro is wheelchair accessible, and each station should have an ATM. Children under 90cm (3ft) tall travel free if accompanied by an adult. Note that photography is strictly prohibited on the metro.

City and regional tours

The DTTDC tourist office (see opposite), daily except Monday, organizes a/c bus **tours** of New Delhi (9am–1.30pm; Rs150) and Old Delhi (2.15–5.45pm; Rs150), plus a full-day tour which covers both (9am–5.45pm; Rs250). All start outside the DTTDC office opposite the Hanuman Temple on Baba Kharak Singh Marg. From the same place, they run a "Delhi by Evening" tour (Tues–Sun; Rs150), which includes sound and light at the Red Fort, and an Agra day-trip (Wed, Sat & Sun; depart 7am, return 10pm; Rs950). Delhi Transport Corporation (☎011/2884 4192) run one-day tours for Rs100, starting from New Delhi rail station at 9.15am, Scindia House in Connaught Place (corner of Janpath) at 9.30am, or the Red Fort at 9.45am. All the five-star hotels offer their own, door-to-door packages, and many hotels in and around Paharganj, such as *Namaskar* and *Metropolis*, can arrange city tours by taxi for Rs500–600, which is good value when shared between three or four people.

Buses

With auto- and cycle rickshaws so cheap and plentiful, only hardened shoestring travellers will want to use Delhi's confusing and overcrowded **buses**. However, one **useful route** is the #505 from Ajmeri Gate and Connaught Place (Super Bazaar and the corner of Kasturba Gandhi Marg) to the National Museum, Safdarjang's Tomb, Hauz Khas and the Qutb Minar. It is possible to check bus routes **online** at ⓦ delhigovt.nic.in/dtcbusroute/dtc/Find_Route/getroute.asp, but the lists of bus stops do not always use location names that will be familiar to tourists (stops in Connaught Place, for example, are listed individually as "Regal Cinema", "Super Bazaar" and so on).

Auto-rickshaws and cycle rickshaws

Auto-rickshaws ("autos") – India's three-wheeler taxis – are the most effective form of transport around Delhi, although their drivers are notoriously anarchic. Some auto-wallahs will offer to use the meter, but in general you'll need to negotiate a price before getting in, and try to have the exact change ready; prices for foreigners vary considerably according to your haggling skills and the mood of the driver, but as a sample fare, it should cost about Rs40 from Connaught Place to Old Delhi. Auto stands, which dot the city, are the best places to pick up auto-rickshaws, though they can also be hailed in the street.

Cycle rickshaws are not allowed in Connaught Place and parts of New Delhi, but are handy for short journeys to outlying areas and around Paharganj. They're also nippier than motorized traffic in Old Delhi. Rates should be roughly half that demanded by autos.

While auto- and rickshaw-wallahs may well try to take advantage of you by overcharging, do bear in mind that cycle rickshaw-wallahs in particular are among the city's poorest residents, and it really isn't worth haggling them down to the absolute minimum fare or arguing with them over what will amount in the end to a trifling sum. Most tourists accept that they are going to pay a bit more than local residents, and when you see how hard your rickshaw-wallah has to work, you may well feel he deserves a hefty tip on top of that.

Taxis

Delhi's **taxis** (white, or black and yellow) cost around fifty percent more than auto-rickshaws and are generally safe and reliable. Drivers belong to local taxi stands, where you can make bookings and fix prices; if you flag a taxi down on the street you're letting yourself in for some hectic haggling. A surcharge of around 25 percent operates between 11pm and 5am. Alternatively, Mega Cabs (☎1929) offer a 24hr call-a-cab service with air-conditioned cars (in summer at least), and tamper-proof digital meters, though expect to pay a bit more than usual.

Car and cycle rental

For local sightseeing and journeys beyond the city confines, **chauffeur-driven cars** are very good value, especially for groups of three to four. Many budget hotels offer cars and drivers, as does the DTTDC transport office on Aurobindo Marg at Kidwai Nagar West, by Dilli Haat (☎011/2467 4153), and the booths at the southern end of the Tibetan Market on Janpath. DTTDC rates are Rs955 for an eight-hour day within Delhi (Rs1972 in an a/c vehicle), which includes 80km mileage. Alternatively, there's Kumar Tourist Taxi Service,

K-14 Connaught Place (☎011/2341 5390). Driving yourself in Delhi can be dangerous, so is not advisable.

Cycling in the large avenues of New Delhi takes some getting used to and can be hazardous for those not used to chaotic traffic. **Bicycle rental** is surprisingly difficult to come by; try Mehta Cycles (☎011/2358 9239) at 5109–10 Main Bazaar, Paharganj, a few doors from *Kholsa Cafe*, who rent bikes for Rs60 a day.

Accommodation

Delhi has a vast range of **accommodation**, from dirt-cheap lodges to extravagant international hotels. Bookings for upmarket hotels can be made at airport and railway station tourist desks; budget travellers will have to hunt around independently.

The hotels in **Connaught Place** cover all price ranges, are handy for banks, restaurants and shops, and have good transport connections to all the main sights. North of Connaught Place, the busy market area of **Paharganj** and the adjacent **Ram Nagar**, close to New Delhi railway station, feature the best of the budget accommodation. There will always be budget rooms available in Paharganj – don't believe anyone who tells you otherwise, and **avoid** all hotels in Karol Bagh that are recommended by touts (see box, p.103). The main youth hostel is in the **south**, where you'll also find most of Delhi's top **luxury hotels**. Fifteen minutes north of Old Delhi by auto-rickshaw, the Tibetan colony of **Majnu Ka Tilla** also has a few good places to stay.

Finally, for those leaving on early flights, we've included reviews of dependable hotels out near the international airport.

Connaught Place and central New Delhi

You pay a premium to stay on **Connaught Place** itelf, so if you want value for money, stay elsewhere. To its south, grander hotels on and around **Janpath** and along **Sansad Marg** cater mainly for business travellers and tourist groups, but there are some very good ones among them. Most upmarket hotels have plush restaurants and swimming pools, and some require non-Indian residents to pay in foreign currency. Of the budget travellers' lodges that used to dot the lanes off the northern end of Janpath, only a few remain, and they're often full, so book ahead.

Unless otherwise stated, the hotels listed below are marked on the Connaught Place **map** on p.108.

Alka 16/90 P-Block, Connaught Place ☎011/2334 4000, ⓦwww.hotelalka.com. "The best alternative to luxury", they reckon, but the rooms, though a/c and carpeted, are pretty poky – the cheaper ones don't even have a window, though they do try to make up for it with mirrors to create an illusion of more space. The staff, on the other hand, don't give out any smiles to create an illusion of friendliness. On the plus side, there's a reasonable veg restaurant, and an annexe on M-block for when the main hotel is full. Doubles from $110. ⓭

Bright M-85, Connaught Place ☎011/4151 7766, ⓔhotelbright@hotmail.com. A mixed bag of rooms, some attached, at this slightly ramshackle but decent enough city-centre hotel. The best room is no.11, spacious with big windows, but others are a bit on the dingy side, so try before you buy. Upstairs, *Blue* (☎011/2341 6666, ⓔhotelbluedelhi@hotmail.com) has the benefit of a terrace and is a decent fallback option. ⓹

🏃 **Imperial** Janpath, Connaught Place end ☎011/2334 1234, ⓦwww.theimperialindia .com. See also New Delhi map, p.115. Delhi's classiest hotel, in a beautiful 1933 Art Deco building set amid large, palm-shaded gardens. The rooms are stylish, as is the cool lobby done out in cream and gold, while corridors double up as galleries depicting rather fascinating eighteenth- and nineteenth-century prints of India. Staff

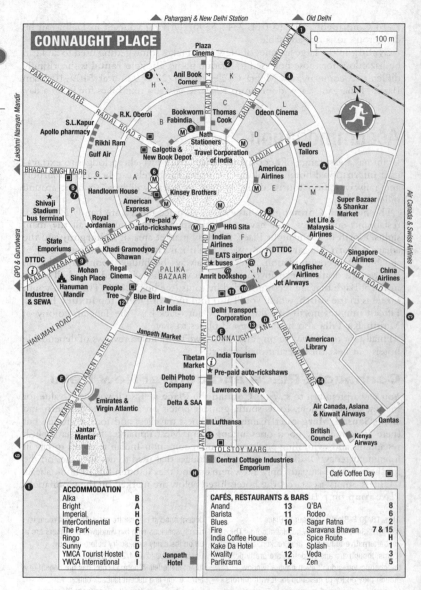

▲ Paharganj & New Delhi Station   ▲ Old Delhi

CONNAUGHT PLACE

0   100 m

Lakshmi Narayan Mandir

PANCHKUIN MARG

RADIAL ROAD 3

BHAGAT SINGH MARG

GPO & Gurudwara

BABA KHARAK SINGH

RADIAL RD 2

RADIAL RD 1

HANUMAN ROAD

SANSAD MARG (PARLIAMENT STREET)

JANPATH

JANPATH

MINTO ROAD

RADIAL RD 4

RADIAL RD 5

RADIAL RD 6

RADIAL RD 7

RADIAL RD 8

BARAKHAMBA ROAD

KASTURBA GANDHI MARG

CONNAUGHT LANE

TOLSTOY MARG

Air Canada & Swiss Airlines

N

Plaza Cinema
Anil Book Corner
R.K. Oberoi
S.L.Kapur
Apollo pharmacy
Rikhi Ram
Gulf Air
Bookworm
Fabindia
Galgotia & New Book Depot
Thomas Cook
Nath Stationers
Travel Corporation of India
Odeon Cinema
Vedi Tailors
American Airlines
Super Bazaar & Shankar Market
Shivaji Stadium bus terminal
Handloom House
American Express
Royal Jordanian
Pre-paid auto-rickshaws
Kinsey Brothers
HRG Sita
Jet Life & Malaysia Airlines
State Emporiums
DTTDC
Khadi Gramodyog Bhawan
Mohan Singh Place
Regal Cinema
Indian Airlines
EATS airport buses
PALIKA BAZAAR
Amrit bookshop
DTTDC
Kingfisher Airlines
Jet Airways
Singapore Airlines
China Airlines
Hanuman Mandir
Industree & SEWA
People Tree
Blue Bird
Air India
Delhi Transport Corporation
Janpath Market
Tibetan Market
India Tourism
Pre-paid auto-rickshaws
Connaught Lane
American Library
Delhi Photo Company
Lawrence & Mayo
Delta & SAA
Lufthansa
Emirates & Virgin Atlantic
Jantar Mantar
Air Canada, Asiana & Kuwait Airways
Qantas
British Council
Kenya Airways
TOLSTOY MARG
Central Cottage Industries Emporium
Café Coffee Day ▣
Janpath Hotel

ACCOMMODATION	
Alka	B
Bright	A
Imperial	H
InterContinental	C
The Park	F
Ringo	E
Sunny	D
YMCA Tourist Hostel	G
YWCA International	I

CAFÉS, RESTAURANTS & BARS			
Anand	13	Q'BA	8
Barista	11	Rodeo	6
Blues	10	Sagar Ratna	2
Fire	F	Saravana Bhavan	7 & 15
India Coffee House	9	Spice Route	H
Kake Da Hotel	4	Splash	1
Kwality	12	Veda	3
Parikrama	14	Zen	5

maintain just the right degree of courteousness, and there are a number of excellent restaurants including the renowned *Spice Route* (see p.132). Doubles from US$636. ⑨

InterContinental off Barakhamba Rd and Tolstoy Marg, southeast of Connaught Place ☎011/4444 7777, ⓦwww.intercontinental.com. See also New Delhi map, p.115. Brash and monolithic upmarket

hotel frequented by business travellers, that's all opulence and mod cons, conference meetings and general comings and goings. Has a choice of restaurants, bars and a disco, and lots of shops. When the hotel's at its busiest, doubles start from US$565, but prices are lower when business is slack. ⑨

Le Meridien Windsor Place, Raisna Rd ☎011/2371 0101, ⓦwww.starwoodhotels.com/lemeridien. See

New Delhi map, p.115. Busy five-star with glass-walled elevators that take you up to bedrooms set around a massive atrium. The whole ensemble looks like a housing scheme in a sci-fi movie, though the rooms are spacious and comfortable within, and service is excellent. Facilities include a swimming pool, health club, choice of restaurants and bars, wheelchair access throughout, including a room adapted for wheelchair users. Prices start from US$427 per double. **⑨**

Master R-500 New Rajendra Nagar ☏011/2874 1089, ⓦwww.master-guesthouse.com. See Delhi map, pp.98–99. A lovely little *pension*-style guesthouse, comfortable, secure and family-run, with only four a/c double rooms of different sizes (a bathroom between each pair), and a secluded roof terrace. Located on the edge of the green belt only 10min by auto-rickshaw from Connaught Place (or bus #910 from Shivaji Terminal behind Block P) and not far from Karol Bagh metro. Veg meals are available. Book ahead. **⑥**

The Park 15 Sansad Marg ☏011/2374 3000 or 1800/117 275, ⓦwww.theparkhotels.com. See also New Delhi map, p.115. They don't come much snazzier than this place, from the super-cool lobby to the ultra-modern rooms, the decor is state-of-the-art, down to the LCD TV in each room and the frosted glass walls that screen off the en-suite bathrooms. Service is snappy, the atmosphere is relaxed, and all the facilities you'd expect are here, including a bar, a good restaurant and a pool. A cut above your run-of-the-mill five-star. Doubles from US$455. **⑨**

Ringo 17 Scindia House, Connaught Lane ☏011/2331 0605, ⓔringo_guest_house@yahoo.co.in. An old backpacker favourite that's traded in its dorms for single and double rooms, which are plain but decent, some attached, and arranged around a central terrace that makes a pretty congenial little hangout. **③**

Sunny 152 Scincia House, Connaught Lane ☏011/2331 2909, ⓔsunnyguesthouse123@hotmail.com. Another former backpacker dorm hotel that now offers cheap but rather box-like single and double rooms, some attached, with hot water at 20 minutes' notice. **③**

YMCA Tourist Hostel Jai Singh Marg, southwest of Connaught Place ☏011/2336 1915, ⓦwww.newdelhiymca.org. See also New Delhi map, p.115. A rather staid establishment popular with American budgeteers (though it isn't all that cheap), the institutional corridors belie the spacious if simple rooms, and there are good restaurants, a large swimming pool (open April–Oct only) and attractive gardens. Rates include breakfast and supper. **⑦**

YWCA Blue Triangle Ashok Rd, southwest of Connaught Place ☏011/2336 0133, ⓦwww.ywcaindia.org. See New Delhi map, p.115. Open to men and women, rooms here are nice and big, with large attached bathrooms. The whole place is clean, quiet and respectable, with lawns outside to relax on. Rooms bookable in advance, dorms (Rs410) day-by-day depending on availability, with groups given preference. Rates include breakfast. **⑥**

YWCA International 10 Sansad Marg, southwest of Connaught Place ☏011/2336 1561, ⓦwww.ywcaindia.org. See also New Delhi map, p.115. Clean and airy a/c rooms with private bathrooms, though not as nice as at the *Blue Triangle* (and pricier); set meals are available in the restaurant. Women are given priority but men can also stay. Rates include breakfast, and you even get a free copy of *The Times of India* every morning. **⑥–⑦**

Paharganj

Running west from New Delhi railway station, the **Paharganj** area is prime backpacker territory, with innumerable lodges offering inexpensive and mid-range accommodation. Some are extremely good value; others offer very little for very little, and most can suffer from slamming-door syndrome and people shouting till dawn (especially if windows face inwards onto the communal stairwell), so choose carefully if you value quiet. Some hotels here run a 24-hour checkout system, which means you check out at the same time you checked in – good if you arrived late, but bad if you arrived early.

Unless otherwise stated, the hotels listed below are marked on the Paharganj **map** on p.110.

Ajay 5084-A Main Bazaar ☏011/2358 3125, ⓦwww.anupamhoteliersltd.com/html/ajay.htm. Tucked away down an alley off the Main Bazaar, this well-run place with marble decor has clean rooms, some a/c, most with baths and TV, but not all with windows. There's a pool table, Internet access, and a 24hr bakery downstairs, next to a big café area for breakfast or snacks. 24hr checkout. **③**

Camran 1116 Main Bazaar ☏011/3297 4474, ⓔsubhashthakur@yahoo.com. A small, somewhat

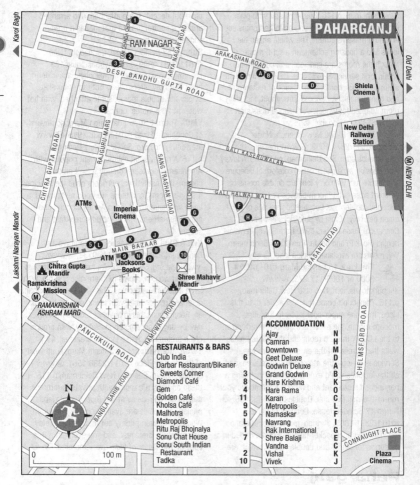

PAHARGANJ

ACCOMMODATION

Ajay	N
Camran	H
Downtown	M
Geet Deluxe	D
Godwin Deluxe	A
Grand Godwin	B
Hare Krishna	K
Hare Rama	O
Karan	C
Metropolis	L
Namaskar	F
Navrang	I
Rak International	G
Shree Balaji	E
Vandna	C
Vishal	K
Vivek	J

RESTAURANTS & BARS

Club India	6
Darbar Restaurant/Bikaner	
Sweets Corner	3
Diamond Café	8
Gem	4
Golden Café	11
Kholsa Café	9
Malhotra	5
Metropolis	L
Ritu Raj Bhojnalya	1
Sonu Chat House	7
Sonu South Indian	
Restaurant	2
Tadka	10

run-down lodge in part of a late-Mughal period mosque, with some character and a panoramic rooftop terrace. The cheapest single rooms are box-like cubicles (though they are cheap); double rooms have attached bathrooms. Dorm beds also available (Rs90). ②

Downtown 4583 Main Bazaar ☎011/4154 1529, ℮ltctravel@rediffmail.com. This friendly lodging, just off the Main Bazaar, is bright and breezy, and not bad value, but it's worth asking for a room with an outside window. There's also a dorm (Rs60). Minus points for its 11am checkout. ②

Hare Krishna 1572–3 Main Bazaar ☎011/4154 1341, ℗www.anupamhoteliersltd.com/html/hare .htm. A friendly and reasonably cosy place. The rooms vary, but the best are spacious, most are

attached, and they're all clean. There's hot running water and a pleasant rooftop café-restaurant, but the lower floors can be pretty noisy. 24hr checkout. ③

Hare Rama T-298 off Main Bazaar ☎011/3536 1301 or 2, ℮harerama_2000@hotmail.com. Decent, clean attached rooms at this busy, good-value hotel down an alley off the Main Bazaar. 24hr checkout. ③

Metropolis 1634 Main Bazaar ☎011/2358 5766, ℗www.metropolistravels.com. Main Bazaar's most upmarket and comfortable hotel, though somewhat overpriced for what you get. A few double rooms have large windows and bathtubs; others don't have a window. All are a/c with a TV, fridge and balcony, and there's a good restaurant and bar, with seating downstairs or on the roof terrace. ⑤–⑥

Namaskar 917 Chandiwalan, Main Bazaar ☎011/2358 2233, ✉namaskarhotel@yahoo.com. Popular family-run budget hotel off the Main Bazaar with a variety of attached rooms, some with a/c, but not all the cheaper ones have hot showers or outside windows. The staff are very attentive and helpful, but they also run tours which they can be pushy about selling. ③

Navrang Tooti Chowk, 820 Main Bazaar ☎011/2352 1965. More like a down-at-heel lodge in a remote small town than a city hotel in the middle of Delhi, but it's very friendly, if somewhat basic. On the other hand, you get what you pay for, and at these rates it isn't bad value. Some rooms have bathrooms, but there's no hot running water (they'll bring you a bucket for Rs20). ①

Rak International Tooti Chowk, 820 Main Bazaar ☎011/2358 6508, ⓦwww.hotelrakinternational .com. One of the most consistently popular Paharganj choices, in a small square off the Main Bazaar, good value with large, cool rooms, a/c, TV, fridge and hot water, and a nice rooftop too, but it could definitely do with a lick of paint. ③–④

Shree Balaji 2204 Rajguru Marg, Chuna Mandi ☎011/2353 2212. Between the Main Bazaar and

Ram Nagar, this is one of the better hotels along this street in terms of comfort and cleanliness. All rooms have en-suite bathrooms with hot water on tap, but most have no shower. ②

Vishal 1575–80 Main Bazaar ☎011/2356 2123, ✉vishalhotel@hotmail.com. There's a choice here between rather bare, cheap rooms with outside bathroom, and much nicer large attached ones, and there's a good restaurant too, but check the sheets before you take a room. ③

Vivek 1534–50 Main Bazaar ☎011/4154 1435 or 6, ⓦwww.vivekhotel.com. A longstanding travellers' favourite, with a 24hr rooftop restaurant, and decent if unremarkable rooms, most with attached baths and hot water, some a/c; the best have windows facing the street. There's even room service. ②–③

Yatri 3/4 Jhansi Rd, off Punchkuin Rd, by Delhi Heart and Lung Institute ☎011/2362 5563, ⓦwww.yatrihouse.com. See Delhi map, pp.98–99. This guesthouse, tucked away up a small residential street ten minutes' walk from Paharganj, is like staying in a private home, with clean and quiet attached rooms, hot water, TV and a small enclosed garden for breakfast or just for relaxing, though it's a bit pricey for what you get. Book well in advance if you want to stay here. ⑨

Ram Nagar

Directly north of Paharganj, five minutes' walk from New Delhi railway station and just beyond the flyover section of Desh Bandhu Gupta Road, **Ram Nagar** is lined with hotels and a few restaurants. It's within easy reach of the Main Bazaar, but you're spared the incessant noise and commercial atmosphere. The area's accommodation tends to be a little more expensive than in Paharganj, but the rooms are generally bigger, brighter and cleaner.

The hotels listed below are marked on the Paharganj **map** opposite.

Geet Deluxe 8570 Arakashan Rd ☎011/2361 6140 to 43. A cut above the other mid-range options in this area, well kept with nice touches and a certain charm, and clean, decent-sized rooms, all with TV, and either a/c or air-cooled. ④

Godwin Deluxe 8501/15 Arakashan Rd ☎011/2351 3795 to 8, ⓦwww.godwinhotels.com. Well-run hotel with bright, clean a/c rooms, 24hr room service, TV, and excellent staff. If an ordinary "deluxe" room isn't good enough, you can opt for a bigger "super deluxe" version. ④–⑤

🏃 **Grand Godwin** 8502/41 Arakashan Rd ☎011/2354 6891 to 8, ⓦwww .godwinhotels.com. As its name suggests, a slightly grander sister hotel to the *Godwin Deluxe*. Rooms start at merely "semi-deluxe" (on the ground floor and slightly smaller than the rest), but they're all well appointed and well kept, and there are even

suites, as well as a multi-cuisine restaurant. Rates include a buffet breakfast. ⑤–⑦

Vandna and **Karan** 47 Arakashan Rd ☎011/2362 8821 to 3. Two hotels next to each other and jointly run. The *Karan* has smaller and simpler rooms, while the *Vandna* – with mosaics of Krishna and the Qutb Minar flanking the doorway – has slightly larger rooms, though currently the same price; all the rooms in both hotels are attached with hot water and TVs, but mattresses are rather hard. ③

Woodland 8235/6 Multani Danda, Arakashan Rd ☎011/4154 1304 to 6, ⓦwww.hotelwoodland .com. Popular hotel with a choice of big a/c, or less expensive smaller, non-a/c rooms. If you want a cheaper room still, they'll send you to their sister establishment, the *Dreamland*, just across the street. ③

Old Delhi

Few tourists stay in **Old Delhi**: it's less central than Connaught Place and Paharganj, and it's dirtier, noisier and more crowded, with hotels geared mostly to Indian visitors rather than foreigners. The hotels around Old Delhi station in particular are bad value. On the other hand, there are a couple of good upmarket options on the area's fringes, and some reasonable budget hotels around the Jama Masjid, and of all the areas in town to stay in, this is the most colourful, with lots of character.

The hotels listed below appear on the Old Delhi **map** on p.120.

Ambar 6477 Katra Bariyan ☎011/2382 2059. This tourist-friendly hotel behind Fatehpuri Mosque is one of the area's better offerings, although hot water comes in buckets rather than out of the shower, and the windows all face inward. ❸
Broadway 4/15A Asaf Ali Rd ☎011/2327 3821 to 5, ✉broadway@vsnl.net. On the southern edge of Old Delhi, close to Delhi Gate, this mid-range hotel has a lot of old-fashioned charm, and an excellent restaurant specializing in Kashmiri feasts (see p.133), plus two bars, and tours through Old Delhi are available. Rooms are a little bit sombre, but they're clean and well equipped, and some look out to the Jama Masjid. Prices include breakfast. ❼–❽
Diamond Palace 3696 Netaji Suhaj Marg ☎011/2324 3786 or 7, ☏011/2314 3789. Comfortable carpeted a/c rooms above the hubbub of Netaji Subhaj Marg on the east side of Old Delhi. 24hr checkout. ❹

Maidens 7 Sham Nath Marg, Civil Lines; metro Civil Lines ☎011/2397 5464, ⓦwww.maidenshotel.com. See Delhi map, pp.98–99. A nice bit of understated luxury in a lovely old colonial mansion dating back to Company days; quiet and relaxing with comfortable period rooms, big bathrooms and leafy gardens as well as a swimming pool and a good restaurant. Doubles from $285. ❾
New City Palace 726 Jama Masjid Motor Market ☎011/2327 9548, ✉newcitypalace@hotmail.com. Though it doesn't quite live up to its billing of "a home for palatial comfort", this budget hotel is clean and well situated, directly behind the Jama Masjid (reserve ahead if you want a room with a view). Showers are hot and the best rooms have a/c, though not all the cheaper ones have outside windows. 24hr checkout. ❸–❹

South Delhi

Most of the accommodation **south of Connaught Place** lies firmly in the luxury category, although there are a few guesthouses in Sunder Nagar, the odd mid-range hotel tucked away in a residential area and a modern youth hostel near the exclusive diplomatic enclave in Chanakyapuri.

The hotels listed below appear on the New Delhi **map** on p.115.

Ambassador Sujan Singh Park, off Subramaniam Bharti Marg ☎011/2463 2600, ⓦwww.tajhotels .com. Low-key but well-run and classy, this is a friendly place with comfortable-sized rooms and huge bathrooms, plus a couple of good restaurants and free use of the pool and health club at the other Taj Group hotel, *Taj Mahal.* Doubles start from US$375. ❾
The Claridges 12 Aurangzeb Rd ☎011/4133 5133, ⓦwww.claridges-hotels.com/delhi. One of Delhi's oldest and finest establishments, oozing elegant 1930s style from its facade to its rooms and even its bathrooms. Facilities include tennis courts, restaurants and a swimming pool. Doubles start at US$395. ❾
La Sagrita 14 Sunder Nagar ☎011/2435 9541, ⓦwww.lasagrita.com. Tucked away down a quiet

side street in an exclusive colony, opposite a small park and next door to the Grenadian high commission, this small guesthouse might just suit if you want to escape the din of central Delhi. The rooms are cosy, carpeted, attached and tastefully done out, and there's a little garden out front to relax in. ❽–❾
Maurya Sardar Patel Marg, Chanakyapuri ☎011/2611 2233, ⓦwww.itcwelcomgroup.in. An extremely plush hotel on the edge of Chanakyapuri, opposite the Ridge forest, with an imposing range of luxury rooms, and some of the best dining in Delhi (see p.134). It regularly hosts visiting heads of state, with Bill Clinton and Jacques Chirac among those who have stayed here. Full-price room rates start at US$612 (including breakfast), but promotional rates are often available. ❾

Youth Hostel 5 Nyaya Marg, off Kautilya Marg, Chanakyapuri ☎011/2611 6285, ⓦwww.yhaindia .org. Away from the bustling city centre, this ultra-modern and ecofriendly grey concrete building, with dorms (a/c Rs270; non-a/c Rs90) and a/c or non-a/c singles and doubles, is the showpiece-cum-administration centre of the Indian YHA. You need to be an HI member to stay here (maximum stay seven days) but you can join on the spot (Rs250). Rates include breakfast. ❸–❹

Majnu Ka Tilla

If you want to avoid Delhi's hustle and bustle, or to have a change from Indian culture and cuisine, the Tibetan colony at **Majnu Ka Tilla** offers excellent-value budget hotels with immaculately kept rooms, much nicer than what you'd get for the same price in Paharganj, in a relatively quiet district with Tibetan food, Internet facilities and money changers close at hand, but it isn't very convenient for central Delhi (Connaught Place is Rs80 away by auto, Vidhan Sabha metro Rs20 by rickshaw). Book ahead if you intend to stay here as hotels are often full. There's only one main drag in Majnu ka Tilla, so everything's pretty easy to find.

Lhasa House 16 New Camp, just east of the main street ☎011/2393 9777 or 9888, ⒺIhasahouse @rediffmail.com. The rooms are a little bit smaller and simpler than at *Wongdhen House* next door, but all are attached, with TV and fan. Cheapest rooms are on the top floor. ❶–❹
White House 44 New Camp ☎011/2381 3544 or 3644 or 3944, Ⓔwhitehouse02@radiffmail.com. On the Tibetan colony's main street (such as it is), 100m north of the other two hotels mentioned here; the rooms are quite large, attached, with TV, and certainly well kept, but the mattresses are a bit on the hard side. ❸

🏃 Wongdhen House 15-A New Camp, just east of the main drag, next to *Lhasa House* ☎011/6415 5330, Ⓔwongdhenhouse@hotmail .com. Friendly guesthouse with a choice of rooms, some attached and some overlooking the Yamuna river. There's also a good restaurant (Tibetan food, or breakfast items) and a terrace with a great river view. ❷–❹

Near IGI Airport

If you have a long wait between flights and don't want to head into town, you could try the hotels near the **international airport** in Mahipalpur, most of them on the Gurgaon Road, which is part of NH-8, the main highway to Jaipur. Several good *dhabas* can be found around there too, and the *Radisson* boasts a cake shop and seven cafés, bars and restaurants where you can while away the time agreeably. Mahipalpur is 4km from IGI Airport, or about Rs50 by auto.

The hotels listed below appear on the Delhi **map** on pp.98–99.

Ashok Country Resort 30 Rajokri Rd, Kapashera ☎011/2506 4590 to 99, ⓦwww .ashokcountryresort.com. Elegant, stylish establishment just off the NH-8, set amid spacious gardens (ask for a room with a garden view), with a 24hr restaurant and a pool, but service could be better for the price. Doubles from US$232 including breakfast. ❾
Radisson NH-8, Mahipalpur ☎011/2677 9191, ⓦwww.radisson.com. The most luxurious choice in the area, aimed at businesspeople flying in and out of IGI, and equipped with all mod cons including Wi-Fi, pool and health club, squash courts, bowling alley, bars, and Italian, Chinese and Indian restaurants. Doubles from $481: free airport transfers. ❾
Star A-288 NH-8, Mahipalpur ☎011/2678 4092 to 5, ⓦwww.indiamart.com/hotelstar. Well-kept, clean and professionally staffed, this is the best of the mid-range hotels along this stretch of road. All rooms have a/c. ❻–❽

The City

Delhi is both daunting and alluring, a sprawling metropolis with a stunning backdrop of ancient architecture. Once you've found your feet and got over the initial impact of the commotion, noise, pollution and sheer scale of the place, the city's geography slowly slips into focus. Monuments in assorted states of repair are dotted around the city, especially in **Old Delhi** and in southern enclaves such as Hauz Khas. The British-built modern city centres on Connaught Place, the heart of **New Delhi** (though actually on its northern edge), from which it's easy – by taxi, bus, auto-rickshaw or metro – to visit pretty much anywhere else in town.

New Delhi

The modern area of **NEW DELHI**, with its wide tree-lined avenues and solid colonial architecture, has been the seat of central government since 1931. At its hub, the royal mall, **Rajpath**, runs from the palatial **Rashtrapati Bhavan**, in the west, to the **India Gate** war memorial in the east. Its wide grassy margins are a popular meeting place for families, picnickers and courting couples. The **National Museum** is located just south of the central intersection. At the north edge of the new capital lies the thriving business centre, **Connaught Place**, where neon advertisements for restaurants, bars and banks adorn the flat roofs and colonnaded verandas of the white buildings that circle its central park.

Rashtrapati Bhavan and Rajpath

After George V, king of England and emperor of British India, decreed in 1911 that Delhi should replace Calcutta as the capital of India, the English architect **Edwin Lutyens** was commissioned to plan the new governmental centre. **Rashtrapati Bhavan**, the official residence of the president of India, is one of the largest and most grandiose of the Raj constructions, built by Lutyens and Sir Herbert Baker between 1921 and 1929. Despite its classical columns, Mughal-style domes and chhatris, and Indian filigree work, the whole building is unmistakably British in character. Its majestic proportions are best appreciated from India Gate to the east – though with increasing pollution, the view is often clouded by a smoggy haze. The apartments inside are strictly private, but the **gardens** at the west side are open to the public for two weeks each February (free). Modelled on Mughal pleasure parks, with a typically ordered square pattern of quadrants dissected by waterways and refreshed by fountains, Lutyens' gardens extend beyond the normal confines to include tennis courts, butterfly enclosures, vegetable and fruit patches and a swimming pool.

Vijay Chowk, immediately in front of Rashtrapati Bhavan, leads into the wide, straight **Rajpath**, flanked with gardens and fountains that are floodlit at night, and the scene of annual **Republic Day** celebrations (Jan 26). Rajpath runs east to **India Gate**. Designed by Lutyens in 1921, the high arch, reminiscent of the Arc de Triomphe in Paris, commemorates 90,000 Indian soldiers killed fighting for the British in World War I, and bears the names of more than 3000 British and Indian soldiers who died on the Northwest frontier and in the Afghan War of 1919. The extra memorial beneath the arch honours the lives lost in the Indo-Pakistan War of 1971.

Connaught Place and around

New Delhi's commercial hub, **Connaught Place** (known as "CP"), with its classical colonnades, is radically different from the bazaars of Old Delhi, which

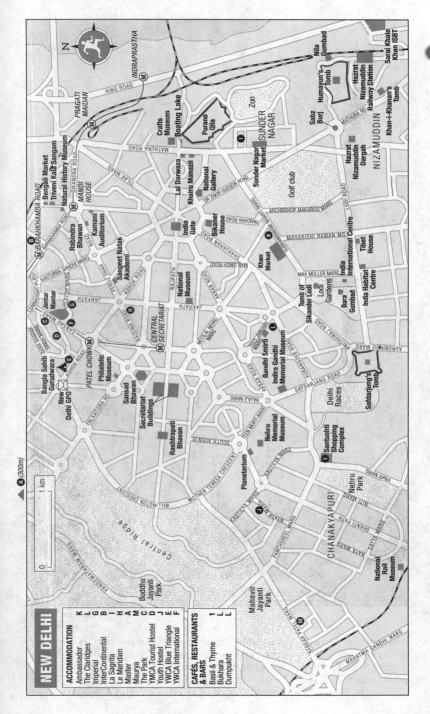

▲ Rashtrapati Bhavan

it superseded. Named after a minor British royal of the day, it takes the form of a circle, divided by eight radial roads and three ring roads into blocks lettered A–N. The term Connaught Place originally referred to the inner circle (now renamed Rajiv Chowk after Rajiv Gandhi), the outer one being Connaught Circus (now Indira Chowk, after Rajiv's mum). CP is crammed with restaurants, bars, shops, cinemas, banks and airline offices (there's a good online index at ⓦwww.connaughtplacemall.com). For a **map** of Connaught Place, see p.108.

Jantar Mantar

South of Connaught Place on Sansad Marg, the **Jantar Mantar** (daily sunrise–sunset; Rs100 [Rs5]) was built in 1725, the first of five open-air observatories designed by the ruler of Jaipur, Jai Singh II, and precursor to his larger one in Jaipur (see p.160). Huge red and white slanting stone structures looming over palm trees and neat flowerbeds were used to calculate time, solar and lunar calendars and astrological movements with an admirable degree of accuracy.

Two tourist-friendly temples

Southwest of Connaught Place, on Ashok Road by the GPO, the vast white marble structure of **Bangla Sahib Gurudwara** is Delhi's biggest Sikh temple, topped by a huge, golden, onion-shaped dome which is visible from some distance. The temple commemorates a 1664 visit to Delhi by the eighth Sikh guru, Hare Krishan, and welcomes visitors; deposit shoes at the information centre near the main entrance, where you can also enlist the services of a free guide. Remember to cover your head and dress conservatively. Live devotional music (vocals, harmonium and tabla) is relayed throughout the complex, and everybody is invited to share a simple meal of dhal and chapatis, served three times daily.

  Lakshmi Narayan Mandir (daily 4am–1.30pm & 2.30–9pm; deposit cameras, shoes and mobile phones at the entrance), northwest of the GPO and directly west of Connaught Place on Mandir Marg, is a modern Hindu temple which also welcomes tourists. With its white, cream and red brick domes, it was commissioned by a wealthy merchant family, the Birlas (hence its alternative name, Birla Mandir). The main shrine is dedicated to Lakshmi, goddess of wealth (on the right), and her consort Narayana, aka Vishnu, the preserver of life (on the left, holding a conch). At the back is a tiny ornate chamber decorated with coloured stones and mirrors and dedicated to Krishna, one of Vishnu's earthly incarnations. Devotional music is played throughout, and quotes from Hindu scriptures adorn the walls, many translated into English.

Paharganj

North of Connaught Place and directly west of New Delhi railway station, **Paharganj**, centred around Main Bazaar, provides the first experience of the Subcontinent for many budget travellers. Packed with cheap hotels, restaurants, cafés and *dhabas*, and with a busy fruit and vegetable market halfway along, it's also a paradise for shoestring shoppers seeking psychedelic clothing, joss sticks, bags, and oils of patchouli or sandalwood. For a **map** of Paharganj and neighbouring Ram Nagar, see p.110.

  There is also a less-visible underside to life in Paharganj, in the shape of the **street children**. Most are runaways who've left difficult homes, often hundreds of kilometres away, and the majority sleep on the streets and inhale solvents to numb their pain. The Salaam Baalak Trust (ⓦwww.salaambaalaktrust.com) has been set up by one of the local NGOs working to help them, which organizes **walking tours** of Paharganj conducted by former street children, who will show you the district and its hidden side. Tours last for two hours and usually start at 10am, and cost Rs200. For bookings, contact ☏09873 130383 or Ⓔsbttour@yahoo.com. Proceeds go towards providing shelter, education and healthcare for the area's street children.

National Museum

The **National Museum** (Tues–Sun 10am–5pm; Rs300 [Rs10]; cameras Rs300 [Rs20]; ⓦwww.nationalmuseumindia.gov.in), just south of Rajpath at 11 Janpath, provides a good overview of Indian culture and history. The foreigners' entry fee includes a free audio tour (Rs150 in English for Indian citizens), but you need to leave a passport, driving licence, credit card or Rs2000 (or US\$40/£40/€40) as a deposit, and the exhibits it covers are rather random. At a trot, you can see the museum in a couple of hours, but to get the best out of your visit you should set aside at least half a day.

The most important exhibits are on the ground floor, kicking off in **room 4** with the Harappan civilization. The Gandhara sculptures in **room 6** betray a very obvious Greco-Roman influence. **Room 9** has some very fine bronzes, most especially those of the Chola period (from south India in the ninth to the thirteenth century), and a fifteenth-century statue of Devi from Vijanaraya in south India, by the left-hand wall. Among the late medieval sculptures in **room 10**, is a fearsome, vampire-like, late chola dvarapala (a guardian figure built to flank the doorway to a shrine), also from south India, and a couple of performing musicians from Mysore. **Room 12** is devoted to the Mughals, and in particular their miniature paintings. Look out also for two paintings depicting a subject you wouldn't expect – the nativity of Jesus. It's worth popping upstairs to the **textiles**, and the **musical instruments** collection on the second floor is outstanding. The **Central Asian antiquities** collection includes a large number of paintings, documents, ceramics and textiles from Eastern Turkestan (Xinjiang) and the Silk Route, dating from between the third and twelfth centuries. Finally, on your way out, take a look at the massive twelve-tiered temple chariot from Tamil Nadu, an extremely impressive piece of woodwork in a glass shelter just by the southern entrance gate.

Memorial museums

The **Nehru Memorial Museum** (Tues–Sun 9am–5.30pm; free) on Teen Murti Marg was home to India's first prime minister, Jawaharlal Nehru, and is now preserved in his memory. One of Nehru's passions was astronomy, and there's a **planetarium** (Rs2; 40min astronomy shows in English Tues–Sun 11.30am & 3pm, Rs15) in the grounds of the house.

Nehru's daughter, Indira Gandhi, despite her excesses during the 1975–77 Emergency (see p.191), is still remembered by many with respect and affection. The **Indira Gandhi Memorial Museum** (Tues–Sun 9.30am–4.45pm; free), 1 Safdarjang Rd, was the house where she was assassinated by her Sikh bodyguards in 1984; her bloodstained sari, chemically preserved, is on display, and there's a section devoted to her son Rajiv, including the clothes he was wearing when he was in turn assassinated by Sri Lankan Tamil separatists in 1991.

Still more tragic than the deaths of Rajiv and Indira was the 1948 assassination of the nation's founder, Mahatma Gandhi, who shared their surname but was not related. The **Gandhi Smriti** (Tues–Sun 10am–5pm; free), 5 Tees January Marg, is the house where the Mahatma lived his last days. He had come to Delhi to quell the sectarian rioting that accompanied Partition, but Hindu sectarian extremists hated him for protecting Muslims, and on 30 January 1948, one of them shot him dead. Visitors can view an exhibition about his life, and follow in his last footsteps to the spot where he died.

National Gallery of Modern Art

Once the residence of the Maharaja of Jaipur, the extensive **National Gallery** (Tues–Sun 10am–5pm; Rs150 [Rs10]) housed in Jaipur House near India Gate, is a rich showcase of Indian contemporary art. The permanent displays, focusing on post-1930s work, exhibit many of India's most important works of modern art, including pieces by the "Bengali Renaissance" artists Abanendranath Tagore and Nandalal Bose, the great poet and artist, Rabindranath Tagore, and Jamini Roy, whose work, reminiscent of Modigliani, reflects the influence of Indian folk art. Also on show are the romantic paintings and etchings of Thomas Daniell and his nephew William, British artists of the Bombay or Company School, which combined Indian delicacy with Western realism. The ground-floor galleries are used for temporary exhibitions.

Crafts Museum

Immediately north of Purana Qila on Bhairon Marg, the **Crafts Museum** (Tues–Sun 10am–5pm; free) is a dynamic exhibition of the rural arts and crafts of India, divided into three sections. The **exhibition galleries** show a range of textiles, carvings, ceramics, painting and metalwork from across India, while the **village complex** displays an assortment of traditional homes from different parts of the country. The **craft demonstrations** do feature a few artisans actually at work, but mostly they are more like shops selling crafts typical of different Indian regions. There's also a library and a fixed-price museum **shop**.

Old Delhi (Shahjahanabad)

Though it's not in fact the oldest part of Delhi, the seventeenth-century city of **Shahjahanabad**, built for the Mughal emperor Shah Jahan, is known as **OLD DELHI**. Construction began on the city in 1638, and within eleven years it was substantially complete, surrounded by over 8km of ramparts pierced by fourteen main gates. It boasted a beautiful main thoroughfare, **Chandni Chowk**, an imposing citadel, the **Red Fort** (Lal Qila), and an impressive congregational mosque, the **Jama Masjid**. Today much of the wall has crumbled, and of the fourteen gates only four remain, but it's still a fascinating area, crammed with interesting nooks and crannies, though you'll need stamina, patience, time and probably a fair few chai stops along the way to endure the crowds and traffic. Old Delhi is served by metro stations at Chandni Chowk (actually nearer Old Delhi train station), Chawri Bazaar, and the Ajmeri Gate side of New Delhi train station (the metro stop's name of "New Delhi" is in this instance misleading).

The Red Fort (Lal Qila)

The largest of Old Delhi's monuments is Lal Qila, known in English as the **Red Fort** because of the red sandstone from which it was built (Tues–Sun sunrise to sunset, museums 10am–5pm; Rs100 [Rs5]). It was commissioned by Shah Jahan to be his residence, and modelled on the fort at Agra. Work started in 1638, and the emperor moved in ten years later. The fort contains all the trappings you'd expect at the centre of Mughal government: halls of public and private audience, domed and arched marble palaces, plush private apartments, a mosque, and elaborately designed gardens. The ramparts, which stretch for over 2km, are interrupted by two gates – **Lahori Gate** to the west, through which you enter, and Delhi Gate to the south. Shah Jahan's son, Aurangzeb, added barbicans to both gates. In those days, the Yamuna River ran along the eastern wall, feeding both the moat and a "stream of paradise" which ran through every pavilion. As the Mughal Empire declined, the fort fell into disrepair. It was attacked and plundered by the Persian emperor Nadir Shah in 1739, and by the British in 1857. Nevertheless, it remains an impressive testimony to Mughal grandeur. Keep your ticket stub as you will have to show it several times (for example, to enter the museums).

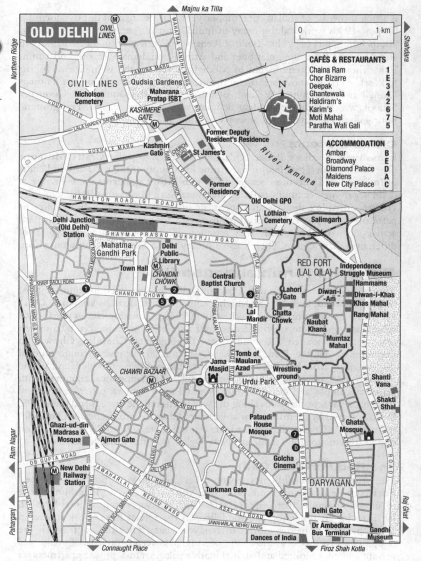

CAFÉS & RESTAURANTS	
Chaina Ram	1
Chor Bizarre	E
Deepak	3
Ghantewala	4
Haldiram's	2
Karim's	6
Moti Mahal	7
Paratha Wali Gali	5

ACCOMMODATION	
Ambar	B
Broadway	E
Diamond Palace	D
Maidens	A
New City Palace	C

The main entrance to the fort from Lahori Gate opens onto **Chatta Chowk**, a covered street flanked with arched cells that used to house Delhi's most talented jewellers, carpet-makers, goldsmiths and silk-weavers, but is now given over to souvenir sellers. At the end, a path to the left leads to the **Museum of the Struggle for Independence**, depicting resistance to British rule.

The **Naubhat Khana** ("Musicians' Gallery") marked the entrance into the royal quarters. Beyond it, a path leads ahead through wide lawns to the **Diwan-i-Am**, or Hall of Public Audience, where the emperor used to meet commoners and hold court. In those days it was strewn with silk carpets and partitioned with hanging tapestries. Its centrepiece is a marble dais on which sat the emperor's throne, surrounded by twelve panels inlaid with precious stones, mostly depicting birds and flowers. The most famous of them, in the middle at the top (and not easy to see), shows the mythological Greek Orpheus with his lute. The panels were made by a Florentine jeweller and imported from Italy, but the surrounding inlay work was done locally.

The pavilions along the fort's east wall face spacious gardens and overlook the banks of the Yamuna. Immediately east of the Diwan-i-Am, **Rang Mahal**, the "Palace of Colour", housed the emperor's wives and mistresses. Originally, its ceiling was overlaid with gold and silver and reflected onto a central pool in the marble floor. Unfortunately, it suffered a lot of vandalism when the British used it as an Officers' Mess after the 1857 uprising. The similar **Mumtaz Mahal**, south of the main *zenana*, or women's quarters, and probably used by princesses, now houses an **Archeological Museum**, displaying manuscripts, paintings, ceramics and textiles, with a section devoted to the last Mughal emperor, Bahadur Shah II, whose exhibits include his silk robes and silver hookah pipe.

On the northern side of Rang Mahal, the marble **Khas Mahal** was the personal palace of the emperor, split into separate apartments for worship, sleeping and sitting. The southern chamber, **Tosh Khana** ("Robe Room"), has a stunning marble filigree screen on its north wall, surmounted by a panel carved with the scales of justice. The octagonal tower projecting over the east wall of the Khas Mahal was where the emperor appeared daily before throngs gathered on the riverbanks below.

North of Khas Mahal, in the large **Diwan-i-Khas** ("Hall of Private Audience"), the emperor would address the highest nobles of his court. Today it's the finest building in the fort, a marble pavilion shaded by a roof raised on stolid pillars meeting in ornate scalloped arches and embellished with exquisitely delicate inlays of flowers made from semiprecious stones. On the north and south walls you can still make out the inscription of a couplet in Persian attributed to Shah Jahan's prime minister, which roughly translates as: "If there be paradise upon this earthly sphere / It is here, oh it is here, oh it is here". More than just a paean, the verse refers to the deliberate modelling of the fort's gardens on the Koranic description of heaven.

A little further north are the **hammams**, or baths, sunk into the marble floor inlaid with patterns of precious stones, and dappled in jewel-coloured light that filters through stained-glass windows. The western chamber contained hot baths while the eastern apartment, with fountains of rosewater, was used as a dressing room. Next to the hammams, the sweetly fashioned **Moti Masjid**, or Pearl Mosque, triple-domed in white marble, was added by Aurangzeb in 1659, but unfortunately it's currently closed to the public.

Jama Masjid

A wonderful piece of Mughal pomp, the red-and-white **Jama Masjid** (8am–12.15pm & 1.45pm till 30min before sunset; closed for 30min in the afternoon

Sound-and-light shows

Each night except Monday, a **sound-and-light show** takes place in the **Red Fort**: the palaces are dramatically lit, and a historical commentary blares from crackly loudspeakers. The show starts after sunset and lasts an hour (in English Feb–April & Sept–Oct 8.30pm, May–Aug 9pm, Nov–Jan 7.30pm; Rs50; ☏011/2327 4580). The mosquitoes are ferocious, so bring repellent. Heavy monsoon rains may affect summer shows.

for afternoon prayers; in summer opens at 7am; free; Rs200 for cameras; no shorts, short skirts or sleeveless tops) is India's largest mosque. Its courtyard is large enough to accommodate the prostrated bodies of 25,000 worshippers. It was designed by Shah Jahan and built by a workforce of 5000 people between 1644 and 1656. Originally called Masjid-i-Jahanuma ("mosque commanding a view of the world"), this grand structure stands on Bho Jhala, one of Shahjahanabad's two hills, and looks east to the sprawling Red Fort, and down on the seething streets of Old Delhi. Broad, red-sandstone staircases lead to gateways on the east, north and southern sides, where worshippers and visitors alike must remove their shoes (the custodian will guard them for you for a small tip).

Once inside the courtyard, your eyes will be drawn to the three bulbous marble domes crowning the **main prayer hall** on the west side (facing Mecca), fronted by a series of high cusped arches, and sheltering the mihrab, the central niche in the west wall indicating the direction of prayer. The pool in the centre is used for ritual ablutions. At each corner of the square yard a slender minaret crowned with a marble dome rises to the sky, and it's worth climbing the **tower** (Rs20; women must be accompanied by a man) south of the main sanctuary for a view over Delhi. In the northeast corner a white shrine protects a collection of Muhammad's relics, including his sandals, a hair from his beard, and his "footprint" miraculously embedded in a marble slab.

Chandni Chowk

Old Delhi's main thoroughfare, **Chandni Chowk** was once a sublime canal lined with trees and some of the most opulent bazaars in the whole of Asia. The British paved over the canal after 1857. Recently, congestion has been eased with a daytime (8am–8pm) ban on cycle rickshaws along the street, and their replacement by a fleet of green minibuses (fare Rs5), but the best way to take it in is on foot. Along it, look out for numbered "heritage buildings" signposted at intervals, with placards outside explaining their historical importance, especially during the 1857 uprising.

At Chandni Chowk's eastern end, opposite the Red Fort, the **Lal Mandir** Jain temple is not as ornate as the Jain temples in Rajasthan, but it does boast detailed carvings, and gilded paintwork in the antechambers surrounding the main shrine. Remove your shoes, and leave any leather articles at the kiosk before entering. The attached **bird hospital** (no charge but donations appreciated) puts into practice the Jain principle that all life is sacred by rescuing injured birds, with each species having its own ward. The sparrow ward is largely occupied by victims of ceiling fans, with which these poor critters apparently collide quite often.

Raj Ghat

When Shah Jahan established his city in 1638, its eastern edges bordered the River Yamuna, and a line of *ghats*, or steps leading to the water, was installed along the riverbanks. *Ghats* have been used in India for centuries, for mundane things like washing clothes and bathing, but also for worship and funeral cremation. **Raj Ghat** (daily: April–Sept 5am–7.30pm; Oct–March 5.30am–7pm; free), east of Delhi Gate – really more a park than a *ghat* – is the place where Mahatma Gandhi was cremated, on the day after his assassination in 1948. The Mahatma's *samadhi* (cremation memorial), a low black plinth inscribed with his last words, "Hai Ram" ("Oh God"), receives a steady stream of visitors, and he is remembered through prayers here every Friday evening at 5pm, and on the anniversaries of his birth and death (Oct 2 & Jan 30). Opposite Raj Ghat's southwest corner, the small **Gandhi Memorial Museum** (daily except Mon and every other Sun 9.30am–5.30pm; free) houses some of Gandhi's photographs and writings, and at weekends you can watch films on his political and personal life (English Sat 4pm; Hindi Sun 4pm).

North of Raj Ghat, memorials also mark the places where Jawaharlal Nehru (at Shanti Vana), his daughter Indira Gandhi (at Shakti Sthal), and his grandson Rajiv Gandhi (at Vir Bhumi) were cremated.

Firoz Shah Kotla

Supposedly, Firoz Shah, sultan of Delhi from 1351 to 1358, had a whole fifth city of Delhi built – Firozabad, founded in 1354. Today few traces survive of what was in any case probably never more than a suburb of the main city, but what does remain is the fortified palace of **Firoz Shah Kotla** (Tues–Sun sunrise to sunset; Rs100 [Rs5]), now a crumbling ruin with ornamental gardens, 500m east of Delhi Gate. Its most incongruous and yet distinctive element is the third century BC polished sandstone **Ashokan pillar**, carried down the Yamuna by raft from Ambala. For a reasonable view of the column, you'll need to climb to the top of the building, entering the compound through a gate on the west side, then mounting a stairway in the northeast corner. From the top you also get a view of the neighbouring mosque and *baoli* (step-well), as well as the lawns which make the site such a pleasant place to visit.

North of the Red Fort

Netaji Subhash Marg leads north from the Red Fort and under a railway bridge to Old Delhi GPO. Just before the post office, on the east side of the road, **Lothian Cemetery**, the burial ground for officers of the East India Company from 1808 until just after the 1857 uprising, had become very run-down, but was being renovated at last check. In the middle of the road in front of the post office, the remains of the East India Company's **Magazine** or arsenal is now used mainly as an unofficial public toilet, so watch your step if you cross the street to explore it. Another part of the magazine, with a memorial plaque, stands on a second traffic island just to the north.

Continuing north along Lothian Road, you'll pass another remnant of Company days on your right in the form of the old **Residency**, now the Archeology Department of Guru Gobind Singh Indraprastha University. A couple of hundred metres further is the rather fine cream-and-white baroque facade of **St James's Church** (daily 8.30am–1pm & 2–5pm, or whenever you can find the caretaker), commissioned in 1836 by **James Skinner**, the son of a Scottish Company-wallah and a Rajput princess. Because of his mixed ancestry, and the increasing racism of the British regime, Skinner was refused a commission in the Company's army, but set up his own irregular cavalry unit (Skinner's Horse, also called the Yellow Boys after their uniform) and made himself pretty much indispensable to the Company in northern India. Though he was continually snubbed over pay and rank, his astounding victories over the forces of the Maharajah of Jaipur and the great Sikh leader Maharajah Ranjit Singh eventually forced the Company to begrudgingly grant him the rank of Lieutenant Colonel and absorb his cavalrymen into its ranks. Skinner died in 1842 and is buried just in front of the altar.

Immediately north of the church, Church Road leads to the offices of the Northern Railway, where the East India Company's **Deputy Resident's Residence** is now the office of the railway's chief engineer. If you ask at the gate, you'll probably be allowed in to admire the bow-fronted veranda and balustrades, but you probably won't be permitted to take photos or to venture inside. A plaque to the left of its front door explains the building's history.

The double-arched **Kashmiri Gate**, on the west side of Lothian Road just 300m north of the church, was where the Mughal court would leave Delhi every summer bound for the cool valley of Kashmir. To its north is Maharana Pratap Inter-state Bus Terminal, beyond which, across the busy Lala Hardev Sahai Marg, is the district known as the **Civil Lines**. This area was created after the events of 1857, when the British no longer felt safe living among the Indian residents of Old Delhi and moved up here for a more secluded location. Immediately north of Lala Hardev Sahai Marg, the peaceful **Qudsia Gardens** are a fading remnant of the magnificent pleasure parks commissioned in the mid-eighteenth century by Queen Qudsia, favourite mistress of Muhammad Shah, and mother of Ahmed Shah. Just west of the gardens, on Qudsia Road, is Delhi's oldest burial ground, **Nicholson Cemetery**, named after Brigadier General John Nicholson, who was shot down while leading the British attack to regain Delhi from the 1857 insurgents.

South Delhi

Most of the early settlements of Delhi, including its first city at Qila Rai Pithora (around the Qutb Minar), are to be found not in "Old Delhi" but in **South Delhi**, the area south of Lutyens' carefully planned boulevards, where the rapid expansion of suburban Delhi has swallowed up what was previously countryside. Whole villages have been embedded within it, and the area is littered with monuments from the past. Meanwhile, as the centre becomes more and more congested, South Delhi's housing enclaves and colonies are increasingly home to the newest shopping centres and the most happening locales.

Purana Qila

The majestic fortress of **Purana Qila** (daily sunrise to sunset; Rs100 [Rs5], whose crumbling ramparts dominate busy Mathura Road, east of India Gate, is thought to stand on the site of Indraprastha, the Pandava city of Mahabharata fame. Considered the sixth city of Delhi, it was begun by Humayun, the second Mughal emperor, as Din-Panah, and renamed Shergarh by Sher Khan, who displaced him in 1540 and oversaw most of the construction. Purana Qila is served by **buses** between Delhi Gate and Sunder Nagar, including #423 and #438 (ask for the zoo, which is the same stop).

Most of the inside of the fortress is taken up by pleasant lawns and gardens, but two important buildings survive. Of them, the **Qila-i-Kuhna Masjid** is one of Sher Khan's finest monuments. Constructed in 1541 in the Afghan style, it has five elegant arches, embellished with white and black marble to complement the red sandstone. The geometric patterns and carved Arabic calligraphy around the main doorway all represent a more sophisticated degree of decorative artwork than on anything seen before in Delhi. Previous decorative carving on buildings was in plaster, but here it's in stone, a more serious affair as it's obviously much harder to work.

The Purana Qila's other main building, the **Sher Mandal**, is a red-sandstone octagonal observatory and library built for Sher Khan. It was here in 1556 that the emperor Humayun died. He stumbled down its treacherously steep steps while hurrying to answer the *muezzin*'s call to prayer, just a year after he had defeated Sher Khan's son Sikander Suri and regained power.

Humayun's Tomb

Close to the medieval Muslim centre of Nizamuddin and 2km from Purana Qila, **Humayun's Tomb** (daily sunrise to sunset; Rs250 [Rs10]) stands at the crossroads of the Lodi and Mathura roads, 500m from Nizamuddin railway station (one stop from New Delhi Station on the suburban line), and easily accessible from Connaught Place by bus (#181, #966 and #893) or pre-paid auto (Rs50). Late afternoon is the best time to photograph it. Delhi's first Mughal mausoleum, it was constructed to house the remains of the second Mughal emperor, Humayun, and was built under the watchful eye of Haji Begum, his senior widow and mother of Akbar, who camped here for the duration, and is now buried alongside her husband. The grounds were later used to inter several prominent Mughals, and served as a refuge for the last emperor, Bahadur Shah II, before his capture by the British in 1857.

The tomb's sombre, Persian-style elegance marks this as one of Delhi's finest historic sites. Constructed of red sandstone, inlaid with black and white marble, on a commanding podium looking towards the Yamuna, it stands in the centre of the formal *charbagh*, or quartered garden. The octagonal structure is crowned with a double dome that soars to a height of 38m. Though it was the very first Mughal garden tomb – to be followed by Akbar's at Sikandra (see p.287) and of course the Taj Mahal at Agra (see p.279), for which it can be seen as a prototype – Humayun's mausoleum has antecedents in Delhi in the form of Ghiyas-ud-din Tughluq's tomb at Tughluqabad (see p.128), and that of Sikandar Lodi in Lodi Gardens (see p.126). From the second of those it adopted its octagonal shape and the high central arch that was to be such a typical feature of Mughal architecture – you'll see it at the Taj, and in Delhi's Jama Masjid (see p.121), for example.

Within the grounds southeast of the main mausoleum, another impressive square mausoleum, with a double dome and two graves bearing Koranic inscriptions, is that of Humayun's barber, a man considered important because he was trusted with holding a razor to the emperor's throat. Nearby but outside the compound (so you'll have to walk right round for a closer look) stands the **Nila Gumbad** ("blue dome"), an octagonal tomb with a dome of blue tiles, supposedly built by one of Akbar's nobles to honour a faithful servant, and which may possibly predate Humayun's Tomb. On your way round to the Nila Gumbad (depending on your route), you pass the **tomb of Khan-i-Khanan**, a Mughal general who died in 1626 (daily sunrise to sunset; $2 [Rs5]); unfortunately, the tomb looks rather ragged as the facing was all stripped for use in Safdarjang's tomb, and the garden that surrounded it has mostly gone. The blue-domed structure in the middle of the road junction in front of the entrance to Humayun's tomb is a seventeenth-century tomb called **Sabz Burj** – the tiles on its dome are not original, but the result of a recent restoration.

Nizamuddin

Just across the busy Mathura Road from Humayun's Tomb, and now engulfed by a busy road network and plush suburbs, the self-contained *mahalla* (village) of **Nizamuddin**, with its lack of traffic, ancient mosques and tombs, and slow pace of life, is so different from the surrounding city that to enter it is like passing through a time warp. At its heart, surrounded by a tangle of narrow alleyways lined with shops and market stalls, lies one of Sufism's greatest shrines, the **Hazrat Nizamuddin Dargah**, which draws a constant stream of devotees from far and wide.

The marble *dargah* is the tomb of Sheikh Nizam-ud-din Aulia (1236–1325), fourth saint of the Chishtiya Sufi order (followers of Khwaja Muin-ud-din Chishti of Ajmer; see p.199), was built the year the sheikh died, but has been through several renovations, and the present mausoleum dates from 1562. Lattice screens and arches in the inner sanctum surround the actual tomb (closed to women), which is surrounded by a marble rail and a canopy of mother-of-pearl. Sheikh Nizam-ud-din's disciple, the poet and chronicler

Amir Khusrau – considered to be the first Urdu poet and the founder of *khyal*, the most common form of north Indian classical music – lies in a contrasting red-sandstone tomb in front of his master's mausoleum.

Religious song and music play an important role among the Chishtiyas, as among several Sufi orders, and *qawwals* (bards) gather to sing in the evenings (especially on Thurs and feast days). Comprising a chorus led by solo singing accompanied by clapping and usually a harmonium combined with a *dholak* (double-membraned barrel drum) and tabla (paired hand-drums), the hypnotic rhythm of their **qawwali music** is designed to lull its audience into a state of *mast* (spiritual intoxication), which is believed to bring the devotee closer to God.

The oldest building in the area, the red-sandstone mosque of **Jamat Khana Masjid**, looms over the main *dargah* on its western side. It was commissioned in 1325 by Khizr Khan, the son of the Khalji sultan Ala-ud-din. Enclosed by marble lattice screens next to Amir Khusrau's mausoleum, the tomb of **Princess Jahanara**, Shah Jahan's favourite daughter, is topped by a hollow filled with grass in compliance with her wish to have nothing but grass covering her grave. Just east of the *dargah* compound, the elegant 64-pillared white marble **Chausath Khamba** was built as a mausoleum for the family of a Mughal politician who had been governor of Gujarat, and the building, with its low, wide form and elegant marble screens, bears the unmistakable evidence of a Gujarati influence. The compound containing the Chausath is usually locked, but the caretaker should be on hand somewhere nearby to open it up if you want to take a closer look.

Lodi Gardens

Two kilometres west of Nizamuddin along Lodi Road, the leafy, pleasant **Lodi Gardens** (daily 5am–8pm; free) form part of a belt of fifteenth- and sixteenth-century monuments that now stand incongruously amid golf greens, large bungalows and elite estates. The park is especially full in the early mornings and early evenings, when fitness enthusiasts come for brisk walks or to jog through the manicured gardens against a backdrop of much-graffitied medieval monuments; it's also a popular lovers' hangout. The gardens, a Rs40 auto-ride from Connaught Place, also contain the **National Bonsai Park**, which has a fine selection of diminutive trees. The best time to come is at sunset, when the light is soft and the tombs are all lit up.

Near the centre of the gardens, the imposing **Bara Gumbad** ("large dome") is a square, late fifteenth-century tomb capped by the eponymous dome, its monotonous exterior relieved by grey and black stones and its interior adorned with painted stuccowork. **Shish Gumbad** ("glazed dome"), a similar tomb 50m north, still bears a few traces of the blue tiles liberally used to form friezes below the cornice and above the entrance. Inside, plasterwork is inscribed with ornate Koranic inscriptions.

The octagonal **tomb of Muhammad Shah** (1434–44) of the Sayyid dynasty stands 300m southwest of Bara Gumbad, surrounded by verandas and pierced by arches and sloping buttresses. Enclosed within high walls and a square garden, 300m north of Bara Gumbad, the **tomb of Sikandar Lodi** (1517–18) repeats the octagonal theme, with a central chamber encircled by a veranda. **Athpula** ("eight piers"), a sixteenth-century ornamental bridge, lies east, in the northwest corner of the park.

Safdarjang's Tomb

The tomb of **Safdarjang** (daily dawn to dusk; Rs100 [Rs5]), the Mughal viceroy of Avadh under Muhammad Shah (1719–48), stands at the junction of

Lodi Road and Aurobindo Marg, 5km southwest of Connaught Place; from Ajmeri Gate or Connaught Place (Kasturba Gandhi Marg), or from Connaught Place by pre-paid auto-rickshaw (Rs50). Constructed between 1753 and 1774, the double-storeyed mausoleum, built of red and buff sandstone and relieved by marble, rises on a dramatic platform overlooking the adjacent airport of the Delhi Flying Club. It was the very last of India's great Mughal garden tombs, dating from the period after Nadir Shah's sacking of the city, by which time the empire was reduced to a fraction of its former size and most of the capital's grander buildings lay in ruins. Emblematic of the decadence and degeneracy that characterized the twilight of the Mughal era, the mausoleum sports an elongated, tapered dome and absurdly ornate interior filled with swirling plasterwork. In *City of Djinns*, William Dalrymple aptly describes its quirky design as "blowzy Mughal rococo" typifying an age "not so much decaying into impoverished anonymity as one whoring and drinking itself into extinction".

National Rail Museum

The cream of India's royal coaches and oldest engines are on permanent display at the **National Rail Museum** (Tues–Sun: April–Sept 9.30am–1pm & 1.30–7.30pm; Oct–March 9.30am–1pm & 1.30–5.30pm; Rs10, video Rs100) in the Embassy enclave of Chanakyapuri, southwest of Connaught Place; take bus #620 from Shivaji Stadium terminal by Connaught Place, or a pre-paid auto (Rs50). Some 27 locomotives and 17 carriages – including the ornate 1886 gold-painted saloon car of the Maharaja of Baroda (Rs50 to go inside), the teak carriage of the Maharaja of Mysore, trimmed in gold and ivory, and the cabin used by the Prince of Wales in 1876 – are kept in the grounds. A steam-hauled miniature "Joy Train" does a circuit of the grounds (Rs10) whenever it has enough passengers.

The covered section of the museum houses models of famous engines and coaches, displays of old tickets, and even the skull of an elephant hit by a train near Calcutta in 1894. The pride of the collection, however, is a model of India's very first train, a steam engine which made its inaugural journey of 21 miles from Mumbai to Thane in 1853.

Hauz Khas

Set amid parks and woodland 4km south of Safdarjang's Tomb, the wealthy suburban development of **Hauz Khas** is typical of South Delhi in being a thoroughly modern area dotted with remnants of antiquity. The modern part takes the form of Hauz Khas village, a shopping area packed with chic boutiques and smart restaurants. There's also a very pleasant deer park and a rose garden, but of most interest to visitors, apart from the upmarket shopping possibilities (see pp.137–139), are the ruins of a fourteenth-century reservoir at the western end of the village.

Sultan Ala-ud-din Khalji had the reservoir (or "tank") built in 1304 to supply water to his citadel at Siri, Delhi's "second city", and it was known after him as **Hauz-i-Alai**. Half a century later, it was expanded by Firoz Shah, who added a two-storey *madrasa* (seminary), and a mosque at its northern end. Among the anonymous tombs scattered throughout the area is that of Firoz Shah himself, directly overlooking the southern corner of the tank. Its high walls, lofty dome, and doorway spanned by a lintel with a stone railing outside, are fine examples of Hindu Indian traditions effectively blended with Islamic architecture.

Siri itself was located a couple of kilometres east of Hauz Khas, and the remains of its ramparts can be seen from Khel Gaon Marg. Much of the site has been given over to parkland, which makes it pleasant enough to visit, but part of it has been subsumed by a village built to house athletes competing in the 1982 Asian Games.

Baha'i Temple

Often compared visually to the Sydney Opera House, Delhi's 1986 **Baha'i Temple** (Tues–Sun: April–Sept 9am–7pm; Oct–March 9.30am–5.30pm; you may be asked to wait briefly outside during services, which are on the hour 9am–noon & 3–5pm) is an iconic piece of modern architecture that attracts a steady stream of visitors. Dominating the surrounding suburban sprawl, 27 spectacular giant white petals of marble in the shape of an unfolding lotus spring from nine pools and walkways, to symbolize the nine unifying spiritual paths of the Baha'i faith; each petal alcove contains an extract of the Baha'i holy scriptures. Set amid well-maintained gardens, the temple is at its most impressive at sunset. It'll cost you Rs75 to get here by pre-paid auto from Connaught Place, or you can take bus #440 from New Delhi Station (gate 1) or Connaught Place (the stop in Kasturba Gandhi Marg) to the Outer Ring Road by Kalkaji bus depot, a short walk from the temple.

Ashoka's Rock Edict

Northwest of the Baha'i Temple, just off Raja Dhirsain Marg, **Ashoka's Rock Edict** is a ten-line epigraph inscribed in ancient Brahmi script on a smooth, sloping rock. The rock, now protected by a shelter in its own little park, was used as a slide by neighbourhood kids until 1966, when local residents noticed the ancient inscription, which was promulgated by the Mauryan emperor Ashoka the Great in the third century BC, and shows there must have been an important settlement nearby. It states that the emperor's exertions in the cause of dharma (righteousness) had brought the people closer to the gods, and that through their efforts this attainment could be increased even further.

Tughluqabad

Fifteen kilometres southeast of Connaught Place on the Mehrauli–Badarpur Road (the entrance is a kilometre east of the junction with Guru Ravidas Marg), a rocky escarpment holds the crumbling 6.5-kilometre-long battlements of the third city of Delhi, **Tughluqabad** (daily sunrise to sunset; Rs100 [Rs5]), built during the short reign of Ghiyas-ud-din Tughluq (1320–24). After the king's death the city was deserted, probably due to the lack of a clean water source nearby. The most interesting area is the high-walled **citadel** in the southwestern part of the site, though only a long underground passage, the ruins of several halls and a tower now remain. The grid pattern of some of the city streets to the north is still traceable. The palace area is to the west of the entrance, and the former bazaar to the east.

The southernmost of Tughlaqabad's thirteen gates still looks down on a causeway, breached by the modern road, which rises above the flood plain, to link the fortress with **Ghiyas-ud-din Tughluq's tomb** (same hours and ticket as Tughlaqabad). The tomb is entered through a massive red-sandstone gateway leading into a courtyard surrounded by cloisters in the defensive walls. In the middle, surrounded by a well-kept lawn, stands the distinctive mausoleum, its sloping sandstone walls topped by a marble dome, and in its small way a precursor to the fine series of garden tombs built by the Mughals, which began here in Delhi with that of Humayun (see p.124). Inside the mausoleum are the graves of Ghiyas-ud-din, his wife and their son Muhammad Shah II. Ghiyas-ud-din's chief minister Jafar Khan is buried in the eastern bastion, and interred in the cloister nearby is the sultan's favourite dog.

The later fortress of **Adilabad** (free entry), built by Muhammad Shah II in much the same style as his father's citadel, and now in ruins, stands on a hillock to the southeast.

Tughluqabad is served by buses #34, #525 and #717 along the Mehrauli–Badarpur road from Lado Sarai near the Qutb Minar, and by #430 from Kalkaji near the Baha'i Temple. From Connaught Place, the easiest way to get there is by pre-paid auto-rickshaw (around Rs100). By bus, the most direct route from New Delhi Station (gate 1) or Connaught Place (the stop in Kasturba Gandhi Marg) is #440 to the junction of Guru Ravidas Marg with the Mehrauli–Badarpur Road at Hamdard Nagar, and from there you can either walk (1km) or take an eastbound bus along the Mehrauli–Badarpur Road.

Qutb Minar Complex

Above the foundations of Lal Kot, the "first city of Delhi" founded in the eleventh century by the Tomar Rajputs, stand the first monuments of Muslim India, known as the **Qutb Minar Complex** (daily sunrise to sunset; Rs250 [Rs10]). You'll find it 13km south of Connaught Place off Aurobindo Marg, easy to reach by bus #505 from Ajmeri Gate, Connaught Place (Super Bazaar) or Kasturba Gandhi Marg, or by pre-paid auto from Connaught Place (Rs70). One of Delhi's most famous landmarks, the fluted red-sandstone tower of the **Qutb Minar** tapers upwards from the ruins, covered with intricate carvings and deeply inscribed verses from the Koran, to a height of just over 72m. In times past it was considered one of the "Wonders of the East", second only to the Taj Mahal – in the words of Victorian historian James Ferguson, "the most beautiful example of its class known anywhere"; but historian John Keay was perhaps more representative of the modern eye when he claimed that the tower had "an unfortunate hint of the factory chimney and the brick kiln; a wisp of white smoke trailing from its summit would not seem out of place".

Work on the Qutb Minar started in 1202; it was Qutb-ud-Din Aibak's victory tower, celebrating the advent of the Muslim dominance of Delhi (and much of the Subcontinent) that was to endure until 1857. For Qutb-ud-din, who died four years after gaining power, it marked the eastern extremity of the Islamic faith, casting the shadow of God over east and west. It was also a minaret, from which the *muezzin* called the faithful to prayer. Only the first storey has been ascribed to Qutb-ud-din's own short reign; the other four were built under his successor Iltutmish, and the top was restored in 1369 under Firoz Shah, using marble to face the red sandstone.

Adjacent to the tower lie the ruins of India's first mosque, **Quwwat-ul-Islam** ("the Might of Islam"), commissioned by Qutb-ud-din and built using the remains of 27 Hindu and Jain temples with the help of Hindu artisans whose influence can be seen in the detail of the masonry and the indigenous corbelled arches. Steps lead to an impressive courtyard flanked by cloisters and supported by pillars unmistakably taken from a Hindu temple and adapted to accord with strict Islamic law forbidding iconic worship – all the faces of the decorative figures carved into the columns have been removed. Especially fine ornamental arches, rising as high as 16m, remain of what was once the prayer hall. Beautifully carved sandstone screens, combining Koranic calligraphy with the Indian lotus, form a facade immediately to the west of the mosque, facing Mecca. Iltutmish and his successors had the building extended, enlarging the prayer hall and the cloisters and introducing geometric designs, calligraphy, glazed tiles set in brick, and squinches (arches set diagonally to a square to support a dome).

The Khalji sultan Ala-ud-din had the mosque extended to the north, and aimed to build a tower even taller than the Qutb Minar, but his **Alai Minar** never made it beyond the first storey, which still stands, and is regarded as a monument to the folly of vain ambition. Ala-ud-din also commissioned the **Alai Darwaza**, an elegant mausoleum-like gateway with stone lattice screens, just to the south of the Qutb Minar.

In complete contrast to the mainly Islamic surroundings, an **Iron Pillar** (7.2m) stands in the precincts of Qutb-ud-din's original mosque, bearing fourth-century Sanskrit inscriptions of the Gupta period attributing it to the memory of King Chandragupta II (375–415 AD). Once topped with an image of the Hindu bird god, Garuda, the extraordinarily pure but rust-free pillar has puzzled metallurgists. Its rust resistance is apparently due to it containing as much as one percent phosphorous, which has acted as a chemical catalyst to create a protective layer of an unusual compound called misawite (FeOOH) around the metal. The pillar was evidently transplanted here by the Tomars, but it's not known where from.

Archeological Park

The area south of the Qutb Minar Complex, rich with remains from all sorts of historical periods, has been turned into an **Archeological Park** (daily sunrise to sunset; free). Here, within a very pleasant stroll of each other, you'll find: the tomb of Ghiyas-ud-din Balban, one of the Slave Dynasty sultans (reigned 1265–87), believed to be the first building in India constructed with true arches; the beautiful 1528 mosque and tomb of the poet Jamali Kamali (you may need to find the caretaker to open up the tomb for you); and the octagonal Mughal tomb of Muhammad Quli Khan, one of Akbar's courtiers, which was occupied in the early nineteenth century by Sir Thomas Metcalfe, the East India Company's resident at the Mughal court, who rather bizarrely converted it into a country house. Metcalfe made his mark on the area in other ways too, restoring a Lodi-period dovecote and constructing "follies" – mock-ancient pavilions, a typical feature of English country estates of the time, except that Metcalfe's were Indian in style. The park extends over more than a hundred hectares and contains over eighty monuments, including tombs, mosques, gateways and *baolis*, dating from every century between the thirteenth and the twentieth.

Akshardham Temple

Across Nizamuddin Bridge on the east side of the Yamuna River (Rs60 by pre-paid auto from Connaught Place), the opulent **Akshardham Temple** (daily: April–Sept 9am–7pm; Oct–March 9am–6pm; free; Ⓦwww.akshardham .com) is Delhi's newest tourist attraction, and in terms of visitor numbers, one of its biggest. Built in 2005 by the Gujarat-based Shri Swaminarayan sect, the temple is a stunning piece of art, embellished with wonderful carvings made using the same tools and techniques as in ancient times. Cameras, mobile phones, mirrors and any electronic equipment, including USB keys, are prohibited and should be deposited at the cloakroom outside. Visitors may not enter wearing shorts or skirts above the knee. The **main shrine** is surrounded by a pink sandstone relief (you must walk round it clockwise) whose theme is elephants; wild, domesticated or in legend. Inside, the centrepiece and main object of devotion is a three-metre-high gold statue of the sect's founder, Bhagwan Shri Swaminarayan, attended by four disciples. Behind it are paintings depicting scenes from his life, and also some personal objects such as his sandals and even some of his hair and nail clippings. The four subsidiary shrines are devoted to conventional Hindu gods.

Coronation Park

Now just a windblown piece of waste ground on the city's northern fringes, 10km north of Connaught Place, **Coronation Park** once showpieced the pomp and might of the British Raj. The British held three **durbars** (huge imperial pageants) here: in 1887 on Queen Victoria's assumption of the title "Empress of India"; in 1903 to mark the coronation of her successor Edward VII; and in 1911 when George V came to be crowned in person as emperor. The high point of the durbar was a procession of elephants bearing all the princes of India, headed by the Nizam of Hyderabad, to pay homage to the British ruler, in the same way that they had previously to the Mughals. All but forgotten nowadays (your auto-wallah or taxi driver won't have heard of the place so they'll need clear instructions on how to get here), the park is centred around a **granite obelisk** commemorating the 1911 coronation. In an enclosure close by, a grandiose statue of the king-emperor George, which once graced what is now the Rajpath, stands Ozymandias-like among other nameless and forgotten rulers from an empire fast receding into history. The park is located on Nirankari Marg, just south of the Outer Ring Road NH-1 bypass (Dr K.B. Hedgewar Marg) near Sant Nagar. It costs Rs75 by pre-paid auto from Connaught Place, or around Rs120 from town if you don't pre-pay.

Eating

Delhi has quite an eating culture, and enough prosperous foodies to sustain a large variety of **restaurants** and worldwide cuisines, while less rarified establishments cater for office workers in need of somewhere to fill up cheaply at lunchtime or after work. The result is something for every budget, with excellent food on offer at humble roadside *dhabas* and unassuming diners, and truly magnificent Indian and foreign cuisine in Delhi's more renowned restaurants.

Most restaurants close around 11pm, but those with bars usually stay open until midnight. If you're looking for a **late-night** meal, you have a number of choices: eat in one of the restaurants in a top hotel, or the 24-hour coffee shops in *Le Meridien*, the *Intercontinental*, *The Park* or *The Claridges*, or the *Marina* at G-59 Connaught Place; try a snack in Paharganj's round-the-clock rooftop cafés; or head to Pandara Road market (south of India Gate, open till 1.30am). Old Delhi railway station also has a couple of 24-hour places.

Connaught Place

Connaught Place ("CP") is dominated by upmarket restaurants and Western-style fast-food places, with a few cheap and cheerful eateries hidden away if you know where to look. The **Bengali Market**, on Tansen Marg, off Barakhamba Road, is a good place for sweets and snacks.

The restaurants and cafés listed below are marked on the Connaught Place **map** on p.108.

Anand Connaught Lane, three doors from *Sunny Guest House*. Good, cheap non-veg eats including great biriyanis, with non-veg dishes at Rs80–85 a throw (thali Rs95).

Barista N-16 Connaught Place. Popular coffee bar, the first of what is now a nationwide chain that claims to do the best espresso in India (100 percent Arabica), plus cakes and muffins to accompany. Rival chain *Café Coffee Day* has numerous CP outlets (almost one on every block).

Fire *Park Hotel*, 15 Sarsad Marg ☎ 011/2374 3000. Scintillating if expensive modern restaurant whose contemporary Indian cuisine bears a strong hint of European influence. Menu depends on the season, with lighter dishes in summer, fierier ones in winter. Main non-veg dinner dishes are

Rs625–1000, but at lunchtime there are set menus (Rs550–900). Booking advisable.

India Coffee House 2nd floor, Mohan Singh Place Shopping Complex, Baba Kharak Singh Marg. Down-at-heel canteen with a large roof terrace, part of a mainly south Indian co-op chain, serving filter and espresso coffee, snacks and basic meals (thalis Rs34, everything else less) to an eclectic cross-section of downtown New Delhi's daytime population.

Kake Da Hotel 74 Municipal Market, Outer Ring, Connaught Place. A small, cramped diner (the term "hotel" does not imply accommodation) that's been here so long it's become a Delhi institution, known for unpretentious but reliably good Punjabi curries, mostly non-veg, such as butter chicken or sag meat (palak mutton), at around Rs60 a plate. Takeaway available.

Kwality 7 Regal Building, Sansad Marg. Originally set up to serve American GIs during World War II, this is one of CP's better mid-market choices (non-veg mains Rs175–300), quite elegantly decorated with lots of mirrors and chandeliers (though the odd mouse has been spotted scurrying across the floor). Good choices include chicken tikka with green peas, and mutton *shahi kurma*.

Parikrama Kasturba Gandhi Marg ☎011/2372 1616. Novel and expensive Indian (mainly tandoori) and Chinese cuisine in a revolving restaurant affording superb views over Delhi; a single rotation takes ninety minutes. Main dishes cost Rs170–310 (specials Rs480). Specialities include *murg pasandey parikrama* (chicken breast stuffed with minced chicken and nuts in a cashew-nut sauce) and *murg tikka parikrama* (chicken tikka in a spicy cashewnut marinade). Booking advisable.

Q'BA E-42/3 Connaught Place. Cool and stylish upmarket bar-restaurant on two floors and two terraces, with views over CP, though its "world cuisine" actually boils down to Indian, Italian and Thai, with pizza, pasta, green and red curry, and specialities such as *Q'BA raan* (char-grilled leg of lamb with herbs) and *fish tikka methi malai* (tandoori fish kebabs in a ginger and fenugreek marinade). Main courses go for Rs300–500.

Sagar Ratna K-15 Connaught Place. The CP branch of the renowned Defence Colony restaurant (see p.134), great for *vadas*, *dosas* or a south Indian veg thali (Rs100). Main dishes Rs45–90.

Saravana Bhavan P-15 Connaught Place and 46 Janpath. Excellent low-priced south Indian snacks and meals, including thalis (Rs98) and quick lunches (Rs72), as well as the usual *dosas*, *iddlis* and *uttapams*. The mini tiffin (Rs72) has a taste of everything.

Spice Route *Hotel Imperial*, Janpath. This beautifully decorated restaurant, rarified and expensive, if perhaps a little overpriced (non-veg main dishes Rs650–775), specializes in spicy Southeast Asian and Keralan cuisine. If you want to eat well in the CP vicinity, this is one of your best bets.

Veda H-27 Connaught Place ☎011/4151 3535. CP's swankiest restaurant, heavy on the "ambience" (all smoochy red and black decor with low lights), which is what you pay for here, though the food isn't at all bad (main dishes such as Peshawari kebabs and malai fish tikka at Rs200–300; a mixed platter for Rs375 veg, Rs495 non-veg).

Zen B-25 Connaught Place. Excellent Chinese meals (as well as a few Thai and Japanese dishes) served in a relaxed and traditional style, plus Western snacks (3–7pm), and a broad selection of wines, spirits and beers. Most non-veg main dishes are Rs240–290 (prawns Rs560).

Paharganj and Ram Nagar

With so much good food on offer in Delhi, it's a shame to dine in **Paharganj**, even if that's where your hotel is. Most of the restaurants on the Main Bazaar are geared to unadventurous foreign tastebuds, offering poor imitations of Western, Israeli, Japanese, and even Thai dishes, or sloppy, insipid versions of Indian curries for foreigners who can't handle chilli. Most serve breakfasts of toast, porridge, muesli and omelettes, though they'll do you a *paratha* as well. Eating options in **Ram Nagar** are more indigenous. If you decide to eat in any of the *dhabas* opposite New Delhi Station, especially those with waiters outside trying to hustle you in, and unless you can read the price list in Hindi, always ask the price of a dish before ordering, or you're likely to be overcharged.

The restaurants listed below are marked on the Paharganj **map** on p.110.

Club India 4797 Main Bazaar. First-floor and rooftop restaurant with the best views over central Paharganj, lively music, and the usual travellers' breakfast options plus Israeli, Japanese, Tibetan and even tandoori dishes. Non-veg main courses go for Rs90–175, thalis and meal combos Rs100–275.

Darbar Restaurant and Bikaner Sweets Corner 9002 Multani Dhanda Chowk, just off D B Gupta Rd

①011/2351 6666. Upstairs, it's a no-nonsense moderately priced veg restaurant, serving tasty thalis (Rs85) and Punjabi veg curries (Rs38–78); it also has a take-away service, and delivers orders over Rs100 within a kilometre radius. Downstairs, it's a wonderful sweets emporium, with all sorts of multicoloured Bengali and Rajasthani confections.
Diamond Café 5069 Main Bazaar. Small, friendly restaurant with a good if typical backpackers' menu (main dishes Rs80–150 non-veg), thalis (Rs60–100), a choice of set breakfasts (Continental, Indian, American, Israeli; Rs60–80), and Indian/fusion music on the sound system. *Kholsa Cafe*, down the street at no. 5024, is very similar, but slightly cheaper, and opens earlier for breakfast.
Golden Café 1 Nehru Bazaar, Ramdwara Rd, opposite Sri Mahavir Mandir. Cheap and cheerful café popular with Korean and Japanese travellers, serving Chinese, Korean and European food with dishes at Rs30–100.
Malhotra Laksmi Narain Rd. One of the better restaurants in Paharganj, offering passable tandoori and Mughlai dishes at reasonable prices (Rs90–165 for non-veg dishes). There's a basement, and an a/c upstairs section, plus a veg south Indian branch two doors down.
Metropolis 1634 Main Bazaar. Cosy a/c ground-floor restaurant in the hotel of same name

(downstairs, or on the roof terrace). Paharganj's priciest venue serves full breakfasts, reasonable curries and tandoori specials, plus Western dishes, beer, spirits, cocktails and nonalcoholic "mocktails". Main dishes are Rs150–225 veg, Rs250–375 non-veg.
Ritu Raj Bhojnalya Arakashan Rd, below *Delhi Continental Hotel*. Cheap, popular *dhaba* serving excellent Indian breakfasts, simple veg curries, and south Indian snacks (Rs20–50). A great place for *chana* rice or *iddli sambar*.
Sonu Chat House 5046 Main Bazaar. Popular cheap diner serving noodles, soup, samosas, curries, and even masala dosa to the backpacker crowd. Set breakfasts Rs60–80, non-veg main dishes Rs65–120.
Sonu South Indian Restaurant 8849/2 Multani Dhanda Chowk, off C B Gupta Rd, Ram Nagar. Basic south Indian grub (masala dosa, *iddlis*, *vadas* and the like) at low prices (Rs25–60 a go, or Rs50–65 for a thali).
Tadka 4986 Ramdwara Rd (Nehru Bazaar) ①011/3291 5216. The best dining in Paharganj: a clean, bright, modern little restaurant serving low-priced Indian veg dishes (main dishes Rs40–60, thalis Rs55–75). They'll deliver to any address within 2km.

Old Delhi

Old Delhi's crowded streets contain numerous simple food-halls that serve surprisingly good, and invariably fiery, Indian dishes for as little as Rs20. Upmarket eating is thin on the ground, but some of the mid-range restaurants serve food every bit as good as the posh eateries of South Delhi, and the sweets and snacks in Old Delhi are the best in town.

The restaurants listed below are marked on the Old Delhi **map** on p.120.

Chaina Ram 6499 Fatehpuri Chowk, next to Fatehpuri Mosque. Established in Karachi in 1901, and forced to relocate in 1947, this little shop is well known for its Sindhi-style sweets; the delicately aromatic Karachi halwa, with almonds and pistachios, is the best in town.
Chor Bizarre *Hotel Broadway*, 4/15 Asaf Ali Rd. A wide selection of excellent Indian cuisine including specialities from around the country, but above all from Kashmir. Eccentric, delightful decor featuring a four-poster bed, sewing table and a servery made from a 1927 vintage Fiat. Non-veg main dishes go for Rs255–395. The speciality is a Kashmiri sampler (*tarami*).
Deepak Chandni Chowk. A *dhaba* in the bazaar opposite the Jain temple, serving inexpensive south Indian snacks (*iddli sambar*, *dosas*, *uttapams*, at Rs15–50) and thalis (Rs28–32).

Ghantewala 1862-A Chandni Chowk. Established in 1790, this famous confectioner supplied sweets to the last Mughal emperors; its *ladoo* was already renowned in the nineteenth century, and the cashew fancies are out of this world, but their speciality is a nutty, butterscotch-like sweet called *sohan halwa*.
Haldiram's 1454 Chandni Chowk. Super-hygienic low-priced snack-bar and takeaway with sweets and samosas downstairs, drinks and snacks (Rs26–48) upstairs, including excellent *puris*, lassis, lime sodas, kulfis and thalis (Rs74–102). If you've never tried one, check the *raj kachori* (Rs38), a crunchy pastry shell enclosing a tangy chickpea curry with yoghurt.
Karim's Gali Kababian. A perennial Delhiite favourite, located in a passage down a side street, opposite the south gate of the Jama Masjid, consisting of four eating halls (same kitchen) offering the best meat dishes in the old city, at

moderate prices, with delicious fresh kebabs, hot breads and great Mughlai curries. Full dishes cost Rs100–400, but half dishes are also available. **Moti Mahal** Netaji Subhash Marg. Renowned for its tandoori chicken, this medium-priced restaurant is another local favourite – one of the first Punjabi restaurants in town – with both indoor seating and a large open-air courtyard. Main dishes go for Rs125–275, or Rs370 for the speciality, *murg musallam* (chicken stuffed with mincemeat).

Paratha Wali Gali Off Chandni Chowk, opposite the Central Bank. Head down this alleyway by Kanwarji Raj Kumar Sweet Shop (itself pretty good), and you'll be rewarded with *parathas* filled with anything from *paneer* and *gobi* to *mutter* and *mooli*, all cooked to order and served with a small selection of curries for around Rs30. There are three *paratha*-wallahs in the alley, all good, but the most renowned is the first one, *Pandit Babu Ram*.

South Delhi

The enclaves and villages spread across the vast area of **South Delhi** offer countless eating options, and most of its upmarket shopping zones (Hauz Khas, Defence Colony, Ansal Plaza, and the like) contain several good restaurants. **Dilli Haat**, the tourist market in Safdarjang has 25 food stalls offering dishes from nearly every state in India. **Pandara Road Market**'s restaurants and snack bars, just south of India Gate, stay open until 1.30am.

Unless otherwise stated, the restaurants listed here are marked on the Delhi **map** on pp.98–99.

Basil & Thyme Santushti Shopping Complex. See New Delhi map, p.115. Bistro-style Mediterranean eating with dishes like shitake risotto, lamb couscous and asparagus tart, and desserts including blueberry crêpes or tiramisu, mains Rs285–345. The 6pm closing time however, means it's lunch not supper, unless you want to make that tea. Closed Sun.

Bukhara *Maurya Hotel*, Sardar Patel Marg, Chanakyapuri ☎011/2611 2233. See New Delhi map, p.115. Delhi's top restaurant, specializing in succulently tender tandoori kebabs, with a menu that's short but very sweet, and a kitchen separated from the eating area by a glass partition, so you can watch the chefs at work. The *murgh malai* (chicken in curd) is wonderful, or you can get an "express platter" with three different kebabs (Rs2000). Bill Clinton is among the celebs who flock here. Most non-veg main dishes are Rs1250. The *Maurya Sheraton* also has another fine restaurant, *Dum Pukht* (evenings only, except at weekends), which specializes in the *dum* (slow-cooked casserole) cuisine of Avadh (eastern Uttar Pradesh), with non-veg main dishes at Rs975–1250.

Ego 4 Community Centre, Friends Colony, Mathura Rd. A saloon-style bar serving authentic and imaginative Italian food, with good beer, cocktails and loud music. Main dishes go for around Rs300. There's also a very good Thai-food branch, *Ego Thai*, close by at no. 53.

Flavors C-52 Defence Colony. Run by a Mizo–Italian couple, this is one of Delhi's very best Italian eateries, where you'll find excellent risotto, great pasta and pizzas, and wonderful tiramisu. Main dishes cost Rs300–500.

Park Balluchi Deer Park, Hauz Khas ☎011/2685 9369. Kebabs and Baluchi dishes (veg Rs160–210, non-veg Rs255–325) amid pleasant sylvan surroundings, with a choice of smoking (and drinking) or nonsmoking (and alcohol-free) areas.

Punjabi by Nature Priya Cinema Complex, Basant Lok, Vasant Vihar ☎011/4151 6666. It's quite a haul from the centre (Rs100 by pre-paid auto from CP), but this restaurant has made a big name for itself among Delhiite foodies with its fabulous Punjabi and north Indian cuisine – expensive, but worth it (most main dishes Rs295–515). The Amritsari fish tikka is succulent, the tandoori prawns (Rs595) wonderful, but for something really special, try the *raan-e-Punjab* (leg of lamb, Rs695). There's now a more easily accessible branch at TF-06, third floor, Square Mall, Raja Garden (☎011/4222 5656 or 5757), by Rajaouri Garden metro.

Sagar 18 Defence Colony Market. Delicious, inexpensive south Indian vegetarian food (main dishes Rs43–70), with *vadas*, *iddlis*, *ravas* and *dosas*, plus great thalis (Rs85). They've also opened a north Indian restaurant a few doors down at no. 24, and they have branches all over town, but the original is still the best.

Swagath 14 Defence Colony Market. A non-veg off-shoot of *Sagar*, a few doors away. There are Indian and Chinese meat dishes on the menu, but ignore them and go for the Mangalore-style seafood – the *Swagath* special (chilli and tamarind), *gassi* (coconut sauce) and *sawantwadi* (green masala) dishes are all great, at Rs235–245 a throw with pomfret, Rs325–535 for versions made with prawns.

Nightlife and entertainment

With an ever-increasing number of pubs and clubs, Delhi's **nightlife** scene is in full swing. During the week, lounge and dance bars are your best bet, but come the weekend the **discos** really take off. Most, if not all, of the discos popular with Delhi's young jet-set are in the luxury hotels, and many don't allow "stag entry" (men unaccompanied by women), which makes them a whole lot more comfortable for women, but is tough luck if you're male and alone; the big exception is *Elevate* – Delhi's nightclub for serious clubbers. India Gate and Rajpath attract nightly "**people's parties**" where large crowds mill about, snacking and eating ice cream; these are not advisable for women on their own, as you're likely to get hassled.

For **drinking**, the five-star hotels all have plush and expensive bars, and many of the better ones have dance floors. Lounge bars with laid-back music have become very popular of late, and there are some good ones scattered about the southern suburbs. Note that the drinking age in Delhi is 25, though there are proposals to lower it to 21.

Bars

Blues N-17 Connaught Place. See map, p.108. Snazzy bar and restaurant, offering an eclectic range of loud music (Thurs is rock night, retro on Sun). The bar staff are all pros at mixing extravagant cocktails. Happy hour (buy 1, get 1 free) is 4–8pm, after which entry is Rs200 and lone males are not allowed in.

Gem 1050 Main Bazar, Paharganj. See map, p.110. Not a place to seek out from elsewhere in town, but handy if you're in Paharganj and don't want to venture too far afield for a beer, though women won't be comfortable drinking here without a male escort; for a classier drink in Paharganj, try the *Metropolis Hotel* (see p.110).

Lizard Lounge E-5, 1st Floor, South Extension II. See Delhi map, p.110. Lounge music (what else?) and hookah pipes (21 flavours) at this well-established, but still trendy lounge bar, with Mediterranean and Middle Eastern food.

Rodeo A-12 Connaught Place. See map, p.108. Saloon-style bar with Wild West waiters, swinging-saddle bar stools, pitchers of beer, tequila slammers, and Mexican-style bar snacks (tacos, enchiladas, fajitas, quesadillas).

Shalom N-18, N-Block Market, Greater Kailash Part I ☏011/5163 2280 or 83. See Delhi map, pp.98–99. An upmarket, trendy lounge bar with laid-back music, a Mediterranean theme, Spanish and Lebanese food (tapas meets mezze), hookah pipes, and tables for all, but you'll need to book, especially at weekends.

Splash Minto Rd (Viveknand Marg), just north of the rail bridge. See Connaught Place map, p.108. Quite a civilized bar with food and reasonably priced beer, and quite often dance parties, a stone's throw from Connaught Place.

Clubs

Elevate 6th floor, Center Stage Mall, Sector 18, Noida ☏0120/251 3904, ⓦ www.elevateindia.com. See Delhi map, pp.98–99. Across the river, and indeed just across the state line in UP, this is the biggest and most kicking club in town, modelled on London's Fabric, with three floors (dance floor, chill-out and VIP), a roof terrace, and Indian and international DJs playing bhangra, filmi, hip-hop, trance or techno, depending on the night. Wed–Sat till 3.30am (check the website for what's on), and "stag entry" is permitted.

Royale Mirage *Crowne Plaza Hotel*, New Friends Colony ☏011/2683 5070. See Delhi map, pp.98–99. A long-time favourite, with a French–Arab theme (hummus is among the snacks available), table dinner service, dancing podiums, state-of-the-art light show and a hip, young crowd. Open Fri & Sat, 9.30pm–1am.

Dance and drama

Dances of India Parsi Anjuman Hall, Bahadur Shah Zafar Marg, near Delhi Gate ☏011/2623 4689 or 2642 9170. See Old Delhi map, p.120. Excellent classical, folk and tribal dance featuring six to seven items every night from different parts of India, usually including Bharatnatyam, Kathakali, Bhawai and the graceful dance of the northeastern state of Manipur. Daily 6.45pm; Rs200.

India Habitat Centre Lodi Rd ☏011/2468 2001 to 9, ⓦ www.indiahabitat.org. See New Delhi map, p.115. Popular venue near Lodi Gardens for dance, music and theatre as well as talks and exhibitions.

India International Centre 40 Max Müller Marg, Lodi Estate ☏011/2461 9431. See New Delhi map, p.115. Films, lectures, dance and music performances.

Kamani Auditorium Copernicus Marg ☏011/2338 8084. Bharatnatyam and other dance performances.

Sangeet Natak Akademi Rabindra Bhavan, 35 Firoz Shah Rd ☏011/2338 7246 to 8, ⓦwww .sangeetnatak.com. See New Delhi map, p.115. Delhi's premier performing-arts institution.

Triveni Kala Sangam 205 Tansen Marg, just south of the Bengali Market ☏011/2371 8833. See map, p.115. Bharatnatyam dance shows, also art exhibitions.

Cultural centres and libraries

American Library 24 Kasturba Gandhi Marg, southeast of Connaught Place ☏011/2331 6841, ⓦnewdelhi.usembassy.gov/americanlibrary.html. American newspapers and periodicals, plus books on current affairs, trade, politics and economics.

British Council 17 Kasturba Gandhi Marg, southeast of Connaught Place ☏011/2371 1401. See Connaught Place map, p.108. Talks, film shows and concerts, plus a good library and reading room.

Delhi Public Library SP Mukherjee Marg, opposite Old Delhi Station, with branches around town ☏011/2396 2682, ⓦwww.dpl.gov.in. See Old Delhi map, p.120. Reading rooms open to all. Daily 8.30am–8pm.

India International Centre 40 Max Müller Marg, near Lodi Gardens ☏011/2461 9431, ⓦwww.iicdelhi.nic.in. See New Delhi map, p.115. Exhibitions, lectures, films and a library.

Lalit Kala Galleries Rabindra Bhavan, 35 Firoz Shah Rd, by Mandi House Chowk ☏011/2338 7241 to 3. See New Delhi map, p.115. Delhi's premier art academy, with an extensive collection of paintings, sculpture, frescoes and drawings. Also shows films and stages seminars and photographic exhibitions.

Sahitya Akademi Rabindra Bhavan, 32 Firoz Shah Rd, by Mandi House Chowk ☏011/2338 7246. See New Delhi map, p.115. An excellent library devoted to Indian literature through the ages, with some books and periodicals in English.

Tibet House 1 Institutional Area, Lodi Rd ☏011/2461 1515, ⓦwww.tibet.net/tibethouse /eng. See New Delhi map, p.115. A library on all aspects of Tibetan culture, plus a small museum of Tibetan artefacts (Rs10). Mon–Fri 10am–5.30pm.

Cinemas

Bollywood movies are shown at **cinemas** such as the Plaza (☏011/4151 3787) and Regal (☏011/2336 2245) in Connaught Place, the Shiela (☏011/2352 2100) on D B Gupta Road, near New Delhi railway station, or the Imperial (☏011/3130 7111) on Rajguru Marg in Paharganj. Ticket prices vary – in a down-at-heel flea-pit like the Imperial, they're Rs20–25, whereas a posh picture palace like the Plaza charges Rs125–200. Films are usually in Hindi without subtitles, though an alternative branch of Bollywood has recently emerged, producing films in English that ooze attitude, with sex scenes and lots of designer clothing. Suburban cinemas more often show American movies, often with digital surround sound and popcorn. In addition, some of the cultural centres listed above occasionally run international film festivals. If you want to see Hindi films with English subtitles, your best bet is to head down to shops like Blue Bird (see p.139), and buy them on DVD.

Sports and outdoor activities

The recreational activity most likely to appeal to visitors in the pre-monsoon months has to be a dip in one of Delhi's **swimming pools**. The main public baths (open 16 March to 30 Sept, minimum membership Rs400 for a month) are the NMDC Pool at Nehru Park in Chanakyapuri (☏011/2611 1440; see New Delhi map, p.115), on Mandir Marg near **Lakshmi Narayan Mandir** (☏011/2336 3629; see Delhi map, pp.98–99), and on Avenue 1, Sarojini Nagar (☏011/2412 1581; see Delhi map, pp.98–99) and the Talkatora Pool, Park Road (☏011/2301 8178; see New Delhi map, p.115). Most luxury hotels restrict their pools to residents only, but may allow outsiders to join their health clubs.

Other local diversions include **bowling**, **golf** and even, during the cooler months, **rock climbing** on the outskirts of the city.

Delhi Golf Club Dr Zakir Hussein Marg ☎011/2436 2768. Busy and beautiful 220-acre golf course on the fifteenth-century estate of the Lodi dynasty; with more than two hundred varieties of trees, it also acts as a bird sanctuary. Monuments and mausoleums, such as the ruined *barakhamba* on a hillock next to the seventh green, dot the grounds. Temporary membership is available.

Delhi Lawn Tennis Association R K Khanna Tennis Stadium, 1 Africa Avenue ☎011/2619 3955, ⓦwww.dltatennis.in. There are 21 courts and a pool at this complex near Hauz Khas village. Courts should be booked a day in advance.

Delhi Races Kamal Ataturk Rd ☎011/2379 2869. Regular horse racing Tues from 1.30pm, sometimes other days too. Men usually Rs50, women Rs20. Mobile phones not allowed in (you can deposit them at the entrance).

Delhi Riding Club Safdarjang Rd ☎011/2301 1891. Rides at 6.30am, 7.30am, 8.30am, 9.30am, 2.45pm; open to the public by prior arrangement through the Club Secretary (children afternoons only).

Indian Mountaineering Foundation 6 Benito Juárez Marg ☎011/2411 1211, ⓦwww.indmount .org. Official organization governing mountaineering and permits throughout India, with a library and an outdoor climbing wall. Some equipment can be rented here, and you can get information on local crags and climbing groups.

Siri Fort Sports Complex Siri Fort ☎011/2649 7482, ⓦwww.dda.org.in. An olympic-sized swimming pool, a toddlers' pool, plus tennis, squash and badminton courts are among the facilities here, at the most central of the Delhi Development Authority's 14 sports complexes. Out-of-towners can use it for Rs100 [Rs40] a day.

Shopping

Although the traditional places to **shop** in Delhi are around **Connaught Place** (particularly the underground Palika Bazaar) and **Chandni Chowk**, a number of suburbs created by the rapid growth of the city are emerging as fashionable shopping districts. To check prices and quality for crafts, you can't do better than the **state emporiums** on Baba Kharak Singh Marg.

Unlike the markets of Old Delhi, most shops in New Delhi take credit cards, and beware of touts who'll try to drag you into false "government shops" for a commission. In all bazaars and street markets, the rule is to **haggle**.

Art, antiques, crafts and jewellery

Sunder Nagar Market near Purana Qila is a good upmarket place to shop for **art**, **antiques** and **jewellery**; shops 5, 7, 9, 14 and 26 have the best variety. **Hauz Khas Village** also has some interesting art and antiques shops and galleries. Remember that it's illegal to take art objects more than one hundred years old out of the country.

The **Tibetan Market** at the north end of Janpath remains popular with tourists, though only a few of the stalls are still run by Tibetans. You can find statues, incense, shawls, paintings and Tibetan artefacts including jewellery and semiprecious stones. Remember that not all white metal is silver, and drive a hard bargain. A number of **state government emporiums** with fixed but fair prices can be found along Baba Kharak Singh Marg near Connaught Place, where artisans sell their own wares.

Central Cottage Industries Emporium Jawahar Vyapar Bhawan, Janpath, opposite *Imperial Hotel* ☎011/2372 5035, ⓦwww.cottageemporiumindia .com. Popular and convenient multistorey government-run complex, with handicrafts, carpets, leather and reproduction miniatures at fixed (if

fractionally high) rates. Jewellery ranges from tribal silver anklets to costume pieces and precious stones. **Cottage of Arts and Jewels** 50 Hauz Khas Village ☎011/2696 7418. Interesting, eccentric mix of jewellery, curios and papier-mâché crafts. The best of the collection, including miniatures and precious stones, is not on display: you'll have to ask to see it.

Dilli Haat Aurobindo Marg, Safdarjang ☏ www .dillihaat.org. You have to pay to visit this market, but it's only Rs15, and it keeps out the beggars and the touts. It's full of stalls selling crafts from across the country, and the range and quality is excellent. It can be a bit touristy, but it's a great place to buy souvenirs, and have a bite to eat, with food stalls from almost every Indian state.

Neemrana Shop upper floor, 12 Khan Market, New Delhi ☏ 011/2462 0262. Run by the renowned

hotel group of the same name, the shop has a chic clientele and offers a range of home furnishings and knick-knacks, as well as a small collection of antiques and *objets d'art*.

Plutus 10 Hauz Khas Village ☏ 011/2653 6898, ☏ www.plutusexports.com. An attractively presented shop selling replica antiques, bronze statues and an assorted collection of silver and gold jewellery. Ethnic Silver, two doors down at 9A, has a nice selection of jewellery and silverware.

Books

Delhi has a wide selection of places to buy **books**. Connaught Place has many good general bookshops, including Amrit (N-21), Galgotia & Sons (B-17), New Book Depot (B-18), Bookworm (B-29) and Rajiv Book House (30 Palika Bazaar). RS Books & Prints at A-40 South Extension II (☏ 011/2625 7095) sells antiquarian books, and interesting old maps and prints. **Second-hand bookstalls** include Jacksons at 5106 Paharganj Main Bazaar, opposite *Vishal* hotel, and Anil Book Corner by the Plaza Cinema on Connaught Place; on Sundays there's also Daryaganj Market by Delhi Gate in Old Delhi.

Fabrics and clothes

Delhi's **fabric** and **clothes** shops sell anything from high-quality silks, homespun cottons, saris, Kashmiri shawls and traditional *kurta* pyjamas to multi-coloured tie-dyed T-shirts and other hippy gear. For T-shirts and tie-dyed clothing (not to mention joss sticks and chillums), try **Paharganj** or the **Tibetan Market**. For bargain Western-style trousers, skirts and shirts the export-surplus market at **Sarojini Nagar** (see Delhi map, pp.98–99) is very good. Roadside stalls behind the Tibetan Market off Janpath sell lavishly embroidered and mirrored spreads from Rajasthan and Gujarat, but silks and fine cotton are best bought in **government emporiums** on Baba Kharak Singh Marg.

Anokhi 5 & 6 Santushti Shopping Complex and 9 & 32 Khan Market ☏ 011/2462 8253, ☏ www .anokhi.com. Soft cotton and raw silk clothes and soft furnishings; particularly renowned for hand-block printed cottons combining traditional and contemporary designs.

Fabindia 5, 7, 9 & 14-N, N-Block Market, Greater Kailash ☏ 011/2923 2183, ☏ www.fabindia.com. Spread over several shops in the market, with a range from furnishings and interiors to chic cotton clothing for men, women and children and wearable block-printed cottons, sourced from villages across India; also sells organic spices, jams and pickles, and has branches around town including Khan Market (central hall, above nos. 20 & 21) and B-28 Connaught Place.

Handloom House A-9 Connaught Place ☏ 011/2332 3057. Roll after roll of fine hand-woven cotton and silk textiles, plus cotton and linen shirts and silk saris.

Khadi Gramodyog Bhawan 24 Regal Building, corner of Sansad Marg and Connaught Place ☏ 011/2336 0902, ☏ www.kvic.org.in. Government-run and a great place to pick up hardy, lightweight travelling clothes. Reasonably priced, ready-made traditional Indian garments include *salwar kameez*, woollen waistcoats, pyjamas, shawls and caps, plus rugs, cloth by the metre, tea, incense, cards and tablecloths.

People Tree 8 Regal Building, Sansad Marg, Connaught Place ☏ 011/2334 0699, ☏ www .peopletreeonline.com. An interesting selection of alternative designs, with an emphasis on T-shirts, ethnic chic and jewellery.

SEWA Trade Facilitation Centre 5 Rajiv Gandhi Bhawan, between the two state emporium buildings, Baba Kharak Singh Marg ☏ 011/3948 9374, ☏ www.sewa.org. Lovely clothes, accessories and furnishings made by self-employed

women, mostly working at home, and sold through their own cooperatively run outlet.
Vedi Tailors M-60 Connaught Place ☏011/2341 6901. Originally established in Rangoon in 1926, this gents' tailor can run you up a made-to-measure suit for Rs4500–20,000, depending on fabric and cut. They usually take a week, but for Rs1500 extra they can do it in 24 hours. S.L. Kapur at G-7 is an equally reputable firm offering a similar service.

Musical instruments, cassettes and CDs

Delhi is a good place to buy classical Indian **instruments** as well as **recorded music**. The listings below are some of the better options amongst the huge array of outlets.

Blue Bird 9 Regal Building, Sansad Marg, Connaught Place ☏011/2334 2805. An excellent range of classical and modern Indian music on CD and cassette, plus Hindi movies on DVD.
Lahore Music House Netaji Subhash Marg, Old Delhi (next-door to *Moti Mahal* restaurant) ☏011/ 2327 1305, ⓦwww.lmhindia.com. Long-established north Indian musical instrument makers with a reputation for quality.

The Music Shop 18 Khan Market ☏011/2461 7797. Wide range of CDs, cassettes and videos, featuring both Indian and Western music, with helpful, well-informed staff.
Rikhi Ram G-8, Outer Circle, Connaught Place ☏011/2332 7685, ⓦwww.rikhiram.com. Once sitar makers to the likes of renowned musician Ravi Shankar, and still maintaining an exclusive air, with prices to match. Check out the display of their own unique instrumental inventions.

Miscellaneous

Gujrat Art Gallery 22A Hauz Khas Village ☏011/5521 9649. Despite the name, old film posters – both Hollywood and Bollywood – are the speciality here, mostly in the Rs300–1000 range. You can buy them framed, but it's generally easier, if you're transporting them, to have them rolled up and slipped into a protective tube.
Industree 8 Rajiv Gandhi Bhawan, between the two state emporium buildings, Baba Kharak Singh Marg ☏011/6597 0850, ⓦwww.industreecrafts .com. A light, bright shop with equally light, bright designs, including mats, blinds, boxes and bags

made of natural fibres such as jute, reeds and rattan, crafted by small producers mostly working from home and sold by a fair-trade NGO.
Jain Super Store 172 Palika Bazaar, Connaught Place ☏011/2332 1031, ⓦwww.jainperfumers .com. Essential oils, natural perfumes and their own in-house fragrances, as well as joss sticks, scented candles and aroma diffusers.
Nath Stationers (The Card Shop) B-38 Connaught Place. A small shop with a big selection of greetings cards featuring Indian artwork and designs.

Listings

Airlines Aeroflot, N-1 Tolstoy House, 15–17 Tolstoy Marg ☏011/2331 0426; Air Canada, 202, 2nd floor, Ansal Bhawan, 16 Kasturba Gandhi Marg ☏011/4152 8181; Air France, airport ☏95124/272 0272 from Delhi, or 0124/272 0272 from outside Delhi; Air Deccan, G-11, G Block Market, Hauz Khas ☏011/3900 8888 or 080/4114 8190 to 99; Air India, 2nd floor, Tower 1, Jeevan Bharati Building, 124 Connaught Circus at Sansad Marg ☏1800/227722 or 95124/234 8888 from Delhi or ☏0124/234 8888 from outside Delhi; Alitalia, 7th floor, Golf View Tower, Sector 42, Gurgaon, Haryana ☏95124/402 6000 from Delhi, or 0124/402 6000

from outside Delhi; American Airlines, E-9 Connaught Place ☏1800/180 7300 or 011/2341 6930; Asiana Airlines, 2 Ansal Bhawan, ground floor, 16 Kasturba Gandhi Marg ☏011/2331 5631; British Airways, DLF Plaza Tower, DLF Qutab Enclave, Gurgaon, Haryana ☏95124/412 0747 from Delhi, or 0124/412 0747 from outside Delhi; Cathay Pacific, c/o G.C. Nanda, 107–110,1st Floor, Kanchenchunga Building, 18 Barakhamba Rd ☏011/2332 1286; China Airlines, c/o Ascent Air, upper ground floor, Kanchenchunga Building, 18 Barakhamba Rd ☏011/2332 7131; Continental, 2nd floor, Tower C, Cyber Greens, DLF Phase 3,

Gurgaon, Haryana ☎95124/431 5500 from Delhi, or 0124/431 5500 from outside Delhi; Delta, c/o Interglobe Enterprises, Thapar House, 124 Janpath ☎011/4351 3140 or 41; Emirates, 7th floor, DLF Centre, Sansad Marg ☎011/6631 4444; GoAir, airport ☎011/6541 0030 to 33; Gulf Air, airport ☎1800/221122; Indian Airlines, Malhotra Building, Janpath, at F-Block Connaught Place ☎1800/180 1407 or 011/1407; IndiGo, 124 Thapar House, near *Imperial Hotel*, Janpath ☎011/4351 3185 or 86; Indus Air, airport ☎011/2567 1370; Jet Airways, N-40 Connaught Place ☎011/3984 1111; JetLite, ground floor, Dr Gopaldas Bhawan, 28 Barakhamba Rd ☎1800/223 020 or 011/3030 2020; Kenya Airways, c/o Jetair, C-28 Connaught Place ☎011/2341 1953; Kingfisher, N-42 Connaught Place ☎1800/223020 or 1800/3030 2020 or 011/6458 7557; KLM, Tower 8-C, Cyber City, DLF Phase Pt 2, Gurgaon, Haryana ☎95124/272 0272 from Delhi, or 0124/272 0272 from outside Delhi; Kuwait Airways, 4 Ansal Bhawan, ground floor, 16 Kasturba Gandhi Marg ☎011/2335 3933; Lufthansa, 56 Janpath ☎011/2372 4200; Malaysia Airlines, 16th floor, Dr Gopaldas Bhawan, 28 Barakhamba Rd ☎011/4151 2121; Qantas, 511 Prakash Deep Building, 7 Tolstoy Marg ☎011/2373 0940; Qatar Airways, ground floor, Dr Gopaldas Bhawan, 28 Barakhamba Rd ☎011/4151 5763; Royal Jordanian, G-56 Connaught Place ☎011/2332 7418; SAA, 66 Janpath ☎011/2335 4422; Singapore Airlines, 9th floor, Ashoka Estate Building, 24 Barakhamba Rd ☎011/2332 6373; SpiceJet, airport ☎1800/180 3333; Swiss, 5th floor, World Trade Tower, New Barakhamba Lane ☎011/2341 2929; SyrianAir, 1st floor, Amba Deep Building, 14 Kasturba Gandhi Marg ☎011/4351 3184; Thai, *Park Royal Hotel*, American Plaza, Nehru Place ☎011/4149 7777; Virgin Atlantic, 8th floor, DLF Centre, Sansad Marg ☎011/5150 1314.

Archeological Survey of India 11 Janpath (☎011/2301 5954, 🖳asi.nic.in). Responsible for the maintenance of India's numerous heritage sites and for the entry tariffs.

Banks and currency exchange At the international airport, you can change money at the 24hr State Bank of India and at Thomas Cook. Almost every block on Connaught Place has ATMs that take Visa or MasterCard, as do metro stations, and there are several along Chandni Chowk and Asaf Ali Rd in Old Delhi. There's an ATM opposite the *Metropolis Hotel* on Paharganj Main Bazaar, one a few doors west of the *Metropolis*, and a couple more just up Rajguru Marg beneath the *Roxy Hotel*. You can also change money at numerous other exchange offices in Connaught Place and Paharganj (but if you're changing traveller's cheques, make sure before

signing that they're not going to mess you around demanding receipts and such like, or sting you with unmentioned commissions). All major hotels have exchange facilities; the *Ajanta*, near the *Grand Godwin* on Arakashan Rd in Ram Nagar has a 24hr bureau. The central branch of Thomas Cook is upstairs at C-33 Connaught Place (☎011/2345 6585; Mon–Fri 9.30am–6pm, Sat 10am–5.30pm), and there's a branch on the Ajmeri Gate side of New Delhi Station (by VIP parking, near platform 12; ☎011/2321 1819; daily 10am–5pm). American Express is at A-1 Connaught Place (☎011/2332 7602; Mon–Fri 9am–4pm, Sat 10am–1pm).

Bus enquiries Haryana Roadways ☎011/2386 1262; Himachal Roadways ☎011/2386 3473; Punjab Roadways ☎011/2386 7842; Rajasthan Roadways ☎011/2386 3469; UP Roadways ☎011/2386 8709. Delhi Transport Corporation (☎011/2386 8836) can provide enquiry numbers for other state transport corporations.

Embassies, consulates & high commissions Call ahead for opening hours before you visit. Afghanistan, 5/50-F Shanti Path, Chanakyapuri ☎011/2688 3601; Australia, 1/50-G Shanti Path, Chanakyapuri ☎011/4139 9900; Bangladesh, E-39, D Radha Krishan Marg, Chanakyapuri ☎011/2412 1389; Bhutan, Chandragupta Marg, Chanakyapuri ☎011/2688 9230; Burma, 3/50-F Shanti Path, Chanakyapuri ☎011/2688 9007; Canada, 7/8 Shanti Path, Chanakyapuri ☎011/5178 2000; China, 50-D Shanti Path, Chanakyapuri ☎011/2611 2345; Denmark, 11 Aurangzeb Rd ☎011/2301 0700; European Commission, 65 Golf Links ☎011/2462 9237 or 8; Indonesia, 50-A Kautilya Marg, Chanakyapuri ☎011/2611 8642 to 5; Iran, 5 Barakhamba Rd ☎011/2332 9600 to 02; Ireland, 230 Jor Bagh-3 (near Safdarjang's Tomb) ☎011/2462 6733; Malaysia, 50-M Satya Marg, Chanakyapuri ☎011/2611 1291 to 3; Maldives, E-45 Greater Kailash II ☎011/4143 5701; Nepal, Barakhamba Rd by Mandi House Chowk, southeast of Connaught Place ☎011/2332 9969; Netherlands, 6/50-F Shanti Path, Chanakyapuri ☎011/2419 7600; New Zealand, 50-N Nyaya Marg ☎011/2688 3170; Norway, 50-C Shanti Path, Chanakyapuri ☎011/4177 9200; Pakistan, 2/50-G Shanti Path, Chanakyapuri ☎011/2467 6004; Singapore, E-6 Chandragupta Marg, Chanakyapuri ☎011/4600 0800; South Africa, B-18 Vasant Marg, Vasant Vihar, ☎011/2614 9411; Sri Lanka, 27 Kautilya Marg, Chanakyapuri ☎011/2301 0201 to 3; Sweden, Nyaya Marg, Chanakyapuri ☎011/2419 7100; Thailand, 56-N Nyaya Marg, Chanakyapuri ☎011/2611 8103 or 4; UK, Shanti Path, Chanakyapuri ☎011/2687 2161; USA, Shanti Path, Chanakyapuri ☎011/2419 8000.

Hospitals All India Institute of Medical Sciences (AIIMS), Ansari Nagar, Aurobindo Marg (℡011/2658 8500), has a 24hr emergency service and good treatment, as does Lok Nayak Jai Prakash Hospital, Jawaharlal Nehru Marg, Old Delhi (℡011/2332 2400), near Delhi Gate. Dr Ram Manohar Lohia Hospital, Baba Kharak Singh Marg (℡011/2336 5525), is another government hospital. Private clinics include East West Medical Centre, B-28 Greater Kailash Part 1 (℡011/2629 3701 to 3).

Internet access Reliable places include: Sunrise N-9/II Connaught Place (Rs35/hr); Shivam, 651 Tooti Chowk, just off Main Bazaar, Paharganj (Rs20/hr); Kesri, 5111 Main Bazaar, Paharganj (near *Kholsa Café*; Rs20/hr).

Left luggage Rs10–15/day at the railway stations. In addition, most hotels in Paharganj offer a left-luggage service.

Money transfers Western Union agents include several post offices, most conveniently Old Delhi and New Delhi GPOs, but if having money sent to a post office, be sure to specify the name correctly ("Delhi GPO" means Old Delhi GPO, but specify "Old Delhi" just to be sure, and add the street name, Lothian Rd). WU agents also include the Bank of Baroda at B-3 and M-9 Connaught Place and the Centurion Bank of Punjab at L-40 and N-47. Money-Gram's agents can be found in branches of Thomas Cook (such as *Hotel Imperial*, in New Delhi station or at C-33 Connaught Place), and the South Indian Bank including 22 Regal Building, Connaught Place.

Motorcycles The Karol Bagh area has many good bike shops selling new or secondhand Enfields. Reliable dealers include Inder Motors, 1744-A/55 basement, Hardhyan Singh Nalwala St, Abdul Aziz Rd (℡011/2572 8579, @www .lallisingh.com), two blocks east of Ajmal Khan Rd, turning right at the *chowki*, then the third alley on the left; closed Mon. Also worth trying is Ess Aar Motors, 1-E/13 Jhandewalan Extension, between Karol Bagh and Paharganj (℡011/2367 8836). In Paharganj, there's Bulletwallas on Rajguru Marg by Imperial Cinema (℡09810 902872, @www.bulletwallas.com).

Opticians Lawrence & Mayo, 76 Janpath; R.K. Oberoi, H-14 Connaught Place.

Pharmacies Nearly every market has at least one pharmacy. Apollo, G-8 Connaught Place, and the pharmacy at the All India Medical Institute, Ansari Nagar, Aurobindo Marg (℡011/2696 7546), are open 24hr.

Photography Delhi Photo Company, 78 Janpath, offers high-quality developing, printing, and slide processing. It's second only to Kinsey Brothers beneath the *India Today* offices at 2-A Block, Connaught Place.

Police ℡100 (national number). Delhi now has a dedicated squad of tourist police based at the airport, main stations and major tourist sights and hotel areas, whose aim is specifically to help tourists in trouble. If you have a problem that needs to involve the police, your hotel reception or the Government of India tourist office will direct you to the appropriate station.

Postal services Poste restante (Mon–Sat 10am–5pm) is available at the GPO (known as Gole PO) on the roundabout at the intersection of Baba Kharak Singh Marg and Ashoka Rd and the Foreign Post Office, nearby on Bhai Vir Singh Marg, five minutes' walk from Connaught Place. You must show your passport to claim mail or check the register for parcels. Have mail addressed to "Poste Restante, New Delhi GPO", as letters sent to "Poste Restante, Delhi" will go to Old Delhi GPO, north of the railway line on Mahatma Gandhi Rd. There is a useful branch office at A-6 Connaught Place (Mon–Sat 8am–7.30pm).

State tourist offices Andaman and Nicobar Islands, 12 Chanakyapuri ℡011/2687 1443, @tourism .andaman.nic.in; Andhra Pradesh, AP Bhawar, 1 Ashoka Rd ℡011/2338 1293, @www.aptourism .In; Arunachal Pradesh, Arunchal House, opposite Chanakya Cinema, Bir Tikendrajit Marg, Chanakyapuri ℡011/2611 7728, @www.arunachaltourism.com; Assam, State Emporia Complex, B-1 Baba Kharak Singh Marg ℡011/2334 5897, @www .assamtourism.org; Bihar, Room #6, *Hotel Janpath*, Janpath ℡011/2336 8371, @bstdc.bih.nic.in; Chandigarh, 21-B Harish Chandra Mathur Lane, off Kasturba Gandhi Marg behind Max Muller Bhawan ℡011/2335 3359, @www.citcochandigarh.com; Daman and Diu, F-308 Curzon Road Hostel, Kasturba Gandhi Marg ℡011/2338 5369; Goa, Goa Sadan, 18 Amrita Shergil Marg, near Khan Market ℡011/2462 9968, @www.goa-tourism.com; Gujarat, A-6 State Emporia Building, Baba Kharak Singh Marg ℡011/2374 4015, @www.gujarattourism.com; Haryana, Chanderlok Building, 36 Janpath ℡011/2332 4910 or 11, @www.haryanatourism .com; Himachal Pradesh, Chanderlok Building, 36 Janpath ℡011/2332 5320, @www.hptdc.nic.in; Jammu & Kashmir, 512–512A Tolstoy House, Tolstoy Marg ℡011/2371 4948, @www.jktourism.org; Karnataka, C-4 State Emporia Building, Baba Kharak Singh Marg ℡011/2336 3863, @kstdc.nic.in; Kerala, Travancore Palace, Kasturba Gandhi Marg ℡011/2338 2067, @www.keralatourism.org; Lakshadweep, F-301 Curzon Road Hostel, Kasturba Gandhi Marg ℡011/2338 6807, @lakshadweeptourism.nic.in; Madhya Pradesh, Room #12, *Hotel Janpath*, Janpath ℡011/2334 1187, @www.mptourism.com; Maharashtra, Room

#10, *Hotel Janpath*, Janpath ☏011/2334 1413, ⓦwww.maharashtratourism.gov.in; Manipur, C-7 State Emporia Building, Baba Kharak Singh Marg ☏011/2374 6359, ⓦmanipur.nic.in/tourism.htm; Meghalaya, Meghalaya House, 9 Aurangzeb Rd ☏011/2301 4417, ⓦmegtourism.gov.in; Mizoram, Mizoram Bhawan, Circular Rd, Chanakyapuri ☏011/2301 5951, ⓦmizotourism.nic.in/home.htm; Nagaland, Government of Nagaland, 29 Aurangzeb Rd ☏011/2301 5638, ⓦnagaland.nic.in/potential /tourism.htm; Orissa, B-4 State Emporia Building, Baba Kharak Singh Marg ☏011/2336 4580, ⓦwww.orissa-tourism.com; Puducherry, 3 Sardar Patel Marg, Chanakyapuri ☏011/2611 8195, ⓦtourism.pondicherry.gov.in; Punjab, 214–215 Kanishka Shopping Plaza, Ashoka Rd ☏011/2334 3025, ⓦpunjabgovt.nic.in/tourism/tour1.htm; Rajasthan, Bikaner House, Pandara Rd, near India Gate ☏011/2338 3837, ⓦwww.rajasthan tourismindia.com; Sikkim, New Sikkim House, 14 Panchsheel Marg, Chanakyapuri ☏011/2611 5171, ⓦsikkim.nic.in/sws/tour_off.htm; Tamil Nadu, C-1 State Emporia Building, Baba Kharak Singh Marg ☏011/2336 6327, ⓦwww.tamilnadutourism.org; Tripura, Tripura Bhavan, Kautilya Marg, Chanakyapuri ☏011/2301 5157, ⓦtripura.nic.in/ttourism1.htm;

Uttarakhand, 102 and 103 Indraprakash Building, 21 Barakhamba Rd, GMVN (Garhwal) ☏011/2335 0481, KMVN (Kumaon) ☏011/2371 2246, ⓦgov.ua.nic.in /uttaranchaltourism/index.html; Uttar Pradesh, Chanderlok Building, 36 Janpath ☏011/2332 2251, ⓦwww.up-tourism.com; West Bengal, A-2 State Emporia Building, Baba Kharak Singh Marg ☏011/2374 2840, ⓦwww.wbtourism.com.

Visa extensions and permits The first place to go if you need to extend your visa is the Ministry of Home Affairs, Foreigners Division, Jaisalmer House, 26 Man Singh Rd (Mon–Fri 10am–noon). This is also the place to apply for permits to visit restricted areas. If your total stay will exceed six months, you will also need to go to the Foreigners Regional Registration Office (FRRO), East Block 8, Level 2, Sector 1, Ramakrishna Puram (Mon–Fri 9.30am– 1.30pm & 2–4pm; ☏011/2671 1348). Forms can be downloaded from ⓦwww.immigrationindia .nic.in. If you've been in India more than 120 days, before leaving you'll need to fill in a tax clearance certificate, obtainable from the Foreign Section, Income Tax Office, Central Revenue Building, Vikas Bhawan, Indraprastha Estate (Mon–Fri 10am–1pm & 2–5pm; ☏011/2337 9161); have your foreign exchange certificates to hand.

Moving on from Delhi

Delhi has good international and domestic **travel connections**; it seldom takes more than a day to arrange an onward journey. Scores of **travel agents** (see box opposite) sell bus and air tickets, while many hotels (budget or otherwise) will book private buses for you. There's an ever-expanding network of internal flights, but it's still best to book as far ahead as possible; bear in mind that at peak times such as Diwali, demand is very high.

If leaving India for a country that requires a **visa** (including Pakistan, Nepal and Bangladesh), make sure you have obtained the necessary documentation from the embassy concerned (see p.140); call in advance to check opening hours, specific requirements (such as how many photos you'll need), and the likely waiting period.

By air

Indira Gandhi International Airport (international flight enquiries ☏011/2569 6021, domestic flight enquiries ☏011/2567 5181, ⓦwww.newdelhiairport.in) is 20km southwest of the city centre. Most tourists on night-flights book a **taxi** to the airport in advance (around Rs250; 30–60min) through their hotel. By **auto-rickshaw** it's around Rs100–150. Otherwise, three daily **EATS airport buses** run from F-block on Connaught Place, by the Indian Airlines office (Rs50, plus Rs10 per item of baggage; 45min); departures are at 3.30pm, 7pm and 9pm. You can book tickets in advance at the small office next to Indian Airlines (☏011/2331 6530).

    Domestic flights leave from Terminal 1 (☏011/2566 1000). Tickets can be bought through travel agents or direct from the airlines. **International flights**

Travel agents and tour operators

The Rajasthan Tourism Development Corporation, Bikaner House, Pandara Road (☏011/2338 3837 or 6069), organize **package tours** including wildlife tours and trips on the *Palace on Wheels* and *Heritage on Wheels* trains. The Delhi Tourism and Transport Development Corporation (DTTDC), N-36, Bombay Life Building, Middle Circle, Connaught Place (☏011/5152 3073), offer day-trips to Agra (Rs950) and three-day "Golden Triangle" excursions to Agra, Ajmer, Bharatpur and Jaipur (Rs3200). For competitively priced car tours around Rajasthan try *Hotel Namaskar*, Paharganj (☏011/2358 2233, ⓔnamaskarhotel@yahoo.com). The India Tourism Development Corporation's commercial arm, Ashok Travels, *Janpath Hotel*, Janpath (☏011/2334 8745, ⓔtravel@attindiatourism.com), sells excursions and air tickets.

For **ticketing**, recommended operators specializing in international and domestic flights include: HRG Sita, F-12 Connaught Place (☏011/2331 1409); STA Travel, upstairs at G-55 Connaught Place (☏011/2373 1480, ⓦwww.statravel.co.in); and Travel Corporation of India, C-35 Connaught Place (☏011/2341 6082 to 5, ⓦwww.tcindia.com). Aa Bee Travel, in the lobby of *Hare Rama Guest House* (☏011/2356 2171 or 2117, ⓔaabee@mail.com) at T-298 off Main Bazaar, Paharganj, are a reliable firm for competitively priced air and private bus tickets. The Student Travel Information Centre, STIC Travels, 1st floor, West Wing, Chandralok Building, opposite *Imperial Hotel*, 36 Janpath (☏011/2332 1487, ⓦwww.stictravel.com), can issue or renew ISIC cards.

It's a very bad idea to book flights or excursions through any agency that you're directed to by a street tout, and that goes double for any agency spuriously trying to pass itself off as a tourist information office.

leave from Terminal 2 (☏011/2566 2000). If you don't already have a ticket for a **flight** out of India, you'll have little trouble finding one, except between December and March when it may be difficult at short notice. While you can buy tickets directly from the airlines (addresses on p.139), it saves time and leg-work to book through an **agency** (see box above). Remember that most airlines require you to reconfirm your flight between a week and 72 hours before leaving.

By train

New Delhi Station has regular departures to all corners of India, and a very efficient **booking office** (Mon–Sat 8am–8pm, Sun 8am–2pm) for foreign tourists, on the first floor (above ground) of the main departure building. Staff will give you advice on the fastest trains, and you should have little difficulty finding a seat or berth: **women** travelling alone in second class may prefer to ask for a berth in the ladies' carriage. Foreigners must show passports, and pay in foreign currency or in rupees backed up by exchange certificates. Ignore roadside advice to book train tickets elsewhere, and don't try buying one at the reservations building down the road – you'll be faced with a confusion of queues and crowds. Also, ignore claims that the tourist booking office has moved or is closed (see p.103 for more on scam merchants).

Most southbound trains leave from New Delhi, but all trains to Rajasthan, except those to Bharatpur, Kota and Sawai Madhopur, leave from either **Old Delhi** or **Sarai Rohilla** stations. A few trains to south and central India leave from **Hazrat Nizamuddin** Station, so check carefully when you buy your ticket. Bookings for all trains can be made at New Delhi Station.

See the box on p.144 for recommended trains from Delhi, and the "Travel details" on p.145 for a summary of the main train services from the capital.

Recommended trains from Delhi

The trains below are recommended as the fastest and/or most convenient for specific cities. Daily unless marked.

Destination	Name	No.	From	Departs	Total time
Agra	Shatabdi Express*	#2002	ND	6.15am	2hr (except Fri)
	Taj Express	#2180	HN	7.15am	2hr 52min
	Mangala Express	#2618	HN	9.20am	3hr
	Kerala Express	#2626	ND	11.30am	2hr 50min
Ahmedabad	Ashram Express	#2916	OD	3.05pm	16hr 35min
	Rajdhani Express	#2958	ND	8pm	14hr 05min (except Tues)
Ajmer	Shatabdi Express*	#2015	ND	6.10am	6hr 50min (except Wed)
	Ahmedabad Mail	#9106	OD	10.40pm	8hr 45min
Chandigarh	Shatabdi Express*	#2011	ND	7.40am	3hr 20min
	Paschim Express	#2925	ND	11.10am	4hr 35min
	Shatabdi Express*	#2005	ND	5.15pm	3hr 07min
Chennai	Tamil Nadu Express	#2622	ND	10.30pm	32hr 40min
	Sampark Kranti	#2652	HN	7.30am	34hr 23min (Tues & Thurs only)
Haridwar	Shatabdi Express*	#2017	ND	6.50am	4hr 35min
	Mussoorie Express	#4041	OD	10.15pm	7hr 30min
Jaipur	Shatabdi Express*	#2015	ND	6.10am	4hr 35min (except Wed)
	Ashram Express	#2916	OD	3.05pm	5hr 20min
Jhansi	Shatabdi Express*	#2002	ND	6.15am	4hr 28min
Kolkata (Calcutta)	Kolkata Rajdhani*	#2302	ND	5pm	16hr 55min (except Fri)
	Sealdah Rajdhani*	#2306	ND	4.45pm	17hr 30min
	Howrah–Poorva Express	#2304	ND	4.25pm	24hr 30min (W, Th, Sa, Su)
	Kalka Mail	#2304	OD	7.30am	23hr 50min
Mumbai	Rajdhani Express*	#2952	ND	4.30pm	16hr 05min
Udaipur	Mewar Express	#2963	HN	7pm	12hr
Varanasi	Varanasi Special	#2458A	OD	6.15pm	11hr 15min
	Shiv Ganga Express	#2560	ND	6.30pm	11hr
Vasco da Gama	Goa Express	#2780	HN	3pm	39hr 30min
OD Old Delhi	ND New Delhi	HN Hazrat Nizamuddin		SR Sarai Rohilla	

*a/c only

By bus

Delhi is the hub of a **bus** network covering the neighbouring states. Buses are of most use for travelling to mountainous areas not served by trains, but they may also be faster than trains on shorter routes. On longer routes there's usually a choice between the ramshackle state-run buses and more comfortable private buses, which some see as potentially more dangerous, as they travel faster and often overnight.

The vast majority of **state-run buses** depart from the **Maharana Pratap ISBT** (☎011/2386 8836; see Old Delhi map, p.120) by Kashmiri Gate metro and Rs60 from Connaught Place by auto. Be sure to arrive up to an hour before departure to allow time to find the correct counter (there are thirty or so) and book your ticket. Ask for the numbers of both platform and licence plate to ensure you board the right bus.

Services for Uttarakhand (Uttaranchal) hill stations like Nainital, Almora and Ramnagar (for Corbett National Park) leave from **Anand Vihar ISBT** in East Delhi (☎011/2215 2431; bus #85, or Rs75 by pre-paid auto from Connaught Place). Buses to Agra, Mathura, Ajmer and Jaipur leave from the **Sarai Kale Khan ISBT** (☎011/2435 8092; see New Delhi map, p.115) east of Hazrat Nizamuddin Station. However, for Jaipur, Udaipur, Jodhpur and Ajmer, the **Rajasthan Roadways terminal** at Bikaner House, India Gate (☎011/2338 3469; see New Delhi map, p.115), has by far the best service, with a range that includes comfortable deluxe buses.

Private **deluxe buses** usually depart from near the Ramakrishna Mission at the end of Main Bazaar, Paharganj, but some pick up passengers at hotels. Popular destinations include Kullu, Manali and Dharamsala, which are not accessible by train, as well as Pushkar and the Uttarakhand (Uttaranchal) hill stations. You can book tickets a day or two in advance at the agencies in Paharganj or Connaught Place.

The only **international service** is to Lahore in Pakistan, leaving from Dr Ambedkar Terminal on Jahwaharlal Nehru Marg near Delhi Gate on Tuesdays, Wednesdays, Fridays and Saturdays at 6am (☎011/2331 8180, ⓦdtc .nic.in/lahorebus.htm).

Travel details

Trains

To **Central India**: Bhopal (12–17 daily; 7hr 50min–13hr 5min); Gwalior (17–20 daily; 3hr 16min–6hr 5min); Indore (2 daily; 13hr 25min–17hr 30min); Jhansi (13–18 daily; 4hr 28min–7hr 50min).

To **the east**: Bhubaneshwar (2–4 daily; 24hr 20min–40hr 5min); Cuttack (2–4 daily; 22hr 5min–39hr 15min); Gaya (4–7 daily; 7hr 26min–17hr 30min); Guwahati (4–5 daily; 27hr 20min–43hr 40min); Kolkata (Calcutta) (Howrah/Sealdah) (3–5 daily; 16hr 55min–35hr 25min); Puri (2–3 daily; 30hr 45min–41hr 50min); Vijayawada (4–7 daily; 22hr 20min–33hr 50min).

To **Gujarat and Maharashtra**: Ahmedabad (3–7 daily; 14hr 5min–18hr 55min); Mumbai (10–11 daily; 16hr 5min–30hr 20min); Pune (2–3 daily; 25hr 30min–28hr 15min).

To **Punjab and Himachal Pradesh**: Amritsar (10–14 daily; 5hr 55min–12hr 5min); Chandigarh (6–7 daily; 3hr 7min–5hr 10min); Kalka, for Shimla (5 daily; 4hr–6hr 45min); Pathankot (3–6 daily; 9hr 40min–11hr 55min).

To **Rajasthan**: Abu Road (3–4 daily; 10hr 20min–14hr); Ajmer (4–6 daily; 6hr 50min–8hr 45min); Bharatpur (8–9 daily; 2hr 29min–4hr); Bikaner (4 weekly; 12hr 5min); Chittaurgarh (2 daily; 9hr 40min–13hr 20min); Jaipur (6–9 daily; 4hr 35min–6hr); Jodhpur (2 daily; 11hr 10min–12hr 5min); Kota (10–14 daily; 4hr 25min–9hr 30min); Sawai Madhopur (8–10 daily; 4hr 33min–6hr 25min); Udaipur (1 daily; 12hr).

To **the south**: Bengaluru (Bangalore) (1–2 daily; 36hr 25min–40hr 25min); Chennai (2–3 daily; 32hr 40min–35hr 35min); Ernakulam (2 daily; 46hr 5min–49hr 40min); Hyderabad/Secunderabad (2–3 daily; 24hr 10min–30hr 40min); Thiruvananthapuram (1 daily; 50hr 50min); Vasco Da Gama (1 daily; 39hr 30min).

To **Uttar Pradesh and Uttarakhand**: Agra (14–18 daily; 2hr–4hr); Allahabad (16–23 daily; 6hr 47min–14hr 20min); Gorakhpur (8–9 daily; 13hr 25min–17hr 15min); Haridwar (6–7 daily; 4hr–9hr 25min); Kanpur (16–20 daily; 4hr 35min–8hr 30min); Lucknow (15–19 daily; 6hr 15min–10hr 55min); Mathura (15–19 daily; 1hr 20min–3hr 25min); Varanasi/Mughal Sarai (19–27 daily; 8hr 45min–18hr).

145

Buses

Only state buses are included in this summary; for details of private buses, see p.145.

In the listings below, for points of departure, **A** means Anand Vihar ISBT in East Delhi, **B** is the Rajasthan Roadways terminal at Bikaner House, **M** is Maharana Pratap ISBT at Kashmiri Gate, and **S** is Sarai Kale Khan ISBT at Nizamuddin.

To **Rajasthan**: Ajmer (B 3 daily, M 8 daily, S 10 daily; 9hr); Jaipur (B 28 daily, M every 20min, S every 45min; 6hr); Jodhpur (B 1 daily, S 2 daily; 12hr); Udaipur (B 1 daily, M 3 daily; 20hr).

To **Uttar Pradesh and Uttarakhand**: Agra (S hourly; 5hr), Almora (A 4 daily; 12hr); Dehra Dun (M every 30min; 7hr); Haridwar (M every 30min; 6hr); Mussoorie (M 2 daily; 9hr); Nainital (A 6 daily; 9hr); Ramnagar, for Corbett National Park (A hourly; 7–8hr); Rishikesh (M hourly; 6hr 30min).

To **Punjab** and **Himachal Pradesh**: Amritsar (M every 20–40min; 8–10hr); Chandigarh (M every 15–30min; 5–6hr); Dharamsala (M 10 daily; 11–12hr); Manali (M 15 daily; 14hr); Shimla (M 25 daily; 8–9hr).

Flights

(**AI** = Air India, **IC** = Indian Airlines, **IT** = Kingfisher, **DN** = Air Deccan, **SG** = SpiceJet, **S2** = JetLite, **9W** = Jet Airways, **6E** = IndiGo, **G8** = Go Air)

Delhi to: Ahmedabad (IC, DN, SG, 9W, G8; 10 daily; 1hr 25min); Allahabad (S2; 3 weekly; 2hr 20min); Amritsar (AI, IC, DN, 9W; 3–4 daily; 50min); Aurangabad (IC; 1 daily; 3hr 40min); Bagdogra (for Siliguri and Darjeeling) (IC, DN, 9W; 2–3 daily; 1hr 50min–3hr 55min); Bengaluru (Bangalore) (IC, IT, DN, SG, S2, 9W, 6E, G8; 30–31 daily; 2hr 30min–4hr 10min); Bhopal (IC, DN, 9W; 3–4 daily; 1hr 40min–3hr); Bhubaneshwar (IC, DN, S2; 4 daily; 2hr); Chandigarh (IC, DN, 9W; 3 daily; 40–45min); Chennai (IC, IT, DN, SG, S2, 9W, 6E, G8; 20 daily; 2hr 30min–7hr 05min); Coimbatore (IC, SG, S2; 3 daily; 4hr–4hr 45min); Goa (IC, IT, DN, SG, S2, 6E, G8; 9–10 daily; 2hr 20min–4hr 05min); Gorakhpur (S2; 3 weekly; 1hr 20min); Guwahati (IC, DN, SG, S2, 9W, 6E; 7–8 daily; 2hr 15min–3hr 30min); Gwalior (DN; 1 daily; 50min); Hyderabad (IC, IT, DN, SG, 9W, 6E; 17–18 daily; 2hr–3hr 55min); Imphal (IC, 6E; 1–2 daily; 3hr 35min); Indore (IC, DN, S2, 9W; 4–5 daily; 1hr 20min–2hr 55min); Jaipur (IC, IT, DN, S2, 9W, G8; 6 daily; 40–45min); Jabalpur (DN; 1 daily; 2hr–2hr 45min); Jaisalmer (IC; 1 daily; 1hr 10min); Jodhpur (IC, DN, 9W; 2–3 daily; 1hr 20min–2hr 25min); Khajuraho (IC, 9W; 1–2 daily; 1hr 05min–2hr 45min); Kochi (IC, SG, S2, 6E, G8; 9 daily; 3hr 05min– 5hr 25min); Kolkata (IC, IT, DN, S2, 9W, 6E; 18 daily; 2hr–9hr 40min); Kozhikode (IC; 1 daily; 5hr 55min); Kullu (IC, DN; 1–2 daily; 1hr 10min–1hr 15min); Leh (IC, DN, 9W; 1–4 daily; 1hr 15min–1hr 30min); Lucknow (AI, IC, DN, S2, 9W; 8–9 daily; 55min–1hr 25min); Mumbai (AI, IC, IT, DN, SG, S2, 9W, 6E, G8; 65 daily; 1hr 55min–4hr 10min); Nagpur (IC, S2, 9W, 6E; 4 daily; 1hr 25min–2hr 55min); Pathankot (DN; 1 daily; 1hr 20min); Patna (IC, DN, S2; 4 daily; 1hr 25min–3hr 05min); Pune (IC, IT, DN, SG, S2, 9W, 6E; 9–12 daily; 1hr 55min–5hr); Raipur (IC, DN, 9W; 3–4 daily; 1hr 40min–1hr 50min); Ranchi (IC, DN, S2; 3–4 daily; 1hr 35min–1hr 45 min); Shimla (DN; 1 daily; 1hr 15min); Surat (IC; 1 daily; 1hr 30min); Thiruvananthapuram (IC, DN, S2, 9W; 5 daily; 4hr 10min–4hr 50min); Tirupati (IC; 1 daily; 3hr 50min); Udaipur (IC, DN, 9W; 3–4 daily; 1hr 10min–2hr 25min); Vadodara (IC, 9W, 6E; 4 daily; 1hr 25min–2hr 15min); Varanasi (IC, IT, SG, S2, 9W; 5–6 daily; 1hr 10min–2hr 40min).

Rajasthan

AFGHANISTAN

CHINA
(TIBET AUTONOMOUS
REGION)

0   400 km

PAKISTAN

BHUTAN

NEPAL

BANGLADESH

MYANMAR
(BURMA)

ARABIAN
SEA

BAY OF BENGAL

N

SRI
LANKA

INDIAN OCEAN

The International boundaries on this map are neither purported to be correct
nor authentic by Survey of India directives. Publisher.

CHAPTER 2 # Highlights

✳ **Keoladeo National Park, Bharatpur** Flocks of rare birds – and bird-watchers – travel from across Asia and Europe each winter to visit this remarkable wetland sanctuary. See p.191

✳ **Ranthambore National Park** India's most popular wildlife park and one of the easiest places in the world to see tigers in the wild, thanks to its large and exhibitionist population of big cats. See p.192

✳ **Savitri Temple, Pushkar** For optimum views of the famous lake and whitewashed holy town, climb to the hilltop Savitri Temple at sunset. See p.206

✳ **Meherangarh Fort, Jodhpur** Rajasthan's showcase citadel, offering maximum-impact views of the blue city below and an unparalleled museum. See p.213

✳ **Camel trekking** There's no better way to experience the Thar Desert than by riding a camel through it. See p.223

✳ **Jaisalmer Fort** India's greatest inhabited fort, with more than two thousand people still occupying its golden sandstone homes. See p.224

✳ **Udaipur** Rajasthan's – if not India's – most romantic city: a fairy-tale ensemble of lakes, floating palaces and sumptuous Rajput architecture ringed by dramatic green hills. See p.239

▲ Jaisalmer Fort

2

Rajasthan

The state of **RAJASTHAN** emerged after Partition from a mosaic of twenty-two feudal kingdoms, known in the British era as Rajputana, "Land of Kings". Running northeast from Mount Abu, near the border with Gujarat, to within a stone's throw of the ruins of ancient Delhi, its backbone is formed by the bare brown hills of the Aravalli Range, which divide the fertile Dhundar basin from the shifting sands of the mighty Thar Desert, one of the driest places on earth.

Rajasthan's extravagant **palaces**, **forts** and finely carved **temples** comprise one of the country's richest crop of architectural monuments. But these exotic buildings are far from the only legacy of the region's prosperous and militaristic history. For visitors, Rajasthan's strong adherence to the traditions of the past is precisely what makes it a compelling place to travel. Swaggering moustaches, heavy silver anklets, bulky red, yellow or orange turbans, pleated veils and mirror-inlaid saris may be part of the complex language of **caste**, but to most outsiders they epitomize India at its most exotic.

Colour also distinguishes Rajasthan's most important tourist cities. **Jaipur**, the chaotic state capital, is known as the "Pink City" thanks to the reddish paint applied to its ornate facades and palaces. **Jodhpur**, the "Blue City", is centred on a labyrinthine old walled town, whose sky-blue mass of cubic houses is overlooked by India's most imposing hilltop fort. Further west, the magical desert city of **Jaisalmer**, built from local sandstone, is termed the "Golden City". In the far south of the state, **Udaipur** hasn't gained a colour tag yet, but it could be called the "White City": coated in decaying limewash, its waterside palaces and havelis framed by a distant vista of sawtooth hills.

As an extension to the "Golden Triangle" of Delhi–Agra–Jaipur, the route stringing together these four cities has become the most heavily trodden tourist trail in India. But it's easy to escape into more remote areas. Northwest of Jaipur, the desert region of **Shekhawati** is littered with atmospheric market towns whose richly painted havelis are beginning to attract increasing numbers of visitors, while the desert city of **Bikaner** is also well worth a stopover for its fine fort, havelis and the unique "rat temple" at nearby Deshnok. The same is true of **Bundi**, in the far south of the state, with its magnificent, muralled fort, as well as the superb fort at **Chittaurgarh** nearby, not to mention the engaging hill station and remarkable Jain temples of **Mount Abu**.

Another attraction is Rajasthan's wonderful **wildlife sanctuaries**. Of these, the famous tiger-sanctuary at **Ranthambore** is deservedly the most famous, while the **Keoladeo National Park** at **Bharatpur**, on the eastern border of Rajasthan near Agra, is unmatched in South Asia for its incredible avian

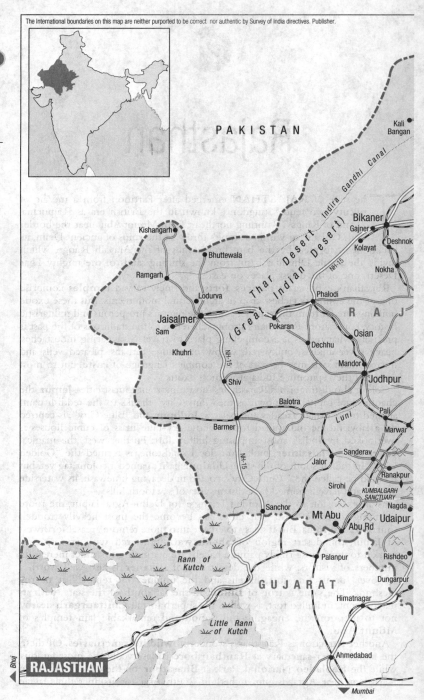

The International boundaries on this map are neither purported to be correct nor authentic by Survey of India directives. Publisher.

PAKISTAN

Kali Bangan

Bikaner
Gajner
Deshnok
Kolayat
Kishangarh
Nokha

Bhuttewala

Ramgarh
Lodurva
Phalodi

R A J

Jaisalmer
Pokaran
Sam
Osian
Khuhri
Dechhu
Mandor
Shiv
Jodhpur
Balotra
Pali
Luni
Barmer
Marwar

Sanderav
Jalor
Ranakpur
Sirohi
KUMBALGARH
SANCTUARY
Nagda
Sanchor
Udaipur
Mt Abu
Abu Rd

Rann of
Kutch
Palanpur
Rishdeo

GUJARAT
Dungarpur
Himatnagar

Little Rann
of Kutch

Ahmedabad

Bhuj

RAJASTHAN

Mumbai

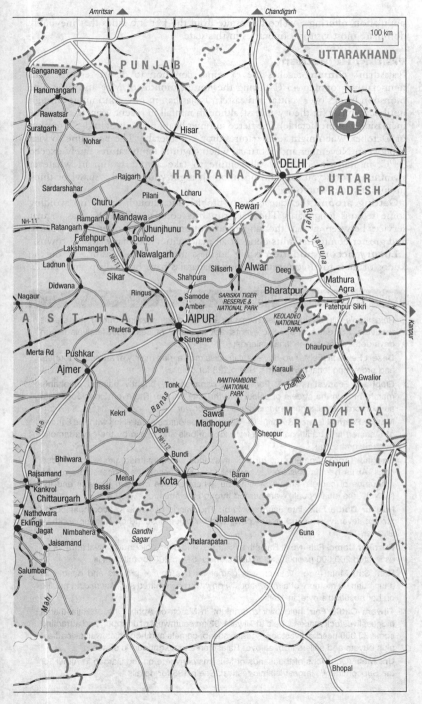

population, offering a welcome respite from the frenetic cities that inevitably dominate most visitors' itineraries in this state.

Visiting Rajasthan

Rajasthan's **climate** reaches the extremes common to desert regions, with temperatures topping 45°C during the hottest months of May and June. The monsoon breaks over central and eastern Rajasthan in July, continuing through until September (in theory at least, although rainfall in recent years has become increasingly unpredictable). The fierce summer heat lingers until mid–September or October, when night temperatures drop considerably. The best time to visit is between November and February, when daytime temperatures rarely exceed 30°C; in midwinter, you'll still venture to take a midday dip in whatever swimming pools you can find open, but at night you'll need a shawl or thick jumper if you're outdoors.

Getting around the state is rarely problematic, though there's no avoiding some tedious long hauls. The state-run **bus** company, RSTDC, has regular services between cities, although **private operators** often offer faster services and greater comfort. **Trains** connect all major cities and many smaller towns.

Luxury accommodation is big business in Rajasthan. Cashing in on the kudos of their royal connections, local maharajas have opened up their family

Festivals and fairs in Rajasthan

Rajasthan's vibrant local costumes are at their most dazzling during the state's **festivals**. For dates of specific events, ask at tourist offices; most festivals fall on days determined by the lunar calendar.

Desert Festival (Feb). Two-day event in Jaisalmer, aimed mainly at attracting tourists and promoting local handicrafts. See p.228 for details.

Elephant Festival (March). Parades of caparisoned, brightly painted elephants march through the streets of Jaipur into the City Palace. The event concludes with an extraordinary elephant versus *mahout* tug of war.

Mewar Festival (March & April). The ranas of Udaipur celebrate Holi with the lighting of a sacred fire, traditional dance from local tribals and music by the city's famous bagpipe orchestra.

Gangaur (April). Women pray for their husbands and unmarried girls wish for good ones. At its best in Jaisalmer, when the local raja heads the procession amid an entourage of camels, and in Mount Abu, where effigies of Gauri (Parvati) and Isa (Shiva) – the ideal couple – are carried through the streets.

Nagaur Cattle Fair (late Jan/early Feb). Thousands of farmers, accompanied by around seventy thousand steers, cows and bullocks, descend on Nagaur, south of Bikaner.

Pushkar Camel Fair (Nov). Rajasthan's largest and most colourful festival attracts an estimated 200,000 people and 50,000 camels. See p.208 for full details.

Rani Sati Mela (Aug). Vast crowds gather for this day of prayers and dances in Jhunjhunu, in memory of a merchant's widow who committed sati, sacrificing her life on her husband's pyre, in 1595.

Tilwara Cattle Fair (held over a fortnight in March or April). One of Rajasthan's biggest livestock markets, held at Tilwara, 93km southwest of Jodhpur, and attracting some 80,000 head of livestock – goats, sheep, camels and horses as well as cattle – plus buyers and sellers from all over Rajasthan and neighbouring states.

Urs Mela (Oct). Tens of thousands of Muslims converge on the Dargah in Ajmer for the Subcontinent's largest Islamic festival. See p.198 for details.

homes as "heritage" or **palace hotels**. At the opposite end of the scale, the state's laudable **paying guest scheme**, Rajasthan's equivalent of B&B accommodation, provides a great opportunity to get to know an Indian family. Tourist offices across the state keep names and addresses of local families who take part in the scheme For online information, visit Ⓦ www.rajasthantourism.gov.in.

Some history

The turbulent history of Rajasthan only really begins in the sixth and seventh centuries AD, with the emergence of warrior clans such as the Sisodias. Chauhans, Kuchwahas and Rathores – the **Rajputs** ("sons of princes"). Never exceeding eight percent of the population, they were to rule the separate states of **Rajputana** for centuries. Their code of honour set them apart from the rest of society – as did the genesis myth that they descended from the sun and moon – but did not invite excessive hostility. The Rajputs provided land, employment and trading opportunities for their subjects, and are still today praised as gods in some communities.

The Rajput codes of chivalry that lay behind endless clashes between clans and family feuds found their most savage expression in battles with Muslims. **Muhammad of Ghori** was the first to march his troops through Rajasthan, eventually gaining a foothold that enabled him to establish the **Sultanate** in Delhi. During the 350 years that followed, much of central, eastern and western India came under the control of the sultans, but, despite all the Muslims' efforts, Rajput resistance precluded them from ever taking over Rajputana.

Ghori's successors were pushed out of Delhi in 1483 by the Mughal Babur, whose grandson **Akbar** came to power in 1556. Aware of the futility of using force against the Rajputs, Akbar chose instead to negotiate in friendship, and married Rani Jodha Bai, a princess from the Kuchchwaha family of Amber. As a result, Rajputs entered the Mughal courts, and the influence of Mughal ideas on art and architecture remains evident in palaces, mosques, pleasure gardens and temples throughout the state.

When the Mughal empire began to decline after the accession of Aurangzeb in 1658, so too did the power of the Rajputs. Aurangzeb sided with a new force, the **Marathas**, who plundered Rajput lands and extorted huge sums of protection money. The Rajputs eventually turned for help to the Marathas' chief rivals, the **British**, and signed formal treaties as to mutual allies and enemies. Although in theory the residents who represented British authority in each state were supposed to be neutral communicators, they soon wielded more power than the Rajput princes. However, the Rajputs were never denied their royal status, and relations were so amicable that few joined the Mutiny of 1857. Wealth from overland trade enabled them to festoon their palaces with silks, carpets, jewels and furnishings far beyond the imagination of most ordinary citizens, while the prosperous **Marwari** merchants of the northwest built and decorated stylish mansions, temples and meeting halls.

The nationwide clamour for Independence in the years up to 1947 eventually proved stronger in Rajasthan than Rajput loyalty; when British rule ended, the Rajputs were left out on a limb. With persuasion from the new Indian government including the offer of "privy purses", they agreed one by one to join the Indian Union, and in 1949 the 22 states of Rajputana finally merged to form the state of **Rajasthan**.

Apart from three brief years of Janata domination from 1977 to 1980, Congress held sway over Rajasthan from its first democratic elections in 1952 until 1994, when the **BJP** won a decisive victory. Central control soon exposed the Rajputs' neglect of their subjects, whom they had entrusted to power-thirsty landowners (*jagirdars*), and village councils (*panchayats*) were set up to organize local affairs. Since 1991 no state has come even close to matching Rajasthan's tripling of the male literacy rate – though the literacy rate for women remains one of the worst in India. Several universities have also been established, new industries have benefited from an increased electricity supply that now reaches most villages, while irrigation schemes have improved crop production in this notoriously dry region, although the entire state was crippled by years of drought from the late 1990s through to 2004, which drove hundreds of thousands of people off the land and even dried up the famous Lake Pichola in Udaipur. Water – or the lack of it – remains a pressing problem throughout the state.

Modern Rajasthan remains among the poorest and most staunchly traditional regions of India, and although the need for economic development is modernizing the state faster than ever, the state's firmly held attitudes and customs are unlikely to disappear any time soon. As Rajasthanis themselves are apt to remind you: *Delhi door ast* – "Delhi is far away."

Jaipur and around

A flamboyant showcase of Rajasthani architecture, **JAIPUR** has long been established on tourist itineraries as the third corner of India's "Golden Triangle". At the heart of Jaipur lies the **Pink City**, the old walled quarter, whose **bazaars** rank among the most vibrant in Asia, renowned above all for hand-dyed and embroidered textiles and jewellery. For all its colour, however, Jaipur's heavy traffic, dense crowds and pushy traders makes it a taxing place to explore, and many visitors stay just long enough to catch a train to more laid-back destinations further west or south. If you can put up with the urban stress, however, the city's modern outlook and commercial hustle and bustle offer a stimulating contrast to many other places in the state.

If you're anywhere near Jaipur in March, don't miss the **Elephant Festival** (see p.152), one of India's most flamboyant parades, celebrated with full Rajput pomp.

Some history

Established in 1727, Jaipur is one of Rajasthan's youngest cities, founded by (and named after) **Jai Singh II** of the **Kachchwaha** family, who ruled a sizeable portion of northern Rajasthan from their fort at nearby Amber. The Kachchwaha Rajputs had been the first to ally themselves with the Mughals, in 1561, and the free flow of trade, art and ideas had by the time of Jai Singh's accession won them great prosperity.

Jai Singh's fruitful 43-year reign was followed by an inevitable battle for succession, and the state was thrown into turmoil. Much of its territory was lost to Marathas and Jats, and the British quickly moved in to take advantage of Rajput infighting. Unlike their neighbours in Delhi and Agra, the rulers of Jaipur remained loyal to the British during the 1857 uprising. Following Independence, Jaipur merged with the states of Mewar, Bikaner, Jodhpur and Jaisalmer, becoming **state capital** of Rajasthan in 1956.

Today, with a population of around 2.5 million, Jaipur is the state's most advanced commercial and business centre and its most prosperous city – some estimates put it amongst the world's 25 fastest growing cities, with an annual population growth of over 3.5 percent. More than anywhere else in Rajasthan,

Jaipur evinces the jarring paradox of India's development: while glistening new shopping malls are being erected for a newly emboldened middle class, poverty from the city's poorer districts is spilling over into the streets and the entire city is choked with traffic, frequently approaching gridlock during the morning and evening rush hours.

Arrival and information

Jaipur's **railway station** lies 1.5km west of the Pink City, close to the main concentration of hotels around the western end of MI Road; state buses from all over Rajasthan and further afield pull in at the **Inter-state Bus Terminal** on Station Road. Buses arriving from Delhi or Agra skirt the southern side of the city, stopping briefly at Narain Singh Circle, where rickshaw-wallahs frequently board the bus and, with the connivance of the bus driver, announce that it's the end of the line ("bus going to yard"); this is a ploy to get you on to their rickshaws and into a hotel that pays generous commission. The city's modern Sanganer **airport**, 15km south of the centre, is served by domestic flights from Ahmedabad, Delhi, Mumbai, Udaipur, Jodhpur, Panjim, Hyderabad and Kolkata (Calcutta). An airport bus into town costs around Rs30, a rickshaw Rs150 and a taxi Rs250–300.

The **RTDC** has several tourist information offices around town. The most convenient are on Platform 1 of the railway station (daily 24hr; ℡0141/231 5714); at the *Tourist Hotel* on MI Road opposite the GPO (daily 8am–8pm; ℡0141/237 5466); and on platform 3 at the state bus terminal (daily 9.30am–5pm). There's a third, rather difficult-to-find, office on Station Road (daily 10am–5pm; ℡0141/511 4768) on the north side of the roundabout directly in front of the station (go down the small driveway past the *Hotel Chitra Palace*); this is where you'll need to come to make bookings for the *Palace on Wheels* and *Fairy Queen* trains (see p.47). **RTDC tours** (see below) can be booked through any of these offices. There's an **India Tourism** office at the *Khasa Kothi* hotel (Mon–Fri 9am–6pm, Sat 9am–2pm; ℡0141/237 2200), with a good range of leaflets and countrywide information. To find out **what's on**, you're best off consulting the monthly *Jaipur City Guide* (Rs30), available at some hotels, bookshops and newspaper stalls.

City transport and tours

Jaipur is very spread out, and although it's possible to explore the Pink City on foot (despite the crowds), you may need some form of transport to get you there from your hotel. It's best to avoid the morning and evening rush hours, especially within the Pink City. **Auto-rickshaws** are available all over the city, although prices are relatively high, as are **cycle rickshaws**, though these can take forever to get anywhere in the heavy traffic.

Unmetered yellow-top **taxis** have a stand on MI Road outside the RTDC tourist office; **radio taxis** charge Rs8–10/km and rarely take more than ten minutes for a pick-up; try Pink City (℡0141/222 5000). **Cars with driver** can be rented through most hotels and guesthouses, or through any RTDC office. Typical costs are around Rs400 return to Amber, or Rs700 to Samode.

One very inexpensive, though also very rushed, way to see Jaipur's main attractions is on one of the two **guided tours** run by the RTDC (5hr half-day tour, Rs120; 9hr full-day tour, Rs170; entrance fees not included), which cram in most of the major city sights. They also run a "Pink City by Night" tour (6.30–10.30pm; Rs200), which includes dinner at Nahargarh Fort. Tours can be booked through any of the RTDC offices listed above.

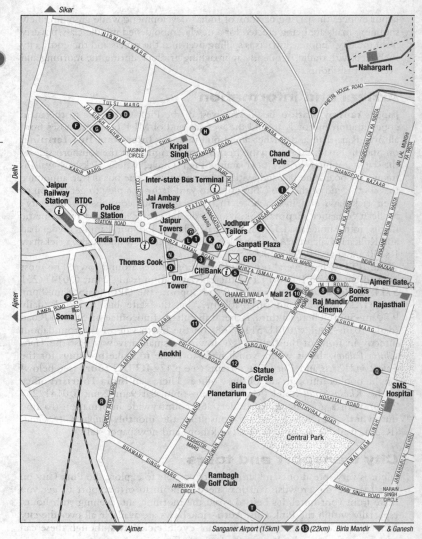

Accommodation

Jaipur has a wide range of **accommodation**, mostly found west of the city centre, along (or close to) MI Road and in the upmarket suburb of Bani Park. Standards are high, as are prices. Wherever you choose to stay, it's a good idea to **book ahead**, particularly around the Pushkar camel *mela* (early Nov) and the Elephant Festival (first half of March). Most places offer **free pick-up** from bus or train stations – check when you book ahead. All the following places also offer **Internet access**.

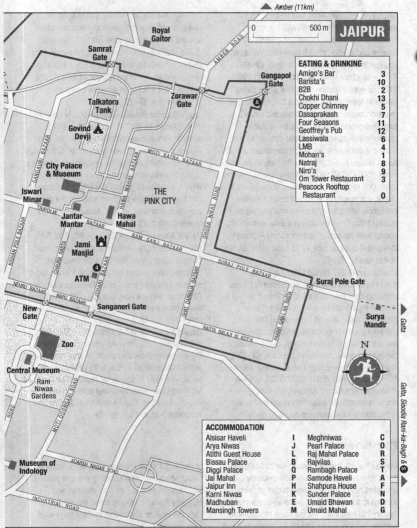

Amber (11km)

JAIPUR

0   500 m

EATING & DRINKING

Amigo's Bar	3
Barista's	10
B2B	2
Chokhi Dhani	13
Copper Chimney	5
Dasaprakash	7
Four Seasons	11
Geoffrey's Pub	12
Lassiwala	6
LMB	4
Mohan's	1
Natraj	8
Niro's	9
Om Tower Restaurant	3
Peacock Rooftop Restaurant	0

THE PINK CITY

ACCOMMODATION

Alsisar Haveli	I	Meghniwas	C
Arya Niwas	J	Pearl Palace	O
Atithi Guest House	L	Raj Mahal Palace	R
Bissau Palace	B	Rajvilas	S
Diggi Palace	Q	Rambagh Palace	T
Jai Mahal	P	Samode Haveli	A
Jaipur Inn	H	Shahpura House	F
Karni Niwas	K	Sunder Palace	N
Madhuban	E	Umaid Bhawan	D
Mansingh Towers	M	Umaid Mahal	G

Mandir (500m)

Budget to mid-range

Arya Niwas Sansar Chandra Rd ☎0141/237 2456, ⓦwww.aryaniwas.com. Dependable old hotel, arranged around a couple of intimate courtyards and a spacious lawn flanked by a spacious veranda. The whole place has a certain faded charm, although some of the rooms (doubles with a/c, singles with fan) are decidedly drab, and the in-house cafeteria looks like it should be in a hospital. Popular with tour groups. ⑤

Atithi Guest House 1 Park House Scheme, just off MI Rd ☎0141/237 8679, ⓔatithijaipur@hotmail .com. Long-established guesthouse and still one of the nicer budget places in town, with attractive and spotlessly clean tiled rooms (fan and a/c), an attractive rooftop terrace and a small garden. ④

Diggi Palace SMS Hospital Rd ☎0141/237 3091, ⓦwww.hoteldiggipalace.com. One of the city's best-value heritage hotels, occupying a characterful old haveli set amidst attractive gardens in a conveniently central location. The more expensive rooms (with a/c) are nicely furnished. The budget rooms (air-cooled) are smaller and plainer, though reasonable value when you factor in the atmospheric setting. ④—⑦

Jaipur Inn Shiv Marg, Bani Park ☎0141/220 1121, ⓦwww.jaipurinn.com. One of the oldest places in town, much improved following recent refurbishments, with comfortable and nicely furnished rooms with TV and a/c – it's still relatively expensive, though you may be able to wangle a discount if you opt to do without a/c. ⑤

Karni Niwas C-5 Motilal Atal Rd (behind *Neelam Hotel*) ☎0141/236 5433, ⓦwww.hotelkarniniwas .com. One of the longest-running guesthouses in Jaipur, this simple little place retains a homely ambience, with pleasant communal seating on outside balconies overlooking a small garden and comfortable air-cooled and a/c rooms – though they aren't quite as nice, or as good value, as other places nearby. ④—⑤

Madhuban D-237 Behari Marg, Bani Park ☎0141/220 0033, ⓦwww.madhuban.net. Less imposing than the city's other heritage hotels (it's more of an overgrown suburban villa than a genuine palace), though better-value than most, and with plenty of quaint Rajput decorative touches and attractively furnished rooms, plus a pleasant garden and small pool round the back. ⑤—⑧

🏃 **Pearl Palace** Hari Kishan Somani Marg, Hathroi Fort ☎0141/237 3700, ⓦwww .hotelpearlpalace.com. Arguably the best guest-house in Rajasthan, beautifully decorated with eye-catching local artefacts adorning every

available surface and a selection of spacious, spotless and excellent-value modern air-cooled and a/c rooms, plus a dorm (Rs100). The well-drilled staff can take care of all your needs, plus there's a handy in-house 24hr money exchange and an excellent rooftop restaurant (see p.165). Usually fills up early, so advance bookings recommended. ②—④

🏃 **Sunder Palace** Sanjay Marg, Hathroi Fort, Ajmer Rd ☎0141/236 0178 or 0878 ⓦwww.sunderpalace.com. Along with the *Pearl Palace*, this sparkling new guesthouse is the city's standout budget option. The spacious and spotless modern rooms (air-cooled and a/c) are a bargain, there's a choice of garden and rooftop restaurants, and the two friendly brothers who run the place provide outstanding service. Advance bookings recommended. ③—④

Umaid Bhawan D1-2A Off Bank Rd, Bani Park ☎0141/220 6426, ⓦwww.umaidbhawan.com. One of Jaipur's most flamboyantly decorated heritage hotels, full of eye-catching murals, old wooden furnishings and other Rajasthani artefacts. Rooms (all a/c) are spacious and cool, and there's also a pool, Wi-Fi in the lobby and a rooftop restaurant. ⑥—⑧

Umaid Mahal C-20/B-2 Bihari Marg, Bani Park ☎0141/220 1952, ⓦwww.umaidmahal.com. Extravagantly decorated place centred around a pretty little arcaded atrium, with virtually every surface covered in traditional murals. The spacious a/c rooms are nicely furnished with antique-style wooden furniture. There's also Wi-Fi access and a basement pool and bar. ⑥—⑦

Expensive

Alsisar Haveli Sansar Chandra Rd ☎0141/236 8290, ⓦwww.alsisar.com. An unexpectedly upmarket haven in a ramshackle part of town, occupying a large and immaculately modernized century-old haveli. It's not the most atmospheric heritage hotel in Jaipur, though it's comfy and well-run, and the pool (non-guests Rs100/hr) is one of the prettiest in town. ⑧

Bissau Palace Khetri House Rd ☎0141/230 4371, ⓦwww.bissaupalace.com. Tucked away in a down-at-heel part of town, this attractive heritage hotel is less flash than others in Jaipur but has plenty of old-world atmosphere, especially the gorgeous Sheesh Mahal and the antique library; modern facil-ities include a decent-sized pool and a Jacuzzi. Discounts of fifty percent in summer. ⑦—⑧

Jai Mahal Jacob Rd, Civil Lines ☎0141/222 3636, ⓦwww.tajhotels.com. One of the smartest addresses in the city, this palatial former residence

of the Jaipur state PM offers a genuine taste of Rajput splendour, with rambling red and yellow buildings set around beautiful gardens and elegantly furnished rooms (from around $390). Facilities include a spa, pool (guests only), and yoga sessions. ⑨

Mansingh Towers Sansar Chandra Rd ☎0141/237 8771, ⓦwww.mansinghhotels.com. Modern hotel occupying an attractive red-sandstone building with graceful Rajput decorative touches, offering cosy rooms and a conveniently central location. Guests can use the pool, health club and spa at the *Mansingh Hotel* next door. Prices from around US$200. ⑨

Meghniwas C-9 Sawai Jai Singh Highway, Bani Park ☎0141/220 2034, ⓦwww.meghniwas .com. Small, modern hotel with spacious a/c rooms (although some suffer from slight road noise) and a nice little pool and garden around the back. Very comfortable, though relatively expensive. ❼–❽

Raj Mahal Palace Sardar Patel Marg ☎ 0141/510 5666, ⓦ www.royalfamilyjaipur.com. This former palace of Jai Singh's favourite maharani has plenty of period charm, with a grand old banqueting hall, wood-panelled library and spacious lawns, plus a medium-size pool (non-guests Rs150). Rooms (all a/c) are large and old-fashioned and a bit past their best, but still decent value at current rates. ❽

Rajvilas Goner Rd, 7km from the city centre ☎ 0141/268 0101, ⓦ www.oberoihotels.com. This dreamy resort occupies a superb fake Rajasthani fort-style complex beautifully landscaped with pools and pavilions. Accommodation is either in delectable creamy rooms (US$750) with private ornamental gardens or in luxury a/c tents (US$870) with Burmese teak floors. There are all the mod cons and facilities you'd expect at this price, including a beautiful spa. ❾

🏋 **Rambagh Palace** Bhawani Singh Marg ☎ 0141/221 1919, ⓦ www.tajhotels.com. This opulent palace complex, set amid 47 acres of beautiful gardens, is indisputably the grandest hotel in Jaipur, and one of the most romantic places to stay in India, with superbly equipped rooms featuring Rajasthani artworks, reproduction antique furniture and all mod-cons. Even if you can't afford to stay, call in for tea (from around Rs300). Doubles from around US$530. ❾

🏋 **Samode Haveli** Gangapole ☎ 0141/263 2407, ⓦ www.samode.com. In an unbeatably central location on the northeastern edge of the Pink City, this superb old haveli is brimful of atmosphere, centred on an idyllic central courtyard and with the prettiest pool in town (guests only). Rooms are a mishmash: some are functional, modern and fairly characterless; others are pure museum pieces; and others are a bit of both – ask to see several before you make a choice. Rooms from around US$190. A good deal in summer (May–Sept), when rates can fall by up to forty percent. ❾

🏋 **Shahpura House** Devi Marg, Bani Park ☎ 0141/220 3392, ⓦ www.shahpurahouse .com. The most characterful of the heritage hotels in this part of town, superbly decorated throughout with lavish murals and with lovely Rajput architectural touches. Rooms all come with a/c, minibar and bathtub, and are attractively furnished with old wooden furniture; there's also a small pool. ❽

The city

Jaipur's attractions fall into three distinct areas. At the heart of the urban sprawl, the historic **Pink City** is where you'll find the fine City Palace, along with myriad teeming bazaars stuffed with enticing Rajasthani handicrafts. The much leafier and less hectic area **south of the Pink City** is home to the Ram Niwas Gardens and Central Museum, while the city's **outskirts** are dotted with a string of intriguing relics of royal rule, most notably Nahargarh Fort, the cenotaphs at Royal Gaitor, and the temples (and monkeys) of Galta.

The Pink City

At the heart of Jaipur lies Jai Singh's original city, popularly known as the **Pink City**, enclosed by walls and imposing gateways which were designed to offer it some measure of protection against hostile forces, and which still serve to physically demarcate it from the sprawling modern suburbs around. One of the Pink City's most striking features is its regular **grid-plan**, with wide, dead-straight streets, laid out at right angles and broadening to spacious plazas at major intersections. The design was created in accordance with the *Vastu Shastras*, a series of ancient Hindu architectural treatises, whereby the entire layout can be read as a kind of mandala, or sacred diagram, in which the city becomes a divinely ordained element of the overreaching cosmic design. The city's other striking feature is its uniform **pink colour**, intended to camouflage the poor-quality materials from which its buildings were originally constructed (the uniform colour scheme was briefly tampered with in the 1860s before being restored to its original pink, an event which led to the widely held but erroneous belief that this was a nineteenth-century innovation, rather than part of the city's original design).

City Palace

The magnificent **City Palace** (daily 9.30am–5pm; Rs180, Indian residents Rs35, video Rs200; same ticket also valid for Jaigarh Fort at Amber if used within 24hr), open to the public as the **Sawai Man Singh Museum**, stands enclosed by a high wall in the centre of the city. The palace was originally built by Jai Singh in the 1720s and has lost none of its original pomp and splendour. Each door and gateway is heavily decorated, each chandelier intact and each hall guarded by turbaned retainers decked out in full royal livery.

The royal family still occupies part of the palace, advancing in procession on formal occasions through the grand **Tripolia Gate** in the centre of the southern wall. Less exalted visitors must enter through the **Udaipole Gate** on the northwest side of the complex. Official guides wait outside the ticket booth offering one-hour tours of the complex (Rs150 for up to four people). On the far side of the Udaipole Gate lies the small **Diwan-i-Am courtyard**, with a collection of old carriages tucked into one end.

Continue straight ahead across the courtyard and through another gate to reach the first of the palace's two main courtyards, painted a deep salmon pink and centred on the raised **Diwan-i-Khas** (Hall of Private Audience). Open-sided, with its roof raised on marble pillars, this was the place in which all important decisions of state were taken by the maharaja and his advisors. The hall contains two silver urns, or *gangajalis*, listed in the *Guinness Book of Records* as the largest crafted silver objects in the world, each more than 1.5m high with a capacity of 8182 litres. When Madho Singh II went to London to attend the coronation of King Edward VII in 1901, he was so reluctant to trust the water in the West that he had these urns filled with Ganges water and took them along with him. On the far (west) side of the Diwan-i-Khas courtyard, a small corridor leads through to the **Pritam Niwas Chowk**, known as the "Peacock Courtyard". This courtyard gives the best view of the soaring yellow **Chandra Mahal**, the residence of the royal family (closed to the public), its heavily balconied seven-storey facade rising to a slope-shouldered summit, with the maharaja's flag flying from the topmost pavilion.

On the opposite (east) side of the Diwan-i-Khas courtyard, beneath the large clocktower, another door takes you into the ornate **Diwan-i-Am** (Hall of Public Audience). A sequence of ornate palanquins occupies the centre of the room, while miniature paintings and Jai Singh's translations of astronomical treatises are displayed in glass cases, along with some superb early manuscripts, scrolls and palm-leaf books, some written in text of microscopic fineness.

An ornate gateway, its southern side guarded by a pair of fine stone elephants, leads from the Diwan-i-Khas courtyard into the second main courtyard, the **Sarvatobhadra**, painted a rich red with yellow trimmings. At the centre of the courtyard lies the elegant **Mubarak Mahal**, with finely carved stone arches and a veranda encircling the whole of the upper storey. Built as a reception hall in 1899, the building now holds the museum's **textile collection**, housing examples of the tie-dyed, block-printed and elaborately woven and brocaded fabrics from the royal wardrobe. On the north side of the courtyard, a further series of rooms is given over to the museum's **Armoury**, filled with the usual collection of blood-curdling, albeit beautifully decorated, knives, swords and guns.

Jantar Mantar

Immediately south of the City Palace lies the remarkable **Jantar Mantar** (daily 9am–4.30pm; Rs10, camera Rs50, video Rs100), a large grassy enclosure containing eighteen huge stone astronomical measuring devices constructed between 1728 and 1734 at the behest of Jai Singh, many of them his own invention, their strange, abstract shapes lending the whole place the look of a weirdly futuristic sculpture park. The Jantar Mantar is one of five identically named observatories created by the star-crazed Jai Singh across North India (including the well-known example in Delhi), though his motivation was astrological rather than astronomical. Astrology has always played a key practical role in Indian culture, and it was in order to more accurately map events in the heavens – and thus more precisely predict their effects on earth – that the observatory was constructed, rather than from any abstract love of science per se.

It's a good idea to pay (Rs100–150) for the services of a **guide** to explain the workings of the observatory, which was able to identify the position and movement of stars and planets, tell the time and even predict the intensity of the monsoon. The time calculated is unique to Jaipur, between ten and forty-one minutes (depending on the time of year) behind Indian standard time. Probably the most impressive of the observatory's constructions is the 27-metre-high sundial, the **Samrat Yantra**, which can calculate the time to within two seconds. A more original device, the **Jaiprakash Yantra**, consists of two hemispheres laid in the ground, each composed of six curving marble slabs with a suspended ring in the centre, whose shadow marks the day, time and zodiac symbol – vital for the calculation of auspicious days for marriage.

Hawa Mahal

Jaipur's most acclaimed landmark, the tapering **Hawa Mahal**, or "Palace of Winds" (daily 9am–4.30pm; Rs5, camera Rs30, video Rs70), stands to the east of the City Palace – best appreciated from the outside during the early morning, when it exudes an orangey-pink glow in the rays of the rising sun. Built in 1799 to enable the women of the court to watch street processions while remaining in purdah, its five-storey facade, decked out with hundreds of finely screened windows and balconies, makes the building seem far larger than it really is; in fact, it's little more than a facade. To get inside the palace itself you'll need to walk for five minutes around the rear of the building, following the lane which runs north from Tripolia Bazaar. Once inside, you can climb up the back of the facade to the screened niches from which the ladies of the court would once have looked down, and which still offer unparalleled views over the mayhem of Jaipur below.

Govind Devji

North of the City Palace is the Govind Devji, the family temple of the maharajas of Jaipur, although it also remains enduringly popular with the hoi polloi of Jaipur, who flock here in droves for the evening puja around 6pm. The temple is dedicated to Krishna in his character of Govinda, while the principal shrine houses an image of Govinda brought from Vrindavan (near Agra) in 1735, which is considered the guardian deity of the rulers of Jaipur. The temple building itself occupies an unusual open-sided pavilion, more like a Mughal audience hall than a traditional Hindu temple. Local tradition states that it was originally a palace pavilion, but that Krishna appeared to Jai Singh in a dream and expressed a fondness for the building, after which the dutiful maharaja had it converted into a temple.

Iswari Minar Swarg Suli

Rising from the centre of the Pink City is the slender **Iswari Minar Swarg Suli** (Heaven-piercing Minaret; daily 9am–4.30pm; Rs10, camera Rs2), whose summit offers the definitive view of old Jaipur, with fascinating glimpses down into the tangled labyrinth of alleyways and courtyards which honeycomb the city in the spaces between the major roads, and which remain largely invisible at street level. The minaret was built by Jai Singh II's son and successor, Iswari Singh, who erected this excessively grandiose monument to celebrate his army's minor victory over a combined Maratha–Rajput force in 1747. The entrance is around the back of the minaret, which can be reached through the small arch about 50m to the west of the minaret along Tripolia Bazaar (or, alternatively, via a second arch around 100m east of the minaret).

South of the Pink City

The leafy, low-key suburbs south of the Pink City offer a welcome respite from the crowds of the centre, dotted with a handful of quirky museums and temples including the dusty **Central Museum** and the bizarre little **Museum of Indology**.

Central Museum

Immediately south of the Pink City, the road leading out from New Gate is flanked by the lush **Ram Niwas Gardens**, named after their creator, Maharaja Ram Singh (1835–1880). The gardens' centrepiece is the florid **Albert Hall** of 1867, designed in a whimsical mix of Venetian and Mughal styles. This eye-catching structure houses the city's **Central Museum** (daily except Fri 10am–4.30pm; Rs30, Indian residents Rs5; photography prohibited inside the museum, though photos are allowed from the rooftop for an additional Rs30). The museum is a real colonial period piece, from the dilapidated Victorian-era decor to the mildewed exhibits themselves, which appear not to have been dusted since the nineteenth century. The **ground floor** features displays on assorted Rajasthani ethnic groups, plus examples of the region's myriad artisanal traditions, while the first-floor **library** has a good selection of miniature paintings. From here you can climb up to the fancifully decorated rooftop, with breezy views out over the surrounding parkland.

Museum of Indology

Further south, off Jawaharlal Nehru Road, the **Museum of Indology** (daily 8am–4pm; Rs20 including guided tour, plus tip) holds assorted curiosities collected by the late writer and painter Acharya Vyakul stuffed into a rambling suburban house. Exhibits include oddities such as a map of India painted on a grain of rice, letters written on a hair and a glass bed, along with enormous quantities of junk, all heaped up together in great mouldering piles – it's all fairly unedifying, and whatever one might get out of the strange little collection is largely negated by the resident caretaker, whose whistle-stop tour and largely incomprehensible "explanations" are followed by inevitable demands for further cash.

Outlying sights

The rocky hills that overlook Jaipur to the north and east are home to a string of spectacularly situated forts and temples, all reachable via steep paths climbing up from the city (or, for the less energetic, via longer roads around the back of the hills).

Nahargarh

Teetering on the edge of the hills north of Jaipur is **Nahargarh**, or "Tiger Fort" (open 24hr; free). Built by Jai Singh II in 1734, it is an eye-catching structure, though the main reason for visiting is to sample the superb views of Jaipur, best enjoyed towards dusk. The imposing walls of the fort sprawl for the best part of a kilometre along the ridgetop, although the only significant surviving structures within are the **palace apartments** (daily 10pm–5pm; Rs5, camera Rs30, video Rs70), built inside the old fort by Madho Singh II between 1883 and 1892 as a love nest in which he housed a selection of his most treasured concubines away from the disapproving eyes of his courtiers and four official wives. The large and rather plain pale-pink structure is filled with dozens of virtually identical rooms and a disorienting labyrinth of corridors and stairwells, allegedly designed to allow the canny Madho Singh to come and go at will without anyone being aware of his movements.

Vehicles of any kind can only get to the fort along a road that branches off Amber Road, a fifteen-kilometre journey from Jaipur. It's simpler to **walk** to the fort along the steep path that climbs up from the north side of the city centre, a stiff fifteen- to twenty-minute walk, although the path is a bit tricky to find, so you might want to take a rickshaw to the bottom. At the top of the path, go through the first gate and then head left, up the steps opposite a large bathing pool and through a second gate into the palace area, then head around to the left to reach the palace itself. It's best to avoid going up too late in the day or returning after dark – the fort is popular with delinquent teenagers and other unsavoury types, and the atmosphere can be a tad seedy at the best of times. There are a couple of **cafés** in the palace complex.

Royal Gaitor

On the northern edge of the city centre, the walled funerary complex of **Royal Gaitor** (daily 9am–4.30pm; free, camera Rs10, video Rs20) contains the stately marble mausoleums (chhatris) of Jaipur's ruling family. The compound consists of two main courtyards, each crammed full of imposing memorials. The first (and more modern) courtyard is dominated by the grandiose twentieth-century cenotaph of **Madho Singh II** (d. 1922), a ruler of famously gargantuan appetites, whose four wives and fifty-odd concubines bore him a grand total of "around 125" children (two of the wives and fourteen children are entombed in smaller chhatris directly behind). To the left of Madho Singh II's cenotaph lies that of Man Singh II (d. 1970), the most recent addition to the royal cemetery.

The second, older, courtyard is dominated by the elaborate tomb of **Jai Singh II** (d. 1743), the founder of Jaipur and the first ruler to be interred at Gaitor. This is the finest of the chhatris, its base decorated with delicately carved elephant- and lion-hunting scenes. Further memorials to Ram Singh II (d. 1880), Madho Singh I (d. 1768), Pratap Singh (d. 1803) and Jagat Singh (d. 1819) lie close by.

On the ridgetop above Gaitor (and reachable from it via a steep path) lies the **Ganesh Mandir**, the second of the city's two major Ganesh temples – a huge and eye-catching building instantly recognizable from the huge swastika painted on its side.

Galta

Nestling in a steep-sided valley 3km east of Jaipur, **Galta** (daily sunrise–sunset; free, camera Rs30, video Rs70) comprises a picturesque collection of 250-year-old temples squeezed into a narrow rocky ravine. Galta owes its sacred status in large part to a freshwater spring which seeps constantly through the rocks in the otherwise dry valley, keeping two **tanks** full. These putrid-smelling ponds are now the domain of over five thousand macaque monkeys, which have earned Galta its nickname of the "Monkey Palace". For many tourists the sight of the splashing monkeys outstrips the attraction of the temples themselves, though the assorted shrines are attractively atmospheric – a tiny shrine in the last (the one closest to the entrance on the north side of the path) is lit by a candle whose flame is claimed to have been kept burning continuously since a visit by Akbar more than four centuries ago. It's also worth walking up to the spectacularly situated **Surya Mandir**, perched above the tanks on the ridgetop overlooking Jaipur and commanding dramatic views of the city below.

The best way to reach Galta **by vehicle** is to drive the 10km or so along the road past Sisodia Rani-ka-Bagh (see below) around the hills behind Jaipur, passing through beautiful countryside en route – remarkably quiet and unspoilt given its proximity to the city. You can also **walk** to Galta, following the path beyond Suraj Pole gate on the eastern edge of the Pink City and climbing steeply up to the Surya Mandir on the crest of the hill above the main temple complex – a stiff thirty-minute walk.

Sisodia Rani-ka-Bagh

The road to Galta runs past a sequence of pleasure gardens, most of them now sadly dilapidated, established by the ruling nobility to serve as retreats from the city. The best preserved of these is the former royal palace and gardens of **Sisodia Rani-ka-Bagh** (daily 8am–5pm; Rs10, or Rs20 5–8pm). The palace is a small and rather chintzy building covered in painted floral decorations, whilst below stretches a sequence of walled and terraced gardens, dotted with small kiosks, marble fountains and water channels (usually dry) – a pleasant enough spot, though of no particular architectural or horticultural distinction.

Eating

Jaipur has Rajasthan's best selection of quality **restaurants**, both veg and non-veg, albeit at higher-than-average prices.

Barista's Das Rd, opposite the Raj Mandir cinema. Smart coffee house serving up excellent, freshly ground coffee – as popular with Jaipur's affluent twenty-somethings as it is among caffeine-crazed foreigners. The well-stocked, little attached bookshop is a bonus.

Chokhi Dhani 22km south of Jaipur on the Tonk Rd ☏0141/277 0554. This Rajasthani theme-park-cum-restaurant attracts droves of well-heeled Jaipuris, especially at weekends, when the whole place gets wildly busy. The Rs270 entrance fee includes an evening meal plus access to a wide range of attractions (though tips are expected at many) – elephant, camel and bullock-cart rides, folk dances, drumming, puppet shows, archery, chapati-making demonstrations and a superb magician, to name just a few. When you've done with the entertainment, head off to the mud-walled restaurant where you'll be sat on the floor and served an authentically original (albeit very salty) Rajasthani village thali quite unlike anything you'll find in the restaurants of Jaipur, with lots of rustic rural delicacies like cornflour chapatis, *gatta* and unusual curried vegetables. It's all a bit hokey, but fun, in a rather kitsch way. A radio taxi charges Rs600 for the round trip, including wait

(auto-rickshaw Rs300). Open Mon–Sat 6–11pm & Sun from 11am.

Copper Chimney MI Rd. Plush glass-fronted restaurant with a good range of north Indian standards (albeit sometimes a bit heavy on the oil and spices), plus local specialities like *laal maans* (special Rajasthani desert-style mutton) and *gatta*, and a few Chinese and continental dishes. Mains Rs85–205. Licensed.

Dasaprakash MI Rd. This unpretentious a/c restaurant serves up a tasty range of classic south Indian veg fare – *iddlis*, vadas, uttapams, *upuma*, thalis, and no less than seventeen types of *dosa* – plus a selection of sweet-toothed ice-cream sundaes in various colourful combinations. Mains from around Rs80.

Four Seasons Bhagat Singh Marg. The most popular veg restaurant in town among locals, with top-notch *dosas* and uttapams along with a large selection of moreish north Indian curries, plus some Chinese. Big portions cater to local tastes and can be a bit spicy. Expect a short wait for a table.

Lassiwala Opposite *Niro's*, MI Rd. A Jaipur institution for its sublime lassis, served in old-style, hygienic terracotta mugs. Its popularity has sparked a small lassi-wallah-war, with two impostors setting up shop to the right (as you face it) of the original. Open 8am–4pm only.

LMB Johari Bazaar. The only proper restaurant in the Pink City, and the best-looking place to eat in town, with stylish chrome and coloured-glass fittings. Sadly, the food (mains from around Rs90) is over-spiced and pedestrian, while service is irritatingly intrusive. There's a good sweet-counter outside.

Mohan's Cosy and unpretentious little veg restaurant, popular with locals thanks to its well-prepared and excellent-value food, with virtually everything under Rs60. There's not much room, so you might end up sharing a table.

Natraj MI Rd. Long-established pure-veg restaurant offering a big range of north Indian standards, plus thalis, *dosas* and superb sweets piled up at the counter by the door. Mains Rs110–160.

Niro's MI Rd. Some of the best non-veg food in Jaipur, with Rajasthani specialities such as *sula*

(lamb), *lal maans* (mutton) and *gatta* along with a big choice of tandooris, tikkas and other meat and veg curries, plus Western and Chinese dishes. Mains from Rs110–200. Licensed.

Om Tower Restaurant Om Tower, MI Rd. Rajasthan's first revolving restaurant, on the 14th floor of the landmark Om Tower. The head-spinning views, of course, are the main attraction, but the food (veg only) is quite presentable, with a good selection of the usual north Indian standards at somewhat above-average prices (mains around Rs160–190), but no alcohol.

Peacock Rooftop Restaurant *Pearl Palace* hotel, Hari Kishan Somani Marg, Hathroi Fort. The lovely little rooftop restaurant gives the city's fancier restaurants a real run for their money. The fairy-tale decor is an attraction in its own right, and there's a big menu of veg and non-veg curries (Rs40–80), as well as a few Chinese dishes, Western snacks, pizzas, and cold beer. Purified water is used to wash all fruit and veg.

Drinking and entertainment

For **drinks**, *Amigo's Bar*, on the ninth floor of the Om Tower, is a popular spot, the slightly gloomy decor offset by fine city views, a reasonable drinks list (including a few cocktails). *Geoffrey's Pub* in the *Hotel Park Plaza* on Prithviraj Road is the city's most appealing English-style pub, complete with oak bar and sporting memorabilia, and with a good range of imported and domestic beers and spirits.

B2B (Fri & Sat only 8.30pm–2am; couples only), at the *Country Inn* on MI Road, is Jaipur's best stab at a Western-style **club** and attracts a mix of locals and foreigners with its good live DJs and big drinks list. Entrance is Rs1000 (Rs700 redeemable in food and drink). Alternatively, there's the fancy and much more expensive *Steam*, at the *Rambagh Palace Hotel*, built inside an old locomotive.

If you go to the **cinema** just once while you're in India, it should be at the Raj Mandir on Bhagwan Das Road just off MI Road, which boasts a stunning Art Deco lobby and 1500-seat auditorium. Most movies have four daily showings (usually at 12.30pm, 3.30pm, 6.30pm and 9.30pm), and there's always a long queue, so get your tickets (Rs39–93) an hour or so before the show starts.

Shopping

If you come across an Indian **handicraft** object or garment abroad, chances are it will have been bought in Jaipur. Foreign buyers and wholesalers flock to the city to shop for textiles, clothes, jewellery and pottery. As a regular tourist, you'll find it harder to hunt out the best merchandise, but as a source of souvenirs, perhaps only Delhi can surpass it.

In keeping with Maharaja Jai Singh's original city divisions, different streets are reserved for purveyors of different goods. **Bapu Bazaar**, on the south side of the Pink City, is the best place for clothes and textiles, including Jaipur's famous **block-print** work and *bandhani* **tie-dye**. On the opposite side of town, along Amber Road just beyond Zorawar Gate, rows of emporiums are stacked with gorgeous patchwork wall-hangings and **embroidery**; these places do a steady trade with bus parties of wealthy tourists, so be prepared to haggle hard.

Jewellery and gemstones in Jaipur

The two best places for silver jewellery are **Johari Bazaar**, the broad street running north of Sanganeri Gate in the Pink City, and **Chameliwala Market**, just off MI Road in the tangle of alleyways behind the *Copper Chimney* restaurant. The latter also has the city's best selection of gems, though it's also one of the hardest places to shop in peace, thanks to a particularly slippery breed of scam merchant, known locally as *lapkars* – usually smartly dressed young men speaking excellent English – whose offers of trips to local beauty spots are invariably followed by a stop at a "relative's" art studio, pottery or carpet-weaving workshop, with accompanying credit-card fraud should you purchase anything. If buying gemstones, be extremely suspicious of anyone offering an address in your own country where, it is claimed, you'll be able to sell them at a huge profit. This is nonsense, of course, but by the time you realize this you'll be thousands of miles away wondering where the mysterious entries on your credit-card bill came from. If you're paying for gemstones or jewellery with a credit card in Jaipur, don't let it out of your sight, and certainly don't agree to leaving a docket as security.

For old-style Persian-influenced vases, plus tiles, plates and candleholders, visit the outlets of the city's renowned **blue potteries** along Amber Road or the workshop of the late Kripal Singh (see below). Bear in mind though that Jaipur's blue pottery is essentially decorative; none of it – in spite of what some shop owners tell you – should be used for hot food as the glazes are unstable and poisonous. For **bookshops**, see "Listings" opposite.

Anokhi 2nd Floor, KK Square Mall, Prithviraj Rd ⓦwww.anokhi.com. Started by a British designer, and recently relocated to a spacious new showroom, this is the place to buy high-quality "ethnic" Indian evening wear, *salwar kameez* and shirts. They also do lovely bedspreads, quilts, tablecloths and cushion covers. Daily 9.30am–8pm.
Jodhpur Tailors Behind the *Neelam Hotel* near Ganpati Plaza, just off MI Rd. One of the best tailors in town, patronized by no less than the maharaja himself. Hand-stitched suits run from around Rs7500 and up, or you could just pick up a shirt (from Rs700) or a pair of trousers (Rs1200) or jodhpurs (Rs1400). Mon–Sat 10.30am–9.30pm, Sun 2–6pm.

Kripal Kumbh Shiv Marg, near the *Jaipur Inn*. The former workshop-cum-home of Jaipur's most famous ceramist, the late Kripal Singh, full of attractive and affordable examples of traditional blue-and-white Jaipuri pottery. Daily 9.30am–8pm.
Rajasthali MI Rd, just south of Ajmer Gate. This large, government-run emporium (Mon–Sat 11am–7.30pm) is a good place to get a sense of the range of handicrafts available and to gauge approximate costs – although you'll probably find similar items at cheaper prices in the Pink City bazaars.
Soma 5 Jacob Rd, near the *Jai Mahal* hotel ⓦwww.somashop.com. Similar range of clothes and fabrics to Anokhi, though at slightly cheaper prices. Mon–Sat 10am–8pm, Sun 10am–6pm.

Listings

Airlines Jaipur Towers on MI Rd is home to dozens of airline agents, not all of them particularly reliable. The best place to head for is Travel-Care (open 24hr; ☎0141/237 1832, ⓦwww.travelcareindia .com), on the ground floor around the right-hand side of the building, who act as agents for virtually every domestic airline and most major international operators, including Air India, BA, Air France, KLM, Lufthansa, Thai Airways, Singapore Air and Gulf Air.
Banks and exchange There are plentiful ATMs around town, especially along MI Rd. There are many private exchange places in Jaipur offering more or less the same rates as the banks; these include two branches of Thomas Cook on MI Rd (both Mon–Sat 9.30am–5.30pm), one on the ground floor of Jaipur Towers, the other opposite Ganpati Plaza, where you can also get cash advances on credit cards. Many of the guesthouses and hotels listed on pp.157–159 can change money (though rates can be poor); the *Pearl Palace Hotel* has 24hr money-changing facilities.
Bookshops Bookwise, in Mall 21, opposite the Raj Mandir cinema, has an excellent selection of English-language fiction and India-related titles; there's also a

handy little bookstall attached to the *Barista* coffee house in the same building. Close by on MI Rd, Books Corner (a couple of doors west of *Niro's* restaurant) has a passable selection of India-related titles crammed into a poky little shop. There are lots of newspaper and magazine stalls along the south side of MI Rd east of here, heading towards Ajmer Gate.

Hospitals For emergencies, the government-run SMS Hospital (T 0141/256 0291), on Sawai Ram Singh Rd, is best; treatment is usually free for foreigners. The best private hospital is the Santokba Durlabhji Memorial Hospital (SDMH), Bhawani Singh Marg T 0141/256 6251.

Internet access All the guesthouses and hotels listed on pp.157–159 have Internet access. If you can't get online where you're staying (or at another guesthouse), the iWay Internet café (daily 9am–11pm; Rs40/hr), near the *Atithi Guest House*, is one of the few reliable alternatives.

Meditation The Dhamma Thali Vipassana Centre (T 0141/268 0220, W www.dhamma.org), located in beautiful countryside on the road to Galta, is one of fifty centres across the world set up to promote the practice of Vipassana meditation. Courses (3–45 days; see website for schedule and details) are free, but a donation is expected.

Photography Sentosa Colour Lab (daily 10am–8pm), Ganpati Plaza (on the side facing MI Rd), and Goyal Colour Lab, next to *Lassiwalla* on MI Rd. Both can download digital images to CD and develop print film.

Police stations The main police post is on Station Rd opposite the railway station T 0141/220 6324.

Post and couriers For poste restante, go to the GPO on MI Rd (Mon–Sat 10am–6pm). Parcels and registered mail are kept at the sorting office behind the main desks; packages are cotton-wrapped and sewn at the concession (Mon–Sat 10am–4pm) by the main entrance. There's a DHL office on Vinobha Marg, which runs south off MI Rd just west of *Dasaprakash* restaurant, though you can save money by going to the *Pearl Palace* hotel (see p.158), whose owner is a DHL agent and who offers 10% discounts on standard rates.

Swimming pools The nicest hotel pool in Jaipur currently open to non-guests is at the *Alsisar Haveli* (Rs100).

Travel agents It's usually easiest to arrange something through your hotel or guesthouse. Alternatively, try the reputable Rajasthan Travel Service, on the ground floor of Ganpati Plaza on MI Rd (T 0141/238 9408, W www.rajasthantravelservice .com) or Travel-Care (see "Airlines", opposite).

Yoga Rajasthan Swasth Yog Parishad, New Police Academy Rd (T 0141/239 7330); the Rajasthan Yoga Centre, 2km north of Bani Park in Shastri Nagar; and Madhavanand Ashram (T 0141/220 0317), also in Bani Park.

Moving on from Jaipur

Jaipur is Rajasthan's main **transport hub** and has frequent bus and train services to all major destinations around the state, as well as good air connections. Short journeys to destinations like Bharatpur, Ajmer (for Pushkar) and towns in Shekhawati are usually best made by bus; one exception is Sawai Madhopur, which is most easily reached by train.

For details of **flights** from Jaipur's Sanganer Airport, see travel details on p.268. Flights to **Jaisalmer** were due to begin in late 2008/early 2009, so may have started by the time you read this.

RSRTC government buses leave from the Inter-state Bus Terminal on Station Road, with frequent, direct services to pretty much every major town in Rajasthan and beyond. For longer routes, faster (but less frequent) deluxe services guarantee seats (enquiries on T 0141/511 6031, bookings up to 24hr in advance on T 0141/220 5790) but for express services it's less hassle to turn up at the bus stand and head for the relevant booking office; destinations are listed outside each cabin. The deluxe services have their own separate booking hatch on platform 3 (open 24hr). There's an RTDC bus for **Pushkar** daily at 1pm; otherwise catch one of the regular buses for Ajmer and change there, or take a private bus (see below). For full details of RSRTC buses, see **travel details** on p.268.

Private bus services can tend to cram too many passengers on board and make excessive chai stops along the way. A reliable company for direct buses to **Pushkar** is Jai Ambay Travels (daily 7.30am–9am; T 0141/220 5177), on Station Road near the junction with MI Road, whose comfortable deluxe coaches leave at 9.30am; you can buy tickets (Rs120, or Rs180 a/c bus) just prior to departure, but it's a good idea to get them in advance (you can also book by phone). The same outfit also runs buses to Ajmer (6 daily; 2hr 30min; Rs70), Jodhpur (3 daily, including 10.30pm sleeper; 6–7hr; Rs160, or Rs210 sleeper bus), Jaisalmer (1 nightly; 12hr; Rs200 sitting, Rs300 sleeper), Udaipur (2 nightly; 9hr; Rs150 sitting, Rs220 sleeper) and Agra (every 1–2hr but making frequent stops; 5hr 30min; Rs100).

Bookings for **trains** should be made at least a day in advance at the computerized reservations hall just outside the main station (Mon–Sat 8am–8pm, Sun 8am–2pm; ☏0141/220 1401); go to the special "Foreign Tourist and Freedom Fighter" counter.

Around Jaipur

Forts, palaces, temples and assorted ruins from a thousand years of Kachchwaha history adorn the hills and valleys near Jaipur. As big a draw as Jaipur's more modern palace complex, the superb palace at **Amber** provides the most

Recommended trains from Jaipur

The trains below are recommended as the fastest and/or most convenient for specific cities.

Destination	Name	No.	Departs	Arrives
Abu Road	Aravalli Express	9708	(daily) 8.45am	4.50pm
Agra	Gwalior Intercity	2987	(daily) 6.10am	10.15am
	Marudhar Express	4864/4854	(daily) 3.50pm	9.10pm
Ajmer	Shatabdi Express	2015	(daily except Wed) 10.50am	1pm
	Aravali Express	9708	(daily) 8.45am	11.15am
Alwar	Jammu Tawi Express	2413	(daily) 4.35pm	6.56pm
	Shatabdi Express	2016	(daily except Wed) 5.45pm	7.26pm
Bikaner	Bikaner Intercity Express	2468	(daily) 3.50pm	10.45pm
	Bikaner Express	4737	(daily) 10.10pm	6.55am
Chittaurgarh	Udaipur Express	2965	(daily) 10.25pm	5.20am
Delhi	Jaisalmer Express	4060	(daily) 5am	11.10am
	Shatabdi Express	2016	(daily except Wed) 5.45pm	10.45pm
Jaisalmer	Jaisalmer Express	4059	(daily) 11.57pm	1pm
Jodhpur	Marudhar Express	4853	(Mon, Wed, Sat) 11.50am	6.20pm
	Ranthambore Express	2465	(daily) 5.40pm	11pm
	Delhi Express	4059	(daily) 11.57pm	5.50am
Kota	Mumbai Superfast	2956	(daily) 2.10pm	5.25pm
	Dayodaya Express	2182	(daily) 5.25pm	9.10pm
Sawai Madhopur (for Ranthambore National Park)	Mumbai Superfast	2956	(daily) 2.10pm	4pm
	Intercity Express	2466	(daily) 10.55am	1.15pm
Udaipur	Udaipur Express	2965	(daily) 10.25pm	7.45am
Varanasi	Marudhar Express	4864/4854	(daily) 3.50pm	8.15am/9.30am

obvious destination for a day-trip, easily combined with a visit to the impressive fort of **Jaigarh**.

Amber

On the crest of a rocky hill 11km north of Jaipur, the Rajput stronghold of **AMBER** (or Amer) was the capital of the leading **Kachchwaha** Rajput clan from 1037 until 1727, when Jai Singh established his new city at Jaipur. Amber's palace buildings are less impressive than those at Jaipur (or many other places in Rajasthan), though the natural setting, perched high on a narrow rocky ridge above the surrounding countryside and fortified by natural hills, high ramparts and a succession of gates along a cobbled road, is unforgettably dramatic – a suitably imposing stronghold for one of Rajputana's most eminent families.

Regular **public buses** to Amber leave from outside Jaipur's Hawa Mahal (every 5–10min; 20–30min), stopping on the main road below the palace. Arrive early in the day if you want to avoid the big coach parties. There's a small **tourist office** (daily 8am–4pm) at the bottom of the path to the palace; it's a pleasant fifteen-minute uphill walk from here to the palace. Alternatively you could hire a Jeep (they hang out along the main road and around the tourist office and charge Rs200 for the return trip, including 1hr waiting time) or waddle up on the back of an elephant (Rs550 for up to two people).

The palace complex

The path from the village leads up to Suraj Pole (Sun Gate) and the large **Jaleb Chowk** courtyard at the entrance to the main **palace complex** (daily 8am–6pm; Rs100, India residents Rs20, video Rs200); this is where you'll find the ticket office and assorted official guides, who offer tours of the palace for around Rs200. On the left-hand side of the courtyard is the **Shri Sila Devi temple**, dedicated to Sila, an aspect of Kali. The revered statue of Sila Devi within is one of the most important in Jaipur, framed by an unusual arch formed from stylized carvings of banana leaves.

Next to the Shri Sila Devi temple, a steep flight of steps leads up to **Singh Pole** (Lion Gate), the entrance to the main palace. The architectural style is distinctly Rajput, though it's clear that Mughal ideas also crept into the design – the practice of covering walls with mirrored mosaics, for example, is pure Mughal. Passing through Singh Pole leads into the first of the palace's three main courtyards, on the far side of which stands the **Diwan-i-Am** (Hall of Public Audience), constructed in 1639. This open-sided pavilion is notably similar in its overall conception to contemporary Mughal audience halls in Delhi and Agra, even if the architectural details are essentially Rajput.

Diagonally opposite, the exquisitely painted **Ganesh Pole** leads into a second courtyard, its right-hand side filled with a miniature fountain-studded garden, behind which lie the rooms of the **Sukh Mahal**, set into the side of the courtyard. The marble rooms here were cooled by water channelled through small conduits carved into the walls, an early and ingenious system of air-conditioning – the central room has a particularly finely carved example.

On the opposite side of the courtyard, the dazzling **Sheesh Mahal** houses what were the private chambers of the maharaja and his queen, its walls and ceilings decorated with intricate mosaics fashioned out of shards of mirror and coloured glass. On the far side of the courtyard beyond the Sheesh Mahal, a narrow stairwell leads up to the small **Jas Mandir**, decorated with similar mosaics and guarded from the sun by delicate marble screens.

From the rear of the Sheesh Mahal courtyard, a narrow corridor leads into a further expansive courtyard at the heart of the **Palace of Man Singh I**, the oldest part of the palace complex. The buildings here are notably plain and austere compared to later structures, though they would originally have been richly decorated and furnished. The pillared *baradari* in the centre of the courtyard was once a meeting area for the maharanis, shrouded from men's eyes by flowing curtains.

Jaigarh

Perched high on the hills behind Amber Palace, the rugged **Jaigarh** fort (daily 9am–5pm; Rs50, Indian residents Rs20; same ticket also valid for Jaipur City Palace if used within 24hr) offers incredible vistas over the hills and plains below. The fort was built in 1600, though as the Kachchwahas were on friendly terms with the Mughals, it saw few battles.

At the centre of the fort, a small **museum** has a rather dusty display of the usual old maps and photographs, plus a good little selection of cannons dating back to 1588 – Jaigarh was an important centre for the manufacture of these highly-prized weapons. None of them, however, can hold a candle to the immense **Jaivana** cannon, the largest in Asia, which sits in solitary splendour at the highest point of the fort, five minutes' walk beyond the museum. Needing one hundred kilos of gunpowder for one shot, the Jaivana could purportedly shoot a cannonball 35km – though its true military value was never accurately gauged since it was never fired in anger.

Most people walk to Jaigarh from Amber Palace, a steep fifteen- to twenty-minute climb. The path to the fort goes from just below the entrance to the palace, branching off from near the top of the zigzagging road (the one used by elephants; not the pedestrian path). By car or Jeep, you'll need to descend to the valley and follow the much longer road that leads to both Jaigarh and Nahargarh; Jeeps can be hired in Amber village for the return trip to the fort (Rs400, including 2hr waiting time). If you've walked up you'll arrive at the Awani Gate – go through the gate and head left to reach the museum; if you've driven, you'll arrive on the opposite side of the fort, near the Jaivana cannon, where you'll also find several **cafés**.

▲ Elephant bathing near the Amber Fort

Amber town

Below the palace, the atmospheric but little-visited **Amber town** is full of remnants of Kachchwaha rule including a small lake, crumbling havelis and chhatris, and almost four hundred temples – a good place for an idle wander. One of the most striking local landmarks is the unusual **Jagat Shiromani Temple**, built by Man Singh after the death in battle of his son and would-have-been successor, a large and florid structure, its shrine topped by an enormous *shikhara* and fronted by an unusually large, two-storey *mandapa* with a curved roof inspired by those on Mughal pavilions. The image of Krishna within is said to have been rescued by Man Singh from Chittaurgarh after that fort had been sacked by Akbar. Behind the temple stands the small **palace** which was the original home of the Kachchwaha rulers before the construction of Amber palace proper.

The town is also home to an excellent new **Anokhi Museum of Hand Printing** (Tues–Sat 10.30am—5pm, Sun 11am–4.30pm; closed May to mid-July; Rs30, camera Rs50, video Rs150; Ⓦwww.anokhimuseum.com) at Kheri Gate, a ten-minute walk from the fort. Housed in the attractive old Anokhi Haveli, the museum has an interesting collection of hand block-printed textiles and garments, along with live demonstrations of printing and carving by two resident craftsmen.

Samode

Hidden among the scrubby Aravalli Hills, **SAMODE**, on the edge of Shekhawati, is notable for its impeccably restored eighteenth-century **palace**, now an award-winning heritage hotel, the *Samode Palace* (Ⓣ01423/240014, Ⓦwww.samode.com; from around US$300; rates drop by 30 percent May–Sept; ❾). It's possible to come here on a day-trip from Jaipur, 42km southeast, but if your budget can stretch to it, spend a night in one of the palace's uncompromisingly romantic rooms, plastered with murals and filled with antiques and ornate stonework. Non-guests have to shell out a hefty Rs500 (recoverable against food and drink inside) to visit, but it's worth it just to see the beautiful **Sheesh Mahal** on the south side of the building. Three hundred steps lead up from the palace to a hilltop **fort**, with impressive views over the surrounding countryside.

The owners of the hotel also have fifty richly appointed tents, 3km southeast of Samode at *Samode Bagh* (around $200 per double tent; ❾), with their own swimming pool.

Sanganer

SANGANER, 16km south of Jaipur, is the busiest centre for handmade **textiles** in the region, and the best place to watch traditional block printers in action (much of what's on offer can be bought in Jaipur). There are a couple of large factories here, but most of the printing is done in family homes as a cottage industry. Sanganeri craftsmen and -women also decorate **pottery** in Rajasthan's distinctive style – floral designs in white or deep sea-green on a traditional inky-blue glaze. Within the town itself, there are ruined palaces and a handful of elegant Jain **temples**, most notably the Shri Digamber temple near the Tripolia Gate.

Minibuses, buses and *tempos* for Sanganer (including *tempos* #11 and #55 and buses #210 and #404) leave from various places in Jaipur including Chand Pole, the railway station and Ajmeri Gate. Services run roughly every ten to fifteen minutes.

North of Jaipur: Shekhawati

North of Jaipur, small sand-blown towns nestle between sprawling expanses of parched land and dunes at the easternmost edges of the Thar Desert. Known as **Shekhawati**, this region lay on an important caravan route connecting Delhi and Sind (now in Pakistan) with the Gujarati coast. Having grown rich on trade and taxes from the through traffic, the merchant Marwari and landowning thakur castes of its small market towns spent their fortunes competing with each other to build grand, ostentatiously decorated **havelis** (see box, p.174). Many have survived, and now collectively comprise one of Rajasthan's most unusual artistic and architectural legacies: an incredible concentration of mansions, palaces and cenotaphs plastered inside and out with elaborate and colourful **murals**, executed between the 1770s and the 1930s.

Shekhawati is crossed by a mainline railway, but services are hopelessly slow and inconvenient, and you're better off travelling by bus. Fairly regular local buses, always overcrowded, connect Shekhawati's main towns; Jeeps also shuttle between towns and villages around the region, picking up as many passengers as they can cram in. Alternatively, it's possible to hire your own Jeep or taxi through most of the region's hotels and guesthouses.

Some history

Shekhawati's history is an unusual blend of Muslim and Rajput influences. The district's major town, **Jhunjhunu** was ruled first by the Rajput Chauhans of Ajmer until 1450, when it was taken over by Muslim nawabs of the Khaimkani clan, who also gained control of nearby **Fatehpur**. The Khaimkanis ruled for almost three centuries and parts of Jhunjhunu, in particular, still retain a distinctly Islamic flavour. At about the same time that the Khaimkanis were taking possession of Jhunjhunu, **Rao Shekhaji** (1433–1488), a grandson of the Kachchwaha maharaja of Amber, was carving out his own small kingdom in the region, named **Shekhawati**. Muslim Jhunjhunu was incorporated into Rajput Shekhawati in 1730 when **Sardul Singh** took over Jhunjhunu following the death of the last nawab. Two years later he consolidated Shekhawat rule by helping his brother to seize Fatehpur from its Muslim ruler.

Shekhawati is best known, however, for its **Marwari merchants**, who were responsible for the magnificent havelis that adorn every town in the region. Even though many of the Marwaris subsequently moved to Bombay, Madras and, especially, Calcutta, they continued to send their earnings back to Shekhawati. Following independence, a number of Marwaris bought British industries, and Marwari families such as Birla and Poddar remain prominent in business today. Many merchant families now live outside the region, with the result that their old mansions have been allowed to fall into a state of disrepair, though renewed tourist interest in the region's heritage has encouraged some owners to embark on much-needed restoration work. Considering the wealth of traditional art here, and the region's proximity to Jaipur, however, most of Shekhawati still feels surprisingly far off the tourist trail.

Nawalgarh

At the centre of Shekhawati, surrounded by desert and *khejri* scrub, the lively little market town of **NAWALGARH** – along with nearby Mandawa – makes the most convenient and congenial base for exploring Shekhawati, with a bumper crop of painted havelis and a picturesque bazaar, along with good transport connections and a decent range of accommodation.

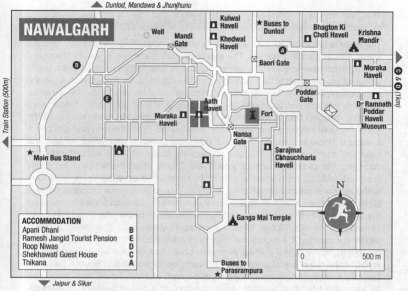

NAWALGARH

Dunlod, Mandawa & Jhunjhunu

Train Station (500m)

Well
Mandi Gate

Kulwal Haveli
Khedwal Haveli

Buses to Dunlod

Bhagton Ki Choti Haveli
Krishna Mandir

Baori Gate

Moraka Haveli

C & D (1km)

Aath Haveli

Muraka Haveli

Poddar Gate

Dr Ramnath Poddar Haveli Museum

Fort

Nansa Gate

Surajmal Chhauchharia Haveli

Main Bus Stand

N

Ganga Mai Temple

ACCOMMODATION

Apani Dhani	B
Ramesh Jangid Tourist Pension	E
Roop Niwas	D
Shekhawati Guest House	C
Thikana	A

0   500 m

Buses to Parasrampura

Jaipur & Sikar

Arrival and information

Nawalgarh's **bus** and **Jeep** stand, about 2km west of town, is served by buses from Jhunjhunu (every 30min; 1hr) via Dunlod (15min), Mandawa (every 30min; 45min); and Ajmer (daily at 10am; 5hr). Travelling on to **Jaipur** there are RSRTC buses every 15min (3hr 30min) and a deluxe bus service at 8am; there are also some private buses, though these drop passengers 5km outside the centre of Jaipur. Hourly buses run to Delhi (8hr) in the morning. The **train station** is a further kilometre west from the bus stand, but the only remotely useful service is the daily train to Jaipur at 6.06am (arrives 10.20am).

For trips around the region, you can either jump on and off cheap, cramped village-to-village **Jeeps** or rent a vehicle through *Apani Dhani* (see below) or the *Ramesh Jangid Tourist Pension* (see p.175). The owners of these two guesthouses also run socially responsible **tours** of Shekhawati (and the rest of Rajasthan and India; see Ⓦwww.apanidhani.com) including Jeep tours of nearby towns and other places of interest (Rs1500–2000), walking tours of Nawalgarh (Rs350 per person) and tours by camel cart (Rs1500/day). The *Roop Niwas* hotel (see p.175) can also arrange short excursions by camel (Rs400/hr) and horseback (Rs450/hr), and also runs more extended horse and camel safaris through the region – see Ⓦwww.royalridingholidays.com for full details. **Cycles** can be rented at *Apani Dhani* and the *Ramesh Jangid Tourist Pension* (Rs50 per day).

Accommodation and eating

Nawalgarh has a reasonable selection of **places to stay**, several of which also do good organic vegetarian home-cooking. There are no restaurants though, apart from the usual town-centre *dhabas*, and you'll almost certainly end up **eating** where you're staying.

Apani Dhani Northwest edge of town, on the main Jhunjhunu road ☎01594/222239, Ⓦwww.apanidhani.com. Occupying a fetching cluster of mud-walled Rajasthani village-style huts, this pretty little eco-resort offers an exemplary example of sustainable local tourism. Rooms (especially those in the slightly more expensive superior category) have plenty of rustic charm, and

The havelis of Shekhawati

The **havelis** (after the Persian word for "enclosed space") of Shekhawati typically follow a fairly standard pattern. The **entrance** from the street is usually through a grandly decorated gateway with carved doors; this is sometimes placed at the top of a large ramp, designed to be broad enough to be ridden up on an elephant, when the occasion required. Inside, most havelis consist of two main courtyards. As you enter, you step into the first courtyard, the **mardana**, or men's, courtyard; visitors were normally received here in the **baithak**, an open-sided meeting room, usually to the left of the main entrance and often finely embellished. From the *mardana* courtyard, a second doorway (usually the most richly decorated in the entire haveli, and generally surmounted by a figure of Ganesh) leads into the second principal courtyard, the **zenana**, or women's courtyard. This is where the ladies of the house lived in purdah, shielded from the eyes of the street, although a latticed window next to the *zenana* entrance allowed them to spy on proceedings in the *mardana*, while in some havelis there is also an upper storey above the *mardana* courtyard reserved for the use of women to observe proceedings in the *baithak* below. The *zenana* was also home to the haveli's kitchen, often recognizable by the areas of smoke-blackened plaster surrounding it. Although the majority of havelis consist of just these two main courtyards, some of the grander examples boast four or even six separate courtyards, while there are also occasional examples of so-called **"double havelis"**, basically two separate havelis joined together, each of which would have been used by two related families, typically those belonging to a pair of brothers. In addition, many also have a subsidiary courtyard to one side which was used for stabling animals – horses, camels or even elephants.

Murals

The flamboyant **murals** that characteristically cover both the interior and exterior walls of Shekhawati's havelis typically include a mix of religious and secular themes. Religious subjects, especially episodes from the life of **Krishna**, were often depicted along the lintels above the main exterior doors to cultivate faith among the uneducated masses, as well as on walls inside the havelis. What sets the murals of Shekhawati apart from those elsewhere in India, however, are not their religious paintings but the incongruous and often charmingly naive depictions of contemporary machines, fashions and outlandish foreigners, from pictures of early aeroplanes, steam trains and boats to Edwardian memsahibs in big hats. Quaintly old-fashioned now, at the time when they were painted these exotic images represented everything that was most modern and exotic about the outside world, one which the women and poor townsfolk of Shekhawati had no hope of ever seeing with their own eyes (nor, for that matter, the artists themselves, most of whom had probably never seen the newfangled European novelties they were asked to depict). Nowadays, most of the murals are faded, defaced, covered with posters or even just whitewashed over, though in some ways this simply adds to their haunting appeal.

Visiting Shekhawati's havelis

A small number of havelis have now been restored and opened as museums. Most, however, remain in a state of picturesque dilapidation and are still occupied by local families, while others have been abandoned, and are now empty apart from a solitary **chowkidar** (caretaker-cum-guard). Visitors are welcome to look around inside some havelis in return for a small tip (Rs10–20 is sufficient), while others remain closed to outsiders. If in doubt just stick your head in the front door and ask, but remember that you're effectively entering someone's private home, and never go in without permission.

there's excellent organic food, tie-dye and cookery classes, plus tours (see p.173). Book ahead. ❹

Ramesh Jangid Tourist Pension On the western edge of town, just north of Maur Hospital ☎01594/224060, ⊛www.apanidhani.com. Homely guesthouse offering simple but spotless and good-value rooms in a sociable Brahmin family home; the more expensive rooms have solar-heated water and beautiful murals. There's also excellent pure-veg food, Internet access, Jeep tours, plus tie-dye, cooking and Hindi classes. ❸–❹

Roop Niwas 1km east of the town centre ☎01594/222008, ⊛www.roopniwaskothi.com. This rambling Raj-era hotel is Nawalgarh's closest thing to an upscale resort, with old-fashioned rooms and a certain faded elegance – although beds can be a bit hard. Horse- and camel-riding tours can be arranged (see p.173). ❼–❽

Shekhawati Guest House 1km east of the town centre, 200m south of the *Roop Niwas* ☎01594/224658, ⊛www.shekhawatirestaurant .com. Friendly family guesthouse offering accommodation either in the clean but somewhat gloomy rooms in the main house or in the slightly fancier garden cottages. Fresh organic produce is used in the superb food (veg and non-veg), and guests also get free cookery lessons. ❹

Thikana 100m west of the Bhagton ki Haveli ☎01594/222152, ✉heritagethikana@rediffmail .com. Pleasant hotel in the heart of town, with friendly female management and lovely views from the upstairs terrace. It's a nice enough spot, though the slightly chintzy pink modern building doesn't really live up to its billing as a so-called "heritage" hotel. ❹–❺

The Town

The logical place to start a tour of Nawalgarh is on the east side of town at the magnificent Anandi Lal Poddar Haveli, which now houses the **Dr Ramnath A. Poddar Haveli Museum** (daily 8.30am–5.30pm; Rs85, camera Rs30). Built in 1920 and now doubling up as a school, this is one of the few havelis in Shekhawati to have been restored to its original glory, and boasts the most vivid murals in town. These include the usual scenes from the life of Krishna along with more modern subjects including steam trains and soldiers drilling with rifles, plus a clever 3D-like panel of a bull's head that transmogrifies into an elephant's as you move from left to right. The haveli also houses a mildly diverting series of **exhibits** showcasing various aspects of Rajasthani life.

A short walk to the north lies the fine **Moraka Haveli** (daily 8am–6.30pm, winter until 7.30pm; Rs40), whose principal courtyard boasts murals of Shiva, Parvati and Krishna and a *baithak* complete with a fine old hand-pulled fan (*punkah*). The beautiful second courtyard is decorated with friezes showing scenes from the Ramayana and other pictures from Hindu mythology around the top of its arches. Directly opposite the Moraka Haveli lies the eye-catching **Krishna Mandir**, dating from the mid-eighteenth century, a florid mass of delicate chhatris.

About 200m east of the Moraka Haveli, the unrestored, 150-year-old **Bhagton ki Choti Haveli** (no set hours, though the resident chowkidar can usually be found sitting on the doorstep waiting for visitors; Rs40) boasts an unusually varied selection of murals including a European-style angel and Queen Victoria (over the arches by the right of the main door) along with Krishna and Radha on a swing. On the left, a *trompe-l'oeil* picture shows seven women in the shape of an elephant, while other pictures show Europeans riding bicycles along with a steamboat and a train.

A further fine pair of havelis lie west of here, side by side, due north of the Nansa Gate. The first, the **Khedwal Haveli**, is still inhabited and can usually only be viewed from the outside; look through the main entrance and you can catch a glimpse of the lovely mirrorwork (plus train) on the upper storey of the main courtyard. A few metres north, the **Kulwal Haveli** is also inhabited, though open for visitors on payment of a small baksheesh. Pictures of Gandhi and Nehru adorn the entrance porch, while a European woman sits above the main door applying her lipstick.

The fort and eastern havelis

Central Nawalgarh has plenty of old-fashioned, small-town charm, with dozens of tiny shops and lots of street vendors hawking piles of merchandise. At the heart of the town, the **fort** (Bala Qila) has more or less vanished under a clutch of modern buildings huddled around a central courtyard which now hosts the town's colourful vegetable market. The dilapidated building on the far left-hand side of the courtyard (by the Bank of Baroda) boasts a magnificent, eerily echoing **Sheesh Mahal**, covered in mirrorwork, which once served as the dressing room of the maharani of Nawalgarh, its ceiling decorated with pictorial maps of Nawalgarh and Jaipur. You'll have to pay the usual Rs10–20 baksheesh to see the room; if no one's around, ask at the sweet factory on the opposite side of the courtyard.

The havelis on the eastern side of Nawalgarh are less striking than those on the west, though this part of town is generally more peaceful. Heading west through the Nansa Gate (signed, confusingly, as the "Rambilas Podar Memorial Gate") and following the road around brings you to the so-called Aath Haveli (Eight Havelis, built by eight brothers, although only six were actually completed), a complex of heavily decorated mansions featuring murals in a range of styles depicting the usual mishmash of subjects both ancient and modern. The Muraka Haveli, opposite, also boasts a richly painted exterior, with elephants, horses and a pair of fine blue carriages, plus miniatures showing scenes from the life of Krishna, framed in a mass of florid decoration.

Further havelis dot the streets south and southeast of the Nansa Gate, one of the quietest and most atmospheric parts of town. These include the Surajmal Chhauchharia Haveli, whose murals include a picture of Europeans floating past in a hot-air balloon. The painter took some playful licence as to the mechanics involved: the two passengers blow into the balloon to power their journey.

Dunlod and Parasrampura

The most obvious target for a day-trip from Nawalgarh is **DUNLOD**, 7km north and the site of an old fort and some large havelis. It's possible to get there by bus, but most people walk across the fields – a leisurely two-hour amble that's enjoyable save for the last couple of kilometres along the track linking the village with the main road, which you'll have to share with a small amount of passing traffic. The musty old **fort** (Rs20) is worth a quick visit for its atmospheric Diwan-i-Khana, a fine old drawing room painted a vivid orange and filled with antique European furniture and books. The fort has been converted into a hotel, the *Dunlod Castle* (☎01594/252519 or 0141/221 1276, ⒲www.dundlod.com; ❼), though the rather shabby and tackily restored rooms lack the atmosphere of those at Mandawa and Mahansar. Radiating from the southeastern walls of the fort, the **village** harbours several interesting havelis, painted around the start of the twentieth century, and the delicate chhatri of Ram Dutt Goenka, a cenotaph erected in 1888 with vibrant friezes lining its dome.

More painted buildings are dotted around the serene hamlet of **PARAS-RAMPURA**, 20km southeast of Nawalgarh, set amid rolling hills dotted with janti trees that makes for some of the most attractive desert scenery in Rajasthan. Buses run every thirty minutes or so, or you could cycle (although be warned that several stretches of the track degenerate into soft sand). Monuments include the **Gopinath temple**, built in 1742, whose murals depict the torments of hell alongside images of the famous local Rajput ruler,

Sardul Singh, with his five sons. Some of the paintings are unfinished, as the artists were diverted to decorate the chhatri of Rajul Singh, who died that same year. The large dome of his exquisite **cenotaph** contains a flourish of lively and well-preserved murals, once again including images of hell, and of Sardul Singh with his sons. Parasrampura's modest **fort** in reasonable repair, is on the west bank of the dry riverbed.

Jhunjhunu

Spreading in a mass of brick and concrete from the base of a rocky hill, **JHUNJHUNU** is a busy and fairly unprepossessing town, though it preserves an interesting old central bazaar and a fine collection of havelis decorated with vigorous murals. Jhunjhunu is usually visited as a day-trip from nearby Nawalgarh or Mandawa, though it has a few good accommodation options if you want to stay.

Arrival and information

Buses from the government stand in the south of town run to Nawalgarh (every 30min; 1hr) and towns throughout Shekhawati, as well as to Bikaner (hourly; 5hr 30min), Jaipur (every 30min; 4hr–4hr 30min) and Delhi (hourly; 7hr 30min). Buses to Mandawa (every 30min; 45min) also stop briefly on Mandawa Circle near the RTDC *Tourist Bungalow*.

There's a **Tourist Reception Centre** (Mon–Sat 10am–5pm, closed every second Sat; ℡01592/232909) by the RTDC *Tourist Bungalow* on Mandawa Circle at the western edge of town. Jhunjhunu is quite spread out and walking around can be tiring; **rickshaws** operate as taxis, picking up as many passengers as they can. **Taxis** gather at a rank outside the government bus stand, charging around Rs4 per kilometre. Laxmi Jangid, the owner of the *Jamuna Resort* (see below), offers full-day **tours** around Shekhawati by car or Jeep for Rs2000, as well as shorter camel tours (2hr; Rs600 per person).

Accommodation and eating

The following are the best of Jhunjhunu's limited supply of **accommodation** options. There are no good restaurants in town, and you'll almost certainly end up **eating** where you're staying, unless you fancy braving one of the down-at-heel *dhabas* around the government bus stand.

Jhunjhunu

Fresco Palace Paramveer Path, off Station Rd ℡01592/395233. Neat modern hotel with comfortable, slightly chintzy rooms, all with a/c and TV, and a relaxing garden restaurant. The *Hotel Shekhawati Heritage* next door is similarly priced though less attractive. ❺

Jamuna Resort Delhi–Sikar Rd ℡01592/232871, ⓦwww.shivshekhawati.com. This lovely village-style resort on the eastern edge of town comprises a cluster of thatch-roofed cottages (all with a/c and TV) set amid extensive grounds complete with pool and garden restaurant. The more expensive rooms are exquisitely decorated with mirrorwork and traditional murals. They also run courses in Indian cooking and art, plus free yoga classes. Also a good place to arrange tours. ❹–❼

Sangam Paramveer Path, opposite the government bus stand ℡01592/232544. Basic cheapie with large but bare and slightly shabby rooms – make sure you get one away from the noisy main road. ❷–❸

Shiv Shekhawati Khemi Shakti Rd, near Muni Ashram ℡01592/232651 or 32651, ⓦwww .shivshekhawati.com. Well-maintained modern sister hotel to *Jamuna Resort* with large, clean rooms (all with a/c and TV), restaurant and Internet access. ❹–❺

Around Jhunjhunu

Alsisar Mahal Alsisar Village, 15km north of Jhunjhunu ℡01595/275271, ⓦwww.alsisar.com. The ancestral home of the thakurs of Alsisar, this grand old fort has recently been spruced up and reopened as a luxurious hotel, complete with spotless traditional-style rooms, lofty courtyards and a good-sized swimming pool. Good value. ❽ **Piramal Haveli** Bagar Village, 15km northeast of Jhunjhunu ☎ 01592/221220, ⊛ www.neemrana hotels.com. Intimate, self-styled "non-hotel" with just eight rooms in an unusual 1920s Rajasthani-cum-Italianate villa set in a peaceful rural location well away from the hustle and bustle of Jhunjhunu. Rooms are simple but comfortable, and there's a lovely garden. ❻–❼, with 20–40% discounts from May to Aug.

The Town

Hidden away in the alleyways behind the main bazaar is Jhunjhunu's most striking building, the magnificent **Khetri Mahal** of 1760 (entrance Rs20), a superb, open-sided sandstone palace with cusped Islamic-style arches which wouldn't look out of place amidst the great Indo-Islamic monuments of Fatehpur Sikri. The whole edifice seems incongruously grand amidst the modest streets of central Jhunjhunu, but now stands empty. A covered ramp, wide enough for horses, winds up to the roof, from where there are sweeping views over the town and across to the massive ramparts of the sturdy **Badalgarh Fort** (currently closed to the public) on a nearby hilltop.

Stretching east of the Khetri Mahal is Jhunjhunu's main bazaar, centred around **Futala Market**, a fascinating (and hopelessly confusing) tangle of narrow streets crammed with dozens of tiny, charmingly old-fashioned shops painted in pastel greens and blues, many of them owned by the town's sizeable Muslim population. On the northern edge of the bazaar, facing each other across the small square of Chabutra Chowk, lie the two so-called **Modi havelis**, boasting the usual range of murals – the one on the eastern side of the *chowk* is the most impressive, entered via a grand, three-metre-high ramp (a common feature of havelis in Jhunjhunu).

Along Nehru Bazaar

Jhunjhunu's finest havelis are spread out along **Nehru Bazaar**, immediately east of the main bazaar. Heading east, you'll first reach the striking **Kaniram Narsinghdas Tibrewala Haveli** of 1883, perched on a platform above the surrounding vegetable stalls and sporting a fine selection of paintings inside (the entrance is around the back). Further east down Nehru Bazaar, the **Mohanlal Ishwardas Modi Haveli** has a good selection of entertainingly naive portrait murals. Unusual oval miniatures of various Indian notables frame the entrance to the *zenana* courtyard, whose arches are topped by a quaint selection of portraits showing assorted European and Indian personages sporting a range of flouncy costumes, silly hats and magnificent moustaches. Immediately north of here, the striking little **Bihari temple** features some of the oldest murals in Shekhawati, painted in 1776 in black and brown vegetable pigments, including a dramatic depiction inside the central dome of the scene from the Ramayana in which Hanuman's monkey army takes on the forces of the many-headed demon king Ravana.

Outlying sights

West of the Khetri Mahal at the foot of the craggy Nehara Pahar lies the **Dargah of Kamaruddin Shah**, an atmospheric complex comprising a mosque and *madrasa* arranged around a pretty courtyard (still retaining some of its original murals), with the ornate *dargah* (tomb) of the Sufi saint Kamaruddin Shah in the centre.

North of the town centre lies the **Mertani Baori**, one of the region's most impressive step-wells, while further east is the extraordinary **Rani Sati Mandir**, dedicated to a merchant's wife who commited *sati* in 1595. The shrine is reputedly the richest temple in the country after Tirupati in Andhra Pradesh (although similar claims are made for the Nathdwara temple near Udaipur), receiving hundreds of thousands of pilgrims each year and millions of rupees in donations, its immense popularity bearing witness to the enduring awe with which *satis* are regarded in the state. Although banned by the British in 1829 in areas under their rule, the practice has survived in parts of rural Rajasthan; forty cases are known to have occurred since Independence, the most infamous being that of **Roop Kanwar**, an 18-year-old Rajput girl who committed *sati* in 1987 in the village of Deorala, near Jaipur, sparking off nationwide controversy.

Mandawa

Rising from a flat, featureless landscape roughly midway between Jhunjhunu and Fatehpur, **MANDAWA** was founded by the Shekhawats in 1755 and is now the most tourist-oriented place in Shekhawati, although the handicraft shops, touts and guides detract very little from the town's profusion of beautifully dilapidated mansions.

Arrival and information

Buses from Jhunjhunu (every 30min; 1hr) and Nawalgarh (every 30min; 45min), as well as Jaipur and Bikaner, stop at Sonthaliya Gate in the east of town. From Fatehpur, most buses pull in at a stand in the centre, just off the main bazaar. **Jeeps** ply the same routes. The town is so small that both bus stands are within walking distance of most hotels. There are various places along the main bazaar offering **Internet** access – try the Deshnok Money Changer (Rs50 per hour; open 24hr), opposite the *Mandawa Haveli* hotel; they also **change cash**, traveller's cheques and give cash advances against Visa and MasterCard.

Taking a **walking tour** to see Mandawa's havelis is recommended; guides can be arranged through your hotel, or at Classic Shekhawati Tours (℡01592/223144, ⓔclassicshekhamnd@yahoo.co.in), by the entrance to the fort (Rs200–250 for a 2–3hr walk). Most guesthouses and hotels can also arrange tours out into the surrounding desert either by Jeep or on horseback, camel-back or in camel-drawn carts. Prices for all these activities vary wildly, but are usually cheapest if booked through the *Hotel Shekhawati* (see p.180), who also run overnight camel safaris camping out in the desert. Classic Shekhawati Tours also arranges more upmarket day and overnight **camel safaris**, though you'll need to book five days in advance.

Accommodation and eating

Mandawa has the best selection of **hotels** in Shekhawati, although prices are quite steep, with only one real budget option. You'll probably **eat** at your hotel or guesthouse; meals at most places are served alongside tacky puppet shows and folk dancing. If you want to venture out, you could try the *Hotel Shekhawati* which has cheap and tasty food, along with plenty of cold beer, while the *Mandawa Haveli* serves up above-average buffets on its atmospheric rooftop terrace.

Castle Mandawa ℡01592/223124, ⓦwww .castlemandawa.com. Mandawa's fanciest accommodation, set in the old town fort, with an atmospheric mishmash of buildings around a sand-filled courtyard. All rooms are different, so look at several before you decide, since standards of comfort and decor vary considerably. Amenities include a spa, gym, pool (guests only) and spacious gardens. ❽–❾

The Desert Resort Mukandgarh Rd, 1.5km from Mandawa ℡01592/223151, ⓦwww.mandawa hotels.com. Just outside Mandawa, this attractively rustic – though surprisingly pricey – little resort occupies a tangle of mud-walled traditional village-style Rajasthani cottages in a soothingly peaceful rural setting. Cottages (all a/c) are nicely decorated, if a bit dark, and there's also a pool. ❽–❾

Heritage Mandawa Off Mukandgarh Rd south of the bus stand ☎01592/223742, ⓦwww .hotelheritagemandawa.com. Brightly painted, late nineteenth-century mansion with a/c rooms of varying standards, some of them absolutely covered in murals – nice enough, albeit relatively expensive. ⑤–⑦

Mandawa Haveli Near Sonthaliya Gate ☎01592/223088, ⓦhttp://hotelmandawa.free.fr. Occupying a superb old haveli, this place is rather more atmospheric and significantly better value

than the *Heritage Mandawa* nearby. Rooms (all a/c in summer) are quaint, although those downstairs are a bit dark; the upstairs suites are significantly brighter and more spacious. ⑥–⑧

Shekhawati Off Mukandgarh Rd south of the bus stand ☎0931469 8079, ⓔhotelshekwati@sify .com. Mandawa's only budget option – and fortunately it's very good, with spacious and spotless rooms (some with a/c and pretty murals) in an eye-catchingly painted house. There's also good food, Internet access, and cheap tours. ②–④

The Town

Tours usually begin with the **Naveti Haveli** (now the State Bank of Bikaner & Jaipur), on the main bazaar in the centre of town. Duck through the metal gate to the right of the bank (no charge) for a look at Mandawa's most entertaining wall of murals, including well-preserved images of a primitive flying machine, the Wright Brothers' aeroplane, a man using a telephone and a strongman pulling a car.

A ten-minute walk west from here brings you to an interesting cluster of buildings centred around the **Nand Lal Murmuria Haveli**. The murals here are relatively modern, dating from the 1930s and executed in a decidedly flowery and sentimental style, perhaps influenced by contemporary European magazines, with images of various Venetian scenes (the Grand Canal, Rialto and San Marco), along with George V, Nehru riding a horse and the legendary Maratha warrior Shivaji. Next door, the sun-faded **Goenka Double Haveli** (comprising the Vishwanath Goenka Haveli and Tarkeshwar Goenka Haveli – and not to be confused with either of the town's other Goenka havelis nearby) is one of the largest and grandest in Mandawa, with two separate entrances and striking elephants and horses on the facade. The **Thakurji temple** opposite has a rather odd mural (on the right-hand side of the facade) showing soldiers being fired from the mouths of cannon, a favoured British method of executing mutinous sepoys during the 1857 uprising.

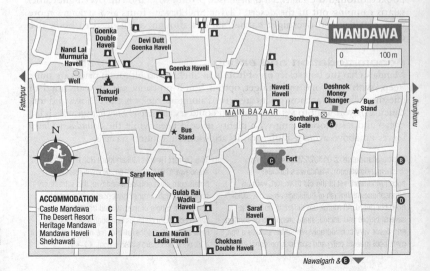

South of the main bazaar, the **Gulab Rai Wadia Haveli** is one of the finest in town. The south-facing exterior wall is particularly interesting, with unusually racy (albeit modestly small) murals depicting, amongst other things, a Kama Sutra–like scene in a railway carriage. The interior of the haveli is entered via a grand ramp, with Belgian-glass mirrorwork over the finely carved door leading into the *zenana* courtyard.

Immediately south of here lies the almost equally fine **Laxmi Narain Ladia Haveli**. The *zenana* courtyard boasts naive paintings of a plane and a steamship, along with a cannon being pulled by horses and a tiger attacking a centaur. Some 100m further south, the unusually large **Chokhani Double Haveli** (Rs10) consists of two separate wings built for two brothers; look for the miserable British soldiers and chillum-smoking sadhu facing one another in the recess at the centre of the facade.

Fatehpur

Lying just off NH-11, **FATEHPUR** is the closest town in Shekhawati to Bikaner, 116km west, and a convenient place to stop if you're taking the northern route across the Thar to or from Jaisalmer. The town itself is fairly run-down and its accommodation uninspiring, but it does boast several elaborately painted mansions.

The most celebrated of Fatehpur's havelis is the **Nadine Le Prince Haveli** (daily 8am–7pm; Rs100), an 1802 mansion restored to its original splendour by its current owner Nadine Le Prince, a French artist who purchased the haveli in 1998. Some local aficionados complain about the manner in which the haveli has been restored – with large-scale repainting of murals, rather than the simple cleaning and preservation of existing art – but the overall effect is undeniably impressive, and the haveli as a whole is one of the few in Shekhawati where you get a real sense of how these lavish mansions would originally have looked, complete with superbly carved wooden doors and beams and a dense array of murals.

Several further fine havelis lie clustered immediately around the Nadine Le Prince Haveli. Next door on the west side, the **Saraf Haveli** boasts fine exterior murals (albeit missing large chunks of plaster – a common sight in Fatehpur), while opposite lies the expansive **Devra Lal Haveli** (closed to visitors), fronted by an unusually elaborate sequence of arched porches, their undersides covered with well-preserved medallion portraits.

Northeast of the Nadine Le Prince Haveli, the imposing **Jagannath Singania Haveli** (also closed to visitors) towers over the main road. Most of the exterior paintings have faded, though there are still some fine paintings of elephants and other subjects on the smaller western facade around the back. South from here, the **Geori Shankar Haveli** (next to an unusually fine bangle stall) is the polar opposite of the Nadine Le Prince Haveli, dilapidated but hugely atmospheric, and still inhabited by a number of impoverished local families. There's fine mirrorwork in the ceiling of the main entrance arch and around the doorway into the *zenana* courtyard, plus fine religious paintings in the *mardana* courtyard.

Just east of here lies the small but exquisite **Mahavir Prasad Goenka Haveli** (not to be confused with a second and relatively uninteresting Goenka Haveli signposted from opposite the Geori Shankar Haveli), built in the mid-nineteenth century by a Jain merchant, Mahavir Prasad, and currently being restored. The inner courtyard is beautifully painted, and the first-floor room is dazzling, its walls and ceiling decorated in the finest detail with myriad colours, gold leaf and mirrors.

Practicalities

Fatehpur has two **bus stands**, near each other in the centre of town on the main Sikar–Churu (north–south) road. Buses from the government Roadways stand, furthest south, serve Jaipur (every 30min; 3hr 30min), Ramgarh (hourly; 30min), Bikaner (14 daily; 3hr 30min–4hr) and Delhi (5 daily; 6hr). Private buses run from the stand further north along the bazaar to Mandawa (every 30min; 45min), Jhunjhunu (every 30min; 1hr), Mahansar (4 daily; 45min) and Ramgarh (hourly; 30min). Arriving in Fatehpur, note that many buses drop passengers off at the NH-11 intersection, about 1km south of town.

Just off NH-11, the modern RTDC *Hotel Haveli* (℡01571/230293; ❸–❹) is the town's only plausible hotel, though its large and light rooms (some with a/c) don't quite compensate for the dodgy plumbing and general air of neglect. For **food**, you've a less than inspiring choice between the RTDC *Hotel Haveli*'s hit-and-miss overpriced menu, or the row of basic *dhabas* near the bus stand.

Mahansar, Ramgarh and Lakshmangarh

Some of the most outstanding murals and Hindu monuments in the region are scattered across three small towns in the far north and west of Shekhawati: **Mahansar**, **Ramgarh** and **Lakshmangarh**. Only Mahansar has any accommodation, but you can reach the other two on day-trips from Fatehpur, Mandawa or Nawalgarh. The easiest way to visit them is to hire your own vehicle, although they can also be reached, albeit a lot more slowly, on inter-village Jeeps and occasional buses – ask at your hotel or guesthouse about local transport connections.

Mahansar

The relative inaccessibility of **MAHANSAR**, marooned amid a sea of scrub and drifting sand 27km northeast of Fatehpur, has ensured that its attractions rank among the least visited in the region. A ribbon of hopelessly potholed tarmac leads out here from Mandawa, and another runs due west to Ramgarh, but aside from sporadic buses, the only traffic along them are camel carts and herds of goats, making Mahansar a peaceful place to hole up for a day or two.

Another reason to come is to **stay** at the quirky *Narayan Niwas Castle* (℡01595/264322; ❺), a destination in itself. Managed by Mahansar's royal family in their crumbling 1768 abode, it consists of twelve rooms of varying standards (#1 is the most romantic). It's a more informal establishment than other heritage hotels in the area, but this lends it a certain charm – and affordability. Be sure to peruse the family heirlooms and sample the royal moonshine. The food is excellent, too.

Mahansar's most beautiful murals are locked away out of sight in the **Sona Ki Dukan Haveli**, next to the main crossroads (ask around the shops for the key). The ceiling of the entrance hall to this mansion is exquisitely decorated with painted and richly gilded scenes from the Ramayana and Jayaveda's classic twelfth-century life of Krishna, the *Gita Govinda*, though you'll need a torch to fully appreciate the colours and mass of detail. The *Narayan Niwas* can arrange tours.

Ramgarh

RAMGARH, 20km north of Fatehpur, was founded in 1791 and developed as something of a status symbol by disaffected members of the wealthy Poddar merchant family, who made every effort for the town to outshine nearby Churu, which they left following a dispute with the local thakur over the wool tax. They succeeded in their aim: Ramgarh is one of the most beautiful – but also one of the least-visited – towns in Shekhawati, with the usual fine havelis along with an exceptional array of religious architecture as well.

Starting from the bus stand on the west side of town, follow either of the two roads east into the town centre. After about five minutes' walk you'll reach the **Poddar family havelis**, a superb cluster of ornate mansions that cover the entire area immediately west of the main town square. The streets here form one of the most architecturally perfect ensembles in Shekhawati, the havelis' patrician ochre facades decorated with scenes from local folk stories and a frequently repeated motif, comprising three fishes joined at the mouth, which is unique to Ramgarh.

Just beyond here lies the town's main square, surrounded by the disintegrating remains of further lavishly painted havelis. Turn left here and head through the Churu Gate, beyond which the road is lined with a dense cluster of extraordinarily ornate **temples and chhatris** erected by various members of the Poddar clan, all fantastically domed and pavilioned, while many also sport the remains of elaborate murals. Walking along the road you'll pass (on your right) the Ganga Temple (with two fine elephant statues flanking either side of entrance steps) followed by (on your left) the Hanuman and Ganesh temples (the latter with a richly painted forecourt). These are followed by a number of elaborate chhatris erected to commemorate assorted Poddar notables, and the diminutive Shani Mandir (dedicated to Saturn), decorated with elaborate mirrorwork.

Lakshmangarh

The small town of **LAKSHMANGARH**, 20km south of Fatehpur, is another archetypal, but seldom visited, Shekhawati destination, its neat grid of streets (a layout inspired by that of Jaipur's Pink City) dotted with dozens of ornate havelis, virtually all of them in various stages of picturesque decay. The town is dominated by its dramatic nineteenth-century **fort**, which crowns a rocky outcrop on the west side of town; it's now closed to the public, though you can walk up the steep track to the entrance to enjoy the fine views over town. Looking down from here you can also see the extensive **Char Chowk Haveli** (Four-Courtyard Haveli), off to the left, the finest in town and one of the largest in Shekhawati. Most of the haveli's exterior paintings have faded, although the paintings under the eaves remain well preserved. The haveli remains inhabited, and the interior is generally off-limits to visitors.

Walk east from here past the attractive Radha Murlimanohar Temple to reach the nearly derelict **Sanganeeria Haveli**, whose entertaining murals include a Ferris wheel, a pair of wrestlers and a lady on a swing. There are several other fine havelis along this street. Just south of here, opposite the Oriental Bank of Commerce, the **Chokhani Haveli** sports a particularly fine and colourful crop of animals, as well as rifle-wielding soldiers on horseback and a picture of Dhola and Maru shooting a bow and arrow from the back of a camel.

Head south to reach the town's clock tower, the centre of a lively little vegetable market. There's a further crop of interesting havelis in the sandy backstreets southeast of here, including a particularly fine (though apparently nameless) haveli two blocks east and one block south of the clock tower, with well-preserved murals showing Krishna being driven to his wedding in a bullock cart by Hanuman next to a fine European carriage with two musket-wielding soldiers.

East of Jaipur

The fertile area **east of Jaipur**, interspersed with the forested slopes of the
Aravalli Hills, holds an inviting mixture of historic towns and wildlife sanctuaries. To the northeast is the fortified town of **Alwar**, jumping-off point for the
Sariska Tiger Reserve and National Park. Further east are the former
princely capitals of **Deeg** and **Bharatpur**, and India's finest bird sanctuary,
Keoladeo National Park, worth a visit even for novice birders. The wildlife
sanctuary at **Ranthambore**, in idyllic scenery southeast of Jaipur, offers the best
chance in India of spotting wild tigers.

Alwar

Roughly 140km northeast from Jaipur towards Delhi, the large, bustling town
of **ALWAR** sprawls across a valley beneath one of eastern Rajasthan's larger
and more impressive **forts**, whose massive ramparts straggle impressively
along craggy ridges above. Traditionally the northern gateway to Rajasthan,
Alwar's strategic position on the Rajput border resulted in incessant warfare
from the tenth to the seventeenth centuries between the Jats of Bharatpur and
the Kachchwahas of Amber. Jai Singh, the flamboyant and eccentric great-
grandfather of the present maharaja, became notorious during the British era
for his outrageous behaviour. Official reports from the 1930s describe various
instances of maharajal madness, including Jai Singh's habit of burying his
luxury Hispano-Suiza cars once he had tired of them and the occasion on
which he doused his favourite polo pony in petrol and set fire to it; rumours
also circulated suggesting a predilection for young boys.

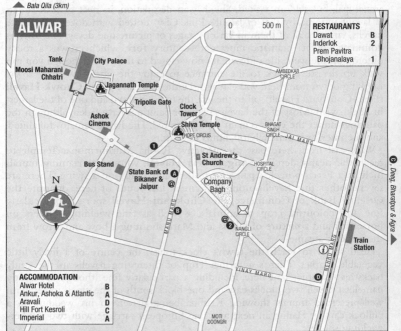

Arrival and information

Alwar's **bus stand** is conveniently located in the middle of town; the **railway station** is around 1.5km east of the centre. Note that there are hardly any auto-rickshaws in town, though cycle rickshaws are plentiful.

The **tourist office** (Mon–Sat 10am–5pm; ☎0144/234 7348) is just south of the station; staff here can arrange transport (they charge Rs1000 for a full-day tour to Sariska). You can **change currency** and traveller's cheques at the State Bank of Bikaner & Jaipur, in the centre of town. There are a couple of **ATMs** a few doors east from here operated by ICICI and Dena banks. For **Internet** access, try the well-equipped Cyberland (daily 8am–8pm; Rs20/hr) on the south side of Company Bagh, or Manish Cyber on Manu Marg (daily 8.30am–10pm; Rs20/hr).

Accommodation

Alwar

Alwar Hotel 26 Manu Marg ☎0144/270 0012, @ukrustagi@rediffmail.com. This trim little mid-range hotel is easily the nicest place to stay in Alwar itself, with smart and spacious a/c rooms set around a neat garden. The in-house *Dawat* restaurant (see p.186) is another major bonus. ⑤–⑥
Ankur, Ashoka, Atlantic and **Imperial** hotels. Clustered together on the corner of Manu Marg, a 5min walk from the bus station, this group of four adjacent and more or less indistinguishable hotels offers a range of simple but cheap, tolerably clean and reasonably comfortable fan and a/c rooms, and there are always plenty of vacancies. ①–④
Aravali Just south of the railway station on Nehru Marg ☎0144/233 2883. The town's only plausible budget alternative to the *Ankur* group of hotels. It's definitely seen better days, and the wide variety of rooms (fan, air-cooled and a/c) are all rather run-down, though reasonably clean. There's also a bar, Internet access, and a pool (guests only) in summer. ②–⑦

Around Alwar

Amanbagh Ajabgarh around 50km from Alwar ☎01465/223333, @www.amanresorts.com One of the most alluring boltholes in Rajasthan, set in a verdant oasis in a remote corner of the Aravalli Hills. The resort has all the style you'd expect at the price (room rates from US$720), set in a lavish contemporary re-creation of a Mughal-style palace. There's also a gorgeous spa. ⑨
Hill Fort Kesroli 12km east of Alwar ☎01468/289352, @www.neemranahotels.com. India's oldest heritage hotel, occupying a rugged old fifteenth-century fort impeccably restored and centred on a lush inner courtyard filled with plants and birds. Rooms are pleasantly rustic and have great views over Kesroli village and the surrounding countryside. ⑦–⑨

The Town

Alwar's principal attraction is its rambling and atmospheric **City Palace**, or Vinai Vilas Mahal, a sprawling complex of ornate but now decidedly dilapidated buildings, covered in crumbling ochre plaster and studded with endless canopied balconies. Construction of the palace began under Bhaktawar Singh, Pratap Singh's successor, though most of the palace's innumerable rooms are now put to more mundane use as government offices – their dimly lit interiors piled high with musty mounds of official documents – while the courtyard in front provides open-air office space for dozens of typists, lined up behind clanking old antique metal machines, and lawyers, who prosecute their business under the trees. The palace's **museum** (daily except Fri 10am–4.30pm; Rs3), on the top floor of the palace, houses a haphazard collection of objects belonging to former maharajas including musical instruments, miniature paintings, weapons and stuffed animals.

Go up the steps at the left-hand end of the main facade to reach the large **tank** which bounds this end of the palace, a beautiful spot, overlooked on one side by the palace's delicate balconies, and flanked by symmetrical *ghats* and pavilions. On the terrace overlooking the tank stands the **Moosi Maharani**

Chhatri, built in memory of Bhaktawar Singh's mistress, who immolated herself on his funeral pyre. Steps lead up (take off your shoes) to the ornate marble monument, at the centre of which the former maharaja and his mistress are represented by two pairs of marble feet, strewn with flower petals.

Bala Qila

Perched high above Alwar is **Bala Qila** fort (Mon–Fri 10am–5pm; free), whose well-preserved walls climb dramatically up and down the thickly wooded hillsides that rise above the town. There's not much actually to see inside the fort – besides a temple and a few old cannons – but it's a pleasant walk up from town, with fine views and fresh hill breezes. It takes about two hours to make the return trip on foot up to the fort's outermost gate, or about twice that to reach the topmost point of the fortifications. If you don't want to walk, you'll have to arrange for a taxi through your hotel or the tourist office – the road up is far too steep for a cycle rickshaw to tackle.

Eating

Alwar is famous throughout Rajasthan for its cavity-causing **milk cakes**, which you can buy at the stalls around Hope Circus.

Dawat Hotel Alwar, Manu Marg. This reliable little a/c restaurant serves up a good range of north Indian dishes at moderate prices, plus better-than-average Chinese food. They should also have a beer licence by the time you read this. Most mains Rs55–100.
Inderlok Near Nangli Circle. Unpretentious a/c veg restaurant, popular with locals, serving up good North and south Indian standards along with a few Chinese dishes. Mains Rs50–80.

Prem Pavitra Bhojanalya Near Hope Circus. This cosy little restaurant dishes up the best food in town, with a very short, very cheap menu of basic north Indian standards (all mains under Rs40). The entrance is easily missed: go up the road roughly opposite the State Bank of Jaipur & Bikaner, past the petrol station. It's on the left about 50m up.

Moving on from Alwar

From Alwar, there are **bus** services to Bharatpur via Deeg (every 15min; 4hr), Sariska (every 30min; 1hr–1hr 30min), Delhi (every 30min; 5hr) and Jaipur (hourly; 4hr). **Trains** run to and from Delhi, Jaipur, Jodhpur, Ajmer and Ahmedabad (but not Bharatpur). For Jaipur, the best service is the Ajmer Shatabdi (#2015; daily except Wed; dep. 8.37am, arr. 10.45am); for Delhi, the Jaisalmer–Delhi Express (#4060; daily; dep. 07.37am, arr. 11.10am) and the Ajmer Shatabdi (#2016; daily except Wed; dep. 7.28pm, arr. 10.45pm) are two of the faster services.

Sariska Tiger Reserve and around

Alwar is the access point for **Sariska Tiger Reserve and National Park**, a former maharaja's hunting ground managed since 1979 by Project Tiger. Accustomed to being overshadowed by the more famous Ranthambore, Sariska was unwittingly thrust into the headlines in 2005 when it was discovered that its tiger population, estimated at around 28 in 2003, had all but vanished. Prime Minister Manmohan Singh ordered a high-profile police investigation following rumours that a famed taxidermist, in collusion with corrupt wardens, had orchestrated a mass poisoning. Regardless of where blame lies, activists see the decimation of Sariska's tiger population as one of India's biggest conservation scandals.

One silver lining from the whole affair is that the number of visitors to the sanctuary has dwindled significantly, and for birders and wildlife enthusiasts put off by the crowds and hassle of Ranthambore, Sariska's relative serenity comes as a welcome relief. The 881-square-kilometre sanctuary encompasses acres of woodland that are home to abundant **wildlife** including *sambar*, *chital*, wild boar, nilgai and other antelopes, jackals, mongooses, monkeys, peacocks, porcupines, and numerous birds. The park is also dotted with a number of evocative ruins and other man-made structures, including the old **Kankwari Fort**, and a **Hanuman temple** deep within the park that gets surprisingly lively on Saturdays and Tuesdays, when visitors to the temple are allowed into the park for free.

Practicalities

Sariska is **open** daily (July to mid-Sept 8am–3pm; April–June & mid-Sept to Oct 6am–4pm; Nov–March 7am–3.30pm). The park lies 35km southwest of Alwar on the main Alwar–Jaipur road; express **buses** between the two stop briefly to drop off and pick up passengers, on request, at the *Sariska Palace* hotel, a five-minute walk from the park. **Taxis** to the park can be booked through the tourist office in Alwar (see p.185) and cost Rs500 for a half-day trip, or Rs1000 for a full day, which also gives you time to visit Siliserh (see below) on the way back. Alternatively, you might be able to book transport through your hotel.

  Entrance to the park costs Rs200 per person plus Rs125 per vehicle (and Rs200 for a video camera). **Jeeps with guide** can be hired at the entrance and cost Rs700 for a diesel Jeep, Rs800 for a petrol Jeep (the latter are quieter, and so less likely to scare off wildlife) for a three-hour drive around the park, or Rs1300/1500 (diesel/petrol) for the longer ride to the ruined Kankwari Fort, deep in the heart of the park, which is where the Mughal emperor Aurangzeb imprisoned his brother and rival for the throne, Dara Shikoh. Because Sariska gets so few visitors, lone travellers should be prepared for a long wait if looking for a ride-share. You can also go on **guided walks** around the entrance with reserve guides (Rs100/hr).

  Most travellers choose **to stay** in Alwar, but there are a couple of places close to the reserve. Conveniently situated right next to the park entrance, the RTDC *Hotel Tiger Den* (☎0144/284 1342; ❻) is attractive, if rather overpriced, with spacious old-fashioned fan and a/c rooms, plus a nice garden out the front, though service can be awful. A couple of minutes' drive down the main road is the far grander, but again significantly overpriced (from US\$125), *Sariska Palace* (☎0144/284 1322; ❾). This former maharaja's residence has plenty of atmosphere, though rooms in the main building are disappointingly shabby given the price, while those in the various modern annexes scattered around the grounds are poky and boring. There's also a pool, and large swathes of manicured lawns to loll around on.

Siliserh Palace

Fifteen kilometres south of Alwar along the road to Sariska, the little-visited **Siliserh Palace** is easily visited en route to or from Sariska if you've got your own vehicle (there's no public transport here). Maharaja Vijay Singh had the palace built in 1845 to win over a beautiful commoner, a certain Sheela, who agreed to marriage on the condition that she live within sight of her family's modest home. The whitewashed palace itself is fairly humdrum, but the Shangri-La setting, on the edge of a ten-square-kilometre lake ringed by uninhabited, jungle-clad hills, is idyllic. The palace now houses the disappointingly shabby and expensive RTDC *Lake Palace Hotel* (☎0144 288/6322; ❹–❻; Fri–Sun half-board rates only ❻). It's a nice spot to while away an afternoon, even so, and you can also rent out paddle-boats (Rs80/30min) and motorboats (Rs400/15min) if you want to get out onto the water – which also offers the best views of the palace itself, rising high above the lake.

Deeg

DEEG, 30km northwest of Bharatpur (see below), is an anarchic and dust-choked little market town which, as the second capital of the local ruling Jats, was the scene of bloody encounters with the Mughal overlords in the mid-eighteenth century. The only reason you might want to come here these days is to see the town's lavish **palace** (daily 8am–5pm; Rs100). Construction of this began in 1730, when the Jat ruler Badan Singh established Deeg as the second capital of Bharatpur state, though most of the palace was built by his successor Surajmal in 1756. The extensive complex comprises a large number of finely carved buildings scattered around extensive *charbagh*-style gardens dotted with thirty-odd water jets – though sadly, the water channels are dry and the fountains are only switched on during local festivals.

Entering the palace, the first and largest of the various *bhawans*, the **Gopal Bhawan** (closed Fri) lies immediately ahead and to the right, a spacious and plushly furnished hall which served as Surajmal's summer residence. Behind it lies the first of the palace's two large tanks, the **Gopal Sagar**. On the opposite side of the gardens lies the ornate **Kesav Bhawan**, or "Monsoon Palace", a richly carved open-sided pavilion surrounded by a deep water channel dotted with hundreds of tiny fountains. This unusual structure was designed to re-create the cool ambience of the rainy season, with water released from rooftop pipes to imitate a shower of monsoon rain, whilst metal balls were agitated by further streams of pressurized water to simulate the sound of thunder. Immediately behind here is the second of the palace's **tanks**, its stepped *ghats* usually covered in washing laid out by local housewives, while beyond rise the enormous walls of the town's huge fort. At the rear of the gardens lies the third of the palace's main buildings, the **Kishan Bhawan**. A walkway here leads up to a rooftop terrace, from where there are fine views over the whole complex.

Deeg is served by **bus** (every 15min; 3hr) and **train** (daily; 2hr) from Alwar, and by bus from Bharatpur (every 15min; 1hr). The town is easily visited as a day-trip from Bharatpur, or en route between Bharatpur and Alwar.

Bharatpur and Keoladeo National Park

The walled town of **BHARATPUR** is just a stone's throw from the border with Uttar Pradesh, 150km east of Jaipur, and a mere 18km from the magnificent abandoned city of Fatehpur Sikri. The town itself has an interesting mix of traditional bazaars, temples, mosques, palaces and a massive fort, but the real reason to come here is to visit India's most famous bird sanctuary, the **Keoladeo National Park**, on the town's southern edge, one of India's, if not the world's, top ornithological destinations.

Arrival and information

Bharatpur's **bus stand** is in the west of town. If you're arriving from Fatehpur Sikri you'll save yourself time (and a rickshaw fare) by getting off the bus at the crossroads on the southeast side of town near the park gates and guesthouses – look out for the prominent Rajasthan government tourist office right on the crossroads, or the large RTDC *Hotel Saras* opposite. The **railway station** is a couple of kilometres northwest of the town centre, a Rs40–50 ride from Keoladeo National Park and the nearby guesthouses.

The town's **tourist office** (Mon–Sat 10am–5pm; ☏05644/222542, ⓦwww.bharatpur.nic.in) is at the crossroads near the park entrance where Fatehpur Sikri buses pull in. Nearby, on New Civil Lines, The Perch and the Royal Guest House Forex (both open till around 10/11pm) offer **Internet** access (Rs40/hr)

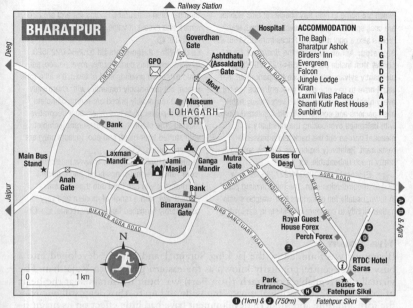

BHARATPUR

ACCOMMODATION	
The Bagh	B
Bharatpur Ashok	I
Birders' Inn	G
Evergreen	E
Falcon	D
Jungle Lodge	C
Kiran	F
Laxmi Vilas Palace	A
Shanti Kutir Rest House	J
Sunbird	H

and also change cash and traveller's cheques; The Perch also gives cash advances on credit cards.

Accommodation and eating

All the town's best **hotels** and **guesthouses** are located near the entrance to Keoladeo National Park, some 3km south of the town centre itself. Bharatpur's reputation as a tourist-friendly oasis has made it an attractive base for day-trippers to Agra and the Taj Mahal – a day-trip by taxi to Agra and back should cost about Rs1000. It's a good idea to **book rooms** in advance, especially from mid-November to late February. Most guesthouses also rent bikes (Rs25–50 per day) and binoculars (Rs50–70 per day). There are no independent restaurants in Bharatpur. Most people **eat** where they're staying.

Budget

Evergreen ☎05644/225917. One of the cheapest options in Bharatpur, with simple but clean rooms with fan and private bathroom (though hot water comes in a bucket in some rooms). ❶–❷

Falcon ☎05644/223815, ⓔfalconguest_house @hotmail.com. Attractive modern guesthouse with a selection of spotless, comfortable and good-value fan, air-cooled and a/c rooms, plus a small garden restaurant with excellent food. Internet access available. ❶–❺

Jungle Lodge ☎05644/225622, ⓦwww .junglelodge.dk. Run by a knowledgeable naturalist, this friendly place has a range of clean and spacious modern rooms (fan, air-cooled and a/c) overlooking a tranquil flower-filled garden. The pleasant little terrace restaurant and evening fires

(in winter) give the place a pleasantly sociable feel, and there are bikes and binoculars for rent, plus Internet access. ❶–❹

Kiran ☎05644/223845, ⓦwww .kiranguesthouse.com. Run by an extremely friendly and helpful pair of brothers, this place offers a range of clean and comfortable fan, air-cooled and a/c rooms at rock-bottom prices. There's free pick-up and drop-off from bus and train stations, plus binoculars for rent, and a small library. ❶–❹

Mid-range to expensive

The Bagh Agra Rd, 1km past *Laxmi Vilas Palace* ☎05644/228333, ⓦwww.thebagh.com. This idyllic upmarket hotel occupies a cluster of pink, low-rise buildings scattered around *charbagh*-style gardens which are home to over fifty species of bird. Rooms are cool, spacious and attractively furnished, and there's also a pool and gym. Prices from US$165. ⑨

Bahratpur Ashok (formerly the *Bharatpur Forest Lodge*) 1km inside park ☎05644/222760. In a pleasantly sylvan setting inside the park (note that you'll have to pay one day's park entrance fee for every night you stay here), this very sleepy hotel has spacious and comfortable old-fashioned rooms with balconies overlooking the sanctuary, a pleasant garden out the back and a passable restaurant. Relatively expensive, but the setting is pretty much unbeatable. ⑦

Birders' Inn ☎05644/227346, ⓦwww .thebirdersinn.com. The most inviting place in town, usually full of serious bird-watchers who gather nightly to compare checklists in the inviting

thatch-roofed restaurant. Rooms (all a/c) are large, smart, and excellent value. Internet access available. ⑤

Laxmi Vilas Palace Agra Rd ☎05644/223523, ⓦwww.laxmivilas.com. Former royal palace, set amid extensive grounds east of town. It's all a trifle kitsch, but undeniably romantic, with charmingly OTT and reasonably priced a/c rooms complete with four-poster beds and other regal decorative touches. The old-fashioned restaurant (complete with stuffed tiger head) and pool (guests only) are further bonuses. ⑧

Sunbird ☎05644/225701, ⓦwww.hotelsunbird .com. Attractive mid-range hotel, and a decent alternative if you can't get into the adjacent *Birders' Inn*, with a range of modern and very comfortably furnished fan and a/c rooms. ④–⑥

The Town

Bharatpur was founded by the Jat king Surajmal, and quickly developed into a busy market centre, popularly known as the eastern gateway to Rajasthan. The virtually impregnable **Lohagarh** (Iron Fort) was built by Surajmal at the heart of town in 1732; the original moat, 45m wide and up to 15m deep, still encircles the fort, and time and modern development have had little effect on its magnificent eleven-kilometre-long bastions – the British spent four months in 1805 trying in vain to breach them, before suffering their heaviest defeat in Rajasthan. You're most likely to enter the fort from the south, though it's worth continuing across the fort to the impressive **Ashtdhatu** (or Eight-Metal) **Gate**, named on account of the number of different types of metal that apparently went into the making of its extremely solid-looking doors.

The fort is home to no less than three large royal palaces in various stages of dereliction, all built by the Jats between 1730 and 1850. The best preserved is the large orange **Kamra Khas Mahal**, on the west side of the fort, which now serves as the town's mildly diverting **museum** (daily except Fri 10am–4.30pm; Rs3, camera Rs10, video Rs20), home to a large collection of finely carved sculptures, including some exquisitely detailed Jain statues and a superb little marble *hamman* (baths), along with the usual ragtag collection of miniature paintings, weaponry and other regal memorabilia.

Turn left as you exit the museum and follow the narrow road up around the edge of the palace to reach the lofty **Jawahar Burj** next door. This small, elevated platform is topped with four delicately carved pavilions and an unusual iron pole embellished with the family tree of the maharajas of Bharatpur, though its principal attraction is the superb panorama over the fort and modern town.

Immediately south of the fort lies the unusual **Ganga Mandir**, a large Hindu temple dedicated to the proprietary goddess of India's most sacred river, though the elaborately carved sandstone building itself looks more like a Neoclassical French chateau than a Subcontinental temple. Beyond here, narrow roads snake southwest through Bharatpur's characterful bazaar district to reach the imposing **Jama Masjid**, fronted by a fine arched portal and set high on a raised platform above the busy surrounding streets. A short distance further east lies the finely embellished **Laxman Mandir**, dedicated to the family deity of the maharajas of Bharatpur, Laxman, one of the brothers of Lord Rama, after whose other brother, Bharat, the town itself was named.

Moving on from Bharatpur

Buses run from the main bus stand to Jaipur (every 30min; 4hr), Delhi (every 30min–1hr; 5hr), Agra (hourly; 1hr 30min–2hr) and Fatehpur Sikri (every 30min–1hr; 30–45min). Bharatpur's **railway station** lies on the main Delhi–Mumbai line. There are four services daily to Agra Fort (the most convenient being the Jaipur–Gwalior Intercity #2987; daily; dep. 9.05am, arr. 10.15am); eight services to Sawai Madhopur (the best being the Golden Temple Mail #2904; daily; dep. 10.45am, arr. 1.05pm, which continues to Kota, arriving at 2.30pm), and four inconveniently timed services to Jaipur, for which you're better off taking the bus.

Keoladeo National Park

Keoladeo National Park (daily April–Sept 6am–6pm; Oct–March 6.30am–5pm; Rs200, Indian residents Rs25, video Rs200) is India's premier bird-watching sanctuary – an avian wonderland that attracts vast numbers of feathered creatures thanks to its strategic location, protected status and extensive wetlands (although the last are currently much reduced - see below). Dedicated ornithologists also flock to the park in droves, though it's a richly rewarding place to visit even for novices who don't know one end of a pair of binoculars from the other.

Keoladeo (also known as Keoladeo-Ghana – *ghana* meaning "thick forest") was for sixty years a royal hunting reserve, a past memorialized inside the park by a plaque recounting the murderous exploits of former "illustrious" visitors. (On one particularly gruesome day, in 1938, the party of viceroy Lord Linlinthgow bagged a staggering 4273 birds.) Despite the depredations of such trigger-happy hunters, the reserve's avian population continued to thrive. The area became a sanctuary in 1956 and a national park in 1982, and was declared a **UNESCO World Heritage Site** in 1985.

Today, Keoladeo's 29 square kilometres, including extensive areas of swamp and lake, constitute one of the world's most important ornithological breeding and migratory areas, with a staggering number of birds packed into a comparatively small area. Some 375 species have been recorded here, including around two hundred year-round residents along with 150-odd migratory species from as far afield as Tibet, China, Siberia and even Europe, who fly south to escape the northern winter. Keoladeo is probably best known for its stupendous array of **aquatic birds**, which descend en masse on the park's wetlands following the dramatic arrival of the monsoon in July. These include the majestic saras crane and a staggering two thousand painted storks, whose nesting cries create a constant background din, as well as snake-necked darters, spoonbills, pink flamingos, white ibis and grey pelicans (although sadly the extremely endangered Siberian cranes which were formerly one of the park's most prized visitors have not been seen in significant numbers since the early 1990s, apart from a single pair who last visited in 2002). An added bonus is the number of large **mammals** who frequent the park; you stand a good chance of glimpsing wild boar, mongoose, *chital*, nilgai and *sambar* along the paths, as well as hyenas, jackals and otters, and perhaps even elusive jungle cats. Rock pythons sun themselves at Python Point, just past Keoladeo temple, and in the bush land off the main road close to the entrance barrier.

The **best time to visit** is following the monsoon (roughly Oct–March), when the weather is dry but the lakes are still full and the migratory birds in residence (although mists in December and January can hinder serious bird-watching). Unfortunately, the **drought** suffered by Rajasthan in the past decade has taken a massive toll on Keoladeo. Diminished monsoon rains over recent years have left the park's lakes at a fraction of their customary size, with a huge consequent reduction in the number of aquatic birds in residence. A plan to artificially irrigate the park may have improved the situation by the time you read this, but don't hold your breath. For the time being, even a waterless Keoladeo is still an extremely enjoyable place to visit.

Park practicalities

The park entrance is around 4km south of Bharatpur railway station; free **maps** are available here. A single road passes through the park, while numerous small paths cut around lakes and across marshes and provide excellent cover for bird-watching. You can hire a **guide** at the gate (Rs70/hr for up to five people), who will probably have binoculars for you to borrow. The best way to get around is by **bike**, available at the main entrance (Rs25) if you haven't hired one at your guesthouse, or by cycle rickshaw (Rs50/hr) – drivers are trained by the park authorities and very clued up. During the winter, gondola-style **boats** (Rs100) offer short rides across the wetlands, assuming there's enough water in the park, providing a superb opportunity to get really close to the birds. The *Bahratpur Ashok Hotel* (see p.190) at the north end of the park is a reliable place to get a drink or something **to eat**.

Ranthambore National Park

No Indian nature reserve can guarantee a tiger sighting, but at **RANTHAM-BORE NATIONAL PARK** the odds are probably better than anywhere else. This has less to do with the size of the population, which is perilously small due to poaching, than because the tigers themselves are famously unperturbed by humans, hunting in broad daylight and rarely shying from cameras or Jeep-loads of tourists. Combine the big cats' bravado with the park's proximity to the Delhi–Agra–Jaipur "Golden Triangle", and you'll understand why Ranthambore attracts the numbers of visitors it does.

Arrival and information

Ranthambore National Park is reached via the small town of **Sawai Madhopur**, which is served by **trains** on the main Mumbai–Delhi line, and is thus easily accessible from Bharatpur, Agra, Jaipur and Delhi, as well as destinations further south, such as Kota. The **station** is right in the middle of town, close to the **bus stand**. The helpful **tourist office** (Mon–Sat 10am–5pm; ☎07462/220808) in the station hands out free **maps** of the town. There are **exchange** facilities at many hotels and in the State Bank of Bikaner & Jaipur in Sawai Madhopur. There are lots of ad hoc **Internet** places along the main road to the park, including a cluster just before you reach the *Ankur Hotel*; rates vary wildly, though connections at all places can be hair-tearingly slow. The town's indus-trial zone, rather confusingly known as **Sawai Madhopur City**, lies south of the main town, though is of no interest to visitors except as the departure point for buses to Shivpuri in Madhya Pradesh.

Three kilometres beyond the turning for the park, near the village of Kutalpura, it's worth popping into the excellent **Dastkar Crafts Centre**, which trains local low-caste woman to make patchwork quilting and appliqué – a laudable attempt to combat poverty in villages bordering the park, lessening the hardships that, in the past, have pushed villagers into illegal poaching. A small shop on site showcases their exceptional work, and there's another outlet immediately north of *Ranthambore Regency Hotel* in Ranthambore itself.

Accommodation and eating

Most of the area's numerous **hotels and guesthouses** are strung out along the 14km road between Sawai Madhopur and the national park; some of the better places are featured on Ⓦ www.hotelsranthambhore.com. Accommodation **prices** in Ranthambore are significantly higher than average, despite the fierce competition and number of places in business (hotel owners claim that they only really see six months' business every year – and that they therefore have to charge double prices). Genuine budget accommodation is almost non-existent, although there's plenty of choice of lower mid-range places. Try bargaining hard wherever you go.

Food in Ranthambore is very average, unless you want to push the boat out and go for a meal at one of the area's top-end places, like the lovely *Vanyavilas* or the *Sawai Madhopur Lodge* (which does a lunch and dinner buffet for Rs600). For budget food, the rooftop restaurant at the *Tiger Safari* hotel is cheap and reasonably tasty, and usually as lively as anywhere in town.

Budget to mid-range

Aditya Resort Ranthambore Rd, 3km north of town ☏ 0/941 472 8468. One of the best-value cheapies in Ranthambore at the time of writing, offering simple but clean and comfortable modern rooms (some with shared bath) with hot water and TV. ❶–❸

Ankur Resort Ranthambore Rd, 2km from town ☏ 07462/220792, ✉ ankurresort@yahoo.com. A wide range of accommodation, from rather shabby budget rooms in the main building up to smart cottages in the gardens behind; the cheaper fan and air-cooled options are better value than the more expensive a/c cottages and rooms. There's also a small pool and a passable restaurant. ❸–❼

Anurag Resort Ranthambore Rd, 2.5 km from town ☏ 07462/220751, Ⓦ www.anuragresort.com. Sprawling pink resort with slight Rajput decorative touches and a nice big lawn out the front. Rooms (all air-cooled) are uninspiring but modern and spacious, and there are also some slightly more expensive a/c cottages set around the attractively meandering gardens at the back. ❼–❽

Hammir Wildlife Resort Ranthambore Rd, 7km from town ☏ 09414 446566, Ⓦ www.nivalink .com/hammir. Popular with Indian tourists, this is one of the more sensibly priced places in town (though the rooms are much better value than the garden cottages). Facilities include a pool (non-guests Rs100) and money exchange. ❺–❼

Raj Palace Resort Ranthambore Rd, 2km from town ☏ 07462/224793, Ⓦ www.hotelraj-palace .com. One of the best-value places in Ranthambore, with spacious and clean (though rather bare) modern rooms with TV (some also with a/c) plus some slightly more homely a/c cottages around the gardens at the back, plus a pool. ❷–❸

Tiger Safari Ranthambore Rd, 2.5 km from town ☏ 07462/221137, Ⓦ www.tigersafariresort.com.

The best of Ranthambore's cheaper hotels, with helpful service and comfortably furnished rooms (all with TV; some with a/c) plus spacious cottages around the rear garden. There's also Internet access, a pool, free pick-up/drop-off from the station, and a good rooftop restaurant. ❹–❺

Expensive

Aman-i-Khás On the edge of the national park ☏ 07462/252052, Ⓦ www.amanresorts.com. Situated in a very quiet rural setting, this place rivals *Vanyavilas* (see p.194) for tasteful opulence (and even outdoes it for wallet-crunching expense). Accommodation is in ten superb, cavernous luxury tents, and there's also a traditional step-well for swimming, fresh produce from the on-site organic farm, and a spa tent. Closed May to Sept. US$880 (plus US$120 "board" charge per person per day). ❾

Nahargarh 2km south of park entrance, Khilchipur Village, Ranthambore Rd ☏ 07462/252281, Ⓦ www.alsisar.com. Superbly theatrical-looking hotel, built in the style of an old-fashioned Rajput palace and looking every inch the regal retreat. Rooms are sumptuously decorated in traditional style and there's also a large pool. Rooms from around $200. ❾

RTDC Castle Jhoomar Baori On a hillside 7km out of town ☏ 07462/220495, Ⓦ www .hotelsranthambhore.com. Former royal hunting lodge on a lofty hilltop site inside the park, with superb views from the roof terrace and large, and atmospheric – albeit slightly shabby – rooms. ❼–❽ full board

🏃 **Sawai Madhopur Lodge** Ranthambore Rd, 1.5km from town ☏ 07462/220541, Ⓦ www.tajhotels.com. Occupying an atmospheric 1930s hunting lodge, this luxury heritage hotel has bags of charm, with pleasantly leafy grounds and accommodation in beautifully appointed colonial-style rooms (from around $270), plus a pool (non-guests Rs750) and attractive restaurant. ⓿ **Vanyavilas** Ranthambore Rd, about 7km from town ☎07462/223999, ⓦwww.oberoihotels.com. Superbly stylish (and expensive) jungle resort offering a real splash of class in dusty

Ranthambore. The resort is centred around a lavishly decorated building in the style of a royal hunting palace, with accommodation scattered around the rustic grounds in beautifully equipped wooden-floored a/c tents. Non-guests can visit for a romantic terrace dinner (Rs1000). Rooms from around US$960. ⓿

The park

In comparison to the tranquil tiger sanctuaries in the neighbouring state of Madhya Pradesh, the crowds at **Ranthambore National Park** can be off-putting, to say the least – the park is one of India's most popular, with more than eighty thousand visitors a year, and can get ridiculously busy throughout the cool winter months, especially around holiday periods such as Diwali and New Year. The summer months from April to June are a lot quieter, but obviously very hot.

Ranthambore has been controlled by the Rajputs for most of its existence, and was set aside by the rulers of Jaipur for royal hunting jaunts. Soon after Independence the area was declared a sanctuary, becoming a fully fledged national park under **Project Tiger** in 1972. There are currently around 28 adult tigers and ten cubs in the park, plus healthy populations of *chital*, nilgai, jackals, leopards, jungle cats and a wide array of birds.

Note that **Ranthambore is closed** annually from 1 July to 30 September; the **best time to visit** is during the dry season (Oct–March), when the lack of water entices the larger animals out to the lakeside. During and immediately after the monsoons, they are more likely to remain in the forest. More information can be gleaned from Project Tiger's excellent booklet, *The Ultimate Ranthambore Guide* (Rs250), on sale in local souvenir shops.

Park practicalities

Rules about **visiting Ranthambore** seem to change every couple of years, so don't be surprised if the following information has become obsolete by the time you arrive. At present, the number of vehicles allowed into the park is strictly controlled, with a maximum of around seventeen six-seater **Jeeps** (also known as "Gypsys") and twenty **Canters** (open-top buses seating twenty people) being allowed in during each morning and afternoon session. Obviously, most visitors prefer the much smaller and quieter Jeeps, although demand usually outstrips supply, and a lot of tourists find themselves having to make do with a place on a Canter instead. **Safaris** run daily every morning and afternoon, and last around three hours. Departure times vary slightly depending on sunrise, leaving between 6.30am and 7am and between 3pm and 3.30pm. Dress in layers: mornings can be surprisingly cool.

Seats officially cost Rs460 in a Canter and Rs566 in a Jeep (both prices include the park entrance fee which is Rs200 for foreigners and Rs25 for Indian residents). There's also a charge for video cameras of Rs200. If you want to book your own seat, the best option is to **reserve on line** at ⓦwww.rajasthantourism .gov.in. The alternative is to battle the crowds at the frequently chaotic **Tourist Reception Centre** (ticket office open 5–6.30am & noon–1pm) at the RTDC *Hotel Vinayak*, about 7km along Ranthambore Road, where you can buy tickets for tours on the day, though you'll be very lucky to bag a seat in a Jeep, which usually get bought up by hotels and safari operators way in advance.

A much easier option is to book a seat in a Jeep or Canter through your hotel or a local tour operator. You'll pay a surcharge for this, which can be anything from Rs75 for a seat in a Canter booked through a budget guesthouse up to Rs2000 for a place in a Jeep booked through a top-end hotel. In practice, seats in a Canter usually go for around Rs540, while prices for seats in Jeeps fluctuate wildly according to demand, anything from Rs750 to Rs1200 or more. You shouldn't have any problems getting a seat in a Canter if you book the day before (except possibly on Sundays between 1 Oct and 15 April, when six Canters are block-booked by the *Palace on Wheels*). If you want to go in a Jeep it's best to book ahead, although you might get lucky, especially from around April through to June, when visitor numbers fall significantly. Your chances drop considerably closer to Diwali, New Year and around any other public holiday.

Ranthambore Fort

It's well worth setting aside some time from the tigers to visit the dramatic **Ranthambore Fort** (daily 6am–6pm; free), set atop a rocky crag near the entrance to the national park. The fort was founded as early as 944 by the Chauhan Rajputs and, following the decisive defeat of Prithviraj III by Muhammad of Ghor in 1192, became a key strategic focus in Rajput resistance to the expanding power of the Delhi Sultanate. The fort changed hands on several occasions, and was conquered by Ala-ud-din Khalji's army in 1301, and by Akbar in 1559, before finally passing into the hands of the Kachchwahas of Amber in the seventeenth century.

A few kilometres along the road into the park, a twisting flight of around two hundred eroded stone steps lead up through a sequence of impressively large gateways and crumbling fortifications to reach the fort, enclosed by some 7km of walls and bastions which snake around the ridgetop, offering fine views over the surrounding countryside. The numerous remains within the fort include a mosque, a large tank, assorted chattris and several temples, including a particularly revered one dedicated to Ganesh; people from all over the country write to the elephant-headed god's shrine here to invite him to their weddings.

The easiest way to **visit the fort** is to go on a tour; these can be arranged through the *Tiger Safari* hotel (Rs600 per person), or just ask at your hotel to see if they can arrange a Jeep. Note that you don't have to pay the park entry fee if you're just going to the fort.

Moving on from Ranthambore

There are virtually no **rickshaws** in Ranthambore, so you'll have to arrange transport to the bus or train station through your hotel when you come to leave.

Sawai Madhopur straddles the main Delhi–Mumbai railway line and is well served by **trains**. There are daily services for Jaipur (7am, 10.20am, 10.45am & 3.05pm; 2hr 10min–2hr 45min), Bharatpur (12.40pm; 2hr 30min), Jodhpur (3.05pm; 8hr) and Kota (1.10pm, 1.30pm, 4.10pm, 6.05pm; 1hr 20min–1hr 30min). For Bundi, it's easiest to take a train to Kota and then catch a bus, or catch a direct bus all the way (see below).

Ongoing improvements to the previously awful roads around Ranthambore are gradually making **bus** travel a quicker and more comfortable option, although taking the train is still preferable for most destinations. Services run to Jaipur (every 90min; 4–5hr), Bundi (4 daily; 4–5hr), and Ajmer (2 daily; 8hr). Buses depart from one of the two bus stands close to one another in the middle of Sawai Madhopur; check with the person who's taking you that you're at the right stand.

Ajmer

The Nag Pahar ("Snake Mountain"), a steeply shelving spur of the Aravallis west of Jaipur, forms an appropriately epic backdrop for **AJMER**, home of the great Sufi saint **Khwaja Muin-ud-din Chishti**, who founded the Chishtiya Sufi order. To this day, his tomb, the **Dargah Khwaja Sahib**, remains one of the most important Islamic shrines in the world. The streams of pilgrims and dervishes (it is believed that seven visits here are the equivalent to one to Mecca), especially pick up during Muharram (Muslim New Year) and Id, and for the saint's anniversary day, or **Urs Mela** (see box, p.198).

For Hindu pilgrims and foreign travellers, Ajmer is important primarily as a jumping-off place for **Pushkar**, a twenty-minute bus ride away across the Nag Pahar, and most stay only for as long as it takes to catch a bus out, but as a day-trip from Pushkar it's a highly worthwhile excursion, and as a stronghold of Islam, Ajmer is unique in Hindu-dominated Rajasthan.

History

A local Rajput chieftain, Ajay Pal Chauhan, established a fort at Ajmer in the tenth century, and it became the capital of a territory carved out by his

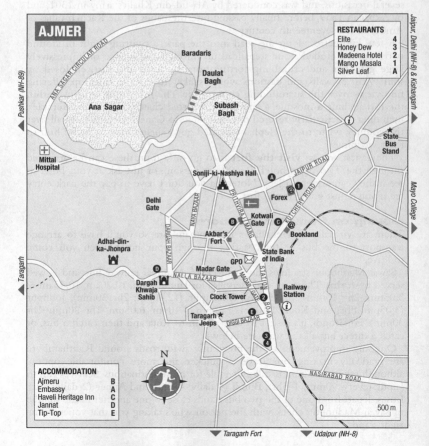

AJMER

RESTAURANTS
Elite	4
Honey Dew	3
Madeena Hotel	2
Mango Masala	1
Silver Leaf	A

ACCOMMODATION
Ajmeru	B
Embassy	A
Haveli Heritage Inn	C
Jannat	D
Tip-Top	E

Pushkar (NH-89)

ANA SAGAR CIRCULAR ROAD

Baradaris

Daulat Bagh

Ana Sagar

Subash Bagh

Mittal Hospital

Soniji-ki-Nashiya Hall

Delhi Gate

MAYA BAZAAR

PRITHVIRAJ MARG

JAIPUR ROAD

Forex

Kotwali Gate

KUTCHERY ROAD

Adhai-din-ka-Jhonpra

DARGAH BAZAAR

Akbar's Fort

State Bank of India

Bookland

Taragarh

GPO

Madar Gate

NALLA BAZAAR

Dargah Khwaja Sahib

MADAR GATE

STATION ROAD

Railway Station

Clock Tower

Taragarh Jeeps

DIGGI BAZAAR

N

NASIRABAD ROAD

State Bus Stand

Jaipur, Delhi (NH-8) & Kishangarh

Mayo College

0   500 m

Taragarh Fort   Udaipur (NH-8)

Chauhan clan. The Chauhans went on to become the dominant power in eastern Rajasthan, but were beaten in 1193 by Muhammad of Ghor (see p.1338), who had invaded from Afghanistan. The Delhi sultans allowed the Chauhans to carry on ruling as their tributaries, but in 1365, with Delhi on the wane as a regional power, Ajmer fell to the kingdom of Mewar (Udaipur).

During the sixteenth century, the city became the object of rivalry between Mewar and the neighbouring kingdom of Marwar (Jodhpur). The Marwaris took it in 1532, but the presence of Khwaja Muin-ud-din Chishti's *dargah* (see p.198) made Ajmer an important prize for the Muslim Mughals, and Akbar's forces marched in only 27 years later.

The Mughals held onto Ajmer for over two centuries, but as their empire began to fragment, the neighbouring Rajput kingdoms once again started giving the city covetous looks. It was eventually taken in 1770 by the Marathas, who subsequently sold the city to the East India Company for fifty thousand rupees in 1818. Thus, while most of Hindu-dominated Rajasthan retained internal independence during the Raj, Ajmer was a little Muslim enclave of directly-ruled British territory, only reunited with Jodhpur and Udaipur, its former overlords, when it became part of Rajasthan in 1956.

Arrival and information

Ajmer's **railway station** is slap-bang in the centre of town, but the **State Bus Stand**, with an exhaustive array of routes, is inconveniently situated on the Jaipur Road, 2km to the northeast. *Tempos* and auto-rickshaws connect the two; auto-rickshaws cost around Rs30. If you're heading straight on to **Pushkar**, buses depart from the state bus stand every 15min or so until around 9pm.

The RTDC runs **tourist offices** near the state bus stand next to the RTDC *Hotel Khadim* (Mon–Sat 10am–5pm; ☏0145/262 7426) and at the railway station (daily 9am–5pm; no phone – it's just inside the station's smaller, southern entrance).

Accommodation

Ajmer's **hotels** are not great value and you're really better off staying in Pushkar and commuting in. Lower-priced hotels tend to operate a 24-hour checkout system. Accommodation also tends to get chock-full during Urs Mela.

Ajmeru Khailand market, off Prithviraj Marg, just inside Kotwali Gate ☏0145/243 1103, ⓦwww .hotelajmeru.com. This comfortable modern hotel is one of the best-value places to stay in town, with bright, clean and well-kept rooms. 24hr checkout. ❹–❺

Embassy Jaipur Rd ☏0145/242 5519, ⓦwww .hotelembassyajmer.com. Pleasant, modern three-star. All rooms come with a/c, TV and minibar, and there's also the good in-house *Silver Leaf* restaurant (see p.201). ❺–❼

Haveli Heritage Inn Kutchery Rd, Phul Nawas ☏0145/262 1607, ⓔhaveliherit –ageinn@hotmail.com. In an old house from the 1870s that was once used as the state HQ of the Congress Party – Nehru and Ghandi both stayed here. It actually sounds grander than it is, but if you think of this as a pension rather than a haveli,

you'll get the right idea – the big attractions are the peaceful atmosphere and the delightful family that run it. Rooms (air-cooled and a/c) are bright, spacious and attractively furnished, and there's great home-cooking too. ❹–❻

Jannat Dargah Bazaar, near Nizam Gate ☏0145/243 2494, ⓦwww.ajmerhoteljannat.com. A stone's throw from the Dargah Khwaja Sahib, and the best hotel in the area, it fills up quickly on Thurs and Fri, but usually has space the rest of the week. There's a range of rooms, all modern and clean, some a/c, plus a good restaurant and friendly service. 24hr checkout. ❹–❺

Tip-Top Cinema Rd, off Diggi Bazaar ☏0145/510 0241 or 1241. Best of the hotels around the station, in a lively market area and good value by Ajmer standards, with a/c or non-a/c attached rooms. 24hr checkout. ❷–❹

The Town

Although Ajmer's dusty main streets are choked with traffic, the narrow lanes of the bazaars and residential quarters around the **Dargah Khwaja Sahib** retain an almost medieval character, with lines of rose-petal stalls and shops selling prayer mats, beads and lengths of gold-edged green silk offerings. Finely arched Mughal gateways still stand at the main entrances to the **old city**, whose skyscape of mosque minarets and domes is overlooked from on high by the crumbling **Taragarh** – for centuries India's most strategically important fortress.

Dargah Khwaja Sahib

The revered Sufi saint, Khwaja Muin-ud-din Chishti (see box opposite), who died in Ajmer in 1236, was buried in a small brick tomb that is today engulfed by a large complex known as the **Dargah Khwaja Sahib**, or Dargah Sharif (Ⓦ www.dargahajmer.com; daily 5am to midnight; no cameras allowed inside). Founded in the thirteenth century, the *dargah* contains structures financed by many Muslim rulers, but it was under the imperial patronage of the three great Mughals – Shah Jahan, Jahangir and, most crucially, Akbar – that this became the most important Muslim shrine in India. It remains massively popular, with thousands of pilgrims passing through the gates every day, and the continual murmur of prayer and the sound of *qawwali* music being performed before the shrine, exactly as it has been for seven hundred years, still create an unforgettable atmosphere.

You enter the *dargah* through the lofty **Nizam Gate**, donated by the Nizam of Hyderabad in 1911. Once inside, you may be accosted by stern-looking young men claiming they are "official guides". In fact, they are *khadims*, hereditary priests, leading pilgrims through rituals in the sacred precinct in exchange for donations. Their services are not compulsory, although you may wish to employ one as a guide. If you do, agree a fee in advance and don't be afraid to say no if you think they're asking too much. It's also worth being aware that you might be pressed for further donations at various places inside the shrine.

Immediately beyond the Nizam Gate is a smaller gateway, the **Shajahani Gate**, so called because it was commissioned by the Mughal emperor Shah Jahan, through which is a courtyard where, to your right, a small flight of steps lead up to the **Akbari Masjid**, donated by the emperor Akbar, though the large, plain building shows little evidence of its Mughal origins. Akbar had come to the *dargah* to pray for a son; when his prayer was granted with the birth of Salim (subsequently the emperor Jahangir), Akbar had this mosque built here in gratitude.

Just past the Shajahani Gate is a third gateway, the imposing, blue-and-green **Buland Darwaza**. After passing through it, you'll see, resting on raised platforms on either side, two immense cauldrons, known as **degs**, into which

The Urs Mela

The Urs Mela, held on the sixth day of the Islamic month of Rajab (approximately 29 June 2009, 18 June 2010) is predominantly a religious celebration in honour of the city's Sufi saint, Khwaja Muin-ud-din Chishti (see opposite), on the anniversary of his death. Pilgrims flock to the town to honour the saint with *qawwali* (Sufi devotional) chanting. *Kheer* (rice pudding) is cooked in huge vats at the *dargah* and distributed to visitors. At night religious gatherings called *mehfils* are held. It isn't really an affair for non-religious tourists, but the city does take on a festive air, with devotees from across the Subcontinent and beyond converging on Ajmer for the week leading up to it.

Khwaja Muin-ud-din Chishti

In 1992–93, following the demolition by Hindu fundamentalists of the mosque at Ayodha (see p.1350), sectarian riots swept across India as Hindus turned on their Muslim neighbours nationwide, but Ajmer – a Muslim city in a Hindu fundamentalist state, and an obvious flashpoint – escaped unscathed. No one had any doubt that peace prevailed because of the enduring influence of the Sufi saint enshrined at the heart of the city, **Khwaja Muin-ud-din Chishti**.

Born in 1156, in Afghanistan, Muslim India's most revered saint began his religious career at the age of thirteen, when he distributed his inheritance among the poor and adopted the simple, pious life of an itinerant Sufi *fakir* (the equivalent of the Hindu sadhu). On his travels, he soaked up the teachings of the great Central Asian Sufis, whose emphasis on mysticism, ecstatic states and pure devotion as a path to God were revolutionizing Islam during this period.

Khwaja Sahib's growing reputation as a saint and a sage snowballed after he and his disciples settled in Ajmer at the beginning of the thirteenth century. Withdrawing into a life of meditation and fasting, he preached a message of renunciation, affirming that personal experience of God was attainable to anyone who relinquished their ties to the world. More radically, he also insisted on the fundamental **unity of all religions**: mosques and temples, he asserted, were merely material manifestations of a single divinity, with which all men and women could commune. In this way, Khwaja Sahib became one of the first religious figures to bridge the gap between India's two great faiths. After he died at the age of 97, his followers lauded the Bhagavad Gita as a sacred text, and even encouraged Hindu devotees to pray using names of God familiar to them, equating Ram with "Rahman", the Merciful Aspect of Allah. The spirit of acceptance and unity central to the founder of the Chishti order's teachings explains why his shrine in Ajmer continues to be loved by adherents of all faiths.

pilgrims throw money to be shared among the poor. The one on the right, the larger of the two, was donated by Akbar in 1567; the other was a gift from Jahangir upon his accession in 1605.

Beyond the *khanas* is an inner courtyard where the Tomb of Khwaja Sahib lies inside a domed mausoleum, the marble **Mazar Sharif**. Nightly recitations of *qawwali* are held in the courtyard here, an exuberant form of religious singing accompanied by harmonium and drums which aims to lull the participants into a trance-like state called *mast* – the desire to enter into personal communion with God being a central tenet of Sufism. The **tomb** inside (closed daily 3–4pm except Thurs when it's shut 2.30–3.30pm) is surrounded by silver railings and surmounted by a large gilt dome. Devotees file past carrying brilliant *chadars*, gilt-brocaded silk covers for the saint's grave, on beds of rose petals in flat, round head-baskets. Visitors are blessed, lightly brushed with peacock feathers and given the chance to touch the cloth covering the tomb in return for a suitable offering.

Subsidiary shrines in the inner courtyard include those belonging to daughters of Khwaja Sahib and Shah Jahan, plus a handful of generals and governors, and some Afghani companions of the saint. The delicately carved marble mosque behind the saint's tomb, the **Jama Masjid** or Shahjahani Masjid, was commissioned by Shah Jahan in 1628 and took nine years to build. Despite its grand scale, the emperor deliberately had it built without a dome so as not to upstage the saint's mausoleum next door.

Other Islamic monuments

Often overlooked by visitors, the **Adhai-din-ka-Jhonpra**, or "two-and-a-half-day hut", is the oldest surviving monument in the city and unquestionably one of the finest examples of medieval architecture in Rajasthan. Originally built in 660 AD as a Jain temple, and converted in 1153 into a Hindu college, it was destroyed forty years later by the invading Afghan chieftain Muhammad of Ghor, who later had it renovated as a mosque. Tradition holds that its name derives from the speed with which it was constructed, but in fact the reconstruction took fifteen years, using materials plundered from Hindu and Jain temples; the name actually refers to a *fakirs'* festival which used to be held here in the eighteenth century, a *jhonpra* (hut) being the abode of a *fakir* (Sufi mendicant). Defaced Hindu motifs are still clearly discernible on the pillars and ceilings, but the mosque's most beautiful feature is the bands of Koranic calligraphy that decorate its seven-arched facade. The monument is about 400m west of the *dargah*, reached via a small and easy-to-miss alleyway off the main bazaar; by the time you can see the shrine's walls rising on your right, you've already walked past the entrance.

A more recent Islamic relic is the small but attractive **Akbar's Fort**, which encloses a rectangular pavilion made of golden sandstone that was used by Akbar and his son Jahangir; it was here in 1616 that Jahangir received Sir Thomas Roe, the first British ambassador to be granted an official audience, after four years of trailing between the emperor's encampments. Today, the old palace houses a small **museum** (daily 10am–4.30pm; Rs3, camera Rs10, video Rs20), displaying mainly Hindu and Jain statues including a striking twelfth-century sculpture of Varaha (Vishnu in his incarnation as a boar).

Laid out in the twelfth century, the artificial lake northwest of Ajmer, known as **Ana Sagar**, is today little more than a pond, but worth a visit to see the line of exquisite white-marble pavilions called **baradaris**, or summer shelters, erected by Shah Jahan on the lake's southwest shore. Modelled on Red Fort in the Diwan-i-Am in Delhi, four of the five pavilions remain beautifully preserved, standing in the shade of trees and ornamental gardens laid out by Jahangir – particularly beautiful an hour or so before sunset.

Taragarh Fort

Three kilometres to the south, and just visible on the ridge high above the city, **Taragarh** (the Star Fort) was for two thousand years the most important strategic objective for invading armies in northwest India. Any ruler who successfully breached its walls, rising from a ring of forbidding escarpments, effectively controlled the region's trade. The fort is now badly ruined but is still visited in large numbers by pilgrims, who come to pay their respects at what must be one of the few shrines in the world devoted to a tax inspector, the **Dargah of Miran Sayeed Hussein Khangsawar** – Muhammad of Ghor's chief revenue collector was one of many slain in the Rajput attack of 1202 when, following one of the fort's rare defeats, the entire Muslim population of the fort was put to the sword.

The best way of getting to Taragarh is to take a ninety-minute **hike** along the ancient paved pathway from Ajmer, which offers superb **views** across the plains and neighbouring hills. To pick up the trailhead, follow the lane behind the Dargah Khwaja Sahib, past the Adhai-din-ka-Jhonpra and on towards the saddle in the ridge visible to the south. Alternatively, you can take an auto (Rs150–200 return) or one of the **Jeeps** (Rs20) that leave from behind the Plaza Cinema on Diggi Chowk, west of the train station; ask for the "Ta-ra-garh jeeps", pronouncing all the syllables clearly, or you may end up at the main Khwaja Sahib Dargah. To return to Ajmer, you can either follow the path back downhill, or catch a Jeep from the lot at the northeast side of the village, near the Dargah.

Other attractions

While most of Rajasthan consisted of princely states, Ajmer was under British rule, and relics of the colonial period can be found scattered across the city, among them the **Jubilee clock tower** opposite the railway station and the **King Edward Memorial Hall** a little to the west. The famous **Mayo College**, originally built as a school for princes, and now a leading educational institution is known in society circles as the "Eton of the East".

Perhaps the most bizarre sight in Ajmer is the mirrored **Soniji-ki-Nashiya** hall adjoining the **Nashiyan Jain temple**, or "Red Temple" (daily 8.30am–5.30pm; Rs5, camera Rs15). Commissioned in the 1820s by an Ajmeri diamond magnate, the hall contains a huge diorama-style display commemorating the life of Rishabha (or Adinath), the first Jain *tirthankara*, believed to have lived countless aeons in the past. The glowing tableau (containing a tonne of gold) features a huge procession of soldiers and elephants carrying the infant *tirthankara* from Ayodhya to Mount Sumeru to be blessed, while musicians and deities fly overhead. Admission to the main temple alongside is restricted to Jains.

Eating

In addition to the snack and fruit-juice places around Dargah Bazaar and Delhi Gate, Ajmer has a handful of larger **restaurants**. Note that none of the following serve alcohol; if you want a **drink** you'll have to find a local bottle shop or try room service in your hotel.

Elite Station Rd. Reliable veg restaurant serving moderately priced curries and thalis (most around Rs40–50), plus a sprinkling of vegetarian Chinese, Continental and south Indian options. You can eat either inside in the white-tablecloth dining room or outside at a table in the garden. The *Honey Dew* restaurant, a few doors to the north, is very similar.

Madeena Hotel Station Rd. Muslim establishment serving very tasty non-veg Mughlai curries, mostly involving "mutton" (ie, goat), in the form of korma, mughlai, *keema*, masala or biriyani, in full or half portions (Rs30–55) with freshly baked tandoori breads. There are also chicken, egg and veg options.

Mango Masala Sardar Patel Marg. Popular, trendy establishment serving pizzas, snacks, veg burgers, salads, shakes, mocktails and ice-cream sodas, as well as veg set-meals and thalis, and lots of *paneer* curries. Mains Rs45–95.

Silver Leaf *Embassy Hotel*, Jaipur Rd. Sedate veg restaurant, with a big selection of curries (most around Rs50–75), plus an assortment of Chinese and Continental dishes, as well as snacks and breakfasts.

Listings

Banks and exchange There's a State Bank of India ATM opposite the GPO on Prithviraj Marg, a Bank of Baroda ATM between the *Elite* and *Honey Dew* restaurants, and ICICI and HDFC ATMs at either end of Sardar Patel Marg (the road which *Mango Masala* restaurant is on). If you need a forex bureau, UAE Money Exchange at 10 Sardar Patel Marg (Mon–Sat 9am–1.30pm & 2–6pm) changes cash and traveller's cheques, and also receives MoneyGram money transfers.
Bookshop Bookland, 75 Kutchery Rd, opposite *Haveli Heritage Inn*.

Hospital Mittal Hospital, Pushkar Rd ☏0145/260 3600, is well equipped and has a 24hr emergency department.
Internet access Satguru, at 61 Kutchery Rd (daily 9am–10pm; Rs20/hr) near *Haveli Heritage Inn*, and at 10 Sardar Patel Marg (daily 11am–9pm; Rs15/hr).
Left luggage There's a left-luggage office (open 24hr) directly opposite the tourist information office in the train station.
Post office Southern end of Prithviraj Marg (Mon–Sat 10am–6pm, Sun 10am–4pm).

Recommended trains from Ajmer

The trains below are recommended as the fastest and/or most convenient for specific cities.

Destination	Name	No.	Departs	Arrives
Abu Road	Ahmedabad Mail	9106	7.40am (daily)	12.43pm
	Aravali Express	9708	11.25am (daily)	4.50pm
Chittaurgarh	Udaipur Express	2992	3.55pm (daily)	6.55pm
	Ratlam Express	9654	1.10pm (daily)	5.25pm
Jaipur	Shatabdi Express	2016	3.50pm (exc W)	5.35pm
	Ajmer–Jaipur Intercity	9652	6.40am (daily)	9.45am
	Aravali Express	9707	4.15pm (daily)	6.45pm
Jodhpur	Fast passenger train	2JA	3pm (daily)	10pm
New Delhi	Shatabdi Express	2016	3.50pm (exc W)	10.45pm
	Rajdhani Express	2957	12.35am (exc Tue)	7.35am
Udaipur	Udaipur Express	2992	3.55pm (daily)	9.20pm

Moving on from Ajmer

Ajmer station (℡0145/243 2535) is on the main Delhi–Ahmedabad **train line**, but there are considerable variations between the journey times of services passing through here (see box above for recommendations). The computerized **reservations** hall is on the first floor of the railway station's south wing; get there early in the morning to avoid queues or shell out a little extra for a travel agent.

For details of buses from Ajmer, see **"Travel details"** on p.267. State buses – including services to **Pushkar** (roughly every 15min until about 9pm) – depart from the **State Bus Stand** (℡0145/242 9398) on Jaipur Road, about 2km northeast of the city centre. Seats on private buses – many of which have connecting services from Pushkar – can be reserved at travel agents along Kutchery Road towards Prithviraj Marg.

Pushkar

According to legend, **PUSHKAR**, 15km northwest of Ajmer, came into existence when Lord Brahma, the Creator, dropped a lotus flower (*pushpa*) to earth from his hand (*kar*). At the three spots where the petals landed, water magically appeared in the midst of the desert to form three small blue lakes, and it was on the banks of the largest of these that Brahma subsequently convened a gathering of some 900,000 celestial beings – the entire Hindu pantheon. Surrounded by whitewashed temples and bathing *ghats*, the lake is today revered as one of India's most sacred sites: *Pushkaraj Maharaj*, literally "Pushkar King of Kings". During the auspicious full-moon phase of October/November (the anniversary of the gods' mass meeting, or *yagya*), its waters are believed to cleanse the soul of all impurities, drawing pilgrims from all over the country. Alongside this annual religious festival, Rajasthani villagers also buy and sell livestock at what has become the largest **camel market** (*unt mela*) in the world, when more than 150,000 dealers, tourists and traders fill the dunes to the west of the lake.

The beautiful desert scenery and heady religious atmosphere has inevitably made Pushkar a prime destination for foreign tourists ever since the 1960s, and the budget hotels and cafés set up to cater for them have kept it firmly on the

▲ The lake in Pushkar at sunset

backpacker trail. The main bazaar is now a kilometre-long line of shops offering hippy trinkets, forex and Internet, while the streetside cafés churn out banana pancakes, pizzas and bhang-laced "special lassis".

Arrival and information

Pushkar does not have a railway station, and most long-distance journeys to and from Pushkar, even by bus, have to be made via Ajmer, though there are also direct buses from Delhi, Jaipur, Jodhpur and Bikaner. The **Ajmer Bus Stand** in the east of town is served by local buses from Ajmer. Services from destinations further afield, such as Delhi, Jaipur, Jodhpur and Bikaner (most of which also stop en route at Ajmer), arrive in the north of town at **Marwar Bus Stand**. Make sure you know which stand you've arrived at if you're walking to your guesthouse unaccompanied or you could get lost. There are virtually no rickshaws in Pushkar, so you'll have to walk to your hotel (though there are hand-carts for transporting luggage).

Pushkar's **tourist office** (daily 10am–5pm; 24hr during camel fair; ☎0145/277 2040) is conveniently located inside the main gate of the RTDC *Hotel Sarovar*, a short walk from the Ajmer Bus Stand.

Accommodation

Note that prices rise dramatically during the **camel fair**: increases of up to five times the usual rates are common, and there's considerable pressure, especially at budget hotels, to pre-pay for your entire stay or risk having your reservation lost – you should resist doing this as you won't get your money back if the fair disappoints and you decide to beat a hasty retreat.

Budget

Amar Holika Chowk (back entrance on Main Bazaar) ☎0145/277 2809, ⓔamar-hotel @yahoo.com.in. Very central but pleasantly peaceful place, with rooms set around a large garden. Maintains reasonable prices during camel fair. ❶–❸

Bharatpur Palace Main Bazaar ☎0145/277 2320, ⓔbharatpurpa ace_pushkar@yahoo.co.in. A bit run-down and overpriced for what you get,

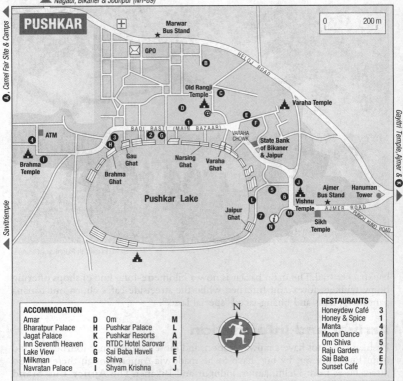

PUSHKAR

▲ *Nagaur, Bikaner & Jodhpur (NH-89)*

Marwar Bus Stand
GPO
Old Rangji Temple
Varaha Temple
BADI BASTI (MAIN BAZAAR)
VARAHA CHOWK
State Bank of Bikaner & Jaipur
ATM
Brahma Temple
Gau Ghat
Narsing Ghat
Varaha Ghat
Brahma Ghat

Pushkar Lake

Jaipur Ghat
Ajmer Bus Stand
Hanuman Tower
Vishnu Temple
AJMER ROAD
Sikh Temple
PUNCH KUND ROAD

Gaytiri Temple, Ajmer & K ►

0 — 200 m

ACCOMMODATION			
Amar	D	Om	M
Bharatpur Palace	H	Pushkar Palace	L
Jagat Palace	K	Pushkar Resorts	A
Inn Seventh Heaven	C	RTDC Hotel Sarovar	N
Lake View	G	Sai Baba Haveli	E
Milkman	B	Shiva	F
Navratan Palace	I	Shyam Krishna	J

RESTAURANTS	
Honeydew Café	3
Honey & Spice	1
Manta	4
Moon Dance	6
Om Shiva	5
Raju Garden	2
Sai Baba	E
Sunset Café	7

but the location's wonderful, right on the lake, with views across the *ghats* from some rooms. Cheaper rooms have shared bathroom. ❶–❹

Lake View Main Bazaar ☏0145/277 2106, ⓦwww.lakeviewpushkar.com. Fairly basic and overpriced rooms (even the ones with a/c and private bathroom), but you do get great views over the lake from the terrace and the rooftop restaurant (which gets crowded at sunset). ❶–❹

Milkman Maili Mohalla ☏0145/277 3452. Intimate and sociable little family-run place hidden away in the backstreets with a range of cosy, well-kept rooms (fan and air-cooled; some with shared bath) and a nice rooftop café and terrace. ❶–❹

Navratan Palace Near Brahma Temple ☏0145/277 2145, ⓦwww.pushkarnavaratanpalace .com. Aimed at Indian rather than foreign visitors, this modern place has fresh, spotless rooms (some with a/c), well-kept gardens and one of the best pools in town (non-guests Rs50). Great value. ❸–❹

Om Ajmer Rd ☏0145/277 2672, ⓔom_deepak2004@yahoo.com. Pleasantly

tranquil hotel with a wide variety of rooms (all attached; some with TV) and a relaxing garden with hammocks for lounging, though the pool is about as inviting as the lake. ❶–❹

Sai Baba Haveli Off Varaha Chowk ☏0145/510 5161. Run by a French–Indian couple, this place offers a range of rooms (some with shared bath) in a lovely old house set around a pleasant garden patio. There's also a good restaurant (see p.207). ❷–❹

Shiva Off Varaha Chowk ☏0145/277 2120. Friendly, dependable little place, with bright, clean and very cheap rooms (the cheapest with shared bath), set around a small courtyard with a *champa* tree and five tortoises. Does not take advance reservations. ❶

Shyam Krishna Guest House Main Bazaar near Vishnu temple ☏0145/277 2461. Attractively tranquil guesthouse with a variety of rooms (some with shared bathroom) set around a garden in a lovely old blue-washed former temple compound. Excellent value, especially during the camel fair. ❶–❸

Mid-range to expensive

Inn Seventh Heaven Chhoti Basti
☎0145/510 5455, ⓦwww.inn-seventh
-heaven.com. Beautiful hotel in a fine old haveli,
mixing traditional and contemporary styles to
memorable effect, with vine-draped balconies
around a spacious interior courtyard and a range of
beautifully furnished rooms. Superb value at
current rates. ❸–❻

Jagat Palace Ajmer Rd ☎0145/277 2953,
ⓦwww.hotelpushkarpalace.com. Well-run luxury
hotel in a slightly inconvenient location on the
outskirts of town. The impressive buildings incorporate masonry plundered from an old fort,
decorated with elaborate wall paintings and period
fittings. Sweeping views, a huge pool, steam bath,
Jacuzzi and walled garden add to the allure. ❽

Pushkar Palace ☎0145/277 3001, ⓦwww
.hotelpushkarpalace.com. Newly renovated hotel
occupying a characterful old maharaja's palace in a
great location overlooking the lake. The whole
place has lots of charm, with period-style rooms
(most with lake views), a pretty garden restaurant
and a beautiful lake-facing veranda. Rooms from
around $140. ❾

Pushkar Resorts Motisar Rd, Ganehara
☎0145/277 2017 or 277 2944, ⓦwww
.pushkarresorts.com. Modern resort, inconveniently
situated 5km (a Rs100 taxi ride) out of town in the
desert, with forty swish a/c cottages in pristine
gardens and a kidney-shaped pool. Their restaurant
is the only one hereabouts that serves meat and
alcohol. Advance booking recommended. ❻–❾

RTDC Hotel Sarovar ☎0145/277 2040. State-run
hotel, a bit institutional and with miserable staff,
but boasting a nice lakeside setting, pleasant
garden and pool and spacious rooms (fan, air-
cooled or a/c; the cheapest ones have shared
bath). ❷–❻

The Town

There are more than five hundred **temples** in and around Pushkar; many had
to be rebuilt after pillaging during the merciless rule of Mughal emperor
Aurangzeb (1656–1708), while others are recent additions. Some, like the
splendid **Vishnu Temple**, on your right as you enter the village from the Ajmer
Bus Stand, are out of bounds to non-Hindus. Pushkar's most important shrine,
the **Brahma Temple**, houses a four-headed image of Brahma in its main
sanctuary, and is one of the few temples in India devoted to him. Raised on a

---

Brahma, Savitri and Gayitri

Although **Brahma**, the Creator, is one of the trinity of top Hindu gods, along with
Vishnu (the Preserver) and Shiva (the Destroyer), his importance has dwindled since
Vedic times and he has nothing like the following of the other two. The story behind
his temple here in Pushkar serves to explain why this is so, and also reveals the
significance of the temples here named after Brahma's wives, **Savitri** and **Gayitri**.

The story goes that Lord Brahma was to marry Savitri, a river goddess, at a sacrificial
ritual called a *yagna*, which had to be performed at a specific, astrologically auspicious
moment. But Savitri, busy dressing for the ceremony, failed to show up on time.
Without a wife, the Creator could not perform the *yagna* at the right moment, so he had
to find another consort quickly. The only unmarried woman available was a shepherdess
of the untouchable Gujar caste named Gayitri, whom the gods hastily purified by
passing her through the mouth of a cow (*gaya* means "cow", and *tri*, "passed through").
When Savitri finally arrived, she was furious that Brahma had married someone else
and cursed him, saying that henceforth he would be worshipped only at Pushkar. She
also proclaimed that the Gujar caste would gain liberation after death only if their ashes
were scattered on Pushkar lake – a belief which has persisted to this day. After casting
her curses, disgruntled Savitri flew off to the highest hill above the town. To placate her,
it was agreed that she should have her temple on that hilltop, while Gayitri occupied
the lower hill on the opposite, eastern side of the lake, and that Savitri would always
be worshipped before Gayitri, which is exactly how pilgrims do it, visiting Savitri's
temple first, and Gayitri's temple afterwards

stepped platform in the centre of a courtyard, the always crowded chamber is surrounded on three sides by smaller subsidiary shrines topped with flat roofs providing views across the desert to **Savitri Temple** on the summit of a nearby hill. The one-hour climb to the top of that hill is rewarded by matchless vistas over the town, surrounded on all sides by desert, and is best done before dawn, to reach the summit for sunrise, though it's also a great spot to watch the sun set. The temple itself is modern, but the image of Savitri is supposed to date back to the seventh century. **Gayitri Temple** (Pap Mochini Mandir), set on a hill east of the town, also offers great views, but especially at sunrise.

The lake and ghats

Pushkar **lake** is ringed by five hundred beautiful whitewashed temples, connected to the water by 52 *ghats* – one for each of Rajasthan's maharajas, who built separate guesthouses in which to stay during their visits here. Each is named after an event or person, and three in particular bear special significance. Primary among them is **Gau Ghat**, sometimes called Main Ghat, from which ashes of Mahatma Gandhi, Jawaharlal Nehru and Shri Lal Bahadur Shastri were sprinkled into the lake. **Brahma Ghat** marks the spot where Brahma himself is said to have worshipped, while at the large **Varaha Ghat**, just off the market square, Vishnu is believed to have appeared in the form of Varaha (a boar), the third of his nine earthly incarnations. At all the *ghats* visitors should remove their shoes at a reverential distance from the lake and refrain from smoking and taking photos.

Indian and Western tourists alike are urged by local Brahmin priests to worship at the lake; that is, to make **Pushkar Puja**. This involves the repetition of prayers while scattering rose petals into the lake, and then being asked for a donation, which usually goes to temple funds, or to the priest who depends on such benefaction. On completion of the puja, a red thread taken from a temple is tied around your wrist. Labelled the "Pushkar passport" by locals, this simple token means that you'll no longer attract pushy Pushkar priests and can wander unhindered onto the *ghats*. Indians usually give a sum of Rs21 or Rs51; the latter should suffice for a foreign tourist. A favourite trick of (usually phoney) priests is to ask how much you want to pay, then say a blessing for assorted members of your family, and demand the amount you stated times the number of family members blessed; don't be bullied by such cheap tricks into giving any more than you agreed.

Eating

As Pushkar is sacred to Lord Brahma, all food within city limits is strictly veg: meat, eggs and alcohol are banned, as are drugs other than bhang. Most **restaurants** tend to cater for foreign rather than Indian palates, offering pizza, falafel and chow mein along with the usual curries. Pushkar's sweet speciality is **malpua**, which is basically a chapati fried in syrup, sold at sweetshops around town, and on Halwai Gali, the street directly opposite Gau Ghat.

Honey & Spice Laxmi Market Main Bazaar. A bit more imaginative than your your average Pushkar backpacker café, with good filter coffee and a short but sweet menu of tasty vegetarian wholefood dishes (Rs45–65) featuring lots of brown rice and tofu. Closes 7pm.

Honeydew Café Main Bazaar near *Bharatpur Palace* hotel. A hole-in-the-wall place that's been a hippy hang-out since the days of the overland trail. It still knocks out a decent breakfast, especially if you like filter coffee, and its pasta dishes (Rs30–50) aren't bad either.

Manta near Brahma Temple. This is where a lot of Pushkar's Indian visitors come to eat, as it serves up some of the best veg curries (Rs25–50) and thalis (Rs45–55) in town. What's available depends on what vegetables are in season, but there's always a good selection. Not to be confused with the *Mamta* restaurant next door.

Moon Dance Pleasant garden restaurant-cum-bakery opposite the Vishnu temple dishing up pizzas, pasta, Chinese dishes and a reasonable range of Indian food (mains Rs30–110).

Om Shiva On the lane heading down to *Pushkar Palace* from Main Bazaar. The all-you-can-eat buffets here (different for breakfast, lunch and supper) are good value considering the Rs50 price tag, unchanged in over a decade.

Raju Garden Main Bazaar, near Ram Ghat. Above-average Indian, Chinese and Western food in a lovely lakeside setting. Particularly renowned for its veg shepherd's pie and baked potatoes, but does a good range of veg curries too. Mains Rs35–75.

Sai Baba Haveli Off Varaha Chowk. The usual Indian veg curries (Rs36–60) plus great pasta and the best pizzas in Pushkar (the tandoor doubles as a pizza oven). You can sit out front or, more atmospherically, in the garden. There's Rajasthani dancing on Saturdays at 8pm, when there's an excellent Rs150 buffet.

Sunset Café East side of the lake. The perfect place to enjoy Pushkar's legendary lakeside sunsets, with great views (though the outside seats fill up quickly towards dusk) and an impressive selection of juices, lassis, shakes, and even non-alcoholic beer and organic tea, plus the inevitable pizzas and cakes. Mains Rs50–100.

Listings

Banks and exchange There's a useful State Bank of Bikaner & Jaipur ATM near the Brahma Temple. Alternatively, you can change cash or traveller's cheques or get cash advances on credit cards quickly at any of the dozens of forex offices in the Main Bazaar. Two reliable places are the Thomas Cook office (Mon–Sat 9.30am–6.30pm) opposite the *Shyam Krishna* guesthouse, and NL Forex in Laxmi Market, by the *Honey & Spice* café (daily 9.30am–7pm), which is also open Sun.

Bicycle rental Malakar Bicycle Shop, by the Ajmer Bus Stand (the unsigned pink shop next to EKTA Travels), has basic bikes for Rs25/24hr.

Camel safaris A number of places around town offer camel safaris into the desert around Pushkar. Maharaja Camel Safari, on the road just before the *Om Shiva* restaurant (☎0/982 827 3366), runs 3hr (Rs250) and full-day trips (Rs350), and can also arrange longer safaris as well as excursions by camel-cart (Rs300/3hr) and horse-riding (Rs250/hr).

Hospital Government Hospital, opposite the GPO near Marwar Bus Stand ☎0145/277 2029.

Internet access Numerous small places around town charge Rs20–30 per hour. There's a cluster along the road near the Old Rangji Temple, including the well-equipped KK Internet (daily 9.30am–11pm; Rs20/hr).

Laundry Chhotu just off Varaha Chowk (daily 7am–9pm). Bring clothes early for same-day service.

Motorcycle rental Bhagwati, at the Ajmer Bus Stand, has bikes for Rs100–200/day.

Police Next to the GPO ☎0145/277 2046.

Post office In the north of town near the Marwar Bus Stand (Mon–Sat 9am–5pm).

Shopping Though it isn't a craft centre as such, Pushkar is a good place to pick up touristy souvenirs, with its shops conveniently strung out along the Main Bazaar. As well as lots of hippy-type clothes, T-shirts and silver jewellery, not to mention ceramic chillums (Pushkar's rival those of Hampi and Pondicherry in the south), you'll find lac bangles, Rajasthani textiles, incense, essential oils and – always handy for a paint fight – Holi dyes. For new and used books, there's a slew of shops on the Main Bazaar just south of Varaha Chowk.

Swimming pools The *Navratan Palace* hotel charges non-guests Rs50 to use theirs.

Moving on from Pushkar

Government and private intercity **buses** leave from the **Marwar Bus Stand** (☎0145/242 9398), north of town, for Bikaner (9 daily; 6hr 30min), Bundi (2 daily, or hourly from Ajmer), Delhi (5 daily; 9hr), Jaipur (8 daily; 3hr 30min), Jodhpur (3 daily; 5hr) and Udaipur (1 nightly, or 2 daily from Ajmer; 7hr 30min). Two of the **Delhi** buses are overnight sleeper services. For **Jaisalmer** you'll need to catch a bus from Ajmer (2 daily and 1 nightly; 11hr). To get to **Ajmer**, take a bus (every 30min; 30min) from the **Ajmer Bus Stand**. Further destinations are served from Ajmer (see "Travel details" on p.267), and connecting services are available, but it is not unknown for people who have

Kartika Purnima and Pushkar camel fair

Hindus visit Pushkar year-round to take a dip in the redemptory waters of the lake, but there is one particular day when bathing here is believed to relieve devotees of all their sins, and ultimately free them from the endless cycle of death and reincarnation. That day is the full moon (*purnima*) of the **Kartika** month (usually Nov). The five days leading up to and including the full moon, Pushkar hosts thousands of celebrating devotees, following prescribed rituals on the lakeside and in the Brahma Temple. To add to the flurry of colour and activity, a large week-long **camel fair** is held at around the same time in the sand dunes west of the town, with hordes of herders from all over Rajasthan gathering to parade, race and trade over forty thousand animals.

Once trading is under way, camels and cattle are meticulously groomed and auctioned, while women dressed in mirrored skirts and vivid shawls lay out embroidered cloth, jewellery, pots and ornaments beside the herds. Cattle, poultry, sheep and goats are entered for competitions, and prizes are given for the best displays of fruit and vegetables. Away from the main activity, the dusty ground is stirred up by vigorous **camel races**, urged on by gamblers. Aside from its overwhelming size, the most striking feature of the fair from a foreign visitor's point of view is that it is attended by equal numbers of men and women. With the harvest safely in the bag and the surplus livestock sold, the villagers, for this brief week or so, have a little money to spend enjoying themselves, which creates a lighthearted atmosphere that's generally absent from most other Rajasthani livestock fairs.

The popularity of Pushkar's fair has – inevitably – had an effect on the event, with camera-toting package tourists now bumping elbows with the event's traditional pilgrims and camel traders. But while the commercialism can be off-putting, the festive environment and coming together of cultures does produce some spontaneous mirth: the second prize in the moustache contest was recently won by a Mancunian. To avoid the worst of the tomfoolery **come at least a week before the final weekend**, when most of the buying and selling is done. By the full moon, the bulk of the herders have packed up and gone home.

Practicalities

Hotels hike their rates sometimes a fortnight before the full moon and still fill up quickly. Though it's best to book a room as far ahead as possible, if you arrive early in the day – and with a bit of hunting – securing **accommodation** shouldn't be a problem. RTDC usually sends its package guests out to **tented compounds** close to the fairgrounds, where there's a choice between dormitory beds (Rs300), deluxe tents (⑨), or huts (④) complete with private bathrooms. Book well ahead by contacting the RTDC office in Jaipur (☎0141/511 4768, ✉cro@rajasthantourism.gov .in) or check their website for more details (⊛www.rajasthantourism.gov.in). Additional luxury camping, complete with carpets, furniture, running water and Western toilets, is offered by the maharaja of Jodhpur's *Royal Camp* (for reservations contact WelcomHeritage ☎0291/257 2321, ⊛www.welcomheritagehotels.com; ⑨), or *Royal Desert Camp* (for reservations contact the *Jagat Palace* hotel; ⑨).

The **dates** of the next few camel fairs are: 5–13 Nov 2008, 25 Oct–2 Nov 2009, and 13–21 Nov 2010. It's best to get here for the first two or three days to see the *mela* in full swing – most of the camels have left by the last few days of the fair.

bought tickets at agencies in Pushkar to find their seats double-booked when they try boarding in Ajmer. If possible, it's best to make bookings for bus journeys from Ajmer in Ajmer itself. Services to Delhi in particular are often reserved days ahead.

For recommended **trains from Ajmer**, see p.202. EKTA Travels act as Indian Railways' agents in Pushkar and can arrange tickets for train journeys out of any station in India for a Rs40 charge, and also book, cancel or confirm air tickets.

They have offices at both the Marwar (☎0145/277 2131) and Ajmer bus stands (☎0145/277 2888)

Jodhpur and around

On the eastern fringe of the Thar Desert, **JODHPUR**, dubbed "the Blue City" after the colour-wash of its old town houses, sprawls across the arid terrain, overlooked by the mighty **Meherangarh Fort**, whose ramparts rise from a sheer-sided sandstone outcrop. It was once the centre of Marwar, the largest

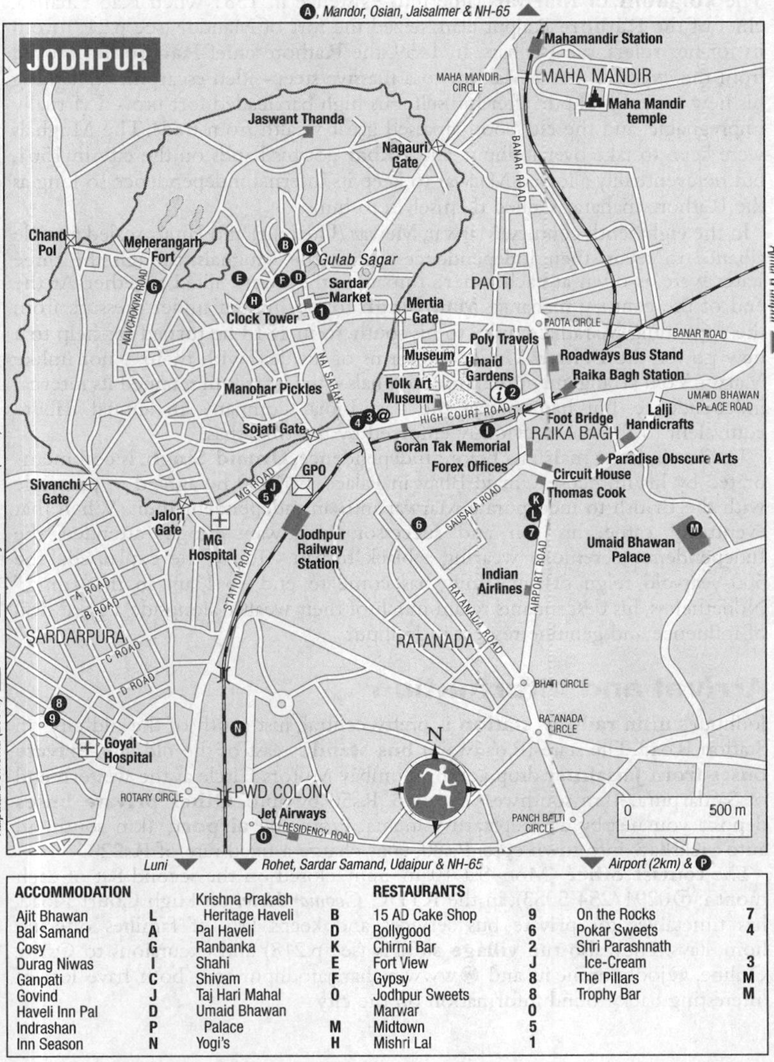

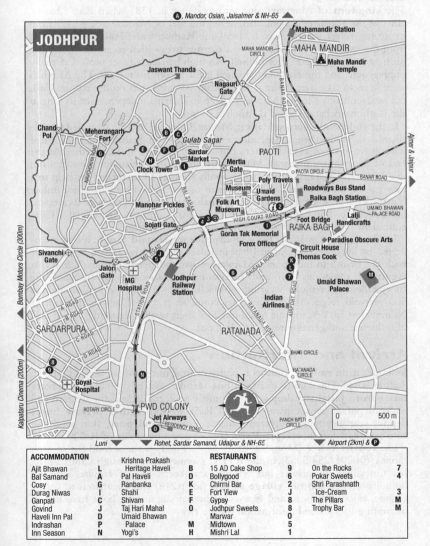

ACCOMMODATION				RESTAURANTS			
Ajit Bhawan	L	Krishna Prakash Heritage Haveli	B	15 AD Cake Shop	9	On the Rocks	7
Bal Samand	A	Pal Haveli	D	Bollygood	6	Pokar Sweets	4
Cosy	G	Ranbanka	K	Chirmi Bar	2	Shri Parashnath Ice-Cream	3
Durag Niwas	I	Shahi	E	Fort View	J	The Pillars	M
Ganpati	C	Shivam	F	Gypsy	8	Trophy Bar	M
Govind	J	Taj Hari Mahal	O	Jodhpur Sweets	8		
Haveli Inn Pal	D	Umaid Bhawan Palace	M	Marwar	0		
Indrashan	P	Yogi's	H	Midtown	5		
Inn Season	N			Mishri Lal	1		

princely state in Rajputana, and today has a population of around a million. But despite its size and importance, Jodhpur is barely a pit-stop for most travellers en route between Jaisalmer to the west and Jaipur to the east, and only that by virtue of the fort. It's a shame to rush the place, though. Getting lost in the blue maze of the old city you'll stumble across Muslim tie-dyers, puppet-makers and traditional spice markets, while Jodhpur's famed cubic roofscape, best viewed at sunset, is a photographer's dream. In addition, the encroaching desert beyond the blue city is dotted with small settlements where you can escape the congestion for a true taste of rural Rajasthan.

Some history

The **kingdom of Marwar** came into existence in 1381 when Rao Chanda, chief of the **Rathore** Rajput clan, seized the fort of Mandor (see p.217) from its former rulers, the Parihars. In 1459, the Rathore chief **Rao Jodha** moved from the exposed site at Mandor to a massive steep-sided escarpment, naming his new capital Jodhpur, after himself. His high barricaded fort proved virtually impregnable, and the city soon amassed great wealth from trade. The Mughals were keen to take over Jodhpur, and **Akbar** got his hands on the city in 1561, but he eventuallly allowed Marwar to keep its internal independence so long as the Rathore maharajas allied themselves to him.

In the eighteenth century, Marwar, Mewar (Udaipur) and Jaipur sealed a triple alliance to retain their independence against the Mughals, though the three states were as often at each other's throats as they were allied together. At the end of the century, maharaja **Man Singh** found himself under pressure from the expanding Maratha empire to his south, so in 1818 he turned for help to a new power, the **British**. Under the terms of his deal with them – not unlike Marwar's old arrangement with the Mughals – the kingdom retained its internal independence, but had to pay the East India Company an annual tribute equivalent to the one previously enforced by the Marathas.

The last but one maharaja before Independence, **Umaid Singh**, is commemorated by his immense Umaid Bhawan Palace. In 1930 he agreed in principle with the British to incorporate Marwar into an independent India. When that eventually came, his son and successor, Hanuwant Singh, attended the Independence ceremony wearing a black turban. "Today," he explained, "the 500-year-old reign of my family has come to end, so I am in mourning." Nonetheless, his descendants retain much of their wealth, alongside a great deal of influence and genuine respect in Jodhpur.

Arrival and information

Jodhpur's main **railway station** is pretty central, just south of the old city on Station Road. The state (Roadways) **bus stand** is east of the old city. **Private buses from Jaisalmer** drop you by Bombay Motors Circle at the western end of Sardarpura, 4km southwest of town, Rs50 by auto. **Other private buses** deposit you nearby at Kalpataru Cinema. From the **airport**, 4km south, an auto-rickshaw into town costs Rs80; taxis charge a fixed rate of Rs220.

The **tourist office** (Mon–Sat 10am–5pm, closed on the second Sat of each month; ☎0291/254 5083), in the RTDC *Goomar Hotel* on High Court Road, has timetables for private bus services and keeps lists of families offering homestays. They also run **village safaris** (see p.218) and excursions to Osian. Online, ⓦjodhpur.nic.in and ⓦwww.maharajajodhpur.com both have lots of interesting background information on the city.

Accommodation

Jodhpur has plenty of good accommodation in all brackets, but auto-wallahs will invariably find ways to avoid taking you to any hotel that doesn't pay them commission. Some guesthouses offer free pick-ups; alternatively, take an auto to a point nearby and then walk.

Budget

Cosy Bhram Puri, Chuna ki Choki, Navchokiya ☎0291/261 2066, ⊛www.cosyguesthouse.com. A steep climb (signposted) from Navchokiya Road, but it's friendly and fun, and the upper terraces have killer views of the fort, as well as cheap tents (❶) – though you'll have to reserve ahead to get one. ❶–❸

Durag Niwas 1 Old Public Park, Raika Bagh ☎0291/251 2385, ⊛www.durag-niwas.com. Very friendly and well-run little place, great value and socially responsible too, with a volunteer programme helping disadvantaged local women.

The plumbing is temperamental, however, so check the hot water before taking a room. ❷–❹

Ganpati Makrana Mohalla (exit Sardar Market through the northern gateway, then turn left then first right) ☎0291/263 1686, ⊜ganpatigh@yahoo .co.uk. Bright and comfortable rooms (all attached; some with a/c) in a nice modern guesthouse with fine fort views from the rooftop restaurant and the more expensive rooms. The same family's older and shabbier *Shivam Guest House*, just down the road, has a further selection of rooms at slightly cheaper rates. ❷–❹

Heritage hotels in the Jodhpur region

Bal Samand Lake Palace (8km north of Jodhpur) ☎0291/257 2321, ⊛www.welcom heritagehotels.com. Among the most attractive heritage hotels in the state, converted from the maharaja's lakeside summer palace. The standard rooms are nothing special, but the nine suites in the main building are huge, airy and exquisitely furnished. ❸

Fort Chanwa Luni Luni (36km south of Jodhpur) ☎02931/284216, ⊛www .fortchanwa.com. Set in an 1895 red-sandstone fort, with all the usual deluxe heritage-hotel trappings. The standard rooms aren't all that old-fashioned, however, so it's worth forking out more to get one that's a bit special. ❻–❾

Fort Khejarla Khejarla (84km east of Jodhpur) ☎02930/258311, ⊛www.nivalink .com/fortkhejrala. A mightily imposing fort with lots of carved red sandstone, taste-fully furnished rooms and views over the surrounding countryside. The best rooms are in the turrets. ❼–❽

Jhalamand Garh Jhalamand (7km south of Jodhpur) ☎0291/274 0481. This eighteenth-century palace of the thakurs (barons) of the village of Jhalamand is close enough to Jodhpur that you can actually see the city from it. The whole building is rather elegant, and the lobby was formerly the thakur's Diwan-i-Am (audience hall). ❻

Khimsar Fort Khimsar (80km northeast of Jodhpur) ☎01585/262345, ⊛www .nivalink.com/khimsar. There's a variety of rooms (from Rs6000) in different styles – some traditional, some Art Deco – plus a pool, tennis courts, a croquet lawn and golf practising facilities at this former sixteenth-century fort. ❾

Rohet Garh Rohet (39km south of Jodhpur) ☎02936/268231 or 531, ⊛www .rohetgarh.com. This sleek palace hotel offers cool, spacious rooms, candle-lit poolside dinners, royal-style picnics with liveried attendants, plus culinary workshops, horse riding and bird-watching expeditions. ❽–❾

Sardar Samand Palace Pali (65km southeast of Jodhpur) ☎02960/245001 to 3, ⊛www.welcomheritagehotels.com. Bird-watchers and fans of Art Deco will love this hunting lodge built in 1930 for the maharaja of Jodhpur. On the highest piece of land for miles, with magnificent panoramic views, the palace has retained many of its original features. Activities include bird-watching, nature walks and village safaris. Doubles from Rs5100. ❾

Govind Station Rd ☎ 0291/262 2758, ⓦ www.govindhotel.com. A long-standing travellers' favourite, with jolly rooms in pretty colours, a clean dorm (Rs90), good rooftop restaurant (see p.215) and a very helpful owner. He doesn't pay commission, so auto-wallahs won't want to bring you here, but it's easy to find – look for the trees outside. ③–④

Mid-range

Haveli Inn Pal near Gulab Sagar Lake (exit the north gate of Sardar Market, turn right and first left) ☎ 0291/261 2519, ⓦ www.haveliinnpal.com. Large, well-appointed rooms (all with a/c and TV; some with fort or lake views) in an eighteenth-century haveli. Reservations recommended. ⑦

Indrashan 593 High Court Colony, 3km south of town ☎ 0291/244 0665, ⓦ www.rajputana discovery.com. Eight thoroughly comfortable rooms in an authentic homestay, with sumptuous cooking classes that draw amateur chefs from around the world. Non-guests are welcome for dinner if they call ahead (Rs350). ④–⑤

Inn Season PWD Rd ☎ 0291/261 6400, ⓦ www .innseasonjodhpur.com. Boutique hotel whose Art Deco rooms pay homage to the owner's love affair with vintage cars. A loyal clientele of handicraft exporters chill out at night to vinyl on a vintage gramophone. One drawback: it's noisy during wedding season (approx Oct–March) due to the wedding ground next door. Book ahead. ⑤–⑧

Krishna Prakash Nayabas (it's straight up the road past the *Shivam Guest House*) ☎ 0/982 924 1547,

Expensive

Ajit Bhawan Airport Rd ☎ 0291/251 1410, ⓦ www.ajitbhawan.com. Despite the Flintstones-like theme-park design, this self-contained resort – built to resemble a dhani village – gets rave reviews for its try-hard attitude and relaxing environment. Accommodation is in cute little round chalets or more conventional rooms, and there's a quaint waterfall-fed pool (non-guests Rs500), thatch-roofed outdoor restaurant and spa. Rooms from around $140. ⑨

Ranbanka Airport Rd ☎ 0291/251 0162, ⓦ ranbankahotels.com. In the other half of the palace occupied by *Ajit Bhawan*, this is more authentic in some ways (the rooms are actually inside the palace), but less professional and a bit creakier, though it has a nice pool (non-guests Rs500), a health spa and a garden restaurant. ⑧–⑨

Yogi's Manak Chowk, Nayabas (about 50m down the road in front of the *Krishna Prakash Haveli*) ☎ 0291/264 3436, ⓦ www.yogiguesthouse.com. Right in the heart of the old city, this is one of Jodhpur's pricier guesthouses, but with an excellent location, pleasant rooms (some with a/c) and excellent fort views from the rooftop terrace, which is one of Rajasthan's best chill-out spaces. ③–⑤

ⓦ www.kpheritage.com. Heritage hotel in a superbly located haveli right below the fort walls. The building itself isn't that exciting, but rooms (almost all with a/c and TV) are nicely furnished with antique bric-a-brac and rates are surprisingly inexpensive. ⑤–⑦

Pal Haveli near Gulab Sagar Lake ☎ 0291/329 3328, ⓦ www.palhaveli.com. In the same compound as *Haveli Inn Pal*, and owned by the same family, this is a more upmarket affair, with statelier rooms – a low-priced heritage hotel rather than a guesthouse. ⑦–⑧

Shahi Gandhi St, City Police district, off Katla Bazaar opposite Narsingh Temple ☎ 0291/262 3802, ⓔ shahigh@rediffmail.com. Welcoming family guesthouse occupying a quirky 350-year-old haveli buried deep in the warren of lanes beneath the fort's southwest wall – and with superb views of it from the roof. The six rooms (air-cooled and a/c) are brimful of character, decorated with a medley of quaint murals and assorted curios. Call for directions. ④–⑤

Taj Hari Mahal 5 Residency Rd, less than 1km south of town ☎ 0291/243 9700, ⓦ www.tajhotels .com. All the luxury you'd expect from a five-star Taj hotel, including good restaurants and a huge pool, but it lacks the charm and personality of the heritage and boutique alternatives. Rooms from around US$210. ⑨

Umaid Bhawan Palace southeast of town ☎ 0291/251 0101 or 1600/111 825, ⓦ www .tajhotels.com. The Maharaja of Jodhpur's princely pile (also see p.214) ranks among the world's grandest hotels, with celebrity guests and lashings of trendy Art Deco. But being king or queen for a day can be a solitary experience – some find the oversized suites, stately salons and dark, marbled passageways a bit foreboding. Rooms start at around US$850. ⑨

The City

Life in Jodhpur focuses very much around the fort, which dominates the walled old city. The blue wash applied to most of the houses huddled beneath it originally denoted high-caste Brahmin residences, and resulted from the addition of indigo to their lime-based whitewash, thought to protect buildings from insect pests, and to keep them cool in summer. Over time the distinctive colour caught on – there's now even a blue-wash mosque on the road from the Jalori Gate, west of the fort.

The bazaars of the old city, with different areas assigned to different trades, radiate out from the 1910 **Sardar Market** with its tall **clock tower**, a distinctive local landmark marking the centre of town. Most of the ramparts on the south side of the old city have been dismantled, leaving **Jalori Gate** and **Sojati Gate** looking rather forlorn as gates without a wall.

Meherangarh Fort

Jodhpur's **Meherangarh Fort** (daily: summer 8.30am–5.30pm; winter 9am–5pm; Rs250 entry includes audio tour if you leave ID, credit card or deposit; camera Rs50, video Rs200; elevator Rs15; guide Rs100; ⓦ www.mehrangarh .org) provides a taste of the war, honour and extravagance that characterized Rajputana. Huge and imposing, it dominates the city, though unlike the fort in Jaisalmer it is uninhabited, its paths trodden only by visitors.

The walk up to the fort from the old city is pretty steep, but you can reach the entrance by taxi or auto along the road from Nagauri Gate. The outstanding audio tour takes about two hours to complete. You enter the fort through **Jai Pol**, constructed in 1806, and the first of seven defensive gates on the way up to the fort's living quarters. The sixth of the seven gates, **Loha Pol**, has a sharp right-angle turn and sharper iron spikes to hinder the ascent of charging enemy elephants. On the wall just inside it you can see the handprints of Maharaja Man Singh's widows, placed there in 1843 as they left the palace to commit *sati* on his funeral pyre – the last mass *sati* by wives of a Marwari maharaja.

Beyond the final gate, the massive **Suraj Pol**, lies the **Coronation Courtyard** (Shangar Chowk), where maharajas are crowned on a special marble throne. Looking up from the courtyard, you can see the fantastic *jali* (lattice) work that almost entirely covers the surrounding sandstone walls. The adjoining apartments now serve as a **museum** showcasing solid silver *howdahs* (elephant seats), palanquins and assorted armaments including Akbar's own sword. Upstairs are some fine **miniature paintings** of the Marwari school, mostly featuring Maharaja Man Singh.

The most elaborate of the royal apartments, the magnificent 1724 **Phool Mahal** (Flower Palace), with its jewel-like stained-glass windows and gold filigree ceiling, was a pleasure hall used by the maharajas to listen to music or poetry, or watch dancers perform. Maharaja Takhat Singh, on the other hand, preferred his own nineteenth-century apartment, **Takhat Vilas**, its ceiling hung with huge Christmas-tree balls, while the walls are painted with murals reminiscent of those in Shekhawati (see p.174). In the **Jhanki Mahal**, or Queen's Palace, there's a colourful array of cradles of former rulers. The **Moti Mahal** (Pearl Palace) was used for councils of state. The five alcoves in the wall opposite the entrance are in fact concealed balconies where the maharaja's wives could listen in secretly on the proceedings.

Beyond the Moti Mahal is the **Zenana**, or women's quarters. From here, you descend to the **Temple of Chamunda**, the city's oldest temple, dedicated to Jodhpur's patron goddess, an incarnation of Durga.

Jaswant Thanda

Some 500m north of the fort, and connected to it by road, **Jaswant Thanda** (daily 9am–5pm; Rs20, camera Rs25, video Rs50) is a pillared marble memorial to the popular ruler Jaswant Singh II (1878–95), who purged Jodhpur of bandits, initiated irrigation systems and boosted the economy. The cenotaphs of members of the royal family who have died since Jaswant are close to his memorial; those who preceded him are remembered by chhatris at Mandor (see p.217). In the morning, this southwest-facing spot is an excellent place from which to photograph the fort.

Umaid Bhawan Palace

Dominating the city's southeast horizon is the **Umaid Bhawan Palace**, a colossal Indo-Saracenic heap commissioned by Maharaja Umaid Singh in 1929 as a famine relief project. It kept three thousand labourers gainfully employed for sixteen years and cost nearly 95 lakh (nine and a half million) rupees. When completed in 1944, it boasted 347 rooms, including a cinema and indoor swimming pool. Its furniture and fittings, ordered from Maples in London at the height of World War II, were sunk by a U-boat en route to India, and the maharaja had to turn instead to a wartime Polish refugee, Stephen Norblin, who gave the palace its fabulous Art Deco interiors. Umaid Singh unfortunately had little time to enjoy his new home; he died three years after it was finished.

The present incumbent, Maharaja Gaj Singh, occupies only one-third of the palace; the rest is given over to a luxury **hotel** (see p.212) and a **museum** (daily 9.30am–5pm; Rs50; no photography). The museum contains an exhibition on the building of the palace, a gallery of crockery and glassware, a salon with a peeling gold gilt ceiling, and a gallery of clocks and barometers, some in the form of railway locomotives, lighthouses and windmills. Far more interesting (and expensive) than the museum is the palace itself, its Art Deco furniture and fittings nearly all original, enlivened with lashings of typically Rajasthani gilt and sweeping staircases. To see them, non-guests will need to spend a minimum of Rs2000 at the hotel's bar or restaurant (see opposite). It's also a good idea to reserve in advance.

Umaid Gardens

On High Court Road, the **Umaid Gardens** are home to the city's depressing **zoo** (daily except Tues 8am–5.30pm; Rs50, camera Rs10, video Rs40), whose animals are housed in enclosures scattered around the park, and the **Sardar Government Museum** (daily 10am–4.30pm; Rs3), exhibiting the usual collection of skinned, stuffed, decapitated and pickled animals, along with a few other Rajasthani artefacts. Just outside the gardens, the Rajasthan Sangeet Natak Akademi runs a **Folk Art Museum** (Mon–Sat 11am–5pm; free) with a slightly moth-eaten collection of Rajasthani musical instruments and puppets.

Eating and drinking

Jodhpur's **restaurants** cater for all tastes and all budgets. Local **specialities** include *mirchi bada*, a big chilli covered in wheatgerm and potato and then deep-fried like a pakora. Jodhpuri sweets, often made with *mawa* (milk that's been boiled down until solid), include *makhan wada* (made from wheatflour, semolina and sugar, fried in ghee) and *mawa kachori* (a *kachori* filled with *mawa* and drizzled with syrup). In winter, there's *doodh feni*, consisting of wheat strands (sweet or plain) in hot milk.

Bars are pretty thin on the ground in Jodhpur, but most of the restaurants listed below are licenced. If you don't want to pay Rs2000 to visit the *Umaid Bhawan Palace Hotel's Trophy Bar*, you could try the uninspiring but quiet *Chirmi Bar* at the RTDC *Hotel Goomar*, next to the tourist office, or the dimly lit, male-dominated bars around the *Midtown* restaurant on Station Road.

Cafés, sweets and snacks

Jodhpur Sweets C Rd, Sardarpura, next to *Gipsy*. The best sweet shop in town, and an excellent place to try *makhan wada*, *mawa kachori*, or any other Rajasthani or Bengali sweets.

Mishri Lal in the eastern arch of the south gate to Sardar Market. The most famous purveyor of *makhania* lassi, made with cream, saffron and cardamom, very rich and thick, but those with delicate stomachs should take note that they use crushed ice made from tap water. They also do good *doodh feni*.

Pokar Sweets corner of Nai Sarak with High Court Rd. Known for their *makhan wada*, and their *mirchi bada*'s pretty hot too. This is also a good place to try *doodh feni*.

Shri Parashnath Ice-Cream High Court Rd. Jodhpur's best address for juices and ice cream. Their Marwari kulfi (kulfi with nuts and saffron) is outstanding.

Restaurants

Bollygood Khaas Bagh, Ratanada. A fun, movie-themed restaurant with indoor or garden dining, veg or non-veg. Tandoori dishes are the mainstay. Main courses around Rs100–150.

Fort View *Govind Hotel*, Station Rd. A cut above the usual tourist places, with good, reasonably priced veg curries and thalis (Rs55–110), local specialities such as *makhania* lassi and *gulab jamun* (not the Bengali sweet, but a savoury Rajasthani dish made with *mawa*), plus some Chinese items and good breakfast options, including real coffee. Also has Wi-Fi coverage, and you can hang out here while waiting for a bus or train (baggage storage facilities are available).

Gypsy C Rd, Sardarpura. Downstairs it's a diner selling south Indian, Chinese and Continental snacks (Rs30–60). Upstairs it's an immaculate restaurant serving one thing only: an unlimited and very delicious veg thali (Rs90) which they keep refilling for as long as you can keep eating. There's another branch on PWD Rd, next to *Inn Season* hotel.

Marwar At the *Taj Hari Mahal* hotel ☎0291/243 9700. Pricey, but the best place in town to sample traditional Marwari cuisine, such as Jodhpuri *mas*

(a spicy mutton dish) or *gatta di subzi* (its veg equivalent). Mains Rs210–400.

Midtown on a branch off Station Rd leading from opposite the station to Raj Ranchodji Temple. Bright, clean and friendly, with a delicious range of pure-veg curries (Rs55–100), south Indian dishes, Gujarati and Rajasthani thalis (Rs70–100) and other Rajasthani specialities, as well as pizza and pasta.

On the Rocks Next to *Ajit Bhawan* hotel, Airport Rd ☎0291/230 2701. Attractive garden restaurant specializing in kebabs and tandoori cuisine. Fun and festive at night, though the lunch crowd is mostly tour groups. Mains Rs75–110 veg, Rs120–200 non-veg.

The Pillars *Umaid Bhawan Palace* hotel ☎0291/251 0101. A visit to this veranda café-restaurant gives you the excuse to wander around the hotel's opulent Art Deco interior – and it's also a great place for a sundowner. Sandwiches are available all day and there's a dinner menu of mostly Western food from 7.30pm, or take a seat on an elephant-foot footstool and have a drink in the *Trophy Bar*. Rs2000 minimum charge, payable on entry.

Jodhpurs

The city of Jodhpur gives its name to a type of **trouser** – baggy around the thigh but narrow around the calf – designed for **horseback riding**. They were invented for his own personal use by Sir Pratap Singh, brother of Maharaja Jaswant Singh II, in 1887, and his custom-made riding trousers caught on big-time among Britain's aristocracy, who were soon flocking to Savile Row to get their own jodhpurs made.

Shopping

Jodhpur's first-rate **antique reproductions** – everything from chests of drawers to sculptures of Jain *tirthankaras* – attract dealers from around the world. There's a line of shops selling them along Umaid Bhawan Palace Road east of the Circuit House. Other good buys in town are **textiles**, including mirrorwork dresses, patchwork bedcovers, and *Bandhani* (tie-dye) fabric and saris, not to mention **Jodhpur riding britches**. For bookshops, see Listings, below.

India Tailors High Court Rd, 75m east of the junction with Nai Sarak. Despite its small and unprepossessing appearance, this little shop can't be beaten for custom-made suits or Jodhpur riding britches, and counts the maharaja amongst its customers. They can run you up a pair of jodhpurs within 8hr for around Rs4000.

Mohanlal Verhomal's (MV) Spice Shop 209-B Kirana Merchant Vegetable Market, west of the clock tower ⊛ www.mvspices.com. Lots of spices and unique spice mixes for different types of curry, as well as a range of masala chais.

Paradise Obscure Arts Umaid Bhawan Palace Rd. A treasure-trove of superior bric-a-brac, including old tin boxes, enamel signs, silverware, glassware,

little brass gods, metal toys, doorknobs and so on. The nearby Lalji Handicrafts has an even bigger selection of quirky collectibles (plus a fair amount of junk) and is also worth a look.

Raju's MG Rd, almost opposite Sojati Gate. Embroidered and *bandhani* saris and *salwar kameez* suits: very classy, very colourful, very Rajasthani. Lucky Silk Stores, a few doors away on MG Rd, is also worth checking.

Shriganesham Pal Haveli, north of Sardar Market, opposite the eastern arch of the north gate. Wonderful Rajasthani fabrics, old and new, including *dhurries*, mirrorwork dresses, patchwork bedspreads made from recycled garments, and some sumptuous embroidered coats and dresses.

Listings

Airlines Indian Airlines, East Patel Nagar, Airport Rd ☏ 0291/251 0758; Jet Airways, Osho Apartments, Residency Rd ☏ 0291/510 3333.
Banks and exchange There are ATMs at 151 & 157 Nai Sarak; on MG Rd 100m east of Sojati Gate; on the little street off MG Rd opposite Sojati Gate; on Station Rd near *Govind Hotel*; and next to the tourist office. Forex offices can be found north of the clock tower in Sardar Market and on Hanwant Vihar just north of Circuit House (there's also a Thomas Cook on Airport Rd).
Bicycle rental Hind Silk Store, 30m west of *Midtown* restaurant on Station Rd (☏ 0291/261 2953), rents bicycles for Rs25–35 a day.
Bookshops Sarvodaya Bookstall, opposite Raj Ranchodji Temple on the same side-road off Station Rd as *Midtown* restaurant; and Krishna Book Depot, upstairs at Krishna Art and Export in Sardar Market, just east of the north gate.
Festival Jodhpur's annual two-day Marwar Festival, held at the full moon of the Hindu month of Ashvina (3–4 Oct 2009, 21–22 Oct 2010, 10–11 Oct 2011) is a showcase of performing arts, mainly music and dance.

Hospital The best private hospital is the Goyal on Residency Rd in the Sindhi Colony, 2km south of town (☏ 0291/243 2144).
Internet access Internet (usually Rs30–40 an hour) is widely available, even amid the medieval labyrinth of the old city. Handy Internet stations include The Net (daily 9am–10pm; Rs25/hr) on High Court Rd by *Shri Parashnath Ice-Cream*, *Govind Hotel's* Internet office on Station Rd (daily 24hr) and Sify I-Way (daily 9am–11pm; Rs30/hr), opposite the north gate from Sardar Market.
Motorcycle rental Jodhpur Travels, Station Road (a few doors south of the *Govind Hotel*) has motorbikes and mopeds for rent for Rs200–500/day.
Police ☏ 0291/265 0777. There's a police tourist assistance booth by the clock tower in Sardar Market.
Post office The GPO is opposite the *Govind Hotel* on Station Road. Stamps can be bought in the section through the right-hand entrance (Mon–Sat 9am–5pm, Sun 11am–4pm). For poste restante and parcel packing head through the left-hand entrance (Mon–Fri 9am–1pm & 2–3pm, Sat 9am–1pm).
Swimming pools Non-guests can use the lovely pool at the *Ajit Bhawan* hotel (see p.212) for Rs500.

Moving on from Jodhpur

Jodhpur stands at the nexus of Rajasthan's main **tourist routes**, with connections northeast to Jaipur, Pushkar and Delhi, south to Udaipur and Ahmedabad, and west to Jaisalmer. Buses for most destinations are faster than the train.

Recommended trains from Jodhpur

All the following depart daily unless otherwise stated. Note that there are no direct trains to **Udaipur** or **Chittaurgarh**.

Destination	Name	No.	Departs	Arrives
Abu Road	Ahmedabad Express	9224	6.35am	11.25am
	Ranakpur Express	4707	3.00pm	8pm
Agra	Howrah Superfast	2308	7.45pm	6.35am
Ajmer	Fast passenger train	1JA	7.15am	12.35pm
Alwar	Jaisalmer–Delhi Express	4060	10.30pm	7.35am
Bikaner	Ranakpur Express	4708	10.05am	4pm
	Barmer-Kalka Express	4888	10.30am	4.20pm
	Bhatinda passenger train	340	2.05pm	9.20pm
Delhi	Mandor Express	2462	7.30pm	6.20am
	Jaisalmer–Delhi Express	4060	10.30pm	11.10am
Jaipur	Jaipur Intercity Express	2466	5.55am	10.47am
	Marudhar Express	4854	9.15am	3.30pm
			(M, Th, Sat only)	
Jaisalmer	Delhi–Jaisalmer Express	4059	6.20am	1pm
	Jaisalmer Express	4810	11.25pm	5.30am
Sawai Madhopur	Intercity Express	2466	5.55am	1.15pm
	Bhopal passenger train	492	7.25am	8.25pm

The **airport** is 4km south of town (auto Rs50, taxi Rs220); for details of flights, see **"Travel details"** on p.268.

For full details of buses from Jodhpur, see **"Travel details"** on p.268. **Private buses** for most destinations leave from Kalpataru Cinema, 4km southwest of town, reached by auto for Rs30; private buses for Jaisalmer (of which there are a dozen a day) leave nearby, from Bombay Motors Circle. You can book private buses at most travel agents and a lot of hotels (for a Rs50 fee). **Government buses** leave from the Roadways Bus Stand just east of town. For timetable information, it's best to ask your hotel or guesthouse to ring on your behalf (☎0291/254 4686). There are Silver and Gold Line buses to Delhi, Agra, Ajmer, Jaipur and Udaipur.

The **railway station** is on Station Road, 300m south of Sojati Gate. There's a computerized **reservations office** (Mon–Sat 8am–8pm, Sun 8am–2pm), just north of the station behind the GPO. *Govind Hotel* allows customers at its *Fort View* restaurant (see p.215) to leave baggage free of charge and use toilet facilities while waiting for a train. Recommended services are listed in the box above; there's also the once-weekly Thar Express to Karachi in **Pakistan** (Fri at 11.30pm; 25hr).

Mandor

The royal cenotaphs at **MANDOR** (free; 24hr), 9km north of the city, are set in a little park full of monkeys, and can be reached on minibuses #1, #5 and #7 from Sojati Gate. Between the sixth and fourteenth centuries, Mandor was capital of the Parihar Rajputs, who were ousted by Rathore Rao Chauhan in 1381. His successors moved their capital to Jodhpur in 1459, but once they had been cremated their cenotaphs were erected here in Mandor. Temple-like in their sombre, dark red sandstone (the canopy-like chhatris next to them are for lesser royals), the cenotaphs grew in size and grandeur as the Rathore kingdom prospered. The largest is Ajit Singh's, built in 1724. His six queens, along with assorted mistresses, concubines, maids and entertainers – 84 women in all – committed *sati* on his funeral pyre.

At the end of the gardens, on the far side of the chhatris, you'll find the octagonal **Ek Thamba Mahal** (Single Pillared Palace), a three-storey pagoda-like affair built at the beginning of the eighteenth century for royal ladies to watch public events without breaking their purdah. Behind it is a small **museum** (daily except Fri 10am–4pm; Rs3), home to a few dull sculptures and paintings. Much more interesting are the extensive remains of **Mandor Fort**, citadel of the Parihar and Rathore Rajputs when Mandor was their capital, reached via a flight of steps behind the museum.

If you'd like to **stay** in Mandor, try the pleasantly sylvan little *Mandore Guest House*, close to the gardens on Dadawari Lane (T0291/254 5210, W www .mandore.com; ⑥). It's actually more of a miniature resort than a guesthouse, with accommodation in a mix of air-cooled and a/c rooms and (rather dark) round huts set in a tree-studded garden.

The Bishnoi villages

Jodhpur's surroundings can be explored on organized "**village safaris**", which take small groups of tourists out into rural Rajasthan, usually stopping at four or five **Bishnoi villages** where you can taste traditional food, drink opium tea and watch crafts such as spinning and carpet-making. You'll also probably spot nilgai (bluebull) antelopes and gazelles.

The Bishnois – a religious sect rather than an ethnic group in the usual sense – are among the world's earliest tree-huggers. Their origins go back to a drought in the year 1485. Observing that this was caused largely by deforestation, a guru by the name of Jambeshwar Bhagavan formulated 29 rules for living in harmony with nature and the environment – his followers are called Bishnoi after the Marwari word for twenty-nine. As well as enforcing strict vegetarianism, Jambeshwar's rules forbid the killing of animals or felling of live trees. In particular, Bishnoi hold the **khejri** tree sacred. In 1730, at the village of **Khejadali**, workers sent by the maharaja of Marwar to make lime for the construction of a palace started felling *khejri* trees to burn the local limestone. A woman by the name of Amrita Devi put her arms around a tree and declared that if they wanted to cut it down, they would have to cut her head off first. The leader of the working party ordered her decapitation, upon which her three daughters followed her example, and were similarly beheaded. Bishnoi people from the whole of the surrounding region then converged on the site to defend the trees – 363 of them gave their lives doing so. When news reached the maharaja, he ordered the felling to cease and banned cutting down trees and hunting animals in Bishnoi territory. Today, a small temple marks the place where all this happened, while in its grounds, 363 *khejri* trees commemorate the martyrs.

Although it is possible to go to Khejadali by bus, you'll be hard put to find a villager who speaks English, and it's a lot better to go with a tour group, which will also visit other villages. Most tours stop at Khejadali for lunch. This is usually followed by an **opium ceremony** in which opium is dissolved in water in a specially designed wooden vessel, and poured through a strainer into a second receptacle. The process is repeated twice more, and the resulting tea is drunk from the palm of a hand. Strictly speaking, it's illegal, but blind eyes are turned to this kind of traditional opium use, though in fact opium addiction is something of a social problem in rural Rajasthan.

Good and inexpensive **tours** of the Bishnoi villages are run by several guest-houses in Jodhpur including *Durag Niwas*, *Govind Hotel* and *Yogi's Guest House*. Rates start at around Rs600 per couple (cheaper in larger groups).

Osian

Rajasthan's largest group of early Jain and Hindu temples lies on the outskirts of the small town of **OSIAN**, 64km north of Jodhpur. RSTDC buses drop you at the bus stand on the main road just south of town. The temples date from the eighth to the twelfth centuries when Osian was a regional trading centre. The town's ruler and population apparently converted to Jainism in the eleventh century, and the town is still an important Jain pilgrimage centre.

The town centre is dominated by the imposing twelfth-century **Sachiya Mata Temple**, overlooking the whole of Osian from its elevated hilltop position. At the very top of the complex, the main shrine to Sachiya (an incarnation of Durga) is unusually decorated with multicoloured mirrorwork and topped by a cluster of finely carved *shikharas*.

A five-minute walk from the Sachiya Mata Temple lies Osian's most beautiful monument, the **Mahavira Jain Temple** (Rs5, Rs40 camera, Rs100 video; no leather items permitted, and women should not enter during menstruation). Built in the eighth century, renovated in the tenth, and restored quite recently, the temple's beautifully carved central shrine is fronted by twenty elegant pillars and surrounded by shrines to further *tirthankaras*. A trio of smaller temples lies nearby, including a pair of Surya temples and the unusual **Peeplaj Temple**, surrounded by gargoyle-like projecting elephants, along with a massive Pratihara-period step-well.

Just south of the bus stop lies Osian's oldest collection of temples, centred on the **Vishnu and Harihara temples**, built in the Pratihara period (eighth and ninth centuries). The nine temples in this group retain a considerable amount of decorative carving, particularly in the surrounding friezes.

Most people **stay** at the basic but welcoming *Priest Bhanu Sarma Guesthouse* (☎0/941 444 0479; ❸) opposite the Mahavira temple, run by the (Hindu) priest who looks after the (Jain) temple, who can also provide information and arrange camel safaris and tours of local Bishnoi villages. More upmarket accommodation can be found at the luxury *Camel Camp Osian*, perched on a sand dune overlooking the railway line west of town (book in advance through the *India Safari Club* in Jodhpur on ☎0291/243 7023, ⓦwww.camelcamposian .com; ❾), with carpeted tents and a pool. The daily rate of around $225 includes three meals and a camel safari.

Jaisalmer

In the remote westernmost corner of Rajasthan, **JAISALMER** is the quintessential desert town, its sand-yellow ramparts rising out of the arid Thar like a scene from the *Arabian Nights*. Rampant commercialism has dampened the romantic vision somewhat, but even with all the touts, hustling merchants and tour buses, the town deservedly remains one of India's most popular destinations. Villagers from outlying settlements, dressed in dazzling red and orange *odhnis* or voluminous turbans, still outnumber foreigners in the bazaar, while the exquisite sandstone architecture of the "Golden City" is quite unlike anything else in India.

JAISALMER

Bada Bagh ▲

Amar Sagar, Lodurva & Sam ▲

Khuhri ▲

ACCOMMODATION

Artist Hotel	A
Fort Rajwada	J
Jawahar Niwas Palace	F
Mandir Palace	H
Nachana Haveli	G
Ratan Palace	C
Renuka	B
Residency Centre Point	E
Shahi Palace	E
Swastika	D

RESTAURANTS, BARS & SNACKS

Chandan Shree	4
Dhanraj Ranmal Bhatia	7
Narayan Niwas Palace	1
Natraj	8
RK Juice Center	5
RTDC Moomal Hotel	6
Saffron	6
Shree Bikaner	2
Trio	3

N

0　　　250 m

JODHPUR ROAD (NH-15)

BARMER ROAD (NH-15)

Railway
Station

Gadi Sagar
Tank

GARROOP SAGAR ROAD

GADI SAGAR LANE

Tilon-ki-Pol

Gadi
Sagar
Pol

Desert Culture
Museum

Folklore
Museum

i

GADI SAGAR ROAD

Desert Bikes

Malka Pol

Patwa Haveli

Salim Singh ki
Haveli

8

Adventure
Travels

Private Buses

Sunset Point

A

1

E

Nathmalji-
ki-Haveli

BHATIA BAZAAR

7

GOPA
CHOWK

Fort

MAIN CHOWK

Jain
Temples

See 'Jaisalmer Fort' map

AIR-
FORCE
CIRCLE ★

B

C

D

Local
Buses

Amar
Sagar Pol

Rajasthali

★

G

H

3

4

5

Bhatia
News
Agency

GANDHI
CHOWK

COURT RD

Laxminath
Temple

Palace

1

SHIV MARG

ATM

2

HANUMAN
CIRCLE

AMAR SAGAR ROAD

State Bus
Stand ★

Hospital

✚

ATM

District
Magistrate

SAM ROAD

BADA BAGH ROAD (RAMGARH ROAD)

F

Government
Museum

6

Jaisalmer in jeopardy

Erected on a base of soft bantonite clay, sand and sandstone, the foundations of **Jaisalmer Fort** are rapidly eroding because of huge increases in water consumption. At the height of the tourist season, around 120 litres per head are pumped into the area – twelve times the quantity used only a couple of decades ago. Due to problems with the drainage system, a large proportion of this water seeps into the soil beneath the fort, weakening its foundations. The result has been disastrous: houses have collapsed and significant damage has been done to the sixteenth-century Maharani's Palace. In 1998 six people died when an exterior wall gave way, and five more bastions fell in 2000 and 2001. Jaisalmer is now listed among the World Monument Fund's 100 Most Endangered Sites.

An international campaign, JiJ, has now been set up to facilitate repairs throughout the fort. JiJ has already upgraded more than half of the 350 homes in the fort with underground sewerage, as well as restoring their facades and replacing grey cement with traditional material. Despite these repairs, city authorities still think the best way to save the fort is to evacuate the two thousand people who live there and start repairs to the drainage system from scratch, an expensive and time-consuming venture much opposed by the guesthouse owners inside whose earnings depend on tourism. The JiJ campaign relies substantially on donations. If you'd like to help, contact JiJ at 3 Brickbarn Close, London SW10 0UJ, UK (☏+44 (0)20/7352 4336, ⊛www.jaisalmer-in-jeopardy.org). Bear in mind, too, that you can make a small difference by not staying in the fort or, if you do, by conserving water as much as possible while you're there.

Some history

Rawal Jaisal of the Bhati clan founded Jaisalmer in 1156 as a replacement for his less easily defensible capital at Lodurva. Constant wars with the neighbouring Rajput states of Jodhpur and Bikaner followed, as did conflict with the Muslim sultans of Delhi. In 1298, a seven-year siege of the fort by the forces of Ala-ud-din Khalji (see p.1339) ended when the men of the city rode out to their deaths while the women committed *johar* – although with no local food supplies, Ala-ud-din's forces were unable to continue their occupation and the Bhatis soon resumed their rule. The city was again besieged by Sultanate forces in 1326, resulting in another desperate act of *johar*, but Gharsi Bhati managed to negotiate the return of his kingdom as a vassal state of Delhi, after which it remained in Bhati hands.

In 1570 the ruler of Jaisalmer married one of his daughters to Akbar's son, cementing an alliance between Jaisalmer and the Mughal Empire, of which it nonetheless remained a vassal state. Its position on the overland route between Delhi and Central Asia made it an important entrepôt for goods such as silk, opium and spices, and the city grew rich on the proceeds, as the magnificent havelis of its merchants bear witness. However, the emergence of Bombay and Surat as major ports meant that overland trade diminished, and with it Jaisalmer's wealth. The death blow came with Partition, when Jaisalmer's life-line trade route was severed by the new, highly sensitive Pakistani border. The city took on renewed strategic importance during the Indo-Pakistani wars of 1965 and 1971, and it is now a major **military outpost**, with jet aircraft regularly roaring past the ramparts.

Arrival and information

Jaisalmer's **railway station** is 2km east of the city. Touts and rickshaw drivers are held at bay outside the terminal, while reservationless travellers can calmly enquire among the sandwich-board toting hoteliers lined up in the parking lot. The majority offer free rides; otherwise an auto-rickshaw into town will cost around Rs20–30. **Government buses** stop briefly at a stand near the railway station before continuing to the more convenient new **State Bus Stand** southwest of the fort. **Private buses** will drop you at Air Force Circle south of the fort. A **tourist tax** of Rs20 (Rs10 for Indian residents, plus Rs10 per car) is levied on all foreign visitors by the municipal council. You'll be charged on arrival at either the bus stand or train station, or in your vehicle if arriving by private transport.

RTDC's **tourist office** (Mon–Sat 10am–5pm; ☎02992/252406), southeast of town near Gadi Sagar Pol, is of little use, and its "recommended" operators pay for the privilege. **Online**, it's worth having a look at ⊛www.jaisalmer.org .uk and ⊛jaisalmer.nic.in.

Accommodation

Jaisalmer has plenty of places to stay in all categories, but do think twice before staying in the **fort**, for the reasons outlined in the box on p.221. Almost all accommodation offers **camel treks**, which vary in standard and price, and some managers even at reputable hotels can be uncomfortably pushy if you don't arrange a safari through them.

In the fort

The hotels listed below are shown on the Jaisalmer Fort map on p.225.

Desert ☎02992/250602, ⊛ajitdeserthotel @hotmail.com. Friendly if slightly shabby little budget place with cheaper rooms (some with shared bath) downstairs and brighter, airier rooms upstairs. ❶–❸

Desert Haveli ☎02992/251555. Simple but popular budget guesthouse offering variously sized stone-walled rooms with attached bathrooms. Free pick-up from bus or railway station. Excellent value. ❶–❹

Moti Palace ☎02992/254693, ⊛kailash_bissa @yahoo.co.uk. Friendly budget option, with a range of good-value rooms (all attached) and unbeatable views over the main gate. ❶–❹

Paradise ☎02992/252674, ⊛www.paradiseonfort .com. Atmospheric old haveli with a leafy courtyard and a wide selection of rooms, ranging from cheap downstairs rooms with common baths to prettily decorated upstairs rooms with a/c. ❶–❺

Suraj ☎02992/251623, ⊛hotelsurajjaisalmer @hotmail.com. This superbly carved sandstone haveli is one of the nicest places to stay in the fort, with a friendly family atmosphere, characterful old rooms (including a spectacular painted room) and a rooftop view of the Jain temples. ❹–❺

Surja ☎0/941 439 1149. A range of basic attached fan rooms – those without view are much better value than those with – and a relaxing rooftop terrace with one of the best views in town. Not to be confused with the less appealing Surya next door. ❶–❹

In town

Unless otherwise stated, the hotels listed below are shown on the Jaisalmer map, p.220.

Artist Hotel Manganyar colony ☎02992/252082, ⊛artisthotel@yahoo.com. Run by an Austrian expat as a co-op for members of the Manganyar (minstrel musician) caste, who play here most evenings. The rather rustic stone-walled rooms are comfortable enough, if a bit gloomy and shabby, and there's a nice rooftop restaurant with good food. ❸–❹

Mandir Palace Gandhi Chowk ☎02992/252788, ⊛www.welcomheritagehotels.com. Occupying part of the exquisite Mandir Palace (see p.226), although the hotel doesn't quite live up to the setting. Rooms are modern and comfortable, but surprisingly characterless, service is hit-and-miss and a strange air of neglect hangs over the whole place – although rates are surprisingly modest given the setting. ❽

Nachana Haveli Gandhi Chowk ☎02992/251910, ⊛nachana_haveli@yahoo.com. Run by a cousin of the maharaja, this venerable old haveli is one of the best choices in its class. The atmospheric stone-walled ground-floor rooms (all a/c) are virtually windowless but attractively decorated with antique fittings; the suites upstairs are brighter. There's also the good Saffron rooftop restaurant (see p.227). ❼–❽

Camel safaris from Jaisalmer

Few visitors who make it as far as Jaisalmer pass up the opportunity to go on a **camel trek**, which provides an irresistibly romantic chance to cross the barren sands and sleep under one of the starriest skies in the world. Sandstorms, sore backsides and camel farts aside, the safaris are usually great fun.

Although you can travel for up to two weeks by camel from Jaisalmer to Bikaner, treks normally last from one to four days, with **prices** varying from Rs400 to Rs1500 per night. For most travellers, the highlight is spending the evening under the desert stars and you usually find that departing around 3pm one day and returning the next at noon is sufficient. Unfortunately, the price you pay is not an adequate gauge of the quality of services you get. Hotels are notorious for sizing up potential clients and charging prices on a whim, so it pays to shop around, ask other travellers for recommendations and bargain appropriately. We've listed a few dependable operators below, though the list is far from exhaustive and not every trip they offer is the same. A lot depends on what expectations you have, whether the guides are friendly and how big the group is. Make sure you'll be provided with your own camel, an adequate supply of blankets (it can get very cold at night), food cooked with mineral water, and a campfire. As a precaution, have the deal fixed on paper, giving the maximum size of the group, details of the food you'll be getting, transport and anything else you've arranged. If you're only going for a day, none of this applies, but wear a broad-brimmed hat and take high-factor sun-protection lotion and plenty of water, especially in summer.

Following government restrictions on **routes**, most safaris head out to the assorted villages west of Jaisalmer, typically visiting Amar Sagar, Bada Bagh, Lodurva, Sam and Kuldera. Some visitors find these places, especially the dunes at Sam, overrun with other tourists and barely more than a scenic trash-pit. However, it's possible to arrange a few days' amble through the desert without stopping at the popular sights. Taking a **Jeep** at the start or end of the trek enables you to go further in a short time, and some travellers prefer to begin their trek at Khuhri (see p.230). Longer treks to Pokaran, Jodhpur or Bikaner can also be arranged. Firms running treks into restricted areas (see p.229) should fix the necessary permits for you, but check in advance.

However much you intend to spend on a trek, don't book anything until you get to Jaisalmer. Touts trawl the train from Jodhpur, but they, and the barrage of operators combing the streets, usually represent dodgy outfits, most of which are based at one or other of the small budget hotels north of the fort. Some offer absurdly cheap rooms if you agree to book a camel trek with them, but guesthouse notice-boards (not to mention our postbags) are filled with sorry stories by tourists who accepted. As a rule of thumb, any firm that has to tout for business – and that includes hotels – is worth avoiding.

Recommended operators

Adventure Travel (℡0/941 414 9176, @www.adventurecamels.com), just south of the First Fort Gate, gets rave reviews for seeking out remote locations and providing fringe amenities, like real mattresses and sheets, at low prices. Slightly cheaper, but equally dependable, is **Sahara Travels** in Gopa Chowk (℡02992/252609, @www.mrdesertjaisalmer.com), run by the instantly identifiable "Mr. Desert," a former truck driver turned Rajasthani model and movie star. "Don't make a booking until you see the face," is his motto.

Of the **hotels** that organize camel safaris, *Shahi Palace* has a deservedly good reputation and virtually guarantees you won't see another tourist, though their prices are known to fluctuate. Among the budget alternatives, the friendly *Renuka* offers excellent value for money. They've been running trips for more than a decade into a stretch of drifting dunes south of Sam that only a couple of other operators are allowed into.

Ratan Palace Off Gandhi Chowk ☎02992/252757, ⓔhotelrenuka@rediffmail.com. One of the best cheapies in this part of town, with a friendly owner and spotless, hassle-free accommodation in spacious rooms with large bathrooms. They run good camel treks and have even cheaper rooms (❶–❸; some with shared bath) in the slightly older *Renuka* across the street. ❸–❹

Residency Centre Point Khumbara Para ☎0/941 476 0421. Small, family-run guesthouse in the backstreets near Patwa Haveli and Nathamal ki Haveli. Rooms (a couple with a/c) are comfortable and good value, and there's home-cooked food and nice town views from the rooftop. Advance booking recommended. ❸–❹

🏃 **Shahi Palace** off Shiv Marg ☎02992/255920, ⓦwww.shahipalacehotel.com. See also Fort

map opposite. Outstanding little hotel tucked away just south of the fort in a stylish modern sandstone building with stunning fort views from the rooftop terrace restaurant and immaculate and beautifully decorated rooms. The only caveat is that the cheaper rooms are a bit small – it's well worth coughing up for one of the superb larger rooms (which also have a/c and TV). The same family also run the neighbouring *Oasis Haveli* and *Star Haveli*, which have further rooms of a similar standard. ❸–❻

Swastika Off Gandhi Chowk ☎02992/252152, ⓔswastikahotel@yahoo.com. Long-running budget hotel offering simple modern fan and a/c rooms, though not as good value as the nearby *Ratan Palace*. ❷–❹

Out of town

Fort Rajwada off Jodhpur Rd, 3.5km east of town ☎02992/253233 or 533, ⓦwww.fortrajwada.com. Best by a long chalk of the new resort hotels on the outskirts of town. Its massive marble lobby includes chunks of richly filigreed sandstone plundered from havelis in the old city. Has all the facilities of a five-star (pool, bar, good restaurant

and grand coffee shop). Double rooms start at around US$200. ❾

Jawahar Niwas Palace 1 Bada Bagh Rd ☎02992/252208 or 288. Late nineteenth-century royal guesthouse with turreted sandstone exterior, large and graceful rooms, and a good pool (Rs250 for non-guests). ❻–❼

The Town

Getting lost in the narrow winding streets of Jaisalmer is both easy and enjoyable, though the town is so small that it never takes long to find a familiar landmark.

Jaisalmer Fort

Every part of **Jaisalmer Fort**, from its outer walls to the palace, temples and houses within, is made of soft yellow Jurassic sandstone. Inside the fort the narrow winding streets are flanked with carved golden facades, and from the barrel-sided bastions, some of which still bear cannons, you can see the thick walls that drop almost 100m to the town below. Two thousand people live within its walls; seventy percent of them are Brahmins and the rest, living primarily on the east side, are predominantly Rajput.

A paved road punctuated by four huge gateways winds up to the fort's **main chowk** (square) – large round stones lie atop the ramparts above the entrance road, waiting to be pushed down onto any enemy army trying to force its way in. The main chowk was the scene of the terrible acts of *johar* that took place here three times during the fourteenth and fifteenth centuries. Choosing death rather than dishonour for themselves and their children if their husbands were ever defeated on the battlefield, the women of the royal palace, which overlooks the *chowk*, had a huge fire built, and jumped from the palace walls into it.

Palace of the Maharawal

The main *chowk* is dominated by the Palace of the Maharawal, open to the public as the **Fort Palace Museum** (daily: summer 8am–6pm; winter 9am–6pm; Rs250 including audio tour if you leave ID, credit card or deposit;

JAISALMER FORT

ACCOMMODATION
Desert	B
Desert Haveli	F
Moti Palace	A
Paradise	E
Shahi Palace	C
Suraj	G
Surja	D

RESTAURANTS
Bhang shop	2	Little Italy	3
Joshi's German		Little Tibet	5
Bakery	1	Monica	4
July 8	7	Vyas Meals	6
Krishna's Boulangerie	8		

Gandhi Chowk

GOPA CHOWK

Ganesh Pol

Suraj Pcl

Sahara Travels

First Fort Gate (Akhai Pol)

KUND PARA CHOWK

Laxminath Temple

Palace of the Maharawal

Hawa Pcl

MAIN CHOWK

Jain Temples

SHIV MARG

Salim Singh's Haveli

All Force Circle

RSTDC Bus Stand

N

0   50 m

Rs150 video). The palace's five-storey facade of balconies and windows displays some of the finest masonry in Jaisalmer, while the ornate marble throne to the left of the palace entrance is where the monarch (known in Jaisalmer as the maharawal rather than the maharaja) would have addressed his troops and issued orders. Inside, the museum offers an interesting snapshot of the life of Jaisalmer's potentates through the ages, with artefacts ranging from a fancy silver coronation throne through to more homely items, such as the bed and thali dish of a nineteenth-century ruler. There's also an interesting array of other exhibits – from fifteenth-century sculptures (including an unusual bearded Rama) through to local stamps and banknotes, while the rooftop terrace gives unrivalled views over the city and the surrounding countryside.

Hindu and Jain temples

The fort has a number of Hindu temples, including the venerable **Laxminath Temple** of 1494, dedicated to Laxmi. None, however, is as impressive as the complex of seven **Jain temples** (daily 7am–noon; Rs20, plus Rs50 for camera, Rs100 video, Rs30 camera phone; usual entry restrictions apply). The temples, connected by small corridors and stairways, were built between the twelfth and fifteenth centuries with yellow and white marble shrines and exquisite sculpted motifs covering the walls, ceilings and pillars. Two of the seven temples are open between 7am and noon; the other five only open from 11am to noon, when the whole place gets very busy with coach parties, so it's best to visit before 11am to see the first two temples, then come back later to see the rest.

The havelis

The streets of Jaisalmer are flanked with numerous pale honey-coloured facades, covered with latticework and floral designs, but the city's real showpieces are its **havelis**, commissioned by wealthy merchants during the eighteenth and nineteenth centuries.

Just north of Bhatia Bazaar (take the small road between the Ajanta Photo Studio and Dev Handicrafts), the **Nathmalji-ki-Haveli** was built in 1885 for Jaisalmer's prime minister by two brother stonemasons, one of whom built the left half, the other his right, as a result of which the two sides are subtly different. It's guarded by two elephants and the first-floor bay window above the main doorway is surmounted by a frieze of little figures including elephants, horses, a steam train, and a bicycle and a horse-drawn carriage.

Even more finely decorated, the large **Patwa Haveli**, or Patwon-ki-Haveli (daily 8am–6.30pm; Rs50, Indian residents Rs30, camera Rs20, video Rs40), down a street to the right a couple of blocks north from the Nathmalji-ki-Haveli, was constructed in the first half of the nineteenth century by five brothers from a Jain family who were bankers and traders in brocade and opium. Traces of stylish wall paintings survive in some rooms, but the building's most striking features are its exuberantly carved *jharokhas*, or protruding balconies. As well as visiting the interior of the Patwa Haveli, it's worth taking a little stroll down the street whose entrance it bridges, to check out the stonework on four impressive neighbouring havelis.

The third of Jaisalmer's famous trio of havelis, the **Salim Singh ki Haveli** (daily summer 8am–7pm; winter 8am–6pm; Rs15), lies on the east side of town and is immediately recognizable thanks to its lavishly carved overhanging rooftop balcony which gives the whole building a strangely top-heavy appearance.

In addition to these havelis, parts of the **Mandir Palace**, now partly converted into a heritage hotel (see p.222), can be visited (daily 10am–5pm; Rs10), though its most striking feature, the elegant **Badal Vilas tower**, is best seen from the west, just outside Amar Sagar Pol.

Gadi Sagar Tank and museums

South of town through an imposing triple gateway lies **Gadi Sagar Tank**, once Jaisalmer's sole water supply, flanked with sandstone *ghats* and temples – a peaceful spot, staring out into the desert. It's possible to rent boats here (daily 8am–9pm; 30min; Rs50–100 for 2–4 people). The nearby little **Folklore Museum** (daily 8am–6pm; Rs20) has displays of folk art, textiles and paraphernalia relating to the consumption of opium and betel nuts. You'll find a slightly larger selection of local curiosities, including musical instruments, fossils, manuscripts, tools and utensils, at the **Desert Culture Museum** (daily 10am–1.30pm & 3.30–8pm; Rs20), just up the road next to the tourist office. The main exhibit is a cloth painting depicting the life of local folk hero Pabuji, a legendary figure credited with introducing the camel to Rajasthan. The museum also puts on a half-hour puppet show (Rs30) at 6.30pm and 7.30pm each evening, using traditional Rajasthani puppets.

Eating and drinking

Jaisalmer's tourist **restaurants**, usually rooftop affairs with fort views, offer pizza, pancakes, apple pie and cakes on their menus alongside Indian dishes, and some of them are pretty good. Most restaurants serve beer. The *Narayan Niwas Palace*, between Nathmalji-ki-Haveli and Malka Pol, has one of the better **bars** in town; the bar at the RTDC *Moomal Hotel* on the western edge of town is less refined but cheaper. The *Nachana Haveli* on Gandhi Chowk should have opened a bar in its former stables by the time you read this.

Unless otherwise indicated, all the following are shown on the Jaisalmer map on p.220.

Restaurants

Chandan Shree Restaurant on the outside of the city wall, just south of Amar Sagar Pol. Popular diner for inexpensive veg curries (Rs20–75) and thalis (Rs50–100), as well as Rajasthani specialities such as *govind gatta* and *malai jamun*.

July 8 Main Chowk, in the fort. See Fort map, p.225. Recommended for its privileged terrace view of the fort's bustling main *chowk* and palace rather than for its food, though it has a good selection of smoothies, lassis, juices and *jaffels*, along with Indian, Italian and Chinese mains (Rs50–85). Good spot for breakfast.

Little Italy just inside first fort gate. See Fort map, p.225. Italian restaurant with great pasta dishes (Rs90–120), served in heaped portions at reasonable prices (the pizzas make a stab at authenticity, but don't really cut it) and a superb terrace directly opposite the main ramparts – wonderful when they're floodlit at night.

Little Tibet In the Fort. See map, p.225. Run by a team of young Tibetans, this travellers' café serves up all the usual Indian and Chinese choices, plus enchiladas, pasta, and a range of Tibetan food including *momos*, *thukpa* and *thantuk*. Also a good venue for breakfast. Mains Rs55–85.

Monica Near the first Fort gate. See Fort map, p.225. Moderately priced Rajasthani and tandoori dishes, plus delicious veg and non-veg Rajasthani thalis (Rs125/175). Mains Rs70–140.

Natraj Opposite the Salim Singh ki Haveli. Friendly rooftop non-veg restaurant, popular for its excellent, gently spiced Mughlai chicken, *malai kofta* and other Indian dishes (mains Rs65–130).

Saffron *Nachana Haveli*, Gandhi Chowk ☏02992/251910. Slightly upmarket restaurant with fine tandoori and Mughlai food, plus some Continental and Chinese options (mains Rs50–140) and live music in the evenings.

Shree Bikaner Restaurant north of Hanuman Circle, near Geeta Ashram. Punjabi veg curries (Rs35–80), a choice of Rajasthani, Gujarati and Bengali thalis (Rs50–90), and a wonderful *dal bati churma* (a traditional Rajasthani dish consisting of baked wheatflour balls served with dhal and sweet *churma* sauce; Rs90), which they'll keep refilling till you've had enough.

Trio Gandhi Chowk ☏02992/252733. Slightly upscale choice known for its sumptuous tandoori food (most mains around Rs130), plus some Rajasthani specialities like *gatta* (gram-flour dumplings) and *lal maas* (spicy lamb marinaded in chilli). Book early for the best tables overlooking the Mandir Palace and fort.

Vyas Meals In the fort near the Jain temples. See Fort map, p.225. Hole-in-the-wall place run by an elderly couple who do superb home-style veg thalis and snacks at unbeatable prices (Rs20–40). Eat in or take away, but expect a long wait for either.

Drinks and snacks

Bhang shop Gopa Chowk. See Fort map, p.225. If you like bhang, this is one of the best places in the country to get it, with a whole menu of bhang-laced drinks and sweets, and a choice of different strengths.

Joshi's German Bakery Gopa Chowk. See Fort map, p.225. Scrumptious range of fresh cakes, croissants and cookies, especially in the morning. Too bad the coffee's instant.

Krishna's Boulangerie in the fort, near the Jain temples. See Fort map, p.225. A handy place to stop for a breather in the fort, with excellent coffee, reasonable cakes, and more substantial food, including pizzas.

RK Juice Center Bhatia Bazaar. Wonderful, freshly pressed juices including pomegranate, pineapple and banana, or carrot and ginger. No ice or tap water.

Listings

Banks and exchange There's an ATM just inside Amar Sagar Pol, one directly opposite the gate on the outside, one by the District Magistrate's office on Sam Road, and one on Shiv Chowk south of the *Shahi Palace* hotel. There's a cluster of forex bureaux on Gandhi Chowk.

Bicycle rental Naran Thaker, in the street directly opposite *Nachana Haveli* hotel (no sign in English; it's 75m up on the left, just where the street starts to bend); Rs5/hr.

Bookshops Bhatia News agency on Court Rd, just beyond Gandhi Chowk, plus numerous stalls in the fort.

Doctor Dr S.K. Dube (℡02992/251560) speaks good English; Rs500 per consultation.

Festival Jaisalmer's Desert Festival is held over three days at the full moon in the lunar month of Magha (7–9 Feb 2009, 28–30 Jan 2010, 16–18 Feb 2011). This fun festival of performing arts features folk dancing, turban-tying and moustache competitions, camel racing and camel-polo matches. Main events are held at Dedansar Polo Ground. Hotels tend to get full at this time, but they don't generally increase their prices. There's usually a programme of events posted at ⓦjaisalmer.nic.in.

Hospital The small, private Maheshwari Hospital (℡02992/250024), off Sam Rd opposite the court and District Magistrate's office, is the best place in town.

Internet access Internet is widely available but mostly slow. The *Chai Bar*, inside the fort just beyond Ganesh Gate, has the best machines (Rs40/hr). Nearby, slower and cheaper, there's Joshi Cyber Café (Rs20/hr) in the *Joshi's German Bakery*.

Motorbike rental Desert Bikes, south of Gopa Chowk (℡0/941 415 0033). Bikes and scooters for Rs300/day.

Police Amar Sagar Rd ℡02992/252322.

Post office The main post office, with poste restante, is on Amar Sagar Rd 200m south of Hanuman Circle (Mon–Sat 9am–3.30pm); there's a smaller office opposite the fort wall behind Gopa Chowk (Mon–Sat 10am–5pm).

Shopping Jaisalmer is one of the best places in India to shop for souvenirs. Prices are comparatively high and the salesmen push hard, but the choice of goods is excellent. As well as embroidered patchwork tapestries and other Rajasthani textiles, good buys include woven jackets, tie-dyed cloth, puppets, wooden boxes and ornaments, camel-leather slippers and Western-style (or at least, hippy-style) clothes made from Indian fabrics with Indian designs. Rajasthali, the official Rajasthan state crafts emporium outside Amar Sagar Pol, is rather dry and unattractively arranged, and not always the very best quality, but handy for checking prices as they're fixed and marked.

Swimming pool There's a trio of package hotels 2km west of town on the Sam road, all of which allow outsiders to use their pools for a price.

Moving on from Jaisalmer

The **train station** is east of town on the Jodhpur road, around Rs40 from town by auto. Note that **night trains** can get very cold – close to freezing in winter. The #4060 **Jaisalmer–Delhi** Express departs daily at 4pm and stops at Pokaran (5.28pm), Phalodi (6.46pm), Osian (8.01pm), Jodhpur (10pm), Jaipur (4.50am) and Delhi (11.10am). The overnight #4809 **Jaisalmer–Jodhpur** Express departs at 11.15pm, arriving in Jodhpur at 5.30am. There are two services to **Bikaner**, departing at 11am and 10.45pm and arriving at 5.20pm and 4.40am respectively.

For details of **bus** services, see **travel details** on p.268. The bus stands are both just south of the old city. The **State Bus Stand** is at the southern end of Amar Sagar Road (℡02992/251541), while **private buses** leave from Air Force Circle. Tickets for private buses can be purchased from any of the numerous travel agents around town – try Swagat Travels or Hanuman Travels, just north of Hanuman Circle. **Local buses** to Lodurva, Khuhri and Sam leave from the stand northeast of Hanuman Circle, though there are plans to move this stand to a location further out of town along the main road north of Hanuman Circle during 2008/09 – check the latest situation at your guesthouse.

Jaisalmer's new **domestic airport**, 9km west of town, is scheduled to come into operation sometime in late 2008/early 2009, with flights to Jaipur, Delhi, Udaipur and Mumbai. Check with the tourist office or ask at your guesthouse for latest details.

Around Jaisalmer

The barren desert terrain around Jaisalmer harbours some unexpected monuments, dating from the Rajput era when the area lay on busy caravan routes. Infrequent buses negotiate the dusty roads, or you can rent a Jeep through RTDC or your hotel; the best way to visit these places, however, and see villages and abandoned towns inaccessible by road, is on a **camel trek** (see box, p.223). Being close to the Pakistani border, the area west of Highway NH-15 is **restricted**. Tourists are currently allowed to visit **Bada Bagh**, **Amar Sagar**, **Lodurva**, **Sam**, **Kuldara** and **Khuhri**, but if you want to travel beyond those areas, you'll need a **permit**, for which you apply to the District Magistrate's Office, just west of Hanuman Circle in Jaisalmer (☎02992/252201; Mon–Fri 10am–5pm).

Bada Bagh, Amar Sagar and Lodurva

Six kilometres north of Jaisalmer, in the fertile area of **Bada Bagh**, a cluster of **cenotaphs** (daily summer 6am–7/8pm; Rs50, camera or video Rs50) built in memory of Jaisalmer's rulers stands incongruously on a hill amidst a cluster of modern wind turbines. The green oasis below is where most of the area's fruit and vegetables used to be grown.

Seven kilometres northwest of Jaisalmer is **AMAR SAGAR**, a small and peaceful town set around a large artificial lake (empty during the dry season) where you'll find the eighteenth-century Amar Singh Palace and three Jain temples (Rs10 entry, Rs50 camera), including the Adeshwar Nath Temple, commissioned in 1928 by a member of the same family who put up the Patwa Haveli in Jaisalmer.

A further 10km northwest of Amar Sagar, **LODURVA** was the capital of the Bhati Rajputs from the eighth century until the twelfth, when it was sacked by Mohammed Ghori, after which the Bhatis moved their capital to Jaisalmer. Only a few **Jain temples**, rebuilt in the seventeenth century, remain. The main temple (daily 6am–8pm; Rs20, camera Rs50, video Rs100), dedicated to Parshvanath, features an ornately carved eight-metre *toran* (arch), just inside the entrance to the main temple compound, perhaps the most exquisite in Rajasthan, plus

▲ Local women in the Rajasthani desert

detailed tracery work and a finely carved exterior. To the right of the temple is a structure built in a series of diminishing square platforms, out of which springs the Kalpataru tree, made from an alloy of eight metals, with copper leaves.

There are four daily **buses** to Lodurva, but taking a **taxi** is a more leisurely option (Rs400 round trip including stops at Amar Sagar and Bada Bagh), or you could **cycle**.

Kuldara

South of the Sam road, around 25km west of Jaisalmer, the ghost village of **Kuldara** (daily sunrise–sunset; Rs50, vehicles Rs50) was one of 84 villages abandoned, for unknown reasons, simultaneously one night in 1825 by the Paliwal Brahmin community, which had settled here in the thirteenth century. The Paliwals' sense of industry and order is attested by their homes, each with its living quarters, guest room, kitchen and stables, plus a parking space for a camel. You can take an atmospheric stroll through them to the temple at the heart of the village.

Sam

The huge, rolling sand dunes 40km west of Jaisalmer are known as **SAM**, though strictly this is the name of a small village further west. The dunes are a prime attraction for tourists, who come here in droves to watch the sunset, although the romance is significantly diluted by the hoardes of hawkers, musicians, bus parties and piles of rubbish. There are also **camel rides** available (Rs80/30min, plus Rs70 for a camel driver and Rs10 tax). Jeeps pay Rs20 to enter the dunes area.

Most camel safaris decamp nearby, but there are a few **accommodation** options in the village itself, the most reliable of which is the simple RTDC *Hotel Sam Dhani* (reservations via RTDC *Moomal Hotel* in Jaisalmer ☎02992/252392; ❺). There are four **buses** daily to Sam (1hr 30min). Alternatively, the tourist office can arrange a **car or Jeep** (Rs150pp) for sunset viewing.

Khuhri

A less-touristed place to watch the sun set over the dunes is the village of **KHUHRI**, 42km south of Jaisalmer – though even this formerly peaceful village is now attracting significant crowds. Most safaris time their arrival so visitors can see flamboyantly dressed women arriving to collect water at caste-specific wells. The village is also quite a charming, sleepy little place to stay, many of its homes still made of mud and thatch rather than concrete, their exterior surfaces beautifully decorated with ornate white murals, and with superb moulded mud shelves and fireplaces, inlaid with mica and mirrorwork, inside (if you're lucky enough to be invited in for a look).

Khuhri can be reached by four daily **buses** (1hr 30min) from the local bus stand in Jaisalmer, or by Jeep (Rs500 for the round trip from Jaisalmer) or taxi (Rs250 round trip). There's a growing number of **guesthouses**, too; prices include supper and breakfast. All the following places can arrange camel safaris. Note that the **phone code** if calling from Jaisalmer is ☎935014; from anywhere else it is ☎03014. The *Mama* (☎935014/274042, ✉gajendra_sodha2003@yahoo.com; ❹–❺), hosted by the charismatic former mayor and slap bang in the middle of the village, has a mix of air-conditioned attached cottages and more simple rooms with shared bathrooms and bucket hot water; they can also arrange local camel safaris. Across the street is the peaceful and relaxed *Badal House* (☎935014/274120; ❸), which is much more like staying with a local family, and a good place to chill out for a few days and get a feel for local village life. Alternatively, try *Fort Khuhri* (☎935014/274123; ❻), a kilometre out of town, where all the rooms are attached with hot showers, some have a/c, and there's an unimpeded view of the dunes (it isn't actually a fort, but a fort-style compound).

Pokaran

Some 110km east of Jaisalmer at the road and rail junctions between Jodhpur, Bikaner and the west is the quiet and little-visited town of **POKARAN**. Pokaran became the centre of international attention in May 1998 when three massive **nuclear explosions** were detonated 200m beneath the sands of the Thar Desert, 20km northwest of the town, announcing India's arrival as one of the world's fully-fledged atomic powers. A huge international outcry followed the blasts, while two weeks later Pakistan detonated its own thermonuclear devices in reply. Hundreds of poor families fell ill shortly after the detonations, and although no fatalities have been directly attributed to the blasts, scientists warn that the environmental hazards may take years to materialize.

Despite its brief and unwelcome moment of international fame, Pokaran remains something of an outpost, but does offer excellent **accommodation** at its sixteenth-century **fort** (☎02994/222274, ⓦwww.fortpokaran.com; ❼–❽), a wonderful old sandstone building that feels more authentic for having only been partly restored. The only other accommodation is the RTDC *Motel Godavan* at the road junction on the edge of town (☎02994/222275; ❸–❹). The State Bank of Bikaner and Jaipur in the middle of town has an **ATM**.

Phalodi and Keechen

The main highway and train line wind in tandem east from Jaisalmer across the desert, separating at the small junction settlement of **PHALODI**, almost exactly midway between Jaisalmer and Bikaner. This scruffy salt-extraction colony would be entirely forgettable were it not the jumping-off place for one of Rajasthan's most beautiful natural sights. Around 6km east of Phalodi, the village of **Keechen** hosts a four-thousand-strong flock of **demoiselle cranes** which migrate here each winter from their breeding grounds in Central Asia. Known locally as *kurja*, the birds are encouraged to return by the villagers, who scatter grain for them twice a day – a custom that has persisted for 150 years or more. At feeding times (5–7am & 5–6pm), the flock descends en masse on a fenced-off area just outside the village, where you can watch them at close quarters.

From Phalodi, the best way to **get to Keechen** is to rent a bicycle from one of the stalls near the bus stand – a pleasant, mostly flat ride on well-surfaced roads. Alternatively, jump in an auto-rickshaw (Rs100) or taxi (Rs200); Ambassador taxis queue outside the railway station. For **accommodation**, *Hotel Chetnya Palace* (☎02925/223945; ❷–❹), next to the Jaisalmer Bus Stand, is the best budget option, with a decent restaurant and a variety of rooms, though the cheaper ones look a bit moth-eaten. Your other option is *Lal Niwas* (☎02925/223813, ⓦwww.lalniwas.com; ❼–❽), a three hundred-year-old red-sandstone haveli converted into a low-key heritage hotel, with slightly dog-eared a/c rooms, a tiny pool and a little attached **museum** (daily 10.30am–7pm; Rs50), with a well-presented but unexciting collection of coins, manuscripts and miniatures. If you're only stopping for a couple of hours, **check bus times** before you head off to Keechen, as services can be sporadic, though theoretically there are buses roughly hourly to Jaisalmer and Bikaner. For Jaisalmer, **trains** depart at 8.58am and 9.55am; to Jodhpur at 6.51pm; and to Bikaner (Lalgarh Junction) at 2.20pm.

Bikaner and around

The smoggy city of **BIKANER** has little of the aesthetic magic of neighbouring Jaisalmer, Jodhpur or Jaipur, but is worth a visit thanks to the impressive **Junagarh Fort**, as well as for the chance to explore its atmospheric old city, dotted with quirky havelis, as well as the nearby government **camel-breeding farm**. It's also the jumping-off point for the remarkable **rat temple** at Deshnok.

The city was founded in 1486 by **Bika**, one of fourteen sons of Rao Jodha, the Rathore king who established Jodhpur, as a link in the overland trading route. In the early 1900s, new agricultural schemes, irrigation work, town planning and

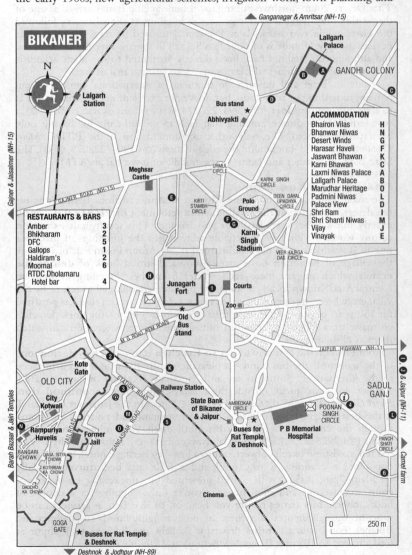

▲ Ganganagar & Amritsar (NH-15)

BIKANER

N

Lalgarh Station

Bus stand
★ Abhivyakti

Lallgarh Palace

GANDHI COLONY

ACCOMMODATION

Bhairon Vilas	H
Bhanwar Niwas	N
Desert Winds	G
Harasar Haveli	F
Jaswant Bhawan	K
Karni Bhawan	C
Laxmi Niwas Palace	A
Lallgarh Palace	B
Marudhar Heritage	O
Padmini Niwas	L
Palace View	D
Shri Ram	I
Shri Shanti Niwas	M
Vijay	J
Vinayak	E

Gajner & Jaisalmer (NH-15)

GAJNER ROAD (NH-15)

Meghsar Castle

URMUL CIRCLE

KIRTI STAMBH CIRCLE

KARNI SINGH CIRCLE

DEEN DAYAL UPADHYA CIRCLE

Polo Ground

Karni Singh Stadium

VEER DURGA DAS CIRCLE

RESTAURANTS & BARS

Amber	3
Bhikharam	2
DFC	5
Gallops	1
Haldiram's	2
Moomal	6
RTDC Dholamaru Hotel bar	4

Junagarh Fort

Courts

Old Bus stand

Zoo

M G ROAD (KEM ROAD)

JAIPUR HIGHWAY (NH-11)

& Jaipur (NH-11)

SADUL GANJ

Kote Gate

OLD CITY

STATION ROAD

Railway Station

City Kotwali

State Bank of Bikaner & Jaipur

AMBEDKAR CIRCLE

POONAN SINGH CIRCLE

PANCH SHATI CIRCLE

Barah Bazaar & Jain Temples

JAIL ROAD

Rampuriya Havelis

Former Jail

GANGASHAR ROAD

Buses for Rat Temple & Deshnok

P B Memorial Hospital

Camel farm

RANGARI CHOWK

DAGA SITYA CHOWK

KOTHRIAN KA CHOWK

DADDHO KA CHOWK

Cinema

0   250 m

GOGA GATE

★ Buses for Rat Temple & Deshnok

▼ Deshnok & Jodhpur (NH-89)

the construction of a rail link with Delhi helped Bikaner's economic advance; it has long since outgrown the confines of the city walls, and the population has more than tripled in size since 1947 to over six hundred thousand.

Arrival and information

Bikaner is very spread out, with widely scattered accommodation. The **State Bus Stand** is north of town near the Lallgarh Palace; the **old bus stand** (used by some private buses) and **railway station** and are both centrally located. (Note though that the new Lalgarh Express #4703 from Jaisalmer terminates at Lalgarh railway station, on the northeast edge of town). Auto-wallahs can be a nuisance; some will employ all the usual tricks to avoid taking you to any establishment that doesn't pay them commission. A ride across town from the state bus stand to the **railway station** should cost around Rs30.

The helpful **tourist office** (daily 10am–5pm; ☏0151/222 6701), in the RTDC *Dholamaru Hotel* at Pooran Singh Circle, can suggest **homestays**. There's useful **online information** at ⓦ www.realbikaner.com.

Accommodation

Bikaner boasts a surprisingly large selection of **hotels**, though the cheap flophouses along Station Road are insalubrious and best avoided.

Budget

Desert Winds 200 metres east of Kirti Stambh Circle ☏0151/254 2202, ⓦ www.hoteldesertwinds .in. Functional, medium-sized hotel with clean and comfy rooms (the more expensive with a/c and TV) and a decent veg restaurant. A slightly more low-key alternative to the very similar *Harasar Haveli* next door, minus the tour groups. ❸–❺

Harasar Haveli next to *Desert Winds* ☏0151/220 9891, ⓦ www.harasar.com. Not a haveli, but a functional, medium-sized modern hotel, with a range of bright, comfortable and spotlessly clean rooms (the more expensive with a/c and TV), plus rooftop and terrace restaurants offering good veg and non-veg food. Popular with tour groups. ❷–❺

Marudhar Heritage Gangashahar Rd ☏0151/252 2524, ⓔ hmheritage2000@yahoo .co.in. Friendly, tranquil hotel near the station with a variety of air-cooled and a/c rooms, all attached. Free pick-up. ❸–❹

Shri Shanti Niwas Gangashahar Rd ☏0151/252 4231. The cleanest of the ultra-cheapies near the station. The various rooms include some very inexpensive singles (Rs80) with shared bath. Doubles are all attached. 24hr checkout. ❶–❹

🏃 **Vijay** Opposite Sophia School, 5km east of centre along the Jaipur Highway ☏0151/223 1244, ⓦ www.camelman.com. Slightly eccentric, pleasantly scruffy and very affordable family guesthouse with just eight attached rooms. There's also camping space, plus a nice garden and free bicycles. ❶–❹

Vinayak Old Ginani ☏0151/220 2634, ⓔ vinayakguesthouse@gmail.com. Hidden away in the backstreets north of the fort, this welcoming little family guesthouse offers cheap attached doubles (with hot water in a bucket). Free pick-up. ❶–❸

Mid-range

Bhairon Vilas Next to Junagarh Fort ☏0151/254 4751, ⓦ hotelbhaironvilas.tripod.com. Stylish heritage hotel in an old royal haveli, surrounded by an attractive garden and kitted out with funky antiques and family curios. Rooms (all a/c) are a mixed bag: the cheaper ones are rather poky, the more expensive ones are spacious and atmospheric. ❹–❻

Jaswant Bhawan Alakhsagar Rd (go out of the rear exit of the train station) ☏0151/254 8848, ⓦ www.hoteljaswantbhawan.com. Relaxing hotel in a nice old house very close to the station. Surprisingly quiet given the location, with comfortable fan, air-cooled and a/c rooms. ❹–❺

Padmini Niwas 148 Sadul Ganj, off Jaipur Rd 1.5 km east of the city centre ☏0151/252 2794, ⓔ padmini_hotel@rediffmail.com. A little bit out of the way, but quiet and good value, with carpeted rooms (some with a/c, all with TV), as well as a pool. ❸–❹

Palace View Lallgarh Palace Campus ☏0151/254 3625, ⓔ hotelpalacev ew@gmail.com. Welcoming guesthouse in a quiet location, with comfortable and pleasantly old-fashioned rooms (some a/c), a homely little dining room and views of Lallgarh Palace. ❹–❺

Camel safaris from Bikaner

Although lacking Jaisalmer's edge-of-the-desert feel, **camel treks** in Bikaner can be just as rewarding. This eastern part of the desert, while just as scenic as the western Thar, is not nearly as congested with fellow trekkers, with the result that local people in the villages along the route don't wait around all day for the chance to sell Pepsi to tourists. Wildlife is also abundant, with plentiful blackbuck, nilgai, and desert foxes.

Your choices of **operator** are somewhat limited, but the same advice applies as that outlined in the Jaisalmer camel safaris box, p.223. Most hotels work with a single guide, who usually hails from one of the villages you'll visit. The best all-round value safaris out of Bikaner are usually offered by Vijay Singh Rathore (aka "Camel Man"), based at *Vijay Guest House*, 5km out of town along the Jaipur road (T 0151/223 1244, W www.camelman.com). Full details and rates of his various treks are posted on his website; a full-day safari goes for Rs900 per person. Another similarly affordable and dependable operator is Thar Camel Safari (c/o the *Meghsar Castle* hotel or on T 0/935 120 6093). Another possibility is the safaris arranged by the *Vinayak Guest House* (see p.233). These are led by Jitu Solanki, a trained zoologist, whose trips offer fascinating insights into the wildlife and enivronment of the desert, as well as visits to remote Bishnoi villages.

Shri Ram Sadul Ganj, 1.5 km east of the city centre T 0151/252 2651, W www.hotelshriram .com. This suburban guesthouse doubles as Bikaner's youth hostel. Second-floor suite rooms are preferable to the cramped rooms out back, or there are 5-bed dorms (Rs100). ❹–❺

Expensive

Bhanwar Niwas Old city T 0151/220 1043, W www.bhanwarniwas.com. Bikaner's most ostentatious haveli, built for a textile tycoon in the late 1920s and crammed with kitsch fittings and furniture, complete with a 1927 Buick in the lobby, an atmospheric *fin de siècle* dining room and an array of memorably chintzy rooms. ❽–❾

Karni Bhawan Palace Gandhi Colony, 1km east of Lallgarh Palace T 0151/252 4701 to 5, or 1800/180 2933 or 2944, W www.hrhindia.com. On the outside it looks like an oversized English suburban house, but the interior is period and wonderful, with superb (if overpriced) Art Deco suites in the main building, complete with original

1930s furniture (but don't bother with the standard rooms in the annexe). ❼–❽

Laxmi Niwas Palace Lallgarh Palace T 0151/220 2777, W www.laxminiwaspalace.com. The better of two palatial hotels in the Lallgarh Palace complex, offering large rooms with period English furniture – the best is #108, which has hosted British monarchs Queen Victoria, George V and Elizabeth II. Rates from around $190. Rooms at the neighbouring *Lallgarh Palace Hotel* (❽) are almost half the price and less impressive, though still boast plenty of old colonial character. ❾

Around Bikaner

Gajner Palace Hotel 32km southwest of Bikaner T 01534/275 061, W www.hrhindia.com. This grand affair in red sandstone was built in the early twentieth century as a hunting lodge for the maharajas of Bikaner. The hotel overlooks a lake, and staff can arrange jaunts through the surrounding Gajner Wildlife Sanctuary. Rooms from around $175. ❾

The City

Bikaner's main sight is the impressive **Junagarh Fort**, but it's also worth making time for a wander through the **old city**, with its rich array of quirky, early twentieth-century havelis.

Junagarh Fort

Built on ground level and defended only by high walls and a wide moat, **Junagarh Fort** (daily 10am–4.30pm; foreign visitors Rs100, Indian residents Rs20; camera Rs30, video Rs100) isn't as immediately imposing as the mighty hill forts elsewhere in Rajasthan, but its richly decorated interiors are as magnificent as anywhere in the state. The entrance price includes a 1hr **compulsory guided tour**, though it's easy enough to break away from the tour and make your own way around.

The fort was built between 1587 and 1593 during the rule of Rai Singh, and progressively enlarged and embellished by later rulers. Although never conquered, the bastion was attacked on several occasions by armies from Marwar (Jodhpur) handprints set in stone near the second gate, **Daulat Pol**, bear witness to the *satis* of various royal women.

From the entrance, a passageway climbs up to the small Vikram Vilas courtyard, beyond which you'll find the main courtyard. Opening onto the main courtyard is the **Karan Mahal**, built in the seventeenth century to commemorate a victory over the Mughal emperor Aurangzeb. The *mahel*'s pillars and walls are adorned with gold-leaf painting, while from the ceiling hangs an old *punkah* (fan). Next to here in the **Rai Niwas** are Maharaja Gaj Singh's ivory slippers, one of Akbar's swords, and a set of regal insignia including a representation of the Pisces zodiac sign which looks remarkably like a dinosaur in a headscarf.

The **Anup Mahal** (Diwan-i-Khas) is the grandest room in the palace, with stunning red and gold filigree decorative painting and a red satin throne framed by an arc of glass and mirrors. The carpet was made by inmates of Bikaner jail – a manufacturing tradition that has only recently ceased. After such a hectic display of opulence, the **Badal Mahal** ("cloud palace"), built in the mid-nineteenth century for Maharaja Sardar Singh (1851–72) and painted with blue sky and clouds, is pleasantly understated. Upstairs, a room exhibits beds of nails, sword blades and spear heads used by sadhus to demonstrate their immunity to pain, while across the terrace in the **Gaj Mandar** is the maharaja's chaste single bed and the maharani's more accommodation double.

The next part of the palace, the twentieth-century **Ganga Niwas**, created by Maharaja Ganga Singh (1887–1943), can be reached either via a long passageway from the Gaj Mandar or, more directly, from the Vikram Vilas courtyard (see above). Exhibits include seven German machine guns seized during World War I, when Bikaner troops fought in Europe alongside the British, and a sandalwood throne of 1212 in the **throne room**, though the room itself, decorated with reliefs of trees and animals, dates from 1937. Next door, the **Diwan-i-Am** is dominated by a World War I Haviland biplane, a present from the British to Bikaner's state forces.

Also in the fort complex, the **Prachina Museum** (daily 9am–6pm; foreign visitors Rs50, Indian residents Rs10, camera Rs20, video Rs75; Ⓦ www.prachina-museum.com) houses a pretty collection of objects (glassware, crockery, cutlery and walking sticks) demonstrating the growing influence of Europe on Rajasthani style in the early twentieth century. A whole circa-1900 salon has been re-created, and there's also an interesting collection of Rajasthani textiles and clothing.

The old city

Bikaner's labyrinthine **old city** is notable for its profusion of unusual **havelis** whose idiosyncratic architecture demonstrates an unlikely fusion of indigenous sandstone carving with *fin-de-siècle* Art Nouveau and red-brick municipal Britain. The city is confusing to navigate, so accept getting lost as part of the experience.

Entering the old city through Kote Gate, bear left (south) down Jail Road. After 300m, a right turn just before a fort-like pink-and-white girls' school takes you past the City Kotwali (the old city's central police station) to the three striking **Rampuriya Havelis**, commissioned in the 1920s by three brothers from a Jain trading family and faced with reliefs of a mixture of personages both religious and secular, including Maharaja Ganga Singh, Britain's George V and Queen Mary, and Krishna and Radha.

The most interesting cluster of havelis lies southeast of here, around a sequence of tiny *chowks* (squares). Just south of the Rampuriya Havelis is **Rangari Chowk**, in the middle of which stands an odd little building with four painted figures in relief between its first-floor windows. Proceed along the right-hand side of the building and straight ahead is **Kothrion ka Chowk**, lined by handsome havelis. Continue round to the left and then take the first left past the **Kothari Building** (on your right), with five wonderfully extravagant Art Nouveau balconies, to reach the small **Daga Sitya Chowk**. A house on the left still has fading murals of steam trains, while Diamond House, on the right, gets wider as it goes up, each storey overhanging the one below it. Retrace your steps back to the street you were originally on, then turn left and left again to reach the **Punan Chand Haveli** boasting an amazingly carved floral facade. Retrace your steps and head left again to reach the large **Daddho ka Chowk** (Dhadha Chowk), surrounded by fine havelis.

Cross the square, to where the street ends at a T-junction, then turn right and continue for around 400m to reach **Barah Bazaar**, centred on a large pillar painted in the colours of the Indian flag that appears to sprout out of a gaggle of auto-rickshaws. Follow the street round to the left and you'll eventually reach the **Bhandreshwar (Bhandasar) Temple**, unusual amongst Jain temples in being covered in a rich, almost gaudy, array of paintings. Porcelain tiles imported from Victorian England decorate the main altar, and steps lead up the unusually large tower, where you get a great view over the old city. Building started in 1468, before Bikaner itself was founded, but the temple wasn't finished until 1504. The mortar for the foundations was apparently made with ghee instead of water. Immediately to the rear on the edge of the high city wall lies the large Hindu **Laxminath Temple**, commissioned in the early sixteenth century by

Recommended trains from Bikaner

For **Delhi**, the #2464A Sampark Kranti Express to Sarai Rohilla Station runs on Tuesdays, Thursdays and Sundays only; on other days, you'll have to get the #2308 Howrah Superfast to Merta Road (arrives 9.40pm) and wait there till 12.10am for the #4060 Jaisalmer–Delhi Express, which gets you in to Old Delhi at 11.05am. There are no direct trains **to Ajmer**, but if you take the #2467 Jaipur Intercity at 5am, you can change at Phulera (arrive 10.45am) for the #2414A Link Express, which leaves for Ajmer at 11.11am, getting in at 12.45pm. For Sawai Madhopur, Kota and Chittaurgarh, take train #2467 and change at Jaipur.

Destination	Name	No.	Departs	Arrives
Abu Road	Ranakpur Express	4707	9.45am (daily)	8pm
	Ahmedabad Express	9224	12.55am (daily)	11.25am
Agra	Howrah Superfast	2308A	6.30pm (daily)	6.35am
Delhi (SR)	Sampark Kranti Express	2464A	5.20pm (T, Th, S)	5.40am
Jaipur	Jaipur Intercity	2467	5am (daily)	11.40am
Jaisalmer	Lalgarh Express	4704	6.55am (daily)	1.45pm
	Jaisalmer Express	4702	11.25pm (daily)	6.10am
Jodhpur	Ranakpur Express	4707	9.45am (daily)	2.45pm
	Kalka–Barmer Express	4887	11.30am (daily)	4.50pm
	Ahmedabad Express	9224	12.55am (daily)	6.20

Lunkaran Singh, the third ruler of Bikaner. In a small park just beyond (follow the road between the Laxminath and Bhandreshwar temples) is a second Jain temple, the **Sandeshwar (Neminath) Temple** of 1536, also profusely but more sobrely painted in dark greens and reds. A large model behind the temple shows the huge Jain religious complex at Palitana in Gujarat.

Lallgarh Palace and Shri Sadul Museum

The sturdy red-sandstone **Lallgarh Palace** in the north of the town is home to the royal family of Bikaner, although parts have now been converted into a pair of hotels. It was built during the reign of Ganga Singh, who lived here from 1902, and the sheer scale and profusion of the exterior decoration is impressive, even if it lacks the romantic allure of older Rajasthani palaces. The **Shri Sadul Museum** (Mon–Sat 10am–5pm; Rs20, Indian residents Rs10, camera Rs20, video Rs50) houses an enormous and surprisingly engrossing collection of old photographs showing various viceregal visits, pictures of Ganga Singh at the signing of the Versailles Treaty and royal processions.

The camel farm

What claims to be Asia's largest camel-breeding farm, the **National Research Centre on Camels** (daily 2–5pm; Rs10, Indian residents Rs5, camera Rs20; camel ride Rs40, guided tour Rs100) lies out in the desert 10km south of Bikaner (around Rs80 round-trip by auto including 30min waiting time). Although Bikaner has long been renowned for its famously sturdy beasts – the camel corps was a much-feared component of the imperial battle formation – growing proliferation of the internal combustion engine has severely reduced their traditional role as a means of rural transport. It's best to take a guided tour of the farm; aim to be here at 3.30–4pm, when you'll be wowed by the sight of three hundred stampeding dromedaries arriving from the desert for their daily chow. The small **museum** has little of interest, but the camel milk parlour next door sells an assortment of camel milk-based products such as lassis and kulfi.

Eating and drinking

Restaurants are thin on the ground in Bikaner and most visitors eat at their hotels. For a **drink**, try the bar of the RTDC *Dholamaru Hotel* at Pooran Singh Circle or the more expensive bar at the *Lallgarh Palace* hotel. Bikaner is famous for its **sweets** such as *kaju katli*, made with cashew nuts, and *tirangi*, a three-coloured confection made with cashews, almonds and pistachios.

Amber Station Rd. Simple but clean local restaurant that's popular with Westerners, with a long menu of Indian veg standards along with a few snacks. Most mains Rs50–70.

Bhikharam Chandmal Bhujiawala just off Station Rd on the road to Kote Gate (the English sign is very small and easy to miss). Top *mithai* shop, known for its excellent Bengali and Rajasthani sweets, though it also has a good range of savoury snacks.

DFC (Dwarika Food Cuisine) Station Rd, by Silver Square mall. Clean and pleasant restaurant offering a big list of veg mains (most Rs50–65), thalis (Rs40–75) and even train tiffins (Rs60) to take with you on a rail journey.

Gallops Court Rd. Good veg and non-veg in a rather smart restaurant opposite the fort – normally full of tour groups at lunchtime, though usually quieter in the evenings. Food includes Rajasthani specialities like *gatta Bikaner*, a local version of the pan-Rajasthani dish. Mains Rs90–175. Licenced.

Moomal Panch Shati Circle. Popular with well-heeled locals, this white-linen restaurant serves sumptuous south Indian veg food – the punchy cashew and cherry Moomal Special alone is worth the trip. Mains around Rs90–180.

Shopping

Bikaner is famous for its skilled lacquerwork and handicrafts, sold in the bazaar for a fraction of Jaisalmer's inflated "tourist prices", and for its hand-woven woollen *pattu* (a kind of shawl-cum-blanket). The best place to buy the latter is the **Abhivyakti** handicrafts shop on Ganganar Road, near the bus stand, whose manager can also arrange visits to villages to see how the textiles are woven by Oxfam-supported women's co-ops. **Vichitra Arts**, at *Bhairon Vilas*, sells vintage royal garb and miniature paintings.

Listings

Banks and exchange There are ATMs directly opposite the station, and another one 100m south; on Station Rd almost opposite the road from Kote Gate; about halfway along MG Rd on the south side; and between RTDC *Hotel Dhola Maru* and Panch Shati Circle. There are several forexes on Lallgarh Palace Rd between the fort and Kirti Stambh Circle including LKP Forex (daily 9am–8pm), which also gives cash advance on credit cards. Thomas Cook (Mon–Sat 9am–6pm), inside the entrance to the fort, also changes cash and credit cards.

Bicycle rental Basic bikes are available from a row of shacks just south of the main post office, opposite the southwest corner of the fort, for Rs3/hr.

Festival Though not as renowned or as touristed as those of Pushkar or Jaisalmer, Bikaner's camel fair (10–11 Jan & 30–31 Dec 2009, 18–19 Jan 2011) still has plenty of colour, with camel races,

camel hairstyle competitions and camel acrobatics, plus fire dancing and fireworks. Most of the action takes place at the polo ground north of town near *Harasar Haveli* hotel. Advance accommodation booking recommended.

Hospital PB Memorial Hospital by Ambedkar Circle ☎ 0151/222 6334.

Internet access Internet is widely available for around Rs20/hr but generally slow. There are lots of places around Kirti Stambh Circus; alternatively, try New Horizons behind the *Amber Restaurant* on Station Rd (daily 9am–9pm; Rs20/hr).

Police Station Rd ☎ 0151/252 2225.

Post office The main post office is just west of the fort (Mon–Fri 10am–3pm, Sat 10am–1pm).

Swimming pool The *Padmini Niwas Hotel* allows non-guests to use theirs for Rs100.

Moving on from Bikaner

For full details of buses from Bikaner, see **travel details** on p.268. **RSTRC government buses** operate out of the main bus stand on the north side of town (☎ 0151/252 3800). Buses to Deshnok and Nagaur start at the state bus stand but can be picked up at Ambedkar Circle and Goga Gate Circle. **Private buses** are run by a handful of firms, most of which have offices at the old bus stand – shop around until you find a service that suits.

The **railway** station is on Station Road, just east of the old city. Recommended services are listed in the box on p.236.

Deshnok

The **Karni Mata Temple** (daily 6am–10pm; free; Rs20 camera, Rs50 video; ⓦ www.karnimata.com) in **DESHNOK**, 30km south of Bikaner, is one of India's more bizarre attractions. Step inside the Italian-marble arched doorway and everywhere you'll see free-roaming rats, known as *kabas*, which devotees believe are reincarnated souls saved from the wrath of Yama, the god of death. The innermost shrine, made of rough stone and logs cut from sacred *jal* trees, houses the yellow-marble image of Karniji (see box opposite). This in turn is encased by a much grander marble building erected by Rao Bika's grandson after he defeated the Mughals. Pilgrims bring offerings for the rats to eat inside the main shrine, and it's considered auspicious to eat the leftovers after they've been nibbled by the *kabas*. Some pilgrims spend hours searching for a glimpse

The Deshnok Devi

Members of the Charan caste of musicians believe that incarnations of the goddess Durga periodically appear among them, one of whom was **Karni Mata**, born at a village near Phalodi in 1387, who went on to perform such miracles as water divination and bringing the dead back to life, eventually becoming the region's most powerful cult leader.

According to legend, one of Karni Mata's followers came to her because her son was grievously ill, but by the time they got to him, he had died. Karni Mata went to Yama, the god of the underworld, to ask for him back, but Yama refused. Knowing that of all the creatures upon the earth, only rats were outside Yama's dominion, Karni Mata decreed that all Charans would henceforth be reincarnated as rats, thus escaping Yama's power. It is these sacred rats (*kabas*) that inhabit the Deshnok temple.

Rao Bika, the founder of Bikaner, realized that he and Karni could forge a formidable alliance, and wooed her with financial and religious promises in return for giving his clan her stamp of approval. When her eventual endorsement came it turned Bika's fortunes, quadrupling the size of his army. Bika regularly consulted her throughout his reign – a connection with the ruling family that has endured to this day. The Bikaner flag sports Karni's colours, and she is the patron goddess of the Bikaner camel corps, who still march into battle crying "Shree Karniji!"

of the temple's venerated white rat, while it's also considered fortunate for a rat to run over your feet (stand still for a while – preferably next to some food), but whatever you do don't step on one, or you'll have to donate a gold model of a rat to placate the deity. Shoes have to be removed at the gate, leaving you to wander among the rat droppings barefoot or in your socks.

Directly in front of the temple, the easily overlooked **Shri Karni Sixth Centenary Auditorium** contains a collection of oil paintings recounting the major events in Karniji's life, with English captions. A few kilometres away on the edge of town, the rarely visited **Nahrij Temple**, although lacking in rodents, has encased in marble the tree where Karniji in her last years came to make butter and await nirvana.

Buses from Bikaner leave for Deshnok (roughly every 15min; 40min) from the main bus stand, stopping on the east side of Ambedkar Circle near PB Memorial Hospital, and just south of Goga Gate Circle, near the southeast corner of the old city. There are also **trains** at 9.45am and 11.30am, with return services from Deshnok at 2.59pm and 3.39pm.

Udaipur

Few people forget their first sight of **UDAIPUR**. Spreading around the shores of the idyllic Lake Pichola and backdropped by a majestic ring of craggy green hills, the city seems to encapsulate India at its most quintessentially romantic, with its intricate sequence of ornately turreted and balconied palaces, whitewashed havelis and bathing *ghats* clustered around the waters of the lake – or, in the case of the *Lake Palace* hotel and Jag Mandir, floating magically upon them. Not that the city is quite as perfect as the publicity would have you believe. The drought which recently emptied Lake Pichola for several years has mercifully ended, and water levels have now been restored to their original levels, but insensitive modern lakeside development, appalling traffic and vast hordes of tourists mean that the city is far from unspoilt or undiscovered. Even so, Udaipur remains

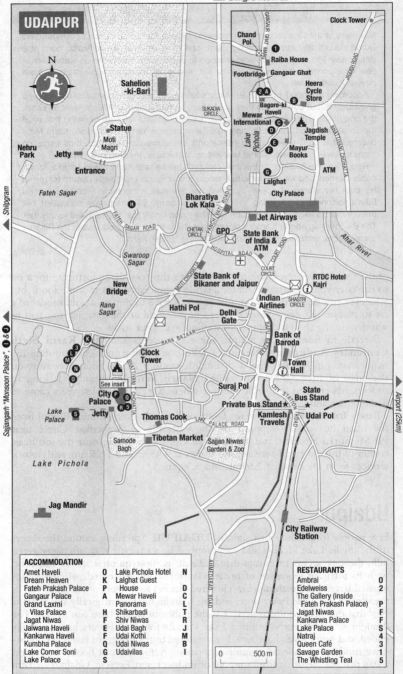

Eklingji & Mount Abu

UDAIPUR

N

Sahelion-ki-Bari

Statue
Moti Magri

Nehru Park

Jetty

Entrance

Fateh Sagar

Shilpgram

Bharatiya Lok Kala

SUKADIA CIRCLE

PANCH VATI ROAD

Swaroop Sagar

New Bridge

Rang Sagar

CHETAK CIRCLE

GPO

HOSPITAL ROAD

State Bank of India & ATM

State Bank of Bikaner and Jaipur

COURT CIRCLE

COURT ROAD

RTDC Hotel Kajri

SHASTRI CIRCLE

Hathi Pol

Delhi Gate

Indian Airlines

Jet Airways

Ahar River

Sajjangarh "Monsoon Palace"

MOTI CHOHTTA

BARA BAZAAR

Clock Tower

BHATTIYANI CHOHTTA

BAPU BAZAAR

CITY STATION ROAD

Bank of Baroda

Town Hall

Suraj Pol

State Bus Stand

Private Bus Stand

Kamlesh Travels

Udai Pol

Airport (25km)

City Palace

Jetty

Thomas Cook

Lake Palace

LAKE PALACE ROAD

Tibetan Market

Samode Bagh

Sajjan Niwas Garden & Zoo

Lake Pichola

AHMEDABAD ROAD

City Railway Station

Jag Mandir

Inset (top right):

Clock Tower

GANGAUR GHAT MARG

Chand Pol

Raiba House

Footbridge

Gangaur Ghat

Heera Cycle Store

Mewar International

Bagore-ki Haveli

Lake Pichola

Jagdish Temple

Mayur Books

BHATTIYANI CHOHTTA

ATM

Lalghat

City Palace

ACCOMMODATION

Amet Haveli	O	Lake Pichola Hotel	N
Dream Heaven	K	Lalghat Guest	
Fateh Prakash Palace	P	House	D
Gangaur Palace	A	Mewar Haveli	C
Grand Laxmi		Panorama	L
Vilas Palace	H	Shikarbadi	T
Jagat Niwas	F	Shiv Niwas	R
Jaiwana Haveli	E	Udai Bagh	J
Kankarwa Haveli	F	Udai Kothi	M
Kumbha Palace	Q	Udai Niwas	B
Lake Corner Soni	G	Udaivilas	I
Lake Palace	S		

RESTAURANTS

Ambrai	O
Edelweiss	2
The Gallery (inside	
Fateh Prakash Palace)	P
Jagat Niwas	F
Kankarwa Palace	F
Lake Palace	S
Natraj	4
Queen Café	3
Savage Garden	1
The Whistling Teal	5

0   500 m

① & Ahmedabad

a richly rewarding place to visit, and although it's possible to take in most of the sights in a few days, many people spend at least a week exploring the city and the various attractions scattered about the surrounding countryside.

Some history

Udaipur is a relatively young city by Indian standards, having been established in the mid-sixteenth century by Udai Singh II of the **Sisodia** family, rulers of the state of **Mewar**, which covered much of present-day southern Rajasthan. The Sisodias are traditionally considered the foremost of all the Rajput royal dynasties. The present Sisodia maharana is the seventy-sixth in the unbroken line of Mewar suzerains, which makes the Mewar household the longest lasting of all royal families of Rajasthan, and perhaps the oldest surviving dynasty in the world.

The state of Mewar was established by Guhil in 568 AD. His successors set up their capital first at Nagda and then, in 734, at the mighty fort of Chittaurgarh, from where they established control over much of present-day southern Rajasthan (for a brief history of the Sisodias at Chittaurgarh, see p.259). By the time **Udai Singh II** inherited the throne of Mewar in 1537, however, it was clear that Chittaurgarh's days were numbered. Udai began looking for a location for a new city, to be named Udaipur, eventually chosing a swampy site beside Lake Pichola, protected on all sides by outcrops of the Aravalli range. The Mughal emperor Akbar duly captured Chittaurgarh after a protracted seige in 1568, but by then Udai was firmly established in his new capital, where he remained unmolested until his death in 1572. His son, the heroic **Pratap Singh**, continued to defy Akbar and spent much of his reign doggedly defending his kingdom's freedom against the overwhelming military muscle of the Mughal army.

Following Akbar's death, peace finally ensued, and the city prospered until 1736, when Mewar suffered the first of repeated attacks by the **Marathas**, who gradually reduced the city to poverty until being finally driven off by the British in the early eighteenth century. The Sisodias thenceforth allied themselves to the British, while preserving their independence until 1947, when the famous old state of Mewar was finally merged into the newly created nation of India.

Arrival, information and city transport

The **bus stand** is on the east side of the centre, a Rs20–30 rickshaw ride from the City Palace area. **Trains** pull in at Udaipur City Station, southeast of the city centre (don't get off at Udaipur Station, much further north). **Flights** arrive at **Dabok Airport** (☎0294/265 5453), 25km east of Udaipur, a Rs200 taxi ride from the city. The main **tourist office** (Mon–Sat 10am–5pm; ☎0294/241 1535) is inconveniently situated on the east side of the city.

Auto-rickshaws are the usual means of transport; there are no cycle rickshaws in town. Renting a **bicycle** is another possibility (see "Listings" on p.248), although traffic around the city is fairly awful. The RTDC office, in the RTDC *Hotel Kajri* on Shastri Circle, arranges city sightseeing trips and other cheap **tours** to Ranakpur, Kumbalgarh, Nathdwara and Eklingji. Similar tours are offered by some of the innumerable **travel agents** dotted around the city centre (see "Listings", p.248), as well as car rental (usually around Rs1200 per day for up to 300km).

Accommodation

Most accommodation is on the **east side of Lake Pichola,** although there are a growing number of places on the far more peaceful **northwestern side** of the lake, just across the bridge by Chand Pol.

East of Lake Pichola

Fateh Prakash Palace City Palace ℡0294/252 8016, ⓦwww.hrhindia.com. The best location in the city, right in the heart of the City Palace complex, with prices to match. Most of the rooms (from around US$380) have superb lake views, although some are rather small and characterless for the price. ❾

Gangaur Palace Gangaur Ghat Marg ℡0294/242 2303, ⓦwww.ashokahaveli.com. Popular budget hotel in an atmospheric traditional haveli. There's a wide range of rooms of varying standards (fan and a/c), including some with lake views, though prices for the smarter rooms can be a bit steep – try bargaining. Facilities include in-house palmist, painting lessons and German bakery. ❷–❺

Jagat Niwas 23–25 Lalghat ℡0294/242 2860, ⓦwww.jagatniwaspalace.com. Beautifully restored seventeenth-century haveli right on the lakeside, with pleasant a/c rooms (some with lake views) and a good restaurant (see p.247), though not as peaceful or as good value as the nearby *Kankarwa* and *Jaiwana* havelis. Popular with tour groups. ❺–❾

Jaiwana Haveli 14 Lalghat ℡0294/241 1103, ⓦwww.jaiwanahaveli.com. Good-value lakeside haveli accommodation with a range of spotless modern rooms; some have a/c, and the more expensive ones have fine lake views, as does the good rooftop restaurant. ❸–❻

Kankarwa Haveli 26 Lalghat ℡0294/241 1457, ⓔkhaveli@yahoo.com. Romantically restored haveli right on the waterfront. Not quite as pristine as the nearby *Jagat Niwas*, but more atmospheric and much better value, with colourful, antiquey rooms (all a/c; some with superb lake views). There's also excellent veg food (see p.247). ❹–❼

Kumbha Palace 104 Bhatiyani Chohatta ℡0294/242 2702, ⓔkumbha01@hotmail.com. Friendly, Dutch-owned guesthouse hidden under the east walls of City Palace and backed by a bougainvillea-strewn garden. Rooms (a few with a/c) are simple but bright and clean, and the whole place is refreshingly peaceful. ❷–❹

Lake Corner Soni Paying Guest House Lalghat ℡0294/252 5712. This simple little guesthouse, run by a charming elderly couple, offers some of the cheapest lodgings in Udaipur. Rooms (some with shared bathroom) are basic but clean and peaceful, and there are fine lake views from the rooftop terrace and some rooms. ❶

Lake Palace Lake Pichola ℡0294/252 8800, ⓦwww.tajhotels.com. One of India's most famous and romantic hotels, sailing in magnificent isolation on its own island amidst the serene waters of Lake Pichola. Accommodation is in a selection of rooms and suites, which range from the merely luxurious to the opulently theatrical, while facilities include a spa, pool, butler service and limousine rental. Non-guests can visit for a pricey lunch or dinner (see p.247). Room rates start at $850, though check the website for discounts. ❾

Lalghat Guest House Lalghat ℡0294/252 5301, ⓔlalghat@hotmail.com. One of the oldest guesthouses in Udaipur, and still going strong thanks to its superb lakeside position and cheapish rates. There's a mix of rooms (all attached, some a/c, and some with lakeside views), plus a nicer-than-average ten-person dorm (Rs100pp). ❸–❺

Mewar Haveli 34–35 Lalghat ℡0294/252 1140, ⓦwww.mewarhaveli.com. Spotless and well-run modern mid-range hotel in a very central location. Rooms (some with a/c and lake views) are chintzy but comfortable, and there are further lake views from the attractive rooftop restaurant. ❺–❻

Shiv Niwas City Palace ℡0294/252 8016, ⓦwww .hrhindia.com. This upmarket heritage hotel trades on its superb location inside the City Palace complex, with grand public areas, a dreamy pool (non-guests Rs300) and a brand-new spa. The viewless standard ("palace") rooms are disappointingly small and ordinary given the US$325 price tag; suites (from around US$650) are far more memorable, with genuine old-world atmosphere and marvellous lake views. 20% discounts in summer. ❾

Udai Niwas Gangaur Ghat Marg ℡0294/241 4303, ⓦwww.hoteludainiwas.com. Bright modern high-rise hotel with a range of smart rooms in various price categories (the more expensive ones with a/c), although road noise and the periodic outbursts of massively amplified music from the nearby Jagdish Temple mean that it's not particularly peaceful. ❷–❹

Northwestern side of Lake Pichola

Amet Haveli Chand Pol ℡0294/243 4009, ⓔamethaveli@sify.com. This fine old white haveli is one of the best lakefront properties in town. All rooms are beautifully decorated with traditional touches and come with a/c, TV and fine lake views, though you might want to spend a little bit extra to get one of the superb suites, with big windows right over the water. Also home to the excellent *Ambrai* restaurant (see p.247). ❽

Dream Heaven Chand Pol ℡0294/243 1038, Ⓔdeep_rg@yahoo.co.uk. A decent alternative to the nearby *Panorama*, with a good range of clean, cheap and competitively priced rooms; some have superb lake views, as does the rooftop restaurant. ❶–❹

Lake Pichola Hotel Chand Pol ℡0294/243 1197, Ⓦwww.lakepicholahotel.com. This long-established hotel won't win any design awards but the lakeside location and City Palace views are just about perfect, and prices quite reasonable. Don't bother with the viewless economy rooms, though. All rooms with a/c and TV. ❻–❾

🏃 Panorama Chand Pol ℡0294/243 1027, Ⓔkrishna2311@rediffmail.com. The best

budget hotel in Udaipur, very efficiently run and with cheap, cosy and excellent-value rooms (some with slight lake views; a few with a/c). There's also a nice rooftop restaurant with superb lake views and better-than-average food. Book ahead. ❶–❹

Udai Kothi Chand Pol ℡0294/243 2810, Ⓦwww.udaikothi.com. Smart and spotless modern hotel in traditional style, with lots of flowery murals and chintzy little architectural touches. Rooms all come with TV, a/c and plenty of slightly twee furnishings; there's also a pool (non-guests Rs300) and a lovely garden. ❽–❾

Outside the city centre

Grand Laxmi Vilas Palace Off Fateh Sagar Rd ℡0294/252 9711, Ⓦwww.thegrandhotels.net. Luxury hotel occupying a nineteenth-century hilltop guesthouse above Fateh Sagar Lake. It's strong on creature comforts, with well-equipped rooms and a huge pool, although a bit lacking in atmosphere compared to the similarly priced hotels in the City Palace. Rooms from US$380, but check the website for special offers. ❾

🏃 Udaivilas ℡0294/243 3300, Ⓦwww.oberoihotels.com. Udaipur's most opulent hotel, occupying a sprawling palace, embellished with acres of marble and a novel "moated pool" which flows around the outside of the main building. Suites come with their own infinity swimming pools and private butler, and the spa is pure indulgence. Rates from around US$700. ❾

Around Udaipur

🏃 Devi Garh Delwara Village, 25km north of Udaipur ℡02953/289211, Ⓦwww.deviresorts.com. Hidden away in the Aravalli Hills a 40min drive north of Udaipur, this luxury hotel occupies the magnificent seventeenth-century Devi Garh palace, mixing traditional Rajasthani palace opulence with contemporary style to memorable effect. Facilities include a superb spa and a spectacular pool. Rooms from around US$540; 20% discounts April–Sept. ❾

Shikarbadi Goverdhan Vilas, 5km south of Udaipur on the NH-8 ℡0294/258 3201,

Ⓦwww.hrhindia.com. Former royal hunting lodge with its own pool, lake, deer park and stud farm – less ostentatious (and significantly cheaper) than the palaces in town. Suites in the old 1930s block have more character than the newer a/c rooms. Rooms from around $160. ❾

Udai Bagh 6km from the city centre. Idyllic retreat in a surprisingly peaceful rural location close to Udaipur. Accommodation is in luxurious permanent tents complete with antique furniture and tiled bathrooms, and there's a big pool and spa (under construction). Rooms from around $160. ❾

The City

The original settlement of Udaipur grew up around the grand **City Palace**, on the east shore of **Lake Pichola** and bounded to the north by the **old city**'s maze of tightly winding streets. North of here stretches the second of Udaipur's two major lakes, **Fateh Sagar**, while outlying attractions include the crafts village of **Shilpgram** and the so-called "Monsoon Palace" of **Sajjangarh**.

Lake Pichola

Udaipur's idyllic **Lake Pichola** provides the city with virtually all of its most memorable views, offering a beautiful frame for the superb City Palace buildings, havelis, *ghats*, temple towers and myriad other structures which crowd its eastern side – best seen from a boat trip around the lake (see p.244). The

Note that to reach certain parts of the City Palace, including the *Fateh Prakash Palace* and *Shiv Niwas* hotels, the Durbar Hall, Crystal Gallery and the jetty for boats around Lake Pichola and over to the *Lake Palace* hotel, you'll have to fork out Rs25 for a **general entrance ticket** to the City Palace complex. You don't have to buy this ticket if you're just visiting the City Palace Museum or the courtyard outside, or if you're actually staying at any of the three aforementioned hotels.

lake's two **island palaces** are amongst Udaipur's most famous features. **Jag Niwas**, now the *Lake Palace* hotel, was built in amalgamated Rajput–Mughal style as a summer palace during the reign of Jagat Singh (1628–52), after whom it was named, although if you aren't staying there the only way of visiting is to splash out on lunch or dinner (see p.247). The **Jag Mandir** palace, on the island to the south, is arranged around a large garden guarded by stone elephants. The main building here is the **Gol Mahal**, which has detailed stone inlay work within its domed roof and houses a small exhibition on the history of the island. The young Shah Jahan once stayed here and was apparently so impressed by the building that he used it as one of the models for his own Taj Mahal, though it's difficult to see the resemblance.

Boat rides around the lake depart from the jetty towards the south end of the City Palace complex, offering unforgettable views of the various palaces. Choose between a quick thirty-minute circuit of the lake (Rs200) or the same trip with an additional stop at the Jag Mandir (Rs300). Both tours depart hourly on the hour from 10am to 6pm. To make the most of them, sit on the side of the boat facing the palace (they usually run anticlockwise around the lake). You can also hire your own boat (seating up to 7 people) here for Rs2000. Alternatively, you can rent pedalos or motorboats on the waterfront betweeen the *Jaiwana* and *Kankarwa* havelis (2-seater Rs75/20min, 4-seater Rs150/20min, motorboats from Rs450/20min).

City Palace museum

Udaipur's fascinating **City Palace** stands moulded in soft yellow stone on the northeast side of Lake Pichola, its thick windowless base crowned with ornate turrets and cupolas. The largest royal complex in Rajasthan, the building comprises eleven different *mahals* (palaces) constructed by successive rulers over a period of three hundred years. Part of the palace is now a **museum** (daily 9.30am–4.30pm; Rs50, camera Rs200, video Rs200, audioguide Rs250, guided tours Rs100–150). Narrow low-roofed passages connect the different *mahals* and courtyards, creating a haphazard effect designed to prevent surprise intrusion by armed enemies – the layout of the whole complex is incredibly labyrinthine and confusing, although fortunately visitors are directed around a clearly signed one-way circuit, so your opportunities for getting lost are pretty limited.

The entrance to the museum is on the far side of the **Moti Chowk** courtyard (look out for the large portable tiger trap in the middle of the courtyard), past the palace's small **armoury**. Go in, past propitious statues of Ganesh and Lakshmi, and head upstairs to reach the first of the palace's myriad courtyards, the **Rajya Angan**. A room off on one side is devoted to the exploits of Pratap Singh, one of Udaipur's most famous military leaders. From here, steps lead up to pleasantly sylvan **Badi Mahal** (Garden Palace; also known as Amar Vilas after its creator, Amar Singh II, reigned 1695–1755), its main courtyard embellished with finely carved pillars and a marble pool and dotted with trees which flourish despite being built some 30m above ground level.

From the Badi Mahal, twisting steps lead down to the **Dilkushal Mahal**, whose rooms house a superb selection of paintings depicting festive events in the life of the Udaipur court and portraits of the maharanas, as well as the superb **Kanch ki Burj**, a tiny little chamber eye-catchingly walled with red zigzag mirrors. Immediately past here, the courtyard of the **Madan Vilas** (built by Bhim Singh, reigned 1778–1828) offers fine lake and city views; the lakeside wall is decorated with quaint inlaid mirrorwork pictures.

Stairs lead down to the **Moti Mahal** (Pearl Palace), another oddly futuristic-looking little mirrored chamber, its walls entirely covered in plain mirrors, the only colour being supplied by its stained-glass windows. Steps lead around the top of the Mor Chowk courtyard (see below) to the **Pitam Niwas** (built by Jagat Singh II, reigned 1734–1790) and down to the small **Surya Choupad**, dominated by a striking image showing a kingly-looking Rajput face enclosed by a huge golden halo – a reference to the belief that the rulers of the house of Mewar are descended from the sun.

Next to here, the wall of the fine **Mor Chowk** courtyard is embellished with one of the palace's most flamboyant artworks, a trio of superb mosaic peacocks (*mor*), commissioned by Sajjan Singh in 1874, each made from around five thousand pieces of glass and coloured stone. On the other side of the courtyard is the opulent little **Manek Mahal** (Ruby Palace), its walls mirrored in rich reds and greens.

From here a long corridor winds past the kitschly decorated apartments of the queen mother Shri Gulabkunwar (1928–73) and through the **Zenana Mahal** (Women's Palace), whose long sequence of rooms now houses a huge array of paintings depicting royal fun and frolics in Mewar. Continue onwards to emerge, finally, into the last and largest of the palace's courtyards, **Lakshmi Chowk**, the centrepiece of the Zenana Mahal. The exit is at the far end.

The rest of the City Palace complex

The small **Government Museum** (daily 10am–4.30pm; Rs3; no photography), opposite the entrance to the City Palace Museum, is mainly of interest for its impressive sculpture gallery of pieces from Kumbalgarh, including some outstanding works in black marble. More interesting in many ways – and certainly far more atmospheric – is the vast **Durbar Hall** in the Fateh Prakash Palace (the building immediately behind the main City Palace building which now houses the *Fateh Prakash Palace* hotel). This huge, wonderfully time-warped Edwardian-era ballroom was built to host state banquets, royal functions and the like, and remains full of period character, complete with huge chandeliers, creaky old furniture and fusty portraits. You can have afternoon tea here as part of a visit to *The Gallery* café (see p.247). In a gallery overlooking the hall is the eccentric **Crystal Gallery** (daily 9am–7pm; Rs500), housing an array of fine British crystal ordered by Sajjan Singh in the 1880s and featuring outlandishly kitsch items including crystal chairs, tables and lamps – there's even a crystal hookah and a crystal bed. The extortionate entrance charge is a bit of a turn-off, though it does include a free audioguide and also gets you a drink at *The Gallery* cafe.

Jagdish Temple

Just north of the City Palace, **Jagdish Temple** is one of Udaipur's most popular and vibrant shrines. Built in 1652 and dedicated to Lord Jagannath, an aspect of Vishnu, its outer walls and towering *shikhara* are heavily carved with figures of Vishnu, scenes from the life of Krishna and dancing *apsaras* (nymphs). The circular *mandapa* leads to the sanctuary where a black stone image of Jagannath sits shrouded in flowers, while a small raised shrine in front of the temple protects a bronze Garuda. Subsidiary shrines to Shiva, Ganesh, Surya and Durga stand at each corner of the main temple.

Bagore-ki-Haveli

North of Jagdish Temple, a lane leads to Gangaur Ghat and the **Bagore-ki-Haveli**, a 138-room lakeside haveli of 1751. A section of the building has been converted into a worthwhile **museum** (daily 10am–5.30pm; Rs25, camera Rs10, video Rs50), arranged on two floors around one of the rambling haveli's several courtyards. The upper floor has several immaculately restored rooms with original furnishings and artworks, plus some fine murals. The lower floor has rooms full of women's clothes, musical instruments, kitchen equipment and – the undisputed highlight – what is claimed to be the world's largest turban. Traditional **music and dance** shows (Rs60, camera Rs50, video Rs50) are staged here nightly at 7pm.

Bharatiya Lok Kala

Just north of Chetak Circle in the new city, the hoary old **Bharatiya Lok Kala** museum (daily 9am–6pm; Rs35, Indian residents Rs20, camera Rs10, video Rs50) is home to a mildly interesting collection of exhibits covering the folk traditions of Rajasthan and India, with dusty displays of colourful masks, puppets and musical instruments. Short, amusing **puppet shows** (tip expected) are staged throughout the day on demand (the performers will probably hunt you down and drag you into the theatre shortly after your arrival), while there's an hour-long show, with music, dancing and more puppets, daily at 6pm (Rs50, camera Rs10, video Rs50).

Sahelion-ki-Bari

Northeast of Moti Magri, **Sahelion-ki-Bari** (daily 9am–7.30pm; Rs5), the "garden of the maids of honour", was laid out by Sangram Singh (1710–34) as a summer retreat for the entertainment of the ladies of the royal household – though the eye-catching fountains weren't installed until the reign of Fateh Singh (1884–1930). The gardens are centred on a peaceful courtyard enclosing a large pool and surrounded by attractive formal walled gardens, at the back of which four elephant statues surround Udaipur's most striking fountain – a fanciful tiered creation which looks a bit like a huge, multicoloured cake stand.

Shilpgram

Some 5km west of town, the popular rural arts and crafts centre of **Shilpgram** (daily 11am–7pm; Rs25, camera Rs10, video Rs50) was set up as a crafts village to promote the traditional architecture, music and crafts of the tribal people of western India, with displays dedicated to the diverse lifestyles and customs of the region's rural population. Around thirty replica houses and huts in traditional style are arranged in a village-like compound, with examples of buildings from various states. Musicians, puppeteers and dancers – *hijras* (eunuchs) among them – hang out around the houses and strike up on the approach of visitors (tip expected), while you may also see people weaving, potting and embroidering as they would in their original homes – though most of the actual handicrafts on sale are fifth-rate, if that. Despite its honourable intentions, many tourists find the atmosphere contrived and resent the hustling by musicians and their ilk. Even so, it's well worth a visit if only for the scenic journey out along the road around Fateh Sagar Lake, best done by bicycle. Alternatively, the return journey by auto-rickshaw costs around Rs100 including waiting time.

Sajjangarh

High on a hill 5km west of the city, the so-called "Monsoon Palace", **Sajjangarh**, was begun in 1883 by Maharana Sajjan Singh to serve as a summer retreat, complete with a nine-storey observatory from which the royal family proposed to watch the monsoon clouds travelling across the countryside below. Unfortunately, the maharana's untimely death the following year put paid to the planned observatory, and although the palace itself was finished by Singh's successor, Maharana Fateh Singh, it was found to be impossible to pump water up to it, and the whole place was abandoned shortly afterwards. The large though rather plain building is now a somewhat melancholy sight, but the views over Udaipur, more than 300m below, are unrivalled. The journey up to the palace takes a good fifteen minutes by rickshaw or taxi (around Rs200 for the round trip); the climb is too steep to tackle comfortably by bicycle, though some people try. The palace is located inside the **Sajjangarh Wildlife Sanctuary** (foreign visitors Rs80, Indian residents Rs10, plus Rs20 for a rickshaw or Rs65 for car). It's open daily from 9am, with last entry at 5.30pm, although you can come down after sunset.

Eating, drinking and entertainment

Bagore-ki-Haveli (see opposite) has nightly **dance** performances, while Shilpgram (see opposite) often hosts out-of-town performers. Alternatively, many of Udaipur's backpacker cafés run free screenings of the camp James Bond classic **Octopussy**, partly set in Udaipur, every evening, usually at 7pm.

Restaurants and cafés

Ambrai *Amet Haveli*, Chand Pole. In a superlative setting facing the City Palace, this is one of the few lakeside restaurants where the cooking lives up to its location. The menu features an extensive selection of north Indian veg and non-veg dishes (including top-notch tandooris), as well as a few Chinese and European offerings. Or just come for a sundowner and watch the sun set over the lake. Mains from around Rs140.

Edelweiss 71 Gangaur Ghat Marg, next to *Gangaur Palace*. Excellent hole-in-the-wall bakery and pastry shop that receives a steady stream of customers thanks to its tasty home-baked apple pie, chocolate cake and fresh ground coffee.

The Gallery City Palace. Buried away in the innards of the *Fateh Prakash Palace* hotel (just finding it is half the fun), this is Udaipur's most memorable spot for a classic English-style high tea (daily 3–6pm), served either on a sunny terrace overlooking the lake or in the grandiose Durbar Hall (see p.245). Cream teas cost Rs285 and Rs340, or just come for a tea or coffee.

Jagat Niwas 23–25 Lalghat. Popular restaurant in the hotel of the same name, serving up well-prepared north Indian standards (mains around Rs100), with nice views over the lake from its comfy window seats and discreet live sitar music.

Kankarwa Haveli 26 Lalghat. The low-key rooftop restaurant at this excellent hotel offers a welcome

alternative to your average tourist menu, with a choice of just two thalis featuring authentic and delicious home-cooked dishes like sweet aubergine and pumpkin curries. Cold beer and panoramic lake views complete the ambience.

Lake Palace Lake Pichola ☎ 0294/252 8800. If your budget won't stretch to a stay at the iconic *Lake Palace* hotel, the next best thing is to book in for lunch (Rs2800) or the four-course à la carte dinner (Rs3375) at what must rank among the world's most romantic restaurants. Call to reserve a table at least a day in advance.

Natraj New Bapu Bazaar, behind Ashok Cinema. Udaipur's top thali joint for over twenty years but well off the tourist trail and fiendishly hard to find (head to Suraj Pol and then ask for directions). Easily the best cheap meal in town – just Rs50 for unlimited portions of five different vegetables.

Queen Café Chand Pol. This homely and unpretentious little café offers a refreshing alternative to Udaipur's mainstream tourist restaurants, with an authentic taste of home-style vegetarian Indian cooking including coconut-flavoured banana, mango and pumpkin curries – all at giveaway prices, with most mains at around Rs45.

Savage Garden Chand Pol. Stylish restaurant set in an old haveli given a funky modern makeover, with loads of blue and white paint and minimalist decor. Food is mainly Indian (veg and non-veg),

247

with slight gourmet pretensions, plus a few European dishes including good pastas, salads and soups. Mains Rs110–210.

The Whistling Teal *Raj Palace* hotel, 103 Bhattiyani Chohatta. Attractive, tented garden restaurant serving well-prepared north Indian and Rajasthani veg and non-veg dishes from around Rs115 – pricier than average, but worth it. There's also a decent selection of shishas (Rs250), plus good coffee.

Listings

Airlines Indian Airlines, LIC Building, Delhi Gate (Mon–Sat 10am–5pm; ☏0294/241 0999); Jet Airways, Blue Circle Business Centre, 1-C Madhuban (Mon–Sat 9.30am–6pm, Sun 10am–3pm; ☏0294/256 1105); Kingfisher Airlines, airport ☏0294/510 2468.

Banks and exchange There are ATMs all over the new city, plus a particularly handy 24hr machine on the street leading to the City Palace. There are lots of places offering forex around the Jagdish Temple. Mewar International (daily 8am–11pm), on Lalghat, changes cash and all brands of traveller's cheques, as well as giving cash advances on Visa and MasterCard. Another option is Thomas Cook (Mon–Sat 9am–6pm), on Lake Palace Rd, which changes cash and all traveller's cheques.

Bicycle and motorbike rental Heera Cycle Store (daily 7.30am–9pm; ☏0/982 852 0466), at 86 Gangaur Ghat Marg by the Jagdish Temple, rents out basic bicycles for Rs25/day, and mountain bikes for Rs50/day. They also have mopeds (Rs150–200/day), 150cc Vespa motorcycles (Rs300/day) and 350cc Enfield Bullets (Rs400/day).

Bookshops Mayur Book Paradise, on a small side road behind the Jagdish Temple, is particularly good, while the bookshop on the main courtyard outside the City Palace complex (no ticket required) has a fine selection of India-related titles. Mewar International, on Lalghat behind the Jagdish Temple, buys and exchanges secondhand books.

Cooking lessons Available at numerous places around town. Good options include the *Panorama Guest House* (see p.243; Rs400 for 3hr classes) or, more expensive, the homely little *Queen Café* (see p.247; Rs900 for 4hr).

Horse riding Various places around town offer horse-riding expeditions into the surrounding countryside. The reputable *Hotel Kumbha Palace* (see p.242; ⊛www.krishnaranch.da.ru) runs half- and full-day excursions (Rs750/Rs1500), as well as longer trips. Princess Trails (☏0/982 904 2012, ⊛www.princesstrails.com) specializes in more extended, 4- to 8-day safaris on thoroughbred Mawari mounts.

Hospital The (private) Aravalli Hospital, at 332 Ambamata Rd (☏0294/242 0222 or 241 8787).

Internet access There are dozens of places offering Internet around Lalghat and Gangaur Ghat. The going rate is currently Rs30 per hour. Two of the best-equipped places are Mewar International, on Lalghat near the Jagdish Temple, which also allows you to upload material; and the cybercafé on the ground floor of the *Udai Niwas* hotel.

Music The enthusiastic Rajesh Prajapat at the Prem Musical Instrument shop (☏0294/243 0599), opposite the *Gangaur Palace* hotel, offers sitar and tabla lessons (Rs250 for 90min) and can also arrange flute lessons with his brother, or musical appreciation classes if you just want to learn more about Indian music. Count on around Rs250 for a 90min lesson.

Painting lessons Lessons in traditional Indian painting are offered by many places around town; the *Gangaur Palace* guesthouse is a reliable option (Rs100/hr on paper, or Rs150/hr on silk).

Palm readings The resident palmist at the *Gangaur Palace* guesthouse charges Rs250 for a 20min reading.

Photography Mewar International, on Lalghat behind the Jagdish Temple, burn CDs and DVDs, sell memory cards and have equipment to download photos from most types of digital cameras; they also offer back-up and photo recovery from defective memory cards.

Post office Parcels are best sent from the GPO (Mon–Fri 10am–4pm & Sat 10am–3pm), located at Chetak Circle. Note that poste restante mail is held at the post office at Shastri Circle, not at the GPO.

Shopping Udaipur is one of Rajasthan's top shopping destinations, with an eclectic array of local artisanal specialities along with other crafts from across the state. The city's particular speciality is miniature painting, with numerous shops selling traditional Mewari-style works on paper and silk. Many places also do a good line in leather- and cloth-bound stationery using handmade paper. Udaipur is well known for its silver jewellery – Jagdish Street, Bara Bazaar and Moti Chohatta, around the clock tower, are home to lots of shops. For bookshops, see above.

Travel agents Virtually every shop and guesthouse around the Jagdish Temple seems to offer bus and rail ticketing. Reliable agents include Mewar International, on Lalghat behind the Jagdish

Recommended trains from Udaipur

The trains below are recommended as the fastest and/or most convenient for specific cities.

Destination	Name	No.	Departs	Arrives
Ahmedabad	Ahmedabad Fast Passenger	431	9.20am daily	8.55pm
	Ahmedabad Express	9943	7.45pm daily	4.20am
Ajmer	Ajmer Express	2991	7.05am daily	12.30pm
Chittaurgarh	Mewar Express	2964	6.35pm daily	8.30pm
Delhi (HN)	Mewar Express	2964	6.35pm daily	6.10am
Jaipur	Jaipur Superfast Express	2966	9.40pm daily	7.10am
Kota	Mewar Express	2964	6.35pm daily	11.40pm

Temple; Gangaur Tour 'n' Travels, close by on Gangaur Ghat Marg; and the travel agency inside the *Udai Niwas* hotel.

Volunteer work The Animal Aid Society (☎0294/251 3359, ⊛www.animalaidsociety.org), run by a friendly American expat couple, maintains a pet hospital about 1km from Shilpgram. Volunteers and visitors are encouraged and no special skills are required – just a willingness to work with animals, usually including street dogs, cows, donkeys, cats and monkeys.

Yoga Ashtanga Yoga Ashram (aka "Raiba House"), Chand Pol (☎0294/252 4872). Daily 90min hatha yoga classes for all standards at 8/8.30am and 5/6pm (also at 10.30pm from Aug–March). Free, but donations appreciated – proceeds go to a local animal charity. Individual lessons also available.

Moving on from Udaipur

For details of **flights** from Udaipur's Dabok Airport, see "Travel details" on p.268. Local contact details are given in the "Listings" opposite. Flights to **Jaisalmer** were due to begin in late 2008/early 2009, assuming completion of the new airport there has run to schedule.

A full breakdown of bus services from Udaipur is given in **"Travel details"** on p.268. **Government buses** leave from the main RSTRC bus stand at Udai Pol. **Private buses** depart from Udai Pol, opposite the government bus stand, and run to a similar range of destinations, plus Jaisalmer and Pushkar. Private buses are often a bit faster and more comfortable than government services, and are probably a better option for longer and (especially) overnight journeys – most night buses are sleepers, and there are also fast nightly a/c super-deluxe sleeper services to Mumbai, Delhi and Jaipur. It's easiest to book **tickets** for private buses through one of the many travel agents in town (usually for a modest surcharge of around Rs20). If you want to book your own ticket you'll need to make a reservation with one of the various bus-company offices clustered around Udai Pol – try the reliable Kamlesh Travels (☎0294/248 5823). **Local buses** to destinations such as Nagda, Eklingji, Nathdwara and Kankroli leave from the main government bus stand at regular intervals throughout the day.

Train services from Udaipur are surprisingly limited; those listed below are the best of a bad bunch. Note that there are no direct services to Jodhpur, Bundi (take a bus to Chittaurgarh and pick up the 2.15pm or 2.55pm train) or Mumbai (change at Ahmedabad). There are a couple of direct services to Sawai Madhopur and Kota, but at horrible times. You can save yourself a trip to the station by booking railway tickets through any of the city's numerous travel agents (see "Listings", opposite) for a surcharge of around Rs50–75.

Around Udaipur

North of the city are the historic temples of **Nagda**, **Eklingji**, **Nathdwara** and **Kankroli**, while to the northwest, en route to Jodhpur, lie the superb Jain temples of **Ranakpur** and the rambling fort at **Kumbalgarh**. Renting a car or motorcycle saves time, though local buses serve both routes.

Nagda and Eklingji

Dating back to 626 AD, the ragged remnants of the ancient capital of Mewar, **NAGDA**, stand next to a lake 20km northeast of Udaipur. Buses from Udaipur travelling north along the main road to Eklingji set passengers down at the turn-off for Nagda, next to a small bicycle shop (bike rental Rs5/hr). Nagda itself is a further 1km away down this side-road. Most of the buildings here were either destroyed by the Mughals or submerged by the lake, which has expanded naturally over the centuries. All that survives is a fine pair of tenth-century Vaishnavite temples known as **Saas-Bahu** – literally "mother-in-law" and "daughter-in-law". The more impressive mother-in-law temple has lost its *shikhara* (tower) but preserves a wealth of carving inside, while within the *mandapa* a marriage area is marked by four ornate pillars to which couples must pay homage.

Returning to the main road, you can continue to **EKLINGJI** via the road or along a path that leads behind the old protective walls and downhill. Ask for directions at the bike shop. The god **Eklingji**, a manifestation of Shiva, has been the protective deity of the rulers of Mewar ever since the eighth century, when Bappa Rawal was bestowed with the title *darwan* (servant) of Eklingji by his guru. To this day, the maharana of Udaipur still visits the 108-temple complex every Monday evening (the day traditionally celebrated all over India as being sacred to Shiva) and the whole place is usually lively with local pilgrims seeking his blessings. The milky-white marble main temple (daily 10.30am–1.30pm & 5.15–7.45pm), is crowned by an elaborate two-storey *mandapa* guarded by stone elephants; inside, a four-faced black marble lingam marks he precise spot where Bappa Rawal received his accolade. Frequent **buses** leave for Eklingji from Udaipur's main bus stand, dropping passengers off close to the temple.

Nathdwara

The temple dedicated to Krishna – known also as **Nath**, the favourite avatar (incarnation) of Vishnu – at **NATHDWARA**, "Gateway to God", is said to be the second-richest temple in India after Tirupati in Andhra Pradesh (although similar claims are made for the Rani Sati Mandir in Jhunjhunu), and can get incredibly crowded during major religious festivals. The temple dates back to the seventeenth century when a chariot laden with an image of Krishna – which was being carried from Mathura to Udaipur to save it from destruction by Aurangzeb – became stuck in the mud here. Its bearers inter-preted the event as a divine sign, establishing the new **Shri Nathji Temple** where it had stopped.

The temple lies about 1km south of the town's bus stop, surrounded by a fascinating tangle of narrow streets where stalls display incense, perfumes and small Krishna statues. The temple opens for worship eight times daily, when the image is woken, dressed, washed, fed and put to bed. Don't miss the radiant *pichwai* paintings in the main sanctuary, made of hand-spun cloth and coloured with strong vegetable pigments. You could also ask a guide to show you the "footsteps of Krishna", a process that requires rubbing rose petals on the marble floor. Nathdwara is on NH-8, and sees a constant flow of buses en route north and south.

Ranakpur

Some 90km north of Udaipur, the spectacular **Jain temples** at **RANAKPUR** boast marble work on a par with that of the more famous Dilwara shrines at Mount Abu (see p.256). The temples are hidden away in a beautiful wooded valley, deep in the Aravalli Hills, that was originally gifted to the Jain community in the fifteenth century by Rana Kumbha, the Hindu ruler of Mewar.

Arrival and information

Ranakpur is a bumpy three-hour journey on regular **buses** from Udaipur (around six daily) or from Jodhpur (5–6 daily; 4–5hr) via the market town of Falna (the nearest railway station) on the NH-14; there are also a couple of express buses daily to Abu Road (5–6hr). Getting from the bus stop to the village's hotels can be tricky. Buses stop right outside the Jain temples, between 2km and 4km away from the various hotels. If you're lucky, you might find a rickshaw or Jeep available for hire at the bus stop; if not you'll have to ring your hotel and ask to be picked up or (worst-case scenario) walk.

Ranakpur can also be visited as a day-trip from Udaipur, either on its own or in combination with nearby Kumbalgarh; count on around Rs1200 for the round trip by **car**. If you're intending to visit Kumbalgarh as well, though, think about **trekking** between the two sites, a beautiful hike through an unspoilt section of the Aravalli Hills. As Kumbalgarh is on the top of the range, it's much easier to hike from there down to Ranakpur (for more on this route see p.252), but guides may be arranged through any of the hotels listed below for the six-hour uphill climb in the other direction.

Accommodation and eating

For budget **accommodation** in Ranakpur, you can stay for a Rs10 donation with the Jain pilgrims at the temple complex, but don't expect anything more than a mattress on a cold, cement floor. This option excepted, accommodation in the village is relatively expensive. There are no restaurants outside the hotels and guesthouses, and virtually everyone **eats** where they are staying.

Aranyawas 11km from Ranakpur on the road to Kumbalgarh ☏0294/258 3148, ⓦwww .aranyawas.com. Small jungle lodge with rustically elegant rooms and cottages overlooking a watering hole frequented by leopards – an ideal place to recharge your batteries in complete isolation. ⑦
Fateh Bagh 4km south of the temples ☏02934/286186, ⓦwww.hrhindia.com. Ranakpur's top accommodation option, this 200-year-old palace was painstakingly disassembled piece by piece, transported 50km, and then rebuilt here. Rooms are comfy and characterful, and facilities include a pool, spa and Ayurveda centre. Rooms from around $160. ⑨
Maharani Bagh Orchard 3.5km south of the temples ☏02934/285105, ⓦwww.nivalink.com /maharanibagh. Pleasantly low-key resort, with attractively furnished rooms (all a/c) in red-brick cottages around rambling gardens. There's also a pool. ⑧
Ranakpur Hill Resort 3km south of the temples ☏02934/286411, ⓦwww.ranakpurhillresort.com. Chintzy pink little resort with a range of rooms (air-cooled and a/c) of varying standards, and some less appealing tents (available Oct–March only). Also has a decent-size pool and a small Ayurveda centre, and can arrange half-day horse safaris. Rooms ⑥–⑦, tents ⑥
Shivika Lake Hotel 2km south of the temples ☏02934/285078. The only real budget option in Ranakpur, although the cheaper rooms are disappointingly basic given the price; the more expensive rooms (some with a/c) are relatively better value. Local treks (Rs300pp) and Jeep safaris (Rs600pp) can be arranged here. ❸–❺

The temples

The **main temple** (noon–5pm; free, camera Rs50, video Rs100) was built in 1439 according to a strict system of measurement based on the number 72 (the age at which the founder of Jainism, Mahavira, achieved nirvana). The entire temple sits on a pedestal measuring 72 yards square and is held up by 1440 (72 x 20) individually carved pillars. Inside, there are 72 elaborately carved shrines, some octagonal in shape, along with the main deity (a 72-inch-tall image of the four-faced Adinath, the first *tirthankara*) encased in the central sanctum. The carving on the walls, columns and the domed ceilings is superb. Friezes depicting the life of the *tirthankara* are etched into the walls, while musicians and dancers have been modelled out of brackets between the pillars and the ceiling.

Three smaller temples nestle among the trees in the enclosure in front of the main temple. The most impressive is the **Parshwanath Temple**, around 100m from the main temple, with a small but finely carved shrine, while a further 100m walk brings you to the simpler **Neminath Temple**. Close by (a short walk across the car park) is a contemporary Hindu temple dedicated to **Surya**.

Kumbalgarh

The remote hilltop fort of **KUMBALGARH** (daily 9am–6pm; Rs100, Indian residents Rs5), 80km north of Udaipur, is the most formidable of the 32 constructed or restored by Rana Kumbha of Chittaurgarh in the fifteenth century. Protected by a series of monumental walls and bastions, it was only successfully besieged once, when a confederacy led by Akbar poisoned the water supply. Aside from the fort itself, Kumbalgarh is worth a visit to experience the idyllic Aravalli countryside, dotted with tribal villages, and magnificent views.

The most memorable panorama of all is from the pinnacle of the rather plain **palace** building, crowning the summit of the fort, with striking bird's-eye views over the numerous Jain and Hindu **temples** clustered around the main gate and scattered over the hills below. The oldest are thought to date from the second century; the **tombs** of the great Rana Kumbha himself (murdered by his eldest son) and his grandson Prithviraj (poisoned by his brother-in-law) stand to the east. Some 36km of crenellated ramparts wind around the rim of the hilltop, and it's possible to walk around them in two comfortable days, sleeping rough midway around. You won't need a guide, but be sure to take food and water.

Lining the deep valley that plunges west from the fort down to the plains, the **Kumbalgarh Wildlife Sanctuary** comprises a dense area of woodland that offers a refuge for wolves and leopards. With a local guide, you can trek through it to Ranakpur, a rewarding and easy hike of between four and five hours (the alternative is a long journey on an infrequent country bus). Entry to the sanctuary costs Rs80 (plus Rs200 for camera); foreigners need **permits**, obtainable from the District Forest Officer at nearby **Kelwara**. Local guides, contactable through the hotels listed below, can also obtain your permit for you – and stop you getting lost – for around Rs600–1000. To save money you can try to find a guide on your own – it's not easy, but if you ask around at the café just inside the fort gates you might get lucky.

Practicalities

Kumbalgarh and Ranakpur can easily be visited as a (longish) day-trip from Udaipur (around Rs1200 for the round trip by taxi). A direct **bus** currently leaves Udaipur's RSRTC stand at 12.45am, arriving at the *Aodhi* hotel in Kumbalgarh around 5pm; there are also Jeeps and slow local buses (roughly every hour) either from Udaipur's RSRTC stand or from Chetak Circle to the town of **Kelwara**, 7km down the road, from where you should be able to pick up a Jeep or rickshaw to Kumbalgarh.

Accommodaton

There's no budget accommodation in Kumbalgarh.

Aodhi 1km below the fort ☎02954/242341, ⓦwww.hrhindia.com. Peaceful and welcoming heritage hotel with accommodation in stylishly furnished rooms in a cluster of attractive little thatched granite buildings. There's also a big pool and Jeep safaris to local villages. Rooms from around $160. ⑨

Kumbalgarh Fort Hotel 5km along the Kelwara road ☎02954/242057 ⓦwww.hotelhilltoppalace.net.

Recently renovated upmarket modern hotel with superb views from its garden terrace and pool, and marbled a/c rooms. ⑦–⑧

Kumbhal Castle 1.5km below the fort ☎02954/242171, ⓦwww.nivalink.com /kumbhalcastle. Pleasant modern hotel, with spacious and nicely furnished air-cooled and a/c doubles, plus a pool. You can also arrange Jeep and car hire here. ⑤–⑦

Mount Abu

Rajasthan's only bona fide hill station, **MOUNT ABU** (1220m) is a major Indian resort, popular above all with honeymooners who flock here during the winter wedding season (Nov to March) and with visiting holiday-makers from nearby Gujarat. Mount Abu's hokey commercialism is aimed squarely at these local vacationers rather than foreign tourists, but the sight of lovestruck honeymooners shyly holding hands and jolly parties of Gujarati tourists on the loose lends the whole place a charmingly idiosyncratic holiday atmosphere quite unlike anywhere else in Rajasthan – and the fresh air is exhilarating after the heat of the desert plains. The town also occupies an important place in Rajput history, being the site of the famous *yagna agnikund* fire ceremony, conducted in the eighth century AD, from which all Rajputs claim mythological descent.

Note that during the peak months of April to June, and at almost any major festival time (especially Diwali in Nov) the town's population of thirty thousand mushrooms, room rates skyrocket, and peace and quiet are at a premium.

Arrival and information

Mount Abu is accessible only by road. The nearest railhead is at **Abu Road**, from where buses make the 45-minute ascent up to Mount Abu itself. Entering Mount Abu, you have to pay a Rs10 fee (or Rs21 if entering in your own vehicle).

The **tourist office** (Mon–Sat 10am–1.30pm & 2–5pm) is opposite the main bus stand; there's also information online at ⓦwww.mountsabu.com. To **change traveller's cheques** the best bet is the Union Bank of India, hidden away in the bazaar just behind the **post office**. There's a handy State Bank of India **ATM** (24hr; Visa and MasterCard) in front of the tourist office. For **Internet** access try the *Shri Ganesh* guesthouse, the Yani-Ya Cyber Zone, just south of the post office, or the Shree Krishna Cybercafe in the lane just behind the Yani-Ya (all Rs30/hr). **Tours** can be arranged through the *Shri Ganesh* guesthouse, whose owner organizes Jeep tours (Rs350 for the vehicle for a half-day trip) out to places like Achalgarh and Guru Shikar.

Accommodation

The steady stream of pilgrims and honeymoon couples ensures that Mount Abu has plenty of **hotels**, lots of them offering luxuries for newlyweds in special "couple rooms". Prices rocket in **high season** (April–June &

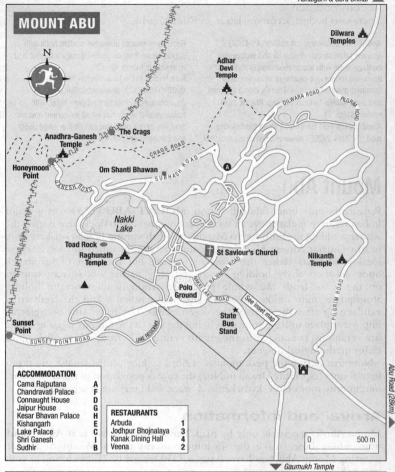

Achalgarh & Guru Shikar ▲

MOUNT ABU

N

Dilwara Temples

Adhar Devi Temple

DILWARA ROAD

PILGRIM ROAD

Anadhra-Ganesh Temple

The Crags

CRAGS ROAD

Honeymoon Point

GANESH ROAD

Om Shanti Bhawan

SUBHASH ROAD

A

Nakki Lake

St Saviour's Church

Nilkanth Temple

Toad Rock

Raghunath Temple

RAJENDRA ROAD

NAKKI LAKE ROAD

Polo Ground

See inset map

State Bus Stand

Sunset Point

SUNSET POINT ROAD

LAKE RESIDENCY

PILGRIM ROAD

Abu Road (28km) ▶

ACCOMMODATION

Cama Rajputana	A
Chandravati Palace	F
Connaught House	D
Jaipur House	G
Kesar Bhavan Palace	H
Kishangarh	E
Lake Palace	C
Shri Ganesh	I
Sudhir	B

RESTAURANTS

Arbuda	1
Jodhpur Bhojnalaya	3
Kanak Dining Hall	4
Veena	2

0   500 m

▼ Gaumukh Temple

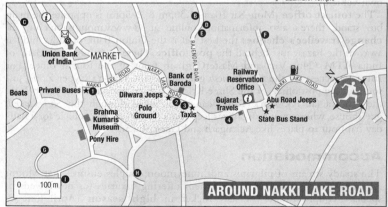

C

i

✉

@

Union Bank of India

MARKET

NAKKI LAKE ROAD

B

D

E

RAJENDRA ROAD

F

Boats

Private Buses ★1

Bank of Baroda

Dilwara Jeeps ★ 2 3 ★

Taxis ★

Polo Ground

Brahma Kumaris Museum

Pony Hire

Railway Reservation Office

Gujarat Travels i

NAKKI LAKE ROAD

Abu Road Jeeps ★

State Bus Stand

4

N

G

H

I

0   100 m

AROUND NAKKI LAKE ROAD

Nov–Dec), reaching their peak during Diwali. The price codes given below are for high season.

Cama Rajputana Adhar Devi Rd ☎02974/238205, ⓦwww.camahotelsindia.com. Attractive resort-style place occupying a neatly refurbished granite colonial building located in sprawling grounds. Rooms (all a/c) are cool and spacious, while the extensive facilities include a gym, massage centre and a big pool (guests only). Popular with tour groups. ❽–❾

Chandravati Palace 9 Janta Colony ☎02974/238219. Excellent and very good-value little guesthouse on a quiet side-road. The small, bright modern rooms are impeccably maintained and have good-sized balconies and hill views. ❷

🏃 **Connaught House** Rajendra Rd ☎02974/238560, ⓦwww.welcomheritage hotels.com. Mount Abu's most memorable accommodation option, occupying a time-warped colonial-era retreat set in a flower-filled garden with sweeping views. Rooms (all a/c) in the old house are beautifully preserved, with period furniture and decor; those in the modern block on the hill above are much less atmospheric. ❽

Jaipur House South of the lake ☎02974/235176, ⓦwww.nivalink.com/jaipurhouse. Perched on a hilltop above town, this fine old summer palace offers some of the town's best accommodation in tastefully decorated suites with wooden furnishings – although the so-called "deluxe" rooms, occupying an ugly modern block halfway down the drive, are dull and overpriced. ❽

Kesar Bhavan Palace Sunset Rd ☎02974/238647, ⓦwww.kesarpalace.com. Functional modern hotel rather than the promised "palace", though rooms (some with a/c) are pleasantly spacious and sunny, with views over the tree tops from large individual verandas. The rooms

in the new annexe (same price) are darker and less appealing. ❼–❽

Kishangarh House Rajendra Rd ☎02974/238092, ⓦwww.royalkishangarh.com. Not as memorable as the neighbouring *Connaught House*, but still offering a modest helping of colonial-era charm. Accommodation is in neatly furnished rooms (mostly a/c) in the old building itself, or in cheaper but fairly characterless "cottage" rooms in a new block outside. ❼–❽

Lake Palace Nakki Lake Rd ☎02974/237154, ⓦwww.savshantihotels.com. One of the town's best mid-range options, in a scenic position facing Nakki Lake, with good service and a range of well-maintained modern rooms (all a/c, the more expensive ones with lake view and balcony). Reasonable value, especially in low season. ❺–❻

🏃 **Shri Ganesh** southwest of the polo ground, near Sophia High School ☎02974/237292, ⓔlalit_ganesh@yahoo.co.in. Easily the best budget hotel in town, and the only one geared towards foreign backpackers. There are plenty of simple, clean rooms with TV (some with shared bathroom), plus dorm beds (Rs60–100 per person), while the owner and his Irish wife offer Indian cooking lessons (Rs150) and guided walks; also has reliable Internet access. Free pick-up from bus stand. ❷–❹

Sudhir Opposite *Connaught House*, Rajendra Rd ☎02974/235120. Functional modern hotel with bright and spacious rooms: choose between the rather bare "semi-deluxe" and the significantly nicer "deluxe" categories. Rather expensive during high season (May–July & Oct–Dec), but good value at other times. ❺–❼

The town and around

At the centre of town, the ever-popular **Nakki Lake** is where everyone converges in the late afternoon for pony and pedalo rides. Of several panoramic viewpoints on the fringes of town above the plains, **Sunset Point** is the favourite – though the hordes of holiday-makers and hawkers also make it one of the noisiest and least romantic. **Honeymoon Point**, also known as Ganesh Point (after the adjacent temple), and **Anadhra Point** offer breathtaking views over the plain at any time of day, and tend to be more peaceful; 4pm is a good time to visit.

The **Brahma Kumaris Museum** (daily 8am–8pm; free), between the polo ground and the lake, is devoted to the spiritual ideals of the Brahma Kumaris ("children of Brahma"), whose headquarters are situated nearby. The Brahma Kumaris preach that all religions reach for the same goal, but label it differently. The museum is filled with freakish, life-sized mannequins including blue monsters wielding long knives. Each personifies greed, sex-lust and other vestiges of the so-called "iron age" that temple leaders promise deliverance from.

Hiking in Mount Abu

Down in Mount Abu's market area, you gain little sense of the wonderfully wild **landscape** enfolding the town, but head for a few minutes up one of the many trails threading around the sides of the plateau, and it's easy to see why the area has inspired sages, saints and pilgrims for centuries. Unfortunately **hiking alone** is not recommended, thanks to a few unscrupulous characters who have taken to robbing unaccompanied visitors – tourist police will turn back anyone spotted heading out alone. There's also a small but significant chance of running into bears and leopards – bears, in particular, can be dangerous if surprised, or when with young.

Two good local **guides** are Lalit Kanojia at the *Shri Ganesh* hotel, who leads 5hr treks every morning (Rs100 per person); and Mahendra Dan, better known as "Charles" (⊛www.mount-abu-treks.blogspot.com), who runs a range of half-day (Rs300) and full-day (Rs450) walking tours focusing on village life, wildlife spotting and local Ayurvedic plants, as well as overnight camping expeditions. He can be contacted via the *Lake Palace* hotel or on ☎0/941 415 4854, or emailed on Ⓔmahendradan @yahoomail.co.in.

If it all sounds somewhat cultish you'll understand why many locals try to keep foreigners from entering into the sect's clutches.

Dilwara temples

The **Dilwara temples** (daily noon–6pm; free, but donation requested; no photography, usual restrictions apply), 3km northeast of Mount Abu, are some of the most beautiful Jain shrines in India. All five are made purely from marble, and the carving is breathtakingly intricate. Entrance to the temples is by guided tour only – you'll have to wait until sufficient people have arrived to make up a group – though once inside it's easy enough to break away and look around on your own.

The oldest temple, the **Vimala Vasahi**, named after the Gujarati minister who funded its construction in 1031, is dedicated to Adinath, the first *tirthankara*. Although the exterior is simple – as, indeed, are the exteriors of all the temples here – inside not one wall, column or ceiling is unadorned, a prodigious feat of artistry which took almost two thousand labourers and sculptors fourteen years to complete. There are forty-eight intricately carved pillars inside, eight of them supporting a domed ceiling arranged in eleven concentric circles alive with dancers, musicians, elephants and horses, while a sequence of 57 subsidiary shrines run around the edge of the enclosure. In front of the entrance to the temple the so-called "Elephant Cell" (added after the construction of the temple itself in 1147) contains ten impressively large stone pachyderms. A more modest pair of painted elephants, along with an unusual carving showing stacked-up tiers of *tirthankaras*, flank the entrance to the diminutive **Mahaveer-swami Temple**, built in 1582, which sits by the entrance to the Vimala Vasahi.

The second of the two great temples at Dilwara, the **Luna Vasahi Temple** was built in 1231 and is dedicated to Neminath, the 22nd *tirthankara*. The temple follows a similar plan to the Vimala Vasahi, with a central shrine fronted by a minutely carved dome and surrounded by a long sequence of shrines (a mere 48 this time). The carvings, however, are perhaps even more precise and detailed, especially so in the magnificently intricate dome covering the entrance hall.

The remaining two temples, both dating from the fifteenth century, are less spectacular. The **Bhimasah Pittalhar Temple** houses a huge gilded image of the first *tirthankara*, Adinath, installed in 1468, which measures over eight foot high and weighs in at around 4.5 tons. The large three-storey **Khartar Vasahi Temple** (near the entrance to the temples) was built in 1458 and is consecrated to Parshvanath. The temple is topped by a high grey stone tower and boasts some intricate carving in places, though overall it's only a pale shadow of the earlier temples

To **get to Dilwara**, you can charter a Jeep (Rs50 one way or Rs150 return) from the corner by the *Jodhpur Bhojnalaya* restaurant, or take a place in a shared one (Rs5); the latter leave from in front of the large Chacha Museum (a shop, incidentally, not a museum), a few doors down from the *Veena* restaurant. The hour-long walk up there is also pleasant, though many prefer to save their energy for the downhill walk back into town.

Hindu temples

On the north side of town, en route to the Dilwara temples, a flight of more than four hundred steps climbs up to the **Adhar Devi Temple** (dedicated to Durga). The small main shrine is cut into the rocky hilltop and entered by clambering under a very low overhang. There are fine views from the terrace above, where there's another tiny shrine cut out of solid rock. The milk-coloured water of the **Doodh Baori** well at the foot of the steps is considered to be a source of pure milk (*doodh*) for gods and sages.

A further 8km northeast, the temple complex at **ACHALGARH** is dominated by the **Achaleshwar Mahadeo Temple**, believed to have been created when Lord Shiva placed his toe on the spot to still an earthquake. Its sanctuary holds a yoni with a hole in it that is said to reach into the nether-world. Nearby, the **Jamadagni Ashram** is site of the *yagna agnikund*, where the sage Vashishtha presided over the fire ritual that produced the four Rajput clans (the Parmars, Parihars, Solankis and Chauhans).

The lesser visited, but more dramatically situated, **Gaumukh Temple** lies 7km south of the market area. Reached via a steep flight of 750 steps, the small pool inside the shrine – which continues to flow even during times of drought – is believed to hold water from the sacred Sarawati Ganga River. Pilgrims come here to perform puja, to invoke the blessings of India's two greatest *rishis* (sages), Vashishtha and Vishwamitra, who are thought to have meditated and debated here.

The last important Hindu pilgrimage site on Mount Abu is the Atri Rishi Temple at **Guru Shikar**, 15km northeast of town, which at 1772m above sea level marks the highest point in Rajasthan. You can enjoy superb panoramic vistas either from the temple itself, or from the drinks stall at the bottom of the steps leading up to it. There's no public transport there, however, so you'll have to hire a Jeep (around Rs400).

Eating and drinking

Mount Abu's predominantly middle-class Gujarati visitors are typically hard to please when it comes to food, so standards are exceptionally high and prices low. Meat is fairly rare in Mount Abu; if you get carniverous cravings, there are a couple of Punjabi restaurants in the bazaar.

Arbuda Nakki Lake Rd. Perennially popular spot with a huge veggie menu ranging from pizzas, burgers and sandwiches through to Chinese and Indian, as well as good fresh juices. Lightning-fast, friendly service and a popular, airy terrace.
Jodhpur Bhojnalaya Nakki Lake Rd. The only place in town where you can eat authentic Rajasthani food, very heavy on ghee and spices. It's famous for its definitive *dhal bati churma* (a traditional Rajasthani dish consisting of baked wheatflour balls served with dhal and sweet *churma* sauce), and also has the usual big list of veg North and south Indian dishes.

🏃 **Kanak Dining Hall** Nakki Lake Rd. Friendly place offering arguably the best Gujarati thalis in town – a superb array of subtly spiced veg delicacies for a very modest Rs60 per head. Come hungry – portions are literally limitless. They also have a big range of North and south Indian veg dishes, plus a few Chinese options.

Veena Nakki Lake Rd. Open-air seating next to the main road. Quintessentially tacky Mount Abu (bright lights and the latest *filmi* hits blaring out), but the fast food is second to none and they have a welcome open fire on the terrace most evenings. Try a tangy *pau bhaji* or melt-in-the-mouth *dosas*.

Moving on from Mount Abu

Government buses run from the State Bus Stand on Nakki Lake Road. **Private buses** are run by a string of operators along Nakki Lake Road west of the State Bus Stand (Gujarat Travels is a reliable option). There are currently services to Ajmer (1 nightly; 7hr), Ahmedabad (3 daily; 6hr), Chittaurgarh (1 daily; 10hr), Jaipur (1 nightly; 11hr), Jodhpur (1 daily; 6hr) and Udaipur (4 daily; 5hr).

There's a computerized **train booking office** (daily 8am–2pm) upstairs at the tourist office. Buses leave Mount Abu for **Abu Road**, the nearest railhead, every hour until 9pm; Jeeps leave when full (from opposite the bus stand), and taxis can be hired at the corner by the *Jodhpur Bhojnalaya* restaurant for Rs250.

Chittaurgarh, Kota and Bundi

The belt of hilly land east of Udaipur is the most fertile in Rajasthan, watered by several perennial rivers and guarded by a sequence of imposing forts perched atop the craggy ridges that crisscross the region. Heading east, the first major settlement is the historic town of **Chittaurgarh**, capital of the kingdom of Mewar before Udaipur and site of one of Rajasthan's most spectacular and historic forts. Further east, the tranquil town of **Bundi** boasts another atmospheric fort and picturesque old bazaars and havelis, while an hour away by bus, **Kota** is home to another impressive palace.

A prime crop in this area for centuries has been **opium**. Although grown for the pharmaceutical industry according to strict government quotas, the legal cultivation masks a much larger illicit production overseen by Mumbai drug barons. An estimated one in five men in the area are addicts.

Recommended trains from Abu Road

The trains below are recommended as the fastest and/or most convenient for specific cities.

Destination	Name	No.	Departs	Arrives
Ahmedabad	Ahmedabad Express	9224	11.45am (daily)	4.10pm
	Ahmedabad Mail	9106	12.48pm (daily)	5.35pm
Ajmer	Aravali Express	9707	9.58am (daily)	4.05pm
	Haridwar Mail	9105	2.05pm (daily)	8.10pm
Delhi	Ashram Express	2915	9.20pm (daily)	10.15am
Jaipur	Aravali Express	9707	9.58am (daily)	6.45pm
	Haridwar Mail	9105	2.05pm (daily)	10.45pm
Jodhpur	Jammu Tawi Express	9223	3.27pm (daily)	8.15pm
Mumbai	Ajmer–Mumbai Express	2990	00.25am (W, F & Su only)	1.05pm

Chittaurgarh

Of all the former Rajput capitals, **CHITTAURGARH** (or Chittor), 115km northeast of Udaipur, was the strongest bastion of Hindu resistance against the Muslim invaders. No less than three mass suicides (*johars*) were committed over the centuries by the female inhabitants of its **fort**, and an air of desolation still hangs over the honey-coloured old citadel. As a symbol of Rajput chivalry and militarism only Jodhpur's Meherangarh Fort compares.

Some visitors squeeze a tour of Chittaurgarh into a day-trip, or en route between Bundi and Udaipur, but it's well worth stopping overnight to give yourself time to explore the fort properly.

Some history

The origins of Chittor Fort are obscure, but probably date back to the seventh century. It was seized by **Bappa Rawal**, founder of the Mewar dynasty, in 734, and remained the Mewar capital for the next 834 years, bar a couple of brief interruptions. Despite its commanding position and formidable appearance, however, Chittor was far from invincible, and was sacked three times over the centuries, by **Ala-ud-din-Khalji** (1303), **Sultan Bahadur Shah** (1535) and **Akbar** (1568). It was this last attack which convinced the then ruler of Mewar, Udai Singh, to decamp to a more remote and easily defensible site at Udaipur. Chittaurgarh was

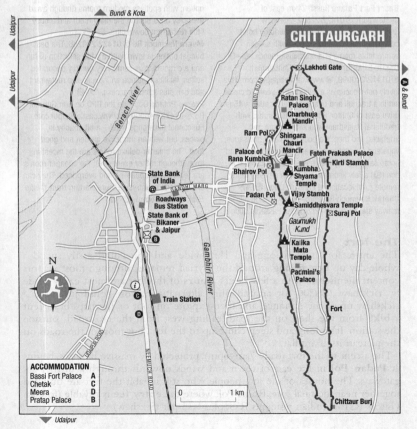

eventually ceded back to the Rajputs in 1616 on condition that it was never refortified, but the royal family of Mewar, by now firmly ensconced in Udaipur, never resettled there, and the entire fort, which once boasted a population of many thousands, is now home to no more than a few hundred people.

Arrival and information

Chittaurgarh's **railway station** is in the western corner of the city. From here it's about 2km north to the **Roadways** (aka "**Kothwali**") **Bus Stand** on the west bank of the Ghambiri, and a further 2km east to the base of the fort. The RTDC **tourist office** (Mon–Sat 10am–5pm; ☎01472/241089) stands just north of the railway station on Station Road and has details of government-registered guides (Rs230 for up to 4hr). There are **ATM**s at the State Bank of India and the State Bank of Bikaner & Jaipur. **Internet** access is available at Megavista Internet, on the way into town.

Accommodation and eating

Accommodation in Chittor is relatively pricey; the only really cheap places are the slightly grim hotels around the train station and in the middle of town. You'll probably end up **eating** where you're staying, unless you fancy trying one of the rough-and-ready *dhabas* in the town centre or around the train station.

Bassi Fort Palace Bassi, 24km east of Chittaurgarh ☎01472/225321, ⓦwww .bassifortpalace.com. Attractive heritage hotel, occupying Bassi's florid palace, with sixteen comfortable rooms and spacious grounds. ❼–❽

Castle Bijaipur 32km east of Chittaurgarh ☎01472/240099, ⓦwww.castlebijaipur.com. This lovely hotel occupies a superb 350-year-old castle set in a tranquil and unspoilt rural location a 45min drive east of Chittor. Rooms are decorated with traditional Rajasthani wooden furniture and artefacts, and there's a pool, Ayurvedic massages, yoga and meditation classes, plus cycle, Jeep and horse safaris. They also have tented accommodation (❺) a few kilometres away in an even more remote rural location at Pangarh Lake. ❽–❾

Chetak Neemuch Rd, immediately outside the railway station ☎01472/241679. Passable budget option, with spotless modern rooms (though avoid the noisy ones next to the main road) and a busy little restaurant downstairs. ❸–❺

Meera Neemuch Rd ☎01472/240266. The best budget option in town, with a wide selection of fan and a/c rooms, plus some very quirkily decorated suites; facilities include an inexpensive restaurant and bar, plus Internet access. ❸–❺

Pratap Palace Opposite the GPO on Shri Gurukul Rd ☎01472/240099, ⓦwww.castlebijaipur.com. Functional mid-range hotel – a bit shabby in places, but with an attractive garden and good food. The smarter deluxe rooms are the nicest in town (though rather expensive); the cheaper rooms are relatively unappealing and overpriced. They can also arrange countryside tours starting from *Castle Bijaipur* (see above). ❻–❼

The fort

The entire fort is 5km long and 1km wide, and you could easily spend a whole day up here nosing around the myriad remains, although most visitors content themselves with a few hours. **Tours** of the fort are most easily made by rickshaw (Rs200 for around 3hr); alternatively, you could just take a rickshaw up to the entrance, and then explore on foot or (perhaps best) rent a **bike** from the shop on the road leading west from the crossroads outside the station. It's a long and steep climb up to the fort, but most of the roads on the plateau itself are flat.

The ascent to the fort (daily 7am–6pm), protected by massive bastions, begins at **Padan Pol** in the east of town and winds upwards through a further six gateways. The houses of the few people who still inhabit the fort are huddled together near the final gate, Rama Pol, where the **entry fee** is payable (foreign visitors Rs100, Indian residents Rs5; plus Rs5 per rickshaw).

Entering the fort, you first reach the slowly deteriorating fifteenth-century **Palace of Rana Kumbha** (reigned 1433–68), built by the ruler who presided over the period of Mewar's greatest prosperity. The main palace building still stands five storeys high, though it's difficult to now make much sense of the confusing tangle of partially ruined walls and towers. Opposite the palace stands the intricately carved fifteenth-century **Shingara Chauri Mandir**, a small but lavishly adorned Jain temple dedicated to Shantinath, the sixteenth *tirthankara*. Nearby, the modern **Fateh Prakash Palace**, a large, plain edifice built for the maharana of Udaipur in the 1920s, is home to a small **archeological museum** (daily except Fri 10am–5pm; Rs3), containing a fine array of Jain and Hindu carvings recovered from various places around the fort.

A couple of hundred metres further on lies the imposing **Kumbha Shyama Temple**, constructed by (and named after) Rana Kumbha. A black statue of Garuda stands in its own pavilion in front of the shrine, while an image of Varaha, the boar incarnation of Vishnu, occupies a niche at the rear. A second shrine stands close by within the small walled enclosure, dedicated to **Meerabai**, a Jodhpur princess and poet famed for her devotion to Krishna.

The Vijay Stambh and beyond

The main road within the fort continues south to its focal point, **Vijay Stambh**, the soaring "tower of victory" erected by Rana Kumbha to commemorate his 1440 victory over the Muslim sultan Mehmud Khilji of Malwa. This magnificent sand-coloured tower, whose nine storeys rise 36m, took a decade to build; its walls are lavishly carved with mythological scenes and images from all Indian religions, including Arabic inscriptions in praise of Allah. You can climb the dark narrow stairs to the very summit for free.

The area around the Vijay Stambh is littered with an impressive number of further remains, including a pair of monumental gateways and a number of florid temples, including the superbly decorated **Samiddhesvara Temple**, whose shrine houses an image of the *trimurti*, a composite, three-headed image of Shiva, Brahma and Vishnu. A path leads from here down to the **Gaumukh Kund**, a large reservoir fed by an underground stream that trickles through carved mouths (*mukh*) of cows (*gau*) and commands superb views across the plains.

Buildings further south include the **Kalika Mata Temple**, and **Padmini's Palace**, its rather plain buildings enclosing a series of attractive little walled gardens leading to a tower overlooking the small lake. The road continues south to the point once used for hurling traitors to their deaths, then returns north

Recommended trains from Chittaurgarh

The trains below are recommended as the fastest and/or most convenient for specific cities.

Destination	Name	No.	Departs (daily)	Arrives
Ajmer	Udaipur–Ajmer Express	2991	9.20am	12.30pm
	Ratlam–Ajmer Express	9653	10.10am	2.30pm
Bundi	Nimach–Kota Express	9019A	2.55pm	5.10pm
Delhi (HN)	Mewar Express	2964	8.50pm	6.10am
Jaipur	Jaipur Superfast	2966	11.50pm	7.10am
Kota	Nimach–Kota Express	9019A	2.55pm	6pm
Udaipur	Mewar Express	2963	5am	7am
	Jaipur–Udaipur Express	2965	5.40am	7.45am

along the eastern ridge to **Suraj Pol** gate, with spectacular vistas across a patchwork of farmland. Several temples line the route, but the most impressive monument is **Kirti Stambh**. The inspiration for the tower of victory, this smaller "tower of fame" was built by Digambaras as a monument to the first *tirthankara* Adinath, whose unclad image appears throughout its six storeys.

Moving on from Chittaurgarh

Trains are generally quicker than buses when leaving Chittor – the most useful services are listed in the box on p.261. There are **buses** to Udaipur (hourly; 3hr–3hr 30min); Ajmer (hourly; 5hr), Kota (6 daily; 4hr 30min), and Bundi (4 daily; 5hr).

Bundi

The walled town of **BUNDI**, 37km north of Kota, lies in the north of the former Hadaoti state, shielded by jagged outcrops of the Vindhya Range. The site was the capital of the Hadachauhans, but although settled in 1241, 25 years before Kota, Bundi never amounted to more than a modest market centre, and

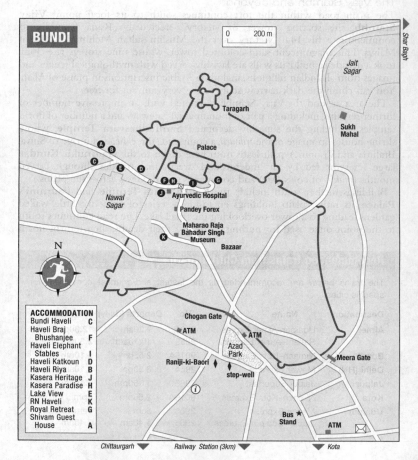

ACCOMMODATION
Bundi Haveli	C
Haveli Braj Bhushanjee	F
Haveli Elephant Stables	I
Haveli Katkoun	D
Haveli Riya	B
Kasera Heritage	J
Kasera Paradise	H
Lake View	E
RN Haveli	K
Royal Retreat	G
Shivam Guest House	A

remains relatively untouched by modern developments. The palace alone justifies a visit thanks to its superb collection of **murals**, while the well-preserved **old town**, crammed with crumbling havelis, makes this one of southern Rajasthan's most appealing destinations – a fact recognized by the ever-increasing numbers of foreign tourists who are now visiting the place.

Arrival and information

Buses arrive in the southeast part of town near the post office, from where it's about Rs20–30 by rickshaw to the palace and guesthouses; the train station is around 5km south of town (Rs40–50 by rickshaw). Bundi's **tourist office** (Mon–Sat 10am–5pm; ☎0747/244 3697) is south of town near the *Ishwari Niwas* hotel. You can **change money** at Pandey Forex, about 100m south of the palace, and at the *Kasera Heritage* guesthouse; there are also several ATMs in the southern end of town (see the map for locations). Dozens of places offer **Internet** access for around Rs40 per hour, while lots of places also rent out **motorbikes** (around Rs250/day), and a few also have **bicycles** (or try *Kasera Heritage*, which has both).

If you're in the area around mid-November try to arrive for the annual **Bundi Festival**, a celebration of Hadaoti heritage with a very local, country-fair feel.

Accommodation and eating

Much of Bundi's **accommodation** is in old havelis, with a wide range of standards and prices. Most people **eat** where they're staying. If you want to go out, the *Bundi Haveli* (see below) has good veg and non-veg Indian food (mains 70–150) and real coffee in a stylishly laid-back setting, while the terrace at the *Royal Retreat* (see p.264) has fine town views and is a nice place for a sundowner.

Bundi Haveli ☎0/941 493 5209, ⓦwww .hotelbundihaveli.com. Traditional old haveli given a stylish contemporary makeover, with beautifully furnished rooms (most with a/c), a good restaurant and facilities including Internet access and money exchange. Excellent value at current rates. ⑤–⑧

Haveli Braj Bhushanjee ☎0747/244 2322, ⓦwww.kiplingsbundi.com. Wonderfully atmospheric 150-year-old haveli, with original murals, antiques and assorted artworks adorning virtually every surface. Rooms (some with a/c and TV) are similarly engaging, and immaculately maintained. On the down side, there's not much in the way of food, and no alcohol or meat. ④–⑧

Haveli Elephant Stables ☎0/992 815 4064. Just three rooms (2 doubles and 1 single) in the palace's former elephant stables, occupying a pretty and very peaceful spot underneath the fort's huge walls. Rooms are fairly basic, but at this price and in this location you can't really complain. A couple of more expensive rooms are planned for 2008. ①

Haveli Katkoun ☎0747/244 4311, ⓦhavelikatkoun.free.fr. Formerly the most popular budget guesthouse in town, the *Haveli Katkoun* was being rebuilt at the time of writing and is due

to reopen in 2008 with a range of spacious and smart new modern rooms. ③–⑤

Haveli Riya ☎0/925 259 0312. Friendly family guesthouse with a small selection of neat, comfortable and well-kept rooms at bargain prices, plus a nice little rooftop cafe. ①–②

Kasera Paradise ☎0747/244 4679, ⓦwww .kaseraparadise.com. Tucked away in a peaceful little lane just behind the *Braj Bhushanjee*, this attractive guesthouse occupies a meticulously restored sixteenth-century haveli with a range of variously priced a/c rooms, all nicely furnished and decorated with traditional murals. There are similar rooms at slightly cheaper prices in the same owner's *Kasera Heritage* (④–⑧), just over the road. ⑥–⑧

Lake View ☎0747/244 2326, ⓔlakeviewbundi _@yahoo.com. Slightly scruffy guesthouse in an old lakeside haveli. It's not the cleanest place in town, but compensates with cheap rates and a fine terrace overlooking Nawal Sagar. The cheap garden rooms are pretty basic; the more expensive ones in the haveli itself have faded old murals and lake views. ①–③

RN Haveli ☎0747/512 0098, ⓔrnhavelibundi @yahoo.co.in. Possibly the only guesthouse in Rajasthan run entirely by women, and deservedly popular amongst female travellers. The 200-year-old haveli itself is a bit run-down and the rooms are very basic, but they're cheap and clean, and the home-cooked meals are excellent. ❶–❷ **Royal Retreat** ☎0747/244 4426, Ⓔroyalretreat bhati@yahoo.com. Just four comfortable rooms (all air-cooled) in a superb and peaceful location in the lower part of the palace complex – although

the place can feel a mite lonely after dark, especially if there's no one else staying. There's decent food in the terrace restaurant. ❷–❹ **Shivam Tourist Guesthouse** ☎0747/244 7892, Ⓔshivam_pg@yahoo.com. Extremely sociable little family guesthouse with friendly female management, six clean and pleasantly decorated attached rooms, and good home-cooking. ❶–❹

The Town

Bundi's **palace** (daily 7am–5pm; foreign visitors Rs50, Indian residents Rs10; camera Rs50, video Rs100) was one of the few royal abodes in Rajasthan untouched by Mughal influence, and its appearance is surprisingly homogenous considering the number of times it was added to over the years. If you want a **guide**, the extremely informative Keshav Bhati (☎0/941 439 4241, Ⓔbharat _bhati@yahoo.com) charges around Rs200 for a tour of the entire palace, and also offers visits to local rock-painting sites and of Kota.

A short steep path winds up to the main gateway, **Hathi Pol**, surmounted by elephant carvings, beyond which lies the palace's principal courtyard. On the right-hand side, steps lead up to the **Ratan Doulat**, the early seventeenth-century Diwan-i-Am, or Hall of Public Audience, an open terrace with a simple marble throne overlooking the courtyard below.

At the far end of the Ratan Daulat, further steps lead up to the **Chhatra Mahal**. Go through the open-sided turquoise-painted pavilion on the southern side of the courtyard and the room beyond to reach a superb little **antechamber** (or "dressing room"), every surface covered in finely detailed murals from the 1780s embellished with gold and silver leaf. The opposite side of the courtyard is flanked by a pavilion with columns supported on the backs of quaint black trumpeting elephants, at the back of which you'll find a well-preserved old squat toilet, offering possibly the best view from any public convenience in Rajasthan.

From the Chattra Mahal courtyard, a narrow flight of steps leads up to an even smaller courtyard flanked by the superbly decorated **Phool Mahal** (built in 1607, though the murals date from the 1860s), whose murals include a vast procession featuring regiments of soldiers in European dress and a complete camel corps. From here, further narrow steps ascend to the **Badal Mahal** (Cloud Palace), home to what are often regarded as the finest paintings in the whole of southern Rajasthan. A vividly coloured ring of Krishnas and Radhas dance around the highest part of the vaulted dome, flanked by murals showing Krishna being driven to his wedding by Ganesh, and Rama returning from Sri Lanka to Ayodhya.

There are further outstanding murals in the **Chittra Sala** (sunrise–sunset; Rs60), just above the palace. At the rear left-hand corner of the garden inside, steps lead up to a small courtyard embellished with an outstanding sequence of murals painted in an unusual muted palette of turquoises, blues and blacks, the majority devoted to magical depictions of scenes from the life of Krishna.

A steep twenty-minute climb above the Chittra Sala, the monkey-infested **Taragarh** fort offers even more spectacular views over Bundi, its palace and the surrounding countryside.

The rest of the town

Right in the centre of town, the recently opened **Maharao Raja Bahadur Singh Museum** (daily 9am–1pm & 2–5pm; Rs100, camera Rs50) houses a

Crafts to go

No country in the world produces such a tempting array of arts and crafts as India. Intensely colourful, delicately worked, exquisitely ornate and immensely varied, India's crafts have the added advantage of being amazingly inexpensive. Every part of the country has its specialities – textiles in Rajasthan, metalwork in Karnataka, carpets in Kashmir – but everywhere you'll see beautiful things that you'll find hard to resist buying. Whether it's sumptuous fabrics, exquisite carvings or garish knick-knacks, India offers a feast of artistic creations that you'll want to indulge in.

Thangka painting ▲

Meenakari jewellery box ▼

Paintings

Most Tibetan **thangkas** (Buddhist religious paintings mounted on brocaded silk) are mass produced (usually in Nepal) and modern, whatever the seller says, but even the cheapest boast the dense Buddhist symbolism inherent in the form. You'll find them mostly in the north, where there are Tibetan communities, and they come in quite an array of different styles.

Miniature paintings, on cotton, silk or paper, are a tradition in Rajasthan, where you'll find them on sale in almost every tourist centre in the state. Some of them are very fine and rather pricey but, at the other end of the scale, **leaf skeleton paintings**, originally from southern Kerala, are cheap as chips, and often sold in the form of greeting cards which you can post straight home.

Metalwork

Brass and **copperware** can be very finely worked into trays, plates, ashtrays, cups and bowls. In the north, particularly in Rajasthan, enamel inlay (*meenakari*) is common. **Bidri** work from Karnataka is made by inlaying a gunmetal alloy with fine designs in brass or silver, then blackening the gunmetal with sal ammoniac, to leave the inlay work shining. *Bidri* jewellery boxes, dishes and hookah pipes, among other things, are particularly good in Karnataka and Andhra Pradesh. In Orissa, filigree *tarakashi* is worth looking out for.

Especially in the south, brass statues of Hindu gods are still produced by the **lost-wax process**, in which a model is carved out of wax, surrounded in clay and fired. The wax melts to leave a terracotta mould from which the brass model is cast.

Carpets

Kashmiri rugs are among the best in the world, and given a little caution and scepticism, you can get yourself a bargain, though you can also get shafted if you're not careful. A pukka Kashmiri carpet should have a label on the back stating that it is made in Kashmir and what it is made of (wool, silk or "silk touch", which is wool with a little silk to give it a sheen). Choose your shop carefully, and remember that the best way of ensuring a carpet reaches home is to take it or post it yourself.

Dhurries (woven carpets or kilims), traditionally made of wool, are an older art form, and a less expensive one. UP is the main centre for these, particularly Agra and Mirzapur, but they are also made in Rajasthan, Gujarat, the Punjab and Andhra Pradesh. Tibetan rugs are available in areas with large Tibetan communities, such as Himachal Pradesh.

▲ Traditionally made dhurries

▼ Sandals at Anjuna flea market, Goa

Leatherware

Leatherware can be very cheap and well made, though the leather doesn't normally come from cows, of course. Rajasthani camel-hide **mojadi** slippers are extremely comfortable, though **chappals** (sandals) – and particularly the distinctive slipper-like **kolhapuri** variety from Maharashtra – will need to be broken in (dunking them in water for a minute or so should do the job); pointed **jootis**, popular around Delhi and the Punjab, also need some perseverance. Otherwise, buffalo-hide belts and bags can be very reasonable compared to similar items made of cowhide in the West; Chennai and Puducherry are good places to go looking. Upmarket shops offer a range of high-quality leather goods from handbags to briefcases at very reasonable prices.

Tailors in Jodhpur ▲

Tie-dyed fabrics on a Goa beach ▼

Clothing and textiles

Textiles are so much a part of Indian culture that Gandhi wanted a **spinning wheel** put on the national flag. The kind of cloth he had in mind was the plain white homespun fabric called **khadi**, sold in government shops (Khadi Gramodyog) nationwide. Methods of dyeing and printing this and other cloth vary from the tie-dyeing (*bandhani*) of Rajasthan to block printing and screen printing of calico cotton (from Calicut – now Kozhikode – in Kerala) and silk.

Saris are normally made of cotton for everyday use, although silk is used for special occasions. Though Varanasi silk is world famous, the best silk nowadays comes from the south of India: Kanchipuram and Madurai in Tamil Nadu, famous for their brightly coloured saris, and Mysore in Karnataka, where the silk shines with its own particularly scintillating sheen.

Rajasthan's heavy **mirror-embroidered** cloth is sumptuous and luxuriant, but it's far from being India's only fabulous brocaded fabric. Bengal's wonderful **baluchari** silk brocade is decorated with scenes from Indian mythology. Alternatively, there's *ikat* and *batik* cloth from Orissa, Madhya Pradesh and Gujarat, thick Tibetan sweaters from Darjeeling, and *salwar kameez*, the elegant pyjama suits worn by Muslim women, with trousers (pyjamas) of various styles. **Block-printed bedsheets**, as well as being useful, make great wall-hangings, as do Punjabi *phulkari* (originally wedding sheets), and *lunghis* from the south (as much sheets as garments), but every region has its own fabrics and its own methods of colouring them and making them up – the choice is endless.

skull-crackingly tedious collection of self-congratulatory portraits of assorted maharajas of Bundi, plus a gallery of stuffed tigers and other dumb animals massacred in the name of sport by notables ranging from Lord Mountbatten to Haile Selassie. Save your cash.

On the south side of town is the much more rewarding **Raniji-ki-Baori** (no set hours), one of Rajasthan's most spectacular step-wells. Built in 1699, the well is reached by a flight of steps punctuated by platforms and pillars embellished with sinuous S-shaped brackets and elephant capitals. As you descend, look for the beautifully carved panels showing the ten avatars of Lord Vishnu, which line the side walls.

Northeast of the town on the southern shore of Jait Sagar tank is the pretty but now rather neglected **Sukh Mahal** – Rao Raja Vishnu Singh's summer palace – where Rudyard Kipling (who stayed here for a few months at the invitation of the raja) wrote parts of *Kim* and the *Jungle Book*. The building itself is closed to visitors but it's a pleasant spot, and you can walk for a short distance along the lakeshore on either side of the palace. Some 1.5km further along the side of the lake, **Shar Bagh** encloses sixty crumbling royal cenotaphs. If the door is locked, ask for the key at the *chowkidar's* hut on your left just after the gateway over the main road some 100m north of the cenotaphs. Count on around Rs60 return by auto to Sukh Mahal, and Rs100 to Shar Bagh.

Moving on from Bundi

Heading south, there are regular buses to **Kota** (every 30min; 45min–1hr), but no convenient trains. There are two fast trains to **Chittaurgarh** daily at 7.21am (#282 Haldighati Passenger) and 9.38am (#9020A Dehra Dun Express), arriving at 10.35am and noon respectively; Chittaurgarh is also served by four buses daily (4–5hr). There are four buses daily to **Udaipur** (7–8hr) but no trains.

Heading north, **Sawai Madhopur** (for Ranthambore National Park) is most easily reached by catching a bus to Kota and then picking up a train (see p.266 for details). Alternatively there are a few direct buses daily (4hr). Buses are also the best way of reaching **Ajmer** (hourly; 4hr), **Jaipur** (hourly; 5hr), **Jodhpur** (three daily; 10hr) and **Pushkar** (3 daily; 5hr).

Kota

KOTA, 230km south of Jaipur on a fertile plain fed by Rajasthan's largest river, the Chambal, is one of the state's dirtier and less appealing cities. With a population nudging 700,000, it is one of Rajasthan's major commercial and industrial hubs, with hydro, atomic and thermal power stations lining the banks of the Chambal, alongside Asia's largest fertilizer plant, whose enormous chimneys provide a not-very-scenic backdrop to many views of the town. Kota is worth a visit if only for its city palace, which houses one of the better museums in Rajasthan, while the old town has a commercial hustle and bustle which makes a nice contrast to somnolent Bundi, just down the road.

Arrival and information

Kota's **railway station** is in the north of town, a few kilometres from the central **bus stand** on Bundi Road. The **tourist office** (Mon–Sat 10am–5pm; ✆0744/232 7695) is in the RTDC *Chambal Hotel*, just north of the Kishor Sagar. The best place for changing **traveller's cheques** is the inconveniently located State Bank of Bikaner & Jaipur in the south of town. There are several **ATMs** scattered around the road intersection by the *Navrang* hotel.

Accommodation and eating

Kota's **hotels** cater mainly for passing business travellers; if you can't afford to stay in one of the places below, it's better to base yourself in Bundi. For **eating**, the modern *Venue* pure-veg restaurant, attached to the *Navrang* hotel, has a good selection of north Indian veg mains (most around Rs50) plus *dosas*, pizzas and Chinese dishes.

Brijraj Bhawan Civil Lines ☎0744/245 0529, ⓦwww.nivalink.com/brijrajbhawan. An idyllic retreat in the heart of noisy Kota, occupying a fine old colonial mansion set in a peaceful spot overlooking the river. Rooms are pure Victorian period pieces, all scrupulously maintained and very comfortable. ⑦–⑧
Navrang Station Rd ☎0744/232 3294. The nicest cheap hotel in town, with a mix of simple air-cooled and more attractively furnished a/c rooms, all with TV. The adjacent *Phul Plaza* is reasonable too, but not quite so appealing. ③–④

Sukhdham Kothi Civil Lines ☎0744/232 0081, ⓦwww.sukhdhamkothi.com. Marvellously atmospheric guesthouse located in a hundred-year-old stone mansion set amid extensive gardens. Comfy and atmospheric rooms with old wooden furniture and assorted nineteenth-century bric-a-brac. ⑥
Umed Bhawan Palace Station Rd, Khelri Phatak ☎0744/232 5262, ⓦwww.welcomheritagehotels .com. Occupying a huge and rather ugly former royal residence, this fancy hotel offers upmarket comforts (and a fair bit of chintz) at a reasonable price. ⑦–⑧

The Town

Kota is a surprisingly large and sprawling city, and you'll need a rickshaw to cover the sights below, especially if arriving at the train station, on the far northern side of town. Arriving at the bus station, it's possible to walk across the city centre and through the main bazaar to the City Palace, although even this is a longish and potentially disorienting walk.

The City Palace

On the southern side of the town centre, around 2km from the bus station, lies the **City Palace**, a well-preserved cluster of blue and pink royal residences; construction on them began in 1625 and continued sporadically until the early years of the twentieth century. The palace now houses the excellent **Maharao**

Recommended trains from Kota

The trains below are recommended as the fastest and/or most convenient for specific cities.

Destination	Name	No.	Departs	Arrives
Bundi	Dehra Dun Express	9020A	9.05am (daily)	9.36am
Chittaurgarh	Dehra Dun Express	9020A	9.05am (daily)	noon
Delhi (Hazrat Nizamuddin)	Kota Shatabdi	2059	6am (daily)	12.25pm
	Rajdhani Express	2431	7.05am (Tu & Th)	12.35pm
	Golden Temple Mail	2903	11.25am (daily)	6.25pm
	Mewar Express	2964	11.55pm (daily)	6.10am
Jaipur	Dayodaya Express	2181	8.35am (daily)	12.30pm
	Mumbai–Jaipur Express	2955	8.55am (daily)	12.55pm
Mumbai	Mumbai Rajdhani	2952	9.05pm (daily)	8.35am
	Kranti Rajdhani	2954	9.55pm (daily)	10.15am
Sawai Madhopur	Dayodaya Express	2181	8.35am (daily)	10am
	Golden Temple Mail	2903	11.25am (daily)	12.35pm
	Avadh Express	9037	2.55pm (Tu, W, F, Su)	4.20pm

Madho Singh Museum (daily except Fri 10am–4.30pm; combined entrance to museum and palace Rs100, Indian residents Rs10; camera Rs50, video Rs100). The first room is filled with a selection of luxury items belonging to the maharaja, while diagonally across the courtyard lies the dazzling **Raj Mahal**, built by Rao Madho Singh (ruled 1625–49), richly decorated with paintings and mirrorwork, which served as the ruler's public audience hall. From the Raj Mahal, a corridor leads into a further sequence of rooms housing a well-stocked armoury and a small art gallery, and a depressing wildlife gallery, filled with the mothy remains of various leopards and tigers.

Exit the museum then follow the steps up past the Raj Mahal to reach a series of finely painted palace buildings. Three storeys up is the **Barah Mahal**, one of whose rooms is richly decorated with dozens of square miniatures placed together on the wall like tiles and depicting a range of religious and contemporary scenes, from Krishna lifting Mount Goverdhan to exotic-looking European ladies and gentlemen.

The rest of the city

Kishore Sagar, an artificial lake built in 1346, gives some visual relief from the city's grim industrial backdrop; the red-and-white palace in its centre, **Jag Mandir**, was commissioned by Prince Dher Deh of Bundi in 1346. On the northern edge of the lake the dusty **Government Museum** (daily 10am–5pm; Rs3) serves as the dispiriting home for an excellent collection of local stone carvings (signs in Hindi only, if at all).

On the edge of the river a few kilometres south of the fort, crocodiles and gharial sun themselves in a shallow pond in the **Chambal Gardens** (Rs2); boats depart from here for fifteen minute tours (Rs15) of the crocodile-infested River Chambal.

Moving on from Kota

Buses leave regularly from the stand near Nayapura Circle to Bundi (every 30min; 45min–1hr), Ajmer (every 30min; 6hr), Chittor (6 daily; 4hr 30min), Jaipur (12 daily; 6hr) and Udaipur (10 daily; 6hr). Kota also has good **train** connections; see the box opposite.

Travel details

Trains

Jaipur to: Abu Road (4–6 daily; 5hr 30min–8hr); Agra (4–5 daily; 4hr–5hr 30min); Ahmedabad (3–4 daily; 9hr–13hr 30min); Ajmer (5–8 daily; 2hr–2hr 30min); Alwar (8–10 daily; 1hr 40min–4hr); Bikaner (3–5 daily; 6hr 45min–11hr); Chittaurgarh (2 daily; 7hr 40min–8hr 15min); Delhi (8–10 daily; 5hr–6hr 30min); Jaisalmer (1 daily; 13hr); Jodhpur (5–8 daily; 5hr 30min–9hr 20min); Kota (6–8 daily; 3hr 15min–5hr 20min); Mumbai (2 daily; 17hr 30min–22hr); Sawai Madhopur (6–8 daily; 1hr 50min–3hr); Udaipur (1 daily; 9hr 20min).

Jodhpur to: Abu Rd (3 daily; 5hr); Agra (1–2 daily; 12hr); Ahmedabad (3 daily; 9–10hr); Bikaner (5 daily; 5hr–7hr 15min); Delhi (2 daily; 11–13hr); Jaipur (5–8 daily; 5hr 30min–9hr); Jaisalmer (2 daily; 6hr–6hr 40min).

Udaipur to: Ahmedabad (2 daily; 8hr 30min–13hr 30min); Ajmer (1 daily; 5hr 30min); Chittaurgarh (3 daily; 2hr); Delhi (1 daily; 12hr); Jaipur (1 daily; 9hr 30min); Kota (2 daily; 5hr).

Buses

Ajmer to: Agra (9 daily; 9hr); Bikaner (15 daily; 7hr); Bundi (hourly; 4–5hr); Chittaurgarh (hourly; 5hr); Delhi (every 30–45min; 9hr); Jaipur (every 30min; 2hr 30min); Jaisalmer (2 daily, 1 nightly; 11hr); Jodhpur (half-hourly; 5hr); Kota (half-hourly; 6hr); Udaipur (hourly; 7hr).

Bikaner to: Ajmer (15 daily; 7hr); Chittaurgarh
(1 daily; 10hr 30min); Delhi (6 daily; 10hr);
Fatehpur (14 daily; 3hr 30min–4hr); Jaipur
(11 daily; 7hr 30min); Jaisalmer (8 daily; 7hr);
Jodhpur (8 daily; 6hr); Kota (2 daily; 10hr); Pushkar
(12 daily; 6hr 30min); Udaipur (4 daily; 12hr).

Jaipur to: Agra (every 1–2hr; 5hr); Ahmedabad
(1 daily; 16hr); Ajmer (8 daily; 2hr–2hr 30min);
Alwar (hourly; 4hr); Bharatpur (every 30min;
4hr 30min); Bikaner (11 daily; 7hr 30min);
Chittaurgarh (2 daily; 7hr 15min); Delhi (every
45min–1hr; 6hr); Gwalior (1 nightly; 7hr); Jaisalmer
(1 nightly; 13–15hr); Jhunjhunu (every 30min; 5hr);
Jodhpur (7 daily; 7–8hr); Kota (4 daily; 6hr); Mount
Abu (1 daily; 11hr; 1 nightly; 12hr); Nawalgarh
(every 30min; 3hr); Pushkar (1 daily; 3hr
30min–4hr); Sawai Madhopur (2 daily; 4hr 30min);
Shimla (1 nightly; 15hr); Udaipur (5 daily; 10hr).

Jaisalmer to: Ajmer (3 daily; 10hr); Bikaner
(9 daily; 7–8hr); Jaipur (3 daily; 12–15hr); Jodhpur
(10 daily; 5hr 30min); Lodurva (4 daily; 40min);
Mount Abu (1 daily; 13hr); Udaipur (1 daily;
12–14hr).

Jodhpur to: Abu Road (every 30min–1hr; 6–9hr);
Agra (3 daily; 14hr); Ajmer (half-hourly; 5hr);
Bharatpur (2 daily; 10hr); Bikaner (every
30min–1hr; 6hr); Bundi (3 daily; 10hr); Chittaurgarh
(3 daily; 9hr); Delhi (6 daily; 11–12hr); Jaipur
(every 30min–1hr; 7–8hr); Jaisalmer (every
30min–1hr; 5hr 30min); Kota (5 daily; 11hr);
Mount Abu (1 daily; 6–9hr 30min); Osian (every
30–45min; 2hr); Pushkar (3 daily; 4hr 30min–6hr

30min); Ranakpur (5–6 daily; 4–5hr); Udaipur
(hourly; 7–9hr).

Udaipur to: Agra (3 daily; 14hr); Ahmedabad
(hourly; 4–6hr); Ajmer (hourly; 7hr); Bikaner
(1 nightly; 13hr); Bundi (10 daily; 7hr 30min);
Chittaurgarh (hourly; 3hr–3hr 30min); Delhi
(6 daily; 13–15hr); Jaipur (hourly; 7–10hr);
Jaisalmer (1 nightly; 12hr); Jodhpur (14 daily;
6–10hr); Kota (10 daily; 6hr); Mount Abu (10 daily;
5–7hr); Mumbai (3 daily; 14–15hr); Pushkar
(1 nightly; 6hr 30min); Rajkot (1 nightly; 9hr).

Flights

(**AI** = Indian Airlines, **IT** = Kingfisher Airlines, **9W** =
Jet Airways, **6E** = IndiGo, **DN** = Air Deccan, **SG** =
SpiceJet, **S2** = JetLite)

Jaipur to: Ahmedabad (SG, S2; daily; 1hr 10min);
Delhi (DN, AI, 9W, S2, IT; daily; 40min–1hr);
Hyderabad (6E; daily; 1hr 45min); Jodhpur (DN, IT;
daily; 55min–1hr); Kolkata (6E; daily; 2hr 15min);
Mumbai (DN, AI, 6E, IT, SG; daily; 1hr 5min–1hr
50min); Panjim (IT; daily; 2hr 20min); Udaipur (DN,
9W, IT; daily; 1hr 5min).

Jodhpur to: Delhi (AI, 9W; daily; 55min–1hr
30min); Jaipur (DN, IT; daily; 1hr); Mumbai (AI, 9W;
daily; 1hr 50min–2hr 25min); Udaipur (AI, 9W, IT;
daily; 50min–1hr 10min).

Udaipur to: Delhi (AI, 9W; daily; 2hr–2hr 15min);
Jaipur (DN, 9W, IT; daily; 1hr–1hr 20min); Jodhpur
(AI, IT; daily; 50min); Mumbai (AI, 9W, IT; daily;
1hr 10min).

Uttar Pradesh

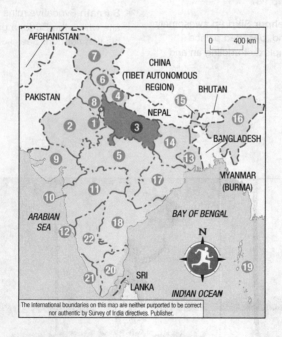

AFGHANISTAN

CHINA
(TIBET AUTONOMOUS
REGION)

BHUTAN

PAKISTAN

NEPAL

BANGLADESH

MYANMAR
(BURMA)

ARABIAN
SEA

BAY OF BENGAL

N

SRI
LANKA

INDIAN OCEAN

0   400 km

The international boundaries on this map are neither purported to be correct
nor authentic by Survey of India directives. Publisher.

CHAPTER 3 # Highlights

✳ **Taj Mahal** The highest expression of Mughal culture, and one of the most stunning buildings in the world. See p.279

✳ **Akbar's mausoleum, Sikandra** The great Mughal's tomb looks just as it does in old miniatures, with tame monkeys and deer wandering in its ornamental gardens. See p.287

✳ **Fatehpur Sikri** An awesomely grand, deserted palace complex, straddling an arid ridge near the Rajasthani border. See p.291

✳ **Kalinjar Fort** Remote fortifications in Uttar Pradesh's dusty badlands, far from the tourist trail. See p.318

✳ **Varanasi** Take a boat on the Ganges before dawn to watch the sun rise over India's most ancient and sacred city. See p.318

✳ **Sarnath** Evocative ruins on the site where the Buddha gave his first sermon. See p.333

▲ Dawn ceremony at Dashoswamedh Ghat, Varanasi

Uttar Pradesh

U TTAR PRADESH, or "the Northern State" – formerly the United Provinces, but always **UP** – is the heartland of Hinduism and Hindi, dominating the nation in culture, religion, language and politics. A vast, steamy plain of the Ganges, its history is very much the history of India, and its temples and monuments – Buddhist, Hindu and Muslim – are among the most impressive in the country.

Western UP, which adjoins Delhi, has always been close to India's centre of power. Its main city, **Agra**, once the Mughal capital, is home to the **Taj Mahal**, the most famous and prominent of its stupendous monuments. Nearby, the abandoned Mughal city of **Fatehpur Sikri** remains perfectly preserved in the desert-like air, and just to the north, somehow sheltered from successive waves of Muslim conquest, the much-mythologized Hindu land of **Braj** – centred on **Mathura** and **Vrindavan** – was the childhood playground of the god Krishna.

Large tracts of **central UP**, along the fertile flood plains of the Doab, constituted the **Kingdom of Avadh**, the last centre of independent Muslim rule in northern India until the British unceremoniously took it over, fuelling the resentment that led to the great uprising of 1857, in which its capital **Lucknow** (now UP's state capital), played such a celebrated role. Today, central UP is a Hindu stronghold, with **Allahabad**, where the Ganges meets the Yamuna, being one of Hinduism's holiest sites, and home to the enormous twelve-yearly **Kumbh Mela**, the world's biggest religious fair.

Bundelkhand – the area north of the craggy Vindhya Mountains, which stretch across northeastern Madhya Pradesh – was part of a ninth-century kingdom carved out by the Chandella Rajputs. The same kingdom included Khajuraho in Madhya Pradesh (see p.430), for which **Jhansi**, whose nineteenth-century fort remains a symbol of the struggle for independence, is a convenient jumping-off point.

In **eastern UP** lies the holiest Hindu city of all – the sacred *tirtha* (crossing-place) of **Varanasi**, where it's believed death transports the soul to final liberation. This land has been sacred since antiquity; Buddha himself, and the founder of Jainism, Mahavira, frequented Varanasi, while the whole state – from Mathura to **Sarnath** on the outskirts of Varanasi, and beyond to the great schools of learning in Bihar – was long under Buddhist influence.

Although UP was once a thriving centre of Islamic jurisprudence and culture, many Muslims departed during the years after Independence, and the Muslim population now comprises just sixteen percent. As the heart of what is known as the "cow belt" (equivalent to America's "bible belt"), UP has been plagued by caste politics and was for some years dominated by the Hindu sectarian BJP. The state acquired an unfortunate reputation as the focus of bitter communal

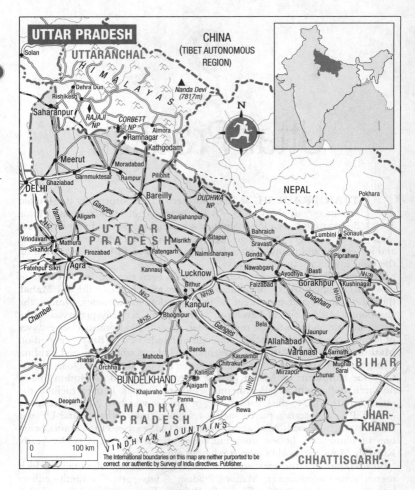

tensions, most notoriously in the wake of the 1992 destruction of the Babri Masjid mosque in **Ayodhya** (east of Lucknow, near Faizabad), which sparked off sectarian riots across India. In recent years, state politics has been dominated by two largely local leftwing parties, of whom the socialist Samajwadi Party (SP) lost control of the state government in 2007 to the low-caste Bahujan Samaj Party (BSP). What effect this will have on caste and sectarian politics in UP remains to be seen.

With an efficient if basic state bus system and an excellent railway network, **travelling around** the state is generally straightforward (except in Bundelkhand in the south). The major tourist cities, Agra and Varanasi, have been coping with visitors and pilgrims for centuries, and today have good transport connections and all the facilities a traveller might need. **UP Tourism** (Ⓦ www.up-tourism .com) have offices in most major towns.

Agra

The splendour of **AGRA** – capital of all India under the Mughals – remains undiminished, from the massive fort to the magnificent **Taj Mahal**. Along with Delhi, 204km northwest, and Jaipur in Rajasthan, Agra is the third apex of the "Golden Triangle", India's most popular tourist itinerary. It fully merits that status; the Taj effortlessly transcends all the frippery and commercialism that surrounds it, and continues to have a fresh and immediate impact on all who see it. That said, Agra city itself can be an intense experience, even for seasoned India hands. Years of corruption and political neglect have reduced its infrastructure to a shambles: filthy water and open sewers are ubiquitous, power cuts routine and the traffic pollution appalling (some mornings you can barely see the sun through the fog of fumes). Moreover, as a tourist you'll have to contend with often overwhelming crowds at the major monuments, absurdly high admission fees, and some of Asia's most persistent touts, commission merchants and rickshaw-wallahs. Don't, however, let all this put you off. Although it's possible to see Agra on a day-trip from Delhi, the Taj alone deserves so much more – a fleeting visit would miss the subtleties of its many moods, as the light changes from sunrise to sunset – while the city's other sights and Fatehpur Sikri can easily fill several days.

Some history

Little is known of the pre-Muslim history of Agra; one of the earliest chronicles, dated to the Afghan invasion under Ibrahim Ghaznavi in 1080 AD, describes a robust fort occupying a chain of hills, with a flourishing city strategically placed at the crossroads between the north and the centre of India. However, Agra remained a minor administrative centre until 1504, when the Sultan of Delhi, **Sikandar Lodi**, moved his capital here so as to keep a check on the warring factions of his empire. The ruins of the Lodis' great city can still be seen on the eastern bank of the Yamuna. After defeating the last Lodi sultan, Ibrahim Lodi, at Panipat in 1526, **Babur**, the founder of the Mughal Empire, sent ahead his son **Humayun** to capture Agra. In gratitude for their benevolent treatment at his hands, the family of the Raja of Gwalior rewarded the Mughal with jewellery and precious stones – among them the legendary **Koh-i-noor Diamond**, now one of Britain's crown jewels.

Agra's greatest days arrived during the reign of Humayun's son, **Akbar the Great** (1556–1605), with the construction of Agra Fort. The city maintained its position as the capital of the empire for over a century; even when **Shah Jahan**, Jahangir's son and successor, built a new city in Delhi – Shahjahanabad, now known as Old Delhi – his heart remained in Agra. He pulled down many of the earlier red-sandstone structures in the fort, replacing them with his hallmark – exquisite marble buildings. Although the empire flourished under his heir Aurangzeb (1658–1707), his intolerance towards non-Muslims stirred a hornets' nest. Agra was occupied successively by the Jats, the Marathas, and eventually the British.

After the uprising in 1857, the city lost the headquarters of the government of the Northwestern Provinces and the High Court to Allahabad and went into a period of decline. Its Mughal treasures have ensured its survival, and today the city is once again prospering, as an industrial and commercial centre as well as a tourist destination.

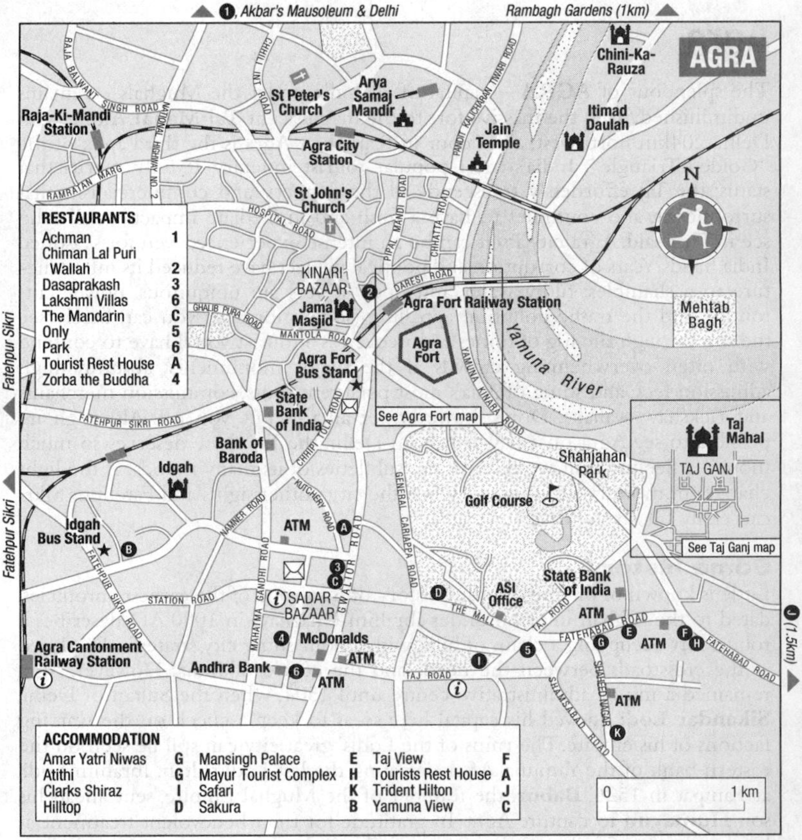
1, Akbar's Mausoleum & Delhi
Rambagh Gardens (1km)
AGRA
RESTAURANTS
Achman 1
Chiman Lal Puri Wallah 2
Dasaprakash 3
Lakshmi Villas 6
The Mandarin C
Only 5
Park 6
Tourist Rest House A
Zorba the Buddha 4
ACCOMMODATION
Amar Yatri Niwas G
Atithi G
Clarks Shiraz I
Hilltop D
Mansingh Palace E
Mayur Tourist Complex H
Safari K
Sakura B
Taj View F
Tourists Rest House A
Trident Hilton J
Yamuna View C
Raja-Ki-Mandi Station
St Peter's Church
Arya Samaj Mandir
Agra City Station
Jain Temple
Itimad Daulah
Chini-Ka-Rauza
St John's Church
KINARI BAZAAR
Jama Masjid
Agra Fort Railway Station
Agra Fort
See Agra Fort map
Yamuna River
Mehtab Bagh
Agra Fort Bus Stand
State Bank of India
Bank of Baroda
Idgah
Idgah Bus Stand
Taj Mahal
TAJ GANJ
See Taj Ganj map
Shahjahan Park
Golf Course
ASI Office
SADAR BAZAAR
McDonalds
Andhra Bank
ATM
Agra Cantonment Railway Station
Fatehpur Sikri
J (1.5km)
RAJA BALWANT SINGH ROAD
NATIONAL HIGHWAY NO. 2
RAMRATAN MARG
CHHILI INT ROAD
HOSPITAL ROAD
PIPAL MANDI ROAD
CHHATTA ROAD
PANDIT KALICHARAN TIWARI ROAD
DARESI ROAD
GHALIB PURA ROAD
MANTOLA ROAD
FATEHPUR SIKRI ROAD
CHHIPI TOLA ROAD
YAMUNA KINARA ROAD
KUTCHERY ROAD
NAMNER ROAD
GWALIOR ROAD
MAHATMA GANDHI ROAD
GENERAL CARIAPPA ROAD
STATION ROAD
THE MALL
TAJ ROAD
FATEHABAD ROAD
SHAHEED NAGAR
SHAMSABAD ROAD
0 1 km
N

Arrival and information

Agra has no less than six **railway stations**, though visitors are only likely to use two of them. The busiest is **Agra Cantonment** ("Cantt"), in the southwest, which serves Delhi, Gwalior, Jhansi and most points south. Trains from Rajasthan pull in close to the Jama Masjid at **Agra Fort Station** (a few also stop at Agra Cantt). Agra Cantt is more convenient for the hotels around Sadar Bazaar, while Agra Fort Station is slightly closer to the Taj Ganj area; both are a fair way from the hotels along Fatehabad Road.

There's a pre-paid auto-rickshaw/taxi booth at Agra Cantonment Station (Rs50/150 to anywhere in town); drivers may collar you on your way out, trying to grab you before you reach the pre-paid booth so as to overcharge you or work some commission scam. Cycle rickshaws wait in the forecourt outside, but are slow if you're going to Fatehabad Road or Taj Ganj. As ever, cycle rickshaw and auto drivers will try to earn commission by taking you to a hotel of their choosing, and may therefore tell you (falsely) that the hotel of your choice is closed.

Buses from Rajasthan and express services from Delhi terminate at **Idgah Bus Stand** close to Agra Cantonment Station; a few services from other destinations arrive at the more chaotic **Agra Fort Bus Stand**, just west of the fort.

In addition, some buses from Delhi stop outside the fort gate, where you'll have no trouble finding a rickshaw.

One common **scam** to look out for applies to buses that stop in the suburbs, about 6km out from Idgah, for locals to get off. Rickshaw drivers (sometimes in collusion with the bus drivers) may get on and insist that your vehicle has reached the end of the line, and that you need to disembark; if there are other passengers still sitting on the bus, sit tight till you get to Idgah.

Information

Agra has two **tourist offices**, India Tourism at 191 The Mall (Mon–Fri 9am–5.30pm, Sat 9am–2pm; ☏0562/222 6368), and UP Tourism at 64 Taj Road (Mon–Sat 10am–5pm; ☏0562/222 6378); there is also an information booth (daily 8am–9pm; ☏0562/242 1204) at Cantonment Station. UP Tourism runs a whistlestop **tour** (daily except Friday) of Agra aimed mainly at day-trippers from Delhi. The tour leaves the India Tourism office at around 9.45am, and Agra Cantonment Railway station at around 10.20am, coinciding with the Taj Express from Delhi, which arrives at 10.07am. The full-day tour (Rs1700 including all entrance and guide fees) whisks you at breakneck speed around the Taj, Agra Fort and Fatehpur Sikri, ending at around 6pm in time for the Taj Express back to Delhi at 6.55pm; you can also join the tour just for the afternoon visit to Fatehpur Sikri (Rs550). Tours can be booked either through the UP Tourism or India Tourism offices.

City transport

Agra is very spread out and its sights too widely separated to explore on foot, so wherever you're staying you'll end up spending a fair amount of time in rickshaws or taxis. Getting from one part of the city to another can prove surprisingly time-consuming thanks to the sheer volume of traffic and the poorness of the roads, and crossing from one side of the Yamuna River to the other is particularly tedious, given the condition of the city centre's two massively over-used and under-maintained bridges.

Cycle rickshaws are good for short trips and provide a livelihood for some of the city's poorest inhabitants, as well as being cleaner and greener than autos, but can be unbearably slow for longer journeys. Rickshaw drivers are also the single biggest source of hassle in Agra – attempt to walk anywhere, and these persistent folk will be on your case, following you down the street. There are also some **tongas** (horse-drawn carriages) around Taj Ganj, but the sight of these skinny and near-lame horses tends to put most people off; if you do take a ride, expect to pay about the same as you would in a cycle rickshaw.

Auto-rickshaws are faster and fares, including waiting time, are very reasonable if you don't mind bargaining: sample fares from Taj Ganj are Rs30–40 to Sadar Bazaar, Rs50–60 to Agra Cantt Station, and Rs15–20 to the fort. **Taxis** are handy for longer trips to Sikandra or Fatehpur Sikri; agree a fare before you set off. There are taxi ranks at the stations, or your hotel should be able to arrange a vehicle. There's also a cheap and environmentally friendly **electric bus** (Rs5) which shuttles back and forth between the fort and the west gate of the Taj Mahal, though you could easily spend twenty or thirty minutes waiting for it to arrive.

Whichever form of transport you choose, expect to haggle hard. Agra sees so many "fresh" tourists that drivers will almost always quote significantly inflated prices to start with (the best policy, if a rickshaw driver names a silly price, is simply to walk away – they'll usually chase after you and offer a more realistic fare). Also, note that the main agenda for many rickshaw- and taxi-drivers is to get you into shops that pay them **commission**, added to your bill of course.

Many locals get around by **bicycle**, but for foreigners unused to the anarchic traffic and treacherous road surfaces, travel on two wheels can be stressful and potentially dangerous. You're better off hiring a cycle rickshaw and getting someone else to do the pedalling for you.

Note that motorized vehicles are excluded from a small area on each side of the Taj, supposedly to protect it from pollution. This makes the roads beside the Taj quite peaceful, but it may mean your taxi or auto will have to drop you short of your hotel if it's within the exclusion zone.

Accommodation

Taj Ganj, the jumble of narrow lanes immediately south of the Taj, is where most budget travellers end up in Agra. With their unrivalled rooftop views, laid-back cafés and low room rates, the little guesthouses here can be great places to stay, though some are quite basic. There are more modern and upmarket lodgings along **Fatehabad Road**, southwest of Taj Ganj, while the leafier **Cantonment** area and the adjacent **Sadar Bazaar** have places to suit every budget, as well as offering a convenient location more or less at the centre of the city.

The Taj Ganj hotels and guesthouses listed below are marked on the Taj Ganj map opposite; all other accommodation appears on the Agra map on p.274.

Taj Ganj

Amarvilas East Gate ☎0562/223 1515, ⓦwww.oberoihotels.com. Easily the loveliest (and most expensive) hotel in Agra, virtually a work of art in its own right, constructed in a serene blend of Mughal and Moorish styles around a gorgeous *charbagh*-style courtyard water garden – particularly magical by night. Most rooms have Taj views (prices start at US$780. Facilities include a large pool, idyllic terraced gardens, two smart restaurants and a very chichi bar. ❾

Host West Gate ☎0562/233 1010. It looks a bit run-down, but rooms – though small and often windowless – are clean and perfectly comfortable; most have air-coolers and all have cable TV, and there's also a fine view of the Taj from the roof. ❷–❸

Kamal Chowk Kagzi, South Gate ☎0562/233 0126, ⓔhotelkamal@hotmail.com. Right in the thick of the Taj Ganj action, with well-maintained rooms (but no hot showers in the cheapest ones) and a great view from the rooftop restaurant. ❷–❹

Raj 2/26 South Gate ☎09358 107023. Undoubtedly correct in its claim to have the best view of the Taj from its rooftop restaurant, its rooms are pretty plain, but decent enough, certainly for the price, and all have hot running water. ❷–❸

Shah Jahan Chowk Kagzi ☎0562/320 0240. Looks grotty at first glance, but the rooms are fresh, clean and good value, and even the cheapest have hot showers. There's a rooftop restaurant, and a well-equipped Internet downstairs. ❶–❸

Shanti Lodge Chowk Kagzi, South Gate ☎0562/233 1973, ⓔshantilodge2000@yahoo.co.in.

Popular backpacker lodge with superb Taj views from the rooftop restaurant, but rooms (some with a/c and Taj views) are a mixed bag: those in the old block are poky and not great value; those in the new annexe are larger and smarter. ❸–❹

Sheela East Gate ☎0562/233 1973, ⓦwww.hotelsheelaagra.com. Clean and spacious rooms ranged around a lovely little garden, with fan, air-cooled and a/c options, friendly staff and a good restaurant, but the cheapest rooms aren't such great value, with hot water in buckets only. ❸–❹

Shyam Palace West Gate ☎0562/233 1599, ⓦwww.hotelshyampalace.com. This rather dog-eared establishment has large but slightly shabby rooms plus a peaceful courtyard garden that doubles as a low-key restaurant. ❸–❹

Sidhartha West Gate ☎0562/233 0901, ⓦwww.hotelsidhartha.com. Bigger and better rooms than the other Taj Ganj budget joints, set around a restaurant in a leafy courtyard that includes fragments of Mughal-era walls, but cheapest rooms lack hot running water. ❸–❹

Taj Plaza East Gate ☎0562/223 2515, ⓦwww.hoteltajplaza.com. A slightly more upmarket alternative to the nearby Taj Ganj guesthouses, this small modern hotel has a range of clean, bright air-cooled and a/c rooms with cable TV; the more expensive ones also have good Taj views. Prices are a bit steep, though *Rough Guide* readers are promised a forty percent discount on published rates (ask when booking). ❺–❼

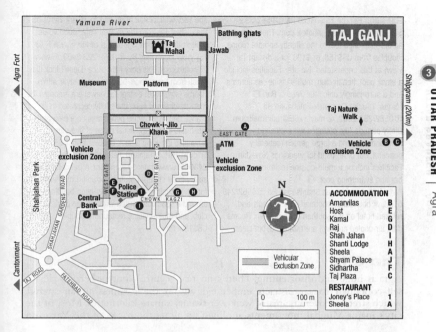

TAJ GANJ

Yamuna River

Mosque

Taj Mahal

Bathing ghats

Jawab

Museum

Platform

Agra Fort

Chowk-i-Jilo Khana

Taj Nature Walk

EAST GATE

Vehicle exclusion Zone

ATM

Vehicle exclusion Zone

A

B C

Vehicle exclusion Zone

Shilpgram (200m)

Shahjahan Park

WEST GATE

SOUTH GATE

E
F

Police Station

D

Central Bank

J

I

CHOWK KAGZI

G H

Cantonment

SHAHJAHAN GARDENS ROAD

TAJ ROAD

FATEHBAD ROAD

N

Vehicular Exclusion Zone

0   100 m

ACCOMMODATION

Amarvilas	B
Host	E
Kamal	G
Raj	D
Shah Jahan	I
Shanti Lodge	H
Sheela	A
Shyam Palace	J
Sidhartha	F
Taj Plaza	C

RESTAURANT

Joney's Place	1
Sheela	A

Cantonment and Sadar Bazaar

Clarks Shiraz 54 Taj Rd ☎0562/222 6121, ⓦwww.hotelclarksshiraz.com. Sprawling five-star in a pleasant cantonment setting with small but cosy rooms; the more expensive ones with distant Taj views. Facilities include two multi-cuisine restaurants, a bar, swimming pool, basic gym, steam bath, Jacuzzi and beauty salon. Rooms start at US$137. ❾

Hilltop 21 The Mall ☎0562/222 6836, ⓔhotelhilltopagra@yahoo.com. Very run-down but the rooms aren't too bad; all double rooms have hot running water, the cheapest are pretty poky, but the smarter ones are better value. If you're utterly strapped for cash, there are also some ultra-basic cell-like singles with shared bath for just Rs60, and you can camp for Rs100. *Rough Guide* readers are promised a twenty percent discount. ❷–❹

Sakura Near Idgah Bus Station ☎0562/242 0169, ⓦwww.hotelsakuraagra.com. Well-run and good-value guesthouse on the west side of town. Rooms (all with air-coolers) are large, bright, spacious and nicely furnished, and the helpful owner is a mine of local information. The only drawback is the rather inconvenient location: handy for bus and train stations, but a bit of a hike from everywhere else. ❷–❹

Tourists Rest House Kutchery Rd, Baluganj ☎0562/246 3961, ⓔdontworrychicken curry@hotmail.com. One of Agra's top budget options, with a range of bright, competitively priced rooms around a tranquil leafy courtyard; all have hot running water. There's also a phone booth, Internet facilities, back-up generator and free pick-up from bus or train stations with a day's notice (rickshaw drivers may try to take you to one of the commission-paying "soundalikes"). ❷–❸

Yamuna View 6-B The Mall ☎0562/246 2989, ⓦwww.hotelyamunaviewagra.com. Conveniently central but run-of-the-mill five-star. Rooms are rather plush, though showing a little wear and tear. Facilities include a pool, a bar and a couple of smart restaurants, including the snazzy *Mandarin* (see p.288). Doubles from US$116. ❾

Fatehabad Road and around

Amar Yatri Niwas Fatehabad Rd ☎0562/223 3030, ⓦwww.amaryatriniwas.com. Good-value mid-range hotel with well-maintained rooms (the cheaper ones small but still very comfortable) and a multi-cuisine restaurant. ❺–❼

Atithi Fatehabad Rd ☎0562/233 0880, ⓦwww .hotelatithiagra.com. Good-sized rooms, not plush but well turned-out, and there's a pool in a yard round the back. A bit impersonal, but the staff aim to please. ❻–❼

Mansingh Palace Fatehabad Rd ☎0562/233 1771, ⓦwww.mansinghhotels.com. There's quite an old-fashioned feel to the slightly sombre rooms (doubles from US$158, or $198 for a distant Taj view) at this understated five-star. Facilities include a small pool, health club, multi-cuisine restaurants and a surprisingly chic little *Tequila Bar*. ❾

Mayur Tourist Complex Fatehabad Rd ☎0562/233 2302, ⓔmayur268@rediffmail.com. Dinky pagoda-like cottages with attached bathrooms around a large garden (generally peaceful, but often used for weddings Nov–Jan). Facilities include a multi-cuisine restaurant, dingy bar and swimming pool. ❻

Safari Shaheed Nagar, Shamsabad Rd ☎0562/248 0106, ⓔhotelsafari@hotmail.com. Friendly and relaxed hotel on the southern side of town. Rooms (fan, air-cooled and a/c) are rather old, but clean and very well looked after, and there are views of the distant Taj from the rooftop café. Good value, though the location is a bit out of the way. ❸–❹

Taj View Fatehabad Rd ☎0562/223 2400, ⓦwww.tajhotels.com. This boxy little place doesn't look like much from the outside, but has lots of style within. Rooms (some with distant Taj views) are amongst the most attractive in Agra, cheerfully decorated in orange and white, while public areas are pleasantly plush and there's the usual range of five-star amenities including a pool. Doubles from US$198. ❾

Trident Hilton Tajnagri, Fatehabad Rd ☎0562/233 2400, ⓦwww.trident-hilton.com. A peaceful five-star, whose cheerful rooms (including two adapted for wheelchair users) are in low-lying buildings around a spacious garden with a large pool, kids' club, and multi-cuisine restaurant. Doubles start at US$186. ❾

The City

Agra is huge and disorienting. There's no real "centre", but rather a series of self-contained bazaar districts embedded within the formless urban sprawl, which stretches over an area of well over twenty square kilometres. Most of the city's major Mughal monuments are lined up along the banks of the **Yamuna**

Kabootars

Look up from any Taj Ganj roof terrace around 4pm, when the sun is low and the city's bulbous onion domes and minarets glow pale orange, and you'll see a side of local life of which few tourists are aware. Pigeons, or **kabootars**, wheel above clusters of men and boys staring skywards from their flat rooftops, shouting, whistling and waving sticks at the birds. Agra's pigeon fanciers, known as *kabootar baz*, don't race their pigeons, but fly them in flocks, controlling them with a code of high-pitched whistles and calls that are as much a feature of Muslim districts like Taj Ganj as the *muezzin*'s call to prayer. The waving of sticks is supposed to keep the lazier pigeons in the air, although a couple of sleepy specimens can usually be spotted hiding on nearby satellite dishes, waiting for their owners to scatter soaked grain for them to feed on. When this happens, the rest of the flock drops back to ground in a cloud, and pecks around the roof of their coop, or *kabootar khana*, for the grain. This five- or ten-minute cycle is then repeated for an hour or so until the pigeons have been well exercised. Four or five flocks fly above Taj Ganj each day, best watched from the area's myriad rooftop terraces and cafés.

Pigeon fancying is an established tradition in Agra, and in cities such as Old Delhi and Lucknow, where there are sizeable Muslim communities (Hindus rarely indulge in the sport). Its techniques were set down by Akbar's poet laureate, Abu'l Fazl, for the Mughal court who considered it a noble pastime, and to this day men and boys across Urdu-speaking parts of India still take their *kabootar* flying very seriously. Thoroughbred birds change hands for more than Rs5000, around six months' wages for most *kabootar baz*. Owning a large flock brings with it a certain cachet, and the coveted title of *Barra Kabootar Baz*, literally "Big Pigeon Fancier". Once a man is deemed to have mastered the plethora of tricks and subtleties of this ancient sport, he may even be known among his peers as a *Khalifa*, or "Great Master". Only *Khalifas* can direct their flocks in perfect parabolic curves, or single files across the sky, or command them to encircle a neighbour's flock and drive it to ground.

The secret symbolism of the Taj Mahal

Inextricably associated with the royal love legend of Shah Jahan and his wife Mumtaz, the **Taj Mahal** is regarded by most modern visitors as *the* symbol of eternal love. Historical research, however, suggests the world's most famous tomb complex encodes a somewhat less poetic and poignant vision – one more revealing of the Mughal emperor's megalomania and unbridled vanity than his legendary romantic disposition.

The clues to the Taj's **hidden symbolism** lie in the numerous Islamic inscriptions which play a key part in the overall design of the building. Fourteen chapters of the Koran are quoted at length here, dealing with two principal themes: the Day of Judgement, and the pleasures of Heaven. The first appears in the broad band of intricate calligraphy over the main gateway. Citing the last phrase of chapter 89, it invites the faithful to "Enter thou My Paradise". This is one of only two occasions in the Islamic scriptures when God speaks directly to man, and the quotation stresses the dual function of the Taj as both a tomb garden and replica of Heaven, complete with the four Rivers of Paradise and central Pool of Abundance.

In a dramatic break with tradition, the actual tomb is situated not in the middle of the gardens, as was customary, but at the far end of a rectangle. Recently, the theory of symbolic association has been taken a step further with the rediscovery of an enigmatic diagram contained in an **ancient Sufi text**, *The Revelations of Mecca* by renowned medieval mystic, Ibn al 'Arabi. Entitled *The Plain of Assembly on the Day of Judgement*, the diagram, which scholars know Shah Jahan's father Jahangir had a copy of in his library, corresponds exactly to the layout of the Taj Mahal complex, proving beyond doubt, they now claim, that the tomb was intended as a reproduction of God's throne. Given that the emperor's remains are enshrined within it, the inevitable conclusion is that, aside from being an extravagant romantic, Shah Jahan possessed an opinion of his own importance that knew no bounds.

River, which bounds the city's eastern edge, including the Taj Mahal. Clustered around the Taj, the tangled little streets of **Taj Ganj** are home to most of the city's cheap accommodation and backpacker cafés. A couple of kilometres to the west, on the far side of the leafy **Cantonment** area, lies **Sadar Bazaar**, linked to Taj Ganj by **Fatehabad Road**, where you'll find many of the city's smarter places to stay, as well as numerous restaurants and crafts emporia. Northwest of Taj Ganj lies **Agra Fort** and, beyond, the third of the city's main commercial districts, **Kinari Bazaar**, centred on the massive Jama Masjid.

The monuments in Agra date from the later phase of Mughal rule and the reigns of Akbar, Jahangir and Shah Jahan – exemplifying the ever-increasing extravagance which, by Shah Jahan's time, had already begun to strain the imperial coffers and sow the seeds of political and military decline.

The Taj Mahal

Described by Bengali poet Rabindranath Tagore as "a teardrop on the face of eternity", the **Taj Mahal** (daily 6am–7pm, closed Fri; Rs750 [Rs20]) is undoubtedly the zenith of Mughal architecture. Volumes have been written on its perfection, and its image adorns countless glossy brochures and guidebooks; nonetheless, the reality never fails to overwhelm all who see it, and few words can do it justice.

The magic of the monument is strangely undiminished by the crowds of tourists who visit, as small and insignificant as ants in the face of the immense mausoleum. That said, the Taj is at its most alluring in the relative quiet of early morning, shrouded in mist and bathed with a soft red glow. As its vast marble surfaces fall into shadow or reflect the sun, its colour changes, from soft grey

▲ Detail of the Taj mahal

and yellow to pearly cream and dazzling white. This play of light is an important decorative device, symbolically implying the presence of Allah, who is never represented in physical form.

Overlooking the Yamuna, the Taj Mahal stands at the northern end of a vast walled garden. Though its layout follows a distinctly Islamic theme, representing Paradise, it is above all a monument to romantic love. **Shah Jahan** built the Taj to enshrine the body of his favourite wife, Arjumand Bann Begum, better known by her official palace title, **Mumtaz Mahal** ("Chosen One of the Palace"), who died shortly after giving birth to her fourteenth child in 1631 – the number of children she bore the emperor is itself a tribute to her hold on him, given the number of other wives and concubines which the emperor would have been able to call on. The emperor was devastated by her death, and set out to create an unsurpassed monument to her memory – its name, "Taj Mahal", is simply a shortened, informal version of Mumtaz Mahal's palace title. Construction by a workforce of some 20,000 men from all over Asia commenced in 1632 and took over twenty years, not being completed until 1653. Marble was brought from Makrana, near Ajmer in Rajasthan, and semi-precious stones for decoration – onyx, amethyst, lapis lazuli, turquoise, jade, crystal, coral and mother-of-pearl – were carried to Agra from Persia, Russia, Afghanistan, Tibet, China and the Indian Ocean. Eventually, Shah Jahan's pious and intolerant son Aurangzeb seized power, and the former emperor was interned in Agra Fort, where as legend would have it he lived out his final years gazing wistfully at the Taj Mahal. When he died in January 1666, his body was carried across the river to lie alongside his beloved wife in his peerless tomb.

The complex

The south, east and west **entrances** all lead into the **Chowk-i-Jilo Khana** forecourt. The main entrance into the complex, an arched gateway topped with delicate domes and adorned with Koranic verses and inlaid floral designs, stands at the northern edge of Chowk-i-Jilo Khana, directly aligned with the Taj, but shielding it from the view of those who wait outside.

Once through the gateway, you'll see the Taj itself at the end of the huge **charbagh** (literally "four gardens"), a garden dissected into four quadrants by waterways (usually dry), evoking the Koranic description of Paradise, where rivers flow with water, milk, wine and honey. Introduced by Babur from Central Asia, *charbaghs* remained fashionable throughout the Mughal era. Unlike other Mughal mausoleums such as Akbar's (see p.287) and Humayan's (see p.124), the Taj isn't at the centre of the *charbagh*, but at the northern end, presumably to exploit its riverside setting (see box, p.279).

The Taj's **museum**, in the enclosure's western wall (in theory daily except Fri 9am–5pm, although it sometimes shuts for no apparent reason; Rs5), features exquisite miniature paintings, two marble pillars believed to have come from the fort, and portraits of Mughal rulers including Shah Jahan and Mumtaz Mahal, as well as architectural drawings of the Taj and examples of *pietra dura* stone inlay work.

Steps lead from the far end of the gardens up to the high square marble platform on which the **mausoleum** itself sits, each corner marked by a tall, tapering minaret. Visitors must remove or cover their shoes before climbing to the tomb (hence the shoe-covers which foreign visitors are given free with their entrance tickets). West of the tomb is a domed red-sandstone **mosque** and to the east a replica **jawab**, which was probably used to house visitors, though its main function was to complete the architectural symmetry of the complex (it cannot be used as a mosque since it faces away from Mecca).

The Taj itself is essentially square in shape, with pointed arches cut into its sides and topped with a huge central dome which rises for over 55m, its height accentuated by a crowning brass spire almost 17m high. On approach, the tomb looms ever larger and grander, but not until you are close do you appreciate both its sheer size and the extraordinarily fine detail of relief carving, highlighted by floral patterns of precious stones. Arabic verses praising the glory of Paradise fringe the archways, proportioned exactly so that each letter appears to be the same size when viewed from the ground.

The south face of the tomb is the main entrance to the **interior**: a high octagonal chamber whose weirdly echoing interior is flushed with pale light. A marble screen, decorated with precious stones and cut so finely that it seems almost translucent, protects the cenotaph of Mumtaz Mahal in the centre, perfectly aligned with the doorway and the distant gateway into the Chowk-i-Jilo Khana, and that of Shah Jahan crammed in next to it – the only object which breaks the perfect symmetry of the entire complex. The inlay work on the marble tombs is the finest in Agra, and no pains were spared in perfecting the inlay work – some of the petals and leaves are made of up to sixty separate stone fragments. Ninety-nine names of Allah adorn the top of Mumtaz's tomb, and set into Shah Jahan's is a pen box, the hallmark of a male ruler. These cenotaphs, in accordance with Mughal tradition, are only representations of the real coffins, which lie in the same positions in a crypt below.

Taj Mahal viewing practicalities

India's most famous monument became the centre of heated controversy in December 2000, when the Agra Municipality and Archeological Survey of

India (ASI) jointly imposed a hike in **admission charges** for foreign visitors from Rs15 to a whopping Rs960 for a day ticket; it's since been reduced to its present level of Rs750 for foreign visitors (Rs250 for the ASI, Rs500 in local tax). Further disputes followed the announcement, in January 2001, that the Taj would be **closed on Fridays** (instead of Mondays, as it had been previously) – a move strongly resisted by Agra's vociferous Muslim community, many of whom visit the Taj to pray on the Islamic day of communal prayer. The profit-boosting measures would, it was claimed, generate revenue for "essential renovation work", but in a city renowned throughout India for its corrupt politicians, little of the extra cash has been "ploughed back into the upkeep of the Taj" (or any other of the 3606 monuments on India's critical list).

Galling though the price increase is, comparatively few visitors refuse to pay it; fewer still regard the expense as money wasted once they are inside. That said foreign tourists these days rarely visit the Taj on several consecutive days. To appreciate the famous play of light on the building, you'd have to stick around from dawn until dusk (ticket valid all day, but only for one entrance). Note that you are not allowed to enter with food (and none is available inside), nor with a mobile phone or a travel guidebook (not even this one) – those can be deposited at lockers near the entrances. Foreigners are given a free bottle of water and a pair of shoe covers on entry. The Taj entrance ticket also entitles you to tax-free entry at a few other sites if used on the same day, giving you

The Taj Mahal: a monument under threat

Despite the seemingly impregnable sense of serenity and otherworldliness which clings to the Taj, in reality, India's most famous building faces serious threats from traffic and industrial **pollution**, and from the millions of tourists who visit it each year. Marble is all but impervious to the onslaught of wind and rain that erodes softer sandstone, but it has no natural defence against the sulphur dioxide that lingers in a dusty haze and shrouds the monument; sometimes the smog is so dense that the tomb cannot be seen from the fort. Sulphur dioxide mixes with atmospheric moisture and settles as sulphuric acid on the surface of the tomb, making the smooth white marble yellow and flaky, and forming a subtle fungus that experts have named "marble cancer".

The main sources of pollution are the continuous flow of vehicles along the national highways that skirt the city, and the 1700 **factories** in and around Agra – chemical effluents belched out from their chimneys are well beyond recommended safety limits. Despite laws demanding the installation of pollution-control devices, the imposition of a ban on all petrol- and diesel-fuelled traffic within 500m of the Taj Mahal, and an **exclusion zone** banning new industrial plants from an area of 10,400 square kilometres around the complex, pollutants in the atmosphere have continued to rise (many blame the diesel generators of nearby hotels), and new factories have been set up illegally.

Cleaning work on the Taj Mahal rectifies the problem to some extent, but the chemicals used will themselves eventually affect the marble – attendants already shine their torches on "repaired" sections of marble to demonstrate how they've lost their translucency. Hopes for proper care of the Taj Mahal have been raised since the government turned its attention to the plight of India's greatest monument, though it now appears the UP government have more than just the threat of pollution damage to worry about. In early 2005, they launched an investigation into claims that decreased water levels in the Yamuna have led to dangerous **tilts** in the Taj's minarets, and fears that unless something is done to restore the river to previous levels, the entire building could collapse. It would seem that for the moment, the fate of the Taj Mahal hangs in the balance.

Rs50 off the admission fee at Agra Fort, and Rs10 off at Sikandra, Itimad-ud-daulah and Fatehpur Sikri.

The Taj is particularly beautiful after dark, when the moonlight shimmers on the facade; it is open to visitors in two half-hour slots (8.30–9pm and 9–9.30pm, but not Fridays or during Ramadan) on the night of the full moon, two days preceding and two days following it. Tickets (Rs750 [Rs510]) have to be purchased a day in advance from the Archeological Survey of India office, 22 Mall Rd (Mon–Sat 10am–5pm; ☎0562/222 7261). Night visitors are not allowed to move freely around the site but are confined to a viewing platform.

The only ways to **see the Taj for free** are by climbing onto a Taj Ganj hotel rooftop or, better still, by heading across the Yamuna to **Mehtab Bagh**. From the opposite bank of the river, the view is breathtaking, especially at dawn. **Boats** ferry foot passengers across from the *ghats* just east of the Taj at first light, charging what they can get away with (anything from Rs100 to Rs1000, depending on the size of your camera). Alternatively, hire a rickshaw-wallah for the trip, or cycle there yourself. You cross the river on the road bridge north of Agra Fort, and turn right when you reach the far bank, following the metalled road until it enters the village of Katchpura; here, it becomes a rough track that eventually emerges at a small Dalit shrine on the riverside, directly opposite the Taj and next to the entrance of the Mehtab Garden (daily sunrise to sunset; Rs100 [Rs5]). You can see the Taj from the garden's floodlit walkways, and from outside the gardens on the riverbank.

Agra Fort

The high red-sandstone ramparts of **Agra Fort** (sunrise to sunset; Rs300 [Rs20], video Rs25) dominate a bend in the Yamuna River 2km northwest of the Taj Mahal. Akbar laid the foundations of this majestic citadel, built between 1565 and 1573 in the form of a half moon, on the remains of earlier Rajput fortifications. The structure developed as the seat and stronghold of the Mughal Empire for successive generations: Akbar commissioned the walls and gates, his grandson, Shah Jahan, had most of the principal buildings erected, and Aurangzeb, the last great emperor, was responsible for the ramparts.

The curved sandstone bastions reach a height of over twenty metres and stretch for around two and a half kilometres, punctuated by a sequence of massive gates, (although only the **Amar Singh Pol** is currently open to visitors). The original and grandest entrance, however, was through the western side, via the **Delhi Gate** and **Hathi Pol** or "Elephant Gate", now flanked by two red-sandstone towers faced in marble, but once guarded by colossal stone elephants with riders which were destroyed by Aurangzeb in 1668. Access to much of the fort is restricted, and only those parts open to the public are described below.

Note that there's nowhere to buy drinks inside the fort, and exploring the complex can be thirsty work, so unless you're happy to take your chances at the public drinking taps, it's a good idea to take water in with you.

Diwan-i-Am and the great courtyard

Entrance to the fort is through the **Amar Singh Pol**, actually three separate gates placed close together and at right angles to one another to disorientate any potential attackers and to deprive them of the space in which to use battering weapons against the fortifications. From here a ramp climbs gently uphill flanked by high walls (another defensive measure), through a second gate to the spacious courtyard, with tree-studded lawns, which surrounds the graceful **Diwan-i-Am** ("Hall of Public Audience"). Open on three sides, the pillared hall, which

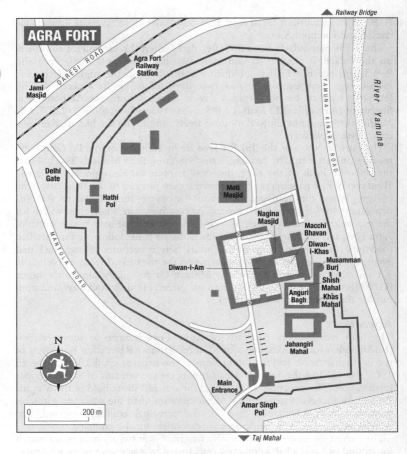

▲ Railway Bridge

AGRA FORT

▼ Taj Mahal

replaced an earlier wooden structure, was commissioned by Shah Jahan in 1628. The elegance of the setting would have been enhanced by the addition of brocade, carpets and satin canopies for audiences with the emperor.

The ornate throne alcove – built to house a gem-encrusted Peacock Throne, which was eventually moved to Delhi, only to be looted from there by Nadir Shah and finishing up in Tehran – is inlaid in marble decorated with flowers and foliage in bas-relief, and connects to the royal chambers within. In front of the alcove, the **Baithak**, a small marble table, is where ministers would have sat to deliver petitions and receive commands. This is also where trials would have been conducted, and justice speedily implemented.

The area to the north of the Diwan-i-Am courtyard is, sadly, closed to visitors, though you can make out the delicate white marble domes and chattris of the striking, if rather clumsily proportioned, **Moti Masjid** ("Pearl Mosque") rising beyond the courtyard walls, best seen from the Diwan-i-Am itself. Directly in front of the Diwan-i-Am an incongruously Gothic Christian tomb marks the **grave of John Russell Colvin**, lieutenant governor of the Northwestern Provinces, who died here during the 1857 uprising, when Agra's British population barricaded themselves inside the fort.

The royal pavilions

Heading through the small door to the left of the throne alcove in the Diwan-i-Am and climbing the stairs beyond brings you out onto the upper level of the **Macchi Bhavan** (Fish Palace), a large but relatively plain two-storey structure overlooking a spacious, grassy courtyard. This was once strewn with fountains and flowerbeds, interspersed with tanks and water channels stocked with fish on which the emperor and his courtiers would practice their angling skills, though the Maharaja of Bharatpur subsequently removed some of its marble fixtures to his palace in Deeg, and William Bentinck (governor general from 1828 to 1835) auctioned off much of the palace's original mosaics and fretwork.

On the north side of the courtyard (to the left as you enter) a small door leads to the exquisite little **Nagina Masjid** (Gem Mosque), made entirely of marble. Capped with three domes and approached from a marble-paved courtyard, it was commissioned by Shah Jahan for the ladies of the *zenana* (harem). At the rear on the right, a small balcony with beautifully carved lattice screens offers a discreet viewpoint from where ladies of the harem were able to inspect luxury goods – silks, jewellery and brocade – laid out for sale by merchants in the courtyard below, without themselves being seen.

The raised terrace on the far side of the Macchi Bhavan is adorned by two **thrones**, one black slate, the other white marble. The white one was used by Shah Jahan, the black one by the future emperor Jahangir to watch elephant fights in the eastern enclosure. It now serves, somewhat less gloriously, as a favoured perch for couples posing for photos against the backdrop of the Taj.

To your right (as you face the river), a high terrace overlooking the Yamuna is topped with a sequence of lavish royal apartments designed to catch the cool breezes blowing across the waters below. The first is the delicate **Diwan-i-Khas** (Hall of Private Audience), erected in 1635, where the emperor would have received kings, dignitaries and ambassadors, and is one of the most finely decorated buildings in the fort, with paired marble pillars and peacock arches inlaid with lapis lazuli and jasper.

A passageway behind it leads to the tiny **Mina Masjid**, a plain white marble mosque built for Shah Jahan and traditionally said to have been used by him during his imprisonment here. Beyond, the passageway leads to a two-storeyed pavilion known as the **Musamman Burj**, famous as the spot where he is said to have caught his last glimpse of the Taj Mahal before he died, and the most elaborately decorated structure in the fort. Its lattice-screen balustrade is dotted with ornamental niches and with exquisite *pietra dura* inlay covering almost every surface. In front of the tower a courtyard, paved with marble octagons, centres on a **pachisi board** where the emperor, following his father's example at Fatehpur Sikri (see p.294), played *pachisi* (a form of ludo) using dancing girls as pieces.

Past the Musamman Burj, another large courtyard, the **Anguri Bagh** (Grape Garden), is a miniature *charbagh*, its east side flanked by the marble building known as **Khas Mahal** (Private Palace), possibly a drawing room or the emperor's sleeping chamber. The palace is flanked by two so-called **Golden Pavilions**, their curved roofs covered with gilded copper tiles in a style inspired by the thatched roofs of Bengali village huts. In front of the Khas Mahal, steps descend into the northeast corner of the Anguri Bagh and the **Shish Mahal** (Glass Palace), where royal women bathed in the soft lamplight reflected from the mirror-work mosaics that covered the walls and ceiling; unfortunately the building is currently locked, so you can only peek in through the windows.

The Jahangiri Mahal

Immediately beyond the Shah Jahani Mahal lies the huge **Jahangiri Mahal** (Jahangir's Palace), although the name is misleading since it was actually built for Jahangir's father, Akbar, and probably served not as a royal palace, but as a harem. Compared to the classic Mughal designs of the surrounding buildings, this robust sandstone structure has quite a few Hindu elements mixed up with traditional Mughal and Islamic motifs.

From the central courtyard, a gateway leads out through the main gateway into the palace, whose impressive facade shows a characteristic mix of Mughal and Indian motifs, with Islamic pointed arches and inlaid mosaics combined with Hindu-style overhanging eaves supported by heavily carved brackets. Immediately in front of the palace sits **Jahangir's Hauz** (Jahangir's Cistern), a giant bowl with steps inside and out, made in 1611 from a single block of porphyry and inscribed in Persian. Filled with rosewater, it would have been used by the emperor as a bathtub, whilst it's also believed that the emperor took it with him on his travels around the empire – though it seems difficult to credit this, given the bath's size and weight.

Jama Masjid and the bazaars

Opposite the fort, and overlooking Agra Fort railway station is the city's principal mosque, the soaring red-sandstone **Jama Masjid** (Friday Mosque). Built in 1648 it was originally connected directly to the fort's principal entrance, the Delhi Gate, by a large courtyard, but the British ran a railway line between the two, leaving the mosque stranded in no-man's land on the far side of the tracks.

Standing on a high plinth above the chaotic streets of the surrounding bazaar (of which it affords fine views), the mosque is crowned by three large sandstone domes covered in distinctive zigzagging bands of marble. Five huge arches lead into the main prayer hall, topped by a prettily inlaid band of sandstone decorated in abstract floral patterns, while inside the mihrab is surrounded by delicate flourishes of Koranic script, inlaid in black, a design mirrored in the principal archway.

The space around the base of the mosque is now filled with the crowded – but refreshingly hassle-free – streets of **Kinari Bazaar**, a fascinating warren of streets crammed full with shops and stalls, though the numbers of people, scooters, cycle rickshaws and cows pushing their way through the streets make exploring it a slow and tiring business. Opposite the northeast corner of the complex, look out for the **petha-wallahs**, purveyors of Agra's most famous sweet (see p.288).

Itimad-ud-daulah

On the east bank of the Yamuna some 3km north of Agra Fort, the beautiful **Itimad-ud-daulah** (pronounced "Artma Dollar"; daily sunrise to sunset; Rs110 [Rs10]), is the tomb of Mirza Ghiyas Beg, *wazir* (chief minister) and father-in-law of Emperor Jahangir, who gave him the title of Itimad-ud-daulah, or "Pillar of the State". The tomb is popularly known among Agra's rickshaw-wallahs as the "Baby Taj", and though it's much smaller and less successfully proportioned than its more famous relative, it does foreshadow the Taj in being the first building in Mughal Agra to be faced entirely in marble, with lavish use of *pietra dura* inlay to decorate its translucent exterior walls.

As usual, the tomb sits at the centre of a *charbagh* garden, though here entered from the eastern (rather than the usual southern) side, presumably to highlight its setting against the backdrop of the Yamuna River – another element of its design which anticipates that of the Taj. The building's undersized rooftop pavilion replaces the usual dome, and has four stocky minarets stuck onto each corner. However, these imperfections seem unimportant given the superbly intricate **inlay work** which covers virtually the entire tomb – an incredible profusion of floral and geometrical patterning in muted reds, oranges, browns and greys that give it the appearance of an enormous, slightly hallucinogenic experiment in medieval op-art. Elegant inlaid designs showing characteristic Persian motifs including wine vases, trees and honeysuckles adorn the arches of the four entrances, and inside the walls are largely covered in rather eroded and clumsily restored paintings of further vases, flowers and cypresses.

Chini-ka-rauza and Rambagh

Around 1km north of Itimad-ud-daulah is the **Chini-ka-rauza**, built between 1628 and 1639 as the mausoleum of Afzal Khan, a Persian poet from Shiraz who was one of Shah Jahan's ministers. As befits his origins, Afzal Khan's tomb is of purely Persian design, the only such building in Agra.

A kilometre or so north of the Chini-ka-Rauza, amidst the dusty sprawl of northern Agra, the **Rambagh** gardens (daily sunrise to sunset; Rs100 [Rs5]) are one of the very few surviving physical remains in India from the reign of the Mughal dynasty's founder Babur, though there's little left to see here now. The gardens were originally laid out in 1526 following the Persian *charbagh* plan, which would subsequently prove the prototype for all later Mughal gardens in the Subcontinent.

Akbar's mausoleum: Sikandra

Given the Mughal tradition of magnificent tombs, it comes as no surprise that the mausoleum of the most distinguished Mughal ruler was one of the most ambitious structures of its time. **Akbar's mausoleum** (daily sunrise to sunset; Rs110 [Rs10]) borders the side of the main highway to Mathura at **SIKANDRA**, 10km northwest of Agra. Rickshaws charge at least Rs120 for the round trip, or hop on a Mathura-bound bus from Agra Fort Bus Stand.

The complex is entered via its huge **Buland Darwaza** (Great Gate), surmounted by four tapering marble minarets, and overlaid with marble and coloured tiles in repetitive geometrical patterns, bearing the Koranic inscription "These are the gardens of Eden, enter them and live forever". Through the gateway, extensive, park-like **gardens** are divided by fine raised sandstone walkways into the four equal quadrants of the typical Mughal *charbagh* design. Langur monkeys may be seen along the path, while deer roam through the tall grasses, just as they do in the Mughal miniature paintings dating from the era when the tomb was constructed, lending the whole place a magically peaceful and rural atmosphere.

The **mausoleum** itself sits in the middle of the gardens, at the centre of the *charbagh* and directly in front of Buland Darwaza. The entire structure is one of the strangest in Mughal Agra, its huge square base topped not by the usual dome but by a three-storey open-sided sandstone construction crowned with a solid-looking marble pavilion. The mishmash design may be attributable to Jahangir, who ordered changes in the mausoleum's design halfway through its construction, Akbar himself having neglected to leave finished plans for his mausoleum. By the standards of India's other Mughal buildings, it's architecturally a failure, but not without a certain whimsical charm, and much of the inlay work around the lower storey is exquisite.

A high marble gateway in the mausoleum's southern facade frames an elaborate lattice screen shielding a small vestibule painted with rich sea-blue frescoes and Koranic verses. From here a ramp leads down into a large, echoing and absolutely plain subterranean **crypt**, lit by a single skylight, in the centre of which stands Akbar's grave, decorated with the pen-box motif, the symbol of a male ruler, which can also be seen on Shah Jahan's tomb in the Taj Mahal.

Just north of Sikandra lies the altogether more modest **Mariam's tomb** (daily sunrise to sunset; Rs100 [Rs5]), the mausoleum of Akbar's wife and Jahangir's mother Mariam Zamani.

Eating

In culinary terms, Agra is famous as the home of **Mughlai cooking**. Imitated in Indian curry houses throughout the world, the city's traditional Persian-influenced cuisine is renowned for its rich cream- and curd-based sauces, accompanied by naan and tandoori breads roasted in earthen ovens, pulao rice dishes and milky sweets such as *kheer*. Mughlai specialities can be sampled in many of the town's better restaurants, the majority of which can be found in **Sadar Bazaar** and along **Fatehabad Road**. There are also innumerable scruffy little travellers' cafés around **Taj Ganj**, though standards of hygiene are often suspect and the food is generally uninspiring, with slow service the norm. Taj Ganj's saving grace is the **rooftop cafés**, many with fine Taj views, which cap most of its buildings – the best views are from the *Kamal* and *Shanti Lodge* guesthouses – though of course you can't see anything after dark, except on or around full-moon days.

Local **specialities** of Agra are *petha* (crystallized pumpkin) – the best is the Panchi brand, available at various outlets all over Agra, particularly in the row of *petha* shops in Kinari Bazaar along the northeast side of the Jami Masjid (past *Chimman Lal Poori Wale* café). Look out too for *ghazak*, a rock-hard candy with nuts, and *dalmoth*, a crunchy mix made with black lentils.

Agra's restaurants – including even apparently reputable establishments – are not immune to the epidemic of **credit-card fraud** (see p.81). It's best not to pay with credit card except in the city's five-star establishments, or, if you do, to supervise the operation carefully.

Other than *Sheela* and *Joney's Place*, which are shown on the Taj Ganj map (p.277), all the places listed below are marked on the Agra map, p.274.

Achman Agra–Delhi Highway (NH-2), Dayal Bagh, 5km out of town. Highly rated among Agra-wallahs in the know, famous for its navratan korma (a mildly spiced mix of nuts, dried fruit and *paneer*), malai kofta and chickpea masala, as well as wonderful stuffed naans. Well off the tourist trail in the north of the city, but ideally placed for dinner on your way home from Sikandra (to which it's about halfway). Mains Rs55–105.

Chiman Lal Puri Wallah Opposite northeast wall of Jami Masjid. An Agra institution for five generations, this much-loved little café-restaurant looks a touch grubby from the outside, but serves delicious *puri*-thalis, with two veg dishes and a sweet – all for Rs25. Ideal pit-stop after visiting the Jami Masjid.

Dasaprakash Meher Theatre Complex, 1 Gwalior Rd, close to the *Tourists Rest House*. Offshoot of the famous Chennai restaurant, serving a limited menu of top-notch South Indian food and an extensive ice-cream menu – the "hot fudge bonanza split" wins by a nose. Most mains Rs65–95, thalis Rs80–180.

Joney's Place Chowk Kagzi, Taj Ganj. Oldest and best of the Taj Ganj travellers' cafés, going since 1978, and open from 5am in case you need breakfast ahead of a dawn visit to the Taj. The Indian breakfast (*puris*, chickpea curry, *jalebi* and chai) is pretty good, or there's spaghetti, macaroni, veg or non-veg curries, even (on occasion) hummus and falafel. Main dishes Rs25–50.

Lakshmi Villas 50-A Sadar Bazaar. Unpretentious but deservedly popular South Indian café in the middle of Sadar Bazaar offering the usual *iddli*-*dosa-uttapam* menu, plus a couple of thalis – a good, and much cheaper, alternative to *Dasaprakash*, with most dishes at a bargain Rs30–66.

The Mandarin *Yamuna View Hotel*. One of the best non-Indian restaurants in town, this rather snazzy-looking Chinese offers a possibly welcome change from Mughlai curries and masala dosas. The large (though rather expensive) menu features a good selection of delicately prepared dishes like stir-fried vegetables in almond sauce and chicken in honey chilli, with the emphasis on light ingredients and subtle flavours. Non-veg mains Rs325–375 (prawns Rs550).

Only Corner of The Mall and Taj Rd. One of Agra's most popular north Indian restaurants, usually packed with local families and tourist groups and known for its well-prepared tandoori and Mughlai creations, though there's also a wide selection of more mainstream north Indian meat and veg standards, plus a few Chinese and Continental offerings. There's seating in an indoor a/c dining room or in the pleasant courtyard. Non-veg mains Rs110–400.

Park Restaurant Taj Rd, Sadar Bazaar. A long-established favourite with both locals and tourists, this simple a/c restaurant dishes up an excellent range of classic Mughlai chicken dishes, along with more mainstream tandooris and meat and veg curries accompanied by superb naan breads, plus a modest selection of Continental and Chinese favourites. Mains Rs70–170.

Sheela East Gate, Taj Ganj. The most dependable and pleasant place to eat near the Taj, with outside seating in the shady garden or inside the narrow café. The menu features a good choice of simple (mostly veg) Indian dishes, as well as drinks and snacks, and the fruit lassis are more of a yoghurty dessert than a drink. Mains Rs40–70.

Tourist Rest House Baluganj. Atmospheric, candle-lit garden restaurant serving a modest selection of breakfasts and Indian veg dishes to a clientele of foreign backpackers. Try the tasty malai kofta, rounded off with banana custard. All mains under Rs50.

Zorba the Buddha E-19 Shopping Arcade, Sadar Bazaar. Aimed unashamedly at foreign tourists, though you'll find Indian people eating here too, this prettily decorated little place promises no chilli unless you ask for it, and offers, along with Indian veg dishes, odd specialities such as a Hawaiian spree (vegetables and pineapple in pineapple sauce) or a fiesta (vegetables in tomato and cashew sauce), but tasty and well presented, at Rs90–150 a throw. Closed June.

Shopping

Agra is renowned for its **marble** tabletops, vases and trays, inlaid with semi-precious stones in ornate floral designs, in imitation of those found in the Taj Mahal. It is also an excellent place to buy **leather**: Agra's shoe industry supplies all India, and its tanneries export bags, briefcases and jackets. **Carpets** and **dhurries** are manufactured here too, and traditional embroidery continues to thrive. *Zari* and *zardozi* are brightly coloured, the latter building up three-dimensional patterns with fantastic motifs; *chikan* uses more delicate overlay techniques.

There are several large emporiums such as the official-sounding Cottage Industries Exposition on the Fatehabad Road, which is well presented but outrageously expensive; it is one of the places you're likely to be taken to by a commission-seeking driver. Shops in the big hotels may be pricey, but their quality and service are usually more reliable. State emporiums round the Taj include UP's Gangotri, which has fixed prices. Close to the East Gate, Shilpgram is an extensive crafts village with arts and handicrafts from all over India, and occasional live music and dance performances.

Shopping or browsing around The Mall, MG Road, Munro Road, Kinari Bazaar, Sadar Bazaar and the Taj Complex is fun, but you need to know what you're buying and be prepared to haggle; you should also be wary of ordering anything to be sent overseas. It's advisable never to let your credit card out of your sight, even for the transaction to be authorized, and you should make sure that all documentation is filled in correctly and fully so as not to allow unauthorized later additions. A large number of serious cases of **credit-card fraud** have been reported in Agra, even in some of the most popular tourist restaurants. A list of stores against whom complaints have been lodged is maintained by the local police department.

Listings

Airlines Indian Airlines, *Hotel Clarks Shiraz* ☏0562/222 6821; Jet, *Hotel Clarks Shiraz* ☏0562/222 6527.

Banks and exchange There are two ATMs in Cantonment train station, and a few dotted around the city (marked on the maps on p.274 & p.277). The State Bank of India is just south of Taj Rd in the Cantonment (Amex traveller's cheques not accepted); Allahabad Bank is in the *Hotel Clarks Shiraz*. There are several private exchange offices in Taj Ganj, or in the Tourist

A scam to make you sick

Agra has long been renowned for its con-merchants, but in the late 1990s some dodgy operators in Taj Ganj came up with a scam so cynical it makes phoney policemen and fake gemstone peddlers look pedestrian. Typically, shortly after a meal at a Taj Ganj café, the victim, a tourist, would suddenly fall ill. As luck would have it, the rickshaw-wallah taking them back to their hotel, or some other seemingly sympathetic person such as the hotel manager, would happen to know a good doctor nearby, who would make a prompt diagnosis, check the victim into a private "clinic" and prescribe some pills, while contacting the medical insurers and claiming a huge sum of money for daily health-care costs. What the victim wouldn't know is that the pills were the reason why, days later, they were still ill, and the "doctor" had all along been in cahoots with the rickshaw driver, the hotelier and the restaurant.

In November 1998, dozens of "clinics" were raided and their records scrutinized after a young British couple who'd been poisoned went to the Agra press with their experience. The story was soon picked up by the national dailies in Delhi and an investigation began, leading to the arrests of several doctors and co-conspirators, but no one was convicted. No further incidents have since been reported, but it's still a good idea to be wary of Taj Ganj restaurants (though the ones listed in our "Eating" reviews should be all right). If you do get sick, go to a reputable hospital (such as those listed below), not a backstreet clinic.

Complex Area around *Amar Yatri Niwas* and *Mansingh Palace* hotels (LKP Forex, opposite the *Amar Hotel* on the Fatehabad Rd, are reliable and fast).

Hospitals Clean and dependable, with English-speaking doctors: Essar, Namner Cross Roads ☎0562/226 5587; GG Nursing Home, 106/2 Sanjay Place ☎0562/285 3952; Pushpanjali, Delhi Gate ☎0562/252 7566 to 8.

Internet access There's plenty of Internet access available around town, particularly in Taj Ganj; rates virtually everywhere are Rs30–40 per hour. Many hotels and guesthouses have their own Internet connections too (the *Tourists Rest House* and *Shah Jahan* for example).

Photography A number of places around Taj Ganj can download and burn digital images to disc or make prints – try Moonlight Studio on the corner of West Gate and Chowk Kagzi.

Police There are police stations on Chowk Kagzi in Taj Ganj (☎0562/233 1015) and on Mahatma Ghandi Road in Sadar Bazaar, slightly south of the intersection with Fatehpur Sikri Rd (☎0562/222 6561).

Post The Head Post Office is on The Mall, near India Tourism, though the poste restante service has a very poor reputation.

Swimming The pools at most of Agra's hotels are usually reserved for the use of hotel guests only, though a few places admit outsiders on payment of a fee. These currently include the *Amar* (near *Amar Yatri Niwas*; Rs250), *Mansingh Palace* (Rs400), *Yamuna View* (Rs350), *Mughal Sheraton* (Rs450) and *Clarks Shiraz* (Rs500).

Moving on from Agra

For a rundown of frequencies and journey times, see "Travel details", p.339. Kheria airport, 7km out of town, is not currently used for passenger flights, but has been in the past and may again be in the future.

By train

Train tickets, especially to the capital, should be booked well in advance at either Agra Cantonment or Agra Fort stations, which both have fully computerized booking offices with separate tourist counters. Trains for Delhi leave from Cantonment Station, the fastest, most comfortable and most expensive being the Shatabdi Express #2001 (8.30pm except Friday; 2hr); in the other direction, as #2002 (8am except Friday), it travels to **Gwalior** (1hr 15min) and on to **Jhansi** (2hr 30min), where you can catch a bus to **Khajuraho**. A convenient but relatively slow early-morning service to New Delhi is the Intercity

Express #4211 (6am; 4hr); the fastest midday train is the Kerala Express #2625 (10.03am; 3hr 18min). Jaipur trains from Agra Fort include the 6.20pm #2988 Jaipur Intercity (arrives 10.20pm); the 6.15am #4863 Marudhar Express (arrives 11.30am) runs only on Monday, Wednesday, Friday and Saturday. The best service to Jodhpur is the daily #2307 Howrah–Jodhpur Express at 7.35pm, which arrives at 7.20am next morning. For **Kolkata**, the Jodhpur–Howrah Express #2308 (6.45am from Agra Fort; 21hr 15min) is the fastest. There is currently no daily train to **Lucknow**, the most convenient service being the four-times-weekly #9037 Avadh Express (leaves Agra Fort Monday, Wednesday, Thursday and Saturday 10pm; arrives 6.25am). The best train for **Varanasi** is the nightly #4854 Marudhar Express (9.15pm from Agra Fort, arriving 9.30am). For **Goa**, the #2780 Goa Express leaves Agra Cantonment at 5.50pm, pulling in at Vasco 37hr 40min later; the two night departures for **Chennai** (the #2616 GT Express at 9.50pm and the #2622 Tamil Nadu Express at 1.10am) are faster, the #2622 taking only 30hr.

By bus

Travelling by **bus** along the main highways, especially to the capital on the Grand Trunk road and to Jaipur on NH-11, is considerably more hair-raising than travelling the same routes by train. Accidents, most of them head-on collisions with other buses or trucks, are disconcertingly frequent.

Agra has two bus stands: **Idgah Bus Stand**, near Cantonment station in the southwest of town, has services to Fatehpur Sikri, Delhi, Jhansi, Madhya Pradesh and Rajasthan. For Rajasthani destinations beyond Jaipur, take a bus to Jaipur (via Bharatpur) and pick up a connecting service (an exception is Ajmer, which has a direct service). Deluxe and a/c services for Jaipur leave from the forecourt of *Hotel Shakpura*, next to the bus stand. The 12hr ride to Khajuraho (leaving at 5am) is a bit gruelling – it's better to take a train to Jhansi (3hr) and pick up a bus there (5hr).

Chaotic **Agra Fort Bus Stand** has services to UP destinations such as Lucknow and Varanasi, as well as to Mathura, Haridwar, Rishikesh and Dehra Dun.

Hotels and travel agents can book seats on **private buses** to Delhi, Gwalior, Khajuraho, Lucknow and Nainital.

Fatehpur Sikri

The ghost city of **FATEHPUR SIKRI**, former imperial capital of the great Mughal emperor **Akbar**, straddles the crest of a rocky ridge 40km southwest of Agra. The city built here between 1569 and 1585 as a result of the emperor's enthusiasm for the local Muslim divine **Sheikh Salim Chishti** (see p.295), though the move away from Agra may also have had something to do with Akbar's weariness of the crowds and his desire to create a new capital that was an appropriate symbol of imperial power. The fusion of Hindu and Muslim traditions in its architecture says a lot about the religious and cultural tolerance of Akbar's reign.

Fatehpur Sikri's period of pre-eminence amongst the cities of the Mughal Empire was brief, however, and after 1585 it would never again serve as the seat of the Mughal emperor. The reasons for the **city's abandonment** remain enigmatic. The theory that the city's water supply proved incapable of sustaining its population is no longer widely accepted – even after the city had been deserted, the nearby lake to its northwest still measured over 20km in circumference and yielded good water. A more likely explanation is that the city was simply the victim of the vagaries of the empire's day-to-day military contingencies. Shortly after the new capital was established, the empire was threatened by troubles in the Punjab, and Akbar moved to the more strategically situated Lahore to deal with them. These military preoccupations kept Akbar at Lahore for over a decade, and at the end of this period he decided, apparently for no particular reason, to return to Agra rather than Fatehpur Sikri.

The Royal Palace

Shunning the Hindu tradition of aligning towns with the cardinal points, Akbar chose to construct his new capital following the natural features of the terrain, which is why the principal thoroughfare, town walls, and many of the most important buildings face southwest or northeast. The mosque and most private apartments do not follow the main axis, but face west towards Mecca, according to Muslim tradition, with the palace crowning the highest point on the ridge.

There are two **entrances** to the **Royal Palace** and court complex (daily sunrise to sunset; Rs260 [Rs20], video Rs25). Independent travellers will most likely use the one on the west side, by Jodhbai's Palace; organized tours tend to use that on the east, by the Diwan-i-Am. Official **guides** offer their services at the booking office for Rs50–100. Note that there's nowhere to buy drinks in the palace, so take water in with you; you're not allowed to eat inside.

Diwan-i-Am

A logical place to begin a tour of the palace complex is the **Diwan-i-Am**, where important festivals were held, and where citizens could exercise their right to petition the emperor. Unlike the ornate pillared Diwan-i-Am buildings at the forts in Agra and Delhi, it is basically just a large courtyard, surrounded by a continuous colonnaded walkway with Hindu-style square columns and capitals, and broken only by the small pavilion, flanked by elaborately carved *jali* screens, in which the emperor himself would have sat – the position of the royal platform forced the emperor's subjects to approach him from the side in an attitude of humility.

The Diwan-i-Khas courtyard

A doorway in the northwest corner of the Diwan-i-Am leads to the centre of the *mardana* (men's quarters), a large, irregularly shaped enclosure dotted with a strikingly eclectic range of buildings. At the far (northern) end of the enclosure stands the tall **Diwan-i-Khas** (*Hall of Private Audience*), topped with four chattris and embellished with the heavily carved Hindu-style brackets, large overhanging eaves and corbelled arches which are typical of the architecture of Fatehpur Sikri.

The interior of the building consists of a single high hall (despite the appearance outside of a two-storey building) centred on an elaborately corbelled column known as the **Throne Pillar**, supporting a large circular platform from which four balustraded bridges radiate outwards. Seated upon this throne, the emperor held discussions with representatives of diverse religions, aiming to synthesize India's religions into one. The pillar symbolizes this project by incorporating motifs drawn from Hinduism, Buddhism, Islam and Christianity.

Next to the Diwan-i-Khas lies the three-roomed **Treasury**, its brackets embellished by mythical sea creatures, guardians of the treasures of the deep; it's also known as Ankh Michauli, after the game (hide and seek) of the same name, which it's said used to be played here – in fact both names are probably just fanciful inventions, and the building most likely served as a multi-purpose pavilion which could be used for a variety of functions, as could most buildings in Mughal palaces. Attached to it is the so-called **Astrologer's Seat**, a small pavilion adorned with elaborate Jain carvings.

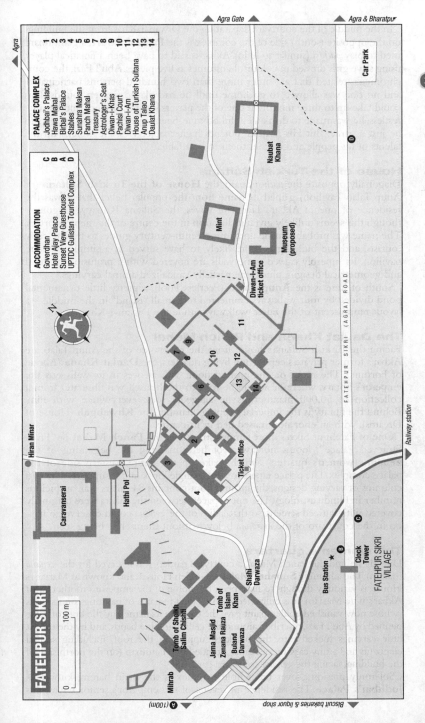

FATEHPUR SIKRI

0 ─────── 100 m

ACCOMMODATION

Goverdhan	C
Hotel Ajay Palace	B
Sunset View Guesthouse	A
UPTDC Gulistan Tourist Complex	D

PALACE COMPLEX

Jodhbai's Palace	1
Hawa Mahal	2
Birbal's Palace	3
Stables	4
Sunahra Makan	5
Panch Mahal	6
Astrologer's Seat	7
Diwan-i-Khas	8
Pachisi Court	9
Diwan-i-Am	10
House of Turkish Sultana	11
Anup Talao	12
Daulat Khana	13
	14

Agra

Agra Gate

Agra & Bharatpur

Car Park

Naubat Khana

Mint

Museum (proposed)

Diwan-i-Am ticket office

FATEHPUR SIKRI (AGRA) ROAD

Railway station

Hiran Minar

Caravanserai

Hathi Pol

Ticket Office

Mihrab

Tomb of Sheikh Salim Chishti

Jama Masjid
Zenana Rauza
Buland Darwaza

Tomb of Islam Khan

Shahi Darwaza

Bus Station

Clock Tower

FATEHPUR SIKRI VILLAGE

Biscuit bakeries & liquor shop

(100m)

In the middle of the courtyard, separating the Diwan-i-Khas from the buildings on the opposite (south) side of the complex is the **Pachisi Court**, a giant board used to play *pachisi* (similar to ludo). Akbar is said to have been a fanatical player, using slave girls dressed in colourful costumes as live pieces. Abu'l Fazl, the court chronicler, related that at "times more than two hundred persons participated, and no one was allowed to go home until he had played sixteen rounds. This could take up to three months. If one of the players lost his patience and became restless, he was made to drink a cupful of wine. Seen superficially, this appears to be just a game. But His Majesty pursues higher objectives. He weighs up the talents of his people and teaches them to be affable."

House of the Turkish Sultana

Diagonally opposite the *pachisi* board, the **House of the Turkish Sultana** (or Anup Talao Pavilion) gained its name from the popular belief that it was the residence of one of Akbar's favourite wives, the Sultana Ruqayya Begum – though this seems unlikely given its location in the centre of the men's quarters. The name was probably made up by nineteenth-century guides to titillate early tourists, and the building is more likely to have served as a simple pleasure pavilion. Its superbly carved stone walls are covered with a profusion of floral and geometrical designs, plus some partially vandalized animal carvings.

South of here is the **Anup Talao** (Peerless Pool), a pretty little ornamental pond divided by four walkways connected to a small "island" in the middle – a layout reminiscent of the raised walkways inside the Diwan-i-Khas.

The Daulat Khana and Panch Mahal

Facing the Turkish Sultana's house from the other side of the Anup Talao are Akbar's former private sleeping and living quarters, the **Daulat Khana** (Abode of Fortune). The room on the ground floor with alcoves in its walls was the emperor's library, where he would be read to (he himself was illiterate) from a collection of 50,000 manuscripts he allegedly took everywhere with him. Behind the library is the imperial sleeping chamber, the **Khwabgah** (House of Dreams), with an enormous raised bed in its centre.

One of Fatehpur Sikri's most famous structures, the **Panch Mahal** or "Five-Storeyed Palace", looms northwest of here, marking the beginning of the **zenana** (women's quarters) which make up the entire western side of the palace complex. The palace tapers to a final single kiosk and is supported by 176 columns of varying designs; the ground floor contains 84 pillars – an auspicious number in Hindu astrology. The open spaces between the pillars were originally covered with latticed screens, so that ladies of the *zenana* could observe goings-on in the courtyard of the *mardana* below without themselves being seen.

The women's quarters

Directly behind the Panch Mahal, a courtyard garden was reserved for the *zenana* (harem). The adjoining **Sunahra Makan** (Golden House), also known as Mariam's House, is variously thought to have been the home of the emperor's mother or of Akbar's wife Mariam. It is enlivened by the faded remains of paintings on its walls (whose now vanished golden paint gave the pavilion its name), by the lines of verse penned by Abu'l Fazl, inscribed around the ceiling in blue bands, and by the quaint little carvings tucked into the brackets supporting the roof, including several elephants and a tiny carving of Rama attended by Hanuman (on the north side of the building, facing the *zenana* courtyard garden).

Solemnly presiding over the whole complex is the main harem, known as **Jodhbai's Palace**. The residence of several of the emperor's senior wives, this striking building is perhaps the grandest and largest in the entire city, and looks decidedly Hindu even in the eclectic context of Fatehpur Sikri, having been modelled after Rajput palaces such as those at Gwalior and Orchha.

On the north side of the palace, the **Hawa Mahal** (Palace of the Winds), a small screened tower with a delicately carved chamber, was designed to catch the evening breeze, while a raised covered walkway, lined with five large chattris, leads from here to a (now vanished) lake.

Northwest of Jodhbai's Palace lies a third women's palace, known as **Birbal's Palace** – though this is another misnomer, as Birbal, Akbar's favourite courtier, was a man and would have been most unwelcome in the middle of the *zenana*. It's more likely to have been the residence of two of Akbar's senior wives.

Jama Masjid

At the southwestern corner of the palace complex, with the village of Fatehpur Sikri nestling at its base, stands the **Jama Masjid** (daily dawn to dusk) or Dargah Mosque, one of the finest in the whole of India. Unfortunately, the mosque is rife with self-appointed "guides" (around Rs20 for a tour) who make it all but impossible to enjoy the place in peace. The mosque was apparently completed in 1571, before work on the palace commenced, showing the religious significance which Akbar accorded the entire site. This was due to its connections with the Sufi saint Sheikh Salim Chishti, who is buried here, and who played a crucial role in the founding of Fatehpur Sikri by prophesying the birth of a son to the emperor: when one of Akbar's wives Rani Jodhabai, a Hindu Rajput princess from Amber, became pregnant she was sent here until the birth of her son Salim, who later became the emperor Jahangir. Fatehpur Sikri was constructed in the saint's honour.

The neck-cricking **Buland Darwaza** (Great Gate), a spectacular entrance scaled by an impressive flight of steps, was added around 1576 to commemorate Akbar's military campaign in Gujarat. Flanked by domed kiosks, the archway of the simple sandstone memorial is inscribed with a message from the Koran: "Said Jesus Son of Mary (peace be on him): The world is but a bridge – pass over without building houses on it. He who hopes for an hour hopes for eternity; the world is an hour – spend it in prayer for the rest is unseen." The numerous horseshoes nailed to the doors here date from the beginning of the twentieth century – an odd instance of British folk superstition in this very Islamic place.

The gate leads into a vast cloistered courtyard, far larger than any previous mosque in India. The **prayer hall**, on the west (left) side, is the focus of the mosque, punctuated by an enormous gateway. More eye-catching is the exquisite **Tomb of Sheikh Salim Chishti**, directly ahead as you enter the courtyard. Much of this was originally crafted in red sandstone and only later faced with marble: the beautiful lattice screens – another design feature probably imported from Gujarat, though it would later become a staple of Mughal architecture – are unusually intricate, with striking serpentine exterior brackets supporting the eaves.

Practicalities

Buses to the palace leave from the bus station in the centre of the village, but can be flagged down at the bypass junction a few hundred metres beyond Agra Gate (about Rs10 by tonga from the village), which is the best place to pick up buses to Bharatpur or Jaipur, including vehicles coming through from Agra. If you're in a rush, you can hire a Jeep at the bus stand to Agra for around

Akbar's harem

Although remembered primarily for his liberal approach to religion, Akbar was typically Mughal in his attitudes to women, whom he collected in much the same way as a philatelist amasses stamps. At its height of splendour, the **royal harem** at Fatehpur Sikri held around five thousand women, guarded by a legion of eunuchs. Its doors were closed to outsiders, but rumours permeated the sandstone walls and several notable travellers were smuggled inside the Great Mughals' seraglios, leaving for posterity often lurid accounts of the emperors' private lives.

The size of Akbar's harem grew in direct proportion to his empire. With each new conquest, he would be gifted by the defeated rulers and nobles their most beautiful daughters, who, together with their maidservants, would be installed in the luxurious royal **zenana**. In all, the emperor is thought to have kept three hundred wives; their ranks were swollen by a constant flow of concubines (*kaniz*), dancing girls (*kanchni*) and female slaves (*bandis*), or "silver bodied damsels with musky tresses" as one chronicler described them, purchased from markets across Asia. Screened from public view by ornately pierced stone *jali* windows were women from the four corners of the Mughal empire, as well as Afghanis, Turks, Iranis, Arabs, Tibetans, Russians and Abyssinians, and even one Portuguese, sent as presents or tribute.

The **eunuchs** who presided over them came from similarly diverse backgrounds. While some were hermaphrodites, others had been forcibly castrated, either as punishment following defeat on the battlefield, or after having been donated by their fathers as payment of backdated revenue – an all too common custom at the time.

Akbar is said to have consumed prodigious quantities of Persian wine, *araq* (a spirit distilled from sugar cane), bhang and opium. The lavish dance recitals held in the harem, as well as sexual liaisons conducted on the top pavilion of the Panch Mahal and in the *zenana* itself, would have been fuelled by these substances. Over time, Akbar's hedonistic ways incurred the disapproval of his highest clerics – the *Ulema*. The Koran expressly limits the number of wives a man may take to four, but one verse also admits a lower form of marriage, known as *muta*, which was more like an informal pact, and could be entered into with non-Muslims. Akbar's abuse of this long-lapsed law was heavily criticized by his Sunni head priest during their religious disquisitions.

What life must actually have been like for the women who lived in Akbar's harem one can only imagine, but it is known that alcoholism and drug addiction were widespread, and that some also risked their lives to conduct illicit affairs with male lovers, smuggled in disguised as physicians or under heavy Muslim veils. If the reports of a couple of foreign adventurers who secretly gained access to Jahangir's seraglio are to be believed, the eunuchs were also required to intercept anything (other than the emperor) that might excite the women's passion.

In fact, the notion that the harem was a gilded prison whose inmates whiled their lifetimes away in idle vanity and dalliance is something of a myth. Many of the women in the *zenana* were immensely rich in their own right, and wielded enormous influence on the court. Jahangir's wife, Nur Jahan, virtually ran the empire from behind the screen of purdah during the last five years of her husband's ailing reign, while her mother-in-law owned a ship that traded between Surat and the Red Sea, a tradition continued by Shah Jahan's daughter, who grew immensely wealthy through her business enterprises.

Partly as a result of the money and power at the women's disposal, jealousies in the harem were also rife, and the work of maintaining order and calm among the thousands of foster mothers, aunties, the emperor's relatives and all his wives, minor wives, paramours, musicians, dancers, amazons and slaves, was a major preoccupation. As Akbar's court chronicler wryly observed, "The government of the kingdom is but an amusement compared with such a task, for it is within the (harem) that intrigue is enthroned."

Rs400–500. **Tongas** (horse-drawn carriages) are the staple means of transport around the village (there are no rickshaws at present), expect to pay about the same as you normally would for a cycle rickshaw. There are no useful **trains**, but the station has a usually queue-free booking office.

Of the **hotels**, the *Goverdhan* on Buland Gate Road, just east of the bus stand (℡05613/282643, Ⓦwww.hotelfatehpursikriviews.com; ❷) has a range of old but spacious and well-maintained fan, air-cooled and a/c rooms arranged around a neat lawn, as well as good food (meals are made with filtered or mineral water, Fatehpur Sikri's ground water being rather salty). The *Ajay Palace* in the village (℡05613/282950; ❷) is slightly more basic, with simple and rather small rooms, but very clean (though hot water comes in buckets), plus a nice little rooftop. The *Sunset View*, 100m west of the Jama Masjid (℡0123 84416; ❶–❸), has neat, clean rooms, including some extremely cheap (Rs75) non-attached ones, and superb views over the mosque and the countryside beyond. If none of these are posh enough, you'll want the *Gulistan Tourist Complex*, 1km out of town on the Agra Road (℡05613/282490; ❸–❹), a low-rise, modern building in red sandstone that looks rather like an academic institution, with decent but functional rooms, a restaurant, pool room and small bar.

You'll probably eat where you stay. If you want to go out, try the *Goverdhan* or the *Ajay Palace* hotel. Fatehpur Sikri's delicious **biscuits** are not to be missed – you can savour them hot out of the oven each evening at the bakeries on the lane leading up from the bazaar to the Jami Masjid.

Braj: Mathura, Vrindavan and around

The holy land of **BRAJ**, in the southwestern corner of the Gangetic valley, is the mythological land where **Krishna** – Vishnu's eighth earthly incarnation and a major character in the Mahabarata epic (see p.1360) – spent his idyllic childhood. Early texts on Braj mention only his birthplace **Mathura**, the forest tract of **Vrindavan**, the hill of **Govardhan**, and the **Yamuna River**. However, in the sixteenth century, Krishna devotees "rediscovered" the geographical features and boundaries of the holy area and identified it with his legendary pastoral playground.

Braj became, and remains, one of the most important pilgrimage centres for devotees of Krishna, who tour on foot twelve forests where he is supposed to have played, though they are now reduced to groves on the outskirts of towns and villages. This great circular pilgrimage, known as the **Ban Yatra** (forest pilgrimage), or the **Chaurasi Kos Parikrama** (which refers to the circumambulatory distance of 84 *kos*, equivalent to 224km), can take several weeks. Less energetic or devout visitors may prefer to explore the major sites by bus.

Mathura

The sprawling city of **MATHURA**, 141km south of Delhi and 58km northwest of Agra, is celebrated as the place where Krishna was born, on the banks of the Yamuna River that features so prominently in tales of his boyhood. Hindu mythology claims that it was founded by Shatrugna, the youngest brother of Ramayana hero and earlier Vishnu avatar Rama, while Mathura's earliest historical records date back around 2500 years. Buddha himself founded monasteries here, in what was known to the Greeks, after Alexander the Great's conquests, as Madoura ton Theon (Mathura of the Gods). The city reached an early peak under the Indo-Bactrian Kushan people, whose greatest ruler Kanishka came to power in 78 AD. Fa Hian, the Chinese pilgrim, reported that in 400 AD it held twenty Buddhist monasteries with about three thousand resident monks. The enduring prosperity and sophistication of Mathura, which lay on a busy trade route, attracted such adventurers as the Afghan Mahmud of Ghazni in 1017, whose plundering and destruction signalled the death knell of Buddhism. Sikandar Lodi from Delhi wrought further havoc in 1500, as did Aurangzeb. In recent years, Mathura has expanded rapidly, incorporating the teeming old city with its many Krishna-associated sites, a vast British military cantonment known as the **Civil Lines** to the south, and haphazard industrial development on the outskirts.

The Town

The sandstone **Holi Gate** at the entrance to the old city is Mathura's major landmark, surrounded by similarly decorative temples boasting Mughal cusped arches and intricate carvings of flowers and deities. To the east, the riverfront, with temples crowding the *ghats*, is minute compared with Varanasi. Flanking each temple are shops selling Krishna dolls, outfits to dress them in, and other devotional paraphernalia. North along the river, little is left of **Kans Qila**, a fort commissioned by Raja Man Singh of Jaipur and rebuilt under Akbar.

To the south, the brightly coloured **Vishram Ghat** is the "*ghat* of rest", where Krishna is said to have recuperated after killing his evil uncle Kamsa. You must remove your shoes before entering the temple complex or visiting the *ghats*, no matter how muddy they are. **Boats** for river excursions (Rs100 per boat) can be rented here.

Heading through the network of lanes from Vishram Ghat you come to Radha Dhiraj Bazaar and Mathura's most popular shrine, the large and ostentatious **Dwarkadhish Temple**, dating from 1815. A little way north on a plinth raised above street level, the **Jama Masjid**, completed in 1661, has long since lost its original glazed tiles, but still has its four minarets and assorted outer pavilions. Around 500m west stands the impressive red-sandstone **Katra Masjid**, a mosque erected on the foundations of the once-famous Kesava Deo temple – destroyed by Aurangzeb – which had itself been built on the ruins of a Buddhist monastery. Some traces of the Hindu temple can be seen around the back, where the **Shri Krishna Janmasthan** or Janmabhoomi complex (daily 3am–8pm) now stands. Directly behind the mosque, approached through a corridor, a shrine marks Krishna's exact birthplace (*janmasthan*); its cage-like surround signifies that he was born in captivity, when his parents were prisoners of the tyrant King Kamsa. Inside the adjacent **Bhagwat Bhawan** – a flamboyantly modern, towering hulk also known as **Gita Mandir** – a garishly painted ceiling depicts scenes from Krishna's life. No cameras are allowed into the complex, where, although the shops and shrines combine to produce a park-like atmosphere, nothing obscures the heavy paramilitary presence – a reminder of underlying Hindu–Muslim tensions. Nearby, the impressive stepped sandstone tank of **Potara Kund** is believed to have been used to wash Krishna's baby clothes.

Close to the centre of Mathura in Dampier Park, the **Archeological Museum** (Tues–Sat 10.30am–4.30pm; Rs25 [Rs5]) places a particular emphasis on Buddhist and Jain sculpture dating from the Kushan (first to third centuries AD) and Gupta periods (fourth to sixth centuries). Known collectively as the **Mathura School**, it is characterized by its spotted red sandstone and reflects the assimilation of early primitive cults within the successive Jain, Buddhist and Hindu pantheons. The museum's highlight, one of the finest examples of Gupta art, is a miraculously intact standing Buddha with a beautifully benign expression, an ornate halo and delicate fluted robes, making the *Abhaya mudra* (fearless) hand gesture. Both this and a seated Buddha, also in the museum, are thought

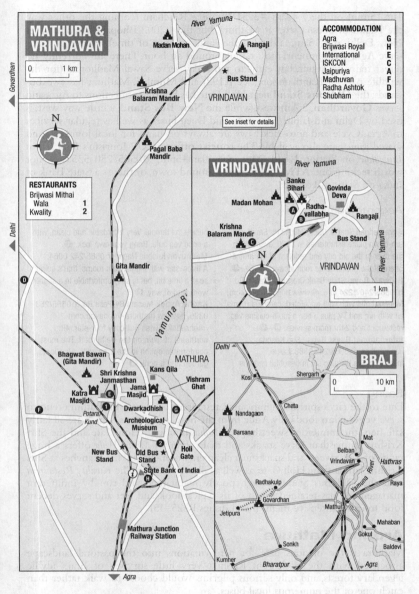

MATHURA & VRINDAVAN

0   1 km

River Yamuna

Madan Mohan

Rangaji

★ Bus Stand

Krishna
Balaram Mandir

VRINDAVAN

See inset for details

ACCOMMODATION

Agra	G
Brijwasi Royal	H
International	E
ISKCON	C
Jaipuriya	A
Madhuvan	F
Radha Ashtok	D
Shubham	B

N

◄ Govardhan

◄ Delhi

Pagal Baba
Mandir

RESTAURANTS

Brijwasi Mithai Wala	1
Kwality	2

VRINDAVAN

River Yamuna

Banke
Bihari

Govinda
Deva

Madan Mohan

Ⓐ Radha-
  vallabha

Ⓑ   Rangaji

Krishna
Balaram Mandir

Ⓒ

★ Bus Stand

N

VRINDAVAN

0   1 km

Gita Mandir

Yamuna R

Ⓓ

Yamuna Riv

Bhagwat Bawan
(Gita Mandir)

Shri Krishna
Janmasthan

Kans Qila

Katra
Masjid   Ⓔ

Jama
Masjid

Vishram
Ghat

Delhi

BRAJ

0   10 km

Ⓕ

Potara
Kund

⓵

Dwarkadhish   Ⓖ

Archeological
Museum

MATHURA

Kosi

Shergarh

Nandagaon

Chata

Barsana

Mat

New Bus
Stand

Old Bus
Stand ★

⓶

Holi
Gate

Belban

State Bank of India

Ⓗ

Radhakulp

Vrindavan

Hathras

Raya

Mathura Junction
Railway Station

Jetipura

Govardhan

Mahaban

Gokul

▼ *Agra*

Kumher

Sonkh

Bharatpur

Baldevi

Yamuna River

Mathura

Agra

UTTAR PRADESH | Braj: Mathura, Vrindavan and around

to have been created by a monk named Dinna around 434 AD. Kushana art on display includes a headless image of King Kanishka in a central Asian tunic and boots, and some exquisite railings carved with floral motifs and human figures.

Practicalities

The city's principal **railway station**, Mathura Junction, 4km south of the centre, is on the main Delhi–Agra line. You can get to New Delhi (journey time

299

1hr 15min) on the 7.47am #2951 Mumbai Rajdhani (coming the other way, the Rajdhani doesn't stop at Mathura, but the #2002 Bhopal Shatabdi leaves New Delhi at 6.15am, and takes the same amount of time). Plenty of trains serve Agra Cantonment, most taking around an hour. There are currently no direct trains to Jaipur, but eight to ten a day serve Sawai Madhopur (for the wildlife park of Ranthambore; see p.192) and Mumbai. Mathura has two bus stands; the **Old Bus Stand** near Holi Gate has hourly connections to Agra and serves **Govardhan**, 25km west, while the **New Bus Stand**, a little way west, is used by Delhi and Jaipur, Bharatpur and Deeg buses as well as regular services to Agra. Cycle and auto-rickshaws are always on hand for local journeys, and shared *tempos* are also available. The **tourist office**, in UP Tourism's *Rahi Tourist Bungalow* on Station Road (Mon–Sat 10am–5pm; ☎0565/250 5351), is not worth seeking out; **ATMs** are scattered around town, or there's a State Bank of India on Station Road.

Accommodation

Agra Bengali Ghat ☎0565/240 3318. Small, rather run-down place established in 1930, overlooking the river in the old city and redolent of the atmosphere of the *ghats*. Some rooms have a/c. ❸–❹

Brijwasi Royal State Bank Crossing, Station Rd ☎0565/240 1224 to 6, ⓦwww.brijwasiroyal.com. Modern hotel with well-appointed, carpeted rooms, all with a/c and TV, plus a bar, a multi-cuisine veg restaurant and 24hr room service. ❻–❽

International Guest House Shri Krishna Janmasthan ☎0565/242 3888. Large, institution-like building set in beautiful gardens beside the temple. Very affordable and clean, with a good veg café. Bring your own lock. ❶

Madhuvan Krishna Nagar ☎0565/242 0064. A three-star with biggish, a/c rooms, that's going to seed a little bit, but is still comfortable in a slightly worn kind of way. ❻

Radha Ashok Masani By-Pass Rd ☎0565/253 0395, ⓦwww.mathura-vrindavan.com /radhashok. Swish but cosy four-star, 4km northeast of town on the Delhi road. The most comfortable option in the area, with a/c rooms, garden and a pool. ❽

Eating

Due to the city's spiritual significance, restaurants and cafés in Mathura tend to serve **vegetarian** food only. Aside from the hotel restaurants, which are all fairly safe bets, the numerous sweetshops and *dhabas* around Holi Gate and the Shri Krishna Janmasthan serve snacks and thalis. *Brijwasi Mithai Wala* offers a huge range of fresh sweets and snacks in a clean environment and has branches at Shri Krishna Janmasthan, Holi Gate, as well as all over the city. The *Kwality Restaurant* near the Old Bus Stand, though poorly maintained and run by indifferent management, has retained much of its typical look and feel and serves decent food from an extensive menu (main dishes Rs25–45).

Around Mathura

Mathura is the obvious base for peregrinations into the pastoral landscape associated with the adolescent Krishna. Very little survives of Braj's idyllic legendary forests, and only serious pilgrims would choose to walk rather than catch one of the numerous local buses.

Mahaban and Gokul

Ten kilometres southeast of Mathura, across the Yamuna, and reachable by boat, rickshaw or bus, **Mahaban** and **Gokul** are associated with Krishna's foster parents, Nanda and Yashoda. Of the cluster of temples at **MAHABAN**, "the Great Forest", the most interesting is **Nanda's Palace**, also known as **Assi Khamba** or "Eighty Pillars", an amalgam of several influences including Buddhist, which was rebuilt as a mosque under Aurangzeb. The eponymous pillars date back to the tenth century and are rather reminiscent of Delhi's Qutb Minar.

Krishna was the son of Princess Devaki, whose brother had seized the throne from their father, but feared a prophecy that he would die at the hands of Devaki's son, so he had her imprisoned and all her children killed. However, Devaki managed to get the newborn Krishna smuggled out to **GOKUL**, then a cowherd encampment, 2km from Mahaban, on a high bank overlooking the river, where he was brought up by foster-parents. Gokul was also the headquarters for followers of the sixteenth-century saint Vallabha, but its sixteenth- and seventeenth-century temples are all in a pretty bad state of repair.

Govardhan

GOVARDHAN, 25km west of Mathura, is famous for its hill, which Krishna is said to have lifted on the tip of one finger to shelter the inhabitants of Braj from a deluge caused by the wrath of his fellow god Indra; every year, thousands of pilgrims come to circumambulate the hill in celebration. Govardhan town lies in a gap towards the hill's northern end, near a masonry tank called Mansi Ganga, which is directly opposite two impressive **cenotaphs** commemorating two Bharatpur rajas; the nearby temple of **Hari Deva** dates from the reign of Akbar.

Barsana and Nandagaon

The hill sites of **Barsana** and **Nandagaon**, 25km and 32km north of Govardhan respectively, were originally dedicated to Brahma and Shiva before being appropriated into the Krishna myth. An impressive stone staircase leads from the town at the base of the hill at **BARSANA** to an extensive ridge, where temples include that of **Lali ji**, a local name for Krishna's mistress, Radha.

The eighteenth-century temple of **Nand Rae** dominates the smaller hill and town of **NANDAGAON**, identified as the village of Krishna's foster-father Nanda. A curious local ritual takes place each year during the spring festival of Holi. First the menfolk of Nandagaon invade Barsana, to taunt the women with lewd songs and be beaten with long wooden staffs for their pains; then on the next day the procedure is reversed, and the men of Barsana pay courting calls to the women of Nandagaon.

Vrindavan

VRINDAVAN, a dusty little town on the Yamuna, 11km north of Mathura, attracts half a million pilgrims every year, mostly during the spring Holi festival, which lasts for up to a month here, and during the two months of celebrations for the birthdays of Krishna and his mistress Radha, starting in August.

Although Vrindavan is in theory a *tirtha* or holy crossing place on the Yamuna, the town has in fact been progressively abandoned by the river, as it meanders away from the original two-kilometre-long waterfront – all but five of its 38 *ghats* are now without water. Neither is there much trace of the forests of the Krishna legend, and only a few sacred basil groves remain at the spot where he cavorted with the *gopis* (female cowherds; see p.1362). Nevertheless, as a *tirtha*, the town attracts elderly Vaishnavas who believe that to die here earns them instant *moksha* or liberation. Along with its many *dharamshalas*, Vrindavan holds several "**widow houses**", maintained by wealthy devotees, which provide food and shelter for widows (see box, p.302) of whom two thousand congregate twice daily in the Mirabai Ashram to sing *bhajans* (devotional songs).

Though it may not boast the several thousand temples of popular exaggeration, the town does hold numerous shrines, many now neglected and crumbling or overrun with monkeys. Close to the centre, on the main Mathura–Vrindavan road, **Govinda Deva**, erected in 1590 and known locally as "Govindji", is one of northern India's most impressive medieval Hindu edifices, though worship here is low-key in comparison to some of the other shrines of Vrindavan. Its main tower is said to have once been seven storeys high; the three storeys that survived Aurangzeb's depredations leave it with a squat, truncated look.

Although of much later design, and rebuilt in the nineteenth century, **Banke Bihari** (winter 8.45am–1pm & 4.30–8.30pm; summer 7.45am–noon & 5.30–9.30pm; ⓦ www.bankeybihari.info), off Purana Bazaar, is the town's most popular shrine, renowned for impressive floral decorations inside the temple. A kilometre down the road, the lavish South Indian-style temple of **Shri Ranganatha**, also known as **Rangaji Temple**, sports gold-plated embellishments atop its lofty *shikhara*, and a gold-plated **Dhwaja Stambha** column in the inner courtyard (no admittance to non-Hindus).

The International Society of Krishna Consciousness or **ISKCON**, has a lavish new temple complex in Vrindavan, the **Krishna Balaram Mandir**, around 3km west of town at Raman Reti. Built in Bengal Renaissance style with bright frescoes depicting episodes from Krishna's life, the temple incorporates a marble mausoleum in honour of the society's founder, Swami Prabhupada, who died in 1977.

Among the new temples springing up along the Mathura–Vrindavan road is the **Gita Mandir** which houses the Gita Stambh, a pillar with the entire *Bhagavad Gita* carved on its surface. The imposing temple, financed by one of the country's leading industrial families, the Birlas, is overshadowed by the outrageous multistorey, spaceship-like edifice known as the **Pagal Baba Mandir** just down the road.

Practicalities

Buses, shared *tempos* and Jeeps run out to Vrindavan from Mathura for Rs10 per head one-way. Five daily local **trains** also cover the same route. Besides the numerous *dharamshalas*, several ashrams offer good-value **accommodation** at

The widows of Vrindavan

The large numbers of shaven-headed women dressed in ragged white-cotton saris, who shuffle between shops, shrines and ashrams with their begging bowls, are the **widows of Vrindavan** – women who, after the deaths of their husbands, have left home so as not to be a burden on their families, or who have been forced into destitution by cruel relatives.

In Hindu tradition, a widow is cursed. She is expected to destroy her marriage bangles and jewellery, abstain from wearing colour and *kohl* under her eyes, *kunkum* vermilion in her hair parting and *mehendi* on her hands, and to spend the rest of her days in fasting and prayer for her deceased spouse.

When the ostracization and ignominy of life among the in-laws gets too much, Vrindavan is one of the religious centres to which widows travel in search of succour. Here, by chanting in ashrams and begging for alms from pilgrims, they can at least expect to obtain a bowl of rice and a few rupees. As many as nine thousand women subsist in this way in Vrindavan alone, living off the charity of ashrams, in whose huge halls you can see them intoning mantras and *kirtans* for eight-hour shifts. Some of the ashrams are said to be fronts for money laundering, and the widows are also vulnerable to unscrupulous landlords and the sex industry. Women's rights and support groups from the capital have tried to alleviate the suffering of Vrindavan's widows, but their efforts are swamped by the ever-increasing numbers of women pouring in.

fixed rates, as well as **food**, but some open only to Hindu pilgrims. In the centre of town, around Ahir Para, try the *Jaipuriya Guest House* (no sign in English; ☏0565/244 2388; ❹), with clean, light and airy rooms built around a pleasant garden courtyard. Rooms at the ISKCON's *Guest House* (☏0565/254 0023 or 4, ✉ganpati.gkg@pamho.net; ❸–❹), immediately behind their temple, get booked up quickly, so reserve in advance. The vegetarian restaurant serves decent meals, pitched at the Western palate (mains Rs40–60, thali Rs95). If you prefer a hotel as such, the *Shubham* at Vidyapeeth Crossing (☏0565/244 3011; ❹) is clean if rather impersonal, with some a/c rooms and a restaurant.

Jhansi

Despite its seventeenth-century fort, the rail- and road-junction town of **JHANSI**, in an anomalous promontory of UP that thrusts south into Madhya Pradesh, is not very exciting. Most visitors stop only long enough to catch a connecting bus to **Khajuraho**, 175km further southeast in Madhya Pradesh. Like Avadh (see p.271), Jhansi was an independent state until the British summarily annexed it in 1854, and was consequently a major centre of support for the 1857 uprising, under the leadership of **Rani Lakshmibai**, its last ruler's widow, who was one of the uprising's great heroines.

In common with many former British cities, Jhansi is divided into two distinct areas: the wide tree-lined avenues, leafy gardens and bungalows of the **Cantonment** and **Civil Lines** to the west, and the clutter of brick and concrete cubes, narrow lanes, minarets and *shikharas* of the **old town** to the east. Dominating it all from a bare brown craggy hill, **Jhansi Fort** (daily sunrise to sunset; Rs100 [Rs5], video camera Rs25) was built in 1613 by one of the Orchha rajas, Bir Singh Joo Deo, and is worth visiting primarily for the **views** from the lofty ramparts – down to the densely packed old town on one side, and out across a dusty *maidan* and the Cantonment to the other. Rani Lakshmibai is supposed to have leapt over the west wall on horseback to escape the British, though she must have had a very athletic horse to do so. Inside the fort are a couple of unremarkable temples, plus an old cistern and the ruins of a palace.

Two minutes' walk from the roundabout directly below the fort, the **Rani Lakshmi Mahal** (daily 9.30am–5.30pm; Rs100 [Rs5], no photography allowed) is a small stately home in "Bundela style" (lots of ornate balconies and domed roofs), built as the palace of the Rani of Jhansi. It was the scene of a brutal massacre in 1858, when British troops bayoneted all its occupants (they murdered some five thousand people in all after recapturing Jhansi from the insurgents). These days, the building is a memorial museum-cum-archeological warehouse, with unlabelled fragments of antique stone sculpture littered around its attractive interior courtyard.

The grounds of a pleasant seminary in the Cantonment area between the station and the GPO hold one of the most important Catholic pilgrimage sites in India, **St Jude's Shrine**. A bone belonging to Jude the Apostle, the patron saint of hopeless causes, is said to be buried in the foundations of the sombre grey and white cathedral. On his feast day, October 28, thousands come to plead their own special causes.

Practicalities

Trains on both of the Central Railway branches that converge on Jhansi pull in at the station on the west side of town, near the Civil Lines area. There are

UP and MP **tourist information** kiosks on platform 1; UP (Mon–Sat 10am–5pm) gives town plans, while MP (daily 10am–5pm; ☎0510/244 2622) has information about getting to Khajuraho. In town, the **UP Tourist Office** at the *Hotel Veerangana* on Shivpuri Road (Mon–Sat 10am–5pm; ☎0510/244 1267) provides information on Bundelkhand and the route to Khajuraho. There's a pre-paid auto booth in front of the station, where you'll pay Rs30 to the fort, Rs40 to the bus stand.

Jhansi is the most convenient main railway station for Khajuraho and Orchha. Buses to Khajuraho go from the **bus stand** 3km east – private buses (6 daily; 4hr 30min; Rs98) are faster and more comfortable than the state buses (3 daily; 5hr 30min; Rs90). Shared **tempos** for **Orchha** (45min; Rs10) wait alongside the bus stand, or you can take an auto (Rs100). **Car rental** is available through the larger hotels, as well as the helpful Baghel Travels (☎0510/244 1255), opposite Dunro Cinema, off Elite Cross, the busy intersection in the middle of town. There are two **ATMs** next to Dunro Cinema, or there's a State Bank of India 200m east on Jhokan Bagh Road.

Accommodation and eating

With Orchha just down the road, few people **stay** in Jhansi. Options if you do want to stay include the *Jhansi* on Shastri Marg, opposite the GPO (☎0510/247 0360, ✉jhansihotel@sancharnet.in; ❹), a former haunt of British burra-sahibs, with a well-stocked and atmospheric colonial bar and restaurant, and a small garden, and the *Dreamland* on Station Road in the Civil Lines district (☎0510/233 3088; ❸–❹), with pleasant if basic bungalow accommodation, including some a/c rooms, set around a small garden and very handy for the station. Most Jhansi **hotels** operate 24-hour checkout.

For a cheap alternative to hotel **restaurants**, try the *Railway Refreshment Rooms* in the station, which serve freshly cooked Rs22 thalis and budget breakfasts. Otherwise, there's a row of places on Shastri Marg including the *Holiday*, a posh but not too expensive a/c restaurant with low lights, tablecloths, attentive service and classy Indian and Western food (non-veg mains Rs75–120) including Amritsar-style tandoori fish, *handi* chicken and *paneer* pulao, or the *Nav Bharat*, a few doors up, which has veg or non-veg thalis, *dosas*, curries, burgers and sizzlers (non-veg mains Rs70–100; closed Tues). Next door, Sharma Sweets is a good spot for a bit of *mithai* confectionery – the nutty dry fruit *ladoo* is wonderful.

Lucknow

UP's state capital **LUCKNOW** is best remembered for the ordeal of its British residents during a five-month **siege** of the Residency in 1857. Less remembered are the horrific atrocities perpetrated by the British following their recapture of the city. Lucknow had earlier witnessed the last heady days of Muslim rule in India, and the summary British deposition in 1856 of Wajid Ali Shah, the last Nawab of **Avadh** (Oudh, as the British spelt it), was one of the main causes of the 1857 uprising.

Avadh broke away from the Mughal Empire in the mid-eighteenth century after its nawab, Safdarjang, was thrown out of office in Delhi for being a Shi'ite, but as the Mughal Empire declined, Avadh became the centre of Muslim power. The later nawabs are a byword for indolence and decadence, but under their rule the arts flourished. Lucknow, the Avadhi capital, became a magnet for artisans. Courtesans took on the roles of poets, singers and dancers, and under the last nawab's patronage the amorous musical form called *thumri* emerged here (see p.1387). The city was also an important repository of Shi'a culture and Islamic jurisprudence, its Farangi Mahal law school attracting students from China and Central Asia.

The patronage of the Shi'a nawabs also produced new expressions of the faith, notably in the annual **Muharram** processions. Held in memory of the martyrdom of Muhammad's grandson Hussain (the second Shi'ite Imam) at Karbala in Iraq, these developed into elaborate affairs with **tazia**, ornate paper reproductions of Hussein's Karbala shrine, being carried through the streets. During the rest of the year the *tazia* images are kept in Imambara (houses of the Imam); these range from humble rooms in poor Shi'a households to the **Great Imambara** built by Asaf-ud-daula in 1784.

Extraordinary sandstone monuments, now engulfed by modern Lucknow, still testify to the euphoric atmosphere of this unique culture. European-inspired edifices, too, are prominent on the skyline, often embellished with flying buttresses, turrets, cupolas and floral patterns, but the brick and mortar with which they were constructed means that they are not ageing as well as the earlier stone buildings, and old Lucknow is, literally, crumbling away.

Arrival, information and transport

From **Amausi airport**, 16km south on the Kanpur Road, a taxi to the centre of Lucknow costs around Rs350. Lucknow's extremely busy **Charbagh railway station** (with a computerized reservations office), 4km southwest of the central hub of Hazratganj (Rs25–35 by rickshaw or auto), is itself a remarkable building, with prominent chhatris above the entrance arcade and a roof

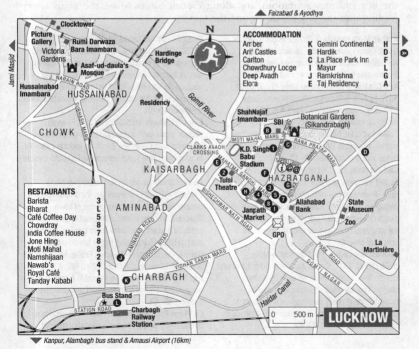

inspired by chess pieces. Intercity **buses** pull in at **Alambagh Bus Stand**, 3km southwest of the station, Rs50 from Hazratganj by auto.

The **UP Tourism office** is at *Hotel Gomti*, 6 Sapru Marg (Mon–Sat 10am–5pm; T0522/261 2659). There are plenty of **ATMs** around town (at the station and the bus stand, on MG Road, and a whole slew on Shah Najaf Road); otherwise, there's Allahabad Bank on Park Road in Hazratganj and the State Bank of India on Moti Mahal Marg. For **Internet** connections, try i-way, on the second floor of the building next to the UP office on Sapru Marg, or Meeting Point, about 100m east near the junction with Ashok Marg. The **Lucknow Festival**, held in February, gives visitors an excellent opportunity to sample the city's vibrant traditions of music and dance. For information, contact UP Tourism.

Multi-seater **tempos** and **Vikrams**, their diesel engines sounding like hundreds of loud rattles, have more or less taken over from city buses, plying regular routes such as from Charbagh to the GPO, with depots at Janpath Market, Clarks Avadh Crossing and the Chowk. Adding to the chaos are legions of cycle rickshaws. **Cars** can be rented from various operators, including *Hotel Clarks Avadh*, 8 MG Marg (T0522/261 6500), and UP Tours at the *Hotel Gomti* (see above; T0522/261 2659). Comprehensive daily **city tours** (Rs520 including most entry fees), which must be booked in advance through UP Tours, and only run if they have five or more takers, leave the *Hotel Gomti* at 9.30am and return at 2.30pm. You can also be picked up from the station (at 9.00am) and from various other hotels. Guide and entrance fees are included in the price except for the Residency (Rs100).

Accommodation

Budget and mid-range **hotels** are concentrated in the **Charbagh** area, around the bus and railway stations, and along Vidhan Sabha Marg, the main artery feeding into the city centre around the GPO.

Amber Naka Hindola T0522/268 3201, F268 3404. Good value near the station: spacious air-cooled rooms (some have a/c), and clean Indian-style toilets. 24hr checkout. ❸–❹
Arif Castles 4 Rana Pratap Marg T0522/221 1313 to 7, Earifcastles@hotmail.com. Quite well-appointed in marble, brass and light blue, though it could do with a lick of paint, this "business class hotel", as it calls itself, has cool rooms, a/c, cable TV and an Italian restaurant. Rates include breakfast. ❼–❽
Carlton Shah Najaf Rd T0522/222 4021. Fabled Lucknow address, a *fin-de-siècle* Euro–Avadhi edifice with big rooms, ancient plumbing and musty hunting trophies. It was getting run-down, but was closed at last check for total refurbishment, so should emerge all spanking new. ❽
Chowdhury Lodge 3 Vidhan Sabha Marg T0522/222 1911. Grimy, *paan*-stained but friendly city-centre cheapie down an alley by a filling station. The attached doubles (hot water in buckets) aren't really as cheap as they ought to be, but it's very central, and there are non-attached singles for only Rs120. ❸–❹

Deep Avadh Aminabad Rd, Naka Hindola T0522/268 4381 to 7, Edeepavadh@sify.com. Huge range of rooms from sparse and simple to a/c, as well as two restaurants, bar and travel desk, in an interesting part of town close to the station and on the edge of bustling Aminabad. 24hr checkout. ❸–❻
Elora 3 Lalbagh T0522/221 1307. Friendly, popular place with a good range of clean rooms, including some with a/c. Facilities include cable TV in all rooms, 24hr room service and a multi-cuisine restaurant. ❸–❺
Gemini Continental 10 Rani Laximbai Marg T0522/401 1111, Wwww.geminicontinental.com. Snazzy, upscale hotel in the centre of town. Spacious, modern rooms with great views, minibar, cable TV and a/c, and 24hr room service. Doubles start at US$145 including buffet breakfast. ❾
Hardik Guest House 16 Rana Pratap Marg, near Jopling Rd Crossing T0522/220 9497. A range of rooms in this clean and comfortable family-run guesthouse. Friendly, helpful staff and good home-cooking. ❹–❼
La Place Park Inn 6 Shah Najaf Rd, Hazratganj T0522/400 4040, Wwww.sarovarhotels.com.

Small but smart modern business hotel crackling with brisk efficiency. Facilities include Wi-Fi, a business centre, executive offices, but no pool. ❽ **Mayur** Subhash Marg by the junction with Station Rd, Charbagh (above *Bharat Restaurant*) ☎0522/245 1824. Unattractive cheaper rooms, but those at the other end of the range are much better value. Opposite the station so handy for early morning get-aways and late-night arrivals by train. ❸–❹

Ramkrishna Ashok Marg ☎0522/228 0099. Best-value cheapie in the Hazratganj vicinity, but very often full, as is its similar neighbour the *New Ram Krishna* (☎0522/262 4225). ❷–❹

Taj Residency Vpin Khand, Gomti Nagar ☎0522/239 3939, ⓦwww.tajhotels.com. Built in Avadhi style, this is easily Lucknow's most elegant and comfortable hotel, with a swimming pool and a range of restaurants, but inconveniently situated 3km out of town. Doubles from US$198. ❾

The Town

Most of Lucknow's monuments are spread along or near the southern bank of the Gomti River, which is sluggish and weed-covered except at monsoon time, when its waters swell enough to accommodate hordes of local fishermen's dugout boats. Close to the main central bridge lies the modern commercial

▲ Hussainabad Imambara

centre of **Hazratganj**, with the **Shah Najaf Imambara** to its north near the riverbank. Further west, beyond the ruins of the **Residency**, the road passes the majestic **Bara Imambara**, leading through the large gate of **Rumi Darwaza** to the **Hussainabad Imambara**. South of Hussainabad, between Hazratganj and Charbagh, the old city sector of **Aminabad** holds a maze of busy streets and fascinating markets.

Hussainabad

In the west of the city, in the vicinity of Hardinge Bridge around "old" Lucknow, lie several crumbling relics of the nawabs of Avadh. Chief among them is the Great or **Bara Imambara** (daily 6am–6pm, closed during Muharram; Rs300 [Rs25], ticket includes Hussainabad Imambara and Picture Gallery), which boasts one of the largest vaulted halls in the world – 50m long and 15m high. Flat on top, slightly arched inside, and built by Asaf-ud-daula in 1784 without the aid of a single iron or wooden beam, the roof was constructed using a technique known as *kara dena*, in which bricks are broken and angled to form an interlocking section and then covered with concrete – here several metres thick. The arcaded structure is approached through what must have been an extravagant gate, now pockmarked and on the verge of collapse. Two successive courtyards lead from the gates to the unusually festive-looking Imambara itself. Steps lead up to a labyrinth of chambers known as *bhulbhulaiya* – the "maze". Adjacent to the Bara Imambara and overlooking it is **Asaf-ud-daula's Mosque**, set upon a two-tiered arcaded plinth with two lofty minarets. Closed to non-Muslims, it can be readily viewed from the Victoria Gardens that adjoin it to the west (daily except Fri dawn to dusk; free).

Straddling the main road west of the main gates, the colossal **Rumi Darwaza** is an ornamental victory arch modelled on one of the gates to Asia Minor in Istanbul (known to the Islamic world in Byzantine times as "Rumi"). Now decaying, it sports elaborate floral patterns and a few extraordinary trumpets; steps lead up to open chambers that command a general prospect of the monuments of Hussainabad.

A short distance further west, the lavish **Hussainabad Imambara** (same hours and ticket as Bara Imambara) is also known as the Chhota (small) Imambara, or the Palace of Lights, thanks to its fairy-tale appearance when decorated and illuminated for special occasions. The raised bathing pool in front of it, which is approached via a spacious courtyard, adds to the overall atmosphere. A central gilded dome dominates the whole ensemble, busy with minarets, small domes and arches and even a crude miniature Taj Mahal. Built in 1837 by Muhammad Ali Shah (1837–42), partly to provide famine relief through employment, the Imambara houses a silver-faced throne, plus the tombs of important Avadhi personalities. The dummy gate opposite the main entrance was used by ceremonial musicians, while the unfinished watchtower is known as the Satkhanda or "Seven Storeys", even though only four were ever constructed. West of the Imambara, and surrounded by ruins, are the two soaring minarets and three domes of the **Jami Masjid** (no admission to non-Muslims), completed after the death of Muhammad Ali Shah.

Beyond the Hussainabad Tank, east of the Hussainabad Imambara, is the isolated 67-metre-high **Hussainabad Clocktower**, an ambitious Gothic affair completed in 1887 which carries the largest clock in India. Close to this bizarre monolith lies **Taluqdar's Hall**, built by Muhammad Ali Shah to house the offices of the Hussainabad Trust and the dusty **Picture Gallery**, also known as the **Muhammad Ali Shah Art Gallery** (same hours and ticket as Bara Imambara). Arranged chronologically, the portraits of nawabs graphically demonstrate the decline of their civilization, as the figures become progressively portlier. In a famous image, the androgynous-looking last nawab, Wajid Ali Shah (1847–56), is shown in a daringly low-cut top that reveals his left nipple.

The Residency

The blasted **Residency** (daily sunrise to sunset; Rs100 [Rs5], video cameras Rs25) rests in peace amid landscaped gardens southeast of Hardinge Bridge – a battle-scarred ruin left exactly as it stood when the siege was finally relieved by Sir Colin Campbell on November 17, 1857 (see box below). Its cannonball-shattered tower became a shrine to the tenacity of the British in India, and continued to be maintained as such even after Independence.

During the siege, every building in the complex was utilized for the hard-fought defence of the compound. The **Treasury**, on the right through the **Baillie Guard Gate**, served as an arsenal, while the sumptuous **Banqueting Hall**, immediately west, was a makeshift hospital, and the extensive single-storey **Dr Fayrer's House**, just south, housed women and children. Most of the original structures, such as **Begum Kothi**, were left standing to impede direct fire from the enemy. On the lawn outside Begum Kothi, a large cross honours the astute Sir Henry Lawrence, responsible for building its defences, who died shortly after hostilities began.

The pockmarked Residency itself holds a small **museum** (Tues–Sun 9am–4.30pm; Rs5, buy ticket at Residency main gate). On the ground floor, the **Model Room**, the only one with its roof intact, houses a large model of the defences and of the Residency and a small but excellent collection of images,

---

The Lucknow Residency siege

The insurgent sepoys who entered Lucknow on June 30, 1857, found the city rife with resentment against the recent British takeover of the kingdom of Avadh. The tiny and isolated **British garrison**, under the command of Sir Henry Lawrence, took refuge in the **Residency**, which became the focus of a fierce struggle.

Less than a third of the three thousand British residents and loyal Indians who crammed into the Residency survived the four-and-a-half-month siege. So unhygienic were their living conditions that those who failed to succumb to gangrenous and tetanus-infected wounds often fell victim to cholera and scurvy. While a barrage of heavy artillery was maintained by both sides, the insurgents attempted to tunnel under the defences and lay mines, but among the British were former tin-miners in the 32nd (Cornish) Regiment, who were far more adept at such things, and were able to follow the sounds of enemy chipping, defuse mines, and even blow up several sepoy-controlled buildings on the peripheries of the complex.

Morale remained high among the 1400 **noncombatants**, who included fifty school-boys from La Martinière, and class distinctions were upheld throughout. While the wives of European soldiers and noncommissioned officers, children and servants took refuge in the *tikhana* (cellar), the "ladies" of the Residency occupied the higher and airier chambers, until the unfortunate loss of one Miss Palmer's leg on July 1 persuaded them of the gravity of their predicament. Sir Henry Lawrence was fatally wounded the next day. The wealthier officers managed to maintain their own private hoard of supplies, living in much their usual style. Matters improved when, after three months, Brigadier General Sir Henry Havelock arrived with reinforcements, and the normal round of visits and invitations to supper was resumed despite the inconvenient shortage of good food and wine. Not until November 17 was the siege finally broken by a force of Sikhs and Highlanders under Sir Colin Campbell. Their offers of tea, however, were turned down by the Residency women; they were used to taking it with milk, which the soldiers could not supply.

including etchings showing wall breaches blocked up with billiard tables and a soldier blacking up in preparation for a dash across enemy lines.

Hazratganj

Along the river, opposite the *Carlton Hotel* on Rana Pratap Marg, squats the huge dome of the **Shah Najaf Imambara** (daily except Fri dawn to dusk; donations), named after the tomb of Ali in Iraq and at its best when adorned with lights during Muharram. Its musty interior holds some incredibly garish chandeliers used in processions, several *tazia*, and the silver-faced tomb of the decadent and profligate Ghazi-ud-din-Haidar (1814–27), buried with three of his queens.

The Imambara was commandeered as a sepoy stronghold in 1857, and the crucial battle that enabled the British to relieve the Residency was fought in the adjacent pleasure gardens of **Sikandrabagh** on November 16. It took one and a half hours of bombardment by Sir Colin Campbell's soldiers to breach the defences of the two thousand sepoys; then the Sikhs and 93rd Highlanders poured through. There was no escape for the terrified sepoys, some of whom are said to have believed the bloodstained, red-faced, kilted Scots to be the ghosts of the murdered European women of Kanpur. Driven against the north wall, they were either bayoneted or shot, and the dead and dying piled shoulder-high. Tranquil once again, Sikandrabagh is now home to the National Botanical Research Institute and the beautiful **Botanical Gardens** (Mon–Fri 6am–7pm; Rs1), with manicured lawns, conservatories, nurseries and herb, rose and bougainvillea gardens.

Towards the east of Lucknow, an extraordinary chateau-like building has become almost a symbol of the city – **La Martinière** remains to this day an exclusive public school in the finest colonial tradition. It was built as a country retreat by Major-General Claude Martin, a French soldier-adventurer taken prisoner by the British in Puducherry. The enigmatic Martin later joined the East India Company, made his fortune in indigo, and served both the British and the nawabs of Avadh. The building is an outrageous but intriguing amalgam, crowned by flying walkways; Greco-Roman figures on the parapets give it a busy silhouette, gigantic heraldic lions gaze across the grounds, and a large bronze cannon graces the front. Martin himself is buried in the basement. During the siege, La Martinière was occupied by rebels, while its boys were evacuated to the Residency.

Close to the centre of Hazratganj, its grounds dotted with derelict Avadhi monuments, Lucknow's small **zoo** also serves as an amusement park with a miniature train to view the animals (Tues–Sun 8.30am–5.30pm; Rs15). Head through the large zoo gardens to reach the **State Museum** (Tues–Sun 10.30am–4.30pm; Rs100 [Rs5], camera Rs20), with its delicate, speckled-red-sandstone sculpture from the Mathura school of the Kushana and Gupta periods (first to sixth centuries AD). Besides sculpture from Gandhara, Mahoba, Nalanda and Sravasti, it boasts a gallery of terracotta artefacts and even an Egyptian mummy. Musical instruments, paintings and costumes provide atmosphere in the Avadh Gallery, while the natural history section is a taxidermist's dream.

Eating

The rich traditional **Lucknavi cuisine** – featuring Mughlai dishes as well as the local *dum pukht* (steam casserole) style, sometimes known as *handi* after the pot it's cooked in – is available from food stalls throughout the city, in places such as Shami Avadh Bazaar, near the K.D. Singh Babu Stadium, the Chowk, Aminabad and behind the Tulsi Theatre in Hazratganj. The bazaars are also the place to get Lucknow's popular breakfast speciality *paya-khulcha*, a spicy mutton soup served with hot breads.

Bharat Subhash Marg by the junction with Station Rd, Charbagh. Cheap *dhaba* opposite the station serving good *dosas* and curries (veg Rs35–60, non-veg Rs40–160).

Chowdray MG Marg, Hazratganj. Excellent Lucknavi cuisine in a busy restaurant (main dishes Rs38–70); locals say that this is *the* place to come to for lunch.

India Coffee House Ashoka Marg. Once a hotbed of Lucknow's political intelligentsia, nicknamed the "maternity ward" for the ideas it gave birth to, now so run-down it looks like a squatted warehouse, it still serves filter coffee and cheap South Indian and breakfast snacks. If you prefer to take your coffee in slicker surroundings, *Café Coffee Day* is a few doors away on the corner of MG Marg, with *Barista* just 100m down MG Marg.

Jone Hing MG Marg, Hazratganj. Chinese restaurant serving the usual sweet and sour, chop suey and chow mein, plus specialities such as ginger chicken and Manchurian fish. Main dishes are Rs60–75 for meat, Rs105 for fish, Rs195 for prawns.

Moti Mahal MG Marg, Hazratganj. The sweet shop at the front has some great milky confections, including sugar-free ones; the family restaurant upstairs serves excellent veg curries (Rs50–110), including three types of *dum aloo* (Lucknavi, Banarsi or Kashmiri).

Namshijaan China Gate. One of a number of open-air diners in this little street by UP Press Club, with kebabs, tandoori chicken, biriyanis, and local specialties such as chicken *dum pukht*. Main dishes Rs40–120

Nawab's in *Capoor's* hotel, MG Marg, Hazratganj. A refined eatery, with live *qawwali* music in the evening (except Tues). Top dishes include *murg nawabi*, a mild, creamy dish of chicken in cashew butter, or there's a great mushroom tikka masala. Non-veg main dishes are Rs100–250.

Royal Café Shahmajaf Rd. Lively place that's popular amongst Lucknavi families. Muglai non-veg main dishes go for Rs90–160, *handi dum* biriyanis at Rs105–135. There's another branch by *Capoor's* hotel on MG Marg.

🏃 **Tanday Kababi** Naaz Cinema Rd, just off Aminabad main chowk. For an authentic Avadhi gastronomic experience, head to this popular cheap eatery, the best in a street of them, where the tandoori chicken, and mutton or (shock horror!) beef kebabs are prepared out front and served up within. Main dishes Rs30–60.

Shopping

Chikan is a long-standing Lucknavi tradition of embroidery, in which designs are built up to form delicate floral patterns along edges on saris and on necklines and collars of *kurtas*. Workshops can be found around the Chowk, the market area of old Lucknow, and shops and showrooms in Hazratganj (especially Janpath Market), Nazirabad and Aminabad. The fixed prices at **Gangotri**, the UP government emporium on MG Marg in Hazratganj (a block west of Lalbagh), are more expensive than those in the markets, but the quality is assured and you don't have to haggle.

Lucknow is also renowned for its **ittar** (or *attar*), concentrated perfume sold in small vials – an acquired (and expensive) taste. Small balls of cotton wool are daubed with the scent and placed neatly within the top folds of the ear; musicians believe that the aroma heightens their senses. Popular *ittar* include *ambar* from amber, *khus* from a flowering plant and rose-derived *ghulab*. A well-established dealer is Sugandhco at D-4 Janpath Market (on the south side of the market).

Moving on from Lucknow

Amausi **airport** is 16km south of town, around Rs200 by auto, Rs350 by taxi. Airlines include: Indian Airlines, 9 Rani Laxmi Bai Marg (near *Gemini Continental* hotel) ☎0522/262 0927; Air India, FF-7 Chintels House, 16 Station Rd ☎0522/263 8700; Jet Airways and JetLite, 6 Park Rd ☎0522/223 9612.

All **buses** leave from Alambagh Bus stand, 3km southwest of the train station (Rs50 by auto from Hazratganj).

Trains to **Delhi** tend to be overnight: the #2229 Lucknow Mail, which departs at 10pm is one of four evening services to New Delhi (arrives 7am), while for Old Delhi the #2225 Kaifiyat Express leaves at 11pm (arriving

Bundelkhand

The harshness of the terrain in the **Bundelkhand** region, south of Lucknow along the Madhya Pradesh border, and the all but unbearable heat in the summer, make it the most difficult, if intriguing, part of the state to control, and even today, its labyrinthine hills and valleys are home to infamous bands of outlaw **dacoits**. Many of these have become folk-heroes among local villagers, who shelter them from the almost equally brutal police force. The most celebrated in recent years was **Phoolan Devi**, the "Bandit Queen", from a village near Behmai who was kidnapped by a dacoit gang, became the leader's lover, and took over from him after he was killed. She eventually surrendered to the police, was released in 1994, and even became an MP for the socialist Samajwadi Party before being assassinated in 2001.

6.50am). There are no daily trains to **Agra**, but the #4863 Marudhar Express leaves Monday, Wednesday, Friday & Saturday mornings (Sun, Tues, Thurs & Fri nights) at five past midnight, arriving in Agra Fort at 6.10am. The Pushpak Express #2533 is the most convenient service to **Mumbai** (daily 7.45pm; 23hr). The fastest daily service to **Kolkata** is the #3006 Amritsar–Howrah Mail (leaves 10.55am, arriving 7.30am next day). The #4258 Kashi–Vishwanatha Express leaves at 11.15pm for **Varanasi**, if you don't mind arriving at 5.50am; daytime services include the #3006 Amritsar–Howrah Mail (leaves 10.55am, arrives 4.45pm). The #4265 Varanasi–Dehra Dun Express at 8.15pm for **Dehra Dun** (arrives 9.40am) via **Haridwar** (arrives 7.10am) is the best service up to Uttarakhand, especially as part of it splits off to serve Ramnagar (arrives 6am). Also to Uttarakhand, the #3019 Bagh Express leaves at 12.41am to reach Kathgodam, the railhead for Nainital, at 9.30am. For **Khajuraho**, the #5009 Chitrakoot Express at 5.30pm gets in to Satna at a bleary 4.15am, well in time to catch an onward bus.

For **Nepal**, daily overnight trains to Gorakhpur – where you can get a bus to the Sonauli border, and then buses to Kathmandu and Pokhara on the other side – include the #5708 Amritsar–Katihar Express (12.55am, arriving 5.50am), and the #1015 Kushinagar Express (1.55am, arriving 7.25am). There are also buses direct to Sonauli, but it's a gruelling twelve-hour journey.

Agents for air, rail and bus tickets include Travel Corporation of India, 13-A Jopling Rd (℡0522/220 7554), and UP Tours, *Hotel Gomti*, 6 Sapru Marg (℡0522/221 2659).

Finally, if you're heading for Uttaranchal, Lucknow holds offices of both **GMVN**, at 4-7-RF Khushnuma Complex, Bahadur Marg (℡0522/220 7844), and **KMVN**, 3rd floor, Sarang Menor, Shah Nzaf Road (℡0522/223 9434), who organize tours of, and accommodation in, **Garhwal** and **Kumaon** respectively.

For more on transport from Lucknow see "Travel details", p.340.

Allahabad and around

The administrative and industrial city of **ALLAHABAD**, 135km west of Varanasi and 227km southeast of Lucknow, is also known as **Prayag** ("confluence"): the point where the rivers Yamuna and Ganges meet the mythical Saraswati. Sacred to Hindus, the **Sangam** (which also means "confluence"), east of the city, is one of the great pilgrimage destinations of India. Allahabad comes alive during its *melas* (fairs) – the annual **Magh Mela** (Jan/Feb), and the colossal **Maha Kumbh Mela**, held every twelve years (the next is due to take place in 2013).

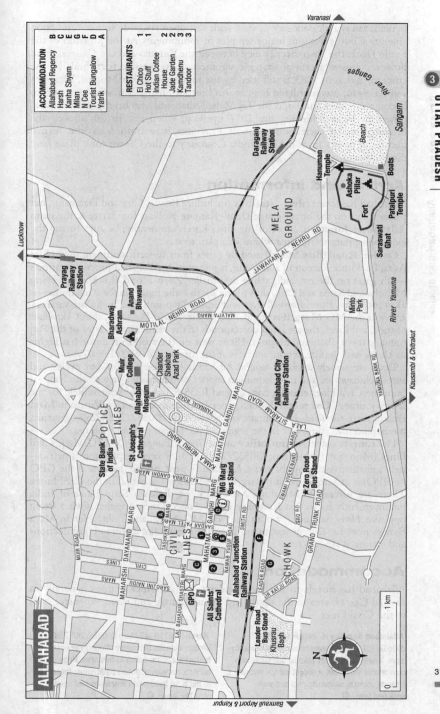

ALLAHABAD

ACCOMMODATION
Allahabad Regency	B
Harsh	C
Kanha Shyam	E
Milan	G
N Cee	F
Tourist Bungalow	D
Yatrik	A

RESTAURANTS
El Chico	1
Hot Stuff	1
Indian Coffee House	2
Jade Garden	2
Kamdhenu	3
Tandoor	3

Varanasi

River Ganges

Sangam

Beach

Boats

Hanuman Temple

Ashoka Pillar

Fort

Patalpuri Temple

Saraswati Ghat

Daraganj Railway Station

MELA GROUND

JAWAHARLAL NEHRU RD

River Yamuna

Minto Park

MALVIYA MARG

Kausambi & Chitrakut

YAMUNA BANK RD

Allahabad City Railway Station

LALA SITARAM ROAD

Lucknow

Prayag Railway Station

Bharadwaj Ashram

Anand Bhavan

MOTILAL NEHRU ROAD

Muir College

Chander Shekhar Azad Park

Allahabad Museum

PANNALAL ROAD

KAMLA NEHRU MARG

MAHATMA GANDHI MARG

State Bank of India

POLICE LINES

St Joseph's Cathedral

CIVIL LINES

KASTURBA GANDHI MARG

TASHKENT MARG

MAHATMA GANDHI MARG

SARDAR PATEL MARG

NABAB YUSUF ROAD

SMITH RD

SWAMI VIVEKANAND MARG

Zero Road Bus Stand

CHBO RD

MG Marg Bus Stand

MUIR ROAD

CIVIL LINES

MAHARSHI DAYANAND MARG

SAROJINI NAIDU MARG

LAL BAHADUR SHASTRI MARG

GPO

All Saints' Cathedral

Allahabad Junction Railway Station

LEADER ROAD

Leader Road Bus Stand

Khusrau Bagh

GRAND TRUNK ROAD

DR KATJU ROAD

CHOWK

Barmauli Airport & Kanpur

N

1 km
0

Allahabad is a pleasant city to visit, with vast open riverside scenery and good amenities, but is without major temples or monuments. At the junction of the fertile Doab, the "two-river" valley between the Yamuna and the Ganges, it did however possess a crucial strategic significance; its massive **fort**, built by the emperor Akbar in 1583, is still used by the military. Another Mughal, Jahangir's son Khusrau, was murdered here by his brother Shah Jahan, who went on to become emperor and build the Taj Mahal. Allahabad was briefly the centre of power in India following the 1857 uprising, when the British moved the headquarters of their Northwestern Provinces here from Agra; the formal transfer of power from the East India Company to the Crown took place here the following year.

Arrival and information

Allahabad has four **railway stations** (including Prayag, City and Daraganj), but major trains on the broad-gauge Delhi–Kanpur–Kolkata line arrive at the main **Allahabad Junction**. Most of the city's hotels are nearby; be sure to use the exit appropriate to the area where you plan to stay.

Leader Road Bus Stand, used by buses from western destinations such as Agra, Lucknow, Kausambi and Delhi, is just outside Allahabad Junction station's south gates on the city side, while the smaller **Zero Road** Bus Stand, serving Mahoba and Satna and Chitrakut to the south – the railheads for Khajuraho – is 1km southeast. Buses from all over and especially points east, including Varanasi, arrive at the **MG Marg** Bus Stand, next to the *Tourist Bungalow*, about 1km east of the Civil Lines, the area that corresponds to the residential quarter of the Raj military town. Bamrauli **airport**, 18km west on the road to Kanpur, has flights to Delhi with JetLite, whose office is at the airport (℡0532/258 0796).

Taxis are widely available around Allahabad Junction Station, but cycle- and auto-rickshaws are the most common modes of transport; a trip to the Sangam from the Civil Lines crossing costs around Rs35 (hang on to your vehicle for the return journey). **Car rental** through general travel agencies such as Varuna in Maya Bazaar, next to *Tandoor* restaurant on MG Marg ℡0532/242 7259, Ⓔvaruna travels@hotmail.com), cost in the region of Rs550 per day plus mileage.

The **tourist information office** at the *Tourist Bungalow*, 35 MG Marg, Civil Lines (Mon–Sat 10am–5pm; ℡0532/260 1873), is very helpful and is particularly informative during the *melas*. Allahabad's **post office** (known as the GPO or HPO) is at Sarojini Naidu Marg, near All Saints' Cathedral in the Civil Lines. There are several **ATMs** along MG Marg, or there's a State Bank of India inconveniently located at Kutchery Road, Police Lines. Angelica Cyber Point opposite *Hotel Sangam* down an alley off MG Marg, and Vishal Net in Maya Bazaar, next to *Tandoor* restaurant, have reasonably fast **Internet** connections and charge Rs15–20/hr.

Accommodation

Allahabad has **hotels** to suit most budgets, with cheaper options generally in the old Chowk area to the south, and the mid-range and more expensive ones in the Civil Lines.

Allahabad Regency 16 Tashkent Marg ℡0532/261 1110, ⓦwww.hotelallahabadregency .com. Nineteenth-century colonial bungalow with comfortable a/c rooms, a decent garden restaurant, a sauna, Jacuzzi, swimming pool and well-equipped gym. ⑧

Harsh 118/116 MG Marg ℡0532/242 7897. Shabby colonial bungalow offering the best budget accommodation in this area. Huge tatty rooms with attached bathrooms; those at the front have small fireplaces and open onto the lawn. ❶

Kanha Shyam Strachey Rd, Civil Lines ☎ 0532/256 0123 to 32, ⓦ www.hotelkanhashyam.com. Classy four-star with quite stately rooms done out in burgundy and dark wood (though the latter's getting a bit scuffed). There's a bar, a coffee shop and a rooftop restaurant overlooking the city, and a pool under construction. ❽

Milan 46 Leader Rd ☎ 0532/240 3776 or 7, ⓦ www.milanhotels.in. A cut above the other hotels in the area south of the station, and not a bad mid-market choice. The cheaper rooms are a bit shabby, and the mattresses a little hard, but there are better a/c rooms if you don't mind spending a little bit more. ❹–❺

N Cee 108 Leader Rd ☎ 0532/240 1166. Popular budget hotel south of the railway line in the busy bazaar area. The rooms are small,

but it's a pleasant and friendly place. 24hr checkout. ❷

Tourist Bungalow (Ilawart) 35 MG Marg ☎ 0532/260 1440, ⓔ rahiilawart@up-tourism.com. The comfortable newer block here, built around a central well, overlooks the bus stand, so choose your room carefully to avoid round-the-clock noise. Now showing its age, the older block is quieter. As well as rooms, there's a dorm (Rs125), a restaurant with haphazard service but good food, and a popular bar. Run by UP Tourism. ❹–❺

Yatrik 33 Sardar Patel Marg ☎ 0532/226 0921 to 6, ⓦ www.hotelyatrik.com. Best of the upmarket places, with more character than its rival the Kanha. Popular, well run and with a beautiful garden graced with elegant palms, and a pool. Sometimes booked out by tour groups. 24hr check-out. ❼

The Town

Central Allahabad is split in two by the railway line, with the chaotic and congested **Old City** or **Chowk** south of the main Allahabad Junction Station, and the well-defined grid of the **Civil Lines** to the north.

One kilometre north of Allahabad Junction Station, the yellow-and-red sandstone bulk of the Gothic **All Saints' Cathedral** dominates the surrounding avenues. Designed by Sir William Emerson, architect of Kolkata's Victoria Memorial, the cathedral retains much of its stained glass, and an impressive altar of inlaid marble. Plaques provide interesting glimpses of Allahabad in the days of the Raj, while flying buttresses and snarling gargoyles on the exterior add to

The Kumbh Mela

Hindus traditionally regard river confluences as auspicious places, and none more so than the **Sangam** at Allahabad, where the Yamuna and the Ganges meet the River of Enlightenment, the mythical subterranean Saraswati. According to legend, Vishnu was carrying a *kumbha* (pot) of *amrita* (nectar), when a scuffle broke out between the gods, and four drops were spilled. They fell to earth at the four *tirthas* of Prayag, Haridwar, Nasik and Ujjain. The event is commemorated every three years by the **Kumbh Mela**, held at each *tirtha* in turn; the Allahabad Sangam is known as Tirtharaja, the "King of *tirthas*", and its *mela*, the **Maha Kumbh Mela** or "Great" Kumbh Mela, is the greatest and holiest of all.

The largest religious fair in India, Maha Kumbh Mela was attended by an astonishing **seventeen million** pilgrims in 2001 (the next is in 2013). The vast flood plains and riverbanks adjacent to the confluence were overrun by tents, organized in almost military fashion by the government, the local authorities and the police. The *mela* is especially renowned for the presence of an extraordinary array of religious ascetics – sadhus and *mahants* – enticed from remote hideaways in forests, mountains and caves. Once astrologers have determined the propitious bathing time or *kumbhayog*, the first to hit the water are legions of Naga Sadhus or Naga Babas, the ferocious-looking members of the "snake sect" who cover their naked bodies with ash and wear their hair in dreadlocks. The sadhus, who see themselves as guardians of the faith, approach the confluence at the appointed time with all the pomp and bravado of a charging army.

Although the Kumbh Mela is only triennial, and not always in Allahabad, there is a smaller annual bathing festival, the Magh Mela, held here every year in the month of Magha (Jan–Feb).

the effect of an English county town – though the impression is subverted by the palm trees in the garden. Sunday services continue to attract large congregations; so too do Masses at the flamboyant **St Joseph's Roman Catholic Cathedral**, a short distance northeast.

On the edge of the pleasant **Chandra Shekhar Azad Park**, also in the Civil Lines, the grounds of the **Allahabad Museum** (Tues–Sun 10.15am–4.30pm, closed the Sun following the second Sat of the month; Rs100 [Rs5]) are dotted with pieces of ancient sculpture. Inside, you'll find early terracotta artefacts, eighth-century sculptures from the Buddhist site of Kausambi, and a striking twelfth-century image from Khajuraho of Shiva and Parvati. A copious collection of modern Indian art includes work by Haldar, Sajit Khastgir and Rathin Mitra, as well as Jamini Roy, who was inspired by folk art. European paintings concentrate on spiritual themes, with bright, naive canvases by the Russian artist Nicholas Roerich, and pieces by the Tibetologist Lama Angarika Govinda. A natural history section features stuffed animals and birds, while photographs and documents cover the Independence struggle.

North of the museum rise the nineteenth-century sandstone buildings of **Allahabad University**, and the Gothic **Muir College**, built in 1870. A 61m-high tower accompanies domes clad with blue and white glazed tiles (some of which are missing), and a quadrangle with tall and elegant arches. Just beyond the college, in beautiful grounds roughly 1km northeast of the museum, is **Anand Bhawan** (Tues–Sun 9.30am–5pm; Rs5 allows entry to the first floor; no tickets sold 12.45–1.30pm). This ornate Victorian building, crowned by a chhatri and with Indo-Saracenic effects finished in grey-and-white trim, was the boyhood home of the first prime minister of an independent India, **Jawaharlal Nehru**. It's now maintained as a museum, allowing queues of visitors to peer through plate glass into the opulent interior and see how well the first family lived. More diverting than Nehru's spoons and trousers is the stuffy English court document recording his trial for making salt. Nehru's daughter Indira Gandhi was born here, and Mahatma Gandhi (no relation) stayed here when he visited the city. Also within the grounds, as at the Nehru Memorial Museum in Delhi, is a **planetarium**, which puts on five hour-long shows per day (11am, noon, 2pm, 3pm, 4pm; Rs15, all in Hindi with a 30min lecture prior to the show).

A short way south of Allahabad Junction railway station, a lofty gateway leads to the attractive walled gardens of **Khusrau Bagh**, where the remains of Jahangir's tragic son Khusrau rest in a simple sandstone mausoleum, completed in 1622. Khusrau made an unsuccessful bid for power that ended in death at the hands of his brother Shah Jahan, and is buried far from the centre of Mughal power. His mother's two-storeyed mausoleum is a short way west, beyond a tomb reputed to be that of his sister. Once Jahangir's pleasure garden, today much of Khusrau Bagh has been made into an orchard, famous for its guavas, and a rose nursery, but parts are unkempt and overgrown.

The river frontage

Most of Allahabad's river frontage is along the Yamuna, to the south, where women perform *arati* or evening worship at **Saraswati Ghat** by floating *diya* downstream. Immediately to the west, in **Minto Park**, a memorial marks the exact spot where the British Raj came into being, when India was taken away from the East India Company in 1858 and placed under the auspices of the Crown.

East of Saraswati Ghat, close to the Sangam, loom the huge battlements of Akbar's **Fort** – best appreciated from boats on the river (see box opposite).

The Sangam

Around 7km from the centre of the Civil Lines, overlooked by the eastern ramparts of the fort, wide flood plains and muddy banks protrude towards the sacred **Sangam**. At the point at which the brown Ganges meets the greenish Yamuna, *pandas* (priests) perch on small platforms to perform puja and assist the devout in their ritual ablutions in the shallow waters. Beaches and *ghats* here are littered with the shorn hair of pilgrims who come to offer *pind* for their deceased parents, and women sit around selling cone-shaped pyramids of bright red and orange *tilak* powder.

Boats to the Sangam, used by pilgrims and tourists alike, can be rented at the *ghat* immediately east of the fort, for the recommended government rate of Rs25 per head. However, most pilgrims pay around Rs50 and you can be charged as much as Rs150. Official prices for a whole boat are between Rs100 and Rs120 but can soar to more than Rs250 during peak seasons and Rs1000 during the *melas*. On the way to the Sangam, high-pressure aquatic salesmen loom up on the placid waters selling offerings such as coconuts for pilgrims to discard at the confluence. Once abandoned, the offerings are fished up and sold on to other pilgrims.

Much of the fort remains in military occupation, and public access is restricted to the leafy corner around the **Patalpuri Temple**, approached through any one of the three massive gates that puncture the fort's defences. Much of the super-structure of the fort is neglected; the **Zenana** with its columned hall does survive, but can only be viewed with prior permission. At the main gates to the fort stands a poorly restored polished stone **Ashoka Pillar**, inscribed with the emperor's edicts and dated to 242 BC.

Where the eastern battlements of the fort meet the river, a muddy *ghat* is busy with boatmen jostling for custom from the steady stream of pilgrims heading to the Sangam. Inland along the base of the fort, with the vast flood plain of the Sangam to the right, a road leads past rows of stalls catering to pilgrims to the brightly painted **Hanuman Temple**. Unusually, the large sunken image of the monkey god inside is reclining rather than standing erect; the story goes that during the annual floods the waters rise to touch his feet before once again receding.

Eating

Most of the better **cafés** and **restaurants** are in the Civil Lines area, within walking distance from each other close to the main crossing. In the early evening, the snack stalls along MG Marg entice the populace with their individual and often legendary specialities.

El Chico 24 MG Marg. One of the city's best, a smart place with good Indian, Chinese and Western cuisine, including grills, sizzlers, Szechuan-style pork or baked fish in cheese sauce. Non-veg mains Rs165–260.

Hot Stuff 21 Sardar Patel Marg. Popular hang-out for Allahabad's young and trendy, offering burgers, shakes, Chinese food and ice cream. Main dishes Rs50–100.

Indian Coffee House MG Marg, set back from the road. Allahabad branch of the South Indian co-op, serving great filter coffee and basic cheap snacks (nothing over Rs30) with no frills or pretensions.

Jade Garden MG Marg. Small, thatched garden restaurant, offering Chinese food of the chop suey, chow mein and sweet-and-sour variety, plus veg and non-veg Indian dishes (mains Rs90–150).

Kamdhenu 37 MG Marg. Famous Allahabad sweetshop, where the delicious local specialities include milk cakes stuffed with almonds.

Tandoor MG Marg. Upmarket non-veg restaurant and one of the best places in the city for Indian food, serving all the tandoori classics including chicken or fish tikka, kebabs and Muglai curries. Mains dishes are Rs65–100.

Around Allahabad

Just 63km south of Allahabad, on the banks of the Yamuna, are the extensive ruins of **Kausambi**, a major Buddhist centre where Buddha himself once preached. The city flourished between the eighth century BC and the sixth century AD; archeological evidence suggests even earlier habitation. According to legend, it was founded by descendants of the Pandavas, after floods destroyed their city of Hastinapur. Mud ramparts (originally faced with brick) tower over the fields, running along an irregular 6km perimeter, and sections remain of a defensive moat. Within the complex, excavations have revealed a paved road, brick houses, wells, tanks and drains, a monastery with cloisters and a large stupa, and the ruins of a palace in the southeast corner. The only standing feature is a damaged sandstone column ascribed to **Ashoka** – a second column, moved by the Mughals, now graces the gates of the fort at Allahabad. If you have your own vehicle or hire a taxi (around Rs1000), Kausambi is a straightforward day-trip from Allahabad. Otherwise, there is a direct bus every day from Leader Road bus station (Rs30).

Allahabad also makes a good base from which to venture into the remoter parts of **Bundelkhand** to the south. The sprawling pilgrimage town of **CHITRAKUT (also called Sitapur)** is 128km southwest, and easily accessible by both train and bus. It's also a good place to catch onward transport to Kalinjar and Khajuraho. Together with its twin town of **Karbi**, 8km east (where there are train connections to Allahabad, Kolkata and Delhi), Chitrakut is a major Vaishnavite pilgrimage centre. Most of its religious and leisure activity revolves around the charming central **Ramghat**, where boats with electric-blue mattresses and pillows create a pretty picture against a backdrop of ashrams and *ghats* to either side of the narrow, slow-moving river.

Eighty-eight kilometres southwest of Chitrakut, the abandoned star-shaped fortress of **KALINJAR** looks down on the Gangetic valley from the final escarpments of the craggy Vindhya hills, above the town of the same name. Much of the fort has been reclaimed by dry shrubby forest, populated by monkeys; once-grand avenues are now rocky footpaths that wind through the few crumbling yet ornately carved buildings that remain. Kalinjar has no tourist facilities to speak of – most of those who do come are either on day-trips from Chitrakut or Allahabad, or stay in Banda, which is on major train and bus routes and is connected to Kalinjar by local buses. Steep steps lead straight up for 3km from Kalinjar village to the fort's main gate, **Alam Darwaza**, but the southern **Panna Gate** has rock carvings depicting seven deer (like the fort's seven gates, these represent the then-known planets). Beneath **Bara Darwaza**, the "Large Gate", in the artificial cave of Sita Sej, a stone couch dating from the fourth century holds some of Kalinjar's earliest inscriptions. The fort's colossal rambling **battlements** provide sweeping views of the Gangetic plain to the north and the Vindhya hills to the south.

Varanasi

Older than history, older than tradition, older even than legend, and looks twice as old as all of them put together.

Mark Twain

The great Hindu city of **VARANASI**, also known as **Banaras** or **Benares**, stretches along the crescent of the River Ganges, its waterfront dominated by long flights of stone *ghats* where thousands of pilgrims and residents come for their daily ritual ablutions. Known to the devout as **Kashi**, the Luminous – the

City of Light, founded by Shiva – Varanasi is one of the oldest living cities in the world. It has maintained its religious life since the sixth century BC in one continuous tradition, in part by remaining outside the mainstream of political activity and historical development of the Subcontinent, and stands at the centre of the Hindu universe, the focus of a religious geography that reaches from the Himalayan cave of Amarnath in Kashmir, to India's southern tip at Kanniyakumari, Puri to the east, and Dwarka to the west. Located next to a ford on an ancient trade route, Varanasi is among the holiest of all *tirthas* – "crossing places", that allow the devotee access to the divine and enable gods and goddesses to come down to earth. It has attracted pilgrims, seekers, sannyasins and students of the *Vedas* throughout its history, including sages such as Buddha, Mahavira (founder of the Jain faith) and the great Hindu reformer Shankara.

Anyone who dies in Varanasi attains instant *moksha* or enlightenment. Widows and the elderly come here to seek refuge or to live out their final days, finding shelter in the temples and assisted by alms given by the faithful. Western visitors since the Middle Ages have marvelled at the strangeness of this most alien of Indian cities: at the tight mesh of alleys, the accoutrements of religion, the host of deities – and at the proximity of death.

Arrival, information and city transport

A pre-paid taxi from **Babatpur airport**, 22km northwest of the city, costs Rs350. Autos charge Rs175 for the same journey.

Varanasi lies on the main east–west axis between Delhi and Kolkata (Calcutta), and is served by two main railway stations: **Varanasi Cantonment** in the town itself, and **Mughal Sarai**, 17km east of town. Cantonment is the most conveniently located, but depending on where you are travelling from, you may find yourself using the Mughal Sarai line. There are retiring rooms at Mughal Sarai and local buses and taxis run regularly into Varanasi. Most **buses** terminate a couple of hundred metres east of the railway station along the main Grand Trunk Road and at the **Roadways bus station**. Buses from Nepal are met by the rickshaw mafia – see box below.

Tout dodging

Like Agra and Delhi, Varanasi is rife with **touts**, and you'll have to be careful of scams, especially on arrival. Most hotels pay a **commission** of up to eighty percent of the room rate (for every day you stay) to whoever takes you to the door – a cost that is passed on to you.

All English-speaking rickshaw drivers are part of this racket, and avoiding it takes persistence. At Cantonment railway station, first visit the very helpful tourist office (see p.322) and telephone your hotel of choice. They'll send someone to pick you up. If you want to make your own way to the hotels of the old town, walk away from the bus or railway station to the main road, find a non-English-speaking rickshaw driver, and ask to be taken to Godaulia, 3km southeast – a Rs15–20 cycle-rickshaw ride. Rickshaws are unable to penetrate the maze of lanes around Vishwanatha Temple and are banned from the central part of Godaulia. Again, you should telephone a hotel from here and they'll come and find you – if you attempt to get to a hotel yourself, touts may try to attach themselves and claim a commission on arrival. The only hotels in the old town that don't pay commission to touts are the *Vishnu*, *Shanti* and *Yogi Lodge* (see box, p.322), so it's common to hear that these places have "burned down" or "flooded"; touts also try to remove signs directing guests to the properties.

VARANASI

Mughal Sarai

Mughal Sarai

Sarnath

Gorakhpur

Lucknow

Lucknow

Lucknow

Allahabad

Lucknow

Adi Keshava Ghat

Malaviya Bridge

Kashi Railway Station

Trilochana Ghat

Gaya Ghat

Panchganga Ghat

Sankata Ghat

Manikarnika Ghat

City Railway Station

KOTWALI

Bus Stand

GPO

Mosque of Alamgir

CHOWK

OLD CITY

See Godaulia map

Varuna River

RAJGHAT ROAD

RABINDRANATH TAGORE ROAD

KABIR CHAURA ROAD

Chhavi Mahal Cinema

CHATTGANJ ROAD (NAI SARAK)

LUXA RD

Sanskrit University

Roadways Bus Station

STATION ROAD

Mehrota Silk

Bharat Mata Temple

VIDYAPEETH ROAD

SIGRA

Handloom House

SHRI RAMAKRISHNA ROAD

MAGBUL ALAM ROAD

RAJA BAZAR RD

CANTONMENT

Air India

TV Tower

Indian Airlines

Bihar Tourist Office

Varanasi Cantonment Railway Station

GRAND TRUNK ROAD (NH-2)

THE MALL

RESTAURANTS

Annapurna	2
Ashiyana	1
Bread of Life	6
El Parador	3
Haifa	7
Kerala Café	5
Lotus Lounge	4
Poonam	G
Vaatika	8

ACCOMMODATION

Ajay & Elena	J
Clarks	D
Ganges View	N
Gautam Grand	H
India	F
MM Continental	B
Palace on Ganges	N
Pradeep	G
Radisson Varanasi	A
Raj Kamal	H
Shiva Ganga	M
Surya	C
Taj Ganges	E
Tiwari Lodge	L
UPTDC Tourist Bungalow	I
Vishnu	K

Rana Ghat
Chaumsathi Ghat
Pandey Ghat
Raja Ghat
Narada Ghat
Mansarowar Ghat
Dhobi Ghat
Chauki Ghat
Kedara Ghat
Harishchandra Ghat
Hanuman Ghat
Shivala Ghat
Tulsi Ghat
Asi Ghat

River Ganges

SONAPURA RD
BHADANI ROAD
DURGA KUND ROAD

Harmony Books

Ramnagar Fort

Pontoor Bridge (dry season)

See Inset map

River Ganges

SONAPURA RD
BHADANI ROAD
DURGA KUND ROAD
ASI RD
SANKAT MOCHAN ROAD
RAMNAGAR ROAD
UNIVERSITY ROAD
HARISCHANDRA MARG
PANCH KOSHI ROAD

BHELPURA

Pilgrims Book House
Durga (Monkey) Temple
Tulsi Manas Temple

Sir Sundarlal Hospital

Bharat Kala Bhawan Museum

BANARAS HINDU UNIVERSITY

New Vishwanatha Temple

River Asi

Allahabad

0   500 m

What's in a name?

The **Yogi Lodge** (near Vishwanatha Temple), **Vishnu Rest House** (overlooking the river) and **Shanti Guest House** (near Manikarnika Ghat) are three of the oldest and best-run places in the Old City. Unfortunately they are all facing dubious competition from other hotels copying their names and paying rickshaw-wallahs to divert customers. Four other bogus Vishnu lodges have sprung up – the *Old Vishnu Lodge*, the *Vishnu Guest House*, the *Real Vishnu Guest House* and the *New Vishnu Guest House*. And several more "Shanti" lodges and "Yogi" lodges are playing the same name game. Legal battles are being fought between some of these similarly named hotels although the outcome is uncertain as no one owns the copyright to such universal Indian words as "Yogi", "Vishnu" and "Shanti". Only the original hotels are listed in the accommodation section.

Information

The main **UP Tourism office** is at their *Tourist Bungalow*, on Parade Kothi 500m southwest of Cantonment railway station (Mon–Sat 9am–5.30pm; ☏0542/220 6638), though their **tourist information counter** (daily 7am–7pm; ☏0542/250 6670) inside the railway station is their main office for giving out information – the boss, Uma Shankar, is extremely helpful and seems to regard protecting tourists as a personal crusade. The shabby **Bihar Government tourist office** at Englishia Market, Sher Shah Suri Marg, Cantonment (☏0542/234 3821), is useful if you're heading east into that state.

The **India Tourism office** languishes in the leafy suburbs of the Cantonment, a long way from the main attractions of the Old City and the *ghats*, just off The Mall on Stranger Road (Mon–Fri 9am–5.30pm, Sat 9am–2pm; ☏0542/250 1784). Its primary function is to dish out information on the whole of India, but the staff can assist with booking accommodation and car hire, and they'll also hold mail. They maintain a booth at the airport during flight times.

To experience the *ghats* at sunrise, or the peace of Sarnath, you're best off eschewing guided tours and making your own arrangements. If your time is very limited, official tour **guides** can be organized through the India Tourism office (Rs600 a day for up to five people, slightly more for bigger groups).

The local branch of the National Informatics Centre have some interesting information about Varanasi on their **website** at ⓦwww.varanasi.nic.in, and there's a commercial site on Varanasi at ⓦwww.visitvaranasi.com.

City transport

Cycle rickshaws are the easiest way to get around Varanasi, and often defy death and traffic jams by cycling up the wrong side of the road; a ride from Godaulia to Cantonment railway station costs Rs30. Auto–rickshaws should be faster, but due to the volume of traffic they rarely are for short rides across town. Godaulia to the railway station should cost Rs50.

Accommodation

Most of Varanasi's better and more expensive hotels lie on its peripheries, though to experience the full ambience of the city, stay close to the *ghats* and the lanes of the **Old City**. The top floors of Old City places, with views and more light, generally offer the best value, but can be hard to find during and shortly after the monsoons, when the swollen Ganges waters render them inaccessible from the waterside. Long-term tourists tend to stay around Asi *ghat* – rooms here are usually simple and cheap, and the atmosphere is laid-back.

If you want to stay with a local family, UP Tourism run a **paying guesthouse** scheme – ask at their station office.

Places listed below under the Godaulia heading appear on the Godaulia map (p.330); all others appear on the main Varanasi map (pp.320–321).

Godaulia

Alka D-3/23 Mir Ghat ☏ 0542/239 8445, ⓔ hotelalka@hotmail.com. Often booked up by tour groups, but a good mid-market riverside choice, with a big variety of well-maintained quality rooms, plus a terrace and a pleasant little lawn overlooking the river. ❶–❹

Ganga Fuji D-7/21 Sakarkand Gali ☏ 0542/232 7333, ⓔ raj327333@yahoo.com. Well-run family guesthouse near the Golden Temple, with a range of tastefully decorated rooms, scrupulously clean (though it's down a rather dirty alley), some with a/c, clean bathrooms and hot showers. ❶–❹

Ganpati D-3/24 Mir Ghat ☏ 0542/239 0059, ⓔ gghouse@satyam.net.in. Rooms here overlook the Ganges or are arranged around a courtyard, and there's a restaurant and a sociable balcony overlooking the river. The 10am checkout time is a bit inconvenient. ❷–❺

Golden Lodge D-8/35 Kalika Gali ☏ 0542/239 8788, ⓔ thegoldenlodge@yahoo.co.in. A friendly little place with a wide range of rooms – with and without bathrooms or a/c – of which the best value are on the roof. There's also a good restaurant. ❶–❸

La-Ra India Dashaswamedh Rd ☏ 0542/245 1805, ⓦ www.hotellaraindia.com. Genteel but shabby mid-range hotel in the heart of Godaulia, with a mainly Indian clientele, and a restaurant serving Banarsi (local) cuisine. ❸–❹

Puja D-1/45 Lalita Ghat ☏ 0542/240 5027, ⓦ www.pujaguesthouse.com. Ugly concrete building overlooking the Nepali Temple, with a rooftop restaurant and excellent views. Offers a range of rooms, of which those at the top of the steep stairs are the best, with a/c and balconies. ❶–❹

Scindhia Scindia Ghat ☏ 0542/242 0319. Near Manikarnika Ghat, this guesthouse is easy to find at low tide but well hidden after the monsoon, when the riverside path is closed. Clean rooms, some with balconies and river views. ❸–❺

Shanti Ck 8/129 Garwasi Tola, near Manikarnika Ghat ☏ 0542/239 2568, ⓔ varanasishanti@yahoo.com. An old favourite – though in need of a lick of paint – tucked away near the burning *ghats*. Large building with loads of (generally) clean rooms with attached bathrooms, as well as dorm beds (Rs50). Excellent views from the lively rooftop restaurant. ❶–❷

Sri Venkateswar D-5/64 Dashaswamedh Rd ☏ 0542/239 2357, ⓔ venlodge@yahoo.com. Simple but clean and close to the *ghats* and to Vishwanatha Temple, capturing the ambience of

the Old City. Airy rooms, nice courtyard, friendly staff and a strict no-drugs policy. ❷

Yogi Lodge D-8/29 Kalika Gali ☏ 0542/239 2588, ⓔ yogilodge@yahoo.com. An old budget-traveller favourite in the heart of the Old City that's been going for years; very well run, with a safe for valuables. Spotless restaurant, clean rooms and dorms (Rs60). ❶

South of Godaulia, near the river

Ajay and **Elena** D-21/11 Rana Ghat ☏ 0542/245 0970, ⓔ hotel_elena_vns@yahoo.com. Two neighbouring hotels (separated by a big banyan tree), each effectively the other's annexe, with rooms ranging from budget to a/c, but all immaculate, some giving views over the *ghats*. ❶–❹

Ganges View Asi Ghat ☏ 0542/231 3218, ⓦ www .hotelgangesview.com. A great veranda looking out onto the river, a lobby full of good books, a pleasant ambience and an interesting landlord mean this popular place is often booked up. The rooms are small but tastefully and stylishly decorated. You pay a premium to stay on the upper floor, with better views. ❸–❼

Palace on Ganges B-1/158 Asi Ghat ☏ 0542/231 5050, ⓔ palaceonganges@indiatimes.com. The only luxury hotel on the Ganges, with 22 individually decorated rooms representing the states of India – Gujarati is particularly colourful. Facilities include central a/c, TV, minibar, tour desk and rooftop restaurant. ❸

Shiva Ganga B-3/155 Niranjani Akhara, Shivala Ghat ☏ 0542/227 7755. Peaceful place with simple rooms, a veranda and a lush enclosed garden. Next to the Shiva Temple and affording great river views. ❶

Tiwari Lodge Asi Ghat ☏ 0542/231 5129. Appealing family-run place, built around a shrine and aimed at long-term guests. The rooms are simple, but spacious and squeaky clean, with shiny tile floors, and there's a German bakery on the premises. ❶

Vishnu Rest House D-24/17 Pandey Ghat ☏ 0542/245 0206. One of the nicest of the riverside lodges, with rooms, dorms (Rs50) and a lovely patio and café overlooking the Ganges; popular and often booked up. Best approached via the *ghats*, south of Dashaswamedh. ❶–❹

Cantonment and around

Clarks The Mall, Cantonment ☏ 0542/234 8501, ⓦ www.clarkshotels.com. Not really as posh as a five-star ought to be, a little bit worn in places, with horrible laminated floors in the rooms, but it does have a swimming pool, bar, restaurant and coffee shop. Doubles from US$132. ❾

Gautam Grand Parade Kothi, Cantonment ☎0542/220 8288. A new hotel, and better value than its pricier neighbours on this street near the station; the rooms (some a/c) are not huge, but they're reasonably well-kept, each with a balcony, there's 24hr room service, and the staff are eager to please. ❸–❹

India 59 Patel Nagar ☎0542/250 7593. A three-star hotel that makes a pretty good attempt at being stylish. The rooms are quite smart and modern (cool white with pinewood – even the laminated floor doesn't look too naff) with attached bathrooms and a/c; and a health and fitness centre, a rooftop bar and four restaurants, including the excellent *Palm Springs*. ❼–❽

MM Continental The Mall, Cantonment ☎0542/250 0172, ⓦwww.hotelmmcontinental .com. Tucked away behind *Clarks*. Ordinary rooms with baths and deluxe rooms without, not tremendously well kept, but there's a restaurant and rooftop coffee shop. ❼

Pradeep Kabir Chaura Rd, Jagatganj ☎0542/220 7231 or 2, ⓦwww.hotelpradeep.com. Comfortable, quite stylish and popular with tour groups; away from the *ghats* but within striking distance. Enticing multi-cuisine restaurant on site. ❺–❼

Radisson Varanasi The Mall, Cantonment ☎0542/250 1515, ⓦwww.radisson.com/varanasi.in. One of Varanasi's best-value luxury places, with classy and well-appointed rooms, stylish but not huge, plus a swimming pool, two restaurants, a bar and a coffee shop. Rates (doubles from US$172) include a huge buffet breakfast. ❾

Raj Kamal Parade Kothi, Cantonment ☎0542/220 0071. Budget option near the railway station, just outside the *Tourist Bungalow* gates. Useful for early and late train departures, but often full. ❷

Surya S-20/51, A5 The Mall, Cantonment ☎0542/250 8465 or 6, ⓦwww.hotelsuryavns .com. Well-run, comfortable and relaxing hotel arranged around a small lawn that doubles up as an alfresco restaurant. Rooms are small but well kept with modern bathrooms; many have balconies. Facilities include Internet, tour desk, foreign exchange, a pool (Rs100 for guests, Rs200 for non-guests) and a decent restaurant. You can also camp (Rs150 per person). ❹–❺

Taj Ganges Nadesar Palace Grounds, Raja Bazaar Rd, Cantonment ☎0542/250 3001 to 19, ⓦwww .tajhotels.com. The poshest gaff in town, set among vast grounds (explore them by buggy, or on a birdwatching walk), with stately rooms, fine dining, a pool and fitness centre naturally, and also yoga classes. Double rooms start at US$198, or take an executive suite for $265. ❾

UPTDC Tourist Bungalow Parade Kothi, Cantonment ☎0542/220 8413, ⓔrahitbvaranasi @up-tourism.com. Large institutional complex with a garden, bar, restaurant and a wide range of rooms including a dorm (Rs75). Handy for the bus and railway stations. ❷–❹

The ghats

The great riverbanks at Varanasi, built high with eighteenth- and nineteenth-century pavilions and palaces, temples and terraces, are lined by stone steps – the **ghats** – which stretch along the whole waterfront, changing dramatically in appearance with the seasonal fluctuations of the river level. Each of the hundred *ghats*, big and small, is marked by a lingam, and occupies its own special place in the religious geography of the city. Some have crumbled over the years while others continue to thrive, visited by early-morning bathers, brahmin priests offering puja, and people practising meditation and yoga. Hindus regard the Ganges as *amrita*, the elixir of life, which brings purity to the living and salvation to the dead, but in reality the river is scummy with effluent, so don't be tempted to join the bathers; never mind the chemicals and human body parts, it's the level of heavy metals, dumped by factories upstream, that are the real cause for concern. Whether Ganga water still has the power to absolve sin if sterilized is a contentious point; current thinking has it that boiling is acceptable but chemical treatment ruins it.

For centuries, pilgrims have traced the perimeter of the city by a ritual circumambulation, paying homage to shrines on the way. Among the most popular routes is the **Panchatirthi Yatra**, which takes in the *pancha* (five) *tirthi* (crossings) of Asi, Dash, Manikarnaka, Panchganga, and finally Adi Kesh. To gain

Boat trips on the Ganges

All along the *ghats*, and especially at the main ones such as Dashaswamedh, the prices of **boat** (*bajra*) **rental** are highly inflated, with local boatmen under pressure from touts to fleece tourists and pilgrims. There's a police counter at the top of Dashaswamedh, but the lack of government tourist assistance means that renting a boat to catch the dawn can be a bit of a free-for-all, and haggling is essential. There is an official rate, determined by UP Tourism, of Rs50 per hour for a small (one- to four-person) boat, Rs75 for a larger (five- to ten-person) one, but you won't find a boatman who'll agree to it.

merit or appease the gods, the devotee, accompanied by a *panda* (priest), recites a *sankalpa* (statement of intent) and performs a ritual at each stage of the journey. For the casual visitor, however, the easiest way to see the *ghats* is to follow a south–north sequence either by boat or on foot.

Asi Ghat to Kedara Ghat

At the clay-banked **Asi Ghat**, where the River Asi runs into the Ganges, pilgrims bathe prior to worshipping at a huge lingam under a peepal tree. A small marble temple just off the *ghat* houses another lingam called **Asisangameshvara**, the "Lord of the Confluence of the Asi". Traditionally, pilgrims continued from these to **Lolarka Kund**, the "Trembling Sun", a rectangular tank 15m below ground level, approached by steep steps, but it's now almost abandoned – except during the Lolarka Mela fair (Aug/Sept), when thousands come to propitiate the gods and pray for the birth of a son. It is actually one of Varanasi's earliest sites, and was attracting bathers in the days of Buddha. Equated with the twelve *adityas* or divisions of the sun, it is one of only two remaining sites in Varanasi that are linked with the origins of Hinduism, when worship of the sun god Surya predominated over that of the modern deities Shiva and Vishnu.

Much of the adjacent **Tulsi Ghat** – originally Lolarka Ghat, but renamed in honour of the poet Tulsi Das, who lived nearby in the sixteenth century – has crumbled. **Hanuman Ghat**, to its north, is believed by many to be the birthplace of the fifteenth-century Vaishnavite saint, Vallabha, who was instrumental in reviving the worship of Krishna (Vishnu's human incarnation in the Mahabarata). As well as a new South Indian temple, the *ghat* also has a striking image of **Ruru**, the dog, one of the eight forms of **Bhairava**, a ferocious and early form of Shiva.

The next set of steps northwards is **Harishchandra Ghat**, named after a legendary king who gave up his entire kingdom in a fit of self-abnegation. One of Varanasi's two **burning ghats** (*ghats* used for cremation, that is, the other being Manikarnika Ghat), it is easily recognizable from the smoke of its funeral pyres.

Further north still, **Kedara Ghat** is connected mythologically to Kedarnath, Shiva's home in the Himalayas. Pilgrims on the Panchatirthi Yatra don't visit it, but it's always busy and becomes a hive of activity in the sacred month of Shravana (July/Aug), at the height of the monsoon. Above its steps, a red-and-white-striped temple houses the **Kedareshvara lingam**, made of black rock shot through with a vein of white.

Chauki Ghat to Chaumsathi Ghat

Northwards along the river, **Chauki Ghat** is distinguished by an enormous tree that shelters small stone shrines to the *nagas*, water-snake deities, while at the unmistakable **Dhobi** ("Laundrymen's") **Ghat**, clothes are still rhythmically pulverized in pursuit of purity. Past smaller *ghats* such as **Manasarowar**, named after the holy lake in Tibet, and **Narada**, honouring the divine musician and sage, lies **Chaumsathi Ghat**, where impressive stone steps lead up to the small temple of the **Chaumsathi** (64) **Yoginis**. Images of Kali and Durga in its inner sanctum represent a stage in the emergence of the great goddess as a single representation of a number of female divinities. Overlooking the *ghats* here is Peshwa Amrit Rao's majestic sandstone haveli (mansion), built in 1807 and currently used for religious ceremonies and occasionally as an auditorium for concerts.

Dashaswamedh Ghat

Dashaswamedh Ghat is Varanasi's most popular and accessible bathing *ghat*, with rows of *pandas* sitting on wooden platforms under bamboo umbrellas, masseurs plying their trade and boatmen jostling for custom. It's the second and busiest of the five *tirthas* on the Panchatirthi Yatra. Its **Brahmeshvara** lingam is supposed to have been planted by the god Brahma. South of Dashaswamedh Ghat, a flat-roofed building houses the shrine of **Shitala**, which is likewise extremely popular, even in the rainy season when devotees have to wade to the temple or take a boat.

Man Mandir Ghat to Lalita Ghat

Man Mandir Ghat is known primarily for its magnificent eighteenth-century observatory, built for the Maharaja of Jaipur and equipped with ornate window casings. Pilgrims pay homage to the important lingam of Someshvara, the lord of the moon, alongside, before crossing **Tripurabhairavi Ghat** to **Mir Ghat** and the **New Vishwanatha Temple**, built by conservative brahmins who claimed that the main Vishwanatha lingam was rendered impure when Harijans (Untouchables) entered the sanctum in 1956. At Mir Ghat, the **Dharma Kupa**, the Well of Dharma, surrounded by subsidiary shrines and the lingam of **Dharmesha**, where it is said that Yama, the Lord of Death, obtained his jurisdiction over all the dead of the world – except here in Varanasi.

To the north is **Lalita Ghat**, renowned for its **Ganga Keshava** shrine to Vishnu and the **Nepali Temple** (daily 5am–8pm; Rs10), a Kathmandu-style wooden structure which houses an image of **Pashupateshvara** – Shiva's manifestation at Pashupatinath, in the Kathmandu Valley – and sporting a small selection of erotic carvings.

Manikarnika Ghat

North of Lalita lies Varanasi's pre-eminent cremation ground, **Manikarnika Ghat**. Such grounds are usually held to be inauspicious, and located on the fringes of cities, but the entire city of Shiva is regarded as **Mahashamshana**, the Great Cremation Ground for the corpse of the entire universe. The *ghat* is perpetually crowded with funeral parties, as well as the **Doms**, its Untouchable guardians, busy and preoccupied with facilitating final release for those lucky enough to pass away here. Seeing bodies being cremated so publicly has always exerted a great fascination for visitors to the city, but photography is strictly taboo; even having a camera visible may be construed as intent, and provoke hostility. Wood touts descend on tourists at the *ghat* explaining the finer metaphysical points of transmutation ("cremation is education") before subtly shifting to the practicalities of how much wood is needed to burn one body, the never-ending cycle of inflation and would you like to give a donation. The amounts written down in their "ledgers" are unbelievable.

Lying at the centre of the five *tirthas*, Manikarnika Ghat symbolizes both creation and destruction, epitomized by the juxtaposition of the sacred well of **Manikarnika Kund**, said to have been dug by Vishnu at the time of creation, and the hot, sandy ash-infused soil of cremation grounds where time comes to an end. In Hindu mythology, Manikarnika Kund predates the arrival of the Ganga and has its source deep in the Himalayas. Vishnu carved the *kund* (water tank) with his discus, and filled it with perspiration from his exertions in creating the world at the behest of Shiva. When Shiva quivered with delight, his earring fell into this pool, which as Manikarnika – "Jewelled Earring" – became the first *tirtha* in the world. Every year, after the floodwaters of the river have receded to leave the pool caked in alluvial deposits, the *kund* is re-dug. Its surroundings are cleaned and painted with bright folk art depicting the presiding goddess, **Manikarni Devi**.

Bordering Manikarnika to the north is the picturesque **Scindia Ghat**, its tilted Shiva temple lying partially submerged in the river, after falling in as a result of the sheer weight of the *ghat's* construction in the mid-nineteenth century. Above the *ghat*, several of Varanasi's most influential shrines are hidden within the tight maze of alleyways of the area known as **Siddha Kshetra** (the "Field of Fulfilment").

Panchganga Ghat to Adi Keshava Ghat

Beyond Lakshmanbala Ghat, with its commanding views of the river, lies one of the most dramatic – and contentious – *ghats*, **Panchganga**, dominated by Varanasi's largest riverside building, the great **Mosque of Alamgir**, known locally as Beni Madhav-ka-Darera. With its minarets now much shortened, the mosque stands on the ruins of the **Bindu Madhava**, a Vishnu temple that extended from Panchganga to Rama Ghat before it was destroyed by Aurangzeb and replaced with the mosque. Panchganga also bears testimony to more favourable Hindu–Muslim relations, being the site of the initiation of the medieval saint of the Sufi-Sant tradition, Kabir, the son of a humble Muslim weaver who is venerated by Hindus and Muslims alike. Along the riverfront lies a curious array of three-sided cells, submerged during the rainy season, some with lingams, others with images of Vishnu, and some empty and used for meditation or yoga. Above **Trilochana Ghat**, further north, is the holy ancient lingam of the three (*tri*)-eyed (*lochana*) Shiva. Beyond it, the river bypasses some of Varanasi's oldest precincts, now predominantly Muslim in character; the *ghats* themselves gradually become less impressive and are usually of the *kaccha* (clay-banked) variety. At **Adi Keshava Ghat** (the "Original Vishnu"), on the outskirts of the city, the Varana flows into the Ganga. Unapproachable during the rainy season, when it is completely submerged, the *ghat* marks the place where Vishnu supposedly landed as an emissary of Shiva, and stands on the original site of the city before it spread southwards; around Adi Keshava are a number of Ganesha shrines.

The Old City

At the heart of Varanasi, between Dashaswamedh Ghat and Godaulia to the south and west and Manikarnika Ghat on the river to the north, lies the maze of ramshackle alleys that comprise the **Old City**, or Vishwanatha Khanda. The whole area buzzes with the activity of pilgrims, *pandas* and stalls selling offerings to the faithful, and there are lingams and shrines tucked into every corner. If you get lost just head for the river.

Approached through labyrinthine alleys and the **Vishwanatha Gali** (or Lane), the temple complex of **Vishwanatha** or Visheshwara, the "Lord of All", is popularly known as the **Golden Temple**, due to the gold plating on its massive *shikhara* (spire). Hidden behind a wall, the opulent complex is closed to non-Hindus, who have to make do with glimpses from adjacent buildings.

Vishwanatha's history has been fraught. Sacked by successive Muslim rulers, it was repeatedly rebuilt and destroyed; in 1785, Queen Ahilyabai Holkar of Indore built the temple that stands today. Its simple white domes tower over the **Jnana Vapi** ("Wisdom Well"), immediately north, housed in an open-arcaded hall built in 1828, where Shiva cooled his lingam after the construction of Vishwanatha. Adjacent to the temple, guarded by armed police to protect it from Hindu fanatics, stands the **Jnana Vapi Mosque**, also known as the Great Mosque of Aurangzeb. Close by, the temple of **Annapurna Bhavani** is dedicated to Shakti, the divine female energy. Manifest in many forms, including the awesome Kali and Durga with their weapons and gruesome garlands of skulls, she's seen here as the provider of sustenance and carries a cooking pot. Nearby is a stunning image, faced in silver against a black surround, of **Shani** or Saturn. Slightly north, across the main road, the thirteenth-century **Razia's Mosque** stands atop the ruins of a still earlier Vishwanatha temple that was destroyed under the Sultanate.

Bharat Mata

About 3km northwest of Godaulia, outside the Old City, the modern temple of **Bharat Mata** ("Mother India"), inaugurated by Mahatma Gandhi, is unusual in that it has a huge relief map in marble of the whole of the Indian Subcontinent and the Tibetan plateau, with mountains, rivers and the holy *tirthas* all clearly visible. Pilgrims circumambulate the map before viewing it in its entirety from the second floor. The temple can be reached by rickshaw from Godaulia for around Rs20.

South of the Old City

The nineteenth-century **Durga Temple** – stained red with ochre, and popularly known as the Monkey Temple, thanks to its aggressive and irritable monkeys – stands in a walled enclosure 4km south of Godaulia, not far from Asi Ghat. It is devoted to Durga, the terrifying aspect of Shiva's consort, Parvati, and the embodiment of **Shakti** (divine female energy), and was built in a typical north Indian style, with an ornate *shikhara* in five segments, symbolizing the elements. The best views of the temple are from across Durga *kund*, the adjoining tank. A forked stake in the courtyard is used during some festivals to behead sacrificial goats. Non-Hindus are admitted to the courtyard, but not the inner sanctum.

Access to the neighbouring **Tulsi Manas Temple**, on the other hand, is unrestricted (daily 5am–noon & 4pm–midnight). Built in 1964 of white-streaked marble, its walls are inscribed with verses by the poet and author of the Ramcharitmanas, the Hindi equivalent of the great Sanskrit epic Ramayana.

A little further south, the **Bharat Kala Bhawan** museum (Mon–Sat: May & June 7.30am–1pm; July–April 10.30am–4.30pm; Rs100 [Rs10], camera Rs50) has a fabulous collection of miniature paintings, sculpture, contemporary art and bronzes. A gallery dedicated to the city of Varanasi, with a stunning nineteenth-century map, has a display of the recent Raj Ghat excavations and old etchings of the city. Along with Buddhist and Hindu sculpture and Mughal glass, further galleries are devoted to foreign artists who found inspiration in India, such as Nicholas Roerich and Alice Boner; the Bengali renaissance painter, Jamini Roy, so influenced by folk art, is also well represented.

Bharat Kala Bhawan forms part of Banaras Hindu University, the campus of which also holds the **New Vishwanatha Temple** (daily 4am–noon & 1–9pm), distinguished by its lofty white-marble *shikhara*. The temple was the brainchild of Pandit Malaviya, founder of the university and a great believer in an egalitarian and casteless Hindu revival, and was built by the Birlas, a wealthy Marwari industrial family. Although supposedly modelled on the original temple destroyed by Aurangzeb, the building displays characteristics of the new wave of temple architecture, amalgamating influences from various parts of India with a garish interior. Outside the gates a small market with teashops, flower-sellers and other vendors caters for the continuous flow of visitors.

Ramnagar Fort

South of Asi Ghat, on the opposite side of the river, the residence of the Maharaja of Varanasi, **Ramnagar Fort** looks down upon the Ganges. The best views of the fortifications – especially impressive in late afternoon – are to be had from the rickety pontoon bridge that crosses the river to the fort on the south bank, which is reached by a road heading south from the BHU area. During the monsoon the bridge is dismantled and replaced by a ferry, still preferable to taking the long main road that crosses the main Malaviya Bridge to the north before heading down the eastern bank of the river. The fort can also be reached by chartering a boat from Dashaswamedh Ghat.

Inside, the fort bears testimony to the wealth of the maharaja and his continuing influence. A dusty and poorly kept **museum** (daily 10am–5pm; Rs12) provides glimpses of a decadent past: horse-drawn carriages, old motor cars, palanquins, ornate gilded and silver *howdahs* (elephant seats), hookahs, costumes and old silk in a sorry state are all part of the collection, along with an armoury, some minute ivory carvings, an astronomical clock and hunting trophies. Some visitors have reported having tea with the affable maharaja after chance encounters.

Varanasi is renowned for its **Ram Lila**, held during Dussehra (Oct), during which episodes from the Ramayana are re-enacted throughout the city and the maharaja sponsors three weeks of elaborate celebrations. Across the courtyard, a section is devoted to the Ram Lila procession and festivities.

Eating

Most of the Old City **cafés** are veg, and alcohol is not tolerated, but the newer Cantonment area is less constrained, and some of the more expensive hotels have bars. After a trip on the boats in the early morning, try the traditional snack of *kachori*, savoury deep-fried pastry bread sold in the Old City next to the *ghats* – but avoid the chai stalls here as the cups are washed in the river.

Stomach disorders are a common phenomenon in Varanasi, so stick to bottled or treated water and be careful when choosing where you eat. Among hotel restaurants, *Vishnu Rest House* on Pandey Ghat does excellent thalis and the *Yogi Lodge* near Vishwanatha Temple must have the cleanest kitchen in the Old City, and dishes out all the travellers' favourites with not a lot of spice. Places listed below under the Godaulia heading appear on the Godaulia map (p.330); all others appear on the main Varanasi map (pp.320–321).

Godaulia

Ayyar's Dashaswamedh Rd. Small, inexpensive café at the back of a shopping arcade, serving South Indian food (Rs15–30), including great masala dosas, excellent filter coffee and delicious milk drinks.

Ganga Fuji D5/8 Kalika Gali, Dashaswamedh. Pleasant little restaurant near Vishwanatha, with a friendly host who guides diners through the multi-cuisine menu (main dishes Rs60–80 veg, Rs100–150

non-veg) – north Indian dishes are particularly good. Live classical music every evening from 7.30pm.

Keshari D-14/8, Teri Neem, off Dashas-wamedh Rd. The menu lists a huge variety of veg curries at Rs45–80, "all items available", they say. The *paneer* tomato and the mushroom masala are its specialities, but every dish is delicious.

Madhur Milan Dashaswamedh Rd, just past Vishwanatha Lane. Cheap and very popular café, great for *dosas*, sweets, *kachoris* and samosas

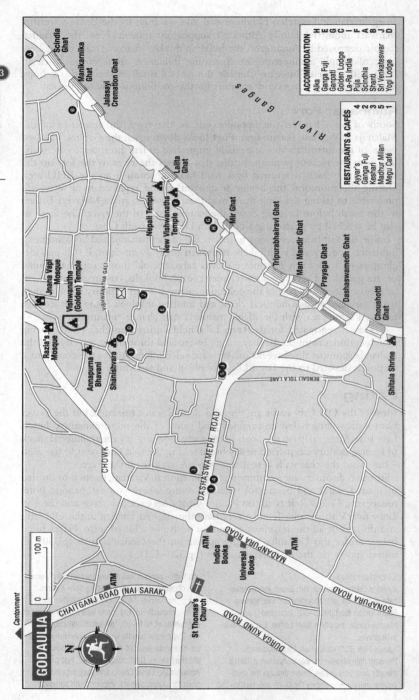

GODAULIA

Cantonment

River Ganges

Scindia Ghat

Manikarnika Ghat

Jalasayi Cremation Ghat

Lalita Ghat

Nepali Temple

New Vishwanatha Temple

Mir Ghat

Tripurabhairavi Ghat

Man Mandir Ghat

Prayaga Ghat

Dashaswamedh Ghat

Choushotti Ghat

Shitala Shrine

Jnana Vapi Mosque

Vishwanatha (Golden) Temple

VISHWANATHA GALI

Razia's Mosque

Annapurna Bhavani

Shanishvara

BENGALI TOLA LANE

DASHASWAMEDH ROAD

CHOWK

CHAITGANJ ROAD (NAI SARAK)

ATM

Indica Books

Universal Books

St Thomas's Church

MADANPURA ROAD

SONAPURA ROAD

DURGA KUND ROAD

ATM

ATM

N

0   100 m

ACCOMMODATION	
Alka	H
Ganga Fuji	E
Ganpati	G
Golden Lodge	C
La-Ra India	I
Puja	F
Scindhia	A
Shanti	B
Sri Venkateswar	J
Yogi Lodge	D

RESTAURANTS & CAFÉS	
Ayyar's	4
Ganga Fuji	2
Keshari	3
Madhur Milan	5
Megu Café	1

(watch them being fried out front, and grab them while they're piping hot). Main dishes Rs20–50, thalis Rs35–90.

Megu Café D-8/1 Kalika Gali. Down the alley leading to the *Golden Lodge* and *Yogi Lodge*, this small place run by a Japanese–Indian couple (shoes off at the door), serves a short menu of Japanese treats including veg sushi rolls, veg tempura and ginger chicken (mains dishes Rs60–80). Closed Sundays.

The rest of the town

Annapurna J-12/16A Ramkatora ☎0542/220 0151. Doesn't look promising on the outside, but gleaming within, this multi-cuisine restaurant serves Continental, Subcontinental and Chinese veg food (main dishes Rs45–100), and also does home delivery. Has a good selection of thalis (Rs75–110) and mini-meals (Rs65).

Ashiyana Major Singh Place, Lt Rohan Marg, Cantonment. Chinese and Indian meals, snacks and drinks served in an a/c lounge or on a rather noisy lawn, with non-veg mains at Rs45–120, including *nargisi kofta* (mincemeat stuffed with eggs), chicken dilruba (with *paneer* and dried fruit), even chicken tikka masala.

Bread of Life B3/322 Sonapura Rd. Bakery providing brown bread, cinnamon rolls, muffins and confectionery, with a small, clean restaurant serving Western food such as tuna burgers and crème caramel. Main dishes Rs80–120; profits go to charity, but service is slow.

El Parador Maldahia Rd. Remarkable restaurant round the corner from the *Tourist Bungalow*, serving outstanding Mexican, Italian, Greek and French cuisine in a bistro atmosphere. All the pasta is home-made, main dishes Rs165–225.

Haifa 1/108 Asi Rd. Laid-back place serving approximations of Middle Eastern dishes – including hummus, fresh-baked pittas and falafel – as well as the more usual Indian fare, in a congenial atmosphere. Main dishes Rs45–70, breakfasts Rs50–70. The "Middle Eastern thali" (a selection of mezze with pitta) is a great deal at Rs70.

Kerala Café Durga Kund Rd, Bhelpura Thana. A very popular South Indian restaurant with good snacks (*dosas*, vadas, uttapams and the like, at Rs20–30) and lemon rice, tamarind rice, sambar rice or curd rice (Rs30).

Lotus Lounge 14/21 Mansarowar Ghat. Not a lounge at all, but a bright and breezy terrace restaurant overlooking the *ghats*, and serving an eclectic mix of international cuisine from chicken satay to Thai red curry to moussaka, plus pastas and salads, with main dishes at Rs70–140.

Poonam *Hotel Pradeep*, Kabir Chaura Rd, Jagatganj. Good, if expensive (Rs150–225), Mughlai food served in a comfortable air-conditioned environment.

Vaatika Asi Ghat. A leafy terrace right on the *ghat*, serving good pizza (Rs65–100) and pasta (Rs50–70), plus wonderful freshly made juices and salads (all vegetables sterilized in permanganate, all water boiled and filtered).

Shopping

With hustlers and rickshaw drivers keen to drag tourists into stores offering commission, **shopping in Varanasi** can be a nightmare – but it's worth seeking out the city's rich silk-weaving and brasswork. The best **areas to browse** are the Thatheri Bazaar (for brass), or Jnana Vapi and the Vishwanatha Gali in Godaulia with its Temple Bazaar (for silk brocade and jewellery). State-run emporiums in Godaulia, Lahurabir and the Chowk – the three UP Handlooms outlets at Lahurabir, and Nichi Bagh, and Mahatex in Godaulia – offer fixed prices and assured quality. The CIE, housed in a former palace opposite the *Taj Ganges Hotel* in the Cantonment, has a large and impressive selection but, despite its official-sounding name, is an outrageously expensive Kashmiri-run chain aimed exclusively at the five-star market. **Open Hand Café and Shop**, B1/128-3 Dumraun Bagh, Colony Asi, near *Haifa* restaurant and *Tiwari Lodge*, is a community-run project selling bed linen, clothes, bags, cards, and it doubles up as a café, so you can enjoy filter coffee and chocolate cake while you shop.

Sales pitches tend to become most aggressive when it comes to **silk**, and you need to be wary of the hard sell. Qazi Sadullahpura, near the Chhavi Mahal Cinema, lies at the heart of a fascinating Muslim neighbourhood devoted to the production of silk. Mehrotra silk factory, 21/72 Englishia Lane, off Station Road near the railway station is highly recommended, and will happily run you up a shirt and deliver it to your hotel, as well as selling ready-made scarves, shawls and bedsheets. Upica, the government-run emporium, has outlets at

Godaulia and opposite the *Taj Ganges* hotel, and Handloom House, D64/132K Sigra, is another government-sponsored chain. Nearby Paraslakshmi Exports, 71 Chandrika Colony, offer a wide range of silk fabrics as well as scarves, shawls and bedspreads at fixed prices.

Listings

Airlines Air India, Sridas Foundation Building, 4 The Mall (next to *Radisson* hotel), Cantonment ☎0542/250 9195; Indian Airlines, 52 Jadunath Marg, just off The Mall, Cantonment ☎0542/250 2527 to 29; Jet Airways and JetLite, at the airport ☎0542/262 2795.

Banks and exchange There are plenty of ATMs around town (one on Godaulia roundabout for example). In addition several of the cheap hotels, as well as the upmarket ones, will change money, as well as NL Forex on Dashaswamedh Rd and near *Taj Ganges* hotel. The State Bank of India by *Hotel Surya* in the Cantonment (Mon–Fri 10am–4pm, Sat 10am–1pm) also changes cash and traveller's cheques.

Bookshops A few doors away, Universal Book Company has a large selection of fiction, reference and art books. Pilgrims Book House on Durgakund Rd has a good range especially on Buddhism and Hinduism. Harmony, B1/158 Asi Ghat, have a superb selection of books on all things Indian as well as fiction and philosophy.

Car rental Rental at around Rs2000–3000 per day for a car with driver from Travel Corporation of India (see "Travel agencies" below); India Tourism (see p.322) ☎0542/250 1784.

Hospitals Sir Sunderlal Hospital, Benares Hindu University (☎0542/230 7565); Shiv Prasad Gupta Hospital (government-run), Kabir Chaura (☎0542/221 4720 to 3); Marwari Hospital, Godaulia (☎0542/239 2611); Ram Krishna Mission Hospital, Luxa (☎0542/245 1727).

Internet access Internet cafés aimed at travellers cluster around Kachauri Lane and Bengali Tola Lane in the Godaulia area, charging Rs20–25/hr. In the Cantonment (across the st

from the *Taj Ganges* hotel, for example), they cost Rs30–50/hr.

Motorcycles Mechanics and workshops specializing in Enfields are clustered in the Jagatganj area, near the Sanskrit University; ask around for a secondhand bike.

Music The International Music Ashram, D33/81 Kalishpura in the Old City (☎0542/245 2302, ✉keshvaraonayak@hotmail.com), is an excellent place to get a few lessons in tabla, sitar and theory.

Pharmacies Singh Medical pharmacy near Prakash Cinema, Lahurabir (a couple of kilometres north of Godaulia), opens late; the pharmacy at the Apollo Hospital in Sigra is open 24hr.

Post The main post office in the Old City is on Kabir Chaura Rd near Kotwalli police station at the top end of the Chowk district. The one in the Cantonment is off Raja Bazaar Rd near the big TV mast at its top end. Branch offices are located in *Clarks* hotel in the Cantonment, on Dashaswamedh Rd near the river, and on Sakarkand Gali near *Ganga Fuji* restaurant.

Travel agencies General travel agencies, selling train, plane and bus tickets, include the friendly Nova International on Shubhash Nagar, near Parade Kothi ☎0542/220 8361, and the Travel Corporation of India, Sridas Foundation Building, 4 The Mall (next to *Radisson* hotel) ☎01542/250 0310, ⊛www.tcindia.com.

Yoga There is a yoga institute at the Benares Hindu University, but the Yoga Ashram Academy (D5/4 *Ganesha Guest House*, Saraswati Phatak ☎0542/240 2814) in Godaulia is more central; alternatively there's Yogi Rakesh Pandeep, B-4/35 Hanuman Ghat (☎09415 817882), and Swami Shwam Yogacharya, K-4/35 Lal Ghat (☎0542/243 6006).

Moving on from Varanasi

To get to the **airport** through the gridlock (around Rs350 by taxi, Rs175 by auto), allow at least ninety minutes from the Old City.

From the Roadways Bus Stand on GT Road (☎0542/220 3476), UPSRTC run morning and evening **buses**, including overnight services, to the **Nepal** border at Sonauli (10hr) via Gorakhpur, and there are good and regular buses for Allahabad, making road a better option than rail for that destination. For Bihar on the other hand, bus services are now few and far between, and road conditions not great, so rail is your best bet.

As always, check **train** times before you travel (@www.indianrail.gov.in). Varanasi Station has a reservations desk (Mon–Sat 8am–1.50pm & 2–8pm, Sun 8am–2pm). Many trains on the main east–west Delhi–Kolkata line bypass Varanasi but stop at Mughal Sarai, around 45 minutes away by road or rail. The fastest train to Agra and Jaipur, for example, is the daily #2307 Howrah–Jodhpur Express, which leaves Mughal Sarai at 9.50am, getting in to Agra at 7.25pm, Jaipur at midnight, and Jodhpur at 7.20am the next morning, but there's also a thrice-weekly overnight service from Varanasi itself, the #4853 Marudhar Express (Mon, Wed & Sat 5.20pm, arriving Agra 6.10am, Jaipur 11.30am, Jodhpur 6.20pm). For Delhi, though a couple of Rajdhanis pass through Mughal Sarai around 1am, the most convenient trains leave from Varanasi, including the #2559 Shiv Ganga Express (leaves 7.15pm, arrives in New Delhi at 7.25am). The best daytime service, the #2875 Neelachal Express (leaves 7.38am, arrives in New Delhi at 9.40pm) runs Monday, Wednesday and Saturday only. To Kolkata, convenient overnight services include the #3006 Howrah Mail, leaving Varanasi at 5pm, for a chirpy 7.30am arrival at Howrah; you can get a faster service from Mughal Sarai (the 1.55am #2302 Rajdhani takes only eight hours), but it isn't worth the extra effort. The Mahanagri Express #1094 is the fastest train to Mumbai (departs 11.30am, arriving at Kalyan 12.55pm next day), and if you're heading further south, the twice-weekly #2670 Gangakaveri Express leaves Monday & Wednesday at 8.25pm for the 38-hour haul to Chennai.

The most convenient train to **Patna**, though it arrives relatively late, is the Vibhuti Express #2334, which leaves at 6pm, arriving in Patna at 10.20pm. Earlier services are much slower. For **Gaya** the best train is the Doon Express #3010, which should leave at 4.25pm and arrive at 9.40pm.

To **Uttranachal**, the #3009 Doon Express (10.35am arriving Dehra Dun 7.10am next day) is the best option for Dehra Dun, but the #4265 Dehra Dun Express (departs 8.30am) also serves Ramnagar (arrives 6am next day). For Khajuraho, take a train to Satna (the 4-weekly #1062 Lokmanyatilak Express does it overnight, departing Mon, Wed, Fri & Sun 11.15pm, arriving at 6.15am, otherwise the daily #1094 Mahanagri Express at 11.30am will get you in at 6.15pm), where you can pick up regular state buses for the four-hour journey.

For a rundown of frequencies and journey times, see "Travel details", p.340.

Sarnath

Ten kilometres north of Varanasi, the cluster of ruins and temples at **SARNATH** is a place of pilgrimage for Buddhists, and has also become popular with day-trippers from Varanasi who picnic among the ruins and parklands. It was here, at some time around 530 BC, just five weeks after he had found enlightenment, that Buddha gave his first ever sermon. According to Buddhist belief, this set in motion the Dharmachakra ("Wheel of Law"), a new cycle of rebirths and reincarnations leading eventually to ultimate enlightenment for everybody. During the rainy season, when the Buddha and his followers sought respite from their round of itinerant teaching, they would retire to Sarnath. Also known as **Rishipatana**, the place of the *rishis* or sages, or **Mrigadaya**, the deer park, Sarnath's name derives from Saranganatha, the Lord of the Deer.

Over the centuries, the settlement flourished as a centre of Buddhist (particularly Hinayana) art and teaching. Seventh-century Chinese pilgrim Xuan Zhang recounted seeing thirty monasteries, supporting some 3000 monks, and a life-sized brass statue of the Buddha turning the Wheel of Law, but Indian

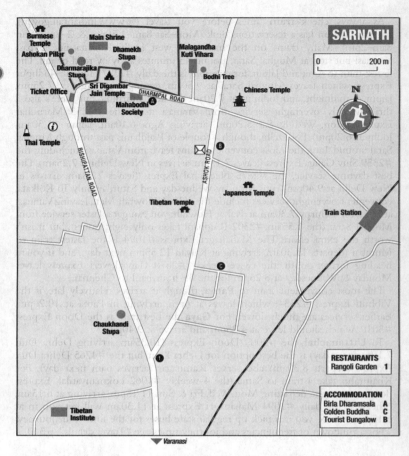

▼ Varanasi

Buddhism floundered under the impact of Muslim invasions and the rise of Hinduism. Sarnath's expanding Buddhist settlement eventually dissolved in the wake of this religious and political metamorphosis – except for the vast bulk of the Dhamekh Stupa, much of the site lay in ruins for almost a millennium. Prey to vandalism and pilfering, Sarnath remained abandoned until 1834, when it was visited by Alexander Cunningham, then head of the Archeological Survey, who excavated the site. Today it is once more an important Buddhist centre, and its avenues house missions from all over the Buddhist world.

The main site and the Dhamekh Stupa

Dominated by the huge bulk of the Dhamekh Stupa, the extensive archeo-logical excavations of the main site of Sarnath are maintained within an immaculate park (daily sunrise to sunset; Rs100 [Rs5], video camera Rs25). Entering from the southwest, the pillaged remains of the **Dharmarajika Stupa** lie immediately to the north: within its core the stupa holds a green marble casket containing relics of Buddha (Ashoka gathered these up from seven original locations and redistributed among numerous stupas nationwide including this one) and precious objects, including decayed pearls and gold leaf. Commemorating the spot where the Buddha delivered his first sermon, Dharmarajika is attributed to the reign of Ashoka in the third century BC, but was extended a further six times.

Adjacent to Dharmarajika Stupa are the ruins of the **Main Shrine**, where Ashoka is said to have meditated. To the west stands the lower portion of an **Ashoka Pillar** – minus its famous capital, now housed in the museum. The ruins of four monasteries, dating from the third to the twelfth centuries, are also contained within the compound; all bear the same hallmark of a central courtyard surrounded by monastic cells.

The most impressive of the site's remains is the **Dhamekh Stupa**, also known as the **Dharma Chakra Stupa**, which stakes a competing claim as the exact spot of Buddha's first sermon. The stupa is composed of a cylindrical tower rising 33.5m from a stone drum, ornamented with bas-relief foliage and geometric patterns; the eight-arched niches halfway up may once have held statues of the Buddha. It dates from the Gupta period, but with evidence of earlier Mauryan construction; some archeologists have conjectured that the stupa's upper brickwork may originally have been plastered over.

In its own enclosure outside the park, so accessible for free, the **Sri Digamber Jain Temple**, or Shreyanshnath Temple, is believed to mark the birthplace of Shreyanshnath, the eleventh Jain *tirthankara*. Built in 1824, the interior houses a large image of the saint, as well as attractive frescoes depicting the life of Mahavira, contemporary of Buddha and founder of the Jain religion.

The museum

Opposite the gates to the main site, the **museum** (daily except Fri 10am–5pm; Rs2; leave cameras and mobiles in lockers at the entrance) is designed to look like a *vihara* (monastery). Its small but renowned collection of Buddhist and brahmanist antiquities consists mostly of sculpture made from Chunar sandstone. The most famous exhibit is the **lion capital**, removed here from the Ashoka column on the main site. Constructed by Ashoka (273–232 BC), the great Mauryan king and convert to the *dharma*, it has become the emblem of modern India: four alert and beautifully sculpted lions guard the four cardinal points, atop a circular platform. Belonging to the first and second centuries AD are two impressive life-size standing *bodhisattvas* – one has a stone parasol with fine ornamentation and emblems of the faith. Among the large number of fifth-century figures is one of **Buddha**, cross-legged and with his hands in the *mudra* gesture. Perfectly poised, with his eyes downcast in deep meditation and a halo forming an exquisite nimbus behind his head, the Buddha is seated above six figures, possibly representing his companions, with the Wheel of Law in the middle to signify his first sermon. Later sculptures, dating from the tenth to twelfth centuries, include an exceptionally delicate image of the deity **Avalokiteshvara** with a lotus, and another of **Lokeshvara** holding a bowl.

Chaukhandi Stupa, Mulagandha Kuti Vihara and the modern sites

The dilapidated brick remains of the **Chaukhandi Stupa**, 1km south of the main site along Ashoka Marg, date from the Gupta period (300–700 AD), and are said to mark the spot where Buddha was reunited with the Panchavargiya Bikshus, his five ascetic companions who had previously deserted him. The stupa, standing atop a terraced rectangular plinth, is capped by an incongruous octagonal Mughal tower, which was built by Akbar in 1589 AD to commemorate his father's visit to the site.

Northeast of the Dhamekh Stupa, the lofty church-like **Mulagandha Kuti Vihara** monastery (no set hours; free entry) was built in 1931 with donations from the international Buddhist community. Run by the Mahabodhi Society, it drew devotees from all over the world to witness its consecration, and has become one of Sarnath's greatest attractions for pilgrims and tourists alike. The entrance foyer is dominated by a huge bell – a gift from Japan – and the interior houses a gilded reproduction of the museum's famous image of the Buddha, surrounded by fresco-covered walls depicting scenes from his life.

A little way east, shielded by a small enclosure, Sarnath's **bodhi tree** is an offshoot of the tree at Bodhgaya in Bihar, under which Buddha attained enlightenment. Sangamitra, Emperor Ashoka's daughter, took a branch from the original tree in 288 BC and planted it in Anuradhapura, in Sri Lanka, where its offshoots have been nurtured through the ages.

Buddhist communities from other parts of the world are well represented in Sarnath. In addition to the long-established **Mahabodhi Society**, the **Central Institute of Higher Tibetan Studies** (℡0542/258 5242, ⓦwww.cihts.ac.in), just out of Sarnath toward Varanasi, offers degree courses in Tibetan philosophy and the ancient language of Pali. Close to the post office is the traditional-style **Tibetan Temple** with frescoes and a good collection of *thangkas* (Tibetan Buddhist paintings): its central image is a colossal Shakyamuni, or "Buddha Calling the Earth to Witness" (his enlightenment). Two hundred metres to the east of the main gates is the **Chinese Temple**, while to the northwest, the **Burmese Temple** houses a white marble image of the Buddha flanked by two disciples. Behind the *Tourist Bungalow* is the **Japanese Temple**, run by the Mrigdayavana Mahavihara Society.

Practicalities

Sarnath-bound blue **buses** depart regularly from outside Varanasi Cantonment railway station and cost Rs8, but can get crowded. An auto-rickshaw from Varanasi will cost around Rs60–75 each way. Once you are in Sarnath, the sites are easy, and pleasant, to visit on foot.

Opposite the post office, southeast of the park, the UPTDC-run *Tourist Bungalow* (℡0542/259 5965, ⓔrahimrigdava@up-tourism.com; ❹) has reasonable **rooms** and a **dorm** (Rs125). Some of the monasteries, such as the pleasant *Burmese Vihara*, northwest of the main site, have basic rooms where visitors can stay for a donation. Right in front of the Mahabodhi Society gates, the *Birla Dharamsala* (℡09839 245096; ❶) is a central option with very basic facilities. Further out of town, a ten-minute walk south from the Japanese temple, *Hotel Golden Buddha* (℡0542/258 7933, ⓦwww.goldenbuddhahotel.com; ❹–❺) is the most comfortable option in the area, with some very chic rooms and a decent restaurant serving good home-cooking. There are a few simple **cafés** and **restaurants** outside the main gates near the Mulagandha Kuti Vihara, and a rather institutional restaurant serving thalis at the *Tourist Bungalow*. *Rangoli Garden Restaurant*, just past Chukhandi Stupa, at the crossroad on the way from Varanasi, is popular for inexpensive Indian food and has an outdoor sitting area.

Gorakhpur

Some 230km north of Varanasi, **GORAKHPUR** rose to prominence as a waystation on a pilgrims' route linking Kushinagar (the place of Buddha's enlightenment) and **Lumbini** (his birthplace, across the border in Nepal), and is now known primarily as a gateway to Nepal. It was named after the Shaivite yogi **Gorakhnath**, and holds a large ashram and temple dedicated to him. Tourists and pilgrims tend to hurry through, their departure hastened by the town's infamous flies and mosquitoes; if you do get stranded, there's a bustling bazaar, adequate amenities and a few passable hotels.

Practicalities

Gorakhpur has three **bus** stands – the Railway Bus Stand, near the station, for services from the Nepalese border at **Sonauli** and **Kushinagar**; the Kacheri Bus Stand, 1km southwest of the station, for buses from **Allahabad**, **Lucknow** and **Varanasi**; and the main bus stand for **Varanasi** (6hr) which is 2km southeast of the station at Pedleyganj, though one or two Varanasi services use the Railway Bus Stand.

Daily **trains** from Gorakhpur include the #2555 Gorakdam Express at 4.30pm for **Lucknow** (9.45pm) and **New Delhi** (5.45am), and the #5018 Gorakhpur–Lokmanyatilak Express at 5.45am for **Mumbai** (arrives at Kayan 5.30pm next day) via Varanasi (11am); other trains to **Varanasi** (6hr) include the overnight #549 Gorakhpur–Manduadih passenger train (it has sleepers), which leaves at 11.10pm, arriving 6.10am. Station facilities include pleasant retiring rooms, a basic restaurant and a tourist information booth (theoretically Mon–Sat 9am–5pm, but usually closed).

The **airport** (currently served only by JetLite) is 7km east of Gorakhpur towards Kushinagar. Taxis at the stand charge Rs100 into town.

Cycle rickshaws are the main means of **transport** around town, with few hotels more than 2km from the station. Beware of ticket touts and poor service from the travel agents opposite the station. There are **ATMs** in Golghar (1km southwest of the station) and directly outside the station (alongside Railtel Cyber Express, which has Rs23/hr **Internet access**); the State Bank of India on Bank Road will change traveller's cheques. The **GPO** is in Golghar.

Getting to Nepal

Gorakhpur is a convenient jumping-off point for western **Nepal**, offering access to Pokhara and even Kathmandu. Direct buses to or from Kathmandu and Pokhara are not a good deal – it's much better to get a bus to Sonauli, cross over, and pick up onward transport connections on the other side.

Buses for Sonauli (3hr) depart from Gorakhpur's Railway Bus Stand between 4.30am and 9pm: deluxe buses leave from in front of the railway station. Take one of the earliest if you want to get a connecting bus to **Pokhara** or **Kathmandu** (both 10hr) in daylight, to enjoy the views; night buses also ply the routes. Private buses leave Sonauli almost hourly in the mornings, between 5am and 11am. The most popular bus service for Kathmandu actually operates from **Bhairawa**, 4km away in Nepal; the booking office is near Bhairawa's *Yeti Hotel*. Local Jeeps cover the 24km from Bhairawa to Lumbini (Nepal), the birthplace of the Buddha.

If you want to **break your journey**, UPTD's *Hotel Niranjana* (☎05522/238201; ❷–❹) in Sonauli, 1km short of the border, has air-cooled rooms and a dorm (Rs100). There's more choice over the border in Nepal; and in Bhairawa, 4km up the road from the border, the *Yeti* and the *Himalayan Inn* are popular.

Nepalese visas (valid for one month) are available at the border for US$30. There is a State Bank of India on the Indian side of the border; moneychangers across the border will also cash traveller's cheques. Note that Indian Rs500 notes are illegal in Nepal; yours may be "confiscated".

Accommodation and eating

Gorakhpur has a wide range of **hotels**, from the budget-type near the station to the mid-range in the dull commercial hub around Golghar, 1km southwest. Cheap *dhabas* can be found in the vicinity of the station; a row of them stand outside the station gates. Elsewhere, the best **restaurants** are in the more expensive hotels or the multi-cuisine *Bobis* in Golghar (mains Rs40–90 veg, Rs80–130 non-veg). All the following hotels have 24hr checkout.

Accommodation

Bobina Nepal Rd, Niyamachak, 1.5km west of the station ☎ 0551/233 6663, ✉ bobina@ndb.vsnl.net .in. Good a/c rooms, a decent restaurant and bar, even a pool. ⑤–⑦

Elora Station Rd, opposite the railway station ☎ 0551/220 0647. One of the best station hotels, with a range of rooms (including some with a/c), of which the better ones are at the back, away from the noise. ②–④

Ganges Tarang Cinema crossing, towards Gorakhnath Temple, Niyamachak, 2km west of the station ☎ 0551/329 5091. Pronounced "gang-ez", this is one of Gorakhpur's better hotels, though the decor isn't hugely inspired. All the mod cons, including two good restaurants and friendly staff. ④–⑤

Ganges Deluxe Cinema Rd, Golghar ☎ 0551/233 6330. Sister hotel to the *Ganges*, with only a/c rooms, all spacious and spotless, plus a bar and restaurant. ④

Marina Golghar ☎ 0551/233 7630. Tucked away behind the *President Hotel* in the same compound, this place is older, less ostentatious and more pleasant. Clean rooms – some of those with a/c are real bargains. ③–④

Retiring Rooms Gorakhpur railway station. Good value, offering rooms with or without a/c, or dorms (Rs75); recommended if you need to catch an early train. ①–③

Upvan Nepal Rd, Niyamachak, 1.5km west of the station ☎ 0551/233 8003. Generally neat and tidy rooms with hot water for the winter and a/c for the summer, arranged around a central garden courtyard. One of the few places that will accommodate very late night arrivals. ④

Yark Inn M.P. Building, Golghar ☎ 0551/233 8233. One of several similarly and reasonably priced establishments along this busy stretch of road, offering clean and well-kept rooms with TV. ②–④

Kushinagar

Set against a pastoral landscape 53km west of Gorakhpur, the small hamlet of **KUSHINAGAR** is revered as the site of Buddha's death and cremation, and final liberation (**Mahaparinirvana**) from the cycles of death and rebirth. During his lifetime, **Kushinara**, as it was then called, was a small kingdom of the Mallas, surrounded by forest. It remained forgotten until the late nineteenth century, when archeologists rediscovered the site and began excavations based on the writings of the seventh-century Chinese pilgrims.

Set in a leafy park in the heart of Kushinagar, the **Mahaparinirvana Temple** (or **Nirvana Stupa**), dated to the reign of Kumaragupta I (413–455 AD), was extensively rebuilt by Burmese Buddhists in 1927. The large gilded **reclining Buddha** inside the shrine was reconstructed from the remains of an earlier Malla image. At the road crossing immediately southwest, the **Matha Kuwar** shrine holds a tenth-century blue schist Buddha, also covered in gilt, and usually locked up (you can look in through the windows), though the caretaker may offer to open it up for you if he's around. Just round the corner, there's a "Bauddha Museum" (Tue–Sat and most Sun 10.30am–4.30pm; Rs4), housing a so-so collection of ancient Buddhist sculpture, not all original; the most interesting exhibits are the small pieces in a case of antiquities unearthed locally. The crumbling bricks of the **Ramabhar Stupa**, about 1.5km southeast of the main site (around Rs50 for the round trip by rickshaw), are thought to be the original **Mukutabandhana Stupa**, erected to mark the spot where Buddha was cremated.

Today Kushinagar is rediscovering its roots as a centre of international Buddhism, and is home to several monasteries sponsored by Buddhists from countries such as Tibet, Burma, Thailand, Sri Lanka and Japan. The strikingly simple **Japanese Temple** consists of a single circular chamber housing a great golden image of Buddha, softly lit through small, stained-glass windows. In stark contrast, the recently constructed **Thai Monastery** is a large complex of lavish, traditionally styled temples and shrines.

Practicalities

Regular **buses** link Kushinagar with **Gorakhpur** (2hr). **UP Tourism** maintains an office (Mon–Sat 10am–5pm) by the Birla Dharamshala. Both India Tourism and UP Tourism run comprehensive tours of the whole "Buddhist Circuit" of Uttar Pradesh, which can be booked in Kushinagar, or at UP Tourism in Delhi (see p.142). There's a moneychanger next to *Yama Café*, and you can also change money at the *Lotus Nikko* hotel.

Most of the temples offer **accommodation** for visiting pilgrims in return for a donation (in the region of Rs200). Of these, the Linh Son (Chinese) Temple (T09936 132062) has clean, spacious doubles with attached baths and hot water; the *Shree Birla* opposite (T05564/273090), and the *International Buddhist Guest House*, next to the Tibetan *gompa*, are more basic. The relatively expensive state-run tourist bungalow, *Pathik Niwas* (T05564/273045, E rahipathikniwas @up-tourism.com; ❹–❻), has a/c rooms, luxury cottages called "American Huts", dorm beds (Rs100), and a canteen-like restaurant. *Lotus Nikko* (T05564/272250, W www.lotusnikkohotels.com; ❽), next to the Japanese Temple is a three-star with a/c rooms and moneychanging facilities, but it is sometimes booked up by tour groups.

Restaurants are scarce, but the pleasant and clean 🍴 *Yama Café* next to Linh Son Temple, has a small menu of home-cooked Indian, Tibetan and Chinese food (main dishes Rs30–50) – the vegetable or chicken-noodle soup is particularly recommended. It opens for breakfast but closes around 8pm. Food stalls at the Kasia crossing also provide inexpensive snacks. Ask at the *Yama Café* about their 9km half-day hike to surrounding villages and holy sites.

Travel details

Trains

Note that some important trains for Varanasi stop at Mughul Sarai, requiring a change of trains or a connecting bus or taxi.

Agra to: Ahmedabad (1 weekly; 25hr 45min); Bhopal (13–16 daily; 5hr 48min–9hr 55min); Bhubaneshwar (1–2 daily; 28hr 35min–36hr 40min); Chennai (2 daily; 30hr–32hr 25min); Delhi (14–18 daily; 2hr–6hr 5min); Gwalior (15–19 daily; 1hr 14min–1hr 55min); Haridwar (1–2 daily; 9hr 35min); Indore (1–2 daily; 13hr 25min–14hr); Jaipur (1 daily; 4hr 40min); Jalgaon (4 daily; 13hr 28min–18hr 10min); Jhansi (12–16 daily; 2hr 26min–3hr 35min); Jodhpur (1–3 daily; 10hr 45min–12hr 5min); Kanpur (2–6 daily; 3hr 55min–6hr 35min); Kolkata

(3–4 daily; 21hr 15min–30hr 15min); Lucknow (10 weekly; 5hr 30min–8hr 25min); Mathura (15–19 daily; 33min–1hr 5min); Mumbai (3–4 daily; 19hr 20min–25hr 45min); Puri (1 daily; 38hr 25min); Satna (1 daily, 11hr 15min); Thiruvananthapuram (1–2 daily; 47hr 55min–49hr 20min); Ujjain (1–2 daily; 11hr 35min–12hr 20min); Varanasi (8 weekly; 11hr–13hr 5min); Vasco da Gama (1 daily; 37hr 40min).

Jhansi to: Agra (20–26 daily; 2hr 52min–4hr 40min); Chennai (2–4 daily; 24–30hr 30min); Delhi (13–17 daily; 5hr–8hr); Indore (1 daily; 10hr 23min); Kalyan (for Mumbai) (5–6 daily; 17hr 45min–21hr 55min); Kolkata (Calcutta) (1 weekly; 21hr 53min); Ujjain (1–2 daily; 8hr 43min–11hr 20min); Vasco da Gama (Goa) (1 daily; 33hr 23min).

Lucknow to: Agra (12 weekly; 6hr 5min–7hr 45min); Dehra Dun (2–3 daily; 11hr 25min–13hr 25min); Delhi (13–20 daily; 6hr 25min–10hr); Gorakhpur (14–18 daily; 4hr 45min–7hr 20min); Haridwar (2 daily; 9hr 55min–10hr 55min); Kanpur (13–20 daily; 1hr 5min–2hr 10min); Kolkata (4–5 daily; 18hr 5min–30hr 15min); Kathgodam for Nainital (1 daily; 8hr 49min); Mumbai (2–6 daily; 23hr 50min–30hr 48min); Patna (3–6 daily; 9hr 55min–14hr 30min); Varanasi (13–17 daily; 4hr 20min–10hr 25min).

Mughal Sarai to: Agra (2 daily; 9hr 35min–11hr 50min); Delhi (10–17 daily; 8hr 50min–14hr 50min); Jaipur (1 daily; 14hr 10min); Jodhpur (1 daily; 21hr 30min); Kolkata (11–16 daily; 8hr–18hr 55min); New Jalpaiguri (for Siliguri and Darjeeling) (3–5 daily; 7hr 15min–16hr); Puri (1–2 daily; 17hr 55min–18hr 25min).

Varanasi to: Agra (3 weekly; 10hr 30min); Allahabad (10–13 daily; 2hr 35min–4hr 45min); Chennai (2 weekly; 37hr 25min); Dehra Dun (2 daily; 20hr–25hr 10min); Delhi (7–10 daily; 12hr–29hr 5min); Gaya (3–4 daily; 4hr–5hr 15min); Gorakhpur (4–5 daily; 3hr 40min–8hr 25min); Gwalior (1 daily; 17hr 5min); Haridwar (2 daily; 17hr 45min–22hr 40min); Jabalpur (2–5 daily; 8hr 40min–12hr 30min); Jaipur (3 weekly; 18hr 10min); Jalgaon (3–4 daily; 19hr 23min–23hr 27min); Jhansi (1–2 daily; 11hr 45min–15hr 15min); Kanpur (5–9 daily; 5hr 40min–9hr 30min); Kolkata (5–7 daily; 12hr 55min–20hr 20min); Lucknow (12–16 daily; 5hr 14min–12hr 45min); Mughal Sarai (8–14 daily; 40–55min); Mumbai (3–4 daily; 25hr 25min–30hr 15min); Patna (6–10 daily; 4hr 5min–7hr); Satna (4–7 daily; 6hr 15min–8hr 30min).

Buses

Agra to: Ajmer (hourly; 10hr); Bharatpur (hourly; 2hr); Dehra Dun (8 daily, 13hr); Delhi (hourly; 5–6hr); Fatehpur Sikri (every 30min; 1hr–1hr 30min); Gwalior (15 daily; 3hr 30min); Haridwar (8 daily; 10hr); Jaipur (every 20min; 5–6hr); Jhansi (8 daily; 5hr 30min); Khajuraho (1 daily; 12hr); Lucknow (hourly; 9hr 30min); Mathura (hourly; 1hr 30min); Rishikesh (1 daily, 12hr); Varanasi (1 daily; 14hr).

Jhansi to: Agra (8 daily; 5hr 30min); Khajuraho (9 daily; 4hr 30min–5hr 30min); Lucknow (5 daily; 8hr).

Lucknow to: Agra (3 daily; 10hr); Allahabad (every 45min; 4hr 30min); Dehra Dun (1 daily, 10hr 30min); Delhi (2 daily; 9hr); Haridwar (1 daily; 10hr); Jhansi (5 daily; 8hr); Kanpur (every 30min; 2hr); Sonauli (2 daily; 12hr); Varanasi (6 daily; 8hr).

Varanasi to: Agra (1 daily; 14hr); Allahabad (every 20min; 3hr); Jaunpur (15 daily; 2hr); Kanpur (14 daily; 10hr); Lucknow (6 daily; 8hr); Patna (1 daily; 8hr).

Flights

(**AI** = Air India, **IC** = Indian Airlines, **IT** = Kingfisher, **DN** = Air Deccan, **SG** = SpiceJet, **S2** = JetLite, **9W** = Jet Airways)

Allahabad to: Delhi (S2; 3 weekly; 2hr 20min).

Gorakhpur to: Allahabad (S2; 3 weekly; 30min); Delhi (S2; 3 weekly; 2hr 25min).

Lucknow to: Delhi (AI, IC, DN, S2, 9W; 8–9 daily; 55min–1hr); Kolkata (S2; 1 daily; 2hr 20min); Mumbai (IC, S2; 3 daily; 2hr 5min–4hr 05min); Patna (S2; 1 daily; 55min).

Varanasi to: Delhi (AI, IC, IT, SG, S2, 9W; 6–7 daily; 1hr 15min–2hr 30min); Kathmandu (IC; 4 weekly; 1hr); Khajuraho (IC, 9W; 3–4 daily; 40min); Kolkata (IT; 1 daily; 4hr 50min); Mumbai (IC, SG, S2; 3 daily; 2hr 20min–4hr 15min).

4

Uttarakhand

AFGHANISTAN

CHINA
(TIBET AUTONOMOUS
REGION)

BHUTAN

PAKISTAN

NEPAL

BANGLADESH

MYANMAR
(BURMA)

ARABIAN
SEA

BAY OF BENGAL

N

SRI
LANKA

INDIAN OCEAN

0   400 km

The International boundaries on this map are neither purported to be correct
nor authentic by Survey of India directives. Publisher.

CHAPTER 4 # Highlights

❋ **Char Dham** The pilgrim circuit around the four holy sites of Garhwal reveals a cross-section of the Indian Himalayas' most superb scenery. See p.346

❋ **Rishikesh** This busy pilgrimage place on the banks of the turquoise Ganges is a renowned yoga and meditation centre. See p.358

❋ **Gangotri** Hole up at the source of the Ganges, high in the mountains, where sadhus offer accommodation for spiritual retreats. See p.366

❋ **Valley of the Flowers** A hidden valley, only discovered in 1931 by Europeans, whose lush meadows are a botanist's dream: hike here after the monsoons. See p.373

❋ **Curzon Trail** A ten-day trail over the Kuari Pass, offering stunning views of the Great Himalayan Watershed. See p.375

❋ **Corbett Tiger Reserve** Established in the 1930s, India's most famous nature reserve is renowned for its population of tigers. See p.379

❋ **The Panchulis** The magnificent "Five Cooking Pots" peaks, plumes of snow perennially blowing from them, are visible from Munsiyari. See p.389

▲ On the way from Gangotri to Gomukh

Uttarakhand

Northeast of Delhi, bordering Nepal and Tibet, the mountains of Garhwal and Kumaon rise from the fertile sub–Himalayan plains. Together they form the state of **UTTARAKHAND**, which was shorn free from lowland Uttar Pradesh in 2000 after years of agitation, and changed its name from Uttaranchal in 2007. The region has its own distinct languages and cultures, and successive deep river valleys shelter fascinating micro–civilizations, where Hinduism meets animism and Buddhist influence is never too far away. Although not as high as the giants of Nepal, further east, or as the Karakoram, the snow peaks here rank among the most beautiful mountains of the inner Himalayas, forming an almost continuous chain that culminates in **Nanda Devi**, the highest mountain in India at 7816m.

Garhwal is the more visited region, busy with pilgrims who flock to its holy spots. At **Haridwar**, the Ganges thunders out from the foothills on its long journey to the sea. The nearby ashram town of **Rishikesh** is familiar from one of the classic East-meets-West images of the 1960s; it was where the Beatles came to stay with the Maharishi. From here pilgrims set off for the high temples known as the Char Dham – **Badrinath**, **Kedarnath**, **Yamunotri** and **Gangotri**, the source of the Ganges. Earthier pursuits are on offer at **Mussoorie**, a British hill station that's now a popular Indian resort. The lesser–visited **Kumaon** region is more unspoilt, and boasts pleasant small towns famed for mountain views and hill walks, such as **Kausani** and **Ranikhet**, as well as its own Victorian hill station, **Nainital**, whose promenade throngs with refugees from the heat of the plains. Further down, the forests at **Corbett Tiger Reserve** offer the chance to go tiger-spotting from the back of an elephant. Both districts abound in classic **treks**, many leading through the high alpine meadows known as *bugyals* – summer pastures, where rivers are born and paths meet.

Facilities are good in the big towns of the foothills, but not upcountry, so if you're aiming to ascend, you should make the most of foreign exchange services, Internet cafés and satellite TV beforehand. In the mountains, roads are good – maintained by the army, which has a large presence up here thanks to the proximity of the Tibetan border – but **getting around** is not always easy as the monsoon (Aug–Sept) causes landslides and avalanches which block the roads; similar troubles occur during the winter snow season (Dec–Feb). There are buses, but, especially high up, most locals get around by shared Jeep, with many vehicles crammed to bursting (women and foreigners inside, local youths hanging off the back). Compared to the plains, there's little caste strife (most mountain people are high-caste rajput or brahmin) and you'll see few beggars other than religious mendicants. A few words of Hindi are certainly handy as the mountain people usually speak little English. **Uttarakhand Tourism**

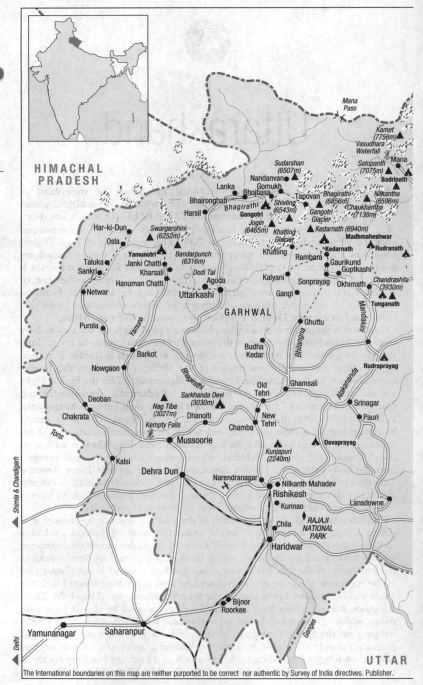

HIMACHAL
PRADESH

Mana
Pass

Kamet
(7756m)
Vasudhara
Waterfall
Mana

Satopanth
(7075m)

Badrinath

Sudarshan
(6507m)
Nandanvan
Gomukh
Bhojbasa
Lanka
Bhaironghati
Harsil
Bhagirathi
Gangotri
Jogin
(6465m)
Shivling
(6543m)
Tapovan
Bhagirathi
(6856m)
Gangotri
Glacier
Khatling
Glacier
Nilkantha
(6596m)
Chaukhamba
(7138m)
Kedarnath (6940m)
Madhmaheshwar

Har-ki-Dun
Osla
Swargarohini
(6252m)
Taluka
Sankri
Yamunotri
Janki Chatti
Kharsali
Hanuman Chatti
Netwar
Bandarpunch
(6316m)
Dodi Tal
Agoda
Uttarkashi
Khatling
Rambara
Kedarnath
Kalyani
Gangi
Gaurikund
Guptkashi
Sonprayag
Okhimath
Rudranath
Chandrashila
(3930m)
Tunganath

Purola

GARHWAL

Ghuttu

Barkot
Nowgaon
Budha
Kedar
Ghamsali
Rudraprayag

Deoban
Chakrata
Tons
Nag Tiba
(3027m)
Sarkhanda Devi
(3030m)
Dhanolti
Old
Tehri
New
Tehri
Srinagar
Pauri

Kalsi
Kempty Falls
Mussoorie
Chamba
Kunjapuri
(2240m)
Devaprayag

Dehra Dun
Narendranagar
Nilkanth Mahadev
Rishikesh
Kunnao
Chila
RAJAJI
NATIONAL
PARK
Lansdowne

Haridwar

Bijnor
Roorkee

Yamunanagar
Saharanpur

UTTAR

Shimla & Chandigarh

Delhi

Ganges

The International boundaries on this map are neither purported to be correct nor authentic by Survey of India directives. Publisher.

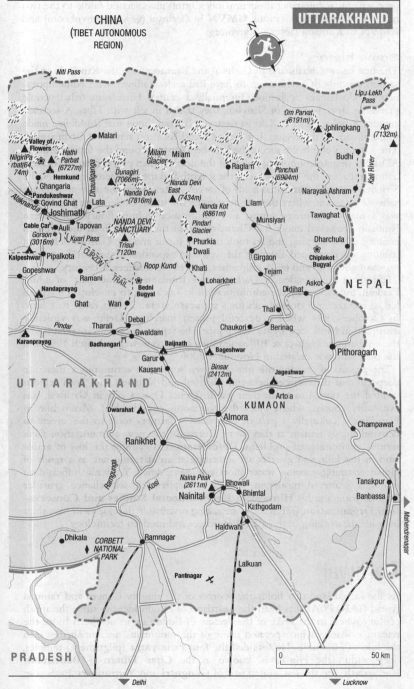

Mount Kailash

CHINA
(TIBET AUTONOMOUS
REGION)

Niti Pass

Lipu Lekh
Pass

Valley of
Flowers

Malari

Om Parvat,
(6191m)

Johlingkang

Api
(7132m)

NilgiriPa
rbat(64
74m)

Hathi
Parbat
(6727m)

Hemkund

Milam
Glacier

Milam

Budhi

Ghangaria

Dunagiri
(7066m)

Ragla ti

Panchuli
(6904m)

Narayan Ashram

Pandukeshwar
Govind Ghat

Nanda Devi
(7816m)

Nanda Devi
East
(7434m)

Lilam

Tawaghat

Joshimath

Lata

Nanda Kot
(6861m)

Munsiyari

Dharchula

Cable Car

Tapovan

NANDA DEVI
SANCTUARY

Pindari
Glacier

Chiplakot
Bugyal

Auli

Gorson
(3016m)

Kuari Pass

Phurkia

Dwali

Kalpeshwar

Pipalkota

Trisul
7120m

Girgaon

Askot

NEPAL

Gopeshwar

Roop Kund

Khati

Tejam

Didihat

Ramani

Loharkhet

Nandaprayag

Bedni
Bugyal

Ghat

Wan

Debal

Thal

Chaukori

Berinag

Tharali

Gwaldam

Karanprayag

Pindar

Badhangari

Baijnath

Bageshwar

Pithoragarh

Garur

Kausani

Binsar
(2412m)

Jageshwar

UTTARAKHAND

Dwarahat

Arto a

KUMAON

Almora

Champawat

Ranikhet

Naina Peak
(2611m)

Bhowali

Tanakpur

Nainital

Bhimtal

Banbassa

Kathgodam

Dhikala

CORBETT
NATIONAL
PARK

Ramnagar

Haldwani

Lalkuan

Pantnagar

PRADESH

0   50 km

Delhi

Lucknow

(@gov.ua.nic.in/uttaranchaltourism/index.html) plays second fiddle to the two regional tourism organizations, **GMVN** in Garhwal (@www.gmvnl.com) and **KMVN** in Kumaon (@www.kmvn.org).

Some history

The first known inhabitants of Garhwal and Kumaon were the **Kuninda** in the second century BC, who seem to have had a close affinity with contemporaneous Indo-Greek civilization. Essentially a central Himalayan tribal people practising an early form of Shaivism, they traded in salt with Tibet. A second-century Ashokan edict at Kalsi in western Garhwal shows that Buddhism made some inroads in the region, but Garhwal and Kumaon remained Brahmanical. The Kuninda eventually succumbed to the **Guptas** around the fourth century AD, who, despite controlling much of the north Indian plains, failed to make a lasting impact in the hills. Between the seventh and the fourteenth centuries, the Shaivite **Katyuri** dominated lands of varying extent from the Katyur-Baijnath valley in Kumaon, where their stone temples still stand. Under them **Jageshwar** was a major pilgrimage centre, and Brahmanical culture flourished. Eastern Kumaon prospered under the **Chandras**, from the thirteenth to the fifteenth century, when learning and art took on new forms and the Garhwal school of painting was developed. Later on, the westward expansion of the Gurkha empire was brought to an end by British annexation in the nineteenth century.

Following Independence, Garhwal and Kumaon became part of Uttar Pradesh, but failure by the administration in Lucknow to develop the region led to increasingly violent calls for a **separate state**. Things came to a head in October 1994 when a peaceful protest march to Delhi was violently disrupted in Mussoorie by the UP police. The separatist cause was taken up by the sympathetic high-caste BJP when they came to power in March 1998 and the new state was created in November 2000.

The process of creating this new state was somewhat acrimonious; there are deep cultural **differences** between Garhwal and Kumaon, and both regions wanted the capital to sit in their patch (Dehra Dun, a city in Garhwal, was eventually chosen, which upset the Kumaonis considerably). Meanwhile in Haridwar – culturally a part of the plains – farmers took to the streets to demand things remain as they were. Currently, the new administration faces serious environmental problems. **Deforestation** is causing the loss of arable land in the hills, and glaciers are retreating at an alarming rate as a result of global warming, causing water shortages lower down. Yet while officialdom founders, scattered mountain villages – inspired by self-reliance crusader Dr Anil Joshi and his **Himalayan Environmental Studies and Conservation Organization** (HESCO) – are taking sustainable development into their own hands, working to meld local resources and modern technology.

Garhwal

As the sacred land that holds the sources of the mighty Ganges and Yamuna rivers, **GARHWAL** has been the heartland of Hindu identity since the ninth century when, in the wake of the decline of Buddhism in northern India, the reformer Shankara incorporated many of the mountains' ancient shrines into the fold of Hinduism. He founded the four main **yatra** (pilgrimage) temples, deep within the Himalayas, known as the **Char Dham** – **Badrinath**, **Kedarnath**, and the less-visited pair of **Gangotri** and **Yamunotri**. Each year, between May and November, once the snows have melted, streams of pilgrims penetrate high into the mountains, passing by way of **Rishikesh**, the land of *yogis* and ashrams.

For more than a millennium, the *yatris* (pilgrims) came on foot. However, the annual event has been transformed in the last few years; roads blasted by the military through the mountains during the war against China in the early 1960s are now the lifelines for a new form of motorized *yatra*. Eastern Garhwal in particular is getting rich, and the fabric of hill society is changing rapidly – visitors hoping to experience the old Garhwal should spend at least part of their time well away from the principal *yatra* routes. In addition to their spiritual significance, the hills are now becoming established as a centre for **adventure sports**, offering all levels of trekking, whitewater rafting, paragliding, skiing and climbing.

Garhwal is a challenging place to **travel** around, with extremely long and often nerve-wracking bus and Jeep rides being the order of the day. However, you are rewarded with spectacular views of snowy peaks offset by gaudily painted Garhwali villages in deep valleys. All of the tourist bungalows are operated by Garhwal Mandal Vikas Nigam – **GMVN** (ⓦwww.gmvnl.com). Most are concentrated along the pilgrimage routes, although their network has been expanding both in areas right off the beaten track and in new destinations such as the ski resort of **Auli**. Standards vary widely, but most bungalows offer a range of rooms and dorms to suit most budgets, along with a restaurant. GMVN also organizes Char Dham **tours** (often overpriced and inefficient), and offers expensive **car rental**. The GMVN headquarters is in Dehra Dun (ⓣ0135/274 6817), although you will get more help from their office in Delhi (ⓣ011/2335 0481). The GMVN Trekking and Mountaineering Division, based in Rishikesh (ⓣ01364/243 0799, ⓔmountdivision@gmvnl.com), is the office to contact for adventure-sports packages such as skiing and trekking.

Dehra Dun

Capital of Uttarakhand since 2000, **DEHRA DUN**, 255km north of Delhi, is pleasantly located at just below 700m, as the Himalayan foothills begin their dramatic rise, so it never gets too hot in summer, and snows rarely appear in winter. It stands at the centre of the 120km-long **Doon Valley** (*dun* or *doon* literally means "valley"), famous for its basmati rice and hemmed in by the Yamuna to the west and the Ganges at Rishikesh to the east. A popular retirement spot, renowned for its elite public schools, Dehra Dun has been occupied in turn by Sikhs, Mughals and Gurkhas, but it is the British influence that is most apparent.

Arrival and information

The **Inter-state Bus Terminal** (ISBT) is located in the far southwest of town, a Rs50 auto-rickshaw ride (Rs4 on shared Vikram #5) from the **railway station** and the budget hotels on Gandhi Road. Gandhi Road doglegs east then north at Princes Chowk towards the **post office** and Clock Tower in the centre of town, from where Rajpur Road heads north, with the Astley Hall area branching off to the east. There's no shortage of ATMs in town (several surround the Clock Tower for example), and the State Bank of India on Convent Road changes travellers' cheques, as do many of the **banks** along Rajpur Road. Dehra Dun is the best place in the state for **Internet** access as Garhwal's only server is here. The GMVN's helpful **regional tourist office**, in the *Hotel Drona*, 45 Gandhi Rd (Mon–Sat 10am–5pm; ⓣ0135/265 3217), covers Dehra Dun; in the same complex, Drona Travels (ⓣ0135/265 3309) books GMVN accommodation and tours throughout Garhwal, and also rents cars. Another helpful source of information is the GMVN Head Office, 74/1 Rajpur Rd (℡0135/274 6817, 🖂gmvn@sacharnet.in), who can also advise about trekking.

If you're looking to fix up a **trek**, try Garhwal Adventure Tours, 151 Araghar (℡0135/267 7769, 🖂garhwaltrekking@rediffmail.com), an established and experienced organization used to working with tour groups such as Exodus. Paramount, off Paltan Bazaar south of the Clock Tower at 16 Moti Market, and Mountain Equipment, 200m further south at 53 Moti Market, with Cliff Climbers opposite, are the best trekking and mountaineering **equipment** dealers in the entire region.

Accommodation

Dehra Dun has a good selection of mid-range **hotels**, many of them strung along Rajpur Road as it heads north to Mussoorie. What little budget accommodation there is can be found between the railway station and the Clock Tower – or in the old-fashioned railway retiring rooms.

Ashrey 10 Tyagi Rd ℡0135/262 3388, ⓦwww .ashrey.com. In a quiet, but still central spot, 3min walk south of Princes Chowk; the private lawn in front complements the spotless, spacious and well-furnished new rooms. Good value. ❹–❺
Great Value 74-C Rajpur Rd, 2.5km north of the Clock Tower ℡0135/274 4086, ⓦwww .greatvaluehotel.com. Large, well-run chain hotel with good facilities including a nice garden, bar and in-room broadband Internet connections (Rs100 per hour). ❽–❾
Madhuban 97 Rajpur Rd ℡0135/274 0066 or 77, ⓦwww.hotelmadhuban.com. A large, imposing upmarket hotel with a popular restaurant, bar, steam room and gym, considered the best in town, and the most expensive at $80–160, though the *Comfotel Inn* annexe has cheaper rooms. ❼–❾
Moti Mahal 7 Rajpur Rd ℡0135/265 1277, 🖂hotelmotimahal@yahoo.co.in. A bright, modern

hotel where smoked-glass double-glazing in the immaculate a/c rooms keeps the noise and fumes out. ❼
Shalimar 43/7 Gandhi Rd ℡0135/271 3956, 🖂hotel_shalimar2001@yahoo.co.in. Small rooms but well-kept and clean, some with a/c, though the busy road is a minus point. ❹–❺
Victoria 70 Gandhi Rd ℡0135/262 3486. Basic lodge near the railway station, established in 1936, far from deluxe (hot water comes in buckets), and actually a bit overpriced for what it is, but it has a certain ramshackle charm. ❷
🏃 **White House** 15/7 Subhash Rd (aka Lytton Rd) ℡0135/265 2765. Atmospheric old Art Deco Raj residence near Astley Hall, with huge verandas, lofty ceilings, sturdy furniture (rather hard beds) and moody plumbing. A peaceful retreat from the centre of Dehra Dun, yet only a few minutes' walk away. ❸

The town and around

Driven by Dehra Dun's status as state capital, increasing local investment has resulted in a mini-boom – and accompanying noise and traffic problems – within the city centre. Most of Dehra Dun's bustling markets lie near the tall Victorian **Clock Tower**, from where Rajpur Road, the lifeline to Mussoorie, stretches northwards. Four kilometres along is the vast leafy colony occupied by the **Survey of India**, founded in 1767. Its greatest achievement was to determine the height of Mount Everest and name it after the surveyor general, Sir George Everest, but the Survey isn't a place to shop for **maps**; stock is paltry and the 1:250,000 scale trekking maps pretty useless. Natraj **bookshop** at 17 Rajpur Rd is one of the best in the country for wildlife books.

Crossing the rainy-season riverbed of Bindal Rao, Kaulagarh Road progresses northwest past Dehra Dun's top private school, the **Doon School**, to the expansive grounds of the chateau-like **Forest Research Institute** (Mon–Fri 9.30am–5pm; Rs10), devoted to the preservation of India's much-threatened woodlands. There's a large and interesting **museum** here holding wood samples, insects, furniture, pickled animal embryos and the like. The **Botanical Survey of India**, in the next building, is only of interest to the specialist.

Somewhat further afield, **Rajpur**, 12km to the north, past the Survey of India and accessible by shared Vikrams, has a sizeable Tibetan community. Its striking *gompa* – the **Shakya Centre** – decorated with ornate frescoes, stands next to a centre of Tibetan medicine next door. There's another *gompa* on the main road around 5km towards Mussoorie.

Eating

Dehra Dun has several commendable mid-priced **eating places** and a bunch of adequate cheaper cafés around Gandhi Road. Posh espresso cafés include *Barista* next to *Kumar Veg*, and *Coffee Day* opposite the *Madhuban* hotel. *Kumar Sweets* by the Clock Tower is the town's favourite *mithai* centre.

Countdown Fast Food Subhash Rd, behind Astley Hall. Options include pizzas, burgers and quite a range of chopsuey-style Chinese dishes, veg and non-veg (Rs35–70).

Kumar Veg 15B Rajpur Rd. Excellent veg cooking at reasonable prices (mains Rs70–130), and comfortable surroundings. There's a separate south Indian menu, including lemon, tamarind or sambhar rice (Rs50–60).

Kundan Palace 72 Rajpur Rd, nearly opposite the *Madhuban* hotel. Popular but rather run-down open-air multi-cuisine eatery serving inexpensive Indian and south Indian fare (mains Rs30–50), plus sandwiches and snacks, mostly veg but they do omelettes.

Moti Mahal 7 Rajpur Rd. Attached to the hotel of the same name, this is the place for a spot of posh nosh, especially chicken and *paneer*; non-veg dishes (Rs150–250) include chicken karahi, chicken muglai, and that great Anglo-Bangladeshi contribution to Indian cuisine, chicken tikka masala.

Tirupati 27-B Rajpur Rd. Clean and friendly multi-cuisine restaurant, particularly strong on south Indian dishes. A north Indian or south Indian thali will set you back Rs99, or for Rs90 you can try a south Indian combination featuring dosa, *iodli* and vada. Otherwise, most main dishes are Rs65–100.

Yeti 55-A Rajpur Rd. Interesting Chinese and Thai menus, including spicy Szechuan cuisine. Main dishes (non-veg) are Rs75–150, or Rs120–250 for seafood.

Moving on from Dehra Dun

Jolly Grant **airport** is 24km east of Dehra Dun, but has no passenger flights at present. The modern **Inter-state Bus Terminal (ISBT)** lies 5km southwest of town and can be reached on shared Vikram #5 from Princes Chowk or the Clock Tower. Frequent buses to Delhi include a regular Rs192 deluxe service.

From the station off Gandhi Road, the best daily **trains** to Delhi are the overnight Mussoorie Express #4042 (leaves 9.30pm, arrives Old Delhi 7.20am), or to New Delhi, the a/c Shatabdi Express #2018 at 5pm (arrives 10.45pm), or the Janshatabdi Express #2056 at 5.10am (arrives 11.15am). The Doon Express #3010, leaving at 8.25pm, is the most convenient service to Lucknow (arrives 8.15am) and Varanasi (arrives 4.10pm), and continues to Kolkata. The Ujjain Express #4310, on Tuesdays and Wednesdays only, leaves at 6am and reaches Agra at 4.55pm.

See p.390 for a rundown of frequencies and journey times.

Mussoorie

Spreading for 15km along a high serrated ridge, **MUSSOORIE** is the closest hill station to Delhi, just 278km north of the capital and 34km north of Dehra Dun (from where it is visible on a clear day). At an altitude of 2000m, it gives travellers from the plains their first glimpse of the snow-covered Himalayan **peaks** of western Garhwal, as well as dramatic views of the Dehra Dun valley below.

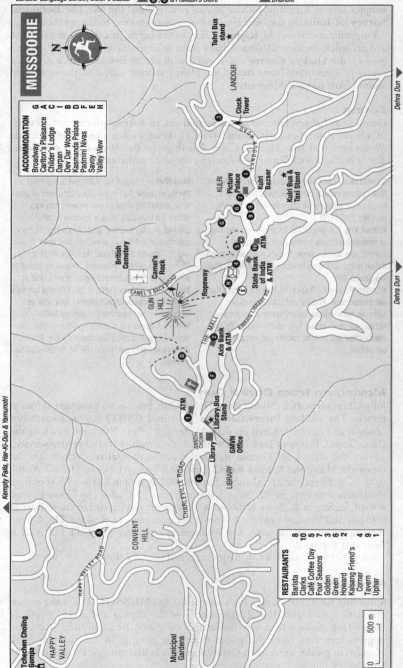

Landour Language School, Sister's Bazaar ▲ **B**, **C** & Prakash's Store ▲ Dhanolti

MUSSOORIE

N

ACCOMMODATION
Broadway   G
Carlton's Plaisance A
Childer's Lodge   I
Darpan   B
Dev Dar Woods   D
Kasmanda Palace   F
Padmini Nivas   E
Savoy   H
Valley View

Tehri Bus stand ★

LANDOUR

Clock Tower

Dehra Dun ▶

KULRI
Picture Palace
Kulri Bazaar
Kulri Bus & Taxi Stand ★

British Cemetery

Camel's Rock
Ropeway
State Bank of India & ATM

CAMEL'S BACK ROAD
GUN HILL
THE MALL
Axis Bank & ATM

Dehra Dun ▶

CHARLEVILLE ROAD

ATM
Library Bus Stand ★
GANDHI CHOWK
Library
GMVN Office
LIBRARY

CONVENT HILL

Kempty Falls, Har-Ki-Dun & Yamunotri ◀
HAPPY VALLEY ROAD

Tchechen Choling Gompa
HAPPY VALLEY

Municipal Gardens

RESTAURANTS
Barista   8
Clarks   10
Café Coffee Day   5
Four Seasons   7
Golden   3
Green   6
Howard   2
Kaisang Friend's   4
Corner
Tavern   9
Uphar   1

0   500 m

350

These days, Mussoorie is a very popular weekend retreat for middle-class Indians up from the plains. Most foreign visitors come to Mussoorie to **study** Hindi at the excellent Landour Language School, but the town is also a useful base camp for **treks** into the western interior of Garhwal. Dominated by the long Bandarpunch Massif (6316m), with Swargarohini (6252m) in the west and the Gangotri group in the east, Mussoorie's mountain panorama may not be as dramatic as some other hill stations, but it forms a pleasant backdrop to the busy holiday town.

Arrival and information

As Mussoorie's two-kilometre-long **Mall** is closed to motor vehicles during the tourist season, its two ends – the **Library** area at the west end, and the **Kulri** area in the east – serve as **transport hubs**. Cycle rickshaws operate mostly on the flat Library end. Buses (Rs28) and shared taxis (about Rs100) from Dehra Dun, the plains and the rest of Garhwal arrive either at the **Library Bus Stand** at Gandhi Chowk, or the **Kulri** Bus Stand (which is also called the **Masonic Lodge Bus Stand**). At the smaller **Tehri Bus Stand**, east of Landour 5km from the Mall, buses pull in from New Tehri and Chamba (where you have to change buses if travelling between Mussoorie and Uttarkashi). Shared taxis and cars are available at the bus stands, while ponies and hand-drawn carriages – glorified rickshaws – run along the Mall itself. Ponies can also carry you around the Camel's Back Road.

Facilities along the Mall include the **tourist bureau** (Mon–Sat 10am–5pm; ☎0135/263 2863) next to the cable car, where you can get a small booklet of local information; a **post office** at the Kulri end, and a **GMVN transport office** (Mon–Sat 10am–5pm; ☎0135/263 1281) next to the Library Bus Stand, which runs tours of the town and further afield. The State Bank of India and Apex Bank both change money and have **ATM**s, of which there are two more along the Mall. **Internet** access is available at FastTrack across the Mall from *Clarks* restaurant and at the *Tavern* restaurant (both Rs60/hr). Trek Himalaya, on the steep street opposite the cable car (☎0135/263 0491, ⊛www.trekhimalaya .com), can put together trekking packages, while Kulwant Travels (☎0135/263 2717) at Kulri Bus Stand are approved tour and **car rental** operators, and the taxi office opposite has services to destinations including Dehra Dun (Rs400), Delhi (Rs4000), Gangotri and Yamunotri (both Rs5000).

Accommodation

Mussoorie's **hotel** rates fluctuate between three rather vague **seasons**; low (Jan–March & July–Sept, when the rains come), shoulder or mid-season (Christmas, April and the "Bengali season" of Oct & Nov), and peak (May–early July), when prices quadruple and a dingy room can cost over Rs1000. The town suffers from occasional **water shortages**, which may affect some of the cheaper hotels. Check-out time in Mussoorie is 10am.

Porters from either the Library or the Kulri Bus Stands charge under Rs50 to carry luggage to most locations along the Mall.

BroadwayCamel's Back Rd ☎0135/263 2243. Rambling old guesthouse perching on the edge of Kulri Bazaar with charming, bright window boxes, lovely views and a friendly atmosphere. A good bet for budget travellers, indeed the only budget hotel in season, although the more commercial *Hotel Deep* (☎0135/263 2470, ℮deephotel@hotmail.com) next door has some better-value rooms off-season. ❷–❸

Carlton's PlaisanceHappy Valley Rd, 1.5km from town ☎0135/263 2800. ⊛www.geocities.com/carltonhotels_india. Atmospheric Raj-era house plus a more modern annexe, both stuffed full of period memorabilia. Edmund Hillary stayed here and loved it, and George Everest's house is just up the road. Lovely gardens and an ideal base for gentle rambles away from the town. Book two weeks ahead in season. ⑦–⑧

Darpan Landour Rd, near Picture Palace, Kulri ⑦0135/263 2483. Reasonable and clean, with hot showers, mountain views from some rooms, and a good Gujarati veg restaurant. ④–⑦

Dev Dar Woods Sister's Bazaar ⑦0135/263 2644, ⓔanilprakash56@yahoo.com. Craggy old hotel on a secluded site, often full due to its proximity to the language school, so book well in advance – you may even get picked up from the bus stop. Rates include breakfast. ⑤

Kasmanda Palace The Mall ⑦0135/263 2424, ⓦwww.welcomeheritage.com. A short, stiff climb up from the Mall leads to this ex-maharaja's summer palace, now opened as a heritage hotel. Comfortable and quiet with beautiful gardens and rhino heads on the walls. Book a month ahead in season. ⑧–⑨

Neelam International Kulri ⑦0135/263 2195. Centrally located and good value, even in high season; it looks a bit tatty, but the rooms are cosy and clean. ⑤

Padmini Nivas Library ⑦0135/263 1093, ⓦwww .hotelpadmininivas.com. Just below the Mall, with a beautiful rose garden and fruit trees plus excellent views and lovely, fresh rooms, most with a veranda. It was founded by a British colonel in the 1840s, and was subsequently home to a Gujarati queen (Padmini), hence the name. ⑦

Savoy The Mall ⑦0135/263 2010. Reached via a long driveway, this collapsing Victorian pile above the Library is atmospheric and steeped in history. Agatha Christie based her first novel, *The Mysterious Affair at Styles*, on a celebrated poisoning that took place here. It was closed at last check for major refurbishment, but should be the best hotel in town when it reopens. ⑨

Valley View The Mall ⑦0135/263 2324. Friendly, clean place towering over the Mall and close to all amenities, with a good restaurant and sunny terraces overlooking the Doon Valley. ④–⑦

The Town

Surprisingly, the Mall and the town's main hub face away from the snows towards Dehra Dun; the distant peaks can best be seen from the flat summit of **Gun Hill**, which rises like a volcano from central Mussoorie. This can be ascended on foot or pony on a bridle path that forks up from the Mall, or on the 400-metre "Ropeway" **cable car** from the Mall (Rs55 return). Alternative prospects of the mountains can be seen on a peaceful stroll or ride around the three-kilometre-long **Camel's Back Road**, which girdles the northern base of Gun Hill, passing by the distinctive Camel's Rock and an old **British cemetery** (closed to visitors). Another vantage point, the highest in the immediate vicinity, is **Childer's Lodge**, 5km east of the Mall above Landour.

At the eastern end of the Mall, beyond the bustling Kulri Bazaar, the road winds steeply upwards for 5km through the fascinating market of **Landour**, where you'll find shops overflowing with relics of the Raj, silver jewellery and books. At the top of Landour Bazaar, a square surrounded by cafés attracts both travellers and the local intelligentsia. Nearby, the lovely forested area of **Sister's Bazaar** is excellent for walks, especially to the **Haunted House**, a deserted Raj-era mansion, and around the famous **Landour Language School** (⑦0135/263 1487, ⓦwww.landourlanguageschool.com; one-on-one Hindi lessons Rs275 per 50-minute lesson, plus enrolment and textbook fees; open mid-Feb to mid-Dec).

Away from the noise and bustle, close to Convent Hill and 3km west of the Library, the Tibetan settlement of **Happy Valley** holds a large school, a shop selling hand-knitted sweaters and the small but beautiful **Tchechen Choling** *gompa* overlooking the Doon Valley and surrounded by gardens. It makes an enjoyable walk from the Mall along wooded roads, but you can also catch a taxi (around Rs120 return).

Eating

Cafés and **restaurants** all along the Mall and around Kulri serve everything from hotdogs to Chinese specialities; in addition to those recommended below, there are good restaurants in many of the hotels. Espresso chains **Barista** and

A relatively undemanding but superb trek **from Mussoorie** takes three days (plus one on the bus) to reach the sparsely populated "Valley of the Gods", **HAR-KI-DUN**, in the **Fateh Parvat** region of northwestern Garhwal. The valley trails are open from mid-April until mid-November, but the mountain passes only from mid-June to mid-September. All the trails on the trek are clear, and villagers will happily point you in the right direction. Recommended maps of the trail and region include those published by Leomann – sheet 8 covers Garhwal – and the Ground Survey of India map of the area available from any major Uttarakhand tourist office. In the valley itself, if not higher in the mountains, accommodation is widely available, and food can usually be bought. This area is being developed as a national park, so there are **fees** to be paid if you pass the forest checkpoint at Netwar: Rs350 in total for the first three days, plus Rs175 for each extra day, and a daily camping fee of Rs100.

The rivers and streams of Har-ki-Dun drain the glaciers and snowfields of the peaks of **Swargarohini** (the "Ascent to Heaven"; 6252m) and **Bandarpunch** (the "Monkey's Tail"; 6316m). Local people trace their lineage back to the Mahabharata, claiming descent from Duryodhana and his brothers. Like the Pandavas of the epic, they practise a form of polyandry and follow intriguing religious customs, including witchcraft. Worship at Taluka's Duryodhana temple, for example, consists of throwing shoes at the idol; at Pakola, the image has its back to the congregation. Their distinctive alpine buildings have beautifully carved wooden doors and windows, with the mortar construction punctuated by wooden slats.

The trek to Har-ki-Dun

Starting out from Mussoorie on **Day 1**, catch a Yamunotri bus (1 daily; 10am) at the Library Bus Stand and change at Nowgaon (9km short of Barkot, from where a road climbs to Hanuman Chatti) and take a bus or jeep from there to **Purola** and (changing vehicles at Purola if necessary) on to Netwar – a total of 148km. Set amid a patchwork of wheat and rice terraces in Netwar is a **PWD** bungalow with rooms; you can also obtain permission here or at the PWD office in Purola to stay at the forest bungalows further on. Simple cafés can be found around the bus stand.

Early the next morning – **Day 2** – take the bus to the roadhead at **Sankri**, which also has a bungalow. A jeepable road from here leads 12km through *deodar* and sycamore woods to **Taluka** (1900m), where there is another bungalow serving simple food.

On **Day 3**, the trail descends to follow the River Tons through beautiful forests. Although you can get tea at the hamlet of Gangar, no food is available until you've walked the full 11km to **Osla** (2259m). The forest bungalow, GMVN hotel and *dhaba* stalls are all on the main trail in an area known as Seema, below Osla; from here on you have to carry your food, so stock up.

A steep climb of 14km from Osla on **Day 4** finally brings you to the campground at **Har-ki-Dun** (3560m) – an excellent base from which to explore the *bugyals* below the Swargarohini to the east, and the Jaundhar Glacier (3910m) at the head of the valley.

Café Coffee Day both have branches in town. Prakash's Store, in Sister's Bazaar, is a wonderful place to shop if you're in the neighbourhood, with homemade breads, jams, peanut butter, cheddar cheese and even Marmite.

Clarks The Mall, Kulri. Multi-cuisine restaurant that manages to maintain a period atmosphere of sorts. Non-veg Indian and Chinese menus. Main dishes Rs75–120.

Four Seasons The Mall. Not as much fun as the *Tavern* across the street, but locals claim its mostly Indian menu is the best in town. Free delivery to your hotel. Non-veg mains Rs100–300.

Golden Landour Bazaar. A popular if unremarkable local place next to the Clock Tower, serving Tibetan, Chinese and Indian dishes, and breakfasts. Mains Rs40–70 veg, Rs80–100 non-veg.

Green The Mall, Kulri. Justifiably popular veg (but licensed) restaurant serving Indian and Chinese food and snacks; in season, you may have to queue. Main dishes Rs60–80.

Howard The Mall. Rickety-looking revolving restaurant (non-veg mains Rs50–100) offering all-round views.

Kalsang Friend's Corner The Mall, by the post office. Hearty Tibetan fare (including *momo* dumplings and *thukpa* soup) as well as Chinese, Indian and the odd Thai dish, all tasty, with non-veg mains at Rs50–100.

Tavern The Mall. Hip and recently renovated place near the Picture Palace, offering pricey Western, Thai, Chinese and Indian dishes. There's a small bar and live music and dancing on some Saturdays. Billiards hall and Internet café upstairs. Non-veg main dishes are Rs150–260.

Uphar Gandhi Chowk. Clean, friendly North and south Indian veg food joint with an ice-cream bar. One of the best in the Library area. Main dishes Rs30–80.

Haridwar

At **Haridwar** – the Gates (*dwar*) of God (*Hari*) – 214km northeast of Delhi, the **River Ganges** emerges from its final rapids past the Shivalik Hills to start the long slow journey across northern India to the Bay of Bengal. Stretching for roughly 3km along a narrow strip of land between the craggy wooded hills to the west and the river to the east, Haridwar is especially revered by Hindus, for whom the **Har-ki-Pairi** *ghat* (literally the "Footstep of God") marks the exact spot where the river leaves the mountains. As a road and rail junction, Haridwar links the Gangetic plains with the mountains of Uttarakhand and their holy pilgrimage (*yatra*) network. Along with Nasik (see p.748), Ujjain (see p.462) and Allahabad (see p.312), Haridwar is one of the four holy *tirthas* or "crossings" that serve as the focus of the massive **Kumbh Mela** festival (see p.315). Every twelve years (in 2010 and 2022 for example), thousands of pilgrims come to

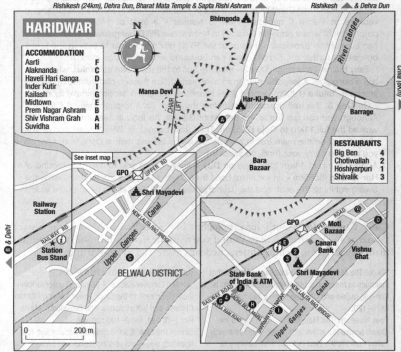

bathe at a preordained moment in the turbulent waters of the channelled river around Har-ki-Pairi.

Arrival and information

Haridwar's **railway station** and **Station Bus Stand** face each other across the town's main thoroughfare, just southwest of the centre. **Tourist information** is available at a booth inside the station, from the more helpful **GMVN tourist office** (℡01334/224240) near Lalita Rao Bridge on Upper Road, or from the **state tourism office** at *Rahi Motel* on Railway Road by the bus stand (℡01334/265304); all open Monday to Saturday 10am to 5pm. Konark Tourist Service on Jassa Ram Road (℡01334/227210, ⓦwww.konarktravels.com) offer **tours** of the state by bus or car.

There's a **post office** on Upper Road. The most central ATM is the State Bank of India's on Railway Road by Sadhu Bela Marg, on which you'll find the bank itself (handy if you need to change cash). Canara Bank on Railway Road also changes travellers' cheques and cash, and has an ATM. Upper Street has two more ATMs and an LPK Forex, with an attached **Internet office**.

Accommodation

Although it has no luxury hotels, Haridwar has **accommodation** to suit most budgets, but none of it is very good value compared to Rishikesh, 24km north (see p.358). The rates below are subject to change with seasonal discounts and hard bargaining.

Aarti Railway Rd ℡01334/226365. A bit grimy, but convenient for the railway station and bus stand, with fifty percent discounts off-season. The priciest rooms have a/c. ④–⑤

Alaknanda Belwala, on the main island ℡01334/226379, ⓔalaknanda@up-tourism.com. The former Tourist Bungalow, still owned by UP State though current litigation may change this. It's a bit institutional, its rooms floored with lino tiles, and not really very spic and span, but it's quiet and has a pleasant garden overlooking the river. ⑤–⑧

Haveli Hari Ganga 21 Ramghat ℡01334/265207, ⓦwww.havelihariganga.com. A beautiful haveli set up by two merchant brothers in 1917, now converted into a beautiful heritage hotel. Double rooms start at $200 for foreigners. ⑨

Inder Kutir Guest House Sharwan Nath Nagar ℡01334/226336. Near the river, with small rooms and hard beds, a terrace, great rooftop views, a friendly vibe and hot water in buckets (though geysers are promised in the near future). Best value in this price range. ②

Kailash Railway Rd ℡01334/227789. Central hotel near the railway station, with a range of rooms, the better ones air-cooled. Up to fifty percent discounts off-season. ③–⑤

Midtown In an alley off Upper Rd, opposite *Chotiwallah* restaurant ℡01334/227507, ⓔhotelmidtown@gmail.com. Haridwar's best-value mid-range hotel, with clean rooms and friendly staff. Rooms at the front have balconies. ④

Prem Nagar Ashram Jawalapur Rd, 2km west of the station ℡01334/226345, ⓦwww .manavcharam.org. Very calm and peaceful, if rather removed from town (Rs5 by shared Vikram). The staff are charming and the rooms clean and cheap (Rs75 per person). ①

Shiv Vishram Grah Lodge Upper Rd, near Har-ki-Pairi ℡01334/227618, ⓦwww.svgl.co.in. The budget rooms are air-cooled and pretty spacious; the deluxe ones have TVs and balconies overlooking a sunny courtyard (which is used for parking), and the location is bang in the heart of town. ④

Suvidha Sharwan Nath Nagar, behind Chitra Talkies cinema ℡01334/227023. Comfortable, plush place with a pleasant location near the river, away from the bustle of the bazaars and main roads. A/c and non-a/c rooms – make sure yours has a geyser. ⑤–⑦

The Town

Split by a barrage north of Haridwar, the **Ganges** flows through the town in two principal channels, divided by a long sliver of land. The natural stream lies to the east, while the embankment of the fast-flowing canal to the west holds *ghats* and ashrams. Promenades, river channels and bridges create a pleasant riverfront ambience, with the major *ghats* and religious activity clustered around the **Har-ki-Pairi temple**, which looks like a railway station. Bridges and walkways connect the various islands, and metal chains are placed in the river to protect bathers from being swept away by swift currents.

The clock tower opposite Har-ki-Pairi *ghat* is an excellent vantage point, especially during evening worship. At dusk, the spectacular daily ceremony of **Ganga Arati** – devotion to the life-bestowing goddess Ganga – draws a crowd of thousands onto the islands and bridges. Lights float down the river and priests perform elaborate choreographed movements while swinging torches to the accompaniment of gongs and music. As soon as they've finished the river shallows fill up with people looking for coins thrown in by the devout. The *ghat* area is free to visit, although a donation is required to visit the section at the bottom of the first staircase.

Haridwar's teeming network of **markets** is the other main focus of interest. **Bara Bazaar**, at the top of town, is a good place to buy a *danda* (bamboo staff) for treks in the mountains. Stalls in the colourful **Moti Bazaar** in the centre of town on the Jawalapur road sell everything from clothes to spices.

High above Haridwar, on the crest of a ridge, the gleaming white *shikhara* of the **Mansa Devi** temple dominates both town and valley. The temple is easily reached by **cable car** (daily: April–Oct 7.30am–7pm; Dec–March 8.30am–5pm; Rs48 return), from a base station off Upper Road in the heart of town, though the steep 1.5-kilometre walk is pleasant enough early in the morning. None of the shrines and temples up top holds any great architectural interest, but you do get excellent views along the river. An elaborate queuing system leads pilgrims to a *darshan* of the main image, showing Mansa Devi – a triple-headed image of Shakti as the goddess Durga. Photography is forbidden.

The modern, seven-storeyed **Bharat Mata** temple – 5km north of Haridwar and reachable in shared Vikrams from next to *Shivalik* restaurant for Rs10 – is dedicated to "Mother India". A temple with a similar name and purpose can be found in Varanasi, but this one is much newer and much more garish. Each of its various floors – connected by lifts – is dedicated to a celestial or political theme, and populated by lifelike images of heroes, heroines and Hindu deities.

Eating

As a holy city, Haridwar is strictly **vegetarian** and booze-free.

Big Ben Railway Rd, next to the *Kailash* hotel. Hotel restaurant with a good range of veg curries (Rs60–100), set meals (Rs100–125), breakfasts (Rs85–115) and a few Chinese and Continental dishes including cheese steak or veg steak (they mean "cutlets").
Chotiwala Upper Rd. Established in 1937, this comfortable, dimly lit place is still one of the best around, offering good Indian food (main dishes Rs40–75) as well as breakfast (tea, coffee, toast and the like, but no omelettes of course), and some south Indian and Chinese dishes.

Hoshiyarpuri Upper Rd. Busy and friendly *dhaba*-like restaurant close to Har-ki-Pairi. Delicious Indian (especially Punjabi) and Chinese mains (Rs22–70), and great *kheer* (creamed rice pudding).
Shivalik Railway Rd. A small hotel restaurant whose chef prides himself on his small selection of Chinese dishes (try the chop suey). Tasty south Indian snacks, including *dosas*, are also on offer. Mains are Rs40–100, breakfasts Rs70–120, thalis Rs80–100.

Moving on from Haridwar

Major **trains** passing through Haridwar include the overnight Mussoorie Express #4042 to **Delhi**, which leaves town at 11.20pm, reaching Old Delhi at 7.20am. The a/c Janshatabdi Express #2056, which leaves at 6.20am, gets to New Delhi at 11.15am. For **Agra**, the Kalingautkal Express #8478, leaving daily at 6am, reaches Agra Cantonment at 4pm. The Doon Express #3010, leaving at 10.15pm, is the most convenient service to Lucknow (arrives 8.15am), Varanasi (arrives 4.10pm) and Kolkata (arrives Howrah 7am second morning). Local trains on the branch line to **Rishikesh** aren't that useful in view of the excellent and more frequent road connections.

The **Station Bus Stand** has half-hourly services to Delhi and Rishikesh from 4am till 11pm, and to Dehra Dun from 5am till 7.30pm. Shared Vikrams to Rishikesh from next to *Shivalik* restaurant provide a cramped alternative for much the same price. The **Taxi** Association near the railway station sets prices slightly higher than those quoted elsewhere, charging Rs2500 for a taxi to Delhi, Rs450 to Rishikesh, Rs310 to Chila. Travellers heading into the mountains should go to Rishikesh to pick up onward transport. See p.390 for frequencies and journey times.

Rajaji National Park and around

Around 830 square kilometres of the Himalayan foothills immediately east of Haridwar are taken up by **RAJAJI NATIONAL PARK** (Rs350 [Rs40] for three days, Rs175 [Rs25] each additional day, plus Rs100–500 per vehicle, Rs100 for a camera; ⓦ www.rajajinationalpark.in), which belongs to the same forest belt as Corbett Tiger Reserve, 180km east. Although not geared up to tourism to the same extent as Corbett, the park is absolutely beautiful, with a similar range of **wildlife** – most notably elephants, but also antelope, leopard and even a rare species of anteater – although no tigers. The **Van Gujjars**, a nomadic tribe whose summer homes lie within the park, have long been engaged in a land-rights dispute with the forestry department over designation of the forest for wildlife use, but a July 2007 state high court ruling upheld a petition allowing those already resident within the park to remain under the terms of the federal government's 2006 Forest Rights Act.

There are eight **entry gates** into the national park, including **Kunnao** close to Rishikesh and the main gates at **Chila** (see below), 9km east of Haridwar by road and across the Ganges. **Accommodation** is available at ten forest rest houses within the park and is bookable through the Rajaji National Park Office, 5/1 Ansari Marg, Dehra Dun (☎0135/262 1669). However, visitors don't have to go into the core area to experience the jungles – it's possible to venture in from Chila or Rishikesh, or from the road between the two, which runs parallel to the canal marking the boundary of the huge fringe forest.

Chila

To get to **CHILA** from Haridwar, catch one of the Rishikesh-bound buses which leave hourly 7am to 2pm from the GMOU office by the bus stand, take a taxi (about Rs300–350 one way, or Rs500–600 for the round trip), or even **walk** (Chila is visible from Haridwar, and taking a short cut from Har-ki-Pairi via the riverbeds and a bridge makes it a journey of just 4km east). The town itself is neither attractive nor interesting, located right beside the Ganges barrage and its massive electricity pylons. However, it makes a good base for explorations of the park, and **Chila Beach** – occasionally used by large river turtles – lies within walking distance through the woods, 1km north along the Ganges. **Elephant rides** from here cost around Rs300 per head for two hours; to arrange one, just ask the trainers who tout for business.

Accommodation is available at the large GMVN *Chila Tourist Bungalow* (☎01382/266678; ❺–❻), which has an overpriced dorm (Rs150), deluxe and a/c rooms, huts and grassy camping facilities. Rooms here can also be reserved through the Haridwar GMVN office.

Rishikesh and around

RISHIKESH, 238km northeast of Delhi and 24km north of Haridwar, lies at the point where the wooded mountains of Garhwal rise abruptly from the low valley floor and the Ganges crashes onto the plains. The centre for all manner of New Age and Hindu activity, its many ashrams – some ascetic, some opulent – continue to draw devotees and followers of all sorts of weird and wonderful gurus, with the large **Shivananda Ashram** in particular renowned as a yoga centre. Rishikesh is also emerging as an **adventure-sports** hub, with rafting, trekking and mountaineering all on offer.

Rishikesh has one or two ancient shrines, but its main role has always been as a way-station for *sannyasin*, *yogis* and heading for the high Himalayas. The arrival of the Beatles, who came here to meet the Maharishi in 1968, was one of the first manifestations of the lucrative expansion of the *yatra* pilgrimage circuit; these days it's easy to see why Ringo thought it was "just like Butlin's". By far the best times to visit are in winter and spring, when the mountain temples are shut by the snows – without the *yatra* razzmatazz, you get a sense of the tranquillity that was the original appeal of the place. At other times, a walk upriver leads easily away from the bustle to secluded spots among giant rocks ideally suited for yoga, meditation or an invigorating dip in the cold water (but not a swim: fast currents make that too dangerous).

Confusingly, the name Rishikesh is applied to a loose association of five distinct areas, encompassing not only the town but also hamlets and settlements on both sides of the river: **Rishikesh** itself, the commercial and communications hub; sprawling suburban **Muni-ki-Reti**; **Shivananda Nagar**, just north; the assorted ashrams around **Swarg Ashram** on the east bank; and the riverbank temples of **Lakshmanjhula**, a little further north.

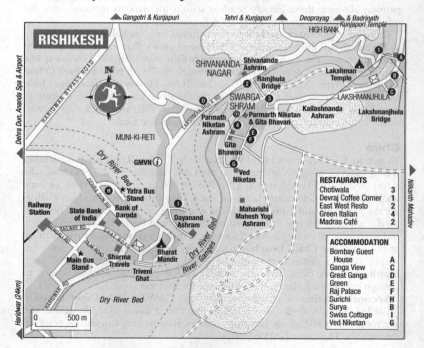

The **telephone code** for Rishikesh is ⑦0135 unless you're dialling from within a 75km radius, in which case the ⑦0135 code changes to ⑦95135.

Arrival and information

The **Main Bus Stand**, used by Haridwar and Dehra Dun government buses, as well as services from Delhi, is on Bengali Road, close to the centre; buses for the Garhwal hills use the **Yatra Bus Stand**, also known as the **Tehri Bus Stand**, off the Dehra Dun Road. Rishikesh is at the end of a small branch **railway** line from Haridwar, served by six trains daily. The airport, 18km west, is not currently served by commercial flights.

Local transport connecting the main areas includes cycle and auto-rickshaws and shared Vikrams; the fare from Rishikesh to Lakshmanjhula is Rs25 (Rs5 shared ride). There are also shared Vikrams to Haridwar. Reliable agencies for renting **cars** and **taxis** include Ajay Travels, at the *Hotel Neelkanth*, Haridwar Road (⑦0135/243 0644), and Mahayama Travels, Urvasi Complex, Dehra Dun Road (⑦0135/243 2968, ⓦwww.himalayantour.com). Rishikesh, like many of the hill towns, is increasingly turning to seasonal tourism, and a negative impact of this has been the dramatic rise of unregulated tour and **travel operators** with no insurance cover for their drivers and cars, or for you. Ask for recommended travel agents at your hotel or at the tourist office. Long-distance journeys can be booked at Triveni Travels, Shop No. 1, opposite Punjab National Bank, Haridwar Road (⑦0135/243 0989).

The **Uttarakhand Tourist Office** and **GMVN Yatra Office** on Haridwar Bypass Road can provide local information, though GMVN in practice restrict themselves to selling their own tours or to booking accommodation in their tourist lodges. Their **Mountaineering and Trekking** division on Lakshmanjhula Road, Muni-ki-Reti (⑦0135/243 0799), however, rents basic equipment, arranges guides, and can also organize ski trips to Auli (see p.371). Most of the established river camps on the Ganges above Rishikesh operate from the end of September to mid-December, and from mid-February until late April. **Rafting excursions** vary in length from half-day runs to extended camping–rafting expeditions; expect to pay around Rs700 per head for a half-day raft trip, or Rs4500 for three days all-in. Unfortunately, cowboy operators abound, so beware; a reliable local firm is Red Chilli on Lakshmanjhula Road in High Bank (⑦0135/243 4021, ⓦwww.redchilliadventure.com).

Banks in town include the Bank of Baroda, 70 Dehra Dun Road, and Apex Bank very near by, both with ATMs. There are other ATMs on Haridwar Road at the corner of Ghat Road, on Lakshmanjhula Road by the GMVN trekking office, and on the east bank near Ramjhula Bridge. A number of travel agents in Lakshmanjhula will change cash and traveller's cheques. The main post office is on Ghat Road, with branch offices in Lakshmanjhula, and near both sides of Ramjhula Bridge. **Internet** cafés abound; one of the best is Blue Hill Travel and Cyber Café (Rs20/hr) in the Swarg Ashram area near Parmarth Niketan; their travel agency, however, has a bad reputation.

Accommodation

Rishikesh town has plenty of hotels but it's a noisy and polluted place and the only reason to stay here is to be near the bus station and amenities. **Muni-ki-Reti** is not too far and slightly more pleasant. New Agers tend to stay around **Swarg Ashram** and the east bank of the river, away from the noise and near the ashrams, while backpackers head for the cheap little guesthouses of **Lakshmanjhula**.

Bombay Guest House Lakshmanjhula ☎0135/325 0038. Basic accommodation with shared baths off a leafy courtyard, handy for exploring the unspoilt upper reaches of this stretch of the river, and popular with hippy travellers. ❶

Ganga View Lakshmanjhula ☎0135/244 0320. A good-value choice among the many, generally similar, small budget hotels in the area – this one has nice fresh rooms (all with attached bathrooms and hot water), and it's off the main drag, so reasonably quiet. ❶

The Great Ganga Lakshmanjhula Rd, Shivananda Nagar ☎0135/244 2243, ⓦwww.thegreatganga .com. It's worth braving the steep and very grotty pathway to reach this comfortable upmarket hotel whose fresh rooms have river-facing balconies and good views; there's also a good restaurant. If you really want to push the boat out, go for an executive suite ($110). ❼

Green Swarg Ashram ☎0135/243 1242. Popular little travellers' hotel tucked behind Gita Bhavan Ashram. All rooms have attached bathrooms, most with running hot water, there's a roof terrace and a restaurant which serves under-spiced Indian and Italian food. The sister-hotel *Green View* behind is a slightly more upmarket option and also recommended. ❶–❺

Omkarananda Gita Sadan Lakshmanjhula Rd, Shivananda Nagar ☎0135/243 6346 or 7, ⓔswami.kumarananada@gmail.com. Run by the ashram of the same name, this lovely guest-house has a relaxed atmosphere, plain but spacious and immaculately clean rooms, great views over the river, and even a four-person family suite, but you'll need to book ahead. ❺

Raj Palace Swarg Ashram behind Parmarth Niketan ☎0135/244 0079. Well-managed hotel popular with yoga students due to its location near the ashrams and large, sunny yoga room. Rooftop café. Discounts up to fifty percent off-season. ❷–❻

Suruchi Yatra Bus Stand ☎0135/243 2602. Friendly but rather dingy hotel whose main attraction is that it's convenient for early Char Dham buses. ❶–❸

Surya Lakshmanjhula Rd ☎0135/243 3211, ⓔhotelsurya@hotmail.com. Clean and marble-floored double rooms, the best (and priciest) being at the front with river views, though the darker back rooms are quieter. There's also a rooftop restaurant. ❶–❷

Swiss Cottage Chandra Bhaga ☎0135/243 5012, ⓔshivgangamylove @rediff.mail.com. Near the bridge and down unnamed lanes towards the river is Rishikesh's first guesthouse, founded in 1961 by Swami Brahmananda, one of Swami Shivananda's inner group of disciples. It's a small but peaceful haven with a motley assortment of rooms. Popular with long-term visitors and extremely good value, so often booked up. ❶–❸

Ved Niketan Swarg Ashram ☎0135/243 0279. Enormous orange ashram on the east bank of the river, with cheap accommodation that is very popular with low-budget travellers. ❶

The Town

Most of the pilgrims who pass through Rishikesh on their way to the Himalayan shrines of the Char Dham pause for a dip and puja at what is left of the large sandy expanse of **Triveni Ghat**, close to the centre of town. The river here looks especially spectacular during *arati* (evening worship), when *diya* lights float on the water. Nearby, at **Bharat Mandir**, Rishikesh's oldest temple, a black stone image of Vishnu is supposed to have been consecrated by the great ninth-century Hindu revivalist Shankara; the event is commemorated during Basant Panchami, to mark the first day of spring.

The dense-knit complex of cafés, shops and ashrams collectively known as **Swarg Ashram**, opposite Shivananda Ashram, backs on to forest-covered hills where caves are still inhabited by sadhus. The river can be crossed at this point either on the Ramjhula footbridge, or on **ferries**, which operate between 8am and 7pm according to demand (Rs5 one way, Rs8 return). Put away any thoughts about swimming across; reports of people drowning in these swift waters are not uncommon. Swarg Ashram itself, popularly referred to as Kale Kumbli Wale, was founded in honour of Swami Vishudhanand, who came here in 1884 and habitually wore a black (*kala*) blanket (*kumble*). The most conspicuous of the other ashram-temples is **Parmarth Niketan**, whose large courtyard is crammed with brightly clad gods and goddesses. **Gita Bhavan**, next door, runs an Ayurvedic dispensary up the street (Tues–Sun 10am–noon; first three days of medicine free), where they also sell books and *khadi* handloom cloth.

▲ Sitting on the banks of the Ganges

Around 2km north of Swarg Ashram, a path skirts the east bank of the river and beautiful sandy beaches sheltered by large boulders, en route to **Lakshman-jhula**. A footbridge spans the river here as it negotiates its final rocky course out of the mountains. It's the most appealing part of Rishikesh, featuring the enormous, gaudy **Kailashnanda Ashram**. The attractive landscape and turquoise river are best appreciated from the *Devraj Coffee Corner* on the west side where travellers spend days watching daredevil monkeys cavorting on the bridge and pouncing on unsuspecting passers-by.

Eating

Rishikesh has plenty of worthy **restaurants** and *dhabas*, many with pleasant river views and tourist-orientated menus. Expect only vegetarian food in this holy town.

Chotiwala Swarg Ashram. Two neighbouring establishments with the same name vie for custom and constantly attempt to outdo each other. The one closest to the river has slightly better service and a congenial roof terrace. Both places are large, busy and open at 7am for breakfast; the extensive menus (main dishes Rs35–85) include ice cream, sweets and cold drinks.

Devraj Coffee Corner Lakshmanjhula, just above the bridge on the town side of the river. Enjoy cinnamon rolls, muesli fruit curd and superb cakes, or dine on pizzas, veg sizzlers, curries, veggie-burgers, or even the odd attempt at a Mexican dish, as you watch the Ganges and the pilgrims flow past. Most dishes are in the Rs50–100 range.

East West Resto Directly opposite ferry quay, Ramjhula. Tiny, cheap café serving up strong coffee and healthy, tasty lunches such as brown basmati rice with veg (main dishes Rs40–90).

Green Italian Restaurant Swarg Ashram. Pizzas and pastas head the list of treats at this offshoot of the *Green Hotel*'s in-house Italian eatery. There's a choice of spaghetti or penne with a range of veg sauces, or cannelloni with a choice of three veg fillings (Rs80–95), plus a range of set breakfasts (Rs35–90).

Madras Café Directly opposite ferry quay, Ramjhula. Busy, welcoming restaurant, with great filter coffee, and reasonably priced south Indian food (main dishes Rs40–90, thali Rs60). The "Himalayan Health Pullao" (Rs75) is made with vegetable sprouts and ayurvedic herbs.

Ashrams, yoga and meditation

Due to an ongoing dispute with the government, Maharishi Mahesh Yogi's beautifully situated ashram, home to the Beatles in 1968, stands empty on a high forested bluff above the river. Although there are no classes here, it's a wonderfully atmospheric place to wander around – but don't come alone, as there have been reports of muggings. Yoga Niketan Ashram should also be avoided as there have been incidents of theft and worse; indeed, complaints about theft and harassment in ashrams are surprisingly common. However, a number of reputable ashrams in Rishikesh welcome students of yoga, offering courses of varying duration – from one day to several months – and cost.

Ananda Spa ☏01378/227500, ⊛www.anandaspa.com. Not an ashram but an internationally renowned luxury resort on the outskirts of Rishikesh, offering yoga, spa and Ayurvedic-based beauty treatments. Rooms, suites and villas from $530 to $1855 per night.

Dayanand Ashram ☏0135/243 0769. Irregular courses on Vedanta as well as yoga classes. Near *Swiss Cottage* guesthouse.

Parmarth Niketan Ashram ☏0135/244 0077 or 88, ⊛www.parmarth.com. Runs regular yoga classes and, in association with Uttarakhand Tourism, sponsors a yoga week in late Feb/early March. There are a range of courses to choose from, with accommodation at a variety of hotels throughout Rishikesh.

Shivananda Ashram ☏0135/243 0040, ⊛www.divinelifesociety.org. Large institution, with branches all over the world, run by the Divine Life Society and founded by the remarkable Swami Shivananda (who passed into what his followers refer to as *maha samadhi*, final liberation, in 1963). It has a well-stocked library, a forest retreat and a charitable hospital. Sessions in meditation and yoga, plus other activities, are always going on. To arrange a long-term stay, contact the Secretary two months in advance (Divine Life Society, PO Shivanandanagar 249192, Tehri District, Garhwal, Uttarakhand).

Ved Niketan Ashram ☏0135/243 0279. Across the river south of Swarg Ashram. Month-long courses run by the charismatic Swamiji Dharmananda, introducing students to all aspects of yoga. Hatha yoga classes held every morning (8–9.30am) and evening (4–5.30pm).

Yoga Study Centre ☏0135/243 3837. Reputable school for the Iyengar form of Hatha yoga, 1km south of central Rishikesh at Ganga Vihar.

Moving on

All **trains** from Rishikesh go to Haridwar (though it's easier by bus or Vikram), and the 7am #372 passenger train even continues to Delhi, but it's very slow and you're better off taking the bus to Haridwar to pick up the 11.20pm overnight Mussoorie Express. Advance reservations can be made at Rishikesh Station, but it only gets a small quota of seats.

Buses to lowland destinations such as Dehra Dun and Delhi leave from the main bus stand on Bengali Road. During the April-to-October pilgrimage season, when the **Char Dham** temples are open in the Garhwal hills, direct buses connect Rishikesh's Yatra Bus Stand with **Badrinath** (297km), **Kedarnath** (210km, via Gaurikund), **Gangotri** (250km) and **Yamunotri** (280km, via Hanuman Chatti). Book at least a day in advance. Buses start to leave around 4am and only the early ones complete the journey in a day; the roads are treacherous and tedious, so you might prefer to break the journey along the way.

Every morning, from around 5am, a fleet of **press Jeeps** heads up into the mountains to deliver the day's newspapers, and they also act as share-taxis, leaving from Haridwar Road in front of Nagar Palika Parashad (just south of

Tilak Road). Advance bookings for at least some of them can be made at Sharma Travels (aka Kaushik Telecom), 86 Haridwar Road, by *Akash Ganga Hotel* (℡0135/243 0364). They cost more than the bus (Rs300 to Joshimath, for example), but are a lot faster, and they may agree to pick you up at your hotel if you book in advance and are staying on the west side of the river.

GMVN in Muni-ki-Reti (see p.359) organizes **package tours** (a four-day trip to Badrinath, including bus, food and lodging, costs around Rs3300), as well as very expensive car rental.

Around Rishikesh: local treks

Although a road has now been blasted through the forest to the small Shiva shrine in the hamlet of **Nilkanth Mahadev** (Nilkantha), east of Rishikesh, it's still possible to walk there along the older and shorter pilgrim path. This beautiful forest track rises through the forests behind Swarg Ashram, passes Mahesh Yogi's ashram, and eventually crosses a spur before descending to Nilkantha. There's a chance you may encounter wildlife along the way; keep a safe distance from wild elephants. Nilkantha itself is changing, as an ever-growing number of pilgrims travel along the new road that has cut a swathe through the forests.

You can also follow the river along the motorable track north of Lakshman-jhula, passing several good beaches before arriving at the beautiful ashram of **Phulcchatti** (10km), which lies on a bend in the river and has giant boulders and excellent swimming.

Another hike leads high above Lakshmanjhula for 10km to the small white Shakti temple of **Kunjapuri**, at the sharp point of an almost perfectly conical hill with stupendous views of the Himalayas to the north and towards Haridwar to the south. Try to catch the sunrise from the top, before the haze seeps into the atmosphere. A less strenuous alternative is to take the bus to Hindola Khal on the road to Tehri and walk the remaining 3km to the temple. Bring a guide or partner in any of these areas as incidents of **robbery** along the trails have been reported.

The trek to Yamunotri

Cradled in a deep cleft in the lap of Bandarpunch, and thus denied mountain vistas, the temple of **Yamunotri** (3291m), 223km northeast of Rishikesh, marks the source of the Yamuna, India's second holiest river after the Ganges. The least dramatic but most beautiful of the four *dhams* (temples) of Garhwal, it's also the least spoiled and commercial. **Access** (mid-April to early November only; exact dates vary annually) has become easier following road improve-ments; from the roadhead at Janki Chatti it's a mere 5km along a trail that follows the turbulent ice-blue river as it runs below rocky crags, with snowy peaks in the distance. The walk can also be combined with the **Dodi Tal trek** linking nearby Hanuman Chatti to Uttarkashi (see box, p.365).

Janki Chatti and around

The enchanting little village of **JANKI CHATTI** marks the end of a motorable road connected by bus with Dehra Dun, Mussoorie and Rishikesh. Some routes require a change at **BARKOT**, a four-hour bus ride (Rs100) beyond Mussoorie, which has a GMVN *Tourist Bungalow* (℡013752/24236; ❸–❹) but very little to eat. Jeeps and buses (Rs40) travel another two and a half hours to reach the small riverside hamlet of **HANUMAN CHATTI**, which has an excellent GMVN *Tourist Bungalow* (℡01375/223 3371; ❺) with river-facing rooms and a comfort-able dorm (Rs150). Crossing a bridge at the edge of town, a brand-new road weaves into the mountains for 9km until it reaches Janki Chatti, home to a GMVN *Tourist Rest House* (☎013752/235639; ❺, dorms Rs150), and a travellers' lodge (❹). The *Ganga Yamuna* (☎01375/223 3301; ❸) and the *Arvind Ashram* (❷) are alternatives, both along the main trail, and there are a number of decent **restaurants** offering thalis, cold drinks and snacks. While you're in Janki Chatti, it's worth making the one-kilometre detour across the river to the traditional Garhwali village of **KHARSALI**, home to the *pandas* (pilgrim priests) of Yamunotri. Among the drystone buildings with their beautifully carved wooden beams stands a unique three-storey Shiva temple – dedicated to Someshwar, lord of the mythical intoxicant Soma. If travelling to Gangotri the same day (an eleven-hour journey), it is best to take the first bus (at 5.30am) if you want to be sure of arriving the same day, though the second bus (at 7am) should also reach Gangotri that evening; buses usually leave from Hanuman Chatti, but may serve Janki Chatti too.

Yamunotri

A short way beyond Janki Chatti, the trail becomes much steeper but increasingly dramatic and beautiful as it passes through rocky forested crags to **YAMUNOTRI**. Sited near the river, around three piping-hot sulphur springs, Yamunotri's temple is new and architecturally uninteresting; it has to be completely rebuilt every few years due to the impact of heavy winter snows and monsoon rains. Its main shrine – actually part of the top spring, worshipped as the source of the river – holds a small silver image of the goddess Yamuna, bedecked with garlands. The daughter of Surya, the sun, and Sangya, consciousness, Yamuna is the twin sister of Yama, the lord of death; all who bathe in her waters are spared a painful end, while food cooked in the water is considered to be *prasad* (divine offering). Most pilgrims also bathe in the **hot spring** (free); both male and female pools have been built. If you choose to **stay** in Yamunotri, there's a simple dormitory (Rs150) at the GMVN *Tourist Bungalow* near the temple. The best of the few *dharamshalas* is the *Ramananda Ashram* (❷), commanding good views from the hill above the temple, and owned by the head priest. Simple **food** arrangements can be made through the ashrams and the bungalow.

Technically, the source of the Yamuna is the glacial lake of **Saptarishi Kund**. This is reached via a hard twelve-kilometre trek, which heads straight up the mountain alongside the river until finally easing towards the base of Kalinda Parbat. Both this trek and the route over the challenging Yamunotri Pass to Har-ki-Dun (see p.353) necessitate at least one day's acclimatization, adequate clothing, supplies and a guide.

Uttarkashi

The largest town in the interior of Garhwal, **UTTARKASHI** made the news when it was hit by an earthquake in 1991, but this was neither the first nor the last disaster to hit it. It suffered severe floods in 1978, and in 2003 a massive landslide wiped out several hotels on the main road, as well as the tourist office and the bus stand. Miraculously nobody was hurt, but it left a large gap in the middle of town, which has still to be rebuilt – the hillside is first being secured against further landslides.

The town occupies the flat and fertile valley floor of the Bhagirathi; most pilgrims and tourists stop here to break the long journey between Rishikesh, 148km south, and Gangotri, 100km northeast. Uttarkashi's busy and well-stocked **market** is ideal for picking up supplies before high-altitude treks, and

The Dodi Tal trek

The relatively short **Dodi Tal trek**, which links the Gangotri and Yamunotri regions without straying into high glacial terrain, is one of Garhwal's all-time classics. It's not a difficult hike, but local villagers are keen to offer their services as porters or guides, and you should definitely avail yourself of their help if you want to wander off the beaten track and visit the villages. Carry as much of your own food as possible, and also your own tent. The best maps for this trek are the Ground Survey map of Garhwal, and Leomann map (sheet 7 in the India Series), both available from major Uttarakhand Tourism offices.

The trek is described below from east to west, starting from **Uttarkashi** on the way to Gangotri, and ending at **Hanuman Chatti**, 14km south of Yamunotri.

On **DAY ONE**, catch one of the three daily buses or an hourly Jeep from Uttarkashi to **Kalyani** (1829m) via Gangotri (the first is at 7am; 1hr). From Kalyani, it's a gentle 7km climb through fields and woodland to **Agoda** (2286m), where the *Tourist Bungalow* at the far end of the village is currently in a state of disrepair, so you will have to put up a tent for the night.

On **DAY TWO**, the trail from Agoda climbs beside a river and then zigzags steadily upwards through lush pine and spruce forests, with a couple of chai shops en route. After 14km and a final undulation, it arrives at **Dodi Tal** (3024m), a lake set against a backdrop of thickly forested hills. Near the basic forest bungalow in the clearing are chai shops and areas for camping.

Some trekkers consider the full 18km from Dodi Tal to Shima on **DAY THREE** too long and arduous, and prefer to split it into two days. Follow the well-marked path along (and often across) the stream that feeds Dodi Tal, which can get steep and entail scrambling; continue straight ahead, ignoring tracks that cross the trail, until you emerge above the treeline. After a further 1.5km the trail heads left to a small pass then zigzags up scree to **Darwa Pass** (4130m), about halfway to Shima. This is the highest point of the trek, providing superb panoramas of the Srikanta Range. If you're ready to rest here, a leftward path beyond the top leads to camping and water. The main route goes down to a valley and then climbs sharply again. It takes about four more hours to reach **Shima**, where you rejoin the treeline. There's basic hut accommodation, but bring your own food.

The beautiful twelve-kilometre trail down from Shima on **DAY FOUR** kicks off with a steep 1.5km scramble alongside a stream, then eases past forest and *bugyal*, where shepherds have their huts. A well-defined rocky path drops steadily through two villages and zigzags down to the Hanuman Ganga River. It emerges at **Hanuman Chatti** (see opposite) from where buses run via Barkot to Uttarkashi, Mussoorie and other points in Garhwal. The Dodi Tal trek can easily be tied in with hikes in the **Har-ki-Dun** and **Yamunotri** areas; see also p.353.

the town is also a good place to contact experienced **mountain guides** – mostly graduates of its highly esteemed Nehru Institute of Mountaineering (☎01374/222123, ⓦwww.nimindia.org). The going rates stand at around Rs200 per porter and Rs300–500 for a guide. Specialist operators include Mount Support, PO Box 2, B.D. Nautial Bhawan, Bhatwari Road (☎01374/222419, ⓔmountsupport@rediffmail.com), on the main road, who also have equipment for rent and porters for hire.

Practicalities

All **buses** to and from Uttarkashi – which has regular services to both Gangotri (until 2pm) and Rishikesh between May and November – park up by the main road in the centre of town (for Mussoorie, take a Rishikesh-bound bus and change at Chamba). **Taxis** can be picked up in the market area; a seat in a shared Jeep to Gangotri costs around Rs100 per person. There is an **ATM** two doors from the *Bandhari* hotel, and **Internet** access is available around town at a pricey Rs60/hr.

On the main road, the *Bandhari* (☎01374/222203; ❷–❸) has a range of double **rooms**, some with hot water and TV. Their annexe (☎01374/ 222384; ❸–❹), 300m up the road on the left, is newer, cleaner and brighter, with balconies overlooking the road. In the lanes by the market you'll find the simple but well-kept *Amba* (☎01374/222150; ❶), and the GMVN *Tourist Bungalow* (☎01374/222271; ❹), with spacious rooms and a dorm (Rs150), set around a small lawn. By far the best accommodation and food is 2km from the centre at the delightful ⚓ *Monal Tourist Home* (☎01374/222270, ⓔmonaluttarkashi@rediffmail.com; ❹). The friendly owner, a graduate of the Nehru Institute of Mountaineering, will pick you up from the bus stand if you phone in advance, and is more than happy to provide information (and company) if you're interested in trekking in the region. In town, the best place to **eat** is the restaurant of the *Bandhari* hotel, which serves breakfast items and basic veg curries at Rs30–50 a go.

Gangotri and around

Set amid tall *deodar* pine forests at the head of the Bhagirathi gorge, 248km north of Rishikesh at 3140m, **Gangotri** is the most remote of the four *dhams* (pilgrimage sites) of Garhwal, and is closed from early November till mid-April. Although the wide Alaknanda, which flows past Badrinath, has in some ways a better claim to be considered the main channel of the Ganges, Gangotri is for Hindus the spiritual source of the great river, while its physical source is the ice cave of **Gomukh** on the Gangotri Glacier, 14km further up the valley. From here, the **River Bhagirathi** begins its tempestuous descent through a series of mighty gorges, carving great channels and cauldrons in the rock and foaming in white-water pools.

From Uttarkashi, frequent buses, taxis and Jeeps head up to Gangotri. A shared Jeep (3hr 30min) should cost around Rs100 per head and is probably the most enjoyable way of making the journey; buses stop frequently and can take more than five hours to make the trip. Parts of the road beyond Gangnani, where the vast and fertile Bhagirathi flood plain is famous for its apple orchards, were damaged by the earthquake in 1992; gigantic blocks of rock almost dammed the river and created a lake. Ten kilometres beyond the uninspiring village of **Harsil**, the road crosses the deep Bhagirathi gorge at **Lanka**, on a dramatic bridge said to be among the highest in the world. This is an army area, so don't take any photographs. At the hamlet of **Bhaironghati**, 3km further on and 11km short of Gangotri, the Rudragaira emerges from its own gorge to meet the Bhagirathi. A small temple stands in towering *deodar* forests, and there are a few teashops as well as a barely used GMVN *Tourist Bungalow* (❸–❹).

Gangotri

Although most of the nearby snow peaks are obscured by the desolate craggy mountains looming immediately above **GANGOTRI**, the town itself is redolent of the atmosphere of the high Himalayas, populated by a mixed cast of Hindu pilgrims and foreign trekkers. Its unassuming **temple**, overlooking the river just beyond a small market on the left bank, was built early in the eighteenth century by the Gurkha general Amar Singh Thapa. Capped with a gilded roof, consisting of a squat *shikhara* surrounded by four smaller replicas, it commemorates the legend that the goddess Ganga was enticed to earth by acts of penance performed by King Bhagirath, who wanted her to revitalize

Gangotri ashrams

Although most of the so-called "ashrams" in Gangotri are in reality boarding houses, a few sadhus offer rooms on a donation basis for visitors looking for a quiet retreat. The simple, atmospheric **Kailash Ashram**, overlooking the confluence of the Kedar Ganga and the Bhagirathi, is run (along with a small Ayurvedic clinic) by the affable Bhim Yogi, who welcomes guests for medium- and long-term stays. Nearby, **Nani Mata's Ashram** belongs to an Australian *mataji* (female sadhu), who has lived in Gangotri for many years and is held in high esteem.

the ashes of his people. Inside the temple is a silver image of the goddess, while a slab of stone adjacent to the temple is venerated as **Bhagirath Shila**, the spot where the king meditated. Steps lead down to the main riverside *ghat*, where the devout bathe in the freezing waters of the river to cleanse their bodies and souls of sin.

Across the river, a loose development of ashrams and guesthouses dwarfed by great rocky outcrops and huge trees leads down to **Dev Ghat**, overlooking the confluence with the Kedar Ganga. Not far beyond, at the impressive waterfall-fed pool of **Gaurikund**, the twenty-kilometre-long gorge starts to get into its stride. Beautiful forest paths lead through the dark *deodar* woods and past a bridge along the edge of the gorge to a flimsy rope-bridge, commanding great views of the ferocious torrent below.

GMVN's *Tourist Bungalow* (☎013772/22221; ❸–❺), over the footbridge from the bus stand, offers rooms and a reasonably cheap dorm (Rs150). Next to the main cantilever bridge, the large and popular *Ganga Niketan* (☎013772/22219; ❹) has a café and shop overlooking the river, while the *Himalayan Sadan* (no phone; ❶–❷), along the riverside opposite the temple, offers basic, friendly accommodation with fantastic views up the valley to the snow peaks. A number of *dhabas* and cafés on both sides of the river serve thalis, good breakfasts and much-needed, warming chai. For pilgrims heading toward Gomukh, the market area also marks the last chance to buy gloves and woolly hats.

Gomukh and Gangotri Glacier

A flight of steps alongside the temple at Gangotri leads up to join a large pony path that rises gently, providing gorgeous mountain vistas, towards the **Gangotri Glacier**, long regarded as one of the most beautiful and accessible glaciers in the inner Himalayas. Sadly, it is retreating hundreds of metres per year. Two kilometres into the trek, the forest **checkpoint** takes a Rs150 park entry fee (valid for three days, plus Rs150 for each additional day) and confiscates any potential plastic rubbish you may be carrying in your rucksack.

Approaching the oasis of **Chirbasa**, 7km out of Gangotri, the skyline is dominated by magnificent buttresses and glass-like walls, culminating in the sharp pinnacles of Bhagirathi 3 (6454m) and Bhagirathi 1 (6856m). Chirbasa amounts to no more than a few chai stalls, which can also provide you with a roof and simple food. The path then climbs above the treeline, continuing along the widening valley to enter a high mountain desert. Just beyond Chirbasa, the trail across a cliff face has badly deteriorated and gusts of wind can send small rocks cascading down onto the narrow path, so great care is called for. Soon after crossing a stream, the path rounds a shoulder to offer a glimpse of the glacier's snout near **Gomukh** ("the cow's mouth"), the ever-present Bhagirathi peaks and the huge expanse of the Gangotri Glacier – 23km long, and up to 4km wide – sweeping like a gigantic highway through the heart of the mountains.

Down below on the flat valley bottom, 5km from Chirbasa, is the cold grey hamlet of **Bhojbasa**, cowering in the shadow of the beautiful **Shivling Peak** (6543m), where most visitors spend the night before heading on to Gomukh and beyond. If you're planning on trekking any further than Gomukh, this is a good point at which to stop and acclimatize. The GMVN *Tourist Bungalow* here (no phone) provides a **dorm** (Rs250) but no private rooms. Guests huddle in the evening in the small, friendly café, which is the place to arrange a mountain guide if you plan to cross the glaciers. Accommodation is also available at *Lal Baba's Ashram* (no phone; ❷), which offers only sheets and the odd floor mattress – though food is included in the price. There is a good **campground** down by the river if you have your own tent.

If you've stayed in Bhojbasa, it really is worth braving the cold to walk to Gomukh for **sunrise**. A good track continues from Bhojbasa for 5km to Gomukh, where the river emerges with great force from a cavern in the glacier. The ice is in a constant state of flux, so the huge greyish-blue snout of the glacier continually changes appearance as chunks of ice tumble into the gushing water. Be careful of standing above or below the cave; many pilgrims have been crushed to death by falling ice while attempting to collect water. Two or three chai shops near here provide food and basic shelter, and there are many flat areas for camping.

Tapovan and Nandanvan

The campsites of **Tapovan** and **Nandanvan**, 6km beyond Gomukh on slightly divergent glacier-side routes, are popular objectives for lightweight trekking and mountaineering, and as a rule best attempted using guides engaged from Gangotri or Bhojbasa.

A difficult track leads past the last teashop at Gomukh to ascend the moraine on the left edge of the glacier, following it for 1km before crossing the glacier diagonally towards a high point in the middle, in line with Shivling. Depending on the season, this stage can be confusing and dangerous; heavy snow can conceal deep crevasses and the cairns that mark the way. From the high point, you should be able to see a stream coming down the high bank opposite. Use this as a marker; an extremely steep and strenuous climb up unstable ground runs to its left, to top out eventually on the grassy meadow of **TAPOVAN**, where you're greeted by the fantastic sight of Shivling (6543m) towering above. With its herds of grazing, almost tame *bharal* (mountain goats), and a tranquil stream, the meadow makes a bizarre contrast to the sea of ice below.

Many trekkers arrive in Tapovan without camping equipment, expecting to shelter in either of its two ashrams. However, although Mataji, a female sadhu who lives here throughout the year, and Shimla Baba do indeed have small hermitages with blankets, and are prepared to feed visitors, their resources are greatly stretched. Whether or not you stay with them, carry supplies, which will always be welcome, and bring camping and cooking equipment if you plan to be here more than a day or two.

NANDANVAN lies on a similar but less frequented meadow below the Bhagirathi Peaks, at the junction of the glacier known as the Chaturang Bamak and the Gangotri Glacier. From here you get magnificent views of Bhagirathi, Shivling and the huge snowy mass of **Kedar Dome** (6831m), hiding a steep sheer rocky face. The trail up follows the same path from Gomukh, but instead of the diagonal slant towards Tapovan, continues across the Raktaban Glacier and follows the left bank of the Gangotri Glacier. If you do get confused and find yourself in Nandanvan by mistake, an indistinct 3km trail across Gangotri Glacier leads back to Tapovan.

The route to Kedarnath

It's hard to imagine a more dramatic setting for a temple than **Kedarnath**, 223km northeast of Rishikesh, close to the source of the Mandakini at 3583m above sea level, and overlooked by tumbling glaciers and huge buttresses of ice, snow and rock. Kedarnath, the third of the sacred Char Dham sites, is the most important shrine in the Himalayas and as one of India's twelve *jyotrilinga* – lingams of light – attracts hordes of Hindu pilgrims (*yatri*) in the summer months, but is closed from early November to early April. The area makes a refreshing change from the rocky and desolate valleys of west Garhwal, with lush hanging gorges, immaculately terraced hillsides and abundant apple orchards. Kedarnath is also a good base for short treks to the beautiful lakes of Vasuki Tal and Gandhi Sarovar.

Gaurikund

GAURIKUND, a friendly and bustling small town perched above the roadhead for Sonprayag, marks the starting point of the trek up to the **temple of Kedarnath**, although there are plans to extend the road as far as Rambara.

Direct **buses** run to Gaurikund all the way from Rishikesh, but most visitors arrive on local buses and taxis from the larger bus terminal at **Guptkashi**, 29km lower down. This receives services from **Rudraprayag**, 109km south on the busy main Rishikesh–Joshimath–Badrinath route, and **Gopeshwar**, 138km southeast.

Inexpensive *dharamshalas* and **hotels** in Gaurikund itself include the *Vijay Tourist Lodge* (☎01364/269242; ❷), which is on the main bazaar road and has clean if basic rooms. Opposite, the *Annapurna* (☎01364/269209; ❷) has large carpeted doubles with sunny balconies and dorms. The squat GMVN *Tourist Bungalow* (☎01364/269202; ❹) has pricier but cosy doubles, a cheap dorm (Rs150) and a **restaurant** offering soup and salad.

The trail from Gaurikund

So popular is Kedarnath on the *yatra* trail that the path up from Gaurikund is being slowly stripped of its vegetation, which is used for fuel and to feed the ponies that carry wealthier pilgrims. You can hire a horse for the trip for Rs300 – a bargain compared to the Rs2500 that some pilgrims pay to be hauled up by a four-man team of *doli*-wallahs.

The large pony track that climbs from Gaurikund is dotted with chai shops and traverses the hillside through the disappearing forests to the village of **Rambara**, 7km up and halfway to Kedarnath. With its many cafés and rest houses (and open sewers), Rambara signals the end of the treeline and the start of the alpine zone. Several conspicuous short-cuts scar the hillside as the track rises steeply to **Garur Chatti**, then levels off roughly 1km short of Kedarnath. Suddenly, rounding a corner, you come face to face with the incredible south face of the peak of Kedarnath (6940m) at the end of the valley, with the temple town dwarfed beneath it and almost insignificant in the distance.

Kedarnath: town and treks

KEDARNATH is not a very attractive town – in fact it's almost unbearable at the height of the pilgrimage season (May, June & Sept). It's a grey place, whose central thoroughfare stretches 500m between the temple and the bridge, lined with resthouses and *dharamshalas*, pilgrim shops and administrative offices. However, the sheer power of its location tends to sweep away any negative impressions, and it's always possible to escape to explore the incredible high-altitude scenery.

At the head of the town, the imposing **temple** is constructed along simple lines in stone, with a large *mandapa* (fore-chamber) housing an impressive stone image of Shiva's bull, Nandi. Within the inner sanctum, open to all, *pandas* (pilgrim priests) sit around a rock considered to be Shiva's upraised bottom, left here as he plunged head-first into the ground. Mendicant sadhus congregate in the elevated courtyard in front of the temple.

A solid path from near the main bridge, before the town, crosses the Mandakini to the left of the valley, and ends 4km away at the **glacier**. At its edge, the **Chorabari Tal** lake is now known as **Gandhi Sarovar**, as some of the Mahatma's ashes were scattered here. Close by, around 800m before the lake, is the source of the Mandakini; it emerges from a hole in the moraine on extremely suspect ground, which should not be approached. You could also cross the river by the small bridge behind the temple, and scramble up the rough boulder-strewn moraine to meet the main track.

East of town, a well-marked path rises diagonally along the hillside to the prayer flags that mark a small shrine of the wrathful emanation of Shiva – **Bhairava**. The cliff known as **Bhairava Jhamp** is said to be somewhere nearby; until the British banned the practice in the nineteenth century, fanatical pilgrims used to leap to their deaths from it in the hope of gaining instant liberation.

Practicalities

Kedarnath's GMVN *Tourist Bungalow* (☎01364/263218; ❸–❻), located close to the centre of town, offers large, anonymous double **rooms** and a dorm (Rs150). Alternatives include the clean, comfortable *Bharat Seva Ashram* (☎01364/27213; ❸), a large red building beyond the temple on the left, and the pleasantly located bungalow of *Modi Bhavan* (no phone; ❹), behind and above the temple near the monument, which has large rooms and kitchenettes.

Food in the cafés along Kedarnath's main street is simple but expensive, as all supplies have to be brought up from the valley on horseback. The one most familiar with the needs of the western palate is *Kedar Mishthan Bhandar*, which can rustle up passable salads and potato dishes. The canteen run by the temple committee, *Shri Badrinath Kedarnath Mandi Samiti*, behind the temple, serves curries and *aloo paratha*.

Joshimath

The scattered administrative town of **JOSHIMATH** clings to the side of a deep valley 250km northeast of Rishikesh, with tantalizing glimpses of the snow peaks high above and the prospect, far below, of the road disappearing into a sunless canyon at Vishnu Prayag, the confluence with the Dhauli Ganga. Few of the thousands of pilgrims who pass through en route to Badrinath linger, but Joshimath has close links with **Shankara**, the ninth-century reformer, who attained enlightenment here beneath a mulberry tree, before going on to establish **Jyotiramath**, one of the four centres of Hinduism (*dhams*) at the four cardinal points. In winter, when Badrinath is closed, the Rawal, the head priest of both Badrinath and Kedarnath, resides at Joshimath. The town itself consists of a long drawn-out **upper bazaar**, and, around 1km from the main square on the Badrinath road, a **lower bazaar** that holds the colourful Narsingh, Navadurga, Vasudev and Gauri Shankar **temples**.

Practicalities

Most **buses** and **Jeeps** up to Joshimath stop in the upper bazaar. For **trekking** and skiing advice, head for Eskimo Adventure Company (☎01389/222864, ✉aeskimoadventures@rediffmail.com), opposite *Hotel Sriram*, which is run by two graduates of the Nehru Institute of Mountaineering who can organize treks, rock climbing, skiing and river rafting, as well as provide permits, guides and equipment. They also have **Internet** access (Rs100/hr), as does KCE Uniyal Infotech (Rs60/hr), further along Upper Bazaar by the Badrinath Jeep stand. There is a **tourist office** (℡01389/222181; Mon–Fri and usually Sat 10am–5pm) by the new GMVN block.

Rooms at the grim GMVN *Tourist Rest House* (℡01389/222118; ❹), up a short lane at the north end of the upper bazaar, include a dorm (Rs150); a café serves simple meals. The new block, up above the old (accessed by the lane opposite the GMOU office), is much better but still not great value (℡01389/222226; ❹, dorm Rs150). Next to the old GMVN block the *Hotel Sriram* (℡01389/222332; ❸) has better-value rooms; the deluxe include a TV and hot water geyser while standard rooms have hot bucket. Up the lane, the *Shailja* (℡01389/222208; ❸), owned by UP Tourism, was closed for renovation at last check, but is also generally good value. South of the centre, *Dronagiri* (℡01389/222254; ❺–❼) is the most comfortable hotel in town, with good views, a clean restaurant and satellite TV. **Food** options in Joshimath are not exciting: the restaurants at the *Dronagiri* and *Sriram* are the best; of the *dhabas* the busy *Marwari* on the main square has good special thalis (Rs60), while the *New Star*, on Upper Bazaar near the GMVNs and *Sriram*, opens early for breakfast.

Auli

A rough road winds 15km up through the *deodar* forest from Joshimath to **AULI**, which has recently been developed as a **ski** resort, partly in the hope of replacing the ski areas rendered inaccessible by the war in Kashmir. To get there, you can either walk 4km straight up the hill, or take a 22-minute ride on India's highest and longest cable car (made in Austria), known as the **ropeway**, which connects Joshimath (1906m) with **Gorson** (3016m), above Auli (every 25min 8am–5pm; Rs400 round trip). You can also hire a Jeep (Rs600). Energetic skiers haul themselves up Gorson Top, a nearby hill, to increase their ski runs – in summertime, this makes for a pleasant walk with excellent views of the Nanda Devi, Kamet and Dunagiri mountain peaks.

As a ski destination, Auli actually has little to offer – a short season (Jan–March), a solitary chairlift (Rs200 round trip) and one long T-bar to cover 3km of beginner and intermediate runs; but if you're interested, GMVN offers various ski packages (a 7-day course is Rs10,000). Equipment can be hired through Eskimo Adventure Company in Joshimath. For up-to-date information contact the GMVN **Mountaineering and Trekking** division in Rishikesh (℡0135/243 0799). For skiers it's just as convenient to **stay** in Joshimath as Auli, and take advantage of the ropeway. At the top end of the chairlift, the *Cliff Top Club Resort* (℡01389/223217, ⓦwww.nivalink.com/clifftop; ❽–❾) has huge wood-panelled en-suite rooms with kitchenettes, and also offers ski packages ($425 for a couple for three nights), but meals are outrageously priced at Rs1200. The GMVN *Tourist Centre* (℡01389/223305; ❹–❺) near the base of the chairlift has cosy but scruffy double rooms and basic huts, and two dorms with lockable cubicles (Rs150). The friendly staff in the dining hall try their best, but don't expect any après-ski activity.

Badrinath

BADRINATH, "Lord of the Berries", just 40km from the Tibetan border, is the most popular of Garhwal's four main pilgrimage temples, and one of Hinduism's holiest sites. It was founded by Shankara in the ninth century, not far from the source of the Alaknanda, the main tributary of the holy Ganges. Although the temple boasts a dazzling setting, deep in a valley beneath the sharp snowy pyramid of Nilkantha (6558m), the town that has grown up around it is grubby and unattractive. All motorized transport from Joshimath – and there are plenty of buses during the *yatra* season – is obliged to move in **convoys**; a gate system controls traffic in each direction, in two equal 24-kilometre stages – the first between Joshimath and Pandukeshwar, the second between Pandukeshwar and Badrinath. Several convoys leave Joshimath each day, the first at 6.30am and the last at 4.30pm. At night the road is closed, and Badrinath itself remains closed from mid-November to early April.

Badrinath is still presided over by a Nambudiri brahmin from Kerala – the Rawal, who also acts as the head priest for Kedarnath. According to myth, the two temples were once close enough together for the priest to worship at both on the same day. The **temple** itself, also known as **Badri Narayan**, is dedicated to Vishnu, who is said to have done penance in the mythical Badrivan ("Forest of Berries"), that once covered the mountains of Uttarakhand. Unusually, it is made of wood; the entire facade is repainted each May, once the snows have receded and the temple opens for the season. From a distance, its bright colours, which contrast strikingly with the concrete buildings, snowy peaks and deep blue skies, resemble a Tibetan *gompa*; there's some debate as to whether the temple was formerly a Buddhist shrine. Inside, where photography is strictly taboo, the black stone image of **Badri Vishal** is seated like a *bodhisattva* in the lotus position (some Hindus regard Buddha as an incarnation of Vishnu). *Pandas* (pilgrim priests) sit around the cloisters carrying on the business of worship and a booth enables visitors to pay in advance for *darshan* (devotional rituals) chosen from a long menu.

This site, on the west bank of the turbulent Alaknanda, may well have been selected because of the sulphurous **Tapt Kund** hot springs on the embankment right beneath the temple, which are used for ritual bathing. Immediately south of the temple, the old **village** of Badrinath is still there, its traditional stone buildings and a small market seeming like relics from a bygone age. The main road north of Badrinath heads into increasingly border-sensitive territory, but visitors can normally take local buses and taxis 4km on to the end of the road where the intriguing Bhotia village of **Mana** nestles – check the current situation before setting out. It's also possible to walk to Mana along a clear footpath by the road. The village itself consists of a warren of small lanes and buildings piled virtually on top of each other; the local Bhotia people, Buddhists of Tibetan origin who formerly traded across the high Mana Pass, now tend livestock and ponies and sell yak meat and brightly coloured, handmade carpets. Past the village and over a natural rock bridge, a path leads up the true left bank of the river towards the mountain of Satopanth (7075m) on the divide between the Mana and Gangotri regions, to the base of the impressive high **waterfall** of **Vasudhara**. Dropping from a hanging valley, this is considered to be the source of the Alaknanda, where it falls from heaven. Walking time is just an hour and a half but, unusually, there are no chai stalls en route, so bring some snacks.

Practicalities

Badrinath is awash with rough, flea-bitten budget **hotels** strung along the main road. A better choice is the GMVN *Devlok* (☎01381/22212; ④–⑤), behind the post office, with pleasant rooms, a restaurant and excellent local advice. There are two other GMVN establishments near the bus stand, both contactable via the *Devlok*: *Yatri Niwas* (aka the *Tourist Hotel*) has five hundred dorm beds (Rs80), while the *Travellers Lodge* has cosy and carpeted doubles (③). *Gujarat*

Bhavan (☎01381/22266; ❺) overlooks the river and temple but gets its loudspeaker noise. *Hotel Narayan Palace* (☎01381/22380; ❻–❼) isn't bad, but the worn carpets and lack of heating don't quite merit the price. The poshest hotel in town is the plush new *Sarovar Portico* (☎01381/222267, ⓦwww.sarovar hotels.com; ❽). The most atmospheric area for **cafés** and chai shops is the old section close to the temple, but the more commercial east bank holds a few more upmarket neon-lit restaurants, such as *Laxmi* and *Saket*, along with numerous *dhabas*, none of them very special.

Traffic back down to Joshimath, including the regular local **buses**, moves in the same convoy system as on the way up, the last one departing at 3.30pm. Long-distance buses run direct to Rishikesh – the nearest railway station – with an overnight halt en route, and to Gaurikund near Kedarnath (14hr), bookable at the bus-stand office above the town.

Hemkund and the Valley of the Flowers

Starting from the hamlet of **Govind Ghat**, 28km south of Badrinath on the road to Joshimath (local buses will stop on request), an important pilgrim trail winds for 21 steep kilometres up to the snow-melt lake of **Hemkund** (4329m). In the Sikh holy book, the *Guru Granth Sahib*, Govind Singh recalled meditating at a lake surrounded by seven high mountains; only in the twentieth century was Hemkund discovered to be that lake. A large *gurudwara* (Sikh temple) and a small shrine to Lakshmana, the brother of Rama of Ramayana fame, now stand alongside. However, to protect the *deodar* forests along the trail, visitors can no longer spend the night here.

Instead, the overgrown village of **Ghangaria**, 6km below Hemkund, serves as a base for day-hikes. It has several chai shops, a small tourist information centre, basic lodges, *gurudwaras* and a GMVN *Tourist Bungalow*, complete with dormitory (mid-April to early Nov; ❹, dorm Rs150). Govind Ghat also has a large *gurudwara*, run on a donations system.

An alternative trail forks left from Ghangaria, climbing 5km to the mountain *bugyals* of the Bhyundar valley – the **Valley of the Flowers**. Starting at an altitude of 3352m, the valley was discovered in 1931 by the visionary mountaineer, Frank Smythe, who named it for its multitude of rare and beautiful plants and flowers. The meadows are at their best towards the end of the monsoons, in early September; they too have suffered at the hands (or rather feet) of large numbers of visitors, so camping is not allowed here either. As a result, it is not possible to explore the ten-kilometre valley in its entirety in the space of a day's hike from Ghangaria. At the entrance of the valley, foreigners must pay Rs350 for a three-day **permit**.

Nanda Devi National Park

East of Joshimath and visible from Auli, the majestic twin peaks of **Nanda Devi** – at 7816m, the highest mountain that is completely in India – dominate a large swathe of northeastern Garhwal and Kumaon. The eponymous goddess is the most important deity for all who live in her shadow, a fertility symbol also said to represent Durga, the invincible form of Shakti. Surrounded by an apparently impenetrable ring of mountains, the fastness of Nanda Devi was long considered inviolable; when mountaineers Eric Shipton and Bill Tilman finally traced a way through, along the difficult **Rishi Gorge**, in 1934, it was seen as a defilement of sacred ground. A string of catastrophes followed, and in 1976 an attempt on the mountain by father and daughter team Willi and Nanda Devi Unsoeld ended in tragedy when Nanda Devi died below the summit after which she was named.

The beautiful wilderness around the mountain now forms the **Nanda Devi Sanctuary**. This is the core zone of the 5860-kilometre-square **Nanda Devi National Park**, which was declared a UNESCO Biosphere Reserve in October 2004. Access into the core zone has been prohibited since 1982 for environmental reasons, and trekking in the National Park is restricted to a limited number of visitors between May and October on a single route from the roadhead village of Lata to Dharansi Pass, which has fabulous views over to the twin peaks of Nanda Devi. The nine-day trek can be arranged through the GMVN M**ountaineering and Trekking** division in Rishikesh (℡0135/243 0799), and costs Rs24,150 per person all-in, in groups of three to five only. Further information on getting permits can be obtained from the Forestry Office in Joshimath (up two lots of steps to the left of the *Dronagiri* hotel, and then right).

Gwaldam

Straddling a pass between Garhwal and Kumaon, surrounded by pine forests 61km east of Karnprayag, the peaceful hamlet of **GWALDAM** looks down upon the beautiful valley of the Pindar, a world away from the hectic *yatra* trails. This picturesque spot, with fabulous views of the triple-pointed peak, **Trisul** (7120m), used to be a tea plantation; now, thanks to its position on the main road to Almora, 90km southeast, it makes an ideal base for treks, especially following the ten-day **Curzon Trail** across the high mountain *bugyals* of north-eastern Garhwal, over **Kuari Pass** to Tapovan and Joshimath. The unassuming little Buddhist **Khamba Temple**, or **Drikung Kagyu Lhundrup Ling**, stands alongside orchards in the middle of a Tibetan settlement about 1.5km from Gwaldam's main crossroads. On the ridge above the village, the small shrine of **Badhangari**, dedicated to the goddess Durga and not far from the remnants of a Chand stone fort, commands superb views of the mountains of Kumaon and Garhwal. To reach it, take a bus for 4km to the village of Tal, then trek another 4km – some of which is quite steep – through rhododendron forests.

The GMVN *Tourist Rest House* (℡01363/274244; **❷–❹**), above the crossroads in Gwaldam, has an old cottage equipped with two exceptionally comfortable suites, as well as ordinary **rooms** and dorms (Rs100); only limited food is available. Alternatively try the good-value and traveller-friendly *Trishul* (℡09412 117721; **❶–❷**), where a sunny terrace offers views of the snows, if you sit in the right place. The helpful owner also operates the nearby *Mid Point Sweet and Fast Food Centre*, which is a good place for a bite to eat or to stock up on post-trekking goodies, such as beer and soya ice cream. If you're passing through Gwaldam en route to Almora, Pithoragarh or Munsiyari, better value rooms, with even better views of Trisul, are available just 20km further down the road, at **Baijnath** (see p.388).

Kumaon

The Shaivite temples of **Kumaon** do not attract the same fervour as their equivalents in Garhwal, so there is far less tourist traffic, villages are largely unspoilt and trekking routes unlittered. To the east, Kumaon's border with Nepal follows the Kali valley to its watershed with Tibet; threading through it is the holy trail (closed to foreigners) to the ultimate pilgrimage site, Mount Kailash in Tibet, the abode of Shiva and his consort Parvati. Kumaon Mandal Vikas Nigam, or **KMVN** (🌐www.kmvn.org), are in charge of tourism in Kumaon, providing a similar (and equally patchy) range of services to GMVN in Garhwal. Note too that Kumaon's **electricity** supply can be capricious, with frequent power cuts, and that, ATMs apart, the only banks that **change cash** are in Nainital, though you can change traveller's cheques in Ranikhet and Almora.

Kuari Pass and the Curzon Trail

The long route over **KUARI PASS** (4268m) in northeastern Garhwal provides some stunning mountain views. It is known as the **Curzon Trail** after a British Viceroy who trekked along parts of it, though officially it was renamed the **Nehru Trail** after Independence. Traversing the high ranges without entering the permanent snowline, the ten-day trail starts on the border with Kumaon at Gwaldam above the River Pindar and ends around 150km north, at the hot springs of Tapovan in the Dhauli Ganga Valley near Joshimath. There are numerous alternative paths and shorter trails to approach the pass, including one of around 24km from Auli. The whole route, and connected hikes, is mapped out on the Leomann map of Kumaon–Garhwal (sheet 8 in the India Series). The best time to go is from May to June and mid-September to November.

An ideal expedition for those not equipped to tackle glacial terrain, the trail over Kuari Pass follows alpine meadows and crosses several major streams, skirting the outer western edge of the Nanda Devi National Park. Along the way you'll get excellent views of Trisul (7120m), the trident, Nanda Ghunti (6309m), and the elusive tooth-like Changabang (6864m), while to the far north on the border with Tibet rises the unmistakable pyramid of Kamet (7756m).

On a major bus route between Karnprayag and Almora and with comfortable accommodation, **Gwaldam** makes a good base for the start of the trek. Camping equipment is needed, especially on the pass. Guides can be negotiated here or at several points along the route. You can either take local transport from Gwaldam, including shared Jeeps via Tharali, or trek down through beautiful pine forests and cross the River Pindar to **Debal** 8km away, where there is a forest resthouse and a tourist lodge. Motorized transport is available from Debal to **Bagrigadh**, just below the beautiful hamlet of Lohajung, which has a pleasant tourist lodge. Also here is the shrine of *lohajung* – a rusted iron bell suspended from a cypress tree and rung to announce your arrival to the *devta* or local spirit.

Following the River Wan for 10km from Debal, the trail arrives at the large village of **Wan**, where there's a choice of accommodation, including a GMVN *Tourist Bungalow* (dorm Rs80) and a forest resthouse. The small village of **Sutol** is 14km from Wan, along a trail following pleasant cypress and *deodar* forests. From Sutol to **Ramani**, a gentle 10km trail passes through several villages. A steep trail rises for 4km through dense forest from Ramni to the pass of **Sem Kharak** before descending for a further 9km to the small village of **Jhenjhenipati**, from where a rough track continues to the village of Panna 12km away, passing the beautiful **Gauna Lake**. From Panna a relentlessly steep trail rises for 12km to **Kuari Pass** (4298m) on the high divide between the lesser and the greater Himalayas, with rewarding views of Nanda Devi and Trisul.

Using Kuari Pass as a base, a climb to the peak of **Pangerchuli** (5183m), 12km up and down, is thoroughly recommended – the views from the summit reveal almost the entire route, including breathtaking mountain vistas. Although snow may be encountered on the climb, it is not a technical peak and no special equipment is necessary, save a good stick. From Kuari, a gruelling, knee-grinding 22-kilometre descent brings you straight down to the small village of **Tapovan**, overlooking the Dhauli Ganga, which has a hot-spring-fed tank. From here, local buses run to Joshimath, 11km away with several bus connections back down towards Karnaprayag and Rishikesh. An alternative descent from Kuari Pass is the long but picturesque route through forest to the ski centre of **Auli** via Chitrakantha – a trek of 24km – that avoids the dramatic decrease in altitude to Tapovan.

Nainital

The dramatic, peanut-shaped crater lake of Nainital (*tal* means lake), set in a mountain hollow at an altitude of 1938m, 277km north of Delhi, gives its name to the largest town in Kumaon. Discovered for Europeans in 1841 by Mr Barron, a wealthy sugar merchant, **NAINITAL** swiftly became a popular escape from the summer heat of the lowlands, and continues to be one of India's main hill stations. Throughout the year, and especially between March and July, hordes of tourists and honeymooners pack the **Mall**, the promenade that links **Mallital** (head of the lake), the older colonial part of Nainital at the north end, with **Tallital** (foot of the lake).

Nainital's position within striking range of the inner Himalayas – the peaks are visible from vantage points above town – makes it a good base for exploring Kumaon: Corbett Tiger Reserve, Almora and Ranikhet are all within easy access. When the town's commercialism gets a bit much, it's always possible to escape into the beautiful surrounding country, to lakes such as **Sat Tal** where the foothills begin their sudden drop towards the plains to the south, or to the forested ridges around **Kilbury**.

Arrival and information

Most Jeeps and buses arrive in Tallital; a rickshaw from here up the lakeside Mall to Mallital, where most of the hotels are, costs Rs5 – buy your ticket from the office by Parvat Tours at the beginning of the Mall. Buses from Ramnagar mostly arrive at a stand in Sukhatal, north of town, from where Mallital is a Rs50 taxi ride, or a longish but downhill walk.

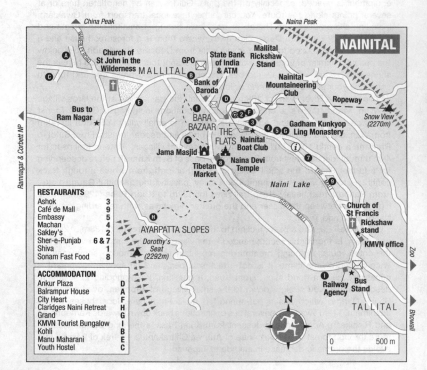

The **KMVN** representative, Parvat Tours, on the Mall in Tallital (☎05942/235656), organizes tours and car rental, and books accommodation at KMVN lodges. Cars can also be rented from agencies along the Mall, such as Hina Tours (☎05942/235860). There's an **Uttarakhand Tourism office** on the Mall near Mallital (Mon–Sat 10am–5pm; ☎05942/235337), but you'll find better information online at ⓦwww.nainitaltourism.com. For more advice on **trekking** and **mountaineering**, call in at Nainital Mountaineering Club, CRST Inter College Building, opposite *City Heart* hotel (☎05942/235119). Anil Tiwari (☎05942/235526) is a government-registered trekking guide (Rs500 per day).

There are a handful of **ATMs** along the Mall and in Mallital. The State Bank of India and the Bank of Baroda change cash and travellers' cheques, and it's a good idea to do that here if you are moving on into the mountains, as no banks further north will change cash. The best place for **Internet access** is Cyberia, by the path to the ropeway (Rs30/hr).

Accommodation

As a holiday town, Nainital is full of **hotels**, but budget accommodation is hard to come by in season. **Rates** are highest between March and July, peaking between mid-April and mid-June. Off-season however, there are bargains to be had as rates come down substantially. On the whole, rooms are cheaper in Tallital than in Mallital.

Ankur Plaza Mallital, by the ropeway station ☎05942/235448, ⓔankurplaza@yahoo.co.in. High prices in season, but friendly management and good bargains off-season, when this is among the best budget options. Rooms are cosy, and plastic flowers show attention to detail if not great taste. ⑥–⑧
Balrampur House Waverley Rd, Mallital ☎05942/236236 or 011/2338 4495, ⓔbalrampurhouse_ntl@rediffmail.com. Period mansion with echoes of grandeur (despite the laminated floors) still owned by the Maharaja of Balrampur, whose sepia pictures hang in the hallways. Food is good but preparation can be slow; prices ($185–238) are for half-board. ⑨
City Heart Mallital rickshaw stand ☎05942/235228, ⓦwww.cityhearthotel.netfirms .com. Expensive in high season but reasonable otherwise, and has some of the best lake views in town, especially from the upper rooms and rooftop restaurant. The manager is a wildlife photographer and bass guitarist in a hard rock band. ⑤–⑦
Claridges Naini Retreat Ayarpatta Slopes ☎05942/235105, ⓦwww.leisurehotels.in. Beautifully situated high above the lake, with extensive and immaculate grounds and a great terrace for barbecues. The best rooms in town ($158—383). ⑨
Grand The Mall ☎05942/235406. One of Nainital's oldest establishments, where time seems to stand still. A good location and plenty of period atmosphere in the large, high-ceilinged rooms, some of which are showing their age a bit. Closed Nov–March. ⑦–⑧
KMVN Tourist Bungalow Tallital, booked through Parvat Tours, The Mall ☎05942/235656. Lodge with a welcoming reception area, functional rooms and a cheap dorm (Rs100) in a quiet part of Tallital, but not far from the bus stand. ⑤
Kohli Bara Bazaar, Mallital ☎05942/236368. Another place whose prices drop to budget levels off-season, about 10min walk from the lake. Rooms at the top overlook the lake. Hot showers in the morning; bucket hot water any time. There's a similarly priced sister hotel, *Kohli Cottage* (☎05942/233279) on the road to the zoo. ⑤
Manu Maharani Grasmere Estate ☎05942/237341. Luxury hotel with modern rooms, complete with heating, a/c and flat-screen TVs, as well as a bar, disco and good Szechuan food in the *Lotus Garden* restaurant. Rates include an excellent buffet breakfast. Rooms from $132. ⑨
Youth Hostel Mallital ☎05942/236353. Fifty dorm beds (Rs40 for YHA members, otherwise Rs60) in a charming, secluded spot with a lovely garden 1.5km above Mallital; likely to be either deserted or jammed with schoolkids. Friendly staff and excellent value – but no generator.

The Town

Most of the activity in Nainital takes place along the 1.5-kilometre-long **Mall**, a promenade of restaurants, hotels and souvenir shops. Cycle rickshaws charge a fixed Rs5 from one end to the other (tickets from offices by Parvat Tours or *Ashok* restaurant). A favourite pastime for day-trippers is to **rent a boat** on **the lake** by the boat club on the northeast corner; rates start at Rs85 per hour, but can shoot up to Rs200 in summer. The boat club stands on the large plain known as the **Flats**, the result of a huge landslide in 1880, which buried the *Victoria Hotel* along with 150 people. The Flats now hosts sporting events and a **Tibetan Market**. Overlooking the town is Nainital's excellent **High Altitude Zoo** (Tues–Sun 10am–4.30pm; Rs25, Rs25 for camera), a steep 1.5km climb from the southern end of the Mall, and home to all sorts of exotic creatures such as Siberian tigers, Tibetan wolves, leopards and Himalayan black bears. It's well managed, with detailed explanations in English and a tiny Shiva temple tucked away at the top.

A ropeway (daily: summer 7am–7pm; winter 10am–5pm) climbs from near the *Mayur* restaurant on the Mall to **Snow View** (2270m); the Rs70 return ticket covers a one-hour stay at the top. Otherwise it's a two-kilometre hike along a choice of steep trails, which can also be undertaken on ponies for Rs200. At the top, which gets overcrowded in season, you'll find a promenade, cafés and a viewpoint; views of the snow peaks are most likely early in the morning. Trails lead on for five kilometres to **Naina Peak** (2611m), one of the best vantage points around, and to the isolated **China Peak** (pronounced "Cheena"), the craggy rise to the west. About halfway up to Snow View, conspicuous thanks to its abundant prayer flags, lies the small Tibetan *gompa* (temple) of **Gadhan Kunkyop Ling**, which has recently been rebuilt in traditional *gompa* style. Three kilometres out of town along the Almora Road, **Hanuman Garh**, a temple teeming with monkeys and young priests monkeying around, is a popular place to watch the sunset.

Eating

Nainital has plenty of places to **eat**, with restaurants and fast-food options along the Mall geared to tourists (some closed in the low season), and everyday *dhabas* (which serve cheap and tasty fish curry) in the bazaars at either end.

Ashok The Mall, Mallital. Good inexpensive veg *dhaba*. Main dishes (Rs35–70) include malai kofta, veg korma and *paneer* butter masala, but it also does a good line in breakfast dishes (toast and omelette, or samosa and chickpeas).

Café de Mall The Mall ⓦ www.cafedemall.com. A restaurant rather than a café, though it does offer coffee of a sort (instant), and has an open eating area overlooking the lake. There are south Indian snacks, pizzas and sizzlers, and thalis (Rs90–110). Non-veg mains go for Rs70–130.

Embassy The Mall, Mallital. One of Nainital's better restaurants, with a wood-panelled interior. Strongest on Mughlai dishes (Rs80–100), as well as pizzas (Rs72–105) and sizzlers (Rs120–180).

Machan The Mall. Just west of the *Embassy*, boasting "Bronze Age chic" decor and good service, this is a well-run upstairs restaurant that's good for people-watching on the promenade below as well as for excellent Indian

cuisine and some Chinese dishes (non-veg mains Rs80–120).

Sakley's The Mall, Mallital. Quite posh if pricey international cuisine (main dishes Rs175–350) including seafood dishes such as steamed fish delight and fierce (spicy) dragon prawns. Alternatively, pop in for a tea and a pastry – very civilized.

Sher-e-Punjab The Mall. Good non-veg Indian food including chicken sagwala, karahi, handi and, of course, butter chicken (Rs60–90). A second, bigger branch, near Bara Bazaar, is just as good, and popular with locals.

Shiva Bara Bazaar, Mallital. Cheap, good and popular *dhaba* with tasty *paneer* and mushroom dishes among other veg options (Rs36–75). The next-door clone is equally good.

Sonam Fast Food Tibetan Market, Mallital. Small café up an alley in the market selling veg *momos* (steamed dumplings), noodles and *thukpa* (soup), all at around Rs20, but without much in the way of seating.

Moving on from Nainital

Most **buses** leave from Tallital Bus Stand. For several Kumaon destinations, such as Ranikhet and Almora, you'll need to get a bus (every half-hour from 7am to 6pm) or shared Jeep to Bhowali to pick up onward transport there (buses and Jeeps to Almora are frequent). To get to Song – the start of the route to Pindari Glacier – there's a direct bus from Bhowali. Buses to Ramnagar mostly leave from a stand in Sukhatal, north of Mallital, but one morning service leaves from Tallital.

The **Railway Reservation Office** (Mon–Sat 9am–noon & 2–5pm, Sun 9am–2pm; ☎05942/231010) is by the Tallital Bus Stand. The nearest railhead is at Kathgodam, served by buses from Tallital (half-hourly 5am–7pm). Among **trains** from Kathgodam, the Raniket Express #5014 at 8.40pm to Old Delhi (arrives 4.10am), and the Dehra Dun Express #4119 at 7.40pm to Haridwar (arrives 2.20am) and Dehra Dun (arrives 4.20am), drop you off at rather uncivilized hours of the night; the Kathgodam–Howrah Express #3020 at 9.55pm to Lucknow (arrives 5.55am), Gorakpur (arrives 12.40pm) and Kolkata (arrives Howrah 12.40pm next day) has rather more convenient arrival times.

Corbett Tiger Reserve

Based at **Ramnagar**, 250km northeast of Delhi and 63km southwest of Nainital, **Corbett Tiger Reserve** is one of India's premier wildlife reserves. Established in 1936 by Jim Corbett (among others) as the Hailey National Park, India's first, and later renamed in his honour, it is one of Himalayan India's last expanses of wilderness. Almost the entire 1288-square-kilometre park, spread over the foothills of Kumaon, is sheltered by a buffer zone of mixed deciduous and giant *sal* forests, which provide impenetrable cover for wildlife. Most of the core area of 520 square kilometres at its heart remains out of bounds, and safaris on foot are only permissible in the fringe forests.

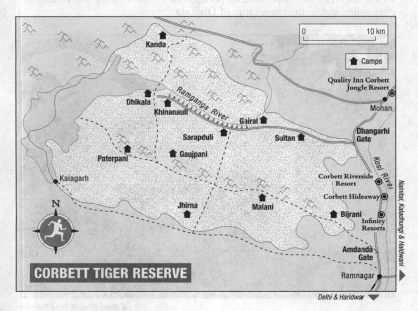

CORBETT TIGER RESERVE

Corbett is most famous for its big cats, and in particular the **tiger** – this was the first designated Project Tiger Reserve, in 1973 – but its 112 or so tigers are extremely elusive. Sightings are very far from guaranteed, and should be regarded as an unlikely bonus. Nonetheless, although there have been problems elsewhere with the project, and with the very survival of the tiger in India in serious jeopardy (see Contexts, p.1376), Corbett does at least seem to be prioritizing the needs of tigers over those of other wildlife and of tourists. Still, **poaching** is not unheard of, though it's Corbett's **elephants** that face the most serious threat. Around two dozen are killed each year in and around the park; poisoned by plantation workers or shot by farmers for hide, meat and, most importantly, their valuable tusks. The park's 627 elephants – 100 of them males with tusks – have been confined within its boundaries since the construction of the Ramganga reservoir in 1974 blocked migratory routes that formerly ranged as far as Rajaji National Park, 200km west. The best place to see them is around the picturesque Dhikala camp near the reservoir; spring is the best time, when the water level drops and the animals have more space to roam. The reservoir also shelters populations of **gharial**, a long-snouted, fish-eating crocodile, and **maggar**, a large marsh crocodile, as well as other reptiles. Jackal are common, and wild boar often run through the camps in the evenings. The grasslands around Dhikala are home to deer species such as the spotted **chital**, hog and barking **deer** and the larger **sambar**, while rhesus and common langur, the two main classes of Indian **monkey**, are both abundant, and happy to provide in-camp entertainment. Bird life ranges from water birds such as the pied kingfisher to **birds of prey**, including the crested serpent eagle, Pallas's fishing eagle and Himalayan greyheaded fishing eagle.

The closest of the various **gates** into the park, 1km from central Ramnagar, is Amdanda on the road to **Bijrani camp**, 11km away, a base for day-trips. **Dhangarhi Gate**, 18km along the highway north to Ranikhet, provides access to the northern and northwestern portions of the park along the Ramganga river valley, and to the main camp of **Dhikala**.

▲ Tiger, Corbett Tiger Reserve

Ramnagar

Situated in the rich farm-belt of the *terai*, on the southeastern fringes of the great forests, the busy market town of **RAMNAGAR** is the administrative hub for **Corbett Tiger Reserve**. **Permits** and **accommodation reservations** are issued at the **reception centre**, about 100m north of the bus stand on the other side of the road (see box, p.382). There's little to do around Ramnagar itself except go **fishing** (Oct 1–June 30; permits from the park reception centre). At Lohachaur, 15km north along the River Kosi, good anglers are in with a chance of landing the legendary *mahseer*, a redoubtable battling river carp. Fishing permits must be sought from the Corbett Tiger Reserve reception centre; most resorts also arrange all-inclusive fishing trips.

Although most tourists head straight to Dhikala in the park as soon as they arrive, Ramnagar does have some **accommodation**. The KMVN *Tourist Lodge* (℡05947/251225; ④), next to the Corbett Tiger Reserve reception, is as institutional as usual, with a dorm (Rs100) as well as spartan doubles. A further 200m south on the main road, down the street opposite *Govind* restaurant, the basic *Everest* (℡05947/251099; ①) has rooms with sunny balconies, but no running hot water in the attached bathrooms; a little further, in quite a handsome building with verandas, the *Rameshwaram* (℡05947/252664; ②–③) costs slightly more but has better rooms, some with hot showers. The immaculate *Corbett Kingdom*, 400m south on the main road (℡05947/251601, ⓦwww.corbett kingdom.com; ⑦), is the best hotel in town. On the main road, 100m south of the bus stand, *Govind* is a good **restaurant**, non-veg, but strongest on veg dishes such as stuffed tomato or peppers (main dishes Rs30–150). *Green Valley*, 300m south of *Govind*, offers fine open-air eating (main dishes Rs45–120).

There are a couple of **ATMs** 200m south of the *Govind*, and across the road; 100m further south, Anuradha confectionary store will change sterling, euros and dollars. A handful of cybercafés are located around the ATMs, mostly charging Rs40/hr, and a little bit slow.

Moving on from Ramnagar, there are half-hourly buses to Delhi, nine a day to Haridwar and Dehra Dun, and four to Nainital. From the train station (1.5km south of town – bear right at *Corbett Kingdom* hotel and again after 100m at the filling station), the Corbett Park Link Express #5014A leaves at 9.40pm for Old Delhi (arrives 4.10am). For faster trains and connections to other parts change at Moradabad (served by seven daily trains).

Dhikala

Beautifully situated overlooking the Ramganga reservoir and the forested hills beyond, Corbett's main camp, **DHIKALA**, lies 49km northwest of Ramnagar. As you can only stray beyond the confines of the camp on elephant-back or in a car or Jeep, the whole place has something of the air of a military encampment. **Accommodation**, all bookable via the Corbett Tiger Reserve reception in Ramnagar, ranges from the 24 rather uncomfortable bunk beds in the *Log Huts* (Rs200) to slightly better bungalows and cabins (⑤–⑦) which sleep two. Indian and Western **food** is available in the KMVN-run *Parvat* restaurant, which also has a reading room and outdoor area where you can watch film shows on wildlife (in Hindi). The same-quality food is served at cheaper prices and minus the eight percent sales tax at a *dhaba* at the other end of the camp, which is frequented by the park staff and drivers.

It's normally possible to see plenty of animals and birds from the Dhikala **watchtower**, which is a 1km wander down the path near the restaurant (turn left where the path meets a junction); bring binoculars, remain quiet and don't wear bright colours or perfume. Chital, sambar and various other

Organizing entry into Corbett Tiger Reserve

Safaris in Corbett Tiger Reserve take place in the morning (around 6.30–9.30am) and afternoon (around 1.30–5.30pm). Half-day or one-day safaris from Ramnagar to the fringes of the park (around Jhirna or Bijrani) are possible, but if you want to visit the heart of the park, around Dhikala (the best place for wildlife viewing), you will have to book **accommodation**. This should be done at least thirty days in advance (twenty days for Indian nationals), via the **Ramnagar reception centre** (daily 6–8am & 11am–4pm; ℡&℻05947/251489), where you also obtain your entry permit (Rs450 [Rs50] for three days and two nights plus Rs200 [Rs30] for each additional day) and pay vehicle and driver entry fees and guide fees. A tariff sheet at the centre lists all the prices. If you've turned up on the off-chance of getting accommodation, poor communication between the tourist zones in the reserve, the Delhi booking office and the HQ means you may well be told that rooms and dorms are fully booked, when they are in fact empty, so booking thirty days ahead saves a lot of hassle.

Jeeps, the most convenient way to travel to and around the reserve, can only be rented at Ramnagar. Reckon on Rs1500 per day for up to five people. Girish at *Govind* restaurant (℡05947/251615) is one person who can arrange this; other operators can be found outsice the bus stand – shop around and be clear about what you're getting for your money (fuel, driver's accommodation and a specific number of 3hr safaris should all be included). A petrol 4WD, such as a Maruti Gypsy, is best as it is quiet (if the brakes are well maintained) and built for the terrain. All Jeep safaris must be accompanied by a **guide** (another Rs150 per day) – who may or may not be able to identify wildlife and speak English, and is allotted to your Jeep by a rota system. If you require a guide with specific knowledge (eg for birding), write or fax the Field Director one month in advance with your request (Corbett Tiger Reserve, Ramnagar 244715, Nainital, Uttarakhand ℻05947/251489).

Note that Corbett (apart from the area around Jhirna) is only **open** between 15 October and 15 June, and the zone around Dhikala from 15 November to 15 June. Between June and October the monsoons flood the riverbanks and cut the fragile road links. One way to avoid all the restrictions and bureaucracy is by going on safari instead to a forest area outside the park such as Sitabani – again Girish at the *Govind* can arrange this – this would also allow you to choose your own guide.

deer species find refuge in the savannah grasslands known as the *chaur*, behind the camp to the south, and tigers are occasionally drawn in looking for prey. Two-hour **elephant rides from the camp** (Rs250 per person; first-come-first-served) explore this sea of grass, rarely penetrating far into the deep jungles beyond; try to convince your *mahout* (elephant driver) to venture in, as they can be quite magical.

On the way to Dhikala from the Dhangarhi gate, the road passes through magnificent forest – if you have your own transport, stop at the **High Bank** vantage point, and try to spot crocodiles or even elephants on the river below. You can stop for a night en route at the *Sultan* (❹), *Gairal* (❺) and *Sarapduli* (❺) forest resthouses, bookable through the Reserve reception centre. The bungalows are surrounded by deep forest; as movement on foot is prohibited, you'll only see wild animals that stray close to or into the compound.

Resort accommodation around Corbett

A number of self-contained **resorts** have sprung up on the fringes of Corbett, providing a higher standard of accommodation than in Dhikala or Ramnagar – at a price – as well as guides for expeditions in the neighbouring forests, which can be as rich in wildlife as the park, without the restrictions.

Corbett Hideaway Garija, Ramnagar ☎05947/284132 or 011/4652 0000, ⊛www .corbetthideaway.com. Luxurious terracotta-coloured huts ($152–192) with all mod cons, dotted around a pleasant orchard on a bluff overlooking the river and pretending to be rustic without success. Safaris and the usual tours arranged. ❾

Corbett Riverside Resort Garija, Ramnagar ☎05947/284125, ⊛www.corbettriverside.com. A picturesque setting, 10km north of Ramnagar looking across the River Kosi to forest-covered cliffs. Riverfront suites have a veranda directly above the river beach. Full board $142–198; off-season discounts available. ❾

Infinity Resorts Garija, Ramnagar ☎05947/2804103, ⊛www.infinityresorts.com.

Corbett's most ostentatious resort overlooks the Kosi and the forested hills beyond, with large comfortable rooms ($210–263), a library, a well-stocked bar and a swimming pool. Activities include nature trails with the resort's own naturalists, jungle rides, fishing, trekking and films. ❾

Quality Inn Corbett Jungle Resort Kumeria Reserve Forest, Mohan ☎05947/287820, ⊛corbettjungleresort.net. Wood-panelled stone cottages ($132 ful board) in a leafy mango orchard above the Kosi, 29km from Ramnagar on the road north to Ranikhet, 9km beyond the Dhangarhi gate. Elephant rides into the forest and safaris into the park itself; food is included in the rates, and there are good off-season discounts. ❾

Ranikhet

The small and deliberately undeveloped hill station of **RANIKHET**, 50km west of Almora, is essentially an army cantonment, the home of the Kumaon Rifles. New construction is confined to the **Sadar Bazaar** area, while the rest of the town above it, climbing up towards the crest of the hill, retains atmospheric leafy pine woods. Beautiful forest trails abound, including short cuts from the bazaar to the Mall; leopards still roam some of the more remote areas within the town boundaries, despite efforts by army officers to prove their hunting skills.

Ranikhet's Mall – something of a misnomer, as it's a quiet road with few buildings apart from officers' messes – starts just above the town and continues for 3km along the wooded crest of the ridge. Above the Narsingh Stadium Parade Ground, at the very start of the Mall, the **KRC Shawl and Tweed Factory** (summer Mon–Sat 9am–7pm, Sun 10am–5pm; winter Mon–Sat 10am–6pm, Sun 10am–5pm), in an old church equipped with looms and wheels, offers the opportunity to watch the weavers in action, a fascinating display of concentration, dexterity and counting. The herringbone and houndstooth tweeds are sold in the shop next door. For a taste of Indian military life, men and women can join the **Ranikhet Club** (☎05966/220611; Rs50/day), 1km up the Mall, which has a rather fine bar, restaurant and billiards room, and features men with grand moustaches calling each other chaps.

Practicalities

Buses from all over Kumaon, including the railhead at Kathgodam, 84km away, arrive at the bazaar, at either of two bus stops. The KMOU stand, on the Haldwani road, is the base for buses to Haldwani (7 daily; 4hr), via Bhowali (where you can change for Nainital) and Kathgodam (the nearest railhead). The Kausani–Pithoragarh bus (2 daily; 4hr) also departs from this stand. There is only one direct bus a day to Nainital, but you can change at Bhowali; frequent shared Jeeps also ply this route. The Roadways (Almora) Bus Stand, 500m on, is used by regular bus and shared Jeep services to Almora (2hr). The **taxi rank** is just above the KMOU Bus Stand.

The **Uttarakhand Tourism bureau**, above the Almora Bus Stand (Mon–Sat 10am–5pm; ☎05966/220227; no sign), has little information to offer. The **rail reservation office** (Mon–Sat 9am–noon & 2–5pm) is just above it. The main **post office** is on the Mall, not far beyond the Ranikhet Club. There's a trio of **ATMs** in town, and the State Bank of India will change travellers' cheques (Mon–Fri 10am–4pm), but not cash.

Jim Corbett (1875–1955)

Hunter of man-eating tigers, photographer, conservationist and author, **Jim Corbett** was born in Nainital of English and Irish parentage. A childhood spent around the Corbett winter home of Kaladhungi (halfway between Nainital and Ramnagar) brought young Jim into close communion with nature and to an instinctive understanding of jungle ways. After working on the railways, he joined the Indian army in 1917 at the age of forty, rising to the rank of Lieutenant Colonel and seeing action in Flanders at the head of the 70th Kumaon Company.

Known locally as "Carpet Sahib", a mispronunciation of his name, Jim Corbett was called upon time and time again to rid the hills of Kumaon of **man-eating tigers** and leopards. Normally shy of human contact, such animals become maneaters when infirmity brought upon by old age or wounds renders them unable to hunt their usual prey. Many of those killed by Corbett were found to have suppurating wounds caused by porcupine quills embedded deep in their paws; tigers always seem to fall for the porcupine's simple defensive trick of walking backwards in line with its lethal quills.

One of Corbett's most memorable exploits was the killing of the **Champawat tiger**, which was responsible for a documented 436 human deaths, and was bold enough to steal its victims from the midst of human habitation; he also terminated the careers of the Chowgarh tigress, the Talla Des and the Mohan man-eaters. By the mid-1930s, though, Corbett had become dismayed with the increasing number of hunters in the Himalayas and the resultant decline in wildlife, and diverted his energies into conservation, swapping his gun for a movie camera and spending months capturing tigers on film. His adventures are described in books such as *My India*, *Jungle Lore* and *Man-Eaters of Kumaon*; Martin Booth's *Carpet Sahib* is an excellent biography of a remarkable man. Unhappy in post-Independence India, Jim Corbett retired to East Africa, where he continued his conservation efforts until his death at the age of eighty.

Accommodation and eating

If you're just passing through Ranikhet, **hotels** in the busy bazaar are sufficient, while the Mall is better for an extended stay. Most places offer big discounts (thirty to fifty percent) off-season. **Eating** choices are pretty limited; the best food is found in the better hotels, but there are a few simple cafés and *dhabas* in the market area.

KMVN Tourist Bungalow 500m off the Mall (uphill left just after *Hotel Meghdoot* if coming from town) ☎05966/220893. A reasonably well-kept complex of bungalows (clean, but a bit worn round the edges) and a cheap dorm (Rs100) in a beautiful wooded spot. ❺

Meghdoot The Mall, 1.5km from town ☎05966/220475, ✉hotelmeghdoot@yahoo.com. Comfortable suites set back from balconies full of potted plants and flowers, with running hot water, parking and room service, plus a good mid-price restaurant that serves up a range of tasty biriyani, pulao and other non-veg dishes (mostly Rs40–85). ❹–❺

Norton's off the Mall (right just after *Hotel Meghdoot* if coming from town) ☎05966/220377. Eccentric, family-run hotel established in 1880, homely but slightly run-down, with a friendly manager who still remembers the Raj, and a choice of rooms, suites or cottages. ❸–❹

Rajdeep Bazaar ☎05966/220017, ⓦwww .hotelrajdeep.com. The best budget hotel in the bazaar area and nearly always busy. A bit noisy, but clean, with long verandas facing the snow peaks. ❸–❻

Rosemount 1km off the Mall (sharp left just after *Hotel Meghdoot* if coming from town) ☎05966/221391, ⓦwww.chevronhotels.com. A beautifully restored 1897 colonial mansion, deep in the woods, all pine and teak with lovely rooms ($225–316), a restaurant, and gardens complete with tennis, croquet, badminton and snow views from the lawn. There's also a four-person cottage ($396). ❾

Almora and around

ALMORA, 67km north of Nainital and set at a pleasant altitude of 1646m, was founded by the Chand dynasty in 1560, and occupied successively by the Gurkhas and the British. It remains a major market town, considered the cultural capital of the region, and has attracted an eclectic assortment of visitors over the years, including Swami Vivekananda, Timothy Leary and the Tibetologist author of *The Way of the White Clouds*, Lama Angarika Govinda.

Arrival and information

Access to much of the centre, including the market area, is restricted to pedestrians. Most **buses** arrive and depart from the **bus stand** in the middle of Almora's main street, the Mall, which has a **taxi stand** close by. Bus tickets for Dehra Dun, Haridwar and Delhi are sold from an office 50m east of the bus stand, down some steps by Deewan's Sweets, though Lion Tours, a few doors from the KMVN office (℡05962/232922), sometimes runs a luxury bus to Delhi. Another bus stand at Dharanaula, on the Bypass Road beyond the market above the Mall, is for buses for areas to the east such as Munsiyari and Pithoragarh. There's a computerized **railway reservation centre** (Mon–Sat 9am–noon & 2–5pm) at the KMVN *Holiday Home* hotel, up the Mall 1km west of the centre.

Uttarakhand Tourism maintains a **tourist office** next to the *Savoy Hotel* (Mon–Sat 10am–5pm; ℡05962/230180). The KMVN office (no sign in English) is on the upper floor of the row of shops east of the Boshi Sen clock tower opposite the Gandhi statue on the Mall (Mon–Sat 10am–5pm; ℡05962/230706). The best places to find out about taxi excursions, **treks** or equipment hire and guides are Discover Himalaya (℡05962/231470, ✉discoverhimalaya@indiatimes.com) and High Adventure (℡05962/232277, ⓦwww.binsarecotrek.com), both on the Mall by *Hotel Kailas*. Discover Himalaya also offer yoga meditation packages (from Rs300 per day) at their holiday camp at Jalna, 25km east of Almora, and rock-climbing courses. There are four ATMs along the Mall; otherwise, the State Bank of India (Mon–Fri 10am–1pm) will change travellers' cheques (preferably Amex), but not cash – Nainital is the nearest town for that. A lot of places along the Mall offer **Internet** access – the going rate is around Rs30, but all offices close around 8pm.

Should you need a **doctor**, there's a good clinic run by Dr Gusain (daily: summer 9am–4pm & 5.30–7.30pm; winter 9.30am–3.30pm & 4.30–6.30pm; ℡05962/231423) in a grey and white building on the Mall 100m west of the Boshi Sen clock tower (the sign is in Hindi only); a consultation costs Rs50.

Accommodation

Accommodation in Almora itself is largely centred along the Mall. However, there's a thriving long-term travellers' scene around Kasar Devi (nicknamed "hippyland" by some locals; Rs20 by shared Jeep from the Bharat filling station just west of *Hotel Shikhar*), where you can ask at the chai shops about rooms to rent.

Bansal Lala Bazaar ℡05962/230864. At the top of the steep lane opposite *Hotel Shikhar*, and next door to the espresso bar (see p.386). Spotless, simple rooms with en-suite bath (free hot bucket water), fantastic rooftop views and very friendly management, who'll deliver lassis to your room. The top room is the best. Fixed price year round. ➋

Deodar Holiday-Inn Sister Nivedita Cottage, the Mall ℡05962/231295. Time seems to have forgotten this friendly place, home to Swami Vivekananda and his disciple Nivedita between 1890 and 1898. The rooms are simple – the pricier ones have geysers and a TV – and there's a lovely sunny terrace and tranquil patio with a log fire at night. Fixed prices year round. ➌–➍

Kailas The Mall, above the GPO ℡05962/230624, ✉jawaharlalshah@india.com. They aren't kidding when they call this ramshackle heap "a hotel like no other". One way of looking at it is that it's (almost literally) a dump; another view is that it's a charming old place inspired by Nek Chand's rock garden in Chandigarh (see p.597), and run by the equally charming Mr Shah, who'll happily regale guests with fascinating tales of times gone by. ❸–❹

Konark The Mall ☎05962/231217. The rooms are simple, but clean and good value, especially with off-season discounts. The bigger rooms upstairs have geysers, with hot water in a bucket for the cheaper downstairs rooms. ❸

Savoy Police Line, above the GPO ☎05962/230329. A quiet place, away from the

noise of the Mall but still central, and with pleasant gardens, a veranda and good restaurant. Spacious, dim rooms – geysers upstairs, hot water in buckets downstairs. ❸

Shikhar The Mall ☎05962/230253. Don't be put off by the exterior or expensive reputation at what is Almora's central landmark. There's a wide range of rooms, some at very reasonable prices, most with balconies. The welcoming, cavernous restaurant serves good breakfasts, and there's an Internet café (Rs30/hour). Fixed prices year round, and a generator. ❷–❹

The Town

Although most of Almora's official business is conducted along the **Mall**, the **market area**, immediately above and parallel to it along the crest of the saddle, holds much more of interest. Exploring its well-stocked bazaars, knitted together with lanes flanked by beautifully carved wooden facades, at times you feel as though you're drifting into the distant past. Among items you might want to buy are *khadi* (home-spun) cotton textiles and ready-mades from the Khadi Bhawan just west of the Boshi Sen clock tower, scarfs and shawls from Panchachuli on the Mall near *Hotel Shikhar*, and local woollens from Kumaon Woollens, further west by *Hotel Himsagar*. However, the great local tradition is the manufacture of **tamta**, beaten copper pots plated with silver, which are sold in the busy Lala Bazaar and the Chowk area at the northeast end of the market.

Towards the top of town, beyond Chowk, a compound holds a group of Chand-period stone **temples**. The main one, a squat single-storey structure, is dedicated to **Nanda Devi**, the goddess embodied in the region's highest mountain. More typical of Kumaoni temple architecture are two larger Shaivite painted stone temples, capped with umbrella-like wooden roofs covering their stone *amalaka* (circular crowns). During September a large fair is held here in honour of Nanda Devi.

Eating

Cafés and **restaurants** are strung along the Mall, especially around the bazaar area; locally grown and prepared Kumaon rice and black dhal are particularly delicious. Hotels such as the *Savoy* can produce a feast of Kumaoni dishes, if given plenty of advance warning.

Bansal Expresso Bar Lala Bazaar. Despite its name, the coffee is instant, but this place does serve up the best lassis and shakes in town – their banana lassis in particular are legendary. It also opens for breakfast before 6am, which is very handy if you've got an early bus to catch.

City Heart The Mall, by the Gandhi statue. Reasonable attempts at pizza, south Indian, Tibetan and Chinese dishes (Rs30–75), but snacks rather than meals.

Glory The Mall, near *Shikhar Hotel*. Multi-cuisine café-cum-restaurant, strong on north Indian

cooking (veg dishes Rs35–60, non-veg Rs70–100), and also good for breakfast.

New Dolma Kasa Devi, 5km west of the town. A café run by Tibetans that shows the locals how it's done. Located at a beauty spot with a view of the Himalayas. *Momos, thukpa* rice and chow mein at Rs25–50 a throw, with breakfasts too, and rooms upstairs (Rs300) in case you want to stay.

New Soni Dhaba The Mall, near the bus stand. Excellent, Sikh-run *dhaba*: famed for its chicken dishes (Rs120, but half-dishes also available), it can get crowded.

Binsar and Jageshwar

Both **Binsar** and **Jageshwar** are in easy reach of Almora and can be visited as a day-trip (around Rs450 return for a taxi), though it's well worth overnighting at both places as they are lovely spots. **BINSAR**, known locally as Jhandi Dhar ("hill top"), 34km north of Almora, rises in isolation to a commanding 2412m. A steep road leads 11km up from the main Almora–Bageshwar highway to a tourist complex near the top of the hill (☎05962/280176; ❹), offering bland but comfortable **accommodation**. This was the summer capital of Kumaon's kings, the Chandras, but today little remains in the area except the bulbous stone Shiva temple of **Bineshwar** 3km below the summit. Most visitors come to see the 300-kilometre panorama of Himalayan peaks along the northern horizon, including, from west to east Kedarnath, Chaukhamba, Trisul, Nandaghunti, Nanda Devi, Nandakot and Panchuli. Closer at hand, you can enjoy quiet forest walks through oak and rhododendron woods. Recently designated a nature reserve, Binsar is rich in alpine flora, ferns, hanging moss and wild flowers.

JAGESHWAR, 34km northeast of Almora, is the very heart of Kumaon, a place where language and customs seem to have resisted change. An idyllic small river meanders through dark pines for 3km off the main road from **Artola** (Rs30 bus from Almora), stumbling onto a complex of 124 ancient shrines and temples which cluster at the base of venerable *deodar* trees. Jageshwar village retains much of its traditional charm, with stone-paved lanes and beautifully carved wooden doors and windows painted in green, turquoise and other striking colours. **Accommodation** can be found either in the large, comfortable KMVN *Tourist Bungalow* (☎05962/263028; ❹), which also has a dorm (Rs100), or up the hill at *Tara Guesthouse* (☎05962/263068; ❶); there is also a sprinkling of simple **dhabas**. Good local **walks** include the steep three-kilometre ascent through beautiful pine forests to the small hamlet and stone temples of **Vriddha** or **Briddh Jageshwar** (Old Jageshwar), with an extensive panorama from the mountains of Garhwal to the massifs of western Nepal. A trail from here leads 12km along an undulating ridge to Binsar (see above); the trail finally emerges from the woods near the stone temple of **Bineshwar**.

Kausani and around

Spreading from east to west along a narrow pine-covered ridge, 52km northwest of Almora, the village of **KAUSANI** has become a popular resort thanks to its spectacular Himalayan panorama. It's a simple day-trip from Almora, though as the peaks – Nanda Choti, Trisul, Nanda Devi and Panchol – are at their best at dawn and dusk, it's worth staying overnight. The tourist scene is growing and a number of new hotels and restaurants have sprung up in recent years to cater for the very seasonal demand. There are several **ashrams**, including one that once housed Mahatma Gandhi, who walked here in 1929, thirty years before the road came through. There are numerous possibilities for short **day-hikes** in the woods and valleys around Kausani, as well as longer excursions to the important pilgrimage sites of **Baijnath** and **Bageshwar**. Kausani is connected by **bus and shared Jeep** to Almora and Gwaldam (see p.374).

Practicalities

Hill Queen Café near Snow View Point above town offers **Internet** access (Rs30/hr), and telescopes for admiring the peaks and the stars. The State Bank of India has an **ATM**. The *Ashoka* **restaurant** near Snow View Point serves inexpensive multi-cuisine dishes (Rs35–60) including local Kumaoni specialities and great *kheer*; the *Uttarkhand Tourist Lodge* has a wonderful terrace and imported goodies like olive oil and parmesan (main dishes Rs50–120).

Accommodation

The prices below are for the **high season** (April 15–June 15 & Oct 1–Nov 15), but can go down by as much as fifty percent off-season. Rooms with views are much more expensive than those without.

Anashakti Ashram Snow View Rd, looking down on the Mall ☎05962/258028. Guests prepared to observe ashram rules, such as attending compulsory prayers and not smoking, are welcome to stay at Gandhi's pleasant but spartan former ashram. Even if you don't stay it's worth visiting the main prayer hall which doubles as a Gandhi museum (daily 8am–6pm). Good views, but no generator. ❶

Himalaya Mount View 1km north of town downhill towards Baijnath ☎05962/258080. Very quiet and rather pleasant, with chunky but elegant wooden furnishings and tile floors. Little English is spoken. ❹–❼

Hotel Uttarkhand Up the steps that head north from the bus stand ☎05962/258012. Foreigner-friendly place that can offer good hiking advice and makes a great place to hang out. Clean doubles and a great terrace with Himalayan views; the second-storey rooms with satellite TV and flush bidet toilets are the best value. ❹–❻

Krishna Mountview ☎05962/258008, ⓦwww.kumaonindia.com. Huge place next to the Gandhi Ashram with lovely gardens, comfortable rooms, a gym and an expensive restaurant. Friendly management, and good views of the snows. ❼–❽

Baijnath and Bageshwar

BAIJNATH is halfway between Kausani, 20km southeast, and Gwaldam (see p.374) to the west. The road, served by buses and shared Jeeps, drops down to a broad valley and to eleventh-century stone temples, standing at a bend in a beautiful river. This was once an important town of the Katyurs, who ruled much of Garhwal and Kumaon; now it's more like a park. Unusually, the main temple is devoted to Parvati, the consort of Shiva, rather than Shiva himself; its 1.5-metre image of the goddess is one of the few in the complex to have withstood the ravages of time. The only **amenities** are KMVN's modern *Tourist Rest House* (☎05963/250101; ❶–❸) – which has large en-suite rooms, a dorm (Rs50), garden and great views of Trishul – and a couple of simple cafés.

BAGESHWAR, nestled in a steamy valley 90km north of Almora, is one of Kumaon's most important pilgrimage towns. The lush Gomti River valley around is lovely, the market is a good place to stock up on provisions, and it's used by hikers as the base for the trek to Pindari. Most foreigners stay at the rooms or dorm (Rs70) at the large, ugly KMVN *Tourist Bungalow* (☎05963/220034; ❶–❸), 2km south of the bus station across a bridge; there are basic *dharamshalas* and *dhabas* around the temple.

Pithoragarh

Occupying the beautiful sprawling Sore valley, 188km northeast of Nainital, **PITHORAGARH** is the headquarters of the easternmost district of Kumaon and a busy administrative and market town that acts as a gateway to the mountains. While the town itself is not attractive, and only worth stopping at to stock up on provisions for expeditions, the fringes remain charming with terraced cultivation at an altitude of around 1650m offering glimpses of Panchuli and the remote mountains of western Nepal. Above Pithoragarh, in the pine-wooded slopes of the **Leprosy Mission** at Chandag (7km north), a large cross overlooks the valley, commanding views of the Saipal and Api massifs in western Nepal. It makes a pleasant walk up from the *Tourist Bungalow*, or you can take local buses en route for Bans.

Despite Pithoragarh's proximity to **Nepal**, the nearest official border crossing for foreigners is a four-hour drive south at **Banbassa**, where sixty-day visas are available for $30 and public transport can shuttle you across the frontier.

Trekking restrictions in eastern Kumaon

With the gradual shrinking of the Inner Line and the removal of restrictions, the mountains of Pithoragarh District are being opened up to trekkers. Ironically, while foreigners do not require **permits** on certain routes, Indians – including trekking agents – still do. Starting at Tawaghat, the trail via Nue to Johlingkang near the base of Om Parvat (6191m) aka Chotta ("small") Kailash, is currently open. Although the main Kailash trail to Tibet also starts at Tawaghat, access is allowed, via the idyllic Narayan Ashram, only as far as Budhi. Milam Glacier north of Munsiyari (see below) has also been derestricted. If the local tourist office and local trekking agencies can't provide the necessary information regarding current regulations, contact the Sub-Divisional Magistrates (SDM) at Pithoragarh, Dharchula or Munsiyari, who are responsible for issuing permits.

Practicalities

Uttarakhand Tourism's low-key **tourist office**, toward the top of the town, just beyond the BRO roundabout at Siltham (Mon–Sat 10am–5pm; ☎05964/225527), has information on current trekking restrictions. Hill **buses** and shared **taxis** stop at the main **Roadways Bus Stand**, near the centre below the bazaar; the smaller **KMOU Bus Stand**, 1km to the north, also services hill destinations. Private bus companies and USRTC buses connect the town with **Nainital** (8hr; 1 daily) and **Almora** (3 daily; 6hr), as well as the railheads of **Tanakpur**, 151km south, and **Kathgodam**, 212km southeast. Although amenities in town remain limited, Pithoragarh's busy markets are worth a browse for trek supplies.

Hotel **accommodation** is basic and, for once, the KMVN *Tourist Lodge* (☎05964/225434; dorm Rs100; ❸–❹), tucked away in the woods 1.5km above the bazaar on the Chandag Road, comes out tops. The more central *Ulka Priya-darshani* (☎05964/225596; ❶–❸), in the top bazaar between the Roadways Bus Stand and BRO roundabout, is a decent, clean budget hotel. A couple of doors down, Pithoragarh's best **restaurant**, the first-floor *Shagun*, serves wonderful Indian food and is a respite from the crowded bazaar. *Meghna*, in Simalgair Bazaar, a large, popular, noisy snack bar, specializes in sweets and masala dosa.

Munsiyari

The sprawling village of **MUNSIYARI** stands at the threshold of the inner Himalayas, 154km north of Pithoragarh, looking down on the Gori River gorge and deep valleys branching up into the high mountains. Vantage spots throughout the area offer breathtaking views of the five almost-symmetrical **Panchuli Peaks**, which owe their name – the "five cooking pots" – to their plumes of wind-blown snow. These are notorious for their bad weather, but on clear days at Munsiyari you feel you could almost reach out and touch them.

Among spectacular local high-mountain walks that you can do from here, which are being increasingly derestricted (see box above), is the gentle 11km trail up to the **Kalika Pass** (2700m), where a small Shakti temple stands amid dark pines. More difficult trails lead, via the small village of **Matkot**, 12km away, to the glaciers in the Panchuli group, and 30km away to the large alpine meadows of **Chiplakot Bugyal**, dotted with tiny lakes, as well as up to the Milam Glacier and the Johar valley.

Many of the local people are **Bhotias** of Tibetan stock. They've absorbed Indian religious and cultural practices over the ages, though their origins can be seen in their weaving of carpets, adorned with the ubiquitous dragon motif, and in cultural practices such as animal sacrifice – a festive and bloody picnic for all and sundry.

Practicalities

Munsiyari is at the end of the road, so few **buses** come this way and those that do are very basic; there are daily departures to **Pithoragarh** and **Almora**. Most people arrive here from those places by shared Jeep. Along with KMVN's *Tourist Lodge* (☎059612/22339; ➍), which has dorms (Rs100) as well as rooms, there are a couple of simple **lodges** near the bus stand, the best of which is the *Hansling* (☎059612/22321; ➌). Great views, friendly owners and a range of comfy and recently renovated rooms has made this a popular choice with foreign trekkers. A handful of **trekking agencies** are cropping up around the bazaar, while Prem Ram, of Gram Bunga, Tala, Nayabasti, is a recommended guide who can organize treks, including cooks and porters, from around Rs350 per head per day. He's contactable via all local hotels.

Travel details

Trains

Haridwar to: Dehra Dun (10–11 daily; 1hr 12min–2hr 15min); Delhi (6–8 daily; 4hr 05min–8hr 50min); Kathgodam (1 daily; 7hr 10min); Kolkata (1 daily; 32hr 45min); Mumbai (1 daily; 37hr 11min); Rishikesh (6 daily; 55min–1hr 30min).

Kathgodam (railhead 3hr from Nainital) to: Delhi (2 daily; 6hr 10min–7hr 30min); Lucknow (1 daily; 7hr 30min).

Ramnagar to: Delhi (1 daily; 6hr 30min); Lucknow (1 daily; 11hr 10min); Varanasi (1 daily; 22hr).

Buses

Almora to: Bhowali (for Nainital) (every 30min 6.30am–2.30pm; 2hr 30min); Dehra Dun (3 daily; 12hr); Delhi (4 daily; 11hr); Kathgodam (every 30min 6.30am–2.30pm; 3hr); Munsiyari (1 daily; 11hr); Pithoragarh (3 daily; 6hr); Ranikhet (7 daily; 2hr).

Dehra Dun to: Delhi (every 30min; 7hr); Haridwar (every 30min; 1hr 15min); Kullu/Manali (2 daily; 14hr); Mussoorie (hourly; 1hr 30min); Nainital (5 daily; 12hr); Rishikesh (every 30min; 1hr); Shimla (3 daily; 9hr).

Haridwar to: Agra (8 daily; 10hr); Dehra Dun (every 30min; 1hr 15min); Delhi (every 30min; 6hr); Nainital (6 daily; 10hr); Rishikesh (every 30min; 30min); Shimla (6 daily; 10hr).

Mussoorie to: Chamba (for Uttarkashi) (5 daily; 2hr 30min); Dehra Dun (every 30min; 1hr); Delhi (2 daily; 9hr).

Nainital to: Almora (1 daily; 3hr); Bhowali (every 30min; 20min); Dehra Dun (8 daily; 10hr) via Haridwar (8hr 30min); Delhi (4 daily; 8hr); Kathgodam (every 30min; 1hr 30min); Pithoragarh (1 daily; 8hr); Ramnagar (4 daily; 3hr).

Rishikesh to: Dehra Dun (every 30min; 1hr 30min); Haridwar (every 30min; 30min); Janki Chatti (4 daily; 10hr); Joshimath (3 daily, 10hr); Nainital (1 daily; 9hr); Uttarkashi (5 daily; 7hr).

CHAPTER 5

Madhya Pradesh and Chhattisgarh

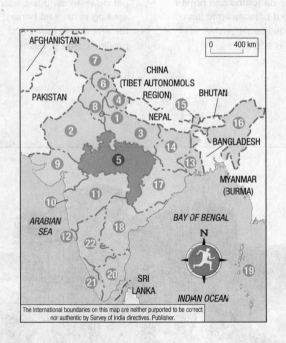

CHAPTER 5 · Highlights

* **Sanchi** A finely restored Buddhist stupa complex, complete with intricately carved gateways. See p.404

* **Pachmarhi** Central India's only hill station, where you can trek to the top of a sacred Shiva peak, hunt out prehistoric rock art or just relax in the cool air. See p.414

* **Orchha** Madhya Pradesh at its most exotic: crumbling riverside tombs and ornate Rajput palaces amid lush, tranquil countryside. See p.426

* **Khajuraho** Temples swathed in blatantly erotic sculpture, lost for centuries in thick jungle but now beautifully restored. See p.430

* **Kanha and Bandhavgarh national parks** Archetypal Kipling country, teeming with wildlife, notably tigers. See p.446 & p.450

* **Mandu** A medieval fort atop a plateau where the emperor got down to serious pleasure-seeking in his vast harem, theatre, steam baths and pavilions. See p.458

▲ Deserted palace at Orchha

Madhya Pradesh and Chhattisgarh

Hot, dusty **MADHYA PRADESH** is a vast landlocked expanse of scrub-covered hills, sun-parched plains and one third of India's forests. Stretching from beyond the headwaters of the mighty **River Narmada** to the fringes of the Western Ghats, it's a transitional zone between the Gangetic lowlands in the north and the high, dry **Deccan plateau** to the south.

Despite its diverse array of exceptional attractions, ranging from ancient **temples** and hilltop **forts** to some of India's best **tiger reserves**, Madhya Pradesh receives only a fraction of the tourist traffic that pours between Delhi, Agra, Varanasi and the south. For those who make the effort, this gem of a state is both culturally rewarding and largely hassle-free. While interest from tour groups is rising, the only places you're likely to meet more than a handful of **tourists** are the palace at Orchha, Khajuraho, one of India's most celebrated temple sites, and the tiger reserves of Kanha and Bandhavgarh.

Any exploration of central India will be illuminated if you have a grasp of its long and turbulent **history**. Most of the marauding armies that have swept across the peninsula over the last two millennia passed through this corridor, leaving in their wake a bumper crop of monuments. The very first traces of settlement in Madhya Pradesh are the 10,000-year-old paintings on the lonely hilltop of **Bhimbetka**, a day-trip south of the sprawling capital **Bhopal**. Aboriginal rock art was still being created here during the Mauryan emperor Ashoka's evangelical dissemination of Buddhism, in the second century BC. Nearby, the immaculately restored stupa complex at **Sanchi** is the most impressive relic of this era, ranking among the finest early Buddhist remains in Asia, while the rock-cut Jain and Hindu caves at **Udaigiri** recall the dynasties that succeeded the Mauryans, from the Andhras to the Guptas in the fourth century.

By the end of the first millennium AD, central India was divided into several kingdoms. The Paramaras, whose ruler Raja Bhoj founded Bhopal, controlled the southern and central area, known as **Malwa**, while the **Chandellas**, responsible for some of the Subcontinent's most exquisite temples, held sway in the north. Lost deep in the countryside, equidistant from Agra and Varanasi, their magnificent erotica-encrusted sandstone shrines at **Khajuraho** were erected sufficiently far from the main north–south route to have been overlooked by the iconoclastic warriors who marched past in the eleventh and twelfth centuries. Today, the site is as far off the beaten track as ever; its many visitors either fly in, or make the four- to five-hour bus journey from the nearest railheads at **Satna**, to the east, or **Jhansi**, in an anomalous sliver of Uttar Pradesh to the west. Just south of Jhansi, the atmospheric ruined capital of the Bundella rajas at **Orchha** merits a detour from the highway.

Monuments associated with the long Muslim domination of the region are much easier to visit. The romantic ghost town of **Mandu**, capital of the Malwa sultans, can be reached in a day from the industrial city of Indore, in western Madhya Pradesh. Meanwhile **Gwalior**, whose hilltop fort-palace was the linchpin of both the Delhi Sultanate's and the Mughals' southward expansion, straddles the main Delhi–Mumbai railway in the far north.

Under the **British**, the middle of India was known as the "Central Provinces", and administered jointly from Nagpur (now in Maharashtra), and the summer capital **Pachmarhi** near Bhopal, the state's highest hill station. Madhya Pradesh, or **MP**, only came into being after Independence, when the Central Provinces were amalgamated with a number of smaller princedoms. Since then, the 90 plus-percent-Hindu state, with a substantial rural and tribal population, has remained far more stable than neighbouring Uttar Pradesh and Bihar. Major

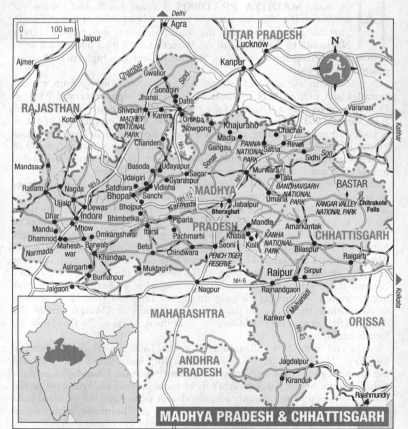

MADHYA PRADESH & CHHATTISGARH

civil unrest was virtually unheard of until the Bhopal riots of 1992–93, sparked off by events in Ayodhya, Uttar Pradesh. Despite this sudden assertion of Hindu fundamentalism, a subsequent backlash against the BJP-led central government in 1998 resulted in Congress reasserting itself as the leading local party. Now that Hindu-Muslim relations in MP are relatively cordial again, the state has turned to focus on the latest enemy – recurring **drought** across the poverty-stricken plains and the social and environmental consequences of the damming of the great River Narmada.

Since 2000, the BJP has returned to dominate the state's political scene, leaving Congress trailing in its wake. This stability, however, has not translated into economic prosperity: the state remains one of India's poorest, despite flourishing automotive, cement and soybean industries. Moreover, alongside Bihar and Jarkhand, Madhya Pradesh has the highest rate of child malnutrition in India. Female literacy is also lower than the national average, itself depressingly low.

Attracting more tourists is seen by officials as one way of boosting the state's economic prospects. In addition to its historic sites, Madhya Pradesh boasts a number of **wildlife reserves**. In the sparsely populated east, remote savannah grasslands are an ideal habitat for deer and bison, while the shady *sal* forests and *tarai* swamplands that surround the *maidans* provide perfect cover for larger predators such as the tiger. Of the **national parks** hidden away in this area, **Kanha** is deservedly popular, though there are more chances of seeing the big cats at **Bandhavgarh National Park** to the north, while the appealing **Pench** and **Panna** have the advantage of far fewer visitors.

In November 2000, sixteen districts seceded from Madhya Pradesh to form **Chhattisgarh**, which has rich mineral resources but is badly affected by violent Naxalite activity. While there is little in the way of stand-out attractions, the state has fascinating tribal groups, particularly in the Bastar region, and offers the opportunity to travel in an area barely touched by foreign tourists.

Visiting Madhya Pradesh

Getting around Madhya Pradesh without your own vehicle normally involves a lot of bone-shaking bus journeys, usually under the auspices of MPSRTC, the state road transport authority, although deluxe buses ply the main tourist routes too. For longer distances, **trains** are the best way to go. The Central Railway, the main broad-gauge line between Mumbai and Kolkata (Calcutta), scythes straight through the middle of the state, forking at **Itarsi** junction. One branch veers north towards Bhopal, Jhansi, Gwalior and Agra, while the other continues northeast to Varanasi and eastern India via Jabalpur. In the far west, at Indore and the holy city of **Ujjain**, you can pick up the Western Railway, which heads up through eastern Rajasthan to Bharatpur and Delhi.

The **best time to visit** Madhya Pradesh is during the relatively cool winter months (Nov–Feb). In April, May and June the region heats up like a furnace, and daytime temperatures frequently exceed 40°C, but if you can stand the heat, this is the best time to catch glimpses of tigers in the parks. The increasingly meagre rains finally sweep in from the southeast in late June or early July.

Madhya Pradesh Tourism (commonly known as MP Tourism or occasionally MPSTDC) has **hotels**, **lodges** and the odd **hostel** scattered throughout the state, of variable standards but often in excellent locations; you can book any of them at any MP Tourism office or online at Ⓦ www.mptourism.com, as well as directly.

Central Madhya Pradesh

All roads through **central Madhya Pradesh** lead to the state's capital, **Bhopal**. Although synonymous with the Union Carbide gas disaster, these days the state's fastest growing city is an upbeat cultural centre whose museums, galleries and nineteenth-century Islamic architecture, as well as its parks, lakes and markets, provide ample incentive to break any long journey across central India. Moreover, only a couple of hours away is one of India's most famous archeological sites, the Buddhist stupa complex at **Sanchi**, and there are numerous other ancient monuments scattered around the area. The prehistoric site of **Bhimbetka** lies just 45km south of Bhopal, while further southeast, at the attractive but rarely visited hill station of **Pachmarhi**, enjoyable hikes lead through craggy mountains and thick forests littered with ancient rock art.

Bhopal

With well over a million inhabitants, **BHOPAL**, the capital of Madhya Pradesh, sprawls from the eastern shores of a huge artificial lake, its packed old city surrounded by modern concrete suburbs and green hills. The nineteenth-century **mosques** bear witness to its enduring Muslim legacy, while the packed **bazaars** of the walled old city are well worth a visit. Elsewhere, a couple of good archeological **museums** house hoards of ancient sculpture and **Bharat Bhavan**, on the lakeside, ranks among India's premier centres for performing and visual arts, with an unrivalled collection of contemporary painting, sculpture and *adivasi* (tribal) art. In the **Museum of Man** on the city's outskirts, you can also visit the country's most comprehensive exhibition of *adivasi* houses, culture and technology, spread around an open-air hilltop site. Despite all this, however, Bhopal will always be known for the tragic 1984 **gas disaster**, which still casts a long shadow over the city and its people.

Some history

Bhopal's name is said to have come from the eleventh-century **Raja Bhoj**, who was instructed by his court gurus to atone for the murder of his mother by linking up the nine rivers flowing through his kingdom. A dam, or *pal*, was built across one of them, and the ruler established a new capital around the two resultant lakes – **Bhojapal**. By the end of the seventeenth century, **Dost Mohammed Khan**, an opportunistic ex-soldier of fortune and erstwhile general of Aurangzeb, had occupied the now-deserted site to carve out his own kingdom from the chaos left in the wake of the Mughal Empire. The Muslim dynasty he established became one of central India's leading royal families. Under the Raj, its members were among the select few to merit the accolade of a nineteen-gun salute from the British – a consequence of the help given to General Goddard in his march against the Marathas in 1778. In the nineteenth century, Bhopal was presided over largely by women rulers. Holding court from behind the wicker screen of purdah, successive begums revamped the city with noble civic works, including the three sandstone **mosques** which still dominate the skyline.

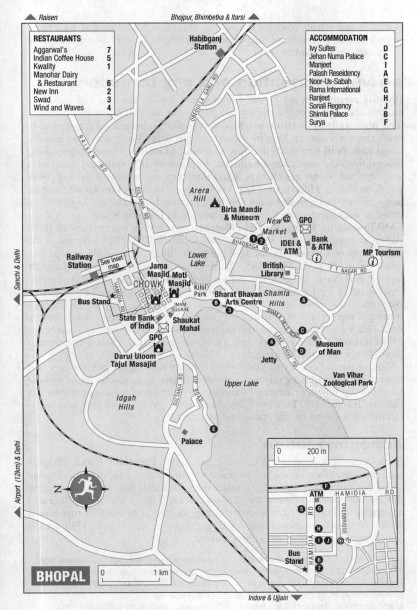

RESTAURANTS

Aggarwal's	7
Indian Coffee House	5
Kwality	1
Manohar Dairy	
& Restaurant	6
New Inn	2
Swad	3
Wind and Waves	4

ACCOMMODATION

Ivy Suites	D
Jehan Numa Palace	C
Manjeet	I
Palash Reseidency	A
Noor-Us-Sabah	E
Rama International	G
Ranjeet	H
Sonali Regency	J
Shimla Palace	B
Surya	F

Raisen

Bhojpur, Bhimbetka & Itarsi

Habibganj Station

OBEDULLA GANJ RD

RAISEN RD

SULTANIA RD

Arera Hill

Birla Mandir & Museum

New Market

GPO

BHADBADA RD

IDEI & ATM

Bank & ATM

MP Tourism

Railway Station

See inset map

Sanchi & Delhi

Lower Lake

Jama Masjid

Moti Masjid

CHOWK

Kilol Park

British Library

T T NAGAR RD

Bus Stand

HAMIDIA RD

IMAM SQUARE

Bharat Bhavan Arts Centre

Shamla Hills

State Bank of India

Shaukat Mahal

GPO

Darul Uloom Tajul Masajid

Jetty

Museum of Man

SHAMLA HILLS RD

LAKE DRIVE RD

Van Vihar Zoological Park

Airport (12km) & Delhi

Idgah Hills

SULTANIA RD

VIP ROAD

Upper Lake

N

Palace

BHOPAL

0   1 km

Indore & Ujjain

ATM

HAMIDIA RD

OVERBRIDGE RD

HAMIDIA RD

Bus Stand

0   200 m

Today, Bhopal carries the burden of the appalling Union Carbide factory gas disaster of 1984 (see box, p.400), with residents still quick to remind you of their continuing legal and medical plight. In 1992, Hindu-Muslim rioting broke out following the destruction of the Babri Masjid in Ayodhya. In spite of the inter-communal violence, however, the many tales of Hindus sheltering their Muslim friends from the mobs at this time and vice versa demonstrate the long tradition of religious tolerance which exists in the city. In the last few years, Bhopal – and Madhya Pradesh in general – has remained true to its lenient nature, with little of the political and religious intolerance that bedevils many other north Indian states.

Arrival, information and city transport

Bhopal's **airport**, served by daily flights from Delhi, Mumbai and Indore, is around 12km north of the city; by taxi (Rs350) or auto-rickshaw (Rs150–200). The main **railway station** is within easy walking distance of the centre; to reach the hotel district, leave by the exit on platforms 4 or 5 and head past the tonga rank until you reach the busy corner of **Hamidia Road**. Approaching Bhopal from the south, most trains also stop briefly at **Habibganj Station**, a long way out – only get off here if you intend to stay in one of the expensive hotels in Shamla Hills or the New Market area. The main **bus stand**, used by long-distance buses from Indore, Jabalpur, Pachmarhi, Sanchi and Ujjain is ten minutes' walk southwest of the railway station on Hamidia Road.

MP Tourism has helpful **tourist information** offices in the arrivals hall at the railway station (platform 1 exit; daily 10am–5pm; ☎0755/274 6827) and at the airport (opens to meet incoming flights). The head office (daily except Sun 10am–5pm; ☎0755/277 8383, ✆info@mptourism.com), inconveniently located in Paryatan Bhawan, Bhadbhada Road, 2km south of New Market, has a ticket office for Jet Airways and Indian Airlines, but no maps. They also hire out cars with driver (Rs5.50/km, minimum 250km, plus Rs250 for an overnight stop), run a **city tour** (daily except Mon 11am–3pm; Rs60) leaving from *Palash Residency* and can organize trips to Sanchi, Bhojpur and Bhimbetka. MP Tourism's Boat Club operates speedboat trips (Rs35/5min) and cruises (Rs75/45min) on the Upper Lake.

Most of Bhopal's principal places of interest are so far apart that the best way of **getting around** is by metered **auto-rickshaws**. Taxis can be found outside all of the top hotels, or arranged through MP Tourism or private operators like Garuda Travels (☎0755/254 0609). There's also a pre-paid taxi and auto-rickshaw booth outside the station on Hamidia Road.

Accommodation

If you're not bothered by traffic noise and fumes, **Hamidia Road**, Bhopal's busy main thoroughfare, is the best **place to stay**, within easy walking distance of the bus and railway stations and crammed with hotels. Shoestring options are thin on the ground and even the dingiest dives will slap a ten percent "luxury" tax onto your bill (and often a service charge too). Most of Bhopal's **top hotels** favour congenial locations close to Upper Lake in the Shamla Hills area, a fifteen-minute ride from the railway station.

Ivy Suites A. Nadir Colony, Shamla Hills ☎0755/423 4753, ⊛www.ivysuites.com. This pleasant guesthouse, tucked away in an upmarket housing estate, provides a wonderfully relaxed atmosphere. There are ten spacious, homely rooms; those upstairs have ivy-filled balconies overlooking the Upper Lake. Rates include meals. ❼

Jehan Numa Palace 157 Shamla Hills Rd ☎0755/266 1100, ⊛www.hoteljehanumapalace .com. Bhopal's top heritage hotel is a palazzo-style building set around a central courtyard covered by bougainvillea-clad walkways. The luxurious rooms are of a high standard, as are the three fabulous restaurants (Rs600/dinner), particularly the trattoria. ❼–❾

Manjeet 3 Hamidia Rd ☎0755/267 9039, ✆hmanjeet@sancharnet.in. Carpeted rooms, a warming orange and peach decor and cable TV make this a solid, if unspectacular, choice. ❸–❹

Noor-Us-Sabah Palace Grounds, VIP Rd ☎0755/522 3333, ⊛www.noorussabahpalace .com. "The Light of Dawn" is an impeccably renovated nawab's palace, built in the 1920s and perched on a hill overlooking the Upper Lake. Opulent rooms come with elegant mirrors, regal red furniture and private balconies, and there's a pool and fine restaurant. ⑧–⑨

Palash Reseidency TT Nagar, near New Market ☏0755/255 3006, ✉palash@mptourism.com. A notch above most other MP Tourism properties with chic rooms – including tea- and coffee-making facilities and baskets of toiletries – and a small garden area. Rates include breakfast. Bookings are advised. ⑦

Rama International Hamidia Rd ☏0755/253 5542. Walk through a courtyard off the main road to this relatively peaceful, rambling hotel. The rooms are simple, clean and inexpensive; some also have a/c. ②–④

Ranjeet Hamidia Rd ☏0755/274 0500, ✉ranjeethotels@sancharnet.in. The green marble lobby gives off a subterranean feel, but the rooms are bright enough and come with complimentary breakfast. Those at the front are very noisy, so ask for one at the back. ③–④

Shimla Palace 31 Shamla Rd ☏0755/266 1427. A ramshackle hotel in desperate need of a little loving care: however, some rooms have lake views and the peaceful location in leafy Shamla Hills is a world away from the Hamidia Road hotels in the same price bracket. ③

Sonali Regency Just off Hamidia Rd ☏0755/274 0880, ⊛www.sonalihotel .com. Quieter than the other hotels in this area, and although its rooms are a little boxy they do boast marble floors, cable TV and mini sofas. Nice touches like free newspapers, a travel desk and superb service elevate *Sonali* above the competition. ③–④

Surya Hamidia Rd ☏0755/274 1701, ⊕424 2503. Behind the tinted glass lobby is a good-value business-style hotel. The a/c en suites at the front are noisy, but the standard rooms at the back, with snooker-table-green carpets and brown leather seats, are a particularly good deal. ③–④

The City

Bhopal has two separate centres. Spread over the hills to the south of the lakes, the **New Market** area – much of it recently pedestrianized – is a modern mix of shopping arcades, Internet cafés, ice-cream parlours, cinemas and modern office blocks. Once you've squeezed through the strip of land that divides the Upper and (smaller) Lower lakes, sweeping avenues, civic buildings and pleasure gardens quickly give way to the more heavily congested **old city**. This area includes the **Jama Masjid** and the bazaar, centred on **Chowk**, a dense grid of streets between the **Moti Masjid** and Hamidia Road. The art **galleries** and **museums** are tucked down side-roads off New Market, or along the hilly southern edge of the Upper Lake.

Chowk

Bhopal's lively **bazaar** (Tues–Sat) provides a welcome splash of colour after the dismal, traffic-filled streets around the railway station. Famous for "*zarda, purdah, garda and namarda*" (tobacco, veils, dust and eunuchs), it retains a strong Muslim ambience, with overhanging balconies intricately carved with Islamic geometric designs. Each of the narrow streets radiating from the central square specializes in a different type of merchandise, including "Chanderi" silk saris, bass drums and clarinets, tussar silk, silver jewellery and Bhopal's famous beaded purses. At the heart of the market loom the rich red-sandstone walls and stumpy minarets of the **Jami Masjid**. Built in 1837 by Kudsia Begum, its whitewashed domes and gleaming gilded pinnacles lend an exotic air to proceedings in the square below.

Imam Square to the Tajul Masajid

Southwest of Chowk, **Imam Square** was once the epicentre of royal Bhopal. Nowadays, it's little more than a glorified traffic island, only worth stopping at to admire the **Moti Masjid** on its eastern edge. The "Pearl

The Bhopal gas tragedy

Late at night, on December 2, 1984, a lethal cloud of Methyl Iso-Cynate (MIC), a toxic chemical used in the manufacture of pesticides, exploded at the huge, US-owned **Union Carbide** (UCIL) plant on the northern edge of the city.

MIC is highly reactive and must be kept under constant pressure at a temperature of 0°C. Cost-conscious officials, however, had reduced the pressure to save some $40 a day. When water entered Tank 610 through badly maintained and leaking valves to contaminate the MIC, a massive reaction was triggered. Wind dispersed the gas throughout the densely populated residential districts and shanty settlements. There was neither a warning siren nor adequate emergency procedures put in place, leaving the thick cloud of burning gas to blind and suffocate its victims. The leak killed 1600 instantly (according to official figures) and between 7000 and 10,000 in the aftermath, but the figure now totals over 20,000 in the years since the incident. More than 500,000 people were exposed to the gas, of whom about one-fifth have been left with chronic and incurable health problems, often passed on to children born since the tragedy. As if the suffering was not already enough, the water in the community pumps of the affected residential areas continues to be contaminated with dangerous toxic chemicals that seeped out from the now-deserted factory.

Though the incidence of TB, cancers, infertility and cataracts in the affected area remains way above the national average, the factory officials and their "medical experts" initially said that the effect of MIC was akin to tear gas, causing only temporary health problems. They accepted moral responsibility for the accident, but blamed the Indian government for inadequate safety standards when it came to the issue of compensation. Only in 1989 did UCIL agree to pay an average of Rs15,000 to each adult victim – a paltry sum that didn't even cover loans for the medical bills in the first five years, let alone compensate for the loss of life and livelihoods, and other consequences of the disaster. Relatives of only 6000 of the victims who died have received compensation. Finally, in 2001, the Bhopal Memorial Hospital and Research Centre (set up from the proceeds of Union Carbide's sale of its shares in UCIL) opened to treat patients.

Government and factory authorities have been keen to sweep the whole catalogue of mistakes and failures under the carpet – both US and Indian officials charged with serious offences, including manslaughter, have escaped their sentences to date. In 2002, a Bhopal court directed the Central Bureau of Investigation to pursue the extradition of Warren Anderson, the CEO of Union Carbide in the US; since then, however, Anderson has gone "missing" from his home in the US. Today, the factory stands desolate and overgrown though campaigners say it still contains around 170 tonnes of toxic waste.

In 2005 the government, after much lobbying, launched a legal case to recoup money from Dow Chemical, which bought Union Carbide in 2001 but denies ongoing liability. To date, little progress has been made but people in Bhopal continue to stage regular protests and rallies to ensure the issue remains fresh in people's minds.

If you're interested in learning more about the disaster or **volunteering** your services, contact the Sambhavna Trust at Bafna Colony, Berasia Road, Bhopal ☎0755/273 0914, ✉sambavna@sancharnet.in. *Five Past Midnight in Bhopal* by Dominique Lapierre and Javier Moro, and the 2007 Booker Prize–nominated novel *Animal's People* by Indra Sinha are both highly recommended further reading.

Mosque", erected in 1860 by Sikander Begum, Kudsia's daughter, is a diminutive and much less imposing version of Shah Jahan's Jami Masjid in Old Delhi, notable more for its slender, gold–topped minarets and sandstone cupolas than its size.

Lining the opposite, northern side of the square near the ceremonial archway is a more eccentric nineteenth-century pile. An unlikely fusion of Italian, Gothic and Islamic influences, the **Shaukat Mahal** palace was originally designed by a French architect (allegedly descended from the Bourbon royal family). Unfortunately, both it and the elegant **Sadar Manzil** ("Hall of Public Audience") have been converted into government offices and are closed to visitors.

Leaving Imam Square by the archway to the west, a five-minute walk brings you to Bhopal's most impressive monument. With its matching pair of colossal pink minarets soaring high above the city skyline, the **Darul Uloom Tajul Masajid** (daily except Fri and during Id-ul-Fitr) certainly lives up to the epithet of "mother of all mosques", as denoted by the extra "a" in its name. Whether it also deserves to be dubbed the biggest in India, as locals claim, is less certain. Work on the building commenced under the auspices of Sultan Jehan Begum (1868–1901), the eighth ruler of Bhopal. After the death of her domineering husband, the widow queen embarked on a spending spree that left the city with a postal system, new schools and a railway, but which all but impoverished the state – and the Tajul Masajid was never actually completed.

The Birla Mandir museum

To the east of Lower Lake, the **Birla Mandir** collection (Tues–Sun 9.30am–8pm; Rs51 [Rs5]) comprises some of the finest stone sculpture in Madhya Pradesh, informatively displayed with explanatory panels in English in the main galleries. The museum is housed in a detached mansion beside Birla Mandir, the garish modern Hindu Lakshmi Narayan temple that stands high on Arera Hill overlooking Lower Lake. Aside from the museum itself, the **temple gardens**, which overlook the city sprawl, are a fine place to watch the sun setting behind the minarets.

The exhibition is divided between Vishnu, the mother goddesses and Shiva. The **Vishnu** section contains some interesting representations of the god's diverse and frequently bizarre reincarnations (avatars), while in the **Devi** gallery next door, a cadaverous Chamunda (the goddess Durga in her most terrifying aspect) stands incongruously amid a row of voluptuous maidens and fertility figures. The **Shiva** room, by contrast, is altogether more subdued. Finally, have a look at the replicas of the 3500-year-old **Harappan** artefacts encased under the stairs. One of the seals bears an image of the pre-Aryan god Rudra, seated in the lotus position; archeologists believe he was the ancient forerunner of Shiva.

Bharat Bhavan

Bharat Bhavan (Tues–Sun: Feb–Oct 2–8pm; Nov–Jan 1–7pm; Rs10, Rs20–50 for stage plays and performances) was set up in 1982 as part of a wider government project to promote visual and performing arts in state capitals throughout India. The initiative fizzled out after the then prime minister Indira Gandhi's death, but Bhopal's contribution has become established as provincial India's most outstanding arts centre.

Inside Goan architect Charles Correa's campus of concrete domes and dour brickwork are **temporary exhibitions** as well as a large split-level **permanent collection** of modern Indian painting and sculpture. Rather incongruously placed in the midst of the latter, look out for an eighteenth-century gilt-framed "landscape" by the Daniells – the uncle-nephew duo employed as a part of the "Company School of Painting" during the Raj, which churned out romantic paintings of India for those back in Britain. Bharat Bhavan has a gallery devoted exclusively to **adivasi art**, in search of which talent scouts spent months roaming remote regions. Among their more famous discoveries was the Gond painter **Jangarh Singh Shyam**, featured by veteran BBC correspondent Mark Tully in his book *No Full Stops In India*. A number of Jangarh's works are on display here, along with a colourful assemblage of masks, terracottas, woodcarvings and ritual paraphernalia. The absence of background information is intentional – the exhibition is intended to represent the objects as works of art in their own right, rather than merely anthropological curios.

The Museum of Man

The story of India's indigenous minorities – the *adivasis*, literally "original inhabitants" – is all too familiar. Dispossessed of their land by large-scale "development" projects or exploitative moneylenders, the "tribals" have seen a gradual erosion of their traditional culture – a process hastened by proselytizing missionaries and governments that tend to regard tribal people as anachronistic or even an embarrassment. The **Museum of Man**, properly known as the Rashtriya Manav Sangrahalaya (Tues–Sun: March–Aug 11am–6.30pm; Sept–Feb 10am–5.30pm; Rs10, plus Rs10 for a vehicle and Rs50 for video), is an enlightened attempt to redress the balance.

Overlooking New Market on one side and the majestic sweep of Upper Lake on the other, the two-hundred-acre hilltop site includes a reconstructed Keralan coastal village, and a winding, mythological trail where each tribal group from the state has contributed their own interpretation of the creation. A large exhibition hall draws on all the daily and ritual elements in the *adivasi* lifestyle. Dotted amongst the forest scrub are botanical trails, a research centre and, as its centrepiece, a permanent open-air exhibition of traditional *adivasi* houses, compounds and religious shrines collectively known as the **"tribal habitat"**.

Before tackling the exhibition, have a quick look at the **introductory gallery** in the small building opposite the main entrance (the approach from New Market). From here, a flight of steps leads underneath a thatched gateway (a structure adapted from the "youth dormitory" of the Ao-Naga from Nagaland) up to the top of the hill, where the seventeen or so dwelling complexes are scattered. Of particular note are the multicoloured paintings of horses adorning the walls of the Rathwa huts (look out for the picture of the train that carried the artists from their village in Gujarat); the ochre, red, black and yellow rectangular designs inside the Gadaba buildings (from Orissa); and the famous Worli wedding paintings of northern Maharashtra, which show the tribal fertility goddess Palghat framed by complex geometrical patterns.

The only way to **get to the museum** without your own vehicle is by autorickshaw; it's best to negotiate a flat rate for the round trip, including at least an hour's waiting time (around Rs150).

Van Vihar Zoological Park

If you haven't made it to Madhya Pradesh's bona fide national parks, or if you have but missed the big cats, it's well worth visiting the **Van Vihar Zoological Park** (daily: March–Sept 8am–5.30pm; Oct–Feb 6.30am–5.30pm; Rs200 [Rs15]; plus Rs40 for camera, Rs300 for video; for transport around the park, a rickshaw is Rs150 plus Rs20 entrance fee for the driver, bicycle Rs10). A trip round the five-square-kilometre sanctuary ties in nicely with a visit to the Museum of Man next door – keep the same rickshaw for the whole trip. The stars of the park are two regal **white tigers**, but there are also long-nosed gharial, leopards, Himalayan bears, Indian tigers and deer. The best chance of sightings is from 4pm onwards, when the animals wait for their daily feed. You can get a longer and more peaceful look at the birds – there are 207 species, including the black ibis and the brainfever bird – by taking a boat from the jetty half a kilometre northeast of the park gate (9am to sunset; pedal boats Rs30/30min).

Eating

Restaurants in Bhopal's larger hotels serve uniform multi-cuisine menus; the strip-light-and-formica cafés opposite the bus stand do thalis and hot platefuls of *subzi*, rice and dhal for next to nothing. For breakfast try the state's favourite food, *poha* – a light steamed rice cake served piping hot in newspaper from every street corner, followed by *katchoris* (a fried, lentil-stuffed snack) and chai.

Aggarwal's Hamidia Rd. A cheerful local stalwart with lively Hindi music, flashing light, religious shrines and an absolute bargain Rs30 bottomless veg thali.

Indian Coffee House Hamidia Rd. Big breakfast venue for south Indian snacks, eggs and filter coffee served with great style at rock-bottom prices (Rs20–70).

Kwality New Market. Bhopal branch of the reliable national chain with outdoor seating, a busy canteen area and a more sedate a/c dining room. There is a vast array of snacks like *bhel puri*, pizzas, Chinese and Indian main meals (Rs30–70).

Manohar Dairy & Restaurant Hamidia Rd. Glitzy fast-food-style joint popular with families, where yellow-shirted waiters dish up south Indian snacks like *dosas*, veg burgers, pizzas, pastries and ice cream (Rs20–50). Try the north Indian favourite

cholle bhatura: piping hot, fluffy bread pockets with rich, spicy chickpeas.

New Inn Bhadbhada Rd, New Market. Despite the large glass frontage – decorated with an incongruous yellow and green dragon design – this eatery has a slightly gloomy exterior. However, the food, particularly the mutton and chicken kebabs, comes up trumps (mains Rs50–90).

Swad Bharat Bhavan Arts Centre. Attracting a refreshingly mixed crowd of students, artists and visitors with its economically-priced samosas, pakoras and mini meals (Rs3–30), *Swad*'s terrace is a great place to watch the sunset, but don't forget the mosquito repellent.

Wind and Waves Lake Drive Rd. Sample the same old MP Tourism menu (mains Rs60–120) in a much better than usual setting conveniently close to the lakeside museums and the boat-rental jetty.

Listings

Airlines Indian Airlines has an office in the Gangotri complex on TT Nagar Rd, New Market (Mon–Sat 9am–5pm, Sun 9am–noon; ☎0755/255 0480), and a booking counter at the airport. Jet Airways, Ranjit Towers, MP Nagar (☎0755/276 0371), also has a booking counter at the airport (☎0755/264 5676), as does Air Deccan (☎0755/264 5676).

Banks and exchange Apart from the top hotels, only the main banks in New Market offer foreign exchange. IDBI has ATMs which accept Visa and MasterCard. In the Chowk, the ICICI in the petrol station on the corner of Hamidia Rd has an ATM, while the State Bank of India is next to the GPO.

Bookstores Variety Book House at the top of Bhadbhada Rd in New Market and Book's World

opposite, stock a wide selection of English-language books and magazines at very reasonable prices.

Hospital Bhopal's main Hamidia hospital (☎0755/254 0222) is on Sultania Rd, between Imam Square and the Darul Uloom Tajul Masajid. The small, private Hajela Hospital (☎0755/277 3392) on TT Nagar is excellent. Doctors are best arranged through the top hotels.

Internet access Internet cafés abound in the Chowk, Hamidia Rd and New Market areas: try Surfing Point on Overbridge Rd (Rs15/hr) or Hub, opposite the State Bank of India in New Market, (Rs20/hr).

Library The British Council has a library in the GTB Complex on Roshanpura Naka, New Market (Tues–Sat 11am–7pm), where non-members are welcome to peruse the collection of British newspapers and magazines. However, at the time of writing there were controversial plans to close the place down.

Post office Have poste restante mail sent to the Head Post Office on TT Nagar in New Market well in advance; the GPO on Sultania Rd near the Darul Uloom Tajul Masajid is less reliable.

Shopping Chowk (bazaar Mon–Sat) is the best place for silk and silver. The New Market area has some bigger stores, including Mrignayani for handicrafts, men's calico shirts, *salwar kameez*, batiks, dokra metalwork, *khadi* clothes, bedspreads and silk saris, though the fixed prices are not cheap. The MP State Emporium on Hamidia Rd has similar wares to Mrignayani, also with fixed prices. Check the street stalls on Overbridge Rd for bargains.

Moving on from Bhopal

Bhopal is on one of the two broad-gauge train lines between Delhi and Mumbai. Heading **north** via Jhansi (for Orchha/Khajuraho), Gwalior or Agra, you have a choice between twelve or so regular services, and the superfast Shatabdi Express #2001, which leaves Bhopal daily at 2.40pm and arrives in Delhi a mere seven hours fifty minutes later. The one train to avoid on this route is the super-slow Dadar–Amritsar Express #1057. In the other direction, the 5pm Punjab Mail #2138 is the best for **Mumbai** (12hr 35min). The nightly service to **Jabalpur**, Narmada Express #8233, leaves 11.35pm and gets in 6.25am, in time to pick up a connecting bus to Kanha. Other services to Jabalpur include the excellent a/c Jan Shatabdi Express #2061 (daily 5.40pm; 5hr 15min), which departs from Habibganj Station and calls at **Itarsi Junction**, 92km south, where you can pick up a connection for Kolkata (Calcutta) and Varanasi.

Most journeys from Bhopal are easier and quicker by train, but the city's good **bus** connections are especially useful for **Indore**, which can be reached either on frequent state buses or on the quicker MP Tourism daily express services (5 daily; 4hr); **for Ujjain**, get off at Dewas and pick up a local bus for the remaining 37km. MP Tourism also has a daily bus to **Pachmarhi** (6.30am; 5hr); all MP Tourism services leave from *Palash Residency*, where you can reserve tickets. Half-hourly buses leave for Sanchi (1hr 30min) from the state bus stand on Hamidia Road. Jet Airways has two daily **flights** to Delhi ($130) and Indore ($90), and one to Mumbai ($150); Indian Airlines has similarly priced daily services to Delhi and Indore and four weekly to Gwalior ($90). Air Deccan's daily flight to Delhi is often cheaper.

For more on transport from Bhopal, see "Travel details" on p.473.

Around Bhopal

A wealth of impressive ancient monuments lie within a couple of hours' journey from Bhopal. To the northeast, the third-century BC stupas at **Sanchi** are an easy day-trip. Its peaceful setting also makes an ideal base for visits to more stupas at **Satdhara** or **Udaigiri**'s rock-cut caves and the nearby Column of Heliodorus at **Besnagar**. Close to the main road south towards Hoshangabad and the Narmada Valley, the prehistoric cave paintings at **Bhimbetka** can be visited in a day by bus.

Sanchi

From a distance, the smooth-sided hemispherical object that appears on a hillock overlooking the main train line at **SANCHI**, 46km northeast of Bhopal, has the surreal air of an upturned satellite dish. In fact, the giant stone mound stands as testimony to a much older means of communing with the cosmos. Quite apart from being India's finest Buddhist monument, the **Great Stupa** is one of the earliest religious structures in the Subcontinent. It presides over a complex of ruined temples and monasteries that collectively provide a rich and unbroken record of the development of Buddhist art and architecture from the faith's first emergence in central India during the third century BC, until it was eventually squeezed out by the resurgence of Brahmanism during the medieval era.

A visit to Sanchi, however, is no dry lesson in South Asian art history. The main stupa is surrounded by some of the richest and best-preserved ancient **sculpture** you're ever likely to see in situ, while the site itself, floating serenely above a vast expanse of open plains, has preserved the tranquillity that attracted its original occupants. Most visitors find a couple of hours sufficient to explore the ruins, though you could spend several days poring over the four exquisite gateways, or **toranas**, surrounding the Great Stupa. Paved walkways and steps lead around

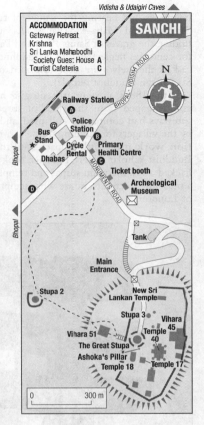

the hilltop enclosure (daily 8am–6pm; Rs250 [Rs5], video Rs25, car Rs10), dotted with interpretative panels and shady trees.

Once you've bought an entrance **ticket** from the roadside booth outside the museum, head up the winding path on the right for ten minutes to the main entrance. From here, the central walkway runs alongside the new Sri Lankan Buddhist temple and cold drinks stalls, before leading to the Great Stupa.

Some history

Unlike other famous Buddhist centres in eastern India and Nepal, Sanchi has no known connection with Buddha himself. It first became a place of pilgrimage when the Mauryan emperor **Ashoka**, who married a woman from nearby Besnagar (see p.413), erected a polished stone pillar and brick-and-mortar stupa here midway through the third century BC. The complex was enlarged by successive dynasties, but after the eclipse of Buddhism Sanchi lay deserted and overgrown until its rediscovery in 1818 by General Taylor of the Bengal Cavalry. In the following years, a swarm of heavy-handed treasure hunters invaded the site, eager to crack open the giant stone eggs and make off with what they imagined to be their valuable contents. However, the explorer Sir Alexander Cunningham was the only one to find anything more than rubble. In 1851, he unearthed two soapstone relic boxes, containing bone fragments and bearing the names of two of Buddha's most noted followers, Sariputra and Maha-Mogalanasa. As author John Keay writes: "It was like finding the graves of Saints Peter and Paul." This discovery transformed Sanchi, for centuries neglected, into a Buddhist place of pilgrimage once again. (The caskets themselves are now displayed once a year, in late November, in the Sri Lankan Buddhist temple).

By the 1880s, amateur archeologists had left the ruins in a sorry state. Deep gouges gaped from the sides of stupas 1 and 2, a couple of ceremonial gateways had completely collapsed, and much of the masonry was plundered by the villagers for building to use as a roller in his sugar cane press. **Restoration work** made little impact until the archeologist John Marshall and the Buddhist scholar Albert Foucher took on the job in 1912. The jungle was hacked away, the main stupas and temples rebuilt, lawns and trees planted and a museum erected to house what sculpture had not been shipped off to Delhi or London.

▲ Stupa 3, Sanchi

Stupas

The hemispherical mounds known as **stupas** have been central to Buddhist worship since the sixth century BC, when Buddha himself modelled the first prototype. Asked by one of his disciples for a symbol to help disseminate his teachings after his death, the Master took his begging bowl, teaching staff and a length of cloth – his only worldly possessions – and arranged them into the form of a stupa, using the cloth as a base, the upturned bowl as the dome and the stick as the projecting finial, or spire.

Originally, stupas were simple burial mounds of compacted earth and stone containing relics of the Buddha and his followers. As the religion spread, however, the basic components multiplied and became imbued with **symbolic significance**. The main dome, or **anda** – representing the sacred mountain, or "divine axis" linking heaven and earth – grew larger, while the wooden railings, or **vedikas**, surrounding it were replaced by massive stone ones. A raised ambulatory terrace, or **medhi**, was added to the vertical sides of the drum, along with two flights of stairs and four ceremonial entrances, carefully aligned with the cardinal points. Finally, crowning the tip of the stupa, the single spike evolved into a three-tiered umbrella, or **chhattra**, standing for the Three Jewels of Buddhism: the Buddha, the Law and the community of monks.

The *chhattra*, usually enclosed within a low square stone railing, or **harmika** (a throwback to the days when sacred *bodhi* trees were surrounded by fences) formed the topmost point of the axis, directly above the reliquary in the heart of the stupa. Ranging from bits of bone wrapped in cloth to fine caskets of precious metals, crystal and carved stone, the reliquaries were the "seeds" and their protective mounds the "egg". Excavations of the 84,000 stupas scattered around the Subcontinent have shown that the solid interiors were also sometimes built as elaborate **mandalas** – symbolic patterns that exerted a beneficial influence over the stupa and those who walked around it. The ritual of circumambulation, or **pradhakshina**, which enabled the worshipper to tap into cosmic energy and be transported from the mundane to the divine realms, was always carried out in a clockwise direction from the east, in imitation of the sun's passage across the heavens.

Of the half-dozen or so giant stupa sites dotted around ancient India, only **Sanchi** has survived to the present day. To see one in action, however, you have to follow in the footsteps of Ashoka's missionaries southwards to Sri Lanka, northwards to the Himalayas and the Tibetan plateau, or across the Bay of Bengal to Southeast Asia, where, as "**dagobas**", "**chortens**" and "**chedis**", stupas are still revered as repositories of sacred energy.

Arrival and information

There are three daily trains from Bhopal to Sanchi, starting at 8.10am (45min); on the return leg the first train leaves at 10am. The nearest mainline station is **Vidisha**, 10km northeast and connected by plenty of local buses; there are daily trains from here to Mumbai and Delhi. **Buses** from Bhopal to Sanchi (90min) depart every half-hour from the main city bus stand. To catch a bus back to Bhopal, wait opposite the *Gateway Retreat* (see p.411) and flag one down.

A handful of wooden stalls surround the bus stand, constituting Sanchi's tiny bazaar, where there's also an **Internet** booth (Rs20/hr). There is no **tourist office**, but staff at the *Gateway Retreat* can provide local information. The low, whitewashed houses of the village proper are on the other side of the main road, huddled below the stupa-covered hill. **Bicycles** – good for a trip to the nearby Udaigiri caves – can be rented for around Rs5/hr from a hut in the bazaar. **Power cuts** happen frequently in Sanchi, so bring a torch.

The Great Stupa

Stupa 1, or the **Great Stupa**, stands on a stretch of level ground at the western edge of the plateau. Fragments of the original construction, a much smaller version built in the third century BC by Ashoka, lie entombed beneath the thick outer shell of lime plaster added a century later. The **Shungas** were responsible for the raised processional balcony, and the two graceful staircases that curve gently around the sides of the drum from the paved walkway at ground level, as well as the aerial-like *chhattra* and its square enclosure which crown the top of the mound. Four elaborate gateways were added by the **Satavahanas** in the first century BC, followed by the four serene meditating **Buddhas** that greet you as you pass through the main entrances. Carved out of local sandstone, these were installed during the Gupta era, around 450 AD, by which time figurative depictions of Buddha had become acceptable (elsewhere in Sanchi, the Master is euphemistically represented by an empty throne, a wheel, a pair of footprints or even a parasol).

As you move gradually closer to the stupa, the extraordinary wealth of sculpture adorning the **toranas** slips slowly into focus. It's easy to see why archeologists believe them to have been the work of ivory craftsmen. Every conceivable space on the eight-metre upright posts and three curving cross-bars teems with delicate figures of humans, demigods and goddesses, birds, beasts and propitious symbols. Some of the larger reliefs depict narratives drawn from the lives of Gautama Buddha and his six predecessors, the *Manushis*, while others recount Ashoka's dissemination of the faith. In between are purely decorative panels and illustrations of heaven intended to inspire worshippers to lead meritorious lives on earth. Start with the *torana* on the south side, which is the oldest, and, as is the custom at Buddhist monuments, proceed in a clockwise direction around the stupa.

Southern torana

Opening directly onto the ceremonial staircase, the **southern torana** was the Great Stupa's principal entrance, borne out by the proximity of the stump of Ashoka's original stone pillar. Over the years, some of the panels with the best sculpture have dropped off the gateway (and are now housed in the site museum), but those that remain on the three crossbeams are still in reasonable condition. A carved frieze on the middle architrave shows Ashoka, complete with royal retinue, visiting a stupa in a traditional show of veneration. On the reverse side, the scene switches to one of the Buddha's previous incarnations. For the **Chhaddanta Jataka**, the *bodhisattva* adopts the guise of an elephant who, in extreme selflessness, helps an ivory hunter saw off his own (six) tusks.

Western torana

The **western torana** collapsed during the depredations of the nineteenth century, but has been skilfully restored and has some of Sanchi's liveliest sculpture. In the top right panel, a troupe of monkeys scurries across a bridge over the Ganges, made by the *bodhisattva*, their leader, from his own body to help them escape a gang of soldiers (seen below). According to the **Mahakapi Jataka**, the troops were dispatched by the local king to capture a coveted mango tree from which the monkeys had been feeding. You can also just about make out the final scene, where the repentant monarch gets a stern ticking-off from the *bodhisattva* under a *peepal* tree.

One of the most frequently represented episodes from the life of Buddha features on the first two panels of the left-hand post facing the stupa. In the

Temptation of Mara, Buddha, who has vowed to remain under the *bodhi* tree until he attains enlightenment, heroically ignores the attempts of the evil demon Mara to distract him with threats of violence and her seductive daughters.

Northern torana

Crowned with a fragmented Wheel of the Law and two tridents symbolizing the Buddhist trinity, the **northern torana** is the most elaborate and best preserved of the four gateways. Scenes crammed onto its two vertical posts include Buddha performing an aerial promenade – one of many stunts he pulled to impress a group of heretics – and a monkey presenting the Master with a bowl of honey. Straddling the two pillars, a bas-relief on both faces of the lowest crossbeam depicts the **Vessantara Jataka**, telling of a *bodhisattva*-prince banished by his father for giving away a magical rain-making elephant. A better view of the inner, south-facing side of the plaque can be had from the balcony of the stupa's raised terrace. Note the little tableau on the far right showing the royal family trudging through the jungle; the prince's son is holding his father's hand, while his daughter clings to her mother's hip.

Eastern torana

Leaning languorously into space from the right capital of the **eastern torana** is Sanchi's most celebrated piece of sculpture, the sensuous **salabhanjika**, or wood-nymph. The full-breasted fertility goddess is one of several such figures that once blessed worshippers as they entered the Great Stupa. Only a few, however, still remain in place, others having been removed to museums in Los Angeles and London.

Panels on the inner face of the pillar below the *salabhanjika* depict scenes from the life of the Buddha, including his conception when the *bodhisattva* entered the body of his mother, Maya, in the form of a white elephant, shown astride a crescent moon. The front face of the middle architrave picks up the tale some years later, when the young Buddha, represented by a riderless horse, makes his **Great Departure** from the palace where he grew up to begin the life of a wandering ascetic. The reverse side shows the fully enlightened Master, now symbolized by an empty throne, with a crowd of celestial beings and jungle animals paying their respects.

Elsewhere around the enclosure

Of the dozens of other numbered ruins around the 400-metre enclosure, only a handful are of more than passing interest. Smaller, plainer and graced with only one ceremonial gateway, the immaculately restored **Stupa 3**, immediately northeast of Stupa 1, is upstaged by its slightly older cousin in every way but one. In 1851, a pair of priceless reliquaries was discovered deep in the middle of the mound. Turned on a lathe from fine marble-like soapstone called steatite, the caskets were found to contain relics belonging to two of Buddha's closest disciples. In one, fragments of bone were encased with beads made from pearls, crystal, amethyst, lapis lazuli and gypsum, while on the lid, the initial of the saint they are thought to have belonged to, Sariputra, was painted in ink. Once in London's British Museum, along with other treasures pilfered from Sanchi, both are now safely locked in the new Buddhist temple outside the stupa enclosure, and are brought out for public view for one day in late November (ask at any MP Tourism office for details). On this day, Sanchi is transformed from a lonely open-air museum into a bustling pilgrimage site, with devotees from as far afield as Sri Lanka and Japan.

From Stupa 3, pick your way through the clutter of pillars, small stupas and exposed temple floors nearby to the large complex of interconnecting raised terraces at the far **eastern edge** of the site. The most intact monastery of the bunch, **Vihara 45**, dates from the ninth and tenth centuries and has the usual layout of cells ranged around a central courtyard. Originally, a colossal, richly decorated sanctuary tower soared high above the complex, but this collapsed, leaving the inner sanctum exposed. The river goddesses Ganga and Yamuna number among the skilfully sculpted figures flanking the entrance to the shrine itself – testimony to the mounting popularity of Brahmanism at the start of the medieval era. Inside, however, Buddha still reigns supreme. Regally enthroned on a lotus bloom, his right hand touches the ground to call upon the earth goddess to witness the moment of his enlightenment.

The enclosure's tenth-century eastern **boundary wall** is the best place from which to enjoy Sanchi's serene **views**, especially at sunset. To the northeast, a huge, sheer-sided rock rises from the midst of Vidisha, near the site of the ancient city that sponsored the monasteries here (traces of the **pilgrimage** trail between Besnagar and Sanchi can still be seen crossing the hillside below). South from the hill, a wide expanse of well-watered wheat-fields, dotted with clumps of mango and palm trees, stretches off towards the angular sandstone ridges of the Raisen escarpment on the distant horizon.

The southern area

The **southern area** of the enclosure harbours some of Sanchi's most interesting temples. Pieces of burnt wood dug from the foundations of **Temple 40** prove that the present apsidal-ended *chaitya* was built on top of an earlier structure contemporary with the Mauryan Stupa 1. **Temple 17** is a fine example of early Gupta architecture and the precursor of the classical Hindu design developed later in Orissa and Khajuraho. Its small, flat-roofed sanctum is entered via an open-sided porch held up by four finely carved pillars with lion capitals.

Before leaving the enclosure, hunt out the stump of **Ashoka's Pillar** on the right of Stupa 1's southern *torana*. The Mauryan emperor erected columns such as this all over the empire to mark sacred sites and pilgrims' trails (see p.1333 in Contexts). Its finely polished shaft (made, like all Ashokan pillars, with a sandstone known as Chunar after a quarry on the Ganges near Varanasi) was originally crowned with the magnificent lion capital now housed in the site museum. The inscription etched around its base is in the Brahmi script, recording Ashoka's edicts in Pali, the early Buddhist language and forerunner of Sanskrit.

The western slope

A flight of steps beside Stupa 1 leads down the **western slope** of Sanchi hill to the village, passing two notable monuments. The bottom portions of the thick stone walls of **Vihara 51** have been carefully restored to show its floorplan of 22 cells around a paved central courtyard. Further down, the second-century BC **Stupa 2** stands on an artificial ledge, well below the main enclosure – probably because its relics were less important than those of stupas 1 and 3. The ornamental railings and gateways around it are certainly no match for those up the hill, although the carvings of lotus medallions and mythical beasts (including some bizarre horse-headed women) that decorate them are worth close scrutiny. The straps that dangle from some of the horse-riders' saddles are believed to mark the first appearance in India of stirrups.

The archeological museum

Sanchi's small **archeological museum** (daily except Fri 10am–5pm; Rs5), to the left of the road up to the hilltop, houses a modest collection of artefacts, mostly fragments of sculpture, jewellery, pottery, weapons and tools recovered during successive excavations. Its **main hall** contains the most impressive pieces, including the famous Ashokan lion-capital (see opposite) and two damaged *salabhanjikas* from the gateways of Stupa 1. Also of note are the distinctive Mathuran red-sandstone Buddhas, believed to have been sent to Sanchi from Gandhara in the far northwest of India – source of the first figurative representations of the Master.

Practicalities

For inexpensive **accommodation** try the *Sri Lanka Mahabodhi Society Guest House* (☎07482/266699; ❶–❸), primarily aimed at visiting Buddhists, but tourists are very welcome, offering spartan rooms with shared facilities facing a shady garden, or more comfortable carpeted rooms with attached bathrooms. The friendly family-run *Krishna* (☎07482/266610; ❷) above the Jaiswal chemist shop on the Bhopal–Vidisha Road, has the best setup for travellers, with clean tiled rooms, hot water bucket and a roof terrace facing the stupas. Food such as pancakes, sandwiches, noodles and main meals (Rs25–50) is also available. MP Tourism's *Gateway Retreat*, also on the Bhopal–Vidisha Road, (☎07482/266723; ❹–❻), is Sanchi's smartest option, with slightly overpriced white-washed en suites in neatly-tended gardens. There's also a computerised train-reservation office and a new meditation centre. It's often busy, so book ahead. MP Tourism's *Tourist Cafeteria* has two plain en-suite doubles (☎07482/266743; ❹), and serves unimaginative but generally well-executed **food**, including soups, tandoori chicken, Chinese, and fish and chips from Rs40–130, in a pleasant garden, with monkeys crashing about in the trees, the faint call from the nearby mosque drifting across and views of the stupas. *Gateway Retreat* has exactly the same menu and is a better bet for an evening meal, particularly as it has Sanchi's only **bar**. The *dhabas* and stalls by the bus stand serve cheap thalis, *puri*, *sabzii* and *jalebi*; try the local speciality, sweet coconut *nariyal* samosas.

Satdhara

Perched on the edge of a dramatic ravine amid rolling hills 30km north of Bhopal, **SATDHARA** ("seven streams") is well worth the detour for stupa enthusiasts, though you'll need your own vehicle to get there. Heading north from Bhopal, a signpost about 13km south of Sanchi points west down a motorable seven-kilometre dirt-track leading to the excavated site. There are no less than 34 **stupas** dating from the Mauryan period in the third century BC, and fourteen monasteries, three of which have substantial foundations still visible. Under the auspices of UNESCO, a number of the stupas and two of the **monasteries** have now been reconstructed using original methods and materials, and others are currently under excavation and renovation.

A path down to the left of the makeshift car park leads directly to the site, which is normally devoid of visitors. No human bones have been discovered in any of the stupas, the most impressive of which is **Stupa 1**, standing 13m high and with a *medhi* (broad circumambulatory path) around the base. Some of its sculpted **toranas** (gateways) have been moved a short distance away for restoration work, but remain on view. Immediately behind it is the imposing three-metre-tall foundation platform of **Monastery 1**, while to the right are two circular **mills**, where oxen still push a great stone around a rut to crush the lime, sand and stone rubble for cement – the technique used by the original architects.

Alongside the numerous subsidiary stupas and monasteries, the remains of **apsidal temples** from the second-century BC Gupta period bear inscriptions in Brahmi script.

Vidisha

The main reason to call in at the bustling railway and market town of **VIDISHA**, a straightforward 56-kilometre train or bus ride from Bhopal, and also served by buses from nearby Sanchi, is to hop on a tonga to the archeological sites at **Udaigiri** and **Besnagar**. However, if you're not pushed for time, the place merits a closer look. Head first for the small **museum** (Tues–Sun 10am–5pm; Rs20 [Rs2]), hidden away behind the railway station in the east of town. The majority of its prize pieces, such as Kubera Yaksha, the three-metre, pot-bellied male fertility figure in the hallway, are second-century Hindu artefacts unearthed at Besnagar. Attractive Jain *tirthankaras* and lumps of masonry salvaged from the district's plethora of ruined Gupta temples litter the garden. Otherwise, occupy yourself with a wander into the brightly painted **Hindu temple** opposite the station, or take a meander through the cheerful **bazaar** in the old town.

Vidisha is also known for financing a prolific third-century BC spate of stupa construction, including much of the work at Sanchi. By the sixth century AD, however, it lay deserted and in ruins, remaining so until the arrival of the Muslims three hundred years later when a settlement, called Bhilsa, was founded around the flat-topped hill in the centre of the modern town. Vidisha's other rather tenuous claim to fame is that the bricks of a nearby second-century BC Vishnu temple were stuck together with lime mortar, believed to be the world's oldest cement.

Udaigiri and Besnagar

A modest collection of ruined temples and fifth-century rock-cut caves stand just 6km west of Vidisha at **UDAIGIRI**. The caves, many decorated by Hindu and Jain mendicants, lie scattered around a long, thin outcrop of sandstone surrounded by a patchwork of wheat fields. It's a congenial area to explore, particularly on one of the tongas that hang around outside Vidisha's bus stand (Rs40–50 round trip), though the site is also an easy cycle ride from town (bikes are available for rent from shops on the outskirts of the bazaar) or, if your legs are up to it, from Sanchi (1–2hr). Bring food and water as there are no shops after Vidisha.

Heading out from town, a left turn just after crossing the Betwa River leads along a gently undulating tree-lined avenue for 2–3km. As it approaches the hillside, the road takes a sharp left turn towards the village. Stop at this corner, at the base of the near-vertical rock face, to climb a steep flight of steps to **Cave 19**, which has worn but attractive reliefs of gods and demons around the doorways, and a **Jain cave temple** on the northern edge of the ridge. An ASI *chowkidar* should be around to unlock the doors for you.

The site's *pièce de résistance*, a four-metre image of the boar-headed hero Varaha, stands carved into **Cave 5**. Vishnu adopted the guise of this long-snouted monster to rescue the earth-goddess, Prithvi (perched on a lotus next to his right shoulder) from the churning primordial ocean. Varaha's left foot rests on a Naga king wearing a hood of thirteen cobra heads, while the river goddesses

Ganga and Yamuna hold water vessels on either side. In the background you can see Brahma and Agni, the Vedic fire-god, plus sundry sages and musicians. The scene, prominent in many contemporary Hindu monuments, is seen as an allegory of the emperor Chandra Gupta II's conquest of northern India.

The ruins of ancient **BESNAGAR**, known locally as **Khambaba**, lie couched in a tiny village down the main road from Vidisha, 5km after the Udaigiri turn-off. During the time of the Mauryan and Shunga empires, between the third and first centuries BC, a thriving provincial capital overlooked the confluence of the Beas and Betwa rivers. The emperor Ashoka himself was governor here at one time and even married a local banker's daughter. Nowadays, a few mounds and some scattered pieces of masonry are all that remain of the houses, stupas, temples and streets. One small monument, however, makes the short detour worthwhile. According to the inscription etched around its base and sixteen-sided column, the stone pillar in an enclosed courtyard, known as the **Column of Heliodorus**, was erected in 113 BC by a Bactrian-Greek envoy from Taxila, the capital city of Gandhara (now the northwest frontier region of Pakistan), who converted to the local Vaishnavite cult during his long diplomatic posting here. The shaft, dedicated to Krishna's father Vasudeva, was originally crowned with a statue of Vishnu's vehicle Garuda. Most of the other archeological finds dug up on the site – including a colossal fertility god, Kubera Yaksha – are now at the museum in Vidisha and the archeological museum in Gwalior.

Bhimbetka

Shortly after NH-12 peels away from the main Bhopal–Hoshangabad road, 45km southeast of the state capital, a long line of boulders appears high on a scrub-covered ridge to the west. The hollows, overhangs and crevices eroded over the millennia from the crags of this malleable sandstone outcrop harbour one of the world's largest collections of **prehistoric rock art**. Discovered accidentally in 1957 by the Indian archeologist Dr V.S. Wankaner. **BHIMBETKA** (sunrise to sunset; Rs10 [Rs2]) makes a fascinating day-trip, although you'll need a car to get there (take along a supply of food and drink). From Bhopal, take NH-12; 7km beyond the market town of Obaidullaganj take a left when you see a sign in Hindi with "3.2" written on it. Cross the railway line and the caves are 3km further along the road.

Of the thousand **shelters** so far catalogued along the ten-kilometre hilltop, around half contain rock paintings. These date from three different periods, each with its own distinctive style. The oldest fall into two categories: green outline drawings of human figures, and large red images of animals. Lumps of hematite (from which the red pigment was manufactured) unearthed amid the deepest excavations on the site have been carbon-dated to reveal origins in the Upper Paleolithic era, around 10,000 years ago. The second and more prolific phase accounts for the bulk of Bhimbetka's rock art, and took place in the **Late Mesolithic** era – the "Stone Age" – between 8000 and 5000 BC. These friezes depict dynamic hunting scenes full of rampaging animals, initiation ceremonies, burials, masked dances, sports, wars, pregnant women, an arsenal of different weapons and even what seems to be a drinking party. One theory for why hunter-gatherers decorated their abodes in this way is that the cave art served the ritual or **magical** function of ensuring a plentiful supply of game; but while abundant depictions of bison, wild boar, antelope and deer lend credence to that notion, animals that were not on the Mesolithic menu, such as tigers and elephants, also appear. Shards of pottery found amid the accumulated detritus on the rock-shelter floors show that Bhimbetka's third and final spate of cave painting took place during the early historic period, after its inhabitants had begun to trade with settled agriculturalists. Their stylized, geometric figures bear a strong resemblance to the art still produced by the region's *adivasi*, or tribal groups.

From the car park at the top of the hill, a paved pathway winds through the jumble of rocks containing the most striking and accessible of Bhimbetka's art. Some of the paintings can be difficult to find and decipher, but the *chowkidars* sitting at the entrance will show you around for a bit of baksheesh. As you progress through the site, look out for the Paleolithic images in green, the wonderful "X-ray" animals filled in with cross-hatching and complex geometric designs, and the recurrent image of a bull chasing a human figure and a crab – a motif believed to represent a struggle between the totemic heroes of three different tribes.

Pachmarhi

Among the last tracts of central India mapped by the British, the **Mahadeo Hills** weren't explored until 1857, when big-game hunter Captain J. Forsyth and his party of Bengal Lancers stumbled upon an idyllic saucer-shaped plateau at the heart of the range, strewn with huge boulders and crisscrossed by perennial clear-water streams. Five years later a road was cut from the railhead at **Piparia**, and by the end of the century **PACHMARHI** had become the summer capital of the entire Central Provinces, complete with a military sanatorium, churches, clubhouses, racecourse and inevitable polo pitch.

Aside from the faded Raj atmosphere and walks to waterfalls and viewpoints around the hill station itself, the main incentive to travel up here is the chance to scramble around the surrounding forest in search of **prehistoric rock art**. Nearby, the **Satpura National Park** is home to Indian bison (*gaur*), barking deer, sambar, *barasingha* swamp deer, jackals, wild dogs and a handful of elusive tigers and leopards.

Popular during the summer, mainly with Bengali, Gujarati and Maharashtrian families who come here to escape the heat of the cities, Pachmarhi remains sleepy for the rest of the year. In winter, things liven up during the annual **Shivratri Mela** (Feb/March), when lakhs of pilgrims pour through en route to the top of nearby Chauragarh Mountain. Out of season, the *yatra* route they follow is one of Central India's classic **hikes**.

The best **time to visit** Pachmarhi is between October and March, when the cool, clear mountain air makes a refreshing change from the heat and dust at lower elevations. It's especially worth trying to be here for Shivratri, although the bus journeys up from the plains can be nightmarish when the *mela* is in full swing. It is also best to avoid long holiday weekends, when popular spots such as **Bee Falls** and **Dhupgarh** (famed for its sunsets) attract crowds.

Arrival, information and accommodation

The easiest way to get to Pachmarhi is on MP Tourism's daily 6.30am express bus from Bhopal, via the busy market town of **Piparia** (5hr); it leaves on the return journey at 2.30pm. Piparia is the nearest railhead for Pachmarhi, 52km northeast and one hour away by frequent buses. It is on the Mumbai–Howrah (via Allahabad, Varanasi and Itarsi) line. If you're coming from Bhopal, the north or the south, you will need to get off at **Itarsi Junction** and catch a bus (3hr) or train (several daily; 1–2hr) to Piparia. The last bus for Pachmarhi leaves at 7.30pm but shared taxi-Jeeps keep running till late. MP Tourism's *Tourist Motel* (☎07576/222299; ❸) behind the station is the only decent **place to stay**. State buses also connect Pachmarhi with Bhopal (6–7 daily; 6–8hr), Chindwara (2 daily; 4–5hr) en route to Nagpur, and Indore (2 daily; 12hr).

Pachmarhi's small bus stand has an MP Tourism **information** office (Mon–Fri 10am–5pm; ☎07578/252100), which has wildly inaccurate **maps** but can rent out cars with driver (around Rs850 per day), as can the major hotels. It also runs a one-day **bus tour** (Rs100), covering most of Pachmarhi's main sights. The State Bank of India has an **ATM**, but no foreign exchange facilities. Bagri **Internet** Centre (Rs40/hr) is opposite *Khalsa Restaurant*, but the connection is erratic.

Accommodation

Accommodation in Pachmarhi is in short supply during the *melas*, over the Christmas and New Year period, and May to June, during which times you'd be well advised to book in advance. Outside these times, you will be able to negotiate a good discount almost everywhere. Most budget accommodation lies a short walk up the hill in the bazaar and in a cluster close to the bus stand, but a few of the more comfortable MP Tourism hotels (it has eight) are a five-minute Jeep or rickshaw ride south on the far side of a lotus-filled lake, near the military training area, Tehsil.

Amaltas Near Tehsil ☎07578/252098, ✉amaltas@mptourism.com. MP Tourism hotel in an old British-built building with ten spacious, minimalist doubles; room 5 is particularly good, with curved walls, marble fireplace and sweeping private veranda. ❺

Evelyn's Own Near *Satpura Retreat* ☎07578/252056, ✉evelynsown@gmail.com. A colonial-era bungalow with homely rooms (they vary in quality, so ask to see a few), games room, pool and tennis court. However, the real draw is owner, and former army colonel, Bunny Rao and wife Pramila, who are a mine of information and play golf and tennis with guests. ❺–❼

Golf View 2km from the bus station, overlooking the golf course ☎07578/252115, ⊛www.welcomheritagehotels.com. Pachmarhi's priciest option (US$125–175) has fifteen suites, each with 1920s-style furniture, fireplaces and modern features like whirlpool baths. Outside you find

manicured lawns, mango trees and, unexpectedly, a running track. ❾

Hotel Highlands Near SADA Barrier, about 600m before the bus stand ☎07578/252099, ✉highland@mptourism.com. The most affordable MP Tourism hotel has no-nonsense cottages with private verandas and little gardens. The attached bathrooms, however, are decidedly chilly in the winter. ❹

Rock End Manor Near Tehsil ☎07578/252079, ✉rem@mptourism.com. MP Tourism's well-restored British bungalow is a long-established favourite of visiting VIPs for its pukka rooms and stately atmosphere. Easy chairs on the veranda give views over the hills and the flower garden. ❽

Saket Patel Marg ☎07578/252165. Close to the State Bank of India in the heart of the bazaar, 5min from bus stand. Friendly, clean and very good value; the more expensive rooms have a/c and bath tubs. ❶–❹

The town and hikes

At over 1000m above sea level, Pachmarhi **town** is clean, green and relaxed, despite the presence of a large military cantonment in its midst. It has retained a distinctly colonial ambience enhanced by the elegant British bungalows and Victorian church spires that nose incongruously above the tropical tree line. In the evenings families stroll and picnic in the parklands, while army bands and scout troupes march around the *maidans*.

The web of forest tracks and pilgrim trails that thread their way around Pachmarhi's widely dispersed archeological and religious sites make for excellent

walking. However, few, if any, of the paths are marked in English, and if you aim to attempt any routes more ambitious than those outlined below, consider employing a local **guide**. One reliable agency is the Tola Trekking Club (☎07578/252256), run by Vinay Sahu from hotel *Saket*, which will organize day-treks from Rs200 per person. The guides are all young tribal men with expert knowledge of the area, and the fees go directly to them and their villages. Kamal Dhoot from *Hotel Kachnar* (☎07578/252547) is another reliable source of information on trekking and the area's flora and fauna. **Bikes**, available from the bazaar or the repair shop just below the Government Gardens for around Rs30 per day, are an alternative way of getting to the trailheads, but make sure you carry a chain and padlock and hide the bicycle in the bushes while you are trekking to stop them from being pinched.

Satpura National Park

The 524-square-kilometre **Satpura National Park**, around 3km southwest of town and dominated by the rugged Mahadeo Hills, is worth a visit to see the Indian bison (*gaur*), barking deer, sambar, *barasingha* swamp deer, jackals and wild dogs, although you're highly unlikely to spot the handful of tigers and leopards. Buy **permits** (Rs200/day; vehicle Rs40, video Rs300) at the office of the Director of the Forestry Commission (Mon–Sat 10am–5pm), next door to the *Amaltas* hotel; separate permits are needed for overnight trips – ask at the office for more information. The office's small museum (Mon–Sat 9am–1pm & 3–7pm) gives a good introduction to the park's flora and fauna.

Pachmarhi Hill and the Jatashankar cave

Two popular short excursions you can safely attempt without a guide include the fifteen-minute climb from the whitewashed Muslim shrine in the Babu Lines area of town (1km southwest of the bus stand) to the top of **Pachmarhi Hill**. From here you have a fine panoramic view over the town on one side and the thickly forested valley of **Jambu Dwip** on the other. The craggy cliffs lining the north side of the uninhabited gorge below are riddled with hidden rock-shelters and caves.

Alternatively, a thirty-minute walk follows a well-beaten track from the bus stand, twisting north from the main bazaar into the hillside through a narrow steep-sided canyon to **Jatashankar**, a sacred cave that's a prominent point in the Shivratri *yatra*. En route, in a small cluster of prehistoric rock-shelters just off the path, look out for **Harper's cave**, named for its naturally formed seated figure of a man playing a harp. Beyond it, at the head of a dark chasm, the Jatashankar cave itself lurks at the foot of a long flight of stone steps. Lord Shiva is said to have fled here through a secret passageway under the Mahadeo range to escape the evil demon Bhasmasur. The grotto's name, which literally means "Shiva's hairstyle", derives from the rock formation around a natural lingam on the cave floor, supposed to resemble the god's matted dreadlocks.

Pandav caves, Fairy Pool and Big Falls

A two- to three-hour walk around the eastern fringes of the plateau strings together a small cluster of interesting sights. First head up to the **Pandav caves** (40min), which occupy a knobbly sandstone hillock just east of the road between the ATC cantonment and the petrol pump. Hindu mythology tells these five (*panch*) simple cells (*marhi*) sheltered the Pandava brothers of Mahabharata fame during their thirteen-year exile. Archeologists, however, maintain that the bare stone chambers and pillared verandas were excavated by a group of Buddhist monks around the first century BC.

Rejoin the road in front of the caves and head around the back of the hill to the melancholy **British cemetery**. Beyond that, the road becomes a dirt track leading to a small car park. From here, take the footpath down the hill through the woods for about twenty minutes till the trail flattens out, and turn right at a fork to descend to **Apsara Vihar**, or "Fairy Pool" – an often crowded bathing place and picnic spot at the foot of a small waterfall. Troupes of black-faced langur monkeys crash through the canopy overhead as you approach the 150-metre **Rajat Prapat**, or "Big Falls", about a five-minute scramble over the boulders downstream from the Fairy Pool. If you walk back to the fork and continue along the trail, a five-minute walk brings you to a railing facing the 105-metre-high falls. Beyond this point you will need a guide to find the two-kilometre trail down to the deep, cold pool at the bottom, best swum in when the sun is directly on it in the mornings.

Chauragarh

The 23-kilometre climb to the sacred summit of **Chauragarh Mountain**, on the south rim of the plateau, follows the main *yatra* trail used by pilgrims during the Shivratri *mela*. The first 8km can be covered by bike. From the bazaar, head south across the lake towards the crossroads in front of *Amaltas* hotel, then take the road to **Mahadeo cave**, passing a vantage point above the narrow **Handi Kho** ravine, and leave your bike hidden in the bushes just before the road makes its first sharp descent at the turn-off for **Priyadarshini**, or "Forsyth's Point".

The **footpath** proper begins at the very bottom of the valley, after the road has plunged down a sequence of hairpin bends. Before setting off, make a brief diversion up the *khud* behind the modern **temple** to the Mahadeo cave, where pilgrims take a purifying dip in the cool perennial springwater that gushes through its pitch-black interior. From here, a strenuous two-hour climb follows an ancient trail to the top of the holy mountain, crammed with tens of thousands of worshippers and sadhus during the Shivratri festival. At the summit, where a temple houses the all-powerful Chauragarh lingam, a thicket of orange tridents surrounds a bright blue statue of Shiva. The view over the verdant Satpuras, to the scrubland and distant flat-topped mountains, is suitably sublime.

Eating

All the **MP Tourism** hotels have **restaurants** serving the same unimaginative but reliable Indian and Chinese menu at reasonable prices. The charming *Rock End Manor* has the edge if you've come here in search of Raj-era atmosphere; book a table in advance. Less expensively, the *dhabas* along the main road serve generous and very cheap thalis, although hygiene is not always a priority.

China Bowl Near *Panchvati*. Good mutton, chicken, *paneer* and *kofta* dishes with a few soups, chop sueys and chow meins thrown in for good measure (mains Rs30–90).
Indian Coffee House Main Rd, just before the bus stand. This local favourite opens from 8.30am for masala dosas, good coffee and south Indian fast-food lunches (mains Rs20–70).

Khalsa Bottom end of bazaar, off the main road. Inexpensive, delicious Punjabi and Chinese dishes from Rs40–130, served inside in a frantic, strip-lit atmosphere, or in the calmer garden. Beer is available in a side room.
Mrignayani Gandhi Chowk. The cleanest of the inexpensive thali joints in the bazaar serves giant portions of fiery pure veg curries and piping hot *rotis* from Rs5–40.

Northern Madhya Pradesh

The remoteness of the famous temples at **Khajuraho**, with their superbly carved erotic sculptures, means many visitors find themselves passing through a large tract of **northern Madhya Pradesh**. Few choose to linger, however, preferring to return to the main Delhi–Agra artery or move onto Varanasi. Yet this much-trodden trail passes within striking distance of several other sights which are well worth taking time out to see. Foremost among them is the spectacular hill-fort at **Gwalior**, below which an extravagant European-style palace is crammed with quirky art treasures and curios.

To the east, Jhansi, in UP (see p.303), is the jumping-off point both for Khajuraho and the medieval ghost-village of **Orchha**, a wonderfully atmospheric former capital whose decaying monuments rise from the banks of the Betwa River. Looming above a lively little market town, the fort-palace at **Datia**, 27km northwest of Jhansi, is another forgotten architectural treasure.

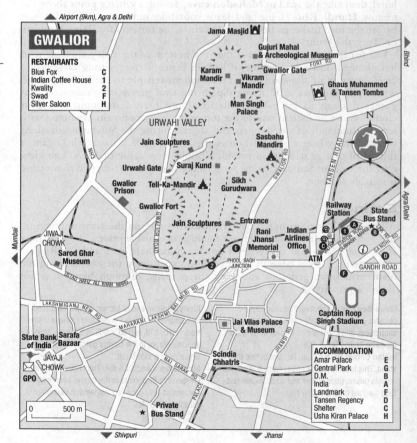

▲ Airport (9km), Agra & Delhi

GWALIOR

RESTAURANTS
Blue Fox	C
Indian Coffee House	1
Kwality	2
Swad	F
Silver Saloon	H

Jama Masjid

Gujuri Mahal & Archeological Museum

Karam Mandir

Gwalior Gate

Vikram Mandir

Ghaus Muhammed & Tansen Tombs

Man Singh Palace

URWAHI VALLEY

Jain Sculptures

Sasbahu Mandirs

Urwahi Gate

Suraj Kund

Teli-Ka-Mandir

Sikh Gurudwara

Gwalior Prison

Gwalior Fort

Jain Sculptures

Entrance

Railway Station

State Bus Stand

JIWAJI CHOWK

Rani Jhansi Memorial

Indian Airlines Office

Sarod Ghar Museum

PHOOL BAGH JUNCTION

ATM

GANDHI ROAD

LAKSHMIGANJ NEW RD

MAHARANI LAKSHMI BAI (MLB) RD

Captain Roop Singh Stadium

State Bank of India

Sarafa Bazaar

JAYAJI CHOWK

GPO

Jai Vilas Palace & Museum

Scindia Chhatris

ACCOMMODATION
Amar Palace	E
Central Park	G
D.M.	B
India	A
Landmark	F
Tansen Regency	D
Shelter	C
Usha Kiran Palace	H

0   500 m

★ Private Bus Stand

▼ Shivpuri   ▼ Jhansi

▶ Bhind
▶ Agra/Delhi
◀ Mumbai

The region's major rail and road routes arc north from Bhopal, passing through the jigsaw joint with neighbouring Uttar Pradesh at Jhansi, before continuing north to Agra and Delhi. In the east, the Central Railway connects the state capital with **Satna**, the nearest railhead to Khajuraho, before veering northeast towards Varanasi and the Ganges basin.

Gwalior

Straddling the main Delhi–Mumbai train line, **GWALIOR** is the largest city in northern Madhya Pradesh and the site of one of India's most magnificent hilltop forts – dubbed "the Gibraltar of the East" by artist William Hodges. The old sandstone citadel, with its temples and palaces, peers down from the edge of a sheer-sided plateau above a haze of petrol fumes, busy streets and cubic concrete houses. The city's other unmissable attraction is the extraordinarily flamboyant **Jai Vilas Palace**, owned by the local ruling family, the **Scindias**. Their personalities and influence are everywhere, from the grand hospital and the **chhatris** (memorial halls) north of Jayaji Chowk to the excellent **Sarod Ghar** museum that celebrates the long tradition of royal patronage of classical music in the city.

Despite its proximity to Agra, 119km north, Gwalior sees few foreigners and with its drab modern centre, it lacks the charm of its counterparts in nearby Rajasthan. Nevertheless, it is a worthwhile place to pause for a day, particularly around late November/early December, when the old **Mughal tombs** in the Muslim quarter host one of the premier Indian classical music events, the four-day **Tansen festival**.

Some history

A donative inscription unearthed in a now-defunct sun temple proves that Gwalior was first occupied in the sixth century BC by Hun invaders from the north. Local legend, however, attributes the founding of the fort to the Kuchwaha prince **Suraj Sen**, said to have been cured of leprosy during the tenth century by the hermit **Gwalipa** after whom the city is named. The Kuchwahas' successors, the Parihars, were brutally overthrown in 1232 by **Iltutmish**, following an eleven-month siege. Before the fort eventually fell to the Muslim army, the Rajput women trapped inside committed mass suicide by self-immolation.

A third Rajput dynasty, the **Tomars**, retook Gwalior in 1398, and ushered in the city's "golden age". Under **Man Singh**, who ascended to the Tomar *gadi* (throne) in 1486, the hilltop gained the magnificent palaces and fortifications that were to earn it the epithet "the pearl in the necklace of the castles of Hind". Skirmishes with neighbouring powers dogged the Rajputs' rule until 1517, when the **Lodis** from Delhi besieged the fort for a second time and Man Singh was slain. Thereafter, Gwalior was ruled by a succession of Muslim overlords, including Babur, Humayun and Sher Shah, before falling to Akbar.

With the decline of the Mughals, Gwalior became the base of the most powerful of the four Maratha clans, the **Scindias**, in 1754. Twenty-six years later, wily British East India Company troops conquered the fort in an audacious night raid. Within hours, the citadel was overrun, and Gwalior became a British feudatory state ruled by a succession of puppet rajas. The most famous of these, the immensely rich Jayaji Rao Scindia (1843–86), remained loyal to the British during the 1857 uprising, although 6500 of his troops joined the opposing forces led by Tantia Tope and **Rani Lakshmi Bai** of Jhansi (see p.303). Both rebel leaders were killed in the ensuing battle, and the maharaja quickly resumed his role as host of some of the grandest viceregal dinners, royal visits and tiger hunts ever witnessed by the Raj. The Scindias remained influential after Independence, and still live in Gwalior; the late Maharaja was a high-ranking minister in the Congress Party and other members of the family have also enjoyed political power in the BJP or the Congress. Their political fortunes, quarrels and marriages continue to provide fodder for voracious gossip columnists. Another native of Gwalior, **Atal Vajpayee**, was BJP leader and prime minister from 1998 to 2003.

Arrival and information

Gwalior's main-line **railway station**, linked to Delhi, Agra, Jhansi and Bhopal by the fast Shatabdi Express, lies in the east of the city, just around the corner from the **state bus stand**, which has regular buses to Agra, Jhansi and Shivpuri (all 2hr 30min–3hr). Most of the decent accommodation is within walking distance, with more places an auto-rickshaw ride away to the west, down busy MLB (Maharani Lakshmi Bai) Road. If you're travelling light, you could save on the fare by squeezing into one of the inexpensive *tempos* that run along Station Road. The **private bus stand** is inconveniently situated on the south-western edge of town. The airport is 9km north of the city from which Indian Airlines (℡011/2463 1337) has four weekly **flights** to Bhopal and Delhi, and Air Deccan (℡0751/247 9851) has daily services to Indore and Delhi. For more on transport from Gwalior, see "Travel details" on p.473.

MP Tourism's helpful **information** office at *Tansen Residency* (daily except Sun 10am–5pm; ℡0751/223 4557), less than ten-minutes' walk south of the railway station on Gandhi Road, also has daily **tours** of the main sights (10am–1pm & 4–7pm; Rs75) in a retro yellow bus. There is also an MP Tourism booth in the railway station on platform 1 (daily except Sun 9.30am–3pm; ℡0751/407 0777). To book onward transport, accommodation and flights, authorized **travel agents** include Travel Bureau (℡0751/234 0103), 220 Jiwaji Chowk, and Touraids Travel Service (℡0751/242 3293), in the Moti palace area, southeast of Phool Bagh Junction. If you need to **change money**, and your hotel has no foreign exchange facility, head for the State Bank of India, at the heart of the bazaar district near the **GPO** on Jayaji Chowk. There is an ICICI **ATM** next to the *Shelter* hotel, which also has several **Internet** centres nearby, including Gwala's Cyber Zone (Rs10/hr) and R.J. Cyber Zone (Rs30/hr).

Accommodation

Standards at the cheaper end of the **hotel** market are particularly low, with cramped windowless cells the norm; those listed below have attached baths (but not necessarily hot water) and noon checkout. Most of the moderate to expensive hotels whack a ten percent "luxury" tax and ten percent service charge on top of the tariff.

Amar Palace Phool Bagh Junction ℡0751/232 5843. The no-frills rooms are a little pokey but come with marble floors and phones. Pay more for one with a small balcony, some with fort views, and a/c. ❸–❹

Central Park City Centre, off Ghandi Rd ℡0751/223 2440, ⓦwww.thecentralpark.net. Excellent business-orientated hotel. Rooms come with swish bathrooms, comfy beds, Wi-Fi access and complimentary breakfast. There's also a pastry shop, restaurant, health club and pool. ❼–❽

D.M. Near the state bus stand ℡0751/234 2083. Miniscule but clean and quiet rooms; the cheaper ones have squat toilets. The ancient TVs are locked inside glass and wood cabinets, lest you were thinking of pinching one. ❸–❹

India Station Rd ℡0751/234 1983. Very popular no-frills lodge run by the Indian Coffee Workers'

Co-op. Clean, but the rooms overlook the noisy main street and only deluxe units have western toilets. ②–④

Landmark Manik Vilas ☎0751/401 1271, ⓦwww.hotellandmarkgwalior.com. The 42 centrally a/c rooms are comfortable, but are let down by their dull brown decor. There's a 24-hour coffee shop, restaurant and bar. ⑥

Shelter Padav Rd ☎0751/232 6209, ⓦwww .hotelsheltergwalior.com. Behind the hotel's wood-panel-effect exterior are large, scrupulously clean a/c doubles with bath tubs, a swimming pool and a fine restaurant (see below). ⑥

Tansen Residency 6-A Gandhi Rd ☎0751/234 0370, ⓔtansen@mptourism.com. MP Tourism's large, efficient hotel, in its own gardens near the station, has well-furnished but somewhat cramped rooms, plus a good restaurant and bar. It's popular, so book in advance. ⑥

Usha Kiran Palace Jayendraganj, Lakshar ☎0751/244 4000, ⓦwww.tajhotels.com. Romantic 120-year-old palace set in nine acres of landscaped gardens. Charming deluxe rooms (US$150–200) have Indian-style divans, 1930s furniture and silk cushions. There's a pool and spa, and cookery, yoga and aerobic classes are available. ⑨

The fort

Gwalior's imposing **fort** (daily sunrise to sunset; Rs100 [Rs5]) sprawls over a 3km-long outcrop of sandstone to the north of the modern city. Its mighty turreted battlements encompass no less than six palaces, three temples and several water tanks and cisterns, as well as a prestigious public school and a Sikh *gurudwara*.

Two routes wind up the hill. In the west, a motorable track just off Gwalior Road climbs the steep gorge of the **Urwahi valley** to the **Urwahi Gate**, passing a line of rock-cut Jain statues along the way. The other, more accessible **Gwalior Gate** is on the northeast corner of the cliff, at the head of a long, stepped ramp. The two can be combined by taking a rickshaw to the Urwahi Gate from the city centre, then walking up and across the plateau, taking in the fort and its various sights, before heading down to the Gwalior Gate, from where it's easier to pick up a rickshaw or *tempo* back into town.

Official **guides** (Rs200/3hr) tout for trade at the Urwahi Gate and the cold drinks shop at the entrance to the palace complex. You can also swot up on the fort's history via the nightly 45-minute **son-et-lumière** show (English show starts at 8.30pm; Rs100 [Rs40]) at the Man Mandir.

The Gwalior Gate approach and museum

Just beyond the Gwalior Gate is the modest **Gujuri Mahal**, built by Man Singh to woo his favourite rani, Mrignayani, when she was still a peasant girl. The elegant sandstone palace now houses Gwalior's **archeological museum** (Tues–Sun 10am–5pm; Rs30 [Rs5]), where the large exhibition of sculpture, inscriptions and painting is well worth a look, even if the labels are woefully uninformative. Highlights include the twin Ashoka lion capitals from Vidisha in gallery two, and gallery nine's erotic bas-relief, in which a prince is shown gently removing the top of his beloved's sari. However, the most famous piece here is the exquisite **salabhanjika**, a small, exquisitely carved female figurine found in the ruins of the temple at Gyaraspur. Noted for her sensuous curves and sublime facial expression, the statue is often dubbed "India's Mona Lisa".

The Man Singh Palace

Entered via the **Hathiya** ("elephant") **Paur** gateway, with its twin turrets and ornate blue tilework, the **Man Singh Palace** was declared "the noblest specimen of Hindu domestic architecture in northern India" by nineteenth-century explorer Sir Alexander Cunningham. Built between 1486 and 1517 by the Tomar ruler Man Singh, it's also known as the Chit Mandir ("painted palace") for the rich ceramic **mosaics** that encrust its facade. The best-preserved fragments of tilework, on its south side, can be seen from the bank left of the main Hathiya Paur gateway. Spread in luxurious bands of turquoise, emerald green and yellow across the ornate stonework are tigers, elephants, peacocks, banana palms and crocodiles brandishing flowers.

By contrast, the **interior** of the four-storeyed palace is very plain. However, there are some fine pierced-stone *jali* screens, behind which the women of the palace would assemble to receive instruction from Gwalior's great music gurus. The circular chambers in the lower storeys were formerly dungeons. Prisoners incarcerated here in Mughal times were fed on a preparation made with boiled poppy heads called *poust* – which ensured a protracted and painful death from malnourishment and drug addiction.

The Teli-ka-Mandir and Suraj Kund

The thirty-metre-tall **Teli-ka-Mandir**, on the south side of the plateau, is the oldest surviving monument in the fort. Dating from the mid-eighth century, it consists of a huge rectangular sanctuary tower capped with an unusual vaulted-arch roof, whose *peepal*-leaf shape derives from the *chaitya* windows of much earlier rock-cut Buddhist caves. In the aftermath of the Indian uprising in 1857, the temple, dedicated to Vishnu, was used by the British as a soda factory. The Archeological Survey of India is now carrying out extensive restoration work. Set back from the road at the head of the Urwahi ravine, just north of the Teli-ka-Mandir, the **Suraj Kund** is the hundred-metre-long tank whose magical waters are supposed to have cured the tenth-century ruler Suraj Sen, later Suraj Pal, of leprosy.

The Sasbahu mandirs and Sikh gurudwara

The **Sasbahu**, or "mother-and-daughter-in-law", temples overlook the city from the eastern edge of the fort, near the unsightly TV mast. The larger of the pair has a three-storey *mandapa* (assembly hall), supported by four intricate pillars, while the smaller one consists of an open-sided porch with a pyramidal roof. Both were erected late in the eleventh century and are dedicated, like the Teli-ka-Mandir, to Vishnu.

The huge, gold-tipped, white-domed marble building to the south is a modern **Sikh gurudwara**. Built to commemorate a Sikh hero who was imprisoned in the fort, the temple attracts a constant stream of pilgrims. Along the road leading to it, you'll pass groups of men clad in the traditional garb of Sikh warriors – long blue *kurtas*, bulky turbans, daggers, and spears held over their shoulders – filing along like foot-soldiers from a bygone era. Before entering the *gurudwara*, make sure you cover your arms, legs and head, remove your socks and shoes, and wash your feet in the tank at the bottom of the steps. Tobacco is strictly prohibited inside the complex.

The Jain sculptures

The sheer sandstone cliffs around the fort harbour some imposing rock-cut **Jain sculptures**. Carved between the seventh and fifteenth centuries, most of the large honey-coloured figures depict the 24 Jain teacher-saviours – the *tirthankaras*, or "Crossing Makers" – in characteristic poses: standing with their arms held stiffly at their sides, or sitting cross-legged, the palms of their hands upturned, staring serenely into the distance. Many lost their faces and genitalia when Mughal emperor Babur's iconoclastic army descended on the city in 1527.

The larger of the two main groups lines the southwestern approach to the fort, along the sides of the **Urwahi** ravine. The largest image, to the side of the road near Urwahi Gate, portrays Adinath, 19m tall, with decorative nipples, a head of tightly curled hair and drooping ears, standing on a lotus bloom beside several smaller statues. A little further from the fort, on the other side of the road, another company of *tirthankaras* enjoys a more dramatic situation, looking over a natural gorge. All have lost their faces, save a proud trio sheltered by a delicate canopy.

The third collection stands on the southeast corner of the plateau, overlooking the city from a narrow ledge. To get there, follow Gwalior Road north along the foot of the cliff from Phool Bagh junction, near the **Rani Jhansi memorial**, until you see a paved path winding up the hill from behind a row of houses on the left. Once again, the *tirthankaras*, which are numbered, occupy deep recesses hewn from the rock wall. One of the few not defaced by the Muslim invaders, no. 10, is still visited by Gwalior's small Jain community as a shrine.

The old town and south of the fort

A number of interesting Islamic monuments are tucked away down the narrow, dusty backstreets of Gwalior's predominantly Muslim **old town**, clustered around the north and northeast corners of the hill. The **Jama Masjid** stands close to the Gujuri Mahal, near the main entrance to the fort. Erected in 1661 by Mohammad Khan, using sandstone quarried from the plateau above, the beautifully preserved mosque sports two slender minarets and three bulbous onion domes crowned with golden spires.

The city's most famous Muslim building, however, is set amid balding lawns 1km further east. The sixteenth-century **Tomb of Ghaus Mohammed**, an Afghan prince who helped Babur take Gwalior fort, is a fine specimen of early Mughal architecture, and a popular local shrine. Elegant hexagonal pavilions stand at each of its four corners; in the centre, the large central dome retains a few remnants of its blue-glazed tiles. The tomb's walls are inlaid with exquisite pierced-stone *jali* screens, whose complex geometric patterns are best admired from the incense-filled interior.

The second and smaller of the tombs in the gardens is that of the famous Mughal singer-musician **Tansen**, one of the "Nine Jewels" of Emperor Akbar's court. Every year, performers and aficionados from all over India flock here for Gwalior's annual **music festival** (Nov/Dec). At other times, impromptu recitals of *qawwali*, Islamic devotional singing accompanied on the harmonium, take place on the terrace outside. Local superstition holds that the leaves of the **tamarind tree** growing on the plinth nearby have a salutary effect on the singing voice, which explains why its bottom branches have been stripped bare. **To get there** from the station, take a rickshaw (Rs20) or a *tempo* bound for Hazira (Rs2).

The Jai Vilas Palace

Due south of the fort, in the heart of Gwalior's upper-class neighbourhood, the **Jai Vilas Palace** (daily except Wed 10am–5.30pm; Rs200 [Rs30], plus Rs30 camera, Rs80 video) is one of India's most grandiose and eccentric nineteenth-century relics, although the steep entry fee and lack of labelling and information make it an unsatisfactory experience. **Guides** hang out by the entrance and charge about Rs50 per tour.

The palace was built in 1875 during the reign of Maharaja Jayaji Rao Scindia. Wanting his residence to rival those of his colonial overlords in Britain, he dispatched his friend Colonel Michael Filose on a grand tour of Europe to seek inspiration. A year or so later, Filose returned with a vast shipment of furniture, fabric, paintings, tapestries and cut glass, together with the blueprints for a building that borrowed heavily from Buckingham Palace, Versailles, and a host of

Greek ruins and Italian-Baroque stately homes. The result is an improbable and shamelessly over-the-top blend of Doric, Tuscan and Corinthian architecture.

The Scindias, who still occupy a part of the palace, have opened two wings to the public. Eager to maintain the sense of a family home, they have placed innumerable photographs of their richly clad clan members on every available surface throughout the first wing, a **museum** of the more valuable and extraordinary artefacts accumulated by the rulers of Gwalior. Collecting dust in the dozens of rooms and creaky wood-panelled corridors are countless Mughal paintings, Persian rugs, gold and silver ornaments, and antique furniture that had originally belonged to the estate of Louis XVI before the French Revolution. Elsewhere, you'll come across a swing made from Venetian cut glass which the royal family used to celebrate Krishna's birthday, and, upstairs, a room full of erotic art.

A still more extravagant wing lies across the courtyard from the museum. The **durbar hall** was where the maharaja entertained important visitors, among them the Prince of Wales (later Edward VII), who descended on Gwalior in 1875 with an entourage of a thousand people. Displayed in the banquet hall on the ground floor is a silver toy train used by Jayaji Rao Scindia to dispense brandy and cigars after dinner; the maharaja would tease anyone he didn't like by not stopping the electric locomotive when it reached them. A sweeping Belgian glass staircase leads from the lobby to the gargantuan assembly hall upstairs. Suspended from its ceiling are the world's biggest chandeliers. At over three and a half tonnes apiece, they could not be installed until the strength of the roof had been tested with eight elephants – a feat that necessitated the construction of a 500-metre-long earth ramp. The rug lining the floor of the hall is equally enormous. Woven by inmates of Gwalior jail, it took twelve years to complete and, at over 40m in length, is the largest handmade carpet in Asia.

Sarod Ghar

Tucked away in the west of the city, the **Sarod Ghar** music museum (Tues–Sun 10am–1pm & 2–4pm; ⓦ www.sarod.com) is on Ustad Hafiz Ali Khan Marg, Jiwaji Ganj. Take a rickshaw directly to the house, or a *tempo* (Rs3) to Jiwaji, a five-minute walk north of Jayaji Chowk. The museum occupies the beautiful ancestral home of the Bangash family, with its rose-sandstone walls aligned in pure symmetry and delicate sculptural detail around a marble courtyard, still used for musical recitals (check newspaper listings or at the tourist office). The Bangash ancestors were originally Afghan horse-traders who settled in India and produced a dynasty of musical virtuosos, including **Ustad Hafiz Ali Khan** and his son **Ustad Amjad Ali Khan.**

The museum traces Gwalior's rich musical legacy from Tansen, who performed in the court of Mughal emperor Akbar, to the invention by Gulam Ali Khan Bangash of the **sarod** (for more on which, see Contexts, p.1383), whose ethereal tones accompany you as you progress through the galleries. The exhibition culminates with a display of instruments donated by famous musicians, and there's also a small shop.

The Scindia chhatris

Two typically ostentatious tombs belonging to the Scindia family stand a short rickshaw ride north of Jayaji Chowk. Enclosed inside a walled courtyard, the **chhatris** (cenotaphs) are worth a look for their intricate stone work and ornately painted scenes of life inside the Maratha royal court in the nineteenth century. Built in 1817 to commemorate Maharaja Jiyaji Rao Scindia, the larger of the pair is most remarkable for the intricate outside panelling of interwoven flowers.

The second *chhatri* is reached through a yellow-and-white arch to the left of the courtyard, and is a more compact and finely detailed version of the former. Constructed in 1843 for the newly departed Maharaja Janakaji Scindia, sculptures and carvings depict the hectic lifestyle of a king. There are little stone elephants, each bejewelled and covered with a unique silk canopy, plodding in a line around the platform to symbolize the power of the maharaja, and the door is guarded by two solemn soldiers in full Maratha regalia. As an antidote to the warring reputation of the Maratha rulers, numerous panels outside depict the life of Krishna surrounded by his many pleasure-seeking beauties, while inside the *chhatri* are painted frescoes of princesses and court dances, as well as life-sized marble effigies of the maharaja and his three wives.

Eating

With a couple of exceptions, all the **best places to eat** in Gwalior are in the mid- and top-range hotels. More basic and much cheaper dhal, *subzi* and roti are doled out on stainless-steel plates at the row of *dhabas* outside the railway station. Look out too for the **juice bars** dotted around the station and Jayaji Chowk, over in the west end of town, which serve glasses of refreshing, freshly squeezed fruit juice (ask for no ice).

Blue Fox *Shelter* hotel. Chatty staff serve hearty meals in contemporary surroundings: grab a cosy booth and tuck into chicken *shashlik*, masala chips and sweet *falooda* (mains Rs60–150).

Indian Coffee House Station Rd. Low-key eatery with white-turbaned waiters that consistently produces the goods: toast and cornflakes, south Indian snacks and more substantial meals (Rs20–70).

Kwality MLB Rd. The long menu inexplicably omits *cholle bhatura*, the snack for which the chain became famous. Nevertheless there are still a number of appealing veg and non-veg options (Rs50–100), with the *paneer* dishes particularly recommended.

Silver Saloon Usha Kiran Palace. If you can't afford to stay at the hotel, a visit to its exemplary restaurant is the next best thing. Gourmet Indian, Nepalese and international dishes are impeccably served in evocative surroundings. Expect to pay around Rs550 for dinner.

Swad *Landmark* hotel. As well as tasty Mughal and south Indian dishes, this is the place to come for comfort food like baked beans on toast, porridge and French toast (Rs90–200).

Datia

Constructed by Bir Singh Deo at the height of the Bundela's "golden age", the majestic palace at **DATIA**, 30km northwest of Jhansi, is regarded as one of the finest Rajput buildings in India. Although few of the visitors who spy the exotic hulk of yellow-brown ramparts, cupolas and domed pavilions from the nearby train line actually stop here, those that do are rarely disappointed. Presiding over a mass of white- and blue-washed brick houses from its seat atop a rock outcrop, the **Nrsing Dev Palace** (dawn to dusk) stands in the north of town. Half the fun of visiting the labyrinthine palace is trying to find a path from its pitch-black subterranean chambers, hewn out of the solid base of the hill for use during the hot season, to the rani's airy apartment on the top floor. In between, a maze of cross-cutting corridors, flying walkways, walls encrusted with fragments of ceramic tiles, latticed screens and archways, hidden passages, pavilions and suites of apartments lead you in ever-decreasing circles until you eventually run out of staircases. The views from the upper storeys are breathtaking.

Practicalities

Datia, on the main Delhi–Mumbai train line, is most often visited as a day-trip from Jhansi, or as a break in the journey to Gwalior, 71km to the northwest. Buses run from both cities every thirty minutes and there are ten trains daily. If you're coming from Shivpuri, 97km west, you'll have to change buses at Karera. Tongas and cycle rickshaws ferry passengers into town from the small **railway station**, 2km southwest, while **buses** pull in at a lot on the south side of the centre. Bicycles can be hired at minimal cost from a shop on the corner of the main road and the road to the bus stand, near Raj Garh Palace. You can get simple **food** and cold drinks in the *dhabas*.

Shivpuri

Shivpuri, 112km south of Gwalior and the summer capital of the city's former Scindia rulers, is worth a stop-off to see the **Madhav Rao Scindia Chhatri** (cenotaph), a white marble synthesis of Hindu and Islamic architectural styles with spires and pavilions (daily 8am–noon & 3–8pm; Rs2, camera Rs10). There are also several other lesser *chhatris* and tranquil gardens, complete with Victorian lamps and ornamental balustrades. Nearby is the 156-square-kilometre **Madhav National Park** (daily 6am–11am & 3–6pm; Rs150 [Rs15], camera Rs40, video Rs300, vehicle Rs75, guide Rs40), with its wooded hills and grassland home to deer, and rather less common leopards, sloth bears and blackbucks. Crocodiles, pythons and monitor lizards inhabit the area around and in the artificial lake, and there are various Scindia-era constructions, including a hunting lodge, a boat club and a castle. If you want to stay a night in Shivpuri, MP Tourism's *Tourist Village* (☎07492/223760, ✉tvshivpuri@mptourism.com; ⑤), situated beside a lake, has a slightly overpriced collection of a/c **rooms** with complimentary breakfast and a laid-back ambience. The manager can also organize Jeeps for Madhav National Park. Shivpuri is linked to Gwalior by **train** (4hr), but the regular state **buses** (3hr) are quicker.

Orchha

An essential stop en route to or from Khajuraho, **ORCHHA** ("hidden place") certainly lives up to its name, residing amid a tangle of scrubby *dhak* forest 18km southeast of Jhansi. In spite of its generally tumbledown state, the fortified and now deserted medieval town is a former capital of the Bundela rajas and remains an architectural gem, its guano-splashed temple *shikharas*, derelict palaces, havelis and weed-choked sandstone cenotaphs floating serenely above the banks of the River Betwa. Clustered around the foot of the exotic ruins, the sleepy village of neatly painted houses, market stalls and a couple of attractive hotels makes an excellent spot to unwind after the hassle of northern cities. However, it's firmly established on the tour-group trail these days, and it's worth spending a night or two here to see Orchha after the bus parties have moved off.

Some history

After being chased by several generations of Delhi sultans from various capitals around central India, the Bundela dynasty finally settled at the former Malwan fort of **Orchha** in the fifteenth century. Work on Orchha's magnificent fortifications, palaces and temples was started by Raja **Rudra Pratap**, and continued after he was killed in 1531 trying to wrestle a cow from the clutches of a tiger. Thereafter, the dynasty's fortunes depended on the goodwill of their mighty neighbours, the **Mughals**. After being defeated in battle by Akbar, the proud and pious **Madhukar Shah** nearly signed his clan's death warrant by showing up at the imperial court with a red *tilak* smeared on his forehead – a mark at that time banned by the emperor. Madhukar's bold gesture, however, earned Akbar's respect, and the two became friends – an alliance fostered in the following years by Orchha's most illustrious raja. During his 22-year rule, **Bir Singh Deo** erected a total of 52 forts and palaces across the region, including the citadel at Jhansi, the rambling Nrsing Dev at Datia and many of Orchha's finest buildings. In 1627, he was killed by bandits while returning from the Deccan with a camel train full of booty. Afterwards, relations with the Mughals rapidly deteriorated. Attacks by the armies of Shah Jahan, Aurangzeb and the Marathas ensued, and a spate of eighteenth-century Jat peasant uprisings finally forced the Bundelas to flee Orchha for the comparative safety of **Tikamgarh**. Apart from the Sheesh Mahal, now converted into a small hotel, the magnificent monuments have lain virtually deserted ever since.

Arrival and information

Tightly packed **tempos** from Jhansi bus station run frequently to Orchha's main crossroads, 18km away, or there are five daily **buses**. Both take twenty to forty minutes (depending on the number of stops), and cost Rs10 (plus Rs10 for luggage in a *tempo*). An **auto-rickshaw** from Jhansi railway or bus station costs around Rs150, a taxi Rs350; both are more expensive at night. Coming from **Khajuraho**, you can ask to be dropped at the Orchha turning on the main road and pick up a *tempo* for the remaining 7km.

If you're heading in the other direction, **towards Khajuraho**, don't bank on being able to flag down one of the quick private buses (6 daily; 4hr) on the highway, as they're often full. Instead, get to Jhansi railway station, where they depart, early and arrange a ticket before the Delhi/Agra trains pull in. There are also three daily public buses (5–6hr) from Jhansi Bus Stand. **Cars** (with drivers) cut the journey time to Khajuraho – they cost Rs1400 (one way), and can be hired through the MP Tourism **information** office (daily 6am–10pm; ☎07680/252624) at the *Sheesh Mahal*, which also organizes **river rafting** trips (Rs1200/90min; Rs3000/3hr, including lunch). You can change **traveller's cheques** at Canara Bank in the main square and there is a State Bank of India **ATM** on Tikamgarh Road, ten minutes south of the market. There are several **Internet** centres around town; try Cyber Café (Rs30/hr) next to *Bhola* restaurant, which also burns digital photos onto disks and offers Skype phone calls (Rs70/hr). As with all of Orchha's Internet cafés, take promises of a "speedy connection" with a hefty pinch of salt. AR Tours and Travel, Tikamgarh Road, rents out **bikes** (of varying quality) for Rs50/day.

Accommodation

Amar Mahal Bypass Rd, 200m south of the market ☎07680/252202, ⬤www.amarmahal.com. Mughal-themed rooms with tiled floors, dark wood furnishings and elaborately painted ceilings (some even have chandeliers). There's a pool, bar, café and pricey restaurant. ❼–❽
Betwa Retreat Off Tikamgarh Rd ☎07680/252618, Ⓒbetwa@mptourism.com. MP Tourism lodge has a

selection of salmon-coloured cottages and comfy a/c tents – each with TV, fridge and marble bathroom – in a peaceful garden close to the river. It's a 10min walk south of the town centre. ❹–❺
Ganpati Main Rd ☎07680/252765, Ⓒganpati_vinod@yahoo.com. A wide range of en suites set around a small garden, from which there are spectacular views of the old fortifications.

All the rooms are immaculately clean, freshly painted and come with smart bathrooms; the more expensive have a/c and vistas of their own. ②–④
Orchha Resort Off Tikamgarh Rd, close to *Betwa Retreat* ☎ 07680/252677, ⊛ www.orchharesort .com. Attractive, if garishly painted, riverside resort with all mod cons including foreign exchange, pool, and tennis and badminton courts. The luxury a/c tents are more affordable. ⑤–⑧
Sheesh Mahal Jehangir Mahal Rd, next to the Raj Mahal ☎ 07680/252624, smorchha@mptourism .com. The local raja's former country bolthole in the heart of the fort is now an atmospheric hotel with a handful of rooms and a personalised approach. If you can afford it, treat yourself to a romantic night

in the royal suite – perks include candlelit dinner on your private veranda, a vast marble bathtub and the ultimate loo with a view. Advance booking recommended. ⑤–⑨
Shri Mahant Guesthouse Overlooking the market ☎ 07680/252715. Run by the same people as *Hotel Shri Mahant*, this place is aimed at backpackers. Rooms are a little claustrophobic, and the most basic have squat toilets, but for a few more rupees you get air-coolers, TV and Western toilets. ①–②
Shri Mahant Hotel Lakshmi Narayan Temple Rd, 200m northwest of the market ☎ 07680/252341. Welcoming family-friendly hotel with huge pale pink rooms decorated with plastic flowers, spotless bathrooms (some with tubs) and balconies. ④

The monuments

The best-preserved of Orchha's scattered **palaces**, **temples**, **tombs** and **gardens** (daily 7.30am–6pm; "day passport" for all monuments Rs250 [Rs10], Rs25 camera) lie within comfortable walking distance of the village and can be seen – at breakneck speed – in a day, but to get the most out of a trip you should plan on staying the night. English-speaking guides can be hired at the main gate for around Rs100 for a short tour of the fort, or near the main square for Rs200–250 for a half-day tour of Orchha.

The Raj Mahal and the Rai Praveen Mahal

The first building you come to across Orchha's medieval granite bridge is the well-preserved ruin of the royal palace, or **Raj Mahal** (unrestricted access), started by Rudra Pratap and completed by one of his successors, the indomitable Madhukar Shah. From the end of the bridge, bear left at the main entrance, and then right to reach the *Sheesh Mahal* hotel. Of the two rectangular courtyards inside, the second, formerly used by the Bundela ranis, is the most dramatic. Opulent royal quarters, raised balconies and interlocking walkways rise in symmetrical tiers on all four sides, crowned by domed pavilions and turrets; the apartments projecting into the quadrangle on the ground floor belonged to the most-favoured queens. As you wander around, look out for the fragments of mirror inlay and vibrant **painting** plastered over their walls and ceilings. Some of the friezes are still in remarkable condition, depicting Vishnu's various outlandish incarnations, court and hunting scenes, and lively festivals involving dancers, musicians and jugglers. The resident *chowkidar* is an excellent guide.

Reached via a path that leads from the Raj Mahal around the northern side of the hill, the **Rai Praveen Mahal** is a small, double-storeyed brick apartment built by Raja Indramani for his concubine in the mid-1670s. The gifted poetess, musician and dancer, Rai Praveen, beguiled the Mughal emperor Akbar when she was sent to him as a gift, but was eventually returned to Orchha to live out her remaining days. Set amid the well-watered lawns of the **Anand Mahal gardens** (unrestricted access), it has a main assembly hall on the ground floor (used to host music and dance performances), a boudoir upstairs and cool underground apartments.

The Jahangir Mahal

Orchha's single most admired palace, the **Jahangir Mahal** was built by Bir Singh Deo as a monumental welcome present for the Mughal emperor when he paid a state visit here in the seventeenth century. Jahangir had come to invest his old ally with the sword of Abdul Fazal – the emperor's erstwhile enemy whom Bir Singh had murdered some years earlier. Entered through an ornate ceremonial gateway, the main, east-facing facade is still encrusted with turquoise tiles. Two stone elephants flank the stairway, holding bells in their trunks to announce the arrival of the raja, and there are three storeys of elegant hanging balconies, terraces, apartments and onion domes piled around a central courtyard. This palace, however, has a much lighter feel, with countless windows and pierced stone screens looking out over the exotic Orchha skyline to the west, and a sea of treetops and ruined temples in the other direction.

The Sheesh Mahal

Built during the early eighteenth century, long after Orchha's demise, the **Sheesh Mahal** ("Palace of Mirrors") was originally intended as an exclusive country retreat for the local raja, Udait Singh. Following Independence, however, the property was inherited by the state government, who converted it into a hotel. The rather squat palace stands between the Raj Mahal and the Jahangir Mahal, at the far end of an open-sided courtyard. Covered in a coat of whitewash and stripped of most of its Persian rugs and antiques, the building retains little of its former splendour, though it does offer stunning views from its upper terraces and turrets. The only rooms worth a peep – assuming they're not occupied (check with reception) – are the palatial nos. 1 and 2, which contain original bathroom fittings.

Around the village

Dotted around the **village** below the hill are several other interesting monuments. The **Ram Raja Mandir** stands at the end of the small bazaar, in a cool marble-tiled courtyard. Local legend has it Madhukar Shah constructed the building as a palace for his wife, Rani Ganesha, and it only became a temple after a Rama icon, which the queen had dutifully carried all the way from her home town of Ayodhya, could not be lifted from the spot where she first set it down; it remains there to this day, and the temple is a popular pilgrimage site.

   With its huge pointed *shikharas* soaring high above the village, **Chatturbuj Mandir** is the temple originally built to house Rani Ganesha's icon. In cruciform shape, representing the four-armed Vishnu, with seven storeys and spacious courtyards ringed by arched balconies, it epitomizes the regal Bundelkhand style, inspired by the Mughals, with Rajput, Persian and European touches. It's unusual for a Hindu temple, with very few carvings and a wealth of space – perhaps to accommodate followers of the **bhakti** cult (a form of worship involving large congregations of people rather than a small elite of priests). You can climb up the narrow staircases between storeys to the temple's roof, pierced by an ornate *shikhara* whose niches shelter nesting vultures.

   On the other side of Ram Mandir, a path leads through the Mughal-style **Phool Bagh** ornamental garden to **Hardaul ka Baithak**, a grand pavilion where Bir Singh Deo's second son, Hardaul, ally of Jahangir and romantic paragon, once held court. Newlyweds come here to seek blessing from Hardaul, who, despite being poisoned by his jealous brother who accused him of intimacy with his sister-in-law, is thought to confer good luck. The tall towers rising above the gardens like disregarded bridge supports are *dastgirs* (literally "wind-catchers"), Persian-style cooling towers that provided air-conditioning for the neighbouring palace, Palkhi Mahal; they're thought to be the only ones of their kind surviving in India.

A solemn row of pale brown weed-choked domes and spires, the riverside **chhatris** are Orchha's most melancholy ruins. The fourteen cenotaphs, memorials to Bundelkhand's former rulers, are best viewed from the narrow road bridge or, better still, from the boulders on the opposite bank, where you get the full effect of their reflection in the still waters of the Betwa.

The Lakshmi Narayan Mandir

The solitary **Lakshmi Narayan temple** crowns a rocky hillock just under 1km west of Orchha village, at the end of a long, paved pathway. From the square directly behind the Ram Raja temple, a leisurely fifteen-minute stroll is rewarded with fine views, and excellent seventeenth- and nineteenth-century paintings. For a small tip, the resident *chowkidar* will lead you through the galleries inside the temple. Look out for the frieze depicting the battle of Jhansi, in which the rani appears in an upper room of the fort next to her horse, while musket-bearing British troops scuttle about below. Elsewhere, episodes from the much-loved Krishna story crop up alongside portraits of the Bundela rajas and their military and architectural achievements, while a side pillar bears a sketch of two very inebriated English soldiers.

Eating

A smart **place to eat** and hang out in the evenings is the colonnaded dining hall in the *Sheesh Mahal* hotel, which often has live music in the evening and serves a mix of veg and non-veg food, and tandoori specials at lunch time (Rs40–140). *Betwa Retreat* offers the same menu in less evocative surroundings. *Bhola* on the approach to the Fort Bridge is the first in a trio of traveller haunts (mains in all three Rs20–80) and has an eclectic array of Chinese, Korean, Israeli and Indian dishes, as well as, of course, banana pancakes. Closer to the bridge is *Milan*, a good breakfast spot for hash browns and porridge. Next door is *Ram Raja*, which matches pink walls with yellow plastic chairs, and dishes up omelettes, Chinese, so-so pasta and a super-sweet concoction, the surreally-named "Hello to the Queen". The veg Indian food at all these places is generally the most reliable option. *Betwa Tarang*, also on the Fort Bridge, is an excellent spot for a drink, though the food gets mixed reviews. If you tire of the international menus, head to *Neeraj*, a popular stall just west of the market, which does a brisk trade in Rs40 thalis. The delicious local speciality, *kalakand* (milk cake), can be bought from the small stalls opposite the *Shri Mahant Guesthouse*.

Khajuraho

The resplendent Hindu temples of **KHAJURAHO**, immaculately restored after almost a millennium of abandonment and neglect, are an essential stop on any itinerary of India's historic monuments. Famed for the delicate sensuality – and forthright **eroticism** – of their sculpture, they were built between the tenth and twelfth centuries AD as the greatest architectural achievement of the **Chandella** dynasty.

Waves of Afghan invaders soon hastened the decline of the Chandellas, however, who abandoned the temples shortly after they were built for more secure ground. The temples gradually fell out of use and by the sixteenth century had been swallowed by the surrounding jungle. It took "rediscovery" by the British in 1838 before these masterpieces were fully appreciated in India, let alone internationally.

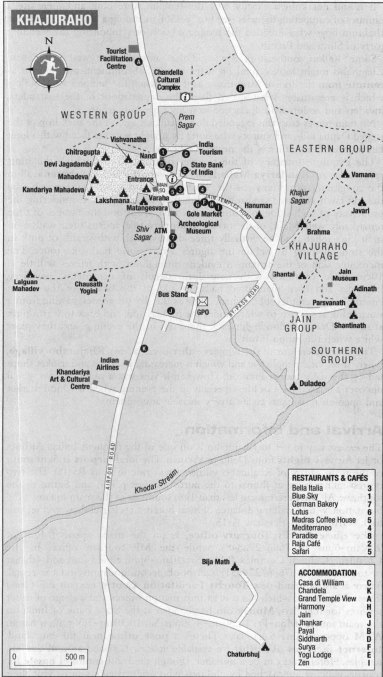

KHAJURAHO

N

Rajnagar (5km)

Tourist
Facilitation
Centre ■ A

Chandella
Cultural
Complex

ⓘ

B

WESTERN GROUP

Prem
Sagar

Vishvanatha

Chitragupta
Nandi
India
Tourism

Devi Jagadambi
Mahadeva
Entrance
Kandariya Mahadeva
Lakshmana
Matangesvara

① C
D ② E
State Bank
of India
ⓘ
MAIN
SQ
⑤ ③
Varaha
⑥
G

EASTERN GROUP

Vamana

State Bank
of India

④
JAIN TEMPLES ROAD
Hanuman

H I

Khajur
Sagar

Javari

Brahma

Shiv
Sagar
ATM
⑦
⑧

Gole Market
Archeological
Museum

KHAJURAHO
VILLAGE

Lalguan
Mahadev

Chausath
Yogini

Ghantai

Jain
Museum

Adinath

Bus Stand

GPO

BY-PASS ROAD

Parsvanath

Shantinath

JAIN
GROUP

J

Indian
Airlines

Khandariya
Art & Cultural
Centre

K

SOUTHERN
GROUP

Duladeo

Khodar Stream

AIRPORT ROAD

Bija Math

Chaturbhuj

0   500 m

RESTAURANTS & CAFÉS	
Bella Italia	3
Blue Sky	1
German Bakery	7
Lotus	6
Madras Coffee House	5
Mediterraneo	4
Paradise	8
Raja Café	2
Safari	5

ACCOMMODATION	
Casa di William	C
Chandela	K
Grand Temple View	A
Harmony	H
Jain	G
Jhankar	J
Payal	B
Siddharth	D
Surya	F
Yogi Lodge	E
Zen	I

Airport (1km), Jhansi & Panna National Park

It is still not known exactly why the temples were built and there are a number of competing theories (see box, p.436), including a "how to" guide for Brahmin boys who attended the temple schools or symbolizing the wedding party of Shiva and Parvati.

Some 400km southeast of Agra and the same distance west of Varanasi, Khajuraho might look central on maps of the Subcontinent, but remains as **remote** from the Indian mainstream as it was when the temples were built – which is presumably what spared them the depredations of the marauders, invaders and zealots who devastated so many early Hindu sites.

No train routes cross this extended flood plain, set against the backdrop of the jagged Dantla hills, and visitors who don't fly straight here are faced with a long bus journey from either of the nearest railheads.

The exquisite intricacy of the temples themselves – of which the most spectacular are **Kandariya Mahadeva**, **Vishvanatha** and **Lakshmana**, all in the conglomeration known as the **Western Group** – was made possible by the soft fawn-coloured sandstone used in their construction. Considering the propensity of such stone to crumble, they have withstood the ravages of time remarkably well. Much of the ornate **sculpture** that adorns their walls is in such high relief as to be virtually three-dimensional, with strains of pink in the stone helping to imbue the figures with gentle flesh-like tones. The incredible skill of the artisans is evident throughout, with friezes as little as 10cm wide crammed with naturalistic details of ornaments, jewellery, hairstyles and even manicured nails. To add to the beauty of the whole ensemble, the temples subtly change hue as the day progresses, passing from a warm pink at sunrise, to white under the midday sun, and back to warm pink at sunset. Dramatic floodlights pick them out in the evening, and they glow white when the moon is out.

The sheer splendour of the temples rather overshadows **Khajuraho village**, where most local people live and which is increasing in hotels and trinket shops fed by the daily tourist invasion. However, if you stay a night or two, you'll discover a relaxed pace of life, especially in the evening when the local market and open-air restaurants create a very sociable atmosphere.

Arrival and information

The easiest way to get to Khajuraho is on one of the frequent Indian Airlines or Jet Airways **flights** from Delhi or Varanasi. The local **airport** is 5km south of the main square of Khajuraho village; a taxi ride in costs Rs100. The two nearest railheads are at **Jhansi** to the northwest (see p.303) and **Satna** to the southeast. All **buses** terminate less than 1km southeast of the main square at the bus station, within walking distance of most hotels; a cycle rickshaw will set you back Rs10, an auto-rickshaw Rs15.

The efficient India **Tourism office**, is on the main square (Mon–Sat 9.30am–6pm; ☏07686/272348), while the MP tourism office, in the Chandella Cultural Complex (Mon–Sat 10am–5pm; closed 2nd and 4th Sat of the month; ☏07686/274051), can book accommodation and car rental. There is also a brand-new **Tourist Facilitation Centre** next to the *Grand Temple View* hotel, which has tourist information offices and a range of other services for travellers. **Money** can be changed at the State Bank of India on the main square (Mon–Fri 10.30am–4.30pm, Sat 10.30am–1.30pm); it has an **ATM** opposite Shiv Sagar lake. There's a **post office** near the bus stand. **Internet facilities** (Rs40/hr) are available at *Raja Café* and around the Jain temples. Hotel touts can be a nuisance, though the most common **hassle** for tourists is being approached by children who offer to take you to visit their school or village, a visit that ends with demands for money. There's a **Tourist Police** booth on Main Road, if you have any serious problems.

Getting around

Khajuraho is an overgrown cluster of tiny villages, and has no public **transport**, so visitors are dependent on various rentable vehicles. **Taxis** and **cars** are available at the main square, through *Raja Café*, and from operators such as Sanjay Jain of *Hotel Jain*, Khajuraho Tours (℡07686/272343) in the Maqbara building, Tour Aids (℡07686/274060) in the Khandariya Art and Cultural Centre, and Travel Bureau (℡07686/274037), on Jain Temples Road. A taxi to Orchha costs around Rs1500, to Satna Rs1200 and to Panna National Park Rs1500; ignore requests from drivers for extortionate "road tolls" and firmly agree a price first. **Cycle rickshaw** drivers ask for around Rs40 per hour; trips to the Eastern or Southern groups from the main square are Rs40, and a tour of all the temples costs Rs100. **Auto-rickshaws** charge Rs150 for a half-day, or Rs250 for a full day of temple-spotting. With virtually empty roads, a **bicycle** is by far the most enjoyable way of getting around; Mohammad Bilal, on Jain Temples Road, charges Rs50 per day.

Among the recommended and highly experienced **guides** who can help you make sense of Khajuraho are Ganga, owner of the *Harmony* hotel; the reputable Mr D.S. Rajput, Mr Mama and Mr Chandel, all three of whom can be contacted through the *Raja Café*; and Raghuvir Singh, who can be contacted at the Tour Aids office. Guide rates are set by the government at Rs350 for one to five people for a half-day, Rs500 for a full day; there's a Rs180 surcharge for tours in languages other than Hindi and English.

Accommodation

For travellers coming from elsewhere in Madhya Pradesh, Khajuraho's **touts** and commission system can be a shock. Avoid going into **hotels** with taxi or auto-rickshaw drivers and be firm about where you want to stay. The sheer number of hotels means competition is fierce, standards high in all price ranges and substantial **discounts** can be negotiated, especially if you're staying several nights or visiting in the slow summer season.

Casa di William Just off Main Rd ℡07686/274244, @hotelcasediwilliam@hotmail.com. An easygoing establishment with a handful of keenly priced spick-and-span en suites: perfectly decent, but on the whole a little uninspiring. **③**

Chandela Airport Rd ℡07686/272355, @www.tajhotels.com. Sophisticated en-suite cottages (US$95–150) in eleven acres of neatly tended gardens, with all the hallmarks of the Taj Group: mini-golf, tennis and croquet, fitness centre, pool (Rs300 for non-guests), coffee shop, bar and two restaurants. **③–⑨**

Grand Temple View Main Rd ℡07686/272111, @www.thegrandhotels.net. If money is no object, this is the place to stay. Sumptuous rooms (from US$330) look out onto an enticing curvy pool and shaded groves of *mahua* trees. The spa treatments, however, are the real selling point, and include yoga, Ayurvedic and Thai massage, reflexology and meditation. Just make sure you squeeze in a visit to the temples as well. **⑨**

Harmony Jain Temples Rd ℡07686/274135, @www.hotelharmonyonline.com. The Mediterranean influence in the design lends an air of spaciousness to this hotel, which has a range of budget and mid-range rooms – each one airy and surgically clean – and a bird-filled courtyard. You can even sample "cornflakes and foot curd" at the restaurant. **②–⑤**

Jhankar By-Pass Rd ℡07686/274063, @jhankar@mptourism.com. Away from the tourist and tout scrum near the Western Group, this gleaming MP Tourism hotel is justifiably popular, particularly with Indian tourists. En-suite a/c doubles come with free breakfast, and the cubby-hole bar has a 20-percent-off happy hour (3pm–7pm) **⑤**

Payal Across the fields northeast of the centre ⊕07686/274064, ⓔpayal@mptourism.com. MP Tourism's cheaper option has drab standard rooms and better a/c doubles, with verandas opening out onto pleasant gardens. The adjacent campsite can be booked through reception. ④–⑤

Siddharth Opposite the Western Group ⊕07686/274627, ⓔhotelsiddharth@rediffmail.com. A respectable mid-range choice with amiable staff and appealing rooms, although the decor could do with a little jazzing up. The a/c deluxe double has wonderful temple views and the restaurant produces some of the best Indian food in town. ④–⑤

Surya Jain Temples Rd ⊕07686/274145, ⓦwww.hotelsuryakhajuraho.com. This efficiently run hotel has forty immaculate, variously priced rooms, a lush garden, yoga and massage sessions, and an alfresco eating area. ①–④

Yogi Lodge In a cul-de-sac between the row of shops behind *Raja Café* ⊕07686/274158, ⓔyogi_sharm@yahoo.com. While the pinkish rooms with attached bathrooms are somewhat austere, you can't argue with the price, particularly as it includes free yoga and meditation sessions. ①

Zen Jain Temples Rd ⊕07686/274228, ⓔoshozen62@hotmail.com. Good-value rooms around a peaceful Zen-influenced garden, complete with lotus pond. The pricier options are bigger and have more extravagant colour schemes. Bear in mind that if the owner asks you to join him for food in his home, you will be expected to pay. ②–⑤

The village

Facilities for visitors are concentrated in the uncluttered avenues of the small village of **Khajuraho**; the gates of the Western Group of temples open immediately onto its main square, which is surrounded by budget hotels, cafés and curio shops where you should brace yourself for some hard selling. If you aren't up to the haggling, head instead for the **Khandariya Art and Cultural Centre**, 1km south of the centre, an upmarket emporium offering quality goods at fixed price; in the same complex, an auditorium hosts evening dance shows (daily 7 & 8pm; Rs300). On the south side of the main square, the small **Archeological Museum** (daily except Fri 10am–5pm; Rs5) is principally noteworthy for a remarkable sculpture of a pot-bellied dancing Ganesh. The **Adivart State Museum of Tribal and Folk Art** in the Chandella Cultural Complex (Tues–Sat 10am–5pm; Rs50) has a small but interesting collection of paintings, sculptures and artwork by Madhya Pradesh's many tribal groups. Keep an eye out for the exquisitely carved wooden doors and delicate pieces of terracotta.

Khajuraho is transformed into a bustling epicentre during **Phalguna** (Feb/March), when the festival of **Maha Shivratri** draws pilgrims from all over the region to commemorate the marriage of Shiva; many believe Khajuraho's erotic sculptures represent the union of Shiva and Parvati. It also sees one of India's premier dance events, the **Khajuraho Festival of Dance** – a showcase for all forms of classical dance with some performances staged against the stunning backdrop of the Western Group (though most take place at the more prosaic Chandella Cultural Complex). Precise dates for the festival tend to be confirmed late, so check with Government of India tourist authorities, and book early. Tickets for specific events cost between Rs40 and Rs200.

The Western Group

Stranded like a fleet of stone ships amid pristine lawns and flowerbeds fringed with bougainvillea, the **Western Group** of temples (daily sunrise to sunset; Rs250 [Rs20]) is Khajuraho's prime attraction. With the exception of Matangesvara, just outside the main complex, all are now virtually devoid of religious significance, and only spring back to life during Shivratri (see above). Visitors must remove their shoes before entering individual temples. MP Tourism offers informative **audio tours** of the Western Group (Rs60 plus Rs500 deposit; 45min), which are available from any of their hotels, the tourist offices or at the temple booking office.

An excellent **son-et-lumière** show in the grounds of the Western Group uses Indian classical music and impressive coloured floodlighting to give ambience to the history of the temples, as narrated by the "master sculptor" (nightly English show: March–Oct 7.30pm; Nov–Feb 6.30pm; 50min; Rs300 [Rs50]).

Varaha

Just inside the complex a small open *mandapa* pavilion, built between the tenth and eleventh centuries, houses a huge, highly polished sandstone image of **Vishnu** as the boar – **Varaha**. Carved in low relief on its body, 674 figures in neat rows represent the major gods and goddesses of the Hindu pantheon. Lord of the earth, water and heaven, the alert boar straddles Shesha the serpent, accompanied by what T.S. Burt (see box, p.436) conjectured must have been the most beautiful form of **Prithvi**, the earth goddess – all that remains are her feet, and a hand on the neck of the boar. Above the image the lotus ceiling stands out in relief.

Lakshmana

Beyond Varaha, adjacent to the Matangesvara temple across the boundary wall, the richly-carved **Lakshmana** temple, dating from around 950 AD, is the oldest of the Western Group. It stands on a high plinth covered with processional friezes of horses, elephants and camels, as well as soldiers, domestic scenes, musicians and dancers. Among explicit sexual images is a man sodomizing a horse, flanked by shocked female onlookers. The sheer energy of the work gives the whole temple an astounding sense of movement and vitality.

While the plinth depicts the human world, the temple itself, the *adhisthana*, brings one into contact with the celestial realm. Two tiers of carved panels decorate its exterior, with gods and goddesses attended by *apsaras*, "celestial nymphs", and figures in complicated sexual acts on the lower tier and in the recesses. Fine detail includes a magnificent dancing Ganesh on the south face, a master architect with his students on the east, and heavenly musicians and dancers.

Successive pyramidal roofs over the *mandapa* and the porch rise to a clustered tower made of identical superimposed elements. Small porches with sloping eaves project from the *mandapa* and passageway, with exquisite columns, each with eight figures, at each corner of the platform supported by superb brackets in the form of *apsaras*. The inner sanctum, the *garbha griha*, is reached through a door whose lintel shows Vishnu's consort **Lakshmi**, accompanied by **Brahma** and **Shiva**; a frieze depicts the **Navagraha**, the nine planets. Inside, the main image is of Vishnu as the triple-headed, four-armed Vaikuntha, attended by his incarnations as boar and man-lion.

Kandariya Mahadeva

Sharing a common platform with other temples in the western corner of the enclosure, the majestic **Kandariya Mahadeva** temple, built between 1025 and 1050 AD, is the largest and most imposing of the Western Group. A perfect consummation of the five-part design instigated in Lakshmana and Vishvanatha, this Shiva temple represents the pinnacle of Chandellan art, its ornate roofs soaring dramatically to culminate 31m above the base in a *shikhara* that consists of 84 smaller replicas.

Kandariya Mahadeva is especially popular with visitors for the extraordinarily energetic and provocative erotica that ornaments its three tiers, covering almost every facet of the exterior. Admiring crowds can always be found in front of a particularly fine image of a couple locked in **mithuna** (sexual intercourse) with a maiden assisting on either side. One of Khajuraho's most familiar motifs, it

The erotic art of Khajuraho

Prurient eyes have been hypnotized by the unabashed **erotica** of Khajuraho ever since its "rediscovery" in February 1838. A young British officer of the Bengal Engineers, **T.S. Burt**, alerted by the talk of his *palki* (palanquin) bearers, had deviated from his official itinerary when he came upon the ancient temples all but engulfed by jungle – "They reared their sun-burnt tops above the huge trees by which they were surrounded, with all the pride of superior height and age. But the chances are, the trees (or jungle rather) will eventually have the best of it."

Frank representations of oral sex, masturbation, copulation with animals and such acts may have fitted into the mores of the tenth-century Chandellas, but, as Burt relates, were hardly calculated to meet with the approval of the upstanding officers of Queen Victoria:

I found . . . seven Hindoo temples, most beautifully and exquisitely carved as to workmanship, but the sculptor had at times allowed his subject to grow a little warmer than there was any absolute necessity for his doing; indeed some of the sculptures here were extremely indecent and offensive, which I was at first much surprised to find in temples that are professed to be erected for good purposes, and on account of religion... The palki bearers, however, appeared to take great delight at those, to them, very agreeable novelties, which they took care to point out to all present.

Burt found the inscription on the steps of the Vishvanatha temple that enabled historians to attribute the site to the Chandellas, and to piece together their genealogy, but it was several more years before Major General Sir Alexander Cunningham produced detailed plans of Khajuraho, drawing the distinction between "Western" and "Eastern" groups that is still applied today. For Cunningham, "All [the sculptures] are highly indecent, and most of them disgustingly obscene."

The erotic images remain the subject of a disproportionate amount of controversy and debate among academics and curious tourists alike. The task of explanation is made more difficult by the fact that even the Chandellas themselves barely mentioned the temples in their literature, and the very name "Khajuraho" may be misleading, simply taken from that of the nearby village.

Among attempts to account for the sexual content of the carvings have been suggestions of links with **Tantric** cults, which use sex as a pivotal part of worship. Some claim they were inspired by the **Kama Sutra**, and similarly intended to serve as a manual on love, while others argue that the sculptures were designed to entertain the gods, diverting their wrath and thus protecting the temples against natural calamities. Alternatively, the geometric qualities of certain images have been put forward as evidence that each represents a *yantra*, a pictorial form of a mantra, for use in meditation.

The sixteen large panels depicting sexual union that appear along the northern and southern aspects of the three principal temples – Kandariya Mahadeva, Lakshmana and Vishvanatha – are mostly concerned with the junction of the male and the female elements of the temples, the *mandapa* and the *garbha griha* (the "womb"). They might therefore have been intended as a visual pun, elaborated by artistic licence.

A radical new approach that ties history and architecture with living traditions has been proposed by Shobita Punja in her book *Divine Ecstasy*. Citing historic references to Khajuraho under the name of Shivpuri – the "City of Shiva" – she uses ancient Sanskrit texts to suggest that the dramatic temples and their celestial hordes represent the **marriage party of Shiva and Parvati**, taking place in a mythical landscape that stretches along the Vindhya hills to Kalinjar in the east. Thus Punja argues that the lower panel on Vishvanatha's southern walls shows Shiva as a bridegroom accompanied by his faithful bull, Nandi, while the intertwined limbs of the panel above – the couple locked in *mithuna*, assisted by a maiden to either side – show the consummation, with the lustful Brahma a pot-bellied voyeur at their feet.

seems to defy nature, with the male figure suspended upside down on his head; only when considered as if from above do the sinuous intertwined limbs begin to make sense.

An elaborate garland at the entrance to the temple, carved from a single stone, acts as a *torana*, the ritual gateway of a marriage procession. Both inside and out, lavish and intricate images of gods, goddesses, musicians and nymphs celebrate the occasion; within the sanctuary a dark passage leads to the *garbha griha* and its central *shivalingam*. Niches along the exterior contain images of **Ganesh**, **Virabhadra** and the **Sapta Matrikas**, the Seven Mothers responsible for dressing the bridegroom, Shiva. Wrathful deities and fearsome protectors, the seven consist of Brahmi, a female counterpart of Shiva, seated on the swan of Brahma; a three-eyed Maheshvari on Shiva's bull Nandi; Kumari; Vaishnavi, seated on the bird Garuda; Varahi, the female form of Vishnu as the boar; Narasimhi, the female form of Vishnu as man-lion; and the terrifying Chamunda, the slayer of the *asuras* or "demons" Chanda and Munda, and the only one of the Sapta Matrikas who is not a female representation of a major male god.

Devi Jagadambi

North of Kandariya Mahadeva along the platform, the earlier **Devi Jagadambi** temple is a simpler structure, whose outer walls lack projecting balconies. Originally dedicated to Vishnu, its prominent *mandapa* is capped by a massive pyramidal roof. Three *bhandas* (belts) bind the *jangha* (body), adorned with exquisite and sensuous carvings; the erotica on the third is arguably the finest in Khajuraho. Vishnu appears throughout the panels, all decorated with sinuous figures of nymphs, gods and goddesses, some in amorous embrace. Some consider the image in the temple sanctum to be a standing Parvati, others argue that it is the black goddess Kali, known here as Jagadambi.

Between Kandariya Mahadeva and Jagadambi, the remains of **Mahadeva** temple shelter a metre-high lion accompanied by a figure of indeterminate sex. Recurring throughout Khajuraho, the highly stylized lion motif, seen here rearing itself over a kneeling warrior with drawn sword, may have been an emblem of the Chandellas.

Chitragupta

Beyond the platform, and similar to its southern neighbour, Jagadambi, the heavily (and in places clumsily) restored **Chitragupta** temple is unusual in being dedicated to **Surya**, the sun god. Ornate depictions of hunting scenes, nymphs and dancing girls accompany processional friezes, while on the southern aspect a particularly vigorous ten-headed Vishnu embodies all his ten incarnations. Within the inner chamber, the fiery Surya rides a chariot driven by seven horses. The small and relatively insignificant temple in front of Chitragupta, also heavily restored and now known as **Parvati**, may originally have been a Vishnu temple, but holds an interesting image of the goddess Ganga riding on a crocodile.

Vishvanatha

Laid out along the same lines as Lakshmana, **Vishvanatha**, in the northeast corner of the enclosure – the third of the three main Western Group shrines – can be precisely dated to 1002 AD as the work of the ruler Dhangadeva. Unlike some other temples at Khajuraho, which may have changed their presiding deities, Vishvanatha is most definitely a Shiva temple, as confirmed by the open *mandapa* pavilion in front of the main temple, where a monolithic seated **Nandi** waits obediently. Large panels between the balconies once more show *mithuna*, with amorous couples embracing among the sensuous nymphs.

Idealized representations of the female form include women in such poses as writing letters, playing music and cuddling babies. Decorative elephant motifs appear to the south of Vishvanatha, and lions guard its northern aspect.

Matangesvara

The simplicity of the **Matangesvara** temple, outside the complex gates, shows it to be one of Khajuraho's oldest structures, but although built early in the tenth century it remains in everyday use. Deep balconies project from the walls of its circular sanctuary, inside which a pillar-like *shivalingam* emerges from the pedestal yoni, the vulva – the recurring symbol of the union of Shiva. During the annual festival of Shivratri, the great wedding of Shiva and Parvati, the shrine becomes a hive of activity, drawing pilgrims for ceremonies that hark back to Khajuraho's distant past.

Chausath Yogini

Southwest of Shiv Sagar lie the remains of the curious temple of **Chausath Yogini** – the "Sixty-Four Yoginis". Dating from the ninth century, it consists of 35 small granite shrines clustered around a quadrangle; there were originally 64 shrines, with the presiding goddess's temple at the centre. Only fourteen other temples, all in northern India, are known to have been dedicated to these wrathful and bloodthirsty female attendants of the goddess Kali. Around 1km further west lie the ruins of Lalguan Mahadev, a small temple dedicated to Shiva.

The Eastern Group

The two separate networks of temples that make up Cunningham's **Eastern Group** (daily sunrise to sunset) are reached via the two forks of the road east of town. One is the tightly clustered **Jain Group**, while slightly north there are a number of shrines and two larger temples, **Vamana** and **Javari**, both dating from the late eleventh century.

On the north side of Jain Temples Road a more modern temple is home to a two-metre-high image of the monkey god **Hanuman** that may predate all of Khajuraho's temples and shrines. As the road forks left along the eastern shore of the murky Khajur Sagar lake, at the edge of Khajuraho village, it passes the remains of a single-room temple erroneously referred to as the **Brahma** temple. Often considered to be a Vishnu temple, it is in fact a shrine to Shiva, as demonstrated by its *chaturmukha* – "four-faced" – lingam. While the eastern and western faces carry benign expressions, and the north face bears the gentler aspect of Uma, the female manifestation of Shiva, the ferocious southern face is surrounded by images of death and destruction. Crowning the lingam is the rounded form of **Sadashiva**, Shiva the Infinite at the centre of the cosmos.

The dirt road continues to the small **Javari** temple. It may not have the exuberance seen elsewhere but nevertheless contains some fine sculpture, including nymphets in classic Khajuraho style.

The largest of the Khajuraho village temples, **Vamana**, stands alone in a field 200m further north. Erected slightly earlier than Javari, in a fully evolved Chandella style, Vamana has a simple uncluttered *shikhara* that rises in bands covered with arch-like motifs. Figures including seductive celestial nymphs form two bands around the *jangha*, the body of the temple, while a superb doorway leads to the inner sanctum, which is dedicated to Vamana, an incarnation of Vishnu. On the way to the Jain Group, the road runs near what survives of a late tenth-century temple, known as **Ghantai** for its fine columns sporting bells (*ghantai*), garlands and other motifs.

The temple of **Parsvanath**, dominating the walled enclosure of the **Jain Group**, is probably older than the main temples of Khajuraho, judging by its relatively simple ground plan. Its origins are a mystery; although officially classified as a Jain monument, and jointly administered by the Archeological Survey and the Jain community, it may have been a Hindu temple that was donated to the Jains, who settled here at a later date. Certainly, the animated sculpture of Khajuraho's other Hindu temples is well represented on the two horizontal bands around the walls, and the upper one is crowded with Hindu gods in intimate entanglements. Among Khajuraho's finest work, they include Brahma and his consort; a beautiful Vishnu; a rare image of the god of love, **Kama**, shown with his quiver of flower arrows embracing his consort **Rati**; and two graceful female figures, one applying kohl to her eyes and another removing a thorn from her foot. A narrow strip above the two main bands depicts celestial musicians (*gandharvas*) playing cymbals, drums, stringed instruments and flutes. Inside, beyond an ornate hall, a black monolithic stone is dedicated to the Jain lord Parsvanath, inaugurated as recently as 1860 to replace an image of another *tirthankara*, Adinath.

Immediately north of Parsvanath, **Adinath**'s own temple, similar but smaller, has undergone drastic renovation. Three tiers of sculpture surround its original structure, of which only the sanctum, *shikhara* and vestibule survive; the incongruous *mandapa* is a much later addition. Inside the *garbha griha* stands the black image of the *tirthankara* Adinath himself. The huge 4.5-metre-high statue of the sixteenth *tirthankara*, **Shantinath**, in his newer temple, is the most important image in this working Jain complex. With its slender beehive *shikharas*, the temple attracts pilgrims from all over India, including naked sadhus.

Sculpture in the small circular **Jain Museum** (Mon–Sat 7am–6pm; Rs5), at the entrance to the Jain temples, includes stone carvings of all twenty-four *tirthankaras*.

The Southern Group

Khajuraho's **Southern Group** consists of three widely separated temples. The nearest to town, **Duladeo**, is down a dirt track south of the Jain Group, 1.5km from the main square. Built early in the twelfth century, Duladeo bears witness to the decline of temple architecture in the late Chandellan period, noticeable above all in its sculpture, which lacks Khajuraho's hallmark fluidity. Nonetheless, its main hall does contain some exquisite carving, and the angular rippled exterior of the main temple is unique to Khajuraho.

Across the Khodar stream and south along Airport Road, a small road leads left to the disproportionately tall, tapering **Chaturbhuj** – the *shikhara* is visible for miles above the trees. A forerunner to Duladeo, built around 1100 AD and bearing some resemblance to the Javari temple of the Eastern Group, Chaturbhuj is plainer than Duladeo and devoid of erotica. A remarkable 2.7-metre-high image of Vishnu graces its inner sanctum.

To reach the third temple, **Bija Math**, return to the cluster of houses before Chaturbhuj and take a right along the dirt track through the hamlet. The structure lay below a suspiciously large mound of mud (*tela*) until 1998, when the ASI undertook an excavation project and discovered the delicately carved platform. Unfortunately, the temple itself has disintegrated into the debris of ornate sculpture lying strewn around the site. You can go and watch the archeologists at work, patiently brushing the mud away to reveal parading elephants, intertwined lovers and rearing horses.

Eating

Khajuraho has an abundance of **restaurants**, from simple and cheap rice and *sabzi* joints to sophisticated and expensive multi-cuisine and Italian places. At the top of the range, hotels like *Chandela, Holiday Inn, Jass Trident* and *Grand Temple View* offer fine dining for very reasonable prices. Note that many rooftop restaurants erroneously claim you can see the evening sound-and-light shows from their establishments – what you actually get are occasional flashes of light and muffled voices.

Bella Italia Jain Temples Rd. A fine – and more economical – alternative to *Mediterraneo* (see below) for home-made pizzas, pastas, hygienically prepared salads and crepes. During the early evening, hundreds of parrots congregate in the trees opposite to make an almighty racket, before settling down for the night around 8pm. Mains Rs95–190.

Blue Sky Main Rd. This rooftop restaurant offers a unique experience: a table in a treehouse high above the other diners (just ring the bell for service). Even if you don't have a head for heights, the thalis, Chinese meals and decent stabs at gnocchi and risotto make it worth a visit. The refreshing *jeevan rakshak ghol* (mineral water, lime juice, sugar and salt) is hard to beat on a hot day. Mains Rs45–130.

German Bakery Main Rd. A tiny shop-front, with four plastic stools, a rickety table and tempting home-baked croissants, *pain au chocolat*, rolls, cookies and brownies all for around Rs10–30, plus it does filter coffee. Those with more adventurous palates can try the Nepalese yak's-milk cheese sandwiches.

Lotus Jain Temples Rd. Relaxed rooftop eatery with bright red tablecloths, good breakfast options like *aloo paratha*, and Indian and Chinese staples for later on. Mains Rs60–150.

Madras Coffee House Jain Temples Rd. Straightforward canteen serving south Indian food like *dosas*, *vadas* and *uttapams* at (more expensive) north Indian prices (Rs30–80).

Mediterraneo Jain Temples Rd ☏07686/272246. Authentic thin-crust pizzas from a wood-fired oven, homemade pasta, home-baked brown bread with their own marmalade, chocolate cake, muffins and unparalleled cappuccinos make the delightful *Mediterraneo* the top joint in town. Bookings advised. Mains Rs150–260.

Paradise Airport Rd. Typical pancake and non-spicy thali menu (Rs35–100), with little tables and lanterns on a roof terrace that overlooks the waterlily-covered Shiv Sagar lake.

Raja Café Main Square. Khajuraho's buzzing one-stop shop: as well as offering official guides, Internet access and a bookstore, *Raja* also does a good line in rostis, stroganoff, goulash and the ever-popular southern fried chicken, as well as Indian and Chinese options and cold beer. Mains Rs60–100.

Safari Jain Temples Rd. Travellers' hangout, serving chicken and chips, extensive breakfasts, and a big range of lassis to the strains of Bob Marley. Mains Rs50–100.

Moving on from Khajuraho

There are six daily private **buses** to Jhansi (4hr), 174km west, as well as three slower public buses (5–6hr). There are regular services to Gwalior, daily buses to Agra (8hr) and Bhopal (12hr), and three weekly to Varanasi (14hr). You will need to catch the 11am service to Jhansi to connect with night trains north and express services running to Delhi and Agra, or Bhopal and Mumbai. The super-fast a/c Shatabdi Express #2001 **train** via Gwalior and Agra to Delhi departs from Jhansi at 5.56pm. Most hotels display bus and train timetables.

There are three daily buses to Satna (3hr 30min–4hr), 125km east, which is served by trains on the Mumbai–Varanasi–Kolkata network, as well as to **Gorakhpur**, from where buses head for the Nepal border. If you're heading to **Varanasi**, 415km east, either take the 4.30pm overnight bus from Khajuraho, or expect a long wait in Satna: night trains (8hr) leave daily at 7.50pm, while the daily morning departure (7–8hr) leaves at 7.05am. The best train for Jabalpur is the Mahanagiri Express #1094, which leaves Satna daily at 5.55pm (3hr). An alternative route to Varanasi is to take one of the eleven daily buses north to Mahoba (first bus 6am, last 10.30pm; 3hr), from where the Bundelkhand Express #1107 train to Varanasi departs at 10.35pm (12hr).

There is a computerized **train booking office** at the bus stand (daily 9am–noon & 2–4pm), which saves the long queues in Jhansi, Mahoba or Satna.

Indian Airlines (office ☎07686/274035; airport ☎07686/274036) has six **flights** a week to Varanasi (US$140) and three to Delhi (US$180). Jet Airways (airport ☎07686/274407) flies daily to Delhi via Varanasi. There are fewer services in the monsoon season. Flights can be heavily booked, and note that with a late reservation you may be promised a confirmation, but can only be sure of a place on the flight at the airport, shortly before departure; allow a little leeway in case your flight is delayed.

For more on transport from Khajuraho, see "Travel details" on p.474.

Panna National Park

Panna National Park (Nov to end June 6.30–10.30am & 2.30–4pm; Rs2000 [Rs500] per vehicle with up to eight people per safari, compulsory guide Rs150 per safari, elephant ride Rs600 [Rs100]), 26km southeast of Khajuraho, is a quiet alternative to Madhya Pradesh's more popular tiger reserves. Although tigers are the main draw – sightings are common – the 543-square-kilometre park also has wolves, sloth bears, pythons and 200 species of bird. There's an **Interpretation Centre** (daily 6am–6pm; Rs50 [Rs5]) 2km west of the park gate. A **car** and driver for the 37km journey from Khajuraho costs Rs700 one way, Rs1800 day-trip. Alternatively, catch a **bus** from Khajuraho to Madla, and then a shared Jeep to the park. *Ken River Lodge* (☎07732/275235, ⓦwww .kenriverlodge.com; ❽), has rustic **huts** with concrete bathrooms and small dressing rooms as well as smarter cottages in thirty acres of grounds beside the Ken River. The lodge offers a "Jungle Plan" deal (US$100 for two), which includes accommodation, meals and safaris.

Eastern Madhya Pradesh

The so-called "tribal belt" of **eastern Madhya Pradesh**, homeland of the Gond and Barga *adivasi* minorities, holds few historic sites of note but is justifiably famous for the **Kanha**, **Bandhavgarh** and **Pench** reserves. In the few remaining fragments of a forest that, until 150 years ago, extended right across central India, the parks are among the last strongholds for many endangered species of birds and mammals, including the **tiger** – reason enough for thousands of visitors each year to make the long journey across the area's rolling terraced plains.

Two major **rail networks** cut through the region. The **Central Railway** heads straight through the Narmada Valley from Bhopal to Jabalpur, the spring-board for Kanha National Park, before veering north to Satna (4hr from Khajuraho) and the Gangetic plains. The other main route, traced by the **Southeastern Railway**, skirts the top of Bastar district (the remote and poor southern extension of the state, dovetailing with Maharashtra, Andhra Pradesh

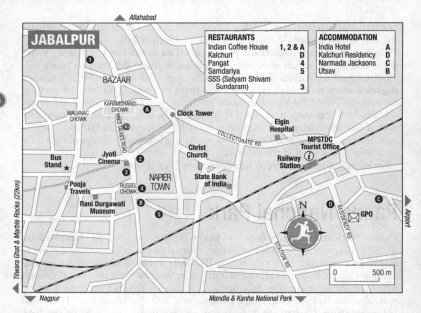

RESTAURANTS		ACCOMMODATION	
Indian Coffee House	1, 2 & A	India Hotel	A
Kalchuri	D	Kalchuri Residency	D
Pangat	4	Narmada Jacksons	C
Samdariya	5	Utsav	B
SSS (Satyam Shivam Sundaram)	3		

and Orissa), passing through the grim industrial cities of Raipur and Bilaspur at the head of the Chhattisgarh Valley.

Jabalpur and around

After running in tandem across an endless expanse of wheat fields and tribal villages, the main Kolkata (Calcutta) to Mumbai road and train lines converge on eastern Madhya Pradesh's largest city. Though an important provincial capital, **JABALPUR**, 330km east of Bhopal, harbours little of interest, and is only really worth visiting en route to the **Marble Rocks**, gouged by the River Narmada nearby, or to the national parks and tiger reserves, Kanha, Bandhavgarh and Pench, all half a day's journey away.

If you do have some time to kill in Jabalpur, jump in an auto-rickshaw to the **Rani Durgawati Museum** (daily except Mon 10am–5pm; Rs30 [Rs5], camera Rs20, video Rs50), about 2km west of the railway station, which houses a predictable assortment of ancient temple sculpture, bronze plates and seals recording regional dynastic histories. It also boasts a better-than-average display on the state's *adivasi* minorities. Three kilometres further west in the direction of the Marble Rocks, the main highway skirts a large moraine of enormous granite boulders, on the top of which stand the ruins of the **Madan Mahal** – a fortress-cum-pleasure-palace built by the Gond ruler Madan Shah in 1116. Another kilometre west, you reach an impressive bridge spanning the River Narmada. Known locally as **Tilwara Ghat**, the handful of shrines near the water's edge below marks one of the sacred places where Mahatma Gandhi's ashes were scattered.

Arrival and information

Central Railway trains arrive at Jabalpur's **railway station**, 2km east of the centre. From here, it's a five-minute auto-rickshaw ride (Rs30) into town. The shambolic city **bus stand** is more in the thick of things, a short way south of the bazaar and west of Naudra Bridge, site of several cheaper hotels.

MP Tourism's **information office** is inside the main arrivals hall at the railway station (daily 10am–5pm; ✆0761/267 7690), provides the usual range of hand-outs and runs a bus **tour** (10am–6pm; Rs200) of the city's sights and the Marble Rocks. The **post office** is a five-minute walk south of the railway station. If you need to **change money** (there are no exchange facilities in the reserves), you can cash traveller's cheques at the State Bank of India, just under 1km west of the railway station, or at the *Rishi Regency* hotel opposite, which has a 24-hour exchange counter.

Jabalpur teems with **auto-** and **cycle rickshaws**, while the rarer Ambassador taxis can usually be found on Russel Chowk in front of the *Samdariya* hotel. Vehicles for day-trips can be rented through the top hotels (from Rs800/day). The dilapidated **tempos** and **minibuses** that chug through the centre of town serve outlying suburbs and are only useful for travelling to the Marble Rocks. The Cyber Junction offers **Internet** access in the comfort of (someone else's) home for Rs20/hr.

Accommodation

The majority of Jabalpur's **hotels** are within easy reach of the bus stand – handy for early departures to Kanha. Watch out for "luxury taxes" and "service charges" levied by the pricier places.

India Near Karamchand Chowk ✆0761/248 0093, ✉icwcsltdjbp@rediffmail.com. Owned by the cooperative society behind the *Indian Coffee Houses* – and run with the same quiet professionalism – this hotel has well-appointed, clean en suites. So new, the chairs are still covered in plastic. ④–⑤

Kalchuri Residency Residency Rd ✆0761/267 8491, ✉kalchuri@mptourism.com. MP Tourism's welcoming hotel, around the corner from the railway station, has care-worn but amply sized a/c rooms and an appealing restaurant–bar. ⑤

Narmada Jacksons Civil Lines ✆0761/400 1122, ✉info@narmadajacksons.com. Bijou heritage hotel with centrally a/c modern rooms, an inviting pool and the finest bar in Jabalpur. ⑦–⑧

Utsav Russel Chowk ✆0761/401 7269, ☜www.hotelutsav.com. Keenly priced, if grungy, rooms with attached bathrooms and over a hundred cable TV channels. The hotel, bang in the centre of town, is on the corner of a busy junction, so bring earplugs. ②–④

Eating

Indian Coffee Houses Bazaar district, opposite Jyoti Cinema and in the *India* hotel. Each branch serves wallet-friendly south Indian breakfasts, snacks and meals (Rs15–70) with the minimum of fuss. The one in *India* is smarter than average, with funky black-leather chairs and glass walls.

Kalchuri Residency *Kalchuri Residency* hotel. While the usual MP Tourism menu – standard meat, veg and Chinese dishes from Rs50–100 – is unlikely to generate too much excitement, *Kalchuri* is a good place for a cold beer in the evening.

The Options Vined Talkies Rd. Fashionable a/c joint with frosted-glass-shaded booths, bow-tied waiters and an enticing bar area; sadly it only serves "mocktails". The veg sizzlers, pizzas and Indian snacks (Rs30–60) are all good choices.

Pangat *Shikhar Palace* hotel, Russel Chowk. With orange walls, multicoloured cube-shaped lights and gold-flecked plastic tablecloths, it's perhaps fortunate this a/c restaurant is dimly lit. The food, by contrast, is reassuringly straightforward, with well-prepared pure-veg north Indian and Chinese dishes (Rs30–75).

Samdariya *Samdariya* hotel, just off Russel Chowk. Hotel restaurant with attentive service and quality veg food such as *aloo palak* (Rs40–80); the Chinese *paneer* dishes however, are a fusion step too far. A western-style coffee shop also does delicious south Indian favourites.

SSS (Satyam Shivam Sundaram) Near Jyoti Cinema, Naudra Bridge. Understated local pure-veg favourite for its superior thalis, wide range of dhals and specials like mushroom curry, all at unbeatable prices (Rs28–50).

Moving on from Jabalpur

Kanha National Park is most travellers' next stop after Jabalpur. Direct state **buses** leave three times daily (7am, 11am and noon, returning 6am, 8am and 1pm; 5–7hr) from the central bus stand for the main gate at Kisli; the first buses of the day are invariably the quickest. Buses to Mandla, halfway to the park, leave hourly. Bandhavgarh is harder to reach; you need to catch a train (4–6 daily; 1hr 20min) or bus (hourly; 2hr) to Murwara, then travel down the Eastern Railway line to Umaria, where you can pick up a local bus to the park gate.

To get to **Khajuraho**, there are several daily **trains** to Satna (3hr), from where you can pick up direct state buses. **Varanasi** is on the main Mumbai–Kolkata (Calcutta) line; aim for the Varanasi Express #2165 (Mon, Thurs and Fri; departs 9.20pm, arrives 8am), as the other services leave in the early hours or entail a long day journey. Daily trains from Jabalpur to Patna help travellers en route to **Nepal**.

Of the five or six daily **express trains** to Mumbai, the Howrah–Mumbai Mail #2321 is the most convenient (departs 5.50pm, arrives 11.25am). For Delhi, take the daily Gondwana Express #2411 (departs 3.55pm, arrives 7.15am) or the daily all-a/c Jan Shatabdi Express #2062 (departs 6am, arrives Bhopal 11.35am) and then catch the 2.40pm Shatabdi Express #2001 to Delhi (daily except Fri: departs 2.40pm, arrives 10.30pm; Fri departs 2.55pm, arrives 11.05pm). There are 1–2 daily trains to Chennai (23hr 45min–32hr). Pooja Travels (T0761/261 0118), run by the obliging Mr Jain, is a reputable agency with **cars** (and drivers) for hire; a journey to Kanha costs around Rs2000. Budget carrier Kingfisher Airlines (T1800/233 3131) has a daily **flight** to Indore.

For more on transport from Jabalpur, see "Travel details on p.473.

The Marble Rocks

In a bustling, dusty, Oriental land, the charm of coolness and quiet belonging to these pure cold rocks, and deep and blue yet pellucid waters, is almost entrancing.

Captain J. Forsyth, *The Highlands of Central India* (1889)

West of Jabalpur, the Narmada River suddenly narrows, plunges over a series of dramatic waterfalls, then squeezes through a seam of milky white marble before continuing on its westward course across the Deccan. The thirty-metre cliffs and globulous shapes worn by the water out of the rock may not exactly rank as one of the seven wonders of the natural world, but the **Marble Rocks**, known locally as Bheraghat, are as good a place as any to while away an idle afternoon.

BHERAGHAT village itself, overlooking the gorge, is a sleepy little place, with few signs of activity beyond the ringing of chisels in the workshops of its many **marble-carvers**. Most pieces on display in the shop fronts are heavy-duty Hanumans, *shivalingams* and other deities, destined for sites around India – the local translucent white marble is much in demand for new temples and shrines.

From the main street, a flight of steps leads down to the river and the **ghats**, where **rowing boats** (Rs20 per head on a shared basis) are on hand to ferry visitors up the gorge, although these don't run during the monsoon (July to mid-Oct). Trips take thirty to forty minutes, depending on the water level (if the dams upstream are open, the current can be too strong for boats to pass), though you're more likely to spend at least that long waiting for a minimum of fifteen passengers to show up. Avoid the boatmen who try and squeeze in twenty-five: the boats are old and are theoretically designed only for ten people.

Once underway, the boatman begins his spiel, in Hindi, pointing out the more interesting **rock formations**. The most appreciative noises from the other passengers are not reserved for the "footprint of the celestial elephant", however, or even the "monkey's leap" (jumped over by Hanuman on his way to Lanka), but for the places where Bollywood movie-stars posed in well-known films shot on location here. Look out for the enormous **bees' nests** dangling from the crevices in the rock. One nineteenth-century guidebook urged its readers to refrain from "smoking or firing guns" in the gorge, as an angry swarm once attacked a party of English army engineers who were carrying out survey work for a new railway here. A memorial plaque, still visible on top of the cliffs, was erected to one of their number who drowned trying to shake the bees off. The formations are floodlit after dark.

Bheraghat is also something of a **religious site**. From the fork in the river, 107 stone steps lead up to the tenth-century **Mandapur temple**, a circular building known for the 64 beautifully carved Tantric goddesses, or Chausath Yogini, which stand in its enclosure. Beyond the temple, at the far end of the gorge, the Dhuandhar, or "Smoke Cascade" waterfall, is particularly dramatic when shrouded in spray after the monsoons. It's reached either by following the main street out through the village, or else via the goat-track that twists along the top of the cliffs below the MP Tourism motel. Just above the waterfall, you pass a string of stalls loaded with locally carved marble goods.

Practicalities

Getting to Bheraghat from Jabalpur involves picking up a **tempo** (Rs10) from the bus stand next to the museum. The 45-minute stop-and-start trip on a *tempo* can be excruciating; you need to clamber off when you see a row of cold drink and souvenir stalls lining a sharp left-hand bend in the main street. Auto-rickshaws (Rs350 return) can be negotiated anywhere in Jabalpur, or a private taxi can be arranged in any of the hotels or at Pooja Travels (see above), for Rs500.

If you want to **stay** the night, head for the pleasant MP Tourism's *Motel Marble Rocks* (℡0761/283 0424, ✉mmr@mptourism.com; ❹–❺), a converted colonial bungalow just off the road out to the falls, complete with veranda, well-kept lawn and easy chairs. The garden looks out over the gorge and a small **restaurant** serves a standard veg and non-veg menu. The only other option is at the slightly cheaper *Shagun Resort* (℡0761/329 6061; ❸–❹), a motley collection of little huts, each with a veranda, air-cooler and attached bath, in a scrubby garden opposite the brightly painted Jain temple on the main street (sign in Hindi). There is a basic veg restaurant in the garden, if you don't mind being surrounded by adolescent couples escaping here for some privacy.

From Jabalpur to Kanha

From Jabalpur, the bone-shaking journey to Kanha takes you into some of eastern Madhya Pradesh's most isolated rural districts. When Captain J. Forsyth and his Bengal Lancers pushed through en route to the uncharted interior at the end of the nineteenth century, this landscape was a virtually unbroken tract of *sal* forest teeming with Indian bison, deer and tigers. Since then, the local Barga tribals have taken up the plough, and all but a few patches of forest clinging to the ridges of nearby hillsides have been logged, cleared for farmland or simply burned as firewood by the burgeoning populations of sharecroppers.

The only major town en route to Kanha is **MANDLA**, worth a brief pause to visit the sacred confluence of **Triveni Sangam**, at the bottom of town beyond the bazaar. Said to form the shape of the auspicious "Om" symbol, it's a magical spot, distinguished by a couple of temples (among them one with oddly tapering towers dedicated to Rama). If you're rushing through en route to Kanha, note that the last bus to the park departs at 4.15pm. Heading in the opposite direction, buses to Jabalpur leave every thirty minutes throughout the day. The State Bank of India will exchange cash only, and is the nearest place to Kanha with this facility.

Kanha National Park

Widely considered the greatest of India's wildlife reserves, **KANHA NATIONAL PARK** encompasses some 940 square kilometres of deciduous forest, savannah grassland, hills and gently meandering rivers – home to hundreds of species of birds and animals, including **tigers**. Despite the arduous overland haul to the park, few travellers are disappointed by its beauty, particularly striking at dawn. Tiger sightings are not guaranteed but even a fleeting glimpse of one of the big cats should be considered a great privilege. Moreover the wealth of other creatures and some of central India's most quintessentially Kiplingesque countryside make it a wonderful place to spend a few days.

Central portions of the Kanha Valley were designated a wildlife sanctuary as long ago as 1933. Prior to this, the whole area was one enormous viceregal hunting ground, its game the exclusive preserve of high-ranking British army officers and civil servants seeking trophies for their colonial bungalows. Not until the 1950s though, after a particularly voracious hunter bagged thirty tigers in a single shoot, did the government declare Kanha a bona fide national park. Kanha was one of the original participants in Indira Gandhi's **Project Tiger** (see p.1377), which helped numbers recover. The forest department claims figures in excess of 130 tigers, but guides and naturalists say 50 is a more accurate estimate (for most of India's tiger reserves, halving the official figures will generally give you a more realistic idea). As part of a long-term project, the park has expanded to encompass a large protective buffer zone – a move not without its opponents among the local tribal community, who depend on the forest for food and firewood. Over the years, the authorities have had a hard time reconciling the needs of the villagers with the demands of conservation and tourism; but for the time being at least, an equitable balance seems to have been struck.

However, serious challenges remain: in recent years **poaching** has become a serious problem again and traps have even been discovered in the park's "tourist zone" (the area frequented by safaris). Illegal timber felling is also problematic, the buffer zone is increasingly being encroached upon and there is little effort to check the growth of new hotels – by contrast, at the time of writing, there were plans to open a third gate at the park, which would only fuel further development.

The park

From the main gates, at **Kisli**, in the west, and **Mukki**, 35km away in the south, a complex network of motorable dirt tracks fans out across the park, taking in a good cross-section of its diverse terrain. Which animals you see from your open-top Jeep largely depends on where your guide decides to take you. Kanha is perhaps best known for the broad sweeps of grassy rolling meadows, or

maidans, along its river valleys, which support large concentrations of deer. The park has several different species, including the endangered "twelve-horned" **barasingha** (swamp deer), plucked from the verge of extinction in the 1960s. The ubiquitous **chital** (spotted deer – the staple diet of Kanha's tigers) congregates in especially large numbers during the rutting season in early July, when it's not uncommon to see around four thousand at one time.

The **woodlands** carpeting the spurs of the Maikal Ridge that taper into the core zone from the south consists of *sal*, teak and moist deciduous forest oddly reminiscent of northern Europe. Troupes of black-faced langur monkeys crash through the canopy, while **gaur**, the world's largest wild cattle, forage through the fallen leaves. Years of exposure to snap-happy humans seem to have left the awesome, hump-backed bulls impervious to camera flashes, but it's still wise to keep a safe distance. Higher up, you may catch sight of a **dhol** (wild dog) as well as porcupines, pythons, sloth bears, wild boar, mouse deer or the magnificent **sambar** – the latter a favourite snack for the nocturnal predators that prowl through the trees. You might even spot a **leopard**, although these shy animals tend to steer well clear of motor vehicles. Kanha also supports an exotic and colourful array of **birds**, including Indian rollers, bee-eaters, golden orioles, paradise flycatchers, egrets, some outlandish **hornbills** and numerous kingfishers and birds of prey.

Kanha's **tigers**, though, are its biggest draw, and the Jeep drivers, who are well aware of this, scan the sandy tracks for pug marks and respond to the agitated alarm calls of nearby animals. Tigers are often spotted via a "tiger show" (Rs600 [Rs100]): when a tiger is spotted sleeping or sitting, trained elephants wait nearby and visitors disembark from their Jeeps to take a short elephant ride to see the big cat. Some, however, find the experience a little contrived. If you're intent on **seeing a tiger**, plan on spending three nights at the park and taking around five excursions; the cats are most often spotted lounging among camouflaging brakes of bamboo or in the tall elephant grass lining streams and waterholes.

Park practicalities

Kanha is **open** (6am–noon & 3–5.30pm (Rs2000 [Rs500] per vehicle with up to eight people per safari, Rs12,0000 [Rs1600] per vehicle with between nine and 32 people per safari, compulsory guide Rs150 per safari) from November 1 until the monsoon arrives at the end of June. During peak season (Nov–Feb), the nights and early mornings can get very **cold**, and there are frequent frosts, so bring warm clothing. The heat between March and June keeps visitor numbers down, but tiger sightings are more common then, when the cats are forced to come out to the waterholes and streams.

The most straightforward way to **get to Kanha** is via Jabalpur, which is well connected by **rail** to most other parts of the country. If you're coming from **Orissa**, take a direct train to Katni on the main Mumbai–Kolkata (Calcutta) line and change onto one of the many southbound services such as the Howrah–Mumbai mail #2321 (daily 4.20pm; 1hr 20min) to Jabalpur, the park's nearest railhead. The nearest airports with scheduled domestic flights are at Jabalpur and Nagpur, 226km away. Daily **buses** leave Jabalpur for **Kisli** (via Mandla) at 7am, 11am and noon (5–7hr). Both stop briefly at the barrier in **Khatia**, 4km down the road from Kisli; you must register with the park office here. Buses back to Jabalpur leave Khatia at 6am, 8am and 1pm. There's also a daily bus to and from Nagpur (6hr 30min). You can arrange to visit the park by car (around Rs2500 for the round trip from Jabalpur, with a night halt) via the MP Tourism office in Jabalpur (see p.443).

If you're not staying on a "Jungle Plan" package, which includes accommo-dation, food and safaris, you will have to hire an open-top Jeep – or "Gypsy" – (around Rs14/km; in a day you can expect to cover 50–70km, spread over a morning and an afternoon safari) to **get around the park**. These are available through most hotels, private operators in Khatia or at the main gates: try and get a group together and book at least a day in advance. Jeeps can comfortably sit four people (excluding guides/driver), although you can squeeze on eight at a push. There are plans to introduce minibuses seating up to 32 people, although this experience is unlikely to compare to that in a Jeep. Given the increasing popularity of Kanha – and Madhya Pradesh's other tiger reserves – vehicle restrictions may be introduced in the not too distant future. Walking inside the park is strictly forbidden – a park worker, on foot, was killed by a tiger in December 2007 – but you can ask at the gates about arranging an evening **elephant ride**.

Accommodation and eating

MP Tourism has two **lodges** in **Kisli**, atmospherically situated inside the park proper, and one close to **Mukki** gate. Private hotels outside the west gate, in and around the village of **Khatia**, range from walk-in budget lodges to five-star resorts, those close to Mukki are largely high-end places; all should be booked at least five days in advance (and up to three months in the high season). However, at any hotel it's worth asking about possible discounts; if the hotel is having a lean patch they may negotiate a good reduction.

The Khatia hotels are scattered along a six-kilometre stretch of road that sees very little traffic during the day, so make sure you are dropped off at the right place. To reach the Mukki hotels from Khatia, you will require your own transport or a pick-up. Avoid visiting during **Indian holidays** like Diwali and Holi, when hotels are packed and park fees double.

Baghira Log Huts/Tourist Hostel Kisli
☎07649/277227, ✉blh@mptourism.com. MP Tourism's lodge, in the core zone, has spacious chalets with attached bath (US$75–90 full board per double; **7**; nos 1–8 overlook a meadow where animals come to graze. There's also a decent restaurant and bar. The nearby *Tourist Hostel* (same ☎, ✉thk@mptourism.com), with 24 dorm places (Rs490 full board), is a great choice for budget travellers. **3**

Kanha Safari Lodge Mukki ☎07637/226029, ✉ksl@mptourism.com. MP Tourism's tree-filled lodge on the quieter side of the park overlooks the river and has pristine a/c and non-a/c rooms with blue bathrooms and rather redundant TVs. Rates include full board. **7**

Kipling Camp 4km south of Khatia
☎07649/277218, ⊛www.kiplingcamp.com. British-run camp in a secluded forest location offering a rustic experience with five-star comfort, plus the company of Tara, the elephant made famous by Mark Shand's book (see Contexts, p.1394). Beautiful cottages (US$175 person, including full board, safaris and guides) have exposed wooden beams and private verandas. **9**

Krishna Jungle Resort 4.5km south of Khatia
☎07649/277 207, ⊛www.jungleresort.in. Established and rightly popular complex with colonial-style rooms, pool, heavenly food and an enthusiastic manager (a wildlife expert). Room only, B&B and Jungle Plan packages available. **6**

Pug Mark Resort Khatia ☎07649/277291, ⊛www.pugmarkresort.com. Cheerful turquoise and green rooms in lush gardens with a campfire at the centre, around which naturalists give evening talks. There's also an attractive restaurant filled with images of classical Indian dancers, open to non-guests. It's a winding 10min walk from the main road; follow the signs. **5–6**

Shergarh Mukki ☎07637/226215, ⊛www.shergarh.com. Katie and Jehan Bhujwala run a wonderfully intimate, environmen-tally and socially responsible camp of six comfortable tents, each with a slick attached stone and marble bathroom (LPG units provide constant hot water) and private veranda, on which staff light a small log fire each night. The kitchen makes use of organic produce from the camp's butterfly-filled gardens, while the small lake in the centre is home to kingfishers and cormorants. Jungle Plan US$235 per person. **9**

▲ Rhesus monkeys

Singinawa Mukki ☎07636/200031, ⓦwww
.singinawa.in. Brand-new lodge that combines an
ecofriendly "plastic free" ethos with luxury: 12
cottages, some with wheelchair access, 55 acres of
wildlife-filled grounds, a pool and the fascinating
company of Nanda SJB Rana, a wildlife photographer
and film-maker, and his wife Latika, a leading wildlife
biologist. Jungle Plan US$360 per person. ❾

Van Vihar Khatia ☎07649/277241,
ⓕ07649/277277. This welcoming, family-run
place, 500m off the main road at Khatia Gate,
has a collection of rooms, ranging from the
ultra-basic to comfortable a/c attached rooms an
economical restaurant and Jeeps/guides
available. ❶–❺

Bandhavgarh National Park

With Kanha becoming ever more popular, Madhya Pradesh's second national park, **BANDHAVGARH**, tucked away in the hilly northeast of the state, is receiving increasing attention from tourists. The draw is that it has the highest relative density of **tigers** of any of India's reserves, shelters a collection of fascinating ruins, and offers the chance of trekking through the jungle on elephant-back. It's a long haul to Bandhavgarh from either Jabalpur (195km) or Khajuraho (237km), but worth it – not only to track tigers and deer but also, as all the accommodation is close to the park gates, to watch the array of birdlife without even entering the park.

Bandhavgarh may be one of India's newer national parks, but it has a long history. Legend dates the construction of its hilltop **fort** to the time of the epic Ramayana (around 800 BC), when monkey architects built Rama a place to rest on his return from his battle with the demon king of Lanka. Excavations of caves tunnelled into the rock below the fort have revealed inscriptions scratched into the sandstone in the first century BC, from which time Bandhavgarh served as a base for a string of dynasties, among them the **Chandellas**, responsible for the temples at Khajuraho. They ruled from here until the **Bhagels** took over in the twelfth century, staking a claim to the region that is still held by their direct descendant, the Maharaja of Rewa. The dynasty shifted to Rewa in 1617, allowing Bandhavgarh to be slowly consumed by forest and by the bamboo and grasslands that provided prime hunting ground for the Rewa kings. The present maharaja ended his hunting days in 1968 when he donated the area to the state as parkland. In 1986, two more chunks of forest were added to the original core zone, giving the park a total area of 448 square kilometres.

The park

Though there are flat grassy *maidans* in the south of the park, Bandhavgarh is predominantly rugged and hilly, clad in *sal* trees in the valleys, and mixed forest in the upper reaches, which shelter a diverse avian population. Bandhavgarh's headquarters are in the tiny village of **Tala**, a stone's throw from the main gate in the north, connected to Umaria, 32km southwest, by a road slicing through the park's narrow midriff. Jeep tracks wind through the park from the north gate in Tala, circling below the central **fort** through forest and grassland, and passing watering holes and streams – good spots for viewing wildlife.

On the whole, Jeep safaris tend to stick to the core area where the chances of spotting one of the fifty or so **tigers** are high, and glimpses of deer and monkeys guaranteed. Deer species include shy but animated gazelle and small barking deer, as well as the more common *nilgai* (blueball) and *chital* (spotted deer). Sloth bears, porcupines, *sambar* and muntjac also hide away in the forest, while hyenas, foxes and jackals appear occasionally in the open country. If you're very fortunate, you may catch sight of an elusive leopard. Look out too for some very **exotic birds** like red jungle fowl, white-naped woodpecker, painted spurfowl, long-billed vultures, lesser adjutant stork, brown fish owl, jungle owlet, Malabar pied hornbill, eagles, falcons and flycatchers. Perhaps the most enjoyable way of viewing game is to take an **elephant ride** in the misty dawn, tramping through the undergrowth as the *mahout* hacks through spider webs and overhanging branches.

The crumbling ramparts of the **fort** crown a hill in the centre of the park, 300m above the surrounding terrain. Its ramparts offer spectacular views over the valley and by far the best birdwatching in the park. Beneath the fort are a few modest temples, the rock-cut cells of monks and soldiers, and a massive stone Vishnu reclining on his cobra near a pool that dates from the tenth century and still defies the undergrowth. The exotic plant life hereabouts attracts numerous species of insects that may make your skin crawl, but not as much as the thought that tigers may be watching you as you wander the sites. They're more likely to stick to the lower levels nearer their favourite prey, and there are no instances of people actually being harmed by tigers or even suddenly coming across them – but the risks are real nonetheless.

Park practicalities

Bandhavgarh is **open** from November to end of June (dawn to dusk; Rs2000 [Rs500] per vehicle with up to eight people per safari, Rs12,0000 [Rs1600] per vehicle with between nine and 32 people per safari, compulsory guide Rs150 per safari). For wildlife-spotting the **best time to visit** is during the hotter months between March and June, when thirsty tigers and their prey are forced out to the waterholes and the park's three perennial streams; the heat can be trying at this time, however. Visiting in the cooler months, when wildlife viewing is still good, is more comfortable.

Without your own vehicle, **getting there** can be tricky. The easiest option by rail is to catch the daily overnight Narmada Express #8233 which goes through Indore, Bhopal, Jabalpur and Bilaspur (if you are coming from Orissa) to Umaria, the nearest railhead, from where regular shared Jeeps and taxis (Rs15/300) make the one-hour trip to Tala. Approaching from Khajuraho or Varanasi, make your way to **Satna** on the main train line and pick up a train straight to Umaria (there is currently no bus service between Satna and Umaria). If you're coming from Delhi (or Agra), the best train is the Utkal Express #8478, which leaves Delhi's Nizamuddin Station at 12.50pm and arrives in Umaria early the next day (going the other way, it leaves Umaria 8.45pm). The Narmada Express #8233 leaves Jabalpur 6.35am, arriving Umaria 10.30am (the return journey leaves Umaria at 4.25pm). Travelling by rented car either from Khajuraho or Jabalpur takes roughly five hours, and will cost upwards of Rs2500 for the round trip, plus an extra Rs250–300 for each night you stay.

To cover a reasonable distance within the park, book a **Jeep** at the headquarters at the park gate (Rs700 per safari) or through your hotel. Up to five people can share a Jeep (though four is more comfortable). **Elephant rides** can also be arranged at the park office or your hotel (Rs600 [Rs100]). Elephants and their *mahouts* wait in any area where a tiger or two has been spotted lurking deep in the forest; the lure of a quick jaunt into the jungle to get a virtually guaranteed sighting is hard to resist.

For the serious wildlife enthusiast, there are a few very experienced naturalists in Tala, all of whom can be contacted through your hotel. S.K. Tiwari of Skay's Camp (℡07653/265355, ℻07653/265309) specializes in nature photography, and has an impressive knowledge of Indian flora and fauna.

Accommodation and eating

Most of Bandhavgarh's hotels, all of which are in and around **Tala**, cater for travellers on a higher budget, and offer Jungle Plan prices – deals including accommodation, meals and two Jeep safaris per person. However, there are a few mid-priced hotels and budget lodges for those on a lower budget. The only places to eat outside the hotels are the friendly, inexpensive *dhabas* on Tala's main road.

Bandhavgarh Jungle Lodge Close to the river ☏07627/265317, ⓦwww.welcomheritagehotels.com. Huts with rustic mud walls and thatched roofs (but eminently cosy interiors) and lush gardens give this lodge plenty of character, as do the enthusiastic manager and resident wildlife experts. Jungle Plan US$300 for two. ❾

Kum Kum Home Umaria Rd, next to *White Tiger Forest Lodge* ☏07653/265324. This guesthouse is the most popular budget choice and offers a warm welcome, extremely basic rooms with hot bucket and unlimited (Rs25) thalis eaten round a camp fire. ❷–❸

Tiger's Den Resort Umaria Rd ☏011/2704 9446, ⓦwww.tigerdenbandhavgarh.com. This efficient and friendly lodge has a cluster of pretty cottages with soothing decor and bathtubs in flower-filled gardens. Jungle Plan US$130 for two; full-board packages also available. ❾

Tiger Trails 2.5km beyond Tala; book through Indian Adventures, C257, SV Rd, Bandra West, Mumbai 400050 ☏022/2640 8742, ⓦwww.indianadventures.com. One of the best-value deals in Tala: en-suite cottages have tiled roofs and exposed brickwork, while the alfresco dining room overlooks a little lake, which is great for birdwatching. Jungle Plan US$125 for two. ❻

🏃 **Treehouse Hideaway** Ketkiya Village ☏011/2588 9516, ⓦwww.treehouse hideaway.com. Blending seamlessly into the surrounding jungle, these five stunning treehouses, made from local materials, are far removed from anything you may have played in as a child, combining top-end comforts with a sense of adventure. The recently opened camp has 21 acres of forest and even its own watering hole, which is sometimes visited by tigers. Jungle Plan US$450 for two; full-board packages also available. ❾

White Tiger Forest Lodge Umaria Rd, next to the barrier over the main road ☏07653/265308, ⓔwtfl@mptourism.com. MP Tourism's large complex has snug en suites, some with a/c, linked by raised walkways, and a restaurant/bar. Rooms 17–21 are in bungalows with large verandas overlooking the river, which attracts myriad birds and – very occasionally at the height of summer – tigers. Rates (US$65–90 per double) include full board, but not safaris. ❼–❽

Pench Tiger Reserve

Named after the river that runs through it, **Pench Tiger Reserve** (Nov–July dawn to dusk; Rs2000 [Rs500] per vehicle for up to eight people per safari, compulsory guide Rs150, elephant ride Rs600 [Rs100]) has around 25 big cats – down from 41 in 1997 – and sightings are common. The 758-square-kilometre park, largely tropical deciduous forest crisscrossed with streams, is also home to leopards, jackals, deer and 250 species of birds, and is far quieter than its more famous counterparts. Daily buses link Jabalpur (192km; 4–5hr) and Nagpur (92km; 2hr 30min) with Khawasa, from where you can catch a shared Jeep to Turia, 2km from the main gates and location of the hotels; alternatively, hire a car and driver from either Jabalpur (around Rs2500) or Nagpur (around Rs1500). In Turia, MP Tourism's *Kipling's Court* (☏97695/232830, ⓔkcpench @mptourism.com; ❼–❽) offers no-nonsense lodgings in a/c and non-a/c **rooms**, plus ten dorm places (Rs490). All rates include full board. The attractive *Pench Jungle Camp* (☏07695/232817, ⓦwww.wildlife-camp-india.com; ❾) has 12 "safari" tents with wicker furniture and attached tiled bathrooms, a handful of appealing cottages and a library for talks and slide shows (Jungle Plan US$350 for two).

Western Madhya Pradesh

The geography of **western Madhya Pradesh** is dominated by the Narmada River, which drains westwards through a wide alluvial valley, bounded in the south by the Satpura hills and the Maharashtran border, and in the north by the rugged Vindhya Range. Forming the major trade corridor between the Ganges plains and the west coast, the region – known as **Malwa** – was for nearly a thousand years an independent princely state ruled from the sprawling hilltop fort complex at **Mandu**. The former capital, now deserted, is the area's outstanding tourist attraction, with its ruined mosques, tanks and palaces, and spectacular panoramic views.

Most visitors travel to Mandu via the industrial city of **Indore**, then continue northeast to Bhopal, or south on the main Delhi–Mumbai train line towards Jalgaon, the jumping-off point for the Ellora and Ajanta caves. The sacred city of **Ujjain**, 55km north of Indore, boasts a bumper crop of modern Hindu temples, but little else. You could, nevertheless, choose to pause here on your way to or from southern Rajasthan on the Western Railway, the most direct land link with Delhi. Alternatively, head south to the Narmada and the fascinating Hindu pilgrimage centres of **Omkareshwar** and **Maheshwar**.

Indore and around

The state's economic powerhouse, **INDORE** is huge, modern, heavily industrialized and generally dull. If you find yourself with time to kill en route to or from **Mandu**, 98km southwest, however, a couple of worthwhile sights lie hidden among its tangle of ferroconcrete flyovers, expressways and crowded bazaars.

Situated at the confluence of the Kham and Saraswati rivers, the city was for centuries merely a stopover on the pilgrimage trails to Omkareshwar and Ujjain, 55km north. In the eighteenth century, however, it became the capital of Malhar Rao's **Holkar** dynasty, whose chief, Malhar Rao, had previously managed to scrounge several choice scraps of land from the Marathas during their northward advance against the Mughals. Later, Rao's daughter-in-law, **Ahilya Bai**, took over control of the state, which then stretched as far as the Ganges and the Punjab. Described by a contemporary British diplomat as "the most exemplary ruler that ever lived", the rani was a kind of central Indian Queen Victoria, who, in addition to founding the modern city of Indore, built palaces, temples, *dharamshalas* and charitable institutions all over the country. When she died in 1795, the state plunged into a series of bloody conflicts, which only ended in 1818 when the dynasty secured a small but rich dominion with Indore as the capital. The city's expansion gained momentum in the nineteenth century, fuelled by a lucrative trade in cotton and opium, and the maverick Holkar maharajas remained in power until Independence.

Indore is now the region's biggest business and commercial centre today. The nearby industrial estate of **Pithampur**, hyped as "the Detroit of India", hosts numerous giant steel and auto manufacturers. The resulting **affluence** has made a big impact: satellite dishes, luxury hotels and American-style shopping malls are popping up all over, while the nouveaux riches swan ostentatiously around town on brand-new cars and Japanese scooters.

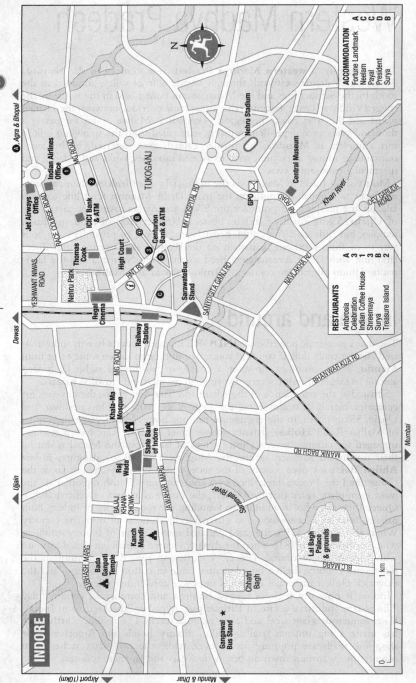

INDORE

Ujjain ◀   *Dewas* ◀   *Agra & Bhopal* ▲

Mumbai ▶

Mandu & Dhar ▼   *Airport (10km)* ▼

ACCOMMODATION
Fortune Landmark	A
Neelam	C
Payal	D
President	D
Surya	B

RESTAURANTS
Ambrosia	A
Celebration	3
Indian Coffee House	1
Shreemaya	B
Surya	B
Treasure Island	2

Nehru Stadium

Central Museum

Khan River

DEV GARUDA ROAD

AB ROAD

NAVLAKHA RD

GPO

TUKOGANJ

MY HOSPITAL RD

SANYOGITA GANJ RD

Sarawate Bus Stand

MG ROAD

Indian Airlines Office

Jet Airways Office

RACE COURSE ROAD

ICICI Bank & ATM

Centurion Bank & ATM

Thomas Cook

High Court

RNT RD

YESHWANT NIWAS ROAD

Nehru Park

Regal Cinema

Railway Station

MG ROAD

BHAN WAH KUA RD

MANIK BAGH RD

Khala-Ma Mosque

State Bank of Indore

Raj Wada

BAJAJ KHANA CHOWK

JAWAHAR MARG

Saraswati River

Kanch Mandir

SUBHASH MARG

Bada Ganpati Temple

Chhatri Bagh

Gangawal Bus Stand

Lal Bagh Palace & grounds

BLC MARG

1 km

0

Arrival and information

Trains arriving on the Central Railway pull in at the mainline station in the middle of the city. The principal **bus stand**, Sarawate (℡0731/246 5688), is a short walk south from platform 1, beyond the overpass. Buses for **Mandu** use the less convenient Gangawal Bus Stand (℡0731/248 0688), 3km west towards the domestic **airport**, which is 10km out of town.

MP Tourism's helpful **information** office on Rabindranath Tagore Road (RNT Rd) in the Jhabua Tower (daily 10am–5pm; ℡0731/252 8653) has cars with drivers for rent, available for two-day **tours** to Mandu and trips to Omkareshwar and Maheshwar (all Rs50/hr of driving plus Rs250 per night halt).

The State Bank of Indore has a **foreign exchange** office opposite their main branch on Raj Wada. ICICI Bank, 576 MG Rd, is an efficient alternative and has an ATM accepting both Visa and MasterCard. Another ATM can be found at Centurion Bank on RNT Road. Thomas Cook (Mon–Sat 9.30am–6pm; ℡0731/254 2525) has an office on Yeshwant Niwas Road. There's a 24-hour **pharmacy** (℡0731/252 8301) in the MY Hospital compound, off AB Road. **Internet cafés** are rife; try Taha Cyber City in the Silver Mall (Rs15/hr). The most convenient means of **getting around** is by metered auto-rickshaw, or rather more cheaply by the ancient *tempos*.

Accommodation

Most of Indore's **hotels** cater for business visitors and are scattered around the prosperous suburb of **Tukoganj**, 1km east of the railway station. Competition here is stiff, so standards tend to be high and prices reasonable. The same can't be said of the cheaper accommodation, much of which is in the noisy area between Sarawate and the railway station. Ignore the touts who try to drag you off to the dire lodges opposite the bus stand, and head instead for the better-value budget hotels along **Chhoti Gwaltoli**, a lane just east of the railway station beneath the big Patel flyover. All but the absolute rock-bottom lodges levy a mandatory ten percent **luxury tax**, and all have noon checkout unless noted otherwise.

Fortune Landmark Vijaynagar, 3km from the centre of town off AB Rd near Meghdoot Gardens ℡0731/255 7700, ⓦwww.fortunehotels.in. Indore's top hotel, aimed squarely at the international business circuit, has snazzy rooms, complete with cool yellow decor and lazy chairs, a pool, fitness centre and several dining choices, including an open-air terrace grill and a sports pub. ⓫

Neelam 33/2 Patel Bridge Corner ℡0731/246 6001, Ⓕ251 8774. Despite the dingy exterior, *Neelam* is probably the pick of the backpacker options. The pale blue rooms, lining a central courtyard, are clean enough and have TVs and attached bathrooms (with squat toilets). A friendly welcome is guaranteed and there's 24-hour checkout. ❷

Payal 38 Chhoti Gwaltoli ℡0731/504 5151. A decent alternative to *Neelam*: the rudimentary

rooms all have attached shower-toilets but it's worth shelling out an extra Rs50 for a larger deluxe room with cable TV. ❷–❸

President 163 RNT Rd ℡0731/252 8866, ⓦwww.hotelpresidentindore.com. A pink building housing identikit – and a little soulless – mid-range a/c rooms, all with fridge and TV, a recommended in-house travel agent, rooftop café, and a motley library of airport thrillers and potboilers in the lobby. ❺

Surya 5/5 Nath Mandir Rd ℡0731/2517701, ⓦwww.suryaindore.com. Outstanding, personalized service elevates this three-star way above the others in its class (as well as several of Indore's more expensive options). The attractive en suites come with all mod cons, including a cute dressing area, and there's an excellent multi-cuisine restaurant and bar to boot. ❹–❺

The City

Indore's sights lie west of the train line, in and around the **bazaar**. Two broad thoroughfares, MG Road and Jawahar Marg, form the north and south boundaries of this cluttered and chaotic district, which is interrupted in the east by the confluence of the Saraswati and Khan rivers. The city's principal landmark is the former Holkar palace of **Raj Wada**, an eighteenth-century mansion that presides over a palm-fringed square in the heart of the city and boasts a lofty, seven-storey gateway. Its upper four floors were originally made of wood, which made it particularly prone to fire; most of the palace collapsed after the last one, in 1984. Only the facade and the family temple, immediately inside the main courtyard, survive.

Indore's **bazaars** are great for a stroll, with rows of stalls and open-fronted shops jammed beneath picturesque four-storeyed houses with overhanging wooden balconies. The Jain **Kanch Mandir** or "Mirror Temple" (daily 10am–5pm; no photos), tucked away deep in the bazaar district, is one of the city's more eccentric religious monuments; surprisingly, for a faith renowned for its austerity, the interior is decked with multicoloured glass **mosaics**. If you're in a shopping mood, the Sarafa Bazaar, around the corner from the Mirror Temple, is a good place to pick up gold and silver **jewellery**; cloth is sold by weight at the massive wholesale textile market nearby. Also worth seeking out are shops on Bajaj Khana Chowk that specialize in traditional embroidered and beadwork costumes, and the atmospheric fruit and vegetable market on the riverbank beneath the lime-green **Khala-Ma mosque**.

The **Central Museum of Indore** (daily except Mon 10am–5pm; Rs30 [Rs5]) on AB Road was founded in 1929 and houses Holkar-era swords, shields and armour, as well as terracotta, coins, paintings and inscriptions from throughout the state.

The Lal Bagh palace

Set in its own grounds on the banks of the River Kham, the **Lal Bagh Palace** (daily except Mon 10am–5pm; Rs100 [Rs5], camera Rs10) is another of the extravagant Neoclassical creations so beloved by rich maharajas of the nineteenth and early twentieth centuries. The building took two generations of the Holkar family around thirty years to complete, and was, in its day, rivalled only by the Scindias' Jai Vilas Palace in Gwalior. Granted carte blanche and a limitless budget, its British architects and interior decorators produced a vast stately home dripping with Doric columns, gilt stucco, crystal chandeliers, and piles of replica Rococo furniture.

Lal Bagh's main entrance is via a pair of grandiose wrought-iron gates, modelled on those at Buckingham Palace, which bear the Holkar family arms – note the wheat and poppies in the background, symbolizing the two main sources of the dynasty's prosperity. **Inside**, a vast array of family heirlooms is housed in the former durbar hall, banquet rooms and the ballroom, with its specially sprung herringbone dance-floor. Check out the jewel-encrusted portrait of Tukoji Rao (1902–25) – the ruler responsible for completing the palace – in the billiards room, and the underground passage leading down to the kitchens. One of the rooms hidden away in this vault contains a modest but very colourful collection of **tribal artefacts**, including terracotta votive statues, clothes, jewellery, murals and brass sculpture. At the maharaja's private **planetarium** (Rs5) visitors are shown the position of planets, important stars and constellations in the Indore night sky on the day of their visit.

Eating

Eating out is popular among Indore's middle classes, and there are plenty of quality restaurants around the city centre to choose from. Inexpensive meals are available in canteens and *dhabas* near Sarawate Bus Stand; stick to those doing brisk business and you shouldn't go far wrong. **Snack stalls** near Raj Wada and in the markets serve local favourites like *parathas, poha, chaat,* samosas and *katchoris,* and sweets including *jaleoi* and *gulab jamun.* Indore is also known for its salty nibbles called *namkeens* – some, like the Ratlami Sev, are fiery and spicy.

Ambrosia *Fortune Landmark.* The grand dining room, with red-cushioned-chairs and delicately folded napkins, has the air of a stately home, and the extensive Indian, Chinese and international menu (try the mutton *rogan josh*) is suitably lofty too. Not quite the food of the gods, but pretty darn close. Mains Rs100–200.

Celebration RNT Rd, in the annexe to the right of *Shreemaya* hotel. A student hangout known for its sweet goodies, including a cavity-inducing chocolate truffle cake, as well as savoury snacks like samosas (Rs10–20).

Indian Coffee House next to Rampura Building, off MG Rd. Come for a south Indian breakfast (Rs20–70), served by waiters in turbans and cummerbunds, and a leisurely read of the papers. There's another branch set in peaceful grounds behind the high court.

Shreemaya *Shreemaya* hotel, RNT Rd. Contemporary peach-coloured dining room with a curvy Art Deco-style ceiling, frosted glasswork and mouthwatering food: the mutton *bhuna, missi* roti and – if you have any space left – chocolate brownie and ice cream are not to be missed.

Surya *Surya* hotel. The kitchen keeps up with the hotel's exacting standards by producing memorable Continental dishes such as goulash and roast lamb, as well as masterful tandoori items (Rs80–125).

Treasure Island MG Rd. This vast shopping mall is the place for anyone hankering after a fast-food fix: *McDonald's, Pizza Hut* and *Baskin Robbins* are all present and correct, and there's a decent food court and – a real rarity for MP – authentic espresso at the *Barista* coffee shop.

Moving on from Indore

Tickets for daily Indian Airlines flights to Delhi (US$155), Bhopal (US$75) and Mumbai (US$130) from **Indore airport** (℡0731/241 1758) can be booked at the company's office (℡0731/243 1595) on Race Course Road, 2km northeast of the station. Jet Airways (℡0731/262 0454) also fly twice daily to Bhopal and Mumbai; tickets can be booked either at the airport or their city office, opposite Indian Airlines on Race Course Road. Kingfisher Airlines (℡1800/233 3131) has daily flights to Ahmedabad, Hyderabad, Jabalpur and Kolkata, and two daily to Mumbai, while Air Deccan (℡0731/262 0047) has daily flights to Delhi (via Gwalior). There's no airport bus, but plenty of taxis (Rs200) and auto-rickshaws (Rs90) ply the route into town.

As for **trains**, two broad-gauge branches of the Western Railway connect Indore to cities in northern India. The fastest service to Delhi, the daily Indore–Nizamuddin Express #2416 (departs 4.20pm, arrives 5.40am) heads north via Ujjain, Kota and Bharatpur. The other branch, serviced by the daily Malwa Express #2919 (departs 12.25pm, arrives 4.55am next day), runs east to Bhopal, then north to New Delhi on the Central Railway via Jhansi, Gwalior and Agra. For Rajasthan, the daily Ranthambore Express #2465 leaves 6.45am, arriving Jaipur 5.20pm. The daily 5pm (11hr 25min) Narmada Express #8233 is the only train to Jabalpur, for connections to Kanha, Bandhavgarh and Pench.

To get to Mandu by **bus** from Indore, there are a couple of daily direct services (3hr 30min–4hr) from Gangawal Bus Stand. Failing that, take any of the frequent services from Gangawal Bus Stand to Dhar (2hr), which is connected to Mandu by half-hourly buses (1hr 30min–2hr). Less frequent services run to

Dhar from Sarawate Bus Stand. MP Tourism operates five daily "luxury" buses to Bhopal (6am, 8am, noon, 3.30pm and 6pm; 4hr); you have to catch the 6am bus if you want to make the 2.50pm daily Delhi-bound Shatabdi Express.

Reliable **travel agents** include the excellent President Travels at *Hotel President*, 163 RNT Rd (☎0731/253 3472).

For more on transport from Indore, see "Travel details" on p.474.

Mandu

Set against the rugged backdrop of the Vindhya hills, the medieval ghost-town of **MANDU**, 98km southwest of Indore, is one of central India's most atmospheric historical monuments. Come here at the height of the monsoons, when the rocky plateau and its steeply shelving sides are carpeted with green vegetation, and you'll understand why the Malwa sultans christened their capital **Shadiabad** – "City of Joy". Even during the relentless heat of the dry season, the ruins make an exotic spectacle. Elegant Islamic palaces, mosques and onion-domed mausoleums crumble beside large medieval reservoirs and precipitous ravines, while below, an endless vista of scorched plains and tiny villages stretches off to the horizon. Mandu can be visited as a day-trip from Indore, but you'll enjoy it more if you spend a couple of nights, giving you time not only to explore the ruins, but to witness the memorable sunsets over the Narmada Valley.

Some history

Archeological evidence suggests that the remote hilltop was fortified around the sixth century AD, when it was known as Mandapa-Durga, or "Durga's hall of

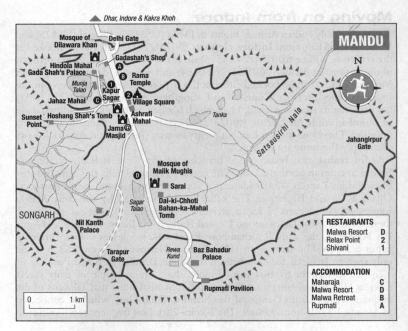

worship" – in time corrupted to "Mandu". Four hundred years later, the site gained in strategic importance when the powerful **Paramaras** moved their capital from Ujjain to Dhar, 35km north. The plateau's natural defences proved, however, unable to withstand persistent attacks by the Muslim invaders and the fort eventually fell to the sultans of Delhi in 1305.

While the Sultanate was busy fending off the Mongols on their northern borders a century or so later, Malwa's Afghan governor, Dilawar Khan Ghuri, seized the chance to establish his own independent kingdom. He died after only four years on the throne, however, leaving his ambitious young son at the helm. During **Hoshang Shah**'s illustrious 27-year reign, Mandu was promoted from pleasure resort to royal capital, and acquired some of the finest Islamic monuments in Asia.

Mandu's golden age continued under the **Khaljis**, who took over from the Ghuri dynasty in 1436, when Mahmud Shah Khalji poisoned Hoshang Shah's grandson. Another building boom and several protracted wars later, Mandu settled down to a lengthy period of peace and prosperity under **Ghiyath Shah** (1469–1500). Famous for his love of cooking and beautiful women, Ghiyath amassed a harem of 15,000 courtesans, and a bodyguard of a thousand Turkish and Abyssinian women, whom he accommodated in the appropriately lavish Jahaz Mahal. The sybaritic sultan was poisoned by his son shortly after his eightieth birthday. His successor, Nasir Shah, died of guilt ten years later, and Mandu, dogged by feuds and the threat of rebellion, became an easy target for the militaristic Sultan of Gujarat, who invaded in 1526. In the centuries that followed, control over the fort and its rapidly decaying monuments passed between a succession of independent rulers, and the Mughals. By the time King James I's ambassador, **Sir Thomas Roe**, followed the mobile court of Emperor Jahangir here in 1617, most of the city lay in ruins, its mansions and tombs occupied by Bhil villagers whose descendents continue to scratch a living from the surrounding fields. Mandu today is a tranquil backwater that sees far fewer visitors than it deserves, save for the busloads of exuberant Indian day-trippers who breeze in from Indore at weekends.

The monuments

Mandu's monuments derive from a unique school of Islamic architecture that flourished here, and at Dhar, between 1400 and 1516. The elegantly simple buildings are believed to have exerted a considerable influence on the Mughal architects responsible for the Taj Mahal. Mandu's platform, a 23-kilometre-square plateau, is separated from the body of hills to the north by the **Kakra Khoh**, literally "deep ravine". A narrow causeway forms a natural bridge across the gorge, carrying the present road across and up via a series of subsidiary gates to the fort's modern entrance, beside the original, and very grand, Delhi Gate.

If you don't have your own vehicle, the most pleasant way of getting around the fort and its widely dispersed monuments is to rent a **bicycle** (Rs30/24hr) from your hotel or one of the hire shops near the *Shivani Hotel*. A decrepit old **tempo** runs regularly between the village square near the village group of monuments) and the Rewa Kund Group (in the far south of the site). Alternatively, rent an **auto-rickshaw** for a complete tour (around Rs150).

The Royal Enclave
Reached via the lane that leads west off the village square, **the Royal Enclave** (daily except Fri sunrise to sunset; Rs100 [Rs5], video Rs25) is dominated by Mandu's most photographed monument, Ghiyath Shah's majestic **Jahaz Mahal**

or "Ship Palace". The name derives from its unusual shape and elevated situation on a narrow strip of land between two large water tanks. A breezy rooftop terrace, crowned with four domed pavilions, overlooks **Munja Talao** lake to the west, and the square, stone-lined **Kapur Sagar** to the east. From the northern balcony, you also get a good view of the geometric sandstone bathing pools.

The next building along the lane is the **Hindola Mahal**, or "Swing Palace" – so-called because its distinctive sloping walls supposedly look as though they are swaying from side to side. The design was, in fact, purely functional, intended to buttress the graceful but heavy stone arches that support the ceiling inside. At the far end of the T-shaped assembly hall, a long stepped ramp allowed the sultan and his retinue to reach the upper storey on elephant-back.

Sprawling over the northern shores of Munja Talao are the dilapidated remains of a second royal pleasure palace. The **Champa Baodi** boasts an ingeniously complex ventilation and water-supply system, which kept its dozens of *tykhanas* (subterranean chambers) cool during the long Malwan summers. Immediately to the north stands the venerable **Mosque of Dilawara Khan**, dating from 1405. The chunks of Hindu temple used to build its main doorway and colonnaded hall are still very evident.

The **Hathi Pol**, or "Elephant Gate", with its pair of colossal, half-decapitated elephant guardians, was the main entrance to the Royal Enclave but is now closed. To reach the edge of the plateau and the grand **Delhi Gate** you will have to return to the bazaar and follow the road out of Mandu. Built around the same time as Dilawara Khan's mosque, this great bastion, towering over the cobbled road in five sculpted arches, is the most imposing of the twelve that stud the battlements along the fort's 45-kilometre perimeter.

The village group

Some of the fort's best-preserved buildings are clustered **around the village** to the south of Jahaz Mahal (all daily sunrise to sunset; Rs100 [Rs5], video Rs25). Work on the magnificent pink-sandstone mosque, the **Jama Masjid** on the west side of the main square, commenced during the reign of Hoshang Shah and took three generations to complete. Said to be modelled on the Great Mosque at Damascus, it rests on a huge raised plinth pierced by rows of tiny arched chambers – once used as cells for visiting clerics. Beyond the ornate *jali* screens and bands of blue-glazed tiles that decorate the main doorway, you emerge in the Great Courtyard, where a prayer hall at the far end is decorated with finely carved inscriptions from the Koran.

Hoshang Shah's tomb (c.1440), behind the Jama Masjid, is this group's real highlight. It stands on a low plinth at the centre of a square-walled enclosure, and is crowned by a squat central dome and four small corner cupolas. Now streaked with mildew and mud washed down from the bats' nests inside its eaves, the tomb is made entirely from milky-white marble – the first of its kind in the Subcontinent. The interior is very plain, except for the elaborate pierced-stone windows that illuminate Hoshang's sarcophagus.

The **Ashrafi Mahal**, or "Palace of Coins", was a theological college (*madrasa*) that the ruler Muhammad Shah later converted into a tomb. The complex included a giant marble mausoleum and a seven-storey *minar*, or victory tower, of which only the base survives.

Around the Sagar Talao

En route to the Rewa Kund Group, a further handful of monuments are scattered around the fields east of Sagar Talao lake. Dating from the early fifteenth century, the **Mosque of Malik Mughis** is the oldest of the bunch, once again constructed using ancient Hindu masonry. Note the turquoise tiles and fine Islamic calligraphy over the main doorway. The high-walled building opposite was a *caravanserai*, where merchants and their camel trains would rest during long treks across the Subcontinent.

A short way south, the octagonal tomb known as the **Dai-ki-Chhoti Bahan-ka-Mahal** looms above the surrounding fields from a raised plinth, still retaining large strips of the blue ceramic tiles that plastered most of Mandu's beautiful Afghan domes. Young couples from the nearby village sneak off here during the evenings for a bit of privacy, so make plenty of noise as you approach.

The Rewa Kund Group

The road to the **Rewa Kund Group** (daily sunrise to sunset; Rs100 [Rs5], video Rs25) heads past herds of water buffalo grazing on the muddy foreshores of the lake, then winds its way gently through a couple of Bhil villages towards the far southern edge of the plateau; stately old baobabs line the roadside, like giant upturned root vegetables. The **Rewa Kund** itself, an old stone tank noted for its curative waters, lies 6km south of the main village. Water from it used to be pumped into the cistern in the nearby **Baz Bahadur Palace**. Bahadur, the last independent ruler of Malwa, retreated to Mandu to study music after being trounced in battle by Rani Durgavati. Legend has it that he fell in love with a Hindu singer named Rupmati, whom he enticed to his hilltop home with an exquisite palace. The couple eventually married, but did not live happily ever after. When Akbar heard of Rupmati's beauty, he dispatched an army to Mandu to capture her and the long-coveted fort. Bahadur managed to slip away from the ensuing battle, but his bride, left behind in the palace, poisoned herself rather than fall into the clutches of the attackers.

The romantic **Rupmati Pavilion**, built by Bahadur for his bride-to-be, rests on a ridge high above the Rewa Kund; beneath its lofty terrace, the plateau plunges a sheer 300m to the Narmada Valley. The view is breathtaking, especially at sunset or on a clear day, when you can just about make out the sun-bleached banks of the sacred river as it winds west towards the Arabian Sea.

Practicalities

Although there are a few direct private **buses** to Mandu from Indore (3hr 30min–4hr), it's often quicker to travel to Dhar and pick up the half-hourly local service to the fort from there – a bone-shaking 35-kilometre journey that takes over an hour. **Taxis** can be arranged at all hotels in Indore (see p.455), and charge around Rs800 for the round trip, plus a hefty Rs250 waiting charge if you stay overnight; the same service from MP Tourism office in Indore (see p.455) is generally a little more expensive. There is nowhere to **change money** in Mandu; the nearest bank is in Indore. Vinayak on Main Road offers painfully slow **Internet** access (Rs10/hr). The disorganized post office, on the main road near the Rama temple, is not recommended for poste restante.

Accommodation options are decidedly limited. *Hotel Rupmati* (℡07292/263270; ❹–❺), at the north end of the plateau near the Nagar Panchayat barrier, has good-value a/c rooms, each with a private balcony overlooking the ravine; there's a decent garden restaurant and a bar serving cold beers. It's a one-kilometre hike from the main square where the buses pull in, however, so ask to be dropped off en route. Round towards the Royal Enclave, the *Maharaja* (℡07292/263288; ❷) is pretty dirty and only worth trying as a last resort; its restaurant is just a drinking den. *Malwa Resort* (℡07292/263235, ⓔmresortm@mptourism.com; ❺–❻), 2km south of the square, is Mandu's most comfortable and expensive hotel; book the a/c cottages, each with private lake-facing verandas, in advance. MP Tourism's other establishment, *Malwa Retreat* (T07292/263221, Emretreatm@mptourism.com; 5), is a couple of rungs down in quality but still a reasonable choice.

The semi-open-air restaurant is one of the most appealing **places to eat** in the fort, with a moderately priced menu, limited to Indian veg dishes. *Shivani*, halfway between the square and the Nagar Panchayat barrier, has a range of north and south Indian dishes. *Relax Point* on the square offers chai, cold drinks, samosas and substantial all-you-can-eat thalis. It's best to avoid meat and *paneer*, as frequent power-cuts mean that even places with refrigerators can have problems keeping perishables fresh.

Ujjain

Situated on the banks of the sacred River Shipra, **UJJAIN**, 55km north of Indore, is one of India's seven holiest cities. Like Haridwar, Nasik and Prayag, it plays host every twelve years to the country's largest religious gathering, the **Kumbh Mela** (see p.315), which in 2004 drew an estimated thirty million pilgrims here to bathe; naked sadhus are among the millions jamming the waterfront, waiting to wash away several lifetimes of bad karma. Outside festival times, Ujjain is a great place for people-watching, as pilgrims and locals alike go about the daily business of puja, temple visiting and chai drinking. Around the main temples, you see modern Hinduism at its most kitsch, with all types of devotional paraphernalia, gaudy lighting and plastic flower garlands for sale. Down at the *ghats*, women flap wet saris dry while their soapy children splash in the water, and sleepy *pujaris* ply their trade beneath the rows of orange- and whitewashed riverside shrines. A mini-Varanasi Ujjain is not, but nonetheless the temples rising behind the *ghats* are majestic at dusk, and with the ringing of bells and incense drifting around, this atmospheric place can feel timeless.

Some history

Excavations north of Ujjain have yielded traces of settlement as far back as the eighth century BC. The ancient city was a major regional capital under the Mauryans (Ashok was governor here for a time during the reign of his father), when it was known as **Avantika** and lay on the main trade route that linked northern India with Mesopotamia and Egypt. According to Hindu mythology, Shiva later changed its name to **Ujjaiyini**, "He Who Conquers With Pride", to mark his victory over the demon king of Tripuri. Chandra Gupta II, renowned for his patronage of the arts, also ruled from here in the fourth and fifth centuries AD. Among the Nava Ratna, or "Nine Gems", of his court was the illustrious Sanskrit poet **Kalidasa**, whose much-loved narrative poem *Meghduta* ("Cloud Messenger") includes a lyrical evocation of the city and its inhabitants. (In 1914, **E.M. Forster** visited Ujjain, determined to get an image in his head of what the town looked like in Kalidasa's day. He soon admitted defeat, declaring: "Old buildings are buildings, ruins are ruins.")

Ujjain was sacked in 1234 by Iltutmish, of the Delhi Slave Dynasty, who razed most of its temples. Thereafter, the Malwan capital was governed by the sultans of Mandu, by the Mughals, and by **Raja Jai Singh** from Jaipur, who designed, along with many renovation projects elsewhere in India, the Vedha Shala observatory (Ujjain straddles the Hindu first meridian of longitude). Ujjain's

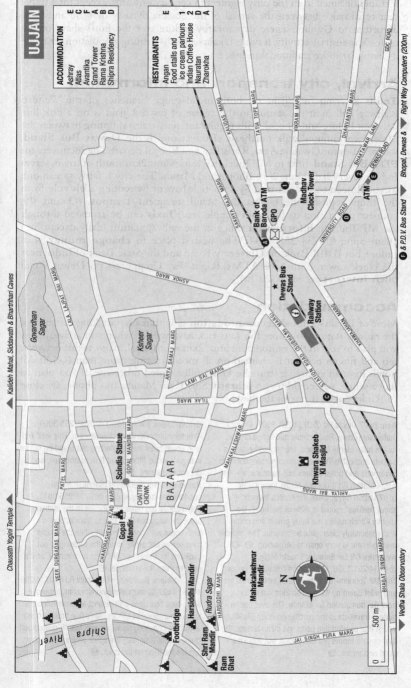

UJJAIN

ACCOMMODATION
Ashray   E
Atlas   C
Avantika   F
Grand Tower   A
Rama Krishna   B
Shipra Residency D

RESTAURANTS
Angan   E
Food stalls and
ice cream parlours 1
Indian Coffee House 2
Nauratan   D
Zharokha   A

◀ Chausath Yogini Temple   ◀ Kalideh Mahal, Siddavath & Bhartrihari Caves

Shipra River

Govardhan Sagar

Ksheer Sagar

BAZAAR

Scindia Statue

Gopal Mandir

Ram Ghat
Shri Ram Mandir
Footbridge
Harsiddhi Mandir
Rudra Sagar
Mahakaleshwar Mandir

Khwara Shakeb Ki Masjid

Bank of Baroda ATM
GPO
Madhav Clock Tower

Dewas Bus Stand

Railway Station

ATM E

▶ Bhopal, Dewas &   ▶ Right Way Computers (200m)

▶ & P.D.V. Bus Stand

▶ Vedha Shala Observatory

N

0   500 m

KALIDAS MARG
TATA TOPE MARG
VIKRAM MARG
SAKHYA RAJA MARG
DHANVANTRI MARG
BHAKTAWAR GANJ
DEWAS ROAD
GDC ROAD
UNIVERSITY ROAD
ASHOK MARG
LALA LAJPAT RAI MARG
ARYA SAMAJ MARG
LAMI SAI MARG
TILAK MARG
STATION ROAD (SUBHASH MARG)
NANAKHEDA MARG
MAHAKALESHWAR MARG
AHILYA BAI MARG
BHAGAT SINGH MARG
JAI SINGH PURA MARG
HARSIDDHI MARG
CHANDRASHEKHER AZAD MARG
GOPAL MANDIR MARG
PATEL MARG
VEER DURGADAS MARG
CHATTRI CHOWK

fortunes declined from the early eighteenth century onwards, except for a sixty-year renaissance between the arrival of the Scindia dynasty in 1750 and their departure to Gwalior. These days, nearby Indore sees the lion's share of the region's industrial activity, leaving Ujjain's 367,000-strong population to make its living by more traditional means.

Arrival, city transport and information

Trains arriving in Ujjain on both broad-gauge branches of the Western Railway pull in at the station in the centre of town; Ujjain is on a link line between Indore and Bhopal, with regular intercity trains shunting between the three. Two-minutes' walk northeast of the station is the **Dewas Bus Stand**, where buses for Gwalior, Agra, Rajasthan and Bhopal depart. The inconvenient **PDV Bus Stand**, next to MP Tourism's *Yatri Niwas* 2km south of town, serves Indore (every half-hour; 2hr), Bhopal and Mandu. The city is fairly spread out, so you'll need to **get around** by auto-rickshaw or by renting a **bicycle** from the shop opposite the Dewas Bus Stand. Frequent **tempos**, #2 and #9, connect the station to the main temple area. **Taxis** can be arranged through the MP Tourism **information** office in the railway station (daily except Sun 10am–5pm; ☎0734/256 1544). The nearest place to **change money** is in Indore, but IDIBI Bank on University Road and the State Bank of India, near the clock tower, both have **ATMs**. Right Way Computers on Dewas Road offers **Internet** access (Rs20/hr).

Accommodation

Most of Ujjain's limited **accommodation** is within easy walking distance of the railway station, so ignore the auto-rickshaw-wallahs when you arrive, unless you plan to stay in the cantonment area, 2km southeast. Luxury tax of between ten and fifteen percent is charged on all rooms costing more than Rs100. All hotels have an annoying 9am checkout, unless stated otherwise. If you plan to stay a while, you could try an **ashram**; Shri Ram Mandir (no phone; ❶) close to Rudra Sagar, is one of the best.

Ashray 77 Devas Rd ☎0734/251 9301, ⓦwww .hotelashray.com. Respectable mid-range choice: rooms have plenty of space, unimaginative brown carpets and cable TV. The more expensive ones are cavernous and boast fridges and bathtubs. ❸–❺
Atlas Station Rd (Subhash Marg), Indore Gate ☎0734/256 0473. While the hotel's hyperbole about "deluxe" rooms is wide of the mark, the slightly kitsch rooms are fairly priced and come with reasonably clean pink bathrooms. The amiable management is very open to bargaining. ❸–❹
Avantika Off Lal Bahadur Shastri Marg ☎0734/251 1398, ⓔavantika@mptourism.com. This MP Tourism-run hotel has an institutional feel and is let down by its location 2km out of town, near the bus station for Mandu. The best bet for budget travellers is the partitioned dorm (Rs90), which has comfortable beds and clean sheets; the four private rooms are overpriced, but there's a good restaurant. ❹

Grand Tower Vikram Marg ☎0734/255 3699, ⓔhotelgrandtower@sancharnet.com. This well-run lime green hotel has comforting but bland en suites with pale wood fittings and firm mattresses, and a decent restaurant. ❹–❺
Rama Krishna Station Rd (Subhash Marg), opposite the railway station ☎0734/255 3017. A notch above the other flophouses in the station area; the large but tired rooms have attached bathrooms with hot water. But while the rooms themselves are pretty clean, the bedding is not. Look out for the large "RK" sign on the roof, as it's easy to miss the entrance. ❸
Shipra Residency University Rd ☎0734/255 1495, ⓔshirpa@mptourism.com. A tranquil, white-tiled courtyard with distinct Moorish influences is the centrepiece of MP Tourism's fine hotel, around which are charming en suites with fancily-quilted bed clothes. Complimentary breakfast and noon checkout provide the icing on the cake. ❺

The City

The Western Railway cuts straight through the **centre** of Ujjain, forming a neat divide between the spacious and affluent residential suburbs to the south and the more interesting, densely packed streets northwest of the station. Unless you spend all day wandering through the **bazaar**, sightseeing in Ujjain usually means treading the **temple** trail, with a brief foray south of the *ghats* to visit the **Vedha Shala observatory**.

The Mahakaleshwar and the Harsiddhi mandirs

Ujjain's chief landmark, the **Mahakaleshwar Mandir**, crowning a rise above the river, is the logical place to start a tour of the town. Its gigantic saffron-painted sanctuary tower, a modern replacement built by the Scindias in the nineteenth century for the one destroyed by Iltutmish in 1234, soars high above a complex of marble courtyards, water tanks and fountains, advertising the presence below of one of India's most powerful *shivalingams*. Housed in a claustrophobic subterranean chamber, the deity is one of India's twelve **jyotrilingam** – "lingam of light" – whose essential energy, or *shakti*, is "born of itself", rather than from the rituals performed around it, and is considered particularly potent, especially by Tantric followers, due to its unusual south-facing position.

From the Mahakaleshwar Mandir, head west down the hill past the Rudra Sagar tank to the auspicious **Harsiddhi Mandir**, which Hindu mythology identifies as the spot where Parvati's elbow fell to earth while Shiva was carrying her burning body from the *sati* pyre. Its main shrine, erected by the Marathas in the eighteenth century, houses (from left to right) images of Mahalakshmi (the goddess of wealth), Annapurna (goddess of food and sustenance), and Saraswati (the goddess of wisdom).

The Gopal Mandir

Northwest of **Chattri Chowk**, a chaotic market square in the heart of the bazaar, the picturesque **Gopal Mandir** was erected by one of the Scindia ranis in the early nineteenth century. With its distinctive blend of Mughal domes, Moorish arches and lofty Hindu sanctuary tower, the temple is a fine example of late Maratha architecture. Inside, the sanctum's silver-plated doors were placed here by Mahaji Scindia, who rescued them from Lahore after they had been carried off by Muslim looters. The shrine room itself, lined with marble, silver and mother-of-pearl, contains icons of the presiding deity, Gopal (Krishna), together with his parents, Shiva and Parvati.

The Vedha Shala observatory

In addition to being a major religious centre, Ujjain was the birthplace of mathematical astronomy in India, research into the motion of the stars and planets having been carried out here since the time of Ashok. Later, Hindu astronomers fixed both the **first meridian** of longitude and the Tropic of Cancer here – the reason why Raja Jai Singh of Jaipur, governor of Malwa under the Mughal emperor Mohammad Shah, chose it as the site for another of his surreal open-air observatories. Built in 1725, the **Vedha Shala observatory** (daily dawn to dusk; Rs2) lies 1km southwest of the railway station, overlooking a bend in the River Shipra. The complex is nowhere near as large as its more famous cousins in Delhi and Jaipur, the Jantar Mantars, but remains in excellent condition with very informative guides (free but they may expect a tip) and labelling. Local astronomers continue to use its five instruments, or *yantras*, to formulate ephemeredes (charts predicting the positions of the planets), which you can buy at the site. An auto-rickshaw from the town centre costs around Rs30.

Eating

Ujjain suffers from a dearth of decent **places to eat**. Most visitors either stick to their hotel restaurant or head to a cluster of food stalls on the eastern side of the clock tower; potato cakes with chickpeas and tomatoes, and deep-fried sweet potato chips are two of the highlights on offer, although as with the inexpensive *dhabas* opposite the railway station, only frequent the most popular ones. There are also several ice-cream parlours close to the clock tower.

Angan *Ashray* hotel. Alongside the tandoori and Chinese staples are a few surprising options, including fish fingers with tartare sauce. Service is painfully slow but cold beers (Rs100 per bottle) are available to help pass the time. Mains Rs45–80.

Indian Coffee House Durga Plaza, Dewas Rd. Unpretentious spot for a moderately priced masala dosa or light meal (Rs25–60); although a little harassed during the breakfast rush, staff noticeably relax as the day wears on.

Nauratan *Shipra Residency* hotel. Typical MP Tourism menu – veg, Mughal, tandoori and Chinese dishes, plus some western options (Rs40–100) – in above-average surroundings, plus Ujjain's widest choice of alcoholic drinks.

Zharokha *Grand Tower* hotel. A varied menu of north Indian favourites, with particularly rich sauces, plus a few obligatory Chinese dishes thrown in for good measure (Rs40–60).

Maheshwar

Overlooking the north bank of the mighty Narmada River, 91km southwest of Indore, **MAHESHWAR** has been identified as the site of King Kartvirajun's ancient capital, **Mahishmati**, a city mentioned in both the Mahabharata and Ramayana. In the eighteenth century, Maharani **Ahilya Bai** built a palace and several temples here, giving the town a new lease of life. Today, it's a prominent port of call on the Narmada Hindu pilgrimage circuit, but well off the tourist trail.

The waterfront **ghats** that line the river below an old sandstone palace, however, make a quintessentially Indian spectacle. Parties of *yatris* take holy dips, drying their clothes in the breeze blowing off the river, while *pujaris* and groups of sadhus sit around murmuring prayers under raffia sunshades. For the best view of them, head for the overhanging balcony of the eighteenth-century **Ahilya Bai Mandir**, reached via steps under the facade of the palace behind.

The palace and fort complex itself, further up the steps, houses the workshops of the Rewa Society, established by the maharani 250 years ago to promote the local handloom industry. Maheshwari **saris** are famous all over India for their distinctive patterns and superior quality; check out the designs for yourself by visiting the weavers' workshops (Mon–Fri 10am–5pm), which are sponsored by a German aid project. Though descendants of the old ruling family still occupy parts of the building, a couple of rooms around the entrance courtyard have been given over to a small and eminently missable museum.

Practicalities

All roads leading to Maheshwar are in a terrible state, so allow extra time if you are in a private car – the journey from Mandu can take up to four hours, and from Indore, at least three. There is a shady car park in the fort area (Rs10), just near the entrance to the museum. **Buses** also run from Dhar (every 20–30min; 2hr). From Indore, services are fairly frequent, taking three and a half hours, with a change at the market town of Dhamnod, 76km southwest of Indore on the NH-3. The nearest railhead is at **Barwah**, 39km west.

A recent spate of building means that finding decent **accommodation** is relatively easy. Conveniently situated in the centre of town, the welcoming *Aakash Deep Rest House* (☎07283/273326; ❶), to the right of the fort car park, has a handful of threadbare rooms with attached bathrooms. MP Tourism's *Narmada Retreat* (☎07283/273455, ✉maheshwar@mptourism.com; ❹–❺), 1km outside town, beside the river, has cosy cottages and an appealing restaurant, but don't forgot the mozzie repellent. ⚘*Ahilya Fort* (☎011/4155 1055, ⓦwww.ahilyafort .com; ❾) is a heritage hotel run by the son of the last maharaja of Indore. The fort dates back to the sixteenth century and the ornate rooms (US$240) have stone walls and colonial-era furnishings. The price includes exquisite Indian and European meals, which are worth staying a night just to sample.

Places to eat are thin on the ground, as the majority of visitors are pilgrims who cook their own food. The best option is the *Cottage Garden*, although it is inconveniently situated 1km from the fort, next to *Hotel Kumal* on the main road.

Omkareshwar

East of the main river crossing at Barwah, the Narmada dips southwards, sweeps north again to form a wide bend, and then forks around a two-kilometre-long wedge-shaped outcrop of sandstone. Seen from above, the island, cut by several deep ravines, bears an uncanny resemblance to the "Om" symbol. This, coupled with the presence on its sheer south-facing side of a revered *shivalingam*, has made **OMKARESHWAR**, 77km south of Indore, one of the most sacred Hindu sites in central India. Since ancient times, pilgrims have flocked here for *darshan* and a holy dip in the river, but in recent years, the town's remoteness and loaded religious feel have made it a favourite with hard-core Western and Israeli dope-heads, vying with local sadhus in the chillum-smoking and dreadlock-growing stakes. However, a more authentic atmosphere is preserved among the temples, wayside shrines, bathing places and caves strung together by an old paved pilgrims' trail.

From the bus stand at the bottom of the village on the mainland, Omkareshwar's only street runs 400m uphill to a ramshackle square, where you'll find most of the *dharamshalas* and chai shops, and a handful of stalls hawking lurid puja paraphernalia (including the excellent stylized **maps** taken home by pilgrims as souvenirs of their visits). To get to the island itself, cross the high concrete footbridge or take one of the flat-bottomed ferries that shuttle between the *ghats* crouched at the foot of the river gorge. Once across, you're soon swallowed up by the crowded narrow lane leading to the main temple.

The prominent white *shikhara* that now soars above the **Shri Omkar Mandhata Mandir** is a relatively new addition to the dense cluster of buildings on the south side of the island. Below it, the ornate pillars in the assembly hall, or *mandapa*, are more representative of the shrine's great antiquity. Myths relating to the origins of the deity in the low-ceilinged sanctum date back to the second century BC. Another of India's twelve **jyotrilingams** ("lingams of light"), it is said by Hindus to have emerged spontaneously from the earth after a struggle between Brahma, Vishnu and Shiva.

Around the island

Traditionally, the *parikrama* (circular tour) of Omkareshwar begins at the *ghats* below Shri Mandhata and proceeds clockwise **around the island**. The walk takes at least a couple of hours, so carry plenty of water if you plan to do the whole thing in one go.

The first section of the trail is a leisurely half-hour stroll from the footbridge to the pebble-strewn western tip of the island, where you'll find a small chai stall and a couple of insignificant shrines. The **Triveni Sangam**, or "Three-rivers Confluence", is an especially propitious bathing place where the Narmada forks as it merges with the Kaveri. From here, the path climbs above the fringe of fine white sand lining the northern shore until it reaches level ground. The ruins of the **Gaudi Somnath temple** stand in the middle of the plateau, surrounded by a sizeable collection of sculpture mounted on concrete plinths. The sanctuary houses a colossal *shivalingam*, attended by an equally huge Nandi bull. At this point, drop down a steep flight of steps to the village, or continue east towards the old fortified town that crowned the top of the island before it was ransacked by Muslims in the medieval era. Numerous chunks of temple sculpture, lying discarded among the rubble, include a couple of finely carved gods and goddesses, used for shade by families of black-faced langur monkeys.

After scaling the sides of a gully, the trail leads under the large ornamental archway of the **Surajkund Gate**, flanked by three-metre figures of Arjun and Bheema, two of the illustrious Pandava brothers. The tenth-century **Siddhesvara temple** stands five minutes' walk away to the south, on a patch of flat ground overlooking the river. Raised on a large plinth decorated with rampaging elephants, it has some fine *apsaras*, or celestial dancers, carved over its southern doorway.

Of the two possible routes back to the village, one takes you along the top of the plateau before dropping sharply down, via another ruined temple and the **maharaja's palace**, to the Shri Mandhata temple. The other follows a flight of steps to the riverbank, and then heads past a group of sadhus' caves to the main *ghats*.

Practicalities

Omkareshwar is connected by state **bus** to Indore (3–5hr) and Maheshwar (2hr). Omkareshwar Road is the nearest railhead, but only slow passenger services stop here. Barhawa, on the north bank of the Narmada, is the closest main-line railway station.

The State Bank of India on the main street changes US dollars only (at abysmal rates) and has an ATM. The best option is to **change money** before you arrive; Indore is the nearest place with foreign exchange facilities. A small **post office** on the main street offers reliable poste restante.

Omkareshwar has a good range of **accommodation**. For those seeking the ascetic experience, the central *dharamshalas* in the mainland village are inexpensive (Rs30–60), and offer close-hand experience of pilgrim culture. On the down side, *dharamshala* rooms tend to be windowless cells, with washing facilities limited to a standpipe in the yard (to encourage people to use the river) and communal toilets. One of the best is *Jat Samaj*, facing the river, to the right of the bridge on the main square – look for the rooftop figure on horseback. Another favourite is *Ahilya Bai*, tucked away behind the Vishnu temple off the road to Mamaleshwar temple and the *ghats*. This and its close neighbour, *Tirole Kunbi Patel*, have great views over the river to the Om island from their balconies and roof terraces. If you can't face a spell in a *dharamshala*, there are a few alternatives. The peaceful *Yatrika Niwas* (no phone; ❷), behind the bus stand, has clean but spartan rooms with attached bathrooms; the distance from the *ghats* reduces the impact of devotional music played there early each morning.

Opposite the Shri Omkar Mandhata Mandir, the *Hotel Aishwarya* (☎07280/271325; ❷–❸), probably the best choice in town, has functional, clean doubles with attached bathrooms and hot bucket, plus a restaurant. *Gita Shri Guest House* (☎07280/271560; ❶–❷) has good-value rooms with attached baths and squat toilets, in the main market area.

Long-stay visitors and pilgrims tend to opt for cooking their own **meals** using stoves provided by the *dharamshalas* or bought at minimal cost in the bazaar, where you can also get basic provisions. The alternatives are the good, pure-veg restaurant at *Hotel Aishwarya*, or the garden restaurant of *Ganesh Guest House*, directly behind the *Tirole Kunbi Patel*, which offers travellers' favourites including good egg-free pancakes, pizza, hummus and falafel. It also has no-nonsense digs (❶).

Chhattisgarh

A meagre trickle of foreign visitors come to **CHHATTISGARH**, formed in November 2000 when sixteen districts seceded from Madhya Pradesh. Rich in mineral resources and productive agricultural land, the new state is endowed with few attractions of the kind that usually entice travellers to India. Part of Chhattisgarh's undeniable appeal, however, lies in getting very much off the beaten track, where you'll encounter none of the frenzied competition for custom that exists elsewhere.

The thickly forested southern district of **Bastar** is most rewarding; here you'll find exceptional landscapes and fascinating *adivasi* cultures, but before travelling anywhere south of the capital, Raipur, you must obtain up-to-date information about the **state of security** around your intended destination (Raipur's CTDC tourist office can help with this). **Violent conflict** between Naxalite guerrillas and state-sponsored militias periodically blights parts of southern Chhattisgarh, with some remote areas more or less permanently controlled by the rebels.

The **best time to visit** is during the cooler winter months between November and February, when the average daytime temperature on the central plains (including Raipur) is around 25°C; during the summer months of April, May and June it is frequently 40°C or hotter. In the higher elevations north and south of the central plains temperatures are generally 5°C lower throughout the year.

Getting around involves a straightforward choice between bus and car transport. Chhattisgarh doesn't have its own state bus service, but buses operated by the Madhya Pradesh State Road Transport Corporation (MPSRTC) and private firms run between cities and the major towns. The service is often patchy away from the major highways, particularly in Bastar, leaving no alternative but to hire a car.

Raipur

Despite being an important centre of administration and commerce, the burgeoning city of **RAIPUR** offers few cultural or historical attractions. A further disincentive to pause here is the acute air pollution, a consequence of

Tribes of Bastar

In the thickly forested district of Bastar, over seventy percent of the population belong to one of a number of indigenous tribes, collectively known as **adivasis** (literally, "original inhabitants"), whose ancestors may have been present in India anywhere between 10,000 and 65,000 years ago. Historically, the inaccessibility of the region, its distance from important centres of trade, and the partial success of the *adivasis'* resistance to invaders, provided an environment favourable for the retention of traditional *adivasi* ways of life.

A number of different tribes – as distinct from one another as from "mainstream" society – live within a day's drive of Jagdalpur. Most *adivasi* people are friendly and are as curious about you as you are about them; they will welcome your interest, as long as you do not treat them as exotic exhibits. Asking questions, taking a genuine interest in their customs and showing an appreciation of their crafts is acceptable; gawping, taking photographs without permission and doling out money is not.

You should not attempt unplanned exploration of tribal areas outside of Jagdalpur on your own. *Adivasi* people usually speak little if any Hindi, and no English, and you may be met with anger or even violence if you arrive uninvited on their land. Some areas require **permits**; others may be off-limits altogether – the situation can change quickly. **Naxalites** are active in parts of Bastar and do sometimes indiscriminately target buses, while **state security forces** are unlikely to welcome foreigners – whom they may believe to be unsympathetic reporters – in areas where there has been conflict between *adivasis* and the police. For these reasons it is essential that you discuss your plans with the Chhattisgarh Tourist Board office in Jagdalpur, which can arrange **permits**, **guides** and **transport**.

One way to experience *adivasi* culture is to attend one of the two hundred weekly **haats** held throughout Bastar, at which *adivasi* people from different tribes, often after a trek of many kilometres, gather to socialize and sell or barter their produce. Some *haats* only offer specific types of goods; others are large general markets, such as the one held each Friday at the village of **Lohandiguda**, 18km from Jagdalpur. By late afternoon the event becomes a little unruly, due to everyone having consumed much *landa* (rice beer), *salphi* (sago palm wine) and other liquors, which the *adivasis* traditionally use to lubricate every kind of social occasion.

---

ongoing vigorous industrial expansion fuelled by cheap labour and plentiful raw materials. However, Raipur is a useful base; it's centrally located within the state, and has facilities for changing money and arranging transport and accommodation for trips into the hinterland.

Practicalities

Buses to Raipur terminate at the **New Bus Stand**, in the Pagaria Complex, slightly north of the city centre. From here, regular services connect the capital with all cities and major towns in Chhattisgarh and a number of destinations in Orissa, Madhya Pradesh and Maharashtra. The **railway station**, which operates an efficient ticket-booking service, lies 2km west of the New Bus Stand. It receives regular direct interstate trains from the north, east and west; when travelling to or from southern India it's often quicker to change trains at Visakhapatnam, in northern Andhra Pradesh. Raipur's **airport** is 10km southeast of the city; taxis to the city centre cost around Rs250.

There is a **CTDC tourist office** in Paryatan Bhawan, on G.E. Road, 5km from the New Bus Stand (Mon–Sat 10am–5pm; ℡0771/406 6415, ⓦwww .chhattisgarhtourism.net), which can organize car-hire, book tours and provide advice about the security situation in **Bastar**. The **Chhattisgarh Tourist**

Board has tourist offices at the railway station (℡0771/645 6336) and the airport (℡0771/654 3336). The State Bank of India on Jaistambh Chowk (Mon–Fri 10.30am–4.30pm) changes major foreign currencies and traveller's cheques, and has an ATM. Ice Cubes, 3 Vallabh Nagar, approximately 4km south of Jaistambh Chowk (℡0771/404 3700, Ⓦwww.icecubes.in), specializes in customized archeological, wildlife and tribal tours, and can book air tickets and arrange car hire throughout Chhattisgarh.

Raipur's most inexpensive places to stay are mainly grouped around either the railway station or the New Bus Stand; opposite the latter is the welcoming *Jyoti* (℡0771/242 8777; ❸–❹), which offers clean, good-value rooms. Half a kilometre from the railway station, on MG Road, is *Allnear* (℡0771/253 9832; ❸–❹), which has unexceptional but well-maintained rooms, and a decent restaurant. A convenient and relatively inexpensive three-star option is the *Celebration*, on Jail Road (℡0771/409 2990, Ⓦwww.celebrationworld .in; ❻–❽), where facilities include a travel agent, Internet café, health club and a popular, high-class restaurant.

There are good inexpensive **restaurants** dotted around the city, and several *dhabas* near the New Bus Stand and the railway station offer thalis. *Girnar*, opposite the State Bank of India on Jaistambh Chowk, is deservedly popular and serves a wide range of Indian dishes (from Rs90), while *Oberoi's Gulshan*, VIP Road, Rajiv Gandhi Marg, is a large, glitzy place offering Indian, Chinese and international cuisine (from Rs100). *Bageecha*, Indravati Colony, 1km from the New Bus Stand, specializes in Chinese and Thai cuisine.

Sirpur

The town of **SIRPUR**, 78km northeast of Raipur, is home to the impressive seventh-century Vaisnavite **Laxman Temple**, one of the oldest and best-preserved brick-built temples in India. Constructed at a time when Sirpur was the capital of the kingdom of South Kosala, the temple is the earliest example known to have featured a *shikhara*, in this case beautifully adorned with erotic sculpture, and thus marks a significant turning-point in Indian temple architecture. A **museum** (Mon–Sat 10am–5pm; foreigners Rs100, Indian residents Rs5) run by the Archeological Survey of India houses a collection of rare statues and other relics significant to the Shaiva, Vaishnava, Buddhist and Jain faiths, including a recently unearthed 1.8-metre *Shivalinga*.

Close-by lie extensive remains of **Buddhist vihars**, or monasteries, some of which are still undergoing excavation, with many more sites in the area still to be worked. Successive rulers of South Kosala are known to have been Hindus, particularly Shaivites, but their patronage of the monasteries led to the area becoming an important centre of Buddhism between the sixth and tenth centuries.

Regular **buses** ply the route along NH-6 from Raipur to Sirpur; journey time is around an hour and thirty minutes, cut to an hour if you hire a **taxi** from Raipur CTDC at a cost of around Rs400, including waiting time of around two hours.

Jagdalpur

Bounded by the Indravati River to the north and surrounded by thick forest, **JAGDALPUR** is the largest outpost for hundreds of miles around and is therefore a convenient springboard for visits to points of interest throughout the Bastar district, for which it is the administrative headquarters.

A royal capital until 1948, when the princely state of Bastar was absorbed into the Indian Union, Jagdalpur has since grown from little more than a jungle clearing into a modest town containing a handful of interesting diversions. The **Tribal Museum** (Mon–Fri 10am–12.30pm and 2.30–5.30pm; free), run by the Anthropological Survey of India, is located at Dharampura, on Chitrakote Road. Exhibits include some fascinating nineteenth-century photographs, *adivasi* craftwork and models of dwellings, and there's a reading room with a good selection of English-language books. Next to Bastar Palace the **Danteshwari Temple** is architecturally uninspiring but becomes the focus of colourful devotional activity each September during **Bastar Dusshera**, the region's most important – and unique – religious festival, when deities from the surrounding tribal villages are brought to its shrine. A stroll along the shore of **Dalpat Sagar**, an artificial lake created over four hundred years ago, close to the Indravati River in the north of town, is a relaxing way to start or end a day. Early in the morning you'll be joined by bathers and fishermen; in the evening pedal-boats can be hired from the pier on the eastern shore.

Practicalities

Jagdalpur is connected to Visakhapatnam, in northern Andhra Pradesh, by the highest **broad-gauge railway line** in India. The daily Kirandul–Visakhapatnam 2VK service departs at 9.45am, although Naxalite activity renders it subject to periodic disruption. **Buses** to Raipur and other destinations in Chhattisgarh leave from the old bus stand in the city centre. From the Interstate Bus Stand, close to the Indra Stadium in the southwest corner of the city, services run to destinations in Orissa, Madhya Pradesh and Andhra Pradesh.

Tourist information, car hire (Rs1200/day) and guides (Rs500/day) are available from the Chhattisgarh Tourist Board office (Mon–Sat 10am–6pm), at the *Rainbow Hotel*, Sanjay Market (Mon–Sat 10am–6pm). The State Bank of India (Mon–Fri 10.30am–4.30pm), at the old bus stand, has an ATM but no exchange facilities.

The choice of **hotels** in Jagdalpur is limited to a handful of mid-range and a larger number of inexpensive options. Some have an aversion to foreign guests; book ahead if you can. ✯ *Rainbow*, Sanjay Market (☎07782/229740; ❸–❺), is a friendly, centrally located hotel with capacious rooms and an in-house travel service; it's often full so book in advance. A reasonable alternative is *Atithi* (☎07782/225275, ✉atithihotel@rediffmail.com; ❸–❹), half a kilometre from the old bus stand, on Bodh Ghat Road, though rooms are smaller. The most-upmarket hotel in the city is *Akanksha*, Bodh Ghat Road (☎07782/226102, ⓦwww.hotelakanksha.com; ❹–❻), where the best rooms overlook a lake. Aside from the odd grubby *dhaba*, the only **restaurants** are in the hotels. The best is at the *Rainbow*, which serves Indian and international cuisine (mains from Rs70) and is blessed with a bar.

Kanger Valley National Park

Situated in a transition zone marking the southern limit of *sal* and the northern limit of teak, the ancient mixed forests that make up the 200-square-kilometre **Kanger Valley National Park** (Nov–June 8am–4pm; Rs200 [Rs25], camera Rs25, video camera Rs200, vehicle charge Rs50) abound with myriad flora and fauna. Species present include tigers, leopards, wild pigs, deer, boars, sloths and many varieties of birds and reptiles. A small lake, Bhaimsa Darha, provides a habitat for crocodiles and turtles. **Tirathgarh Falls**, 4km from the park entrance, where the Kanger River tumbles a hundred metres by stages into a glistening arcadian pool, makes a good place to stop for lunch. The **Kailash**, **Kutumsar** and **Dandak limestone cave networks** (8am–3pm; compulsory guide Rs50) contain some impressive stalactites and stalagmites; markings on some of the latter suggest they were once worshipped as *shivalingams*. Kutumsar is home to a species of blind albinic cave-fish.

Private **taxis** in Jagdalpur (27km away) charge around Rs1500 for a full day's visit to the park and back. Alternatively, it's possible to **stay overnight** in the park at one of the very basic forest lodges (❷–❸); enquiries should be made at the Chhattisgarh Tourist Board office in Jagdalpur (see opposite).

Travel details

Trains

Bhopal to: Agra (15–19 daily; 5hr 20min–9hr 30min); Chennai (3–7 daily; 19hr 25min–32hr); Delhi (18–21 daily; 8–14hr); Goa (2 daily; 34hr–40hr 30min); Gwalior (17–21 daily; 4hr 5min–6hr 40min); Indore (3–6 daily; 5hr–8hr 15min); Jabalpur (2–6 daily; 6–7hr 20min); Jalgaon (2–3 daily; 7–9hr); Jhansi (22–26 daily; 3hr–5hr 40min); Mumbai (6–12 daily; 14hr 55min–18hr); Nagpur (12–15 daily; 5hr 30min–8hr 30min); Pune (2 daily; 16–17hr); Sanchi (3 daily; 40–55min); Ujjain (3–6 daily; 3–5hr); Vidisha (3–4 daily; 40–50min).

Gwalior to: Agra (20–28 daily; 1hr 10min–2hr 20min); Chennai (2–3 daily; 28–40hr); Delhi (18–22 daily; 3hr 30min–6hr 35min); Goa (2 daily; 30hr–37hr); Indore (3 daily; 13hr); Jabalpur (2 daily; 11hr 12min–13hr 20min); Jalgaon (2–3 daily; 12hr 30min–16hr 30min); Jhansi (22–26 daily; 1hr 10min–2hr 45min); Kolkata (Calcutta; 4 weekly; 24hr 20min); Mumbai (5–6 daily; 20hr–25hr); Pune (2–3 daily; 21–24hr); Satna (1–2 daily; 10hr); Ujjain (1–2 daily; 11hr); Vidisha (5–6 daily; 4hr 30min–6hr).

Indore to: Agra (1–2 daily; 14hr 30min–16hr); Ajmer (2 daily; 13hr 30min–16hr); Chennai (1 weekly; 34hr); Chittaurgarh (2 daily; 7hr 30min–8hr 35min); Delhi (2–3 daily; 13hr–19hr 10min); Jabalpur (1 daily; 15hr 35min); Jaipur (1–2 daily; 12–16hr); Jhansi (1 daily; 11hr 35min); Kolkata (Calcutta; 3 weekly; 34hr); Kota (1–2 daily; 6hr 30min–7hr 40min); Mumbai (1 daily; 14hr 35min); Ujjain (4–6 daily; 1hr 30min–2hr).

Jabalpur to: Bhopal (2–6 daily; 6hr–7hr 20min); Chennai (1–2 daily; 23hr 45min–32hr); Delhi (2 daily; 15hr 40min–19hr 40min); Gwalior (2 daily; 11hr 12min–13hr 20min); Indore (1 daily; 15hr 35min); Jhansi (2 daily; 8hr 50min–11hr); Kolkata (Calcutta; 2 daily; 23–25hr); Mumbai (3–5 daily; 18–20hr); Nagpur (8 weekly; 9hr 15min–10hr 30min); Patna (2–4 daily; 12hr 30min–18hr

30min); Satna (3–4 daily; 3hr); Ujjain (2–3 daily; 11hr–13hr); Varanasi (4–6 daily; 10hr 30min–12hr).

Jagdalpur to: Visakhapatnam (daily; 10hr).

Raipur to: Bhopal (2–4 daily; 11hr 20min–5hr 30min); Chennai (Wed, Sat & Sun only; 22hr 30min–24hr); Delhi (1–3 daily; 20hr–7hr 45min); Kolkata (Calcutta; 4–6 daily; 12hr 40min–16hr 10min); Mumbai (2–3 daily; 19hr 10min–20hr 30min); Puri (daily, except Thurs & Fri; 16hr 20min–16hr 50min); Thiruvananthapuram (Wed & Sat; 42hr); Visakhapatnam (1–2 daily; 10hr 50min–11hr 50min).

Ujjain to: Agra (2–3 daily; 12–16hr); Ahmedabad (1 daily; 9hr 30min); Chennai (6 weekly; 32hr 30min–33hr 30min); Delhi (2–3 daily; 12hr–21hr 30min); Gwalior (1–2 daily; 11hr); Indore (4–6 daily; 1hr 30min–2hr); Jabalpur (1–2 daily; 10hr 40min–13hr); Jaipur (6 weekly; 8hr 45min–10hr); Jhansi (2–4 daily; 9–10hr); Kolkata (Calcutta; 3 weekly; 32hr); Mumbai (1 daily; 12hr 25min); Nagpur (4 weekly; 12hr); Varanasi (3 weekly; 31hr 35min).

Buses

Bhopal to: Indore (every 30min; 4–6hr); Jabalpur (3–4 daily; 8–10hr); Nagpur (2–3 daily; 7–10hr); Pachmarhi (4–5 daily; 5–8hr); Sanchi (every 30min; 1hr 30min); Ujjain (hourly; 5–6hr); Vidisha (every 30min; 2hr–2hr 30min).

Gwalior to: Agra (every 30min; 3hr–3hr 30min); Datia (every 30min; 1hr 30min–2hr); Delhi (4 daily; 8hr); Jhansi (every 30min; 3hr); Khajuraho (4–5 daily; 7–9hr); Kolkata (Calcutta; 1–3 daily; 23–29hr 29hr 35min); Shivpuri (every 30min; 2hr 30); Ujjain (3 daily; 12hr).

Indore to: Agra (1–2 daily; 16hr); Aurangabad (3 daily; 14hr); Chittaurgarh (1 daily; 10hr); Dhar (every 30min; 2–3hr); Jaipur (3 nightly; 14–15hr); Kota (4 daily; 8–9hr); Mandu (3 daily; 4hr); Mumbai (2 daily; 16hr); Nagpur (2–4 daily; 11hr–14hr);

Omkareshwar (3 daily; 3–5hr); Udaipur (5–6 daily; 15hr); Ujjain (every 15min; 1hr 30min–2hr).

Jabalpur to: Khajuraho (5 daily; 7–9hr); Kisli (for Kanha; 3 daily; 5–7hr); Kolkata (Calcutta; 2 daily; 19hr 30min–27hr 45min); Mandla (hourly; 3hr); Murwara (for Bandhavgarh; 8–10 daily; 2hr); Nagpur (10–12 daily; 7hr); Satna (6–8 daily; 8hr).

Jagdalpur to: Brahmapur (Berhampur; 1–2 daily; 10hr); Hyderabad (1–2 daily; 16hr); Raipur (4–6 daily 7hr); Visakhapatnam (daily; 11hr 50min).

Khajuraho to: Agra (1 daily; 12hr); Bhopal (1 daily; 12hr); Gwalior (4–5 daily; 7–9hr); Jhansi (9 daily; 4–6hr); Mahoba (11 daily; 2hr 30min–3hr); Satna (3 daily; 3hr 30min–4hr); Varanasi (3 weekly; 14hr).

Raipur to: Bhubaneswar (2–4 daily; 12hr); Jabalpur (3–5 daily; 12–14hr); Jagdalpur (4–6 daily; 7hr); Nagpur (3–5 daily; 7hr); Puri (2–4 daily, 13hr); Sambalpur (2–4 daily; 9hr).

Ujjain to: Agra (2 daily; 15hr); Delhi (1 daily; 21hr); Dhar (5 daily; 4hr); Gwalior (3 daily; 12hr); Kota (8–10 daily; 8hr); Maheshwar (4 daily; 5hr);

Mumbai (1 daily; 17hr); Omkareshwar (3 daily; 6–7hr).

Flights

Bhopal to: Delhi (3 daily; 1hr 10min–2hr); Gwalior (4 weekly; 1hr); Indore (3 daily; 30min); Mumbai (1–2 daily; 2hr 5min).

Indore to: Ahmedabad (1 daily; 1hr 15min); Delhi (3–4 daily; 2hr 10min); Gwalior (1 daily; 1hr 10min); Jabalpur (1 daily; 1hr); Mumbai (3 daily; 2hr 5min).

Khajuraho to: Delhi (1–2 daily; 1hr 50min); Varanasi (1–2 daily; 40min).

Raipur to: Bhubaneswar (daily; 1hr); Chennai (Mon, Wed, Fri & Sun; 2hr 20min); Delhi (2–3 daily; 1hr 40min–2hr 40min); Indore (daily; 2hr); Kolkata (Calcutta 1–2 daily; 2hr 10min); Mumbai (3 daily; 1hr 30min–1hr 40min); Nagpur (Tues, Thurs & Sat; 40min); Visakhapatnam (Mon, Wed, Fri & Sun; 2hr 25min).

Himachal Pradesh

AFGHANISTAN

CHINA
(TIBET AUTONOMOUS
REGION)

BHUTAN

PAKISTAN

NEPAL

BANGLADESH

MYANMAR
(BURMA)

ARABIAN
SEA

BAY OF BENGAL

N

SRI
LANKA

INDIAN OCEAN

0   400 km

The International boundaries on this map are neither purported to be correct
nor authentic by Survey of India directives. Publisher.

CHAPTER 6 # Highlights

* **Narrow-gauge railway**
  A rattly ride through stunning mountain scenery to the Raj-era hill station of Shimla.
  See p.482

* **Rewalsar** Buddhist pilgrimage site based around a sacred lake, with monasteries, temples, caves and hermitages. See p.498

* **Dharamsala** This relaxing hill station, home of the Dalai Lama, is an ever-popular place for rest, meditation retreats and trekking.
  See p.502

* **Dharamsala trek** A fantastic five-day trek leading through Dhauladhar forest to the Indrahar Pass, visiting traditional villages. See p.509

* **Manikaran hot springs**
  Sacred to Sikhs and Hindus, this steamy settlement stands at the gateway to the spectacular Parvati Valley.
  See p.522

* **Manali** Travellers en route to Ladakh chill out at this honeymoon capital, enjoying Himalayan panoramas from flower-filled gardens.
  See p.525

* **Spiti Valley** Tiny Tibetan villages and beautiful white *gompas* dot Spiti's lunar landscape. See p.537

* **Manali–Leh Highway** The second-highest road in the world, passing through a vast wilderness. See p.543

▲ Prayer flags in the Spiti Valley

Himachal Pradesh

Ruffled by the lower ridges of the Shivalik Range in the far south, cut through by the Pir Panjal and Dhauladhar ranges in the northwest, and dominated by the great Himalayas in the north and east, **HIMACHAL PRADESH** (HP) is India's most popular and easily accessible hill state. Sandwiched between the Punjab and Tibet, its lowland orchards, subtropical forests and maize fields peter out in the higher reaches where pines cling to the steep slopes of mountains whose inhospitable peaks soar in rocky crags and forbidding ice fields to heights of more than 6000m.

Together with deep gorges cut by rivers crashing down from the Himalayas, these mountains form natural boundaries between the state's separate districts. Each has its own architecture, from rock-cut shrines and *shikhara* temples to colonial mansions and Buddhist monasteries. Roads struggle against the vagaries of the climate to connect the larger settlements, which are way outnumbered by remote villages, many of which are home to semi-nomadic **Gaddi** and **Gujjar** shepherds.

An obvious way to approach the state is to head north from Delhi to the state capital, **Shimla**, beyond the lush and temperate valleys of **Sirmaur**. The former summer location of the British government, Shimla is a curious, appealing mix of grand homes, churches and chaotic bazaars, with breathtaking views. The main road **northeast** from Shimla tackles a pass just north of **Narkanda**, then follows the River Sutlej east to **Sarahan**, with its spectacular wooden temple, and enters the eastern district of **Kinnaur**, most of which is accessible only to those holding **Inner Line permits** (see p.480). Alpine and green in the west, Kinnaur becomes more austere and barren as it stretches east to the Tibetan plateau, its beauty enhanced by delicate timber houses, temples and fluttering prayer flags.

Another road from Shimla climbs slowly northwest to **Mandi**, a major staging post for the state. To the north is Himachal's most popular tourist spot, the **Kullu Valley**, an undulating mass of terraced fields, orchards and forests overlooked by snowy peaks. Its epicentre is the continuously expanding tourist town of **Manali** – long a favourite hangout of Western hippies – set in idyllic mountain scenery and offering trekking, whitewater rafting and relaxing hot springs in nearby **Vashisht**. The sacred site of **Manikaran** in the Parvati Valley also has hot sulphur-free springs.

Beyond the Rohtang Pass in the far north of Kullu district, the high-altitude desert valleys of **Lahaul and Spiti** stretch beneath massive snowcapped peaks and remote settlements with Tibetan *gompas* dotting the landscape. **Permits** are needed for travel through to Kinnaur, but **Ki**, **Kaza** and **Tabo** have unrestricted access, as does the road through Lahaul to Leh in Ladakh.

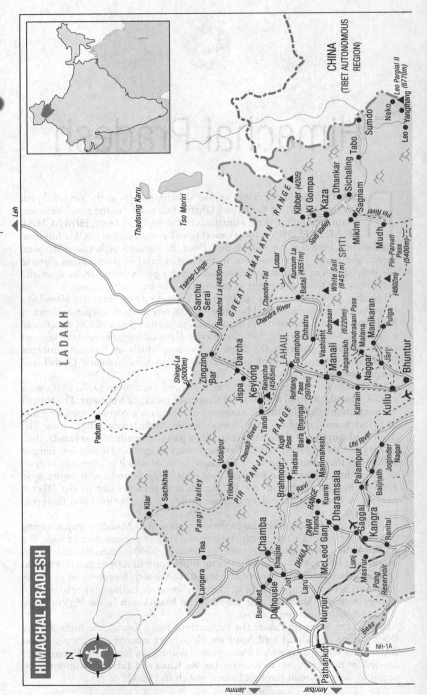

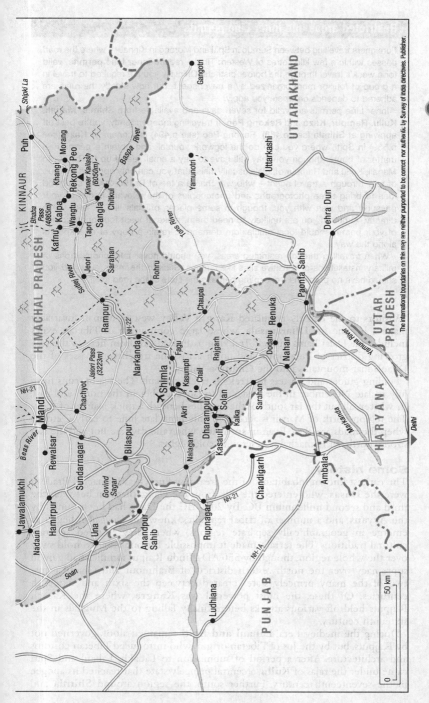

The international boundaries on this map are neither purported to be correct nor authentic. by Survey of India directives. Publisher.

Restricted areas and Inner Line permits

Foreigners travelling between Sumdo in Spiti and Morang in Kinnaur – where the road passes within a few kilometres of Western Tibet – require **Inner Line permits**, valid for a week's travel through the border districts. Officially you are required to travel in a group of four or more organized by a travel agent, but how strictly the rules are adhered to depends on where you apply.

Inner Line permits are valid for seven days and available from **Shimla**, **Manali**, **Kullu**, **Rampur**, **Kaza** and **Rekong Peo**. If travelling independently, you're best off applying at **Shimla** (see p.488), Rekong Peo (see p.494) in Kinnaur or **Kaza** (see p.539) in Spiti, where you can do the legwork yourself and obtain a permit in a matter of hours, though you may still have to pay a small fee of up to Rs150. In Manali, Kullu and Rampur officials usually insist that you can only apply as a group of four through a travel agent – who will charge a fee of Rs150–200. It's a good idea to bring three photographs and photocopies of the relevant pages of your passport and visa with you, though in some places officials like to take these directly. Although you are unlikely to need them, make at least four photocopies of your permit should local officialdom demand to retain a copy at checkpoints along the way.

When travelling through restricted areas, you should never take photographs of military installations or sensitive sites like bridges. Stick to the main route and you should have no problems – excepting perhaps the state of the road itself.

Visitors to the densely populated **Kangra Valley** west of Manali invariably make a beeline for **Dharamsala**, whose large community of Tibetan exiles includes the Dalai Lama himself. Trekking paths lead east from here to the tea-growing district of **Palampur**, and north across the treacherous passes of the Dhauladhar mountains into the **Chamba Valley**.

Finding guides and porters for **treks** is rarely difficult. The season runs from July to late November in the west, and to late October in the north and east. In **winter**, all but the far south of the state lies beneath a thick blanket of snow. The region north of Manali is accessible only from late June to early October when the roads are clear. Even in **summer**, when the days are hot and the sun strong, northern Himachal is beset with cold nights.

Some history

The earliest known inhabitants of the area now known as Himachal Pradesh were the **Dasas**, who entered the hills from the Gangetic plain between the third and second millennium BC. By 2000 BC the Dasas had been joined by the **Aryans**, and a number of tribal republics, known as *janapadas*, began to emerge in geographically separate regions, where they fostered separate cultural traditions. The terrain made it impossible for one ruler to hold sway over the whole region, though by 550 AD Hindu Rajput families had gained supremacy over the northwestern districts of Brahmour and Chamba, just two of the many princely states created between the sixth and sixteenth centuries. Of these, the most powerful was **Kangra**, where the Katoch Rajputs held off various attacks before finally falling to the Mughals in the sixteenth century.

During the medieval era, **Lahaul and Spiti** remained aloof, governed not by Rajputs, but by the Jos of Tibetan origin, who introduced Tibetan customs and architecture. After a period of submission to Ladakh, Lahaul and Spiti came under the rajas of **Kullu**, a central princely state that reached its apogee in the seventeenth century. Further south, the region around **Shimla** and

Sirmaur was divided into over thirty independently governed *thakurais*. In the late seventeenth century, the newly empowered **Sikh** community, based at **Paonta Sahib** (Sirmaur), added to the threat already posed by the Mughals. By the eighteenth century, under **Maharaja Ranjit Singh**, the Sikhs had gained strongholds in much of western Himachal, and considerable power in both Kullu and Spiti.

Battling against Sikh expansion, Amar Singh Tapur, the leader of the **Gurkha** army, consolidated Nepalese dominion in the southern Shimla hill states. The *thakurai* chiefs turned to the **British** for help, and forced the last of the Gurkhas back into Nepal in 1815. Predictably, the British assumed power over the south, thus tempting the Sikhs to battle in the **Anglo-Sikh War**. With the signing of a treaty in 1846 the British annexed most of the south and west of the state, and in 1864 pronounced Shimla the summer government headquarters.

After Independence, the regions bordering present-day Punjab were integrated and named Himachal Pradesh ("Himalayan Provinces"). In 1956 HP was recognized as a Union Territory and ten years later the modern state was formed, with Shimla as its capital. Despite being a political unity, Himachal Pradesh is culturally very diverse. With more than ninety percent of the population living outside the main towns, and many areas remaining totally isolated during the long winter months, Himachal's separate districts maintain distinct customs, architecture, dress and agricultural methods. Though Hinduism dominates, there are substantial numbers of Sikhs, Muslims and Christians, and Lahaul, Spiti and Kinnaur have been home to Tibetan Buddhists since the tenth century. This may explain why the state is usually a **stronghold** for the more inclusive Congress Party.

Shimla and around

Shimla, Himachal's capital, is India's largest and most famous hill-station, where much of the action in Rudyard Kipling's colonial classic *Kim* took place. While the city is a favourite spot for Indian families and honeymooners, its size does little to win it popularity among Western tourists who tend to pass through on their way to Manali. It is however, a perfect halfway house if you're heading to the Kullu Valley, or back in the other direction towards the plains of Haryana and Punjab. It's also the starting post for forays into the remoter regions of Kinnaur and Spiti.

The southernmost area of the state, **Sirmaur**, is Himachal's most fertile area. **Nahan**, the capital, holds little of interest, but the major Sikh shrine in **Paonta Sahib** and **Renuka wildlife sanctuary** are worth visiting. Southeast of Shimla, **Kasauli** is a peaceful place to break your journey from Chandigarh in Punjab, whilst nearby **Nalagarh Fort** has been converted into the finest hotel in the state.

Northeast of Shimla, **Sarahan**, site of the famous **Bhimakali temple**, set against a backdrop of the majestic Himalayas, can be visited in a two- or three-day round trip from Shimla, or en route to Kinnaur.

Shimla

Whether you travel by road or rail from the south, the last stretch of the climb up to **SHIMLA** seems interminable. Deep in the foothills of the Himalayas, the hill station is approached via a sinuous route that winds from the plains at Kalka across nearly 100km of precipitous river valleys, pine forests, and mountainsides swathed in maize terraces and apple orchards. It's not hard to see why the British chose this inaccessible site as their summer capital. At an altitude of 2159m, the crescent-shaped ridge over which it spills is blessed with perennially cool air and superb **panoramas** across verdant country to the snowy peaks of the Great Himalayan range.

Named after its patron goddess, Shamla Devi (a manifestation of Kali), the tiny village that stood on this spot was "discovered" by a team of British surveyors in 1817. Glowing reports of its beauty and climate gradually filtered to the imperial capital, Calcutta, and within two decades the settlement had become the Subcontinent's most fashionable summer resort. The annual migration was finally rubber-stamped in 1864, when Shimla – by now an elegant town of mansions, churches and cricket pitches – was declared the Government of India's official hot-season HQ. With the completion of the **Kalka–Shimla Railway** in 1903, Shimla lay only two days by train from Delhi. Its growth continued after Independence, especially after becoming state capital of Himachal Pradesh in 1966.

Today, Shimla is still a major holiday resort, popular mainly with nouveau riche Punjabis and Delhi-ites who flock here in their thousands during the May–June run-up to the monsoons, and then again in September and October. Its jaded colonial charm also appeals to foreigners looking for a taste of the Raj. The *burra-* and *memsahibs* may have moved on, but Shimla retains a decidedly **British feel**: pukka Indian gentlemen in tweeds stroll along the Mall smoking pipes, while neatly turned-out schoolchildren scuttle past mock-Tudor shop-fronts and houses with names like Braeside. At the same time, the pesky monkey troupes and chaotic mass of corrugated iron rooftops that make up Shimla's **bazaar** lend an unmistakably Indian aspect to the town.

The **best time to visit** is during October and November, before the Himachali winter sets in, when the days are still warm and dry, and the morning

The Viceroy's toy train

Until the construction of the **Kalka–Shimla Railway**, the only way to get to the Shimla hill station was on the so-called **Cart Road** – a slow, winding trail trodden by lines of long-suffering porters and horse-drawn tongas. By the time the 96-kilometre narrow-gauge line was completed in 1903, 103 tunnels, 24 bridges and 18 stations had been built between Shimla and the railhead at Kalka, 26km northeast of Chandigarh. These days, buses may be quicker, but a ride on the "toy train" is far more memorable – especially if you travel first-class, in one of the glass-windowed rail cars. Hauled along by a tiny diesel locomotive, they rattle at a leisurely pace through stunning scenery, taking between five and a half and seven hours to reach Shimla.

Along the route, you'll notice the guards exchanging little leather pouches with staff strategically positioned on the station platforms. The bags they receive in return contain small brass discs, which the drivers slot into special machines to alert the signals ahead of their approach. **"Neal's Token System"**, in place since the line was first inaugurated, is a fail-safe means of ensuring that trains travelling in opposite directions never meet face to face on the single-track sections of the railway.

For information about train times and ticket booking, see p.488.

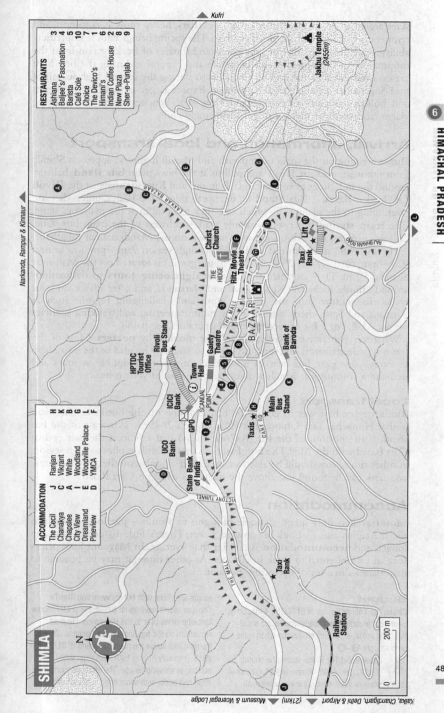

SHIMLA

N

▲ *Kufri*

◄ *Narkanda, Rampur & Kinnaur*

RESTAURANTS

Ashiana	3
Baljee's/ Fascination	4
Barista	5
Café Sole	10
Choice	7
The Devico's	1
Himani's	6
Indian Coffee House	2
New Plaza	8
Sher-e-Punjab	9

ACCOMMODATION

The Cecil	J	Ranjan	H
Chanakya	C	Vikrant	K
Chapslee	A	White	B
City View	G	Woodland	L
Dreamland	E	Woodville Palace	F
Pineview	D	YMCA	D

Jakhu Temple
(2455m)

LAKKAR BAZAAR

Christ Church

THE RIDGE

Ritz Movie Theatre

Gaiety Theatre

THE MALL

BAZAAR

RAJ BHAVAN ROAD

Taxi Rank

Lift

Bank of Baroda

HPTDC Tourist Office

Rivoli Bus Stand

Town Hall

SCANDAL POINT

ICICI Bank

GPO

State Bank of India

UCO Bank

Main Bus Stand

Taxis

CART RD

VICTORY TUNNEL

THE MALL

Taxi Rank

Railway Station

0   200 m

◄ *Kalka, Chandigarh, Delhi & Airport* ▲ *(21km)* ▲ *Museum & Viceregal Lodge*

skies are clear. From December to late February, heavy snow is common, and temperatures hover around, or below zero. The spring brings with it unpredictability: warm blasts of air from the plains and flurries of freezing rain from the mountains. Accommodation can be scarce and expensive during the first high season (mid–April to the end of June), less so during the second high season of mid–September through mid–November. Expect larger crowds on weekends and holidays, notably Christmas and New Year. Whenever you come, bring warm clothes as the nights can get surprisingly chilly.

Arrival, information and local transport

Buses arriving on the main Chandigarh and Manali highways approach Shimla from the west, via Cart Road, and pull in at the busy main **bus stand**, halfway around the hill. Buses from Narkanda, Rampur and Kinnaur arrive at the **Rivoli** (or "Lakkar Bazaar") **Bus Stand** on the north side of the Ridge, unless they are continuing to the plains – in which case they too pull in at the main bus stand. The **train station** is a twenty-minute walk southwest of the main bus stand. Shimla's **airport** lies 21km southwest of town on the Mandi road at Jubarhati.

The HPTDC main **tourist office** (daily: high season 9am–7pm; low season 9am–6pm; ☎0177/265 2561, ⓦwww.hptdc.gov.in) is located on the Mall near Scandal Point. They organize whistle-stop **sightseeing tours** to destinations around Shimla, including Kufri, Chail and Narkanda, and offer advice on local walks. To venture into the more remote and challenging regions such as Kinnaur and Spiti, check out the many mountaineering and trekking agencies on the Mall. For a list of recommended operators, see p.488.

Wherever you arrive in Shimla, you'll be mobbed by **porters**. Most of the town is pedestrianized, and seriously steep, so you may be glad of the extra help to carry your gear, but bear in mind that most porters double as touts and demand a commission which will increase the cost of your room.

Local transport

Taxis are the best way to get to the pricier hotels on the outskirts. The main Vishal Himachal Taxi Union rank (☎0177/265 7645) is 1km east of the bus stand, at the bottom of the **lift** (Rs7 each way) that connects the east end of Cart Road with the Mall. The list of set fares they publish applies to high season; at other times, you should be able to negotiate discounts. Another, more central, taxi rank can be found just above the main bus stand on Cart Road.

Accommodation

Most travellers only spend a couple of nights in Shimla – just long enough to see the sights and to book an onward ticket. There's little to detain you any longer, and **accommodation** is costlier than average. In May and June prices soar and it's essential to book in advance. At other times, it may be possible to negotiate a discount of up to fifty percent.

Budget

Chanakya Lakkar Bazaar ☎0177/265 4465. Cosy, clean and friendly. The cheaper rooms are small but good value, especially off-season when rates drop sharply. ❷–❺

Dreamland The Ridge, above the church ☎0177/280 6897, ⓔvinayakjishtu@hotmail .com. Excellent value during the low season; all

rooms are clean, with hot showers and Star TV. Cheaper rooms have squat toilets, the pricier rooms fantastic views over to the Himalayas. Pleasant restaurant on the top floor and Net access. ❸–❻

Ranjan Just above the main bus stand ☎0177/265 2818. Originally built in 1907, this large white building is showing its age. The attached rooms are large and basic, with some original fittings and a sunny balcony. Good if you can't face the climb with your bags from the bus stand. ❷

Vikrant Cart Rd, near the bus stand ☎0177/265 3602. Large hotel with clean doubles and some singles. The cheaper ones have a common bathroom with hot bucket water. There's also a dorm (Rs100). ❷–❹

YMCA The Ridge. Take the steps to the left of the Ritz movie theatre ☎0177/280 4085, ⓔymcashimla@yahoo.co.in. Large rooms, including seven attached. In-house dining hall (breakfast is included) and sun-terrace, along with Star TV, snooker tables, weights, table tennis and Internet café; low-season rates negotiable. ❸

Mid-range

City View US Club Rd, east of Christ Church ☎0177/281 1666. Not the cleanest, but the owners are friendly, offer good trekking advice and are flexible on the room rates. All rooms are attached with hot showers and colour cable TV. Good sunset views from the small balcony. ❹–❺

Pineview Mythe Estate, on the far side of the Victory tunnel ☎0177/265 8604. A good location in an apple orchard facing north, with a wide choice of comfortable attached rooms. ❹–❺

White Lakkar Bazaar ☎0177/265 5276, ⓦwww.hotelwhiteshimla.com. Well-managed hotel with light rooms overlooking the Himalayas. Cleanliness can vary. The deluxe suite (Rs1700) is excellent. Fixed prices all year. ❹–❻

Woodland Daisy Bank Estate ☎0177/281 1002, ⓔwoodlandshimla@yahoo.com. Quiet place tucked away above the eastern end of the Mall in a concrete jungle. Attentive staff and a range of clean rooms; the pricier ones have bathtubs. Good bazaar views and easy access to Jakhu Peak. ❹–❺

Expensive

The Cecil The Mall ☎0177/280 4848, ⓦwww.oberoihotels.com. Raj-era building, frequented by Rudyard Kipling among others, bought and revamped by the Oberoi group in 1939. It is now opulent but devoid of character, with little but the facade as a reminder of its past. $290–620. ❾

Chapslee Lakkar Bazaar ☎0177/280 2542, ⓦwww.chapslee.com. Exclusive, beautiful old manor house set in its own grounds on the edge of town and stuffed with antiques. Five luxurious suites, one single room, plus a library, card room, tennis court and croquet lawn. You'll need to book in advance; meals are also available to non-guests if booked in advance. $230–290 full board. ❾

Woodville Palace Raj Bhavan Rd ☎0177/262 3919, ⓦwww.woodlandpalacehotel.com. Twenty mintues' walk south from Christ Church, this elegant 1930s mansion lies on the peaceful western side of town, with huge rooms, period furniture, lawns and a badminton court. Members of Shimla's former royal family still live upstairs. Rooms are from $75; the showpiece Royal Suite goes for $225. ❽–❾

The Town

Although Shimla and its satellite districts sprawl over the flanks of five or more hills, the centre is fairly compact, on and immediately beneath a shoulder of high ground known as the "**Ridge**". Shimla's busy social scene revolves around the broad and breezy piazza that straddles the Ridge, overlooking rippling foothills with the jagged white peaks of the Pir Panjal and Great Himalayan ranges on the horizon. During high season the Ridge is a hive of activity, with entertainment provided by brass bands and pony rides. The Victorian Gothic spire of **Christ Church** is Shimla's most prominent landmark. The **stained-glass windows**, the finest in British India, depict (from left to right) Faith, Hope, Charity, Fortitude, Patience and Humility. At the other end of the Ridge, **Scandal Point** is the focus of Shimla's famous mid-afternoon meet when crowds gather here to gossip.

From the Ridge, a tangle of roads and lanes tumbles down in stages, each layer connected to the next by stone steps. **The Mall**, the main pedestrian thoroughfare, curves around the south slope of the hill. Flanked by a long row of unmistakably British half-timbered buildings, Shimla's main shopping street was, until World War I, strictly out-of-bounds to all "natives" except royalty and rickshaw-pullers. These days, rickshaws, man-powered or otherwise, are banned and non-Indian faces are in the minority. The quintessentially colonial **Gaiety Theatre** was undergoing extensive renovation at the time of writing but should be hosting the Shimla Amateur Dramatic Company again by late 2008.

The hike to Jakhu Temple

The early-morning hike up to **Jakhu**, or "Monkey", **Temple** is something of a tradition in Shimla. The top of the hill (2455m) on which it stands offers a superb panorama of the Himalayas – particularly breathtaking before the cloud gathers later in the day. The relentlessly steep climb takes twenty to forty minutes – or you could arrange a horse (there are usually a couple to be hired in the main square opposite the Gandhi statue). The path starts just left of Christ Church; during the season, all you need do is follow the crowds.

After the hard walk up, the temple itself, a red-and-yellow-brick affair crammed with fairy lights and tinsel, comes as something of an anticlimax. The shrine inside houses what are believed to be the footprints of **Hanuman**. Legend has it that the monkey god, adored by Hindus for his strength and fidelity, rested on Jakhu after collecting healing Himalayan herbs for Rama's injured brother, Lakshmana. Watch out for the troupes of mangy monkeys around the temple. Pampered by generations of pilgrims and tourists, they have become real pests; hang on to your bag and don't flash food.

Walk down any of the narrow lanes leading off the Mall, and you're plunged into a warren of twisting backstreets. Shimla's **bazaar** is the hill station at its most vibrant – a maze of dishevelled shacks, brightly lit stalls and minarets, cascading in a clutter of corrugated iron to the edge of Cart Road. Apart from being a good place to shop for authentic souvenirs, this is also one of the few areas of town that feels Himalayan: multicoloured Kullu caps (*topis*) bob about in the crowd, alongside the odd Lahauli, Kinnauri or Tibetan face.

The state museum

The HP state **museum** (Tues–Sun 10am–1pm & 2–5pm, closed 2nd Sat of month; Rs50 [Rs10], camera Rs50) is a 1.5-kilometre hike west from the centre, but well worth the effort. The ground floor of the elegant colonial mansion is given over largely to temple sculpture, and a gallery of magnificent **Pahari miniatures** – examples of the last great Hindu art form to flourish in northern India before the deadening impact of Western culture in the early nineteenth century. An offspring of the Mughal painting tradition, the Pahari or "Hill" school is renowned for subtle depictions of romantic love, inspired by scenes from Hindu epics. Among the museum's **paintings** are dozens of Mughal and Rajasthani miniatures and a couple of fine "Company" water-colours. Produced for souvenir-hunting colonials by the descendants of the Mughal and Pahari masters, the *fakirs*, itinerant sadhus and mendicants they depict could have leapt straight from the pages of Kipling. One room is devoted to Mahatma Gandhi, packed with photos of his time in Shimla and amusing cartoons of his political relationship with the British.

To get there, follow the Mall past the post office and downhill, passing *Dalziel* and *Classic* hotels, then take the right fork at the first intersection and left at the second, where a signpost guides you up the last, short ascent.

The Viceregal Lodge and Prospect Hill

Shimla's single most impressive colonial monument, the old **Viceregal Lodge** (daily 9am–5pm; Rs50 [Rs20]; guided tours every 30min except 1–2pm), summer seat of British government until the 1940s and today home to the **Institute of Advanced Studies**, is a fifteen-minute walk west of the museum. The lodge is Shimla at its most British. The solid grey mansion, built in Elizabethan style with a lion and unicorn set above the entrance porch, surveys trimmed lawns fringed by pines and flowerbeds. Inside is just as ostentatious, though only sections of the ground floor are open to the public: a vast teak-panelled entrance hall, an impressive library (formerly the ballroom) and the guest room. The **conference room**, hung with photos of Nehru, Jinnah and Gandhi, was the scene of crucial talks in the run-up to Independence. On the stone terrace to the rear of the building, a plaque profiles and names the peaks visible in the distance.

The short hike up to **Prospect Hill** (2176m), a popular picnic spot, ties in nicely with a visit to the lodge. By cutting through the woods to the west of the mansion, you can drop down to a busy intersection known as **Boileauganj**, from where a tarmac path climbs steeply up to the small shrine of Kamana Devi. The summit gives fine views across the south side of Shimla ridge, and over the hills and valleys of southern HP towards the plains of the Punjab.

Eating

Few **restaurants** in Shimla retain the colonial ambience you might expect and standards are generally poor, with little variety on offer. Catering mainly for Indian visitors, they are heavily Punjabi-oriented, with an emphasis on rich, spicy, meat-based menus. At the top of the range, try the restaurants at *The Cecil* or *Clarks*, another period hotel at the south end of the Mall. Various **"fast-food"** restaurants along the Mall offer everything from *dosas* and Chinese food to Mughlai cooking, while its many **bakeries** and ice-cream parlours offer comfort for the sweet-toothed. For a really cheap and filling meal, try the fried potato patties (*tikki*) or chickpea curry and *puris* (*channa batura*) at one of the snack bars that line the steps opposite the Gaiety Theatre. Alternatively, the bazaar is good for cheap *dhabas*.

Ashiana The Ridge. HPTDC restaurant in a converted bandstand offering mainly non-veg Indian food, including tasty chicken *makhanwalla*, plus pizzas and a few Chinese dishes. Mains typically Rs100.

Baljee's 26 the Mall. A landmark on Shimla's culinary and social map, this hectic smart-set coffee house does a roaring trade in snacks, sweets and ice cream in the evenings, but serves no alcohol. The swish à la carte *Fascination* restaurant upstairs offers a good selection of Indian and Chinese dishes for around Rs120–200, as well as sausage, egg and chips.

Barista The Mall. Western-style coffee bar, complete with excellent lattes, muffins, chocolate brownies and chirpy service, for a fraction of the price back home.

Café Sole The Mall, on the roof of *Combermere Hotel* below. Slick modern cafeteria-cum-restaurant, serving reasonable Italian and Thai dishes for around Rs150, as well as standard Indian and good bakery items.

Choice Middle Bazaar, down steps from *Baljee's*. Tiny, no-nonsense Chinese restaurant with an exhaustive menu, serving delicious veg and non-veg dishes for Rs50–80.

The Devico's The Mall. Lively Western-style fast food joint with south Indian snacks, veggie-burgers, and shakes. Most items under Rs100. There's an additional restaurant downstairs and a plush bar upstairs.

Himani's 48 the Mall. The ground floor is taken up by a flashy video-game arcade, a lively (mostly male) bar on the first floor and a family-style restaurant, pool den and sundeck on the top floor. Menu includes tandoori (Rs120) and south Indian dishes.

Indian Coffee House The Mall. Atmospheric, faded café with colonial ambience, offering the usual *Coffee House* package of veg snacks and attentive waiter service to the predominantly male clientele.

New Plaza 60/1 Middle Bazaar, down the steps beside *Himani's*. Popular family restaurant. Good-value food including tasty meat sizzlers for Rs100.

Sher-e-Punjab Upper Bazaar. The best of the *dhabas* just below the Mall. Hearty portions of spicy beans, chickpeas and dhal at Rs40–60.

Listings

Airlines Indian Airlines, Air Sahara, Air Deccan and Jagson Air, c/o Ambassador Travels, The Mall ☏0177/265 8014.

Banks and exchange ATMs of Citibank, UCO Bank and ICICI are among half a dozen along the Mall. Only the SBI will cash traveller's cheques, although cash can be exchanged at other banks and agents, who keep longer hours and offer mostly decent rates. Visa encashments can be made at the Bank of Baroda on Cart Rd, five minutes' walk east of the main bus stand.

Bookshops Maria Brothers, an antiquarian bookshop on the Mall, sells old maps and etchings as well as a limited selection of new books – but don't expect a bargain. Asia Bookhouse and Minerva, also on the Mall, both stock paperbacks.

Hospitals Indira Gandhi Medical College Hospital ☏0177/280 4251; Deen Dayal Hospital, near the ISBT ☏0177/265 4071.

Internet access There are several places along the Mall, such as Mr Sood's Internet café, next door to Sindh Tours and below the church. The *Dreamland* hotel has facilities too.

Laundry Snowhite and Whiteway, both on the Mall.

Permits Inner Line permits (see p.480) are issued at the Additional District Magistrate's office (Mon–Sat 10am–5pm, closed 2nd Sat of the month; ☏0177/265 7005) on the first floor of the modern courthouse, one street below the Mall, opposite Sheel SJ Jewellers.

Pharmacies Indu Medical, the Mall (9am–8pm).

Post The green-painted, Swiss-chalet-style GPO (Mon–Sat 10am–6pm), with its poste restante counter, is near Scandal Point on the Mall.

Travel agents Reliable operators include Band Box, 9 the Mall, near Scandal Point (☏0177/265 8157, ✉bboxhy@satyam.net.in), which specializes in tailor-made itineraries, and Great Himalayan Travels (☏0177/265 8934, ⊛www.ghtravels.com). The *YMCA* (☏0177/280 4085) also organizes treks and safaris, as does Silver Dreams (☏09816 008180, ✉silverdreams@gmail.com) at the *Dreamland*.

Moving on from Shimla

The **toy train** leaves Shimla for **Kalka**, where you can change onto the main broad-gauge line for **Chandigarh** and **New Delhi**. The 10.55am departure gets you into Kalka in good time to catch either the Himalayan Queen #4096 at 4.40pm or the faster Shatabdi Express #2012 at 5.30pm, both arriving in New Delhi around 10pm. The other toy-train services depart at 11.35am, 2.30pm, 5.30pm and 5.45pm; they should take around 5hr each, though it's often longer. **Reservations** for onward journeys from Kalka can be made at Shimla Station (☏0177/265 2915, enquiries ☏131). Alternatively, you can catch a bus to Chandigarh and continue to Delhi by train from there.

The **main bus stand** (☏0177/265 8765), on Cart Road below the bazaar, serves Chandigarh, Delhi, Mandi, Kullu, Dharamsala, Manali and elsewhere, while the Rivoli (or Lakkar Bazaar) Bus Stand, reached via the path dropping behind ICICI Bank on Scandal Point, handles departures to Narkanda, Ani, Rampur, Sarahan and Kalpa (for Kinnaur). Passengers for **Manali** or **Delhi** can choose between luxury a/c, deluxe non-a/c, or Himachal's standard bone-shaking state buses. Tickets for the former two should be booked a day in advance at travel agents on the Mall, while state bus tickets can be reserved at the ticket counter (Mon–Sat 10am–4.30pm) outside the HPTDC tourist office near Scandal Point; alternatively, head to the counters at the main bus stand. For **Chandigarh**, services are so frequent there's no need to book.

Flights on small aircraft from Shimla to Delhi (1hr 15min) are operated by Jagson Airlines (daily except Sun) for around Rs2600 and Air Deccan (daily), whose prices vary wildly with demand. The inbound Jagson flight from Delhi continues to Kullu (around Rs1950). Tickets are available from various agents.

See p.545 for more information on journey frequencies and durations.

South of Shimla

On the border with Uttarakhand, the town of **PAONTA SAHIB**, where pastel-yellow houses are packed tightly into the cobbled streets, holds an important shrine dedicated to **Guru Gobind Singh**, the tenth Sikh guru, who lived here in the late 1680s. Paonta Sahib provides good bus connections for travel to Shimla from points such as Mussoorie, Dehra Dun, Haridwar and Rishikesh. Should you decide to stay, the HPTDC *Hotel Yamuna* (℡01704/222341; ❸–❺), on the banks of the River Yamuna, has pleasant rooms, a restaurant and bar. Further northwest lies the secluded lake at **Renuka**, where a **wildlife sanctuary** protects rare deer plus a magnificent pride of Asiatic lions, introduced in the hope of creating a stable breeding population. Tropical forests reach the lakeside, along which trees and reeds shelter colonies of herons, kingfishers and bee-eaters. The HPTDC *Hotel Renuka* (℡01702/267339; ❹–❺), in sloping gardens on the western shore, has rooms opening onto a shady veranda, as well as dorm beds (Rs75). The lake is connected by several daily private buses to Paonta Sahib and is also accessible via Dodahu, 2km away, served by six daily buses from the dull regional capital of Nahan, 45km to the west.

Kasauli

Though it sees few Western tourists, the small, slow-paced town of **KASAULI**, cradled by pine forests 77km southwest of Shimla (3hr by bus), and with a touch of Raj architecture, makes a good stop-off on the way to or from Delhi. Criss-crossed by spindly cobbled streets, spreading along low ridges carpeted with forests and flower-filled meadows, Kasauli offers an abundance of gentle short strolls, such as the one to nearby Sanawar.

The nearest railway station is Dharampur on the Kalka–Shimla line, from where buses travel the 11km up to Kasauli; there are also direct buses from Shimla. From Kasauli, an easy and scenic twelve-kilometre trek leads through forests to **Kalka**, railhead for the **toy train** to Shimla. There is no tourist office in Kasauli but the manager at the HPTDC *Ros Common* will provide information on paths, and train and bus times. You can **change money** at the Bank of Baroda (Mon–Fri 11am–3pm) on Lower Mall.

Aside from the cheaper lodges, of which one of the best is *Gian* (℡01792/272244; ❷–❸) on Post Office Road, most of Kasauli's **hotels** have high-ceilinged rooms with fireplaces, carpets and balconies, in true Raj style. Few have built-in water heaters but supply hot water in buckets. Two good options on the Lower Mall are the classy *Alasia* (℡01792/272008; ⓔalasia @vsnl.com; ❺–❼) and the reliable state-run HPTDC *Ros Common* (℡01792/272005; ❻–❼), which has a cheaper annexe (❺) 500m away. Apart from the larger hotels, **food** options are limited to *dhabas* serving *aloo mutter*, *aloo gobi* and dhal, and fresh *puris* in the morning.

Nalagarh Fort

If you can afford it, the eighteenth-century ☀**Nalagarh Fort** (℡01795/223179, ⓔfortresort@satyam.net.in; ❾), converted into probably the finest **hotel** in Himachal Pradesh, is an excellent place to break the journey between Delhi and Kullu. Towering above the town of the same name, with the Himachal foothills rising steeply behind, the fort – lying 60km from Chandigarh and 12km off the main Chandigarh–Mandi road – played a key role in the Gurkha wars of the early nineteenth century, and is today filled with memorabilia evoking its military past. Accommodation is in beautifully maintained suites, each with period furniture. An atmospheric lounge bar overlooks terraced grounds with a tennis court, croquet lawn and swimming pool, and an Ayurvedic clinic offers massage. Book in advance.

Northeast of Shimla: from Narkanda to Sarahan

A three-hour (65km) bus ride northeast of Shimla, the scruffy hill town of **NARKANDA** (2725m) makes a good resting point on the bumpy, six-hour journey to Sarahan. This former staging post on the Hindustan–Tibet caravan route acts as the roadhead and main market town for the area's widely dispersed apple and potato growers, and is a popular **ski area** (Jan–March) for Indian holiday-makers, although the lone ski hill is little more than a lopsided cricket pitch. A couple of places in town rent skis, including Highlands Travel & Adventure (℡01782/242444, ⓔhta30@hotmail.com), overlooking the bus stand. There are some good rambles through the cedar forests that surround the town, and great **views** of the Himalayas. **Hatu Peak** (3143m), crowned by a lonely hilltop **Durga temple**, 7km east of town, looks out over the River Sutlej winding far below, and a string of white-tipped mountains to the north and east.

Accommodation options include HPTDC's quietly situated *Hotel Hatu* (℡01782/242430; ❹–❺), with large well-appointed rooms, great views from the lawns and a restaurant; and the large attached rooms at the ski centre (℡01782/242426; ❷–❸). For a little more comfort, *Mahamaya Palace* (℡01782/242448; ❸) has reasonable attached rooms and a **restaurant**. Otherwise, the *New Himalayan Dhaba* opposite serves up simple but tasty veg food.

Rampur

Once over the pass at Narkanda, the highway winds steadily down the Sutlej Valley towards **RAMPUR**, a major transport hub 132km northeast of Shimla. Formerly the capital of the princely state of Bhushar, the town today is a gritty and cheerless cluster of concrete houses hemmed in by a forbidding wall of rock. During the local **Lavi Mela** (late Oct or early Nov), hill-people gather to trade bundles of wool and sacks of dried fruit and nuts. Across the main road from the bus stand, a small Buddhist **gompa** houses a huge metal prayer wheel and a rock reputedly bearing ten million minute inscriptions of the mantra "Om Mane Padme Hum".

Rampur has **bus** connections to Rekong Peo and onward all the way to Kaza in Spiti, and – when the Jalori Pass road is open – to Kullu. **Inner Line permits** for Kinnaur can be obtained from the Sub-Divisional Magistrate's office opposite the fire station on the main road, or else in Rekong Peo (see p.494). As you head down the steps from the bus stand, bypass the poky *Rama* and head for the *Amar Jyoti* (℡01782/233185; ❶), left at the bottom of the lane, which has comfortable attached doubles with balconies facing the river and a restaurant. The nearby *Bhagwati* (℡01782/233117; ❶–❸) has some plusher rooms, but top of the range is the HPTDC *Bushehar Regency* (℡01782/234103; ❹–❺), on the Shimla-facing edge of town. For **food**, the *Bhagwati* has the best restaurant; *Café Sutluj*, 200m west of town, makes up for its lack of atmosphere with air-conditioning, a bar and a great terrace overlooking the river.

Sarahan

Secluded **SARAHAN**, erstwhile summer capital of the Bhushar rajas, sits astride a 2000-metre ledge above the River Sutlej, near the Shimla–Kinnaur border. Set against a spectacular backdrop, the village harbours one of the northwestern Himalayas' most exotic spectacles – the **Bhimakali temple**. With its two multi-tiered sanctuary towers, elegantly sloping slate-tiled roofs and gleaming golden spires, it is the most majestic early timber temple in the Sutlej Valley – an area renowned for housing holy shrines on raised wooden platforms. Although most of the structure dates from the early twentieth century, parts are thought to be more than eight hundred years old.

A pair of elaborately decorated metal doors lead into a large courtyard flanked by rest rooms and a small carved-stone **Shiva shrine**. Visitors should leave shoes and any leather articles at the racks, before heading up the steps to a second, smaller yard. Beyond another golden door, also richly embossed with mythical scenes, the innermost enclosure holds the two **sanctuary towers**. The one on the right houses musical instruments, flags, paladins and ceremonial weapons used in religious festivals, a selection of which is on show in the small "museum" in the corner of the courtyard. Non-Hindus who want to climb to the top of the other more modern tower (no photography) to view the highly polished gold-faced deity have to don a saffron cap. Bhimakali herself is enshrined on the top floor, decked with garlands of flowers and tended not by ordinary villagers, as is normally the case in Himachal, but by bona fide Brahmin priests.

Practicalities

Buses from Shimla to Sangla and Rekong Peo pass through the small town of Jeori, from where several buses a day and taxis climb the 17km up the mountainside to Sarahan. There's also a direct bus service from Rampur. Keen walkers might fancy ambling along the well-worn mule track to Sarahan from Jeori. There's a fair choice of **accommodation** for such a small place. HPTDC's *Hotel Srikhand* (☎01782/274234; ④–⑤) is a concrete monster, but has a delightful garden and a restaurant serving good veg meals on a relaxing terrace. The clean, comfortable rooms are overpriced but come with hot water and valley views; there's also a dorm (Rs75) and a cheaper annexe. For more atmosphere, the *Temple Guest House* (☎01782/274248; ①–②), inside the Bhimakali courtyard, has a range of pleasant rooms and a basement dorm (Rs75). The

---

Blood sacrifice in Sarahan

The **Bhimakali** deity, a local manifestation of the black-faced, bloodthirsty Hindu goddess Kali (Durga), has for centuries been associated with **human sacrifice**. Once every decade, until the disapproving British intervened in the 1800s, a man was killed here as an offering to the *devi*. Following a complex ceremony, his newly spilled blood was poured over the goddess's tongue for her to drink, after which his body was dumped in a deep well inside the temple compound. If no victim could be found, it is said that a voice would bellow from the depths of the pit, which is now sealed up.

The tradition of blood sacrifice continues in Sarahan to this day, albeit in less extreme form. During the annual **Astami** festival, two days before the culmination of **Dussehra**, a veritable menagerie of birds and beasts are put to the knife, including a water-buffalo calf, sheep, goat, fish, chicken, crab, and even a spider. The gory spectacle draws large crowds, and is a memorable alternative to the Dussehra procession in Kullu, which takes place at around the same time in mid-October.

slightly faded *Hotel Trehan's* (☎01782/274205, ✉hotel-trehan47@rediffmail
.com;) offers spacious attached rooms with TV. When the temple kitchens aren't
dishing up their usual cheap and delicious meals, try one of the several Tibetan
dhabas around the square outside, such as *Dev Bhumi*.

Kinnaur

Before 1992, the remote backwater of **KINNAUR**, a rugged buffer zone
between the Shimla foothills and the wild western extremity of Chinese-
occupied Tibet, was strictly off-limits to tourists. Although visitors are now
allowed to travel through the "**Restricted Area**", and on to Spiti, Lahaul and
the Kullu Valley, permits are still required (see p.480). Other areas of Kinnaur –
notably the **Baspa Valley** and the sacred **Kinner–Kailash** massif visible from
the mountain village of **Kalpa** are completely open.

Straddling the mighty River Sutlej, which rises on the southern slopes of
Mount Kailash, Kinnaur has for centuries been a major trans-Himalayan corridor.
Merchants travelling between China and the Punjabi plains passed through on the
Hindustan–Tibet caravan route, stretches of which are still used by villagers
and trekkers. The bulk of the traffic that lumbers east towards the frontier,
however, uses the newer fair-weather road, veering north into Spiti just short of
the ascent to Shipki La pass, on the Chinese border, which remains closed.

In the well-watered, mainly Hindu west of the region, the scenery ranges from
subtropical to almost alpine: wood-and-slate villages, surrounded by maize
terraces and orchards, nestle beneath pine forests and vast blue-grey mountain
peaks. Further east, beyond the reach of the monsoons (June–Sept), it grows
more austere, and glaciers loom on all sides. **Buddhism** arrived in Kinnaur with
the tenth-century kings of Guge, who ruled what is now southwestern Tibet.
When **Rinchen Zangpo** (958–1055), the "Great Translator" credited with the
"Second Spreading" of the faith in Guge, passed through here, he left behind
several monasteries and a devotion to a pure form of the Buddhist faith that has
endured here for nearly one thousand years. In the sixteenth century, after Guge
had fragmented into dozens of petty fiefdoms, the **Bhushar kings** took control
of Kinnaur. They remained in power throughout the British Raj, when this was
one of the battlegrounds of the espionage war played out between agents of the
Chinese, Russian and British empires – the "Great Game" evocatively depicted
in the novels of Rudyard Kipling.

Rekong Peo

East of Jeori, the road climbs high above the Sutlej into ever more remote
territory, traversing sheer ravines on cable bridges, while tiny wooden villages,
each with a pagoda-roofed temple, cling to the mountainsides. At **Wangtu**
bridge, the trailhead for the Kinnaur–Pin Valley–Kaza trek (see box opposite),
the highway switches to the north bank of the river. Beyond the village of
Tapri, a right fork leads to **Sangla** in the Baspa Valley, while the main highway
continues to **REKONG PEO**, district headquarters of Kinnaur, 7km above the
main road. Its batch of concrete houses and government buildings around a

Unfrequented mountain trails criss-cross Kinnaur, offering **treks** ranging from gentle hikes to challenging climbs over high-altitude passes. The routes along the **Sutlej Valley**, punctuated with government resthouses and villages, are feasible without the aid of ponies, but away from the main road you need to be completely self-sufficient. **Porters** can usually be hired in Rampur, Rekong Peo and the Baspa Valley except in early autumn (Sept/Oct), when they're busy with the apple harvest.

The Kinner-Kailash circuit

The five- to seven-day *parikrama* (circumambulation) of the majestic Kinner-Kailash massif, a sacred pilgrimage trail, makes a spectacular trek for which you won't need an Inner Line permit. The circuit starts at the village of **MORANG**, on the left bank of the Sutlej, served by buses from Tapri or Rekong Peo. A jeepable track runs southeast from here to **Thangi**, the trailhead, and continues through Rahtak, over the **Charang La** pass (5266m) to **Chitkul** in the Baspa Valley. The trail then follows the river down to the beautiful village of **Sangla**, from where a couple of worthwhile day-hikes can be made – to **Kamru fort** behind the village, or the steep ascent to the **Shivaling La** pass, from where there are superb views of Raldang (5499m), the southernmost peak on the Kinner-Kailash massif. The final stage passes through the lower Baspa Valley, via Shang and Brua to **Karcham**, which overlooks the NH-22 highway. The best time for the Kinner-Kailash *parikrama* is between July and October; August is the most popular month for local pilgrims to complete the circuit.

Kafnu to Kaza, via the Pin Valley

This challenging route across the Great Himalayan range, via the Kalang Setal glacier and the Shakarof La pass, is a dramatic approach to Spiti and the **Pin Valley**, and no restrictions apply. The trail, which is very steep, snow-covered, and hard to follow in places, should definitely not be attempted without ponies, porters, adequate gear and a **guide** – preferably one arranged through a reputable trekking agency. It starts in earnest at Kafnu village, now connected to Wangtu on the main road by a paved surface, continuing via Mulling, Phustirang (3750m), and over the **Bhaba Pass** (4865m), a gruelling slog through snowfields, before dropping down into the beautiful and isolated **Pin Valley**. Kaza (see p.539), the district headquarters of Spiti, lies a further three or four days' hike to the north. On its way to the main road, the trail winds through remote settlements including **Kharo**, from where the ancient Buddhist *gompa* at **Khungri** can be reached. More of this route may become paved, as the delayed Wangtu-to-Mudh road project painfully progresses.

Chitkul to Har-ki-Dun

This ten-day trek to **Garhwal** (see p.346) passes along the edge of the Inner Line and is subject to restrictions. Starting from **Chitkul** and crossing the River Baspa to Doaria, the route then climbs up a side valley to follow a lateral moraine up to the Zupika Gad and then a steep ascent – the final section of which is up a crevassed glacier – to the **Borsu Pass** (5300m). The other side of the pass is down a steep snow and boulder field requiring some scrambling; you arrive a few days later in the beautiful valley of **Har-ki-Dun** in Garhwal. You should be able to link the trek with one over the Yamunotri Pass and Dodi Tal (see p.365) to Uttarkashi but this depends on conditions around the roadhead of Har-ki-Dun and Yamunotri. A guide is essential.

The old Hindustan–Tibet road from Kalpa to the Rupa Valley

Another route to consider is the relatively easy five-day trek starting at **Kalpa** and following the old Hindustan–Tibet road through the remote hamlets of upper Kinnaur (permits needed), past Shi Asu to the Rupa Valley. The views along the route are superb and the villagers are extremely hospitable. The road, now crumbling in places, is also ideal for mountain biking. Although there is a route from the Rupa Valley over the Manirang Pass into Spiti, few locals know it or are willing to guide you across.

small *maidan* gives it the air of an upstart frontier settlement. The only reason to stop is to buy trekking supplies, pick up the trail to Kalpa, or obtain an Inner Line **permit** (see p.480) from the District Commissioner's office; this is actually arranged through the nearby Tourist Info Centre (Mon–Sat 10am–5pm; ☎01786/222857) in the open courtyard below the bazaar bus stop. They charge Rs150 but take your photo and make copies of your passport themselves.

The Rekong Peo **bazaar** is good for crowd-watching, particularly in late afternoon when it fills up with villagers waiting for the bus home. Many of the women don traditional Kinnauri garb for their trip to town – green velvet jackets, heavy home-spun blankets with intricate borders, raw-silk cummerbunds and stacks of elaborate silver jewellery. Around 2km above the bazaar behind the All India Radio complex stands the **Mahabodhi Kinnaur Buddhist temple**, with its large yellow Maitreya statue overlooking an orchard. The temple was consecrated during the Kalachakra initiation ceremony performed here by the Dalai Lama in 1992.

Practicalities

Rekong Peo's **buses** are fairly frequent, considering its relative isolation. Buses drop off and pick up at the bend in the main bazaar before proceeding up the hill on the Kalpa road for 2km to the **main bus stand**. There are several daily services to Shimla, an early morning departure direct to Mandi, direct buses to Chandigarh, Delhi and nearby Sangla, two buses daily to Puh and a morning departure for Kaza. More services can be picked up from the main road at the bottom of the valley, 6km below.

Accommodation in town is overpriced for what you get; the best option around the bazaar is the *Hotel Fairyland* (☎01786/222477; ❸), on the road behind the *Cafeteria on the Roof*, which has modest but clean attached rooms and great views over the bazaar to Kinner Kailash. A reasonable fallback is *Hotel Mehfil* (☎01786/223600; ❸), also above the main bazaar. About 1km up the road to the main bus stand is the new *Hotel City Heart* (☎09418 018615; ❸–❹), which has immaculate, spacious doubles with bath; the pricier rooms have the best views. **Food** options in Peo itself are pretty much limited to the *Cafeteria on the Roof*, 100m east of the lower bus stand, which has sizzlers, pizza, a couple of Kinnauri dishes and a small terrace for people-watching. Also on the bazaar, opposite the Sharma Boot House, is a good, unsigned *dhaba* which serves up cheap mutton *momos* and veg *thukpa*. There is Internet access at Network, 100m beyond the main bus stand. You can get cash from the SBI ATM in the bazaar.

Kalpa (Chini)

Almost 250km northeast of Shimla and 9km along a twisting road from Rekong Peo, **KALPA** can be reached by road, or on foot along various steep tracks. Its narrow atmospheric lanes and dramatic location astride a rocky bluff, high above the right bank of the Sutlej, make the hike worthwhile. The ancient Tibetan *gompa* here was founded by Rinchen Zangpo, and there is also a small Shiva temple. Facing the village, the magnificent **Kinner-Kailash** massif sweeps 4500m up from the valley floor. The mountain in the middle, Jorkaden (6473m), is the highest, followed by the sacred summit of Kinner-Kailash (6050m) to the north, and the needle point of Raldang (5499m) in the south. Up the valley you'll see remains of the Hindustan–Tibet road.

Kalpa is a far more attractive place to stay than Rekong Peo, although finding **accommodation** can involve some walking. On the upper road, the *Kinner Villa* (☎01786/226006, ✆kinnervilla@rediffmail.com; ❺) is the most tasteful place around, with sleek, refurbished rooms, spotless bathrooms and a grassy pitch out front. On the same road the combined HPDTC *Tourist Complex* and *Kinner Kailash Cottage* (☎01786/226159; ④–⑧) contains a range of doubles and larger chalets, as well as a seasonal campsite, while the smart new *Rakpa Regency* (☎09418 245285; ③–⑤) is set in pleasant grounds and the front rooms have balconies with splendid views. In Kalpa itself, the *Blue Lotus Guest House* (☎01786/226001; ③–⑤), a concrete block 100m beyond the lower bus stand, has rooms priced according to their view, as well as a dorm (Rs150). The **restaurant** here offers the widest choice in the village; otherwise there are just a handful of local *dhabas*. Buses and taxis between Kalpa and Rekong Peo run every thirty minutes or so until 6pm; convenient connections include three daily buses to Shimla (6.30am, 11.30am & 2.30pm) and one to Sangla and Chitkul (8.30am).

The Baspa Valley

Hemmed in by the pinnacles of Kinner-Kailash to the north and the high peaks of the Garhwal range to the south, the seventy-kilometre **River Baspa** rises in the mountain wilderness along the Indo-Tibetan border to flow through what was until recently one of Kinnaur's most beautiful and secluded areas. The lower reaches of the valley below Sangla are now dominated by a massive and ugly hydroelectric plant, but beyond Sangla the scenery remains unspoilt. Although the head of the valley is closed to tourists, there are still plenty of walking opportunities exploring side valleys.

The valley's largest settlement, **SANGLA**, is served by daily **buses** from Shimla, Rampur, Rekong Peo and Tapri, and makes an excellent base to visit nearby **Kamru** village, 25 minutes' walk above Sangla, with its warren of lanes and slate-roofed stone houses, and its wood-and-stone gable-roofed **fort**. Tibetan prayer flags flutter in the breeze and the inhabitants retain Buddhist funerary rites, although they are now mostly Hindu and no longer read Tibetan. The inner sanctums of the **temple** below the fort are off limits to visitors unless a goat is paid for and sacrificed. In September and October Sangla fills up with Bengali holiday-makers, and hotel options are increasing every year; the centre is rather crowded and noisy at any time so the best **places to stay** are mostly dotted around the road in. One good choice is the *Monal Regency* (☎01786/242922; ③–④), 500m before town, which has pleasant rooms with a well-tended lawn out front. The next bend in the road leads up a short path to the friendly *Sangla Resorts* (☎01786/242401; ③), offering clean doubles, a dorm (Rs70) and a good restaurant. Just below the main road, the adjacent *Highland Guest House* (☎01786/242285; ②) and *Himalaya Home* (☎01786/242256; ①) both offer basic but clean rooms. **Eating** options are limited to hotel restaurants and several small cafés in the centre; *Sonam*, the middle of three adjacent places just above street level in the middle of the main bazaar, does fair Tibetan and Chinese. The bazaar also includes a Net Café and a snooker hall.

Two daily **buses** head (from the bazaar) further up the increasingly dramatic Baspa Valley to Chitkul (ask about times), though they are usually late and sometimes cancelled, in which case you'll need to hitch or hire a Jeep (Rs500). Eight kilometres beyond Sangla there's a wonderful campsite on the banks of the river, the *Banjara Camp* (☎01786/242536, ⓦ www.banjaracamps.com; ⑧), with luxurious tents, attentive service and meals included for a tad under $100 per night. At quiet **RAKCHAM**, 14km and forty minutes by bus from Sangla, the *Rupin River View Guest House* (☎01786/244225; ②) – offering pleasant wood-panelled rooms with shared bath and hot water – can organize **porters** and **guides** for treks such as the tough three-day hike to Thangi on the Kinner-Kailash circuit.

On a rise with dramatic views of the opening valley, **CHITKUL**, 25km from Sangla, is as far up the valley as you can go without an Inner Line permit (see p.480) – a gate and checkpoint at the far end of the village marks the start of the Inner Line. The bright, friendly *Amar Guesthouse* (**①**), a rickety wooden structure in the upper part of the village west of the fort, is extremely basic but cosier than the blue *Thakur Guesthouse* (☎01786/244320; **②–③**; dorm Rs75), down by the bus stand, which boasts some attached rooms, great views and can give trekking advice. The upstairs *Great Himalayan* restaurant, almost opposite *Thakur*, offers tasty food but service is very slow.

Visible above the village, a trail winds steeply up to a huge saddle below the **Charang La pass** – the route of the Kinner-Kailash *parikrama*, or pilgrimage circuit (see p.493). Throughout the Baspa Valley and especially past Sangla, trekkers and campers need to be self-sufficient in food and fuel so as not to overburden the local subsistence-oriented economy.

Upper Kinnaur

Inner Line permits are required for **upper Kinnaur**, the remote region east of Kalpa. Several hours by Jeep from Rekong Peo and within a day's hike of the frontier, the tiny hamlet of **Puh** is the first main settlement you encounter. Evidence from inscriptions suggest that Puh was, in the eleventh century, an important trading centre that fell under the influence of the Tibetan kingdom of Guge when the Great Translator, Rinchen Zangpo travelled through the area. The temple here is devoted to Sakyamuni, with wooden columns supporting a high ceiling and a circumambulatory path around the altar.

Beyond Puh, the road bends north, crossing the muddy Sutlej for the last time at **Khabo**, where it meets the turquoise waters of River Spiti. To the northeast, Kinnaur's highest peak, **Leo Pargial II** (6770m), rises in a near-vertical 4000-metre wall which marks the border with Tibet and overlooks the old Indo–Tibet road at the **Shipki La pass** (5569m). The NH-22 continues north through the barren wastes of the Hanglang Valley, very similar to parts of Ladakh with its small settlements of dry-stone houses piled high with fuel and fodder.

At **Yangthang**, little more than a string of roadside chai stalls, a road leads off to **NAKO**, the valley's largest village, nestling high above the river at 2950m around a small **lake**. In the northwest corner, the eleventh-century complex of the **Nako Chokhor** is attributed to Rinchen Zangpo; although it's in desperate need of restoration, its exquisite interior paintings are comparable to those of Alchi (see p.579). The finest building of all is the Serkhang or "Golden Hall", dedicated to the Tathagatas or Supreme Buddhas. There are some basic **accommodation** options: the best of the trio of lodges by the bus stand is the *Rio Purguil* (☎01785/236339; **②–③**), where all rooms have bathrooms and balconies. Down by the lake, the *Lake View Guest House* (☎01785/236041; **②–③**) also has decent attached rooms and a restaurant, while the *Natural Lake View Camp Naygo* rents out spacious tents for Rs500.

Frequent public **Jeeps** run up from Yangthang to Nako; going south, three **buses** a day (6am, 6.30am & 2pm; 5hr 30min) head for Rekong Peo from Yangthang. If you are continuing on to Spiti (see p.537), the good news is that there is now a more weather-resistant bypass around the notorious **Malling Slide**, a high-risk landslide zone just north of Yangthang. This makes the journey north far more straightforward; at least one daily bus leaves from Yangthang around 11am to noon for Tabo (5hr) and on to Kaza (7hr). Once beyond Sumdo, the rest of Spiti is open, Inner Line permits are not required and you have more freedom to explore and get off the beaten track.

Northwest Himachal

From Shimla the main road winds west and north to the riverside market town of **Mandi**, an important crossroads linking the Kullu Valley and the hills to **the northwest**. The rolling foothills on this side of the state are warmer and more accessible than Himachal's eastern reaches, though less dramatic and considerably lower. The area sees little tourism outside **Dharamsala**, the British hill station turned Tibetan settlement, home to the Dalai Lama. Dharamsala is an excellent base for treks over the soaring Dhauladhar range to the **Chamba Valley**, which harbours uniquely styled Hindu temples in **Brahmour** and **Chamba**. South of Chamba, the fading hill station of **Dalhousie** still has a certain ex-Raj charm, and is popular with Indian tourists who arrive in droves during the hot season.

Mandi to Dharamsala

The following section traces the River Beas and NH–21 as they weave from Mandi to Dharamsala, linking a string of quiet mountain towns and villages. While most visitors make the six-hour journey to Dharamsala in one go on one of the nine daily **buses**, those with more time can pause at sacred **Rewalsar**, just outside Mandi, or some smaller places of interest around **Palampur** and in the **Kangra Valley**. Even if you don't have time for these, you may decide to stop at **Joginder Nagar** or **Baijnath** to pick up the narrow-gauge train that trundles through patchwork fields and light forest to **Kangra**, just an hour away from Dharamsala.

Mandi

The junction town of **MANDI**, 158km north of Shimla, straddles the River Beas, its riverside *ghats* dotted with stone temples where sadhus and pilgrims pray. Once a major trading post for Ladakhis heading south – *mandi* means market – the town still bustles with commercial activity, now centred on the attractive **Indira Market** and its sunken garden, in the centre of the town square. A collection of sixteenth-century Naggari-style temples sits above the town on **Tarna Hill**. To get there, climb the 160 steps facing the market square, or take the road that winds up from the bridge close to the Bank of Baroda. On the summit is the main Kali temple, decorated with garish paintings of the fierce mother goddess draped in skulls and blood.

The frenetic **bus stand** is a short ride across the river on the east bank; its café does delicious veg food. There are departures every half-hour or so for Rewalsar. Kullu, Manali, Dharamsala and hourly for Shimla, with a possible change in Bilaspur, as well as longer-distance services. The town has plenty of **hotels**, most of them in the Indira Market area. The nicest place to stay is the ramshackle *Raj Mahal* (☎01905/222401; ❸), above the town square, a period-furnished palace set in spacious shady gardens, with a good restaurant and atmospheric gentlemen's bar. Also on the square is the *Shiva* (☎01905/224211; ❷), less atmospheric but cheaper, and the larger *Evening Plaza* (☎01905/225123, Ⓔmalhotralalji@hotmail.com; ❷–❹), which has a range of rooms, some with air-conditioning. The government-run *Café Shiraz*, at the edge of the main square, serves south Indian snacks and can book **bus tickets**. Indira Market is handy for fast-food joints, **Internet cafés** and the computerized **railway ticketing office** on the north end. Apart from a couple of ATMs, both the Bank of Baroda and the Overseas India Bank can **change money** and cash traveller's cheques, but the most convenient exchange is at the *Evening Plaza*.

Rewalsar

If you've any interest in Buddhism it's worth taking a detour 24km southeast of Mandi to **REWALSAR**, where three Tibetan monasteries (Nyingma, Drikung Kagyu and Drukpa Kagyu) mark an important place of pilgrimage. There are also Sikh and Hindu temples here, all of which draw a steady stream of pilgrims and tourists. The devout complete a *chora* around the small sacred lake and along narrow lanes full of shrines and stalls selling Tibetan curios, before lounging beneath the prayer flags on the lake's grassy fringes.

It's believed that Padmasambhava left many footprints and handprints in rocks and caves up in the hills around the lake, and steep paths lead up from the lake to **caves** that are used today as isolated meditation retreats. Of the three monasteries around the lake, **Tso–Pema Ogyen Heruka Gompa**, below the tourist lodge, is the most venerated and atmospheric; check out the tree planted in 1957 by the Dalai Lama, who visited India that year to celebrate the 2500th anniversary of the Buddha's birth, two years before his exile from Tibet. Towering dramatically over the lake and visually dominating the Rewalsar setting is the large but much newer **Drukpa Kagyu Zigar Gompa**.

For **Hindus**, Rewalsar is regarded as the abode of the sage Lomas, for whose sake the lake was created with waters from the Ganga and Yamuna. Three small temples dedicated to Krishna, Lomas and Shiva, along with a Nandi bull statue and lakeside *ghats*, reflect Rewalsar's Hindu connections. On the west shore, the Sikh **gurudwara** attracts pilgrims retracing the steps of Guru Gobind Singh, who came here in 1702; this is one of the few sites associated with his life in Himachal. To the south a small **sanctuary** protects deer and Himalayan black bears.

The HPTDC *Tourist Inn* (℡01905/240252; ❷–❹), a short way back from the north shore, has comfortable rooms with hot showers, as well as a small dorm (Rs75) in the older block. Visitors who plan to stay for a while may well prefer the pleasant **monastery accommodation** at the *Nyingma Gompa* (℡01905/280226; ❶–❷), or the more comfortable *Drukpa Kagyu Gompa* (℡01905/280210; ❶–❷). Local families are also keen to rent out rooms; ask at the *Zigar Tibetan Food Corner* restaurant. **Eating** is limited to several small but reasonable Tibetan restaurants near the lake which serve *thukpa*, *momos* and noodles, and the *dhabas* along the main road serving north Indian food.

Joginder Nagar and Baijnath

JOGINDER NAGAR, 63km northwest of Mandi, is an uninviting little town: little more than two streets flanked by wooden-fronted houses and a crowded bus stand. The main reason to stop here is that it is the eastern terminal of the Kangra Valley **train** (see box, p.501) to Kangra and Pathankot. The bus stand and railway station are 500m apart, and the smart HPTDC *Hotel Uhl* (℡01908/222002; ❸–❹) is at the eastern end of town; enquire here about paragliding at **Bir**, 15km west.

Around 30km northwest of Joginder Nagar, **BAIJNATH** is perhaps a better spot to pick up the toy train, as more services originate here and it gives you a chance to visit the **Baidyanath Shiva temple**, parts of which are intricately carved and supposed to date from 804 AD.

Palampur and around

Further into the Kangra Valley, tree-clad slopes give way to rolling deep-green fields, as the westbound road enters Himachal's prime tea-growing area, around the small town of **PALAMPUR**. Few travellers stop here, though the area has a couple of exceptional places to stay as well as a few sights of interest. Among them, **Tashi Jong**, 12km to the east just off the main highway, is a Tibetan settlement whose mural-filled monastery is dedicated to Sakyamuni. A recent addition to Tashi Jong is the **Dongyu Gatsal Ling Nunnery**, instigated by the Venerable Tenzin Palmo, a British-born nun who spends much of her time on worldwide lecture tours but often returns to Palampur; check out ⓦwww .tenzinpalmo.com. Palampur is also the trailhead for walks to nearby hills and gorges, such as the hike 2km north of the *Hotel T-Bud* to the spectacular 300-metre-wide **Neugal Gorge** on the River Bundla, and treks into the Kullu and Chamba valleys (see box below).

The best of the town's **hotels** is HPTDC *T-Bud* (☏01894/231298; ④—⑤), surrounded by lawns and pine trees 1km north of town, with immaculate, spacious rooms and an excellent restaurant. Further down, at the new bus stand, the *Highland Regency* (☏01894/231222; ②—③) has good-value doubles with balconies and is the best budget option. To sample the delights of life on a **tea estate**, head for *Country Cottage Tea Garden Resort*, Chandpur Tea Estate (☏01894/230647, ⓦwww.countrycottageindia.com; ⑥), around 5km northeast of Palampur, set in fifty acres of tea plantations, orchards and forest. The most luxurious place to stay in the region, however, is the 1930s *Taragarh Palace* (☏01894/242034, ⓦwww .taragarh.com; ⑧—⑨), set in a fifteen-acre wooded estate in **Taragarh**, 8km southeast towards Baijnath. Home to the Raja of Kashmir, the palace has period furnishings, a swimming pool, a new wing with luxury suites (US$150) and a campsite geared to visiting tour groups; advance booking is essential.

Trekking from Palampur district

With its lush tea gardens and alpine meadows, Palampur makes a good base for some lesser-known **treks**; the passes north of town offer unrivalled views of the Kangra Valley. Trek & Tour Himachal, with branches opposite the bus stand and at the *Country Cottage Tea Garden Resort* (see above), offer all-inclusive tailor-made packages with most equipment provided except sleeping bags. See p.500 for a **map** of some of the hiking routes described below.

Treks from Palampur

An easy four-day hike leads from Palampur over **Waru Pass** (3850m), the "gateway of the wind", via Satchali, Thanetar and Dhog to **Hol**; continuing for two more testing days to the sacred **Manimahesh Lake** near Brahmour. From Dhog it's possible to continue east to Barabhangal and as far as Manali.

A pleasant but difficult seven- or eight-day trek from Palampur starts by crossing **Sunghar Pass** (4473m), then leads back across the Dhauladhar ranges at **Jalsu Pass** (3600m) and south to Baijnath. **Baijnath** itself, under 20km from Palampur by road, is a good trailhead for treks to Chamba or Bharabhangal, following paths that traverse glaciers, waterfalls, the high Thamsar Pass (4665m) and the River Ravi.

Other routes

Treks from **Billing** lead via Rajgunda, Palachak, and over the Thansar Pass to **Marhu** from where you can continue west to **Chamba** (3 days) and **Manimahesh** (3 days), or southeast to **Manali** over the Kalihan ("black ice") Pass. The latter is a strenuous route requiring six days and is suitable only for experienced trekkers.

DHAULADHAR TREKS

Baijnath

Palampur

Dhog

Jalsu Pass
(3600m)

Thanetar

Satchali

Deol

Waru Pass
(3850m)

Manimahesh
Lake

Hadsar

Holi

Sunghar Pass
(4473m)

Brahmour

Kuthehar

Toral Pass
(4575m)

Chamnauta

Guntu Got

Tang
Narwana

Macchetar

Kuarsi

Kundli Pass
(4550m)

River Ravi

Indrahar Pass
(4350m)

Illaqa
Got

Lahesh
Cave

Triund

Bhimghasutri
Pass
(4580m)

Bag Pass
(4243m)

Minkiani Pass
(4250m)

Bleni Pass
(3710m)

Dharamkot

Bhagsu

McLeod Ganj

Dharamsala

Norbulingka

Dunali

▲ Chamba

N

0   (Approx.)   5 km

Kangra

Although **KANGRA** is bypassed by most travellers on their way to Dharamsala, 18km further north, it's worth a brief detour. Buses from all over the Kangra Valley and further afield pull into the bus stand 1km north of the town centre, where there are frequent connections to Dharamsala. Kangra can also be reached from Pathankot (see p.602) and from Joginder Nagar by the daily **narrow-gauge railway** service (see box below).

Behind the crowded **central bazaar** stands the **Bajreshwari Devi temple**, sacked and looted several times between the twelfth and fifteenth centuries for its legendary wealth. It was finally laid low by an earthquake in 1905 – what you see today is the result of extensive rebuilding, and holds little architectural appeal. Kangra's crumbling, overgrown **fort** (daily sunrise–sunset; Rs100 [Rs5]) was also damaged by the earthquake and is now inhabited by screeching green parrots that flit through a few simple temples still tended by priests. High gates, some British-built, span a cobbled path to the deserted ramparts. To get there, head 3km south on the road to Jawalamukhi, then turn up the one-kilometre access road just before the bridge.

Places to stay on the road between the bus stand and town include the simple *Hotel Preet* (☎01892/265260; ❷), which has its best rooms on the first floor alongside a cosy little terrace, and the cleaner *Hotel Yatrika* (☎01892/262258; ❸–❺) whose deluxe rooms have a/c. The noisy *Raj*, opposite the bus stand, is not worth staying in, but does have a good **restaurant** and bar.

Masrur

Southwest of Kangra a narrow road skirts low rippling hills for 30km to the tiny hamlet of **MASRUR**, the only place in the Himalayas with **rock-cut Hindu temples** (daily sunrise–sunset; Rs100 [Rs5]) similar to those at Ellora in Maharashtra (see p.732), though they are nowhere near as impressive. Hewn out of natural rock formations during the ninth and tenth centuries, the fifteen temples devoted to Shiva, Sita, Ram and Lakshmi bear eroded carvings of meditating mendicants and buxom maidens guarding dim cavernous sanctuaries. Passages cut into the rocky mounds wind up to a flat roof above the main temple, pierced by a vast *shikhara* adorned with Hindu deities.

The Kangra Valley Railway

India has five of the twenty or so vintage "toy trains" or narrow-gauge mountain railways in the world – three in the Himalayas and two of these in Himachal Pradesh. Most famous is the Kalka–Shimla line (see p.482), but the little-known 163-kilometre **Kangra Valley Railway** is also a magnificent engineering feat. Unlike the Kalka line, with its 103 tunnels and tortuous switchbacks, engineers of this route preferred bridges – 950 in all, many of which are still considered masterpieces – that give passengers uninterrupted views all the way from Pathankot to Joginder Nagar. Although slower than the equivalent road journey, the scenery is far more impressive, particularly the stretch between Kangra and Mangwal.

There are seven trains daily from Pathankot, departing between 2.40am and 5.40pm; the last only goes as far as Jawalamukhi Road (4hr 10min), four others terminate at Baijnath (6hr 30min–7hr), while the first and one other (9.25am) go all the way to Joginder Nagar (9hr). In the opposite direction there are departures from Joginder Nagar at 7.20am and 12.25pm, four more from Baijnath between 4.20am and 6pm, while one train originates at Jawalamukhi Road at 4.50am. All services pass through Kangra.

If you don't have your own vehicle, you can get to Masrur from Kangra by catching a **direct bus** to Pir Bindu, and getting off at the tiny hamlet of Nagrota Suriyan, from where you walk 1.5km up to the temples.

Jawalamukhi

A simple whitewashed temple in the otherwise nondescript town of **JAWALAMUKHI**, 35km south of Kangra, protects one of north India's most important Hindu shrines. The sanctuary, crowned with a squat golden spire, contains a natural blue gas flame emitted from the earth, revered as a manifestation of the goddess of fire, Jawalamukhi. Priests are eager to light emissions of gas in smaller chambers for expectant devotees, but only the main flame is kept alight continuously. A three-kilometre *parikrama*, or circumambulation, starts from the temple, climbing steeply up into the wooded hills and taking in several shrines on the way.

Frequent **buses** (1hr) depart from Kangra, but it's quicker to hitch or take a taxi. In the other direction several buses travel direct to Dharamsala, 53km north. The two best **hotels** are the plush HPTDC *Hotel Jwalaji* (℡01970/222280; ❹–❻) on the outskirts, and *Mata Vaishno Devi Hotel* (℡01970/222135; ❹–❻), 250m north of the bus stand, though a basic cell at the *Geeta Bhawan Ashram* (℡01970/222242; ❶) is much cheaper.

Dharamsala and McLeod Ganj

Home to the Dalai Lama and Tibetan government in exile, and starting point for some exhilarating treks into the high Himalayas, **DHARAMSALA**, or more correctly, its upper town **McLEOD GANJ**, is one of Himachal's most irresistible destinations. Spread across wooded ridges beneath the stark rock faces of the Dhauladhar Range, the town is divided into two distinct and separate sections, separated by 10km of perilously twisting road and almost a thousand metres in altitude. Originally a British hill station, **McLeod Ganj** has been transformed by the influx of **Tibetan refugees** fleeing Chinese oppression in their homeland. Tibetan influence here is subsequently very strong, their achievements including the construction of temples, schools, monasteries, nunneries, meditation centres and the most extensive library of Tibetan history and religion. As well as playing host to hordes of foreign and domestic tourists, McLeod Ganj is a place of pilgrimage that attracts Buddhists and interested parties from all over the world, including Hollywood celebrities Richard Gere, Uma Thurman and Goldie Hawn. Many people visit India specifically to come here, and its relaxed and friendly atmosphere can make it a difficult place to leave.

Despite heavy snows and low **temperatures** between December and March, McLeod Ganj receives visitors year round. Summer brings torrential rains – this being the second wettest place in India – that return in bursts for much of the year. Daytime temperatures can be high, but you'll need warm clothes for the chilly nights.

Arrival and information

State-run **buses** from Shimla, Manali, Mandi, Pathankot, Kangra and Delhi pull into the bus stand in the very south of the lower town, though a very few private and deluxe buses from Delhi and Manali continue to McLeod Ganj.

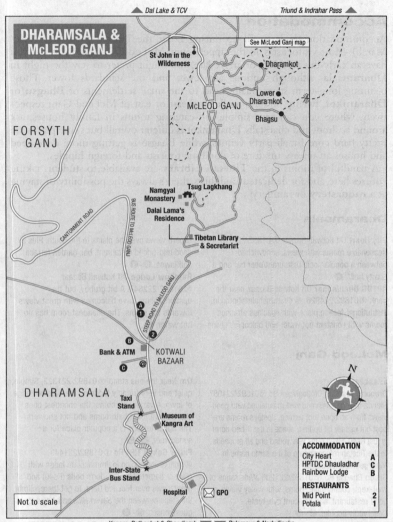

Kangra, Pathankot & Chandigarh ▼   ▼ *Palampur & Norbulingka*

Dharamsala's **airport** is 11km south at Gaggal. See p.546 for further transportation details. McLeod Ganj's **tourist office** (Mon–Sat 10am–5pm), on South End, opposite Bookworm, provides basic accommodation and transport information. A good source of entertainment and other local listings is the free monthly magazine *Contact*, available in restaurants.

From 7.45am onwards numerous **buses** run between Dharamsala and McLeod Ganj (40min), though a **shared taxi** (Rs7) is much quicker; both McLeod Ganj and Dharamsala have unions with fixed prices clearly displayed. An ordinary taxi from McLeod Ganj to Dharamsala costs Rs120. Autorickshaws travel frequently from McLeod Ganj Bus Stand to Bhagsu (Rs30) and the chai shop at Dharamkot (Rs40).

Accommodation

Accommodation tends to fill up during Losar, the Tibetan New Year (Feb/March). Most visitors stay in the upper town, **McLeod Ganj**; however, if you have an early bus to catch, or arrive late, you might prefer to stay the night in **Dharamsala**, although options are fewer and the standards lower. Those planning long-term stays usually head to the small settlements of **Bhagsu** or **Dharamkot**, twenty minutes' walk northeast or east of McLeod Ganj respectively, where you can rent simple self-catering rooms in family houses; ask around at shops and chai stalls. Dharamkot is quieter overall but some places are pretty hard core Israeli party venues, while Bhagsu is getting more developed and houses an uneasy mixture of domestic tourists and foreign hippies.

A handful of rooms in the **Tibetan Library** are available to students taking courses here, and for dedicated Buddhists, there's always the possibility of staying at a **monastery** or nunnery.

Dharamsala

City Heart Off Kotwali Bazaar ☎01892/223761. Reasonable rooms with views, sandwiched between a popular local restaurant/beer bar and a "party hall". ❸

HPTDC Dhauladhar Off Kotwali Bazaar, near the bank ☎01892/224926, ✉dharamshala@hptdc.in. Institutional-feeling place with spacious attached rooms with constant hot water and balconies giving superb views over the plains to the south. Plus a good mid-priced restaurant, bar, garden terrace and lawns. ❺–❼

Rainbow Lodge Off Kotwali Bazaar ☎01892/222647. A bit grubby, but the upstairs rooms have balconies with great views towards the plains. The cheapest room has no hot water. ❷

McLeod Ganj

Budget

Drepung Loseling Off Jogiwara Rd ☎01892/221087. Standard lodge, plain and well maintained with good views from an open roof terrace. Upstairs rooms are best but usually fill up first; space in the 3-bed dorm is just Rs40. Fixed rates year round and all proceeds to the Tibetan refugee camp of the same name in Mundgod, south India. ❶

Green Bhagsu Rd ☎01892/221200. Wide range of well-kept, comfortable rooms, with valley views, a good restaurant, and adjacent cybercafé. Deservedly popular. ❶–❷

Kunga's Bhagsu Rd ☎01892/221180, ✉tenzin_dhonyo@yahoo.co.in. Clean and centrally located with a variety of rooms and a fantastic sun deck; larger rooms are spacious and light, with big balconies. The down-to-earth owner Mr Tenzin (aka Nick) caters to the needs of all guests and manages one of the best restaurants in town. ❶–❸

Ladies Venture Jogiwara Rd, past the *Chocolate Log* ☎01892/221559, ✉shantiazad@yahoo.co.in. Well-appointed rooms of varying size in a welcoming Tibetan-run hotel. Dorm beds Rs80. Quiet location, with a garden and a small café. Fixed price year round. ❷–❸

Om Near the bus stand ☎01892/221322. Simple, quiet and very friendly lodge on the western edge of town. A variety of rooms; the cheapest ones share squat toilet bathrooms and hot showers. The upper terrace is a popular place for a sundowner. ❶–❸

Paljor Gakyil TIPA Rd ☎01892/221443, ✉ngapal@yahoo.co.in. Immaculate lodge with plain or carpeted rooms, dorm beds (Rs40) and great views over McLeod Ganj. To get there, climb the steps between the *Seven Hills* and *Kalsang* guesthouses. ❶–❷

Tibetan Ashoka Jogiwara Rd ☎01892/221763. Friendly, congenial and popular place. Rooms vary from Rs55 cubes with shared facilities to larger attached rooms with hot water. Superb views from the balcony. ❶–❷

Zilnon Kagyeling Monastery Bhagsu Rd ☎01892/220581. Basic and extremely cheap single and double rooms with shared facilities in an active *gompa*. ❶

Mid-range and expensive

Asian Plaza Main Chowk ☎01892/220685, ⓦwww.asianplazahotel.com. Snazzy new hotel with well-decorated rooms and huge suites, right in the heart of town. Also has rooftop restaurant. 6–8

Cheryton Cottage Jogiwara Rd, reception in *Chocolate Log* ⓣ01892/221237. Cute and comfortable double-storey cottage set in a pleasant garden. Upper rooms are lighter and airier. There's a top-floor apartment for Rs1600. Fixed rates all year. 4–6

Chonor House Near Thekchen Choeling Gompa, South End ⓣ01892/221006, ⓔchonorhs@norbulingka.org. Part of the Norbulingka Institute for Tibetan Culture, with very well presented rooms decorated by artists, combining traditional Tibetan decor with modern comfort. There's also an excellent restaurant, with garden seating. All proceeds go to Norbulingka. 6–7

Glenmoor Cottages above Mall Rd ⓣ01892/221010, ⓦwww.glenmoorecottages.com. Five luxurious cottages with impressive wood panelling and less expensive rooms in the main building, set in picturesque woodlands about 1km above the main bazaar. 4–8

HPTDC Bhagsu South End, 250m south of the information centre ⓣ01892/221091, ⓔdharamshala@hptdc.in. Large flagship hotel with indifferent management but comfortable carpeted rooms, some en suite, and small gardens in a quiet location. 5–7

Kareri Lodge South End ⓣ01892/221132, ⓔkarerhl@hotmail.com. Five spotless rooms, two with superb balcony views, in a quiet location. Preference is given to long-term guests, who are also offered discount rates. 4–5

Pema Thang South End ⓣ01892/221871, ⓦwww.pemathang.net. Friendly hotel, the best maintained on South End. Rooms all have heaters and hot showers; you'll pay more for a good view. Popular with well-off Westerners interested in Buddhism. 4–5

Surya Resorts South End ⓣ01892/221418, ⓦwww.suryaresorts.com. Big, brash, modern hotel, with some large glass-fronted rooms facing west over the plains, aimed at businessmen and domestic tourists. 6–8

Tibet Bhagsu Rd ⓣ01892/221587, ⓔhtdshala@sancharnet.in. Excellent hotel with a superb restaurant; the downstairs valley-facing rooms offer the best value. Popular and central. Fixed prices all year. 4–5

Dharamkot

Dev Cottages Off the main road before the teashop ⓣ01892/221558. Smart and spacious new cottages, comfortably furnished with fine valley views. 6

New Blue Heaven Off the main road before the teashop ⓣ01892/221005, ⓔsandeep74gill@yahoo.co.in. Two-storey family house with sociable terrace and garden. All rooms are simple but attached. 2

Bhagsu

Sky Pie Guest House Off the left turning as you approach temple ⓣ01892/220497, ⓔdenisraaz8@gmail.com. Friendly and lively place with standard budget rooms, some with shared bathrooms. 2–3

Trimurti Guest House Upper Bhagsu towards Dharamkot ⓣ01892/221364, ⓦwww.trimurtimusic.com. A few rooms in a quiet family place with a lawn and colourful shrine. The owner runs a small music school; see p.508. 2–3

Dharamsala

It's easy to see why most visitors bypass Dharamsala itself, a haphazard jumble of shops, offices and houses. The only place of interest is the **Museum of Kangra Art** (Tues–Sun 10am–5pm), with a small collection of Kangra miniatures and some modern art. On foot, the quickest route up to McLeod Ganj is up a steep 3km track that starts from behind the vegetable market, passing the Tibetan Library and Secretariat.

McLeod Ganj

The ever-expanding settlement of **McLeod Ganj** extends along a pine-covered ridge with valley views below and the near vertical walls of the Dhauladhar range towering behind. Despite being named after David McLeod, the Lieutenant Governor of Punjab when the hill station was founded in 1848,

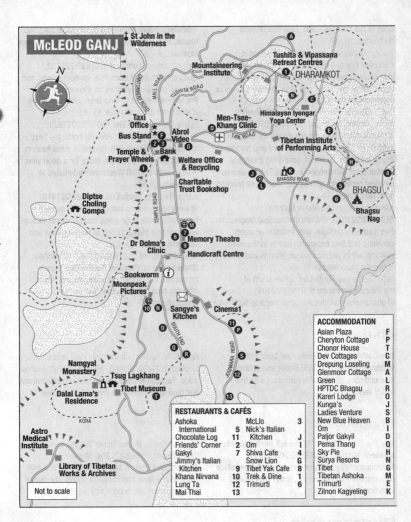

St John in the Wilderness

Mountaineering Institute

Tushita & Vipassana Retreat Centres

DHARAMKOT

Himalayan Iyengar Yoga Center

Men-Tsee-Khang Clinic

Tibetan Institute of Performing Arts

Taxi Office

Abrol Video

Bus Stand

Temple & Prayer Wheels

Bank

Welfare Office & Recycling

Charitable Trust Bookshop

BHAGSU ROAD

BHAGSU

Diptse Choling Gompa

Bhagsu Nag

Dr Dolma's Clinic

Memory Theatre

Handicraft Centre

Bookworm

Moonpeak Pictures

Sangye's Kitchen

Cinema1

Namgyal Monastery

Tsug Lagkhang

Tibet Museum

Dalai Lama's Residence

KORA

Astro Medical Institute

Library of Tibetan Works & Archives

Not to scale

CANTONMENT ROAD
MALL ROAD
TUSHITA ROAD
TIPA ROAD
TEMPLE ROAD
SOUTH END
JOGIWARA ROAD

RESTAURANTS & CAFÉS

Ashoka International		McLlo	3
Chocolate Log	11	Nick's Italian Kitchen	J
Friends' Corner	2	Om	I
Gakyi	7	Shiva Cafe	4
Jimmy's Italian Kitchen		Snow Lion	G
Khana Nirvana	10	Tibet Yak Cafe	8
Lung Ta	12	Trek & Dine	1
Mai Thai	13	Trimurti	6

ACCOMMODATION

Asian Plaza	F
Cheryton Cottage	P
Chonor House	T
Dev Cottages	C
Drepung Loseling	M
Glenmoor Cottage	A
Green	L
HPTDC Bhagsu	R
Kareri Lodge	O
Kunga's	J
Ladies Venture	S
New Blue Heaven	B
Om	I
Paljor Gakyil	D
Pema Thang	Q
Sky Pie	H
Surya Resorts	N
Tibet	G
Tibetan Ashoka	M
Trimurti	E
Zilnon Kagyeling	K

little evidence of British occupation remains. Intersected by two narrow potholed roads, the focal point of McLeod Ganj is its Buddhist **temple**, ringed with spinning red and gold prayer wheels. Today, Indian residents are outnumbered by Tibetans, who bedeck their ramshackle buildings with fluttering prayer flags: McLeod Ganj is not simply a political haven for them, but also home to their spiritual leader, the Dalai Lama, and to the Tibetan government in exile.

It's easy to **find your way around** McLeod Ganj. At its northern end, the road up from the lower town arrives at a small square that serves as the bus stand. Roads radiating from here head south to the Dalai Lama's Residence and the **Library of Tibetan Works and Archives**, north to the village of Dharamkot, the Tushita Retreat Meditation Centre and to the Tibetan Children's Village next to Dal Lake, and east to the hamlet of Bhagsu.

You may not notice it, but efforts are being made to clean up McLeod Ganj. The **Welfare Office** in particular has initiated several schemes to tackle environmental issues, including a **Green Shop** on Bhagsu Road, which sells boiled filtered water in an effort to deal with the plague of plastic bottles.

The Dalai Lama's Residence and the Tibet Museum

The Dalai Lama settled temporarily in McLeod Ganj in 1960; nearly five decades later he's still there, and his **Residence** on the south edge of town has become his permanent home in exile. His own quarters are modest, and most of the walled compound overhanging the valley is taken up by government offices. In front of the private enclosure, Dharamsala's main Buddhist temple, **Tsug Lakhang**, shelters images of Sakyamuni (the historical Buddha), Padmasambhava (who introduced Buddhism to Tibet) and Avalokitesvara (the *bodhisattva* of compassion) seated in meditation postures, surrounded by offerings from devotees. After paying homage to the Buddha inside, devotees complete a *kora*, a circumambulation of the temple complex (clockwise, starting at the trailhead below the monks' quarters), turning the numerous prayer wheels to send prayers out in all directions. Every afternoon monks from the nearby **Namgyal monastery** hold fierce but disciplined debates in the courtyard opposite the temple. The small *Namgyal Café* provides quality meals and snacks (Tues–Sun 11am–8.30pm).

Next to the monastery, the **Tibet Museum** (Tues–Sun 9am–5pm; Rs5; Ⓦ www.thetibetmuseum.org) displays in graphic detail the plight of the Tibetan people since China invaded Tibet in 1949. Using photographs and video clips, the self-guided tour describes how Tibetan freedom fighters, backed by the CIA, waged an impossible guerrilla war against China that lasted into the 1970s. The upstairs hall features profiles of the museum curators – all refugees and ex-political prisoners – and a memorial to the 1.2 million Tibetans who have died in the conflict.

Library of Tibetan Works and Archives

The **Library of Tibetan Works and Archives** (Mon–Sat 9am–1pm & 2–5pm; closed 2nd & 4th Sat of month; ☎01892/222467) has one of the world's most extensive collections of original Tibetan manuscripts of sacred

Meeting His Holiness the Dalai Lama

The **Dalai Lama** is in great demand. Tibetans fleeing their homeland come to him for blessing and reassurance; monks and nuns from all over India and Nepal look to him for spiritual guidance; and an ever-increasing number of Westerners arrive in Dharamsala hoping for a moment of his attention. Twenty years ago it might have been possible for people to meet His Holiness on an individual basis; now casual visitors should count on attending a **public audience**, when he greets and shakes the hands of several hundred people. These are held every few weeks if His Holiness is in town, though there are no fixed dates or timings. Ask the Branch Security Office (above the Welfare Office on Bhagsu Road ☎01892/221560) when the next audience will be, but note that they themselves only know a couple of days in advance. You'll need to register here too; bring a passport and some passport photos, and expect to wait. If you're interested in attending His Holiness's **public teachings**, check Ⓦ www.tibet.com for dates, locations and what to expect. **Private audiences** are granted to a select few, and can only be arranged by writing at least four months in advance. The Dalai Lama's secretary receives hundreds of such letters each day, and each case is reviewed on its merits.

texts and prayers, books on all aspects of Tibet, information on Indian culture and architecture, and a rich archive of historical photos. Decorated with bright Tibetan motifs, it is housed in the Tibetan Central Administration compound, below the southern end of McLeod Ganj. Tibetan language and philosophy **courses** are held each weekday (see "Listings", p.511), and a small **museum** on the first floor of the library (Rs10) displays Buddhist statues, finely moulded bronzes and mandalas (symmetrical images, used in meditation to symbolize spiritual journeys and the pattern of the universe).

An information centre in the **Tibetan Secretariat**, beside the entrance to the compound, provides up-to-date news about the Tibetan community in Tibet and around the world. Just outside, the small **Astro Medical Institute** (daily 9am–1pm & 2–5pm; free) is staffed by monks who diagnose symptoms by examining the eyes, pulse and urine, and prescribe pills made of herbs, precious stones and sometimes animal products, mixed on particularly auspicious lunar dates. You can also have your horoscope prepared here.

North and east of McLeod Ganj

A minor road winds northwards from the McLeod Ganj Bus Stand to the **Mountaineering Institute** (Mon–Sat 10am–1.30pm & 2–5pm; closed 2nd Sat of month; ℡01892/221787), which provides information on the region, including books and maps on the Dhauladhar Range, and organizes trekking expeditions. Continuing up the road you approach two Buddhist retreat centres, both beautifully situated in the midst of forests: the **Tushita** Tibetan Buddhist Centre was founded in 1972 by Lama Thubten Zopa Rinpoche, while just around the corner is **Dhamma Sikhara**, a Theravadan Vipassana centre (see under "Meditation" on p.511 for details of courses at both centres). From here the road continues to Dharamkot, starting point for walks to **Triund** (2975m) and treks over the high passes to the Chamba Valley. Taking a path down through the wooded slopes from Dharamkot brings you to the small, murky **Dal Lake**, the scene of an animal fair and Shaivite festival in September. It stands behind the **Tibetan Children's Village** (TCV), a huge complex providing education and training in traditional handicrafts for around two thousand students, many of whom are orphans or have been brought to safety by parents who have returned to Tibet.

Bhagsu Road heads east from McLeod Ganj's main square, skirting the hillside for 2km before reaching the village of **Bhagsu** with its ancient Shiva temple. The last few years have seen big changes here, with the construction of several hotels catering primarily for the domestic tourist market. However it's still a pleasant enough place, with a few cafés near the temple complex. Beyond the temple a path meanders up the boulder-strewn slopes of a small stream up to a **waterfall**. If you're interested in studying tabla, contact Ashoka at the *Trimurti Guest House* (see p.505); he runs the **Trimurti International Music School** from his home. Note: there have been several **attacks** on women walking between Bhagsu and McLeod Ganj in the past few years. Don't walk it alone.

Tibetan Institute of Performing Arts

The **Tibetan Institute of Performing Arts** was founded in 1959 to preserve the Tibetan identity in exile. Around 150 people live on its campus, in the forests above McLeod Ganj overlooking Bhagsu, including artists, teachers, musicians and administrators. The TIPA troupe perform traditional *lhamo* operas, which derive from ancient masked dance dramas, and have played a morale-building role at Tibetan refugee camps throughout India, while also sharing Tibet's cultural heritage with international audiences. Visit its office for information on upcoming events and tours (Mon–Sat 9am–noon & 1–5pm, closed 2nd & 4th Sat of month; ☎01892/221478, ⓦwww.tibetanarts.org).

South of McLeod Ganj: the Norbulingka Institute

Eight kilometres (30min) from Dharamsala, near the village of Sidpur, the **Norbulingka Institute** (Mon–Sat 8am–5pm; ☎01892/246402, ⓦwww .norbulingka.org) is dedicated to preserving literary and artistic Tibetan culture. The complex of Tibetan-style buildings, built in 1985, is set amidst peaceful Japanese gardens, and centres on the two-storey **Deden Tsugla-khang temple**, which houses 1173 images of the Buddha and frescoes of the fourteen Dalai Lamas in the upper gallery. The gilded copper statue of Sakyamuni in the hall downstairs is the largest of its kind outside Tibet. Elsewhere in the complex, the **Losel Doll Museum** shows colourful dioramas packed with traditionally clothed dolls. If you'd like to **stay**, the *Norling Guest House* (☎01892/246406; ❻–❼) in the gardens is clean and well decorated; even if you don't stop over it's worth a look for its upstairs gallery of fifty drawings that chronicle the life of the fourteenth Dalai Lama.

Trekking from Dharamsala

Dharamsala is one of the most popular starting points for **treks** over the rocky ridges of the Dhauladhar Range, which rise steeply from the Kangra Valley to 4600m. Trails pass through forests of *deodar*, pine, oak and rhododendron, cross streams and rivers and wind along vertiginous cliff tracks passing the occasional lake waterfall and glacier. Unless you are very experienced, you'll need a guide as the routes are steep and memorial stones testify to those who didn't make it. The **Mountaineering Institute** on Dharamkot Road (see opposite) can help arrange guides and porters, and stocks maps. Despite the availability of rough huts and caves, it's best to take a tent. The best **season** to trek here is September to November, when the worst of the monsoon is over and before it gets too cold. Winter climbing should only be attempted by mountaineers experienced in the use of crampons and ice axes. See p.500 for a **map** of the hiking routes described below.

Dharamsala to Chamba over Indrahar Pass

The most frequented route from Dharamsala to the Chamba Valley, over the **Indrahar Pass** (4350m), is arduous in places, but most trekkers manage it in around five days. The first section, from Dharamkot, winds through thick forest and steep rocky terrain for 9km to a grassy plateau at **Triund**. From here the path climbs to **Laqa Got**, and then on a seriously steep section up to the knife-edged Indrahar Pass where, weather permitting, you'll enjoy breathtaking views south to the plains and north to the snowy Pir Panjal peaks and Greater Himalayas. The descent is difficult in places and will take you via the Gaddi villages of **Kuarsi** and **Channauta** to the main road, from where you can pick up transport to Brahmour and Chamba by road.

Other routes from Dharamsala to Chamba

Several **other routes** cross the Dhauladhar Range, including the **Toral Pass** (4575m) which starts from **Tang Narwana** (1150m), 10km from Dharamsala. The most difficult route north is the five- or six-day trek across **Bhimghasutri Pass** (4580m), covering near-vertical rocky ascents, sharp cliffs and dangerous gorges. A much easier four- or five-day trek from Dharamsala crosses **Bleni Pass** (3710m) in the milder ranges to the northwest, weaving through alpine pastures and woods and crossing a few streams, before terminating at **Dunali**, on the Chamba road.

Eating

McLeod Ganj is one of those places where sitting, chatting and philosophizing in **restaurants** is the favoured activity. Tibetan dishes such as *thukpa* and *momos* are prominent, along with Chinese egg noodles, chow mein and stir-fry. Fresh-baked Tibetan bread and cakes are widely available, and you'll also come across omelettes, chips, toast, veggie-burgers and plenty of Israeli dishes. If you fancy making some Tibetan food, *Sangye's Kitchen* near the Post Office on Jogiwara Road holds **cooking lessons** (Sun–Fri 11am–1pm & 5–7pm; Rs150). In **Dharamsala**, there's no shortage of snack stalls, but less choice of cuisine: your best bets for Indian and Western dishes are the *Mid Point* and the *City Heart* hotels. For Tibetan food, try the *Potala*, a small but clean café with a simple menu. In **Dharamkot**, *Trek and Dine*, a ten-minute walk uphill from the chai stall at the junction, is a good place to grab a bite with pizza and pies. In **Bhagsu**, the *Ashoka International* serves up some of the best Indian food in town to cushion-seated diners; the great-value *Trimurti*, next to the temple (not in the guesthouse of the same name), is an excellent Indian veg café with a rooftop terrace. Past the Bhagsu Nag temple, a path winds up to the popular *Shiva Café*, situated next to a waterfall and the scene of many an all-night rave.

Chocolate Log Jogiwara Rd. Delicious cakes, pies and truffles plus savouries such as spinach pizza. Eat inside or laze on deck chairs in a pleasant garden. Most items Rs50–100. Daily except Tues.

Friends' Corner Temple Rd. Popular, comfortable place by the bus stop, with a range of food (around Rs100) and beers, a good sound system and a roller-skating rink upstairs.

Gakyi Jogiwara Rd. Humble and homely, with great Tibetan and Western veg dishes, plus the town's best fruit muesli and Tibetan bread. All items under Rs100.

Jimmy's Italian Kitchen Jogiwara Rd. Snug café decorated with classic film posters. Good salads, baked potatoes, lattes and home-made desserts; dinners mainly Rs100–150. A brand new upstairs branch 30m towards the temple from here has live music on Wed and Sat.

Khana Nirvana Temple Rd. Great hang-out place above Stitches in Time, popular with the expat volunteer crowd. Wonderful views over the plains, with healthy tofu burgers (Rs80) and fresh juices. Wed-night jam sessions; movies on Thurs.

Lung Ta Jogiwara Rd. Japanese vegetarian place with a constantly changing menu that usually includes miso soup, sushi, tempura vegetables and tofu steak; main courses around Rs100. Profits go to assisting former Tibetan political prisoners. The Korean restaurant next door, *Dokebi Nara*, offers hotpot dishes in a cozy atmosphere.

Mai Thai Jogiwara Rd. At the southern edge of town, this cosy place serves up pretty authentic Thai curries and other SE Asian fare for around Rs100.

McLlo Central Square. Massive neon-lit monstrosity overlooking the bus stop. Large selection of good Western food (from Rs100), an official *Baskin-Robbins* ice-cream parlour and a second-floor drinking den which is pleasant early evening but can get very rowdy later on.

Nick's Italian Kitchen *Kunga's*, Bhagsu Rd. Excellent pasta (Rs80–120), to-die-for brownies and lemon-curd cake. The sunny back-deck is one of McLeod's best.

Om *Om Hotel*, near the bus stand. Friendly, comfortable restaurant jutting out over the hillside with the town's only west-facing roof terrace. Generous portions of good Tibetan and Chinese veg food, and a few Mexican items. Rs60–100.

Snow Lion *Tibet* hotel, Bhagsu Rd. One of the best venues in Dharamsala for Tibetan and Chinese food, veg and non-veg; main dishes over Rs100. You can also drink at the *Dragon Bar*.

Tibet Yak Cafe Jogiwara Rd. Tiny, simple restaurant, popular with locals, serving good Tibetan food for Rs40–60.

Listings

Banks and exchange The Punjab National Bank (Mon–Fri 10am–2pm, Sat 10am–noon) in McLeod Ganj near the bus stand will change traveller's cheques and cash, as will the upper branch of State Bank of India in Dharamsala. Both also have ATMs. There are several authorized exchange agencies in McLeod Ganj, such as Thomas Cook and LKP Forex on Temple Rd, who provide cash advances on credit and debit cards.

Bookshops The Tibetan Bookshop and Information Office is a good place to browse for books on Tibetan Buddhism, as is the Charitable Trust Shop, both on Jogiwara Rd in McLeod Ganj's main bazaar. Bookworm, opposite the tourist office, South End, is small but has a very good selection, especially on Buddhism, and also stocks second-hand books.

Cinema Cinemaa1, Abrol Video and Memory Theatre, all on Jogiwara Rd, show Hollywood flicks, often with a Tibetan or Indian theme.

Courses Numerous courses are available in McLeod Ganj, including *dharma* teachings, Tibetan language, Hindi, ancient Thai massage, yoga, tabla, karate, Xi Gung, Tai Chi, Reiki, and Indian vegetarian and Tibetan cooking. Check listings in *Contact* (see p.503) for further details. Free classes on *dharma* are given in translation by Buddhist monks from 11am until noon most weekdays at the Library of Tibetan Works and Archives. Philosophy courses and three-month Tibetan language courses (beginning March, June & Sept) are also run from the library (contact the Secretary for Tibetan Studies ☎01892/222467).

Hospitals The Tibetan Delek Hospital (☎01892/222053), above the Astro Medical Institute, is one of the best hospitals in the state and has Western physicians on call.

Internet access McLeod Ganj now has a multitude of Internet cafés, either attached to hotels such as the *Green* or in separate establishments, mainly on Bhagsu Rd or Jogiwara Rd. Most charge Rs30/hr. Down in Dharamsala, the first-floor Cyber World is marginally cheaper.

Meditation Tibetan Buddhist meditation courses are held at the Tushita Meditation Centre in Dharamkot (office Mon–Sat 9.30–11.30am & 1–4.30pm; ☎01892/221866, ⊛www.tushita.info). Courses range from short retreats of eight to ten days to an intensive three-month summer purification retreat (Vajrasattva). Accommodation is available in simple rooms and dorms and there's also an excellent library. Book well in advance. The Vipassana Centre, next door, follows teachings more akin to Theravada Buddhism. They run ten-day silent retreats and daily sittings (register in person Mon–Sat 4–5pm or contact ☎01892/221309, ⊛www.sikhara.dhamma.org).

Photography Moonpeak Pictures on Temple Rd (☎01892/220375, ⓔ moonpeak@rediffmail.com) sells slide film and can develop prints. They also print from digital memory cards and burn CDs.

Post office McLeod Ganj's post office, on Jogiwara Rd, has a poste restante counter that holds letters for up to one month. Letters not addressed to McLeod Ganj, Upper Dharamsala, end up in the GPO in the lower town.

Shopping Stalls and little shops along the main streets stock Tibetan trinkets, inexpensive warm clothing, incense, prayer bells, rugs and books. The large handicrafts shop on Jogiwara Rd sells *thangkas* of all sizes, along with prayer flags, and you can have a *bakku* (a Tibetan women's dress) stitched here for around Rs600 plus the cost of the cloth. The Green Shop, Bhagsu Rd, sells recycled painted cards, hand-painted T-shirts, books on the environment and filtered boiled water for Rs5.

Teaching The Yong Ling School, Jogiwara Rd on the left past the post office, welcomes volunteer teachers. An excellent resource for jobs is Volunteer Tibet (⊛www.volunteertibet.org), whose office is opposite the school.

Tibetan settlement For enquiries about the Tibetan settlement, call in either at the Welfare Office on Bhagsu Rd in McLeod Ganj or directly at the Reception Centre below the post office, where donations of clothes, books, blankets and pens for new Tibetan arrivals are always gratefully accepted. Another good place for information is the Tibetan Bookshop and Information Office on Jogiwara Rd near McLeod Ganj's main bazaar.

Travel agents Himachal Travels, Jogiwara Rd (☎01892/221428), books local and private buses, trains from Pathankot and domestic flights, and confirms or alters international flights. You can also rent taxis for journeys within Himachal Pradesh or beyond, and enquire about treks. Ways Tours & Travels, Temple Rd (☎01892/221910), is a well-organized agency that handles international flights, organizes tailor-made itineraries around India and changes money. Yeti Trekking, on the road to the Mountaineering Institute (☎01892/221032), offers treks and has plenty of equipment for rent.

Yoga The Himalayan Iyengar Yoga Centre (⊛www.hiyogacentre.com) in Dharamkot runs five-day courses in hatha yoga, starting every Thurs.

Moving on from Dharamsala

Air Deccan operate a daily **flight** to Delhi, with deals going from as little as Rs1200 one way, but flights are often cancelled in bad weather, so it's wise not to cut it fine with any international connections. HRTC run numerous **buses** to destinations in Himachal Pradesh and beyond from the main bus stand in the lower town, including half-hourly buses from Gaggal, for the airport. Buses to

Pathankot, handy for **train** connections, also leave every thirty minutes. Three buses a day (6am, 8am & 8pm) travel to Manali, and two run to Delhi (6pm & 7pm) via Chandigarh, although more are put on according to demand. There are two daily government buses to Dalhousie (8am & noon). Many tourists prefer to book private "deluxe" buses through agents in McLeod Ganj (see "Listings", p.511), especially the new sleeper buses to Delhi (Rs650).

See p.546 for more information on journey frequencies and durations.

Dalhousie and around

The quiet, relaxed hill station of **Dalhousie** spreads over five low-level hills at the western edge of the Dhauladhar Range. While the town itself, mostly modern hotels interspersed with Raj-era buildings and low-roofed stalls, is unremarkable, the pine-covered slopes around it are intersected with paths and tracks ideal for short undemanding walks.

From Dalhousie the road east zigzags through forests to **Khajjiar**, a popular local day out, before descending through terraced mountain slopes to **Chamba**, perched above the rushing River Ravi. It's a slow and relaxed place with some fascinating temples and a small art museum. **Brahmour**, three hours further east by bus and the final settlement on the road into the mountains, holds more Hindu temples – both towns make good bases for **treks** into the remote **Pangi Valley**.

Dalhousie

DALHOUSIE owes its name to Lord Dalhousie, Governor General of Punjab (1849–56), who was attracted by the cool climate to establish a sanatorium here for the many British, who, like himself, suffered ill health. Early in the twentieth century, it was a popular alternative to crowded, expensive Shimla, but thereafter declined. Today Dalhousie is a favourite summer retreat for holidaying Punjabis, but receives only a handful of Western tourists, few of whom stay longer than a day or two. A small population of Tibetans has lived here since the Chinese invasion of Tibet in 1959.

The town is spread over a series of hills with winding roads connecting the two focal points, the chowks. **Gandhi Chowk**, with its restaurants and post office, is the busiest section. From here the Mall and Garam Sarak dip and curve 2km to **Subhash Chowk**, at the top end of the largely Muslim Sadar Bazaar. North of here, the bus stand and information office mark the main road out of town.

Practicalities

Dalhousie is usually approached by **bus** from Pathankot in the Punjab, 80km southwest, or Chamba, 47km east; the journey through the Himalayan foothills from Dharamsala (6hr) and Shimla (18hr) is made via Nurpur. Transport to Chamba (2hr 15min) usually goes via Banikhet, though four buses also travel via Khajjiar. The **tourist information office** (Mon–Sat 10am–5pm; ☎01899/242136), 50m from the bus stand, provides transport information. A steep path leads up from the bus stand to the Mall; if you don't fancy the walk, local Maruti taxis (Rs50) ply the route. The State Bank of India at the bus stand has foreign **exchange** facilities and an ATM. Eva's Cyber Café, in the Tibetan Lhasa market above the bus stand, has Internet facilities.

Numerous **hotels** cater for Dalhousie's hot-season hordes and most offer substantial **discounts** in the off-season. The *Silverton*, above the Circuit House on the Mall (☎01899/240674, ⊛www.heritagehotels.com/silverton; ➍–➐), is an old-world manor house with large rooms and immaculate lawns set within private woodlands. *Aroma-N-Claires* (℡01899/242199, ℻242639; ➍–➎), a rambling 1930s building south of Subhash Chowk on Court Road is atmospheric, cluttered and eccentric, with a library and leafy patios. Half a kilometre along a footpath from Subhash Chowk, ➑ *Hotel Crags* on Garam Sarak Road (℡01899/242124; ➌–➍) is a quiet and exceptionally friendly hotel with a large terrace, tasty food and great views down to the plains. The basic **youth hostel** (℡01899/242189, ✉yh_dalhousie@rediffmail.com; ➋), five minutes' walk behind the *dhabas* from the bus stand, has dorm beds (Rs60) and doubles. Apart from the hotel restaurants and scattered *dhabas*, **places to eat** include *Food Junction* at the bus stand, *Kwality's* at Gandhi Chowk, and *Moti Mahal* and *Sher-e-Punjab* at Subhash Chowk.

Khajjiar

Heading east towards Chamba, the road descends through *deodar* forests to the meadow of **Khajjiar** where the small twelfth-century temple of **Khajjinag** looks down over a vast rolling green with a small lake cupped in the centre. Khajjiar is a popular day-trip from Dalhousie for Indian tourists who come to have their pictures taken and to take pony rides. If you want to stay, the *Shining Star Resort* (℡01899/236336, 🌐www.shiningstarresort.com; ➎–➏) is a plush hotel with a decent restaurant and fine views. The road past Khajjiar dips across denuded and terraced hillsides down towards Chamba. Prince Travels at the bus stand in Dalhousie runs a tourist **bus** to Khajjiar and Chamba, departing at 10am and returning to Dalhousie at 6.30pm; alternatively, four Chamba-bound buses travel via Khajjiar every day.

Chamba

Shielded on all sides by high mountains, **CHAMBA** was ruled for an entire millennium by kings descended from Raja Sahil Varma, who founded it in 920 AD and named it after his daughter Champavati. Unlike Himachal states further south, it was never formally under Mughal rule and its distinct Hindu culture remained intact until the first roads were built to Dalhousie in 1870.

Chamba festivals

Chamba's annual four-day **Suhi Mata Festival**, in early April, commemorates Rani Sunena, the wife of the tenth-century Raja Sahil Verma. A curious legend relates that when water from a nearby stream failed to flow through a channel supposed to divert it to the town, local brahmins advised Raja Verma that either his son or his wife would have to sacrifice themselves. The queen obliged; she was buried alive at the head of the channel, and the water flowed freely. Only women and children participate in the festival, dancing on the *chaugan* before processing with an image of Champavati (Rani Sunena's daughter who gave her name to the town) and banners of the clan's solar emblem to the Suhi Mata temple in the hills behind the town.

Minjar, a week of singing and dancing at the start of August to celebrate the growth of maize, is also peculiar to Chamba. Its climax comes on the last day, when a rowdy procession of locals, Gaddis and Gujjars, dressed in traditional costumes, leaves the palace and snakes down to the riverbank, where bunches of maize are thrown into the water. Before Independence, locals had the custom of pushing one male buffalo into the river; its drowning was an auspicious sign but if the beast managed to swim to the opposite bank bad fortune was expected for the coming year.

When the state of Himachal Pradesh was formed in 1948, Chamba became the capital. Today, only a handful of visitors make it out here, passing through before or after trekking, or stopping off to see the unique **temples**.

The *chaugan*, a large green used for sports, evening strolls and festive celebrations, marks the centre of town, overlooked by the **Rang Mahal** palace, now a government building. At the south end of the *chaugan*, the **Bhuri Singh museum** (Tues–Sun 10am–5pm; free) holds a reasonable display of local arts and crafts. Its eighteenth- and nineteenth-century **Kangra miniature paintings**, depicting court life, amorous meetings and men and women smoking elaborate hookahs, are much bolder than their Mughal-influenced Rajasthani equivalents. The museum's best feature is its small cache of **rumals**. Made by women since the tenth century, *rumals* are like embroidered paintings, depicting scenes from popular myth. Today only a few women continue this tradition, but a weaving centre in the old palace is attempting to revitalize the art.

The temples

The intimate complex of **Lakshmi Narayan temples**, behind Dogra Bazaar west of the *chaugan*, is of a style found only in Chamba and Brahmour. Three of its six earth-brown temples are dedicated to Vishnu and three to Shiva, all with profusely carved outer walls and curious curved *shikharas*, topped with overhanging wooden canopies and gold pinnacles added in 1678 in defiance of Aurangzeb's order to destroy all Hindu temples in the hill states. Niches in the walls contain images of deities, but many stand empty, some statues lost in the earthquake of 1905 and others looted more recently.

Entering the compound, you're confronted by the largest and oldest temple, built in the tenth century and enshrining a marble idol of Lakshmi Narayan. The buxom maidens flanking the entrance to the sanctuary, each holding a water vessel, represent the goddesses Ganga and Yamuna, while inside a frieze depicts scenes from the Mahabharata and Ramayana. Temples dedicated to Shiva fill the third courtyard. In the inner sanctuary, you'll see sturdy brass images of Shiva, Parvati and Nandi, inlaid with silver and copper brought from mines nearby. Outside the temple complex, **coppersmiths** manufacture curved ceremonial trumpets and brass hookahs.

Of Chamba's other temples, the most intriguing is the tenth-century **Chamunda Devi temple** high above the town in the north, a steep half-hour climb up steps that begin near the bus stand. Decorated with hundreds of heavy brass bells and protecting a fearsome image of the bloodthirsty goddess Chamunda, the temple is built entirely of wood, and commands an excellent view up the Ravi gorge. Back in town, south of the *chaugan* near the post office, the small, lavishly carved eleventh-century **Harirai temple** contains a smooth brass image of Vaikuntha, the triple-headed aspect of Vishnu.

Practicalities

Buses arrive at the cramped bus stand in the north of town, close to several **lodges**, the best of which is the slightly shabby *Chamunda View* (☎01899/224067; ❸), below the bus stand. The HPTDC *Hotel Iravati* (☎01899/222671; ❹–❺) on the nearest corner of the *chaugan*, has comfortable, carpeted attached rooms; their cheaper annexe, *Champak* (☎01899/222774; ❷), has reasonable doubles and a dorm (Rs75). The best hotel in town is the modern *City Heart* (☎01899/225930, ⓦhotelcityheart chamba.com; ❺–❻), above the far end of the *chaugan*.

The best **food** can be found at the *Khaatir* in the *City Heart*, though the *Rishi* in Dogra Bazaar and *Park View* on Museum Road are decent alternatives.

Try the local speciality, *madhra*, a rich, oily and slightly bitter mix of beans and curd. The uninspiring **tourist office** (Mon–Sat 10am–5pm; ☎01899/224002) is part of the *Iravati* complex. **Internet** access is available at Mani Mahesh Travels. The Punjab National Bank on Hospital Road cannot change **money** but will cash American Express traveller's cheques.

From Chamba, there is one **bus** a day for Dharamsala (9.30pm; 8–9hr), and two for Shimla (4am & 5pm; 15–16hr). There are buses every half-hour to **Banikhet** and hourly to **Pathankot**, and a daily departure to **Amritsar** (11pm; 8hr).

Brahmour

BRAHMOUR is a one-horse town of slate-roofed houses, apple trees and small maize fields, shadowed on all sides by high snowy peaks. The **temples**, whose curved *shikharas* dominate the large, neatly paved central square, are more dramatic and better preserved than their rivals at Chamba. The sanctuaries are unlocked only for puja in the mornings and evenings, permitting a glimpse of bold bronze images of Ganesh, Shiva and Parvati, unchanged since their installation in the seventh and eighth centuries when Brahmour was capital of the surrounding mountainous region.

Treks around Chamba and Brahmour

The most popular treks from Chamba lead south over the **Dhauladhar** via the Minkiani or Indrahar pass to Dharamsala. **Equipment** can be rented and porters and **guides** hired in Chamba and Brahmour. Mani Mahesh Travels in Chamba (☎01899/222507) organizes and equips treks. See map, p.500, for some of the routes below.

Treks in the Pangi Valley to Lahaul

Few trekkers make it to the spectacular, all but inaccessible **Pangi Valley**, between the soaring Greater Himalayan Range in the north and the Outer Himalayan Range in the south. Several peaks within it have never been climbed, and onward paths lead to Kashmir, Lahaul and Zanskar. The trek to Lahaul takes nine or ten days from **Traila** (90km north of Chamba) via Satraundhi (3500m) over the Sach Pass to Killar, Sach Khas, and finishing in Purthi from where you can take a bus via Tindi to **Udaipur**. Buses run from here to Keylong, capital of Lahaul, for connections northwards to Leh or south over the Rohtang Pass and down to Manali.

Treks from Brahmour

Trekking routes lead north from **Brahmour** (2130m) over the Pir Panjal range across passes that are covered with snow for most of the year. The challenging six- to seven-day trek over **Kalichho Pass** (4990m), "The Abode of Kali", ends in the village of **Triloknath**, whose ancient temple to three-faced Shiva is sacred to both Hindus and Buddhists. Buses run from here to Udaipur, and on to Keylong and Manali.

Another demanding five- to six-day route crosses the **Kugti Pass** (5040m). From **Hadsar**, an hour by bus from Brahmour, the path follows the River Budhil for 12km to **Kugti**, then up to **Kuddi Got**, a vast flower-filled meadow (4000m). The next stage, over the pass, requires crampons and ice axes for an incredibly taxing six-hour climb. Having enjoyed views of the towering peaks of Lahaul and Zanskar from the summit, you plummet once again to the head of a glacier at **Khardu**, continuing down to Raape, 7km from **Shansha**, which is linked to Udaipur and Keylong by road.

Finally, a delightful three-day trek to the sacred lake of **Manimahesh** (4183m) starts from and returns to Hadsar. The awesome Manimahesh Kailash massif, with its permanent glaciers and ice fields, overlooks the lake.

Except during the September *yatra* or pilgrimage when everywhere is booked up, you can find **rooms** at a handful of guesthouses. Best choices are *Divya Cottage* (☎01090/275033; ❷) – probably the best in Brahmour – and *Shanti Guesthouse* (☎01090/225018; ❶) nearby. There isn't much choice of **food**; the *Chourasi* restaurant is a notch above the handful of stalls lining the main road between the bus stand and the square. The efficient Mountaineering Institute has details of local **treks**, reliable guides and porters, and equipment for rent.

The Kullu Valley

The majestic **KULLU VALLEY** is cradled by the Pir Panjal to the north, the Parvati Range to the east, and the Barabhangal Range to the west. This is Himachal at its most idyllic, with roaring rivers, pretty mountain villages, orchards and terraced fields, thick pine forests and snow-flecked ridges.

Known in the ancient Hindu scriptures as **Kulanthapitha**, or "End of the Habitable World", the Kullu Valley extends 80km north from the mouth of the perilously steep and narrow **Larji Gorge**, near Mandi, to the foot of the **Rohtang Pass** – gateway to Lahaul and Ladakh. For centuries, it formed one of the major trade corridors between Central Asia and the Gangetic plains, and local rulers, based first at **Jagatsukh** and later at **Naggar** and Sultanpur (now **Kullu**), were able to rake off handsome profits from the through traffic. This trade monopoly, however, also made it a prime target for invasion, and in the eighteenth and early nineteenth centuries the Kullu rajas were forced to repulse attacks by both the Raja of Kangra and the Sikhs, before seeing their lands annexed by the British in 1847. Over the following years, colonial families crossed the Jalori Pass from Shimla, making the most of the valley's alpine climate to grow the **apples** that, along with **cannabis** cultivation, today form the mainstay of the rural economy. The first road, built in 1927 to export the fruit, spelled the end of the peace and isolation, prompting many settlers to pack up and leave long before Independence. The population expanded again in the 1950s and 1960s with an influx of **Tibetan refugees**.

In spite of the changes wrought by roads, immigration and, more recently, mass tourism, the Kullu Valley's way of life is maintained in countless timber and stone villages. Known as **paharis** ("hill people"), the locals – high-caste landowning Thakurs, and their (low-caste) sharecropping tenant farmers – still sport the distinctive Kullu cap, or *topi*. The women, meanwhile, wear colourful headscarves and *puttoos* fastened with silver pins and chains. Venture into the lush meadows above the tree line and you'll cross paths with nomadic **Gaddi** shepherds.

Most tourists make a beeline for **Manali** after a gruelling bus ride from either Leh or Delhi. With its vast choice of hotels and restaurants, there is something here for everyone. Still an evergreen hippy hangout, it's India's number-one honeymoon spot too, and is also popular with outdoors enthusiasts taking advantage of the fine **trekking** opportunities – everything from day-hikes up the River Beas's side valleys (or *nalas*) to challenging long hauls over high-altitude passes and glaciers. Few travellers actually stay in **Kullu town** and the

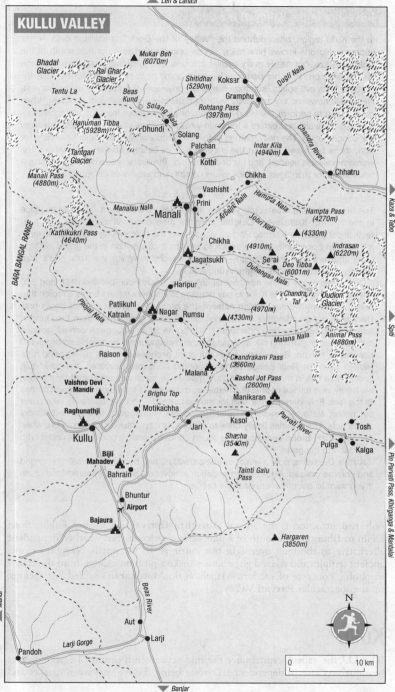

KULLU VALLEY

Bhadal
Glacier
Rai Ghar
Glacier
Tentu La
Beas
Kund
▲ Mukar Beh
(6070m)
Shitidhar
(5290m)
Koksar
Gramphu
Solang Nala
Rohtang Pass
(3978m)
Dugli Nala
Chandra River
Hanuman Tibba
(5928m)
Dhundi
Solang
Palchan
Kothi
Indar Kila
(4940m) ▲
Tantgari
Glacier
Manali Pass
(4880m)
Chikha
Chhatru
BARA BANGAL RANGE
Manalsu Nala
Vashisht
Prini
Hampta Nala
Hampta Nala
Manali
Arbaju Nala
Jobri Nala
Hampta Pass
(4270m)
Kathikukri Pass
(4640m)
Chikha
(4910m)
▲ (4330m)
Indrasan
(6220m) ▲
Jagatsukh
Se ai
Deo Tibba
(6001m)
Duhangan Nala
Chandra
Tal
Oudion
Glacier
Haripur
Patlikuhl
Piojai Nala
▲ (4970m)
Chandra
Glacier
Katrain
Nagar
Rumsu
▲(4330m)
Animal Pass
(4880m)
Malana Nala
Raison
Chandrakani Pass
(3560m)
Malana
Rashol Jot Pass
(2600m)
Vaishno Devi
Mandir
Brighu Top
Manikaran
Tosh
Raghunathji
Motikachha
Jari
Kasol
Parvati River
Kullu
Shacha
(3540m)
Pulga
Kalga
Bijli
Mahadev
Bahrain
Tainti Galu
Pass
Bhuntur
Airport
Bajaura
Hargaren
(3850m)

◀ Mandi

Beas River

Aut
Larji

Pandoh
Larji Gorge

N

0   10 km

Dussehra in the Valley of the Gods

In the Kullu region, often dubbed the **"Valley of the Gods"**, the village deity reigns supreme. No one knows how many *devtas* and *devis* inhabit the hills south of the Rohtang Pass, but nearly every hamlet has one. The part each one plays in village life depends on his or her particular **powers**; some heal, others protect the "parish" borders from evil spirits, summon the rains, or ensure the success of the harvest. Nearly all, however, communicate with their devotees by means of **oracles**. When called upon to perform, the village shaman, or **gaur** – drawn from the lower castes – strips to the waist and enters a trance in which the *devta* uses his voice to speak to the congregation. The deity, carried out of the temple on a ceremonial palanquin, or *rath*, rocks back and forth on the shoulders of its bearers as the *gaur* speaks. His words are always heeded, and his decisions final; the *devta*-oracle decides the propitious dates for marriages, and for sowing crops, and arbitrates disputes.

Dussehra

The single most important outing for any village deity is **Dussehra**, which takes place in the town of **Kullu** every October after the monsoons. Although the week-long festival ostensibly celebrates Rama's victory over the demon-king of Lanka, Ravana, it is also an opportunity for the *devtas* to reaffirm their position in the grand pecking order that prevails among them – a rigid hierarchy in which the Kullu raja's own tutelary deity Rama, alias **Raghunathji**, is king.

On the tenth day of the new, or "white" moon in October, between 150 and 200 *devtas* make their way to Kullu to pay homage to Raghunathji. As befits a region that holds its elderly women in high esteem, the procession proper cannot begin until **Hadimba**, the grandmother of the royal family's chief god, arrives from the Dunghri temple in Manali. Like her underlings, she is borne on an elaborately carved wooden *rath* swathed in glittering silk and garlands, and surmounted by a richly embroidered parasol, or chhatri. Raghunathji leads the great **procession** in his six-wheeled *rath*. Hauled from the Rupi palace by two hundred honoured devotees, the palanquin lurches to a halt in the middle of Kullu's *maidan*, to be circumambulated by the raja, his family, and retinue of priests. Thereafter, the festival's more secular aspect comes to the fore. **Folk dancers** perform for the vast crowds, and the *maidan* is taken over by market stalls, sweet-sellers, snake charmers, astrologers, sadhus and tawdry circus acts. The revelries finally draw to a close six days later on the full moon, when the customary **blood sacrifices** of a young buffalo, a goat, a cock, a fish and a crab are made to the god.

Kullu's Dussehra, now a major tourist attraction, has become increasingly staged and commercialized. Book accommodation in advance, and be prepared for a crush if you want to get anywhere near the *devtas*.

---

only real attraction is the annual **Dussehra festival** in October. Flights from Delhi to Bhuntur, just south of Kullu, offer a welcome but weather-dependent alternative to the long overnight bus journeys. To the north, **Naggar**'s castle, ancient temples and relaxed guesthouses make a pleasant change from the claustrophobic concrete of modern Manali, as do **Manikaran**'s sacred hot springs, up the spectacular **Parvati Valley**.

Kullu

KULLU, the valley's capital since the mid-seventeenth century, became district headquarters after Independence. Despite being the region's main market and transport hub it has been eclipsed as a tourist centre by Manali, 40km north. Kullu is noisy, polluted and worlds away from the tranquil villages that peer down from the surrounding hillsides, even though a bypass now diverts some of the traffic from the centre. Kullu makes a handy **transport hub** if you're travelling onwards to the Parvati Valley, and there are several **temples** dotted around town, some of which provide fine valley views. In October, when the entire population of the valley comes to town to celebrate **Dussehra**, the city takes on a life of its own.

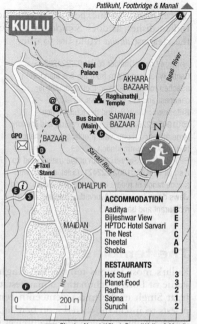

Arrival and information

All long-distance **buses** pull in at the **main bus stand** in **Sarvari Bazaar**, on the north side of the Sarvari River, which flows through the town from the west. Local services heading north also drop and pick up passengers at the top of **Dhalpur maidan**, close to most of the hotels and restaurants and the District Commissioner's office (Mon–Sat 10am–5pm, closed 2nd Sat of month; ☎01902/222727) – the place to apply for **Inner Line permits** (see p.480). HPTDC's **tourist office** (daily 10am–7pm; ☎01902/222349), on the west side of Dhalpur *maidan*, can book tickets on HPTDC's deluxe buses to Delhi, Shimla and Chandigarh. **Flights** to Kullu from Delhi and Shimla arrive in **Bhuntur**, thirty minutes south of Kullu by bus. Taxis to the airport (Rs200) should be booked in the union office (☎01902/222322) on the main road close to the tourist office. Indian Airlines are handled by Ambassador Travels (☎01902/225286), in the LAC Building opposite the Dhalpur *maidan*, and Jagsons (☎01902/265222) in Bhuntur, who are cheaper at just under $100 one-way to or from Delhi. The most convenient **Internet** café is next to the *Aaditya*.

If you're travelling on to **Naggar**, catch one of the frequent Manali-bound buses that run north along the main road, on the west side of the valley, and jump off at **Patlikuhl**, 5km north of Katrain, where you can pick up a shared taxi or local bus for the remaining 6km. Buses also run direct to Manali via Naggar, from the end of the Tapu suspension bridge, across the river from Akhara Bazaar. This service, which leaves more or less hourly, is slower, but far more scenic.

Accommodation and eating

Kullu has a reasonable choice of **accommodation**, although during Dussehra most places are booked way in advance and prices can quadruple. The rates quoted below are for high season; at other times discounts of up to fifty percent may be given. Apart from hotel **restaurants**, the best places to eat are at *Planet Food* and *Hot Stuff*, two similarly priced mixed-menu joints close to the tourist office. *Sapna*, an inexpensive sweets-shop in Akhara Bazaar, also offers south Indian dishes, as does *Suruchi*, on the town side of the footbridge near *Radha*, the cleanest *dhaba* Kullu has to offer.

Aaditya Lower Dhalpur ☎01902/224263. Centrally located 200m from the bus stand, with attached rooms; the basic rooftop double is cheapest and has good views. ❸–❹
Bijleshwar View Behind the tourist office ☎01902/222677. Quiet, clean, central and friendly; large attached rooms with fireplaces, and cheaper bungalow accommodation. ❷–❹
HPTDC Hotel Sarvari South of the *maidan* and up a small lane ☎01902/222471. Quiet location with a wide range of rooms in old and new blocks. Good views down the valley, Ayurvedic massage, and a restaurant and bar. ❹–❻

The Nest Next to the main bus stand ☎01902/222685, ✉hotelnest@rediffmail.com. The best option near the bus stand, with clean, very good value doubles. The cheapest ground-floor rooms have bucket hot water; two of the pricier second-floor rooms have attached bathrooms with tubs. Fixed rates all year. ❶–❸
Sheetal Akhara Bazaar ☎01902/224548. Pleasant little guesthouse with rooms overlooking the river. Excellent value. ❷
Shobla Dhalpur ☎01902/222800, ⓦwww .shoblainternational.com. Kullu's top hotel, which has recently had a major revamp. Large rooms, a good mixed-cuisine restaurant and a relaxing lawn. ❻–❽

The temples

Kullu's most famous temple, the **Raghunathji Mandir** is home to a sacred statue of Lord Raghunathji, a manifestation of Rama, brought to Kullu by Raja Jagat Singh in the mid-seventeenth century. The raja had been advised by his priests to install the sacred icon here and crown it king in his place, and to this day the Kullu rajas consider themselves mere viceroys of Raghunathji, the most powerful *devta* in the valley and the focus of the Dussehra procession. The temple is tucked away behind the Kullu raja's **Rupi Palace** above the bus station. Half an hour's walk further up, the paved trail leads beyond the village of Sultanpur to a high ridge, with excellent views over the Beas River to the snow peaks in the east. **Vaishno Devi Mandir**, a small cave-temple that houses an image of the goddess Kali (Durga), is a stiff 3km further on.

Another important temple, the **Bijli Mahadev Mandir**, stands 8km southeast of town, atop the bluff that overlooks the sacred confluence of the Beas and Parvati rivers. Although it's closer to Bhuntur than Kullu, you have to approach the temple via the Akhara Bazaar–Tapu suspension bridge and a well-worn track south along the left bank of the Beas. Bijli Mahadev is renowned for its extraordinary **lingam**. Bolts of lightning, conducted into the inner sanctum by means of the twenty-metre, trident-tipped pole, are said to periodically shatter the icon, which later, with the help of invocations from the resident *pujari*, magically reconstitutes itself. From the temple there are superb panoramic views of the Parvati and Kullu valleys and Himachal's highest peaks. You can **stay** in the temple resthouse (donations welcome), a simple affair with a single cold tap and no toilets, and walk down into the Parvati Valley the next day.

The Parvati Valley

Hemmed in by giant-pinnacled mountain peaks, the **Parvati Valley**, which twists west from the glaciers and snowfields on the Spiti border to meet the Beas at Bhuntur, is the Kullu Valley's longest tributary. It's a picturesque place, with quiet hamlets perching precariously on its sides amid lush terraces and old pine forests. Though the landscape around **Jari** has been scarred by the ugly

Parvati disappearances

For over a decade the Parvati Valley has seen the mysterious **disappearance** of up to thirty travellers. Most were travelling alone, although one incident in August 2000 involved three campers who were brutally attacked in their tent, thrown into the gorge and left for dead – one survived. Most of the vanished have never been found, including the Israeli who went missing in the most recently publicized case in August 2005. Several theories have been put forward to explain these disappearances, from drug-related accidents on the treacherous mountain trails, to attacks by bears or wolves or foul play by the numerous cannabis cultivators in the region; some even claim that the disappeared may have joined secret cults deep in the mountains. Most likely, however, they were victims of bandit attacks, motivated solely by money, with the wild waters of the River Parvati conveniently placed for disposing of bodies. Individual travellers should **take heed** and only use recognized guides on treks across the mountains. Don't attempt solo treks – even along the relatively simple trail over the Chandrakhani Pass between Naggar and Malana and the straightforward trek to the hot springs at Khirganga. There are many trekking agencies in Kullu and Manali who can put you in touch with a reputable guide.

Malana hydro project, there is strong local pressure to at least camouflage the site. Visitors to the valley are an incongruous mix – a combination of Western hippies (there's a big Israeli scene here) and van-loads of Sikh pilgrims bound for the *gurudwara* at **Manikaran**, 32km northeast of the Beas–Parvati confluence. Crouched at the foot of a gloomy ravine, this ancient religious site, sacred to Hindus as well as Sikhs, is famous for the **hot springs** that bubble out of its stony river banks.

To make the most of Parvati's stunning scenery you'll have to **hike**. Two popular trails thread their way up the valley: one heads north from the fascinating hill village of **Malana** (see box, p.531), over the Chandrakani Pass to Naggar; the other follows the River Parvati east to another sacred hot spring and sadhu hang-out, **Khirganga**. The trail continues from Khirganga to **Mantalai** with its Shiva shrine and over the awesome 5400m Pin–Parvati pass into **Spiti**. This serious snowfield is riddled with crevasses and takes several hours to cross. A guide is absolutely essential (see box, p.530).

Jari, Mateura and Kasol

Spilling over the main road and down the south side of the Parvati Valley, **JARI**, 15km from Bhuntur, looks across to the precipitous Malana *nala* in the north, and to the snow-flecked needles of the Baranagh Range on the eastern horizon. Like many of its lookalike cousins, the tatty settlement supports a small transient population of stoned Westerners, attracted by the top-quality *charas*. For basic **accommodation**, the *Dharma Guest House* (℡01902/276059; ❶), just above the bus stand, and the cleaner *Om Shiva* (℡01902/276202; ❶–❷), on the left-hand side as you enter the village, are simple and welcoming. The best place to eat is *Deepak* restaurant at the bus stand. Those wanting a shortcut to **Malana** (see box, p.531), can hire a vehicle up to the Malana hydro project roadhead, from where the village is a mere 4km trek.

Just ten minutes' walk up the hill from the bus stand is the unspoilt hamlet of **MATEURA**, which has spectacular views over the Parvati Range and is home to the small but important Kali Anagha temple. The *Village Guest House* (℡01902/276070; ❷) is a traditional wooden-balconied house, whose immaculate rooms have satellite TV; set in a wonderful garden, it's popular year-round. The roof terrace of the nearby *Rooftop Restaurant & Guest House* (℡01902/275434; **①**) overlooks the village. All the Mateura guesthouses offer food.

Beyond Jari, the road winds down towards the rushing grey-green Parvati, which it meets at **KASOL**, a pleasant village straddling a mountain stream and surrounded by forest. A mere 4.5km from Manikaran and a nice walk along a wooded road, Kasol has grown in popularity, and now has a large resident population of *charas*-smoking travellers, mostly Israelis – earning it the nickname of "little Israel" from the locals. A trickle of trekkers also plod through on their way to or from the pass of Rashol Jot (2440m), a hard day's climb up the north side of the valley which provides an alternative approach to Malana and the Chandrakani route to the Kullu Valley. You can **change money** here at Swagtam Tourism, who will also give cash advances against credit cards for a three percent fee. **Accommodation** ranges from basic rooms in village houses and simple guesthouses such as *Deep Forest* (℡01902/273048; **②**), up the hill just beyond the bridge, to the plush *Hotel Sandhya Kasol* (℡01902/273745; **④–⑤**), 300m beyond the village, with comfortable rooms and discounts up to seventy percent in the off-season. The best value is offered by the two-storey *Alpine Guest House* (℡01902/273710, ✉alpinehimachal@gmail.com; **③**), with spacious rooms set in wooded grounds by the river. Kasol's **travellers' cafés** are cheap and plentiful. The *Moondance Restaurant and German Bakery* has an excellent location near the bridge; it faces the pleasant *Sasi Palace* on the opposite bank. Further down the road to Manikaran is the popular *Evergreen*, which has a varied international menu; the dope-free restaurant is less popular than its fragrant floor-cushioned backroom. Sadhus and Western hippies pass *charas* round at the *Nutan Tea Stall*.

Manikaran and around

A short distance beyond Kasol, clouds of steam billowing from the rocky riverbank herald the Parvati Valley's chief attraction. Hindu mythology identifies **MANIKARAN** as the place where the serpent king Shesha stole Parvati's earrings, or *manikara*, while she and her husband Shiva were bathing in the river. When interrogated, the snake flew into a rage and snorted the earrings out of his nose. Ever since, boiling water has poured out of the ground. The site is also venerated by Sikhs, who have erected a massive concrete *gurudwara* over the springs.

Boxed in at the bottom of a vast, sheer-sided chasm, Manikaran is a damp, dark and claustrophobic place where you're unlikely to want to spend more than a night. Most of the action revolves around the springs themselves, reached via the lane that leads through the village from the footbridge. On the way, check out the finely carved pale-grey stone **Rama temple** just beyond the main square, and the pans of rice and dhal cooking in the steaming pools on the pavements. Down at the riverside **Shiva shrine**, semi-naked **sadhus** sit in the scalding waters smoking chillums. Sikh pilgrims, meanwhile, make their way to the atmospheric **gurudwara** nearby, where they take a purifying dip in the underground pool, sweat in the hot cave and then congregate upstairs to listen to musical recitations from the Sikhs' holy book, the *Guru Granth Sahib*. If you visit, keep your arms, legs and head covered; tobacco is prohibited inside the complex.

Practicalities

Buses leave Bhuntur at least hourly for Manikaran (1hr 30min). The last bus back to Kullu, via Bhuntur, leaves around 6pm. You can also hire Maruti-van **taxis**. Except during May and June, when Manikaran fills up with Punjabi visitors, **accommodation** is plentiful and inexpensive. Most hotels have a steaming indoor hot tub but the abundance of moisture has left many of them feeling rather damp and dirty. *Hotel Shivalik* (℡01902/273817; ❸–❹), on the main road at the turn-off to the bus stand, has large rooms, TV and balconies with river views. Just before the bus stand itself, the *Country Charm* (℡01902/273703; ❹–❺) is a comfortable mid-range place catering mainly for domestic tourists, with kitsch rooms and a hot pool. Crossing the footbridge brings you to a clutch of cheap guesthouses and overcrowded temple dorms. First up is the *Sharma Sardar Guest House* (℡01902/273703; ❷), which has a hot pool and the best-value doubles in town, with great river views. At the far end of the bazaar the *Sharma Guest House* (℡01902/273742; ❶–❷) is the better of the two near the *gurudwara*. The best **restaurant** is the *Holy Palace*, on the main lane between the Rama Temple and the *gurudwara*. Down a lane towards the bridge, the tiny *Iris Café*, a smokers' hang-out, also has good food, while *Sharma Sweets*, by the Rama Temple, is the spot for chai and snacks.

East of Manikaran

Fourteen kilometres beyond Manikaran, the paved road swivels up the valley and peters out just beyond **Barshani**, from where it's a thirty-minute walk to the villages of Tulga, Pulga and Kalga, all visible across the river. Bridging the dramatic gorge is an ugly hydroelectric dam – still a few years away from completion, but already dominating the once pristine landscape. Despite this, the trio of beautiful villages remains relatively unscathed, resembling Manali in the late 1960s.

PULGA, the westernmost of the three, is lined with narrow stone-covered lanes and rickety wooden houses, most of which sport "room for rent" boards. The *Blue Diamond* (❶–❷), on the far edge of the village nudging against the woods, is the most secluded option. **KALGA**, perched above the dam project, already has more guesthouses than local homes; the *Pink House* (❶), run by a friendly sadhu, is popular. At **TULGA**, really just a hamlet of private homes between the aforementioned villages, you can stay at the woodsy *Peace Place Hotel* (❶).

Naggar

Stacked up the lush, terraced lower slopes of the valley as they sweep towards the tree line from the left bank of the Beas, **NAGGAR**, 6km from the main road junction at Patlikuhl, is the most scenic and accessible of the hill villages between Kullu and Manali. Clustered around an old **castle**, this was the regional capital before the local rajas decamped to Kullu in the mid-1800s. A century or so later, European settlers began to move in. Seduced by the village's ancient **temples**, peaceful setting and unhurried pace, visitors often find themselves lingering in Naggar – a far less hippified village than those further north – longer than they intended. Numerous tracks wind up the mountain to more remote settlements, providing a choice of enjoyable **hikes**.

Arrival and information

Naggar is equidistant (21km) from Kullu and Manali and connected to both by regular **buses**. The direct services that ply the road on the eastern side of the valley are slower (1hr 30min from Manali or Kullu), but more scenic and straightforward than the more frequent services along the main highway on the opposite, west side. The latter drop at **Patlikuhl** (6km from Naggar), from where taxis, auto-rickshaws and hourly buses cross the Beas to climb up to Naggar. If you arrive in daylight and are not weighed down with bags, you can also walk from Patlikuhl on the old mule track – a hike of up to an hour.

Naggar village proper, its sights and accommodation lie a way above the small bazaar on the main road where the buses pull in. If you have your own vehicle, you can drive all the way up to the Roerich Gallery at the top of the village. If you are thinking of **trekking** around Naggar, you are advised to use guides, especially if crossing the **Chandrakhani Pass** to Malana (see p.531). Himalayan Mountain Treks at *Poonam Mountain Lodge* (see below) have equipment, will arrange porters and guides, and can fix up Jeep trips to Lahaul and Spiti. Local guides are also easy to find, though make sure they are reputable.

Accommodation

Alliance Guest House Halfway between the village and the Roerich Gallery ☎01902/248263. Popular guesthouse with simple, clean rooms (four new in 2005), a small lending library and a warm family atmosphere. ❷–❹

Chanderlok Guest House in adjoining Chanalti village below Naggar ☎01902/248213. Simple guesthouse with attached rooms in a quiet location. Korean restaurant also on premises. ❶–❷

HPTDC Hotel Castle ☎01902/248316. Atmospheric castle with well-furnished attached doubles, some offering superb views from spacious wooden balconies, plus dorm beds (Rs75). Book in advance at any HPTDC tourist office to secure one of the more expensive rooms in the west wing. ❸–❼

Karbo Shin Guesthouse Ghourdor village ☎01902/248342, ⓔawhitecloud46@hotmail.com. Dutch-owned guesthouse with four rooms, a

shared bathroom with hot shower, excellent food and superb views. They can also arrange local and long-distance treks. To get there follow the forest road from Naggar to Bijli Mahadev Mandir temple; the guesthouse is down the path signed off the road (10–15min). ❷

Poonam Mountain Lodge Below the castle ☎01902/248248, ⓦwww.poonamlodge .com. Cosy doubles, three with fireplaces for winter stays, Internet access, a lovely outside seating area and a good veg restaurant serving local specialities such as red rice. Extremely welcoming and knowledgable owner too. ❶

Sheetal Guest House ☎01902/248250, ⓔsheetal _hotel_naggar@yahoo.com. An alternative to the nearby *Castle*, offering better-value rooms of similar standard, with balconies, a roof-top restaurant and substantially reduced rates off-season. ❸–❺

The Town

Naggar is a very pleasant place, often sadly overlooked by travellers making a beeline for Manali. The relaxed atmosphere, refreshing elevation, stunning views and a variety of interesting sites combine to make it an excellent spot to while away a couple of days.

The castle

Since it was erected by Raja Sidh Singh (*c.*1700), Naggar's central **castle**, astride a sheer-sided bluff, has served as palace, colonial mansion, courthouse and school. It is now a hotel, but nonresidents can wander in for Rs15 to admire the views from its balconies. Built in the traditional "earthquake-proof" *pahari* style (layers of stone bonded together with cedar logs), the castle has a central courtyard, a small shrine and a shop selling local handicrafts downstairs. The **Jagti Patt temple**'s amorphous deity, a triangular slab of rock strewn with rose petals and rupee notes, is said to have been borne here from its home on the summit of Deo Tibba by a swarm of wild honeybees – the valley's *devtas* in disguise.

The Nicholas Roerich Gallery

Perched on the upper outskirts of the village, the **Nicholas Roerich Gallery** (Tues–Sun: May–Aug 10am–1pm & 1.30–6pm; Sept–March 10am–1pm &

1.30–5pm; Rs30, Rs25 extra for camera, Rs60 extra for video; ⓦwww.roerich trust.org) houses an exhibition of paintings and photographs dedicated to the memory of its former occupier, the Russian artist, writer, philosopher, archeologist, explorer and mystic. Around the turn of the twentieth century, Roerich's atmospheric landscape paintings and esoteric philosophies – an arcane blend of Eastern mysticism and *fin-de-siècle* humanist-idealism – inspired a cult-like following in France and the United States. Financed by donations from devotees, Roerich was able to indulge his obsession with Himalayan travel, eventually retiring in Naggar in 1929 and dying here eighteen years later.

A path winds further up above the road through the forest for around 100m to **Urusvati-Himalayan Folk Art Museum** (same ticket). Founded by Roerich's wife in 1928, the museum features a collection of local folk art, costumes, more of Roerich's paintings, several paintings by his Russian followers, and a gallery of Russian folk art.

The temples

The largest and most distinctive of Naggar's ancient Hindu **temples** and shrines, the wooden pagoda-style **Tripuri Sundri** stands in a small enclosure at the top of the village, just below the road to the Roerich Gallery. Like the Dunghri temple in Manali, it is crowned with a three-tiered roof, whose top storey is circular. Its *devta* is the focus of an annual *mela* (mid-May) in which deities from local villages are brought in procession to pay their respects.

Ten minutes' walk further up the hill – follow the stone steps that lead right from the road – brings you to a clearing where the old stone **Murlidhar** (Krishna) **Mandir** looks down on Naggar, with superb views up the valley to the snow peaks around Solan and the Rohtang Pass. Built on the ruins of the ancient town of Thawa, the shrine, set in a large courtyard, is strictly off-limits to non-Hindus.

Finally, on your way to or from the bus stand at the bottom of the village, look out for the finely carved stone *shikharas* of the **Gaurishankar Mandir**. Set in its own paved courtyard below the castle, this Shiva temple, among the oldest of its kind in the valley, houses a living lingam, so slip off your shoes before approaching it.

Eating

The *Cinderella* **restaurant**, above the *Sheetal Guest House*, serves good food, including grilled trout if ordered a few hours in advance. Other options include the *Mountain View Café*, which offers a standard Indian and Western menu at the start of the road towards the Roerich Gallery. The nearby *La Purezza* serves excellent Italian cuisine and rainbow trout specials in a downstairs room and more pleasant roof terrace.

Manali and around

Himachal's main tourist resort, **MANALI**, stands at the head of the Kullu Valley, 108km north of Mandi. Despite lying at the heart of the region's highest mountain range, it remains easily accessible by road from the plains; after one hour on a plane and a short hop by road, or sixteen hours on a bus from Delhi, you could be staring from your hotel veranda across apple orchards and thick pine forests to the snowfields of Solang Nala, which shine a tantalizing stone's throw away to the north. With the continuing troubles in Kashmir, Manali has

OLD MANALI

Rohtang Pass, Keylong & Leh

& Manu Mandir

Manalsu Nala

Club House

VASHISHT

Temple & Tank

LOG HUT ROAD

OLD MANALI ROAD

Reserve Forest

HPTDC Hot Baths Complex

Hadimba Temple

Deodar Woods

Gardens

ACCOMMODATION

Arohi	K
Amrit	G
Ashok Mayur	F
Bhrigu	K
Dharma	J
Dragon	D
Godfather Palace Ashram	L
Hadimbaway	Q
HPTDC Log Huts	N
Jamuna	X
Johnson Lodge	T
Kalptaru	H
Laxmi	C
Lhasa	U
Meridien	W
Mount View	V
Negi's Hotel Mayflower	
Pinewood	S
Rajhans	R
Retreat Cottages	P
Rockway Cottage	O
Snowcrest Manor	B
Surabhi	M
Tiger Eye	I
Veer	A
	E

HPTDC

Mission Rd

GPO

Bus Stand

The Mall

Model Town Rd

Taxi Stand

MODEL TOWN

Gochi Rd

Beas River

Nagar Road

RESTAURANTS & CAFÉS

Café Amigos	13
Café Mahalsu	5
Chopsticks	16
Freedom Café	10
Il Forno	14
Green Forest Café	12
Johnson's Café	T
Manu Café	1
Mayur	15
Moondance	6
Mountain Café	2
Phuntsak Café	11
Pizza Olive	4
Rainbow Café	7
River Music Café	8
Shiva Café	3
Tibet Kitchen	9
Treat	16
World Peace Café	I

Gadhan Thekchhokling gompa

State Bank of India

Kullu

Aleo, Nagar, Jagatsukh & Mountaineering Institute

become increasingly popular with domestic tourists, giving rise to an eclectic mix of honeymooners, holiday-makers, hippies, trekkers and traders.

The Manali that lured travellers in the 1970s has certainly changed, although the majestic mountain scenery, thermal springs and quality *charas* can still be enjoyed. **Old Manali** retains some of its atmosphere, and the village of **Vashisht** across the valley, with its increasing choice of guesthouses and cafés, has become a popular place to chill out. For those preferring to venture into the mountains, Manali makes an ideal **trekking** base for short hikes and serious expeditions, and countless agencies can help put a package together for you. The relaxing hotels in Manali's cleaner, greener outskirts, and dozens of sociable cafés and restaurants ranged around a well-stocked **bazaar**, provide a welcome relief from the rigours of the mountain trails. For more on treks around Manali and the Kullu Valley, see box, p.530.

Arrival and information

Coming from Delhi, most private buses pull into the bus stand 100m south of the State Bank of India at the bottom of town; government buses pull in to Manali's **bus stand** in the middle of the Mall, a short walk from the friendly **tourist office** (daily: 8am–8pm high season; 10am–1.30pm & 2–5pm rest of year; ☎01902/252175). You can make reservations for the town's state-run hotels at the HPTDC offices, two doors down. Manali's **Taxi Operators' Union kiosk** (☎01902/252450) lies just up from the tourist office; the taxis have fixed rates which are negotiable off-season. If you need to **change money**, the State Bank of India is on the main road 250m south of the Mall. There are also a handful of authorized private agencies open longer hours but these usually offer lower rates. There are also two SBI and one UCO Bank ATMs on the Mall. The main **post office**, off Model Town Road, has a reliable poste restante counter (Mon–Sat 9am–1pm & 1.30–5pm); broadband **Internet** facilities are available at several places on the Mall and more in Old Manali. Although most people apply for **Inner Line permits** either in Kaza (see p.539), or if travelling south–north, in Rekong Peo (see p.494), if you want to get one in Manali, you must do so through a registered travel agent (see p.529 for recommendations). Take along three photos, and a photocopy of your passport and visa details.

Accommodation

There are three main accommodation areas in Manali. Most longer-stay budget places are clustered in **Old Manali**, where rough-and-ready family-run guest-houses, joined by a handful of less appealing modern hotels, nestle amid the orchards. A *charas*-induced torpor hangs over many of them, but the peace and quiet and views from their flower gardens make the two-kilometre hike (or Rs30 Vikram ride) from New Manali worthwhile. Most of Manali's classic hotels with gardens and character are dotted around the **northern and western outskirts**, midway between Old Manali and the Mall. In town, tucked away behind the Mall, is a cluster of identikit concrete hotels known as **Model Town**. Mostly mid-range and seriously lacking character, they are conveniently located, invariably have hot water and TV in their attached rooms, and offer discounts of up to 75 percent off-season (July, Aug & Nov–March).

Tariffs rocket in Manali during **high season** (April–June & Sept–Oct). At other times, a fifty percent reduction on the advertised rates for more expensive hotels is standard. The few hotels that stay open in **winter** cater mainly for skiing parties. All prices listed below are for high season.

Old Manali

Ashok Mayur ☎01902/252868. Small, basic (verging on dingy) and friendly guesthouse opposite *Shiva* café, with balconies warmed by the morning sun. ❶–❷

Dragon ☎01902/252790, ⊛www.dragontours .com. Newer hotel with brash exterior but comfortable, spacious attached rooms with hot water and balconies. The top floor has some great wooden-floored duplexes for Rs800–1500. Useful Internet café and travel centre. ❸–❺

Laxmi Guest House ☎01902/253569. Small, friendly place with rickety wooden rooms and shared bathrooms, which stay cheap in high season. Uninterrupted valley views and a small garden are the best features. ❶

Rockway Cottage 500m along the track starting just past the *Mahalsu Café* ☎01902/253428. Pleasant rooms, some with wood heaters, in an idyllic setting. Good food in the garden café, set above the river. Well worth the effort, but bring a torch. ❸–❹

Tiger Eye Tucked into lanes at top of village but signposted ☎01902/252718, ⓔtigereyeindia @yahoo.com. Peaceful, newly built family guesthouse run by friendly Indian–Dutch couple. Immaculate rooms and balconies with great views. ❸

Veer ☎01902/252410. Simple place with fine views down the valley from a lovely leafy garden and communal eating area. Some attached bathrooms, too. ❶–❷

Northern and western outskirts

Hadimbaway Log Huts Area ☎01902/251552, ⓔhadimbaway@yahoo.co.in. Best value of the several places in this quiet little enclave near the Hadimba Temple. Unusually, the upstairs rooms are cheaper. ❹

HPTDC Log Huts Overlooking Manalsu Nala ☎01902/253225, ⓔmanali@hptdc.in. Comfortable but overpriced timber holiday cottages tucked away in the woods, with one or two double bedrooms, kitchens and most comforts including Star TV. ❽

Johnson Lodge Old Manali Rd ☎01902/253023, ⊛www.johnsonslodge .com. Three-star comfort in an old colonial building. Spacious and neat wooden-floored rooms overlook the garden; the carpeted downstairs rooms are cheaper, with wood-burning heaters for winter. ❼–❽

Negi's Hotel Mayflower Old Manali Rd ☎01902/252104, ⓔnegismayflower@sancharnet .in. One of Manali's most agreeable hotels. The large rooms are new, but feel traditional with wood

panelling and views over the pine forests. Balconies out front catch the afternoon sun. ❻–❼

Pinewood Old Manali Rd ☎01902/250118. Colonial building with furniture, fireplaces and garden to match. All rooms with balcony. Big off-season discounts. ❻

Rajhans Off Old Manali Rd ☎01902/252209, ⓔhotelrajhans@gmail.com. Stylish new four-storey brick building with valley views from the more luxurious higher rooms; all attached with TV. ❹–❻

Retreat Cottages Log Hut Rd ☎01902/252042, ⓔtibetemporium@hotmail.com. Immaculate, huge self-catering two- and three-bedroom (Rs7000) suites with baths in a tastefully designed building. Recommended for groups of 6–8. Meals can also be ordered. ❽–❾

Snowcrest Manor Above the *Log Huts* ☎01902/253351, ⓔsnowcrestmanor@hotmail .com. Aimed at business-class tourists, with luxury rooms, all mod cons, central heating and a large terrace overlooking the valley from its perch on a ridge. ❼–❽

Model Town

Jamuna Gompa Rd ☎01902/252506. Old-style hotel but the rooms are clean and spacious enough and about as cheap as it gets in Model Town. ❸

Lhasa Just off Model Town Rd ☎01902/252134. One of the friendlier and better-value places in the area. Slightly faded decoration and furnishings but all rooms have bathrooms and TV. ❹

Meridien Model Town Rd ☎01902/250484, ⊛www.hotelhollywoodmanali.com. Pristine new five-storey hotel, with glitzy attached rooms, with TV. Also a roof terrace and multi-cuisine restaurant. ❹–❻

Mount View Far end of Model Town Rd ☎01902/252465. Pleasant ivy-clad building in a quieter area with decent-sized doubles and a rooftop terrace with splendid views. ❸–❹

The Town

Manali's main street, **the Mall**, quite unlike its namesake in Shimla, is a noisy scene of constant activity, fronted by the bus stand, several shopping markets, travel agents, and a line of hotels and restaurants. It's a great place to watch the world go by – locals in traditional caps, Tibetan women in immaculate rainbow-striped pinafores, Nepali porters, Buddhist monks, the odd party of Zanskaris swathed in fusty woollen *gonchas*, souvenir-hunting Indian tourists and a curious mix of Westerners.

Manali's days as an authentic *pahari* bazaar ended when the mule trains were superseded by Tata trucks, but it's still great for souvenir **shopping**. Woollen goods are the town's real forte, particularly the brilliantly patterned **shawls** for which Kullu Valley is famous. Genuine pure-wool handloom shawls with embroidered borders start at around Rs500, but those made from finest pashmina cost several thousand rupees. Shop around and check out the fixed-price factory shops to get an idea of what's available: the government-sponsored Bhutico on the Mall opposite the tourist office, the Bodh Shawl factory shop just off the Mall south of the bus stand and The Great Hadimba

Tours and adventure sports around Manali

Weather and road conditions permitting, HPTDC (℡01902/252116), two doors down from the tourist office, run daily bus **tours** to the **Rohtang Pass** (10am–5pm; Rs220) and day-trips to **Manikaran** in the Parvati Valley (9am–6.30pm; Rs250). Tickets can be bought in advance from their transport counter.

Considering the fierce white-water that thrashes down the Kullu Valley during the spring melt, Manali's **rafting** scene is surprisingly low-key. Raft trips down the River Beas are offered between the end of May and early July, when water levels are highest, beginning at Piridi (above Bhuntur) around 15km downstream at Jhiri. The price (around Rs1200) should include meals, lifejackets, helmets, and return travel; check exactly what you're paying for, as some unscrupulous operators expect you to make your own way back after the trip.

Skiing in the Solang Valley is popular from January to April – but the slope isn't much bigger than a cricket pitch. A new ski centre in conjunction with the Finnish government is being planned for the Rohtang Pass. The valley was also one of the biggest **paragliding** centres in India, though in 2004 paragliding was banned pending new safety and insurance regulations and its status is still uncertain. One of the best ways to explore Kullu is by **mountain biking**, which is possible from mid-June to mid-October. The best local guide is Raju Sharma (℡09816 056934, @www.magicmountainadventures.com), who can arrange bike hire (Rs300 per day for a European bike , Rs500 with Raju as guide), and suggest routes around Manali as well as expeditions up to Leh. Popular routes include the descent from Rohtang, the forest trail to the Bijli Mahadev Temple and the back road to Naggar.

If you're planning a trekking or rafting trip, shop around to compare prices and packages; many agencies are fly-by-night operators who make their money from mark-ups on long-distance bus tickets to Delhi, Chandigarh and Leh. Long-established, **reputable agents** include the very experienced Rup Negi at Himalayan Adventurers (℡01902/253050), opposite the tourist office, and Himanshu Sharma at Himalayan Journeys (℡01902/252365), next to *Café Amigos*. They can organize trekking, rock climbing, rafting and ski packages at Solang. Other recommended agents include Nirvana Travels (℡01902/253222), on Old Manali Road before the bridge, and Northern Adventures Tours (℡01902/254382), back on the Mall. A number of agents also operate **Jeep safaris** to remote regions such as Spiti.

Shop & Factory next to the Manu Temple in Old Manali are recommended; the NSC (New Shopping Centre) market near the bus stand also has a good selection.

Elsewhere around the bazaar, innumerable stalls are stacked with handwoven goods and pillbox Kullu **topis**. Those with gaudy multicoloured up-turned flaps and gold piping are indigenous to the valley, but you can also pick up the plain-green velvet-fronted variety favoured by Kinnauris. Manali's other specialities are **Tibetan curios** such as prayer wheels, amulets, *dorjees* (thunderbolts), masks, musical instruments, jewellery and **thangkas**. Few of the items hawked as antiques are genuine, but it takes an expert eye to spot a fake. The same

Treks around Manali and the Kullu Valley

The Kullu Valley's spectacular alpine scenery makes it perfect for **trekking**. Trails are long and steep, but more than repay the effort with superb views, varied flora and the chance to visit remote hill stations. Within striking distance of several major trailheads, **Manali** is the most popular place to begin and end treks. While **package deals** (around Rs1800 per person for three days with a group of four) offered by the town's many agencies can save time and energy, it is relatively easy to organize your own trip with maps and advice from the tourist office and the Mountaineering Institute at the bottom end of town. Porters and horsemen can be sought out in the square behind the main street. Always take a reliable **guide**, especially on less-frequented routes, as you cannot rely solely on **maps**. Some trekkers have reported difficulties when descending from the Bara Bangal Pass, as maps don't do the terrain justice.

The optimum trekking **season** is right after the monsoons (mid-Sept to late Oct), when skies are clear and pass-crossings easier. From June to August, you run the risk of sudden, potentially fatal snow, or view-obscuring cloud and rain.

Manali to Beas Kund

The relatively easy trek to Beas Kund, a glacial lake at the head of Solang *nala*, is the region's most popular short hike. Encircled by 5000-metre-plus peaks, the well-used campground beside the lake, accessible in two days from Manali, makes a good base for side-trips up to the surrounding ridges and passes.

From **Palchan**, a village 30min north of Manali by bus, follow the Jeep track up the valley to **Solang**, site of a small ski station, resthouse and the Mountaineering Institute's log huts. The next two hours take you through pine forests and grassy meadows to the campground at **Dhundi** (2743m). A more strenuous walk of 5–6hr the next day leads to **Beas Kund**. The hike up to the **Tentu La** Pass (4996m) and back from here can be done in a day, as can the descent to Manali via Solang.

Manali to Lahaul, via the Hampta Pass

The three-day trek from the Kullu Valley over the Hampta Pass to Lahaul, the old caravan route to Spiti, is a classic. Rising to 4330m, it is high by Kullu standards; do not undertake it without allowing good time to acclimatize. **Day one**, from the trailhead at **Jagatsukh** or Hampta (both villages near Manali) to the campground above **Sethen**, is an easy hike (4–5hr) up the verdant, forested sides of the valley. **Day two** (5hr) brings you to **Chikha**, a high Gaddi pasture below the pass; stay put for a day or so if you're feeling the effects of altitude. The ascent (700m) on **day three** to the **Hampta Pass** (4330m) is gruelling, but the views from the top – of Indrasan and Deo Tibba to the south, and the moonscape of Lahaul to the north – are sublime recompense. It takes six to seven hours of relentless rock-hopping and stream-crossing to reach **Chhatru**, on the floor of the Chandra Valley. From here, you can turn east towards Koksar and the **Rohtang Pass**, or west past the world's largest glacier, **Bara Shigri**, to **Batal**, the trailhead for the Chandratal–Baralacha trek (see p.543).

applies to silver **jewellery** inlaid with turquoise and coral, which can nonetheless be attractive and relatively inexpensive.

The Hadimba Temple

Resting on a wide stone platform fifteen minutes' walk northwest of the bazaar, the **Hadimba Temple** is Manali's oldest shrine and the seat of Hadimba (or "Hirma Devi"), wife of Bhima. Considered to be an incarnation of Kali, Hadimba is worshipped in times of adversity, and also plays a key role in the Dussehra festival (see p.518). Hadimba is supposed to have given the kingdom of Kullu to the forefathers of the rajas of Kullu, and in veneration and affection

Naggar to Malana via the Chandrakani Pass and onwards

The trek to Jari in the Parvati Valley from Naggar, 21km south of Manali, is quintessential Kullu Valley trekking with superb scenery and fascinating villages. The round trip can be completed in three days, but you may be tempted to linger in **Malana** and explore the surrounding countryside. A **guide** is essential for several reasons: the first stage of the trek involves crossing a maze of grazing trails; Malana is culturally sensitive and requires some familiarity with local customs; and several people have **disappeared** in the Parvati Valley over the last few years in suspicious circumstances (see p.521). The descent to the Parvati Valley is too steep for pack ponies, but porters are available in Naggar through the guesthouses, including Himalayan Mountain Treks at *Poonam Mountain Lodge* (see p.524).

The trail leads through the village of Rumsu and then winds through wonderful old-growth forests to a pasture just above the tree line, which makes ideal camping ground. From here, a climb of 4km takes you to the **Chandrakani Pass** (3660m), with fine views west over the top of the Kullu Valley to the peaks surrounding Solang *nala* and north to the Ghalpo mountains of Lahaul. Some prefer to reach the base of the pass on the first day and then camp below the final ascent.

The inhabitants of **MALANA**, a steep 7km descent from the pass, are known for their frostiness and staunch traditions. Plans by regional developers to extend a paved road here are vehemently opposed by the insular locals. Although notions of **caste pollution** are not as strictly adhered to as they once were, you should observe a few basic "**rules**" in Malana: approach the village quietly and respectfully; stick to paths at all times; keep away from the temple; and above all, don't touch anybody or anything, especially children or houses. If you do commit a cultural blunder, you'll be expected to make amends: usually in the form of a Rs1000 payment for a sacrificial offering of a young sheep or goat to the village deity, **Jamlu**, one of the most powerful Kullu Valley gods. His **temple**, open to high-caste Hindus only, is decorated with lively folk carvings, among them images of soldiers – the villagers claim to be the area's sole remaining descendents of Alexander the Great's army. Popular **places to stay** include the *Renuka Guest-house* (➊), which has hot water, and the *Himalaya Guesthouse* (➊), run by the former village headman. The owner of *Santu Ram's* (➊) is an authority on local trails. All the guesthouses offer simple meals. The official camping ground lies 100m beyond the village spring.

The **final stage** of the trek takes you down the sheer limestone sides of Malana *nala* to the floor of the Parvati Valley – a precipitous 12km drop that is partially covered by a switchback road. From the hamlet of **Rashol** you have a choice of three onward routes: either head east up the right bank of the river to **Manikaran** (see p.522); follow the trail southwest to the sacred **Bijli Mahadev Mandir**; or climb the remaining 3km up to the road at **Jari**, from where regular buses leave for Bhuntur, Kullu and Manali.

the family to this day refer to her as "grandmother". The massive triple-tiered wooden pagoda crowned by crimson pennants and a brass ball and trident (Shiva's *trishul*), dates from 1553, and is a replica of earlier ones that burned down in successive forest fires. The facade writhes with wonderful woodcarvings of elephants, crocodiles and folk deities. Entered by a door surmounted by wild ibex horns, the gloomy **shrine** is dominated by several large boulders, one of which shelters the stone on which goats and buffalo are sacrificed during important rituals. The hollow in its middle, believed to be Vishnu's footprint, channels the blood to Hadimba's mouth.

Soft-drinks stands, curio stalls and yak rides cater for visitors while the presiding deity looks on. The nearby **Kullu Cultural Museum** (Rs10) displays detailed models of the valley's temples.

Old Manali

Old Manali, the village from which the modern town takes its name, lies 2km north of the Mall, on the far side of the Manalsu Nala. Built in the old *pahari* style, most of the houses of Old Manali have heavy stone roofs and wooden balconies hung with bushels of drying herbs and tobacco. Unlike its crowded, concrete offspring, the settlement retains an unhurried and traditional feel – out of season. In summer, travellers on throaty Enfields roar through its lanes, guesthouses blare trance music and the cafés are thick with chillum smoke. In the wake of the tourists come the Kashmiris, Rajasthani tailors and other opportunists, eager to make good business before returning to Goa in the autumn.

To get there, head north up Old Manali Road, bear right at the fork in the road, and keep going through the pine woods until you reach the iron bridge across the river. A bit of leg work will bring you to the village proper, clustered on top of a steeply shelving ledge of level ground above the *nala*. It is also known as **Manaligarh** after its ancient citadel – now a ruined fort surrounded by a patchwork of maize terraces and deep-green orchards. At the centre of the village is an unusual, brash new temple dedicated to **Manu**, who laid the foundations of Hindu law that continues to today, as well as *varna* or "colour" – the basis of the caste system. Inscribed stones dating from the Middle Ages embedded into the concrete paving reveal the site's antiquity. Although Manali itself is considered safe, women should be wary of walking along the lane from town to Old Manali after dark; it has been the scene of several attempted **rapes** over the last decade.

The gompas

Manali harbours the highest concentration of **Tibetan refugees** in the Kullu Valley, hence the prayer flags fluttering over the approach roads into town, and the presence, on its southern edge, of two **gompas**.

Capped with polished golden finials, the distinctive yellow corrugated-iron pagoda roof of the **Gadhan Thekchhokling Gompa** is an exotic splash of colour amid the ramshackle huts of the Tibetan quarter. Built in 1969, the monastery is maintained by donations from the local community and through the sale of **carpets** handwoven in the temple workshop. When they are not looking after the **shop**, the young lamas huddle in the courtyard to play *cholo* – a Tibetan dice game involving much shouting and slamming of wooden *tsampa* bowls on leather pads. Beside the main entrance, a roll of honour recounts the names of Tibetans killed during the violent political demonstrations that wracked China in the late 1980s.

The smaller and more modern of the two *gompas* stands nearer the bazaar, in a garden that in late summer blazes with sunflowers. Its main shrine, lit by dozens of bare electric bulbs and filled with fragrant Tibetan incense, houses a colossal gold-faced Buddha, best viewed from the small room on the first floor.

Eating and drinking

Manali's wide range of **restaurants** reflects the town's melting-pot credentials: Tibetan *thukpa* joints stand cheek-by-jowl with south Indian coffee houses, Gujarati thali bars and Nepalese-run German pastry shops. Whatever their ostensible speciality, though, most offer mixed menus that include Chinese and Western dishes alongside standard north Indian favourites and many do traveller-friendly **breakfasts** of eggs, porridge, pancakes, toast and jam. Competition and a preponderance of domestic tourists and foreign backpackers keep prices reasonable so, unless indicated, most places charge in the Rs60–100 range for main courses. For rock-bottom budget food, head for one of the *dhabas* opposite the bus stand. Stock up on energy-rich **trekking food** at the local produce stores and bakeries in the bazaar. The state-sponsored co-op, near the temple on the Mall, sells sacks of nuts, dried fruit and pots of pure honey at fixed prices. One legendary spot, 5km away in Jagatsukh (Rs50–60 by auto-rickshaw), is the laid-back Brit-run *Alchemy Bar*, serving health-conscious Western food among creature comforts such as sofas, videos, world music and a pool table.

The Mall and around

Café Amigos The Mall. Wooden tables, colourful pottery, chilled-out music and a fantastic range of cakes and brownies, as well as main meals.

Chopsticks The Mall. Very popular Tibetan-run restaurant with a pleasant atmosphere and varied menu. Try the filter coffee and the great muesli, fruit and curd.

Green Forest Café Off Log Hut Rd. Small local restaurant, serving the best *momos* in Manali for only Rs40–50.

Il Forno Hadimba Rd. A traditional building that has been successfully converted into an Italian-run restaurant serving excellent pizzas, pasta, salads and tiramisu. Main dishes in the Rs100–150 range. Good views.

Johnson's Café Part of *Johnson Lodge*. A great café, with garden seating and an inviting menu including beer, fresh trout and crème caramel. Some items top Rs200 but they are worth it.

Mayur Mission Rd, just off the Mall. Exciting and extensive Indian menu featuring dishes from all over the Subcontinent – try the excellent *jalfrezi*. Candles, serviettes and classical Indian music create a pleasant vibe.

Treat The Mall. Good first-floor Indian/Chinese joint, serving up copious amounts of rice- and noodle-based dishes with views of the street action below.

Old Manali

Café Mahalsu Popular restaurant overlooking the river, with the usual mixed menu but the benefit of satellite radio, English-language magazines and Internet access.

Manu Café A local house with a small upstairs café, which despite the usual travellers' menu is best for local food. Most veg items Rs50 or less.

Moondance Popular garden café and meeting place above the river with a varied menu that includes Mexican and Italian dishes.

Mountain Café Set away from most of the guest-houses, with extensive views of the surrounding mountains. Simple yet varied menu; open 24hr in season or when there's sufficient demand.

Pizza Olive Great pizzas and delicious snacks like bruschetta.

River Music Café Hang-out place by the bridge with tables on the terrace or floor-cushion seating under shelter. Usual menu and a good sound-system.

Shiva Café Sociable, laid-back balcony, an open fire most evenings, and Chinese, Indian and pasta dishes make this popular among budget travellers.

Tibet Kitchen Near the Club House. A comfortable and popular restaurant with a mixed menu serving great Tibetan food as well as the odd Japanese dish.

Moving on from Manali

Manali is well connected by **bus** to other Himachali towns and major cities on the plains. HPSRTC run luxury, deluxe and ordinary buses, all of which can be booked at the bus stand. During the summer, demand invariably outstrips supply, particularly for the faster services, so book as far in advance as possible. The numerous travel agents dotted around town also sell tickets for **private** "deluxe" services to Delhi, Shimla and Dharamsala. Consider breaking your journey in Mandi (for Rewalsar) or using the **Kangra Valley Railway** to reach Dharamsala or Pathankot from where you can pick up trains for Amritsar, Delhi and Rajasthan. Buses also cross the Rohtang La to Kaza, capital of Spiti, from where you can continue to Shimla, although **permits** are required to travel beyond Sumdo. Harisons Travels (☎01902/253519), Monal Himalayan Travels (☎01902/254215), Swagtam (☎01902/253990) and Valleycon (☎01902/253776), at the bus stand and at *Mayur* restaurant, all sell tickets.

See p.545 for more information on journey frequencies and durations.

Transport to Leh

The **Rohtang Pass** at the head of the Kullu Valley is only open from June to October when buses travel to Keylong, capital of Lahaul. It can be difficult to book onward transport from Keylong to Leh as buses nearly always arrive full, so try to reserve a seat in advance. It is quite easy to book single places in mini-vans and Maruti Gypsy taxis to **Leh** from Manali – prices start from Rs1200, though front seats cost a bit more and all prices rise in the early summer high season. This is the fastest way, as most vehicles try to cover it in 17–19hr after a 2am start but that means you do miss the scenery at the beginning and end of the ride. There are also frequent complaints of the drivers, who often lack sleep, taking unnecessary risks on the sharp bends and long sections of unpaved road. Many backpackers, therefore, still travel the 485km to Leh by bus – an arduous but unforgettable two-day trip, involving a night halt under canvas en route. HPTDC's "super-deluxe" bus, bookable through the tourist office, runs on alternate days and costs Rs1600, which includes accommodation and a meal at the tent colony in Keylong. Otherwise, choice is limited to the beaten-up buses operated by HPSRTC and their J&K equivalents.

Officially, the **Manali–Leh Highway** (see p.543) is only open from mid-June until September 15, after which state authorities absolve themselves of responsibility and emergency services aren't available for civilian traffic. Some of the private companies, however, continue to operate until late September. 4WD taxis continue to ply the route well into October, but again you risk getting stuck and having to spend a few extra freezing cold nights on the road. Whenever and however you travel, avoid the bumpy back seat of the bus and take food and lots of water (at least 2–3 litres) to reduce the risk of dehydration and **altitude sickness**.

Vashisht

Famous for its sweeping valley views and sulphurous hot-water springs, the ever-expanding village of **VASHISHT**, 3km north of Manali, is an amorphous jumble of traditional timber houses and modern concrete cubes, divided by paved courtyards and narrow muddy lanes. It is the epicentre of the local budget travellers' scene, with a good choice of guesthouses and cafés. The tranquil and traditional atmosphere is only interrupted by the occasional rave that takes place in the woods, or if the weather is poor, in one or two obliging hotels.

You can get to Vashisht from Manali by road, or along the footpath from the main highway that passes the **HPTDC hot baths complex** – which has been closed for several years now due to a dispute between the villagers and the Himachal government. In the meantime, the only place for a **hot soak** is in the bathing pools of Vashisht's ancient temple (free), which is far more atmospheric anyway. Divided into separate sections for men and women, they attract a decidedly mixed crowd of Hindu pilgrims, Western hippies, semi-naked sadhus and groups of local kids.

Vashisht boasts two old stone **temples**, opposite each other above the main square and dedicated to the local patron saint Vashishta, guru of Raghunathji. The smaller of the two opens onto a partially covered courtyard and is adorned with elaborate woodcarvings. Those lining the interior of the shrine, blackened by years of oil-lamp and *dhoop* smoke, are worth checking out.

If you're up for more than just leaning back with a chillum, the **Himalayan Extreme Centre** (☎09816 174164, ⓦ www.himalayan-extreme-center.com), on the road into the village, organizes days out snowboarding, kite-surfing and rock climbing; it also has its own lodge (❷–❸).

Accommodation

Vashisht is packed with budget **guesthouses**, many of them old wooden buildings with broad verandas and uninterrupted vistas up the valley. If you don't mind primitive plumbing, grungy beds and dope smoke, the only time you'll not be spoilt for choice is during high season (May–June & Sept–Oct), when even floor-space can be at a premium. On the outskirts, a couple of larger **hotels** offer good-value, comfortable rooms. The places below are marked on the Manali & Vashisht map on p.526.

Amrit The uppermost hotel, tucked away behind the temples ☎01902/254209. A turquoise wooden house with basic facilities, including bucket hot water. Grubby but atmospheric with rickety balconies affording fine views. ❶

Arohi Just up from the *Bhrigu* ☎01902/254421. Immaculate rooms with cable TV, intercom and balconies overlooking the river. The ex-army owner speaks excellent English and gives up to fifty percent discounts off-season. ❹

Bhrigu Hotel On the main road into the village ☎01902/253414. Large hotel whose west-facing rooms all have attached bathrooms and superb views from their spacious balconies. ❸

🏃 **Dharma** 5min walk up the lane behind the temples ☎01902/252354, ⓦ www .hoteldharma.com. Complete with new wing, most rooms have fantastic views, as does the marble terrace with a swing and loungers. There's even a tiny swimming pool, filled by the hot springs. ❸

Godfather Palace Ashram 50m before the village square, signed off the road ☎01902/254069. Large attached rooms with hot showers, cannabis growing in the garden and a basement for raves. ❷

Kalptaru Overlooking the temple tanks ☎01902/253443. You can't get any closer to the baths – with reasonable rooms, all attached, with hot bucket water. Small garden and veranda from which to watch the world go by. ❶

Surabhi Halfway up the main road ☎01902/252796, ⓦ www.surabhihotel.com. The airy, smart new rooms upstairs all have views of the valley. The cheaper ground-floor rooms are colder and darker. ❸–❺

Eating

A backpackers' paradise, Vashisht has numerous **cafés** serving the typical fried rice, noodles, omelettes, pancakes and lassis, all at standard rates. In addition, bakeries provide wholemeal bread, apple pies and a variety of sticky things. Most of the cafés are hang-out places and several have open-air terraces with views, but there is little to choose between them.

Freedom Café On the main road past *Bhrigu Hotel*. Floor seating and a grassy deck with good views; food is Mexican, Tibetan and Italian.

Phuntsok Café On the river banks, on the outskirts of the village. Outdoor café serving delicious and wholesome home-cooked Tibetan food. One of Vashisht's best.

Rainbow Café Near *Kalptaru* hotel. Traveller-friendly offerings such as pancakes, pasta and spring rolls, with terrace views of the temple tanks.

World Peace Café On the main road, above the *Surabhi* hotel. The food is a fairly standard Indian/Western mix but there's Turkish coffee, as well as movies, board games and frequent live gigs. There's a roof terrace too.

Lahaul and Spiti

Few places on earth can mark so dramatic a change in landscape as the **Rohtang Pass**. To one side, the lush green head of the Kullu Valley; to the other, an awesome vista of bare, chocolate-coloured mountains, hanging glaciers and snowfields that shine in the dazzlingly crisp light, with just flecks of flora deep in the valley to soften the stark image. The district of **Lahaul and Spiti**, Himachal's largest, is named after its two subdivisions, which are, in spite of their numerous geographical and cultural similarities, distinct and separate regions.

Lahaul

Lahaul, sometimes referred to as the Chandra-Bhaga Valley, is the region that divides the Great Himalayas and Pir Panjal ranges. Its principal river, the Chandra, rises deep in the barren wastes below the **Baralacha Pass**, a major landmark on the Manali–Leh road, and flows south towards its confluence with the River Bhaga near Tandi. Here, the two rivers become the Chenab, and crash north out of Himachal to Kishtwar in Kashmir. Lahaul's **climate** is very similar to that of Ladakh and Zanskar, which border it to the north. The valley receives precious little rain, and during the summer the sun is very strong and the nights cool. Between late October and late March, heavy snow closes the passes, and seals off the region. Even so, its inhabitants, a mixture of Buddhists and Hindus, enjoy one of the highest per capita incomes in the Subcontinent. Using glacial water channelled through ancient irrigation ducts, Lahauli farmers manage to coax a bumper crop of **seed potatoes** from their painstakingly fashioned terraces. The region is also the sole supplier of **hops** to India's breweries, and harvests prodigious quantities of wild herbs, used to make perfume and medicine. Much of the profit generated by these cash crops is spent on lavish jewellery, especially seed-pearl necklaces and coral and turquoise-inlaid silver plaques, worn by the women over ankle-length burgundy or fawn woollen dresses. Lahaul's traditional costume and Buddhism are a legacy of the Tibetan influence that has permeated the region from the east.

State **buses** run from Manali up the Chandra and Bhaga valleys to Keylong and Darcha from whenever the Rohtang Pass is cleared, usually in late June, until it snows up again in late October. You can also travel through Lahaul on private Leh-bound buses if there are free seats.

Keylong

Lahaul's largest settlement and the district headquarters, **KEYLONG**, 114km north of Manali, is a good place to pause on the long road journey to Ladakh. Although of little interest itself, the village lies amid superb scenery, within a day's climb of three Buddhist **gompas**, one visible on the opposite (south) side of the grandiose Bhaga Valley. A couple of **stores** in the busy market sell trekking supplies if you are heading off to Zanskar.

Lahauli Buddhists consider it auspicious to make a clockwise circumambulation – known as the **Rangcha Parikarma** – of the sacred **Rangcha Mountain** (4565m), which dominates the confluence of the Bhaga and Chandra rivers. A well-worn trail that makes a long day-hike from Keylong, the route is highly scenic, and takes in the large **Khardung gompa** along the way. Rising over 1000m from its base elevation (3348m), the trail is a hard slog if you haven't acclimatized. Carry plenty of food, water and warm clothing, and be prepared to turn back if you start to feel dizzy and/or acutely short of breath. A rough motorable road leads to Khardung *gompa* (10km), but closer to Keylong and on the same side of the valley are two quiet and picturesque *gompas* high up the mountainside, **Shasher Gompa** (3km) and **Gungshal Gompa** (5km).

Practicalities

Keylong is connected by regular state **buses** to Manali, and (in summer) by private buses to all points north along the main highway. Note that onward **transport to Leh** can be difficult to arrange in high season (July & Aug), as most buses are full by the time they get there. Travellers frequently find themselves having to ride on the roof, or hitch a lift on one of the trucks that stop at the *dhabas* on the roadside above the village – neither legal, nor particularly safe. There are eight buses daily to Manali, the first one leaving at 5.30am and the last at 1.30pm.

Keylong's **hotels** can be found along the main road above the town and strung out along the Mall that runs through the bazaar below the main highway. A steep path leads down to the bazaar from the main road just past where the buses pull in. Aside of the grubby lodges by the bus stand, the *Tashi Deleg* (℡01900/222450; ❸–❹) on the Mall has a range of clean and comfortable attached rooms with hot showers. The *Gyespa*, also on the Mall (℡01900/222207; ❸), has attached rooms with hot showers, a dorm (Rs50), and a small *chorten* in the garden. Back up on the main road, 1km towards Darcha, the HPTDC *Chander Bhaga* (℡01900/222393; ❺–❻, dorm Rs150) is comfortable but bland and typically overpriced. Below it, on a path between the main road and the bus stand, the *Nordaling* (℡01900/222294; ❸) has bright rooms with bathrooms and TV. All these hotels have inspiring views of Khardung Gompa. Apart from the *dhabas*, the best **eating** is at the *Chander Bhaga* and the *Lamayuru* hotel, down on the Mall.

The **post office** is on the main road a little way beyond the bus stand. Down on the Mall, Global Info Tech and Cyber Media Services offer slower and more expensive **Internet** access than in Manali. There are no official foreign **currency facilities** here, but *Tashi Deleg* will change money for a poor rate.

Spiti

From its headwaters below the **Kunzum Pass**, the River Spiti runs 130km southeast to within the flick of a yak's tail of the border of Chinese-occupied Tibet, where it meets the Sutlej. The valley itself, surrounded by huge peaks and with an average altitude of 4500m, is one of the highest and most remote inhabited places on earth – a desolate, barren tract scattered with tiny mud-and-timber hamlets and lonely lamaseries. Until 1992, Spiti in its entirety lay off-limits to foreign tourists. Now, only its far southeastern corner falls within the **Inner Line** – which leaves upper Spiti, including the district headquarters **Kaza**, freely accessible from the northwest via Lahaul. If you are really keen to complete the loop through the restricted area to or from Kinnaur (see p.492), you will need a **permit** (see p.480). The last main stop before reaching the restricted zone is the famed **Tabo** *gompa*, which harbours some of the oldest and most exquisite Buddhist art in the world.

Although the old trade routes to Ladakh and Tibet are now sealed with tarmac, most of this remote and spectacular region is still only accessible on foot. Its trails, though well frequented in high season, are long, hard and high, so you must be self-sufficient and have a guide. Packhorses and provisions are most readily available in **Manali**, or in **Keylong** and **Darcha** (Lahaul) and **Kaza** (Spiti) if you can afford to wait a few days. A good rope for river crossings will be useful on many of the routes, particularly in summer when the water levels are at their highest.

The **best time** to trek is July to early September, when brilliant blue skies make this an ideal alternative to the monsoon-prone Kullu Valley. By late September, the risk of snowfall deters many visitors from the longer expeditions. Whenever you leave, allow enough time to acclimatize to the **altitude** before attempting any big passes: AMS (Acute Mountain Sickness) claims victims here every season (see Basics, p.41).

Lahaul: Darcha to Padum via the Shingo La Pass

The most popular trek is from **Darcha** over the **Shingo La** pass (5000m) to **Padum** in Zanskar. The trail passes through **Kargyak**, the highest village in Zanskar, and follows the Kargyak Valley down to its confluence with the Tsarap at **Purne**. There is a small café, shop, and camping ground here and it's a good base for the side trip to **Phuktal gompa**, one of the most spectacular sights in Zanskar. During the high season (July & Aug), a string of chai stall–tent camps spring up at intervals along the well-worn trail through the Tsarap Valley to Padum, meaning that you can manage without a guide or ponies from here on. Do not bank on finding food and shelter here at the start or end of the season.

Lahaul: Batal to Baralacha Pass

Lahaul's other popular trekking route follows the River Chandra north to its source at the **Baralacha Pass** (4830m) and makes a good extension to the Hampta Pass hike described on p.530. Alternatively, catch a Kaza bus from Manali to the trailhead at **Batal** (3960m) below the **Kunzum La** (4551m). The beautiful milky-blue **Chandratal** ("Moon") **Lake** is a relentless ascent of 7hr from Batal, with stunning views south across the world's longest glacier, **Bara Shigri**, and the forbidding north face of the **White Sail** massif (6451m). The next campground is at **Tokping Yongma** torrent. **Tokpo Yongma**, several hours further up, is the second of the two big side-torrents and is much easier to ford early in the morning; from here it is a steady climb up to the **Baralacha Pass**. You can then continue to Zanskar via the Phirtse La, or pick up transport (prearranged if possible) down to Keylong and Manali or onwards to Leh. Alternatively, if you're biking down from Leh and are confident off-road, this is a fantastic detour.

Spiti: Kaza via the Pin Valley to Manikaran or Wangtu

One of the best treks in **Spiti** is up the **Pin Valley**. The track alongside the River Pin, which passes a string of traditional settlements and monasteries, is now motorable as far as Mudh, around 40km south of Kaza. Over the next few years it is expected to be paved right through to Wangtu, but for now it forks beyond Mudh into two walking paths; the northern path over the Pin–Parvati Pass (5400m) to **Manikaran** in the Parvati Valley (see p.522), and the southern one to Wangtu in **Kinnaur** via the Bhaba Pass (4865m). The last section to Wangtu itself has also fallen to the roadbuilders, so you might decide just to hitch a ride.

In summer, once the **Rohtang La** and **Kunzum La** (4550m) are clear of snow, two buses leave Manali for Spiti every morning. It is also possible to hire **Jeeps** from Manali (through HPTDC or any other travel agency) and to trek in from the Kullu Valley or south from the Baralacha La. Soon after crossing the Kunzum La the road passes through the tiny village of **LOSAR**, where there is a police checkpoint and a couple of basic guesthouses: the *Sam Song* (➊–➋) and the *Serchu* (➊). From here Kaza is a mere 58km further down the Spiti Valley. A great portion of the road from the Rohtang La to Kaza is unsealed and makes for a bumpy, gruelling ride.

Kaza and around

KAZA, the subdivisional headquarters of **Spiti**, lies 76km southeast of the Kunzum Pass, and 201km from Manali. Overlooking the left bank of the River Spiti, it's Spiti's least picturesque town, but as the region's main market and roadhead it's a good base from which to head off on two- or three-day treks to monasteries and remote villages such as Kibber Rates for porters and ponymen are comparable to those in Kullu (see p.518). It is also possible to trek to Dhankar (32km) and on to Tabo (43km). Those planning to continue on to Kinnaur can pick up **Inner Line permits** from the Additional Deputy Commissioner's office in the new town. You will need three passport-sized photos and copies of the relevant pages in your passport, as well as a police stamp, obtainable from the police station down the hill from the DC office towards the river (look for the green roof near the stadium). If they are enforcing the "group of four" rule, you can get a permit for around Rs150 through a travel agent such as Spiti Holiday Adventures (℡01906/222711), which also does currency exchange.

Practicalities

Two daily **buses** depart for Tabo (2hr) in the morning and early afternoon, and a lone bus leaves for Mudh in the Pin Valley in the late morning (2hr 30min), returning almost straight away. Double-check the bus times for these destinations, as they change frequently. Hiring a **Jeep** in Spiti – where the roads are dangerous and public transport unreliable – is a good idea. You can pick them up near the bus stand; expect to pay Rs1200 return for the Pin Valley, Rs700–800 for Tabo or around Rs4500 for Manali. The road beyond Sumdo, where the Inner Line starts, has been upgraded and now bypasses the worst of the landslides at Malling, but if you do have your own vehicle it's still wise to check road conditions.

Most **places to stay** overlook the (usually dry) creek that divides the new and old quarters. On the main road, *Sakya's Abode* (℡01906/222254; ➌–➍) is a good-looking place offering a wide range of rooms and a cheap dorm (Rs80). Nearby, in the same compound as the Sakya Monastery, the *Banjara Khunphen Retreat* (℡01906/222236; ➎) has twelve comfortable double rooms and a good restaurant. Still in this modern area, and a few steps down the creek, *Phuntsok Palbar* (℡01906/222360; ➊) is the best value in town, with spotless rooms and hot bucket showers; it also has a warm sitting room, sunny yard and free luggage storage. Old Kaza, connected by a footpath across the riverbed, has a few more budget choices, including the *Zangchuk Guest House* (℡01906/222510; ➊), with basic facilities but excellent views from its peaceful terrace on the creek, and, for a tad more comfort, the *Khangasar Hotel* (℡01906/222276; ➌–➍), with large, pleasant attached rooms. Most visitors eat in the hotel **restaurants**, best of which are the *Banjara Khunphen Retreat* and new *Sanchen Kunga Nyingpo*, not far from the bus stand, or in the handful of tourist cafés such as *Little Italy* and *Echi Wan*, both in Old Kaza. The predictable *German Bakery* in the village square has a decent Internet connection.

Ki Gompa

Set against a backdrop of snow-flecked mountains and clinging to the steep sides of a windswept conical hillock, **Ki Gompa** is a picture-book example of Tibetan architecture and one of Himachal's most exotic spectacles. Founded in the sixteenth century, Ki is the largest **monastery** in the Spiti Valley, supporting a thriving community of lamas whose Rinpoche, Lo Chien Tulkhu from Shalkar near Sumdo, is said to be the current incarnation of the "Great Translator" Rinchen Zangpo. His glass-fronted quarters crown the top of the complex, reached via stone steps that wind between the lamas' houses below. A labyrinth of dark passages and wooden staircases connect the prayer and assembly halls, home to collections of old *thangkas*, weapons, musical instruments, manuscripts and devotional images (no photography). Many of the rooms have seen extensive renovation since an earthquake struck in 1975; a new prayer hall, dedicated by the Dalai Lama, was also added in 2000. During the new moon towards late June or early July, Ki plays host to a large **festival** celebrating the "burning of the demon" when *chaam* dances are followed by a procession that winds its way down to the ritual ground below the monastery where a large butter sculpture is set on fire.

Ki village lies 12km northwest of Kaza on the road to Kibber, and Ki Gompa is a steep 1km walk up from the town. The most scenic approach is to take the 7am bus from Kaza to Kibber; get off at Ki village and walk the last section to appreciate the full effect of the *gompa's* dramatic southern aspect. Alternatively, the 9am bus from Kibber detours to the monastery on its way down to Kaza. **Accommodation** in Ki is scant: you can stay at the monks' quarters for Rs100 (including food) or try the welcoming *Tashi Khangsar Guesthouse* (℡01906/226277; ❶), located after the first bend in the road and marked with a small green sign.

Kibber

KIBBER (4205m) is reputedly the highest settlement in the world with a motorable road and electricity. Jeep tracks, satellite dishes and the odd tin-roofed government building aside, its smattering of a hundred or so old Spitian houses is truly picturesque. Surrounded in summer by lush green barley fields, Kibber also stands at the head of a trail that picks its way north across the mountains, via the high **Parang La** pass (5578m) to Ladakh. Before the construction of roads into the Spiti Valley, locals used to lead ponies and yaks this way to trade in Leh bazaar. Some Manali-based trekking companies offer a seventeen-day trek from here to the lake of **Tso Moriri** in Ladakh (see p.571).

The 7am **bus** from Kaza to Kibber (1hr) is often delayed, and only waits until 9am before making the return journey. Alternatively you could hire a **Jeep**, hitch with a tour group, or forego transport altogether and walk the 16km of trails, although the outbound trip is nearly all uphill. Kibber's fabulous location makes for a great overnight stop, and it's easy to end up staying longer than you planned in one of the congenial **guesthouses**, all very simple with hot bucket shared baths. Opposite the school at the start of the village the *Norling* (℡01906/226242; ❶–❷) is slightly better than the adjoining *Rainbow* (℡01906/226309; ❶) and has a better restaurant. Further into the village itself, the quaint *Sargong* (℡01906/226222; ❶) is even scruffier but usually full.

Dhankar and the Pin Valley

Nearly a third of the way between Kaza and Tabo, near the meeting of the Pin and Spiti rivers, a rough road veers off to the east for 8.5km to the village of **DHANKAR** (3890m). The **Dhankar Gompa** on the uppermost peak behind the village is famed for its brilliant murals, probably painted in the seventeenth century, depicting the life of the Buddha. Although some of the work has been vandalized, the scenes depicting the Buddha's birth, rebirth and life in Kapilavastu and his rejection of worldly ways are spectacular. The *gompa* also affords superb views down to the confluence of the main River Spiti and the Pin tributary. Dhankar is not on a bus route so you will have to arrange your own transport (a taxi from **Sichaling** on the main road is Rs160) or walk – the shortcut starts from the storm shelter by the main road under the *gompa* 3km before Sichaling. Visitors are welcome to **stay** at the monastery for a donation but bring your own sheets – Dhankar's bedbugs are merciless.

The Pin Valley

Thirty minutes east of Kaza a bridge at Attargu crosses the Spiti and begins a sixteen-kilometre run up the **Pin Valley** to **GULLING**, above which stands the important Nyingma *gompa* of Gungri, believed to date back to the eighth or ninth centuries. There's a simple hotel here, the *Himalaya* (❶), a couple of cafés serving *thukpa* and *momos*, and a camping ground. Tiny **Mikim** lies 3km beyond Gulling at the confluence of the Pin and Parahio rivers; the slightly larger settlement of **SAGNAM** across the river has a few basic places to stay including a *PWD Resthouse* (❶), the *Norzang Guesthouse* (❶) and the *Shambala Guesthouse* (☎01906/224221; ❶).

Beyond Sagnam the road deteriorates rapidly, but vehicles can push ahead another 14km to **MUDH**, an enchanting hamlet with a tiny nunnery that peers over a breathtaking valley, the end of which is flanked by the pyramid-shaped Tordang Mountain. There are several **guesthouses** for the increasing number of trekkers passing through, though conditions remain pretty rough and none currently have private bathrooms. The *Dawa* (❶) is the nicest, and offers a huge dorm (Rs50); food is served in the main house and a new wing under construction promises attached rooms. Also recommended are the friendly *Himalayan Pin Parvati Guest House* (❶) and *Tara Guest House* (☎09418 441453; ❶). Check times for the one crowded and oft-delayed daily **bus** between Kaza and Mudh. A motorable road beyond Mudh is being plowed through the virgin landscape and by 2010 should cross the Bhaba Pass down to Wangtu, thus creating a shortcut between Kaza and Shimla via lower Kinnaur.

Tabo

One of the main reasons to brave the rough roads of Spiti is to get to **Tabo Gompa**, 43km east of Kaza. The mud and timber boxes that nestle on the steep north bank of the Spiti may look drab, but the multi-hued murals and stucco sculpture they contain are some of the world's richest and most important ancient Buddhist art treasures – the link between the cave paintings of Ajanta and the more exuberant Tantric art that flourished in Tibet five centuries or so later. According to an inscription in its main assembly hall, the monastery was established in 996 AD, when **Rinchen Zangpo** was disseminating *dharma* across the northwestern Himalayas. In addition to the 158 Sanskrit Buddhist texts he personally transcribed, the "Great Translator" brought with him a retinue of Kashmiri artisans to decorate the temples. The only surviving examples of their exceptional work are here at Tabo, at Alchi in Ladakh, and Toling and Tsaparang *gompas* in Chinese-occupied western Tibet.

Enclosed within a mud-brick wall, Tabo's **Chogskhar**, or "sacred enclave", contains eight temples and 24 *chortens* (stupas). The largest and oldest structure in the group, the **Sug La-khang**, stands opposite the main entrance. Erected at the end of the tenth century, the "Hall of the Enlightened Gods" was conceived

▲ Mudh

in the form of a three-dimensional *mandala*, whose structure and elaborately decorated interior functions as a mystical model of the universe complete with deities. There are three distinct bands of detail – the lower-level paintings depict episodes in the life of the Buddha and his previous incarnations; above are stucco gods and goddesses; and the top of the hall is covered with meditating Buddhas and *bodhisattvas*. Bring a torch to see the full detail of the murals.

The other temples date from the fifteenth and eighteenth centuries. Their contents illustrate the development of Buddhist iconography from its early Indian origins to the Chinese-influenced opulence of medieval Tibetan Tantricism that still, in a more lurid form, predominates in modern *gompas*. The new *gompa*, inaugurated by the Dalai Lama in 1983, houses nearly fifty lamas and a handful of *chomos* (nuns), some of whom receive training in traditional painting techniques under a *geshe*, or teacher from eastern Tibet. Visitors are welcome to attend daily 6.30am puja and must be guided around the *gompa* by a monk, usually in the morning only. It's also worth exploring the caves across the main road, one of which houses more paintings, but you need to be let in by the *gompa* caretaker.

Practicalities

There are a number of **accommodation** options in Tabo. The friendly, atmospheric *Millennium Monastery Guest House*, outside the main monastery gates (℡01906/223333; ❶–❷), has simple rooms, some attached, and a dorm (Rs70). Behind the monastery near the river, the welcoming *Tashi Khangsar Hotel* (℡01906/233346; ❷–❸) has bland but good-value attached rooms, while three places in the village centre under the same ownership offer a range of rooms: *Panma Guest House*, *Zion Café* and *Trojan* (℡01906/223419; ❷–❹). The *Millennium Monastery* restaurant and the *Tibetan Dish*, down the lane towards the bus stand, offer basic Tibetan and Indian **food**; the former also provides good trekking advice and organizes recycling and eco-projects. Three **buses** per day travel to Kaza, the 4am departure going all the way to Manali. Another bus passes through at around 11am on its way from Kaza to Rekong Peo in Kinnaur.

The Manali–Leh Highway

Since it opened to foreign tourists in 1989, the famous **Manali–Leh Highway** has replaced the old Srinagar–Kargil route as the most popular approach to Ladakh. In summer, a stream of vehicles set off from the Kullu Valley to travel

---

Cycling the Manali–Leh Highway

Motorbikers and **cylists** revere Manali–Leh as one of the most spectacular rides in the world and the number of two-wheelers on the route is a real surprise. After cycling the second-highest road in the world, the highest one awaits you north of Leh (see p.572). While the **gradients** are rarely very steep, the long, slow slogs, rough road **conditions** and, most crucially, **altitude** demand respect and some preparation. Hauling a fully laden bike up climbs of 50km isn't everyone's idea of fun, especially at over 5000m, but the rewards for your efforts are outstanding – especially if you bring camping equipment and sufficient food and water supplies for the remoter stretches. To enjoy yourself, you'll need waterproof clothing, a warm fleece, sunglasses and a good supply of chocolate bars. Check the bike has a suitably easy gear for grinding up the passes, enough wear left in the brake pads for bombing down them, and make sure that you can attach your belongings securely. As for clothing, loose cotton trousers and T-shirts are more suitable than Lycra. Most people start from Manali and take eight to ten days to cover the 485km, though it has been done in as little as four. Don't fret about you, or your bike, packing up halfway though – as remote as it feels, you'll always be able to hitch a lift during the day. If riding solo is a daunting prospect, see p.529 for **mountain-bike tour operators** in Manali. For more information, see ⓦ www.pocketsprocket.com.

THE MANALI–LEH HIGHWAY

Not to scale
Distances are shown from Manali

N

Leh *(3505m)*
(485km)

Karu
(450km)
Upshi
(436km)

Indus River

Taglang La
(5360m)
(376km)
Dibring
Camp

JAMMU &
KASHMIR

Moray
Plains

Tso Morni

ZANSKAR
Lachuglang La
(5019m)
(276km)
PANG
(4500m)
(301km)

Nakeela La
(4740m)
(262km)

Shingo La
(5100m)

Zingzing
Bar
Sarchu
Serai
(222km)

Keylong
(3348m)
(113km)
Darcha
(145km)
Jispa
Baralacha La
(4830m)
(186km)

HIMACHAL
PRADESH

Rangcha *(4565m)*

Tandi
(107km)
Koksar
(71km)
CB10
(6227m)

Sikar Beh
(6248m)
Chandra River
Kunzum La
Pass
(4551m)

Spiti

Marrhi
(36km)
Rohtang
Pass
(3978m)
(51km)
White Sail
(6451m)

Manali
(1896m)

Shimla & Delhi

along the second-highest road in the world, which reaches a dizzying altitude of 5328m. Its surface varies wildly from fairly smooth asphalt through potholes of differing depths to dirt tracks sliced by glacial streams, traversing a starkly beautiful lunar wilderness. Depending on road conditions and type of vehicle, the 485-kilometre journey can take anything from seventeen to thirty hours' actual driving. Bus drivers invariably stop for a short and chilly night in one of the overpriced **tent camps** along the route. These, however, are few and far between after September 15, when the highway officially closes; in practice, all this means is that the Indian government won't airlift you out if you get trapped in snow. Yet some companies run regardless of this until the passes become blocked by snowfall in mid to late October. For more details on **transport** between Manali and Leh, see p.534 and p.565.

Manali to Keylong

Once out of **Manali**, the road begins its long ascent of the **Rohtang Pass** (3978m) and, annoyingly, often gets clogged only an hour or so up, when trucks get bogged down in wet weather; it's not uncommon to have an unscheduled wait of up to four hours when this happens. Buses pull in for breakfast (or brunch) 17km before the pass at a row of makeshift *dhabas* at Marhi (3360m). Though not all that high by Himalayan standards, the pass itself is one of the most treacherous in the region and every year Gaddis and mountaineers are caught unawares by sudden weather changes – hence Rohtang's name, which literally means "piles of dead bodies". The road descends from Rohtang to the floor of the **Chandra Valley**, finally reaching the river at **Koksar**, little more than a scruffy collection of chai stalls with a **checkpoint** where you have to enter passport details in a ledger – one of several such stops on the road to Leh. The next few hours are among the most memorable on the entire trip. Bus seats on the left are best, as the road runs across the northern slopes of the valley through the first Buddhist settlements, hemmed in by towering peaks and hanging glaciers towards **Keylong** (see p.536). The HPTDC super-deluxe and some other buses break the journey here, leaving the bulk of the journey to the second day (the opposite obviously applies if travelling to Manali from Leh).

Keylong to Sarchu Serai

Beyond Keylong, the Bhaga Valley broadens, but its bare sides support very few villages. By the time you reach **Darcha**, a lonely cluster of dry-stone huts and dingy tent camps, the landscape is utterly denuded. All buses stop here for passengers to grab a hot bowl of Tibetan *thukpa* from a wayside *dhaba*. There's little else to do in Darcha, though the Shingo La trailhead – the main trekking route north to Zanskar (see p.538) – is on the outskirts. If you are not on one of the through Manali–Leh buses, you're better off stopping at **JISPA** 7km south, a pleasant little hamlet with ample camping along the river as well as the upmarket *Hotel Jispa* (T01900/233203; ⑥), whose breakfasts are legendary among passing cycle tourists; they also have dorm beds for Rs200. One kilometre before the *Jispa*, the Mountaineering Institute arranges mountaineering and rescue courses in summer through tour agencies in Manali, and may also provide accommodation.

From Darcha, the road climbs steadily northeast to the **Baralacha La** pass. On the other side, some buses stop for the night at **SARCHU SERAI**, where HPTDC's *Tent Camp* (③), a rather ordinary affair, serves steaming plates of rice, dhal and veg, as do a handful of similarly priced *dhabas* nearby. There are several more expensive camps dotted along the road charging up to Rs800 per person including food. Note that Sarchu Serai is 2500m higher than Manali, and travellers coming straight from Manali might suffer from the higher altitude here.

Sarchu Serai to Taglang La

Sarchu Serai packs up for the season from September 15. Northbound buses that haven't overnighted in Keylong thereafter press on over **Lachuglang La** (5019m), the second-highest pass on the highway, to the tent camp at **PANG** (4500m), which stays open longer. Unfortunately, this means that the drive through one of the most dramatic stretches of the route, through an incredible canyon, is in darkness. North of Pang, the road heads up to the fourth and final pass, the **Taglang La**, the highest point on the Manali–Leh Highway at a literally breathtaking 5328m. Drivers pull in for a quick spin of the prayer wheels and a brief photo session alongside the altitude sign and small shrine. If the weather's clear enough, you can gaze north beyond the multicoloured tangle of prayer flags across Ladakh to the Karakoram Range, just visible on the horizon.

Taglang La to Leh

From Taglang La, 40km of switchbacks deliver you from the windswept pass through a purple-hued gorge to the neat, kidney-shaped barley fields and the white *chortens* of Ladakhi villages. At **Upshi**, the road reaches the dramatic Indus Valley, tracing the **Indus River** past slender poplars, sprawling army camps and ancient monasteries. Traffic builds as you approach **Choglamsar**, then climb the final dusty kilometres to **Leh** – past the world's highest golf-course – through the modern outskirts to the haberdashers, canny traders and wrinkled apricot-sellers of Leh's Main Bazaar.

Travel details

Trains	Buses
Baijnath to: Pathankot (6 daily; 6hr 30min–7hr).	Chamba to: Amritsar (1 daily; 8hr); Brahmour
Joginder Nagar to: Pathankot (2 daily; 9hr).	(7 daily; 3hr); Dalhousie (10 daily; 2hr 30min);
Shimla to: Kalka (5 daily; 5hr).	Khajjiar (4 daily; 1hr 30min); Mandi (1 daily; 14hr);

Pathankot (hourly; 5hr 30min); Shimla (1 daily; 15–16hr).

Dalhousie to: Amritsar (1 daily; 6hr); Dharamsala (2 daily; 6–7hr); Khajjiar (4 daily; 1hr); Pathankot (hourly; 3hr); Shimla (1 daily; 14–15hr).

Dharamsala to: Baijnath (hourly; 3hr 30min); Chamba (1 daily; 8hr); Chandigarh (8 daily; 7–8hr); Dalhousie (2 daily; 6–7hr); Dehra Dun (1 daily; 14–15hr); Delhi (6 daily; 15–16hr); Haridwar (1 daily; 16–17hr); Jawalamukhi (8 daily; 2hr 30min); Kangra (every 15min; 45min–1hr); Kullu (4 daily; 8hr); Manali (3 daily; 10hr); Mandi (8 daily; 6hr); McLeod Ganj (every 20min; 40min); Pathankot (every 30min; 3hr); Shimla (6 daily; 10hr).

Kullu to: Amritsar (1 daily; 16hr); Bhuntur (every 10min; 30min); Chandigarh (hourly; 7–8hr); Dehra Dun (1 daily; 13–14hr); Delhi (8 daily; 15hr); Haridwar (1 daily; 14–15hr); Manali (every 10min; 1hr–2hr); Mandi (every 30min; 3hr); Manikaran (6 daily; 2hr); Naggar (hourly; 1hr 30min).

Manali to: Amritsar (1 daily; 17hr); Chandigarh (hourly; 8–9hr); Dehra Dun (1 daily; 16hr); Delhi (8 daily; 16–17hr); Dharamsala (3 daily; 10hr); Haridwar (1 daily; 17hr); Kaza (2 daily; 12hr); Keylong (8 daily; 6hr); Kullu (every 10–15min; 1–2hr); Mandi (every 30min; 4hr); Manikaran

(every 30min; 4hr); Naggar (hourly; 1hr 30min); Pathankot (1 daily; 12hr).

Mandi to: Dharamsala (hourly; 6hr); Kullu (every 30min; 3hr); Manali (every 30min; 4hr); Shimla (8 daily; 5hr).

Shimla to: Chandigarh (every 15min; 4hr); Dalhousie (1 daily; 14–15hr); Dehra Dun (3 daily; 9–10hr); Delhi (hourly; 10hr); Dharamsala (6 daily; 10hr); Haridwar (3 daily; 10–11hr); Kalka (every 30min; 3hr); Kangra (8 daily: 8hr); Kasauli (hourly; 2hr 30min); Kullu (8 daily; 7–8hr); Manali (8 daily; 8–9hr); Mandi (8 daily; 5hr); Narkanda (hourly; 3hr); Pathankot (4 daily; 13hr); Rampur (hourly; 6hr); Rekong Peo (6 daily; 9–10hr); Sarahan (2 daily; 7–8hr).

Flights

(AI = Indian Airlines, IT = Kingfisher Airlines, 9W = Jet Airways, 6E = IndiGo, DN = Air Deccan, SG = SpiceJet, S2 = JetLite)

Dharamsala (Gaggal) to: Delhi (DN; 1 daily; 1hr 30min).

Kullu (Bhuntur) to: Delhi (IC, JA; 1 daily Mon–Sat; 2hr 15min); Shimla (IC, JA; 1 daily Mon–Sat; 30min).

Shimla to: Delhi (IC, JA; 1–2 daily; 1hr 15min); Kullu (IC, JA; 1–2 daily Mon–Sat; 30min).

Ladakh

The International boundaries on this map are neither purported to be correct nor authentic by Survey of India directives. Publisher.

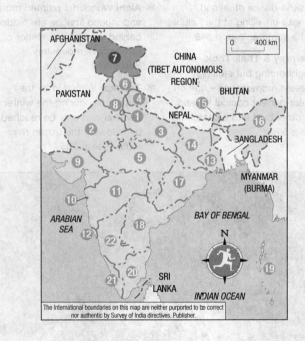

CHAPTER 7 # Highlights

* **Leh** Medieval streets, a Tibetan-style palace, bazaars and looming snowy peaks. See p.555

* **Tikse** Along with Lamayuru, the Indian Himalayas' most impressive monastery complex. See p.568

* **Hemis** Ladakh's largest monastery hosts its annual masked-dance ritual and *thangka* unveiling at the height of the summer. See p.568

* **Chemrey & Thak Thok** Neighbouring but strikingly different monasteries – one on a near-perfect conical hill and the other built into a catacomb. See p.570

* **Tso Moriri** This exquisite high-altitude lake inhabited by nomadic herders features snow-fringed desert mountains and rare migratory birds. See p.571

* **Nubra Valley** Sand dunes, Bactrian camels and views of the mighty Karakorams await across the world's highest motorable road. See p.572

* **Alchi** Wonderful painted murals and stucco images are hidden behind the simple exterior of this ancient monastery. See p.579

* **Zanskar** Walled in by the Himalayas, during the winter Zanskar can only be reached by following the frozen river route. See p.585

▲ Details from mural, Alchi

Ladakh

L ADAKH, the far-flung eastern corner of Jammu and Kashmir state, is India's most remote and sparsely populated region, a high-altitude snow desert cradled by the Karakoram and Great Himalayas ranges, and criss-crossed by a myriad razor-sharp peaks and ridges. To the many thousands of military personnel charged with guarding its craggy frontiers with China and Pakistan, this barren, breathless land is a punitive and potentially dangerous posting. For tourists, however, it offers a window on a unique Himalayan landscape and culture that, until 1974, had only been glimpsed by a few intrepid Western travellers.

Variously described as "Little Tibet" or "the last Shangri-La", **La–Dags** – "land of high mountain passes" – is one of the last enclaves of Mahayana **Buddhism**, Ladakh's principal religion for nearly a thousand years, now brutally suppressed by the Chinese in its native Tibet. Except near the Kashmiri border, the outward symbols of Buddhism are everywhere: strings of multi-coloured prayer flags flutter from the rooftops of houses, while bright prayer wheels and whitewashed *chortens* (the regional equivalent of stupas; see p.560) guard the entrances to even the tiniest settlements. More mysterious still are Ladakh's medieval **monasteries**. Perched on rocky hilltops and clinging to sheer cliffs, **gompas** are both repositories of ancient wisdom and living centres of worship. Their gloomy prayer halls and ornate shrines harbour remarkable art treasures: giant brass Buddhas, *thangkas*, libraries of antique Tibetan manuscripts, weird musical instruments and painted walls that writhe with fierce Tantric divinities.

The highest concentration of monasteries is in the **Indus Valley** near **Leh**, the region's capital. Surrounded by sublime landscapes and crammed with hotels, guesthouses and restaurants, this atmospheric little town, a staging post on the old Silk Route, is most visitors' point of arrival and an ideal base for side trips. North of Leh, across the highest motorable pass in the world – **Khardung La**, lies the valley of **Nubra**, where sand dunes carpet the valley floor in stark contrast to the towering crags of the Karakoram Range. It is also possible to visit the great wilderness around the lake of **Tso Moriri** in **Rupshu**, southeast of Leh, and to glimpse Tibet from the shores of **Pangong Tso** in the far east of Ladakh. For these areas you will, however, need a permit (see p.552). West of Leh, beyond the windswept **Fatu La** and **Namika La** passes, Buddhist prayer flags peter out as you approach the predominantly Muslim district of **Kargil**. Ladakh's second largest town, at the mouth of the breathtakingly beautiful **Suru Valley**, marks the halfway stage of the journey to or from Srinagar, and is the jumping-off point for **Zanskar**, the vast wilderness in the far south of the state that forms the border with Lahaul in Himachal Pradesh.

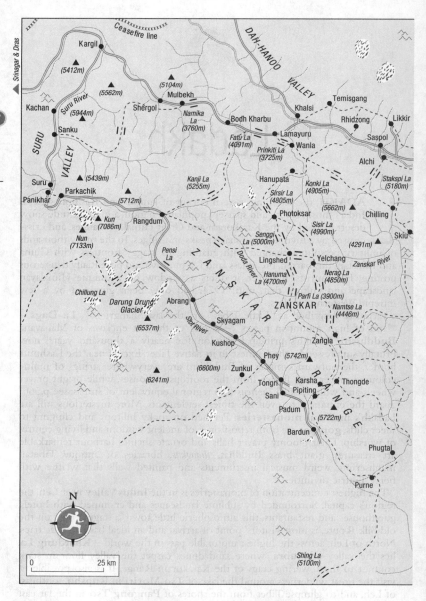

Far beyond the reach of the monsoons, Ladakh receives little snow, especially in the valleys, and even less rain (just four inches per year). Only the most frugal methods enable its inhabitants to **farm** the thin sandy soil, frozen solid for eight months of the year and scorched for the other four. Nourished by meltwater channelled through elaborate irrigation ditches, a single crop of barley (roasted to make the staple *ngamphe*) is sown and harvested between late June and the first October frosts. At lower altitudes,

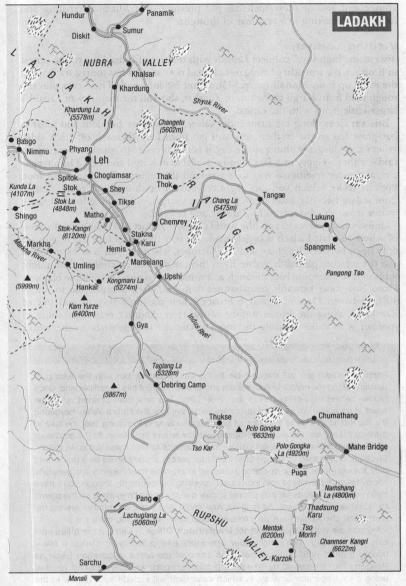

LADAKH

Hundur
Panamik
Diskit
Sumur

NUBRA VALLEY
Khalsar
Khardung
Khardung La (5578m)
Shyok River

Changetu (5602m)

Basgo
Nimmu
Phyang
Leh
Spitok
Choglamsar
Shey
Thak Thok

Kunda La (4107m)
Stok
Tikse
Chang La (5475m)
Tangse

Shingo
Stok La (4848m)
Matho
Chemrey
Lukung

Stok-Kangri (6120m)
Stakna
Karu
Spangmik

Markha
Markha River
Hemis
Marselang

Umling
Kongmaru La (5274m)
Upshi
Pangong Tso

(5999m)
Hankar
Kam Yurze (6400m)

Gya
Indus River

Taglang La (5328m)
Debring Camp

(5867m)

Thukse
Polo Gongka (6632m)
Chumathang

Tso Kar
Polo Gongka La (4920m)
Mahe Bridge

Puga

Namshang La (4800m)

Pang
Lachuglang La (5060m)
RUPSHU
Thadsung Karu

VALLEY
Mentok (6200m)
Tso Moriri

Sarchu
Karzok
Chanmser Kangri (6622m)

Manali ▼

where neat terraced fields provide vivid green splashes against the bare rock
and mica-flecked scree slopes, this is supplemented by fast-growing strains of
wheat, garden vegetables, apricots and walnuts. Higher up, the relentless chill
and steep gradients render agriculture impossible, and villagers depend on
animals – yaks, goats, sheep and *dzo* (a hybrid of the yak and the domestic
cow) – for wool, milk and butter to barter or sell for grain and fuel. In recent
years, **global warming** has meant drier winters with even less snow; the

consequent loss of snow-melt has put pressure on traditional farming and irrigation, resulting in a real fear of drought.

Visiting Ladakh

Two main "highways" connect Ladakh with the rest of India. Due to the unrest in Kashmir, the legendary Srinagar–Leh road now sees far less tourist traffic than the route up from **Manali** (see p.543), almost 500km south. These two, plus the rough road from Kargil to Padum in Zanskar, also link the majority of Ladakh's larger settlements with the capital.

Bus services along the main Indus Valley highway are frequent and reliable, but grow less so the further away you get from Leh. To reach off-track side-valleys and villages within a single day, it is much easier to splash out on a Jeep **taxi** – either a Gypsy or a Tata Sumo – available in Kargil and Leh. The alternative, and more traditional way to get around the region, of course, is on foot. Popular **treks**, which you can organize yourself or through an agency, range from sedate two-day hikes through roadless villages, to gruelling long-distance routes across the mountains to Zanskar, and beyond.

Unless you fly direct to Leh (the world's highest airport at 3505m), the decision of **when to visit** Ladakh is largely made for you: the passes into the region are only open between late June and late October, when the sun is at its strongest and the weather pleasantly warm. Even then, nights can be chilly, so you might want to take a sleeping bag, although accommodations provide multiple blankets. From November onwards, temperatures drop fast, often plummeting to minus 40°C between December and February, when the only way in and out of Zanskar is along the frozen surface of the river. Another reason to come in summer is to make arguably the most spectacular road journey in the world.

Restricted areas and permits

Parts of Ladakh are still inaccessible to the casual tourist, but with the easing of tensions along the border between India and China, much of this incredible land, once hidden behind the political veil of the "Inner Line", has now been opened up. Three areas in particular are now firm favourites with travellers: the **Nubra Valley** bordering the Karakoram Range to the north of Leh; the area around **Pangong Tso**, the lake to the east of Leh; and the region of **Rupshu** with the lake of **Tso Moriri**, to the southeast of Leh. Both Indian and foreign visitors need **permits** to visit these areas. In theory, these are only issued to groups of at least four people accompanied by a guide, and only through a local tour operator. However, in practice travel agents are generally happy to issue permits to solo individuals travelling independently, though you'll have three imaginary friends (usually people applying at the same time) listed on the permit to bump up the numbers. As long as your name and passport number are on the permit, the checkpoints are quite relaxed about how many of you there are.

Permits are issued by the **District Magistrate's Office** in **Leh** but the office now only deals through Leh's many **tour operators** (see p.565), who charge a **fee** – usually around Rs50–100 per head. As some of the areas in question (such as Pangong Tso) are served by infrequent public transport, you may well find yourself using a tour operator anyway, in which case they will include your permit in the package. You will need two photocopies of the relevant pages of your passport and visa. Provided you apply in the morning, permits are usually issued on the same day. Once you have your permit, usually only valid for a maximum period of seven days, make at least five copies before setting off, as checkpoints often like to keep a copy when you report in. They may also occasionally spot-check to see the original copy. If you go on an organised trip, however, the driver takes care of all this and you may never even handle your permit.

The hour-long flight over the Himalayas may be memorable, but is no substitute for the two-day trip from Manali (see p.543) – a crash course in just how remote and extraordinary this lonely mountain kingdom really is.

Some history

The first inhabitants of Ladakh are thought to have been a mixture of nomadic herdsmen from the Tibetan plateau and a small contingent of early Buddhist refugees from northern India called the Mons. Some time in the fourth or fifth century, these two groups were joined by the **Dards**, a tribe of Indo-Aryan origin who migrated southeast along the Indus Valley, bringing with them irrigation and settled agriculture.

The first independent kingdom in the region was established in the ninth century by the maverick nobleman Nyima Gon, taking advantage of the chaos after the collapse of the Guge empire of western Tibet. **Buddhism**, meanwhile, had also found its way across the Himalayas from India. Disseminated by the wandering sage-apostles such as Padmasambhava (alias "Guru Rinpoche"), *dharma* gradually displaced the pantheistic shamanism of the Bon cult, which still holds sway in remote villages north of Khalsi, near Lamayuru. The eastward expansion of the faith towards the Tibetan plateau continued in the tenth and eleventh centuries – the period later dubbed the "**Second Spreading**". Among its key proselytizers was the "Great Translator" **Rinchen Zangpo**, a scholar and missionary associated with the foundation of numerous monasteries in Ladakh and in neighbouring Spiti (see p.540).

Around the fourteenth century, Ladakh passed through a dark age during which, for reasons that remain unclear, its rulers switched allegiance from Indian to Tibetan Buddhism, a form of the faith deeply invested with esoteric practices drawn from the **Tantra** texts, and possibly influenced by the animated celebrations common to Bon (the pre-Buddhist indigenous religion). This coincided with the rise to prominence in Tibet of **Tsongkhapa** (1357–1419), who is accepted as founder of the **Gelug-pa** or "Yellow Hat" school. With the Dalai Lama at its head, Gelug-pa is today the most popular school in Ladakh. Under **Tashi Namgyal** (1555–70), who reunified the kingdom, Ladakh became a major Himalayan power, and the ascent to the throne of the "Lion", **Sengge Namgyal**, in the seventeenth century, signalled further territorial gains. After being routed by the Mughal-Balti army at Bodh Kharbu in 1639, he turned his energies to civil and religious matters, founding a new capital and palace at Leh, as well as a string of monasteries that included Hemis, seat of the newly arrived **Drukpa** sect.

Sengge's building spree created some fine monuments, but it also drained the kingdom's coffers, as did the hefty annual tribute paid to the Mughals after the Bodh Kharbu debacle. Finances were further strained when Deldan, Sengge's successor, picked a quarrel with his ally, Tibet. The fifth Dalai Lama dispatched an army of Mongolian horsemen to teach him a lesson, and three years of conflict only ended after the Mughal governor of Kashmir intervened on Ladakh's behalf. This help, however, came at a price: Aurangzeb demanded more tribute, ordered the construction of a mosque in Leh, and forced the Ladakhi king to convert to Islam.

Trade links with Tibet resumed in the eighteenth century, but Ladakh never regained its former status. Plagued by feuds and assassinations, the kingdom teetered into terminal decline, and was an easy target for the **Dogra** general Zorawar Singh, who annexed it for the Maharaja of Kashmir in 1834. The Ladakhi royal family was banished to Stok Palace, where their descendants reside to this day.

Festivals in Ladakh

Most of Ladakh's Buddhist **festivals**, in which masked **chaam** dance dramas are performed by lamas in monastery courtyards, take place in January and February, when roads into the region are snowbound. This works out well for the locals, for whom the festivals relieve the tedium of the relentless winter, but it means that few outsiders get to experience some of the northern Himalayas' most vibrant and fascinating spectacles. Recently, however, a few of the larger *gompas* around Leh have followed the example of **Hemis**, and switched their annual festivals to the **summer** to attract tourists. Proceeds from ticket sales go towards maintenance and restoration work, and the construction of new shrines. The precise dates of these monastic events over a five-year period, which vary according to the Tibetan lunar calendar, are published in the useful local guide, *Reach Ladakh*, available from most bookshops in Leh; the description of the Hemis festival programme is also very useful in providing an insight into the proceedings. Alternatively, the tourist office in Leh produces a listings booklet called *Ladakh*.

Gompas that hold their *chaams* (dance festivals) in winter or spring include **Matho** (mid-Feb to mid-March), **Spitok** (mid-Jan), **Tikse** (late Oct to mid-Nov) and **Diskit** (mid-Feb to early March) in Nubra. Other important festivals in Ladakh include **Losar** (the Tibetan/Ladakhi New Year), which falls any time between mid-December and early January.

Summer festivals

Hemis Tsechu: July 12–13, 2008; July 1–2, 2009; June 21–22, 2010. See p.569.

Karsha Gustor, Zanskar: July 29–30, 2008; July 18–19, 2009; July 8–9, 2010. See p.587.

Thak Thok Tsechu Aug 11–12, 2008; July 30–31, 2009; July 20–21, 2010. See p.570.

Sani Nasjal, Zanskar: Aug 15–16, 2008; Aug 3–4, 2009; July 24–25, 2010. See p.589.

Phyang Tsedup Aug 3–4, 2008; July 23–24, 2009; July 13–14, 2010. See p.578.

Festival of Ladakh Sept 1–15. This popular J&K Tourism–sponsored two-week event, held principally in Leh, is designed to extend the tourist season, featuring archery contests, polo matches, Bactrian camels from Nubra and traditional Ladakhi dance accompanied by some tedious speeches.

Ladakh became a part of Jammu and Kashmir state in independent India in 1948, following the first of the four Indo-Pak wars fought in the region. However, both the international frontier and the so-called **"Ceasefire Line"** that scythes through the top of the state remain "unauthenticated" and a source of continued tension both locally and between Delhi and Islamabad. Indeed, sporadic fighting from 1999 to 2002 just outside **Kargil** nearly led to all-out war (see box, p.1355). The situation there has now improved but the two sides still take occasional pot-shots at each other across the disputed Siachen Glacier, 100km north in the Karakorams. When you consider the proximity of China, another old foe who annexed a large chunk of Ladakh in 1962, it's easy to see why this is India's most sensitive border zone.

Today, Ladakh, along with Zanskar, comprises around seventy percent of the state of Jammu and Kashmir (J&K) as it stands. Long dissatisfied with the state government based in Srinagar, and after years of agitation, the Ladakhis finally saw the establishment of their region as the **Ladakh Autonomous Hill Development Council** (LAHDC) in September 1995, localizing – in theory – government control. Still unhappy with the reality of continuing central control, Ladakhi Buddhist and Muslim parties formed a new unified party in 2002, the **Ladakh Union Territory Front**, the goal of which is to split from Jammu and Kashmir and gain Union Territory recognition from Delhi. Although some Muslim factions oppose separation from Jammu and Kashmir, the Front scored a major victory by winning 24 of the 26 LAHDC seats in the 2005 state elections. Despite that, the Congress-led state government has repeatedly blocked moves to set up the Union Territory status, so the campaign and frequent protests continue.

Leh

As you approach **LEH** for the first time, via the sloping sweep of dust and pebbles that divide it from the floor of the Indus Valley, you'll have little difficulty imagining how the old trans-Himalayan traders must have felt as they plodded in on the caravan routes from Yarkhand and Tibet: a mixture of relief at having crossed the mountains in one piece, and anticipation of a relaxing spell in one of central Asia's most scenic towns. Spilling out of a side valley that tapers north towards eroded snow-capped peaks, the Ladakhi capital sprawls from the foot of a ruined Tibetan-style palace – a maze of mud brick and concrete flanked on one side by cream-coloured desert and on the other by a swathe of lush, irrigated farmland.

Leh only became regional capital in the seventeenth century, when Sengge Namgyal shifted his court here from Shey, 15km southeast, to be closer to the head of the Khardung La–Karakoram corridor into China. The move paid off: within a generation the town had blossomed into one of the busiest markets on the Silk Road. During the 1920s and 1930s, the broad bazaar that still forms its heart received more than a dozen pony- and camel-trains each day. Leh's prosperity, managed mainly by the Sunni **Muslim** merchants whose descendants live in its labyrinthine old quarter, came to an abrupt end with the closure of the Chinese border in the 1950s. Only after the Indo-Pak wars of 1965 and 1971, when India rediscovered the hitherto forgotten capital's strategic value, did its fortunes begin to look up. Today, khaki-clad *jawans* (soldiers) and their families from the nearby military and air force bases are the mainstay of the local economy in winter, when foreign visitors are few and far between.

Undoubtedly the most radical shake-up, however, ensued from the Indian government's decision in 1974 to open Ladakh to foreign **tourists**. From the start, Leh bore the brunt of the annual invasion, as busloads of backpackers poured up the road from Srinagar. Over thirty years on, Leh has more than

---

Health in Leh: altitude sickness and dirty water

As Leh is 3505m above sea level, some travellers, and especially those who arrive by plane from Delhi, experience mild **altitude sickness**. The best way to avoid the symptoms – persistent headaches, dizziness, insomnia, nausea, loss of appetite or shortness of breath – is to rest for at least 48 hours on arrival. Drink 3–4 litres of water a day, avoid alcohol, and don't exert yourself. Overdo it in the first few days and you'll feel off-colour for up to a week. For more information, see p.41, or contact the SNM hospital (℡01982/252014 or 252360).

A health problem that affects far more travellers, however, is diarrhoea. **Dirty water** is invariably the culprit – a consequence of Leh's grossly inadequate sewage system, which can't cope with the massive summer influx of visitors. Redouble your normal health precautions while you are here: take extra care over what you drink, and avoid salads and raw vegetables unless you know they have been cleaned in sterilized water. Many hotels now filter their own water, making it perfectly safe to drink, and the Dzomsa Laundry provides safe water in recycled plastic bottles (see p.557).

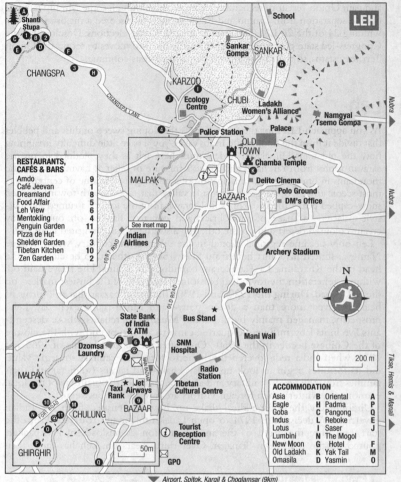

LEH

RESTAURANTS, CAFÉS & BARS

Amdo	9
Café Jeevan	1
Dreamland	8
Food Affair	5
Leh View	6
Mentokling	4
Penguin Garden	11
Pizza de Hut	7
Shelden Garden	3
Tibetan Kitchen	10
Zen Garden	2

ACCOMMODATION

Asia	B	Oriental	A
Eagle	H	Padma	P
Goba	C	Pangong	Q
Indus	L	Reboke	E
Lotus	I	Saser	J
Lumbini	N	The Mogol	
New Moon	G	Hotel	F
Old Ladakh	K	Yak Tail	M
Omasila	D	Yasmin	O

Airport, Spitok, Kargil & Choglamsar (9km)

doubled in size and is a far cry from the sleepy Himalayan town of the early 1970s. The provision stores and old-style outfitters on the main street have been squeezed out by Kashmiri handicraft shops, Internet cafés, art emporiums and Tibetan restaurants. A rapid increase in the number of Kashmiri traders, who have little choice but to seek business outside Kashmir, has in recent years led to bouts of unrest in Leh's bazaar, the first communal violence ever seen in normally peaceful Ladakh.

The abiding impression of Leh, however, remains that of a lively yet laid-back place to unwind after a long bus journey. Attractions in and around the town itself include the former **palace** and **Namgyal Tsemo gompa**, perched amid strings of prayer flags above the narrow dusty streets of the **old quarter**. A short walk away north across the fields, the small monastery at **Sankar** harbours accomplished modern Tantric murals and a thousand-headed Avalokitesvara deity. Leh is also a good base for longer **day-trips** out into the Indus Valley.

Environmental issues

Damage to the **environment** has become an issue of paramount importance in Ladakh. Although plastic bags are officially banned in Leh, as they clog up the vital river systems that the state so depends on, shopkeepers continue to use them. Plastic mineral-water bottles are a particular headache; you are advised to bring your own filtration system (see p.36) with you, or refill your plastic water bottles at Leh's Dzomsa Laundry (see below) or at guesthouses with filtered water. You are also advised to leave all unnecessary packaging behind before arriving in Ladakh.

Situated on a strategic corner between Upper Thaka Road and Old Fort Road at one end of the market square, the **Dzomsa Laundry** provides a vital service in ecology-sound washing, using biodegradable detergent and water at a safe distance from habitation. It also serves as a co-op for rural, semi-literate people. Dzomsa, which literally means "meeting point", serves delicious fresh apricot and seabuckthorn juices which you can drink while sitting outside watching the world go by. You can also recycle your plastic bottles and refill them with **safe drinking water** here.

For more on environmental issues in Ladakh, see the accounts of the **Ecology Centre** (see p.561) and local **voluntary organizations** (see p.562). For tips on **trekking** sensitively, see p.576.

Among the string of picturesque villages and *gompas* within reach by bus are **Shey**, site of a derelict seventeenth-century palace, and the spectacular **Tikse gompa**. Until you have adjusted to the altitude, however, the only sightseeing you'll probably feel up to will be from a guesthouse roof terrace or garden, from where the snowy summits of the majestic **Stok-Kangri massif** (6120m), magnified in the crystal-clear Ladakhi sunshine, look close enough to touch.

Arrival, information and local transport

A taxi from Leh **airport**, 5km southwest of town on the main Srinagar highway, will set you back a fixed fare of Rs110 to the bazaar, or Rs150 to Changspa, in the northwest of town, where many of the hotels are located. State and private **buses** pull into the dusty town bus stand, fifteen minutes' walk or a Rs50 taxi ride south of the bazaar and most of the hotels. Manali buses terminate on Fort Road, near the *Hotel Dreamland*.

The main J&K **tourist reception centre** (Mon–Sat 10am–4pm; ☏01982/252094, ⊚www.jktourism.org), 3km from the bazaar on the airport road, is too far out of town and hardly worth visiting. The summer-only **tourist information centre** on Fort Road in the bazaar (May–Sept Mon–Sat 10am–4pm; ☏01982/253462) is a bit more helpful. Two banks offer **money-changing** facilities: try the J&K Bank, 1st Floor, Himalaya Shopping Complex, Main Bazaar or the State Bank of India on the main market square, which also has an ATM, as does the nearby Punjab National Bank. Elsewhere, private licensed foreign exchange, including many hotels and travel agents around Fort Road and along Changspa Lane, invariably offer lower rates but are accessible after hours and on weekends.

The **taxi** rank (daily 6am–7pm; ☏01982/253039) is almost directly opposite the tourist information centre. Each driver carries a list of fixed fares to just about everywhere you might want to visit in Ladakh, taking into account waiting time and night halt charges. These rates apply to peak season; reductions of up to forty percent can be had at other times. Prices are high as the season is so short – expect to pay around Rs60 to Changspa, Rs420 to Tikse, Rs900 to Hemis and Rs4900 to Pangong Lake, with an additional Rs300 for a night's stay. Hunt around the tour operators in the bazaar and you can get cheaper deals for long-distance rides, especially if you don't mind a Maruti (Suzuki) Gypsy, which is a bit more cramped and bumpy on Ladakh's rough roads.

Accommodation

Leh is glutted with **accommodation**, most of it refreshingly neat, clean and excellent value, mainly due to strict regulation. Budget travellers in particular are in for a treat. Most of the town's **cheap guesthouses** are immaculately whitewashed traditional houses, set on the leafy outskirts, especially in the area of **Changspa** to the west; they usually have sociable garden terraces looking onto green fields. Simple double rooms with common baths go from around Rs150, even in high season, and from Rs300 for attached. For a little more, you can often find a sunny en-suite "glass room" with a view all to yourself. More in the thick of things are central hotels and lodges, as well as converted houses in the mainly Muslim **old town**, below Leh palace.

Rooms in Leh's few **mid-range hotels** come with attached bathrooms and piped hot water; the standard of **upmarket** accommodation options has improved with the opening of some new places, though these are sometimes booked up with tour groups. The prices below are for high season; off-season, prices can be slashed by as much as sixty percent. For homestays outside Leh, see "Listings" on p.564.

Budget

Asia Changspa Lane ☎01982/253403. Large riverside guesthouse with a spanking new block. Sociable roof terrace-cum-café and meditation classes, but limited views. ❷–❹

Eagle Changspa Lane, across from the Mahabodhi centre ☎01982/253074, ✉ladakh_adv@yahoo.co.in. The friendly and helpful owner Motuup runs a pleasant guesthouse with a large garden and can arrange excellent trekking tours. ❶–❷

Goba Down path off Changspa Lane ☎01982/253670. Well-maintained traditional house with a pleasant garden. Rooms are immaculate, and those in the new block have attached bathrooms. ❶–❸

🏃 **Indus** Malpak, off Fort Rd ☎01982/252502. Cheap singles and a few doubles, all with attached bathrooms and solar-heated water. Central, pleasant, with a family atmosphere and open in winter. ❸–❹

Old Ladakh Old town ☎01982/252951, ✉old_ladakh@rediff.com. Ladakh's first-ever guesthouse is homely and central, and offers a choice of rooms: the kitsch "deluxe" one (pink pillows and Tibetan rugs) is a real winner. Cross-check any trekking prices they quote though. *Tak*, across the lane, handles overflow. ❶–❸

🏃 **Oriental** Below the Shanti Stupa, Changspa ☎01982/253153, ⊛www.oriental-ladakh.com. Congenial, extremely popular guesthouse with spotless rooms (many now with attached bath), free filtered water, an Internet café, superb views, nourishing home-cooked meals and a

genuinely warm welcome, even in winter. Booking advisable in summer. ❶–❹

Reboke Changspa Lane ☎01982/253230. Small, simple, friendly guesthouse, which also has a couple of rooms with attached baths, at the far end of a narrow lane past the ugly *Sun & Sand*. If, full try the simple rooms at *Chunka* (☎01982/253382) next door. ❷

Saser Karzoo, up the path from the Ecology Centre ☎01982/250162, ✉nam_gyal@rediffmail.com. Modern hotel that successfully embraces elements of traditional architecture, with a pleasant garden courtyard and comfortable rooms with baths – a bargain off-season. ❸–❹

Mid-range

New Moon Guest House Sankar Rd, Chubi ☎01982/250296, ✉angchok@india.com. New place built in traditional style with spacious rooms and a good location below Namgyal Tsemo Gompa. ❹

Padma Ghirghir, off Fort Rd ☎01982/252630, ⊛www.padmaladakh.net. There are two parts to this hotel: a traditional old building with immaculate rooms with shared baths, a beautiful kitchen, a garden and mountain views; and a modern annexe with comfortable doubles and attached baths and a rooftop restaurant. ❹–❼

Yak Tail Fort Rd ☎01982/252118. Large, central hotel with thirty-odd high-standard rooms, all with cable TV, arranged around a courtyard. ❻

Yasmin Off Fort Rd ☎01982/252405, ⊛www.yasminladakh.com. Clean, comfortable rooms in a custom-built guesthouse with a sunny garden. It's convenient, owned by one of Ladakh's literary figures and impeccably managed. Good value. ④–⑥

Expensive

Lotus Upper Karzoo ☎01982/250265, ⓔhotellotus@vsnl.net. The laid-back staff and leafy location make this a relaxing and welcoming option, although the rooms are better at other places. It's done in a traditional style and the more expensive rooms have mountain views. ⑦

Lumbini Fort Rd ☎01982/252528. Owned by one of the abbots of Phyang, this well-designed building has airy, pleasant rooms and a lovely courtyard that makes for excellent lounging. ⑦

The Mogol Hotel Changspa Lane ☎01932/253438, ⓔhotelmogol@rediffmail.com. Smart new place with welcoming staff and large, nicely furnished rooms, half of them with TV. ⑦

🏃 **Omasila** Changspa Lane ☎01982/252113, ⓦwww.hotelomasila.com. Friendly, accommodating 35-room hotel, including five suites and six centrally heated rooms. The large terrace offers sweeping views of the mountains and the lovely dining room serves excellent dishes featuring vegetables grown in the garden outside. Open year round. ⑦–⑧

Pangong Chulung ☎01982/254655, ⓦwww.pangongladakh.com. Pleasant hotel built around a courtyard garden with spacious, well-priced rooms and an inviting balcony. ⑦

The Town

With the mighty hulk of the **palace** looming to the north, it's virtually impossible to lose your bearings in Leh. The broad **main bazaar** runs north to south through the heart of town, dividing the labyrinthine **old town** and nearby polo ground from the greener and more spacious residential districts of **Karzoo** and **Suki** to the west. **Fort Road**, the other principal thoroughfare, turns west off the main street and then winds downhill past the taxi rank and a host of hotels, restaurants and shops, towards the Indian Airlines office on the southern outskirts.

The bazaar and old town

After settling into a hotel or guesthouse, most visitors spend their first day in Leh soaking up the atmosphere of the **bazaar**. Eighty or so years ago, this bustling tree-lined boulevard was the busiest market between Yarkhand and Kashmir. Merchants from Srinagar and the Punjab would gather to barter for pashmina wool brought down by nomadic herdsmen from western Tibet, or for raw silk hauled across the Karakorams on Bactrian camels. These days, though the street is awash with kitsch curio shops and handicraft emporiums, it retains a distinctly Central Asian feel. Even if you're not shopping for trekking supplies, check out the **provision stores** along the street, where bright pink, turquoise, and wine-red silk cummerbunds hang in the windows.

When you've had enough of the bazaar, head past the new green-and-white-painted **Jama Masjid** at the top of the street, and follow one of the lanes that lead into the **old town**. Apart from the odd electric cable and concrete path, nothing much has changed here since the warren of flat-roofed houses, crumbling *chortens* and *mani* walls (see box, p.560) was laid down in the late sixteenth century – least of all the plumbing. One place definitely worth walking through the putrid-smelling puddles to visit, however, is the **Chamba temple**. It's not easy to find on your own; when you get to the second row of shops on the left beyond the big arch ask for the key-keeper (*gonyer*), who will show you the way. Hemmed in by dilapidated medieval mansions, the one-roomed shrine houses a colossal image of Maitreya, the Buddha to come, and some wonderful old wall paintings.

The palace

Lording it over the old town from the top of a craggy granite ridge is the derelict **palace** (daily sunrise to sunset; Rs100 [Rs5]) of the sixteenth-century ruler Sengge Namgyal. A scaled-down version of the Potala in Lhasa, it is a textbook example of medieval Tibetan architecture, with gigantic sloping buttressed walls and projecting wooden balconies that tower nine storeys above the surrounding houses. Since the Ladakhi royal family left in the 1940s, damage inflicted by nineteenth-century Kashmiri cannons has caused large chunks of it to collapse. Take a torch, and watch where you walk: in spite of restoration work, holes gape in the floors and dark staircases. Also, the ticket booth is often unmanned, in which case ignore the demands for money from the street urchins who man the entrance for pocket money.

Namgyal Tsemo Gompa

Once you are acclimatized to the altitude, the stiff early-morning hike up to **Namgyal Tsemo Gompa** (daily 7–9am & 5–8pm), the monastery perched precariously on the shaly crag above Leh palace, is a great way to start the day. Two trails lead up to "the Peak of Victory", whose twin peaks are connected by giant strings of multicoloured prayer flags; the first and most popular path zigzags across its south side from the palace road, while a second scales the more gentle northern slope via the village of Chubi, the route followed by the lama from Sankar *gompa* (see opposite) who tends to the shrine each morning and evening. Alternatively, you could drive there along the dirt track that turns left off the main Khardung La highway, 2km north of the bus stand.

Approaching the *gompa* from the south, the first building you come to is the red-painted **Maitreya temple**. Thought to date from the fourteenth century, the shrine houses a giant Buddha statue flanked by *bodhisattvas*. However, its wall

Chortens and mani walls

Among the more visible expressions of Buddhism in Ladakh are the chess-pawn-shaped **chortens** at the entrance to villages and monasteries. These are the Tibetan equivalent of the Indian stupa (see p.407) – large hemispherical burial mounds-cum-devotional objects, prominent in Buddhist ritual since the third century BC. Made of mud and stone (now also concrete), many *chortens* were erected as acts of piety by Ladakhi nobles, and like their southern cousins, they are imbued with mystical powers and **symbolic significance**: the tall tapering spire, normally divided into thirteen sections, represents the soul's progression towards nirvana, while the sun cradled by the crescent moon at the top stands for the unity of opposites, and the oneness of existence and the universe. Some contain sacred manuscripts that, like the *chortens*, wither and decay in time, illustrating the central Buddhist doctrine of impermanence. Those enshrined in monasteries, however, generally made of solid silver and encrusted with semiprecious stones, contain the ashes or relics of revered *rinpoches* (incarnate lamas). Always pass a *chorten* in a clockwise direction: the ritual of circumambulation mimics the passage of the planets through the heavens and is believed to ward off evil spirits. The largest array is to be found in the desert east of **Shey**, the former capital (see p.567), but look out for the giant, brightly painted specimen between the bus station and Leh bazaar, whose red spire stands out against the snowy Stok-Kangri mountains to the south.

A short way downhill from the big *chorten*, near the radio station, stands an even more monumental symbol of devotion. The 500-metre **mani wall**, erected by King Deldan Namgyal in 1635, is one of several at important religious sites around Ladakh. Ranging from a couple of metres to over a kilometre in length, the walls are made of hundreds of thousands of stones, each inscribed with prayers or sacred mantras – usually the invocation *Om Mani Padme Hum*: "Hail to the Jewel in the Lotus". It goes without saying that such stones should never be removed and visitors should resist the urge to climb onto the walls to have photographs taken.

paintings are modern and of less interest than those in the **Gon-khang** (temple of protector deities) up the hill.

The Shanti Stupa

A relatively new addition to the rocky skyline around Leh is the toothpaste-white **Shanti Stupa** above Changspa village, nearly 3km west of the bazaar by road. Inaugurated in 1983 by the Dalai Lama, the "Peace Pagoda", whose sides are decorated with gilt panels depicting episodes from the life of the Buddha, is one of several such monuments erected around India by a "Peace Sect" of Japanese Buddhists. It can be reached by car, or on foot via a steep flight of more than five hundred steps, which winds up from the end of Changspa Lane to the café just below the stupa – a welcome respite for those not fit or acclimatized. Its broad terrace makes an excellent spot to watch the sunrise, and is popular with early morning *yogis*.

The Ecology Centre

Five minutes' walk north of the main bazaar, the rather dusty and sometimes unmanned **Ecology Centre** (Mon–Sat 10am–4.30pm; ☏01982/253221) is the headquarters of LEDeG (the Ladakh Ecological Development Group) – a local nongovernmental organization that aims to counter the negative impact of Western-style "development" by fostering economic independence and respect for traditional culture. This involves promoting "appropriate" technologies such as solar energy, encouraging organic farming and cottage industries, and providing education on environmental and social issues through drama workshops and seminars in the village. The garden hosts an open-air exhibition of solar gadgets, hydraulic pumps, water mills and other ingenious energy-saving devices that have proved successful throughout Ladakh. There's also a small **library** and a **handicraft shop**, selling locally made clothes, *thangkas*, T-shirts, books and postcards. Try to catch a screening of LEDeG's **video**, *Ladakh: the Forbidden Wilderness* (Mon, Wed & Fri 4pm; Rs50), a well-made documentary focusing on Tso Moriri Lake and the plants, animals and people that live around it.

There's a second branch of the centre in Ribook, just below the Shanti Stupa, which also has a workshop, training centre and basic, solar-heated accommodation; email ⓔ ledeg@vsnl.net for details.

Sankar Gompa

Nestled amid the shimmering poplar coppices and terraced fields of barley that extend up the valley behind Leh, **Sankar Gompa**, 2km north of the town centre, is among the most accessible monasteries in central Ladakh – hence its restricted visiting hours for tourists (daily 7am–6pm; Rs20). You can get there either by car or on foot: turn left at the *Antelope Guesthouse* and then right onto the concrete path that runs alongside the stream. Sankar appears after about fifteen minutes' walk, surrounded by sun-bleached *chortens* and a high mud wall. You can also work your way through the fields behind the burgeoning tourist area of Karzoo.

The monastery, a small under-*gompa* of Spitok, is staffed by twenty monks, and is the official residence of the **Kushok Bakula**, Ladakh's head of the Gelug-pa sect. Since the highly respected previous incumbent's death in 2004, the spiritual leader's new incarnation has been diligently sought but not yet identified. Above the **Du-khang** (main prayer hall) stands the *gompa*'s principal deity, Tara, in her triumphant, one-thousand-armed form as Dukkar, or "Lady of the White Parasol", presiding over a light, airy shrine room whose walls are adorned with a Tibetan calendar and tableaux depicting "dos and don'ts" for monks – some of which are very arcane indeed. Another flight of steps leads to the *gompa*

Voluntary organizations

With limited resources at their disposal, a handful of **voluntary organizations**, including LEDeG (see p.561), battle to protect Ladakh's delicate environment and ancient culture.

Helena Norberg Hodge, the Swedish-born founder of LEDeG, is also behind the International Society for Ecology and Culture (**ISEC**) website (ⓦ www.isec.org.uk), devoted to promoting sustainable ways of living in both "developing" and "developed" countries. ISEC employs **volunteers** in Ladakh on the **Farm Project** to help local farmers maintain traditional farming methods. Closely aligned to the Farm Project, the co-operative Women's Alliance of Ladakh (**WAL**), based in Chubi, north of central Leh, works to reinforce traditional Ladakhi culture. One of their more noticeable achievements was to ban plastic bags from Leh in 1998; the alliance now boasts more than five thousand members in one hundred villages. The best time to visit them is during one of their **fêtes**, where you can sample local produce, pick up handicrafts and catch exhibitions of colourful traditional costume and folk dance performances. They also show a number of **videos**, including *Ancient Futures: Learning From Ladakh* (Mon–Sat 3pm), which gives an insightful account of Ladakhi culture and the sweeping changes of the past thirty or so years, many of them direct results of tourism. On Wednesdays, when she's in town, Norberg Hodge leads the discussion that follows the video. Other screenings are *Paradise with Side Effects* (Mon & Thurs 4.30pm), a documentary that follows two Ladakhi women on a tour of London, *Local Futures* (Tues 4.30pm) and *The Future of Progress* (times vary), a thirty-minute series of interviews with leading critics of globalization. Norberg Hodge has also written an excellent **book** on Ladakh, *Ancient Futures*, available at the Women's Alliance and the Ecology Centre handicraft shop.

Another group is **LEHO** (Ladakh Environment and Health Organization), which places its emphasis on the proper utilization of land and water resources and the management of livestock on a sustainable basis. Their office and showroom is on the first floor of the Himalaya Complex, beneath the *Amdo* restaurant, on Main Bazaar (Mon–Sat 10am–5pm; ☏01982/253691, ⓔsultanaleho@yahoo.com).

library and, eventually, a roof terrace with fine views towards the north side of Namgyal Tsemo hill and the valley to the south.

Eating and drinking

As Leh's thriving restaurant and café scene has been cornered by the refugee community, **Tibetan food** has a high profile alongside tourist-oriented Chinese and European dishes. Tibetan specialities include *momos* – crescent-shaped dumplings stuffed with meat, cheese or vegetables, and (if you're lucky) ginger, then steamed and served with hot soup and spicy sauce. Fried *momos* are sometimes called *kothays*. *Thukpa*, another wholesome favourite, is broth made from fresh pasta strips, meat and vegetables. These, and dozens of variations, are dished up in tourist restaurants and backstreet *momo* kitchens alike.

Visitors have **breakfast** either in their hotel or guesthouse, where the host family cook small round loaves of Ladakhi wheat-flour bread (*tagi shamos*), eaten piping hot with butter and honey or jam, or in the tourist cafés. Trekkers and cyclists will appreciate the slow energy release of *tsampa* (barley) porridge, which is often sweetened with honey and makes a fantastic start to the day. Apple pie and chocolate brownie **pastry shops**, most of them owned by the Sikh-run *German Bakery* chain, are dotted all over town; pop in for filled baguettes, croissants and muesli breakfasts. **Beer** is widely available in most of Leh's tourist restaurants while **chang**, a local barley brew, is harder to come by:

ask at your guesthouse if they can get some in for you. A handful of bars cater to the tourist trade, including the *Ibex* near the taxi stand on Fort Road.

Amdo Main Bazaar. Popular Tibetan restaurant, with freshly prepared food that is generally excellent but can take up to an hour to appear; main courses Rs50–80. There's a second *Amdo* across the street, which catches the morning sun and serves hearty *tsampa* porridge.

Café Jeevan Changspa Lane. Modern pure-veg Sikh-run restaurant featuring a variety of cuisines in the Rs60–100 range. Lovely decor both downstairs and in the partially enclosed roof terrace.

Dreamland Fort Rd, near the hotel of the same name. One of the most popular late-night haunts in town for a mixed menu of food and beer. The chicken platter (Rs120) is recommended.

Food Affair Main Bazaar. A great outdoor café on the square with a mix of baked and cooked food. It's especially good for breakfast and snacky lunches for around Rs50. It shares its terrace with the authentic *Ladakhi Kitchen*, where you can eat for Rs30–40.

Leh View Restaurant Main Bazaar. The best 360-degree views in town from the roof terrace is offset by painfully slow service, making this a better bet for a drink than a meal.

Mentokling Changspa Lane, near Mission School. One of the best of the garden cafés along this road,

with a fine all-round menu that's especially strong on Indian food. Dinners Rs80–120.

Penguin Garden Restaurant Old Rd, just off Fort Rd. A great place for a beer, *German Bakery* snacks or a meal (around Rs80–100) in a leafy garden location.

Pizza de Hut Main Bazaar, almost opposite SBI. Good for breakfast or for a beer in the evenings, with a great rooftop location in the centre of town. The mixed menu includes wood-fired pizzas and tandoori dishes (Rs100–150). Better than adjacent *La Terrasse*.

Shelden Garden Restaurant Changspa Lane. Specializes in succulent barbecued meat and fish for around Rs150, served in a pleasant courtyard or in a tent where a nightly DVD is shown.

Tibetan Kitchen Down alley off Fort Rd. Considered by many, locals and visitors alike, to be the best Tibetan food in town. Great mutton *thukpas* for Rs60. Large parties are advised to book.

Zen Garden Changspa Lane. Seasonal, open-air restaurant with a barbecue under willow trees. Varied menu of Indian, Chinese and Western food, including pasta and Israeli dishes.

Shopping

Between June and September, Leh is swamped by almost as many transient Tibetan and Kashmiri **traders** as souvenir-hungry tourists. Most of the merchandise hawked in their temporary boutiques and stalls comes from outside the region: papier-mâché bowls, shawls and carpets from Srinagar, jewellery and miniature paintings from Jaipur, and "Himalayan" handicrafts, including *thangkas*, churned out in Nepal and by Tibetan refugees in Old Delhi. Prices tend to be high, so haggle hard, and don't be conned into shelling out for cleverly faked "antiques". Much of the "silver" on sale is in fact cheap white metal.

Tibetan and Ladakhi **curios** account for the bulk of the goods on sale in Leh's emporiums, though most of these are run by Kashmiris from the Srinagar Valley. The Ladakh Art Palace off the main bazaar, one of the very few locally run souvenir stores, is a good place to browse. If money is no object, you could splash out on a **perak**, a long Ladakhi headdress, encrusted with turquoise, which cost upwards of Rs5000. **Turquoise** is sold by the *tolah* (there are eighty *tolahs* to a kilogram), and quality and age determine the price. You'll find vendors sitting on the main road; otherwise try the locally owned Potala – an atmospheric old-world shop well worth a rummage – down Nowshara Lane, off the main road close to the Jama Masjid. Next door, Himalayan Art is also locally owned, with an extensive selection of curios, ranging from stones to *thangkas*.

For **authentic Ladakhi souvenirs**, try the outfitters and provision stores dotted along the main bazaar. Worth browsing is Konchok Lobzang's shop, a few doors north of the Lehling bookshop, which makes its own Ladakhi-style handicrafts, including wonderfully carved tables and *thangkas*.

The lanes running off the bazaar towards old town offer hole-in-the-wall seamstress shops that can produce custom-fit **local clothing**, including the dapper stovepipe hats (*tibi*), hand-dyed *gonchas*, raw silk cummerbunds, tie-dyed rope-soled shoes (*pabbu*) and Bhutanese cross-button shirts. Try the Lonpo Shop up the lane across from *Amdo* restaurant, or around the corner to the right at the *Namgail* Dorjey and Tsereng Yangskit shops. The handicraft shops at the **Ecology Centre** (see p.561) and **Women's Alliance** (see p.562) are other sources of quality traditional clothing, including hand-knitted woollen jumpers, hats and socks. Most of the wool gathered in Ladakh lands up in the Kashmir Valley for milling and weaving, and few of the **pashmina shawls** on offer in the shops along Fort Road are genuine. However, a couple of Ladakhi co-operatives are trying to break the Kashmiri monopoly of the business and are producing pashmina shawls in Ladakh itself. Try the Ladakh Environment and Health Organization (LEHO; see p.562) for plush but plain shawls for around Rs5000.

Of the **bookshops** in Leh, Ladakh Bookshop, on the first floor below the *Leh View* restaurant in the Main Bazaar, and Book Lovers Retreat on Changspa Lane both have a fine selection of literature, reference and souvenir books. Secondhand paperbacks are sold or part-exchanged at Parkash Stationers opposite the vegetable market. Fairdeal Stationers near the Jami Masjid, Main Bazaar Square, is good for **newspapers**.

Listings

Bike rental Mountain bikes can be rented from Luna Ladakh Travel, Zangsti Rd (50m from Dzomsa Laundry), for Rs250/day.

Homestays Homestays can be arranged in remote villages, which offer a dinner, bed and breakfast for Rs400/person (Rs600/couple), with ten percent of the proceeds going towards village development programmes. The scheme is currently running in the areas between Likkir and Temisgang, and Stok and Chilling. For more information contact Snow Leopard Trails (☎01982/252188, ⊛www .snowleopardtrails.com) in the *Hotel Kanglhachhen* complex off Fort Road.

Hospital Leh's overstretched, poorly equipped SNM Hospital (☎01982/252014) is 1km south of the centre on the main road. For urgent medical treatment, contact a doctor through any upmarket hotel. PT Alamdar Chemist & Clinic (☎01982/252587), off the lower end of the Bazaar, has a good English-speaking morning surgery from 9am.

Internet access Now that most places have a satellite connection, broadband Internet cafés have popped up all over the main bazaar, Fort Road and Changspa Lane. Charges start at Rs1.50/min.

Laundry Dzomsa Laundry (see p.557).

Libraries The Ecology Centre's excellent library (Mon–Sat 10am–4pm) keeps books on everything from agriculture to Zen Buddhism, as well as periodicals, magazines and files of articles on Ladakh and development issues. Students of Buddhism should check out the collection of books

at the Chokhang Vihara Monastery, across from the State Bank of India, or the Tibetan Cultural Centre in the south of town.

Massage Indian Vedyashala on Changspa Lane (☎09906 999502) offers a range of Ayurvedic massages for around Rs500–1000.

Meditation, yoga and alternative therapy In high season small classes are run by the Mahabodhi Society in Changspa which specializes in Vipassana ☎01982/253689; their extensive complex in Devachan (☎01982/244155, ⊛www .mahabodhiladakh.org) towards Choglamsar, 3km south of Leh, includes a meditation centre with courses ranging from three to seven days. The *Asia Guesthouse*, Changspa Lane, houses a German-run Vajrayana Meditation and Healing Arts Centre. Numerous posters and flyers advertise classes and sessions in yoga, reiki, shiatsu and other alternative therapies.

Motorbikes Although several places now hire motorcycles, with the going rate of around Rs800/day for an Enfield, you should check the bikes carefully. By far the most reliable of the agencies is Enntrax Tours (☎01982/250603), a few doors down from the *Khangri Hotel*; mopeds here are Rs600/24hr.

Paragliding Try Indus Himalayan Explorers, Fort Rd (☎01982/252788), across from the *Yak Tail Hotel*.

Pharmacy Het Ram Vinay Kumar at the top of the main bazaar sells a range of allopathic pills and potions, as well as batteries and tampons. For Tibetan medicine, two *amchis* at the LSTM Amchi Clinic,

Changspa Lane (daily: July–Sept 8am–8pm; Oct–June 10am–4pm), speak English and charge Rs50 for a consultation using traditional diagnostic techniques.

Photography The Sonu Color Lab next to the Tibet Handicraft Emporium on the main street sells transparency and print film. Internet places can burn digital photos onto CDs.

Police ☎01982/252018 or 252200. ☎100 for the operator.

Post The post office is in the main bazaar (Mon–Sat 10am–1pm & 2–5pm). For parcels, go to the GPO (Mon–Sat 10am–4.30pm), out of town on Airport Rd, whose unreliable poste restante counter is tucked around the back. You can also receive letters through the Tourist Information Centre on Fort Rd.

Tour operators Reliable agents recommended for trekking and Jeep safaris include: Yama Adventures, Changspa Lane (☎01982/250833, ⓦwww .yamatreks.com); Mountain Trails, 2 Hemis Complex, Zangsti Rd (☎01982/254855); Footprints, Fort Rd (☎01982/251799 ⓦwww.footprintsindia.com); and Dreamland Trek & Tours, Fort Rd (☎01982/250784, ⓦwww.dreamladakh.com). Alternatively, smaller agencies such as Oriental Travels, at the *Oriental Guest house* in Changspa (☎01982/253153), offer a more personalized service. Some agents also offer rafting on the River Indus (see p.575).

Moving on from Leh

As befits India's remotest Himalayan town, Leh is singularly hard to get to, and even harder to leave. Fragile road and air links mean visitors all too often find themselves stranded waiting for passes to open or planes to appear. Wherever and however you travel, book your onward ticket as far in advance as possible, be prepared for delays if the weather changes, and allow plenty of time to connect with onward flights.

The quickest way out of Leh is **by plane**. During the summer, weather permitting, Indian Airlines (Tues–Sun), Jet Airways (daily except Sat) and Air Deccan (3–4 weekly) all operate flights to **Delhi**. IA also flies to **Jammu** (Fri & Sun) and **Srinagar** (Wed). The rest of the year, flights are less frequent and reliable. Tickets can be booked and confirmed at the Indian Airlines/Tushita Travels office on Fort Road (daily 10am–5pm; ☎01982/252076). The Jet office is located in the main bazaar (Mon–Sat 10am–5pm, Sun 10am–3pm; ☎01982/250999, ⓦwww.jetairways.com), not far down from the mosque. As usual, Air Deccan tickets must be obtained through any travel agent. One-way summer ticket prices to Delhi range from under $100 with Air Deccan to over $200 with the other carriers at peak times.

The overland route to **Manali** in Himachal Pradesh (see p.543) is officially open until September 15, but invariably a sense of panic sets in towards the end of the season and some bus operators such as HPTDC fold up earlier. Private buses continue to ply the route through to early October as long as the weather holds, as do 4WD Gypsies and Sumos. The 485km journey across the Himalayas generally takes two days, with buses halting for the night at a tent camp en route – though if the road has been recently cleared of snow or landslides the journey can take three or four days. A full account of the route, starting at Manali, is given on p.543. Tickets for **HPTDC**'s alternate-days "super-deluxe" bus (Rs1600 including overnight stop and meal in Keylong) can be booked at their office upstairs on Fort Road. Under half the price are the ramshackle **state transport** corporation buses run by HPSRTC and J&KSRTC, bookable the day before departure at the town bus stand. Several agencies along Fort Road, including Dreamland Trek & Tours (☎01982/250784), sell tickets for **private buses** to Manali for around Rs800–900. They will also help arrange a Sumo or Gypsy **4WD** taxi to Manali for Rs1100–1600 per person. This is by far the most comfortable option and, if you don't mind leaving at 2am, they usually get to Manali that evening. The downside of this is that you will miss some of the spectacular scenery by travelling in the dark and the drivers are often accused of reckless driving, not good on potholed mountain roads.

J&KSRTC buses to **Srinagar** run from mid-June to late October, stopping overnight at Kargil before grinding up the bleak Zoji La pass (3540m), the threshold of Ladakh and Kashmir, and descending steeply into an alpine scene of birch, fir and flowers – the fabled Vale of Kashmir. It's a scenic route, and one which is becoming more and more popular with travellers, but you must check the current situation before you decide to visit (see p.1354 for more on Kashmir).

For information regarding **local bus services** to destinations in Ladakh, see the relevant account, or see the "Travel details" at the end of this chapter.

Southeast of Leh

Southeast of Leh, the Indus Valley broadens to form a fertile river basin. Among the spectacular Buddhist monuments lining the edges of the flat valley floor are **Shey**, site of a ruined palace and giant brass Buddha, and the stunning monastery of **Tikse**. Both overlook the main highway and are thus served by regular buses.

With the exception of **Stok Palace**, home of the Ladakhi queen, sights on the opposite (south) side of the Indus, linked to the main road by a relatively infrequented and partly surfaced road, are harder to reach by public transport. South of Stok, **Matho** *gompa* is more famous for its winter oracle festivals than its art treasures, but is well worth a visit, if only for the superb views from its roof terrace. Further south still, either cross the Indus and rejoin the highway, calling in at **Stakna** *gompa* en route, or continue down the left bank to **Hemis**, Ladakh's wealthiest monastery and the venue for one of the region's few summer religious festivals. To side-step your fellow tourists without spending a night away from Leh, head up the austerely beautiful tributary valley opposite Hemis to the *gompas* of **Chemrey** and **Thak Thok**, the latter built around a fabled meditation cave.

Further east and south, the easing of restrictions has opened up new areas. East of Thak Thok, the road crosses the Chang La and then veers east to the high mountain lake of **Pangong Tso**, most of which lies in Tibet. Far more relaxing and inviting is the vast wilderness of **Rupshu** with trekking possibilities around the shores of **Tso Moriri**. Permits are required for all these areas; for full details see the box on p.552.

Stok

Just beyond the Tibetan refugee camp at **Choglamsar**, at the head of a huge moraine, the elegant four-storey **Stok Palace** stands in the shadow of an intrusive TV mast, overlooking barley terraces studded with whitewashed farmhouses. Built early in the nineteenth century by the last ruler of independent Ladakh, it has been the official residence of the Ladakhi royal family since they were ousted from Leh and Shey two hundred years ago.

The present Gyalmo or "queen", Deskit Angmo, a former member of parliament, still lives here during the summer, and has converted one wing of her 77-roomed palace into a small **museum** (daily 8am–6pm; Rs30). The fascinating collection comprises some of the royal family's most precious heirlooms, including exquisite sixteenth-century **thangkas** illuminated with paint made from crushed rubies, emeralds and sapphires. The *pièces de résistance*, however, are the Gyalmo's **peraks**. Still worn on important occasions, the ancient headdresses, thought to have originated in Tibet, are encrusted with slabs of flawless turquoise, polished coral, lapis lazuli and nuggets of pure gold. **Stok gompa** (dawn–dusk; Rs20), twenty minutes' walk up the valley, boasts a collection of dance-drama masks and some lurid modern murals painted by lamas from Lingshet *gompa* in Zanskar, the artists responsible for the Maitreya statue in Tikse (see p.568).

If you have time, it's also worth exploring the beautiful **side-valley** behind the village, which is the trailhead for the Markha Valley trek (see pp.576–577).

Practicalities

A half-day in **Stok** is enough to do it, and its side valley, justice. **Buses** leave Leh for Stok (40min) at 8am, 2pm and 5pm. The last bus returning to Leh leaves at 5pm; if you miss it or are tempted to **stay**, try the *Hotel Highland* (☎01982/242005, ✉tangdul@yahoo.co.in; ❼), a palatial two-storey house with fine views from its well-furnished attached rooms. About 2km down the road towards Leh is the imposing *Hotel Skittsal* (☎01982/242049, ⓦskittsal .com; ❸–❻), with panoramic views over the Indus Valley. Both of these close in early September, unlike the small and basic *Kalden Guest House* (☎01982/242057; ❷) at the foot of the palace.

Shey

SHEY, 15km southeast of Leh and once the capital of Ladakh, is now all but deserted, the royal family having been forced to abandon it by the Dogras midway through the nineteenth century. Only a semi-derelict palace, a small *gompa* and a profusion of *chortens* remain, clustered around a bleached spur of rock that juts into the fertile floor of the Indus Valley The ruins overlook the main highway, and can be reached on the frequent minibuses between Leh Bus Stand and Tikse. Alternatively, you could walk to Shey from Tikse monastery along a winding path that passes through one of Ladakh's biggest *chorten* fields with hundreds of whitewashed shrines of varying sizes scattered across the surreal desert landscape.

The **palace**, a smaller and more dilapidated version of the one in Leh, sits astride the ridge, below an ancient fort. Crowned by a golden *chorten* spire, its pride and joy is the colossal metal Shakyamuni Buddha housed in its ruined split-level temple (daily 6–9am; Rs20). Installed in 1633, the twelve-metre icon allegedly contains a hoard of precious stones, mandalas and powerful charms. Entering from a painted antechamber, you come face to face with the Buddha's huge feet, soles pointing upwards. Upstairs, a balcony surrounding the statue's torso surveys the massive Buddha in better light. Preserved for centuries by thick soot from votary butter lamps, the gold-tinted murals coating the walls are among the finest in the valley.

Five minutes' walk from the *Shikhar Restaurant* at the base of the palace, and past an area of walled-in *chortens,* stands a **temple**, enshrining another massive Shakyamuni statue (daily 7–9am & 5–6pm). Best viewed from the mezzanine veranda on the first floor, it is slightly older than its cousin up the hill. The descendants of the Nepali metalworkers who made it, brought here by Sengge Namgyal, still live and work in the isolated village of **Chilling** (on the River Zanskar), famous for its traditional silverwork.

Easily missed as you whizz past on the road is Shey's most ancient monument. The **rock carving** of the five Tathagata or "Thus gone" Buddhas, distinguished by their respective vehicles (*vahanas*) and hand positions (*mudras*), appears on a smooth slab of stone on the edge of the highway; it was probably carved soon after the eighth century, before the "Second Spreading" (see p.553). The large central figure with hands held in the gesture of preaching (turning the wheel of *dharma*), is the Buddha Resplendant, Vairocana, whose image is central in many of the Alchi murals (see p.579).

Practicalities

Rooms are available at the *Besthang Hotel*, a converted traditional Ladakhi house (℡01982/252792; ❸) with attached rooms, a pleasant garden and simple home cooking, located a few minutes' walk down the lane behind the roadside *Shilkhar Restaurant*. The only eating option in Shey, the *Shilkhar*, opposite the path leading up to the palace, has a varied menu of Indian and Western food. Buses arrive every couple of hours from Leh (30min), the last one at around 6.30pm. Returning to Leh, buses pass by every hour until 6.15pm, or you can hitch.

Tikse

Ladakh's most photographed and architecturally impressive *gompa* is at **TIKSE**, 19km southeast of Leh. Founded in the fifteenth century, its whitewashed *chortens* and cubic monks' quarters rise in ranks up the sides of a craggy bluff, crowned by an imposing ochre- and red-painted temple complex whose gleaming golden finials are visible for miles in every direction.

Tikse's reincarnation as a major tourist attraction has brought it mixed blessings: its constant stream of summer visitors spoils the peace and quiet necessary for meditation, but the income generated has enabled the monks to invest in major refurbishments, among them the **Maitreya temple** immediately above the main courtyard. Inaugurated in 1980 by the Dalai Lama, the shrine is built around a gigantic fourteen-metre gold-faced Buddha-to-come, seated not on a throne as is normally the case, but in the lotus position. The bright murals on the wall behind, painted by monks from Lingshet *gompa* in Zanskar, depict scenes from Maitreya's life.

For most foreign visitors, however, the highlight of a trip to Tikse is the view from its lofty **roof terrace**. A patchwork of barley fields stretches across the floor of the valley, fringed by rippling snow-flecked desert mountains and a string of monasteries, palaces, and Ladakhi villages. To enjoy this impressive panorama accompanied by primeval groans from the *gompa*'s gargantuan Tibetan trumpets – played on the rooftop at the 7am puja – you'll have to stay overnight or arrange an early Jeep from Leh.

Practicalities

An asphalted road cuts up the empty west side of the hill from the main highway to the monastery's small car park. If you arrive by **minibus** from Leh (hourly, from the town bus stand), pick your way across the wasteground below the *gompa* and follow the footpath up through its lower buildings to the main entrance, where monks issue tickets (Rs20). The last bus back to Leh leaves at 6pm. You can **stay** in the rooms behind the monastery's restaurant (℡01982/267005, ⓦwww.thiksey.com; ❸); they are spacious and clean but only have shared facilities. *Chamba Hotel* (April–Sept; ℡01982/267005; ❷–❸) offers decent attached rooms at lower rates, and there is a good garden **restaurant** serving a varied menu from Tibetan food to pancakes, as well as a Rs220 buffet.

Matho

MATHO, 27km south of Leh, straddles a spur at the mouth of an idyllic side-valley that runs deep into the heart of the Stok-Kangri massif. Though no less interesting or scenically situated than its neighbours, it sees comparatively few visitors. The *gompa* is the only representative in Ladakh of the **Sakyapa** sect, which held political power in thirteenth-century Tibet. As it's relatively isolated from the main highway, **buses** aren't all that frequent: services leave Leh daily at 7.30am, 2pm and 4.30pm, returning at 7.30am, 4pm and 4.30pm. By car, Matho also makes an ideal halfway halt on the journey along the little-used left-bank road between Stok and Hemis.

Despite its collection of 400-year-old *thangkas*, the monastery is best known for its **oracle festival**, Matho Nagran, held on the twenty-fifth and twenty-sixth day of the second Tibetan month (Feb/March). Two oracles, known as *rongzan*, are elected by lot every three years from among the sixty or so resident lamas. During the run-up to the big days, the pair fast and meditate in readiness for the moment when they are possessed by the spirit of the deity. Watched by crowds of rapt onlookers, they then perform all manner of death-defying stunts that include leaping blindfold around the *gompa's* precipitous parapets while slurping kettle-fulls of *chang*, and slashing themselves with razor-sharp sabres without drawing blood. The events are rounded off with colourful *chaam* dances in the monastery courtyard, and a question-and-answer session in which the *rongzan*, still under the influence of the deity, make prophecies about the coming year.

You can admire the costumes and masks worn by the monks during the festivals in Matho's small **museum**, tucked away behind the Du-khang. Men are also permitted to visit the eerie **Gon-khang** on the roof (strictly no photography), where the oracles' weapons and ritual garb are stored. The floor of the tiny temple lies under a deep layer of barley brought as harvest offerings by local villagers.

Hemis

Thanks to its famous festival – one of the few held in summer, when the passes are open – **HEMIS**, 45km southeast of Leh, is visited in greater numbers than any other *gompa* in Ladakh. Every year in mid-July (see p.554 for dates), hundreds of foreigners join the huge crowds of locals, dressed in their finest traditional garb, which flock to watch the colourful two-day pageant. However, at other times, the rambling and atmospheric seventeenth-century **monastery** (daily 8am–6pm; Rs30) can be disappointingly quiet. Although one of the region's foremost religious institutions, only a skeleton staff of monks and novices are resident off-season.

The main entrance opens onto the large rectangular courtyard where the festival **chaam dances** are performed. Accompanied by cymbal crashes, drum rolls and periodic blasts from the temple trumpets, the culmination of the event on the second day is a frenzied dismemberment of a dummy, symbolizing the destruction of the human ego, and thus the triumph of Buddhism over ignorance and evil. Once every twelve years, the Hemis festival also hosts the ritual unrolling of a giant *thangka*. The *gompa's* prize possession, which covers the entire facade of the building, it was embroidered by women whose hands are now revered as holy relics. Decorated with pearls and precious stones, it was last displayed in 2004. There is a **museum** (8am–6pm; Rs100 [Rs50]) in the corner of the courtyard but the modest collection of *thangkas*, masks and musical instruments barely justifies the inflated fee.

Practicalities

By car, Hemis is an easy day-trip from Leh. By **bus**, services are only frequent during the festival; at other times a single morning service leaves Leh at 9.30am and returns at noon, but there are ten daily shared minibuses, the last of which returns at 6pm. Another bus leaves Leh at 4pm but stays the night at Hemis, returning the next morning at 7am. An overnight stay means you can attend the 7am puja, and there is now more choice in the basic **accommodation** available, all with shared bathrooms. You can camp for free below nearby Chomoling village or for Rs100 at the *Hemis Restaurant* (T01982/249072; ●), which also has a couple of tatty rooms below the *gompa*, run by young *carrom*-playing monks. The newer *Hemis Spiritual Retreat* (T01982/249011; ●) has slightly better rooms and also serves **food** in its garden. Both the *Hemis Restaurant* and the *Parachute Restaurant* in Chomoling serve simple meals; the latter is cheaper, has a selection of pancakes and is a useful stop-off for trekkers heading for the Markha Valley. Pause here for last-minute tips and a weather update; day-hikers can enquire about guides to explore the mountains around Hemis.

Chemrey

Clinging like a swallow's nest to the sides of a shaly conical hill, the magnificent *gompa* of **CHEMREY** (Rs20) sees very few visitors because of its location – tucked up the side valley that runs from Karu, below Hemis, to the Chang La pass into Pangong. If you don't have your own vehicle, you'll have to be prepared to do some walking to get here. It takes around fifty minutes to follow the dirt track down to the river and up to the monastery after the Leh–Thak Thok bus drops you off beside the main road.

Founded in 1664 as a memorial to King Sengge Namgyal, the monastery is staffed by a dwindling community of around twenty Drugpa monks and their young novices. Its main **Du-khang**, off the courtyard on the lower level, boasts a fine silver *chorten* and a set of ancient Tibetan texts whose title pages are illuminated with gold and silver calligraphy. Upstairs in the revamped **Guru-La-khang** sits a giant brass statue of Padmasambhava.

Thak Thok

A few kilometres up the valley from Chemrey above the village of **Sakti**, **THAK THOK** (pronounced *Tak-Tak* and meaning "rock roof") *gompa* shelters a cave in which the apostle Padmasambhava is said to have meditated during his epic eighth-century journey to Tibet. Blackened over the years by sticky butter-lamp and incense smoke, the mysterious grotto is now somewhat upstaged by the monastery's more modern wings nearby. As well as some spectacular 35-year-old wall paintings, the **Urgyan Photan Du-khang** harbours a collection of multicoloured yak-butter candle-sculptures made by the head lama. For a glimpse of state-of-the-art Buddhist iconography, head to the top of Thak Thok village, where a shiny new temple houses a row of huge gleaming Buddhas, decked out in silk robes and surrounded by garish modern murals.

Apart from during the annual **festivals** (see p.554), the village of Sakti is a tranquil place, blessed with serene views south over the snowy mountains behind Hemis. Accommodation is available in the J&K *Tourist Bungalow* (❷) on the road directly below the *gompa*. There are also plenty of ideal camping spots beside the river, although as ever you should seek permission before putting up a tent on someone's field. Three minibuses a day leave Leh for Sakti (8.30am, 2.30pm and 3.30pm); the last one back to Leh departs at 4pm.

Pangong Tso

Pangong Tso, 154km southeast of Leh, is one of the largest saltwater lakes in Asia, a long narrow strip of water stretching from Ladakh east into Tibet. Only a quarter of the 134-kilometre-long lake is in India, and the army, who experienced bitter losses along its shores in the war against China in 1962, jealously guard their side of the frontier. Until the mid-1990s, it was off limits to visitors, and tourists still need a permit to come here (see box, p.552). The lake, at an altitude of 4267m, with the dramatic glacier-clad Pangong Range to its south and the Changchenmo Range reflected in its deep blue-green waters to the north, measures 8km across at its widest point and provides a tantalizing view of Tibet in the distance, although the bitter winds blowing over the brackish water make it one of the coldest places in Ladakh. Occasional public **buses** from Leh will drop off visitors at the village of **Spangmik** before continuing to the restricted border area; return buses come through the next morning at around 7.30am. There is basic **accommodation** and food at Spangmik, but most tourists come here on an organized two-day **Jeep safari**. Tour operators in Leh (see p.565) provide all the necessary facilities, including camping and food at **Lukung**, 15km north of the lake, or at the tent camp by the lake itself. Jeep-safari prices start at around Rs5500 for up to five people plus a driver and guide. To add further interest to the trip, take in the monasteries of Chemrey and Thak Thok en route.

Tso Moriri

Famous for the large herds of *kiang*, or wild ass, which graze on its shores, the lake of **Tso Moriri**, 210km southeast of Leh, lies in the sparsely populated region of **Rupshu**. You need a permit to travel here (see box, p.552), which most visitors do via a Jeep safari out of Leh.

Nestling in a wide valley flanked by some of the highest peaks in Ladakh – **Lungser Kangri** (6666m) and **Chanmser Kangri** (6622m) – the twenty-kilometre-long lake is home to flocks of migratory *nangpa* or bar-headed geese, as well as occasional herds of pashmina goats and camps of nomadic herders. Located on the shores of the lake at an altitude of 4595m, **Korzok** – the only large village in the area – is a friendly place with a small *gompa*. To help protect the fragile ecosystem against the influx of tourists, a new directive stipulates that no habitation can be built within 700m of the shoreline. Visitors should bring their own food supplies and make sure they take all their rubbish away.

The open spaces around Tso Moriri make for some pleasant **trekking**, including the relatively easy – if you are acclimatized – three-day, forty-kilometre circuit of the lake. Another route gaining popularity is the trail from Rumtse near Upshi via Tso Kar to Tso Moriri. Some trekking operators in Manali and Leh can arrange more ambitious routes such as the ancient trade route linking **Spiti** to Tso Moriri and Leh via Kibber. Treks start from around $40 per person per day in a group of four, which usually includes transport, food and tents.

Practicalities

From Leh, three **buses** depart for Tso Moriri on the 10th, 20th and 30th of each month at 6am, returning the following day. Another option is to hitch a ride on a truck, or to visit on a **Jeep safari** (see p.565 for details of tour operators in Leh), which start at around Rs7000 for a two-day trip. These usually follow a circular itinerary through Upshi and Mahe Bridge, winding up at Korzok. From there they then continue on towards the Manali–Leh Highway, passing the lake of Tso Kar and Thukse village along the way. **Accommodation** is in local homestays and in Korzok, at the Delhi-run and fairly grotty and overpriced *Lake View* (⑤), just below the bus stand. Similarly overpriced is the tent colony, where a bed costs a whopping Rs1000. Anyone headed this way should first check out the **video** on Tso Moriri, *Forbidden Wilderness*, shown at Leh's Ecology Centre (see p.561).

North of Leh: Nubra Valley

Until 1994, the lands north of Leh were off limits to tourists and had been unexplored by outsiders since the nineteenth century. Now, the breathtaking **Nubra Valley**, unfolding beyond the world's highest stretch of motorable road as it crosses the **Khardung La** (5602m), can be visited with a seven-day **permit** (see p.552), which gives you enough time to explore the stark terrain and trek out to one or two *gompas*. The valley's mountain backbone looks east to the Nubra River and west to the Shyok River, which meet amid silver-grey sand dunes and boulder fields. To the north and east, the mighty Karakoram Range marks the Indian border with China and Pakistan. In the valley it's relatively mild, though **dust storms** are common, whipping up sand and light debris in choking clouds above the broad riverbeds.

Before the region passed into the administrative hands of Leh, Nubra's ancient kings ruled from a palace in **Charasa**, topping an isolated hillock opposite Sumur, home to the valley's principal monastery. Further up the Nubra River, the hot springs of **Panamik**, once welcomed by footsore traders, are blissfully refreshing after all day on a bumpy bus. By the neighbouring Shyok River, **Diskit**, surveyed by a hillside *gompa*, lies just 7km from **Hundur**, known for its peculiar high-altitude double-humped Bactrian camels.

The route north to Nubra, a steep and rough road that forces painful groans from buses and trucks, keeps Leh in sight for three hours before crossing the Khardung La, and ploughing down more gently towards the distant Karakoram Range. Due to its strategic importance as the military road to the battlefields of the Siachen Glacier, the road to Nubra is kept open all year round but conditions can be treacherous at any time.

Practicalities

Buses leave Leh on Tuesdays at 6am for Panamik via Sumur (7–8hr) and Hunder via Diskit (Thurs & Sat 6am; 6–7hr). The buses return to Leh the next day and you should book your return journey on arrival. Alternatively, **Jeeps** for a maximum of five people can be rented from Leh taxi rank or any tour operator (see p.565). A complete three-day itinerary, including a visit to Diskit and Panamik, costs in the region of Rs6500 for the Jeep plus driver. Once in the valley, **hitching** on military or road-builders' trucks is an option, though it's inadvisable for lone travellers. The few **taxis** at Diskit charge from around Rs1000 for a day's exploration of the valley, with trips to Sumur and Panamik adding up. **Buses** between Diskit and Panamik travel daily, leaving Panamik at 7am and returning at 4pm.

Sumur

Beyond the confluence of the Shyok and Nubra rivers, **SUMUR**, a sleepy oasis spread over a large area, is home to the valley's most influential monastery, **Samstem Ling gompa**, a pleasant forty-minute walk behind the village. Built in 1841, the *gompa* accommodates just under a hundred Gelug-pa monks of all ages. To catch the morning or evening pujas, you'll have to **stay** in Sumur. Most of the guesthouses are on the sand lane that leads off from the bus stop at the prayer wheel. Closest to the main road is the *AO Guesthouse* (℡01980/223506; ❶–❷), which has basic doubles including six with attached baths, a garden, vegetarian café and camping (Rs50); two newer alternatives, 500m further down the lane, are *K-Sar Guest House* (℡01980/223574; ❷), where all the spruce rooms are attached and you can camp for Rs300 in their spacious tents or Rs100 in your own, and *Saser Guest House* (℡01980/223584; ❶–❷), which has shared and attached rooms and allows camping for Rs100. It's a 1.5km trek to the *gompa*; equally convenient for catching the pujas, but overpriced, the *Yarab Tso* (℡01980/223544, ✉rimo@vsnl.com; ❺ full board) is at Teggar village, twenty minutes' walk up the main road to Panamik.

Panamik

A one-hour bus journey (22km) up the valley from Sumur, **PANAMIK** (aka Pinchimik), a dusty hamlet overlooked by the pin-point summit of Charouk Dongchen, marks the most northerly point in India accessible to tourists. A kilometre past the **hot springs**, beyond the stone walls that line the pitted road, is the village proper. Splitting into wide rivulets at this point, the sapphire Nubra seems shallow and tame, but it's not – heed local advice not to ford it as there have been several reported accidents involving travellers.

Don't expect much from Panamik's hot springs – they're no more than a stone shack on the hillside, 100m past the J&K tourism hut. In fact, once you're here, there's little to do but walk. A dot on the mountainside across the river, **Ensa gompa** makes an obvious excursion. The route, three hours each way, passes through the village and crosses a bridge beyond the vast boulder field 3km upstream, then joins a wide Jeep track above the river for several kilometres. The final haul up a precipitous gorge hides the *gompa* from view until you stumble upon it, couched in an unexpected valley of willow and poplar trees fed by a perennial sweet-water stream. Though the *gompa* is usually locked, the views from rows of crumbling *chortens* nearby make the climb worthwhile. If one of the few semi-resident monks is there, however, you'll be shown inside to see the old wall paintings in the temples, and the footprint of Tsong-kha-pa, allegedly imprinted at this spot when he journeyed from Tibet to India in the fourteenth century.

The *Hot Spring Guesthouse* (❷) just beyond the hot springs themselves, and the unsigned *Bangka Guesthouse* (❷), 600m further along, comprise Panamik's unexciting **accommodation** options. All **buses** passing through Sumur originate from or terminate in Panamik. Direct buses to Leh depart Friday and Sunday at 6am.

Diskit and Hundur

DISKIT feels rather dull on first impressions, but it does possess an appealing old town, whose low, balconied houses lie below the main road before the diversion to the centre. For the guesthouses, get off at the first bus stop, next to the prayer wheel, from where a road runs down through the old quarter to the bazaar. The main road climbs on past the newly constructed 30m statue of the seated Buddha up the hillside above the town to Diskit's picturesque **gompa**, built in 1420. If you're on foot, follow the long *mani* wall, which continues on the other side of the road, and trace the path that winds upwards from its end to the monastery – a steep walk of around thirty minutes. The *gompa*'s steps climb past the monks' quarters to the first of a group of temples (Rs20). Local legend has it that a Mongol demon, a sworn enemy of Buddhism, was slain nearby, but his lifeless body kept returning to the *gompa*. What are reputed to be his wrinkled head and hand are now clasped by a pot-bellied protector deity in the spooky **Gon-khang**.

The diminutive **Lachung temple**, higher up, is the oldest here. Soot-soiled murals face a huge Tsong-kha-pa statue, topped with a Gelug-pa yellow hat. In the heart of the *gompa*, the **Du-khang**'s remarkable mural, filling a raised cupola above the hall, depicts Tibet's Tashilhunpo *gompa*, where the Panchen Lama is receiving a long stream of visitors approaching on camels, horses and carts. Finally, the **Kangyu Lang** (bookroom) and **Tsangyu Lang** temples act as storerooms for hundreds of Mongolian and Tibetan texts.

HUNDUR, a tiny village in a wooded valley beyond some impressive sand dunes, 7km north, is as far as one is allowed to go along this part of the Nubra Valley. The main monastery lies just below the main road, near the bridge and the end of the route. Further down and across the brook is a creaky, cobweb-filled old manor that once belonged to the local Zimskhang royal family, and is now occasionally unlocked by a key-keeper at the *Goba Guesthouse*. The village is renowned for its herd of Bactrian camels (a vestige of its days on the old trans-Karakoram trade route), which you will invariably encounter if you walk out onto the dunes. **Camel rides** start around Rs150 for a short lope across the sand.

Practicalities

Buses stop on Diskit's main road by the prayer wheel where the road descends through the old quarter to the bazaar, and then again on the new road to the bazaar, before continuing to Hundur.

Accommodation in Diskit is simple but ample. By the upper bus stop close to the prayer wheel on the main road, *Olthang Guest House* (℡01980/220025; ❸–❹) has a range of attached rooms and camping for Rs300; home-grown vegetables from the picturesque garden are served for dinner in the dining hall (around Rs50), which doubles as a bar in the evenings. Follow the road down from the prayer wheel and along the *mani* wall on your right through a *chorten* gate to cosy *Sunrise* (℡01980/220011; ❷) which has cheap beds, shared bathrooms and a pleasant garden. Further down, along a lane beyond the second prayer wheel, the pleasant *Thachung* (℡01980/220002; ❷) has beautiful sunny glass rooms and clean bathrooms. Nearing the village centre, the newest and smartest option is the ⚇ *Hotel Sangam* (℡01980/220404; ❶–❸), which has spacious rooms, both with attached and shared baths. All the guest-houses will provide food or you can eat authentic Tibetan dishes at the upstairs *Sangam View* **restaurant** right in the centre.

Accommodation in **Hundur** is even more laid back; the most popular hang-out is the friendly *Goba Guesthouse* (℡01983/221083; ❶–❸), 400m down from the roadside *gompa*, a quaint, low-key affair with a sunny yard and hundreds of flowers. More secluded and excellent value, the *Snow Leopard* (℡01980/221097; ❷–❹) is set in a beautiful vegetable garden, has great views and offers some rooms with bath; it is signposted from the main road through the back of the village. Back on the road in from Diskit, handy for the dunes, the more basic *Semba Guest House* (℡01980/221348; ❶) has just three rooms with shared facilities and the village bar.

Buses return to Leh from Diskit and Hundur at 9am on Wednesdays. Make sure you buy a ticket from the driver the day before, otherwise you're unlikely to be let on; there's a daily bus to Sumur and Panamik, usually in the afternoon but check with your guesthouse. If you're not alone, **hitching** is a good alternative. You can usually get a lift with one of the slow military vehicles running up and down the valley.

West of Leh

Of the many *gompas* accessible by road **west of Leh**, only **Spitok**, piled on a hilltop at the end of the airport runway, and **Phyang**, which presides over one of Ladakh's most picturesque villages, can be comfortably visited on day-trips from the capital. The rest, including **Likkir** and the temple complex at **Alchi**, with its wonderfully preserved eleventh-century murals, are usually seen en route to or from **Kargil**. The 231km journey, which takes in a couple of high passes and some mind-blowing scenery, can be completed in a single eight-hour haul, slightly less by Jeep. To do this stretch of road justice, however, you should spend at least a few days making short forays up the side valleys of the Indus, where idyllic settlements and *gompas* nestle amid barley fields and mountains.

One of the great landmarks punctuating the former caravan route is the monastery of **Lamayuru**. Reached via a nail-biting sequence of hairpin bends as the highway climbs out of the Indus Valley to begin its meandering ascent of **Fotu La**, it lies within walking distance of some extraordinary lunar-like rock formations, at the start of the main trekking route south to Padum in Zanskar. Further west still, beyond the dramatic **Namika La** pass, **Mulbekh** is the last Buddhist village on the highway. From here on, *gompas* and *gonchas* give way to onion-domed mosques and flowing *salwar kameez*.

There is, on average, an accident a day on the narrow, high and twisting Leh–Kargil road. Tata trucks are the most prone to toppling off the tarmac, and it can take hours for the rescue vehicles from Leh and Kargil to arrive and then clear the road. In summer, **transport** along the highway is straightforward as ramshackle state and private buses ply the route; getting to more remote spots, however, can be hard. Some travellers resort to paying for a ride on one of the countless Tata trucks that lumber past, or hitch with an army convoy, but getting a group together to rent a **Jeep** from tour operators in Leh (p.565), while expensive, will be safer, save time and give more access to the side valleys.

Spitok

SPITOK gompa, rising incongruously from the end of the airport runway, makes a good half-day foray from Leh, 10km up the north side of the

---

Rafting and kayaking on the River Indus

While water levels are high, between the end of June and late August, Leh's more entre-preneurial travel agents operate **rafting** trips on the River Indus. The routes are tame in comparison with Nepal's, but floating downstream in a twelve-seater rubber inflatable is a hugely enjoyable way to experience the valley's most rugged and beautiful landscape. Two different stretches of the river are used: from **Spitok** to the Indus–Zanskar confluence at **Nimmu** (3hr), and from Nimmu to the ancient temple complex at **Alchi** (2hr 30min). Experienced rafters may also want to try the more challenging route between Alchi and Khalsi, which takes in the kilometre-long series of rapids at **Nurla**. The annual multi-day expedition down the River Zanskar to the Indus is by far the most rewarding as it also includes the spectacular road approach to Padum.

Several adventure-tour operators in Leh offer whitewater rafting or kayaking on the Indus. **Tickets** should be booked at least a day in advance. One of the best operators is Splash Adventure Tours, Changspa Lane (①01982/254970, ⑩www.kayakindia .com); **prices** start from around Rs1000 for one-day trips. Make sure when you book that the price includes transport to and from the river, rental of life jackets and helmets, and meals, and that there is a waterproof strongbox for valuables.

The ancient footpaths that crisscross **Ladakh** and **Zanskar** provide some of the most inspiring **trekking** in the Himalayas. Threading together remote Buddhist villages and monasteries, cut off in winter behind high passes whose rocky tops bristle with prayer flags, nearly all are long, hard and high – but never dull. Whether you make all the necessary preparations yourself, or pay an agency to do it for you, **Leh** (see p.555) is the best place to plan a trek; the **best time** to trek is from June to September.

Trekking **independently** is straightforward if you have a copy of *Trekking in Ladakh* (see below), don't mind haggling and are happy to organize the logistics yourself. To find ponies and guides, head for the Tibetan refugee camp at Choglamsar, 3km south of Leh. Count on paying around Rs300 per horse and Rs200 per donkey each day – two people trekking through the Markha Valley for example would pay around $30 each for the entire week. By contrast, a **package trek** sold by a trekking agent in Leh will cost around $50 per day, and more if your group is less than four people.

You can **rent equipment**, including high-quality tents, sleeping bags, sleeping mats and duck-down jackets, either through your chosen agency or at places like **Frontier Adventure Company**, across from the taxi stand on Fort Road (℡01982/253011), or Spiritual Trek, Changspa Lane (℡01982/251701, ℮spiritualtrek @yahoo.com). Both also act as trek operators, supplying guides, porters, transport and food. Expect to pay around Rs100–150 a day for a tent, Rs70–100 for a sleeping bag and Rs30–40 for a gas stove; if you're intending to climb Stok-Kangri you may need to dish out Rs40 for an ice axe. Independent trekkers might consider buying Indian equipment in the bazaar, which could be resold.

Minimize your impact in culturally and ecologically sensitive areas by being as **self-reliant** as possible, especially with food and fuel. Buying provisions along the way puts an unnecessary burden on the villages' subsistence-oriented economies, and encourages strings of unsightly "tea shops" (often run by outsiders) to sprout along the trails. Always burn kerosene, never wood – a scarce and valuable resource. Refuse should be packed up, not disposed of along the route, no matter how far from the nearest town you are, and plastics retained for recycling at the Ecology Centre in Leh. Always bury your faeces and burn your toilet paper afterwards. Finally, do not defecate in the dry-stone huts along the trails; local shepherds use them for shelter during snow storms. For more details about environmental issues in Ladakh, see p.557.

An excellent **book** covering everything you need to know to undertake an expedition in the region is Trailblazer's *Trekking in Ladakh* by Charlie Loram, on sale in bookstores in Leh. For information about trekking to **Zanskar** from the south, see "Trekking in Lahaul and Spiti" (p.538).

The Markha Valley

The beautiful **Markha Valley** runs parallel with the Indus on the far southern side of the snowy Stok-Kangri massif, visible from Leh. Passing through cultivated valley floors, undulating high-altitude grassland and snow-prone passes, the winding trail

Indus Valley. If you can't afford the taxi fare (around Rs100), the easiest way to get there is to stroll down to the crossroads above the GPO and the tourist reception centre and then flag down any of the **buses** heading west along the main Srinagar highway. Travellers who walk the whole way invariably regret it, as the route is relentlessly dull, passing through a string of unsightly military installations hemmed in by barbed-wire fences. A break in the monotony appears 1km before Spitok in the form of the **Museum of Ladakh, Culture and Military Heritage** (Rs20), a self-congratulatory montage of Indian military achievements in Ladakh, with tributes to the heroic road-builders who risked their lives to open Ladakh to

along it enables trekkers to experience life in a roadless region without having to hike for weeks into the wilderness – as a result, it has become the most frequented route in Ladakh. Do not attempt this trek without adequate wet- and cold-weather gear: snow flurries sweep across the higher reaches of the Markha Valley even in August.

The circuit takes six to eight days to complete, and is usually followed anticlockwise, starting from the village of **Spitok** (see p.575), 10km south of Leh. A more dramatic approach via **Stok** (see p.566) affords matchless views over the Indus Valley to the Ladakh and Karakoram ranges, but involves a sharp ascent of **Stok La** (4848m) on only the second day; don't try it unless you are already well acclimatized to the altitude.

Likkir to Temisgang

A motorable road along the old caravan route through the hills between **Likkir** and **Temisgang** makes a leisurely two-day hike, which takes in three major monasteries (Likkir, Rhizong and Temisgang) and a string of idyllic villages. It's a great introduction to trekking in Ladakh, the perfect acclimatizer if you plan to attempt any longer and more demanding routes. Ponies and guides for the trip may be arranged on spec at either Likkir or Temisgang villages, both of which have small guesthouses and are connected by daily buses to Leh.

Lamayuru to Alchi

Albeit short by Ladakhi standards, the five-day trek from **Lamayuru** to **Alchi** is one of the toughest in the region, winding across high passes and a tangle of isolated valleys past a couple of ancient *gompas*, and offering superb panoramic views of the wilderness south of the Indus Valley. It's very hard to follow in places, so don't attempt it without an experienced guide, ponies and enough provisions to tide you over if you lose your way.

Padum to Lamayuru

The trek across the rugged Zanskar Range from **Padum** to **Lamayuru** on the Srinagar–Leh highway, usually completed in ten to twelve days, is a hugely popular but very demanding long-distance route, not to be attempted as a first-time trek nor without adequate preparation, ponies and a guide.

Stok-Kangri

Visible from most of Leh, **Stok-Kangri** (6120m) is reputed to be the easiest peak above 6000m in the world. Several agents in Leh advertise five-day **climbing expeditions** via the village of Stok with a non-technical final climb for around $40 per head per day for a group of four. If you've got *Trekking in Ladakh* in your rucksack, it's straightforward to walk up it independently, though you'll need to carry enough food for three or four days.

the world. A couple of token rooms cover the other two thousand years of Ladakhi history.

The fifteenth-century **monastery**, which tumbles down the sides of a steep knoll to a tight cluster of farmhouses and well-watered fields, is altogether more picturesque. Approached by road from the north, or from the south along a footpath that winds through Spitok village, its spacious rooftops command superb views. The main complex is of less interest than the **Palden Lumo** chapel, perched on a ridge above. Although visiting soldiers from the nearby Indian army barracks consider the deity inside the temple to be Kali Mata, the key-keeper will assure visitors that what many consider to be the black-faced and bloodthirsty Hindu goddess of death and destruction is actually **Yidam Dorje Jigjet**. Coloured electric lights illuminate the cobwebbed chamber of veiled guardian deities whose ferocious faces are only revealed once a year. If you have a torch, check out the 600-year-old paintings on the back wall, partially hidden by eerie *chaam* masks used during the winter festival season.

Phyang

A mere 17km west of Leh, **PHYANG gompa** looms large at the head of a secluded side-valley that tapers north into the Ladakh Range from the Srinagar highway. Eight daily **buses** serve the *gompa* from Leh; if you miss your return bus, just walk down the paved access road to the main highway (30min) and flag down a vehicle bound for Leh.

The *gompa* itself houses a fifty-strong community of lamas, but few antique murals of note, most having recently been painted over with brighter colours. Its only treasures are a small collection of fourteenth-century Kashmiri bronzes (locked behind glass in the modern Guru-Padmasambhava temple), and the light and airy **Du-khang**'s three silver *chortens*, one of which is decorated with a seven-eyed **dzi stone**. The gem, considered to be highly auspicious, was brought to Phyang from Tibet by the monastery's former head lama, whose ashes the *chorten* encases. Tucked away around the side, the shrine in the *gompa*'s gloomily atmospheric **Gon-khang** (Rs20) houses a ferocious veiled protector deity and an amazing collection of weapons and armour plundered during the Mongol invasions of the fourteenth century. Also dangling from the cobweb-covered rafters are various bits of dead animals, including most of a vulture and several sets of yak horns, believed to be 900-year-old relics of the Bon cult.

Phyang's annual **festival**, Phyang Tsedup, held in summer (between mid-July and early Aug; see p.554) to coincide with the tourist season, is the second largest in Ladakh after Hemis (see p.569). Celebrated with the usual masked *chaam* dances, the event is marked with a ritual exposition of a giant ten-metre brocaded silk *thangka*.

Likkir

Five kilometres to the north of the main Leh–Srinagar highway, shortly before the village of Saspol, the large and wealthy *gompa* of **LIKKIR**, home to around one hundred monks, is renowned for its new 23-metre-high yellow statue of the Buddha-to-come which towers serenely above the terraced fields. A pleasant break from the bustle of Leh, the village of Likkir offers a small but adequate choice of accommodation that, along with the sheer tranquillity of the surroundings, tempts many travellers to linger a few days.

The *gompa*, 3km up the valley from the village, was extensively renovated in the eighteenth century and today shows little sign of the antiquity related to the site. It overlooks the starting point for the popular two-day hike to Temisgang via Rhizong, which provides a comparatively gentle introduction to trekking in Ladakh.

The direct **minibus** from Leh (4pm; 3hr) goes past the village and makes the 3km haul up the valley to the *gompa*, returning to Leh at 7am the next morning. Otherwise, take any west-bound vehicle, get dropped off on the main Leh–Kargil highway (by the solitary chai stall) and walk the short but treeless one-kilometre road to the village, where you can hire a taxi for the *gompa*. Simple **rooms** are available at the *gompa* itself and next door at the monastic school; both ask for a donation. The pleasant *Gaph-Chow* (℡01982/252748; ❷) in the lower village has simple, comfortable rooms with attached baths, camping space in the lovely vegetable garden, email facilities, a garden café and traditional Ladakhi kitchen. The other option is the friendly *Norboo Spon* (❸ full board), easily spotted from the road to the monastery; the owner offers woodcarving and *thangka*-painting lessons to his guests. He can also give good trekking advice – aided by the scale model of the Likkir–Temisgang trek in his garden.

Alchi

Driving past on the nearby Srinagar–Leh highway, you'd never guess that the spectacular sweep of wine-coloured scree 3km across the Indus from **Saspol**, conceals one of the most significant historical sites in Asia. Yet the low pagoda-roofed *Chos-khor*, or "religious enclave", at **ALCHI**, 70km west of Leh, harbours an extraordinary wealth of ancient wall paintings and wood sculpture, miraculously preserved for more than nine centuries inside five tiny mud-walled temples. The site's earliest murals are regarded as the finest surviving examples of a style that flourished in Kashmir during the "Second Spreading". Barely a handful of the monasteries founded during this era escaped the Muslim depredations of the fourteenth century; Alchi is the most impressive of them all, the least remote and the only one you don't need a special permit to visit. Nestled beside a bend in the muddy River Indus amid some dramatic scenery, it's also a serene spot to break a long journey to or from the Ladakhi capital.

Legend tells that Rinchen Zangpo, the "Great Translator" (see p.553), stuck his walking stick in the ground here en route to Chilling and upon his return found it had become a poplar, an auspicious sign that made him build a temple on the spot. One tree near the entrance to the *Chos-khor*, denoted with a signboard, is symbolic of this event. The *Chos-khor* itself consists of five separate temples, various residential buildings and a scattering of large *chortens*, surrounded by a mud-and-stone wall. If you are pushed for time, concentrate on the two oldest buildings, the **Du-khang** and the **Sumtsek**, both in the middle of the enclosure. Entrance **tickets** (Rs30) are issued by a caretaker lama from nearby Likkir *gompa*, who will unlock the doors for you. Newly installed lights mean you can no longer use a torch to examine the paintings' vibrant colours close up, nor are you allowed to take photographs (even without flash).

The Du-khang

An inscription records that Alchi's oldest structure, the **Du-khang**, was erected late in the eleventh century. Its centrepiece is an image of Vairocana, the "Buddha Resplendent", flanked by the four main Buddha manifestations that appear all over Alchi's temple walls, always presented in their associated colours: Akshobya ("Unshakeable"; blue), Ratnasambhava ("Jewel Born"; yellow), Amitabha ("Boundless Radiance"; red) and Amoghasiddhi ("Unfailing Success"; green). The other walls are decorated with six elaborate mandalas, interspersed with intricate friezes.

The Sumtsek

Standing to the left of the Du-khang, the **Sumtsek** marks the high watermark of early medieval Indian-Buddhist art. Its woodcarvings and paintings, dominated by rich reds and blues, are almost as fresh and vibrant today as they were nine hundred years ago when the squat triple-storey structure was built. The heart of the shrine is a colossal statue of **Maitreya**, the Buddha-to-come, his head shielded from sight high in the second storey. Accompanying him are two equally grand **bodhisattvas**, their heads peering serenely down through gaps in the ceiling. Each of these stucco statues wears a figure-clinging *dhoti*, adorned with different, meticulously detailed motifs. Avalokitesvara, the *bodhisattva* of compassion (to the left), has pilgrimage sites, court vignettes, palaces and pre-Muslim style stupas on his robe, while that of Maitreya is decorated with episodes from the life of Gautama Buddha. The robe of Manjushri, destroyer of falsehood, to the right, shows the 84 masters of Tantra, the *mahasiddhas*, adopting complex yogic poses in a maze of bold square patterns.

Among the exquisite **murals**, some repaired in the sixteenth century, is the famous six-armed green goddess Prajnaparamita, the "Perfection of Wisdom". Amazingly, this, and the multitude of other images that plaster the interior of the Sumtsek, resolve, when viewed from the centre of the shrine, into a harmonious whole.

Other temples

The *Chos-khor's* three **other temples** all date from the twelfth and thirteenth centuries, but are nowhere near as impressive as their predecessors and the lama will need to be cajoled into unlocking them. Tucked away at the far, river end of the enclosure, the **Manjushri La-khang** is noteworthy only for its relatively recent "Thousand Buddha" paintings and gilded four-faced icon of Manjushri that fills almost the whole temple. Next door, the **Lotsawa La-khang**, with its central image and mural of Shakyamuni, is one of a handful of temples dedicated to Rinchen Zangpo; his small droopy-eared image sits on the right of Shakyamuni. **La-khang Soma**, the small square shrine south of the Sumtsek, is decorated with three large mandalas and various figures including an accomplished *yab-yum*: the Tantric image of the copulating deities symbolizes the union of opposites on a material and spiritual level.

Practicalities

An alternative to hiring a taxi from Leh is to catch the 8am or 4pm private **bus**, which takes three hours to cover the 70km and returns at 3.45pm or 7am the next day. Otherwise you can board any Kargil-bound vehicle, get off at the metal truss bridge west of **Saspol** and walk across the river and up the remaining 6km.

Of the growing selection of **guesthouses** in Alchi, the *Lotsava* (T01982/227129; ●–❷), down below the group-oriented *Alchi Resort* as you approach the taxi stand, is pleasant and simple with good views; with a little warning, the owner will serve filling breakfasts and evening meals in the small garden. On both sides of the lane that leads to the *gompa*, the *Zimskhang* (T01982/227086, @zimskhang@yahoo.com; ❷–❺) has two identities: to the right a modern hotel, and to the left a cheaper guesthouse with a pleasant garden. More upmarket is the purpose-built *Samdupling* (T01982/221704; ❾), 100m above the taxi stand, approached by following the stream behind the adequate *gompa*-owned *Hotel Potala* (T09419 178747, @angchok1@rediffmail .com; ❸). The only **restaurant**, apart from a couple of cheap *dhabas* near the taxi stand, is the *Golden Oriole German Bakery* just above the *gompa*, which does a standard mixture of Western and Indian dishes. If you've a real appetite, you might try the quality veg buffet at the *Zimskhang*.

Lamayuru

If one sight could be said to sum up Ladakh, it would have to be **LAMAYURU gompa**, 130km west of Leh. Hemmed in by a moonscape of scree-covered mountains, the whitewashed medieval monastery towers above a scruffy cluster of tumbledown mud-brick houses from the top of a near-vertical, weirdly eroded cliff. A major landmark on the old silk route, the *gompa* numbers among the 108 (a spiritually significant number, probably legendary) founded by the Rinchen Zangpo in the tenth and eleventh centuries. However, its craggy seat,

▲ Gompas, Lamayuru

believed to have sheltered Milarepa during his religious odyssey across the Himalayas, was probably sacred long before the advent of Buddhism, when local people followed the shamanistic Bon cult. Just thirty lamas of the Brigungpa branch of the Kagyu school are now left, as opposed to the four hundred that lived here a century or so ago. Nor does Lamayuru harbour much in the way of art treasures. The main reason visitors make a stop on this section of the Srinagar–Leh road is to photograph the *gompa* from the valley floor, or to pick up the trail to the Prikiti La pass – gateway to Zanskar – that begins here.

The steep footpath from the highway above town brings you out near the main entrance to the monastery, where you should be able to find the lama responsible for issuing entrance tickets (Rs20) and unlocking the door to the **Du-khang**. Lamayuru's newly renovated prayer-hall houses little of note other than a **cave** where Naropa, Milarepa's teacher, is said to have meditated, and a collection of colourful yak-butter sculptures. If you're lucky, you'll be shown through the tangle of narrow lanes below the *gompa* to a tiny **chapel**, whose badly damaged murals of mandalas and the Tathagata Buddhas date from the same period as those at Alchi (see p.579).

Practicalities

Lamayuru lies too far from either Leh or Kargil, 107km west, to be visited in a day-trip, so you either have to call in en route between the two, or spend the night here. The daily Leh–Kargil and Kargil–Leh **buses** both depart around 5.30am from their respective towns of origin and pass through Lamayuru between 9am and 10am, stopping near the central chai stalls. Some private buses also pass through up to early afternoon. **Trekkers** in search of reliable guides and ponies could ask at the *Dragon Guest House* (see below) or try arranging them in advance through their office in Leh (℡01982/253164).

Dominating the village skyline by the *gompa* entrance, the four-storey *Niranjana Hotel* (℡01982/224555; ❹) has twenty concrete **rooms** with good views of the surrounding valleys; the shared bathrooms have hot running water. Alternatively, the welcoming, family-run ⚐ *Dragon Guest House*

(☎01982/224510, ⓕ01982/252414; ❶–❸) has a range of rooms, including one coveted glass room, and a pleasant garden restaurant, which is the best place to **eat** in Lamayuru. The *Siachen Guesthouse* (☎01982/224538; ❶), on the opposite side of the footpath into the village, is a decent fallback. All accommodation prices double during the **festival** (late June/early July).

Mulbekh

West of Lamayuru, the main road crawls to the top of **Fotu La** (4091m), the highest pass between Leh and Srinagar, then ascends **Namika** ("Sky-Pillar") **La** (3760m), so called because of the jagged pinnacle of rock that looms above it to the south. Once across the windswept ridge, it drops through a dramatic landscape of disintegrating desert cliffs and pebbly ravines to the wayside village of **MULBEKH** – the last sizeable Buddhist settlement along the road before the Muslim Purki settlements around Kargil. The village is scattered around the banks of the River Wakha, lined with poplars and orchards of walnut and apricot trees.

Formerly an outpost of the Zangla kingdom of western Ladakh (the deposed monarchs, King Nyima Norbu Namgyal Dey and his queen, Tashi Deskit Angmo, still live in a dilapidated four-storey mansion on the western outskirts of the village), Mulbekh would be a sleepy hamlet were it not for the endless convoys of trucks and tourist buses that thunder through while the passes are open. Those visitors who stop at all tend only to stay long enough to grab a chai at a roadside *dhaba* and to have a quick look at the seven-metre-high **Maitreya** ("Chamba" in Tibetan) **statue** carved from the face of a gigantic boulder nearby. The precise origins of the shapely four-armed Buddha-to-be are not known, but an ancient inscription on its side records that it was carved between the seventh and eighth centuries, well before Buddhism was fully established in Tibet. The single-chambered *gompa* (Rs10), in front of the statue and decorated with particularly beautiful murals, is dedicated to the thousand-armed Chenrazig (Avalokiteshvara).

Accommodation in Mulbekh itself is limited to shabby rooms above basic restaurants such as the *Paradise* (☎01985/270010; ❶) and the *Tsomo Riri* (☎01985/270013; ❶) on the main road opposite the Chamba statue; serving *thukpa*, dhal, rice, *momos* and butter tea during the day, they later turn into cheap drinking dens. More comfort and attached rooms can be found 1km west along the main road at *Maitreya Guest House* (☎01985/270035; ❹).

Kargil

Though it is surrounded by awesome scenery, most travellers don't spend more than a few hours in **KARGIL**, capital of the area dubbed "Little Baltistan", which rises in a clutter of corrugated-iron rooftops from the confluence of the Suru and Drass rivers. As a halfway point between Leh and Srinagar, its grubby hotels fill up at night-time with weary bus passengers, who then get up at 4am and career off under cover of darkness. Although the town has expanded several kilometres along and above the riverside, the central area around the main bazaar, which loops round into a northerly orientation, is very compact and walkable. While Kargil has no attractions, it is an atmospheric place to pass a day or more while waiting for a bus to Zanskar (see p.585). Woolly-hatted and bearded old men and slick youths stroll the streets past old-fashioned wholesalers with their sacks of grains, spices and tins of ghee, Tibetans selling Panasonic electricals and butchers displaying severed goats' heads on dusty bookshelves. The town feels more Pakistani than Indian, and the faces (nearly all male) and food derive from Kashmir and Central Asia. Tourists are unusual, and Western women should keep their arms and legs covered; those walking around alone will probably encounter both giggling teenage boys and curious elderly Kargili gentlemen.

The majority of Kargil's eighty thousand inhabitants, known as Purki, are strict **Muslims**. Unlike their Sunni cousins in Kashmir, however, the locals here are orthodox **Shias**, which not only explains the ubiquitous Ayatollah photographs, but also the conspicuous absence of women from the bazaar. You might even spot the odd black turban of an Agha, one of Kargil's spiritual leaders, who still go on pilgrimage to holy sites in Iran and have outlawed male–female social practices such as dancing. Descendants of settlers and Muslim merchants from Kashmir and Yarkhand, Purkis speak a dialect called **Purig** – a mixture of Ladakhi and Balti. Indeed, had it not been for the daring Indian reconquest of the region during the 1948 Indo-Pak War, Kargil would today be part of Baltistan, the region across the Ceasefire Line which it closely resembles. Indeed, Kargil is so close to the Ceasefire Line and Pakistani positions that it served as the logistics centre in the 1999 war, (see p. 1355) and was repeatedly targeted by Pakistani artillery. Aside from the odd building destroyed, however, much of the town escaped unscathed as the army bases and airport lie on the outskirts of town. Since further conflict in the summer of 2002 the dust has settled markedly and, as dialogue continues between India and Pakistan on Kashmir, tourist numbers have been steadily increasing. It's still wise, however, to check the current situation before setting out.

Practicalities

State buses arriving in Kargil from Leh, Srinagar and Padum pull in to the compact main bus stand, just below the bazaar, towards its northern end, while private buses, minibuses and Jeeps share the larger **taxi stand** compound further south, around 100m off the bazaar. Buses for Mulbekh leave at 3pm, 3.30pm and 4pm every day. In the mornings you may be able to catch a shared Matador minibus. If you're wanting to head south, the government service to Padum in Zanskar is still suspended, so you'll need to try your luck with the private buses. These are patchy at best, generally running three times a week (but not on fixed days), and, due to the lack of alternatives, tend to be very busy. If you don't mind hitching, you could catch a bus to Panikhar (daily 7am & 2pm) and wait by the *Kayoul*. Hiring a taxi is much less hassle; the one-way fare to Padum is around Rs8000 (Rs1600 per person). For **Leh**, several buses depart daily between 4am and 5am (Rs200), but the quick and easy option is to book a seat the day before in a Tata Sumo (Rs500–600), which also tend to depart early in the day.

The J&K **tourism reception centre** (Mon–Sat 10am–4pm;℡01985/232721) is on the east side of town, on the river side of the **taxi stand**. As well as the usual leaflet on Ladakh, they rent out Norwegian **trekking equipment**, including four-season sleeping bags, tents, coats and boots. The J&K Bank has an **ATM**, while the *Siachen Hotel* can exchange sterling or dollars. Kargil has several **Internet** places (Rs80/hr), the best being the one on the corner of the main bazaar and the road to the state bus stand.

Accommodation

The Kashmir crisis, which reduced tourist traffic to a trickle, squeezed half of Kargil's **hotels** out of business, and perhaps surprisingly, it's the more salubrious ones that survived. Consequently, budget options are very limited and room tariffs soar in July and August when most travellers pass through; these are the rates below but discounts are usually available at other times.

Crown Next to the taxi stand. Rambling old budget hotel that's seen better days but still attracts backpackers. Some rooms come with attached bathrooms and there's a dirt-cheap dorm (Rs20). Running water on request. ➋

Greenland Just off the lane heading down to the taxi stand ℡01985/232324. A notch above rock-bottom, with a restaurant and reasonable rooms (all with bath); those on the first floor are more spacious. ➌

J&K Tourist Bungalow unit no.1 A 5min walk uphill from the crossroads above the bus stand ℡01985/232328. Clean rooms, clean sheets and peaceful atmosphere, with a small dining room. By far the best budget deal in town but needs to be booked in advance through any J&K office. Unit no.2 in the tourist office complex is shabbier but has river views. ➊

Kargil Continental Next to the *Greenland* ℡01985/232304. Open all year, with large comfortable rooms and a pleasant garden. A bit soulless and overpriced, though they plan a makeover by 2009. ➍

Siachen On a lane down to taxi stand ℡01985/233055, ℮hotel-siachen-kargil @rediffmail.com. One of the best downtown hotels, large and comfortable with attached rooms, a few cheaper options on the first floor, and a good restaurant. ➏–➐

Eating

Besides upmarket hotels like the *Siachen*, finding somewhere to **eat** in Kargil is a toss-up between the small tourist-oriented joints and local *dhabas* that are dotted on and around the main bazaar. Most restaurants are closed for **breakfast**, but the street food can be delicious – chai, chapatis and omelettes, with hot Kashmiri bread slathered with butter. Spicy shish kebabs go for just Rs10 later in the day.

Karan Singh Punjabi Janata South end of Main Bazaar. One of the town's better *dhabas*: spicy Indian sauces spooned onto groaning platefuls of rice. Eat well for around Rs50.

Las Vegas On the lane from the taxi stand to Main Bazaar. One of the more salubrious places, serving mainly non-veg Indian, Kashmiri and Chinese fare for around Rs80–100.

Rubby South end of Main Bazaar. Popular restaurant serving local specialities including *yakhani* (meat boiled in yoghurt) and *gustaba* (meat balls), both of which can be daunting if you're not adjusted to Central Asian cuisine. Most items well under Rs50.

Tibetan Food Restaurant Main Bazaar. All the favourites like *momo* and *thukpa*, dished up for around Rs40–60. Very authentic atmosphere in this attractive upstairs dining room.

Zojila Bakery Main Bazaar. A good place to stop for a morning tea, or to pick up bread and cookies. One of the few places for a sit-down brekky.

The Suru Valley

Dividing two of the world's most formidable mountain ranges, the **Suru Valley** winds south from Kargil to the desolate Pensi La – the main entry point for Zanskar. The first leg, usually undertaken in the pre-dawn darkness by bus, leads through the broad lower reaches of the Suru Valley, strewn with Muslim villages clustered around metal mosque domes. As you progress southwards, the pristine white ice-fields and pinnacles of **Nun–Kun** (7077m) nose over the horizon. Apart from a brief disappearance behind the steep sides of the valley at **Panikhar**, this awesome massif dominates the landscape all the way to Zanskar.

Shortly beyond Panikhar, the Suru veers east around the base of Nun-Kun, passing within a stone's throw of the magnificent **Parkachik Gangri** glacier. Having wound across a seemingly endless boulder field, closed in on both sides by sheer mountain walls, the road then emerges at a marshy open plain surrounded by snow peaks and swathes of near-vertical strata. **Juldo**, a tiny settlement whose fodder-stacked rooftops are strung with fluttering prayer flags, marks the beginning of Buddhist **Suru**.

The climb to the pass from **Rangdum gompa**, across the flat river basin from Juldo, is absolutely breathtaking. One glistening 6000-metre peak after another appears atop a series of side valleys, many lined with gigantic folds of rock and ice. The real high point, though, is reserved for the dizzying descent from **Pensi La** (4401m), as the road's switchbacks swing over the colossal S-shaped **Darung Drung Glacier**, whose milky-green meltwaters drain southeast into the Stod Valley, visible below.

Panikhar

Although by no means the largest settlement in the Suru Valley, **PANIKHAR**, three hours' bus ride south of Kargil, is a good place to break the long journey to Padum. Before the Kashmir troubles, it was a minor trekking centre, at the start of the Lonvilad Gali–Pahalgum trail. These days, the scruffy collection of roadside stalls and poor mud-brick farmhouses sees far fewer tourists, even in high season.

The main reason to stop is to hike to nearby **Parkachik La**, for panoramic views of the glacier-gouged north face of the mighty **Nun-Kun massif**. The **trail** up to the pass begins on the far side of the Suru, crossed via a suspension bridge thirty minutes south of the village. It may look straightforward from Panikhar, but the four-hour round-trip climb to the ridge gets very tough indeed towards the top, especially for those not used to the altitude. However, even seasoned trekkers gasp in awe at the sight that greets them when they finally arrive at the cairns. Capped with a plume of cloud and with snow streaming from its huge pyramidal peak, Nun sails 3500m above the valley floor, draped with heavily crevassed hanging glaciers and flanked by its sisters, multipinnacled Kun and saddle-topped Barmal.

There are only two **places to stay** in Panikhar. The *Kayoul* (☎01985/ 259080; ❶), directly opposite the bus stand, has a couple of very basic rooms with fold-away *charpois* and shared "earth" latrines, plus a ramshackle roadside café. For a bit more comfort, try the modest J&K *Tourist Bungalow* (❶), 100m further down the road on the left, where a large attached room with running water sets you back a mere Rs80. **Buses** to Kargil leave from the *Kayoul* at 7am and 11am. If you're looking for a lift to Padum, collar the truckers as they leave the *dhaba* after their lunch; the one-way fare costs around the same as the bus (Rs200).

Zanskar

Walled in by the Great Himalayan Divide, **ZANSKAR**, literally "Land of White Copper", has for decades exerted the allure of Shangri-La on visitors to Ladakh. The region's staggering remoteness, extreme climate and distance from the major Himalayan trade routes has meant that the successive winds of change that have blown through the Indus Valley to the north had little impact here. The annual influx of trekkers and a motorable road have certainly quickened the pace of development, but away from the main settlement of Padum, the Zanskaris' way of life has altered little since the sage Padmasambhava passed through in the eighth century.

The nucleus of the region is a Y-shaped glacial valley system drained by three main rivers: the **Stot** (or Doda) and the **Tsarap** (or Lingit) join and flow north as the **Zanskar**. Lying to the leeward side of the Himalayan watershed, the valley sees a lot more snow than central Ladakh. Even the lowest passes remain blocked for seven or eight months of the year, while midwinter temperatures can drop to a bone-numbing minus 40°C. Fourteen thousand or so tenacious souls subsist in this bleak and treeless terrain – among the coldest inhabited places on the planet – muffled up for half the year inside their smoke-filled whitewashed crofts, with a winter's-worth of fodder piled on the roof.

Until the end of the 1970s, anything the resourceful Zanskaris could not produce for themselves (including timber for building) had to be transported into the region over 4000- to 5000-metre passes, or, in midwinter, carried along the frozen surface of the Zanskar from its confluence with the Indus at Nimmu – a ten- to twelve-day round trip that's still the quickest route to the Srinagar–Leh road from Padum. Finally, in 1980, a motorable dirt track was blasted down the Suru and over Pensi La into the Stod Valley. Landslides and freak blizzards permitting (Pensi La can be snowbound even in August), the bumpy journey from Kargil to Padum can now be completed in as little as thirteen hours.

Most visitors come to Zanskar to **trek**. Numerous trails wind their way north from Padum to central Ladakh, west to Kishtwar and south to neighbouring Lahaul – all long, hard hikes (see box, p.538). If you're travelling down here hoping to use the district headquarters as a comfortable base from which to make short day-trips, you'll be disappointed. Only a handful of Zanskar's widely scattered *gompas* and settlements lie within striking distance of the road. The rest are hidden away in remote valleys, reached after days or weeks of walking.

Improved communications may yet turn out to be a mixed blessing for Zanskar. While the new road has undoubtedly brought a degree of prosperity to Padum, it has already forced significant changes upon the rest of the valley – most noticeably a sharp increase in tourist traffic – whose long-term impact on the region's fragile ecology and **traditional culture** has yet to be fully realized. Increased tourism has, in fact, done little to benefit the locals financially, with agencies in Leh, Manali, Srinagar and even Delhi pocketing the money paid by trekking groups. Zanskaris, weary of seeing their region come second to Kargil (which lies in the same administrative district), have been campaigning for several years for a sub-hill council status with more control over **development**, and a road following the Zanskar river gorge to Nimmu; the road project is going ahead, but painfully slowly. Buddhist concerns have also been heightened in the face of state government mismanagement and occasional communal tensions with their Muslim neighbours.

Padum

After a memorable trek or bus ride, **PADUM**, 240km to the south of Kargil, comes as a bit of an anticlimax. Instead of the picturesque Zanskari village you might expect, the region's administrative headquarters and principal roadhead turns out to be a desultory collection of crumbling mud and concrete cubes, oily truck parks and tin-roofed government buildings. The settlement's only real appeal lies in its superb location. Nestled at the southernmost tip of a broad, fertile river basin, Padum presides over a flat patchwork of farm land enclosed on three sides by colossal walls of scree and snow-capped mountains.

Straddling a nexus of several long-distance trails, Padum is an important **trekking hub** and the only place in Zanskar where tourism has thus far made much of an impression. During the short summer season, you'll see almost as many weather-beaten Westerners wandering around its sandy lanes as locals – a mixture of indigenous Buddhists and Sunni Muslims. Even so, facilities remain very basic, limited to a small tourist office and a handful of temporary teashops and guesthouses, as well as the inevitable rash of Kashmiri handicraft stalls. Nor is there much to see while you are waiting for your blisters to heal. The only noteworthy sight within easy walking distance is a small **Tagrimo gompa** fifteen minutes' walk to the west.

Practicalities

Arriving in Padum by **bus**, you'll be dropped in the dusty square at the far south end of the village, close to the old quarter and a couple of the cheaper guest-houses. Going the other way, a bus ticket for Kargil costs around Rs250. The J&K **Tourist Complex** (July–Sept Mon–Sat 10am–4pm; ℡01983/245017) lies 1km north of the square in Mane Ringmo, on the side of the main road, two minutes' walk from the other main concentration of guesthouses; it's good for general advice, though it doesn't rent out trekking gear. Due to the short season and the limited tourist trade, renting a car in Padum (through the Padum Taxi Union office near the bus stand) is expensive: a trip to Karsha and back costs at least Rs1000. As yet, there is nowhere in Padum to change money, although you can mail letters from the **post office** next door to the tourist centre.

Basic **trekking supplies** are sold at the hole-in-the-wall stores above the bus stand. Prices are much higher than elsewhere, so it pays to bring your own provisions with you from Kargil. Most trekkers arrange **ponies** through the tourist office or guesthouse owners, or you could try Zanskar Trek (℡01983/245053), who also supply guides (Rs500 per day). Expect to pay Rs200–300 per pony per day, depending on the time of year (ponies transport grain during the harvest, so they're more expensive in early September). If you have trouble finding a horse-wallah in Padum, ask at a neighbouring village, such as Pipiting, a thirty-minute walk north across the fields from Padum, where many of them live.

Accommodation

Accommodation in Padum is limited to a handful of grotty guesthouses and rooms in private family homes. In both cases, bathrooms are usually shared, and toilets are of the "long-drop" variety. One exception is the simple but comfort-able J&K *Tourist Complex* (℡01983/245017; ❶), whose well-maintained attached doubles have running cold water. The *Hotel Ibex* (℡01983/245012; ❸), with doubles set around a courtyard, is one of the better alternatives. Other options, both near the bus stand, include the friendly French-run *Mont Blanc* (❷–❸, tent pitch Rs50) and the *Chorala* (℡01983/245035; ❶), which offers reasonable doubles and even has a travel desk. Alternatively, **camping** pitches near the tourist centre cost Rs50 per night, though don't leave valuables in the tent – there have been recent reports of theft. Trekkers arriving from Shingo La sometimes camp beside the stream in the Tsarap Valley.

Eating

Finding **food** in Padum only tends to be a problem towards the end of the trekking season; by mid-October, stocks of imported goods (virtually every-thing except barley flour and yak butter) are low, and even a fresh egg can be a cause for celebration. Earlier in the year, temporary teashops and cafés ensure a supply of filling and inexpensive meals – one of the best is the *Lhasa*. For cheap Chinese and Tibetan food, try the *Changthang* near the *Tourist Bungalow*, or the *Gakyi Café* near the post office. Most guesthouses also provide half-board if given enough warning; the *Hotel Ibex* has the best restaurant.

Around Padum

Public transport around the Zanskar Valley is erratic, although one public bus travels from Padum to Zangla on Wednesday and Friday, leaving in the morning and returning the same afternoon. Otherwise you will have to shell out for the vastly inflated fares demanded by Padum's taxi union. Determined trekkers can alternatively set out on foot; the hike across the fields to **KARSHA gompa**,

Zanskar's largest Gelug-pa monastery, is the most rewarding objective. This cluster of whitewashed mud cubes clinging to the rocky lower slopes of the mountain north of Padum dates from the tenth to the fourteenth century. Of the prayer halls, the recently renovated Du-khang and Gon-khang at the top of the complex are the most impressive, while the small Chukshok-jal, set apart from the *gompa* below a ruined fort on the far side of a gully, contains Karsha's oldest wall paintings, contemporaneous with those at Alchi (see p.579).

The quickest way to get to Karsha on foot is to head north from Padum to the cable bridge across the Stot, immediately below the monastery. Set off early in the morning; the violent icy storms that blow in from the south across the Great Himalayan Range around mid-afternoon make the ninety-minute hike across the exposed river basin something of an endurance test. Karsha is a far more pleasant place to stay than Padum and some villagers rent **rooms** to tourists. Try the wonderful glass room belonging to Thuktan Thardot in Sharling Ward just below the *gompa* (❶) or the basic *Lobzang Guest House* (❶).

Karsha can also be reached by road, via the bridge at **Tungri**, 8km northwest of Padum. En route, you pass another large *gompa*, **SANI**, lauded as the oldest in Zanskar, and the only one built on the valley floor. Local legend attributes its foundation to the itinerant Padmasambhava (Guru Rinpoche) in the eighth century. Set apart from the temples a little to the north is a two-metre-high Maitreya figure, carved out of local stone some time between the eighth and tenth centuries.

Travel details

Buses

The bus details here apply during the **tourist season** between July 1 and September 15 only, after which date the Manali–Leh Highway is officially closed. Most other roads, including the highway from Leh to Srinagar via Kargil, remain open until the end of October. Despite heavy snow falls, the road from Leh to the Nubra Valley over the incredibly high Khardung La is kept open all year.

Leh to: Alchi (1 daily; 3hr); Diskit (Nubra) (2 weekly; 7–8hr); Hemis (2 daily; 1hr 45min); Kargil (2–4 daily; 8–9hr); Lamayuru (2–4 daily; 5hr); Manali (4 daily; 2 days); Matho (3 daily; 1hr); Panamik & Sumur (Nubra) (1 weekly; 8–9hr); Phyang (3 daily; 1hr 15min); Shey (hourly; 30min); Spitok (every 30min–1hr; 20min); Srinagar (1–2 daily except Sun; 2 days); Stok (3 daily; 40min); Tikse (hourly; 45min).

Kargil to: Drass (2 daily; 2hr); Leh (2–4 daily; 9hr); Mulbekh (3 daily; 1hr 30min); Padum (3 weekly; 14–15hr); Panikhar (2 daily; 3hr); Sankhu (3 daily; 1hr 30min); Srinagar (1–2 daily; 11–12hr).

Flights

(**AI** = Indian Airlines, **IT** = Kingfisher Airlines, **9W** = Jet Airways, **6E** = IndiGo, **DN** = Air Deccan, **SG** = SpiceJet, **S2** = JetLite)

Leh to: Delhi (IC, 9W, DN; daily, 1–3 daily in high season; 1hr 15min–3hr); Jammu (IC; 2 weekly; 50min); Srinagar (IC; 1 weekly; 45min).

Haryana and Punjab

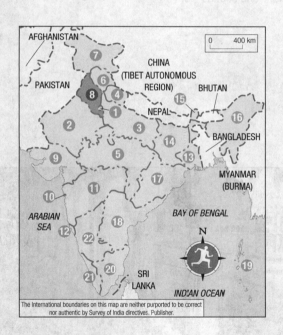

The International boundaries on this map are neither purported to be correct nor authentic by Survey of India directives. Publisher.

CHAPTER 8

Highlights

* **Rock Garden, Chandigarh** This bizarre and seemingly haphazard sculpture garden, assembled from industrial debris by a local eccentric, offers curious contrast to the ordered city that surrounds it. See p.597

* **The Golden Temple, Amritsar** One of the great sights – and sounds – of India; *kirtan* (devotional songs) are performed throughout the day and into the night. See p.605

* **Border ceremony, Wagha** Shorter and more colourful than a cricket match, the border ceremony is a highly charged event, especially on Sundays, when hundreds of people gather. See p.608

▲ Sikh elder, Golden Temple of Amritsar

8

Haryana and Punjab

The prosperous states of **HARYANA** and **PUNJAB** occupy the fertile river plain that extends northwest from Delhi towards the mountains of Kashmir and the Pakistani border. Crossed by the five major tributaries of the **Indus**, the former British-administered region of Punjab ("Land of Five Rivers") was split down the middle at Independence. Indian Muslims fled west into Pakistan, and Hindus east, in an exodus accompanied by horrific massacres. The Sikhs, meanwhile, threw in their lot with India, which they considered a safer option than the homeland of their Muslim arch-enemies. In 1966 prime minister Indira Gandhi, in response to Sikh pressure, moved the Punjab Hills into Himachal Pradesh and divided the rest of the state into two semi-autonomous districts: the predominantly Sikh Punjab, and the 96-percent Hindu Haryana, both governed from the newly built capital of **Chandigarh**.

There is little of tourist interest in the two states other than the beautiful Golden Temple in Amritsar and the wacky Rock Garden of Chandigarh, but the region – known as India's "bread basket" – is very important to the nation's **economy**. Punjabi farmers produce nearly a quarter of India's wheat and one-third of its milk and dairy foods, while Ludhiana churns out ninety percent of the country's woollen goods. Helped by remittance cheques from millions of expatriates in the UK, US and Canada, the state's per capita income is now almost double the national average.

Most travellers simply pass through the region en route to Himachal Pradesh, or to the Indo-Pak border at **Wagha**, but a visit to the Golden Temple in **Amritsar** is well worth the effort. If you want to linger longer, there's also Le Corbusier's experimental city of **Chandigarh**, the Mughal monuments at **Sirhind** and **Pinjore**, the great *gurudwara* at **Anandpur Sahib**, the European-inspired **Kapurthala** or any of the countless brick villages. The inhabitants are extremely hospitable, and many turn out to have family in Toronto or Southall. Crossing Haryana and Punjab en route to, or from, Delhi, you're bound to travel at some stage along part of the longest, oldest and most famous highway in India – the NH-1, alias the **Grand Trunk Road**, stretching 2000km from Peshawar near the rugged Afghan–Pakistan frontier to Kolkata (Calcutta) on the River Hooghly. The first recorded mention of this trade corridor dates from the fourth century BC, when it was known as the Uttar Path (the "North Way").

Some history

Punjab's first urban settlement, dating back to 3000 BC and now known as the **Harappan** Civilization, was invaded by the Aryans around 1700 BC.

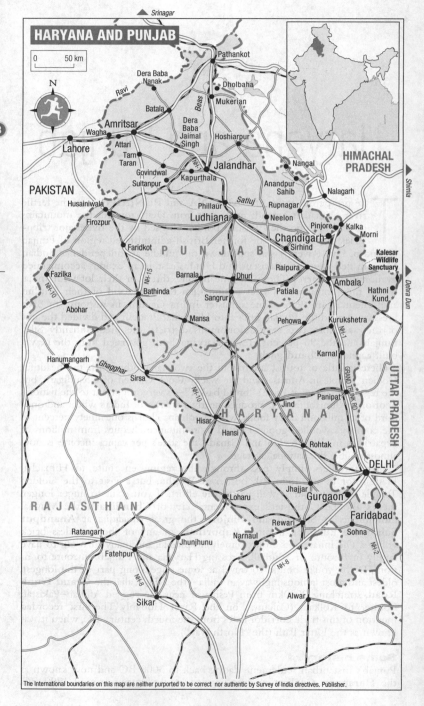

HIMACHAL PRADESH

PAKISTAN

PUNJAB

HARYANA

RAJASTHAN

UTTAR PRADESH

0   50 km

N

Srinagar

Pathankot

Dera Baba Nanak

Dholbaha

Mukerian

Ravi

Beas

Batala

Dera Baba Jaimal Singh

Hoshiarpur

Amritsar

Wagha

Nangal

HIMACHAL PRADESH

Lahore

Attari

Tarn Taran

Jalandhar

Shimla

Govindwal

Kapurthala

Anandpur Sahib

Sultanpur

Nalagarh

Husainiwala

Phillaur

Satluj

Rupnagar

Firozpur

Ludhiana

Neelon

Pinjore

Kalka

Morni

Faridkot

Chandigarh

Sirhind

Dehra Dun

Fazilka

Barnala

Dhuri

Raipura

Kalesar Wildlife Sanctuary

Bathinda

Sangrur

Patiala

Ambala

Abohar

Hathni Kund

Mansa

Pehowa

Kurukshetra

Hanumangarh

Ghagghar

Karnal

Sirsa

Jind

Panipat

Hisar

Hansi

Rohtak

DELHI

Loharu

Jhajjar

Gurgaon

Faridabad

Ratangarh

Rewari

Sohna

Fatehpur

Jhunjhunu

Narnaul

Sikar

Alwar

NH-15

NH-10

NH-1

GRAND TRUNK RD.

NH-8

NH-2

The International boundaries on this map are neither purported to be correct nor authentic by Survey of India directives. Publisher.

Among the Sanskrit scriptures set down in the ensuing **Vedic** age was the **Mahabharata**, whose epic battles drew on real-life encounters between the ancient kings of Punjab at Karnal, 118km north of Delhi. Conquered by the Mauryans in the third century BC, it saw plenty more action as various invading Mughal armies passed through on their way from the Khyber Pass to Delhi – including Babur, who routed Ibrahim Lodi at Panipat in 1526.

Meanwhile, further north, **Sikhism** was beginning to establish itself under the tutelage of Guru Nanak (1469–1539). Based on the notion of a single Formless God, the guru's vision of a casteless egalitarian society found favour with both Hindus and Muslims, in spite of Mughal emperor Aurangzeb's attempts to stamp it out. Suppression actually strengthened the Sikh faith in the long run, inspiring the militaristic and confrontational tenth guru **Gobind Singh** to introduce the Five Ks, part of a rigorous new orthodoxy called the **Khalsa**, or "Community of the Pure" (see p.1371).

Having survived repeated seventeenth-century Afghan invasions, the Sikh nation emerged to fill the power vacuum left by the collapse of the Mughals. Only in the 1840s, after two bloody wars with the British, was the Khalsa army finally defeated. Thereafter, the Sikhs played a vital role in the Raj, helping to quash the Mutiny of 1857. The relationship only soured after the **Jallianwalla Bagh massacre** of 1919 (see p.606), which also ensured that the Punjab's puppet leaders (who hailed the general responsible as a hero) were discredited, leaving the way open for the rise of radicalism.

After the Partition era and Independence, things calmed down enough to allow the new state to grow wealthy on its prodigious agricultural output. As it did, militant Sikhs began to press for the creation of the separate Punjabi-speaking state they called Khalistan. A compromise of sorts was reached in 1966, when the Hindu district of Haryana and the Sikh-majority Punjab were nominally divided. However, the move did not silence the separatists, and in 1977 Indira Gandhi's Congress was trounced in state elections by a coalition that included the Sikh religious party, the **Akali Dal**.

A more sinister element entered the volatile equation with the emergence of an ultra-radical separatist movement led by **Sant Jarnail Singh Bhindranwale**. Covertly supported by the national government (who saw the group as a way to defeat the Akali Dal), Bhindranwale and his band waged a ruthless campaign of sectarian terror in the Punjab which came to a head in 1984, when they occupied Amritsar's Golden Temple; Indira's brutal response, **Operation Blue Star** (see p.603), plunged the Punjab into another ugly bout of communal violence. Four years later, history repeated itself when a less threatening occupation of the temple was crushed by **Operation Black Thunder**. Since then, the Punjabi police have gone on to make considerable advances against the terrorists – helped, for the first time, by the Punjabi peasant farmers, the **Jats**, who had grown tired of the inexorable slaughter. Most Akali Dal factions boycotted the 1992 elections, which saw Congress returned on a 22 percent turnout. Chief minister **Beant Singh** was killed by a car bomb in 1995, but this was the militants' last gasp. Public support had ebbed, and the police, using strong-arm tactics, were able to wipe out the paramilitary groups that had burgeoned during the 1980s. Subsequent state elections have seen a **return to normality**. An Akali Dal/BJP coalition that was thrown out by Congress in 2002 regained power in 2007, with voter turnout back to normal and no paramilitary violence on either occasion. From a tourist point of view, Punjab has regained its political stability, and is quite safe to travel in.

Chandigarh

Chandigarh is the state capital of both Punjab and Haryana, but part of neither, being a Union Territory administered by India's federal government. Its history begins in 1947, when Partition placed the Punjab's main city of Lahore in Pakistan, leaving India's state of Punjab without a capital. Nehru saw this as an opportunity to realize his vision of a city "symbolic of the future of India, unfettered by the traditions of the past, [and] an expression of the nation's faith in the future". The job of designing it went to controversial Swiss-French architect Charles-Edouard Jeanneret, alias **Le Corbusier**.

Begun in 1952, **CHANDIGARH** was to be a ground-breaking experiment in town planning. Le Corbusier's blueprints were for an orderly grid of sweeping boulevards, divided into 29 neat blocks, or **Sectors**, each measuring 800 by 1200 metres, and interspersed with extensive stretches of green. The resulting city has been a source of controversy since its completion in the 1960s. Some applaud Le Corbusier's brainchild as one of the great architectural achievements of the twentieth century, but detractors complain that the design is self-indulgent and un-Indian. Le Corbusier created a city for fast-flowing traffic at a time when few people owned cars, while his cubic concrete buildings are like ovens during the summer – all but uninhabitable without expensive air-conditioning. The city has expanded from the first phase comprising sectors 1 to 30 (there is no Sector 13), through a second phase – sectors 31 to 47 – and is now into the third phase with (half-size) sectors 48 to 61. Satellite towns emulating Chandigarh's grid plan and sterile concrete architecture have also sprung up on either side, with Panchkula in Haryana and Mohali in Punjab easing the pressure on a city left with nowhere else to grow.

Despite Chandigarh's shortcomings, its inhabitants are proud of their capital, which is cleaner, greener and more affluent than other Indian cities of comparable size, and boasts a Rock Garden said to be India's second most visited tourist site after the Taj Mahal.

Arrival, information and city transport

The **Inter-state Bus Terminus** (**ISBT**) is on the south edge of the main commercial and shopping district, Sector 17, but services from Punjab and Himachal Pradesh (Shimla excepted) may leave you at Sector 43 bus stand, connected to the ISBT by regular local buses. Chandigarh's **airport** is 11km south of the city centre, its **railway station** 8km southeast. Both have pre-paid auto-rickshaw counters with fixed rates, as does the ISBT (the booth is at its northern corner). A pre-paid auto to the ISBT from the airport costs Rs83 (a taxi is around Rs200), or Rs51 from the railway station; a pre-paid auto from the ISBT to the Rock Garden is Rs29. There's a rail reservation centre at the ISBT (Mon–Sat 8am–2pm & 2.15–8pm, Sun 8am–2pm).

The **tourist office** at the ISBT (daily 9.30am–1pm & 1.30–5.30pm; ☎0172/270 0054, ⓦchandigarhtourism.gov.in) is helpful, friendly and a good place to check bus and train times as well as any other information, and to get a permit to visit the Capital Complex (see p.597). Their Tour and Travel Wing, CITCO (Chandigarh Industry and Tourism Development Corporation; ☎0172/270 7267, ⓦcitcochandigarh.com), is in the same office. Himachal Pradesh's office (Mon–Sat 10am–5pm; ☎0172/270 8569), next door to the tourist office, is useful for booking HP Tourist Development Corporation tours and buses to HP destinations such as Manali and Shimla. Punjab Tourism have an office at 3 Sector 38-A (☎0172/269 9140); Haryana Tourism's office is at 17–19 Sector 17-B (☎0172/270 2955).

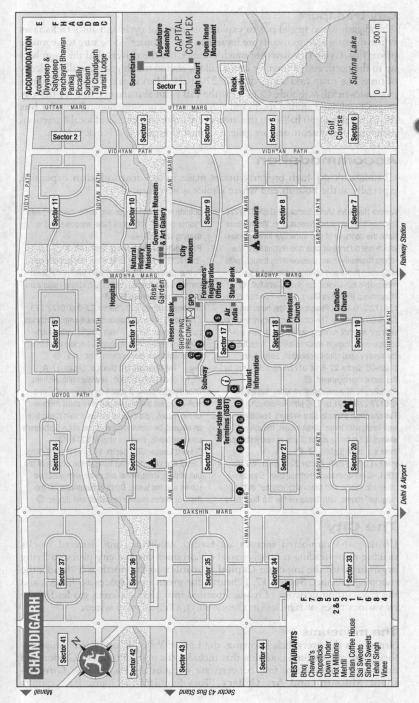

CHANDIGARH

ACCOMMODATION

Aroma	E
Divyadeep & Satyadeep	F
Panchayat Bhawan	H
Panjki	A
Piccadilly	G
Sunbeam	D
Taj Chandigarh	B
Transit Lodge	C

Sector 1

CAPITAL COMPLEX

Legislature Assembly
Secretariat
High Court
Open Hand Monument
Rock Garden
Sukhna Lake

0   500 m

UTTAR MARG
UTTAR MARG

Sector 2
Sector 3
Sector 4
Sector 5
Sector 6
Golf Course

VIDHYAN PATH
VIDHYAN PATH

VIDYA PATH
UDYAN PATH

Sector 11
Sector 10
Sector 9
Sector 8
Sector 7

Government Museum & Art Gallery
Natural History Museum
City Museum

Gurudwara

HIMALAYA MARG
SAROVAR PATH

MADHYA MARG
MADHYA MARG

Hospital
Rose Garden
Reserve Bank
SHOPPING PRECINCT
GPO
Foreigners' Registration Office
State Bank
Air India
Subway
Tourist Information

Sector 15
Sector 16
Sector 17
Sector 18
Sector 19

Catholic Church
Protestant Church

SUKHNA PATH

UDYOG PATH

Sector 24
Sector 23
Sector 22
Sector 21
Sector 20

Inter-state Bus Terminus (ISBT)

JAN MARG
HIMALAYA MARG
SAROVAR PATH

DAKSHIN MARG

Sector 37
Sector 36
Sector 35
Sector 34
Sector 33

Sector 41
Sector 42
Sector 43
Sector 44

Railway Station ▶
Delhi & Airport ▶
▲ Manali
▲ Sector 43 Bus Stand

RESTAURANTS

Bhoj	F
Chawla's	7
Chopsticks	9
Down Under	5
Hot Millions	2 & 5
Mehfil	3
Indian Coffee House	1
Sai Sweets	F
Sindhi Sweets	6
Tehal Singh	8
Vinee	4

595

City transport

Chandigarh is too spread out to explore on foot, but cycle and auto-**rickshaws** cruise the streets. Auto meters are invariably "out of order" so be sure to negotiate prices first. Cycle rickshaws are much cheaper, but the drivers find the long haul up to the north end of town or to the railway station tough going, so allow plenty of time. The main **taxi** stand (℡0172/270 4621; 24hr) is next to the ISBT's pre-paid auto-rickshaw booth. CITCO at the ISBT can also arrange half- or full-day excursions in and around town, and also operates a hop-on, hop-off **tourist bus** (Rs75 full day, Rs50 half-day) that runs every hour on a circuit of local attractions including the museum and art gallery, Capital Complex and Rock Garden.

Accommodation

Chandigarh's sky-high property prices make its **accommodation** expensive, especially at the bottom end where choice is very limited.

Aroma Himalaya Marg, Sector 22-C ℡0172/270 0047 or 8, ⊛www.hotelaroma.com. Vintage cars flank the doorway of this attractive-looking hotel, which has a range of bars and restaurants. The rooms themselves are disappointing though, with laminated floors and scuffed walls, but it's a reasonable fall-back if the *Sunbeam*'s full. ❼

Divyadeep Himalaya Marg, 1090–1 Sector 22-B ℡0172/270 1169. Pleasant budget hotel run by Sai Baba devotees. The rooms are decent enough, with a/c and hot running water, and there's a large rooftop area, though liquor is barred. If it's full, try the nearby (and slightly cheaper) *Satyadeep*, 1102–03 Sector 22-B (℡0172/270 3103), run by the same management. ❹

Panchayat Bhawan Madhya Marg, Sector 18 ℡0172/278 0701 or 2, ✉pbhutchd@yahoo.co.in. The cheapest place to stay in town, hostel-like but well-kept, with large, clean rooms, though not always hot running water. If you're really strapped, there's a dorm (Rs50). ❷–❹

Pankaj Udyog Path, Sector 22-A ℡0172/270 9891, ✉colharsharan@hotmail.com. Squeaky-clean a/c rooms and fancy showers but of the "regular" rooms, only those on the top floor have outside windows; bigger and better "deluxe" and "super deluxe" rooms all have windows and a seating area. ❺–❼

Piccadily Himalaya Marg, Sector 22-B ℡0172/270 7571 or 2, ⊛www.thepiccadily.com. Rather plush establishment with thickly carpeted corridors and rooms, central a/c, classy restaurant, bar and coffee shop. ❼–❽

Sunbeam Udyog Path, Sector 22-B ℡0172/270 8100 to 07, ⊛www.hotelsunbeam.com. Upmarket hotel opposite the ISBT with swish marble lobby and comfortable rooms, though brickwork in front of the windows makes them a bit dark. ❼

🏃 **Taj Chandigarh** Block 9, Sector 17-A ℡0172/661 3000, ⊛www.tajhotels.com. Chandigarh's poshest option by a long chalk, in a well-designed building whose minimalist modern decor in cool, light colours makes it something like an elegant, beautiful version of one of Le Corbusier's concrete boxes. Doubles start at $214. ❾

Transit Lodge ISBT, Sector 17 ℡0172/464 4485. Cheap and cheerful, slap bang in the middle of the bus station, institutional but clean with attached rooms and hot water. Dorm accommodation too (Rs175). Rates include breakfast and dinner. ❹

The City

Chandigarh's numbered **sectors** are further subdivided into lettered blocks, making route-finding relatively easy. Le Corbusier saw the city plan as a living organism, with the imposing **Capital Complex** to the north as a "head", the shopping precinct, **Sector 17**, a "heart", the green open spaces as "lungs", and the crosscutting network of roads, separated into eight different grades for use by various types of vehicles (in theory only), a "circulatory system".

The museums

Situated in the green belt known as the Leisure Valley, Chandigarh's museums form part of a cultural complex that includes the adjoining Rose Garden and open-air theatre where free concerts are occasionally staged. The **Government Museum and Art Gallery** (Tues–Sun 10am–4.30pm; Rs2, camera

Rs5), in Sector 10, houses a sizeable and informatively displayed collection of textiles, Harappan artefacts, miniature paintings and contemporary Indian art, including five original Roerichs and a couple of A.N. Tagore's atmospheric watercolours. The ancient sculptures are the compelling exhibits, notably the Gandhara Buddhas with their delicately carved "wet-look" *lunghis* and distinctly Hellenic features – a legacy of Alexander the Great's conquests. Next door, the small but appropriately modernist **City (Architecture) Museum** (Tues–Sun 10am–5pm; free) illustrates the planning and construction of Chandigarh, with models and photographs in a concrete pavilion based on one of Le Corbusier's designs. Beyond that, the **Natural History Museum** (Tues–Sun 10am–4.45pm; Rs2, camera Rs5) has a few stuffed animals, some bits of fossilized mammoths and diorama depictions of early humans.

The Capital Complex

Tight security following the 1995 assassination (in front of the Assembly building) of Punjab chief minister Beant Singh by Sikh nationalist hardliners means you'll need a letter of permission from the tourist office at the ISBT (see p.594) to visit the **Capital Complex** in Sector 1. The Complex's most imposing edifice is the eleven-storey **Secretariat**, Chandigarh's highest building, which houses ministerial offices for both Haryana and Punjab, and has a roof garden with good views over the city. The resemblance of the **Legislature Assembly Building**, or Vidhan Sabha (home to the legislatures of both states) to a power station is no coincidence: Le Corbusier was allegedly inspired by a stack of cooling towers he saw in Ahmedabad. Opposite the Secretariat is the most colourful building in the Complex, the **High Court** (also serving both states), which is said to incorporate elements of the Buland Darwaza in Fatehpur Sikri, and is decorated inside with huge woollen tapestries. North of this is the black, thirteen-metre-high **Open Hand monument**, Chandigarh's adopted emblem. Weighing all of 45 tonnes, it revolves on ball bearings like a weather vane and stands for "post-colonial harmony and peace".

The Rock Garden

Close to the Capital Complex, the **Rock Garden** (daily: April–Sept 9am–7pm; Oct–March 9am–6pm; Rs10) is a surreal fantasyland fashioned from fragments of shattered plates, neon strip-lights, pots, pebbles, broken bangles and assorted urban-industrial junk. The open-air exhibition is the lifelong labour of retired Public Works Department road inspector **Nek Chand**. Inspired by a recurrent childhood dream, he began construction in 1965. His intention was to create just a small garden, but by the time it was discovered in 1973 – to widespread astonishment – it covered 12 acres. Though it was completely illegal, the city council recognized it as a great artistic endeavour and, in a conspicuously enlightened decision, awarded Chand a salary to continue his work, and a workforce of fifty labourers to help. Opened to the public in 1976, the garden now covers 25 acres and contains several thousand sculptures.

Now over 85, Nek Chand continues to oversee expansion of the site, a labyrinth of more than a dozen different enclosures interconnected by narrow passages, arched walkways, streams, bridges, grottos, waterfalls, battlements and turrets. Stick to the path, or you could end up wandering the maze until the *chowkidar* finds you at closing time.

Eating

Chandigarh has no shortage of **places to eat**. As with everywhere in Punjab, the most popular foodstuff is chicken, cooked in a variety of ways. Sai Sweets,

▲ Rock garden, Chandigarh

below the *Satyadeep* hotel in Sector 22-B, and Sindhi Sweets, 110 Sector 17-B, are two of the best sweet shops in town (Sai Sweets also does great *chana puri*).

Bhoj *Hotel Divyadeep*, 1090–1 Sector 22-B. Classy pure-veg joint run by Sai Baba devotees, serving only thalis at Rs70 and Rs100.

Chawla's Himalaya Marg, Sector 22-C. Small tandoori restaurant renowned for its wonderful, rich cream chicken (Rs220 for a whole one, but a Rs120 half portion will be more than enough).

Chopsticks Near *Hotel Piccadily*, Himalaya Marg, Sector 22. A reasonable Chinese restaurant offering mains, including some pork dishes, at Rs90–170.

Hot Millions Sector 17-D (upstairs). Part of the successful fast-food chain, selling everything from *dosas* to pizzas. This branch also has a good salad bar, and there's an all-you-can-eat lunch and dinner buffet (Rs145 veg/Rs175 non-veg). *Hot Millions 2* in Sector 17-C near *Mehfil* has a popular pub – *Down Under*.

Indian Coffee House Sector 17-E. Budget co-op chain with a limited and predictable menu, including *dosas*, sandwiches and coffee. All dishes are under Rs35.

Mehfil 183–5 Sector 17-C. Preserve of Chandigarh's smart set, and *the* place to sample rich Mughlai and Punjabi cuisine in a/c comfort. Non-veg main dishes are Rs160–200. For dessert, *Baskin-Robbins* is directly opposite.

Tehal Singh Himalaya Marg, 1116–7 Sector 22-B. Very popular tandoori restaurant (main dishes Rs60–130). *Singh's Chicken* right next door provides competition.

Vinee Udyog Path, Sector 22-B, opposite the bus stand. Karahi dishes (chicken or *paneer*) are the speciality at this low-priced restaurant where the kitchen is behind glass, so you can watch them cook up your meal. Non-veg mains Rs65–125.

Listings

Airline offices Air India, 107–8 Sector 17-B
☎0172/270 3510; Indian Airlines, SCO 162–4,
Sector 34 ☎0172/262 4943; Indus Air, airport
☎0172/265 0318; Jet SCO 14–15, Madhya
Marg, Sector 9-D ☎0172/274 1465. Bajaj
Travels, 96–7 Sector 17-C (☎0172/270 8677)
are agents for several international and
domestic airlines.

Banks and exchange Several banks around
Bank Square on the northwest side of Sector 17
change money, including UCO Bank, Punjab
National Bank and State Bank of India. ATMs are
common around town, including one at the station
and two at the ISBT.

Bookshops Capital Book Depot, 3 Sector 17-E;
English Bookshop 30 Sector 17-E.

Hospitals Chandigarh's General Hospital is in
Sector 16 (☎0172/276 8265 or 6), but is not as
good as the PGI, Sector 12 (☎0172/274 6018).

Internet access e-net, Sector 17-E (upstairs from
the *Indian Coffee House*; Rs25/hr).

Left luggage There is a cloakroom in the bus
stand (Rs4/day; 24hr except 12.30–1pm &
8.30–9pm).

Pharmacies Apollo Pharmacy, 1617 Sector 34-A
☎0172/260 4383 (24hr).

Police ☎0172/274 1900.

Shopping Several states run handicraft emporiums
in the Sector 17 shopping complex, among them
Punjab, whose Phulkari store (27 Sector 17-E)
stocks a good range of embroidered silk, woodwork
and traditional painted Punjabi shoes. For quality
handloom products, try the UP emporium in the
building opposite (139–41 Sector 17-C), or the
Khadi Gramodyog in the arcade at the *Shivalikview*
hotel just to the west of the shopping area (28
Sector 17-E): both are strong on block-printed
calico garments, especially *salwar kameese*.

Moving on from Chandigarh

The **railway station**, 8km southeast of the centre, has direct services to Delhi,
Jodhpur, Mumbai, Kolkata (Calcutta), and even, once a week, to Chennai. The
superfast a/c Shatabdi Express runs to Delhi (#2006 & #2012 departing at
7.10am & 6.20pm). Second-class tickets cost Rs430, four times the bus price,
but the journey is far more comfortable and almost twice as fast. Other useful
daily trains include the #4096 Himalayan Queen (dep. 5.28pm, arr. New Delhi
10.15pm), the #4535 Kalka–Amritsar Express (dep. 4.58pm, arr. Amritsar
11.20pm) and the #4887 Kalka–Jodhpur Express (dep. 10.10pm, arr. Jodhpur
5.55pm next day).

Most travellers move on from the city by **bus** from the Inter-state Bus
Terminus (ISBT) in Sector 17. Tickets can be pre-booked at the counters on
the ground floor, or just pay on the bus. Daytime departures to Punjab and
Himachal Pradesh (except Shimla) leave from bus station no. 2 in Sector 43,
which is connected to the ISBT by city bus #8.

The **airport** is 11km south of town (Rs83 by pre-paid auto from the ISBT,
Rs200 by taxi). Indian Airlines fly to Leh, Delhi (also served by Jet Air) and
Mumbai.

Chandigarh is an important transport hub for **Shimla**. The quickest way to
get to Shimla is by bus (4hr): either with the direct Himachal Pradesh or
Haryana Roadways ordinary "express" buses or with more comfortable
deluxe buses, departing every 15min from the ISBT. You can also get there
on the slower but more congenial Viceroys' "Toy Train" (see p.482) from
Kalka 26km to the northeast, and connected to Chandigarh by trains
and frequent buses. The scenic 75-kilometre journey from Kalka to Shimla
takes around 5hr (dep. 4am, 5.30am, 6.30am & 12.10pm). See p.488 for
Shimla–Kalka times.

See p.610 for journey frequencies and durations.

Around Chandigarh

While Chandigarh's architecture may be of limited interest to most travellers, the ornamental Mughal gardens in **Pinjore**, on the northern outskirts of the city, have a much more universal appeal. Southwest of Chandigarh, there are further Mughal ruins at **Sirhind**, a good place to stop overnight between Delhi and Amritsar. **Anandpur Sahib**, the home of the Khalsa movement and one of Sikhism's most venerated shrines, lies just off the Chandigarh–Mandi highway and makes a worthwhile detour, especially during the festival of Holi.

Pinjore

PINJORE, 22km north of Chandigarh and 7km south of Kalka on the Shimla road, is best known for its walled **Yadavindra Gardens**, one of many sites associated with the exile of the Pandavas as chronicled in the Mahabharata. The gardens originally belonged to the rajas of Sirmaur, but under the Mughals Pinjore was taken over by Aurangzeb's foster brother, Fidai Khan, who erected three pleasure palaces for his wife amid the cypress trees. Legend tells that the raja reclaimed his summer retreat by sending a female fruit-seller with a goitre to the imperial impostors. On being told that the woman's unsightly swelling was caused by the local water, the begum and her entourage fled.

These days, the walled gardens harbour a small otter sanctuary, aviary, and zoo, and are popular places for a picnic. One of the three palaces has been converted by Haryana Tourism into a comfortable **hotel** (T01733/230759; ⑤–⑥), which boasts a range of rooms including a dorm (Rs150). Frequent local **buses** connect Pinjore with Chandigarh and Kalka.

Sirhind

Close to the Grand Trunk Road (NH-1) and Northern Railway, **SIRHIND** (the name derives from *Sir-i-Hind*, "the Head or Frontier of Hind or Hindu India"), 48km southwest of Chandigarh, was the capital of the Pathan Suri sultans and the site of an important *caravansarai*. Today, only a couple of minor-league Mughal palaces, hot baths and pleasure pavilions remain from the illustrious past, but it's still a pleasant overnight stop between Delhi and Amritsar.

The site of the Mughal ruins, **Aam-Khas-Bagh**, lies 2.5km north of the town proper. Here you'll see Sirhind's best-preserved monuments, encircled by the high walls of Sher Shah Suri's sixteenth-century fort. Approached via a tree- and fountain-lined walkway, the ruins of the old baths, or **hammam**, enclose a giant circular well whose water was channelled into geometric bathing pools outside. Nearby stand the ruins of Emperor Shah Jahan's residence, the **Daulat Khana**. Just behind the tourist complex, in much better shape, is the seventeenth-century **Sheesh Mahal** or "Palace of Mirrors". **Fatehgarh Sahib**, a pristine white *gurudwara* 1.5km north of the tourist complex, stands in memory of Guru Gobind Singh's two youngest sons who were bricked up alive in the fort by the Mughal emperor Aurangzeb for not embracing Islam. Cover your head to enter the *gurudwara*. Next door to Fatehgarh Sahib, the fourteenth-century *dargah* (burial shrine), dedicated to a Sufi saint, attracts busloads of Muslim pilgrims and provides a sharp reminder of the friction caused by the proximity of religions so fundamentally opposed.

Practicalities

Regular **buses** run between Chandigarh and Sirhind, a stopping-point on the main Delhi–Amritsar **railway**. The railway station lies 5km from the tourist complex. Buses from Amritsar usually drop passengers at the Grand Trunk Road intersection, 7km south of Aam-Khas-Bagh – catch a local bus into town or take a shared auto-rickshaw (Rs10).

The PTDC's *Maulsarai Tourist Complex*, in a small eighteenth-century summer palace overlooking gardens and the Sheesh Mahal, was closed at last check pending transfer to new management. The **PTDC Bougainvillea Tourist Complex** (℡01763/229170; ❸–❹), 3km up the GT Road towards Amritsar, has ordinary, air-cooled and a/c rooms, as well as a restaurant. Visitors are welcome to stay overnight at the *gurudwara* on a donation basis.

Anandpur Sahib

The gleaming-white, citadel-like *gurudwara* at **ANANDPUR SAHIB** ("The City of Bliss") stands 75km north of Chandigarh. Known as the **Gurudwara Kesgarh Sahib**, it is one of the holiest Sikh shrines, commemorating the birth of the Khalsa movement by Guru Gobind Singh three hundred years ago. With surrounding citadels, gates and ramparts, its fortress-like appearance hints at its difficult past and the long years of struggle against Muslim domination and jealous Hindu kingdoms.

Guru Gobind Singh's father, Guru Tegh Bahadur, laid the foundations in 1664, but was beheaded by the zealous Mughal emperor Aurangzeb in Delhi for refusing to convert to Islam. His head was brought back to Anandpur Sahib and cremated at the spot now marked by the shrine of **Gurudwara Sis Ganj**. Guru Gobind Singh built the fortifications which withstood a string of onslaughts from hostile neighbours, and, on March 30, 1699, initiated five disciples into the Khalsa, whose goals were to support the poor, fight oppression, discard dogma, superstition and caste, and be warriors of their faith.

All are welcome inside the *gurudwara* (cover your head and remove shoes) to listen to the devotional singing *(kirtan)* and accompanying readings by *granthis* from the Sikh holy book, the *Guru Granth Sahib*. Every year on the first day of Chaitra (11 March 2009, 1 March 2010, 20 March 2011), the festival of **Hola Mohalla** takes place below Kesgarh Sahib, attracting thousands of people. It celebrates Khalsa and reinterprets the Hindu festival of colour, Holi; the festivities include displays of horsemanship and swordsmanship by the *nihangs* – an orthodox sect devoted to the great guru.

Practicalities

Accommodation at Anandpur Sahib is limited to the *gurudwara*, though further afield at **Rupnagar** (also called Ropar), 45km south on the Chandigarh–Mandi highway, there's the *Pinkcassia Tourist Complex* (℡01881/222097; ❹), set in pleasant riverside grounds. Local **buses** run between Chandigarh, Rupnagar and Anandpur Sahib and a new railway line between Anandpur Sahib and New Delhi via Sirhind is "in the pipeline".

Pathankot

The dusty town of **PATHANKOT**, 270km north of Chandigarh and 101km to the northeast of Amritsar, is an important cantonment and railway junction, close to the frontier with Pakistan and near the borders with Himachal Pradesh and Jammu. Many travellers pass through to pick up bus connections to Dharamsala, Dalhousie, Chamba and Kashmir, or to take the slow train east through the picturesque Kangra Valley.

Pathankot has a few **hotels**, should you need to spend the night. The *Atlas Guest House*, 50m east of the station on Railway Road (℡0186/222 1397; ❷), is a good budget option with clean but bare rooms, failing which, the *Tourist Hotel* (℡0186/222 0660; ❷), a few metres further along Railway Road, has reasonable rooms including some tiny singles (❶). The well-kept railway retiring rooms (℡0186/222 0046; ❶) are better value, with a choice of ordinary or a/c rooms, the latter containing sofas, carpets and private bathrooms with hot water. The *Venice*, south of the station on Dhangu Road (℡0186/222 5061, Ⓦ www.venice hotelindia.com; ❹–❻), is Pathankot's top business hotel, but lacks atmosphere.

Himachal Pradesh Tourism has a downbeat but friendly **tourist office** at the railway station (Mon–Fri and every other Sat 10am–5pm, but often closed for no apparent reason; ℡0186/222 0316). The slow narrow-gauge passenger **trains** to Jogindernagar (daily 2.15am & 9.20pm; 7hr 15min–9hr 25min; plus four trains to Baijnath only) wind through the scenic Kangra Valley and make a pleasant alternative to the busy road to both Dharamsala (change at Kangra) and the Kullu Valley (bus from Jogindernagar). Other useful trains include the daily #3152 Jammu–Sealdah Express to Lucknow, Varanasi and Kolkata (Calcutta), and the overnight #4646 Shalimar Express to New Delhi. **Taxis** to Dharamsala cost around Rs1000 (3hr). Pathankot also has a busy **bus station**, on Railway Road, 300m west of the rail station, with frequent departures to Amritsar, Jammu and various parts of Himachal Pradesh (see p.610 for details).

Amritsar

The Sikhs' holy city of **AMRITSAR** is the largest city in Punjab: noisy, dirty and hopelessly congested. Its one saving grace is the fabled **Golden Temple**, whose domes soar above the teeming streets. Amritsar is also an important staging-post for those crossing the Indo–Pakistani frontier at Wagha, 29km west (see p.610).

Some history

Amritsar was founded in 1577 by **Ram Das**, the fourth Sikh guru, beside a bathing pool famed for its healing powers. The land around the tank was granted in perpetuity by the Mughal Akbar to the Sikhs (who paid off the local Jat farmers to avoid any future dispute over ownership). When merchants moved in to take advantage of the strategic location on the Silk Route, Amritsar expanded rapidly, gaining a grand new temple under Ram Das's son and heir, **Guru Arjan Dev**. Sacked by Afghans in 1761, the shrine was rebuilt by the Sikhs' greatest secular leader, **Maharaja Ranjit Singh**, who also donated the gold used in its construction.

Amritsar's **twentieth-century** history has been blighted by a series of appalling **massacres**. The first occurred in 1919, when thousands of unarmed civilian demonstrators were gunned down without warning by British troops in **Jallianwalla Bagh** (see box, p.606) – an atrocity that inspired Gandhi's Non-Co-operation Movement. Following the collapse of the Raj, Amritsar experienced some of the worst communal blood-letting ever seen on the Subcontinent. The Golden Temple, however, remained unaffected by the volatile politics of post-Independence Punjab until the 1980s, when as part of a protracted and bloody campaign for the setting up of a Sikh homeland, heavily armed fundamentalists under the preacher-warrior Sant Jarnail Singh **Bhindranwale** occupied the Akal Takht, a building in the Golden Temple complex that has traditionally been the seat of Sikh religious authority.

The siege was brought to an end in early June 1984, when prime minister Indira Gandhi ordered an inept paramilitary attack on the temple, code-named **Operation Blue Star**. Bhindranwale was killed along with two hundred soldiers and two thousand others, including pilgrims trapped inside.

Widely regarded as an unmitigated disaster, Blue Star led directly to the assassination of Indira Gandhi by her Sikh bodyguards just four months later, and provoked the worst riots in the city since Partition. Nevertheless, the Congress government seemed to learn little from its mistakes. In 1987, Indira's son, Rajiv Gandhi, reneged on an important accord with the Sikhs' main religious party, the Akali Dal, thereby strengthening the hand of the separatists, who retaliated by occupying the temple for a second time. This time, the army responded with greater restraint, leaving **Operation Black Thunder** to the Punjab police. Neither as well provisioned nor as well motivated as Bhindranwale's martyrs, the fundamentalists eventually surrendered.

Arrival, information and city transport

Amritsar's **airport**, served by Indian Airlines and Air India flights from Delhi, as well as some international flights, lies 12km northwest of the city. Taxis (around Rs200) and auto-rickshaws (Rs100) run to the town centre. The **railway station** is conveniently located in the centre of town, north of the old

city. The large, new **bus stand** is off GT Road on the eastern edge of the city centre. PTDC's **tourist office** (Mon–Sat 9am–5pm; ☎0183/240 2452), at the *Pegasus/Palace Hotel* opposite the railway station on Queens Road, is friendly enough, but its staff are not always very well informed, and the nearby *Grand Hotel* is sometimes a better bet for information.

You may find Amritsar too large and labyrinthine to negotiate on foot; if you're crossing town or are in a hurry, flag down an **auto–rickshaw**. Otherwise, stick to **cycle rickshaws**, which are the best way to get around the narrow, packed streets of the old quarter.

Accommodation

Amritsar's numerous **hotels** are spread out all over the city. While mid–range and upmarket accommodation is plentiful, budget options are limited; one solution is to stay in one of the Golden Temple's *gurudwaras* (see box opposite).

Bharat off Railway Link Rd ☎0183/222 7536, ✉bharat_hotel@yahoo.com. Clean, reasonably priced and handy for the station, offering a range of rooms of varying size, all with attached bathrooms (the best rates with hot showers; bucket hot water in the cheapest). Touts in the street below will try to steer you into soundalikes. ②–④

Blue Moon Mall Rd ☎0183/222 0759, ✉hotelbluemoon@gmail.com. Friendly, helpful place, much better value than its more expensive competitors. There's a decent restaurant (see p.609) open to nonresidents. ⑤–⑥

Grand Queens Rd, opposite the railway station ☎0183/256 2977, ⊛www.hotelgrand.in. Neat, clean, convenient and central with rooms around a pleasant garden courtyard, though windows all face inward. There's an adjacent bar decorated with Hollywood movie posters. The friendly manager can organize a share-taxi to Wagha for the border ceremony. ④–⑤

Mohan International Albert Rd ☎0183/222 7801, ⊛www.mohaninternationalhotel.com. One of Amritsar's top hotels but overpriced, though it does have a/c, room service, a 24hr coffee shop and a pool. Popular in season (Nov–March) for Punjabi wedding receptions which are colourful but noisy. Rates include breakfast. ⑧

Mrs Bhandari's Guest House 10 Cantonment ☎0183/222 8509, ⊛bhandari_guesthouse.tripod .com. Wonderful old-fashioned rooms with wood fires and bathtubs in a colonial home with lawns, gardens and a small swimming pool. "British-style" three-course meals are available but pricey. You can

camp in the grounds for Rs170 per person. Popular with overlanders, it's become an Amritsar institution, as has the centegenarian Mrs Bhandari. ⑥–⑦

Pegasus/Palace Opposite the railway station ☎0183/256 5111. This place has seen better days, but it's conveniently located and reasonably priced. Rooms are attached, with geysers in the pricier ones and bucket hot water in the cheaper ones. Discounts in winter. ③–④

Ritz Plaza 45 Mall Rd ☎0183/256 2836. Low-key but reasonably classy establishment, though it gets mixed reviews, with central a/c, good-sized rooms and a relaxed atmosphere, surrounded by lawns; facilities include a pool, lounge bar, 24hr coffee shop and international restaurant. Wheelchair friendly with an adapted room. ⑧

Sita Niwas 61 Sita Niwas Rd ☎0183/254 3092, ✆256 2762. A good-value and popular budget option near *Guru Ram Das Niwas* and the Golden Temple, with wide range of rooms, most en suite, and 24hr hot water. ②–④

Skylark 79 Railway Link Rd ☎0183/265 2053. One of the better hotels on this street opposite the station; the rooms, if slightly shabby, are huge, with comfortable beds and hot water round the clock. ④

Tourist Guest House Hide Market, near Bhandari Bridge, GT Rd ☎0183/255 3830, ✉bubblesgoolry @yahoo.com. Popular with budget travellers since the "hippy trail" days, offering a variety of rooms. The cheapest are rather dingy with shared bathrooms; attached ones with hot water are quite nice and still not pricey. Ignore commission-hungry rickshaw-wallahs telling you it's full. ②–③

The City

The Golden Temple stands in the heart of the **old town**, itself a maze of narrow lanes and bazaars. Eighteen fortified **gateways** punctuate the aptly named **Circular Road**, of which only one (to the north) is original. Skirting the edge of the old quarter, the railway line forms a sharp divide between

The gurudwaras

Undoubtedly the most authentic places to stay in Amritsar are the Golden Temple's five **gurudwaras**. Intended for use by Sikh pilgrims, these charitable institutions also open their doors to foreign tourists, who are sometimes limited to a maximum of three nights. Lodging at *gurudwaras* is free, as is the Sikh custom, but donations are expected. The first building as you approach the *gurudwaras*, which are on the east side of the temple, is the *Guru Arjan Dev Niwas*, which has the check-in counter for all the *gurudwaras* and simple but spacious rooms. The most comfortable of the five *gurudwaras* is the new, clean and excellent-value *Guru Hargobind Niwas*. The *Sri Guru Nanak Niwas* was where Bhindranwale and his men holed up prior to the Golden Temple siege in 1984.

Apart from the inevitable dawn chorus of throat-clearing, the downside of staying in a *gurudwara* is that facilities can be basic (*charpoi* beds and communal wash-basins in the central courtyard are the norm) and **security** can be a problem. During festivals, rooms and beds are at a premium and tourists are less likely to find space here.

the bazaar and the more spacious British-built side of the city. Further north, long straight tree-lined streets eventually peter out into leafy residential suburbs. The neat military barracks of the **cantonment** form the north-western limits of the city.

The Golden Temple

Even visitors without a religious bone in their bodies cannot fail to be moved by Amritsar's resplendent **Golden Temple**, spiritual centre of the Sikh faith and open to all. Built by **Guru Arjan Dev** in the late sixteenth century, the richly gilded **Harmandir** rises from the middle of an artificial rectangular lake, connected to the surrounding white-marble complex by a narrow causeway. Every Sikh tries to make at least one pilgrimage here during their lifetime to listen to the sublime music (*shabad kirtan*), readings from the *Adi Granth* and also to bathe in the purifying waters of the temple tank – the **Amrit Sarovar** or "Pool of Immortality-Giving Nectar".

The best time to visit is early morning, to catch the first rays of sunlight gleaming on the bulbous golden domes and reflecting in the waters of the Amrit Sarovar. Sunset and evenings are an excellent time to tune in to the beautiful music performed in the Harmandir. The helpful information office (daily 7am–8pm) to the right of the main entrance organizes **guided tours**, provides details on temple accommodation and has books and leaflets about the temple and Sikh faith.

The Parikrama

The principal north entrance to the temple, the **Darshini Deori**, leads under a Victorian **clocktower** to a flight of steps, from where you catch your first glimpse of the Harmandir, floating serenely above the glassy surface of the Amrit Sarovar. Dropping down as a reminder of the humility necessary to approach God, the steps end at the polished marble **Parikrama** that surrounds the tank, its smooth white stones set with the names of those who contributed to the temple's construction.

The shrines on the north edge of the enclosure are known as the **68 Holy Places**. Arjan Dev, the fifth guru, told his followers that a visit to these was equivalent to a pilgrimage around all 68 of India's most sacred Hindu sites. Several have been converted into a **Gallery of Martyrs**, in which paintings of glorious but gory episodes from Sikh history are displayed.

The Jallianwalla Bagh massacre

Only 100m northeast of the Golden Temple, a narrow lane leads between two tall buildings to **Jallianwalla Bagh** memorial park (daily: summer 6am–9pm; winter 7am–8pm), site of one of the bloodiest atrocities committed by the British Raj.

In 1919, a series of one-day strikes, or *hartals*, was staged in Amritsar in protest against the recent **Rowlatt Act**, which enabled the British to imprison without trial any Indian suspected of sedition. When the peaceful demonstrations escalated into sporadic looting, the lieutenant governor of Punjab declared martial law and called for reinforcements from Jalandhar. A platoon of infantry arrived soon after, led by **General R.E.H. Dyer**.

Despite a ban on public meetings, a mass demonstration was called by Mahatma Gandhi for April 13, the Sikh holiday of Baisakhi. The venue was a stretch of waste ground in the heart of the city, hemmed in by high brick walls and with only a couple of alleys for access. An estimated twenty thousand people gathered in Jallianwalla Bagh for the meeting. However, before any speakers could address the crowd, Dyer and his 150 troops, stationed on a patch of high ground in front of the main exit, opened fire without warning. By the time they had finished firing, ten to fifteen minutes later, hundreds of unarmed demonstrators lay dead and dying, many of them shot in the back while clambering over the walls. Others perished after diving for cover into the well that still stands in the middle of the *bagh*.

No one knows exactly how many people were killed. Official estimates put the death toll at 379, with 1200 injured, although the final figure may well have been several times higher. Indian sources quote a figure of two thousand dead. Hushed up for over six months in Britain, the Jallianwalla Bagh massacre caused an international outcry when the story finally broke. It also proved seminal in the Independence struggle, prompting Gandhi to initiate the widespread civil disobedience campaign that played such a significant part in ridding India of its colonial overlords.

Moving first-hand accounts of the horrific events of April 13, 1919, and contemporary pictures and newspaper reports are displayed in Jallianwalla Bagh's small **martyrs gallery**. The **well**, complete with chilling bullet holes, has been turned into a memorial to the victims.

Four glass-fronted booths punctuate the Parikrama. Seated in each is a priest, or **granthi**, intoning verses from the *Adi Granth*. The continuous readings are performed in shifts; passing pilgrims touch the steps in front of the booths with their heads and leave offerings of money.

At the east end of the Parikrama, the two truncated **Ramgarhia Minars** – brick watchtowers whose tops were blasted off during Operation Blue Star – overlook the Guru-ka-Langar and the main bathing **ghats**. Hang around here long enough and you'll see a fair cross-section of modern Sikh society parade past: families of Jat farmers, NRIs (Non-Resident Indians) on holiday from Britain and North America, and the odd group of fierce-looking warriors carrying lances, sabres and long curved daggers. Distinguished by their deep-blue knee-length robes and saffron turbans, the ultra-orthodox **nihangs** (literally "crocodiles") are devotees of the militaristic tenth guru, Gobind Singh.

The Guru-ka-Langar

For Sikhs, no pilgrimage to the Golden Temple is considered complete without a visit to the **Guru-ka-Langar**. The giant communal canteen, which overlooks the eastern entrance to the temple complex, provides **free food** to all comers, regardless of creed, colour, caste or gender. Sharing meals with strangers in this way is intended to reinforce one of the central tenets of the Sikh faith, the principle of equality, instigated by the third guru, **Amar Das**, in the sixteenth century to break down caste barriers.

Some ten thousand chapati and black dhal dinners are dished up here each day in an operation of typical Sikh efficiency, which you can witness for yourself by joining the queues that form outside the hall (open 24hr). Thousands of pilgrims at a time pile in to take their places on the long coir floor-mats. The meal begins only after grace has been sung by a volunteer, or *sevak*, and continues until everyone has eaten their fill. By the time the tin trays have been collected up and the floors swept for the next sitting, another crowd of pilgrims has gathered at the gates, and the cycle starts again. Although the meals are paid for out of the temple's coffers, most visitors leave a small donation in the boxes in the yard outside.

The Akal Takht

Directly opposite the ceremonial entrance to the Harmandir, the **Akal Takht** is the second most sacred shrine in the Golden Temple complex. A symbol of God's authority on earth, it was built by Guru Hargobind in the seventeenth century and came to house the Shiromani Gurudwara Parbandhak Committee, the religious and political governing body of the Sikh faith founded in 1925.

During the 1984 siege, **Bhindranwale** and his army used this golden-domed building as their headquarters, fortifying it with sandbags and machine-gun posts. When Indian paratroopers tried to storm the shrine, they were mown down in their hundreds while crossing the courtyard in front of it: the reason why the army ultimately resorted to much heavier-handed tactics to end the siege. Positioned at the opposite end of the Amrit Sarovar, tanks pumped a salvo of high-explosive squash-head shells into the delicate facade, reducing it to rubble within seconds. The destruction of the Akal Takht offended Sikh sensibilities more than any other aspect of the operation. The shrine has been largely rebuilt and now looks almost the same as it did before June 6, 1984. Decorated with elaborate inlay, its ground floor is where the *Adi Granth* is brought each evening from the Harmandir, borne in a gold and silver paladin.

The Jubi Tree

The gnarled old **Jubi Tree** in the northwest corner of the compound was planted 450 years ago by the Golden Temple's first high priest, or *Babba Buddhaya*, and is believed to have special powers. Barren women wanting a son hang strips of cloth from its branches, while marriage deals are traditionally struck in its shade for good luck – a practice frowned upon by the modern temple administration.

The Harmandir

Likened by one guru to "a ship crossing the ocean of ignorance", the triple-storey **Harmandir**, or "Golden Temple of God" was built by Arjan Dev to house

---

Golden rules

Visitors of all nationalities and religions are allowed into the Golden Temple provided they respect a few basic **rules**, enforced by patrolling guards. Firstly, tobacco, alcohol and drugs of any kind are forbidden. Before entering, you should also leave your shoes at the free cloakrooms, cover your head (cotton scarves are available outside the main entrance – or wear your Kullu hat) and wash your feet in the pool below the steps. **Photography** is permitted around the pool, but not inside any of the shrines.

the *Adi Granth* (Original Book), which he compiled from teachings of all the Sikh gurus; it is the focus of the Sikh faith. The temple has four doors indicating it is open to people of all faiths and all four caste divisions of Hindu society. The large dome and roof, covered with 100kg of gold leaf, is shaped like an inverted lotus, symbolizing the Sikhs' concern for temporal as well as spiritual matters.

The long causeway, or **"Guru's Bridge"**, which joins the *mandir* to the west side of the Amrit Sarovar, is approached via an ornate archway, the **Darshani Deorh**. As you approach the sanctum check out the amazing Mughal-style inlay work and floral gilt above the doors and windows.

The **interior** of the temple – decorated with yet more gold and silver, adorned with ivory mosaics and intricately carved wood panels – is dominated by the enormous **Adi Granth**, which rests on a sumptuous throne beneath a jewel-encrusted silk canopy. Before his death in 1708, Guru Gobind Singh, who revised the *Adi Granth*, declared that he was to be the last living guru, and that the tome would take over after him – hence its full title, the *Guru Granth Sahib*. *Granthis* intone continuous readings from the text as the worshippers file past, accompanied by singers and musicians – all relayed by loudspeakers around the complex. Known as Shri Akhand Path, a single continuous reading of the *Guru Granth Sahib* is carried out in three-hour shifts and takes around 48 hours to complete.

Eating

For cheaper food, try the simple vegetarian **dhabas** around the Golden Temple and bus stand, which serve cheap and tasty *puris* and *chana* dhal. Local specialities include **Amritsari fish** (fillets of river fish – sole fish is the best, but *singara* is cheaper – fried in a spicy batter), as well as *dal pinni* and *matthi*, sweets made from lentils that are sold at places such as *Mahajan* on Hall Bazaar.

Bharawan da Dhaba Near the City Hall. One of the best *dhabas* in Amritsar, though it's now grown into a full-sized restaurant, serving simple and inexpensive but good veg curries (Rs30–70).
Bubby Vaishno Dhaba Opposite the Golden Temple main entrance. A handy place for veg curries (Rs20–70), thalis (Rs40–70) and breakfast options such as *parathas* or *puris*, plus a few south Indian dishes for good measure.
Chicken King and **Chicken Inn** 1 Pink Plaza Market, outside Hall Gate. Two grubby and insalubrious-looking *dhabas* which double up as drinking dens, but they cook all the food out front. The Amritsari fish (Rs80 per quarter kilo) is

Bedlam at the border

Every evening as sunset approaches, the **India-Pakistan border** closes for the night with a spectacular and somewhat Pythonesque show. It takes place at a remote little place 27km west of Amritsar called **Wagha** (the nearest town, 2km away, is Attari), connected by frequent minibuses to Amritsar. Hundreds, if not thousands, of Indians make their way westwards to Wagha (and Pakistanis eastwards) to watch the popular tourist attraction from specially erected stands.

Indian guards sporting outrageous moustaches and outlandish hats perform synchronized speed marching along a 100-metre walkway to the border gate where they turn and stomp back. Raucous cheering, clapping and much blowing of horns accompanies the spectacle. Guards on the Pakistan side then emulate their neighbours' efforts to much the same sort of cacophony on the other side of the gate. The guards strut their military catwalk several times and then vanish into the guardhouse. Flags are simultaneously lowered, the gates slammed shut and the crowds on either side rush forward for a massive and congenial photo session. On both sides, more empathy than ever occurs on a cricket pitch permeates the air; photos are taken with the stone-faced guards and then everyone heads home – back to business as usual.

succulent and the tandoori chicken's pretty good too (Rs100 for a plate of chicken tikka).

Crystal Crystal Chowk. One of the city's most popular restaurants, with Indian, Chinese and Western dishes (non-veg mains Rs150–200) served in comfortable surroundings, or from "fast-food" outlets on the street.

Kesar da Dhaba Between Golden Temple and Durgiana Temple. A limited menu of basic veg curries (Rs20–60) in an establishment that's been going since 1916.

Makhan Fish House Lawrence Rd. A little *dhaba* ("old and famous", it proclaims) where you can tuck into tasty Amritsari fish (*singara*) at Rs120 for a quarter kilo.

New Punjabi Rasoli By Jallianwalla Bagh. Indian vegetarian dishes, plus some Chinese and Continental, at reasonable prices (Rs40–65). Most of the Indian dishes involve *paneer* (the *paneer* tomato is good), but there's also a delicious mushroom tikka.

Prakash Meet Shop, Sunder Meat Shop and **Mama Meat Shop** Maqbool Rd, 500m north of Mall Rd. This trio of locally renowned *dhabas* are an Amritsar institution, frying up spicy mutton tikka or (for the brave) brain curry, on *tawas* (griddles) out front, at Rs70 a throw.

Sindhi Coffee House Opposite Ram Bagh. Tinted windows and tablecloths, and a menu that includes thalis, biriyanis and some Sindhi specialities, with dishes in the Rs80–110 range.

Spice Room *Blue Moon Hotel*, Mall Rd. Mainly Chinese dishes, with the accent on spicy, plus some Indian and Western options. Main dishes go for Rs110–195.

Listings

Airlines Air India, *MK International Hotel*, Ranjit Ave ℡0183/250 8122 or 33; Indian Airlines, 39-A Court Rd ℡0183/221 3392 or 3; Indus Air, airport ℡0183/221 4061; Jet, airport ℡0183/250 8003 or 4.

Banks and exchange There are ATMs across town, including two at the train station and several around Jallianwalla Bagh. There's a clutch of forex bureaux opposite the train station on Railway Link Rd, many of which will change Pakistani rupees.

Hospitals The best in the city are Kakkar Hospital, Green Avenue ℡0183/250 6015, and Munilal Chopra Hospital, 361 Mall Rd ℡0183/222 2072.

Internet access Railtel Cyber Express, outside the train station (Rs25/hr).

Left luggage Baggage can be left for short periods at the Golden Temple's *gurudwaras*, or at the railway station cloakroom.

Shopping Tablas (hand-drums), harmonia and other musical instruments are available at the shops outside the Golden Temple, where you can also buy cheap cassettes of the beautiful *kirtan* played in the shrine itself. Other possible souvenirs include a pair of traditional *Arabian Nights*-style Punjabi leather slippers, sold at stalls east of the temple's main entrance.

Swimming pools The *Mohan International* and *Ritz Plaza* hotels allow nonresidents discretionary use of their pools (Rs130–200).

Moving on from Amritsar

Amritsar is a major hub for traffic heading northeast to Kashmir, southeast towards Delhi and Chandigarh (the main jumping-off place for Shimla and central HP), and west to the Pakistani border at Wagha.

The **bus station** is on GT Road (NH-1), north of the old city. Private buses, including a/c services, leave from around the railway station or outside Hall Gate (that is, on the street just north of Hall Hate/Gandhi Gate). Agencies outside Hall Gate and on Queens Road operate deluxe and a/c buses to **Delhi** (8hr) and **Chandigarh** (4–5hr). For **Pathankot** (3hr) and other connections to Himachal Pradesh, you are restricted to state transport buses. Delhi, 475km away, is a long and tiring road journey – most travellers prefer to go by train.

The best **trains** for Delhi are the daily superfast all-a/c chaircar Amritsar–New Delhi Shatabdis – the #2014 (dep. 5.10am, arr. 11.05am) and the #2030/2032 (dep. 5pm, arr. 10.50pm). If you prefer to travel overnight, there's the #2904 Golden Temple Mail (dep. 9.35pm, arr. 7.10am), which continues to Mumbai (arr. 6.30am the following day). Other trains include the daily #3050 Amritsar–Howrah Express (dep. 6.15pm) via Varanasi (arr. 7pm next day) to Kolkata (arr. Howrah 3.45m the day after that), and the twice-weekly #9782

Amritsar–Jaipur Express (Tues & Thurs 6pm), which is a little bit faster than the #9772 (Wed & Sun 2.30pm) – both arrive in Jaipur at 9.35am.

The **airport** is 12km northwest of town (Rs200 by taxi, Rs100 by auto). A rundown of destinations, frequencies and journey times can be seen below.

To Pakistan

For **Pakistan**, take one of the frequent buses to **Attari**, from where it's just 2km to the border at **Wagha**, or hire a taxi or auto from Amritsar. Rickshaws are available between Attari and Wagha. You'll have to cross into Pakistan by foot – it can take up to two hours to complete formalities. Tourists just wishing to watch the bizarre border spectacle can rent taxis (Rs400) or auto-rickshaws (Rs200) for the round trip. Depending on the political situation, **cross-border train** operations are sometimes suspended, but if all is well, the #4607 Amritsar–Lahore Samjhauta Express train (Mon & Thurs) leaves Amritsar for Lahore at 9.30am, reaching Attari for Indian border formalities at 10.10am. On the Pakistani side, it is scheduled to leave Wagha at 11.30am, to reach Lahore at 4.15pm but is invariably delayed. In the other direction, the #4608 Lahore–Amritsar Express (Tues & Fri) departs at 8.35am, reaching Wagha at 9.10pm, and is scheduled to depart from the Indian side at 2.20pm, arriving in Amritsar at 3pm.

Travel details

Trains

Amritsar to: Agra (3–4 daily; 10hr 55min–16hr 55min); Ambala (for Chandigarh 12–18 daily; 3hr 19min–6hr 45min); Delhi (10–14 daily; 5hr 50min–11hr 55min); Jaipur (2 weekly; 19hr 5min); Kolkata (2 daily; 36hr 45min–45hr 25min); Mumbai (3 daily; 30hr 5min–42hr 5min); Pathankot (2 daily; 2hr 25min–2hr 50min); Varanasi (2–3 daily; 20hr 45min–24hr 45min).

Chandigarh to: Ambala (for Amritsar 8–10 daily; 38min–1hr); Delhi (6–8 daily; 3hr 10min–5hr); Jodhpur (1 daily; 18hr 15min); Kalka (for Shimla 7 daily; 45min–1hr); Kolkata (1 daily; 30hr); Mumbai (1–2 daily; 20hr 15min–26hr 50min).

Pathankot to: Amritsar (2 daily; 2hr 5min–2hr 20min); Delhi (4–5 daily; 10hr 10min–11hr 50min); Jodhpur (1 daily; 19hr 15min); Jogindernagar (2 daily; 7hr 15min–9hr 25min); Kolkata (1 daily; 42hr); Varanasi (1 daily; 27hr 45min).

Buses

Amritsar to: Chandigarh (every 10min; 5–6hr); Delhi (32 daily; 8–10hr); Pathankot (every 15min; 3hr); Wagha/Attari (every 20min; 45min).

Chandigarh to: Agra (1 daily; 10hr); Amritsar (every 10min; 5–6hr); Anandpur Sahib (8 daily; 2–3hr); Chamba (3 daily; 12hr); Dehra Dun (4 daily; 4hr); Delhi (43 daily; 6hr); Dharamsala (19 daily; 7–8hr); Haridwar (8 daily; 6hr); Jaipur (8 daily; 11hr); Kalka (22 daily; 40min); Kullu (10 daily; 9hr); Manali (hourly; 10hr); Pathankot (every 30–40min; 6hr); Pinjore (every 20min; 30min); Rishikesh (2 daily; 6hr); Shimla (every 10min; 4hr–4hr 30min); Sirhind (hourly; 1hr 30min).

Pathankot to: Amritsar (every 15min; 3hr); Chamba (14 daily; 5hr); Chandigarh (every 30–40min; 6hr); Dalhousie (12 daily; 3hr 30min); Delhi (11 daily; 11hr); Dharamsala (11 daily; 4hr); Jammu (every 30min; 3hr); Kangra (every 15–30min; 3–4hr); Manali (6 daily; 12hr); Mandi (5 daily; 8hr); Shimla (5 daily; 12hr).

Flights

(**AI** = Air India, **IC** = Indian Airlines, **DN** = Air Deccan, **9W** = Jet Airways)

Amritsar to: Delhi (AI, IC, DN, 9W; 3–4 daily; 55min–1hr 25min); Mumbai (AI; 5 weekly; 2hr 30min).

Chandigarh to: Delhi (IC, DN, 9W; 3 daily; 40min–1hr); Mumbai (IC, 9W; 1 daily; 2hr–3hr 40min).

Gujarat

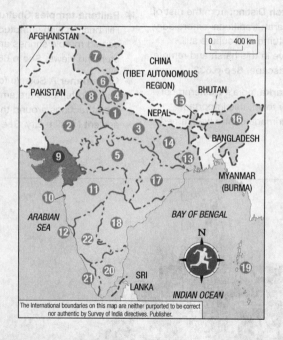

AFGHANISTAN

CHINA
(TIBET AUTONOMOUS
REGION)

BHUTAN

PAKISTAN

NEPAL

BANGLADESH

MYANMAR
(BURMA)

ARABIAN
SEA

BAY OF BENGAL

N

SRI
LANKA

INDIAN OCEAN

0   400 km

The International boundaries on this map are neither purported to be correct
nor authentic by Survey of India directives. Publisher.

CHAPTER 9

Highlights

✱ **Ahmedabad** Superb Indo-Islamic architecture, bustling bazaars and Mahatma Gandhi's Sabarmati Ashram. See p.618

✱ **Sun temple, Modhera** A beautiful eleventh-century temple, set in peaceful gardens: the finest example of Solanki architecture. See p.630

✱ **Kutch** Distinct from the rest of Gujarat; traditional embroidery, costume and culture still thrive in this harsh and remote landscape. See p.632

✱ **Dwarka** India's westernmost holy town, this important pilgrimage centre was famed in legend as Krishna's capital. See p.645

✱ **Sasan Gir** This protected forest is the last remaining habitat of the rare Asiatic lion. See p.654

✱ **Diu** West India's most congenial beach venue, this relaxed island has a Portuguese flavour in its colonial architecture. See p.656

✱ **Palitana temples** Shatrunjaya Hill bristles with sumptuously carved marble shrines and stunning views. See p.664

✱ **Champaner** A Solanki fortress and Jain temples are among the attractions around this ancient Muslim city. See p.668

▲ Jain temple, Palitana

Gujarat

Heated in the north by the blistering deserts of Pakistan and Rajasthan, and cooled in the south by the gentle ocean breeze of the Arabian Sea, **GUJARAT** forms India's westernmost bulkhead. The diversity of its topography – forested hilly tracts and fertile plains in the east, vast tidal marshland and desert plains in the Rann of Kutch in the west, with a rocky shoreline jutting into its heartland – is challenged only by the multiplicity of its politics and culture. Home to significant populations of Hindus, Jains, Muslims and Christians, as well as tribal and nomadic groups, the state boasts a patchwork of religious shrines and areas steeped in Hindu lore. Gujarat is the homeland of **Mahatma Gandhi**, the father of modern India, who was born in Porbandar and worked for many years in Ahmedabad. Having long lived by his credo of self-dependence, Gujaratis are consistently at or near the top of the chart in terms of India's economic output, and like Punjabis they have also fanned around the world to settle abroad. The region's **prosperity** dates as far back as the third millennium BC, when the Harappans started trading shell jewellery and textiles, with the latter Jain-dominated industry remaining an important source of income to the state. India's most industrialized state, Gujarat also boasts some of the Subcontinent's biggest oil refineries; thriving cement, chemicals and pharmaceutical manufacturing units; and a vast and lucrative ship-breaking yard at Alang. Kandla is one of India's **largest ports**, while most of the country's diamond cutting and polishing takes place in centres such as Surat, Ahmedabad, Bhavnagar and Palanpur. Rural poverty remains a serious problem, however, and health and education developments have not kept pace with the economic growth.

Gandhi's primary mission – to instigate political change through nonviolent means – has not always been adhered to in Gujarat and Muslim-Hindu tensions boil over to violence on a cyclical basis. In 2002, the state suffered India's worst **communal rioting** since Partition, with up to two thousand people, mostly Muslims, killed. The fighting came on the heels of an equally traumatic and deadly event, the January 2001 **earthquake** centred in Kutch, which levelled whole towns. These events added to the woes of a state already beleaguered by severe **water shortages** and **drought**.

Nevertheless, Gujarat has plenty to offer those who take time to detour from its more famous northerly neighbour Rajasthan, and it's free of the hard-sell and hassle that tourists often encounter there. The lure of important **temple cities**, **forts** and **palaces** is balanced by the chance to search out unique **crafts** made in communities whose way of life remains scarcely affected by global trends. As so often in India, Gujarat's **architectural diversity** reflects the influences of its many different rulers – the Buddhist Mauryans, Hindu rajas and Muslim

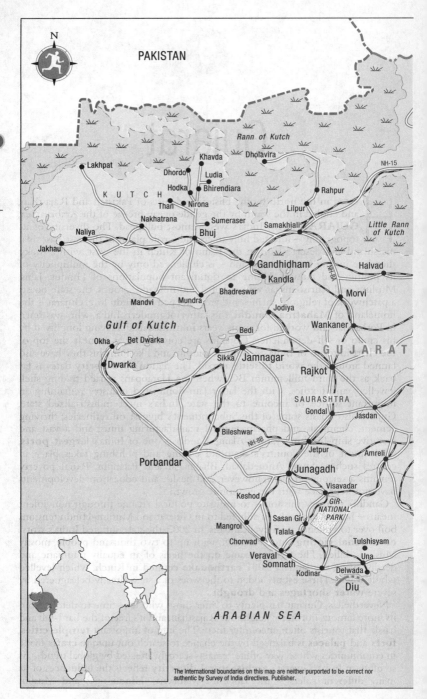

The International boundaries on this map are neither purported to be correct nor authentic by Survey of India directives. Publisher.

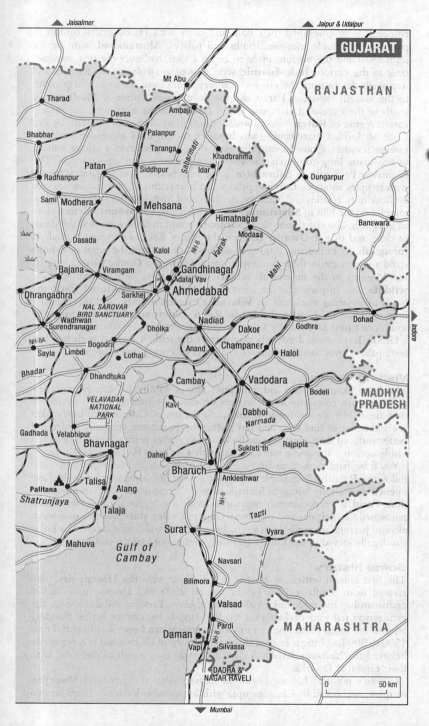

9

emperors who combined their skills and tastes with Hindu craftsmanship to produce remarkable mosques, tombs and palaces. **Ahmedabad**, state capital until 1970 and the obvious place to begin a tour, harbours the first mosques built in the curious **Indo-Islamic** style, as well as richly carved temples and step-wells dating from the eleventh century. From here, it's an easy trip north to the ancient capital of **Patan** and the Solanki sun temple at **Modhera**, or south to the excavated Harappan site at **Lothal**. In the northwest, the largely barren region of **Kutch** – occasionally cut off from the rest of the state by vast tracts of flooded marshland – was bypassed by Gujarat's successive waves of foreign invaders. Consequently, this intriguing area preserves a village culture where crafts long forgotten elsewhere are practised with age-old skill. The Kathiawar Peninsula, or **Saurashtra**, is the true heartland of Gujarat, scattered with temples, mosques, forts and palaces that bear testimony to centuries of rule by Buddhists, Hindus and Muslims. Architectural highlights include superb Jain temples on the hills of **Shatrunjaya**, near Bhavnagar, and **Mount Girnar**, close to Junagadh. The coastal temple at **Somnath** is said to have witnessed the dawn of time, and that at **Dwarka** built on the site of Krishna's ancient capital. At **Junagadh**, rocks bearing 2000-year-old inscriptions from the reign of Ashoka stand a stone's throw from flamboyant mausoleums and Gothic palaces built by the Muslims in the nineteenth century. There's plenty of scope for spotting **wildlife**, too, in particular the lions in the forested **Gir National Park**, the herds of strutting blackbuck at **Velavadar National Park**, and the chestnut brown Indian wild ass in the **Little Rann Sanctuary**. Separated from the south coast near Delwada by a thin sliver of the Arabian Sea, the island of **Diu**, a Union Territory and not officially part of the state, is fringed with beaches, leafy palm groves and the whitewashed spires of Portuguese churches.

Visiting Gujarat

Thanks to extensive road and train links, **travel** within the state presents few problems, but communication barriers do require a little effort to overcome (few timetables are written in English, and the use of Gujarati numbers makes it challenging to find train and bus platforms). Roads are generally wider and better surfaced than elsewhere in India, which makes getting around by **taxi** a viable option – the going rate for a car with a driver is Rs1200–1600 a day.

You'll be hard pushed to find a luxury **hotel** outside the major cities, but following Rajasthan's example a number of local maharajas and nawabs have opened their family homes as heritage hotels offering good-value accommodation. **Food** is predominantly vegetarian with the region's good-value thalis renowned for their size and sweetness. Gujarat is a **dry state**, but free one-week alcohol permits are available from the bigger hotels and liquor shops. Alcohol is also legally served in the Union Territory enclaves of Daman and Diu.

Some history

The first known settlers in what is now Gujarat were the **Harappans**, who arrived from Sindh and Punjab in around 2500 BC. Despite their skilful craftsmanship and trade links with Africans, Arabs, Persians and Europeans, the civilization fell into decline in 1900 BC, largely because of severe flooding around the Indus delta; some of its oldest remains can be seen at Lothal. From 1500 to 500 BC, little is known about the history of Gujarat but it is popularly believed the **Yadavas**, Krishna's clan, held sway over much of the state, with their capital at Dwarka.

Gujarat's political history begins in earnest with the powerful **Mauryan empire**, established by Chandragupta with its capital at Junagadh (then known as Girinagar) and reaching its peak under Ashoka. After his death in 226 BC, Mauryan power dwindled; the last significant ruler was Samprati, Ashoka's grandson, a Jain who built fabulous temples at *tirthas* (pilgrimage sites) such as Girnar and Palitana.

During the first millennium AD, control of the region passed between a succession of warring dynasties and nomadic tribes, including the **Gurjars**, from whom the state eventually derived its name, and the Kathi warriors of Saurashtra. Gujarat eventually came under the sway of the **Solanki** (or **Chalukyan**) dynasty in the eleventh and twelfth centuries, a golden period in the state's architectural

Godhra and Gujarat's communal violence

When the BJP shocked India with its landslide victory over its Congress rivals in the December 2002 election, analysts needed only to point to a single word to find an answer for the victory – **Godhra**. The town was an anonymous train depot until February 27, 2002, when a Muslim mob set fire to train cars filled with Hindu pilgrims returning from the controversial temple at Ayodhya, killing 59.

The incident sparked huge **riots** across Gujarat. Muslim neighbourhoods burned while sword- and stick-wielding Hindus rampaged, looted and raped. In many cases police forces allegedly stood by and watched. Officially, more than 1000 people died in the weeks following the Godhra incident, although human rights organizations estimate the real figure at more than 2000, most of them Muslims, while thousands more moved to refugee camps, too frightened to go back to their own homes.

The violence was politicized after the Congress Party accused the government of not doing enough to ensure the safety of Muslim citizens. Gujarat's BJP chief minister **Narendra Modi** earned the moniker "Muslim killer" for his seemingly passive attitude as the violence continued, and his lack of support for the survivors. Just days after the New York–based Human Rights Watch reported Gujarat state officials "were directly involved in the killings of hundreds of Muslims since February 27 and are now engineering a massive **cover-up** of the state's role in the violence", Parliament attempted to censure the BJP government. At the end of the sixteen-hour debate Prime Minister Atal Bihari Vajpayee apologized for not having "tried harder" to end the riots and announced a $31 million rehabilitation package.

With the state elections approaching, Modi intensified his *Hindutva* rhetoric and campaign "to prevent" another Godhra. While he avoided any direct anti-Muslim statements, it was clear the minister was battling to haul in as many Hindu votes as possible in the midst of so much ethnic tension. Yet it wasn't until the December 12 election that his cult status among ordinary Gujaratis was at last verified by his surprising landslide win.

The 2004 national elections, however, saw a turnaround, ushering in the Congress-led UPA government with Manmohan Singh of Congress as Prime Minister. Though BJP retained the majority in Gujarat, the elections were closely contested. Following protests that the violence had been government-supported and that the authorities were biased, the Supreme Court ruled the cases of the violence-affected families be moved to courts in other states for their safety and ordered investigations into the riots. As yet, none of the investigations have been able to come to any conclusion regarding the train-burning at Godhra.

In October 2007, in the run-up to the state elections, respected news magazine *Tehelka* published secretly-filmed footage of senior Gujarati Hindu politicians, mainly from the BJP, describing in graphic detail how they took part in and helped to orchestrate the riots. The report alleged Modi allowed the violence to continue unabated, ordered the police to side with Hindu rioters and sheltered the perpetrators from justice. Thus far no attempt has been made to investigate the claims at a judicial or political level, and Modi was resoundingly re-elected in December 2007.

history as the rulers commissioned splendid Hindu and Jain **temples** and **step-wells**. Many of these structures suffered during the raids of Mahmud of Ghazni in 1027, but Muslim rule was not actually established until the Khalji conquest in 1299. Eight years later, Muzaffar Shah's declaration of independence from Delhi marked the foundation of the **Sultanate of Gujarat**, which lasted until its conquest by the Mughal emperor Akbar in the sixteenth century. In this period Muslim, Jain and Hindu styles were melded to produce remarkable **Indo-Islamic** mosques and tombs. Contrary to impressions encouraged by recent sectarian violence, particularly in Ahmedabad, Islam never eclipsed Hinduism or Jainism, and the three have lived side by side for centuries.

In the 1500s, the **Portuguese**, already settled in Goa, turned their attention to Gujarat, aware of the excellent potential of its ports. Having captured Daman in 1531, they took Diu four years later, building forts and typically European towns. Fending off Arab and Muslim attacks, the Portuguese governed the ports until they were subsumed into India in the 1960s.

The **British East India Company** set up its headquarters in Surat in 1613, and soon established their first "factory", a self-contained village of labourers' and merchants' houses and warehouses, sowing the seeds of a prospering textile industry. When British sovereignty was established in 1818, governor-generals moved into some of Gujarat's main cities and signed treaties with about two hundred princely and petty states of Saurashtra. Under British rule the introduction of machinery upgraded textile manufacture, which brought substantial wealth to the region but put many manual labourers out of business. Their cause was valiantly fought by Gujarat-born **Mahatma Gandhi** (see box, p.648), whose campaigns for independence and social equality brought international attention to his ashram in Ahmedabad. After Partition, Gujarat received an influx of Hindus from Sind and witnessed terrible sectarian fighting as Muslims fled to their new homeland.

In 1960, after the Marathi and Gujarati **language riots** (demonstrators sought the redrawing of state boundaries according to language, as had happened in the south), Bombay state was split and Gujarat created. The Portuguese enclaves, along with Goa, were forcibly annexed by the Indian government in 1961. After Independence Gujarat was a staunch Congress stronghold, apart from a brief defeat by the Janata party in 1977, until the fundamentalists of the BJP took control in 1991. The communal violence of 2002, which resulted in one to two thousand deaths, reopened an old chapter of history by pitting Muslim and Hindu neighbours against one another. The tensions and violence started suspiciously near the beginning of the state election campaign; theories that the problems were politically generated appeared to be verified when the BJP rode a dramatic wave of Hindu nationalism to victory over Congress by a margin of 126 seats to 51. Six years on, the communal tensions continue to cast a long shadow over the state, with neighbourhoods often divided along religious lines and Muslims increasingly marginalized.

Ahmedabad

A tangled mass of factories, mosques, temples and skyscrapers, Gujarat's commercial hub, **AHMEDABAD** (also known as Amdavad), sprawls along the banks of the River Sabarmati, 90km from its mouth in the Bay of Cambay. The state's largest city, with a population of around five million, is appallingly polluted, renowned for its dreadful congestion and repeated outbreaks of

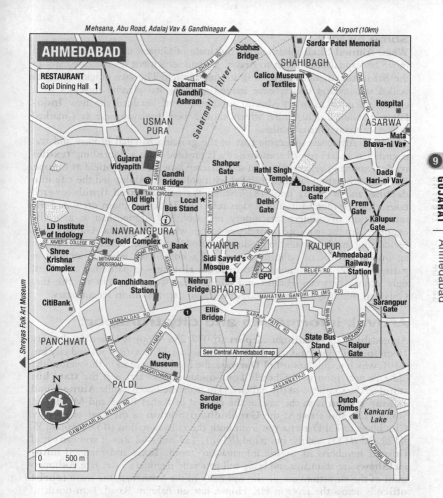

AHMEDABAD

RESTAURANT
Gopi Dining Hall   1

Subhas Bridge

Sardar Patel Memorial

SHAHIBAGH

Sabarmati (Gandhi) Ashram

Calico Museum of Textiles

USMAN PURA

Hospital

ASARWA

Mata Bhava-ni Vav

Gujarat Vidyapith

Shahpur Gate

Hathi Singh Temple

Gandhi Bridge

INCOME TAX CIRCLE

Old High Court

Local Bus Stand

Dariapur Gate

Dada Hari-ni Vav

Delhi Gate

Prem Gate

Kalupur Gate

LD Institute of Indology

ST. XAVIER'S COLLEGE RD

NAVRANGPURA

City Gold Complex

Bank

KHANPUR

KALUPUR

Shree Krishna Complex

MITHAKALI CROSSROAD

Sidi Sayyid's Mosque

Ahmedabad Railway Station

GPO

RELIEF RD

CitiBank

Gandhidham Station

Nehru Bridge

BHADRA

MAHATMA GANDHI RD (MG RD)

Sarangpur Gate

PANCHVATI

MANGALDAS RD

Ellis Bridge

State Bus Stand

Raipur Gate

City Museum

See Central Ahmedabad map

N

0   500 m

PALDI

Sardar Bridge

Dutch Tombs

Kankaria Lake

Shreyas Folk Art Museum

GUJARAT | Ahmedabad

9

communal violence. Give it a little time, however, and the mix of medieval and modern makes the city a compelling place to explore.

A wander through the bazaars and pols (residential areas) of the bustling **old city** is rewarding, but Ahmedabad is also packed with diverse architectural styles, with over fifty **mosques** and **tombs**, plus Hindu and Jain **temples** and grand **step-wells** (*vavs*). The **Calico Museum of Textiles** is one of the world's finest, while Gandhi's **Sabarmati Ashram** is an essential stop for anyone with even a passing interest in the Mahatma and the Indian Freedom Movement.

Particularly in the old city, it's advisable to cover your mouth and nose with a bandana or handkerchief to reduce inhalation of **carbon monoxide**. In 2002, a controversial **canal project** diverted water from the River Narmada into the Sabarmati, which previously had virtually dried up outside the monsoon. This has given the city a cooler feel, but Ahmedabad has a long way to go before it can breathe easily.

In mid-January the city plays host to a famed **international kite festival**, the largest of its kind in the world.

619

Some history

When **Ahmed Shah** inherited the Sultanate of Gujarat in 1411, he chose to move his capital from Patan to Asawal, a small settlement on the east bank of the Sabarmati, modestly renaming it after himself. The city quickly grew as skilled artisans and traders were invited to settle. Its splendid mosques were clearly intended to assert Muslim supremacy, and heralded the new **Indo-Islamic** style of architecture, which, though best displayed here, is a marked feature of many Gujarati cities.

In 1572, Ahmedabad became part of the growing Mughal Empire and was regarded as India's most handsome city. It profited from a flourishing **textiles trade**, exporting velvets, silks and shimmering brocades as far afield as Europe. But two devastating famines coupled with political instability led the city into **decline**, and it wasn't until 1817, when the newly-arrived British lowered taxes, that the merchants and traders returned. Trade in opium grew and the introduction of modern machinery re-established Ahmedabad as a textile exporter. In the run-up to Independence, while **Mahatma Gandhi** was revitalizing small-scale textile production, the "Manchester of the East" became an important seat of political power and a hotbed for religious tension as parties vied for pre-eminence. **Communal rioting** – in particular a series of ugly clashes between Hindus and Muslims, as well as attacks on the tiny Christian minority – have sullied Ahmedabad's reputation in recent years.

Arrival, information and city transport

Ahmedabad's **international airport** (☏079/286 9266) is linked to the city, 10km south, by pre-paid taxi (Rs250–300), auto-rickshaw (Rs150) and city bus #101, which terminates at **Lal Darwaja**, the local bus station in the west of the old city, near most of the hotels. Long-distance buses arrive at the **state bus stand** in the southeast of the old city, 1km from the hotels, while **Ahmedabad railway station** is to the east, at the far end of Relief Road and MG Road. Some trains also arrive at the **Gandhidham Station** in the west of the city. City buses to Lal Darwaja run from both the railway station (#37, #56, #135, #122 and #133) and the bus stand (#13/1, #32 and #52/2) – if you can't read Gujarati numbers, ask at the information booth. **Taxis** and metered **auto-rickshaws** are abundant and both will generally negotiate a day rate. Although most of the attractions are on the east bank of the Sabarmati, the main **tourist office** is across the river in HK House, just off Ashram Road, 1km north of Nehru Bridge (Mon–Sat 10.30am–1.30pm & 2–6pm, closed 2nd & 4th Sat of month; ☏079/2658 9172, ⓦwww.gujarattourism.com). The Municipal Transport Service runs **city bus tours** (9am–1pm & 1.30–5.30pm; Rs60; ☏079/2550 7739) from the bus stand at Lal Darwaja; to see Jama Mosque, Manek Chowk and the pols not accessible by bus, take the Municipal Corporation's informative **heritage walk** (daily at 8am; 2hr 30min; Rs50 [Rs20]; ☏079/2539 1811, ⓔheritagewalkme@gmail.com), which leaves from the Swaminarayan Temple (see p.623).

Accommodation

Most of Ahmedabad's **hotels** are conveniently located in the **west end of the old city**, within walking distance of the bazaars, the local bus station and many of the sights. Others are clustered around the **railway station**, while north of Nehru Bridge, in the classy **Khanpur** area, accommodation tends to be more upmarket.

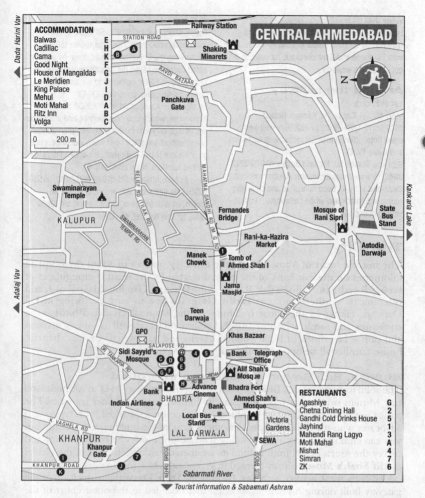

ACCOMMODATION

Balwas	E
Cadillac	H
Cama	K
Good Night	F
House of Mangaldas	G
Le Meridien	J
King Palace	I
Mehul	D
Moti Mahal	A
Ritz Inn	B
Volga	C

0   200 m

CENTRAL AHMEDABAD

Railway Station

STATION ROAD

Shaking
Minarets

RAVDI BAZAAR

Panchkuva
Gate

Dada Harini Vav

Adaaj Vav

Kankaria Lake

Swaminarayan
Temple

KALUPUR

RELIEF RD (TILAK RD)

SWAMINARAYAN TEMPLE RD

MAHATMA GANDHI RD (M G RD)

Fernandes
Bridge

Mosque of
Rani Sipri

State
Bus
Stand

Rani-ka-Hazira
Market

Astodia
Darwaja

Manek
Chowk

Tomb of
Ahmed Shah I

Jama
Masjid

SARDAR PATEL RD

Teen
Darwaja

GPO

SALAPOSE RD

Khas Bazaar

DR TANKARIA RD

Sidi Sayyid's
Mosque

Bank   Telegraph
Office

Alif Shah's
Mosque

ADVANCE CINEMA RD

Advance
Cinema

Bhadra Fort

Bank

Indian Airlines

BHADRA

Ahmed Shah's
Mosque

Local Bus
Stand

Bank

Victoria
Gardens

K VAGHELA RD

KHANPUR

Khanpur
Gate

KHANPUR ROAD

LAL DARWAJA

SEWA

NEHRU BRIDGE

ELLIS BRIDGE

Sabarmati River

RESTAURANTS

Agashiye	G
Chetna Dining Hall	2
Gandhi Cold Drinks House	5
Jayhind	1
Mahendi Rang Lagyo	3
Moti Mahal	A
Nishat	4
Simran	7
ZK	6

▼ Tourist information & Sabarmati Ashram

Lal Darwaja

Balwas 6751 Relief Rd, opposite Relief Cinema
☎079/2550 7135, ℱ2550 6320. A modern
establishment with the best and quietest rooms
in a separate back building. Most have a/c and TV,
and all have clean private bathrooms with hot
water. ❹

Cadillac Advance Cinema Rd, near Sidi Sayyid's
Mosque ☎079/2550 7558. The best shoestring
option has small, colourful rooms, some with
private bath, and a men-only dorm (Rs60). ❶–❷

Good Night Dr Tankaria Rd, opposite Sidi Sayyid's
Mosque ☎079/2550 7181, ℱ2550 6998. Neat
and tidy rooms come with smart white-tiled
bathrooms and small TVs. The triples are
particularly good value. ❹

House of Mangaldas Dr Tankaria Rd,
opposite Sidi Sayyid's Mosque ☎079/2550
6946, ⊛www.houseofmg.com. Formerly the home
of a wealthy industrialist, this 1920s heritage hotel
has spacious, individually decorated rooms ($100),
most with four-poster beds. Courtyards have period
furniture, and old photos of eminent visitors to the
family home – including Mahatma Gandhi – line
the walls. Two excellent restaurants, an indoor pool
and audio-guide tours complete the package. The
only downside is the 9am checkout. ❽

Mehul Just off Relief Rd, opposite Electricity House
☎079/2550 6525. Behind the tinted-glass
reception area, the rooms are plain but decent,
with cramped bathrooms. Rooms vary in quality, so
ask to see a few. ❹

Volga Just off Relief Rd, opposite Electricity Houses ⑦ 079/2550 9497. Friendly service is matched by spotless pastel-shaded en-suites, each with TV, phone and 24hr checkout; as quiet as it gets in Lal Darwaja. ④

Around the railway station

Moti Mahal Station Rd, Kapasia Bazaar ⑦ 079/212 1881, ⑦ 213 6132. Very well-kept, clean hotel offering identikit rooms with bathroom and cable TV. ④

Ritz Inn Station Rd, Kapasia Bazaar ⑦ 079/2212 3842, ⑩ www.hotelritzinn.com. A recommended three-star with Art Deco flourishes and charming rooms with black and white bathrooms, TVs and writing desks. ⑦

Khanpur district

Cama Khanpur Rd ⑦ 079/2550 1234, ⑩ www .camahotelsindia.com. The large rooms ($90–115) overlooking the Sabarmati are let down by slightly dated decor. However, the garden terrace, pool, top restaurant and 24hr coffee shop are ample compensation. 9am checkout. ⑧–⑨

Le Meridien Khanpur Rd ⑦ 079/2550 5505, ⑩ www.starwoodhotels.com. Service and standards are as high as you'd expect from this international chain, with an excellent restaurant, indoor pool and gym. Rooms ($195–280) feature wooden floors and leather furniture. Noon checkout. ⑨

King Palace Khanpur Rd ⑦ 079/550 0280, ⑦ 550 0275. This three-star has smart, comfortable rooms, all with big beds, cable TV and a/c. Good value for this bracket. ⑤–⑥

The City

The historic heart of Ahmedabad is the **old city**, an area of about three square kilometres on the east bank of the river, dissected by the main thoroughfares of Relief Road (also called Tilak Road) and Mahatma Gandhi (MG) Road, and reaching its northern limits at **Delhi Gate**. It's best to start exploring in Lal Darwaja, taking in the squat buildings of the original citadel, **Bhadra**, the **mosques** and tombs of Ahmedabad's Muslim rulers, as well as vibrant bazaars and pols – labyrinths of high wooden havelis and narrow cul-de-sacs that still house families all belonging to the same caste or trade.

Bhadra, Sidi Sayyid's Mosque and around

The solid fortified citadel, **Bhadra**, built of deep red stone in 1411 as Ahmedabad's first Muslim structure, is relatively plain in comparison to the later mosques. The palace inside is now occupied by offices and its courtyard packed with typists and advocates who use it like an open-air office. Most of the building is off-limits, but you can climb to its roof via a winding staircase just inside the main gateway and survey the streets below from behind its weathered bastions. In front of the citadel is **Alif Shah's Mosque**, gaily painted in green and white. Further east, beyond the odoriferous meat market in **Khas Bazaar**, is **Teen Darwaja**, a thick-set triple gateway built during Ahmed Shah's reign that once led to the outer court of the royal citadel. A trio of pointed arches engraved with Islamic inscriptions and detailed carving spans the busy road below and shelters cobblers and peddlers.

A prominent feature on the front of glossy city brochures, **Sidi Sayyid's Mosque** (1573), famed for the ten magnificent *jali* (lattice-work) screens lining its upper walls, sits in the centre of a busy traffic circle to the east of Nehru Bridge. The two semicircular screens high on the western wall are the most spectacular, with floral designs exquisitely carved out of the yellow stone so common in Ahmedabad's mosques. Stonework within depicts heroes and animals from popular Hindu myths – one effect of Hindu and Jain craftsmanship on an Islamic tradition that rarely allowed the depiction of living beings in its mosques. Women cannot enter this mosque, but the gardens around it afford good views of the screens.

Ahmed Shah's Mosque

West of Bhadra, not far from Victoria Gardens, **Ahmed Shah's** small and attractively simple **mosque** was the private place of worship for the royal household.

Sections of an old Hindu temple, perhaps dating back to 1250 AD, were used in its construction – hence the incongruous Sanskrit inscriptions on some of the pillars in the sanctuary. Look out for the *zenana*, or women's chamber, hidden behind pierced stone screens above the sanctuary in the northeast corner.

Jama Masjid

A short walk from Teen Darwaja along MG Road leads to the spectacular **Jama Masjid**. Completed in 1424, it stands today in its entirety, except for two minarets destroyed by an earthquake in 1957. Always buzzing with people, the mosque is busiest on Fridays, when thousands converge to worship. The 260 elegant pillars supporting the roof of the domed prayer hall (*qibla*) are covered with profuse, unmistakably Hindu, carvings, while close to the sanctuary's principal arch a large black slab is said to be the base of a Jain idol inverted and buried as a sign of Muslim supremacy.

Manek Chowk

East of Jama Masjid, the jewellery and textiles market **Manek Chowk** is filled with craftsmen hard at work in narrow alleys amid newly dyed and tailored cloth. Immediately outside the east entrance of the mosque, the square **Tomb of Ahmed Shah I**, who died in 1442, stands surrounded by pillared verandas. Women are not permitted to enter the central chamber, site of his grave, and those of his son and grandson. Further into the market area is the mausoleum of Ahmed Shah's queens, **Rani-ka-Hazira**, surrounded by the dyers' colourful stalls. Its plan is identical to Shah's own tomb, with pillared verandas clearly inspired by Hindu architectural tastes. Inside, the graves are elaborately decorated with faded metal inlay and mother-of-pearl.

Swaminarayan Temple

Heading north from Rani-ka-Hazira along Temple Road, a narrow street of fabric shops, and crossing Relief Road brings you to the **Swaminarayan Temple**. A delicate contrast to the many hard-stone mosques in the city, both the temple and the houses in the courtyard surrounding it are of finely carved wood, with elaborate and intricate patterns typical of the havelis of north and west Gujarat. The temple's main sanctuary is given over to Vishnu and his consort Lakshmi.

Mosque and Tomb of Rani Sipri

Near Astodia Darwaja in the south of the city, the small, elegant **mosque of Rani Sipri** was built in 1514 at the queen's orders. Her grave lies in front, sheltered by a pillared mausoleum. The stylish mosque shows more Hindu influence than any other in Ahmedabad: its pillared sanctuary has an open facade to the east and fine tracery work on the west wall.

Shaking minarets

South of the railway station, opposite Sarangpur Darwaja, **Sidi Bashir's minars** are all that remain of the mosque popularly named after one of Ahmed Shah's favourite slaves. More than 21m high, these are the best existing example of the "**shaking minarets**" – built on a foundation of flexible sandstone, probably to protect them from earthquake damage – once a common sight on Ahmedabad's skyline. At least two European visitors, Robert Grindlay (1826) and Henry Cousens (1905), reported climbing to the top storey of one minaret, shaking it hard, and causing its twin to shake, but as entry is restricted you'll be lucky to be able to try this yourself.

Dada Hari-ni Vav and Mata Bhava-ni Vav

Northern Gujarat abounds with remarkable **step-wells** – deep, with elaborately carved walls and broad flights of covered steps leading to a shaft – but **Dada Hari-ni Vav**, in the northeast of the city just outside the old boundaries, is among the finest. It can be reached by taking bus #111 to Asarwa; ask to be dropped nearby, and either walk or take an auto-rickshaw to the well. An auto-rickshaw from Lal Darwaja should cost around Rs50. While it's a Muslim construction, built in 1500 for Bai Harir Sultani, superintendent of the royal harem, the craftsmen were Hindu, and their influence is clear in the lavish and sensuous carvings on the walls and pillars. The best time to visit is an hour or so before noon when the sculpted floral patterns and shapely figurines inside are bathed in sunlight. **Bai Harir**'s lofty mosque and lattice-walled tomb stand west of the well.

A couple of hundred metres north, the neglected **Mata Bhava-ni Vav** was probably constructed in the eleventh century, before Ahmedabad was founded. It's profoundly Hindu in character, and dedicated to Bhava-ni, an aspect of Shiva's consort Parvati, whose modest shrine is set in the back wall of the well shaft.

Hathi Singh Temple

The Svetambara **Hathi Singh Temple** (daily 10am–noon & 4–7.30pm), north of Delhi Gate, is easily distinguished by its high carved column. Built entirely of white marble embossed with smooth carvings of dancers, musicians, animals and flowers, this serene temple is dedicated to Dharamnath, whose statue stands in the main sanctuary. He is the fifteenth *tirthankara*, or "ford-maker", one of twenty-four great teachers sanctified by the Jains.

Calico Museum of Textiles

Nobody should leave Ahmedabad without taking a tour of the **Calico Museum of Textiles** (℡079/2786 8172), in the Sarabhai Foundation, 3km north of Delhi Gate opposite Shahibagh Underbridge (bus #101, #101/1, #103, #105); it's simply the finest collection of textiles, clothes, furniture and crafts in the country. Highlights of the **morning tour** (daily 10.30am–12.30pm) include a number of exquisite pieces made for the British and Portuguese, while from India's royal households there's an embroidered tent and the robes of Shah Jahan. Look out too for the *patola* saris, woven in Patan (see p.631), as well as the extravagant *zari* work that gilds saris in heavy gold stitching and can bring their weight to almost nine kilos. Other galleries are dedicated to embroideries, *bandhani* tie-and-dye, textiles made for overseas trade and woollen shawls from Kashmir and Chamba. In addition, tribal crafts such as Kutchi silk-and-cotton *mashru* weaving are displayed in spectacular wooden havelis from Patan and Siddhpur in northern Gujarat. The **afternoon tour** (daily 2.45–4.45pm) includes the galleries of *pichwais* and other temple paintings and decorations, including Jain statues housed in a replica haveli temple and centuries-old manuscripts and mandalas painted on palm leaves. Arrive early for the tours, as they fill up quickly and it's not possible to look round on your own.

City Museum

Just west of Sardar Bridge in the modern Sanskar Kendra on Bhagatcharya Road, the **City Museum** (Tues–Sun 10am–6pm) is well worth a visit, covering subjects such as the history of the city, urban growth, sociological development and the activities of Gandhi and the freedom movement. There is also a **Kite Museum** (same hours) in the basement.

SEWA

Almost ninety percent of women who work in India are self-employed. Existing outside the protection of labour laws and the minimum wage, they are particularly subject to exploitation, often at the hands of unscrupulous banks and private lenders. Ahmedabad, however, has maintained a tradition of self-help since the days of Gandhi, achieving global recognition as the home base of the ground-breaking **Self-Employed Women's Association**, **SEWA** (℡079/2550 6444, ⊛www.sewa.org), founded in the early 1970s. SEWA offers legal advice, provides training and child care, and negotiates with police and local government for vendors' licences and education for members' children, as well as running its own co-operative **Mahila Bank**, the first to offer women low-interest loans, savings and deposit accounts and insurance. SEWA is now involved with projects throughout Gujarat, India and overseas.

In 1984 a major textile industry slump affected 35,000 families, mostly Harijans and Muslims, and many had to resort to rag- and paper-picking. Setting up training centres in weaving, sewing, dyeing and printing, and providing efficient machinery, SEWA helped to re-establish many women in the textile labour force, and provided an outlet for their products. SEWA (now with 319,000 members nationwide, 206,000 in Gujarat) has trained its members in a variety of skills including accountancy and office administration. In 1987, 2000 women registered a protest against *sati* (widow burning) and a campaign to have verbal divorce and polygamy banned in Gujarat resulted in a change in the law. SEWA also strongly opposes the sex determination tests that lead to female foeticide, a particularly widespread practice in Gujarat. SEWA has two **craft shops** (both Mon–Sat 10am–8pm, Sun 10am–6.30pm): one on the east side of Ellis Bridge, in the organization's reception centre, another on CG Road at the Banascraft Chandan Complex.

Sabarmati (Gandhi) Ashram

At the northern end of Ashram Road, the **Sabarmati Ashram** (daily 8.30am–6.30pm) is where the Mahatma lived from 1917 until 1930, holding meetings with weavers and Harijans as he helped them find security and re-establish the manual textile industry in Ahmedabad. In keeping with the man's uncluttered lifestyle, the collection of his personal property is modest but poignant – wooden shoes, white seamless clothes and a pair of round spectacles. The ashram itself is no longer operating, but many people come here simply to sit and meditate. Regular evening **sound–and–light shows** are also held.

Other museums

The informative **Shreyas Folk Art Museum**, way out to the west near the city limits (Fri–Tues 10am–1.30pm & 2–5.30pm; Rs45 [Rs7]; bus #34/2 or 34/3 from Lal Darwaja), displays the traditional work of Gujarat's many tribes. Also illuminating is the **Tribal Museum** (daily except Mon 11am–5pm) in Gujarat Vidyapith, north of Income Tax Circle on Ashram Road, detailing the various peoples of the state and their customs. The **N.C. Mehta Gallery** in the **LD Institute of Indology** in the west of town (Tues–Sun: May & June 8.30am–12.30pm; July–April 10.30am–5.30pm) has a superb collection of miniature paintings from all over India; an **Indology Museum** in the same complex is strong on Jain sculpture and manuscripts. Take bus #52/1 from Lal Darwaja.

Eating

Ahmedabad's most popular **restaurants** are clustered around Relief Road, Salapose Road and Badhra; for **snack** food, there are good stalls at Khas Bazaar.

If you are making only a brief stop in Gujarat, make sure you sample the state's delicious thali.

Agashiye *House of Mangaldas* (see p.621). One of the best restaurants in Gujarat, with a rooftop terrace, floor cushions to sit on and an open kitchen where you can watch the chefs at work. Prices are steep by local standards (Rs195–255), but the mouthwatering thalis are as good as it gets.

Chetna Dining Hall Relief Rd. Don't be put off by the dusty exterior, inside is a busy veg place with excellent, inexpensive South Indian dishes and sumptuous Gujarati thalis.

Gandhi Cold Drinks House Khas Bazaar. Third-generation hole-in-the-wall serving up refreshing milk and ice-cream concoctions, including Indonesian-style "Royal Faluda", unique to Ahmedabad, and saffron-flavoured *kesar* milkshake.

Gopi Dining Hall Pritamrai Rd ℡079/657 6388. Welcoming, tourist-friendly veg place on the west side of Ellis Bridge, offering Gujarati and Kathiawadi thalis at unbeatable prices (Rs40–65). Very popular, so reserve or wait in line.

Green House *House of Mangaldas* (see p.621). Cheaper than *Agashiye* (Rs50–100), but almost as appealing: sit on wooden benches under an ivy-covered pavilion and tuck into snacks, light meals and ice creams (including unusual flavours like dried fig).

Havmor Relief Rd. Fast-food-style joint popular with families and teenagers for its sandwiches, *dosas*, burgers, milkshakes and ice creams (Rs15–70).

Jayhind Manek Chowk. One of the best places to sample Ahmedabad's famous sweets, *Jayhind* has been producing wonderful dry-fruit halwa and *kaju pista roll* since 1948 (Rs5–30).

Mahendi Rang Lagyo Fruit Juice House Relief Rd. A bustling roadside stall with a loyal local following for its vast array of fresh juices and milkshakes (Rs10–20).

Moti Mahal *Moti Mahal* hotel (see p.622). This non-veg restaurant and sweet centre is renowned for its great biriyanis (Rs30–80) and refreshing salted lassi flavoured with cumin.

Nishat Khas Bazaar. The non-veg thali (Rs85) – with chicken tikka, mutton curry and biriyani – is a firm favourite at *Nishat*, which has a hectic downstairs dining room and a calmer, if slightly more expensive, a/c area above.

Ritz Inn *Ritz Inn* hotel (see p.622). A peaceful hotel restaurant with stained-glass windows, chandeliers and a menu of delectable veg Indian and Chinese dishes (Rs65–90).

Simran Khanpur Rd. An a/c restaurant handy for those staying at the big hotels on this road: good choices include *tawa jhinga* (shrimp/prawn curry), chicken tikka masala, mutton kebabs, *shahi raan* (tandoori leg of lamb) and fish curries (Rs45–130).

ZK Relief Rd. A dimly-lit restaurant with a pink-and-maroon colour scheme and an ancient fish tank. Trawling through the exhaustive menu – well over 200 dishes – certainly builds up an appetite: the tandoori items (Rs65–80) are particularly good.

Listings

Airlines, Domestic Air Deccan (airport ℡079/3092 5213); Air Sahara (airport ℡079/2285 8002 or 2285 8003 or 5545 5969); Indian Airlines, on the road from Sidi Sayyid's Mosque to Nehru Bridge ℡079/2658 5382; Jet Airways, Ashram Rd opposite Gujarat Vidyapith ℡079/2754 3304; Kingfisher Airlines (airport ℡1800/233 3131).

Airlines, International Air India, near the old High Court ℡079/2658 5622; Air France, Madhuban House near Ellis Bridge town hall ℡079/2644 6886; Alitalia and Kenya Airways, c/o Ajanta Travels, behind City Gold movie complex, off Ashram Rd ℡079/2658 5077; British Airways, Centre Point Building, Panchwati Circle, CG Rd ℡079/2656 5957; Cathay Pacific, Ratnanabh Complex, opposite Gujarat Vidyapith ℡079/2754 5421; KLM, in the Shefali Centre, Paldi ℡079/2657 7677; Malaysia Airlines, CG Rd, near Ellis Bridge ℡079/5561 3355; Singapore Airlines, SP Nagar Rd, just off CG Rd ℡079/5525 9933.

Banks and exchange Facilities for US or sterling cash and traveller's cheques are available at the Bank of India in Khas Bazaar, the Central Bank of India opposite Sidi Sayyid's Mosque and the State Bank of India opposite Lal Darwaja bus station (all Mon–Fri 11am–3pm, Sat 11am–1pm). For Visa encashment, go to the Bank of Baroda's Ashram Rd branch on the west side of the river, 300m north of Nehru Bridge. There's a branch of Thomas Cook at 208 Sakar III, off Ashram Rd near the old High Court. CITIBank has a branch on CG Rd at B/201 Fairdeal House, near Swastik Four Rd.

Bookshops For maps, guides and books try Crossword, a megastore with a coffee shop in the Shree Krishna Complex, near the Mithakali crossroad. Also good are Sastu Kitab Ghar on Relief Rd, 100m east of Salapose Rd, and People's Book House, 100m further down.

Cinemas Modern multi-screen cineplexes like City Gold Cinema (℡079/2658 7782), above

McDonald's near the tourist office on Ashram Rd, Fun Republic (☎079/5530 0000), west of town on the Sarkhej–Gandhinagar Highway and the nearby Wide Angle show English and Hindi films. **Hospitals** VS General, Ellis Bridge (☎079/657 7621), is a large government hospital; for traditional treatments, try Akhandanand Ayurvedic, Akhandanand Rd (☎ 079/550 7796). **Internet access** Facilities available at Relief Cyber Café, opposite the Relief Rd cinema, and Wizard

Online 50m down an alley, just north of Income Tax Circle, on the west side of the Ashram Rd. **Photography** Gujarat Mercantile Co, 100m south of the GPO on Salapose Rd; One Hour Photo, Ashram Rd, northwest corner of Income Tax Circle. For transparencies, the best is Sukruti (☎079/2658 7355) at Jaldarshan Apartments opposite Natraj Cinema. **Post office** Salapose Rd (Mon–Sat 10am–8pm, Sun 10am–4pm).

Moving on from Ahmedabad

As a main station along the Delhi–Mumbai train line, Ahmedabad sees plenty of through traffic. It's also the jumping-off point for nearly all destinations within Gujarat, and, if you're heading north, to Mount Abu, Jodhpur and Udaipur in Rajasthan. For more on transport from Ahmedabad see "Travel details" on p.673.

The **state bus stand** serves local destinations including Gandhinagar (every 15min; 1hr), Dholka (for Lothal, every 30min; 1hr 30min), Mehsana (every 10min; 2hr), and Dhrangadhra (every 30min; 3hr), as well as Rajasthan, Maharashtra and Madhya Pradesh. More comfortable and expensive **private buses** to places both in Gujarat and around are run by a cluster of agencies in Paldi, west of Sardar Bridge, from where most services leave for Bhavnagar, Rajkot, Bhuj and Mumbai.

Daily **flights** to Delhi and Mumbai are operated by Jet Airways and Indian Airlines; the latter also serves Bengaluru, Hyderabad and Vadodara, while Jet Airways flies to Kolkata. Air Deccan serves Bangalore, Mumbai and Delhi, while Kingfisher Airlines has flights to Bangalore, Pune, Delhi, Indore, Jaipur, Kolkata and Nagpur. A number of reliable IATA-approved travel agencies on Ashram Road and CG Road can book all tickets.

The main **railway station** is in the east of town at the end of Relief Road. Gandhigram Station, in the west, serves destinations across Saurashtra, including a direct train to Delwada (for Diu). There are computerized **reservation centres** (Mon–Sat 8am–8pm & Sun 8am–2pm) at both stations.

Recommended daily trains from Ahmedabad

The serives listed below are the most convenient and/or fastest trains from Ahmedabad.

Destination	Name	No.	Departs	Total time
Bhavnagar	Bhavnagar Express	#2971	6am	5hr 30min
Bhuj	Nagari Express	#9115	11.25pm	7hr 35min
Delhi	Ashram Express	#2915	5.45pm	16hr 30min
Dwarka	Saurashtra Mail	#9005	5.30am	10hr 30min
Jamnagar	Saurashtra Mail	#9005	5.30am	6hr 51min
Jodhpur	Ranakpur Express	#4708	12.25pm	9hr 20min
Mumbai	Shatabdi Express	#2010	2.30pm	7hr 5min
	Gujarat Mail	#2902	10pm	8hr 40min
Porbandar	Saurashtra Express	#9215	8pm	10hr 5min
Udaipur	Udaipur City Express	#9944	11.05pm	8hr 35min

Around Ahmedabad

The most obvious day-trips from Ahmedabad are north to **Adalaj**, with its impressive step-well, and beyond to the new capital of **Gandhinagar**, with its extraordinary Swaminarayan religious complex. South of town, the lake, pavilions and mausoleums of **Sarkhej** make a pleasant break from the crowded city, while further south, the excavated ancient Harappan site at **Lothal**, dating back four thousand years, is well worth a visit.

Adalaj Vav

One of Gujarat's most spectacular step-wells, **Adalaj Vav** (daily 8am–6pm), stands in lovingly tended gardens about 1km from a bus stop on the route between Ahmedabad, 19km away, and Gandhinagar. The monument, built in 1498 and now out of use, is best seen around noon, when sunlight penetrates to the bottom of the five-storey octagonal well shaft. Steps lead down to the cool depths through a series of platforms raised on pillars. Alive with exquisite sculptures, the walls, pillars, cornices and niches portray erotica, dancing maidens, musicians, animals and images of Shiva in his terrible aspect, Bhairava. Stone elephants, horses and mythical animals parade around the sides of the shaft, where green parrots swoop down to rest in the shade.

Gandhinagar

The second state capital after Chandigarh to be built from scratch since Independence, the uninspiring city of **GANDHINAGAR** is laid out in thirty residential sectors in an ordered style influenced by the work of **Le Corbusier**. Its near-symmetrical numbered streets are wide and strangely quiet, lined with a total of sixteen *lakh* trees – 26 per head of the city's population. There's little to warrant spending much time here, save the headquarters of the Swaminarayan sect, **Akshardham**. This Hindu revivalist movement, established in 1907, promotes Vedic ideals pronounced by Lord Swaminarayan (1781–1830), who proclaimed his presence would continue through a succession of saints.

Swaminarayan Complex

The Akshardham may advocate simplicity and poverty, but the colossal **Swaminarayan complex** on J Road, Sector 20 (daily except Mon 9.30am–7pm, Sat & Sun 9.30am–6.30pm) is hugely extravagant. Built of pink sandstone, all six thousand tonnes of it brought from Rajasthan, with domed roofs raised on almost one hundred profusely carved pillars, it houses the gold-leaf-coated statues of Swaminarayan and two other prominent gurus. The rest of the complex is a surreal **theme park**, with a Hall of Holy Relics containing possessions of Swaminarayan and a state-of-the-art audiovisual show using fourteen screens.

From the tone of the place, you'd never guess Akshardham witnessed one of the most appalling massacres in recent Indian history, when 33 innocent people were killed and 72 injured during a fourteen-hour **armed siege** by Pakistani suicide terrorists (the previously unknown Movement for Taking Revenge) on September 24, 2002. Links were quickly made between the attack and the post-Godhra rioting. Today, the only evidence of the massacre is a few scattered bullet holes and a heavy security presence at the entrance.

Practicalities

Regular **buses** run between Gandhinagar and Ahmedabad (45min), but there's only one train a day in each direction (1hr) and the station is inconveniently placed, out in Sector 14. Should you want to **stay**, the *Capital Guest House*, next to the tourist office in Sector 16 (entrance round the back ☎079/323 2651; ☺), has airy but dull rooms with attached bathrooms. Alternatively, there's a **youth hostel** about 1km up the lane behind it (☎079/322 2364) with barren 10–12-bed dorms (Rs60; linen Rs10).

Sarkhej

Just under 10km southwest of Ahmedabad (bus #31 from Lal Darwaja), **Sarkhej** holds a complex of beautifully fashioned monuments arranged around an artificial **lake**. On the southwest side of the lake, the square **tomb** of the revered saint Sheikh Ahmed Khattu, the spiritual mentor of Ahmed Shah, who died in 1445, is the largest mausoleum in Gujarat, with scores of pillars inside supporting the domed roof. It was constructed by Ahmed Shah's successor, Mohammed Shah, in 1446. The later Sultan Mohammed Beghada (died 1511) so deeply admired Sheikh Ahmed that he added palaces, a harem and a vast lake to the site, and finally chose to build his own tomb here as well. Sarkhej became a retreat of Gujarati sultans, who added gardens, pavilions and tombs to the elaborate complex. While some of the buildings are falling into ruin, it remains a charming place, usually teeming with Gujarati holiday-makers.

Lothal

Remains of the **Harappan** (Indus Valley) Civilization that once spread across what is now western India and eastern Pakistan have been discovered in more than fifty places in Gujarat. The largest excavated site is at **Lothal** (daily dawn to dusk), close to the mouth of the River Sabarmati, roughly 100km south of Ahmedabad, and an easy journey by bus (change at Dholka) or train (3hr). Foundations, platforms, crumbling walls and paved floors are all that remain of the prosperous sea-trading community that dwelt here between 2400 and 1900 BC, when a flood all but destroyed the settlement. A walk around the **central mound** reveals the old roads that ran past ministers' houses and through the acropolis, where you can see the remains of twelve baths and a sewer. The lower town, evident today from a scattering of fragmented bricks and foundations, comprised a bazaar, workshops for coppersmiths, bead-makers and potters, and residential quarters. On the eastern edge of the site, shattered walls enclosing a rectangle indicate the existence of a dock – the only one discovered of its kind, suggesting that Lothal was probably a port serving a number of Harappan towns. Evidence has been found here of an even older culture, perhaps dating from the fourth millennium BC, known because of its red pottery as the **Red Ware Culture**. You can see remains from this period and from the Indus Valley Civilization in the illuminating **museum** (daily except Fri 10am–5pm; Rs3).

Northern Gujarat

North of Gandhinagar, the district of Mehsana was the Solankis' seat of government between the eleventh and thirteenth centuries. Some remains of their old capital – including the extraordinary **Rani-ki-Vav** step-well – still stand at **Anhilawada Patan**, just outside the modern city of **Patan**, home to Gujarat's last remaining *patola* weavers. From the city of **Mehsana**, at the province's centre, it's easy to get to the ancient and well-preserved sun temple at **Modhera**. A Jain temple in the hills at **Taranga** can be reached from Mehsana, or directly from Ahmedabad.

The Indus Valley Civilization

Before the Mauryan empire took hold in the fourth century BC, the greatest empire in India was the **Indus Valley Civilization**. Well-planned, sophisticated settlements dating back to 2500 BC were first discovered in 1924 on the banks of the River Indus in present-day Sind (in Pakistan), at **Mohenjo Daro**. Further excavations in 1946 in Punjab revealed the city of **Harappa**, from the same era, on which archeologists based their knowledge of the entire Indus Valley Civilization. In its prime, this great society spread from the present borders of Iran and Afghanistan to Kashmir, Delhi and southern Gujarat. It lasted until 1900 BC when a series of heavy floods swept away the towns and villages in the delta regions of major rivers in Sind, Saurashtra and southern Gujarat.

A prosperous and literate society, importing raw materials from regions as far west as Egypt and trading ornaments, jewellery and cotton, it also had a remarkable, centrally controlled **political system**. Each town was almost identical, with separate areas for the ruling elite and the "workers", and all buildings built with bricks measured according to a system distinctly similar to that laid out in the Vedic *Shastras* (the earliest Hindu treatises). The complex, efficient drainage systems were unmatched by any other pre-Roman civilization.

Lothal, close to the Gulf of Cambay in southern Gujarat, was a major port, and also the source of shells which the Harappans made into jewellery. Although much about this complex society remains unknown – including their impenetrable script – similarities exist between the Indus Valley Civilization and present-day India. Like Hindus, there was a strong custom of worshipping a mother goddess. The *peepal* tree was revered as it is by Buddhists today, and there is evidence of phallic worship, still strong among Shaivites.

Mehsana

The crowded residential city of **MEHSANA**, 100km north of Ahmedabad, is the centre of the huge dairy industry, one of the largest in Asia. The only building of any interest is the old **Rajmahal** palace, now used as government offices, but the city makes a useful overnight halt if you are exploring northern Gujarat. About 3km from the station on the Ahmedabad–Palanpur highway, the *Savera Guesthouse* (℡02762/256710; ❸–❹) is the best **accommodation** Mehsana has to offer, with reasonably clean, spacious doubles, hot bucket water and some a/c rooms. If you're coming from Modhera you'll arrive on the other side of town; ask a rickshaw driver to take you to the "highway". Across the road is the flash *Navjivan* **restaurant**, with a pure-veg menu and refreshing sweet lassis. The **budget lodges** in town are some of the worst in Gujarat – the *A-One Guesthouse* (℡02762/51394; ❶) near the station is the best of a poor bunch. The nearby Janta Supermarket has a **post office** and three **banks**. **Trains** link Mehsana to Ahmedabad (2–3hr), Abu Road (2hr), Ajmer (7hr) and Jodhpur (7hr 30min). There are also very slow passenger trains to Patan (2hr). **Buses** tend to be faster and serve cities in Rajasthan and Gujarat including Bhuj.

Modhera

If you visit only one town in northern Gujarat, make it **MODHERA**, where the eleventh-century **Sun Temple** (daily 8am–6pm; Rs100) is the best example of Solanki temple architecture in the state. Almost a thousand years old, the temple has survived earthquakes and Muslim iconoclasm; apart from a missing *shikhara* and slightly worn carvings, it remains largely intact. The Solanki kings were probably influenced in their temple design by Jain traditions; deities and their vehicles, animals, voluptuous maidens and complex friezes adorn the sandy brown walls and pillars. Within the *mandapa*, or pillared entrance hall, twelve *adityas* set into niches in the wall portray the transformations of the sun in each month of the year – representations found only in sun temples. Closely associated with the sun, *adityas* are the sons of Aditi, the goddess of infinity and eternity, and represent the constraints under which the universe can exist. According to Indian convention, Modhera's sun temple is positioned so that at the equinoxes the rising sun strikes the images in the sanctuary, which at other times languishes in a dim half-light.

Modhera is linked by road to Mehsana (40min) and Ahmedabad (2–3hr). If you are coming from Ahmedabad by **bus** and want to save time, ask to get out at Mehsana highway and you can head off the hourly Modhera buses at the junction without going all the way into town. The return fare for a **taxi** from Mehsana is around Rs300. There are also direct buses from Modhera to Patan. There's nowhere to **stay** in Modhera, but the *Toran Cafeteria* in the temple grounds sells **snacks**. If you are here in January, ask about Modhera's **dance festival**, staged against the backdrop of the sun temple.

Patan and Anhilawada Patan

Founded in 1796, **PATAN**, roughly 40km northwest of Mehsana, has few monuments, but the streets of its older quarters are interesting enough, overlooked by the carved balconies of Muslim havelis and the marble domes of Jain temples. In the **Salvivad** area you can watch the complex weaving of silk *patola* saris, once the preferred garment of queens and aristocrats, and an important export of Gujarat, now made by just one extended family. Each sari, sold for Rs50–70,000, takes from four to six months to produce. Two **trains** leave Mehsana for Patan each day at 8.30am and 1.45pm, returning at 2.30pm and 6pm.

The big-city bustle of Patan is a far cry from the old Gujarati capital at **ANHILAWADA PATAN**, 2km northwest, which served several Rajput dynasties, including the Solankis, between the eighth and the twelfth centuries, before being annexed by the Mughals. It fell into decline when Ahmed Shah moved the capital to Ahmedabad in 1411. Little remains now except traces of fortifications scattered in the surrounding fields, and the stunning **Rani-ki-Vav** (daily 8am–6pm; Rs100 [Rs5]), Gujarat's greatest **step-well**. It was built for the Solanki queen Udaimati in 1050 and extensively restored during the 1980s, re-creating as perfectly as possible the original extravagant carving. Its most distinctive carving lines the well shaft, dominated by sculptures of Vishnu and his various avatars, or incarnations. Not far from the well is **Sahastraling Talav**, the "thousand-lingam tank" built at the turn of the twelfth century, but razed during Mughal raids. Only a few pillars of the Shiva temples that surrounded it still stand. This is part of the same **complex** (daily 8am–6pm) that includes a small open-air **museum** displaying a modest collection of sculpture from the area. Sparse ruins of Rani Udaimati's house crumble nearby on a hill that affords excellent views over the surrounding plains. It's a Rs30 rickshaw ride out to Rani-ki-Vav from the station. Less than a ten-minute walk from the station, the *Gujary Hotel* (℡02766/230244; ❸) is one of a few hotels in this neighbourhood offering reasonable rooms, some of them a/c, with attached bath, and a restaurant.

The Jain temple at Taranga

Well off the tourist trail, the **hilltop temple complex** at **TARANGA**, 60km or so northeast of Mehsana and easily visitable by bus, was built during the

Solanki period. The shrines are particularly striking, and better preserved than more famous sites such as Mount Abu, Girnar and Shatrunjaya. Pilgrims and white-clad monks and nuns gather here year-round to take blessings and pray. The **main temple**, built of durable sandstone, is dedicated to Ajitanath, the second of twenty-four *tirthankaras*. His image gazes out from the main sanctuary, while the rest of the temple is alive with a tangle of voluptuous maidens and musicians in smooth carved stone round the walls, pillars and ceilings. There is little in the way of tourist facilities here, although you can get a remarkably inexpensive lunch at the Jain *dharamshalas*.

Kutch

Bounded on the north and east by marshy flats and on the south and west by the Gulf of Kutch and the Arabian Sea, the province of **KUTCH** (also Kuchchh or Kachchha) is a place apart. All but isolated from neighbouring Saurashtra and Sind, the largely arid landscape is shot through with the colours of the heavily embroidered local dress. Kutchi legends can be traced in sculptural motifs, and its strong folk tradition is still represented in popular craft, clothing and jewellery designs. Few tourists make it to this region, but those who do are invariably enchanted. With a little effort, you can head out from the central city of **Bhuj** – whose population and medieval centre were devastated by the 2001 earthquake – to villages, ancient fortresses, medieval ports and isolated monasteries. The treeless marshes to the north and east, known as the Great and Little **Ranns of Kutch**, can flood completely during a heavy monsoon, effectively transforming the region into an island. Home to the rare wild ass, the Ranns are also the only region in India where flamingos breed successfully, during July and August, out of reach of any but the most determined bird-watchers who can cross the marshes by camel. The southern district of **Aiyar Patti** was once among India's most fertile areas, and though drier today, still supports crops of cotton, castor-oil plants, sunflowers, wheat and groundnuts. Northern Kutch, or **Banni**, by contrast, is semi-desert with dry shifting sands, arid grasslands and no perennial rivers; the villagers rely on their livestock and the income drawn from traditional crafts.

Some history

Remains from the third millennium BC in eastern Kutch suggest that migrating Indus Valley communities crossed the Ranns from Mohenjo Daro in modern Pakistan to Lothal in eastern Gujarat. Despite being so cut off, Kutch felt the effect of the Buddhist Mauryan empire, later coming under the control of Greek Bactrians, the Western Satraps and the powerful Guptas. The Arab invasion of Sind in 720 AD pushed refugees into Kutch's western regions, and tribes from Rajputana and Gujarat crossed its eastern borders. Later in the eighth century the region fell under the sway of the Gujarati capital Anhilawada (now Patan), and by the tenth century the Samma Rajputs, later known as the Jadejas, had infiltrated Kutch from the west and established themselves as rulers. Their line continued until Kutch was absorbed into the Indian Union in 1948, though the region has retained its customs, laws and a thriving maritime tradition, built originally on trade with Malabar, Mocha, Muscat and the African coast.

Bhuj

In the heart of Kutch, the narrow streets and old bazaars of the walled town of **BHUJ** retain a medieval flavour unlike any other Gujarati city, although much

Kutch has the most significant population of **pastoral communities** in Gujarat, most of whom migrated from east and west since the seventh century. Each tribe can be identified from its costume, and gains income from farming or crafts such as weaving, painting, woodcarving and dyeing. Traditionally, each concentrated on different crafts, although the distinctions today are less clear-cut.

The **Rabari,** the largest group, rear cattle, buffalo and camels, sell ghee, weave, and are known for their fine **embroidery.** Most of the men sport a white turban, and wear white cotton trousers tight at the ankle and in baggy pleats above the knee, a white jacket (*kehdiyun*), and a blanket thrown over one shoulder. Rabari women dress in black pleated jackets or open-backed blouses, full black skirts and tie-dyed head cloths, usually black and red, and always deck themselves with heavy silver jewellery and ivory bangles around the upper arms. Child marriages, customary among the Rabari, are performed over a four-to-five-day period in the summer; immediately upon the birth of a daughter, a mother starts embroidering cloth to form the most valuable basis of her dowry. In **Bhujodi**, near Bhuj, the Rabari weave camel wool on pit looms into blankets and shawls.

Claiming descent from Krishna, the **Bharvad** tribes infiltrated Gujarat from Vrindavan, close to Mathura in Uttar Pradesh. The men are distinguishable by the peacock, parrot and flower motifs sewn into their *khediyun*, and the women by their bright backless shirts, *kapadun*, rarely covered by veils. Both wear a thick *bori* cloth around the waist. Mass marriages take place among the Bharvad every few years, a custom originating as a form of protection in the Muslim period when single girls were frequently victims of abduction (the kidnapping of married girls was heavily punished). In the first week of each September the Bharvads gather at the Trinetresvar temple in **Tarnetar,** 65km from Rajkot, celebrating with dances and songs and sheltering under the shade of embroidered umbrellas made especially for the occasion.

The wandering **Ahir** cattle-breeders came to Gujarat from Sind, and settled as farmers. Baggy trousers and *khediyun* are worn by the men, together with a white loosely wound headcloth; the women dress like the Rabaris, with additional heavy silver nose-rings. The children's bright *topis*, or skull-caps, overlaid with neat fragments of mirrors, are like those common in Pakistan. During Diwali, Ahirs lead their cattle through the streets to be fed by other local communities, which bestows merit on the giver and is good for karma. Today the Ahirs are prospering as entrepreneurs, operating much of the truck transport in Kutch.

The **Charans,** long-established bards of Gujarat, encompass in their clans the Maldharis, who raise prize cattle in southern Kutch and the Gir Forest, and the leather-workers known as Meghavals. They claim descent from a celestial union between Charan and a maiden created by Parvati. The women are often worshipped by other tribes, since their connection with Parvati links them closely to the mother goddess, Ashpura, who is popular in Kutch. The men's curses were once considered so powerful that they drove their opponents to kill themselves in the hope that the curse would be deflected upon the Charans: such "heroes" are remembered by stone monuments around Kutch depicting a man piercing his neck with a dagger.

Said to have migrated from Pakistan, the **Jats** are an Islamic pastoral group. The men can be identified by their black dress, while young Jat girls have dainty plaits curving round the sides of their faces, and wear heavy nose-rings. Traditionally semi-nomadic camel- and cattle-rearers, with houses made of reed (*pakha*) that are easily folded and carried from place to place, they have recently begun to settle more permanently.

of it was reduced to rubble in the **earthquake** of January 2001 (which killed around 20,000 people and destroyed 1.2 million homes in the region). The section immediately behind the famed **Aina Mahal** ("Palace of Mirrors")

Kutch is known for its distinctive traditional crafts, particularly its **embroidery**, practised by pastoral groups like Hindu Rabaris and Ahirs, and Muslim Jats and Muthwas, as well as migrants from Sind including the Sodha Rajputs and Meghwal Harijans. Traditionally, each community has its own stitches and patterns, though these distinctions are becoming less apparent as time goes on.

The northern villages of Dhordo, Khavda and Hodko are home to the few remaining communities of **leather embroiderers**, who stitch flower, peacock and fish motifs onto bags, fans, horse belts, wallets, cushion covers and mirror frames, which are then sold in villages throughout the region. Dhordo is also known for its **woodcarving**, while Khavda is one of the last villages to continue the printing method known as **ajrakh**. Cloth is dyed with natural pigments in a lengthy process similar to batik, but instead of wax, a mixture of lime and gum is used to resist the dye in certain parts of the cloth when new colours are added. Women in Khavda also paint **terracotta pots**, using cotton rags and brushes made from bamboo leaves.

Rogan painting is practised only by a few artisans at Nirona in northern Kutch. A complex process turns hand-pounded castor oil into coloured dyes which are used to decorate cushion covers, bedspreads and curtains with simple geometric patterns. Craftsmen also make melodic **bells** coated in intricate designs of copper and brass; these were once used for communication among shepherds. Silver jewellery is common, featuring in most traditional Kutchi costumes, but Kutchi **silver engraving**, traditionally practised in Bhuj, is a dwindling art form. The anklets, earrings, nose rings, bangles and necklaces are similar to those seen in Rajasthan; many of them are made by the Ahir and Rabari communities who live in both areas. The main centres for silver are Anjar, Bhuj, Mandvi and Mundra.

Kutchi clothes are distinctive not only for their fine embroidery but also their bold designs. The most common form of **cloth** printing is **bandhani**, or tie-dye, practised in most villages, but concentrated in Mandvi and Anjar. One craft unique to the area is *mushroo*-weaving (*ilacha*), practised today by only a handful of artisans. The yarn used is silk, carefully dyed before it is woven in a basic striped pattern, with a complex design woven over the top in such fine detail that it seems to be embroidered.

suffered the most damage and is still being redeveloped. Since the earthquake, however, Bhuj has got a new airport, railway line and university, while the region's road infrastructure has been greatly improved. The multi-million-dollar reconstruction has created new jobs, and businesses are increasingly moving to the city. Locals are generally positive about the changes, although the process has been far from smooth: reconstruction was slow to start; there have been persistent concerns about how aid money is being spent; and the prices of staple goods have risen, in some cases dramatically. Reconstruction is ongoing and parts of the city still resemble a building site, but the city looks finally to be emerging from the tragedy.

Bhuj was established as the capital of Kutch in the mid-sixteenth century by Rao Khengarji, a Jadeja Rajput. The one interruption before 1948 in his family's continuous rule was a brief period of British domination early in the nineteenth century. When the governance of the state was handed back to the rightful ruler, Maharao Desal, in 1834, the import of slaves from Africa was banned and Africans were given homes in the north of the city. With the establishment of the city of Gandhidham and the port of Kandla southeast of the capital, the economic centre of gravity shifted away from Bhuj, leaving it to carry on its traditions little affected by the modernizations of the twentieth century.

Arrival and information

Bhuj **airport** is 5km north of town, fifteen minutes away by auto-rickshaw. The **railway station** is 1.5km north of the Aina Mahal, while the **bus stand** is on ST Station Road on the southern edge of the old city. Bhuj has no official tourist office, so your best bet for **information** is the tourist desk at Aina Mahal (daily except Sat 9am–noon & 3–6pm; ☎02832/222004, ✉pkumar_94@yahoo.com), manned by the friendly and well-informed caretaker, Pramod Jethi, who also organizes heritage walks around Bhuj (8.30am–1.30pm; Rs500).

A good way to get round the city is by **bicycle** (Rs25/day), which can be rented from Assa Cycles, Shop 40, 100m east of the *VRP Guesthouse* on Station Road; **motorcycles** can be rented to explore the surrounding Kutchi villages from MK Auto (☎02832/250077), below the *VRP Guesthouse*, for around Rs300 per 24 hours – although most are in a poor state of repair, with unreliable brakes and lights. The State Bank of India on Hospital Road **changes money** and traveller's cheques, as does ICICI across the street. Most of the **Internet** cafés are located on Hospital Road, less than 1km south of the bus stand: try Funworld (Rs20/hr) in the Jay Somnath Apartments opposite Ganatra Hospital, or Orbitt Cyber Shoppy, opposite PPC Club (Rs20/hr).

Bhuj is one of the cheapest places in western India to pick up **handicrafts** and there are shops all over town, especially at Shroff Bazaar and Vaniyawad near the old railway station around 1km north of town. In the old city, on Darbargadh Road near the Aina Mahal, Anand Handicrafts sells embroidered fabrics, woollen shawls, wall hangings, saris and *bandhani* (tie-dye).

Accommodation

City Guest House Langa St, just off Shroff Bazar, ☎02832/221067. The place to head to if rupees are tight: threadbare but super-clean rooms – some with attached bathrooms – are set around a small courtyard. ●

Gangaram Behind the Aina Mahal in the old city ☎02832/222948. The obliging Rajesh Jethi runs this travellers' stalwart, which has clean and cosy rooms, Internet access and a restaurant. ●

Garha Safari Lodge 14km north of Bhuj overlooking the Gorudra Reservoir, Ahmedabad ☎079/657 9672, ✉gbglad1@sancharnet.in. A good option for those with their own transport, this camp has 17 white concrete huts resembling traditional *bhungas* (mud-brick and straw homes) and a restaurant that often features live musical entertainment. ●

Ilark Station Rd ☎02832/258999, ✇www.hotelilark.com. Brand-new hotel with a hyper-modern red and black glass exterior and the chicest rooms in town (all have wooden floors, large beds and swanky bathrooms). There are also two smart restaurants, a small bookshop and – somewhat incongruously – a tree in the lobby. ●–●

KBN east of the bus stand on Station Rd ☎02832/227251, ✇www.hotelkbn.com. Simple mid-range rooms with wooden fittings, TV and safe; the more expensive options have a/c, and there's a decent restaurant. ●

Prince 450m east of the bus stand on Station Rd ☎02832/220370, ✉princad1@sancharnet.in. Long-established mid-range choice, with large, tastefully decorated attached rooms, welcoming staff, a foreign exchange counter and two fine restaurants. ●–●

The Town

Bhuj is overlooked from the east by the old, crumbling fort on Bhujia Hill, closed to the public as it lies in a military area, while the vast **Hamirsar Tank**, with a small park on an island in its centre, stands on its western edge. The remnants of the **old city** form an intricate maze of streets and alleyways leading to the **palace complex**, guarded by sturdy walls and high heavy gates, enclosing the Aina and Prag mahals. Built in the eighteenth century during the reign of Maharao Lakho, and later turned into a museum showcasing the opulence of the royal dynasty, the **Aina Mahal** suffered much damage in the 2001 earthquake.

Fortunately, despite its roof collapsing, the famed **Hall of Mirrors** (daily except Sat 9am–noon & 3–6pm; Rs10, camera Rs35, video camera Rs100) remains intact, and full renovation of the palace is planned, provided the budget can be secured. The chief architect of the palace, Ram Singh Malam, was an Indian seafarer who studied in Europe for seventeen years after being rescued from a shipwreck by Dutch sailors off the coast of Africa. His masterpiece was the tiled pleasure-chamber at the heart of the palace where the maharaja, soothed by an ingenious system of fountains, used to compose poetry and listen to music. Royal heirlooms on display include a couple of original Hogarths, a portrait of Catherine the Great and some priceless antique embroidery.

The nearby **Prag Mahal**, built in the 1860s and combining Mughal, British, Kutchi and Italian architectural styles, also suffered damage during the quake, and visitors are currently only allowed inside the main hall (Mon–Sat 9am–noon & 3–6pm; Rs10, camera Rs30, video camera Rs100). Movie buffs may recognize the palace as one of the locations used in Aamir Khan's 2001 hit crossover movie, *Lagaan*.

On the southwest corner of Hamirsar Tank, the **Sharad Bagh Palace** (daily 9am–noon & 3–6pm; Rs10, camera Rs20, video camera Rs100) was built in 1867 as the retreat of the last maharao. Its small porticoed buildings are delicately proportioned and include a plush drawing room, decked with hunting trophies, photographs and old clocks, and a dining room containing Maharao Madansinjhi's coffin. The palace's most appealing feature, however, is its well-tended garden. The **Kachchh Museum** at the southeast corner of Hamirsar Tank is currently being renovated, but is due to reopen in early 2008.

Just south of Hamirsar Tank and west of College Road, a path leads to the 250-year-old bone-dry **Ramkund Tank**, made of hard grey stone and shaded by trees. Decorated with skilfully crafted images of Kali, Vishnu, Nag and Ganesh, the tank also has small niches in the walls where oil lamps would glitter in the dusk as devotees prayed at the evening puja. Nearby is a set of sixteenth-century *sati* stones.

Bhuj's private **Folk Museum**, on Mandvi Road 100m west of the Collectors' Office (Mon–Sat 9am–noon & 3–6pm; Rs10, camera Rs50), contains fine examples of Kutchi pottery, embroidery, games and wall hangings.

Eating

There's an excellent crop of restaurants and juice shops along **Station Road**, while the **Hospital Road/Kalapataru Road** area southwest of the bus stand is dotted with inexpensive food stalls and snack bars. A five-minute walk north in the **Jubilee Ground** area, you'll find several ice-cream parlours.

Hotel Nilam, across from the *Prince*, is a popular veg place with a large bright dining room, attentive waiting staff and a varied menu, which includes a tasty sweetcorn curry (Rs30–70). The *Prince* has two a/c restaurants: *Jesal* offers passable international dishes like chicken stroganoff and better Indian food (Rs50–170), while *Toral* serves a memorable all-you-can-eat Rs100 thali. Station Road is also the place to pick up the local favourite **snack**, *dhabeli* (spiced lentils and peanuts in a bun), for about Rs10 each. The *Bharat Juice and Cold Drinks Shop*, 50m east of the station, and *Gopi's Parlour* on the other side of the station near the *VRP Guesthouse*, serve refreshing milkshakes and ice-cream coffees. Opposite the bus stand, the air-conditioned, family-orientated *Green Rock* has delicious Gujarati thalis as well as Punjabi dishes, south Indian *dosas* and pizzas (Rs45–60).

In the **old city**, the delightful *Green Hotel*, 200m east of the palace tucked away in an alley off Shroff Bazaar, across from the vegetable market, has been serving good-value meals (Rs45) since 1948. A popular travellers' hang-out is *Annapurna* at Bhid Gate, where Kutchi thalis (Rs45) are available in an unpretentious dining hall with coffee-table books and maps of the region – the owners are friendly and well informed. *Vijay*, 20m from the Aina Mahal entrance on Shroff Bazaar, is a quintessential Indian teashop, where locals – mainly men – gather round metal tables to drink small cups of frothy sweet tea and debate the issues of the day.

Moving on from Bhuj

Jet Airways has daily **flights** to Mumbai; book through their offices near Bank of Baroda on Station Road (℡02832/253671) or at the airport (℡02832/244101). H.M. Menon & Sons (℡02832/252286), 200m west of the station opposite the *Sagar Guesthouse*, is a recommended travel agent.

The best way to go to Ahmedabad is by **train**: take either the #9116 Nagari Express (departs 10.30pm, arrives 5.15am) or the #9032 Kutch Express (departs 8pm, arrives 2.45am) before continuing to Mumbai (11.45am). Five trains daily travel to Gandhidham, but it's easier to take the bus.

There are state **buses** to Ahmedabad (8–9hr), Rajkot (6–7hr) and Jamnagar (8hr), as well as Kutchi towns like Mandvi and Mundra. More sparse connections serve some villages in northern Kutch: call ℡02832/220002 for timings. Private bus operators are strung along Station Road: Ashapura Travels (℡02832/252491), opposite the bus stand, has a daily bus to Barmer (Rajasthan), which continues to Jaisalmer every other day, as well as a bus to Ajmer (for Pushkar); Patel Tours and Travels (℡02832/657781), 100m west of the station, has two night-sleeper buses to Ahmedabad.

For more on transport from Bhuj see "Travel details" on p.674.

Around Bhuj

Bhuj is a useful base for visiting the **outlying craft villages**. Exploring the area by **taxi** or **motorcycle** (see p.635 for rental details) gives you the most freedom. Should you opt for the slow and infrequent public **buses**, services run from Bhuj to Nirona (8–9 daily), Dhordo (2 daily) and Khavda (7 daily). For advice on which settlements to visit, chat to Pramod Jethi at the Aina Mahal museum (see p.635), who has written a useful guidebook on Kutch (Rs50), available in English and French, and runs tours to the surrounding craft villages (8.30am–5pm; Rs1300).

Earthquake damage in the places mentioned below was minimal, with the exception of the toppled Jain temples at Bhadreswar. **Permits** are required for many of the outlying villages, available from the District Superintendent of Police's Office, a five-minute walk southeast of the Hamirsar Tank (daily except Sun; 11am–2pm & 3–6pm); the permits are free, but the process takes about an hour and you'll need two copies of your passport and visa, as well as the originals.

Mandvi

The compact town of **MANDVI**, on the west bank of a wide tidal estuary 60km southwest of Bhuj, faces the Arabian Sea to the south and supports a dwindling *dhow*-building industry. Merchants, seamen and later the British settled in this once-flourishing port; though few remained long, they left behind grand mansions, painted and carved in a style clearly influenced by European tastes.

Mandvi today has a leisurely feel, with cluttered shops stretching west of the estuary and **markets** stocked with *bandhani* and silver. The estuary is blocked on the south side by shifting sands, forming a long, uncrowded **beach** good for swimming. Beside the estuary you can see the **dhows** being hand-built from long wooden planks, with nails up to 1m long forged by local blacksmiths. Fifty men spend two years building each ship, the largest of which cost around Rs2 crore (around $500,000); they're commissioned by wealthy Gulf Arabs for use as pleasure vessels, floating hotels or casinos.

Mandvi's neglected and little-visited **Vijay Vilas Palace** (daily 9am–6pm; Rs15, camera Rs50, video camera Rs200), 8km west of town (turn left after 4km), is a sandy-white domed building in almost 700 acres of land, built as a summer retreat by Kutch's maharao in the 1940s, and now often used as a film set. Inside, European furniture fills the high-ceilinged carpeted rooms, hunting trophies deck the walls and a grand stairway leads to the ladies' quarters on the first floor. The palace estate has a private beach (Rs50) with a royal pavilion offering unending sea views.

Practicalities

Hourly **buses** run between Bhuj and Mandvi (1hr 30min); crammed shared **taxis** also make the journey when full for Rs25 a head. Of the town's few **guesthouses**, the clean, modern *Sahara*, adjoining the city wall some 300m west of the bus stand (☏02834/220272; ❸), is one of the best, with a dorm (Rs50) and 24-hour checkout. Alternatively, try the *Hotel Sea View*, on ST Road on the waterfront (☏02834/224481; ❹–❺), which has homely rooms and wonderful views, or the *Vijay Vilas Palace* (☏02834/222543), with a sea-facing restaurant on its own private beach: it has a choice of unkempt rooms (❺) that are full of character, or a more expensive, luxurious tented camp (❽). The best bet for **food** is *Zorba the Buddha* on KT Shah Road, west of the bus stand behind an old town gate, where the renowned veg thalis include more than ten dishes plus fresh chutneys, pickles and sweets.

Mundra

The lively fishing port of **MUNDRA**, 44km east of Mandvi, has few sights of its own, but is a pleasant place to catch the sea breezes and buy local crafts – batik prints, silver jewellery, unusual woollen *namadas*, floor coverings and wall-hangings. A bus ride and a short walk will get you to several small Rabari and Jat villages nearby and, to the east, the Jain temple site at **Bhadreswar**, which was levelled in the 2001 earthquake but is set for complete reconstruction using the original stones and salvaged artwork. Mundra is served by slow **buses** from Mandvi (hourly; 1hr 30min) and Bhuj (hourly; 1hr 30min). Rudimentary **accommodation** is available at the unsigned *Saheb* (☏02838/222356; ❶) and *Eshant* (☏02838/222737; ❶–❷), both near the central crossroads.

Southeast to Kandla

The fifty-kilometre journey southeast from Bhuj to **KANDLA**, India's busiest port, takes you past dry scrubland. In the small village of **Bhujodi**, about 7km out of Bhuj, artisans weave thick shawls and blankets on pit looms dug into the floors of squat mud houses decorated with *gargomati*. You can buy their products from the small shop run by the Bhujodi Handweaving Co-op Society, or the Shrujan showroom, which sells a variety of Kutchi handicrafts. Further along on this road are the villages of **Paddhar**, known for Rabari embroidery, and **Dhaneti**, a centre for Ahir embroidery (ask for artisan Radhaben Ahir or for Laxmiben, who runs a small co-operative). **Dhamadka** is still an important centre for Ajrakh block-printing, though after the earthquake many artisans were moved to a new village, **Ajrakhpur**, around 10km east of Bhuj on the main highway.

The first main town beyond Bhuj, **ANJAR**, was the capital of Kutch until 1548. It was badly affected by the earthquake; recovery here has been much slower than in Bhuj, and traditional craftsmaking – Ahir embroidery, *bandhani*, batik and nut-crackers – was seriously disrupted, although a market is now held once or twice a week. Further east is **GANDHIDHAM**, the city planned for Sind refugees who came to Kutch after Partition. For tourists it serves mainly as a place to change buses or trains; it is also a good place to buy cheap handicrafts, at the market stalls along Court Road near the bus station. A state bus to Barmer (Rajasthan) passes through here daily at 3.30pm; buses run every fifteen minutes between Bhuj and Gandhidham (1hr); and the rail connections around the state include the #4312 Ala Hazrat Express to Palanpur (for Abu Rd), departing at 12.50pm and arriving at 11.50pm (Mon, Thurs, Sat & Sun).

North of Bhuj

A resurfaced road leads north of Bhuj to the craft centres of **HODKA**, **DHORDO** and **KHAVDA**, where clusters of grass-roofed mud huts are decorated with traditional clay and whitewash patterns. Around **LUDIA** – a Rabari village where NGOs unnecessarily flexed their muscles in the wake of the earthquake, building expensive and unwanted modern *bhunga* housing at a site called Ghandigram – there's a fairly commercial attitude towards tourists, so expect insistent sales pitches. Embroidery and patchwork centres include **BHIRENDIARA**, where some houses feature beautiful mud-work (*liponkan*) interiors, and **SUMERASER SHEIKH**, where NGO **Kala Raksha** (☎02808/277238, ⓦwww.kala-raksha.org) maintains an archive of antique textiles, a handicraft workshop, a small museum and a fixed-price shop. Originally established to preserve and foster traditional arts in Kutch, most of Kala Raksha's participants are women from marginalized communities, and this is a great place for travellers interested in textile design to learn about local embroidery, tie-dying, patchwork and inlay techniques. Call ahead if you want a tour of the village, where you'll be able to watch painstaking embroidery techniques like *soof* and *paako*, which create intricate symmetrical patterns. Kala Raksha's work is particularly important as the future of many of the craft villages is in some doubt: the post-earthquake reconstruction has created a great number of – largely unskilled labouring – jobs, which have attracted many craft workers with higher wages.

In the village of **Hodka**, 50km north of Bhuj, the *Shaam-e-Sarhand Rural Resort* (☎2832/654124, ⓦwww.hodka.in; ❻–❼) is a sustainable tourism project run by the local Halepotra people. Meaning "Sunset at the Border", it offers accommodation in circular mud huts or luxury tents, craft workshops, bird-watching excursions and trips to local villages. The price includes all meals and an evening musical performance. You will need a permit to visit (see p.637).

Than and Dhinodar

The monastery at **THAN**, 60km northwest of Bhuj, is home to a Tantric order of Hindu sadhus known as Kanphata ("split-ear") after the heavy agate rings they traditionally wear in their ears. Surrounded by impressive walls (to protect its occupants from attack by marauding Sindhi pirates), the whitewashed complex at the foot of the hill encloses a handful of medieval temples, tombs and domed dwellings. You can spend the night in its *dharamshala* (or up on the flat rooftop) for a small donation. Facilities are extremely basic, but worth enduring for the atmosphere: the site lies deep amid idyllic Kutchi countryside, close to the Rann, and wild peacocks congregate around the main temple at dawn to be fed by the last remaining Kanphata *sadhu*.

From Than, you can walk up a rocky ravine via an ancient pilgrims' trail to the mountaintop behind, where Dharamnath performed his yoga austerities.

Dhinodar is now the site of a neatly painted little temple, home to a single Kanphata yogi, Hiranath Baba, and his acolytes; it's a popular low-key pilgrimage destination for Kutchis during the winter. Allow three hours for the round trip from Than and take along enough water as there's little shade along the route.

Dholavira

In the far north of Kutch, on an island surrounded by snow-white salt flats, the tiny village of **DHOLAVIRA** is strewn around the remnants of a once-thriving city which, six thousand or more years ago, maintained trade links with Persia and the Euphrates Delta. Of all the so-called "Indus Valley" or "Harappan" archeological centres so far unearthed, only Mohenjo Daro and Harappa, in neighbouring Pakistan, surpass this in scale and sophistication. Yet Dholavira – which is currently being considered for UNESCO World Heritage site status – attracts barely a trickle of visitors. A bumpy 250km trip from Bhuj, it requires a major effort and sense of adventure to reach, and offers little in the way of facilities when you get there. The reward, however, is the chance to see a world-class ancient site virtually on your own.

Archeological digs started here in the 1970s after a local farmer ploughed up a small terracotta seal and sent it to Delhi. Soon, the existence of a major planned city with a citadel at its centre was revealed, complete with monumental structures, palace complex and extraordinary water management system. Uniquely among Indus Valley sites, a large ten-lettered **inscription** was found on a stone near the entrance to the citadel, which archeologists claim is the "world's oldest signboard". Unfortunately it's covered over, though a facsimile version is on display at the nearby Survey Office.

Visits to Dholavira (daily 9am–dusk) are carefully managed by a resident *chowkidar* who zealously enforces the inexplicable **no photography** rule. The "visitors centre" at the main gate is nothing of the kind, providing accommodation only for archeologists and visiting dignitaries. Instead, most people travel up here by taxi and return the same day. **Buses** do run from Bhuj, but arrive late in the evening, in which case you'll have no option but to seek out local postmaster and farmer, Mr Sambhu Dan (who found the first Dholavira seal), and request a *charpoi* in his yard. As in most Kutchi villages, offers of payment will at first be refused out of politeness, but you should persevere until they're accepted; give what you'd pay for a simple hotel room (around Rs250 per person, plus Rs100–150 for a meal).

Little Rann Wild Ass Sanctuary

Spanning 4850 square kilometres, the **Little Rann Wild Ass Sanctuary**, a vast salt-encrusted desert plain that becomes inundated during the rains (July–Sept), is home to an abundance of wildlife, including the endangered Indian **wild ass**. Usually seen in loosely knit herds that scatter when disturbed, this handsome chestnut-brown and white member of the horse family is capable of running very fast; despite strict penalties imposed by the forest department, some visitors still persist in chasing them in their cars for fun. The best way to approach the ass, which can only be found in this sanctuary (the closest relative is the Kiang, seen in Ladakh) is on foot; once they get accustomed to your presence they will pretty much continue their peaceful existence. The sanctuary is also home to wolves, Indian and desert foxes, jackals, jungle and desert cats, nilgai and blackbuck antelopes, the chinkara gazelle and a wide variety of birds. Large flocks of flamingo, pelicans and winter-visiting cranes can be seen at Bajana Lake; visit October to March if you want to see the migratory birds.

The sanctuary headquarters is at Dhrangadhra in Saurashtra, but most tourist facilities are at **Dasada**, a bumpy six-hour bus-ride east from Bhuj and 33km fromViramgam (on the Bhuj–Ahmedabad train line). From Dasada (or any of the resorts below) you can rent a 4WD (Rs1500 per day) and guide to take a tour of the sanctuary. Entrance fees (Rs250 [Rs5], camera Rs20) are paid at the entrance to the sanctuary near **Bajana** village, about thirty minutes' drive from Dasada. All the **accommodation** options in the area can arrange to pick you up at the station on arrival: try *Rann Riders* (T02757/280257, Wwww.rannriders.com, F280457; ⑥), 2km from Dasada and a half-hour drive from the station, with thirteen comfortable a/c *kooba* mud huts with tiled or grass roofs, a restaurant and swimming pool. Its all-in package (Rs2100 per person) includes all meals and two daily tours of the sanctuary and nearby villages. Another 12km on towards the sanctuary gates, *Camp Zainabad* (aka "Desert Coursers"; T0257/241333, Wwww.desertcoursers.net; ⑧) is in a similar vein, only slightly cheaper, with all-in packages from Rs1800 per person. However, the best option is wildlife photographer Devjibhai Dhamecha's excellent 🜂 *Eco Tour Camp* (T02754/280560, Wwww.littlerann.com; ❹), in Jogad village, close to Sumera lake, which has traditional thatched-roof huts for Rs1000 per couple, with all meals included.

Saurashtra

SAURASHTRA, or the **Kathiawar Peninsula**, forms the bulk of Gujarat state, a large knob of land spreading south from the hills and marshes of the north out to the Arabian Sea, cut into by the Gulf of Cambay to the east and the Gulf of Kutch to the west. This is Gujarat at its most diverse, populated by cattle-rearing tribes and industrialists, with Hindu, Jain, Buddhist and Muslim architecture, modern urban centres and traditional bazaars. Saurashtra boasts India's finest Jain temple city at **Shatrunjaya** near **Palitana**, Krishna temples at **Dwarka** and **Somnath** and Ashoka's Buddhist capital, **Junagadh**. Lions can still be found in the national park in **Gir Forest**, while in the flat yellow grassland northeast of Bhavnagar, India's largest herd of blackbuck live in a national park at **Velavadar**. Gandhi's birthplace is still honoured in **Porbandar**; he is also remembered by a museum in **Rajkot**, where he lived for some years. The best place to head for sun, sea, beaches and beer is the formerly Portuguese island of **Diu**, just off the south coast.

Rajkot

Founded in the sixteenth century, **RAJKOT** was ruled by the Jadeja Rajputs until merging with the Union of Saurashtra after Independence, since when it has become a successful industrial centre – resulting in its high levels of pollution – with a large middle class. Best known for its association with **Mahatma Gandhi**, there is little to attract tourists save a museum and Gandhi's family home. Rajkot's central position, however, makes it a good base for trips to nearby princely towns.

Arrival and information

Three main roads radiate from the busy road junction at Sanganwa Chowk in the centre of Rajkot: **Dhebar Road** heads south, past the state bus stand, 100m away; **Lakhajiraj Road** goes east, through the old city; and **Jawahar Road** runs north, past Alfred High School (Gandhi's former school, and now officially named Mahatma Gandhi High School, though most people still use its old name) and Jubilee Gardens towards **Rajkot Junction Station**, 2km northeast (get off here rather than at City Station if arriving by train), and the airport 4km northwest.

There are regular state **buses** to Jamnagar (2hr), Junagadh (2hr), Porbandar (5hr) and Veraval (5hr). Eagle Travels on Ring Road, opposite the Adani Hyper Market (☎0281/554444) has more comfortable a/c bus services to Ahmedabad, Porbandar and Vadodara. Jet Airways (opposite *Lord's Banquet* ☎0281/247 9623) has a daily **flight** to Mumbai. Rajkot's rather redundant **tourist office** (Mon–Sat 10.30am–1.30pm & 2–6pm, closed 2nd and 4th Sat of month; ☎0281/223 4507) is off Jawahar Road, north of Sanganwa Chowk behind the **State Bank of Saurashtra** (Mon–Fri 11am–3pm & 3.30–4.45pm; look for the blue ATM signs as the bank's name is in Gujarati). You'll find the **post office** on Sadar Road, off Jawahar Road opposite Jubilee Gardens. I-way **Internet centres** all over Rajkot offer fast connections (Rs30/hr).

Accommodation

Rajkot has a clutch of **hotels** around the bus stand; the cheapest leave much to be desired, so it's worth spending a little more to escape the noise and dirt of the city. In contrast to the rest of the state, **room rates** are rigidly fixed.

Bhabha Guest House Panchnath Rd, off Jawahar Rd just south of Alfred High School ☎0281/222 0861, ⊛www.hotelbhabha.com. A reasonable budget option with small singles, doubles, triples and quads; the more expensive rooms come with bathtubs, carpets and a/c. 24hr checkout. ❸–❹

Galaxy Jawahar Rd, 100m north of Sanganwa Chowk ☎0281/222 2905, ⊛www.thegalaxy hotelrajkot.com. Rooms have a drab 1970s' B&B feel but are comfortable enough, with plenty of space. The hotel is on the third floor of a shopping complex, with the only access via a creaking lift. ❹–❺

Imperial Palace Hotel Dr Yagnik Rd ☎0281/248 0000, ⊛www.theimperialpalace.biz. Rajkot's classiest hotel attracts visiting cricketers and Bollywood stars with its sumptuous rooms ($75–130) set around a central atrium, excellent restaurant, beauty centre and fitness suite. ❾

Harmony Opposite Shastri Maidan, near Limda Chowk ☎0281/224 0950, ⊛www.hotelharmony rajkot.com. Upmarket hotel in the town centre with a warming apricot colour-scheme. Attached rooms come with fridges, TVs and bathtubs, breakfast is included and there's a good restaurant. ❻–❼

Jyoti Kanak Rd, 200m north of the bus stand ☎0281/222 5472. The best of the scruffy and poky lodges in the area, thanks largely to its welcoming manager. ❶

Kavery Kanak Rd ☎0281/223 9331, ⊛www .hotelkavery.com. This mid-range hotel has neat and tidy rooms with pale wood fittings. Perks include free airport pick-up and minibar. ❻

The Town

Rajkot's most appealing area is the **old city**, where you'll see plenty of typical Gujarati wooden-fronted houses with intricately carved shutters and stained-glass windows. The Gandhis moved here from Porbandar in 1881. Tucked away in the narrow streets on Ghitaka Road, off Lakhajiraj Road about 300m east of Sanganwa Chowk – the turning is marked by a blue signpost, but it's not easily spotted – the family house **Kaba Gandhi no Delo** (Mon–Sat 9am–noon & 3–5.30pm) has a small display of artefacts and photographs. In a robust nineteenth-century building in Jubilee Bagh, the **Watson Museum** (daily except Sun and 2nd & 4th Sat of month, 9am–1pm & 2–6pm; Rs50 [Rs2]) is named after Colonel Watson, British Political Agent from 1886 to 1893 and displays relics from 2000 BC to the nineteenth century, including findings from Indus Valley sites, medieval statues and manuscripts.

Eating

Rajkot has a number of **restaurants** serving the Kathiawadi version of the Gujarati thali, spiced with ginger and garlic. It is also known for milk **sweets** like *thabdi halwas* and the saffron-flavoured *kesar pedas*, best sampled at one of the city's *Jai Siyaram* outlets.

Adingo Limda Chowk, next door to *Hotel Harmony*. Sleek eatery decked out with red tables and chairs and dishing up Gujarati and Chinese fare; the *paneer* tikka stands out (Rs45–80).

Bukhara *Kavery Hotel*, Kanak Rd. Smart-looking restaurant with good north Indian, south Indian and Mexican dishes (around Rs80 each) as well as Gujarati thali lunches.

City Fast Food 37 Karanpura. Hygienic café behind the bus stand serving meals and south Indian snacks, including wonderful masala dosas (Rs20–60).

Grand Regency Debar Rd. Recommended multi-cuisine hotel restaurant; the glass-walled kitchen is an attraction in itself, as diners get to see Indian breads like naan being prepared on the spot (Rs80).

Havmor Jawahar Rd, opposite Alfred High School. Low-key eatery with Punjabi, Chinese and Western options (including delicious chicken tikka) and its own-brand ice cream, although the snacks are overpriced – a puny chicken sandwich costs Rs40.

Lord's Banquet Kasturba Rd, opposite Dharam Cinema. Where locals go when they want a treat, this efficient place serves superior north Indian food (Rs60–130) in a/c comfort. You can get Western and Chinese snacks at their food court on the first floor of the neighbouring building.

Around Rajkot

The princes of Rajkot district left a rich legacy of elaborate **residences** whose architectural styles range from the delicate detail of the seventeenth century to bold 1930s Art Deco. Most of the buses between Rajkot and Ahmedabad stop at **SAYLA**, 87km east of Rajkot, where a colonial bungalow has been converted into the heritage hotel, *Old Bell Guest House* (T 02755/280017, F 280357; ⑥) with ten large, comfortable a/c rooms and a fine restaurant. The relaxing grounds are home to a giant chessboard and an aged tennis court. At Sayla, you can see a range of Saurashtran handicrafts, including beadwork and weaving; it is also a good base if you want to visit **Wadhwan**, known for its *bandhani* tie-dye and brassware.

Wankaner

The flamboyant **Ranjit Vilas Palace** (call ahead for permission to visit; T 02828/220000) at **WANKANER**, 39km northeast of Rajkot, is still home to the family who once ruled the old state of the same name. Built between 1899 and 1914, the symmetrical building can be seen from far across the flat Saurashtran plains. Up close, its fancy arched facade shows a frenzy of Mughal, Italianate, Moorish and Victorian Gothic styles with stained-glass windows, domed towers, chandelier-lit hallways and scores of hunting trophies looming from the walls. You can **stay** in Art Deco splendour at the family's nearby summer home, the *Royal Oasis* (T 02828/220000, F 220002; ⑦). Nightly rates include a tour of the family museum, stables, garage and step-well, use of the beautiful indoor swimming pool, and all meals. The hotel lies near the highway heading northwest to Bhuj.

Gondal

GONDAL, 39km south of Rajkot and served by half-hourly buses (1hr), was one of the most progressive of the princely states of Saurashtra, known for its wide-ranging educational and social reforms. Gondal is a centre for beadwork embroidery, handloom weaving, silverware, handmade brass-boxes called *pataras* and Ayurvedic medicine. Good places for **shopping** include the market on Darbargadh Road and the Udyog Bharati emporium near the palace. The former royal family still lives at the Huzoor Palace and have converted their guest wing into the *Orchard Palace Hotel* (T 02825/224550, E ssibal@ad1.vsnl .net.in; ⑨). Facing onto groves of fruit trees, it's a great place to stay, with large high-ceilinged rooms ($125), four-poster beds, period furniture and nice hot showers. Prices include delicious meals and **tours** of the beautifully carved 1748

Naulakha Palace, the Maharaja's vintage car collection, rail saloon and horse-drawn carriages, and the estate's bird-rich lakes and grasslands.

Jamnagar

Close to the northwest coast of Saurashtra, the busy, noisy city of **JAMNAGAR** has some fabulous architectural surprises. Founded in the sixteenth century, the walled city was built to the east of Ranmal Lake, centred on the circular Lakhota Fort. **K.S. Ranjitsinhji**, the famously elegant cricketer who played for England alongside W.G. Grace, ruled Jamnagar at the turn of the twentieth century, improving commercial contacts and replacing run-down buildings with attractive constructions that remain as testimony to a prosperous and efficient rule. The city is renowned for excellent *bandhani* (tie-dye), sold in the markets near the Darbargadh.

Arrival and information

From the **state bus station**, it's a 2km walk or rickshaw ride west, past Ranmal Lake, to **Bedi Gate** and the **New Super Market**, the unofficial centre of town. Coming from Rajkot, your bus will pass through town before arriving at the bus station, so ask to be dropped off at Bedi Gate; if departing to Rajkot, you can flag down a bus outside the *President Hotel*. From the **main railway station**, it's a six-kilometre ride southeast into town, past **Teen Batti**, an important square; most trains also stop at the smaller **Gandhinagar railway station**, 2km from the centre. There are frequent state buses to Rajkot (2hr), Junagadh (4hr), Porbandar (4hr) and Dwarka (3–4hr). **Private buses** leave from Pancheshwar Tower near Teen Batti: Patel Tours & Travels (☎0288/255 2419) has regular services to Ahmedabad, Gandhidham and Bhuj. For air tickets and other travel queries, try Savetime Travel (☎0288/255 3137) on Bedi Gate Road. The **airport** is 8km west of the bus stand: Indian Airlines (Bhid Bhanjan Rd ☎0288/255 0211) has a daily **flight** to Mumbai. The State Bank of India in New Super Market will **change cash** or traveller's cheques. There are numerous **Internet** cafés; try Venus (Rs20/hr) in a shopping complex opposite the Teen Batti **post office**.

Accommodation

Acceptable **accommodation** in Jamnagar is limited: the inexpensive places in and around New Super Market are noisy and substandard, while the more expensive hotels are better value, though more spread out.

Aram Nand Niwas, Pandit Nehru Marg ☎0288/255 1701, ⊛www.hotelaram.com. Palatial white building with blue awnings, giving it something of the feel of a British seaside hotel. The large rooms inside, nostalgic for the days of the Raj and filled with European antiques, have a faded charm. ❹–❺
Ashiana Third Floor, New Super Market ☎0288/255 9110, ℗255 1155. The rooms are spacious for a downtown budget hotel and come with TV and attached hot water bathroom – choose from carpeted deluxe rooms or grubbier ordinary ones. ❸–❹
Dreamland Teen Batti ☎0288/254 2569, ℮hoteldreamland@yahoo.co.uk. Currently under-going renovation, *Dreamland* has a number of good-alue, contemporary rooms with smart wooden fittings and bathtubs. ❹

Gayatri Guest House Sumer Club Rd ☎0288/256 4727. A 5min walk south of the bus stand, on the second floor across from Rathi Hospital; reasonably comfy rooms, some with a/c and TV, good-value singles and 24hr checkout. ❸
President Teen Batti ☎0288/255 7491, ⊛www.hotelpresident.in. A well-managed hotel, home to plain, white-walled rooms with dark wood furniture, a currency exchange and a good restaurant. Staff can also organize sailing trips. ❸–❺
Punit Pandit Nehru Marg, just northwest of Teen Batti ☎0288/255 9275, ℗255 0561. A popular place with a small but pleasant roof terrace and airy turquoise-coloured rooms, which come with carpets and slightly dated decor. ❹

The City

The most remarkable of Ranjitsinhji's constructions is **Willingdon Crescent**, the swooping arches of its curved façade overlooking the wide streets of Chelmsford Market and the old palace, the **Darbargadh**. In the heart of town, just off Ranjit Road southwest of Bedi Gate, stands the late nineteenth-century **Ratan Bai Mosque**. This grand domed prayer-hall, its sandalwood doors inlaid with mother-of-pearl, is the unlikely neighbour to a magnificent pair of **Jain temples**, both decorated with extraordinary **murals**. The most spectacular of the two, **Shantinath Mandir**, is a maze of brightly coloured columns. The outer side of the large dome over **Adinath Mandir** is inlaid with gold and coloured mosaic and both temples have cupolas enriched with a design of mirrors above the entrance porch. The temples form the hub of **Chandni Bazaar**, an almost circular market area enlivened by carved wooden doors, mosaics and balconies.

Stretching west towards the bus stand, Ranmal Lake and **Lakhota Palace** (daily except Wed and 2nd & 4th Sat of month, 10.30am–5.30pm; Rs 50 [Rs2]) were part of an employment-generating measure during a spell of drought in Jamnagar state during the 1750s. The palace is connected to solid land in both directions by a causeway but only accessible from the north side. Thick circular walls studded with gun-holes protect the inner building. On entering you'll pass a guardroom containing muskets, swords and powder flasks; the **museum** on the upper floor holds a mediocre display of paintings, sculpture, folk art and coins. South of the lake stands the solid **Bhujia Fort**, one of the few casualties of the earthquake in Jamnagar and closed ever since. To its northwest, on the edge of the old city, the **Bala Hanuman Temple** has been the scene of round-the-clock nonstop chanting ("Shree Ram, Jay Ram, Jay Jay Ram") since 1964, for which feat it is cited in the *Guinness Book of Records*.

Jamnagar's **Ayurvedic University** (☎0288/277 0103, ⊛www.ayurveduniversity.com), around 1km northwest of Teen Bati, runs a vast array of courses, lasting from a week to several months, and offers massage and mud-therapy sessions. Opposite the town hall, the **Tibet Refugee Lhasa Market** is a great place to shop for inexpensive clothes and other items.

Eating

7 Seas *Hotel President*. Continuing the hotel's vaguely nautical theme with a porthole-like door and paintings of ships on the walls, *7 Seas* also serves up some of the best non-veg food (Rs50–110) in town: the roast mutton curry stands out and don't miss the pineapple lassi.
Brahmaniya Dining Hall Teen Batti. Dark and cool a/c restaurant, serving one of Jamnagar's most famous Gujarati thalis (Rs50). Closed Sat evening.

Fresh Point Near the Town Hall. Popular with locals for its Punjabi and other north Indian dishes (Rs30–70), and laid-back atmosphere.
Kalpana Teen Batti. The decor's ageing, but the tempting veg snacks – burgers, *dosas*, milkshakes and ice cream (Rs20–50) – certainly hit the spot.
Madras Teen Batti. A cramped dining room, with separate a/c area, but great Punjabi, south Indian, Jain and Chinese dishes, including a mean veg *jalfrezi* (Rs20–65).

Dwarka

In the far west of the peninsula, fertile wheat, groundnut and cotton fields emerge in vivid contrast to the arid expanses further inland. According to Hindu legend, Krishna fled Mathura to this coastal region, declaring **DWARKA** his capital. A labyrinth of narrow winding streets cluttered with temples, the town resonates today with the bustle of eager saffron-clad pilgrims and the clatter of celebratory drums. Dwarka really comes to life during the major

Hindu **festivals**; the most fervent are the Shivratri Mela, dedicated to Shiva (Feb/March), and Janmashtami, Krishna's birthday (Aug/Sept).

The elaborately carved tower of the sixteenth-century **Dwarkadish Temple** (daily 9am–12.30pm & 5–9.30pm) looms 50m above the town. Non-Hindus can enter the shrine only on signing a form declaring, at the very least, respect for religion. Get small change for donations from the change-wallahs at the east entrance.

When Krishna came to Dwarka with the Yadava clan, he eloped with Princess Rukmini. One kilometre east of town, the small twelfth-century **Rukmini Temple** is, if anything, more architecturally impressive than the Dwarkadish temple, with carvings of elephants, flowers, dancers and Shiva in several of his aspects covering every wall. For great **views** over the town and the sea beyond, climb to the top of the **lighthouse** (daily 5pm–6.30pm; Rs6), near the *Toran Guest House*.

Practicalities

Trains from Jamnagar arrive at the station north of town, from where tongas or auto-rickshaws ferry visitors to hotels and the temple. The **bus stand** on the road to Okha has regular services to Jamnagar (3–4hr), Porbandar (3hr), Junagadh (5–6hr) and Veraval (6hr). Dwarka Darshan (☎02892/234093) in the vegetable market runs five-hour **tours** (Rs40) at 8am and 2pm to the underground *jyotrilingam* at the Nageshwar Temple, 16km from Dwarka. **Internet** access is available at Shreeji Cybercafe (Rs40/hr) opposite the *Hotel Uttam*. **Acco-mmodation** in Dwarka is, for the most part, inexpensive. *Gurupreena* (☎02892/235512; ❹), just off the approach road leading from the highway to the bus stand, has clean, comfortable rooms with hot water. The clean, modern *Hotel Rajdhani* on Hospital Road (☎02892/234070; ❹), just off the main road between the bus stand and the temple, has good-value rooms with TV; the more expensive also have a/c. *Meera* (☎02892/234031; ❶–❹) on the approach road has simple, clean rooms along with a dining hall that does a brisk turnover in Rs30 **thalis**.

Porbandar

Once an international port and princely state capital, **PORBANDAR**, between Veraval and Dwarka, is famed as the birthplace of Mahatma Gandhi. The city is also linked with the legends of **Krishna** – in ancient times the settlement was called Sudampuri, after one of Krishna's comrades. Today, shrouded in a dim haze of excretions from the cement and chemical factories on its outskirts, Porbandar is grimier than ever, despite the flow of remittance cheques from its emigrants overseas; this is where much of Gujarat's **diaspora** originate and "NRIs" (Non-Resident Indians) from Britain, Canada and East Africa are often here on visits to family and friends.

Arrival and information

Porbandar's main street, **Mahatma Gandhi (MG) Road**, runs from a fountain at its eastern end – northeast of which is the **railway station** – to a triple gateway at its western end, near Gandhi's house. In the middle, at the **main square**, it is bisected by Arya Sumaj Road, which runs northwards across Jubilee Bridge, and southwards to the **GPO**. Just east is the **State Bus Stand** (connected to MG Road by ST Road) and, to its south, the main beach. Thankys Tours and Travels, on MG Road near Dreamland Cinema (☎0286/224 4344), can book taxis, domestic and international flights, along with tickets on the #9216 Saurashtra Express **train**, which departs 8.10pm, arriving in

Ahmedabad at 6am and Mumbai at 7.10pm. Eagle Travels (☎0281/221 2089) runs regular **buses** to Rajkot (5hr), Ahmedabad (10hr) and Junagadh (3hr); there are also slower state buses. Jet Airways has a daily **flight** to Mumbai and six weekly to Diu; the airport is 5km from town. **Banks** along MG Road change foreign currency and traveller's cheques as does Thankys Tours and Travels (see opposite). Below the *Indraprasth Hotel*, Shiny the Cyber Hut and Skyline (both Rs25/hr) offer **Internet** access.

Accommodation

Indraprasth Off ST Rd ☎286/224 2681, ⓦwww.hotelindraprasth.biz. A pale pink and burgundy exterior gives way to a more tasteful interior, with original murals by local artists brightening the walls. There are a wide range of rooms with all mod cons, and the service is good. ❸–❻
Moon Palace MG Rd, 100m east of the main square ☎0286/224 1172, ⓔhmppbr@hotmail.com. Somewhat sombre but comfortable and spotless rooms, all with attached bathrooms and TV. ❷–❹

Natraj MG Rd, close to Moon Palace ☎0286/221 5658, ⓦwww.hotelnatrajp.com. Porbandar's best hotel is a notch above the competition, with cool, minimalist rooms – at bargain prices – a top restaurant and noon checkout. ❸–❹
Silver Palace Silver Complex, just off MG Rd ☎0286/225 2591, ⓦwww.silverpalacehotel.com. Another good choice; rooms are spick and span and come with TVs, fridges and various superfluous pieces of furniture (such as padded stools and mini tables). Ask to see a few rooms, as some have lurid colour schemes. ❹

The Town

The town harbours little of note, except, of course, **Gandhi's birthplace** (daily 7.30am–7.30pm; free but guides expect a donation), in the west of town. The place is empty, though some of the walls in the reading and prayer rooms on the upper floors bear faded traces of paintings. The Kirti Mandir, a memorial to the Mahatma and his wife erected in the 1950s, has photographs and artefacts from his life. The former Maharajas' palaces can be seen near the Chowpatty Seaface. **Huzoor Palace** is occupied by the family when they visit from their present home in London, while the **Daria Rajmahal Palace** near the lighthouse is now a college. **Grishmabhawan**, near the bus stand, is an impressive pavilion, adorned with arches and carvings, built for the eighteenth-century poet Maharaja Sartanji. Porbandar's lake is a designated bird sanctuary, but you can actually see more **flamingos** – along with *dhow*-builders – at the creeks along the coast than here. Over a thousand **whale sharks** visit the Gujarati coast each year, close to Porbandar and Veraval: the Wildlife Trust of India (☎011/2632 6025, ⓦwww.wildlifetrustofindia.org) works with local fishermen – who used to hunt the creatures for oil and meat – to monitor them and can help organize dives (although you will need your own equipment) or trips on research boats.

Eating

Although Porbandar is known in Gujarat for its **seafood**, you'll have a job finding it, and outside the main hotels there's a fairly uninspiring choice of **restaurants**. However, *dhabas* like *Raghuvanshi* just off MG Road have tasty and cheap Gujarati dishes (Rs25–40), while *Aarti Sweets* on MG Road is popular for packaged nibbles and freshly made sweets.

Moon Palace *Moon Palace* hotel. Justifiably popular restaurant serving Gujarati thalis (Rs50–70), Punjabi dishes and Western snacks. It also opens early for breakfast.

National MG Rd. This unassuming Muslim-run place serves skimpy but delicious meat and veg meals (Rs30–90) to a steady stream of contented customers.

Natraj *Natraj* hotel. Run with the same style and quiet efficiency as the hotel, *Natraj* has a bright dining room and varied menu of Indian, Chinese and even decent pizzas and pasta dishes – the latter a real rarity for Gujarat (Rs40–80).

Swagat MG Rd, 250m east of the main square. Softly-lit place serving excellent, mid-priced Punjabi and south Indian veg dishes (Rs20–80. It gets very busy at weekends.

Mahatma Gandhi – India's great soul

Gujarat's most famous son **Mohandas Karamchand Gandhi** was born on October 2, 1869, in Porbandar. Although merchants by caste – Gandhi means grocer – both his grandfather and father rose to positions of political influence. Young Mohandas was shy and sickly, only an average scholar, but from early on questioned the codes of power around him and even flouted accepted Hindu practice: he once ate meat for a year believing it would give him the physical edge the British appeared to possess. As a teenager, he began to develop an interest in spirituality, particularly the Jain principle of **ahimsa** (nonviolence).

Gandhi moved to London to study law at 19, outwardly adopting the appearance and manners of an English gentleman, but also keeping to his mother's wish that he resist meat, alcohol and women. Avidly reading the Bible alongside the *Bhagavad Gita*, he started to view different religions as a collective source of truth from which everyone could draw spiritual inheritance.

After a brief spell back in India, Gandhi left again to practise law in South Africa, where the plight of fellow Indians – coupled with his own indignation at being ejected from a first-class rail carriage – fuelled his campaigns for racial equality. His public profile grew and he gained crucial victories for minorities against the practices of indentured labour. During this time he also opted to transcend material possessions, dressing in the handspun *dhoti* and shawl of a peasant, and took a vow of celibacy. This turn to ascetic purity he characterized as *satyagraha*, which derived from Sanskrit ideas of "truth" and "firmness", and would become the touchstone of **passive resistance**. Returning to India with his messianic reputation well established – the poet Tagore named him **"Mahatma"** (Great Soul) – Gandhi travelled the country campaigning for **swaraj** (home rule). He also worked tirelessly for the rights of women and untouchables, whom he called **Harijans** (children of God), and founded an ashram at Sabarmati outside Ahmedabad where these principles were upheld. Gandhi stepped up his activities in the wake of the brutal massacre of protesters at Amritsar, leading a series of self-sufficiency drives during the 1920s, which culminated in the great **salt march** from Ahmedabad to Dandi in 1930. This month-long 386-kilometre journey led a swelling band of followers to the coast, where salt was made in defiance of the British monopoly on production. It drew worldwide attention: although Gandhi was promptly imprisoned, British resolve was seen to have weakened and on release he was invited to a round-table meeting in London to discuss home rule. The struggle continued for several years and Gandhi served more time in jail – his wife Kasturba dying by his side.

As the nationalist movement gained strength, Gandhi grew more concerned about the state of Hindu–Muslim relations. He responded to outbreaks of **communal violence** by subjecting his own body to self-purification and suffering through fasting. When Britain finally guaranteed independence in 1947, it seemed Gandhi's dream of a united and free India was possible after all. But **Partition** left him with a deep sense of failure. Once more he fasted in Calcutta in a bid to stem the violence as large numbers of Hindus and Muslims flowed between the new countries. Gandhi's commitment to the fair treatment of Muslim Indians and his intention to visit and endorse Pakistan as a neighbour enraged many Hindu fundamentalists. He survived an attempt on his life on January 20, 1948, only to be shot dead from close range by a lone Hindu gunman in Delhi ten days later. Prime Minister Nehru announced the loss on national radio: "Friends and comrades, the light has gone out of our lives and there is darkness everywhere."

Junagadh and around

The small town of **JUNAGADH** (or Junagarh), around 160km from Diu (via Veraval), is an intriguing place, with a skyline broken by domes and minarets and narrow streets whose shopfronts are piled high with pyramids of spices. With its lively bazaars, Buddhist monuments, Hindu temples, mosques, bold Gothic archways and faded mansions – not to mention the magnificent Jain temples on **Mount Girnar** – Junagadh is an exciting city to explore for anyone with an interest in architecture and a taste for history.

From the fourth century BC to the death of Ashoka (*c.*232 BC), Junagadh was the capital of Gujarat under the Buddhist Mauryas. The short reigns of the Kshatrapas and the Guptas came to an end when the town passed into the hands of the Hindu Chudasanas, who in turn soon lost out to Muslim invaders. Muslim sovereignty lasted until Independence when, although the leaders planned to unite Junagadh with Pakistan, local pressure ensured that it became part of the Indian Union. Because of the sanctity of Mount Girnar, 4km away, the **Shivratri Mela** (Feb/March) assumes particular importance in Junagadh, when thousands of saffron-clad sadhus come to camp around the town. Fireworks, processions, chanting, chillum-smoking and demonstrations of body-torturing ascetic practices continue for nine days and nights, and performances of folk dances and Bhawai theatre are staged. Meanwhile, every November up to one million people take part in the **Parikrama**, a five-day 36km walk around the base of the Girnar and the surrounding hills. Tourists arriving in Junagadh at either of these times are in for a memorable experience, though rooms should be booked well in advance.

Arrival and information

Arriving in Junagadh by bus or train, you're within easy walking distance of nearly all the hotels. Local transport is provided by **auto-rickshaws**, though bicycles are great for getting around; with a bit of legwork you can even cycle to the foot of Mount Girnar. Run-of-the-mill bikes can be rented from a shop just west of Chittakhana Chowk, or from the *Relief Hotel*, where staff also give the best **information** on the town's sites and Sasan Gir. The **GPO** (with poste restante) is 2km south of town; there's also a smaller branch next to the local bus stand. The State Bank of India opposite the Durbar Hall Museum **changes** dollar and sterling cash; to exchange traveller's cheques, head for the nearby State Bank of Saurashtra or the Bank of Baroda in Azad Chowk Bazaar. The Indian Cyber Café in the same shopping complex as *Ashiyana* and *Madhuvanti* offers **Internet** access (Rs20/hr).

Accommodation

Junagadh's budget **accommodation** is pretty good, though there's little in the way of luxury or mod cons.

Ashiyana Jayshree Rd, just west of Kalwa Chowk ☏0285/262 4299. Excellent-value uniform rooms with bath and cable TV on the second floor of a mini shopping complex. It's very popular with Indian tourists, so book ahead. ❷

Lotus Station Rd, close to the railway station ☏0285/265 8500, ⓦwww.thelotushotel.com. This sparkling new hotel is the most comfortable in town. The cool, swish rooms are enlivened by black and white marble floors and beige furniture. If you spend a little more you get a bathtub and a flat-screen TV as well. ❺–❻

Madhuvanti Jayshree Rd, just west of Kalwa Chowk ☏0285/262 0087. One floor down from the *Ashiyana*, *Madhuvanti* is a decent alternative to its neighbour, with hyper-plain rooms set around a central courtyard. Great if you hate clutter. ❶–❸

President Opposite the railway station ☏0285/262 5661. Handy if you want to catch an early train, this place has spotless, comfortable rooms with hot water. The larger and more expensive rooms face the noisy main road, so opt for those facing the courtyard. ❹

🏃 **Relief** Dhal Rd, Chittakhana Chowk
☎0285/262 0280, ⓦwww.reliefhotel.com.

Welcoming and knowledgeable staff, clean, bright and homely rooms, and a superior restaurant make this the best bet for backpackers, even though the plumbing sometimes leaves a little to be desired. ❷–❹

The Town

Junagadh is fairly compact, focused on the busy market area around **Chittakhana Chowk**. To the north, near the railway station, quiet wide roads lead past the majestic **Maqbara monuments**, while in the south, congested streets surround Circle and Janta *chowks*. The former comprises a fine semicircular terrace between towering Gothic gateways, while the latter is dominated by **Durbar Hall** with its modest museum. MG Road continues further south to Kalwa Chowk, another hub of activity.

In the east is the imposing fortified citadel of **Uperkot** (daily except 2nd and 4th Sat of month 6.30am–6.30pm; Rs2), perched on a thickly walled mound and colonized by eagles, egrets and squirrels. Legend dates the fort's origins to the time of the Yadavas (Krishna's clan) who fled Mathura to settle in Dwarka, but

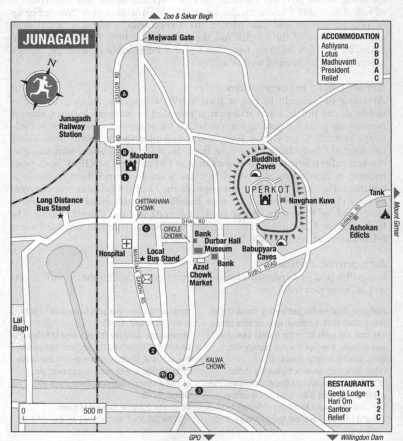

JUNAGADH

ACCOMMODATION
Ashiyana   D
Lotus   B
Madhuvanti   D
President   A
Relief   C

RESTAURANTS
Geeta Lodge   1
Hari Om   3
Santoor   2
Relief   C

historians believe it was built by Chandragupta Maurya in 319 BC. Rediscovered and repaired in 976 AD by Muslim conquerors, it regained its defensive importance, withstanding sixteen sieges over the next eight hundred years.

A grand sequence of three high gateways cut into solid rock during the Muslim occupation stands at the entrance to the citadel, spanning a cobbled walkway that winds upwards to the summit of the raised fort, where the **Jama Masjid** stands abandoned. The two fierce cannons opposite the mosque were used at Diu fort in defence against the Portuguese in 1530 and were brought here in 1538.

Heading north from the Jama Masjid, you come to a complex of small cells arranged around courtyards cut down into the rock. These **Buddhist Caves** (daily 8am–6pm; Rs100 [Rs5]) were built in the third or fourth century AD – worn traces of figurines and foliage can still be made out on the columns in the lower level. Nearby, more than 170 steps descend to the well **Adi Chadi Vav**, believed to date from the fifteenth century. The more impressive eleventh-century **Navghan Kuva**, in the southeast of the citadel, consists of a superb staircase that winds around the well shaft to the dimly-lit water level over 52m below.

Below the southern wall of the fort, the **Babupyara Caves** (Rs100 [Rs5]), hewn from the rock between 200 BC and 200 AD, were used by Buddhists until the time of Ashoka, and then by Jains. A little to the north of Uparkot, the slightly later, plainer **Khapra Kodia Caves** remain in good condition, intersected with staircases, colonnades and passages.

West of the main entrance to Uparkot, in Janta Chowk, the **Durbar Hall Museum** (daily except Wed and the 2nd & 4th Sat of each month, 9am–12.15pm & 3–6pm; Rs5) takes up part of the former palace of the nawabs. Silver chairs in the great hall stand in regal splendour around a large carpet, valuable silver clocks encase scruffy stuffed birds and huge coloured chandeliers hang from the ceiling. Surrounding rooms contain silver *howdahs* (elephant seats), weaponry, portraits and a collection of textiles.

Junagadh's chief Muslim monuments are the boldly decorated **maqbara** – quite unlike any other in Gujarat – on MG Road opposite the High Courts. Built for Muslim rulers in the nineteenth century, these squat and square mausolea are crowned with a multitude of bulbous domes. The most opulent tomb is the 1892 sepulchre of Mahabat Khan I, but more outstanding, for its complex design, is that of Vizir Sahib Baka-ud-din Bhar, completed four years later and flanked on each corner by tall minarets hugged with spiral staircases. Next to the *maqbara* is a mosque whose multicoloured pillars and gaily painted walls are oddly reminiscent of a *cassata*.

An eighteenth-century group of **smaller memorials** to earlier nawabs stands in a peaceful graveyard shielded by shops on Chittakhana Chowk. Delicate in both size and design, they boast fine carving on the graves and stone latticework cut from the walls; the rooftop of the adjacent *Amdavad* restaurant gives good aerial views.

Ashokan edicts

Two kilometres east of town on the road to Girnar, a rock engraved with the Buddhist **edicts of Ashoka** (daily 8am–1pm & 2–6pm; Rs100 [Rs5]), Junagadh's most famous monarch, remains where it was placed in the third century BC, its impact somewhat marred by a modern shelter and concrete platform. Written in the Prakrit dialect, the worn verses etched into the granite encourage the practice of *dharma* and equality and beseech different religious sects to live in harmony and repent the evils of war. Situated on the route taken by pilgrims to the sacred hill of Girnar, Ashoka's edicts had a lasting influence: even as late as the seventh century AD there were about three thousand

Buddhists in Junagadh, and over fifty convents. Sanskrit inscriptions on the same rock were added during the reigns of King Rudraman (150 AD) and Skandagupta (455 AD).

Mount Girnar

Rising to a height of more than 1100m, **Mount Girnar** (bus #4 and #6 from the GPO, or take an auto-rickshaw for Rs35), a steep-sided extinct volcano 4km east of Junagadh, is a major pilgrimage centre for both Jains and Hindus, and has been considered sacred since before the third century BC. It's best to start the ascent, which takes at least two hours, well before 7am, when the scorching sun starts to rise from behind the peak. The path of five thousand irregular steps climbs through eucalyptus forests before zigzagging across the sheer rock face, and there's a ready supply of chai and biscuits at stalls along the way.

On a plateau below the summit, roughly ninety minutes' climb from the base of the steps, the picturesque huddle of Jain temples has been slightly renovated since its erection between 1128 and 1500. Neminath, the 22nd *tirthankara* who is said to have died on Mount Girnar after seven hundred years of meditation and asceticism, is depicted as a black figure sitting in the lotus position holding a conch in the marble **Neminath temple**, the first on the left as you enter the "temple city". It's well worth making the effort to climb the final two thousand steps to the summit of Mount Girnar; the views on the way are breathtaking. At the top, a temple dedicated to the Hindu goddess **Amba Mata** attracts both Hindu and Jain pilgrims, particularly newlyweds who come here to be blessed by the mother goddess and to pray for a happy marriage. Steps lead down from this temple and then up again along a narrow ridge towards **Gorakhnath Peak**, where a small shrine covers what are supposedly the footprints of the pilgrim Gorakhnath, and further to a third peak where the imprints of Neminath's feet are sheltered by a small canopy. At the most distant point of the ridge, a shrine dedicated to the fierce Hindu goddess **Kalika**, the eternal aspect of Durga, is a haunt for near-naked **Aghora ascetics** who express their absolute renunciation of the world by ritually enacting their own funerals, living among corpses on burial grounds, and smearing themselves with ash from funeral pyres.

Eating

Kalwa Chowk is the place to head for most of Junagadh's Punjabi and south Indian restaurants and snack stalls, while **Dhal Road** has Gujarati thali restaurants and cheap non-veg *dhabas*.

Geeta Lodge Opposite the railway station. Great-value all-you-can-eat thalis (Rs 45) in this bustling low-key joint.

Hari Om Datar Rd, opposite the *National Hotel*. A friendly spot for a south Indian breakfast of *dosas* and uttapams, or a more filling Punjabi or Chinese meal (Rs50).

Santoor North of Kalwa Chowk on MG Rd.

Delicious, reasonably priced south Indian and Punjabi dishes (Rs20–60), plus locally-grown fruit milkshakes and juices, including Junagadh's famous *kesar* (saffron) mangos.

Relief *Relief Hotel.* Recently revamped restaurant where sharply-dressed bow-tie-wearing waiters serve up above-average chicken and mutton, as well as a tempting fish tikka (Rs60–100).

Moving on from Junagadh

Trains to Rajkot, Ahmedabad and the south coast all call at Junagadh. For Ahmedabad, the Jabalpur Express #1465 departs 11.45am (6hr 30min), calling at Rajkot at 1.50pm. There are also daily services to Veraval, Sasan Gir and Delwada (for Diu); for the latter two destinations, buses are quicker, but less comfortable. **Buses** from the long-distance bus stand, just west of Chittakhana Chowk, serve destinations around the state, including regular services to Una, for Diu (the 7.45am and 2.30pm go direct to Diu; 5hr). Mahasagar Travels (☎0285/262 6085) near the railway station sells tickets for private buses, notably to Mumbai (18hr); it has another office at Kalwa Chowk (☎0285/262 1913). See "Travel details" on p.673 for more information on transport from Junagadh.

Veraval and Somnath

Midway between Porbandar and Diu, the fishing port of **VERAVAL** is the jumping-off point for trips to **Somnath**, 5km east, whose temple is one of the twelve *jyotrilingams* of Shiva (see Contexts). Its shrines to Vishnu and connection with Krishna – who is said to have lived here with the Yadavas during the time of the Mahabharata – make it equally important for Vaishnavites.

Veraval practicalities

Veraval's **bus stand** (☎02876/221666) is a ten-minute walk west of town. The town is well connected to Junagadh, Porbandar and Dwarka; local buses also run to Diu, but the service is slow and the roads are rough – consider hiring a taxi. Services to Sasan Gir (1hr) start at 8am and continue every two hours thereafter. Buses to Somnath (every 15–30min) terminate a few hundred metres east of the Shiva temple. **Trains** from Junagadh (2hr), Rajkot (5hr) and Ahmedabad (12hr) pull in at the station (☎02876/220444) just over 1km north of town. For long journeys by train from Veraval it's quicker to change at Rajkot. The most convenient train for Sasan Gir (2hr) departs at 9.40am.

Veraval has a wider choice of **accommodation** than Somnath, although the smell and dirt may be enough to dissuade you from staying. *Hotel Kaveri* in Akar Complex on ST Road (☎02876/220842, ☎240140; ❹–❺) is the best in town, with clean, comfortable and well-appointed a/c and non-a/c rooms with TV and hot showers. *Tourist Bungalow* on College Road (☎02876/220488; ❸–❹), on the outskirts near the shore and the lighthouse, offers a dorm (Rs125) and spacious rooms, a so-so restaurant and a stingy 9am checkout. *Hotel Utsav*, opposite the bus stand (☎02876/22306; ❷–❹), is grubby but habitable for those on a tight budget.

Though Veraval is one of the largest fishing ports in India few places serve seafood. The comfortable a/c *Sagar* **restaurant**, near the clock tower, provides a varied veg menu of Indian, Chinese and some continental dishes, while the *Prakash Dining Hall* nearby is popular for Gujarati thalis. If you're hankering after a fishy feast, head for the *Hotel Park* on the approach road from Junagadh (Rs25 auto-rickshaws from ST Road), which has veg and non-veg restaurants.

Somnath

SOMNATH consists of only a few streets and a bus stand – even its famed sea-facing **temple** (daily 6am–9.30pm; photography prohibited) is little to look at, despite its many-layered history. Legend has it the site, formerly known as **Prabhas Patan**, was dedicated to Soma, the juice of a plant used in rituals and greatly praised for its enlightening powers (and hallucinogenic effects) in the RigVeda. The temple of Somnath itself is believed to have appeared first in gold, at the behest of the sun god, next in silver, created by the moon god, a third time in wood at the command of Krishna and, finally, in stone, built by Bhimdeva, the strongest of the five Pandava brothers from the Mahabharata tale. The earliest definite record, however, dates the temple to the tenth century when it became rich from devotees' donations. Unfortunately, such wealth came to the attention of the brutal iconoclast Mahmud of Ghazni who destroyed the shrine and carried its treasure (including elaborate sandalwood gates) off to Afghanistan. The next seven centuries saw a cycle of rebuilding and sacking, though the temple lay in ruins for over two hundred years after a final sacking by Aurangzeb before the most recent reconstruction began in 1950. Very little of the original structure remains and, although planned in the style of the Solanki period, the temple is built from unattractive modern stone. The main pujas are held at 7am, noon and 7pm. An **architectural museum** (daily except Wed and 2nd & 4th Sat of month, 10.30am–5.30pm) north of the temple, contains a hoard of its treasures – statues, lintels, sections of roof pillars, friezes and *toranas* from the tenth to twelfth centuries.

Somnath's **museum** (daily except Wed and 2nd & 4th Sat of month, 10.30am–5.30pm; Rs50 [Rs2]), housed inside a hideous pile of concrete across from the bus stand, is loaded up with seaworthy artefacts. Tongas and rickshaws gather outside the bus station, ready to take pilgrims to **temple sites east of Somnath**. Most important of these is **Triveni Tirth**, at the confluence of the Hiran, Saraswati and Kapil rivers as they flow into the sea: a peaceful place with a couple of unspectacular new temples. Before reaching the confluence, the road passes the ancient **Surya Mandir**, probably built during the Solanki period and now cramped by a newer temple and concrete houses built almost against its walls.

Practicalities

Somnath's best place to **stay** is the modern *Shivam* (☏02876/233086; ❸–❹), tucked away in the side streets near the temple, where you'll get clean rooms with the option of air-conditioning. Slightly cheaper prices push *Mayuram* (☏02876/231286; ❷–❸), southeast of the bus stand, with a Gujarati sign, into second place, ahead of *Nandi* (☏02786/231839; ❸–❹) near the architectural museum. The temple trust dishes up good-value veg **thalis** at their simple dining area near the parking lot in front of the temple.

Gir National Park

The **Asiatic lion** which, thanks to hunting, forest-cutting and poaching, has been extinct in the rest of India since the 1880s, survives in the wild in just 1150 square kilometres of the gently undulating Gir Forest. **Gir National Park** (mid-Oct or Nov to mid-June daily 7–11am & 3–5.30pm), entered from **Sasan Gir**, 60km southeast of Junagadh and 45km northeast of Veraval, holds around 350 Asiatic lions in its 260 square kilometres. They share the land with Maldhari cattle-breeders, whose main source of income is buffalo milk. Many families have been relocated outside the sanctuary, but those who remain are paid compensation by the government for the inevitable loss of buffalo to marauding lions. Gir also shelters two hundred **panthers**, which you are more likely to see here than in any other Indian park.

The best place to get acquainted with the park is the well-presented **Gir Orientation Centre** (9am–6pm) to the right as you enter the walled-in park headquarters. Across the road, behind the gift shop, **permits** can be obtained at the **park information centre**. Entry is Rs250 [Rs30], plus Rs250 [Rs50] for a camera. Furthermore, you'll be slapped with a Rs500 [Rs100] permit for vehicles (good for three days) and a mandatory **guide fee** of Rs500 [Rs50]. You'll need to hire a Jeep, available at the orientation centre (Rs500/2hr 30min–3hr trip; max 6 passengers). Though sightings are far from certain, the lions are accustomed to human noise, and seem not to be disturbed by Jeeps. Summer is the best time to spot them, when they gather at waterholes to drink.

For a guaranteed sighting, head for **Dewaliya** (daily except Wed 8–11am & 3–5pm; Rs250 [Rs30], Jeep Rs500 [Rs100], guide Rs500 [Rs50]), a partially

The Asiatic lion

The rare **Asiatic lion** (*panthera leo persica*) is paler and shaggier than the more common African breed, with longer tail tassles, more prominent elbow tufts and a larger belly fold. Probably introduced to India from Persia, the lions were widespread in the Indo-Gangetic plains at the time of the Buddha. In 300 BC Kautilya, the minister of Chandragupta Maurya, offered them protection by declaring certain areas *abharaya aranyas*, "forests free from fear". Later, in his rock-inscribed edicts, **Ashoka** admonished those who hunted the majestic animals – the emblem of Ashoka, printed on all Indian currency notes, shows four Asiatic lions standing back to back.

The Asiatic lion was favourite game for India's nineteenth-century rulers and by 1913, not long after it had been declared a protected species by the Nawab of Junagadh, its population was reduced to twenty. Since then, Gir Forest has been recognized as a sanctuary (1969), and a national park (1975), and their number has swelled to around 350. However, they remain under very serious threat. In March 2007 poachers killed eight cats, while illegal timber-felling in the forest is still common. Three major roads and a railway line bisect the park, which also has four temples that attract over 80,000 pilgrims each year; all this produces noise, pollution and littering. Moreover, when lions stray from the sanctuary – an increasingly common occurrence – there have been attacks on both human and livestock, and villagers often leave poison out for them. Plans, meanwhile, to create another reserve – possibly outside the state – to reduce the risk of the cats being wiped out by a particularly contagious disease or infection, continue to be resisted. For more info, see ⓦwww.asiatic-lion.org.

fenced-off area of the park known as the Gir Interpretation Zone. Regular Jeeps (Rs200 return) leave from Sasan Gir; once in the centre, visitors are driven in a minibus past docile lions. You get a surprisingly good impression of them "in the wild" here – they still have to hunt their food even if the deer have limited space to escape.

Practicalities

Buses and **trains** connect Sasan Gir to Junagadh (1hr 30min–2hr 30min) and Veraval (1–2hr). From Diu, head to Una and then catch a bus (2hr 15min). Sasan Gir itself is little more than a litter-strewn street fronted by chai stalls and ugly concrete blocks, and swarming with touts. One of the better inexpensive choices is *Umang* (ⓣ02877/285590; ❸–❹), close to the Forest Department's mediocre and wildly overpriced *Sinh Sadan Forest Lodge*, with freshly-painted but spartan rooms. The best place to stay near the bus stand is the elegant, Taj-run *Gir Lodge* (ⓣ02877/285521, ⓔsasan_gir@tajhotels.com; ❾), down a lane to the right of the orientation centre and backing onto the park. It's worth paying a little extra for the "superior" rooms ($80–90), which come with mini verandas overlooking the river. There is also the chance of occasional evening views of lions drinking at the nearby waterhole.

If you have your own vehicle, consider heading out to one of two hotels in the mango orchards around the park. At the sanctuary's Bambaphor Gate, the *Gir Birding Lodge* (ⓣ079/2630 2019, ⓔnwsafaris@hotmail.com; ❾) has rooms ($85–95) in a main building and in cottages. There's a natural-history library and a friendly naturalist-guide who takes guests for bird-watching walks along the nearby river. The restaurant, overlooking the sanctuary, serves good Indian and continental food. Around 4km from Sasan Gir, just off the main road from Junagadh, however, is ⚘ *Anil Farmhouse* (ⓣ02877/285590; ❹) with lovely gardens. Its excellent-value rooms are clean and comfortable with hot water, and you can enjoy all-you-can-eat meals in the unpretentious dining room for

Rs100. Note that high-season (Dec) hotel **prices** can drop by up to seventy percent in the low season (June/July).

Diu

Set off the southern tip of Saurashtra, the island of **DIU**, less than 12km long and just 3km wide, was still under Portuguese control only forty years ago. Today, governed along with Daman as a Union Territory from Delhi, it has a relaxed atmosphere quite different from anywhere in Gujarat. While its smallish beaches are not as idyllic as Goa's, most visitors stay longer than intended, idling in cafés, cycling around the island or strolling along the cliffs. The leisurely pace is also due in part to the lack of alcohol restrictions.

Diu Town in the east is the focus: a maze of alleys lined with distinctive Portuguese buildings form the hub of the **old town**, while the **fort** stands on the easternmost tip of the island, staring defiantly out at the Gulf of Cambay. Along the northern coast, the island's main road runs past salt pans that give way to mud flats sheltering flocks of water birds, including flamingos that stop to feed in early spring. The route skirting the south coast passes rocky cliffs and beaches, the most popular of which is **Nagoa Beach**, before reaching the tiny fishing village of **Vanakbara** in the very west of the island.

Some history

The earliest records of Diu date from 1298, when it was controlled by the Chudasana dynasty. Soon after, like most of Gujarat, it fell into the hands of invading Muslims and by 1349 was ruled by Mohammed bin Tughluq who successfully boosted the shipbuilding industry. Diu prospered as a Gujarati harbour and in 1510 came under the government of the Ottoman Malik Ayaz, who repelled besieging **Portuguese** forces in 1520 and 1521. Aware of Diu's strategic position for trade with Arabia and the Persian Gulf, and having already gained a toehold in Daman, the Portuguese did not relent. Under **Nuno da Cunha**, they once more tried, but failed, to take the island in 1531. However, in 1535 Sultan Bahadur of Gujarat, who had agreed to sign a peace accord, was murdered and the Portuguese took control, immediately building the fort and a strong wall around the town. While local traders and merchants continued to thrive, many resented paying taxes to boost Portuguese coffers. In defiance, local seamen made a series

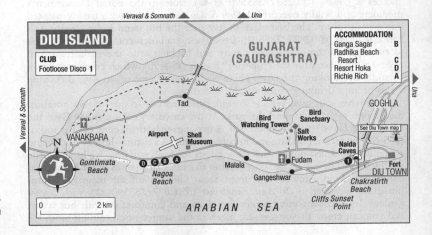

of unsuccessful raids on Portuguese ships. Mughal and Arab attacks were resisted, too, but the Portuguese were finally forced out in 1961 by the Indian government which, after a swift bombing campaign, declared Diu part of India.

Arrival and information

The usual point of entry to Diu island is by road, via **Goghla**, the small fishing village on the mainland that forms the northern edge of Diu territory. The hotels here are nothing special and most people head straight on to the island across the new bridge that links it to the northwestern edge of Diu Town. If arriving directly from points west, you may come across the other bridge in the centre of the island.

Buses pull in to the stand by the bridge, from where it's less than ten minutes' walk into town. There are state services to Porbandar, Rajkot, Jamnagar and Veraval; for Palitana, take the daily bus to Bhavnagar and change at Talaja. A number of private tour operators, including Shivshakti and Swaminarayan, operate more comfortable buses to Bhavnagar, Rajkot, Ahmedabad, Porbandar and Mumbai from the main bus stand. Far better transport connections, however, are found on the mainland, at **Una** Bus Stand and **Delwada** railway station, both connected to Diu by *tempos*, auto-rickshaws and half-hourly buses. Jet Airways (☎02875/253542) operates a **flight** every day but Saturday to Mumbai, via Porbandar ($110); their office is at the airport. Panchmurthi Travels (☎02875/252515) is a reliable agency for booking bus tickets, while convenient air, bus and train **bookings** can be made at Goa Travel (☎02875/252180).

Diu's **tourist office** (Mon–Sat 9am–1.30pm & 2.30–6pm; ☎02875/252653, ⓦwww.diuindia.com), in the port opposite the main square, offers maps but little else. The **GPO** is on the west side of the main square, upstairs, and the State Bank of Saurashtra, near the square, will **exchange money**; there are also several ATMs. Uma Cyber Café (Rs40/hr), below the *Uma Shakti* hotel and restaurant, is one of several **Internet** access points, as is the useful A–Z Tourist Centre (Rs30/hr) in the Old Portuguese District, which can also organize car, moped or **bike rental** (around Rs50/day), plus train, bus and flight tickets. Babu at the *Apana Hotel* (see below) can arrange **scooter** and **motorbike rental** (Rs125–200/day). Taxis and auto-rickshaws are also widely available. Diu-by-Night **boat cruises** (daily in high season; Rs110, including a drink) leave from the jetty at 7.30pm.

Accommodation

The price codes below represent high-season **tariffs**; during festival periods, particularly Diwali and Holi, you can expect to pay even more, while in the off-season prices can come down by as much as seventy percent. Some people, especially women, may also be put off at festival times by the rowdy atmosphere, fuelled by freely available cheap booze.

Diu Town

Apana Fort Rd ☎02875/252650, ⓕ252309. "The Peacock" is a large, professionally-run hotel that offers sizeable off-season discounts. The best rooms have sea-facing balconies, while the cheaper options are tucked away behind the restaurant and come with laminate flooring and high ceilings. ④–⑥

Cidade de Diu Off Collectorate Rd, behind *Samrat* ☎02875/254595, ⓦwww.cidadediu .com. Diu Town's top hotel is a pink, white and purple wedding cake of a building, illuminated by flashing neon lights at night. Thankfully inside, up the marble staircase, the rooms are much more tasteful and come with all mod cons. ⑥–⑦

Jay Shankar Jallandhar Beach ☎02875/252424. Remains a popular travellers' haunt for its sociable upstairs restaurant and location close to the beaches, but the rooms are beginning to show signs of wear and tear. ②–③

Samrat Collectorate Rd ☎02875/252354, ⓔsamrat_diu@yahoo.com.in. If you don't mind the clashing decor – one room boasts orange walls and tartan bedclothes – this is a fine mid-range choice, particularly as the manager is very open to bargaining. ⑤

Sanman Palace Fort Rd ☎02875/253031.This refurbished colonial mansion has an evocative exterior, which sadly does not translate to the rooms. Nevertheless they are comfortable and the a/c double is a bargain. ⑥

São Tome Retiro St Thomas's Church ☎02875/253137. A classic place to soak up the chilled Diu vibe, with a handful of straightforward rooms in an atmospheric, old Portuguese church. If it's full, you can sleep on the roof (Rs100), and the D'Souza family, who run the place, throw legendary all-you-can-eat BBQs (Rs100) every other night, open to non-guests. ②–③

Super Silver Super Silver Marketing Complex ☎02875/252020, ⓔhotel_supersilver@rediff.com. Attracts many foreign tourists with good-value, clean rooms – including triples and claustrophobic quads – all with TV; some have garish blue stripes

so ask to see a few. There is also a book exchange and a lovely roof terrace. ②–④

The rest of the island

Ganga Sagar Nagoa Beach ☎02875/252249. A great location right on the beach, but the economically-priced tiled rooms are a little worn at the seams. ④

Radhika Beach Resort Nagoa Beach ☎02875/252553, ⓦwww.radhikaresort.com. The most upmarket option outside Diu Town has attractive attached rooms, some with sea views, set around a neatly-tended garden, as well as a pool, small gym and restaurant/bar. ⑦–⑧

Resort Hoka Behind Nagoa Beach ☎02875/253036, ⓦwww.resorthoka.com. Pleasant hotel with enticing rooms, hammocks hanging in the communal areas, groves of palm trees, pool and a restaurant serving delicious fish dishes. ⑥–⑦

Richie Rich Nagoa Beach ☎02875/255355, ⓦwww.richirichresort.com. Low-rise resort that has a range of slightly boxy rooms, all with cable TV and hot showers. ⑤

Diu Town

Little **Diu Town** is protected by the fort in the east and a wall in the west. **Nagar Seth's Haveli**, one of the grandest of the town's distinctive Portuguese mansions, is on Makata Road, hidden in the web of narrow streets that wind through the residential Old Portuguese District. Fisherfolk make daily trips from the north coast in wooden boats; women lay the silvery catch out on rugs to sell in the market near the mosque.

Although the Christian population is dwindling along with the old language, a few **churches** built by the former European inhabitants are still used. Portuguese Mass is celebrated beneath the high ceilings and painted arches of **St Paul's**, though the church of **St Thomas**, to the northwest, is now a museum (daily 8am–9pm; donation expected) and guesthouse, and that of **St Francis of Assisi**, to the south, is partly occupied by the local hospital.

Diu's serene **fort** (daily 8am–6pm) stands robust, resisting the battering of the sea on three sides and sheltering birds, jackals and the town jail. Its wide moat and coastal position enabled the fort to withhold attack by land and sea, but there are obvious scars from the Indian government's air strikes in 1961 – notice the hole above the altar of the church in the southwest corner. Now abandoned almost completely to nature, and littered with centuries-old cannonballs, it commands excellent views out to sea and over the island. Just offshore, the curious, ship-shaped **Panikotha Fort** – connected to the mainland by tunnel, according to lore – is off limits, but you can hire a fishing boat (Rs60) from the dock for a closer look.

Around the island

Cliffs and rocky pools make up much of the southern coast of the island, giving way to the occasional sandy stretch. South of Diu Town is an idyllic stretch of sand called **Jallandhar Beach**; the larger **Chakratirth Beach**, overlooked by a high mound, is a little to the west, just outside the city walls. In many ways this is the most attractive beach and it's usually deserted, making it the best

DIU TOWN

Una

GOGHLA

Panikotha

N

Vegetable
Market

Main
Square

Port

Fish
Market

GPO

★ Bus
Stand

FORT RD

St Thomas's
Church

Deer
Park

St Paul's
Church

Fort

Bank

Nagar Seth's
Haveli

OLD
PORTUGUESE
DISTRICT

St Francis
of Assisi
Church

Bike
Shops

Chakratirth
Beach

Circuit
House

Jallandhar
Beach

ARABIAN SEA

0   250 m

Nagoa

Gangeshwar

RESTAURANTS & BARS	
Apana	A
Dee Pee Bar	1
Casa Luxo	1
Heranca Goesa	5
O'Couqueiro	4
Shri Ram Vijay	2
Uma Shakti	3

ACCOMMODATION	
Apana	A
Cidade de Diu	E
Jay Shankar	G
Samrat	C
Sanman Palace	B
São Tome Retiro	F
Super Silver	D

option for an undisturbed swim, especially for female travellers. At its western end, **Sunset Point** provides the regular spectacle of a golden disc sinking into the waves. The longest and only developed beach is at **Nagoa**, 7km west of town, where there are several hotels, as well as stalls, camel rides and the like, but sunbathers, especially women, are more likely to get hassled here. Buses leave Diu Town for Nagoa, but times change frequently so check with the tourist office. With a vehicle, the invariably deserted **Gomtimata Beach**, between Nagoa and Vanakbara, lies within reach.

Not far out of town, a turning off the Nagoa Road leads to **FUDAM**, an attractive village of Portuguese houses washed in pale yellow and sky grey where a church has been converted into a medical clinic. One small outdoor **bar**, shaded by twisted palm fronds, stands in the centre of the village. Further along the main road, on the right just before the airport, the **Shell Museum** (daily 9am–6pm; Rs10) is the personal collection – 42 years in the making – of Captain Fulbari, an old sailor who spent a lifetime on the ocean picking up shells wherever he weighed anchor.

Eating and drinking

Sadly, the main vestige of Portuguese influence on the dining scene in Diu is the availability of **alcohol**. *Dee Pee Bar*, guarded by mini canons, and the nearby *Casa Luxo*, which has been caught in a 1960s' time-warp, are decent drinking spots, while Diu's only nightclub, *Footloose Disco* at the *Hotel Kohinoor*, has a tiny

▲ Vanakbara fishing village

dancefloor and pop standards. Stalls in Diu Town's main square sell snacks all day; look out for the break-dancing, juggling lassi-wallah.

Apana *Apana Hotel*, Fort Rd. A busy garden terrace, overlooking the sea, with popular all-day options: the tandoori chicken dishes, in particular, stand out (Rs80–140).

Herancca Goesa Close to Diu Museum ☏02875/253851. An intimate eatery in a family home, and one of the only places to sample Portuguese- and Goan-style food in Diu: try the chicken *peri peri* and the toothsome *bebinca* pudding (Rs40–100). Book a table for dinner. If you enjoy the family atmosphere, there's also a cosy double room (❷).

O'Couqueiro On lane behind *Cidade de Diu*. A family-run garden restaurant with hanging lanterns and palm trees, serving muesli and

yoghurt for breakfast, pasta dishes made with Italian olive oil and parmesan, and some of the best fish and chips in town (Rs90–140). If you bring an MP3 player, the owners will let you play your music through their speakers.

Shri Ram Vijay Just off the main square. A wonderful piece of small-town Americana transported to Diu Town, this tiny parlour has homemade ice cream (Rs12–20/scoop), sundaes, banana splits and milkshakes.

Uma Shakti Behind the market. The rooftop terrace catches the breeze and offers views over Diu Town; it's a good place for a breakfast of pancakes and cornflakes, or a more substantial meal later on (Rs60–90).

Bhavnagar

The port of **BHAVNAGAR**, founded in 1723 by the Gohil Rajput Bhavsinghji, whose ancestors came to Gujarat from Marwar (Rajasthan) in the thirteenth century, is an important trading centre whose principal export is cotton. With few sights of its own, Bhavnagar does, however, boast a fascinating bazaar in the old city, and is an obvious place to stay for a night or two before heading southwest to the wonderful Jain temples of Palitana. For Gujarati industrialists, it serves as the jumping-off point for the massive and controversial ship-breaking yard at **Alang**, where 20,000 highly-paid labourers literally tear ships apart by hand and with explosives. The yard has been off limits to foreigners since Greenpeace red-flagged it for environmental damage, toxic spills and hazardous work. Bhavnagar is Saurashtra's **cultural capital** and the city has produced a string of artists and writers, notably the poet **Jhaverchand Meghani**, who played a prominent role in the Indian Freedom Movement. Locals also claim to speak the most grammatically-correct (or "pure") form of Gujarati.

Arrival and information

The **airport** is 5km southeast of town; auto-rickshaws into the centre cost Rs150. Arriving by **train**, the way into town is straight ahead along Station Road. From the state **bus stand**, turn right up ST Station Road for the town centre. The State Bank of Saurashtra and the Bank of India have **exchange** facilities; they're on Amba Chowk between the hotels *Shital* and *Vrindavan*. The **GPO** is next to the High Court on High Court Road, with branches just off Station Road a block south of the station, and opposite the southeastern corner of Ganga Jalia Tank. You can rent **bikes** (Rs5/hr) from a shop less than 100m south of the *Mini Hotel* on Station Road. **Internet** access is not widespread but you can surf at *Jupiter Cyber Café*, close to the State Bank of Saurashtra, for Rs15/hr.

Accommodation

Apollo ST Station Rd, opposite the bus stand ☎0278/251 5655. The cheaper rooms in this mothballed hotel are shabby, but those with a/c are a much better bet; all come with TVs and complimentary breakfast. **④**

Bluehill Opposite Pil Gardens ☎0278/242 6951, ✉bluehillad1@sancharnet.in. Staff are a little harassed, but the rooms are spacious and come with blue furniture, tubs and cute separate seating areas. **⑤**

Jubilee Opposite Pil Gardens ☎0278/243 0045, ℱ242 1744. Next door to *Bluehill*, and with similar views of the stork-filled park, *Jubilee* has good-value rooms, though the bathrooms are grungy (particularly in the a/c rooms). **③–④**

Mini Station Rd ☎0278/242 4415, ✉mahipat _mini@yahoo.com. Unkempt but sizeable rooms and friendly management make this the best budget choice. **②**

Nilambagh Palace ST Station Rd ☎0278/242 4241, ℱ242 8072. Built in 1859 by a German architect for the local crown prince, *Nilambagh Palace* is the most luxurious hotel in Bhavnagar, with vast rooms, peaceful gardens and remnants of the European influence in the chandeliers and period furniture. **⑦–⑧**

Sun 'n' Shine ST Station Rd ☎0278/251 6131, ℱ251 6130. The high expectations generated by the red-turbaned doorman and the elegant marble lobby are matched by swish rooms with carpets and bathtubs. Breakfast and free airport pick-up are included in the price. **⑤–⑥**

Vrindavan Darbargadh ☎0278/251 8928. Hidden away in the hectic streets around the market, this economy hotel has no-frills, fairly clean rooms – worth trying if the *Mini* is full. **②**

The Town

The focus of interest is the **old city**, its vibrant markets overlooked by delicate wooden balconies and the plush, pillared fronts of former merchants' houses. Local handicrafts include *bandhani* and the elaborate beadwork characteristic of the region. The marble temple, **Ganga Devi Mandir**, by the Ganga Jalia Tank in the town centre has a large dome and intricate latticework on its walls, while the otherwise unspectacular **Takhteshwar Temple**, raised on a hill in the south of town, affords a good view over to the Gulf of Cambay in the east. Southeast of the town centre, on the road to Diamond Chowk, the **Gandhi Smriti Museum** (Mon–Sat 9am–6pm, closed 2nd and 4th Sat of the month; Rs3) exhibits old sepia photos of the Mahatma, who studied here at the Shamaldas Arts College & Sir PP Science Institute for some time – a plaque in his honour can be seen in the forecourt of the imposing 1880s building. The **Barton Museum** downstairs (Mon–Sat 9am–6pm, closed 2nd and 4th Sat of the month; Rs3) haphazardly

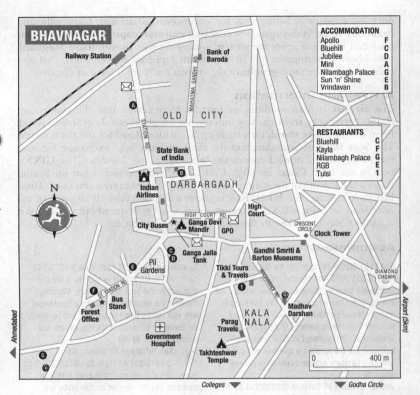

BHAVNAGAR

Railway Station

Bank of
Baroda

OLD   CITY

STATION RD

MAHATMA GANDHI RD

State Bank
of India

Indian
Airlines

DARBARGADH

HIGH COURT RD

City Buses ★ Ganga Devi
Mandir   GPO

High
Court

CRESCENT
CIRCLE   Clock Tower

Pil
Gardens

Ganga Jalia
Tank

Gandhi Smriti &
Barton Museums

Tikki Tours
& Travels

WAGHAWADI RD

DIAMOND
CHOWK

ST STATION RD

Bus
Stand

Forest
Office

KALA
NALA

Parag
Travels

Madhav
Darshan

Government
Hospital

Takhteshwar
Temple

0   400 m

Colledges ▼   ▼ Godha Circle

N

Ahmedabad ◀

▶ Airport (5km)

ACCOMMODATION

Apollo	F
Bluehill	C
Jubilee	D
Mini	A
Nilambagh Palace	G
Sun 'n' Shine	E
Vrindavan	B

RESTAURANTS

Bluehill	C
Kayla	F
Nilambagh Palace	G
RGB	E
Tulsi	1

9

GUJARAT | Saurashtra

shows off Buddhist, Jain and Hindu statues, medieval bronzes and Harappan terracotta, farming implements, coins of the princely states of Saurashtra and Kutch, weapons, and a collection of handicrafts from all over India. The **Khadi Gramodyog** shop in the same building has a good selection of Gujarati cotton shirts. Bhavnagar also has a number of impressive buildings – including the government hospital, with its huge domes and arches – commissioned by the maharajas from prominent architects like Sir William Emerson whose works include the Victoria Memorial and Crawford Market in Mumbai.

Eating

The streets on the west side of Pil Gardens are filled with stalls serving simple veg meals and snacks, although if you sit at the tables you'll have to block out the road noise. Salty nibbles called *ganthias* and *farsans*, and sweets like the famous Bhavnagar *pedas*, can be bought at *Das* on the approach road from Ahmedabad and at *Khattri* on Waghawadi Road. There is also an excellent unnamed **restaurant** behind Police Chowk on Gandhi Road, which stays open all day for low-priced local thalis.

Bluehill *Bluehill Hotel.* There are two high-class restaurants here: *Nilgiri*, serving Indian, Chinese and Western food; and the slightly cheaper *Gokul*, which serves Gujarati thalis (Rs50–90).
Kayla *Apollo Hotel.* Brand-new shiny orange dining area with glass partitions between the tables and

an interesting selection of north Indian, Punjabi and Chinese meals (Rs60–90).

🏃 **Nilambagh Palace** *Nilambagh Palace* hotel. Superb and competitively-priced chicken, mutton, fish and prawn dishes (Rs50–200). The real draw, however, is the atmosphere in the stately dining room and the peaceful gardens, where the hassles of the city seem a world away.

RGB *Sun 'n' Shine* hotel. Excellent veg Gujarati, Jain and Chinese dishes, sizzlers, and ice-cream sundaes (Rs60–110). Serving staff are professional and happy to adjust spicing levels to suit personal tastes.

Tulsi Kalanala Chowk. Indian, Chinese and a couple of continental dishes, as well as soups and salads (Rs40–70). It's a calm, quiet and dimly lit place, providing a welcome respite from the noise outside.

Moving on from Bhavnagar

The usual way to get anywhere from Bhavnagar is by **bus**. Services run from the state bus stand to Ahmedabad (hourly; 5hr), Mumbai, Bhuj, Rajkot, Junagadh and Veraval, plus Vadodara (8 daily; 6hr) and Surat (5 daily; 9hr). There's no direct service to Diu but five to Una (6hr), where you can pick up buses to Diu Town every 30min. There are buses to Palitana (every 30min; 1hr 15min) but only two daily services direct to Velavadar (1hr). **Private buses**, operated by firms such as Tanna Travels (℡0278/2425218) at Crescent Circle and any of those on Waghawadi Road, serve destinations in-state – a/c buses to Ahmedabad take 4hr, to Vadodara 5hr. Some pricier sleeper buses (with berths) are available for longer journeys. There are several **trains** to ', but most leave or arrive in the early hours. **Flights** to Mumbai (50min) are operated four days a week by Indian Airlines (northwest of Ganga Jalia Tank; ℡0278/242 6503); tickets can also be bought from Parag Travels (℡0278/251 4700) at Madhav Hill complex near the turn for Takteshwar Temple, and Tamboli Travels (℡0278/242 3400) and Tikki Tours and Travels (℡0278/243 1477) in the Prithvi Complex in Kalanala. For more on transport from Bhavnagar, see "Travel details" on p.673.

Velavadar Blackbuck National Park

Outside the tiny village of **Velavadar**, 65km north of Bhavnagar, the 34-square-kilometre **Blackbuck National Park** (mid-Oct to mid-June) shelters the highest concentration of this Indian antelope anywhere in the country. Prior to Independence their number stood at some 8000, but habitat loss and hunting cut this figure down to 200 by 1966; they now number over 3400. The park is also home to the endangered Indian wolf, nilgai antelopes, jackal foxes and jungle cats, as well as Indian fox along the periphery. Bird-watchers can spot rare species like the Stoicka's bushchat and a large roost of harrier hawks.

There are no Jeeps available for hire on site, so it's best to have your own vehicle (a **taxi** costs around Rs1000 for a day-trip from Bhavnagar). If you arrive by **bus** (2–3 daily from Bhavnagar; 1hr), it is possible to walk to one of the watchtowers near the entrance and get a good view, but it's not the same.

The park's 23-kilometre western **access road** runs via Velabhipur (on the Ahmedabad road); while its ten-kilometre eastern access road is via the tiny truck stop called Adelhai (on the road to Vadodara). **Entry** to the park is Rs250 [Rs10], plus Rs250 [Rs20] per vehicle and Rs250 [Rs5] for a still camera. On top of this you are required to take a **guide** (Rs250 [Rs30]/4hr), though few speak English and most of them are in a hurry to get back to the entrance post. **Accommodation** is decidedly limited; there are only four basic rooms (●) in the park itself, which can be booked through Bhavnagar's Forest Office (Mon–Fri 11am–6pm; ℡0278/242 6425), in the cream-and-brown concrete Bahumaliya Multi-Storey Building, Annexe F/10, just west of the bus stand. Alternatively contact the park directly (℡0278/283 0342). Meals are available and reservations are recommended.

Shatrunjaya and Palitana

For many visitors, the highlight of a trip to Saurashtra is a climb up the holy hill of **Shatrunjaya** (daily 6.30am–7.45pm, photography permits Rs40), India's principal Jain pilgrimage site, just outside the dull town of **PALITANA**, 50km southwest of Bhavnagar. More than nine hundred temples – many made of marble – crown this hill, said to be a chunk of the mighty Himalayas from where the Jains' first *tirthankara*, Adinath, and his chief disciple gained enlightenment. While records show that the hill was a *tirtha* as far back as the fifth century, the existing temples date only from the sixteenth century, anything earlier having been lost in the Muslim raids of the 1500s and 1600s.

Climbing the wide steps up Shatrunjaya takes one to two hours, though, as with all hilltop pilgrimage centres, *dholis* (seats on poles held by four bearers) are available for those who can't make it under their own steam. The views as you ascend are magnificent; spires and towers swoop upwards, hemmed in by mighty protective walls. You should allow at least two more hours to see even a fraction of the temples.

The individual *tuks* – temple enclosures – are named after the merchants who funded them. Together they create a formidable city, laid over the two summits and fortified by thick walls. Each *tuk* comprises courtyards chequered in black-and-white marble and several temples whose walls are exquisitely and profusely carved with saints, birds, animals, buxom maidens, musicians and dancers. Many are two or even three storeys high, with balconies crowned by perfectly proportioned pavilions. The *shikharas* (spires) are hollow on the inside, their conical ceilings swarming with carved figures that flow in concentric circles outwards from a central lotus blossom. The largest temple, dedicated to Adinath, in the Khartaravasi *tuk* on the northern ridge is usually full of masked Svetambara nuns and monks, dressed in white and carrying white fly-whisks. The southern ridge and the spectacular Adishvara temple in its western corner are reached by taking the right-hand fork at the top of the path. On a clear day the view from the summit takes in the Gulf of Cambay to the south, Bhavnagar to the north and the mountain range which includes Mount Girnar to the west.

The **museum** (daily 8am–noon & 4–8.30pm; Rs5), located 400m before the start of the steps at the bottom of the hill, displays a collection of Jain artefacts, labelled in Gujarati but well worth seeing.

A path leads along the ridge and down into the valley of Adipur, 13km away; it's open for one day only, during the festival of **Suth Tera** (Feb/March), when up to 50,000 pilgrims come to Shatrunjaya for this unique display of devotion.

Practicalities

Buses to Palitana depart from Bhavnagar (hourly; 1hr–1hr 30min), Junagadh (2 daily; 6hr) and Una (1 daily; 5hr). Auto-rickshaws (Rs30) and tongas run from Palitana to the foot of Shatrunjaya (10min).

There is no **accommodation** on Shatrunjaya, so you'll have to stay in Palitana, either at one of many Jain *dharamshalas* in the old part of town (all of which oblige guests to observe strict vegetarianism) or in one of the hotels on the bus stand side of town. *Hotel Sumeru* (℡02848/252327; ❸–❹), on Station Road between the bus stand and the railway station, has acceptable if scruffy rooms, some with a/c, dorm beds (Rs90) and a 9am checkout; its restaurant serves lunchtime thalis and, surprisingly, excellent pasta. *Hotel Shavrak* (℡02848/252428; ❹), opposite the bus stand, has adequate, fairly clean rooms and 24hr checkout; there is also a men-only dorm (Rs100; 9am checkout). *Vijay Vilas Palace Hotel* (℡02848/282371, ✉ssibal@ad1.vsnl.net.in; ❺) at Adpur, 4km from the bus station, is a good alternative for those who have a bit of cash and their own vehicle (alternatively an auto-rickshaw costs Rs50 one way). This converted 1906 European-style palace guesthouse is run by Yashpal, great-grandson of Prince Vijay Singh of Palitana who built it, and his wife. The rooms boast four-posters, old dressers and other early twentieth-century paraphernalia, there's a tennis court in the grounds and delicious home-cooked food is on offer.

For **food** outside the hotels, head for the narrow alley next to *Hotel Shavrak* where the basic, busy and very cheap *Jagruti Restaurant* serves excellent Gujarati meals and snacks.

Southeastern Gujarat

The seldom-visited **southeastern** corner of Gujarat, sandwiched between Maharashtra and the Arabian Sea, harbours few attractions to entice you off the road or railway line to or from Mumbai. There's little to recommend **Vadodara** (Baroda), former capital of the Gaekwad rajas, other than its proximity to the old Muslim town of **Champaner** and the ruined forts and exotic Jain and Hindu temples that encrust **Pavagadh Hill**. Further south, dairy pastures gradually give way to a swampy, malaria-infested coastal strip of banana plantations and shimmering saltpans cut by silty, sinuous rivers. The area's largest city is **Surat**, a sprawling modern industrial centre sporting a handful of colonial monuments. The only place of real interest in the far south of the state is the former Portuguese territory of **Daman**. Although nowhere near as appealing as its colonial cousins Goa and Diu, the 12km-long enclave does boast some impressive colonial architecture.

The west coast's main **transport** arteries, the NH-8 and Western Railway, run in tandem between Mumbai and Ahmedabad. The train is always more comfortable, especially between Ahmedabad and Vadodara, where the undivided highway is one of the most nail-bitingly terrifying roads in India.

Vadodara (Baroda)

The area between Ahmedabad and **VADODARA** (or Baroda) is primarily agricultural, but Vadodara itself is a congested industrial city with few attractions. However, its old core retains some interest, with beautiful havelis and traditional bazaars, and the 100,000-strong student population at the respected MS University gives it a youthful feel. **Vadodara** is also the most convenient place to stay for a trip to the ruined city of **Champaner**. If you are here at the time of the **Navratri** festival (late Sept/early Oct), you can join the throngs watching thousands of colourfully dressed women, men and children dancing into the small hours.

Arrival and information

The **railway station** and **bus stand** are close together in the west of town, within easy walking distance of most of the hotels. The airport is 6km northeast (Rs35 by auto-rickshaw). **Gujarat Tourism** (Mon–Sat 10.30am–6pm, closed 2nd and 4th Sat of month; ℡0265/242 7489) is a couple of kilometres from the station at C-Block, Ground floor, Narmada Bhavan, Jail Road. Sterling and dollars cash or **traveller's cheques** can be changed at the Bank of Baroda in Sayaji Gunj behind Kadak Bazaar, the Bank of South India opposite or the State Bank of India on RC Dutt (Racecourse) Road close to *WelcomHotel Vadodara*. The Trade Wings agency behind *Hotel Amity* in Sayaji

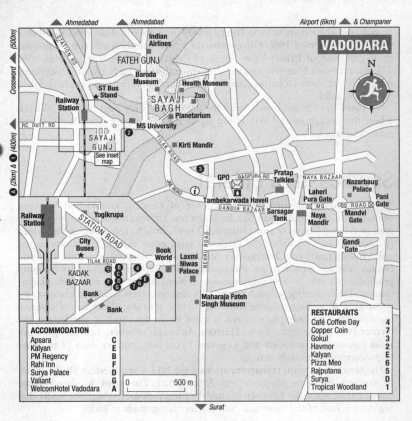

Gunj also runs an efficient exchange service and is open later than the banks. The **GPO** is off Raopura Road in the centre of town. The best **bookstore** is the excellent Crossword at Annapurna Society in Alkapuri, west of town, and there is a small selection at Book World near the Sardar Patel statue. There's an abundance of **Internet** cafés around Sayaji Gunj; try New Speedy Cyber Café (Rs15/hr), opposite the *Apsara* hotel, which also offers cheap international phone calls.

Accommodation

Vadodara has dozens of mainly mid-range hotels, but they're often full, particularly when a conference is in town, so booking ahead is advised. There are only a handful of budget options, the vast majority of which are in serious need of some loving care. Most hotels are in the **Sayaji Gunj** area just south of the railway station.

Apsara ☎0265/554 9600. Probably the best of the shoestring options – not really a ringing endorsement – with ramshackle but (just about) habitable rooms and a friendly welcome. ①–②
Kalyan Sayaji Gunj ☎0265/236 2211, ⓦwww .kalyanhotel.com. This super-clean, efficient hotel has slick, well-furnished rooms. Staff will also book train or flight tickets. ④

PM Regency Sayaji Gunj ☎0265/236 1616, ⓔpmregency@hotmail.com. Smart, modern, good-value multistorey hotel with all mod cons and 24hr checkout. ④–⑤
Rahi Inn Sayaji Gunj, opposite BBC Tower ☎0265/222 6016, ⓔhotel_rahi_inn@yahoo.co.in. New mid-range hotel with big rooms elevated by several quirky touches: fancily-painted doors,

flurescent stars on the ceiling and a lift that plays an electro version of the *Lambada*. Sheets could be cleaner, however. ❸–❹

🏃 **Surya Palace** Sayaji Gunj ☎0265/222 6000, ⊛www.suryapalace.com. The pick of the Sayaji Gunj accommodation options has smart rooms with all mod cons, an established in-house travel agent, complimentary breakfast and free Internet access. Advance bookings are highly recommended. ❻–❼

Valiant 7th floor BBC Tower, Sayaji Gunj ☎0265/236 3480, ⓕ236 2502. Another good, but somewhat impersonal business traveller–orientated hotel; all the rooms come with cable TV, fridge and clean bathrooms. ❹

WelcomHotel Vadodara RC Dutt (Racecourse) Rc ☎0265/233 0033, ⊛www.itcwelcomgroup.in. Vadodara's only five-star hotel has predictably swanky and well-maintained rooms ($125) plus a quality restaurant, swimming pool and even an in-house astrologer, should you need one. ❾

The City

Vadodara's chief attractions are in **Sayaji Bagh**, a large green park with a number of museums, the planetarium, zoo and a vintage toy train; the main entrance is on Tilak Road. Leave yourself one or two hours to get round the large Indo-Saracenic **Baroda Museum** (daily 10.30am–5pm; Rs10), reached from University Road, which holds art and textiles from all over the world, Gujarati archeological remains and Mughal miniatures.

From Sayaji Bagh, Tilak Road continues east across the river past **Kirti Mandir** (the mausoleum of Vadodara's rulers) towards the old city, the centre of which is MG Road, bounded at its western end by **Laheri Pura Gate** and **Naya Mandir** (literally "New Temple"), a fine Indo-Saracenic building, now a law court. There's another gate (Pani Gate) at the eastern end of MG Road, near the late nineteenth-century **Nazarbaug Palace** and, halfway between the two, the four-way **Mandvi Gate**, originally Mughal but much altered since.

To the west of MG Road is an artificial lake, the **Sarsagar Tank** (check out Pratap Talkies, an over-the-top Art Deco theatre at the northeastern corner), surrounded by glorious painted havelis and with a huge modern statue of Shiva in the middle. Other buildings worth a look include **Laxmi Niwas Palace** in the south of town, the most extravagant of Vadodara's palaces. If you wish to tour the palace's impressive Durbar Hall, armoury and palm-filled mosaic courtyards (Rs100), head to the **Maharaja Fateh Singh Museum** (Tues–Sun 10.30am–5.30pm; Rs15) in the palace grounds; the museum itself holds a range of Japanese, Chinese, Indian and European arts collected by the maharajas.

Eating

With a large student population and a constant influx of business people, Vadodara has a wide choice of **restaurants** in all price ranges. The cheapest places to eat are in the market and shopping centres opposite Sarsagar tank, along Dandia Bazaar and at the *dhabas* near the railway station.

Café Coffee Day Opposite the Sardar Patel statue. Vadodara's branch of the national chain draws a youthful crowd for snacks, light meals and, of course, pukka coffee (Rs25–60).

Copper Coin World Trade Centre, Sayaji Gunj. An a/c restaurant with faded charm, a fish tank and fine non-veg options, including a wonderful butter chicken (Rs80–120).

Gokul Koti Char Rasta. Small snack-bar serving excellent south Indian dishes, Punjabi and Gujarati

thalis, and ice cream at low, low prices (Rs20–60).

Havmor Tilak Rd. Tasty but fairly pricey Indian, Chinese and Western food (Rs35–150) with a/c and good service. Try the tandoori prawns or mutton kebab. There's also an ice cream and juice centre facing the main road outside.

Kalyan Sayaji Gunj. Lively fast-food-style joint with multicoloured stools where students come to chat and tuck into Mexican, Chinese and Indian snacks (Rs20–80).

Pizza Meo Sayaji Gunj. Like the ambitious Renaissance-style painted ceiling, this Italian's pizzas and pastas (Rs95–155) are good efforts, if not entirely authentic.

Rajputana Sayaji Gunj. A busy pure-veg Kutch/Rajasthani restaurant serving what many locals consider the best food in town (Rs50–90).

Surya *Surya Palace* hotel. The restaurant is the place to go for hearty buffet lunches, the chic café

serves light meals like wraps and sandwiches, while the cake shop has plenty of sugary goodies for dessert (Rs20–160).

Tropical Woodland 139 Windsor Plaza. One of the top eateries in town, with excellent south Indian food, including no less than 17 different types of *dosas*, main meals and milkshakes: try the *chikoo* flavour (Rs70–125).

Moving on from Vadodara

Vadodara **railway station** is often crowded and queues for tickets can be long (the reservation office is upstairs); you can bypass the hassle for a Rs20–30 fee if you buy your ticket from Yogikrupa Travel Service opposite (daily 8.30am–8.30pm; ℡0265/279 4977). All trains travelling along the main Delhi–Mumbai line stop here.

The **bus stand** on Station Road, a little north, has regular, state-run services to other Gujarati towns, including Champaner (hourly; 1hr 30min). Mumbai (14hr) is served by eight buses, all in the evening, but none start at Vadodara, so they may be full when they arrive – the train is far better. Stalls selling tickets for **private buses** (to Mumbai, Rajasthan and Madhya Pradesh) line Station Road.

Jet Airways and Indian Airlines have daily **flights** to Mumbai (55min); the latter also flies daily to Delhi (1hr 25min). The Indian Airlines office is in Fateh Gunj, just north of Sayaji Bagh (℡0265/279 4747); Jet Airways (℡0265/234 3441) is opposite the *WelcomHotel Vadodara* on RC Dutt (Racecourse) Road.

If you need to hire a **car and driver**, Sweta Travels (℡0265/278 6917), opposite the railway station, is a reliable operator.

For more on transport from Vadodara, see "Travel details" on p.673.

Pavagadh and Champaner

The hill of Pavagadh, 45km northeast of Vadodara, rises 820m above the plains, overlooking the almost forgotten Muslim city of **CHAMPANER**, now a World Heritage Site. Champaner (daily 10am–6pm; Rs100 [Rs5]) today has a strange, time-warped atmosphere. The massive city walls with inscribed gateways still stand, encompassing several houses, exquisite mosques and Muslim funerary monuments, as well as newer Jain *dharamshalas* to accommodate and feed pilgrims visiting Pavagadh. The largest mosque, the exuberant **Jama Masjid**, is east of the walls. Towering *minars* stand either side of the main entrance, and the prayer halls are dissected by almost two hundred pillars supporting a splendid carved roof raised in a series of domes. Save your entrance ticket, as it's also valid for the **Shahr-ki Matchi temple**, located inside the city wall near the bus stand.

For **Pavagadh**, take a bus (Rs10) from Champaner, or walk up the path that ascends through battered gates and past the old walls of the Chauhan Rajput fortress to a mid-point where you can get snacks, souvenirs and chai. You can take the cable car to the top (Rs70 return), or follow a well-trodden path on foot. On top of the hill a number of Jain temples sit below a Hindu temple dedicated to Mataji, which also has a shrine to the Muslim saint Sadan Shah on its roof.

While the view is Pavagadh's top draw, the most interesting part of the area is the ruined **fort**, opposite the main bus stand. In 1297 the Chauhan Rajputs made Pavagadh their stronghold, and fended off three attacks by the Muslims before eventually losing to Mohammed Begada in 1484. All the women and children committed *johar* (ritual suicide by self-immolation) and the men who survived the battle were slain when they refused to embrace Islam. After his conquest, Begada set to work on Champaner, which took 23 years to build. The town was the political capital of Gujarat until the death of Bahadur Shah in 1536, when the courts moved to Ahmedabad and Champaner fell into decline.

Buses from Vadodara leave hourly (via Halol; 1hr 30min) for Champaner. There are also several daily services to and from Ahmedabad, as well as shared taxis. Halfway up Pavagadh, *Hotel Champaner* (☎02676/245641; ❷–❹) has a dorm (Rs75) and adequate **rooms** with magnificent views over the vast plains of south Gujarat, as well as a **restaurant** that serves decent veg thalis. However, the ⚑ *Jambughoda Palace* (☎02676/241258, ⓦwww.jambughoda.com; ❺), 25km outside Champaner, is a much swisher option. The rooms are filled with personal touches, and the home-cooked meals (Rs250–350) make use of organic fruit and vegetables grown in the gardens. The family pile of the former Maharaja of Jambughoda, the palace overlooks the 130-sq-km Jambughoda Wildlife Sanctuary, a haven for birds, including the Paradise Fly Catcher.

Surat

Packed around a tight bend in the River Tapti, 19km before it dumps its silty waters into the Gulf of Cambay, sprawling **SURAT** was the west coast's principal port before the meteoric rise of Bombay. These days, it is one of India's fastest growing industrial centres – known for its textile, chemical and diamond-cutting businesses – of real interest only to colonial-history buffs, who come to inspect what few vestiges remain of the East India Company's first foothold on the Subcontinent, as well as some relics of Dutch and Portuguese settlers in the city before it fell to the British.

In 1994, following severe floods, the city was gripped by an outbreak of the plague, which killed more than 60 people. This proved a wake-up call and Surat has since become one of the cleanest cities in India, with an attendant rise in living standards. There is a "zero garbage" system in place for its major roads – littering is punished with a fine – which are cleaned every night by 1600 sweepers.

Surat's two main sights can be seen in an hour if you take an auto-rickshaw between them. Start at **Chowk**, a busy riverside intersection at the foot of Nehru Bridge, where the **castle** is the city's oldest surviving monument. Erected in 1540 by the Sultan of Gujarat, it was occupied by the Mughals and British, but now houses government offices. The other historic remnant of note lies fifteen minutes northeast across town beside Kataragama Road, beyond the fortified gateway of the same name. Hemmed in by modern blocks of flats, the domed mausolea of the weed-choked **English cemetery** could easily be mistaken for an oriental tomb garden. Its most impressive sepulchre is that of General Oxinden, who defeated the Marathas. Another – that of the factor Francis Breton, at the time the East India Company's most senior representative in India – was admired by the architect John Vanbrugh when he was a young factor in Surat, and is believed to have inspired his famous domed mausolea at British country seats such as Castle Howard and Blenheim.

Practicalities

Surat has very good **train and bus** connections; both stations are on the eastern edge of the city centre. Private buses dump you about 50m from the railway station. Hidden away at 1/847 Athugar St in Nanpura, the **tourist office** (Mon–Sat 10.30am–6pm, closed 2nd & 4th Sat of month; ☎0261/347 6586) can arrange visits to diamond-cutting workshops. A Rs25 auto-rickshaw ride from the railway station takes you 4km up the Ring Road to the riverbank, from where you eventually curve left towards the **tourist office**; the State Bank of India is on the same street.

Surat is a major hub for business travellers and finding a room can be hard on weekdays, so book ahead. There are plenty of **hotels** near the station, many along Sufi Baug, the street running straight ahead opposite the entrance. To the right of Sufi Baug, *Embassy* (☎0261/744 3170, ℉744 3173; ❺) is a stylish three-star and the best hotel in its price bracket. All rooms come with carpets, bathtubs and cable TV. In Khand Bazaar near the railway station, *Hospice* (☎0261/254 2424, ℉254 8484; ❹) is a welcoming high-rise with clean, comfortable rooms and complimentary breakfast, while budget travellers should head to the busy *Omkar* (☎0261/741 9329; ❶–❷), eighth floor, Omkar Chambers, Sufi Baug, which has unfussy rooms with great views over Surat (admittedly not the most picturesque of cities). There are plenty of cheap eateries in the station area, while most of the big hotels have quality **restaurants**; try *Mossam* in *Hotel Yuvraj* near the station or *Copper Chimney* at *Lords Park Inn* on the Ring Road, for good buffet deals. Surat is known for its local shortbread cookies called *nankatai*; they're available at *Mazda* in the Lalgate area and *Dotiwala* at Nanpura.

Daman

Ask any Gujarati what they associate with **DAMAN** and they'll probably say "liquor". As a Union Territory, independent of the dry state that surrounds it, Daman has liberal licensing laws and low duty on booze, making it a target at weekends for busloads of Gujarati men who drink themselves senseless and stagger around the main street. The rest of the time Daman is quieter, but generally disappointing, with a rather forlorn feel and a couple of uninspiring beaches. It does, however, offer excellent **seafood** and some immaculately preserved **Portuguese churches, houses** and **forts**.

Straddling the mouth of the **Damanganga River**, which rises in the Sahyadri Range on the Deccan plateau, Daman made an obvious target for the Portuguese, who took it in 1531 from the Sultan of Gujarat's Ethiopian governor, Siddu Bapita. The governor of Goa, Dom Constantino de Bragança, cajoled the Sultan into ceding the territory 28 years later, after which it became the hub of the Portuguese trans-Arabian Sea trade with East Africa. The town's economic decline was precipitated by the British occupation of Sind in the 1830s, which effectively strangled its **opium** business. Colonial rule, however, survived until 1961 when Nehru lost patience with Portuguese refusal to negotiate a peaceful handover and sent in the troops.

Today Daman is administered from New Delhi as a Union Territory, along with the nearby ex-Portuguese colonies of Diu, Dadra and Nagar Haveli. Apart from alcohol production and sales, its chief sources of income are coconuts, salt and smuggling. In recent years, the local tourist office has been trying to promote the area as a mini-Goa. Don't be taken in – the unbroken stretch of palm-fringed sand that runs along its twelve-kilometre coastline may look idyllic in the brochures, but is in fact grubby and subject to massive tides.

The town of Daman is made up of two separate districts. On the north side of the Damanganga River is **Nani** ("Little") **Daman**, where you'll find most of the hotels, restaurants, bars and markets; **Moti** ("Great") **Daman**, the old Portuguese quarter, lies to the south, its Baroque churches and Latinate mansions encircled by imposing stone battlements.

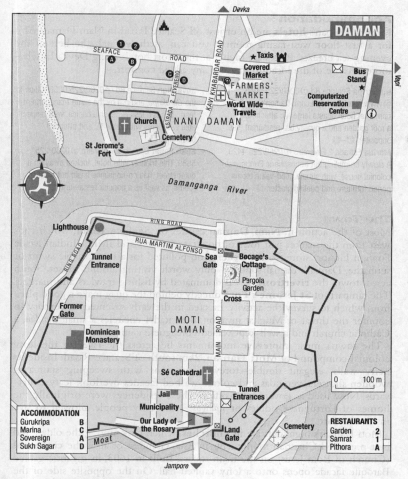

Map labels:

▲ *Devka*

SEAFACE
ROAD

Taxis
Covered
Market
FARMERS'
MARKET
World Wide
Travels

Bus
Stand

Computerized
Reservation
Centre
(i)

Church
NANI DAMAN
Cemetery

St Jerome's
Fort

N

Damanganga River

Lighthouse
RING ROAD
RUA MARTIM ALFONSO

Tunnel
Entrance
Sea
Gate
Bocage's
Cottage
Pergola
Garden
Cross

Former
Gate

MOTI
DAMAN

Dominican
Monastery

MAIN ROAD

Sé Cathedral

Jail
Municipality
Our Lady of
the Rosary
Tunnel
Entrances

Land
Gate
Cemetery

Moat

0   100 m

ACCOMMODATION
Gurukripa   B
Marina   C
Sovereign   A
Sukh Sagar   D

RESTAURANTS
Garden   2
Samrat   1
Pithora   A

▼ *Jampore*

Arrival and information

The nearest **railhead** to Daman is 12km east at **Vapi**, ranked one of the ten most polluted places in the world. Share **taxis (**Rs10) will drop you on Daman's Seaface Road, close to most of the hotels – if none is waiting in the square in front of the station, walk to the main road, take a right and continue 500m until the next main junction. Just beyond the flyover is Vapi's state **bus station**, with half-hourly buses to Daman, or you can take an auto-rickshaw (Rs70). **Leaving Daman**, there are no direct buses to anywhere further than Vapi. You can reserve **train tickets** at the computerized reservation centre (daily 8am–4pm), opposite the **tourist office** (Mon–Fri 9.30am–1.30pm & 2–6pm; ☎0260/225 5104), which is in the pink administrative building just south of the bus stand. There are two **post offices**: one north of the Damanganga Road bridge, the other in Moti Daman, opposite the Municipal Council building. World Wide Travels in the basement of the *Hotel Maharaja* (9am–9pm; ☎0260/225 5734) is the best place to **change money**. **Internet** access is available in the same building at Net City (Rs35/hr).

Accommodation

Most of Daman's **hotels** are on or just off Seaface Road in Nani Daman. Aim for a first-floor west-facing room if you can, as these catch the best of the evening sea breezes. Prices are higher at the resort hotels along Devka Beach – more because of the location than for any added comfort.

Gurukripa Seaface Rd ⓉⒹ0260/225 5046, ⓌⓌwww.hotelgurukripa.com. Daman's most upmarket hotel boasts large a/c attached, a roof garden and a quality bar-restaurant (see opposite). ⑤–⑥

Marina Estrada 2 Fevereiro ⓉⒹ0260/225 4420. A slowly crumbling but atmospheric Portuguese-colonial house, with simple good-value rooms, period furniture and peeling plaster. ④

Sovereign Seaface Rd ⓉⒹ0260/225 0236. Close to the *Gurukripa*, and run by the same management team, this is a less expensive choice, with respectable a/c rooms with cable TV and attached bathroom. ④

Sukh Sagar Estrada 2 Fevereiro ⓉⒹ0260/225 5089. This friendly little hotel, tucked away on a quiet street, has no-nonsense basic but clean rooms, as well as a popular restaurant. ③

The Town

Most of the action in **Nani Daman** centres on **Seaface Road**, which runs west from the market past rows of hotels, seedy bars and IMFL (Indian Made Foreign Liquor) stores to the **beach**. Too polluted for a comfortable swim or sunbathe, Daman's dismal strand is only worth visiting around sunset. South across town, the **riverfront** area is dominated by fishing trawlers and markets. The ramparts of **St Jerome's Fort**, directly behind the quay, make a good place from which to survey the activity. Erected in the early seventeenth century to counter the threat of Mughal invasion, the citadel encircles a small *maidan*, a Catholic church and a well-kept walled Portuguese cemetery.

The town's most impressive monuments lie across the river in the leafy colonial compound of **Moti Daman**, 2km south of Seaface Road. Inside its hefty walls, elegant double-storeyed mansions with sweeping staircases, wooden shutters, verandas and colour-washed facades overlook leafy courtyards. Now used as government offices, these residences were originally the homes of Portuguese nobles or *fidalgos* – the only people allowed to live inside the fort.

Moti Daman's highlights are its **churches**, which rank among the oldest and best-preserved Christian monuments in Asia. Grandest of all is the **cathedral** (Church of Bom Jesus) on the main square. Built in 1603, its gigantic gabled Baroque facade opens onto a lofty vaulted hall. On the opposite side of the square, the **Church of Our Lady of the Rosary** is crammed with ornate woodwork, notably some fine tableaux of the life of Jesus by the altar.

Main Road links Moti Daman's two **gates**, installed in the 1580s following a Mughal invasion. A small cottage next to the northern ("sea") gate was once the home of the eighteenth-century Portuguese poet Bocage, while atop the bastion facing the southern ("land") gate is the cell where prisoners condemned to death in Portuguese times spent their final days. A vivid account of the appalling conditions in which those interred in them were kept has been preserved in the chronicle of **Charles Dellon**, an unfortunate young French physician who found himself at the mercy of the Inquisition in 1673 after the governor suspected him of having an affair with his wife. Dellon recalls how rather than endure the squalour, forty Malabar pirates hanged themselves with their own turbans. Transferred to Goa, the Frenchman survived three more years in solitary confinement before being released as a galley slave. His account of the ordeal, published in 1687, became an international bestseller and remains one of the most harrowing accounts of captivity ever written.

Eating and drinking

The disproportionately large number of **places to eat** in Daman is due to the town's liquor laws, which oblige all bars to serve food with alcohol. Most of the "bar-restaurants" along Seaface Road are restaurants in name only and best avoided. **Seafood**, on offer all year except during the monsoons, is especially good from late September to early November, when the fish market is glutted with fresh crabs, prawns and lobsters. Also seasonal is *papri*, a street snack consisting of beans baked in a pot with potatoes, sold with a special masala between January and April.

Garden Seaface Rd. A terrace restaurant-bar serving reasonably priced tandoori pomfret and lobster, as well as Goan and Damanese meat and veg specialities (Rs40–200).

Gurukripa *Gurukripa* hotel. The place to come for a slap-up meal: choose from an extensive seafood menu – pomfret stuffed with prawns and rich fish curries are highlights (Rs50–200) – and finish with a nip of potent Goan *feni* (coconut spirit).

Samrat Seaface Rd. Spotless roadside restaurant specializing in eat-till-you-burst Gujarati thalis, which come with *namkeens* (salty titbits), a couple of different dhals and mouthwatering mild veg dishes (Rs40–70). Strictly "pure-veg" (read "no alcohol").

Pithora *Sovereign* hotel. south Indian snacks, thalis, Chinese dishes and cold beers served indoors or alfresco on a breezy balcony done up like a Gujarati village (Rs40–90).

Travel details

Trains

Ahmedabad to: Abu Rd (7 daily; 3hr 30min–4hr 30min); Agra (4 weekly; 27hr 45min); Ajmer (4 daily; 7hr 5min–10hr 55min); Bengaluru (Bangalore) (6 weekly; 35hr 55min–37hr 40min); Bhavnagar (2 daily; 3hr 30min–7hr); Chennai (1 daily; 37hr 30min); Delhi (2–4 daily; 13hr–31hr 35min); Dwarka (1–2 daily; 10hr); Jaipur (7 daily; 9hr–14hr); Jamnagar (4 daily; 7hr); Jodhpur (2 daily; 9hr–9hr 55min); Junagadh (1–3 daily; 8hr 20min–9hr 55min); Kolkata (Calcutta; 1 daily; 41hr); Mumbai (10 daily; 7hr 5min–12hr); Porbandar (1–2 daily; 10hr); Rajkot (5–6 daily; 4hr 5min–5hr 35min); Surat (11–14 daily; 3hr 30min–4hr 30min); Thiruvananthapuram (2 weekly; 40hr 15min); Udaipur (2 daily; 8hr 45min); Vadodara (14–17 daily; 1hr 35min–2hr 25min); Varanasi (4 weekly; 41hr); Veraval (3 nightly; 10hr 25min–12hr).

Bhavnagar to: Ahmedabad (2 daily; 3hr 30min–7hr); Veraval (1 daily; 9hr).

Dwarka to: Ahmedabad (1–2 daily; 10hr); Jamnagar (2–3 daily; 2hr 20min–4hr 40min); Mumbai (1 daily; 17hr 45min); Rajkot (3–4 daily; 4hr 50min–7hr 30min).

Junagadh to: Ahmedabad (1–3 daily; 8hr 20min–9hr 55min); Delvada (for Diu; 1 daily; 6hr); Rajkot (4 daily; 3hr 20min–5hr); Sasan Gir (1 daily;

2hr 30min); Veraval (3 daily; 2hr–3hr 30min).

Porbandar to: Ahmedabad (1–2 daily; 10hr); Jamnagar (2–3 daily; 2hr 25min–4hr); Mumbai (1 daily; 23hr 30min); Rajkot (2–3 daily; 4hr 40min–6hr); Surat (1 daily; 16hr 40min); Vadodara (1 daily; 13hr 35min).

Rajkot to: Ahmedabad (5–6 daily; 4hr 5min–5hr 35min); Junagadh (4 daily; 3hr 30min–5hr 05min); Porbandar (2–3 daily; 4hr 25min–5hr 35min); Veraval (1 daily; 5hr 15min).

Vadodara to: Ahmedabad (14–17 daily; 1hr 35min–2hr 30min); Baruch (every 30min daily; 48min–1hr 15min); Delhi (6 daily; 12–24hr); Indore (2 daily; 8hr 10min); Jaipur (1 daily; 11hr 50min); Kolkata (Calcutta; 1 daily; 42hr); Mumbai (16–20 daily; 7hr); Porbandar (1 daily; 13hr 40min); Pune (1 daily; 10hr 20min–11hr); Surat (every 30min; 1hr 50min–2hr 30min); Vapi (for Daman; 10 daily; 4hr).

Vapi to: Ahmedabad (7 daily; 6–7hr); Jamnagar (1 daily; 15hr); Mumbai (10 daily; 3–4hr); Rajkot (1 daily; 12hr 30min); Surat (9–10 daily; 1hr 45min–3hr); Vadodara (13–14 daily; 4–5hr).

Buses

Ahmedabad to: Abu Rd (5–6 daily; 6hr); Ajmer (1 daily; 14hr); Bhavnagar (hourly; 5hr); Bhuj (10–12 daily; 8–9hr); Diu (2–4 daily; 11hr–12hr); Dwarka (6 daily; 11hr) Indore (1–2 nightly; 10hr); Jaipur (1 daily; 16hr); Jamnagar (hourly; 7hr);

Jodhpur (3 daily; 12hr); Junagadh (hourly; 8hr); Mumbai (2–3 daily; 14hr); Porbandar (4–5 daily; 10hr); Rajkot (every 15min; 5–6hr); Surat (every 30min; 5hr 30min); Udaipur (hourly; 7–8hr); Una (4 daily; 10hr); Vadodara (every 10min; 2hr 30min); Veraval (7 daily; 10hr).

Bhavnagar to: Ahmedabad (hourly; 5hr); Bhuj (2 daily; 8hr); Junagadh (5 daily; 7hr); Mumbai (2 daily; 17hr); Palitana (hourly; 1hr 15min); Rajkot (14 daily; 4hr); Una (5 daily; 6hr); Vadodara (8 daily; 6hr).

Bhuj to: Ahmedabad (hourly; 8–9hr); Bhavnagar (2 daily; 8hr); Gandhidham (every 30min; 1hr); Jamnagar (5 daily; 7hr); Palanpur (4–5 daily; 8hr); Rajkot (8–10 daily; 7hr).

Diu to: Ahmedabad (2–4 daily; 11–12hr); Junagadh (4 daily; 5hr 30min); Rajkot (4 daily; 7hr 30min); Una (every 30min; 30–40min); Veraval (4 daily; 3hr).

Dwarka to: Ahmedabad (6 daily; 11hr); Jamnagar (8 daily; 3hr); Junagadh (3 daily; 5hr); Porbandar (hourly; 2hr 30min–3hr); Veraval (hourly; 5–6hr).

Junagadh to: Ahmedabad (hourly; 8hr); Jamnagar (hourly; 5hr); Porbandar (10 daily; 3hr); Rajkot (hourly; 2hr 30min); Veraval (every 30min; 2hr).

Porbandar to: Ahmedabad (6 daily; 10hr); Dwarka (hourly; 3hr); Jamnagar (hourly; 2hr 30min); Rajkot (10 daily; 5hr).

Rajkot to: Ahmedabad (every 15min; 5hr); Jamnagar (every 30min; 2hr); Junagadh (hourly; 2hr 30min); Porbandar (10 daily; 5hr); Una (6 daily; 8hr); Vadodara (12–16 daily; 8hr); Veraval (hourly; 5hr).

Vadodara to: Ahmedabad (every 10min; 2hr 30min); Baruch (every 30min; 2hr); Indore (1–2 daily; 12hr); Mumbai (7 daily; 14hr); Pune (3 daily; 14hr); Rajkot (12–16 daily; 8hr); Surat (every 30min; 3hr).

Flights

Ahmedabad to: Bengaluru (Bangalore) (2 daily; 3hr 15min); Delhi (5–6 daily; 1hr 25min–2hr 35min); Hyderabad (5 weekly; 1hr 40min); Jaipur (1 daily; 1hr); Kolkata (1 daily; 2hr 15min–3hr 35min); Mumbai (6–7 daily; 1hr); Vadodara (1 daily; 30min).

Bhavnagar to: Mumbai (2–3 daily; 50min–1hr 15min).

Bhuj to: Mumbai (1 daily; 1hr 5min).

Diu to: Porbandar (6 weekly; 30min); Mumbai (6 weekly; 2hr 45min).

Jamnagar to: Mumbai (1 daily; 2hr 15min).

Porbandar to: Diu (6 weekly; 30min); Mumbai (daily; 1hr 30min).

Rajkot to: Mumbai (3 daily; 50min–1hr).

Vadodara to: Delhi (1 daily; 1hr 25min); Mumbai (3 daily; 55min).

Mumbai

CHAPTER 10

Highlights

✳ **The Gateway of India** Mumbai's defining landmark, and a favourite spot for an evening stroll. See p.692

✳ **Chhatrapati Shivaji Museum** A fine collection of priceless Indian art, from ancient temple sculpture to Mughal armour. See p.694

✳ **Maidans (parks)** Where Mumbai's citizens escape the hustle and bustle to play cricket, eat lunch and hang out. See p.696

✳ **CS (Victoria) Terminus** A fantastically eccentric pile, perhaps the greatest railway station ever built by the British. See p.698

✳ **Haji Ali's Tomb** Mingle with the crowds of Muslim worshippers who flock to the island tomb of Sufi mystic Haji Ali to listen to *qawwali* music on Thursday evenings. See p.701

✳ **Elephanta Island** Catch a boat across Mumbai harbour to see one of ancient India's most wonderful rock-cut Shiva temples. See p.703

✳ **Bollywood blockbusters** Check out the latest Hindi mega-movie in one of the city centre's gigantic Art-Deco cinemas. See p.708

▲ The Gateway of India by night

10

Mumbai

E ver since the opening of the Suez Canal in 1869, the principal gateway
to the Indian Subcontinent has been **MUMBAI (Bombay)**, the city
Aldous Huxley famously described as "the most appalling… of either
hemisphere". Travellers tend to regard time spent here as a rite of passage
to be survived rather than savoured. But as the powerhouse of Indian business,
industry and trade, and the source of its most seductive media images, the
Maharashtrian capital can be a compelling place to kill time. Whether or not
you find the experience enjoyable, however, will depend largely on how well
you handle the heat, humidity, hassle, traffic fumes, relentless crowds and
appalling poverty of India's most dynamic, Westernized city.

First impressions of Mumbai tend to be dominated by its chronic **shortage
of space**. Crammed onto a narrow spit of land that curls from the swamp-
ridden coast into the Arabian Sea, the city has, in less than five hundred years'
metamorphosed from an aboriginal fishing settlement into a megalopolis of
over sixteen million people – the biggest urban sprawl on the planet. Being
swept along broad boulevards by endless streams of commuters, or jostled by
coolies and hand-cart pullers in the teeming bazaars, you'll continually feel as if
Mumbai is about to burst at the seams.

The roots of the population problem and attendant poverty lie, paradoxi-
cally, in the city's enduring ability to create **wealth**. Mumbai alone generates
one third of India's tax income, its port handles half the country's foreign
trade, and its movie industry is the biggest in the world. Symbols of prosperity
are everywhere: from the phalanx of office blocks clustered on Nariman

Mumbai or Bombay?

In 1996 Bombay was renamed **Mumbai**, as part of a wider policy instigated by the right-
wing Maharashtrian nationalist Shiv Sena Municipality to replace names of any places,
roads and features in the city that had connotations of the Raj. The Shiv Sena asserted
that the British term "Bombay" derived from the Marathi title of a local deity, the
mouthless "Maha-amba-aiee" (Mumba Devi for short; see p.699). In fact, historians are
unanimously agreed that the Portuguese, who dubbed the harbour "Bom Bahia" ("Good
Bay") when they first came across it, were responsible for christening the site and that
the later British moniker had nothing to do with the aboriginal Hindu earth goddess.

The name change was widely unpopular when it was first imposed, especially
among the upper and middle classes, and non-Maharashtrian immigrant communities, who doggedly stuck to Bombay. More than a decade on, however, "Mumbai"
seems to have definitively taken root with the dotcom generation and even outgrown
the narrow agenda of its nationalist originators – just as "Bombay" outlived the Raj.

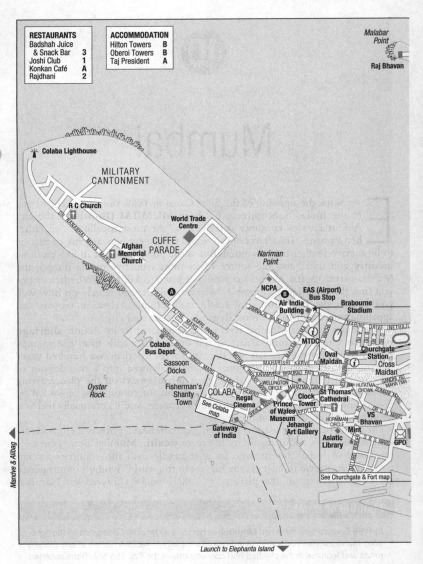

RESTAURANTS	
Badshah Juice & Snack Bar	3
Joshi Club	1
Konkan Café	A
Rajdhani	2

ACCOMMODATION	
Hilton Towers	B
Oberoi Towers	B
Taj President	A

Malabar Point

Raj Bhavan

Colaba Lighthouse

MILITARY CANTONMENT

R C Church

World Trade Centre

Afghan Memorial Church

CUFFE PARADE

Nariman Point

NCPA

EAS (Airport) Bus Stop

Air India Building

Brabourne Stadium

MTDC

MARINE DRIVE (NETHAJI

Colaba Bus Depot

Oval Maidan

Churchgate Station

Cross Maidan

Sassoon Docks

MAHARISHI KARVE RD

Oyster Rock

Fisherman's Shanty Town

WELLINGTON CIRCLE

St Thomas' Cathedral

HUTATMA CHOWK

COLABA

Regal Cinema

See Colaba map

Prince of Wales Museum

Clock Tower

DR D N MARG

HORNIMAN CIRCLE

VS Bhavan

Jehangir Art Gallery

Gateway of India

Asiatic Library

Mint

GPO

See Churchgate & Fort map

Mandve & Alibag

Launch to Elephanta Island ▼

Point, Maharashtra's Manhattan, to the expensively dressed teenagers posing in Colaba's trendiest nightspots.

The flip side to the success story is the city's much-chronicled **poverty**. Each day, an estimated five hundred economic refugees pour into Mumbai from the Maharashtrian hinterland. Some find jobs and secure accommodation; many more end up living on the already overcrowded streets, or amid the squalor of some of Asia's largest slums, reduced to rag-picking and begging from cars at traffic lights.

However, while it would definitely be misleading to downplay its difficulties, Mumbai is far from the ordeal some travellers make it out to be. Once you've

MUMBAI

0 _____ 1 km

ARABIAN SEA

Banganga Tank

Walukeshwar Temple

WALUKESHWAR MARG

N DABHOLKAR MARG

JAGMOHANDAS MARG

Jain Temple

Malabar Hill

PM (Hanging) Gardens

Towers of Silence

Breach Candy Hospital

BHULABHAI DESAI RD

Crossword Bookshop

Mahalakshmi Temple

Haji Ali's Tomb

Kamla Nehru Park

KEMPS CORNER

Bulbunath Mandir Temple

DR G DESHMUKH MARG

VATSALABAI DESAI CHOWK

BALBUNATH MARG

SITARAM PATKAR MARG

Back Bay

Chowpatty Beach

PANDITA RAMABAI

DR R A THADANI MARG

NANAC HOWK

Mani Bhavan (Mahatma Gandhi Museum)

TARDEO RD

K BADODAWALA MARG

LA LAJPATRAI MARG

KASHINATH KHADE MARG

Tarporevala Aquarium

Opera House

Grant Rd Railway Station

DR D BHADKAMKAR MARG

NAIK CHOWK

TADDEV RD

Willingdon Golf Course

Mahalakshmi Racecourse

Gymkhanas

SUBHASH CHANDRA MARG

MAHARISHI KARVE MARG

JAGANNATH SHANKERSHETH MARG

DR D N ROAD

Alfred Talkies

Mumbai Central

Bus Stop for Downtown

Mumbai Central Inter-state Bus Stand

SANE GURUJI MARG

SANT GADGE MAHARAJ CHOWK

Municipal Dhobi Ghats

Wankhede Stadium

Bombay Hospital

Metro Cinema (Buses to Goa)

Mumba Devi Temple

Bhuleshwar Market

Red Light District

Maratha Mandir Cinema

SANT SAVTA MARG

Azad Maidan

Zaveri Bazaar

MEMON ST

Chor Bazaar

MAULANA AZAD RD (SOUTH)

MAULANA AZAD RD (NORTH)

MIRZA GALIB ST

Mahalakshmi Station

Crawford Market

ABDUL REHMAN ST

MOHAMMED ALI RD

SIR J JEEJIBHOY ROAD

N M JOSHI MARG

DR BABASAHEB AMBEDKAR MARG

Jami Masjid

Minara Masjid

Panjrapool Animal Sanctuary

MAULANA SHAUKAT ALI RD

JOHAR CHOWK

BAPURAO JAGTAP MARG

Chatrapathi Shivaji Terminus (Victoria Terminus)

NANDALAL JANI RD

P D'MELLO RD

SHIVDAS CHAMPSI MARG

V J B Udyan (Victoria Gardens)

Veermata Jeejamata (Victoria & Albert) Museum

NATH PAI MARG (REAY RD)

---

overcome the major hurdle of finding somewhere to stay, you may begin to enjoy its frenzied pace and crowded, cosmopolitan feel.

Some history

Mumbai originally consisted of seven **islands**, inhabited by small Koli fishing communities. The town of Gharapuri on **Elephanta** is thought to have been the major settlement in the region until the early fourteenth century, when the Yadava ruler, King Bhima, founded a new capital at nearby Mahim after the old one in north India had been threatened by the Khalji sultans of Delhi. In 1534, Sultan Bahadur of Ahmedabad ceded the land to the **Portuguese**, who felt it to be of little importance and concentrated development in the areas further north at Vasai, which they would rechristen Baçaim (modern-day Bassein). The largest island was handed to the English in 1661, as part of the dowry when the Portuguese Infanta Catherine of Braganza married Charles II; four years later Charles received the remaining islands and the port, and the town took on the anglicized name of Bombay (see box, p.677). This was the first part of India that could properly be termed a colony; elsewhere on the Subcontinent the English had merely been granted the right to set up "factories", or trading posts. Because of its natural safe harbour and strategic position for commerce, the **East India Company**, based at Surat, wanted to buy the land; in 1668 a deal was struck, and Charles leased Mumbai to them for a pittance.

The English set about an ambitious programme of fortifying their outpost, living in the area known today as Fort. However, life was not easy. Malaria, "Chinese Death" (cholera), beriberi and "fluxes" (dysentery) culled many of the first settlers, prompting from the colony's chaplain the declaration that "two monsoons are the age of a man". **Gerald Aungier**, the fourth governor (1672–77), began planning what he stated was "the city which by God's assistance is intended to be built", and by the start of the eighteenth century the town was the capital of the East India Company. Aungier is credited with encouraging the mix that still contributes to the city's success, welcoming Hindu traders from Gujarat, Goans, Muslim weavers and, most visibly, the business-minded Zoroastrian **Parsis**.

Much of the British settlement in the old Fort area was destroyed by a devastating fire in 1803, prompting substantial rebuilding. The arrival of the **Great Indian Peninsular Railway** half a century or so later improved communications, encouraging yet more immigration from elsewhere in India. This crucial artery, coupled with the cotton crisis in America following the Civil War, gave impetus to the great Bombay **cotton boom** and established the city as a major industrial and commercial centre. With the opening of the Suez Canal in 1869, and the construction of enormous docks, Bombay's access to European markets improved further. **Sir Bartle Frere**, governor from 1862 to 1867, oversaw the construction of the city's distinctive colonial-Gothic buildings; the most extravagant of all, **Victoria Terminus** railway station – now officially Chhatrapati Shivaji Terminus or CST – is a fitting testimony to this extraordinary age of expansion.

As the most prosperous city in the nation, Bombay was at the forefront of the **Independence** struggle; Mahatma Gandhi used a house here, now a museum, to coordinate the struggle through three decades. Fittingly, the first British colony took pleasure in waving the final goodbye to the Raj, when the last contingent of British troops passed through the Gateway of India in February 1948. Since Independence, Mumbai has prospered as India's commercial and cultural capital and the population has grown tenfold to more than sixteen million.

However, the resultant overcrowding has done little to foster relations between the city's various minorities and the past two decades have seen repeated outbursts of **communal tensions** among the poorer classes. Strikes and riots paralysed the metropolis throughout the 1980s and early 1990s as more and more immigrants from other regions of the country poured in. The mounting discontent fuelled the rise of the extreme right-wing Maharashtrian party, the **Shiv Sena**, founded in 1966 by the former cartoonist, Bal "the Saheb" Thackery, a self-confessed admirer of Hitler. Many people blamed Sena cadres for orchestrating the attacks on Muslims that followed in the wake of the Babri Masjid destruction in Ayodhya in 1992–93, when thousands were murdered by mobs as the city descended into anarchy for ten days.

Record rains

On July 26, 2005, Mumbai sustained the **heaviest rainfall** ever to have been recorded in a city over a 24-hour period: a staggering 942mm. The storm caused havoc – landslides and flooding killed an estimated one hundred people in the city and stranded 150,000 more. It also provoked a downpour of criticism for the Mumbai Municipality, whose corrupt management was blamed for the failure of the city's infrastructure to cope with the crisis.

Only a few months later, on March 12, 1993, ten massive **bomb blasts** killed 260 people and damaged several landmark buildings. The involvement of Muslim godfather Dawood Ibrahim and the Pakistani secret service was suspected – as, indeed, it was a decade or so later in the wake of two other bloody bomb attacks that brought the city to a standstill: the first, in August 2003, killed 107 tourists right outside the **Gateway of India** itself; the second, on July 7, 2006, simultaneously blew apart seven packed commuter trains at points across the city.

After each of these terrible blows, however, the city bounced back with amazing ebullience, and in the popular imagination it continues to be identified less with terrorist outrages than with the **glamour** purveyed by its movie and satellite-TV industries. Bollywood starlets, VJs and playboy heirs to industrial fortunes provide the staple for the gossip columns and fanzines lapped up across the country, while hundreds of Hindi blockbusters are shot in its streets and suburban studios each year.

Rajiv Gandhi's reforms of the early 1990s paved the way for a consumer boom across India, but nowhere has **economic liberalization** been more passionately embraced than in Mumbai. Following decades of stagnation, the textiles industry has been supplanted by rapidly growing IT, finance, healthcare and back-office support sectors. Whole suburbs have sprung up to accommodate the affluent new middle-class workforce, with shiny shopping malls, multiplex cinemas and car showrooms to relieve them of their income.

Far from keeping up with the boom, however, the city's infrastructure continues to deteriorate – as the chaos that ensued after the 2005 floods vividly demonstrated (see box above). Corruption in politics and business has drained away investment from socially deprived areas. Luxury apartments in Bandra may change hands for half a million dollars or more, but an estimated seven to eight million people (just under fifty percent of Mumbai's population) live in slums with no toilets, on just six percent of the land.

Arrival

Unless you arrive in Mumbai by train at **Chhatrapati Shivaji Terminus** (formerly Victoria Terminus), be prepared for a long slog into the centre. The international and domestic **airports** are way north of the city, and ninety minutes or more by road from the main hotel areas, while from **Mumbai Central** railway or **bus station**, you face a laborious trip across town.

By air

Mumbai's busy **international airport**, **Chhatrapati Shivaji** (30km north; ⓦ www.csia.in), is divided into two "modules", one for Air India flights and the other for foreign airlines. Once through customs and the lengthy immigration formalities, you'll find a 24-hour State Bank of India exchange facility and ATM, government (ITDC) and state (MTDC) tourist information counters, car rental kiosks, cafés and a pre-paid taxi stand in the arrivals concourse. There's also – very usefully – an **Indian Railways booking office** which you should make use of if you know your next destination; it'll save you a long wait at the reservation offices downtown. If you're on one of the few flights to land in the afternoon or early evening – by which time most hotels tend to be full – it can be worth paying on the spot for a room at the **accommodation booking desk** in the arrivals hall. All of the domestic airlines also have offices outside the main entrance, and there's a handy 24-hour **left luggage** "cloakroom" in the car park nearby (Rs70 per day, or part thereof; maximum duration ninety days).

Many of the more upmarket hotels, particularly those near the airport, send out **courtesy coaches** to pick up their guests. **Taxis** are not too extravagant. To avoid haggling over the fare or being duped by the private taxi companies outside the airport, go to the "Pre-Paid" taxi desk in the arrivals hall. The price on the receipt, which you hand to the driver on arrival at your destination, is slightly more than the normal meter rate (Rs375 to Colaba or Nariman Point, or Rs180 to Juhu), but at least you can be sure you'll be taken by the most direct route. Taxi-wallahs sometimes try to persuade you to stay at a different hotel from the one you ask for. Don't agree to this; their commission will be added onto the price of your room.

Internal flights land at Mumbai's **domestic airport** (26km to the north of downtown and 2km west of the international airport), officially also called Chhatrapati Shivaji, but still, somewhat confusingly, referred to by many Mumbaikars by its old name, "Santa Cruz". It is divided into separate terminals: the cream-coloured one (Module 1A) for the government-run Indian Airlines, and the blue-and-white (Module 1B) for private carriers. If you're transferring directly from here to an international flight take the free "fly-bus" that shuttles every fifteen minutes between the two; look for the transfer counter in your transit lounge.

The ITDC and MTDC both have 24-hour **information counters** in the arrivals hall, and there's a foreign exchange counter and accommodation desk tucked away near the first-floor exit. The official "Pre-Paid" taxi counter on the arrivals concourse charges around Rs400 to Colaba. Don't be tempted by the cheaper fares offered by touts outside, and avoid **auto-rickshaws** altogether, as they're not allowed downtown and will leave you at the mercy of unscrupulous taxi drivers on the edge of vile-smelling Mahim Creek, the southernmost limit of their permitted area.

In transit

If you're only passing through Mumbai between flights and need to sit out half the night, it's worth knowing that the *Leela Kempinski* and *Royal Meridien* five-stars are both a short, complimentary transfer bus ride from the international terminal to CST. Their air-conditioned restaurants, coffee shops and bars make much more comfortable places to kill time than the departure lounge at the grungy airport – and their toilets are in a different league.

The domestic airport is being gradually upgraded and its new **retiring rooms** are an option worth considering if you'd like to get some shut-eye between planes – though they're rarely available at short notice. Check at the information desk on the Arrivals concourses in terminals 1 or 2.

Malaria warning

Due to the massive slum encampments and bodies of stagnant water around the **airports**, both the international and domestic terminals are major **malaria** black spots. Clouds of mosquitoes await your arrival in the car park, so don't forget to smother yourself with strong insect repellent before leaving the terminal.

By train

Trains to Mumbai from most central, southern and eastern regions arrive at **Chhatrapati Shivaji Terminus** or **CST** (formerly **Victoria Terminus**, or **VT**), the main railway station at the end of the Central Railway line. From here it's a ten- or fifteen-minute ride to Colaba; taxis queue at the busy rank outside the south exit, opposite the new reservation hall.

Mumbai Central, the terminus for Western Railway trains from northern India, is a half-hour ride from Colaba; take a taxi from the forecourt, or flag one down on the main road – it should cost around Rs175–200.

Some trains from South India arrive at more obscure stations. If you find yourself at **Dadar**, way up in the industrial suburbs, and don't want to shell out on a taxi, cross the Tilak Marg road bridge onto the Western Railway and catch a suburban train into town (remembering to purchase a ticket at the hatch on platform 1 beforehand). **Kurla** station, where a few Bengaluru (Bangalore) trains pull in, is even further out, just south of the domestic airport; taking a suburban train for Churchgate is the only reasonable alternative to a taxi. From either, it's worth asking at the station when you arrive if there is another long-distance train going to Churchgate or CST (Victoria Terminus) shortly after – it's far preferable to trying to cram into either a suburban train or bus.

▲ Chhatrapati Shivaji Terminus (formerly Victoria Terminus)

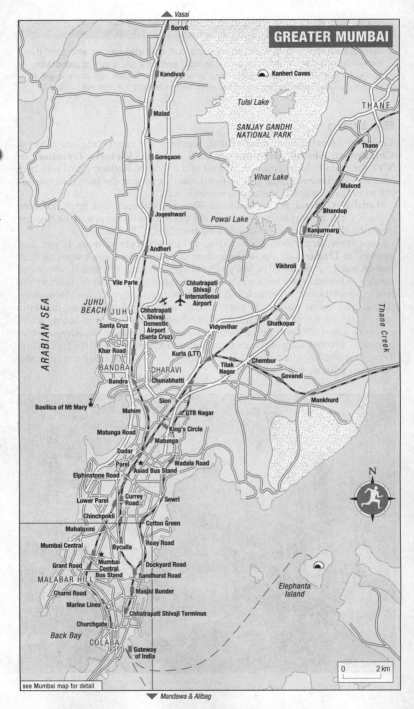

▲ Vasai

Borivli

Kandivali

◉ Kanheri Caves

Tulsi Lake

THANE

Malad

SANJAY GANDHI
NATIONAL PARK

Thane

Goregaon

Vihar Lake

Mulund

Bhandup

Jogeshwari

Powai Lake

Kanjurmarg

Andheri

Vikhroli

Vile Parle

Chhatrapati
Shivaji
International
Airport

JUHU
BEACH   JUHU

Chhatrapati
Shivaji
Domestic
Airport
(Santa Cruz)

Santa Cruz

Vidyavihar

Ghatkopar

Khar Road

Kurla (LTT)

BANDRA   DHARAVI

Tilak
Nagar

Chembur

Govandi

Bandra

Chunabhatti

Basilica of Mt Mary

Mahim

Sion

GTB Nagar

Matunga Road

King's Circle

Matunga

Dadar

Parel

Wadala Road

Asiad Bus Stand

Elphinstone Road

Lower Parel   Currey
Road

Sewri

Chinchpokli

Cotton Green

Mahalaxmi

Mumbai Central   Byculla

Reay Road

Grant Road   Mumbai
Central
Bus Stand

Dockyard Road

MALABAR HILL   Sandhurst Road

Charni Road

Masjid Bunder

Marine Lines

Chhatrapati Shivaji Terminus

Churchgate

Back Bay

COLABA   Gateway
of India

ARABIAN SEA

Thane Creek

Mankhurd

Elephanta
Island

N

MUMBAI   10

0   2 km

see Mumbai map for detail

▼ Mandawa & Alibag

By bus

Nearly all interstate **buses** arrive at **Mumbai Central** Bus Stand, a stone's throw from the railway station of the same name. Government services use the main **Maharashtra State Road Transport Corporation (MSRTC)** stand itself; private ones operate from the roadside next to Mumbai Central railway station, two minutes' walk west on the opposite side of busy Dr AN Marg (Lamington Road). To get downtown, either catch a suburban train from Mumbai Central's local platform, over the footbridge from the mainline, or jump in a cab at the rank in front of the station.

Note that while most MSRTC buses terminate at Mumbai Central, those from **Pune** (and surrounding areas) end up at the **ASIAD** bus stand, a glorified parking lot near the **Dadar** railway station. Again, you can travel onwards by suburban train or taxi.

Information

The best source of **information** in Mumbai is the excellent **India Tourism** (Mon–Fri 8.30am–6pm, Sat 8.30am–2pm; ℡022/2203 3144, ✉indiatourism @vsnl.com) at 123 M Karve Rd, opposite Churchgate Station's east exit. The staff here are exceptionally helpful and hand out a wide range of leaflets, maps and brochures on both Mumbai and the rest of the country.

The **Maharashtra State Tourism Development Corporation (MTDC) office**, on Madam Cama Road opposite the LIC Building in Nariman Point (Mon–Sat 8.30am–7pm; ℡022/202 6731, ⓦwww.maharashtratourism.gov.in), can reserve rooms in MTDC resorts and also sells tickets for city sightseeing tours (see p.687).

For detailed **listings**, the most complete source is Mumbai's *Time Out* (ⓦwww .timeoutmumbai.net), which carries full details of what's on and where, just like its London and New York counterparts. Alternatively, check out the "Metro" page in the *Indian Express* or the "Bombay Times" section of the *Times of India*. All are available from street vendors around Colaba and the downtown area.

City transport and tours

Transport congestion has eased slightly since the opening of the huge flyover that now scythes straight through the heart of the city from just north of CST station. During peak hours, however, gridlock is the norm and you should brace yourself for long waits at junctions if you take to the roads by taxi, bus or auto. Local **trains** get there faster, but can be a real endurance test even outside rush hours.

Trains

Mumbai's local **trains** carry an estimated 6.1 million commuters each day between downtown and the sprawling suburbs in the north – half the entire passenger capacity of Indian Railways (see box, p.686). One line begins at CST (VT), running up the east side of the city as far as Thane. The other leaves Churchgate, hugging the curve of Back Bay as far as Chowpatty Beach, where it veers north through Mumbai Central, Dadar, Santa Cruz and Vasai, beyond the city limits. Services depart every few minutes from 5am until midnight, stopping at dozens of small stations. Carriages remain packed solid virtually the

A "Super-dense" Crush

The **suburban rail network** in Mumbai is officially the busiest on the planet. No other line carries as many passengers, nor crams them into such confined spaces. At peak times, as many as 4700 people may be jammed into a nine-carriage train designed to carry 1700, resulting in what the rail company, in typically jaunty Mumbai style, refers to as "Super-dense Crush Load" of 14–16 standing passengers per square metre. Not all of these actually occupy floor space, of course: ten percent will be dangling precariously out of the doors.

The busiest stretch, a sixty-kilometre segment between Churchgate Terminus and Virar in north Mumbai, transports nearly 900 million people each year, the highest of any rail network in the world. **Fatalities** are all too frequent: on average, 3500 die on the rail network annually, from falling out of the doors, crossing the tracks or because they're hit by overhead cables while riding on the roof.

whole time, with passengers dangling precariously out of open doors to escape the crush, so start to make your way to the exit at least three stops before your destination. Peak hours (approximately 8.30–10am & 4–7pm) are the worst of all. Women are marginally better off in the "ladies carriages"; look for the crowd of colourful saris and *salwar kameezes* grouped at the end of the platform.

Buses

BEST (Brihanmumbai Electric Supply and Transport; ☎022/2285 6262, ⊛www.bestundertaking.com) operates a **bus** network of labyrinthine complexity, extending to the furthest-flung corners of the city. We've listed bus numbers for Mumbai's sights in our accounts, but you can easily check all the routes on the BEST website, which has an excellent "point-to-point" facility (from drop-down menus you specify your starting and finishing points, and it will generate the bus numbers). Recognizing the bus numbers in the street, however, can be more problematic, as the numerals are written in Marathi (although in English on the sides). Aim, wherever possible, for the "Limited" ("Ltd") services, which stop less frequently, and avoid rush hours at all costs. Tickets should be bought from the conductor on the bus.

Taxis and car rental

With rickshaws banished to the suburbs, Mumbai's ubiquitous black-and-yellow **taxis** are the quickest and most convenient way to nip around the city centre. In theory, all should have meters and a current "tariff card" (to convert the amount shown on the meter to the correct fare); in practice, particularly at night or early in the morning, many drivers refuse to use them. If this happens, either flag down another or haggle out a fare. As a rule of thumb, expect to be charged Rs10 per kilometre after the minimum fare of around Rs20, plus a small sum for heavy luggage (Rs5–10 per article). The latest addition to Mumbai's hectic roads is the **Cool Cab** (☎022/2824 6216), a blue taxi that boasts air-conditioning and tinted windows, and charges around forty percent higher rates for the privilege.

Cars with drivers can be rented per eight-hour day (Rs1200–1500 for a non-a/c Ambassador, upwards of Rs1500 for more luxurious a/c cars), or per kilometre, from ITDC. They have an (occasionally) staffed counter at the Government of India tourist office and on the eleventh floor of the Nirmal Building at Nariman Point. Otherwise, go through any good travel agent (see p.714). Ramniranjan Kedia Tours and Travels (☎022/2437 1112, ⊛www.rnk.com)

are recommended if you want to book a vehicle on arrival at Chhatrapati Shivaji international airport.

Boats

Ferryboats regularly chug out of Mumbai harbour, connecting the city with the far shore and some of the larger islands in between. The most popular with visitors is the **Elephanta Island** launch (see p.703), which departs from the Gateway of India (see p.692), as do frequent boats to **Mandawa Jetty**, for Alibag, the transport hub for the rarely used **coastal route south** (see p.718).

Tours

MTDC's whistlestop "City" tour (Tues–Sun 2–6pm; Rs150, not including admission charges) is an inexpensive way to cram south Mumbai's touristic highlights into half a day, with stops at the Museum, Marine Drive, Chowpatty Beach, the Hanging Gardens and Mani Bhavan. The trip starts at the company's booth in front of the Gateway of India, where you can purchase advace tickets.

A more leisurely alternative, focusing mainly on period buildings and the city's colonial history, is to follow the excellent guided walks organized by architects Abha Bahl and Brinda Gaitonde of the **Mumbai Heritage Walks Society**. The tours are run every Sunday (except during the monsoons), cost Rs1500 for a minimum of three people (and Rs500 per additional person) and last ninety minutes. Further details and advance booking are available on ⊤022/2369 0992 or 2683 5856, or at ⓦwww.bombayheritagewalks.com.

Finally, the outfit **Reality Tours and Travels** operate compelling trips out to the Dharavi shantytown in north Mumbai, one of Asia's largest slums. For more details, see the box on p.702.

Accommodation

Finding **accommodation** at the right price when you arrive in Mumbai can be a real problem. Budget travellers, in particular, can expect a hard time: standards at the bottom of the range are grim and room rates exorbitant. The best of the relatively inexpensive places tend to fill up by noon, which can often mean a long trudge in the heat with only an overpriced fleapit at the end of it, so you should really phone ahead as soon as (or preferably well before) you arrive. Prices in upmarket places are especially high for India, and rising fast (at nearly fifty percent per year); state-imposed "**luxury tax**" (between four and thirty percent depending on how expensive the room is), and "**service charges**" levied by the hotel itself further bump up bills; both add-ons are included in the price symbols used in the following reviews.

Colaba, down in the far southern end of the city, is where the majority of foreign visitors head first. A short way across the city centre, **Marine Drive**'s accommodation is generally a little more expensive, but more salubrious, with Back Bay and the promenade right on the doorstep. If you're arriving by train and plan to make a quick getaway, a room closer to **CST** (VT) station is worth considering. Alternatively, **Juhu**, way to the north near the airports, hosts a string of flashy four- and five-stars, with a handful of less expensive places behind the beach. For those who just want to crawl off the plane and straight into bed, a handful of overpriced options are also available in the suburbs around the **airports**, a short taxi ride from the main terminal buildings.

Colaba and Kala Ghoda

A short ride from the city's main commercial districts, railway stations and tourist office, **Colaba** makes a handy base. It also offers more in the way of food and entertainment than neighbouring districts, especially along its busy main thorough-fare, "**Colaba Causeway**" (Shahid Bhagat Singh – SBS – Marg). The streets immediately south and west of the Gateway of India are chock-full of accommo-dation, ranging from grungy guesthouses to India's most famous five-star hotel, the *Taj Mahal Palace & Tower*. Avoid at all costs the nameless lodges lurking on the top storeys of wooden-fronted houses along **Arthur Bunder Road** – the haunts of touts who depend on commission to finance their heroin habits.

The hotels below are marked on the map of Colaba and Kala Ghoda on p.693, except for the *Taj President*, which is on the main Mumbai map (p.679).

Budget

Aga Bheg's & Hotel Kishan Ground, 2nd & 3rd floor, Shirin Manzil, Walton Rd ☎022/2284 2227 or 2202 1534. Muslim-run pair of budget guesthouses on different floors of the same building. Both are a bit noisy and rough looking, but acceptably clean, and among the cheapest options in Colaba. ④–⑤

Lawrence 3rd floor, 33 Sri Sai Baba Marg (Rope Walk Lane), off K Dubash Marg, behind *TGI's* ☎022/2284 3618 or 6633 6107. Strictly speaking in the arty Kala Ghoda district rather than Colaba proper, close to the Jehangir Art Gallery, this is arguably south Mumbai's best rock-bottom choice. Six well-scrubbed doubles (one single) with fans, and not-so-clean shared shower-toilet; breakfast included in the price. Advance booking essential. ④

Red Shield Red Shield House, 30 Boram Behram (Mereweather) Rd, near the *Taj* ☎022/2284 1824 or 2282 4613, ⓔredshield@vsnl.net. Ultra-basic bunk beds (Rs165) in cramped, stuffy dorms (lockers available), or larger good-value doubles (Rs600 without a/c, Rs1000), fully en suite. Rates include three meals, served in a sociable travellers' canteen. Priority is given to women, and your stay is limited to one week or less. ①–⑤

Sea Shore 4th floor, 1-49 Kamal Mansion, Arthur Bunder Rd ☎022/2287 4237. Among the best budget deals in Colaba. The sea-facing rooms with windows (Rs600) are much nicer than the airless cells on the other side. Friendly management and free, safe baggage store. Common baths only, though some rooms have a/c. If it's full try the wooden-partitioned rooms at the less salubrious *India* (☎022/2283 3769; ④–⑤) or the grubby but bearable *Sea Lord* (☎022/2284 5392; ④–⑤) in the same building. ④–⑤

Mid-range

Ascot 38 Garden Rd ☎022/6638 5566, ⓦwww.ascothotel.com. One of the oldest and most comfortable small hotels in Mumbai, dating from the 1930s but with state-of-the-art glass-and-marble designer interiors. The rooms are centrally air-conditioned and very spacious for the price, plus they're fitted with CD players. Doubles from Rs5500. ⑨

Bentley's 17 Oliver Rd ☎022/2284 1474, ⓦwww.bentleyshotel.com. Dependable old Parsi-owned favourite in four different colonial tenements, all on leafy backstreets. The rooms are quiet, secure and spacious, if a little worn. Some have a/c and small balconies overlooking rear gardens, but the overall shabbiness isn't compen-sated for by the rates, which are higher than you'd expect for the level of comfort. ⑥–⑦

Godwin Jasmine Building, 41 Garden Rd ☎022/2287 2050, ⓦwww.mumbainet.com/hotels /godwin. Top-class three-star with large, international-standard rooms and great views from upper floors (ask for 804, 805 or 806 when you book). The *Garden* (☎022/2283 1330, ⓔgardenhotel@mail.com) next door is similar but slightly inferior. Both ⑧

Moti International 10 Best Marg ☎022/2202 1654, ⓔhotelmotiinternational@yahoo.co.in. British-era building with original painted stucco and woodwork. It's quiet and clean with friendly management, though frayed around the edges. The rooms range from non-a/c doubles (Rs1700) to pricier deluxe triples with a/c, fridges and TVs. ⑥–⑦

Regent 8 Best Marg ☎022/2287 1854, ⓔhotelregent@vsnl.com. Smart, international-standard hotel on a small scale, popular mainly with Gulf Arabs; the rooms aren't large, but good value in this bracket, with large cable TVs, fridges and Internet access. Rates include breakfast. ⑧

Sea Palace Kerawalla Chambers, 26 PJ Ramchandani Marg (Apollo Bunder) ☎022/2284 1828, ⓦwww.seapalacehotel.com. Comfortable, well-maintained hotel at the quiet end of the harbour front. All rooms are a/c but sea views cost extra. Breakfast and light meals are served on a sunny terrace at the front. ⑧–⑨

🏃 **Strand** PJ Ramachandani Marg (Apollo Bunder) ☎022/2288 2222, ⓦwww .hotelstrand.com. Deservedly popular mid-scale option on the seafront that's nicely situated, respectable and efficiently run. The rooms are plain, but well aired, with higher ceilings than usual, and a few surviving Art-Deco features add character. Their "Super-Deluxe" frontside rooms have the best harbour views. ⑧

🏃 **YWCA** 18 Madam Cama Rd ☎022/2202 5053, ⓦwww.ywcaic.info. Relaxing, secure and quiet hostel with spotless attached rooms (recently renovated and with windows and TVs) and same-day laundry service. Rates include membership, breakfast and generous buffet dinner – a bargain for south Mumbai. Advance booking (by money draft) obligatory. ⑥

Luxury

Fariyas 25 Arthur Rd ☎022/2204 2911, ⓦwww .fariyas.com. Compact luxury hotel, overlooking the Koli fishing *basti* on one side, with all the trimmings of a five-star but none of the grandeur. Doubles from $255. ⑨

Gordon House 5 Battery St ☎022/2287 1122, ⓦwww.ghhotel.com. Ultra-chic designer boutique place behind the Regal cinema. Each floor is differently themed: "Scandinavian" (the easiest to live with), "Mediterranean" and "American Country"; CD players in every room, but no pool. Doubles from $275. ⑨

Taj Mahal Palace & Tower PJ Ramchandani Marg ☎022/5665 3366, ⓦwww.tajhotels.com. The stately home among India's top hotels (see p.692), and the haunt of Mumbai's *beau monde*, with 546 luxury rooms, shopping arcades, a huge outdoor pool, nine bars and restaurants, plus one of the city's favourite nightclubs (*Insomnia*; see p.708). Prices vary according to view: if your budget can stretch to it, go for a sea-facing suite in the old wing, where rates range from $400 to $3300; in the *Tower*, count on half that. ⑨

Taj President 90 Cuffe Parade ☎022/5665 0808, ⓦwww.tajhotels.com. Modern, business-oriented five-star occupying an eighteen-floor skyscraper just south of Colaba. A much more competitively priced option than its sister concern, the *Taj Mahal Palace & Tower*, though lacking old-world style and atmosphere. The pool is outdoors and large, with a multi-gym and steam room adjacent. Rates start at around $300–650. ⑨

Marine Drive and Nariman Point

At the western edge of the downtown area, Netaji Subhash Chandra Marg, or **Marine Drive**, sweeps from the skyscrapers of Nariman Point in the south to Chowpatty Beach in the north. Along the way, four- and five-star hotels take advantage of the panoramic views over Back Bay and the easy access to the city's commercial heart, while a couple of inexpensive guesthouses are worth trying if Colaba's cheap lodges don't appeal.

The hotels below are marked on the Churchgate and Fort map on p.695, apart from *Hilton Towers* and the *Oberoi*, which are marked on pp.678–679.

Ambassador VN Rd ☎022/2204 1131, ⓦwww .ambassadorindia.com. Ageing four-star whose scruffy concrete exterior and slightly worn furnishings are redeemed by its choice location, close to the sea and main shopping and café strip. Even if you're not staying, pop up to the revolving *Pearl of the Orient* restaurant (see p.707) for the matchless city views. Doubles from $220. ⑨

Astoria Jamshedji Tata ☎022/6654 1234, ⓦwww.astoriamumbai.com. Smart business hotel in refurbished 1930s Art-Deco building near the Eros cinema. The rooms are nowhere near as ritzy as the lobby but offer good value this close to the centre. Doubles from $165–215. ⑨

Bentley 3rd floor, Krishna Mahal, Marine Drive ☎022/2281 5244. Not to be confused with *Bentley's* in Colaba (see opposite), this small, friendly guesthouse is across town on the corner of D Rd/Marine Drive, near the cricket stadium. The marble-lined rooms are clean and comfortable for the price, though most share shower-toilets. Rates (from Rs1000) include breakfast. ⑤

🏃 **Chateau Windsor** 5th floor, 86 VN Rd ☎022/2204 4455, ⓦwww.chateauwindsor .com. Impeccably neat and central, with unfailingly polite staff and a choice of differently priced, 1950s-style rooms, squeezed onto three floors and accessed via an old cage lift and narrow landings. Very popular, so reserve well in advance. ⑧

Hilton Towers Nariman Point ☎022/6632 4343, ⓦwww.hilton.com. This north wing of the former *Oberoi* was recently acquired by the Hilton Group and serves, along with its former sibling next door (see p.690), as the city's premier business hotel. It offers all the facilities and trimmings you'd expect of an international five-star, including a gigantic lobby and sea views from its pool. From around $400. ⑨

Intercontinental 135 Marine Drive ☎ 022/3987 9999, ⓦ www.mumbai.intercontinental.com. This ultra-chic boutique hotel is currently one of India's most stylishly modern addresses. The rooms have huge sea-facing windows and state-of-the-art gadgets (such as 42-inch plasma screens, DVD players, safes with laptop rechargers and broadband connections), while the rooftop pool, bars and restaurants (including the famous *Dome* – see p.708) rank among Mumbai's most fashionable. Doubles from $450. ❾

Marine Plaza 29 Marine Drive ☎ 022/2285 1212, ⓦ www.hotelmarineplaza.com. Ritzy but small luxury hotel on the seafront, with (pseudo-) Art-Deco atrium lobby, glass-bottomed rooftop pool and the usual five-star facilities. Rooms $450–575. ❾

Oberoi Towers Nariman Point ☎ 022/2232 5757, ⓦ www.oberoihotels.com. India's tallest hotel enjoys a prime spot overlooking Back Bay (the views from the 35th-floor conference room are stupendous). Glitteringly opulent throughout, and – together with its northern wing, now managed by the Hilton Group – the first choice of business travellers, though lacking the heritage character of the *Taj*. Rooms $450–3000 per night. ❾

Sea Green/Sea Green South 145 Marine Drive ☎ 022/6633 6525, ⓦ www.seagreenhotel.com & 145-A Marine Drive 022/2282 1613, ⓦ www .seagreensouth.com. Jointly owned and enduringly popular pair of green-and-white-painted hotels on the seafront. Rates are quite high for the rooms, which are fitted with threadbare coir carpets and thirty-year-old furniture, but on the plus side, they do both have great views of the bay and retain a period feel lacking in most mid-range places. ❻–❼

Around Chhatrapati Shivaji (Victoria) Terminus

Arriving in Mumbai at **CST** (VT) after a long train journey, you may not feel like embarking on a room hunt around Colaba. Unfortunately, the area around the station and the nearby GPO, though fairly central, has little to recommend it. The majority of places worth trying are mid-range hotels grouped around the crossroads of P. D'Mello (Frere) Road, St George's Road and Shahid Bhagat Singh (SBS) Marg, immediately southeast of the post office (5min on foot from the station). CST (VT) itself also has **retiring rooms** (Rs250), although these are always booked up by noon, or even days in advance. The following are all marked on the Churchgate and Fort map on p.695.

City Palace 121 City Terrace ☎ 022/2261 5515, ⓦ www.hotelcitypalace.net. Large and popular hotel bang opposite the station. "Ordinary" rooms are tiny and windowless, but have a/c and are perfectly clean. The pricier ones higher up the building have bird's-eye views over Nagar Chowk. There's a reliable left-luggage facility for guests. ❻–❼

Grand 17 Shri SR Marg, Ballard Estate ☎ 022/6658 0506, ⓦ www.grandhotelbombay.com. British-era three-star out near the old docks and former financial district. Recently refurbished and offering some of the best-value deals downtown (from around Rs3700). ❽

Oasis 276 SBS Marg ☎ 022/3022 7886, ⓦ www .hoteloasisindia.com. Very well placed for CST station, and the best-value budget option in this area: non-a/c attached doubles have good beds, clean linen and TVs. It's worth splashing out on a top-floor "deluxe" room as they offer better views. ❹–❺

Residency 26 Rustom Sidhwa Marg DN Rd ☎ 022/2262 5525, ⓦ www.residencyhotel .com. This is a great little mid-priced hotel, and one of the few commendable options in the bustling Fort district, close to the best shopping areas and only a short taxi ride from Colaba. Its variously priced rooms (all with safes and Internet points) offer unbeatable value, especially the no-frills "standard" options, though you'll have to book at least a couple of weeks ahead to get one. ❼

Juhu and around the airports

Hotels in the congested area around the international and domestic **airports** cater predominantly for transit passengers, business executives and flight crews, at premium rates. If you can face the thirty-minute drive across town and afford the first-world room tariffs, head for **Juhu**, one of the city's swisher suburbs, which faces the sea and is a lot less hectic. Nearly all the hotels below have courtesy buses to and from the terminal building, or at worst can arrange for a car and driver to meet you.

Hyatt Regency Airport Rd, Andheri (East)
⊕022/6696 1234, ⓦwww.mumbai.regency.hyatt
.com. Ancient Hindu precepts on architecture and
design were incorporated into the plans for this
ultra-luxurious five-star, right next to the airport.
The results are impressive, and a notch more
stylish than the competition, with extensive use of
Malaysian teak, floor-to-ceiling windows, step-
down rain showers and polished dark marble
floors. From $440–550. ❾

ISKCON Juhu Church Rd, Juhu ⊕022/2620 6860,
ⓦwww.iskconmumbai.com. Idiosyncratic hotel run
by the International Society for Krishna Consciousness. The building itself is a hotch-potch of mock
Mughal, Gujarati and Western styles, and the rooms
are very large for the price, though certain restrictions apply (no alcohol, meat or caffeine may be
consumed on the premises). Forty days' advance
booking recommended. ❼

JW Marriott Juhu Tara Rd, Juhu ⊕022/6693
3000, ⓦwww.marriott.com. Palatial five-star
complex, hemmed in by high walls and a tighter-
than-average security cordon. Inside lie five opulent
restaurants, three pools (one of them filled with

treated salt water) and blocks of luxury rooms
looking through landscaped grounds and rustling
palms to the beach. From around $350. ❾

Lotus Suites Andheri Kurla Rd, International Airport
Zone, Andheri (East) ⊕022/2827 0707, ⓦwww.lotus
suites.com. An "Eco-Four-Star at Three-Star prices" is
how this environment-friendly hotel describes itself.
Designed with energy-saving building materials, a/c
and fittings, it features "green" trimmings such as pot
plants instead of cut flowers, jute slippers and
recycling bins in the rooms. A very comfortable option
for under $300 if you book online. ❾

Midland Jawaharlal Nehru Rd, Santa Cruz (East)
⊕022/2611 0414, ⓦwww.hotelmidland.com.
Dependable two-star with well-furnished twin-
bedded rooms. Rates (from Rs4400) include
courtesy bus and breakfast. ❽

Orchid 70-C Nehru Rd, Vile Parle (East)
⊕022/2616 4040, ⓦwww.orchidhotel.com.
Award-winning "Eco-Five-Star", built with organic
or recycled materials and using low-toxin paints.
Every effort is made to minimize waste of natural
resources, with a water-recycling plant and "zero
garbage" policy. Rooms from around $400. ❾

The City

Nowhere reinforces your sense of having arrived in Mumbai quite as emphati-
cally as the **Gateway of India**, the city's defining landmark. Only a five-minute
walk north, the **Prince of Wales Museum** should be next on your list of sightseeing priorities, as much for its flamboyantly eclectic architecture as for the art
treasures inside. The museum provides a foretaste of what lies in store just up the
road, where the cream of Bartle Frere's Bombay – the University and High
Court – line up with the open *maidans* on one side, and the boulevards of **Fort**
on the other. The commercial hub of the city, Fort is a great area for aimless
wandering, with plenty of old-fashioned cafés, department stores and street stalls
crammed between the Victorian piles. But for the fullest sense of why the city's
founding fathers declared it Urbs Prima in Indis, you should press further north
still to visit the **Chhatrapati Shivaji Terminus**, formerly the **Victoria
Terminus**, the high-water mark of India's Raj architecture.

Few visitors venture into the bazaars and Muslim neighbourhoods beyond VT,
but **central Mumbai** certainly possess plenty of intensity, with the recently
revamped Dr Bhau Dadji Lad Museum in Byculla the main visitor attraction.

Possibilities for an escape from the crowds include: an evening stroll along
Marine Drive, bounding the western edge of the downtown area; the Muslim
tomb of Haji Ali, especially atmospheric on Thursday and Friday evenings;
Elephanta, a rock-cut cave on an island in Mumbai harbour containing a
wealth of ancient art; and the thousand-year-old **Kanheri Cave** complex,
carved from a forested hillside on the outskirts.

Colaba

At the end of the seventeenth century, **Colaba** was little more than the last in
a straggling line of rocky islands extending to the lighthouse that stood on

Mumbai's southernmost point. Today, the original outlines of the promontory (whose name derives from the Koli fishermen who first lived here) have been submerged under a mass of dilapidated colonial tenements, hotels, bars, restaurants and handicraft emporia. If you never venture beyond the district, you'll get a very distorted picture of Mumbai; even though it's the main tourist enclave and a trendy hang-out for the city's rich young things, Colaba has retained the sleazy feel of the port it used to be.

The Gateway of India

Commemorating the visit of King George V and Queen Mary in 1911, India's own honey-coloured Arc de Triomphe, the **Gateway of India**, was built in 1924 by George Wittet, the architect responsible for many of the city's grandest constructions. Blending indigenous Gujarati motifs with high Victorian pomp, it was originally envisaged as a ceremonial disembarkation point for passengers alighting from the P&O steamers, but – ironically – is today more often remembered as the place the British chose to stage their final departure from the country. On February 28, 1948, the last battalion of troops remaining on Indian soil slow-marched under the arch to board the waiting ship back to Tilbury. Nowadays, the only boats bobbing about at the bottom of its stone staircase are the launches that ferry tourists across the harbour to Elephanta Island (see p.703).

On evenings and weekends, crowds gather in the piazza fronting the arch to feed the pigeons, be snapped by the posses of strolling photographers, ride silver horse-drawn *gaddis* around the *Taj*, or just to people-watch.

Behind the Gateway

Directly behind the Gateway, the older hotel in the **Taj Mahal Palace & Tower** complex (see p.689) stands as a monument to local pride in the face of colonial oppression. Its patron, the Parsi industrialist J.N. Tata, is said to have built the old *Taj* as an act of revenge after he was refused entry to what was then the best hotel in town, the "whites only" *Watson's*. The ban proved to be its undoing. *Watson's* disappeared long ago, and the *Taj* still presides imperiously over the seafront, the preserve of Mumbai's air-kissing jet set. Lesser mortals are allowed in to experience the tea lounge, shopping arcades and vast air-conditioned lobby – a good place to cool down if the heat of the harbourfront has got the better of you (there's also a fabulously luxurious loo off the corridor to the left of the main desk).

Southwards along Colaba Causeway

Reclaimed in the late nineteenth century from the sea, the district's main thoroughfare, **Colaba Causeway** (this stretch of Shahid Bhagat Singh Marg), leads south towards the military cantonment. Few tourists stray much further down it than the claustrophobic hawker zone at the top of the street, but it's well worth doing so, if only to see the neighbourhood's earthy **fresh produce market**, a

---

Bombay duck

Its name suggests some kind of fowl curry, but **Bombay duck** is actually a fish – to be precise, the marine lizard fish (*Harpalon nehereus*), known in the local dialect of Marathi as *bummalo*. How this long, ribbon-like sea creature acquired its English name no one is exactly sure, but the most plausible theory holds that the Raj-era culinary term derives from the Hindustani for mail train, *dak*. The nasty odour of the dried fish is said to have reminded the British of the less salubrious carriages of the Calcutta–Bombay *dak* when it pulled into VT after three days and nights on the rails, its wooden carriages covered in the stinking mould that flourished in the monsoonal humidity.

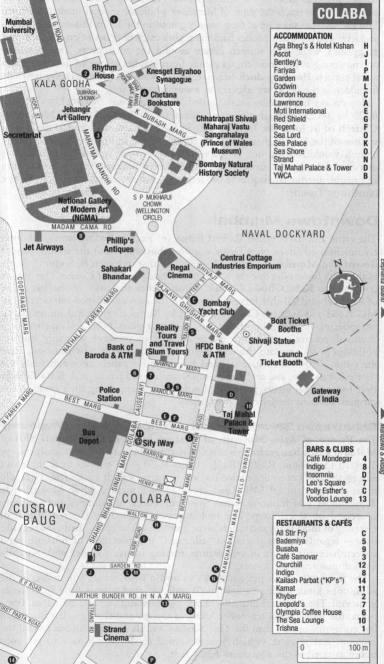

COLABA

ACCOMMODATION

Aga Bheg's & Hotel Kishan	H
Ascot	J
Bentley's	I
Fariyas	P
Garden	M
Godwin	L
Gordon House	C
Lawrence	A
Moti International	E
Red Shield	G
Regent	F
Sea Lord	O
Sea Palace	K
Sea Shore	O
Strand	N
Taj Mahal Palace & Tower	D
YWCA	B

Mumbai University

Rhythm House

Knesget Eliyahoo Synagogue

KALA GHODA

SUBHASH CHOWK

Chetana Bookstore

Jehangir Art Gallery

Secretariat

Chhatrapati Shivaji Maharaj Vastu Sangrahalaya (Prince of Wales Museum)

Bombay Natural History Society

National Gallery of Modern Art (NGMA)

S P MUKHARJI CHOWK (WELLINGTON CIRCLE)

MADAM CAMA RD

NAVAL DOCKYARD

Jet Airways

Phillip's Antiques

Sahakari Bhandar

Regal Cinema

Central Cottage Industries Emporium

SHIVAJI MARG

Bombay Yacht Club

RAJKAVI GHUSHAN

Reality Tours and Travel (Slum Tours)

Boat Ticket Booths

Shivaji Statue

HFDC Bank & ATM

Launch Ticket Booth

Bank of Baroda & ATM

NAWROJI F MARG

Gateway of India

Police Station

MANDLIK MARG

BEST MARG

Taj Mahal Palace & Tower

Bus Depot

@Sify iWay

BARROW RC

HENRY RD

COLABA

CUSROW BAUG

WALTON RD

OLIVER ROAD

GARDEN RD

S B ROAD

ARTHUR BUNDER RD (H N A A MARG)

FIRST PASTA ROAD

Strand Cinema

Elephanta Island

Mandwa & Alibag

N

BARS & CLUBS

Café Mondegar	4
Indigo	8
Insomnia	D
Leo's Square	7
Polly Esther's	C
Voodoo Lounge	13

RESTAURANTS & CAFÉS

All Stir Fry	C
Bademiya	5
Busaba	9
Café Samovar	3
Churchill	12
Indigo	8
Kailash Parbat ("KP's")	14
Kamat	11
Khyber	2
Leopold's	7
Olympia Coffee House	6
The Sea Lounge	10
Trishna	1

0   100 m

couple of blocks south of the Strand cinema. From here, return to the main road and turn left to reach the gates of Mumbai's wholesale seafood market, **Sassoon Docks**. The quaysides are at their most vigorous in the hours immediately before and after sunrise, when coolies haul the night's catch in crates of crushed ice over gangplanks, while Koli women cluster around the auctioneers. The stench, as overpowering as the noise, comes mostly from bundles of one of the city's traditional exports, **Bombay duck** (see box, p.692). Note that **photography** is strictly forbidden as the docks are adjacent to a sensitive navy area.

Hop on any bus heading south down Colaba Causeway (#3, #11, #47, #103, #123 or #125) through the cantonment to reach the **Afghan Memorial Church of St John the Baptist**, built in 1847–54 as a memorial to the British victims of the First Afghan War. With its tall steeple and tower, the pale yellow church wouldn't look out of place in Worcester or Suffolk. If the door is unlocked, take a peep inside at the battle-scarred military colours on the wall and marble memorial plaques to officers who died in various campaigns on the Northwest Frontier.

Downtown Mumbai

The critic and travel writer Robert Byron (of *Road to Oxiana* fame), although a wholehearted fan of New Delhi, was unenthusiastic about the architecture of **downtown Mumbai**, which he described as "that architectural Sodom". Some of the city's finest piles line the streets immediately north of Colaba. The district is known as **Kala Ghoda** ("Black Statue"), after the large equestrian statue of King Edward VII that formerly stood on the crescent-shaped intersection of MG Road and Subhash Chowk. Flanked by Mumbai's principal museum and art galleries, the neighbourhood has in recent years been re-launched as a "cultural enclave" – as much in an attempt to preserve its many historic buildings as to promote the contemporary visual arts that have thrived here since the 1950s. Fancy stainless-steel interpretative panels now punctuate the district's walkways, and on Sundays in December and January, the **Kala Ghoda Fair** sees portrait artists, potters and *mehendi* painters plying their trade in the car park fronting the Jehangir Art Gallery.

Chhatrapati Shivaji Museum (Prince of Wales Museum)

The **Prince of Wales Museum of Western India**, or **Chhatrapati Shivaji Maharaj Vastu Sangrahalaya** as it was renamed by the Shiv Sena (daily except Tues 10.15am–6pm; Rs300 [Rs6], camera Rs30 – no tripods or flash), ranks among the city's most distinctive Raj-era constructions. It stands rather grandly in its own gardens off MG Road, crowned by a massive white Mughal-style dome, under which one of India's finest collections of paintings and sculpture is arrayed on three floors. The building was designed by George Wittet, of Gateway of India fame, and stands as the epitome of the hybrid **Indo–Saracenic** style – regarded in its day as an "educated" interpretation of fifteenth- and sixteenth-century Gujarati architecture, mixing Islamic touches with typically English municipal brickwork.

The foreigners' ticket price includes an **audio tour**, which you collect at the admissions kiosk inside, though you'll probably find it does little to enhance your visit. The heat and humidity inside the building can also be a trial. For a break, the institutional tea-coffee kiosk in the ground-floor garden is a much less congenial option than the *Café Samovar* outside (see p.705), but to exit the museum and re-enter (which you're entitled to do) you'll have to get your ticket stamped in the admissions lobby first.

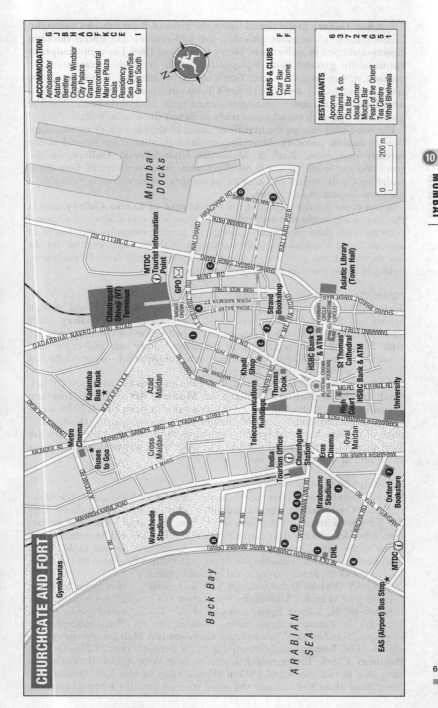

CHURCHGATE AND FORT

ACCOMMODATION
Ambassador	G
Astoria	J
Bentley	B
Chateau Windsor	H
City Palace	A
Grand	D
Intercontinental	F
Marine Plaza	K
Oasis	C
Residency	E
Sea Green/Sea Green South	I

BARS & CLUBS
Czar Bar	F
The Dome	F

RESTAURANTS
Apoorva	6
Britannia & co.	3
Cha Bar	7
Ideal Corner	2
Mocha Bar	4
Pearl of the Orient	G
Tea Centre	5
Vithal Bhelwala	1

Mumbai Docks

Chhatrapati Shivaji (VT) Terminus

MTDC Tourist Information Point

GPO

Asiatic Library (Town Hall)

Strand Bookshop

HSBC Bank & ATM

St Thomas' Cathedral

HSBC Bank & ATM

University

Kadamba Bus Kiosk

Azad Maidan

Khadi Shop

Thomas Cook

High Court

Telecommunications Building

Metro Cinema

Buses to Goa

Cross Maidan

India Tourism Office

Churchgate Station

Eros Cinema

Oval Maidan

Oxford Bookstore

Wankhede Stadium

Gymkhanas

Brabourne Stadium

DHL

MTDC

EAS (Airport) Bus Stop

Back Bay

ARABIAN SEA

0   200 m

The **Key Gallery** in the central hall of the **ground floor** provides a snapshot of the collection's treasures, including the fifth-century AD stucco Buddhist figures unearthed by archeologist Henry Cousens in 1909. The main **sculpture room** on the **ground floor** displays other fourth- and fifth-century Buddhist artefacts, mostly from the former Greek colony of Gandhara. Important Hindu sculptures include a seventh-century Chalukyan bas-relief depicting Brahma seated on a lotus, and a sensuously carved torso of Mahisasuramardini, the goddess Durga, with tripod raised ready to skewer the demon buffalo.

The main attraction on the **first floor** has to be the museum's famous collection of **Indian painting**. More fine medieval miniatures are housed in the recently inaugurated **Karl & Meherbai Khandalavala Gallery**, on the renovated east wing of this floor, along with priceless pieces of Ghandaran sculpture, Chola bronzes and some of the country's finest surviving examples of medieval Gujarati woodcarving.

Indian **coins** are the subject of the new **House of Laxmi Gallery**, also in the east wing, while the **second floor** showcases a vast array of Oriental ceramics and glassware. Finally, among the grizzly **weapons** and pieces of armour stored in a small side-gallery at the top of the building, look out for the cuirass, helmet and jade dagger which the museum only recently discovered belonged to no less than the Mughal emperor Akbar.

Kala Ghoda art galleries

Technically in the same compound as the Prince of Wales Museum, though approached from further up MG Road, the **Jehangir Art Gallery** (daily 11am–7pm; free) is Mumbai's longest-established venue for contemporary art, with five small halls specializing in twentieth-century arts and crafts from around the world. You never know what you're going to find – most exhibitions last only a week and exhibits are often for sale.

On the opposite side of MG Road, facing the museum and Mukharji Chowk, stands the larger **National Gallery of Modern Art** (NGMA; Tues–Sun 11am–5pm; Rs150 [Rs20]), housed in a converted concert hall. It holds a mix of permanent and temporary exhibitions on three storeys, charting the development of modern Indian art from its beginnings in the 1950s to the present day. The installations, in particular, tend to be a lot more adventurous than those you'll find in the Jehangir across the road.

Around Oval Maidan

Some of Mumbai's most important Victorian buildings flank the eastern side of the vast green **Oval Maidan**, where impromptu cricket matches are held almost every day (foreign enthusiasts are welcome to take part, but should beware the *maidan's* demon bowlers and less-than-even pitches). The dull yellow old **Secretariat** now serves as the City Civil and Sessions Court. Indian civil servant G.W. Forrest described it in 1903 as "a massive pile whose main features have been brought from Venice, but all the beauty has vanished in transshipment".

Across AS D'Mello Road from the Old Secretariat are two major buildings belonging to **Mumbai University** (established 1857), which were designed in England by Sir Gilbert Scott, architect of the Gothic extravaganza that is London's St Pancras railway station. Funded by the Parsi philanthropist Cowasjee "Readymoney" Jehangir, the **Convocation Hall** greatly resembles a church. The **library** (daily 10am–10pm) is beneath the 79.2-metre-high **Rajabhai Clock Tower**, which is said to have been modelled on Giotto's campanile in Florence. Until 1931, it chimed tunes such as *Rule Britannia* and *Home Sweet Home*. You can scale the grand staircase from the lobby to enter the

Mumbai's size and inconvenient shape create all kind of hassles for its working population – not least having to stew for over four hours each day in slow municipal transport. One thing the daily tidal wave of commuters does not have to worry about, however, is where to find an inexpensive and wholesome home-cooked lunch. In a city with a wallah for everything, it will find them. The members of the **Nutan Mumbai Tiffin Box Suppliers Charity Trust (NMTSCT)**, known colloquially, and with no little affection, as **"dabawallahs"**, see to that. Every day, around 4500 to 5000 *dabawallahs* deliver freshly cooked meals from 175,000 to 200,000 suburban kitchens to offices in the downtown area. Each lunch is prepared early in the morning by a devoted wife or mother while her husband or son is enduring the crush on the train. She arranges the rice, dhal, *subzi*, curd and *parathas* into cylindrical aluminium trays, stacks them on top of one another and clips them together with a neat little handle. This **tiffin box**, not unlike a slim paint tin, is the lynchpin of the whole operation. When the runner calls to collect it in the morning, he uses a special colour code on the lid to tell him where the lunch has to go. At the end of his round, he carries all the boxes to the nearest railway station and hands them over to other *dabawallahs* for the trip into town. Between leaving the wife and reaching its final destination, the tiffin box will pass through at least half a dozen different pairs of hands, carried on heads, shoulder-poles, bicycle handlebars and in the brightly decorated handcarts that plough with such insouciance through the midday traffic. Tins are rarely, if ever, lost – a fact recently reinforced by the American business magazine, *Forbes*, which awarded Mumbai's *dabawallahs* a 6-Sigma performance rating, the score reserved for companies who attain a 99.9 percentage of correctness. This means that only one tiffin box in 6 million goes astray, in efficiency terms putting the illiterate *dabawallahs* on a par with bluechip firms such as Motorola.

To catch them in action, head for **CST (VT)** or **Churchgate** stations around late morning, when the tiffin boxes arrive in the city centre. The event is accompanied by a chorus of "*lafka! lafka!*" – "hurry! hurry!" – as the *dabawallahs*, recognizable in their white Nehru caps and baggy pyjama trousers, rush to make their lunch-hour deadlines. Nearly all come from the same small village near Pune and are related to one another. They collect around Rs350–400 from each customer, or Rs5000–6000 per month in total – not a bad income by Indian standards. One of the reasons the system survives in the face of competition from trendy fast-food outlets is that *daba* lunches still work out a good deal cheaper, saving precious paise for the middle-income workers who use the system.

Business leaders who have taken more than a passing interest in the *dabawallah* phenomenon include Sir Richard Branson: the Virgin tycoon spent a day accompanying a tiffin carrier on his round. If you'd like to do the same, contact the NMTSCT via its website, ⑩www.mydabbawala.com, and look for the link to their "Day With a Dabbawala" scheme.

magnificent vaulted reading-room, whose high Gothic windows and stained glass still evoke a reverential approach to learning.

Hutatma Chowk (Flora Fountain)

A busy five-point intersection in the heart of the Fort area, the roundabout formerly known as **Flora Fountain** has been renamed **Hutatma Chowk** ("Martyrs' Square") to commemorate the freedom fighters who died to establish the state of Maharashtra in the Indian Union. The *chowk* centres on a statue of the Roman goddess **Flora**, erected in 1869 to commemorate Sir Bartle Frere. It's hard to see quite why they bothered – the Raj architecture expert, Philip Davies, was not being unkind when he said, "The fountain was designed by a committee, and it shows."

Horniman Circle and the Town Hall

Horniman Circle, formerly Elphinstone Circle, is named after the editor of a pro-Independence newspaper. It was conceived in 1860 as the centrepiece of a newly-planned Bombay by the then Municipal Commissioner, Charles Forjett, on the site of Bombay "Green". Later, the space served as a cotton market and parade ground.

Flanking the east side of the circle, the impressive **Town Hall** on SBS Marg was among the few buildings in Mumbai that pleased Aldous Huxley: "(Among) so many architectural cads and pretentious bounders," he wrote in 1948, "it is almost the only gentleman." The Doric edifice, dating from 1833, was originally built to house the vast collection of the **Asiatic Society Library**, still open to the general public (Mon–Sat 10am–7pm). Save for the addition of electricity, little has changed here since the institution was founded. Inside reading rooms, lined with wrought-iron loggias and teak bookcases, scholars pour over mouldering tomes dating from the Raj. Among the ten thousand rare and valuable manuscripts stored here is a fourteenth-century first edition of Dante's *Divine Comedy*, said to be worth around US$3 million, which the Society famously refused to sell to Mussolini. Visitors are welcome but should sign in at the Head Librarian's desk on the ground floor.

St Thomas' Cathedral

The small, simple **St Thomas' Cathedral** (daily 6.30am–6pm) on Tamarind Street is reckoned to be the oldest British building in Mumbai, blending classical and Gothic styles. After the death of its founding father, Governor Aungier, the project was abandoned; the walls stood 5m high for forty-odd years until enthusiasm was rekindled by a chaplain to the East India Company in the second decade of the eighteenth century. It was finally opened on Christmas Day, 1718, complete with the essential "cannon-ball-proof roof". In those days, the seating was divided into useful sections for those who should know their place, including one for "Inferior Women".

St Thomas' whitewashed and polished brass-and-wood interior looks much the same as when the staff of the East India Company worshipped here in the eighteenth century. Lining the walls are memorial tablets to British parishioners, many of whom died young, either from disease or in battle.

Chhatrapati Shivaji Terminus (Victoria Terminus)

Inspired by St Pancras Station in London, F.W. Stevens designed **Victoria Terminus**, the most barmy of Mumbai's buildings, as a paean to "progress". Built in 1887 as the largest British edifice in India, it's an extraordinary amalgam of domes, spires, Corinthian columns and minarets that was succinctly defined by the journalist James Cameron as "Victorian-Gothic-Saracenic-Italianate-Oriental-St Pancras-Baroque". In keeping with the current re-Indianization of the city's roads and buildings, this icon of British imperial architecture has been renamed **Chhatrapati Shivaji Terminus**, in honour of a Maratha warlord. However, the new name is a bit of a mouthful and the locals mostly still use **VT** (pronounced "vitee" or "wee-tee") when referring to it.

Few of the two million or so passengers who fill almost a thousand trains every day notice the mass of decorative detail. A "British" lion and Indian tiger stand guard at the entrance, and the exterior is festooned with sculptures executed at the Bombay Art School by the Indian students of John Lockwood Kipling, Rudyard's father. Among them are grotesque mythical beasts, monkeys, plants and medallions of important personages. To minimize the sun's impact, stained glass was employed, decorated with locomotives and elephant images. Above it all, "Progress" stands atop the massive central dome.

An endless frenzy of activity goes on inside: hundreds of porters in red with impossibly oversized headloads; TTEs (Travelling Ticket Examiners) in black jackets and white trousers clasping clipboards detailing reservations; spitting checkers busy handing out fines to those caught in the act; chai-wallahs with trays of tea; trundling magazine stands; crowds of bored soldiers smoking *beedis*; and the inexorable progress across the station of sweepers bent double. Amid it all, whole families spread out on the floor, eating, sleeping or just waiting and waiting.

Crawford Market and the bazaars

A kilometre or so north of CST (VT) station, lining the anarchic jumble of streets beyond Lokmanya Tilak Road, is Mumbai's bustling **central bazaar district** – a fascinating counterpoint to the wide and Westernized streets of downtown. In keeping with traditional divisions of guild, caste and religion, most streets specialize in one or two types of merchandise. If you lose your bearings, the best way out is to ask someone to wave you in the direction of **Mohammed Ali Road**, the busy road through the heart of the district (now surmounted by a gigantic flyover), from where you can hail a cab.

Crawford (aka Mahatma Phule) **Market**, ten minutes' walk north of CST, is an old British-style covered market dealing in just about every kind of fresh food and domestic animal imaginable. Before venturing inside, stop to admire the **friezes** wrapped around its exterior – a Victorian vision of sturdy-limbed peasants toiling in the fields designed by Rudyard Kipling's father, Lockwood, as principal of the Bombay School of Art in 1865. The **main hall** is still divided into different sections: pyramids of polished fruit and vegetables down one aisle, sacks of nuts or oil-tins full of herbs and spices down another. Around the back of the market, in the atmospheric wholesale wing, the pace of life is more hectic. Here, noisy crowds of coolies mill about with large reed-baskets held high in the air (if they are looking for work) or on their heads (if they've found some).

North of Crawford Market

Dominated by the pale green domes and minarets of the **Jama Masjid**, or "Friday Mosque" (c.1800), the streets immediately **north of Crawford Market** and west of **Mohammed Ali Road** form one vast bazaar area. **Memon Street**, cutting north from the mosque, is the site of the **Zaveri Bazaar**, the jewellery market where Mumbaikars come to shop for dowries and wedding attire.

Further north, the **Mumba Devi temple**'s cream-and-turquoise tower rises above a maze of twisting lanes hemmed in by tall, wooden-balconied buildings. One of the most important centres of Devi worship in India, the temple was built early in the nineteenth century, when the deity was relocated from her former home to make way for CST (VT) station. Mumba Devi's other claim to fame is that her name is the original root of the city's modern name.

Marine Drive and Chowpatty Beach

Netaji Subhash Chandra Marg, better known as **Marine Drive**, is Mumbai's seaside prom, an eight-lane highway with a wide pavement built in the 1920s on reclaimed land. The whole three-kilometre stretch – still often referred to by Mumbaikars as the "Queen's Necklace", after the row of lights which illuminates its spectacular curve at night – is a favourite place for a stroll; the promenade next to the sea has uninterrupted views virtually the whole way along, while the peeling, mildew-streaked Art-Deco apartment blocks on the land side remain some of the most desirable addresses in the city.

Chowpatty Beach, at the top of Marine Drive, is a Mumbai institution. On evenings and weekends, Mumbaikars gather in large numbers – not to swim (the sea is foul) but to wander, sit on the sand, munch *kulif* and *bhel puri*, get their ears cleaned and gaze across the bay while the kids ride a pony or a rusty Ferris wheel. Once a year in September the **Ganesh Chathurthi** festival draws gigantic crowds as idols, both huge and small, of the elephant-headed god Ganesh are immersed in the sea.

Mani Bhavan (Mahatma Gandhi Museum)

A ten-minute walk north from the middle of Chowpatty Beach (along P Ramabai Marg), **Mani Bhavan**, at 19 Laburnum Rd (daily 9.30am–6pm), was Gandhi's Bombay base between 1917 and 1934. Throughout the campaign for Independence, the Mahatma spent long spells here, organizing strikes among the city's textile workers, addressing mass rallies and negotiating with British officials. Set in a leafy upper-middle-class road, Mani Bhavan has now been converted into a permanent memorial to the Mahatma with an extensive research library. Within the lovingly maintained polished-wood interior, the walls are covered with photos of historic events and artefacts from the man's extraordinary life – the most disarming of which is a friendly letter to Hitler suggesting world peace. Gandhi's predictably simple sitting room-cum-bedroom is preserved behind glass. Laburnum Road is a few streets along from the Bharatiya Vidya Bhavan music venue on KM Munshi Marg – if coming by taxi ask for the nearby Gamdevi Police Station.

Malabar Hill

Its shirt-tails swathed in greenery and brow bristling with gigantic skyscrapers, the promontory enfolding Chowpatty Beach at the north end of Back Bay has been south Mumbai's most desirable neighbourhood almost since the city was founded. The British were quick to see the potential of its salubrious breezes and sweeping sea views, constructing bungalows at the tip of what was then a separate island – the grandest of them the Government House, originally erected in the 1820s and now the seat of the serving Governor of Maharashtra, **Raj Bhavan**.

The Towers of Silence

High on Malabar Hill, screened from prying eyes by a high wall and dense curtain of vegetation, stand the seven **Towers of Silence**, where the city's dwindling Zoroastrian community (better known as Parsis) dispose of their dead. Pollution of the four sacred elements (air, water, earth and, holiest of all, fire) contradicts the most fundamental precepts of the 2500-year-old Parsi faith, first imported to India when Zoroastrians fled from Sassanid Persia to escape Arab persecution in the seventh century. So instead of being buried or cremated, the bodies are laid out on top of open-topped, cylindrical towers, called *dokhmas*, for their bones to be cleaned by **vultures** and the weather. The remains are then placed in an ossuary at the centre of the tower.

Recent decades have seen a sharp decline in the number of Parsis choosing this traditional funerary rite, one reason for which is the disappearance of India's vultures – a result of their exposure to the anti-inflammatory drug, Diclofenac, which is fed to cattle and therefore found in the carcasses on which the birds more commonly feed. Solar panels have instead been installed in the towers, to use the sun's rays to dispose of the corpses; captive vultures are being considered as another solution. The Towers of Silence are strictly closed to visitors.

Although none of Malabar's landmarks might be classed as unmissable, its Hindu shrines and surviving colonial-era residences form an interesting counterpoint to the modernity towering on all sides. Bal Gangadhar Kher Marg (formerly Ridge Road) is the district's main artery. You can follow it from Mumbai's principal **Jain Temple** (see map, p.678), with its mirror-encrusted interior dedicated to Adinath, all the way to the tip of the headland, where the famous **Walukeshwar Temple** stands as the city's oldest Hindu shrine surviving *in situ*. According to the Ramayana, Rama fashioned a lingam out of sand to worship Shiva here, which over the centuries became one of the Konkan's most important pilgrimage centres. Today's temple, erected in 1715 after the original had been destroyed by the Portuguese, is of less note than the **Banganga Tank** below it – a rectangular lake lined by stone *ghats* and numerous crumbling shrines.

Central Mumbai: Mahalakshmi to Byculla

The centre of Mumbai, beyond Malabar Hill, is mostly made up of working-class neighbourhoods: a huge mosaic of dilapidated tenements, markets and industrial eyesores left over from the Victorian cotton boom. For relief from the urban cauldron, residents travel west to the seashore to worship at the **Mahalakshmi Temple** (if they're Hindus) or the island **tomb of Haji Ali** (if they're Muslims). Both make great excursions from south Mumbai, and can be combined with a foray across town to the recently revamped **Dr Bhau Dadji Lad Museum** in Byculla, calling en route at the **Mahalakshmi dhobi ghats** – one of the city's more offbeat sights.

Buses #83, #132 or #133 will take you from Colaba to Haji Ali, within a stone's throw of the Mahalakshmi Temple. To continue east from here to Byculla, your best option would be to catch a cab, though bus #124 will take you as far as the *dhobi ghats*. These are also easily accessible from south Mumbai by train or bus.

Mahalakshmi Temple

Mahalakshmi Temple, just off Bhulabhai Desai Road, is approached via an alley lined with stalls selling spectacular floral offerings and devotional pictures. Gifts for Mumbai's favourite *devi*, **Lakshmi**, goddess of beauty and prosperity – the city's most sought-after attributes – pile so high that the temple *pujaris* run a money-spinning sideline reselling them. While you're here, find out what your future holds by joining the huddle of devotees pressing rupees onto the rear wall of the shrine room. If your coin sticks, you'll be rich.

Haji Ali's Tomb

Occupying a small islet in the bay just north of the Mahalakshmi is the mausoleum of the Muslim saint, Afghan mystic **Haji Ali Bukhari**. The tomb is connected to the mainland by a narrow concrete **causeway**, only passable at low tide. When not immersed in water, its entire length is lined with beggars supplicating passers-by and chanting verses from the Ko'ran. The white Mughal domes and minarets of the tomb itself look a lot less exotic close up than when viewed from the shore, silhouetted against the sun as it drops into the Arabian Sea. But the site is a great place to head for on Thursday and Friday evenings, when large crowds gather around the headland to watch the sunset and listen to live **qawwali** music. Non-Muslims are welcome, but you'll need to keep well covered up (a headscarf should be worn by women).

The traditional way to round off a trip to the mausoleum is a glass or two of fresh fruit juice at the legendary **Haji Ali Juice Centre**, just to the right of the

Dharavi: the £700 million slum

Flying into Mumbai airport, your plane's undercarriage will almost skim the corrugated-iron rooftops of the vast shantytown spread across the middle of one of India's largest slums. Sprawling over 550 acres, **Dharavi**'s maze of dilapidated shacks and narrow, stinking alleyways is home to more than a million people. An average of 15,000 of them share a single toilet. Infectious diseases such as dysentery, malaria and hepatitis are rife; and there aren't any hospitals. Yet Dharavi was recently described by the UK's *Observer* newspaper as "one of the most inspiring economic models in Asia": hidden amid the warren of ramshackle huts and squalid open sewers are an estimated 15,000 single-room factories, employing around a quarter of a million people and turning over a staggering £700 million (US$1.4 billion) annually.

The majority of small businesses in Dharavi are based on **waste recycling** of one kind or another. Slum residents young and old scavenge materials from across the city and haul them back in huge bundles to be reprocessed. Aluminium cans are smelted down, soap scraps salvaged from schools and hotels are reduced in huge vats, leather reworked, disused oil drums restored and discarded plastic reshaped and remoulded. An estimated ten thousand workers are employed in the plastics sector alone. Ranging from Rs3000–15,000 per month, wages are well above the national average, and though Dharavi may not have any health centres, it does hold a couple of banks, and even ATMs.

The economic miracle, however, is living in the shadow of a massive $40billion **redevelopment project**, spearheaded by the Municipality and private financiers, which aims to bulldoze the entire slum to make room for a radical makeover of central Mumbai. In return for agreeing to eviction, Dharavi's residents will be entitled to 225 square feet of apartment space per family in new multistorey tower blocks. Schools, roads, hospitals and other amenities have also been promised. Yet opposition to the scheme among Dharavites is all but unanimous. The slum dwellers insist any future development should focus not on erecting a swanky new suburb but improving existing conditions. For the time being, the initiative remains deadlocked.

You can visit Dharavi yourself by joining one of the **"Slum Tours"** run by Reality Tours and Travels out of Colaba. Tickets for these engaging guided trips cost Rs300 (including transport), or you can also opt for a longer and more comfortable version with an a/c car for Rs600. For more details, contact Krishna Pujari on ☎022/2283 3872, or ☎m09820/822253, check out ⊛www.realitytoursandtravel.com, or just drop in to their booking office (Mon–Fri 10.15am–8.35pm, Sat 10.15am–3.45pm) off Colaba Causeway (SBS Marg), on the first floor of Akbar Hose Nawroji Fardonji Marg, opposite the *Laxmi Vilas Hotel* (see map, p.693 – but note that to find the place you'll need further directions by phone or their website as it's hidden behind a shop).

entrance to the causeway. Customers either cram into the tiny dining hall or else order from their cars.

Mahalakshmi dhobi ghats

On the face of it, the idea of going out of your way to ogle Mumbai's dirty washing sounds like a very perverse pastime. If you're passing, however, the **municipal dhobi ghats**, near Mahalakshmi suburban railway station, are a sufficiently memorable spectacle to break a trip across town to see. Washing from all over the city is brought here each morning to be soaked in concrete vats and thumped by the resident *dhobis*. A trickle of curious foreign tourists gathers on Mahalakshmi road bridge for this uniquely Indian photo opportunity every morning; even Bill Clinton found time to slot in a visit in 2005.

Much the easiest way to get to Mahalakshmi is to jump on a suburban train from Churchgate. Emerging from the station, turn left and follow the road over the rail tracks – the *ghats* will be below you on your left (the hawkers from the nearby slums who work the spot will show you the way). Bus #124 from Colaba and Haji Ali will also drop you there.

The Dr Bhau Dadji Lad Museum

The only reason you might wish to venture into the postindustrial wasteland of Byculla, in central Mumbai, would be to visit the **Dr Bhau Dadji Lad Museum** (daily except Wed 10.30am–4.30pm; admission Rs20) in Byculla-East. When it opened in 1872, the **Victoria and Albert Museum**, as it was then, was hailed as "one of the greatest boons the British have conferred on India" – an elegant, fashionably decorated edifice in high Palladian style, set amid classically planned botanical gardens (which these days accommodate a rather depressing zoo). A century or more of neglect took its toll, but the building was recently restored to its former glory. Its collection of lithographs, prints, documents, uniforms and models relating to the development of Bombay don't perhaps quite live up to the promise of their sumptuous Victorian surroundings, but will interest aficionados of colonial history. In the adjacent garden, the carved stone pachyderm after which the Portuguese are said to have named Elephanta Island presides over a collection of forlorn British statues, moved here during Independence beyond the reach of angry mobs.

Elephanta

An hour's ride northeast across Mumbai harbour from Colaba, the island of **Elephanta** offers the best escape from the seething claustrophobia of the city – as long as you time your visit to avoid the weekend deluge of noisy day-trippers. Populated only by a small fishing community, it was originally known as **Gherapura**, the "city of Ghara priests", until the island was renamed in the sixteenth century by the Portuguese in honour of the carved elephant they found at the port (now on display outside the Dr Bhau Dadji Lad – formerly Victoria and Albert – Museum in Byculla). Its chief attraction is its unique **cave temple**, whose massive **Trimurti** (three-faced) **Shiva sculpture** is as fine an example of Hindu architecture as you'll find anywhere.

"**Deluxe**" **boats** set off from the Gateway of India (Oct–May Tues–Sun hourly 9am–2.30pm; Rs150 return including government guide; book through the kiosks near the Gateway of India). Ask for your guide at the cave's ticket office on arrival – tours last thirty minutes. **Ordinary ferries** (Oct–May Tues–Fri hourly 9am–3pm; Rs125 return), also from the Gateway of India, don't include guides and are usually more packed. Cool drinks and souvenir stalls line the way up the hill, and, at the top, the MTDC *Chalukya* restaurant offers substandard food and warm beer, served on a terrace with good views out to sea, Note that you cannot stay overnight on the island and that the caves are closed on Mondays.

The cave

Elephanta's impressive excavated eighth-century **cave** (Tues–Sun 9.30am–5pm; Rs250 [Rs10]), covering an area of approximately 5000 square metres, is reached by climbing more than one hundred steps to the top of the hill, lined by souvenir and knick-knack stalls. Inside, the massive columns, carved from solid rock, give the deceptive impression of being structural. To the right as you enter, note the panel of **Nataraj**, Shiva as the cosmic dancer. Though spoiled by the Portuguese who, it is said, used it for target practice, the panel remains magnificent: Shiva's face is rapt, and with one of his left hands he removes the veil of ignorance. Opposite is a badly damaged panel of Lakulisha, Shiva with a club (*lakula*).

Each of the four entrances to the simple square main **shrine** – unusually, it has one on each side – is flanked by a pair of huge fanged *dvarpala* guardians (only those to the back have survived undamaged), while inside a large lingam is surrounded by coins and smouldering joss left by devotees. Facing the northern wall of the shrine, another panel shows Shiva impaling the demon Andhaka, who wandered around as though blind, symbolizing his spiritual blindness. The panel behind the shrine on the back wall portrays the marriage of Shiva and Parvati, but the cave's outstanding centrepiece is its powerful six-metre bust of **Trimurti**, the three-faced Shiva, whose profile has become almost as familiar to Indians as that of the Taj Mahal.

From Cave 1 you can follow a paved path around the north flank of the hillside past a string of other, unfinished excavations, which exemplify how the caves were originally dug out and carved. If you've the stamina, follow the dirt path that leads from the end of the paved trail beyond these to the summit of Elephanta Hill, a stiff hike of fifteen minutes. At the top you'll be rewarded with an encounter with a couple of rusting Portuguese cannons and a magnificent view back over Mumbai harbour to the distant city beyond.

The outskirts: Kanheri Caves

Overlooking the suburb of Borivli, 42km out at the northern limits of Mumbai's sprawl, are the Buddhist **Kanheri Caves** (Tues–Sun 9am–5.30pm; Rs100 [Rs5]), ranged over the hills in virtually unspoilt forest. It's an interminable journey by road, so catch one of the many **trains** (50min) on the suburban line from Churchgate (marked "BO" on the departure boards; "limited stop" trains are 15min faster) to Borivli East. When you arrive, take the Borivli East exit, where a **bus** (for Kanheri Caves via SG Parles; Rs20), **auto-rickshaw** (about Rs125) or **taxi** (about Rs150) will take you the last 15km. Bring water and food as the stalls here only sell warm soft drinks.

Kanheri may not be as spectacular as other cave sites, but some of its sculpture is superb – though to enjoy the blissful peace and quiet that attracted its original occupants you should **avoid the weekends**. Most of the caves, which date from the second to the ninth century AD, were used simply by monks for accommodation and meditation during the four months of the monsoon, when an itinerant life was impractical. They are connected by steep winding paths and steps; engage one of the friendly local guides at the entrance to find your way about, but don't expect any sort of lecture as their English is limited. The risk of muggings in some of the remoter caves means it is not advisable to venture off the beaten track alone.

Eating

Mirroring its cosmopolitan make-up, Mumbai is crammed with interesting **eating places**. In the south of the city, Colaba's cafés, bars and restaurants encompass just about the full gamut of gastronomic possibilities. The majority – among them the popular travellers' haunts, *Leopold's* and the *Café Mondegar* (see p.706 & p.708) – line the north end of the Causeway. However, don't be discouraged by the heat and traffic from venturing outside Colaba for a meal. A short walk or taxi ride north to **Kala Ghoda** and into **Fort** are some of the best cafés and restaurants in the Mumbai, among them the last surviving traditional Parsi diners, whose menus and decor have changed little over three or four generations.

Street food

Mumbai is renowned for distinctive street foods – and especially **bhel puri**, a quint-essentially Mumbai masala mixture of puffed rice, deep-fried vermicelli, potato, crunchy *puri* pieces, chilli paste, tamarind water, chopped onions and coriander. More hygienic, but no less ubiquitous, is **pao bhaji**, a round Portuguese-style bread roll served on a tin plate with griddle-fried, spicy vegetable stew, and **kanji vada**, savoury doughnuts soaked in fermented mustard and chilli sauce. And if all that doesn't appeal, a pit-stop at one of the city's hundreds of **juice bars** probably will. There's no better way to beat the sticky heat than with a glass of cool milk shaken with fresh pineapple, mango, banana, *chikoo* (small brown fruit that tastes like a sweet pear) or custard apple. Just make sure they hold on the ice – which may be made with untreated water.

Restaurants and cafés are listed by district. Phone numbers have been given where we recommend you reserve a table. Beware of service charges levied on your bill by some of the more expensive places. Except where noted, places listed under Colaba and Kala Ghoda can be found on the map on p.693, and those under Churchgate and Fort on p.695; the rest are found on the map on pp.678–679.

Colaba and Kala Ghoda

All Stir Fry *Gordon House Hotel.* Build-your-own wok meal from a selection of fresh veg, meat, fish, noodles and sauces, flash-cooked in front of you (Rs275–375 per bowl). The satay and dim sum are particularly good. Trendy minimalist decor, glacial a/c and snappy service.

Bademiya Behind the *Taj* on Tulloch Rd. Legendary Colaba kebab-wallah serving delicious flame-grilled chicken, mutton and fish steaks, as well as veg alternatives, wrapped in paper-thin, piping hot rotis, from benches on the sidewalk. Rich families from uptown drive here on weekends, eating on their car bonnets, but there are also little tables and chairs if you don't fancy a take-away.

Busaba 4 Mandlik Marg ☎ 022/2204 3779. Sophisticated bar-restaurant specializing in Far-Eastern cuisine – Thai, Korean, Burmese, Vietnamese and Tibetan staples, with exotic salads (green mango and glass noodle). One of *the* places to be seen (if you can't quite afford to eat at *Indigo* next door). Count on Rs800–1400 per head for the works.

Café Samovar Jehangir Art Gallery, MG Rd ☎ 022/2284 8000. Very pleasant, peaceful semi-alfresco café opening onto the museum gardens, with a good-value lunch menu (Rs75) featuring pilau, stuffed *parathas* and biriyanis, as well as plenty of à la carte choices (prawn curry, roti kebabs and fresh salads and dhansak. They also serve delicious chilled guava juice and beer (Rs120), but note no alcohol served 1–3pm.

Churchill 103 Colaba Causeway. Tiny 26-seater Parsi diner, with a bewildering choice of dishes,

including salads, pastas and burgers, mostly meat-based and served in mild sauces alongside a blob of mash and boiled veg – ideal if you've had your fill of spicy food. No alcohol. Main courses around Rs175–225.

Indigo 4 Mandlik Marg ☎ 022/2236 8999. One of the city's most fashionable restaurants, and for once deserving of the hype. The Italian-based cooking has a Konkan–Keralan twist (Kochi oysters with saffron ravioli, for example). House flambée is extremely popular, as much for its head-turning potential as anything else. Count on Rs1000-plus for three courses. Reservations essential.

Kailash Parbat ("KP's") 1 Pasta Lane, near the Strand cinema. Uninspiring on the outside, but the breakfast *aloo parathas*, pure veg nibbles, hot snacks and sweets (across the road) are worth the walk. A Colaba institution – try their famous *makai-ka* (corn) rotis.

Kamat Colaba Causeway. Friendly little eatery serving unquestionably the best South Indian breakfasts in the area, as well as the usual range of southern snacks (*iddli*, vada, *sambar*), delicious spring *dosas* and (limited) thalis for Rs50–120. The best option in the area for budget travellers with big appetites.

Khyber opposite Jehangir Art Gallery ☎ 022/2267 3227. Opulent Arabian Nights interior and uncom-promisingly rich "Northwest Frontier" cuisine, served by black-tie waiters. The chicken tikka is legendary, but their tandoori dishes and kebab platter are superb too. Count on Rs1000–1300.

Konkan Café *Taj President Hotel,* Cuffe Parade (see map, pp.678–679) ☎ 022/5665 0808. Just the place to push the boat out: a sophisticated five-star hotel restaurant serving fine regional cuisine from coastal Maharashtra, Goa, Karnataka and Kerala. You can choose from their thali platters (Rs500–6500) or go à la carte: butter-pepper-garlic crab is to die for. Quite simply some of the most mouthwatering South Indian food you'll ever eat.

Leopold's Colaba Causeway. A Mumbai institution for decades, Leopold's is the number-one hangout for India-weary Western travellers, who cram onto its small tables for overpriced, largely uninteresting food. Among the white faces you might spot are Gregory David "Shantaram" Roberts, who immortalized the place in his best-selling biog-novel and still drops in from time to time. Three hundred items feature on the menu from scrambled eggs to "chilly chicken"; cold beers cost Rs150. There's also a gloomy a/c bar upstairs (not recommended for women).

Olympia Coffee House Colaba Causeway. *Fin-de-siècle* Irani café with marble tabletops, wooden wall panels, fancy mirrors and a mezzanine floor for women. Waiters in Peshwari caps and *salwar kameezes* serve melt-in-the-mouth kebabs and delicious curd-based dips. It gets packed out at breakfast time for cholesterol-packed "mutton mince and fried eggs", which regulars wash down with bright orange chai. A quintessential (and inexpensive) Bombay experience.

The Sea Lounge *Taj Mahal Hotel.* Spacious 1930s-style lounge café on the first floor of the *Taj* with a backdrop of the Gateway and harbour. Come for afternoon tea or a late breakfast – it's worth splashing out on for the atmosphere. Opens at 7am for breakfast; closes at midnight. Pastries Rs350–400; coffees and teas Rs175–250; breakfast Rs740.

Saurabh 136 SBS Marg (Colaba Causeway). Small Udipi joint 10min walk south down Colaba Causeway from the main shopping area, which would be undistinguished were it not for the fact that Madonna and her husband, Guy Richie, accompanied by Shantaram author, Gregory David Roberts, made a pit stop here in Jan 2008, after visiting a local slum. The food – South Indian veg staples, *wada pao*, and some Gujarati and Marathi specialities – is fresh, cheap and tasty.

Trishna 7 Sai Baba Marg (Ropewalk Lane), Kala Ghoda ☎022/2261 4991 or 2270 3213. Visiting dignitaries and local celebs, from the President of Greece and Imran Khan to Bollywood stars, have eaten in this dimly lit Mangalorean, tucked away down a narrow sidestreet on the south edge of Fort. It serves wonderful fish dishes in every sauce going, with prices to match the clientele (main courses from Rs550). Butter-pepper-garlic crab (sold by weight, average cost around Rs650–750) is their

signature dish, but the pomfret stuffed with green masala is great too. Very small, so book in advance.

Churchgate and Fort

Apoorva Vasta House (Noble Chambers), SA Brelvi Rd ☎022/2287 0335. Currently the city's busiest Mangalorean, hidden up a side street off Horniman Circle (look for the tree trunk wrapped with fairy lights). The cooking's completely authentic and the seafood – simmered in spicy coconut-based gravies – fresh off the boats each day. Try their definitive Bombay duck, *surmai* (kingfish) in coconut gravy or sublime prawn *gassi*, served with perfect *sanna* and *appams*. Beers and spirits available on the ground floor; there's also a less male-dominated a/c "family room" upstairs.

Britannia & Co Opposite the GPO, Sprott Rd, Ballard Estate. Quirky little Parsi restaurant, famous as much for its quaint period atmosphere as its wholesome Irani food. Most people come for the sublime "berry pulao" (chicken, mutton or vegetable), made with deliciously tart dried berries imported from Tehran (Rs180, but portions are gigantic). For afters, there's the house "caramel custard". One of the city's unmissable eating experiences. Open 11.30am–3.30pm.

Cha Bar Oxford Bookstore, 3 Dinsha Wacha Rd, Churchgate. Chic a/c café accessed via downtown's top bookshop, popular mainly with well-heeled students. They serve an exhaustive range of single-estate regional teas and coffees, from high-fired Darjeeling to Kashmiri *kawa* and Ladhaki butter tea, as well as trendy Ayurvedic brews and house "tea cocktails"; and there's a tempting menu of (pricey) light snacks and toasties.

Ideal Corner 12 F/G Hornby View, Gunbow St ☎022/2262 1930. Another Parsi café with a cult following, but more in the thick of things than *Britannia* and less old-world since its recent facelift. Go for one of their delicious home-made Parsi specialities: *kchchidi* prawn, lamb dhansak or chicken *farcha*, rounded off with the legendary *lagan* custard. Most mains Rs50–75. Closed eves and Sun.

Joshi Club 31-A Narottamwadi, Kalbadevi Rd (see map, pp.678–679) ☎022/2205 8089. Also known as *The Friends Union Joshi Club*, this eccentric thali canteen serves what many aficionados regard as the most genuine and tasty Gujarati–Marwari meals in the city, on unpromising Formica tables against a backdrop of grubby walls. Rs95 buys you unlimited portions of four vegetable dishes, dhals and up to four different kinds of bread, with all the trimmings (and banana custard). Finding it requires some effort: walk or catch a cab to the bottom of Kalbadevi Rd (opposite the Metro cinema; see map, p.695); head north across

Vardhaman Chowk, and continue up Kalbadevi Rd for 5min until you see a signboard on your right for "Bhojanalaya", below a first-floor window.

Mocha Bar VN Rd. Chilled terrace café where swarms of north Mumbai bratpackers order American-style coffees, Mediterranean mezes and outrageously expensive New World wines, crashed out on bolster cushions and smoking fruit-flavoured tobacco on hookah pipes: very much the zeitgeist.

The Pearl of the Orient *Ambassador Hotel*, VN Rd ☏ 022/229 1131. Revolving Oriental restaurant in this faded four-star hotel. The cooking's nothing special (and expensive at around Rs750–1000 for three courses), but the views over the city are extraordinary.

The Tea Centre Resham Bhavan, 78 VN Rd. Another vestige of colonial days, which, despite a lavish refit, has retained its Raj-era charm, with paddle fans, comfy furniture and waiters wearing old-style "ice-cream-wafer" *pugris*. Fine tea is its *raison d'être*, but they also serve delicious Continental snacks (try the fluffy cheese omelettes) and cakes, as well as a good-value "Executive Lunch" (Rs225).

Vithal Bhelwala 5 AK Naik Marg (Baston Rd), close to CST (VT). Mumbai's favourite *bhel puri* outlet, open since 1875 and still doing a roaring trade. No fewer than 25 kinds of *bhel* are on offer, including one pitched at British palates, with "boiled veg and cornflakes". They also do delicious potato cutlets, served with crunchy *puri* and yoghurt. Handy for the movie houses and the station.

Crawford Market and the central bazaars

Badshah Juice and Snack Bar Opposite Crawford Market, Lokmanya Tilak Rd. Mumbai's most acclaimed *falooda* joint also serves delicious kulfi, ice creams and dozens of freshly squeezed fruit juices. The ideal place to round off a trip to the market, though expect to have to queue for a table.

Rajdhani Mangaldas Rd (in the silk bazaar opposite Crawford Market). Outstanding, eat-till-you-burst Gujarati thalis. Very cramped and more expensive than usual (Rs175 on weekdays, or Rs225 for the "Special" Sun lunch), but they don't stint on quality. Closed Sun evenings.

Bars and nightlife

Mumbaikars have an unusually easy-going attitude to alcohol; popping into a **bar** for a beer is very much accepted (for men at least), even at lunchtime. Colaba Causeway, where you'll find *Leopold's* (see opposite) and *Café Mondegar* (see p.708), forms the focus of the travellers' social scene but if you want to sample the pulse of the city's nightlife, venture up to Bandra and Juhu.

In 2005, the killjoy Mumbai Municipality, in a bid to crack down on what its Shiv Sena mandarins perceived as out-of-control Western decadence, slapped a 1.30am **curfew** on the city's nightlife. The effect was instant and a catastrophe for smaller, niche venues playing more experimental music, few of which could make ends meet with such limited opening hours. The law, however, proved a boon for the bigger clubs hosted by Mumbai's five-star hotels, which are allowed to stay open until 3am.

Despite the 2005 curfew, Mumbai's **nightclub** scene remains the most full-on in India. Tiny, skin-tight outfits that show off razor-sharp abs and pumped-up pecs are very much the order of the day, especially in venues frequented by Bollywood's movers and shakers – and the pretty young things desperate to break into the industry. Dominated by *filmi* pop mixes, the music is far from cutting edge by the standards of London or New York, but no one seems to mind. Dance floors get as rammed as a suburban commuter train and the cover charges are astronomical. Door policies and dress codes tend to be strict ("no ballcaps, no shorts, no sandals"), and, in theory, most clubs have a "couples-only" policy – they charge per couple on the door (with a portion of the entrance cost redeemable at the bar). In practice, if you're in a mixed group or don't appear sleazy you shouldn't have any problems. At the five-star hotels, entry can be restricted to hotel guests and members.

Bollywood

The home of the Hindi blockbuster, the "all-India film", is Mumbai, famously known as **Bollywood**. Visitors to the city should have ample opportunity to sample the delights of a Hindi movie, traditional or otherwise. To make an educated choice, buy *Time Out Mumbai* magazine, which contains extensive **listings** and reviews. Alternatively, look for the biggest, brightest hoarding, and join the queue. Seats in a comfortable air-conditioned cinema cost Rs100–195, or less if you sit in the stalls (not advisable for women).

Of the two hundred or so **cinemas**, only a dozen or so regularly screen **English-language** films. The most central and convenient are the gloriously Art-Deco halls dating from the twilight of the Raj: the Regal in Colaba; the Eros opposite Churchgate station, and the Metro (Ⓦwww.adlabscinemas.com) at Dhobi Talao junction – the latter was recently converted into a state-of-the-art multiplex. Down on Nariman Point, near Express Towers, the Inox (Ⓦwww.inoxmovies.com) is another big multi-screen venue, built only a few years ago in retro Mumbai-Art-Deco style.

For more on Bollywood, see "*Bollywood and beyond*" colour section.

Bars

Café Mondegar Colaba Causeway (see map, p.693). Draught beer by the glass or pitcher (both imported and Indian) and deliciously fruity cocktails are served in this small café-bar. The atmosphere is very relaxed, the music tends towards cheesy rock classics and the clientele is a mix of Westerners and students; murals by a famous Goan cartoonist give the place a cheerful ambience.

Czar Bar *Hotel Intercontinental*, 135 Marine Drive (see map, p.695). Trendy vodka bar with chic, minimalist decor, clever lighting and 24 brands on offer (from Rs250/shot), plus a full range of other drinks and cocktails. Music is lounge until around 11pm, then picks up. Quiet on weekday nights, but popular on weekends.

The Dome *Hotel Intercontinental*, 135 Marine Drive (see map, p.695). Easily south Mumbai's most alluring spot for a sundowner, on the rooftop of this smart boutique hotel. Plush white sofas and armchairs line up alongside the candle-lit tables, spread in front of the eponymous domed rotunda and a very sexy raised pool. The views over Back Bay can occasionally make the sky-high drink prices (Rs350 for beer; Rs450 for a shot and mixer) feel worth it. Popular mainly with overpaid expats.

Indigo 4 Mandlik Rd, Colaba (see map, p.693). The coolest hang-out in Colaba, frequented by young media types and would-be wine buffs. Its funky, stripped-bare decor set a new trend in the city. See also p.705.

Leo's Square 1st floor, *Leopold's*, Colaba Causeway (see map, p.693). Pretty much the same drinks menu and prices as *Leopold's* downstairs, but here you can enjoy a/c, a back-lit bar and quality sound system.

Olive 4 Union Park Rd, Pali Hill. Nowhere pulls in Bollywood's A-list like *Olive*. If you want to rub shoulders with Hrithik, Abhishek and Aishwarya, Preity and Shilpa, this is your best bet, though dress to kill – and come armed with a flexible wallet. Although basically just a pretext to crowd-watch, the food is fine gourmet Mediterranean.

Nightclubs

Enigma *JW Marriott Hotel* (see map, pp.678–679), Juhu Tara Rd. This is what Hindi film stars and hip young Indian millionaires do for kicks: the sexiest outfits, latest Bolly-bhangra mixes, most gorgeous decor and stiffest entrance cost (from Rs1500 per couple).

Insomnia *Taj Mahal Palace & Tower* (see map, p.693). Well-heeled yuppies and their NRI (Non-Resident Indian) relatives strut their stuff in this warren of illuminated bars, hardwood dance floors and chill-out spaces beneath the *Taj*, featuring one of the city's heftiest sound systems. Open to non-members, but you'll have to look your best. Cover Rs1300–1800 per couple. Punters start arriving at 11pm and it usually stays open until 3am.

Polly Esther's *Gordon House Hotel*, Battery St, Colaba (see map, p.693). Retro club with brightly coloured Seventies/Eighties decor, leather upholstery and a Nineties night on Thurs, where the waiters wear ludicrous fluoro-coloured Afro wigs; pop, rock, disco and Motown on the weekend. Rs9000–1200 per couple.

Squeeze 5th Rd, Khar. Bandra's funkiest nightspot is aptly named: it's packed seven nights a week, and bursting at the seams on weekends, when the music's less dominated by Hindi pop than elsewhere. Fridays hosts Submerge – the city's original and best House night (they usually throw in plenty of hip-hop and R&B for good measure). Admission Rs1200–1500 per couple.

Voodoo Lounge Arthur Bunder Rd, Colaba (see map, p.693). This cavernous, but delightfully louche, little dive off Colaba Causeway plays host to Mumbai's one and only gay club, from 9pm on Sat (it's dead and depressing the rest of the week). The atmosphere's restrained by Western standards, but welcoming and sociable for both gay and straight men and women, though most of the punters do come to cruise. Admission Rs250–300/head.

Shopping

Mumbai is a great place to shop, whether for last-minute souvenirs or essentials for the long journeys ahead. Locally produced **textiles** and export-surplus clothing are among the best buys, as are **handicrafts** from far-flung corners of the country. With the exception of the swish arcades in the five-star hotels, prices compare surprisingly well with other Indian cities. In the larger shops, rates are fixed and **credit cards** are often accepted; elsewhere, particularly dealing with street vendors, it pays to haggle. Uptown, the **central bazaars** – see p.699 – are better for spectating than serious shopping. The **Zaveri** (goldsmiths') **Bazaar** opposite Crawford Market is the place to head for new gold and silver **jewellery**. **Tea** lovers should check out the Tea Centre on VN Road (see p.707), which sells a wide range of quality tea, including the outrageously expensive "fine tippy golden Orange Pekoe" (Rs1350 per 250g).

Antiques

The **Chor Bazaar** area, and Mutton Street in particular, is the centre of Mumbai's **antique trade**. Another good, if much more expensive, place is **Phillip's** famous antique shop, on the corner of Madam Cama Road, facing SP Mukharji Circle, and opposite the Regal cinema in Colaba. Brass, bronze and wood Hindu sculpture, silver jewellery, old prints and aquatints form the mainstay of its collection. Most of the stuff on sale dates from the twilight of the Raj – a result of the Indian government's ban on the export by foreigners of items more than a century old.

In the **Jehangir Art Gallery** basement, a branch of the antiques chain Natesan's Antiqarts offers a tempting selection of antique (and reproduction) sculpture, furniture, paintings and bronzes.

Clothes

Mumbai produces the bulk of India's **clothes**, mostly the lightweight, light-coloured "shirtings and suitings" favoured by droves of uniformly attired office-wallahs. For cheap Western clothing, you can't beat the long row of stalls on the pavement of MG Road, opposite the Mumbai Gymkhana. "**Fashion Street**" specializes in reject and export-surplus goods ditched by big manufacturers, selling off T-shirts, jeans, summer dresses and sweatshirts. Better-quality

---

Performing arts in Mumbai

Mumbai is a major centre for traditional performing arts, attracting the finest **Indian classical musicians** and **dancers** from all over the country. Frequent concerts and recitals are staged at venues such as Bharatiya Vidya Bhavan, KM Munshi Marg (☎022/2363 0224), the headquarters of the international cultural (Hindu) organization, and the National Centre for the Performing Arts, Nariman Point (NCPA; ⦾www .ncpamumbai.com).

cotton clothes (often stylish designer-label rip-offs) are available in shops along **Colaba Causeway**, such as Cotton World, down Mandlik Marg.

If you're looking for **traditional Indian clothes**, look no further than the Khadi Village Industries Emporium at 286 Dr DN Marg, near the Thomas Cook office. As Whiteaway & Laidlaw, this rambling Victorian department store used to kit all the newly arrived *burra-sahibs* out with pith helmets, khaki shorts and quinine tablets. These days, its old wooden counters and shirt and sock drawers stock dozens of different hand-spun cottons and silks, sold by the metre or made up as vests, *kurtas* or block-printed *salwar kameezes*. Other items include the ubiquitous white Nehru caps, *dhotis*, Madras-check *lunghis* and fine brocaded silk saris.

Handicrafts

Regionally produced **handicrafts** are marketed in assorted state-run emporia at the World Trade Centre, down on Cuffe Parade, and along Sir PM Road, Fort. The quality is consistently high – as are the prices, if you miss out on the periodic holiday discounts. The same goes for the **Central Cottage Industries Emporium**, 34 Shivaji Marg, near the Gateway of India in Colaba, whose size and central location make it the single best all-round place to hunt for souvenirs. Downstairs you'll find inlaid furniture, wood- and metalwork, miniature paintings and jewellery, while upstairs specializes in toys, clothing and textiles – Gujarati appliqué bedspreads, hand-painted pillowcases and Rajasthani mirror-work, plus silk ties and Noël Coward dressing gowns. **Mereweather Road** (now officially B Behram Marg), directly behind the *Taj*, is awash with Kashmiri handicraft stores stocking overpriced papier-mâché pots and bowls, silver jewellery, woollen shawls and rugs. Avoid them if you find it hard to shrug off aggressive sales pitches.

Perfume is essentially a Muslim preserve in Mumbai. Down at the south end of Colaba Causeway, around Arthur Bunder Road, shops with mirrored walls and shelves are stacked with cut-glass carafes full of syrupy, fragrant essential oils. **Incense** is hawked in sticks, cones and slabs of sticky *dhoop* on the pavement nearby (check that the boxes haven't already been opened and their contents sold off piecemeal). For bulk buying, the hand-rolled, cottage-made bundles of incense sold in the Khadi Village Industries Emporium on Dr DN Marg (see above) are a better deal; it also has a handicraft department where, in addition to furniture, paintings and ornaments, you can pick up glass bangles, block-printed and calico bedspreads and wooden votive statues produced in Maharashtrian craft villages.

Books

Mumbai's excellent English-language **bookshops** and bookstalls are well stocked with everything to do with India, and a good selection of general classics, pulp fiction and travel writing.

Crossword Bookstore Mohammed Bhai Mansion, Huges Rd, Kemp's Corner, a 10min walk north of Chowpatty Beach ☎ 022/2384 2001. Mumbai's largest retailer, in smart new a/c premises, complete with its own coffee bar. Open Mon–Fri 10am–8pm, Sat & Sun 10am–9pm.

Nalanda Ground floor, *Taj Mahal Palace & Tower*. An exhaustive range of coffee-table tomes and paperback literature, though at top prices.

Oxford Bookstore Apeejay House, 3 Dinsha Vacha Rd, Churchgate. Not quite as large as Crossword, but almost, and much more easily accessible if you're staying downtown or in Colaba. It also has a very cool a/c café, the *Cha Bar* (see p.706).

Search Word SBS Marg (Colaba Causeway). The best bookshop in Colaba, with shelves full of guides and a great range of Indian fiction – at discounts only rivalled by the Strand in Fort. Gregory David "Shantaram" Roberts numbers among the regulars.

Strand Next door to the Canara Bank, off PM Rd, Fort. The best-value bookshop in the city centre, with the full gamut of Penguins and Indian literature, sold at amazing discounts.

Music

The most famous of Mumbai's many **musical instrument shops** are near the Moti cinema along SV Patel Road, in the central bazaar district. Haribhai Vishwanath, Ram Singh and RS Mayeka are all government-approved retailers, stocking sitars, sarods, tablas and flutes. For guaranteed top quality, however, it's advisable to make the trek north to Bhargava's Musik, at 4/5 Imperial Plaza, 30th Rd in Bandra, which numbers among its clients some of India's top classical performers.

For **cassettes and CDs** a good first stop if you're based down in Colaba is Rhythm House, on Subhash Chowk opposite the Jehangir Art Gallery. This is a veritable Aladdin's cave of classical, devotional and popular music from all over India, with a reasonable selection of Western rock, pop and jazz, as well as DVDs of classic and contemporary Hindi movies. A ten-minute walk further north along Dr DN Rd in Fort, Planet M is a Virgin/HMV-style megastore stocking an array of music CDs and computer games to rival any in the country.

Sports

In common with most Indians, Mumbaikars are crazy about **cricket**. Few other spectator sports get much of a look-in, although the **horse racing** at Mahalakshmi draws large crowds on Derby days. Further down the social scale, more **traditional games**, like kabadi and *kho kho*, form the focus of weekend activities at Shivaji Park in central Mumbai. Previews of all forthcoming events are posted on the back pages of the *Times of India*, and in *Time Out Mumbai*.

Cricket

Cricket provides almost as much of a distraction as movies in the Maharashtrian capital, and you'll see games in progress everywhere, from impromptu sunset knockabouts on Chowpatty Beach to more formal club matches in full whites at the gymkhanas lined up along Marine Drive. In south Mumbai, **Oval Maidan** is the place to watch local talent in action, set against a wonderfully apt backdrop of imperial-era buildings. Something of a pecking order applies here: the further from the path cutting across the centre of the park you go, the better the wickets and the classier the games become.

Pitches like these are where Mumbai's favourite son, **Sachin Tendulkar**, cut his cricketing teeth. The world's most prolific batsman (in one-day cricket) still lives in the city and plays regularly for its league-winning club side at the **Brabourne Stadium**, off Marine Drive. A kilometre or so further north, 45,000-capacity **Wankhede Stadium** is where major test matches are hosted, amid an atmosphere as intense, raucous and intimidating for visiting teams as any in India.

The Indian cricket season runs from October through February. Tickets for big games are almost as hard to come by as seats on commuter trains, but foreign visitors can sometimes gain preferential access to quotas through the Mumbai Cricket Association's offices on the first floor of Wankhede.

Horse racing and horse riding

The **Mahalakshmi Racecourse**, near the Mahalakshmi Temple just north of Malabar Hill, is the home of the **Royal Western India Turf Club** – a throwback to British times that still serves as a prime stomping ground for the

Laughter Yoga

On the principle that laughter is the best medicine, Mumbai doctor Madan Kataria and his wife Madhuri – aka "the Giggling Gurus" – have created a new kind of therapy: *hasya* (laughter) yoga. There are now over three hundred **Laughter Clubs** in India and many more worldwide; around 50,000 people join the Laughter Day celebrations in Mumbai on the first Sunday of May each year, with tens of thousands more participating worldwide.

Fifteen-minute sessions start with adherents doing yogic breathing whilst chanting "Ho ho ha ha", which develops into spontaneous "hearty laughter" (raising both hands in the air with the head tilting backwards), "milkshake laughter" (everyone laughs while making a gesture as if they are drinking milkshake), and "swinging laughter" (standing in a circle saying "aaee-oo-eee-uuu") before the rather fearsome "lion laughter" (extruding the tongue fully with eyes wide open and hands stretched out like claws, and laughing from the tummy). The session then winds up with holding hands and the chanting of slogans ("We are the laughter club member [sic]... Y... E... S!").

Laughter Clubs take place between 6am and 7am at various venues around the city, including Colaba Woods in Cuffe Parade and Juhu Beach. For the full story, go to ⓦwww.laughteryoga.org.

city's upper classes. Race meets are held twice weekly, on Wednesdays and Saturdays between November and March, and big days such as the 2000 Guineas and Derby attract crowds of 25,000. Entrance to the public ground is by ticket on the day. Seats for the colonial-era stand, with its posh lawns and exclusive *Gallops Restaurant* are, alas, allocated to members only. Race cards are posted in the sports section of the *Times of India*, and can be downloaded (along with form guides) from ⓦwww.rwitc.com.

On non-race days, the Mahalakshmi ground doubles as a riding track. Temporary membership of the **Amateur Riding Club of Mumbai**, another bastion of elite Mumbai, entitles you to use the club's thoroughbreds for classes. Full details on how to do this, along with previews of forthcoming club **polo** matches, are posted at ⓦwww.arcmumbai.com.

Listings

Airlines, domestic Air Deccan ⓣ98925/77008; Air India Express, Air India Building, Nariman Point ⓣ022/227 6330, airport ⓣ022/2831 8888; Go Air ⓣ1800 222111, airport ⓣ022/6741 0000; Indian Airlines, Air India Building, Nariman Point ⓣ022/2202 3031, airport ⓣ022/2682 9328 or toll free ⓣ1800/180 1407; IndiGo Airlines, 17 Jolly Maker Chambers II, 255 Nariman Point ⓣ099/1038 3838 or toll free ⓣ1800 180 3838; Jet Airways, Amarchand Mansion, Madam Cama Rd ⓣ022/2285 5788; Jet Lite, Terminal 1-B Domestic Airport, Santa Cruz East ⓣ022/26156567; Kingfisher, First Floor, Arrivals Hall, Terminal 1-A, domestic airport ⓣ022/2729 3030, or toll free ⓣ1800/233 3131; SpiceJet, c/o Akbar Travels, Terminus View, 169 DN Rd, opp CST Station, toll free ⓣ1800/180 3333.

Airlines, international Aeroflot, ground floor, 14 Tulsiani Chambers, Free Press Journal Rd, Nariman Point ⓣ022/2285 6648; Air France, 201-B Sarjan Plaza, 100 Dr Annie Besant Rd, Worli, North Mumbai ⓣ022/2346 6276; Air India, 1st Floor, Air India Building, Nariman Point ⓣ022/2548 9999 or toll free ⓣ1800 227722; Alitalia, 5th Floor, CG House, Annie Besant Rd, Prabhadevi, Worli, North Mumbai ⓣ022/5663 0800; British Airways, 4th Floor, CG House, Annie Besant Rd, Prabhadevi, Worli, North Mumbai ⓣ08925 77470; Cathay Pacific, 3rd floor, Bajaj Bhavan, 226 Nariman Point ⓣ022/5657 2222; Delta, Interglobe Enterprises Limited, 12th Floor, Bajaj Bhavan, Nariman Point ⓣ022/2826 7007; Egypt Air, Oriental House, 7 J Tata Rd, Churchgate ⓣ022/2283 3798; Emirates, 228 Mittal

Gigantic film posters in Old Delhi ▲

Actress Ashwini Iyer in dance rehearsals ▼

A chaste on-screen kiss ▼

Made in Mumbai

Although sometimes used to refer to all Indian-made movies, strictly speaking the name **Bollywood** refers only to Hindi-language films made in Mumbai, whose studios churn out around nine hundred films every year. There are numerous other regional schools of cinema throughout India, most importantly the huge Tamil-language movie industry based in Chennai (see box, p.1104). But only Bollywood films attract nationwide audiences. Bollywood films have an estimated global audience of 3.6 billion, compared to Hollywood's 2.5 billion.

Music and masalas

Bollywood films traditionally follow the so-called **masala** format, typically featuring an eclectic blend of romantic entanglements, rip-roaring action sequences and light-hearted comedy, and featuring stock characters like corrupt politicians, scheming villains and star-crossed lovers. **Music** also plays a vital role in most Bollywood films, with numerous songs (or *filmi*, for more on which, see p.1389) and elaborate dance sequences – indeed, many films live or die by the quality of their musical set pieces.

The traditional Bollywood masala formula has moved closer to the mainstream Hollywood model in recent years. The all-singing, all-dancing flicks of yesteryear are increasingly giving way to more adventurous and challenging films depicting emerging new classes within **Indian society**, such as Westernized urban youngsters and Indians living overseas, along with an increasingly liberal portrayal of sexual relations – even if the famous taboo against showing on-screen kissing is still widely observed.

Ten Bollywood classics

Devdas (1955). Vintage Bollywood tale of tragic love, starring the great Dilip Kumar as doomed lover Devdas.

Dil Chahta Hai ("The Heart Desires", 2001). Stylish and genre-breaking movie depicting the lives and loves of India's new and well-heeled urban elite.

Dilwale Dulhania Le Jayenge ("The Brave-hearted will take the Bride", 1995). One of the biggest hits of all time, this was one of the first Bollywood movies to be set overseas.

Lagaan ("Land Tax", 2001). Emotive Raj-era drama in which a group of impoverished villagers attempt to beat the local British at cricket in exchange for a remission in punitive taxes.

Mother India (1957). Classic rural epic highlighting the immemorial troubles and travails of an Indian mother living in an impoverished village.

Mr India (1987) Brilliantly quirky action-movie featuring the battles between Mr India (Anil Kapoor) and megalomaniac arch-villain Mogambo.

Mughal-e-Azam (1960). One of the most spectacular historical epics ever created, *Mughal-e-Azam* was nine years in the making and remains unrivalled in its lavish depiction of love and intrigue at the court of Mughal emperor Akbar.

Munna Bhai M.B.B.S. ("Brother Munna M.B.B.S.", 2003). Light-hearted comedy starring Sanjay Dutt as the aimiably roguish Mumbai gangster Munna Bhai.

Salaam Bombay! (1988). Internationally acclaimed feature chronicling the lives of children living hand-to-mouth on the streets of Mumbai.

Sholay ("Embers", 1975). Widely regarded as the greatest Bollywood film ever, this action-packed tale of warring outlaws stars the young Amitabh Bachchan, one of Bollywood's greatest living actors.

▲ Poster for Mother India

▼ Cinema-goers queuing for tickets

Celebrity gossip, Bollywood style

Pick up virtually any magazine or newspaper in India and you'll be regaled by news and pictures of the latest doings of Bollywood's A-list, featuring images of celluloid stars such as Amitabh Bachchan, Bollywood's elder statesman, or forty-something icon Salman Khan, regularly voted India's most eligible bachelor and recently immortalized in wax at London's Madame Tussauds. Meanwhile, the exploits of young male heart-throbs like John Abraham, Hrithik Roshan and Emraan Hashmi, or their female counterparts Rani Mukerji, Kareena Kapoor and Preity Zinta, continue to fill the gossip columns, not to mention the latest doings of India's biggest celebrity couple, star actor Abhishek Bachchan and his wife Aishwarya Rai, herself a leading Bollywood actress.

The wonderful whiff of scandal and controversy is never far away from many of Bollywood's stars. Stellar actor Sanjay Dutt, for instance, lived up to his bad-boy image by being convicted of the illegal possession of firearms in 2002, while Salman Khan has also been in trouble over assorted misdemeanours. These, however, paled into global insignificance compared to the controversy surrounding the UK's *Celebrity Big Brother* TV show in 2007, when the relatively low-profile Bollywood starlette Shilpa Shetty suffered alleged racist bullying by fellow contestants, leading to nationwide protests throughout India, questions in the UK's House of Parliament and a distinct cooling in Anglo–Indian relationships – at least until Shetty emerged victorious from the show.

Sanjay Dutt arrives for his court hearing ▲

Abhishek Bachchan and Aishwarya Rai ▼

Chambers, Nariman Point ☏022/2879 7979; Gulf Air, Ground Floor, Maker Chamber V, Nariman Point ☏022/2202 1626; Japan Airlines, 9th Floor, 911 Raheja Centre, Nariman Point ☏022/2283 3136; KLM, 201-B Sarjan Plaza, 100 Annie Besant Rd, Worli, North Mumbai toll free ☏1800/114777; Kuwait Airways, 901 Nariman Bhavan, 9th Floor, Nariman Point ☏022/6655 5655; Lufthansa, 3rd floor, Express Towers, Nariman Point ☏022/6630 1940; Qantas Airways, 2nd floor, Godrej Bhavan, Home St ☏022/2200 7440; Qatar Airways, Bajaj Bhavan, Nariman Point ☏0124/456 6000; Saudi Air, 3rd floor, Express Towers, Nariman Point ☏022/2202 0199; Singapore Airlines, *Taj Mahal Palace & Tower*, Apollo Bunder (PJ Ramachandani Marg), Colaba ☏022/2202 8316; South African Airways, Podar House, 10 Marine Drive, Church-gate ☏022/282 3450; Sri Lankan Airlines, 2nd Floor, Vaswani Mansion, 12 Dinshaw Vachha Rd, Churchgate ☏022/282 3288; Thai Airways, Ground Floor, Maker Chamber IV, Nariman Point ☏022/5637 3737.

Airport enquiries Chhatrapati Shivaji international airport ☏022/2681 3000, ⓦwww.csia.in; Chhatrapati Shivaji (Santa Cruz) domestic airport ☏022/2626 4000; ⓦwww.csia.in.

Ambulance ☏101 for general emergencies; but you're nearly always better off taking a taxi. See also Hospitals, see below.

Banks and currency exchange The most convenient place to change money when you arrive in Mumbai is at the State Bank of India's 24hr counter in Chhatrapati Shivaji international airport. Rates here are standard but you may have to pay for an encashment certificate – essential if you intend to buy tourist-quota train tickets or an Indrail pass at the special counters in Churchgate or CST (VT) stations. All the major state banks downtown change foreign currency (Mon–Fri 10.30am–2.30pm, Sat 10.30am–12.30pm); some (eg the Bank of Baroda) also handle credit cards and cash advances. Most now have 24hr ATMs that can handle international transactions; the closest if you're staying in Colaba is the Bank of Baroda's at the north end of SBS Marg (Colaba Causeway). Thomas Cook's big Dr DN Marg branch (Mon–Sat 9.30am–7pm; ☏022/2204 8556), between the Khadi shop and Hutatma Chowk, can also arrange money transfers from overseas.

Consulates and high commissions Although the many consulates and high commissions in Mumbai can be useful for replacing lost travel documents or obtaining visas, most of India's neighbouring states, including Bangladesh, Bhutan, Burma, Nepal and Pakistan, only have embassies in New Delhi and/or Kolkata (Calcutta). All of the following are open

Mon–Fri only: Australia, 16th Floor, 36 Maker Tower V, Nariman Point (9am–5pm; ☏022/5669 2000); Canada, 41/42 Maker Chambers VI, Nariman Point (9am–5.30pm; ☏022/2287 6027); China, 1st floor, 11 ML Dahanukar Marg (10am–4.30pm; ☏022/2282 2662); France, 2nd floor, Datta Prasad, N Gamadia Cross Rd (9am–1pm & 2.30–5.30pm; ☏022/2495 0918); Germany, 10th floor, Hoechst House, Nariman Point (8–11am; ☏022/2283 2422); Indonesia, 19 Altamount Rd, Cumbala Hill (10am–4.30pm; ☏022/2351 1678); Netherlands, 1st Floor, Forbes Building, Chiranjit Rai Marg, Fort (9am–5pm; ☏022/2201 6750); Poland, 2nd Floor Manavi Apt, 36 BG Kher Marg, Malabar Hill (☏022/2363 3863); Republic of Ireland, 38 Western Indian House, Sir PM Rd (9.30am–1pm; ☏022/2287 1931); Singapore, 10th floor, Maker Chamber IV, 222 Jamnal Bajaj Marg, Nariman Point (9am–noon; ☏022/2204 3205); South Africa, Gandhi Mansion, 20 Altamount Rd (9am–noon; ☏022/2389 3725); Sri Lanka, Sri Lanka House, 34 Homi Modi St, Fort (9.30am–11.30am; ☏022/2204 5861); Sweden, 85 Sayani Rd, Subash Gupta Bhawan, Prabhedavi (10am–12.30pm; ☏022/2436 0493); Thailand, Malabar View, 4th floor, Dr Purandure Marg, Chowpatty Sea Face (9–11.30am; ☏022/2363 1404); United Kingdom, 2nd floor, Maker Chamber IV, Nariman Point (8am–11.30am; ☏022/2283 0517); USA, Lincoln House, 78 Bhulabhai Desai Rd (8.30am–11am; ☏022/2363 3611).

Hospitals The best hospital in the centre is the private Bombay Hospital, New Marine Lines (☏022/2206 7676, ⓦwww.bombayhospital.com), just north of the government tourist office on M Karve Rd. Breach Candy Hospital (☏022/2367 1888, ⓦwww.breachcandyhospital.org) on Bhulabhai Desai Rd, near the swimming pool, is also recommended by foreign embassies.

Internet access A couple of cramped 24hr places (Rs40/hr) can be found in Colaba on Nawroji F Marg, though it's worth paying the Rs5 extra at Sify iWay, near *Leopold's* (see map, p.693), which is faster and more comfortable.

Left luggage If your hotel won't let you store bags with them, try the cloakrooms at the airports (see p.682), or the one in CST (VT) Station (Rs12/day). Anything left here, even rucksacks, must be securely fastened with a padlock and can be left for a maximum of one month.

Libraries Asiatic Society (see p.698), SBS Marg, Horniman Circle, Ballard Estate (Mon–Sat 10.30am–7pm); British Council (for British newspapers and magazines), A Wing, 1st floor, Mittal Tower, Nariman Point (Tues–Sat 10am–6pm); Mumbai Natural History Society, Hornbill House

Since the advent of low-cost airlines, easily the best-value way to travel the 500km from Mumbai to Goa has been by **plane**. With most carriers, it's straightforward to purchase tickets online and prices often compare favourably with the cost of the same journey via the Konkan Railway, which sees two departures daily. Whatever your budget, however, think twice before attempting the hellish overnight bus journey.

By air

Between 15 and 21 flights leave daily from Chhatrapati Shivaji (aka Santa Cruz) domestic airport, 30km north of the city, for Goa's Dabolim airport. The cheapest fares are offered by Kingfisher (ⓦwww.flykingfisher.com), Air Deccan (ⓦwww.airdeccan.net), IndiGo (ⓦwww.goindigo.in), SpiceJet (ⓦwww.spicejet.com) and Go Air (ⓦwww.goair.in), who sell tickets on their websites from as low as Rs650, though the normal rate is more like US$70–100. Flying with Indian Airlines (ⓦwww.indian-airlines.nic.in), Jet Lite (ⓦwww.jetlite.com), Jet (ⓦwww.jetairways.com) or Air India (ⓦwww.airindia.com) will typically set you back upwards of $100, though to compete with their low-cost rivals, they too have started to offer discounted fares online.

Demand for seats can be fierce around Diwali and Christmas/New Year, when you're unlikely to get a ticket at short notice. At other times, one or other of the carriers should be able to offer a seat on the day you wish to travel – though perhaps not at the lowest fares. If you didn't pre-book when you purchased your international ticket, check availability with the airlines as soon as you arrive; tickets can be bought directly from their offices (see p.712), through any reputable travel agent in Mumbai (bearing in mind that an agent may charge you the dollar fare at a poorer rate of exchange than that offered by the airline company), by phone or direct via the Internet (though note that some low-cost airlines refuse payments by credit or debit cards not registered in India.

All Goa flights leave from Chhatrapati Shivaji (aka Santa Cruz) domestic airport, 30km north of the city centre.

By train

The **Konkan Railway** line runs daily express trains from Mumbai to Goa. **Fares** for the twelve-hour journey from CST start at Rs293 for standard sleeper class, rising to

---

(Mon–Fri 10am–5pm, Sat 10am–1pm, closed 1st & 3rd Sat of the month), has an international reputation for the study of wildlife in India. Visitors may obtain temporary membership, which allows them access to the library, natural history collection, occasional talks and the opportunity to join organized walks and field trips.

Pharmacies Bombay Chemist, 39–40 Kakad Arcade, opposite Bombay Hospital, New Marine Lines (ⓣ022/2207 6171) opens daily 8am–11pm. Kemps in the *Taj Mahal* also opens late.

Police The main police station in Colaba (ⓣ022/2285 6817) is on the west side of Colaba Causeway, near the crossroads with Best Marg.

Postal services The GPO (Mon–Sat 9am–8pm, Sun 9am–4pm) is around the corner from CST (VT)

Station, off Nagar Chowk. The parcel office (10am–4.30pm) is behind the main building on the first floor. Packing-wallahs hang around on the pavement outside. DHL (ⓣ022/2850 5050) has eleven offices in Mumbai, the most convenient being the 24hr one under the *Sea Green Hotel* at the bottom of Marine Drive.

Travel agents The following travel agents are recommended for booking domestic and international flights, and long-distance private buses where specified: Cox and Kings India, 271/272 Dr DN Marg ⓣ022/2207 3065, ⓦwww.coxandkings.com; Sita World Travels, 8 Atlanta Building, Nariman Point ⓣ022/2286 0684, ⓔbom@sitaincoming.com; Thomas Cook, 324 Dr DN Rd, Fort ⓣ022/2204 8556, ⓦwww.thomascook.co.in.

Rs1242 for second-class a/c or Rs2345 for luxurious first-class a/c. However, these services are not always available at short notice from the booking halls at CST and Churchgate. If you're certain of your travel dates in advance (ie if you're flying into Mumbai and want to catch the train to Goa soon after arriving), consider **booking online** at ⓦ**www.irctc.co.in**. There are downsides to this: you're only entitled to relatively expensive three-tier a/c fares (Rs1242 one way) and must make your booking between seven and two days before your date of departure – but all in all, online reservation is a much more convenient way to secure a seat than leaving it until you arrive in Mumbai. You could also make the reservation through an Indian Railways agent in your home country; see Basics, p.47.

Don't, whatever you do, be tempted to travel "unreserved" class on any Konkan service, as the journey as far as Ratnagiri (roughly midway) is overwhelmingly crushed. The most convenient of the Konkan services is the overnight Mumbai–Madgaon Express (see box, p.716). The other, only slightly faster, train is the Mandovi Express (#KR0103), leaving at 6.55am from CST.

By bus

The Mumbai–Goa bus journey ranks among the very worst in India. Don't believe travel agents who assure you it takes thirteen hours. Depending on the type of bus you get, appalling road surfaces along the sinuous coastal route make sixteen to eighteen hours a more realistic estimate.

Fares start at around Rs320 for a push-back seat on a beaten-up Kadamba (Goan government) or MSRTC coach. Tickets for these services are in great demand in season with domestic tourists, so book in advance at Mumbai Central or Kadamba's kiosks on the north side of Azad Maidan, near St Xavier's College (just up from CST station). Quite a few **private overnight buses** (around a dozen daily) also run to Goa, costing from around Rs275/450 (low/high season) for no-frills buses to Rs750/850 for swisher a/c Volvo coaches with berths (which bizarrely you may have to share). Tickets should be booked at least a day in advance through a reputable travel agent (see opposite), or direct through the bus company. The largest operator for Goa is Paulo Travels (ⓦwww.paulotravels.com).

Moving on from Mumbai

Most visitors aim to escape Mumbai as soon as possible, and the city is equipped with "superfast" services to make **onward travel** speedy and painless (by Indian standards). All the major international and domestic **airlines** have offices downtown, the **railway** networks operate special tourist counters in the main reservation halls, and dozens of **travel agents** and road transport companies are eager to help you on your way by **bus**. In addition to the information here, see "Travel details", p.718.

By air

Indian Airlines and other **domestic carriers** fly out of Chhatrapati Shivaji domestic airport (aka Santa Cruz; ⓦwww.csia.com) to destinations all over India. Availability on popular routes should never be taken for granted – check with the airlines as soon as you arrive. **Tickets** can be bought directly from airline offices (see p.712), via the Internet, or through any reputable travel agent.

Recommended trains from Mumbai

The services listed below are the most direct and/or the fastest. This list is by no means exhaustive and there are numerous slower trains that are often more conven ient for smaller destinations. All the details listed below were correct at the time of writing, but departure times, in particular, should be checked when you purchase your ticket, or in advance via the Indian Railways website: ⓦwww.indianrail.gov.in.

Destination	Name	No.	From	Departs	Journey time
Agra	Punjab Mail	#2137/38	MC	Daily 6.25am	24hr 10min
Ahmedabad	Shatabdi Express	#2009	CST	Daily 7.40pm	6hr 55min
Aurangabad	CSTM UMD Express	#1005	CST	Daily 10.20pm	7hr 05min
	Tapovan Express	#7617	CST	Daily 6.10am	7hr 20min
Bengaluru (Bangalore)	Udyan Express	#6529	CST	Daily 8.05am	24hr
Bhopal	Punjab Mail	#2137	CST	Daily 7.40pm	14hr
Chennai	Mumbai–Chennai Express	#6011	CST	Daily 2pm	26hr 45min
Delhi	Rajdhani Express	#2951	MC	Daily 4.40pm	15hr 50min
	Golden Temple Mail	#2903	MC	Daily 9.25pm	21hr 25min
Goa (Margao)	Mumbai–Madgaon Express	#KR0111	CST	Daily 11pm	11hr 45min
Hyderabad	Hussain-sagar Express	#2701	CST	Daily 9.50pm	14hr 20min
Jaipur	Mumbai–Jaipur Express	#2955	MC	Daily 6.50pm	18hr
Jodhpur	Ranakpur Express	#4708	Bandra	Daily 3pm	19hr 25min
Kochi (Cochin)	Netravati Express	#6345	LTT (Kurla)	Daily 11.40am	26hr 25min
Kolhapur	Sahyadri Express	#1023	CST	Daily 5.50pm	12hr 15min
Kolkata (Calcutta/ Howrah)	Gitanjali Express	#2859	CST	Daily 6am	31hr 35min
	Mumbai–Howrah Mail	#2809	CST	Daily 8.40pm	33hr 45min
Lonavala	Udyan Express	#6529	CST	Daily 8.40am	2hr 50min
Mysore	Sharavathi Express	#1035	Dadar	Tues 9.30pm	23hr 40min
Pune	Udyan Express	#6529	CST	Daily 8.40am	3hr 35min
Thiruva-nanthapuram	Netravati Express	#6345	LTT (Kurla)	Daily 11.40am	31hr
Udaipur	Saurashtra Express**	#9215	MC	Daily 8.20am	23hr 45min
Varanasi	Mahanagiri Express	#1093	CST	Daily 12.10am	28hr 20min

**change trains at Ahmedabad

By train

The quickest and most convenient place for foreign nationals to make reservations is at the efficient tourist counter on the first floor of the **Western Railway's booking hall**, next door to the Government of India tourist office in **Churchgate** (Mon–Fri 9.30am–4.30pm, Sat 9.30am–2.30pm; ☎022/2209 7577). This counter, at the far (bottom) end of the booking hall, has access to special "tourist quotas", which are released the day before departure if the train leaves during the day, or the morning of the departure if it leaves after 5pm. If the quota is "closed" or already used up, you will have to join the regular queue. As elsewhere in the country, periods before major national holidays (notably **Diwali**, when half of India is on the move) should be avoided at all costs. But if you do find yourself having to travel when there don't seem to be any tickets left, bear in mind you can pay extra for a special Tatkal seat (see p.46) – an option well worth considering, for example, if you want to get to Goa on the oversubscribed Konkan Railway route.

Mumbai's other "Tourist Ticketing Facility" is in the snazzy air-conditioned **Central Railway booking office** to the rear of **CST** (VT; Mon–Sat 8am–1.30pm & 2–3pm, Sun 8am–2pm; ☎022/2262 2859), the departure point for most trains heading east and south. Indrail passes can also be bought here, and there's an MTDC tourist information kiosk in the main concourse if you need help filling in your reservation slips.

Tickets for seats on the **Konkan Railway** can be booked at either Churchgate or CST booking halls; for more information on getting to Goa by rail, see box, p.214. Just to complicate matters, some **Central Railway** trains to **South India** – notably those running via the Konkan Railway to **Kerala** – do not depart from CST at all, but from **Kurla Station** (aka Lokmanya Tilak Terminus, or **LTT**), up near the airports. Others leave from **Dadar**, also way north of the centre. Getting to either on public transport can be a major struggle, though many long-distance trains from CST (VT) or Churchgate stop there and aren't as crowded.

By bus

The main departure point for long-distance **government buses** leaving Mumbai is the frenetic **Central Bus Stand** on JB Behram Marg, opposite Mumbai Central railway station. States with bus company **counters** (daily 8am–8pm) here include Maharashtra, Karnataka and Goa. Few of their services compare favourably with train travel on the same routes. Reliable timetable information can be difficult to obtain, reservations are not available on standard buses, and most long-haul journeys are gruelling overnighters. Among the exceptions are the deluxe buses run by MSRTC to Pune and Kolhapur; the small extra cost buys you more leg-room, fewer stops and the option of advance booking. The only problem is that most leave from the ASIAD bus stand in Dadar, or the new MSRTC stand in Thane, thirty and sixty minutes respectively by road or rail north of Mumbai Central.

Private buses cover most of the same routes. They tend to be faster, more comfortable and easier to book in advance – though again, long distance services invariably depart at night. Tickets are sold from a row of booths on busy Dr Anadao Nair Marg, just outside Mumbai Central railway station, on the opposite side of the main (north–south) road from the Central Bus Stand (see map, pp.678–679). Note that fares on services to popular tourist destinations such as Goa and Mahabaleshwar increase by as much as 75 percent during peak season.

By boat

Three companies operate boat services from the Gateway of India to **Mandawa jetty**, on the far side of Mumbai harbour, from where buses shuttle to nearby **Alibag**, transport hub for the route southwards down the Konkan coast. Ranging from comfortable air-conditioned catamarans (Rs110) to bog-standard launches (Rs65), the ferries leave roughly every hour; tickets should be purchased in advance from the PNP, Ajanta or Maldar company booths, on the north side of Shivaji Marg, near the MTDC information counter.

Travel details

Trains

Mumbai to: Agra (3 daily; 23hr 15min–27hr); Ahmedabad (11–15 daily; 6hr 55min–16hr); Aurangabad (2 daily; 7hr 45min); Bengaluru (Bangalore) (2–5 daily; 24hr–26hr 10min); Bhopal (6–7 daily; 14hr); Chennai (3 daily; 24–29hr); Delhi (9–12 daily; 15hr 50min–33hr); Hyderabad (4–5 daily; 15–17hr); Indore (1 daily; 14hr 35min); Jaipur (2 daily; 18–23hr); Jodhpur (1 daily; 19hr 25min; change at Ahmedabad); Kolhapur (3 daily; 11–12hr); Kolkata (Calcutta) (2–4 daily; 32–40hr); Nagpur (4 daily; 14–15hr); Nasik (15 daily; 4hr); Neral Junction (hourly; 1hr 30min–2hr 15min); Pune (25 daily; 3hr 25min–5hr); Thiruvananthapuram (2 daily; 42hr); Udaipur (1 daily; 24hr 40min; change at Ahmedabad); Ujjain (1 daily; 12hr 25 min); Varanasi (2 daily; 29–36hr).

Buses

Only state bus services are listed here; for details of private buses, see above.
ASIAD Dadar to: Kolhapur (4–6 daily; 9–11hr); Nasik (17 daily; 5hr); Pune (half-hourly; 3hr 30min–4hr).
Mumbai Central to: Ahmedabad (12–16 daily; 12–13hr 30min); Aurangabad (2 daily; 10hr); Bangalore (3 daily; 24hr); Bijapur (3 daily; 12hr); Goa (2 daily; 18–19hr); Indore (2 daily; 16hr); Ujjain (1 daily; 17hr).

Flights

For a list of airline addresses and travel agents, see p.712 & p.714.

AI = Air India, **AIE** = Air India Express, **DN** = Air Deccan, **G8** = Go Air, **IC** = Indian Airlines, **IT** = Kingfisher, **S2** = JetLite, **SG** = Spicejet, **6E** = IndiGo, **9W** = Jet Airways)
Chhatrapati Shivaji (Santa Cruz) Domestic Airport to: Ahmedabad (DN, AI, IA, 9W, SG 7–9 daily; 1hr); Allahabad (S2 3 weekly; 6hr); Aurangabad (AD, IC, 9W 5 daily; 45min); Bengaluru (Bangalore) (DN, IC, AI, 6E 9W, IT, S2, SG 23–25 daily; 1hr 30min); Bhopal (IC, 9W 2 daily; 2hr 05min); Bhubaneshwar (DN, IC, S2 3–34 daily; 2hr); Bhuj (IC, 9W, IT 3 daily; 1hr 15min); Chennai (DN, AI, IC, 6E, 9W, IT, SG 13–15 daily; 1hr 45min); Cochin (see "Kochi"); Delhi (DN, IC, 6E, AI, 9W, S2, SG 52–57 daily; 1hr 55min); Coimbatore (IC, IT, 9W, S2, SG 5 daily; 1hr 45min–2hr); Goa (DN, AI, G8, IC, 6E, 9W, S2, IT, SG 14–15 daily; 45min–1hr); Guwahati (IC, IT, S2 4 daily; 3hr 15min); Hyderabad (DN, IC, 9W, S2, IT, SG 14–21 daily; 1hr 15min); Indore (IC, 9W, S2, IT 6 daily; 1hr 05min); Jaipur (DN, IC, 6E, 9W, IT, SG 8 daily; 1hr 35min); Jodhpur (IC, 9W 2 daily; 2hr 10min); Kochi (DN, AI, IC, 6E, S2, IT 5–7 daily; 1hr 45min); Kolkata (Calcutta; IC, AI, 6E, 9W, S2, IT, SG 15–17 daily; 2hr 40min); Kolhapur (DN 1 daily; 1hr 05min); Lucknow (S2 3 daily; 2hr); Madurai (IC 1 daily; 3hr 20min); Mangalore (DN, 9W, IC, IT 4–5 daily; 1hr 15min); Nagpur (DN, IC, 6E, 9W 4 daily; 1hr 20min–1hr 55min); Patna (2 daily; 3hr 35min–4hr 40min); Pune (IC, 9W, S2 5 daily; 35min); Srinagar (S2 1 daily; 4hr); Thiruvananthapuram (DN, AI, IC, 9W 3–4 daily; 2hr); Udaipur (IC 2–3 daily; 1hr 10min); Varanasi (IC, S2, SG 3 daily; 2hr 35min–4hr 55min).

Maharashtra

AFGHANISTAN

CHINA
(TIBET AUTONOMOUS
REGION)

PAKISTAN

NEPAL

BHUTAN

BANGLADESH

ARABIAN
SEA

MYANMAR
(BURMA)

BAY OF BENGAL

N

SRI
LANKA

INDIAN OCEAN

0   400 km

The International boundaries on this map are neither purported to be correct
nor authentic by Survey of India directives. Publisher.

CHAPTER 11

Highlights

✴ **Daulatabad** One of India's most spectacular hill-forts, presiding over an epic desert landscape of table-topped mountains. See p.730

✴ **Ellora caves** Breathtaking Hindu, Buddhist and Jain caves carved from solid volcanic rock. See p.732

✴ **Ajanta caves** Hidden in a remote horseshoe-shaped ravine, Ajanta's murals are the finest storehouse of art to have survived from any ancient civilization. See p.739

✴ **Lonar** Centred on a saltwater lake and dotted with temples, this massive meteorite crater, lost in the wilds of northeastern Maharashtra, makes an unforgettable escape. See p.746

✴ **Trimbakeshwar** Scale flights of rock steps cut into sheer cliffs of the Sahyadri Hills to reach the sacred source of the Goadvari River. See p.750

✴ **Miniature train to Matheran** Fantastic views across the Western Ghats are revealed during the two-hour ride to this quintessentially British hill-station. See p.758

▲ Ellora caves

Maharashtra

Vast and rugged, the modern state of **MAHARASHTRA**, the third largest in India, was created in 1960 from the Marathi-speaking regions of what was previously Bombay State. As soon as you leave its seething port capital, **Mumbai**, you enter a different world with a different history.

Undoubtedly, Maharashtra's greatest treasures are its extraordinary **cave temples** and **monasteries**. The finest of all are found near **Aurangabad**, renamed after the Mughal emperor Aurangzeb and still home to a sizeable Muslim population (as well as "the poor man's Taj Mahal", the **Bibi-ka-Maqbara**). The busy commercial city is the obvious base for visits to the caves at **Ajanta**, with their fabulous and still-vibrant murals, and the monolithic temples of **Ellora**, where the Hindu **Kailash temple** may look like a regular structure but was carved in its entirety from one single rock. From the second century BC, this region was an important centre of Buddhism; artificial caves were excavated to shelter monks, and the finest artists sculpted magnificent cathedral-like halls for congregational worship. Around 100km east of Aurangabad lies fascinating **Lonar Lake**, situated in a meteorite crater.

Hinduism later supplanted Buddhism as the region's principal religion, which it remains, despite the efforts of the successive Muslim rulers to introduce Islam to Maharashtra – around eighty percent of the population is Hindu. Balancing modern industry alongside ancient associations with the Ramayana, the main pilgrimage centre has always been **Nasik**, 187km northeast of Mumbai en route to Aurangabad. As one of the four locations of the Kumbh Mela, when up to four million devotees battle to bathe simultaneously in the holy River Godavari, the town is always a hive of devotional activity, even during less auspicious times. A short distance west, one of India's most sacred Shiva shrines lies close to the source of the Godavari, reached by a short trek from **Trimbak**.

Away from the cities, the most characteristic feature of the landscape is a plenitude of **forts** – as the western borderland between north and south India, Maharashtra's trade routes were always important, but could also bring trouble. Inland, parallel to the sea, and never further than 100km from it, the mighty **Western Ghats** rise abruptly. The areas of level ground that crowned them, endowed with fresh water, were easily converted into forts where small forces could withstand protracted sieges by large armies. Modern visitors can scale such windswept fortified heights at **Pratapgadh** and **Daulatabad**, the latter of which – briefly, bizarrely and disastrously – replaced Delhi as capital in the fourteenth century.

During the nineteenth century, the mountains found another use. When the summer proved too much for the British in Bombay, they sought refuge in

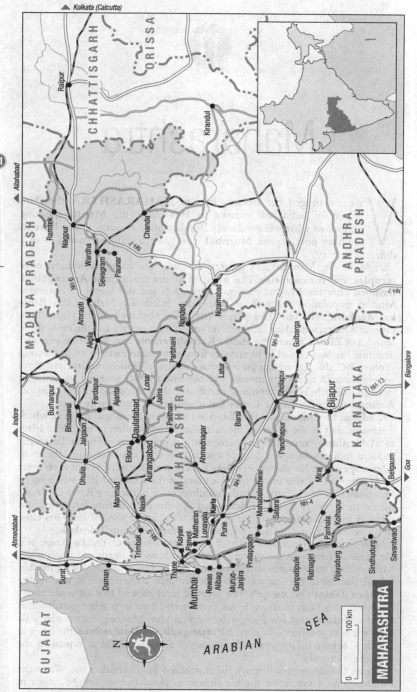

▲ Kolkata (Calcutta)

CHHATTISGARH

ORISSA

Raipur

Kirandul

MADHYA PRADESH

ANDHRA PRADESH

Ramtek

Nagpur

Wardha

Chanda

Sevagram

Paunar

NH-7

▲ Allahabad

Amraoti

Nanded

Nizamabad

NH-7

Akola

Parbhani

Gulbarga

NH-9

Burhanpur

Lonar

Latur

Sholapur

Bijapur

NH-13

Bhusawal

Fardapur

Ajanta

Jalna

Bangalore

Jalgaon

Ellora

Daulatabad

Paithan

MAHARASHTRA

Barsi

▲ Indore

Dhulia

Aurangabad

Ahmednagar

Pandhepur

KARNATAKA

Manmad

Belgaum

Nasik

NH-9

Miraj

Goa

Trimbak

Matheran

Karla

Mahabaleshwar

Panhala

Kolhapur

▲ Ahmedabad

Kalyan

Lonavala

Pune

Satara

NH-4

Panvel

Thane

Pratapgadh

Vijayadurg

Sindhudurg

Savantwadi

Surat

Daman

Rewas

Alibag

Ganpatipule

Ratnagiri

GUJARAT

Mumbai

Murud-Janjira

SEA

ARABIAN

N

MAHARASHTRA

0   100 km

nearby **hill stations**, the most popular of which, **Mahabaleshwar**, now caters for droves of Indian holiday-makers. **Matheran**, 108km east of Mumbai and 800m higher, has a special attraction: a rickety miniature train that twists up the hill on a sinuous track. Beyond the Ghats, the modern city of **Pune**, site of the internationally famous **Osho ashram** founded by the New Age guru Bhagwan Rajneesh, presides over a semi-arid tableland of flat-topped hills and dusty wheat fields. Maharashtra extends 900km further east across the Deccan plateau to the geographical centre of the Subcontinent, an area largely populated by several different tribal groups and where Mahatma Gandhi set up his headquarters at **Sevagram** during the Independence struggle.

To the west, Maharashtra occupies 500km of the **Konkan coast** on the Arabian Sea, from Gujarat to Goa. The palm-fringed coast winds back and forth with countless inlets, ridges and valleys, studded with forts. Incentives to break the journey down to Goa include **Murud-Janjira**, an extraordinary island fort flanked by beaches, and, in the far south, the interesting little seaside Ganesh temple of **Ganpatipule**, with its almost deserted stretch of beach.

Some history

Although some Paleolithic remains have been discovered, Maharashtra enters recorded history in the second century BC, with the construction of its first Buddhist caves. These lay, and still lie, in peaceful places of great natural beauty, but could never have been created without the wealth generated by the nearby caravan trade routes between north and south India.

The region's first Hindu rulers – based in Badami, Karnataka – appeared during the sixth century. Buddhism was almost entirely supplanted throughout the country by the twelfth century, in what has been characterized as a peaceful people's revolution attributable largely to the popular songs and teachings of poet-saints. The tradition they established continued to flourish throughout the thirteenth and fourteenth centuries, even when forced underground by Islam, reaching its zenith in the simple faith of **Ramdas** (1608–81), the "Servant of Rama".

Ramdas, ascetic and political activist, provided the philosophical underpinning behind the campaigns of Maharashtra's greatest warrior, **Shivaji** (1627–80). The fiercely independent Maratha chieftain united local forces to place insurmountable obstacles in the way of any prospective invader; so effective were their guerrilla tactics that he could even take on the mighty Mughals. Shivaji progressively fought his way northwards, at a time when the Mughals, who had got as far as capturing Daulatabad in 1633, were embroiled in protracted family feuds. A year after he succeeded in sacking the great port of Surat (Gujarat), in 1664, he was defeated in battle and imprisoned by **Aurangzeb** in Agra, from which he is said to have escaped by hiding in a package which the prison guards imagined was a gift intended for local Brahmins. Once outside, Shivaji simply walked away, disguised as a religious mendicant. By the time he died, in 1680, he had managed to unite the Marathas into a stable and secure state, funded by the plunder gleaned through guerrilla raids as far afield as Andhra Pradesh.

To be better placed to subdue the Marathas, Aurangzeb moved his court and capital south to the Deccan, first to Bijapur (1686) and then Golconda (1687). But after 25 years of relentless campaigns, he had still failed to subdue Shivaji's dynasty, which had meanwhile become a confederacy with a dominion extending as far east as Orissa. By the end of the eighteenth century, however, the power of both had weakened and the British were able to take full control.

Maharashtra claims a crucial role in the development of a nationalist consciousness. An organization known as the Indian National Union, originally

convened in Pune, held a conference in Bombay in 1885, which was thereafter known as the **Indian National Congress**. This loose congregation of key figures from local politics around the country was to change the face of Indian politics. At first, its aim was limited to establishing a national platform to raise the status of Indians, and it remained loyal to the British. In the long term, of course, it was instrumental in the achievement of Independence 62 years later, with many of the Congress's factional leaders over the years hailing from Maharashtra. Of late, the modern Congress has reasserted its power in the state assembly, as the influence of the BJP and Shiv Sena has waned.

With Independence, the Bombay Presidency, to which most of Maharashtra belonged, became known as Bombay State. Maharashtra as such was created in 1960. Its manufacturing industries, centred on Mumbai and to a lesser extent cities such as Nagpur, Nasik, Aurangabad, Sholapur and Kolhapur, now account for a quarter of the nation's output. Textiles have long been important, but this is now also one of the premier high-tech industry regions, especially along the Mumbai–Pune corridor. However, the majority of Maharashtra's population of over one hundred million are still engaged in agriculture: main crops include sugar cane, cotton, turmeric, peanuts, sunflowers, tobacco, pulses, wine grapes, fruit and vegetables.

Northern Maharashtra

Beyond the seemingly endless concrete housing projects, petrochemical works and mosquito-infested swamplands of Greater Mumbai, a wall of bare bluish-brown hills dominates the horizon. The **Western Ghats** – or the "Sahyadri Hills" as they are also known – form a series of huge steps that march up from the narrow, humid coastal strip to the edge of the **Deccan** plateau. **Northern Maharashtra**'s main transport arteries, the NH-3 and Central Railway line, wind in tandem through a landscape of arid, flat-topped table mountains, following an ancient trade route that once linked the western ports with the prosperous cities further north. Over the centuries, a number of pilgrimage sites sprang up to take advantage of the lucrative through-traffic, and these form the principal points of interest in the region today.

The holy city of **Nasik** is a handy place to break journeys to or from Mumbai, four hours away by road. Amid impressive scenery, the town of **Trimbak**, 10km west at the start of a steep half-day hike to the source of the sacred River Godavari, makes a more atmospheric overnight stop. Most foreign visitors, however, head straight for the regional capital, **Aurangabad**, the jumping-off point for the world-famous rock-cut **caves** at **Ellora** and **Ajanta**. Among **Muslim monuments** to seek out here are Aurangabad's answer to the Taj Mahal, the **Bibi-ka-Maqbara**, the dramatic hilltop fort at **Daulatabad** and the tiny tomb-town of **Khuldabad**, 5km from Ellora, where the last of the great Mughal emperors, Aurangzeb, is buried.

From Aurangabad, a well-beaten track cuts through the middle of Madhya Pradesh, via **Jalgaon**, towards Varanasi and Nepal. Alternatively, you could head across central India to **Wardha** and **Nagpur**, in the far northeastern corner of

the state, where a couple of **Gandhi ashrams**, and the picturesque white-washed Hindu temple complex at **Ramtek** make pleasant pauses on long cross-country hauls.

Aurangabad and beyond

It's easy to see why many travellers regard **AURANGABAD** as little more than a convenient, though largely uninteresting, place in which to kill time on the way to **Ellora** and **Ajanta**. First impressions seem to confirm its reputation; yet, given a little effort, northern Maharashtra's largest city can compensate for its architectural shortcomings. Scattered around its ragged fringes, the remains of fortifications, gateways, domes and minarets – including those of the most ambitious Mughal tomb garden in western India, the **Bibi-ka-Maqbara** – bear witness to an illustrious imperial past; the small but fascinating crop of **rock-cut**

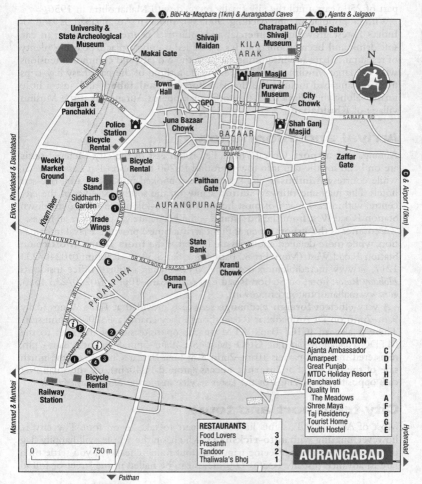

▲ **A**, Bibi-Ka-Maqbara (1km) & Aurangabad Caves ▲ **B**, Ajanta & Jalgaon

ACCOMMODATION
Ajanta Ambassador	C
Amarpeet	D
Great Punjab	I
MTDC Holiday Resort	H
Panchavati	E
Quality Inn	
The Meadows	A
Shree Maya	F
Taj Residency	B
Tourist Home	G
Youth Hostel	E

RESTAURANTS
Food Lovers	3
Prasanth	4
Tandoor	2
Thaliwala's Bhoj	1

AURANGABAD

Buddhist caves, huddled along the flanks of the flat-topped, sandy yellow hills to the north, are remnants of even more ancient occupation.

The city, originally called **Khadke**, or "Big Rock", was founded in the early sixteenth century by **Malik Amber**, an ex-Abyssinian slave and prime minister of the independent Muslim kingdom of the Nizam Shahis, based at Ahmadnagar, 112km southwest. It was a perfect spot for a provincial capital: on the banks of the **River Kham**, in a broad valley separating the then-forested Sahyadri range to the north from the Satharas to the south, and at a crossroads of the region's key trade routes. Many of the **mosques** and palaces erected by Malik Amber still endure, albeit in ruins.

Aurangabad really rose to prominence, however, towards the end of the seventeenth century, when **Aurangzeb** decamped here from Delhi. At his behest, the impressive city walls and gates were raised in 1682 to withstand the persistent Maratha attacks that bedevilled his later years. Following his death in 1707, the city was renamed in his honour as it changed hands once again. The new rulers, the **Nizams of Hyderabad**, somehow staved off the Marathas for the greater part of 250 years, until the city finally merged with Maharashtra in 1956.

With a population approaching 900,000, modern Aurangabad is one of India's fastest growing commercial and industrial centres, specializing in car, soft drink and beer production. It's a decidedly upbeat place, boasting plenty of restaurants, bars and interesting shops in the old city, and communal tensions with the large Muslim minority seem to be a thing of the past. Easy day-trips from Aurangabad include the dramatic fort of **Daulatabad**, and, just a little further along the Ellora road, the tomb of Emperor Aurangzeb at the Muslim village of **Khuldabad**.

Arrival and information

Aurangabad's **airport**, Chikal Thana, lies 10km east of the city. Metered **taxis** are on hand for the trip into town (around Rs200 to Station Rd East or West), while courtesy **minibuses** whisk away guests booked into the nearby five-star hotels. The mainline **railway station** stands on the southwest edge of the city centre, within easy reach of most hotels, and a 2.5-kilometre ride south down Station Road West from the **bus stand** – the hectic arrival point for all buses.

A counter at the airport (open at flight arrival times) provides arrival information, while more detailed enquiries are fielded at the **India Tourism office** on Station Road West (Mon–Fri 8.30am–6pm, Sat 8.30am–1.30pm; ☎0240/233 1217, ⓦwww.incredibleindia.org). The MTDC runs a tourist office inside its *Holiday Resort* hotel on Station Road East (daily 6am–10pm; ☎0240/233 1513, ⓦwww.maharashtratourism.gov.in).

A very efficient **foreign exchange** service is provided at Trade Wings (daily 9am–7pm) on Dr Ambedkhar Road, though they charge a Rs100 commission. There is also an ICICI Bank **ATM** on the opposite side of the road to the MTDC *Holiday Resort*. The **GPO** (Mon–Sat 10am–5pm, Speedpost 8am–7pm, registered mail and parcels 10am–2pm) is at Juna Bazaar Chowk, on the north side of the old city. For **Internet access** (around Rs40/hr), try the small Net café opposite Trade Wings, or the faster service inside the *Shree Maya Hotel*.

City transport and tours

Most of Aurangabad's sights lie too far apart to take in on foot. The city is, however, buzzing with **auto-rickshaws**, which, on the whole, will happily flag their meters; longer sightseeing trips work out much cheaper if you settle on a fare in advance (usually Rs500–600). Taxis can be hailed in the street or found

at the railway station and **cars with drivers** can be hired through travel agents such as the efficient Classic Travel (℡0240/233 5598, 🌐www.aurangabadtours .com), opposite MTDC's *Holiday Resort* on Station Road East. Expect to pay Rs1000–2000 (depending on the size and comfort of the car) for an eight-hour day with an additional overnight charge of around Rs200.

Much the cheapest and most satisfying way to get around the city, however, is by **bicycle**. While the busy main streets and market can be hair-raising at times, a ride out to the sights in the north of town makes an enjoyable alternative to public transport. Two stalls just north of the bus stand have the best bikes (Rs5/hr), and there's another near the railway station.

Various companies run daily guided **tours** of Aurangabad and the surrounding area, all operating to the same itineraries and departure times, and all generally rushed; the only difference is the price. **Ellora and City** tours usually take in the Bibi-ka-Maqbara, Panchakki, Daulatabad Fort, Aurangzeb's tomb at Khuldabad and the Ellora caves (though not the Aurangabad ones). **Ajanta** tours go to the caves only, but it's a long round trip to make in a day. Classic Travel (see above) runs the best of the tours (Ellora and City Rs200, Ajanta Rs300), using smaller vehicles with a greater level of comfort, and depart from the MTDC *Holiday Resort*. If you want to spend more time at the site, stay in the caveside MTDC accommodation (see p.746), at Fardapur (see p.746), or travel on to Jalgaon (see p.747).

Accommodation

Aurangabad's proximity to some of India's most important monuments, together with its new "boom-city" status, ensures a profusion of **hotels**. On the whole, standards tend to be high and prices very reasonable, particularly in the **budget** places, most of which are near the bus stand or the railway station. All have 24-hour checkout unless otherwise stated.

Ajanta Ambassador Chikalthana ℡0240/248 5211, 🌐www.ambassadorindia.com. Luxurious five-star near the airport, with ersatz traditional interior and a good-sized outdoor pool. Doubles from Rs5000. 🄋

Amarpeet Jalna Rd ℡0240/621 1133, 🌐www.amarpreethotel.com. Recently revamped mid-scale place, on a main road just south of the old city, offering smart, modern rooms. Good value given the level of comfort, and you get discounts online. 🄇

Great Punjab Station Rd East ℡0240/233 6482, ℱ233 6131. Business-oriented hotel very near the railway station. All 42 rooms have bathrooms, balconies and TVs. Bland but good value. 🄄–🄅

MTDC Holiday Resort Station Rd East ℡0240/233 4259, ℱ233 1198. Spacious, comfortable rooms, showing signs of wear and tear, within easy walking distance of the train station. Mosquito nets over the beds. 8am checkout. 🄅

Panchavati off Station Rd West, Padampura. ℡0240/232 8755. A couple of dozen neat, clean rooms (all attached) on the western edge of the city centre, just opposite the YHA. The best choice at this end of the scale, and the staff are very welcoming. 🄌–🄍

Quality Inn The Meadows off Mumbai–Aurangabad Highway ℡022/6654 8361, 🌐www.themeadowsresort.com. Set amid 13 acres of lush gardens on the outskirts, this luxury, green-oriented resort offers a choice of differently priced chalets, suites and cottages, the nicest of them sporting gleaming marble floors and cane furniture. Meals are served alfresco by the poolside, surrounded by abundant birdlife. From Rs4000 (tariffs include airport transfers). 🄈

Shree Maya Bharuka Complex, Padampura Rd, off Station Rd West ℡0240/333093, ℮shrimay_agd @sancharnet.in. Friendly place with large, cleanish rooms (some a/c; all attached). There's also a sociable rooftop terrace restaurant where meals and snacks are served. 🄋

Taj Residency Ajanta Rd ℡0240/238 1106, 🌐www.tajhotels.com. Business-orientated branch of the famous chain, about 3km north of Delhi Gate, and convenient for sights on the north side of town. Large swimming pool, tennis courts, gardens and health suite. From $250 a night. 🄎

Tourist Home Station Rd West ☎ 0240/233 7212. Rock-bottom travellers' hostel with basic, worn dorms or attached rooms, and sociable communal terrace. A bit on the grubby side, but the most commendable of the ultra-cheapos. Dorm beds from Rs75. ❷

Youth Hostel Off Station Rd West ☎ 0240/233 4892. Run-down, segregated dorms (Rs50 under 35s, Rs70 over 35s) with mosquito nets, and a handful of private, attached doubles. Checkout 9am, closed 11am–4pm, and a 10pm curfew is imposed. ❷

The City

The old walled city, laid out on a grid by Malik Amber in the sixteenth century, still forms the core of Aurangabad's large **bazaar** area. It's best approached via **Gulmandi Square** to the south, along any of several streets lined with colourful shops and stalls. The bazaar lacks the character and intensity of those in larger Indian cities, but has a pleasant, workaday feel, and you'll not be approached by too many zealous salesmen.

The unremarkable eighteenth-century **Shah Ganj Masjid** that presides over the main square directly east of City Chowk is surrounded on three sides by small shops and a congested roundabout. Anyone keen to see other remnants of Aurangabad's Mughal splendour should make for the city's largest and most impressive mosque, the **Jama Masjid**, 1km northwest of Shah Ganj Masjid. Its amalgam of parts was begun by Malik Amber in 1612 and added to by Aurangzeb nearly a century later. To the east of the mosque lie the ruins of Aurangzeb's former imperial headquarters, the **Kila Arak**. Once this was a complex of palaces, battlements, gateways, tanks and gardens that housed three princes and a retinue of thousands.

On the left bank of the Kham River, on Panchakki Road, the **Dargah** of Baba Shah Muzaffar (daily sunrise–8pm; Rs5) is a religious compound built by Aurangzeb as a memorial to his spiritual mentor, a Chishti mystic. The principal point of interest is not so much the mosque, the modest tomb or ornamental gardens nearby, pleasant as they are, but the unusual adjoining water-mill known as the **Panchakki**. Water pumped underground from a reservoir in the hills 6km away collects in a tank, now teeming with enormous carp, to drive a small grind-stone once used to mill flour. The complex makes a lively place to wander around in the early evening with lots of chai shops, *mehendi* (henna hand-painting) artists and souvenir shops. South of the Panchakki, also on the left bank of the river, an excellent **weekly market** is held every Thursday. Villagers from outlying areas pour in all morning on bullock carts to buy and sell livestock and fresh produce. The market gets into its stride by noon, winding up around 5pm.

The Bibi-ka-Maqbara

Completed in 1678, Aurangabad's Mughal tomb-garden, the **Bibi-ka-Maqbara** (daily 8am–sunset; $2 [Rs5]), was dedicated by **Prince Azam Shah** to the memory of his mother **Begum Rabi'a Daurani**, Aurangzeb's wife. Lack of resources dogged the 25-year project, and the end result fell far short of expectations. Looking at the mausoleum from beyond the ornamental gardens and redundant fountains in front of it, the truncated minarets and ungainly entrance arch make the Bibi-ka-Maqbara appear ill-proportioned compared with the elegant height and symmetry of the Taj, built fifty years earlier by Aurangzeb's father. The impression is not enhanced by the abrupt discontinuation of marble after the first 2m – allegedly a cost-saving measure.

An enormous brass-inlaid **door** – decorated with Persian calligraphy naming the maker, the year of its installation and chief architect – gives access to the archetypal *charbagh* (quadrangular) garden complex. Of the two entrances to the mausoleum itself, one leads to the inner balcony while the second drops

through another beautiful door to the **vault** (since a suicidal student jumped from a minaret, visitors may no longer climb them). Inside, an exquisite octagonal **lattice-screen** of white marble surrounds the raised plinth supporting Rabi'a Daurani's grave. Like her husband's in nearby Khuldabad, it is "open" as a sign of humility. The unmarked grave beside it is said to be that of the empress's nurse.

The caves

Carved out of a steep-sided spur of the Sahyadri range, directly overlooking the Bibi-ka-Maqbara, Aurangabad's own **caves** (Tues–Sun 8.30am–5pm; $2 [Rs5]) bear no comparison to those in nearby Ellora and Ajanta, but their fine **sculpture** makes a worthwhile introduction to rock-cut architecture. In addition, the infrequently visited site is peaceful and pleasant in itself, with commanding views over the city and surrounding countryside.

The caves, all Buddhist, consist of two groups, eastern and western, numbered 1 to 9 by the Archeological Survey of India. The majority were excavated between the fourth and eighth centuries, under the patronage of two successive dynasties: the **Vakatkas**, who ruled the western Deccan from Nasik, and the **Chalukyas**, a powerful Mysore family who emerged during the sixth century. All except the much earlier Cave 4, which is a *chaitya* hall, are of the *vihara* (monastery) type, belonging to the Mahayana school of Buddhism.

Unless you cycle, the only practical way of **getting to the caves** is by auto-rickshaw or taxi; you'll be expected to pay for waiting time, or the return fare. Alternatively, drop down on foot to the Bibi-ka-Maqbara and pick up an auto-rickshaw back into town from there.

Eating and drinking

Food in Aurangabad tends to be an incongruous mixture of strictly vegetarian **Gujarati** and meat-oriented north Indian Muslim dishes. As elsewhere in the state, "non-veg" is synonymous with dim lights, drawn curtains and a male clientele, while the veg restaurants attract families and are particularly popular on Sunday evenings, when booking is recommended. **Drinking** is an exclusively male preserve, carried out in the many specially segregated bars (aka "permit rooms"), with the exception of the larger and more tourist-oriented hotels and restaurants.

Food Lovers Station Rd East, opposite MTDC office. A kitsch wonderland of bamboo, plastic waterfalls and fish tanks – all illuminated by candles – with a non-seedy bar. The mid-price Indian and Manchurian food is consistently tasty, making this a popular choice among travellers. Most mains Rs75–250.
Prasanth Siddharth Arcade, Station Rd East, opposite MTDC office. A cheaper alternative to nearby *Food Lovers*, serving exclusively vegetarian dishes (mainly Punjabi and Chinese), indoors or on an external terrace, against a barage of *filmi* music and coloured lights. The food's freshly prepared and inexpensive, though the service can be slow.

Tandoor Shyam Chambers, Station Rd East ☎0240/232 8481. Upmarket a/c bar/ restaurant, dominated by an imposing bust of Egyptian pharaoh Tutankhamen, but offering some of the city's most delectable non-veg Mughlai food. Tandoori chicken and mutton kebabs are the house specialities, while for monster appetites there's the full-on "sizzling tandoori platter" (Rs475 and copious enough for two). Mains Rs80–225.
Thaliwala's Bhoj Opposite *Hotel Kartiki*, Dr Ambedkhar Rd. An old favourite, pure-veg restaurant renowned for its meticulously prepared, good-value Rajasthani and Gujarati thalis (Rs75).

Moving on from Aurangabad

Aurangabad's Chikal Thana airport, 10km east of the city, is most easily reached by taxi (around Rs200 one way). En route, you pass the offices of Indian Airlines

(☎0240/248 5421) and Jet Airways (☎0240/244 1392), both on Jalna Road; Kingfisher Airlines (☎1800 2333 131) and Air Deccan (☎0240/3900 8888) maintain counters at the airport.

All the state transport corporation (MSRTC) buses leave from the Central Bus Stand, including good-value "luxury" daily **night buses** to **Mumbai**. If you feel like a little more comfort, there are a couple of companies running more expensive a/c buses to most of the larger destinations; tickets can be booked through travel agents. Getting to **Pune** is easy, on MSRTC's "express"; **Nasik** buses are also frequent, as are services to Jalgaon. A couple of private bus companies run buses to **Indore**, **Nasik**, **Pune**, **Udaipur**, **Ahmedabad** and **Jalgaon**, which can be booked through most travel agents.

Trains to and from Aurangabad are very limited, as the city is not on the main line. Of the four to five daily services to Mumbai, the most convenient is the heavily booked Devgiri Express #7058, which departs at 11.30pm and arrives early the next morning in CST (VT) at 7.10am. Note, however, that this train is often subject to lengthy delays as it originates across country in Secunderabad. A marginally more dependable alternative is the #7618 Tapovan Express, leaving Aurangabad daily at 2.40pm and arriving in CST at 10.05pm.

Otherwise, the nearest mainline station, at **Jalgaon**, 108km north, is served by far more trains to many destinations, including Mumbai, Delhi, Agra, Bhopal, Kolkata (Calcutta) and Chennai.

See "Travel details" at the end of this chapter for information on journey frequencies and durations.

Daulatabad (Deogiri)

Dominating the horizon 13km northwest of Aurangabad, the awesome hilltop citadel of **DAULATABAD** crowns a massive conical volcanic outcrop whose sides have been shaped into a sheer sixty-metre wall of granite. The fort's forbidding appearance is further accentuated by the enormous minaret rising out of the ruins of the city that once sprawled from its base. If only for the panoramic **views** from the top of the hill, Daulatabad makes a rewarding pause en route to or from the caves at Ellora, 17km northwest.

Aside from the inevitable Buddhist and Jain hermits, occupation of the site – then known as **Deogiri**, "Hill of the Gods" – dates from its ninth-century role as bastion and capital of a confederacy of Hindu tribes. The **Yadavas** were responsible for scraping away the jagged lower slopes of the mount to form its vertical-cliff base, as well as the fifteen-metre-deep moat that still encircles the upper portion of the citadel. Their prosperity eventually aroused the interest of the acquisitive Delhi sultans, who stormed the fortress in 1294 and carried off a hoard of gold, silver and precious stones.

Muslim occupation of Deogiri began in earnest with the arrival in 1327 of Ghiyas-ud-din **Tughluq**. Convinced that the fort was the perfect base for campaigns further south, the sultan decreed that his entire court should decamp here from Tughluqabad, the "third city" of Delhi. The epic 1100-kilometre march cost thousands of lives. But within seventeen years, drought, famine and the growing threat of a full-scale Mughal invasion on his northern borders forced the beleaguered ruler to return to Tughluqabad. His governor, Zafar Khan, took the opportunity to mount a rebellion and established the **Bahmani** dynasty. Thereafter, the fortress fell to a succession of different regimes, including Shah Jahan's **Mughals** in 1633, before it was finally taken by the **Marathas** midway through the eighteenth century.

The fortress

Daulatabad's labyrinthine **fortress** (daily 6am–6pm; $2 [Rs5]) unfolds around the **Chandminar**, or "Victory Tower", erected by Ala-ud-din Bahmani to celebrate his conquest of the fort in 1435. The Persian blue-and-turquoise tiles that once plastered it in complex geometric patterns have disappeared, but it remains an impressive spectacle.

The Jama Masjid, directly opposite, is Daulatabad's oldest Islamic monument. Built by the Delhi sultans in 1318, the well-preserved mosque comprises 106 pillars plundered from the Hindu and Jain temples which previously stood on the site. It was recently converted into a Bharatmata temple, much to the chagrin of local Muslims. Nearby, the large stone-lined "Elephant" **tank** was once a central component in the fort's extensive water-supply system. Two giant terracotta pipes channelled water from the hills into Deogiri's legendary fruit and vegetable gardens.

Once beyond the open ground surrounding the tower, the main walkway heads through a series of interlocking bastions, fortified walls, moats and drawbridges before emerging to the **Chini Mahal**, or "Chinese Palace". The impressive ram-headed **Kila Shikan** ("Fort Breaker") cannon, inscribed with its name in Persian, rests on a stone platform nearby. From here onwards, a sequence of macabre traps lay in wait for the unwary intruder, including a moat infested with man-eating crocodiles and a maze of passageways with iron covers that could be heated to generate toxic gases.

At the end of the final tunnel, a broad flight of rock-cut steps climbs to an attractive twelve-pillared pavilion. The **Baradari** is thought to have been the residence of a Yadavi queen, though it was later used by the emperor Shah Jahan during his visits to Daulatabad. The **views** from the flat roof of the building are superb, but an even more impressive panorama is to be had from the **look-out post** perched on the summit of the hill, marked with another grand cannon and a cave that in Mughal times sheltered a famous holy man.

Practicalities

Although Daulatabad features on the guided **tours** of Ellora from Aurangabad (see p.727), you'll have more time to enjoy it by travelling there on one of the hourly shuttle **buses** between Aurangabad and the caves. From Daulatabad, it is easy to catch another bus onto Khuldabad and Ellora; the stop is directly opposite the main entrance to the fort, beside the string of chai and souvenir stalls and the small MTDC-run **restaurant**. If you're not on a tour, it's a good idea to hire a guide, as some of the passages in the fort are pitch-black and hopelessly confusing.

Khuldabad (Rauza)

Nestled on a saddle of high ground, 22km from Aurangabad and a four-kilometre ride from Ellora, **KHULDABAD**, also known as **Rauza**, is an old walled town famous for a wonderful crop of onion-domed **tombs**. Among the Muslim notables deemed worthy of a patch of earth in this most hallowed of burial grounds ("Khuldabad" means "Heavenly Abode"), were the emperor Aurangzeb, a couple of nizams, and a fair few of the town's Chishti founding fathers – the seven hundred mystic missionaries dispatched by the saint Nizam-ud-din Aulia to soften up local Hindus before the Sultanate's invasion in the fourteenth century.

MSRTC **buses** run every half-hour from Aurangabad to Khuldabad's small bus stand, a short walk west of the walls, en route to the Ellora caves just down

the hill. There is no **accommodation** in the village, nor anywhere decent to **eat**, so you'll need to bring your own supplies.

The Dargah of Sayeed Zain-ud-din

Khuldabad is encircled by tall granite battlements and seven fortified **gateways** raised by Aurangzeb before his death in 1707. The last of the great Mughals' tomb lies inside a whitewashed **dargah** (sunrise–10pm; free), midway between the North and South gates. The grave itself is a humble affair decorated only by the fresh flower petals scattered by visitors, open to the elements instead of sealed in stone. The devout emperor insisted that it be paid for not out of the royal coffers, but with the money he raised in the last years of life by selling his own hand-quilted white skullcaps. The pierced-marble **screen** and walls that now surround the spot were erected much later by the British viceroy, Lord Curzon, and the Nizam of Hyderabad.

Aurangzeb chose this as his final resting place primarily because of the presence, next door, of **Sayeed Zain-ud-din**'s tomb. The mausoleum of the Muslim saint, or *pir*, occupies a quadrangle separating Aurangzeb's grave from those of his wife and second son, Azam Shah. The steps leading to it are encrusted with highly polished semiprecious stones donated by the wandering Muslim ascetics, or *fakirs*, who formerly came here on pilgrimages. Locked away behind a small door is Khuldabad's most jealously guarded relic, the **Robe of the Prophet**, revealed to the public once a year on the twelfth day of the Islamic month of Rabi-ul-Awwal (usually around November), when the tomb attracts worshippers from all over India.

The Dargah of Sayeed Burhan-ud-din

Directly opposite Zain-ud-din's tomb is the **Dargah of Sayeed Burhan-ud-din** (same hours), a Chishti missionary buried here in 1334. The shrine is said to contain hairs from the Prophet's beard which magically increase in number when they are counted each year. At the end of the fourteenth century, when a financial crisis had left the saint's disciples unable to provide for upkeep of the *dargah*, a pair of "**silver trees**" miraculously sprouted in its central courtyard. The attendant will point out the two innocuous-looking lumps in the pavement nearby where the fabled trees once stood, and which are still said to secrete the odd drop of silver.

Ellora

Palaces will decay, bridges will fall, and the noblest structures must give way to the corroding tooth of time; whilst the caverned temples of Ellora shall rear their indestructible and hoary heads in stern loneliness, the glory of past ages, and the admiration of ages yet to come.

Captain Seely, *The Wonders of Ellora*

Maharashtra's most visited ancient monument, the **ELLORA** caves, 29km northwest of Aurangabad, may not enjoy as grand a setting as their older

---

Admission to the caves

Admission to the Ellora caves (Wed–Mon, dawn to dusk) costs Rs250 for Indians, or $5 (or the rupee equivalent) for foreigners. Entrance tickets should be purchased on arrival at the kiosk outside the Kailash temple. Note that the complex is **closed on Tuesdays.**

cousins at Ajanta, but the amazing wealth of **sculpture** they contain more than compensates, and this is an unmissable port of call if you're heading to or from Mumbai, 400km southwest. In all, 34 Buddhist, Hindu and Jain caves – some excavated simultaneously, in competition – line the foot of the two-kilometre-long Chamadiri escarpment as it tumbles down to meet the open plains. The site's principal attraction, the colossal **Kailash temple**, rears from a huge, sheer-edged cavity cut from the hillside – a vast lump of solid basalt fashioned into a spectacular complex of colonnaded halls, galleries and shrines.

The original reason why this apparently remote spot became the focus of so much religious and artistic activity was the busy **caravan route** that passed through here on its way between the prosperous cities to the north and the ports of the west coast. Profits from the lucrative trade fuelled a five-hundred-year spate of excavation, beginning midway through the sixth century AD at around the same time that Ajanta, 100km northeast, was abandoned. This was the twilight of the **Buddhist** era in central India; by the end of the seventh century, **Hinduism** had begun to reassert itself. The Brahmanical resurgence gathered momentum over the next three hundred years under the patronage of the Chalukya and Rashtrakuta kings – the two powerful dynasties responsible for the bulk of the work carried out at Ellora, including the eighth-century Kailash

ELLORA

temple. A third and final flourish of activity on the site took place towards the end of the first millennium AD, after the local rulers had switched allegiance from Shaivism to the Digambara sect of the **Jain** faith. A small cluster of more subdued caves to the north of the main group stand as reminders of this age.

Unlike the isolated site of Ajanta, Ellora did not escape the iconoclasm that accompanied the arrival of the **Muslims** in the thirteenth century. The worst excesses were committed during the reign of Aurangzeb who ordered the demolition of the site's "heathen idols". Although Ellora still bears the scars from this time, most of its best pieces of sculpture have remained remarkably well preserved, sheltered from centuries of monsoon downpours by the hard basalt hillside.

All the **caves** are numbered, following a roughly chronological plan. Numbers 1 to 12, at the south end of the site, are the oldest, from the Vajrayana Buddhist era (500–750 AD). The Hindu caves, 13 to 29, overlap with the later Buddhist ones and date from between 600 and 870 AD. Further north, the Jain caves – 30 to 34 – were excavated from 800 AD until the late

Rock-cut caves of the northwestern Deccan

The **rock-cut caves** scattered across the volcanic hills of the northwestern Deccan rank among the most extraordinary religious monuments in Asia. Ranging from tiny monastic cells to elaborately carved temples, they are remarkable for having been hewn by hand from solid rock. Their third-century BC origins seem to have been as temporary shelters for Buddhist monks when heavy monsoon rains brought their travels to a halt. Modelled on earlier wooden structures, most were sponsored by **merchants**, for whom the casteless new faith offered an attractive alternative to the old, discriminatory social order. Gradually, encouraged by the example of the Mauryan emperor Ashoka, the local ruling dynasties also began to embrace Buddhism. Under their patronage, during the second century BC, the first large-scale monastery caves were created at **Karla**, **Bhaja** and **Ajanta**.

Around this time, the austere **Hinayana**, or "Lesser Vehicle", school of Buddhism predominated in India. Caves cut in this era were mostly simple worship halls, or **chaityas** – long, rectangular apsed chambers with barrel-vaulted roofs and two narrow colonnaded aisles curving gently around the back of a monolithic **stupa**. Symbols of the Buddha's Enlightenment, these hemispherical burial mounds provided the principal focus for worship and meditation, circumambulated by the monks during their communal rituals.

By the fourth century AD, the Hinayana school was losing ground to the more exuberant **Mahayana**, or "Greater Vehicle", school. Its emphasis on an ever-enlarging pantheon of deities and **bodhisattvas** (merciful saints who postponed their accession to nirvana to help mankind towards Enlightenment) was accompanied by a transformation in architectural styles. *Chaityas* were superseded by lavish monastery halls, or **viharas**, in which the monks both lived and worshipped, and the once-prohibited image of the Buddha became far more prominent. Occupying the circumambulatory recess at the end of the hall, where the stupa formerly stood, the colossal **icon** acquired the 32 characteristics, or **lakshanas** (including long dangling ear-lobes, cranial protuberance, short curls, robe and halo) by which the Buddha was distinguished from lesser divinities. The peak of Mahayanan art came towards the end of the Buddhist age. Drawing on the rich catalogue of themes and images contained in ancient scriptures such as the **Jatakas** (legends relating to the Buddha's previous incarnations), Ajanta's exquisite wall **painting** may, in part, have been designed to rekindle enthusiasm for the faith, which was, by this point, already starting to wane in the region.

Attempts to compete with the resurgence of **Hinduism**, from the sixth century onwards, eventually led to the evolution of another, more esoteric religious movement. The **Vajrayana**, or "Thunderbolt" sect stressed the female creative principle, **shakti**, with arcane rituals combining spells and magic formulas. Ultimately, however, such modifications were to prove powerless against the growing allure of Brahmanism.

The ensuing shift in royal and popular patronage is best exemplified by **Ellora** where, during the eighth century, many old *viharas* were converted into temples, their shrines housing polished *shivalinga* instead of stupas and Buddhas. Hindu cave architecture, with its dramatic mythological **sculpture**, culminated in the tenth century with the magnificent **Kailash temple**, a giant replica of the freestanding structures that had already begun to replace rock-cut caves. It was Hinduism that bore the brunt of the iconoclastic medieval descent of Islam on the Deccan, Buddhism having long since fled to the comparative safety of the Himalayas, where it still flourishes.

eleventh century. Because of the sloping hillside, most of the cave entrances are set back from the level ground behind open courtyards and large colonnaded verandas or porches.

To see the oldest caves first, turn right from the car park where the buses pull in and follow the main pathway down to Cave 1. From here, work your way gradually northwards again, avoiding the temptation to look around Cave 16, the Kailash temple, which is best saved until late afternoon when the bus parties have all left and the long shadows cast by the setting sun bring its extraordinary stonework to life.

The Buddhist group

The **Buddhist caves** line the sides of a gentle recess in the Chamadiri escarpment. All except Cave 10 are *viharas*, or monastery halls, which the monks would originally have used for study, solitary meditation and communal worship, as well as the mundane business of eating and sleeping. As you progress through them, the chambers grow steadily more impressive in scale and tone. Scholars attribute this to the rise of Hinduism and the need to compete for patronage with the more overtly awe-inspiring Shaivite cave-temples being excavated so close at hand.

Caves 1 to 5

Cave 1, which may have been a granary for the larger halls, is a plain, bare *vihara* containing eight small cells and very little sculpture. In the much more impressive **Cave 2**, a large central chamber is supported by twelve massive, square-based pillars while the side walls are lined with seated Buddhas. The doorway into the shrine room is flanked by two giant *dvarpalas*, or guardian figures: an unusually muscular Padmapani, the lotus-holding *bodhisattva* of compassion, on the left, and an opulent bejewelled Maitreya, the "Buddha-to-come", on the right. Both are accompanied by their consorts. Inside the sanctum itself, a stately Buddha is seated on a lion throne, looking stronger and more determined than his serene forerunners in Ajanta. **Caves 3** and **4**, slightly older and similar in design to Cave 2, are in rather poor condition.

Known as the "Maharwada" cave because it was used by local Mahar tribespeople as a shelter during the monsoon, **Cave 5** is the grandest single-storeyed *vihara* in Ellora. Its enormous 36-metre-long rectangular assembly hall is thought to have been used by the monks as a refectory, and has two rows of benches carved from the stone floor. The Buddha inside the central shrine is seated, this time on a stool, his right hand touching the ground in the *mudra* denoting the "Miracle of a Thousand Buddhas" (performed by the Master to confound a gang of heretics).

Cave 6

The next four caves were excavated at roughly the same time in the seventh century, and are mere variations on their predecessors. On the walls of the antechamber at the far end of the central hall in **Cave 6** are two of Ellora's most famous and finely executed figures. **Tara**, the female consort of the *bodhisattva* Avalokitesvara, stands to the left, with an intense, kindly expression. On the opposite side, the Buddhist goddess of learning, Mahamayuri, is depicted with her emblem, the peacock, while a diligent student sets a good example at his desk below. The parallels with Mahamayuri's Hindu counterpart, Saraswati, are strong (the latter's mythological vehicle is also a peacock), and show the extent to which seventh-century Indian Buddhism incorporated elements from its rival faith in an attempt to rekindle its waning popularity.

Caves 10, 11 and 12

Excavated in the early eighth century, **Cave 10** is one of the last and most magnificent of the Deccan's rock-cut *chaitya* halls. Steps lead from the left of its large veranda to an upper balcony, where a trefoil doorway flanked by flying threesomes, heavenly nymphs and a frieze of playful dwarfs leads to an interior balcony. The stone "rafters" carved out of the ceiling, imitations of the beams that would have appeared in earlier freestanding wooden structures, are the source of this cave's popular name, the **Sutar Jhopadi**, or "Carpenter's Workshop".

In spite of the rediscovery in 1876 of its hitherto hidden basement, **Cave 11** continues to be known as the **Dho Tal**, or "Two Floors" cave. Its top storey is a long columned assembly hall housing a Buddha shrine and, on its rear wall, images of Durga and Ganesh, the elephant-headed son of Shiva – evidence that the cave was converted into a Hindu temple after being abandoned by the Buddhists.

Cave 12 next door – the **Tin Tal**, or "three floors" – is another triple-storeyed *vihara*, approached via a large open courtyard. Again, the main highlights are on the uppermost level. The shrine room at the end of the hall, whose walls are lined with five large *bodhisattvas*, is flanked on both sides by seven Buddhas – one for each of the Master's previous incarnations.

The Hindu group

Ellora's seventeen **Hindu caves** are grouped around the middle of the escarpment, to either side of the majestic Kailash temple. Excavated at the start of the Brahmanical revival in the Deccan during a time of relative stability, the cave-temples throb with a vitality absent from their restrained Buddhist predecessors. In place of benign-faced Buddhas, huge **bas-reliefs** line the walls, writhing with dynamic scenes from the Hindu scriptures. Most are connected with **Shiva**, the god of destruction and regeneration (and the presiding deity in all of the Hindu caves on the site), although you'll also come across numerous images of Vishnu (the Preserver) and his various incarnations.

The same tableaux crop up time and again, a repetition that gave Ellora's craftsmen ample opportunity to refine their technique over the years leading up to their greatest achievement, the **Kailash temple** (Cave 16). Covered separately (see opposite), the temple is the highlight of any visit to Ellora, but you'll appreciate its beautiful sculpture all the more if you visit the earlier Hindu caves first. Numbers 14 and 15, immediately south, are the best of the bunch if you're pushed for time.

Cave 14

Dating from the start of the seventh century AD, and among the last of the early excavations, **Cave 14** was a Buddhist *vihara* converted into a temple by the Hindus. The entrance to the sanctum is guarded by two impressive river goddesses, Ganga and Yamuna, while in an alcove behind and to the right, seven heavy-breasted fertility goddesses, the **Sapta Matrikas**, dandle chubby babies on their laps. Shiva's elephant-headed son, Ganesh, sits to their right beside two cadaverous apparitions, Kala and Kali, the goddesses of death. Superb **friezes** adorn the cave's long side-walls.

Cave 15

Like its neighbour, the two-storeyed **Cave 15**, reached via a long flight of steps, began life as a Buddhist *vihara* but was hijacked by the Hindus and became a Shiva shrine. Skip the largely uninteresting ground floor, and make for the

upper level to find some of Ellora's most magnificent sculpture. The cave's name, **Das Avatara**, is derived from the sequence of panels along the right wall, which show five of **Vishnu**'s ten incarnations (*avatars*).

A carved panel in a recess to the right of the antechamber shows Shiva emerging from a lingam. Brahma and Vishnu, stand before the apparition in humility and supplication – symbolizing the supremacy of Shaivism in the region at the time the conversion work was carried out. Finally, halfway down the left wall of the chamber as you're facing the shrine, the cave's most elegant piece of sculpture shows Shiva, as Nataraja, poised in a classical dance pose.

Caves 17 to 29

Only three of the Hindu caves strung along the hillside north of the Kailash temple are worth a visit. **Cave 21** – the **Ramesvara** – was excavated late in the sixth century. Thought to be the oldest Hindu cave at Ellora, it harbours some well-executed sculpture, including a fine pair of river goddesses on either side of the veranda, two wonderful door guardians and some sensuous loving couples, or *mithunas*, dotted around the walls of the balcony. **Cave 25**, further along, contains a striking image of the sun-god **Surya** speeding in his chariot towards the dawn.

From here, the path picks its way past two more excavations, then drops steeply across the face of a sheer cliff to the bottom of a small river gorge. Once under the seasonal **waterfall**, the trail climbs the other side of the gully to emerge beside **Cave 29**, the **Dhumar Lena**. Dating from the late sixth century, the cave boasts an unusual cross-shaped floor plan similar to the Elephanta cave in Mumbai harbour. Pairs of rampant lions guard its three staircases while, inside, the walls are covered with huge **friezes**. Left of the entrance, Shiva skewers the Andhaka demon; in the adjacent wall panel he foils the many-armed Ravana's attempts to shake him and Parvati off the top of Mount Kailash (look for the cheeky dwarf baring his bum to taunt the evil demon). On the south side, a dice-playing scene shows Shiva teasing Parvati by holding her arm back as she prepares to throw.

The Kailash temple (Cave 16)

Cave 16, the colossal **Kailash temple** (daily except Tues 9am–5.30pm; $5 [Rs10]), is Ellora's masterpiece. Here, the term "cave" is not only a gross understatement but a complete misnomer. For although the temple was, like the other excavations, hewn from solid rock, it bears a striking resemblance to earlier freestanding structures in south India. The monolith is believed to have been the brainchild of the Rashtrakuta ruler **Krishna I** (756–773). One hundred years and four generations of kings, architects and craftsmen elapsed, however, before the project was completed. Climb up the track leading along the lip of the compound's north-facing cliff to the ledge overlooking the squat main tower, and you'll see why.

The sheer scale is staggering. Work began by digging three deep trenches into the top of the hill using pickaxes and lengths of wood which, soaked with water and stuffed into narrow cracks, expanded to crumble the basalt. Once a huge chunk of raw rock had been exposed in this way, the royal sculptors set to work. In all, a quarter of a million tonnes of chippings and debris are estimated to have been cut from the hillside, with no room for improvisation or error. The temple was conceived as a giant replica of Shiva and Parvati's Himalayan abode, the pyramidal **Mount Kailash** – a Tibetan peak, said to be the "divine axis" between heaven and earth. Today, all but a few fragments of the thick coat of white-lime plaster that gave the temple the appearance of a

snowy mountain have flaked off, to expose elaborately carved surfaces of grey-brown stone beneath. Around the rear of the tower, these have been bleached and blurred by centuries of erosion, as if the giant sculpture is slowly melting in the fierce Deccan heat.

The temple

The main **entrance** to the temple is through a tall stone screen, intended to mark the transition from the profane to the sacred realms. After passing between two guardian river goddesses, Ganga and Yamuna, you enter a narrow passage that opens onto the main forecourt, opposite a panel showing **Lakshmi**, the goddess of wealth, being illustrated by a pair of elephants. Custom requires pilgrims to circumambulate clockwise around Mount Kailash, so descend the steps to your left and head across the front of the courtyard towards the near corner.

From the top of the concrete steps in the corner, all three principal sections of the complex are visible: first, the shrine above the entrance housing Shiva's vehicle, **Nandi**, the bull; next, the intricate recessed walls of the main assembly hall, or **mandapa**, which still bear traces of the coloured plaster that originally coated the whole edifice; and finally, the sanctuary itself, surmounted by the stumpy, 29-metre, pyramidal tower, or **shikhara** (best viewed from above). These three components rest on an appropriately huge raised platform, borne by dozens of lotus-gathering elephants. As well as symbolizing Shiva's sacred mountain, the temple also represented a giant **chariot**. The transepts protruding from the side of the main hall are its wheels, the Nandi shrine its yoke, and the two life-sized, trunkless elephants in the front of the courtyard (disfigured by Muslim raiders) are the beasts of burden.

Most of the main highlights of the temple itself are confined to its sidewalls, which are plastered with vibrant **sculpture**. Lining the staircase that leads up to the north side of the *mandapa*, a long, lively narrative panel depicts scenes from the Mahabharata. Below this are featured episodes from the life of **Krishna**. Continuing around the temple in a clockwise direction, the majority of the panels around the lower sections of the temple are devoted to **Shiva**. On the south side of the *mandapa*, in an alcove carved out of the most prominent projection, you'll find the relief widely held to be the finest piece of sculpture in the compound. It shows Shiva and Parvati being disturbed by the multi-headed demon **Ravana**, who has been incarcerated inside the sacred mountain and is now shaking the walls of his prison with his many arms. Shiva is about to assert his supremacy by calming the earthquake with a prod of his toe. Parvati, meanwhile, looks nonchalantly on, reclining on her elbow as one of her handmaidens flees in panic.

At this point, make a short detour up the steps at the bottom (southwest) corner of the courtyard, to the "**Hall of Sacrifices**", with its striking frieze of the seven mother goddesses, the Sapta Matrikas, and their ghoulish companions Kala and Kali (shown astride a heap of corpses). The sixteen-columned assembly hall is shrouded in a gloomy half-light designed to focus worshippers on the presence of the deity within. Using a portable arc light, the *chowkidar* will illuminate fragments of painting on the ceiling, where Shiva, as **Nataraja**, performs the dance of death.

The Jain group

Ellora's small cluster of four **Jain caves** is north of the main group, at the end of a curving asphalt road. They can be reached either from Cave 29, by dropping down to the T-junction and bearing right, or directly from the Kailash temple.

Either way, the two-kilometre round trip is quite a hike in the heat, and you may feel like taking a rickshaw.

Excavated in the late ninth and tenth centuries, after the Hindu phase had petered out, the Jain caves are Ellora's swansong. After the exuberance of the Kailash temple, their modest scale and subdued interiors lack vitality and inspiration, although some of the decorative carving is very fine. Only one of the group is of any real note. **Cave 32**, the **Indra Sabha** ("Indra's Assembly Hall"), is a miniature version of the Kailash temple. The lower of its two levels is plain and incomplete, but the upper storey is crammed with elaborate stonework, notably the ornate pillars and the two *tirthankaras* guarding the entrance to the central shrine. The naked figure of Gomatesvara, on the right, is fulfilling a vow of silence in the forest. He is so deeply immersed in meditation that creepers have grown up his legs, and animals, snakes and scorpions crawl around his feet.

The Grishneshwar Mandir

Rising above the small village west of the caves, the cream-coloured *shikhara* of the eighteenth-century **Grishneshwar Mandir** pinpoints the location of one of India's oldest and most sacred deities. The lingam enshrined inside the temple's cavernous inner sanctum is one of the twelve "self-born" **jyotirlingas** ("linga of light"), thought to date back to the second century BC. Non-Hindus are allowed to join the queue for *darshan*, but men have to remove their shirts before entering the shrine itself.

Ellora practicalities

Most visitors use Aurangabad as a base for day-trips to the caves, **getting to Ellora** either via the half-hourly MSRTC buses or on one of MTDC's popular guided **tours** (see p.727). These tours are very rushed, however; if you prefer to take in the caves at a more leisurely pace and climb Daulatabad Hill, either spend the night at Ellora or leave Aurangabad early in the morning. Official multilingual **guides** are on hand to take you on a tour (1–4hr) of the most interesting caves (groups of up to four people Rs650).

Ellora offers a couple of decent **places to stay**, including the *Hotel Kailas* (T02437/245443, Wwww.hotelkailas.com; **G–T**), a small campus of self-contained chalets insensitively positioned opposite the caves, with a few cheaper rooms by the road, and a restaurant and a/c bar.

Tasty, moderately priced **food** is available at the MTDC Ellora restaurant. In addition to the usual veg and non-veg Indian dishes, they serve Chinese, good-value lunchtime thalis and cold beer – indoors under the fan or alfresco on the shady terrace. You can also order meals and filled rolls in the *Kailas's* slightly pricier *Heritage* restaurant, but their turnover is sluggish, especially during the week. Roadside *dhabas* opposite the bus stand sell *bhajis*, pakoras and other snacks as well as inexpensive rice-plates.

Ajanta

Hewn from the near-vertical sides of a horseshoe-shaped ravine, the caves at **AJANTA** occupy a site worthy of the spectacular ancient art they contain. Less than two centuries ago, this remote spot was known only to the local Bhil tribespeople; the shadowy entrances to its abandoned stone chambers lay buried deep under a thick blanket of creepers and jungle. The chance arrival in 1819 of a small detachment of East India Company troops, however, brought the caves'

▲ Wall painting at the Ajanta Caves

obscurity to an abrupt end. Led to the top of the precipitous bluff that overlooks the gorge by a young "half-wild" scout, the tiger-hunters spied what has now been identified as the facade of Cave 10 protruding through the foliage.

The British soldiers had made one of the most sensational archeological finds of all time. Further exploration revealed a total of 28 colonnaded caves chiselled out of the chocolate-brown and grey basalt cliffs lining the River Waghora. More remarkable still were the immaculately preserved **paintings** writhing

Admission to the Ajanta Caves

Admission to the Ajanta Caves (Tues–Sun 9am–5.30 pm) costs Rs250 for Indians or $5 (or rupee equivalent) for foreigners. Tickets are sold at the main entrance, beyond the MTDC restaurant. Note that the complex is **closed on Mondays**.

over their interior surfaces. For, in addition to the rows of stone Buddhas and other **sculpture** enshrined within them, Ajanta's excavations are adorned with a swirling profusion of murals, depicting everything from battlefields to sailing ships, city streets and teeming animal-filled forests to snow-capped mountains. Even if you aren't wholly familiar with the narratives they portray, it's easy to see why these paintings are regarded as the finest surviving gallery of art from any of the world's ancient civilizations.

In spite of its comparative remoteness, Ajanta receives an extraordinary number of visitors. If you want to enjoy the site in anything close to its original serenity, avoid coming on a weekend or public holiday – it takes a fertile imagination indeed to picture Buddhist monks filing softly around the rough stone steps when riotous schoolkids and holiday-makers are clambering over them. The best **seasons to visit** are either during the monsoon, when the river is swollen and the gorge reverberates with the sound of the waterfalls, or during the cooler winter months between October and March. At other times, the relentless Deccan sun beating down on the south-facing rock can make a trip around Ajanta a real endurance test. Whenever you go, take a hat, some dark glasses, a good torch and plenty of drinking water. Flash photography of the paintings is strictly forbidden, but the caretakers usually turn a blind eye to visitors who discretely take pictures using digital cameras (by cranking up the ISO light sensitivity).

Some history

Located close enough to the major trans-Deccan trade routes to ensure a steady supply of alms, yet far enough from civilization to preserve the peace and tranquillity necessary for meditation and prayer, Ajanta was an ideal location for the region's itinerant Buddhist monks to found their first permanent monasteries. Donative inscriptions indicate that its earliest cave excavations took place in the second century BC.

In its heyday, Ajanta sheltered more than two hundred monks, as well as a sizeable community of painters, sculptors and labourers employed in excavating and decorating the cells and sanctuaries. Sometime in the seventh century, however, the site was abandoned – whether because of the growing popularity of nearby Ellora, or the threat posed by the resurgence of Hinduism, no one knows. By the eighth century, the complex lay deserted and forgotten, overlooked even by the Muslim iconoclasts who wrought such damage to the area's other sacred sites during the medieval era.

Early attempts to document the amazing rediscovery of the site met with such little success that Ajanta has ever since been associated with a sinister **curse**. In 1866, after spending 27 years faithfully copying the paintings from his field-camp nearby, the artist **Robert Gill** lost his entire collection when London's Crystal Palace burned to the ground. The same fate befell another batch of facsimiles in the 1870s, which went up in smoke with London's Victoria and Albert Museum, while the efforts of a Japanese team were dramatically foiled when their rice-paper impressions of Ajanta's sculpture were crushed in an earthquake. Even **restoration** work has been dogged with misfortune. In 1920,

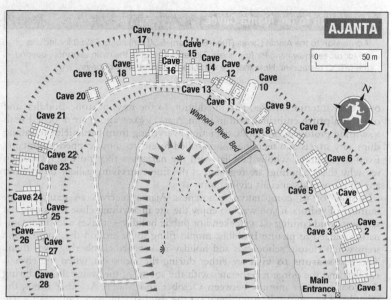

Ticket Booth, Green buses & MTDC Ajanta Travellers Lodge ▼

the Nizam of Hyderabad (who then ruled the region) employed a pair of Italian experts to patch up some of the more badly damaged paintings. Unfortunately, the varnish they used to seal the flakier fragments of plaster to the cave walls darkened and cracked over time, causing further irreparable deterioration.

Nowadays, the job of restoration has fallen to the Archeological Survey of India (ASI). Among measures to minimize the impact of the hundreds of visitors who daily trudge through is a ban on **flash photography**, and strict limits on the numbers allowed into a single cave at any given time – another reason to avoid weekends. A new move to reduce the ecological impact on the area is the recent creation of the Ajanta T-junction – see "Ajanta practicalities" on p.745. For more information on the rock-cut caves of the northwestern Deccan, see the box on p.734.

An obvious path leads from the admissions kiosk to the grand **Mahayana** *viharas*; if you'd prefer to see the caves in chronological order, however, start with the smaller **Hinayana** group of *chaitya* halls at the bottom of the river bend (caves 12, 10 & 9), then work your way back up, via Cave 17. For help getting up the steps, sedan-chair porters (around Rs150/hr), or *dhooli*-wallahs, stand in front of the stalls below. Official **guides** make two-hour tours which can be arranged through the ticket office; most deliver an interesting spiel (it's difficult to follow the pictorial stories without them) but you may well feel like taking in the sights again afterwards at a more leisurely pace.

Cave 1

Cave 1 contains some of the finest and stylistically most evolved paintings on the site. By the time work on it began, late in the fifth century, *viharas* served not only to shelter and feed the monks, but also as places of worship in their own right. In common with most Mahayana *viharas*, the extraordinary murals lining the walls and ceilings depict episodes from the *Jatakas*, tales of the birth and former lives of the Buddha.

Left of the doorway into the main shrine stands another masterpiece. **Padmapani**, the lotus-holding form of Avalokitesvara, is surrounded by an entourage of smaller attendants, divine musicians, lovers, monkeys and a peacock. His heavy almond eyes and languid hip-shot *tribhanga* (or "three-bend") pose exudes a distant and sublime calm. Opposite, flanking the right side of the doorway, is his counterpart, **Vajrapani**, the thunderbolt holder. Between them, these two *bodhisattvas* represent the dual aspects of Mahayana Buddhism: compassion and knowledge.

The real focal point of Cave 1, however, is the gigantic sculpted Buddha seated in the shrine room – the finest such figure in Ajanta. Using portable electric spotlights, guides love to demonstrate how the expression on the Buddha's exquisitely carved face changes according to where the light is held.

On the way out, you may be able to spot this cave's other famous trompe l'oeil, crowning one of the pillars (on the third pillar from the rear as you face the shrine): the figures of four apparently separate stags which, on closer inspection, all share the same head.

Cave 2

Cave 2 is another similarly impressive Mahayana *vihara*, dating from the sixth century. Here, the ceiling, which seems to sag like a tent roof, is decorated with complex floral patterns, including lotus and medallion motifs. The design clearly takes its cue from ancient Greek art – perhaps a legacy of Alexander the Great's foray into the Subcontinent half a millennium earlier. Sculpted friezes in the small subsidiary shrine to the right of the main chapel centre on a well-endowed fertility goddess, **Hariti**, the infamous child-eating ogress. When the Buddha threatened to give her a taste of her own medicine by kidnapping *her* child, Hariti flew into a frenzy (upper right), but was subdued by the Buddha's teachings of compassion (upper left). Below, a schoolroom scene shows a teacher waving a cane at a class of unruly pupils.

The side walls teem with lively **paintings** of the *Jatakas* and other mythological episodes. A frieze on the left veranda shows the birth of the Buddha, emerging from under his mother's arm, and his conception when a white elephant appeared to her in a dream (bottom left).

Caves 3 to 9

Caves 3, 4 and 7 hold little of interest, but take a quick look into **Cave 6**, a double-storeyed *vihara* with a finely carved doorjamb above its shrine room and some peeling paintings above the entrances to its cells. Cave 8 is always closed; it contains the generator for the lights.

Cave 9, which dates from the first century BC, is the first *chaitya* you come to along the walkway. Resting in the half-light shed by a characteristic *peepal*-leaf-shaped window in the sculpted facade, the hemispherical **stupa**, with its inverted pyramidal reliquary, forms the devotional centrepiece of the fourteen-metre-long hall. The fragments of painting that remain, including the procession scene on the left wall, are mostly superimpositions over the top of earlier snake-deities – *nagarajas*.

Cave 10

Though partially collapsed, and marred by the unsightly wire meshing erected by the ASI to keep out bats, the facade of **Cave 10**, a second-century BC *chaitya* hall – the oldest and most impressive of its kind in the ravine – is still a grand sight. The cave's main highlights, however, are far smaller and more subdued. With the help of sunlight reflected from a mirror held by an attendant, you may

Cave painting techniques

The basic **painting techniques** used by the artists of Ajanta to transform the dull rock walls into lustrous kaleidoscopes of colour changed surprisingly little over the eight centuries the site was in use, from 200 BC to 650 AD. First, the rough-stone surfaces were primed with a six- to seven-centimetre coating of paste made from clay, cow-dung, and animal hair, strengthened with vegetable fibre. Next, a finer layer of smooth white lime was applied. Before this was dry, the artists quickly sketched the outlines of their pictures using red cinnabar, which they then filled in with a coating of *terre verte*. The **pigments**, all derived from natural water-soluble substances (kaolin chalk for white, lamp soot for black, glauconite for green, ochre for yellow and imported lapis lazuli for blue), were thickened with glue and added only after the undercoat was completely dry. Thus the Ajanta paintings are not, strictly speaking, frescoes (always executed on damp surfaces), but **tempera**. Finally, after they had been left to dry, the murals were painstakingly polished with a smooth stone to bring out their natural sheen.

The artists' only sources of **light** were oil-lamps and sunshine reflected into the caves by metal mirrors and pools of water (the external courtyards were flooded expressly for this purpose). Ironically, many of them were not even Buddhists but Hindus employed by the royal courts of the day. Nevertheless, their extraordinary mastery of line, perspective and shading, which endows Ajanta's paintings with their characteristic other-worldly light, resulted in one of the great technical landmarks in Indian Buddhist art history.

be able to pick out the fading traces of painting along the left wall (now encased in glass). The scene in which a raja and his retinue approach a group of dancers and musicians surrounding a garlanded *bodhi* tree – a symbol of the Buddha (the Hinayanas preferred not to depict him figuratively) – is believed to be the earliest surviving Buddhist mural in India. Elsewhere on the wall is graffiti scrawled by the British soldiers who rediscovered the caves in 1819.

The apsidal-ended hall itself, divided by three rows of painted octagonal pillars, is dominated by a huge monolithic **stupa** at its far end. If there's no one else around, try out the *chaitya*'s amazing acoustics.

Cave 16

The next cave of interest, **Cave 16**, is another spectacular fifth-century *vihara*, with the famous painting known as the "**Dying Princess**" near the front of its left wall. The "princess" was actually a queen named **Sundari**, and she isn't dying, but fainting after hearing the news that her husband, King Nanda (Buddha's cousin), is about to renounce his throne to take up monastic orders. The opposite walls show events from Buddha's early life as **Siddhartha**.

Cave 17

Cave 17, dating from between the mid-fifth and early sixth centuries, boasts the best-preserved and most varied paintings in Ajanta. As with caves 1 and 2, only a limited number of visitors are allowed in at any one time. While you wait, have a look at the frescoes on the **veranda**. Above the door, eight seated Buddhas, including Maitreya, the Buddha-to-come, look down. To the left, an amorous princely couple share a last glass of wine before giving their worldly wealth away to the poor. The wall that forms the far left side of the veranda features fragments of an elaborate "Wheel of Life".

Inside the cave, the murals are, once more, dominated by the illustrations of the *Jatakas*, particularly those in which the Buddha takes the form of an animal

to illustrate certain virtues. This is also where you'll find the exquisite and much-celebrated portrait of a sultry, dark-skinned princess admiring herself in a mirror while her handmaidens and a female dwarf look on. The *chowkidars* will demonstrate how, when illuminated from the side, her iridescent eyes and jewellery glow like pearls against the brooding, dark background.

Cave 19

Excavated during the mid-fifth century, when the age of Mahayana Buddhism was in full swing, **Cave 19** is indisputably Ajanta's most magnificent *chaitya* hall, its **facade** teeming with elaborate sculpture. Hindu influence is discernible in the friezes that line the interior of the **porch**. Inside the hall, the faded frescoes are of less note than the sculpture around the tops of the pillars. The standing Buddha at the far end, another Mahayana innovation, is even more remarkable. Notice the development from the stumpier stupas enshrined within the early *chaityas* (caves 9 & 10) to this more elongated version. Its umbrellas, supported by angels and a vase of divine nectar, reach right up to the vaulted roof.

Caves 21 to 26

Caves 21 to 26 date from the seventh century, a couple of hundred years after the others, and form a separate group at the far end of the cliff. Apart from the unfinished **Cave 24**, whose roughly hacked trenches and pillars give an idea of how the original excavation was carried out here, the only one worth a close look is **Cave 26**. Envisaged on a similarly grand scale to the other large *chaitya*, Cave 19, this impressive hall was never completed. Nevertheless, the sculpture is among the most vivid and dramatic at Ajanta. In the "**Temptation of Mara**" frieze (on your left as you enter the cave), Buddha is ensconced under a *peepal* tree as seven tantalizing sisters try to seduce him. Their father, the satanic Mara, watches from astride an elephant in the top left corner. The ruse to lead the Buddha astray fails, of course, eventually forcing the evil adversary and his daughters to retreat (bottom right). In contrast, the colossal image of **Parinirvana** (Siddhartha reclining on his deathbed) along the opposite wall is a pool of tranquillity. Note the weeping mourners below, and the flying angels and musicians above, preparing to greet the sage as he drifts into nirvana. The soft sunlight diffusing gently from the doorway over Buddha's fine, sensuously carved features completes the appropriately transcendent effect.

The viewpoint

The stiff thirty-minute climb to the "**viewpoint**", from where the British hunting party first spotted the Ajanta Caves is well worth the effort – the panorama over the Waghora gorge and its surrounding walls of bare, flat-topped mountains is spectacular. The easiest way to pick up the path is to head through the souvenir stalls outside the entrance to the caves and ford the river; alternatively, drop down the steps below caves 16 and 17 and follow the walkway until you reach a concrete footbridge. Turn left on the far side of the river, and then right when you see steps branching uphill. A right turn at the end of the bridge will take you further into the ravine, where there's an impressive waterfall. Don't attempt this during **monsoon**, though, as water levels can be dangerously high.

Ajanta practicalities

The only way of **getting to Ajanta**, unless you have your own transport, is by **bus**. All vehicles (including taxis) must now stop at **Ajanta T-junction**, 5km from the caves on the main Aurangabad–Jalgaon road, where you'll find an

MTDC reception centre (with five smart a/c rooms, bookable only through MTDC head office in Mumbai; see p.685), refreshments, toilets and souvenirs. It costs Rs5 to enter the complex; once inside, ecofriendly green buses regularly ply the route to and from the caves (return fare Rs12 non-a/c, Rs20 a/c). All **MSRTC buses** between **Aurangabad**, 108km southwest, and the nearest railhead at **Jalgaon**, 58km north, stop at the T-junction on request. Provided you catch an early enough service up here, it's possible to see the caves, grab a bite to eat, and then head off again in either direction. Alternatively, you could do the round trip from Aurangabad on one of the rushed **tours** (see p.727).

Apart from MTDC's new luxury guestrooms at the T-Junction reception centre, no **accommodation** is available in Ajanta proper – visitors tend to stay in Aurangabad, or Jalgaon, to catch a train early the following day. If you want to stay within striking distance of the caves, however, you can do so in the village of **Fardapur**, a few kilometres down the Jalgaon road, where MTDC's upscale *Holiday Resort* (☎02438/244230; ❹–❺) offers comfortable rooms in a newly built complex facing the main highway. Close by, the *Padmapani Park* (☎02438/244280 or 09422 81838; ❸) is a pleasant, well-run budget alternative, with simple but clean attached rooms; phone ahead from the bus stand when you arrive and they'll pick you up. Other privately run guesthouses in the village include the *Murli Manohar* (☎02438/244289; ❸), 1km north of the MTDC *Holiday Resort*, in a shabby roadside block that served as MTDC's budget annexe until it was recently taken over, and the friendly *New Ajanta Hotel* (aka "Mustak House"; ☎02438/244360; ❹–❺), a basic, family bed-and-breakfast place in the heart of the village proper, close to the old fort on Jama Masjid Road.

Places to eat at Ajanta are limited to the uninspiring MTDC restaurant just outside the entrance to the caves, which serves veg and non-veg Punjabi dishes and thalis (until 6pm). The *Holiday Resort* in Fardapur serves an identical menu in its small restaurant (open to nonresidents). However, you'll eat fresher, tastier, and much cheaper food, at the nearby *Hotel Ajanta*, a typical Maharashtran roadside *dhaba* two minutes' walk north along the main highway, which rustles up delicious chicken, fish and mutton masala with hot rotis freshly baked over a shigdi (charcoal) brazier.

Lonar

Few visitors reach the unique crater at **LONAR** but those who do find this **meteorite-formed lake** an amazing and tranquil place. Referred to as "Taratirth" in the Hindu legend that correctly claimed it was created by a shooting star, the gigantic hole in the ground was formed about fifty thousand years ago when a lump of space rock survived its fiery descent through the atmosphere to bury itself here. The biggest of its kind in the world, the crater has a diameter of 1800m and depth of 170m.

The steep **path** down to the lake from the rim begins almost opposite the MTDC *Tourist Bungalow* and emerges in the basin near a twelfth-century temple dedicated to Shiva. A complete circuit of the lake, surrounded by thick forest which is home to scampering monkeys and a rich array of **birdlife**, takes a leisurely hour and a half. En route you will discover other seemingly lost shrines to Surya and Vishnu, as well as a stone lingam on an alternative path up, which marks the spot where, in the Ramayana, Rama and Sita are said to have bathed during their exile. On the lake itself you are likely to see flamingos, moorhens and reed warblers among the wallowing buffalo.

Practicalities

The easiest way to get to Lonar is by **taxi** from Aurangabad, which costs about Rs2000 for a day-trip; it allows you a couple of hours at the crater. There are two daily **buses** direct from Aurangabad at 7.30am and 8.30am, returning at 3pm and 4pm. These cover the 150km in four to five hours, although you can also get a later bus to Jalna and change there. The only **accommodation** is at the MTDC *Travellers Resort* (☎07260/221602; ❹), located next to the crater, where rooms are comfortable enough but **food** is not guaranteed if there are few guests; the only alternative is the basic chai stalls 2km away in the village.

Jalgaon

Straddling an important junction on the Central and Western Railway networks, as well as the main trans-Deccan trunk road, NH-6, **JALGAON** is a busy market town for the region's cotton and banana growers, and a key jumping-off point for travellers heading to or from the Ajanta Caves, 58km south. Even though the town holds nothing of interest, you may find yourself obliged to hole up here to be well placed for a morning departure.

Practicalities

Jalgaon is well served by mainline **trains** between Delhi, Kolkata (Calcutta) and Mumbai, and convenient for most cities to the north on the Central Railway. Express services also pass through en route to join the Southeastern Railway at Nagpur. **Buses** to Indore (257km north) and Pune (336km south) leave from the busy MSRTC bus stand, a ten-minute rickshaw ride across town from the railway station. Private services to Mumbai, Indore, Pune and other towns can be booked through any travel agent, including the reliable and friendly Shivalik Tours, almost opposite the bus stand at 4 Stadium Complex (☎0257/223 8405). If you're heading to Ajanta, the fastest buses are the half-hourly ones to Aurangabad, 160km south, all of which stop at the Ajanta T-junction. For withdrawing **money**, there's a UTI Bank ATM 500m towards the bus stand from the station, while for **Internet** try the Mandora Cyberpoint (Rs30/hr), near the *Arya Nivas*.

You shouldn't have any difficulty finding **accommodation** in Jalgaon. The *Aram Guest House*, on Station Road (☎0257/222 6549; ❷), is comfortable, with reasonably clean – if cramped – attached singles and doubles. One of the best budget hotels in India, however, has to be the very spruce ⚵ *Plaza Hotel* (☎0257/222 7354, ✉hotelplaza_jal@yahoo.com; ❸–❹), two minutes from the station on the left side of Station Road. Its economy rooms are particularly good, brightly decorated with immaculate, tiled bathrooms; there is a spotless air-conditioned dorm (Rs150), while pricier rooms come with cable TV, and they'll provide tea in your room if you're leaving early in the morning. One kilometre further back, past the bus stand, the plush new *Royal Palace* (☎0257/223 3888; ❹–❺) is a decent mid-range fallback.

There's no better place to **eat** than the *Silver Palace*, next to the *Plaza Hotel*, a smart restaurant with an a/c lounge and open terrace, serving quality Chinese and Indian veg and non-veg, including dishes from Hyderabad and Lahore; it also has the only non-seedy bar. *Anjali*, back towards the station on the other side of the road, does a good range of south Indian veg snacks and fairly spicy Punjabi meals. Another pure-veg joint, the north Indian *Hotel Arya*, is a five-minute walk from the station, near the clock tower – turn left at the roundabout

at the top of Station Road, carry on past the Mandora Cyberpoint; take the first left and it's on the left.

Nasik and around

Lying at the head of the main pass through the Western Ghats, **NASIK** makes an interesting stopover on the lengthy journey to or from Mumbai, 187km southwest. The city is one of the four sites of the world's largest religious gatherings, the **Kumbh Mela**, held at different locations in India every three years (see p.315); Nasik is next due to host the gathering in 2015.

Even outside festival times, the *ghat*-lined banks of the **River Godavari** are always animated. According to the Ramayana, Nasik was where Rama (Vishnu in human form), his brother Lakshmana and wife Sita lived during their exile from Ayodhya, and the arch-demon Ravana carried off Sita from here in an aerial chariot to his kingdom, Lanka, in the far south. The scene of such episodes forms the core of the busy pilgrimage circuit – a lively enclave packed with religious specialists, beggars, sadhus and street vendors touting puja paraphernalia. However, Nasik has a surprising dearth of historical buildings – even the famous temples beside the Godavari only date from the **Maratha era** of the eighteenth century. Its only real monuments are the rock-cut caves at nearby **Pandav Lena**. Excavated at the peak of Buddhist achievement on the Deccan, these two-thousand-year-old cells hark back to the days when, as capital of the powerful **Satavahana** dynasty, Nasik dominated the all-important trade routes linking the Ganges plains with the ports to the west.

From Nasik, you can make an interesting day-trip to the highly auspicious village of **Trimbak**, where hordes of Hindu pilgrims come to seek the nectar of immortality, spilt by Vishnu whilst in battle. A steep climb up from Trimbak takes you to **Brahmagiri**, the source of the holy Godavari River. Somewhat in contrast to its religious importance, Nasik is also the centre of Maharashtra's burgeoning **wine region**; permits have been granted for around fifty wineries to open in the next few years. Of those already open, Sula has the best reputation, if you want to try a sample.

Arrival and information

Buses from Mumbai pull in at the **Mahamarga Bus Stand**, a ten-minute rickshaw ride from the city centre. Aurangabad buses terminate at the chaotic central **City Bus Stand**, an easy walk from several cheap hotels and restaurants. Arrival by train is more problematic as the **railway station**, on Nasik Road, lies 8km southeast. Local buses regularly ply the route into town, however, and there is no shortage of shared taxis and auto-rickshaws. If you plan to leave Nasik by train, particularly on a weekend when the city booking counter (Mon–Fri 10am–5pm), off MG Road, is closed, reserve your outward ticket on arrival.

Predictably for a city that sees so few foreign visitors, the MTDC **tourist office**, near the golf course on Old Agra Road (Mon–Fri 10am–5pm; ℡0752/257 0059), is welcoming but not worth the trouble to find. Their daily "Darshan Tour" (7.30am–3pm; Rs90) of the city and its environs will only appeal to those with a passion for ferroconcrete temple architecture. To **change money**, the State Bank of India is just up from the City Bus Stand on Swami Vivekanand Road. The **GPO** is around the corner on Trimbak Road. **Internet** access is available at Matrix (Rs20/hr), down an alley beside the *Hotel Basera*.

Accommodation

Most of Nasik's **hotels** are pitched at middle-class Mumbai business travellers. The few noteworthy exceptions are the lodge-style budget places around the City Bus Stand *chowk*.

Basera Shivaji Rd ☎0253/257 5616, ℱ257 3958. Very close to the City Bus Stand. Airy, comfortable rooms, all with hot water till 11.30am and some with a/c. ❸–❹

Padma Sharampur Rd ☎0253/257 6837. Directly opposite the City Bus Stand. Safe, clean and convenient, with restaurant and permit room. All rooms have attached bathrooms and hot water 6am–noon. ❸

Panchavati 430 Chandak Vadi ☎0253/257 2291, ⓦwww.panchavatihotels.com. This four-part complex, close to the riverside, has rooms to suit most pockets, all of them scrupulously clean, attached, and unbeatable value for money in their

respective categories. At the bottom of the range is the budget *Panchavati Guesthouse* (☎0253/257 8771; ❹), followed by the midscale ⚥*Panchavati Yatri* (☎0253/257 8782; ❹–❺), the slightly swisher *Hotel Panchavati* (☎0253/257 5771; ❺) and, at the top of the range, the flagship *Panchavati Millionaire* (☎0253/231 2318; ❻).

Taj Residency 12km west on Mumbai–Agra Rd ☎0253/560 4499, ⓦwww.tajhotels.com. Primarily a business hotel and the plushest place to stay in the area. Opening on to beautifully landscaped grounds, the lobby is designed in traditional Maratha style. As ever with Taj Group, for the best tariffs book online. ❾

The City

Down on the riverbank, over 1km east of the bus stand, the **Ram Kund** is the reason most people come to Nasik, although it can look more like an overcrowded municipal swimming pool than one of India's most ancient sacred places. Among the Ram Kund's more arcane attributes is its capacity to dissolve bones – whence the epithet of "**Astivilaya Tirth**" or "Bone Immersion Tank". Follow the street opposite Ram Kund up the hill to arrive at the city's second most important sacred site, the area around the **Kala Ram Mandir**, or "Black Rama Temple". Among the well-known episodes from the Ramayana to occur here was the event that led to Sita's abduction, when Lakshmana sliced off the nose of Ravana's sister after she had tried to seduce Rama by taking the form of a voluptuous princess. Sita's cave, or **Gumpha**, a tiny grotto known in the Ramayana as Parnakuti ("Smallest Hut"), is just off the square.

The Kala Ram temple itself, at the bottom of the square, houses unusual jet-black deities of Rama, Sita and Lakshmana; these are very popular with visiting pilgrims, as access is free from all caste restrictions. The best time to visit is around sunset, after evening puja, when a crowd, mostly of women, gathers in the courtyard to listen to a traditional storyteller recount tales from the Ramayana and other epics.

Halfway up one of the precipitous conical hills that overlook the Mumbai–Agra Road, 8km southwest of Nasik, is a small group of 24 rock-cut **caves**, some dating from the first century BC. The **Pandav Lena** site is famous for its well-preserved inscriptions in the ancient Pali language, and fine ancient stone sculpture. The most straightforward way of getting to Pandav Lena without your own vehicle is by auto-rickshaw (around Rs50–75 each way), although the numerous local buses that go there are not too packed most of the time.

Eating and drinking

By and large, Nasik's best-value meals are to be had in its traditional "keep it coming" thali **restaurants**. While they may not always be the cheapest option, for less than the price of a beer you can enjoy carefully prepared and freshly cooked food, often including such regional specialities as *bajra* (wholemeal rotis)

Going doolally

In the days of the Raj, soldiers who cracked under the stresses and strains of military life in British India were packed off to recuperate at a psychiatric hospital in the small Maharashtran cantonment town of **Deolali**, near Nasik. Its name became synonymous with madness and nervous breakdown; hence the English idiom "to go doolally".

and *bakri* (hot oatmeal biscuits), together with an array of tasty vegetable, pulse and lentil dishes. The city's religious associations tend to mean that meat and alcohol are less easily available than elsewhere in Maharashtra, but most of the larger hotels have **bars** and restaurants with permits.

Samrat Swami Vivekanand Rd. Well-known 24hr thali joint, 2–3 minutes from the City Bus Stand, doing a brisk trade in moderately priced, quality Gujarati food.

Shilpa Near the *Panchavati Hotel*, Chandak Vadi. A garden restaurant that offers a small amount of peace and respite amidst the chaos; the usual

range of pure-veg Chinese and particularly good Punjabi tandoori items, with most mains Rs80–125.

Suruchi Under *Basera Hotel*, Shivaji Rd. Cheap, clean, no-nonsense south Indian fast-food café that also serves inexpensive Udipi snacks and cold drinks. Full of crowds of office workers at lunch. Family/ladies' room upstairs.

Trimbak (Trimbakeshwar)

Crouched in the shadow of the Western Ghats, 28km west of Nasik, **TRIMBAK** – literally "Three-Eyed", another name for Lord Shiva, in Marathi – was the exact spot where one of the four infamous drops of immortality-giving *amrit* nectar fell to earth from the *kumbh* vessel during the struggle between Vishnu's vehicle Garuda and the Demons – the mythological origin of the Kumbh Mela (see p.315). Trimbak is also near the source of one of India's longest and most sacred rivers, the Godavari; the spring can be reached via an ancient pilgrim-trail that cuts through a cleft in an awesome, guano-splashed cliff face. En route you pass colourful wayside shrines and a ruined fort (see below).

Numbering among India's most sacred centres for Shiva worship (it houses one of the twelve "self-born" *jyotirlingas* – see Contexts), the **Trimbakeshwar Mandir** temple is unfortunately closed to non-Hindus. Its impressive eighteenth-century *shikhara* (tower), however, can be glimpsed from the backstreets nearby.

The Brahmagiri hike

The round trip to **Brahmagiri**, the source of the Godavari, takes between two and three hours. It's a strenuous walk, particularly in the heat, so make sure you take adequate water. From the trailhead at the bottom of the village, the way is paved and stepped as far as the first level outcrop, where there are some welcome chai stalls and a small hamlet. Beyond that, either turn left after the last group of huts and follow the dirt trail through the woods to the foot of the **rock-cut steps** (20min), or continue straight on to the three **shrines** clinging to the base of the cliff above. The first is dedicated to the goddess Ganga, the second – a cave containing 108 lingams – to Shankar (Shiva), and the third to the sage Gautama Rishi, whose hermitage this once was.

The steps climb 550m above Trimbak to the remains of **Anjeri Fort** – a site that was, over the years, attacked by the armies of both Shah Jahan and Aurangzeb before it fell into the hands of Shaha-ji Raj, father of the legendary rebel-leader Shivaji. The **source** itself is another twenty minutes further on, across **Brahmagiri Hill**, in the otherwise unremarkable Gaumukh ("Mouth of the Cow") temple. From its rather unimpressive

origins, this paltry trickle flows for nearly 1000km east across the entire Deccan plateau to the Bay of Bengal.

Practicalities

Getting to Trimbak from Nasik is easy. Half-hourly **buses** leave from the depot opposite the main City Bus Stand (45min). To return, you can catch a bus (until around 8pm) or one of the shared **taxis** that wait outside Trimbak Bus Stand; there's no difference in price as long as the car is full.

Although Trimbak makes an easy day-trip from Nasik, it's a peaceful and atmospheric place to spend a night, with plenty of basic pilgrim **accommodation**. The modern MTDC *Tourist Bungalow* (☎02594/233143; ❺–❻), opposite the start of the Brahmagiri path, is in a pleasant location on the edge of town, with scruffy (but peaceful) doubles with attached bathrooms. More comfortable rooms are to be had at the *Shri Prasad* (☎02594/233737; ❷–❸), halfway between the bus stand and the temple.

For food, you're more or less limited to one of the two **restaurants** on the main street which both serve adequate thalis and north Indian dishes. There's also **Internet** access at RajNet Café (Rs25/hr) towards the top of the main street.

Nagpur and around

Capital of the "land of oranges" and geographically at the virtual centre of India, **NAGPUR** is the focus of government attempts to develop industry in the remote and tribal northeastern corner of Maharashtra – most foreigners in the city are there for business rather than aesthetic purposes. The trickle of visitors who do stop here tend to do so en route to the Gandhian ashrams at **Sevagram** and **Paunar**, near **Wardha** (77km southwest). The other worthwhile excursion is the ninety-minute bus ride northeast to the hilltop temple complex at **Ramtek**.

In the city itself, the most prominent landmark is the **Sitabuldi Fort**, standing on a saddle between two low hills above the railway station. Strengthened by the British in the wake of the 1857 Mutiny, its ramparts and monuments were later annexed by the Indian army and are now closed to the public. North and west of the fort, the **Civil Lines** district holds some grand Raj-era buildings and bungalows, dating from the era when this was the capital of the vast Central Provinces region.

If you have an evening to fill, take an auto-rickshaw out to the **Ambazari Bagh**, the large artificial lake and gardens 5km southwest of the railway station, for a row and a chai at its waterside cafés.

Practicalities

Nagpur's busy central mainline **railway station**, Nagpur Junction, is a short auto-rickshaw ride from the main hotel and market districts along Central Avenue. MSRTC **buses** pull in at the state bus stand, a further 1.5km southeast of the railway station. Buses to and from Madhya Pradesh use the smaller MPSRTC bus stand, five minutes' walk south down the main road outside the station. If you're in a rush to get away, Indian Airlines (☎0712/253 3962) runs **flights** to Mumbai daily, as does Jet (☎0712/561 7888), and on certain days to Delhi, Kolkata (Calcutta) and Hyderabad.

The MTDC **tourist office** (daily 10am–6pm; ☎0712/253 3325), in the Sanskrutik Bachat Bhavan building, Sitabuldi, can book other MTDC accommodation but will disappoint if you're seeking specific information relating to

Nagpur. At the helpful MPTDC tourist office, on the fourth floor of the Lokmat Building, Wardha Road (Mon–Fri 10am–5pm; ☏0712/252 3324), you can book accommodation for Pachmarhi (see p.414) and for Kanha National Park (see p.446). The **GPO** is on Palm Road, in the Civil Lines, 4km west of the centre. **Banks** that deal in foreign exchange include the State Bank of India on Kingsway, near the railway station.

Accommodation

Most of Nagpur's **places to stay** are across the big railway bridge east of the station, along Central Avenue, or southwest of the fort around Sitabuldi, in the central bazaar.

Blue Moon Opposite Mayo Hospital, Central Ave ☏0712/272 6061, ✉micron@bom3.vsnl.net.in. Nearest to the station and definitely the least seedy of the cheapies; clean enough, and welcoming, with large doubles. ❷–❸

Centre Point 24 Central Bazaar Rd ☏0712/242 0910, ✉rooms@centrepointgroup.org. The most established of Nagpur's top hotels, with all the trimmings you'd expect from a three-star, plus a pool. ❼–❽

Hardeo Dr Munje Margi Marg, Sitabuldi ☏0712/252 9115, ✉hardeo_ngp@sancharnet.in. Three-star business hotel near the fort that's one of the city's top places to stay, though showing signs of wear. Quality restaurant, spacious and comfortable a/c rooms, bar and 24hr coffee shop. ❽

Skylark 119 Central Ave ☏0712/272 4654, ℱ272 6193. Close to railway station and best value in its class, with cable TV in all rooms and a good restaurant, though a tad grubby and marred by traffic noise. Some credit cards accepted. ❹–❺

Eating

While Nagpur's swish hotels boast the majority of its top **restaurants**, a number of smaller, less pretentious places to eat around Central Avenue and Sitabuldi offer excellent food at a fraction of the cost.

The Grill Ground floor of *Skylark Hotel*. Slightly more expensive than average but fine, quality veg and non-veg dishes are served by black-tie waiters in a comfy a/c dining room. Live *ghazals* every evening from 8.30pm. Most mains Rs125–250.

Naivedhyam Off Rani Jhansi Chowk, Sitabuldi. Respectable first-floor family restaurant serving delicious veg food (Chinese, Indian and Continental) to a background of Hindi-Hawaiian music. Mains Rs75–185.

Parnakuti North Ambazari Rd, Daga Layout, on the outskirts near the lake. Attractive restaurant noted for ersatz rustic decor and authentic, village-style Maharashtran cooking. Hard to find (most rickshaw-wallahs know the way) but well worth it. Unlimited thalis Rs175.

Shivraj Central Ave, near *Blue Moon*. Tasty and cheap south Indian snacks and thalis, especially good for breakfast as it opens at 7am.

Ramtek

The picturesque cluster of whitewashed hilltop temples and shrines at **RAMTEK**, 40km northeast of Nagpur on the main Jabalpur road (NH-7), is one of those alluring apparitions you spy from afar on long journeys through central India. According to the Ramayana, this craggy, scrub-strewn outcrop was the spot where Rama, Sita and Lakshmana paused on their way back from Lanka. It is also allegedly the place where the greatest-ever Sanskrit poet and playwright, **Kalidasa**, penned the fifth-century *Meghdoota*, "the Cloud Messenger". Although few traces of these ancient times have survived (most of Ramtek's temples date from the eighteenth century), the site's old paved pilgrim trails, sacred lake, tumbledown shrines and fine views across the endless plains more than live up to its distant promise.

Buses from Nagpur stop short of **Ram Mandir** (the temple complex) at Ramtek town, from whose fringes a flight of stone steps climbs steeply up the

side of Ramtek hill. Built in 1740 by Raghoji I, the Bhonsla ruler of Nagpur, the temple stands on the site of an earlier structure erected between the fourth and fifth centuries, of which only three small sandstone shrines remain. Next to the temple stands the circular Kalidas Smarak (daily 8.30am–8pm; Rs5), a modern memorial to the great poet whose interior walls are decorated with painted panels depicting scenes from his life and works.

Another of Ramtek's sacred sites is **Ambala Lake**, a holy bathing tank 1500m on foot from the hilltop. To pick up the flagstone pathway that leads down to it, head along the concourse opposite the temple's main entrance porch to the edge of the plateau. From here, either turn left towards the small **Trivikarma Krishna temple**, clinging to the north slope of the hill, or continue down the main pilgrims' trail to the **lake**, which lies at the bottom of the gully, enfolded by a spur of parched brown hills. Its main attractions are the temples and *ghats* clinging to its muddy banks. More energetic visitors may wish to combine a look with a *parikrama*, or circular **tour** of the tank, taking in the semi-derelict cenotaphs and weed-choked shrines scattered along the more tranquil north and western shores. A rickshaw (around Rs40–50) will get you back to Gandhi Chowk – the drivers hang around by the chai shop near the entrance.

Practicalities

Direct **buses** leave Nagpur (MSRTC stand) every thirty minutes for the hour-long trip to Ramtek. Long-distance MPSRTC buses also pass by en route to and from Jabalpur, although these will dump you on the main road at Mansar, 6km from Ramtek. If you don't feel like hiking up to the temple, **auto-rickshaws** will whisk you up from the town bus stand via Ambala Lake for Rs80 to Rs100. A pleasant alternative to these is to take a **bicycle**, which are available for rent near the bus stand (Rs5/hr). Ramtek's **railway** station, 4km from the town centre, connects with Nagpur, but this service takes longer than the bus.

Apart from the mosquito-infested pilgrims' *dharamshalas* and ashrams around Ambala Lake, the only **accommodation** near the sights is the *Rajkamal Resort* (☎07114/255620; ❸–❹) on the hill beside the main temple complex, offering simple but clean self-contained rooms, some with air-contioning. The hotel's multi-cuisine restaurant is also the best place to eat for miles.

Sevagram

SEVAGRAM, Gandhi's model "Village of Service", is set deep in the serene Maharashtran countryside, 9km from the railroad town of **WARDHA**. The Mahatma moved here from his former ashram at Sabarmati in Gujarat during the monsoon of 1936, on the invitation of his friend Seth Jamnalal Bajaj. Right at the centre of the Subcontinent, within easy reach of the Central Railway, it made an ideal headquarters for the national, nonviolent *Satyagraha* movement, combining seclusion with the easy access to other parts of the country Gandhi needed in order to carry out his political activities.

These days, the small settlement is a cross between a museum and living centre for the promulgation of Gandhian philosophies. Interested visitors are welcome to spend a couple of days here, helping in the fields, attending discussions and prayer meetings (daily 4.45am, 10am & 6pm; bring mosquito repellent for the last), and learning the dying art of hand-spinning. The older ashramites, or **sadhaks**, are veritable founts of wisdom when it comes to the words of their guru, Gandhiji.

Once past the **visitors' centre** (daily except Tues 10am–6pm), with its photos and documents relating to Gandhi's life, the real focal-point of the ashram is the main compound. These modest rustic **huts** – among them the Mahatma's main residence – have been preserved exactly the way they were when the great man and his disciples lived here in the last years of the Independence struggle.

Practicalities

Half-hourly local **buses** run from Wardha – on the Central Railway and accessible from Mumbai (759km) – to the crossroads outside the Kasturba Gandhi Hospital, from where it's a one-kilometre walk to the ashram. There are frequent "express" buses from Nagpur's MSRTC bus stand (2hr).

Accommodation is limited to the ashram's own *Yatri Niwas* (℡07152/222172; donations), a basic but spotless hostel for those staying at the ashram; it's not really a hotel, but phone to see what they have. If you decide to stay and learn something of Gandhi and the philosophy of nonviolence, you can sleep and eat here for no charge, though you'll be expected to do a couple of hours' communal work a day.

Paunar

Vinoba Bhave's ashram at **PAUNAR**, 10km by road south of Wardha on the Nagpur Road, has an altogether more dynamic feel than its more famous cousin at Sevagram. Bhave, a close friend and disciple of Gandhi, best remembered for his successful Bhoodan or **"land gift"** campaign to persuade wealthy landowners to hand over farmland to the poor, founded the ashram in 1938 to develop the concept of **swarajya**, or "self-sufficiency". Consequently, organic gardening, milk production, spinning and weaving have an even higher profile here than the regular meditation, prayer and yoga sessions. Another difference between this institution and the one up the road is that the *sadhaks* here are almost all female.

In the ashram's living quarters, Bhave's old **room** is kept as a shrine. Stone steps lead down from the upper level to a small terrace looking out over the **ghats**, where two small memorials mark the spots where a handful of Gandhi's, and later Bhave's, ashes were scattered onto the river: Gandhi's is the circular plinth at the end of the long, narrow jetty, Bhave's the brass urn on the small stupa-shaped dome to the right. Every year, on January 30, the *ghats*, which are immersed by floods for four months during the monsoon, are inundated with half a million people who come here to mark the anniversary of Gandhi's death.

Practicalities

Paunar can be reached by **bus** from either Nagpur (67km) or Wardha by hopping off at the old stone bridge near the ashram. Alternatively, you can **walk** the 3km from Sevagram. The path, a cart track that runs over the hill opposite the hospital crossroads, comes out in the roadside village 1km west of the Paunar ashram.

As with Sevagram, it is possible to **stay** at Paunar in one of the visitors' rooms or dorms (donation). These are frequently booked up during conferences or seminars, so check when you arrive. Women are given preference if space is short. **Meals**, made from organic, home-grown produce, are available on request.

Southern Maharashtra

The southern part of Maharashtra, dividing Mumbai and Goa, ranks among the areas of the country least explored by outsiders. Yet its scattered towns and cities hold lots of traditional Maharashtran character, while the landscape – a mix of rugged, table-top hills and palm-fringed coast cut by countless rivers and estuaries – is as diverse as any in south India.

Until the mid-nineteenth century, this was the homeland of the Maratha warlords, who at the peak of their power in the 1700s ruled over a vast swath of the Subcontinent – from the foothills of the Himalayas to the southernmost fringes of the Deccan plateau – and were a thorn in the southern flank of successive Mughal emperors. It wasn't until the British subjugated them in the Battle of Khadki in 1817 that the rich volcanic soils of the Deccan could be opened up and a railway line built through the Sahyadri Hills, supplying the world with cotton when its main source was interrupted by the American Civil War.

The same route, now carved up by an eight-lane "Expressway" and superfast electrified rail line, has been a strategically important trade artery since ancient times. A series of magnificent rock-cut caves dating from the first century BC attest for its former prominence. Along with the quirky, Raj-era hill station of Matheran, these archeological sites, the largest concentration of them around the hill town of Lonvala, provide the main incentive to break the journey inland to Pune, the former Maratha capital and booming, modern industrial centre. Some of the region's most awesome forts crown hilltops around the city, but its principal visitor attractions – a well-stocked museum and Peshwa palace – lie amid the streets of its atmospheric old town, most of whose male residents still wear old-style Nehru caps and *dhotis*.

Maratha citadels also punctuate the journey south via the Konkan Coast, the most striking of them at Murud-Janjira, which rises seamlessly from the waves and was virtually the only fortress never conquered by the Mughals. Further south still, Ganpatipule is the region's chief pilgrimage centre, where you can walk on miles of virtually deserted, palm-fringed beaches. By the time you reach Kolhapur, the main town in the far south of the state, famous for its temple and Raj-era Maharaja's palace, Mumbai feels a world away.

The Konkan Coast

Despite the recent appearance of a string of upscale resorts pitched at wealthy urbanites, the coast stretching south from Mumbai, known as the **Konkan**, remains relatively unspoilt. Empty beaches, backed by casuarina and areca trees and coconut plantations, regularly slip in and out of view, framed by the distant Ghats, while little fortified towns preserve a distinct coastal culture, with its own dialect of Marathi and fiery cuisine. The number of rivers and estuaries slicing the coast meant that for years this little-explored area was difficult to navigate, but the Konkan railway, which winds inland between Mumbai and Kerala via Goa, now renders it easily accessible.

Murud-Janjira

The first interesting place to break the journey south is the quiet port of **MURUD-JANJIRA**, 165km south of Mumbai. A traditional trade centre

formerly belonging to a dynasty of former Abyssinian slaves known as the Siddis, it still features plenty of attractive wood-built houses, some brightly painted and fronted by pillared verandas. The gently shelving beach is wide and safe for swimming, though the sand is cleaner and softer 3km north in **Kashid**. Five kilometres south, an imposing sixteenth-century **fort**, built on an island in the river, was one of the few the Marathas failed to penetrate. You can reach it by local *hodka* boat (around Rs50–75) from the jetty at the southern end of town – an excellent excursion – or by *tempo*. The 1661 Kasa Fort sits in the open sea 2km off the beach but cannot be visited, nor can the impressive nineteenth-century palace of the last Nawab, which dominates the northern end of the bay. Fine views of the coast and surrounding countryside can be had, however, from the hilltop **Dattatreya Temple**, sporting an Islamic-style tower but dedicated to the triple-headed deity comprising Brahma, Vishnu and Shiva.

Murud-Janjira practicalities

The nearest railhead to Murud is Roha, a two-hour bus ride away, which is why most travellers still reach the town by jumping on one of the hydrofoil catamarans or regular diesel launches from the Gateway of India in Mumbai to **Mandawa**, on the southern side of the harbour. Buses meet the boats and shuttle passengers straight to Alibag, from where you can catch regular government buses to Murud. Most direct bus services from Mumbai Central take six hours; there are also two faster ASIAD buses (5.45am & 11am; 4hr 30min) which must be booked in advance. Don't jump out prematurely at the inland bus stand but continue to Murud's main street, Durbar Road, parallel to the coast, where you'll find the tiny post office, covered market, and a handful of basic restaurants.

The best of the accommodation is also lined up along Durbar Road. Slap on the sands, the *Golden Swan Resort* (℡02144/274078, ⊛www.goldenswan .com; ❼–❽) sits on the edge of town and is the most comfortable option, with smart a/c chalets and less appealing non-a/c rooms in an older colonial-style block, plus a restaurant serving local Malvani cuisine. Opposite is the newer *Club Leisure Shoreline* (℡02144/274640; ❻–❼), which has more recently fitted rooms and marginally lower tariffs. Further north up Durbar Road, the *Mirage Holiday Homes* (℡02144/276744; ❺–❻) occupies an attractive period building, with more character than the competition. *The Nest Bamboo House* (℡02144/276144; ❹), which has simple palm-thatch and bamboo huts fitted with beds, lights and fans, is the only decent budget option.

All of these places serve food, but there is no shortage of regular, clean and inexpensive local **eating options** on Durbar Road, including the *Anand Vatika*, south of the *chowk*, which serves south Indian veg snacks and fuller North Indian meals in a shady garden, and the *Hotel Vinayak*, whose menu is more extensive in theory than practice. In addition, a row of seafront stalls south of the *chowk* dish up tasty seafood and veg snacks.

Ganpatipule

Two hundred and fifteen kilometres south of Marud-Janjira lies the Konkan Coast's other commendable stopover, **GANPATIPULE**, a tiny village with a long, golden sandy beach and a modern **Ganapati temple**. Although attracting thousands of Indian pilgrims each year, this sleepy place sees relatively few foreign visitors, with most of the tourists being pilgrims or honeymooners from Mumbai. The temple is built around a Ganapati *omnar*, a naturally formed – though not strictly accurate – image of the elephant god.

There are plenty of accommodation options, the most idiosyncratic of them the *Shiv Sagar Palace* (℡02357/235070, ⊛www.shivsagarpalace.com; ❺–❻), on

a hilltop a kilometre back from the coast. Housed in a sprawling, red-, white-and yellow-painted mansion, complete with ornamental domes, a grand, curved staircase, acres of marble floors and some of the most kitsch interior decor you'll ever set eyes on, the hotel has a surreal quality that some will enjoy. Alternatively, there's the more run-down, government-owned MTDC *Resort* (☎02357/235248, ℱ235328; ❹–❺), offering uninspiring a/c chalet rooms and "cottages", as well as cheaper tent accommodation – all a stone's throw from the beach. Two cheaper options, both on the approach road to the beach, are the *Shri Ganesh Kripa* (☎02357/235229; ❹), with basic attached rooms, and the *Shreesagar* (☎02357/235145; ❺), which has clean compact doubles. For **food**, the *Shiv Sagar* has a mid-price multi-cuisine restuarant (in a typically vast pillared hall) that's open to nonresidents, while the *Shri Ganesh Kripa* rustles up mainly Punjabi specialities; there's also a handful of cheap *dhabas* at the bottom of the village towards the main road.

To get to Ganpatipule, either make your way to Ratnagiri (on the Konkan railway and well connected by state and private buses) and take a local bus (10 daily; 1–1hr 30min) the last 32km, or catch one of the direct MSRTC services from Mumbai, Pune or Kolhapur. All the buses stop outside the MTDC resort.

Matheran

The little hill station of **MATHERAN**, 108km east of Mumbai, is set on a narrow north–south ridge, at an altitude of 800m in the Sahyadri Range. From viewpoints with such names as Porcupine, Monkey and Echo, at the edge of sheer cliffs that plunge into deep ravines, you can see way across the hazy plains – on a good day, so they say, as far as Mumbai. The town itself, shrouded in thick mist for much of the year, has, for the moment, one unique attribute: cars, buses, motorbikes and auto-rickshaws are prohibited. That, added to the journey up, on a **miniature train** that chugs its way through spectac-ular scenery to the crest of the hill, gives the town an agreeably quaint, time-warped feel.

Matheran (literally "mother forest") has been a popular retreat from the heat of Mumbai since the nineteenth century. These days, however, few foreign visitors venture up here, and those that do only hang around for a couple of days, to kill time before a flight or to sample the Raj-era charms of Matheran's colonial-style hotels. The tourist season lasts from mid-September to mid-June (at other times it's raining or misty), and is at its most hectic between November and January, in April and May, and over virtually any weekend. There's really nothing up here to do but relax, wander the woods on foot or horseback, and enjoy the fresh air and views.

757

As the crow flies, Matheran is only 6.5km from Neral on the plain below, but the train climbs up on 21km of track with no less than 281 curves, said to be among the sharpest on any railway in the world. After 1907, the demanding haul was handled by four complex steam engines. Sadly, they puffed their last in 1980 and were replaced by cast-off diesels from Darjeeling, Shimla and Ooty. The two-hour train ride is a treat, especially if you get a window seat, but be prepared for a squash and hard benches.

In 1974, the All India Rail Strike cut Matheran off. To combat the situation, the track from Neral was made passable for Jeeps and finally in 1984 was sealed up to Dasturi Naka, 2km from the town, though any attempts to extend it through the town have been thwarted by the encouragingly ecofriendly local authorities.

Arrival and information

To reach Matheran by **rail**, you must first get to **Neral Junction** (1hr 30min–2hr 15min), served by frequent overground metro trains from CST and Dadar (terminating at Karjat, also spelled "Karghat" or "Karzat"). The only fast service scheduled to stop at Neral is the daily Deccan Express #1007 (dep. 7.10am), which gets there 45 minutes quicker than the metro. Travelling in the opposite direction from **Pune** (2hr 30min–3hr), the Deccan Express #1008 (dep. 3.30pm) is again the only fast train that pauses at Neral, though plenty so stop at Karjat, from where you can backtrack on suburban services.

At the time of writing (after a period of prolonged disruption while work was carried out on the line to repair flood damage) three narrow-gauge trains each day chugged up from Neral to **Matheran** (2hr), departing at 8.50am, 10.15am and 5pm. Two more services are planned, and there is generally an extra one at weekends. All trains are timed to tie in with incoming mainline expresses, so don't worry about missing a connection if one you're on is delayed – the toy train should wait. Matheran **station** is in the centre of the hill station on MG Road, which runs roughly north–south. Leaving town, there is a little halt on the miniature railway near the Dasturi Naka taxi stand but, unless you've already booked a seat, you won't be allowed on.

All **motor transport**, including shared taxis and minibuses from Neral (Rs60 per person, Rs275 for car), parks at the taxi stand next to the MTDC *Holiday Camp* at Dasturi Naka. From here you can walk with a porter (Rs60–70), be led by horse (Rs100–125), or take a hand-pulled rickshaw (Rs130–150) – now the only place left in India where such rickshaws are officially permitted. If you're happy to carry your own bags, follow the rail tracks, which cut straight to the middle of Matheran, rather than the more convoluted dirt road. However you arrive, you must pay a **toll** (Rs25) to enter the town, valid for your entire stay.

Accommodation and eating

Matheran has plenty of **hotels**, though few could be termed cheap. Most are close to the railway station on MG Road and on the road behind it, Kasturba Bhavan. Reduced rates of up to fifty percent often apply to midweek or long stays, and

Money in Matheran

It's worth noting that there is **no ATM** in Matheran, nor anywhere to **change money**. Bring enough cash to see you through your stay, or you could find yourself stranded.

▲ The miniature train to Matheran

during the rainy off-season (when many places close down). Note that 10am or 11am checkouts are standard. Single men travellers should brace themselves for a long room-hunt: in 2005, the local Municipality issued a directive stating that hotels in the town should refuse beds to unaccompanied males ("stags"). The reason: so many were coming to the hill station from Mumbai to kill themselves. This applies in particular to places at the lower end of the scale.

Virtually all the hotels provide **full** or **half-board** at reasonable rates, but if you want to eat out, or are on a tight budget, try one of the numerous thali joints around the station or tasty kebab and tikka dishes at *Hookahs'N'Tikkas*, also on MG Road.

Bombay View north Matheran, southwest of Paymaster Park ☎02148/230453. Housed in a huge converted colonial-era mansion, this place is the best budget option in town; it's a notch pricier than the more basic places down by the station, but well worth the extra. Most of its rooms are enormous, with high ceilings, sit-outs and forest or garden views, and the staff are friendly and

helpful. Advance booking recommended on weekends. ③–④

Hope Hall MG Rd ☎02148/230253, opposite *Lord's Central*. Decent-sized, clean, attached rooms arranged around a secluded yard with badminton and table tennis, at the quiet end of town. Among the few commendable budget options this close to the station. ④

🏃 **Lord's Central** MG Rd ☏ 02148/230228, Ⓦ www.matheran.com. With its verandas, brown-painted woodwork, plaid blankets and friendly spaniel, *Lord's* is the kind of place you imagine the Famous Five might have spent their holidays in the 1930s. Though it does boast spectacular views from its garden (where they've recently installed a pool), it lacks the elegance of *The Verandah in the Forest*. Full board only (Rs1500–2100 per night; 30 percent discounts for stays of 2 nights or more); booking recommended. ❽

Pramod Lodge Just south of the railway station ☏ 09521 48230144. This is where all the porters and touts will try to take you, because it hands out commission. The rooms aren't great, but would do as a fallback option for a night. ❸

🏃 **The Verandah in the Forest** 2km southwest of station ☏ 02148/230296, Ⓦ www.neemranahotels.com. Set in woods a short way above Charlotte Lake, this sumptuously restored nineteenth-century bungalow is reason enough to come to Matheran. Apart from the evocative period decor and furnishings, its greatest asset is a huge west-facing veranda smothered in foliage – one of the most perfect spots in India for afternoon tea and biscuits (though if you eat here beware of the pilfering monkeys). Rooms are reasonably priced. ❽–❾

The points and forest walks

Matheran occupies a long, narrow, semicircular plateau, bounded for most of its extent by sheer cliffs. These taper at regular intervals into outcrops, or **points**, revealing through the tree canopy wonderful panoramas of distant hills and plains. Few visitors manage more than half a dozen in a single outing, but in midwinter when temperatures are pleasantly cool, it's possible to tick off the majority in a long day's trek.

For a quick taster, head south from the main bazaar past *Lord's Central Hotel* on Matheran's eastern flank to Alexander Point, pressing on beyond it to Chowk Point – the most southerly of the mountain's spurs. This shouldn't take more than a couple of hours there and back. Another enjoyable route on an old cart track winds around the western rim, past a series of gorgeous British-era bungalows to Louisa, Coronation and Porcupine Points – a trip best saved for late afternoon.

Accurate topographical maps of the mountain and its many paths are all but impossible to come by, although hanging proudly in the dining room of Lord's Central Hotel is a wonderful old British one, which walkers are welcome to consult.

Lonavala and around

Just thirty years ago, the town of **LONAVALA**, 110km southeast of Mumbai and 62km northwest of Pune, was a quiet retreat in the Sahyadri hills. Since then, the place has mushroomed to cope with hordes of holiday-makers and second-home owners from the state capital, and is now only of interest as a base for the magnificent **Buddhist caves** of **Karla**, **Bhaja** and **Bedsa**, some of which date from the Satavahana period (second century BC).

Arrival and information

Frequent buses arrive at Lonavala's central **bus stand**, just off the old Mumbai–Pune Road, but the train is infinitely preferable. Lonavala is on the main railway line between Mumbai (3hr) and Pune (1hr 30min), and most express trains stop here. The **railway station** is on the south side of town, a ten-minute walk from the bus stand area; take the path right at the end of platform one to get there. With a car, or by taking an early train, it's just about

Bollywood and beyond

Film is massive in India. The country produces more movies than anywhere else in the world (around 1200 every year), while the fact that many Indian households still lack televisions ensures a huge and devoted cinema-going public. Although the traditional image of Indian film as a melodramatic medley of outlandishly choreographed musical sequences, badly dubbed songs, hamfisted overacting and wet saris persists, modern Indian movies are increasingly beginning to challenge these cinematic stereotypes, and to feature acting, scripts and production values that are on a par with anything made in the West.

possible to take in the caves as a day-trip from Mumbai, but it's better to allow yourself a full day to get around.

Several of the banks around town have **ATMs**, though none have foreign exchange facilities. There's a small **Internet** café, Balaji's, on the road running south from the railway station (Rs40/hr).

Accommodation

With a couple of exceptions, Lonavala's limited **accommodation** offers poor value, mainly because demand well outstrips supply for much of the year. Rates drop between October and March, and for longer stays, and you can expect reductions on weekdays. But this isn't somewhere you're likely to want to unpack your bags.

Adarsh Behind the bus stand on Shivaji Rd ☏02114/272353. Clean a/c and non-a/c rooms, some overlooking a central courtyard. Best fallback in this bracket if the *Chandralok* has no vacancies. ❻–❼

Chandralok Opposite the bus stand on Shivaji Rd ☏02114/272294, ⓦwww.hotelchandralok.net. Set back from the market street, this well-run mid-range place has good-sized, well-aired, modern rooms with shiny ceramic tiled floors, plus a quality thali restaurant at ground level. ❺

Ferreira Resort D Shahani Rd, Ward C, nr Telephone Exchange, a 5min rickshaw ride from the train and bus stands ☏02114/272689. The one budget place worthy of mention: a pleasantly old-fashioned place located down a quiet suburban backstreet. Its rooms are all attached, peaceful and clean, and have little balconies opening on to a leafy rear plot. ❹

The Metropole Close to the bus stand on Shivaji Rd ☏02114/273808, ⓦwww.hotelthemetropole.com. This smart new four-star is Lonavala's most comfortable option, boasting central a/c and modern furnishings, as well as a rooftop pool and ersatz "Punjabi-dhaba" restaurant. ❼–❽

Shahani Health Home D Shahani Rd, 5min rickshaw ride east of the railway station ☏02114/272784,. A quirky, not-for-profit place offering 62 large rooms in a worn, rather institutional block on the quiet edge of town; worth trying if the *Ferreira Resort* opposite is full, but not nearly as congenial. ❸–❹

Eating

Most of Lonavala's hotels lay on full board or have serviceable **restaurants**, but you'll eat fresher food in places along the main street, which cater more for the brisk through-trade. The town also holds a bewildering number of shops selling the local sweet speciality, **chikki** – a moreish amalgam of dried fruit and nuts set in rock-solid honey toffee. *Super Chikki* on the main street allows you to sample the many varieties before you buy. Their main competitor, *National Chikki*, further down, is also recommended; this is also the best place to stock up on delicious deep-fried nibbles (*namkeen*), the other local speciality.

Guru Krippa Mumbai–Pune Rd. Sparkling, clean pure-veg joint on the main street: piping-hot south Indian snacks, cheese toasties, and inexpensive thalis with Chinese and Punjabi main meals. Also a good selection of ice creams, kulfi and full-on *faloodas*.

Kumar's Mumbai–Pune Rd. A big, bustling place with surreal English-country-house-theme murals that gets packed out on weekends for its great Mughlai and tandoori specialities: try the delicious *murg handi* (Mughlai-style boneless chicken) mopped up with hot naan bread. Most dishes come in shiny copper *karais*, snappily served by waiters in black ties and baggy tartan waistcoats. They also do cold beers, and terrific mixed dry-fruit and rose-flavoured lassis. Count on Rs200–275 per head.

Shabri *Hotel Rama Krishna*, Mumbai–Pune Rd. Along with *Kumar's*, this is the well-heeled Mumbaikars' favourite, serving a wide range of North and south Indian dishes, and chilled beer, in a large, busy ground-floor dining hall. Most mains under Rs150.

Smokin' Joe's Overbridge Rd, just off the main Mumbai–Pune Rd. A huge range of freshly baked pizzas, from Rs100 to Rs300 (depending on size and toppings), served up on modern wood tables in a snug a/c restaurant with big glass windows.

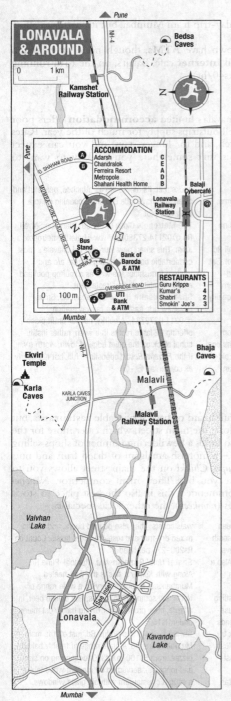

The Buddhist caves of Karla, Bhaja and Bedsa

The three cave sites of **Karla**, **Bhaja** and **Bedsa** comprise some of the finest rock-cut architecture in the northwest of the Deccan region. Though not on nearly such an impressive scale as Ajanta and Ellora, they harbour some beautifully preserved ancient sculpture.

The three sites lie some way from each other, all to the east of Lonavala. As Karla contains the most spectacular sculpture, it's best left until last. Covering Karla and Bhaja under your own steam by bus and/or train is manageable in a day, if you are prepared for a good walk, but if you want to get out to Bedsa, too, the easiest option is to rent an **auto-rickshaw** (around Rs300–400) or **car** (Rs600–700 for 4hr) for the tour, both of which can usually be found at Lonavala railway station. Finally, it's a good idea to avoid weekends if you want to enjoy the caves in peace and quiet; Karla, in particular, gets swamped with noisy day-trippers.

Bhaja

The eighteen **caves** (daily 8.30am–6pm; $2 [Rs10]) at **BHAJA** lie 1.5km from the village of Malavli, to which hourly passenger trains run from Lonavala (9km west). To reach the caves, follow a path up from the village square near the railway station.

The excavations are among the oldest in India, dating from the late second to early first century BC, during the earliest, Hinayana, phase of Buddhism. Most consist of simple halls – *viharas* – with adjoining cells that contain plain shelf-like beds;

many are fronted by rough verandas. Bhaja's apsidal *chaitya* hall, **Cave 12**, which contains a stupa but no figures, has 27 plain bevelled pillars which lean inwards, mimicking the style of wooden buildings. Sockets in the stone of the exterior arch reveal that it once contained a wooden gate or facade. Further south, the last cave, **Cave 19**, a *vihara*, is decorated with superb carvings. Mysteriously, scholars identify the figures as the Hindu gods, **Surya** and **Indra**, who figure prominently in the *Rig Veda* (*c.* 1000 BC).

Karla

KARLA (also Karli) is 3km north of **Karla Caves Junction** on the Mumbai–Pune Road and 11km from Lonavala. Take any bus or *tempo* to the junction (from where it's a Rs30–40 rickshaw ride), or there are five daily **buses** (6am, 9am, 12.30pm, 3pm & 6.30pm) that head for the caves directly from Lonavala, with the last bus returning from Karla at 6.30pm.

The rock-cut Buddhist **chaitya** hall at Karla (daily 8.30am–6pm; $2 [Rs10]), reached by steep steps that climb 110m, is the largest and best preserved in India, dating from the first century AD. As you approach across a large courtyard, itself hewn from the rock, the enormous fourteen-metre-high facade of the hall towers above, topped by a horseshoe-shaped window and with three entrances below, one for the priest and the others for devotees. To the left of the entrance stands a *simhas stambha*, a tall column capped with four lions. On the right is a Hindu shrine to **Ekviri**, a goddess-oracle revered by Koli fishing communities, for whom Karla is a popular weekend day-trip destination (which explains the number of puja-offering stalls and opportunistic political posters lining the steps).

In the porch of the cave, dividing the three doorways, are panels of figures in six couples, presumed to have been the wealthy patrons of the hall. With their expressive faces and sensuous bodies, it's hard to believe these figures were carved around 2000 years ago. Two rows of octagonal columns with pot-shaped bases divide the interior into three, forming a wide central aisle and, on the outside, a hall that allowed devotees to circumambulate the monolithic stupa at the back. Above each pillar's fluted capital kneels a finely carved elephant mounted by two riders, one with arms draped over the other's shoulders. Amazingly, perishable remnants survive from the time when the hall was in use.

Bedsa

It's quite possible that you won't encounter anyone else when visiting the caves at **BEDSA** (daily 8.30am–6pm; $2 [Rs10]), which is one of its great attractions. Once you reach the village, 12km beyond Bhaja on the NH-4, or a three-kilometre bus ride from Kamshet, the nearest railway station, you'll have to ask the way to the unsigned path. The village kids hanging around might scramble up the steep hillside with you, for a fee.

Bedsa's *chaitya* hall, excavated later than that at Karla, is far less sophisticated. The entrance is extremely narrow, leading from a porch which appears to be supported, though of course it is not, by four octagonal pillars more than 7m high, with pot-shaped bases and bell capitals; bulls, horses and elephants rest on inverted, stepped slabs on top. Inside, 26 plain octagonal columns lead to an unadorned monolithic stupa.

Pune (Poona)

At an altitude of 598m, **PUNE**, Maharashtra's second largest city, lies close to the Western Ghat mountains (known here as the Sahyadri hills), on the edge of the Deccan plains as they stretch away to the east. Capital of the Marathas' sovereign state in the sixteenth century, Pune was – thanks to its cool, dry climate – chosen by the British in 1820 as an alternative headquarters for the Bombay Presidency. Since colonial days, Pune has continued to develop as a major industrial city and now ranks along with Hyderabad, Bengaluru (Bangalore) and Chennai as one of south India's fastest growing business centres, with booming software, back-office and call-centre sectors. Signs of the new prosperity abound, from huge hoardings advertising multistorey executive apartment blocks and gated estates, to cappuccino bars, air-conditioned malls and hip clothes stores.

The full-on traffic and ultra-Westernized city centre may come as a shock if all you know about Pune is its connection with India's famously laid-back, New Age guru, Bhagwan Rajneesh, or **Osho** (1931–90). The spiritual teacher founded his ashram in the leafy suburb of Koregaon Park in 1974 and, although its activities nowadays generate a lot less publicity than they did during

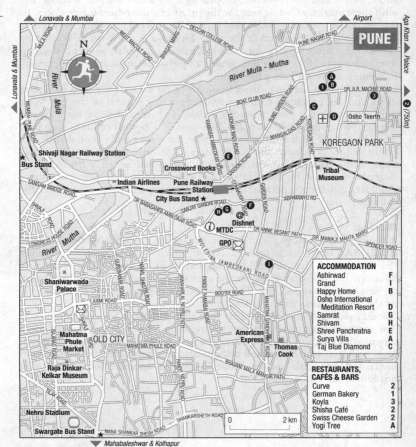

ACCOMMODATION

Ashirwad	F
Grand	I
Happy Home	B
Osho International Meditation Resort	D
Samrat	G
Shivam	H
Shree Panchratna	E
Surya Villa	A
Taj Blue Diamond	C

RESTAURANTS, CAFÉS & BARS

Curve	2
German Bakery	1
Koyla	3
Shisha Café	2
Swiss Cheese Garden	2
Yogi Tree	A

Rajneesh's lifetime, the centre continues to attract followers from all over the world. Pune's other main claim to spiritual fame is the presence on its outskirts of *yogacharya* **BKS Iyengar**'s illustrious yoga centre – a far more sober and serious institution than the Osho ashram (see Basics, p.71).

Arrival and information

From Pune's Lohagaon **airport**, 10km northeast of the centre, pre-paid taxis (around Rs200) and auto-rickshaws (Rs100–150) take between fifteen and thirty minutes to reach the centre, depending on the traffic. Pune is an important staging point on southern express-train routes from Mumbai (3hr 30min–4hr 30min); the main **railway station** is in the centre of town, south of the river.

There are three main **bus stands**: the City Bus Stand, next to the railway station, is split into two sections, one serving Pune itself (with signs and timetables only in Marathi), the other for destinations south and west, including Goa, Lonavala and Mumbai. Swargate Bus Stand, about 5km south, close to Nehru Stadium, services Karnataka and some of the same destinations as City, while the stand next to Shivaji Nagar railway station, 3km west of the centre, runs buses to towns in the north. To establish which station you require for your destination, ask at the enquiries hatch of the City Bus Stand.

Another source of travel information is the **MTDC Tourist Office** (Mon–Sat 10am–5.30pm; ☎0212/2612 6867), inside "I" block of Central Building (enter between Ambedkar Chowk and Sadhu Vaswani Circle). They also have an **information counter** (allegedly Mon–Fri 10am–6pm, Sat 10am–1pm; closed second & fourth Sat of month) opposite the railway station's first-class booking office.

There are ATMs all over the city these days. For changing currency or traveller's cheques, Thomas Cook is at 13 Thacker House, just off General Thimmaya Road (Mon–Sat 9.30am–6pm; ☎0212/613 8188); American Express have an office on MG Road (Mon–Fri 9.30am–6.30pm, Sat 9.30am–2.30pm; ☎0212/2605 5337). The very efficient **GPO** is on Sadhu Vasavani (Connaught) Road.

Manney's Booksellers, at 7 Moledina Rd, Clover Centre, and Crossword, on the first floor of Sohrab Hall (next to the *Hotel Shree Panchratna*), are the city's best bookstores. You can access the **Internet** in many places, including a 24-hour cybercafé on the first floor of the railway station (Rs30/hr), and Dishnet, five minutes' walk from the station on Connaught Road (Rs30/hr). If you're up near the Osho ashram in Koregaon Park, the best option is Zorba Net Surfing, on the ground floor of the *Hotel Surya Villa*, next to the *Yogi Tree Café* (only Rs20/hr).

Accommodation

Pune is short of decent **hotels** across the scale, which explains why, in keeping with most big cities in Maharashtra, prices are high for what you get and vacancies are like gold dust. Options are especially limited at the bottom of the range, where advance booking is all but essential. For information on staying at the Osho International Meditation Resort, see p.768.

Ashirwad 16 Connaught Rd ☎020/2612 8585, ⓔhotelashir@vsnl.com. Despite its proximity to a busy main road, this newish business hotel near the station is a quiet and relaxing choice. Its rooms are well aired, with sparkling white tiled floors and good-sized bathrooms. ❽

Grand MG Rd, near Dr Ambedkar statue at the top of MG Rd ☎020/2636 0728. The colonial-era

Grand, set behind a dimly lit beer garden, used to be most budget travellers' first choice, but it's gone drastically downhill in recent years. Despite the decrepit plumbing and overall shabbiness, the doubles in the rear annexe are bearable for a night or two, but forget the stinky wood-partitioned, bathroom-less singles off reception. ➍

Happy Home 294 Koregaon Park ☎020/2612 2933, ✉happyhomehostel @yahoo.co.im. Pune's nicest budget guesthouse: far more salubrious, better scrubbed, friendlier and more pleasant than anywhere else in its price bracket, *Happy Home* occupies a modern tenement in a surburban backstreet near the ashram – an area dominated by foreign Osho-ites. The rooms are all clean, have attached bathrooms and small balconies. Discounts for stays of more than two days. ➌–➍

Samrat 17 Wilson Garden, opposite railway station ☎020/2613 7964, ✉thesamrathotel@vsnl.com. Smart, centrally a/c tower block, with large, spotless rooms in galleries opening onto a central atrium. It's tucked away down a hidden backstreet a stone's throw from the railway station, but easy to find and offers superb value by Pune standards. ➐

Shivam 12 Wilson Garden, opposite railway station ☎020/2613 7593, ⓕ2605 3472. A lot less appealing inside than its spruce exterior suggests, but clean enough for a short stay, and the beds have good thick mattresses. Some a/c available. ➎–➏

Shree Panchratna 7 Tadiwala Rd ☎020/2605 9999, ⓦwww.hotelshreepanchratna.in. Plain but well-maintained and efficient business hotel close to the railway station, down a quiet side-street. The rooms are all a/c, bright, fresh and simply furnished, with shining tiled floors, small balconies and Wi-Fi-enabled desks. ➑

Surya Villa 284/1 Koregaon Park ☎020/2612 4501. Good-sized, attractively furnished rooms spread over four floors in a peaceful suburban block close to the Osho ashram. It's popular mainly with long-staying, foreign ashram-ites. ➎–➏

Taj Blue Diamond 11 Koregaon Rd ☎020/2612 5555, ⓦwww.tajhotels.com. 2km northeast of railway station near the Osho ashram. Pune's top business hotel offering the usual five-star facilities, including Indian and Thai restaurants, 24hr coffee shop, swimming pool, and shops. ➒

The City

Pune's centre is bordered to the north by the **River Mula** and to the west by the **River Mutha** – the two join in the northwest to form the Mutha-Mula, at Sangam Bridge. The principal shopping area, and the greatest concentration of restaurants and hotels, is in the streets south of the railway station, particularly Connaught and, further south, **MG Road**. The old Peshwa part of town, by far the most interesting to explore, is towards the west between the fortified **Shaniwarwada Palace** and fascinating **Raja Dinkar Kelkar Museum**; old wooden *wadas* – palatial city homes – survive on these narrow, busy streets, and the Victorian, circular **Mahatma Phule Market** is always a hive of activity.

Raja Dinkar Kelkar Museum

Dinkar Gangadhar Kelkar (1896–1990), aside from being a celebrated Marathi poet published under the name Adnyatwass, spent much of his life travelling and collecting arts and crafts from all over the country. In 1975, he donated his collection to the Maharashtran government for the creation of a museum dedicated to the memory of his son, Raja, who had died at the age of 12. Housed in a huge old-town mansion, the **Raja Dinkar Kelkar Museum** (daily 9.30am–6pm; Rs150 [Rs20]) at 1378 Shukrawar Peth (buses #72 or #74 from the railway station to Mahatma Phule Market) is a wonderful potpourri in which beauty and interest is found in both artistic and everyday objects. Paraphernalia associated with paan, the Indian passion, includes containers in every conceivable design, made from silk, wood, brass and silver: some mimic animals or fish, or are egg-shaped and in delicate filigree; others are solid, heavy-duty boxes built to withstand constant use. Also on show are musical instruments, superb Marathi textiles and costumes, toys, domestic shrines and furniture, beauty accessories and a model of Shaniwarwada Palace.

Shaniwarwada Palace

In the centre of the oldest part of town, only the imposing high walls of the **Shaniwarwada Palace** (daily 8am–noon & 2–6pm; US$2 [Rs10]) survived three fires in the eighteenth and nineteenth centuries. Founded by the Peshwa ruler Bajrao I in 1730 and the chief residence of the Peshwas until the British arrived in 1817, the building has little to excite interest today, though there's a daily **sound-and-light** show in English (7pm; Rs100). The entrance is through the Delhi gate on the north side, one of five set into the perimeter wall, whose huge teak doors come complete with nasty elephant-proof spikes. The interior of the palace is now grassed over, the seven-storey building entirely absent. Only one of the guides, usually available in the afternoons, speaks English. Bus #3 runs the 2km southwest from the railway station to the palace.

Aga Khan Palace and Gandhi Memorial

In 1942, Mahatma Gandhi, his wife Kasturba and other key figures of the freedom movement were interned at the **Aga Khan Palace** (daily 9am–5.30pm; Rs100 [Rs5]), which is set in quiet leafy gardens across the River Mula, 5km northeast of the centre (buses #1, #158 & #156). The Aga Khan donated the palace to the state in 1969, and it is now a small Gandhi museum, typical of many all over India, with captioned photos and simple rooms unchanged since they were occupied by the freedom fighters. A memorial behind the house commemorates Kasturba, who died during their imprisonment. A small *khadi* shop sells hand-loomed cloth and products made by village co-operatives.

Tribal Museum

The Tribal Research and Training Institute, which runs the **Tribal Museum** on Koregaon Road (Mon–Sat 10am–5pm; free), 2km east of the railway station, is dedicated to the protection and documentation of Maharashtra's numerous tribal groups, such as the Wagdheo, Bahiram, Danteshwari and Marai, who number more than five million. The museum's faded photos, costumes and artefacts serve as an excellent introduction to this little-known world, but the highlights are the wonderful collections of dance masks and Worli wedding paintings. Talk to the director of the museum if you're interested in guided (but culturally sensitive) **tours** to tribal areas.

Osho International Meditation Resort

Pune is the headquarters of the infamous **Osho International Meditation Resort**, 17 Koregaon Park Rd (☏0212/2401 9999, ⊛www.osho.com), 2km east of the railway station. Set amid forty acres of landscaped gardens and woodland, the ashram of the now-deceased New Age guru, Shri Bagwan Rajneesh (aka "Osho"; see box, p.768), comprises a dreamy playground of cafés, marble walkways, swimming pools, saunas and clinics, with a shop selling the Master's enormous list of books, DVDs and CDs. Courses at its Multiversity, mostly one to three days in duration (US$80–100 per day), are offered in a variety of therapies and meditation techniques. Forty-five-minute lunchtime demos are also available if you just want to dip your toe in. There are a host of other courses ranging from primal screaming to meditation techniques and more offbeat workshops with titles such as "Zen For Billionaires", "Chakra Magic" and "A Taste of Inner Chocolate".

This ecofriendly bubble follows a strict door policy: visitors who wish to spend longer than the short **guided tours** (daily 9.15am & 2pm; book the day before 9.30am–1pm & 2–4pm; Rs10) must produce two passport photos and an HIV-negative certificate no less than thirty days old. If you don't have one

Osho

It is nearly forty years since followers began to congregate around **Bhagwan Rajneesh**, the self-proclaimed New Age guru better known to his tens of thousands of acolytes worldwide as simply **Osho**. Underpinned by a philosophical mishmash of Buddhism, Sufism, sexual liberationism, Tantric practices, Zen, yoga, hypnosis, Tibetan pulsing, disco and unabashed materialism, the first Rajneesh ashram was founded in Pune in 1974. It rapidly attracted droves of Westerners, and some Indians, who adopted new Sanskrit names and a uniform of orange or maroon cottons and a bead necklace (*mala*) with an attached photo of the enlightened guru, in classic style, sporting long greying hair and beard.

Few early adherents denied that much of the attraction lay in Rajneesh's novel approach to fulfilment. His dismissal of Christianity ("Crosstianity") as a miserably oppressive obsession with guilt struck a chord with many, as did the espousal of liberation through sex. Rajneesh assured his devotees that material comfort was not to be shunned. Within a few years, satellite ashrams were popping up throughout Western Europe, and by 1980 an estimated 200,000 devotees had liberated themselves in six hundred meditation centres across eighty countries.

To protect itself from pollution, nuclear war and the AIDS virus, the organization poured money into a utopian project, **Rajneeshpuram**, on 64,000 acres of agricultural land in Oregon, USA. It was at this point that the tabloids and TV documentary teams really got interested in Rajneesh, now a multimillionaire. Infiltrators leaked stories of strange goings-on at Rajneeshpuram and before long its high-powered female executives became subject to police interest. Charges of tax evasion, drugs, fraud, arson and a conspiracy to poison several people in a neighbouring town to sway the vote in local elections provoked further sensation. Although he claimed to know nothing of this, Rajneesh pleaded guilty to breaches of US immigration laws and was deported in 1985. Following protracted attempts to resettle in 21 different countries, and now suffering complications of the chronic fatigue, ME, the Valium-addicted Rajneesh returned home to Pune, where he died in 1990, aged 59.

The ashram went through a period of internal squabbles and financial trouble in the 1990s. At his death, Rajneesh appointed an inner circle to manage the group, though several departed and the Osho "brand" – which sells around four million books each year, supplemented by CDs, DVDs, paintings and photos – is now controlled from Zurich and New York. The Pune ashram wasn't seeing enough of this to meet its costs and consequently has had to re-launch and re-style itself, changing both its name (from Osho Commune International to **Osho International Meditation Resort**) and the pattern of life inside its walls; whereas in its heyday an average stay was three to six months, today people typically stay no more than two weeks and few followers live on site.

and still want to stay there, you'll have to take an on-the-spot HIV test at the ashram clinic as part of your induction – the registration, HIV test and initial day-pass package costs Rs1350 for foreigners, after which it's Rs500 per day. You'll also need two robes (maroon for daywear, white for evenings). If you want to actually stay inside the ashram, the smart *Osho Guest House* (☎020/6601 9900; ❽) offers stylish, minimalist, Zen rooms – though be warned that the accommodation is situated above the main auditorium, which, as the ashram likes to put it, "can make the 6am Dynamic Meditation hard to resist".

The beautiful gardens laid out to the east of the main Osho complex, known as Osho Teerth, are open to the public (daily 6–9am & 3–6pm; admission free; no photography), and make a serene place for a stroll, with babbling streams, stands of giant bamboo, mature trees and Zen sculpture artfully placed amid the greenery.

Eating and drinking

Pune's affluent young things have money to burn these days, and new, innovative places to eat and drink open up every month to relieve them of their info-tech salaries. The largest concentration is up in Koregaon Park, where **ABC Farms**, a ten-minute rickshaw ride from the *Taj Blue Diamond*, encompasses seven or eight of the hippest cafés, bars and restaurants, grouped in a single enclave. The best of them are reviewed below, along with Pune's more established eateries. As with most Indian boom cities, everywhere of note gets jam-packed on weekends, when you'll need to book well in advance to be sure of a table.

Curve ABC Farms, Koregaon Park. Candle-lit outdoor pub, famous for its funky architecture and trademark curved bar, decorated with mosaics and rope. It has a friendly vibe, but the atmosphere is often compromised by cheesy Western pop. Cocktails Rs200, shorts Rs50; they also do grilled meats and kebabs to order.

German Bakery 291 Koregaon Park. One of the oldest branches of this chain of faded hippy cafés, providing light meals and heavy pastry snacks and breads, to a mixed clientele of cellphone-wielding, cigarette-smoking students and clean-living ashram-ites.

Juice World 2436/B East Street Camp. Freshly squeezed fruit juices (Rs25–40) and shakes (try the fabulous dried fruit and *badam*) are the mainstay of this central Mumbai-style place just east of the top of MG Rd. They also serve piping-hot snacks such as *aloo paratha* and, throughout the afternoon and evening, tangy Bombay-style *pao bhaji*, which bubbles away on a huge counter griddle.

Koyla Mira Nagar Corner, North Main Rd, Koregaon Park ☏020/2612 0102. Pune's most extravagantly decorated restaurant, featuring twinkling, mirror-inlaid Arabian Nights murals. The waiters sport long Muslim djellabas and fez caps, and serve Hydera-badi cuisine as sumptuous as the surroundings: complicated, creamy curries and huge, slow-baked biriyanis, rounded off with traditional saffron, cardamom and pistachio-accented desserts. Count on Rs750–900 for three courses. Reservation recommended on weekends.

The Place (Touche the Sizzler) 7 Moledina Rd. Succulent sizzlers (veg, fish, pork or beef) and door-stopper steaks, dished up with huge piles of perfect fries and salad, are the house specialities of this popular Parsi-run restaurant in the city centre. Mains Rs200–300.

Ram Krishna 6 Molecina Rd, opposite West End Theatre. Top-notch North and south Indian veg food, including some fantastic Punjabi tandooris, dished up in a high-ceilinged dining hall with black-tie service, but at restrained prices (most mains Rs70–150). Open 9am–11.15pm.

🏃 **Shisha Café** ABC Farms, Koregaon Park. Currently Pune's trendiest watering-hole: a cavernous gastro-bar on stilts, capped with a huge thatched roof. The interior is lined with Turkish rugs and low platforms strewn with cushions to lounge on. Iranian food dominates the menu, but the music's Cuban and BeeBop. They also serve beer and shorts, and hookahs with strawberry-flavoured tobacco.

Swiss Cheese Garden ABC Farms, Koregaon Park. From Fri–Sun you'll be lucky to get a table at this quirky Swiss-themed place. Against a backdrop of warm red brickwork and pretty glass mosaic lanterns, or out in a garden wrapped in fairy lights, you can enjoy scrumptious rösti potatoes, fondues (Rs425–600 depending on ingredients), raclettes (Rs450) and wood-baked pizzas (Rs125–250).

Yogi Tree Ground floor, *Hotel Surya Villa*, 284/1 Koregaon Park. This is the favourite hang-out of health-conscious ashram-ites, serving pure, hygienic juices, grilled sandwiches, tofu steaks (Rs150) and delicious koftas (Rs100), in addition to a very popular stir-fried pak choi (Rs150). And their desserts are great too.

Moving on from Pune

Pune's prominence as a business capital means that it's well connected to towns and cities in southern India. However, demand for seats on planes, trains and buses far exceeds demand and you'd do well to book onward transport as soon as possible. See "Travel details" at the end of this chapter for a roundup of routes, journey frequencies and durations.

As Pune is one of the last stops for around twenty long-distance **trains** to and from Mumbai, rail services are excellent. Many depart early morning, however,

11

Recommended trains from Pune

The following trains are recommended as the fastest and/or most convenient. Reservations for all trains should be made as far in advance as possible at the **Reservation Centre** next to the main station (Mon–Sat 8am–8pm, Sun 8am–2pm).

Destination	Name	No.	Frequency	Departs	Journey time
Bengaluru (Bangalore)	Udyan Express	#6529	Daily	11.45pm	9hr
Chennai	Chennai Express	#2163	Daily	12.10am	22hr
Ernakulam (Kochi)/ Thirvananthapuram (Trivandrum)	Udyan Express	#6529	Daily	7.25pm	33hr/39hr
Goa	Goa Express	#2780	Daily	4.40pm	13hr
Hyderabad	Hyderabad Express	#7031	Daily	4.40pm	13hr 5min
Kolhapur	Sahyadri Express	#1023 CST	Daily	10.05pm	8hr
Mumbai	Mumbai Express	#6012	Daily	9.45am	4hr

and some terminate at Dadar or (worse still) Kurla, so always check first online at Ⓦ www.indianrail.gov.in, or at the station.

Seek advice from the MTDC Tourist Information Counter at the railway station for information on **state bus** services, as the bus stands display none in English. Services from the long-distance section of the City stand (next to Pune railway station) head west and west, to Mahabaleshwar, Kolhapur, Goa and Lonavala. ASIAD buses to Mumbai also leave here every fifteen minutes between 5.30am and 11.30pm. Additional services in these directions work out of the Swargate stand 5km south. Literally dozens of private buses also operate on most popular routes, including to Goa and Mahabaleshwar; you'll find their agents lined up opposite the train and bus stations. If you book onto one, be sure to check the departure point.

For Mumbai, 24-hour **taxis** leave from agencies at the taxi stand in front of Pune railway station, charging around Rs300 per passenger – though note that they'll only get you as far as Dadar. Pricier a/c "cool cabs" operate from the same place (Rs360 per passenger).

Mahabaleshwar and around

MAHABALESHWAR, 250km southeast of Mumbai and rivalling Matheran as the most visited hill-resort in Maharashtra, is easily reached from Pune, 120km northeast. The highest point in the Western Ghats (1372m), it is subject to extraordinarily extreme **weather** conditions. The start of June brings heavy mists and a dramatic drop in temperature, followed by a deluge of biblical proportions: up to seven metres of rain can fall in the hundred days up to the end of September. As a result, tourists only come here between November and May; during April and May, at the height of summer, the place is packed. There is a Rs10 per head entry fee for visitors, collected at toll booths at each end of town.

For most foreign visitors, Mahabaleshwar's prime appeal is its location midway between Mumbai and Goa, but it holds enough good **hiking trails** to keep walkers here for a few days, with tracks through the woods to waterfalls and assorted vantage points overlooking the peaks and plains. You can also take **boats** out on the central **Yenna Lake**, and **shop** for strawberries, raspberries, locally made jams and honey in the lively market. One enjoyable short route is the walk to **Wilson's Point**, the highest spot on the ridge, which you should aim to reach well before dusk. To pick up the (driveable) trail, head south through the bazaar (away from the bus stand) and straight over the crossroads at the end past the *Mayfair* hotel; ten minutes further up the hill, you reach a red-and-white sign pointing left off the road. Wilson's Point lies another stiff ten minutes up, crowned by a gigantic radio transmitter that is visible for miles. The sunset **panoramas** from here can be breathtaking.

Practicalities

The central **State Bus Stand** at the northwest end of the bazaar serves Pune, the most convenient railhead, as well as Kolhapur and Satara, which is 17km from Satara Road railway station, connected to Mumbai via Pune and Goa via Miraj. There are five daily buses from Mumbai, the best option being the MSRTC semi-luxury bus which departs from the Mumbai Central Bus Stand at 7am (7hr). The single daily direct service to Panaji in Goa departs at 9am (12hr). There are a couple of unreliable **Internet** joints in the bazaar, and ATMs at the Bank of Maharashtra in the Main Bazaar (Dr Sabne Rd) and the State Bank of India on Masjid Street.

As in many hill stations, despite an abundance of hotels, prices in Mahabaleshwar are well above average. The cheapest **places to stay** are on the Main Bazaar and the road parallel to it, Murray Peth; with a little haggling, you can pick up rooms for under Rs400 midweek or off-season. Accommodation is scarce during the monsoon (mid-June to mid-Sept), when most hotels close, and during peak times like Diwali and over Christmas and New Year, when tariffs double. Apart from the hotel restaurants and ubiquitous thali joints, two worthwhile **eateries** on the Main Bazaar are *Dragon Chinese Den* and *Tinklers-The Taste Bud*, which does excellent, if slightly pricey, south Indian and other snacks.

Hotels

Blue Star 114 Dr Sabne Rd ☎02168/260678. Offers as competitive off-peak deals as you'll find for a basic attached room close to the centre of town, but with correspondingly low standards. ❹
Deluxe Dr Sabne Rd ☎02168/260202. Clean, new-ish lodge above a fabrics shop. One of the better budget deals and within easy reach of the bus stand. ❹–❺
Dreamland Directly below the State Bus Stand ☎02168/260228, ⓦwww.hoteldreamland.com. Large, established resort hotel in extensive gardens. Rooms range from simple chalets ("cottages") to new a/c poolside apartments with stupendous views. The congenial garden café serves decent espresso and the restaurant fine Indian, Continental, Mexican and Chinese cooking. ❻–❽

MTDC Holiday Camp 2km southwest of the centre ☎02168/260318. Wide range of good-value, no-frills accommodation, including cottages to sleep four, doubles and group accommodation, in a peaceful location on the edge of the resort. ❸–❹
Paradise International Main Rd, near bus stand ☎02168/260084. Ramshackle but acceptable mid-range lodge whose saving grace is a pleasant courtyard. ❹–❺
Valley View Resort Valley View Rd, off Murray Peth Rd ☎02168/260066. Most congenial of Mahabaleshwar's upscale options: a modern, 80-room campus right in the middle of town, but set in lush gardens and boasting spectacular views. Facilities include a smart, pure-veg restaurant (no alcohol), large indoor pool and health club. Non-a/c doubles from around Rs3000. ❽–❾

Pratapgadh

An hour's bus ride away from Mahabaleshwar, the seventeenth-century **fort** of **PRATAPGADH** (daily dawn to dusk; free) stretches the full length of a high ridge affording superb views over the surrounding mountains. Reached by a flight of five hundred steps, it is famously associated with the Maratha chieftain, **Shivaji**, who lured the Mughal general Afzal Khan here from Bijapur to discuss a possible truce. Neither, it would seem, intended to keep to the condition that they should come unarmed. Khan attempted to knife Shivaji, who responded by killing him with the gruesome *wagnakh*, a set of metal claws worn on the hand. Modern visitors can see Afzal Khan's tomb, a memorial to Shivaji, and views of the surrounding hills.

Taxis charge around Rs750, plus waiting time, for the run out to Pratapgadh. State buses also do the journey each day, starting at 9.30am from Mahabaleshwar Bus Stand, but only pause for an hour before turning around.

Kolhapur

KOLHAPUR, on the banks of the River Panchaganga 225km south of Pune, is thought to have been an important centre of the Tantric cult associated with Shakti worship since ancient times. The town probably grew around the sacred site of the present-day **Mahalakshmi temple**, still central to the life of the city, although there are said to be up to 250 other shrines in the area. With a population of more than half a million, Kolhapur has become a major industrial centre, but has retained enough Maharashtran character to make it worthy of a stopover.

The City

The **Mahalakshmi temple**, whose cream-painted sanctuary towers embellish the western end of the city, is thought to have been founded in the seventh century by the Chalukyan king Karnadeva, though what you see today dates from the early eighteenth century. It is built from bluish-black basalt on the plan of a cross, with the image of the goddess Mahalakshmi beneath the eastern and largest of five domed towers. Presiding over the square just up the road from the Mahalakshmi temple, the **Rajwada**, or Old Palace, is still occupied by members of the former ruling Chhatrapati family. Visitors can see the entrance hall (daily 10am–6pm; free) by passing under a pillared porch which extends out into the town square.

Kolhapur is famous as a centre for traditional wrestling, or *kushti*. On leaving the palace gates, turn right and head through the low doorway in front of you, from where a path picks its way past a couple of derelict buildings to the sunken *motibaug*, or **wrestling ground**. Come here between 5.30am and 5.30pm, and you can watch the wrestlers training. The main season is between June and September, the coolest time of year, but you may see them active at other times. Hindus and Muslims train together, and it's fine to take photographs.

The maharaja's **New Palace** (Tues–Sun 9.30am–1pm & 2.30–6pm; Rs20), 2km north of the centre, was built in 1884, following a fire at the Rajwada. Designed by Major Mant, its style fuses Jain and Hindu influences from Gujarat and Rajasthan and local touches from the Rajwada while remaining indomitably Victorian, with a prominent clock tower. The present maharaja lives on the first floor, while the ground floor holds an absorbing collection of costumes, weapons, games, jewellery, embroidery and paraphernalia such as silver elephant saddles.

Practicalities

Kolhapur **airport**, served by daily flights from Mumbai, lies 8km southeast of the town centre. Two direct express **trains** leave Mumbai CST for Kolhapur via Pune each evening: the Mahalaxmi Express #1011 and the Sahyadri Express #1023. Heading in the other direction, the Mahalaxmi Express, bound for Pune and Mumbai, leaves Kolhapur at 7.35pm. The **railway station** is 500m from the **bus stand** on Station Road, near the centre of town. A five-minute walk from here (turn right) brings you to the **MTDC tourist office**, in the Kedar Complex on Station Road (Mon–Sat 8.30am–6.30pm; ☎0231/269 2935), where you can sign up for a guided **tour** of Kolhapur (Mon–Sat 10am–5.30pm; Rs75). The only place in town to **exchange** traveller's cheques is at the State Bank of India at Dasara Chowk Bridge, near Shahamahar railway station, which also has an ATM; other cash machines can be found at most of the major banks, including the dependable UTI, on Station Road. If you need to get online, Balaji Net Café (Rs20/hr), on Station Road between the bus stand and railway station, is reliable.

There's no shortage of decent, reasonably priced **accommodation** in Kolhapur, most within easy reach of the bus stand along Station Road. The *Maharaja*, at 514 Station Rd (☎0231/265 0829; ❸), is a basic lodge, directly opposite the bus stand, with dozens of good-value, no-frills, clean rooms, and a veg restaurant. If it's full, try the *Sony* (☎0231/265 8585; ❷–❸), diagonally across the square inside the Mahalaxmi Chambers complex. A more comfortable option in a peaceful suburb a five-minute rickshaw drive away is the *Hotel Woodlands*, at 204E Tarabai Park (☎0231/265 0941, ℉263 3378; ❺–❻), which has a range of a/c and non-a/c rooms with TV, plus a 24-hour coffee shop, multi-cuisine restaurant, garden and bar. On the outskirts of town, overlooking the shores of Rankala Lake, the ⚘ *Shalini Palace* (☎0231/263 0401; ❼) was once the Maharaja's summer residence. Fitted with enormous four-poster beds and upholstered furniture, its suites are an uneasy mishmash of period and modern features, but are far and away the most luxurious options in Kolhapur, and the grounds have acres of green space for evening strolls. Even if you don't stay here, it's worth considering a trip out to the *Shalini* to eat in its enormous restaurant, located in the former Durbar Hall.

Outside the hotels, the best **food** is to be had in *Subraya* at the top of Station Square, a comfortable a/c restaurant with a varied menu including good Maharashtran thalis, breakfast and cheaper south Indian–style snacks such as tasty *dosas*, *vada pao* and filling *pani puris*.

Travel details

Trains

Aurangabad to: Delhi (1 daily; 22hr 20min); Mumbai (4–5 daily; 7hr 20min–8hr).
Jalgaon to: Agra (4–5 daily; 15hr–18hr 20min); Bengaluru (Bangalore; 1 daily; 23hr 30min); Bhopal (7 daily; 7hr–8hr 30min); Chennai (1 daily; 23hr); Delhi (4 daily; 18hr 15min–22hr 50min); Gwalior (4–5 daily; 13hr 30min–16hr 20min); Mumbai (11–13 daily; 7hr 45min–9hr 30min); Nagpur (8–9 daily; 7hr 45min–9hr 15min); Pune (4 daily; 8hr 45min–11hr 15min); Varanasi (2–3 daily; 19hr 25min–23hr 15min); Wardha (5–7 daily; 6hr 30min–7hr 45min).

Kolhapur to: Bengaluru (Bangalore; 1–3 daily; 21hr–25hr 45min); Mumbai (2–3 daily; 11–12hr 15min); Pune (4 daily; 7hr 30min–7hr 50min).
Nagpur to: Bhopal (7–17 daily; 5hr 30min–8hr 30min); Chennai (3–6 daily; 15hr 15min–23hr 30min); Delhi (10–13 daily 14hr–21hr 45min); Hyderabad (2–5 daily; 8hr–14hr 45min); Indore (1 daily; 11hr 45min); Jabalpur (1–3 daily; 9hr 15min–10hr 20min); Jalgaon (8–9 daily; 7hr 45min–9hr 15min); Kolkata (Calcutta; 3–5 daily; 18hr 40min–24hr 10min); Mumbai (6–8 daily; 17hr 15min–19hr); Nasik (6 daily; 11–13hr); Pune (2 daily; 17hr 20min–19hr); Varanasi (1 weekly; 18hr 45min–19hr 50min); Wardha (hourly; 2hr).
Nasik to: Agra (3–4 daily; 17hr 20min–21hr 15min); Bhopal (4–5 daily; 10hr–12hr 20min); Delhi (3 daily; 21hr 20min–25hr 50min); Jabalpur (5–6 daily; 12hr 20min–14hr 55min); Mumbai (8–10 daily; 4–6hr); Nagpur (6 daily; 11hr–13hr).
Pune to: Bengaluru (Bangalore; 2–5 daily; 19hr 15min–22hr 40min); Chennai (3 daily; 20hr–25hr 45min; 55min); Delhi (3 daily; 26hr 30min–29hr 15min); Hyderabad (3–4 daily; 11hr–14hr); Jalgaon (3–4 daily; 8hr 20min–11hr); Kolhapur (4 daily; 7hr 30min–7hr 50min); Margao (1 daily; 14hr); Mumbai (20–23 daily; 3hr 25min–5hr 10min); Nagpur (1–2 daily; 17hr 20min–19hr).

Buses

Aurangabad to: Ahmedabad (1 nightly; 14–15hr); Ajanta (every 30min–1hr; 3hr); Bijapur (1 daily; 12hr); Ellora (every 30min; 40min); Indore (2 daily; 12hr); Jalgaon (every 30min–1hr; 4hr); Lonar (2 daily; 4–5hr); Mumbai (6–8 nightly; 8–10hr); Nagpur (4 daily; 12hr); Nasik (8 daily; 4hr 30min–5hr); Pune (10 daily; 5hr).
Jalgaon to: Ajanta (every 30min; 1hr); Aurangabad (every 30min–1hr; 4hr); Mumbai (1 daily; 10hr 30min); Nagpur (2 daily; 8–9hr); Pune (5 daily; 9hr).
Kolhapur to: Bijapur (2 daily; 4hr); Mahabaleshwar (3–4 daily; 5hr); Pune (4 daily; 5hr 30min–7hr);

Nagpur to: Aurangabad (4 daily; 12hr); Indore (4 daily; 11–12hr); Jabalpur (9 daily; 7–8hr); Jalgaon (2 daily; 8–9hr); Pune (5 daily; 16hr); Ramtek (hourly; 1hr); Wardha (hourly; 2hr).
Nasik to: Aurangabad (8 daily; 5hr); Mumbai (hourly; 4–5hr); Pune (every 30min; 3–4hr); Trimbak (hourly; 45min).
Pune to: Aurangabad (10 daily; 5hr); Bijapur (1 daily; 11–12hr); Goa (4 daily; 15–16hr); Kolhapur (4 daily; 5hr 30min–7hr); Mahabaleshwar (9 daily; 3hr 30min–4hr); Mumbai (every 15min; 4hr–4hr 30min); Nasik (every 30min; 3–4hr).

Flights

(**AI** = Air India, **I7** = Paramount Airways, **IC** = Indian Airlines, **IT** = Kingfisher, **IX** = Air India Express, **DN** = Air Deccan, **S2** = JetLite, **9W** = Jet Airways, **G8** = Go Air)
Aurangabad to: Delhi (IA 1 daily, via Mumbai; 3hr 35min); Mumbai (DN, IA, 9W 4 daily; 45min–1hr); Udaipur (IT 1 daily; 1hr 45min).
Kolhapur to: Mumbai (DN 1 daily; 1hr 10min).
Nagpur to: Ahmedabad (IT, SG 1 daily; 2hr); Bengaluru (Bangalore) (6E & S2 2 daily; 2–4hr); Bhubaneshwar (S2 1 daily; 3hr); Delhi (IA, 6E, 9W, S2 4 daily; 1hr 25min–1hr 40min); Hyderabad (IA, IT 2 daily; 1hr–1hr 35min); Indore (IT 1 daily; 1hr 20min); Jaipur (6E daily via Mumbai; 4hr); Kochi (Cochin) (S2 1 daily; 4hr 30min); Hyderabad (S2 & IT 2 daily; 1hr); Kolkata (Calcutta) (6E daily; 1hr 30min); Mumbai (IX, IA, 6E, IT, 9W 6–7 daily; 1hr 20min–1hr 35min); Pune (6E & S2 2 daily; 1hr–2hr 30min).
Pune to: Ahmedabad (IT, SG 2 daily; 1hr 20min); Bengaluru (Bangalore) (DA, IA, 9W, IT & SG 8–9 daily; 1hr 20min–2hr 25min); Chennai (GO, 9W, IT & SG 3–4 daily; 1hr 35min–3hr 10min); Delhi (IC, 6E, 9W, S2, IT & SG 7–9 daily; 2hr–5hr); Goa (IC 1 daily; 50min); Hyderabad (DA, IC, IT & SG 4–5daily; 1hr–1hr 30min); Indore (IT 1 daily; 1hr 20min); Kolkata (Calcutta) (9W, IT 3 daily; 4hr 30min–6hr 20min); Mumbai (9W 2 daily; 35min); Nagpur (6E & S2 2 daily; 1hr 10min–2hr 30min).

Goa

AFGHANISTAN

CHINA
(TIBET AUTONOMOUS REGION)

0   400 km

⑦

⑥

PAKISTAN

⑧   ④

①

NEPAL

⑮

BHUTAN

⑯

②

③

BANGLADESH

⑨

⑤

⑭

⑬

MYANMAR
(BURMA)

⑰

ARABIAN
SEA

⑩

⑪

⑱

BAY OF BENGAL

N

⑫   ㉒

⑳

SRI
LANKA

⑲

㉑

INDIAN OCEAN

The International boundaries on this map are neither purported to be correct
nor authentic by Survey of India directives. Publisher.

CHAPTER 12

Highlights

✳ **Old Goa** The belfries and Baroque church facades looming over the trees on the banks of the Mandovi are all that remains of this once splendid colonial city.
See p.788

✳ **Ingo's Night Bazaar, Arpora** Cooler and less frenetic than the flea market, with better-quality goods on sale and heaps more atmosphere.
See p.803

✳ **Flea market, Anjuna** Goa's famous tourist bazaar is the place to pick up the latest party gear, shop for souvenirs, and watch the crowds go by.
See p.806

✳ **Nine Bar, Vagator** The epicentre of hip Goa, where trance music accompanies the sunsets over the beach.
See p.812

✳ **Arambol** An alternative resort with exquisite beaches and some of Asia's best budget restaurants. See p.817

✳ **Braganza-Perreira house, Chandor** The region's most extravagant colonial-era mansion, crammed with period furniture and fittings.
See p.823

✳ **Beach shacks** Tuck into a fresh kingfish, tandoori pomfret or lobster, washed down with a *feni* cocktail or an ice-cold Kingfisher beer. See p.827

✳ **Sunset stroll, Palolem** Tropical sunsets don't come much more romantic than at this idyllic palm-fringed cove in the hilly deep south. See p.829

▲ View over Arambol beach

12

Goa

f one word could be said to encapsulate the essence of **GOA**, it would have
to be the Portuguese *sossegado*, meaning "laid back". The pace of life in this
former colonial enclave, midway down India's southwest coast, has picked
up over the past twenty years, but in spite of the increasing chaos of its
capital, beach resorts and market towns, Goa has retained the relaxed feel that
has traditionally set it apart from the rest of the country. Its 1.4 million inhabitants are unequivocal about the roots of their distinctiveness; while most of the
Subcontinent was colonized by the stiff-upper-lipped British, Goa's European
overlords were the **Portuguese**, a people far more inclined to enjoy the good
things in life than their Anglo-Saxon counterparts.

Goa was Portugal's first toe-hold in Asia, and served as the linchpin for a
vast **trade network** for over 450 years. However, when the Lusitanian
empire began to founder in the seventeenth century, so too did the fortunes
of its capital. Cut off from the rest of India by a wall of mountains and
hundreds of miles of unnavigable alluvial plain, it remained aloof from the
wider Subcontinent – while India was tearing itself to pieces in the run-up
to Independence in 1947, the only machetes wielded here were cutting
coconuts. Not until 1961, after exasperated Prime Minister Jawaharlal Nehru
gave up trying to negotiate with the Portuguese dictator Salazar and sent in
the army, was Goa finally absorbed into India.

Those who visited in the late 1960s and 1970s, when the overland travellers'
trail wriggled its way south from Bombay, found a way of life little changed in
centuries: Portuguese was still very much the lingua franca of the well-educated
elite, and the coastal settlements were mere fishing and coconut cultivation
villages. Relieved to have found somewhere inexpensive and culturally
undemanding to recover from the travails of Indian travel, the "freaks" got
stoned, watched the mesmeric sunsets over the Arabian Sea and partied madly
on full-moon nights, giving rise to a holiday culture that soon made Goa
synonymous with hedonistic **hippies**.

Since then, the state has shaken off its reputation as a drop-out zone, but
hundreds of thousands of visitors still flock here each winter, the vast majority
to relax on Goa's beautiful **beaches**. Around two dozen stretches of soft white
sand indent the region's coast, from spectacular 25-kilometre sweeps to secluded
palm-backed coves. The level of development varies wildly; while some are
lined by ritzy Western-style resorts, the most sophisticated structures on others
are palm-leaf shacks and old wooden outriggers that are heaved into the sea
each afternoon.

Wherever you travel in Goa, vestiges of former Portuguese domination are
ubiquitous, creating an ambience that is at once exotic and strangely familiar.

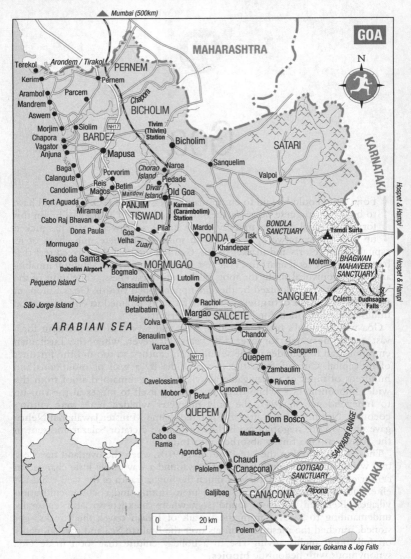

GOA

▲ Mumbai (500km)

MAHARASHTRA

N

PERNEM

Terekol • *Arondem / Tirakol*
Kerim •
Arambol •   Parcem •   • Pernem
Mandrem •
Aswem •   *Chapora*
                             BICHOLIM
Morjim • • Siolim   NH17 Tivim
Chapora • BARDEZ   (Thivim)
Vagator •   Station
Anjuna •   • Mapusa   • Bicholim   SATARI
Baga •   Naroa
Calangute • Porvorim *Chorao* • Sanquelim
Reis   • Betim *Island* Piedade   Valpoi •
Candolim Magos *Divar* *Old Goa*
Fort Aguada •   *Mandovi* *Island* Karmali
Miramar •   PANJIM   (Carambolim)
Cabo Raj Bhavan • TISWADI   Station
Dona Paula • Goa   • Pilar Mardol   BONDLA
Mormugao •   Velha *Zuari*   Tisk   SANCTUARY ▲ Tamdi Surla
            Vasco da Gama • PONDA Khandepar
Dabolim Airport •   MORMUGAO Ponda   Molem • BHAGWAN
Bogmalo •   MAHAVEER
Pequeno Island Cansaulim • Lutolim •   SANCTUARY

São Jorge Island Majorda • • Rachol   SANGUEM
            Betalbatim • Margao   Colem • Dudhsagar
ARABIAN SEA Colva • SALCETE   Falls
            Benaulim •   Chandor •
            Varca •   NH17
                         Quepem •   • Sanguem
                         • Zambaulim
            Cavelossim •   • Rivona
            Mobor • Cuncolim •
                    QUEPEM   • Dom Bosco
            Cabo da
            Rama • *Mallikarjun* ▲
            Agonda • Chaudi
            Palolem • (Canacona)
                                COTIGAO
            Galjibag   CANACONA SANCTUARY *Talpona*

            0   20 km

            • Polem

KARNATAKA

Hospet & Hampi ▶

SAHYADRI RANGE

KARNATAKA

▼ ▼ Karwar, Gokarna & Jog Falls

This is particularly true of Goan **food** which, blending the Latin love of meat and fish with India's predilection for spices, is quite unlike any other regional cuisine in Asia. Equally unique is the prevalence of **alcohol**. Beer is cheap, and six thousand or more bars around the state are licensed to serve it, along with the more traditional tipple, *feni*, a rocket-fuel spirit distilled from cashew fruit or coconut sap.

Travelling around the Christian heartland of central Goa, with its whitewashed churches and wayside shrines, it's all too easy to forget that **Hinduism** remains the religion of more than two-thirds of the state's population. Unlike in many parts of the country, however, religious intolerance is rare here, and traditional practices mingle easily with more recently implanted ones. Faced by the threat of merger with neighbouring states, Goans have always put regional cohesion before communal differences at the ballot box. A potent stimulus for regional identity was the campaign through the 1980s to have **Konkani**, the language spoken by the vast majority of Goans, recognized as an official state language, which it eventually was in 1992. Since then, the **immigration** issue has come to dominate the political agenda. Considerably more prosperous than neighbouring states, Goa has been deluged over the past couple of decades with economic refugees, stirring up fears that the region's cultural distinctiveness will disappear. Among the main employers of migrant labour in recent years has been the **Konkan Railway**, completed in 1997 to form a super fast land-link with Mumbai – another conduit of economic prosperity that has brought lasting changes.

Which beach you opt for when you arrive largely depends on what sort of holiday you have in mind. More developed resorts such as **Calangute** and **Baga** in the north, and **Colva** and **Benaulim** in the south, offer more "walk-in" accommodation and tourist facilities than elsewhere. Even if you're looking for a less touristy scene, it can be worth heading for these centres first, as finding places to stay in less commercialised corners is often difficult. **Anjuna**, **Vagator** and **Chapora**, where accommodation is generally more basic and harder to come by, are the beaches to aim for if you've come to Goa to party. However, the bulk of budget travellers taking time out from tours of India end up in **Palolem**, in the far south, or **Arambol**, both beyond the increasingly long reach of the charter buses. That said, Palolem, in particular, has become a major resort in its own right, with thousands of long-stay visitors in peak season.

Some 10km from the state capital, **Panjim**, the ruins of the former Portuguese capital at **Old Goa** are foremost among the attractions away from the coast – a sprawl of Catholic cathedrals, convents and churches that draw crowds of Christian pilgrims from all over India. Another popular day excursion is to Anjuna's Wednesday **flea market**, a sociable place to shop for souvenirs and dance wear. Further inland, the thickly wooded countryside around **Ponda** harbours numerous temples, where you can experience Goa's peculiar brand of Hindu architecture. The district of Salcete, and its main market town, **Margao**, is also littered with Portuguese mansions, churches and seminaries. Finally, wildlife enthusiasts may be tempted into the interior to visit the nature reserve at **Cotigao** in the far south.

The **best time to come** to Goa is during the dry, relatively cool winter months between mid-November and mid-March. At other times, either the sun is too hot for comfort, or the monsoon rains and clouds make life miserable. During peak season, from mid-December to the end of January, the weather is perfect, with temperatures rarely nudging above 32°C. Finding a room or a house to rent at that time, however – particularly over Christmas and New Year when tariffs double, or triple – can be a real hassle.

Some history

Goa's sheer inaccessibility by land has always kept it out of the mainstream of Indian history; on the other hand, its control of the seas and the lucrative spice trade made it a much-coveted prize for rival colonial powers. Until a century before the arrival of the Portuguese, Goa had belonged for over a thousand years to the kingdom of **Kadamba**. They, in turn, were overthrown by the Karnatakan Vijayanagars, the Muslim Bahmanis, and Yusuf Adil Shah of Bijapur, but the capture of the fort at Panjim by **Afonso de Albuquerque** in 1510 signalled the start of a Portuguese occupation that was to last 451 years.

As Goa expanded, its splendid capital (now Old Goa) came to hold a larger population than Paris or London. Though Ismail Adil Shah laid siege for ten

White Maruti van **taxis** are how most foreign visitors travel between beach resorts in Goa. You'll find them lined up outside charter hotels, where a board invariably displays "fixed rates" to destinations in and around the region. These fares only apply to peak season, however, and at other times you should be able to negotiate a hefty reduction.

A cheaper alternative is to rent either a **bicycle** (gearless, Indian-made cycles are on offer in all the resorts for around Rs75–100 per day) or, for longer trips, a **motorbike**. Buzzing around Goa's tropical backroads on a scooter or motorcycle gives an unrivalled sense of freedom, but it can be perilous. Every season, an average of one person a day dies on the roads; many are tourists on two-wheelers. Make sure, therefore, that the lights and brakes are in good shape, and be especially vigilant at night: Goan roads can be appallingly pot-holed and unlit, and stray cows, dogs and bullock carts can appear from nowhere.

Officially, you need an **international driver's licence** to rent and ride anything, but in practise a standard licence will suffice if you're stopped and asked to produce your papers by the local police. In 2006, a new law was introduced in Goa requiring that all rented motorcycles carry special **yellow-and-black licence plates**, for which the vehicle's owners pay a couple of thousand rupees extra. This slightly increases the cost of the bike (typically by around Rs50 per day), but the new plates ensure you can ride free from harassment by Goa's notoriously corrupt traffic cops. Go for a cheaper bike with regular black-and-white plates, on the other hand, and you'll be pulled over with frustrating regularity.

Helmets are also compulsory these days while riding on the highways. The owner of your rented motorbike should provide an Indian-made one, but it may not fit and isn't likely to be of the best quality. **Rates** for motorbikes vary according to season, duration of rental and vehicle; most owners also insist on a deposit and/or passport as security. The cheapest bike, a scooter-style Honda Activa 100cc, which has automatic gears, costs Rs200 per day (with yellow plates). Other options include the perennially stylish Enfield Bullet 350cc, although these are heavy, unwieldy and – at upwards of Rs300 per day – the most expensive bike to rent. For all-round performance and maneuverability, you can't beat the fast and light Honda Splendours and Baja Pulsars, which go for Rs250–300, depending on what kind of shape the vehicle is in and how long you rent it for.

Fuel is sold at service stations (known locally as "petrol pumps") in Panjim, Mapusa, Vagator/Anjuna, Margao, Chaudi, and at Arambol in the far north. In smaller settlements, including the resorts, it's sold in mineral-water bottles at general stores or through backstreet suppliers – but you should avoid these as some bulk out their petrol with low-grade kerosene or industrial solvent, which makes engines misfire and smoke badly.

Tours

On paper, guided **tours** (daily; Rs200) run by the local tourism authority **GTDC** (ⓦ www.goa-tourism.com) from Panjim, Margao, Calangute and Colva seem like a good way of stringing together Goa's highlights in a short time. However, they're far too rushed for most foreign tourists, appealing essentially to Indian families wishing to combine a peek at the resorts with a whistle-stop puja tour of the temples around Ponda. Most also include a string of places inland that you wouldn't otherwise consider visiting. Leaflets giving full itineraries are available at any GTDC office.

months in 1570, and the Marathas under Shivaji and later chiefs came nail-bitingly close to seizing the region, the greatest threat was from other European maritime nations, principally Holland and France. Meanwhile, conversions to **Christianity**, started by the Franciscans, gathered pace when St Francis Xavier founded the **Jesuit** mission in 1542. With the advent of the **Inquisition** soon afterwards, laws were introduced censoring literature and banning any faith other than Catholicism. Hindu temples were destroyed, and converted Hindus adopted Portuguese names, such as da Silva, Correa and de Sousa, which remain common in the region. Thereafter, the colony, whose trade monopoly had been broken by its European rivals, went into gradual decline, hastened by the unhealthy, disease-ridden environment of its capital.

Despite certain liberalization, such as the restoration of Hindus' right to worship and the final banishment of the dreaded Inquisition in 1820, the nineteenth century saw widespread civil unrest. During the British Raj many Goans moved to Bombay, and elsewhere in British India, to find work.

The success of the post-Independence Goan struggle for freedom owed as much to the efforts of the Indian government, which cut off diplomatic ties with Portugal, as to the work of freedom fighters such as **Menezes Braganza** and **Dr Cunha**. After a "liberation march" in 1955 resulted in a number of deaths, the state was blockaded. Trade with Bombay ceased, and the railway was cut off, so Goa set out to forge international links, particularly with Pakistan and Sri Lanka: that led to the building of Dabolim airport, and a determination to improve local agricultural output. In 1961, Prime Minister Jawaharlal Nehru finally ran out of patience with his opposite number in Lisbon, the right-wing dictator Salazar, and sent in the armed forces. Mounted in defiance of a United Nations resolution, "**Operation Vijay**" met only token resistance, and the Indian army overran Goa in two days. Thereafter, Goa (along with Portugal's other two enclaves, Daman and Diu) became part of India as a self-governing **Union Territory**, with minimum interference from Delhi.

Since Independence, Goa has continued to prosper, bolstered by iron-ore exports and a booming tourist industry. Dominated by issues of statehood, the status of Konkani and the ever-rising levels of immigration, its political life has been dogged by chronic **instability**. In the 1990s, no fewer than twelve chief ministers held power and, in May 2004, after a spate of failed confidence votes rendered the state ungovernable, New Delhi stepped in to declare **President's Rule**, effectively suspending the State Legislature. The deadlock between the BJP and Congress dominated national headlines for months, until fresh elections could be organized. These eventually returned Congress to power, with **Pratapsingh Rane** as Chief Minister, and since 2005 an uneasy peace has reigned. In the interior, meanwhile, the spectre of communal violence, virtually unheard of in Goa, raised its head in March 2006, when **anti-Muslim riots** erupted in the mining town of Sanvordem.

At the start of the twenty-first century, as ever-improving infrastructural links with the rest of India render Goa's borders more porous, the survival of the state as a culturally distinct region hinges on the extent to which its government is able to resist the drift towards communal politics and establish democratic policies. If the past decade is anything to go by, the chances of this happening seem remote, although the embarrassment of President's Rule does seem to have galvanized the state's leaders.

Panjim and central Goa

Stacked around the sides of a lush terraced hillside at the mouth of the River Mandovi, **PANJIM** (also known by its Marathi name, **Panaji** – "land that does not flood") was for centuries little more than a minor landing stage and customs house, protected by a hilltop fort and surrounded by stagnant swampland.

It only became state capital in 1843, after the port at Old Goa had silted up and its rulers and impoverished inhabitants had fled the plague. Although the last Portuguese viceroy managed to drain many of Panjim's marshes, and erected imposing public buildings on the new site, the town never emulated the grandeur of its predecessor upriver – a result, in part, of the Portuguese nobles' predilection for constructing their mansions in the countryside rather than the city. Panjim expanded rapidly in the 1960s and 1970s, without reaching the unmanageable proportions of other Indian capitals. After Mumbai, or even Bengaluru (Bangalore), its uncongested streets seem refreshingly parochial. Sights are thin on the ground, but the backstreets of the old quarter, **Fontainhas**, have retained a faded Portuguese atmosphere, with colour-washed houses, Catholic churches and shopfronts sporting names such as De Souza and Pinto.

Some travellers see no more of Panjim than its noisy bus terminal – which is

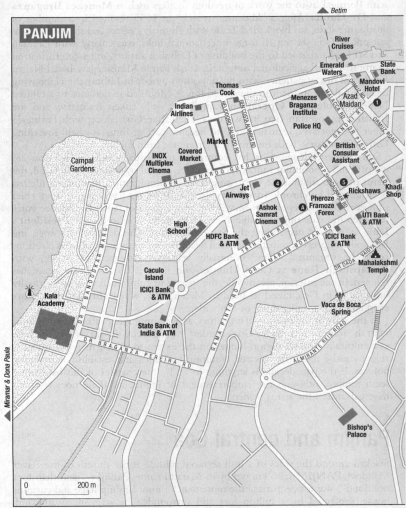

a pity. Although you can completely bypass the town when you arrive in Goa, either by jumping off the train or coach at Margao (for the south), or Mapusa (for the northern resorts), or by heading straight off on a local bus, it's definitely worth spending time here – if only a couple of hours en route to the ruined former capital at **Old Goa**.

The area **around Panjim** attracts far fewer visitors than the coastal resorts, yet its paddy fields and wooded valleys harbour several attractions worth a day or two's break from the beach. **Old Goa** is just a bus ride away, as are the unique temples around **Ponda**, an hour or so southeast, to where Hindus smuggled their deities during the Inquisition. Further inland still, the forested lower slopes of the Western Ghats, cut through by the main Panjim–Bengaluru (Bangalore) highway, shelter the impressive **Dudhsagar falls**, reachable only by four-wheel-drive Jeep.

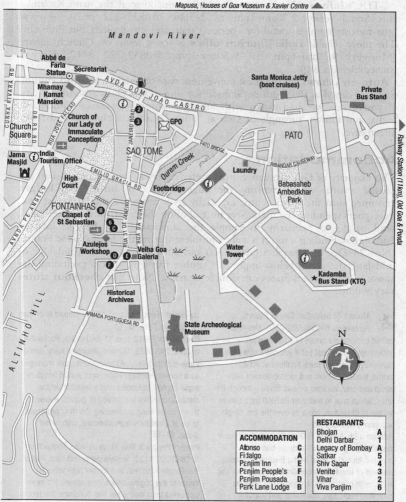

Mapusa, Houses of Goa Museum & Xavier Centre

Mandovi River

Abbé de Faria Statue
Secretariat
CUNHA RIVARA RD
DR. R.S. RD
Mhamay Kamat Mansion
RUA JOSÉ FALCAO
Church Square
Church of our Lady of Immaculate Conception
GPO
SÃO TOMÉ
AVDA DOM JOAO CASTRO
31 JANEIRO ROAD
FATO BRIDGE
Ourem Creek
Santa Monica Jetty (boat cruises)
Private Bus Stand
PATO
Jama Masjid
India Tourism Office
High Court
EMILIO GRACIA RD
Footbridge
Laundry
RIBANDAR CAUSEWAY
Babasaheb Ambedkhar Park
Railway Station (11km), Old Goa & Ponda
AVDA PE ANGELO
FONTAINHAS
Chapel of St Sebastian
RUA 31 DE JANEIRO
RUA DA OUREM
Azulejos Workshop
Velha Goa Galeria
Water Tower
Kadamba Bus Stand (KTC)
ALTINHO HILL
Historical Archives
ARMADA PORTUGUESA RD
State Archeological Museum
N

ACCOMMODATION	
Afonso	C
Fidalgo	A
Panjim Inn	E
Panjim People's	F
Panjim Pousada	D
Park Lane Lodge	B

RESTAURANTS	
Bhojan	A
Delhi Darbar	1
Legacy of Bombay	A
Satkar	5
Shiv Sagar	4
Venite	3
Vihar	2
Viva Panjim	6

Bambolim (hospital), Vasco Da Gama, Dabolim Airport (29km) & Margao

Arrival, information and local transport

European charter planes and domestic flights arrive at **Dabolim airport** (℡0832/254 0788), 29km south of Panjim on the outskirts of Vasco da Gama, Goa's second city. Pre-paid taxis into town (45min; Rs495), booked at the counter in the forecourt, can be shared by up to four people.

There's no **train** station in town itself; the nearest one, on the Konkan Railway, is at **Karmali** (11km east of Panjim at Old Goa). State buses to central Panjim await arrivals.

Long-distance and local **buses** pull into Panjim's busy Kadamba Bus Stand, 1km east of the centre in the district of Pato. Ten minutes' walk, across Ourem Creek to Fontainhas, brings you to several budget hotels. For the more modern west end of town, jump into an auto-rickshaw at the rank outside the station concourse (Rs25–40).

GTDC's **information** counter, inside the concourse at the main Kadamba Bus Stand (daily 9.30am–1pm & 2–5pm; ℡0832/222 5620, ⓦwww .goa-tourism.com) is useful for checking train and bus timings, but little else. The more reliable **India Tourism office** is across town on Church Square (Mon–Fri 9.30am–6pm, Sat 9.30am–1pm; ℡0832/222 3412, ⓦwww .incredibleindia.org).

Auto-rickshaws are the most convenient way of **getting around** Panjim; flag one down at the roadside or head for one of the ranks around the city. If you're not weighed down with luggage, motorcycle taxis – unique in India, and known throughout Goa as "pilots" – offer a cheaper and faster alternative.

Accommodation

The majority of Goa's Indian visitors prefer to stay in Panjim rather than the coastal resorts, which explains the huge number of **hotels** and **lodges** crammed into the town centre, especially its noisy, more modern west end. Foreigners spending the night here instead of on the coast, on the other hand, tend to do so primarily to sample the atmosphere of the old quarter, Fontainhas. Finding a room is only a problem during the festival of St Francis (Nov 24–Dec 3), Dussehra (Sept/Oct) and during peak season (mid-Dec to mid-Jan); the codes below apply to October through March, excluding the above periods, when prices can double or triple. Note that **checkout times** vary wildly.

Afonso St Sebastian Chapel Square, Fontainhas ℡0832/222 2359. This refurbished colonial-era house in a picturesque backstreet is your best bet if you can't afford the *Panjim Inn* down the road. Spotless attached rooms, friendly owners and rooftop terrace with views and cool, ceramic mosaic floors – though the rates, which soar to well over Rs1000 for a simple double at Christmas, are a bit over the top. Single occupancy available. ❹

Fidalgo 18th June Rd ℡0832/222 6291, ⓦwww .hotelfidalgo-goa.com. Affordable business-oriented four-star hotel in the bustling commercial end of town. It's a comfortable option for the price, with central a/c, a good-sized open-air pool, Ayurvedic spa, bookshop and popular six-outlet "Food Enclave" on the ground floor (see "Eating", p.787). ❼–❽

Panjim Inn E-212, Rua 31 de Janeiro, Fontainhas ℡0832/243 5628, ⓦwww.panjiminn.com. Grand three-hundred-year-old townhouse, now managed as a homely Heritage Hotel, with period furniture, sepia photos, balconies and a veranda where meals and drinks are served to guests. A new three-storey wing overlooking the river promises to be of a similarly high standard, with better views. ❻–❼

Panjim People's Rua 31 de Janeiro, Fontainhas ℡0832/222 1122, ⓦwww.panjiminn.com. Part of the *Panjim Inn* line, in a former high school opposite the original house (see above). It's more upmarket than their other two buildings: the rooms are huge, fitted with antique rosewood furniture, gilded pelmets and lace curtains, and the bathrooms feature the Sukhija family's trademark crazy-mosaic tiling. Tariffs mid-season start at around Rs5000 ($110) per night. ❾

🏃 **Panjim Pousada** Rua 31 de Janeiro, Fontainhas ☎0832/243 5628, ⓦwww .panjiminn.com. Within an old Hindu house with oodles of period character, this is another sister concern of the *Panjim Inn* across the road. Ask for a room on the first floor, where a lovely wooden

balcony, shaded by a breadfruit tree, overlooks the inner courtyard. ❻–❼

Park Lane Lodge Near the Chapel of St Sebastian, Fontainhas ☎0832/222 7154, ⓔpklaldg @sancharnet.in. Cramped but clean and friendly family guesthouse in a rambling 1930s home. Pepper and coffee plants add atmosphere to the narrow communal terrace, and there's a TV lounge upstairs; also safe deposit facilities, Internet access and laundry service. Rates are high in season, but discounts are available at other times. ❺

The Town

The leafy rectangular park opposite the India Government tourist office, known as **Church Square** or the **Municipal Gardens**, forms the heart of Panjim. Presiding over its southeast side is the town's most distinctive landmark, the whitewashed Baroque facade of the **Church of Our Lady of the Immaculate Conception**. At the head of a crisscrossing laterite walkway, the church was built in 1541 for the benefit of sailors arriving here from Lisbon. The weary mariners would stagger up from the quay to give thanks for their safe passage before proceeding to the capital at Old Goa – the original home of the enormous bell that hangs from its central gable.

Running north from the church, Rua José Falcao brings you to the riverside, where Panjim's main street, Avenida Dom Joao Castro, holds the town's oldest surviving building. With its sloping tiled roofs, carved-stone coats of arms and wooden verandas, the stalwart **Secretariat** looks typically colonial. Yet it was originally the summer palace of Goa's sixteenth-century Muslim ruler, the Adil Shah. Later, the Portuguese converted it into a temporary resthouse for the territory's governors (who used to overnight here en route to and from Lisbon) and then a residence for the viceroy. Today, it houses municipal offices.

A hundred metres east, a peculiar statue of a man holding his hands over the body of an entranced reclining woman represents **Abbé de Faria** (1755–1819), a Goan priest who emigrated to France to become one of the world's first professional hypnotist.

Just behind the esplanade, 500m west of the Abbé de Faria statue, stands another grand vestige of the colonial era, the **Menezes Braganza Institute**. Now the town's Central Library (Mon–Fri 9.30am–1pm & 2–5.30pm), this Neoclassical building was erected as part of the civic makeover initiated by the Marquis of Pombal and Dom Manuel de Portugal e Castro in the early nineteenth century. Its entrance lobby on Malacca Road is lined with panels of blue-and-yellow-painted ceramic tiles, known as **azulejos**, depicting scenes from Luis Vaz Camões' epic poem, *Os Luisiades*.

Fontainhas

Panjim's oldest and most interesting district, **Fontainhas**, comprises a dozen or so blocks of Neoclassical houses rising up the sides of leafy Altinho Hill on the eastern edge of town, near the bus stand. Many have retained their traditional coat of ochre, pale yellow, green or blue – a legacy of the Portuguese insistence that every Goan building (except churches, which had to be white) should be colour-washed after the monsoons. While some have been restored, most remain in a state of charismatic decay.

The **Chapel of St Sebastian** stands at the centre of Fontainhas, at the head of a small square where the Portuguese-speaking locals hold a lively annual street *festa* to celebrate their patron saint's day in mid-November. The eerie crucifix inside the chapel, brought here in 1812, formerly hung in the Palace of the Inquisition in Old Goa. Unusually, Christ's eyes are open – allegedly to inspire fear in those being interrogated by the Inquisitors.

Just off the bottom of the square is a small workshop where you can watch traditional Goan *azulejos* being made. The main sales room, **Galeria Velha Goa**, is a couple of blocks away, next door to the *Panjim Inn*.

The State Archeological Museum

The most noteworthy feature of Panjim's **State Archeological Museum** (Mon–Fri 9.30am–1.15pm & 2–5.30pm; Rs20; ⓦ www.goamuseum.nic.in) is its impressive size, which stands in glaringly inverse proportion to the collections inside. In their bid to erect a structure befitting a state capital, Goa's bureaucrats ignored the fact that there was precious little to put in it. The only rarities to be found amid the half-hearted array of temple sculpture and dowdy colonial-era artefacts are a couple of Jain bronzes rescued by Customs and Excise officials from smugglers and, on the first floor, the infamous Italian-style table used by Goa's Grand Inquisitors, complete with its original, ornately carved tall-backed chairs.

The Houses of Goa Museum

Across the river, near the new hilltop suburb of **Porvorim**, the quirky **Houses of Goa Museum** (Tues–Sun 10am–7.30pm; Rs25; ⓦ www.archgoa.org), 5km from Panjim, aims to showcase the region's way of life as it used to be before the protective shield of Portuguese rule was lifted in 1961. The triangular building itself resembles a modern ark, with themed displays divided between four levels

---

Goan food and drink

Not unnaturally, after 451 years of colonization, Goan **cooking** has absorbed a strong Portuguese influence – palm vinegar (unknown elsewhere in India), copious amounts of coconut, tangy *kokum* and fierce local chillies also play their part. Goa is the home of the famous **vindaloo** (from the Portuguese *vinho d'alho*, literally "garlic wine"), originally an extra-hot and sour pork curry, but now made with a variety of meat and fish. Other **pork** specialities include *chouriço* red sausages, *sorpotel*, a hot curry made from pickled pig's liver and heart, *leitao*, suckling pig and *balchao*, pork in a rich brown sauce. Delicious alternatives include mutton *xacutti*, made with a sauce of lemon juice, peanuts, coconut, chillies and spices. The choice of **seafood**, often cooked in fragrant masalas, is excellent – clams, mussels, crab, lobster, giant prawns – while **fish**, depending on the type, is either cooked in wet curries, grilled, or baked in tandoori clay ovens. *Sanna*, like the south Indian *iddli*, is a steamed cake of fermented rice flour, but here made with palm toddy. Sweet tooths will adore *bebinca*, a rich, delicious solid egg custard with coconut.

As for **drinks**, locally produced wine, spirits and beer are cheaper than anywhere in the country, thanks to lower rates of tax. The most famous and widespread **beer** is Kingfisher, which tastes less of glycerine preservative than it does elsewhere in India, but you'll also come across pricier Fosters, brewed in Mumbai and nothing like the original. Goan **port**, a sweeter, inferior version of its Portuguese namesake, is ubiquitous, served chilled in large wine glasses with a slice of lemon. Local **spirits** – whiskies, brandies, rums, gins and vodkas – come in a variety of brand names for less than Rs30–50 a shot, but, at half the price, local speciality **feni**, made from distilled cashew or from the sap of coconut palms, offers strong competition. Cashew *feni* is usually drunk after the first distillation, but you can also find it double-distilled, flavoured with ginger or cumin to produce a smooth liqueur.

interconnected by spiral staircases. After a whistle-stop graphic resumé of Goan history, the exhibitions are largely given over to domestic houses. Pieces of traditional colonial-era houses – from wonderful old doors and oyster-shell windows, to carved railings, ceramic tiles, furniture and masonry – are assembled to explain construction processes and changes in decor and style.

The Houses of Goa Museum is most easily reached by taxi or auto-rickshaw. With your own transport, head north over the Mandovi bridge and keep going until you reach the big Alto-Porvorim Circle roundabout. Take a right here and follow the road until it forks, then bear left and drop downhill for 750m or so, until you reach a second fork, where you bear left again.

Eating and drinking

Catering for the droves of tourists who come here from other Indian states, as well as fussy, more price-conscious locals, Panjim is packed with good **places to eat**. Most are connected to a hotel, but there are also plenty of other independently run establishments offering quality food for far less than you pay in the coastal resorts. If you're unsure about which regional cooking style to go for, head for *The Fidalgo Food Enclave*, in the *Hotel Fidalgo* on 18th June Road, which hosts six different outlets, from Goan to Gujarati, with a great general Indian joint (*Mirch Masala*).

Bhojan *Hotel Fidalgo*, 18th June Rd. Authentic, pure-veg Gujarati thali joint, in the ground-floor restaurant complex of a popular upscale hotel. You won't eat finer Indian vegetarian cuisine anywhere in Goa. Rs125 for the works.

Delhi Darbar Mahatma Gandhi Rd, behind the *Hotel Mandovi*. A provincial branch of the famous Mumbai restaurant, and the best place in Panjim – if not all Goa – to sample traditional Mughlai cuisine of mainly meat steeped in rich, spicy sauces (try their superb *rogan ghosh* or melt-in-the-mouth chicken tikka). For vegetarians, there's a generous choice of fresh veg dishes, including a delicious *malai kofta*. Most mains Rs175–250.

Legacy of Bombay *Hotel Fidalgo*, 18th June Rd. Basically an upmarket Udupi, only with black bow ties instead of grubby cotton tunics. Their menu features the usual *dosas*, south Indian snacks, *pao bhaji* and tasty spring rolls, as well as spiced teas and delicious lassis.

Satkar 18th June Rd. Popular South-Indian snack and juice joint. There's a huge range of dishes, including Chinese and North Indian, but most people go for their fantastic masala dosas and piping hot, crunchy samosas – the best in town.

Shiv Sagar Mahatma Gandhi Rd. Smarter-than-average Udupi café that does a brisk trade

with Panjim's middle classes for its consistently fresh, delicious pan-Indian food and fresh fruit juices. The northern dishes aren't so great, but their Udupi menu is superb (try the delicious *palak dosa*, made with spinach), and their fiery *pao bhaji* is a real crowd-puller on weekends. No alcohol.

Venite Rua 31 de Janeiro. With its wooden floors and romantic, candle-lit balcony seats, this tourist-oriented place is one of the most atmospheric places to eat in Panjim. Continental and Goan seafood dishes dominate the menu. Most mains are Rs125–150.

Vihar Around the corner from *Venite*, on Avenida Dom Joao Castro. One of the best South-Indian snack cafés in Panjim, and more conveniently situated than its competitors if you're staying in Fontainhas. Try their tasty *rawa* masala dosas or cheese uttapams. The only drawback is the traffic noise, so avoid it during rush hours.

Viva Panjim 178 Rua 31 de Janeiro, behind Mary Immaculate High School, Fontainhas. Traditional Goan home-cooking – *xacutis*, vindaloo, prawn *balchao*, *cafreal*, *amotik* and fantastic freshly grilled fish – served by a charming local lady in an atmospheric colonial-era backstreet. Mains Rs80–150.

Listings

Airlines All airlines flying to Goa (for a full list, see "Travel details", p.836) have counters at Dabolim airport. Carriers with offices in downtown Panjim include: Air France, Air Seychelles, American Airlines, Biman Bangladesh, Cathay Pacific, Gulf Air, Kenyan Airways, Royal Jordanian, Sri Lankan

Airlines, all c/o Jet Air, 102 Rizvi Chambers, 1st floor, H Salgado Rd ☎0832/223172; Air India, Colvacar Centaur, Campal ☎0832/243 1100; British Airways, DKI Airlines Service, DKI Travel Services Pvt Ltd 102, Shiv Towers, Plot 14, Patto Plaza ☎0832/243 8055; Alitalia, Globe Trotters International, G-7 Shankar Parvati Building, 18th June Rd ☎0832/223 0940; Indian Airlines, Dempo House, Dr D Bandodkar Rd ☎0832/242 8787 or 223 7826; Jet Airways, Sesa Ghor, Patto Plaza, next to GTDC *Panjim Residency*, Pato ☎0832/243 8792.

Banks and ATMs Thomas Cook, near the Indian Airlines office at 8 Alcon Chambers, Dr Bandodkar Rd (Mon–Sat 9am–6pm, Oct–March also Sun 10am–5pm); Pheroze Framroze Exchange Bureau on Dr P Shirgaonkar Rd (Mon–Sat 9.30am–7pm, Sun 9.30am–1pm). Nearly all the banks in town also have ATMs.

Bookshops The bookshops in the *Hotel Fidalgo* and the *Hotel Mandovi* stock English-language titles, but the best selection of Goa-related books is at the Broadway Book Centre on 18th June Rd, near the Caculo Island intersection. It sells a great range of old texts in facsimile editions and lots of architecture and photographic tomes in hardback at discounted prices.

British Consular Assistant The British High Commission of Mumbai has a Tourist Assistance Office in Panjim – a useful contact for British nationals who've lost passports, got into trouble with the law or need help dealing with a death. It's over near the Kadamba Bus Stand at 13/14 Dempo Towers, Patto Plaza ☎0832/243 8734 or 8897, ⊕664 1297, ✉assistance@goaukconsular.org, ⊛www.ukinindia.com. Office opening hours are Mon–Fri 9am–1pm & 2.30–3.30pm. Outside these times, you should contact the main British Consulate in Mumbai ☎022/6650 2222, which in theory has a duty officer on call 24/7.

Cinema Panjim's swanky multiplex, the 1272-seater Inox, is in the northwest of town on the site of the old Goa Medical College, Dayanand Bandodkar (DB) Marg (☎0832/242 0999, ⊛www .inoxmovies.com). It screens all the latest Hindi blockbusters, and some English-language Hollywood movies; see the local press or their websites for listings and booking details.

Hospital The state's main medical facility is the new Goa Medical College, aka GMC (☎0832/245 8700–07), 7km south on NH-17 at Bambolim, where there's also a 24hr pharmacy. Ambulances (☎102) are likely to get you there a lot less quickly than a standard taxi. Conditions are grim by Western standards. Less serious cases can receive attention at the Vintage Hospital, next to the fire brigade headquarters in Panjim's St Inez district (☎0832/564 4401–05).

Internet access Hotels and guesthouses, including the *Park Lane Lodge* and *Panjim Inn* (see p.784), offer Internet access to guests. Otherwise, Cozy Nook Travels, at No.6 Municipal Bldg, 18th June Rd, has a fast ADSL connection.

Music and dance Regular recitals of classical Indian music and dance are held at Panjim's school for the performing arts, the Kala Academy in Campal (⊛www.kalaacademy.org), at the far west end of town on Dr Devanand Bandodkar Rd. For details of forthcoming concerts, consult the listings pages of local newspapers.

Pharmacies Hindu Pharma, near the tourist office on Church Square (☎0832/222 3176), stocks a phenomenal range of Ayurvedic, homeopathic and allopathic medicines.

Police The Police Headquarters is on Malacca Rd, central Panjim. In an emergency, call ☎100.

Travel agent AERO Mundial, ground floor, *Hotel Mandovi*, Dr Devanand Bandodkar Rd ☎0832/222 3773.

Old Goa

A one-time byword for splendour with a population of several hundred thousand, Goa's erstwhile former capital, **OLD GOA**, was virtually abandoned following malaria and cholera epidemics from the seventeenth century onwards. Today you need considerable imagination to picture the once-great capital as it used to be. The maze of twisting streets, piazzas and ochre-washed villas has gone, and all that remains is a score of cream-painted churches and convents. Granted World Heritage Status by UNESCO, Old Goa today attracts busloads of foreign tourists from the coast, and as many Christian pilgrims from around India. While the former come to admire the gigantic facades and gilt altars of the beautifully preserved churches, the main attraction for the latter is the tomb of **St Francis Xavier** (see p.790), the legendary sixteenth-century missionary, whose remains are enshrined in the **Basilica of Bom Jesus**. If you're staying on the coast and contemplating a day-trip inland, this is the most obvious and accessible option.

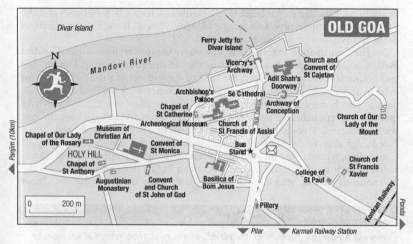

Just thirty minutes by road from the state capital, Old Goa is served by buses every fifteen minutes from Panjim's Kadamba Bus Stand; alternatively, hop into an auto-rickshaw (Rs100), or rent a taxi (Rs275–300). There is nowhere commendable to eat in Old Goa; for a snack or coffee, head a couple of kilometres back along the road to Panjim, where the lifestyle store **Casa de Goa**, housed in a beautifully converted, late sixteenth-century *palacio*, has an excellent **café**.

The Viceroy's Archway and the Church of St Cajetan

On arriving at the river landing stage to the north, seventeenth-century visitors passed through the **Viceroy's Archway** (1597), constructed to commemorate Vasco da Gama's arrival in India and built from the same porous red laterite as virtually all Old Goa's buildings. Above it a Bible-toting figure rests his foot on the cringing figure of a "native", while its granite facade, facing the river, holds a statue of da Gama himself. It's hard to imagine today that these overgrown fields and simple streets were once the focus of a lively market, with silk and gem merchants, horse dealers and carpet weavers. The one surviving monument, known as **Adil Shah's Doorway**, predates the Portuguese and possibly even the Muslim period. Hindu in style, it consists simply of a lintel supported by two columns in black basalt. You can find it by turning left at the crossroads immediately above the Arch of the Viceroys.

A short way up the lane from the Gate, the distinctive domed **Church of St Cajetan** (1651) was modelled on St Peter's in Rome by monks from the Theatine Order. While it boasts a Corinthian exterior, non-European elements are also evident in the decoration, such as the cashew-nut designs in the carving of the pulpit. Hidden beneath the church is a crypt where the embalmed bodies of Portuguese governors were once kept in lead coffins before they were shipped back to Lisbon. Forgotten for over thirty years, the last batch (of three) was only removed in 1992 on the eve of the state visit to Goa by the then Portuguese president.

The Sé (St Catherine's Cathedral)

The Portuguese viceroy Redondo (1561–64) commissioned the **Sé**, or **St Catherine's Cathedral**, southwest of St Cajetan's, to be "a grandiose church worthy of the wealth, power and fame of the Portuguese who dominated the seas from the Atlantic to the Pacific". Today it stands larger than any church in Portugal, although it was beset by problems, not least a lack of funds and the motherland's temporary loss of independence to Spain. It took eighty years to build and was not consecrated until 1640.

On the Tuscan-style exterior, the one surviving tower houses the **Golden Bell**, cast in Cuncolim (south Goa) in the seventeenth century. During the Inquisition its tolling announced the start of the gruesome tos-da-fé that were held in the square outside, when suspected heretics were subjected to public torture and burned at the stake. The scale and detail of the Corinthian-style interior is overwhelming; no fewer than fifteen altars are arranged around the walls, dedicated among others to Our Ladies of Hope, Anguish and Three Needs. An altar to St Anne treasures the relics of the **Blessed Martyrs of Cuncolim**, whose failed mission to convert the Mughal emperor Akbar culminated in their murder, while a chapel behind a highly detailed screen holds the **Miraculous Cross**, which stood in a Goan village until a vision of Christ

St Francis Xavier

Francis Xavier, the "Apostle of the Indies", was born in 1506 in the old kingdom of Navarre, now part of Spain. After taking a masters' degree in philosophy and theology at the University of Paris, where he studied for the priesthood until 1535, he was ordained two years later in Venice. He was then recruited by (Saint) **Ignatius Loyola** (1491–1556) along with five other priests into the new "Society of Jesus", which later became known as the **Jesuits**.

When the Portuguese king, Dom Joao III (1521–57), received reports of corruption and dissolute behaviour among the Portuguese in Goa, he asked Ignatius Loyola to dispatch a priest who could influence the moral climate for the better. In 1541 Xavier was sent to work in the diocese of Goa, constituted seven years earlier, and comprising all regions east of the Cape of Good Hope. Arriving after a year-long journey, he embarked on a busy programme throughout southern India. Despite frequent obstruction from Portuguese officials, he founded numerous churches, and is credited with converting thirty thousand people and performing such miracles as raising the dead and curing the sick with a touch of his beads. Subsequently he took his mission further afield to Sri Lanka, Malacca (Malaysia), China and Japan, where he was less successful.

When Xavier left Goa for the last time, it was with the ambition of evangelizing in China; however, he contracted dysentery aboard ship and died on the island of San Chuan (Sancian), off the Chinese coast, where he was buried. On hearing of his death, a group of Christians from Malacca exhumed his body – which, although the grave had been filled with lime to hasten its decomposition, they found to be in a perfect state of preservation. Reburied in Malacca, his body was later removed and taken to Old Goa, where it has remained ever since, enshrined in the **Basilica of Bom Jesus**.

However, St Francis's incorruptible corpse has never rested entirely in peace. Chunks of it have been removed over the years by **relic hunters** and curious clerics: in 1614, the right arm was dispatched to the pope in Rome (where it allegedly wrote its name on paper), a hand was sent to Japan, and parts of the intestines to Southeast Asia. One Portuguese woman, Dona Isabel de Caron, even bit off the little toe of the cadaver in 1534; apparently, so much blood spurted into her mouth, it left a trail to her house and she was discovered.

Every ten years, the saint's body is carried in a three-hour ceremony from the Basilica of Bom Jesus to the Sé cathedral, where visitors file past, touch and photograph it. During the 2004–05 "**exposition**", around 256,000 pilgrims flocked for *darshan* or ritual viewing of the corpse, these days a shrivelled and somewhat unsavoury spectacle.

appeared on it. Said to heal the sick, it is kept in a box; a small opening on the side allows devotees to touch it. The staggeringly ornate, gilded main **altar** comprises nine carved frames and a splendid crucifix. Panels depict episodes from the life of St Catherine of Alexandria (died 307 AD), including an interchange of ideas with the pagan Roman emperor Maxim, who wished to marry her, and her subsequent flogging and martyrdom.

The Archbishop's Palace

Adjoining the Sé cathedral – an exact contemporary – the **Archbishop's Palace** is unique as the last surviving civil building of colonial Goa's golden era. Presenting its most austere aspect to the river, the two-winged building formerly dominated the skyline of the waterfront. These days it houses a missable collection of contemporary Christian art in the recently inaugurated Kristu Kala Mandir Art Gallery (daily 10am–6pm; free) – not to be confused with the similar gallery at the Santa Monica Convent (see p.792).

The Church of St Francis of Assisi and Archeological Museum

Southwest of the cathedral is the ruined **Palace of the Inquisition**, in operation up until 1774, while to the west stands the **Convent of St Francis of Assisi**, built by Franciscan monks in 1517 and restored in the mid-eighteenth century. Today, the core of its **Archeological Museum** (daily except Fri 10am–5pm; Rs5) is a gallery of **portraits** of Portuguese viceroys, painted by local artists under Italian supervision. Other exhibits include coins, domestic Christian wooden sculpture, and downstairs in the cloister, pre-Portuguese Hindu sculpture. Next door, the **Church of St Francis** (1521) features fine decorative frescoes, *hidalgos'* tombstones in the floor paving, and paintings on wood showing the life of St Francis of Assisi.

Basilica of Bom Jesus

Close to the Convent of St Francis, the 1605 church of **Bom Jesus**, "Good" or "Menino Jesus" (Mon–Sat 9am–6.30pm, Sun 10am–6.30pm), is known principally for the **tomb of St Francis Xavier**. In 1946, it became the first church in India to be elevated to the status of Minor Basilica. On the west, the three-storey Renaissance facade encompasses Corinthian, Doric, Ionic and Composite styles.

The interior is entered beneath the choir, supported by columns. On the northern wall, in the centre of the nave, is a cenotaph in gilded bronze to **Dom Jeronimo Mascarenhas**, the Captain of Cochin and benefactor of the church. The main altar, extravagantly decorated in gold, depicts the infant Jesus under the protection of St Ignatius Loyola (founder of the Jesuit Order); to each side are subsidiary altars to Our Lady of Hope and St Michael. In the southern transept, lavishly decorated with twisted gilded columns and floriate carvings, stands the **Chapel and Tomb of St Francis Xavier**. Constructed of marble and jasper in 1696, it was the gift of the Medici, Cosimo III, the Grand Duke of Tuscany; the middle tier contains panels detailing the saint's life. An ornate domed reliquary in silver contains his remains; for a week around his feast day, December 3, tens of thousands of pilgrims – Hindus as well as Christians – queue for *darshan* (ritual viewing) of the casket before attending open-air Mass in the square outside.

Holy Hill

A number of other important religious buildings and a museum stand opposite Bom Jesus on **Holy Hill**. The **Convent of St Monica**, constructed in 1627, destroyed by fire in 1636 and rebuilt the following year, was the only Goan convent at the time and the largest in Asia. It housed around a hundred nuns, the Daughters of St Monica, and also offered accommodation to women whose husbands were called away to other parts of the empire. The **church** adjoins the convent on the south. As they had to remain away from the public gaze, the nuns attended mass in the choir loft and looked down upon the congregation. Inside, a **Miraculous Cross** rises above the figure of St Monica at the altar. In 1636, it was reported that the figure of Christ had opened his eyes, motioned as if to speak, and blood had flowed from the wounds made by his crown of thorns. The last Daughter of St Monica died in 1885, and since 1964 the convent has been occupied by the Mater Dei Institute for nuns.

Next door to the Chapel of the Miraculous Cross stands Goa's foremost **Museum of Christian Art** (daily 9.30am–5pm; Rs15). Exhibits include processional crosses, ivory ornaments, damask silk clerical robes and some finely sculpted wooden icons dating from the sixteenth and seventeenth centuries, among them an unusual statue of John the Baptist wearing a tiger-skin wrap (in the style of the Hindu god Shiva).

Nearby, the **Convent of St John of God**, built in 1685 by the Order of Hospitallers of St John of God to tend to the sick, was rebuilt in 1953. At the top of the hill, the **Chapel of Our Lady of the Rosary**, constructed in 1526 in the Manueline style (after the Portuguese king Manuel I, 1495–1521), features Ionic plasterwork with a double-storey portico, cylindrical turrets and a tower that commands fine views across the river from the terrace where Albuquerque surveyed the decisive battle of 1510. Its cruciform interior is unremarkable, except for the marble tomb of **Catarina a Piró**, believed to have been the first European woman to set foot in the colony. A commoner, she eloped here to escape the scandal surrounding her romance with Portuguese nobleman Garcia de Sá, who later rose to be governor of Goa. Under pressure from no less than Francis Xavier, Garcia eventually married her, but only *in articulo mortis* as she lay on her deathbed. Her finely carved tomb, set in the wall beside the high altar, incorporates a band of intricate Gujarati-style ornamentation, probably imported from the Portuguese trading post of Diu.

Ponda and around

PONDA, 28km southeast of Panjim and 17km northeast of Margao, is Ponda district's administrative headquarters and main market town. Straddling the busy Panjim–Bengaluru (Bangalore) highway (NH-4), it's not a place to spend any time. However, scattered among the lush valleys and forests **around Ponda** are a dozen or so **Hindu temples** founded during the seventeenth and eighteenth centuries, when this hilly region was a Christian-free haven for Hindus fleeing persecution by the Portuguese. Although the temples are fairly modern by Indian standards, their deities are ancient and held in high esteem by both local people and thousands of pilgrims from Maharashtra and Karnataka.

The temples are concentrated in two main clusters: the first to the north of Ponda, on the NH-4, and the second deep in the countryside, around 5km west of the town. Most people only manage the **Shri Manguesh** and **Shri Mahalsa** (⑩ www.mahalsa.org), between the villages of **Mardol** and **Priol**. Among the most interesting temples in the state, they lie just a stone's throw from the main highway and are passed by regular **buses** between Panjim and Margao via Ponda. The others are farther off the beaten track, although they are not hard to find on motorbikes; locals will wave you in the right direction if you get lost.

Mardol and Priol

Although the **Sri Manguesh** temple originally stood in a secret location in Cortalim, and was moved to its present site between **MARDOL** and **PRIOL** during the sixteenth century, the structure visitors see today dates from the 1700s. A gateway at the roadside leads to a paved path and courtyard that gives onto a water tank, overlooked by the white temple building, raised on a plinth. Also in the courtyard is a seven-storey *deepmal*, a tower for oil lamps. Inside, the floor is paved with marble, and bands of decorative tiles emblazon the white walls. Flanked by large *dvarpala* guardians, embossed silver doorways with floriate designs lead to the sanctum, which houses a *shivalingam*.

Two kilometres south, the **Mahalsa Marayani** temple was also transferred from its original site, in this case Salcete *taluka* further south, in the seventeenth century. Here, the *deepmal* is exceptionally tall, with 21 tiers rising from a figure of Kurma, the tortoise incarnation of Vishnu. Original features include a marble-floored wooden *mandapa* (assembly hall) with carved pillars, ceiling panels of parakeets and, in the eaves, sculptures of the incarnations of Vishnu.

Dudhsagar waterfalls

Measuring a mighty 600m from head to foot, the famous **Dudhsagar waterfalls**, on the Goa–Karnataka border, are some of the highest in India, and a spectacular enough sight to entice a steady stream of visitors from the coast into the rugged Western Ghats. After pouring across the Deccan plateau, the headwaters of the Mandovi River form a foaming torrent that fans into three streams, then cascades down a near-vertical cliff face into a deep green pool. The Konkani name for the falls, which literally translated means "sea of milk", derives from clouds of foam kicked up at the bottom when the water levels are at their highest. Overlooking a steep, crescent-shaped head of a valley carpeted with pristine tropical forest, Dudhsagar is set amid breathtaking **scenery** that is only accessible on foot or by Jeep; the recently upgraded Margao–Castle Rock railway actually passes over the falls on an old stone viaduct, but services along it are infrequent.

One you've reached Dudhsagar, there's little to do beyond enjoying the views and clambering over the rocks below the falls in search of pools to swim in. The **best time to visit** is immediately after the monsoons, from October until mid-December, when water levels are highest, although the falls flow well into April. Unfortunately, the train line only sees two services per week in each direction, neither of them returning the same day. As a result, the only practicable way to get there and back is by four-wheel-drive **Jeep** from **Colem** (reachable by train from Vasco, Margao and Chandor, or by taxi from the north-coast resorts for around Rs1300). The cost of the onward thirty- to forty-minute trip from Colem to the falls, which takes you across rough forest tracks and two or three river fords, is Rs700 per person; the drive ends with an enjoyable ten-minute hike, for which you'll need a sturdy pair of shoes. Finding a Jeep-wallah is easy; just turn up in Colem and look for the "Controller of Jeeps" near the station. However, if you're travelling alone or in a couple, you may have to wait around until the vehicle fills up, or else fork out to cover the cost of hiring the whole Jeep yourself. Alternatively, if you've travelled here **by motorcycle** you may – water levels permitting – ride to within easy reach of the falls: Enfields and Pulsars have enough clearance to ford the streams en route, but not Honda Activas and other small-wheeled scooters. Anyone who's ridden all the way to Colem on these bikes, and is determined not to stump up the Jeep fare, should follow the dirt track that runs alongside the main railway line for approximately 8km until it meets the Jeep route, thus bypassing the stream crossings – the way local stall-holders make the journey each day.

North Goa

Beyond the mouth of the Mandovi estuary, the Goan coast sweeps **north** in a near-continuous string of beaches, broken only by the odd saltwater inlet, rocky headland and three tidal rivers – the most northerly of which, the Arondem, still has to be crossed by ferry. Development is concentrated mainly behind the seven-kilometre strip of white sand that stretches from the foot of **Fort Aguada**, crowning the peninsula east of Panjim, to Baga creek in the north. Encompassing the resorts of **Candolim**, **Calangute** and **Baga**, this is Goa's prime charter belt and an area most independent travellers steer clear of.

Since the advent of mass tourism in the 1980s, the alternative "scene" has drifted progressively north away from the sunbed strip to **Anjuna** and **Vagator** – site of some of the region's loveliest beaches – and scruffier **Chapora**, a workaday fishing village. Further north still, **Arambol** has thus far escaped any large-scale development, despite the completion of the new road bridge across the Chapora River. What little extra traffic there is since the new road link tends to focus on the low-key resorts just south of Arambol, namely **Aswem** and **Mandrem**, where facilities remain basic by modern standards.

North Goa's market town, **Mapusa**, is this area's main jumping-off place, with bus connections to most resorts on the coast. If you're travelling here by train via the **Konkan Railway**, get off the train at **Tivim** (☏0832/229 8682), 19km west of Margao, from where you'll have to jump in a bus or taxi for the remaining leg.

Mapusa

MAPUSA (pronounced "Mapsa") is the district headquarters of Bardez *taluka*. A dusty collection of dilapidated, mostly modern buildings ranged around a busy central square, the town is of little more than passing interest, although it does host a lively **market** on Friday mornings. Anjuna's market may be a better place to shop for souvenirs, but Mapusa's is much more authentic. Local specialities include strings of spicy Goan sausages (*chouriço*), bottles of toddy (fermented palm sap) and large green plantains from nearby Moira.

Practicalities

Tivim (Thivim), the nearest railway station to Mapusa, is 12km east in the neighbouring Bicholim district. Buses should be on hand to transport passengers into town, from where you can pick up local services to Calangute, Baga, Anjuna, Vagator, Chapora and Arambol. These leave from the **Kadamba Bus Stand**, five minutes' walk west of the main square, where all state-run services from Panjim also pull in. **Motorcycle taxis** hang around the square to whisk lightly laden shoppers and travellers to the coast for around Rs50–65. **Taxis** charge considerably more (around Rs150), but you can split the fare with up to five people.

The Konkan Railway's Konkan–Kanya Express (#KR0111) arrives in Tivim at around 9.30am, leaving plenty of time to find **accommodation** in the coastal resorts west of Mapusa. Avoid staying in the town if possible, but if you can't, try GTDC's *Mapusa Residency* (☏0832/226 2794, ⓦwww.goa-tourism .com; ④–⑤), on the roundabout below the square, which has spacious and clean rooms and a Goa **tourist information** counter. Best of the **eating** options on or around the main square is the *Ruchira*, within the *Hotel Satyaheera* on the north side of the main square, which serves a standard multi-cuisine menu and cold beer. For quick, authentically Goan food, you won't do better than the recently revamped *FR Xavier* café over in the Municipal Market, which has been here since the Portuguese era.

Candolim and Fort Aguada

Compared with Calangute, 3km north along the beach, **CANDOLIM** is a surprisingly relaxed resort, attracting mainly middle-aged package tourists from the UK and Scandinavia. Over the past few years, however, its ribbon development of hotels and restaurants has sprouted a string of holiday complexes, and during peak season the few vestiges of authentically Goan culture that remain here are drowned in a deluge of Kashmiri handicraft stalls, luridly lit terrace cafés and shopping arcades. On the plus side, Candolim has lots of pleasant places to stay, many of them tucked away down quiet sandy lanes and better value than comparable guesthouses in nearby Calangute, making this a good first stop if you've just arrived in Goa and are planning to head further north after finding your feet.

Immediately south, **Fort Aguada** crowns the rocky flattened headland at the end of the beach. Built in 1612 to protect the northern shores of the Mandovi estuary from Dutch and Maratha raiders, the bastion encloses several natural springs, the first source of drinking water available to ships arriving in Goa after the long sea voyage from Lisbon. The ruins of the fort can be reached by road; follow the main drag south from Candolim as it bears left, past the turning for the *Taj Holiday Village*, and keep going for 1km until you see a right turn, which runs uphill to a small car park. Nowadays, much of the site serves as a prison, and is therefore closed to visitors. It's worth a visit, though, if only for the panoramic views from the top of the hill where a four-storey Portuguese **lighthouse**,

ACCOMMODATION

Antonio	D
Casa Sea Shell	D F
Dioro's	C
Dona Florina	A G E
Marbella	G
Pretty Petal	E
Shanu	B

RESTAURANTS & BARS

Amigo's	4
Bomra's	8
Café Chocolatti	5
Cinnabar Café	6
Pete's Shack	2
Sheetal	3
Stone House	7
Viva Goa	1

CANDOLIM & FORT AGUADA

erected in 1864 and the oldest of its kind in Asia, looks down over the vast expanse of sea, sand and palm trees.

From the base of Fort Aguada on the northern flank of the headland, a rampart of red-brown laterite juts into the bay at the bottom of picturesque **Sinquerim Beach** (in effect the southernmost reach of Calangute Beach). This was among the first places in Goa to be singled out for upmarket tourism. The Taj Group's *Fort Aguada* resorts, among the most expensive hotels in India, lord over the sands from the slopes below the battlements.

In addition to its nearby fort, Candolim also harbours a bumper crop of wonderful **old mansions** and typically Goan houses, some of the best of them in the excellent folk and architectural museum, **Calizz** (daily 10.30am–11.30pm; admission Rs1200, includes meal; ⓦwww.calizz.com), on the south side of the village near Acron Arcade. Comprising half a dozen beautifully restored period buildings spread over a site of several acres, the complex showcases various styles of traditional Goan houses – both Christian and Hindu – from humble mud structures dating from pre-colonial times to sumptuous Portuguese *palacios* with chapels attached. On display inside them is a superb array of antiques, furniture, religious icons and daily artefacts. Visits kick off with an engaging ninety-minute guided tour, after which you're served a traditional Indo-Portuguese-Goan feast, comprising dishes that would have been prepared in the houses you've looked at.

Practicalities

Buses to and from Panjim stop every ten minutes or so at the stand opposite the *Casa Sea Shell*, in the middle of Candolim. A few continue south to the *Fort Aguada Beach Resort* terminus, from where services depart every thirty minutes for the capital via Nerul village; you can also flag down buses from anywhere along the main drag to Calangute. **Taxis** are ubiquitous but during the season there is often a shortage of **motorcycles for rent** here, and you may find yourself having to search for a bike in Calangute.

There are several ATMs dotted along the main drag (see map, p.795) and you can **change money** at any number of private exchange places dotted around Candolim, although their rates are unlikely to be as competitive as those on offer in Calangute. For **Internet** access, Sify-I-Way, at the north end of the village on the main road, offers a fast broadband connection.

Accommodation

Candolim is charter-holiday land, so **accommodation** tends to be expensive for most of the season. That said, if bookings are down you can find some great bargains here.

Antonio Camotim Waddo ☎0832/248 9735, ☎9822 3381214. Spacious and comfortable chalet-style rooms, some with kitchenettes, all with good-sized balconies, in a two-storey block between the road and the beach, well away from the strip. ❹

Casa Sea Shell Fort Aguada Rd, near *Bom Successo* ☎0832/247 9879. A modern block with its own pool, picturesquely situated beside a small chapel. The rooms are large, with spacious tiled bathrooms, and the staff and management unfailingly welcoming and courteous. If they're full, ask for a room in the identical and slightly cheaper (but

pool-less) *Sea Shell Inn* (☎0832/248 9131) up the road. ❺

Dioro's Camotim Waddo ☎0832/329 0713, or 09823 269376, ⓔdiorosgoa@yahoo.com. Very large, tiled, spotless rooms with huge balconies and fridges, in a quiet residential area well back from the main road and close to the beach. Great value for money, considering the space and comfort, even at Christmas; and there's a well-kept garden. ❹

Dona Florina Monteiro's road, Sequeira Waddo ☎0832/248 9051, ⓦwww .donaflorina.com. Large guesthouse in a superb location, overlooking the beach in the most secluded corner of the village. A breezy rooftop terrace with ceramic mosaic floors provides an ideal spot for yoga practise. Well worth paying a little extra for if you want idyllic sea views. No car access. **❹–❺**

Marbella Sinquerim ☎0832/247 9551, ⓦwww .marbellagoa.com. Individually styled suites and spacious rooms (from Rs2600) in a beautiful house built to resemble a traditional Goan mansion. The decor, fittings and furniture are gorgeous, especially in the top-floor "Penthouse" (Rs4500), and the whole place is screened by a giant mango tree. **❻–❽**

Pretty Petal Camotim Waddo ☎0832/348 9184, ⓦwww.prettypetalsgoa.com. Not as twee as it sounds: very large, modern rooms, all with fridges and balconies, and relaxing, marble-floored communal areas overlooking lawns. Their top-floor apartment, with windows on four sides and a huge balcony, is the best choice, though more expensive. **❺–❻**

Shanu Escrivao Waddo ☎0832/248 9899. Good-sized, well-furnished rooms with narrow balconies right on the dunes, some of them with uninterrupted views of the sea (a real rarity). Ask the hospitable owners for #120 (or failing that #118, #111, #110 or #107). Breakfast is served in your room. **❹**

Eating and drinking

Candolim's numerous beach **cafés** are a cut above your average seafood shacks, with pot plants, high-tech sound systems and prices to match. The further from the *Taj* complex you venture, the lower the prices become.

Amigo's 3km east of Candolim at Nerul bridge ☎0832/240 1123, or 09822 104920. Though well off the beaten track, this rough-and-ready riverside shack, tucked away under the bridge that Jason Bourne's girlfriend sped off in *The Bourne Supremacy*, is famed locally for its superb fresh seafood, served straight off the boats. *Tamoso* (red snapper) is their speciality, but they also do stuffed pomfret, calamari chilli-fry, barramundi and, best of all, Jurassic-sized crabs in butter-garlic sauce (order the day before). Count on Rs250–350 for the works, with drinks. You can phone in your order in advance.

Bomra's Souza Waddo, Fort Aguada Rd, south Candolim ☎09822 149633 or 09822 1306236. Understated, relaxed place, on a dimly lit gravel terrace by the roadside. From the outside you'd never know this was one of Goa's gastronomic highlights, but the food – contemporary Burmese and Kachin cuisine – is superb. Try their spinach wraps in fragrant tahini sauce for starters, or the beef in peanut curry.

Café Chocolatti near Acron Arcade. Goa's answer to Juliette Binoche's "Vianne Rocher" in the movie *Chocolat*, the British-raised owner of this delightful café in south Candolim, Nazneen, has conjured up a Mecca for chocoholics. Over a perfect cup of freshly ground coffee in the garden, you can indulge in gourmet Belgian-style truffles, tinged with chilli, mocca and orange, and crunchy almond-flavoured Italian biscuits.

Cinnabar Café Acron Arcade, Fort Aguada Rd. Hip new café, with Italian-style glass- and wood-panelled interior, serving what we reckon

is Goa's best cappuccino. Occasional DJs add to the ambience. Opens at 8am for cooked breakfasts.

Pete's Shack Sequeira Waddo. One beach shack that deserves singling out because it's always professional and serves great healthy salads (Rs85–225) with real olive oil, mozzarella and balsamic vinegar. All the veg is carefully washed in chlorinated water first, so the food is safe and fresh. The same applies to their seafood sizzler and tandoori main courses. For dessert, try the wonderful chocolate mousse or cooling mint lassis.

Sheetal Murrod Waddo. One of the few restaurants in Goa specializing in authentic Mughlai cuisine. Served in copper *karais* with braziers by a team of snappy waiters dressed in traditional *salwars*, the menu features a long list of chicken, mutton and vegetarian dishes steeped in rich sauces. Count on Rs300–400 per head, plus drinks.

Stone House Fort Aguada Rd. Blues-nut Chris D'Souza hosts this lively, low-lit bar-restaurant, spread in front of a gorgeous bare-laterite Goan house. Prime cuts of beef and kingfish served with scrumptious baked potatoes are their most popular dishes. Blues enthusiasts should come just for the CD collection. Most mains under Rs250.

Viva Goa! Fort Aguada Rd. Succulent, no-nonsense Goan food fresh from the market – mussel fry, barramundi (*chonok*), lemonfish (*modso*) and sharkfish steaks fried *rechado* style in chilli paste or in millet (*rawa*) – served on a roadside terrace. Tourists are welcome, but it's essentially local food at local prices.

Calangute

A 45-minute bus ride up the coast from Panjim, **CALANGUTE** was, in Portuguese times, where well-to-do Goans would come for their annual *mudança*, or change of air, in May and June, when the pre-monsoonal heat made life in the towns insufferable. It remains the state's busiest resort, but has changed beyond recognition since the days when straw-hatted musicians in the beachfront bandstand would regale smartly dressed strollers with Lisbon *fados* and Konkani *dulpods*.

Beach parties of a less genteel nature first started to become a regular feature of life here in the late 1960s. Stoned out of their brains on local *feni* and cheap *charas*, the tribes of long-haired Westerners lying naked on the vast white sandy beach soon became tourist attractions in their own right, pulling in bus-loads of visitors from Mumbai, Bengaluru (Bangalore) and beyond. Calangute's flower-power period, however, is decidedly long gone.

Nowadays, the owners of swish resort hotels look back on the hippy era with a mixture of amusement and nostalgia. But they and their fellow Colongutis have paid a high price for the recent prosperity. Mass package tourism, combined with a huge increase in the number of Indian visitors (for whom this is Goa's number-one beach resort), has placed an impossible burden on the town's rudimentary infrastructure. Hemmed in by four-storey buildings and swarming with traffic, the market area, in particular, has taken on the aspect of a typical makeshift Indian town of precisely the kind that most travellers used to come to Goa to get away from. In short, this is somewhere to avoid, although most people pass through here at some stage, to change money or shop for essentials. The only other reason to endure the chaos is to eat: Calangute boasts some of the best **restaurants** in the whole state.

Practicalities

Buses from Mapusa and Panjim pull in at the small bus stand-cum-market square in the centre of Calangute. Some continue to Baga, stopping at the crossroads behind the beach en route.

For **changing money**, Thomas Cook have a branch in the main market area (Mon–Sat 9.30am–6pm), where there's also an efficient ICICI Bank with 24hr ATM. Private currency changers on the same street include Wall Street Finances (Mon–Sat 9.30am–6pm), opposite the petrol pump and in the shopping complex on the beachfront, who exchange both cash and traveller's cheques at bank rates. At the Bank of Baroda (Mon–Fri 9.30am–2.15pm, Sat 9.30am–noon, Sun 9.30am–2pm), just north of the market on the Anjuna road, you can make encashments against Visa cards; commission is one percent of the amount changed, plus Rs125 for the authorization phone-call.

There are innumerable cafés scattered around town offering broadband **Internet** access, notably Sify-I-Way: Rs60/hr for drop-ins, or Rs35/hr for members. One of Goa's best bookshops, The Oxford Bookstore, stands on the south side of town, directly opposite St Anthony's Chapel on the main Candolim road. Down in Gauro Waddo near *Gabriel's*, on the edge of Candolim, Café Literrati (10am–7pm; closed Wed) has a more off-beat, bibliophile feel about it, with a great collection of paper- and hard-backs shelved in a converted Portuguese-era house.

Accommodation

In spite of the encroaching mayhem, plenty of budget travellers return to Calangute year after year, staying in little family guesthouses in the fishing *waddo* where the pace of life remains remarkably unchanged.

Camizala 5-33B Maddo Waddo ☎0832/227 9530, ☎09822 986544. Lovely, breezy place with only four rooms, common verandas and sea views. About as close to the beach as you can get, and the *waddo* is very quiet. Cheap considering the location. ❸–❹

Casa Leyla Maddo Waddo ☎0832/227 6478 or 227 9068, ⓦwww.cocobananagoa.com. This is a great place if you're a family looking for somewhere with plenty of space for a longish let, say of at least one week. The rooms are huge and well furnished, with fridges, kid-friendly beds and chairs, and basic self-catering facilities, while the house itself is set deep in the secluded fishing ward, behind the quietest stretch of the beach. ❹–❻

CoCo Banana 1195 Umta Waddo ☎0832/227 6478 or 227 9068, ⓦwww.cocobananagoa.com. Very comfortable, spacious chalets, all with bathrooms, fridges, mosquito nets, extra-long mattresses and verandas, around a central garden – but no a/c. Down the lane past *Meena Lobo's* restaurant, it's run by a very sorted Swiss–Goan couple, Walter and Marina Lobo, who have been here for nearly twenty years. ❺

Gabriel's Gauro Waddo ☎0832/227 9486. A congenial guesthouse very close to the beach, midway between Calangute and Candolim, run by a gorgeous family who go out of their way

to help guests. The rooms are large, with quiet fans, lockable steel cupboards and decent mattresses; the rear side ones have balconies looking across the toddy groves and dunes. ❹

Indian Kitchen Behind Our Lady of Piety Church ☎0832/227 7555, ⓔikitchen2602@yahoo.co.in. Jazzily decorated guesthouse with crazy mosaic tiling, brightly patterned walls and lanterns. The rooms, all attached, have fridges and music systems. ❸–❹

Kerkar Retreat Gauro Waddo ☎0832/227 6017, ⓦwww.subodhkerkar.com. Colour-themed "boutique hotel", artfully decorated with original paintings (by local artist and owner, Subodh Kerkar), Goan *azulejos* and designer furniture creating an effect that's modern, but definably Goan. The only downside is the roadside location. ❼

Pousada Tauma Porba Waddo ☎0832/227 9061, ⓦwww.pousada-tauma.com. Small luxury resort complex, comprising double-storey laterite villas ranged around a pool. It's near the middle of Calangute, but screened from the din by lots of vegetation. Understated decor and repro-antique furnishings, and a very exclusive atmosphere, preserved by five-star prices. Their big draw is a first-rate Keralan Ayurvedic health centre (open to non-residents). From $360–550 per night (including taxes). ❾

Eating and drinking

Ever since *Souza Lobo* opened on the beachfront to cater for Goan day-trippers in the 1930s, Calangute has been somewhere people come as much to eat as for a stroll on the beach, and even if you stay in resorts elsewhere you'll doubtless be tempted down here for a meal.

A Reverie Near *Hotel Goan Heritage*, Gauro Waddo ☎09823 174927, 093261 14661. Unashamedly over-the-top gourmet place on the south side of Calangute, centred on a grand terracotta-tiled canopy. Both the gastronomic menu and ambience are about as extravagant as Goa gets, but the prices remain within reach of most budgets (around Rs800 per head, plus drinks). Reservation recommended.

Casandre Beach Rd. Housed in a smartly renovated Portuguese-era home, with a deep veranda fronting the main drag, this popular roadside restaurant is run by three enthusiastic Goan brothers and their Swiss/British wives. The menu is gigantic, but the seafood, steak and sizzler specials listed on a blackboard tend to be the best bets.

Florentine's 4km east of Calangute church at Saligao, next door to the Ayurvedic Natural Health Centre. It's well worth venturing

inland to taste Florence D'Costa's legendary chicken *cafreal*, made to a jealously guarded family recipe that pulls in crowds of locals and tourists from across north Goa. The restaurant is a down-to-earth place, with prices to match, serving only chicken, some seafood and vegetarian snacks.

Infantaria Pastelaria Next to St John's Chapel, Baga road. Roadside terrace café run by *Souza Lobo's* that gets packed out for its stodgy croissants, freshly baked apple pie and traditional Goan sweets (such as *dodol* and home-made *bebinca*). Top of the savoury list, though, are the prawn and veg patties, which locals buy by the boxload.

Oriental Royal Thai 2min walk south off the main crossroads on the beach road, at the *Hotel Mira* ☎0832/3292809 or 098221 21549. Sumptuous Thai cuisine prepared by master chef Chawee, who turns out eighteen house sauces to accompany choice cuts of seafood, meat and poultry, as well

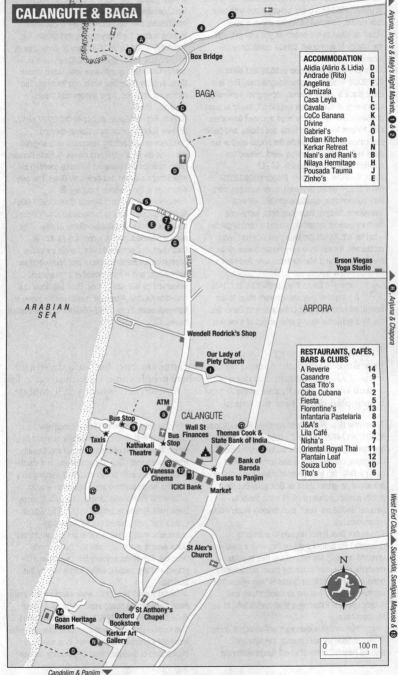

▲ *Anjuna*

CALANGUTE & BAGA

BAGA

Box Bridge

Titó's Lane

BAGA ROAD

Erson Viegas Yoga Studio

ARPORA

ARABIAN SEA

Wendell Rodrick's Shop

Our Lady of Piety Church

CALANGUTE

ATM

Bus Stop

Taxis

Wall St Finances

Bus Stop

Kathakali Theatre

Thomas Cook & State Bank of India

Vanessa Cinema

Bank of Baroda

ICICI Bank

Buses to Panjim

Market

St Alex's Church

St Anthony's Chapel

Goan Heritage Resort

Oxford Bookstore

Kerkar Art Gallery

N

0   100 m

▼ *Candolim & Panjim*

▶ *Anjuna, Ingo's & Maky's Night Markets,* **1** & **2**

▶ *H, Anjuna & Chapora*

▶ *West End Club,* ▲ *Sangolda, Saligao, Mapusa &* **13**

ACCOMMODATION

Alidia (Alirio & Lidia)	D
Andrade (Rita)	G
Angelina	F
Camizala	M
Casa Leyla	L
Cavala	C
CoCo Banana	K
Divine	A
Gabriel's	O
Indian Kitchen	I
Kerkar Retreat	N
Nani's and Rani's	B
Nilaya Hermitage	H
Pousada Tauma	J
Zinho's	E

RESTAURANTS, CAFÉS, BARS & CLUBS

A Reverie	14
Casandre	9
Casa Tito's	1
Cuba Cubana	2
Fiesta	5
Florentine's	13
Infantaria Pastelaria	8
J&A's	3
Lila Café	4
Nisha's	7
Oriental Royal Thai	11
Plantain Leaf	12
Souza Lobo	10
Tito's	6

as plenty of vegetarian options. Be sure to try their signature dish, *soom tham* (papaya salad). At around Rs800–1000 for three courses, it's good value for cooking of this standard.

Plantain Leaf Market area. The best Udupi restaurant outside Panjim, if not all Goa, where waiters in matching shirts serve the usual range of delicious *dosas* and other spicy snacks in a clean, cool marble-lined canteen, with relentless background *filmi* music. Try their definitive *iddli*-vada breakfasts, delicious masala dosas or the cheap and filling set thalis (Rs65).

Souza Lobo Beachfront. A Calangute institution, even though the food – served on gingham tablecloths by legions of fast-moving waiters – isn't always what it used to be. Stuffed crab, full baby kingfish and crepe Souza are the house specialities. Most main dishes Rs195–300.

Nightlife

Calangute's **nightlife** is surprisingly tame for a resort of its size. All but a handful of the bars wind up by midnight, leaving punters to prolong the short evenings back at their hotels, find a shack that's open late, or else head up to Baga (see p.803).

Down on the south edge of Calangute in Gauro Waddo, the **Kerkar Art Gallery** (☎0832/227 6017, ⓦwww.subodhkerkar.com) hosts evenings of **classical music and dance** (Tues 6.45pm; Rs350), held in the back garden on a sumptuously decorated stage, complete with incense and candlelight. The recitals, performed by students and teachers from Panjim's Kala Academy, are kept comfortably short for the benefit of Western visitors, and are preceded by a short introductory talk.

Baga

BAGA, 10km west of Mapusa, is basically an extension of Calangute. The only difference between this far northern end of the beach and its more congested centre is that the scenery here is marginally more varied and picturesque. Overlooked by a rocky headland draped in vegetation, a small tidal river flows into the sea at the top of the village, past a spur of soft white sand where ranks of brightly coloured fishing boats are moored.

Since the package boom, Baga has developed more rapidly than anywhere else in the state and today looks less like the Goan fishing village it still was in the early 1990s and more like a small-scale resort on the Spanish Costas, with a predominantly young, charter-tourist clientele to match. If you can steer clear of the lager louts, Baga boasts distinct advantages over its neighbours: a crop of excellent **restaurants** and a **nightlife** that's consistently more full-on than anywhere else in the state, if not all India.

Accommodation

Accommodation is harder to arrange in Baga than in Calangute, as most of the hotels have been carved up by the charter companies; even rooms in smaller guesthouses tend to be booked up well before the season gets under way. The majority of family-run places lie around the north end of the beach, where night-times have been a lot more peaceful since Goa's premier club, *Tito's*, acquired soundproofing.

Alidia (Alirio & Lidia) Baga Rd, Saunta Waddo ☎0832/227 6835, ⓔalidia@rediffmail.com. Attractive modern chalet-style rooms with particularly comfy beds and good-sized verandas looking on to the dunes. Most go for Rs1000–1500, but there are a handful of cheaper options on the ground floor for budget travellers. Plus they've recently added a pool. ❹–❺

Andrade (Rita) Just south of Tito's Lane ☎0832/227 9087. Half a dozen sea-facing rooms. Those on the lower floor are smaller, but with larger verandas than the much nicer top-storey ones. Friendly management, and close to the liveliest stretch of beach. ❹

Angelina Saunta Waddo ☎0832/227 9145, ⓔangelinabeachresort@rediffmail.com.

Spacious, well-maintained rooms with large, gleaming tiled bathrooms and big balconies, in the thick of things off Tito's Lane. The best rooms are on the top storey of the newest of the three blocks. A/c available. Unbeatable value for money in this enclave. ③–④

Cavala Baga Rd ☎ 0832/227 7587 or 227 6090, ⓦ www.cavala.com. Modern hotel in tastefully traditional laterite, with a pool surrounded by banana groves; spacious twin-bedded rooms and separate balconies, but a little close to the road for comfort. Rooms range from simple non-a/c doubles to luxurious suites. ⑤–⑧

Divine Near *Nani's and Rani's*, north of the river ☎ 0832/227 9546. Run by a couple of hospitable, animal-loving Gulf returnees, the rooms are on the small side, but impeccably clean; some have attached shower-toilets, and there's a lovely upper terrace with sunbeds and shades, presided over by a menagerie of animal finials on the rooftops. Advance booking essential. ④–⑤

Nani's and Rani's North of the river (House #164) ☎ 0832/227 6313, ⓔ jeshuafern@yahoo.com.

A handful of red-tiled, whitewashed budget cottages in a secluded garden behind a huge colonial-era house. Fans, some attached bathrooms, well water, outdoor showers and Internet access. ⑤

Nilaya Hermitage Arpora Bhati ☎ 0832/227 6793, ⓦ www.nilayahermitage.com. Set on the crest of a hilltop 6km inland from the beach, with matchless views over the coastal plain, this ranks among India's most exclusive hotels, patronized by a very rich international jet set (Richard Gere, Giorgio Armani, Sean Connery and Kate Moss are all rumoured to have stayed here). The complex is a fantasy of rich Indian colours, fiddly ironwork and gilded pillars, opening onto a dreamy pool. Tariffs from $460 for two (or $700 over Christmas–New Year), including meals and airport transfers. ⑨

Zinho's 7/3 Saunta Waddo ☎ 0832/227 7383. Tucked away off the main road, close to *Tito's*. Seventeen modest-sized, clean rooms above a family home; those in the new a/c block are a bit overpriced. ④–⑤

Eating

Nowhere else in the state offers such a good choice of quality **eating** as Baga. Restaurateurs – increasing numbers of them European expats or refugees from upper-class Mumbai – vie with each other to lay on the trendiest menus and most romantic, stylish gardens or terraces. It's all a very far cry indeed from the rough-and-ready beach-shack culture that held sway only seven or eight years ago.

Casa Tito's Opposite Ingo's Night Market, Arpora. Boutique-style restaurant in a stylishly renovated Portuguese *palacio*, filled with wonderfully evocative memorabilia belonging to the *Tito's* family. The menu's dominated by gourmet Mediterranean cuisine, served from a garden grill; it also functions as a lounge bar (see opposite). Most dishes Rs250–300.

Fiesta Tito's Lane ☎ 0832/227 9894, ⓦ www.fiestagoa.com. Run by the glamorous but improbably named Yellow and Maneck Contractor, Baga's most extravagantly decorated restaurant enjoys a perfect spot at the top of a long dune, with sea views from the veranda of a 1930s house. The contemporary Mediterranean food is as delectable as the decor: try their carpaccio of beef for starters, followed by seafood lasagne or the succulent wood-baked pizzas (Rs200). Most starters and mains Rs250–300. Reservations recommended.

J&A's Anjuna Rd ☎ 0832/227 5274 or 09823 139488, ⓦ www.littleitalygoa.com. Mouthwatering, authentic Italian food (down to the imported Parmesan, sun-dried tomatoes and olive oil)

served in the gorgeous candle-lit garden of an old fisherman's cottage. There's an innovative range of salads and antipasti, a choice of sumptuous pasta dishes, wood-fired pizzas and tender steaks (with rosemary potatoes) for mains. For dessert, go for the melt-in-the-mouth hot chocolate soufflé. Count on at least Rs750 per head for three courses, plus drinks.

Lila Café Baga Creek. Laid-back bakery-cum-snack-bar, run by a German couple who've been here for decades. Their healthy home-made breads and cakes are great, and there's an adventurous lunch menu featuring spinach à la crème, aubergine pâté and smoked water-buffalo ham. Open 8am–8pm.

Nisha's Tito's Lane ☎ 0832/227 7588. This little restaurant, occupying a sandy terrace just down from *Tito's*, can't be beaten for simply prepared seafood – snapper, kingfish, tiger prawns and lobster – flame-grilled or tandoori-baked to perfection in front of you by chef Frankie Almon and his crew. Freshness counts more here than fancy sauces. For starters, try calamari in chilli oil with lemon. Most mains are a reasonable Rs275–350.

Nightlife

That Baga's **nightlife** has become legendary in India is largely attributable to one club, *Tito's*. Lured by TV images of skimpy dancewear and a thumping sound-and-light system, hundreds of revellers descend on its long narrow terrace each night to drink, shuffle about and watch the action, the majority of them men from other states who've come to Goa as an escape from the moral confines of life at home. For Western women, in particular, this can sometimes make for an uncomfortably loaded atmosphere, although since a facelift (and a hike in door charges), *Tito's* seems to have put the era of Kingfisher-fuelled brawls behind it. New theme-bars and clubs are also popping up each year, offering increasingly sophisticated alternatives.

For anyone who's been travelling around the rest of the country, Baga by night – complete with all the garishness of a Saturday in British clubland – can come as an unpleasant shock. For more on the area's nightlife, see the accounts of Calangute (p.801) and Anjuna (p.808).

Bars and clubs

Casa Tito's Arpora, opposite Ingo's Night Market. Chic Italian gastro-lounge bar in an old Portuguese-era house, with traditional furniture, family memorabilia, resident DJs, cocktails and gourmet food. Perfect post-Ingo's chillout spot.

Cuba Cubana 82 Xim Waddo, Arpora Hill ⓦ www .clubcubana.net. Glam nightclub on a forested hilltop inland from Baga, spread around an underlit open-air pool. Its high entrance charge – Rs700 for single/accompanied men; Rs500 for women (except Wed, "Ladies Nite" when girls get in free) buys you unlimited drinks from a well-stocked bar – a policy intended to keep out the low-spending riff-raff from down on the strip. R&B, hip-hop and garage (they purposely stay well away from techno) played on a twin-storey dance floor. Open daily 9.30pm–5am.

Kamaki Tito's Lane, Saunta Waddo. Big-screen sports and a state-of-the-art karaoke machine account for the appeal of this a/c, Brit-dominated bar just up the lane from *Tito's*. Rs100 cover charge sometimes applies.

Mambo's Tito's Lane, Saunta Waddo. Large, semi-open-air pub with wooden decor and a big circular bar that gets packed out most nights in season with a lively, mixed crowd. Once again, karaoke is the big draw, though drinks cost well above average, and they slap on a Rs400 cover charge after 11pm, or when there's live entertainment. "Ladies Night", on Wed, means free entry and free drinks for women.

Tito's Tito's Lane, Saunta Waddo ⓦ www.titosgoa .com. Occasional cabarets, fashion shows and guest DJs feature throughout the season at India's most famous nightclub. Music policy is lounge

---

Saturday night bazaars

One of the few positive improvements to the north Goa resort strip in recent times has been the **Saturday Night Bazaar**, held on a plot midway between Baga and Anjuna. The brainchild of an expat German called Ingo, it's run with great efficiency and a sense of fun that's palpably lacking these days from the Anjuna Flea Market. The balmy evening temperatures and pretty lights are also a lot more conducive to relaxed browsing than the broiling heat of mid-afternoon on Anjuna beach; moreover, the laid-back ambience is preserved with a ban on hassling customers.

Although far more commercial than its predecessor in Anjuna, many old Goa hands regard this as far truer to the original spirit of the flea market. A significant proportion of the stalls are taken up by foreigners selling their own stuff, from reproduction Indian pop art to antique photos, the latest trance party-wear, hand-polished coconut shell art and techno DJ demos. There's also a tempting array of ethnic-food concessions to choose from and a stage featuring live music from around 7pm until midnight, when the market winds up. Admission is free.

Somewhat confusingly, a **rival** in much the same mould, called **Macy's**, has opened nearby, closer to Baga by the riverside. Spurned by the expatriate designers and stallholders, this one's not quite as lively as its rival, though in recent years has made an effort to close the gap, with better live acts and more foreign stallholders.

grooves till 11pm, and hip-hop, house, salsa and trance thereafter. See the noticeboard for retro and other theme nights. Admission prices are Rs700 for men, which includes free drinks, and free for women (who also get free drinks). At Christmas, prices can soar to Rs1500 or more depending on the attraction. Open 8pm–late Nov–Dec, and until 11pm out of season. Tues and Sat are busiest.

Anjuna

ANJUNA, the next sizeable village up the coast from Baga, was until a few years back the last bastion of alternative chic in Goa – where the state's legendary full-moon parties were staged each season, and where the Beautiful Set would rent pretty red-tiled houses for six months at a time, make trance mixes and groovy dance-clothes, paint the palm trees in their gardens with fluoro colours and spend months lazing on the beach. A small contingent of fashionably attired, middle-aged hippies still turn up, but thanks to a combination of the Y2K music ban (see p.809) and overwhelming growth in popularity

ANJUNA

▲ Vagator & Chapora   ▲ Siolim

Albuquerque House (Kripa Institute)

DE MELLO WADDO

Police Post
GAUN WADDO

Bus Stop ★ STARCO'S CROSSROADS

St Michael's Pharmacy

Bank of Baroda

Motorcycle Repairs

Orchard Stores

Sports Field

Sacred Heart High School

Oxford Stores

St Anthony's Chapel

MAZAL WADDO

GOENKAR WADDO

Sports Ground

Bruno's Laundry

Flea Market Ground

Sunset Point

DANDO WADDO

0   200 m

Ⓐ Ⓑ Mapusa, Calangute ▶   Assago & Animal Sanctuary ▶   Baga ▶

ACCOMMODATION
Anjuna Beach Resort	C
Arjuna Villa	I
Don João Resort	E
Granpa's Inn	A
Laguna Anjuna	J
Manali	J
Martha's	M
Palacete Rodrigues	F
Peaceland	D
Sea Princess	N
Starco's	G
Villa Anjuna	H
White Negro	L
Yoga Magic	B

RESTAURANTS, BARS & CLUBS
Blue Tao	3
The Jam Connection	4
Martha's Breakfast Home	M
Parasiso de Goa ('Paradiso')	1
Sublime	5
Zoori's	2

▼ Baga   ▼ Calangute

of the flea market, Anjuna has seriously fallen out of fashion. Even the young Israeli hellraisers who inundated the village during the late 1990s – and were largely responsible for the government's crackdown on parties – come in much reduced numbers these days.

As a consequence, the scattered settlement of old Portuguese houses and whitewashed churches, nestled amid a labyrinth of leafy lanes behind a long golden sandy beach, nowadays more closely resembles the place it was before the party scene snowballed than it has for decades. With the airport only an hour's drive away, full-scale tourism development must eventually creep around the headland from neighbouring Baga, but for the time being the village is enjoying a well-earned break from noisy crowds.

The one day of the week when the relative peace and quiet is completely shattered is on Wednesdays, when Anjuna hosts the famous **flea market**, held under a coconut plantation backing the south side of the beach. The big gatherings that used to happen at the *Shore Bar* afterwards are a thing of the past, but the perfect hippy sunset can still be had at *Zoori's* (see p.805), overlooking the north end of the beach, while the *Nine Bar* in Vagator continues to pump out definitive, 120-beats-a-minute Goa Trance each evening from its huge sound system (see p.812).

Arrival

Buses from Mapusa and Panjim drop passengers at various points along the tarmac road across the top of the village, which turns north towards Chapora at the main *Starco's* crossroads. If you're looking for a room on spec, get off here as it's close to most of the guesthouses. The crossroads has a couple of small **stores**, a **motorcycle taxi** rank, and functions as a de facto village square and **bus stand**.

The *Manali* guesthouse (see below) and Oxford Stores **change money** (at poor rates). The Bank of Baroda on the Mapusa road will make encashments against Visa cards, but doesn't do foreign exchange. The **post office**, on the Mapusa road near the bank, has an efficient poste restante counter. The *Manali* guesthouse also offers broadband **Internet access** (Rs40/hr).

Accommodation

After years of **accommodation** shortages, visitors are now spoiled for choice in Anjuna, especially those on more flexible budgets.

Budget

Arjuna Villa #681/1 De Mello Waddo, 4th Lane ☎0832/227 4590, ✉godfreymathia@hotmail.com. Pleasant budget rooms (Rs500–650) with tiled floors and high ceilings, opening on to a deep common veranda (those on the upper storey are much nicer). ❹

Manali South of *Starco's* crossroads ☎0832/227 4421. Anjuna's most popular all-round rock-bottom-budget guesthouse has simple rooms opening onto a yard, with shared toilets and fans. There's a safe deposit, money-changing, library, Internet connection and sociable terrace-restaurant. Good value, so book in advance. ❶–❷

Martha's 907 Montero Waddo ☎0832/227 4194, ✉mpd8650@hotmail.com. Eleven immaculate attached rooms run by a friendly family.

Amenities include kitchen space, fans and running solar-heated water. Two pleasant houses also available. ❹

Peaceland Soronto Waddo ☎0832/227 3700. Simple attached rooms in two blocks (Rs425–550), run by a charming local couple with the help of a pair of friendly dogs. All have high, clay-tiled roofs, mosquito nets, rucksack racks, hammocks, clothes hangers and other nice homely touches that make this easily the best-value place in its class. ❸

Sea Princess House #649 Goenkar Waddo, Dando ☎09890 449090. Simple guesthouse in a prime position in the middle of the beach, near the *Shore Bar*. The rooms are spacious and all have bathrooms with dependable plumbing, but aren't as well maintained as they might be and suffer from mosquitoes. Its main selling point is the location, right on the dunes. **④**

Starco's On the crossroads. No phone. Some of the cheapest rooms in Anjuna: simple, but well-maintained, clean and screened from the road outside. Good value if you're happy with bare-bones amenities. Its unique features are pebble-lined bathroom walls and what must be Goa's only surviving Morris Minor. **③**

White Negro 719 Praia de St Anthony, south of the village, near St Anthony's Chapel ☎ 0832/227 3326, ℮ dsouzawhitenegro@rediffmail.com. A row of twelve spotless back-to-back chalets catching the sea breeze, all with attached bathrooms, tiled floors, safe lockers and mozzie nets. Quiet, efficient and good value. **④**

Mid-range to luxury

Anjuna Beach Resort De Mello Waddo ☎ 0832/227 4499, ℮ fabjoe@sancharnet.com. 32 spacious, comfortable rooms with balconies, fridges, attached bathrooms and solar hot water in a new concrete building ranged around a well-kept pool. Those on the upper floors are best. There's also a block of apartments for long stayers; both are very good value. **⑥–⑦**

Don João Resort Soronto Waddo ☎ 0832/227 4325 or 222 2147, ⓦ www.goacom.org/hotels /donjoao. Large former charter hotel, slap in the middle of the village, with a pool. A bit shabby around the edges, but comfortable enough and a good deal in this bracket. **⑥**

Granpa's Inn Gaun Waddo ☎ 0832/227 3270, ⓦ www.granpasinn.com. Formerly known as

Bougainvillea, this is a lovely 200-year-old house set in half an acre of lush gardens, with a kidney-shaped pool and shady breakfast terrace. They offer three categories of rooms, all fully attached. Very popular, so book well ahead. **⑤–⑦**

Laguna Anjuna De Mello Waddo ☎ 0832/227 4305, ⓦ www.lagunaanjuna.com. Alternative "boutique resort" comprising 25 colourfully decorated, domed laterite cottages with wooden rafters and terracotta tiles, grouped behind a convoluted pool. Restaurant, pool tables and bar. A bit shabby round the edges these days, but popular nonetheless. Doubles from $130 mid-season, rising to $200 for Christmas–New Year. **⑧**

Palacete Rodrigues Near Oxford Stores, Mazal Waddo ☎ 0832/227 3358. Two-hundred-year-old residence converted into a mid-scale guesthouse, with carved wood furniture and a relaxed, traditional-Goan feel. Single occupancy available. The three economy options in a separate block around the back are particularly good value. **⑤**

Villa Anjuna Near Anjuna beachfront ☎ 0832/227 3443, ⓦ www.anjunavilla.com. Modern, efficient resort hotel close to the beach, on the main road through the village. Amenities include a fair-sized pool and Jacuzzi. Popular with clubbers, as it's a short stagger from *Paradiso*. **⑥**

Yoga Magic ☎ 0832/562 3796 ⓦ www .yogamagic.net. Innovative "Canvas Ecotel", offering low-impact luxury on the edge of Anjuna in Rajasthani hunting tents. The structures are all decorated with block-printed cotton, furnished with cushions, silk drapes, coir carpets and solar halogen lights. Open mid-Nov to March. **⑧**

The flea market

Anjuna's Wednesday **flea market**, held in the coconut plantation behind the southern end of the beach is, along with Ingo's Night Market at Arpora, *the* place to indulge in a spot of souvenir shopping. Two decades ago, the weekly event was the exclusive preserve of backpackers and the area's seasonal residents, who gathered here to smoke chillums and to buy and sell party clothes and jewellery: something like a small pop festival without the stage. These days, though, everything is more organized and mainstream. Pitches are rented out by the metre, drugs are banned and the approach roads to the village are choked solid all day with a/c buses and Maruti taxis ferrying in tourists from resorts further down the coast. Even the beggars have to pay baksheesh to be here.

The range of goods on sale has broadened, too, thanks to the high profile of migrant hawkers and stallholders from other parts of India. Each region or culture is allotted its own corner. At one end, ever-diminishing ranks of alternative Westerners congregate around racks of fluoro party-gear and designer beachwear, while in the heart of the site, Tibetan jewellery-sellers preside over orderly rows of turquoise bracelets and Himalayan curios. Most distinctive of all are the Lamani women from Karnataka, decked from head to toe in traditional tribal garb and selling elaborately woven multicoloured cloth, which they fashion into everything from jackets to money belts, and which makes even the

▲ Anjuna flea market

Westerners' party gear look positively funereal. Elsewhere, you'll come across dazzling Rajasthani mirrorwork and block-printed bedspreads, Keralan woodcarvings, Gujarati appliqué, Orissan palm-leaf manuscripts, pyramids of colourful spices and incense, "export-surplus" jeans and tops, spangly miniskirts, sequined shoes and Ayurvedic cures for every conceivable ailment.

What you end up paying for this stuff largely depends on your ability to **haggle**. Prices are sky-high by Indian standards, as tourists not used to dealing in rupees will part with almost anything. Be persistent, though, and cautious, and you can usually pick things up for a reasonable rate.

Yoga in Anjuna

The **Brahmani Centre** (Ⓦ www.brahmaniyoga.com, ☎ 09370 568639) offers drop-in Ashtanga yoga classes by expert teachers at their studio in the garden of the *Granpa's Inn*; all levels of ability are catered for. If you're looking for a fully fledged retreat or course, you won't do better than the **Purple Valley** centre, ten minutes' ride away in Assagao (Ⓦ www.yogagoa.com), which has accommodation for up to forty guests and what must be one of the loveliest yoga *shalas* (practice areas) in India. Their top-drawer teachers include Manju Jois and Sharath Rangaswamy, the eldest son and grandson of the illustrious Ashtanga guru, Shri K.Pattabhi Jois. See also Morjim, p.813.

Eating and drinking

Responding to the tastes of its alternative visitors, Anjuna boasts a good crop of quality **cafés** and **restaurants**, many of which serve healthy vegetarian dishes and juices. If you're hankering for a taste of home, call in at the **Orchard Stores** on the eastern side of the village, which, along with its rival **Oxford Stores**, directly opposite, serves the expatriate community with a vast range of pricey imported delights such as digestive biscuits, Marmite and extra-virgin olive oil.

Blue Tao On the main road through the village. Another Italian-run place, this time an "alternative health restaurant" that offers some of Goa's most delicious breakfasts (sourdough and wholemeal breads, herbal teas, tahini and spirulina spreads). In addition to a full menu of main courses (Rs150–200), they also do a tempting range of juices, including wheatgrass, ginseng and Ayurvedic concoctions. Non-smoking and kid-friendly.

The Jam Connection Near Oxford Stores. Fresh, interesting salads (with real organic rocket and garden herbs), mocha and espresso coffee, homemade ice cream and all-day breakfasts, served in a lovely garden. You can lounge on bamboo easychairs or on tree platforms. Daily except Wed 11am–7pm.

Martha's Breakfast Home *Martha's* guesthouse, 907 Montero Waddo. Secluded, very friendly breakfast garden serving fresh Indian coffee, crepes, healthy juices (including a delicious ABC – apple, beetroot and carrot juice), apple and cinnamon porridge, fruit salads with curd and – the

house speciality – melt-in-the-mouth waffles with real maple syrup.

Sublime near *Martha's* guesthouse, Montero Waddo ☎ m93261 12006. Great little "gastro-bistro" where the food really lives up to the name: chef Chris rustles up superb steaks, seafood, chicken and stir-fried vegetable dishes from an open-counter kitchen. Easily Anjuna's best restaurant, though it's still refreshingly informal and affordable, with mains around Rs300.

Zoori's North end of the beach. Chilled Israeli-run café-restaurant occupying a perfect spot on the clifftops – one of the most beautiful places in Goa for sunset. Screened from the brouhaha of the nearby car park, its terraces step down the hillside, strewn with lounging platforms, beds and big cushions. And the food's as delicious as the views: big, juicy fillet steaks are the house speciality, but they also do tasty Mexican enchilladas, tortillas, pasta and fresh hummus, as well as chocolate soufflé and biscuit cake that regulars drive from far away for. Open 10am–midnight.

Nightlife

Anjuna no longer deserves the reputation it gained through the early 1990s as a legendary rave venue, but at least one big **party** is still held in the area around the Christmas–New Year full-moon period.

For the rest of the season, techno heads have to make do with the rather shabby, mainstream *Paraiso de Goa*, aka *Paradiso*, overlooking the far north end of Anjuna beach, which epitomizes the new, more above-board face of Goa Trance. Presiding over a dance space surrounded by spacey statues of Hindu gods and Tantric symbols, visiting DJs spin text-book trance for a mainly Indian and Russian crowd. *Paradiso* keeps to a sporadic timetable, but should be open most nights from around 10pm; admission charges are Rs250–600, depending on the night. Along similar lines, but with free admission, is the *Nine Bar* (see p.812), above Vagator beach.

Vagator

Barely a couple of kilometres of clifftops and parched grassland separate Anjuna from the southern fringes of its nearest neighbour, **VAGATOR**. Spread around a tangle of winding back lanes, this is a more chilled, undeveloped resort that appeals, in the main, to Israeli and southern European beach bums who've been coming back for years.

With the red ramparts of Chapora fort looming above it, Vagator's broad sandy **beach** – known as "**Big Vagator**" – is undeniably beautiful. However, a peaceful swim or lie on the sand is out of the question here as it's a prime stop

The dark side of the moon

Lots of visitors come to Goa expecting to be able to party on the beach every night, and are dismayed when the only places to dance turn out to be **mainstream clubs** they probably wouldn't look twice at back home. But the truth is that the full-on, elbows-in-the-air beach party of old, when tens of thousands of revellers would space out to huge techno sound-systems under fluoro-painted palm trees, chilling out afterwards in the surf under massive full moons, is well and truly a thing of the past in Goa – thanks largely to the kill-joy attitude of the local government.

Goa's coastal villages saw their first big raves back in 1960s with the influx of hippies to Calangute and Baga. Much to the amazement of the locals, the preferred pastime of these wannabe sadhus was to cavort naked on the sands together on full-moon nights, amid a haze of chillum smoke and loud rock music blaring from makeshift PAs. The villagers took little notice of these bizarre gatherings at first, but with each season the scene became better established, and by the late 1970s the **Christmas and New Year** parties, in particular, had become huge events, attracting travellers from all over the country.

In the late 1980s, the local party scene received a dramatic shot in the arm with the coming of Acid House and techno. Ecstasy became the preferred dance drug as the dub-reggae scene gave way to rave culture, with ever-greater numbers of young clubbers pouring in for the season on charter flights. Goa soon spawned its own distinctive brand of psychedelic music, known as **Goa Trance**. Distinguished by its multilayered synth lines and sub-bass rhythms, the hypnotic style combines the darkness of hard techno with a brighter ambient edge. Cultivated by artists such as Goa Gill, Juno Reactor and Hallucinogen, the new sound was given wider exposure when big-name DJs Danny Rampling and Paul Oakenfold started mixing Goa Trance in clubs and on national radio back in the UK, generating a following among music lovers who previously knew nothing of the place which had inspired it.

The **golden era** for Goa's party scene, and Goa Trance, was in the early 1990s, when big raves were held two or three times a week in beautiful locations around Anjuna and Vagator. For a few years the authorities turned a blind eye to the growing scene. Then, quite suddenly, the plug was pulled. For years, drug busts and bribes had provided the notoriously corrupt Goan cops with a lucrative source of baksheesh. But after a couple of drug-related deaths, a series of sensational articles in the local press and a decision by Goa Tourism to promote upmarket over backpacker tourism, the police began to demand impossibly large bribes – sums that the organizers (many of them drug dealers) could not hope to recoup. Although the big New Year and Christmas events continued unabated, smaller parties, hitherto held in off-track venues such as "Disco Valley" behind Middle Vagator beach and the "Bamboo Grove" in south Anjuna, started to peter out, to the dismay of those local people who'd become financially dependent on the raves and the punters they pulled into the villages.

Against this backdrop, the imposition during the run-up to the Y2K celebrations of an **amplified-music ban** between 10pm and 7am sounded the death knell for Goa's party scene. Seven or so years on, it has virtually disappeared without trace, limited to a couple of established, above-board clubs – notably the *Nine Bar* in Vagator (see p.812) and *Paradiso* in Anjuna (see opposite). The occasional hush-hush house party does from time to time escape the notice of the local police, but don't come to Goa expecting Ko Pha Ngan or Ibiza-on-the-Arabian-Sea, or you'll be sorely disappointed.

for bus parties of domestic tourists. A much better option, though one that still sees more than its fair share of day-trippers, is the next beach south. Backed by a steep wall of crumbling palm-fringed laterite, **Ozran** (or "Little") **Vagator beach** is actually a string of three contiguous coves. To reach them you have to walk from where the bus parks above Big Vagator, or drive to the end of the lane running off the main Chapora–Anjuna road (towards the *Nine Bar*), from where footpaths drop sharply down to a wide stretch of level white sand (look for the mopeds and bikes parked at the top of the cliff). The Israeli- and Italian-dominated scene in the prettiest, southernmost cove here revolves around a string of large, well-established shacks, at the end of which a face carved out of the rocks – staring serenely skywards – is the most prominent landmark. Relentless racquetball, trance sound-systems and a particularly sizeable herd of stray cows are the other defining traits.

Practicalities

Buses from Panjim and Mapusa, 9km east, pull in every fifteen minutes or so at the crossroads on the far northeastern edge of Vagator, near where the main road peels away towards Chapora. From here, it's a one-kilometre walk over the hill and down the other side to the beach. *Bethany Inn*, on the north side of the village, has a **foreign exchange** licence (for cash and traveller's cheques), and efficient **travel agency** in the office on the ground floor.

Accommodation

Accommodation in Vagator is composed of a couple of pricey resort hotels, family-run budget guesthouses and dozens of small private properties rented out for long periods. **Water** is in very short supply here, and you'll be doing the villagers a favour if you use it frugally at all times. Tariffs typically double here between Christmas and New Year.

Bethany Inn Just south of the main road ☎0832/227 3731, ⍇www.bethanyinn.com. Nine clean, self-contained rooms with minibar fridges, balconies and attached bathrooms (Rs600); plus four additional a/c options in a new block, with big flat-screen TVs, larger balconies and more spacious tiled bathrooms. Tastefully furnished throughout, and efficiently managed by a pair of young brothers. ❹–❻

Boon's Ark Near *Bethany Inn* ☎0832/227 4045. Pleasant, clean and well-run place offering modern rooms that open onto small verandas and a well-tended little garden. Room service, money changing and bikes to rent. ❺

Dolrina Vagator Beach Rd ☎0832/227 3382, ⍨dolrina@hotmail.com. Nestled under a lush canopy of trees near the beach, Vagator's largest budget guesthouse features attached or shared bathrooms, a sociable garden café, individual safe deposits and roof space. Single occupancy rates, and breakfasts available. ❹–❺

Jolly Jolly Lester Vagator Beach Rd ☎0832/227 3620, or 09822 488536, ⍇www.hoteljollygoa.com. Eleven pleasant doubles with tiled bathrooms and lockers set in shady woodland, and a garden lovingly protected by owners Lazarus and Remy from marauding monkeys. Small restaurant on site; single occupancy is possible. ❸

Jolly Jolly Roma Vagator Beach Rd ☎0832/227 3005, or 09822 488536. Very smart, good-sized chalet-style rooms with high ceilings, nice furniture and private verandas, again surrounded by a well-tended garden; they also offer laundry, exchange facilities and a small library. ❹

Julie Jolly South side of the village ☎0832/227 3357. One of the most pleasant places in Vagator, set on the edge of a leafy belt and within easy reach of Ozran beach. All rooms are tiled and well aired; self-caterers can stay in larger suites with sitting rooms and kitchenettes. ❹–❺

Leoney Resort On the road to Disco Valley ☎0832/227 3634, ⍇www.leoneyresort.com. Comfortable option, with swish "mock Portuguese" chalets and pricier (but more spacious) octagonal "cottages" on the sleepy side of the village, arranged around a very nice little pool. Restaurant, laundry, lockers, foreign exchange facilities and cyber café on site. No advance bookings Dec–Jan. ❼–❽

Eating, drinking and nightlife

Vagator boasts an eclectic batch of **restaurants**, with wildly varying menus and prices. Western tourists tend to stick to the pricier ones lining the road through the village, while Indian visitors frequent the more impersonal, cheaper places down on the beach itself. For a sundown drink, head to the *Nine Bar*, where big trance sounds attract a crowd for sunset, especially on Wednesdays after the flea market

Bean Me Up near the petrol pump. India's one and only American-run tofu joint – the last word in Goan gourmet healthy eating. Main courses (around Rs200–250) come with steamed spinach, brown bread and hygienically washed salads; try their

delicious Thai-style *tempeh* in spicy cashew sauce. There's also a tempting range of vegan desserts – the banana pudding with soya whip is a winner.
China Town Chapora Crossroads, next to *Bethany Inn*. This small roadside restaurant, tucked away

VAGATOR & CHAPORA

N

Chapora Harbour

Fishing Anchorage

RESTAURANTS, CAFÉS & BARS	
Bean Me Up	7
China Town	5
Italian Pizza	1
Nine Bar	6
Sai Ganesh Café	4
Scarlet Cold Drinks	2
Welcome	3

ACCOMMODATION	
Bethany Inn	G
Boon's Ark	H
Casa de Olga	A
Dolrina	D
Jolly Jolly Lester	E
Jolly Jolly Roma	F
Julie Jolly	J
Leoney Resort	I
Shettor Villa	C
Siolim House	B

Chapora Fort

Chapora River

Muslim Tombstones

Laundry

Banyan Tree **Bus stop**

Big Vagator Beach

Narayan Books

HUDDO WADDO

Siddeshwar Temple

B & Siolim (6km)

Coach Park

Car Park

VAGATOR BEACH ROAD

CHIVAR WADDO

Middle Vagator Beach

DISCO VALLEY

VAGATOR

Buses to Mapusa

Petrol Pump

Mapusa (9km), Petrol Pump &

Rainbow Bookshop

St Anthony's

Ozran Vagator Beach

Jackie's Daynite

0	200 m

Get Well Pharmacy

▼ *Anjuna (3.1km)*

just south of the main drag, is the village's most popular budget eating place, serving particularly tasty seafood dishes in addition to a large Chinese selection, as well as all the usual Goa-style travellers' grub.

Nine Bar above Ozran beach. Boasting a crystal trance sound-system, this clifftop café enjoys a prime location, with fine sea views from its terrace through the palm canopy, where Nepali waiters serve up cold beer and the usual range of budget travellers' grub. The dancing starts after dark and keeps going until the bar closes around 10pm. Entrance is free, but drink prices are stiff (Rs175 for a beer); you'll have your bags searched on the way in for drugs and explosives. Strictly no photography.

Chapora

Huddled in the shadow of a Portuguese fort on the opposite, northern side of the headland from Vagator, **CHAPORA**, 10km from Mapusa, is a lot busier than most north coast villages. Dependent on fishing and boat-building, it has, to an extent, retained a life of its own independent of tourism. That said, the relaxation of Goa's drug laws have made a significant impact here over the past five years or so. Whereas the main street used to retain a workaday indifference to the annual invasion of foreigners, now it's largely given over to budget travellers' cafés, with everyone spliffing up and toking on chillums in public at sunset time. Even so, it's unlikely Chapora will develop much over the coming years; tucked away under a dense canopy of trees on the muddy southern shore of a river estuary, it lacks both the space and the white sand that have pulled crowds to Calangute and Colva. The main drawback to staying here is the general grubbiness of the accommodation on offer, which tends to be booked for long periods to hard-drinking, heavy-smoking hippies.

Chapora's chief landmark is its venerable old **fort**, most easily reached from the Vagator side of the hill. At low tide, you can also walk around the bottom of the headland, via the anchorage and the secluded coves beyond it to Big Vagator, then head up the hill from there. The red-laterite bastion, crowning the rocky bluff, was built by the Portuguese in 1617 on the site of an earlier Muslim structure (thus the village's name – from *Shahpura*, "town of the Shah"). Deserted in the nineteenth century, it lies in ruins today, although the **views** up and down the coast from the weed-infested ramparts are still superb. Also worth a visit is the village's busy little **fishing anchorage**, where you can buy delicious calamari fresh off the boats most evenings.

Practicalities

Direct **buses** arrive at Chapora three times daily from Panjim, and every fifteen minutes from Mapusa, with departures until 7pm from various points along the main road. **Motorcycle taxis** hang around the old banyan tree at the far end of the main street, near where the buses pull in. Air, train and bus **tickets** may be booked or reconfirmed at Soniya Tours and Travels, next to the bus stand.

Much the most congenial place to stay in Chapora is the *Casa de Olga* (℡0832/227 4355, or 09822 157145; ❸–❹), an immaculate, red-and-white-painted little guesthouse near the fishing anchorage. It's run with great efficiency and enthusiasm by a young couple called Edmund and Elifa. Their nicest rooms are the five in a new block to the rear, which are all attached and have good-sized balconies. Cheaper and more basic is *Shettor Villa* (℡0832/227 3766, or 098221 58154; ❷), off the west side of the main street. Half a dozen of its rooms, arranged around a sheltered backyard, come with fans and attached bathrooms; the other eighteen share shower-toilets. The above appear on the map on p.811.

The only luxury place is an elegantly converted *palacio* called ⚑ *Siolim House* (℡0832/227 2138, ⓦwww.siolimhouse.com; ❽) in nearby Siolim (5km east along the estuary from Chapora). The three-hundred-year-old building numbers among the few hotels in the state that manage to recapture the period feel of the Portuguese era. Romantic, beautifully furnished rooms and suites are ranged around a central pillared courtyard, with bathtubs, gorgeous oyster-shell windows, four-poster beds and a twelve-metre pool in the garden.

Out on the road leading towards the fishing anchorage, *Italian Pizza* is Chapora's best **restaurant**, in a small courtyard next to a martial-arts gym. Aside from its delicious home-baked pizzas (Rs75–250), house specialities include Mediterranean standards such as filets of local fish in garlic and olive oil, and squid marinated in lemon sauce. They also do daily specials that include minestrone, ravioli and proper gnocchi. Otherwise, take your pick from the crop of inexpensive little cafés and restaurants lining the main street. The popular *Welcome*, halfway down, offers a reasonable selection of cheap and filling seafood, Western and veg dishes, plus backgammon sets and relentless reggae and techno music. *Scarlet Cold Drinks* and the *Sai Ganesh Café*, both a short way east beyond the banyan tree, knock up fresh fruit juices and milkshakes. All of the above appear on the map on p.811.

The far north

Apart from the fishing village of **Arambol**, which, during the winter, plays host to a large contingent of hippy travellers seeking a less pretentious alternative to Anjuna and Vagator, the beautiful coast of Pernem, Goa's northernmost district, remains the quietest stretch of shoreline in the state. Catch the tide right and it is possible to walk in a couple of hours all the way from the sandy spit at **Morjim**, on the opposite side of the river mouth from Chapora, to Arambol, via the villages of **Aswem** and **Mandrem**, where facilities for visitors are limited to a handful of shacks and small hut camps. In the far north, **Terekol fort**, on the Maharashtrian border, makes a good target for a day-trip by motorbike or taxi.

Travelling north from **Siolim**, on the south bank of the River Chapora, the entry point to Pernem proper is the far side of the new road bridge at **Chopdem**. Head straight on for 200m or so until you arrive at a T-junction. A right turn here will take you along the quick route to Arambol; bear left, and you'll head along one of the few stretches of undeveloped coastline remaining in Goa – an area that looks, since the completion of the bridge, to be living on borrowed time.

Morjim

Viewed from Chapora fort, **MORJIM** (or **Morji**) appears as a dramatic expanse of empty sand sweeping north from a spoon-shaped spit to the river mouth – one of Goa's last remaining nesting sites for Olive Ridley turtles (see box, p.814). Behind it, broken dunes are backed by a dense patch of palms and casuarina trees, sheltering a mixed Hindu–Christian village whose inhabitants still live predominantly from fishing and rice farming. Bypassed completely by the main road north, their settlement has remained a relative backwater. Only in the past three or four years, since the completion of the Siolim bridge, has it started to see many tourists, the majority of them young Russians (whose early-morning fitness routines on the beach are still regarded with puzzled amusement by the straw-hatted handnet fishers working the foreshore).

Tucked away in a fold of the wooded hill just inland from Morjim beach is the secluded **Yoga Village** (☎ 0832/224 4546, ⊛ www.yogavillage.org), where you can study yoga techniques and philosophy under the guidance of **Yogi Manmoyanand**, an upcoming teacher who mastered his art during a seven-year stint in a Himalayan cave. Fourteen-day retreats cover a wide range of yogic techniques, from *pranayama* to *mudras*, *bandhas* and the full range of poses

The turtle wind

When a strong and steady on-shore breeze blows through the night in early November at Morjim – the long, empty beach west of the ferry ramp at Chopdem – the locals call it a **turtle wind** because such weather normally heralds the arrival of Goa's rarest migrant visitors: the **Olive Ridley marine turtles** (*Lepidochelys olivacea*).

For as long as anyone can remember, the spoon-shaped spit of soft white sand at **Temb**, the far southern end of the beach, has been the nesting ground of these beautiful sea reptiles. Each winter, a succession of females emerges from the surf during the night and, using their distinctive flippers, crawls to the edge of the dunes to lay their annual clutch of 105–115 eggs. Just over two months later, the fresh hatchlings clamber out and crawl blinking over their siblings to begin the perilous trek back to the water, guided into the sea by reflected moonlight. Little more is known about how these enigmatic creatures spend the rest of their long lives (turtles frequently live for over a century), but it is thought that the females return to the beaches where they were born to lay their own eggs. Some have been known to travel as far as 4500km to do this.

Once a thriving species, with huge populations spread across the Pacific, Atlantic and Indian oceans, the Olive Ridley is nowadays **endangered**. Aside from a wealth of traditional predators (such as crows, ospreys, gulls and buzzards, who pick off the hatchlings during their dash for the sea), the newborns and their parents are vulnerable to a host of man-made threats. In Morjim, as in most of Asia, the eggs are traditionally considered a delicacy and local villagers collect them to sell in Mapusa market. Many (perhaps as many as 35,000 worldwide) are killed accidentally by fishermen, caught up in fine shrimp nets or attracted by squid bait used to catch tuna. Floating litter, which the hapless turtles mistake for jellyfish, has also taken its toll over the past two decades, as have tar balls from oil spills, which coat the animals' digestive tracks and hamper the absorption of food. The growth of tourism poses an additional danger: electric lights behind the beaches throw the hatchlings off course as they scuttle towards the sea, and sand compressed by sunbathers' trampling feet damages nests, preventing the babies from digging their way out at the crucial time. On average, only two out of a typical clutch of more than one hundred survive into adulthood to reproduce. In Goa, the resulting decline has been dramatic. Of the 150 nesting females that used to return each year to Morjim, for example, only six showed up in 2006–07.

However, under the auspices of the Forest Department, a scheme has been launched to revive turtle populations. Locals are employed to watch out for the females' arrival in November, and guard the nests after the eggs have been laid until they hatch. You'll see them camped under palm-leaf shades on the beach, with the nests fenced in and marked by Forest Department signs. One of the main reasons the fishing families at Temb have so enthusiastically espoused the initiative is that its success promises to bring about the creation of an official **nature sanctuary** at Morjim, forever blocking plans to build unwanted tourist resorts on their beach.

So far, the government-led conservation attempt has not proved all that effective. After an initial leap in hatchling figures, recent results have shown a marked dip, which the Forest Department ascribes to an increase in tourist activity.

Watching the nesting turtles is an unforgettable experience, although one requiring a certain amount of dedication, or luck. No one knows for sure when an Olive Ridley female will turn up, but with a strong turtle wind blowing at the right time, the chances are good. Much more predictable are the appearances of the hatchlings, who emerge exactly 54 days after their mothers laid the eggs. If you ask one of the wardens looking after the nests, they can tell you when this will be.

For more on international attempts to save marine turtles, including the massive synchronized *arribida* (arrival) of around 200,000 at the Bhita Kanika Sanctuary, Orissa, on the east coast of India, visit the website of the World Wildlife Fund (@www.wwf.org).

(*asanas*). Vedic discourse (under an old banyan tree) and relaxing Ayurvedic massages are also included in the cost of the course that, aside from tuition, also includes meals and accommodation (in well set-up cane and palm-leaf huts). For full details, check the website.

Arrival, information and eating

Half a dozen **buses** a day connect Morjim with Panjim, from 7am; heading the other way, you can pick up a direct bus from Panjim at 5pm, and there are frequent services from Mapusa via Siolim. They'll drop you on the main road, five minutes' walk from the beachfront area at **Vithaldas Waddo**. If you're planning to stay anywhere else, keep your eyes peeled for the roadside signboards or you could be in for a long walk – rickshaws are few and far between this far north.

The main turning for Vithaldas Waddo, 1km back from the beach, is where you'll find Morjim's **Internet café**, Amigo's (Rs40/hr). They also have telephone and fax facilities, and are licensed to **change money**.

For **food**, you won't do better than *Britto's*, a small, family-run shack five minutes' walk down the beach, where millet-fried mussels, clams in spicy coconut sauce, vegetable fried rice and Chapora calamari in lime are the specialities; they also serve stupendously good lassis and fresh fruit juices.

Accommodation

Most of the **accommodation** in Morjim is in private houses which get snapped up early in the season, or even the previous one by entrepreneurial Muscovites who then sublet them at inflated rates. But you can usually find vacant rooms in one or other of the small guesthouses that have opened close to the beach, and a couple of higher-end places have recently sprung up.

Camp 69 Vithaldas Waddo ☎0832/224 4458. The oldest established place on the beachfront, now boasting large, well-spaced "log cabins", fitted with beds, sofas, fans and attached bathrooms. **❺**

Montego Bay Vithaldas Waddo ☎0832/224 4222, ⓦ www.montegobaygoa.com. A dozen or so plush Rajasthani tents, stylishly equipped with driftwood beds, fans, coir mats and bathrooms with running water, at a breezy spot in the dunes under coconut trees. The most relaxing option bang on the beach, though overpriced. Breakfast included. **❼**

Morjim Beach Resort Temb Waddo ☎08326 521994, ⓔrahul_goa@hotmail.com. This guesthouse is a long plod south down the beach, midway between the village centre and sandy spit at the end: you'll need at least a bicycle to stay here. But it is perfectly situated and well set-up, with proper rooms and suites as well as leaf huts and "cottages". **❻–❽**

Naga Cottages Rasal-Vithaldas Waddo ☎09822 583240, ⓦ www.nagacottages.com. Spacious suites with large semicircular balconies on both sides, overlooking open fields and palm groves. Gleaming tiled floors, kitchenettes, flat-screen TVs and cane swings make this a luxurious option by local standards. **❻–❼**

Tequila Sunset Hideout Vithaldas Waddo ☎09822 588003. Large, new rooms, with attached bathrooms (closets) and big tiled balconies overlooking a beachfront plot. There's also a first-floor café-restaurant offering great sea views. **❹**

White Feather House #694/A Morjim–Aswem Rd ☎m98502 42011 or 094226 35465, ⓔ whitefeather_gh1@yahoo.co.in. Comfortable, mid-range place just back from the road. Its rates are way over the top, but the rooms are large, breezy and pleasant, and nearly always full. From the roof terrace you get a view across the dunes to the sea. **❺–❻**

Aswem

A solitary whitewashed crucifix rises from the rocks dividing Morjim from **ASWEM**, the next village north. Aside from the odd German nudist or two, you should have the sands pretty much to yourself until you arrive at the burgeoning cluster of shacks and hut camps midway along the beach. Huddled under the canopy of a beautiful coconut *mand*, this ad hoc tourist settlement started to snowball after a couple of French restaurateurs from Baga opened a chic beach café here (*La Plage* – see below).

La Plage excepted, amenities remain basic (leaf huts are the norm as the local council has vigorously enforced the Coastal Protection Zone building ban), but the beach is all the more appealing for that. It's clean, quiet for most of the season and, outside the full-moon period, safe for kids to swim off. Only at the far northern end, where a tidal creek periodically prevents you from continuing north towards Arambol, has package tourism made any discernable inroads: Maruti vans deposit punters here to overnight in purpose-built hut camps on the shoreline, but the setup is relatively low-key.

Practicalities

Sporadic **buses** from Panjim and Mapusa cover the quiet stretch of road running parallel to the beach inland, from where a five-minute walk across the paddy fields brings you to the shacks (signboards indicate the paths). Other than the cafés, there are no facilities whatsoever here. Nearly everyone who stays rents a scooter from somewhere else to get to and around Aswem. The nearest Internet access and shops are at Morjim, an idyllic half-hour plod south.

For **food**, head to ⚓ *La Plage* (℡09850 258543; closed evenings), where light Gallic–Mediterranean, heat-beating snacks and drinks (chilled asparagus soup, mint lassis, Moroccan salads, fresh strawberries and cream), along with sumptuous chargrilled seafood and barbequed main courses, are dished up by Nepalis in black *lunghis* against a diaphanous backdrop of floaty white muslin. It's very pricey by Goan standards, and a surreal counterpoint to the fishing *waddo* down the beach, but a very pleasant breakfast or lunch venue nonetheless. If you're staying in the area and looking for somewhere to hang out in the evenings (when *La Plage* is closed) one option is to wander ten minutes further north to the cluster of hut camps and shacks overlooking the tidal creek opposite Aswem village. With its pretty lanterns and fairy lights, *Arabian Sea* tends to be the liveliest of the bunch, serving the usual multi-cuisine menu and fresh local seafood.

Accommodation

Change Your Mind ℡0832/561 3716 or 09822 389290. Basic huts and treehouses behind a lively shack. ❷–❸

Gopal ℡0832/224 4431, ✉gopal@ingoa.com. In much the same mould as *Change Your Mind*, at identical rates. ❷–❸

Palm Grove ℡0832/224 7440. Pick of the hut camps: further up the beach from the others, and with large treehouses that are not only well spaced but also have sea views. Owners Ratnagar and Nali accept telephone bookings. ❹

🏃 **Yab Yum** ℡0832/651 0392, ⓦwww .yabyumresorts.com. A campus of beautiful domed structures made from palm thatch, mango wood and laterite, with curvy moulded concrete floors and walls, painted pale purple. They're very large and attractively furnished inside – though the alt-chic comes at quite a high price (Rs3550 per double or Rs4700 for suites). They also offer a handful of similarly stylish faux-Portuguese-era cottages, and a wooden deck for yoga. Rates include breakfast. ❽

Mandrem

A magnificent, and largely empty, beach stretches north of Aswem towards Arambol, uninterrupted save for a couple of large-scale hut camps and a single package hotel. Whether or not **MANDREM** can continue to hold out against the rising tide of tourism remains to be seen, but for the time being, nature still has the upper hand. Olive Ridley marine turtles nest on the quietest stretch, and you're more than likely to catch a glimpse of one of the white-bellied fish eagles that live in the casuarina trees – their last stronghold in Pernem. If you can afford it, the best spot from which to savour this last unspoilt strip of the Goan coast is Denzil Sequeira's exclusive beachhouse

Elsewhere (see below), nestled in the dunes just north of the creek and unquestionably the most beautiful hideaway hereabouts. The rest of this area's accommodation is tucked away inland at **Junasa Waddo**, where a handful of small guesthouses and hotels have sprung up.

Practicalities

Any of the buses running north to Arambol will drop you at the nearest bazaar, **Madlamaz–Mandrem**, a typically north-Goan market village straddling the main road a mile or so inland from the beach. Parsekar Stores, in the centre of the village, holds an Anjuna-style stock of tourist-oriented food and drink – including muesli, olive oil and Nilgiri cheese – and natural cosmetics; and there's a tiny **laundry** above a jeweller's shop in the small courtyard just to the east of the main road.

Accommodation

Dunes ☎0832/224 7219 or 224 7071, ⓦwww .dunesgoa.com. Huge "holiday village" of twin-bedded, yellow-painted leaf huts. They're a notch too close together for comfort and are brightly lit, so spoiling the aspect of the beach at night, but this is an efficiently run outfit that fills up in peak season. Pricier attached available. ④–⑤

Elsewhere ☎022/2373 8757 or 09820 037387, ⓦwww.aseascape.com. A handful of exclusive, Portuguese-era cottages, exquisitely converted into dream getaways, with gorgeous sea-facing verandas and traditional wood furniture. Flanked by an empty beach on one side and a tidal creek on the other, the location's as romantic as coastal Goa gets, and very private. Rental costs range from $875–2415 per week, depending on the house and time of year. In the same plot, *Otter Creek* offers less-pricey alternative accommodation in stylish

luxury tents ($450/1200 per week low/high season), each with their own bamboo four-posters, bathroom, colour-washed sit-out and jetty on the river. ⑨

Riva Resort ☎0832/224 7088 or 224 7612, ⓦwww.rivaresorts.com. The other big hut camp, next to *Dunes*. This one's more upmarket, with swisher huts and higher rates. The site centres on a huge bar-restaurant that hosts DJ nights and has big-screen video. ③–⑤

Villa River Cat ☎0822/224 7928 or 09890 15706C, ⓦwww.villarivercat.com. Quirky riverside hotel, screened from the beach by the dunes, with distinctive hippy-influenced decor and furniture. The sixteen rooms are all individually designed: mosaics, shells, devotional sculpture and hammocks set the tone. Host Rinoo Seghal is an animal over, so brace yourself for a menagerie of cats and dogs. Artists and musicians receive a ten percent discount. ⑤–⑧

Arambol (Harmal)

The largest coastal village in Pernem district is **ARAMBOL** (sometimes called **Harmal**), 32km northwest of Mapusa. If you're happy with basic amenities but want to stay somewhere lively, this might be your best bet. The village's two beaches are beautiful and still relatively unexploited. The majority of foreigners who stay in Arambol tend to do so for the season, and over time a close-knit expat community – of mostly ageing hippies who've been coming here for years – has grown up, with its own alternative health facilities, paragliding school, yoga gurus and wholefood cafés.

Strewn with dozens of old wooden boats and a line of tourist café-bars, the gently curving village beach is good for bathing, but much less picturesque than its neighbour around the corner, **Paliem** or "**Lakeside**" **beach**. To reach this, follow the track over the headland to the north; beyond a rocky-bottomed cove, the trail emerges to a broad strip of soft white sand hemmed in on both sides by steep cliffs. Behind it, a small **freshwater lake** extends along the bottom of the valley into a thick jungle. Hang around the banks of this murky green pond for long enough, and you'll probably see a fluorescent-yellow human figure or two appear from the bushes at its far end. Fed by boiling hot springs, the lake is lined with sulphurous mud, which, when smeared over the body, dries to form a surreal, butter-coloured shell. The resident hippies swear it's good for you and spend

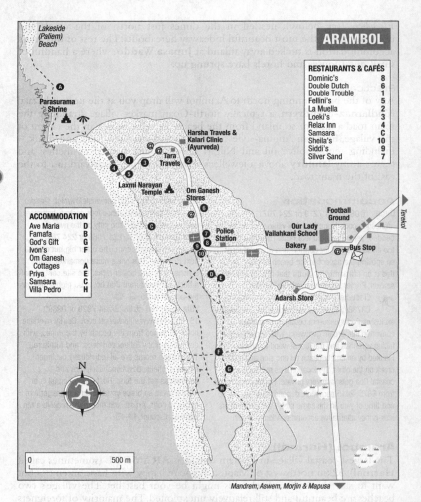

ARAMBOL

RESTAURANTS & CAFÉS	
Dominic's	8
Double Dutch	6
Double Trouble	1
Fellini's	5
La Muella	2
Loeki's	3
Relax Inn	4
Samsara	C
Sheila's	10
Siddi's	9
Silver Sand	7

Lakeside
(Paliem)
Beach

Parasurama
Shrine

Harsha Travels &
Kalari Clinic
(Ayurveda)

Tara
Travels

Laxmi Narayan
Temple

Om Ganesh
Stores

ACCOMMODATION	
Ave Maria	D
Famafa	B
God's Gift	G
Ivon's	F
Om Ganesh	
Cottages	A
Priya	E
Samsara	C
Villa Pedro	H

Football
Ground

Our Lady
Vailahkani School

Police
Station

Bakery

Bus Stop

Adarsh Store

N

0   500 m

Terekol

Mandrem, Aswem, Morjin & Mapusa ▼

much of the day tiptoeing naked around the shallows like refugees from some obscure tribal initiation ceremony – much to the amusement of Arambol's Indian visitors – although in recent years, the banks have been annexed by a local entre-preneur, and you now have to pay for a scraping of what little mud remains.

Arrival and information

Buses to and from Panjim (via Mapusa) pull into Arambol every half-hour until noon, and every ninety minutes thereafter, at the small bus stop on the main road. A faster private **minibus** service from Panjim arrives daily opposite the chai stalls at the beach end of the village. There are plenty of places offering broadband **Internet access**, motorcycle rental and money changing.

Accommodation

Standards of tourist accommodation in Arambol lag well behind the rest of the state, although there are signs of improvement, with a crop of new, family guesthouses on the south side of the village in **Modlo** and **Girkar Waddos**. This area is much more peaceful, but you have to walk down the beach to get there – not such a great idea at night if you're female. The warren of narrow sandy lanes behind the north end of the beach, known as **Khalcha Waddo**, is busier, but – with the exception of those listed below – its guesthouses are uniformly cramped and grotty.

Ave Maria House #22, Modlo Waddo ☎0832/224 2974. Arambol's largest guesthouse offers good-value rooms, with or without bathrooms, and a sociable rooftop restaurant in a three-storey modern building. Tricky to find: turn left on to a *kutcha* track where the main road through the south side of the village makes a sharp right bend. ❸

Famafa Khalcha Waddo ☎0832/229 2516, ⓦwww.travelingoa.com/famafa. Large, ugly concrete place just off the main lane leading to the beachfront; popular with Israelis and correspondingly rowdy, but it usually has vacancies and is very close to the sands. ❸

God's Gift House #411, Girkar Waddo ☎0832/224 2318. Variously priced, sizeable rooms, all tiled and with comfortable verandas; some also have living rooms and kitchens. Rates are good and the proprietors friendly. ❷

Ivon's Girkar Waddo ☎0832/224 2672 or 09822 127398. The pick of the bunch: clean, tiled rooms, all with attached bathroom and fronted by good-sized tiled balconies opening onto a well-groomed family compound or the dunes. ❹

Om Ganesh Cottages ☎0832/224 2957. In the cove between the village and Lakeside beach; book at the Om Ganesh stores on the main drag (☎0832/224 2957). Nicest of the "cottages" stacked up the cliffside just south of Lakeside beach. The sea views from their verandas are superb, but some may find the Israeli chillum scene in the nearby cafés a disincentive. Rates vary wildly according to demand, and advance booking (with a deposit) is all but essential by mid-season. ❹–❺

Priya Modlo Waddo ☎0832/224 2661. Welcoming ten-room guesthouse that's the best fallback if nearby *Ave Maria* is full. ❸

Samsara Arambol beach ☎09822 688471, ⓦwww.samsara.20m.com. Italian-run huts (shared bathrooms) and rooms (attached), slap on the beach. The accommodation's all clean and good value, and they lay on daily yoga classes. For a review of their restaurant, see p.820. ❷–❸

Villa Pedro Girkar Waddo ☎0832/224 7689. Small family place amid the toddy grove just in from the beach – well placed if you want to be near the sea, but a fair way away from the village. The rooms are clean and pleasant, and some have sea views. Good value. ❷

Eating

Thanks to its annually replenished pool of expatriate gastronomic talent, Arambol harbours a handful of unexpectedly good **restaurants** – not that you'd ever guess from their generally lacklustre exteriors. The village's discerning hippy contingent cares more about flavours than fancy decor, and prices reflect the fact that most of them eke out savings to stay here all winter. If you're on a really rock-bottom budget, stick to the "rice-plate" shacks at the bottom of the village. Tasty thalis at *Sheila's* and *Siddi* come with *puris*, and both have a good travellers' breakfast menu of pancakes, eggs and curd. *Dominic's*, also at the bottom of the village (near where the road makes a ninety-degree bend), is popular for its fruit juices and milkshakes.

Double Dutch Main St, halfway down on the right (look for the yellow signboard). Spread under a palm canopy in the thick of the village, this laid-back café is the hub of alternative Arambol. Famous for its delicious apple pie, a tempting range of home-baked buttery biscuits, cakes (Buddha's Dream's a winner), healthy salads and sumptuous main meals (from Rs150), including fresh buffalo steaks and the ever popular "mixed stuff" (stuffed mushrooms and capsicums with sesame pesto).

Double Trouble "Glastonbury Street". Spin-off of *Double Dutch*, offering classy Italian- and French-style seafood dishes from around Rs160–180.

Fellini's "Glastonbury Street". Italian-run place serving delicious wood-fired pizzas (Rs100–150), and authentic pasta or gnocchi with a choice of over twenty sauces. It gets horrendously busy in season, so be here early if you want snappy service.

La Muella In the village, just before the bend in the road. Wholefoody café-restaurant run by Israelis, which is giving *Double Dutch* a run for their money with their delicious quiches, crunchy salads and home-made cakes, in addition to *shak shuka*, hummus, baked aubergines in pitta, falafel and other Israeli staples. Most dishes Rs80–150.

Relax Inn Arambol beach. Top-quality seafood straight off the boats and unbelievably authentic pasta (you get even more expat Italians in here than at *Fellini's*). Try the *vongole* (clam) sauce. Inexpensive, but expect a wait as they cook to order.

Samsara Arambol beach. Very chilled, "double-decked" Italian shack on the beach, done out with hammocks, cushions and attractive lighting. The emphasis is on healthy Italian and macrobiotic food – the smoothies and salads are the best in the village, and at budget traveller–friendly prices.

Silver Sand Opposite Arambol chapel. At the south side of the village, this is another deceptively ordinary streetside café specializing in fresh seafood (including Chapora calamari), home-made pasta, ratatouille for vegans and popular chocolate cake, baked daily. The espresso's top-notch, too, and there can be queues at breakfast for the home-made pineapple jam.

Nightlife and entertainment

Evenings in Arambol tend to revolve around the café-restaurants and whichever bar is hosting **live music**. There are free jam sessions at *Loeki's*, just off "Glastonbury Street", on Sunday and Thursday evenings. Standards vary with whoever happens to blow in, but there have been some memorable impromptu gigs held here over the past few seasons.

Sports and holistic therapies

Posters pinned to palm trees and café noticeboards around Arambol advertise an amazing array of **activities**, from kite surfing to reiki. A good place to get a fix on what's happening is the *Double Dutch* "Bullshit Info" corner, which displays email addresses and meeting details for just about everyone who does anything.

For the adventurous, there's **paragliding** from the clifftops above Lakeside beach, run by a couple of German and British outfits who've been here for the best part of a decade, alternating between Goa and Manali. The cost of the flight includes all the equipment you'll need and full instruction. At the south end of Arambol beach, ask at the Surf Shack for details of **kite-surfing** courses and equipment rental.

Each season, an army of holistic therapists also offer their services and run courses in Arambol, making this a great place to learn new skills. Look out for Iyengar-qualified **yoga** teacher Sharat (Ⓦ www.hiyogacentre.com), who holds five-day classes on the beach (Rs1000), as well as two-week intensives. Prospective students usually have to sign up by Wednesday lunchtime.

Terekol

The tiny enclave of **TEREKOL**, the northernmost tip of Goa, is reached via a clapped-out car ferry (every 30min; 5min) from the hamlet of Querim, 42km from Panjim. If the tide is out and the water levels are too low for the ferry to run, you can either backtrack 5km, where there's another one, or arrange for the boatman at the jetty to run you across (for a negotiable fee).

Set against the backdrop of a filthy iron-ore complex, the old **fort** that dominates the estuary from the north – an ochre-painted building with turreted ramparts that wouldn't look out of place in coastal Portugal – was built by the Marathas at the start of the eighteenth century, but taken soon after by the Portuguese. These days, it serves as a low-key luxury Heritage Hotel, *The Fort Tiracol* (Ⓣ 0832/227 6793, or 02366 227631, Ⓦ www.nilayahermitage.com; Ⓞ), created by the owners of the swish *Nilaya Hermitage* at Arpora (see p.802). The seven rooms are all decorated in traditional ochre and white, with black-oxide floors, black-tiled drench showers and rustic wood and wrought-iron furniture;

tariffs start at $150 per night. Nonresidents are welcome to visit the restaurant and stylish lounge bar, where you can eat authentic Goan cooking while enjoying what must rank among the finest seascapes in southern India.

South Goa

Beyond the unattractive port city of Vasco da Gama and nearby Dabolim airport, Goa's southern reaches are fringed by some of the region's finest **beaches**, backed by a lush band of coconut plantations and green hills scattered with attractive villages. An ideal first base if you've just arrived in the region is **Benaulim**, 6km west of Goa's second city, **Margao**. The most traveller-friendly resort in the area, Benaulim stands slap in the middle of a spectacular 25-kilometre stretch of pure white sand. Although increasingly carved up by Mumbai time-share companies, low-cost accommodation here is plentiful and of a consistently high standard. Nearby Colva, by contrast, has degenerated over the past decade into an insalubrious charter resort. Frequented by huge numbers of day-trippers, and boasting few discernible charms, it's best avoided.

With the gradual spread of package tourism down the coast, **Palolem**, a couple of hours south of Margao along the main highway, has emerged as the budget travellers' preferred resort, despite its relative inaccessibility. Set against a backdrop of forest-cloaked hills, its beach is spectacular, although the number of visitors can feel overwhelming in high season.

Margao and around

The capital of prosperous Salcete *taluka*, **MARGAO** – referred to in railway timetables and on some maps by its official government title, **Madgaon** – is Goa's second city. The town, surrounded by fertile rice paddy and plantain groves, has always been an important agricultural market, and was once a major religious centre, with dozens of wealthy temples and *dharamshalas* – however, most of these were destroyed when the Portuguese absorbed the area into their Novas Conquistas ("New Conquests") during the seventeenth century. Today, Catholic churches still outnumber Hindu shrines, but Margao has retained a cosmopolitan feel due to a huge influx of migrant labour from neighbouring Karnataka and Maharashtra.

If you're arriving in Goa on the Konkan Railway, you'll almost certainly have to pause in Margao to pick up onward transport by road. The other reason to come here is to shop at the town's **market**, whose hub is a labyrinthine covered area. Also worth checking is the little government-run **Khadi Gramodyog** shop, on the main square, which sells the usual range of hand-spun cottons and raw silk by the metre, as well as ready-made traditional Indian garments.

A rickshaw-ride north, the **Church of the Holy Spirit** is the main landmark in Margoa's dishevelled colonial enclave, next to **Largo de Igreja** square. Built by the Portuguese in 1675, it ranks among the finest examples of late-Baroque architecture in Goa, its interior dominated by a huge gilt reredos dedicated to the Virgin. Just northeast of it, overlooking the main Ponda road, stands one of the state's grandest eighteenth-century *palacios*, **Sat Banzam Ghor** ("Seven Gables house"). Only three of its original seven high-pitched roof gables remain, but the mansion is still an impressive sight, its facade decorated with fancy scroll work and huge oyster-shell windows.

For more of Goa's wonderful vernacular colonial architecture, you'll have to head **inland from Margao**, where villages such as **Lutolim**, **Racaim** and

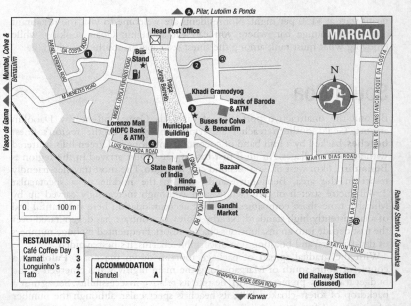

Within the map:

▲ **A**, Pilar, Lutolim & Ponda

MARGAO

Mumbai, Colva & Benaulim ▲◄

Vasco da Gama ▲◄

Head Post Office

RAVEL PEREIRA ROAD

DA COSTA ROAD

1

Bus Stand ★

Praça Jorge Barreto

MIGEL LOYOLA FURADO ROAD

M MENEZES ROAD

2

@

N

RUA DE CONSTANCIO ROQUE DA COSTA

Khadi Gramodyog

Bank of Baroda & ATM

3

Buses for Colva & Benaulim

Lorenzo Mall (HDFC Bank & ATM)

Municipal Building

LUIS MIRANDA ROAD

4

MARTIN DIAS ROAD

(i)

State Bank of India

Hindu Pharmacy

J IGNACIO

DE LOYOLA RD

Bazaar

Bobcards

Gandhi Market

RUA DA SAUDADES

Railway Station & Karnataka ►

0   100 m

STATION ROAD

BHARATKA HEGDE DESAI ROAD

Old Railway Station (disused)

▼ Karwar

RESTAURANTS
Café Coffee Day 1
Kamat 3
Longuinho's 4
Tato 2

ACCOMMODATION
Nanutel A

Rachol are littered with decaying old Portuguese houses, most of them empty – the region's traditional inheritance laws ensure that old family homes tend to be owned by literally dozens of descendants, none of whom are willing or can afford to maintain them.

Another reason to travel into Margao is to catch a movie in south Goa's principal **cinema**, the Osia Multiplex (☎0832/270 1717), out in the north of town near the Kadamba Bus Stand. It screens Hollywood as well as Bollywood releases; tickets cost Rs80–120.

Practicalities

Margao's huge **railway station** lies 3km south of the centre, its reservation office (Mon–Sat 8am–4.30pm, Sun 8am–2pm; ☎0832/271 2940) divided between the ground and first floors. Tickets for trains to Mumbai are in short supply, so make your reservation as far in advance as possible. If you're catching the train to Hospet (en route to Hampi; 4 weekly) get here early to avoid long queues. Several principal trains stop in Margao at unsociable times of night, but there's a 24-hour information counter (☎0832/271 2790) and a round-the-clock pre-paid auto-rickshaw and taxi stand outside the exit.

Local private buses to Colva and Benaulim leave from in front of the *Kamat Hotel*, on the east side of Margao's main square. Arriving on long-distance government services you can get off either here or at the main **Kadamba Bus Stand**, 3km further north, on the outskirts of town. The latter is the departure point for interstate services to Mangalore, via Chaudi and Gokarna, and for services to Panjim and north Goa. Paulo Travel's deluxe coach to and from Hampi works from a lot next to the *Nanutel Hotel*, 1km or so south of the Kadamba Bus Stand on Padre Miranda Road.

GTDC's **information office** (Mon–Fri 9.30am–5.30pm; ☎0832/222 5528), which sells tourist maps and keeps useful lists of current train and bus times, is inside the lobby of the GTDC *Margao Residency*, on the southwest corner of the main square. There are plenty of ATMs dotted around the town centre: try HFDC, in the Lorenzo Mall, on the west side of Praça Jorge Barreto just up from *Longuinho's*, or the Bank of Baroda on the opposite side of the square. Bobcards office in the market sub-branch of the Bank of Baroda, on Station Road, does Visa encashments.

The GPO is at the top of the central municipal gardens. For visitors in need of medical attention, Margao's two main **hospitals** are the Hospicio (℡0832/270 5664 or 270 5754), Rua De Miranda, and the Apollo Victor Hospital, in the suburb of Malbhat (℡0832/272 8888 or 272 6272).

Accommodation

With Colva and Benaulim a mere twenty-minute bus ride away, it's hard to think of a reason why anyone should choose to **stay** in Margao: however, a commendable place in town is the three-star *Nanutel* (℡0832/270 0900, Ⓦwww.nanuindia.com; Ⓞ), a multistorey block north of the main square on Rua Padre Miranda. Pitched at visiting businessmen, it has 55 central a/c rooms and a small pool.

Eating and drinking

After a browse around the bazaar, most visitors make a beeline for *Longuinho's*, the long-established hang-out of Margao's English-speaking middle classes. If you are on a tight budget, try one of the south Indian–style pure-veg cafés along Station Road.

Café Coffee Day Shop 18/19 Vasanth Arcade, near Popular High School. Goa's answer to *Starbucks* has a super-cool a/c branch tucked away off the Municipal Gardens square, popular with local college kids. Aside from a perfect latte, it serves spicy savouries (such as mini-pizzas and salad wraps) and, most memorably, a very sinful "sizzling brownie" (Rs75), which will have chocoholics begging for loyalty cards.

Kamat Praça Jorge Barreto, next to the Colva/Benaulim bus stop. The town's busiest Udupi canteen, serving the usual south Indian selection, as well as hot and cold drinks. More hygienic than it looks, but *Tato* up the road is cleaner.

Longuinho's Luis Miranda Rd. Relaxing, old-fashioned café serving a selection of meat, fish and veg mains, freshly baked savoury snacks, cakes and drinks. The food isn't up to much these days, and the 1950s Goan atmosphere has been marred by the arrival of satellite TV, but it's a pleasant enough place to catch your breath over a beer.

Tato Tucked away up an alley off the east side of Praça Jorge Barreto. The town's brightest and best south Indian café serves the usual range of hot snacks (including especially good samosas at breakfast time, and masala dosas from midday on). A bit cramped downstairs, but well worth the effort to find. For a proper meal, climb the stairs to their cool a/c floor, where you can order wonderful thalis (for Rs45) and a range of North Indian dishes, as well as all the Udupi nibbles dished up on the ground floor.

Chandor

Thirteen kilometres east of Margao across Salcete district's fertile rice fields lies sleepy **CHANDOR** village, a scattering of tumbledown villas and farmhouses ranged along shady tree-lined lanes. The main reason to venture out here is the splendid **Braganza-Perreira/Menezes-Braganza house** (daily except holidays, no set hours; recommended donation Rs100), regarded as the grandest of Goa's colonial mansions. Dominating the dusty village square, the house, built in the 1500s by the wealthy Braganza family for their two sons, has a huge double-storey facade, with 28 windows flanking its entrance. Braganza de Perreira, the great-grandfather of the present owner, was the last knight of the king of Portugal; more recently, Menezes Braganza (1879–1938), a journalist and freedom fighter, was one of the few Goan aristocrats actively to oppose Portuguese rule. Forced to flee Chandor in 1950, the family returned in 1962 to find their house, amazingly, untouched. The airy tiled interiors of both wings contain a veritable feast of **antiques**.

The house is divided into two separate wings, owned by different branches of the old family. Both are open to the public, though there are no set hours as such – just turn up between 10am and noon or 3 and 5pm, go through the main entrance, up the stairs and knock at either of the doors. You'll be expected to leave a donation of at least Rs100. Furniture enthusiasts and lovers of rare Chinese porcelain, in particular, will find plenty to drool over in the Menezes-Braganza wing (to the right as you face the building). Next door in the **Braganza-Pereira** portion, an ornate oratory enshrines St Francis Xavier's diamond-encrusted toenail, retrieved from a local bank vault. The house's most famous feature, however, is its ostentatiously grand ballroom, or **Great Salon**, where a pair of matching high-backed chairs, presented to the Braganza-Perreiras by King Dom Luís of Portugal, occupy pride of place.

Colva

A hot-season retreat for Margao's moneyed middle classes since long before Independence, **COLVA** is the oldest and largest – but least appealing – of south Goa's resorts. Its outlying *waddos* are pleasant enough, dotted with colonial-style villas and ramshackle fishing huts, but the beachfront is dismal: a lacklustre collection of concrete hotels, souvenir stalls and fly-blown snack bars strewn around a bleak central roundabout. The atmosphere is not improved by heaps of rubbish dumped in a rank-smelling ditch that runs behind the beach, nor by the stench of drying fish wafting from the nearby village. Benaulim, only a five-minute drive further south, has a far better choice of accommodation and range of facilities, and is altogether more salubrious.

Benaulim

According to Hindu mythology, Goa was created when the sage Shri Parasurama, Vishnu's sixth incarnation, fired an arrow into the sea from the top of the Western Ghats and ordered the waters to recede. The spot where the shaft fell to earth, known in Sanskrit as Banali ("place where the arrow landed") and later corrupted by the Portuguese to **BENAULIM**, lies in the dead centre of Colva beach, 7km west of Margao. Twenty years ago, this atmospheric fishing and rice-farming village, scattered around the coconut groves and paddy fields between the main Colva–Mobor road and the dunes, had barely made it onto the backpackers' map. Since the completion of the nearby Konkan Railway, however, big-spending middle-class Indians have started to holiday here, in the luxury resorts and time-share apartment complexes that have mushroomed in the rice fields. As a result, the village has lost some of its famously *sossegado* feel. Even so, if you time your visit well (avoiding Diwali and the Christmas peak season), Benaulim is still hard to beat as a place to unwind. Its tourist scene is neither particularly "alternative" nor alcohol-driven. The seafood is superb, accommodation and motorbikes cheaper than anywhere else in the state, and the beach breathtaking, particularly around sunset, when its brilliant white sand and churning surf reflect the changing colours to magical effect. Shelving away almost to Cabo da Rama on the horizon, the beach is also lined with Goa's largest, and most colourfully decorated, fleet of wooden outriggers, and these provide welcome shade during the heat of the day. The only bugbear here is the hawkers: despite repeated clampdowns by shack owners, you can expect to be hassled every five minutes by Karnatakan girls selling *lunghis* and fruit – it's good natured, but intrusive nonetheless.

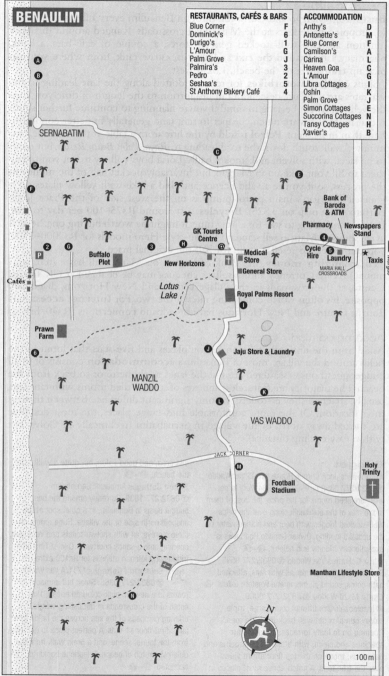

BENAULIM

RESTAURANTS, CAFÉS & BARS	
Blue Corner	F
Dominick's	6
Durigo's	1
L'Amour	G
Palm Grove	J
Palmira's	3
Pedro	2
Seshaa's	5
St Anthony Bakery Café	4

ACCOMMODATION	
Anthy's	D
Antonette's	M
Blue Corner	F
Camilson's	A
Carina	L
Heaven Goa	C
L'Amour	G
Libra Cottages	I
Oshin	K
Palm Grove	J
Simon Cottages	E
Succorina Cottages	N
Tansy Cottages	H
Xavier's	B

SERNABATIM

Cafés

Buffalo Plot

Prawn Farm

GK Tourist Centre

New Horizons

Lotus Lake

Royal Palms Resort

Bank of Baroda & ATM

Pharmacy

Newspapers Stand

Cycle Hire

Laundry

MARIA HALL CROSSROADS

Medical Store

General Store

Taxis

Margao

MANZIL WADDO

Jaju Store & Laundry

VAS WADDO

JACK CORNER

Football Stadium

Holy Trinity

Manthan Lifestyle Store

0   100 m

Varca Cavelossim, Mobor & Palolem ▼

Buses from Margao and Colva roll through Benaulim every fifteen minutes or so, dropping passengers at the Maria Hall crossroads. Ranged around this busy junction are two well-stocked general stores, a couple of café-bars, a bank, pharmacy, laundry and the taxi and auto-rickshaw rank, from where you can pick up **transport** to the beach, 1.5km west.

Signs offering **motorbikes** for rent are dotted along the lane leading to the sea: rates are standard, descending in proportion to the length of time you keep the vehicle. Worth bearing in mind if you're planning to continue further south is that motorbikes are much cheaper to rent (and generally in better condition) here than in Palolem. **Petrol** is sold by the litre from a table at the roadside, two minutes' walk south down the road leading to *Royal Palm Beach Resort*, but tends to be laced with solvent and smokes badly. Local boys will try to get you to pay them to fill your bike up in Margao, but invariably pocket half of the money in the process, so if you've a valid licence and find a bike with yellow plates do it yourself (Margao's main petrol pump is on the west side of the Praça Jorge Barreto – see map on p.825). **Bicycles** cost around Rs75–100 per day to rent. If you're intending to stay for a long time, it might be worth buying one. Several cycle shops in Margao sell standard Indian-style Hero models for Rs2000–2500; you can expect to resell it again for half the original price.

For **changing money**, the Bank of Baroda on Maria Hall has a (temperamental) ATM. Currency and traveller's cheques may be changed at GK Tourist Centre, at the crossroads in the village centre, and New Horizons, diagonally opposite. It's often worth comparing rates at the two. For **Internet access**, GK Tourist Centre and New Horizons have broadband connections (Rs40/hr).

Accommodation

Aside from the unsightly time-share complexes and five-stars that loom in the fields around the village, most of Benaulim's **accommodation** consists of small budget guesthouses, scattered around the lanes a kilometre or so back from the beach. The majority are featureless annexes of spartan tiled rooms with fans and, usually, attached shower-toilets; the only significant difference between them is their location. Of the more comfortable mid-range places, the most desirable are tucked away north of the village in Sernabatim (technically in Colva, but within easy cycling distance).

Budget

Antonette's Jack Corner, House #1695 Vas Waddo ☎0832/277 0358 or 09922 312984. Very large, well-furnished rooms for the price, the best of them to the rear of the building looking over the fields. Well-stocked fridges with beer and bottled water on the upstairs landing. Owner Geraldo Rodrigues is exceptionally friendly and helpful. ❶–❷

Libra Cottages Vas Waddo ☎0832/277 0598. Spartan but clean rooms, all with fans, attached bathrooms, sound plumbing and Western toilets. ❸

Oshin Mazil Waddo ☎0832/277 0069, ✉inaciooshin@rediffmail.com. Large, triple-storey complex set well back from the road. Opening on to leafy terraces, its rooms are spacious and clean, with attached bathrooms and balconies; those on the top floor afford views over the tree tops. A notch above most places in

this area, and good value, but quite a walk from the beach. ❸–❹

Simon Cottages Ambeaxir Sernabatim ☎0832/277 1839. Currently among the best budget deals in Benaulim, in a quiet spot at the unspoilt north side of the village. Huge rooms on three storeys, all with shower-toilets and verandas, opening onto a sandy courtyard. Owner Tina offers fridges and kitchen utensils for Rs100 extra. ❷

Succorina Cottages 1711/A Vas Waddo ☎0832/277 0365. Small but immaculate rooms in a newish, pink-coloured house, 1km south of the crossroads in the fishing village, offering glimpses of the sea across the fields from large first-floor sit-outs. A perfect place to get away from the tourist scene, and a 5min walk from the quietest stretch of beach. Telephone bookings accepted. ❶–❷

Mid-range

Anthy's Sernabatim ☎ 0832/277 1680, ✉ anthysguesthouse@rediffmail.com. Rooms right on the sea, with tiny bathrooms and breezy verandas; there's a Keralan Ayurvedic massage centre on site too. ⑤

Blue Corner Ambeaxir Sernabatim. Popular new hut camp right on the beach, run by an enthusiastic young crew. Large palm-leaf structures with fans, mosquito nets, attached shower-toilets and plywood sit-outs. Quiet and secure, and the bar-restaurant is one of the most happening places on the beach in the evenings. ⑤

Camilson's Sernabatim ☎ 0832/277 1582, ⓦ www.camilsons.in. Small resort of good-sized rooms with private terraces, set very close to the beach amid a manicured garden, well away from the village. The rooms have private terraces and comfy cane chairs; and there are some larger ones set aside for families. ④–⑥

Carina Tamdi-Mati, Vas Waddo ☎ 0832/277 0413, ⓦ www.carinabeachresort.com. Good-value – if somewhat lackadaisical – mid-scale hotel in a tranquil location on the south side of Benaulim, with a pool, garden and bar-restaurant. Some rooms have a/c. ⑤

🏃 **Heaven Goa** 1 Ambeaxir Sernabatim ☎ 0832/277 0365, ⓦ www.heavengoa.co.in. Run by a welcoming Swiss–Keralan couple, this new block of a dozen or so rooms occupies a plum spot, 10min back from the sea beside a lily pond

alive with frogs, egrets and water buffalo. The rooms are spacious and well set up (with wood shelves, mosquito nets, shiny tiled floors and balconies overlooking the water); and they bake fresh pizzas in a wood oven, too. ④–⑤

L'Amour Beach Rd ☎ 0832/277 0404, ⓦ www.lamourbeachresort.com. Benaulim's oldest hotel consists of a comfortable thirty-room cottage complex, with terrace restaurant, travel agent, money changing and some a/c rooms. No single occupancy. Reasonable rates. ④

Palm Grove Tamdi-Mati, 149 Vas Waddo ☎ 0832/277 0059, ⓦ www.palmgrovegoa.com. Secluded hotel surrounded by beautiful gardens, offering two classes of room, some of them a/c; plus there's one of Benaulim's better restaurants on site. A bike ride back from the beachfront, but very pleasant, and the management is helpful. ④–⑤

Tansy Cottages Beach Rd ☎ 0832/277 0574, ✉ tansycottages@yahoo.in. Variously sized apartments, from rooms with self-catering kitchenettes to one- and two-bedroom flats in a two-storey block. The balconies could be more private, but you get lots of space indoors for your money, plus fridges and cooking utensils. ④–⑤

Xavier's Sernabatim ☎ 0832/277 1489, ✉ jovek @sandhar.net. Next door to *Camilson's*, and very similar with well-maintained, large rooms ranged around a lovely garden, virtually on the beach. All rooms have private terraces and low-slung cane chairs to lounge on. ④–⑤

Eating and drinking

Benaulim's proximity to Margao market, along with the presence of a large Christian fishing community, means its **restaurants** serve some of the tastiest, competitively priced seafood in Goa. The best shacks flank the beachfront area, where *Johncy's* catches most of the passing custom. However, you'll find better food at lower prices at places further along the beach, which seem to change chefs annually; the only way to find out which ones offer the best value for money is to wander past and see who has the most customers. An enduring favourite is *Dominick's*, whose extrovert owner hosts bonfire parties one night per week (traditionally on Thursdays), featuring a live band; prices here are on the high side. *Pedro's* on the beachfront is marginally better value and also puts on gigs, mostly on Saturday nights.

Blue Corner Ambeaxir Sernabatim. Great little beachside joint specializing in seafood and authentic Chinese. House favourites include "fish tomato eggdrop soup", scrumptious "dragon potatoes" and, best of all, their "super special steak". Also featured on an eclectic menu are tasty Italian dishes, sizzlers and, for homesick veggies, a pretty good cauliflower cheese. Most mains are Rs120–250.

Durigo's Sernabatim, 2km north of Maria Hall on the outskirts of Colva. This is the locals' favourite place to eat, serving traditional Goan seafood of a

kind and quality you rarely find in the shacks: try their tasty mussels, lemonfish (*modso*) or barramundi (*chonok*), marinated in spicy, sour *rechead* sauce and pan-fried in millet. Some may find the atmosphere a bit rough and ready (though the service is unfailingly polite), in which case follow the example of the village's middle classes and order a takeaway.

L'Amour *L'Amour* hotel. One of Benaulim's slicker restaurants, serving an exhaustive multi-cuisine dinner menu (mains Rs150–200), as well as drinks.

With background noise limited to chinking china and hushed voices, it's also a relaxing place for breakfast: fresh fruit, muesli, yoghurt and pancakes. **Palm Grove** *Palm Grove* hotel. Mostly Goan seafood, with some Indian and Continental options, served in a smart new garden pagoda, against a backdrop of illuminated trees. Main courses Rs175–225.

Palmira's Beach Rd. Benaulim's best tourist breakfasts: wonderfully creamy and fresh set curd, copious fruit salads with coconut, real espresso coffee, warm local bread (*bajri*) and the morning paper. Now open throughout the day.

Seshaa's/St Anthony Bakery Café Maria Hall Crossroads. A local institution, *Seshaa's* is a gloomy and rather cramped lads' café that's great for pukka Goan *channa bhaji* and, best of all, deliciously flaky veg or beef patties. On the opposite side of the road, *St Anthony Bakery* is equally popular (especially in the mornings) serving the same local grub, but is less male-dominated – and its patties come straight out of the ovens.

The far south: Canacona

Ceded to the Portuguese by the Raja of Sund in the Treaty of 1791, Goa's **far south – Canacona** district – was among the last parts of the territory to be absorbed into the Novas Conquistas, and has retained a distinctly Hindu feel. The area also boasts some of the state's most outstanding scenery. Set against a backdrop of the jungle-covered Sahyadri hills (a part of the Western Ghat range), a string of pearl-white coves and sweeping beaches scoop its indented coastline, enfolded by laterite headlands and colossal piles of black boulders.

With the exception of the village of **Palolem**, whose near-perfect beach attracts a deluge of travellers during high season, coastal settlements such as **Agonda**, a short way north, remain rooted in a traditional fishing and toddy-tapping economy. However, the red gash of the **Konkan Railway** threatens to bring its days as a tranquil rural backwater to an end. For the last few years, it has been possible to reach Canacona by direct "superfast" express trains from Mumbai, Panjim and Mangalore: the developers' bulldozers and concrete mixers are sure to follow.

The region's main transport artery is the NH-17, which crawls across the Sahyadri and Karmali ghats towards Karnataka via the district headquarters, **Chaudi**; travellers jump off here for Palolem, a few kilometres across the fields, and the small market at this point is useful for essentials. Bus services to and from Margao are frequent; off the highway, however, bullock carts and bicycles still outnumber motor vehicles. The only way to do the area justice is by motorcycle, although it's advisable to rent one further north (Benaulim's your best bet for this) and drive it down here, as few are available here.

Agonda

AGONDA, 10km north of Chaudi, can only be reached along the sinuous coast road connecting Cabo da Rama with NH-17 at Chaudi. No signposts mark the turning, and few of the tourists that whizz past en route to Palolem pull off here, but the beach is superb – albeit with a strong undertow that weak swimmers should be very wary of (head for the safer cove at the far southern end of the beach, where the fishing boats are moored).

Practicalities

Facilities for visitors are basic, but adequate, and well spaced apart: Agonda never gets too congested, even in peak season. **Places to stay and eat** are dotted along the road behind the beach, and over the past couple of seasons a handful of small guesthouses and treehouse camps have also opened up at the northern end, beyond the church.

For **food**, *Dercy's* is the most enduringly popular option, though it's definitely been exploiting its own success in recent years, serving frozen fish rather than local stuff as it used to. A little further up the road, *La Dolce Vita* is a more sophisticated alternative – an infectiously fun terrace-restaurant run by an energetic Italian couple. Decked out in pretty pastel blue furniture with matching awnings, it serves authentic wood-baked pizzas, delicious house pasta and pesto, and proper chocolate pudding and tiramisu for dessert. For a sundowner, the *Sun Set Bar*, up on a bluff just south of *Dercy's* surveying the bay, is hard to beat.

Accommodation

Common Home South side of beach ☎0832/264 7890. Chic, Brit-owned place with pretensions as a boutique hotel (repro antique wood doors, interesting furniture and floaty mosquito nets). Not at all the kind of place you'd expect to find here, but efficiently run and comfortable, if a touch overpriced. ❻

Dercy's South end of the beach, on the roadside ☎0832/264 7503. Exceptionally clean and relaxing rooms, with tiled floors and good-sized bathrooms. Those on the first floor (front side) have a common sea-facing veranda that catches the breezes; you can lie in bed and hear the waves crashing only 100m away. They also run a couple of rows of (rather overpriced) beach huts on the opposite side of the lane. ❸–❹

Dunhill Beach Resort A short way down the lane beyond *Dercy's* ☎0832/264 7328, ©dunhill-resort@rediffmail.com. All the rooms here are attached with small verandas opening onto a sandy enclosure, where you can eat locally caught fish. Internet access (for guests only). ❸

Fatima South side of beach, next to *La Dolce Vita* ☎0832/264 7477 or 09423 332888. Very good value budget guesthouse offering spacious, squeaky clean attached rooms: shiny tiled floors, bucket hot water, and sea views from the upper floor, plus there's a friendly Great Dane the size of a horse. Best of the cheapies. ❸

Maria Paul Just north of *Dercy's* towards the church ☎0832/264 7606. This modern pink building on the roadside is a bigger and slightly more anonymous guesthouse than the others in the village, which some might prefer. Six large, cool marble-floored rooms. ❹

Palm Beach Lifestyle Resort Behind *Dercy's* ☎0832/264 7783, ⊚www.palmbeachgoa.com. Simple but very pleasant chalets that have painted wood floors, comfy foam mattresses, relaxing decks and uninterrupted sea views. The most restful option in Agonda, and good value. ❺

Sami Near the church ☎09850 453805. Most appealing of the village's small hut camps, right on the beach. The larger-than-average huts are far enough apart, with painted balconies; bikes are available to rent. Also worth trying is the similar nearby *Madhu* (☎0832/264 7116). Both ❷–❸

Palolem

Nowhere else in peninsular India conforms so closely to the archetypal image of a paradise beach as **PALOLEM**, 35km south of Margao. Lined with a swaying curtain of coconut palms, the bay forms a perfect curve of golden sand, arcing north from a giant pile of boulders to the spur of Sahyadri Ghat, which tapers into the sea draped in thick forest. For those foreigners who found their way here before the mid-1990s, however, Palolem is most definitely a paradise lost these days. With the rest of Goa largely carved up by package tourism, this is the first-choice destination of most independent travellers, and the numbers can feel overwhelming in peak season, when literally thousands of people spill across the beach. Behind them, an unbroken line of shacks and Thai-style bamboo- and palm-leaf huts provide food and shelter that grows more sophisticated (and less Goan) with each season – not least because many of the businesses here are now run by expatriates. Thanks to a local law forbidding the construction of permanent buildings close to the beach (enforced by periodic bulldozing of the entire resort), development has been restrained, but it's still a far cry from the idyll of only a few years ago.

Palolem in full swing is the kind of place you'll either love at first sight or want to get away from as quickly as possible. If you're in the latter category, try smaller, less-frequented **Patnem** beach, a short walk south, where the shack scene is more subdued and the sand emptier. Further south still, **Rajbag**, around half an hour's walk from Palolem, used to be one of Goa's last deserted beaches until a vast, seven-star luxury resort was recently built slap behind it.

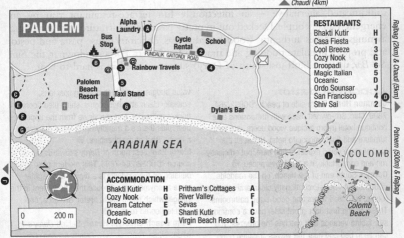

PALOLEM

Alpha Laundry **A**

Bus Stop

Cycle Rental **2**

School

PUNDALIK GAITONDI ROAD

@ 3 Rainbow Travels

4

Palolem Beach Resort

Taxi Stand **★**

6

Dylan's Bar

ARABIAN SEA

Chaudi (4km)

RESTAURANTS

Bhakti Kutir	**H**
Casa Fiesta	**1**
Cool Breeze	**3**
Cozy Nook	**G**
Droopadi	**6**
Magic Italian	**5**
Oceanic	**D**
Ordo Sounsar	**J**
San Francisco	**4**
Shiv Sai	**2**

Rajbag (2km) & Chaudi (5km)

Patnem (500m) & Rajbag

COLOMB

Colomb Beach

0   200 m

ACCOMMODATION

Bhakti Kutir	**H**	Pritham's Cottages	**A**
Cozy Nook	**G**	River Valley	**F**
Dream Catcher	**E**	Sevas	**I**
Oceanic	**D**	Shanti Kutir	**C**
Ordo Sounsar	**J**	Virgin Beach Resort	**B**

Arrival and information

Frequent **buses** run between Margao and Karwar (in Karnataka) via Chaudi (every 30min; 2hr), from where you can pick up an **auto-rickshaw** (Rs50–75) or **taxi** (Rs100–150) for the 2km journey west to Palolem. Alternatively, get off the bus at the Char Rastay ("Four-Way") crossroads, 1.5km before Chaudi, and walk the remaining kilometre or so to the village. Hourly buses also go all the way to Palolem from Margao; these stop at the end of the lane leading from the main street to the beachfront. The last bus from Palolem to Chaudi/Margao leaves at around 4.30pm; check with the locals for the precise times, as these change seasonally. **Bicycles** may be rented from a stall halfway along the main street for the princely sum of Rs15 per hour (with discounts for longer periods). The village has a dozen or more STD/ISD **telephones**; avoid the one in the *Beach Resort*, which charges more than double the going rate for international calls, and head for Bliss Travel, on the left near the main entrance to the beach. This place also has Palolem's fastest Internet connections (Rs50/hr) – go armed with a wrap, as the a/c's fierce.

You can **change money** at any number of agents advertising their services along the lanes through Palolem and on the beach road, though it's worth shopping around for the best rates; LKP Forex in the *Palolem Beach Resort* (on the beachfront behind the taxi stand) was the most competitive when we last checked. The nearest **ATM** (for Visa and MasterCard withdrawals) is in Chaudi. For those wishing to stash valuables, Lalita Enterprises, on the main beach road, offer lockers for Rs35 per day.

Accommodation

Bhakti Kutir Far southern end of the beach, on the hill dividing Palolem from Colom ☎0832/264 3469 or 264 3472, ⓦwww .bhaktikutir.com. Environmentally-friendly, Indian-village-style "Eco Huts" equipped with Western amenities (including biodegradable chemical toilets), set amid mature gardens 5min walk from the south end of Palolem beach. Beautifully situated, discreet

and sensitively designed to blend in with the landscape by its German–Goan owners. The double-storey units (⑧), aimed at families, offer more space, and there's a quality Ayurvedic healing centre on site. ⑦–⑧

Cozy Nook North end of the beach, near the island ☎0832/264 3550. One of the most attractive setups in the village, comprising 25 bamboo huts (sharing seven toilets, but with good mattresses, mosquito nets, safe lockers and fans) opening onto the lagoon on one side and the beach on the other – an unbeatable spot, which explains the higher than average tariffs. ⑥

Dream Catcher North end of the beach behind *Cozy Nook* ☎0832/264 4873 or 09822 137446, ✉lalalandjackie7@yahoo.com. Individually styled, very glam Keralan-style huts, with more space, better mattresses, nicer textiles, bigger windows and sturdier foundations than most, in a plum position by the riverside. The couple who run it have also built a shaded yoga *shala* for classes, and there's a "chillout-ambient bar". Prices are on the high side, to say the least, but so are the standards. ⑦–⑧

Oceanic Tembi Waddo ☎0832/264 3059, ⓦwww.hotel-oceanic.com. 10min walk inland from the beach; also reachable via the backroad to Chaudi. Owned and managed by a resident British couple, its rooms are tastefully fitted out, with large mosquito nets, blockprinted bedspreads and bedside lamps. There's also a pool on a wooded terrace behind and a quality restaurant. Minimum 7-night stay in peak season (Dec 15–Jan 31). ⑨

🏃 **Ordo Sounsar** Far southern end of Palolem beach, on the far side of the creek (look for the rickety footbridge to the right as you head for the island) ☎09822 488769 or 09422 639497, ⓦwww.ordosounsar.com. Run by a hospitable brother and sister team, this is Palolem's most idyllic and friendly hut camp, tucked away on the tranquil side of the river. The huts themselves are a generous size, comfortably furnished and well spaced, with great sit-outs to lounge on and funky thatched roofs; and there's a sociable bar, excellent restaurant and snooker table. ④

Pritham's Cottages Down a lane north of Pundalik Gaitondi Rd ☎0832/264 3320. Quiet two-storey block of budget rooms in the centre of the village: they're bigger than average, have attached bathrooms and share a common veranda. ③

River Valley North end of beach behind *Cozy Nook* ☎09822 155502, ✉srmh2141@hotmail.com. This small hut camp and its young owner, Manju, offer one of the most consistently hospitable and pleasant budget options in the village. The ten bamboo huts (sharing three toilets) are in a nice open compound with beautiful views across the estuary to the hills and forest. Good value for the location, which is a lot more relaxing than comparable sites on the beach. ④

Sevas Far southern end of the beach, on the hill dividing Palolem from Colom ☎09422 065437, ⓦwww.sevaspalolemgoa.com. A cheaper, less sophisticated version of *Bhakti Kutir*, but beautifully done all the same, and the site is peaceful. The "ethnic" cabañas have traditional rice-straw roofs, mud-and-dung floors, hygienic squat-style loos and bucket baths. They also offer massages and yoga classes, and there's a pleasant restaurant serving very good thalis for Rs100. ④–⑤

Shanti Kutir North end of beach behind *River Valley* and *Dream Catcher* ☎09422 450392 or 09960 917150. Keralan-run hut camp of 30 huts (some attached) on stilts; pleasantly secluded and with an appealing location on the river. Rates vary according to proximity to the water. ④

Virgin Beach Resort Palolem village ☎0832/264 3451. Tiled rooms in a modern three-storey block near the lane running from the main junction in the village to the far north end of the beach. Not exactly the kind of architecture that enhances the village's natural feel, but it's an out-of-the-way spot and some may consider the comfort and security a good trade-off; good value. ③–④

Eating and drinking

Palolem's **restaurants** and **bars** reflect the cosmopolitan make-up of its visitors. Each year, a fresh batch of innovative, ever more stylish places open, most of them managed by expats – and both standards, and prices, have increased greatly as a consequence. For those on tight budgets, there are a couple of local cafés along the road running parallel with the beach – the Hindu *Shiv Sai* and Christian *San Francisco* – that serve filling breakfasts of *pao bhaji*, fluffy bread rolls, omelettes and chai for next to nothing, and equally inexpensive fish-curry-rice meals and samosas from lunchtime. Again, you'll find several good options in the *waddo* of Colom, just south of Palolem.

Bhakti Kutir Far southern end of the beach, on the hill dividing Palolem from Colom. Laid-back terrace café-restaurant with rustic wooden tables and an Indo-European fusion menu: sunny tomato and mozzarella salad (with fresh basil), fish from the bay and North Indian vegetarian dishes, all made with local and organically produced ingredients. Most mains around Rs175–250.

Casa Fiesta Pundalik Gaitondi Rd. Funky expat-run place on the main drag, offering an eclectic menu of

world cuisine: hummus, Greek salad, Mexican specialities and fish *pollichatu*; mains (mostly under Rs225) come with delicious roast potatoes.
Cool Breeze Beach Rd. This is one of the classiest restaurants in the village. Their steaks, tandoori chicken and seafood, in particular, have set new standards for Palolem, and the prices are reasonable. Come early, or you could face a long wait for a table – and leave room for the banoffee pie dessert. Most mains are around Rs200–275.
Cozy Nook Far north end of the beach. Wholesome Goan-style cooking served on a small terrace that occupies a prime position opposite the island at the end of the bay. The filling four-course set dinners (7–9pm; Rs175–250) are deservedly popular, offering imaginative and carefully prepared dishes such as pan-fried fish, aubergine with shrimps and fresh beans. They also do a tasty veg equivalent (Rs130), as well as a full seafood and north Indian curry menu, and in high season there's a great (and hygienic) salad bar (eat all you like for Rs150).
Droopadi Beachfront. This place enjoys both a top location and Palolem's best Indian chef, who specializes in rich, creamy Mughlai dishes and tandoori fish. Go for the superb *murg makhini* or crab masala with spinach. With most main courses Rs150–400, prices are low considering the quality of the cooking.

Magic Italian Beach Rd. On the busy approach to the seafront, this is south Goa's number-one Italian restaurant, serving home-made ravioli and tagliatelle, along with scrumptious wood-fired pizzas (Rs175–250).
Oceanic Tembi Waddo. Chilled terrace restaurant, set well back from the beach but worth the walk for the better-than-average food and background music. North and south Indian dishes are the chef's forte (especially *dum aloo* Kashmiri and butter chicken), but there are also great red and green Thai curries, tempting desserts (including lemon-and-ginger cheesecake and banoffee pie) and coffee liqueur.
Ordo Sounsar Far southern end of Palolem beach (for directions see "Accommodation", p.831). With most places using previously frozen fish instead of fresh these days, this laid-back restaurant, on a terrace in a hut camp of the same name, is something special. Seasonal Goan seafood and vegetarian are their specialities: pomfret stuffed with green chilli; papaya curry in coconut juice; green-pea *xacutti*; prawn balchao; shark *ambotik*; white cabbage in lime dressing – all made with the choicest ingredients brought fresh each day. Count on Rs350–450 for two courses. Advance booking advisable.

South of Palolem: Colom, Patnem and Rajbag

Once across the creek and boulder-covered spur bounding the south end of Palolem beach, you arrive at **COLOM**, a largely Hindu fishing village scattered around a series of rocky coves. Dozens of long-stay rooms, leaf huts and houses are tucked away under the palm groves and on the picturesque headland running seawards. This is the best place in the village to start an accommodation hunt – the lads will know of any vacant places; but be warned that most of the rooms here are very basic indeed. Alternatively, there are several good guesthouses reviewed along with Palolem's accommodation (see p.830). Nightlife is pretty laid back, revolving around the beachside bars. The one place worth singling out is *Neptune's Point*, who host popular "silent disco nights". DJs, mostly from the UK, play live until 11pm, after which punters are issued with quality headsets (for a Rs500 refundable deposit); the music winds up around 4am.

A string of small hut camps and shacks line the next beach south, **PATNEM**. The beach, curving for roughly a kilometre to a steep bluff, is broad, with little shade, and shelves quite steeply at certain phases of the tide, though the undertow rarely gets dangerously strong.

There are plenty of good **accommodation** and **eating** options here, though be warned that room rates have gone through the roof over the past few seasons. At the top of the range is *Goyam* (℡09423 821181, Ⓦwww .goyam.net; ⑥–⑦), towards the north end of the beach, which has luxury, double-storeyed wooden bungalows painted pretty pastel colours, right on the sand. Partly screened by casuarina trees, each is smartly furnished and fitted with bathrooms, mosquito nets and swings on sea-facing balconies. The restaurant, an off-shoot of the popular *Droopadi* in Palolem, does superb seafood

▲ Palolem

prepared in rich North Indian style: crab *makhini* and tandoori sea bass (Rs375–425) are their signature dishes. A bit further along, *Home* (℡0832/264 3916, @homeispatnem@yahoo.com; ❺–❼), is a chic little Swiss–British-run guesthouse, comprising an annexe of attached rooms attractively decked out with textiles, lampshades and other cosy touches. They also run Patnem's best beach café, serving mezes, freshly baked bread, Swiss röstis, fresh salads (from around Rs100), Lavazza espresso, proper English tea and wonderful desserts (banoffee pie, warm apple tart with fresh cream, chocolate and walnut cake). It's a particularly pleasant option for breakfast, with Chopin playing over the sound system and sparrows chirping in the palms. Best of the mid-range options here is *Papayas* (℡99230/79447; ❺–❻), which has wood and thatch rooms comparable in comforts to *Goyam*, but at marginally lower rates – plus it remains in the shade all day.

Among the string of **camps** behind the beach shacks, *Namaste* (℡09850 477189; ❹–❺) is a dependable, fun budget option, run by the amiable Satay, most of whose clientele come back season after season. Rates range from Rs600–1000 depending on size of room and time of year; all have shower-toilets attached. In the same bracket, nearby *Casa Fiesta* (℡0832/647 0367; ❹–❺) has a selection of good-sized huts with unobstructed sea views. *Shiva* (no phone; ❶–❸) is the cheapest choice on Patnem, with huts from as low as Rs200 or less, depending on demand.

Among the many shacks lining the beach, *Tantra* does particularly generous evening meals of jumbo prawns, lobster and fresh local fish. Vegetarians on a budget should try the monster biriyanis served at the *Sealands* for around Rs50.

At low tide, you can walk around the bottom of the steep-sided headland dividing Patnem from neighbouring **RAJBAG**, another kilometre-long sweep of white sand. Sadly, its remote feel has been entirely submerged by the massive five-star *Goa Grand Intercontinental* (@www.intercontinental.com; ❾), recently erected on the land behind it – much to the annoyance of the locals, who campaigned for four years to stop the project.

It's possible to press on even further **south from Rajbag**, by crossing the Talpona River via a hand-paddled ferry, which usually has to be summoned from the far bank (fix a return price in advance and only pay once you've completed both legs of the trip, as the boatmen are rumoured to have been holding wealthy tourists from the *Goa Grand* to ransom by refusing to paddle them back unless they hand over huge "tips"). Once across, a short walk brings you to **Talpona Beach**, backed by low dunes and a line of straggly palms. From there, you can cross the headland at the end of the beach to reach **Galjibag**,

Moving on from Goa

The price of seats on planes from Goa fluctuates wildly at certain times of year, especially around Diwali and Christmas. Try and book flights directly through the **airline**, as private agents charge the dollar fare at poor rates of exchange; addresses of airline offices in Panjim are listed on p.787. Tickets for all **Konkan Railway** services can be booked at the KRC reservation office on the first floor of Panjim's Kadamba Bus Stand (Mon–Sat 8am–8pm, Sun 8am–2pm) or at KRC's main reservation hall in Margao Station (Mon–Sat 8am–4.30pm, Sun 8am–2pm; ☎0834/271 2780). Make your reservations as far in advance as possible, and try to get to the offices soon after opening time – the queues can be horrendous. Seats on the Konkan Railway from Goa to Mumbai are in notoriously short supply; peak periods tend to be reserved up to two months in advance. One way around this is to **book online** (✆www.irctc.co.in), though bear in mind if you do you'll only be eligible for the relatively expensive three-tier a/c fares (Rs1250 one way) and must make your booking between seven and two days before your date of departure.

Kadamba **bus tickets** can be bought in advance at their offices in Panjim and Mapusa bus stands (daily 9–11am & 2–5pm); private companies sell through the many travel agents immediately outside the bus stand in Panjim, and at the bottom of the square in Mapusa. **Information** on all departures and fares is available from Goa Tourism's counter inside Panjim's Bus Stand (see p.784).

For a full rundown of destinations reachable from Goa by bus, train and plane, see "Travel details" at the end of this chapter.

To Mumbai

Between fourteen and fifteen **flights** leave Goa's Dabolim airport daily. The cheapest fares are offered by Air Deccan (✆www.airdeccan.net), who can sell tickets from as low as Rs600. Low-cost rivals SpiceJet (✆www.spicejet.com), IndiGo (✆www.goindigo.in) and Kingfisher Airlines (✆www.flykingfisher.com) also offer competitive tickets. Flying with Indian Airlines (✆www.indian-airlines.nic.in) will set you back $105, or $100 with Jet Lite (✆www.jetlite.com) and $100 with Jet (✆www.jetairways.com).

Four to five services run daily on the **Konkan Railway**, the most convenient being the overnight Konkankanya Express (#0112), which departs from Margao at 6pm (or Karmali, near Old Goa, 11km west of Panjim, at 6.30pm), arriving at CST (commonly known as "Victoria Terminus", or "VT") at 5.50am the following day. The other fast train from Goa to Mumbai CST is the Mandvi Express (#0104), departing Margao at 10.10am (or Karmali at 10.37am) and arriving at 9.45pm the same evening.

The cheapest, though far from most comfortable, way to get to Mumbai is by **night bus**, which takes fourteen to eighteen hours, covering 500km of rough road at often terrifying speeds. Fares vary according to levels of comfort, and luxury buses arrive two or three hours sooner. The most popular private services to Mumbai are those run by a company called Paulo Travels, who lay on a range of different services, from no-frills buses for Rs350 to swisher a/c Volvo coaches with berths (which you may have to share) costing Rs700. It's worth pointing out, however, that women travellers have complained of harassment during the journey. For tickets, contact Paulo Travels: at their desk in the *Hotel Fidalgo* on 18th June Road in Panjim, or at the main office just outside the Kadamba Bus Stand, Panjim (☎0832/222 3736, ✆www.paulotravels.com). In south Goa, their main outlet is at the *Hotel Nanutel*, opposite a remote white-sand bay that's a protected nesting site for Olive Ridley marine **turtles**. A strong undertow means swimming isn't safe here.

Cotigao Wildlife Sanctuary

The **Cotigao Wildlife Sanctuary**, 12km southeast of Palolem, was established in 1969 to protect an isolated and vulnerable area of forest lining the

---

Club Harmonia, in Margao (☎0834/272 1516). Information on all departures and fares is available online.

To Pune

Pune is connected to Goa's Dabolim airport by Indian Airlines' daily **flight**. You can also get there by train on the #2779 Goa Express, departing at 3.10pm and arriving early the following morning at 4.05am, and on any number of private night buses from Panjim (tickets for which should be purchased in advance from the companies' offices outside the Kadamba Bus Stand).

To Hampi

The most stress-free and economical way to reach Hospet from Goa is the four-times-weekly **train** service from **Margao**. The Vasco–Howrah Express (#2848) departs every Tuesday, Thursday, Friday and Sunday at 7.50am, arriving six hours later. Fares range from Rs190 for sleeper class to Rs650 for second-class a/c.

The **bus** journey covering the same route is no cheaper than the train (sleeper class) and is far more gruelling. Two or three clapped-out government services leave Panjim's Kadamba stand (platform #9) each morning for Hospet, the last one at 10.30am. Brace yourself for a long, hard slog; all being well, it should take nine or ten hours, but delays and breakdowns are frustratingly frequent. **Tickets** for Kadamba and KSRTC (Karnatakan State Road Transport Corporation) services should be booked at least one day in advance at the hatches in the bus stand. From Margao, you can also travel to Hampi on a swish **night bus** complete with pneumatic suspension and berths. The service, operated by Paulo Travels (⊛www.paulotravels.com), leaves at 8pm from a lot next to the *Nanutel Hotel* on Margao's Rua da Padre Miranda, arriving in Hampi early the next morning at 7am. Tickets cost Rs450–650, depending on the level of comfort, and can be bought from most reputable travel agents around the state. Although the coach is comfortable enough, the coffin-like berths can get very hot and stuffy, making sleep very difficult; moreover, there have been complaints from women of harassment during the night on this service.

To Gokarna, Jog Falls, Mangalore and southern Karnataka

From Goa, the fastest and most convenient way to travel down the coast to Gokarna is via the **Konkan Railway**. At 2.25pm, the Verna–Mangalore Passenger (KR1 DN) leaves Margao, passing through Chaudi at 2.58pm en route to Gokarna Road, the town's railhead, where it arrives at around 4pm. The station lies 9km east of Gokarna itself, but a minibus is on hand to shuttle passengers the rest of the way. As this is classed as a passenger service, you don't have to buy tickets in advance; just turn up at the station 30min before the departure time and pay at the regular ticket counter. As ever, it is a good idea to **check timings** in advance, through any tourist office or travel agent, or via the KRC's website (⊛www.konkanrailway.com).

Buses take as much as two and a half hours longer to cover the same route. A direct service leaves Margao's interstate stand in the north of town daily at 1pm. You can also get there by catching any of the services that run between Goa and Mangalore, and jumping off either at **Ankola**, or at the Gokarna junction on the main highway, from where frequent private minibuses and *tempos* run into town.

Goa–Karnataka border. Best visited between October and March, Cotigao is a peaceful and scenic park that makes a pleasant day-trip from Palolem. Encompassing 86 square kilometres of mixed deciduous woodland, the reserve is certain to inspire tree lovers, but less likely to yield many wildlife sightings: its tigers and leopards were hunted out long ago, while the gazelles, sloth bears, porcupines, panthers and hyenas that allegedly lurk in the woods rarely appear. You do, however, stand a good chance of spotting at least two species of monkey, a couple of wild boar and the odd gaur (the primeval-looking Indian bison), as well as plenty of exotic birdlife, including hornbills. Any of the buses running south on the NH-14 to Karwar via Chaudi will drop you within 2km of the gates. However, to explore the inner reaches of the sanctuary, you really need your own transport. The wardens at the reserve's small **Interpretative Centre** at the main gate, where you have to pay your entry fees (Rs15, plus Rs75 for a car, Rs20 for motorbike, Rs40 for camera permit) will show you how to get to a 25-metre-high tree-top watchtower, overlooking a **waterhole** that attracts a handful of animals around dawn and dusk.

Travel details

Trains

Margao (Madgaon) to: Chaudi (3 daily; 30–50min); Colem (4 weekly; 55min); Delhi (1–2 daily; 26–35hr); Ernakulam/Kochi (4 weekly; 12–15hr 40min); Gokarna (2 daily; 1hr 50min); Hospet (for Hampi) (4 weekly; 6hr); Mangalore (5 daily; 4–6hr); Mumbai (4–5 daily; 9hr 30min–11hr 30min); Pune (1 daily; 14hr; Thiruvananthapuram (1–2 daily; 16hr); Udupi (4 daily; 3hr 40min).

Buses

Benaulim to: Cavelossim (hourly; 20min); Colva (every 30min; 20min); Margao (every 30min; 15min); Mobor (hourly; 25min).
Chaudi to: Gokarna (2 daily; 3hr); Karwar (every 30min; 1hr); Margao (every 30min; 1hr 40min); Palolem (2 daily; 15min); Panjim (hourly; 2hr 15min).
Mapusa to: Anjuna (hourly; 30min); Arambol (12 daily; 1hr 45min); Baga (every 30min); Calangute (hourly; 45min); Chapora (every 30min; 30–40min); Mumbai (6 daily; 13–17hr); Panjim (every 15min; 25min); Vagator (every 30min; 25–35min).
Margao to: Agonda (4 daily; 2hr); Benaulim (every 30min; 15min); Cavelossim (8 daily; 30min); Chandor (hourly; 45min); Chaudi (every 30min; 1hr 40min); Colva (every 15min; 20–30min); Gokarna (2 daily; 4hr 30min); Hampi (1 nightly; 10hr); Karwar (every 30min; 2hr); Mangalore (5 daily; 7hr); Mapusa (10 daily; 2hr 30min); Mobor (8 daily; 35min); Mumbai (2 daily;

16–18hr); Panjim (every 30min; 50min); Pune (1 daily; 12hr).
Panjim to: Arambol (12 daily; 1hr 45min); Baga (every 30min; 45min); Bijapur (7 daily; 10hr); Calangute (every 30min; 40min); Candolim (every 30min; 30min); Chaudi (hourly; 2hr 15min); Gokarna (2 daily; 5hr 30min); Hampi (2 daily; 9–10hr); Hospet (3 daily; 9hr); Hubli (hourly; 6hr); Hyderabad (1 daily; 18hr); Kolhapur (hourly; 8hr); Mahabaleshwar (1 daily; 12hr); Mangalore (4 daily; 10hr); Mapusa (every 15min; 25min); Margao (every 15min; 55min); Morjim (6 daily; 1hr 30min–2hr); Mumbai (6 daily; 14–18hr); Mysore (2 daily; 17hr); Old Goa (every 15min; 20min); Ponda (hourly; 50min); Pune (7 daily; 12hr).

Flights

(AI = Air India, 6G = IndiGo, IC = Indian Airlines, IT = Kingfisher, DN = Air Deccan, S2 = JetLite, 9W = Jet Airways, G8 = Go Air, SG = Spicejet)
Dabolim airport (near Vasco da Gama) to: Bengaluru (Bangalore) (DA, G8, IC, 9W, IT, SG; 6–8 daily; 1hr–4hr 20min); Chennai (IC, 9W, JL; 2–4 daily; 3hr 15min–4hr 30min); Delhi (G8, 6G, IT, SG; 4–5 daily; 3hr 20min); Hyderabad (6G; daily; 1hr 20min); Jaipur (IT; daily; 2hr 10min); Kochi (Cochin) (IC, 6G, IT; 1–3 daily; 1hr 10min–3hr 35min); Kolkata (6G; 1 daily; 4hr 50min); Kozhikode (Calicut) (IC, IT; 1–2 daily; 1hr–2hr 35min); Mumbai (DN, AI, G8, IC, 6G, 9W, JL, IT, SG; 14–15 daily; 50min–1hr); Pune (IC; daily; 50min); Thiruvananthapuram (IT; daily; 5hr 20min).

Kolkata (Calcutta) and West Bengal

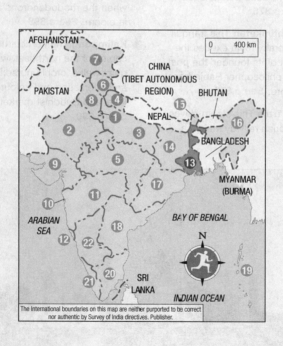

The international boundaries on this map are neither purported to be correct nor authentic by Survey of India directives. Publisher.

CHAPTER 13

Highlights

* **Victoria Memorial** This monument to the British Empire in Kolkata is a dizzying blend of Mughal and Italian architecture. See p.857

* **Eden Gardens** Enjoy the chaos and spectacle of a match at Kolkata's famous cricket ground. See p.859

* **Sunderbans** Float through mangrove forests, home to a profusion of wildlife, including the majestic Bengal tiger. See p.876

* **Shantiniketan** This tranquil university town exudes the spirit of its founder, the poet and philosopher Rabindranath Tagore. See p.879

* **Toy Train** This steam-driven Victorian railway makes a leisurely journey from the steamy plains to the tea gardens that carpet the steep hillsides around Darjeeling. See p.884

* **Darjeeling** A charming hill-station with spectacular views and famously fine tea. See p.888

* **Singalila Trek** This Darjeeling trek features unforgettable mountain vistas, especially beautiful in April and May, when the rhododendrons are in bloom. See p.898

* **Kalimpong** The horticultural capital of the northeast, with quiet walks, orchid nurseries, and interesting and colourful local and Buddhist markets. See p.899

▲ Victoria Memorial

Kolkata (Calcutta) and West Bengal

Unique among Indian states in stretching all the way from the Himalayas to the sea, **WEST BENGAL** is nonetheless explored in depth by few travellers. That may have something to do with the exaggerated reputation of its capital, **KOLKATA** (CALCUTTA), a sophisticated and friendly city that belies its popular image as poverty-stricken and chaotic. The rest of Bengal holds an extraordinary assortment of landscapes and cultures, ranging from the dramatic hill-station of **Darjeeling**, within sight of some of the highest mountains in the world, to the vast mangrove swamps of the **Sunderbans**, prowled by man-eating Royal Bengal tigers. The narrow central band of the state is cut across by the huge River Ganges as it pours from Bihar into Bangladesh; the **Farrakha Barrage** controls the movement of south-flowing channels such as the River Hooghly, the lifeline of Kolkata.

At the height of British rule, in the nineteenth and early twentieth centuries, Bengal flourished both culturally and materially, nurturing a uniquely creative blend of West and East. The **Bengali Renaissance** produced thinkers, writers and artists such as Raja Ram Mohan Roy, Bankim Chandra Chatterjee, and above all **Rabindranath Tagore**, whose collective influence still permeates Bengali society a century later.

Not all of Bengal, however, is Bengali; the current Nepalese-led separatist movement for the creation of a semi-autonomous "Gurkhaland" in the Darjeeling area has highlighted sharp differences in culture. Although the Hindu Nepalese migration eastward from the nineteenth century onwards has largely displaced the indigenous tribal groups of the north, Lamaist Tibetan Buddhism continues to flourish, partly due to an influx of Tibetan refugees. In the southwest, on the other hand, tribal groups such as the Santhals and the Mundas still maintain a presence, and itinerant Baul **musicians** epitomize the region's traditions of song and dance, most often heard around Tagore's university at **Shantiniketan**; Tagore's own musical form, Rabindra Sangeet, is a popular amalgam of influences including folk and classical. Other historical specialities of Bengal include its ornate **terra-cotta temples**, as seen at Bishnupur, and its **silk** production, concentrated around **Murshidabad**, the state's last independent capital.

Bengal's own brand of Hinduism emphasizes the **mother goddess**, who appears in such guises as the fearsome Kali and Durga, the benign Saraswati, goddess of learning, and Lakshmi, the goddess of wealth. The most

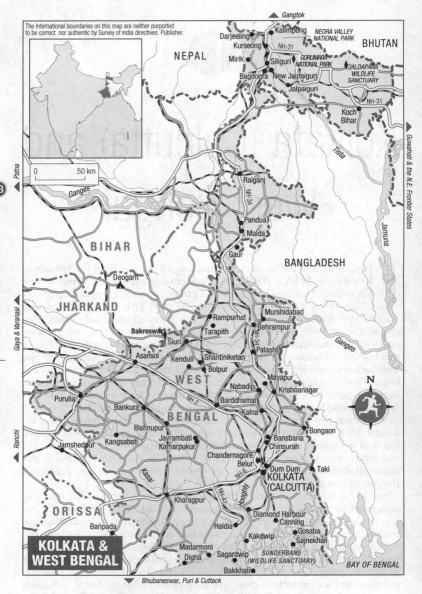

The International boundaries on this map are neither purported
to be correct nor authentic by Survey of India directives. Publisher.

Gangtok

Darjeeling
Kurseong
Mirik
Bagdogra
Kalimpong
NEORA VALLEY
NATIONAL PARK
NH-31
Siliguri
New Jalpaiguri
GORUMARA
NATIONAL PARK
JALDAPARA
WILDLIFE
SANCTUARY
Jalpaiguri
NH-31
Koch
Bihar

BHUTAN

NEPAL

Patna

0   50 km

Ganges

Raiganj

NH-34

Pandua
Malda

Gaur

BANGLADESH

BIHAR

Deogarh

JHARKAND

Murshidabad

Rampurhat
Tarapith
Bakreswar
Siuri
Kendull
Shantiniketan
Bolpur
Behrampur
NH-34
Palashi

Ganges

Gaya & Varanasi

Asansol

WEST

Nabadip
Mayapur
Barddhaman
Krishnanagar
Kalna

N

Purulia
Bankura
NH-2
BENGAL

Ranchi

Bishnupur
Jamshedpur
Kangsabati
Jayrambati
Kamarpukur
Chandernagore
Belur
NH-6
Bansbaria
Chinsurah
Dum Dum
KOLKATA
(CALCUTTA)
Bongaon
Taki

Kasai

Kharagpur
NH-41
Hooghly

Baripada
Haldia
Diamond Harbour
Canning
Kakdwip
Gosaba
Sajnekhali

ORISSA

KOLKATA &
WEST BENGAL

Madarmoni
Digha
Sagardwip
Bakkhali
SUNDERBANS
(WILDLIFE SANCTUARY)

BAY OF BENGAL

Bhubaneswar, Puri & Cuttack

Tista

Guwahati & the N.E. Frontier States

Jamuna

mysterious of all is Tara, an echo of medieval links with Buddhism; her
temple at Tarapith is perhaps the greatest centre of Tantrism in the entire
country. In recent years, however, the prayer flags have given way to red flags,
and the new religion of politics.

Some history

Although Bengal was part of the Mauryan empire during the third century BC,
it first came to prominence in its own right under the Guptas in the fourth

century AD. So dependent was it on trade with the Mediterranean that the fall of Rome caused a sharp decline, only reversed with the rise of the Pala dynasty in the eighth century.

After a short-lived period of rule by the highly cultured Senas, based at **Gaur**, Bengal was brought under Muslim rule at the end of the twelfth century by the first Sultan of Delhi, Qutb-ud-din-Aibak. Sher Shah Suri, who usurped power from the Mughals in the mid-sixteenth century, achieved much in Bengal; it was thanks to him that the Grand Trunk Road was developed, running all the way to the Northwest Province on the borders of his native Afghanistan. Akbar reconquered the territory in 1574, shortly before the advent of the Europeans.

The Portuguese, who were the first to set up a trading community beside the Hooghly, were soon joined by the British, Dutch, French and many others. Rivalry between them – all received some degree of sanction from the Mughal court – eventually resulted in the ascendancy of the **British**, with the only serious indigenous resistance coming from the tutelary kingdom of **Murshidabad**, led by the young Siraj-ud-Daula. His attack on the fledgling British community of Calcutta in 1756 culminated in the infamous **Black Hole** incident, when British prisoners, possibly in error, were incarcerated in a tiny space that caused many to suffocate to death. Vengeance, in the form of a British army from Madras under **Robert Clive**, arrived a year later. The defeat of Siraj-ud-Daula at the **Battle of Plassey** paved the way for British domination of the entire Subcontinent. Bengal became the linchpin of the British East India Company and its lucrative trading empire, until the company handed over control to the Crown in 1854.

Up to 1905, Bengal encompassed Orissa and Bihar; it was then split down the middle by Lord Curzon, leaving East Bengal and Assam on one side and Orissa, Bihar and West Bengal on the other. The move aroused bitter resentment, and the rift it created between Hindus and Muslims was a direct cause of the second Partition, in 1947, when East Bengal became East Pakistan. During the war with Pakistan in the early 1970s that resulted in the creation of an independent **Bangladesh**, up to ten million refugees fled into West Bengal; though most returned, a steady migration from Bangladesh continues. Shorn of its provinces, and with the capital moved from Calcutta to Delhi in 1911, the story of West Bengal in the twentieth century was largely a chronicle of decline.

Economically, the **rice** grown in the paddy fields of the lowlands remains West Bengal's most important cash crop, though **tea** – first introduced by the British from China and grown mainly on the Himalayan foothills around Darjeeling – comes a close second. The other great nineteenth-century industry, **jute**, has not fared so well, the mills along the Hooghly around Kolkata having been cut off from the main growing regions across the border in East Bengal – now Bangladesh.

The state's political life has been dominated by a protracted – and sometimes violent – struggle between the **Congress** and the major left-wing parties: the Marxist Communist Party of India, or **CPI(M)**, and the Marxist-Leninist **Naxalites** (Communist Party of India). In the 1960s and 1970s, the latter launched an abortive but bloody attempt at revolution. Bolstered by a strong rural base, the CPI(M) eventually emerged victorious under the enigmatic Jyoti Basu, weathering the collapse of world communism. However, despite the occasional challenge from the likes of Mamata Bannerjee's **Trinamul Congress**, the CPI(M)'s decades of unassailable rule have been dogged by apathy and decline. Despite a recent sense of optimism, the party has been unable to provide a healthy environment for growth, as illustrated by the fiasco at **Nandigram** in November 2007, when heavily armed CPI(M) cadres sealed off the district to forcibly suppress protest by landowners and farmers against industrial development. Several protesters were killed, and the subsequent discovery of makeshift graves has revealed the true extent of the horror – according to some estimates, the death toll could be in the hundreds. Violent clashes between party activists and frequent strikes occur all too often, while political elements to the north of the state are calling for independence from West Bengal.

Kolkata (Calcutta) and around

One of the four great urban centres of India, **KOLKATA (CALCUTTA)** is, to its proud citizens, the equal of any city in the country in charm, variety and interest. Like Mumbai and Chennai, its roots lie in the European expansion of the seventeenth century. As the showpiece capital of the British Raj, it was the greatest colonial city of the Orient, and descendants of the fortune-seekers who flocked from across the globe to participate in its eighteenth- and nineteenth-century trading boom remain conspicuous in its cosmopolitan blend of communities. Despite this, there has been a recent rise in Bengali nationalism, which has resulted in the renaming of Calcutta as Kolkata (the Bengali pronunciation and official new name), which has yet to be universally embraced – leading English-language paper *The Telegraph* continues to use Calcutta.

Since Indian Independence, mass migrations of dispossessed refugees occasioned by twentieth-century upheavals within the Subcontinent have tested the city's infrastructure to the limit. The resultant suffering – and the work of Mother Teresa in drawing attention to its most helpless victims – has given Kolkata a reputation for **poverty** that its residents consider ill-founded. They argue that the city's problems – the continuing influx of refugees notwithstanding – are no longer as acute as those of Mumbai or other cities across the world. In fact, though Kolkata's mighty Victorian buildings lie peeling and decaying, and its central avenues are choked by traffic, the city exudes a warmth and buoyancy that leaves few visitors unmoved. The booming IT industry has created a renewed sense of optimism, and Kolkata is expanding rapidly, with shopping arcades, restaurants and satellite towns springing up all over the city. The downside of all this development, however, is some of the worst air pollution in the world, which has resulted in a high instance of lung disease, while the increase in traffic has seen the roads become some of the most dangerous in India, especially for pedestrians.

In terms of the city's cultural life, Kolkata's Bengalis exude a pride in their artistic heritage and like to see themselves as the **intelligentsia** of India; a long-standing maxim states that "What Bengal does today, India will do tomorrow." Artistic endeavour is held in high esteem and the city is home to a multitude of **galleries** and huge Indian classical music festivals, with a thriving Bengali-language **theatre** scene and a tradition of **cinema** brought world renown by Satyajit Ray. Adding to the chaos and colour is Kolkata's wonderful tradition of political posters and graffiti, with witty and flamboyant slogans competing with a forest of advertising hoardings to festoon every available surface.

Though Marxists may rule from the chief bastion of imperialism (the **Writers' Building**, which has changed little over the decades), visitors still experience Kolkata first and foremost as a colonial city. Grand edifices in a profusion of styles include the imposing **Victoria Memorial** and the gothic **St Paul's Cathedral**, while the collection at the eclectic **Indian Museum**, one of the largest museums in Asia, ranges from natural history to art and archeology. Among numerous venerable Raj institutions to have survived are the racecourse, the reverence for cricket and several exclusive gentlemen's clubs.

In terms of **climate**, Kolkata is at its best during its short winter (Nov–Feb), when the daily maximum temperature hovers around 27°C, and the markets are filled with vegetables and flowers. Before the monsoons, the heat hangs unbearably heavily; the arrival of the rains in late June brings relief, but usually also floods that turn the streets into a quagmire. After a brief period of post-monsoon high temperatures, October and November are quite pleasant; this is the time of the city's biggest festival, **Durga Puja**.

Some history

By the time the remarkable **Job Charnock** established the headquarters of the **East India Company** at **Sutanuti** on the east bank of the Hooghly in 1690, the riverside was already dotted with trading communities from European countries. Besides the British, previously based at Hooghly on the west bank, there were the French at Chandernagore, the Dutch and Armenians at Chinsurah, the Danes at Serampore, the Portuguese at Bandel, and even Greeks at Rishra and Prussians at Bhadeshwar.

Supported by Armenian funds, the East India Company bought land around Sutanuti, and in 1699 completed its first fort in the area – **Fort William**. A few years later, Sutanuti was amalgamated with two other villages to form the town of **Calcutta**, whose name probably originated from *kalikutir*, the house or temple of Kali (a reference to the **Kalighat** shrine). With trading success came ambitious plans for development; in 1715 a delegation to the Mughal court in Delhi negotiated trading rights, creating a territory on both banks of the Hooghly of around 15km long. The East India Company built a moat around the perimeter, known as the **Maratha Ditch** (marked by today's Circular Rd), to ward off possible Maratha attacks. Later, it became entangled in the web of local power politics, with consequences both unforeseen (as with the Black Hole; see p.859) and greatly desired, as when the Battle of Plassey in 1758 made the British masters of Bengal. Recognized by Parliament in London in 1773, the company's trading monopoly led it to shift the capital of Bengal here from Murshidabad, and Calcutta became a clearing house for a vast range of commerce, including the lucrative export of opium to China.

At first, the East India Company brought young bachelors out from Britain to work as clerks. Known as "writers", they lived in spartan conditions in communal mud huts until the **Writers' Building** was erected to accommodate them. This was the era before the arrival of the British Memsahib, when relations with local women were the norm; many young writers took Indian wives, giving rise to the new **Eurasian** community known as the **Anglo-Indians**. Merchants and adventurers – among them Parsis, Baghdadi Jews, Afghans and Indians from other parts of the country – contributed to the melting pot after the East India Company's monopoly was withdrawn. The ensuing boom lasted for decades,

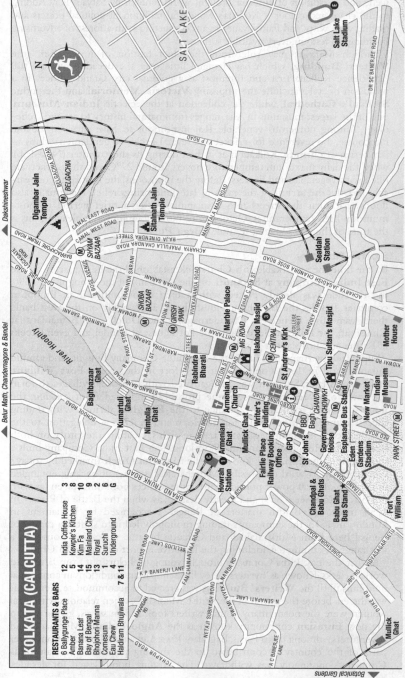

SALT LAKE

Salt Lake
Stadium

E

DR SC BANERJEE ROAD

VIP ROAD

BELGACHIA ROAD
BELGACHIA **M**

CANAL EAST ROAD

CANAL WEST ROAD

Digambar Jain
Temple

Sitalnath Jain
Temple

SHYAM
BAZAAR

MAIN TALA MAIN ROAD

ACHARYA PRAFULLA CHANDRA ROAD

RAJA DINENDRA STREET

ACHARYA JAGADISH CHANDRA BOSE ROAD

Sealdah
Station

B BOSE AVENUE

ARABINDA SARANI

BIDHAN SARANI

VIVEKANANDA ROAD

M G ROAD

KESHAB C SEN ST

COLLEGE STREET

B GANGULY STREET

RABINDRA SARANI

SHOBA
BAZAAR **M**

BEADON ST

GIRISH
PARK **M**

MG ROAD

Marble Palace

Nakhoda Masjid

3

St Andrew's Kirk

CENTRAL **M**

RABINDRA SARANI

N GHAT ST

K K TAGORE STREET

COTTON ST

M G ROAD

2

Armenian
Church

7

Writer's
Building

5

Tipu Sultan's Masjid

LENIN SARANI

S N BANERJI RD

Mother
House

KIDWAI RD

RIDWAI RD

Rabindra
Bharati

RABINDRA SARANI

R K PAUL STREET

STRAND BANK ROAD

MOMAN AV

Baghbazaar
Ghat

Kumartuli
Ghat

Nimtolla
Ghat

River Hooghly

SCHOOL ROAD

Mullick Ghat

Armenian
Ghat

1

BBD
Bagh

CHANDNI
CHOWK **M**

Government
House

Esplanade Bus Stand

Indian
Museum

New Market

RED ROAD

PARK STREET **M**

4

GPO **D**

St John's

Fairlie Place
Railway Booking
Office

i

HOWRAH BRIDGE

M AZAD ROAD

Howrah
Station

C

GRAND TRUNK ROAD

N RY RD

Chandpal &
Babu Ghats

Babu Ghat
Bus Stand

Chandpal
Bus Stand ★

Eden
Gardens
Stadium

STRAND ROAD SOUTH

Fort
William

FORSHORE ROAD

FORSHORE ROAD

VIDYASAGAR SETU

DUKE RD

DLF JRF

N

Dakshineshwar

Belur Math, Chandernagore & Bandel

Botanical Gardens

Mullick Ghat

A C BANERJEE LANE

TICHAPUR ROAD

MAKARDAH ROAD

BELILIOS LANE

K P BANERJI LANE

FAN CHANANTALA ROAD

N SENAPATI LANE

SWAMI VIVEKA NANDA RD

NETAJI SUBHASH ROAD

BELILIOS LANE

BARRACKPORE TRUNK ROAD

GOSSIPORE ROAD

COSSIPORE LOCOGATIC ROAD

GOSSIPORE LOCOGATIC ROAD

KOLKATA AND WEST BENGAL

13

844

KOLKATA (CALCUTTA)

RESTAURANTS & BARS

6 Ballygunge Place	12	India Coffee House	3
Amber	5	Kewpie's Kitchen	8
Banana Leaf	14	Kim Fa	10
Bay of Bengal	9	Mainland China	15
Bhojohri Manna	13	Royal	2
Comesum	1	Suruchi	6
Eau Chew	4	Underground	G
Haldiram Bhujiwala	7 & 11		

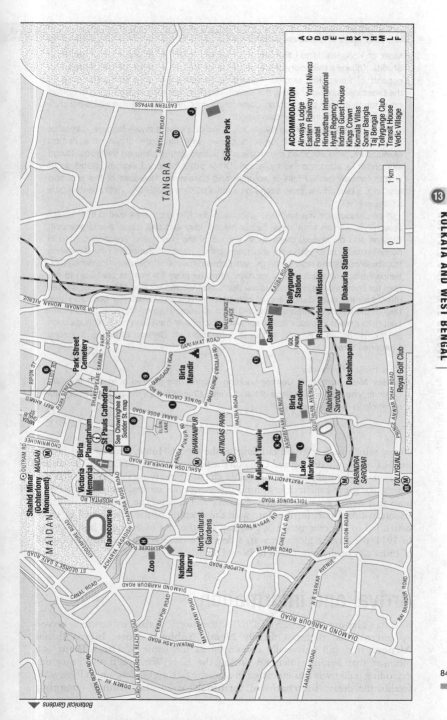

Botanical Gardens ▲

ACCOMMODATION

Airways Lodge	A
Eastern Railway Yatri Niwas	C
Floatel	D
Hindusthan International	G
Hyatt Regency	E
Indrani Guest House	I
Kings Crown	B
Komala Villas	K
Sonar Bangla	J
Taj Bengal	H
Tollygunge Club	M
Transit House	L
Vedic Village	F

0   1 km

Most of Kolkata's Hindu festivals are devoted to forms of the mother goddess, **Shakti**. Kolkata's own deity, the black goddess **Kali**, is an emanation of **Durga**, the consort of Shiva. Kali is most commonly depicted with four arms, standing on the prostrate Shiva after killing the demon Raktviya, her tongue protruding in horror; other forms include the terrifying Chinemasta (torn head), where Kali holds her own severed head and drinks her own blood.

The two-week **Durga Puja** (Sept/Oct) is Kolkata's most lavish festival. A symbol of victory, **Durga**, wife of Shiva, is shown with ten arms slaying the demon Mahisasura, who assumed the shape of a buffalo and threatened the gods. Durga sits on, or is accompanied by, a lion. Other pujas honour **Lakshmi**, goddess of wealth, whose festival falls in autumn, and **Saraswati**, goddess of the arts and learning, a beautiful woman sitting on a lotus playing a sitar-like instrument known as the *veena*.

In preparation for the festivals, artisans in the Kumartuli area (see p.861) sculpt voluptuous women from straw, papier-mâché, clay and *pith* (banana-tree marrow). Clothed and decorated, these lavish images of the goddesses are then carried in noisy procession to elaborate marquees called *pandals*. Supported by donations from businesses and local residents, with popular music blaring through loudspeakers, *pandals* block off small streets for days. After the puja, the images are taken to the river for immersion, a colourful scene that's best viewed via one of the boat cruises offered by the West Bengal tourist office (see p.848); they also offer bus tours that take in the *pandals*. A more traditional form of Durga Puja takes place in purpose-built halls known as *thakur dalan*, set within old manor houses in north Kolkata such as the Than Thani Rajbari, a fabulous mansion off College Street at 1 Bechu Chatterjee Street.

The major festivals

Jaidev Mela (early Jan) Commemorating Joydeb, the revered author of the *Gita Govinda*, and held in the village of Kenduli near Shantiniketan; the place to hear Baul minstrels in their element.

during which such splendid buildings as the Court House, Government House and St Paul's Cathedral earned Calcutta the sobriquet "City of Palaces". In reality, however, the humid and uncomfortable climate, putrefying salt marshes and the hovels that grew haphazardly around the metropolis created unhygienic conditions that were a constant source of misery and disease. The death of Calcutta as an international port finally came with the opening of the Suez Canal in 1869, which led to the emergence of Bombay, and the end of the city's opium trade. In 1911, the days of glory drew to a definitive close when the imperial capital of India was finally transferred to New Delhi.

Arrival and information

Kolkata's **airport** (T033/251 18787), 20km north of the city centre, is served by international flights. Officially **Netaji Subhash Bose International Airport**, it is still universally known by its old name of **Dum Dum** – a moniker that became infamous during the Boer War, when the notorious exploding bullet was manufactured in a nearby factory. Undergoing a long, slow facelift, the dreary **international terminal** has 24-hour **money-changing**

Ganga Sagar Mela (mid-Jan) During the winter solstice of Makar Sankranti, hundreds of thousands of Hindu pilgrims and sadhus travel through Kolkata from all over India for a three-day festival at Sagardwip, 150km south where the Ganges meets the sea.

Dover Lane Music Festival (Jan/Feb) A week-long festival in south Kolkata, attracting many of the country's best musicians.

Saraswati Puja (Jan/Feb) Popular and important *pandal* festival to the goddess of learning staged throughout Bengal.

Chinese New Year (Jan/Feb) Celebrated with a week-long festival of dragon dances, firecrackers and fine food, concentrated around Chinatown and the suburb of Tangra.

Muharram (dates determined by the lunar calendar; see ⓦwww.when-is.com) Shi'ite Muslims mark the anniversary of the martyrdom of Hussein by severe penance including processions during which they flagellate themselves.

Durga Puja (Sept/Oct) At the onset of winter, Durga Puja (known elsewhere as Dussehra) is the Bengali equivalent of Christmas. It climaxes on Mahadashami, the tenth day, when images are immersed in the river.

Laxmi Puja (Oct/Nov) Held five days after Mahadashami on the full moon, to honour the goddess of wealth.

Id ul Fitr (dates determined by the lunar calendar; see ⓦwww.when-is.com) Celebrating the end of the fasting month of Ramadan and heralded by the new moon, the festival is a time of joyousness when people don new clothes and sample wonderful food at the restaurants and stalls around Park Circus.

Diwali and Kali Puja (Oct/Nov) Two weeks after Lakshmi Puja, Kali Puja is held on a moonless night when goats are sacrificed, and coincides with Diwali, the festival of light.

Christmas (Dec 25) Park Street and New Market are adorned with fairy lights and the odd Christmas tree. Plum pudding is sold, and Midnight Mass is well attended.

Poush Mela (late Dec) Held in Shantiniketan around Christmas, the *mela* attracts Bauls, the wandering minstrels who perform to large audiences.

---

facilities including a Thomas Cook, as well as a **pre-paid taxi** booth and an India Tourism information counter; it also has **retiring rooms** (Rs750) booked through the airport manager's office at International Arrivals. The modern **domestic terminal**, 500m to the south, has many amenities, including separate government tourist offices for Kolkata, West Bengal and Tripura, an accommodation booking counter, a railway reservation desk and pre-paid taxi booth. A pre-paid **taxi** to the central Sudder Street area costs around Rs250. Another alternative is to take a taxi (around Rs50) or the shuttle bus to the Dum Dum **Metro** station (5km), and then the Metro (see p.849) into town; Sudder Street is a short walk from Park Street station. Bear in mind that you can't take large items (bikes, sports equipment etc) onto the Metro system. The extension of the **Circular Rail** from the airport travels through Dum Dum railway station to the Strand but runs only twice a day to serve commuters.

Kolkata has two main **railway stations**, neither of them on the Metro system. **Howrah** – the point of arrival for major trains from the south and west, such as the Rajdhani Express from Delhi – stands on the far bank of the Hooghly a couple of kilometres west of the centre. To reach the central downtown area, traffic has to negotiate **Howrah Bridge** – the definitive introduction to the chaos of the city, especially during rush hours, which start late in the mornings. Avoid the touts and **taxis** outside the station building, and head instead straight

The process of reclaiming **Kolkata**'s legacy from its colonial past has its most obvious result in the recent **renaming** of the city. Though most of the old British **street names** were officially changed years ago, old habits die hard and some of the original names continue to be widely used in tandem. The most important of these is Chowringhee or Jawaharlal Nehru Road (which we continue to call Chowringhee). Other name changes to note are Rabindranath Tagore Street (although everyone still calls it Camac St), BBD Bagh (still often referred to by its old name of Dalhousie Square or simply "Dalhousie"), Lenin Sarani (Dharamtala), Mirza Ghalib Street (Free School St), Bepin Bihari Ganguly Street (Bowbazar St), Rabindra Sarani (Chitpore Rd), Ho Chi Minh Sarani (Harrington St), Dr Mohammed Ishaque Road (Kyd St), AJC Bose Road (Lower Circular Rd), Muzaffar Ahmed Street (Ripon St), Shakespeare Sarani (Theatre Rd) and Rafi Ahmed Kidwai Street (Wellesley St).

for the **pre-paid taxi** booth, from where the fare to central Sudder Street and the Park Street areas is Rs65–90. **Minibuses** and buses also operate from Howrah to destinations all over the city, but tend to be very crowded. A good alternative is to follow the signs from the station gate and take a **ferry** (Rs4) across the Hooghly to Babu Ghat or the adjacent Chandpal Ghat, close to BBD Bagh, and pick up a metered taxi, bus or minibus from there.

Sealdah Station, used by trains from the north and with its own **pre-paid taxi** booth in the car park, is on the eastern edge of the centre, and much more convenient as you don't have to cross the river. Long-distance **buses** from the south terminate at **Babu Ghat Bus Stand**, not far from Fort William on the east bank, while most others, such as those from Darjeeling arrive at **Esplanade Bus Stand**, less than 500m north of Sudder Street.

Information

The **India Tourism office**, off the central Chowringhee Road at 4 Shakespeare Sarani (Mon–Fri 9am–6pm, Sat 9am–1pm; ☎033/2282 5813 or 2282 7731, ⓔindtour@cal2.vsnl.net.in), is your best bet for information on Kolkata, West Bengal and destinations further afield, and can assist with itineraries and booking tours. The **Government of West Bengal Tourist Bureau**, near the Writers' Building at 3/2 BBD Bagh East (Mon–Sat 10.30am–4.30pm; ☎033/2248 8271), arranges tours of Kolkata (see below) and package trips around West Bengal. They also issue **permits** and book tours and accommodation at the Sunderbans and Jaldapara wildlife parks (Mon–Fri only). **Tourist information counters** at both the domestic and international terminals of the airport and Howrah Station offer similar services.

English-language **newspapers** such as the *Statesman*, *Telegraph* and *Hindusthan Standard* remain the primary source for information on **what's on**, but the monthlies *Cal Calling* (Rs30) and the useful *City Info* (free), the latter found in some hotel rooms, are excellent for listings and general information on the city.

City tours

The **West Bengal Tourist Bureau** (☎033/2248 8271; Rs200; 7.30am–5pm) offer city tours that also take in Dakshineshwar and Belur; during the pujas, they also run cruises to view the immersions. The best way to see the city, however, are the tailor-made tours and fascinating walks offered by private operators. The walking tours (4–5hr; from Rs250) offered by **Help Tourism** (☎033/2455 0917, ⓦwww.helptourism.com) provide a great insight into the historic heart of the city: the Dalhousie Square tour is usually conducted on Sundays around BBD Bagh, while the similarly priced North Kolkata tour begins and ends at Sovabazaar Rajbari, a mansion close to College Street. The Australian-run **Kali Travel Home** (☎033/2558 7980, ⓦwww.traveleastindia.com) organize tailor-made city tours (from $40 a day), ranging from Raj-themed city walks to riverside strolls that include the artisans of Kumartuli (see p.861); they also offer cooking classes and tours by tram. The Heritage Walk (Sat & Sun 9–11am; Rs250) conducted by architectural preservation group **ARCH** (Action Research in Conservation of Heritage; ☎033/2359 6303, ⓦwww.centrearch .org) concentrates on Dalhousie Square (BBD Bagh), and starts at the Town Hall near the High Court; turn up fifteen minutes early or book ahead. If you want to devise your own walking itineraries, the essential companion is *A Jaywalker's Guide to Calcutta* by Soumitra Das, available at bookshops such as Oxford.

City transport

The **Metro**, India's first and Kolkata's pride and joy, provides a fast, clean and efficient way to get around. It's also very easy to use, as it consists of just the one line running on a north–south axis. The **river** is also used for transport, with the *ghats* near Eden Gardens at the hub of a **ferry** system. You can beat the traffic by jumping on one of the frequent ferries from Chandpal Ghat to Howrah Station (Rs4), though they're crowded at rush hour; other sailings head downriver from Armenian, Chandpal or Babu *ghats* to Shibpur near the Botanical Gardens. Of more use to commuters than tourists, a **circular railway** loops south from Sealdah Station before moving upriver along the Strand and Princep Ghat, past Howrah Bridge and eventually to Dum Dum, with an extension to the airport (see p.847). While using public transport, be wary of **pickpockets**, especially on crowded buses.

The Metro

Despite a few small hiccups, Kolkata's Russian-designed **Metro**, inaugurated in 1984, is every bit as good as its inhabitants proudly claim, with trains operating punctually every few minutes. Services run from 7am to 9.45pm Monday to Saturday and 3pm to 9.45pm on Sundays. Tickets are cheap, starting at Rs4, and you can travel the entire length of the line from Dum Dum near the airport to Tollygunge in the south for just Rs8. The line follows Kolkata's main arteries including Chowringhee Road, with convenient stations such as Park Street, Kalighat, Esplanade and Rabindra Sadan. For more information, visit ⓦwww .kolmetro.com.

Buses and minibuses

Kolkata supports a vast and complicated **bus** network (for route information, check ⓦwww.calcuttaweb.com), in operation each day roughly between 5am and 11pm, and subject to overcrowding and pickpocketing. Useful **bus routes** include: **#8** from Howrah via Esplanade and Gariahat; **#S17** from Chetla near Kalighat via Esplanade to Dakshineshwar; and **#5** and **#6**, which both travel via Howrah and the Esplanade–Chowringhee area, and stop at the Indian Museum at the head of Sudder Street; **#5** goes to Garia in the south via Rabindra Sadan and Kalighat. The **#C6** travels via Chowringhee, passing the top of Park Street before crossing the Vidyasagar Setu (the second bridge over the Hooghly) to the

Botanical Gardens. Buses with an "S" prefix denote special express buses charging marginally more. Of the six Executive (Green Line) bus routes, the **#GL1** runs from Esplanade to the airport. Recently, air-conditioned, white buses called **Whiteliners** have been introduced, with regular services between Tollygunge (via Gariahat) and the airport.

In addition, private brown-and-yellow **minibuses** travel at inordinate speeds on ad-hoc routes; their destinations are usually painted boldly in Bengali and English on their sides; getting on and off can be hazardous, as they tend not to pull over to the kerb to stop.

Taxis

Taxis in Kolkata – painted black and yellow – are extremely good value, especially on long journeys such as to and from the airport (around Rs200 for a twenty-kilometre ride), but a few drivers can be unwilling to take you on short journeys or directions they don't like the sound of. Sudder Street's taxi touts are particularly averse to haggling, and you're better off walking around the corner and flagging down a cab. There's a night-time surcharge between 10pm and 6am; up to two pieces of luggage are free, but there's an additional charge for further pieces and for placing bags in the boot. Most cabs have working **meters** and tend to use them in conjunction with the **conversion charts** they are obliged to carry. Digital meters – very few taxis still operate the old manual ones – start on Rs15 (plus Rs1.50 per 200m) but this can almost double according to the chart, which is published in *Cal Calling*. When fare rises are announced, the Taxi Association finds it cheaper to issue the conversion charts rather than reset each and every meter. Where possible, you could also use the **pre-paid taxi** services found at the main railway stations and the airport. Recently, CNG gas-powered cabs, maroon in colour, offer an alternative to the city's diesel-choking vehicles, while the a/c **Blue Arrow taxis** (☎13658 or 09239 244416) come equipped with tamper-proof meters that produce printed receipts; they can be found outside the airport, railway stations and major hotels. Car-Cab (☎033/2235 3535) is the most established of the **private taxi firms**.

Trams

Kolkata's cumbersome trams (⊛www.calcuttatramways.com), barely changed save for a lick of paint since they started operating in 1873, have been phased down, but certain routes linger on. Despite the general dilapidation, they do have a quirky charm and provide an interesting way of seeing the city; female travellers may well be glad of the rush-hour women-only coaches. Routes include #20, Howrah Bridge via Sealdah to Park Circus; #25, BBD Bagh to Ballygunge via Rafi Ahmed Kidwai Road, Park Circus; and #29, BBD Bagh to Tollygunge via the Maidan and Diamond Harbour Road, Alipore Road and Hazra Mor and Kalighat.

Rickshaws, auto-rickshaws and cycle rickshaws

Despite the fact that they've been officially banned, Kolkata still has **human-drawn rickshaws**, though they're only available in the central areas of the city, especially around New Market where many drivers supplement their meagre income by acting as pimps. Rickshaws come into their own during the monsoons, when the streets get flooded to hip height and the rickshaw-men

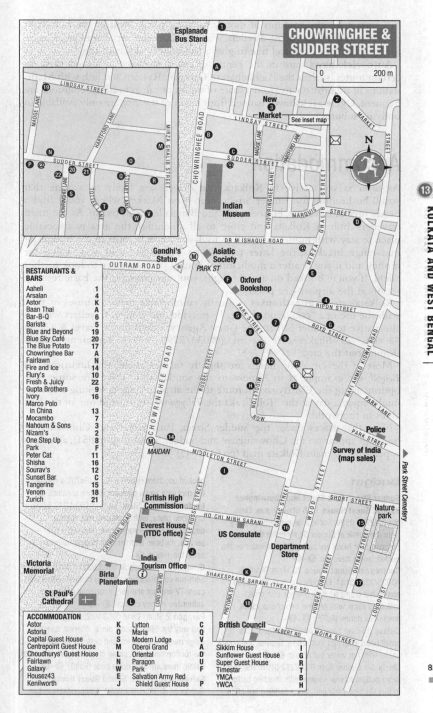

Esplanade
Bus Stand

New
Market

See inset map

LINDSAY STREET

SUDDER STREET

MARQUIS STREET

Indian
Museum

DR M ISHAQUE ROAD

Gandhi's
Statue

Asiatic
Society

OUTRAM ROAD

PARK ST

Oxford
Bookshop

RIPON STREET

ROYD STREET

PARK LANE

Police

PARK STREET

Survey of India
(map sales)

MAIDAN

MIDDLETON STREET

SHORT STREET

Nature
park

British High
Commission

HO CHI MINH SARANI

Everest House
(ITDC office)

US Consulate

Department
Store

India
Tourism Office

Victoria
Memorial

Birla
Planetarium

SHAKESPEARE SARANI (THEATRE RD)

St Paul's
Cathedral

British Council

ALBERT RD

MOIRA STREET

▶ Park Street Cemetery

RESTAURANTS & BARS

Aaheli	1
Arsalan	4
Astor	K
Baan Thai	A
Bar-B-Q	6
Barista	5
Blue and Beyond	19
Blue Sky Café	20
The Blue Potato	17
Chowringhee Bar	A
Fairlawn	N
Fire and Ice	14
Flury's	10
Fresh & Juicy	22
Gupta Brothers	9
Ivory	16
Marco Polo in China	13
Mocambo	7
Nahoum & Sons	3
Nizam's	2
One Step Up	8
Park	F
Peter Cat	11
Shisha	16
Sourav's	12
Sunset Bar	C
Tangerine	15
Venom	18
Zurich	21

ACCOMMODATION

Astor	K	Lytton	C
Astoria	O	Maria	Q
Capital Guest House	S	Modern Lodge	V
Centrepoint Guest House	M	Oberoi Grand	A
Choudhurys' Guest House	L	Oriental	D
Fairlawn	N	Paragon	U
Galaxy	W	Park	F
Housez43	E	Salvation Army Red	
Kenilworth	J	Shield Guest House	P
		Sikkim House	I
		Sunflower Guest House	G
		Super Guest House	R
		Timestar	T
		YMCA	B
		YWCA	H

Inset map streets
LINDSAY STREET
MADGE LANE
HARTFORD LANE
MIRZA GHALIB STREET
SUDDER STREET
CHOWRINGHEE LANE
TOTTEE LANE
STUART LANE
CHOWRINGHEE ROAD

MARKET STREET

CHOWRINGHEE ROAD

CATHEDRAL ROAD

LORD SINHA RD

LITTLE RUSSEL STREET

CAMAC STREET

WOOD STREET

RAFI AHMED KIDWAI ROAD

HUNGER FORD STREET

OUTRAM STREET

LOUDON ST

PRETORIA ST

RUSSEL STREET

MIDDLETON ROW

13

KOLKATA AND WEST BENGAL

0   200 m

N

can extract healthy amounts of money for their pains. Most of the rickshaw-pullers are Bihari pavement-dwellers, who live short and very hard lives. Haggle for a realistic price but feel free to give a handful of baksheesh too.

Auto-rickshaws, rare in the centre of town, are used as shared taxis on certain routes (such as the Rashbehari to Gariahat; Rs4.50) and link with Metro stations in suburbs; try to avoid a share of the front cab as head-on collisions are frequent. **Cycle rickshaws**, banned from much of the city, are only available in outlying suburbs.

Accommodation

As soon as you arrive in Kolkata, taxi drivers are likely to assume that you'll be heading for Sudder Street, near New Market, where you'll find a heady mix of travellers, businessmen and Bangladeshis in transit. As the main travellers' hub in Kolkata and close to all amenities, the area is a sociable place to stay with numerous small to mid-sized hotels, most in the budget or mid-range brackets; the latter tend to be overpriced and poor value for money, and if you're after a modicum of luxury, you may have to look further afield. If you're booked on a night flight, you may consider the basic retiring rooms at the airport (see p.847).

Kolkata's many **guesthouses** – usually comfortable private houses or flats, with the use of a "cook-cum-bearer" – provide mid-budget travellers with an alternative to Sudder Street. The Guest Agency, a division of Travel & Cargo Service, 23 Shakespeare Sarani (℡033/2290 9991), represents places throughout the city.

Most of the city's top hotels are slightly further afield; the luxurious *Taj Bengal*, for example, is in Alipore to the south, while there are some new options along the EM Bypass en route to the airport. Visitors seeking a change might enjoy a stay at the "Tolly", aka the *Tollygunge*, considered one of the best clubs in the world.

Note that places under the Sudder Street, Park Street and Chowringhee headings appear on the Chowringhee and Sudder Street map (p.851); all others appear on the main Kolkata map (pp.844–845).

Budget

Sudder Street, Park Street and Chowringhee

Capital Guest House 11-B Chowringhee Lane ℡033/2252 0598. Set in a large courtyard away from the bustle of Sudder St, rooms in this purpose-built block are plain, with hot water by the bucket; some have a/c. ❸–❹

Centrepoint Guest House 20 Mirza Ghalib St ℡033/2252 8184. Friendly and popular, though somewhat cramped, with a range of rooms, including some with a/c and two cheap, clean single-sex dorms (Rs75). ❸–❹

Galaxy 3 Stuart Lane ℡033/2252 4565. This small hotel, with just four rooms, is clean and good value, with hot water but no a/c. ❷–❸

Maria 5/1 Sudder St ℡033/2252 0860. The good-sized budget rooms – some with attached baths – in this old high-ceilinged, faded building are often

booked up; there is also a dorm (Rs70), a reliable Internet café and a pleasant terrace upstairs. ❷

Modern Lodge 1 Stuart Lane ℡033/2242 5960. Cramped place, with a relaxing roof terrace; despite the surly – sometimes downright rude – service, it's been popular with budget travellers since the 1960s. ❷

Oriental 9-A Marquis St ℡033/2217 4536. Clean, Sikh-run establishment offering modest rooms with cable TV and hot showers (mornings only), and authorized money change. ❸–❹

Paragon 2 Stuart Lane ℡033/2252 2445. Popular and very traveller-friendly place, offering dark and dingy rooms downstairs, and better ones around the rooftop courtyard, some of which have attached baths; there are also dorm beds (Rs80). ❷–❸

Salvation Army Red Shield Guest House 2 Sudder St ℡033/2252 0599. A dependable option that's changed little over the years, screened from the noise and pollution by a large gate. Dorms (from Rs70), and a few doubles including a couple of overpriced a/c ones. ②–④

Timestar 2 Tottee Lane ☎033/2252 8028. The fair-sized rooms in this peeling old villa come with fans and hot water by the bucket; some have TV, too. ②–③

Elsewhere in the city

Airways Lodge No. 2 Airport Gate, Kolkata airport ☎033/2512 7280. An inexpensive place in the vicinity of the airport, with basic but clean rooms. Handy for early departures and late arrivals. ②–④

Eastern Railway Yatri Niwas Howrah Station ☎033/2660 1742. Large place with small dorms (Rs100) and a/c and non-a/c doubles, for travellers holding 200km+ rail tickets only. Maximum stay one night and a 9am checkout. Avoid the dull restaurant in favour of the nearby *Comesum* food hall in Howrah's South Station (see p.867). ③–④

Komala Villas 73 Rashbehari Ave, Lake Market ☎033/2464 1960. A clean and popular south Indian–run hotel, with a good selection of accommodation, from dorms (Rs150) to deluxe a/c rooms, and an excellent restaurant (see p.866). ③–⑤

Mid-range

Sudder Street, Park Street and Chowringhee

Astoria Sudder St ☎033/2252 9679. Popular with businessmen for its convenient location and modicum of comfort, though the old-fashioned a/c rooms are plain and a bit overpriced, and there's room service rather than a restaurant. ⑤–⑥

Choudhurys' Guest House 55 Chowringhee Rd ☎033/2282 1817. Popular with visiting businessmen and a few long-term residents, with old-fashioned rooms and high ceilings; close to the Maidan and quiet at night, yet not far from all amenities. Best to book in advance. ④–⑥

Sikkim House 4/1 Middleton St ☎033/2281 5328. A well-located government guesthouse with a small selection of very competitively priced rooms; it tends to get booked up early, so phone well in advance. Their *Red Panda* restaurant serves great *thukpa*. ⑤

Sunflower Guest House 7 Royd St ☎033/2229 9401. A sizeable and well-maintained old building with most of its guestrooms – all with attached baths – on the top two floors; there's a roof garden and food to order. ④

Super Guest House Opposite Fire Brigade, Sudder St ☎033/2252 0995. One of three good guesthouses tucked around this courtyard, offering good-sized plain rooms, some with a/c, and a restaurant and popular bar; the

neighbouring *Continental* is cheaper, and rooms in *Gulistan* clean but small. ③–④

YMCA 25 Chowringhee Rd ☎033/2249 2192, ⓦwww.calcuttaymca.org. Former grand nightclub near the Indian Museum that's now a faded but popular meeting place, offering a range of shabby rooms, some a/c, on half-board basis. Temporary membership (Rs50 a week) allows access to a well-kept snooker table and table tennis. ④–⑤

YWCA 1 Middleton Row ☎033/2229 7033. Safe for women and especially good for longer stays, this clean, central hostel with plain but adequate rooms off Park St is built around a pleasant courtyard with a tennis court. Rates include breakfast. ④

Elsewhere in the city

🏃 **Indrani Guest House** 3-B Lovelock St ☎033/2486 6712. A comfortable family residence offering B&B and optional home-cooking in a residential part of the city off Ballygunge Circular Rd. There's a limited number of wonderful rooms so book well ahead; popular for longer stays. ⑤

Kings Crown Nazrul Islam Avenue (VIP Rd), near the airport ☎033/2573 1712. On the Ultadunga road, with a good range of accommodation, from plain singles to comfortable a/c rooms, along with a decent restaurant and bar; very convenient for early or late flights. ⑤

Transit House 11-A Raja Basanta Roy Rd ☎033/2466 2700, ⓔtransit1@vsnl.net. Excellent, safe and comfortable guesthouse with good-sized rooms; away from the centre but in an interesting location close to markets and the lakes, and not far from the Metro. ⑤

Expensive

Sudder Street, Park Street and Chowringhee

Astor 15 Shakespeare Sarani ☎033/2282 9950. Comfortable old garden hotel which has managed to retain some of the character of old Calcutta. The comfortable, modernized rooms all have satellite TV, fridge and a/c, and the hotel also houses a nightclub and excellent restaurants (see p.865). ⑧

Fairlawn 13-A Sudder St ☎033/2252 1510, ⓦwww.fairlawnhotel.com. Chock-full of memorabilia, this famous and old-fashioned family-run hotel exudes a charmingly faded and eccentric Raj atmosphere, though the absence of modernization doesn't suit all tastes. Nonresidents can sample a drink in the lush garden. ⑧

Housez43 43 Mirza Ghalib St ☎033/2227 6020, ⓦwww.housez43.com. An old building transformed into a delightful boutique hotel with modern, brightly painted a/c rooms, elegantly decorated in minimalist style. There's also a couple with more traditional elements such as four-poster beds. ⑧–⑨

Kenilworth 1 & 2 Little Russell St ☎033/2282 3939, ⊛www.kenilworthhotels.com. Comfortable and functional business hotel with opulent rooms, a pleasant garden and a convenient location that adds to its popularity. Facilities include a good restaurant, coffee shop, two bars, a barbeque in the garden and a multigym with steam bath and sauna. From $183. ⑨

Lytton 14 Sudder St ☎033/2249 1872, ⊛www .lyttonhotelindia.com. The most modern and comfortable hotel on Sudder St, lacking in character but with a/c, fridges and satellite TV in all rooms. Facilities include a bar and a couple of good restaurants. ⑧

🏃 **Oberoi Grand** 15 Chowringhee Rd ☎033/2249 2323, ⊛www.oberoihotels .com. The white Victorian facade of this luxurious hotel, established in 1938, is very much part of the fabric of the city. Service is attentive, and the interior has been completely revamped in a modern-meets-traditional style; facilities include a swimming pool, and Thai and Indian restaurants. From $246. ⑨

Park 17 Park St ☎033/2249 9000, ⊛www .theparkhotels.com. Modern five-star in a good location on a cosmopolitan street; amenities include swimming pool, health club, late checkout and good food at the three restaurants, including the 24hr *Atrium*; plus a popular nightclub and a bar with live music. Comfortable and stylish rooms. From $194. ⑨

Elsewhere in the city

Floatel 9/10 Kolkata Jetty, Strand Rd South ☎033/2213 7777, ⊛www.floatelhotel.com. A converted ship which has comfortable wood-lined cabins and an expansive deck that's great for watching the world drift by over a sundowner; the food, however, is disappointing. From $143. ⑨

Hindusthan International 235/1 AJC Bose Rd ☎033/4001 8000, ⊛www.hindusthan.com. Recently revamped, though plain and rather overpriced, this is a well-located business hotel with comfortable, conservatively decorated rooms. Facilities are excellent however, and include a travel desk, restaurants, nightclub, health club and an outdoor swimming pool. From $150. ⑨

Hyatt Regency JA-1 Sector 3, Salt Lake City ☎033/2335 1234, ⊛www.kolkata.regency.hyatt .com. Plush hotel on the Eastern Bypass, en route to the airport and handy for the city too. It's built to impress with capacious lobbies, restaurants, a palm-fringed swimming pool and all facilities. From $197. ⑨

Sonar Bangla Eastern Bypass ☎033/2345 4545, ⊛www.itcwelcomgroup.in. Busy hotel whose popularity rests on its convenient location between city and airport and its excellent range of restaurants, bars and nightclubs. All the comforts and services one would expect from a five-star, and a relaxed welcome, though an unflattering exterior. From $270. ⑨

Taj Bengal 24-B Belvedere Rd, Alipore ☎033/2223 3939, ⊛www.tajhotels.com. Opulent showpiece hotel, attempting to amalgamate Bengali features with the usual *Taj* grandeur. Excellent range of restaurants, including Chinese and Indian, and a pool and nightclub. From $226. ⑨

Tollygunge Club 120 Deshapran Sasmal Rd, at the southern end of the Metro line ☎033/2473 2316. The exclusive club offers a choice of cottages or rooms in two modern but characterless blocks; rates include temporary membership and the use of an eighteen-hole golf course, plus riding, swimming, tennis and squash facilities, as well as open-air and indoor restaurants and a good bar. There's an Ayurvedic treatment centre too. You'll need to contact the secretary well in advance, as the club is extremely popular and often full. ⑧

Vedic Village Shikarpur, Rajahat ☎03216/263180, ⊛www.thevedicvillage.com. A sprawling development with beautifully presented modern cottages around a lake and luxurious rooms in the main block. There's also a good restaurant, a swimming pool and an excellent naturopathy health centre. It's 28km from central Kolkata, but only 12km from the airport along slow and winding village roads. ⑧–⑨

The City

Kolkata's crumbling, weatherbeaten buildings and anarchic streets can create an intimidating first impression. With time and patience, though, this huge metropolis starts to resolve itself into a fascinating conglomerate of styles and influences. The **River Hooghly**, which was until recently spanned only by the remarkable cantilever Howrah Bridge, is not all that prominent in the life of the city. Instead its heart is the green expanse of the **Maidan**, which attracts locals from all walks

Although a rich tradition of poetry existed in India long before the arrival of the Europeans – even scientific manuscripts were written in rhyming couplets – prose was all but unknown. Thus the foundation by the British of **Fort William College** in 1800, primarily intended to assist administrators to learn Indian languages by commissioning prose in Bengali, Urdu and Hindi, had the unexpected side-effect of helping to create a vital new genre in indigenous literature. **Bankim Chandra Chatterjee** (1838–99), a senior civil servant who wrote novels of everyday life, became known as the father of Bengali literature, while **Michael Madhusudan Dutt** (1829–73) introduced European conventions into Bengali poetry. Simultaneously, Westernization began to sweep Bengali middle-class society, as people grew disenchanted with their culture and religion.

A leading figure in the new intelligentsia was **Raja Ram Mohan Roy** (1774–1833). Born an orthodox Hindu, he founded the **Brahmo Samaj**, a socio-religious movement that believed in one god and set out to purge Hinduism of its idol worship and rituals, advocating the abolition of *sati* and child marriage. **Keshab Chandra Sen**'s breakaway church Navabidhan (New Dispensation), a synthesis of all the world's major religions, created a split in 1866 over its emphasis on universal Unitarianism and the downplaying of the role of Hinduism. However, no single figure epitomized the Bengali Renaissance more than **Rabindranath Tagore**, a giant of Bengali art, culture and letters, and a Brahmo, who received the Nobel Prize for Literature in 1913. As well as writing several hymns, he set out the principles of the Brahmo Samaj movement in *The Religion of Man*. The intellectual and cultural freedom of the Brahmo Samaj earned it an important influence over the Bengali upper classes that endures to this day, but in recent years extreme Bengali reformists have attacked the movement for having been a corrupting influence on Bengali society.

During and following the period of the Renaissance, Bengal saw a resurgence of Hindu thought through religious leaders such as **Ramakrishna** (1836–86), a great Kali devotee whose message was carried as far as North America by his disciple **Vivekananda**. A formidable spiritual intellect and once a Brahmo himself, Vivekananda inspired generations of Hindu nationalists. After having spent some time in London as a student, **Sri Aurobindo** (1872–1950) returned to India to become a freedom fighter and, finally, emerged as one of the most influential philosophers of twentieth-century India, establishing his own ashram in Pucucherry (see p.1131).

of life for recreation, sports, exhibitions and political rallies. At its southern end stands the white-marble **Victoria Memorial**, and close by rise the tall Gothic spires of **St Paul's Cathedral**. Next to the busy **New Market** area looms the all-embracing **Indian Museum**. Further north, the district centred on BBD Bagh is filled with reminders of the heyday of the East India Company, dominated by the bulk of the **Writers' Building**, built in 1780 to replace the original structure used to house the clerks or "writers" of the East India Company; nearby stand **St Andrew's Kirk** and the pillared immensity of the **GPO**. A little further out, the **Armenian church** stands on the edge of the frenetic, labyrinthine markets of **Barabazaar**, while the renowned and influential temple of **Kalighat** is away to the south. Across the river, south of the marvellous **Howrah railway station**, lies the tranquillity of the **Botanical Gardens**.

The Maidan, New Market and Park Street

One of the largest city-centre parks in the world, the **Maidan** – literally "field" – stretches from the Esplanade in the north to the racecourse in the south, and is bordered by **Chowringhee Road** to the east and the Strand and river to the west. This vast open area stands in utter contrast to the chaotic streets of the surrounding city, and is big enough to swallow up several clubs, including the Calcutta Ladies Golf Club and the immaculate greens of the Calcutta Bowling Club. It was created when the now-inconspicuous **Fort William** was laid out near the river in 1758, and Robert Clive cleared tracts of forest to give its guns a clear line of fire. Originally a haven for the elite, with a strict dress code, today ordinary citizens come to exercise each morning, while shepherds graze their flocks and riders canter along the old bridleways. In the late afternoons, the Maidan plays host to scores of impromptu cricket and football matches, as well as games of kabadi (see p.68).

Esplanade, New Market and Chowringhee

The 46-metre column of **Shahid Minar** (Martyrs' Memorial) towers over busy tram and bus terminals and market stalls at the northeast corner of the Maidan, known here as Esplanade. As the **Ochterlony Monument**, it was built in 1828 to commemorate the memory of David Ochterlony, who led the East India Company troops to victory in the Nepalese Wars of 1814–16. On the east side of Esplanade, the once-elegant colonnaded front of Chowringhee Road, with its long line of colonial villas and palaces, is now in a sorry state of decay and perpetually crowded with hawkers and shoppers. Following endless renovations and changes of management, only the Victorian **Grand Hotel** remains a haven of colonialism, its palm court inspired by the famous *Raffles* of Singapore.

Around the corner to the east, Chowringhee Road leads to the single-storey **New Market**, little changed since it opened in 1874 and with plenty of old-world charm. Its correct name is Sir Stuart Hogg Market; supposedly, the ghost of Sir Stuart roams the corridors at night. Beneath its Gothic red-brick clock tower, the market stocks a vast array of household goods, luggage, garments, textiles, jewellery, nick-nacks and books as well as meat, vegetables and fruit. Among more unique shops, **Chamba Lama** sells Tibetan curios, silver jewellery, bronzes and the occasional antique. The **Symphony** store has a good selection of classical and popular Indian music, while **Sujata's** is known for its silk, and **Nahoum & Sons** is a Jewish bakery and confectioner which does a roaring trade. Further up the corridor, condiment stalls offer cheese from Kalimpong, miniature rounds of salty Bandel cheese and *amshat*, blocks of dried mango; the produce, poultry, fish and meat market nearby is unmistakable by its aroma. Any flicker of uncertainty from the shopper encourages eager coolies with baskets who are only too happy to assist, for the commission offered by retailers.

Indian Museum

At the corner of Chowringhee and Sudder streets, the stately **Indian Museum** (Tues–Sun 10am–5pm; Rs150 [Rs10]) is the oldest and largest museum in India, founded in 1814. Visitors come in their thousands, many of them villagers who bring offerings to what they call the *jadu ghar* or "house of magic", which had its reputation blighted by a blatant theft when, in December 2004, a priceless Buddhist statue was taken during opening hours without anyone noticing.

The main showpiece is a collection of **sculptures** obtained from sites all over India, which centres on a superb Mauryan polished-sandstone **lion capital** dating from the third century BC. One gallery houses the impressive remains of the second-century BC Buddhist **stupa from Bharhut** in Madhya Pradesh, partly reassembled to display the red-sandstone posts, capping stones, railings and gateways. Carvings depict human and animal figures, as well as scenes from the *Jataka* tales of the Buddha's many incarnations. There is also a huge collection of Buddhist schist sculptures, dating from the first to the third centuries, from the Gandhara region. You'll also see stone sculpture from **Khajuraho** and Pala bronzes, plus copper artefacts, Stone-Age tools and terracotta figures from other sites.

Along with an excellent exhibit of Tibetan *thangkas*, the museum holds Kalighat *pats* (see p.862) and paintings by the **Company School**, a group of mid-nineteenth-century Indian artists who emulated Western themes and techniques for European patrons. Finally, there's a spectacular array of fossils and stuffed animals, most of which look in dire need of a decent burial.

Park Street

Around the corner from the museum, the **Asiatic Society** at 1 Park St, established in 1784 by Orientalists including Sir William Jones, houses a huge collection of around 150,000 books and 60,000 manuscripts, some dating back to the seventh century. The society has a **reading room** open to the public (Mon–Fri 10am–8pm, Sat 10am–5pm; free) as well as a **gallery** of art and antiquities that holds paintings by Rubens and Reynolds, a large coin collection and one of Ashoka's stone edicts.

Around 2km east along Park Street from the Maidan, the disused but recently restored **Park Street Cemetery** is one of the city's most haunting memorials to its imperial past. Inaugurated in 1767, it is the oldest in Kolkata, holding a wonderful concentration of pyramids, obelisks, pavilions, urns and headstones, under which many well-known figures from the Raj lie buried. The epitaphs make fascinating reading.

Fort William

The leafy Outram Road leads west through the Maidan from the top of Park Street to the gates of **Fort William**, now home to the military headquarters of the Eastern Command, with restricted public access. Commissioned by the British after their defeat in 1756, it was completed in 1781 and named after King William III. A rough octagon, about 500m in diameter, whose massive, low bunker-like battlements are punctuated by six main gates, it was designed to hold all the city's Europeans in the event of attack. To one side it commanded a view of the Maidan, cleared to give a field of fire; to the other it dominated the river and the crucial shipping lanes. Water from the river was diverted to fill the surrounding moat. Eighteenth- and nineteenth-century structures inside include the Church of St Peter's (now a library), barracks and stables, an arsenal, strongrooms and a prison.

Victoria Memorial and the Calcutta Gallery

The dramatic white-marble **Victoria Memorial** (Tues–Sun 10am–5pm, closed second Saturday of the month; Rs150 [Rs10], Ⓦwww.victoriamemorial -cal.org), at the southern end of the Maidan, with its formal gardens and water courses, continues to be Kolkata's pride and joy (gardens daily 5.30am–7.00pm; Rs4). Other colonial monuments and statues throughout the city have been renamed or demolished, but the popularity of Queen Victoria seems to endure; attempts to change the name of the "VM" have come to nothing. This extraordinary hybrid building designed by Sir William Emerson, with Italianate statues over its entrances, Mughal domes in its corners, and tall elegant open colonnades along its sides, was conceived by Lord Curzon to commemorate the empire at its peak, though by the time it was completed in 1921, twenty years after Victoria's death, the capital of the Raj had shifted to Delhi. A sombre statue of Queen Victoria, flanked by two ornamental tanks, gazes out towards the Maidan from a pedestal lined with bronze panels and friezes. Faced with

Makrana marble from Rajasthan, the building itself is capped by a dome bearing a revolving five-metre-tall bronze figure of Victory.

The main entrance, at the Maidan end, leads into a tall chamber beneath the dome. The 25 **galleries** inside still contain mementoes of British imperialism – statues and busts of Queen Mary, King George V and Queen Victoria; a huge canvas of the future Edward VII entering Jaipur in 1876; French guns captured at the Battle of Plassey in 1758; and the black-marble throne of a nawab defeated by Robert Clive. Well worth seeing, the **Calcutta Gallery** provides a fascinating insight into the history and life of the Indians of the city and the Independence struggle through paintings, documents and old photographs. The evening **sound-and-light** show (Oct–Feb Tues–Sun 7.15pm, March–June 7.45pm; Rs20 [Rs10]) held in the grounds, concentrates on the same theme. After the gardens close the Maidan in front of the gates is transformed by the masses of people who come to enjoy the breeze, roadside snacks, pony and *ikka* (open carriage) rides, and to watch the garish musical fountains.

St Paul's Cathedral and around

A little way from the Victoria Memorial, past the Birla Planetarium, stands the Gothic edifice of **St Paul's Cathedral**, erected by Major W.N. Forbes in 1847. Measuring 75m by 24m, its iron-trussed roof was then the longest span in existence. For improved ventilation, the lancet windows inside extend to plinth level, and tall fans hang from the ceiling. The most outstanding of the many well-preserved memorials and plaques to long-perished imperialists is the stained glass of the west window, designed by Sir Edward Burne-Jones in 1880 to honour Lord Mayo, assassinated in the Andaman Islands. The original steeple was destroyed in the 1897 earthquake; after a second earthquake in 1934 it was remodelled on the Bell Harry Tower at Canterbury Cathedral.

South of the cathedral, the **Academy of Fine Arts** (Tues–Sun noon–8pm; Rs5) on Cathedral Road is a showcase for Bengali contemporary arts. As well as temporary exhibitions, it holds permanent displays of the work of artists such as Jamini Roy and Rabindranath Tagore. A café and pleasant grounds enhance the ambience. **Rabindra Sadan**, the large auditorium nearby, features programmes of Indian classical music and next door, **Nandan**, designed by Satyajit Ray, is a lively film centre with archives, library and auditoria.

Galleries

Bengal has a lively tradition of contemporary art, and with increased prosperity and speculation in fine art, galleries are burgeoning throughout the city showing a high standard of work. Exhibitions are listed in *Cal Calling*; besides the Academy of Fine Arts, the following are worth checking out.

Birla Academy of Art and Culture 108 Southern Ave ☏033/2466 2843, ⓦwww .birlaart.com. Ancient and modern art with regular exhibitions of contemporary Indian artists. (Tues–Sun 3–8pm; Rs5.)

Chemould 12 Park St ☏033/2229 8641. Art gallery and picture framer that stages special exhibitions from time to time. (Mon–Sat 10am–7pm; free.)

CIMA (Centre of International Modern Art), 2nd Floor, Sunny Towers, 43 Ashutosh Chowdhury Ave ☏033/2474 8717, ⓦwww.cimaartindia.com. Prestigious Ballygunge gallery, displaying work by contemporary artists. (Tues–Sun 2–8pm; free.)

Galerie 88 28-B Shakespeare Sarani ☏033/2247 2274. Private gallery showing contemporary Indian paintings plus specialist exhibitions. Also stocks art supplies. (Mon–Sat 10am–7pm; free.)

Central Kolkata

The commercial and administrative hub of both Kolkata and West Bengal is **BBD Bagh**, which die-hard Kolkatans still insist on referring to as **Dalhousie Square**. The new official name, in a fine piece of official rhetoric, commemorates three revolutionaries hanged for trying to kill Lieutenant-Governor General Lord Dalhousie.

Built in 1868 on the site of the original Fort William – destroyed by Siraj-ud-Daula in 1756 – the **GPO** on the west side of the square hides the supposed site of the **Black Hole of Calcutta**. On a hot June night in 1756, 146 English prisoners were forced by Siraj-ud-Daula's guards into a tiny chamber with only the smallest of windows for ventilation; most had suffocated to death by the next morning. By all accounts, the guards were unaware of the tragedy unfolding and, on hearing the news, Siraj-ud-Daula was deeply repentant. A memorial to the victims that formerly stood in front of the Writers' Building was removed in 1940 to the grounds of St John's Church south of the GPO. When Robert Clive regained control of Calcutta, he had learned his lesson: Fort William was not rebuilt here, but in its current location on the Maidan, with clear visibility in all directions.

Beyond the headquarters of Eastern Railways on Netaji Subhash Road, you come to the heart of Kolkata's **commercial district**, clustered around the Calcutta Stock Exchange at the corner of Lyon's Range, which started out as a gathering of traders under a neem tree in the 1830s. The warren of buildings, erected along the same lines as the contemporary business districts of Shanghai, houses all sorts of old colonial trading companies including some still bearing Scottish names.

A trio of eighteenth- and nineteenth-century British **churches** are dotted around this district, the most interesting of them **St John's**, just south of the GPO. Erected in 1787, it houses memorials to British residents, along with an impressive painting of *The Last Supper* by Johann Zoffany, in which prominent Calcuttans are depicted as apostles. In the grounds, Kolkata's oldest graveyard holds the tomb of **Job Charnock**, the city's founding father, who earned eternal notoriety for marrying a Hindu girl he saved from the funeral pyre of her first husband.

Dominating the area south of BBD Bagh, **Government House** (closed to the general public) overlooks the north end of the Maidan and the broad, ceremonial Red Road, which was once used as an airstrip. Until 1911, this was the residence of the British governor-generals and the viceroys of India; now the official home of the Governor of Bengal, it's known as **Raj Bhavan**. Nearby, opposite the **Assembly House** (Rajya Sabha) of West Bengal's Legislative Council, are the All India Radio building, and the sports complex of **Eden Gardens**, site of the world-famous **cricket** ground (officially known as the Ranji Stadium). Watching a test match here is an unforgettable experience as the 100,000-seat stadium resounds to the roar of the crowd and the sound of firecrackers thrown indiscriminately; to avoid the missiles sit in the covered sections. The pleasant palm-fringed **gardens** (daily dawn till dusk) with a lake and a **Burmese pagoda**, are free.

North Kolkata

The amorphous area of **north Kolkata**, long part of the "native" town rather than the European sectors, was where the city's prosperous nineteenth-century Bengali families created their little palaces, or *"raj baris"*, many now in advanced and fascinating states of decay. Its markets continue to thrive, and the occasional church stands as a reminder of days gone by.

North of BBD Bagh, the area known as **Barabazaar** has hosted a succession of trading communities; the Portuguese were here before Job Charnock landed at the fishing village that stood close by, and it later became home to Marwari and Gujarati merchants. The small hectic lanes south of MG Road are lined with shops and stalls selling everything from glass bangles to textiles.

At the northwest corner of Barabazaar, near Howrah Bridge, is Kolkata's oldest church, the **Armenian Church of Our Lady of Nazareth**. Founded in 1724 by Cavond, an Armenian from Persia, it was built on the site of an Armenian cemetery in which the oldest tombstone dates to 1630. The Armenian community was already highly influential at the courts of Bengal by the time the British arrived, and played an important role in the early history of the East India Company. Later they helped start the lucrative jute industry.

East of Barabazaar on Rabindra Sarani (formerly Chitpore Rd), the huge red **Nakhoda Masjid**, whose two lofty minarets rise to 46m, is the great Jamia Masjid (Friday mosque) of the city. Completed in 1942, it was modelled on Akbar's Tomb at Sikandra near Agra; its four floors can hold ten thousand worshippers. The traditional Muslim market that flourishes around the mosque sells religious items along with clothes, dried fruit and sweets such as *firni*, made of rice.

Until relatively recently, the chaotic jumble of streets to the south along Rabindra Sarani housed a thriving **Chinatown**, opium dens and all. A handful of Chinese families continue to live around Chhatawala Gully, where a small early-morning street market (daily 6–7am) offers home-made pork sausages, noodles and jasmine tea.

North of MG Road, on the tiny Muktaram Babu Street off Chittaranjan Avenue, the extraordinary **Marble Palace** (closed Mon & Thurs 10am–4pm; free; no photography) preserves its lavish, sensuous treasures in cramped and dilapidated conditions. To join one of the free guided tours, get a pass from the tourist offices at BBD Bagh or Shakespeare Sarani (see p.848). Built in 1835, the ornate marble-paved palace holds statues, European antiques, Belgian glass, chandeliers, mirrors, Ming vases, and paintings by Rubens, Titian, Reynolds and Gainsborough. To the north of Marble Palace, **Sonagachi**'s warren of lanes comprise Kolkata's largest red-light district.

On Dwarkanath Tagore Lane, a short walk northeast of the Marble Palace, the small campus of Rabindranath Tagore's liberal arts university, **Rabindra Bharati**, preserves the house where he was born and died as the **Rabindra Bharati Museum** (Tues–Sun 10am–4.30pm; Rs50 [Rs10], students Rs25 [Rs5]), otherwise known as Jorasanko Thakurbari or Tagore House. A fine example of a nineteenth-century *raj bari*, the museum holds a large collection of Tagore's paintings. Nearby on College Street, famed for its pavement bookshops, the **Ashutosh Museum of Indian Art** (Mon–Fri 11am–4.30pm; Rs10), housed in University of Calcutta's Centenary Building, is dedicated to the arts of Bengal, from eighth-century Pala-dynasty sculpture to nineteenth-century painted scrolls and contemporary art. Further up College Street past a multitude of book vendors lies the famous **India Coffee House**, which still maintains its reputation as a meeting place for the intelligentsia. Of north Kolkata's two main Jain temples, **Parasnath**, 2km northeast of College Street at Manicktolla, is an extraordinary kitsch homage to the tenth *tirthankara*, Sitalnath, with neoclassical statues in a water garden and, inside, glitzy marble-work studded with silver and illuminated by a collection of ornate chandeliers. The other temple at Belgachia is relatively sedate.

Howrah and the River Hooghly

Although **Howrah** is technically a separate town, it forms an integral part of the city as the home of much of Kolkata's industry, as well as **Howrah Station** – a striking red-brick building built in 1906 and used by millions of passengers each day. Until recently, antiquated **Howrah Bridge** was the only road link across the River Hooghly; since the opening of the elegant **Vidyasagar Setu**, the second Hooghly bridge, the west bank of the river is changing rapidly. Vidyasagar Setu (also referred to as the New or Natun Bridge) provides access to Shibpur and the **Botanical Gardens**, and onwards southwest to the highways toward Orissa.

Until silting rendered it impractical for large ships, the **River Hooghly**, a tributary of the Ganges, was responsible for making Calcutta a bustling port. Unlike those at Varanasi, the *ghats* lining its east bank have no mythological significance; they simply serve as landings and places for ritual ablutions. Around 1.5km north of Howrah Bridge, **Nimtolla Ghat**, one of the city's main cremation grounds, is sealed off from public gaze. The large steps alongside, and a Shiva temple, attract sadhus as they pass through on their way to January's Ganga Sagar Mela (see p.847). Further north, behind **Kumartuli Ghat**, a warren of lanes is home to a community of artisans who make the images of deities used for the major festivals. In the days leading up to the great pujas, especially that of Durga, Kumartuli is a fascinating hive of activity. As you walk north, you come next to **Baghbazaar Ghat**, where overloaded barges of straw arrive for the craftsmen of Kumartuli. Baghbazaar, the Garden Market, stands on the original site of **Sutanuti**, its grand but decaying mansions epitomizing the long-vanished lifestyle of the Bengali gentry, the *bhadra log* (lampooned by Kipling in *The Jungle Book*, whose monkey troupe he called the "bandar log").

South of Howrah Bridge, in its shadow, set behind the busy flower market of **Mullick Ghat**, the **Armenian Ghat** is most animated at dawn, when traditional gymnasts and wrestlers, devotees of Hanuman the monkey god, come to practise. As the Strand – separated from the river by the Circular Railway line – heads south, it passes several warehouses and the recently established **Millennium Park** on the way beyond Fairly Place to another cluster of *ghats*. **Babu Ghat** here, identified by its crumbling colonnade, is used for early morning bathing, attended

Howrah Bridge

One of Kolkata's most famous landmarks and officially Rabindra Setu, though few use this new name, **Howrah Bridge** (@howrahbridgekolkata.gov.in) is 97m high and 705m long, spanning the river in a single leap to make it the world's largest cantilever bridge. It was erected during World War II in 1943 to give Allied troops access to the Burmese front, replacing an earlier pontoon bridge that opened to let river traffic through. With its maze of girders, it was the first bridge to be built using rivets, and is still used by millions of commuters. Despite the removal of the tramlines, its eight lanes are still perpetually clogged with vehicles, and in the 1980s became so worn out that a man pushing his broken-down car is said to have fallen through a hole and disappeared. Don't let that put you off: the bridge has undergone major repairs in recent years, and joining the streams of pedestrians who walk across it each day is a memorable experience. **Vidyasagar Setu**, the second Hooghly bridge, built 3km south to relieve the strain, was 22 years in the making. It's a vast toll bridge with spaghetti-junction-style approaches high enough to let ships pass below. Through sheer incompetence, the agency in charge of managing the tolls, posted a loss of over $7 million in 2006; it has since been privatized.

by *pujaris* (priests) and heavy-handed masseurs. Messy and busy, Babu Ghat's Bus Stand nearby is one of Kolkata's main cross-country terminuses, while frequent ferries (7.30am–8pm) from Chandpal Ghat, a couple of hundred metres north, provide an easy alternative to Howrah Bridge. Further south between Fort William and the river, the Strand comes into its own as a leafy promenade, pleasant during the early evenings with a café, food stalls and boat rides from the small jetty near the café (around Rs150 per hour).

Botanical Gardens

The **Botanical Gardens** (daily 7am–5pm; free) at Shibpur lie 10km south of Howrah Station on the west bank of the Hooghly. Although they were created in 1786 to develop strains of Indian tea, Calcuttans have only started to appreciate these 109 hectares since the opening of the second bridge. Populated by countless bird species, such as waders, cranes and storks, the huge gardens are best seen in winter and spring, and early in the mornings, before the heat of the day sets in. Their most famous feature is the world's largest **banyan tree**, 24.5m high and an astonishing 420m in circumference. The Orchid House, the Herbarium and the Fern Houses are also worth seeing, and there's an attractive riverside promenade.

The gardens are accessible as a tedious road-trip from Esplanade, by minibus or the ordinary ash-coloured #C6 bus. The #T9 runs from Park Street and #6 minibus runs from Dharamtala via Howrah; the ferry service from Chandpal Ghat goes to Shibpur, from where you can get local transport to the gardens. A taxi ride from the central Sudder Street area costs around Rs100 one way and is the easiest way to get there.

South Kolkata

South of the Maidan and Park Street, Kolkata spreads towards **suburbs** such as Alipore and Ballygunge, both within easy distance of the centre. The thoroughfare that starts life as Chowringhee proceeds south from Esplanade past **Kalighat** to **Tollygunge**, following the Metro line which terminates near the luxurious *Tollygunge Club* (see p.854), the mansion of an indigo merchant now surrounded by immaculate golfing fairways and bridle paths. Northeast of Tollygunge, beyond a white-tiled mosque built in 1835 by descendants of Tipu Sultan (see p.1256), lies the parkland of Rabindra Sarobar, known locally as the Lakes, a popular spot for early evening walks.

Alipore

Around 3km south of Park Street, the crumbling nineteenth-century splendour of **Alipore** is being engulfed by a forest of multistorey buildings. Elegant

---

Kalighat paintings

Early in the nineteenth century, Kalighat was in its heyday, drawing pilgrims, merchants and artisans from all over the country. Among them were **scroll painters** from elsewhere in Bengal, who developed the distinctive style now known as **Kalighat pats**. Adapting Western techniques, using paper and water-based paints instead of tempera, they moved away from religious themes to depict contemporary subjects. By 1850, Kalighat *pats* had taken a dynamic new direction, satirizing the middle classes in much the same way as today's political cartoons. They serve as a witty record of the period, filled with images of everyday life, and can be found in galleries and museums around the world, and in the Indian Museum (see p.856) as well as the Birla Academy in Kolkata.

triple-arched gates just south of the popular **Zoo** (daily except Tues 9am–5pm; Rs5) lead to Belvedere, the former residence of the lieutenant-governor of Bengal and now serving as the **National Library** (Mon–Fri 10am–6pm; separate periodical and newspaper reading room on Esplanade Mon–Fri 9am–2pm, Sat & Sun 10am–6pm; free). Presented to Warren Hastings by Mir Jafar, the building's original simplicity was enhanced by double columns and the sweeping staircase leading to the Durbar Hall. When the capital shifted to Delhi, this library was left behind; today it houses a huge collection of books, periodicals and reference material, as well as rare documents in an air-conditioned chamber.

Kalighat

Some 5km south of Park Street along Ashutosh Mukherjee Road (an extension of Chowringhee Rd), Kolkata's most important temple, **Kalighat**, stands at the heart of a diverse and animated area, part residential, part bazaar. The destitute hoping for charity from pilgrims line the temple approaches and prostitutes linger on the thoroughfares and bridges offering their services in tragic, grimy circumstances. The typically Bengali temple itself, built in 1809 of brick and mortar but capturing the sweeping curves of a thatched roof, is dedicated to Kali, the black goddess and form of Shakti. According to legend, Shiva went into a frenzy after the death of his wife Sati, dancing with her dead body and making the whole world tremble. The gods made various attempts to stop him

---

Mother Teresa

Beatified by Pope John Paul II on 19 October 2003, **Mother Teresa**, Kolkata's most famous citizen (1910–97), was born Agnes Gonxha Bojaxhiu to Albanian parents, and grew up in Skopje in the former Yugoslavia. Joining the Sisters of Loreto, an Irish order, she was sent as a teacher to Darjeeling, where she took her vows in May 1931 and became Teresa. In her work at St Mary's School in Kolkata, she became aware of the terrible poverty around her; in 1948, with permission from Rome, she changed her nun's habit for the simple blue-bordered white sari that became the uniform of the **Missionaries of Charity**.

The best known of their many homes and clinics is **Nirmal Hriday** at 251 Kalighat Rd, a hospice for destitutes. In the face of local resistance, Mother Teresa chose its site at Kalighat – Kolkata's most important centre of Hinduism – in the knowledge that many of the poor specifically come here to die, next to a holy *tirtha* or crossing-place. Mother Teresa's piety and single-minded devotion to the poor won her international acclaim, including the Nobel Peace Prize in 1979. Subsequently she also attracted a fair share of controversy with her fierce anti-abortion stance, giving rise to accusations of fundamentalist Catholicism. She was also accused of disregarding advances in medicine in favour of saving the souls of the dying and destitute. Censure, however, seems iniquitous in the light of her immense contribution to humanity.

If you're interested in the work of the Missionaries of Charity, they can be contacted at **Mother House**, near Sealdah Station at 54-A AJC Bose Rd (℡033/2249 7115, closed Thurs), where there is a small museum. Although they occasionally turn casual volunteers away, they run orientation workshops (a brief introduction to their work) on Mondays, Wednesdays and Fridays from 3pm to 5pm. Nearby Shishu Bhavan, 78 AJC Bose Rd, is an orphanage and a dispensary for children.

The appalling poverty highlighted by Mother Teresa has led to a number of NGO charities developing in the city. Established in 1979, **Calcutta Rescue** is a non-religious organization which, with the help of worldwide support groups, runs four clinics, three schools and a creche in Kolkata, as well as an outreach programme to help those in need further afield in West Bengal. For more information visit them online at ⊛www.calcuttarescue.org or call ℡033/2217 5675.

before Vishnu took his solar discus and chopped the disintegrating corpse into 51 bits. The spot where each piece fell became a *pitha*, or pilgrimage site, for worshippers of the female principle of divinity – Shakti. The shrine here marks the place where her little toe fell.

The temple is open all hours, and is always a hive of activity. Avaricious priests will try to whisk you downstairs to confront the dramatic monolithic image of the terrible goddess, with her huge eyes and bloody tongue. The courtyard beyond the main congregational hall is used for sacrificing goats on occasions such as Kali Puja; allegedly, humans were formerly sacrificed here to appease the fertility goddess. To the north of the compound, a lingam is worshipped by women praying for children, while shops all around cater for pilgrims. **Nirmal Hriday**, Mother Teresa's home for the destitute and dying, is nearby.

Eating

Although locals love to **dine out**, traditional Bengali cooking was, until recently, restricted to the home; however some excellent restaurants now offer the chance to taste this wonderful fish-based cuisine. The most popular option for dining out is Chinese food, spiced and cooked to local tastes: the city has a rich tradition including its own Chinatown at **Tangra** (closes early around 10pm) on the road to the airport. You'll also find several good south Indian restaurants, as well as rich Muslim cooking at places like **Royal**; the *kathi* roll, invented at *Nizam's*, is now part and parcel of Kolkata's cuisine. Tibetan cafés on Suburban Hospital Road near Rabindra Sadan Metro offer *momos* and *thukpa*, while brash modern restaurants and cafés have sprung up all over the city, serving everything from vernacular cooking to pizzas, and numerous patisseries and confectioneries work hard to keep abreast of demand. For special occasions, fine dining at one of Kolkata's five-star hotels doesn't have to break the bank.

Restaurants and cafés around **Sudder Street** cater for Western travellers staying in the local hotels, while roadside chai shops and snack vendors offer a tasty alternative. The busy environs around **New Market** include a Muslim quarter with several good restaurants, most with an emphasis on meat. Fast food has caught on with international chains moving in, but despite the queues at its opening, *McDonald's* premier on Park Street came to an abrupt end when a huge explosion, apparently from gas canisters, blew it apart.

New Market and Sudder Street

All the places below appear on the Chowringhee and Sudder Street map, p.851.

Aaheli *Peerless Inn*, 12 Chowringhee Rd ☎033/2288 0301. Excellent Bengali restaurant, where waiters dressed in traditional *dhotis* serve everything from home cooking to festive food; try the rich *maha* thali (grand thali). Around Rs600 per head. No bar.

Arsalan 119-A Ripon St ☎033/6569 9579. Large, new restaurant that serves a selection of Chinese and other food; you're best off sticking to its Mughlai cuisine – such as the kebabs and excellent biriyanis (around Rs250) – for which it is famous.

Baan Thai *Oberoi Grand* hotel, 15 Chowringhee Rd ☎033/2249 2323. Although expensive – Rs1600 per head and up – this in-hotel restaurant offers by far the best Thai cooking in town, with dishes like *poo krapaw* (stuffed crab) as well as standards such as red curry.

Blue and Beyond 9th floor, *Hotel Lindsay*, 8-A Lindsay St. This rooftop bar and restaurant provides an excellent vantage point over New Market and the surrounding city, best seen at dusk; there's good Indian and reasonable Chinese food, plus good-value breakfasts and buffets.

Blue Sky Café Sudder St. Budget travellers' haunt halfway down the strip on a corner, providing all the old favourites. Clean, well run and a popular meeting place.

Fresh & Juicy 2/7 Sudder St. Despite its fruity theme, this small café has a good and varied travellers' menu from breakfasts and "snakes" (snacks) to Chinese *haka*.

Nahoum & Sons F-20, New Market. Legendary Jewish bakery and confectioner selling delicious fruitcake, cashew macaroons, *chala* (Jewish braided bread), cheese straws, chicken patties and bagels with cream cheese.

Nizam's 22–25 Hogg Market. The original restaurant here gave birth to the legendary *kathi* roll – a tasty sheesh kebab, rolled into a *paratha* of white flour. Now with new owners and a garish facelift, its myth has all but died, but it's still worth a visit for a snacky meal.

Zurich 3 Sudder St. Near the *Blue Sky Café* and similarly pitched at travellers; more comfortable and restaurant-like, with good food and a relaxed atmosphere.

Around Park Street

All the places below appear on the Chowringhee and Sudder Street map, p.851.

Astor 15 Shakespeare Sarani ☏033/2242 9950. This hotel houses a bar and several restaurants: the multi-cuisine *Serai*; the *Banyan Tree* serving Bengali food; and, best of all, the *Kebab-e-Que* in the garden, dishing up excellent tandoori meals – try the Moti kebab (mushrooms and *paneer*).

Bar-B-Q 43 Park St. An old and reliable favourite, offering Chinese and much-lauded tandoori cuisine in pleasant air-conditioned surroundings with a bar downstairs; the special lunch menu includes Persian delicacies such as *chelo* kebabs on rice. Mains around Rs300.

Barista 12D Park St. The Kolkata branch of this trendy and popular nationwide chain serves up a range of snacks and good coffee, and has a tiny bookshop upstairs.

The Blue Potato Outram St, 27 Shakespeare Sarani ☏033/3259 7833. Chic, elegant ambience and a celebrity chef from Britain make this the talk of the town, with an international menu including New Zealand lamb, tenderloin, salmon and a mixed grill for Rs1100; there's a good vegetarian selection, too.

Fire and Ice Kanak Building, 41 Chowringhee Rd ☏033/2288 4073, ⓦwww.fireandicepizzeria.com. A trendy bistro and bar with free wireless Internet that serves an excellent and authentic range of Italian cuisine including pizzas and *al fiumé* (fresh river prawns in olive oil); a full meal will set you back around Rs600. Can get packed in the evenings.

Flury's 18 Park St, on the corner of Middleton Row. A Kolkata landmark, this legendary Swiss teashop and patisserie has been completely revamped, swapping its flaky, laid-back atmosphere for a more modern but nouveau-riche style. Still worth visiting for its cakes, patties and Swiss pastries – try the rum balls – and its breakfast. They also make their own chocolates.

Gupta Brothers 42-A Park Mansions, Mirza Ghalib St. Excellent, clean and cheap vegetarian snack bar and sweet counter with a good Rajasthani restaurant upstairs. Try the tandoori *bharwan aloo*.

Ivory Block D, 5th Floor, Pantaloons Department Store, 22 Camac St. Chic dining on the top floor of this monument to consumerism; the mixed menu (from Rs600) is strong on Indian, but there's also Chinese and a "world" selection including the likes of Creole prawns and ratatouille.

Marco Polo in China 24 Park St. Plush restaurant serving good Cantonese and Szechuan food, including dim sum and seafood specialities including lobster and steamed fish; they also offer a good-value lunch buffet for Rs500.

Mocambo 25-B Park St, around the corner on Mirza Ghalib St. A long-standing restaurant that has grown from strength to strength and is now a firm favourite for its smart but relaxed ambience, good cooking and varied menu that runs from Chicken Kiev to pizzas.

One Step Up 18-A Park St. Bright bistro offering a range of options, from sandwiches and light meals to tandoori and pastries. Especially popular at lunch, but also good for an early evening drink.

Park 17 Park St ☏033/2249 3121. This upmarket hotel has developed a reputation for some of the finest dining in town. *Zen* serves dishes from Thailand, China, Japan and Indonesia; *Saffron* specializes in Indian cuisine; while the 24hr *Atrium* coffee bar also provides a good food menu.

Sourav's 20-G Park St, Middleton Row ☏033/2249 4646. Owned by the illustrious cricketer and a place of pilgrimage for Ganguly's fans, this modern complex of restaurants on four floors is topped with a swanky bar and nightclub. *One-Day* serves light meals including sandwiches, *dosas* and pizzas; *Over-Boundary* is a plush and pricey multi-cuisine restaurant, and there's also the vegetarian *Maharaj*.

Tangerine 2/1 Outram St ☏033/2281 5450. The first-floor windows take full advantage of its position opposite a park and give the restaurant a unique ambience, while the mixed menu is full of surprises, from Singapore noodles to *meen molily* (Keralan fish curry), and grilled lobster for Rs635.

Chandni Chowk and around

All the places listed below appear on the Kolkata map, pp.844–845.

Eau Chew P32 Mission Row Extension, Ganesh Chandra Ave ☏09830 141857. A legendary family-run restaurant and a remnant from the heydays of Chinatown, this unassuming place above a petrol station produces authentic Chinese food. The chimney stew, cooked slowly around a metal coal-burning container, is especially good, though you need to order in advance.

Amber 11 Waterloo St ☏033/2248 6520. A Kolkata landmark that refuses to fade away, serving celebrated Mughlai and tandoori cuisine. Plush and dimly lit, it covers three floors, with a bar downstairs.

India Coffee House 15 Bankim Chatterjee St (just off College St). Atmospheric, historic landmark café in the heart of the university area where students and intellectuals continue to meet.

AJC Bose Road and around

All the places listed below appear on the Kolkata map, pp.844–845.

Kewpie's Kitchen 2 Elgin Lane ☏033/2475 9880. Private home with a restaurant annexe, offering rich Bengali feasts fit for a *jamai babu* (son-in-law) first entering his wife's home – try their *lucci* (puris) and the fish and prawn preparations including *malai chingri* (prawns in cream) and *dab-er-chingri* (prawns in a green coconut). Closed Mon.

Suruchi 89 Elliot Rd. Run by the All Bengal Women's Union (®www.abwu.org), a charity for rehabilitated prostitutes and their children, and a good place to taste Bengali home-cooking. Unpretentious atmosphere and reasonable prices; highly recommended for lunch. Closed Sat and Sun evenings.

South Kolkata

All the places listed below appear on the Kolkata map, pp.844–845.

6 Ballygunge Place Ballygunge Place ☏033/2460 3922. One of a new breed of popular Bengali restaurants, with tasteful surroundings and a traditional homely ambience. Start with rice and *shuktoni* (bitter vegetables), follow with *doi bhekti* (fish in yoghurt) and end with *mishti doi* (sweet yoghurt).

Banana Leaf 73 Rashbehari Ave, Lake Market. Plain decor and a fast turnaround for this extremely popular restaurant that cooks up some of the best south Indian food in town.

Bay of Bengal 6 Dr Satyananda Roy Rd, near Menoka Cinema. A good place to taste Bengali home-cooking, with an à la carte menu as well as set platters including the luxurious Mahabhoj menu; specialities include *ilish* (a particularly delicate fish, best eaten in spring), *posto* (vegetables cooked with poppy seeds) and *mangsho jhol* (mutton curry).

Bhojohori Manna 18/1A Hindustan Rd ☏033/2466 3941. Popular chain serving Bengali food, with an emphasis on local cuisine but with a sprinkling of eclectic influences from other parts of the country, including tandoori – try the barbecued

▲ The Indian Coffee House

Sweet shops

Milk-based sweets such as the small and dry *sandesh* are a Bengali speciality. Though the white *rosogulla*, the brown (deep-fried) *pantua* and the distinctive black *kalojam*, all in syrup, are found elsewhere in north India, the best examples are made in Kolkata. Others worth trying are *lal doi* – a delicious red steamed yoghurt made with *jaggery* – or white *mishti doi*, made with sugar. Sweet shops serve savoury snacks in the afternoons such as deep-fried pastry strips called *nimki* (literally "salty"); *shingara*, a delicate Bengali samosa; and *dalpuri*, *paratha*-like bread made with lentils.

Amrita 16-A Sarat Bose Rd. Excellent *mishti doi*.

Bhim Chandra Nag Surya Sen Street, off College Street. Best of several good sweet shops in the area.

Ganguram 46-C Chowringhee Rd. Once-legendary sweet shop near Victoria Memorial, with branches all over the city; try *mishti doi* and *sandesh*.

KC Das 11 Esplanade East and 57-A Ripon St. The city's most famous sweet shop; try their *rosogolla*.

Sen Mahasay 171-H Rashbehari Ave. Next to Gariahat Market, renowned for its *sandesh*; there are several other branches throughout the city.

Vien 34-B Shakespeare Sarani. Small, popular sweet shop, with excellent *sandesh* amongst other offerings.

---

masala *bhekti* or stick to more traditional tastes. Expect to queue; there's another (smaller) branch on nearby Ekdalia Rd.

Elsewhere in the city

All the places listed below appear on the Kolkata map, pp.844–845.

Comesum South Station, Howrah Station. A spotless food-hall in Howrah's relatively placid annexe, offering sandwiches and pizzas as well as south Indian and Chinese food; the *Haldiram* counter offers hot *kachori* and great sweets.

Haldiram Bhujiwala 58 Chowringhee Rd. A snack bar, sweet shop and café all rolled into one, this self-service vegetarian chain offers good if predictable food, with everything from samosas, thalis (from Rs56) and *dosas* to ice cream. Other branches include one in Middleton Row and a

multi-floored supermarket on Gariahat Rd in Ballygunge.

Kim Fa 47 South Tangra Rd ☏033/2329 2895. One of Tangra's best Chinese restaurants – try the Thai soup, garlic prawns and chilli king prawns, which can be quite potent. If full, try *Lily's Kitchen* down the road.

Mainland China 3-A Gurusaday Rd ☏033/2287 2206. Chic Chinese restaurant with elegant service and excellent seafood; widely considered the city's finest, but perhaps a bit overdone, and for some, overcooked.

Royal Near Nakhoda Masjid, Rabindra Sarani. No trip to this area is complete without a visit to this legendary Muslim restaurant for a biriyani or a chicken or mutton *champ* (chop) cooked in aromatic spices and accompanied by rumali roti (thin "handkerchief" bread).

Drinking, nightlife and entertainment

The formerly tense, all–male atmosphere of Kolkata's **bars** is becoming a thing of the past, with designer-style places attracting a young, professional clientele. As well as the places below, the big hotels are a good option for a quiet drink; some of them also have discos. You'll sometimes hear Western live music at restaurants and bars, and Kolkata's spirited **arts scene** is known for its home-grown music – audiences here have a reputation as the most discerning in the country. The main concert season is winter to spring, with the huge week-long **Dover Lane Music Festival**, held in south Kolkata around the end of January and early February, attracting many of India's best musicians. Other popular venues for single- and multi-day festivals include Rabindra Sadan on the junction of AJC Bose Road and Cathedral Road, and Kala Bhavan on Theatre Road (Shakespeare Sarani). One of the country's leading North Indian classical music research institutes, **Sangeet Research Academy** in Tollygunge (℡033/2471 3395, ⓦwww.itcsra.org) offers long-term courses in various music forms, and holds free Wednesday-evening concerts. **All India Radio Calcutta** is a good source for Indian classical music, folk music and Rabindra Sangeet, the songs of Rabindranath Tagore.

Of the many nonreligious festivals each year, the **Ganga Utsav**, held over a few weeks around the end of January at Diamond Harbour, involves music, dance and theatrical events. Rabindra Sadan is Kolkata's theatre and concert hall district, with numerous venues including Nandan next door on AJC Bose Road, the city's leading art-house cinema. *Calcutta This Fortnight*, is a useful source for listings, as is *Cal Calling* and local papers.

Cinemas showing English-language films several times each day can be found along Chowringhee near Esplanade and New Market. All are air-conditioned; some, like the Lighthouse on Humayan Place, are fine examples of Art Deco. Names to look for include Inox, a modern multiplex at the Forum on Elgin Road; Elite, SN Banerjee Road; and Chaplin, Chowringhee Place. Nandan (℡033/2223 1210), behind Rabindra Sadan on AJC Bose Road, is the city's leading art-house cinema with a library, archives and three auditoria.

Bars and clubs

Bar-B-Q 43 Park St. Below the restaurant, this is one of the more stylish bars on the strip and the food is great.

Blue and Beyond 9th floor, *Hotel Lindsay*, 8-A Lindsay St. Best for a drink with the sun setting over the city and the bustle of New Market below.

Chowringhee Bar *Oberoi Grand*, Chowringhee Rd. Plush, quiet and elegant but at a price.

Fairlawn 13-A Sudder St. The beer garden with its nooks and crannies amidst the vegetation makes a pleasant setting for an evening drink.

Park Hotel 17 Park St. The hotel has a choice of bars and discos with *Tantra* still the liveliest nightclub in town where the action starts at 7pm most days and 4pm in the weekends; the dimly lit bar *Someplace Else* gets especially lively in the evenings when live bands belt out familiar Western and Indian covers; the pool-side *Aqua* is as much a

bar as a restaurant and features a DJ in the evenings.

Peter Cat 18-A Park St. Plush and pleasant ambience, with a good reputation as a place for a drink and for its wide-ranging menu.

Shisha 5th Floor, Block D, 22 Camac St. On the top floor of the shopping centre, the *Shisha* nightclub's *Hookah Bar* is the *in* place in Kolkata, with flavoured hookahs served by mock-Arabs and cigars for the less adventurous. There are also cocktails, mocktails and a resident DJ.

Sunset Bar *Lytton Hotel*, Sudder St. Friendly and relaxed bar, popular with travellers.

Underground *Hindusthan International Hotel*, 235/1 AJC Bose Rd. A popular disco with resident DJ, where the action starts late (9pm–3am).

Venom Fort Knox, 6 Camac St. All the rage in the evenings with a lounge bar as well as a dance floor where the DJ pumps out a variety of music from bhangra to hip-hop.

Shopping

Compared to Delhi, Kolkata has limited tourist shopping. However, there are many characterful **markets**, including the wide-ranging **New Market** (see p.856), as well as local institutions such as **Barabazaar** to the north (see p.860) and **Gariahat Market** near the Lakes in south Kolkata, which also has a colourful produce market in the early mornings. Modern **shopping complexes** – good for books, clothes, leather and jewellery – are cropping up all over the city; these include Pantaloons, 22 Camac St; Forum, 10/3 Elgin Rd;

Emami Shoppers City at Lord Sinha Road; the Metro Shopping Centre at 1 Ho Chi Minh Sarani; and the Shree Ram Arcade, opposite the Lighthouse near New Market.

Typical Bengali handicrafts to look out for include **metal** *dokra* items from the Shantiniketan region northwest of the city: animal and bird objects are roughly cast by a lost-wax process to give them a wiry look. Long-necked, pointy eared terracotta horses from Bankura, in all sizes, have become something of a cliché. *Kantha* **fabrics** display delicate line stitching in decorative patterns, while Bengali **leatherwork** features simple patterns dyed in subtle colours. Bengal boasts several good centres of cotton and **silk** weaving resulting in legendary **saris** such as the Baluchari style from Murshidabad.

Books

The month-long Kolkata Book Fair, held on the Maidan near Park Street in January and February, is now among the biggest of its kind in the country, and provides a good opportunity to pick up books at a discount. The shops and the roadside stalls of **College Street** are well worth a browse, with an occasional rare gem turning up.

Crossword 8 Elgin Rd. Large modern bookshop on two floors, with a good selection including novels, illustrated books and travel, plus a music section and a café.
Dey Bros B47 New Market. One of several bookshops in this part of the market selling popular books on India and a selection of novels.
Earthcare Books 10 Middleton St. At the back of a yard, a small and modest but focused bookshop that specializes in books on green issues, and publishes several titles too.
Family Book Shop 1-A Park St. On the Chowringhee end of Park St, this place is small but crammed full of books.

Landmark Emami Shoppers City, 3 Lord Sinha Rd. Modern and extensive bookshop in a popular shopping complex.
Oxford Book & Stationery 17 Park St. An upmarket a/c bookshop with a small music section and the *Cha Bar* café upstairs; despite the ambience the collection of fiction, coffee-table books, maps, guides, magazines, stationery and postcards is limited.
Seagull 31-A SP Mukherjee Rd ☎033/2476 5869, ⓦwww.seagullindia.com. Pleasant little bookshop owned by interesting and creative publishers; their resource centre, a block away, has a library and holds special exhibitions and events.

Emporia

Good selections of most handicrafts, including lace, can be found in various state **emporia**, many of which are located in the large **Dakhsinapan** shopping complex south of Dhakuria Bridge near Gol Park and the Lakes. Offering fixed (if slightly high) prices, these are the simplest places to start shopping.

Assam 8 Russel St. Part of Assam House, selling handicrafts and textiles from Assam including fabrics in *pat* and *moga*, two techniques of silk manufacturing.
Central Cottage Industries 7 Chowringhee Rd, Esplanade. Part of the national chain, with handicrafts, jewellery, silver, and fabrics from all over India, though the stock is a bit faded.
Gurjari Dakhsinapan complex. An outstanding

selection of Gujarati textiles, including handloom and mirrored cushion covers.
Nagaland 13 Shakespeare Sarani. A fine assortment of Naga shawls, with red bands and white and blue stripes on black backgrounds. As with Scots tartan, certain patterns denote particular tribes.
Sasha 27 Mirza Ghalib St. This women's self-help group has a good collection of handicrafts and textiles including *kantha*.

Fabrics and clothing

Kolkata's dress sense tends to be conservative but a wide range of fabric is available and outlets can direct you toward a good (and very cheap) **tailor**; there are several around Mirza Ghalib Street, New Market and Sudder Street. Upmarket boutiques such as Burlington's on Mirza Ghalib Street cater for the city's wealthy, as do department stores such as Pantaloons (see p.868), which have plenty of off-the-peg designer labels. Ritu's, 46-A Rafi Ahmed Kidwai Rd, specializes in chic *salwar kameez*. You can still get shoes made to order at one of the few remaining Chinese shoe shops around Chittaranjan Avenue.

Anokhi 2nd Floor, Forum, 10/3 Elgin Rd. Chic hand-printed cottons from this famous chain.
Balaram Saha 14/6 Gariahat Rd. Tangail, Baluchari and Kantha saris from Bengal.
Fabindia 234/3-A AJC Bose Rd. Good selection of hand-printed *kurtas* and *salwar kameez* as well as

shirts, fabrics and furnishings from this trendy chain boutique; they use natural dyes which run, so wash cool and separate colours. Another branch is at 16 Hindusthan Park near Gariahat.
Henry's New Market. One of Kolkata's better-known Chinese shoe shops.

Musical instruments

Kolkata is renowned for its **sitar** and **sarod** makers – expect to pay upwards of Rs8000 for a decent instrument, much more for a premium one. Shops around Sudder Street are strongest on Western instruments, but their traditional instruments are invariably of inferior quality and may be beyond tuning; Rabindra Sarani (Chitpore Road) has a concentration of shops of varying quality, many catering to the wedding-band trade. Kolkata must produce more tabla players than any other city; tabla makers can be found next to Kalighat Bridge and at Keshab Sen Street off College Street.

Hemen Roy & Sons Rashbehari Ave, Triangular Park. Once master instrument-makers to Ali Akbar Khan, the sarod maestro, though they've lost out to competition in recent years. They now make sitars and tanpuras (the drone instruments used to accompany singing).

Manoj Kumar Sardar & Bros 8-A Lalbazaar St, opposite Lalbazaar Police Station. Ashok Sardar makes very good sitars and sarods to order, with a small selection of off-the-shelf instruments including Indian-made guitars, and will ship them for you.

Sports

Sport is enthusiastically followed in Kolkata, with **football** matches – especially those between the two leading clubs, Mohan Bagan and East Bengal – and **cricket** test matches drawing huge crowds. There are two major stadium complexes, the **Ranji** at Eden Gardens and the new **Salt Lake** on the eastern edge of the city.

The **Maidan**, home to the Calcutta Bowling Club and the Ladies Golf Club, is a favourite venue for impromptu cricket and football matches, and the scene of regular race meetings in winter and spring. These are run by the Calcutta Turf Club, and bets can also be placed at their premises on Russel Street. Also in winter, army teams play **polo** at the grounds at the centre of the racecourse. The curious sport of **kabadi**, a fierce form of tag played by two teams on a pitch the size of a badminton court, can also be seen around the Maidan.

The easiest **swimming pool** for visitors to use is Calcutta Swimming Club, 1 Strand Rd (☎033/2248 2894), where you can apply for temporary membership. The *Hindusthan International Hotel*, 235-1 AJC Bose Rd (☎033/2247 2394), allows nonresidents to use their newly renovated pool on a daily basis (Rs500). Across the road from the superbly equipped *Tollygunge Club*, where (with the right connections) you might get to use the pool and tennis courts, the elite Royal Calcutta Golf Club is the world's second-oldest golf club, after St Andrews in Scotland.

Listings

Airlines, domestic Air Deccan ☏09831 677008; Indian Airlines, 39 Chittaranjan Ave ☏1407 & 033/2211 0730 (24hr with a tourist counter), airport office enquiries ☏033/2511 9272, recorded flight enquiries: general ☏1400, arrival ☏1402, departure ☏1403; Indigo ☏09910 383838; Jet Airways, 18-D Park St ☏033/3984 0000. airport enquiries ☏033/2511 9894; JetLite (Sahara), 2-A Shakespeare Sarani ☏033/3030 2020; Kingfisher Airlines ☏01800/1803333; Spicejet ☏0180 180333.

Airlines, international (* indicates international airlines with flights in and out of Kolkata) General airline/flight enquiries: ☏033/2511 8787 & 2511 9721; Aeroflot, 1st Floor, Lords Building, 7/1 Lord Sinha Rd ☏033/2282 3765; Air France, 230 AJC Bose Rd ☏033/2283 7982; Air India, 50 Chowringhee Rd ☏033/2242 2356–9*; American Airlines, Chitrakoot Building, 230 AJC Bose Rd ☏033/2280 1335; Austrian Airlines, Vasundhara Building, 2/7 Sarat Bose Rd ☏033/2474 5091; Bangladesh Biman, 55B Mirza Ghalib St ☏033/2227 6001*; British Airways ☏09831 377470 & 033/2511 8424*; Cathay Pacific, 1 Middleton St ☏033/2240 3211; Continental Airlines, Stic Travels, East Anglia House, 3C Camac St ☏033/2217 4913; Druk Air, 51 Tivoli Court, 1A Ballygunge Circular Rd ☏033/2280 5376*; Emirates Airlines, Trinity Towers, 83 Topsia Rd (South) ☏1800/233 2030*; Gulf Air, Chitrakoot Building, 230A AJC Bose Rd ☏033/2283 7996*; KLM, Jeevan Deep, 1 Middleton St ☏033/2283 0151*; Kuwait Airlines, Chitrakoot Building, 230 AJC Bose Rd ☏033/2247 4697; Lufthansa, T2 8A Millennium City, IT Park, Salt Lake ☏4002 42000 or 033/2511 2266*; Northwest Airlines, Jeevan Deep, 1 Middleton St ☏033/2283 0151; Qantas, 58 Chitrakoot Building, 230 AJC Bose Rd ☏033/2280 7777*; Royal Jordanian Airlines, Vasudhara Building, 2/7 Sarat Bose Rd ☏033/2474 5094*; Singapore Airlines, DN62, Unit 9A Millennium City, IT Park, Salt Lake ☏033/2367 5422*; Thai Airways International, 8th floor, Crescent Tower, 229 AJC Bose Rd ☏033/2280 1630*.

Ambulance Call ☏102, or the Dhanwantary Clinic ☏033/2449 3734; St John's Ambulance Brigade ☏033/2248 5277; or Bellevue Clinic ☏033/2247 2321.

Banks and currency exchange Kolkata airport has a 24hr branch of the State Bank of India, as well as Thomas Cook at the international terminal. Major banks, concentrated either in the vicinity of BBD Bagh or scattered around Chowringhee Rd, include Bank of America, 8 India Exchange Place; Banque Nationale de Paris, 4-A BBD Bagh East; Citibank, 43 Chowringhee Rd; State Bank of India, 1 Strand Rd and Kolkata airport. The ATM machines at some banks (such as most Axis branches, as well as HSBC at 3-A Shakespeare Sarani, HDFC at BBD Bagh East, and ICICI at 24-B Camac St) take MasterCard, Visa, Cirrus and Maestro. Other currency exchange bureaus include: Thomas Cook, Chitrakoot Building, 230 AJC Bose Rd (☏033/2247 5378), and American Express, 21 Old Court House St, near the West Bengal Tourist Office (☏033/2248 6283). There are numerous private foreign exchange bureaus around Sudder St and New Market.

Car rental Autoriders, 10-A Ho Chi Min Sarani ☏033/2282 3561; Avis, *Oberoi Grand* hotel, 15 Chowringhee Rd ☏033/2217 0147; Wentz, 2 Beck Bagan Row ☏033/3293 4634, and at the airport ☏033/3958 7217; Car-Cab, 2 Manook Lane, off Ezra St ☏033/2235 3535.

Consulates Bangladesh, 9 Circus Ave (Sheikh Mujib Sarani) ☏033/2290 5208; Canada, Duncan House, 31 Netaji Subhash Rd ☏033/2230 8515; France, 4th Floor, Sagar Estate, Clive Ghat St ☏033/2230 4571; Germany, 1 Hastings Park Rd ☏033/2479 1141; Italy, 3 Raja Santosh Rd, Alipore ☏033/2479 2414; Nepal, 1 National Library Ave, Alipore ☏033/2456 1224; Singapore, 8 AJC Bose Rd ☏033/2247 4990; Sri Lanka, Nicco House, 2 Hare St ☏033/2281 5354; Thailand, 18-B Mandeville Gardens ☏033/2440 7836; UK, 1 Ho Chi Minh Sarani ☏033/2242 5171 or 2288 5172; USA, 5/1 Ho Chi Minh Sarani ☏033/2282 3611 or 3984 2400.

Cultural centres International cultural representatives in Kolkata, typically with reading rooms and facilities for performances and film shows, include: the British Council, 16 Camac St ☏033/2282 5370; the Russian Gorky Sadan, Gorky Terrace, near Minto Park ☏033/2283 2742; the German Max Mueller Bhavan, 8 Pramathesh Barua Sarani ☏033/2486 6398; and USIS American Centre, 38-A Chowringhee Rd ☏033/2282 2336.

Homeopaths and herbal medicine Homeopaths include King & Co, 90/6-A MG Rd; Sterling & Co, 91-C Elliot Rd; and Murli Homoeo, 30-A Chowringhee Rd. Tibetan Medical & Astro Institute, 9 East Rd, Jadavpur, offer herbal treatments.

Hospitals Cheap, government-run hospitals are notoriously mismanaged, and private medical care, if expensive by comparison, is infinitely superior. In case of serious illness, you are best advised to contact your consulate. Good private clinics include Belle Vue, 9 Loudon St ☏033/2287 2321; Ruby

General, EM Bypass, Kasba ☎033/2442 0291; Woodlands Nursing Home, 8/5 Alipore Rd ☎033/2456 7075-89.

Internet Net access (from Rs15 an hour) is easily available throughout the city. Of the many places around Sudder St, try *Hotel Maria* and Netfreaks. Around the corner on Mirza Ghalib St, Sify iway is part of a dependable chain; a short walk south, Cyberia, 8 Kyd St, is also consistent.

Libraries Asiatic Society Library, 1 Park St; British Council Library, 16 Camac St (a monthly rate which includes borrowing books, use of the reference section and discounted Internet use); National Library, 1 Belvedere Rd; Ramakrishna Mission Library, Gol Park; University of Kolkata library, College Square. Seagull Arts and Media Resource Centre, 36-CSP Mukherjee Rd, near the Bhowanipur police station, has a small but pleasant and well-organized a/c library.

Permits and visas The Foreigners' Registration Office is at 237-A AJC Bose Rd (☎033/2247 3301).

Pharmacies Deys Medical Stores, 6 Lindsay St & 20-A Nelly Sengupta Sarani; Angel, 151 Park St (24hr); Dhanwantary Clinic, 65 Diamond Harbour Rd (24hr); Welmed, 4–1 Sambhunath Pandit St (24hr Mon & Tues).

Police ☎100. The central police station is on Lal Bazaar St, BBD Bagh ☎033/2241 3230. Others include Park St ☎033/2226 8321.

Postal services The GPO, on the west side of BBD Bagh, houses the poste restante and a philatelic department. If you're staying in the Sudder St area, the New Market Post Office, Mirza Ghalib St, is much more convenient. Sending parcels is easiest from the large and friendly post office on Park St, where enterprising individuals will handle the entire process for you for a negotiable fee. For a quicker service, DHL has several offices including 6 Kedia Villa, Marquis St ☎033/2217 1675. Poste restante is also available from India Tourism, Embassy Building, 4 Shakespeare Sarani, Kolkata 700 071.

State tourist offices The most useful of the many offices representing other states in Kolkata are those that cover the northeastern states (details of permit requirements can be found on p.962), and that of the Andaman and Nicobar islands. Andaman and Nicobar, 3-A Auckland Place ☎033/2283 1932 (permits are issued on arrival, but check before you go); Arunachal Pradesh, Block CE, 109 Sector 1, Salt Lake ☎033/2321 3627; Assam, 8 Russel St ☎033/2229 5094; Manipur, 26 Rowland Rd ☎033/2475 8075; Meghalaya, 120 Shantipally, EM Bypass ☎033/2441 1932; Mizoram, 24 Old Ballygunge Rd ☎033/2461 5887; Nagaland, 11 Shakespeare Sarani ☎033/2282 5247; Orissa, 41 & 55 Lenin Sarani ☎033/2216 4556; Sikkim, 4/1 Middleton St ☎033/2281 5328; Tripura, 1 Pretoria St ☎033/2282 5703. Another useful tourist office is that of the Darjeeling Gurkha Hill Council, India Tourism, 4 Shakespeare Sarani ☎033/2282 1715.

Tour Operators Ethically minded Help Tourism (☎033/2455 0917, ⊛www.helptourism.com) offers a wide range including the Sunderbans and wildlife tours in north Bengal. The flexible Kali Travel Home (☎033/2248 7980, ⊛www .traveleastindia.com) offers guided tours of Bengal and the northeast. Himalayan Footprints (☎033/2243 1063, ⊛www.trekinindia.com) offers informative and flexible wildlife tours, nature treks and trips to the Sunderbans, Sikkim and Darjeeling.

Travel agents Thomas Cook, Chitrakoot Building, 2nd Floor, 230 AJC Bose Rd (☎033/2247 5378), deals with inbound tours and international flights and foreign exchange. For domestic and international flights, there are numerous agents around Sudder St. Chocks-Off, 1 Cockburn Lane, off Royd St (☎033/2246 8780, ©chocks@cal3.vsnl.net.in), is very reliable and efficient for flights. Warren Travels, 31 Chowringhee Rd (☎033/2226 661 & 13), is a well-established service dealing with international and domestic flights, hotel bookings, group tours and travel documents.

Moving on from Kolkata

Transport connections via plane, rail and bus between Kolkata and the rest of India are summarized in "Travel details", p.903. If you're short of time, enlist one of the travel agents listed above to book plane, train or bus tickets. For information on **flights** from Kolkata airport, call ☎033/2511 8787; otherwise call the individual airlines listed on p.871 to confirm departure and arrival times.

Centralized information on train connections is available on ☎033/2230 3545/54 and ☎033/2230 3535. Making reservations to leave Kolkata by train is easy, with computerized booking offices throughout the city; you can also book online (see p.45) or through an agent. The best place to book tourist

⑬

quota train tickets is at the tourist office on the first floor of the Eastern Railways office, in the northwest corner of BBD Bagh at 6 Fairlie Place (Mon–Sat 10am–1pm & 1.30–5pm, Sun & hols 10am–2pm; ☏033/2222 4206). You'll need to bring proof of encashment (an exchange or ATM receipt) to reserve a berth if paying in rupees. Reservations up to sixty days in advance can be made for most trains out of the city.

There are several other booking offices (same hours) including the Booking Office for Eastern and South Eastern Railways, Alexandra Court, 61 Chowringhee Rd, Rabindra Sadan; Howrah Station, 1st Floor; Computerized Booking Office, 3 Koilaghat St; New Koilaghat, 14 Strand Rd; Sealdah Station, 1st Floor. For general reservation enquiries call ☏033/2230 3496, 1331 or 135.

The most famous highway out of the city is the fabled **Grand Trunk Road**, which runs via Varanasi and Delhi all the way to Peshawar in Pakistan. However although there have been some improvements to the highways west of the city, Bengal's roads are notoriously poor. For those willing to brave the 560km overnight journey to Siliguri – handy for Darjeeling and Sikkim – the best bus is the Royal Cruiser service (6.30pm; 12hr; Rs740 a/c) departing from the **Esplanade Bus Stand**. Other services leaving from Esplanade include Behrampur (for Murshidabad), Bishnupur, Malda and Rampurhat (for Tarapith). Several buses from here head to Basanti and the Sunderbans (especially early morning) and for points south to Diamond Harbour and beyond.

Frequent buses for Bhubaneswar and Puri in Orissa leave the **Babu Ghat Bus Stand**, where Orissa Roadways and West Bengal State Transport (☏033/241 6388) have booths.

To Bangladesh

Kolkata is the main gateway to Bangladesh from India. The **Bangladesh Consulate** is at 9 Circus Ave (Mon–Fri 9am–5pm; ☏033/2247 5208 ext 207 for visa section). Visas must be obtained in advance and will be issued on the same day if you submit your passport before 10am.

You can reach Bangladesh by train or road and there are several **flights** daily from Kolkata to Dhaka. Although there is no direct line from Kolkata into Bangladesh, trains from Sealdah take you as far as Bongaon. From here, you can take an auto-rickshaw to Haridaspur, 5km away, and then a rickshaw to Benapal on the border, where you can find inexpensive accommodation. The next morning take one of the frequent buses to Dhaka via Jessore (8hr). **Buses** run from Salt Lake International Karunamoyee terminal (☏033/2359 8448), a Rs120 taxi ride from the centre, to Dhaka (Mon–Sat 6.30am and 7am; 12hr; Rs1000). Several travel agents around Sudder and Marquis streets sell tickets for private buses to Dhaka, which depart from the Esplanade stand, but involve changes at the border.

To the Andaman Islands

Various airlines fly to Port Blair, with several daily services to choose from. Foreigners need permits to enter the Andaman Islands, available on arrival in Port Blair for $30 or the rupee equivalent. To go by sea (there are three to four sailings a month), you'll need to book through the Shipping Corporation of India, 13 Strand Rd (☏033/2248 2354); the journey takes three to five days, so bring plenty to read and food to supplement the dull meals. There are four classes, from bunk beds to a/c dorms and deluxe cabins. Of the three ships that sail the route, MV *Nicobar* is the most luxurious, and MV *Akbar* the cheapest. For more details on sailings, see Chapter 19.

Recommended trains from Kolkata

Destination	Name	No.	From	Departs	Total time
Allahabad	Kalka Mail	#2311	Howrah	7.40pm	13hr 30min
Bhubaneswar	Dhauli Express	#2821	Howrah	6am	7hr 5min
Bolpur	Shantiniketan Express	#2337	Howrah	10.10pm	2hr 15min
Chennai	Coromandel Express	#2841	Howrah	2.50pm	26hr 30min
Delhi	Rajdhani Express*	#2301**	Howrah	4.55pm	17hr 20min
	Rajdhani Express*	#2313	Sealdah	4.50pm	18hr 5min
Gaya	Poorva Express	#2381***	Howrah	8.20am	6hr 37min
	Mumbai Mail	#2321	Howrah	10pm	7hr 25min
Guwahati	Saraighat Express	#2345	Howrah	4pm	17hr 30min
Mumbai	Gitanjali Express	#2860	Howrah	2.10pm	31hr 20min
New Jalpaiguri	Darjeeling Mail	#2343	Sealdah	10.05pm	9hr 55min
(for Siliguri****)	Kanchenjunga Express	#5657	Sealdah	6.45am	11hr 35min
Patna	Lal Qila Express	#3111	Sealdah	8.15pm	10hr 15min
	Jan Shatabdi Express*	#2023**	Howrah	2.05pm	8hr 10min
Puri	Puri Express	#2837	Howrah	10.35pm	8hr 45min
Raxaul (for Birganj in Nepal)	Mithila Express	#3021	Howrah	3.45pm	16hr 40min
Varanasi	Vibhuti Express	#2333	Howrah	8pm	13hr 45min

*A/c only
**Except Sun
***Except Mon
**** Connect here for Darjeeling, Kalimpong and Gangtok; always check planned change in schedule to connect with the Toy Train.

Around Kolkata

For centuries, the River Hooghly served as a lifeline for foreign traders; north of Kolkata, its banks are dotted with the remnants of European settlements such as **Chandernagore**. All these sites, together with the Hindu temples of **Dakshineshwar** and **Belur Math**, and even the great Vaishnavite centres of **Nabadip** and **Mayapur** further north, can be taken in as day-trips on local trains from Kolkata's Sealdah and Howrah stations. Simple hotels are always available should you want to stay.

Dakshineshwar and Belur Math

At the edge of Kolkata, 20km north of Esplanade on the east bank of the river, the popular temple of **Dakshineshwar** stands in the shadow of Bally Bridge.

Built in 1855, it was a product of the Bengali Renaissance, consecrated at a time when growing numbers of middle-class Hindus were questioning their faith. Typical Bengali motifs – a curved roof reminiscent of local village huts, nine chhatris and beehive cupolas – dominate the design. The mystic and influential religious philosopher, **Ramakrishna**, once officiated here, and his room, beside the main gate, now preserves a collection of personal effects. Not far from the main temple, **Yogoday Satsanga Math** is the headquarters of the Self-Realization Fellowship, founded in California in 1925 by the author of *Autobiography of a Yogi*, **Paramahansa Yogananda**.

Across the bridge from Dakshineshwar, 3km south along the west bank of the Hooghly, is the serene forty-acre riverfront campus of **Belur Math** (April–Sept 6–11am & 4–7pm; Oct–March 6.30–11am & 3.30–6pm; free; ⓦ www.belurmath.org). Founded by a disciple of Ramakrishna, **Swami Vivekananda**, and completed (after his death) in 1938, the monastery houses temples and museums dedicated to the Mission. It incorporates elements from several world religions; the gate is inspired by early Buddhist sculpture, the windows by Islamic architecture, and the ground plan is based on the Christian cross. Local trains run from Sealdah to Bally Bridge adjacent to Dakshineshwar, and from Howrah to Belur Math.

Chandernagore

Some 35km north of Howrah, the former French outpost of **CHANDER-NAGORE** still bears traces of its colonial masters, who left in 1949 and officially ceded the town to India in 1952. Crumbling buildings along its grand riverside promenade, formerly the Quai Dupleix and now the **Strand**, include what was once the Hotel de Paris, while the Eglise du Sacré Coeur, set back from the river, houses an image of Joan of Arc. Nearby, the eighteenth-century mansion of the French administrator serves as the **Institut de Chandernagore** (Mon–Wed, Fri & Sat 4–6.30pm, Sun 11am–5pm; free), with a library, a French-language school and an interesting museum of documents, antiques, art and sculpture.

Nabadip

Pilgrims come in thousands to the pleasant little town of **NABADIP** (or Nawadip), on the west bank of the Hooghly, around 100km north of Howrah. Although it was the eleventh-century capital of Bengal under the Sen dynasty, and the home of Hindu sage **Sri Chaitanya** (1486–1533), few of the many temples clustered around its Mayapur Ghat are of any great antiquity. The courtyards of them all, however, are alive with devotees singing *kirtan* (devotional song). A fifty-kilometre *padakrama*, or foot pilgrimage, links Chaitanya with various sites spread across nine islands. It may be a Vaishnava town, but Nabadip's most atmospheric temple is the **Kali Bari** at Poramatolla, dedicated to the goddess, tucked into the folds of one of the most impressive banyan trees you are ever likely to see.

Trains from Howrah run to Nabadip, 2.5km from the main Boral *ghat* (Rs25 by cycle rickshaw).

South of Kolkata: the Sunderbans

South of Kolkata down to the coast, the Hooghly fringes one of the world's largest estuarine deltas, the **Sunderbans**, a 10,000-square-kilometre expanse of marshland, mangrove swamp and islets formed by silt swept down from the Himalayas. Its most southerly and remote districts have been designated a nature reserve to protect the region's abundant wildlife, which includes saltwater crocodiles, Gangetic dolphins, otters and the world's largest population of **tigers**. Closer to the city, on the east bank of the Hooghly, the other obvious target for a trip out of Kolkata is **Sagardwip**, the sacred spot where the Ganges officially debouches into the sea. An important pilgrimage place, it's reached via the former colonial port of **Diamond Harbour**.

Sajnekhali and the Sunderbans Tiger Reserve

The cluster of mangrove-covered islands known as the **Sunderbans**, or "beautiful forest", lie in the Ganges Delta, stretching east from the mouth of the Hooghly to Bangladesh. They are home to the legendary **Royal Bengal tiger**, a ferocious man-eater which has adapted remarkably well to this watery environment, swimming from island to island and covering distances of as much as 40km in one day. Other wildlife include wild boar, spotted deer, Olive Ridley sea turtles, sharks, dolphins and large estuarine crocodiles. Among the half-million or so people who find themselves sharing this delicate ecosystem with the mighty cats are honey collectors, woodcutters and fisherfolk. All, regardless of their official religion, worship Banbibi, the goddess of the forest, and her Muslim consort Dakshin Rai, supreme ruler of the Sunderbans; their occupations are so hazardous that wives remove their marriage ornaments when their husbands go out to hunt, fish or farm, becoming widows until they return. Honey collectors and woodcutters wear masks at the back of their heads in an effort to ward off the tigers, as they tend to attack by creeping up from behind when the victims aren't looking. Meanwhile, the women and children drag nets along the estuary shores to catch prawns – no less hazardous, considering they have to deal with crocodiles and sharks as well as tigers.

Practicalities

Foreigners require a permit (free) to visit the Sunderbans; if you're travelling to the area independently (tour companies will get them for you), get your permit in advance from the WB Tourist Centre in Kolkata (see p.848). You'll also need to book accommodation in the main camp of the **Sunderbans Tiger Reserve** (Rs15 to enter) at **SAJNEKHALI**, a small compound sealed off from the jungle by wire fencing. The *Sajnekhali Tourist Lodge* (☎03219/52562; ❸–❺) is a large, ramshackle forest lodge on stilts; rates include meals. The adjacent Project Tiger compound has a mini-zoo where they hatch turtles and crocodiles, a small museum and a watchtower. Food is left out for wild animals in the late afternoons, which invariably attracts deer and monkeys but rarely tigers. However, the cats have been known to jump the fence and it's advised not to venture out after dark. Other Sunderbans watchtowers stand at Sudhannyakhali, Haldi and Netidhopani, near the ruins of a four-hundred-year-old temple that's approached via caged pathways meant to protect you from the very real threat of tiger attack.

All **transport within the reserve** is by boat; these can be rented with the help of the lodge staff for around Rs1200 per whole day – you have to take along a Project Tiger guide (Rs200) and pay an entry fee (Rs50). The loud diesel motors tend to scare wildlife away, but when they cut their engines the silence is awesome.

The best times to visit are winter and spring. As getting to the Sunderbans from Kolkata is a laborious process, you might want to opt for an all-inclusive package tour booked through the West Bengal Tourist Centre (℡033/2248 5917). Two- and three-day packages with stays either on the boat or at the *Tourist Lodge* start from Rs1150. The cruises can get crowded, so don't expect peace and quiet; this also reduces the likelihood of seeing any animals. Tailor-made tours by private operators are more peaceful and leisurely: try Kali Travel Home (see p.872), or Neil Law of Himalayan Footprints (see p.872). Help Tourism (see p.872) have their own resort, the ⚲ *Sunderbans Jungle Camp* (❾) on Bali Island at the edge of the reserve, a development of thatched cottages tastefully combining local architecture with modern amenities. The camp employs local villagers, some of whom are ex-poachers, as staff and guides in a unique rehabilitation and self-help project; they also have their own boat. Prices (from Rs5000 for a three-day package) are steep, but the opportunity to get deep into the forest and the unique insight into the culture makes it worth a splurge. More commercial and less imaginative, the *Sunderban Tiger Camp* (℡033/3293 5749, ⓦ www.sunderbantigercamp.com; ❼–❽) in Dayapur near Gosaba, is in the core area of the reserve; most guests staying here are on one of the WBTC tours from Kolkata. The range of accommodation includes tents and comfortable a/c cottages. Two-day packages cost from Rs2400 per head including transport.

Getting to the Sunderbans using public transport is complicated, whether by train (from Sealdah; the route is outlined in reverse, below) or by bus. By road, start by catching a bus from Esplanade to Basanti (4 daily; 3hr); aim for the one at 7am. From Basanti, you cross by ferry to Gosaba, an hour-long trip through the delta. Sajnekhali is a six-kilometre cycle rickshaw ride from Gosaba. Finally, to reach the Project Tiger compound itself, and the *Tourist Lodge*, you have to cross the estuarine channel on a country boat from the further back and less likely looking of the two *ghats*. There isn't usually a lot of traffic around here, so you may have to wait or appeal to local boatmen.

Returning to Kolkata, allow plenty of time to make all the connections; the last bus leaves Basanti around 4pm. Alternatively, shared auto-scooters from Basanti can take you to Doc Ghat (30min), to pick up a boat across the river to Canning, and then a local train to Sealdah via Ballygunge station. If you're unlucky enough to find that the tide is out when you get to Canning, you're faced with a laborious 500-metre wade through calf-deep squelchy mud. A short walk through the town brings you to the station, where there are taps to wash off the mud. Your reward is the train ride itself, infinitely faster and more comfortable than the bus.

Along the Hooghly to the sea

The Hooghly reaches the Bay of Bengal at **DIAMOND HARBOUR**, 50km south of Kolkata. The harbour here was used by the East India Company, and a ruined fort is said to date back to Portuguese pirates. A two-week cultural festival, the **Ganga Utsav**, is held here towards the end of January – its theatre and dance performances are advertised in *Cal Calling* and *City Info* (see p.848). The trip down to Diamond Harbour from the city, by bus or train from Sealdah Station, is a popular day's excursion for Calcuttans, though it's also possible to stay the night at the *Sagarika Tourist Lodge* (❷–❺), which has some a/c rooms. Book through the tourist office on BBD Bagh (℡033/2248 8271). For a lot more luxury, the *Ffort Radisson Resort* at nearby Raichak (℡033/2280 0043, ⓦwww.ffort.com; ❾) offers an opulent taste of the Gangetic delta, river cruises, a health spa and fine cuisine; its day-trip packages are popular with middle-class Kolkatans especially at the weekends. Rooms start at $231.

Sagardwip, at the mouth of the Hooghly and accessible by ferry from Harwood Point near Diamond Harbour, is revered by Hindus as the point where the Ganges meets the sea. The confluence is venerated at the **Kapil Muni Temple**, on an island that bears the brunt of the savage Bay of Bengal cyclones and is gradually being submerged. On Makar Sankranti (mid-Jan), during the **Sagar Mela**, hundreds of thousands of pilgrims from all over India descend on the island, cramming into the water to bathe. A selection of small hotels, ashrams and *dharamshalas* offer basic accommodation, while the *Larika Sagar Vihar* (℡03210/240266; ❸–❹) provides slightly more comfort.

Central Bengal

A low-lying rural region where the pace of life is in stark contrast to that of Kolkata, **central Bengal** has a few sights to tempt tourists off the Kolkata–Darjeeling route. **Shantiniketan**, built on the site of Rabindranath Tagore's father's ashram, is a haven of peace, and a must for anyone interested in Bengali music, art and culture. The other highlights of the region include a cluster of exquisite terracotta temples in **Bishnupur**, the ruins of **Gaur**, the region's seventh-century capital, and the palaces of **Murshidabad**, capital of Bengal's last independent dynasty, supplanted by the British.

Bishnupur

BISHNUPUR, a sleepy backwater town 150km northwest of Kolkata, is a famous centre of Bengali learning, renowned above all for its exquisite **terracotta temples**. It was the capital of the Malla rajas, under whose patronage one of India's greatest schools of **music** developed. Largely beyond the sphere of Muslim influence in Bengal, Bishnupur's long tradition of temple-building had its roots in the basic form of the domestic hut. Translated into temple architecture, built of brick (as stone was rarely available) and faced with finely carved terracotta decoration often depicting scenes from the Ramayana, the temples combine striking simplicity of form with vibrant texture.

Several temples (daily 9am–5pm; all Rs100 [Rs5]) lie scattered around a wide area around Bishnupur. **Raas Mancha**, built in 1587 by Bir Hambir in a unique pyramidal style, is used to display the images of Krishna and Radha during the annual Raas festival. Nearby, the well-preserved **Shyamarai**, built in 1643, is a particularly fine example of terracotta art, while the smaller **Jorbangla** has fine detail. The unassuming tenth-century **Mrinmoyee temple** encloses the auspicious nababriksha, nine trees growing as one. To the north of town and dating from 1694, the **Madan Mohan**, with its domed central tower and scenes from the life of Krishna, is one of the largest.

Two express **trains** (#2883 & #2827) a day connect Bishnupur to Kolkata's Howrah Station; the best way to get around is a cycle rickshaw. First choice for **accommodation** in the centre is the extensive *Tourist Lodge* (℡03244/252013, reservations ℡033/2248 5168; ❸–❹), which also has a dorm (Rs80) and serves good meals; otherwise, there's *Udayan Lodge*, College Rd (℡03244/252278; ❸–❹), with a pretty garden.

Shantiniketan and around

Despite rapid growth and encroachment into the tribal Santhal habitat, the peaceful haven of **SHANTINIKETAN**, 136km northwest of Kolkata, remains a world away from the clamour and grime of the city. Founded by **Rabindranath Tagore** in 1921 on the site of his father's ashram, both the settlement and its liberal arts university **Vishwa Bharati** were designed to promote the best of Bengali culture. Towards the end of the Bengali Renaissance, Tagore's vision and immense talent inspired a whole way of life and art; the university and school still operate under this momentum. However, the university's image has been tarnished by the theft, in 2004, of Rabindranath Tagore's Nobel Prize from the museum; the culprit is yet to be found.

Centred around the **Uttarayan** complex of buildings, designed by Tagore, the university is very much in harmony with its surroundings, despite its recent growth as Calcuttans have settled or built holiday homes nearby. Well-known graduates include Indira Gandhi and Satyajit Ray, and departments such as **Kala Bhavan** (art) and **Sangeet Bhavan** (music) still attract students from all

---

Rabindranath Tagore

The Bengali poet and literary giant **Rabindranath Tagore** (1861–1941) has inspired generations of artists, poets and musicians. He developed an early interest in theatre, and set his poems to music – now, as Rabindra Sangeet, one of the most popular musical traditions in Bengal. Introduced to England and the West by the painter William Rothenstein and the poet W.B. Yeats, Tagore had his collection of poems, *Gitanjali*, first published in translation in 1912, and the following year was awarded the Nobel Prize for Literature. Though he preferred to write in Bengali, and encouraged authors in other Indian languages, he was also a master of English prose. Not until he was in his 70s did his talent as an artist and painter emerge, developed from scribblings on the borders of his manuscripts. Tagore was an enormous inspiration to many, including his students, the illustrious painter Nandalal Bose, and later the film-maker Satyajit Ray, who based several of his films on the works of the master.

over the world. The **Kala Bhavan Archive** (daily except Tues 10am–5pm; free, with special permission from the head of department) houses twentieth-century Bengali sculpture and painting, including works by eminent artists such as Abanendranath and Gaganendranath Tagore, Nandalal Bose and Rabindranath Tagore himself, as well as a collection of Chinese and Japanese art. The **Vichitra Museum** (daily 10.30am–1pm & 2–4.30pm, Tues open am only, closed Wed; Rs5), also known as the Rabindra Bhavan Museum, captures the spirit of Tagore's life and work with a collection of his paintings, manuscripts and personal effects.

Some 3km west, **Shriniketan** (daily 10am–4.30pm, Tues open am only, closed Wed; free) is another important subdivision of the university, established by Tagore as a rural reconstruction programme fostering self-reliance, with emphasis on local crafts and agriculture. The crafts and ceramics produced here are sold through the Amarkutir outlet on the Siuri Road; the leather goods are particularly distinctive.

The large fair of **Poush Mela** (also known as Poush Utsav) is held at Shantiniketan's fairground between December 22 and 25 to commemorate the initiation of Rabindranath Tagore's father, Maharishi Debendranath Tagore, into the Brahmo Samaj. It features Santhal sports, dances and music, but is most renowned for the **Bauls**, Bengal's wandering minstrels who have created their own unique style of folk music; their Muslim counterparts, *fakirs*, also perform here. Another good place to hear Bauls is at the informal **shanibarer haat** (Sat market; 3–5pm) held under the trees by Shriniketan's canal; tribals sell produce and crafts.

Practicalities

Bolpur, 3km south of Shantiniketan, is the nearest railway station, on the main line between Kolkata and Darjeeling, served by several trains via Burddhaman (or Burdwan). The best train for Bolpur from Kolkata is the Shantiniketan Express #2337, which leaves Howrah at 10.10am and terminates at Bolpur at 12.25pm, departing for Howrah half an hour later. Baul singers occasionally busk in second-class carriages. and there's a resident Baul in the regular a/c first-class coach.

If you're heading on from Shantiniketan **to Darjeeling**, the best of the many express trains is the Darjeeling Mail, which stops late at night (00.34am) in Bolpur but arrives in New Jalpaiguri (NJP) at 8am the next morning. The best daytime train is the Kanchenjunga Express #5657, which departs at 9.40am and arrives at NJP at 6.20pm, which normally means a night's stay in the Siliguri area before moving on to Darjeeling or Sikkim. **Reservations** are available from the Shantiniketan reservations counter (Mon–Sat 10am–3pm) near the post office; **quotas** from here are tiny but do include some upper-class seats – so book early. There's a computerized reservations counter at Bolpur Station which links you into the national network and offers more choice. Palataka Travels, on Netaji Road in Bolpur (☎03643/254148), arranges air tickets and car rental. The main **bus stand** is at Jamboni, 2km west towards Surul. Cycle rickshaws are the chief means of transport in the area, but the best way to experience Shantiniketan is to cycle – ask at your hotel or at one of the bicycle shops along the main road. If you need **Internet** access there are a couple of slow places at Ratanpalli market.

For **currency exchange**, there's a State Bank of India at the main crossroads in Shantiniketan, and selection of ATM machines on the main road midway between Bolpur and Shantiniketan.

The Shantiniketan area holds a reasonable amount of **accommodation**, with several options along the noisy main Shantiniketan–Bolpur road, and more appealing places around the fringes of the campus. Though some of the better **restaurants** offer multi-cuisine menus, they tend to be strongest on local cuisine, especially fish – try the garden restaurant at the *Park Guest House*. *Ghare Baire* at the Gitanjali Complex on Siuri Road is as smart as it gets in Shantiniketan, with upmarket Bengali cuisine, while at Ratanpalli, the delightful little garden café *Alcha* combines a bookshop, a library (Rs200 for membership), a gallery and a small but excellent boutique selling clothes and furnishings; it's also good for late breakfasts and lunch.

Accommodation

Bolpur Lodge Bolpur ☎03463/252662. Large, long-established and welcoming lodge, set away from the bustle of the main road with a pleasant courtyard, large plain good-value rooms and a reasonable restaurant. ②–③
Bonpulak Shyambati ☎03463/261193. Three pleasant, airy rooms in a friendly family home with a small, colourful garden; meals on request. ③
Chhuti 241 Charu Palli, Jamboni ☎03463/252692, ⑩chhutiresort.com. Comfortable and well laid out cottages with an ethnic touch, some with a/c, and a restaurant. The

most luxurious option around Shantiniketan; credit cards accepted. ⑤–⑥
Hotel Shantiniketan Bhubandanga ☎03463/254434. Bright pink hotel with a pleasant garden and a quiet location down a lane; the cheaper rooms are better value but hot water comes by the bucket and all doubles have twin beds. ③–④
Shantiniketan Tourist Lodge Bolpur Tourist Lodge Rd ☎03463/252699. Large government-run place with some a/c rooms, a dorm (Rs100), very good value cottages, a pleasant garden and a restaurant which once enjoyed a better reputation. ③–⑤

Tarapith

One of the most important centres of Tantric Hinduism, **TARAPITH**, lies 50km north of Shantiniketan. The temple and cremation ground, in a grove beside the river, are popular with Tantric sadhus, and it's not uncommon to witness rituals involving skulls and cremation ashes. The temple itself is a simple building dedicated to Shakti as the mysterious and feared goddess Tara, who appears here with a silver face and large eyes; shrines litter the area, and the grove is populated by monkeys. Of Tarapith's hotels, the friendly *Sathi* (☎03461/253287; ③–⑤) has large attached rooms, while *Sonar Bangla* (☎03461/253827; ③–⑤) offers slightly more comfort and a great restaurant; there's a pleasant *dharamshala* near the temple. Of the several **trains**, the Azimganj Express #3017 departs Howrah at 6.05am and arrives at **Rampurhat** railway station, 8km north of Tarapith, at 10.20am; the 4.45pm Rampurhat Express #2348 returns via Shantiniketan. Buses, shared Vikrams (auto–rickshaw taxis) and taxis make the 10km journey between Tarapith and Rampurhat. There are occasional direct buses from Tarapith to Jasidih in Jharkand; otherwise change at Rampurhat.

Kendubilwa

The town of **KENDUBILWA**, also known as **Kenduli**, on the bank of a wide shallow river 42km from Shantiniketan, is the birthplace of **Jaidev**, the author of *Gita Govinda*, and the spiritual home of the Bauls. Its small terracotta temple is engulfed each year in mid-January when the **Jaidev Mela** attracts streams of pilgrims, as well as a collection of *yogis* and sadhus who gather amongst the banyan trees to hear the Bauls perform through the night. Over the years the *mela* has grown to include a wide range of stalls and a funfair. During the *mela*, special buses leave regularly from Bolpur (2hr).

Murshidabad

Set 219km north of Kolkata in the brilliant green landscape of rural Bengal and close to the commercial town of **Behrampur**, **MURSHIDABAD** represents the grand and final expression of independent Bengal before the arrival of the British. Several eighteenth-century monuments along the banks of the Hooghly stand as melancholic reminders of its days as the last independent capital of Bengal. Established early in the eighteenth century by the **Nawab Murshid Quli Khan**, Murshidabad was soon eclipsed when the forces of Siraj-ud-Daula were defeated by Robert Clive at the Battle of Plassey in 1757, as a result of which the British came to dominate Bengal from the new city of Calcutta. Clive described Murshidabad as equal to London, with several palaces and seven hundred mosques; today it's not even a city, and its past glory lies in ruins, though it is still renowned for cottage industries, especially silk weaving.

Murshidabad's intriguing mixture of cultures is reflected in its architectural styles, which range from the Italianate **Hazarduari**, the nawab's palace, designed by General Duncan Macleod of the Bengal Engineers, to the **Katra Mosque**, built by Murshid Quli Khan in the style of the mosque at Mecca. The palace, with its mirrored banqueting hall, circular durbar room, armoury and library of fine manuscripts, is now a museum (daily except Fri 10am–4.30pm; Rs100 [Rs15]); some of the paintings are in dire need of restoration, but the portrait collection is excellent. A large oxbow lake, the **Moti Jheel** or **Pearl Lake**, guards the desolate ruins of Begum Ghaseti's palace, where Siraj-ud-Daula reigned before his defeat, and which was subsequently occupied for a while by Clive. To the south, across the river, **Khushbagh**, the **Garden of Delight**, holds the tombs of many of the nawabs, including Alivardi Khan and Siraj-ud-Daula.

Practicalities

Accommodation in Murshidabad is limited, with the friendly and welcoming *Hotel Manjusha* near Hazarduari (☎03482/270321; ❷–❹) offering rooms with balconies and a colourful flower garden right on the river. **Behrampur**, 12km away on the busy north–south highway and easily accessible by auto-rickshaw or bus, has far more amenities, including the welcoming *Behrampore Lodge*, 30/31 RN Tagore Rd (☎03482/252952; ❸–❹), which serves meals. The *Samrat* (☎03482/251147; ❷–❺), on the main highway some 3km south of the centre at Panchanantatala, handy for the Murshidabad turn-off, offers a wider range of accommodation, from plain doubles to carpeted a/c rooms, and has an a/c restaurant-bar and a pleasant garden. Transport between Behrampur and Murshidabad includes buses, shared Vikrams and autos. A few **trains** run to Behrampur from Kolkata (Sealdah Station; 4–6hr), including the Lalgola Passenger, which also stops at Murshidabad; there is more choice from Azimganj, 20km and a Rs600 taxi-ride away. Frequent **buses** from Behrampur Station depart for Kolkata's Esplanade (5–6hr), as well as Malda (3hr 30min).

Malda and around

Famous for its mangos, the large, unattractive commercial town of **MALDA**, 340km north of Kolkata, makes a good base to explore the historic sites of **Gaur** and **Pandua**, both earlier capitals of Bengal. Malda is on the main line between Kolkata and north Bengal, served by several good **trains** such as the Kanchenjunga Express #5657/5658. There is a choice of **accommodation** along Station Road, including the budget *Manohar* (☎03512/265515; ❸), which has small rooms with attached baths, and a good if basic restaurant, while on the main NH-34 highway, the *Purbanchal* (☎03512/266183; ❸–❹) offers more comfort, with some a/c rooms, one of the better restaurants in town and a dimly lit bar. Taxis to both Gaur and Pandua charge around Rs1200 for the day.

Gaur

Spread across a landscape of lush paddy fields, 16km south of Malda, **GAUR** was the seventh-century capital of King Sasanka, and then successively belonged to the Buddhist Pals and the Senas. The latter, the last Hindu kings of Bengal, were violently displaced by the Muslims at the start of the thirteenth century. The city was sacked in 1537 by Sher Shah Sur, and its remaining inhabitants wiped out by plague in 1575.

Gaur lay buried in silt for centuries, but excavations have revealed the extensive remains of a city that once boasted over a million inhabitants. Recent finds include a vast brick **palace** complete with waterways and a mint. A *ghat* with chains for anchoring barges suggests that the River Ganges may have once flowed past the palace. Elsewhere, Gaur's sites include various large tanks, such as 1.5km long **Sagar Dighi** from 1126, and the embankments, extending for several kilometres through the rural landscape. From the Muslim period, **Dakhil Darwaza**, an impressive red-brick gateway built in 1425, leads into the **Fort**, in the southeast corner of which a colossal wall encloses the ruins of the old palace. Nearby are the **Qadam Rasul Mosque**, built in 1531 to contain the Prophet's footprint in stone, and the seventeenth-century tomb of Fateh Khan, one of Aurangzeb's generals, in Bengali hut style. Other remains include the elegant **Tantipara Mosque**, with its finely detailed terracotta decoration, the Lattan or **Painted Mosque**, where traces remain of the enamelled bricks that gave it its name, and the massive **Bara Sona Masjid**, "Great Golden Mosque", northeast of the Fort.

Pandua

The splendid **Adina Masjid** at **PANDUA**, 18km north of Malda, built around 1370, was the largest mosque in the Subcontinent in its day. It now lies in ruins, but these still betray the origin of much of the building materials – carved basalt masonry from earlier Hindu temples was used to support 88 brick-built arches and 378 identical small domes, the design following that of the great eighth-century mosque of Damascus. Other monuments include the **Eklakhi mausoleum** – one of the first square brick tombs in Bengal, with a carved Ganesh on the doorway; and **Qutb Shahi Masjid**, or the Golden Mosque, built to honour saint Nur Qutb-ul-Alam whose ruined shrine is nearby together with that of Saint Hazrat Shah Jalal Tabrizi.

North Bengal

NORTH BENGAL, where the Himalayas soar from the flat alluvial plains towards Nepal, Sikkim and Bhutan, holds some magnificent mountain panoramas, and also some of India's most attractive **hill stations**. Most visitors pass as quickly as possible through **Siliguri** en route to **Darjeeling**, **Kalimpong** and the small, mountainous state of Sikkim. If you've time on your hands, it's worth making a detour east of Siliguri to explore the sub-Himalayan **Dooars**, with its patchwork of tea gardens and forests that encompasses the **Jaldapara Wildlife Sanctuary**, home to the one-horned rhino, bison and wild boar.

Besides the occasional strike, few travellers will notice anything of the political turmoil that wracks the region. The Gurkhaland movement, centred around Darjeeling, and the Kamtapuri Liberation Front, which purports to represent most of North Bengal south to Malda, have called for a complete break from the state of West Bengal.

Siliguri and New Jalpaiguri

A major commercial hub and Bengal's second city, ever-expanding **SILIGURI** has a thriving tea-auction centre and serves as the gateway to Darjeeling, Kalimpong, Sikkim and Bhutan. Together with its main railway station, **NEW**

The Darjeeling Himalayan Railway: the Toy Train

Completed in 1881, the small-gauge (2ft or 610mm) **Darjeeling Himalayan Railway** was designed as an extension of the North Bengal State Railway, climbing from **New Jalpaiguri**, via **Siliguri**, for a tortuous 88km up to **Darjeeling**. Given World Heritage status by UNESCO in 1999, the **Toy Train** (as it's affectionately called) follows the Hill Cart Road, crossing it at regular intervals and even sharing it with traffic. Pulled by endearingly ancient blue steam engines, some over 75 years old, the Toy Train is no longer an essential mode of transport, and has survived due to its unique historical importance and tourist appeal.

Weather permitting, first-class coaches with large viewing windows provide magnificent views as the six-hour journey from the plains progresses and the scenery gradually unfolds; second class can be fun but crowded. At the high pass at Jore bungalow near Ghoom (2438m), 7km short of Darjeeling, the dramatic panorama of the Kanchenjunga Range is suddenly revealed. Just beyond Ghoom, the train does a complete circle at the Batasia Loop – the most dramatic of the three loops encountered along the way; another method used to gain rapid height are the **reversing stations** where the track follows a "Z" shape.

Some travellers, however, find this claustrophobic and painfully slow ride a real test of endurance, especially after an overnight journey from Kolkata to Siliguri. An alternative is to take a short ride from Darjeeling to Ghoom, just 7km up the track (see box, p.897) from where you can visit a few monasteries and either walk, take a taxi, bus or the train back to Darjeeling.

For more **information** on the Toy Train, contact Secretary of the Darjeeling Himalayan Railway Society (Ⓦwww.dhrs.org), David Mead, at 43 Geraldine Rd, Malvern, Worcestershire WR14 3NT, UK, or, in India, the Director at Elysia Building, near Himali School, Kurseong 734203 (Ⓣ0354/200 5734 Ⓦwww.dhr.in).

JALPAIGURI – commonly referred to as NJP – and the airport at **Bagdogra**, it forms an unavoidable link between the rail and air connections to Kolkata and Delhi, and the roads up into the mountains. The border with Nepal at **Kakarbitta** nearby is open to tourists, though the bus journey from there to Kathmandu is an arduous one.

Most tourists pass straight through Siliguri, but travel connections may mean that you have to stop overnight. Besides teeming bazaars such as Bidhan Market, there's little of interest to see. A small Tibetan enclave 2km or so from the centre on Sevoke Road houses the impressive **Tashi Gomang Stupa** (daily 5am–noon & 1–5pm) and a traditional Tibetan centre where delicious fragrances rise as medicine-makers pound fresh herbs and spices.

Practicalities

Bagdogra airport, 12km west of Siliguri, is served by flights from Delhi, Kolkata and Guwahati; there's also a helicopter service from here to Gangtok in Sikkim (weather permitting; see p.886). Taxis booked through the **pre-paid** counter run directly to Siliguri (Rs310), Darjeeling (Rs1180), Kalimpong (Rs1040) and Gangtok (Rs1500), though you can negotiate cheaper fares from the stand outside the gates. Siliguri does have its own railway station, used by the Toy Train, but the **New Jalpaiguri** (**NJP**) Station, 4km east, is the main rail junction in the region, with trains to and from Kolkata, Delhi and Assam. Cycle and auto-rickshaws (Rs35 and Rs90) ply the route between NJP and Siliguri, battling through the often-gridlocked market, while shared Vikrams (auto-taxis) charge Rs30 a seat; taxis charge up to Rs300 but should officially be less. Use the pre-paid booth outside the main station for local and long-distance journeys in auto-rickshaws as well as taxis: a reserved taxi to Darjeeling costs Rs1140 and to Gangtok Rs1547, while a seat in a Jeep to Siliguri costs Rs90. Most buses arriving at Siliguri terminate at the **Tenzing Norgay Bus Terminal** on Hill Cart Road at Pradhan Nagar, close to most hotels and taxis to Darjeeling.

The Government of West Bengal's **tourist office** (Mon–Fri 10.30am–4pm; ☏0353/251 1974), opposite the bus station on Pradhan Nagar, provides information and can book rooms in tourist lodges in places like Jaldapara Wildlife Sanctuary. Upstairs, commercial wings WBTDC (Mon–Fri 10.30am–4pm, Sat 10.30am–1pm; ☏0353/251 1974) are far more helpful. There are also tourist office counters at NJP station and the airport. Siliguri's best private tour operator, Help Tourism, First Floor, Malati Bhavan, 143 Hill Cart Rd (☏0353/253 5892, ⓦwww.helptourism.com), organizes wildlife tours, village home-stays, and treks and tours off the beaten track.

Opposite the bus stand in the same compound as Sikkim Nationalized Transport, **Sikkim Tourism** (Mon–Sat 10am–4pm; ☏0353/251 2646), provides information and **Sikkim permits** (see p.932). To **change money**, try the bureau at the *Delhi Hotel* across from the bus terminal on Hill Cart Road, or the State Bank of India, Mangaldeep Building, Hill Cart Road. There are several ATMs which take Visa, Cirrus, Maestro and MasterCard, including the handy HDFC at the Malhotra Towers building, on the approach to Siliguri from the north, and others opposite the *Manila Hotel* on Hill Cart Road and around Sevoke Mor. The main **post office** is on Kacheri Road, with branches near the Central Railway Booking Office and the bus terminal.

The best **restaurants** are located in hotels such as the *Vinayak* and *Saluja* along Hill Cart Road, both serving fine Chinese and Indian cuisine; at the northern end, the *Penguin* at *Hotel Central Plaza* is a cheerful place with a varied menu. There's also the excellent *Khana Khazana* café, at Pradhan Nagar opposite the bus terminal, which has everything from *dosas* to pizzas.

For Bengali cuisine, try the basic but legendary *Kalpataru Pice Hotel*, Rani Tanki More, Sevoke Road, famous for fish; it has a sister branch, *Kalpana Pice*, at Bidhan Market.

In terms of **accommodation**, note that some of the cheap hotels around the bus terminal – the *Delhi* and the *Shere-e-Punjab* in particular – have dubious reputations, especially in their treatment of women guests.

Accommodation

Apsara 18 Patel Rd ☎0353/251 4252. Down a lane parallel to the main road and opposite Tenzing Norgay Bus Terminal, this is a friendly and helpful Tibetan-run budget hotel, handy for transport links and amenities and with basic, clean rooms, all of which have attached baths. ❷–❸

Chancellor Sevoke Mor, corner of Sevoke and Hill Cart roads ☎0353/243 2372. Welcoming and safe Tibetan-run hotel in the busy heart of town, with a quieter block at the back. Rooms are plain but decent, and there's good Tibetan, Chinese and Indian food. ❷–❸

Holydon NJP Station Rd ☎0353/269 1335. Friendly and inexpensive hotel that's the closest decent place to the railway station, with some a/c rooms, a restaurant and a bar that can get busy in the evenings. ❷–❺

Manila Pradhan Nagar ☎0353/251 9342. Spotless modern hotel close to the taxi and bus stand, with attentive service, comfortable rooms, money exchange, and a good restaurant; if it's full, try the similar *Heritage* next door. ❹–❺

Marinas Naxalbari Rd, Bagdogra ☎0353/255 1371. A pleasant garden hotel, handy both for the airport (with free transfers) as well as the Nepal border at Kakarbitta. The reasonably priced rooms all have attached baths, and there's a restaurant and a bar. ❸–❻

Saluja Hill Cart Rd ☎0353/243 1684. Right in the city centre, with a wide range of rooms from budget ones sharing baths to comfortable doubles; the *Parivar* restaurant is excellent, and for a bit more comfort try its big sister, the *Saluja Residency* next door. ❷–❹

Sinclairs Pradhan Nagar ☎0353/251 7674, ⓦwww.sinclairshotels.com. Upmarket old hotel that remains popular for its convenient location on the road to Darjeeling. Comfortable, large refurbished rooms and complementary breakfast, a good restaurant, a garden and a (summer only) swimming pool. ❼–❽

Vinayak Hill Cart Rd ☎0353/243 1130. A reliable mid-range hotel conveniently located in the centre of town yet close to the taxi stands, with a choice of small but adequate rooms including some with a/c. The restaurant downstairs serves good Indian food. ❸–❻

Moving on from Siliguri

Indian Airlines, Jet Airways, Kingfisher and the budget Air Deccan fly from **Bagdogra** to **Kolkata**, **Delhi** and **Guwahati**. For tickets, try Travel & Rental, Sevoke More (☎0353/253 8749); Jet Airways has its own office in the *Hotel Vinayak*, Hill Cart Road (☎0353/243 1495). Helicopter flights to **Gangtok** (Rs2200) leave from Bagdogra around 1.30pm, weather permitting, with a maximum baggage allowance of 10kg; the sole Siliguri agent is the ever-helpful Tourist Service Agency (TSA) in Pradhan Nagar, the lane opposite the bus terminal (☎0353/251 0872) ; they also arrange other flights and tickets on to Kathmandu (see opposite).

All major **trains**, most terminating or starting at Guwahati, use NJP Station, not Siliguri. Reservations can be made at NJP railway station or the **Central Railway Booking Office** (daily 8am–4pm), Bidhan Road, near Kanchenjunga Stadium in Siliguri. The best train to **Kolkata** is the Darjeeling Mail #3143/3144, which terminates at Sealdah, while the most convenient for **Delhi** is the efficient Rajdhani Express #2423 (25hr 30min), which also passes through Patna with connections for Gaya and Bodhgaya; the Rajdhani #2435 (Mon, Tues, Fri & Sat) stops at Varanasi, while on other days take the Rajdhani #2423 and change at Mughal Sarai.

The easiest way to get to **Darjeeling** is by **shared Jeep**. These depart from in front of NJP Station, and Sevoke More and Tenzing Norgay Bus Terminal in Siliguri, where Jeep transport syndicates have their own ticket booths and the prices are fixed. Taxis to Darjeeling depart when full, take 3–5 hours and cost Rs90 per seat. For a bit more comfort, take two seats up in front or a whole taxi (negotiate with returning taxis for reduced rates). Other options include the **Toy Train** (leaving Siliguri at 9am, arriving Darjeeling around 3pm; second class Rs47, first class Rs242), or a bus from Tenzing Norgay Bus Terminal. Regular buses and shared Jeeps also run to **Kalimpong** (Rs80) and to **Gangtok** (Rs120).

Overnight "luxury" **buses** to **Kolkata** (12hr), such as the Rocket Bus and Royal Cruiser, are cheaper than the train (bus tickets Rs300 or Rs740 for a/c), and have the advantage of depositing you in Esplanade, near the central Sudder Street area. However the roads are dire, so be prepared for a severe rattling. Buses also run from Siliguri to Kolkata, Patna and Guwahati. **Sikkim Nationalized Transport**, opposite the bus terminus in Pradhan Nagar (daily 6am–4pm; ☏0353/251 1496), runs a service to **Gangtok** (departures 8.30am, 9.30am & 11.30am), and other points in Sikkim. Get a Sikkim **permit** (see p.932) from Sikkim Tourism next door; shared Jeeps are also obtainable here.

Buses also run to **Phuntsoling**, on the border of **Bhutan**, just 160km away, as well as 176km further on to the capital, Thimpu, and to **Guwahati** in Assam, although the train is far more comfortable. Frequent buses also travel to Chalsa and Madarihat, convenient for the wildlife sanctuaries.

To reach **Kathmandu** in Nepal, travel to **Panitanki**, the crossing (24hrs) on the Indian side of the border, and use a cycle rickshaw (Rs30) to get to the Nepalese side at **Kakarbitta** (6am–7pm). Shared taxis (Rs50), regular buses from the terminal or outside it (from Rs20) and taxis (Rs600) travel to Panitanki, where you can pick up a **Nepalese visa** for $30 in cash. The advantage of pausing in Kakarbitta is that it gives you a greater choice of onward **buses** to Kathmandu (17hrs; Nepalese Rs530); agencies like the TSA in Siliguri offer the convenience of through-connections. For a lot more luxury and around $122, take a **flight** from **Bhadrapur** (25km and a 45-minute taxi ride from Kakarbitta) to Kathmandu with Buddha Air or Yet Airlines. Flights can be booked through agencies like the TSA or at Kakarbitta itself.

Gorumara and Jaldapara

Apart from Darjeeling and the hills, most of North Bengal is well off the beaten track, and few travellers make detours from the Darjeeling–Sikkim–Nepal route. Probably the best reason to do so is to visit one of the string of **wildlife sanctuaries** carpeting the **Dooars** along the southern approaches to the Himalayas. **Gorumara National Park**, 80km to the east of Siliguri, is renowned for its elephants, highly endangered greater one-horned rhinoceros and bison, along with a host of other animals and birds, and has become one of the state's most popular attractions. Closed during the monsoons (mid-June to mid-Sept), Gorumara covers just 80 square kilometres, but together with neighbouring **Chapramari Wildlife Sanctuary**, its varied habitat – from grasslands to deep jungle cover – means a good record of animal sightings; your best chance is from watchtowers like that at Jatraprasad (Rs100). Entry to the park (Rs80 [Rs40]) is by Jeep, arranged at the entry point at **LATAGURI**. **Accommodation** here includes the pleasant *Silver Ridge Resort*

(☎09932 904028; ❹), with a garden and cottages close to the gates. Some 2km from **Chalsa**, a busy town on the main east–west highway, the *Gorumara Jungle Camp* (❼) is a self-help initiative organized by Help Tourism's Siliguri office (see p.885), with rustic cottages ranged around the site of an old saw mill. Rates include food and guided excursions into the forests. If you're after a bit more luxury (such as a swimming pool), there's the *Sinclairs Retreat* (☎03562/260282; ❼), in a gated compound at Chalsa. Buses travel regularly from Chalsa to Siliguri as well as to Lataguri; while Chalsa has a railway station, nearby **New Mal Junction** has better connections with Siliguri.

Further east at 124km from Siliguri, **Jaldapara Wildlife Sanctuary** was established in 1943 to protect wildlife from the encroachment of tea cultivation. Set against a backdrop of forested foothills on the banks of the River Torsa, Jadalpara's 216 square kilometres hold large tracts of tall elephant grass and is home to around fifty one-horned rhinoceros, as well as wild elephants, sambar and hog deer. The park's great charm is its elephant rides (Rs120), which are by far the best way to explore. The sanctuary is open from October to the end of April, with March being the best month to view animals, as they graze on new shoots. A handful of buses and trains run from Siliguri to the town of **Madarihat**, 7km from the reserve and 1km from the sanctuary gates, from where taxis run to **Hollong** in the heart of the forest for around Rs150. **Accommodation** and **food** are available at the *Jaldapara Tourist Lodge* at Madarihat (☎03563/262230; ❺), or at the *Hollong Forest Lodge* (☎03563/262228; ❺); both must be booked through the WB tourist offices in Siliguri, Darjeeling or Kolkata. A pleasant alternative is the private *Traveller's Haven Tourist Lodge* (☎03563/262210; ❹–❺) with cottages and its own watchtower on the edge of the forest. Note that a Rs100 [Rs25] fee is payable at the entrance to the park.

Darjeeling

Part Victorian holiday resort, part major tea-growing centre, **DARJEELING** (from *Dorje Ling*, "the place of the thunderbolt") straddles a ridge 2200m up in the Himalayas and almost 600km north of Kolkata. Over fifty years after the British departed, the town remains as popular as ever with holiday-makers from the plains, and promenades such as the Mall and the Chowrasta still burst with life. The greatest appeal for visitors has to be its stupendous mountain vistas – with Kanchenjunga (the third-highest mountain in the world) and a vast cohort of ice-capped peaks dominating the northern horizon. However, the infrastructure created under the Raj has been unable to cope with the ever-expanding population – there are acute shortages of water and electricity, and chaos on the hopelessly inadequate roads – and despite Darjeeling's cosmopolitan atmosphere and charm, the town is slowly but surely being swamped by its rampant, uncontrolled growth. It remains a colourful and lively place, however, with good shopping and dining, plenty of walks in the surrounding hills and attractions such as the Toy Train and the many thriving Buddhist monasteries. Darjeeling has a considerable **Tibetan** presence and, like Dharamsala in Himachal Pradesh, offers opportunities to study Tibetan culture. The best seasons to visit – and to attempt the magnificent trek to Sandakphu to see Everest – are after the monsoons and before winter (late Sept to late Nov), and spring (mid-Feb to May).

Until the nineteenth century, Darjeeling belonged to **Sikkim**. However in 1817, after a disastrous war with Nepal, Sikkim was forced to concede the right to use

▲ Tea pickers in Darjeeling

the site as a health sanatorium to the **British**, who had helped to broker a peace settlement. Darjeeling soon became the most popular of all hill resorts, especially after the Hill Cart Road was built in 1839 to link it with Siliguri. **Tea** arrived a few years later, and with it an influx of Nepalese labourers and the disappearance of the forests that previously carpeted the hillsides. The town's growing economic significance led Britain to force a treaty on the Sikkimese in 1861, thereby annexing Darjeeling and Kalimpong. In the early 1900s, Darjeeling's reputation as one of the most glamorous and far-flung outposts of the British Empire attracted socialites and adventurers. Subsequently it became a centre for mountaineering and played a key role in the conquest of the greater Himalayas.

After Independence, the region joined West Bengal, administered from Calcutta, but calls for autonomy grew, taking shape in the **Gurkhaland** movement of the 1980s. Led by the **Gurkha National Liberation Front (GNLF)** under Subhash Ghising, a long and frequently violent campaign ended in the late 1980s in what some see as a compromise. Today, the GNLF controls the Darjeeling Gurkha Hill Council (DGHC), under the aegis of the West Bengal government, but running many vital services. Although Darjeeling has been enjoying a period of relative calm fuelled by a buoyant tourism industry, the formation of the **Gorkha Jana Mukti Morcha (GJMM)** in 2007 gave the Ghurka movement a new champion, reinvigorating their cause and challenging Ghising's twenty-year reign via accusations of despotism.

Arrival, information and transport

Virtually all travellers arriving in Darjeeling from the plains come via Siliguri, whether by the Toy Train or road transport. Jeeps and buses stop at the **bus stand** in the lower half of the town, from where it's a bit of an uphill trek to the main hotel area. Most taxis and some Jeeps drop you off at **Clubside** near the **Mall** (officially Nehru Road), at the upper end of town. Porters are available (from Rs60) at the bus stand and bazaar, but be careful as some act as touts. Darjeeling is best explored on foot – in fact much of it, such as the Mall and the Chowrasta, is closed to all vehicles.

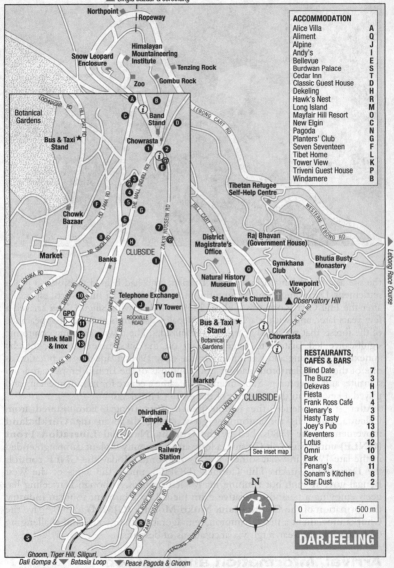

The map contains the following labels:

Singla Bazaar & Jorethang

Northpoint | Ropeway

Snow Leopard Enclosure

Himalayan Mountaineering Institute

Tenzing Rock

Zoo — Gombu Rock

ACCOMMODATION

Alice Villa	A
Aliment	Q
Alpine	J
Andy's	I
Bellevue	E
Burdwan Palace	S
Cedar Inn	T
Classic Guest House	D
Dekeling	H
Hawk's Nest	R
Long Island	M
Mayfair Hill Resort	O
New Elgin	C
Pagoda	N
Planters' Club	G
Seven Seventeen	F
Tibet Home	L
Tower View	K
Triveni Guest House	P
Windamere	B

Botanical Gardens

LOCHNAGAR RD

HILL CART RD

Bus & Taxi Stand

Band Stand

Chowrasta

LEBONG CART RD

WESTERN LEBONG RD

Lebong Race Course

JP SHARMA RD

DR LAMA RD

Chowk Bazaar

THE MALL (NEHRU RD)

ZAKIR HUSSEIN RD

Tibetan Refugee Self-Help Centre

HILL CART RD

Market

NG SEORKA RD

Banks

NB SINGH RD

CLUBSIDE

District Magistrate's Office

Raj Bhavan (Government House)

Bhutia Busty Monastery

Gymkhana Club

HILL CART RD

GANDHI RD

LADEN LA RD

COOCH BEHAR RD

JP SHARMA RD

Telephone Exchange

TV Tower

Natural History Museum

St Andrew's Church

Viewpoint

Observatory Hill

CR DAS RD

GPO

ROCKVILLE ROAD

Rink Mall & Inox

SM DAS RD

Bus & Taxi Stand

Botanical Gardens

Chowrasta

0   100 m

Market

RESTAURANTS, CAFÉS & BARS

Blind Date	7
The Buzz	3
Dekevas	H
Fiesta	1
Frank Ross Café	4
Glenary's	3
Hasty Tasty	5
Joey's Pub	13
Keventers	6
Lotus	12
Omni	10
Park	9
Penang's	11
Sonam's Kitchen	8
Star Dust	2

CLUBSIDE

Dhirdham Temple

LADEN LA RD

GANDHI ROAD

Railway Station

See inset map

N

0   500 m

DARJEELING

HILL CART RD

DB GIRI RD

AC BOSE ROAD

DR ZAKIR HUSSEIN RD

TENZING NORGAY RD

Ghoom, Tiger Hill, Siliguri, Dali Gompa & Batasia Loop

Peace Pagoda & Ghoom

The **Tourist Bureau**, 1 The Mall (Mon–Fri 10am–4.30pm; ☎0354/225 4102), is on Chowrasta above the Indian Airlines office; the more pro-active **DGHC Tourism** has its main office at Silver Fir, 100m to the north of Chowrasta on Bhanu Sarani (daily 9am–5pm; ☎0354/225 4879), where the helpful Micky is a font of knowledge on tours, treks, transport and whitewater rafting on the River Teesta (from Rs350); they also supply a very useful leaflet with maps of the Sandakphu trails. The DGHC booths at Clubside and the railway station are of limited use.

Foreigners planning to head on to **Sikkim** will have to get a **permit**. Travelling to Gangtok, you can get an initial fifteen-day permit instantly at the **Rangpo** border checkpoint (but not at the Naya Bazaar crossing for West Sikkim) and extend it once in Sikkim (see p.932). Getting a permit in Darjeeling allows you the option of travelling directly to West Sikkim on a hair-raising 27-kilometre road descending through tea plantations to Jorethang via Naya Bazaar. To get your permit here, pick up a form from the **District Magistrate's Office** (Mon–Fri 10am–4pm) on Hill Cart Road near Loreto Convent; take it to be stamped at the **Foreigners' Registration Office** (daily 10am–6pm) on Laden La Road, returning to the DM's office for the final stamp. The process is a formality and quite easy but does involve legwork.

Accommodation

Darjeeling has over five hundred hotels, and new ones spring up all the time, placing further strains upon the infrastructure. The main thing to establish before you check in anywhere is the **water** situation; many cheaper places only provide water in buckets, and charge extra if you like it hot. Off-season (late June to Sept & late Nov to April) **discounts** can be fifty percent.

Budget

Aliment 40 Dr Zakir Hussein Rd ☎0354/225 5068. Popular travellers' hang-out with friendly management and Internet access, but plain and somewhat expensive rooms. The restaurant upstairs is the best in this part of town. ❸–❹

Alpine 104/1 Rockville Rd ☎0354/225 6355. A good range of clean rooms with attached baths which, like all the others around here, don't represent good value for money at the height of season. ❹–❺

Andy's 102 Dr Zakir Hussein Rd ☎0354/225 3125. Run by a retired couple, this is the best of the ridge-top guesthouses: safe, with large, immaculate rooms and great views towards Kalimpong and Bhutan, but no restaurant. ❷–❸

Long Island 11/A/2 Dr Zakir Hussein Rd ☎0354/225 2043. Just beyond the *Tower View* and above the road, this is a friendly place with some of the best budget rooms on the ridge-top, most with shared baths and hot water by the bucket. The family-run *Kimchi* café serves genuine Korean food, and there is a good trekking service. ❷–❹

Pagoda 1 Upper Beechwood Rd ☎0354/225 3498. Though the area is no longer the haunt of budget travellers, this is a quiet, central spot close to Laden La Rd and the post office. Keenly priced rooms, a fire in the lounge and free hot water by the bucket. ❷–❸

Tibet Home Manjushree Centre, 12 Gandhi Rd ☎0354/225 6714. The nonprofit cultural centre offers a range of rooms, from basic windowless doubles in the basement with shared baths to large, well-appointed doubles with attached baths and hot water. ❸–❺

Tower View 8/1 Dr Zakir Hussein Rd ☎0354/225 4452. A friendly place near the TV tower, with a restaurant and cheap cubbyholes plus a couple of pleasant wood-lined rooms; there is also a dorm (Rs70). ❷–❸

Triveni Guest House 85/1 Dr Zakir Hussein Rd ☎0354/225 3878. Plain, roomier and a bit cheaper than the *Aliment* opposite, but not as popular. Friendly, with a restaurant and nice views from the sun deck. ❷

Mid-range

Alice Villa 41 HD Lama Rd ☎0354/225 4181. Central and long-established, with a comfortable modern block. The two immaculate duplex suites in the characterful old wing are extremely good value, especially with off-season discounts, so book ahead. ❹–❺

Bellevue The Mall ☎0354/225 4075. Above the tourist bureau, and dominating the Chowrasta, this is not as grand as it once was, but remains pleasant enough, with low-key service and airy wood-lined rooms. ❹–❻

Classic Guest House CR Das Rd ☎0354/225 7025. A handful of clean, comfortable and amply sized rooms with verandas and dramatic views. Conveniently located just a couple of minutes below Chowrasta. ❺–❻

Dekeling 51 Gandhi Rd, above the popular *Dekevas* restaurant ☎0354/225 4159, ✉norbu@dekeling.com. A great central location and comfortable rooms with running hot water – the timbered ones upstairs are charming; good off-season discounts. The Tibetan owners are especially helpful and there is a welcoming log fire. ❹–❻

Travel, trek and tour operators

Clubside Tours and Travels JP Sharma Road ☏0354/225 4646, ⒺＣclubside@satyam .net.in. Established and reliable company dealing with airline tickets, tours and trekking.

Himalayan Adventures Das Studios, 15 Nehru Rd ☏0354/225 4090, Ⓦdastrek.com. Upmarket international agency that organizes treks in Sikkim, Bhutan and Tibet.

Himalayan Travels 18 Gandhi Rd ☏0354/225 6956, or 09434 209847. An efficient organization run by the affable K.K. Gurung, offering tours and treks throughout Darjeeling, Sikkim and Bhutan. Runs the Sandakphu trekking huts and organizes a special Toy Train service from Kurseong.

Pineridge Travels Nehru Road, Chowrasta ☏0354/225 3912. Specialist for domestic and international air tickets including flights to Kathmandu from Kakarbitta/Bhadrapur.

Sandakphu Sikkim Tours & Trek *Hotel Long Island*, 11/A/2 Dr Zakir Hussein Rd ☏09434 467443 & 20 Chowrasta ☏09733 044986. A good local agency for the Sandakphu trek; owner Pritam puts some profits into the Child Welfare Society.

Tenzing Norgay Adventures DB Giri Road ☏0354/225 3058. An efficient, international organization run by Tenzing Norgay's celebrated son, Jamling: excellent for trekking and mountaineering.

Trek-Mate Singalila Arcade, Nehru Road ☏0354/225 6611, or 09832 083241, ⒺＣchagpori@satyam.net.in. Tsewang Trogawa runs this very helpful agency arranging treks to Sandakphu and West Sikkim. They provide guides and porters and rent out sleeping bags, down jackets and day packs, and organize day-treks as well as village homestays near Tukdah.

Planters' Club The Mall ☏0354/225 4348. A local landmark (also known as the *Darjeeling Club*) with old-fashioned rooms, coal fires (Rs100), a billiard room, bar, restaurant and library. Residential guests must take temporary membership (Rs50); non-guests can use the facilities for Rs100. ❺–❻

Seven Seventeen HD Lama Rd ☏0354/225 5099. Extensive, well-run hotel with comfortable airy rooms, despite the location just above the bazaar that means no mountain views. Exchange facilities and credit cards are accepted for un-discounted rooms; there is a cheaper annexe up the road. ❻–❼

Expensive

Burdwan Palace Rosebank ☏09831 196161. Stay in splendour at this blue-domed palace set far below the Hill Cart Rd and approached by a very steep road. The huge rooms stuffed with antiques and hunting trophies are filled with a charm set firmly in the 1930s; the high price includes all meals and transport, including pick-up from the airport. From $350. ❾

Cedar Inn Jalapahar Rd (Dr Zakir Hussein Rd) ☏0354/225 4446, ⒺＣcedarinn@satyam.net.in. An unusual position high above town, a steep 15min walk from the centre, this new mock-gothic hotel has plush wood-lined rooms complete with fireplaces and grand views; there's also a pleasant lounge bar, restaurant and garden. ❽

Hawk's Nest 2 AJC Bose Rd ☏0354/225 3092, Ⓦwww.dekeling.com. Four luxury suites with fireplaces and tasteful decor in a delightful old Tibetan-owned colonial villa; well worth the short walk out of town. Good home-cooking and a warm welcome. ❼

Mayfair Hill Resort Below Government House, The Mall ☏0354/225 6376, ⒺＣdarjeeling @mayfairhotels.com. Once a maharaja's summer retreat, the rooms and garden cottages here offer ostentatious luxury. Facilities include a restaurant and health spa; the gardens are immaculate, with some quirky statuary. From $210. ❾

New Elgin 32 HD Lama Rd ☏0354/225 4114, Ⓦwww.elginhotels.com. Premier hotel, opulent and well maintained, with good facilities and an old-fashioned, formal atmosphere that captures the spirit of Darjeeling. Rates include all meals, and the tea service is the best in town. From $142. ❾

Windamere Observatory Hill ☏0354/225 4041, Ⓦwww.windamerehotel.com. The most iconic and celebrated of Darjeeling's hotels has accommodated a pantheon of rich and famous guests in its old-world cottages decked out with Raj memorabilia; it now has a brand-new wing with comfortable modern suites. Expensive, but well worth a visit for tea on the lawn or the occasional concert. From $188. ❾

The Town

The heart of Victorian Darjeeling is the **Chowrasta**, a traffic-free square above the busy bazaar on Hill Cart Road. One of four main roads leading off it is the **Mall** (also called Nehru Road) which descends from Chowrasta to Clubside, the area below the prestigious **Planters' Club**. Established in 1868, otherwise known as the **Darjeeling Club**, this venerable institution was the centre of Darjeeling high society. Not much seems to have changed since the days when tea planters from all over the territory rode here to attend social occasions. Visitors who take temporary membership are welcome to stay, and facilities such as the bar and snooker room are available for a day-use fee.

Taking the right fork of the Mall from the northern end of the Chowrasta, near the bandstand, brings you to the **viewpoint** from where you can survey the Kanchenjunga massif and almost the entire state of Sikkim. From near the *Windamere Hotel* steps, ascend the pine-covered hillside to the top of **Observatory Hill**, the original site of the Bhutia Busty monastery. Streaming with prayer flags, the shrine at the summit, dedicated to the wrathful Buddhist deity Mahakala, whom Hindus worship as Shiva, reflects a garish hybrid of styles. The picturesque **Bhutia Busty Monastery** was re-established one kilometre downhill from the Chowrasta approached by the steep CR Das Road. Another faded Raj-era institution, the **Gymkhana Club** (☎0354/225 4342), stands near Observatory Hill. Casual visitors drop in to play billiards, snooker, badminton, table tennis, tennis, squash and even to roller-skate (Rs50 for day membership plus nominal game charges), or take advantage of the small library, bar and bridge tables.

Darjeeling tea

Although the original appeal of Darjeeling for the British was as a hill resort with easy access from the plains, inspired by their success in Assam they soon realized its potential for growing **tea**. Today, the Darjeeling tea industry continues to flourish, producing China Jat, China Hybrid and Hybrid Assam. A combination of factors, including altitude and sporadic rainfall, have resulted in a relatively small yield – only three percent of India's total – but the delicate black tea produced here is considered to be one of the finest in the world. It is also some of the most expensive – in 2003 a tea from Makaibari, an estate near Kurseong, sold at auction for an astronomical Rs18,000 a kilo.

Grades such as Flowery Orange Pekoe (FOP) or Broken Orange Pekoe (BOP) are determined by quality and length of leaf as it is withered, crushed, fermented and dried. To watch the process for yourself, call in at the **Happy Valley Tea Estate** (Tues–Sat 8am–noon & 1–4.30pm, Sun 8am–noon; free); it's a 30-minute-walk from town – follow the signs from the Hill Cart Road near the District Magistrate's office. As for **buying**, try the tea stores on the Chowrasta; The House of Tea on the Mall and Tea Cosy at the Rink Mall offer try-before-you-buy, with the latter's menu set clearly by the seasons (otherwise known as "flushes"). However, for the best price and an enthusiastic explanation of tea, explore the labyrinth of Chowk Bazaar to find Radhika & Son near the Laxmi Bhandar. Such vendors usually trade in unblended tea bought directly from tea gardens and are able to pick and choose according to quality. The typical cost of a kilo of good middle-grade tea is Rs600–700. You can get a taste of the opulence of a tea-manager's lifestyle by staying at Glenburn, off the Kalimpong road (☎033/2288 5630, ⓦwww.glenburnteaestate.com; ❾ $400 all-inclusive); for a less exclusive experience of life on a tea estate, try Makaibari **homestays** (book through Help Tourism on ☎033/2485 4584; ❻–❼).

Below the club, the small and little-visited **Natural History Museum** (daily except Thurs 10am–4.30pm; Rs5) holds a large collection of moths and butter-flies, stuffed animals and birds, and a natural-habitat display complete with sound effects. Further away from Chowrasta, a steep drop down from Government House, lies the **Tibetan Refugee Self-Help Centre** (closed Sun). Founded in 1959, it houses seven hundred refugees, most of whom make carpets or Tibetan handicrafts. Tourists are welcome to watch the activities and buy clothes, hats, leatherwork, excellent carpets, and Tibetan boots made of embroidered cloth with leather soles.

A kilometre further north towards the mountains and before the Gothic ramparts of **St Joseph's College**, Darjeeling's **Zoo** (daily except Thurs 8.30am–4pm; Rs100 [Rs10], combined with HMI ticket), with an emphasis on conservation, is well maintained and worth a visit. The zoo's Snow Leopard Breeding Centre (closed to the public), established in 1986, is the only place in the world to have successfully bred this endangered species, while Project Panda has produced several Red Panda; endangered Tibetan wolves have also been bred here.

The **Himalayan Mountaineering Institute** (**HMI**), reached via the zoo and covered by the same ticket, is one of India's most important training centres for mountaineers, holding numerous courses (Indians only). Its first director was **Sherpa Tenzing Norgay**, Sir Edmund Hillary's climbing partner on the first successful ascent of Everest, who lived and died in Darjeeling, and is buried in the Institute's grounds. In the heart of the leafy complex, the **HMI Museum** (daily except Thurs 9am–4.30pm; included in ticket price) is dedicated to the history of mountaineering, with equipment old and new, a relief map of the Himalayas, and a collection of costumes of hill people. The **Everest Museum** in the annexe recounts the history of ascents on the world's highest peak, from Mallory and Irvine's ill-fated 1924 expedition, to Tenzing and Hillary's triumph in 1953 and the record-breaking 20-hour 24-minute climb by Kaji Sherpa in 1998.

Back in town, Lochnagar Road winds down from the bus stand in the bazaar to enter the **Botanical Gardens**, where pines, willows and maples cover the hillside and pleasant walks zigzag down to the slightly dilapidated central green-houses, filled with ferns and orchids. One final prominent sight you're bound to notice is the multi-roofed **Dhirdham Temple**, below the railway station, built as a replica of the great Shiva temple of Pashupatinath on the outskirts of

---

Mountaineering

Although there are plenty of opportunities for trekking around Darjeeling, you can also take things a step further by joining one of the mountaineering courses run by the **HMI** (☎ 0354/225 4087; see above). Lasting 28 days and costing $650, the basic and advanced courses are run with military precision and provide a challenging introduction to climbing in the Sikkim Himalayas. After a short preparation, you trek to their Chaurikhang Base Camp at the foot of Rathong Glacier, where a gruelling programme of acclimatization and climbing on the glacier culminates with an attempt at a sub-6000m summit. The more rewarding advanced course requires previous mountaineering experience; to join either course, you must be aged between 17 and 40. Course fees include accommodation, food, instruction, basic equipment including sleeping bags and transport to and from the start of treks. The HMI also rents cheap and basic equipment to those not on one of their courses; gear rented by Trek-Mate (see p.892) is of better quality; shops in the same arcade sell cheap imitations of big brands including new sleeping bags from Rs800.

Kathmandu. Heading out of town on AJC Bose Road you come to the discreetly hidden **Nipponjan Myohoji Buddhist Temple** (daily 4.30am–7pm; prayers at 4.30am & 4.30pm), usually referred to as the Peace Pagoda, with great views over the valley to Kanchenjunga.

Eating and drinking

Darjeeling has plenty of choice for **eating out**, with the touristy places concentrated around the top of town. Many of the hotels, such as the *Windamere* and *New Elgin*, have good multi-cuisine restaurants, and the latter has a superb tea service; and budget hotels such as the *Triveni* and *Aliment* provide traveller-friendly meals.

Blind Date Fancy Market, 12 NB Singh Rd. Very popular with students and locals as well as Thais, a friendly upstairs restaurant with an open kitchen and great *momos*, *taipao* and crispy chicken.

Dekevas 51 Gandhi Rd. Popular with travellers and locals alike, this no-smoking restaurant with pleasant Tibetan decor offers the usual mixed menu, including a wide range of Tibetan dishes and a very good value breakfast.

Glenary's The Mall. Darjeeling's most reputable eating place serves up tasty sizzlers and the best tandoori in town. There's also a great coffee shop and patisserie with an Internet café; in the basement, *The Buzz* is an American-style bar with a pool table, which also serves burgers and pizzas.

Hasty Tasty The Mall. Offering Indian fast food, and very popular with Indian holiday-makers, this self-service place serves tasty cheese *dosas* and

superb veg thalis. However the service is hardly hasty.

Keventers Clubside. A landmark café serving toasted sandwiches, and fried breakfasts that include bacon and ham. The terrace above the crossroads is excellent for people-watching, even if the service is poor. A delicatessen downstairs sells cheese, ham and sausages.

Lotus Dr SM Das Rd. Good and reasonably priced Chinese food; the pork in rice wine or the chicken with shitaki mushrooms are especially good.

Park 41 Laden La Rd. Darjeeling's finest North Indian and tandoori cuisine, served in plush surroundings; there's also an annexe, *Lemon Grass*, offering good Thai food.

Penang's Opposite the GPO, above Laden La Rd. Cheap, grubby but popular local haunt; as much a bar as a café, serves excellent *momos* and *thukpa*.

Listings

Banks and exchange The State Bank of India (Mon–Fri 10am–4pm, Sat 10am–1pm; Rs100 per transaction), Laden La Rd, is slow and only accepts American Express or Thomas Cook traveller's cheques in US dollars and pounds. Licensed private foreign-exchange vendors are a bit more flexible but charge around four percent more than the bank rate. Amongst these, the *Hotel Mohit* and *Hotel Seven Seventeen* are both on HD Lama Rd. Poddar's, 8 Laden La Rd near the GPO, is also good for cash advances on credit/debit cards. There are several ATMs along Laden La Rd and at the Rink Mall, including ICICI, HDFC and State Bank of India, which also has a handy booth on the Chowrasta.

Bookshops Oxford Books & Stationery, Chowrasta, has an excellent selection of novels and coffee-table books.

Car rental Darjeeling Transport Corporation, Laden La Rd (☎0354/225 2074), is one of the more established operators; numerous others are centred around Clubside.

Cinema Inox, Rink Mall (☎0354/225 7183). A modern new multiplex with three auditoria and the latest from Bollywood and Hollywood.

Hospital Try Planters' Hospital, Planter's Club, The Mall ☎0354/225 4327; Mariam Nursing Home, The Mall ☎0354/225 4327. The Tibetan Medical & Astro Institute, *Hotel Seven Seventeen*, 26 HD Lama Rd (☎0354/225 4735), is part of the Dalai Lama's medical organization, Men-Tsee-Khang, and has a clinic and a well-stocked dispensary. There is also a Women's Clinic (Mon–Sat 1.30–5pm, Sun 10am–1pm) under *Hotel Springburn*, 70 Gandhi Rd.

Internet access Of the numerous Internet cafés, those at *Glenary's* and *Hotel Bellevue* (both Rs30/hr) are the most central and convenient.

Pharmacies Frank Ross & Co, The Mall. There are several more pharmacies clustered around Sadar Hospital above the bus stand.

Photography Das Studios and Darjeeling Photo Stores are both on the Mall, and Photo Stop is near the Chowrasta.

Post office The main post office (Mon–Fri 9am–5pm & Sat 9am–noon) is on Laden La Rd. Shopping The best curio shops are around the Chowrasta including Habib Malik and Jolly Arts. For trekking gear try shops S7 and S4 in the Singalila Market; for arts and crafts and especially carpets, head for Hayden Hall on Laden La Rd and the Tibetan Refugee Centre.

Tibetan studies The Manjushree Centre of Tibetan Culture, 12 Gandhi Rd (☎0354/225 6714, ⓦwww.manjushree-culture.org), founded in 1988 to preserve and promote Tibetan culture, offers both part-time Tibetan language classes (Mon–Sat 4–6pm) and more intensive three-, six- and nine-month courses ($225, $345 and $462). The centre also has a library, holds regular seminars, talks, video shows and exhibitions and is planning a museum. The Chagpori Medical Institute at Takdah (en route to Teesta) runs excellent long courses in Tibetan medicine; ask at Manjushree.

Moving on from Darjeeling

The nearest **airport** to Darjeeling is Bagdogra, 100km to the south (see p.885); allow plenty of time to get there by taxi. Tickets for Jet Airways and other airlines are available through Clubside Tours and Travels, JP Sharma Road (☎0354/225 4646), and Pineridge Travels, Nehru Road, Chowrasta (☎0354/225 3912). Both also handle flights from **Bhadrapur** in Nepal to **Kathmandu** (around $120; see p.887). Indian Airlines have their office on the Chowrasta (☎0354/225 4230).

A handful of **buses** and minibuses (Rs70) run to **Siliguri** from the bus stand near Chowk Bazaar, while shared taxis and Jeeps charge Rs80. For overland bus travel to **Kathmandu**, head to the border town of **Kakarbitta** in Nepal to get a choice of coaches (see p.887); check security conditions with agencies such as Himalayan Travels in Darjeeling and others in Siliguri before starting out. In the mornings, **Jeeps** run regularly to **Gangtok**, **Siliguri**, **Mirik**, **Kalimpong** and **Jorethang** (for West Sikkim; Rs80), and are by far the most efficient way to travel, especially if you pay for two seats in the front for yourself. Book in advance if you can at the Jeep stand (next to the bus stand); each route has its own syndicate, and some have two or three. Gangtok services (4hr 30min; Rs130) run frequently between 7am and 2pm.

The **Toy Train** (see p.884) runs to **Siliguri** and **New Jalpaiguri**, weather and landslides permitting, but takes a leisurely seven to eight hours; the train leaves at 9.15am and costs Rs247 for first class and Rs42 for second to NJP. **Railway reservations** (daily 8am–2pm) for selected **main-line trains** out of NJP can be made at Darjeeling's station a couple of days before departure. They have tourist quotas for trains to Delhi, Kolkata, Bengaluru (Bangalore), Cochin and Thiruvananthapuram. If stuck, try Gupta Tours & Travel, near the station at 5 Chachan Mansion (☎0354/225 4616), who can get tickets (for a commission) when quotas are "full".

Around Darjeeling

One really unmissable part of the Darjeeling experience is the early-morning mass exodus to **Tiger Hill** to watch the sunrise. This can easily be combined with a visit to the old monastery of **Ghoom**, and the huge monastery at **Sonada** on Hill Cart Road towards Siliguri.

Tiger Hill

Jeeps and taxis packed with tourists leave from Clubside in Darjeeling around 4am each morning, careering 12km through Ghoom to catch the sunrise at **TIGER HILL**. This incredible viewpoint (2585m) on the eastern extremity of

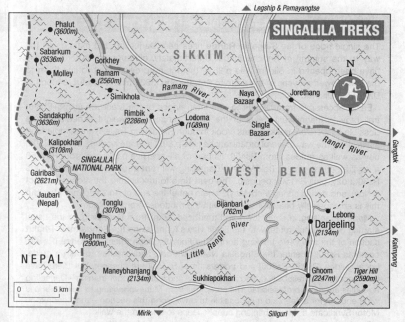

Map labels:

▲ Legship & Pamayangtse

SINGALILA TREKS

SIKKIM

Phalut (3600m)
Sabarkum (3536m)
Molley
Gorkhey
Ramam (2560m)
Simikhola
Ramam River
Naya Bazaar
Jorethang
Sandakphu (3636m)
Rimbik (2286m)
Lodoma (1089m)
Singla Bazaar
Kalipokhari (3108m)
Rangit River
SINGALILA NATIONAL PARK
Gairibas (2621m)
WEST BENGAL
Jaubari (Nepal)
Tonglu (3070m)
Bijanbari (762m)
Lebong
Darjeeling (2134m)
Meghma (2900m)
Little Rangit River
NEPAL
Maneybhanjang (2134m)
Sukhiapokhari
Ghoom (2247m)
Tiger Hill (2590m)
0   5 km
Mirik ▼
Siliguri ▼

▶ Gangtok
▶ Kalimpong

N

the Singalila Range provides a 360-degree Himalayan panorama, with the steamy plains bordering Bangladesh to the south, the Singalila ridge with Everest beyond to the west, Kanchenjunga and Sikkim to the north, and the Bhutan and Assam Himalayas trailing into the distance to the northeast. From left to right, the **peaks** include: Lhotse (which actually looks larger than Everest); Everest itself; Makalu; then, after a long gap, the rocky summit of Kang on the Sikkim–Nepal divide; the prow of Jannu in Nepal; Rathong; tent-like Kabru south and north; Talung; Kanchenjunga main, central and south; Pandim; Simvo; horned Narsing; and the fluted pyramid of Siniolchu. As the sun rises from the plains, it lights each one in turn; not yet obscured by the haze of the day, they are bathed in pastel hues.

In peak season, up to 150 Jeeps leave Darjeeling daily, transporting more than 2000 people to the viewpoint in good weather. A Jeep tour with brief stops at Ghoom, the Gurkha War Memorial (Rs5) and the Batasia Loop, organized with one of the operators around Clubside, will cost Rs700 per vehicle or around Rs75 per seat, less off-season. The **viewing tower** at Tiger Hill provides a warmer but

The Toy Train to Ghoom

Ghoom is the highest point on the **Toy Train** railway (see p.884), just 7km from Darjeeling. In season, two steam-driven tourist trains (Rs265 return trip) leave Darjeeling at 10am and 12.50pm to travel up to Ghoom, where they stop for just fifteen minutes, not enough time to view the monasteries, before returning to Darjeeling with another brief stop at Batasia Loop for views of the Himalayas. The regular 9.15am diesel service from Darjeeling to Siliguri via Ghoom is cheaper (Rs116 first class, Rs25 second class). You could use alternative transport back to Darjeeling or take the top road for a quiet, traffic-free walk back, with stupendous views along the way and a visit to the **Peace Pagoda** in the woods above the Dali Gompa.

The single ridge of the **Singalila Range** rises near Darjeeling and extends all the way to the summit of Kanchenjunga. Unfortunately, although some longer trails have been opened in Sikkim (see p.951), there is no provision yet to link them to the initial lower sections of the ridge to **Sandakphu** (3636m) and **Phalut** (3600m) in Darjeeling District.

Easily accessible from Darjeeling, the later stages of the Maneybhanjang–Phalut trail provide magnificent views of the higher ranges; lightweight expeditions are possible as there are trekking huts (book through Himalayan Travels) and simple food stalls along the way. Several organizations (see p.892) arrange porters, from Rs250 a day as well as **guides**, from Rs400, as part of all-inclusive packages (from Rs1450 a day); amongst others, Trek-Mate in Darjeeling will **rent equipment** (sleeping bags Rs30 a day, plus Rs1500 deposit). The **best time** to trek is after the monsoons (Oct & Nov), and during spring (Feb–May). It gets hot at the end of April and into May, but this is an especially beautiful season, with the rhododendrons in bloom.

Maneybhanjang, a small town and roadhead 27km from Darjeeling, is the usual starting point for the route, with the finest views found along the **Sandakphu–Phalut** section of the trail while trekking north. The Forestry Department levy a fee (Rs100, cameras Rs50) to enter the **Singalila National Park**, and one has to take a guide. Local guides (Rs250–Rs300) and porters (from Rs150) are cheaper, but there have been reports of unreliability due to drunkenness and lack of proper training – Darjeeling agencies are more professional. The steep trail from Maneybhanjang to Sandakphu is wide enough for a Jeep, so it is possible to drive along this section – the Sandakphu Motor Syndicate at Manybhanjang supply Jeeps to shorten the walk.

Foreigners are expected to register with the police at Maneybhanjang; with unrest across the border in Nepal, security is tight and border guards posted along the route are vigilant in checking papers. Taking an early taxi to Maneybhanjang from Darjeeling enables you to start the trek the same day, otherwise you can **stay** in the basic *Pradhans* (❷), *Kanchenjunga* (❷), the *Goperna Lodge* (❷), or the simple but comfortable rooms above *Wangdi* Tibetan restaurant (❷).

often crowded space to see the sunrise from behind glass: it costs Rs40 for the "Super Deluxe" top floor (including coffee), Rs30 for the floor below, or Rs20 for the viewing platform in addition to the Rs10 vehicle fee. The energetic can opt to walk back from Tiger Hill visiting the *gompas* of Ghoom on the way.

Ghoom and other monasteries

Often obscured in cloud, **GHOOM** (2438m), with its charming little railway station and tiny bazaar on the edge of Jorebangla, holds several interesting monasteries. The most venerated of these is **Yiga Choling**, or the Old Ghoom Monastery, tucked off the main thoroughfare above the brash *Sterling Resort*. From Ghoom railway station, head back towards Darjeeling for 200m and turn left into the side road (signposted) and continue through the small market for 500m. Built in 1850 by Sharap Gyatso, a renowned astrologer, the monastery consists of a single chambered temple and a few residential buildings. Inside the prayer hall is a huge figure of Maitreya, the Buddha of the future – a statue of an exceptionally high standard of workmanship, with fine detail above and around the bronze face. Back on the main road, the **Shakya Choling** *gompa* has expanded in recent years, while **Samten Choling**, a small but colourful *gompa* on a bend in the main road to Darjeeling, is sometimes included on the Jeep tours to Tiger Hill. You may prefer to spend time looking around Ghoom when the Jeeps have all returned to Darjeeling.

The normal route

DAY 1 Assuming you start from Maneybhanjang, the first day begins with a sharp climb to **Meghma**, then eases to the hut (●) at **Tonglu** (3070m). One variation bypasses Tonglu to Tumling where there are lodges like the *Shikar* (●), but most strong walkers should be able to press on to Gair bas, or to Kalipokhari where there are a couple of lodges including *Sherpa* (●–●) and *Chewang* (●); otherwise, you'll stay at the Tonglu hut.

DAY 2 From Tonglu head on to **Kalipokhari** and **Bikhebhanjang**. The trail then rises steeply to **Sandakphu** (3636m), which has a trekkers' hut (●), PWD bungalows, the friendly *Sherpa Chalet* (●), and the more comfortable *Namo Buddha* (●–●), where some rooms have attached baths.

DAY 3 The panorama opens out as you leave Sandakphu, and the trek follows the ridge to **Sabarkum**. There's no shelter or food there, but if you drop down to the right for thirty minutes to **Molley**, you'll find an inhospitable trekkers' hut (●).

DAY 4 Retrace your steps to Sabarkum and continue along the ridge to **Phalut** (3600m), where you'll find a trekkers' hut (●), which should be able to rustle up some basic food. The panorama from here is particularly impressive.

DAY 5 Either retrace your steps to Sandakphu, or follow the trail from Phalut via **Gorkhey**, which has a trekkers' hut (●) and the *Shanti Lodge* (●–●) which also has a dorm (Rs100), to **Rammam** (2560m), home of the welcoming *Sherpa Hotel* (●), a trekkers' hut (●) and several other lodges.

DAY 6 The final day leads to **Rimbik** (2286m); check with locals before setting off as the route is confusing. In Rimbik there's the warm and cosy *Sherpa Lodge* (●), where they'll help arrange bus tickets to Darjeeling; the *Sherpa Tenzing* (●) with shared baths, hot water by the bucket and good food; the comfortable *Ganga Prasad* (●), the similar *Greenhill* (●) and a trekkers' hut (●). Rimbik is a roadhead served by buses and Jeeps (Rs110; 6–7am, noon–1pm) heading to Darjeeling, or you can set off on another (long) day's walk to **Bijanbari**, which also has transport to Darjeeling.

Halfway between Ghoom and Darjeeling on the main road stands the imposing **Thupten Sanga Choeling**, otherwise known as the **Dali Gompa**, inaugurated by the Dalai Lama in 1993. This is a very active **Drukpa Kagyu** *gompa* with two hundred monks, including several young lamas. The huge meditation hall is richly decorated with exquisite murals and ceiling mandalas.

South of Ghoom, down the Hill Cart Road towards Kurseong, the influential **Sonada Monastery** or **Samdrub Darjay Choling**, founded in the 1960s, was the seat of **Kalu Rinpoche** who developed a large American and French following. It has recently been extensively renovated to house Kalu Rinpoche's young *tulku* or reincarnation. Rooms (●) are available for retreat and you can dine with the monks for a nominal fee.

Kalimpong and around

Though it may seem grubby at first, the quiet hill station of **KALIMPONG**, 50km east of Darjeeling, has much to offer, including a colourful market, an extraordinary profusion of orchids and other flowers, great views of Kanchenjunga, several monasteries and lots of potential for walks in the surrounding hills, which are still home to the tribal **Lepcha community**. Like Darjeeling, Kalimpong once belonged to Sikkim, and later to Bhutan. Unlike Darjeeling

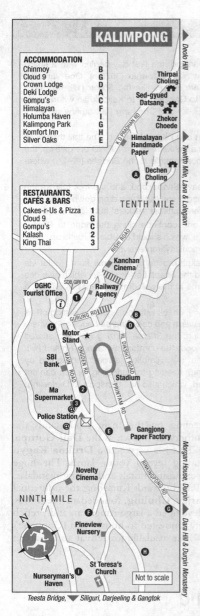

KALIMPONG ▶

ACCOMMODATION

Chinmoy	B
Cloud 9	G
Crown Lodge	D
Deki Lodge	A
Gompu's	C
Himalayan	F
Holumba Haven	I
Kalimpong Park	G
Komfort Inn	H
Silver Oaks	E

Thirpai Choling

Sed-gyued Datsang

Zhekor Choede

Himalayan Handmade Paper

Dechen Choling

TENTH MILE

RESTAURANTS, CAFÉS & BARS

Cakes-r-Us & Pizza	1
Cloud 9	G
Gompu's	C
Kalash	2
King Thai	3

Kanchan Cinema

DGHC Tourist Office ℹ

Railway Agency

SDB GIRI RD

GURUNG RD

Motor Stand ★

SBI Bank

MAIN ROAD

ONGDEN RD

HL DIKSHIT ROAD

Ma Supermarket

Stadium

PRINTAM RD

Police Station

Gangjong Paper Factory

RINKINGPONG RD

Novelty Cinema

NINTH MILE

N

Pineview Nursery

St Teresa's Church

Nurseryman's Haven

Not to scale

K.D. PRADHAN RD

Deolo Hill

Twelfth Mile, Lava & Loilegaon

RISHI ROAD

Morgan House, Durpin

Dara Hill & Durpin Monastery

Teesta Bridge, ▼ *Siliguri, Darjeeling & Gangtok*

this was never a tea town or resort, but a trading centre on the vital route to Tibet – a location that rendered Kalimpong virtually out of bounds for tourists for a couple of decades after the Sino-Indian conflict of the early 1960s. Despite the large military presence, Kalimpong's recent history has been one of neglect, which has led to water shortages and a general decay in the infrastructure. A deep-rooted dissatisfaction has simmered for many years, sometimes breaking out into violence, but political uncertainties and wildcat strikes have not detracted from the charm of Kalimpong's quiet leafy avenues, which offer a breath of fresh air after the razzmatazz of Darjeeling.

The Town

Kalimpong spreads along a curving ridge to either side of its main **market area**, known as **Tenth Mile**. Though there are few of the curio and tourist emporia so abundant in Darjeeling, there are plenty of places selling Buddhist handicrafts and religious paraphernalia, which attract wholesale buyers from all over India. Silk brocade, Tibetan incense, made-to-order monks' attire and silver bowls predominate; of the tourist shops, Kaziratna Shakya on Rishi Road has a good selection and its own workshop, while the wholesale shops are centred around RC Mintri Road. On Wednesdays and Saturdays, Tenth Mile gets very lively as villagers flock in from the surrounding areas for the principal weekly markets. Below the *Silver Oaks Hotel* and down steps off Printam Road, the **Gangjong Paper Factory** (Mon–Sat 9am–4.30pm) welcomes visitors to their handmade paper workshop. Access to **Himalayan Handmade Paper**, at Panlook Compound on KD Pradhan Road near Thirpai (see opposite), is easier and they also have a shop.

Rinkingpong Hill, also known as **Durpin Dara**, looms above the town to the southwest and is firmly in the hands of the army, who allow tourists through in taxis but occasionally stop those on foot. At its highest point, entirely surrounded by the army, **Zong Dog Palri Phodrang Gompa**, also known as Durpin ("telescope") Monastery, built in 1957 to house three copper statues brought from Tibet in the 1940s, was modelled on Guru Rinpoche's mythical "pure realm" palace and consecrated by the Dalai Lama. The beautifully painted building is a scenic four-kilometre hike from the centre of town and, despite the communication masts, its roof is a great place to take in the sunrise accompanied by the chanting of the monks below.

The wooded roads leading up Rinkingpong Hill hide several interesting old manor houses, of which **Morgan House** was built for a British jute merchant but now serves as a tourist lodge, where tea on the lawn captures the atmosphere of the period; the views are stunning. Further up the hill and some 2km above town, **St Teresa's Church** was built in 1929 by a Swiss missionary and borrows heavily from vernacular Buddhist monastic architecture, mimicking a Bhutanese *gompa*. There's beautiful carving inside and out; check out the doors, adorned with the eight sacred Buddhist symbols.

At the other end of town, half an hour's walk up Deolo Hill brings you to the **Thirpai Choling Gompa**, a breakaway Gelugpa monastery founded in 1892 and recently renovated, which hides the controversial image of Dorje Shugden, a deity proscribed by the Dalai Lama. Below and closer to town is **Thongsa Gompa**, a small Bhutanese monastery founded in 1692 and belonging to the Nyingmapa school; its meditation halls are covered with beautiful murals, some new and some fading. The summit of **Deolo Hill** (1704m) is a popular picnic spot (daily 9am–6pm; Rs5) with a DGHC tourist lodge and restaurant, and a superb vista which ranges from the steamy Teesta Valley far below to the summit of Kanchenjunga, with the frontier ridge and the passes of Nathula and Jelepla into Tibet clearly visible.

Kalimpong is renowned for its **horticulture**, especially its orchids, cacti, amaryllis, palms and ferns. Around fifty nurseries, such as Sri Ganesh Mani Pradhan at Twelfth Mile, Nurseryman's Haven (at *Holumba Haven* hotel; see p.902) and Pineview (Rs5) on Atisha Road specialize in exotic cacti. Although Kalimpong blossoms all year long, the best time to see orchids in bloom is between mid-April and mid-May, when the flower festival is usually held.

Practicalities

Kalimpong, only accessible by **road**, is served by regular buses, taxis and Jeeps from Darjeeling, Siliguri and Gangtok. Most transport pulls in at the **Motor Stand** in the central market area, though is slated to be shifted to a new location near the police station on the main road. Here, you can pick up Jeeps and buses to Darjeeling (2hr 30min–4hr; Rs80), Siliguri (2hr 30min; Rs80) and Gangtok (3hr; Rs70); each route has its own syndicate and ticket office. Other destinations include NJP, Lava, Kakarbitta, Pelling and Ghezing, but bear in mind that the last reliable transport links are around mid-afternoon. Dynamic Solutions, Jopa Complex on Main Road (☎03552/257874), are good for all air tickets; for **train tickets**, head to the railway agency on Rishi Road (daily 10am–4pm), although their quota for NJP is low.

Kalimpong's **DGHC tourist office**, Damber Chowkh (daily 9.30am–5pm; ☎03552/257992), has useful general information and leaflets; they also arrange **whitewater rafting** on the Teesta (from Rs350). Private operators offering this popular activity include Johnny Gurkha (☎09832 074341) and White Water Action Adventure (☎09832 097676), both at Teesta, and Murmi White Water Adventures (☎03552/276071) at Melli.

Amongst local **tour operators**, Gurudongma Tours and Treks (☎03552/255204, ⓦ www.gurudongma.com) specializes in ornithological, culinary and trekking trips throughout the northeast and has a farmhouse on the Samthar Plateau (see p.903). The informative Holumba Travel Desk (☎03552/256936) organizes tailor-made itineraries including trips to the Neora Valley, walks and visits to villages throughout the region.

On the Main Road near DGHC office, Soni Emporium **changes money**, as does its neighbour, Kaziratna Shakya. The ATM next to the State Bank of India on the Main Road accepts credit and debit cards. The **post office** is near the town centre, above the bazaar area just behind the police station. There are a few **Internet** cafés; try Odyssey at Ma Supermarket, near the police station on the main road.

Accommodation and eating

Kalimpong's acute water shortages are likely to influence your choice of **accommodation** – few of the lower-range options have running water. Tenth Mile and the area around the Motor Stand hold most of the budget places.

The best **restaurant** is in the *Kalimpong Park* hotel. In a complex on SBG Road near the DGHC office, *Cakes-r-Us* is a pleasant patisserie, while *Pizza* is a bright little bistro with a snacky menu. The best vegetarian restaurant is *Kalash* (signed in Hindi, so ask) on Main Road. The legendary *Gompus*, within the hotel on Damber Chowk, is back after a facelift and is a good place for a long drink and some *momos* and *thukpa*. *King Thai*, upstairs in the Ma Supermarket near the police station, is a popular local bar and restaurant with occasional live bands and a dance floor. If you're after a quiet beer, head up to *Cloud 9* hotel (see below).

Chinmoy Near the Motor Stand ☎03552/256264. A quiet location despite its proximity to the Motor Stand, with a range of pleasant, clean nonsmoking budget rooms; hot water is by the bucket only. ②–③

Cloud 9 Ringkingpong Rd ☎03552/259554. Five spacious, airy and comfortable rooms above a restaurant and bar that's especially lively when the owner Binodh is around – guitar jams and Beatles covers. ⑤

Crown Lodge Below the Motor Stand ☎03552/255846. Handy for early departures, this is a central and popular place with functional, clean rooms, hot running water and a good restaurant. ③–④

Deki Lodge Tirpai Rd ☎03552/255095. 10min walk from the Motor Stand, this clean and very welcoming family-run hotel offers a wide choice, from budget rooms with hot water by the bucket to comfortable doubles with running hot water in the new wing at the rear. ②–④

Gompus Damber Chowk ☎03552/2558181. This legendary hotel in the centre of town has been completely revamped, and offers very comfortable, modern rooms and suites on three floors above a popular restaurant and bar. ④–⑥

Himalayan Upper Cart Rd ☎03552/255248, ⒲www.himalayanhotel.com. Historic and

comfortable family-run hotel full of Tibetan memorabilia, set amid exquisite gardens; the modern cottages are luxurious but lack the ambience of the old house. ⑦

Holumba Haven 8.5 Mile, near the Fire Station ☎03552/256936, ⒲www.holumba.com. Comfortable, beautifully presented cottages set within a stunning orchid nursery with a menagerie of birds and animals. Some have their own kitchens, or you can have home-cooked meals with the informative and extremely welcoming owners. ④–⑥

Kalimpong Park Ringkingpong Rd ☎03552/255305. An old-world garden hotel set above town with panoramic views, the *Park* lacks the grandeur of the *Himalayan* but is more affordable, with a pleasant bar and restaurant. ⑦

Komfort Inn Upper Cart Rd ☎03552/256207. Welcoming family-run hotel in a quiet spot above town, with good-sized rooms, plain but comfortable, with running hot water and room service. ④–⑤

Silver Oaks Ringkingpong Rd ☎03552/255296, ⒲www.elginhotels.com. One of the grandest addresses in town, with a central location, spacious, plush rooms with conservative decor, and a good restaurant; the garden is a pleasant setting for tea or drinks in the evenings. From $124. ⑨

Village tourism and homestays

Offering the chance to explore the rural landscape and experience local culture, organized **village tourism** is becoming increasingly popular hereabouts. The main operators include the excellent Gurudongma and Holumba (see p.901) in Kalimpong, Help Tourism (see p.885) in Siliguri, Himalayan Footprints in Gangtok (☎03592/280433). Gurudongma's *Farm House* (●) is a rustic but luxurious development (rooms from $140 all-inclusive) on the beautiful **Samthar Plateau**, an 80km drive from Kalimpong. Other homestays include *Tinchuley Village House* (☎03542/262236; ●), 28km from Kalimpong near Takdah, a tea and cardamom plantation on the edge of a forest. Across the border into Sikkim, the *Turuk Village House* (☎09434022580; ●), 35km from Kalimpong, is a manor house that dates back to the late nineteenth-century and offers an idyllic stay near the River Teesta.

Around Kalimpong

Although the **Lepchas**, the original inhabitants of the area, have lost their traditional way of life in most parts of Darjeeling and Sikkim, their lifestyle has remained relatively untouched in the unspoilt forest-covered hills and deep river valleys to the south of Kalimpong. Lying on an old trade route to Bhutan, the small town of **LAVA** (2184m), 35km from Kalimpong and accessible by shared Jeep, makes an ideal base for exploring the nature trails of **Neora Valley National Park**, a 880-hectare reserve stretching along a narrow river valley, with a huge variation in wildlife and abundant orchids and birds. Holumba Travel Desk in Kalimpong (see p.901) can arrange the necessary guides and permits as well as transport. Lava is also convenient for approaching the **Rachela Pass** (3152m) on the Sikkim–Bhutan border, which provides excellent views of the Chola Range including Chomalhari (7314m), the sacred mountain of Bhutan on its border with Tibet. The town is very popular with Bengali tourists who come up here directly from Siliguri. There is plenty of basic **accommodation**, including huts at the *Forest Rest House* (●), which should be booked through the Forest Department in Kalimpong, off Rinkingpong Road (☎03552/255780, ⊛www.wbfdc.com); the Forest Department also provide **permits** for visiting the Neora Valley.

Pleasant **trails** lead west from Lava towards **Budhabare**, a market town in the Git River Valley which has a sprinkling of Lepcha, Gurkha and Bhutia villages. The track continues through forest to **Kafer**, where there's an old *Tourist Lodge* with large rooms (●) and a dorm (Rs100). The sunrise from nearby **Lolegaon** is legendary and there is a Heritage Forest walk along a canopy trail. You can get here by road via a rough road from Kalimpong, but if you're fit, you could walk the trail which crosses the Relli River near the village of the same name and returns directly to Kalimpong.

Travel details

Trains

Kolkata to: Agra (1 daily; 30hr); Ahmedabad (1 daily; 41hr); Bhubaneswar (7–8 daily; 7–9hr); Bishnupur (2 daily; 3hr 30min–4hr 20min); Chandernagore (20 daily; 30min); Chennai (2–3 daily; 27hr–32hr 20min); Delhi (9–10 daily; 29hr 45min–35hr 35min); Gaya (4–5 daily; 5hr 30min–7hr 30min); Guwahati (4–5 daily; 18hr–24hr 30min); Haridwar (2 daily; 27hr 15min–32hr 30min); Hooghly (20 daily; 20min); Kalka (Shimla) (1 daily; 33hr); Krishnagar (4 daily;

2–3hr); Lucknow (6–7 daily; 18–30hr); Mumbai (3–4 daily; 30–38hr); Nabadip (6–8 daily; 3hr–4hr 30min); Patna (5–6 daily; 7hr 20min–11hr 15min); Puri (2 daily; 8hr 45min–10hr); Rampurhat (5–6 daily; 4hr 10min–5hr); Raxaul (1 daily; 16hr 40min); Shantiniketan (6–7 daily; 2hr 15min–4hr); Siliguri NJP (7–8 daily; 10–14hr); Thiruvananthapuram (1 weekly; 46hr 30min); Varanasi (3 daily; 12hr–14hr 50min).

Shantiniketan (Bolpur) to: Kolkata (6–7 daily; 2hr 30min–4hr); Siliguri NJP (4–5 daily; 8hr 35min–9hr 15min).

Siliguri New Jalpaiguri (NJP) to: Delhi (5–6 daily; 21hr 40min–30hr 30min); Guwahati (6–8 daily; 7hr 30min–10hr 30min); Kolkata (7–8 daily; 10–14hr); Patna (4–5 daily; 8hr 25min–12hr 20min); Shantiniketan (Bolpur) (4–5 daily; 8hr 35min–9hr 15min); Varanasi and Mughal Sarai (4–5 daily; 11hr 50min–19hr).

Buses

Kolkata to: Basanti (4 daily; 3hr); Behrampur (every 30min; 5hr); Bhubaneswar (4 daily; 8–10hr); Bishnupur (3 daily; 5hr); Bongaon (2 daily; 4hr); Dhaka (2 daily; 12hr); Diamond Harbour (12 daily; 2hr); Digha (8 daily; 5hr); Malda (7 daily; 7hr); Mayapur (4 daily; 3hr 30min); Puri (4 daily; 12hr); Rampurhat (2 daily; 6hr); Siliguri NJP (6 daily; 12hr).

Siliguri to: Gangtok (4 daily; 4hr); Guwahati (4–5 daily; 9hr); Kakarbitta (12 daily; 40min);

Kolkata (6 daily; 12hr); Patna (3–4 daily; 10hr); Phuntsoling (4 daily; 4hr).

Flights

(**AI** = Air India, **AIE** = Air India Express, **BG** = Bangladesh Biman, **DN** = Air Deccan, **G8** = Go Air, **IC** = Indian Airlines, **IT** = Kingfisher, **KB** = Druk Air, **S2** = JetLite, **SG** = SpiceJet, **6E** = IndiGo, **9W** = Jet Airways)

Bagdogra (Siliguri) to: Delhi (IC, 9W, DN, SG, IT 5 daily; 3–4hr); Guwahati (IC, 9W, DN, SG 3–4 daily; 45min); Kolkata (IC, 9W, DN, IT 4 daily; 1hr).

Kolkata to: Agartala (IC, 9W, IT, 6E 3–4 daily; 50min); Ahmedabad (IC, IT 2–3 daily; 2hr); Bagdogra/Siliguri (IC, 9W, DN, IT 4 daily; 1hr); Bhubaneswar (S2, DN, IT 3–4 daily; 55min); Chennai (IC, 9W, DN, IT, 6E 7–8 daily; 2hr); Delhi (IC, DN, 9W, S2, SG, 6E, IT 15 daily; 2hr–2hr 15min); Dhaka (BG, AI 3–4 daily; 1hr); Guwahati (IC, 9W, S2, DN, 6E, IT 8–9 daily; 1hr 10min); Hyderabad (IC, DN, 9W, S2, SG, 6E, IT 6–7 daily; 2–3hr); Imphal (IC, 9W, DN, 6E, IT 6 daily; 1hr 55min–2hr 40min); Jaipur (IC, 6E 1–2 daily; 2hr 20min–4hr); Kathmandu (IC 6 weekly; 1hr 30min); Lucknow (S2 1 daily; 2hr 20min); Mumbai (IC, 9W, S2, AI, DN, SG, IT, AIE, 6E 15 daily; 2hr 30min); Nagpur (6E 3 weekly; 1hr 30min); Paro (Bhutan) (KB 4 weekly; 1hr 10min); Patna (S2, DN 2 daily; 1–2hr); Port Blair (IC, DN, SG, 9W 5–6 daily; 2hr).

Bihar and Jharkhand

The International boundaries on this map are neither purported to be correct nor authentic by Survey of India directives. Publisher.

CHAPTER 14

Highlights

✳ **Sonepur Mela** This month-long festival and cattle fair is a spectacular gathering of pilgrims, sadhus and animals. See p.914

✳ **The Mahabodhi Temple** A cutting from the tree under which the Buddha attained enlightenment is the focal point of Bodhgaya's renowned temple. See p.920

✳ **Rajgir** A dusty Buddhist pilgrimage town filled with shrines and home to one of the region's most unusual hotels. See p.922

✳ **Palamau National Park** A remote national park in western Jharkhand offering elephant rides through tiger country. See p.925

▲ Bodhgaya

14

Bihar and Jharkhand

BIHAR occupies the flat eastern Ganges basin, south of Nepal, between Uttar Pradesh and West Bengal. To its south, **JHARKHAND**, occupying the hilly Chotanagpur plateau north of Orissa, was hewn out of Bihar in 2000, following agitation by its tribal majority. This attempt by the government to arrest the spread of what the author William Dalrymple has called the "Bihar disease" continues to flounder, however, as both states remain seriously troubled by poverty, a lack of infrastructure, inter-caste violence, corruption and general lawlessness (see box, p.909).

The region's plight is all the more tragic considering its proud history. It was at **Bodhgaya** in the sixth century that Prince Gautama settled under a *bodhi* tree and attained enlightenment, following a quest for truth that saw him wandering the kingdoms of the Ganges, including **Vaishali** and **Rajgir**. Today, the region's Buddhist sites draw pilgrims from across the world. As well as being the first centre of Buddhism in north India, Bihar was also its last bastion; **Nalanda University** is a poignant reminder of the extent of the faith. During the sixth century BC, this was the heartland of the **Magadhas**, whose king Bimbisara was converted by the Buddha at his capital of Rajagriha (now Rajgir). Around 321 BC, shortly after the Magadhas shifted their capital to **Patna**, they were overthrown by the dynamic **Chandragupta Maurya**. The next major dynasty to rule the area was the **Guptas**, around the fourth century AD, whose advent marked the return of Hinduism. Remarkably, even after the Muslim Sultanate swept the region at the end of the twelfth century, and the Mughals came to rule northern India from Delhi three hundred years later, the Buddhist centre of Bodhgaya continued to thrive.

Although the ordinary visitor is usually unaffected by Bihar's frequent kidnappings, murders and acts of banditry, Buddhist pilgrims and tourists have on occasion been robbed and few travellers spend much time here. This is a great shame, because the region is refreshingly off the tourist trail and has a fascinating mix of religious history. Check the **safety situation** with your foreign office and the local press (Ⓦwww.patnadaily.com and Ⓦwww.bihartimes.com are good sources of information) before travel; bear in mind that state and tourist authorities tend to downplay safety concerns. Avoid the region during local elections, when tensions run high, and riots and violent crime are not uncommon.

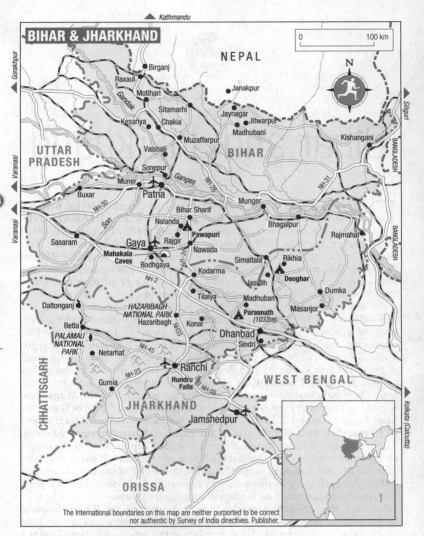

BIHAR & JHARKHAND

▲ Kathmandu

0   100 km

NEPAL

Birganj
Raxaul
Motihari   ● Janakpur
Sitamarhi   Jaynagar   Jitwarpur
Kesariya   Chakia   Madhubani
Muzaffarpur   Madhubani   Kishanganj
Vaishali   BIHAR

UTTAR
PRADESH   Sonepur   *Ganges*   NH-31
Muner   Patna   NH-28
Buxar   NH-30   Munger
Bihar Sharif   Bhagalpur
Nalanda   Pawapuri   Rajmahal
Sasaram   Gaya Rajgir Nawada   Rikhia
Mahakala   Simaltala   Deoghar
Caves   Bodhgaya Kodarma   Jasidih   Dumka
NH-2   Madhuban   Masanjor
Daltonganj   Tilaiya   Parasnath
HAZARIBAGH   (1033m)
NATIONAL PARK Hazaribagh Konar Dhanbad
Betla   Sindri
PALAMAU
NATIONAL   ● Netarhat   WEST BENGAL
PARK   NH-23 Ranchi
Gumia   Hundru
Falls   NH-55

CHHATTISGARH   JHARKHAND
Jamshedpur

ORISSA

The International boundaries on this map are neither purported to be correct
nor authentic by Survey of India directives. Publisher.

Patna and around

Patna, Bihar's capital, is one of the oldest cities in India, dating back to the
sixth century BC. Today, however, it shows few signs of its former glory as the
centre of the Magadhan and Mauryan empires. A sprawling metropolis
hugging the south bank of the Ganges, Patna stretches for around 15km in a
shape that has changed little since Ajatasatru (491–459 BC) shifted the
Magadhan capital here from Rajgir.

The first Mauryan emperor, **Chandragupta**, established himself in what was
then **Pataliputra** in 321 BC, and pushed the limits of his empire as far as the
Indus; his grandson **Ashoka** (274–237 BC), one of India's greatest rulers, held

Lalu and the caste wars: politics in Bihar

Bihar - along with neighbouring Jharkhand - continues to languish at the bottom of almost every measure of development: from literacy rates to GDP. Roads are appalling, buses and trains are ancient, power cuts are common, and even in Patna there are few streetlights. Author William Dalrymple has described Bihar as "the most ungovernable and anarchic state in India", even though it is blessed with ample coal and iron deposits and large tracts of arable land. The problem has been a disastrous combination of virulent intercaste conflict and criminal misgovernance.

Since Independence, Bihar has largely been ruled by a mafia of high-caste landowners, with the lower castes – who together with untouchables and tribal people make up over seventy percent of the state's population – marginalized to the point of persecution. All that seemed set to change in 1991 when a rabble-rouser from a lowly caste of buffalo milkers, **Lalu Prasad Yadav**, united the "backward castes", the Muslims and the untouchables under a banner of social justice, winning that year's state election by a landslide. In power, Lalu delighted with his common touch; he spontaneously unclogged traffic congestion in Patna by walking the streets with a megaphone and filled the grounds of his official residence with buffalo.

Unfortunately Lalu proved little better than his predecessors. His cabinet of caste brethren included men wanted for murder and kidnap, and violence remained the main tool of political persuasion – as one hopeful election candidate said: "Without one hundred men with guns you cannot contest an election in Bihar." Much of the state degenerated into virtual civil war as the upper castes, lower castes, Maoist (Naxalite) guerrillas, police and private armies clashed violently.

Lalu's career appeared over in 1997, when he was imprisoned for a short spell for embezzling billions of rupees. He responded by getting his illiterate wife **Rabri Devi** proclaimed Chief Minister. Even though his RJD party was toppled from power in the 2005 state elections, Lalu has proved his political career is far from over – by contrast he has gone on to gain a national profile as Minister for Railways in the national government.

While he continues to be embroiled in scandal, Lalu has been credited with helping make the lower castes in Bihar – and beyond – more politically conscious, a move compared by some commentators to the US Civil Rights movement in the 1960s. His stated aim of "ending caste", however, looks as far away as ever, while Bihar remains largely untouched by India's "economic miracle".

sway over even greater domains. To facilitate Indo–Hellenic trade, the Mauryans built a Royal Highway from Pataliputra to Taxila, Pakistan, which later became the Grand Trunk Road, as well as highways to the Bay of Bengal and along the east coast. The city experienced two later revivals. The first Gupta emperor, also named **Chandra Gupta**, made Patna his capital early in the fourth century AD, and a thousand years later it was rebuilt by Afghan ruler Sher Shah Suri (1540–45), who constructed the Sher Shahi Mosque in the east of the city. Nearby, the beautiful *gurudwara* of **Har Mandir** was built to honour the birthplace of the tenth and most militant Sikh guru – Guru Gobind Singh. In his honour, the old Patna City quarter is often referred to as **Patna Sahib**.

Every March the city celebrates its illustrious history with several days of music, dancing and public events during the **Pataliputra Mahotsava** festival.

Arrival and information

Patna has three **train stations** but all mainline services arrive at Patna Junction, in the west of the city. Fraser Road (officially "Mazharul-Raq Path" but many still use the old name), immediately north of the station, is the main drag, with

Nalanda & Rajgir ▲

Sonepur, Vaishali, Muzaffarpur & Nepal ▲

PATNA

See inset map

ACCOMMODATION

Akash	F
Chanakya	H
Garden Court Club	B
Kautilya Vihar Tourist Bungalow	G
Maurya Patna	A
Samrat International	E
President	C
Windsor	D

RESTAURANTS

Bansi Vihar	2
Bellpepper	D
Gandhi's	1
Garden Court Club	B
Samrat and Takshila	H

River Ganges

PATNA CITY

Olta House

Har Mandir Sahib

Sher Shahi Mosque

Mahatma Gandhi Bridge

GULZARI BAGH

Old Opium Warehouse

Catholic Church

Gulzar Bagh Railway Station

ASHOK RAJ PATH

NH-19

NEW BYPASS RD

Saif Khan's Mosque

Khuda Baksh Oriental Library

Rajendra Nagar Railway Station

ASHOK RAJ PATH

BAR RD

Mahendra Ghat Ferry Terminal

British Library

Golghar

Gandhi Museum

Gandhi Maidan

Bus Stand

Indian Airlines

Patna Museum

Patna Junction Railway Station

GPO

Mithapur Bus stand

DAK BUNGALOW RD

MOTIWARI RD

FRASER RD

EXHIBITION RD

KANKAR BAGH RD

OLD BYPASS RD

BALEY RD

BEER CHAND PATEL PATH

Muner & Varanasi ▲

Airport ▼

N

0   500 m

Inset map:

State Bank of India

Patna Museum

BUDDHA MARG

IDBI Bank

BUDDHA MARG

GPO

Patna Junction Railway Station

STATION RD

FRASER RD

DAK BUNGALOW RD

HOTEL LANE

EXHIBITION RD

BEER CHAND PATEL PATH

BALEY RD

0   200 m

A B D 1 G F C E 2 G H

as much glamour as the state can muster – although even here you see rag pickers living on the pavement. Patna's **airport** lies 5km to the west; a pre-paid taxi from town costs Rs150–200, an auto-rickshaw around Rs80. **Mithapur**, the main bus station, is 2km south of Patna Junction and has services to Gaya, Ranchi, Varanasi and Raxaul, on the Nepalese border (see p.913). North of Fraser Road, between Gandhi Maidan and the River Ganges, **Gandhi Maidan Bus Stand** is the terminus for state buses. Cycle and auto-rickshaws are the most common means of transport for short journeys. Several huge concrete flyovers were under construction at the time of research, which will do little for Patna's aesthetics but should reduce congestion.

The **Bihar State Tourism Development Corporation** in *Kautilya Vihar Tourist Bungalow* on Beer Chand Patel Path (Mon–Sat 10am–5pm; ☎0612/222 5411, ⊛bstdc.bih.nic.in) can arrange day-trips. It also has a booth at Patna Junction (daily 8am–8pm; ☎0612/220 5755). The inconveniently located **India Tourism** office, close to the railway bridge at Sudama Place, Kankar Bagh Road (Mon–Fri 9.30am–6pm, Sat 9am–1pm; ☎0612/234 5776), runs a guide service. A number of travel agents (see p.913) also arrange tours and **car rental**, but many drivers refuse to take visitors to the more isolated areas because of fear of banditry.

The State Bank of India, West Gandhi Maidan (☎0612/222 6134), handles **foreign exchange**, and **ATMs** are dotted all over the town. The **GPO** is on Buddha Marg. For **Internet access**, try Broadband Internet Café (Rs15/hr) on the second floor of the Jagat Trade Centre, Fraser Road, or the cybercafé at *Hotel Windsor* (Rs25/hr).

At the time of writing, there had been a spate of shootings, robberies and muggings in Patna, and **crime** was generally on the increase: don't walk around on your own after dark.

Accommodation

Most of Patna's better hotels are located on and around Fraser Road in the city centre.

Akash Just off Fraser Rd ☎0612/223 9599. One of Patna's better shoestring hotels, *Akash* has a motley collection of fairly clean, compact rooms; if it's busy try the *New Amar* next door. ❷
Chanakya Beer Chand Patel Path ☎0612/222 3141, ⊛www.hotelchanakyapatna.in. This looming hotel has tastefully furnished beige- and apricot-coloured attached rooms, with nice touches like minibars. There's also a classy bar, a currency exchange and two top restaurants serving a mouthwatering mix of Indian, Chinese, Mughal and Afghan dishes between them. ❽
Garden Court Club SP Verma Rd ☎0612/320 2279. Accessed via an ancient lift, this small hotel in a shopping complex has a handful of neat and tidy rooms with TVs. The best reason to stay, however, is the lovely terrace restaurant. ❸–❺
Kautilya Vihar Tourist Bungalow Beer Chand Patel Path ☎0612/222 5411, ⓔbstdc @sancharnet.in. The Bihar State Tourism Development Corporation's rambling hotel has cavernous, brightly-coloured but somewhat overpriced

doubles, as well as a reasonable dorm (Rs75) and a relaxed rooftop restaurant. ❸–❹
Maurya Patna Fraser Rd, South Gandhi Maidan ☎0612/220 3040, ⊛www.maurya.com. Service can be impersonal at this 5-star, but the luxurious attached room ($150) – decorated in a range of styles, from colonial to oriental – appealing swimming pool (Rs350 for non-guests) and fine eateries more than make up for it. It's particularly popular with tourists from the Far East. ❾
President Just off Fraser Rd ☎0612/220 9203, ⓕ220 9206. Its decor may not have been updated since the 1970s, but *President* remains a good-value option. Although the rooms are a little stuffy, they're clean and boast multicoloured bedspreads. The management is also a good source of transport information. ❸–❹
Windsor Exhibition Rd ☎0612/220 3250, ⊛www .hotelwindsorpatna.com. A reassuringly well-run mid-range hotel, with swish modern attached rooms, reputable in-house travel agent and excellent restaurant serving succulent tandoor dishes. ❺

The City

Patna's most notable monument is the **Golghar**, a huge colonial-era grain storage house, now a symbol of the city. Also known as "the round house", it was built in 1786 in the hope of avoiding a repetition of the terrible famine of 1770. Mercifully, it never needed to be used. Overlooking the river and Gandhi Maidan, the Golghar has two sets of stairs which spiral their way up to its summit; these were designed so coolies could carry grain up one side, deliver their load through a hole at the top, and descend down the other. Sightseers now clamber up for views of the mighty river and the city. Within walking distance, the **Gandhi Museum** (daily except Sat 10am–6pm) is worth a quick visit for its pictures of the Mahatma's life.

The **Patna Museum** on Buddha Marg (Tues–Sun 10.30am–4.30pm; Rs250 [Rs5]), although faded and run-down, has an excellent collection of sculptures. Among its most famous exhibits is a polished sandstone female attendant, or *yakshi*, holding a fly-whisk, dating back to the third century BC. There are also Jain images from the Kushana period, a group of Buddhist *bodhisattvas* from Gandhara (in northwest Pakistan), some freakishly deformed stuffed animals and a gigantic fossilized tree thought to be 200 million years old.

Founded in 1900, the **Khuda Bhaksh Oriental Library** (daily except Fri 9am–5pm), east of Gandhi Maidan, has a remarkable selection of books from across the Islamic world, including manuscripts rescued from the Moorish University in Cordoba, Spain, and a tiny Koran measuring just 25mm in width.

Har Mandir Sahib and beyond

In the most interesting area of Patna – the older part of town, 10km east of Gandhi Maidan – filthy congested lanes lead to **Har Mandir Sahib**, the second holiest of the four great Sikh shrines known as *takhts* (thrones). Set in an expansive courtyard off the main road, the dazzling white onion-domed marble temple is dedicated to Guru Gobind Singh, born in Patna in 1660. Visitors can explore the courtyard and even venture inside where devotional music is often playing. Remove your shoes and cover your head before entering. Shared autorickshaws cost around Rs10 from Gandhi Maidan.

A short way northeast, the private **Qila House** (or Jalan Museum; call ahead for permission; ☎0612/264 2354) on Jalan Avenue holds a fine collection of art, including Chinese paintings and Mughal filigree work in jade and silver. Among the antiques are porcelain items that once belonged to Marie Antoinette and Napoleon's four-poster bed. To the west, the East India Company's **Old Opium Warehouse** at **Gulzaribagh** is now home to a government printing press.

Midway between Har Mandir Sahib and Gandhi Maidan stands **Saif Khan's Mosque** or the "mosque of stone", built by Parwez Shah, son of the great Mughal emperor Jahangir.

Eating

There are several decent **restaurants** strung along Fraser Road, although most double as bars in the evening when the custom is all male. *Bansi Vihar* is a narrow, dimly-lit dining hall packed with locals, who come to sample tasty south Indian snacks, primarily *dosas*, of which there are twenty varieties (Rs28–80). Also on Fraser Road is *Gandhi's*, a polished and super-hygienic pure veg restaurant that serves good-value thalis (Rs45–60), a rich *paneer* butter masala and toothsome *galub jamun*, all of which you can enjoy under incongruous mini-chandeliers. There are also a number of good hotel restaurants, including the 🍴 *Bellpepper* at the *Hotel Windsor* – see "Accommodation", (p.911) for details. While in town, keep an eye out for *littis* – baked balls of spiced chickpea dough – a speciality of Bihar sold by street vendors.

Moving on from Patna

Patna Junction is the most important **railway** station in the region, with connections to Gaya, Delhi, Varanasi, New Jalpaiguri, Guwahati, Kolkata, Mumbai and Chennai. There's a foreigners' reservation counter (No. 7) on the first floor of the booking office. The best train to **Kolkata** (Howrah) is the Shatabdi Express #2024 (Mon–Sat; departs 5.45am, arrives 1.25pm); alternatively take the Vibhuti Express #2334 (daily; departs 10.30pm, arrives 7.55am). For **Varanasi**, the Shramjeevi Express #2401 (daily; departs 10.50am, arrives 3pm) is a good option. The Rajdhani Express #2309 (daily; departs 8.55pm, arrives 9.50am) and the Poorva Express #2303 (Mon, Thurs, Fri and Sat; departs 4.15pm, arrives 7.05am) are the pick of several trains to **Delhi**. The Guwahati–Dadar Express #5646 travels to **Mumbai** and in the other direction, on its way to **Guwahati** it stops at **New Jalpaiguri**, handy for Darjeeling, Kalimpong and Sikkim. The Baidyanathdham Express #8450 (Wed; departs 8.55am; 18hr 25min) travels to **Puri**; a better bet however is the New Delhi–Puri Express #2816, which runs through Gaya rather than Patna (Mon, Wed, Thurs and Sat; departs 9.08pm, arrives 1.15pm). Take the Patna–Hatia #8625 (daily; departs 11.40am, arrives 1.45pm) for the short journey to **Gaya**; the train then continues to **Ranchi** (arrives 8.35pm).

Private travel companies offer bus tickets to **Kathmandu** with a voucher for the bus across the border. However, it's just as easy – and often wiser – to take one of the eighteen or so daily buses to Raxaul (see p.916) on the border and then make your own onward travel arrangements once in Nepal. The Raxaul buses leave from the chaotic **Mithapur bus station**, where there are plenty of vociferous touts to guide you to your bus. **Buses** to Ranchi, Gaya, Vaishali, Rajgir and Varanasi, via Muner, also leave from Mithapur; some services to Vaishali also depart from **Gandhi Maidan Bus Stand**. There are no direct buses to Nalanda or Pawapuri, so you'll have to go via Bihar Sharif. For all destinations it's safer to stick to daytime services. The **Bihar State Tourism Corporation** runs two daily buses to Ranchi (8am and 8pm) and Bodhgaya (7am and 2pm) from *Kautilya Vihar Tourist Bungalow*.

Patna airport has regular flights to Bagdogra, Delhi, Guwahati, Kolkata, Lucknow, Mumbai, Ranchi and Varanasi. The Indian Airlines office is at South Gandhi Maidan (℡0612/222 2554). Reliable **travel agents** include Ashok Travel & Tours in the *Hotel Pataliputra Ashok* (℡0612/222 3238) and the Travel Corporation of India at the *Maurya Patna* (℡0612/222 1699). See "Travel details" at the end of this chapter for more information on journey frequencies and durations.

Around Patna

Patna is a good base for exploring Nalanda, Rajgir and Vaishali (see p.915), but there are also places of interest closer at hand, notably the fabulous hilltop *dargah* (Sufi mausoleum) at **Muner**, 27km west. The imposing but sadly neglected red sandstone shrine of Sufi saint Yahia Muneri, 1km west of Muner, was built in 1605. Every year, around February, a three-day *urs* or festival in the saint's honour attracts pilgrims from far and wide, including *qawwals*, the renowned Sufi minstrels of Delhi and Ajmer. Muner is also known for its **sweets**, particularly lentil *ladoos*.

▲ Pilgrims on the ghats during the Sonepur Mela

If you're in Bihar between early November and early December, don't miss
the **Sonepur Mela**, staged 25km north of Patna across the huge Gandhi Bridge
– reputedly Asia's longest river bridge – at the confluence of the Gandak and
the Ganges. Cattle, elephants, camels, parakeets and other animals are brought
for sale, pilgrims combine business with a dip in the Ganges, *sadhus* congregate,
and festivities abound. The event is memorably described by Mark Shand in his
quixotic *Travels on My Elephant* (see Contexts, p.1394). The Bihar State Tourism

Development Corporation in Patna (see p.911) organizes tours and maintains a tourist village at Sonepur during the *mela* (❶–❹).

North Bihar

The one area of Bihar capable of growing reliable crops is the fertile agricultural belt along the Himalayan foothills north of the Ganges. Other than passing through en route to Nepal, most visitors only pause to explore the remains of the abandoned Buddhist city of **Vaishali**, although the region also has several shrines and temple towns associated with the Ramayana.

Vaishali

Set amid paddy fields 55km north of Patna, the quiet hamlet of **VAISHALI** was the site of the Buddha's last sermon. Named after King Visala, who is mentioned in the Ramayana, Vaishali is also believed by some historians to have been the first city-state in the world to practise a democratic, republican form of government. After leaving Nepal and renouncing the world and his family, Prince Gautama studied here, but eventually rejected his master's teachings and found his own path to enlightenment. He returned to Vaishali three times and on his last visit announced his final liberation – *Mahaparinirvana* – and departure from the world, in around 483 BC. One hundred years later, in 383 BC, the second Buddhist Council was held in Vaishali and two stupas erected.

A small but well-presented **archeological museum** (daily except Fri 10am–5pm; Rs2) provides a glimpse into the ancient Buddhist world. A short path next to the Coronation Tank (Abhishekh Pushkarni) leads off to the remains of the **stupa** where the ashes of the Buddha were reputedly found in a silver urn.

Two kilometres north at **Kolhua** stands the remarkably well-preserved **Ashokan Pillar**, erected by the Mauryan emperor (273–232 BC) to commemorate the site of the Buddha's last sermon. Known locally as Bhimsen-ki-lathi (Bhimsen's Staff), the 18.3-metre-high pillar, made of polished red sandstone, is crowned by a lion sitting on an inverted lotus, which faces north towards Kushinagar, where the Buddha died. Jains of the Svetambara sect, who believe that the last *tirthankara*, **Mahavira**, was born in Vaishali in 599 BC, have erected a **shrine** in the fields 1km east of Kolhua.

Travel agents in Patna can arrange **transport** to Vaishali or you can take a bus as far as Sonepur or Hajipur, and change onto an overcrowded shared taxi. Most

---

Madhubani paintings

Jitwarpur, a village on the outskirts of the small town of **Madhubani**, in northern Bihar, is home to a vibrant tradition of folk art. Madhubani **paintings** by local women were originally decorations for the outside of village huts. The illustrations of mythological themes – including images of local deities as well as Hindu gods and goddesses – the paintings were eventually transferred onto handmade paper, often using bright primary colours to fill the strong black line drawings. **Fabrics** printed with Madhubani designs have become very chic; these days they tend to be professionally made elsewhere, and are sold in the expensive boutiques of India's major cities, although you can still pick them up cheaply in Madhubani itself.

Buses connect Patna to Madhubani (5hr 30min), where there are some basic hotels; rickshaws can take you on to Jitwarpur.

people take in Vaishali as a day-trip from Patna; if you want to stay, try the **Amrapali Vihar** (℡0612/222 2622; ❷), which has habitable doubles, a dorm (Rs70) and a serviceable restaurant.

The road to Nepal

Some 55km north of Vaishali is **KESARIYA**, formerly Kessaputta, which has an impressive five-terraced eighth-century stupa. The stupa is said to have been built on top of one erected by the Buddha's Licchavi disciples after he announced he was about to attain nirvana and gave them his begging bowl as a souvenir. To get to Kesariya, take a bus from Vaishali to **CHAKIA** (3hr), 20km away, then a taxi or rickshaw to the site.

In 1917, **MOTIHARI**, a poor and lawless town 298km north of Patna, was the site of one of Gandhi's first acts of civil disobedience – he refused bail whilst protesting the plight of local farmers, who were being forced to grow indigo for the British textile industry. There's a small **museum** with photos and items such as Gandhi's walking stick and slippers. Motihari was also the birthplace of **George Orwell**, whose father worked here as a government opium agent. Most travellers simply pass through it on the way to Nepal, but there are *dharamshalas* should you wish to stay.

Travellers heading from Patna to **Nepal** have to cross the border at **RAXAUL**, eight hours away by bus. Raxaul is an unattractive, grubby town infested with mosquitoes and with limited amenities – you're better off staying in Birganj just over the border. If you have to spend the night, the functional *Ajanta* **hotel** on Ashram Road (℡06255/222 019; ❷–❸) is just about the best Raxaul has to offer. There's a **café** along the main road by the cinema, serving the local dish of kebab and *muri* (puffed rice).

The border itself, between Raxaul and the Nepalese town of **Birganj**, 5km away (Rs50 by auto-rickshaw), is open 24 hours for foreigners, but visas ($30 in cash; you'll also need two passport photos) are only available from 5.30am to 8pm. Early morning and night buses run from Birganj to Kathmandu (8–12hr) and Pokhara (10–12hr). Minibuses are quicker but cost slightly more – reserve a seat in advance if you can. The foreign exchange facility in Raxaul will only change Indian to Nepalese rupees, but Birganj has facilities to exchange traveller's cheques and US dollars.

Central Bihar

South of the Ganges and north of the hills of the Chotanagpur plateau, **Central Bihar** contains some of North India's most important Buddhist sites, including the great university at **Nalanda** and the small town of **Rajgir**. The greatest shrine of all, however, and a focus for Buddhists from around the world, is the Bodhi Tree at **Bodhgaya** where the Buddha attained enlightenment.

Gaya

The flyblown town of **GAYA**, 100km south of Patna, is a transit point for visitors to **Bodhgaya**, 13km away. Although it's not an appealing place, Gaya is of great significance to Hindus, who come here to honour their parents a year after death by offering *pinda* – funeral cakes – at the massive **Vishnupad temple**, where non-Hindus are forbidden. Pilgrims also come to bathe at the riverside *ghats*. **Brahmajuni Hill**, 1km southeast of the Vishnupad temple, is said to be where the Buddha preached his fire sermon.

Practicalities

Most people arrive at Gaya by **train** and are met by a bewildering array of touts. The best option is take a cycle rickshaw to Kacheri Bus Stand from where you can continue to Bodhgaya by auto-rickshaw or bus (see p.918). If you arrive after dark, stay overnight in Gaya as the route between the two can be unsafe. There is precious little to do in Gaya and tourist facilities are appalling, with staff at the **tourist office** (Mon–Sat 8am–8pm; ☎0361/242 0155), in the railway station, providing a distinct lack of information. Vishal Cyber World on a narrow alley off Station Road has **Internet** access (Rs30/hr).

Most of Gaya's **hotels** are on Station Road near the railway station. *Ajatsatru* (☎0631/243 4584, ⑤243 4202; ❸–❹) has grubby, basic rooms with squat toilets and cleaner, marginally more cheerful, but still overpriced, a/c rooms. The downstairs restaurant, however, has good Indian and Chinese staples (Rs25–80). *Akash* (☎0631/222 2205; ❷), on Laxman Sahay Road, close to *Ajatsatru*, is a much better bet. Simple, clean rooms with squat toilets and mini TVs are set around a vaguely Islamic courtyard. If you have a train ticket, the **railway retiring rooms** are clean and some have air conditioning (Rs75–125).

Bodhgaya

The world's most important Buddhist pilgrimage site, **BODHGAYA**, 13km south of Gaya, is a wonderfully relaxed town, with an array of monasteries, temples and retreats. Its focal point is the **Mahabodhi Temple**, home to the world's most sacred tree, under which the Buddha attained enlightenment.

The temple dates back to the seventh century AD and flourished up to the sixteenth century, when it fell into the hands of Hindu priests, who professed to be baffled by its origins. It was only after British archeologists arrived in the early nineteenth century that the site's significance was rediscovered. Since then Bodhgaya has been rejuvenated by overseas Buddhists, who have built an array of monasteries, temples and shrines.

From November to February, Bodhgaya is home to an animated community of exiled **Tibetans**, often including the Dalai Lama, as well as a stream of international Tibetophiles. Meditation courses attract others (see box, p.920), while large monasteries from places like Darjeeling bring their followers to

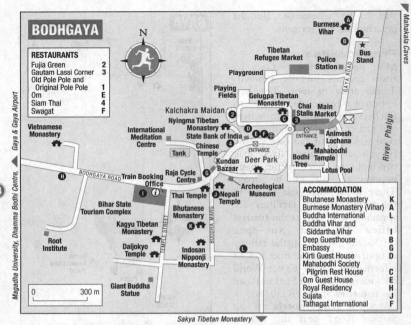

BODHGAYA N

RESTAURANTS
Fujia Green	2
Gautam Lassi Corner	3
Old Pole Pole and	
Original Pole Pole	1
Om	E
Siam Thai	4
Swagat	F

Vietnamese Monastery

International Meditation Centre

Kalchakra Maidan

Nyingma Tibetan Monastery

State Bank of India

Tank

Chinese Temple

Kundan Bazaar

Burmese Vihar

Tibetan Refugee Market

Police Station

Bus Stand

GAYA ROAD

Playground

Playing Fields

Gelugpa Tibetan Monastery

Chai Main Stalls Market

ENTRANCE

Animesh Lochana

ENTRANCE

Deer Park

Bodhi Tree

Mahabodhi Temple

River Phalgu

Lotus Pool

BODHGAYA ROAD Train Booking Office

Raja Cycle Centre

Thai Temple

Nepali Temple

Archeological Museum

Bihar State Tourism Complex

Kagyu Tibetan Monastery

Daijokyo Temple

Bhutanese Monastery

BUDDHA MARG

TEMPLE STREET

Root Institute

Indosan Nipponji Monastery

Giant Buddha Statue

0   300 m

ACCOMMODATION
Bhutanese Monastery	K
Burmese Monastery (Vihar)	A
Buddha International	L
Buddha Vihar and	
Siddartha Vihar	I
Deep Guesthouse	B
Embassy	G
Kirti Guest House	D
Mahabodhi Society	
Pilgrim Rest House	C
Om Guest House	E
Royal Residency	H
Sujata	J
Tathagat International	F

Mahakala Caves ▶

Sakya Tibetan Monastery ▼

attend ceremonies and lectures under the Bodhi Tree. From mid-March to mid-October, the region becomes oppressively hot and Bodhgaya returns to its quiet ways.

The town is not free from problems, however. The Mahabodhi Temple is also sacred to Hindus – the Buddha is seen as a reincarnation of Vishnu – who dominate its management committee, despite strong protests from the Buddhist world. The dispute is exacerbated by the contrasting forms of worship – while Buddhists have a solitary inward approach, Hindus prefer spectacle and noisy ceremony.

Arrival and information

Gaya's international **airport** (☎0631/428081) is around 12km from Bodhgaya. **Buses** connecting Bodhgaya and Gaya leave from outside Gaya railway station and more frequently from Kacheri Bus Stand a couple of kilometres to the south. An **auto-rickshaw** from Gaya costs Rs90–100, while one from the airport will set you back Rs70–80. You'll need to travel back to Gaya to pick up most onward services from Bodhgaya, although two daily buses (7am & 2pm), departing from the Bihar State Tourism Corporation complex, run directly to Patna. Private bus agencies have offices around Kalchakra Maidan; destinations include Varanasi and Siliguri.

The main **tourist office** (daily 10.30am–5pm; ☎0631/220 0672) in the Bihar State Tourism Corporation complex is distinctly unenlightening but has a **computerized train reservation** booth next door. Middle Way Travels (☎0631/220 0648), near the entrance to the temple, can arrange **local tours and car hire**, and book train, bus and flight tickets. The Sri Lankan **Mahabodhi Society** (☎0631/220 0742), responsible for reviving Bodhgaya in the nineteenth century, maintains a small centre northwest of the Mahabodhi Temple and can offer advice on accommodation and **courses**.

The State Bank of India (Mon–Fri 10.30am–4pm, Sat 10.30am–1.30pm) has a tiny **foreign exchange** room and an **ATM**. Niranjana Tours and Travels, close to the Mahabodhi Temple, also changes cash and travellers' cheques, although rates are worse than at the bank. Lotus Gems and Travel, close to *Hotel Tathagat International*, provides **Internet** access (Rs30/hr). The Raja Cycle Centre, next door to the *Embassy Hotel*, is a good place to hire **bikes**.

Accommodation

Outside the pilgrimage season (Nov–Feb) discounts of up to fifty percent are available in most hotels. Many of the **monastery guesthouses** welcome tourists, but you will be expected to adhere to the same rules as the pilgrims, in particular no smoking, alcohol or sex. Monasteries are not allowed to define a fixed rate for accommodation; the price codes below are based on recommended donations.

Monasteries

Bhutanese Monastery Buddha Marg. An old guesthouse, next to the monastery and full of character, with single and family rooms, some with private bathroom and hot water. ❶–❷

Burmese Monastery (Vihar) Gaya Rd. Set in a pleasant garden, the rooms at this guesthouse are boxy but inexpensive. The absence of fans and the prevalence of biting insects will test your Buddhist indifference to personal comfort. ❶

Mahabodhi Society Pilgrim Rest House Bodhgaya Rd ✆ 0631/220 0742. Also known as the *Sri Lankan Guest House*, this Mahabodhi Society-run lodge is very popular with pilgrims and often full. There's a dorm, a handful of private rooms and a modest vegetarian canteen. ❶–❷

Hotels

Buddha International Near the Indosan Nipponji Temple ✆ 0631/220 0506, ✉ buddha_int@yahoo .com. A cool marble lobby – complete with a peculiar mini-stalactite ceiling – gives way to spacious attached rooms with balconies, TVs and telephones. Big off-season discounts are on offer. ❺–❻

Buddha Vihar and **Siddartha Vihar** Bihar State Tourism Corporation complex ✆ 0631/220 0445. The former has decent three- to ten-bed dorms (Rs75–100), while the latter has somewhat shabby but good-value attached doubles. Prices don't rise in the high season, but the management can be curt. ❸–❹

Deep Guesthouse Near the *Burmese Vihar* ✆ 0631/220 0463. One of Bodhgaya's best budget lodges, offering a warm welcome and sociable atmosphere. Rooms are smallish but super-clean; those with private bathrooms have western toilets and TVs. ❶–❷

Embassy Bodhgaya Rd ✆ 0631/220 0127, ✉ embassyhotelbodhgaya@yahoo.com. A fresh lick of paint has breathed new life into this solid mid-range hotel, which has no-frills marble-floored rooms with spotless bathrooms and TVs. ❹

Kirti Guest House Close to Kalchakra Maidan. Run by the Tibetan Monastery, *Kirti* – accessed via a short bridge and covered with climbing plants – has a huge fish tank in the lobby and a serene air. The wood-panelled doubles with green carpets are a little overpriced, but the triples are great value. ❺

Om Guest House Bodhgaya Rd ✆ 09934 057498. Not for anyone vaguely claustrophobic, and without the communal vibe of some of the other traveller places, *Om* nevertheless delivers spic-and-span rooms with attached bathrooms and bright yellow walls at a price that's hard to beat. ❷

Royal Residency Domuhan Rd ✆ 0631/220 1156, ✇ www.theroyalresidency.net. An immaculate but pricey option: the attached rooms ($150) boast sleek wooden floors and fittings, cream-coloured walls and minimalist decor. There's also a communal Japanese bath and the excellent *Amarapali* restaurant. ❾

Sujata Buddha Marg ✆ 0631/220 0481, ✇ www .sujatahotel.com. The a/c attached rooms ($75) are a little plain but come with balconies, gold-flecked bedspreads and sparkling bathrooms with tubs. There's also a restaurant and 24hr coffee shop. ❽

Tathagat International Bodhgaya Rd ✆ 0631/220 0106, ✇ www.hoteltathagatbodhgaya.net. A prominent whitewashed building opposite the deer park, *Tathagat* has slightly cramped but comfortable rooms with mini-sofas, checked curtains and private balconies. Staff can book train and flight tickets. ❺–❻

Meditation courses in Bodhgaya

Especially during the winter high season, **meditation courses** are available in either of the two distinct traditions of Buddhism: Mahayana (the Great Vehicle), epitomized by the various forms of Tibetan Buddhism which spread across China and Japan; and Hinayana (or Theravada), as practised in Sri Lanka, Thailand and other parts of Southeast Asia. Check noticeboards in the various cafés, and ask at the *Root Institute* (see below) or the *Burmese Vihar*.

The **Root Institute for Wisdom Culture** (℡0631/220 0714, Ⓦwww.rootinstitute .com) is a real haven, a semi-monastic *dharma* centre 2km west of the main temple with pleasant gardens, a shrine room, library and accommodation. It organizes residential courses, focusing on the Mahayana tradition. There are drop-in meditation classes, one-day workshops and longer courses on Buddhism, yoga and meditation between October and March. An eight-day course, including fee, food and accommodation, typically costs from $100 – book well in advance. The institute is always looking for volunteers (minimum three months) for general tasks and to help in its charitable school and polio, TB and mobile clinics.

The **Dhamma Bodhi International Meditation Centre** (℡0631/220 0437), a Vipassana centre, is a few kilometres out of town near Magadha University on Dobi Road, and holds regular courses throughout the year. Details of all Vipassana courses are available from the International Academy in Maharashtra (℡02553/228 4076), or you can contact the Vipassana Meditation Centre in the UK (℡01989/730234, Ⓦwww.dhamma.org).

The **International Meditation Centre** (℡0631/220 0707), a couple of hundred metres behind the Chinese temple, also runs Vipassana courses for both beginners and advanced students; donations are accepted as there are no fixed fees.

Another centre of activity is the **Burmese Vihar**. Although not currently running meditation courses they have some useful information and are involved with voluntary social-work projects. **Insight Meditation** (Ⓦwww.bodhgayaretreats.org) runs seven- to ten-day Vipassana retreats with western teachers at the Thai Monastery.

The Mahabodhi Temple and the Bodhi Tree

The elegant single spire of the **Mahabodhi Temple**, rising to a lofty height of 55m, is visible throughout the surrounding countryside. Within the temple complex, which is liberally sprinkled with small stupas and shrines, the main brick temple stands in a hollow encircled by a stone railing dating from the second century BC. Unlike most popular temples in India, this World Heritage Site exudes an atmosphere of peace and tranquillity. Extensively renovated during the nineteenth century, it is supposed to be a replica of a seventh-century structure that in turn stood on the site of Ashoka's original third-century BC shrine. Inside the temple, a single chamber holds a large gilded image of the Buddha, while upstairs is a balcony and a small, plain meditation chamber.

At the rear of the temple to the west, the large **Bodhi Tree** grows out of an expansive base, attracting scholars and meditators. However, the tree is only a distant offshoot of the one under which Buddha attained enlightenment – the original was destroyed by Ashoka before his conversion to Buddhism. His daughter Sanghamitra took a sapling to Sri Lanka and planted it at Anuradhapura, where its offshoots were nurtured. A cutting was later brought back to Bodhgaya and replanted. Pilgrims tie coloured thread to its branches and Tibetans accompany their rituals with long lines of butter lamps. A sandstone slab with carved sides next to the tree is believed to be the **Vajrasana**, or "thunder-seat", upon which the Buddha sat facing east.

The small white **Animesh Lochana Temple** to the right of the compound entrance marks the spot where the Buddha stood and gazed upon the Bodhi Tree in gratitude. Numerous ornate stupas from the Pala period (seventh to twelfth centuries) are littered around the grounds and next to the temple compound to the south is a rectangular lotus pool where the Buddha is believed to have bathed.

Entry to the temple complex (daily 5am–9pm; camera Rs20, video Rs500, audio guide Rs20) is from the east; shoes are tolerated within the grounds but not inside the temple: they can be left at the entrance for a small donation. Guides also congregate at the entrance and charge around Rs100 per hour.

Temples and monasteries

Incongruous modern monasteries and temples have transformed the arid landscape around the Mahabodhi Temple – they are all open from around 7am until noon and between 2pm and 6pm. Some are very simple while others, like the **Thai Temple**, with its unmistakable roof, are elaborate confections. The **Gelugpa Tibetan Monastery**, or *gompa*, is within the Tibetan quarter northwest of the main shrine. The complex includes a central prayer hall, large prayer wheel and residential buildings. The bigger of the two other Tibetan monasteries further west belongs to the **Kagyu** sect; its spacious main prayer hall is decorated with beautiful modern murals, Buddha images and a large Dharma Chakra, or "Wheel of Law". The other two major Tibetan schools also have monastic representation here – there's a **Nyingma** *gompa* next to the Chinese temple and a small **Sakya** *gompa* close to *Hotel Buddha International*.

Next to the Kagyu Monastery, the **Daijokyo Monastery** captures in concrete some elements of a traditional Japanese temple and belongs to the Nichiren sect. Opposite, the **Indosan Nipponji Temple** has an elegant and simple hut-like roof and a beautiful image of the Buddha inside its main hall. Next door, the exquisite **Bhutanese Monastery** features finely painted murals and ceiling mandalas. In a decorative garden at the end of the road, the imposing 25-metre Japanese-style **Giant Buddha Statue** was consecrated by the Dalai Lama in 1989.

Bodhgaya's **Archaeological Museum** (daily except Fri 10am–5pm; Rs2), west of the Mahabodhi Temple complex, has a collection of locally discovered sculptures and ninth-century bronzes of Hindu and Buddhist deities.

Eating

Bodhgaya has Bihar's widest range of eateries, catering to the palates of pilgrims and visitors from all around the world. During the November to February peak season Tibetan tent restaurants spring up throughout town – follow the crowds to find the best ones.

Fujia Green Kalchakra Maidan. An ever-popular Tibetan joint: a cross between a hut and a tent, with plastic chairs and Christmas-style decorations. If you can decipher the erratically spelled menu, you'll find a vast array of *momos* (dumplings) and hearty noodle soups at rock-bottom prices (Rs15–40).

Gautam Lassi Corner Opposite the Mahabodhi Temple entrance. A bustling low-key joint that does a brisk trade in refreshing lassis (try the pineapple flavour), freshly squeezed juices and piping-hot coffee (Rs10–25).

Siam Thai Bodhgaya Rd. Appealing restaurant with authentic Thai food and hospitality. Try the sumptuous red chicken curry or the jumbo prawns in yellow bean sauce (Rs90–300). Beware: the food can be very hot, so ask the kitchen to go easy on the chilli if you prefer it mild.

Swagat *Hotel Tathagat International*. The dining room is a little dim but the menu has a tempting selection of veg and chicken burgers, north Indian dishes like *keema* mutton and decent stabs at Continental mainstays such as chicken Kiev (Rs50–130).

Old Pole Pole and Original Pole Pole Opposite the *Burmese Vihar*. These neighbouring tent restaurants are locked in a dispute over which came first – either way they have similar traveller-oriented menus with big breakfasts, banana pancakes and cinnamon pastries (Rs25–70).

Om Bodhgaya Rd. This canteen is a backpacker stalwart, but come for a quick bite, rather than a leisurely meal. Economically priced Japanese, Korean, Chinese and Indian food, *dosas*, chocolate chip cookies and apple pie (Rs20–70) are all on offer.

Around Bodhgaya: Mahakala Caves

In remote, almost desert-like surroundings on the far side of the Falgu River, 18km northeast of Bodhgaya, sit the **Mahakala** (or Dungeshwari) **Caves**, where the Buddha did the severe penance that resulted in the familiar image of him as a skeletal, emaciated figure. After years of extreme self-denial at Mahakala, he realized its futility and walked down to Bodhgaya, where he eventually achieved nirvana under the Bodhi Tree. A short climb from the base of the impressive cliff leads to a Tibetan monastery and the small caves themselves. A Buddhist shrine inside the main cave is run by Tibetans, although a Hindu priest has also set himself up in competition. Few tourists make it here and the occasional car or bus that does arrive gets mobbed by urchins and beggars.

Rajgir

Eighty kilometres northeast of Bodhgaya, the small market town of **RAJGIR** nestles in rocky hills that witnessed the meditations and teachings of both the Buddha and Mahavira, the founder of Jainism. The capital of the Magadha kingdom before Pataliputra, Rajgir was also where King Bimbisara converted to Buddhism. As well as its religious significance, this pleasant town is also considered a health resort because of its **hot springs**, which can get unpleasantly crowded.

A Japanese shrine at **Venuvana Vihara** marks the spot where a monastery was built for the Buddha to live in, while at **Griddhakuta** (Vulture's Peak), on Ratnagiri Hill, 3km from the town centre, the Buddha set in motion his second "Wheel of Law". The massive modern **Peace Pagoda**, built by the Japanese, dominates Ratnagiri Hill and can be reached by a rickety chairlift (daily 8.15am–1pm & 2–5pm, last ticket 4.30pm; Rs30). Griddhakuta is actually halfway down the hill, so you may prefer to wander down from here rather than climb back up to take the chair lift. Look out for the 26 Jain shrines on top of these hills, reached by a challenging trek attempted almost solely by Jain devotees. On an adjacent hill, in the **Saptaparni cave**, the first Buddhist council met to record the teachings of the Buddha after his death.

Practicalities

Rajgir is connected by **bus** to Gaya, Bodhgaya and Patna; for the latter you sometimes have to change at Bihar Sharif, 25km away. You can also visit Rajgir as part of a long and tiring day-trip, including Nalanda and Pawapuri, from either Patna or Bodhgaya.

The town has several hotels, including the unique 𝒜 *Indo Hokke* (☎0631/220 1156, ⓦwww.theroyalresidency.net; ❾), 2km from Kund Market, which fuses Japanese and Indian architectural influences. It has Japanese- and western-style rooms ($160–180), a communal Japanese bath, and the outstanding *Lotus* restaurant (mains Rs75–400). Moving down the price scale, *Siddharth* (☎06112/255 616; ❹), in Kund Market, a couple of kilometres south of the bus station, is a welcoming place with comfortable carpeted rooms with clean attached bathrooms. Run by the state tourist authority, *Gautam Vihar* (☎06112/255 273; ❸–❹), 300m from the bus station on the road to Nalanda, has spacious rooms with pleasant verandas, a decent dorm (Rs75) and a hit-and-miss garden restaurant. Outside of the hotels, *Green* **restaurant**, opposite the temple complex, offers reasonably priced (Rs25–60) Indian and Chinese food and a relaxed atmosphere on its terrace.

Nalanda and around

The richly adorned towers and the fairy-like turrets, like the pointed hill-tops, are congregated together... The stages have dragon projections and coloured eaves, the pearl-red pillars carved and ornamented, the richly adorned balustrades, and the roofs covered with tiles that reflect the light in a thousand shades.

Hiuen Tsang, who spent twelve years at Nalanda as student and teacher

Founded in the fifth century AD by the Guptas, the great monastic **Buddhist university** of **NALANDA** attracted thousands of international students and teachers until it was sacked by the Afghan invader Bhaktiar Khilji in the twelfth century. Courses included philosophy, logic, theology, grammar, astronomy, mathematics and medicine. Education was provided free, supported by the revenue from surrounding villages and benefactors such as the eighth-century king of Sumatra.

Excavations have revealed nine levels of occupation on the site, dating back to the time of the Buddha and Mahavira in the sixth century BC. Most of it is now in ruins, but the orderliness and scale of what remains is staggering evidence of the strength of Buddhist civilization in its prime. The site is strewn with the remains of stupas, temples and eleven monasteries, their thick walls impressively intact. Nalanda is now part of the modern Buddhist pilgrimage circuit, but even the casual tourist will appreciate taking the time to walk through the extensive site, or climb its massive 31-metre **stupa** for commanding views. Informative booklets available at the ticket booth render the numerous guides unnecessary. A small alfresco bar inside the grounds serves tea, coffee and soft drinks without the hassle of the touts and beggars at the entrance.

Nalanda Museum (daily except Fri 10am–5pm; Rs5) houses antiquities found here and at Rajgir, including Buddhist and Hindu bronzes and a number of undamaged statues of the Buddha. **Nava Nalanda Mahavihara**, the Pali postgraduate research institute, houses many rare Buddhist manuscripts, and is devoted to study and research in Pali literature and Buddhism.

Shared jeeps run regularly between Rajgir and Bihar Sharif, 35km to the northeast, stopping at the turning to Nalanda, from where an assortment of transport, including shared tongas, is available for the remaining 2km to the gates of the site. An old colonial villa 300m past the site is run as a **resthouse** (no telephone; ❶), with large double rooms with verandas, lounge, gardens and simple food.

East of Nalanda

Eighteen kilometres east of Nalanda, at **PAWAPURI**, Mahavira, the founder of Jainism, is said to have attained enlightenment. He died and was cremated here around 500 BC, and the site is now a major draw for pilgrims, who come to visit the **Jalamandir**, a white marble temple in the centre of a lotus pond. Buses to Pawapuri run from Bihar Sharif.

A further 80km east of Pawapuri, at **MUNGER**, is the **Bihar School of Yoga** (☎06344/222430, ⓦwww.yogamag.net) Led by Swami Niranjananda Saraswati, the ashram is the world's first accredited yoga university and runs popular four-month yoga courses in English from October to January, although short stays are also possible. Buses run from Bihar Sharif, or the ashram can help arrange transport. It has a sister school at Rikhia in Jharkhand.

Jharkhand

On the eastern edge of the Vindhya hills, close to the northern fringes of the Deccan, lies the rugged **Chotanagpur plateau** that makes up **JHARKHAND**. An independent state since 2000, after years of agitation by its largely *adivasi* (tribal) population, Jharkhand yields almost forty percent of India's minerals and produces some of the cheapest iron and steel in the country. Roads are noticeably better than in Bihar and residents more upbeat about their future than their northern neighbours. Nevertheless, Jharkhand continues to suffer from inefficient government, extreme poverty and general lawlessness. Although crime has fallen in recent years, numerous Maoist (Naxalite) groups continue to operate in the state – between 2000 and 2007 more than one thousand people were killed in clashes between them and state security forces.

Jharkhand's prime attraction is **Palamau National Park**, but sadly its beautiful forests have been damaged by years of drought and its tigers are now severely endangered. Other forest reserves and parks pepper the state, including **Hazaribagh National Park** in the north. However, bandits and Naxalites are active in these areas, and around Parasnath, so it's vital to check the **security situation** before venturing out, and to avoid travelling at night throughout the state.

Ranchi

Once the pleasant summer capital of Bihar, **RANCHI** is now an ugly and heavily industrialized city, but you'll probably need to stay here on your way to Palamau National Park. One of its few claims to fame is as the birthplace of **MS Dhoni**, India's dashing wicketkeeper-batsman.

The city has a small museum detailing the life and history of the state's tribes at the **Jharkhand Tribal Research Institute** (Mon–Sat 10am–5pm), 4km from the centre, while the seventeenth-century Hindu **Jagannath Temple** is just under 10km away on a hilltop. The pretty **Hundru** and **Jonha waterfalls** can be visited in a morning and offer some respite from the city.

Practicalities

Several major **trains** connect Ranchi with Kolkata, Delhi, Patna, Daltonganj (for Palamau National Park) and Dhanbad, some terminating at Hatia, 7km away. The state **bus stand** near the railway station serves Bodhgaya, Gaya and Patna; Daltonganj is reached from Rathu Road terminus. Services to all other destinations leave from Khadgarh bus station, 3km from the railway station. **Jharkhand Tourism** runs two daily buses to Patna (8am and 8pm) from its tourist office (Mon–Sat 10am–5pm; ☎0651/231 0230) at the *Birsa Vihar* tourist centre. You can fly from Ranchi's **airport** to Delhi, Kolkata, Mumbai and Patna. See "Travel details" at the end of this chapter for more information on journey frequencies and durations.

Ashok Travels at the *Ranchi Ashok* (☎0651/248 0759) and Suhana Travels (☎0651/309 3808) on Station Road can arrange **local sightseeing trips**, excursions to Palamau National Park and car hire. Most of Ranchi's facilities can be found on Main Road including the **post office**, the State Bank of India and an IDBI Bank **ATM**. There are **Internet** places on Station Road including the speedy i-Way (Rs25/hr).

Most of Ranchi's **hotels** are also along, or just off, Main Road. *Embassy* (℡0651/246 0813; ❸–❹) is one of the better options for budget travellers, with straightforward, fairly clean rooms. Close to the railway station and run by the South Eastern Railway, the atmospheric Raj-style 🛪 *BNR Hotel* (Station Rd; ℡0651/246 0584; ❹–❺) dates back almost one hundred years and has an appealing faded grandeur. The sizeable but dated rooms are in bungalows surrounded by pleasant gardens. *Capitol Hill* (℡0651/233 1330, Ⓦwww .hotelcapitolhill.com; ❻) in the Capitol shopping complex, 2km from the railway station, is Ranchi's most stylish hotel. Its pinkish-hued attached rooms all have minibars, Internet access and 24hr room service, while the restaurant serves up outstanding tandoori dishes.

There are plenty of **restaurants** off Main Road, including *Min Min's*, the place to head for reasonably priced Chinese food, and *Masala Planet*, which offers a range of south Indian *dosas*, thalis and ice cream. For north Indian veg staples, try *Vegica's*, also on Main Road, near the Sujata cinema. *The Nook*, in the *Kwality Inn* hotel on Station Road, has tasty meat and fish meals, served up by welcoming staff in a buzzing dining-room.

Palamau (Betla) National Park

In a remote and lawless corner of Jharkhand, 170km west of Ranchi, the beautiful *sal* forests of the **PALAMAU NATIONAL PARK** cover around one thousand square kilometres of hilly terrain. Although part of **Project Tiger**, Palamau has been hard hit by drought and tiger sightings are rare. You are more likely to see elephants, antelope, bison and wild boar. The park is open all year, but October to April is the best time to visit.

Practicalities

The official park headquarters, **Daltonganj**, are served by direct buses and a branch railway line from Ranchi. Regular buses make the 25km journey from Daltonganj to **Betla**, the park's entry point. If you're coming from Ranchi, you could try to change buses at the turn-off and get to Betla without going through Daltonganj.

Next to the Betla gates is an **information centre** where entry tickets can be purchased (℡06562/222 650; Rs80 per vehicle, compulsory guide Rs20/hr, elephant ride Rs100, camera Rs50, video Rs300) and **Jeeps** hired (around Rs200/hr). The state-run *Van Vihar* (℡06567/226 513; ❸–❹), close to the park entrance, is the most comfortable and convenient **accommodation** option, with a wide range of standard rooms, a dorm (Rs100) and even a cosy double in a treehouse. Contact the Field Director to reserve one of the very basic **resthouses** (℡06562/222 650; ❷–❸) inside the reserve. There are a few simple *dhabas* at the park gates.

Travel details

Trains

Gaya to: Allahabad (4 daily; 4hr 20min–6hr 30min); Dehra Dun (1 daily; 25hr); Delhi (9 daily; 12–15hr); Haridwar (1 daily; 23hr); Kolkata; 5–6 daily; 6–13hr); Lucknow (3 daily; 12–13hr); Mughal Sarai (13 daily, 2hr 20min–5hr); Mumbai (1 daily; 31hr); Patna (3–4 daily; 2hr 30min); Puri (1–2 daily;

14hr 5min–18hr 10min); Ranchi (2–3 daily; 4hr–8hr 30min); Sasaram (10 daily; 1–3hr); Varanasi (3 daily; 4hr–5hr 30min).

Jasidih to: Delhi (6 weekly; 15hr 30min–21hr); Kolkata (6 weekly; 5hr 5min–6hr); Patna (6 weekly; 4hr 30min–7hr).

Patna to: Agra (1 daily; 18hr 35min); Allahabad (8–9 daily; 5hr–8hr 45min); Chennai (3 weekly; 38hr 30min–40hr); Delhi (8 daily; 12hr 40min–24hr); Gaya (3–4 daily; 2hr 30min); Guwahati (3 daily; 19–27hr); Kolkata (3–4 daily; 8hr 10min–13hr); Lucknow (4–5 daily; 5hr 30min–15hr); Mumbai (2–3 daily; 30–36hr); Puri (1 weekly; 18hr 25min); Ranchi (3 daily; 8hr 55min–13hr 35min); Varanasi (2–3 daily; 3–5hr).

Ranchi to: Allahabad (2 daily; 13–18hr 30min); Daltonganj (3–4 daily; 5hr 30min–8hr 30min); Delhi (2 daily; 23–29hr); Dhanbad (2–3 daily; 3hr 40min–6hr 10min); Gaya (2–3 daily; 4hr–8hr 30min); Kolkata (5 weekly; 8hr 30min); Patna (3 daily; 8hr 55min–13hr 35min).

Buses

Bodhgaya to: Gaya (hourly; 45min); Patna (2–4 daily; 4hr 30min–5hr 30min); Rajgir (hourly; 2hr 30min); Ranchi (1–2 daily; 9hr); Siliguri (1–2 daily; 15–17hr); Varanasi (1–2 daily; 6–7hr).

Gaya to: Bodhgaya (hourly; 45min); Mughal Sarai (6 daily; 5hr); Patna (hourly; 3hr 30min–4hr 30min); Rajgir (hourly; 2hr 30min–3hr); Ranchi (8 daily; 8hr); Sasaram (8 daily; 3hr); Varanasi (6 daily; 5hr 30min).

Patna to: Bodhgaya (2–4 daily; 4hr 30min–5hr 30min); Gaya (hourly; 3hr 30min–4hr 30min); Rajgir (hourly; 4hr); Ranchi (4–6 daily; 10–14hr); Raxaul (18 daily; 8hr); Vaishali (2 daily; 3hr); Varanasi (4 daily; 6hr 30min).

Rajgir to: Bihar Sharif (hourly; 1hr); Patna (hourly; 4hr–4hr 30min).

Ranchi to: Bodhgaya (1–2 daily; 9hr); Daltonganj (4 daily; 8hr); Dhanbad (6 daily; 5hr); Gaya (8 daily; 8hr); Parasnath (hourly; 6hr); Patna (4–6 daily; 10–14hr).

Vaishali to: Chakia (hourly; 3hr).

Flights

(**IC** = Indian Airlines, **9W** = Jet Airways, **DN** = Air Deccan, **S2** = JetLite)

Gaya to: Bangkok (IC; 3 weekly; 6hr); Guwahati (IC; 1 weekly; 1hr 10min); Kolkata (IC; 1 weekly; 55min); Yangoon (IC; 1 weekly; 3hr 10min).

Patna to: Bagdogra (IC; 3 weekly; 45min); Delhi (IC, 9W, DN, S2; 5–6 daily; 1hr 25min); Guwahati (IC; 3 weekly; 2hr); Kolkata (DN, S2; 1–2 daily; 55min); Lucknow (S2; 1 daily; 55min); Mumbai (IC, S2; 3–4 daily; 3hr 45min–6hr); Ranchi (IC; 1 daily; 45min); Varanasi (S2; 1 daily; 40min).

Ranchi to: Bhubaneshwar (IC; 6 weekly; 50min); Delhi (IC, S2, DN; 3–4 daily; 1hr 35min–3hr 20min); Kolkata (DN; 2 daily; 55min); Mumbai (IC, S2; 2–3 daily; 2hr 30min-4hr 40min); Patna (IC; 1 daily; 45min).

Sikkim

AFGHANISTAN

0   400 km

CHINA
(TIBET AUTONOMOUS
REGION)

PAKISTAN

BHUTAN

NEPAL

BANGLADESH

MYANMAR
(BURMA)

ARABIAN
SEA

BAY OF BENGAL

N

SRI
LANKA

INDIAN OCEAN

The International boundaries on this map are neither purported to be correct nor authentic by Survey of India directives Publisher.

CHAPTER 15

Highlights

✳ **Chaam** Catch this mysterious and colourful lama dance, held in most monasteries around the harvest festival of Losung (early December) to cleanse the world of evil spirits. See p.931

✳ **Rumtek** One of Sikkim's most venerated monasteries, Rumtek is home to the Black Hat sect, and hosts a spectacular festival in February. See p.941

✳ **Maenam mountain** Take a day-trek through an ancient forest to the summit of the mountain – you may be lucky enough to spot deer and red panda. See p.945

✳ **Pemayangtse** A wonderful seventeenth-century mona-stery perched on a high ridge facing Darjeeling. See p.946

✳ **Varshey Rhododendron Sanctuary** Magnificent views and gentle trails through a botanical paradise. See p.948

✳ **Dzongri Trail** Trek through rhododendrons and across high alpine meadows in the shadow of Kanchenjunga, the third-highest mountain in the world. See p.950

✳ **Singalila Ridge** A high alpine meadows trail past remote lakes that offers some of the finest views in the eastern Himalayas, from Kanchenjunga to Everest. See p.951

✳ **Tashiding** A monastic complex on a conical hill with marvellous views. See p.954

▲ Rice terraces, Sikkim

Sikkim

The tiny and beautiful state of **SIKKIM** lies to the south of Tibet, sandwiched between Nepal to the west and Bhutan to the east. Measuring just 65km by 115km, its landscape ranges from sweltering deep valleys just 300m above sea level to lofty snow peaks such as Kanchenjunga (Kanchendzonga to the locals) which, at 8586m, is the third-highest mountain in the world. A small but growing network of tortuous roads penetrate this rugged Himalayan wilderness, but they take a massive battering every monsoon, with large and frequent landslides disrupting communications.

For centuries Sikkim was an isolated, independent Buddhist kingdom, until war with China in the early 1960s led the Indian government to realize the area's worth as a crucial corridor between Tibet and Bangladesh. As a result of its annexation by India in 1975, Sikkim has experienced dramatic changes. Now a fully-fledged Indian state, it is predominantly Hindu, with a population made up of 75 percent **Nepalese Gurungs**, and less than twenty percent **Lepchas**, its former rulers. Smaller proportions survive of **Bhutias**, of Tibetan stock, and **Limbus**, also possibly of Tibetan origin, who gave the state its name – *sukh-im*, "happy homeland". Nepali is now the lingua franca and the Nepalese are socially and politically the most dominant people in the state. However, with the recent civil war across the western border in Nepal and the volatile Nepalese Gurkha movement in neighbouring Darjeeling in West Bengal, the ethnic balance remains delicate. The ruling minority in neighbouring Bhutan, having observed this transition with alarm, has adopted an intransigent and aggressive stance towards the Nepalese, with the final expulsion of ethnic Nepalese from Bhutan. However, due to the recent reopening of the lucrative

The daming of Sikkim's rivers

The ongoing construction programme of **dams** and numerous **hydroelectric projects** on Sikkim's rivers has brought government policy into direct conflict with the interests of the state's diminishing indigenous population. In Dzongu, the heartland of the Lepchas, the dams threaten the lifestyle of the very people the state has claimed to protect, with the Lepchas contending that the huge influx of indentured labourers brought in to work on the projects will result in the rapid destruction of their social and communal heritage. As strikes and political protest are forbidden here, the plight of the Dzongu Lepchas has gone almost unnoticed, though they are trying to make their voice heard by way of hunger strikes outside Sikkim and low-key dissent in Gangtok itself. For more information, visit ⓦ www.weepingsikkim.blogspot.com.

SIKKIM

CHINA
(TIBET AUTONOMOUS
REPUBLIC)

N

0   20 km

Gurudogmar ●

▲ Kangchengyao
(6889m)   ▲ Pauhunri
(7125m)

Chopta
Valley ●   ● Thangu   Chombu   Yumé
Fluted Peak   (6362m)   Samdang ●
(6084m) ▲
Nepal Peak   ● Yumthang
(6910m) ▲   (3645m)

Green Lake
(4850m) ●   G R E A T   H I M A L A Y A

Kanchenjunga   Tangchung   Lama Wangden
(8586m) ▲   Khang   (5868m)
Zemu Glacier   (6010m)   Lachen
Simvo   ▲ Siniolchu   (2977m)   Lachung   ● Lachung
N E P A L   (6812m)   (6887m)   Kyeshong La   (2734m)
(3790m)
Talung Glacier   DZONGU
Kabru   TEESTA
(7338m) ▲   KANCHENDZONGA
Kokthang ▲ Goecha La   NATIONAL   ♜ Tolung   Chungthang
(6147m)   ▲ (4940m)   PARK   (1579m)   CHINA
Zemanthang (4453m) ▲ Pandim   (TIBET
Kangla ▲ Chaurikhang   (6691m) Narsing   Singhik   AUTONOMOUS
(5200m) Dzongri La ▲ Jopuno ▲ (5825m)   ● Tosar Lake   REPUBLIC)
Lampokhari (4400m)   (5935m) Samiti Lake   Mangan ●
Lake ▲ Dzongri   Thansing
Danfeybhir (4030m) (3930m)   Labrang ♜
Tar (4400m) Tsokha   Nathu La
Khecheopalri Bakhim Yoksum   Phodong ♜ ● Phensang ▲ (4328m)
Lake   (1780m)   Lingdum   Serathang
Chewabhanjang   Tashiding ♜ Ralang   Rumtek Tsomgo
(3170m) Pelling ♜   Maenam   ● Gangtok Lake
Uttarey   ● Ghezing Pemayangtse ♜ ▲ (3235m)   (3767m)
(1695m) Legship Kewzing Ravangla Ranipool
Varshey Dentam Rinchenpong   Tendong Singtam ● Assam Lingzey
(3030m) Hilley   ▲ (2757m) Rangpo
Phalut ▲ Soreng Naya   Samdruptse ○   ● Aritar
Sombare Daramdin Bazaar Jorethang Melli   BHUTAN
Namchi   Bazaar Teesta
W E S T   Melli
Darjeeling ●   Teesta Bazaar   Bazaar ● Kalimpong
B E N G A L

The international boundaries on this map are neither purported to be correct nor authentic by Survey of India directives. Publisher.

trade route at **Nathu La** on the border with **Tibet**, Sikkim exudes a growing optimism, and continues to hold a special status within the Indian union, exempt from income tax and attracting government subsidy. Although only Sikkimese can hold major shares in property and businesses, partnerships with Indian (non-Sikkimese) entrepreneurs and subsidies to indigenous Sikkimese light industry have led to prosperity that's evident as soon as you cross the border from West Bengal.

Historically, culturally and spiritually, Sikkim's strongest links are with Tibet. The main draws for visitors are the state's off-the-beaten-track **trekking** and its many **monasteries**, over two hundred in all, mostly belonging to the ancient **Nyingmapa** sect. **Pemayangtse** in West Sikkim is the most historically signifi-cant, and houses an extraordinary wooden mandala depicting Guru Rinpoche's Heavenly Palace. **Tashiding**, a Nyingmapa monastery built in 1717, surrounded by prayer flags and *chortens* and looking across to snowcapped peaks, is considered Sikkim's holiest. **Rumtek** is the seat of the **Gyalwa Karmapa** – head of the **Karma Kagyu** lineage – and probably the most influential monastery in Sikkim. The problems in Nepal have led to a tourism boom in Sikkim, with trekkers searching for alternative Eastern Himalayan routes. The capital, **Gangtok**, is home to a bewildering array of trekking agents only too happy to take your money in dollars – it's also the place to get hold of permits for Sikkim's restricted areas.

Sikkim's gigantic mountain walls and steep wooded hillsides, drained by torrential rivers such as the **Teesta** and the **Rangit**, are a botanist's dream. The lower slopes abound in **orchids**; sprays of cardamom carpet the forest floor, and the land is rich with apple orchards, orange groves and terraced paddy fields (to the Tibetans, this was Denzong, "the land of rice"). At higher altitudes, monsoon mists cling to huge tracts of lichen-covered forests, where countless varieties of rhododendron carpet the hillsides and giant magnolia trees punctuate the deep verdant cover. Higher still, approaching the Tibetan plateau, larch and dwarf rhododendron give way to meadows abundant with gentians and potentilla. Sikkim's forests and wilderness areas are inhabited by a wealth of fauna, including elusive snow leopards, tahr (wild ass on the Tibet plateau), *bharal* or blue sheep, black bear, flying squirrels and the symbol of Sikkim – the endangered **red panda**.

The **best time to visit** is between mid–March and June but especially March, April and May, when the rhododendrons and orchids bloom – although temperatures can be high at this time of year, especially in the valleys. Any earlier than that, and lingering winter snow can make high-altitude trekking arduous. During the monsoons, from the end of June until early September, rivers and roads become impassable, though plants nurtured by the incessant rain erupt again into bloom towards the end of August. October (when orchids bloom once again) and November tend to have the clearest weather of all. Although the colourful harvest festival of **Losung** is in early December, as the month progresses, it gets bitterly cold (especially at high altitudes), and remains that way until early March, despite long periods of clear weather. The impact of global warming is proving tragic for Sikkim, with rapidly receding glaciers and unpredictable weather patterns resulting in excessive rain and the disruption of the state's fragile road systems.

Some history

No one knows quite when or how the **Lepchas** – or the Rong, as they call themselves – came to Sikkim, but their roots can be traced back to the animist Nagas of the Indo-Burmese border. **Buddhism**, which arrived from Tibet in the thirteenth century, took its distinctive Sikkimese form four centuries later, when three Tibetan monks of the old Nyingmapa order, disenchanted with the rise of the reformist Gelugpas, migrated south and gathered at Yoksum in western Sikkim. Having consulted the oracle, they sent to Gangtok for a certain Phuntsog Namgyal, whom they crowned as the first **chogyal** or "righteous king" of Denzong in 1642. Both the secular and religious head of Sikkim, he was soon recognized by Tibet, and set about sweeping reforms. His domain was far larger than today's Sikkim, taking in Kalimpong and parts of western Bhutan.

Over the centuries, territory was lost to the Bhutanese, the Nepalese and the **British**. Sikkim originally ceded Darjeeling to the East India Company as a spa in 1817, but was forced to give up all claim to it in 1861 when the kingdom was declared a protectorate of the British. **Tibet**, which perceived Sikkim as a vassalage, objected and invaded in 1886, but a small British force sent in 1888

Permits and restrictions

Though foreigners need to obtain an **Inner Line Permit** (ILP) to visit Sikkim, getting one is a mere, if irritating, formality. The easiest way is to request one when applying for your Indian visa, though it is also possible to pick up permits in India at the offices listed below. Permits are also instantly available at the **Sikkim border**, but only at Rangpo; go to the tourist office for an application form and then cross the road to have it registered by the police. Shared taxis and buses may not be happy to wait the half-hour or so this process takes. If you're picking up your permit after arrival in India, you'll need two passport photographs, and photocopies of your passport and visa details.

Permits are date-specific and initially valid for fifteen days from entry into the state, which allows enough time to visit the towns and villages at a fairly leisurely pace but places constraints on time if trekking. However, permits are normally renewable for a further fifteen days, and can be extended up to a maximum of sixty days in special cases such as for expeditions. Extensions can be obtained at the Foreigner's Regional Registration Office, Kazi Road, Gangtok (☎03592/223041), and are also available through the superintendents of police at Mangan, Ghezing and Namchi, the capitals of the three other districts. As well as Gangtok and its surroundings in East Sikkim, the general Sikkim permit (ILP) covers all of South Sikkim and most areas in the east and west of the state, apart from the high-altitude treks. Sensitive border areas, like Tsomgo Lake (also known as Changu or Tsangu) in East Sikkim, most of North Sikkim except for Mangan and its immediate vicinity and all high-altitude treks including the Singalila Ridge and Dzongri, require the additional Protected Area Permit (PAP) (see box opposite); foreigners can only enter in groups of at least two accompanied by representatives of approved travel agents, who will themselves arrange the permits. Some areas, such as Nathu La on the border with Tibet in East Sikkim, remain completely off-limits to foreigners.

Offices in India issuing permits

Airport immigration At the four main entry points: Delhi, Mumbai, Kolkata, Chennai.

Foreigners' Regional Registration Offices In Delhi, Mumbai, Kolkata and Chennai. Also in Darjeeling on Laden La Road (see Darjeeling, p.891, for details).

Resident Commissioner Sikkim House, 14 Panchsheel Marg, Chanakyapuri, New Delhi ☎011/2611 5346.

Sikkim Tourist Centre SNTC Bus Stand, Hill Cart Road, Siliguri ☎0354/432646.

Sikkim Tourist Information Centre Sikkim House, 4/1 Middleton St, Kolkata ☎033/2281 5328.

to Lhasa helped the British consolidate their hold. By importing workers from Nepal to work in the tea plantations of Sikkim, Darjeeling and Kalimpong, the British sought to diminish the strong Tibetan influence and helped alter the ethnic make-up of the region, with the new migrants soon outnumbering the indigenous population.

After Indian Independence, the reforming and intensely spiritual eleventh chogyal, **Tashi Namgyal**, strove hard until his death in 1962 to prevent the dissolution of his kingdom. Officially Sikkim was a protectorate of India, and the role of India became increasingly crucial, with the Chinese military build-up along the northern borders that culminated in an actual invasion early in the 1960s. His son **Palden Thondup**, the last chogyal, married as his second wife an American, Hope Cook, whose reforms as gyalmo (queen) did not prove popular and also came to irritate the Indian government. The embattled chogyal eventually succumbed to the demands of the Nepalese majority, and Sikkim was **annexed** by India in 1975 after a referendum with an overwhelming 97-percent majority. The chogyal remained as a figurehead until his death in 1981.

The state continues to be treated with care by the Indian government, partly through a lingering sense of unease amongst the disaffected Sikkimese minority and an increasingly complex ethnic patchwork but, more importantly, because Sikkim remains a bone of contention between India and China despite huge inroads in cross-border diplomacy and trade. Today, the **Sikkim Democratic Front** forms the government of Sikkim; generous government subsidies and loans have helped to ensure that life remains generally contented, while extensive road-building is bringing benefits to remote communities despite the many landslides in recent years.

Trekking in Sikkim

Although the potential is huge, high-altitude **trekking** in Sikkim remains a restricted and expensive business. The government in cahoots with Gangtok-based tour operators, effectively running a cartel by not allowing trekkers to use local guides and amenities and imposing a stringent system of permits, while the fact that foreigners have to pay for the services of the tour operators in US dollars ensures that only the well-heeled get to see certain areas.

Trekking **permits** (aka Protected Area Permits) for high-altitude treks are only available from the Sikkim Tourism offices in Gangtok (see p.935) and Delhi (see p.142). Trekking or tour operators in Gangtok (see p.934) usually make the necessary arrangements; check papers before you set off, as the slightest error can lead to problems later on. Trekking parties consist of a minimum of two people; tour operators charge an official daily rate that ranges from $35 to $150 per head per day depending on the route.

The high-altitude treks most commonly offered by the operators are the **Dzongri–Goecha La** route (plus its variation starting from Uttarey) and the **Singalila Ridge**, both detailed on pp.898–899 and pp.950–951. Treks from **Lachen to Green Lake** are possible, but permission must be obtained from Delhi (most easily arranged through a Gangtok agent) at least three months in advance. At the moment, Dzongri still bears the brunt of the trekking industry in the state, and the pressure is beginning to tell severely on the environment (see p.953). Softer, low-level treks such as the rhododendron trails around **Varshey** are a pleasant alternative (and only require local permits for protected forests), and there are numerous other rewarding possibilities throughout the state that you can do on your own.

While most major peaks require special permits for **mountaineering** and permission from the Indian Mountaineering Foundation in Delhi (see p.137), the Sikkim government, through the appropriate Gangtok trekking operator, hands out permits for Frey's Peak (5830m) near Chaurikhang on the Singalila Ridge; Thingchenkang (6010m) and Jopuno (5935m) in West Sikkim; and Lama Wangden (5868m) and Brumkhangse (5635m) in North Sikkim. On top of operational costs, fees starting at $350 (Rs15000 for Indians) are levied according to group size. Recommended Gangtok agents include Namgyal and Yak & Yeti (see p.934); you will need to submit six photographs and copies of your visa and passport, and plan at least three months ahead.

The **Ecotourism and Conservation Society of Sikkim (ECOSS)** in Gangtok (☎03592/228211, ⊛www.sikkiminfo.net/ecoss) is an independent organization seeking to develop sustainable tourism while protecting natural resources, the environment, and traditional social customs and culture. One of their key aims is to ensure remote and marginalized communities benefit from the part they play in the process.

Gangtok

Capital of Sikkim, the overgrown hill-town of **GANGTOK** (1870m) occupies a rising ridge in the southeast of the state, on what used to be a busy trade route into Tibet. Due to rapid development and new wealth, an ugly assortment of concrete multistorey buildings is growing virtually unchecked, and the town retains only a few traditional Sikkimese elements. However, a short amble soon leads you away

Trekking and tour operators

All high-altitude treks in Sikkim have to be conducted in groups and arranged through the following **travel agents** or **tour operators**, all based in Gangtok, who will also secure the necessary permits. Prices vary a little between agents: high-altitude treks for two to five people cost $45–150 per person per day from established agencies, while low-altitude treks cost between $35 and $80 according to group size. You can get cheaper rates, but ensure that quality is not compromised.

Blue Sky Tours & Travels Tourism Building, MG Marg ☎03592/225113. Very helpful agency which specializes in Jeep safaris, particularly North Sikkim Jeep itineraries.

Himalayan Footprints Pineli Cottage, Upper Syari ☎09832 091078, ⊛www .abouthimalayas.com. Excels in nature tours and treks off the beaten track in East Sikkim, and specializes in village homestays.

Khangri Tours & Treks Tibet Road ☎03592/226050, ⊛www.khangri.com. Owner Tsering Dorjee is an experienced trekking guide and a keen amateur botanist who can arrange cultural and monastic tours and treks throughout Sikkim, and who pioneered routes like the soft trek to Tosar Lake. Recommended.

Marcopolo World Travels PS Road ☎03592/204116, ⊛www.worldmarcopolo.com. The experienced Karma Tashi runs a flexible and reliable tour operation; offerings include high-altitude treks and Jeep safaris to North Sikkim.

Namgyal Treks & Tours Tibet Road ☎03592/203701 or 09434 033122, ⊛www .namgyaltreks.net. Namgyal Sherpa is a highly capable and experienced high-altitude trek and expedition operator, recognized by both the Sikkim and Central Government tourist offices.

Pardick PS Road ☎09434 444837. Inexpensive but reliable trek operator that is often used for outsourcing by the bigger agencies.

Sikkim Adventure 6th Mile, Tadong ☎03592/251250, ✉sikkimorchid@hotmail.com. Sailesh Pradhan runs a plant nursery and is an extremely knowledgeable and enthusiastic botanist and specialist guide for trips focused around Sikkim's rich flora.

Sikkim Tours & Travels Church Road ☎03592/202188, ⊛www.sikkimtours.com. Owner Lukendra is tremendously helpful and experienced, and specializes in nature tours and photography, bird-watching, homestays and treks.

Siniolchu Limbu Bhavan, DPH Road ☎09434 024572. A long-established operator who also specializes in monsoon treks along the Singalila Ridge.

Tashila Tours and Travels Below TNSS School Hall ☎03592/229842, ⊛www .tashila.com. Experienced operator offering trekking, mountain-biking and river-rafting expeditions, as well as yak safaris, angling and monastery tours.

Vajra Adventure Tours Kyitsel House, Arithang Road ☎03592/229676, ✉slg_vatours@sancharnet.in. A very competitively priced and reliable operator, good for transport and treks; the owner comes from Tsokha near Dzongri, and specializes in treks in the area.

Yak & Yeti Zero Point, NH-31A ☎09233 522344, ⊛www.yaknyeti.com. Experienced, reliable and well-equipped expedition specialists in mountaineering; treks available too.

from the hectic central market area, while longer walks out into the surrounding countryside provide glimpses of the full grandeur of the Himalayas. On a good day, you can see Kanchenjunga and the fluted pyramid of Siniolchu.

Although modern Gangtok epitomizes the recent changes in Sikkimese culture and politics, its Buddhist past is the root of its appeal for visitors, evident in the collection at the **Institute of Tibetology** and the charming **Enchey Monastery**, as well as the impressive **Rumtek Monastery**, 24km east of town. However, the **palace** used by the chogyals between 1894 and 1975 is now out of bounds, occupied by the new regime and not acknowledged as part of Sikkimese heritage. Sikkim's pride and joy, the **orchid**, is nurtured at several sites in and around Gangtok, and celebrated at the Flower Show Complex near **White Hall**, the governor's residence on the ridge above town.

Arrival and information

Gangtok is not served directly by rail; most travellers arrive by **Jeep** from **Siliguri** in west Bengal (4hr 30min; see p.887), the transport centre for the railhead at **New Jalpaiguri** (NJP) and for **Bagdogra** airport. Shared Jeeps also run from **Darjeeling** and **Kalimpong**. A **helicopter** service, run in conjunction with Sikkim Tourism, connects Bagdogra airport with Gangtok (Rs2200) but note that the baggage allowance is a mere 10kg.

All **buses** run by **Sikkim Nationalized Transport (SNT)**, the state carrier, use the **SNT Bus Stand** on Paljor Stadium Road, but passengers may prefer to be dropped off earlier at the main crossing on MG Marg near the State Bank of India, which is more convenient for the tourist office and the hotels around the bazaar and Tibet Road. Non-SNT buses stop at the **Private Bus Stand** just off the National Highway (NH-31A) at Deorali, 2km south of the centre. Shared taxis and Jeeps from Kalimpong, Darjeeling, Siliguri, NJP and Bagdogra also stop here; Jeeps and taxis from Eest and South Sikkim terminate at the **Bansilal petrol pump**, adjacent to the National Highway just below MG Marg; taxis and Jeeps from North Sikkim terminate at **Balwakhani**, 1.5km north of the centre near the Vajra Cinema Hall.

With terminals at the Secretariat, Nam Nang and Deorali, the **ropeway** (daily 8am–6pm) provides a spectacular view of the southern city but is an expensive way to get around by local standards (Rs60 round trip, no one-way fare) and is not particularly useful for most accommodation. While it's scheduled to run every twelve minutes, in practice it waits to fill up before moving on. The numerous **shared local taxis** are the most common way of commuting along the main highway, with a ride from central Gangtok Deorali costing around Rs8 per seat. After 9pm, taxis become scarce, but reserved taxis are available from stands near the SNT Bus Stand, the Private Bus Stand at Deorali, the supermarket, Children's Park between MG Marg and Tibet Road, and the Bansilal petrol pump. All taxis carry a rate chart.

Sikkim Tourism's **tourist information centre**, MG Marg (mid-March to early June & mid-Sept to Nov daily 9am–7pm; mid-June to mid-Sept & Dec–Feb Mon–Sat 10am–4pm; ☎03592/221634), provides maps and will advise on arranging transport. This is also the place to extend your Sikkim permit from the initial 15 days. For details of **trekking permits**, see p.933. Sikkim Tourism also sell tickets for their spectacular **helicopter flights** (Rs1200–7000 per seat on demand, or by charter for the entire aircraft at Rs850 per minute) to West Sikkim, Yumthang, Gangtok and, the most breath-taking of them all, a ninety-minute Kanchenjunga trip up the Zemu Glacier. Note that cameras aren't allowed on most routes.

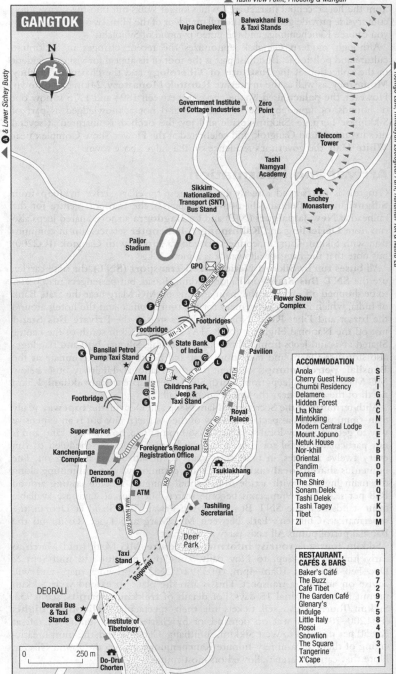

GANGTOK

N

Tashi View Point, Phodong & Mangan

Vajra Cineplex

Balwakhani Bus & Taxi Stands

A & Lower Sichey Busty

Tsomgo Lake, Himalayan Zoological Park, Hanuman Tok & Nathu La

Government Institute of Cottage Industries

Zero Point

Telecom Tower

Tashi Namgyal Academy

Enchey Monastery

Sikkim Nationalized Transport (SNT) Bus Stand

Paljor Stadium

GPO

Flower Show Complex

CHURCH RD

PALJOR STADIUM ROAD

RIDGE ROAD

Footbridges

Footbridge

NH-31A

Bansilal Petrol Pump Taxi Stand

State Bank of India

Pavilion

ATM

TIBET RD

BHANU PATH

M G MARG

Childrens Park, Jeep & Taxi Stand

Footbridge

Royal Palace

Super Market

SECRETARIAT RD

Kanchenjunga Complex

Foreigner's Regional Registration Office

Denzong Cinema

KAZI ROAD

Tsuklakhang

ATM

NAM NANG ROAD

Tashiling Secretariat

Deer Park

Taxi Stand

Ropeway

DEORALI

Deorali Bus & Taxi Stands

Institute of Tibetology

0   250 m

Do-Drul Chorten

Rumtek, Darjeeling & Siliguri

ACCOMMODATION

Anola	S
Cherry Guest House	F
Chumbi Residency	I
Delamere	G
Hidden Forest	A
Lha Khar	C
Mintokling	N
Modern Central Lodge	L
Mount Jopuno	E
Netuk House	J
Nor-khill	B
Oriental	R
Pandim	O
Pomra	P
The Shire	H
Sonam Delek	Q
Tashi Delek	T
Tashi Tagey	K
Tibet	D
Zi	M

RESTAURANT, CAFÉS & BARS

Baker's Café	6
The Buzz	7
Café Tibet	2
The Garden Café	9
Glenary's	5
Indulge	8
Little Italy	4
Rosoi	D
Snowlion	3
The Square	I
Tangerine	
X'Cape	1

Currency exchange is limited to the State Bank of India (SBI) near the tourist office at the junction of NH-31A and MG Marg, which changes most currencies and traveller's cheques, and a couple of licensed private bureaus including Silk Route Tours & Travels at the *Green Hotel* on MG Marg, and Namgyal Treks & Tours off Tibet Road. There are several **ATM**s accepting Visa, MasterCard and Maestro in Gangtok: Axis Bank has ATMs opposite the *Tashi Delek* hotel, near the *Green Hotel* close to Sikkim Tourism, and at Deorali and Tadong. Other banks with ATMs include HDFC and the State Bank. If you're travelling into the interior, it's sensible to change money in Gangtok, as exchange facilities and ATMs are few and far between beyond here.

The STN Memorial Hospital, on the junction of NH-31A and Paljor Stadium Road, has a 24hr emergency wing and an **ambulance** service (☎03592/222944). The main **post office** lies further down Paljor Stadium Road just beyond *Hotel Tibet*. The town is brimming with email services for around Rs30 per hour – try the Web Centre, NH-31A near *Café Tibet*. In case of trouble, contact the **police** on ☎100.

Accommodation

Gangtok's **hotels** are expensive in high season – broadly speaking April to June and September to November – but offer discounted rates at other times. Rooms with views are invariably more expensive. As the town spreads so does the choice of accommodation, with good hotels springing up along the highway at Deorali and Tadong, and a growing number of alternatives away from the bustle but within striking distance of Gangtok.

Central Gangtok

Anola MG Marg, New Market ☎03592/203238. Central, Sikkimese-run hotel on the edge of the market, with plain if somewhat expensive rooms, and a restaurant that serves good Sikkimese food. ❺

Cherry Guest House Rai Cottage Complex, Church Rd ☎03592/205431 or 09932 351925. A short walk from MG Rd and the Bansilal taxi stand, this immaculate place set in a private courtyard offers a wide range of rooms, from plain to beautifully presented doubles opening onto large verandas with views. ❹–❼

Chumbi Residency Tibet Rd ☎03592/226618, ✉slg_chumbi@sancharent.in. A plush, modern hotel close to the centre, offering good service and large, comfortable rooms, most with mountain views; there is an excellent multi-cuisine lounge bar and restaurant. ❼–❽

Delamere Church Rd ☎03592/227646 or 09233 500158, ⊛www.hoteldelamere.com. Central and modern, this lavish new hotel offers well-appointed rooms and good facilities that include a travel desk and a good multi-cuisine restaurant. ❻–❼

Lha Khar Opposite SNT Bus Stand, Paljor Stadium Rd ☎03592/225708. Clean but basic rooms with attached baths in a well-run guesthouse convenient for the SNT Bus Stand; its restaurant is simple but serves wholesome Sikkimese cooking. ❸

Mintokling Bhanu Path (Tashiling Rd) ☎03592/204226, ⊛www.mintokling.com. Run by a Sikkimese family, with a lovely garden and a quiet location near the palace, high above the market. Most of its twelve comfortable, airy rooms have good views over the valley to the mountains. ❺–❻

Modern Central Lodge Tibet Rd ☎03592/224670. A bit run-down but still popular hotel geared towards backpackers, with a traveller-friendly restaurant and some rooms with attached baths and running hot water; there are also dorms from Rs50. ❷–❸

Mount Jopuno Paljor Stadium Rd ☎03592/223502. Government-run place featuring twelve rooms with hot water and attached bathroom, and a rooftop terrace. Well-maintained, central and offers good value (especially with its off-season discount), and there's a decent restaurant and bar. ❹–❻

🐾 **Netuk House** Tibet Rd ☎03592/226778, ✉netukhouse@gmail.com. A family home within easy reach of the centre, with a comfortable hotel anr exe: warm, atmospheric and beautifully presented, with Sikkimese decor and a pleasant roof terrace. The price of Rs3960 for a double includes all meals. ❽

Nor-khill Paljor Stadium Rd ☎03592/225637, ⊛www.elginhotels.com. Luxurious former royal guesthouse of the chogyal, this landmark hotel offers the finest address in town. Plush rooms in grand Sikkimese style, excellent service and a good restaurant, but the location, overlooking the sports stadium, is poor; prices (from $152) include all meals. ⑨

Oriental MG Marg ⓣ03592/221180, ⓦwww
.orientalsikkim.com. A homogenized "oriental" theme in almost doll's-house proportions, with small but immaculate rooms and a good multi-cuisine restaurant; comfortable and a cheaper alternative to *Tashi Delek* across the road. ⑦

Pandim Secretariat Rd ⓣ03592/227540. Friendly and pleasant budget hotel with plain rooms (some on the dark side) and a great location high above town – the rooftop restaurant has lovely views. ③–④

Pomra Secretariat Rd ⓣ03592/226648. A bit more comfy than *Pandim* next door (as is reflected in the price), and a similar great location, although the restaurant is a bit dull (head to *Pandim* instead). There is also a dorm (Rs150). ⑤

Sonam Delek Tibet Rd ⓣ03592/202566. High above the bazaar, this reliable hotel has been recently refurbished and offers a range of comfort-able, clean rooms, a good restaurant and expansive views across the valley to the mountains from the terrace. ④–⑤

Tashi Delek MG Marg ⓣ03592/202991, ⓦwww
.hoteltashidelek.com. An easily missed entrance off the market area hides one of Gangtok's legendary hotels – a plush, extensive complex with spacious, old-fashioned rooms. The multi-cuisine *Blue Poppy* restaurant and adjoining rooftop café serve Sikkimese and Tibetan dishes and club sandwiches. ⑧

Tibet Paljor Stadium Rd ⓣ03592/222523 or 223468. Award-winning hotel linked to the Dalai Lama's trust, with Tibetan decor. The deluxe rooms have Kanchenjunga views but the roadside ones are small and overpriced. The *Snowlion* restaurant (see p.940) is excellent. ⑥–⑧

Zi Near Sadar Thana, Tibet Rd ⓣ03592/205481. Bengali-run place in this popular but sometimes grotty stretch near the town centre, offering plain, clean rooms, some with Western toilets. Overpriced in the peak season. ③–④

Around Gangtok

🏃 **Hidden Forest** Lower Sichey Busty
ⓣ03592/205197, ⓦwww.hiddenforestretreat
.com. A 2km taxi ride from the SNT bus terminus and Paljor Stadium leads away from the noise and bustle of Gangtok to this tranquil horticultural idyll, with organic food and sublimely comfortable cottages in a family-run nursery specializing in orchids and azaleas; recommended. ⑥

The Shire Tshugshing House, Arithang Rd ⓣ03592/202217 or 09832 075920. Close enough to the centre and yet a world away from it, with a small garden and accommodation in a purpose-built modern chalet behind the family home. The rooms are spacious if plain, Sikkimese home-cooking is available and taxis are arranged for those who want to avoid the steep 15min walk up to town. ④–⑤

🏃 **Tashi Tagey** NH-31A, near State Bank of India, Tadong ⓣ03592/231631, ⓦwww
.tashitagey.com. Small, welcoming Tibetan family-run hotel 4km from central Gangtok. Clean and homely, with a good licensed restaurant popular with locals and great for Tibetan home-cooking. It's a steep 15min walk up to Do-Drul *chorten*, and Gangtok is an easy Rs12 taxi ride away; recommended. ③–⑤

The Town

Though central Gangtok – which means "the hilltop" – is concentrated immediately below the palace, its unchecked urban sprawl begins almost as soon as the road rises from the valley floor at Ranipool, 11km southwest. Most of the town itself looks west; one explanation for the lack of development east of the ridge is that tradition dictates that houses face northwest, towards Kanchen-junga, Sikkim's guardian.

The town's best shopping areas are the **Main Market**, stretching for a kilometre along the pedestrianized MG Marg, and the local produce bazaar in the concrete **Kanchenjunga Shopping Complex**. Stalls sell dried fish, yak's cheese (*churpi*), and yeast for making the local beer, *tomba*. At the huge complex run by the **Government Institute of Cottage Industries**, on the National Highway north of the centre, visitors can watch rural Sikkimese create carpets, hand-loomed fabrics, *thangka* paintings and wooden objects, and buy their work at fixed prices. Curio shops on MG Marg and on Paljor Stadium Road sell turquoise and coral jewellery, plus religious objects such as silver ritual bowls and beads.

Right at the top of town just below a colossal telecom tower, 3km from the centre and reached by several roads (the most picturesque follow the west side of the ridge), **Enchey Monastery** is a small two-storey Nyingmapa *gompa*. It was built in the mid-nineteenth century on a site blessed by the Tantric master Druptob Karpo, who was renowned for his ability to fly. Visitors are welcome; the best time to go is between 7am and 8am, when the monastery is busy and the light is good. Surrounded by tall pines, and housing over a hundred monks, it's a real gem of a place. Built by the chogyal on traditional Tibetan lines, its beautifully painted porch holds murals of protective deities and the wheel of law, while the conch shells that grace the doors are auspicious Buddhist symbols. Enchey holds an annual *chaam*, or masked lama dance, during the Losung festival around early December according to the lunar calendar.

The walk down from Enchey leads to the **Flower Show Complex** (daily 10am–5pm; Rs5) at the northern end of Ridge Road near White Hall, where a large well-maintained greenhouse has a good collection of orchids and other Himalayan plants laid out around a set of water features. The complex, with a shop selling seeds, plants and bulbs, used to host the annual **International Flower Festival** in March and April; it's now staged at Saramsa, 14km from Gangtok near Ranipul.

Although in theory guards deny entry to the **Royal Palace** to anyone without permission, visitors not carrying cameras are occasionally granted access to **Tsuklakhang**, the yellow-roofed royal chapel at its far end, to see its impressive murals, Buddhist images and vast collection of manuscripts. Here too there's a lama dance, known as *kagyat*, at the end of December, during which the main gates are open to the public; some years the *kagyat* takes place in Pemayangtse (see p.948) instead.

Beyond the chapel the road meanders down to the small **Deer Park** (also known as the Himalayan Zoological Park; daily 10am–4pm; free) and beyond to Deorali, 3km from the centre on the National Highway, where, set in wooded grounds, is the museum-cum-library of the **Namgyal Institute of Tibetology** (Mon–Sat 10am–4pm, closed second Sat of each month; Rs5). Here you can see an impressive collection of books and rare manuscripts, as well as religious and art objects such as exquisite *thangkas* (scrolls) and a photography archive. You can also get here from the upper town via the new ropeway (see p.935).

A couple of hundred metres beyond the Institute on the brow of the hill, an imposing whitewashed *chorten* (see p.560), known as the **Do-Drul Chorten** – one of the most important in Sikkim – dominates a large, lively monastery. The *chorten* is capped by a gilded tower, whose rising steps signify the thirteen steps to nirvana; the sun and moon symbol at the top stands for the union of opposites and the elements of ether and air. The 108 prayer wheels that surround it – each with the universal prayer *Om mani padme hum*, "Hail to the jewel in the lotus" – are rotated clockwise by devotees as they circle the stupa. Nearby, behind the large monastic complex, a prayer hall houses a large image of **Guru Rinpoche** (Padmasambhava) who brought Buddhism to Tibet at the request of King Trisong Detsen in the eighth century AD. He later travelled through Sikkim hiding precious manuscripts (*termas*) in caves, for discovery at a future date by *tertons*. Curiously, part of the head of the image projects into the ceiling protected by a raised section of roof; belief has it that the image is slowly growing.

Eating, drinking and nightlife

Sikkimese food is a melange of Nepalese, Tibetan and Indian influences; rice is a staple and dhal is readily available, while *gyakho* is a traditional chimney stew served on special occasions. Sikkimese delicacies include *ningro* (fern rings), *shisnu* (nettle soup), *phing* (glass noodles), and *churpi* (yak cheese) cooked with chillies. Some of the best food is served in the restaurants of hotels such as the *Tibet*, and there are several fast-food places and patisseries in town, too.

Most restaurants serve **alcohol**. "Foreign" liquor such as brandy and beer is cheap enough, but look out for **tomba**, a traditional drink consisting largely of fermented millet, with a few grains of rice for flavour, served in a wooden or bamboo mug and sipped through a bamboo straw. The mug is occasionally topped up with hot water; once it's been allowed to sit for a few minutes, you're left with a pleasant milky beer. *Tomba* is usually found in less salubrious places where the mixture might be doctored to make it stronger; for a better-quality brew, try the more expensive hotels. Note that the Sikkimese have alcohol-free days during full moon. The best of Gangtok's **discos** is *X'Cape*, Vajra Cineplex, Balwakhani (Wed–Sun 7pm–midnight; Rs200), sharing the building with a cinema hall; another cinema hall is Denzong in Lall Market.

Baker's Café MG Marg. A modern and spotless patisserie a short walk from the tourist office, with a tempting selection of cakes and pizzas, as well as good filter coffee and a selection of fruit drinks; there's another outlet on the national highway near the Private Bus Stand.

Café Tibet NH-31A, past the hospital. Run by the *Hotel Tibet*, this lively café is popular with students, and serves pizzas and burgers, croissants, cakes and ice cream.

Glenary's and **The Buzz** MG Marg. The patisserie is no longer up to the mark, but the café upstairs is popular and varied, offering pizzas and pastries. On the floor above, *The Buzz* is a modern, lavishly decorated and comfortable pub.

Indulge Children's Park. This chic new upstairs hang-out is *the* place to be in the centre of town. Despite the mood lighting, Nirvana posters and bar-like atmosphere, the food is surprisingly good, from Indian and Chinese to local delicacies.

Little Italy Deorali, next to the petrol pump. Very popular, trendy upstairs bar-restaurant that serves

Italian food and is especially good for pizzas. Occasional live pop music.

Rosoi MG Marg, next to the tourist information office. An old favourite in the heart of town, now reinvented as a good-value, multi-cuisine vegetarian restaurant best for Indian food; there's no bar, however.

Snowlion *Hotel Tibet*, Paljor Stadium Rd ☎03592/222523 or 223468. Still the best restaurant in Gangtok. The superb Tibetan and Indian food, with a selection of Sikkimese and Japanese dishes, is expensive by local standards (from around Rs600 a meal) but highly recommended.

The Square Paljor Stadium Rd, next to Mount Jopuno. Bright little café-bistro which offers a small but varied menu including good Thai, Continental and Nepalese cuisine. There's a bar, and great views.

Tangerine *Chumbi Residency* hotel, Tibet Rd. Plush, elegant yet affordable restaurant serving Indian, Chinese and Sikkimese specialities, including the intriguing *churpi ningro* (cheese and fern). The adjacent lounge bar is good for a relaxing drink.

Moving on from Gangtok

The busiest route in and out of Sikkim is the road between Gangtok and Siliguri in West Bengal, site of the nearest airport (Bagdogra) and railway station (see p.884). **Flights** from Bagdogra can be booked through either Josse & Josse, MG Marg (☎03592/224682), agents for Jet Airways, or through Silk Route Tours and Travels, first floor, *Green Hotel*, MG Marg (☎03592/223354), who also sell tickets for the various airlines flying from Biratnagar (2hr from Siliguri) in eastern Nepal to Kathmandu. Sikkim Tourism sell tickets for the **helicopter** flight (subject to weather conditions; daily 10.30am; Rs2000) to **Bagdogra** to connect with Indian Airlines and Jet flights. **Train reservations** from New Jalpaiguri can be made at the SNT complex on Paljor Stadium Road (Mon–Sat 8am–2pm, Sun 8–11am; ☎03592/222016), but the reservations quota for Gangtok is highly inadequate, so it's better to book in Siliguri.

With the deterioration in Sikkim's roads, shared **Jeeps** are the most popular and efficient mode of transport. Jeeps to Siliguri (Rs120), New Jalpaiguri (NJP; Rs125), Kalimpong (Rs85) and Darjeeling (Rs120) leave from the Private Bus Stand on NH-31A at Deorali. Jeeps to other destinations within Sikkim, such as Ghezing (Rs120), Pelling (Rs150) and Jorethang (Rs98) as well as to Rumtek (Rs30) leave from the Bansilal Pump stand, off NH-31A near MG Marg. Jeeps to North Sikkim depart from Balwakhani. These services are timetabled and require **advance booking** (from the ticket booth at the taxi stand); all taxis and Jeeps carry a rate chart.

Those determined to suffer the **buses** can choose between SNT (Sikkim Nationalized Transport) or a number of private operators; services run to Kalimpong, Darjeeling and Siliguri in West Bengal and Jorethang in South Sikkim. See p.944 for details of bus stands in town.

For more on transport from Gangkok, see "Travel details", p.956

Around Gangtok

The most obvious destinations for day-trips from Gangtok are the great Buddhist monasteries of **Rumtek** to the southwest, and **Phodong** to the north. Closer to Gangtok, there are three popular viewing-points offering panoramas of the **Kanchenjunga Range**. The most accessible is **Ganesh Tok**, a steep one- to two-hour walk from the TV tower and Enchey Monastery. A small Ganesh shrine and views of Gangtok and the mountains reward those that make the climb. Opposite the shrine lies the **Himalayan Zoological Park** (daily 10am–5pm; Rs10) with large open enclosures for red panda and snow leopards. **Hanuman Tok** (2300m), 7km out of town on the road to Tsomgo Lake, is the site of a Hanuman temple, and the cremation ground of the Royal Family, with *chortens* containing relics of the deceased. On the road to Phodong 6km out of Gangtok, **Tashi View Point** provides views of the eastern aspects of Kanchenjunga (whose tent-like appearance here is radically different from the way it looks from Darjeeling) and the snowy pyramid of Siniolchu (6887m), which the pioneering mountaineer Eric Shipton ranked among the most beautiful in the world.

Tsomgo Lake (pronounced "Changu"), 35km northeast of Gangtok and just 20km from the Tibetan border at **Nathu La**, is a scenic spot at an altitude of 3750m, popular with Indian visitors who flock here to sample the high-mountain environment and, hopefully, experience their first thrill of snow in the colder months. While the military dominate the place, tourism still manages to thrive, with yak rides and stalls selling pelts and other curios. It's possible to visit the **Kyongnosla Alpine Sanctuary** (3550m) en route, where a profusion of wild flowers bloom between May and August and migratory birds stop over in winter on their annual pilgrimage from Siberia to India. Tsomgo Lake is now open to foreigners with permits issued from Gangtok through a tour operator, but only Indians are allowed up to Nathu La (4130m), where they can gawk at bemused Chinese soldiers across the rope border marker. Some hotels and many of Gangtok's travel agents (see p.934) run excursions to Tsomgo, Serathang and Nathu La, and can arrange the necessary permits.

Rumtek and around

Visible from Gangtok, and a 24-kilometre road trip southwest of the capital, the large *gompa* of **RUMTEK** is the main seat of the **Karma Kagyu** lineage – also known as the **Black Hat** sect – founded during the twelfth century by the first

Gyalwa Karmapa, Dusun Khyenpa (1110–93). Dusun Khyenpa established the Tsurphu monastery in central Tibet near Lhasa, which became the headquarters of the Karma Kagyu for eight centuries until the Chinese invasion of Tibet in 1959. The sixteenth **Karmapa**, Rangjung Rigpe Dorje, fled Tibet for Sikkim, where he was invited to stay at the old Rumtek *gompa*. Within a couple of years, the Karmapa had begun the work of building a new monastery at Rumtek to become his new seat, on land donated by the Sikkimese king Chogyal Tashi Namgyal. One of the great Tibetan figures of the twentieth century, the sixteenth Karmapa was very influential in the spread of Tibetan Buddhism to the West, setting up over two hundred Karma Kagyu centres and raising funds for the rebuilding of Tsurphu. When he died in 1981, he left behind a wealthy monastery and a huge and lucrative international network, but one bitterly divided by an ugly squabble over his rightful successor. Two reincarnate Karmapas have now emerged as the main contenders to the throne – one blessed by the Dalai Lama and ensconced in Dharamsala, the other in nearby Kalimpong.

The new Rumtek, now heavily guarded against possible raids by the feuding parties, is a large and lavish complex consisting of the main temple, golden stupa, and the Karma Shri Nalanda Institute, with a few smaller shrines and a guesthouse outside the monastery courtyard. The **main temple**, with its ornate facade covered with intricate brightly painted wooden latticework, overlooks the expansive **courtyard**. Large red columns support the high roof of the **prayer hall**, where the walls are decorated with murals and *thangkas*. Visitors can attend daily rituals here, when lines of monks sit chanting. A chamber off the hall, used for Tantric rituals, is painted with gold against a black background and depicts wrathful protective deities (no photography allowed). During Losar, the Tibetan New Year (in February), the main courtyard stages *chaam* dance spectacles, in which ceremonial **Black Hat dancers** spin to the sounds of horns, drums and clashing cymbals.

The **Karma Shri Nalanda Institute of Buddhist Studies**, behind the main temple, built in 1984 in traditional Tibetan style, is the most ornate of all the buildings of Rumtek. Monks spend a minimum of nine years studying here, followed by an optional three-year period of isolated meditation. The main hall on the third floor is decorated with magnificent murals, and holds images including the Buddha Sakyamuni – the historic Buddha – and the sixteenth Karmapa.

The ashes of the sixteenth Karmapa are contained in a gilded four-metre-high *chorten* or stupa, studded with turquoise and coral, that sits in the **Golden Stupa** hall opposite the Institute. Behind the stupa is a central statue of Dorje Chang (Vajradhara) flanked by Tilopa, Naropa, Marpa and Milarepa, the four great Kagyu teachers. Statues of the previous sixteen Karmapas line the side walls. The door to the hall and *chorten* is kept closed so you will need to knock loudly or find a monk to take you in.

Half a kilometre beyond the new monastery and Rumtek village, a path leads to the simple **Old Rumtek Gompa**, the original monastery, founded in 1740 and recently renovated. It's set in an attractive wooded clearing and surrounded by empty outbuildings in traditional Sikkimese alpine style, with latticed wooden windows. Behind the statues in the main prayer hall on the right side is a small shrine room dedicated to the Karma Kagyu protector Mahakala, an image so fierce that it is kept veiled.

The most pleasurable route to Rumtek is via the impressive new *gompa* of **Lingdum**, completed in 1998 and an easy 14km taxi ride (Rs25) from the centre of Gangtok. A haven of peace surrounded by deep woodland, the Lingdum is a grand example of modern monastic architecture, with an expansive terrace and courtyard. Inside, delicate and detailed murals depict the life of the Buddha. The undulating 11km road between Rumtek and Lingdum traverses terraced fields and passes through delightful forest with Gangtok in the distance in sharp contrast.

Practicalities

If you don't arrange your own **transport**, the best way to get to Rumtek is by the shared Jeeps that leave Gangtok from Bansilal Pump when full and cost Rs30 per head and Rs50 in the evenings. Similarly, Jeeps returning to Gangtok do so on demand.

Rumtek has a limited choice of budget **accommodation**, and a growing number of more upscale resorts present a pleasant alternative to the crowded cityscape of Gangtok. Next to a couple of stalls, 100m from the monastery gates, is the atmospheric, rustic and basic *Sangay* (**❶–❷**), with shared bathrooms and, next door, a traditional restaurant with a limited local menu including tasty *momos*. The friendly *Sun-Gay Rumtek Guesthouse* (☎03592/252221; **❷–❸**), close to the main gate of the monastery, is by far the best of the budget options, boasting clean rooms with views in a garden. Their kitchen churns out banana pancakes and other favourites. Of the resorts hereabouts, best choice is the *Martam Village* (☎03592/223314, ⓦwww.sikkim-martam-resort.com; **❼**), 7km beyond Rumtek, in an idyllic rural setting amidst beautiful rice terraces. The landscaped complex consists of fourteen purpose-built, attached thatched cottages with verandas and views, as well as a restaurant; staff can arrange mountain-bike rental and local guides to explore the countryside. Closer to Rumtek, 1km before the monastery gates at Sajong, the *Bamboo Resort* (☎0353/2202049 or 09832 061986, ⓔinfo@sikkim.ch; **❽**) is a boutique hotel in a Swiss chic meets formal Sikkimese style, set against a backdrop of forest with views towards Gangtok and Nathu La in the far distance. There's a herb garden, a herbal bath, library and a meditation room; doubles start at $102 including breakfast and dinner.

In Rumtek itself, noodles and chai are available at the **teashops** clustered near the monastery gate and at the **checkpoint** where foreigners are requested to give passport details before entering the monastery.

Phodong and Labrang

Phodong, 38km north of Gangtok on the Mangan road, is another living monastery, but a far less ostentatious one. Lying on a spur of the hill 1km above the main road, and commanding superb views, it consists of a simple square main temple, plus several outhouses and residential quarters. Built in the early eighteenth century, this was Sikkim's pre-eminent Kagyu monastery until the growth of Rumtek in the 1960s. It too hosts colourful lama dances, similar to the *chaam* of Rumtek, each December. A rough road leads a further 4km up to another renovated old monastery – the unusual octagonal **Labrang**. A cluster of *chortens* between these two monasteries marks the ruins of **Tumlong**, Sikkim's capital city for most of the nineteenth century.

South Sikkim

Ignored by travellers en route to higher trekking trails and the great *gompas* of West Sikkim, southern Sikkim nevertheless offers a quiet charm, its lichen-covered forests draped with a stunning array of orchids and inhabited by rare animals – and now that permit restrictions have eased, it offers many more possibilities for visitors. Traditionally serving as an access point to western Sikkim via border towns like **Jorethang**, the area is dominated by the great forested peak of **Maenam**, famous for its plants and flowers, and for the tremendous view from its summit. Towering above the town of **Ravangla**, Maenam makes a challenging day-trek, while high above the district capital of Namchi, the gigantic statue of **Samdruptse** is clearly visible from as far away as Darjeeling.

Jorethang

The busy market town of **JORETHANG** lies in the very south of the state, just across the River Rangit from Singla Bazaar in West Bengal and a mere 30km north of Darjeeling, which is just visible across the tea plantations. Set on an extensive shelf, which makes it feel oddly flat despite the huge hills that rise in every direction, it's a well-ordered place and a useful transport hub, with a few decent budget **hotels**. The *Namgyal* (☎03595/276852; ❸), next to the bridge and handy for the Darjeeling and SNT bus stands has good-value doubles with running hot water, some with river views; it also has a decent restaurant. *Walk-In* on Street No.2 serves good Indian and Chinese food, and also doubles as a popular bar.

Jorethang is well connected by **bus** with the rest of Sikkim, and there is a direct service to Siliguri daily at 9.30am. Buses for Gangtok leave at 7.30am, for Pelling at 3pm, and Namchi at 8.30am. Shared **Jeeps** make the extraordinarily steep 25-kilometre journey to Darjeeling (Rs90), and go regularly to Legship (change here for Pelling, Ravangla, Yoksum and Tashiding) and to Namchi; there are less frequent services to Ghezing and Varshey. Jeeps travel regularly to Gangtok (Rs98) and Siliguri (Rs100). Few Jeeps leave Jorethang after 1pm and the rule of thumb is to travel early.

Namchi, Samdruptse and around

Some 79km southeast of Gangtok and 24km to the northwest of Jorethang and pleasantly situated on a saddle at 1676m above sea level, busy **NAMCHI** is the administrative centre for South Sikkim, and is rapidly becoming a magnet for domestic tourists due to the large and extraordinary statuary that is springing up around it. High above town, the gigantic 41m statue known as **Samdruptse** ("Guru Rinpoche"; daily 7am–5pm; Rs50 [Rs10]) sits on a high ridge gazing south towards Darjeeling. Constructed by the regional government, the huge edifice has become one of South Sikkim's most popular attractions, its sheer size as much of an attraction as its spiritual significance. Inaugurated by the Dalai Lama in 2004, the statue cost Rs67,600,000 (around US$15,558,112) to build, and contains a meeting hall as well as, somewhat ironically, a window in its back. Samdruptse lies 8km to the north of Namchi along the unfolding ridge; to get there, you'll either need to make the steep, gruelling climb past **Ngadak Monastery**, or take a Jeep (Rs200) to the ornamental **Rock Garden** and then make a 3km climb up steps to the statue; taxis directly to the car park near the statue are Rs250.

Not content with just one statue, the authorities have embarked upon yet another mammoth edifice, a 32m-high statue of the Hindu god Shiva towering on the top of **Solophok**, a hill high above Old Namchi, 5km to the south of town. Due to be completed sometime in 2008, the statue is part of a tourism strategy that, despite misgivings in some quarters, seems to be drawing visitors in ever-larger quantities into what was, until recently, a sleepy backwater.

Away from the statues, Namchi's large **Doling Gompa** is an interesting example of a Nyingmapa monastery, reached via a pleasant walk 1km to the south of town. The more adventurous can opt for the trek up **Tendong Hill** (2623m) to a small monastery used by monks as a retreat. You can walk there from Samdruptse, but the trails are not clear and the best route is from the small town of **DAMTHANG**, 14km to the north of Namchi on the Ravangla road, from where it's a 7km trek along easily followable trails through a beautiful, protected forest. Tendong is especially revered by the Lepchas, who believe that the hill saved them from the great flood that once submerged the earth. On a clear day, the views from the summit stretch from the plains of Bengal to the high Himalayas.

Namchi offers an increasing choice of **accommodation**, much of it within easy proximity to the main square, with its taxi stand and magnificent *pipal* tree. Some 200 metres down the Jorethang road, *Samdruptse* (T03595/264708; ❷–❹) offers a large range of rooms, from basic with shared facilities to more luxurious ones with attached baths and good views from outfacing balconies; the bar and restaurant is one of the best in town, serving local, Indian and Chinese food. *Mayal* (T03595/263588; ❹–❺), nearby in a quiet location on the Jorethang road, has clean rooms and a good restaurant serving Indian and Chinese food. *Kesang* (T03595/263746; ❸–❹) near the *pipal* tree, has a handful of rooms recently renovated to a good standard, and a first-floor bar and restaurant serving excellent mountain cuisine. Namchi has a State Bank of India ATM just off the square, which takes credit and debit cards (Visa and MasterCard). The town is well connected to all points in Sikkim as well as Siliguri, Kalimpong and Darjeeling; shared **Jeeps** travel regularly (6am–2pm) to Gangtok (Rs90) and to Jorethang (Rs25).

Ravangla and Maenam

Spread across a high saddle, 65km west of Gangtok and 52km east of Pelling, the sleepy market town of **RAVANGLA** (also known as Ravang and Rabang) makes for a convenient stopover, especially for those interested in trekking through one of the last remaining **rhododendron forests** in south-central Sikkim where the fabulous **Maenam Sanctuary** remains a botanist's dream, covering the flanks of the gigantic forested peak which looms over the town. The town itself has a sizeable Tibetan settlement, with a handicrafts centre and shop at the **Kheunpheling Carpet Centre** in the refugee camp above town.

The summit of **Maenam** (3235m), 10km from Ravangla bazaar, is home to a small chapel to Guru Rinpoche (Padma Sambhava) and boasts superlative views, weather permitting – the mountain's position on the watershed between the Teesta and the Rangit river systems means that overcast weather can veil the dramatic views of the distant plains to the south, and of the horned summit of Narsing (5825m). Feasible as a day-trek, the stiff 1000-metre **ascent** of Maenam (2hr 30min–4hr) starts with steps rising from the bazaar up to the *gompa* (usually shut) before trailing off the road through the sanctuary. Few come this way, and you may even be lucky enough to glimpse some wildlife including deer, the elusive red panda, black bear and a variety of birds. To catch the sunrise from the summit, take a good sleeping bag and food and water, as there is a dilapidated shelter in which to huddle from the elements, but little else. Locals, who occasionally camp up here, scour the forests for firewood; deforestation is a real worry so use your discretion and bring down your rubbish. The route through the forest is not all that obvious (especially in descent, when a wrong turn can dump you on the wrong side of the mountain) and you may want to take a local guide (Rs300), arranged at the forest gate 1km above town where you pay an entry fee to the sanctuary (Rs25).

Monasteries in the vicinity of Ravangla include the old and the new *gompas* at **Ralang**, 13km to the north, with shared Jeeps travelling the route on demand. The old *gompa*, **Karma Rabtenling**, is linked to the ninth Karmapa and was founded in 1768. The new Ralang monastery, built in 1995 in much the same style as Rumtek, and also part of the Kagyu order, is one of the largest temple buildings in Sikkim. Usually held in December, the *chaam* (lama dance) which commemorates Losung (the end of the harvest) is a particularly colourful and local affair.

In late August, Ravangla hosts the annual three-day **Pang Lhabsol festival**, which celebrates the worship of Kanchenjunga and draws thousands of Sikkimese to enjoy the traditional sports and **Pangtoed Chaam**, a festival of masked dances unique in that it is performed here, not by monks, but by *zigtempas* or lay people. Local villagers come to sell their wares at Ravangla's Wednesday **market**.

Practicalities

Jeeps leave from the stand at the crossroads towards the southern end of the market, heading to Gangtok (Rs80) and Namchi (Rs35), as well as Legship and Ghezing. There are few direct taxis to Pelling (Rs60), so you'll need to change at Ghezing; you can't be assured of regular transport much after midday. **Buses** travel to Ghezing at around 11am and to Gangtok at around 9am and there are two to Namchi (9am & 1pm). The shortest route to Darjeeling is via Namchi, where you may have to change for a Jeep or bus to Jorethang, and again there for Darjeeling.

There's a reasonable choice of **accommodation** on offer. Near the taxi stand and main crossing, the friendly *Hotel 10Zing* (☎03595/260705; ❷) offers small, plain rooms over a popular restaurant; across the square, the Bengali–run *Reegyal* (☎03595/260221; ❸) is slightly more comfortable and has a decent restaurant. Of the several options on the way out of town on the Kewzing road towards Legship, *Zumthang* (☎03595/260870, ✉zumthang@yahoo.com; ❹–❺) is run by a delightful Tibetan family and offers a warm welcome and large,

Homestays

If you're interested in getting a taste of Sikkimese rural life, you might want to try a **homestay**, which provide some interesting insight into local communities and their customs. The Kewzing Tourism Development Committee (KTDC) organizes homestays (Rs1400 per person per night) in the **Kewzing busti** (village), a pleasant rural idyll surrounded by terraced fields just outside the sleepy market town of Kewzing, itself 8km east of Ravangla. As part of the network, fifteen village houses welcome guests on an all-inclusive basis; the best address is that of Sonam Dadul Bhutia, who has two pleasant, well-furnished wood-lined rooms with attached bathrooms and a common veranda. The rather high price is all inclusive of food and cultural show, and for an extra charge you can use a traditional communal hot tub heated by fired stones. For more information contact Chamang R. Bonpo (☎09434 864844).

Aside from Kewzing, there are also homestay options in **Yuksam** (contact Mr Pema Bhutia ☎09832 452527, ✉kcc_sikkim@hotmail.com), **Pastenga** in eastern Sikkim (contact Mr Huna Rai ☎09832 033679) and **Dzongu** (contact Dr N.T. Lepcha ☎09434 179160); for the latter, you'll need a permit arranged by one of the tour operators listed on p.934.

clean rooms, some with balconies; good discounts are available for those visiting Ravangla's Tibetan settlement. If you want to get away from it all, the stunningly located *Mt Narsing Village Resort* (T03595/260558, Eyuksom @gmail.com; 4–7), 3km further on the Kewzing road, offers log chalets and cottages; but for solitude stay at the *Annexe* (same contacts; 4–7), a steep twenty-minute walk (or precarious Jeep drive) up from the road to a plateau with stunning open views. Here, comfortable chalets, built partly of local materials, are ringed around the main lodge, where there's an open fire and a restaurant bedecked with lines of *tomba* vessels.

West Sikkim

This beautiful land, characterized by great tracts of virgin forest and deep river valleys, is home to ancient monasteries such as **Pemayangtse** and **Tashiding** and the attractive but rapidly developing town of **Pelling**. The old capital, **Yoksum**, lies at the start of the trail towards Dzongri and Kanchenjunga. In the far west, along the border with Nepal, the watershed of the Singalila Range rises along a single ridge, with giants such as Rathong and Kabru culminating in Kanchenjunga itself. Only two high-altitude trails are currently easily accessible, and even these are subject to restrictions and high charges; however, several low-altitude treks with numerous variations provide ample opportunities to enjoy the wonderful profusion of orchids, rhododendron forests, waterfalls and terraced hillsides with a backdrop of majestic vistas.

Permit restrictions (see p.932) mean that high-altitude trekkers can only follow well-beaten trails within a limited period of time, but there are numerous alternatives at lower altitudes. If you're coming from Darjeeling and arrange permits and itineraries in advance you could enter Sikkim at Jorethang (see p.944) and go directly to Pelling or Yoksum, saving precious permit time.

Ghezing and Legship

The bustling market town of **GHEZING** (also known as Gyalshing or Geyzing), 110km west of Gangtok, is the administrative centre and transport hub of western Sikkim, and a good place to stock up on provisions and extend **permits**, which you can do through the Superintendent of Police (Mon–Sat 10am–4pm) at **Tikjuk**, midway between Ghezing and Pelling. There are a handful of **hotels** around the main square in the centre of Ghezing, including some basic options and the more comfortable *Attri* (T03595/250602; 3). A few yards from the market on the Tashigang road, *Denkhang* is one of the better restaurants in Ghezing. For a bit of luxury, head for the dramatically situated *Tashigang Resort*, 3km from town at Deecheling (T03595/250340; 5–8), an incongruous multistorey building with stunning views over deep valleys and a landscaped garden with attractive and comfortable cottages.

Shared **Jeeps** leave for Gangtok (Rs120) and Siliguri (Rs125; tickets in advance from the counter near the playground; T03595/250121); there are also regular services to Legship and Jorethang (change here for Darjeeling) on demand. Taxis and Jeeps depart from the main square for Pelling (Rs25) and other local destinations; most have left by midday, with the exception of those to Pelling which continue regularly until dark. If reserving a taxi, Omnis tend to be cheaper as they can travel up the steep short-cut to Pelling, which is closed to Jeeps. An SNT **bus** to Gangtok leaves at 8am and to Siliguri at 8am via Jorethang where there are better connections and Jeeps to Darjeeling.

West Sikkim walks

The numerous trails crisscrossing the countryside of West Sikkim take you into the heart of the Singalila forests. Best visited between mid-April and mid-May, when the rhododendrons are in full bloom, the **Varshey Rhododendron Sanctuary** (aka Barsey or Varsey) covers 104 square kilometres, which range in altitude from 2840m to 4250m and are home to black bear, red panda and pheasant. Entry permits (Rs50 [Rs25]) for the sanctuary are available from forestry departments at **Hilley**, **Soreng**, **Uttarey** and **Gangtok**, and the most popular trail is the 8km round-trip from Hilley to **Varshey** (3030m), which offers majestic views. You can extend the walk to Uttarey (3–4 days with tented accommodation), from where you can either take transport to Jorethang and points en route, or continue on foot to the small town of **Dentam**. From Dentam, a river-valley trail leads to **Rinchenpong** (4–5hr), a good base for West Sikkim treks; another trail from Dentam leads east up the ridge to **Pelling** (4–5hr). There are numerous permutations and possibilities to trekking in this region including an extension, with prior arrangement with tour operators and the appropriate permits, into the long high-altitude **Singalila Ridge trek** to Dzongri and beyond (see pp.950–951).

Walk practicalities

Most Gangtok tour operators (see p.934) can arrange treks and tours of this part of West Sikkim; Sikkim Adventure and Sikkim Tours & Travels are your best bets. Reliable bases convenient to Varshey and Uttarey include the sylvan ⚐ *Yangsum Farm* (☎09733 085196, ⊛www.yangsumfarm.com; ❺) below Rinchenpong, a working hill-farm with large, comfortable rooms furnished in local style, which can arrange all-inclusive treks including transport, food, guides and tents. Cheaper options include the *Trekkers Hut* (no phone; ❷–❸) at Varshey and others at Soreng. Varshey, Rinchenpong and Soreng are connected by **Jeep** services to Jorethang.

The gateway to western Sikkim, **LEGSHIP** sits in the deep and recently dammed Rangit Valley, just under 100km west of Gangtok and 14km south of Ghezing. It's an important regional road junction and one where you could find yourself with an hour or so to spare, but besides a temple and grubby hot springs across the river, it's not an interesting destination. At the crossroads, *Trishna* (☎03595/250887; ❸) has a few rooms and a restaurant. Jeeps and buses connect Legship with Gangtok, Ravangla, Yoksum (via Tashiding) and Pelling, and there are also regular services to Ghezing and Jorethang.

Pemayangtse

Perched at the end of a ridge parallel to (and visible from) that of Darjeeling, the hallowed monastery of **Pemayangtse**, 118km from Gangtok and a mere 2km from Pelling, is poised high above the River Rangit, which snakes towards its confluence with the Teesta on the West Bengal border. It's a nine-kilometre journey along the main road from Ghezing; or you can take a steep, four-kilometre short-cut through the woods past a line of *chortens* and the otherwise uninteresting remains of Sikkim's second capital, **Rabdantse**, now made into a park.

"Perfect Sublime Lotus", founded in the seventeenth century by Lhatsun Chempo, one of the three lamas of Yoksum, and extended in 1705 by his re-incarnation, is one of the most important *gompas* in Sikkim and belongs to the Nyingmapa school. Expansive views of the Kanchenjunga massif and the surrounding woods create an atmosphere of meditative solitude. Surrounded by exquisite outhouses, with intricate woodwork on the beams, lattice windows and doors, the main *gompa* itself is plain in comparison. Built on three floors, it centres around a large hall which contains images of Guru Rinpoche and Lhatsun Chenpo (the latter was an enigmatic Tibetan lama who is the patron saint of Sikkim), and an exquisite display of *thangkas* and murals. On the top floor, a magnificent wooden sculpture carved and painted by Dungzin Rinpoche, a former abbot of Pemayangtse, depicts Sang Thok Palri, the celestial abode of Guru Rinpoche, rising above the realms of hell. The extraordinary detail includes demons, animals, birds, Buddhas and *bodhisattvas*, *chortens* and flying dragons, and took him just five years to complete. The two-day annual Guru Drogma *chaam* is held here during Losar, the New Year (Feb/March), and attracts visitors from all over Sikkim culminating with draping the monastery with a gigantic *thangka*.

In 1980, the **Denjong Padma Choeling Academy** was set up by the monastery to provide for destitute children and orphans; there are currently around 300 children being housed, clothed, fed and educated here. Generous donations have enabled further building and projects including the yak and *dri* dairy project near Dzongri. Volunteer teachers are always welcome, for a minimum of two months, and receive free accommodation in the monastery, and opportunities to study meditation and Buddhism and to learn local crafts. The monastery also runs **courses** at the *International Heritage Meditation Centre* where nine well-furnished rooms are available to students of Buddhism or anyone wanting to experience monastic life. Contact Sonam Yongda at Pemayangste Gompa, West Sikkim 737 113 (℡03595/250760 or 250141).

Pelling and around

The quiet, relatively new yet rapidly swelling town of **PELLING**, situated 2085m above sea level only 2km beyond Pemayangtse, is most notable for its expansive views north towards the glaciers and peaks of Kanchenjunga. High above forest-covered hills, in an amphitheatre of cloud, snow and rock, the entire route from Yoksum over Dzongri La to the Rathong Glacier can be seen. Frenetic building activity hasn't detracted from Pelling's charm, with numerous hotel terraces that allow you to gaze in awe at the world's third-highest peak, as well as easy access to attractive walks in the hinterland. A four-kilometre trail rises from the playing fields near the helipad just above Pelling to reach the small but highly venerated monastery of **Sanga Choling**, one of the oldest *gompas* in Sikkim. It's another of Lhatsun Chenpo's creations, and is held in high esteem among the Nyingmapa. Gutted by fire, it has been rebuilt and houses some of the original clay statues. A trail past the *gompa* continues up the ridge through orchid-clad forest, past a giant hollow tree to the venerated rock of Thikchuyangtse, also known as Rani Dunga (9km).

A scenic low-altitude **trek** along roads and trails to Khecheopalri Lake, Tashiding and Yoksum starts in Pelling. Jeeps run from both Yoksum and Tashiding back to Legship, from where you can continue to Ghezing and eventually back to Pelling. If you have less time on your hands, tour operators such as Simvo Tour and Travels (℡03595/258549) in Upper Pelling and Father Jeep Service (℡03595/258219) can arrange **day-trips** by Jeep (around Rs1600 for a Jeep holding 6–8 people).

Practicalities

From the crossroads of Upper Pelling, shared **Jeeps** travel regularly (6am–4pm) between Pelling and Ghezing; there are also twice-daily services to Gangtok via Ravangla (7am & noon; Rs150), and one Jeep daily for Siliguri (7am; Rs150); one bus (Rs105) leaves at the same time to Siliguri via Jorethang (pre-book at

SNT, *Hotel Pelling*, Lower Pelling ☏03595/250707). The road from Pelling via Rimbi to Yoksum is poor so allow plenty of time; there are no scheduled services, but Jeeps leave from Ghezing and Legship for Tashiding and Yoksum. The **post office** is in Upper Pelling just above the crossroads; nearby, there's a State Bank of India **ATM**, but note there are no official facilities for changing money. For trekking information consult the books at *Hotel Garuda*; other reliable trek and tour operators include Himalayan Heritage (☏09733076469), Upper Pelling; the Tourist Information Centre near the helipad (daily 10am–4pm) is good for general information, as is the local website, Ⓦ www.gopelling.com.

Pelling's **hotels**, whose rates rise steeply in the high seasons (March–May & Sept–Nov) are spread along a 2km stretch of road between Upper, Middle and

West Sikkim high-altitude treks

Two **high-altitude treks** are currently allowed in Sikkim. The first, from **Yoksum** to **Dzongri**, in the shadow of Kanchenjunga, passes through huge tracts of forest and provides incredible mountain vistas; all-inclusive rates from a decent agency are around $50 per head per day. The second, the **Singalila Ridge**, explores the remote high pastures of the Singalila frontier range with breathtaking views of the massif; per-person daily rates are higher, at around $65. Trekkers for either of the two must have special **permits** (see p.933) and travel in groups of at least two organized by authorized agencies (see p.934). Check permits and arrangement for porterage, guides and food before you set off – all should be included in the cost. Bring adequate clothing, including protective headgear to cope with the heat of the river valleys, as well as boots and sleeping bags. The best time to do both treks is between October and mid-November, when the weather is clearest. For general advice on trekking equipment and health issues, see Basics.

The Dzongri Trail

Although Dzongri is the junction of several trails, the prescribed route onwards leads to **Goecha La** via Zemanthang and Samiti Lake. Well-marked and dotted with basic accommodation, the trail, also used by yak herders, is at its best in May when the rhododendrons bloom.

DAY 1 It takes approximately 6hr to climb the 16km from **Yoksum** (1780m) to **Tsokha** (3048m). The trail begins gently and soon reaches deep forest cover before arriving at the Parekh Chu above its confluence with the Rathong. The next 4.5km involve a knee-grinding ascent past the rambling *Forest Rest House* at **Bakhim** (2684m). You have now entered the lichen zone and cloud forests. Tsokha, settled by Tibetan yak herders, has a couple of huts including the *Trekkers Hut*, as well as several rustic houses, where guests are offered Tibetan tea – a salty brew made with rancid butter.

DAY 2 This day can be spent acclimatizing yourself to the altitude at Tsokha, perhaps with a short trek of around 5km towards Dzongri, to a watchtower which (weather permitting) has superb views of Kanchenjunga and Pandim.

DAY 3 The 11km section from **Tsokha** to **Dzongri** (4030) takes at least 5hr, rising through beautiful pine and rhododendron forests to **Phedang Meadows** (3450m), before continuing to the hut on the meadows of Dzongri.

DAY 4 Once again, it's worth staying around Dzongri for further acclimatization. That gives you the opportunity to climb Dzongri Hill above the hut, for early-morning and early-evening views of Kanchenjunga's craggy south summit. Look out for the black tooth of Kabur, a forbidding-looking holy mountain that towers above Dzongri La pass. Several trails meet at the meadows at Dzongri – one crosses Dzongri La (4400m), descends around 450m and rises again to the HMI base camp 12km away at Chaurikhang and the Rathong Glacier.

Lower Pelling, with Lower Pelling's "Bengali Boulevard" gearing itself more towards the domestic market and Upper Pelling offering the finest views, especially from near the helipad.

Most **restaurants** are to be found in hotels, but traditional Sikkimese food is rarer than *dhal bhat* due to the strong Bengali presence. Pelling is a good place to sample a *tomba* (warm millet beer); it's best in Sikkimese-run hotels like *Phamrong*.

Accommodation

Blue Hills Below the helipad, Upper Pelling ☎09733 076211. Friendly, locally-run hotel that's one of the cheaper options in this popular location above town; most of the modest-sized rooms have views, and there is a dorm and lockers (Rs100). **④**

DAY 5 The 8km trek from **Dzongri** to **Thangsing** (3841m) takes around 4hr, descending against an incredible backdrop of peaks to a rhododendron forest, crossing a bridge and continuing through woods to the *Trekkers Hut* at **Thangsing** at the end of a glacial valley.

DAY 6 The 10km short, sharp shock up to **Samiti Lake** (4303m) takes around 3hr through alpine meadows and past a yak-herders' hut, then traverses glacial moraine before arriving at the emerald-green **Samiti Lake** (local name Sungmoteng Tso). If you are still going strong, you could continue to **Zemanthang** (4453m) where there's a *Trekkers Hut*.

DAY 7 Very much the climax of the trek, and also its most difficult section by far simply due to its high altitude. From **Samiti Lake**, the 14km round-trip climb takes around 4hr up to **Goecha La** and 2–3hr back down again. Leaving Samiti, the trail follows glacial moraine, drops to a dry lake at Zemanthang, then makes a final grinding rise alongside cairns decorated with the occasional prayer flag to the narrow defile at Goeche La (5000m), where Kanchenjunga South is clearly visible.

DAY 8 Most of the long 24km hike from **Samiti Lake** back to **Tsokha** is downhill and takes around 8hr, involving a short cut to avoid Dzongri. Crossing the bridge and following the path to a junction signed to the left puts you back above **Tsokha**, to rejoin the trail to Yoksum.

The Singalila Ridge

Itineraries for **Singalila Ridge** treks range between ten and nineteen days and though more expensive due to the area's remoteness, they prove exceptionally rewarding, with views from Everest to the huge Kanchenjunga massif ahead. It's best done from south to north, allowing you views of the undulating ridge as it rises towards the snows through remote alpine pastures and past hidden lakes. From the roadhead at **Uttarey** (1965m), 28km to the west of Pelling, or from **Soreng**, 30km to the west of Jorethang, the trek ascends to **Chewabhanjang** (3170m) on the Sikkim–Nepal frontier. Thereafter, the trail rarely descends below 3500m, crossing steep rocky hillsides and meadows high above the tree line; the highest point of the trail is the **Danfeybhir Tar**, a pass at 4400m. Several lakes such as **Lampokhari**, all considered holy, are encountered along the route, and here and there dwarf rhododendron forests bring a blaze of colour in season (April–May). The route dips down to **Gomathang** (3725m), a yak-herders' shelter on the banks of the Boktochu, then passes through a delightful forest of silver fir and rhododendron before arriving at the welcome sight of the bungalow at **Dzongri**. You could descend from here via Tsokha to Yoksum or continue to **Goecha La**, thus completing a grand and rewarding traverse.

Dubdi Near the helipad ☎03595/258349. This small hotel, pleasantly located in a quiet corner above town and tucked beside the gates to the Norbu Ghang, is a lot cheaper than its neighbour, with very comfortable, large and clean rooms, some with great views. ❹–❺

🏃 **The Elgin Mount Pandim** Just below Pemayangtse monastery ☎03595/250756, ⓦwww.elginhotels.com. Darjeeling-style elegance introduced by its new owners has turned this old government hotel into the most luxurious address in western Sikkim. Every room has a view of the snowy peaks, the multi-cuisine restaurant is excellent and the quiet, unspoilt location makes this an excellent base from which to explore the area. From $152. ❾

Garuda At the crossroads ☎03595/258319. A popular and recommended travellers' haunt and good meeting-place, this well-run family hotel recently underwent major renovation, and offers a range of singles, doubles and dorms (Rs70), and useful comment books have the latest trekking information. The restaurant boasts excellent food, beer and low-key service. ❶–❸

Kabur 200m before the crossroads ☎03595/258504. A welcoming place with Internet access and a helpful local trek and tour operation.

The doubles come with carpets and hot water and there's an expansive rooftop terrace complete with sun loungers and great views. The restaurant offers a healthy range of meals, including Sikkimese cuisine. ❷–❸

Ladakh Upper Pelling ☎09733210355. A rapidly dying breed in Pelling – a traditional, rustic Sikkimese house with two double rooms, one triple and a dorm (Rs50); the common bathrooms are outside but the family-run lodge is being upgraded to add comfort. ❷

Norbu Ghang Resort Near the helipad ☎03595/258245, ⓦwww.sikkiminfo.net /norbughang. Efficient upmarket hotel, with comfortable cottages spread around the manicured gardens; combining vernacular style with modern amenities, each has good views from verandas that take full advantage of the position high above town. ❼–❽

Phamrong Upper Pelling ☎03595/258218, Ⓔmailphamrong@yahoo.com. A wide range of comfortable, clean rooms, running hot water and attentive service; there's a pleasant restaurant serving Sikkimese, Indian and Chinese food, and great views from some of the more expensive rooms. Email is available. ❻–❽

Khecheopalri Lake

Surrounded by dense forests and hidden in a mountain bowl (2000m) 33km northwest of Pelling, **Khecheopalri Lake**, known as the "Wishing Lake", is sacred to the Lepchas. Legend has it that if a leaf drops onto the lake's surface, a guardian bird swoops down and picks it up, thereby maintaining the purity of the water. From the Pelling–Yoksum road, a turn-off diverts at "zero point" to Khecheopalri (11km), with only occasional Jeeps travelling the route (landslides permitting) to the lake. If you want to trek from Pelling to Khecheopalri, there's a shortcut leading down to the river valley, steeply up to the Pelling–Yoksum road and then up to the lake (allow 5hr); you can continue the circuit to Yoksum (see below), but arm yourself with information and a handy map from *Hotel Garuda* (see above) before setting off.

The Khecheopalri *gompa*, 2km from the lake on top of the ridge, provides excellent views of Mount Pandim (6691m), and several sacred caves are scattered through the hills. Guides for visiting these caves and for the trek to Yoksum can be arranged through *Trekkers Hut* (☎09733 076995; ❶), 300m before the village, one of the few places to stay at Khecheopalri – a friendly but very basic option which serves simple meals. It also has some very useful information on the local area and a definitive list for bird-watchers. Tea stalls at the car park serve chai and simple meals. The trail on to Yoksum is 18km long and takes around four hours. Stock up on snacks from Ghezing market or some of the small stalls in Pelling.

Yoksum

The sleepy, spread-out hamlet of **YOKSUM**, which occupies a large shelf at the entrance to the Rathong Chu gorge, 40km north of Pemayangtse at the end of the road, holds a special place in Sikkimese history. This was the spot where three lamas converged from different directions across the Himalayas to enthrone the first religious king of Sikkim, Chogyal Phuntsog Namgyal, in 1642. Named the "Great Religious King", he established Tibetan Buddhism in Sikkim. Lhatsun Chenpo is supposed to have buried offerings in Yoksum's large white **Norbugang Chorten**, built with stones and earth from different parts of Sikkim. From here, a path branches left through the village to a small grove and the simple stone throne of the first chogyal. In front of the throne, an impressive footprint embedded in a rock by one of the lamas no doubt impressed the king too. High above the town, prayer flags announce the site of the Nyingma **Dubdi Monastery**, built in 1701. From the end of the road at the hospital, a path threads past water wheels and a small river and rises through the forest to arrive at the dramatically situated *gompa*, looking out over Yoksum; however there's unlikely to be anyone around to let you have a look inside. **Kathok Lake**, a small scummy pond at the top end of town has nothing of the pristine beauty of Khecheopalri Lake, but has views of the snowcapped peaks in the distance. Above the bazaar, the small **Kathol Wodsal Ling** *gompa*, with its statue of Guru Rinpoche, adds some colour to the scene.

Yoksum's main role these days is as the start of the **Dzongri Trail**. Visitors are welcome in Yoksum itself, but unless you have a Dzongri Trek permit, you're not supposed to venture any further. The police are quite vigilant, so there's not much chance of a surreptitious high-mountain trek, but so long as you're not carrying a backpack they may allow a day-trip along the main trail to the Parekh Chu and its confluence with the Rathong Chu – a 28km round trip. You won't see the high Himalayas, but you do pass through some beautiful forest scenery. Yaks – or rather *dzo*, a more manageable cross between yak and domestic cattle – travel this route carrying supplies for trekking parties and isolated communities.

Practicalities

There are no buses to or from Yoksum itself, but **Jeeps** start to depart at around 6am to Legship via Tashiding, and there are unscheduled services to Ghezing and Jorethang; you're unlikely to get shared transport after 1pm.

Conservation and the Kanchenjunga National Park

Established in 1996 with the help of the Sikkim Biodiversity and Ecotourism Project, the **Khangchendzonga Conservation Committee (KCC)**, a community-based NGO based in Yoksum, aims to promote ecological awareness to locals and visitors alike. The KCC's main concern is the impact of tourism on the fabric of the **Kanchenjunga National Park**, and their methods include planting trees, mobilizing local participation in the planning of ecotourism and organizing clean-up campaigns. Conservation has also been embraced by the Sikkim government, which has put in place a code of conduct, banning the use of wood for fuel in preference to kerosene; however, wood fires continue to be part and parcel of the Sikkim landscape.

One major KCC programme is the uphill battle to keep the Yoksum, Dzongri and Thangsing trails clean – volunteers regularly remove vast amounts of litter and camping debris. Other KCC initiatives include publishing leaflets to promote eco-awareness, training local workers including porters and guides in the ecotourism industry, and organizing self-help initiatives. For more information on the KCC, contact their coordinator Pema Chewang Bhutia at the *Hotel Wild Orchid*, Yoksum (T09832 452527, @kcc_sikkim@hotmail.com).

Internet access is available at the Community Information Centre (Rs50 per hour) above the bazaar.

Accommodation is limited, with several budget options around the small market area, including *Wild Orchid* (☎03595/241212; ❷), an attractively rustic traditional house whose basic rooms have shared bathrooms. Approaching Yoksum's tiny market, *Pemathang* (☎03595/241221; ❸) has clean, airy rooms with attached bathrooms, and a small but picturesque garden. Neighbouring *Yangri Gang* (☎03595/241217; ❷) is not nearly as attractive but is cheaper; most rooms are small, but the better ones have attached baths and hot water, and there's a traveller-friendly restaurant. The *Tashi Gang* (☎03593/241202; ❺), is the plushest of Yoksum's hotels, with Buddhist-themed rooms, and has a decent restaurant. At the Tashi Gang gates, *Pemalingpa Cottage* (☎03593/241214; ❷) offers a taste of village life in a traditional family home with basic wooden rooms and toilets outside.

Besides hotel restaurants, the only other **places to eat** are cafés – such as *Guptas* and the friendly *Yak* – along the main drag, which serve snacks and basic meals.

Tashiding

Considered the holiest in Sikkim, the beautiful *gompa* of **Tashiding** occupies the point of a conical hill 19km southeast of Yoksum, high above the confluence of the Rangit and the Rathong. "The Devoted Central Glory" was built in 1717, after a rainbow was seen to connect the site to Kanchenjunga. While a new road has eaten its way through the forest to the monastery, the climb is still recommended – the well-marked path leaves the main road near an impressive *mani* wall (inscribed with the mantra *Om mani padme hum*: "Hail the jewel in the lotus" in silver paint) and leads steeply past rustic houses and fields and along a final flag-lined approach. The large complex consists of a motley collection of buildings, *chortens*, chapels and the unassuming main temple itself, which was recently rebuilt using some of the features and wooden beams of the original. At the far end of the temple complex, surrounded by numerous multicoloured *mani* stones inscribed with a mantra, is an impressive array of *chortens* containing relics of Sikkim's chogyals and lamas. On the fifteenth day of the first month of the Tibetan New Year, devotees from all over Sikkim gather in Tashiding for the **Nyingmapa Bhumchu festival**, when they are blessed with the holy water from an ancient bowl said by legend never to dry up. Oracles consult the water's level to determine the future.

Around 2km below the *gompa*, Tashiding's tiny bazaar – also known as **Senik Bazaar** – is situated near a saddle that separates the mountainside from the monastery hill. Basic **accommodation** in the bazaar includes the friendly and cosy but very basic *Blue Bird* (no phone; ❶) with a dorm (Rs40) and a restaurant serving simple, wholesome food; and the more spacious, slightly more expensive *Mount Siniolchu Guesthouse* (no phone; ❷) further up the hill; the *Dhakkar Tashiding Lodge* (03595/243249; ❷), between the market and the gates, is more comfortable, though it also has shared baths.

Leaving from the bottom of the bazaar's main street, one or two timetabled **Jeeps** (7–9am) and a handful of unscheduled Jeeps and trucks connect Tashiding to Yoksum (Rs30), Legship (Rs20) and Ghezing (Rs50). The last shared Jeeps depart at 9am. Trails through the forests and along stretches of the main road make trekking an alternative option to public transport; the route to Legship takes around two and a half hours.

North Sikkim

Access to much of spectacular **North Sikkim** is restricted: visitors are allowed in only with the necessary permits, and some areas along the borders remain completely out of bounds. Groups armed with **Protected Area Permits** (see p.933) can go as far north as **Thangu**, at the edge of the Tibetan plateau. Past Mangan, foreigners are only allowed up in groups of two or more and the tours are sold inclusive of transport and accommodation, with the choice of accommodation and food – all limited in these parts – in the hands of tour operators. In general, **permits** for North Sikkim (extendable through the Superintendent of Police in Mangan) are only good for five days and a further seven for trekking. The **Jeep safaris** can prove long and tedious, and due to restrictions on time and movement as well as the lack of infrastructure, the rewards are few. Every year throughout the monsoon, landslides take out stretches of road, making travel even more tedious.

The road north of Gangtok follows the deep Teesta gorge past Phodong across what is said to be the highest bridge in Asia (no photography allowed), before reaching the quiet little town of **MANGAN**, the district capital of North Sikkim. Mangan is the starting point for a few good **treks** including the **Tosar Lake** trail, a very rewarding eight-day trek through forests of bamboo, silver fir and rhododendrons, finally arriving at Tosar Lake, an emerald-green lake cradled in a mountain hollow at an altitude of around 4500m. Offering some grand vistas, the trek captures the very best of Sikkim; contact Khangri Treks & Tours of Gangtok (℡03592/226050) to arrange guides and permits.

There is little of interest in Mangan itself other than a small bazaar and a handful of hotels and cafés. The *Lachen Valley* (℡ 03592/234333; ❷) and *Ganga* (℡ 03592/234333; ❷) both have very basic rooms and shared bathrooms, while on the other end of the scale, *Arcady InHouse* (℡03592/234224; ❹) offers more comfort with attached baths and hot water. The drive down to **Namprikdang**, a popular angling spot at the confluence of the Rangit and Teesta, is both spectacular and hair-raising. A small *gompa* 4km north of Mangan – the northernmost point for those without the additional permits – **Singhik** provides views of the huge east face of Kanchenjunga that are widely considered the best in Sikkim, especially beautiful early in the morning. Singhik is a quiet place to chill out for a day or two, especially at the aptly-named *Friendship Guest House* (℡03592/234278; ❸), a simple village home.

Only recently opened up to visitors, the magnificent valley of **Dzongu** branches northwest from Mangan towards Kanchenjunga. At the heart of the valley, the ancient *gompa* of **Tholung** is home to ancient treasures of the chogyals; these are displayed every three years to the public with the next display in January 2009. A few **homestay** options are now available, arranged, along with permits (see p.932), through tour operators like Sikkim and Khangri in Gangtok (see p.934). A five-day trek starting at Lingza and passing through Tholung, Thizon and across Kyeshong La (3790m) explores the forests and meadows of this unspoilt Lepcha homeland.

A further 40km north of Mangan lies **CHUNGTHANG**, a dark and grubby town set in a deep valley at the confluence of the Lachen and Lachung rivers, beyond which the valleys fork. These are border areas and the military, who maintain the roads, are very sensitive. Photography of bridges, communications and military installations is not allowed. The road to the right climbs rapidly to the small settlement of **LACHUNG**, the "big pass", a mere 15km west of Tibet. Across the river, **Lachung Monastery** is a two-storey Tibetan-style *gompa* belonging to the Nyingmapa sect. The Bhotia people of Lachung and Lachen practice a unique social system known as *Dzumsa* – a sort of gathering of elders that controls everything from grazing to law and order. The **accommodation** here will be pre-booked along with all food and transport through tour operators such as Blue Sky, Marcopolo and Khangri in Gangtok (see p.934); options include the *Apple Valley Inn* and the *Lecoxy*, a large comfortable timber lodge. Food is basic. Twenty-four kilometres further north, the landscape becomes even more spectacular with craggy snow-bound peaks towering to 6000m on either side of **Yumthang** (3645m). This beautiful tree-lined valley boasts hot sulphur springs but no accommodation. The road continues up the valley and emerges on the high plateau at **Yumesamdong** or **Zero Point**, at an altitude of 4770m. Here, the scenery changes dramatically, with icy peaks like **Pauhunri** (7125m) dominating the open grasslands.

The other road from Chungthang leads 26km to **LACHEN** and a further 36km to **THANGU**, tantalizingly close to the Tibetan plateau and as far as foreign tourists are allowed to go. This is the route to the sacred and spectacular **Guru Dongmar Lake**, considered blessed by Guru Rinpoche and the source of the River Teesta. A short day-hike (5km each way) from Thangu (no special trekking permit needed) leads to the picturesque **Chopta Valley** (4400m). Accommodation at Lachen and Thangu is available at several basic lodges, and at the height of the season over 150 tourist-laden Jeeps wind their way up from Gangtok along these northern routes each day.

Several interesting **high-altitude treks** are now open to group tours in this isolated region, including the challenging **Lachen to Green Lake** (4850m) trek, which takes approximately nine days there and back and offers great views of Mount Siniolchu (6887m) across the Zemu glacier. The region abounds with trekking possibilities, such as the challenging route from Yabuk near Green Lake crossing the Zemu and Tholung glaciers, through Dzongu; however red tape invariably proves a dampener. High-altitude **trekking permits** for the north must be sought through Sikkim Tourism in Delhi (see box, p.933) or through one of the Gangtok operators; they take a minimum of three months to process and, despite all that, the final clearance rests with the army at Gangtok, who are known to refuse on a whim; due to logistical headaches, agents charge enormous fees (from $150 per person per day), especially for Green Lake.

Travel details

Jeeps tend to go when full (less frequently after midday), except for long-distance services such as the Gangtok–Ghezing and Pelling routes, with one or two scheduled departures daily. There are no train or plane services available, and the helicopter service from Gangtok only operates to meet flights at Bagdogra. Buses cost a few rupees less than the Jeeps but are much slower and tend to be a lot more uncomfortable.

Jeeps

Gangtok to: Darjeeling (5–6hr); Ghezing (4–5hr); Kalimpong (3–4hr); Pelling (5–6hr); Mangan (2–3hr); Ravangla (3hr); Rumtek (1hr); Siliguri (5–6hr).

Ghezing to: Gangtok (5–6hr); Jorethang (2hr 30min–3hr); Pelling (30min); Tashiding (1hr); Yoksum (2hr 30min–3hr).
Jorethang to: Darjeeling (2hr); Gangtok (4–5hr); Ghezing (2hr); Legship (1hr).

16

The Northeast

AFGHANISTAN

⑦ CHINA
(TIBET AUTONOMOUS
PAKISTAN ⑥ REGION)
⑧ ④ ⑮ BHUTAN
① NEPAL
② ③ BANGLADESH ⑯
⑤ ⑭
⑨ ⑬
MYANMAR
(BURMA)
⑰
⑪
⑩
BAY OF BENGAL
ARABIAN
SEA ⑱ N
⑫ ㉒
⑳ SRI ⑲
㉑ LANKA
INDIAN OCEAN

0   400 km

The International boundaries on this map are neither purported to be correct
nor authentic by Survey of India directives. Publisher.

CHAPTER 16

Highlights

* **Kaziranga National Park, Assam** Encounter the rare one-horned rhino on a dawn elephant ride. See p.969

* **Majuli Island, Assam** Fascinating Vaishnavite sattras (Hindu monasteries) on the world's largest river island. See p.971

* **Khasi Hills, Meghalaya** Explore the impressive caves, dramatic waterfalls and rolling hills of this picturesque state. See p.978

* **Tawang Monastery, Arunachal Pradesh** A spectacular Tibetan Buddhist monastery in one of the most remote locations imaginable. See p.983

* **Namdapha National Park, Arunachal Pradesh** A beautiful park in a stunning setting with clear air, prehistoric trees and pristine vegetation. See p.985

* **Kohima, Nagaland** Proud capital of Nagaland, with a fascinating museum and poignant World War II memorial. See p.986

▲ Monks at Tawang monastery

The Northeast

The least explored and arguably most beautiful region of India, the **NORTHEAST** is connected to the rest of the country by a narrow stretch of land between Bhutan and Bangladesh, and was all but sealed from the outside world until relatively recently. Arunachal Pradesh shares an extremely sensitive frontier with Chinese-occupied Tibet and, together with Nagaland, Manipur and Mizoram, a 1600-kilometre border with Myanmar.

Insurgency has agitated the region since Independence, with tribal groups pushing for various degrees of autonomy as well as fighting each other. A huge influx of Bangladeshis and the displacement of many indigenous people has created further tension. The situation has improved in recent years, although Tripura and Manipur remain unsafe for travel (see p.962) and Restricted or Protected Area Permits are required for four of the seven states (see "Access, permits and tour operators" box, pp.962–963). Tourists are not a target of violence in any state, however, and this fascinating corner of India continues to open up for travellers. An extraordinary diversity of peoples and spectacular landscapes make a visit worth the effort. One of the wettest monsoon belts in the world, the area also boasts an astounding array of flora and fauna, estimated at fifty percent of India's entire biodiversity.

Until the 1960s the region comprised just two states, the North East Frontier Agency (NEFA), now Arunachal Pradesh, and Assam, but separatist pressures further divided it into seven states, known as "the seven sisters". **Assam** consists

Travelling through the Northeast

Much of the region is easiest reached through tour operators (see p.963), but it is increasingly possible – and richly rewarding – for the adventurous to travel independently, though this demands a considerable amount of time, energy and perseverance. Be prepared for bureaucracy, language barriers, long drives on terrible roads, basic accommodation and (except in Assam) extremes in temperature. Consider hiring your own **Jeep and driver**, at least for part of the trip, and using public Tata **Sumos**, Jeeps which operate like shared taxis and are generally much quicker than buses. If travelling in winter, take your own sleeping bag and thermals, as much of the accommodation is not set up for cold weather. People rarely drive at night because of the threat of banditry, and, since the region shares the same time zone as the rest of India despite being so far east, the sun rises and sets early and a lot of places close by 6pm. Outside Guwahati, **money-changing** facilities are few and far between, so bring what cash you need with you. There are regular day-long *bandhs* (strikes) throughout the region when shops, restaurants and public transport shut down – during a typical three-week trip you're likely to lose at least a couple of days to *bandhs*.

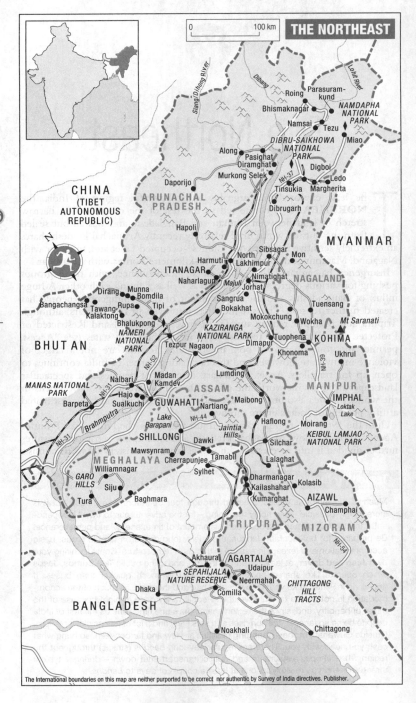

The International boundaries on this map are neither purported to be correct nor authentic by Survey of India directives. Publisher.

of the flat, low-lying Brahmaputra valley. Its capital, **Guwahati**, boasts two of India's most important ancient temples and is the gateway to the region, while a dawn encounter with a one-horned rhino in the magnificent **Kaziranga National Park** is a highlight of any trip to the Northeast.

The other six states occupy the surrounding hills, and are quite distinct from the rest of India in landscape, climate and peoples. **Meghalaya** boasts beautiful lakes and is home to the wettest place on earth. Its capital, **Shillong**, retains some of the colonial atmosphere from its days as East India's summer capital. Majestic **Arunachal Pradesh**, one of the most remote states in India, is inhabited by a fascinating range of peoples, many of Tibetan origin. In the northwestern corner lies the Buddhist monastery of **Tawang**, encircled by awesome mountains, while in the far northeast is the remote wilderness of **Namdapha National Park**. To the south, the lush mountains of **Nagaland** are home to fourteen major tribal groups, each with a strong sense of identity and history. **Mizoram**, in the Lushai hills, was the most peaceful state at the time of writing. Predominantly Christian, it has one of the highest literacy rates in India.

Manipur and **Tripura** were deemed unsafe for travel at the time of writing and the sections on the two states have not been updated for this edition (see boxes, p.993 & p.997). Although tourists are not a direct target, both states continue to suffer from inter-tribal disputes and insurgency involving kidnapping, banditry, village raids, arson and killings. Once an independent princely kingdom, Manipur is at the cultural crossroads where the Subcontinent and Southeast Asia meet, and its people are more closely related to the neighbouring Burmese than the Aryans from the west. Tripura is bordered by Bangladesh on three sides but was cut off from the Bangladeshi plains during the 1947 Partition.

The recommended **time to visit** the Northeast is from November to April, although mountain areas can be extremely cold by December. It rains heavily from May to the end of September. In two weeks you could travel from West Bengal to Guwahati, Shillong and Kaziranga, while three weeks would be enough to cover the main sights of Assam and Meghalaya. A month would enable you to enjoy the two most beautiful and remote states, Arunachal Pradesh and Nagaland – to take in all the states together, including Mizoram, you'll need considerably longer.

Assam

ASSAM is dominated by the mighty **River Brahmaputra**, whose huge, lush valley is sandwiched between the Himalayan foothills to the north and the Meghalayan hills and plateau to the south. An attractive state, Assam is one of India's few **oil** regions as well as producing more than half of the nation's **tea**. Most of its eight hundred tea estates were laid down by the British, who also built one golf club for every fifteen estates. However, the industry is no longer so profitable, and for the marginalized Adivasis – brought from central India by the British to work as indentured labourers on the plantations – depressingly little has changed since colonial times.

This has been one of the major sources of instability in the state, which continues to be plagued by **political violence**. The United Liberation Front of Asom (**ULFA**) began an armed struggle for independence in 1985. In the early 1990s, Assamese nationalism sparked opposition from Bodos, Cachars and other ethnic minorities, giving rise to further insurgence. However, though bombings, *bandhs* and in-fighting continue, the situation has improved and tourists are not a target.

Although the region is increasingly opening up for tourism, **regulations** can change according to the current state of security. Check with the Indian Embassy or tourist office before travelling.

Currently **Assam**, **Meghalaya** and **Tripura** are completely free of restrictions. Foreigners require **Restricted or Protected Area Permits** to visit **Arunachal Pradesh, Nagaland, Mizoram** and **Manipur**. At the time of writing, the UK Foreign Office is advising against all travel to Tripura and Manipur. Arunachal Pradesh is the only state that demands a fee for its permit ($50), though Manipur charges a Rs1500 "royalty fee" when your permit is issued. It is sometimes possible to get an extension to the standard ten-day permits – ask on application or check with a tour operator once you're inside the region.

For all states you are officially required to travel in **groups** of at least four, except in Nagaland, where married couples (or sometimes friends travelling in pairs, if applied for by a travel agent; see opposite) may be allowed to travel on their own. For Arunachal Pradesh, smaller groups, applying through a travel agent, can obtain a permit by paying the full four-person $200 fee. The Mizoram authorities tend to be more flexible, and you can often obtain a permit even if you are travelling alone. When you cross into either Arunachal Pradesh or Mizoram, you may have to tell the guards the other – non-present or fictitious – people on your permit have been "delayed" and that you are meeting a local guide once you reach your destination, regardless of your actual intentions. If you are travelling with a tour operator, expect to pay upwards of $50 per person per day.

Independent travellers should have their permits endorsed at the **Foreigners' Registration Office** (or with the Superintendent of Police) in the state capitals (see p.932). Indian nationals require Inner Line Permits for the aforementioned four states. Permits are not date-stamped when you cross a **border**, so if, as is likely, your travels take you in and out of a state more than once, there may be some confusion as to whether you are allowed back in again. Passes are eligible for the full period they are allocated for, no matter how many times you enter and exit a state, but in practice you may find yourself facing border guards demanding bribes. Stand your ground.

Permits

The quickest and easiest way of getting a **permit** for Mizoram, Nagaland and Arunachal Pradesh is four to six weeks in advance through a well-connected Northeast tour operator (see opposite). You'll have to pay an administration fee – and sometimes a few rupees to "ease" the permit's progress through the state bureaucracy – but they may be able to help put together a group of four people. The alternative is to apply to the Foreigners' Division of the Ministry of Home Affairs, Lok Nayak Bhavan, Khan Market, New Delhi, or the Foreigners' Regional Registration Office, AJC Bose Road, Kolkata. It's also possible to obtain permits from Indian embassies abroad – however, they all have to get permission from Delhi, so apply at least two months in advance. In all cases, applications (attaching two passport

Assam's busy capital, **Guwahati** boasts one of India's most important Kali temples, **Kamakhya**, and is a hub for the whole region, while within easy access of the city the magnificent **Kaziranga National Park** is renowned for its one-horned **rhinos** – the state symbol. Further along the Brahmaputra lies fascinating **Majuli**, the biggest river island in the world and home to unique *sattras* (Hindu monasteries). Another 60km northeast, **Sibsagar** is unusual for its imposing Shivadol Temple, while further north still, **Dibrugarh** is slowly opening up as a second hub for the region.

photos to the form) must be made at least four weeks in advance of your proposed visit. An invitation from someone in one of the states makes the process quicker and more certain.

To obtain **Inner Line Permits**, Indian citizens should apply with two passport photographs to representatives of the state governments concerned. Applications should only take a day to process and are valid for a week in the first instance but can be extended for up to six months in the relevant state capital.

State Government representatives

Arunachal Pradesh Arunachal Bhawan, Kautlya Marg, Chanakyapuri, Delhi ☎011/2301 3915; Block CE-109, Sector 1, Salt Lake, Kolkata ☎033/2334 1243.

Manipur Manipur Bhawan, 2 Sardar Patel Marg, Chanakyapuri, Delhi ☎011/2687 3311; Manipur Bhawan, 26 Rowland Rd, Kolkata ☎033/2475 8075.

Mizoram Mizoram Bhawan, Circular Road (behind the Sri Lankan Embassy), Chanakyapuri, Delhi ☎011/2301 0595; Mizoram House, 24 Old Ballygunge Rd, Kolkata ☎033/2475 7034.

Nagaland 29 Aurangzeb Rd, Delhi ☎011/2301 6411; Nagaland House, 12 Shakespeare Sarani, Kolkata ☎033/2242 5269.

Northeast tour operators

Ashoka Holidays Sanmati Plaza, GS Road, Guwahati, Assam ☎0361/245 7600, ©nwttghy@satyam.net.in. Guwahati-based company organizing adventurous and cultural tours.

Cultural Pursuits Beneath *Hotel Pegasus Crown*, Shillong, Meghalaya ☎09436 303978, ®www.culturalpursuits.com. Friendly and informed Canadian operation arranging off-the-beaten-track trips throughout the region, including tailor-made trips for budget travellers.

Gurudongma Tours & Treks *Gurudongma Lodge*, Hilltop, Kalimpong, West Bengal ☎03552/255204, ®www.gurudongma.com. Highly professional team arranging tailor-made tours, trekking, mountain-biking, tribal, wildlife and bird-watching holidays in Assam, Meghalaya, Nagaland and Arunachal Pradesh, with particular expertise in bird-watching trips (®www.allindiabirding.com).

Himalayan Holidays ABC Building, Main Market, Bomdila, Arunachal Pradesh ☎03782/222017, ®www.himalayan-holidays.com. Local tour agency specializing in cultural and angling trips throughout the Northeast.

Jungle Travels India GNB Road, Silpukhuri, Guwahati, Assam ☎0361/266 0890, ®www.jungletravelsindia.com. Guwahati-based agent organizing quality group and tailor-made tours, including a luxury boat cruise from Guwahati to Kaziranga.

Purvi Discovery Jalannagar, Dibrugarh, Assam ☎0373/230 1120, ®www.purviweb.com. Dibrugarh-based tour operator with excellent guides, arranging tailor-made wildlife, fishing, golfing, horse-riding, war memorial, tribal and tea tours around Dibrugarh and throughout the Northeast.

Guwahati and around

The state capital **GUWAHATI** (or Gauhati) lies on the banks of the **Brahmaputra**, whose swollen sandy channel is so wide that the far shore is often invisible. It's a dirty and crowded city, but as it's the main gateway to the region you will probably need to stay here for at least a night or two. The busy downtown market area contrasts sharply with the rural riverside northeast of the centre, and the surrounding hills beyond. The main attractions are the

GUWAHATI

▶ Hajo, Airport (18km), Saraighat Bridge, Sualkuchi & Manas National Park

Hospital, Assam Tea Auction Centre, Srimanta Sankaradeva Kalakshetra, Dispur, Basistha, Shillong, India Tourism Office,

Zoo & Shillong ▲

RESTAURANTS

Café Coffee Day	1
Delicacy	7
Floating Island	5
Gauhati Dairy	3
JBs	8
Mainland China	4
Sangai	6
Sagar Ratna	6
Royal Woodlands	2

ACCOMMODATION

Dynasty	A
Landmark	G
Nandan	H
Nova	B
Pragati Manor	J
Raj Mahal	E
Siroy Lily	F
Suudarban	C
Tibet	D
Vishwaratha	I

NORTH GUWAHATI

Brahmaputra River

Peacock Island

Umananda Temple

Karmanasa Island

Kamakhya Temple

Navagraha Temple

SILPUKHURI

CHANDMARI

Gandhi Mandap

India Tourism Office

Nehru Stadium

ULUBARI

Bharalu River

Umananda Ghat

Kacheri Ghat

Sukreswar Ghat

Brahmaputra Ashok

Planetarium

State Bank of India

GPO

Telegraph Office

Railway Station

State Museum

Library

State Emporium

Jungle Travels India

ANZ Grindlays Bank

Assam Tourism and Tourist Lodge

State Bus Stand

Network Travels

Rhino Travels

Pan Bazaar Overbridge

Machkowa Bus Stand

PALTAN BAZAR

PAN BAZAAR

FANCY BAZAAR

UZAN BAZAR

N

Kamakhya, Navagraha and **Umananda** temples. Northwest of Guwahati are the famous silk village of **Sualkachi**, the pilgrimage site of **Hajo** and **Manas National Park**.

Arrival and information

The **railway station** is in the town centre, with the **State Bus Stand**, which operates a left-luggage service (daily 4.30am–10.30pm), just behind. The back of the station leads into hectic Paltan Bazaar, where most of the private bus companies are based. Guwahati's **airport** is 18km west of the centre. **Minibuses** for travel all over the city can be flagged down by the roadside.

    Assam Tourism on Station Road (daily except Sun and 2nd & 4th Sat of month: Nov–Feb 10am–4.15pm; March–Oct 10am–5pm; ☎0361/254 7102, Ⓦwww.assamtourism.com) is a good source of information; next door it has a commercial booth offering car hire, flight bookings and excursions to Kaziranga and Hajo (from Rs500 per day). The **India Tourism** office (Mon–Fri 9.30am–5pm; ☎0361/234 1603) is inconveniently located 1km south of Bharalu River on Amarawati Path, just off GS Road, but can advise on travel throughout the Northeast.

Accommodation

Guwahati has a good range of **places to stay** in all price categories.

Dynasty SS Rd, Fancy Bazaar ☎0361/251 6021, Ⓦwww.hoteldynastyindia.com. Expectations are raised by the imposing palm-shaded entrance, water feature and opulent lobby, though not quite matched by the smart but overpriced attached rooms. There's a fine bar and excellent tandoori restaurant. ❽

Nandan GS Rd, Paltan Bazaar ☎0361/254 855, Ⓦwww.hotelnandan.com. This superior mid-range choice has sparkling attached rooms with wood-effect floors, efficient staff and a restaurant specializing in Mexican cuisine. ❺–❼

Nova SS Rd, Fancy Bazaar ☎0361/251 1464. A solid, if unremarkable, option, and a welcome respite from chaotic Fancy Bazaar; rooms are clean and spacious, if a little drab. ❺

Pragati Manor GS Rd, 500m south of Bharalu River ☎0361/234 1261, Ⓦwww.pragatimanor.com. The best upmarket hotel in the city, even though it's a bit of a trek from the centre. The shimmering gold exterior houses swanky, modern attached rooms with red lamps and tribal paintings. There's also a good restaurant and travel desk. ❻–❽

Raj Mahal AT Rd, Paltan Bazaar ☎0361/254 9141, Ⓦwww.rajmahalhotel.com. Big hotel with bright, well-appointed but somewhat character-less rooms – the "deluxe" attached rooms are well worth the extra Rs100–200. There's a slightly grubby pool. ❻–❼

Siroy Lily Solapara Rd, Paltan Bazaar ☎0361/260 8492, Ⓦwww.hotelsiroylily.com. A cut above the others in its price bracket, *Siroy Lily* has cosy, turquoise-coloured, attached rooms with reliable hot water, smart service and complimentary breakfast – some bathrooms, however, suffer from damp. ❹–❺

Suudarban Guest House Just off ME Rd, Paltan Bazaar ☎0361/273 0722, Ⓔkuljitbaruah_sgh@redffmail.com. The pick of Guwahati's backpacker lodges, *Suudarban* has very good value, spotless rooms, with chintzy decor and knowledgeable staff. Bizarrely, a free dental check-up is offered to all guests. ❸–❹

Tibet AT Rd, Paltan Bazaar ☎09864 023296, Ⓔhoteltibet@redimail.com. The best of the budget lodges clustered around the bus station, with clean, boxy rooms. It can be noisy, however, so bring ear plugs. ❷–❹

Tourist Lodge Station Rd ☎0361/254 4475. Assam Tourism's friendly green-and-white hotel has a muzak-playing lift and decent, if dowdy, standard rooms, as well as smarter a/c attached rooms with TVs. ❸–❹

Vishwaratna AT Rd, close to Fancy Bazaar ☎0361/260 7712, Ⓦwww.vishwaratnahotel.com. This smart option boasts roomy centrally air-conditioned attached rooms with mini-fridges and flat-screen TVs, rooftop pool, reputable travel agency and restaurant-bar. ❼

The Town

The bustling markets of **Paltan Bazaar**, **Pan Bazaar** and **Fancy Bazaar**, Guwahati's main shopping areas, are bunched in the centre on either side of the railway, with the older residential areas north of the tracks. Most of the bazaars deal simply in provisions; Assamese **silk**, basketware and other crafts are sold at several good shops on GNB Road, including the **State Emporium**. Assam's main business is tea, and tourists can visit the **Assam Tea Auction Centre** (Tues 9.30am–1pm & 2.30–6pm), in the Dispur suburb, with special permission from the Senior Manager (℡0361/233 1845). The **State Museum** (daily except Mon 10am–4.15pm; Rs5, camera Rs10, video camera Rs250), on GNB Road, is worth a look for its tribal costumes and religious sculptures.

The **Srimanta Sankaradeva Kalakshetra** is an arts complex on Shillong Road, Panjabari district, with a museum, art gallery, open-air theatre and traditional Vaishnavite temple. It's named after the poet and philosopher Sankaradev, who founded the institution of the *sattra* or Hindu monastery in the fifteenth century.

The Shiva temple of **Umananda** stands on Peacock Island in the middle of the Brahmaputra. Its location, atop a steep flight of steps is more dramatic than the temple itself, but you may get to see some rare golden langur monkeys. Ferries leave regularly from Kachari and Umananda Ghat.

On the commanding Nilachal Hill, overlooking the river 8km west of the centre (buses can be picked up along MG Rd), the important Kali temple of **Kamakhya**, with its beehive-shaped *shikhara*, is a good example of the distinctive Assamese style of architecture. As one of the *shakti pithas*, it marks the place where Sati's *yoni* (vulva) landed when her body fell to earth in 51 pieces, and is one of the three most important Tantric temples in India. Animal sacrifice is part of the ritual here and kid goats are bathed in the ceremonial tank before being led to slaughter. A short walk up the hill brings you to a smaller temple with wonderful views of Guwahati and the Brahmaputra.

East of the centre, on another hill, is the atmospheric **Navagraha** temple – the "temple of the nine planets", an ancient seat of astrology and astronomy – with wonderful acoustics. Housed in a single red dome, the central lingam is encircled by a further eight representing the planets, each lit by clusters of candles.

Eating

For breakfast, places around the bus stand open early for tea and omelettes. Most of Guwahati's mid-range and upmarket hotels have good **restaurants**.

Café Coffee Day Taybullah Rd, overlooking the tank. Has the international coffee-shop-chain vibe down to a tee, including excellent coffee, sandwiches and pastries (Rs30–70). There's another branch in the Hub shopping centre, GS Rd.

Delicacy GS Rd, 2km south of Bharalu River. Despite an unprepossessing location beneath an overpass, *Delicacy* dishes up outstanding Northeastern cuisine: huge portions of duck, pigeon, pork, chicken or freshwater fish are served with banana flowers, sesame seeds or bamboo shoots (Rs60–120). Don't miss the *payash*, a sweet rice pudding.

Floating Island MG Rd, south of Sukreswar Ghat. The best of the boat restaurants on the Brahmaputra, *Floating Island* offers hearty Rajasthani thalis (Rs50–90) and a chilled-out ambience.

JBs MG Rd, near the main ferry point. Overlooking the Brahmaputra, *JBs* has a pleasant first-floor a/c restaurant with veg north and south Indian, Mexican and Italian dishes (Rs60–90). Downstairs is a popular bakery and cake shop.

Mainland China Dona Planet mall, GS Rd, 700m south of Bharalu River. Guwahati's most fashionable restaurant wouldn't look out of place in downtown Mumbai. Exquisite and suitably expensive Chinese food (Rs90–450) – including lobster, sea bass and crab dishes – is elegantly served in classy surroundings.

Royal Woodland GNB Rd, close to the State Museum. Modest south Indian eatery with *dosas* – try the *rawa Mysore masala dosa* – vadas and uttapam, as well as a tasty Assamese thali (Rs25–55).

Sagar Ratna MD Shah Rd, Paltan Bazaar. Sleek a/c restaurant with frosted glass, green leather seats and prompt service. The menu is predominantly south Indian – including 22 types of *dosa* – but there are also excellent *paneer* dishes and delectable ice-cream sundaes (Rs40–90).

Sangai *Hotel Siroy Lily*. Understated restaurant specializing in spicy Manipuri cuisine. It also does a great Hyderabadi biriyani (Rs35–120).

Listings

Airlines British Airways c/o Pelican Travels, *Brahmaputra Ashok Hotel*, MG Rd, Uzan Bazaar ☏0361/260 1605; Air India also in the *Brahmaputra Ashok* ☏ 0361/260 2281; Indian Airlines, GS Rd, Ganeshguri Charili, near Assam Assembly ☏0361/226 4425; Jet Airways, GNB Rd, Silpukhuri ☏0361/266 8255.

Banks and exchange ANZ Grindlays, GNB Rd, and the State Bank of India, MG Rd, both change traveller's cheques and foreign currencies. There are ATMs all over town.

Bookshops There are several bookshops in Pan Bazaar, notably Western Book Depot, Josovanta Rd just off HB Rd, with a good selection of fiction, and titles on the Northeast; the Vintage Bookshop on MN Rd opposite *Ananda Lodge*; and the Modern Book Depot on HB Rd near MN Rd.

Hospital Downtown Hospital ☏0361/233 1003; Guwahati Medical College Hospital ☏0361/252 9457.

Internet access I-Way centres on Lamb Lane and MD Shah Rd offer speedy Internet access (Rs25/hr); there are also innumerable cybercafés on GS, GND and MN roads.

Pharmacy There are several chemists on GS Rd around *Hotel Nandan*, including Life Pharmacy, just south of B Barua Rd (8am–10.30pm).

Photography New Frontier Colour Lab, SS Rd, Lakhtokia, 50m west of Pan Bazaar; S Ghoshal, HB Rd, Pan Bazaar.

Police Emergencies ☏100, HB Rd ☏0361/254 0138.

Post office ARB Rd, just round the corner from the State Bank of India.

Travel agents Those at the *Vishwaratna*, *Dynasty* and *Raj Mahal* hotels can book airline tickets, as can Assam Tourism's commercial booth. Rhino Travels, MN Rd, Pan Bazaar (☏0361/254 0666), runs a range of tours, including safaris at Manas. Network Travels, Paltan Bazaar (☏0361/252 2007), can arrange tours and air tickets; it's also one of the region's largest private bus operators. Jungle Travels India (see box, p.963) will book flights, arrange permits and organize tours.

Moving on from Guwahati

State-run buses to destinations throughout the region leave from the ASTC stand on AT Road. Private buses are more comfortable and often quicker; most have booths in Paltan Bazaar.

Several daily trains link Guwahati to Delhi; the Rajdhani Express #2423 (daily at 7am; 27hr 20min) is the fastest. For Kolkata (Howrah), the Kamrup Express #5960 (daily at 7.45am; 23hr 25min) is a good option. For Jorhat, the Shatabdi Express #2067 (daily except Sun at 6.30am, arrives 1.10pm) is the quickest train; it also calls at Lumding (9.15am) and Dimapur (10.50am).

Lok-Priya Airport, 20km southwest of Guwahati, has regular flights to Delhi, Kolkata, Imphal, Agartala and Bagdogra; see Guwahati listings for flight-booking agents. A taxi to the airport costs around Rs400; alternatively, shared minibuses (Rs100) leave when full from outside *Hotel Mahalaxmi*, next to *Hotel Nandan* on GS Road. There are Pawan Hans helicopter flights to Shillong, Tura, Naharlagun (near Itanagar) and Tawang (☏0361/241 6720).

For those with time and money to spare, the Assam Bengal Navigation Company runs sightseeing **cruises** on the Brahmaputra; book through Jungle Travels India (see box, p.963). See "Travel details" at the end of this chapter for more information on journey frequencies and durations.

Around Guwahati

Every home in the village of **SUALKUCHI**, 36km from Guwahati, produces golden *muga* **silk**, named after the rich amber colour of the *muga* cocoon exclusive to Assam. The silk is cheaper than in Guwahati, and you can buy it direct from many villagers' homes. **HAJO**, 2km north, is a pilgrimage site for Hindus, Buddhists and Muslims, worth seeing for its mix of religious temples including the Hindu **Hayagriba-Madhava Mandir**. Muslims believe visiting the **Poa Mecca Mosque** here four times in a lifetime is equivalent to a pilgrimage to Mecca.

The beautiful **MANAS NATIONAL PARK** (Oct–March; Rs250 [Rs20], vehicle Rs200, camera Rs500 [Rs50],), 80km west of Guwahati off the NH-31 on the border with Bhutan, has been on UNESCO's list of endangered World Heritage Sites since 1992. Troubled by insurgency, poachers and staff shortages, the park's population of large mammals has sadly diminished and sightings of tigers and wild elephants are rare. It is still worth a visit for its varied natural beauty however, with water buffalo grazing on expansive stretches of sand and grass, and *sal* forests flanking the Manas River. Moreover there are plans to expand the park's size by a further 365km, create new anti-poaching camps and introduce rhinos from Kaziranga. The *Mathunguri Forest Bungalow* overlooking the river has three atmospheric **rooms** (❸) – for more information contact the Field Director (☎03666/260289). Otherwise try *Bansbari Lodge* just outside the park – book with Jungle Travels India in Guwahati (see box, p.963; ❾). You'll need to hire your own transport to get here.

Tezpur and around

TEZPUR, 174km northeast of Guwahati, is a busy little town on the north bank of the Brahmaputra. Literally meaning "full of blood", it's named after a mythical battle between Vishnu and Shiva. You may need to stay here en route to Arunachal Pradesh.

Chitralekha Udyan (daily 9am–8pm; Rs10, camera Rs20), with its central lake (paddleboats Rs30/15min), is a good place to potter, especially in the early evening when the pathways are lit up with fairy lights. It is still known locally as Cole Park after its founder, the British deputy commissioner. The town's main market, **Chowk Bazaar**, is on MC Road; a little further north lies the ninth-century **Mahabhairav Temple**, dedicated to an incarnation of Shiva. Along the river, 1km to the east, **Agnigarh Hill** (daily 8am–7.30pm; Rs10) commands great views, and is known as the place where Asura, king of the Ban dynasty, protected his beautiful daughter, Usha, from men who wanted to seduce her.

Practicalities

Tezpur's **bus stand**, on Kabarkhana (KK) Road, is 500m north of the **tourist office** (Mon–Sat except 2nd & 4th Sat 10am–5pm; ☎03712/221016), in the *Tourist Lodge* on KP Agarwalla Road. The **GPO** is on Head Post Office Road, parallel to the main road. No banks change foreign currency, but there are plenty of **ATMs**. Elements, 500m southwest of the bus station on SC Road, offers **Internet** access (Rs30/hr). Recently refurbished, Tezpur **airport** serves Delhi and Kolkata; flight tickets can be booked through Anand Travels (☎03712/230693), near the Jonaki cinema. Kabarkhana (KK) Road is lined with **Sumo** stands, with daily services to Bomdila (5–6hr), Dirang (7–8hr) and Tawang (14–18hr) in Arunachal Pradesh.

The *Tourist Lodge* (☎03712/221 016; ❸–❹) is one of the best budget **accommodation** options, with large, slightly musty rooms with clean attached bathrooms and small TVs; the cheaper ones have squat toilets. The venerable *Luit* (☎03712/222 083, ⓔ229 708; ❸–❻), a large white building 100m north of the bus station on a little lane off Ranu Singh Road, has very good value economy rooms in the "old wings" annexe, as well as vast but overpriced attached rooms, with cane furniture and TVs. In Mission Charali, 4km north of the bus station, ⚐ *KF* (☎03712 237 825, ✉skfood@gmail.com; ❼) is something of a surprise: immaculate, contemporary rooms with swanky attached bathrooms, laminate floors, modern art, flat-screen TVs and tea/coffee makers make this "boutique" hotel one of Assam's most stylish. It's also got a great restaurant (see below). For something a little different, a 30km drive north of Tezpur is the *Addabarie Tea Estate Bungalow* (❼–❾), which dates back to 1850 and has comfortable, quiet rooms surrounded by pretty gardens; book through *Wildgrass* in Kaziranga (see p.970).

Tezpur has a handful of decent **restaurants**. *KF* has a cool modern feel and a quality menu, featuring burgers and pizzas, Thai curries, Indian and Chinese favourites (Rs75–130), plus treats from the attached ice-cream parlour. ⚐ *Chinese Villa*, in the Baliram complex on the corner of NB and NC roads, 300m northeast of the bus station, is a classy joint with pink and black marble tables, huge glass windows and red hanging lamps. Tuck into delights such as prawn wantons, shredded lamb and crispy chilli chicken (Rs50–150). Downstairs, *Veggie Foods* is an informal, wallet-friendly eatery serving *dosas*, thalis and fresh juices (Rs15–30).

Nameri National Park

A 35km journey north of Tezpur, accessible only by taxi, the 200-square-kilometre **NAMERI NATIONAL PARK** (Nov–March daily; Rs250 [Rs20]) flanks the River Bharali and is a lovely, quiet place for fishing, rafting, bird-watching or guided walks. There are over three hundred species of bird, including the rare white-winged wood duck, as well as fish eagles and hornbills. You may also see deer, but the park's larger wildlife – tigers, elephants and bison – are rarely spotted. Guides can be hired at the park entrance, while fishing, walking and rafting trips can be arranged via the atmospheric ⚐ *Eco Camp* (☎09435 250052; ❺), 3km from the park, which has comfy tents, protected by thatched roofs, with attached bathrooms, a dorm (Rs100, plus compulsory Rs60 "membership") and restaurant. Alternatively, stay in Bhalukpong (see p.981), 10km from the park entrance. Gurudongma Tours & Treks (see p.963) can arrange specialist bird-watching tours to Nameri, as can *Wildgrass* in Kaziranga (see p.970).

Kaziranga National Park

A World Heritage Site covering 430 square kilometres on the southern bank of the Brahmaputra, **KAZIRANGA NATIONAL PARK**, 217km east of Guwahati, occupies a vast valley floor against a backdrop of the Karbi Anglong hills. Its rivulets, shallow lakes and semi-evergreen forested highlands blend into marshes and flood plains covered with tall elephant grass. A visit here is exhilarating and you are likely to see elephant, deer, wild buffalo and the park's famous one-horned **rhino**. The rhino is best seen from the back of an elephant, first thing on a winter's morning. Jeeps take you deeper into the forest than elephants, but cannot get nearly as close to the rhinos. Although its tigers are very elusive, driving through the park's landscape of open savannah grassland interspersed with dense jungle is a wonderful experience. The abundant birdlife includes egrets, herons, storks, fish eagles, kingfishers and a grey pelican colony.

Kaziranga is open from November to early April. Avoid visiting on Sundays, when it gets busy with noisy groups of Indian tourists. During the monsoons (June–Sept), the Brahmaputra bursts its banks, flooding the low-lying grasslands and causing animals to move to higher ground within the park.

Kaziranga celebrated its centenary in 2005; however land encroachment and **poaching** remain serious threats: at least 21 rhinos were killed in 2007, with a further three killed in January 2008. The under-staffed park authorities appear unable to protect the animals, whose horns fetch astronomical prices as aphrodisiacs. Nevertheless the park has now been named a tiger reserve – as part of Project Tiger – which should result in extra funds: whether this proves enough to make a real difference remains to be seen.

Kaziranga practicalities

Kaziranga is easily accessible by **bus**, with services from Tezpur (80km), Jorhat (97km), Guwahati (220km) and Dibrugarh (220km) in Assam, Itanagar in Arunachal Pradesh and Kohima in Nagaland. State and private buses all stop at **Kohora**, the main gate, on the NH-37 (AT Road), with Network Travels serving as the pick-up and drop-off point – you can arrange transport to and from the park here. The nearest town is **BOKAKHAT**, 20km east.

You pay the **entrance fees** (Rs250 [Rs20], vehicle Rs200, camera Rs500 [Rs50], video Rs1000 [Rs500], elephant ride Rs750 [Rs120], compulsory armed guard Rs50) in the tourist complex in Kohora. Jeeps can be hired (from Rs550) here, or you can get your hotel (see below) to arrange them. For **information**, visit the tourist office (03776/262 423) in *Bonani Lodge* (see below) or contact the Field Director (☎03776/268095).

Kaziranga has a range of **places to stay**. The four state tourist lodges are clustered around the main gate: *Aranya* (☎03776/262429; ❹) is the most comfortable, with clean but characterless attached rooms with balconies, a decent restaurant and bar, and seven acres of neatly tended lawns; *Bonani* (☎03776/262423; ❸) has a handful of good-value airy rooms, some with a/c; *Bonoshree* (❷) has time-worn but acceptable doubles; while *Kunjaban* is the most basic option with several dorms (Rs50, plus Rs25 for bed linen) – ask for one of the three-bed rooms. *Bonoshree* and *Kunjaban* are booked through *Bonani*. There are also two excellent, more expensive, alternatives. Set back from the NH-37 in quiet, peaceful gardens 1km from the park entrance, *Bon Habi Jungle Resort* (☎03776/262675, ⓦwww.bonhabiresort.com; ❺; "Jungle Plan", including accommodation, park fees and safaris $50–80) has large twin-bedded cottages with sofas and private balconies backing onto woodland. Staff are charming and there's a pleasant restaurant. At the foot of the Karbi Hills, 4km east of Kohora and 1.5km off the road, the ecofriendly *Wildgrass* (☎03776/262085, ⓦwww.oldassam.com; ❻–❼) offers cosy colonial-style attached rooms, more economical thatched huts and large permanent tents, all set in lush gardens with 200 types of plants and a swimming pool. Both *Wildgrass* and *Bonhabi* can arrange visits to local Mising and Karbi villages.

Network Travels and *Aranya* provide inexpensive **food**, while *Ashyana Green Resort* on the NH-37 towards the Baguri Range has a spacious restaurant serving Indian and Chinese meals and snacks.

Upper Assam

Around 310km northeast upriver from Guwahati, **Jorhat** has an airport and road connections to Kaziranga, Nagaland and northern Arunachal Pradesh. The unique Vaishnavite culture of **Majuli**, the largest river island in the world, and **Sibsagar**, former capital of the Ahoms, are both close by. Further north, **Dibrugarh** is opening up as a gateway to northern Nagaland and eastern Arunachal Pradesh. The **Dibru–Saikhowa National Park** is worth a visit for its birdlife and wild horses, while **Digboi**'s attractions include an interesting oil museum and war memorial.

Jorhat

Well connected by railway, **JORHAT** is not in itself of great interest but makes a good base for exploring Majuli, Kaziranga and Sibsagar. If you're here in February, check out the **Jorhat Gymkhana Club**'s (call ☎0376/231 1303 for details) annual horse-racing and polo event; keep an eye out for the bareback Mising riders.

The **airport** is 5km from town and served by buses and auto-rickshaws. Indian Airlines and Jet Airways have offices in *Hotel Paradise*, next to *Hotel Heritage* (see below). The state **bus stand** is on AT Road, half a block north of the private companies' offices. The **railway station** is 3km southeast of here. The **tourist office** (Mon–Sat except 2nd & 4th Sat of month 10am–5pm; ☎0376/232 1579) is in the *Tourist Lodge* on MG Road; to get there head east along AT Road from the bus stand and take the third road on your right. Nearby, Jorhat's modest **museum** (Tues–Sun 10am–4.30pm), in the Postgraduate Training College, has a mildly diverting collection of local crafts. The State Bank of India on AT Road, just east of the bus station, has an **ATM** and changes cash and travellers' cheques. Computer Link Cyber Café, just off AT Road, 100m west of the bus stand, offers **Internet** access (Rs15/hr).

The *Tourist Lodge* (☎0376/232 1579; ❸) has a quiet location and very clean **rooms** with tiled floors, little balconies (but no views) and attached bathrooms. Mosquitoes can be a problem, but the beds come with nets. A better option is the attractive white-and-green hotel ⚲ *Heritage* (☎0376/232 7393, ℻230 0008; ❸–❺), on Solicitor Road, next to the bus stand, with mid-range rooms at budget prices: airy apricot-coloured rooms have marble floors, TVs and tiny but spotless attached bathrooms. A 17km-drive south of Jorhat is the delightful *Thengal Manor* (☎0376/233 0268, Ⓦwww.heritagetourismindia.com; ❼), the colonial-style former holiday home of the local Barooah family. It has an impressive white pillar facade and just five rooms, all with fireplaces, four-poster beds and Louis XV-style furniture; the food, however, is variable. The same family also runs the *Sangsua Tea Estate Burra Bungalow* (booking details as above; ❼), a peaceful tea-planter's bungalow 25km southwest of Jorhat with a colonial-style veranda and comfortable, spacious rooms; guests can use the nearby golf course, play croquet, swim in the lake and take tea tours.

Jorhat's **eating** options are limited. *Heritage* has the pick of the Solicitor Road hotel restaurants, with a simple dining room and professional service – try the succulent chicken tikka butter masala or the roasted pomfret (Rs45–140). *Naffy* on AT Road, 100m west of the bus station, has a cheerful – or garish, depending on your point of view – orange-and-yellow colour-scheme, and a tasty, good-value Chinese and North Indian menu (Rs30–130); check out the local fish dishes.

Majuli

The most popular outing from Jorhat is to **MAJULI**, the largest river island in the world and a World Heritage Site. It's a fascinating place, largely because of its unique Vaishnavite *sattras* (Hindu monasteries). The island is also a haven for bird-watchers.

Ferries for Majuli leave twice a day (10.30am & 3pm; 2hr 30min; Rs12) from **Nimatighat**, accessible by bus or taxi (around Rs300; 1hr) from Jorhat. As the ferry timings only give you an hour or so on the island, it is inadvisable to visit as a day-trip – you can hire your own boat for Rs4000 return (contact monk Dulal Saikia (☎03775/273037 for details) but you'll get more out of the island if you stay overnight (see p.972).

Although distances are short, public transport around the island is limited to the occasional bus – running to **Kamalabari** village (5–6 daily; 5km), and beyond to the island's "capital", **Garamur** – and a handful of taxis and auto-rickshaws. For those with plenty of time, the most relaxing way to explore is on foot or bicycle. The best **accommodation** is ⊼ *La Maison de Ananda* (☎03775/274768; ❷–❸), "The House of Joy". Built by a French couple, both architects, these lovely traditional bamboo bungalows, raised on stilts, are set in peaceful gardens. The pillow cases, bedspreads and curtains have all been made by local weavers, and local guide – and poet – Danny Gam ensures everything runs smoothly. A shabby, but acceptable alternative is the *Natun Kamalabari Guesthouse* (☎03775/273302; ❶), with eight cleanish but austere rooms.

There are 22 *sattras* – a temple, monastery, school and centre for the arts – on Majuli: each consists of a prayer hall (*namghar*) surrounded by living quarters for devotees, and *ghats* for bathing. In a day, you could visit **Natun Kamalabari**, and 1.5km away, **Utter Kamalabari**, where Michael Palin pitched up in the BBC television series *Himalaya*. The monks will give you tea, and you can sometimes attend prayer meetings. Four kilometres further west at **Auniati**, another *sattra* keeps royal artefacts from the Ahom kingdom and has an interesting collection of Assamese handicrafts and jewellery. **Bengenati**, 4km east of Auniati, was built in the early seventeenth century, while **Shamaguri**, 6km beyond Bengenati, is renowned for its clay and bamboo masks. **Bongaori**, 8km beyond Shamaguri, and **Dakhinpat**, 5km further south, are also worth a visit.

There are two ferries a day (7.15am & 2pm; 2hr 30min) back to Nimatighat. It is also possible to travel north from Majuli, with two daily ferries from Luhitghat, 3km north of Garamur, to Khabalughat on the north bank, from where there are buses to North Lakhimpur, and from there, buses on to Itanagar or Tezpur, and a train to Guwahati. Allow yourself plenty of time.

Sibsagar

The former capital of the Ahoms and one of the oldest towns in Assam, **SIBSAGAR** – "The Ocean of Shiva" – is 60km northeast of Jorhat. Its cluster of monuments from six centuries of Ahom rule remains significant to modern Assamese culture. A huge **tank**, constructed by Queen Madambika in 1734, lies at the heart of the complex. Rising from its southern shore, the massive 32-metre-high **Shivadol** is India's tallest Shiva temple, flanked by smaller temples dedicated to Durga and Vishnu. Nearly 4km west of the centre of town is the royal **Rang Ghar** pavilion and the ruins of the **Talatal Ghar**, the Ahom's impressive seven-storey palace.

Though best visited as a day-trip, there are a few **accommodation** options: *Kareng* on Temple Road (☎03772/222713; ❷) is one of the better shoestring lodges, with relatively clean, homely rooms, while *Shiva Palace* (☎03772/225184, Ⓔhotel_shiva_palace@rediffmail.com; ❹–❻) on AT Road, 200m from the bus station, is easily Sibsagar's most comfortable hotel with pristine, sparsely-furnished attached rooms and acres of marble. It also has the ⊼ *Sky Chef* a/c restaurant, with an extensive menu of predominantly north Indian fare: standouts include chicken shashlik, *paneer makhani* and an outstanding poppy-seed *paratha* (Rs40–130). You should also pay a visit to the attached *Fahrenheit*, a wonderfully retro 80s-style bar filled with chrome and black leather: grab a cocktail and pretend you're in a Duran Duran video.

Dibrugarh and around

The dusty, little-touristed town of **DIBRUGARH**, 443km north of Guwahati, is surrounded by nine golf courses and lies at the heart of tea-growing country. While there's little to see in the town itself, Dibrugarh is opening up as a gateway to eastern and northern Arunachal Pradesh and northern Nagaland. The town is also a good place to see how **tea** is produced. Purvi Discovery (see "Access, permits and tour operators" box, pp.962–963) offers tea tours on its working tea estate.

Practicalities

Dibrugarh's **airport**, with direct flights to Kolkata and Guwahati, is 16km from town; tickets can be booked at Crown Travels, Mancotta Road (☎0373/232 0007). The **State Bus Stand** is in Chowkidinghee in the town centre, with the **private bus stand** nearby at Phool Bagan. There's a State Bank of India at Thanka Charali, the central commercial district, which cashes **traveller's cheques**. A **car with driver** can be hired from Monikanchan Travel Agency near Chowkidinghee (☎0373/232 5879) or Purvi Discovery (see p.963). There is a daily **ferry** to Oiramghat, near Pasighat (7–8hr; Rs67 per passenger, Rs1500 for a Jeep). The ferry leaves Dibrugarh at 9am – arrive at least an hour before departure to ensure a seat.

Places to stay in town include *Mona Lisa* on Mancotta Road (☎0373/232 0416, ✉paneijonki@sancharnet.in; ⑤), which has a pleasant courtyard, spacious rooms and a bar, or try one of the cool and airy rooms at *Indsurya* on RKB Path (☎0373/232 6322, ⊛www.hotelindsurya.com; ④–⑤). The best option, however, is 5km from the railway station and 15km from the airport, at the peaceful *Chang Bungalows* (book through Purvi Discovery; ⑧) on a tea estate. Built on stilts by British tea planters to protect them from floods and jungle animals, the 150-year-old bungalows have polished wooden floors, elegant dark wood furniture and excellent service.

For **food**, *H20* on the first floor of Amrit Mansion on RNC Path is a trendy bar and restaurant with English-speaking staff serving Thai, Indian, Chinese and Assamese food (Rs50–120).

Dibru-Saikhowa National Park

About 60km north of Dibrugarh, **DIBRU-SAIKHOWA NATIONAL PARK** is rich in birdlife and wild horses. Good rail services run to New Tinsukia Station, 10km from the park's southern entry point at **Guijan**. Information is available from the Range Officer here (☎0374/233 7569). The park is reachable as a day-trip from Dibrugarh, or you can stay in the *Inspection Bungalow* at Guijan (☎0374/233 7569; ②) or campsite (☎0374/233 7666). Purvi Discovery (see p.963) has a simple bungalow which is sometimes available for independent travellers.

Digboi

DIGBOI, 80km northeast of Dibrugarh, is a pleasant place to stop en route to Arunachal Pradesh, with an oil refinery established by the British in 1900, an oil museum, a peaceful World War II cemetery and an eighteen-hole golf course. The *Oil India Guesthouse* has 22 clean and spacious rooms (☎03751/64715; ③–⑤).

South Assam: Silchar

South Assam, divided from the north by the Cachar Hills, is the crossing point to Meghalaya, Tripura, Mizoram and Manipur. Nondescript **SILCHAR** is the region's main transport hub, and is also home to a group of Tibetan traders who run a small wool market on Central Road during the winter. If you need to stay, *Sudakshina* (☎03842/230156; ③–④), on Shillong Patty, has reasonable

rooms and fairly reliable hot water, while *Geetanjali* (☎03842/231738; ❷–❹) on Club Road has scruffy rooms but a decent restaurant. *Kanishka* (☎03842/246764; ❹) in Narsingtola is Silchar's most comfortable hotel with bright and breezy attached rooms.

Silchar's **airport** is 13km from town; Moti Travels on Hospital Road (☎03842/233716) can book flight tickets. The **state bus stand**, near the Devdoot cinema, is the terminus for Assam, Meghalaya and Tripura state services; most **private bus** and **Sumo** companies also run services from here and have agents all over town. The road to Imphal is not recommended because of its bad condition and numerous army checkpoints. The **railway station** is 3km out of town in Tarapur, although services were limited at the time of writing.

Meghalaya

MEGHALAYA, one of India's smallest states, occupies the plateau and rolling hills between Assam and Bangladesh. Its people are predominantly Christian, belonging to three main ethnic groups, the Khasis, Jaintias and Garos. The state has a high literacy rate and teaching is in English.

Much of Meghalaya ("the land of the rain-clouds") is covered with lush forests, rich in orchids. These "blue hills" bear the brunt of the Bay of Bengal's monsoon-laden winds and are among the wettest places on earth. Stupendous waterfalls can be seen near the capital, **Shillong**, but the most dramatic plummet from the plateau to the south, around **Cherrapunjee**.

Meghalaya's hills rise to just under 2000m, making for a pleasantly cool year-round climate. The **Jaintia Hills** in the east offer good walking and caving, and the state is laced with historical sights such as **Nartiang** near **Jowai**, which has an impressive collection of monoliths.

On January 21, 1972, after an eighteen-year struggle for autonomy from Assam, Meghalaya became a full-fledged state. However, the HNLC, the rebel underground movement, regularly calls *bandhs* demanding independence from the rest of India.

Shillong and around

With its rolling hills of pine conifers and pineapple shrubs, **SHILLONG** was known to the British as "the Scotland of the East" – an impression first brought to mind by **Barapani** (or Umiam), the stunning loch-like reservoir on its fringes, and the sight of the local Khasi women wearing gingham and tartan shawls. At an altitude of around 1500m, Shillong became a popular hill-station for the British, who built it on the site of a thousand-year-old Khasi settlement and made it the capital of Assam in 1874.

Sadly, the town has lost some of its charm and the surrounding hills have suffered severe deforestation. The influx of settlers from the plains has placed a strain on natural resources, especially water, and a general lack of planning has resulted in haphazard growth. Much of the original Victorian town, however, is still evident, and the large gardens around the clean and well-kept **Ward Lake** and the buildings surrounding it conjure up images of a colonial past. North of the polo ground, there is an eighteen-hole golf course, founded in 1898 by a group of enthusiastic British civil servants. **Rabindranath Tagore** visited Shillong on several occasions between 1919 and 1927, writing *Raktakarabi* here; the town also features in his masterwork *Shesher Kobita*.

Arrival and information

Shillong (Umroi) airport is 34km west of the city centre, with regular bus connections to town (1hr 30min). Buses from outside the state pull in to Police Bazaar in the heart of town. Central Shillong can easily be explored on foot, though auto-rickshaws and taxis are available. **Meghalaya Tourism** (daily 6.30am–8pm; ☎0364/226220, ⓦwww.meghalayatourism.in), on Jail Road, opposite the bus station, runs good-value day-trips to Cherrapunjee (from Rs200) and Barapani (from Rs210), as well as a city tour (from Rs100). The India Tourism office is nearby on GS Road (Mon–Fri 9.30am–5.30pm, Sat 9.30am–2pm; ☎0364/222 5632). The bookshop opposite stocks town maps and books on the region. The **GPO** is on Kacheri Road, as is the **State Bank of India**, which has foreign exchange facilities. There are **ATMs** and **Internet** places all over town – for the latter, try *Alfies*, opposite *Hotel Centre Point* in Police Bazaar (Rs20/hr).

The highly-recommended Cultural Pursuits (see "Access, permits and tour operators" box, pp.962–963) arranges homestays in Khasi villages outside Shillong, local treks and group tours, including a trip to the Garo Wangala and Khasi Nongkrem Dance religious festivals in October. Those interested in exploring the state's awesome **caves** can contact the Meghalaya Adventurers Association at the Mission Compound near the Synod Complex (☎0364/254 5621).

Accommodation

Shillong has a healthy range of **accommodation**, although staying on GS Road can be noisy.

Baba Tourist Lodge GS Rd ☎0364/221 1285. This long-standing travellers' favourite has cluttered hallways and clean but cramped rooms with TVs and attached bathrooms. Guests are obliged to eat one meal a day in the lodge's (decent) restaurant. ②–③

Boulevard Thana Rd ☎0364/222 9823, ⓔboulevard@yahoo.co.in. An excellent mid-range hotel: even the cheapest rooms boast king-sized beds, swish bathrooms, tea/coffee makers and minimalist decor. ④–⑥

Earle Holiday Home Oakland Rd ☎0364/222 8614. Under renovation at the time of research, *Earle* offers a range of clean, homely rooms in either a traditional Meghalayan house or its modern annexe. ③–⑤

Monsoon GS Rd ☎0364/250 0084, ⓔhotelmonsoon@hotmail.com. Distinctive little hotel filled with plant pots. The blue-carpeted rooms are on the small side, but the best come with gloriously kitsch 60s-style TVs and balconies. ④

Polo Towers Near Polo Ground ☎0364/222 2341, ⓦwww.hotelpolotowers.com. Stylish hotel with contemporary attached rooms, aimed primarily at business travellers. The *Platinum* bar is one of Shillong's liveliest nightlife venues, but the restaurant is hit and miss. ⑦

Ri Kynjai 20km north of Shillong ☎09862 420300, ⓦwww.rikynjai.com. Set in 45 acres of forest in a spectacular location beside Umiam Lake, this five-star is the best in the region. Luxury cottages ($100–150), raised on stilts and with traditional "upturned boat" roofs, come with red pine interiors, fireplaces and Jacuzzi baths. The excellent restaurant specializes in Northeastern cuisine, and often has live folk music. ⑨

Rosaville ☎0364/222 1622. A restful 1930s colonial house a few kilometres east of Shillong, off the National Highway; large comfy rooms come with period furniture, fireplaces, wooden floors and writing desks. ⑥–⑦

Shillong Club Kacheri Rd ☎0364/222 5497, ⓔshillongclubltdresi@hotmail.com. The residential quarters of one of India's famous old clubs still has echoes of the Raj. Its large attached rooms, some with partial lake views, have wicker furniture and shimmering curtains to separate the seating and sleeping areas. You'll have to befriend a member if you want to use the club facilities, however. ⑤–⑥

Tripura Castle (Also known as *Royal Heritage*) Tripura Castle Rd, Cleve Colony ☎0364/250 1111, ⓦwww.royalheritageshillong.com. Beautiful hotel in an inspiring hilltop location 3km south of town, next to the Maharaja of Tripura's former summer home. The charming rooms have wooden floors and brass fireplaces, while the Maharaja Suite has a mahogany bed once slept in by Tagore. ⑥–⑧

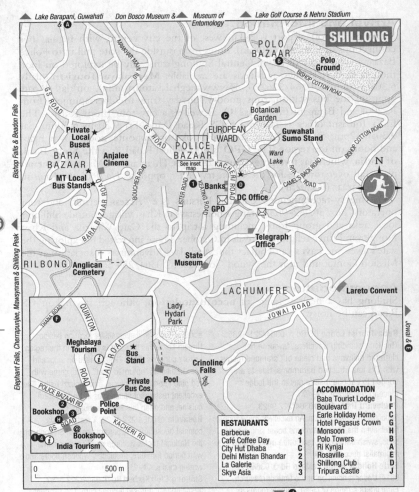

Lake Barapani, Guwahati &Ⓐ   Don Bosco Museum &Ⓐ   Museum of Entomology   Lake Golf Course & Nehru Stadium

SHILLONG

POLO BAZAARⒷ

Polo Ground

BISHOP COTTON ROAD

MAWKHAR MAIN RD

GS ROAD

Botanical Garden

EUROPEAN WARDⒸ

Guwahati Sumo Stand

GS ROAD

Private Local Buses ★

BARA BAZAAR

Anjalee Cinema

POLICE BAZAAR
See inset map

Ward Lake

BISHOP COTTON ROAD

MT Local Bus Stands ★

KACHERI ROAD

BanksⒹ

DC Office

CAMEL'S BACK ROAD

RITA ROAD

BOUCHER ROAD

BARA BAZAAR ROAD

LISTER ROAD

KESTING ROAD

GPO

N

RILBONG

Anglican Cemetery

State Museum

Telegraph Office

LACHUMIERE

Lareto Convent

Lady Hydari Park

JOWAI ROAD

Jowai &Ⓔ

THANA ROAD

QUINTON ROAD

Ⓕ

Crinoline Falls

Meghalaya Tourismⓘ

Bus Stand ★

JAIL ROAD

Private Bus Cos.

Pool

POLICE BAZAAR RD

Police Point

Ⓖ

Bookshop

GS ROAD

Ⓗ

KACHERI RD

Ⓘ ⓘ

Bookshop

India Tourism

0   500 m

RESTAURANTS

Barbecue	4
Café Coffee Day	1
City Hut Dhaba	C
Delhi Mistan Bhandar	2
La Galerie	3
Skye Asia	3

ACCOMMODATION

Baba Tourist Lodge	I
Boulevard	F
Earle Holiday Home	C
Hotel Pegasus Crown	G
Monsoon	H
Polo Towers	B
Ri Kynjai	A
Rosaville	E
Shillong Club	D
Tripura Castle	J

The Town

Life in Shillong used to revolve around the decorative **Ward Lake** (daily except Tues 5.30am–5.30pm; Rs5, camera Rs10) and the exclusive European Ward next to it, with its large bungalows in pine-shaded gardens, and the governor's official residence, Government House. The ambience here is in stark contrast to the narrow streets of **Police Bazaar**, packed with vendors, or, further west, **Bara Bazaar**, where Meghalaya's oldest market, **Iewduh**, is held every eight days: in the days of the Raj, a British officer on horseback patrolled the market to ensure no one littered. The shabby **State Museum** in Lachumiere (Mon–Sat 10am–4pm; closed 2nd & 4th Sat of the month) has exhibits on tribal customs, while the sparkling **Don Bosco Museum** (winter: Mon–Sat 9.30am–5.30pm, Sun 1.30–5.30pm; summer: Mon–Sat 9.30am–4.30pm, Sun 1.30–4.30pm; Rs150 [Rs90]) in Sacred Heart Theological College offers a truly fascinating insight into the region's tribal groups, with displays on culture, music, art, history and religion – just skirt over the woefully one-sided portrayal of Christian mission-aries. To get there, head to *Polo Towers*, then follow the river round to the west for 1.5km until you find the signs pointing uphill to the museum. The **Museum of Entomology** (or Butterfly Museum; Mon–Fri 11am–4pm; Rs25), 2km northwest of Police Bazaar, is dedicated to moths and butterflies.

Shillong is peppered with small booths filled with punters betting on **siat khnam**, an incredibly popular local sport in which Khasi men fire arrows at a target and spectators bet on the final two digits of the successful total. Daily games start at 3.30pm opposite the Nehru Stadium, beyond the golf course.

For some respite from the city, head to *Tripura Castle*, from which a short uphill walk takes you into pine-forested hills, while **Shillong Peak** (1965m), 10km west of town, also offers great views, as well as being home to the last four *ilek khasima*, a high-altitude tree on the verge of extinction.

Eating

Police Bazaar has plenty of places to pick up a snack, and there are some good cheap cafés on Jail Road. In winter, keep an eye out for stalls selling local strawberries.

Barbecue GS Rd. Sumptuous, authentic and very popular Chinese restaurant decked out with paper lamps and oriental trinkets. The pork fried rice and ginger chicken (Rs65–110) are both excellent.

Café Coffee Day Keating Rd. Reliably good coffee and toothsome sweet and savoury snacks (Rs30–70): the hot chocolate brownie "sizzler" is a good way to warm up.

City Hut Dhaba *Earle Holiday Home* complex. A cabin-like dining room with an extravagant water feature, *City Hut Dhaba* has a huge menu of over 300 items, including interesting dishes like spicy duck *chatpata* and hearty thalis (Rs55–140). Wrap up warm, as it can be decidedly cold in the evenings.

Delhi Mistan Bhandar Police Bazaar Rd. A buzzing local joint with a classic range of Indian breakfasts, snacks and sweets (Rs10–40). There's no menu, and staff speak little English, so just point out what you want.

La Galerie and **Skye Asia** *Hotel Centre Point*, Police Bazaar. The former is a low-key canteen, ideal for a quick bite (Rs30–75); try the *cholle bhatura* (puffy dough pockets with chickpeas in a rich gravy). The latter, on the top floor, is more refined, with particularly good Thai food (Rs80–200); it turns into an – occasionally lively – nightclub later on.

Tripura Castle *Tripura Castle* hotel ☏0364/250 1111. Lovely setting for a leisurely meal: book ahead for dinner, and order in advance for Khasi food – dishes on offer include banana flower with sesame seeds and red rice with wild mushrooms (Rs150–300).

Moving on from Shillong

Local buses depart from Bara Bazaar, while Jeeps leave from outside the Anjalee cinema for the same destinations when full. State buses depart from the bus stand on Jail Road, leaving hourly for Guwahati, although Sumos from Kacheri Road are quicker. Private bus firms run services all over the Northeast; there are ticket agents around Police Point. For Aizawl you may prefer to travel to Silchar and then continue by Jeep. Services to Nagaland and Manipur go via Guwahati. The border crossing to Bangladesh at Dawki, southeast of Cherrapunjee, is served by private buses from Bara Bazaar, and a fleet of Sumos, which also run to Cheerapunjee and Mawsynram.

There are flights to Kolkata from Shillong (Umroi) airport, although weather conditions mean delays are common; book with Sheba Travels (☏0364/222 3015) in Police Bazaar. There are also helicopter flights (☏0364/222 3129 or book at the bus stand) to Guwahati and Tura. See "Travel details" at the end of this chapter for more information.

Cherrapunjee and Mawsynram

CHERRAPUNJEE, 56km south of Shillong in the Khasi Hills, achieved fame as the wettest place on earth, with an average annual rainfall of 1205cm. The highest daily rainfall ever recorded fell here in 1876 – 104cm in 24 hours – but Cherrapunjee is close to sharing its watery crown with nearby Mawsynram, whose average annual rainfall is a staggering 1187cm. Cherrapunjee's numerous waterfalls are most impressive during the steamy monsoon season when awesome torrents of water plunge down to the Bangladeshi plains.

The town is spread out over several kilometres. Every eight days a market is held here, with tribal jewellery and local orange-coloured honey on offer. The various nearby points of interest – the **Noh Kalikai waterfall, Bangladesh viewpoint**, and **Mawsmai village and cave** – are all within a few kilometres of Cherrapunjee, though in different directions. An easy way of seeing them all is to join Meghalaya Tourism's (somewhat rushed) **day-trip** (see p.975). Alternatively, regular state buses and Sumos run from Shillong, leaving from the Anjalee cinema bus stand from 7am, though the last bus returns early, at 2.30pm.

Good **accommodation** and food are available at the stunningly located ☆ *Cherrapunjee Holiday Resort* (☎03637/264218, ⓦwww.cherrapunjee.com; ❹), perched on the edge of the East Khasi Hills with excellent views of the Bangladeshi plains below; rooms are clean and homely. From here you can explore some fascinating 150-year-old living root bridges, cool springs, waterfalls, caves and Khasi villages, or take river canyoning or bird-watching trips.You can visit Cherrapunjee on a day-trek along the David Scott Trail from **Mawsphlang**, the site of an ancient sacred grove. Impulse Inc at the NGO Network in Shillong's Lachumiere (☎0364/250 0587) can organize this.

The main attraction at **MAWSYNRAM**, 12km from Cherrapunjee, is the **Mawjinbuin cave**, where a stalagmite resembling a *shivalingam* is perpetually bathed by water dripping from a breast-shaped stalactite. Since there are no direct buses between Mawsynram and Cherrapunjee, you will need to hire a taxi; buses from Shillong leave from Bara Bazaar, or you can visit as part of a Meghalaya Tourism day-trip (see p.975). The only **accommodation** in Mawsynram is the *Inspection Bungalow* (❶); book with the Deputy Commissioner's office in Shillong (☎0364/222 4003).

Dawki

Ninety-six kilometres southeast from Shillong, **DAWKI** is the most important of the Meghalaya–Bangladesh border crossings and has excellent views of the Khasi Hills and Bangladesh. A regular Jeep service from Bara Bazaar serves Dawki.The equivalent border town in Bangladesh is **Tamabil**, two and a half hours from Sylhet.There's no Bangladesh visa office in Meghalaya, so you will need to possess a valid visa before crossing the border – Kolkata has a consulate. Alternatively, there's a Bangladeshi Embassy and a border crossing into Bangladesh in Agartala,Tripura (see p.995). If you are arriving at Dawki from Bangladesh, the last buses and Sumos to Shillong depart around 11am. **Accommodation** is sometimes available at the basic *Inspection Bungalow* (❶); book at the police station.

Jowai and Nartiang

The market town of **JOWAI**, 64km northeast of Shillong in the **Jaintia Hills**, holds the annual Behdienkhlam Festival every July. About 12km north of the town, at **NARTIANG**, are the remains of the Jaintia kings' summer palace and an impressive collection of monoliths and standing stones. A taxi costs about

Rs400 from Jowai. There are caves throughout the area – Cultural Pursuits in Shillong can arrange visits and treks (see p.963). Two daily **buses** run from Shillong to Jowai (4hr), or take a taxi (2hr 30min).

Arunachal Pradesh

ARUNACHAL PRADESH, "the land of the dawn-lit mountains", is one of the last unspoilt wildernesses in India, with a wealth of fascinating cultures and peoples living in a habitat that combines glacial terrain, alpine meadows and subtropical rainforests. It's also home to a staggering 500 species of orchid.

The capital, **Itanagar**, is north of the Brahmaputra across from Jorhat. In the far west of the state, the road from **Bhalukpong** on the Assamese border to **Tawang** climbs steadily through rugged hills, glacial streams and dense primeval forest, crossing the bleak and dramatic **Sela Pass** (4300m) midway. Along the route lie the Buddhist towns of **Bomdila**, **Rupa** and **Dirang**, with their colourful Tibetan monasteries. In the far northeast, the pristine vegetation of **Namdapha National Park** is home to clouded and snow leopards, tigers and elephants. Nearby **Parasuramkund** is one of India's most important and least accessible Hindu pilgrimage sites.

Despite its beauty, tourism has been discouraged due to the extremely sensitive border with Chinese-occupied Tibet in the north and Myanmar in the east. In 1962, the Chinese invaded Arunachal Pradesh, reaching Tezpur in Assam, a 300-kilometre incursion India has never forgotten. Since then, a strong military stance has been adopted in the area. All visitors require a **permit** to enter the state and are encouraged to visit with a **tour operator**, especially as most places are only accessible by Jeep (see box, pp.962–963).

Between December and March, most of the region's hill towns are **extremely cold** and accommodation is not geared up to cope – bring your own winter sleeping bag, a hot water bottle, and a torch, as **power cuts** are very common.

Itanagar

Just under 400km northeast of Guwahati, **ITANAGAR**, the state capital, holds little of interest, though as a transport hub you may need to spend a night here. Surrounded by densely-forested hills, the town itself is little more than a four-kilometre stretch of road running between Zero Point, where the better hotels

---

Arunachal Pradesh's tribal groups

Arunachal Pradesh is stunningly diverse, with 26 major tribal groups, each made up of myriad subgroups. Although most of the tribes are of mongoloid stock, each one has its own distinct culture, dialect, artwork, dress, social structure and traditions. Polygamy remains a common practice among many of them, as does the state's religious blend of Hindu, Buddhist and animist beliefs. The main ethnic groups you're likely to come across include: Wanchos, Noctes, Tangsas, Singphos, Khamptis, Mishmis, Mijis, Galos, Padams, Miwongs, Membas, Tagins and Puroiks. However, within all the groups, tradition is slowly giving way to modern influences, particularly among the younger generation, who increasingly wear western clothes, listen to Bollywood hits and tuck into Chinese food.

are located, and Ganga Market, the main bazaar area where you can find cheaper accommodation around the bus stand.

The **Jawaharlal Nehru State Museum** (daily except Mon 9.30am–5pm; Rs50 [Rs2]) describes the festivals, dances, homes and lifestyles of local tribes. Its impressive ethnographic collection on the first floor has lovely wooden sculptures, musical instruments and esoteric objects like cane penis covers. The dimly lit Government **Sales Emporium** above Zero Point, near *Donyi-Polo Ashok* (see below), sells some interesting handicrafts and cane furniture. Ten kilometres from town, **Gyakar Sinyi** (Ganga Lake; Rs5, camera Rs10) and the lush surrounding jungle provide a taste of the state's magnificent scenery. You can get good views of the surrounding countryside on the hill just above the town from the small **Tibetan Buddhist temple**.

Practicalities

The nearest **airport** is 67km away at **Lilabari**, just outside North Lakhimpur in Assam, although there are plans to build one in Itanagar. There is a Pawan Hans **helicopter** (℡0361/284 0300) between Itanagar and Guwahati (daily except Sun), and irregular shuttle services throughout the region – helicopters run from **Naharlagun**, 10km away. **Trains** from Guwahati run to Harmuti, 33km east in Assam; at the time of writing there were proposals to extend the line to Itanagar. State and private **buses** connect Itanagar with Guwahati (10–11hr) and destinations throughout the state. Taking a **Sumo** will greatly reduce travel times; destinations include Hapoli (5hr), Bomdila (7–8hr), Pasighat (6–7hr) and Along (10hr). Agents around Ganga Market sell tickets. In town, there's a **tourist office** behind the Akash Deep complex.

Itanagar's most expensive **hotel** is the overpriced *Donyi-Polo Ashok*, above Zero Point (℡0360/221 2626, ⓦwww.theashokgroup.com; ➐), part of the lacklustre government chain. There are great views and the worn rooms are comfortable, if soulless, though you should bring ear-plugs, as there's a very noisy disco-cum-bar. A better choice is the *Arun Subansiri*, just below Zero Point (℡0360/221 2806; ➍), which has a cool marble interior, huge rooms with hot water and TVs, friendly staff and a generator for the inevitable power cuts. Buddhist-run *Samsara* (℡0360/221 1266; ➌–➍), in the Akash Deep complex, has adequate if shabby rooms, a relaxing rooftop space as well as indoor and outdoor restaurants, while the *Blue Pine* on APST Road (℡0360/221 1118; ➋–➍) has clean and simple economy rooms for those on a real budget.

Donyi-Pol's **restaurant**, *Bhismak*, serves standard north Indian food, as well as surprisingly good Punjabi dishes; filling buffet lunches and dinners cost Rs300. *Aane Hotel* on Banktinali Road and *Dragon*, 1st Floor Akash Deep, are less expensive alternatives, serving straightforward Indian and Chinese meals.

West Arunachal

Bordered by Bhutan and Tibet, the isolated hills and valleys of western Arunachal climb to some of the remotest glaciers and peaks in the Himalayas. With the exceptions of **Gori Chen** (6858m) and **Nyegi Kangsang** (7047m), most of the 6000-metre-plus mountains remain completely unknown. The solitary road serving the region runs from **Bhalukpong** on the Assamese border to **Tawang**, ending bone-shakingly high in the mountains at one of Asia's largest monasteries. On this spectacular journey you pass through the market town of **Bomdila**, home to three Tibetan monasteries, and **Dirang**, a fortress town a couple of hours up the valley. To the west of the Tawang road lie picturesque **Rupa**, with its colourful Tibetan monastery; **Chillipam**, whose monastery and temple offer astounding views; and the fascinating Buddhist settlements of **Tenzingang** and **Kalaktang**. Beyond Tawang and very close to the Tibetan border stretches the lake district of **Bangachangsa**. Throughout the region, make sure you sample the delicious **fresh fish**, particularly the trout.

Bhalukpong

The **Kameng River** emerges from a deeply forested valley at **BHALUK-PONG**. All public transport services from Tezpur, 56km away, to Bomdila stop here for border formalities. **Accommodation** options include the friendly and peaceful *Bhalukpong Tourist Lodge* (℡03872/234037; ❷–❹), just before the border, in Assam, which has clean and spacious rooms in cottages overlooking the river and surrounding hills. The lodge can arrange rafting and angling – the Kameng River is famed for its fighting *mahseer* fish. Alternatively, *Hotel Solu* (℡03782/234955; ❹), in upper Bhalukpong, 1km from the border gate, has bright and clean attached rooms with TVs. Food at the restaurant is served in little thatched huts. From **Tipi**, 7km north of Bhalukpong, with a small orchidarium, the narrow highway winds up through dense and beautiful mountain forests to Bomdila, 100km away.

Bomdila

BOMDILA is a friendly town (2530m) set on a spur of the Thagla Ridge, the dividing line between rainforests to the south and subalpine valleys to the north. There are a handful of **Tibetan Buddhist monasteries**: the largest of these, a Gelugpa *gompa* high above town, was inaugurated by the Dalai Lama in 1997. The older *gompa* below houses a large blue statue of the Medicine Buddha – Sangye Menhla. A few kilometres beyond Bomdila on the Tawang road, the snow-covered peaks of Gori Chen (5488m) and Kangto (7042m) come into view.

The **tourist office** (℡03782/222049) is based in the *Tourist Lodge* (see below). The professional Himalayan Holidays (℡03782/222017, Ⓦwww .himalayan-holidays.com), on the main market street, can arrange local **sight-seeing trips** and treks, including to Gori Chen's base camp. Next door, Wange's Computer World offers **Internet** access (Rs30/hr).

Most of Bomdila's budget **hotels** are also situated on the main market street. *Passang* (℡03782/222627; ❶–❷) is the pick of the bunch, with simple, clean rooms with attached bathrooms. Nearby *Him-Land* (03782/790001; ❷) is a good alternative: boxy but clean rooms come with lino floors and attached toilets. The *Tourist Lodge* (℡03782/222049; ❸), 1km uphill from the main market street, near the stadium, is a step up in quality, with large but tatty rooms set around a central pond; the heaters are well worth the extra Rs100.

Eating options include *China Town*, on the main market street, 100m south of Himalayan Holidays, a welcoming place serving hearty bowls of chow mein, fried chicken and pork, and warming soups (Rs30–60). About 150m downhill from *China Town* is *Himalaya*, a tiny eatery with just three tables that feels like you're eating in someone's home: it serves hot *thukpas* (thick noodle broths), *momos* (dumplings), noodles and fried fish (Rs20–40). *Siphiyang Phong*, opposite the stadium, dishes up tasty curries and soups (Rs30–70) and closes later than most, at around 9pm.

There are just two **routes** out of Bomdila: onward and upward towards Tawang, and back down towards Bhalukpong. State buses run from the bus station in the lower part of town to **Tezpur** (1–2 daily; 7–8hr); slightly faster **private buses** for Tezpur (1–2 daily) depart from outside Himalayan

Holidays, though **Sumos** are the best way to negotiate the region's steep switchback roads. Daily early morning services run via Rupa to Tezpur, and north to Tawang; book tickets in advance from the offices on the main market street.

Rupa and beyond

The picturesque settlement of **RUPA**, 17km below Bomdila, is the centre of the Sherdukpen people, who occupy the hills that stretch all the way to Bhutan. Rupa has an attractive Tibetan *gompa* and a colourful riverside *lhakang* (chapel) a little further up the valley. Places to stay include *Sawme* (no telephone; ❶), which is clean with basic facilities and buckets of hot water.

About 14km beyond Rupa further off the main road, **Chillipam** has a peaceful monastery and an impressive new temple with astounding views. A further 40km takes you to the influential Tibetan refugee settlement of **Tenzingang**. The Gelugpa monastery here houses nearly four hundred lamas and is one of only two Tantric Gelugpa centres in India. Another 15km beyond Tenzingang lies the end-of-the-road settlement of **Kalaktang**, surrounded by densely forested hills dotted with villages, and close to the Bhutanese border. The small Nyingma Zangdo Peri *gompa* houses some wacky sculptures. There is a basic government *Inspection Bungalow* here where you can sometimes stay; ask at the tourist office in Bomdila.

Dirang and beyond

Ninety minutes beyond Bomdila, the ancient fortress town of **DIRANG** stands over the narrow valley at an altitude of 1690m. Although most of Dirang's original **fort** lies in ruins, it's worth checking out, as is the five-hundred-year-old *gompa* above the village. New Dirang is 5km further up the valley, with an interesting modern **monastery** (small donation requested) belonging to the Red Sect, the oldest Tibetan Buddhism sect. About 8km away, the **Sangti Valley** is the winter home of the black-necked crane and a popular place for bird-watching.

The best **place to stay** is the attractive ✈ *Hotel Pemaling* (☎03780/242615; ❺), halfway between Old Dirang and the new town, with wood-panelled rooms, hot showers and a restaurant with wonderful mountain vistas; local treks and bird-watching can be arranged here. The adjacent *Tourist Lodge* (☎03780/242157; ❸), now run by Himalayan Holidays, is a good alternative, with straightforward rooms and great views.

The road from Dirang to Tawang (a 10–16hr drive) is truly spectacular, with alpine trees, glacial waterfalls and lakes, grazing yaks and mellow villages with two-storey wooden houses. Signs along the way declare you have reached "rough and tough country", and you'll pass several army bases. En route is a war memorial dedicated to those who lost their lives during the 1962 Chinese invasion. A series of extraordinary switchbacks climbs up to the dramatic 4300m **Sela Pass**, where you can take tea in front of a *bakari* (wood-fired oven) at the tiny *Tenzing Restaurant*.

Thirteen kilometres on from Sela Pass, most buses and Sumos stop at the **Jaswant Singh Memorial**, dedicated to an Indian soldier. Conflicting stories abound, but most claim he held off the invading Chinese army single-handedly for several days in 1962 by racing from bunker to bunker, firing constantly. He was eventually captured and killed and the Chinese continued almost all the way to Tezpur before retreating to Tibet.

If you're feeling adventurous, you can stay at the *Dzongrila Rest House* (no telephone; ❷), in a small mountain hamlet before the last stretch to

Tawang. You'll need your own sleeping bag, but there's a friendly owner and fantastic views.

Tawang

Some 180km beyond Bomdila, the great Buddhist monastery of **TAWANG**, the largest in India, dominates the land of the Monpas. Perched at around 3500m and looking out onto a semicircle of peaks, snow-capped for much of the year, the town feels very much like the end-of-the-road place it is. It is cold here most of the time, so bring your thermals.

Tawang Monastery (daily dawn to dusk; camera Rs20, video Rs100) was established in the seventeenth century when this area was part of Greater Tibet, and was the birthplace of the sixth Dalai Lama. The colourful fortress-like complex, a couple of kilometres beyond the town, is home to around five hundred monks and renowned for its collection of manuscripts and *thangkas*. There is a small **museum** (Rs20) filled with Buddhist ornaments and relics, including jewellery belonging to the sixth Dalai Lama's mother, and a library. The main shrine room is richly decorated and houses several statues including a beautiful thousand-armed Chenrezig (or Avalokitesvara). If you're lucky the monks may invite you in for a cup of salted yak-butter tea.

Two *ani gompas* (nunneries) are visible from the main gate, clinging to the steep mountain slopes in the distance. They can be reached on foot in a couple of hours or by vehicle on a road that passes through a military camp and therefore requires a permit.

Tawang is a friendly town, with **festivals** held throughout the year. The monastic three-day Torgya celebration is staged every January to protect the community from evil spirits and natural disasters. The week-long Losar (Buddhist New Year) festival is held in February or early March, with more dancing and festivities.

Beyond Tawang and very close to the Tibetan border is the lake district of **Bangachangsa**. Dotted with pristine high-altitude lakes, small *gompas* and Guru Rinpoche caves, it is sacred to Tibetan Buddhists and Sikhs – Guru Nanak visited the region twice, hence the small Sikh *gurudwara*. There is no public transport but challenging treks and overnight camping can be arranged at *Hotel Pemaling* in Dirang or the tourist office in Bomdila.

Practicalities

Daily **Sumos** and private **buses** run from Tawang to Bomdila, Dirang and Tezpur – book in advance from ticket agents in the bus stand square. There are twice-weekly **helicopter** flights to Guwahati (℡0361/284 0300) from Lumla, 27km west of Tawang, with plans afoot to make this a daily service. A **taxi rank** is on the lane next to *Hotel Gorichen* (see below); a one-way trip to the monastery costs Rs50 but it's worth paying the driver to wait as it can be difficult to find one for the return journey. The *Tourist Lodge* has a small **tourist office**, but Himalayan Holidays (℡03794/223151), opposite *Gorichen*, is a better source of information. Maryul Cyber Café, just east of the prayer wheels on the main market road, provides **Internet** access (Rs50/hr).

The best of the **hotels** is *Tawang Inn* (℡03794/224096; ❹–❺), a pale pink building 400m southwest of the main market road with comfortable attached rooms; those on the top floor boast wonderful views. *Gorichen* (℡03794/224151, ℻222327; ❹), on the main market road, is a good alternative, with large wood-panelled doubles, unreliable electric heaters, big beds and plastic flowers. The slightly run-down *Tourist Lodge* (℡03794/222359; ❸–❹), 300m uphill from the main market road, has spacious green-carpeted rooms with small heaters and attached bathrooms – the beds are in a raised alcove, accessed via some rickety stairs. Near the bus terminus, *Shangri La* (T03794/222275; **①**–**③**) doesn't live up to its name, but is a decent choice for backpackers: rooms are spartan but clean and have attached bathrooms.

Gorichen has a modest **restaurant**, decorated with Avril Lavigne posters and with a menu featuring chow mein, *momos*, chicken curries and thalis (Rs30–70). *Dragon*, on the main market road, has a smart tinted-glass exterior and some of Tawang's best Chinese food (Rs40–70). Diagonally opposite, *Hotel Snowland* offers decent Chinese, Indian and Tibetan dishes, including hearty *thukpas* (Rs20–50). Shops and restaurants tend to close around 6pm.

Central Arunachal

The hill station of **HAPOLI** (formerly Ziro), 1780m above sea level on the Apatani plateau, is 150km north of Itanagar. Although there is little to see in the town itself, the market area is lively. There are several villages dotted around the plateau – some within walking distance – where you can still see Apatani men with impressive facial tattoos and women with bamboo nose-plugs. **Old Ziro** is a scenic seven-kilometre walk from the town centre, or you can take one of the half-hourly buses. Accommodation is available in Hapoli at the pleasant *Arunachal Guest House* (T03788/224196; **②**), and the more comfortable *Hotel Blue Pine* (T03788/224812; **③**), 2km from the town centre, which also has a good restaurant. Sumo services run to Itanagar, Daporijo, Along and Pasighat. Peak Tour and Travels (T03788/225221) can help with local tours.

To the north and east, **ALONG** and **PASIGHAT**, the district headquarters of West and East Siang respectively, both offer trekking and angling. Near Along, there are a number of Adi villages to explore, while around Pasighat, Arunachal's oldest town, the local population is primarily Mishmi. For **accommodation** in Along, *Hotel Holiday Cottage* (T 03783/222463; **③**) on Hospital Hill is a popular choice with nine comfy doubles. In Pasighat, try the central *Oman Hotel* in the Oman Complex (T0360/222 4464; **③**), where the clean but basic rooms have attached bathrooms and buckets of hot water. The towns can be reached from Itanagar on the NH-52 (7hr to Along; 9hr to Pasighat), via **North Lakhimpur**, which has interesting market stalls and shops and is a good place to break your journey. A thirty-minute taxi drive from Pasighat is **Oiramghat**, from which you can get a daily ferry to Dibrugarh (see p.972).

Eastern Arunachal

In eastern Arunachal, the remote valleys of the **Dibang** and **Lohit** rivers, inhabited by the Mishmi, Singpho and Khampti tribes, descend from snow-covered passes through subtropical forests to the plains of the Brahmaputra. Highlights include Hindu pilgrimage centre **Parasuramkund**, **Bhismaknagar**'s twelfth-century fort, and the pristine **Namdapha National Park**.

Parasuramkund

The sacred Hindu site of **Parasuramkund**, on the banks of the River Lohit, is mentioned in the *Kalika Purana* as the place where Parasuram washed away his act of matricide. Thousands of pilgrims make the arduous journey here on Makar Sankranti (mid-Jan), the most auspicious day of the year to take a dip as it's said to wash away all negative karma accumulated in this lifetime. The nearest town, **TEZU**, about 20 km southwest, acts as the gateway to the site, with accommodation available at the no-frills *Osen* (03804/222776; ❸), or the *Inspection Bungalow* (☎03804/223666; ❶).

Bhismaknagar

At **BHISMAKNAGAR**, northwest of Tezu, you can see the ruins of a twelfth-century hill fort, reputedly Arunachal's oldest archeological site, thought to have been built by the **Chutiyas**, a Mongolian tribe. The nearest significant town is **Roing**, about 25km away, where you can stay at the *Circuit House* (☎03803/222636; ❷), or, 3km outside town, the *Sally Lake Guest House* (☎03803/223061; ❷).

Namdapha National Park

The beautifully remote **NAMDAPHA NATIONAL PARK** (Oct–April; Rs50 [Rs10], Jeep Rs100, cameras Rs100, video cameras Rs500), covering almost 2000 square kilometres, is unique for its massive range of altitude (200–4500m). Close to the Myanmar border, Namdapha is home to tigers, leopards (clouded and snow), elephants, red pandas, deer and the endangered Hoolock gibbon, although you are unlikely to spot any big wildlife on a short visit. The journey here is long and uncomfortable, so it's advisable to visit the park with a tour operator or your own Jeep.

The park headquarters are at **Miao** (☎03807/222249, ⓕ222249), where you can book to stay at the *Forest Rest House* (❸–❹) in **Deban**, the main camp, from where there are wonderful views over the river valley. The two top rooms with adjoining veranda are the most comfortable, and have attached bathrooms. Short daytime elephant rides are available, and it's also possible to take a guided elephant trek with overnight camping inside the park – contact the Field Director at Miao. Alternatively, both Purvi Discovery and Gurudongma Tours & Treks (see p.963) arrange well-organized camping and bird-watching trips.

Buses to and from Miao pass through **Margherita**, 64km southwest, and **Tinsukia**, 40km further southwest in Assam, where rail services run to Guwahati (see "Travel details", p.1000). **Dibrugarh** is a further 47km beyond Tinsukia.

Nagaland

On the border with Myanmar, south of Arunachal Pradesh and east of Assam, **NAGALAND** is physically and conceptually at the very edge of the Subcontinent. Home to the fiercely independent Nagas, its hills and valleys were only opened up to tourism in 2000. It is arguably one of India's most beautiful states – a glimpse of the Naga hills in the mist is enough to give respite to any weary traveller. Once renowned for its tribes of fierce head-hunters (see box, p.986), the state is now ninety percent Christian.

When the British arrived in neighbouring Assam in the mid-nineteenth-century, they initially left the fierce warrior tribes of Nagaland well alone. But after continued Naga raids on Assamese villages, the British sought to push them back into the hills. The Angami warriors defeated the British twice, but were finally overcome in 1879, and a truce was declared. The British later came to hold a certain authority among the tribes; the Nagas remained loyal during World War II and fought valiantly against the Japanese invaders. At the time of Independence, the Nagas pleaded with the British to grant them an independent homeland, but instead found their land divided into two, with the larger area

There are fourteen main tribal groups in Nagaland, most of them inhabiting villages perched high on mountain ridges. **Naga warriors** have long been feared and respected throughout the Northeast and head-hunting was practised within living memory. The Nagas originally lived in northeast Tibet, before moving through southwest China into Myanmar, Malaya and Indonesia, as well as eastern Assam. They are skilful farmers, growing twenty different species of rice.

Nagas differentiate between the soul, a celestial body, and the spirit, a supernatural being. The human soul resides in the nape of the neck, while the spirit, in the head, holds great power and brings good fortune. Heads of enemies and fallen comrades were once collected to add to those of the community's own ancestors. Some tribes decorated their faces with tattoos of swirling horns to mark success in **head-hunting**. The heads were kept in the men's meeting house (*morung*) in each village, which was decorated with fantastic carvings of animals, elephant heads and tusks – you can still see examples in many villages. The Nagas also constructed megalithic monuments which lined the approaches to villages personifying those who erected them after death. **Menhirs** honour fame and generosity or enhance the fertility of a field. Traditionally, relations between the sexes were conducted with great openness and equality. Although each tribe has its own dialect, a hybrid language drawn from various local languages and Assamese has developed into the common Nagamese tongue.

falling to Burma. After Independence, Gandhi asked them to remain within India for ten years, promising them choice of destiny thereafter. His promise was never fulfilled.

Sixty years on, the Nagas are still fighting for a homeland. Though a ceasefire has officially been in place for the past few years, violence continues – a bomb in 2004 killed seventy people in Dimapur, and it is unsafe to travel at night. While many Nagas acknowledge that they could not survive independently of India, few feel much affinity with their neighbours in Assam and beyond.

A visit to a Naga village provides a fascinating insight into a rapidly disappearing way of life. Most tour operators will arrange trips here, working with a network of local guides. Be warned, however, that some Nagas are tired of having their homes "on show". If you do visit (and tourism has become a vital source of income), it's a good idea to bring a gift from home and ensure your guide speaks the relevant dialect. You should also offer money for the village to the chief (or *angh*) on arrival.

Traditional Angami villages surround the regional capital of **Kohima**, including **Khonoma**. From **Mon** you can see various Konyak villages including **Shangnyu**, with its impressive fertility sculpture and opium-smoking *angh*. The Ao tribe inhabits **Mokokchung**, while **Tuensang** is home to six different tribes. The state's terrain is also ideal for trekking and other sports – Gurudongma Tours & Treks (see p.963) arranges excellent mountain-biking trips – but note that you'll need a **permit** to enter Nagaland (see "Access, permits and tour operators" box, pp.962–963).

Kohima

The pleasant, busy town of **KOHIMA**, Nagaland's capital, was built alongside the large Angami village of Kohima by the British in the nineteenth century for administrative purposes. Traditional Naga villages, inhabited by tribes such as the Rengma, Zeliang and Kuki as well as the Angami, are just a short drive away. They include **Khonoma**, 20km beyond Kohima, **Jakhema** and **Kigwema**.

Arrival, information and accommodation

Most **private buses** from Imphal are through services to Dimapur and don't go into the centre of town – ask the driver to drop you off at the *Japfu* hotel (see below). **State buses** leave from the bus stand in the town centre, which is small enough to explore on foot, though taxis and minibuses are available. The **tourist office** (Mon–Fri 10am–4pm; ℡0370/224 3124) is on the National Highway, below the *Japfu*. Peak Travels (℡0370/224 2993, Ⓔpeaktravels@rediffmail.com) on PR Hill can arrange transport, local sightseeing and trips around Nagaland.

Kohima has few **accommodation** choices, though standards aren't bad. Its showpiece hotel is the *Japfu* (℡0370/224 0211, Ⓔhoteljapfu@yahoo.co.in; ❺), with great views from PR Hill at the top end of town; it has clean, spacious rooms with big windows, unusually powerful heaters, friendly staff and a decent restaurant. *Fira* (℡0370/224 0940; ❸), nearby, is a budget hotel with adequate if somewhat old-fashioned rooms and a restaurant. *Pine*, on Phool Bari (℡0370/224 3129; ❹), has eight reasonable doubles with TV and attached bathroom, while the *Capital* (℡0370/222 4365; ❶), opposite the bus stand, has clean but decidedly spartan rooms.

The Town

Spread loosely over a saddle joining two large hills, Kohima forms a pass that played a strategic role during World War II. The highway from Imphal to Dimapur – the route along which the Japanese hoped to reach the plains of India – crosses the saddle at the foot of the **World War II Cemetery**, designed by Edwin Lutyens, in a peaceful location overlooking the town. It stands as an emotional memorial to the Allies who died at this spot during the three-month Battle of Kohima, which ended in April 1944 with a death toll of over 10,000 soldiers.

Below the cemetery, on the old NST Road in central Kohima, small shops sell Naga shawls and wraps, spears, bags, and cane and bamboo **handicrafts**. There's also a food **market** behind the bus station, selling everything from dead birds to live maggots (via banana cake). The **Cathedral**, on the way out of town towards the State Museum, contains the largest wooden crucifix in India.

The fascinating **State Museum** (Tues–Sun 10am–4pm; Rs5) in Bayavu Hill Colony, a pleasant twenty-minute walk from Centre Point, houses an excellent collection of Naga jewellery, costumes, spears, beaded corsets and handicrafts. Outside there's an impressive gateway and a log drum, traditionally used in religious rites, during festivals, and for sending messages across the hills.

The large Angami settlement of **Kohima village** is set on a high hill overlooking modern Kohima. Only a few of its buildings are still traditional, with pitched roofs and crossed "house-horns" on the gables, but its tightly knit labyrinth of lanes and houses gives the village a definite Naga feel. Carved heads to signify family status, grain baskets in front of the houses, and troughs used to make rice beer are among the distinctive features. There are less-modernized villages at Jakhema, a few kilometres south on the Manipur road, and Kigwema, a little further on still – go with a guide from an established tour operator.

Eating

Naga food provides a contrast to the strong spices of Indian cuisine, consisting mainly of rice, boiled vegetables and lots of meat, cooked with ginger or chilli. Pomelos, a type of grapefruit, are also widely available here. Naga cuisine is available at the *Bamboo Shoot* and *Sema* hotels; *China Town*, on Old NST Road, and the nearby *Rendez Vous* serve decent Indian and Chinese. Most restaurants and *dhabas* close around 6pm – *Japffs* restaurant is one of the few to stay open later.

Moving on from Kohima

From Kohima, roads lead west to the railhead and airport at **Dimapur**, north to Mokokchung and south to Imphal. From Mokokchung, the road continues to Jorhat in Assam. There are state and private **buses** in all directions: state buses run from the Nagaland State Transport stand in the centre of town; tickets for private buses can be bought from agents in the centre or on Phool Bari. State buses to Dimapur run every half-hour from 6am to 4pm, and daily to Mokokchung and Imphal. Frequent **Sumo** services to Dimapur depart when full from the taxi stand 200m up from the bus station. See "Travel details" at the end of this chapter for more information.

Khonoma and Tuophema

KHONOMA, 20km northwest of Kohima, is where the Angami warriors made their final stand against the British in 1879. Magnificent rice terraces surround the village, irrigated by a complex system of bamboo water pipes. Its highest point, approached through a carved gate and up a flight of steps, provides excellent views of the Naga hills and neighbouring villages of Mezoma and Secuma.

Over the densely forested ridge behind the village lies the scenic Dzoukou valley, part of the Khonoma Nature Conservation and Tragopan Sanctuary, and graced with waterfalls and wonderful viewpoints. Guides can be hired in Khonoma for a popular four-day **trek** into the sanctuary.

Public buses leave three times a day to Khonoma from Kohima NST stand, while **private buses** leave every afternoon from the TCP Gate; there's also a daily bus from Dimapur. Khonoma boasts one guesthouse, which can be booked through Peak Travels in Kohima (see p.987). Taxis are the best bet for a day-trip, as buses can be unreliable.

Forty-one kilometres north of Kohima on the way to Mokokchung, **TUOPHEMA** is a genuine Angami village; the adjoining **Tourist Village** was built by locals and has a small museum displaying Naga artefacts, jewellery and clothing. Guided walks in the surrounding countryside can be arranged here. **Accommodation** is available in one of twelve comfortable Naga huts with hot showers (℡0370/227 0786; ❸). Regular **buses** run from Kohima (1hr 30min) and Dimapur (2hr), though hiring a taxi is preferable if you're visiting as a day-trip.

Dimapur

DIMAPUR, "city of the river people", 74km northwest of Kohima, is Nagaland's most industrialized town. Noisy and polluted, it bears little resemblance to the rest of Nagaland and functions primarily as a gateway to the state. If you have time to kill, visit the **Kachari ruins**, fertility symbols dating back to the Kachari kingdom on the riverside edge of town.

The sole railhead in Nagaland, Dimapur is served by **trains** to Simaluguri (for Sibsagar), Tinsukia and Dibrugarh in Upper Assam. The best service for Guwahati is the Shatabdi Express #2068 (daily except Sun; departs 4.15pm, arrives 8.40pm). State and private **buses** run to Kohima (3hr) from the Nagaland Bus Stand as do **Sumos** (2hr–2hr 30min) from the main drag outside. Private buses to Jorhat, Guwahati and Itanagar leave from the Assam bus stand in Golaghat Road across the railway tracks. Dimapur's **airport** is 6km out of town.

The best **accommodation** option is the *Saramati*, sister hotel to Kohima's *Japfu* (☎03862/234761; ❹–❺); cheaper places to stay, with clean if uninspiring rooms, include the *Tourist Lodge* (☎03862/226355; ❶), beside the Nagaland Bus Stand, and the *Fantasy* (☎03862/232013; ❸) next door.

Mon and around

In the far northeast of Nagaland, 200km south of Dibrugarh in Assam, **MON** is the regional capital of the Konyak tribe. Its main attraction is as a base for visits to the surrounding villages. Look out for older Konyaks with elaborate facial tattoos and goat-horn earrings. Sennunger Imsong, based in Mokokchung (see below), is a reliable young guide who can arrange day-trips.

Shangnyu is a typical village, a bumpy drive 23km from Mon, with a small museum housing fascinating village artefacts including an impressive wooden fertility sculpture. Outside is a huge log drum that the villagers used for festivals and to send messages to each other across the hills. There's also a set of eerie tall stones on which the villagers once displayed hunted heads. The friendly opium-smoking *angh* here may offer you tea in his home, the front of which is packed with horns and animal skulls to indicate his status.

Mon's only **hotel** is the *Mountain View* (☎03869/221730, ✉phejin@yahoo .com; ❸–❹), which has large, clean rooms in an ugly building on Mon's noisy main street; while there is no restaurant, the owners can provide tasty meals. **Buses** to Mon run from Dibrugarh via Sibsagar in Assam, though trips to Mon are best undertaken in a Jeep with a tour operator; Jeeps take seven hours from Dibrugarh, buses considerably longer. In late March or early April, the whole area celebrates its spring **festival**.

Mokokchung and around

A vibrant hill-town southwest of Mon and 160km (5hr by Jeep) north of Kohima, **MOKOKCHUNG** is a good place to soak up Naga town life. There is a small **museum** and shops here sell Naga shawls and bamboo-woven footstools. The town makes a good base for a visit to surrounding Ao villages, including **Longkhum**, 17km away, which has a small museum depicting Ao tribal culture and a guesthouse. Day-trips – including to Tuensang (see below) – can be arranged by Sennunger Imsong, whose aunt Apokla Imsong rents out a pleasant double room with attached bathroom in *Tongpok Abode*, her home at Dilong Ward in Mokokchung (☎0369/222 7030, ✉imsong2003@rediffmail .com; ❸, including meals).

TUENSANG, 115km southeast of Mokokchung, lies at the centre of a region inhabited by six different tribes – you can visit villages belonging to the Phom, Khiamniungan, Chang, Yimchunger and Sangtam. From here it's a two-day drive to **Thanamir**, and the start of a stunning two-day trek between tribal villages to **Mount Saramati**, the highest peak in Nagaland (3826m), near the Burmese border. En route, there are basic places to stay at **Kiphere** – contact the Imsongs to arrange (see above).

WOKHA, 80km south from Mokokchung, is a good place to stop on the NH-61 route to Kohima. Just down the hill on the left after entering the town, the tiny *Tea Hotel* serves good samosas, *momos*, omelettes and mugfuls of decent tea. Cultural and mountain-biking trips in the area are run by Gurungdoma Tours & Treks (see p.963).

Mizoram

Heading south from Assam into the hills of **MIZORAM**, "land of the highlanders", a winding mountain road takes you into forests and bamboo-covered hills. Mizoram is a gentle pastoral land, and the **Mizos** are a friendly and welcoming people who see very little tourism. Whitewashed churches dot the landscape, giving it more of a Central American feel than a state squashed between Myanmar and Bangladesh.

The Mizos, who migrated from the Chin Hills of Burma, were regularly raiding tea plantations in the Assam Valley right into the late nineteenth century; only in 1924 did the British administration finally manage to bring about some semblance of control. They opened up what was then the **Lushai Hills** to missionaries who, with great zeal, converted much of the state to Christianity. **Aizawl**, the busy capital, is a large sprawling city built on impossibly steep slopes which have necessitated stilted housing. In the heart of the state, traditional Mizo communities occupy the crests of a series of ridges, each village dominated by its chief's house and *zawlbuk*, or bachelors' dormitory. An egalitarian people, without sex or class distinctions, the Mizos remain proud of their age-old custom of *Tlawmgaihna*, a code of ethics which governs hospitality, and the weaving of local costumes such as the *puan*, characterized by white, black and red stripes. They enjoy a 95 percent literacy rate, and many speak English and are culturally more influenced by the Christian West than by India.

Tourism remains restricted due to the sensitive border with Myanmar, and **permits** are still required, but the opening of an airport at Lengpui has made the state more accessible.

Aizawl

One of India's remotest state capitals, **AIZAWL** perches precariously on the steep slopes of a sharp ridge, straddling the watershed between the Tlawng and the Tuirial river valleys. At an altitude of 1250m, it enjoys a comfortable year-round climate. Although the views are of hills rather than snowy mountains, it has something of the feel of a Himalayan hill station. There's little to see in the way of monuments and temples, but the markets are interesting. Everything (including restaurants) closes on Sunday, when everyone goes to church. Aizawl's rural surroundings are within easy reach by bus or on foot.

Zarkawt is the main downtown area, where you'll find a host of inexpensive hotels on the upper of two parallel streets which form part of Aizawl's complex road network. They are connected by a series of ridiculously long and steep stairways. **Bara Bazaar** (daily except Sun 6am–3pm) is Aizawl's main attraction: everything from recordings of Mizo music to bespoke shoes made by Chinese cobblers is on sale. Further up the hill, Solomon's Cave in **Zodin Square** is an indoor market selling fabrics, garments and music; traditional stuff is notably absent. The District Industries Centre in Upper Bazaar stocks local handicrafts such as shawls and bags. The **Mizoram State Museum**, on MacDonald Hill (Mon–Fri 11am–3.30pm, Sat 9am–1pm; Rs5), has a small but interesting collection of traditional Mizo costumes.

Due to its precipitous setting, much of Aizawl is deprived of sun for significant parts of the day, with the depth of the shade increased by the multistorey concrete edifices clinging to the hillsides. But there are many vantage points offering great views of the lush green hills surrounding the town – two of the best are **Chaltlang Hill**, high above Chandmari in the north, and the Theological College, perched above the dramatic cleft on the road into Aizawl.

Bamboo, rats and revolution

Mizoram's two main species of bamboo flower every 48–50 years, attracting hordes of rats and boosting their fertility rate fourfold. The rats devour crops in the fields, leaving famine in their wake. The first time this happened, in 1959, the newly independent governments in Delhi and Assam were unprepared, which led a council clerk, **Laldenga**, to found the **Mizo Famine Front** (MFF). Set up initially to combat famine, it transformed into the **Mizo National Front** (MNF), a guerrilla group fighting for secession. The government's heavy-handed response in 1967, rounding up Mizos from their homes into guarded villages under curfew, sought to wipe out the traditional way of life, and boosted support for the MNF. Bangladeshi independence was a bitter blow to the MNF, however, who had relied on Pakistani support, and moderates on both sides eventually brought the MNF to the negotiating table, where statehood was granted in 1986 in return for an end to the insurgency. Mizoram is now the most peaceful of the "seven sisters." However, in 2007 the bamboo began to flower again, the rat population grew and crops were devastated. Although the authorities are better prepared this time – rice supplies have been provided on credit and Rs2 offered for every rat tail collected – the Mizo people continue to suffer serious hardships.

The **Durtlang Hills** immediately north of Aizawl, and **Luangmual**, 7km west, provide pleasant **walking** country – both are easy day-trips from the centre. Buses leave for Luangmual from outside the Salvation Army Temple.

Practicalities

The **tourist office**, in the Chandmari district (Mon–Fri 9am–5pm; ☎0389/231 2475), provides advice and transport, and can book tourist lodges throughout Mizoram. The **post office** is on Treasury Square. The State Bank of India, near First AR Ground, has a **foreign exchange** counter, though it's best to bring what cash you need with you. Of the **minibuses** running between central Aizawl and the suburbs, the most useful head from the top of town near the GPO and Zodin Square to Chandmari in the north – otherwise a tiring two-kilometre walk.

There's a good range of budget and mid-range **hotels** (see below), but you'll struggle to find anything more comfortable. A number of simple **restaurants** in Bara Bazaar serve traditional Mizo food: fish, lentils, rice and bamboo shoots are common ingredients and dishes tend to be quite mild. There are also several cheap and cheerful local *dhabas* on Zodin Square. Aizawl's top restaurant is *David's Kitchen* in Zarkawt, which serves a mix of Indian and international dishes (Rs70–200), including a succulent mutton *rogan josh*. *Hotel Chief*, also in Zarkawt, has a good multi-cuisine restaurant (Rs50–100), but disappointing rooms.

Ahimsa Zarkawt ☎0389/234 1133. One of Aizawl's better hotels, bang in the centre of town, with sizeable attached rooms, rooftop views and a decent restaurant. ❸–❹

Berawtlang Tourist Complex Zemabawk, 6km out of town ☎0389/235 2067. In a serene middle-of-nowhere location, these rustic cottages have wonderful views, with excellent food served in the restaurant. ❸–❹

Chawlhna Zarkawt ☎0389/234 6418. A traveller stalwart, *Chawlhna* has adequate and wallet-friendly rooms with either cleanish shared facilities or attached bathrooms. ❶–❹

Luangmual Tourist Lodge 7km out of town ☎0389/233 2263. This welcoming budget lodge has simple, clean rooms around a garden courtyard and four dormitories (Rs30). ❶

Ritz Bara Bazaar, near Machhunga Point ☎0389/231 0409. A good option, popular with visiting businessmen: the staff are friendly and helpful, and there's a range of rooms, some with attached bathrooms and TVs, as well as a fine restaurant. ❸–❹

State Guest House Chaltlang ☎0389/234 9979. About as smart as Aizawl gets, the *State Guest House* has modern attached rooms and a popular Indian and Chinese restaurant. ❹

Moving on from Mizoram

The only recommended road out of Mizoram leads to **Silchar**, 180km north in Assam; **Sumos** are the best way to travel, taking four to six hours. There are several Sumo agents around Sumkuma Point in Zarkawt. **Private bus** companies also run services to Silchar (12hr), including Capital Travels (℡0389/234 0166) and Jagannath Travels (℡0389/234 2092), also in Zarkawt. Sumo services are available direct to Shillong and Guwahati, as are buses run by Mizoram State Transport, which are cheaper, but slower and less comfortable.

Aizawl's **airport** at **Lengpui**, 35km west, handles flights to Guwahati, Imphal and Kolkata. Book through Quality Tour & Travels, A–51, Chanmari (℡0389/234 1265), a couple of minutes' walk down from the tourist office. A taxi to the airport costs Rs500; alternatively take the 9am bus (Rs100) from outside the *Ritz* (see p.991). See "Travel details" at the end of this chapter for more information.

Tripura

Surrounded by Bangladesh on three sides, the lush green mountains and valleys of **TRIPURA** became part of India in 1949; since then, its fate has been entwined with that of Bengal. Partition and the subsequent creation of East Pakistan (now Bangladesh) in 1948, followed by war, famine and military regimes drove millions of Bangladeshis to flee into Tripura, where they now outnumber by four to one the indigenous people, many of whom feel their land and resources have been stolen and exploited. Tripura is more like India proper than the other Northeastern hill states and its connections with the Bangladeshi plains are strong. The biggest tribal groups are the Tripuris, who account for more than half the tribal population, and the Reangs, originally from the Chittagong Hill Tracts.

Agartala, the state capital, is a relaxed city with a palace and a few temples; **Udaipur** and the fairy-tale palace at **Neermahal** are easy day-trips. Tripura's **forests** were once famed for their elephants, but sadly, due to the widespread and uncontrolled practice of slash-and-burn agriculture, and to general pressure on the land, its wildlife is under severe threat. A handful of sanctuaries such as Gumti, Rowa, Trishna and **Sepahijala** strive to protect the few forests that remain.

The **history** of Tripura and its Manikya rulers, who claimed descent from far-off Rajput *kshatriyas*, is told in the Bengali poem, the *Rajmala*. Udai Manikya (1585–96) founded Udaipur on the site of the old capital of Rangamati, adorning it with beautiful tanks, buildings and temples. The Tripura Sundari temple here is one of India's most important *shakti pithas*. After staving off the Muslim rulers of Bengal, the Manikyas finally submitted to the Mughals, but continued to rule the kingdom until it was subsumed into British India. Maharaja Birchandra Manikya, who came to the throne in 1870 and was heavily influenced both culturally and spiritually by Bengal – and his close friend Rabindranath Tagore – established Bengali as the language of the court. You will also see lots of quite graphic clay sculptures of **Kali**, Bengal's favourite goddess.

Agartala and around

AGARTALA, Tripura's capital, is a laid-back administrative centre reminiscent of the low-level towns of Bangladesh, whose border is just 2km away. Its main attraction is the gleaming white **Ujjayanta Palace**, completed in 1901. Set

Although Tripura is open to tourism, **insurgency** and **ethnic conflict** remain a problem, particularly in the north. At the time of writing, travel to Tripura was deemed **unsafe**, and the UK Foreign and Commonwealth Office was advising against all visits to the state. The information in this section has therefore not been updated for this edition, and it is essential to check the security situation before you travel. Buses from Silchar to Agartala travel in convoy, with a military escort from Kumarghat as far as Teliamura. Although you're unlikely to meet trouble in the tourist spots, it's sensible to heed the advice of local people.

The **NLFT** (National Liberation Front of Tripura) and the **ATTF** (All Tripura Tiger Force) are fighting for tribal rights, autonomy, independence and the expulsion of Bangladeshis. Other insurgents have a financial agenda. In the run-up to elections, kidnapping and extortion help raise large sums of money which can then buy political clout: a successful group may promise to step down from the election in exchange for payments from the competing political parties. Another common event is the mass surrender of militants after elections – followed by their appointment in well-paid jobs. The **UBLF** (United Bengal Liberation Front) has also joined the fray with vicious reprisals against tribals to quell the activities of the other two groups.

amid formal gardens and artificial lakes, this huge building, whose main block now houses the State Legislative Assembly, covers around eight hundred acres. One of many temples nearby and open to the public, the **Jagannath Temple** with its orange tower rises from an octagonal plinth across the road.

Most of Agartala's amenities, bazaars, bus stands and administrative offices are concentrated in the centre, immediately south of the palace. Opposite the GPO, the **State Museum** (Mon–Sat 10am–5pm) displays interesting ethnographic and archeological exhibits (Mon–Sat 10am–5pm; free). The Tribal Cultural Research Institute and Museum (11am–1pm) at Supari Bagan lies well hidden in the backstreets of Krishna Nagar district, near the Jagannath Temple.

Practicalities

Arriving by bus, you'll probably be dropped off at one of the private company offices on Laxmi Narayan Bari (LN Bari) Road, or at the State Bus Stand at Krishna Nagar. Buses and taxis ply the 12km from the **airport** to the centre of town. The local **tourist office** (Mon–Sat 10am–5pm, Sun 3–5pm; ☏0381/222 5930) can be found in a wing of the palace. They also organize **tours** and arrange transport for sightseeing. Cycle and auto-rickshaws are plentiful, while **Jeeps** can be chartered at the bus stand. The **post office** (Mon–Sat 7am–6pm) is at Post Office Chowmuhani. For **Internet** access, head to Star Graphics, on BK Road, 50m past the *Rajdhani* hotel, or to Cyber Masti on Durga Bari Road, next to the telegraph office. There are no foreign exchange facilities in Agartala.

Agartala has a small but good selection of **hotels**: all the places listed below provide mosquito nets. Choices for **eating** are more limited: *Abhishek* on Durga Bari Road is the best in town, with indoor and garden tables; *Ambar*, next to the hotel of the same name, is another option, serving inexpensive basic, filling non-veg dishes.

Ambar SD Barman Sarani ☏0381/222 3587. Central location with reasonably-priced rooms. ❷
Brideway JB Rd, near the west side of the palace ☏0381/220 7298. Friendly place. Reasonable rooms with large attached bathrooms. ❸

Deep Guest House LN Bari Rd ☏0381/220 4718. Small homely hotel on main road. Carpets and attached bathrooms, though the single rooms lack windows. ❷
Moonlight LNB Rd ☏381/220 0813. Basic and

friendly, if a little noisy, with attached bathrooms and a good, cheap veg restaurant. ❶

Rajarshi Badshah Airport Rd ☎0381/220 1034. A couple of kilometres out of town through the north gate. Pleasant, peaceful rooms, lawn, gardens and restaurant. ❸–❺

Rajdhani BK Rd, near Indian Airlines office ☎0381/222 3387. Friendly and comfortable mid-range hotel near the palace. ❷–❺

Royal Guest House Palace Compound West ☎0381/222 5652. Down a side street near the palace. Roomy and comfortable, with a good restaurant. ❸–❹

Welcome Palace HGB Rd ☎0381/238 4940, Ⓔabanik@sancharnet.in. The best hotel in town: its *Kurry Klub* restaurant serves Thai, Chinese and Indian food. ❺

Moving on from Agartala

State buses leave from the terminus on the corner of Hospital and LN Bari Roads for the gruelling stop-start convoy to Silchar, Shillong and Guwahati. It's well worth paying extra for the more comfortable **private buses** run by Network, Capital, Tania, Green Valley and Sagar that depart from LN Bari Road, 100m east of the palace. All buses heading north from Agartala have to travel in thrice-daily army-escorted convoys from Teliamura to Kumarghat, leaving at the same times – 6am, 8am and 11.30am. Buses to Udaipur (every 30min; 2hr) leave from the Battala Bus Stand at the western end of HGB Road, as do shared **Jeeps**, which also serve Melaghar (for Neermahal) and Kamala Sagar. Kumarghat, seven hours away, is the nearest **railhead** to Agartala.

Agartala's **airport**, 12km north of the centre, can be reached by bus or taxi from the motor stand, by bus from the beginning of Airport Road, or by

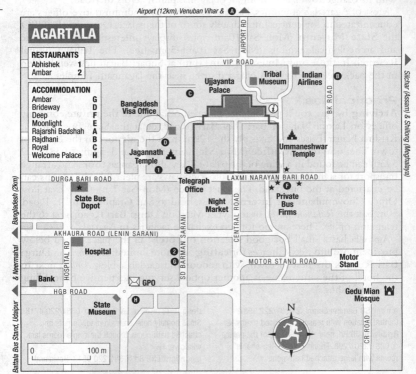

Airport (12km), Venuban Vihar & Ⓐ

AGARTALA

RESTAURANTS
Abhishek 1
Ambar 2

ACCOMMODATION
Ambar G
Brideway D
Deep F
Moonlight E
Rajarshi Badshah A
Rajdhani B
Royal C
Welcome Palace H

Silchar (Assam) & Shillong (Meghalaya)

VIP ROAD

AIRPORT RD

BK ROAD

Tribal Museum
Indian Airlines Ⓑ
Ujjayanta Palace Ⓒ
Bangladesh Visa Office
ⓘ
Ummaneshwar Temple
Jagannath Temple
Ⓓ
❶
Ⓔ
DURGA BARI ROAD
Telegraph Office
LAXMI NARAYAN BARI ROAD
★★Ⓕ★
Private Bus Firms
Night Market
State Bus Depot
★
CENTRAL ROAD
SD BARMAN SARANI
AKHAURA ROAD (LENIN SARANI)
HOSPITAL RD
Hospital
❷
Ⓖ
MOTOR STAND ROAD
Motor Stand
Bank
GPO ✉
HGB ROAD
Gedu Mian Mosque
State Museum
Ⓗ
N
CR ROAD
Bangladesh (2km)
Battala Bus Stand, Udaipur
& Neermahal
0   100 m

auto-rickshaw. The Indian Airlines office is on VIP Road, just west of BK Road (☎0381/222 5470).

See "Travel details" at the end of this chapter for more information on journey frequencies and durations.

To Bangladesh

Agartala is just 2km from the **border with Bangladesh**, and you can easily walk or take a rickshaw to the checkpoint on Akhaura Road. Rickshaws on the Bangladeshi side can take you to Akhaura Junction, 4km away, from where there are trains to Comilla, Sylhet and Dhaka (2hr 30min). Although there are seven official border crossings from Tripura to Bangladesh, this one is the most convenient.

The **Bangladeshi Embassy** (Mon–Thurs 8.30am–1pm & 2–4.30pm, Fri 8.30am–noon; ☎0381/222 4807), next to the *Brideway* hotel, issues visas on the spot. Two passport photos are needed and prices vary according to nationality.

Around Agartala

On the border with Bangladesh, 27km south of Agartala, the large lake of **Kamala Sagar** is overlooked by a small but important Kali temple. Its twelfth-century sandstone image of Mahishasuramardini, a form of Durga, has a *shivalingam* in front of it. Buses leave from Battala Bus Stand in Agartala to the lake (5 daily; 1hr).

On the road to Udaipur, 35km south of Agartala, the nature reserve at **Sepahijala** extends over eighteen square kilometres, with a lake, zoo and botanical gardens, and is home to primates including the Hoolock gibbon and golden langur and around 150 species of bird. The beautiful *Abasarika Bungalow* (❶) offers comfortable rooms in jungle surroundings; book in advance at the Forestry Office (☎0381/222 2224) in Agartala, 2km up Airport Road on the left. All buses to Udaipur travel past the park gate.

Udaipur

The former capital of the Manikyas, **UDAIPUR** retains an atmosphere of antiquity not found in Agartala. An important market town, it is surrounded by paddy fields and low forested hills. On the southwest bank of **Jagannath Dighi** tank, stand the ruins of the **Jagannath** temple, while the seventeenth-century **Mughal Masjid** marks the furthest outpost of the Mughal Empire. **Tripura Sundari**, the most important temple in the area, stands 5km outside Udaipur, on a small hillock in front of a holy lake which teems with carp and turtles. Built in typical Bengali-hut style with a square sanctum and large meeting hall in front, this is one of the 51 *shakti pithas* sacred to the Tantras, marking the spot where Sati's right leg is supposed to have fallen when Shiva was carrying her body from the funeral pyre. Animal sacrifices are performed here daily.

Most people visit Udaipur on a long day-trip from Agartala, but **accommodation** is available at the *Pantha Niwas Tourist Lodge* (❶–❷). There's also a small tourist office (☎0381/222432). **Buses** run from Agartala every thirty minutes (2hr), and there are also frequent shared **Jeeps**.

Neermahal

The romantic water palace of **NEERMAHAL**, in the middle of **Rudrasagar Lake**, 55km south of Agartala, was built in 1930 as a summer residence for Maharaja Bir Bikram Kishore Manikya. Inspired by Mughal architecture, the

▲ Neermahal water palace

palace (daily 9am–6pm) is rather derelict inside, but the exterior and gardens have been restored, and the sight of the domes and pavilions reflected in the lake, especially under the early evening floodlights, is impressive. You can rent boats to cross the lake to the palace from just opposite the tourist lodge (motor-boats Rs125/hr, punts Rs60/30min), a very pleasant journey among lily pads, dragonflies, ducks and cormorants.

The lake is 1km from the town of **Melaghar**, which has bus connections with Agartala (every 30min; 2hr) and Udaipur (every 30min; 30min). Neermahal can be visited together with Udaipur as a day-trip from Agartala, provided you're steeled for a long hard day – the round trip covers 130km along seriously pot-holed roads. Should you prefer to break up the journey, the lakeside *Sagarmahal Tourist Lodge* (℡0381/264418; ❸) has large rooms, some affording great views across the lake, along with seven-bed dorms (Rs60). Food is available at the lodge and at a nearby **restaurant** run by the local fishermen's co-operative.

Manipur

MANIPUR, stretching along the border with Myanmar, centres on a vast lowland area watered by the lake system south of its capital **Imphal**. This almost forgotten region is home to the **Meithei**, who have created in isolation their own fascinating version of Hinduism. Manipur feels closer to Southeast Asia than India, and many locals speak neither English nor Hindi.

Although the area around Imphal is now all but devoid of trees, the outlying hills are still forested, and shelter exotic birds and animals like the spotted linshang, Blyth's tragopan, the curiously named Mrs Hume's bar-backed pheasant, slow loris, Burmese pea-fowl and the beautifully marked clouded leopard, as well as numerous unclassified varieties of orchid. The unique natural habitat of **Loktak Lake**, with its floating islands of matted vegetation, is home to the sangai deer.

Manipur's **history** can be traced back to the founding of Imphal in the first century AD. Despite periodic invasions from Burma, it enjoyed long periods of independent and stable government until the end of the Indo-Burmese war in 1826 when it was incorporated into India. It came under British rule in 1891 after the Battle of Kangla. During World War II, most of Manipur was occupied by the Japanese, with 250,000 British and Indian troops trapped under siege in Imphal for three months. Thanks to a massive RAF air-lift operation from Agartala, they held out, and when Japanese troops received the order to end the Imphal campaign, it was in effect the end of the campaign to conquer India. Manipur became a fully-fledged Indian state in 1972.

Imphal and around

Circled by distant hills, the capital of Manipur, **IMPHAL**, lies on a plain at an altitude of 785m. Though lacking dramatic monuments, its broad avenues give it an open feel. The small centre is sandwiched between the stately avenue of Kanglapat to the east and the somewhat stagnant River Nambu to the west. The town's **Polo Ground** dominates the area; according to popular legend, the Manipuri game of *Sagol Kangjei* is the original form of the modern game of polo. In one corner, the **Shaheed Minar** memorial commemorates the Meithei revolt against British occupation in 1891, while just southeast, the **Manipur State Museum** (daily except Mon 10am–4.15pm; Rs2) focuses on tribal costumes, jewellery and weapons along with geological, archeological and natural history displays.

At the heart of Imphal, along Kangchup Road, the fascinating daily market of **Khwairamband** – also known as Nupi Keithel and Ima Bazaar (mothers' market) – is run by more than 3000 Meithei women, making it the largest of its kind in Asia. One section is devoted to textiles – shawls and fabrics including the *moirangphee*, the traditional Meithei dress. This striped skirt comes in two pieces, which for a small fee will be stitched together on the spot with amazing speed. Across the road, the other section of the market sells local fish, vegetables, and other provisions. Smaller markets nearby sell handicrafts, including cane and wicker. If you prefer not to haggle, there are a few fixed-price shops around, including Eastern Handloom and Handicrafts, at GM Hall, near the clock tower, and the Handloom House in Paona Bazaar.

South of the old palace complex, the golden dome of **Shri Govindjee**, Manipur's pre-eminent Vaishnavite temple, can be seen amongst the palm trees. The temple has a large prayer hall and pleasant ambience; the early morning pujas, complete with conch blowing, drumming and procession, are well worth attending – aim to be there by 7.30am. The **British War Cemetery**, 500m north of the *Tourist Lodge*, is the resting place of British and Indian soldiers killed during the Burma campaign, and is beautifully maintained by the Commonwealth War Graves Commission.

Safety in Manipur

Since Independence, Manipur has seen waves of violence as a result of self-rule campaigns and a brutal **conflict** between the Kukis and Nagas. Disturbances are still common. At the time of writing, the UK Foreign and Commonwealth Office advised against all travel to the state, and this section has not been updated for this edition. Check the security situation before you decide to visit, and even then, tourists are advised not to venture too far from the capital. For permit requirements, see pp.962–963.

The festivals and performing arts of Manipur

Manipuri dance, like the associated colourful traditions of Myanmar, Indonesia and Thailand, is replete with Hindu themes and influences. Now recognized as one of India's main classical dance forms, it centres around the story of Krishna cavorting with the *gopis* (milkmaids). Here the *gopis* are dressed in elaborate crinoline-like skirts, while the accompanying music includes energetic group-drumming, with large barrel drums suspended across the players' shoulders. The Jawaharlal Nehru Manipur Dance Academy, North AOC, Imphal (℡0385/222 0297), Manipur's premier dance institution, arranges occasional recitals and hosts an annual dance festival.

The **martial arts** of Manipur are currently going through something of a revival with performances by men and women being choreographed for the stage. **Thang-Ta** is a dynamic form utilizing *thang*, the sword, and *ta*, the spear. Fast, furious and seemingly extremely dangerous, performances take place each May during **Lai Haraoba**, a ritual dance festival held at Moirang (see opposite).

Finally, the annual **Heikru Hitongba Boat Race** is held every September as part of a celebration to commemorate the founding of the two major Vaishnavite temples of Imphal, Bijoy Govinda and Govindjee. Two teams of rowers, standing in long dugout canoes, race on the Thangapat moat near the Bijoy Govinda temple.

16

Langthabal, set on a small hillock 8km south of Imphal on the road to Burma (Myanmar) overlooking the University of Manipur, has remains of an old palace, together with a few temples and ceremonial houses. The **Khong-hampat Orchidarium**, 12km north of Imphal on NH-39 (the Dimapur road), displays over a hundred varieties of orchid which bloom in April and May in a riot of colours.

Practicalities

State **buses** arrive at the stand next to the Polo Ground and private buses at their individual offices, most of which are along MG Avenue, 200m north of Khwairamband Bazaar. The **Manipur Tourism office** (Mon–Sat 9.30am–5pm, Oct–March 4.30pm; closed 2nd Sat of month; ℡0385/222 0802) is based at *Hotel Imphal*, north of the palace on the main Dimapur road. The **India Tourism** office, on Jail Road (Mon–Sat 9.30am–5.30pm; ℡0385/222 1131), provides information and maps. The **GPO** (Mon–Sat 9am–5pm) is on Secretariat Road, at the southern end of the palace complex. Individual travellers can get permits endorsed at the **Foreigners' Registration Office** along from the GPO. The State Bank of India on MG Avenue has a foreign exchange service. **Internet** facilities are easily accessible; Millennium Link in Paona Bazaar usually has good connections. Auto- and cycle **rickshaws** are the main means of transport within Imphal.

Imphal has a few simple **hotels** in the market area, and a handful of mid-range ones further out. Similarly, the choice of **restaurants** is small – the best in town being the *Host* in the *Anand Continental* hotel. There are no **bars** – this is a dry state.

Anand Continental Khoyathong Rd ℡0385/222 3422. Best in town, with carpets, hot showers, TV in all rooms and an excellent restaurant. ❸–❹

ITDC Imphal North AOC, Dimapur Rd ℡0385/222 0459. Resplendent government-run hotel with large rooms, lawns and restaurant. ❸–❹

Mass Assembly Rd ℡0385/222 2797. Reasonable-sized doubles, some with balconies and attached bathrooms. Central location. ❷–❸

Nirmala MG Ave ℡0385/222 9014. A good-value option with carpeted rooms and hot showers – soap and towels provided. ❸–❺

Pintu North AOC, Dimapur Rd ℡0385/222 4172. Large pink building next to the cinema. Clean and friendly, with a restaurant whose advert declares that "slightly hurried food" is served here. ❷–❸

Moving on from Imphal

Imphal's airport, 6km south of town, is served by Indian Airlines and Jet Airways. The Indian Airlines office is on MG Avenue (☎0385/222 0999), and Jet Airways is in *Hotel Nirmala* (☎0385/223 0835), on the same road.

Bus connections with Guwahati are good, and the 579-kilometre journey takes around twelve hours. Several private bus companies operate from MG Avenue near the State Bank of India, and also have stands on DM Road outside *Hotel Tampha*. National Highway 39 – "The Burma Road" – links Imphal to Kohima in **Nagaland** and continues to Dimapur, the nearest railhead 215km away. You will need a valid permit for Nagaland to travel this route. Buses to Dimapur (6hr) leave daily at 6am and will drop off passengers at Kohima, but on the edge of town, not at the central bus stand. For those heading to Silchar, the 200-kilometre road journey via the border point of Jiribam may look tempting, but military checkpoints and bus searches make it a nightmare trip of around fourteen hours. The twice-weekly thirty-minute flight is recommended.

See "Travel details" at the end of this chapter for more information on journey frequencies and durations.

Loktak Lake

South of Imphal, the huge and complex body of water known as **Loktak Lake**, fed by numerous rivers and dotted with islands, is home to a unique community of fishermen who live on large rafts made of reeds. Rare and endangered sangai, brow-antlered "dancing" deer, live on the floating vegetation that covers much of the lake, sharing their habitat with other species including the hog deer. Much of the lake is taken up by the **Keibul Lamjao National Park**, 53km from Imphal, which attracts a host of waterfowl and migratory birds between November and March. The forty-room hilltop *Tourist Bungalow* (☎0385/222 0802; Rs10 per bed) on **Sendra Island**, 48km from Imphal, provides a good vantage point from which to view the lake and can be booked through the tourist office in Imphal.

On the more populated western shore of Loktak, the small town of **MOIRANG**, 45km south of Imphal, is the traditional centre of Meithei culture, with a temple devoted to the pre-Hindu deity **Thangjing**. In April 1944, the Indian National Army under Netaji Subhas Chandra Bose planted its flag here, having fought alongside the Japanese against the British Indian Army for the cause of Independence. A **memorial** and **museum** commemorating the event includes several photos and Japanese-issued rupee notes from 1943. Guided tours of Loktak, run by Imphal's tourist office, usually include Moirang, or you can take a bus (1hr) from the private stand at Keishampat on Jail Road, near the centre of Imphal. The *Moirang Tourist Home* is currently occupied by the Indian army, so travellers will have to return to Imphal for accommodation.

Travel details

Trains

Dibrugarh to: Chennai (1 weekly; 45hr);
Delhi (1 daily; 51hr); Dimapur (2–3 daily;
5hr 40min–8hr); Guwahati (3–4 daily; 11hr
40min–12hr 15min); Kolkata (daily; 36hr 55min).
Dimapur to: Dibrugarh (2–3 daily; 5hr 40min–8hr);
Guwahati (5–6 daily; 4hr 20min–7hr).
Guwahati to: Chennai (6 weekly; 41hr–56hr
30min); Delhi (4–5 daily; 27hr 20min–43hr);
Dibrugarh (3–4 daily; 11hr 40min–12hr 15min);
Dimapur (5–6 daily; 4hr 20min–7hr); Jorhat
(1–2 daily; 6hr 40min–9hr 35min); Kolkata
(2–4 daily; 18hr 45min–23hr 25min); Mughal Sarai
(for Varanasi; 3–4 daily; 20hr 25min–29hr); Mumbai (3 weekly; 30hr 20min–34hr); Patna
(3 daily; 19–27hr).
Jorhat to: Guwahati (1–2 daily; 6hr 40min–9hr
35min).
Tinsukia to: Dimapur (3 daily; 6–7hr); Guwahati
(3 daily; 15–17hr); Lumding (3 daily 9hr–10hr
30min).

Buses

Agartala to: Guwahati (3–4 daily; 20hr);
Neermahal (every 30min; 2hr); Shillong (2–3 daily;
20hr); Silchar (2–3 daily; 11hr); Udaipur (every
15min; 2hr).
Aizawl to: Silchar (3–4 daily; 12hr).
Dibrugarh to: Digboi (7–8 daily; 4hr); Dimapur
(2–3 daily; 10hr); Guwahati (8–9 daily; 10hr);
Jorhat (12–14 daily; 4hr); Kaziranga (6–7 daily;
6hr); Miao (3 daily; 6–8hr); Tezpur (6–7 daily; 7hr).
Guwahati to: Agartala (3–4 daily; 20hr); Imphal
(2–3 daily; 12–16hr); Itanagar (3 daily; 12hr);
Jorhat (12–14 daily; 7hr); Kaziranga (14–16 daily;
4hr); Kohima (4–5 daily; 11–14hr); Shillong
(12 daily; 3–4hr); Silchar (5 daily; 12hr); Siliguri
(6–7 daily; 12hr); Tezpur (frequent; 5hr).
Imphal to: Dimapur (3–4 daily; 9hr); Guwahati
(2–3 daily; 12–16hr); Kohima (2 daily; 6hr).
Jorhat to: Dimapur (5–6 daily; 5hr); Guwahati
(12–14 daily; 7hr); Itanagar (1–2 daily; 9hr);
Kaziranga (frequent; 1hr 30min); Sibsagar
(frequent; 1hr 30min); Tezpur (14–15 daily; 4hr);
Tinsukia (frequent; 5–6hr).
Kohima to: Dimapur (12–14 daily; 3hr); Guwahati
(4–5 daily; 11–14hr).

Shillong to: Agartala (2–3 daily; 20hr); Aizawl
(3 weekly; 18hr); Cherrapunjee (2–3 daily; 2hr);
Guwahati (12 daily; 3–4hr); Jowai (2–3 daily;
3–4hr); Mawsynram (2 daily; 3hr); Silchar
(3–4 daily; 10hr); Tura (4–5 daily; 12hr).
Tezpur to: Bomdila (1 daily; 7hr); Dibrugarh
(6–7 daily; 7hr); Dirang (1 daily; 9hr); Guwahati
(frequent; 5hr); Itanagar (2–3 daily; 5hr); Jorhat
(frequent; 4hr).

Flights

(**IC** = Indian Airlines, **DN** = Deccan, **IT** = Kingfisher,
S2 = JetLite, **9W** = Jet Airways)
Agartala to: Guwahati (IC, DN, IT 9W 4–5 daily;
40–55min); Kolkata (IC, DN, IT, 9W 5–6 daily;
50min–1hr 5min); Silchar (IC 3 weekly; 50min).
Aizawl to: Guwahati (DN 1 daily; 1hr 10min);
Imphal (IC 3 weekly; 30min); Kolkata (DN 2 daily;
1hr 30min).
Dibrugarh to: Guwahati (DN, S2 1–2 daily; 50min);
Kolkata (IC 1 daily; 1hr 25min).
Dimapur to: Guwahati (IC 6 weekly; 50min);
Imphal (IC 4 weekly; 50min); Kolkata (IC, DN
2 daily; 1hr 5min).
Guwahati to: Agartala (IC, DN, IT, 9W 4–5 daily;
40–55min); Aizawl (DN 1 daily; 1hr 10min);
Bagdogra (IC, DN, 9W 1–2 daily; 55min); Delhi
(IC, DN, 9W, S2 4–6 daily; 2hr–2hr 15min);
Dibrugarh (DN, S2 1–2 daily; 50min); Dimapur
(IC 6 weekly; 50min); Imphal (IC, 9W, DN 2–3 daily;
50min); Jorhat (IC, 9W 1–2 daily; 35min); Kolkata
(IC, 9W, IT 5–6 daily; 1hr 10min); Mumbai (9W
1–2 daily; 4hr 40min); Pune (S2 1 daily;
1hr 20min); Silchar (IC, DN 3–4 daily; 45min).
Imphal to: Aizawl (IC 3 weekly; 30min); Delhi
(IC 2 weekly; 3hr 45min); Dimapur (IC 4 weekly;
50min); Guwahati (IC, 9W, DN 2–3 daily; 50min);
Kolkata (9W 6 weekly; 40min); Mumbai (9W
5 weekly; 6hr 10min); Silchar (IC 5 weekly; 35min).
Jorhat to: Guwahati (IC, 9W 1–2 daily; 35min);
Kolkata (IC, 9W 1–2 daily; 1hr–2hr 15min).
Lilabari to: Guwahati (IC, DN 6 weekly; 1hr).
Shillong to: Jorhat (IC 2 weekly; 50min); Kolkata
(IC 3 weekly; 3hr 25min).
Silchar to: Agartala (IC 3 weekly; 50min); Guwahati
(IC, DN 3–4 daily; 35min); Imphal (IC 5 weekly;
35min); Kolkata (IC 1–2 daily; 1hr 30min).

Orissa

CHAPTER 17

Highlights

* **Bhubaneswar** Hidden in the city's suburbs are five hundred or so temples, with unique architecture and elaborate sculptures. See p.1006

* **Olive Ridley turtles** These endangered creatures find their way to Gahirmatha beach for one night in February to lay eggs – an unforgettable scene. See p.1019

* **Similipal National Park** Tigers, leopards and elephants among the sylvan splendour of the Megasani Hills. See p.1019

* **Puri** Pilgrims flock to the vast temple devoted to Lord Jagannath, particularly during the frenetic midsummer Car Festival. See p.1021

* **Konark** An elegant thirteenth-century Hindu temple sitting astride a huge stone chariot. See p.1031

▲ Olive Ridley turtle

Orissa

Despite being one of India's poorest regions, **ORISSA** boasts a distinctive and rich cultural heritage. The coastal plains claim the highest concentration of historical and religious monuments – Orissa's principal tourist attractions. **Puri**, site of the famous **Jagannath temple** and one of the world's most spectacular devotional processions, the Rath Yatra, combines the heady intensity of a Hindu pilgrimage centre with the more hedonistic pleasures of the beach. Just a short hop off the main Kolkata (Calcutta)–Chennai road and railway, Puri sees its fair share of backpackers, who are enticed by plenty of budget accommodation near the beach and a laid-back social scene. **Konark**, a short hop up the coast, has the ruins of Orissa's most ambitious medieval temple. Hidden for years under a gigantic sand dune, its surfaces writhe with exquisitely preserved sculpture, including some eyebrow-raising erotica. The ancient rock-cut caves and ornate sandstone temples of **Bhubaneswar**, the state capital – all too often skipped by visitors – hark back to an era when it ruled a kingdom stretching from the Ganges delta to the mouth of the River Godavari.

Away from the central "golden triangle" of sights, foreign travellers are few and far between, though you'll see plenty of Bengalis travelling in family groups throughout coastal Orissa. Visitors to these outlying districts, with their minimal infrastructure and overtaxed public transport, tend to have a specialist interest, such as bird or animal life, temples or tribal culture. The **Similipal National Park**, deep in the *sal* forests of the far northeast, boasts some spectacular scenery, as well as tigers, elephants and hundreds of other species of animals, birds and reptiles. In winter, the small islands dotted around **Chilika Lake**, a huge salt-water lagoon south of Bhubaneswar, become a bird-watcher's paradise. Further north, in the **Bhitarkanika Sanctuary** at the end of Orissa's river delta, a remote stretch of beach is the nesting site for Olive Ridley marine **turtles** that migrate here in February and March.

From the number of temples in Orissa, you'd be forgiven for thinking Brahmanical Hinduism was its sole religion. In fact, almost a quarter of the population are **adivasi**, or "tribal" (literally "first") people, thought to have descended from the area's pre-Aryan aboriginal inhabitants. In the more inaccessible corners of the state many of these groups have retained unique cultural traditions and languages. So-called "ethnic" tourism is the latest encroachment on the *adivasis'* way of life, following in the wake of dam builders, missionaries and "advancement programmes" initiated by the state government. In Puri you'll come across signboards advertising "tribal tours" for top dollars, few of which ever trickle down to the *adivasi* villagers themselves.

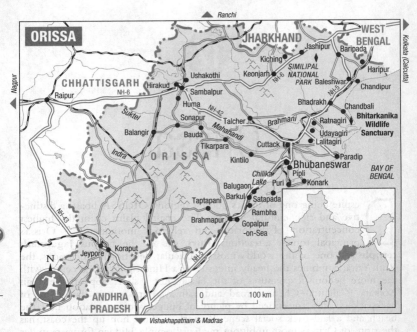

Vishakhapatnam & Madras

Getting around presents few practical problems if you stick to the more populated coastal areas. National Highway 5 and the Southeast Railway, which cut in tandem down the coastal plain via Bhubaneswar, are the main arteries of the region. A metre-gauge branch line also runs as far as Puri, connecting it by frequent, direct express **trains** to Delhi, Kolkata (Calcutta) and Chennai. Elsewhere, **buses** are the best way to travel. Regular government and ever-expanding private services (which tend to be faster and more comfortable) cover all the main routes and most of the more remote stretches.

Some history

Other than scattered fragmentary remains of prehistoric settlement, Orissa's earliest archeological find dates from the fourth century BC. The fortified city of **Sisupalgarh**, near modern Bhubaneswar, was the capital of the **Kalinga** dynasty, about which little is known. In the third century BC, the ambitious Mauryan emperor **Ashoka** descended on ancient Kalinga with his imperial army and routed the kingdom in a battle so bloody that the carnage was supposed to have inspired his legendary conversion to **Buddhism**. Rock edicts erected around the empire extol the virtues of the new faith, dharma, as well as the principles that Ashoka hoped to instil in his vanquished subjects. With the demise of the Mauryans, Kalinga enjoyed something of a resurgence. Under the imperialistic **Chedi** dynasty, which espoused the Jain faith, vast sums were spent expanding the capital and on carving elaborate monastery caves into the nearby hills of **Khandagiri** and **Udaigiri**. In the course of the second century BC, however, the kingdom gradually splintered into warring factions and entered a kind of Dark Age. The influence of Buddhism waned, Jainism all but vanished, and **Brahmanism**, disseminated by the teachings of the Shaivite zealot Lakulisha, started to resurface as the dominant religion.

Orissa's golden age, during which the region's prosperous Hindu rulers created some of South Asia's most sophisticated art and architecture, peaked in the twelfth century under the **Eastern Gangas**. Fuelled by the gains from a thriving trade network (extending as far east as Indonesia), the Ganga kings erected magnificent **temples** where Shiva worship and arcane tantric practices adopted by earlier Orissan rulers were replaced by new forms of devotion to Vishnu. The shrine of the most popular royal deity of all, Lord Jagannath, at Puri, was by now one of the four most hallowed religious centres in India.

In the fifteenth century, the **Afghans of Bengal** swept south to annex the region, with Man Singh's **Mughal** army hot on their heels in 1592. That even a few medieval Hindu monuments escaped the excesses of the ensuing iconoclasm is miraculous, and **non-Hindus** have never since been allowed to enter the most holy temples in Puri and Bhubaneswar. In 1751 the **Marathas** from western India ousted the Mughals as the dominant regional power. The East India Company, meanwhile, was also making inroads along the coast, and 28 years after Clive's victory at Plassey in 1765, Orissa finally came under **British rule**.

Since **Independence**, the state has sustained rapid **development**. Discoveries of coal, bauxite, iron ore and other minerals have stimulated considerable industrial growth and improvements to infrastructure. Despite such urban progress, however, Orissa remains essentially a poor rural state, heavily dependent on agriculture to provide for the basic needs of its 37 million inhabitants.

Orissan festivals

Chances of coinciding with a **festival** while in Orissa are good, since the region celebrates many of its own as well as all the usual Hindu festivals.

Makar Mela (mid-Jan). Pilgrims descend on a tiny island in Chilika Lake to leave votive offerings in a cave for the goddess Kali.

Adivasis Mela (Jan 26–Feb 1). Bhubaneswar's "tribal" fair is a disappointing cross between Coney Island and an agricultural show, though it does feature good live music and dance.

Magha Saptami (Jan & Feb). During the full-moon phase of Magha, a small pool at Chandrabhaga beach, near Konark, is swamped by thousands of worshippers in honour of Surya, the sun god and curer of skin ailments.

Panashankranti (early April). In various regions, on the first day of Vaisakha, saffron-clad penitents carrying peacock feathers enter trances and walk on hot coals.

Chaitra Parba (mid-April). Santals (the largest of Orissa's many *adivasi* ethnic groups) perform *Chhou* dances at Baripada in Mayurbhunj district, northern Orissa.

Ashokastami (April & May). Bhubaneswar's own Car Festival (procession of temple chariots), when the Lingaraj deity takes a dip in the Bindu Sagar tank.

Sitalasasthi (May & June). Celebration of the marriage of Shiva and Parvati, celebrated in Sambalpur and Bhubaneswar.

Rath Yatra (June & July). The biggest and grandest of Orissa's festivals. Giant images of Lord Jagannath, his brother Balabhadra and his sister Subhadra make the sacred journey from the Jagannath temple to Gundicha Mandir in Puri.

Bali Yatra (Nov & Dec). Commemorates the voyages made by Orissan traders to Indonesia. Held at full moon on the banks of the River Mahanadi in Cuttack.

Konark Festival (early Dec). A festival of classical dance featuring Orissan and other regional dance forms in the Sun Temple at Konark.

Bhubaneswar

On first impression, **BHUBANESWAR**, with its featureless 1950s architecture, may strike you as surprisingly dull for a city with a population approaching half a million and a history of settlement stretching back over two thousand years. Beyond the confines of the modern planned city, however, the backstreets and wastegrounds of the southern suburbs harbour the remnants of some of India's finest medieval **temples**. These are indisputably the main attractions, made all the more atmospheric by the animated religious life that continues to revolve around them, particularly at festival times.

Bhubaneswar first appears in history during the fourth century BC, as the capital of ancient **Kalinga**. It was here that Ashoka erected one of the Subcontinent's best-preserved rock edicts – still in place 5km south of **Dhauli**. Under the **Chedis**, ancient Kalinga gained control over the thriving

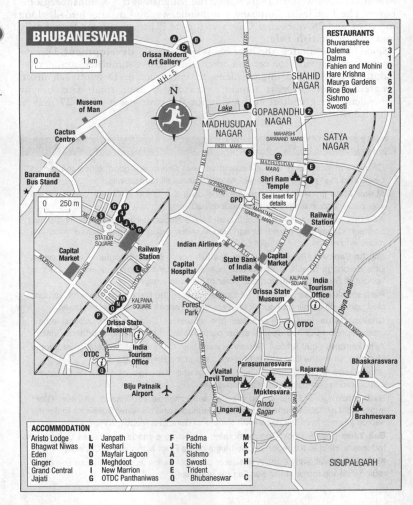

mercantile trade in the region and became the northeast seaboard's most formidable power.

Bhubaneswar then went into decline, re-emerging as a regional force only in the fifth century AD, when – as home to the revolutionary Pasupati sect – it became an important Shaivite centre. Coupled with the formidable wealth of the **Sailodbhavas** two centuries later, the growing religious fervour fuelled an extraordinary spate of temple construction. Between the seventh and twelfth centuries some 7000 shrines are believed to have been erected in the sacred enclave around the **Bindu Sagar** tank. Most were razed in the Muslim incursions of the medieval era, but enough survived for it to be possible in even a short visit to trace the evolution of Orissan architecture from its small, modest beginnings to the gigantic, self-confident proportions of the **Lingaraj** – the seat of Trimbhubaneshwara, or "Lord of Three Worlds", from which the modern city takes its name. A relative backwater until after Independence, Bhubaneswar was only declared the new state capital after nearby Cuttack reached bursting point in the 1950s.

Arrival, information and city transport

There's no regular bus service from Biju Patnaik **airport** into town but taxis and auto-rickshaws cover the 2–3km journey to the centre. Long-distance **buses** terminate at the inconveniently situated Baramunda Bus Stand, 5km out on the western edge of town, though not before making a whistle-stop tour of the centre. Ask to be dropped at **Station Square** (look for a statue of a horse in the middle of a large roundabout), which is near most hotels.

The **OTDC tourist office** on Lewis Road, next to the *Panthaniwas Hotel* (Mon–Sat 10am–5pm, ☎0674/243 1299, ⓦwww.orissa-tourism.com), and the counters at the railway station (24hr) and the airport (☎0674/240 4006), can arrange taxis for local sightseeing and help with hotel bookings. The Lewis Road office also offers rather rushed **tours** of the city (Tues–Sun 9am–5.30pm; Rs130, a/c Rs180), and a similarly hurried trip to Puri, Konark and Pipli (daily 9am–6.30pm; Rs150, a/c Rs180). The India Tourism office behind the museum at B-21 BJB Nagar (Mon–Fri 10am–5pm; ☎0674/243 2203) stocks leaflets and city plans for other parts of the country.

Modern Bhubaneswar is too spread out to explore on foot and is best seen by auto- or cycle **rickshaw**. Sights outside the city, such as Dhauli or the Udaigiri and Khandagiri caves, can be reached by local **buses** from the old city bus stand near Capital Market, by auto-rickshaw or on one of OTDC's **luxury bus tours**. Private Ambassador **taxis** can be arranged through most travel agents and upmarket hotels (Rs900–1200 per day), although far better value are the taxis at the OTDC tourist office.

Accommodation

As state capital, Bhubaneswar offers a typical range of accommodation. While the better-class hotels are spread out all over the city, the inexpensive places tend to be grouped around the **railway station**, or near the busy **Kalpana Square** junction at the bottom of Cuttack Road, a five-minute rickshaw ride away.

Aristo Lodge Kalpana Square ☎0674/231 1093. Very basic, but friendly; some rooms have TV and all have attached bath. ❶–❷

Bhagwat Niwas 9 Buddha Nagar ☎0674/231 3708. Managed by an Aurobindo devotee, the hotel is safe and welcoming. A range of simple, clean rooms, some with balcony and a/c; there's an in-house ISD booth for international calls, and a good restaurant. ❷–❺

Eden 77 Buddha Nagar ☎0674/231 1178. The budget rooms here are larger and cleaner than most others in the area near the railway station. There's also a restaurant and bar. ①–④

Ginger Jaidev Vihar ⓣ0674/230 3933, ⓦwww .gingerhotels.com. Situated 4km from the railway station, the decor and styling is ultra-modern, if somewhat bland. Rooms are large and flawlessly clean; each has a flat-screen TV and Wi-Fi. Staff are courteous and efficient. ⑥

Grand Central Old Station Rd ⓣ0674/231 3411, ⓦ www.hotelgrandcentral.com. Convenient location, minibar and Wi-Fi in every room, travel agent and a superb restaurant serving some of the best masala dosas you're likely to come across. Some of the rooms at the front have balconies. Recommended. ⑥–⑦

Jajati MG Marg ⓣ0674/250 0352. Modern hotel at the top end of Station Square. A little frayed around the edges, but the a/c rooms are comfortable and good value. ②–④

🏃 **Janpath** 29 Jan Path ⓣ0674/253 1547, ⓔhoteljanpath@gmail.com. One kilometre north of the railway station: the cheerful staff are helpful and welcoming, there's a travel agent, Internet access and a good restaurant. The best rooms are at the front and overlook the Shri Ram Temple; all are large and comfortable. The free daily newspaper delivered each morning is a nice touch. Excellent value. ③–⑤

Keshari Station Square ⓣ0674/253 4994, ⓕ253 5553, ⓔkeshari@orissaindia.com. Friendly staff and very close to the railway station. The rooms are dark but clean and comfortable, and the restaurant serves local specialities. Also has a good travel agency. ④–⑤

Mayfair Lagoon 8-B Jaydev Vihar ⓣ0674/236 0101, ⓦwww.mayfairhotels.com. Luxurious villas and cottages surrounding a delightful ornamental lake, with attractive grounds enlivened by life-sized models of crocodiles, deer and sundry other beasts. There's something of the theme park about this hotel, but it's tastefully done, and the facilities are excellent. Cottages from $80; villas from $310. ⑨

Meghdoot 5-B Sahid Nagar ⓣ0674/250 7243, ⓕ251 2168. Some distance away in the north of

town, but well appointed. All rooms, from high-quality doubles to luxurious suites, have bathtubs and colour TV. Good pool, restaurant, coffee shop and foreign exchange. ⑦

New Marrion 6 Jan Path ⓣ0674/238 0850, ⓕ238 0860, ⓔmarrion@sancharnet.in. Upmarket and welcoming hotel with a pool, foreign exchange, travel agent and two good restaurants, one serving Chinese food. The 24hr bar (open to non-residents) has intriguing frescos around the walls. ⑦–⑧

OTDC Panthaniwas Lewis Rd ⓣ0674/243 2314. Institutional government hotel close to the museum and temples. Nothing fancy, but the rooms are large and comfortable. Non-a/c rooms are over-priced, especially in peak season (Oct–Feb). There are two good restaurants on site. The 8am check-out is negotiable if they are not too busy. ③–⑤

Padma Kalpana Square ⓣ0674/231 3330, ⓕ231 0904. A busy little place with cheap and simple rooms; a good fall-back if others are full. No restaurant. ①

Richi Station Square ⓣ0674/253 4619, ⓕ539 418. Large efficient place opposite the station, with cable TV in all rooms. The price includes breakfast. ③–④

Sishmo 86/A-1 Gautam Nagar ⓣ0674/243 3600, ⓦwww.hotelsishmo.com. Plush four-star in the centre of town with pleasant rooms, a bar, pool, 24hr coffee shop and excellent restaurant. Rates include morning tea and breakfast. ⑧

Swosti 103 Jan Path ⓣ0674/253 4678, ⓦwww.swosti.com. Grand four-star hotel bang in the centre of town. Luxurious rooms, travel agency, two top-class restaurants and a bar. Doubles from $125. ⑨

Trident Bhubaneswar Nayapalli ⓣ0674/230 1010, ⓦwww.trident-hilton.com. Indisputably the city's top hotel, part of the Oberoi chain, in the north of town. Exquisitely furnished using antique textiles, stone and metalwork; facilities include an excellent restaurant, an efficient travel centre, foreign exchange, Internet access, and a pool. Doubles from $140. ⑨

The temples

Of the five hundred or so **temples** that remain in Bhubaneswar, only a handful are of interest to any but the most ardent templo-phile. They are quite spread out in the south of the city, but it's possible to see the highlights in a day by rickshaw: allow Rs200–250 for a tour of the main sites (including waiting time). Visiting the temples in chronological order gives a sense of the way styles developed over the years, and leaves the most impressive monuments until last. The majority are active places of worship, so dress appropriately, remove your shoes (and any leather items) at the entrance and seek permission before taking photographs, particularly inside the buildings. The resident priest will expect a donation if he's shown you around, but don't necessarily believe the astronomical amounts recorded in the ledgers you'll be shown. Entry is free to all temples except Rajarani.

The central group

The compact **central group**, just off Lewis Road, includes some of Bhubaneswar's most celebrated temples.

The best preserved and most beautiful early example, the lavishly decorated **Parasuramesvara Mandir**, stands in the shade of a large banyan tree. Dating from around 650 AD, the shrine's plain, rectangular assembly hall (*jagamohana*), simple stepped roof and squat beehive-shaped tower (*deul*) typify the style of the late seventh century. Besides the sheer quality of the building's exterior sculpture, Parasuramesvara is significant in marking the then-recent transition from Buddhism to Hinduism. Look out for panels depicting Lakulisha, the proselytizing Shaivite saint whose sect was largely responsible for the conversion of Orissa to Hinduism in the fifth century. More graphic assertions of Hindu

▲ Rath Yatra

supremacy mark corners of the *deul*, where rampant lions crouch or stand above elephants, symbols of the beleaguered Buddhist faith.

Erected in the mid-tenth century, the **Muktesvara Mandir** is often dubbed "the gem" of Orissan architecture for its compact size and exquisite sculptural detail. It stands in a separate walled courtyard, beside the small **Marichi Kund** tank (whose murky green waters are believed to cure infertility). The temple was constructed two hundred years after the Parasuramesvara, and represents the new, more elaborate style that had evolved in Bhubaneswar. Its *jagamohana* sports the more distinctively Orissan pyramidal roof, while the *deul*, though similar in shape to earlier sanctuary towers, places more emphasis on vertical rather than horizontal lines. Directly facing the main entrance, the ornamental **torana** (gateway), topped by two reclining female figures, is Muktesvara's masterpiece.

Orissan temples

Orissan temples constitute one of the most distinctive regional styles of religious architecture in South Asia. Like their counterparts elsewhere in the Subcontinent, they were built according to strict templates set down a thousand or more years ago in a body of canonical texts called the *Shilpa Shastras*. These specify not only every aspect of temple design – from the proportions of the sanctuary tower to the tiniest sculptural detail – but also the overall symbolic significance of the building. Unlike Christian churches or Islamic mosques, Hindu shrines are not simply places of worship but objects of worship in themselves – re-creations of the "Divine Cosmic Creator-Being" or the particular deity enshrined within them. For a Hindu, to move through a temple is akin to entering the very body of the god glimpsed at the moment of *darshan*, or ritual viewing, in the shrine room. In Orissa, this concept also finds expression in the technical terms used in the *Shastras* to designate the different parts of the structure: the foot (*pabhaga*), shin (*jangha*), torso (*gandi*), neck (*kantha*), head (*mastaka*) and so forth.

Most temples are made up of two main sections. The first and most impressive of these is the **deul**, or sanctuary tower. A soaring, curvilinear spire with a square base and rounded top, the *deul* symbolizes Meru, the sacred mountain at the centre of the universe. Its intricately ribbed sides, which in later buildings were divided into rectangular projections known as *raths*, usually house images of the accessory deities, while its top supports a lotus-shaped, spherical *amla* (a motif derived from an auspicious fruit used in Ayurvedic medicine as a purifying agent). Above that, the vessel of immortality, the *kalasha*, is crowned by the presiding deity's sacred weapon, a wheel (Vishnu's *chakra*) or trident (Shiva's *trishul*). The actual deity occupies a chamber inside the *deul*. Known in Oriya as the **garbha griha**, or inner sanctum, the shrine is shrouded in womb-like darkness, intended to focus the mind of the worshipper on the image of God.

The **jagamohana** ("world delighter"), which adjoins the sanctuary tower, is a porch with a pyramidal roof where the congregation gathers for readings of religious texts and other important ceremonies. Larger temples, such as the Lingaraj in Bhubaneswar and the Jagannath in Puri, also have structures that were tacked on to the main porch when music and dance were more commonly performed as part of temple rituals. Like the *jagamohana*, the roofs of the **nata mandir** (the dancing hall) and **bhoga-mandapa** (the hall of offerings) are pyramidal. The whole structure, along with any smaller subsidiary shrines (often earlier temples erected on the same site), is usually enclosed in a walled courtyard.

Over the centuries, as construction techniques and skills improved, Orissan temples became progressively grander and more elaborate. It's fascinating to chart this transformation as you move from the earlier buildings in Bhubaneswar to the acme of the region's architectural achievement, the stunning Sun Temple at **Konark**. Towers grow taller, roofs gain extra layers, and the **sculpture**, for which the temples are famous all over the world, attains a level of complexity and refinement unrivalled before or since.

On the edge of Muktesvara's terrace, the unfinished **Siddhesvara** was erected at around the same time as the Lingaraj, but is far less imposing; the lesser deities around the tower, Ganesh and Kartikeya (Shiva's sons) are its only remarkable features.

The eastern group

Even though it was never completed, the twelfth-century **Rajarani Mandir** (daily sunrise to sunset; Rs100 [Rs5], video camera Rs25) ranks among the very finest of Bhubaneswar's later temples. From the far end of the well-watered gardens in which it stands, the profile of the *deul* dominates first impressions. The best of the sculpted figures for which Rajrani is famous surround the sides of the tower, roughly 3m off the ground, where the **dikpalas** ("guardians of the eight directions"), separated from one another by exquisite female *nayikas*, protect the main shrine.

Unlike most of its neighbours, the eleventh-century shrine within **Brahmesvara Mandir** still houses a living deity, as indicated by the saffron pennant flying from the top of the sanctuary. Here too *dikpalas* preside over the corners, with a fierce Chamunda on the western facade (shown astride a corpse and holding a trident and severed head), while curvaceous maidens admire themselves in mirrors or dally with their male consorts. An inscription, now lost, records that one Queen Kovalavati once made a donation of "many beautiful women" to this temple, recalling that **devadasis**, the dancers-cum-prostitutes who were to become a prominent feature of Orissan temple life in later years (see p.1033), made an early appearance here. Non-Hindus are barred from the central shrine – whose majestic Nandi bull has testicles well polished by years of propitious rubbing from worshippers.

The Bindu Sagar group

The largest group of temples is clustered around the **Bindu Sagar** ("ocean drop tank"), 2km south of the city centre. This small artificial lake, mentioned in the *Puranas*, is said to contain nectar, wine and water drawn from the world's most sacred rivers. It's the main bathing place both for pilgrims visiting the city and for the Lingaraj deity, who is taken to the pavilion in the middle once every year during Bhubaneswar's annual **Car Festival** (Ashokastami) for his ritual purificatory dip. The hours around sunrise and sunset are the most evocative time for a stroll here, when the residents of the nearby *dharamshalas* file through the smoky lanes to pray at the *ghats*.

Lingaraj Mandir

Immediately south of the Bindu Sagar stands the most stylistically evolved temple in all Orissa. Built early in the eleventh century by the Ganga kings, one hundred years before the Jagannath temple at Puri, the mighty **Lingaraj Mandir** has remained a living shrine. For this reason, foreign visitors are not permitted inside, but there is a **viewing platform** overlooking the north wall of the complex, from where all four of the principal sections of the building are visible. The two nearest the entrance, the *bhoga-mandapa* (Hall of Offering) and the *nata mandir* (Hall of Dance, associated with the rise of the *devadasi* system – see p.1033) are both later additions. Beautiful **sculpture** depicting the music and dance rituals that would once have taken place inside the temple adorns its walls.

The immense 45-metre *deul* is the literal and aesthetic high-point of the Lingaraj. The rampant lion projecting from the curved sides of the tower, and the downtrodden elephant beneath him, again symbolize the triumph of Hinduism over Buddhism. On the top, the typical Orissan motif of the flattened, ribbed sphere (*amla*) supported by gryphons, is crowned with Shiva's trident. As in the Brahmesvara temple, the long saffron pennant announces the living presence of the deity below.

The **shrine** inside is unusual. The powerful 2.5-metre-thick Svayambhu (literally "self-born") lingam that it contains, one of the twelve *jyotirlingas* in India, is known as "Hari-Hara" because it is considered half Shiva, half Vishnu – an extraordinary amalgam thought to have resulted from the ascendancy of Vaishnavism over Shaivism in the twelfth and thirteenth centuries. Unlike other lingams, which are bathed every day in a concoction prepared from hemlock, Svayambhu is offered a libation of rice, milk and bhang by the brahmins.

Vaital Deul Mandir

The **Vaital Deul** temple, one of the group's oldest buildings, is a real feast of Tantric art. The building was erected around 800 AD in a markedly different style from most of its contemporaries in Bhubaneswar, drawing heavily on earlier Buddhist influences. Among the panels of Hindu deities encrusting its outer walls, you can make out examples of some of India's earliest erotic sculpture.

Once past the four-faced lingam post at the main entrance (used for tethering sacrificial offerings), your eyes soon adjust to the darkness of the **interior**, whose grotesque images convey the macabre nature of the esoteric rites once performed here. Durga, in her most terrifying aspect as **Chamunda**, peers out of the half-light from behind the grille at the far end of the hall – her withered body, garlanded with skulls and flanked by an owl and a jackal, stands upon a rotting corpse. In front of her a man picks himself up from the floor, having filled his skull-cup with blood from the decapitated body nearby.

Around the town

The **Orissa State Museum**, at the top of Lewis Road (Tues–Sun 10am–5pm; Rs50), has a collection of "tribal" artefacts, illuminated manuscripts and various archeological finds. On display in the downstairs galleries are pieces of religious sculpture, including pre-twelfth-century Buddhist statues. The upstairs rooms feature ethnographic material from indigenous Orissan societies, including reproductions of **chitra muriya**, the folk murals seen on walls and floors in village houses around Puri. The museum's real highlight, however, is its collection of antique **painting** and illuminated **palm-leaf manuscripts** (see p.1029). Only the National Museum in New Delhi holds finer examples of this traditional Orissan art form.

Close to the Baramunda Bus Stand on NH-5, in the northwest of town, is the Tribal Research Institute's anthropological **Museum of Man** (Mon–Sat 10am–5pm; free), with exhibits on the distinctive cultures and art of the 62 different tribal groups spread throughout Orissa, mostly in the southern hinterlands. Filling the gardens outside are somewhat idealized replicas of *adivasi* dwellings, decorated with more authentic-looking murals. The **library** behind the main institute building reputedly holds copies of all the books and journals ever compiled on the *adivasi* groups of Orissa. Opposite the Museum of Man, in the Acharya Vihar building, is Asia's largest **cactus collection** (daily 10am–5pm; free): it's home to over a thousand species of cacti displayed in polyhouses spread over 20,000 square feet.

The Orissa Modern Art Gallery (Mon–Sat 11am–1.30pm & 4–8pm; free), 132 Forest Walk, in Surya Nagar, showcases the work of the state's best contemporary and most underprivileged artists. Original works are available to buy from Rs200 to Rs15,000.

Capital Market, situated in a residential area along Jan Path, is the place to buy typical Orissan handlooms, handicrafts and jewellery. All the material shops claim to be the official government outlet, so the prices for lengths of beautifully woven cloth and ready-made garments are very competitive.

Eating

With one or two exceptions, **eating** out in Bhubaneswar is limited to the predictable five-star food dished up in the a/c comfort of hotels such as the *Sishmo* or *Swosti*, or the cheap and chilli-ful south Indian dishes served in rather less salubrious cafés such as the *Venus Inn*. The one or two restaurants that specialize in traditional **Orissan cuisine**, or include some Orissan dishes on their menus, are worth seeking out (you will have to order at least eight hours in advance at the big hotels). Look out for *chenna poda* (cheesecake stuffed with almonds), and other sweets like *raswadi* (thickened milk with balls of curd) and *gajjar halwa* (a rich sweet made from grated carrots).

Bhuvanashree At the top of Station Square next to the *Jajati* hotel. Excellent, clean veg restaurant with some south Indian food, a choice of thalis and good coffee. Closed Tues.

Dalema Bhouma Nagar. Dark, simple place offering authentic Orissan dishes like *macha bhaja* (fish curry), *chengudli tarkari* (prawn curry), *dahi machho* (river fish in yoghurt sauce) and a variety of vegetables. Main courses are inexpensive at about Rs45 each.

Dalma Sachivalaya Marg. This modest but celebrated eatery, named after Orissa's most popular traditional vegetarian dish, is one of the few places in Bhubaneswar providing authentic and complete Oriya meals. The *dalma* (potato, brinjal and other vegetables cooked in dhal) is complemented by *bharta* (mixed vegetable curry), *besara* (very hot curry) and a variety of fish dishes. Generally regarded by city residents as *the* place to go for traditional regional cuisine. Mains from Rs60. Highly recommended.

Fahien and **Mohini** At the OTDC *Panthaniwas*, Lewis Rd. *Fahien* and *Mohini* offer identical multi-cuisine menus, but the former is more comfortable.

Hare Krishna Jan Path, just north of the junction with MG Marg, entrance up a flight of stairs in a small market. Quite expensive, with waiters in dinner jackets rather than *dhotis*, but the food is strictly ISKCON-style (the Hare Krishna movement's unique cuisine, without garlic or onions): vegetarian and delicious.

Maurya Gardens 122-A Station Square, next to and part of the *Richi*. Smart interior and reasonable prices. Serves Indian and Chinese food, specializing in tandoor dishes.

Rice Bowl Shahid Nagar. Excellent prawn and fish curries, as well as Chinese cuisine that's a cut above much of the budget-range competition. Mains from Rs70.

Sishmo *Sishmo Hotel*. High-quality food with a wide variety of Indian tandoori dishes in classy surroundings. Pricey, but not as expensive as it looks (around Rs1000 a head with wine).

Swosti *Swosti Hotel*. Ultra-reliable place for good, moderately priced authentic Orissan dishes, such as the mouthwatering *dahi machho*); order at least two or three hours ahead.

Listings

Airlines Indian Airlines' main booking office is on Raj Path, near New Market (℡0674/253 0533, airport office ℡0674/253 5743, ⊛www.indian-airlines.nic.in). JetLite's main office is on Jan Path (℡0674/253 5007, airport office ℡0674/253 5729, ⊛www.jetlite.com). Bookings for Kingfisher Airlines (⊛www.flykingfisher.com) or Air Deccan (⊛www.airdeccan.net) should be made through a travel agent.

Banks and exchange The State Bank of India (Mon–Fri 10am–4pm and Sat 10am–2pm, closed 2nd Sat of every month) on Raj Path has an efficient foreign exchange counter and accepts all major currencies, as does Thomas Cook (Mon–Fri 9am–5pm, Sat 10am–2pm, closed 2nd Sat of every month), 130 Ashok Nagar, Jan Path. A number of ATMs are available around Kalpana Square, on Jan Path, and throughout the city.

Bookshops The Modern Book Depot at the top of Station Square has a rack of pulp fiction and a section dedicated to history, dance, economy, geography and natural history of Orissa. Across the square in Ashoka Market, the Bookshop stocks a wide range of Western literature, Indian literature in translation, and books on politics, religion and history.

Dance Visits or lessons can be arranged through the Orissa Dance Academy, 64 Kharwal Nagar, Unit 3 (℡ 0674/234 0124). The Rabindra Mandap auditorium on Sachivalaya Marg (℡ 0674/241 7677), the Suchana Bhavan building, near the old bus stand (℡ 0674/22253 0794), and the Utkal Sangeet Mahavidyalaya, Orissa's premier college of performing arts, on Sachivalaya Marg (℡ 0674/241 0234), all play host to regular music, dance and drama events.

Hospital The Capital Hospital and Homeopathic Clinic (℡ 0674/240 1983) is near the airport; for casualty, call ℡ 0674/240 0688. The Municipal Hospital, in Lingaraj Square, also has a casualty unit; call ℡ 0674/259 1237. There's an Ayurvedic hospital between the *Panthaniwas* hotel and the Ramesvara temple (℡ 0674/243 2347). For a Red Cross ambulance, call ℡ 0674/240 2384.

Internet access There are plenty of Internet cafés around Station Square, as well as along Cuttack Rd and Jan Path. Iway, in the building next to the *Swosti* hotel, and beside the exhibition ground near

the Shri Ram Temple, charges Rs35/hr for a fast connection.

Photography Fotomakers, 28 West Tower, New Market; Photo Express, 44 Ashok Nagar; Unicolor Photo Lab, 133 Ashok Nagar.

Police station Raj Path, near the State Bank of India (℡ 0674/253 3732).

Post office On the corner of MG Marg and Sachivalaya Marg (Mon–Sat 9am–7pm). For poste restante ask at "enquiries" on the middle counter. A pan-wallah by the main entrance packs and seals parcels.

Travel agents The *Keshari*, *New Marrion*, *Meghdoot*, *Sishmo* and *Trident Bhubaneswar* hotels all have in-house travel agents. Swosti Travels (℡ 0674/250 8738) in the *Swosti* hotel, 103 Jan Path, does ticketing for Indian Airlines and Jet Airways, and offers upmarket package tours of Bhubaneswar, Puri and Konark. Discover Tours (℡ 0674/243 0477, ⓦ www.orissadiscover.com), 463 Lewis Rd, is probably the most reliable agent for cultural/tribal and wildlife tour packages. Prime Tours and Travels, in the Pushpak Complex on Kalpana Square, can fix up car rental, airline tickets and train reservations.

Moving on from Bhubaneswar

Bhubaneswar lies on the main **Howrah–Chennai** line with many **trains** passing through daily, including the recommended Coromandel Express #2841. Trains to **Delhi** include the Rajdhani Express #2421 on Thursday and Monday (the fastest and most convenient), and a daily service from Puri on either the New Delhi Express #2815 (Mon, Wed, Thurs & Sat) or the Neelachal Express #2875 (Tues, Fri & Sun). The fastest train to **Kolkata (Calcutta)** is the Jan Shatabdi Express #2074 (Mon–Sat; 6hr 50min); the slower Sri Jagannath Express #8410 offers an overnight passage, departing at 0.05am and arriving in Kolkata at 8.10am.

Buses run by Orissa State Transport depart from Baramunda Bus Stand. You can pick up buses to Puri, Pipli and Cuttack from Jayadev Nagar opposite the *Kalinga Ashok* hotel, and from near the railway station. Buses and **minibuses** run to Puri (Rs23 per person) as soon as they are full, but get extremely overloaded and drive dangerously fast.

JetLite has **flights** from Bhubaneswar airport to destinations throughout India, including Chennai, Delhi, Goa, Hyderabad, Jaipur, Kolkata (Calcutta), and Mumbai. Both Air Deccan and Indian Airlines have **services** to Mumbai, Delhi, and Bangalore. Kingfisher Airlines operates a service to Kolkata (Calcutta).

See "Travel details" at the end of this chapter for more information on journey frequencies and durations.

Around Bhubaneswar

A number of places around Bhubaneswar can be easily visited on a day-trip from the city. Fifteen minutes by auto-rickshaw out of the centre, the second-century BC caves at **Khandagiri** and **Udaigiri** offer a glimpse of the region's history prior to the rise of Hinduism. **Dhauli**, just off the main road to Puri, boasts an even older monument: a rock edict dating from the Mauryan era, commemorating the battle of c.260 BC that gave the emperor Ashoka control of the eastern seaports, and thus enabled his missionaries to export the state religion across Asia. **Pipli**, 20km south, is famous for its appliqué work and colourful lampshades.

Udaigiri and Khandagiri caves

Six kilometres west of Bhubaneswar, a pair of low hills rises from the coastal plain. More than two thousand years ago, caves chiselled out of their malleable yellow sandstone were home to a community of **Jain monks**. Nowadays, they're clambered over by troupes of black-faced langur monkeys and occasional parties of tourists. Though by no means in the same league as the caves of the Deccan, **Udaigiri** and **Khandagiri** (daily 8am–5pm; Rs100 [Rs5], video camera Rs25) rank among Orissa's foremost historical monuments.

Inscriptions show that the **Chedi** dynasty, which ruled ancient Kalinga from the first century BC, was responsible for the bulk of the work. There are simple monk's cells for meditation and prayer, as well as royal chambers where the hallways, verandas and facades are encrusted with **sculpture** depicting court scenes, lavish processions, hunting expeditions, battles, dances and a host of domestic details from the daily life of Kalinga's cool set. The later additions (from medieval times, when Jainism no longer enjoyed royal patronage in the region) are more austere, showing the twenty-four heroic Jain prophet-teachers, or *tirthankaras* ("crossing-makers").

From Bhubaneswar, the caves are approached via a road that follows the route of an ancient **pilgrimage path**. As you face the hills with the highway behind you, Khandagiri ("Broken Hill") is on your left and Udaigiri ("Sunrise Hill") is on your right.

Udaigiri

The **Udaigiri** caves occupy a fairly compact area around the south slope of the hill. **Cave 1** (Rani Gumpha or "Queen's Cave"), off the main pathway to the right, is the largest and most impressive of the group. A long frieze across the back wall shows rampaging elephants, panicking monkeys, sword fights and the abduction of a woman, perhaps illustrating episodes from the life of Kalinga's King Kharavela. **Caves 3** and **4** contain sculptures of a lion holding its prey and elephants with snakes wrapped around them, and pillars topped by pairs of peculiar winged animals. **Cave 9**, up the hill and around to the right, houses a damaged relief of figures worshipping a long-vanished Jain symbol. The crowned figure is thought to be the Chedi king, Vakradeva, whose donative inscription can still be made out near the roof. Inside the sleeping cells of all the caves, deep grooves in the stone wall at the back and in the floor were designed to carry rainwater down from the roof as an early air-conditioning system.

To reach **Cave 10**, return to the main steps and climb towards the top of the hill. Its popular name, "Ganesh Gumpha", is derived from the elephant-headed Ganesh carved on the rear wall of the cell on the right. From here, follow the path up to the ledge at the very top of Udaigiri hill for good views and the ruins of an old **chaitya hall**, probably the main place of worship for the Jain monks who lived below.

Below the ruins are **Cave 12**, shaped like the head of a tiger, and **Cave 14**, the Hathi Gumpha, known for the long **inscription** in ancient Magadhi carved onto its overhang. This relates in glowing terms the life history of King Kharavela, whose exploits, both on and off the battlefield, brought in the fortune needed to finance the cave excavation.

Khandagiri

The caves on the opposite hill, **Khandagiri**, can be reached either by the long flight of steps leading from the road, or by cutting directly across from Hathi Gumpha via the steps that drop down from Cave 17. The latter route brings you out at **Caves 1** and **2**, known as Tatowa Gumpha ("Parrot Caves") for the carvings of birds on their doorway-arches. Cave 2, excavated in the first century BC, is the larger and more interesting. On the back wall of one of its cells, a few faint lines in red Brahmi script are thought to have been scrawled two thousand years ago by a monk practising his handwriting. The reliefs in **Cave 3**, the Ananta Gumpha ("Snake Cave"), contain the best of the sculpture on Khandagiri hill, albeit badly vandalized in places. **Caves 7** and **8**, left of the main steps, were former sleeping quarters, remodelled in the eleventh century as sanctuaries. Both house reliefs of *tirthankaras* on their walls as well as Hindu deities which had become part of the Jain pantheon by the time conversion work was done. From the nineteenth-century **Jain temple** at the top of the hill there are clear views across the sprawl of Bhubaneswar to the white dome of Dhauli.

Dhauli

The gleaming, white **Vishwa Shanti Stupa** on **Dhauli Hill**, 8km south of Bhubaneswar on the Pipli road, overlooks the spot where the Mauryan emperor **Ashoka** defeated the Kalingas in the decisive battle of 260 BC. Apart from bringing the prosperous Orissan kingdom to its knees, the victory also led the emperor, allegedly overcome by remorse at having slain 150,000 people, to renounce the path of violent conquest in favour of the spiritual path preached by Gautama Buddha. Built in 1972 by an association of Japanese Buddhists, the modern stupa, which eclipses its older predecessor nearby, stands as a memorial to Ashoka's legendary change of heart, and the massive religious sea-change it precipitated.

After his conversion, Ashoka set about promulgating the maxims of his newly found faith in **rock edicts** installed at key sites around the empire (see "History" in Contexts). One such inscription, in ancient **Brahmi**, the ancestor of all non-Islamic Indian scripts, still stands on the roadside at the foot of Dhauli hill, etched in a rock featuring a beautifully carved figure of an elephant (symbolizing Buddhism). The Dhauli edict includes a mixture of rambling philosophical asides, discourses on animal rights and tips on how to treat your slaves. Particularly of note are the lines claiming the Buddhist doctrine of nonviolence was being recognized by "the kings of Egypt, Ptolemy and Antigonus and Magas", which proved for the first time the existence of a connection between the ancient civilizations of India and the West. The inscription diplomatically omits the account that crops up elsewhere describing how many Kalingas Ashoka had put to the sword before he finally "saw the light".

If you don't have your own vehicle and are not on a tour, **getting to Dhauli** involves a two-kilometre walk. Get off the bus at Dhauli Chowk, the junction on the main Puri–Bhubaneswar road, and make your way along the avenue of cashew trees to the rock edict, from where the road begins its short climb up the hill.

Pipli

Fifteen minutes' drive or so beyond Dhauli, on the Puri road, splashes of bright colour in the shop fronts along the main street announce your arrival in **PIPLI**, Orissa's **appliqué** capital (see box, p.1029). Much of what the artisans produce here nowadays on their hand-powered sewing machines is shoddy kitsch compared with the painstaking work traditionally undertaken for the Jagannath

Sacred spaces and pilgrimage places

For most Indians, the presence of the divine is a daily fact of life. There's scarcely a street in the Subcontinent that doesn't boast its own shrine or temple, while innumerable natural features are also considered sacred, from village trees to entire mountains and rivers. According to some accounts, the country boasts almost two thousand major temples and other places of spiritual significance, stretching from remote Himalayan caves and mountains to the sprawling Dravidian temple complexes of Tamil Nadu.

A Hindu pilgrim in the the holy Gangotri Valley ▲

Hindu morning rituals in the Ganges ▼

On the road to the gods

The Indian tradition of **pilgrimage** dates back to at least the time of the Mahabharata, and remains a popular occupation today among all sections of Indian society, from wandering Hindu saddhus and Jain monks who spend their lives walking barefoot across the country from shrine to shrine, begging for sustenance en route, to the more modern pilgrims, who tear between temples in specially chartered video buses, combining the high-speed accrual of religious merit with sightseeing and shopping.

Crossing points to the divine

Hindus describe sacred places using the Sanskrit word *tirtha*, literally meaning a river crossing, but also understood more generally to signify a spiritual crossing point where earth and heaven meet; where the gods descend to earth, and where humans may transcend *samsara* (see p.1359) and rise towards the gods. The act of pilgrimage is called *tirtha-yatra*, visiting *tirthas* in order to encounter the divine and to experience *darshan* (see p.1364) and accrue religious merit, either for its own sake or in pursuance of a particular goal – which could be anything from praying for the birth of a son to asking for good exam results. Near the end of their lives, many Hindus make one final pilgrimage to **Varanasi**, following the belief that all those who die there will gain instant liberation (*moksha*) from the endless cycle of rebirth.

Pilgrimage traditions are also particularly strong amongst **Jains**, and Jain monks and nuns can often been seen walking between important shrines such as Shatrunjaya and

Sravanabelagola and the Jain temples of Rajasthan. **Buddhists** visit the four places more closely associated with Buddha: Bodhgaya, Sarnath, Kushinagar and Lumbini (just over the border in Nepal). For **Muslims**, of course, the ultimate pilgrimage is the *haj* to Mecca. Failing that, seven trips to the shrine of Khwaja Muin-ud-din Chishti in Ajmer are considered equivalent.

▲ A Hindu woman carries out puja (worship)

▼ Rameshwaram temple colonnade

India's sacred spaces

India's myriad religious sites are grouped into a variety of different categories, most covering local areas or, occasionally, the entire country. At the apex of India's spiritual hierarchy lie the **Seven Sacred Cities**, or *Sapta Puri* (Ayodhya, Mathura, Haridwar, Varanasi, Kanchipuram, Ujjain and Dwarka), which are believed to confer *moksha* on anyone who dies within them, and the **Four Abodes**, or *Char Dham* (Rameshwaram, Puri, Dwarka and Badrinath), at the far compass points of the country (not to be confused with the "little" *Char Dham* linking Badrinath, Kedarnath, Gangotri and Yamunotri in Uttarakhand).

Each of the major deities (except Brahma) also has their own individual pilgrimage circuit and set of religious sites. **Shiva** is represented by no less than three major groups of temples: twelve *jyotir linga* ("lingam of light") temples, five *bhuti linga* temples and 68 *svayambhu linga* temples. There are also extensive temple circuits devoted to Mahadevi and Vishnu, as well as more localized south Indian groups of shrines dedicated to Murugan and those associated with the planets (the *Nava Graha Sthalas*) and natural places of spiritual significance, such as the four sites of the **Kumbh Mela** (Allahabad, Haridwar, Ujjain and Nasik).

▼ Srirangam Temple complex

Hindu pilgrims at the Kumbh Mela ▲

Brightly decorated Hindu shrine ▼

Ten famous pilgrimage places

Varanasi The most famous pilgrimage site in India, sacred to Shiva, and the place where many Indians come to die and be cremated. See p.318.

Haridwar Literally the door (*dwar*) of God (*Hari*). The place where the Ganges leaves the Himalayas for the plains, and one of the four locations of the Kumbh Mela. See p.354.

Allahabad The meeting point of the Ganges and the Yamuna, India's two holiest rivers, and home to the Maha Kumbh Mela, the world's largest religious festival. See p.312.

Shatrunjaya The holiest of all Jain pilgrimage sites, with more than nine hundred temples clustered atop a fragment of mountain on which the first Jain *tirthankara*, Adinath, gained enlightenment. See p.664.

Puri The eastern of the four Char Dham, and home to the great temple of Lord Jagannath, in whose honour the vast Rath Yatra is held. See p.1021.

Tirupati Sacred to Vishnu, this dramatic Andhran hilltop shrine complex is said to attract more pilgrims than either Rome or Mecca. See p.1057.

Sabarimala This remote Keralan shrine is said to be the second most popular pilgrimage site in the world. See p.1219.

Tiruvanamalai One of the twelve *bhuti linga* temples, sacred to Shiva, and the site of his famous manifestation as a lingam of fire. See p.1124.

Srirangam The largest temple complex in India and the most important of the country's 108 principal Vishnu shrines, housing a revered image of the god reclining on the coils of the snake Adisesha. See p.1149.

Rameshwaram One of the finest temples in the south, and one of the most famous of the twelve *jyotir linga* temples, sacred to Shiva. See p.1161.

temple. Express enough interest and you'll be shown some of the better-quality pieces for which Pipli is justly famed. Bedspreads, wall-hangings and small chhatris (awnings normally hung above household and temple shrines) are about the most authentic goods on offer. The shops do not open early; the best time to wander around is in the evening, when gas lamps, devotional music and gentle bargaining make the experience much more atmospheric.

Ratnagiri, Udayagiri and Lalitgiri

Nestled among picturesque verdant hills, 95km northeast of Bhubaneswar, are the remains of three Buddhist universities, **Ratnagiri**, **Udayagiri** and **Lalitgiri** (daily 9am–5pm; Rs100 [Rs5], video camera Rs25). The sites lie around 10km apart and are best reached in a day-trip from Bhubaneswar by hiring a car from the OTDC office (Rs900). They are relatively inaccessible by public transport, which involves catching a bus north along NH-5 as far as **Chandikohl** (60km) and then picking up an auto-rickshaw to take you southeast along NH5a towards the triangle of sites. The roundtrip from Chandikohl to the sites and back is around 60km. If you need to stay overnight before returning to Bhubaneswar, basic accommodation is available at the OTDC *Panthasala* (book through OTDC Cuttack to give the warden notice that food is required; ☎0671/231 2225; ❷), a short way east of the Ratnagiri turn-off on the main road.

Ratnagiri

RATNAGIRI, the most impressive of the sites, lies 20km from the main road, on top of a hill overlooking the River Keluo. When the Chinese chronicler Hiuen T'sang visited the university in 639 AD, it had already been a major Buddhist centre for at least two hundred years. In those days the sea reached much further inland, and would have been visible from this point – which may in part account for the choice of location. **Missionaries** were trained in such places before being sent abroad to spread the Buddha's message in China and Southeast Asia.

Two **monasteries** lie below the enormous stupa at the top of the hill. The larger and better preserved of the pair, dating from the seventh century, has a paved courtyard surrounded by cells and a beautifully carved doorway made from local blue-green chlorite stone. The shrine inside houses a majestic khondalite Buddha. A **museum** (10am–5pm, closed Fri; Rs2) houses the antiquities and architectural remains collected from the excavations at all three sites.

Udayagiri

Ten kilometres back towards the main road, **UDAYAGIRI** is the largest Buddhist complex in Orissa. Its main structure is a large stupa, better preserved than its counterpart at Ratnagiri. Of the two monasteries here, which flourished between the seventh and twelfth centuries, only one has been excavated. It features a large seated Buddha in its central shrine and an intricately carved entrance, along with an inscribed step-well. More rock-cut sculptures adorn the crest of the hill behind the monastery.

Lalitgiri

The turning for **LALITGIRI** is about 10km further along the main road towards Paradip. Most of the ruins of the four monasteries here are thought to date from around the ninth century, although inscriptions on an apsidal temple suggest that the site may have been occupied as early as the first century AD. Excavations in 1982 of the large stupa at the top of the hill revealed a gold casket containing a fragment of bone, believed to be a relic of the Buddha.

The hill-top provides a panoramic across the lush green paddy fields of the plains below to the hills of the sister sites.

Northern Orissa

Cuttack, Orissa's second city, straddles the Mahanadi, its chaotic concrete centre packed on to an island in the river. Devoid of noteworthy historic monuments and with an uncommonly drab bazaar, it detains few travellers on the long journey to or from Kolkata (Calcutta). Once clear of Cuttack's polluted outskirts, however, you soon find yourself amid the flat paddy fields, palm groves and mud-walled villages of the **Mahanadi Delta**. Twisting through it is one of India's busiest transport arteries; the main railway line and NH-5 follow the path of the famous pilgrim trail, the **Jagannath Sadak**, which once led from Calcutta to Puri.

The two attractions for which it's worth venturing off the main drag are **Similipal National Park**, close to the border with West Bengal, and the **Bhitarkanika Wildlife Sanctuary**, 130km northeast of Bhubaneswar. Both offer outstanding natural scenery, an abundance of fauna and flora, and an opportunity to escape the perpetual crowds of Orissa's towns and cities.

Bhitarkanika Wildlife Sanctuary

Covering an area of 672 square kilometres overlying the Brahmani-Baitarani delta, the mangrove forests and wetlands of the **BHITARKANIKA WILDLIFE SANCTUARY** constitute one of the richest ecosystems of its type in India. As well as over 200 species of bird, it's a refuge for saltwater crocodiles, monitor lizards, rhesus monkeys and a host of other reptiles and mammals, and incorporates the Olive Ridley turtle nesting beaches at Gahirmatha, Rushikulya and Devi.

Practicalities

Bhitarkanika is open throughout the year, but the best time to visit is November to March, when most of the migratory birds that flock to the sanctuary are in situ, although the nesting season for the herons usually ends around the middle of November. If you're hoping to witness the arrival of Olive Ridley turtles, check first at the OTDC tourist office in Bhubaneswar to find out exactly when – or if – they are expected. Other highlights include the crocodile conservation programme at Dangmar Island and the heronry at Bagagahana.

The hassle of reaching one of Bhitarkanika's entry points, obtaining permits (Rs1000 [Rs20]) and boat transport (expect to pay up to Rs2000 per day) and – if you're staying overnight in the sanctuary – accommodation, means it's easier to take an **organized trip**. Discover Tours in Bhubaneswar (☏0674/243 0477, Ⓦ www.orissadiscover.com) offers a four-day package; Heritage Tours in Puri (☏06752/223656, Ⓦ www.heritagetoursorissa.com) is also reliable.

To keep costs to a minimum it's possible to use the small port of **Chandbali**, reached by bus from Bhubaneswar (190km), or Bhadrak (the nearest railhead; 60km), as a base for day-trips into the sanctuary. There are a number of agents based around the jetty that can arrange permits and transport. If you want to obtain the permit yourself you'll need to contact the somewhat elusive Assistant Conservator of Forests, also based at the jetty (☏06786/220372). Chandbali's best **accommodation** is at the OTDC *Ayanyaniwas* (☏06786/220397; ❶–❸), near the jetty, which has a cheap dorm (Rs90) and a good restaurant. Alternatively,

Sea turtles

Every year around February and March, a strip of beach at the end of Orissa's central river delta witnesses one of the world's most extraordinary natural spectacles. Having swum right across the Pacific and Indian oceans, an average of around 200,000 female **Olive Ridley marine turtles** crawl onto the sand to nest. Almost as soon as the egg laying is complete, they're off again into the surf to begin the journey back to their mating grounds on the other side of the world.

No one knows quite why they travel such distances, but for local villagers the arrival of the giant turtles has traditionally been something of a boon. Turtle soup for breakfast, lunch and tea . . . and extra cash from market sales. Over the years the annual slaughter began to turn into a green gold rush, and turtle numbers plummeted drastically until a wildlife reserve was set up in 1975 at the personal behest of Indira Gandhi. Today, the Bhitarkanika Sanctuary on **Gahirmatha beach**, 130km northeast of Bhubaneswar, is a safe haven for the creatures. Weeks before the big three- or four-day invasion, coastguards monitor the shoreline and armed rangers ensure that poachers are kept at bay. For wildlife enthusiasts it's a field day.

In recent years, however, **environmental threats** have impacted on the turtles' habitat. Several hundred local families have begun to cultivate land within the sanctuary, water quality has been jeopardized by the growth of illegal prawn farms, and trawlers have been caught illegally fishing in the area without "turtle excluder devices" (TEDs). The turtles are further menaced by industrial pollution and the on-going construction of a large seaport at Dhamra, just 15km from Gahirmatha. Several conservation organizations, including Greenpeace and the Worldwide Fund for Nature, are monitoring the area and whilst 2007 saw some 130,000 turtles nesting at Gahirmatha, in other years none come at all.

the *Swagat Lodge* (☎6786/220225; ❶–❷) has diminutive but habitable rooms. Within the sanctuary itself, accommodation is in dormitories or double rooms with shared bathrooms at one of the forest lodges at Dangmal, Ekakula, Gupti or Habalikathi (all ❶–❸). You need to bring your own food and water, which the *chowkidar* will cook for you. Unless you use an agent, the only way to book this accommodation is in advance through the Divisional Forest Officer in the less than accessible outpost of Rajnagar (☎06729/272460).

Similipal National Park

In 1979 an area of 2750 square kilometres west of the town of Baripada was declared a wildlife sanctuary – primarily in an attempt to revive its dwindling population of **tigers** (see "Wildlife" in Contexts). Prior to this it had been the exclusive preserve of the Maharaja of Mayurbhunj, who used the woods as a private hunting ground and source of timber. Six years later **SIMILIPAL** was officially designated a **national park**, and the following year became the site of one of India's first Project Tiger reserves.

One of the last true wildernesses in eastern India, Similipal deserves to be a major attraction. The fact that it isn't has less to do with the amount of wildlife within its borders than with its comparative inaccessibility and the convoluted process of booking the rudimentary accommodation available within the park. If you overcome these obstacles, however, the rewards more than compensate. Apart from the elusive tigers – park rangers, perhaps a touch optimistically, claim they number almost one hundred, alongside a slightly larger number of equally secretive leopards – the reserve boasts sloth bears, *sambar* and spotted deer, barking deer, *gaur*, rhesus and langur monkeys; evening walks near the forest resthouses might yield sightings of mongoose, ratel badgers, porcupines, civets, jungle cats, foxes and jackals. Herds of wild **elephant** are common, and the park's pools and lakes also support marsh crocodiles, pythons, fishing cats and monitor lizards. There are reportedly 231 species of **bird** here, too, including colourful trogons, barbets, hornbills, thrushes, orioles, woodpeckers, parakeets, bee-eaters, spurfowl and jungle fowl. The landscape itself is equally rich, with a backdrop of beautiful granite hills, and a tranquil and pristine old-growth *sal* forest; no less than 1076 species of plant have been recorded here, including an impressive 87 different varieties of orchid. The majority of the tigers and leopards normally reside in the core zone (845 sq km), to which visitors have limited access, but the numerous waterfalls, grazing areas and water holes in the buffer zone (1905 sq km), linked with the lodges by unsurfaced but driveable roads, offer outstanding wildlife-viewing.

Similipal is open from November to mid-June, but the ideal **visiting season** ends in February. Access via either of the two entrance points (Pithabata, 25km from Baripada, and Tulsibani, 15km from Jashipur) requires a day-permit, which can only be purchased on the day of entry, or an accommodation permit allowing you to stay at one of the lodges inside the park for up to three nights, which, except in the case of one lodge, requires advance booking. Either way, the **daily fee** is Rs1000 [Rs40] plus Rs100 per vehicle, and Rs100 camera charge. Without your own vehicle, the only way to get around is to rent a Jeep; expect this to cost Rs1000–1500 per day; a guide will cost a further Rs400–600.

Access to the park by day-permit

Day-permits are available from the entrance gates from 6am to midday, and day-permit holders have to leave the park no later than 5pm. Unless you're coming by car from Kolkata, the more convenient base for access by day-permit is **BARIPADA** on the eastern side. The headquarters of the Mayurbhunj district (pronounced "marvunj"), Baripada is relatively easy to reach from the coastal artery; from Bhubaneswar, the Bhubaneswar-Baripada Express #2892 (Sun, Wed, Fri; 5hr) arrives at 10.30pm. Alternatively, regular buses run from Baleshwar (Balasore) to Baripada (1–2hr). Baripada itself possesses few sights to speak of, though it's a good place to experience small-town Orissan life, with a tumbledown bazaar and whitewashed **Jagannath temple**. Dotted around the outskirts, quietly decaying bungalows and civic buildings survive from the days of the Raj, when Mayurbhunj was a semi-autonomous princely state (one of the last to join independent India). For centuries it remained under the **Bhanja** kings, a reputedly "progressive" ruling family favoured by the British, whose present incumbent still lives in an incongruous Neoclassical mansion overlooking the river in the north of town.

Arriving in Baripada, **buses** pass the temple at the bottom of the broad main street and then head up the hill to the bus stand and market. From here it's a five-minute walk to the most central **hotels**, of which the *Ambika* (☎06792/252557; ❶–❹), with variously priced attached rooms, all with frames for the much-needed mosquito nets, is the best. Alternatively, the *Sibapriya* (☎06792/259103; ❶–❹) is well run, while the simple *Bishram* (☎06792/253535; ❶–❷) is the best-value budget option. Baripada's premier **restaurant** is on the ground floor of the *Ambika*. The OTDC tourist office (Mon–Fri 10am–5pm; ☎06792/252710), five minutes' walk from the bus stand in the opposite direction, is the best place to arrange transport and guides for Similipal, or ask the manager at the *Ambika*.

An alternative base is **JASHIPUR**, three hours' bus ride west of Baripada, which is closer to several points of interest within the park. There are just four

hotels in this small town: the *Sairam* (☎06797/232827; ❶–❹), on the main road, is by far the most comfortable and can help with organizing transport and guides. There's no tourist office in Jashipur, so to organize entry to the park, contact the Jashipur Assistant Conservator of Forests (☎06797/232474).

Staying overnight within Similipal

Staying at one of the seven **lodges** (all ❷–❹) within Similipal allows time to see more of the park. The best from the point of view of spotting wildlife is *Chahala* (83km from Baripada, 35km from Jashipur), one of the maharaja's former hunting lodges, situated just inside the core zone near a salt-lick where animals congregate in the evenings. As with all accommodation in the park, facilities are very basic. You have to bring your own food, though all utensils are provided and the *chowkidar* will cook for you. The other lodges are *Barehipani* (73km from Baripada, 52km from Jashipur), a small wooden lodge with wide verandas near a waterfall, offering impressive views; *Newana* (60km from Jashipur), nestled at the bottom of a deep valley; *Gudugudia* (25km from Jashipur), said to be particularly good for bird-watching and orchids; *Jamuani* (25km from Jashipur), a replica tribal hut in a forest clearing; and *Joranda* (64km from Baripada, 72km from Jashipur), which has a bit of everything and a waterfall. The only lodge not requiring advance permission is the *Aranya Niwas* at Lulung, 35km from Baripada, which should be booked through the OTDC tourist office in Baripada (see opposite). Being just 10km inside the park, you're unlikely to see much wildlife here, but the rooms are pleasant, there's a cheap dorm (Rs90) and a decent restaurant.

Apart from the *Aranya Niwas*, the process for **booking the lodges** involves sending a written application at least 30 days in advance, listing the name, age, sex, nationality, passport number and visa validity for each member of the group, to the Field Director, Similipal Tiger Reserve, Bhanjpur, Baripada, Mayurbhanj, Orissa, 757002 (☎06792/252593, ✉bid_smitig@bsnl.in). You then receive a "Letter of Advice" requesting payment, which has to be made by demand draft. It's much easier to book an **organized tour** through a travel agent that will arrange permits, travel, food and accommodation: Heritage Tours in Puri (☎06752/223656, ⓦwww.heritagetoursorissa.com) or Discover Tours in Bhubaneswar (☎0674/243 0477, ⓦwww.orissadiscover.com) both offer packages, but will still need 30 days' notice.

Puri

As the home of Lord Jagannath and his siblings, **PURI** ranks among Hindu India's most important sacred sites, visited by a vast number of pilgrims each year. The crowds peak during the monsoons for **Rath Yatra**, the famous "Car Festival", when literally millions pour in to watch three giant, multicoloured chariots drawn up the main thoroughfare. At the centre of the maelstrom, the **Jagannath temple** soars above the town's medieval heart and colonial suburbs like some kind of misplaced space rocket. Non-Hindus aren't allowed inside its bustling precincts, but don't let this deter you; Puri's streets and beach remain the focus of intense devotional activity year round, while its bazaars are crammed with collectable religious souvenirs associated with the Lord Jagannath.

Three distinct types of visitor come to Puri: middle-class Bengalis lured by the combined pleasures of puja and promenade; young Western and Japanese backpackers enjoying the low-key travellers' scene; and the thousands of pilgrims from mostly rural eastern India who flock in to pay their respects to Lord Jagannath. Over the years the three have staked out their respective ends of town and stuck to them. It all makes for a rather bizarre and intoxicating atmosphere, where you can be transported from the intensity of Hindu India to the sea and back to the relative calm of your hotel veranda at the turn of a bicycle wheel.

Some history

Until the seventh and eighth centuries, Puri was little more than a provincial outpost along the coastal trade route linking eastern India with the south. Then, thanks to its association with the Hindu reformer **Shankaracharya** (Shankara), the town began to feature on the religious map. Shankara made Puri one of his four *mathas*, or centres for the practice of a radically new, and more ascetic form of Hinduism. Holy men from across the whole Subcontinent came here to debate the new philosophies – a tradition carried on in the town's temple court-yards to this day. With the arrival of the **Gangas** at the beginning of the twelfth century, this religious and political importance was further consolidated. In 1135, Anantavarman Chodaganga founded the great temple in Puri, and dedicated it to **Purushottama**, one of the thousand names of Vishnu – an ambitious attempt to integrate the many feudal kingdoms recently conquered by the Gangas. Under the Gajapati dynasty in the fifteenth century Purushottama's name changed to **Jagannath** ("Lord of the Universe"). Henceforth **Vaishnavism** and the devotional worship of Krishna, an incarnation of Vishnu, was to hold sway as the predominant religious influence in the temple. Puri is nowadays one of the four most auspicious pilgrimage centres, or *dhams*, in India.

Western-style leisure **tourism**, centred firmly on the town's long sandy beach, is a comparatively new phenomenon. The British were the first to spot Puri's potential as a resort. When they left, the Bengalis took over their bungalows, only to find themselves sharing the beach with an annual migration of young, chillum-smoking Westerners attracted to the town by its abundant hashish. Today, few vestiges of this era remain. Thanks to a concerted campaign by the municipality to clean up Puri's image, the "scene" has dwindled to little more than a handful of cafés, and is a far cry from the swinging hippy paradise some still arrive here hoping to find.

Arrival, information and city transport

Trains arriving at Puri's end-of-line **station**, in the north of town, are greeted by fired-up cycle rickshaw-wallahs sprinting alongside in the race to catch a foreigner. You'll encounter similar "rickshaw rage" at the main bus station and the Jagannath temple, caused by competition for the commission offered by the hotels. The bus stand is further in the north of the city, a ten-minute rickshaw ride from the centre through the bumpy back-streets. The OTDC **tourist office** on Station Road (Mon–Sat 10am–5pm, closed 2nd Sat of the month; ☏06752/222664) is friendly and helpful; the 24-hour counter at the railway station is a waste of time. Train travel arrangements are best made or checked directly with the station itself or through a travel agent.

Puri is fairly spread out but flat, so **bicycles** (Rs25–30 per day) are ideal for getting around and exploring the maze of streets around the Jagannath temple. There are several places to rent them on Chakra Tirtha (CT) Road, in the travellers' enclave between the *Gandhara International* and *Love and Life* – try Unique Tours opposite *Z* hotel. **Auto-rickshaws** are thin on the ground,

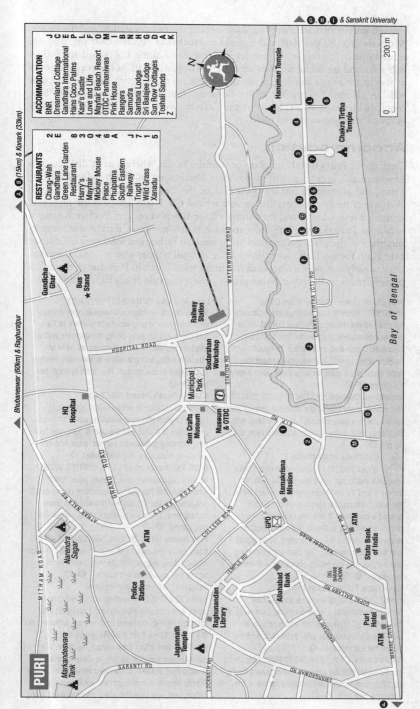

PURI

ACCOMMODATION
BNR	J
Dreamland Cottage	C
Gandhara International	E
Hans Coco Palms	P
Kasi's Castle	L
Love and Life	F
Mayfair Beach Resort	O
OTDC Panthaniwas	M
Pink House	I
Rangers	B
Samudra	N
Santana Lodge	H
Sri Balajee Lodge	G
Sun Row Cottages	D
Toshali Sands	A
Z	K

RESTAURANTS
Chung-Wah	2
Gandhara	E
Green Lane Garden Restaurant	8
Harry's	3
Mayfair	O
Mickey Mouse	4
Peace	A
Phulpatna	6
South Eastern Railway	J
Trupti	7
Wild Grass	1
Xanadu	5

▲ G, H, I & Sanskrit University

Bay of Bengal

Hanuman Temple

Chakra Tirtha Temple

WATERWORKS ROAD

CHAKRA TIRTHA (CT) RD

◀ Bhubaneswar (60km) & Raghurajpur

▲ A, B (15km) & Konark (33km)

Gundicha Ghar

Bus Stand

Railway Station

HOSPITAL ROAD

Sudarshan Workshop

STATION RD

Municipal Park

Museum & OTDC

Sun Crafts Museum

HQ Hospital

GRAND ROAD

CLARKE ROAD

Ramakrisna Mission

COLLEGE ROAD

GPO

ATHAR NAIKA RD

ATM

Narendra Sagar

MITHAM ROAD

Markandesvara Tank

Police Station

Raghunandan Library

Jagannath Temple

GARANTI RD

LOCKNATH RD

TEMPLE RD

Allahabad Bank

DIG BARANI CHOWK

GOPAL BALLABH RD

Puri Hotel

ATM

MARINE DRIVE

SWARGADWAR RD

BADSAHI RD

KACHERI ROAD

VIP RD

State Bank of India

ATM

N

0   200 m

1023

though one or two are always hanging around the railway station and the hotels. **Mopeds** (Rs180 per day) and Enfield **motorbikes** (Rs250–300 per day) are rented out by a couple of travel agents and shops along CT Road for full or half-days and are useful for trips up the coast to Konark. In-house **travel agents** at the larger hotels can help with all transport arrangements, though the most reliable all-round place for ticket booking, flights and car/motorcycle/bike rental is Heritage Tours, based at the *Mayfair Beach Resort* (℡06752/223656, ⓦ www.heritagetoursorissa.com).

Accommodation

Virtually all Puri's **hotels** stand on or near the beach, where a strict distinction is observed: the hotels pitched at domestic tourists are lined up behind Marine Drive, the promenade on the west end of the beach, while budget-conscious Westerners are sandwiched further east around CT Road between the high-rise, upmarket resort hotels and the fishing village; this backpackers' enclave is known locally as **Pentakunta**. The less expensive hotels are quiet during the summer months, but the pricier accommodation tends to be booked solid well in advance over Rath Yatra, which coincides with the Bengali holiday season – make reservations as early as possible. Checkout is 8am for most hotels in Puri due to the influx of early trains to the town, although off-season this rule is less rigidly enforced.

BNR (*South Eastern Railway Hotel*) CT Rd ℡06752/222063, ⓔ bnr@hotmail.com. Recently refurbished but retaining much of the old-world charm that made it the premier bolt-hole for Calcutta's burra- and memsahibs. Turbaned bearers with big belts pad barefoot around the wide verandas. A must for Rajophiles, even if only for dinner. ④–⑤

Dreamland Cottage off CT Rd ℡06752/224122. Not exactly roses around the door, but homely and relaxed, with a leafy secluded garden dotted with birdcages. Five rooms all with attached bath, but no a/c. ①

Gandhara International CT Rd ℡06752/224117, ⓦ www.hotelgandhara .com. Rooms to suit most budgets, all with hot showers and TV, and most giving excellent views of the surrounding area; also has dorms (Rs50) around a courtyard. It has two roof terraces and a restaurant serving authentic Japanese food on request, as well as Internet, a good travel agent, and free poste restante. The staff are welcoming and helpful, and the beach opposite is relatively salubrious. ①–⑥

Hans Coco Palms Marine Drive ℡06752/230038, ⓦ www.hanshotels.com. Modern complex in a superb setting 2km west of the centre; all rooms are a/c and overlook the sea. There's a pool, bar and restaurant, and the beach here is pleasant. ⑧

Kasi's Castle CT Rd ℡06752/224522. Welcoming family house offering irregular but excellent home-cooking. Nine simple, unblemished rooms, each with attached bath. ②–④

Love and Life CT Rd ℡06752/224433, ⓕ 226093, ⓔ loveandlife@hotmail.com. Popular with the many young Japanese visitors to Puri, this place has an easy-going atmosphere and a good restaurant. The clean rooms all have an attached bath, and are either in the main block or in cottages in the garden. The dorm is Rs50 per bed. ①–⑤

Mayfair Beach Resort Off CT Rd ℡06752/227800, ⓦ www.mayfairhotels.com. Luxury chalets and rooms looking down through palm trees to a pool and the beach. Five-star facilities, including a massage parlour, a bar and an excellent restaurant. Recommended. ⑧

OTDC Panthaniwas off CT Rd ℡06752/222562, ⓦ www.panthanivas.com. A good-value hotel, where some of the plain but spacious rooms catch sea breezes; the old Raj-era building has more atmosphere. There's a pleasant restaurant, a bar and garden. ②–⑤

Pink House Off CT Rd ℡06752/222253. Laid-back, pinky-red pad, right on the beach at the edge of the fishing village, with its very own travellers' scene and an adjacent restaurant. ①–②

Rangers Puri-Konark Marine Drive ℡06752/211057, ⓔ freethinker.sanjay@gmail .com. Two cottages (Rs450) and a camping area (pitches; Rs200) secluded among trees adjacent to the beach, 15km from Puri (Rs100 by auto-rickshaw) and 20km from Konark. As close to a lonely beach paradise as you're likely to find around Puri, but less convenient for actually visiting Puri or Konark. A restaurant serves Chinese and Indian food, and bicycles, kites, parasail and fishing equipment can be hired from the knowledgeable and friendly owner, Mr Samantaray. ②–③

Samudra Off CT Rd ☎06752/222705 ℱ06752/228654. One of the best mid-range hotels in Puri. The light and airy rooms all have balconies facing the sea; in the tranquillity of the evening you can hear the waves breaking on the beach. Good restaurant serving excellent Puri bhaji for breakfast. ③–⑤

Santana Lodge At the very end of CT Rd ☎06752/251491, ℮hotelsantana@hotmail.com. Small, pleasant hotel geared up for travellers; especially popular with the Japanese. Prices include breakfast and communal dinner. ①–②

Sri Balajee Lodge CT Rd ☎06752/223388. Some way beyond most of the other hotels, this small lodge has simple rooms around a colourful courtyard. ①–③

Sun Row Cottages CT Rd ☎06752/223259, ℮chitranjan@hotmail.com. Little cottages, each with a private veranda, big cane chairs and attached bath. Rates are reduced for long stays. ①–②

Toshali Sands Konark Rd ☎06752/250571, ℀www.toshalisands.com. Self-styled "ethnic village" 9km north of town, consisting of a/c cottages grouped around a garden and pool. Good restaurant, gym and sauna; ideal for families. Doubles from $45. ⑧–⑨

Z CT Rd ☎06752/222554, ℀www.zhotelindia .com. An institution, the Z (pronounced "jed") made its name by providing cheap, clean and comfortable rooms. Prices are higher now, but the rooms are still pleasant and there are plenty of communal areas, including a large garden and a common room with TV. Women-only dorm (Rs75) also available. ②–③

The Jagannath temple

The mighty **Jagannath temple** in Puri is one of the four holy *dhams*, or "abodes of the divine", drawing pilgrims, or *yatris*, here to spend three auspicious days and nights near Lord Jagannath, the presiding deity. The present temple structure, modelled on the older Lingaraj temple in Bhubaneswar, was erected at the start of the twelfth century by the Ganga ruler Anantavarman Chodaganga.

Non-Hindu visitors, despite the temple's long-standing "caste no bar" rule, are obliged to view proceedings from the flat roof of the **Raghunandan Library** (Mon–Sat 10am–noon & 4–6pm), directly opposite the main gate.

One of the librarians will show you up the stairs to the vantage point overlooking the East Gate. You should make a donation for this service – but don't believe the large sums written in the ledger. From the rooftop a fine view encompasses the immense **deul**, at 65m by far the loftiest building in the entire region. Archeologists have removed the white plaster from the tower to expose elaborate **carving** similar to that on the Lingaraj. Crowning the very top, a long scarlet pennant and the eight-spoked wheel (*chakra*) of Vishnu announce the presence of Lord Jagannath within.

The pyramidal roofs of the temples' adjoining halls, or *mandapas*, rise in steps towards the tower. The one nearest the sanctuary, the *jagamohana* (Assembly Hall), is part of the original building, but the other two, the smaller *nata mandir* (Dance Hall) and the *bhoga-mandapa* (Hall of Offerings) nearest the entrance, were added in the fifteenth and sixteenth centuries. These halls still see a lot of action during the day as worshippers file through for *darshan*, while late every night they become the venue for devotional music. Female and transvestite dancers (*maharis* and *gotipuas*) once performed episodes from Jayadev's *Gita Govinda*, the much-loved story of the life of Krishna, for the amusement of Lord Jagannath and his siblings. Nowadays, piped songs have replaced the traditional theatre.

Outside the main building, at the left end of the walled compound surrounding the temple, are the **kitchens**. The food prepared here, known as *mahaprashad*, and blessed by Lord Jagannath, is said to be so pure that even a morsel taken from the mouth of a dog and fed to a brahmin by a Harijan (an "untouchable") will cleanse the body of sin. Devotees mill around carrying pieces of broken pots full of dhal and rice; they can only offer food to the deity from an imperfect pot as

The Jagannath deities and Rath Yatra

Stand on any street corner in Orissa and you'll probably be able to spot at least one image of the black-faced **Jagannath deity**, with his brother **Balabhadra** and sister **Subhadra**. This faintly grotesque family trio, with glaring eyes, stumpy legless bodies, and undersized arms, seems to crop up everywhere.

The origins of this peculiar symbol are shrouded in **legend**. One version relates that the image of Lord Jagannath looks the way it does because it was never actually finished. King Indramena, a ruler of ancient Orissa, once found the god Vishnu in the form of a tree stump washed up on Puri beach. He carried the lump of wood to the temple and, following instructions from Brahma, called the court carpenter Visvakarma to carve out the image. Visvakarma agreed – on condition that no one set eyes on the deity until it was completed. The king, however, unable to contain his excitement, peeped into the workshop; Visvakarma, spotting him, downed tools and cast a spell on the deity so that no one else could finish it.

Rath Yatra

The Jagannath deities are also the chief focus of Puri's annual "Car Festival", the **Rath Yatra** – just one episode in a long cycle of rituals that begins in the full moon phase of the Oriya month of Djesto (June & July). In the first of these, the **Chandan Yatra**, special replicas of the three temple deities are taken to the **Narendra Sagar** where for 21 consecutive days they are smeared with *chandan* (sandalwood paste) and rowed around in a ceremonial, swan-shaped boat. At the end of this period, in a ceremony known as **Snana Yatra**, the three go for a dip in the tank, after which they head off for fifteen days of secluded preparation for Rath Yatra.

The Car Festival proper takes place during the full moon of the following month, Asadho (July & Aug). Lord Jagannath and his brother and sister are placed in their chariots and dragged by 4200 honoured devotees through the assembled multitudes to their summer home, the **Gundicha Ghar** ("Garden House"), 1.5km away. If you can find a secure vantage point and escape the crush, it's an amazing sight. The immense chariots are draped with brightly coloured cloth and accompanied down Grand Road by elephants, the local raja (who sweeps the chariots as a gesture of humility and equality with all castes) and a cacophony of music and percussion. Each chariot has a different name and a different-coloured cover, and is built anew every year to rigid specifications laid down in the temple's ancient manuals. Balabhadra's *rath*, the green one, leads; Subhadra is next, in black; and lastly, in the thirteen-metre-tall chariot with eighteen wheels and a vivid red and yellow drape, sits Lord Jagannath himself. It takes eight hours or more to haul the *raths* to their resting place. After a nine-day holiday, the sequence is performed in reverse, and the three deities return to the temple to resume their normal lives.

Conventional wisdom has it that the procession commemorates Krishna's journey from Gokhul to Mathura; historians cite the similarity between the *raths* and temple towers to claim it's a hangover from the time when temples were made of wood. Whatever the reason for the Car Festival, its devotees take it very seriously indeed. Early travellers spoke of fanatics throwing themselves under the gigantic wheels as a short cut to eternal bliss (whence the English word "**Juggernaut**", meaning an "irresistible, destructive force"). Contemporary enthusiasts are marginally more restrained, but like most mass gatherings in India, the whole event teeters at times on the brink of complete mayhem.

Lord Jagannath is the only perfection in this world. Among the ten thousand or so daily recipients of the *mahaprashad* are the six thousand employees of the temple itself. These **servants** are divided into 96 hereditary and hierarchical orders known as *chhatisha niyoga*, and include the priests who minister to the needs of the deities (teeth cleaning, dressing, feeding, getting them ready for afternoon siesta, and so forth), as well as the teams of craftspeople who produce all the materials required for the daily round of rituals.

Around the temple

The crowded streets **around the Jagannath temple** buzz with activity – commercial as much as religious. **Grand Road**, Puri's broad main thoroughfare, is lined with a lively **bazaar**, many of its stalls specializing in *rudraksha malas* (Shaivite "rosaries" made of 108 beads), Ayurvedic cures and the ubiquitous images of Lord Jagannath. Look out too for the wonderful "religious maps" of Puri.

Leading south from the main square in the temple surrounds, **Swargadwar** ("Cremation") **Road** leads through a dingy bazaar to the main promenade. The cremation ground itself, situated well beyond the south corner of the beach, is among India's most auspicious mortuary sites, where inquisitive tourists are definitely not welcome.

A more enjoyable foray from the main square is the trip to the **sacred tanks** in the north of town (best attempted by bicycle). Follow the north wall of the Jagannath temple up to the little road junction in the far corner, then turn right and stick to the same narrow twisting backstreet for about a kilometre until you arrive at the **Markandesvara tank**. This large, steep-sided bathing place is said to have been the spot where Vishnu once resided in the form of a neem tree while his temple was buried deep under a sand dune. There's no sign of the tree, but the temples on the south side are worth a look, particularly the smaller of the group, which contains images of the Jagannath trio.

If you retrace your route from here back down the lane as far as the first road junction, then bear left and continue for another kilometre or so, you'll emerge at the **Narendra Sagar**, Puri's most holy tank. A small temple stands in the middle, joined to the *ghats* by a narrow footbridge. During the annual **Chandan Yatra**, a replica deity of Lord Jagannath, Madan Mohan, is brought here every day for his dip. The temple itself is plastered with vivid **murals** that you can photograph on payment of the set fee listed nearby. The list also advertises the range of services offered by the temple *pujaris*, including the unlikely sounding "throw of bone" and "throw of hair" – references to the tank's role as another of Puri's famous mortuary ritual sites.

Museums and the Sudarshan workshop

The **Sun Crafts Museum** (daily 6am–10pm; free) showcases the more commercial side of the Lord Jagannath phenomenon. Run by a Hare Krishna devotee, it houses an extensive collection of images of the deity and his siblings, in various forms. There is also a workshop where little wooden replicas are carved and painted, before being dispatched to ISKCON centres around the world. A more controversial image of Lord Jagannath is the one depicting him mounted on the centre of a Christian crucifix – some regard it as a symbolic demand for religious tolerance in light of recent hostility between Hindus and Christians in Orissa. You may have to ask discreetly to be shown it.

Puri's small **museum** (Tues–Sun 10am–5pm; free), above the tourist office on Station Road, houses tacky reproductions of the Jagannath deities' ceremonial garb and models of the *raths* used in the Car Festival, but little else of note.

Further down the road towards the railway station, the **Sudarshan workshop** is one of the few traditional stone-carvers' yards left in Puri. The sculptors and their apprentices are more interested in pursuing their art than selling it to tourists, but gladly direct potential customers to the factory **shop** next door. Most of the pieces here are large religious icons carved out of khondalite – the multicoloured stone used in the Sun Temple at Konark.

The beach

If a peaceful swim and a lie in the sun are your top priorities, you may be disappointed with **Puri beach**; the stretch in front of the fishing village has become a three-kilometre-long open-air toilet and rubbish dump. For a more salubrious dip, press on beyond the Sanskrit University, 3km further east.

In the west end of town, along **Marine Parade**, the atmosphere is more akin to a British Victorian holiday resort. This stretch is very much the domain of the domestic tourist industry and the beach is much cleaner here. It's a pleasant place to stroll and becomes highly animated after sunset when the nightly souvenir market gets going.

Local fishermen patrol the beach as **lifeguards**; recognizable by their triangular straw hats and *dhotis*, they wade with their punters into the surf and literally hold their hands to keep them on their feet – the **undertow** claims victims every year, so weak swimmers should be careful. When not saving lives, the fishermen are busy at the CT Road end of the beach, engaged in the more traditional industries of mending nets and boats. The **fishing village** is one of the biggest in Orissa, with dozens of tiny sails tacking to and fro off the coast during the day. Once landed, the catch is taken in baskets to the **fish market** in the village.

Eating

Most of the restaurants and cafés along CT Road offer inexpensive thalis, and there's good **fresh fish** to be had, though better food can be found at the

Orissan art and artists

Few regions of India retain as rich a diversity of **traditional art forms** as Orissa. While a browse through the bazaars and emporia in Puri and Bhubaneswar provides a good idea of local styles and techniques, a trip out to the **villages** where the work is actually produced is a much more memorable way to shop. Different villages specialize in different crafts – a division that harks back to the origins of the caste system in Orissa. Patronage from the nobility and wealthy temples during medieval times allowed local artisans, or *shilpins*, to refine their skills over generations. As the market for arts and crafts expanded, notably with the rise of **Puri** as a pilgrimage centre, **guilds** were formed to control the handing down of specialist knowledge and separate communities established to carry out the work. Today, the demand for **souvenirs** has given many old art forms a new lease of life.

- **Stone sculpture** With modern temples increasingly being built out of reinforced concrete, life for Orissa's stone sculptors is getting tougher. To see them at work, head for Pathuria Sahi ("Stonecarvers' Lane") and the famous Sudarshan workshop in **Puri** (see p.1027), where mastercraftsmen and apprentices still fashion Hindu deities and other votive objects according to specifications laid down in ancient manuals.

- **Painting** *Patta chitra*, classical Orissan painting, is closely connected with the Jagannath cult. Traditionally, artists were employed to decorate the inside of the temples in Puri and to paint the deities and chariots used in the Rath Yatra. Later, the same vibrant colour-schemes and motifs were transferred to lacquered cloth or palm leaves and sold as sacred souvenirs to visiting pilgrims. In the village of **Raghurajpur** near Puri, where the majority of the remaining artists, or *chitrakaras*, now live, men use paint made from the local mineral stones. Specialities include sets of *ganjiffa* – small round cards used to play a trick-taking game based on the struggle between Rama and the demon Ravana, as told in the Ramayana.

nearby resort hotels. An interesting alternative to restaurant fare is the sacred food, or *mahaprasad*, the creation of four hundred cooks in the Jagannath temple kitchens, available from stalls in the nearby Anand Bazaar.

Chung-Wah *Hotel Lee Garden*, VIP Rd. Run by a Chinese family from Kolkata, this is one of Puri's most popular Chinese restaurants, with fast, efficient service and a good choice of fish dishes.

Gandhara *Gandhara International Hotel*, CT Rd. Primarily for hotel guests, but nonresidents can book in advance for excellent and authentic Japanese meals. Take a cold beer up onto the high roof terrace and enjoy the sea view.

Green Lane Garden Restaurant off CT Rd. Very good for seafood. The menu lists fewer dishes than are actually on offer, and if the fish of your choice isn't available at lunchtime there's a good chance the chef or one of his relatives will have caught it by evening.

Harry's CT Rd. One of the town's most popular budget places, this pure-veg restaurant serves tasty Indian food made without onions or garlic in Hare-Krishna tradition, and good freshly pressed juices.

Mayfair *Mayfair Beach Resort*, off CT Rd. Sophisticated place with an a/c indoor restaurant and an open-air-veranda dining room, this is Puri's best option for an extravagant evening away from dhal and rice. A top-class chef whips up a delicious and unusually adventurous menu, including Orissan seafood specialities (order 8hr in advance).

Mickey Mouse CT Rd. A popular place for a late-night drink, with the loudest music and the most original lampshades. Very laid-back service and chess sets provided.

Peace CT Rd. Friendly place, with tables in the garden, serving all the usual fare but specializing in seafood

Phulpatna *Toshali Sands*, Konark Rd. The distinguishing feature of the *Phulpatna*'s menu is that it includes recipes revived from Kalingan times. Regardless of their derivation, the dishes are delicious, and tables by the large bay windows give a relaxing view of the gardens below.

South Eastern Railway *BNR* hotel, CT Rd. Idiosyncratic colonial charm, with checked tablecloths,

- **Palm-leaf manuscripts** Palm leaves, or *chitra pothi*, have been used as writing materials in Orissa for centuries. Using a sharp stylus called a *lohankantaka*, the artist first scratches the text or design onto the surface of palm leaves, then applies a paste of turmeric, dried leaves, oil and charcoal. When the residue is rubbed off, the etching stands out more clearly. Palm-leaf flaps are often tied onto the structure so an innocent etching of an animal or deity can be lifted to reveal *Kama Sutra* action. The best places to see genuine antique palm-leaf books, however, are the National Museum in New Delhi or the State Museum in Bhubaneswar.

- **Textiles** Distinctive textiles woven on handlooms are produced throughout Orissa. Silk saris from **Brahmapur** and **Sambalpur** are the most famous, though *ikat*, which originally came to Orissa via the ancient trade links with Southeast Asia, is also typical. It is created using a tie-dye-like technique known as *bandha*, is also employed by weavers from the village of **Nuapatna**, 70km from Bhubaneswar, who produce silk *ikats* covered in verses from the scriptures for use in the Jagannath temple.

- **Appliqué** The village of **Pipli** (see p.1016) has the monopoly on appliqué, another craft rooted in the Jagannath cult. Geometric motifs and stylized birds, animals and flowers are cut from brightly coloured cloth and sewn onto black backgrounds. Pipli artists are responsible for the chariot covers used in the Rath Yatra as well as for the small canopies, or *chhatris*, suspended above the presiding deity in Orissan temples.

- **Metalwork** *Tarakashi* (literally "woven wire"), or silver filigree, is Orissa's best-known metalwork technique. Using lengths of wire made by drawing strips of silver alloy through small holes, the smiths create distinctive ornaments, jewellery and utensils for use in rituals and celebrations. The designs are thought to have come to India from Persia with the Mughals, though the existence of an identical art form in Indonesia, with whom the ancient Orissan kingdoms used to trade, suggests that the technique itself may be even older. *Tarakashi* is now only produced in any quantity in **Cuttack** and is becoming a dying art-form.

silver butter-dishes and waiters in pukka turbans. The poor-value set menus are less memorable. Non-residents should give a couple of hours' warning.

Trupti CT Rd. Indian veg restaurant serving a good range of regional thalis. Especially busy at lunchtime. Also has a sweet counter.

 Wild Grass Corner of VIP Rd and College Rd, 2km from the CT Rd ghetto. Popular with the locals, serving superb tandoori, seafood, vegetarian and Orissan dishes at very reasonable prices, with tables spread around a beautiful leafy garden. Open for lunch and dinner.

Xanadu CT Rd. Easily the best of the cheapies with a pleasant garden and extensive menu, including a special children's breakfast.

Listings

Banks and exchange The State Bank of India (Mon–Fri 10.30am–4pm, Sat 10.30am–1pm) beyond the *Nilachal Ashok Hotel*, on VIP Rd, will change American Express traveller's cheques and cash in US and Australian dollars and sterling, and has an ATM. You can also change money at a branch of the Allahabad Bank (Mon–Fri 10am–5pm, Sat 10am–1pm) on Temple Rd, 200m up from the GPO towards the temple, and Trade Wings above the *Travellers Inn* on CT Rd. There is an ICICI ATM near the Police Station on Grand Rd and Andhra Bank ATM near *Puri Hotel*, both take foreign cards.

Bookshops Loknath Bookshop next to *Raju's* restaurant on CT Rd. Books bought and sold, or you can use the extensive library upon paying a deposit of Rs300, with books lent at Rs12 per day.

Hospitals Puri's main "HQ" hospital (☏06752/223742) is well outside the town centre on Grand Rd. Hotels such as the *Panthaniwas*, or Heritage Tours at the *Mayfair* can help find a doctor in an emergency.

Internet access There are a number of places along CT Rd and on VIP Rd, but services can be slow and unreliable; the *Gandhara* hotel is good value at Rs30/hr, while Nanako.com nearby has a better connection than most others thereabouts.

Police The main station is on Grand Rd, near the Jagannath temple. There is another branch at the Kacheri Rd, VIP Rd junction (☏06952/222025).

Post office The GPO is on Kacheri Rd. For poste restante (Mon–Fri 10.30am–noon & 4–5.30pm, Sat 9am–noon), use the side door on the left of the building.

Shopping and markets Utkalika and the other handloom emporiums, just up from the GPO on Temple Rd, stock a good range of local crafts at fixed prices. Antique India, next to the *Holiday House* on CT Rd is good for antiques and jewellery. Sudarshan on Station Rd (close to the OTDC tourist office) is the best place to buy traditional stone sculpture. For reproductions of the Jagannath deity, look in the bazaar around the temple. For classical Orissan paintings visit the Patta Chitra Centre on Nabakalebar Rd. There's a lively market on the beach off Marine Drive, south of *Puri Hotel*, open every evening until around 10pm. Numerous shops along Marine Drive sell traditional hand-woven Orissan *ikat* saris and textiles.

Tours OTDC runs tour buses from in front of the *Panthaniwas* to nearby attractions including Bhubaneswar and Konark (Tues–Sat 6.30am–7pm; Rs130, a/c Rs160) and Chilika Lake (daily 6.30am–7.30pm; Rs110). Gandhara Travel, at the *Gandhara International Hotel*, does tours and ticketing and organizes trips to Konark during the dance festival. Heritage Tours (☏06752/223656, ⌨www.heritage toursorissa.com), based at the *Mayfair Beach Resort*, is well established and reliable and offers 6- to 10-day tribal tours in Orissa, as well as special-interest tours such as birdwatching and archeology. Grass Routes on CT Rd (☏06752/220560, ⌨www .grassroutesjourneys.com) arranges excellent tours of the area, including to Chilika Lake. It also runs tribal tours, and is one of the few operators in Orissa to show a genuine understanding of the impact of tourism upon *adivasi* communities.

Moving on from Puri

Puri is joined to the main Kolkata (Calcutta)–Chennai routes by a branch line of the busy South East **Train** network and a good metalled road through Bhubaneswar, so it's well connected with most other major Indian cities. Travel agents at major hotels and on CT Road can book tickets.

The Puri–New Delhi Express #2815 leaves at 10.50am (Mon, Wed, Thurs & Sat), calling at **Bhubaneswar**, **Gaya** and **Mughalsarai** (for Varanasi), and arrives in **Delhi** at 5pm the following day. The slower Neelachal Express #2875 (Tues, Fri & Sun) leaves Puri at the same time, calls at the same stations, but arrives in

Delhi at 9.40pm. A convenient train to **Kolkata (Calcutta)** is the Jagannath Express #8410, which leaves Puri at 10.30pm for the 10hr overnight trip. For central Indian destinations such as Nagpur, take one of the Ahmedabad expresses (#2843 on Tues, Thurs, Fri & Sun, or #8405 on Wed). Getting to **Mumbai** involves changing at Bhubaneswar and a total journey time of more than 40hr.

If you're heading for **south India**, it's also best to change at Bhubaneswar or Khurda Road, 44km from Puri, where you can pick up any of a number of daily trains to **Chennai** (20hr–21hr 20min), including the Coromandel Express #2841 or the slightly slower Howrah–Chennai Mail #2603 (both daily). Of the five weekly trains from Bhubaneswar to Thiruvananthapuram in Kerala, the Shalimar–Nagercoil Gurudev Express #2660 (Fri; 36hr 45min) is the fastest. Computerized reservations can be made at the main station in Puri (Mon–Sat 8am–8pm, Sun 8am–2pm) or through a travel agent.

There are hourly buses, although **minibuses** are the easiest way to travel, between Puri and **Bhubaneswar** (both Rs23). Services are fast (1hr) and frequent until 5pm, but make sure that it's "nonstop" before you get on. The same applies to Konark minibuses (Rs15), which also leave when full from the main city bus stand in the northeast of town, near the Gundicha Ghar. **Jeeps** ply the same route hourly for the same price, departing from the bus stand when full.

If you plan to head south by road along the Orissan coast, buses to **Satapada** on Chilika Lake leave every thirty minutes during the day from the main bus stand; some also go from outside the OTDC booking counter on Marine Drive.

See "Travel details" at the end of this chapter for more information on journey frequencies and durations.

Konark and around

Time runs like a horse with seven reins,
Thousand-eyed, unageing, possessing much seed. Him the poets mount; His wheels are all beings.

The *Artharva Veda*

If you see only one temple in Orissa, it should be **KONARK**, one of India's most visited ancient monuments. Standing imperiously in its compound of lawns and casuarina trees, 35km north of Puri, this majestic pile of oxidizing sandstone is considered to be the apogee of Orissan architecture and one of the finest religious buildings anywhere in the world.

The temple is all the more remarkable for having languished under a huge mound of sand since it fell into neglect around three hundred years ago. Not until the dune and heaps of collapsed masonry were cleared away from the sides, early in the twentieth century, did the full extent of its ambitious design become apparent. In 1924, the earl of Ronaldshay wrote of the newly revealed temple as "one of the most stupendous buildings in India which rears itself aloft, a pile of overwhelming grandeur even in its decay". A team of seven galloping horses and 24 exquisitely carved wheels found lining the flanks of a raised platform showed that the temple had been conceived in the form of a colossal chariot for the sun god **Surya**, its presiding deity. Equally sensational was the rediscovery among the ruins of some extraordinary **erotic sculpture**. Konark, like Khajuraho (see p.430), is plastered with loving couples locked in ingenious amatory postures drawn from the *Kama Sutra* – a feature that may well explain the comment made by one of Akbar's emissaries, Abul Fazl, in the sixteenth century: "Even those who are difficult to please," he enthused, "stand astonished at its sight."

Apart from the temple, a small **museum** and a fishing **beach**, Konark **village** has little going for it. Sundays and public holidays are particularly busy here: aim to stay until sunset after most of the tour groups have left, when the rich evening light works wonders on the natural colours in the khondalite sandstone.

Some history

Inscription plates attribute the founding of the temple to the thirteenth-century Ganga monarch **Narasimhadeva**, who may have built it to commemorate his military successes against the Muslim invaders. Local legend attributes its aura of power to the two very powerful magnets said to have been built into the tower, with the poles placed in such a way that the throne of the king was suspended in mid-air.

The temple's seventy-metre tower became a landmark for European mariners sailing off the shallow Orissan coast, who knew it as the "**Black Pagoda**", and the frequent incidence of shipping disasters along the coast was blamed on the effect of the aforesaid magnets on the tidal pattern. The tower also proved to be an obvious target for raids on the region. In the fifteenth century, Konark was sacked by the Yavana army, causing sufficient damage to allow the elements to get a foothold. As the sea receded, sand slowly engulfed the building and salty breezes set to work on the spongy khondalite, eroding the exposed surfaces and weakening the superstructure. By the end of the nineteenth century, the tower had disintegrated completely, and the porch lay buried up to its waist, prompting one art historian of the day to describe it as "an enormous mass of stones studded with a few peepal trees here and there".

Restoration only really began in earnest in 1901, when British archeologists set about unearthing the immaculately preserved hidden sections of the building and salvaging what they could from the rest of the rubble. Finally, trees were planted to shelter the compound from the corrosive winds, and a museum opened to house what sculpture was not shipped off to Delhi, Calcutta and London.

The temple

The main entrance to the **temple** complex (daily 9am–6pm; Rs250 [Rs10]) on its eastern, sea-facing side brings you out directly in front of the **bhoga-mandapa**, or "hall of offerings". Ornate carvings of amorous couples, musicians and dancers decorating the sides of its platform and stocky pillars suggest that the now roofless pavilion, a later addition to the temple, must originally have been used for ritual dance performances.

To get a sense of the overall scale and design, stroll along the low wall that bounds the south side of the enclosure before you tackle the ruins proper. As a giant model of Surya's war chariot, the temple was intended both as an offering to the Vedic sun god and as a symbol for the passage of time itself – believed to lie in his control. The seven **horses** straining to haul the sun eastwards in the direction of the dawn (only one is still intact) represent the days of the week. The **wheels** ranged along the base stand for the twelve months, each with eight spokes detailed with pictures of the eight ideal stages of a woman's day.

With the once-lofty **sanctuary tower** now reduced to little more than a clutter of sandstone slabs tumbling from the western wing, the **porch**, or *jagamohana*, has become Konark's real centrepiece. Its impressive pyramidal roof, rising to a height of 38m, is divided into three tiers by rows of lifelike statues – mostly musicians and dancers serenading the sun god on his passage through the heavens. Though now blocked up, the huge cubic **interior** of the porch was a marvel of medieval architecture. The original builders ran into problems

Even visitors who don't normally enjoy classical dance cannot fail to be seduced by the elegance and poise of Orissa's own regional style, **Odissi**. Friezes in the Rani Gumpha at Udaigiri (see p.1015) attest to the popularity of dance in the Orissan courts as far back as the second century BC. By the time the region's Hindu "golden age" was in full swing, it had become an integral part of religious ritual, with purpose-built dance halls, or *nata mandapas*, being added to existing temples and corps of dancing girls employed to perform in them. **Devadasis**, literally "wives of the god", were handed over by their parents at an early age and symbolically "married" to the deity. They were trained to read, sing and dance and, as one disapproving early nineteenth-century chronicler put it, to "make public traffic of their charms" with male visitors to the temple. Gradually, ritual intercourse (a legacy of the Tantric influence on medieval Hinduism) degenerated into pure prostitution, and dance, formerly an act of worship, grew to become little more than a form of commercial entertainment. By the colonial era, Odissi was all but lost.

Its resurgence followed the rediscovery in the 1950s of the **Abhinaya Chandrika**, a fifteenth-century manual on classical Orissan dance. Like Bharatanatyam, India's most popular dance style, Odissi has its own highly complex language of poses and steps. Based on the *tribhanga* "hip-shot" stance, movements of the body, hands and eyes convey specific emotions and enact episodes from well-known religious texts – most commonly the **Gita Govinda** (the Krishna story). Using the *Abhinaya* and temple sculpture, dancers and choreographers were able to reconstruct this grammar into a coherent form and within a decade Odissi was a thriving performance art once again. Today, dance lessons with a reputed guru have become *de rigueur* for the young daughters of Orissa's middle classes – an ironic reversal of its earlier associations.

Unfortunately, catching a **live performance** is a matter of being in the right place at the right time. The only regular recitals take place in the Jagannath temple. If, however, you're not a Hindu, the annual **festival of dance** at Konark, in the first week of December, is your best chance of seeing Orissa's top performers. If you're keen to learn, a number of dance academies in Bhubaneswar run **courses** for beginners (see p.1014).

installing its heavy ornamental ceiling, and had to forge ten-metre iron beams as support – a considerable engineering feat for the time.

Marvellously elaborate **sculpture** embellishes the temple's exterior with a profusion of deities, animals, floral patterns, bejewelled couples, voluptuous maidens, mythical beasts and aquatic monsters. Some of Konark's most beautiful **erotica** is to be found in the niches halfway up the walls of the porch; look for the telltale pointed beards of sadhus, clearly making the most of a lapse in their vows of chastity. Many theories have been advanced over the years to explain the lascivious scenes here and elsewhere on the temple. The most convincing explanation is that the erotic art was meant as a kind of metaphor for the ecstatic bliss experienced by the soul when it fuses with the divine cosmos – a notion central to **Tantra** and the related worship of the female principle, **shakti**, which were prevalent throughout medieval Orissa.

Moving clockwise around the temple from the south side of the main staircase, you pass the intricately carved **wheels** and extraordinary **friezes** that run in narrow bands above and below them. These depict military processions (inspired by King Narasimhadeva's tussles with the Muslims) and hunting scenes, featuring literally thousands of rampaging elephants. In the top frieze along the south side of the platform, the appearance of a giraffe proves that trade with Africa took place during the thirteenth century.

Beyond the porch, a double staircase leads to a shrine containing a **statue of Surya**. Carved out of green chlorite stone, this serene image – one of three around the base of the ruined sanctuary tower – is considered one of Konark's masterpieces. The other two statues in the series are also worth a look, if only to compare their facial expressions which, following the progress of the sun around the temple, change from wakefulness in the morning (south) to heavy-eyed weariness at the end of the day (north). At the foot of the western wall there's an altar-like platform covered with carvings: the kneeling figure in its central panel is thought to be King Narasimhadeva.

In early December, the temple hosts one of India's premier **dance festivals**, drawing an impressive cast of both classical and folk dance groups from all over the country. For the exact dates, line-up and advance bookings, contact OTDC in Bhubaneswar (℡0674/243 1299) or Delhi (℡011/2336 4580).

The village and around

Some way outside the compound, near the *Yatri Niwas* hotel (see below), the **archeological museum** (10am–5pm, closed Fri; Rs5) has lost most of its best pieces to Delhi, but has retained fragments of sculpture, much of it erotic. Outside, a small shed in the northeast corner of the enclosure houses a stone architrave bearing images of **nine planet deities**, the Navagrahas, which originally sat above one of the temple's ornamental doorways and is now kept as a living shrine.

Chandrabhaga beach, 3km south of the temple, is a quiet and clean alternative to Puri's dirty sands. Although far from ideal for swimming or sunbathing, it's nonetheless a pleasant place to wander in the evening or watch the local fishing fleet at work.

Practicalities

The easiest way to get to Konark **from Puri**, 33km down the coast, is by bus or Jeep. There are regular services in both directions and the journey only takes an hour or so, which makes it possible to do the round trip in a day – the last bus back to Puri leaves at 6.30pm. An auto-rickshaw will do the return journey, including waiting time, for Rs275–350. Buses **from Bhubaneswar** are much less frequent and take between two and four hours to cover the 65km (with a change at Pipli), depending on whether you catch the one direct express "tourist" bus, which leaves Bhubaneswar town stand at 10am. Alternatively, you could join one of OTDC's tours that leave from the *Panthaniwas* in Bhubaneswar (daily 9am–6.30pm; Rs150, a/c Rs200), with stops at Konark, Bhubaneswar and Dhauli. The helpful OTDC **tourist office** in Konark is in the *Yatri Niwas* hotel (℡06758/236821; Mon–Sat 10am–5pm).

With Puri only an hour down the road, few people stay in Konark. The **accommodation** here is convenient, however, if you want to enjoy the temple in peace after the day-trippers have left. Not far from the main entrance to the monuments, the OTDC *Panthaniwas* (℡06758/236831; ❸-❹) offers dark but clean rooms with a/c and hot water. It also runs the reasonable *Travellers' Lodge* (℡06758/236820; ❷-❸), tucked behind the pleasant OTDC *Yatri Niwas* (℡06758/236820; ❸-❺), which has mosquito nets (essential), a restaurant and coloured fountains in the gardens. The manager here boasts an impressive knowledge of local history and the temple itself. The *Labanya Lodge* (℡06758/236824, Ⓔlabanyalodge1@rediffmail.com; ❶-❷), a little out of the village on the beach road, is the most backpacker-friendly place, with a small garden, Internet access and bicycles available for hire.

For **food** you have a choice between the row of thali and tea stalls opposite the temple or a more substantial meal in one of the hotel restaurants. The *Panthaniwas'* very popular and inexpensive *Geetanjali* café serves the usual range of veg and rice dishes. The *Yatri Niwas* is also open to nonresidents and is likely to be packed out at lunchtime with tour parties, all tucking into a good Orissan thali. The *Sun Temple Hotel* is the best of the *dhabas*.

Southern Orissa

Along the stretch of coast between Puri and Andhra Pradesh there are a couple of scenic detours that may tempt you to break the long journey south. Three hours south of the capital, at the foot of a barren, sea-facing spur of the Eastern Ghats, is India's largest saltwater lake. **Chilika's** main attractions are the one million or so migratory birds that nest here in winter, and leisurely boat trips to its islands. Seventy kilometres further on, **Gopalpur-on-Sea** is sufficiently remote to have remained a decidedly low-key beach town. **Brahmapur** (formerly Berhampur), 16km inland, is southern Orissa's biggest market town, and the main transport hub for the sinuous route west through the hills to the spa station of **Taptapani** and "tribal districts" beyond.

Chilika Lake

Were it not for its glass-like surface, **CHILIKA LAKE**, Asia's largest lagoon, could easily be mistaken for the sea; from its mud-fringed foreshore you can barely make out the narrow strip of marshy islands and sand-flats that separate the 1100-square-kilometre expanse of brackish water from the Bay of Bengal. Come here between December and February, though, and you'll see a variety of **birds**, from flamingos, pelicans and painted storks to fish eagles, ospreys and kites, many of them migrants from Siberia, Iran and the Himalayas. Chilika is also one of the few places in India where the Irrawaddy dolphin can be seen. The best way to see the lake and the birds is via a **boat trip**; many of these visit Chilika's **islands** (some inhabited by small subsistence fishing communities, others deserted); the best one to head for in terms of birds is Nalabana, designated a bird sanctuary.

By and large, the fishing villages and fabled island "kingdom" of **Parikud** on the eastern side of the lake are passed up in favour of the boat ride to the *devi* shrine on **Kalijai** island. Legend has it that a local girl once drowned here on the way to her wedding across the lake, and that her voice was subsequently heard calling from under the water. Believing the bride-to-be had become a goddess, local villagers inaugurated a shrine to her that over the years became associated with **Kali** (Shiva's consort Durga in her terrifying aspect). Each year at *makar sankranti*, after the harvest, pilgrims flock to the tiny island from all over Orissa and West Bengal to leave votive offerings in the sacred cave where the deity was enshrined.

Practicalities

SATAPADA, on the coastal side, 45km from Puri and linked by several daily buses, is the best place to stay on the lake; the surrounding waters offer the best chance of seeing dolphins, and it's also home of the informative **visitor centre** (Mon–Sat 10am–5pm; Rs5), run by the Chilika Development Authority. The *Yatri Niwas* (✆06752/262077 ❶–❹) houses the **tourist office** (Mon–Sat 10am–5pm) and provides the best **accommodation** in Satapada; some rooms have private balconies overlooking the well-tended gardens that run down to the lake, and the **restaurant** serves delicious thalis and fresh seafood if given advance notice. Rooms can be booked from Puri's tourist office.

The scenery surrounding **BARKUL** is less impressive than at Satapada, and you're further from most of the islands but it does have the best

accommodation around the lake; the excellent OTDC *Panthaniwas* (☎06756/222 0488; ❹–❻) offers spacious, airy rooms in recently refurbished chalets. It also boasts a fine restaurant serving a variety of appetizing fish dishes; especially recommended is the *chinguri charchari* (shrimp with fried vegetables). To get there, take a bus from Puri or Bhubaneswar towards Brahmapur and get off at Balugaon, where you can get an auto-rickshaw for the remaining 7km to Barkul. If you plan to visit between September and March, it's best to book ahead at the Bhubaneswar OTDC tourist office.

There's a cheap and accessible OTDC *Panthaniwas* (☎06810/278346; ❷) near the railway station at **RAMBHA**, 135km from Bhubaneswar; it's somewhat lacklustre, but well placed for walks around the more scenic southern corner of the lake and for boat rides to Parikud.

If you want to **stay on an island**, *Saga Camp* (☎06810/278518, ℮info @naturesafariindia.com) on Sonakada Island, a short boat ride from Rambha, runs a "luxury jungle retreat"; accommodation is in tents with comfortable cots and attached baths. Rates are a steep Rs6000 per day per person; all meals and two daily boat rides are included.

Gandhara Travel in Puri runs **day-trips** to Chilika, departing at 8am, for Rs550 per head, including lunch and a boat ride. OTDC motor launches, and rowing boats manned by local villagers, operate **boat trips** from Barkul and Satapada; it costs around Rs500 an hour to hire a seven-seater motor launch, or you can book yourself a seat on a twenty- or thirty-seat launch: the round trip to **Kalijai Island**, the most popular option with domestic tourists, takes around two hours (Rs50), while a combination trip to Kalijai and **Nalabana Island** takes four hours (Rs175). The manager at the Barkul *Panthaniwas* can arrange seats. Rowing boats also depart from Rambha, though the fishermen who run them seem to be more intent on attending to their nets than ferrying passengers to the islands.

Gopalpur-on-Sea

Two thousand or more years ago, when the Kalingas were piling up wealth from the pearl and silk trade with Southeast Asia, **GOPALPUR-ON-SEA**, formerly the ancient port of Paloura, must have been a swinging place. Today, the only time you're likely to encounter much action is during festivals and holidays, when the village is temporarily inundated with Bengali holiday-makers. For the rest of the year, its desultory collection of crumbling bungalows and seafront hotels stands idle, left to the odd backpacker blown off-course by the promise of an undiscovered beach paradise, and the armies of industrious fishermen (*katias*) hauling in hand nets on Gopalpur's endless empty shoreline, dressed in traditional pointy straw bonnets. Paradise it certainly isn't, but if you're looking for a spot along the coast to unwind and enjoy the warm sea breezes, this is as appealing a place as any. **Sunbathing** on the beach will quickly make you the centre of attention, but its uncrowded sands, punctuated by coconut groves, sleepy lagoons and tiny creeks, make a good setting for a rejuvenating walk.

Practicalities

Getting here is easiest via the town of Brahmapur (Berhampur); frequent minibuses and Jeeps depart from the central bus stand for the sixteen-kilometre trip. You'll be dumped at the top of Gopalpur's "main street", ten minutes' walk from the seafront and most of the hotels. Tourist information can be had from the friendly folk at the OTDC *Panthaniwas* (see opposite).

Hotel rooms in Gopalpur are comparatively expensive, and it may be worth haggling – only during holiday times are they likely to be full. The rates below all refer to the off-season between October and March. As for **eating**, there's a surprising dearth of seafood in Gopalpur, though some restaurateurs can be cajoled into cooking the odd pomfret or prawn curry, given sufficient warning. The *Seashell* shack, overlooking the beach, has a relaxing ambience and serves up cheap and tasty meals and cold beer.

Holiday Inn Near the lighthouse ☎0680/224 2694. Couldn't be less like its North American namesake – a handful of very basic rooms around a pleasant courtyard, with a communal kitchen. ❶–❷

Kalinga On the main road leading to the seafront ☎0680/224 2067. Clean, pleasant and airy rooms with balconies and TVs. ❷–❺

Mermaid On the north side of the beach ☎0680/224 2050. Friendly place pitched at wealthy Calcuttans, with plain rooms and private sea-facing balconies. With advance notice, non-residents can enjoy delicious Bengali thalis. ❹

OTDC Panthaniwas By the temple ☎0680/224 3931. Clean rooms – none sea-facing, but with attached bath – and a dorm (Rs70); the excellent chef will whip up tasty Indian dishes and breakfast on demand. Checkout 8am. ❶–❹

Rosalin On the seafront ☎0680/224 2071. Chaotic family-run establishment with basic small rooms around a garden courtyard and a restaurant. Cheap and cheerful. ❶

Sea Side Breeze On the seafront at the end of the main road ☎0680/224 2075. Favourable location – the only hotel actually on the beach – large, spotlessly clean rooms, most of which have views of the sea, modest but excellent-value restaurant serving good seafood if you order in advance, and welcoming staff. The manager can arrange trips aboard a fisherman's boat in the backwaters of the nearby "Blue Bay". Good value. ❷–❹

Swosti Palm Beach Near the *Holiday Inn* ☎0680/224 2453. Gopalpur's most upmarket hotel has spacious and comfortably furnished a/c rooms and gardens but no sea views. The restaurant is strong on Indian seafood, such as *chengudi malai* (prawns in coconut cream) and *macha tarkari* (sea-fish curry). Doubles from $80. ❾

Taptapani

One possible foray from the coast, if you're tempted by the lure of the nearby hills, is the trip to the spa village of **TAPTAPANI**, nestled in the *ghats* 51km west of Brahmapur (Berhampur). Little more than a line of dingy snack stalls and mildewed bungalows deep in the forest, it's the kind of place to which government servants pray not to be posted. Pilgrims, however, come here in large numbers for the legendary **hot springs**, which are believed to cure infertility. The boiling sulphurous water bubbles out of a cleft in the mountainside and is piped into a small pool, where little rocks smeared with vermilion and hibiscus petals mark the presence of the living deities believed to reside in the water (which explains why it is prohibited to dip any part of the body in the pool).

You can also enjoy the water in the privacy of your own **hotel**; it's pumped into capacious sunken bathtubs in some of the more expensive rooms at the atmospheric and peaceful OTDC *Panthaniwas* (☎06816/255031; ❷–❹), a short way down the hill from the springs. Despite the fine views it commands over the valley, the *Panthaniwas* is rarely full, which is just as well, as there's nowhere else to stay for miles around (book in advance through an OTDC office or the hotel itself to be on the safe side); it also has a decent restaurant serving inexpensive and delicious Indian food.

Beyond Taptapani

Once over the pass above **Taptapani**, the appearance of pots attached to sago palms and windowless mud huts with low thatched roofs indicates that you've arrived in the traditional land of the **Saoras**, one of Orissa's many *adivasi* minorities. Further west around the Koraput and Jeypore area live the **Dongria Kondh**, the **Koya** and the **Bondas**.

Officially, you're not allowed into the district without first obtaining a **permit** from the local police superintendent. Concern about Naxalites hiding out in the forests along the Andhra Pradesh border, coupled with a marked reluctance to allow foreigners into tribal zones, make these notoriously difficult to obtain. This, coupled with the minimal infrastructure, rudimentary accommodation and infrequent transport around the region, means that if you're really keen to visit *adivasi* villages, the best – though far from cheapest – way is to arrange a **tour** through a specialist travel agent in Bhubaneswar or Puri. They'll take care of the permits, sort out food and rooms and have local contacts to make sure you behave appropriately in the villages and markets. Grass Routes (☎06752/250 560, ⓦ www.grassroutesjourneys.com) in Puri arranges trips of various durations, sometimes involving trekking and camping, and is considered by some NGOs to be one of the more culturally-sensitive operators. Discover Tours (☎0674/243 0477, ⓦ www.orissadiscover.com) in Bhubaneswar has guides with many years' experience and similarly makes every effort not to intrude where outsiders are not welcome. That said, *adivasi* villages see little or no share of the spoils, a situation they feel justifiably angry about, and you may well receive a very frosty reception. Whichever way you look at it, turning up in an isolated and culturally sensitive place with an Ambassador car and a camera has got to be a pretty unsound way of "meeting" the locals, and a glance from a taxi is hardly likely to enlighten you on traditions that have existed for centuries.

Travel details

Trains

Baleshwar (Balasore) to: Bhubaneswar (10–16 daily; 3hr 15min–3hr 50min); Kolkata (Calcutta; 9–13 daily; 4hr 10min–4hr 30min); Puri (5–6 daily; 5–6hr).
Bhubaneswar to: Agra (1–2 daily; 27hr 20min–36hr); Baleshwar (Balasore; 12–15 daily; 3hr 15min–4hr); Bangalore (1–3 daily; 28–29hr); Brahmapur (Berhampur; 10–11 daily; 2hr 30min–3hr 15min); Chennai (2–4 daily; 20hr–21hr 20min); Cochin (3 weekly; 34–35hr); Cuttack (14–15 daily; 20–45min); Delhi (2–3 daily; 23hr 10min–33hr 20min); Gaya (1–2 daily; 11hr 10min–15hr); Guwahati (1–3 daily; 25hr 30min–33hr 20min); Hyderabad (1 daily; 23hr 5min); Kolkata (Calcutta; 10–13 daily; 6hr 50min–8hr 15min); Mumbai (1 daily; 36hr); Puri (7–9 daily; 1hr 40min–2hr 45min); Raipur (1 daily; 13hr 30min); Thiruvananthapuram (Trivandrum; 5 weekly; 36hr 45min–42hr); Varanasi (3 weekly; 19hr).
Puri to: Ahmedabad (daily except Wed; 43hr 30min–49hr); Agra (1 daily; 37hr 50min); Baleshwar (Balasore; 5–6 daily; 4hr 40min–5hr 40min); Bhubaneswar (7–9 daily; 1hr 40min–2hr 45min); Delhi (2 daily; 29hr 40min–34hr 15min); Gaya (2 daily; 14hr 40min–16hr 30min); Kolkata (Calcutta; 2–3 daily; 8hr 45min–9hr 55min);

Mughal Sarai (1–2 daily; 20hr 30min–21hr); Nagpur (5 weekly; 20hr 15min–21hr 10min); Varanasi (3 weekly; 20hr 30min).

Buses

Bhubaneswar to: Baleshwar (Balasore; 6–8 daily; 3hr 30min–5hr); Brahmapur (Berhampur; 6–8 daily; 4hr); Cuttack (every 15min; 45min–1hr); Kolkata (Calcutta; 4 nightly; 10hr); Konark (hourly; 1hr 30min–2hr); Pipli (every 15min; 30min); Puri (every 15–20min; 2hr).
Baleshwar (Balasore) to: Baripada (every 20min; 1hr); Bhubaneswar (6–8 daily; 3hr 30min–5hr); Chandipur (5 daily; 30min); Kolkata (Calcutta; 5 daily; 5–7hr); Puri (4–6 daily; 4hr).
Brahmapur (Berhampur) to: Bhubaneswar (6–8 daily; 4hr); Gopalpur-on-Sea (every 15min; 30min); Koraput (1 daily; 8hr); Rayagada (1 daily; 3hr); Taptapani (hourly; 1hr 15min).
Puri to: Bhubaneswar (every 15–20min; 2hr); Kolkata (Calcutta; 2 daily; 12hr); Konark (hourly; 40min–1hr); Satapada (every 30min; 1hr).

Flights

Bhubaneswar to: Chennai (3 daily; 2hr 30min); Delhi (4 daily; 2hr); Goa (1–2 daily; 5hr); Hyderabad (2–3 daily; 1hr 35min); Kolkata (Calcutta; 5 daily; 55min); Mumbai (4 daily; 2hr).

Andhra Pradesh

AFGHANISTAN

PAKISTAN

CHINA
(TIBET AUTONOMCUS REGION)

NEPAL

BHUTAN

BANGLADESH

MYANMAR
(BURMA)

BAY OF BENGAL

ARABIAN SEA

SRI LANKA

INDIAN OCEAN

N

0 400 km

The International boundaries on this map are neither purported to be correct nor authentic by Survey of India directives. Publisher.

CHAPTER 18

Highlights

* **Hyderabad** A predominately Islamic city offering a compelling combination of monuments, museums and lively bazaars. **See p.1043**

* **Golconda Fort** Set in a lush landscape just west of Hyderabad, the capital of the Qutb Shahi dynasty boasts a dramatic fort. **See p.1048**

* **Warangal** Features two important Hindu monuments: the medieval fort and a thousand-pillared Shiva temple. **See p.1053**

* **Amaravati** At this village on the banks of the Krishna, fine carvings surround the remains of a great Buddhist stupa. **See p.1056**

* **Tirumala Hill, Tirupati** The most visited pilgrimage centre in the world, Tirumala Hill is crowned by the Venkateshwara Vishnu temple. **See p.1058**

* **Puttaparthy** Sai Baba's main ashram attracts modern pilgrims from all over the world, and forms the centrepiece of a thriving community. **See p.1060**

▲ Detail from an archway in Puttaparthy

Andhra Pradesh

Although **ANDHRA PRADESH** occupies a great swathe of eastern India, stretching for more than 1200km along the coast from Orissa to Tamil Nadu and reaching far inland from the fertile deltas of the Godavari and Krishna rivers to the semi-arid Deccan Plateau, it's not a place that receives many tourists. Most foreign travellers pass through en route to its more attractive neighbours, which is understandable as places of interest are few and far between. However, the sights that Andhra Pradesh does have are absorbing and sufficiently well connected to warrant at least a few stops on a longer tour of India.

Now thriving as a major hi-tech hub, the state capital, **Hyderabad**, is an atmospheric city dating from the late sixteenth century. Its endless bazaars, eclectic Salar Jung Museum and the mighty **Golconda Fort** nearby make it an enticing place to spend a day or two. **Warangal**, 150km northeast of Hyderabad, has both Muslim and Hindu remains from the twelfth and thirteenth centuries, while the region's Buddhist legacy – particularly its superb sculpture – is preserved in museums at sites such as **Nagarjunakonda** and **Amaravati**, the ancient Satavahana capital. In the east, the big city of **Vijayawada** has little to recommend it, though it makes a convenient access-point for Amaravati. However, the temple town of **Tirupati** in the far southeast – best reached from Chennai in Tamil Nadu – is one of India's great Hindu phenomena, a fascinating and impossibly crowded pilgrimage site that's said to attract more pilgrims than Mecca or the Vatican. In the southwest of the state, the small town of **Puttaparthy** attracts a more international pilgrim crowd, drawn here by the prospect of *darshan* from spiritual leader Sai Baba.

Although modern industries have grown up around the capital, and shipbuilding, iron and steel are important on the coast, most people in Andhra Pradesh remain poor. Away from the Godavari and Krishna deltas, where the soil is rich enough to grow rice and sugar cane, the land is in places impossible to cultivate, which has contributed to the desperate plight of many farmers (see p.1043).

Some history

Earliest accounts of the region, dating back to the time of **Ashoka** (third century BC), refer to a people known as the Andhras. The **Satavahana dynasty** (second century BC to second century AD), also known as the Andhras, came to control much of central and southern India from their second capital at Amaravati on the Krishna. They enjoyed extensive international trade with both eastern Asia and Europe, and were great patrons of Buddhism. Subsequently, the Pallavas from Tamil Nadu, the Chalukyas from Karnataka, and the Cholas all held sway. By the thirteenth century, the Kakatiyas of Warangal were under constant threat from

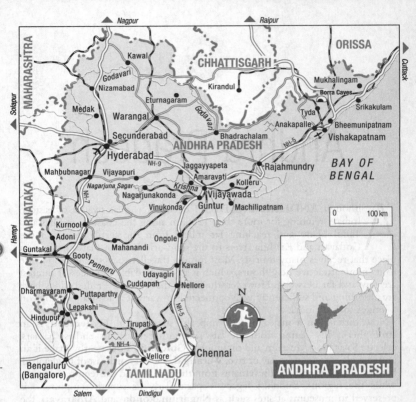

Muslim incursions, while later on, after the fall of their city at Hampi, the Hindu Vijayanagars transferred operations to Chandragiri near Tirupati.

The next significant development was in the mid-sixteenth century, with the rise of the Muslim **Qutb Shahi dynasty**. In 1687, the son of the Mughal emperor Aurangzeb seized Golconda. Five years after Aurangzeb died in 1707, the viceroy of Hyderabad declared independence and established the Asaf Jahi dynasty of **nizams**. In return for allying with the British against Tipu Sultan of Mysore, the nizam dynasty was allowed to retain a certain degree of autonomy even after the British had come to dominate all India.

During the struggle for Independence, harmony between Hindus and Muslims in Andhra Pradesh disintegrated. **Partition** brought matters to a climax, as the nizam desired to join other Muslims in the soon-to-be-created state of **Pakistan**. In 1949 the capital erupted in riots, the army was brought in and Hyderabad state was admitted to the Indian Union. Andhra Pradesh state was created in 1956 from Telugu-speaking regions (although Urdu is widely spoken in Hyderabad) that had previously formed part of the Madras Presidency on the east coast and the princely state of Hyderabad to the west. Today almost ninety percent of the population is Hindu, with Muslims largely concentrated in the capital.

From the late eighties, the pro-business Telugu Desam Party (TDP) grew in strength and eventually wrestled the power long held by Congress in 1999. Over the following five years chief minister Chandrababu Naidu oversaw huge development around Hyderabad, his pride and joy being HITEC City, but he neglected the rural areas, where drought and economic crisis led to hundreds of farmer suicides. In 2004 Congress regained control of the state government, consolidating their grip with further victories in municipal and panchayat elections over the following two years, although they have also been criticized for not doing enough to help the farmers, and suicides have continued with alarming frequency. To complicate matters further, the minority Telangana Rashtra Samithi (TRS) party, which entered a coalition with Congress in 2004, continues pushing for northwestern Andhra Pradesh, known as Telangana, to split off as a separate state.

Hyderabad/Secunderabad

A melting pot of Muslim and Hindu cultures, the capital of Andhra Pradesh comprises the twin cities of **HYDERABAD** and **SECUNDERABAD**, with a combined population of nearly seven million. Secunderabad, of little interest to visitors, is the modern administrative city founded by the British, whereas Hyderabad, the old city, has plenty to offer the visitor, with teeming **bazaars**, **Muslim monuments** and the **Salar Jung Museum**. Hyderabad went into decline after Independence, with tensions often close to the surface due to lack of funding. Nowadays, although the old city is still creaking with overpopulation and substandard amenities, the conurbation as a whole is booming. Recently Hyderabad has overtaken Bengaluru (Bangalore) as the south's hi-tech capital, and is now India's foremost computer and information technology centre; the industry has brought much revenue into the city and given rise to the nickname "Cyberabad".

Hyderabad was founded in 1591 by **Mohammed Quli Shah** (1562–1612), beside the River Musi, 8km east of Golconda, the fortress capital of the Golconda empire which was by this time suffering from overcrowding and a serious lack of water. Unusually, the new city was laid out on a grid system, with huge arches and stone buildings that included Hyderabad's most famous monument, **Charminar**. At first it was a city without walls; these were only added in 1740 as defence against the Marathas. Legend has it that a secret tunnel linked the spectacular **Golconda Fort** with the city, dotted with dome-shaped structures at suitable intervals to provide the unfortunate messengers who had to use it with the opportunity to come up for fresh air.

For the three hundred years of Muslim reign, there was harmony between the predominantly Hindu population and the minority Muslims. Hyderabad was the most important focus of Muslim power in south India at this time; the princes' fabulous wealth derived primarily from the fine gems, particularly diamonds, mined in the Kistna Valley at Golconda. The famous **Koh-i-Noor** diamond was found here – the only time it was ever captured was by Mughal emperor Aurangzeb, when his son seized the Golconda Fort in 1687. It ended up, cut, in the British royal crown.

Arrival and information

The old city of **Hyderabad** straddles the River Musi; most places of interest lie south of the river, while much of the accommodation is to the north. Further north, separated from Hyderabad by the Hussain Sagar lake, is the modern twin city of **Secunderabad**, where some long-distance trains terminate, and where all through-trains deposit passengers. If you do have to get off at Secunderabad, your ticket is valid for any connecting train to Hyderabad;

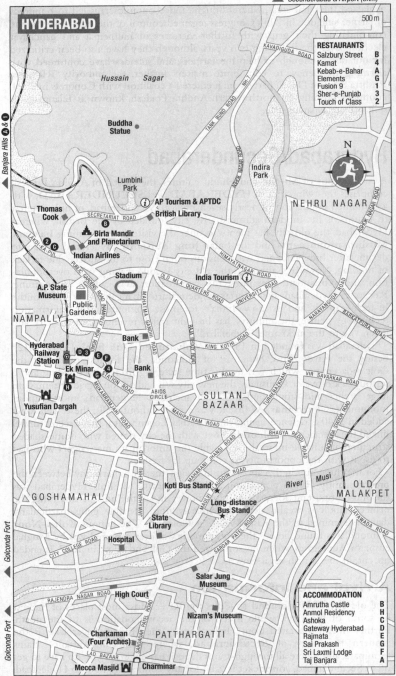

HYDERABAD

RESTAURANTS

Salzbury Street	B
Kamat	4
Kebab-e-Bahar	A
Elements	G
Fusion 9	1
Sher-e-Punjab	3
Touch of Class	2

0   500 m

N

Hussain   Sagar

Banjara Hills A & 1

Buddha
Statue

Lumbini
Park

Indira
Park

NEHRU NAGAR

Thomas
Cook

AP Tourism & APTDC
British Library

SECRETARIAT ROAD

Birla Mandir
and Planetarium

2 C

Indian Airlines

HIMAYATNAGAR ROAD

Stadium

India Tourism

A.P. State
Museum

NAMPALLY

Public
Gardens

OLD MLA QUARTERS ROAD

UNIVERSITY ROAD

MARYANGUDA ROAD

BARKATPURA ROAD

Bank

KING KOTHI ROAD

Hyderabad
Railway
Station

D 3

E F

Ek Minar

4

G

H

Bank

ABIDS
CIRCLE

TILAK ROAD

SULTAN
BAZAAR

VIR SAVARKAR ROAD

Yusufian Dargah

MAHIPATRAM ROAD

BHAGYA REDDY ROAD

Golconda Fort

GOSHAMAHAL

Koti Bus Stand

Long-distance
Bus Stand

River   Musi

OLD
MALAKPET

VIJAYAWADA ROAD

State
Library

Hospital

CITY COLLEGE ROAD

SARDAR PATEL ROAD

Golconda Fort

High Court

RAJENDRA NAGAR ROAD

Nizam's Museum

Salar Jung
Museum

Charkaman
(Four Arches)

PATTHARGATTI

Mecca Masjid

Charminar

Royal Palaces Complex

ACCOMMODATION

Amrutha Castle	B
Anmol Residency	H
Ashoka	C
Gateway Hyderabad	D
Rajmata	E
Sai Prakash	G
Sri Laxmi Lodge	F
Taj Banjara	A

APTDC operates a number of **guided tours** (which can be booked via their two offices, see below). Times quoted below are for when tours set off from the Secunderabad office; pick-up time in Hyderabad is 15–20 minutes later. The **city tour** (daily 7am–6.30pm; Rs240) includes Golconda Fort (entry extra), Qutb Shahi tombs (not Fri), Lumbini Park, the Birla Mandir and planetarium, Salar Jung Museum (not Fri) and Charminar. There is also one to **Golconda Fort's sound-and-light show** (daily 2–9pm; Rs155 including entry), which stops at the Botanical Gardens and drives past HITEC City. **Ramoji Film City** (see p.1050) also has its own tour (daily 7.45am–6pm; Rs465 including entry), although those run by the private agents in Nampally, such as Royal Travels (9.30am–7pm; Rs150, plus Rs300 entry), have more convenient pick-up points and timings.

APTDC's **Nagarjuna Sagar** tour (Sat & Sun 7.30am–9.30pm; Rs360, excluding entry) covers 360km in total, and is rather rushed but is a convenient way to get to this fascinating area (see p.1054). The longer tours to **Tirupati/Tirumala** are not worth considering as they're more conveniently reached from Chennai and further afield in south India.

and if none is imminent, many buses including #5, #8 and #20 ply between both stations. **Hyderabad railway station** (also known as Nampally) is close to all amenities and offers a fairly comprehensive service to major destinations. The well-organized **long-distance bus stand** occupies an island in the middle of the River Musi, 3km southeast of the railway station. The spanking-new Rajiv Gandhi International **Airport** opened in March 2008 at Shamshabad, around 20km south of central Hyderabad, replacing the old one at Begumpet. At the time of writing it was unclear how soon the proposed rail links to the city would be operating; expect dedicated taxis, which are meant to have a fixed rate of Rs15 per km, to cost around Rs300.

The main **tourist office** in Hyderabad is the **AP Tourism office** (daily 8am–7pm; ☏040/2345 3110, ⊛www.aptourism.in), on Secretariat Road just before it becomes Tank Bund Road, near the huge flyover. The **APTDC office** next door (daily 7am–8pm; ☏040/2345 3036, ⊛www.tourisminap .com) and the other APTDC office, at Yatri Nivas, Sardar Patel Road, Secunderabad (☏040/2781 6375), exist principally to book their tours. The **India Tourism office**, 2nd floor, Netaji Bhavan, Liberty Road, Himayatnagar (Mon–Fri 9am–5pm; ☏040/2763 1360), offers a few brochures. The best source of local information is the monthly listings **magazine**, *Channel 6* (Rs15; ⊛www.channel6magazine.com), available from most bookstalls.

Accommodation

The area in front of **Hyderabad railway station** (Nampally) has the cheapest accommodation, but you're unlikely to find anything for less than Rs250. The grim little enclave of five lodges with "Royal" in their name is best avoided. The real **bargains** are more in the mid- to upper-range hotels, which offer better facilities for lower rates than in other big cities. A little over 1km north of Secunderabad railway station, decent places can be found on **Sarojini Devi Road**, near the Gymkhana Ground.

Hyderabad

Amrutha Castle 5-9-16 Saifabad, opposite the Secretariat ☏040/5663 3888, ⊛www.amruthacastle.com. Affiliated to *Best Western*, this extraordinary hotel, designed like a fairy castle with round turret rooms, offers international facilities at fair prices. With its rooftop swimming pool, it's a good place to splash out. ❼–❾

🏃 **Anmol Residency** Adjacent to Ek Minar mosque, Nampally ☎040/2460 8116. Friendly, lower mid-range place, handily placed for the station and offering great value; all rooms are attached and have TV. The deluxe corner rooms have a lot more space and windows covering two walls but cost no more. ❹–❺

Ashoka 6-1-70 Lakdi-ka-Pul ☎040/2323 0105, ℻5551 0220. Standard mid-range hotel with a variety of clean attached rooms with cable TV; the a/c rooms are much better value and cost little more than the non-a/c ones. ❹–❺

Gateway Hyderabad 11-6-242-245 Station Rd, Nampally ☎040/6610 0000, ⓦwww.gateway hyderabad.com. Barely one minute's walk from the station, this sparkling new hotel is the best upper mid-range option in the vicinity. All rooms are well-furnished with a/c and TV; the deluxe ones have fridges and extra space. ❻–❼

Rajmata Nampally High Rd, opposite railway station ☎040/6666 5555, ℻2320 4133. Set back from the road in the same compound as the various *Royal* lodges, with large, clean non-a/c deluxe rooms. Their adjacent *Lakshmi* restaurant offers good south Indian veg food. ❹

Sai Prakash Station Rd ☎040/2461 1726, ⓔhotelsaiprakash@rediffmail.com. Modern hotel, a 5min walk from the station, offering comfortable, carpeted rooms all with cable TV; the non-a/c rooms are good value and very popular. Good restaurants and bar on site. ❻

Sri Laxmi Lodge Gadwal Compound, Station Rd ☎040/5563 4200. Quiet place down a small lane opposite the *Sai Prakash*, with reasonably clean rooms. Good value, especially for singles. ❷

🏃 **Taj Banjara** Main Road No. 1, Banjara Hills, 4km from the centre ☎040/6666 9999, ⓦwww.tajhotels.com. In a pleasant location behind a small lake, with all the usual top-notch facilities including three restaurants (see p.1051) and a 24hr coffee shop. Internet specials are often lower than the official rates, which start at $255. ❾

Secunderabad

Baseraa Sarojini Devi Rd ☎040/2770 3200, ⓦwww.baseraa.com. The plushest hotel within walking distance (15min) of the station. Boasts 77 modern rooms and suites with all mod cons. ❼–❾

National Lodge Annexe Opposite Secunderabad railway station ☎040/2770 5572. No-frills lodge amongst the motley cluster of hotels here, offering very basic rooms; most have their own bathroom. ❷

Ramakrishna St John's Rd ☎040/2783 4567, ℻2782 0933. With some a/c rooms, this comfy mid-range option, in a large concrete block opposite the railway reservation complex, is the smartest place in the immediate station area. ❹–❺

Sri Vinayak off Regimental Bazaar ☎040/2771 0146, ℻2780 2146. Decent lower mid-range lodge tucked away in a quiet lane behind a large white Sikh *gurudwara*, only a few minutes from the station. All rooms have attached bath; some have a/c. ❸–❺

The City

Hyderabad has three fairly distinct sectors: **Hyderabad**, divided between the old city and newer areas towards HITEC City; **Secunderabad**, the modern city (originally called Hussain Shah Pura); and **Golconda**, the old fort. The two cities are basically one big sprawl, separated by a lake, **Hussain Sagar**.

The most interesting area, south of the River Musi, holds the **bazaars**, **Charminar** and the **Salar Jung Museum**. At only a tenth the width of the main bridge to the old city, the river is just a trickle, even after the rains – most of the riverbed is grassed over or planted with palms and rice. North of the river, the main shopping malls are found around **Abids Circle** and **Sultan Bazaar** (readymade clothes, fruit, veg and silk), ten minutes' walk east of the railway station. Abids Circle is connected to MG Road, which runs north to join Tank Bund Road at Hussain Sagar and runs on to Secunderabad, while to the south it metamorphoses into Nehru Road. Four kilometres west of Hyderabad railway station, trendy new shops, restaurants and bars are also springing up in the posh **Banjara Hills** district, and around the exclusive residential area of **Jubilee Hills**. A further six kilometres brings you to the gleaming towers of HITEC City.

Salar Jung Museum

The unmissable **Salar Jung Museum** (daily except Fri 10am–5pm; Rs150 [Rs10]), on the south bank of the Musi, houses part of the huge collection of Salar Jung, one of the nizam's prime ministers, and his ancestors. A well-travelled man of wealth, he bought whatever took his fancy from both East and West, from the sublime to, in some cases, the ridiculous. His extraordinary hoard includes Indian jade, miniatures, furniture, lacquer-work, Mughal opaque glassware, fabrics, bronzes, Buddhist and Hindu sculpture, manuscripts, and weapons. Avoid visiting the museum at the weekend, when it gets very crowded.

Charminar, Lad Bazaar and the Mecca Masjid

A maze of bazaars teeming with people, the old city has at its heart the **Charminar**, or Four Towers, a triumphal arch built at the centre of Mohammed Quli Shah's city in 1591 to commemorate an epidemic. As its name suggests, it features four graceful minarets, each 56m high, housing spiral staircases to the upper storeys. The (now defunct) mosque on the roof is the oldest in Hyderabad; it was built to teach the royal children the Koran. The yellowish colour of the building is due to a special stucco made of marble powder, gram and egg yolk.

Charminar marks the beginning of the fascinating **Lad Bazaar**, as old as the town itself, which leads to Mahboob Chowk, a market square featuring a mosque and Victorian clock tower. Lad Bazaar specializes in everything you could possibly need for a Hyderabadi marriage; it's full of bangle shops, old stores selling rosewater, herbs and spices, and material. You'll also find silver filigree jewellery, antiques, *bidri*-ware, hookah paraphernalia with delicate inlay work and, in the markets near the Charminar, **pearls** – so beloved of the nizams that they not only wore them but also ground them into powder to eat. Today Hyderabad is the centre of India's pearl trade.

Southwest, behind the Charminar, **Mecca Masjid** is the sixth largest mosque in India, constructed in 1598 by the sixth king, Abdullah Qutb Shah, from locally hewn blocks of black granite. Small red bricks from Mecca are slotted over the central arch. The mosque can hold three thousand devotees with up to ten thousand more in the courtyard; on the left of the courtyard are the tombs of the nizams. In May 2007 the mosque was rocked by a powerful bomb; the incident killed fourteen people, five of those shot by police in the ensuing chaos. The perpetrators were never caught and since this and subsequent bombings, security has been very tight at all public places in the city.

The **Charkaman**, or Four Arches, north of Charminar, were built in 1594 and once led to the parade ground of royal palaces (now long gone). The western arch, **Daulat-Khan-e-Ali** (which originally led to the palace), was at one time adorned with rich gold tapestries.

North of the river

Set in a leafy courtyard not far south of the railway station, the **Yusufian Dargah**, with its striking bulbous yellow dome, is the shrine of a seventeenth-century Sufi saint of the venerable Chishti order. You can enter (cover your head) to view the flower-decked tomb. About a kilometre north of the station, set in Hyderabad's tranquil public gardens, the **AP state museum** (daily except Fri and 2nd Sat of each month 10.30am–5pm; Rs10) displays a modest but well-labelled collection of bronzes, prehistoric tools, copper inscription plates, weapons and household utensils. There's a gallery of modern art in the extension.

The **Birla Venkateshwara temple** (daily 7am–noon & 3–9pm) on Kalapahad ("black mountain") Hill, north of the Public Gardens, is open to all. Constructed in Rajasthani white marble in 1976, the temple itself is not of great interest, but it affords fine views. Nearby, and built by the same organization, is the **planetarium** (English: daily except Thurs 11.30am, 4pm & 6pm; Rs20) and a **science centre** (daily 10.30am–8pm; Rs17) with lots of satellite hardware and photos, machines demonstrating sensory perceptions and a small dinosaur display.

Hussain Sagar

Hussain Sagar, the large expanse of water separating Hyderabad from Secunderabad, lends a welcome air of tranquillity to the busy conurbation. The lakeside is a popular place for a stroll, especially at sunset. In the centre of the water stands a large stone statue of the **Buddha Purnima** or "Full Moon Buddha", erected in 1992. Regular **boats** (Rs30 return) chug out to the statue from Lumbini Park, just off Secretariat Road. Two deluxe boats – the *Bhageerathi* and the *Bhagmati* – operated by APTDC, offer hour-long **cruises** of the lake (11am–3pm & 6–8pm; Rs60–90), complete with a hilarious dance show. Unfortunately, the park was the site of one of two bombs that exploded in August 2007, claiming 42 lives between them.

Golconda Fort and the tombs of the Qutb Shahi kings

Golconda, 122m above the plain and 11km west of old Hyderabad, was the capital of the seven Qutb Shahi kings from 1518 until the end of the sixteenth century, when the court moved to Hyderabad. Well preserved and set in thick green scrubland, it is one of the most impressive forts in India. The citadel boasted 87 semicircular bastions and eight mighty gates, four of which are still in use, complete with gruesome elephant-proof spikes.

To get **to the fort**, bus #119 runs from Nampally, while the #66G direct bus from Charminar and #80D from Secunderabad stop outside the main entrance. **For the tombs**, take #123 or #142S from Charminar. From Secunderabad the #5, #5S and #5R all go to Mehdipattanam, where you should hop onto #123. Or, of course, you could take a rickshaw and spare yourself the bother (agree a waiting fee in advance). Set aside a day to explore the fort, which covers an area of around four square kilometres.

Entering the **fort** (daily 9am–5pm; Rs100 [Rs5]) by the Balahisar Gate, you come into the Grand Portico, where guards clap their hands to show off the fort's acoustics; the claps can be clearly heard at the Durbar Hall. To the right is the **mortuary bath**, where the bodies of deceased nobles were ritually bathed prior to burial. If you follow the arrowed anticlockwise route, you pass the two-storey residence of ministers Akkana and Madanna before starting the stairway ascent to the Durbar Hall. Halfway along the steps, you arrive at a small, dark cell named after the court cashier **Ramdas**, who while incarcerated here produced the clumsy carvings and paintings that litter the gloomy room. Nearing the top, you come across the small, pretty mosque of Ibrahim Qutb Shah; beyond here, set beneath two huge granite stones, is an even tinier temple to Durga in her manifestation as Mahakali.

The steps are crowned by the three-storey **Durbar Hall** of the Qutb Shahis, on platforms outside which the monarchs would sit and survey their domains. Their accompaniment was the lilting strains of court musicians, as opposed to today's cacophony of incessant clapping from far below. As you head back down to the palaces and harems, you pass the tanks that supplied the fort's water system.

The ruins of the **queen's palace**, once elaborately decorated with multiple domes, stand in a courtyard centred on an original copper fountain that used to be filled with rosewater. You can still see traces of the "necklace" design on one of the arches, at the top of which a lotus bud sits below an opening flower with a cavity at its centre that once contained a diamond. Petals and creeper leaves

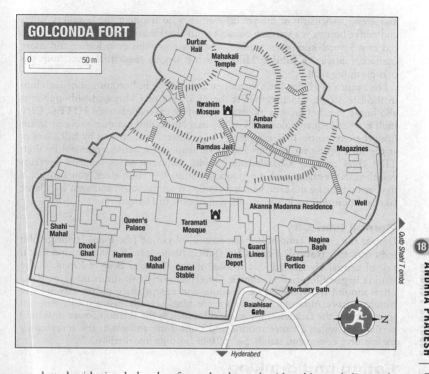

are dotted with tiny holes that formerly gleamed with rubies and diamonds. Today visitors can only speculate how splendid it must all have looked, especially at night, when flaming torches illuminated the glittering decorations. At the entrance to the **palace** itself, four chambers provided protection from intruders. Passing through two rooms, the second of which is overgrown, you come to the **Shahi Mahal**, the royal bedroom. Originally it had a domed roof and niches on the walls that once sheltered candles or oil lamps; it's said that the servants used silver ladders to get up there to light them. Golconda's **sound-and-light** show (English: daily March–Oct 7pm; Nov–Feb 6.30pm; Rs40) is suitably theatrical. It's a good way for foreigners to get into the fort cheaply, though what you see is limited.

There are 82 **tombs** (daily except Fri 9.30am–4.30pm; Rs10) about 1km north of the outer wall. Set in peaceful gardens, they commemorate commanders, relatives of the kings, dancers, singers and royal doctors, as well as all but two of the Qutb Shahi kings. Faded today, they were once brightly coloured in turquoise and green; each has an onion dome on a block, with a decorative arcade. You can reach them by road or, more pleasantly, by picking your way across the quiet grassy verges and fields below the fort's battlements.

The western suburbs

Most of Hyderabad's new-found wealth is concentrated in the city's western suburbs. The nearest of these is the **Banjara Hills**, around 4km from Nampally, which comprises spacious residences in quiet streets surrounding the busy Main Road No. 1, a glitzy business strip that contains many of the city's trendiest shops, bars and restaurants and most luxurious hotels. The western appearance and dress, particularly of the young women who frequent the jewellery shops and coffee houses, is a startling contrast to the burkas and saris ubiquitous in the old city. Several kilometres further west you enter the even leafier and more upmarket district of **Jubilee Hills**, which is largely residential apart from the odd gleaming mall.

The upturn in Hyderabad's fortunes was driven by its becoming a hi-tech hub in the late 1990s, which earned it the nickname of Cyberabad, although it is also home to other growth industries including car manufacture. **HITEC City** itself is several square kilometres of modern blocks and complexes about 10km from the city centre. Its centrepiece, Cyber Towers, was opened by Bill Clinton at the turn of the millennium and its subsequent growth encouraged by then TDP chief minister Chandrababu Naidu. Although strict security prevents casual visits by those with no business within the complexes, you can get a flavour by touring the area, which is bordered on the south and west by a large lake and beautiful rock formations, reminiscent of Hampi.

Ramoji Film City

Despite the greater fame of Bollywood and Tollywood (the Tamil-language film industry), it is **Ramoji Film City** (RFC; 10am–6pm; Rs300), around 25km east of central Hyderabad, that is listed in the *Guinness Book of Records* as the world's largest film studio complex. Covering nearly two thousand acres, RFC offers around five hundred set locations and can produce up to sixty movies simultaneously. Although you cannot see films actually being made, you can tour some of the facades, enjoy a few rides such as the Ramoji Tower simulated earthquake, watch a dance routine and stunt show, and eat at the surprisingly inexpensive concession stands. See p.1045 for tour information.

Eating and drinking

In addition to the hotel restaurants, plenty of "meals" places around town specialize in **Hyderabadi cuisine**, such as authentic biriyanis, or the famously

▲ HITEC City

chilli-hot Andhra cuisine. Hyderabadi cooking is derived from Mughal court cuisine, featuring sumptuous meat dishes with northern ingredients such as cinnamon, cardamom, cloves and garlic, and traditional southern vegetarian dishes with an array of flavourings like cassia buds, peanuts, coconut, tamarind leaves, mustard seeds and red chillies. Though not as abundant as in Bengaluru (Bangalore), **bars** conducive to both sexes have started appearing, mostly along Main Road No.1 in Banjara Hills: try the plush white – leather couches and Indo-Euro pop at *Liquids*, the disco theme-nights at *Cinnabar Redd* (above *Fusion 9*) or the basement rock sounds at *Easy Rider*, further down the road. *Touch*, a futuristic pop and dance club above a new mall on Main Road No. 12 towards Jubilee Hills, is another trendy hang-out.

Hyderabad

Element's *Sai Prakash*, Station Rd. The posher and pricier of the hotel's two restaurants, with comfy armchairs and imaginative daily specials featuring crab and prawns, plus specialities such as Indonesian nasi goreng for around Rs200. The veg *Sukha Sagara* downstairs serves cheaper south Indian snacks and north Indian dishes.

Fusion 9 Main Road no.1, Banjara Hills. Expensive (Rs250–300) but quality cuisine from nine different regions as diverse as Mexico, Europe, the Middle East and Southeast Asia, served in a smart modern lounge overlooking the street through tinted windows.

Kamat Station Rd, opposite *Sai Prakash* hotel. Conveniently located branch of this extremely inexpensive and clean veggie chain. *Dosas* go for around Rs20.

Kebab-e-Bahar Main Road no.1, Banjara Hills. The *Taj Banjara*'s classy lakeside patio restaurant specializes in a range of succulent kebabs and tandoori dishes but also offers delicious curries. Most main courses in the Rs200–400 range.

Salzburg Street *Amrutha Castle*, Secretariat Rd, Saifabad. At the back of the hotel lobby, this restaurant offers a fine evening buffet with unusual items like dim sum and chicken liver salad for Rs350. A la carte main courses Rs100–150.

Sher-e-Punjab Corner of Nampally High Rd and station entrance. Popular basement restaurant offering tasty north Indian veg and non-veg food at bargain prices (Rs40–80).

Touch of Class *Central Court*, Lakdi-ka-Pul. Good Indian, Chinese and a few Continental items like chicken nuggets for Rs100–150. The hotel's other joint, *Salt & Pepper*, does good-value lunch buffets at different times of day (Rs130–275).

Secunderabad

Akbar 1-7-190 MG Rd. A fine range of Hyderabadi dishes – including top-quality biriyanis – at moderate prices.

Paradise-Persis MG Rd. Very popular multi-restaurant complex bashing out fine Hyderabadi cuisine at little expense.

Listings

Airlines, domestic Air Deccan, airport ☏09849 677008; Go Air, Bollywood Tours & Travels, 176 1st floor, B block, Babukhan Estate, Basheerbagh ☏040/5546 4560; Indian Airlines, opposite Assembly, Hill Fort Rd, Saifabad ☏040/2343 0334; IndiGo, 2nd floor, 5-9-86/1 Chapel Rd ☏040/2321 1635; Jet Airways, 6-3-1109/1 GF Nav Bharat Chambers, Raj Bhavan Rd ☏040/3982 4444; Kingfisher Airlines, toll free ☏1800 180 0101; Paramount Airways, airport ☏040/2790 4964; SpiceJet, toll free ☏1800 180 3333.

Airlines, international Air France, Gupta Estate, 1st floor, Basheerbagh ☏040/2323 0947; Air India, 5-9-193 HACA Bhavan, opposite public garden, Saifabad ☏040/2338 9719; British Airways, Nijhawan Travel Services, 5-9-88/4 Ainulaman Fateh Maidan Rd ☏040/2324 1661; Emirates,

Floor F, Reliance Classic Bldg 3 & 4, Main Rd No. 1, Banjara Hills ☏040/2332 1111; Gulf Air, Jet Air, Flat 202, 5-9-58 Gupta Estate, Basheerbagh ☏040/2324 0870; KLM, Ashok Bhoopal Chambers, opposite Anand Talkies. SP Rd ☏040/2772 0940; Lufthansa, 3-5-823 Shop #B1–B3, Hyderaguda ☏040/2323 5537; Malaysia Airlines, 5th Floor, 502 White House, Kundanbagh ☏040/2341 0292; Qantas, Transworld Travels, 3A 1st floor, 5-9-93 Chapel Rd ☏040/2329 8495; Singapore Airlines/ Swissair, Aviation Travels, Navbharat Chambers, 6-3-1109/1 Raj Bhavan Rd ☏040/2340 2664.

Banks and exchange Surprisingly few banks do foreign exchange, two exceptions being the State Bank of Hyderabad, MG Rd. and Federal Bank, 1st floor, Orient Estate, MG Rd; both open Mon–Fri 10.30am–2.30pm, the latter also Sat

10.30am–12.30pm. It's better to head for an agency such as Thomas Cook ☎040/2329 6521 at Nasir Arcade, Secretariat Rd; or LKP Forex ☎040/2321 0094 on Public Gardens Rd, only 10min walk north of Nampally Station; both open Mon–Sat 9.30am–5.30pm. There are an increasing number of ATMs, however, such as the SBI on Nampally High Rd, Syndicate Bank on Station Rd, Oriental Bank at Secunderabad railway station and numerous machines in Banjara Hills.

Bookshops AA Hussian & Co, 5-8-551 Arastu Trust Building, Abid Rd, Hyderabad; Akshara, 8-2-273 Pavani Estate, Road no. 2, Banjara Hills, Hyderabad; Higginbothams, 1 Lal Bahadur Stadium, Hyderabad; Gangarams, 62 DSD Rd, near *Garden Restaurant* in Secunderabad; and Kalaujal, Hill Fort Rd, opposite the Public Gardens, which specializes in art books.

Car rental Air Travels in Banjara Hills (☎040/2335 3099, ✉airtravels@yahoo.com) and Classic Travels in Secunderabad (☎040/2775 5645) both provide a 24hr service, with or without driver.

Dentist Kakade's Dentistree, opposite *Taj Banjara* hotel, Rd No.1 ☎040/2330 2633.

Hospitals The government-run Gandhi Hospital is in Secunderabad ☎040/2770 2222; the private CDR Hospital is in Himayatnagar ☎040/2322 1221; and there's a Tropical Diseases Hospital in Nallakunta ☎040/2766 7843.

Internet access Internet outlets abound throughout both cities: try Modi Xerox opposite Ek Minar mosque (Rs20/hr) or Cyber Railtel in Nampally Station. Several Netphone facilities can be found behind the large Medwin Hospital off Nampally High Rd.

Library The British Library, Secretariat Rd (Tues–Sat 11am–7pm; ☎040/2323 0774), has a wide selection of books and recent British newspapers. Officially you must be a member or a British citizen to get in.

Pharmacies Apollo Pharmacy ☎040/2323 1380 and Health Pharmacy ☎040/2331 0618 are both open 24hr.

Police ☎040/2323 0191. In an emergency call ☎100.

Souvenirs Lepakshi, the AP state government emporium at Gunfoundry on MG Rd, stocks a wide range of handicrafts, including *bidri* metalwork, jewellery and silks. Utkalika (Government of Orissa handicrafts), house no. 60-1-67, between the Ravindra Bharati building and *Hotel Ashoka*, has a modest selection of silver filigree jewellery, handloom cloth, *ikat* tie-dye, Jagannath papier-mâché figures and buffalo bone carvings. Cheneta Bhavan is a modern shopping complex a little south of the railway station, stuffed with hand-loom cloth shops from various states, including Andhra Pradesh. For silks and saris, try Meena Bazaar, Pochampally Silks and Sarees, and Pooja Sarees, all on Tilak Rd.

Travel agents General agents for airline and private bus tickets include: Travel Club Forex ☎040/2323 4180, Nasir Arcade, Saifabad, close to Thomas Cook; and Kamat Travels in the *Hotel Sai Prakash* complex ☎040/2461 2096. There's a host of private bus agents on Nampally High Rd outside Hyderabad railway station.

Moving on from Hyderabad

Daily **train** services from **Hyderabad railway station (Nampally)** include: the Charminar Express #2760 to Chennai (6.30pm; 13hr 45min); the Hyderabad–Ernakulam Sabari Express #7230 (noon; 25hr 40min); the Hyderabad–Mumbai Express #7032 (8.40pm; 16hr 25min); the East Coast Express #8646 to Kolkata (10am; 30hr 15min) via Vijayawada, Vishakapatnam and Bhubaneswar; and the Rayasaleema Express #7429 to Tirupati (5.25pm; 15hr 20min). Almost all northeast-bound services call at Warangal and at Vijayawada. **From Secunderabad,** there are some originating services and many through trains in all directions, including the Konark Express #1020 to Mumbai (11.45am; 16hr 10min). The handy Bangalore Express #2785 (7.05pm; 11hr 25min) departs from **Kacheguda** station, around 6km northwest of Nampally.

The **railways reservations office** at Hyderabad (Mon–Sat 8am–2pm & 2.30–8pm, Sun 8am–2pm) is to the left as you enter the station. Counter #211 (next to enquiry counter) is for tourist reservations, but it's also used for group bookings and lost tickets. The **Secunderabad reservation complex** is by the major junction with St John's Road over 400m to the right as you exit the station. Counter 34 is for foreigners.

From the Central Bus Stand, **regular bus services** run to a host of destinations around the state and beyond. In addition, various **deluxe and video**

buses depart for Bengaluru (Bangalore), Chennai, Mumbai and other major destinations from outside Nampally Station, where you will find a cluster of private agencies, such as National Travels (☎040/2320 3614).

The new **airport** (see p.1045), built to match Hyderabad's commercial expansion, is set to become one of the busiest hubs in South Asia. **International flights**, which were already serving various European, Gulf and Southeast Asian cities, are expected to increase exponentially, as are the number of **domestic schedules**. At the time of writing, all the major and low-cost operators were already operating from the new terminal to a host of destinations within India, including Delhi, Mumbai, Chennai, Bengaluru, Kolkata, Ahmedabad, Kochi, Goa, Tirupati, Coimbatore and Pune.

For specific information on which airlines cover which routes, as well as the frequency and duration of services on all modes of transport, see "Travel details" on p.106.

Around Hyderabad

As you head north from Hyderabad towards the borders of Maharashtra and Madhya Pradesh, the landscape becomes greener and more hilly, sporadically punctuated by photogenic black-granite rock formations. There is little to detain visitors here except the small town of **Warangal**, situated on the main railway line, which warrants a stop to visit the nearby medieval fort and Shiva temple. South of the capital, vast swathes of flat farmland stretch into the centre of the state, where the Nagarjuna Sagar Dam has created a major lake with the important Buddhist site of **Nagarjunakonda**, now an island in its waters.

Warangal

WARANGAL – "one stone" – 150km northeast of Hyderabad, was the Hindu capital of the Kakatiyan empire in the twelfth and thirteenth centuries. Like other Deccan cities, it changed hands many times between the Hindus and the Muslims – something that is reflected in its architecture and the remains you see today.

Warangal's **fort** (daily 9am–5pm; Rs100 [Rs5]), 4km south of town, is famous for its two circles of fortifications: the outer made of earth with a moat, and the inner of stone. Four roads into the centre meet at the ruined temple of **Swayambhu** (1162), dedicated to Shiva. At its southern, freestanding gateway, another Shiva temple, from the fourteenth century, is in much better shape; inside, the remains of an enormous lingam came originally from the Svayambhu shrine. Also inside the citadel is the **Shirab Khan**, or **Audience Hall**, an early eleventh-century building very similar to Mandu's Hindola Mahal (see p.460).

Some 6km north of town, just off the main road beside the slopes of Hanamkonda Hill, the largely basalt Chalukyan-style "**thousand-pillared**" **Shiva temple** (daily 6am–6pm) was constructed by King Rudra Deva in 1163. A low-roofed building on several stepped stages, it features superb carvings and three shrines to Vishnu, Shiva and Surya, the sun god. They lead off the *mandapa*, whose numerous finely carved columns give the temple its name. In front, a polished Nandi bull was carved out of a single stone. A Bhadrakali temple stands at the top of the hill.

Practicalities

If you make an early start, it's just about possible to visit Warangal as a day-trip from Hyderabad. Frequent buses and trains run to the town (roughly 3hr).

Warangal's **bus stand** and **railway station** are opposite each other, served by local buses, auto- and cycle rickshaws. The easiest way to cover the site is to **rent a bicycle** from one of the stalls on Station Road (Rs5/hr). To get to the fort, follow Station Road from the station, turn left just beyond the post office, go under the railway bridge and left again at the next main road. For Hanamkonda, follow the same route from the station but turn right onto JPN Road at the next main junction after the post office, left at the next major crossroads onto MG Road, and right at the end onto the Hanamkonda main road. The temple and hill are on the left.

Accommodation is limited: basic lodges on Station Road include the *Vijaya Lodge* (☏0870/225 1222, 🖷244 6864; ❶–❸), which is close to the station and best value, and *Vaibhav Lodge* (☏0870/694 2895; ❷–❸), just beyond JPN Road, which has some a/c rooms. A new mid-range option even closer to the station on Station Road is *Hotel Surya* (☏0870/244 1834; ❸–❹), while the marginally poshest option is *Hotel Ashoka* (☏0870/285491, Ⓦwww .hotelashoka.in; ❸–❹), not far beyond the thousand-pillared temple on Main Road, Hanamkonda, which has a/c rooms, a restaurant and bar. Several decent **eating places** line Station Road – the *Surabhi* restaurant in the *Hotel Surya* serves good-quality veg and non-veg in cool, comfortable surroundings, while further along on the left, beyond the post office, the much more basic *Bharati Mess* offers help-yourself veg meals, to which you can add chicken or mutton. **Internet** facilities are available at Durga Xerox on Station Road, almost opposite the *Vijaya Lodge*.

Nagarjunakonda

NAGARJUNAKONDA, or "Nagarjuna's Hill", 166km south of Hyderabad and 175km west of Vijayawada, is all that now remains of the vast area, rich in archeological sites, that was submerged when the huge Nagarjuna Sagar Dam was built across the River Krishna in 1960. Ancient settlements in the valley were first discovered in 1926; extensive excavations carried out between 1954 and 1960 uncovered more than one hundred sites dating from the early Stone Age to late medieval times. Nagarjunakonda was once the summit of a hill, where a fort towered 200m above the valley floor; now it's just a small oblong island near the middle of Nagarjuna Sagar lake, accessible by boat from the mainland. Several Buddhist monuments have been reconstructed, in an operation reminiscent of that at Abu Simbel in Egypt, and a **museum** exhibits the more remarkable ruins of the valley. **VIJAYAPURI**, the village on the shore of the lake, overlooks the colossal dam itself, which stretches for almost 2km. Torrents of water flushed through its 26 floodgates produce electricity for the whole region, and irrigate an area of almost 800 square kilometres. Many villages had to be relocated to higher ground when the valley was flooded.

The island and the museum

Boats arrive on the northeastern edge of **Nagarjunakonda island** (daily 9am–5pm), unloading passengers at what remains of one of the gates of the fort, built in the fourteenth century and renovated by the Vijayanagar kings in the mid-sixteenth century. Low, damaged, stone walls skirting the island mark the edge of the fort, and you can see ground-level remains of the Hindu temples that served its inhabitants. Well-kept gardens lie between the jetty and the museum, beyond which nine Buddhist monuments from various sites in the valley have been rebuilt. West of the jetty, there's a reconstructed bathing *ghat*, built entirely of limestone during the reigns of the Ikshvaku kings (third century AD).

The **maha-chaitya**, or stupa, constructed at the command of King Chamtula's sister in the third century AD, is the earliest Buddhist structure in the area. It was raised over relics of the Buddha – said to include a tooth – and has been reassembled in the southwest of the island. Nearby, a towering **statue** of the Buddha stands draped in robes beside a ground plan of a monastery that enshrines a smaller stupa. Other **stupas** stand nearby; the brick walls of the *svastika chaitya* have been arranged in the shape of swastikas, common emblems in early Buddhist iconography.

The **museum** (same hours; Rs100 [Rs5]) houses stone friezes decorated with scenes from the Buddha's life, and statues of Buddha in various postures. Earlier artefacts include stone tools and pots from the Neolithic age (third millennium BC), and metal axe-heads and knives (first millennium BC). Later exhibits include inscribed pillars from Ikshvaku times showing Buddhist monasteries and statues. Medieval sculptures include a thirteenth-century *tirthankara* (Jain saint), a seventeenth-century Ganesh and Nandi, and some eighteenth-century Shiva and Shakti statues, and there is also a model showing the excavated sites in the valley.

Practicalities

Organised **APTDC tours** from Hyderabad to Nagarjunakonda at weekends (see p.1045) – also taking in the nearby Ethiopothala Waterfalls (Rs20) and an engraved Buddhist monolith known as the Pylon – are rushed: if you want to spend more time in the area you can take a bus from Hyderabad (4hr; all the regular Macherla services stop at Vijayapuri) or Vijayawada (6hr; a direct service runs daily at 11am and frequent services leave from Guntur). Tickets for **boats** to the island (daily 9am & 1.30pm; 45min; Rs60) go on sale 25 minutes before departure. Each boat leaves the island ninety minutes after it arrives, which allows enough time to see the museum and walk briskly round the monuments, but if you want to take your time and soak up the atmosphere, take the morning boat and return in the afternoon.

Accommodation at Vijayapuri is limited and there are two distinct settlements 6km apart on either side of the dam. Decide in advance where you want to stay and get off the bus at the best spot. For easy access to the sites it's better to stay near the jetty on the right bank of the dam; ask the bus to leave you at the launch station. The drab-looking concrete *Nagarjuna Motel Complex* (T08642/278188; ❷–❸) has adequate rooms, some with a/c, while 500m away in the village, the *Golden Lodge* (T08642/278148; ❶) is much more basic. APTDC runs two hotels in the area, which can be booked via Ⓦwww .tourisminap.com: the all-a/c *Punnami Vijay Vihar* (T08680/277362; ❺–❻) on the near side of the dam as you approach the lake form Hyderabad, and the *Punnami Ethiopothala* (T08680/276540; ❸–❹), by the waterfalls, which has more modest a/c and non-a/c rooms.

Eastern Andhra Pradesh

Perhaps India's least visited area, **eastern Andhra Pradesh** is sandwiched between the Bay of Bengal in the east and the red soil and high peaks of the Eastern Ghats in the north. Its one architectural attraction is the ancient Buddhist site of **Amaravati**, near the city of **Vijayawada**, whose sprinkling of historic temples is far overshadowed by impersonal, modern buildings. For anyone with a strong desire to explore, however, pockets of natural beauty along the coast and in the hills of eastern Andhra Pradesh can offer rich rewards.

Vijayawada and around

Almost 450km north of Chennai, a third of the way to Kolkata (Calcutta), **VIJAYAWADA** is a bustling commercial centre on the banks of the Krishna delta, 90km from the coast. This mundane city, alleviated by a mountain backdrop of bare granite outcrops and some urban greenery, is seldom visited by tourists, but does, however, make the obvious stop-off point for visits to the third-century Buddhist site at **Amaravati**, 60km west.

The **Kanaka Durga** (also known as Vijaya) **temple** on Indrakila Hill in the east, dedicated to the city's patron goddess of riches, power and benevolence, is the most interesting of Vijayawada's handful of temples. Across the river, roughly 3km out of town, is an ancient, unmodified cave temple at **Undavalli**, a tiny rural village set off the main road and reachable on any Guntur-bound bus, or the local #13 service.

Practicalities

Vijayawada's **railway station**, on the main Chennai–Kolkata (Calcutta) line, is in the centre of town. Buses arriving from Amaravati and as far afield as Hyderabad and Chennai pull into the Pandit Nehru **Bus Stand** 1.5km further west, on the other side of the Ryes Canal which flows through the heart of town. Specific ticket offices cater for each service, and a **tourist office** (℡0866/252 3966) has details on local hotels and sights. APTDC also has an office in the centre of town at the *Hotel Ilapuram* complex, Gandhi Nagar (℡0866/257 0255). You can **change money** at Zen Global Finance, 40-6-27 Krishna Nagar in Labbipet, or use one of the ATMs on Atchutaramaiah Street, which links the railway station to Elluru Road, or at the bus stand.

Vijayawada is a major business centre, with a good selection of mid-range **hotels**, all within 1km of the railway station and bus stand. *Monika Lodge* (℡0866/257 1334; ❷), just off Elluru Road about 300m northeast of the bus stand, is one of the cheapest but a bit grubby. Two better-value places, both on Atchutaramaiah Street, are the *Hotel Narayana Swamy* (℡0866/257 1221, ℻257 2489; ❸–❹) and the *Sri Ram* (℡0866/257 9377, ℻257 7721; ❸–❹), both with spotless rooms, some a/c and cable TV. *Raj Towers* (℡0866/257 1311, ℻556 1714; ❸–❻) on Elluru Road is a tall modern block with good mid-range rooms and a decent **restaurant**. The fourth-floor *Palace Heights* restaurant at the *Hotel Swarna Palace*, where Atchutaramaiah Street meets Elluru Road, also provides large portions of Indian, Chinese and Continental food, and has a bar. Inexpensive Andhra "meals" joints abound.

Amaravati

A small town on the banks of the Krishna 30km west of Vijayawada, **AMARAVATI** is the site of a Buddhist settlement (daily except Fri 10am–5pm; Rs100 [Rs5]), formerly known as Chintapalli, where a stupa larger than those at Sanchi (see p.404) was erected over relics of the Buddha in the third century BC, during the reign of Ashoka. The stupa no longer stands, but its size is evident from the mound that formed its base. There was a gateway at each of the cardinal points, one of which has been reconstructed, and the meticulously carved details show themes from the Buddha's life. A Kalachakra initiation programme was conducted by the Dalai Lama here in January 2006 to commemorate 2550 years since the Buddha's birth.

Exhibits at the small but fascinating **museum** (same hours; Rs2) range in date from the third century BC to the twelfth century AD and include Buddha statues with lotus symbols on the feet, tightly curled hair and long ear lobes – all traditional indications of an enlightened teacher. Other stone carvings show Buddhist symbols such as the *chakra* (wheel of *dharma*), throne, stupa and *bodhi* tree. Later sculptures include limestone statues of the goddess Tara and *bodhisattva* Padmapani, showing that Mahayana teachings had taken over from the earlier Hinayana doctrines.

Practicalities

Buses run at least once an hour from Vijayawada to Amaravati (1hr 45min–2hr) and more frequently from Guntur (every 15min; 45min–1hr), a dull market town in between. The excavated site and museum are under a kilometre from the bus stand. Trishaws – miniature carts attached to tricycles and brightly painted with chubby film stars – shuttle visitors around town. The APTDC *Punnami*, on the bank of the Krishna (℡08645/255332; ❹), has just four a/c rooms and a dorm (Rs100). The only other place to stay is the clean and modern *Sindura Residency* (℡08645/254100; ❸–❹), halfway along the main street. Apart from the standard APTDC canteen, there is a smattering of simple food stalls along the main street.

Southern Andhra Pradesh

The further south you travel from the fertile lands watered by the great Krishna and Godavari rivers, the less hospitable the terrain becomes, especially in the rocky southwest of the state. For Hindus, the main attraction in southern Andhra Pradesh is the tenth-century **Venkateshvara temple**, outside **Tirupati**, the most popular Vishnu shrine in India, where several thousand pilgrims come each day to receive *darshan*. **Puttaparthy**, the home town of the spiritual leader Sai Baba, is the only other place in the region to attract significant numbers of visitors. Both Tirupati and Puttaparthy are closer to Chennai in Tamil Nadu and Bengaluru (Bangalore) in Karnataka than to other points in Andhra Pradesh, and for many tourists, constitute their only foray into the state.

Tirupati and Tirumala Hill

Set in a stunning position, surrounded by wooded hills capped by a ring of vertical red rocks, the **Shri Venkateshvara temple** at Tirumala, 170km northwest of Chennai, is said to be the richest and most popular place of pilgrimage in the world, drawing more devotees than either Rome or Mecca. With its many shrines and *dharamshaias*, the whole area around Tirumala Hill, an enervating drive 700m up in the Venkata hills, provides a fascinating insight into contemporary Hinduism practised on a large scale. The hill is 11km as the crow flies from its service town of **TIRUPATI**, but double that by road.

Just a five-minute walk from the railway station, the one temple in Tirupati itself that's definitely worth a visit is **Govindarajaswamy**, whose modern grey *gopura* is clearly visible from many points in town. Begun by the Nayaks in the sixteenth century, it's an interesting complex with large open courtyards decorated with lion sculptures and some ornate wooden roofs. The inner sanctum is open to non-Hindus and contains a splendid large black reclining Vishnu, coated in bronze armour and bedecked in flowers. A visit during the *darshan* (daily 10am–8.45pm; Rs5) will let you in to glimpse the deity, and participate in fire blessings at the main and subsidiary shrines. In its own compound by the side entrance stands the fine little Venkateshvara Museum of Temple Arts (daily 8am–8pm; Rs1). The temple's impressive tank lies 200m to the east.

Between Tirupati and Tirumala Hill, the **Tiruchanur Padmavati temple** is another popular pilgrimage halt. A gold *vimana* tower with lions at each corner surmounts the sanctuary, which contains a black stone image of goddess Lakshmi with one silver eye. At the front step, water sprays wash the feet of the devotees. A Rs20 ticket allows you to jump the queue to enter the sanctuary.

Tirumala Hill, the Venkateshvara temple and Kapilateertham

The road trip up Tirumala Hill is a lot less terrifying now that there's a separate route down; the most devout, of course, climb the hill by foot. The **trail** starts at Alipuri, 4km from the centre of Tirupati; all the pilgrim buses pass through – look out for a large Garuda statue and the soaring *gopura* of the first temple. The first hour consists of a flight of knee-crunching concrete steps, covered in yellow, orange and red tikka daubed by pilgrims as they ascend. The path then mercifully levels out before the final assault some two hours on. Allow at least four hours to the top – fitter pilgrims might do it half an hour quicker. The trail is covered over for most of the way, affording protection from the blistering sun, and there are drinks stalls all along the route. An early start is recommended. When you get to the top, you will see barbers busying themselves giving pilgrims tonsures as part of their devotions.

The **Venkateshvara temple** (aka Sri Vari) dedicated to **Vishnu** and started in the tenth century, has been recently renovated to provide facilities for the thousands of pilgrims who visit daily; a rabbit warren of passages and waiting rooms wind their way around the complex in which pilgrims interminably shuffle towards the inner sanctum; weekends, public holidays, and festivals are even busier. Unless your visit is intended to be particularly rigorous, on reaching the temple you should follow the signs for the special *darshan* (daily 6–10am & noon–9pm; Rs50) as this may reduce the time it takes to get inside by quite a few hours; you have to sign a declaration of faith in Lord Venkateshvara and give your passport number. You can also obtain these *darshan* tickets from the temple tourism office near the temple bus stand on Station Road. Note that **no electronic devices** are allowed inside the temple so you must either be willing to check them in with your shoes at the free stalls or stow them back at your hotel.

At the entrance is a colonnade, lined with life-sized statues of royal patrons, in copper or stone. The *gopura* gateway leading to the inner courtyard is decorated with sheets of embossed silver; a gold *stambha* (flagstaff) stands outside the inner shrine next to a gold upturned lotus on a plinth. Outside, opposite the temple, is a small museum, the **Hall of Antiquities** (daily 8am–8pm). Your special *darshan* ticket entitles you to enter the museum via a shorter queue opposite the exit and to pick up two free *laddu* sweets. Temple funds support a university, hospital, orphanages and schools at Tirupati as well as providing cheap, and in some cases free, accommodation for pilgrims.

At the bottom of the hill, the **Sri Kapileswaraswami** temple at Kapilateertham is the only Tirumala temple devoted to Shiva, with a small Hindu pleasure garden at the entrance and a sacred waterfall which crashes into a large tank surrounded by colonnades, where pilgrims pile in for a bath.

Chandragiri Fort

In the sixteenth century, **Chandragiri**, 11km southwest of Tirupati, became the third capital of the Vijayanagars, whose power had declined following the fall of the city of Vijayanagar (Hampi) in Karnataka. It was here that the British negotiated the acquisition of the land to establish Fort St George, the earliest settlement at what is now Chennai. The original fort (daily except Fri 10am–5pm; Rs100 [Rs5]), thought to date from around 1000 AD, was taken over by Haider Ali in 1782, followed by the British in 1792. A small **museum** of sculpture, weapons and memorabilia is housed in the main building, the Indo-Saracenic Raja Mahal. Another building, the **Rani Mahal**, stands close by, while behind that is a hill with two freestanding boulders that was used as a place of public execution during Vijayanagar times. A little temple from the Krishna Deva Raya period and a freshwater tank stand at the top of the hill behind the Raja Mahal. In the evening there is a 45-minute **sound-and-light** show (English: Nov–Feb 7.30pm; March–Oct 8pm; Rs30).

Practicalities

The best way of **getting to Tirupati** is by train from Chennai; the trip can just about be done in a day if you get the Saptagiri Express #6057 (6.25am; 3hr 5min). From Hyderabad it takes eleven to fifteen hours by bus or train. The main APTDC **tourist office** is on the second floor of the Sri Devi Complex, Tilak Road (daily 6.30am–9pm; ☎0877/225 5385), and there's also an APTDC counter (daily 8am–9pm; ☎0877/228 9129) at the **railway station**, right in the centre of town. Tirupati's APSRTC Central **bus station** – also with 24-hour left-luggage – is about 1km east of the railway station. Frequent express services run to Chennai (4hr), but the train is far more comfortable. However, if you're travelling south and want to avoid Chennai, there are hourly buses to Kanchipuram (5hr), three of which continue to Mahabalipuram (7hr). There are also three daily flights to Hyderabad and two to Bengaluru from the airport, 14km out of Tirupati. Within town, beautifully decorated **cycle rickshaws**, and auto-rickshaws are available for travelling round town.

A special section at the back of the bus stand has services every few minutes **to Tirumala** and the Venkateshvara temple; you can also access the hill from a separate local bus stand outside the railway station. You shouldn't have to queue for long at either unless it's a weekend or festival. **Taxis** are best organized through the APTDC counter at the railway station rather than the unlicensed ones outside. There are a few **Internet** places in Tirupati, such as Net Hill in the shopping complex at the corner of the bus stand. The Syndicate and ICICI banks both have **ATMs** on Netaji Road, and there are even a couple up on Tirumala Hill.

Accommodation and eating

Unless you're a pilgrim seeking accommodation in the *dharamshalas* near the temple, all the decent **places to stay** are in Tirupati, near the railway station and bus stand: there's a vast array of hotels and lodges to suit all budgets. **Eating** is almost exclusively vegetarian, even in the hotels, and cheap "meals" places abound in town and on Tirumala Hill. If you're in need of meat and booze, head for the *Yalamuri* beer garden, off the traffic circle opposite the bus stand.

Annapurna 349 G Car St, opposite the railway station ☎0877/225 0666. Smart modern hotel with clean, simply furnished rooms and good stand-up snack bar on the ground floor. ❸–❹
Apsara 213 TP Area ☎0877/557 8062. Almost opposite the bus station, this is a pretty standard place offering basic but clean attached rooms of varying sizes. ❶
Balaji Deluxe 291 Railway Station Rd ☎0877/222 5930. Not much deluxe about it, but

this typical basic lodge opposite the station is adequate for a night, with cramped but cleanish attached rooms. ❶
Bhimas Deluxe 34–38 G Car St, near the railway station ☎0877/222 5521, ⦿www.hotelbhimas .com. Decent, comfortable rooms with central a/c, and 12hr "transit rooms" available at half price. The *Mayura* veg restaurant serves North and south Indian food plus some Chinese dishes in the evenings. ❹

Durga Residency 164 TP Area ☎ 0877/222 9111. Spacious mid-range option with some new a/c rooms, on a quiet backstreet between the station and bus stand. ③–④

Mayura 209 TP Area ☎ 0877/222 5925, Ⓔ mayura @nettlinx.com. Best but most expensive of a host of hotels opposite the bus station, offering average mid-range rooms with decent bathrooms and TV. ④–⑤

Sindhuri Park Beside bathing tank ☎ 0877/225 6430, Ⓦ www.hotelsindhuri .com. The smartest place in the centre, this all-a/c hotel has excellent facilities and great views of the tank and temple. The basement *Vrinda* restaurant serves quality veg food, including a range of thalis, and has a Rs100 buffet on weekend evenings. ⑤–⑦

Puttaparthy

Deep in the southwest of the state, amid the arid rocky hills bordering Karnataka, a thriving community has grown up around the once insignificant village of **PUTTAPARTHY**, birthplace of spiritual leader **Sai Baba**, whose followers believe him to be the new incarnation of God. Centring on **Prasanthi Nilayam** (Abode of Peace), the ashram where Sai Baba resides from July to March, the town has schools, a university, hospital and sports centre which offer up-to-date and free services to all. There's even a small airport. The ashram itself is a huge complex with room for thousands, with canteens, shops, a museum and library, and a vast assembly hall where Sai Baba gives *darshan* twice daily (7.45am & 3pm). Queues start more than an hour before the appointed time, and a lottery decides who gets to sit near the front. The museum (daily 10am–noon) contains a detailed, fascinating display on the world's major faiths with illustrations and quotations from their sacred texts, punctuated by Sai Baba's comments.

Practicalities

Buses from Bengaluru (Bangalore), Hyderabad and Chennai stop at the stand outside the ashram entrance. The new **railway station**, named Sri Satya Sai

Shri Satya Sai Baba

Born on November 23, 1926, in Puttaparthy, then an obscure village in the Madras Presidency, **Satyanarayana Raju** is reported to have shown prodigious talents and unusual purity and compassion from an early age. His apparently supernatural abilities initially caused some concern to his family, who took him to Vedic doctors and eventually to be exorcised. Having been pronounced to be possessed by the divine rather than the diabolical, at the age of 14 he calmly announced that he was the new incarnation of **Sai Baba**, a saint from Shirdi in Maharashtra who died eight years before Satya was born.

Gradually his fame spread, and a large following grew. In 1950 the **ashram** was inaugurated and a decade later Sai Baba was attracting international attention; today he has millions of devotees worldwide, a considerable number of whom turn out for his birthday celebrations in Puttaparthy, when he delivers a message to his devotees. Just 5ft tall, with a startling Hendrix-style Afro, his smiling, saffron-clad figure is seen on posters, framed photos and murals all over south India. Though his **miraculous powers** reportedly include the ability to materialize *vibhuti*, sacred ash, with curative properties, Sai Baba claims this to be an unimportant activity, aimed at those firmly entrenched in materialism, and emphasizes instead his message of **universal love**. In recent years a number of ex-followers have made serious accusations about coercion and even sexual abuse on the part of the guru himself, which have been vehemently denied. Whatever your feelings about the divinity of Sai Baba, the atmosphere around the ashram is undeniably peaceful, and the growth of such a vibrant community in this once-forgotten backwater is no small miracle in itself. You can do some research on the guru at Ⓦ www.saibabalinks.com.

Prasanti Nilayam, is 8km from town on the main north–south route, from which you should be able to get a shared auto-rickshaw to the ashram for Rs10. There are more services to and from **Dharmavaram**, 42km away, which is connected to Puttaparthy by regular buses. Indian Airlines runs daily flights to both Mumbai and Chennai from the small airport, 6km from the ashram.

Many visitors choose to **stay** in the ashram accommodation, which is strictly segregated by sex, except for families. Costs are minimal, and though you can't book in advance, you can enquire about availability at the secretary's office (☎08555/287583). Outside the ashram, many of the basic lodges are rather overpriced, but a good cheap option is the friendly *Sai Ganesh Guest House* near the police station (☎08555/287079; ❷). The *Sri Sai Sadan* at the far end of the main street (☎08555/287507, ✉srisaisadan@yahoo.com; ❹) is also decent value; all rooms have fridge, TV and balcony with views of the country-side or the ashram, and there's a meditation room and rooftop restaurant. At the top end, the *Sai Towers*, near the ashram entrance (☎0855/287270, ⓦwww .saitowers.com; ❺–❽), charges a lot for its smallish non-a/c and a/c rooms, but has a good **restaurant** downstairs. The ashram also has a canteen which is open to nonresidents and there are simple snack stalls along the main street outside the ashram; it's also worth trying the delicious Tibetan food at the *Bamboo Nest* on Chitravathi Road or *Little Tibet Kitchen*, a mellow upstairs hang-out just down from *Sai Towers*. As you'd expect of such a cosmopolitan place, there are plenty of exchange bureaus, **ATMs** and **Internet** joints dotted the length of the main drag.

Travel details

Trains

Hyderabad/Secunderabad to: Bengaluru (3–5 daily; 11hr 5min–13hr 25min); Bhubaneswar (4 daily; 18hr 45min–22hr 15min); Chennai (2 daily; 13hr 45min–14hr 10min); Delhi (3–4 daily; 22hr 30min–32hr); Kolkata (2–3 daily; 26hr 45min–30hr 55min); Mumbai (4–5 daily; 13hr 10min–16hr 25min); Tirupati (4–6 daily; 11hr 25min–15hr 20min); Varanasi (2 weekly; 30hr 20min); Vijayawada (10–12 daily; 5hr 25min–7hr 20min); Warangal (9–11 daily; 2hr 5min–3hr 30min).

Tirupati to: Chennai (3 daily; 2hr 55min–3hr 15min); Hyderabad/Secunderabad (4–6 daily; 12hr 15min–16hr 10min); Kolkata (1 daily; 38hr 15min); Mumbai (1–2 daily; 24hr 20min–25hr 35min); Varanasi (1 weekly; 39hr 40min); Vijayawada (3–5 daily; 7hr–8hr 25min).

Vijayawada to: Chennai (7–11 daily; 6hr 25min–8hr 50min); Delhi (4–6 daily; 23hr 10min–32hr 40min); Hyderabad/Secunderabad (10–12 daily; 5hr 20min–8hr 20min); Kolkata (5–7 daily; 21hr 15min–33hr 20min); Tirupati (3–5 daily; 6hr 30min–8hr 35min).

Buses

Hyderabad to: Amaravati (2 daily; 7hr); Bengaluru (hourly; 13hr); Bidar (every 30min–1hr; 4hr); Chennai (3 daily; 16hr); Mumbai (7–10 daily; 17hr); Puttaparthy (3 daily; 10hr); Tirupati (8 daily; 12hr); Vijayapuri (hourly; 4hr); Vijayawada (every 15min; 6hr); Warangal (every 15–30min; 3hr).

Tirupati to: Bengaluru (hourly; 7hr); Chennai (every 15–30min; 3hr 30min–4hr); Hyderabad (8 daily; 12hr); Kanchipuram (hourly; 3hr 30min); Mamallapuram (3 daily; 5hr 30min); Puttaparthy (2 daily; 10–11hr).

Vijayawada to: Amaravati (hourly; 1hr 30min–2hr); Guntur (every 15min; 1hr–1hr 15min); Hyderabad (every 15min; 6hr).

Flights

(**AI** = Air India, **IC** = Indian Airlines, **DN** = Air Deccan, **6E** = IndiGo, **9W** = Jet Airways, **S2** = JetLite, **IT** = Kingfisher, **G8** = Go Air, **I7** = Paramount Airways, **SG** = SpiceJet)

Hyderabad to: Ahmedabad (IC, DN, IT, SG; 4 daily; 1hr 40min); Bengaluru (IC, 6E, 9W, S2, DN, IT, I7, SG; 22 daily; 1hr–1hr 30min); Chennai (IC, 6E, 9W,

S2, DN, IT, G8, I7, SG; 19 daily; 1hr–1hr 30min); Delhi (IC, 6E, 9W, S2, DN, IT, SG: 15 daily; 2hr–4hr 15min); Goa (6E, DN; 2 daily; 1hr 45min); Kolkata (6E, 9W, S2, DN, IT, SG; 8 daily; 2hr–2hr 55min); Mumbai (IC, AI, 9W, S2, DN, IT, G8, SG; 19 daily; 1hr 15min–3hr 30min); Pune (S2, DN, IT, SG; 5 daily; 1hr); Tirupati (IC, DN; 2 daily; 55min).

Puttaparthy to: Chennai (IC; 1 daily; 40min), Mumbai (IC; 1 daily; 2hr).
Tirupati to: Bengaluru (DN, IT; 2 daily; 40min); Hyderabad (IC, DN, IT; 3 daily; 55min).

The Andaman Islands

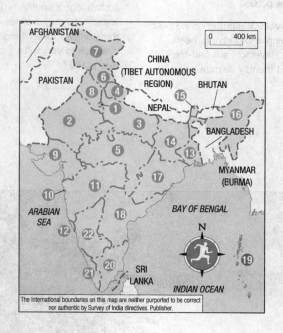

AFGHANISTAN

0   400 km

CHINA
(TIBET AUTONOMOUS
REGION)

PAKISTAN

BHUTAN

⑦
⑥
⑧ ④
① NEPAL
②   ③
⑤
⑨
⑪
⑩
ARABIAN
SEA
⑫ ㉒
㉑ ⑳
SRI
LANKA

⑮
⑯
⑭
⑬
BANGLADESH

MYANMAR
(BURMA)

⑰
⑱
BAY OF BENGAL

N

⑲

INDIAN OCEAN

The International boundaries on this map are neither purported to be correct
nor authentic by Survey of India directives. Publisher.

CHAPTER 19

Highlights

* **Wandoor** The white sandy beach and islets of the Mahatma Gandhi National Marine Park are the most popular day-trip destination from Port Blair, and a good appetizer for more remote parts. See p.1078

* **Scuba diving** The Andamans' beautiful coral reefs teem with vivid underwater life. See p.1080

* **Havelock Island** For the best diving and partying, head for Havelock, still laid-back and friendly despite being the most developed of the Andamans. See p.1081

* **North Andaman** The long haul by bus or boat from Port Blair is worthwhile for the backdrop of thick rainforest and the dazzling tropical beaches when you get there. See p.1086

* **Little Andaman** As very few travellers make it to the archipelago's southernmost island, you may well have the stunning forest-fringed beaches to yourself. See p.1087

▲ Mahatma Gandhi National marine park

The Andaman Islands

Comprising India's most remote state, the **ANDAMAN ISLANDS** are situated over 1000km off the east coast in the middle of the Bay of Bengal, connected to the mainland by flights and ferries from Kolkata, Chennai and Vishakapatnam. Thickly covered by deep green tropical forest, the archipelago supports a profusion of wildlife, including some extremely rare species of bird, but the principal attraction for tourists lies in the beaches and the pristine reefs that ring most of the islands. Filled with colourful fish and kaleidoscopic corals, the crystal-clear waters of the Andaman Sea feature some of the world's richest and least spoilt marine reserves – perfect for **snorkelling** and **scuba diving**. Although parts of the archipelago still see few visitors, the increasing number and decreasing cost of flights mean that the Andamans are now firmly on the tourist circuit. The impending arrival of flights from Thailand and other parts of Southeast Asia might encourage you to go now, before these idyllic islands get overrun.

For administrative purposes, the Andamans are grouped with the **Nicobar Islands**, 200km further south, but these remain strictly off-limits to foreigners, as well as Indians with no direct business there. Approximately two hundred islands make up the Andaman group and nineteen the Nicobar. They are of varying size, the summits of a submarine mountain range stretching 755km from the Arakan Yoma chain in Burma to the fringes of Sumatra in the south. All but the most remote are populated in parts by **indigenous tribes** whose numbers have been slashed dramatically as a result of nineteenth-century European settlement and, more recently, rampant **deforestation**. Today, new felling is supposed to be strictly controlled, confined to mature trees of certain species at least 1km from the coast, but how stringently that is adhered to is a matter for conjecture.

Foreign tourists are only permitted to visit certain parts of the Andaman group, separated by the deep Ten Degree Channel from the Nicobar Islands. The point of arrival for boats and planes is **South Andaman**, where the predominantly Tamil and Bengali community in the small but busy capital, **Port Blair**, accounts for almost half the total population. **Permits**, obtainable on arrival by both sea and air, are granted for a stay of one month. The most beautiful beaches and coral reefs are found on outlying islands. A healthy get-up-and-go spirit is essential if you plan to explore these, as connections and transport can be erratic, frequently uncomfortable and severely limited, especially on the less visited islands. Once away from the settlements, you'll need your own camping supplies and equipment. It's also worth pointing out that a surprising number of travellers fall sick in the Andamans. The dense tree cover, marshy swamps and high rainfall combine

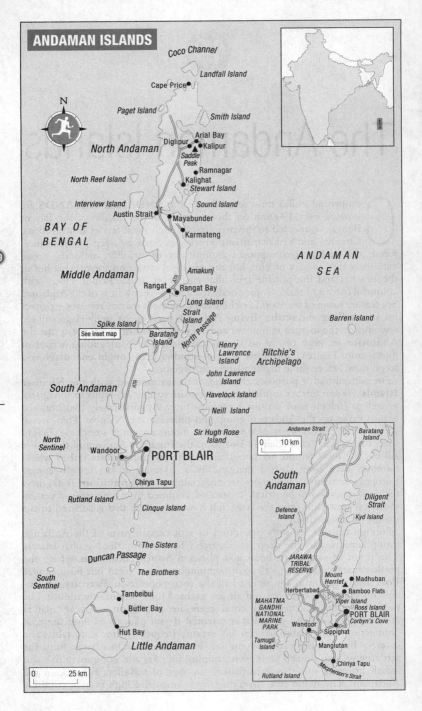

Contrary to the rumours based on the sketchy information that emerged in the days following the devastating **tsunami** of Boxing Day 2004, the island chain did not suffer the total destruction and loss of life at first feared. Most of the damage and death took place in the Nicobars, which lie much closer to the earthquake's epicentre off Indonesia, especially the islands of Car Nicobar, Katchall and Great Nicobar. In all, around three thousand people were confirmed dead there, and a further four and a half thousand declared missing, presumed dead. The only island in the Andamans to suffer extensively was Little Andaman (see p.1087). Indeed, the handful of deaths and structural damage in the Port Blair area – mainly to a few old buildings around town, and the quay and Water Sports Complex at Aberdeen Jetty – were caused by the **earthquake** rather than the ensuing tsunami.

One **positive note** to emerge from the entire episode is that not a single indigenous person of those who are still allowed to live in the traditional way (see box, pp.1070–1071) is said to have perished, even on islands that were badly battered. This is thought to be due to the fact that the tribal people got wind of the impending tragedy by observing the agitation amongst the wildlife and quickly shifted to higher ground. Such a powerful testament to the benefits of living so close to nature provides a sobering lesson to us more "civilized" folk.

to provide the perfect breeding ground for mosquitoes, and **malaria** is endemic in even the most remote settlements. Sandflies are also ferocious in certain places and **tropical ulcer** infections from scratching the bites is a frequent hazard.

The **climate** remains tropical throughout the year, with temperatures ranging from 24°C to 35°C and humidity levels never below seventy percent. By far the best time to visit is between January and April. From mid-May to October, heavy rains flush the islands, often bringing violent cyclones that leave west-coast beaches strewn with fallen trees, while in November and December less severe rains arrive with the northeast monsoon. Despite being so far east, the islands run on Indian time, so the sun rises as early as 4.30am in summer and darkness falls soon after 5pm.

Some history

The earliest mention of the Andaman and Nicobar islands is found in **Ptolemy**'s geographical treatises of the second century AD. Other records from the Chinese Buddhist monk I'Tsing some five hundred years later and Arabian travellers who passed by in the ninth century depict the inhabitants as fierce and cannibalistic. **Marco Polo** arrived in the thirteenth century and could offer no more favourable description of the natives: "The people are without a king and are idolaters no better than wild beasts. All the men of the island of Angamanian have heads like dogs... they are a most cruel generation, and eat everybody they catch..." It is unlikely, however, that the Andamanese were cannibals, as the most vivid reports of their ferocity were propagated by Malay pirates who held sway over the surrounding seas, and needed to keep looters well away from trade ships that passed between India, China and the Far East.

During the eighteenth and nineteenth centuries, **European missionaries** and trading companies turned their attention to the islands with a view to colonization. A string of unsuccessful attempts to convert the Nicobaris to Christianity was made by the French, Dutch and Danish, all of whom were forced to abandon their plans in the face of hideous diseases and a severe lack of food and water. Though the missionaries themselves seldom met with any

THE ANDAMAN ISLANDS

hostility, several fleets of trading ships that tried to dock on the islands were captured, and their crews murdered, by Nicobari people.

In 1777, the British Lieutenant Blair chose the South Andaman harbour now known as **Port Blair** as the site for a **penal colony**. Both this scheme, and an attempt to settle the Nicobar Islands in 1867, were thwarted by the harsh climatic conditions of the forests. However, the third go at colonization was more successful, and in 1858 Port Blair finally did become a penal settlement, where political activists who had fuelled the Mutiny in 1857 were made to clear land and build their own prison. Out of 773 prisoners, 292 died, escaped or were hanged in the first two months. Many also lost their lives in attacks by Andamanese tribes who objected to forest clearance, but the settlement continued to fill with people from mainland India, and by 1864 the number of convicts had grown to three thousand. In 1896 work began on a jail made up of hundreds of tiny solitary cells, which was used to confine political prisoners until 1945. The prison still stands and is Port Blair's prime "tourist attraction" (see p.1074).

In 1919, the British government in India decided to close down the penal settlement, but it was subsequently used to incarcerate a new generation of freedom fighters from India, Malabar and Burma. During World War II the islands were occupied by the **Japanese**, who tortured and murdered hundreds of indigenous islanders suspected of collaborating with the British, and bombed the homes of the Jarawa tribe. British forces moved back in 1945, and at last abolished the penal settlement.

After **Partition**, refugees – mostly low-caste Hindus from Bengal – were given land in Port Blair and North Andaman, where the forest was clear-felled to make room for rice paddy, cocoa plantations and new industries. Since 1951, the population has increased more than ten-fold, further swollen by repatriated Tamils from Sri Lanka, thousands of Bihari labourers, ex-servicemen given land grants, economic migrants from poorer Indian states, and the legions of government employees packed off here on two-year "punishment postings". This replanted population greatly outnumbers the Andamans' indigenous people (see box, pp.1070–1071), who currently comprise around half of one percent of the total. In addition, there exists within Port Blair a clear divide between the relatively recent incomers and the so-called "**pre-42s**" – descendants of the released convicts and freedom fighters whose families settled here before the major influx from the mainland. This small but influential minority, based at the exclusive *Browning Club* in the capital, has been calling for curbs on immigration and new property rules to slow down the rate of settlement, which would be no bad thing.

With the timber-extraction cash cow now partially tethered, the hope is that **tourism** will replace tree-felling as the main source of revenue. However, the extra visitor numbers envisaged are certain to overtax an already inadequate infrastructure, aggravating seasonal water shortages and sewage disposal problems. Given India's track record with tourism development, it's hard to be optimistic. Delhi has already given the go-ahead for air services from Southeast Asia and eventually charter flights from Europe to land on the recently extended airport runway. If only a small percentage of the tourist traffic between Thailand and India is diverted through the Andamans, the impact on this culturally and ecologically fragile region could be catastrophic.

Getting to the Andaman Islands

Port Blair on South Andaman is now served by around half a dozen **flights** daily, from both Kolkata and Chennai, operated by Jet Airways, Kingfisher, Air

Deccan, SpiceJet and Indian Airlines. It's also possible to get to Port Blair by **ship**. Services from Chennai (see p.1111) can be reasonably relied upon to leave in each direction once every week to ten days, while those from Kolkata (see p.873) sail roughly every two weeks; boats from Vishakapatnam are altogether more erratic, averaging once a month – call the Shipping Office on ☏0891/256 5597 for more info. Although cheaper than flying, sea crossings are long (3–5 days), uncomfortable and often delayed by bad conditions. However you get to the islands, thirty-day **permits** are obtainable for free on arrival in Port Blair. Permits are sometimes extendable for fifteen days, but the authorities may only allow you to stay in Port Blair for that period – not an appealing prospect.

South Andaman: Port Blair and around

South Andaman is the most heavily populated of the Andaman Islands – particularly around the capital, **Port Blair** – thanks in part to the drastic thinning of tree cover to make way for settlement. Foreign tourists can only visit its southern and east central reaches – including the beaches at **Corbyn's Cove** and **Chiriya Tapu**, the fine reefs on the western shores at **Wandoor**, 35km southwest of Port Blair, and the environs of **Madhuban** and **Mount Harriet**, on the east coast across the bay from the capital. With your own transport it's easy to find your way along the narrow bumpy roads that connect small villages, weaving through forests and coconut fields, and skirting the swamps and rocky outcrops that form the coastline.

Port Blair

A refreshingly leafy but ultimately characterless cluster of tin-roofed buildings tumbling towards the sea in the north, east and west, and petering out into fields and forests in the south, **PORT BLAIR** merits only a short stay. There's little to see here – just the **Cellular Jail** and a few small **museums** – but as the point of arrival for the islands and the only place with a bank, tourist offices and other facilities, it can't be avoided. If you plan to head off to the more remote islands, this is also the place to stock up on supplies and buy necessary equipment.

Arrival and information

Port Blair has two main jetties: **boats** from the mainland moor at **Haddo Jetty**, nearly 2km northwest of **Phoenix Jetty**, arrival point for inter-island ferries. The Director of Shipping Services at Phoenix Jetty has the latest information on boats and ferries, but you can also check details of forthcoming departures in the shipping-news column of the local newspaper, the *Daily Telegrams* (Rs1.50). Advice on booking ferry tickets appears in the box on pp.1076–1077.

The smart, newly extended **Veer Savarkar airport** terminal is 4km south of town at Lamba Line. **Taxis** and **auto-rickshaws** are on hand for short trips into town (Rs50), but if you've booked a room in any of the middle- or upper-range hotels or do so at the counter in the airport, you should find a shuttle bus waiting outside. Local **buses** also frequently ply the route to town from outside the shop on the far side of the main road, barely 100m from the terminal building.

The counter at the airport (☏03192/232414) hands out a useful general brochure, but trying to get more than basic tour and hotel info from the main **A&N Directorate of Tourism office** (Mon–Fri 10am–5pm, Sat 10am–1pm; ☏03192/232747, ⓦwww.andaman.nic.in), situated in a modern building

Quite where the **indigenous population** of the Andaman and Nicobar islands originally came from is a puzzle that has preoccupied anthropologists since Alfred Radcliffe-Brown conducted his famous field work among the Andamanese at the beginning of the twentieth century. Asian-looking groups such as the Shompen may have migrated here from the east and north when the islands were connected to Burma, or the sea was sufficiently shallow to allow transport by canoe, but this doesn't explain the origins of the black populations, whose appearance suggests African roots. Wherever they came from, the survival of the islands' first inhabitants has long been threatened by traders and colonizers, who introduced disease and destroyed their territories through widespread tree-felling. Thousands also died from addiction to the alcohol and opium which the Chinese, Japanese and British exchanged for valuable shells. Many have had their populations decimated, while others like the Nicobarese have assimilated to modern culture, often adopting Christianity. The indigenous inhabitants of the Andamans, divided into *eramtaga* (those living in the jungle) and *ar-yuato* (those living on the coast), traditionally subsisted as hunter-gatherers, living on fish, turtles, turtle eggs, pigs, fruit, honey and roots.

Although they comprised the largest group when the islands were first colonized, only around forty **Great Andamanese** now survive. In the 1860s, the Rev H. Corbyn set up a "home" for the tribe to learn English on Ross Island, insisting that they wear clothes and attend reading and writing classes. Five children and three adults from Corbyn's school were taken as curiosities to Calcutta in 1864, where they were shown around the sights. The whole experience, however, proved more fascinating for the crowds who'd come to ogle the "monkey men" than for the Andamanese themselves, who, one of the organizers of the trip ruefully remarked, "...never evinced astonishment or admiration at anything which they beheld, however wonderful in its novelty we might suppose it would appear to them". From the foreign settlers, the Andamanese tragically contracted diseases such as syphilis, measles, mumps and influenza, and fell prey to opium addiction. Within three years, almost the entire population had died. In recent years the surviving Great Andamanese were forcibly settled on Strait Island, north of South Andaman, as a "breeding centre", where they were forced to rely on the Indian authorities for food and shelter. In the aftermath of the tsunami they were relocated to Port Blair, though for how long remains uncertain.

The **Jarawas**, who were shifted from their original homes when land was cleared to build Port Blair, currently number around 270 and live on the remote western coasts of Middle and South Andaman, hemmed in by the Andaman Trunk Road (ATR), which since the 1970s has cut them off from hunting grounds and freshwater supplies. During the 1980s and 1990s, encroachments on their land by loggers, road builders and Bengali settlers met with fierce resistance, and dozens, possibly hundreds, of people died in **skirmishes**. In one incident a party of Burmese were caught poaching on Jarawa land; of the eleven men involved, six limped out with horrific injuries, two were found dead, and the other three were never seen again.

diagonally opposite Indian Airlines, can be frustrating. Further southwest on Junglighat Main Road, the **India Tourism office** (Mon–Fri 8.30am–5pm; ☎03192/233006, ⓦwww.incredibleindia.org) is not much better. Note that if you intend to visit Interview Island (see p.1085), you must first attain a free permit from the **Chief Wildlife Warden**, whose office (☎03192/233270) is next to the zoo in Haddo.

Road names are not used much in Port Blair, with most establishments addressing themselves simply by their local area. The name of the busiest and most central area is **Aberdeen Bazaar**, where you'll find the Superintendent

Most incidents occurred on or near the ATR, which is why armed escorts board buses at several points during the journey north from Port Blair to Mayabunder. Some **contact** between settlers and tribals was made for a while through gift exchanges at each full moon, when consignments of coconuts, bananas and red cloth were taken to a friendly band of Jarawas on a boat, but the initiative was later cancelled. These meetings nevertheless led to some Jarawas becoming curious about what "civilization" had to offer, and they started to hold their hands out for goodies to passing vehicles and even visiting Indian settlements near their territory. When the initially generous reception waned, their visits evolved into surreptitious raids culminating in an attack on a police outpost in March 1998. Since then the authorities have tried to minimize contact, and conflicts have ceased. The government has also increased Jarawa land by 180 square kilometres, but has dragged its feet over enforcing a 2002 Indian Supreme Court order to close the ATR, which was passed following protests by international pressure groups such as Survival International. In 2008, the court order was still undergoing a drawn-out official review.

Aside from a couple of violent encounters with nineteenth-century seamen, relations with the **Onge**, who call themselves the **Gaubolambe**, have been relatively peaceful. Distinguished by their white-clay and ochre body paint, they continue to live in communal shelters (*bera*) and construct temporary thatched huts (*korale*) on Little Andaman. The remaining population of around one hundred retain their traditional way of life on two small reserves. The Indian government has erected wood and tin huts for them, dispatched a teacher to instruct them in Hindi, and encouraged coconut cultivation, but to little avail. Contact with outsiders is limited to an occasional trip into town to purchase liquor, and visits from rare parties of anthropologists. The reserves are strictly off limits to foreigners, but you can learn about the Onge's traditional hunting practices, beliefs and rituals in Vishvajit Pandya's wonderful ethnography study, *Above the Forest*.

Only very limited contact is ever had with the isolated **Shompen** tribe of Great Nicobar, whose population of around 380 manage to lead a traditional hunting-and-gathering existence. The most elusive tribe of all the **Sentinelese**, live on North Sentinel Island west of South Andaman. Following the first encounter with Indian settlers in 1967, some contact was made with them in 1990, after a team put together by the local administration left gifts on the beaches every month for two years, but subsequent visits have invariably ended in a hail of arrows. Since the early 1990s, the AAJVS, the government department charged with tribal welfare, has effectively given up trying to contact the Sentinelese, who are estimated to number anywhere between fifty and two hundred. Flying in or out of Port Blair, you pass above their island, ringed by a spectacular coral reef. It's reassuring to think that the people sitting at the bottom of the plumes of smoke drifting up from the forest canopy have for so long resisted contact with the outside world.

For more information on the islands' original inhabitants, visit Survival International's excellent website, ⊕www.survival-international.org.

of Police (for permit extensions), the State Bank of India (Mon–Fri 9am–1pm, Sat 9–11am) and most other facilities. Some hotels will change traveller's cheques, but you'll get faster service and better rates at Island Travels (Mon–Sat 9am–6pm; ☎03192/233034), just up the road from the clock tower in Aberdeen Bazaar. There's an ICICI Bank **ATM** at the lower end of Moulana Azad Road and one at UTI Bank near Netaji Stadium. **Internet** access is available at a number of locations around town, including a couple of anonymous places between the bus stand and clock tower, at CyberNet on the other side of the bus stand and at the *Holiday Resort* (see p.1073).

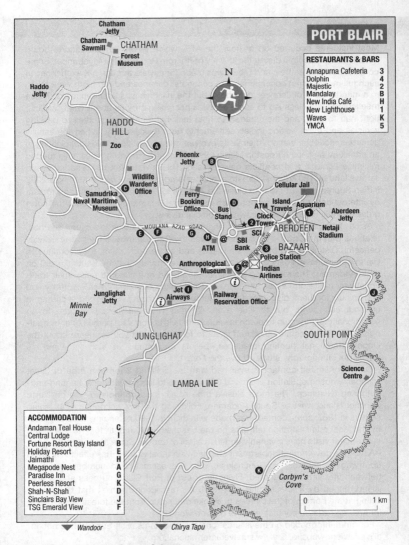

▼ Wandoor   ▼ Chirya Tapu

Local transport and tours

Walking is tiring and time-consuming in hilly Port Blair – even taking into account the minimal amount of sightseeing the place offers – making transport essential. Yellow-top **taxis** gather opposite the bus stand in central Port Blair. They all have meters, but negotiating the price before leaving is the usual practice. Expect to pay at least Rs60 for a trip from the centre of town to Corbyn's Cove; **uto-rickshaws** try to charge just as much as taxis but a ride within town shouldn't cost more than Rs30.

Local **buses** run infrequently from the bus stand to Wandoor and Chiriya Tapu, and can be used for day-trips, though it's best to rely on your own transport to get around South Andaman. **Bicycles** can be rented from Aberdeen

Bazaar, at Rs5 per hour, but the roads to the coasts are most easily covered on a **motorbike** or **scooter**, available for rent at Rs200–250 per day from GDM Tours (℡03192/232999) on Moulana Azad Road or Karishma Tours & Travels, 22 MG Rd, Middle Point (℡09434 274314); you'll need to show a licence and leave a Rs1000 deposit. There are petrol pumps on the crossroads west of the bus stand and on the road towards the airport. Fill up before you leave town, as petrol is hard to come by elsewhere.

The A&N Tourism town **tours** are a complete waste of time but their **harbour cruises** (daily 3–5pm; Rs65) are more worthwhile, departing from Phoenix Jetty for fleeting visits to the floating docks and **Viper Island**; there are also excursions to **Ross Island** (daily 8.30am, 10.30am and 12.30pm; Rs60). They also run **day-trips** to **Mount Harriet** (8am; Rs157) and **Wandoor/Mahatma Gandhi National Marine Park**; the bus tour to Wandoor (8am; Rs105) connects with the 10am boat to the islands of Red Skin and Jolly Buoy (Rs300).

Accommodation

Port Blair boasts a fair selection of places to stay and the abundance of options means availability is only an issue around Christmas and New Year, when prices are also hiked; they drop during monsoon.

Andaman Teal House Delanipur ℡03192/234060. High on the hill above Haddo Jetty, this A&N Tourism place offers great views, spacious and pleasant rooms, and is very good value, although it can be inconvenient without your own transport. ❹

Central Lodge Middle Point ℡03192/233634. Ramshackle wooden building situated in a quiet and secluded corner of town. A rock-bottom option, offering basic rooms, garden space for hammocks and a dorm (Rs80). ❷

Fortune Resort Bay Island Marine Hill ℡03192/234101, ⓦwww.fortuneparkhotels.com. Port Blair's swishest hotel is elegant and airy with polished dark wood. All rooms have carpets and balconies overlooking Phoenix Jetty. There's a quality restaurant, gardens and an open-air sea-water swimming pool. Prices for suites with full board reach $165. ❽–❾

Holiday Resort Premnagar, a 15min walk from the centre ℡03192/230516, ⓔholidayresort88 @hotmail.com. Much better value than most budget places that cost little less; all the rooms are clean and spacious, with TV. There's also a bar and computer room. ❸–❹

Jaimathi Moulana Azad Rd ℡03192/230836. Popular lodge with both Westerners and Indians, offering large, fairly clean rooms with communal balconies. Slightly cheaper than the *Jagannath* next door and more likely to have availability. ❸

Megapode Nest Haddo Hill ℡03192/232380, ⓦwww.aniidco.nic.in. ANIIDCO's upscale

option has 25 comfortable rooms, and pricier self-contained "cottages", ranged around a central lawn; good views, and a quality restaurant. ❻–❼

Paradise Inn Moulana Azad Rd ℡03192/245772, ⓕ233479. Compact modern lodge, where all rooms have TV and phone. Great value and extra off-season discounts. ❸

Peerless Resort Corbyn's Cove ℡03192/229263, ⓦwww.peerlesshotels.com. Lovely setting amid gardens of palms, jasmine and bougainvillea and opposite a white sandy beach, but the balconied a/c rooms and cottages are a bit tatty for the prices they charge. Bar and mid-priced restaurant with an average evening buffet. ❽

Shah-N-Shah Mohanpura ℡03192/233696. Conveniently located between the bus stand and Phoenix Jetty, this is basic but friendly and comfortable, with mostly attached rooms and a sociable terrace. ❸–❹

Sinclairs Bay View On the coast road to Corbyn's Cove ℡03192/227824, ⓦwww.sinclairshotels .com. Clifftop hotel offering spotless carpeted rooms with balconies, large bathrooms and dramatic views, as well as a missable bar and restaurant. Suites in the new wing cost up to $150. ❽–❾

TSG Emerald View 25 Moulana Azad Rd ℡03192/246488, ⓦwww.andamantsg hotels.com. Smart new upper mid-range place with spacious, colourfully furnished rooms, some a/c, boasting all mod cons. ❹–❺

Port Blair's only firm reminder of its gloomy past, the sturdy brick **Cellular Jail** (Tues–Sun 9am–noon & 2–5pm; Rs5), overlooks the sea from a small rise in the northeast of town. Built between 1896 and 1905, its tiny solitary cells were quite different and far worse than the dormitories in other prison blocks erected earlier. Only three of the seven wings that originally radiated from the central tower now remain. Visitors can peer into the 3m-by-3.5m cells and imagine the grim conditions under which the prisoners existed. Cells were dirty and ill-ventilated, drinking water was limited to two glasses per day, and the convicts were expected to wash in the rain as they worked clearing forests and building prison quarters. Food, brought from the mainland, was stored in vats where the rice and pulses became infested with worms; more than half the prison population died long before their twenty years' detention was up. Protests against conditions led to several hunger strikes, and frequent executions took place at the gallows that still stand in squat wooden shelters in the court-yards, in full view of the cells. The **sound-and-light show** (English version Mon, Wed & Fri 6.45pm; Rs20) outlines the history of the prison, and a small **museum** by the entrance gate (same hours as jail) exhibits lists of convicts, photographs and grim torture devices.

About 300m east of the jail near the Water Sports Complex, you can see murky tanks full of fish and coral from the islands' reefs at the **Aquarium** (Tues–Sun except 2nd Sat of each month 9am–1pm & 2–4.45pm; Rs5). Three kilometres out along the coast road towards Corbyn's Cove, Port Blair's newest attraction is the mildly diverting **Science Centre** (Tues–Sun 10am–5.30pm; Rs5), where you can choose to pay an extra Rs2 each to visit the main displays such as the Sky Observatory, Science Magic and other interactive exhibits.

On the south side of the centre, close to the Directorate of Tourism, the **Anthropological Museum** (Mon–Sat 9am–noon & 1–4pm; free) has exhibits on the Andaman and Nicobar tribes, including weapons, tools and rare photo-graphs of the region's indigenous people taken in the 1960s. Among the most striking of these is a sequence featuring the Sentinelese, taken on April 26, 1967, when a party of Indian officials made the first contact with the tribe. After scaring the aborigines, the visitors marched into one of their hunting camps and made off with the bows, arrows and other artefacts now displayed in the museum.

Further northwest in Delanipur opposite ANIIDCO's *Teal House* hotel, the **Samudrika Naval Maritime Museum** (Tues–Sun 9am–5.30pm; Rs10) is an excellent primer if you're heading off to more remote islands, with a superlative shell collection and informative displays on various aspects of local marine biology. One of the exhibits features a cross-section of the different corals you can expect to see on the Andamans' reefs, followed by a rundown of the various threats these fragile organisms face, from mangrove depletion and parasitic starfish to clumsy snorkellers.

Wildlife lovers are advised to steer clear of the grim little **zoo** (Tues–Sun 8am–5pm; Rs2), further down towards Haddo, whose only redeeming feature is that it has successfully bred rare crocodiles and monkeys for release into the wild. Further north, the **Chatham Sawmill** (daily 7am–2.30pm; free) is at the end of the peninsula and marks the northernmost edge of Port Blair. One of the oldest and largest wood-processing plants in Asia, it seasons and mills rare hardwoods taken from various islands – a sad testimony to the continued abuse of international guidelines on tropical timber production, although the authori-ties swear that only fallen trees are processed. Photography is prohibited. The nearby **Forest Museum** (Mon–Sat 8am–noon & 2–5pm; free) is another dismal spectacle, feebly attempting to justify the Indian Forest Service's wholesale destruction of the Andamans' plant life with a series of lacklustre photographs of extraction methods.

Eating and drinking

Between them, Port Blair's **restaurants** offer dishes from north and south India and a wide variety of seafood. There are a few run-of-the-mill "meals" joints in Aberdeen Bazaar: of these, the *Gagan* and *Milan* on AB Road are the best, but steer clear of the *Dhanalakshmi's* notoriously dreadful canteen. **Alcohol** is becoming increasingly easy to come by, either in the upscale hotels or a smattering of less salubrious bars such as the one underneath the *Jaimathi* lodge (see p.1073).

Annapurna Cafeteria Aberdeen Bazaar, towards the post office. Port Blair's best south Indian joint, serving a range of huge crispy *dosas*, plus north Indian and Chinese meals, delicious coffee, and wonderful *pongal* at breakfast. The lunchtime thalis are also great. Mains Rs30–80. Closed Sun.

Dolphin Marthoma Church Complex, Golgha. Pleasantly decorated with cane chairs and blinds, serving carefully prepared Indian and Chinese dishes, as well as some Continental options and a few house specialities involving chicken and seafood (around Rs80–100).

Majestic Aberdeen Bazaar, just up from the bus stand. Simple canteen with a decent range of north and south Indian veg and non-veg dishes for Rs20–60.

Mandalay *Fortune Resort*, Marine Hill. A la carte dishes or a reasonable Rs350 dinner buffet can be enjoyed in the airy open restaurant with great bay views. Service can be a bit lax for its class. The adjacent *Nico Bar* is fine for a drink.

New India Cafe Moulana Azad Rd. In the basement of *Jaimathi* lodge, this cheap restaurant is popular with Westerners and Indians alike. There's a wide menu of veg and meat dishes (Rs40–80), but expect to wait if you order anything that's not already prepared.

New Lighthouse Near Aberdeen Jetty. Popular place with outdoor seating, where you can catch the sea breeze while feasting on some of the cheapest lobster and other seafood (Rs150–250) in India.

Waves *Peerless Resort*, Corbyn's Cove. Slightly pricey but very congenial alfresco hotel restaurant under a shady palm grove, and one of the few places in town you can order a beer with your meal. Most dishes Rs100–150.

YMCA Near the Post Office. North and south Indian standards for under Rs50, served on a pleasant covered terrace; the pure-veg thalis are especially good.

Around Port Blair

At some point, you're almost certain to find yourself killing time in Port Blair, waiting for boats to show up or tickets to go on sale. Rather than wasting days in town, it's worth exploring the **coast** of South Andaman which, although far more densely populated than other islands in the archipelago, holds a handful of easily accessible beauty-spots and historic sites. Among the latter, the ruined colonial monuments on **Viper** and **Ross islands** can be reached on daily harbour cruises or regular ferries from the capital. For **beaches**, head southeast to **Corbyn's Cove**, or cross South Andaman to reach the more secluded **Chiriya Tapu**, both of which are easily accessible on day-trips if you rent a moped or taxi. By far the most rewarding way to spend a day out of town, however, is to catch the tourist boat from **Wandoor** to **Jolly Buoy** or **Red Skin islands** in the **Mahatma Gandhi National Marine Park** opposite, which boasts some of the Andamans' best snorkelling. The other area worth visiting is **Mount Harriet** and **Madhuban** on the central part of South Andaman, north across the bay from Port Blair.

Viper and Ross islands

First stop on the harbour cruise from Port Blair (see p.1073) is generally **Viper Island** (entry Rs5), named not after the many snakes that doubtless inhabit its tangled tropical undergrowth, but a nineteenth-century merchant vessel that ran aground on it during the early years of the colony. Lying a short way off

Port Blair is the departure point for all flights and ferry crossings to the **Indian mainland**; it is also the hub of the Andamans' inter-island bus and ferry network. Unfortunately, booking tickets (especially back to Chennai, Kolkata or Vishakapatnam) can be time-consuming, and many travellers are obliged to come back here well before their permit expires to make reservations, before heading off to more pleasant parts again. For frequencies and durations of all modes of transport, see "Travel details", p.1088.

To the mainland

If you've travelled to the Andamans **by ship**, you'll know what a rough ride the three-day (or more) crossing can be in bunk class, and how difficult tickets are to come by. It's also a good idea to talk to fellow travellers about current conditions, which vary from year to year and vessel to vessel. The one factor you can be sure about is that, at around Rs1550, the ship offers the cheapest route back. The downside is that schedules can be erratic, and accurate information about them difficult to obtain – annoying when you only have a one-month permit. Tickets for all three mainland ports are now handled by the DSS (☎03192/245555) and go on sale, supposedly a week in advance of departure, at the allotted booths within the Computerized Reservation Centre (Mon–Fri 9am–1pm & 2–4pm and Sat 9am–noon) at Phoenix Jetty. It's wise to find out when they are going on sale and be there to join the fray ahead of time. Bear in mind, if your permit is only a week or so from expiring as you read this, that the local police can get heavy with foreigners who outstay their allotted time.

Returning to the mainland by **plane** in just two hours instead of seventy-two can save lots of time and hassle, and though still not cheap, the competition engendered by the arrival of newer airlines such as Air Deccan, SpiceJet and Kingfisher has lowered ticket prices to **Chennai** and **Kolkata** to Rs4000–6000 one way. As there are now up to six flights daily to both Chennai and Kolkata, it's usually possible to book a seat at short notice apart from peak times like Diwali, Christmas and New Year. The Indian Airlines office (☎03192/234744) is diagonally opposite the ANIIDCO office, while Jet Airways (☎03192/236922) is on the first floor at 189 Main Rd, Junglighat, next to the GITO office. Other airlines can be booked through the host of travel agents such as Island Travels (see pp.1070-1071).

Haddo Wharf, it served as an isolation zone for the main prison, where escapees and convicts (including hunger strikers) were sent to be punished. Whipping posts and crumbling walls, reached from the jetty via a winding brick path, remain as relics of a torture area, while occupying the site's most prominent position are the original gallows.

No less eerie are the decaying colonial remains on **Ross Island** (entry Rs20), at the entrance to Port Blair harbour, where the British sited their first penal settlement in the Andamans. Originally cleared by convicts wearing iron fetters (most of them sent here in the wake of the 1857 Mutiny, or First War of Independence), Ross witnessed some of the most brutal excesses of British colonial history, and was the source of the prison's infamy as **Kalapani**, or Black Water. Of the many convicts transported here, distinguished by their branded foreheads, the majority perished from disease or torture before the clearance of the island was completed in 1860. Thereafter, it served briefly as the site of Rev Henry Corbyn's **"Andaman Home"** – a prison camp created with the intention of "civilizing" the local tribespeople – before becoming the headquarters of the revamped penal colony, complete with theatre hall, tennis courts, swimming pool, hospitals and grand residential bungalows. In the end, the entry of the Japanese into World War II, hot on the heels of a massive earthquake in 1941, forced the

Travellers intending to catch onward **trains** from their port of arrival on the mainland should note that Port Blair has an efficient computerized Southern Railways reservation office near the Secretariat (Mon–Sat 8.30am–1pm & 2–4pm).

Inter-island services

Buses connect Port Blair with most major settlements on South and Middle Andaman, mainly via the Andaman Trunk Road. From the mildly chaotic bus-stand in the centre of town, there are two government services to each of **Rangat** (5.45am & 11.45am), **Mayabunder** (5am & 9.45am) and **Diglipur** (4am & 4.30am). Several private companies, including Geetanjali Travels (who sell tickets at *Tillai* teashop by the bus stand) and the cheaper Ananda (☏03192/233252), run deluxe or video coach (ear-plugs essential) services to the same destinations; these usually leave from outside the bus stand around 5am.

Most of the islands open to foreign tourists, including **Neill, Havelock, Middle, North** and **Little Andaman**, are also accessible by **boat** from Phoenix Jetty. Details are posted in the *Daily Telegrams* newspaper, but they only appear two days before departure. The only way to guarantee a passage is to book tickets in advance at the Inter-Island booths in the Computerized Reservation Centre at Phoenix Jetty, though any unsold tickets are issued prior to departure on the quay. Queues at the office can descend into quite a scrum, which can sometimes be avoided by paying an agent, such as Island Travels, to send somebody else in your place. **Fares** are government-subsidized and very cheap, going for as little as Rs20 for the six-hour voyage to Little Andaman, for example; even the two-tier pricing system for islanders and non-islanders in place for more touristy destinations such as Havelock only leaves you Rs150–200 poorer. Schedules change regularly, but during peak season you can expect two boats daily to Havelock, one or two daily to Neill, one daily to both Rangat and Hut Bay on Little Andaman, four a week to Long and five a week to Arial Bay (for Diglipur). Boats can get cramped and uncomfortable, sometimes lacking shade outside and space inside. You should take adequate supplies of food and water with you; only minimal sustenance is sold on the boats. More details of boat services to destinations outside the capital appear in the relevant accounts.

British to evacuate. Little more than the hilltop **Anglican church**, with its weed-infested graveyard, has survived the onslaught of tropical creepers and vines, and the island makes a peaceful break from Port Blair. To get here, jump on one of the regular launches from Phoenix Jetty (daily departing 8.30am, 10.30am & 12.30pm and returning 8.45am, 10.45am & 12.40pm; Rs60).

Corbyn's Cove and Chiriya Tapu

The best beach within easy reach of the capital lies 6km southeast at **Corbyn's Cove**, a small arc of smooth white sand backed by a swaying curtain of palms. There's a large hotel here (see p.1073), but the water isn't particularly clear, and bear in mind that lying around scantily clothed may bring you considerable attention from crowds of local workers.

For more isolation, rent a moped or take a taxi 30km south to **Chiriya Tapu** ("Bird Island"), at the tip of South Andaman. The motorable track running beyond this small fishing village leads through thick jungle overhung with twisting creepers to a large bay, where swamps give way to shell-strewn beaches. Other than at lunchtime, when it often receives a deluge of bus parties, the beach offers plenty of peace and quiet, forest walks on the woodcutters' trails winding inland from it, and easy access to an inshore reef. However, the water here is nowhere near as clear as at some spots in the archipelago. The village can be used to access **Cinque Island** (see p.1087), a couple of hours further south.

Wandoor and the Mahatma Gandhi National Marine Park

Much the most popular excursion from Port Blair is the boat ride from **Wandoor**, 30km southwest, to one or other of the fifteen islets comprising the **Mahatma Gandhi National Marine Park**. Although set up purely for tourists, the trip is worth considering, as it provides access to one of the richest coral reefs in the region. The downside is that entry into the park for foreigners now costs Rs500 [Rs50]. Boats depart at 10am (daily except Mon; Rs300) from Wandoor, which you can reach on A&N Tourism's **tour** (see p.1073) or by local bus, but it's more fun to rent a moped and ride down to meet the boat yourself.

The long white **beach** at Wandoor is littered with the dry, twisted trunks of trees torn up and flung down by annual cyclones, and fringed not with palms, but by dense forest teeming with birdlife. You should only snorkel here at high tide, as the coral is easily damaged when the waters are shallow. From the jetty, the boats chug through broad creeks lined with dense mangrove swamps and pristine forest to either **Red Skin Island** or, more commonly, **Jolly Buoy**. The latter, an idyllic deserted island, boasts an immaculate shell-sand beach ringed by a bank of superb coral. The catch is that the boat only stops for around an hour, which isn't nearly enough time to explore the shore and reef. While snorkelling off the edges of the reef, beware of **strong currents**.

Mount Harriet and Madhuban

The richly forested slopes of **Mount Harriet** make for some decent exercise and can easily be done as a day-trip from Port Blair. You can take one of the passenger ferries (every 30min) from Chatham Jetty to **Bamboo Flats** or, if you want to have your own transport on the other side, one of the eight daily vehicle ferries from Phoenix Bay, which run between 5.30am and 8.30pm. From Bamboo Flats, it's a pleasant seven-kilometre stroll east along the coast and north up a path through trees hung with thick vines and creepers to the 365m summit, which affords fine views back across the bay. An intermittent bus service runs between Bamboo Flats and Hope Town, where the path starts, and saves you 3km. Alternatively, Jeeps and taxis are available to take you all the way to the top, but they charge at least Rs300. There's a charge of Rs250 [Rs25] to enter Mount Harriet National Park, but the checkpost is on the road so you probably won't be asked if you take the path. It's 2.5km from the checkpost up to the resthouse and viewing tower at the summit. If you have strong legs, you can reach **Madhuban** on the coast northeast of the mountain by the sixteen-kilometre round route via Kala Patthar (Black Rock) and back via the coast. There is a decent beach at Madhuban and the area is still used for training logging **elephants**, so you stand a good chance of seeing them learning their trade.

Islands north of Port Blair

Printed on the permit card you receive on arrival in the Andamans is a list of all the other **islands** you're allowed to visit in the archipelago, the majority of which are north of Port Blair. Given the great distances involved, not to mention the sometimes erratic connections between them, it definitely pays to know where to head for as soon as you arrive rather than drift off on the first promising ferry out of Phoenix Jetty. It's surprising how many visitors make a beeline for the only two developed islands in the group, **Neill** and **Havelock**, both within easy reach of Port Blair. An enterprising minority then catch a ferry on to barely developed **Long Island**. To get further north, where tourism has also had very little impact so far, you can take a bus along the infamous **Andaman Trunk Road** (or "ATR") to ramshackle **Rangat** or **Mayabunder**, at the southern and northern ends of **Middle Andaman** respectively, or direct to **Diglipur**, at the top of **North Andaman**. Alternatively, there are ferries to Rangat and Arial Bay, the port of Diglipur. On Middle and North Andaman, and their satellite islands, **accommodation** is scarce, to say the least. Aside from a handful of A&N Tourism hotels (bookable in advance in Port Blair), the only places to stay are a few basic and occasionally grim lodges or the preferable APWD Resthouses (see box, p.1085).

To escape the settled areas you have to be prepared to rough it, travelling on in-shore fishing dugouts, sleeping on beaches or in hammocks and cooking your own food. The rewards, however, are great. Backed by dense forest filled with colourful birds and insects, the beaches, bays and reefs of the outer Andamans teem with wildlife, from gargantuan crabs, pythons and turtles, to dolphins, sharks, giant rays and the occasional primeval-looking dugong. Essential **kit** for off-track wanderings includes a sturdy mosquito net, mats to sleep on (or a hammock), a large plastic container for water, some strong antiseptic for cuts and bites (sandflies are a real problem on many of the beaches) and, most importantly, **water purification** tablets or a water purifier – bottled water is virtually nonexistent. Wherever you end up, preserve the goodwill of local people by packing your rubbish out or burning it, and being sensitive to scruples about dress and nudity.

Neill

Tiny, triangular-shaped **Neill** is the most southerly inhabited island of **Ritchie's Archipelago**, barely two hours northeast of Port Blair on a fast ferry. The source of much of the capital's fresh fruit and vegetables, its fertile centre, ringed by a curtain of stately tropical trees, comprises vivid patches of green paddy dotted with small farmsteads and banana plantations. The beaches are mediocre by the Andamans' standards, but worth a day or two en route to or from Havelock. **Boats** leave Port Blair daily for Neill, all services connecting with Havelock and some with Rangat.

Neill boasts three **beaches**, all of them within easy cycling distance of the small bazaar just up the lane from the jetty (you can rent **cycles** from one of several stallholders for Rs40–50 per day). The best place to swim is **Neill Kendra**, a gently curving bay of white sand which straddles the jetty and is scattered with picturesque wooden fishing boats. This blends into **Lakshmangar**, which continues for 3km north: to get there by road, head right at the A&N hotel (see below) and follow the road for around twenty minutes until it dwindles into a surfaced track, then turn right. Wrapped around the headland, the beach is a broad spur of white-shell sand, with shallow water offering good snorkelling but that makes entry into the water tough at any time other than high tide. Exposed to the open sea and thus prone to higher tides, **Sitapur** beach, 6km south at the tip of the island, is also appealing and has the advantage of a sandy bottom extending into the sea. The ride there (by hourly bus or bicycle) across Neill's central paddy land is pleasant, but there are no facilities when you get there, at least until the new venture by the owners of *Wild Orchid* on Havelock (see p.1082) opens some time in 2009.

The island has four **accommodation** options. From the jetty, a two-minute walk brings you to the A&N Tourism's *Hawabill Nest* (℡03192/282630, ⓦwww.and.nic.in; ❹), a dozen a/c rooms with sit-outs, ranged around a

19

The seas around the Andaman and Nicobar islands are some of the world's most unspoiled. Marine life is abundant, with an estimated 750 species of fish existing on one reef alone, and parrot, trigger and angel fish living alongside manta rays, reef sharks and loggerhead turtles. Many species of fish and coral are unique to the area, and fascinating life-systems exist in ash beds and cooled lava based around the volcanic Barren Island. For a quick taste of marine life, you could start by **snorkelling**; most hotels can supply masks and snorkels, though some equipment is in dire need of replacement. The only way to get really close, however, and venture out into deeper waters, is to **scuba dive**. The experience of weaving in and out of coral beds, coming eye to eye with fish or swimming with dolphin and barracuda is unforgettable.

Apart from one operation at Wandoor (see below), the only organized **diving centres** are currently on Havelock, with three fully certified operators up and running, but it's worth checking if any new outfits have opened up elsewhere. Prices are very similar at all three, with dives for those already certified running around Rs2000 for one tank, Rs3000 for two and Rs4000 for three; more economical packages, often including accommodation and food, are available for multiple dives, and Discover Scuba introductory days go for Rs4500. Courses cost about Rs16,000 for a basic four–five day PADI open-water qualification, Rs12,000 for advanced or Rs30,000 to go all the way up to Divemaster. The current trio are the Indian-run **Andaman Dive Club** (☏09932 17479), whose premises are about 500m from the jetty and who should have a smart 12-cabin sleepover boat by the time you read this, to enable longer trips to more remote islands. Further down the coast at *Café del Mar* on Beach #3, **Barefoot Scuba** (☏03192/282181, ⊛www.barefootindia.com) is the most professional outfit, British-run and manned by mainly Western instructors; it also has the biggest – and newest – range of equipment. Further along at *Island Vinnie's*, **Dive India** (☏09831 802204, ⊛www.diveindia.com) is the second largest of the three. The only reliable place to arrange diving in the Port Blair area is with **Luca Diving** (☏09474 204508), run by legendary ex-navy diver Captain Bhart, who is based in Wandoor.

Underwater in the Andamans, it's not uncommon to come across schools of reef shark, which rarely turn hostile, but one thing to watch out for and avoid is the **black-and-white sea snake**. Though these seldom attack – and, since their fangs are at the back of their mouths, would find it difficult to get a grip on any human – their bite is twenty times deadlier than that of the cobra.

Increased tourism inevitably puts pressure on the delicate marine ecosystem, and poorly funded wildlife organizations can do little to prevent damage from insensitive visitors. You can ensure your presence in the sea around the reefs does not harm the coral by observing the following **Green Coral Code** while diving or snorkelling:

• Never touch, or walk on, living coral or it will die.

• Try to keep your feet away from reefs while wearing fins; the sudden sweep of water caused by a flipper kick can be enough to destroy coral.

• Always control the speed of your descent while diving; enormous damage can be caused by divers landing hard on a coral bed.

• Never break off pieces of coral from a reef, and remember that it is illegal to export dead coral from the islands, even fragments you may have found on a beach.

central courtyard and restaurant; it's best booked in advance from Port Blair. The three private options are all at Lakshmangar or en route to it: the best of the bunch is ⚘ *Tango Beach Resort* (☏03192/282634, ⊜tangobeachresort @rediffmail.com; ❶–❹), a friendly place right on the beach, with two deluxe and ten much more basic bamboo huts. Before *Tango*, little over 500m from the jetty, you pass *Cocon Huts* (☏03192/282528, ⊜coconhuts@yahoo .com; ❶–❸), which has a similar range of huts, although the bar can attract rowdy revellers from the village. The furthest option, 1km north of *Tango*, is *Pearl Park Hotel* (☎03192/282510; ❶–❺), which has some small huts and posher but hugely overpriced a/c bungalows. Although many people stick to the **restaurants** at their beach huts, far and away the best place to eat is the delightful and welcoming ❊ *Gyan Garden*, 500m along the road to Lakshmangar opposite the football pitch, where fresh fish and home-grown veg dishes are a speciality. Of the few tiny eateries in the bazaar, *Hotel Chand* serves up the tastiest, albeit somewhat oily, food.

Havelock

Havelock is the largest island in Ritchie's Archipelago, and the most intensively cultivated, settled – like many in the region – by Bengali refugees after Partition. Thanks to its regular ferry connections with the capital, it is also visited in greater numbers than anywhere else in the Andamans. In recent peak seasons, well over four hundred tourists have been holed up here at one time, yet the locals have only cottoned on to this in the last year, as evidenced by an explosion in accommodation and the opening of the first tourist shops.

Arrival, information and getting around

Havelock's main **jetty** is on the north side of the island, at the village known as **Beach #1**. After registering with the police as you disembark, it's best to make your own way to where you plan to stay, though if you've booked in advance, most places arrange a pick-up. At the time of writing, the Barefoot group were constructing a large ecology and information centre beside the jetty. Five daily buses run to **Radhnagar** (aka beach #7), but only one morning route heads down the east coast, where the bulk of the accommodation is located. Instead, you can take a Rs40–50 auto-rickshaw ride or rent a **scooter**, **motorbike** (both Rs200–250 per day) or **cycle** (Rs50 per day) for a few days. The only place to **change money** is the State Co-operative Bank (Mon–Fri 9am–1pm, Sat 9–11am), at the main bazaar, 2km inland of the main jetty. The **Internet** arrived on the island in 2006, and access available at the ticklishly named Anus Internet in the bazaar, the shop on the corner near *Dolphin Resort* (see p.1082) shop, and two of the guesthouses listed below; all charge an exorbitant Rs100–120 for a slow dial-up connection, which will hopefully have been replaced by satellite broadband by the time you read this.

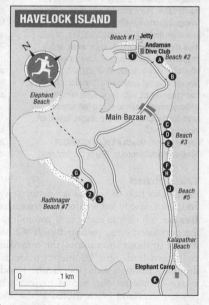

HAVELOCK ISLAND

Beach #1 Jetty
Andaman Dive Club
Beach #2
Elephant Beach
Main Bazaar
Beach #3
Beach #5
Radhnagar Beach #7
Kalapathar Beach
Elephant Camp
0   1 km

ACCOMMODATION

Barefoot at Havelock	G	Emerald Gecko	J	Pooja Paradise	K
Café del Mar	C	Happy Resort	A	Pristine Beach
Dolphin Resort	H	Harmony Resort	I	Resort	D
Eco Villa	B	Island Vinnie's	E	Wild Orchid	F

RESTAURANTS

Arati	3	Mahua	2
Blackbeard's Bistro	J	Nala's Kingdom	1
		Red Snapper	F

Accommodation

As the only fully developed tourist scene in the Andamans, Havelock now has nearly thirty accommodation establishments to choose from, offering everything from the most basic unlockable **huts** to luxuriously furnished **cottages**, although **hotels** in the conventional sense are nonexistent. Price codes here indicate rates through most of the season. They can rise by fifty percent from mid-December to mid-January, and drop considerably between May and October.

Barefoot at Havelock Radnagar ☎03192/220191, ⓦwww.barefootindia.com. Havelock's most luxurious resort, with fan-cooled duplexes, "Nicobari" cottages, and a/c "Andaman" villas. Most of these, and the large restaurant, are attractive timber and thatch structures. ⑧–⑨

Café del Mar Beach #3 ☎03192/282343, ⓦwww.barefootindia.com. Barefoot's budget branch and home to their dive centre. There's a choice of sturdy cottages, all with attached bathrooms, and small tents for rent. ②–⑤

Dolphin Resort Beach #5 ☎03192/282411, ⓦwww.and.nic.in. A&N Tourism's smartest resort is still lacking in atmosphere, though the detached concrete cottages are spacious and comfortable. More popular with Indians than foreign tourists. ④–⑥

Eco Villa Beach #2 ☎03192/282171. All huts have showers, and mostly quite small, with a couple of two-tier structures. Internet available. ③

Emerald Gecko Beach #5 ☎03192/282170, ⓦwww.emerald-gecko.com. The nicest budget to mid-range resort, with ten modest huts (with or withouy private bathroom) and half a dozen superbly designed two-tier cottages. Breakfast included. ③–⑥

Happy Resort Beach #2 ☎03192/282061, ⓔrajhavelock@yahoo.in. One of the best real

cheapies, with a bunch of basic huts, all with shared bathrooms, and a vibe to match the name. ①

Harmony Resort Radnagar ☎03192/282120. Under a kilometre back from the beach on the main road, these huts with shared facilities are a bit overpriced, but are the only cheap option close to Beach #7. ②

Island Vinnie's Beach #3 ☎03192/282187, ⓦwww.islandvinnie.com. Spacious and beautifully constructed Rajasthani tents, some with attached bathroom, which make for a unique and comfortable stay. ③–⑤

Pooja Paradise Kalapathar ☎094742 10549. The most remote place to stay on the island, with a mixture of simple huts and cement cottages. A good fall-back when more popular places are full. ①–③

🏃 **Pristine Beach Resort** Beach #3 ☎03192/282344, ⓦwww .pristinebeachresort.com. One of the friendliest and most sociable options, with a good range of huts, mostly with attached bath, one duplex and an Internet café. ①–⑤

🏃 **Wild Orchid** Beach #5 ☎03192/282472, ⓦwww.wildorchidandaman.com. Easily the best higher-end resort, for its classy cottages (some a/c), splendid restaurant and lounge, and laid-back atmosphere. ⑧

The island

Havelock's hub of activity is not the jetty village, which just has a few stalls, a couple of dowdy lodges, the odd restaurant and the police station, but the **Main Bazaar**, which you come to if you follow the road straight ahead from the jetty for two kilometres, passing Beach #2 on the way. Here you'll find a greater variety of shops and eateries, the only bank and the island's main junction. The right turn leads nine kilometres through paddy fields and other crops before dropping through some spectacular woodland to **Radhnagar** (aka Beach #7), a two-kilometre-long arc of perfect white sand, backed by stands of giant *mowhar* trees and often touted as the most beautiful in India. The water is a sublime turquoise colour and, although the coral is sparse, marine life here is diverse and plentiful, especially among the rocks around the corner from the main beach (accessible at low tide). The main drawback, which can make sunbathing uncomfortable, is a preponderance of pesky sandflies.

As the nesting site for a colony of Olive Ridley **turtles** (see box, p.814), Radhnagar is strictly protected by the Forest Department, whose wardens ensure tourists don't light fires or sleep on the beach. Elephant "jolly rides" (10am–4pm; Rs40) are available from a podium en route to the sand. A couple of kilometres before the road descends to Radhnagar, a path on the right leads over a hill and down through some scattered settlements to far wilder **Elephant Beach**, although the only trunks you are likely to spot are those of huge fallen trees. Snorkelling here is good, and coral reefs are accessible from the shore, but it can be tough to find the way unless somebody takes you; look out for the start of the path at a sharp bend in the road with a Forest Department noticeboard in a small clearing, and then keep asking the way whenever you see a local.

If you take the left turn through the busier strip of Main Bazaar, the road leads on past beaches #3 and #5, where most of the beach huts and resorts are located. As on Neill, these east-facing beaches, though exquisitely scenic, have fairly thin strips of golden-white sand, and when the sea recedes across the lumps of broken coral and rock lying offshore, swimming becomes all but impossible. After Beach #5 the road continues south for several kilometres before turning slightly inland and eventually petering out at **Kalapathar** beach. Here you can visit the Forest Department's elephant training camp, although the sight of the gentle giants being rather ferociously whacked with heavy sticks is hardly an edifying one. The entire southern half of Havelock consists of impenetrable forest.

Eating and drinking

Western travellers' favourites and bland curries are widely available at all the beach hut cafés, but if you want authentic (mainly Bengali) food, then it's better to head for a local restaurant in one of the settlements. **Beer** and basic spirits are sold at most travellers' haunts, but are not cheap and supply of the former from Port Blair can be erratic.

Arati Radhnagar. The best of the row of simple shacks that line the end of the road before the beach, serving cheap, wholesome Bengali dishes for Rs40–80.

Blackbeard's Bistro Emerald Gecko, Beach #5. The lovely open dining area has a bar and furniture created from recycled timber, and offers rare dishes such as ceviche as well as fresh fish cooked in delicious and imaginative sauces for Rs120–200. There is also a stage for regular live shows.

Mahua Just behind Radhnagar beach. Owned by Barefoot but run by a welcoming Italian couple, who serve up delicious Mediterranean cuisine such

as authentic pastas and Greek salad. Main courses from Rs250.

Nala's Kingdom Main Jetty. The most salubrious place in the jetty area, serving Indian, Chinese and fish dishes for Rs50–100.

Poseidon Pristine Beach Resort, Beach #3. Good, convivial restaurant, serving a range of Indian and Western dishes and seafood; the island fish special cooked in a coconut leaf is exquisite and a snip at Rs120.

Red Snapper Wild Orchid, Beach #5. Excellent upmarket seafood, meat and veg menu, served in quality surroundings. Most dinners are in the Rs200–300 range.

Long Island

Just off the southeast coast of Middle Andaman, **Long Island** is dominated by an unsightly plywood mill, but don't let this put you off. Served by only four boats per week from the capital and Rangat, plus two daily launches from Yeratta (7am & 2pm), it sees far fewer visitors than either Neill or Havelock, but boasts a couple of excellent beaches, at **Marg Bay** and **Lalaji Bay**. Both are most easily reached by chartering a fisherman's dinghy from the jetty (around Rs500), as they are a good couple of hours' hike from where the boat docks. The main settlement by the jetty has the island's only facilities, including a couple of tatty lodges – try Kaniappa (☎03192/278529; ❶). Most foreigners head for the beaches with tents, hammocks and supplies; mercifully, plans to develop the beaches into an upscale resort have been shelved, meaning the Robinson Crusoe experience remains viable.

Middle Andaman

For most travellers, **Middle Andaman** is a charmless rite of passage to be endured en route to or from the north. The sinuous Andaman Trunk Road, hemmed in by walls of towering forest, winds through miles of jungle, crossing the strait that separates the island from its neighbour, Baratang, by means of rusting flat-bottomed ferry. The island's frontier feeling is heightened by the presence on the buses of armed guards, and the knowledge that the impenetrable forests west of the ATR comprise the **Jarawa Tribal Reserve** (see p.1070). Of its two main settlements, the more northerly **Mayabunder**, the port for alluring **Interview Island**, is slightly more appealing than characterless inland **Rangat** because of its pleasant setting by the sea, but neither town gives any reason to dally for long.

Rangat and around

At the southeast corner of Middle Andaman, **RANGAT** consists of a ramshackle sprawl around two rows of unsanitary chai shops and general stores divided by the ATR. However, as a major staging-post on the journey north, it's impossible to avoid – just don't get stranded here if you can help it.

The five or six **ferries** per week from Port Blair dock at **Rangat Bay** (aka Nimbutala), 8km east; some stop at Havelock Island (4 weekly) and Long Island (3 weekly), and there are also two daily launches to Long Island from nearby **Yeratta**. In addition, Rangat is served by two daily government buses to Port Blair (6–7hr) as well as some private services, which pass through in the morning en route from further north. The APWD *Rest House* (☎03192/274237; ❸–❹), pleasantly situated up a winding hill from the bazaar with views across the valley, is the best place to stay and eat, providing good, filling fish thalis. The newish *RG Lodge* (☎03192/274237; ❷), just off the main road, is a decent fall-back. The best places to eat are the *Hotel MK*, on the main road, which serves basic Indian and Chinese food; and the *Hotel Star*, on a nearby alley leading to the small market square, for Indian veg and non-veg.

If you do get stuck here, rather than staying put in Rangat jump on a bus heading north, or find a Jeep to take you to **Amakunj beach**, about 9km north, for a swim or snorkel, or head a further 6km to **Cuthbert Bay** (aka RRO), where you can stay at the characterless but comfortable A&N Tourism **hotel**, *Hawksbill Nest* (☎03192/279159; ❸–❹), which is invariably empty. If you have an early ferry out of Rangat Bay, it's better to stay down near the jetty at the friendly *Sea Shore Lodge* (☎03192/274464; ❷). Basic meals can be had from the motley conglomeration of stalls between the lodge and the jetty.

Mayabunder

Only 70km further north by road, perched on a long promontory right at the top of the island and surrounded by mangrove swamps, **MAYABUNDER** is the springboard for the remote northern Andaman Islands. Unfortunately, the bus journey here from Rangat often exceeds three hours due to continual stops on the surprisingly populated route. Home to a large minority of former Burmese **Karen** tribal people who were originally brought here as cheap logging labour by the British, the village is more spread out and more appealing than Rangat. At the brow of the hill, before it descends to the jetty, a small hexagonal wooden structure houses the **Forest Museum/Interpretation**

APWD Rest Houses

Though they are officially set aside for government officials and engineers, travellers are often allowed to stay at the **APWD Rest Houses**, which often constitute the best and sometimes the only accommodation in Middle and North Andaman. To stay in these it is best to get a letter of recommendation from the APWD office (☏03192/232294), just up the road from *Hotel Blair* in Port Blair, but you have to give specific dates. Just turning up is not guaranteed to meet with success even if rooms are free, but you will stand a much better chance of getting in if you can provide staff with photocopies of your permit, Indian visa and personal details pages from your passport. Details on individual locations are given throughout the text, but all *Rest Houses* have standardized prices despite varying standards of comfort: the rooms are doubles but charges are per bed (Rs200 for non-a/c, Rs400 for a/c), so you are not penalized for travelling solo.

Centre (Mon–Sat 8am–noon & 1–4pm; free), which holds a motley collection of turtle shells, snakes in formaldehyde, dead coral, a crocodile skull and precious little information. Next door, the APWD *Rest House* (☏03192/273211; ❸–❹) is large and very comfortable, with a pleasant garden and gazebo overlooking the sea, and a dining room serving good set meals. The only other reasonable **accommodation** nearby is back in the centre of the bazaar at the *Anmol Lodge* (☏03192/262695; ❷), where some of the attached rooms have TV; and nearby *S&S Lodge* (☏03192/273449; ❶), which has clean but unattached rooms; the dilapidated and cockroach-infested *Lakshminarayan Lodge* should be avoided at all costs. Further afield at **Karmateng beach**, 14km southeast, there's another A&N Tourism hotel, the *Swiftlet Nest* (☏03192/273495; ❸–❹) but nothing else. Two buses are supposed to go there daily, failing which there are taxis or auto-rickshaws. Buses from Port Blair now continue over the new bridge to Diglipur on North Andaman at least twice a day. Heading towards the capital, there are a couple of private services, such as Geetanjali Travels, as well as one government bus, all departing very early in the morning.

Interview Island

Mayabunder is the jumping-off place for **Interview Island**, a windswept nature sanctuary off the remote northwest coast of Middle Andaman – if you've come to the Andamans to watch **wildlife**, it should be top of your list. Large and mainly flat, it is completely uninhabited save for a handful of unfortunate forest wardens, coastguards and policemen, posted here to ward off poachers. Foreigners aren't permitted to spend the night on the island, and to do a daytrip you must first obtain permission from the Chief Wildlife Warden in Port Blair (see p.1090). The only way to reach Interview is to charter a private fishing dinghy from Mayabunder jetty for around Rs500. Arrange one the day before and leave at first light. Try to get your boatman to pull up onto the **beach** at the southern tip of the island, which has a perennial freshwater pool inside a low cave; legend has it that the well, a nesting site for white-bellied **swifts**, has no bottom. At the forest post, where you have to sign an entry ledger, ask the wardens about the movements of Interview's feral **elephants**, descendants of trained elephants deserted here by a Kolkata-based logging company after its timber operation failed in the 1950s. **Saltwater crocodiles** are found on the island's eastern coastline.

North Andaman

Shrouded in dense jungle, **North Andaman** is the least populated of the region's large islands, crossed by a single road linking its scattered Bengali settlements. Although parts have been seriously logged, the total absence of motorable roads into northern and western areas has ensured blanket protection for a vast stretch of convoluted coastline, running from Austin Strait in the southeast to the northern tip, Cape Price; it's reassuring to know at least one extensive wilderness survives in the Andamans. That said, the completion of the ATR's final section and the 2002 opening of the bridge from Middle Andaman may herald the start of a new settlement influx. So far, the main settlement of **Diglipur** and its nearby port of **Arial Bay** have existed in remote seclusion. On the other hand, the opening of the bridge may render the village of **Kalighat**, previously the island's entry point from Middle Andaman, virtually redundant.

Kalighat

Although you can now proceed directly to Diglipur by road across the Austin Bridge, a small ferry still chugs once daily (departs 9.30am; returns 12.30pm) through a narrowing mangrove-lined estuary from Mayabunder to **KALIGHAT**, a more relaxed, if slower, point of entry. A cluttered little bazaar unfolds from the top of the slipway, hemmed in by dense mangrove swamps, and when you arrive you should hope a bus is standing here to take you to Diglipur. If there isn't, head for one of the village's dismal little chai stalls and dig in for a wait, or turn right to see if there's space in the three-roomed APWD *Rest House* (℡03192/273360; ❸–❹) on the hill overlooking the end of the street. The only **food** is at chai stalls in the bazaar.

The one worthwhile place to visit in this area is **Ramnagar**, 10km southeast of town and served by hourly buses, where there's a beautiful sandy beach backed by unspoilt forest; camping is feasible. Try to rent a **cycle** from one of the stalls in Kalighat though, as the beach is 2km outside Ramnagar bazaar, the nearest source of refreshments. In principle, four **buses** per day run north from Kalighat to **Diglipur**; they get very full, but the trip takes only 45 minutes.

Diglipur, Arial Bay and around

Known in the British era as Port Cornwallis, **DIGLIPUR**, North Andaman's largest settlement, is another disappointing market where you're only likely to pause long enough to pick up a local bus further north to the coast. On the hill above the main road, the APWD *Rest House* (℡03192/272203; ❸–❹) offers the village's nicest **accommodation**, although the *Maa Yashoda Lodge* on the main street (℡03192/272258; ❷) is a cheaper alternative. Reasonable veg and non-veg fare can be found at the central *Ganga Devi* **restaurant**, while *Ice Cube*, on the road north, serves Chinese and tandoori cuisine. Preferably, head 9km on to **ARIAL BAY**, where a smaller APWD *Rest House* (℡03192/271230; ❸–❹) stands on a hillock overlooking the settlement's tiny bazaar. The best place to while away time with a snack or beer while waiting for a boat is the *Annu* general store. From Arial Bay, the **boat** that has made its way up from the capital returns direct to Port Blair overnight.

Better still, continue another 9km to **Kalipur**, served by several daily buses, where the ⚲ ANIIDCO *Turtle Resort* (℡03192/272553; ❸–❹), occupies a perfect spot on a hilltop with superb views inland and to sea. It's an unfeasibly large hotel for such a remote location, with spacious, clean rooms with fans and a restaurant. Their only competition is the bamboo huts of the *Pristine Jungle Resort* (℡03192/271793; ❶–❹), on the opposite side of the road below. Only five minutes' walk from the *Turtle* down the path by the sharp bend in the road there's an excellent deserted beach, backed by lush forest and covered in photogenic driftwood. Swimming is best at high tide because the water recedes across rocky mudpools.

Locals claim it's possible to walk from Kalipur to **Saddle Peak**, the highest mountain in the Andamans at 737m, which rises dramatically to the south, swathed in lush jungle. Permission to make the three- to four-hour climb must be obtained from the Range Officer at the Forest Check Post near the start of the ascent, but don't attempt it without a guide and plenty of drinking water.

Many tourists find their way up here in order to explore the various **islands** dotted around the gulf north of Arial Bay, particularly **Smith** and **Ross** (not to be confused with its namesake near Port Blair), whose white sandbars, coral reefs and flora are splendid. At the time of writing, Smith was slated to soon be added to the list of places where you can overnight, and a guesthouse was going to be built but, unless a ferry is introduced, you will need to charter a dinghy for around Rs400 to reach the islets. Ross is likely to remain a daytime-only destination.

Other islands

The remaining islands open to foreign tourists in the Andaman group are all hard to get to and, with the exception of **Little Andaman** – where a vestigial population of Onge tribespeople (see p.1071) have survived a massive influx of Indian Tamils and native Nicobars – uninhabited. Two hours' boat ride south of Chiriya Tapu on South Andaman, **Cinque Island** offers superlative diving.

Cinque Island

Cinque actually comprises two islets, joined by a spectacular sand isthmus with shallow water either side that covers it completely at high tide. The main incentive to come here is the superb diving and snorkelling around the reefs. However, heaps of dead coral on the beach attest to damage wreaked by the Indian navy during the construction of the swish "cottages" overlooking the beach. Rumour has it that these were built for the visit of a Thai VIP in 1996, but local government officials now use them as bolt holes from Port Blair. Although there are no **ferries** to Cinque, it is possible to arrange dinghies for around Rs1000 per day from Chiriya Tapu village on the mainland (see p.1077). Currently, overnight stays are prohibited.

Little Andaman

Little Andaman is the furthest point south in the archipelago that foreigners can travel to on their tourist permit. Most of the island has been set aside as a tribal reserve for the **Onge** and is thus off-limits. It was also the only island open to foreigners to sustain extensive damage in the 2004 **tsunami**, but although a number of buildings were destroyed, and sixty-four people died, Little Andaman has recovered well. Very few tourists ever make it down here, however. Daily boats from Port Blair (Rs20–50) arrive at **Hut Bay**, the faster ones making the voyage in under six hours. The main settlement, **INDIRA BAZAAR**, is two kilometres north. The only **places to stay** are here, the best being the two-storey *Sealand Tourist Home* (℡03192/284306; ❶), whose splendid bayfront location is only marred by the fact that the architect inexplicably put all the windows facing the interior. Just a little further along, the *Vvet*

Guest House (℡03192/284155; ❷) has simple rooms that cost a little more but are no better, although the small garden is pleasant enough to relax in and there's an offshoot, the _Cozy Cave_, about 500m away, in the unlikely event that both places are full. Basic **meals** are available at food-only hotels such as the _Snehu_ and _AG Bengali_, while the _Kurinchi Parotta Stall_ offers tasty savoury and sweet snacks. Bicycles can be rented for Rs40 per day from a stall between the two guesthouses, but are in very short supply.

Hut Bay curves gradually round in a majestic eight-kilometre sweep, and the quality of the sand and beauty of the adjacent jungle increase the further you go. The top stretch is named **Netaji Nagar** after the village on the island's only road, which runs behind it. A couple of drink stalls constitute the only facilities. En route, you can detour a kilometre inland at the huge signpost about 2.5km north of Indira Bazaar to see the **White Surf Waterfalls** (daily dawn to dusk; Rs20). Made up of three ten- to fifteen-metre-high cascades, it's a relaxing spot; you can clamber into the right-hand fall for a soothing shower. Crocodiles are supposed to inhabit the surrounding streams, however. Short elephant rides are available for Rs50 per person at the entrance to the falls. Over the headland at the top of Hut Bay, twelve or so kilometres from the jetty, lies the smaller but equally picturesque crescent of **Butler Bay**. There's not much to do here but swim, sunbathe or look around the slightly eerie remains of the government beach resort, which was swept away by the tsunami. That is unless you've brought your surfboard with you: Little Andaman has a cult reputation among surfers for having some of the best conditions anywhere in South Asia.

Travel details

Boats

Arial Bay to: Port Blair (5 weekly; 8–12hr).
Havelock to: Long Island (4 weekly; 2–3hr); Neill Island (1 daily; 1hr–1hr 30min); Port Blair (2 daily; 2hr–4hr 30min); Rangat Bay (4 weekly; 3–5hr).
Mayabunder to: Kalighat (1 daily; 2hr 30min).
Port Blair to: Arial Bay (5 weekly; 8–12hr); Chennai (every 7–10 days; 2.5–3 days); Havelock Island (2 daily; 2hr–4hr 30min); Kolkata (every 2 weeks; 3–5 days); Little Andaman (1 daily; 6–8hr); Long Island (4 weekly; 5–7hr); Neill Island (1–2 daily; 2hr–3hr 30min); Rangat Bay (1 daily; 6–8hr); Vishakapatnam (1 monthly; 3–3.5 days).
Rangat Bay to: Havelock Island (4 weekly; 3–4hr); Long Island (2–3 daily; 1hr–1hr 30min); Neill Island (1–2 weekly; 4–6hr); Port Blair (1 daily; 6–8hr).

Buses

Diglipur to: Arial Bay (every 1–2hr; 20min); Kalighat (4 daily; 45min); Kalipur (every 1–2hr; 40min); Port Blair (2–3 daily; 11–12hr).

Mayabunder to: Karmateng beach (2 daily; 30min); Port Blair (2–4 daily; 9–10hr); Rangat (hourly; 2hr 30min–3hr).
Port Blair to: Chiriya Tapu (3 daily; 1hr 15min); Diglipur (2–3 daily; 11–12hr); Mayabunder (2–4 daily; 9–10hr); Rangat (5 daily; 6–7hr); Wandoor (4 daily; 1hr 15min).
Rangat to: Mayabunder (hourly; 2hr 30min–3hr); Port Blair (5 daily; 6–7hr).

Flights

(IC = Indian Airlines, IT = Kingfisher, 9W = Jet Airways, DN = Air Deccan, SG = SpiceJet)
Port Blair to: Chennai (IC, 9W, IT, SG, DN 5–6 daily; 2hr); Kolkata (IC, 9W, IT, SG, DN 4–5 daily; 2hr).

Tamil Nadu

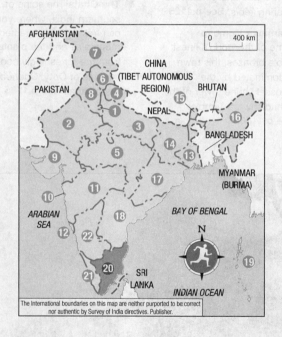

The International boundaries on this map are neither purported to be correct nor authentic by Survey of India directives. Publisher.

CHAPTER 20

Highlights

* **Mamallapuram** Stone-carvers' workshops, a long sandy beach and a bumper hoard of Pallava monuments have made this the state's principal tourist attraction. See p.1112

* **Puducherry** Former French colony that has retained the ambience of a Gallic seaside town: croissants, a promenade and gendarmes wearing *képis*. See p.1126

* **Thanjavur** Home to some of the world's finest Chola bronzes, this town is dominated by the colossal shrine tower of the Brihadishwara Temple. See p.1140

* **Madurai** The love nest of Shiva and his consort Meenakshi, this busy city's major temple hosts a constant round of festivals. See p.1151

* **Kanyakumari** The sacred meeting-point of the Bay of Bengal, Indian Ocean and Arabian Sea, at the southern tip of the Subcontinent. See p.1163

* **The Ghats** The spine of southern India, where you can trek through forested mountains and tea plantations from the refreshingly cool hill-stations of Ooty, Coonoor and Kodaikanal. See p.1165

▲ View over the Ghats

20

Tamil Nadu

W hen Indians refer to "the South", it's usually **TAMIL NADU** they're talking about. While Karnataka and Andhra Pradesh are essentially cultural transition zones buffering the Hindi-speaking north, and Kerala and Goa maintain their own distinctively idiosyncratic identities, the peninsula's massive Tamil-speaking state is India's Dravidian Hindu heartland. Traditionally protected by distance and the military might of the southern Deccan kingdoms, the region has, over the centuries, been less exposed to northern influences than its neighbours. As a result, the three powerful dynasties dominating the south – the Cholas, the Pallavas and the Pandyans – were able, over a period of more than a thousand years, to develop their own unique religious and political institutions, largely unmolested by marauding Muslims. The most visible legacy of this protracted cultural flowering is a crop of astounding **temples**, whose gigantic gateway towers, or *gopuras*, still soar above just about every town large enough to merit a railway station. It is the image of these colossal wedge-shaped pyramids, high above the canopy of dense palm forests, or against patchworks of vibrant green paddy fields, which Edward Lear described as "stupendous and beyond belief". Indeed, the garishly painted gods, goddesses and mythological creatures clinging onto the towers linger long in the memory of most travellers.

The great Tamil temples, however, are merely the largest landmarks in a vast network of **sacred sites** – shrines, bathing places, holy trees, rocks and rivers – interconnected by a web of ancient pilgrims' routes. Tamil Nadu harbours 274 of India's holiest Shiva temples, and 108 are dedicated to Vishnu. In addition, five shrines devoted to the five Vedic elements (Earth, Wind, Fire, Water and Ether) are to be found here, along with eight to the planets, as well as other places revered by Christians and Muslims. Scattered from the pale orange crags and forests of the Western Ghats, across the fertile deltas of the **Vaigai** and **Kaveri** rivers to the Coromandel coast on the Bay of Bengal, these sites were celebrated in the hymns of the Tamil saints, composed between one and two thousand years ago. Today, so little has changed that the same devotional songs are still widely sung and understood in the region.

The Tamils' living connection with their ancient Dravidian past has given rise to a strong **nationalist movement**. With a few fleeting lapses, one or other of the pro-Dravidian parties have been in power here since the 1950s, spreading their anti-brahmin, anti-Hindi proletarian message to the masses principally through the medium of movies. Indeed, since Independence, the majority of Tamil Nadu's political leaders have been drawn from the state's prolific **cinema** industry. Indians from elsewhere in the country love to caricature their southern cousins as "reactionary rice growers" led by "fanatical film stars". While such

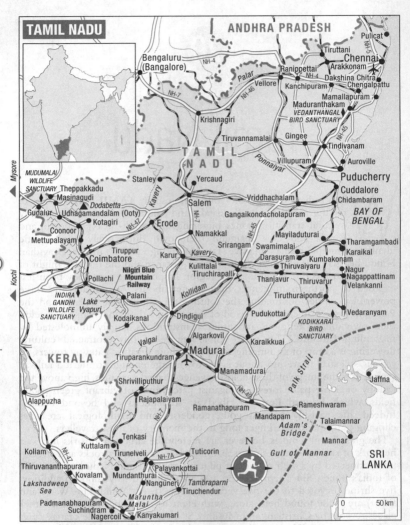

stereotypes should be taken with a pinch of salt, it is undeniable that the Tamil way of life, which has evolved along a distinctive and unbroken path since prehistoric times, sets it apart from the rest of the Subcontinent. This remains, after all, one of the last places in the world where a classical culture has survived well into the present.

Despite its seafront fort, grand mansions and excellence as a centre for the performing arts, the state capital **Chennai** (formerly **Madras**) is a hot, chaotic, noisy Indian metropolis that still carries faint echoes of the Raj. However, it is a good base for visiting **Kanchipuram**, a major pilgrimage and sari-weaving centre, filled with reminders of an illustrious past.

Much the best place to start a temple tour is nearby in **Mamallapuram**, a seaside village that – quite apart from some exquisite Pallava rock-cut architecture – boasts a long and lovely beach. Further down the coast lies the one-time French colony of **Puducherry** (formerly Pondicherry), now home to the famous Sri Aurobindo ashram; nearby, the campus of **Auroville** has carved a role as a popular New Age centre. The road south from Puducherry puts you back on the temple trail, leading to the tenth-century Chola kingdom and the extraordinary architecture of **Chidambaram**, **Gangaikondacholapuram**, **Kumbakonam** and **Darasuram**. For the best Chola bronzes, however, and a glimpse of the magnificent paintings that flourished under Maratha rajas in the eighteenth century, travellers should head for **Thanjavur**. Chola capital for four centuries, the city boasts almost a hundred temples and was the birthplace of Bharatanatyam dance, famous throughout Tamil Nadu.

In the very centre of Tamil Nadu, **Tiruchirapalli**, a commercial town just northwest of Thanjavur, held some interest for the Cholas, but reached its heyday under later dynasties, when the temple complex in neighbouring **Srirangam** became one of south India's largest. Among its patrons were the Nayaks of **Madurai**, whose erstwhile capital further south, bustling with pilgrims, priests, peddlers, tailors and tourists, is an unforgettable destination.

Rameshwaram, on the long spit of land reaching towards Sri Lanka, and **Kanyakumari**, at India's southern tip (the auspicious meeting-point of the Bay of Bengal, the Indian Ocean and the Arabian Sea) are both important pilgrimage centres, and have the added attraction of welcome cool breezes and vistas over the sea.

While Tamil Nadu's temples are undeniably its major attraction, the hill stations of **Kodaikanal** and **Udhagamandalam (Ooty)** in the west of the state are popular destinations on the well-beaten tourist trail between Kerala and Tamil Nadu. The verdant, cool hills offer mountain views and gentle trails through the forests and tea and coffee plantations. You can also spot wildlife in the teak forests of **Mudumalai Wildlife Sanctuary** and bamboo groves of **Indira Gandhi Wildlife Sanctuary**, situated in the Palani Hills.

Visiting Tamil Nadu

Temperatures in Tamil Nadu, which usually hover around 30°C, peak in May and June, when they often soar above 40°C away from the coast and the overpowering heat makes anything but sitting in a shaded café exhausting. The state is barely affected by the southwest monsoon that pounds much of India from June to September: it receives most of its **rain** between October and December, when the odd cyclone may well make an appearance. The cooler, rainy days, however, bring their own problems: large-scale flooding can disrupt road and rail links and imbue everything with an all-pervasive dampness. Note that though the Asian **tsunamis** of December 2004 hit Tamil Nadu hard (see p.1094), the area's tourist infrastructure was soon fully restored and visitor numbers have since returned to pre-tsunami levels.

Accommodation throughout the state is good and plentiful; all but the smallest towns and villages have something for every budget. Most hotels have their own dining halls which, together with local restaurants, usually serve sumptuous and unlimited thalis (known here simply as "meals"), tinged with tamarind and presented on banana leaves. **Indigenous dishes** are almost exclusively vegetarian; for north Indian or Western alternatives, head for the larger hotels or more upmarket city restaurants.

Some history

Since the fourth century BC, Tamil Nadu has been shaped by its majority **Dravidian** population, a people of uncertain origins and physically quite

When the Asian **tsunamis** struck India on December 26, 2004, the coastline of Tamil Nadu bore the brunt of the damage. The waves here averaged 7–10 metres in height, and travelled some 3km inland at Puducherry, causing a huge amount of devastation; in the aftermath, some 8000 people were pronounced dead, while hotels and restaurants in popular resorts such as Mamallapuram were badly damaged. The central coast around Nagapattinam and the pilgrimage centre of Kanyakumari at the southern tip were also badly affected. Cleanup efforts were swift, however, and all the state's resorts and attractions are back in business. In the long term, tourist revenues have become an important supplement to the efforts of aid programmes in rebuilding the region.

different from north Indians. Their language developed separately, as did their social organization; the difference between high-caste brahmins and low-caste workers has always been more pronounced here than in the north – caste divisions that continue to dominate the state's political life. The influence of the powerful *janapadas*, established in the north by the fourth and third centuries BC, extended as far south as the Deccan, but they made few incursions into **Dravidadesa** (Tamil country). Incorporating what is now Kerala and Tamil Nadu, it was ruled by three dynasties: the **Cheras**, who held sway over much of the Malabar coast (Kerala), the **Pandyas** in the far south, and the **Cholas**, whose realm stretched along the eastern Coromandel coast. Indo-Roman trade in spices, precious stones and metals flourished at the start of the Christian era, when **St Thomas** arrived in the south, but dwindled when trade links began with Southeast Asia.

In the fourth century, the **Pallava** dynasty established a powerful kingdom centred in **Kanchipuram**. By the seventh century, the successors of the first Pallava king, Simhavishnu, were engaged in battles with the southern Pandyas and the forces of the Chalukyas, based further west in Karnataka. However, the centuries of Pallava dominion are not marked simply by battles and territorial expansion; this was also an era of social development. **Brahmins** became the dominant community, responsible for lands and riches donated to temples. The emergence of *bhakti*, devotional worship, placed temples firmly at the centre of religious life, and the inspirational *sangam* literature of saint-poets fostered a tradition of dance and music that has become Tamil Nadu's cultural hallmark.

In the tenth and eleventh centuries, the Cholas experienced a period of profound expansion and revival; they soon held sway over much of Tamil Nadu, Andhra Pradesh and even made inroads into Karnataka and Orissa. In the spirit of such glorious victories and power, the Cholas ploughed their new wealth into the construction of splendid and imposing temples, such as those at Gangaikondacholapuram, Kumbakonam and Thanjavur.

The **Vijayanagars**, who gained a firm footing in Hampi (Karnataka) in the fourteenth century, resisted Muslim incursions from the north and spread to cover most of south India by the sixteenth century. This prompted a new phase of architectural development: the building of new temples, the expansion of older ones and the introduction of colossal *gopuras*. In Madurai, the Vijayanagar governors, **Nayaks**, set up an independent kingdom whose impact spread as far as Tiruchirapalli.

Simultaneously, the south experienced its first significant wave of **European settlement**. First came the Portuguese, who landed in Kerala and monopolized Indian trade for about a century before being joined by the British, Dutch and French. Though mostly on cordial terms with the Indians, the Western powers soon found themselves engaged in territorial disputes. The most marked were between the French, based in **Pondicherry**, and the British, whose stronghold since 1640 had been Fort St George in **Madras**. After battles at sea and on land, the French were confined to Pondicherry, while British ambitions reached their apex in the eighteenth century, when the East India Company occupied Bengal (1757) and made firm its bases in Bombay and Madras.

As well as rebellions against colonial rule, Tamil Nadu also saw anti-brahmin protests, in particular those led by the Justice Party in the 1920s and 1930s. **Independence** in 1947 signalled the need for state boundaries, and by 1956 the borders had been demarcated on a linguistic basis; Andhra Pradesh and Kerala were formed, along with Mysore state (later Karnataka) and **Madras Presidency**. In 1965, Madras Presidency became **Tamil Nadu**, the latter part of its name coming from the Chola agrarian administrative units known as *nadus*.

Since Independence, Tamil Nadu's industrial sector has mushroomed. The state was a Congress stronghold until 1967, when the **DMK** (Dravida Munnetra Kazhagam), championing the lower castes and reasserting Tamil identity, won a landslide victory. Anti-Hindi and anti-central government rule, the DMK flourished until the film star "**MGR**" (M.G. Ramachandran) broke away to form the **AIADMK** (**All India Anna Dravida Munnetra Kazhagam**), and won an easy victory in the 1977 elections. Virtually deified by his fans-turned-supporters, MGR remained successful until his death in 1987. Since then power has ping-ponged back and forth between the AIADMK, led by **Srimati Jayalalithaa Jayaram**, an ex-film star and dancer once on close terms with MGR, and her bitter opponent, the DMK leader **M. Karunanidhi**, who is currently back on the Tamil throne as Chief Minister. See the box on p.1104 for more on these dramatic political intrigues.

Chennai (Madras)

In the northeastern corner of Tamil Nadu on the Bay of Bengal, **CHENNAI** (still commonly referred to by its former British name, **Madras**) is India's fourth largest city, with a population nudging six and a half million. Hot, fast, congested and noisy, it's the major transportation hub of the south – the international airport makes a marginally less stressful entry-point to the Subcontinent than Mumbai or Delhi – and most travellers stay just long enough to book a ticket for somewhere else. The attractions of the city itself are sparse, though it does boast fine specimens of **Raj architecture**, pilgrimage sites connected with the apostle **Doubting Thomas**, superb **Chola bronzes** at its state museum, and plenty of **classical music** and **dance** performances.

As capital of Tamil Nadu, Chennai is, like Mumbai and Kolkata (Calcutta), a comparatively modern creation. It was founded by the **British East India Company** in 1639, on a five-kilometre strip of land between the Cooum and Adyar rivers, a few kilometres north of the ancient Tamil port of **Mylapore** and the Portuguese settlement of San Thome; a fortified trading post, completed on St George's Day in 1640, was named **Fort St George**. By 1700, the British had acquired neighbouring territory including **Triplicane** and **Egmore**, while over the course of the next century, as capital of the **Madras Presidency** which covered most of south India, the city mushroomed to include many surrounding villages. The French repeatedly challenged the British, and finally managed to destroy most of the city in 1746. **Robert Clive** ("Clive of India"), then a clerk, was taken prisoner, an experience said to have inspired him to

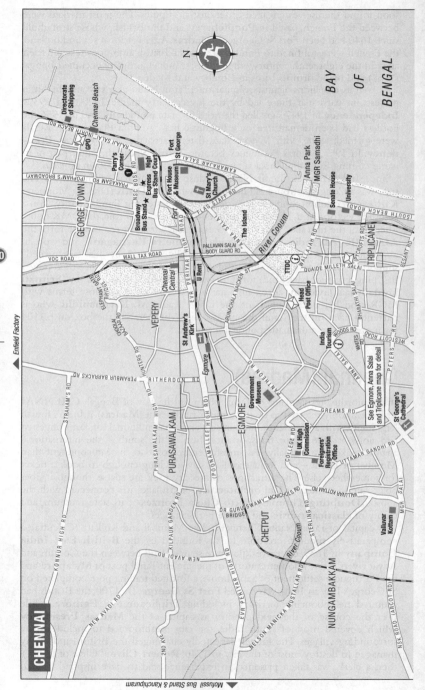

CHENNAI

BAY OF BENGAL

▲ Enfield Factory

▼ Mofussil Bus Stand & Kanchipuram

Directorate of Shipping

Chennai Beach

GPO

Parry's Corner

RAJAJI SALAI (NORTH BEACH RD)

PRAKASAM RD

NSC BOSE RD

POPHAM'S BROADWAY

GEORGE TOWN

Broadway Bus Stand

Express Bus Stand Court

High Court

Fort House & Museum

Fort St George

St Mary's Church

Fort

Fort Road

FLAG STAFF RD

KAMARAJAR SALAI

Anna Park

MGR Samadhi

Senate House

University

SOUTH BEACH ROAD

The Island

River Cooum

PALLAVAN SALAI BODY GUARD RD

ANNA SALAI

WALLAJAH RD

TRIPLICANE

PYCROFTS RD

BESANT RD

QUAIDE MILLETH SALAI

BHARATHI SALAI

WESTCOTT ROAD

TTDC

Head Post Office

India Tourism

WOODS RD

WHITES RD

ANNA SALAI

PETERS RD

See Egmore, Anna Salai and Triplicane map for detail

St George's Cathedral

VOC ROAD

WALL TAX ROAD

Chennai Central

EVR PERIYAR HIGH ROAD

ELEPHANT GATE BRIDGE

COOUM RIVER

EBRAR RD

VEPERY

St Andrew's Kirk

ARUMACHALA MACKEN ST

HUNTERS RD

PERAMBUR BARRACKS RD

RITHERDON RD

Egmore

PANTHEON RD

Government Museum

GREAMS RD

EGMORE

PURASAWALKAM HIGH RD

PURASAWALKAM

STRAHAM'S RD

KONNUR HIGH RD

College RD

UK High Commission

Foreigners' Registration Office

UTTAMAR GANDHI RD

VALLUVAR KOTTAM RD

DR GURUSWAMY BRIDGE

MCNICHOLS RD

NEW AVADI RD

KILPAUK GARDEN RD

CHETPUT

River Cooum

STERLING RD

2ND AVE

NELSON MANICKA MUSTALLAR RD

NSK ROAD (ARCOT RD)

MGR SALAI

Valluvar Kottam

NUNGAMBAKKAM

U Rent

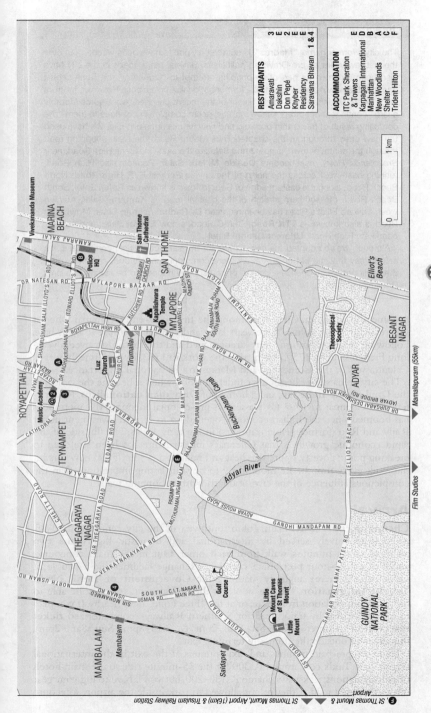

RESTAURANTS

Amaravati	3
Dakshin	E
Don Pepé	2
Khyber	E
Residency	E
Saravana Bhavan	1 & 4

ACCOMMODATION

ITC Park Sheraton & Towers	E
Karpagam International	D
Manhattan	B
New Woodlands	A
Shelter	C
Trident Hilton	F

0 1 km

Vivekananda Museum

MARINA BEACH

San Thome Cathedral

SAN THOME

Police HQ

DR NATESAN RD

MYLAPORE BAZAAR

ROSARY CHURCH RD

KUTCHERY RD

Kapalishvara Temple

MYLAPORE

MANDAVELI ST

MADHA CHURCH ST

HIGH ROAD

Elliot's Beach

BESANT NAGAR

Theosophical Society

ADYAR

ROYAPETTAH

Music Academy

Luz Church

Tirumailai

TEYNAMPET

ST MARY'S RD

Buckingham Canal

Adyar River

THEAGARAYA NAGAR

MAMBALAM

Mambalam

Golf Course

GUINDY NATIONAL PARK

Little Mount Caves of St Thomas Mount

Little Mount

Saidapet

F, St Thomas Mount & Airport (16km) & Trisulam Railway Station

St Thomas Mount, Airport

Mamallapuram (55km)

Film Studios

The city's former name, **"Madras"**, is not the only one to have been weeded out over the last few years by pro-Dravidian politicians. Several major roads in the city have also been renamed as part of an ongoing attempt to **"Dravidify"** the Tamil capital (most of the new names immortalize former nationalist politicians). However, far from all of Chennai's inhabitants are in favour of the recent changes, while some (notably a large contingent of auto-rickshaw wallahs) seem completely oblivious to them. The confusing result of this is that both old and new names remain in use. We have used the new ones throughout the chapter. Thus Mount Road, the main shopping road through the centre of town, is now **Anna Salai**; to the east, Triplicane High Road, near *Broadlands Hotel*, has become **Quaide Milleth Salai**; Poonamallee High Road, running east–west across the north of the city, is **Periyar EVR High Road**; North Beach Road, along the eastern edge of George Town is known as **Rajaji Salai**; South Beach Road, the southern stretch of the coastal road, is **Kamaraj Salai**; running west, Edward Elliot's Road has been renamed **Dr Radhakrishnan Salai**; Mowbray's Road is also known as **TTK Road**; C-in-C Road is now **Ethiraj Salai**; and Nunga-bamkkam High Road, **Uttamar Gandhi Salai**.

Although we've adopted the new names for the sake of political correctness, it's safe to say that the old ones are still more commonly understood, and that using them will not cause offence – unless, of course, you happen to be talking to a pro-Dravidian activist.

become a campaigner. Clive was among the first to re-enter Chennai when it was retaken by the British three years later, and continued to use it as his base. Following this, fortifications were strengthened and the British survived a year-long French siege in 1759, completing the work in 1783. By this time, however, Calcutta was in the ascendancy and Madras lost its national importance.

The city's renaissance began after Independence, when it became the centre of the Tamil **movie industry**, and a hotbed of **Dravidian nationalism**. Rechristened as Chennai in 1997 (to reassert its pre-colonial identity), the metropolis has boomed since the Indian economy opened up to foreign investment under Rajiv and Rao (former prime ministers) in the early 1990s. The flip side of this rapid economic growth is that Chennai's infrastructure has been stretched to breaking point: poverty, oppressive heat and pollution (a scary 5000 new cars hit the roads every month) are more likely to be your lasting impressions than the conspicuous affluence of the city's modern marble shopping malls.

Arrival

Chennai airport in Trisulam, 16km southwest of the city centre on NH-45, is comprehensively served by international and domestic flights; the two terminals are a minute's walk from each other. Out in the main concourse, you'll find a 24-hour post office, currency exchange facilities and a couple of snack bars. If there's anybody manning the **Government of Tamil Nadu Tourist Information Centre** booth at the arrivals exit, you may be able to fix up accommodation from here, or at the "Free Fone" desk nearby. If you plan to leave Chennai by train, head for Southern Railways' computerized **ticket reservation** counter (Mon–Sat 8am–2pm & 2.15–8pm, Sun 8am–2pm), immediately outside the domestic terminal exit.

There are pre-paid minibus and taxi counters at the exit in the international arrivals hall. **Taxis** cost around Rs300 for the 35-minute ride to the main hotels or railway stations; rickshaws charge Rs150–200, but you'll have to lug your gear out to the main road as they're not allowed to park inside the airport forecourt.

A taxi to **Mamallapuram** costs in the region of Rs900. The quickest, cheapest and most efficient way to get into town is by suburban **train**. Services run every ten to fifteen minutes (4.30am–11pm) from **Trisulam** Station, 500m from the airport on the far side of the road, to Park, Egmore and North Beach stations, taking 30–40 minutes. If you want to leave Chennai straight away by bus, catch local bus #70 or #70a to the Moffussil Bus Stand (see below).

By train

Arriving in Chennai by train, you come in at one of two **long-distance railway stations**, 1.5km apart on Periyar EVR High Road, towards the north of the city. **Egmore Station**, in the heart of the busy commercial Egmore district, is the arrival point for most trains from Tamil Nadu and Kerala. On the whole, all the others pull in at **Central Station**, further east, on the edge of George Town, which has multiple food outlets, a 24-hour left-luggage office and pre-paid taxi and rickshaw booths.

By bus

Buses from elsewhere in Tamil Nadu and other states arrive at the huge **Moffussil** Bus Stand, inconveniently situated in the suburb of Koyambedu, over 10km west of the centre – the chaotic old **Express** and **Broadway** bus stands in the centre have been amalgamated and are only used for local services. Moffussil is linked to these and other parts of Chennai by a host of city buses, which depart from the well-organized platforms outside the main terminal: buses #27, #15B, #15F and #17E go to the Egmore/Central area and Parry's Corner; bus #27B also goes on to Triplicane; while bus #70 and #70A link the bus stand to the airport. Note that most buses from Mamallapuram, Puducherry and other towns to the south of Chennai stop at Guindy suburban railway station on their way in and you will save a lot of time by connecting onto the train there.

Information

The highly efficient and very helpful **India Tourism Office** at 154 Anna Salai (Mon–Fri 9am–6pm, Sat 9am–1pm; ☎044/2846 0285), has maps and leaflets, and can arrange accommodation. They also keep a list of approved **guides**.

The **Tamil Nadu Tourism Development Corporation** (TTDC) is based in a smart complex on Wallajah Road, near Anna Park in Triplicane (Mon–Sat 10am–5.30pm; ☎044/2538 3333), where you can also find the tourist offices of many other states including Kerala (☎044/2536 9789). TTDC can book you tours or accommodation in their own hotels across the state. The **India Tourist Development Corporation** (ITDC) office at 29 Dr PV Cherian Crescent, Ethiraj Salai (Mon–Fri 10am–5.30pm; ☎044/2827 8884, ⓦtheashokgroup .com) takes bookings for all its countrywide hotels and services.

The long-established *Hallo! Madras* (monthly; Rs10) is an accurate **directory** to all the city's services, with full-moon dates (useful for estimating temple festivals), a tourist guide to Tamil Nadu, exhaustive flight and train details, and an outline of Chennai bus timetables. Alternatively, the even more comprehensive quarterly directory *Madura Welcome Tamil Nadu* (Rs100) contains even fuller transport, accommodation and tourist information details for Chennai and the rest of Tamil Nadu. Both are available at all book and stationery shops. Unfortunately, neither have a "What's On" section, so for forthcoming music and dance performances, look out for *Chennai: This Fortnight*, available free from all the city's smarter hotels, or check online at ⓦwww.explocity.com/chennai.asp or ⓦwww.chennaionline.com.

City transport

Chennai's sights and facilities are spread over such a wide area that it's impossible to get around without using some form of **public transport**. Most visitors jump in auto-rickshaws, but outside rush hours you can travel around comfortably by **bus** or suburban **train**.

Buses

On Anna Salai and other major thoroughfares **buses** have dedicated stops, but on smaller streets you have to flag them down, or wait with the obvious crowd. Buses in Egmore gather opposite the railway station. Numbers of services to specific places of interest in the city are listed in the relevant accounts, or for a full directory of bus routes, buy *Madura Welcome* (see p.1099). Buses to and from the Moffussil Bus Stand are listed in "Arrival", p.1099.

Trains

If you want to travel south from central Chennai to Guindy (Deer Park) or the airport, the easiest way to go is by **train**. Services run every fifteen minutes (on average) between 4.30am and 11pm, prices are minimal, and you can guarantee a seat at any time except rush hour (around 9am & 5pm). First-class carriages substitute padded seats for wooden slatted benches, and are a little cleaner; buy a ticket before boarding.

City trains travel between: Beach (opposite the GPO), Fort, Park (for Central), Egmore, Nungambakkam, Kodambakkam, Mambalam (for T Nagar and silk shops), Saidapet (for Little Mount Church), Guindy, St Thomas Mount and Trisulam (for the airport).

Taxis and rickshaws

Chennai's yellow-top Ambassador **taxis** gather outside Egmore and Central railway stations, and at the airport. All have meters, but drivers often refuse to use them so prepare yourself for some hard bargaining. At around Rs150 from Central Station to Triplicane, they're practically pricing themselves out of business. For this reason more reliable and economical **radio taxis** such as Bharati Call Taxi (☎044/2814 2233) are becoming more popular.

Auto-rickshaw drivers in Chennai are notorious for demanding high fares from locals and tourists alike. A rickshaw from Triplicane to either of the bus stations, or Egmore and Central railway stations should cost no more than Rs50, but again meters are rarely employed. If you need to get to the airport or station early in the morning, book a rickshaw and negotiate the price the night before. Only take **cycle rickshaws** on the smaller roads; riding amid Chennai traffic on a fragile tricycle seat can be extremely hair-raising.

Tours

One good way to get around the sights of Chennai is on a TTDC **bus tour**; bookings are taken in the relevant offices (see p.1099). They're good value, albeit rushed, and the guides can be very helpful. The TTDC **half-day tour** (daily 8am–1pm or 1.30pm–6.30pm; Rs120 non-a/c, Rs170 with a/c) at their office on Periyar EVR High Road. It takes in Fort St George, the Government Museum, the Snake Park, Kapalishvara Temple, Elliot's Beach and Marina Beach (on Fri, the Government Museum is closed, so the tour goes to the Birla Planetarium instead). TTDC also offer good-value **day-trips**, including visits to Mamallapuram, Kanchipuram and Puducherry, with meals included in the tariff; check at their office for the various itineraries and prices.

Car, motorcycle and bike rental

Car rental with driver is available at many of the city's upmarket hotels or through private agents such as Welcome Tours & Travels at 150 Anna Salai (☎044/2846 0908, ⓦ www.allindiatours.com). An Ambassador car with driver costs Rs1000–1200 per day (or Rs1600–1900 for one with a/c) – rates may be negotiable.

Mopeds and **motorcycles** can be rented at U-Rent Services, 1 1st Main Rd, Gandhinagar, Adyar (Mon–Sat 8am–7pm, Sun 9am–6pm; ☎044/2491 0838). Prices range from Rs200 to Rs400 per day, plus a flat Rs200 annual membership fee regardless of how long you rent a bike for.

Accommodation

Finding a **place to stay** in Chennai can be a problem, as hotels are often full by noon. Demand has pushed prices up, with only a couple of places offering anything for less than Rs250; however, standards in the cheapies are better than in other cities. If you're on a budget, it's advisable to phone and book in advance, at least from the railway station or airport.

Most of the mid-range and inexpensive hotels are around the railway station in **Egmore**, and further east in **Triplicane**, a characterful, busy market and Muslim residential district. The bulk of the top hotels are in the south of the city and several offer courtesy buses to and from the airport. Most hotels have at least one south Indian/multi-cuisine restaurant attached to their premises. Due to frequent shortages, visitors should use **water** as sparingly as possible.

Accommodation listed under the "Outside the centre" heading appears on the main Chennai **map** (pp.1096–1097); all others are marked on the Egmore, Anna Salai and Triplicane map (p.1102).

Egmore

Chandra Park 55 Gandhi Irwin Rd ☎044/2819 1177, ⓦ www.hotelchandra park.com. Newly refurbished business hotel with central a/c, foreign exchange, 24hr coffee shop, bar and rooftop restaurant. The spacious, light and well-furnished standard rooms are an especially good deal. ④–⑥

Masa 15/1 Kennet Lane ☎044/2819 3344, ⓕ 2819 1261. Variously priced rooms with attached bathrooms and TVs in a clean, modern building, close to the station. Good value. The similar *Regal*, tacked onto the back, is marginally cheaper. ③

Nest Inn 55/31 Gandhi Irwin Rd ☎044/2819 2919, ⓦ www.hotelnestinn.co.in. Renovated and renamed business hotel, now with central a/c. The rooms are small but comfortable and pleasantly decorated; there's also a multi-cuisine restaurant and bar. ⑥

Pandian 15 Kennet Lane ☎044/2819 1010, ⓦ www.hotelpandian.com. Pleasant, clean and modern mid-scale place within walking distance of the railway station. Ask for a room on the Church Park side of the building for green views. Rooms with a/c are overpriced, however. ④–⑥

Regent 11 Kennet Lane ☎044/2819 1347, ⓕ 2819 0170. Quiet lodge set around a peaceful courtyard. The fair-sized non-a/c rooms are a bit shabby, though the bathrooms are spotless. ③

Tourist Home 43 Gandhi Irwin Rd ☎044/2819 4679. Popular hotel directly opposite the railway station that could do with a spring clean; nonetheless, it's good value and often full. Rooms (some a/c) have showers and TVs, and clean linen and towels are provided; one room has three beds, another six. Back rooms suffer less from early morning noise. ③

YWCA 1086 Periyar EVR High Rd ☎044/2532 4234, ⓔ ywcamadras @sancharnet.in. Attractive hotel in quiet gardens behind Egmore Station, with spotless, spacious rooms, safe-deposit and a good restaurant. A highly recommended, safe and friendly place; book in advance. Rates include a buffet breakfast. ④–⑤

Anna Salai and Triplicane

Ambassador Pallava 30 Montieth Rd ☎044/2855 4476, ⓦ www.ambassadorindia.com. Colossal four-star close to Anna Salai, with great views from its upper storeys. Amid all the gold-plated mirrors and cool white marble is a sports complex with a pool and health club. All rooms are smartly designed, with fridges; the spacious suites cost over $200. ⑧–⑨

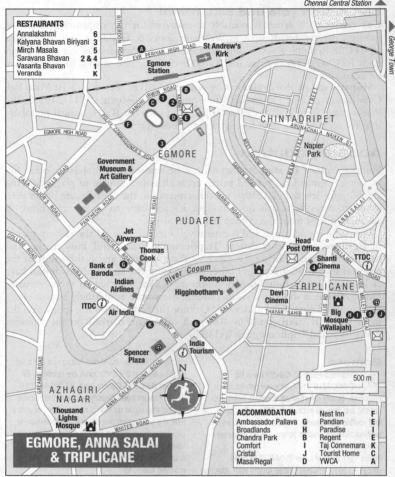

RESTAURANTS

Annalakshmi	6
Kalyana Bhavan Biriyani	3
Mirch Masala	5
Saravana Bhavan	2 & 4
Vasanta Bhavan	1
Veranda	K

ACCOMMODATION

Ambassador Pallava	G	Nest Inn	F
Broadlands	H	Pandian	E
Chandra Park	B	Paradise	I
Comfort	I	Regent	E
Cristal	J	Taj Connemara	K
Masa/Regal	D	Tourist Home	C
		YWCA	A

EGMORE, ANNA SALAI & TRIPLICANE

TAMIL NADU | Chennai (Madras)

Broadlands 18 Vallabha Agraham St, Triplicane ☎044/2854 5573, ⓔbroadlandshotel@yahoo.com. An old whitewashed house, with crumbling stucco and stained glass, ranged around a leafy courtyard, this is the kind of budget travellers' enclave you either love or loathe. There's a large roof terrace and clean rooms, a few with attached bathrooms, private balconies and views of the mosque. ❷–❸

Comfort 22 Vallabha Agraham St, Triplicane ☎044/2858 7661, ⓔhotel-comfort@hotmail.com. Rooms in the new block are simple, but all attached and are worth paying the little extra for, as the dim corridors in the old part are somewhat chaotic. ❹

Cristal 34 CNK Rd, Triplicane ☎044/2858 5605. In a modern building off Quaide Milleth Salai, this is a

safe and friendly place run by a team of brothers; the reception is busy all day with locals sipping coffee. Rooms are tiled and clean, all with attached showers. TVs cost Rs25 extra. As cheap as it gets in Chennai. ❶

Paradise 17/1 Vallabha Agraham St, Triplicane ☎044/2859 4252, ⓔparadisegh@hotmail.com. Very friendly and a dependable choice, offering inexpensive rooms with attached bathroom, TV and a choice of western or Indian loos. There's seating on a large roof terrace, and room service. Good value. ❷–❸

Taj Connemara Binny Rd ☎044/5500 0000, ⓦwww.tajhotels.com. Dating from the Raj era, this whitewashed Art-Deco five-star near Anna Salai is a

Chennai institution. The large "heritage" rooms feature Victorian decor, dressing rooms and verandas overlooking the pool. There is also a health club, 24hr coffee shop, two excellent restaurants (see p.1109) and a bar. Rates start around $200. ⑨

Outside the centre

ITC Park Sheraton & Towers 132 TTK Rd ☎044/2499 4101, ⓦwww.itcwelcomgroup.in. The last word in American-style executive luxury, somehow not too ostentatious despite the bow-tied valets. Three excellent restaurants, a 24hr coffee shop and other five-star facilities. The spacious rooms with plush furnishings make it an excellent choice for business travellers; rates start in excess of $300. ⑨

Karpagam International 41 South Mada St, Mylapore ☎044/2495 9984, ⓕ2464 2299. Very ordinary place whose only outstanding feature is its location overlooking the Kapalishvara Temple. It's also on the right side of the city for the airport, 12km away. Inexpensive single rooms available. ③–④

Manhattan 1 Dr Radhakrishnan Salai ☎044/2844 4546, ⓦwww.thehotelmanhattan.com. Only a few

minutes' walk from Marina Beach, this comfortable modern hotel with central a/c offers decent rooms and a sea view from the rooftop terrace restaurant. ⑥

New Woodlands 72–75 Dr Radhakrishnan Salai ☎044/2811 3111, ⓦwww.newwoodlands.com. Sprawling complex of clean, reasonably sized rooms and more spacious, self-contained apartments (called "cottages"), plus two restaurants and a swimming pool. Rooms ⑤, cottages ⑥–⑦

Shelter 19–21 Venkatesa Agraharam St, Mylapore ☎044/2495 1919, ⓦwww.hotelshelter .com. A stone's throw from the Kapalishvara Temple, this sparklingly clean luxury hotel is better value than most upmarket places with good restaurants and a bar, although the rooms are a little kitsch. ⑦

Trident Hilton 1/24 GST Rd ☎044/2234 4747, ⓦwww.trident-hilton.com. Comfortable five-star in lovely gardens; it's near the airport (3km), but a 12km, albeit complimentary, drive into town. Luxurious rooms (doubles start at $200), swimming pool and good restaurants, one of which serves Thai cuisine. ⑨

▲ Gandhi statue, Chennai

Of movie stars and ministers

One notable difference between the Chennai movie industry and its counterpart in Mumbai is the influence of **politics** on Tamil films – an overlap that dates from the earliest days of regional cinema, when stories, stock themes and characters were derived from traditional folk ballads about low-caste heroes vanquishing high-caste villains. Already familiar to millions, such Robin Hood–style stereotypes were perfect propaganda vehicles for the nascent Tamil nationalist movement, the Dravida Munnetra Kazhagam, or **DMK**. It is no coincidence that the party's founding father, **C.N. Annadurai**, was a top screenplay and script writer. Like prominent Tamil Congress leaders and movie-makers of the 1930s and 1940s, he and his colleagues used the popular film genres of the time to convey their political ideas to the masses. From this politicization of the big screen were born the **fan clubs**, or *rasigar manrams*, that played such a key role in mobilizing support for the nationalist parties in elections.

The most influential fan club of all time was the one set up to support the superstar actor Marudur Gopalamenon Ramachandran, known to millions simply as "**MGR**". By carefully cultivating a political image to mirror the folk-hero roles he played in films, the maverick matinee idol generated fanatical grass-roots support in the state, especially among women, and rose to become chief minister in 1977. His eleven-year rule is still regarded by liberals as a dark age in the state's history, as chronic corruption, police brutality, political purges and rising organized crime were all rife during the period. When he died in 1987, two million people attended his funeral and 31 grief-stricken devotees committed ritual suicide. Even today, MGR's statue, sporting trademark sunglasses and lamb's-wool hat, is revered at tens of thousands of wayside shrines across Tamil Nadu.

MGR's political protégée, and eventual successor, was a teenage screen starlet called **Jayalalitha**, a convent-educated brahmin's daughter whom he spotted at a school dance and, despite an age difference of more than thirty years, recruited to be both his leading lady and mistress. The couple would star opposite each other in 25 hit films, and when MGR eventually moved into politics, Jayalalitha followed him, becoming leader of the AIADMK, the party MGR set up after being expelled from the DMK in 1972. Larger than life in voluminous silver ponchos and heavy gold jewellery, the now portly Puratchi Thalavi ("Revolutionary Leader") has taken her personality cult to extremes brazen even by Indian standards. Jayalalitha's first spell as chief minister, however, was brought to an ignominious end at the 1996 elections, after allegations of fraud and corruption on an appropriately monumental scale. Despite being found guilty by the High Court, she nevertheless later ousted her arch rival, **M. Karunanidhi**, leader of the DMK, regaining her old job as chief minister of Tamil Nadu and wresting back power for two spells in 2001 and from 2002 to 2006. One of her first acts was to exact revenge on Karunanidhi, throwing him and one thousand of his supporters into prison on corruption charges. Predictably, he returned to trump his rival in the elections of 2006.

The City

Chennai divides into three main areas. The northern district, separated from the rest by the River Cooum, is the site of the first British outpost in India, **Fort St George**, and the commercial centre, **George Town**, which developed during British occupation. At the southern end of Rajaji Salai is **Parry's Corner**, George Town's principal landmark and a major bus stop – look for the tall grey building labelled Parry's.

Central Chennai is sandwiched between the Cooum and Adyar rivers, and crossed diagonally by the city's main thoroughfare, **Anna Salai**, the modern, commercial heart of the metropolis. To the east, this gives way to the atmospheric old Muslim quarters of **Triplicane** and a long straight **Marina** where fishermen mend nets and set small boats out to sea, and hordes of Indian tourists hitch up saris and trousers for a quick paddle. South of here, near the coast, **Mylapore**, inhabited in the 1500s by the Portuguese, boasts **Kapalishvara Temple** and **San Thome Cathedral**, both tourist attractions and places of pilgrimage.

Fort St George

Quite unlike any other fort in India, **Fort St George** stands amid state offices facing the sea in the east of the city, just south of George Town on Kamaraj Salai. It looks more like a complex of well-maintained colonial mansions than a fort; indeed many of its buildings are used today as offices, a hive of activity during the week as people rush between the Secretariat and State Legislature.

The fort was the first structure of Madras town and the first territorial posses-sion of the British in India. Construction began in 1640, but most of the original buildings were replaced later that century, after being damaged during French sieges. The most imposing structure is the eighteenth-century colonnaded **Fort House**, coated in deep slate-grey and white paint. Next door, in the more modestly proportioned **Exchange Building** – site of Madras's first bank – is the excellent **Fort Museum** (daily except Fri 10am–5pm; Rs100 [Rs5], video cameras Rs25). The collection within faithfully records the central events of the British occupation of Madras with portraits, regimental flags, weapons, East India Company coins, medals, stamps and thick woollen uniforms that make you wonder how the Raj survived as long as it did. The squat cast-iron cage on the ground floor was brought to Madras from China, where for more than a year in the nineteenth century it was used as a particularly sadistic form of imprisonment for a British captain. The first floor, once the public exchange hall where merchants met to gossip and trade, is now an **art gallery**, where portraits of prim officials and their wives sit side by side with fine sketches of the British embarking at Chennai in aristocratic finery, attended by Indians in loincloths. Also on display are etchings by the famous artist **Thomas Daniells**, whose work largely defined British perceptions of India at the end of the eighteenth century.

South of the museum, past the State Legislature, stands the oldest surviving Anglican church in Asia, **St Mary's** (daily 9am–5pm), built in 1678 and partly renovated after the battle of 1759. Constructed with thick walls and a strong vaulted roof that has withstood the city's many sieges, the church served as a store and shelter in times of war. It's distinctly English in style, crammed with plaques and statues in memory of British soldiers, politicians and their wives. The grandest plaque, made of pure silver, was presented by Elihu Yale, former governor of Fort St George (1687–96), and founder of Yale University in the USA. A collection of photographs of visiting dignitaries, including Queen Elizabeth II, is on display in the entrance porch.

George Town

North of Fort St George, the former British trading centre of **George Town** (reached on bus #18 from Anna Salai) remains the focal area for banks, offices, shipping companies and street stalls. This confusing – if well-ordered – grid of streets harbours a fascinating medley of architecture: eighteenth- and nineteenth-century churches, Hindu and Jain temples and a scattering of mosques, interspersed with grand mansions. In the east, on Rajaji Salai, the **General Post Office** occupies a robust earth-red Indo-Saracenic building constructed in 1884. George Town's southern extent is marked by the bulbous white domes and sandstone towers of the **High Court**, and the even more opulent towers of the **Law College**, both showing strong Islamic influence.

Government Museum

Unfortunately the Chennai **Government Museum** (daily except Fri 9.30am–5pm; Rs250 [Rs10], camera Rs200, video camera Rs500) has joined the ASI sites in charging a ridiculous rate for foreigners, which understandably discourages many visitors from viewing the remarkable archeological finds from south India and the Deccan, stone sculptures from major temples, and its unsurpassed collection of Chola bronzes. To get there, hop on bus #11H from Anna Salai for Pantheon Road, south of Egmore railway station.

The deep-red, circular **main building**, fronted by Italian-style pillars and built in 1851, stands opposite the entrance and ticket office. The first gallery is devoted to archeology and geology; the highlights are the dismantled panels, railings and statues from the second-century AD stupa complex at **Amaravati** (see p.1056). Depicting episodes from the Buddha's life and scenes from the *Jataka* stories from ancient Hinayana Buddhist texts, these sensuously carved marble reliefs are widely regarded as the finest achievements of early Indian art, outshining even the Sanchi *toranas*. To the left of here high, arcaded halls full of stuffed animals lead to the **ethnology gallery**, where models, clothes, weapons and photographs of expressionless faces in orderly lines illustrate local tribal societies, some long since wiped out. A fascinating display of wind and string instruments, drums and percussion includes the large predecessor of today's sitar and several very old tablas. Nearby, a group of wooden doors and window frames from Chettinad, a region near Madurai, are exquisitely carved with floral and geometric designs much like those found in Gujarati havelis.

The museum's real treasure, however, is the modern, well-lit gallery, left of the main building, which contains the world's most complete and impressive selection of **Chola bronzes** (see p.1144). Large statues of Shiva, Vishnu and Parvati stand in the centre, flanked by glass cases containing smaller figurines, including several sculptures of Shiva as **Nataraja**, the Lord of the Dance, encircled by a ring of fire, and standing with his arms and legs poised and head provocatively cocked. One of the finest models is **Ardhanarishvara**, the androgynous form of Shiva (united with Shakti in transcendence of duality); the left side of the body is female and the right male, and the intimacy of detail is astounding. A rounded breast, a delicate hand and tender bejewelled foot are counterpoints to the harsher sinewy limbs and torso, and the male side of the head is crowned with a mass of matted hair and serpents.

Elsewhere, a **children's gallery** demonstrates the principles of electricity and irrigation with marginally diverting, semi-functional models, while the magnificent Indo-Saracenic **art gallery** houses old British portraits of figures such as Clive and Hastings, plus Rajput and Mughal miniatures, and a small display of ivory carvings.

St Andrew's Kirk

Just northeast of Egmore Station, off Periyar EVR High Road, **St Andrew's Kirk**, consecrated in 1821, is a fine example of Georgian architecture. Modelled on London's St Martins-in-the-Fields, it's one of just three churches in India with a circular seating plan, laid out beneath a huge dome painted blue with gold stars and supported by a sweep of Corinthian columns. Marble plaques around the church give a fascinating insight into the kind of people who left Britain to work for the imperial and Christian cause. A staircase leads onto the flat roof, surrounding the dome, from where you can climb further up into the steeple past the massive bell to a tiny balcony affording excellent views of the city.

The Marina

One of the longest city beaches in the world, the **Marina** (Kamaraj Salai) stretches 5km from the harbour at the southeastern corner of George Town to San Thome Cathedral. The impulse to transform Chennai's beach into an attractive and sociable esplanade was conceived by Mountstuart Elphinstone Grant-Duff, governor of Madras from 1881 to 1886, and numerous buildings have sprung up over the years, along with surreal modern memorials to Tamil Nadu's chief political heroes and freedom fighters. Going south, you'll pass the Indo-Saracenic **Presidency College** (1865–71), one of a number of stolid Victorian buildings that make up the **University**. Next door, the nineteenth-century Madras depot of the Tudor Ice Company has been converted into the interesting **Vivekananda Museum** (daily 10am–noon & 3–7pm, closed Wed; free), dedicated to the nineteenth-century saint, Swami Vivekananda. The grand old circular building contains fully annotated photo displays of the peripatetic Hindu master's life, including his study under Ramakrishna, his attendance at the Chicago Conference on World Religions and his later teaching missions.

Today the **beach** itself is a sociable stretch, peopled by idle paddlers, picnickers and pony-riders; every afternoon crowds gather around the beach market. However, its location just a little downstream from the port, which belches out waste and smelly fumes, combined with its function as the toilet for the fishing community detract somewhat from its natural beauty. Consequently, swimming and sunbathing are not recommended. The beach also has a tragic place in recent history, as many young children playing cricket here were swept away by the 2004 tsunami.

Mylapore

Long before Madras came into existence, **Mylapore**, south of the Marina (reached by buses #4, #5 or #21 from the LIC building on Anna Salai), was a major settlement; the Greek geographer Ptolemy mentioned it in the second century AD as a thriving port. During the Pallava period (fifth to ninth centuries) it was second only to Mamallapuram.

An important stop – with Little Mount – on the St Thomas pilgrimage trail, **San Thome Cathedral** (daily 6am–8pm) marks the eastern boundary of Mylapore, lying close to the sea at the southern end of the Marina. Although the present neo-Gothic structure dates from 1896, it stands on the site of two earlier churches (the first possibly erected by Nestorian Christians from Persia during the tenth century) built over the tomb of St Thomas; his relics are kept inside, accessed by an underground passage from the museum at the rear of the courtyard.

The large **Kapalishvara temple** sits just under 1km west of the cathedral. Seventh-century Tamil poet-saints sang its praises, but the present structure, dedicated to Shiva, probably dates from the sixteenth century. Until then, the temple is thought to have occupied a site on the shore; sea erosion or demolition at the hands of the Portuguese led it to be rebuilt inland. The huge (40m) *gopura* towering above the main east entrance, plastered in stucco figures, was added in 1906. Surrounding an assortment of busy shrines, where priests offer blessings for devotees and non-Hindus alike, the courtyard features an old tree where a small shrine to Shiva's consort, Parvati, shows her in the form of a peahen (*mayil*) worshipping a lingam.

A little further west, before you come to TTK Road, the **Luz Church**, on Luz Church Road, is thought to be the earliest in Chennai, built by the Portuguese in the sixteenth century. Its founding is associated with a miracle; Portuguese sailors in difficulties at sea were once guided to land and safety by a light which, when they tried to find its source, disappeared. The church, dedicated to Our Lady of Light, was erected where the light left them.

Little Mount Caves and St Thomas Mount

St Thomas is said to have sought refuge from persecution in the **Little Mount Caves**, 8km south of the city centre (bus #18A, #18B, or #52C from Anna Salai). Entrance to the caves is beside steps leading to a statue of Our Lady of Good Health. Inside, next to a small natural window in the rock, are impressions of what are believed to be St Thomas' handprints, created when he made his escape through this tiny opening. Behind the new circular church of Our Lady of Good Health, together with brightly painted replicas of the *Pietà* and Holy Sepulchre, is a natural **spring**. Tradition has it that this was created when Thomas struck the rock, so the crowds that came to hear him preach could quench their thirst; samples of its holy water are on sale.

Tradition has it that St Thomas was speared to death while praying before a stone cross on **St Thomas Mount**, 11km south of the city centre – take a suburban train to Guindy railway station and walk from there. **Our Lady of Expectation Church** (1523), at the summit of the Mount, can be reached by 134 granite steps marked with the fourteen stations of the Cross, or by a road which curls its way to the top. At the top of the steps, a huge old banyan tree provides shade for devotees who come to fast, pray and sing.

The Theosophical Society headquarters

The **Theosophical Society** was established in New York in 1875 by American Civil War veteran Colonel Henry S. Olcott, a failed farmer and journalist, and the eccentric Russian aristocrat Madame Helena Petrovna Blavatsky, who claimed occult powers and telepathic links with "Mahatmas" in Tibet. Based on a fundamental belief in the equality and truth of all religions, the society in fact propagated a modern form of Hinduism, praising all things Indian and shunning Christian missionaries. Needless to say, its two founders were greeted enthusiastically when they transferred their operations to Madras in 1882, establishing their headquarters near Elliot's Beach in Adyar (buses #5, #5C or #23C from George Town/Anna Salai).

The society's buildings still stand today, sheltering several shrines and an excellent **library** (Mon–Sat 8.30–10am & 2–4pm) of books on religion and philosophy. The collection, begun by Olcott in 1886, comprises 165,000 volumes and nearly 200,000 palm-leaf manuscripts, from all over the world. A selection is housed in an exhibition room on the ground floor. This includes 800-year-old scroll pictures of the Buddha; rare Tibetan xylographs; exquisitely illuminated Korans; a giant copy of Martin Luther's *Biblia* printed in Nuremberg three hundred years ago; and a thumbnail-sized Bible in seven languages. Anybody is welcome to look around, but to gain full use of the library you have to register as a member (Rs30 per year plus Rs200 deposit).

The 270 acres of woodland and gardens surrounding the society's headquarters make a serene place to sit and restore the spirits away from the noise and heat of the city streets. In the middle of the grounds, a vast 400-year-old **banyan tree**, said to be the second-largest in the world, can provide shade for up to three thousand people at a time.

The Enfield factory

India's most stylish home-made motorcycle, the **Enfield Bullet**, is manufactured at a plant on the outskirts of Chennai, 18km north of Anna Salai (bus #1 from LIC Building or Parry's Corner). With its elegant tear-drop tank and thumping 350cc single-cylinder engine, the Bullet has become a contemporary classic – in spite of its propensity to leak oil and break down. Bike enthusiasts should definitely brave the long haul across town to see the **factory**, which is as much a period piece as the machines it turns out. Guided tours, which last around ninety minutes (Mon–Fri 9.30am–5.30pm; Rs500; ℡044/4204 3300, Ⓦwww.royalenfield.com), have to be arranged in advance by phone.

Eating

Chennai runs on inexpensive indigenous fast-food **restaurants** and "meals" (**thali**) joints, in particular the legendary *Saravana Bhavan* chain, which serves superb south Indian food for a fraction of the cost of a coffee at one of the five-stars. Mid-range options also abound.

Unless otherwise stated, the restaurants listed below are marked on the Egmore, Anna Salai and Triplicane **map** on p.1102.

Amaravati Corner of Cathedral and TTK roads (see Chennai map, p.1096). One of four dependable options in this complex of regional speciality restaurants, south of the downtown area. This one does excellent Andhran food, including particularly tasty biriyanis, for Rs100–150.

Annalakshmi 804 Anna Salai. A charitable venture whose profits go to the community, run voluntarily by Sivananda devotees, where you can enjoy a leisurely and expensive (around Rs300 per person) meal in beautiful surroundings. You choose one of several set menus, each with different Ayurvedic properties.

Dakshin/Khyber/Residency *ITC Park Sheraton & Towers*, 132 TTK Rd (see Chennai map, p.1096). ℡044/2499 4101. Three excellent upmarket options in the one hotel: the *Residency* serves Indian, Western and Chinese, and the *Khyber* offers a meaty poolside barbecue, but best of all is the *Dakshin*, one of the country's top south Indian restaurants. It serves up a wide choice of unusual dishes, including seafood in marinated spices, Karnataka mutton biriyani and *appam* made on the spot. Live Carnatic music in the evenings. Book in advance and expect to pay around Rs600 for a meal with starter and drink.

Don Pepé 1st floor, above *Hot Breads*, Cathedral Rd (see Chennai map, p.1096). Swish a/c Tex-Mex joint, serving a predictable menu of fajitas, enchiladas, tortillas and burritos, plus so-so pasta dishes (dubbed "Euro-Mex"). Main courses about Rs120. Hot Breads itself is a great bakery and coffee shop.

Kalyana Bhavan Biriyani 424 Pantheon Rd, Egmore. As the name suggests, this is a biriyani specialist, serving tasty plain, chicken and mutton versions (Rs35–70) on banana leaves, accompanied by aubergine sauce and a semolina sweet.

Mirch Masala Triplicane High Rd, near *Broadlands*. Spotless but plain canteen that dishes up filling veg meals, mutton biriyani and various chicken dishes for Rs50–100. Probably the best option in Triplicane.

Saravana Bhavan Thanigai Murugan Rathinavel Hall, 77 Usman Rd, T Nagar (see both Chennai and Egmore, Anna Salai & Triplicane maps, p.1096 & p.1102). This famous south Indian fast-food chain is an institution among the Chennai middle class, with other branches opposite the bus stand in George Town, in Egmore and in the forecourt of the Shanti cinema (at the top of Anna Salai). Try their delicious *rawa iddlis*, or range of thalis rounded off with some freshly made *ladoo* or *barfi* from the sweets counter outside. Mains Rs30–80.

Vasanta Bhavan 20 Gandhi Irwin Rd. Easily the best "meals" joint among many around Egmore Station, with ranks of attentive waiters and delicious pure-veg food – just Rs30 for an unlimited thali. It's busy, spotlessly clean, and their coffee and sweets are delicious.

Veranda *Taj Connemara*, Binny Rd ℡044/5500 0000. The ideal venue for a posh Sun morning breakfast buffet, with crisp newspapers and fresh coffee served in silver pots. The blow-out lunchtime buffets (around Rs400) are also recommended, and à la carte Italian food is on offer in the evening. Reserve in advance.

Listings

Airlines, domestic Air Deccan, Deshabandu Plaza, 47 Whites Rd ℡044/3297 8596; Go Air ℡1800/222 111; Indian Airlines, 19 Rukhmani Lakshmipathy Rd ℡044/2855 5201 or 1800/180 1407; IndiGo

Airlines, Malavika Centre, 144–145 KH Rd ℡044/6527 2272; Jet Airways, Thaper House, 43–44 Montieth Rd ℡044/3987 2222; Kingfisher Airlines, Spencer Travel Services Ltd,

124 Marshalls Rd ☎044/2858 4366; Paramount Airways, 2nd Floor, Alexander Square, Guindy ☎044/4390 9050; SpiceJet ☎1600180 3333.

Airlines, international Air Canada, Travel Pack, 101 Eldams Rd, Teynampet ☎044/6571 3413; Air France, Thaper House, 40–44 Montieth Rd ☎044/2855 4916; Air India, 19 Rukmani Lakshmipathy Rd ☎044/2855 4477, airport ☎044/2256 0747; Alitalia, Ajantha Travels, 634 Anna Salai ☎044/2434 9822; American Airlines, G-1 Prince Centre, 248 Pathari Rd ☎044/3988 7300; British Airways, 10–11 Dr Radhakrishnan Salai ☎9840 377470; Gulf Air, Thappar House, 43–44 Montieth Rd ☎044/2855 4417; KLM/Northwest, Spencer Travel Services Ltd, 124 Marshalls Rd ☎044/2852 4427; Lufthansa, 167 Anna Salai ☎044/2854 3500; Malaysian Airlines, Arihant Nico Park, 90 Dr R.K. Salai ☎044/4219 9999; Qantas, Eldorado Building, 112 Nungambakkam High Rd ☎044/2827 8680; Singapore Airlines, 108 Dr Radhakrishnan Salai ☎044/2847 3995; Sri Lankan Airlines, Vijaya Towers, Kodambakkam High Rd ☎044/4392 1100; Swissair, Hamid Building, 191 Anna Salai ☎044/2852 4783; Thai Airways, 31 Haddows Rd, Nungambakkam ☎044/4217 3311. Most offices are open Mon–Fri 10am–5pm, Sat 10am–1pm.

Banks and currency exchange Chennai has plenty of banks, though the major hotels offer exchange facilities to residents only. A conveniently central option is American Express, G-17, Spencer Plaza, 769 Anna Salai (Mon–Fri 9.30am–5.30pm, Sat 9.30am–2.30pm). Thomas Cook (Mon–Sat 9am–6pm) has offices at the Ceebros Centre, 45 Montieth Rd, Egmore, at the G-4 Eldorado Building, 112 Uttar Gandhi Salai, and also at the airport (open to meet flights). For encashments on Visa cards, go to Bobcards, next door to the Bank of Baroda on Montieth Rd, near the *Ambassador Pallava Hotel*. There is also an increasing number of 24hr ATMs popping up around town, such as at Citibank, 766 Anna Salai, as well as machines at the airport and both major stations.

Consulates *Australia*, Raheja Towers, 177 Anna Salai ☎044/2860 1160; Canada, Khader Kawaz Khan Rd, Nungambakkam ☎044/2833 0888; New Zealand, 132 Cathedral Rd ☎044/2811 2472 ext 21; Sri Lanka, 196 TTK Rd, Alwarpet ☎044/2498 7897; Thailand, VFS India Ltd, 560–562 Anna Salai ☎044/3298 8660; UK, 20 Anderson Rd, Nungambakkam ☎044/5219 2322; USA, 220 Anna Salai ☎044/2811 2000.

Hospitals Chennai's best-equipped private hospital is the Apollo, 21/22 Greams Rd ☎044/2829 3333. For an ambulance, try ☎044/102, but it's usually quicker to jump in a taxi.

Internet Access is widely available in cybercafés for around Rs20 per hour, or for a bit more in hotel business centres. The snazziest option is the pricier-than-average Net Café at 101/1 Kanakasri Nagar, down an alleyway off Cathedral Rd – look for the neon @ sign. SRIS Netsurfing Café on the first floor of Spencer Plaza is a cheaper, though smaller, alternative. Gee Gee Net in Triplicane, next door to the *Hotel Comfort*, is open 24hr. Egmore options include the 24hr service at the *Pandian* hotel.

Postal services Chennai's main post office is opposite Shanti theatre on Anna Salai (Mon–Sat 8am–8pm, Sun 10am–5pm). If you're using it for poste restante, make sure your correspondents mark the envelope "Head Post Office, Anna Salai". There are smaller branches in both Egmore and Triplicane.

Souvenirs Spencer Plaza on Anna Salai has an excellent selection of boutiques, clothes shops and small souvenir stalls. Across the road at 152 Anna Salai, the Indian Arts Emporium has a good selection of handicrafts, furniture and metalwork.

Travel agents Reliable agents include American Express Travels, 5th Floor, Phase 2, Spencer Plaza, 768–769 Anna Salai ☎044/2852 3592; Surya Travels, F-14 1st Floor, Spencer Plaza ☎044/2852 3937; Thomas Cook, Eldorado Building, 112 Nungambakkam High Rd ☎044/2827 5052; Welcome Tours and Travels, 150 Anna Salai ☎044/2846 0908.

Moving on from Chennai

Chennai's domestic airport stands adjacent to the international terminal, 16km southwest of the centre at **Meenambakkam**; for more on transport to and from it, see p.1098. All the major airlines, such as Jet Airways, Indian Airlines and Kingfisher and a number of the smaller operators, cover multiple routes throughout India. For details on which airlines run to which destinations, along with the frequency and duration of journeys by air and other modes of public transport from Chennai, see "Travel details", p.1177.

All long-distance **buses** leave from the **Moffussil Bus Stand**, over 10km from the centre (see "Arrival", p.1099, for local bus connections). The six platforms are each divided into thirty-odd bays, with frequent services to destinations throughout Tamil Nadu and the neighbouring states. The first stop beyond

Chennai for many people is **Mamallapuram**, for which the fastest services are those marked "ECR" (East Coast Road; every 15–30min; less than 2hr). A myriad other state-run and private services run to all parts of Tamil Nadu and beyond.

Boats leave Chennai every week to ten days for **Port Blair**, capital of the **Andaman Islands**. However, getting a ticket can be a rigmarole, even though the schedule is now more regular. The first thing you'll need to do is contact the Directorate of Shipping on Rajaji Salai, George Town (℡044/2522 6873) to find out when the next sailing is and when tickets go on sale, usually during the week prior to departure. There are no ticket sales on the day of sailing. For more details, see the Andaman Islands chapter.

Trains to Tiruchirapalli (Trichy), Thanjavur, Kodaikanal Road, Madurai and most other destinations in south Tamil Nadu leave from **Egmore Station**, with the occasional service leaving from the suburban **Tambaram** Station. All other trains leave from **Chennai Central** where, left of the main building on the first floor of the Moore Market Complex, the efficient **tourist reservation counter** (Mon–Sat 8am–8pm, Sun 8am–2pm) sells tickets for trains from either station. The booking office at Egmore, up the stairs left of the main entrance (same hours), also handles bookings for both stations, but has no tourist counter.

The northeast

Fazed by the fierce heat and air pollution of Chennai, most visitors escape as fast as they can, heading down the Coromandel coast to India's stone-carving

Recommended trains from Chennai

Destination	Name	No.	From	Departs	Total time
Bengaluru	Shatabdi Express*	#2007	Central	6am**	4hr 50min
(Bangalore)	Bangalore Express	#6523	Central	11.30pm	6hr 25min
Coimbatore	Kovai Express	#2675	Central	6.15am	7hr 40min
	Cheran Express	#2673	Central	10.10pm	8hr
Hyderabad	Charminar Express	#2759	Central	6.10pm	13hr 50min
Kanyakumari	Kanyakumari Express	#2633	Egmore	5.25pm	13hr 5min
Kochi/ Ernakulam	Alleppey Express	#6041	Central	8.15pm	11hr 45min
	Trivandrum Mail	#2623	Central	8pm	10hr 55min
Kodaikanal Road	Pandyan Express	#2637	Egmore	9.30pm	7hr 36min
Madurai	Vaigai Express	#2635	Egmore	12.25pm	7hr 45min
Mettupalayam (for Ooty)	Nilgiri Express	#2671	Central	9pm	9hr 15min
Mumbai	Mumbai Express	#6012	Central	11.45am	26hr
	Dadar Express	#2164	Central	7am	23hr
Mysore	Shatabdi Express*	#2007	Central	6am**	7hr
	Mysore Express	#6222	Central	9.30pm	10hr 35min
Thanjavur	Rock Fort Express	#6177	Egmore	10.30pm	7hr 45min
Thiruvananthapuram	Trivandrum Mail	#2623	Central	8pm	15hr 40min
Tirupati	Sapthagiri Express	#6057	Central	6.25am	3hr 5min

*A/c only
**Except Tues

capital, **Mamallapuram**, whose ancient monuments include the famous Shore Temple and a batch of extraordinary rock sculptures. En route, it's well worth jumping off the bus at **Dakshina Chitra**, a folk museum 30km south of Chennai, where traditional buildings from across south India have been beautifully reconstructed. Further inland, **Kanchipuram** is an important pilgrimage and silk-sari-weaving town from where you can loop southwest to **Tiruvannamalai**, a wonderfully atmospheric temple town clustered at the base of the sacred mountain, Arunachala. On the coast, you can breakfast on croissants and espresso coffee in the former French colony of **Puducherry (Pondicherry)**. A short way north, **Auroville**, the Utopian settlement founded by followers of the Sri Aurobindo Ghose's spiritual successor, The Mother, provides a New Age haven for soul-searching Westerners and an economy for the local population.

Both Mamallapuram and Puducherry are well connected to Chennai by nail-bitingly fast bus services, running along the smooth East Coast Road. You can also get to Puducherry by train, but this usually involves a change at the junction town of **Villupuram**, from where services are slow and relatively infrequent.

Mamallapuram (Mahabalipuram)

Scattered around the base of a colossal mound of boulders, is the small seaside town of **MAMALLAPURAM** (aka Mahabalipuram), 58km south of Chennai. From dawn till dusk, the rhythms of chisels chipping granite resound down its sandy lanes – evidence of a stone-carving tradition that has endured since this was a major port of the Pallava dynasty, between the fifth and ninth centuries. Little is known about life in the ancient city, and it is only possible to speculate about the purpose of much of the boulder sculpture, which includes one of India's most photographed monuments, the **Shore Temple**. It does appear, however, that the friezes and shrines were not made for worship at all, but rather as a showcase for the talents of local artists. Due in no small part to the maritime activities of the Pallavas, their style of art and architecture had wide-ranging influence, spreading from south India as far north as Ellora, as well as to Southeast Asia. This international cultural importance was recognized in 1995 when Mamallapuram was granted World Heritage Site status by UNESCO.

Mamallapuram's monuments divide into four categories: open-air **bas-reliefs**, structured **temples**, man-made **caves** and **rathas** ("chariots" carved *in situ* from single boulders to resemble temples or the chariots used in temple processions). The famous bas-reliefs, **Arjuna's Penance** and the **Krishna Mandapa**, adorn massive rocks near the centre of the village, while the beautiful **Shore Temple** presides over the beach. Sixteen man-made caves and monolithic structures, in different stages of completion, are scattered through the area, but the most complete of the nine *rathas* are in a group, named after the five Pandava brothers of the Mahabharata.

Given the coexistence of so many stunning archeological remains with a long white-sand **beach**, it was inevitable this would become a major destination for Western travellers. Since the 1980s, Mamallapuram has certainly oriented its economy to the needs of tourists, with the inevitable presence of Kashmiri emporia, bus-loads of city dwellers at the weekends, massage-wallahs and hawkers on the beach, burgeoning budget hotels and little fish restaurants. The Shore Temple is now sadly a shadow of the exotic spectacle it used to be when the waves lapped its base, though the atmosphere generated by the stone-carvers' workshops and ancient rock-art backdrop is unique in India. The town recovered quickly after being hit hard by the 2004 tsunami, and is now as busy as ever.

Arrival, information and getting around

Numerous daily **buses** ply to and from Chennai, Tiruvannamalai, Kanchipuram and Puducherry. The bus stand is in the centre of the village.

The nearest **railway station**, at Chengalpattu (Chingleput), 29km northeast on the bus route to Kanchipuram, is on the main north–south line, but not really a convenient access point. **Taxis** to and from Chennai cost Rs1000–1200 or Rs750–800 to and from the airport; book through the tourist office here or in Chennai, or the pre-paid taxi booth at Chennai airport. Mamallapuram suffers badly from aggressive touting by a small number of hotels; ignore the touts and walk briskly to your chosen destination.

The **Government of Tamil Nadu Tourist Office** (Mon–Fri 10am– 5.45pm; ☎044/2744 2232) is one of the first buildings you see in the village, on your left as you arrive from Chennai. It's a good place to find out about local festivals, bus times and pukka hotels. Unless you're staying at one of the upscale hotels, there are only two official places to **change money** in the village: the Indian Overseas Bank, on TK Kunda Road, or the more efficient LKP Forex (Mon–Sat 9.30am–7pm) on East Raja Street.

Mamallapuram itself comprises little more than a few roads. By far the best way to get to the important sites is by **bicycle**, which you can rent from shops on East Raja Street or through your guesthouse for Rs30–40 per day. **Scooters** and Enfield **motorcycles** are also available for Rs200–300 a day, from Poornima Travels, next to *Moonraker's* restaurant, or through guesthouses. Welcome Tours and Travels (☎044/2846 0908) on Othavadai Street can arrange car hire. The going rate for the increasing number of **Net facilities** is Rs40 per hour, though connection speed and reliability can vary; most of them are bunched together along Othavadai and Othavadai Cross streets. If you need **medical treatment**, the Suradeep Hospital on Thirukula Street (☎044/2744 2390) is highly recommended.

Accommodation

Mamallapuram is not short of **accommodation** and, except at the peak Christmas/New Year period, bargaining is the order of the day. All the cheap and mid-range lodges (plus one upper mid-range hotel) are within the village, and there are now two upmarket resorts on the outskirts. All the places listed here are either on the beach or a short stroll from it; there's not much virtue in staying at any of the older resorts up the coast.

Baywatch Fishermens Colony ☎09840 297152, @hotelbaywatch@yahoo.co.in. New place with smartly furnished rooms, the upstairs ones being more expensive. Just one building back from the beach and some sea views. ❸–❹

Chariot Beach Resort 69 Five Rathas Rd ☎044/2498 6364, @www.chariotbeachresorts .com. Brand-new resort with unobstructed sea views, arranged round a 57-metre swimming pool and only 5min walk from Five Rathas. Beautifully furnished, spacious rooms ($175), more luxurious cottages ($225) and sea-facing suites ($400). ❾

Greenwoods Resort Othavadai Cross St ☎044/2744 3318, @greenwoods_resort @yahoo.com. A very friendly family-run place, set in a lush garden that's lovingly tended by the numerous ladies of the house. There's a choice of

a/c or non-a/c rooms with bath, some with a private balcony. Extremely good value. ❷–❺

GRT Temple Bay Beach Resort 1km north of town, off Kovalam Rd ☎044/2744 2251, @www .grttemplebay.com. Great location on the beach, with views of the Shore Temple. Thatched beachside cottages have sea-facing balconies, and there are huge rooms in the main building. There's a swimming pool and restaurant on site. Rates start at $160. ❾

Mamalla Heritage 104 East Raja St ☎044/2744 2060, @2744 2160. Efficient and modern hotel on the main drag through the village. Overlooking a courtyard, the comfortable and spotless a/c rooms have fridge and TV, and there's a very good restaurant on site (see p.1119). ❺

Ramakrishna Lodge 8 Othavadai St ☎044/2744 2331. Clean, well-maintained rooms in the heart of

the tourist enclave, all with bathrooms but no a/c, set round a courtyard filled with pot plants; the newest rooms are on the top storey, and have sea views. There's a back-up generator, and they often have vacancies when everywhere else is full. ❶
Santana Othavadai St ☎09444 290832. Six sizeable and spotless first-floor rooms, of which the seafront one is a gem, sandwiched in between their popular ground-floor beachside restaurant and roof terrace. ❸–❹

🏃 **Sea Breeze** Othavadai Cross St ☎044/2744 3035, ⓔseabreezehotel@hotmail.com. The only bona fide beach resort in the village, featuring comfy and spacious a/c rooms (singles are particularly good value), a smart pool (open to non-residents for Rs200) and an Ayurveda centre. ❻–❽

Siva Guest House 2 Othavadai Cross St ☎044/2744 3234, ⓔsivaguesthouse@hotmail .com. Clean, tidy lodge with choice of a/c and non-a/c rooms. Good value. ❷–❹
Sri Murugan Guest House 42 Othavadai St ☎044/2744 2552. Small and peaceful, with courteous service, clean non-a/c rooms and a rooftop restaurant. One of the nicest options in the area. ❸–❹
Tina Blue View Othavadai St ☎044/2744 2319, ⓦwww.tinablueview.com. Established family guesthouse with simple turquoise and white-washed rooms, all with attached bath and mosquito nets, and a reasonable rooftop restaurant. ❷–❹

The Krishna Mandapa and Arjuna's Penance

A little to the west of the village centre, off Shore Temple Road, the enormous bas-relief known as the **Krishna Mandapa** shows Krishna raising Mount Govardhana aloft in one hand. The sculptor's original intention must have been for the rock above Krishna to represent the mountain, but the seventeenth-century Vijayanagar addition of a columned *mandapa*, or entrance hall, prevents a clear view of the carving. Krishna is also depicted seated milking a cow, and standing playing the flute. Other figures are *gopas* and *gopis*, the cowboys and girls of his pastoral youth. Lions (one with a human face) sit to the left, while above them is a bull.

Another bas-relief, **Arjuna's Penance** (also referred to as the "Descent of the Ganges") is a few metres north, opposite the modern Talasayana Perumal Temple. The surface of this rock erupts with detailed carving, most notably endearing and naturalistic renditions of animals. A family of elephants dominates the right side, with tiny offspring asleep beneath a great tusker. Further still to the right, separate from the great rock, is a freestanding sculpture of an adult monkey grooming its young. On the left-hand side, Arjuna, one of the Pandava brothers and a consummate archer, is shown standing on one leg. He is looking at the midday sun through a prism formed by his hands, meditating on Shiva, who is represented by a nearby statue fashioned by Arjuna himself. The *Shiva Purana* tells that Arjuna made the journey to a forest on the banks of the Ganges to do penance, in the hope that Shiva would part with his favourite weapon, the *pashupatashastra*, a magic staff or arrow. Shiva eventually materialized in the guise of Kirata, a wild forest-dweller, and picked a fight with Arjuna over a boar they both claimed to have shot. Arjuna only realized he was dealing with the deity after his attempts to drub the wild man proved futile; narrowly escaping death at the playful hand of Shiva, he was finally rewarded with the weapon. Not far away, mimicking Arjuna's devout pose, an emaciated (presumably ascetic) cat stands on hind legs, surrounded by mice.

To the right of Arjuna, a natural cleft represents the **Ganges**, complete with *nagas* – water spirits in the form of cobras. Near the bottom, a fault in the rock that broke a *naga* received a quick fix of cement in the 1920s. Evidence of a cistern and channels remain at the top, which at one time must have carried water to flow down the cleft, simulating the great river. It's not known if there was some ritual purpose to all this, or whether it was simply an elaborate spectacle to impress visitors. You may see sudden movements among the carved animals: lazing goats often join the permanent features.

The temples of Tamil Nadu

No Indian state is more dominated by its **temples** than Tamil Nadu, where temple architecture catalogues the tastes of successive dynasties and testifies to the centrality of religion in everyday life. Most temples are built in honour of Shiva, Vishnu and their consorts; all are characterized not only by their design and sculptures, but by constant activity: devotion, dancing, singing, pujas, festivals and feasts. Each is tended by brahmin priests, recognizable by their *dhotis* (loincloths), a sacred thread draped over the right shoulder, and marks on the forehead. One to three horizontal (usually white) lines distinguish Shaivites; vertical lines (yellow or red), often converging into a near-V shape, are common among Vaishnavites.

Dravida, the temple architecture of Tamil Nadu, first took form in the Pallava port of **Mamallapuram**. A step-up from the cave retreats of Hindu and Jain ascetics, the earliest Pallava monuments were **mandapas**, shrines cut into rock faces and fronted by columns. The magnificent Arjuna's Penance **bas-relief** shows the fluid carving of the Pallavas at its most exquisite. This sculptural skill was transferred to freestanding temples, **rathas**, carved out of single rocks and incorporating the essential elements of Hindu temples: the dim inner sanctuary, the *garbhagriha*, capped with a modest tapering spire featuring repetitive architectural motifs. In turn, the Shore Temple was built with three shrines, topped by a **vimana** similar to the towering roofs of the *rathas*; statues of Nandi, Shiva's bull, later to receive pride of place, surmount its low walls. In the finest structural Pallava temple, the Kailasanatha Temple at **Kanchipuram**, the sanctuary stands within a courtyard enclosed by high walls carved with images of Shiva, his consort and ghoulish mythical lions, *yalis*, the prototype for later styles.

Pallava themes were developed in Karnataka by the Chalukyas and Rashtrakutas, but it was the Shaivite **Cholas** who spearheaded Tamil Nadu's next architectural phase, in the tenth century. In **Thanjavur**, Rajaraja I created the Brihadeshvara Temple principally as a status symbol; its proportions far exceed any attempted by the Pallavas. Set within a vast walled courtyard, the sanctuary, fronted by a small *mandapa*, stands beneath a sculpted *vimana* that soars over 60m high. Most sculptures once again feature Shiva, but the *gopuras* each side of the eastern gateway to the courtyard, were an innovation, as were the lions carved into the base of the sanctuary walls, and the pavilion erected over Nandi in front of the sanctuary. The second great Chola temple was built in **Gangaikondacholapuram** by Rajendra I. Instead of a mighty *vimana*, he brought new elements, adding subsidiary shrines and placing an extended *mandapa* in front of the central sanctuary, its pillars writhing with dancers and deities.

By the time of the thirteenth-century **Vijayanagar** kings, the temple was central to city life, the focus for civic meetings, education, dance and theatre. The Vijayanagars extended earlier structures, adding enclosing walls around a series of **prakaras**, or courtyards, and erecting freestanding *mandapas* for use as meeting halls, elephant stables, stages for music and dance, and ceremonial marriage halls (*kalyan mandapas*). Raised on superbly decorated columns, these *mandapas* became known as **thousand-pillared halls**. **Tanks** were added, doubling as water stores and washing areas, and used for festivals when deities were set afloat in boats.

Under the Vijayanagars, the *gopuras* were enlarged and set at the cardinal points over the high gateways to each *prakara*, to become the dominant feature. Rectangular in plan, and embellished with images of animals and local saints or rulers as well as deities, *gopuras* are periodically repainted in pinks, blues, whites and yellows, a sharp and joyous contrast with the earthy browns and greys of halls and sanctuaries beyond. **Madurai** is the place to check out Vijayanagar architecture. Its temples regularly come alive for festivals, in which Shiva and his "fish-eyed" consort are hauled through town on mighty wooden chariots. Outside Tiruchirapalli, the temple at **Srirangam** was extended by the Vijayanagar Nayaks to become south India's largest. Unlike that in Madurai, it incorporates earlier Chola foundations, but the ornamentation, with pillars formed into rearing horses, is superb.

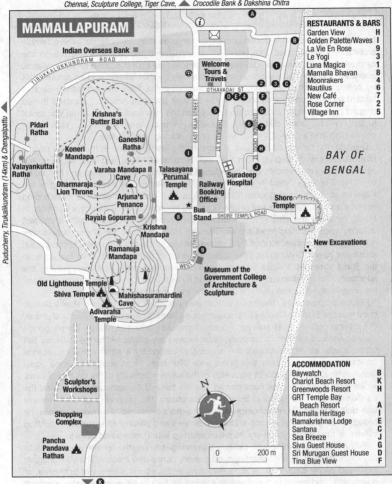

MAMALLAPURAM

Indian Overseas Bank ■

TIRUKKALUKKUNDRAM ROAD

Welcome
Tours &
Travels

OTHAVADAI ST

Krishna's
Butter Ball

Pidari
Ratha

Ganesha
Ratha

Koneri
Mandapa

Varaha Mandapa II
Cave

Talasayana
Perumal
Temple

Dharmaraja
Lion Throne

Railway
Booking
Office

Suradeep
Hospital

Shore
Temple

BAY OF
BENGAL

Arjuna's
Penance

Rayala Gopuram

Krishna
Mandapa

Bus
Stand   SHORE TEMPLE ROAD

Ramanuja
Mandapa

New Excavations

Old Lighthouse Temple

Shiva Temple

Mahishasuramardini
Cave

Adivaraha
Temple

Museum of the
Government College
of Architecture &
Sculpture

Valayankuttai
Ratha

Dharmaraja
Lion Throne

Sculptor's
Workshops

Shopping
Complex

Pancha
Pandava
Rathas

N

0   200 m

Puducherry, Tirukalikundram (14km) & Chengalpattu ◄

RESTAURANTS & BARS

Garden View	H
Golden Palette/Waves	I
La Vie En Rose	9
Le Yogi	3
Luna Magica	1
Mamalla Bhavan	8
Moonrakers	4
Nautilus	6
New Café	7
Rose Corner	2
Village Inn	5

ACCOMMODATION

Baywatch	B
Chariot Beach Resort	K
Greenwoods Resort	H
GRT Temple Bay Beach Resort	A
Mamalla Heritage	I
Ramakrishna Lodge	E
Santana	C
Sea Breeze	J
Siva Guest House	G
Sri Murugan Guest House	D
Tina Blue View	F

Ganesha Ratha and Varaha cave

Just north of Arjuna's Penance a path leads west to a single monolith, the **Ganesha Ratha**. Its image of Ganesh dates from this century; some say it was installed at the instigation of England's King George V. The sculpture at one end, of a protecting demon with a tricorn headdress, is reminiscent of the Indus Valley civilization's 4000-year-old horned figure known as the "proto-Shiva".

Behind Arjuna's Penance, southwest of the Ganesha *ratha*, is the **Varaha Mandapa II Cave**, whose entrance hall has two pillars with horned lion-bases and a cell flanked by two *dvarpalas*, or guardians. One of four **panels** shows the boar-incarnation of Vishnu, who stands with one foot resting on the *naga* snake-king as he lifts a diminutive Prithvi – the earth – from the primordial ocean. Another is of Gajalakshmi, the goddess Lakshmi seated on a lotus being bathed by a pair of elephants. Trivikrama, the dwarf brahmin who becomes huge and bestrides the world in three steps to defeat the demon king Bali, is shown in another panel, and finally a four-armed Durga is depicted in another.

A little way north of Arjuna's Penance, precipitously balanced on the top of a ridge, is a massive, natural, almost spherical boulder called **Krishna's Butter Ball**. Picnickers and goats often rest in its perilous-looking shade.

The Shore Temple

East of the village, the distinctive, soaring silhouette of Mamallapuram's **Shore Temple** (daily sunrise to sunset; Rs250 [Rs10], includes Pancha Pandava *rathas* if visited on the same day) dates from the early eighth century and is considered to be the earliest stone-built temple in south India. The design of its two finely carved towers was profoundly influential: it was exported across south India and eventually abroad to Southeast Asia. Today, due to the combined forces of wind, salt and sand, much of the detailed carving has eroded, giving the whole temple a soft, rounded appearance.

The taller of the towers is raised above a cell that faces out to sea – don't be surprised to see mischievous monkeys crouching inside. Approached from the west through two low-walled enclosures lined with small Nandi (bull) figures, the temple comprises two lingam shrines (one facing east, the other west), and a third shrine between them housing an image of the reclining Vishnu. Recent excavations, revealing a tank containing a structured stone column thought to have been a lantern, and a large Varaha (boar incarnation of Vishnu) aligned with the Vishnu shrine, suggest that the area was sacred long before the Pallavas chose it as a temple site.

The lighthouses and the Mahishasuramardini Cave

South of Arjuna's Penance at the highest point in an area of steep paths, unfinished temples, ruins, scampering monkeys and massive rocks, the **New Lighthouse** affords fine views east to the Shore Temple, and west across paddy fields and flat lands littered with rocks. Next to it, the **Olakanesvara** ("flame-eyed" Shiva), or **Old Lighthouse Temple**, used as a lighthouse until the beginning of the twentieth century, dates from the Rajasimha period (674–800 AD) and contains no image.

Nestling between the two lighthouses is the **Mahishasuramardini Cave**, whose central image portrays Shiva and Parvati with the child Murugan seated on Parvati's lap. Shiva's right foot rests on the back of the bull Nandi, and Parvati sits casually, leaning on her left hand. On the left wall, beyond an empty cell, a panel depicts Vishnu reclining on the serpent, his attitude of repose contrasted with the weapon-brandishing demons, Madhu and Kaithaba. Other figures seek Vishnu's permission to chase them. Opposite, an intricately carved panel shows the eight-armed goddess Durga as Mahishasuramardini, the "crusher" of the buffalo demon Mahishasura. The panel shows Durga riding a lion, in the midst of the struggle. Accompanied by dwarf *ganas*, she wields a bow and other weapons; Mahishasura, equipped with a club, can be seen to the right, in flight with fellow demons.

The tiny **Government College of Architecture and Sculpture Museum** (Mon–Sat 10am–5pm; Rs2, camera Rs10), on West Raja Street near the light-house, has a rather motley collection of unlabelled Pallava sculpture found in and around Mamallapuram.

Pancha Pandava Rathas (Five Rathas)

In a sandy compound 1.5km south of the village centre stands the stunning group of monoliths known for no historical reason as the **Pancha Pandava Rathas** (daily sunrise to sunset; Rs250 [Rs10] which includes the Shore Temple if visited on the same day) the five chariots of the Pandavas. Dating from the period of Narasimhavarman I (c.630–670 AD), and consisting of five separate freestanding sculptures that imitate structured temples plus some beautifully carved life-sized animals, they were either carved from a single gigantic sloping boulder, or from as many as three distinct rocks.

The "architecture" of the *rathas* reflects the variety of styles employed in temple building of the time, and stands almost as a model for much subsequent development in the **Dravida**, or southern, style. Carving was always executed from top to bottom, enabling the artists to work on the upper parts with no fear of damaging anything below. Any unfinished elements are always in the lower areas. Intriguingly, it's thought that the *rathas* were never used for worship. A Hindu temple is only complete when the essential pot-shaped finial, the *kalasha*, is put in place – which would have presented a physical impossibility for the artisans, as the *kalasha* would have had to have been sculpted first. *Kalashas* can be seen next to two of the *rathas* (Dharmaraja and Arjuna), but as part of the base, as if they were perhaps to be put in place at a later date.

The southernmost and tallest of the *rathas*, named after the eldest of the Pandavas, is the pyramidal **Dharmaraja**. Set on a square base, the upper part comprises a series of diminishing storeys, each with a row of pavilions. Four corner blocks, each with two panels and standing figures, are broken up by two pillars and pilasters supported by squatting lions. Figures on the panels include Ardhanarishvara (Shiva and female consort in one figure), Brahma, the king Narasimhavarman I, and Harihara (Shiva and Vishnu combined). The central tier includes sculptures of Shiva Gangadhara holding a rosary with the adoring river-goddess Ganga by his side, and one of the earliest representations in Tamil Nadu of the dancing Shiva, Nataraja, who became all-important in the region. Alongside, the **Bhima** *ratha*, the largest of the group, is the least complete, with tooling marks all over its surface. Devoid of carved figures, the upper storeys, like in the Dharmaraja, feature false windows and repeated pavilion-shaped ornamentation. Its oblong base is very rare for a shrine.

The Arjuna and Draupadi *rathas* share a base. Behind the **Arjuna**, the most complete of the entire group and very similar to the Dharmaraja, stands a superb unfinished sculpture of Shiva's bull Nandi. **Draupadi** is unique in terms of rock-cut architecture, with a roof that appears to be based on a straw thatched hut (a design later copied at Chidambaram). There's an image of Durga inside, but the figure of her lion vehicle outside is aligned side-on and not facing the image, a convincing reason to suppose this was not a real temple. To the west, close to a life-sized carving of an elephant, the *ratha* named after the twin brothers **Nakula and Sahadeva** is, unusually, apsidal ended. The elephant may be a visual pun on this, as the Sanskrit technical name for a curved ended building is *gajaprstika*, "elephant's backside".

The road out to the *rathas* resounds with incessant chiselling from sculptors' workshops. Much of their work is excellent, and well worth a browse – the sculptors produce statues for temples all over the world and are used to shipping large-scale pieces. Some of the artists are horrifyingly young; children often do the donkey work on large pieces, which are then completed by master craftsmen.

Eating and drinking

Mamallapuram is crammed with small restaurants, most of them specializing in **seafood** – tiger prawns, pomfret, tuna, shark and lobster – usually served marinated and grilled with chips and salad. Always establish in advance exactly how much your fish or lobster is going to cost. As this is a traveller's hangout, there are also numerous places offering the usual array of pasta, pancakes, brown bread and bland Indian dishes. If you want to enjoy real Indian food, such as *dosas* or inexpensive fried fish, head to the stalls by the bus stand and on the south side of the Shore Temple complex.

Beer is widely available, but it's on the pricey side (Rs100 or more); the best place for a late-night drink is the pleasant and friendly *Rose Corner*, above a shop on Othavadai Street.

Garden View *Greenwoods Resort*, Othavadai Cross St. Friendly first-floor terrace restaurant which serves delicious sizzlers, seafood and curries – they'll actually make proper hot ones if you ask. There's a choice of views – the relaxed garden or busier street-life. Mains Rs50–100.

Golden Palette *Mamalla Heritage* hotel, 104 East Raja St. Blissfully cool café with a/c and tinted windows, serving the best veg food in the village – Rs60 meals at lunchtime, North Indian tandoori in the courtyard in the evenings – and wonderful ice-cream sundaes. The new rooftop *Waves* restaurant does fish and seafood in the evening, too.

La Vie En Rose West Raja St. Pleasant garden location offering a Westerner-oriented menu including a few unusual salads, great spaghetti and chicken specialities for Rs80–120.

Le Yogi Othavadai St. Run by a French/Indian couple, this welcoming and relaxed place is a good spot to chill. Tasty pastas, and salads can be washed down with good coffee and lassis. Most dishes Rs100–150.

Luna Magica 100m north of Othavadai St. Slap on the beach with top-notch seafood, particularly tiger prawns and lobster, which are kept alive in a tank. The big specimens cost a hefty Rs600–800, but are as tasty as you'll find anywhere, served in a rich tomato, butter and garlic sauce. They also do passable sangria, made with sweet Chennai red

wine, and cold beer, as well as plenty of less expensive dishes – including a good fish curry and "sizzlers" – for budget travellers.

Mamalla Bhavan Shore Temple Rd, opposite the bus stand. Very popular pure-veg and "meals" joint that's invariably packed. Good for *iddli-wada* breakfasts, and evening *dosas* and other snacks. Unlimited lunchtime meals cost around Rs30.

Moonrakers Othavadai St. Cool jazz and blues sounds, great fresh seafood, chess sets and slick service ensure this place is filled year round with foreign tourists; the owners will try and entice you in every single time you pass by. A decent fish meal costs around Rs250

Nautilus Othavadai Cross St. High-quality but reasonably priced eatery, run by an amicable French chef. The menu features fine soups, meat, seafood and veg dishes, grilled or with an array of sauces, plus travellers' favourites, for Rs70–150.

New Café *Lakshmi Lodge*, Othavadai Cross St. Lively upstairs restaurant serving a standard range of Indian and Chinese food, some fish and Western breakfasts. Sometimes stays open late for those wanting to drink. Entrées mainly Rs100–200.

Village Inn Thirukula St. This diminutive thatched eatery serves up seafood grilled on a charcoal fire, as well as a superb butter-fried chicken in a tomato-garlic sauce. Rs150–200 for meat or fish main courses.

Around Mamallapuram

The sandy hinterland and flat estuarine paddy fields around Mamallapuram harbour a handful of sights well worth making forays from the coast to see. A short way north along the main highway, the **Government College of Sculpture** and elaborately carved **Tiger Cave** can easily be reached by bicycle. To get to the **Crocodile Bank**, where rare reptiles from across south Asia are bred for release into the wild, or **Dakshina Chitra**, a museum devoted to south Indian architecture and crafts, you'll need to jump on and off buses or rent a moped for the day.

Government College of Sculpture and the Tiger Cave

A visit to the **Government College of Sculpture**, 2km north of Mamallapuram on the Kovalam (Covelong) Road (℡044/2744 2261; free), gives a fascinating insight into the processes of sculpture training. You can watch anything from preliminary drawing, with its strict rules regarding proportion and iconography, through to the execution of sculpture, both in wood and stone, in the classical Hindu tradition. Contact the college office to make an appointment.

A further 3km north along Kovalam Road from the college, set amid trees close to the sea, the extraordinary **Tiger Cave** (sunrise to sunset; free) contains a shrine to Durga, approached by a flight of steps that passes two subsidiary cells. Following the line of an irregularly shaped rock, the cave is remarkable for its elaborate exterior, which features multiple lion-heads surrounding the entrance to the main cell. If you sit for long enough, the section on the left with seated figures in niches above two elephants begins to resemble an enormous owl.

Crocodile Bank

The **Crocodile Bank** (Tues–Sun 8am–6pm; Rs20, camera Rs10, video camera Rs75) at Vadanemmeli, 14km north of town on the road to Chennai, was set up in 1976 by the American zoologist Romulus Whittaker, to protect and breed indigenous crocodiles. The bank has been so successful (from fifteen crocs to five thousand in the first fifteen years) that its remit now extends to saving endangered species, such as turtles and lizards, from around the world.

Low-walled enclosures in its garden compound house hundreds of inscrutable crocodiles, soaking in ponds or sunning themselves on the banks. Breeds include the fish-eating, knobbly-nosed gharial, and the world's largest species, the saltwater *crocodylus porosus*, which can grow to 8m in length. You can watch feeding time at about 4.30pm on Monday or Thursday or have your own brief feeding session any time for a fee of Rs20. The temptation to take photos is tempered by the sight of those hungry saurians clambering over each other to snap up the chopped flesh, within inches of the top of the wall.

Another important field of work is conducted with the collaboration of local Irula people, whose traditional expertise is with snakes. Cobras are brought to the bank for **venom collection**, to be used in the treatment of snakebites. Elsewhere, snakes are repeatedly "milked" until they die, but here at the bank only a limited amount is taken from each snake, enabling them to return to the wild. This section costs an extra Rs5.

Coastal route buses #117 and #118 stop at the entrance.

Dakshina Chitra

Occupying a patch of sand dunes midway between Chennai and Mamallapuram, **Dakshina Chitra** (daily except Tues 10am–6pm; Rs175 [Rs50]; Ⓦwww.dakshinachitra.net), literally "Vision of the South", is one of India's best-conceived folk museums, devoted to the rich architectural and artistic heritage of Kerala, Karnataka, Andhra Pradesh and Tamil Nadu. Set up by the Chennai Craft Foundation, the museum exposes visitors to many disappearing traditions of the region which you might otherwise not be aware of, from tribal fertility cults and *Ayyannar* field deities to pottery and leather shadow puppets.

A selection of traditional buildings from across peninsular India has been painstakingly reconstructed using original materials. Exhibitions attached to them convey the environmental and cultural diversity of the south, most graphically expressed in a wonderful textile collection featuring antique silk and cotton saris from various castes and regions. To get there, catch any of the buses heading north to Chennai or rent a moped from Mamallapuram (see p.1113). Snacks are available on site.

Kanchipuram

Ask any Tamil what **KANCHIPURAM** (aka "Kanchi") is famous for, and they'll probably say silk saris, shrines and saints – in that order. A dynastic capital throughout the medieval era, it remains one of the seven holiest cities in the Subcontinent, sacred to both Shaivites and Vaishnavites, and among the few

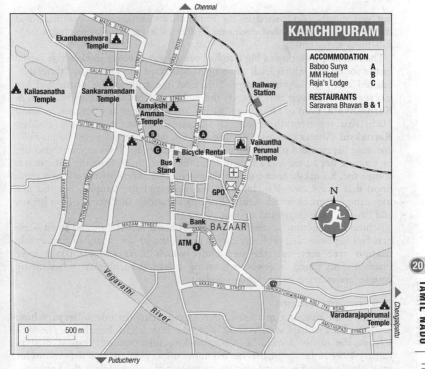

Map labels:
- ▲ Chennai
- KANCHIPURAM
- N MADA STREET
- Ekambareshvara Temple
- CAR STREET
- MOORES ROAD
- SALAI ST
- Kailasanatha Temple
- Sankaramandam Temple
- ODAI STREET
- Kamakshi Amman Temple
- Railway Station
- PUTTERI STREET
- NELLUKKARA ST
- EAST RAJA STREET
- Bicycle Rental
- Vaikuntha Perumal Temple
- Bus Stand
- GPO
- KRISHNARAYAR ST
- PUTHUPALAYAM STREET
- KOSA STREET
- MADAM STREET
- Bank
- BAZAAR
- GANDHI ROAD
- ATM
- Vegavathi River
- VLAKKADI KOIL STREET
- THIRUKATCHININAMBI KOIL (TK) ROAD
- Varadarajaperumal Temple
- AMUTHUPADI STREET
- N
- ▶ Chengalpattu
- ▼ Puducherry
- 0 500 m

ACCOMMODATION
Baboo Surya   A
MM Hotel   B
Raja's Lodge   C

RESTAURANTS
Saravana Bhavan   B & 1

surviving centres of goddess worship in the south. Year round, pilgrims pour through for a quick puja stop on the Tirupati tour circuit and, if they can afford it, a spot of shopping in the sari emporia. For non-Hindu visitors, however, Kanchipuram holds less appeal. Although the temples are undeniably impressive, the town itself is unremittingly hot, with only basic accommodation and amenities. Some people prefer to visit Kanchipuram as a **day-trip** from Chennai or Mamallapuram, both a two-hour bus ride away.

Established by the **Pallava** kings in the fourth century AD, Kanchipuram served as their **capital** for five hundred years, and continued to flourish throughout the Chola, Pandya and Vijayanagar eras. Under the Pallavas, it was an important scholastic forum, and a meeting point for Jain, Buddhist and Hindu cultures. Its **temples** dramatically reflect this enduring political prominence, spanning the years from the peak of Pallava construction to the seventeenth century, when the ornamentation of the *gopuras* and pillared halls was at its most elaborate (for more on Tamil Nadu's temples, see p.1115). All can be easily reached by foot, bike or rickshaw, and shut daily between noon and 4pm. You might need to be a little firm to resist the attentions of pushy puja-wallahs, who try to con foreigners into overpriced ceremonies. If you've come for silk, head for the shops that line Gandhi and Thirukatchininambi roads.

Ekambareshvara Temple
On the north side of town, Kanchipuram's largest temple and most important Shiva shrine, the **Ekambareshvara Temple** (camera Rs10, video Rs20) – also known as Ekambaranatha – is easily identified by its colossal whitewashed *gopuras*, which rise to almost 60m. The main temple contains some Pallava work,

but was mostly constructed in the sixteenth and seventeenth centuries, and stands within a vast walled enclosure beside some smaller shrines and a large fish-filled water tank.

The entrance is through a high-arched passageway beneath an elaborate *gopura* in the south wall which leads to an open courtyard and a majestic "thousand-pillared hall", or *kalyan mandapa*. This faces the tank in the north and the sanctuary in the west that protects the emblem of Shiva (here in his form as **Kameshvara**, Lord of Desire), an "earth" lingam (one of five lingams in Tamil Nadu that represent the elements). Legend connects it with the goddess **Kamakshi** (Shiva's consort, "Wanton-Eyed"), who angered Shiva by playfully covering his eyes and plunging the world into darkness. Shiva reprimanded her by sending her to fashion a lingam from the earth in his honour; once it was completed, Kamakshi found she could not move it. Local myths tell of a great flood that swept over Kanchipuram and destroyed the temples, but did not move the lingam, to which Kamakshi clung so fiercely that marks of her breasts and bangles were imprinted upon it.

Behind the sanctum, accessible from the covered hallway around it, an eerie bare hall lies beneath a profusely carved *gopura*, and in the courtyard a venerable **mango tree** represents the tree under which Shiva and Kamakshi were married. This union is celebrated during a festival each April, when many couples are married in the *kalyan mandapa*.

Sankaramandam

Kanchipuram is the seat of a line of holy men bearing the title **acharya**, whose line dates back perhaps as far as 1300 BC to the saint Adi Sankaracharya. The 68th acharya, the highly revered Sri Chandrasekharendra Sarasvati Swami, died in January 1994 at the age of 101. Buried in the sitting position, as is the custom for great Hindu sages, his mortal remains are enshrined in a *samadhi* at the **Sankaramandam**, a *math* (monastery for Hindu renouncers) down the road from the Ekambareshvara Temple. Lined with old photographs from the life of the former swami, with young brahmin students chanting Sanskrit verses in the background, it's a typically Tamil blend of simple sanctity and garish modern glitz. The *math's* two huge elephants are available to bestow blessings upon visiting pilgrims – just sweeten the mahout's hand with a few rupees. The present incumbent, the 69th acharya, has been embroiled in scandal since November 2004, when he was charged with **murder**; the case is still making its way through the ponderous court system and has seriously tarnished the title's image.

Kailasanatha Temple

The **Kailasanatha Temple**, the oldest structure in Kanchipuram and the finest example of Pallava architecture in south India, is situated among several low-roofed houses just over 1km west of the town centre. Built by the Pallava king Rajasimha early in the eighth century, its intimate size and simple carving distinguish it from the town's later temples. Usually quieter than its neighbours, the shrine becomes the focus of vigorous celebrations during the **Mahashivratri festival** each March. Like its contemporary, the Shore Temple at Mamallapuram, it is built of soft sandstone, but its sheltered position has spared it from wind and sand erosion, and it remains remarkably intact, despite some rather clumsy recent renovation work.

Kamakshi Amman Temple

Built during Pallava supremacy and modified in the fourteenth and seventeenth centuries, the **Kamakshi Amman Temple**, northwest of the bus stand, combines several styles, with an ancient central shrine, gates from the Vijayanagar period, and high, heavily sculpted, creamy *gopuras* set above the gateways.

This is one of India's three holiest shrines to Shakti, Shiva's cosmic energy depicted in female form, usually as his consort. The goddess Kamakshi, a local form of Parvati, shown with a sugar-cane bow and arrows of flowers, is honoured as having lured Shiva to Kanchipuram, where they were married, and thus having forged the connection between the local community and the god. In February or March, deities are wheeled to the temple in huge wooden "cars", decked with robed statues and swaying plantain leaves.

Practicalities

Kanchipuram is situated on the Vegavathi River 70km southwest of Chennai, and slightly less from Mamallapuram on the coast. **Buses** from Chennai, Mamallapuram and Chengalpattu stop at the stand in the town centre just off Kosa Street. The sleepy **railway station** in the northeast sees only four daily passenger services from Chengalpattu (three of them originating in Chennai) and two from Anakkonam.

As most of the main roads are wide and traffic rarely unmanageable, the best way to **get around** Kanchi is by **bicycle** – available for minimal rates (Rs3/hr) at stalls west and northeast of the bus stand. The town's vegetable markets, hotels, restaurants and bazaars are concentrated in the centre of town, near the bus stand.

There is an **ATM** on Gandhi Road, though the nearest official foreign exchange places are in Chennai and Mamallapuram. Fast **Internet** connection is available at Net4U, at the town end of TK Road.

Accommodation and eating

There's no fancy **accommodation** in Kanchipuram, but plenty of good budget and lower mid-range places for a night or two. Best of the bunch is the �‍ *Baboo Surya*, 85 East Raja St (☎044/2722 2556, ⍵www.hotelbaboosoorya .com; ❸–❹), excellent value with immaculate attached rooms (a/c and non-a/c), some with temple views, and its own restaurant. Another good option is *MM*, 65/66 Nellukkara St (☎044/2723 7250, ⍵mmhotels.com; ❸–❹), with clean, good-value rooms. Opposite, at 20-B Nellukkara St, the simple but spotless *Raja's Lodge* (☎044/2722 2603; ❶–❸) is the best real cheapie, with friendly staff and reasonable rooms.

The most highly rated places to **eat** in town are the two branches of *Saravana Bhavan*, an offshoot of the famous Chennai chain of pure-veg restaurants, which offers superb Rs30 "meals" at lunchtime, and a long list of south Indian snacks the rest of the day. One is on Nellukkara Road near *Sri Kusal*, and the other just off Gandhi Road.

Vedanthangal

One of India's most spectacular bird sanctuaries lies roughly 1km east of the village of **VEDANTHANGAL**, a cluster of squat, brown houses set in a patchwork of paddy fields 30km from the east coast and 86km southwest of Chennai. It's a tiny, relaxed place, bisected by one road and with just two chai stalls.

A low-lying area less than half a kilometre square, the **sanctuary** is busiest with birdlife between December and February, when it's totally flooded. The rains of the northeast monsoon, sweeping through in October or November, bring indigenous water birds that nest and settle here until the dry season (usually April), when they leave for wetter areas. Abundant trees on mounds above water level provide perfect nesting spots, alive by January with fledglings. Visitors can watch the avian action from a path at the water's edge, or from a watchtower (fitted out with strong binoculars). Try to come at sunset, when the birds return from feeding. Common Indian **species** to look out for are openbill storks, spoonbills, pelicans, black cormorants, and herons of several types. You may also see ibises, grey pelicans, migrant cuckoos, sandpipers, egrets (which paddle in the rice fields), and tiny darting bee-eaters. Some migrant birds pass through and rest on their way between more permanent sites; swallows, terns and redshanks are common, while peregrine falcons, pigeons and doves are occasionally spotted.

Practicalities

Getting to Vedanthangal can present a few problems. The nearest town is Maduranthakam, 8km east, on NH-45 between Chengalpattu and Tindivanam, from where there are hourly buses to the sanctuary. Alternatively, direct services run every hour or two from Chengalpattu. Taxis make the journey from Maduranthakam for Rs300–350, but cannot be booked from Vedanthangal.

Vedanthangal's only accommodation is the four-room **forest lodge (❸–❹)**, near the bus stand, school and chai stall. The spacious, comfortable rooms (a/c or non-a/c) with attached bath should be booked through the Wildlife Warden in Chennai (☎044/2432 1471 or 09541 520006). It often gets full, especially at weekends, in December and January.

Tiruvannamalai

Synonymous with the fifth Hindu element of fire, **TIRUVANNAMALAI**, 100km south of Kanchipuram, ranks, along with Madurai, Kanchipuram, Chidambaram and Trichy, as one of the five holiest towns in Tamil Nadu. Its name, meaning "Red Mountain", derives from the spectacular extinct volcano, **Arunachala**, which rises behind it, and which glows an unearthly crimson in the dawn light. This awesome natural backdrop, combined with the colossal **Arunachaleshvara Temple** in the centre of town, make Tiruvannamalai one of the region's most memorable destinations. Well off the tourist trail, it's a perfect place to get to grips with life in small-town Tamil Nadu. The countless shrines, sacred tanks, ashrams and paved pilgrim paths scattered around the sacred mountain (not to mention the legions of dreadlocked *babas* who line up for alms outside the main sites) will keep anyone who is interested in Hinduism absorbed for weeks.

Mythology identifies Arunachala as the place where Shiva asserted his power over Brahma and Vishnu by manifesting himself as a lingam of fire, or **agni-lingam**. The two gods had been disputing their respective strengths when Shiva pulled this primordial pyro-stunt, challenging his adversaries to locate the top and bottom of his blazing column. They couldn't (although Vishnu is said to have faked finding the head) and collapsed on their knees in a gesture of supreme submission. The event is commemorated each year at the rising of the full moon in November/December, when a vast vat of ghee and paraffin is lit by priests on the summit of Arunachala. This symbolizes the fulfilment of Shiva's promise to reappear each year to vanquish the forces of darkness and ignorance with firelight.

The sacred Red Mountain is also associated with the famous twentieth-century saint, **Sri Ramana Maharishi**, who chose it as the site for his twenty-three-year meditation retreat. A crop of small ashrams have sprung up on the edge of town below Sri Ramana's Cave, some of them more authentic than others, and the ranks of white-cotton-clad foreigners floating between them have become a defining feature of Tiruvannamalai.

Arunachaleshvara Temple

Known to Hindus as the "Temple of the Eternal Sunrise", the enormous **Arunachaleshvara Temple**, built over a period of almost a thousand years, consists of three concentric courtyards whose gateways are topped by tapering *gopuras*, the largest of which cover the east and north gates. The best spot from which to view the precinct, a breathtaking spectacle against the sprawling plains and lumpy, granite Shevaroy Hills, is the path up to Sri Ramana Maharishi's meditation cave, Virupaksha (see below), on the lower slopes of Arunachala. To enter the temple, however, head for the huge eastern gateway, which leads through the thick outer wall carved with images of deities, local saints and teachers. In the basement of a raised hall to the right before entering the next courtyard is the Parthala lingam, where Sri Ramana Maharishi is said to have sat in a state of Supreme Awareness while ants devoured his flesh.

The caves and Sri Ramanashramam ashram

Opposite the western entrance of the temple complex, a path leads up a holy hill (15min) to the **Virupaksha Cave**, where the Maharishi stayed between 1899 and 1916. He personally built the bench outside and the hill-shaped lingam and platform inside, where all are welcome to meditate in peace. When this cave became too small, constantly crowded with relatives and devotees, Ramana shifted to another, hidden away in a clump of trees a few minutes further up the hill. He named this one, and the small house built onto it, **Skandasraman**, and lived there between 1916 and 1922. The inner cave here is also set aside for meditation, and the front patio affords splendid views across the temple, town and surrounding plains.

The caves can also be reached via the pilgrims' path winding uphill from the **Sri Ramanashramam ashram**, 2km south of the temple along the main road. This simple complex is where the sage lived after returning from his retreat on Arunachala, and where his body is today enshrined. The *samadhi* has become a popular place for Sri Ramana's devotees on pilgrimage, but interested visitors are welcome to stay in the dorms here (T01475/237292, Wwww .ramana-maharshi.org). There's also an excellent bookshop (daily 7.30–11am & 2.30–6.30pm) stocking a huge range of titles on the life and teachings of the guru, as well as quality postcards, calendars and religious images.

Practicalities

Tiruvannamalai is served by regular **buses** from Chennai, Puducherry and Trichy. Coming from the coast, it's easiest to make your way on one of the numerous buses from Tindivanam. The town **bus stand** is just over 1km north of the temple on the main road to Gingee. Half a kilometre east of there, the **railway station** is on the line between Tirupati and Madurai, with a daily

The Pradakshana

During the annual Kartiggai festival, Hindu pilgrims are supposed to perform an auspicious circumambulation of Arunachala, known as the **Pradakshana** (*pra* signifies the removal of all sins, *da* the fulfilment of desires, *ksni* freedom from the cycle of rebirth, and *na* spiritual liberation). Along the way, offerings are made at a string of shrines, tanks, temples, lingams, pillared meditation halls, sacred rocks, springs, trees, and caves related to the Tiruvannamalai legends. Although hectic during the festival, the paved path linking them all together is quiet for most of the year, and makes a wonderful day-hike, affording fine views of the town and its environs.

service in each direction. There is **Internet** access at the Image Computer Centre, 52 Car St, and Sri Sai, 14-A Kadambarayam St.

Accommodation and eating

For such an important pilgrimage place, Tiruvannamalai has surprisingly few decent **hotels**. However the two-star places are fairly comfortable, and the budget options fine for a short stay.

For **food**, you've a choice of a dozen or so typical south Indian "meals" joints just off the bottom of Car Street. Delicious hot ghee chapatis are served here all afternoon, as well as all the usual rice specialities. The *Udipi Brindhavan* and the *Deepam* on Car Street opposite the temple's east entrance are typical *udipi* restaurants, serving, amongst other dishes, excellent *parottas* for under Rs10. The latter also has an adjacent ice-cream and milkshakes parlour. Of the hotels, the *Trisul* has a posh ground-floor restaurant which serves north Indian buffets for around Rs100, and tandoori in the evening, while the *Ramakrishna* does excellent lunchtime thalis and a range of north and south Indian food in the evenings.

Accommodation

Arunachala 5 Vada Sannathi St ☎04175/228300. Large, clean and comfortable hotel, right outside the main temple entrance. Not the quietest place to stay but certainly atmospheric. ❸–❹
NS Lodge 47 Thiruvoodal St ☎04175/225388. Facing the south entrance of Arunachaleshvara Temple. Clean attached rooms (some a/c) with cable TV; great temple view from the roof. ❷–❹
Park 26 Kosmadam St ☎04175/222471. Reliable budget option two minutes' walk northeast of the main temple. All rooms are non-a/c and basic but clean, with singles costing only

Rs70. There's a busy vegetarian canteen on the ground floor. ❶
Ramakrishna 34-F Polur Rd ☎01475/250005, ✉info@hotelramakrishna.com. One of the best places in town, with large rooms with attached bath (a/c or non-a/c) and a decent restaurant. It's a five minute walk north of the bus stand: follow Chinnakadai St north and take the left fork; the hotel is 200m along on the right. ❶–❹
SASA Lodge Chinnakadai St, almost opposite the bus stand ☎04175/253431. One of the best budget lodges, painted bright blue and white, with decent enough rooms, some of which are a/c. ❶–❸

Puducherry (Pondicherry) and Auroville

First impressions of **PUDUCHERRY** (**Pondicherry**, also often referred to simply as Pondy), the former capital of French India, can be unpromising. Instead of the leafy boulevards and *pétanque* pitches you might expect, its messy outer suburbs and bus stand are as cluttered and chaotic as any typical Tamil town. Closer to the seafront, however, the atmosphere grows tangibly more Gallic, as the bazaars give way to rows of houses whose shuttered windows and colourwashed facades wouldn't look out of place in Montpellier. For anyone familiar with the British colonial imprint, the town can induce culture shock to see richly ornamented Catholic churches, French road names and policemen in De Gaulle-style *képis*, not to mention hearing French spoken in the street and seeing *boules* played in the dusty squares. Many of the seafront buildings were damaged by the 2004 tsunami and lives were lost, but Puducherry's tourist infrastructure remained intact.

Known to Greek and Roman geographers as "Poduke", Puducherry was an important staging post on the second-century maritime trade route between Rome and the Far East (a Roman amphitheatre has been unearthed at nearby Arikamedu). When the Roman Empire declined, the Pallavas and Cholas took control and were followed by a succession of colonial powers, from the Portuguese in the sixteenth century to the French, Danes and British, who exchanged the enclave several times after the various battles and treaties of the Carnatic Wars in the early eighteenth century. Puducherry's heyday, however, dates from the arrival of the French governor **Dupleix**, who accepted the governorship in

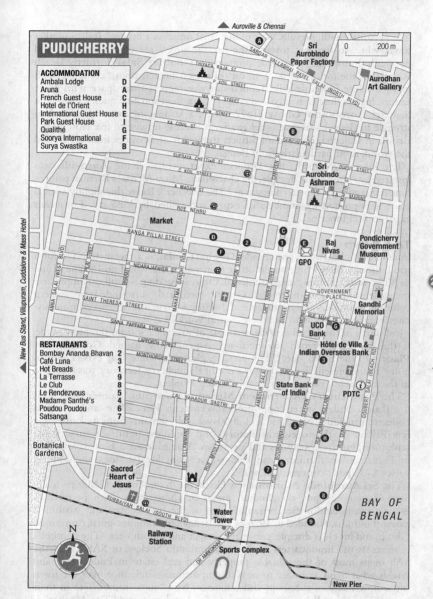

PUDUCHERRY

0   200 m

Sri
Aurobindo
Paper Factory

Aurodhan
Art Gallery

ACCOMMODATION
Ambala Lodge   D
Aruna   A
French Guest House C
Hotel de l'Orient   H
International Guest House E
Park Guest House   I
Qualithé   G
Soorya International F
Surya Swastika   B

THIYAGA RAJA ST
P KOIL STREET
MA KOIL STREET
ID KOIL STREET
KA COVIL ST
SRI AUROBINDO ST
SUPRAYA CHETTIAR ST
C KOIL STREET
A MADAM ST
RUE NEHRU

SARDAR VALLABHAI PATEL SALAI (NORTH BLVD)

L THOLLANDAL ST
B DERICHEMONT ST
DUPUY STREET

Sri
Aurobindo
Ashram

RUE DE LA MARINE

Market

RANGA PILLAI STREET
VELLAJA ST
NIDARAJAPAYER ST.

Raj
Nivas

GPO

Pondicherry
Government
Museum

SAINT THERESA STREET

GOVERNMENT
PLACE

Gandhi
Memorial

SINNA PAPPARA STREET

RUE MAHE DE LABOURDONNAIS

UCO
Bank

LAPPORITH STREET

MONTHORSIER STREET

Hôtel de Ville &
Indian Overseas Bank

RESTAURANTS
Bombay Ananda Bhavan 2
Café Luna   3
Hot Breads   1
La Terrasse   9
Le Club   8
Le Rendezvous   5
Madame Santhé's   4
Poudou Poudou   6
Satsanga   7

SURCOUF ST

C MUDALIAR ST

State Bank
of India

PDTC

LAL BAHADUR SASTRI ST

Botanical
Gardens

Sacred
Heart of
Jesus

SUBBAIAH SALAI (SOUTH BLVD)

Water
Tower

BAY OF
BENGAL

N

Railway
Station

Sports Complex

New Pier

New Bus Stand, Villupuram, Cuddalore & Mass Hotel

20

TAMIL NADU | The northeast

1742 and immediately set about rebuilding a town decimated by its former
British occupants. It was he who instituted the street plan of a central grid
encircled by a broad oblong boulevard, bisected north to south by a canal
dividing the "Ville Blanche", to the east, from the "Ville Noire", to the west.

Although relinquished by the French in 1954 – when the town became the
headquarters of the **Union Territory of Pondicherry**, administering the
three other former colonial enclaves scattered across south India – Puducherry's

split personality still prevails. West of the canal stretches a bustling Indian market town, while to the east, towards the sea, the streets are emptier, cleaner and decidedly European. The seaside promenade, **Goubert Salai** (formerly Beach Road), has the forlorn look of an out-of-season French resort, complete with its own white Hôtel de Ville. Tanned sun-worshippers share space with grave Europeans in white Indian costume, busy about their spiritual quest. It was here that **Sri Aurobindo Ghose** (1872–1950), a leading figure in the freedom struggle in Bengal, was given shelter after it became unwise to live close to the British in Calcutta. His ashram attracts thousands of devotees from all around the world, most particularly from Bengal.

Ten kilometres north, the Utopian experiment-in-living **Auroville** was inspired by Aurobindo's disciple, the charismatic Mirra Alfassa, a Parisian painter, musician and mystic better known as "The Mother". Today this slightly surreal place is populated by numbers of expats and visited by long-stay Europeans eager to find inner peace.

The Town

Puducherry's beachside promenade, **Goubert Salai**, is a favourite place for a stroll, though there's little to do other than watch the world go by. The Hôtel de Ville, today housing the Municipal Offices building, is still an impressive spectacle, and a four-metre-tall Gandhi memorial, surrounded by ancient columns, dominates the northern end. Nearby, a French memorial commemorates French Indians who lost their lives in World War I.

Just north of the Hôtel de Ville, a couple of streets back from the promenade, is the leafy old French-provincial-style square now named **Government Place**. On the north side, the impressive, gleaming white **Raj Nivas**, official home to the present lieutenant governor of Puducherry Territory, was built late in the eighteenth century for Joseph Francis Dupleix.

The **Pondicherry Government Museum** (Tues–Sun 10am–5pm; Rs2) is on Ranga Pillai Street, opposite Government Place. The archeological collection includes Neolithic and 2000-year-old remains from Arikamedu, a few Pallava (sixth- to eighth-century) and Buddhist (tenth-century) stone sculptures, bronzes, weapons and paintings. Alongside are a bizarre assembly of French salon furniture and bric-a-brac from local houses, including a velvet S-shaped "conversation seat".

The **Sri Aurobindo Ashram**, a few blocks north on Rue de la Marine (daily 8am–noon & 2–6pm; no children under 3; photography with permission; ⓦ www.sriaurobindosociety.org.in), is one of the best-known and wealthiest ashrams in India. Founded in 1926 by the Bengali philosopher-guru, Aurobindo Ghosh, and his chief disciple, personal manager and mouthpiece "The Mother", it serves as the headquarters of the Sri Aurobindo Society, or SAS. Today the SAS owns most of the valuable property and real estate in Puducherry, and wields what many consider to be a disproportionate influence over the town (note how many of the shops and businesses have "auro" somewhere in their name). The **samadhi**, or mausoleum, of Sri Aurobindo and "The Mother" is covered daily with flowers and usually surrounded by supplicating devotees with their hands and heads placed on the tomb. Inside the main building, an incongruous and very bourgeois-looking Western-style room complete with three-piece suite and Persian carpet, is where "The Mother" and Sri Aurobindo chilled out. The adjacent bookshop sells a range of literature and tracts, while the building opposite hosts frequent cultural programmes.

In the southwest of town, near the railway station, you can hardly miss the huge cream-and-brown **Sacred Heart of Jesus**, one of Puducherry's finest

Catholic churches, built by French missionaries in the 1700s. Nearby, the shady **Botanical Gardens**, established in 1826, offer many quiet paths to wander (daily 9.30am–6pm; free). The French planted 900 species here, experimenting to see how they would do in Indian conditions; one tree, the *khaya senegalensis*, has grown to a height of 25m. You can also see an extraordinary fossilized tree, found about 25km away in Tiravakarai.

Practicalities

All buses – long and short distance – pull into **New Bus Stand**, which lies on the west edge of town; for a summary of routes, see "Travel details", pp.1177–1178. From here, auto-rickshaws charge at least Rs50 into the old town, taxis double that, but you can jump in a *tempo* to central Ambour Salai for Rs5–10. Puducherry's **railway station** is in the south, five minutes' walk from the sea off Surbaiyah Salai.

The **Puducherry Tourism Development Corporation** office is at 40 Goubert Salai (daily 8.45am–5pm; ☎0413/233 9497, ⓦtourism.pondicherry.gov.in). The staff are extremely helpful, providing leaflets and a city map, and information about Auroville; they can also book you onto their **city tours** (half-day 1.30–5.30pm, Rs90; full-day 9.30am–6pm, Rs110) and help arrange **car rental**. There is a wealth of **ATMs**, and recommended places to **change money** include: the Indian Overseas Bank, in the Hôtel de Ville; the State Bank of India on Surcouf Street; and UCO Bank, Rue Mahe de Labourdonnais. The **GPO** is on Ranga Pillai Street (Mon–Sat 10am–7.30pm). **Internet access** is available throughout central Puducherry; you'll find Net cafés on Ranga Pillai Street, Rue Nehru and Mission Street. Several places, such as the iWay branch at 36 Nidarajapayar St, also offer Netphone facilities.

Puducherry is well served by auto-rickshaws, but for **getting around**, most tourists rent a **cycle** from one of the many stalls dotted about town (Rs25 per day, plus Rs200 refundable deposit). If you're staying at the *Park Guest House*, use one of theirs (they're all immaculately maintained). For trips further afield (to Auroville, for example), you may want to rent a **moped** or **scooter**. Of the rental firms operating in town, both Sri Ganesh Cycle Store, 39 Mission St (☎0413/222 2801), and Sri Sri Durga Pharameshwari Cycle Stores, 106-B Mission St (☎0413/233 4101), have new models such as Honda Kinetics for Rs100 per day, plus a Rs500 deposit.

Accommodation

Puducherry's **basic lodges** are concentrated around the main market area, Ranga Pillai Street and Rue Nehru. Guesthouses belonging to the **Sri Aurobindo Ashram** (ⓦwww.sriaurobindosociety.org.in) offer fantastic value for money, but come with a lot of baggage apart from your own (regulations, curfews and overpowering "philosophy of life" notices). Although supposedly open to all, they are not keen on advertising, or on attracting misguided individuals indulging in "spiritual tourism".

Ambala Lodge 92 Ranga Pillai St ☎0413/233 8910. One of the best and most central cheapies. The rooms, some with common bathrooms, are a little poky but clean enough. ❶

Aruna 3 Zamindar Garden, SV Patel Rd ☎0413/233 7756. Set on a quiet side street, the decent-value attached doubles here are of varying sizes. There is a/c and TV in some, and all have balconies. ❷–❹

French Guest House 38 Ambour Salai ☎0413/420 0853. Clean, spacious rooms, including some family suites, in a welcoming central hotel, better value than its larger competitors. All rooms have optional a/c. ❸–❹

Hotel de l'Orient 17 Rue Romain Rolland ☎0413/234 3067, ☏222 7829. A beautiful, UNESCO heritage-accorded French house with sixteen rooms, individually decorated with French antiques, tiled balconies and long shuttered windows overlooking a leafy courtyard restaurant. Wonderfully romantic. ❼–❾

International Guest House 47 Gingee Salai ☎0413/233 6699, ℮ingh@vsnl.net. The largest Aurobindo establishment, with dozens of very large, clean rooms, some a/c. It's a good budget option but typically institutional, with a 10.30pm curfew. ❷–❸

Park Guest House Goubert Salai ☎0413/233 4412, ℮parkgh@sriaurobindoashram.org. Another Sri Aurobindo Society pad, with strict rules (no alcohol or TVs) and a 10.30pm curfew. Rooms are spotless and very comfortable, with new mosquito nets and sitouts overlooking a well-watered garden and the sea. There's also bike rental, laundry and restaurant. ❸

Qualithé 3 Rue Mahe de Labourdonnais ☎0413/233 4325, ℮rajarathnam8@engineer.com.

Pondy's most characterful budget lodge, in a slightly rickety old French building. Upstairs, big, spotless rooms that fit four lead off a pleasant balcony with wicker chairs and great views over Government Place. Just one cheap single. ❸

Soorya International 55 Ranga Pillai St ☎0413/233 6856, ℮sooryainternational @hotelstamilndu.com. Central hotel with very large, immaculate rooms. An ostentatious exterior, but the tariffs are reasonable. Rates include breakfast. ❹–❺

Surya Swastika 11 ID Koil St ☎0413/234 3092, ℮suryaswastika@sify.com. Traditional Tamil guesthouse in a quiet corner of town, with nine basic rooms around a central courtyard that doubles as a pilgrims' canteen at lunchtime. Incredibly cheap, and cleaner than most of the bazaar lodges. ❶–❸

Eating and drinking

If you've been on the road for a while and are hankering for healthy salads, fresh coffee, crusty bread, cakes and real pastry, you'll be spoilt for choice in Puducherry. Unlike the traveller-oriented German Bakery–style places elsewhere in the country, the Western **restaurants** here cater for a predominantly expatriate clientele, with discerning palettes and fat Euro pay-cheques. **Beer** is available just about everywhere (except the SAS-owned establishments) and is half the regular Tamil Nadu price at Rs45–50 a bottle. The spacious bar at the *Qualithé* hotel is a favourite hang-out.

Bombay Ananda Bhavan 199 Mission St. Good, quiet and very hygienic south Indian veg joint, serving particularly fine masala dosas for around Rs20.

Café Luna Rue Suffren, near the State Bank of India. A little place where old men gather to drink coffee and pass the time of day. The coffee is prepared with great pomp and style, and the ultra-cheap lunch-time plate of lemon rice and vada is superb.

Hot Breads 42 Ambour Salai. Crusty croissants, fresh baguettes, and delicious savoury pastry snacks, served in a squeaky-clean *boulangerie-café* full of French expats.

🏃 **La Terrasse** 5 Subbaiyah Salai. The most popular French restaurant in town amongst European backpackers, who hang out here to devour croissants and cappuccino alfresco. Excellent prawn dishes start at Rs80, pizzas go for Rs70–175, and there's also a range of Indian, Chinese and French food. Closed Wed.

Le Club 33 Rue Dumas. One of the best-known eateries in town, and not quite as expensive as you might expect. The predominantly French menu features their famous coq au vin, steak au poivre, plenty of seafood options (each at around Rs200) and a full wine list, plus cocktails (Rs150). There's also a bistro downstairs (closed Mon) that's great for Sunday brunch, and a decent Vietnamese and Southeast Asian restaurant in the same complex.

Le Rendezvous 30 Rue Suffren. Filling seafood sizzlers, fantastic pizza and tandoori brochettes are specialities of this popular expat-oriented restaurant. They also serve fresh croissants and espresso for breakfast. Dine indoors or up on the more romantic rooftop, where you can relax to eclectic sounds in the evenings. Most main dishes Rs120–250.

🏃 **Madame Santhé's** Rue Romain Rolland. Attractively designed and atmospheric roof terrace serving a mixture of extremely tasty French, Indian and Chinese dishes for around Rs100–200. Their steak in mushroom sauce is a delight. More laid back and better value than the established quality restaurants.

Poudou Poudou 31 Rue Labourdonnais. Upmarket newcomer with trendy decor and a varied *menu du jour* that includes six small entrées for Rs450. There's also an authentic sushi bar, and the gourmet sandwiches are both filling and delicious.

Satsanga 30 Rue Labourdonnais. Devised by the French patron, the menu in this converted colonial mansion is carefully prepared: organic salads with fresh herbs, tzatziki and garlic bread, sauté potatoes, tagliatelle alla carbonara and mouth-watering pizzas, washed down with chilled beer. Check their *plat du jour* for fresh fish dishes. Around Rs400 per head for three courses, with drinks.

Auroville

The most New Age place anywhere in India must surely be **AUROVILLE**, the planned "City of Dawn", 10km north of Puducherry, straddling the border of the Union Territory and Tamil Nadu. Founded in 1968, Auroville was inspired by "The Mother", the spiritual successor of Sri Aurobindo. Around 1700 people live in communes (two-thirds of them non-Indians), with such names as Fertile, Certitude, Sincerity, Revelation and Transformation, in what it is hoped will eventually be an ideal city for a population of 50,000. Architecturally experimental buildings, combining modern Western and traditional Indian elements, are set in a rural landscape of narrow lanes, deep red earth and lush greenery. Income is derived from agriculture, handicrafts, alternative technology, educational and development projects and Aurolec, a computer software company.

Considering how little there is to see here, Auroville attracts a disproportionately large number of day-trippers – much to the chagrin of its inhabitants, who rightly point out that you can only get a sense of what the settlement is all about if you stay a while. Interested visitors are welcomed as paying guests in most of the communes (see p.1129), where you can work alongside permanent residents.

Begun in 1970, the space-age **Matri Mandir** – a gigantic, almost spherical hi-tech meditation centre at the heart of the site – was conceived as "a symbol of the Divine's answer to man's inspiration for perfection". Earth from 124 countries was symbolically placed in an urn, and is kept in a concrete cone in the amphitheatre adjacent to Matri Mandir, from where a speaker can address an audience of three thousand without amplification. The focal point of the interior of the Matri Mandir is a seventy-centimetre crystal ball symbolizing the neutral but divine qualities of light and space. Visitors are allowed in for a fleeting glimpse with strict instructions on behaviour.

Practicalities

Auroville lies 10km north of Puducherry, off the main Chennai road; you can also get there via the coastal highway, turning off at the village of Chinna Mudaliarchavadi. **Bus** services are frequent along both routes, but as Auroville is so spread out, covering some fifty or so square kilometres, it's best to come with your own transport, at the very least a bike. Most people rent a scooter or **motorcycle** from Puducherry and ride up. Alternatively, there's the **Puducherry Tourism Development Corporation**'s half-day **tour** from Puducherry (see p.1129).

In the middle of the site near the **Bharat Niwas**, which holds a permanent exhibition on the history and philosophy of the settlement, the **visitor centre** (daily 9am–5.30pm; ☏0413/262 2239, ⓦwww.auroville.org) is the place to get tickets for the Matri Mandir (daily 10am–noon & 2–4pm). Tickets are available from 9.45am–12.45pm and 1.45–4pm; before they are issued, you're shown a short video presentation about the village. You can also pick up some inexpensive literature on Auroville in the adjacent bookshop and check the notice board for details of **activities** in which visitors may participate (these typically include yoga, reiki and Vipassana meditation, costing around Rs100 per session). In addition, there are a couple of quality handicraft outlets and several pleasant little vegetarian cafés serving snacks, meals and cold drinks.

The information desk at the visitor centre is also the place to enquire about **paying guest accommodation** in Auroville's thirty or so communes. Officially there's no lower limit on the time you have to stay, but visitors are encouraged to stick around for at least a week, helping out on communal projects; tariffs range from Rs100–500 per day, depending on levels of comfort. Alternatively, you can arrange to stay in one of the four a/c **guesthouses**, which have rooms for Rs1500. Beds here and in the communes are always in short supply, especially during the two peak periods of December to March and July to August, when it's advisable to book well in advance (℡0413/262 2704, Ⓔavguests@auroville.org.in). Otherwise, the best of the very limited options nearby is the *Satsanga Guest House* (℡0413/222 5867, Ⓔpierre_satsanga @yahoo.com; ❷–❸), only 500m from the beach, which has a choice of rooms with or without private bathrooms, and a two-bedroom flat (❹). For **food**, you won't do better than the excellent vegetarian "meals" served in Auroville itself.

Central Tamil Nadu: the Chola heartland

To be on the banks of the Cauvery listening to the strains of Carnatic music is to have a taste of eternal bliss

Tamil proverb

Continuing south of Puducherry along the Coromandel coast, you enter the flat landscape of the **Kaveri** (aka Cauvery) **Delta**, a watery world of canals, dams, dykes and rivulets that has been intensively farmed since ancient times. Only a hundred miles in diameter, it forms the verdant rice-bowl core of Tamil Nadu, crossed by more than thirty major rivers and countless streams. The largest of them, the **River Kaveri**, known in Tamil as *Ponni*, "The Lady of Gold" (a form of the Mother Goddess), is revered as a conduit of liquid *shakti*, the primordial female energy that nurtures the millions of farmers who live on her banks and tributaries. The landscape here is one endless swathe of green paddy fields, dotted with palm trees and little villages of thatched roofs and market stalls; it comes as a rude shock to land up in the hot and chaotic towns.

This mighty delta formed the very heartland of the **Chola** empire, which reached its apogee between the ninth and thirteenth centuries, an era often compared to classical Greece and Renaissance Italy both for its cultural richness and the sheer scale and profusion of its architectural creations. Much as the Cholas originally intended, every visitor is immediately in awe of their huge temples, not only at cities such as **Chidambaram**, **Kumbakonam** and **Thanjavur**, but also out in the countryside at places like **Gangaikondacholapuram**, where the magnificent temple is all that remains of a once-great city. Exploring the area for a few days will bring you into contact with the more delicate side of Chola artistic expression, such as the magnificent **bronzes** of Thanjavur.

Chidambaram

CHIDAMBARAM, 58km south of Puducherry, is so steeped in myth that its history is hard to unravel. As the site of the *tandava*, the cosmic dance of Shiva as **Nataraja**, King of the Dance, it's one of the holiest sites in south India, and a visit to its **Sabhanayaka Temple** affords a fascinating glimpse into ancient Tamil religious practice and belief. The legendary king **Hiranyavarman** is said to have made a pilgrimage here from Kashmir, seeking to rid himself of leprosy by bathing in the temple's Shivaganga tank. In thanks for a successful cure, he enlarged the temple. He also brought three thousand brahmins, of the Dikshitar caste, whose descendants, distinguishable by top-knots of hair at the front of their heads, are the ritual specialists of the temple to this day.

Few of the fifty *maths* (monasteries) that once stood here remain, but the temple itself is still a hive of activity and hosts numerous **festivals**. The two most important are ten-day affairs, building up to spectacular finales: on the ninth day of each, temple chariots process through the four Car streets in the

car festival, while on the tenth there is an **abhishekham**, when the principal deities in the Raja Sabha (thousand-pillared hall) are anointed. For exact dates (one is in May/June, the other in Dec/Jan), contact any TTDC tourist office and plan well ahead, as they are very popular Other local festivals include fire-walking and *kavadi* folk dance (dancing with decorated wooden frames on the head) at the Thillaiamman Kali (April/May) and Keelatheru Mariamman (July/Aug) temples.

The town also has a hectic market, and a large student population, based at Annamalai University to the east, a centre of Tamil studies. Among the simple thatched huts in the surrounding countryside, the only solid-looking structures are small roadside temples, most of which are devoted to Aiyannar, the village deity who protects borders, and are accompanied by *kudirais*, brightly painted terracotta or wooden figures of horses.

Sabhanayaka Nataraja Temple

For south India's Shaivites, the **Sabhanayaka Nataraja Temple** (daily 4am–noon & 4–10pm), where Shiva is enthroned as Lord of the Cosmic Dance (Nataraja), is the holiest of holies. Its huge *gopuras*, whose lights are used as landmarks by sailors far out to sea in the Bay of Bengal, soar above a fifty-five-acre complex, divided by four concentric walls. The oldest parts now standing were built under the Cholas, who adopted Nataraja as their chosen deity and crowned several kings here. The rectangular outermost wall, of little interest in itself, affords entry on all four sides, so if you have the time the best way to tackle the complex is to work slowly inwards from the third enclosure in clockwise circles. **Guides** are readily available but tend to shepherd visitors towards the central shrine too quickly. Feel free to roam at your own pace and only make modest donations of small coins for puja blessings; there used to be quite a problem of greedy priests trying to extort vast sums from foreigners, though this has been largely curtailed. However, it's still better to politely refuse those priests who beckon you to sign the temple visitor books.

Frequent **ceremonies** take place at the innermost sanctum, the most popular being at noon and 6pm, when a fire is lit, great gongs are struck and devotees rush forward to catch a last glimpse of the lingam before the doors are shut. On Friday nights before the temple closes, during a particularly elaborate puja, Nataraja is carried on a palanquin accompanied by music and attendants carrying flaming torches and tridents. At other times, you'll hear ancient devotional hymns from the *Tevaram*.

The western *gopura* is the most popular entrance, as well as being the most elaborately carved and probably the earliest (c.1150 AD). Turning north (left) from here, you come to the colonnaded **Shivaganga tank**, the site of seven natural springs. From the broken pillar at the tank's edge, all four *gopuras* are visible. In the northeast corner, the largest building in the complex, the **Raja Sabha** (fourteenth- to fifteenth-century) is also known as "the thousand-pillared hall"; tradition holds that there are only nine hundred and ninety-nine actual pillars, the thousandth being Shiva's leg. During festivals the deities Nataraja and Shivakamasundari are brought here and mounted on a dais for the anointing ceremony, *abhishekha*.

The importance of **dance** at Chidambaram is underlined by the reliefs of dancing figures inside the east *gopura*, demonstrating 108 *karanas* (a similar set is to be found in the west *gopura*). A *karana* (or *adavu* in Tamil) is a specific point in a phase of movement prescribed by the extraordinarily comprehensive Sanskrit treatise on the performing arts, the *Natya Shastra* (c.200 BC–200 AD) – the basis of all classical dance, music and theatre in India. A caption from the

Natya Shastra surmounts each *karana* niche. Four other niches are filled with images of patrons and *stahapatis* – the sculptors and designers responsible for the iconography and positioning of deities.

To get into the square **second enclosure**, head for its western entrance (just north of the west *gopura* in the third wall) which leads into a circumambulatory passageway. Once beyond this second wall it's easy to become disorientated, as the roofed inner enclosures see little light and are supported by a maze of colonnades. The atmosphere is immediately more charged, reaching its peak at the very centre.

The innermost **Govindaraja shrine** is dedicated to Vishnu – a surprise in this most Shaivite of environments. The deity is attended by non-Dikshitar brahmins who, it is said, don't always get along with the Dikshitars. From outside the shrine, non-Hindus can see through to the most sacred part of the temple, the **Kanaka Sabha** and the **Chit Sabha**, adjoining raised structures, roofed with copper and gold plate and linked by a hallway. The latter houses bronze images of Nataraja and his consort Shivakamasundari; behind and to the left of Nataraja, a curtain, sacred to Shiva and strung with rows of leaves from the bilva tree, demarcates the most potent area of all. Within it lies the **Akashalingam**, known as the *rahasya*, or "secret", of Chidambaram: made of the most subtle of the elements, Ether (*akasha*) – from which Air, Fire, Water and Earth are born – the lingam is invisible – signifying the invisible presence of God in the human heart.

A crystal lingam, said to have emanated from the light of the crescent moon on Shiva's brow, and a small ruby Nataraja are worshipped in the Kanaka Sabha. They are ritually bathed in the flames of the priests' camphor fire or oil lamps six times a day. This inner area is where you're most likely to hear **oduvars**, hereditary singers from the middle, non-brahmin castes, intoning verses of ancient Tamil poetry. The songs with which they regale the deities at puja time, drawn from compilations such the *Tevaram* or earlier *Sangam*, are believed to be more than a thousand years old.

Practicalities

Chidambaram revolves around the Sabhanayaka Temple and the busy market area that surrounds it, along North, East, South and West Car streets. At the time of writing, the **railway station**, just over 1km southeast of the centre, was out of commission as the lines through Chidambaram were undergoing gauge conversion. Frequent buses from Chennai, Thanjavur, Mamallapuram and Madurai pull in at the **bus stand**, also in the southeast, but nearer the centre, about 500m from the temple.

Staff at the TTDC **tourist office** (Mon–Fri 9.45am–5.45pm; ☏04144 /238739), next to *Vandayar Gateway Inn* hotel on Railway Feeder Road, are charming and helpful, but only have a small pamphlet to give visitors. None of the **banks** in Chidambaram change money, although the *Saradharam* hotel, near the bus stand, will change cash and there is an ICICI Bank ATM in the forecourt, as well as a couple more on South Car Street. **Internet** is available at the *Saradharam*, as well as at I-Castle, by the east entrance to the temple.

Accommodation and eating

To cope with the influx of tourists and pilgrims, Chidambaram abounds in budget **accommodation**, but few hotels even creep into the mid-range bracket.

As for **eating**, there are plenty of basic, wholesome "meals" places on and around the Car streets – the *Sri Ganesa Bhavan*, on West Car Street, gets the locals' vote. East of the Sabhanayaka Temple, the *Sri Aishwarya*, by the clocktower near the bus stand, is a clean, modern south Indian and Chinese veg restaurant or, close by, there's the airy rooftop restaurant at the *RK Residency*, which serves non-veg food, both Indian and Chinese. Alternatively, the Middle Eastern *Dubai Restaurant* is a tiny hole-in-the-wall place on Venugopal Pillai (VGP) Street serving tasty kebabs, fish and other non-veg fare.

Hotels and guesthouses

Akshaya 17/18 East Car St ☎04144/222592, ⊕akshayhotel@hotmail.com. Pleasant, clean mid-range hotel, with a lawn backing right onto the temple wall. The rooms (a/c and non-a/c) are a decent size but the latter are cheaper and better value, and there are a couple of restaurants. ③–④

Mansoor Lodge 91 East Car St ☎04144/221072. A friendly and good-value cheapie, right opposite the temple. The freshly painted rooms have spotless tiled floors and clean bathrooms, and there are TVs in most. ①–②

Raja Rajan 162 West Car St ☎04144/222690. Close to the west gate of the temple, the clean rooms here have tiled bathrooms and low tariffs; the a/c ones are good value. ①–③

Ritz 2 VGP St, near the bus stand ☎04144/223312, ℉221098. One of the better places in town, this comfortable hotel boasts a convenient location and big rooms (all with TV, and some with a/c), plus a good restaurant. ③–④

Sabanayagam 22 East Sannathi St, off East Car St ☎04144/220896. Despite a flashy exterior, this is a run-of-the-mill budget place, with clean rooms off dim corridors. Some are windowless, and there's a choice of a/c and non-a/c, and Western or Indian loos. Good veg restaurant downstairs. ②–④

Saracharam 19 Venugopal Pillai St, opposite the bus stand ☎04144/221336, ⓦhotelsaradharam .co.in. Large, clean and well-kept rooms (some with a/c and balconies) in modern buildings, with three decent restaurants (including one non-veg), a small garden, bar, laundry and foreign exchange. ③–④

Gangaikondacholapuram

Devised as the centrepiece of a city built by the Chola king Rajendra I (1014–42) to celebrate his conquests, the magnificent **Brihadishwara Temple** stands in the tiny village of **GANGAIKONDACHOLAPURAM**, in Trichy District, 35km northeast of Kumbakonam. The tongue-twisting name means "the town of the Chola who took the Ganges". Under Rajendra I, the Chola empire did indeed stretch as far as the great river of the north, an unprecedented achievement for a southern dynasty. Aside from the temple and the rubble remains of Rajendra's palace, 2km east at Tamalikaimedu, nothing of the city remains. Nonetheless, this is among the most extraordinary archeological sites in south India, outshone only by Thanjavur, and the fact that it's devoid of visitors most of the time gives it a memorably forlorn feel.

Although it is marginally closer to Chidambaram, **bus** connections are better with Kumbakonam, running every fifteen minutes or so. The village is also served by some buses between Trichy and Chidambaram. Be sure not to get stuck here between noon and 4pm when the temple is closed. Facilities are minimal, with little more than a few cool-drinks stands. Parts of the interior are extremely dark, and a torch is useful.

Brihadishwara Temple

Dominating the village landscape, the **Brihadishwara Temple** (daily 6am–noon & 4–8pm; free) sits in a well-maintained grassy courtyard, flanked by a closed *mandapa* hallway. Over the sanctuary, to the right, a massive pyramidal tower (*vimana*) rises 55m in nine diminishing storeys. Though smaller than the one at Thanjavur, the tower's graceful curve gives it an impressive refinement. At the gateway you are likely to meet the ASI caretaker, who is worth taking as a guide, especially if you'd like to climb up onto the roof for views of the vicinity and the tower.

Turning right (north) inside the courtyard, before you reach a small shrine to the goddess **Durga**, containing an image of Mahishasuramardini (the slaying of the buffalo demon), you come across a small well, guarded by a lion statue, known as Simha-kinaru and made from plastered brickwork. King Rajendra is said to have had Ganges water placed in the well to be used for the ritual anointing of the lingam in the main temple. The lion, representing Chola kingly power, bows to the huge Nandi respectfully seated before the eastern entrance of the temple, in line with the shivalingam contained within.

Directly in front of the eastern entrance to the temple stands a small altar for offerings. Two parallel flights of stairs ascend to the *mukhamandapa* or porch, which leads to the long pillared *mahamandapa* hallway, the entrance of which is flanked by a pair of large guardian deities. Immediately inside the temple a guide can show you the way to the tower, up steep steps. On either side of the temple doorway, sculptures of Shiva in his various benevolent (*anugraha*) manifestations include him blessing Vishnu, Devi, Ravana and the saint Chandesha. In the northeast corner, an unusual square stone block features carvings of the nine planets (*navagraha*). A number of **Chola bronzes** (see p.1144) stand on the platform; the figure of Karttikeya, the war god, carrying a club and a shield, is thought to have had particular significance.

The base of the main temple sanctuary is decorated with lions and scrollwork. Above this decoration, running from the southern to the northern entrance of the *ardhamandapa*, a series of sculpted figures in plastered niches portray different images of Shiva. The most famous is at the northern entrance, showing Shiva and Parvati garlanding the saint Chandesha, who here is sometimes identified as Rajendra I. For more on the temples of Tamil Nadu, see p.1115.

Two minutes' walk northeast along the main road (turn right from the car park), the tiny **Archeological Museum** (daily except Fri 10am–1pm & 2–5.45pm; free) contains Chola odds and ends discovered locally. The finds include terracotta lamps, coins, weapons, tiles, bronze, bangle pieces, palm-leaf manuscripts and an old Chinese pot.

Kumbakonam

Sandwiched between the Kaveri (Cauvery) and Arasalar rivers is **KUMBA-KONAM**, 74km southwest of Chidambaram and 38km northeast of Thanjavur. Hindus believe this to be the place where a water pot (*kumba*) of *amrita* – the ambrosial beverage of immortality – was washed up by a great deluge from atop sacred Mount Meru in the Himalayas. Shiva, who just happened to be passing through in the guise of a wild forest-dwelling hunter, for some reason fired an arrow at the pot, causing it to break. From the shards, he made the lingam that is now enshrined in **Kumbareshwara Temple**, whose *gopuras* today tower over the town, along with those of some seventeen other major shrines. A former capital of the Cholas, who are said to have kept a high-security treasury here, Kumbakonam is the chief commercial centre for the Thanjavur region. The main bazaar, **TSR Big Street**, is especially renowned for its quality costume jewellery.

The main reason to stop in Kumbakonam is to admire the exquisite sculpture of the **Nageshwara Swami Shiva Temple**, which contains the most refined Chola stone carving still in situ. The town also lies within easy reach of the magnificent Darasuram and Gangaikondacholapuram temples, both spectacular ancient monuments that see very few visitors. Note that all temples in the area close between noon (or thereabouts) and 4pm. For a change, the village of Swamimalai, only a bike ride away, is the state's principal centre for traditional **bronze casting**.

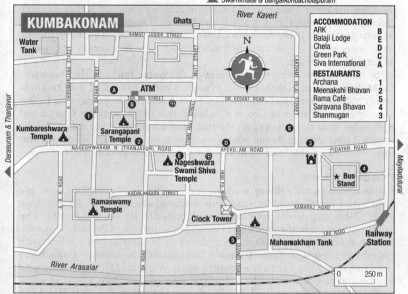

KUMBAKONAM

Ghats

River Kaveri

Water Tank

KAMATI JOSIER STREET

MUTT STREET

N

CHIRUMANJANA STREET

BIG BAZAAR STREET

LAKSHMI VILAI STREET

ACCOMMODATION
ARK   B
Balaji Lodge   E
Chela   D
Green Park   C
Siva International   A

RESTAURANTS
Archana   1
Meenakshi Bhavan   2
Rama Café   5
Saravana Bhavan   4
Shanmugan   3

ⓐ ATM

TSR BIG STREET

DR EESANT ROAD

ⓑ @

Darasuram & Thanjavur

Kumbareshwara Temple

Sarangapani Temple ②

NAGESHWARAM N (THANJAVUR) ROAD

ⓔ @ Nageshwara Swami Shiva Temple

HEAD POST ROAD

AYEKULAM ROAD

PIDAYAR ROAD

ⓓ

ⓒ

③

④

★ Bus Stand

Mayiladuturai

R. R. ROAD

Ramaswamy Temple

KADALANGUDI STREET

KAMARAJ ROAD

Clock Tower

BA ROAD

B.A. ROAD

KUMBI ROAD

⑤

Mahamakham Tank

LBS ROAD

Railway Station

River Arasalar

0   250 m

The Town

Surmounted by a multicoloured *gopura*, the east entrance of Kumbakonam's seventeenth-century **Kumbareshwara Temple**, home of the famous lingam from which the town derived its name, is approached via a covered market selling a huge assortment of cooking pots, a local speciality, as well as the usual glass bangles and trinkets. At the gateway, you may meet the temple elephant, with a painted forehead and necklace of bells. Beyond the flagstaff, a *mandapa* houses a fine collection of silver *vahanas*, vehicles of the deities, used in festivals, and *pancha loham* (compound of five metals) figures of the 63 Nayanmar poet-saints.

The principal and largest of the Vishnu temples in Kumbakonam is the thirteenth-century **Sarangapani Temple**, entered through a ten-storey pyramidal *gopura* gate, more than 45m high. The **central shrine** dates from the late Chola period, with many later accretions. Its entrance, within the innermost court, is guarded by huge *dvarpalas*, identical to Vishnu whom they protect. Between them are carved stone *jali* screens, each different, and in front of them stands the sacred, square *homam* fireplace. During the day, rays of light from tiny ceiling windows penetrate the darkness around the sanctum, designed to resemble a chariot with reliefs of horses, elephants and wheels. A painted cupboard contains a mirror for Vishnu to see himself when he leaves the sanctum sanctorum.

The small **Nageshwara Swami Shiva Temple**, in the centre of town, is Kumbakonam's oldest, founded in 886 and completed a few years into the reign of Parantaka I (907–c.940). First impressions are unpromising, as much of the original building has been hemmed in by later Disney-coloured additions, but beyond the main courtyard, occupied by a large columned *mandapa*, a small *gopura*-topped gateway leads to an inner enclosure where the earliest Chola shrine stands. Framed in the main niches around its sanctum wall are a series of exquisite stone figures, regarded as the finest surviving pieces of **ancient sculpture** in south India. With their languid stance and mesmeric, half-smiling facial expressions, these modest-sized masterpieces far outshine the more monumental art of Thanjavur and Gangaikondacholapuram. The figures show Dakshinamurti (Shiva as a teacher; south wall), Durga and a three-headed Brahma (north wall) and Ardhanari, half-man, half-woman (west wall). Joining them are near-life-size voluptuous maidens believed to be queens or princesses of King Aditya's court.

The most famous and revered of many sacred **water tanks** in Kumbakonam, the **Mahamakham** in the southeast of town, is said to have filled with ambrosia (*amrit*) collected from the pot broken by Shiva. Every twelve years, when Jupiter passes the constellation of Leo, it is believed that water from the Ganges and eight other holy rivers flows into the tank, thus according it the status of *tirtha*, or sacred river crossing. At this auspicious time, as many as four million pilgrims come here for an absolving bathe; the last occasion was in early 2004.

Practicalities

Kumbakonam's small **railway station**, in the southeast of town 2km from the main bazaar, is well served by trains both north and south, and has a left-luggage office (24hr) and decent **retiring rooms** (non-a/c Rs200, a/c Rs400). The hectic bus stand is in the southeast of town, just northwest of the railway station. All the timetables are in Tamil, but there's a 24-hour enquiry office with English-speaking staff. Buses leave for Gangaikondacholapuram, Puducherry and Thanjavur every five to ten minutes, many going via Darasuram. Frequent services run to Chennai, Trichy and several daily to Bangalore. There are a few small **Internet** places on TSR Big Street, where there is also an ICICI ATM machine, 100m east of the *Siva International* hotel.

Accommodation

Kumbakonam is not a major tourist location, and has limited **accommodation**, with only one upper-range hotel, the *Sterling Swamimalai*, over 5km southeast of town on the outskirts of Swamimalai village (see opposite). The good news for budget travellers is that most of the inexpensive places are clean and well maintained.

ARK 21 TSR Big St ☎0435/242 1234. Fifty large, clean rooms (some a/c), on five floors, all with windows; TVs available on request. Bland, but comfortable enough, with an a/c bar serving snacks. ❸–❹

Balaji Lodge 64 Nageshwaram N St ☎0435/243 0546. Good-value budget lodge, offering clean rooms with attached bath and TV, though they are a little dark. ❶

Chela 9 Ayekulam Rd ☎0435/243 0336, ℗243 1592. Large mid-range place, between the bus stand and centre, distinguished by its horrendous mock-classical facade. Soap, fresh towels and TVs are offered as standard. Two restaurants (veg and non-veg) and a bar. ❸–❹

Green Park 10 Lakshmi Vilai St ☎0435/240 3912, ℮hotelgreenpark@dataone.in. Excellent-value business-oriented hotel with spotless doubles, all with TV, some a/c. There's also a coffee shop and the *Peacock* non-veg restaurant. ❹

Siva International 101/3 TSR Big St ☎0435/242 4013, ℮hotelsiva@rediff.com. After the temple *gopuras*, this huge hotel complex is the tallest building in town. Their standard non-a/c is a bargain (ask for #301, which has great views on two sides) and all the spacious, airy doubles are decent value. You can climb onto the roof for incredible views of sunset and dawn behind the *gopuras*. ❷–❹

Eating

There's nothing very exciting about **eating out** in Kumbakonam, and most visitors stick to their hotel restaurant. For a change of scene, though, a few places stand out.

Archana Big Bazaar St. Right in the thick of the market, and popular among shoppers for its good-value south Indian "meals" (Rs30) and great

uttapams, although it can get hot and stuffy inside. Foreigners cause quite a stir here, but are made very welcome.

Meenakshi Bhavan Nageshwaram N St. Excellent, clean south Indian veg joint, which serves some rarer snacks like *adai*, a form of spicy rice cake. Great *dosas* for barely Rs20.
Rama Café Indira Shanti Rd. Simple and wholesome veg "meals" (Rs20–40) and snacks restaurant, in a great setting by the Mahamakham tank.

Saravana Bhavan Just east of bus stand. south Indian veg restaurant serving *iddlis*, vegetable dishes, lunchtime thalis with chai and coffee, and early breakfasts. You can stuff yourself for under Rs50.
Shanmugan Pidayar Rd, opposite the mosque. One of the few places serving non-veg dishes, such as tasty chilli chicken and chicken fried rice (Rs60–90).

Around Kumbakonam

The delta lands around Kumbakonam are scattered with evocative vestiges of the Cholas' golden age, but the most spectacular has to be the crumbling Airavateshwara Temple at **Darasuram**, 6km southwest. Across the fields to the north, the bronze-casters of **Swamimalai** constitute a direct living link with the culture that raised this extraordinary edifice, using traditional "lost wax" techniques, unchanged since the time when Darasuram was a thriving medieval town, to create graceful Hindu deities.

You can combine the two sights in an easy half-day trip from Kumbakonam. The route is flat enough to cycle, although you should keep your wits about you when pedalling the main Thanjavur highway, which sees heavy traffic. To reach Swamimalai from Darasuram, return to the main road from the temple and ask directions in the bazaar. Swamimalai is only 3km north, but travelling between the two involves several turnings, so expect to have to ask someone to wave you in the right direction at regular intervals. From Kumbakonam, the route is more straightforward; cross the Kaveri at the top of Town Hall Street (north of the centre), turn left and follow the main road west through a ribbon of villages.

Darasuram

The **Airavateshwara Temple**, built by King Rajaraja II (*c*.1146–73), stands in the village of **DARASURAM**, an easy five-kilometre bus or cycle ride (on the Thanjavur route) southwest of Kumbakonam. This superb, if little-visited, Chola monument ranks alongside those at Thanjavur and Gangaikondacholapuram; but while the others are grandiose, emphasizing heroism and conquest, this is far smaller, exquisite in proportion and detail and said to have been decorated with *nitya-vinoda*, "perpetual entertainment", in mind. Shiva is called Airavateshwara here because he was worshipped in this temple by Airavata, the white elephant belonging to the king of the gods, Indra.

Darasuram's finest pieces of sculpture are the Chola black-basalt images adorning wall niches in the *mandapa* and inner shrine. These include images of Nagaraja, the snake-king, with a hood of cobras, and Dakshinamurti, the "south-facing" Shiva as teacher, expounding under a banyan tree. Equally renowned is the unique series of somewhat gruesome panels, hard to see without climbing onto the base, lining the top of the basement of the closed *mandapa*. They illustrate scenes from Sekkilar's *Periya Purana*, one of the great works of Tamil literature.

Swamimalai

SWAMIMALAI, 8km west of Kumbakonam, is revered as one of the six sacred abodes of Lord Murugan, Shiva's son, whom Hindu mythology records became his father's religious teacher (*swami*) on a hill (*malai*) here. The site of this epic role-reversal now hosts one of the Tamils' holiest shrines, the **Swaminatha Temple**, crowning the hilltop of the centre of the village, but of more interest to non-Hindus are the **bronze-casters'** workshops dotted around the bazaar and the outlying hamlets.

Known as **sthapathis**, Swamimalai's casters still employ the "lost wax" process perfected by the Cholas to make the most sought-after temple idols in south India. Their finished products are displayed in numerous showrooms along the main street, from where they are exported worldwide, but it is more memorable to watch the *sthapathis* in action, fashioning the original figures from beeswax and breaking open the moulds to expose the mystical finished metalwork inside. For more on Tamil bronze casting, see p.1144.

The nearby hamlet of **Thimmakkudy**, 2km back towards Kumbakonam, is the site of the area's grandest **hotel**, the *Sterling Swamimalai* (℡0435/242 0044, Ⓦwww.sterlingswamimalai.net; ❼), a beautifully restored nineteenth-century brahmins' mansion with all mod cons in its rooms. They also have an in-house yoga teacher, Ayurvedic massage room, and lay on a lively culture show in the evenings.

Thanjavur

As one of the busiest commercial towns of the Kaveri Delta, **THANJAVUR** (aka "Tanjore"), 55km east of Tiruchirapalli and 35km southwest of Kumbakonam, is often overlooked by travellers. However, its history and treasures – among them the breathtaking **Brihadishwara Temple**, Tamil Nadu's most awesome Chola monument – give it a crucial significance to south Indian culture. The home of the world's finest Chola bronze collection, it holds enough of interest to keep you enthralled for at least a couple of days, and is the most obvious base for trips to nearby Gangaikondacholapuram, Darasuram and Swamimalai.

Thanjavur is roughly split in two by the east–west **Grand Anicut Canal**. The **old town**, north of the canal and once entirely enclosed by a fortified wall, was chosen, between the ninth and the end of the thirteenth century, as the capital of their extensive empire by all the Chola kings save one. None of their secular buildings survive, but you can still see as many as ninety temples, of which the Brihadishwara most eloquently epitomizes the power and patronage of Rajaraja I (985–1014), whose military campaigns spread Hinduism to the Maldives, Sri Lanka and Java. Under the Cholas, as well as the later Nayaks and Marathas, literature, painting, sculpture, Carnatic classical music and Bharatanatyam dance all thrived here. Quite apart from its own intrinsic interest, the Nayak **royal palace compound** houses an important library and museums including a famous collection of bronzes.

Of major local **festivals**, the most lavish celebrations at the Brihadishwara Temple are associated with the birthday of King Rajaraja, in October. An eight-day celebration of **Carnatic classical music** is held each January at the Panchanateshwara Temple at **Thiruvaiyaru**, 13km away, to honour the great Carnatic composer-saint, Thyagaraja.

Arrival, information and orientation

Some **buses** from Chennai and Puducherry pull in at the old long-distance State Bus Stand, opposite the City Bus Stand, in the south of the old town. Other services from Madurai, Tiruchirapalli, and Kumbakonam, stop at the New Bus Stand, inconveniently located 4km southwest of the centre, in the middle of nowhere. Rickshaws into town from here cost Rs50, or you can jump on one of the #74 buses that shuttle to and from the centre every few minutes. The **railway station**, just south of the centre, has a computerized system (Mon–Sat 8am–2pm & 2.15–8pm, Sun 8am–2pm & 3–5pm) for booking trains to Chennai, Tiruchirapalli and Rameshwaram (when the line reopens after gauge conversion).

The **GPO** and most of the hotels and restaurants lie on or around **Gandhiji Road** (aka Train Station Rd), which crosses the canal and leads to the railway station in the south. The **TTDC tourist office** (Mon–Fri 10am–5.45pm; ⊕04362/230984) is located in the compound of TTDC *Tamil Nadu* hotel on Gandhiji Road. You can **change money** at Canara Bank on South Main Street and there are a few ATMs around town, including one at the railway station. For **Internet access**, head for Gemini Soft, on the first floor of the *Oriental Towers* hotel, Srinivasam Pillai Road.

Accommodation

Most of Thanjavur's **hotels** are concentrated in the newer part of town, within striking distance of the railway station. They tend to charge higher rates than you'd pay elsewhere in the state, and there's very little choice at the bottom of the market.

Oriental Towers 2889 Srinivasam Pillai Rd ⊕04362/230724, ⓦwww.hotelorientaltowers .com. Huge hotel-cum-shopping complex, with a small swimming pool and luxurious rooms. Good value for the price, with Internet access and three restaurants serving the usual Indian/Chinese/ Western fare. ⑥–⑧

Parisutham 55 Grand Anicut Canal Rd ⊕04362/231801, ⓦwww.hotelparisutham.com. Plush hotel with spacious, centrally a/c rooms ($130), a large palm-fringed pool (residents only), multi-cuisine restaurant, craft shop, foreign exchange and a travel agent. Popular with tour groups, so book ahead. ⑨

🏃 **Sangam** Trichy Rd ⊕04362/239451, ⓦwww.hotelsangam.com. International four-star standards at this luxury hotel with comfortable a/c rooms (from $165), an excellent restaurant (see p.1145), pool (Rs150 for non-residents) and beautiful Tanjore paintings – the one in the lobby is worth a trip here in itself. ⑨

TTDC Tamil Nadu Gandhiji Rd, 10min from the bus and railway stations ⊕04362/231325, ⓦttdconline.com. Once the raja's guesthouse, but now a typically dilapidated state-run hotel, with more character than modern alternatives. Large, comfortable carpeted rooms (some with a/c) are set around a leafy enclosed garden. ❸–❺

Valli 2948 MKM Rd ⊕04362/231580, ⓔarasu_tnj@rediffmail.com. Friendly place with super-clean rooms (some a/c) opening onto bright green corridors; there's a roof terrace and a popular restaurant on the ground floor. The best budget option in town. ❷–❹

Yagappa 1 Trichy Rd ⊕04362/230421. Spacious, well-appointed rooms with sitouts and large, tiled bathrooms. Staff are friendly, there's a bar and restaurant, and the reception features intriguing picture-frames made from coffee roots. Good value. ❸–❹

Brihadishwara Temple

Thanjavur's skyline is dominated by the huge tower of the **Brihadishwara Temple** (daily 6am–8pm), which for all its size lacks the grandiose excesses of later periods. The site has no great significance; the temple was constructed as much to reflect the power of its patron, King Rajaraja I, as to facilitate the worship of Shiva. Profuse **inscriptions** on the base of the main shrine provide incredibly detailed information about the organization of the temple, showing it to have been rich, both in financial terms and in ritual activity. Among recorded **gifts** from Rajaraja, from booty acquired in conquest, are the equivalent of 600lb of silver, 500lb of gold and 250lb of assorted jewels, plus income from agricultural land throughout the Chola empire, set aside for the purpose. No less than four hundred female dancers, **devadasis** (literally "slaves to the gods", married off to the deity), were employed, and each provided with a house. Other staff – another two hundred people – included dance teachers, musicians, tailors, potters, laundrymen, goldsmiths, carpenters, astrologers, accountants, and attendants for all manner of rituals and processions.

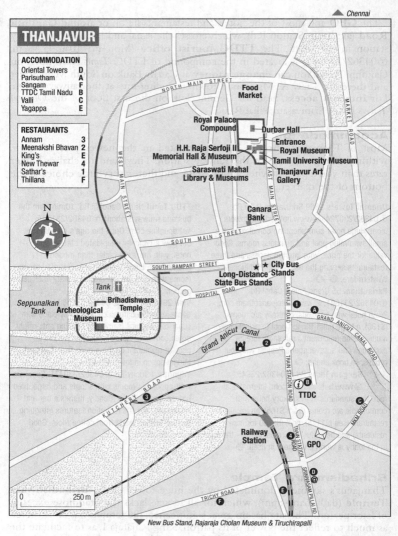

THANJAVUR

ACCOMMODATION

Oriental Towers	D
Parisutham	A
Sangam	F
TTDC Tamil Nadu	B
Valli	C
Yagappa	E

RESTAURANTS

Annam	3
Meenakshi Bhavan	2
King's	E
New Thewar	4
Sathar's	1
Thillana	F

NORTH MAIN STREET

MARKET ROAD

Food Market

Royal Palace Compound — Durbar Hall

WEST MAIN STREET

H.H. Raja Serfoji II Memorial Hall & Museum

Entrance
Royal Museum
Tamil University Museum

Saraswati Mahal Library & Museums

EAST MAIN STREET

Thanjavur Art Gallery

Canara Bank

N

SOUTH MAIN STREET

SOUTH RAMPART STREET

★ City Bus Stands
Long-Distance Stands
State Bus Stands

GANDHIJI ROAD

HOSPITAL ROAD

Tank

Brihadishwara Temple

Seppunalkan Tank

Archeological Museum

GRAND ANICUT CANAL ROAD

Grand Anicut Canal

TRAIN STATION ROAD

TTDC

KUTCHERY ROAD

MKET ROAD

Railway Station

TRAIN STATION ROAD

GPO

SRINIVASAM PILLAI RD

0   250 m

TRICHY ROAD

▼ New Bus Stand, Rajaraja Cholan Museum & Tiruchirapalli

Entrance to the complex is on the east, through two **gopura** gateways some way apart. Although the outer one is the larger, both are of the same pattern: massive rectangular bases topped by pyramidal towers with carved figures and vaulted roofs. At the core of each is a monolithic sandstone lintel, said to have been brought from Tiruchirapalli, over 50km away. The outer facade of the inner *gopura* features mighty, fanged *dvarpala* door guardians, mirror images of each other, and thought to be the largest monolithic sculptures in any Indian temple.

Once inside, the gigantic **courtyard** gives plenty of space to appreciate the buildings. The **main temple**, constructed of granite, consists of a long pillared *mandapa* hallway, followed by the *ardhamandapa*, or "half-hall", which in turn leads to the inner sanctum, the *garbha griha*. Above the shrine, the pyramidal 61m *vimana* tower rises in thirteen diminishing storeys, the apex being exactly one-third of the size of the base. Such a design is quite different from later temples, in which the shrine towers become smaller as the *gopura* entranceways increasingly dominate – a desire to protect the sanctum sanctorum from the polluting gaze of outsiders. This *vimana* is an example of a "structured monolith", a stage removed from the earlier rock-cut architecture of the Pallavas, in which blocks of stone are assembled and then carved. As the stone that surmounts it is said to weigh eighty tonnes, there is considerable speculation as to how it got up there; the most popular theory is that the rock was hauled up a six-kilometre-long ramp. Others have suggested the use of a method comparable to the Sumer Ziggurat style of building, in which logs were placed in gaps in the masonry and the stone raised by leverage. The simplest answer, of course, is that perhaps it's not a single stone at all.

The black *shivalingam*, over 3.5m high, in the **inner sanctum** is called Adavallan, "the one who can dance well" – a reference to Shiva as Nataraja, the King of the Dance, who resides at Chidambaram and was the *ishtadevata*, chosen deity, of the king. The lingam is not always on view, but during puja ceremonies (8am, 11am, noon & 7.30pm), a curtain is pulled revealing the god to the devotees.

Outside, the walls of the courtyard are lined with **colonnaded passageways** – the one along the northern wall is said to be the longest in India. The one on the west, behind the temple, contains 108 lingams from Varanasi and (heavily graffitied) panels from the Maratha period. In the southwest corner of the courtyard, the small **Archeological Museum** (daily 9am–6pm; free) houses an interesting collection of sculpture, including an extremely tubby, damaged Ganesh, before-and-after photos detailing restoration work to the temple in the 1940s and displays about the Cholas. You can also buy the excellent ASI booklet, *Chola Temples*, which gives detailed accounts of Brihadishwara and the temples at Gangaikondacholapuram and Darasuram. For more on Tamil Nadu's temples, see p.1115.

The Royal Palace Compound and around

The **Royal Palace Compound** (all sites daily 9am–6pm), where members of the erstwhile royal family still reside, is on East Main Street (a continuation of Gandhiji Road), 2km northeast of Brihadishwara Temple. Work on the palace began in the mid-sixteenth century under Sevappa Nayak, the founder of the Nayak kingdom of Thanjavur; additions were made by the Marathas from the end of the seventeenth century onwards. Dotted around the compound are several reminders of Thanjavur's past under these two dynasties, including an exhibition of oriental manuscripts and a superlative museum of **Chola bronzes**. Unfortunately, many of the palace buildings remain in a sorry state, despite various promises of funds for renovation.

Durbar Hall and its courtyard

Remodelled by Shaji II in 1684, the **Durbar Hall** (Rs50 [Rs10], camera Rs30, video Rs100), or hall of audience, houses a throne canopy decorated with the mirrored glass distinctive of Thanjavur. Although damaged, the ceiling and walls are elaborately painted. Five domes are striped red, green and yellow, and on the walls, friezes of leaf and pineapple designs, and trumpeting angels in a night sky show European influence. The **courtyard** outside the Durbar Hall was the setting for one of the more poignant moments in Thanjavur's turbulent history when, in 1683, the last of the Nayak kings gave himself up to the king of Madurai. Its most imposing structure, the Sarja Madi or "seven-storey" bell tower, built by Serfoji II in 1800, is closed to the public due to its unsafe condition.

Originally sacred temple objects, **Chola bronzes** are the only art form from Tamil Nadu to have penetrated the world art market. The most memorable bronze icons are the **Natarajas**, or dancing Shivas. The image of Shiva, standing on one leg, encircled by flames, with wild locks caught in mid-motion, has become almost as recognizably Indian as the Taj Mahal.

The principal icons of a temple are usually stationary and made of stone. Frequently, however, ceremonies require an image of the god to be led in procession outside the inner sanctum, and even through the streets. According to the canonical texts known as *Agamas*, these moving images should be made of metal. Indian bronzes are made by the **cire-perdu ("lost wax")** process, known as *madhuchchishtavidhana* in Sanskrit. Three layers of clay mixed with burned grain husks, salt and ground cotton are applied to a figure crafted in beeswax, with a stem left protruding at each end. When that is heated, the wax melts and flows out, creating a hollow mould into which molten metal – a rich five-metal alloy (*panchaloha*) of copper, silver, gold, brass and lead – can be poured through the stems. After the metal has cooled, the clay shell is destroyed, and the stems filed off, leaving a unique completed figure, which the caster-artist, or *sthapathi*, remodels to remove blemishes and add delicate detail.

Knowledge of bronze-casting in India goes back at least as far as the Indus Valley Civilization (2500–1500 BC), and the famous **"Dancing Girl"** from Mohenjo Daro. The earliest produced in the south was made by the Andhras, whose techniques were continued by the Pallavas, the immediate antecedents of the Cholas. The few surviving **Pallava** bronzes show a sophisticated handling of the form; figures are characterized by broad shoulders, thick-set features and an overall simplicity that suggests all the detail was completed at the wax stage. The finest bronzes of all are from the **Chola** period, in the late ninth to the early eleventh century. As the Cholas were predominantly Shaivite, Nataraja, Shiva and his consort Parvati (frequently in a family group with son Skanda) and the 63 Nayanmar poet-saints are the most popular subjects. Chola bronzes display more detail than their predecessors. Human figures are invariably slim-waisted and elegant, with the male form robust and muscular and the female graceful and delicate.

The design, iconography and proportions of each figure are governed by the strict rules laid down in the **shilpa shastras**, which draw no real distinction between art, science and religion. Measurement always begins with the proportions of the artist's own hand and the image's resultant face-length as the basic unit. Then follows a scheme which is allied to the equally scientific rules applied to classical music, and specifically *tala* or rhythm. Human figures total eight face-lengths, eight being the most basic of rhythmic measures. Figures of deities are *nava-tala*, nine face-lengths.

Those bronzes produced by the few artists practising today invariably follow the Chola model; the chief centre is now **Swamimalai** (see p.1139). Original Chola bronzes are kept in many Tamil temples, but as the interiors are often dark it's not always possible to see them properly. Important **public collections** include the Nayak Durbar Hall Art Museum at Thanjavur (see opposite), the Government State Museum at Chennai (see p.1106) and the National Museum, New Delhi (see p.118). Those interested in shopping for bronzes and other handicrafts should check out the Chola Art Galerie (☎04362/277355), a two-minute walk south of the palace entrance at 78/79 East Main St.

Saraswati Mahal Library museum

The **Saraswati Mahal Library** holds one of the most important oriental manuscript collections in India, used by scholars from all over the world. The library is closed to the general public, but a small **museum** (free) displays a bizarre array of books and pictures from the collection. Among the palm-leaf manuscripts is a calligrapher's *tour de force* in the form of a visual mantra, where each letter in the inscription "Shiva" comprises the god's name repeated in microscopically small handwriting. Most of the Maratha manuscripts, produced from the end of the seventeenth century, are on paper; they include a superbly illustrated edition of the Mahabharata. Sadists will be delighted to see the library managed to hang on to their copy of the explicitly illustrated **Punishments in China**, published in 1804. Next to it, full rein is given to the imagination of French artist **Charles Le Brun** (1619–90), in a series of pictures on the subject of physiognomy. Animals such as the horse, bullock, wolf, bear, rabbit and camel are drawn in painstaking care above a series of human faces which bear an uncanny, if unlikely, resemblance to them. You can buy postcards of this scientific study and exhibits from the other palace museums in the **shop** next door.

Thanjavur Art Gallery

A magnificent collection of **Chola bronzes** – the finest of them from the Tiruvengadu hoard, unearthed in the 1950s – fills the **Thanjavur Art Gallery** (Rs20 [Rs5], camera or video camera Rs30), a high-ceilinged audience hall with massive pillars, dating from 1600. The elegance of the figures and delicacy of detail are unsurpassed. A tenth-century statue of Kannappa Nayannar (#174), a hunter-devotee, shows minutiae right down to his embroidered clothing, fingernails and the fine lines on his fingers. The oldest bronze, four cases left of the main doorway (#58), shows Vinadhra Dakshinamurti ("south-facing Shiva") who, with a deer on one left hand, would have originally been playing the *vina* – the musical instrument has long since gone. However, the undisputed masterpiece of the collection shows Shiva as Lord of the Animals (#86), sensuously depicted in a skimpy loin cloth, with a turban made of snakes. Next to him stands an equally stunning Parvati, his consort (#87), but the cream of the female figures, a seated, half-reclining Parvati (#97), is displayed on the opposite side of the hall.

Eating and drinking

For **food**, there's the usual crop of "meals" canteens dotted around town, but only a couple of non-veg places apart from the swish upmarket hotel restaurants.

Annam *Pandiyar Residency* hotel, 14 Kutchery Rd. Small, inexpensive and impeccably clean veg restaurant that's recommended for its cut-above-the-competition lunchtime thalis (Rs30), and evening south Indian snacks (especially the delicious cashew uttapams).

King's *Yagappa*, Trichy Rd. Seven kinds of beer are served in the usual dimly lit room, or on the "lawn" (read: "sandy back yard"), where decor includes stuffed lizards and plastic flowers in fish tanks. They also serve tasty chicken and pakora snacks for Rs40–60.

Meenakshi Bhavan Near corner of Gandhiji and Kutchery roads. Spotless veg restaurant serving excellent *dosas* and other, less common south Indian vegetarian snacks, such as *adai*. You can eat well for Rs20–40.

New Thewar Train Station Rd. Very clean place with an a/c hall, serving a wide range of veg and non-veg curries, as well as some noodle dishes for Rs40–80.

Sathar's Gandhiji Rd. This is the town's most popular non-veg restaurant, and serves a decent variety of chicken dishes. Seating for the predominantly male clientele is downstairs, or on a covered terrace. Dishes are Rs60–80.

Thillana *Sangam*, Trichy Rd. Swish multi-cuisine restaurant that's renowned for its superb lunchtime south Indian thalis (11am–3pm; Rs105). Evenings feature an extensive à la carte menu (their *chettinad* specialities are superb). Worth a splurge just for the live Carnatic music from 7.30–10pm featuring either *vina*, flute or vocals with percussion. Count on Rs300–400 per head.

Tiruchirapalli (Trichy) and around

TIRUCHIRAPALLI – more commonly referred to as **Trichy** – stands in the plains between the Shevaroy and Palani hills, just under 100km north of Madurai. Dominated by the dramatic Rock Fort, it's a sprawling commercial centre with a modern feel; the town itself holds little attraction, but pilgrims flock through en route to the spectacular **Ranganathaswamy Temple** in **Srirangam**, 6km north.

The precise date of Trichy's foundation is uncertain, but though little early architecture remains, it is clear that between 200 and 1000 AD control of the city passed between the Pallavas and Pandyas. The Chola kings who gained supremacy in the eleventh century embarked upon ambitious building projects, reaching a zenith with the Ranganathaswamy Temple. In the twelfth century, the Cholas were ousted by the Vijayanagar kings of Hampi, who then stood up against Muslim invasions until 1565, when they succumbed to the might of the sultans of the Deccan. Less than fifty years later the Nayaks of Madurai came to power, constructing the fort and firmly establishing Trichy as a trading city. After almost a century of struggle against the French and British, who both sought lands in southeast Tamil Nadu, the town came under British control until it was declared part of Tamil Nadu state in 1947.

Arrival and information

Trichy's **airport**, 8km south of the centre, has daily flights to and from Chennai, several weekly to Thiruvananthapuram and Kozhikode, as well as frequent services to Sri Lanka and the Gulf states. The journey into town, by taxi (Rs200) or bus (#7, #28, #59, #63 or #K1) takes less than half an hour. For airport enquiries and bookings go to Indian Airlines, 4-A Dindigul Rd (℡0431/248 0233), or any agent for Air Deccan and the international airlines.

Trichy's main railway station, **Trichy Junction** – which has given its name to the southern district of town – provides frequent rail links with Chennai, Madurai and the eastern coastline. From here you're within easy reach of most hotels, restaurants and banks, as well as the **bus stands**. There are two stands – **Central** and **State Express** – close to each other, but no fixed rules about where a particular bus will depart from, though **private buses** mainly use the Central stand. State Express buses run frequently to major towns such as Madurai, Kodaikanal and Puducherry, right around the clock. The efficient local city service (#1) that leaves from the platform on Rockins Road, opposite the *Shree Krishna* restaurant, is the most convenient way of getting to the Rock Fort, the temples and Srirangam. **Auto-rickshaws** are also widely available.

The **tourist office** (Mon–Fri 10am–5.45pm; ℡0431/246 0136), which proffers travel information but no maps, is opposite the Central Bus Stand, just outside the *Tamil Nadu* hotel. The **State Bank of India** on Dindigul Road **exchanges** American Express and Thomas Cook travellers' cheques, although the Highway Forex office (Mon–Sat 10am–6pm) in the plush Jenne Plaza is more efficient. There are several ATMs in the vicinity of the bus stands. Netpark, also in Jenne Plaza, offers **Internet** and there are several other places to get online around the Central Bus Stand, including two branches of iWay.

Accommodation

Trichy has no shortage of **hotels** to accommodate the thousands of pilgrims that visit the town; dozens cluster around the bus stands and offer good value for money. While most are rather characterless lodges, there are a few more

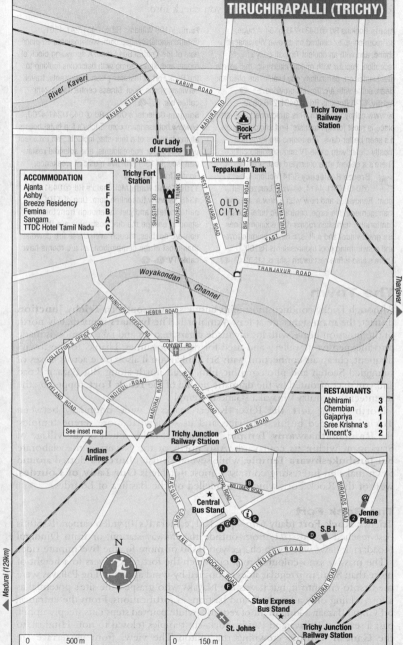

TIRUCHIRAPALLI (TRICHY)

Sri Jambukeshwara Temple, Srirangam & Chennai (315km)

River Kaveri

KABUR ROAD

NAVAB STREET

MADURA RD

Rock Fort

Trichy Town Railway Station

Our Lady of Lourdes

SALAI ROAD

CHINNA BAZAAR

Trichy Fort Station

Teppakulam Tank

MADRAS TRUNK RD

WEST BOULEVARD ROAD

BIG BAZAAR ROAD

OLD CITY

EAST BOULEVARD ROAD

SHASTRI RD

ACCOMMODATION

Ajanta	E
Ashby	F
Breeze Residency	D
Femina	B
Sangam	A
TTDC Hotel Tamil Nadu	C

Woyakondan Channel

THANJAVUR ROAD

Thanjavur ▶

MUNICIPAL OFFICE RD

HEBER ROAD

COLLECTOR'S OFFICE ROAD

CONVENT RD

CLEVELAND ROAD

DINDIGUL ROAD

MADURAI ROAD

RACE COURSE ROAD

See inset map

Indian Airlines

Trichy Junction Railway Station

BYP-ASS ROAD

Madurai (129km) ▼

RESTAURANTS

Abhirami	3
Chembian	A
Gajapriya	1
Sree Krishna's	4
Vincent's	2

0   500 m

Ⓐ

ROYAL ROAD

WILLIAMS ROAD

❶

Ⓑ

BIROADS ROAD

RACQUET COURT LANE

Central Bus Stand ★

ⓘ

Ⓒ

@

Jenne Plaza

❹ @ ❸

❷

S.B.I.

Ⓓ

DINDIGUL ROAD

ROCKINS ROAD

Ⓔ

Ⓕ

N

MADURAI ROAD

State Express Bus Stand ★

St. Johas ✝

Trichy Junction Railway Station

0   150 m

Airport (6km) ▼

comfortable upmarket hotels. Traffic noise is a real problem in this area, so ask for a room at the back of any hotel you check into.

Ajanta Rockins Rd ☎0431/241 5504. A huge, 85-room complex centred on its own Vijayanagar shrine, and with an opulent Tirupati deity in reception. Popular with middle-class pilgrims; rooms (the singles are particularly good value) are plain and clean, some with a/c. Towels provided. ❷–❹

Ashby 17-A Rockins Rd ☎0431/246 0652, ⓦwww.ashbyhotel.com. This atmospheric Raj-era place is most foreign tourists' first choice, though it's seen better days. The rooms are large and mostly clean, with cable TV and mosquito coils. There's a decent little courtyard restaurant. ❸–❹

🏃 **Breeze Residency** 3/14 McDonald's Rd ☎0431/241 4414, ⓦwww.breezehotel .com. Renovated and now with a new name and management, this large, central a/c hotel boasts comfortably furnished rooms (the economy ones are great value) and suites, a nicely painted foyer and a swimming pool (nonresidents Rs100). There's also a fine restaurant (see p.1150). ❹–❽

Femina 109 Williams Rd ☎0431/241 4501, ⓔfeminahotel@yahoo.com. Well-maintained place east of the Central Bus Stand. A sprawling block of rooms and suites, some with balconies looking to the Rock Fort, it features plush restaurants, travel services, shops, pool, fitness centre and a 24hr coffee bar. ❹–❻

Sangam Collector's Office Rd ☎0431/241 4700, ⓦwww.hotelsangam.com. Trichy's top hotel boasts all the facilities of a four-star, including an excellent pool (Rs100 for nonresidents) and splendid restaurant (see p.1150) with live music at weekends. Rooms from $165. ❾

TTDC Tamil Nadu McDonald's Rd ☎0431/241 4346, ⓦwww.ttdconline.com. One of TTDC's better hotels, and just far enough from the bus stand to escape the din. Best value are the non-a/c doubles, though even these are dowdier than most of the competition; all a/c rooms have cable TV. ❸–❹

The Town

Although Trichy conducts most of its business in the southern **Trichy Junction** district, the main sights are at least 4km north. The **bazaars** immediately north of the Junction heave with locally made cigars, textiles and fake diamonds made into inexpensive jewellery and used for dance costumes. Thanks to the town's frequent, cheap air connection with Sri Lanka, you'll also come across boxes of smuggled Scotch and photographic film. Head north along Big Bazaar Road and you're confronted by the dramatic profile of the **Rock Fort**, topped by the seventeenth-century Vinayaka (Ganesh) Temple.

North of the fort, the River Kaveri marks a wide boundary between Trichy's crowded business districts and its somewhat more serene temples; the **Ranganathaswamy Temple** is so large it holds much of the village of Srirangam within its courtyards. Also north of the Kaveri is the elaborate **Sri Jambukeshwara Temple**, while several British **churches** dotted around town make an interesting contrast – most notable is **Our Lady of Lourdes**, west of the Rock Fort, which is modelled on the Basilica of Lourdes.

The Rock Fort

Trichy's **Rock Fort** (daily 6am–8pm; Rs1, camera Rs10, video camera Rs50) is best reached by bus (#1) from outside the railway station, or from Dindigul Road; rickshaws will try to charge you Rs50 or more for the five-minute ride.

The massive sand-coloured rock on which the fort rests towers to a height of more than 80m, its irregular sides smoothed by wind and rain. The Pallavas were the first to cut into it, but it was the Nayaks who grasped the site's potential as a fort, adding only a few walls and bastions as fortifications. From the entrance, off China Bazaar, a long flight of red-and-white painted steps cuts steeply uphill, past a series of Pallava and Pandya rock-cut temples (closed to non-Hindus), to the **Ganesh Temple** crowning the hilltop. The views from its terrace are spectacular, taking in the Ranganathaswamy and Jambukeshwara temples to the north, their *gopuras* rising from a sea of palm trees, and the cubic concrete sprawl of central Trichy to the south.

Sri Ranganathaswamy Temple

The **Sri Ranganathaswamy Temple** at **Srirangam**, 6km north of Trichy Junction, is among the most revered shrines to Vishnu in south India, and also one of the largest and liveliest. Enclosed by seven rectangular walled court-yards and covering more than sixty hectares, it stands on an island defined by a tributary of the River Kaveri. This location symbolizes the transcendence of Vishnu, housed in the sanctuary reclining on the coils of the snake Adisesha, who in legend formed an island for the god, resting on the primor-dial Ocean of Chaos.

Frequent **buses** from Trichy pull in and leave from outside the southern gate. The temple is approached from the south. A gateway topped with an immense and heavily carved *gopura*, plastered and painted in bright pinks, blues and yellows, and completed in the late 1980s, leads to the outermost courtyard, the latest of seven built between the fifth and seventeenth centuries. Most of the present structure dates from the late fourteenth century, when the temple was renovated and enlarged after a disastrous sacking in 1313. The **outer three courtyards**, or *prakaras*, form the hub of the temple community, housing ascetics, priests, musicians and souvenir shops; even vehicles ply the streets within the temple precinct.

At the fourth wall, the entrance to the temple proper, visitors remove footwear and can purchase camera and video camera tickets (Rs50/100) before passing through a high gateway, topped by a magnificent *gopura* and lined with small shrines to teachers, hymn-singers and sages. In earlier days, this **fourth** *prakara* would have formed the outermost limit of the temple, and was the closest members of the lowest castes could get to the sanctuary. It contains some of the finest and oldest buildings of the complex, including a temple to the goddess **Ranganayaki** in the northwest corner where devotees worship before

▲ Details at Sri Ranganathaswamy Temple

approaching Vishnu's shrine. On the eastern side of the *prakara*, the heavily carved "thousand pillared" *kalyan mandapa*, or hall, was constructed in the late Chola period. The pillars of the outstanding **Sheshagiriraya Mandapa**, south of the *kalyan mandapa*, are decorated with rearing steeds and hunters, representing the triumph of good over evil.

To the right of the gateway into the fourth courtyard, a small **museum** (daily 9am–1pm & 2–6pm; Rs1) houses a modest collection of stone and bronze sculptures, and some delicate ivory plaques. For Rs10, you can climb to the roof of the fourth wall from beside the museum and take in the view over the temple rooftops and *gopuras*, which increase in size from the centre outwards. The central dome, crowning the holy sanctuary, is coated in gold and carved with images of Vishnu's incarnations, on each of its four sides.

Inside the gate to the **fifth courtyard** – the final section of the temple open to non-Hindus – is a pillared hall, the **Garuda Mandapa**, carved throughout in typical Nayak style. Maidens, courtly donors and Nayak rulers feature on the pillars that surround the central shrine to Garuda, the man-eagle vehicle of Vishnu.

The dimly lit **innermost (sixth) courtyard**, the most sacred part of the temple, shelters the image of Vishnu in his aspect of Ranganatha, reclining on the serpent Adisesha. The shrine is usually entered from the south, but for one day each year, during the **Vaikuntha Ekadasi festival**, the north portal is opened; those who pass through this "doorway to heaven" can anticipate great merit. Most of the temple's daily festivals take place in this enclosure, beginning each morning with *vina*-playing and hymn–singing as Vishnu is awakened in the presence of a cow and an elephant, and ending just after 9pm with similar ceremonies.

For more on Ranganathaswamy and Tamil Nadu's other great temples, see p.1115.

Eating

To **eat** well in Trichy, you won't have to stray far from the Central Bus Stand, where the town's most popular "meals" joints do a roaring trade all day long.

Abhirami 10 Rockins Rd, opposite Central Bus Stand. Trichy's best-known south Indian restaurant serves up unbeatable value lunchtime "meals" (Rs20), and the standard range of snacks the rest of the day. They also have a fast-food counter where you can get *dosas* and uttapams at any time.

Chembian *Hotel Sangam*, Collector's Office Rd. Excellent restaurant offering a range of delicious Indian dishes, as well as unusually good Western and Chinese cuisine, in an atmospheric, beautifully decorated dining hall. Main dishes around Rs200. Live Carnatic music at weekends.

Gajapriya Royal Rd, on the ground floor of the *Gajapriya* hotel. Non-veg north Indian and noodle dishes are specialities of this small but blissfully cool and clean a/c restaurant. A good place to chill out over coffee.

The Madras *Breeze Residency* 3/14 McDonald's Rd. Worth trying for the excellent-value diner buffet (Rs200), which features a range of mostly Indian and Chinese dishes, with some less common cuisine, such as Mexican, thrown into the mix.

Sree Krishna's 1 Rockins Rd, opposite the Central Bus Stand. Delicious and very filling American or south Indian "set breakfasts", unlimited banana-leaf thalis at lunch time (Rs35) and south Indian specialities in the evenings – all served with a big smile.

Vincent's Dindigul Rd, next to the bakery. An "Oriental" theme restaurant, set back from the road in its own terrace garden, with mock pagodas, concrete bamboo and a multi-cuisine menu that includes tasty chicken tikka and other tandoori dishes. A bit shabby, but it's an escape from the hectic bus-stand area. No alcohol; evenings only.

Madurai

One of the oldest cities in South Asia, **MADURAI**, on the banks of the River Vaigai, has been an important centre of worship and commerce for as long as there has been civilization in south India – indeed, it has long been described as "the Athens of the East". Not surprisingly then, when the Greek ambassador Megasthenes came here in 302 BC, he wrote of its splendour, and described its queen, Pandai, as "a daughter of Herakles". Meanwhile, the Roman geographer Strabo complained at how the city's silk, pearls and spices were draining the imperial coffers of Rome. It was this lucrative trade that enabled the **Pandyan** dynasty to erect the mighty **Meenakshi-Sundareshwarar temple**. Although today surrounded by a sea of modern concrete cubes, the massive *gopuras* of this vast complex, writhing with multicoloured mythological figures and crowned by golden finials, remain the greatest man-made spectacle of the south. Any day of the week no less than 15,000 people pass through its gates, increasing to over 25,000 on Fridays (sacred to the goddess Meenakshi), while the temple's ritual life spills out into the streets in an almost ceaseless round of festivals and processions. The chance to experience sacred ceremonies that have persisted largely unchanged since the time of the ancient Egyptians is one that few travellers pass up.

Madurai's urban and suburban sprawl creates traffic jams to rival India's very worst. Chaos on the narrow, potholed streets is exacerbated by political demonstrations and religious processions, wandering cows – demanding right of way with a peremptory nudge of the haunch – and put-upon pedestrians forced onto the road by ever-increasing numbers of street traders. Open-air kitchens extend from chai shops, where competing *parotta*-wallahs literally drum up custom for their delicious fresh breads with a tattoo of spoon-on-skillet signals. Given the traffic problems, it's just as well that Madurai, with a profusion of markets and intriguing corners, is an absorbing city to walk around.

Some history

Although invariably interwoven with myth, the traceable history and fame of Madurai stretches back well over 2000 years. Numerous natural **caves** in local hills, and boulders often modified by the addition of simple rock-cut beds, were used both in prehistoric times and by ascetics such as the Ajivikas and Jains, who practised withdrawal and penance.

Madurai appears to have been capital of the Pandyan empire without interruption for at least a thousand years. It became a major commercial city, trading with Greece, Rome and China, and *yavanas* (a generic term for foreigners) were frequent visitors to Pandyan seaports. The Tamil epics describe them walking around town with their eyes and mouths wide open with amazement, much as foreign tourists still do when they first arrive. Under the Pandya dynasty, Madurai also became an established seat of Tamil culture, credited with being the site of three **sangams**, "literary academies", said to have lasted 10,000 years and supported some 8000 poets.

The Pandyas' capital fell in the tenth century, when the **Chola** king Parantaka took the city. In the thirteenth century, the Pandyas briefly regained power until the early 1300s, when the notorious **Malik Kafur**, the Delhi Sultanate's "favourite slave", made an unprovoked attack during a plunder-and-desecration tour of the south, and destroyed much of the city. Forewarned of the raid, the Pandya king, Sundara, fled with his immediate family and treasure, leaving his uncle and rival, Vikrama Pandya, to repel Kafur. Nevertheless, the latter returned to Delhi with booty said to consist of "six hundred and twelve elephants,

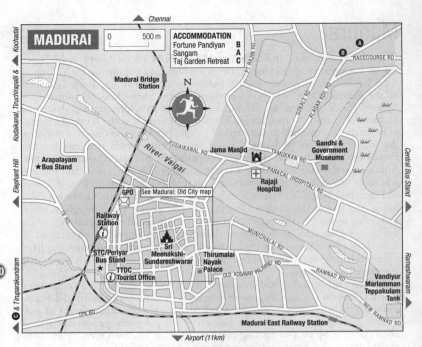

MADURAI

0   500 m

ACCOMMODATION
Fortune Pandiyan   B
Sangam   A
Taj Garden Retreat C

RACECOURSE RD

Madurai Bridge
Station

N

Kodaikanal, Tiruchirapalli & ◄ Kochadai

Elephant Hill ◄

Arapalayam
★ Bus Stand

River Vaigai

KODAIKANAL RD   Jama Masjid

TAMUKKAN RD

Gandhi &
Government
Museums

PANACAL (HOSPITAL) RD

Rajaji
Hospital

GPO   See Madurai: Old City map

Railway
Station
ⓘ

STC/Periyar
Bus Stand   Sri
★   Meenakshi-
TTDC   Sundareshwarar
ⓘ Tourist Office

Thirumalai
Nayak
Palace

OLD KOSAVAR PALINAIL RD

MUNICHALAI RD

RAMNAD RD

Central Bus Stand ►

Rameshwaram ►

Vandiyur
Mariamman
Teppakulam
Tank

TB RD

Ⓒ & Tirupparakundram

TPK RD

NEW RAMNAD RD

Madurai East Railway Station

ninety-six thousand *mans* of gold, several boxes of jewels and pearls and twenty thousand horses".

Shortly after this raid Madurai became an independent Sultanate; in 1364, it joined the Hindu **Vijayanagar** empire, ruled from Vijayanagar/Hampi and administered by governors, the **Nayaks**. In 1565, the Nayaks asserted their own independence. Under their supervision and patronage, Madurai enjoyed a renaissance, being rebuilt on the pattern of a lotus centring on the Meenakshi Temple. Part of the palace of the most illustrious of the Nayaks, **Thirumalai** (1623–55), survives today. The city remained under Nayak control until the mid-eighteenth century when the **British** gradually took over. A hundred years later the British de-fortified Madurai, filling its moat to create the four Veli streets that today mark the boundary of the old city.

Arrival and information

Madurai's small domestic **airport** (℡0452/269 0433), 12km south of the centre, is served by flights to and from Chennai, Mumbai and Bengaluru (Bangalore). Theoretically, you should be able to get information at the **Government of Tamil Nadu tourist information centre** booth by the exit, but it's not always open to meet flights. There's also a bookshop and a branch of Indian Bank. **Taxis** charge fixed rates of around Rs200 for journeys to within the city. City Bus #10A leaves frequently from near the exit and will drop you at Periyar Bus Stand in town.

Arriving in Madurai by **bus**, you come in at one of two stands. The **Central Bus Stand** is 7km from the centre on the east side of the river: it's connected to the centre by, among others, the dedicated city buses #700 and #75. Central is the arrival point of all services except those from towns in the west, including

Kodaikanal and Coimbatore, and Kerala, which terminate at the **Arapalayam Bus Stand** in the northwest, about 2km from the railway station. In the centre, only local city buses operate from either **STC Bus Stand**, or **Periyar stand** next door. Both are on West Veli Street in the west of the old city, and are very close to the railway station and most accommodation. In the main hall of the **railway station** itself you'll find a very helpful branch of the **Tourism Department information centre** (daily 6.30am–8.30pm). The **reservations office** is in a new building to the left of the main hall. There's a small veg **canteen** on Platform 1, and a **pre-paid auto-rickshaw and taxi booth** outside the main entrance, open to coincide with train arrivals.

The **TTDC** tourist office, on West Veli Street (Mon–Fri 10am–5.45pm, plus Sat 10am–1pm during festivals; ☎0452/233 4757), is useful for general information and maps, and can provide information on **car rental and approved guides**. If you want a **taxi** to see the outlying sights, head to the rank at the main railway station, which abides by government set rates; a five-hour city tour will cost Rs600–700.

Madurai's **GPO** is at the corner of West Veli and North Veli streets (Mon–Sat 8am–7.30pm, Sun & hols 9am–4.30pm; Speedpost 10am–7pm). **Internet access** is widely available: try Net Tower, next to the *Hotel International*, Friends, just round the corner at 13/8 Kaka Thoppu St, or the two branches of iWay on West Perumal Maistry Street; both offer Netphone connections.

The best place to **change money** is Tradewings, almost opposite the post office at 168 North Veli St (Mon–Sat 9am–6.30pm). The State Bank of India is at 6 West Veli St, and there are several 24hr ATMs in town, including those at the Canara Bank on West Perumal Maistry Street and the UTI Bank on Station Road. **Bike rental** at low rates is available at SV, West Tower Street, near the west entrance to the temple, or the stall on West Veli Street, opposite the *Tamil Nadu* hotel.

Accommodation

Madurai has a wide range of **accommodation** to cater for the flocks of pilgrims and tourists, from rock-bottom lodges to good, clean mid-range places, with a cluster of hotels on **West Perumal Maistry Street**. Upmarket options lie a few kilometres out of the town centre, north of the Vaigai.

Unless otherwise stated, the hotels listed below are marked on the Old City map (p.1156).

Aarathy 9 Perumal Koil, off South Masi St ☎0452/233 1571, ☎233 6343. Great location overlooking the Kundalagar Temple, so often booked up. All rooms have TV, others have a/c and a balcony – some are better than others, so ask to see a range before checking in. There's an excellent a/c restaurant which extends out into the courtyard where the temple elephant is led through each morning and afternoon. ❸–❹

Fortune Pandyan Racecourse Rd, north of the river (see Madurai map opposite) ☎0452/253 7090, ⓦwww.fortunepandiyanhotel.com. Smart, centrally a/c hotel with large comfortable rooms, all with TV and lavishly decorated with period-style furnishings. It's quiet and relaxed, being some way out of town, and there's a good restaurant, bar, exchange facilities and a travel agency. ❽–❾

International 46/80 West Perumal Maistry St ☎0452/537 7463. Recently renovated lodge with lackadaisical service, but the rooms (some a/c) are decent and all have cable TV. ❷–❹

New College House 2 Town Hall Rd ☎0452/234 2971, ℮info@newcollegehouse.com. This huge, maze-like place has more than 200 rooms (a few with a/c, and one of the town's best "meals" canteens on the ground floor (see opposite). The very cheapest rooms are grubby, but there are likely to be vacancies here when everywhere else is full. ❷–❹

Padmam 1 Perumal Tank West St ☎0452/234 0702, ℮hotelpadmam@hotmail.com. Clean, comfortable and modern hotel, centrally located and with a rooftop restaurant. The views from the front-side rooms, overlooking the ruined Perumal tank, are worth paying extra for. ❹

Prem Nivas 102 West Perumal Maistry St ⓣ0452/234 2532, ⓔpremnivas@eth.net. From the outside this place looks a lot swankier than it is, but the spacious attached rooms (some with a/c) make it among the best deals in the city; singles are especially good value. ❸–❹

Rathna Residency 109 West Perumal Maistry St ⓣ0452/537 4444, ⓦwww.hotelrathnaresidency .com. Standard lower mid-range hotel with decent, clean a/c and non-a/c rooms (the latter are better value), plus two restaurants, one on the rooftop. ❸–❹

Sangam Alagar Koil Rd (see main Madurai map, p.1152) ⓣ0452/253 7531, ⓦwww.hotelsangam .com. Situated in its own grounds on the northern outskirts of town, this plush, centrally a/c hotel has very comfortable rooms (from $165), 24hr room service, bar, currency exchange, swimming pool and pleasant gardens. ❾

🏃 **Sree Devi** 20 West Avani Moola St ⓣ0452/234 7431. Excellent-value, spotless non-a/c doubles right next to the temple mean this place is always filled with foreigners. For a romantic splurge, splash out on their "deluxe" a/c rooftop room, which has matchless views over the western *gopura*. No restaurant, but they will order in food and beer for you. ❶–❹

Supreme 110 West Perumal Maistry St ⓣ0452/234 3151, ⓦwww.supremehotels.com. A large, swish and central hotel, with a great rooftop restaurant, an a/c restaurant on the ground floor and a choice of comfortable a/c and non-a/c rooms in a seven-storey block; the more expensive have temple views. It's a little overpriced, but has good facilities including a 24hr forex desk, Internet access and travel counter. Book in advance. ❹–❺

🏃 **Taj Garden Retreat** 40 TPK Rd, Pasumalai Hills (see main Madurai map, p.1152) ⓣ0452/260 1020, ⓦwww.tajhotels.com. Madurai's most exclusive hotel, in a beautifully refurbished colonial house set within 25 acres of manicured gardens in the hills overlooking the city and temples, albeit 6km out. Of the three categories of room, the superior ones in the old colonial building are the most atmospheric, but the deluxe have the best views. Facilities include a gourmet restaurant, swimming pool, tennis court and bar. Rooms start at $150. ❾

TTDC Hotel Tamil Nadu I West Veli St ⓣ0452/233 7471, ⓦwww.ttdconline.com. Somewhat out on a limb, away from the atmosphere of the temples and the bazaar, but with spacious rooms (some a/c) overlooking a leafy courtyard. The cheapest rooms are especially good value. ❷–❹

The City

Although considerably enlarged and extended over the years, the overall layout of Madurai's **old city**, south of the River Vaigai, has remained largely unchanged since the first centuries AD, comprising a series of concentric squares centred on the massive **Meenakshi Temple**. Aligned with the cardinal points, the street plan forms a giant mandala, or magical diagram, whose sacred properties are believed to be activated during mass circumambulations of the central temple, always conducted in a clockwise direction.

North of the river, Madurai becomes markedly more mundane and irregular. You're only likely to cross the Vaigai to reach the city's more expensive hotels or the Gandhi Museum.

Sri Meenakshi-Sundareshwarar Temple

Enclosed by a roughly rectangular six-metre-high wall, in the manner of a fortified palace, the **Sri Meenakshi-Sundareshwarar Temple** (daily 6am–12.30pm & 4–9.30pm; cameras Rs30, no video cameras) is one of the largest temple complexes in India. Much of it was constructed during the Nayak period between the sixteenth and eighteenth centuries, but certain parts are very much older. The principal shrines (closed to non-Hindus) are those to Sundareshwar (Shiva) and his consort Meenakshi (a form of Parvati); unusually, the goddess takes precedence and is always worshipped first.

For the first-time visitor, confronted with a confusing maze of shrines, sculptures and colonnades, and unaware of the logic employed in their arrangement, it's very easy to get disorientated. However, if you're not in a hurry, this should not deter you. Quite apart from the estimated 33,000 sculptures to arrest your attention, the life of the temple is absolutely absorbing, and many visitors find themselves drawn back to experience it all at different times of the day. Be it the endless round of puja ceremonies, loud *nagaswaram* and *tavil* music, weddings, brahmin boys under religious instruction in the *Vedas*, the prostrations of countless devotees, the glittering market stalls inside the east entrance or, best of all, a festival procession, something is always going on to make this one of the most compelling places in Tamil Nadu.

Approximately fifty priests work in the temple, and live in houses close to the north entrance. They are easily identified – each wears a white *dhoti* (*veshti* in Tamil) tied between the legs; on top of this, around the waist, is a second, coloured cloth, usually of silk. Folded into the cloth, a small bag contains holy white ash. The bare-chested priests invariably carry a small towel over the shoulder. Most wear earrings and necklaces including *rudraksha* beads, sacred to Shiva. As Shaivite priests, they place three horizontal stripes of white ash on the forehead, arms, shoulders and chest and a red powder dot, sacred to the goddess, above the bridge of the nose. Most also wear their long hair tied into a knot, with the forehead shaved. Inside the temple they also carry brass trays holding offerings of camphor and ash.

Madurai takes the **gopura**, so prominent in other southern temples, to its ultimate extreme. The entire complex has no less than twelve such towers; set into the outer walls, the four largest reach a height of around 46m, and are visible for miles outside the city. Each is covered with a profusion of gaily painted stucco gods and demons, with the occasional live monkey scampering and chattering among the divine images. After a referendum in the 1950s, the

Meenakshi the fish-eyed goddess

The goddess **Meenakshi** of Madurai emerged from the flames of a sacrificial fire as a three-year-old child, in answer to the Pandyan king Malayadvaja's prayer for a son. The king, not only surprised to see a female, was also horrified that she had three breasts. In every other respect, she was beautiful, as her name, Meenakshi ("fish-eyed"), suggests – fish-shaped eyes are classic images of desirability in Indian love poetry. Dispelling his concern, a mysterious voice told the king that Meenakshi would lose the third breast on meeting her future husband.

In the absence of a son, the adult Meenakshi succeeded her father as Pandyan monarch. With the aim of world domination, she then embarked on a series of successful battles, culminating in the defeat of Shiva's armies at the god's Himalayan abode, Mount Kailash. Shiva then appeared at the battlefield; on seeing him, Meenakshi immediately lost her third breast. Fulfilling the prophecy, Shiva and Meenakshi travelled to Madurai, where they were married. The two then assumed a dual role, firstly as king and queen of the Pandya kingdom, with Shiva assuming the title Sundara Pandya, and secondly as the presiding deities of the Madurai temple, into which they subsequently disappeared.

Their shrines in Madurai are today the focal point of a hugely popular fertility cult; centred on the gods' coupling, temple priests maintain that it ensures the preservation and regeneration of the Universe. Each night, the pair are placed in Sundareshwarar's bedchamber together, but not before Meenakshi's nose ring is carefully removed so that it won't cut her husband in the heat of passion. Their celestial lovemaking is consistently earth-moving enough to ensure that Sundareshwarar remains completely faithful to his consort (exceptional for the notoriously promiscuous Shiva). Nevertheless, this fidelity is never taken for granted, and has to be ritually tested each year when the beautiful goddess Cellattamman is brought to Sundareshwarar "to have her powers renewed". After she is spurned, she flies into a fury that can only be placated with the sacrifice of a buffalo – one among the dozens of arcane ceremonies that make up Madurai's round of temple rituals.

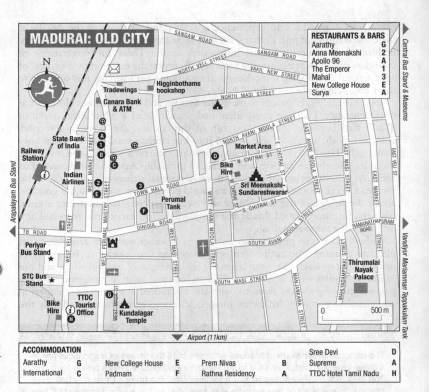

RESTAURANTS & BARS

Aarathy	G
Anna Meenakshi	2
Apollo 96	A
The Emperor	1
Mahal	3
New College House	E
Surya	A

Central Bus Stand & Museums

Vandiyur Mariamman Teppakulam Tank

Arapalayam Bus Stand

N

SANGAM ROAD

SANGAM ROAD

NORTH VELI STREET

VAKIL NEW STREET

NORTH MASI STREET

Higginbothams bookshop

Tradewings

Canara Bank & ATM

NORTH AVANI MOOLA STREET

State Bank of India

Railway Station

Indian Airlines

Market Area

N CHITRAI ST

E CHITRAI ST

Bike Hire

Sri Meenakshi-Sundareshwarar

EAST AVANI MOOLA STREET

EAST MASI STREET

EAST MARKET

EAST VELI ST

TOWN HALL ROAD

S CHITRAI ST

Perumal Tank

WEST CHITRAI ST

DINIGUL ROAD

WEST PERUMAL MAISTRY STREET

WEST AVANI MOOLA STREET

SOUTH AVANI MOOLA STREET

RAMANATHAPURAM ROAD

TB ROAD

Periyar Bus Stand

STC Bus Stand

WEST VELI STREET

WEST MASI STREET

SOUTH MASI STREET

Thirumalai Nayak Palace

MAHILYADAPOKKI STREET

MANJANKARA STREET

Bike Hire

TTDC Tourist Office

WEST MADURAI ST

Kundalagar Temple

0   500 m

▼ Airport (11km)

ACCOMMODATION

Aarathy	G	New College House	E	Prem Nivas	B	Sree Devi	D
International	C	Padmam	F	Rathna Residency	A	Supreme	A
						TTDC Hotel Tamil Nadu	H

gopuras, which had become monochrome and dilapidated, were repainted in the vivid greens, blues, and bright reds you can see today. It is sometimes possible, for a small fee, to climb the southern and tallest tower, to enjoy superb views over the town; for permission, enquire with the guards at one of the gateways.

The most popular **entrance** is on the east side, which leads directly to the Shiva shrine; there is another entrance nearby, through a towerless gate, which leads to the adjacent Meenakshi shrine deep inside. In the **Ashta Shakti Mandapa** ("Eight Goddesses Hallway"), a market sells puja offerings and souvenirs, from fat garlands to sky-blue plaster deities. Sculpted pillars illustrate different aspects of the goddess Shakti, and Shiva's sixty-four miracles at Madurai. Behind this hall, to the south, are stables for elephants and camels.

If you continue straight on from here, cross East Ati Street, and go through the seven-storey **Chitrai gopura**, you enter a passageway leading to the eastern end of the **Pottamarai Kulam** ("Golden Lotus Tank"), where Indra bathed before worshipping the *shivalingam*. From the east side of the tank you can see the glistening gold of the Meenakshi and Sundareshwar *vimana* towers. Steps lead down to the water from the surrounding colonnades, and in the centre stands a brass lamp column. People bathe here, prior to entering the inner shrines, or just sit, gossip and rest on the steps.

The ceiling paintings in the corridors are modern, but Nayak murals around the tank illustrate scenes from the *Gurur Vilayadal Puranam*, which describes Shiva's Madurai miracles. Of the two figures located halfway towards the Meenakshi shrine on the north side, one is the eighth-century king Kulashekhara Pandyan, said to have founded the temple; opposite him is a wealthy merchant patron.

On the west side of the tank is the entrance to the **Meenakshi shrine** (closed to non-Hindus), popularly known as **Amman Koyil**, literally the "mother temple". The immoveable green stone image of the goddess is contained within two further enclosures that form two ambulatories. Facing Meenakshi, just past the first entrance and in front of the sanctum sanctorum, stands Shiva's bull-vehicle, Nandi. At around 9pm, the moveable images of the god and goddess are carried to the **bed chamber**. Here the final puja ceremony of the day, the **lalipuja**, is performed, when for thirty minutes or so the priests sing lullabies (*lali*), before closing the temple for the night

The corridor outside Meenakshi's shrine is known as the **Kilikkutu Mandapa** ("Parrot Cage Hallway"). Parrots used to be kept just south of the shrine as offerings to Meenakshi, a practice discontinued in the mid-1980s as the birds suffered due to "lack of maintenance". Sundareshwar and Meenakshi are brought every Friday (6–7pm) to the sixteenth-century **Oonjal Mandapa** further along, where they are placed on a swing (*oonjal*) and serenaded by members of a special caste, the Oduvars. The black and gold, almost fairground-like decoration of the *mandapa* dates from 1985.

Across the corridor, the small **Rani Mangammal Mandapa**, next to the tank, has a detailed eighteenth-century ceiling painting of the marriage of Meenakshi and Sundareshwar, surrounded by lions and elephants against a blue background. Sculptures in the hallway portray characters such as the warring monkey kings from the Ramayana, the brothers Sugriva (Sukreeva) and Bali (Vahli), and the indomitable Pandava prince, Bhima, from the Mahabharata, who was so strong that he uprooted a tree to use as a club.

Walking back north, past the Meenakshi shrine, through a towered entrance, leads you to the area of the Sundareshwarar shrine. Just inside, is the huge monolithic figure of Ganesh, **Mukkuruni Vinayaka**, believed to have been found during the excavation of the Mariamman Teppakulam tank. Chubby Ganesh is well-known for his love of sweets, and during his annual **Vinayaka Chaturthi festival** (Sept), a special *prasad* (gift offering of food) is concocted from ingredients including 300 kilos of rice, 10 kilos of sugar and 110 coconuts.

Around a corner, a small image of the monkey god **Hanuman**, covered with ghee and red powder, stands on a pillar. Devotees take a little with their finger for a *tilak*, to mark the forehead. A figure of Nandi and two gold-plated copper flagstaffs face the entrance to the **Sundareshwar shrine** (closed to non-Hindus). From here, outsiders can just about see the *shivalingam* beyond the blue-and-red neon "Om" sign (in Tamil).

Causing a certain amount of fun, north of the flagstaffs are figures of Shiva and Kali in the throes of a dance competition. A stall nearby sells tiny **butter balls** from a bowl of water, which visitors throw at the god and goddess "to cool them down". If you leave through the gateway here, on the east, you'll find in the northeast corner the fifteenth-century **Ayirakkal Mandapa**, or thousand-pillared hall, now transformed into the temple's **Art Museum** (daily 10am–5.30pm; Rs5, camera Rs25). In some ways the current function of this gigantic space as a gallery has detracted from its beauty, as the numerous screens and dusty educational displays prevent clear unobstructed view. However, there's a fine, if rather dishevelled, collection of wood, copper, bronze and stone sculpture, and an original nine-metre-high teak temple door. Throughout the hall, large sculptures of strange mythical creatures and cosmic deities rear out at you from the broad stone pillars, some of which have startlingly metallic-like musical tones when tapped.

For more on the temples of Tamil Nadu, see p.1115.

Old Madurai is crowded with **textile and tailors' shops**, particularly in West Veli, Avani Moola and Chitrai streets, and Town Hall Road. At the tailors' shops near the temple, locally produced textiles are generally good value, and tailors pride themselves on turning out faithful copies of favourite clothes in a matter of hours. Unfortunately, most of the **souvenir shops** in the vicinity of the temple employ touts who invite tourists to "come and enjoy temple view free of charge only looking". It's worth doing once as the views from the shops are impressive, but getting back down to street level without making a purchase at hugely inflated prices is quite a challenge.

South Avani Moola Street is packed with **jewellery**, particularly gold shops, and Madurai is also a great place to pick up south Indian **crafts**. Among the best outlets are All India Handicrafts Emporium, 39–41 Town Hall Rd; Co-optex, West Tower Street, and Pandiyan Co-op Supermarket, Palace Road, for handwoven textiles; and Surabhi, West Veli Street, for Keralan handicrafts. For souvenirs such as sandalwood, temple models, carved boxes and oil lamps head for Poompuhar, 12 West Veli St, or Tamilnad Gandhi Smarak Nidhi Khadi Gramodyog Bhavan, West Veli Street, opposite the railway station, which sells crafts, oil lamps, Meenakshi sculptures and *khadi* cloth and shirts.

The old purpose-built, wooden-pillared fruit and vegetable market, between North Chitrai and North Avani Moola streets, provides a slice of Madurai life that doesn't seem to have changed for centuries. Beyond it, on the first floor of the concrete building at the back, the **flower market** (24hr) is a riot of colour and fragrance; weighing scales spill over with tiny white petals and plump pink garlands hang in rows. A variety of flowers such as orange, yellow or white marigolds (*samandi*), pink jasmine (*arelli*), tiny purple spherical *vanameli* and holy *tulsi* plants come from hill areas such as Kodaikanal and Kumili. These are bought in bulk and distributed for use in temples, or to wear in the hair; some are made into elaborate wedding garlands (*kalyanam mala*). The very friendly traders will show you each and every flower, and if you've got a camera will more than likely expect to be recorded for posterity.

Vandiyur Mariamman Teppakulam tank and the floating festival

At one time, the huge **Vandiyur Mariamman Teppakulam** tank in the southeast of town (bus #4 or #4A; 15min) was full with a constant supply of water, flowing via underground channels from the Vaigai. Nowadays, thanks to a number of accidents, it is only filled during the spectacular Teppam **floating festival** (Jan/Feb), when pilgrims take boats out to the goddess shrine in the centre. Before their marriage ceremony, Shiva and Meenakshi are brought in procession to the tank, where they are floated on a raft beautifully decorated with lights, which devotees pull by ropes three times, encircling the shrine. The boat trip is believed to be the overture to a seduction that reaches its passionate conclusion later that night in the temple. This traditionally makes the Teppam the most auspicious time of year for young couples to get married.

During the rest of the year the tank and the central shrine remain empty. Accessible by steps, the tank is most often used as an impromptu cricket green, and the shade of the nearby trees makes a popular gathering place. Tradition states that the huge image of Ganesh, Mukkuruni Vinayaka, in the Meenakshi Temple, was uncovered here when the area was originally excavated to provide bricks for the Thirumalai Nayak Palace.

Thirumalai Nayak Palace

Roughly a quarter survives of the seventeenth-century **Thirumalai Nayak Palace** (daily 9am–1pm & 2–5pm; Rs50 [Rs10]; includes Palace Museum), 1.5km southeast of the Meenakshi Temple. Much of it was dismantled by Thirumalai's grandson, Chockkanatha Nayak, and used for a new palace at Tiruchirapalli; what remains today was renovated in 1858 by the governor of Chennai, Lord Napier, and again in 1971 for the Tamil World Conference. The palace originally consisted of two residential sections, plus a theatre, private temple, harem, royal bandstand, armoury and gardens.

The surviving building, the **Swargavilasa** ('Heavenly Pavilion"), is a rectangular courtyard, flanked by 18m-tall colonnades. As well as occasional live performances of music and dance, the Tourism Department arranges a nightly **Sound-and-Light Show** (in English 6.45–7.30pm; Rs10), which relates the story of the Tamil epic, *Shilipaddikaram*, and the history of the Nayaks. Some find the spectacle edifying, and others soporific – especially when the quality of the tape is poor. In an adjoining hall, the **Palace Museum** (same hours as the palace) includes unlabelled Pandyan, Jain and Buddhist sculpture, terracottas and an eighteenth-century print showing the palace in a dilapidated state.

Tamukkam Palace: the Gandhi and Government museums

Across the Vaigai, 5km northeast of the centre near the Central Telegraph Office (bus #1, #2, #11, #17 or #24; 20min), stands Tamukkam, the seventeenth-century multi-pillared and arched palace of Queen Rani Mangammal. Built to accommodate such regal entertainment as elephant fights, Tamukkam was taken over by the British, used as a courthouse and collector's office, and in 1955 became home to the Gandhi and Government museums. The **Gandhi Memorial Museum** (daily 10am–1pm & 2–5.30pm; free) charts the history of India since the landing of the first Europeans, viewed in terms of the freedom struggle. Generally the perspective is national, but where appropriate, reference is made to the role played by Tamils. Wholeheartedly critical of the British, it states its case clearly and simply, quoting the condemnation by Englishman John Sullivan of his fellow countrymen's insulting treatment of Indians. One chilling artefact, kept in a room painted black, is the bloodstained *dhoti* the Mahatma was wearing when he was assassinated. Next door to the museum, the **Gandhi Memorial Museum Library** (daily except Wed 10am–1pm & 2–5.30pm; free) houses a reference collection, open to all, of 15,000 books, periodicals, letters and microfilms of material by and about Gandhi.

It's not really worth paying the high entrance fee to visit the small **Government Museum** (daily 9am–5pm; Rs100 [Rs5]) opposite. Displays include stone and bronze sculptures, musical instruments, paintings (including examples of Tanjore and Kangra styles) and folk art such as painted terracotta animals, festival costumes and hobbyhorses. There's also a collection of shadow puppets, said to have originated in the Thanjavur area and probably exported to Southeast Asia during the Chola period. A small house in which **Gandhi** once lived stands in a garden within the compound.

Eating

As with accommodation, the range of **places to eat** in Madurai is gratifyingly wide, and standards are generally high, whether you're eating at one of the many utilitarian-looking "meals" places around the temple, or in an upscale hotel – though to make the most of Madurai's exotic skyline you'll have to seek out a **rooftop restaurant**. When the afternoon heat gets too much, head for one of the **juice bars** dotted around the centre, where you can order freshly squeezed pomegranate, pineapple, carrot or orange juice for around Rs15 per glass. Madurai is hardly a drinking town, but most pricier hotels have a bar, the most entertaining being *Apollo 96*, a sci-fi-themed extravaganza at the *Supreme Hotel* (see p.1154).

All of the places below are marked on the Old City map (p.1152).

Restaurants

Aarathy *Aarathy Hotel*, 9 Perumalkoil, West Mada St. Tasty tiffin (*dosas*, *iddlis* and hot *wada sambar*), served on low tables in a hotel forecourt, where the temple elephant turns up twice daily. For more filling, surprisingly inexpensive and excellent lunch-time thalis (Rs40), step into their blissfully cool a/c restaurant.

 Anna Meenakshi West Perumal Maistry St. Arguably the most hygienic and best-value food in the centre, this upmarket branch of *New College House*'s more traditional canteen (see below) serves top tiffin to a discerning, strictly vegetarian clientele. Absolutely delicious coconut or lemon "rice meals" and cheap banana-leaf thalis are served daily, and you can fill up for under Rs50.

The Emperor *Chentoor Hotel*, 106 West Perumal Maistry St. Not as stunning a view as at the *Surya*, but the multi-cuisine food is better and includes some non-veg dishes, such as delicious sizzlers. Rs80–150.

Mahal 21 Town Hall Rd. Nicely decorated street-level restaurant serving small but tasty portions of fish and chips, plus tandoori items and south Indian veg snacks for Rs40–80.

New College House *New College House* hotel, 2 Town Hall Rd. Huge meals-cum-tiffin hall in this old-style hotel. Lunch time, when huge piles of Rs30 pure-veg food are served on banana leaves to long rows of locals, is a real deep-south experience; and the coffee's pure Coorg.

Surya *Supreme Hotel*, 110 West Perumal Maistry St. One of Madurai's most popular rooftop restaurants, with sweeping views of the city and temple. Although the pure-veg food is average and service a little lax, it's still a fine venue for a sundowner. Main courses Rs80–120.

Moving on from Madurai

There are regular **flights** to Chennai, with one Indian Airlines service daily going on to Mumbai and another with Paramount Airways flying on to Bengaluru (Bangalore); Jet and Air Deccan also operate to Chennai. To get to the airport, catch a taxi (around Rs200), or take city bus #10A from the Periyar Bus Stand. Indian Airlines' city office is at 7-A West Veli St, near the post office (℡0452/234 1234); Jet Airways, Air Deccan and Paramount Airways all have offices at the airport.

Bus services to Chennai, Bengaluru (Bangalore), Mysore, Chengalpattu, Chidambaram, Tirupati, Thanjavur, Tiruchirapalli, Kumbakonam, Rameshwaram, Kanyakumari and Thiruvananthapuram (in Kerala) all leave from the **Central Bus Stand**. From the **Arapalayam stand**, buses depart to Coimbatore, Kodaikanal, Kumily (for Periyar Wildlife Sanctuary), and Ernakulam/Kochi via Kottayam. There are no direct services from Madurai to Ooty; change in Coimbatore.

Madurai is on the main broad-gauge **train** line, and is well connected with most major towns and cities in south India. For **timetable** details, ask the Tourism Department Information Centre, to the right of the ticket counters. It's possible to reach the railhead for Kodaikanal by train, but the journey is much faster by express bus. The quickest way to get to **Thiruvananthapuram, Ernakulam** (for Kochi), **Kollam** and **Mettupalayam** (departure point for the Nilgiri Blue Mountain Railway; see p.1174), is to change in **Coimbatore** (see p.1170). The only daily express to Kanyakumari departs at the ungodly hour of 2.10am, so it's better to take the 3pm fast passenger service or go by bus. At the time of writing, the line to Rameshwaram was undergoing gauge conversion and was not due to open until at least the end of 2008.

For journey times and frequencies of all transport out of Madurai, see "Travel details", p.1177.

Destination	Name	No.	Departs	Total time
Bengaluru (Bangalore)	Tuticorin–Mysore Express	#6731	8.05pm	10hr 35min
Chennai	Vaigai Express	#2636	6.45am	7hr 55min
	Pandiyan Express	#2638	8.45pm	9hr
Coimbatore (for Ooty)	Madurai–Coimbatore Express	#6716	10.50pm	6hr 10min
Trichy	Vaigai Express	#2636	6.45am	2hr 20min

Rameshwaram

The sacred island of **RAMESHWARAM**, 163km southeast of Madurai and less than 20km from Sri Lanka across the Gulf of Mannar is, along with Madurai, south India's most important pilgrimage site. Hindus tend to be followers of either Vishnu or Shiva but Rameshwaram brings them together, being where the god Rama, an incarnation of Vishnu, worshipped Shiva in the Ramayana. The **Ramalingeshwara Temple** complex, with its magnificent pillared walkways, is the most famous on the island, but there are several other small temples of interest, such as the **Gandhamadana Parvatam**, sheltering Rama's footprints, and the **Nambunayagi Amman Kali Temple**, frequented for its curative properties. **Danushkodi** ("Rama's Bow") at the eastern end, is where Rama is said to have bathed. The boulders that pepper the sea between here and Sri Lanka, known as "Adam's Bridge", was built by the monkey army so that they could cross over in their search for Rama's wife, Sita after her abduction by Ravana, the demon king of Lanka. The town offers uncommercialized **beaches** (not India's most stunning) where foreigners can unwind or even do a spot of snorkelling.

Rameshwaram, whose streets radiate out from the vast block enclosing the Ramalingeshwara, is always crowded with day-trippers and ragged mendicants who camp outside the Ramalingeshwara and the **Ujainimahamariamman**, the small goddess shore temple. An important part of their pilgrimage is to bathe in the main temple's sacred tanks and in the sea; the narrow strip of beach is shared by groups of bathers, relaxing cows and mantra-reciting *swamis* sitting next to sand lingams. As well as fishing – prawns and lobsters for packaging and export to Japan – shells are a big source of income in the coastal villages.

Ramalingeshwara Temple

The core of the **Ramalingeshwara** (or Ramanathaswamy) **Temple** was built by the Cholas in the twelfth century to house two much-venerated **shiva-lingams** associated with the Ramayana. After rescuing his wife Sita from the clutches of Ravana, Rama was advised to atone for the killing of the demon king – a brahmin – by worshipping Shiva. Rama's monkey lieutenant, Hanuman, was despatched to the Himalayas to fetch a *shivalingam*, but when he failed to return by the appointed day, Sita fashioned a lingam from sand (the *Ramanathalingam*) so the ceremony could proceed. Hanuman eventually showed up with his lingam and in order to assuage the monkey's guilt Rama decreed that in future, of the two, Hanuman's should be worshipped first. The lingams are now housed in the inner section of the Ramalingeshwara, not usually open to non-Hindus. Much of what can be visited dates from the 1600s, when the temple received generous endowments from the Sethupathi rajas of Ramanathapuram.

Ramalingeshwara temple is enclosed by high walls which form a rectangle with huge pyramidal *gopura* entrances on each side. Each gateway leads to a spacious closed ambulatory, flanked to either side by continuous platforms with massive pillars set on their edges. These **corridors** are the most famous attribute of the temple, their extreme length – 205m, with 1212 pillars on the north and south sides – giving a remarkable impression of receding perspective. Delicate scrollwork and brackets of pendant lotuses supported by *yalis*, mythical lion-like beasts, adorn the pillars.

Before entering the inner sections of the temple, pilgrims are expected to bathe at each of the 22 temple **tirthas** (tanks) in the temple – hence the groups of dripping-wet pilgrims, most of them fully clothed, making their way from one tank to the next to be doused in a bucket of water by a temple attendant. Each tank is said to have special benefits: the Rama Vimosana Tirtha provides relief from debt, the Sukreeva Tirtha gives "complete wisdom" and the attainment of *Surya Loka*, the realm of the Sun, and the Draupadi Tirtha ensures long life for women and "the love of their spouses".

Monday is Rama's auspicious day, when the Padilingam puja takes place. **Festivals** of particular importance at the temple include **Mahashivaratri** (ten days during Feb/March), **Brahmotsavam** (ten days during March/April) and **Thirukalyanam** (July/Aug), celebrating the marriage of Shiva to Parvati.

Practicalities

The NH-49, the main road from Madurai, connects Rameshwaram with Mandapam on the mainland via the impressive two-kilometre-long Indira Gandhi Bridge, originally built by the British in 1914 as a railway link, and reopened for road traffic by Rajiv Gandhi in 1988. **Buses** from Madurai, Trichy, Thanjavur, Kanyakumari and Chennai pull in at the bus stand, 2km west of the centre. The railway station, 1km southwest of the centre, is the end of the line for trains from Chennai, Madurai and further afield, but services are suspended until at least late 2008, while the gauge is converted.

Yellow-and-green city bus #1 runs every ten minutes from the bus stand to the main temple; otherwise, **local transport** consists of unmetered cycle and auto-rickshaws. Jeeps are available for rent near the railway station, and bicycles from shops in the four Car streets around the temple.

The main TTDC **tourist office** at the bus stand (daily 10am–5.45pm; ☎04573/221371) gives out information about guides, accommodation and boat trips but opens rather erratically. TTDC also have a counter at the railway station (☎04573/221373), opened to coincide with arriving trains. The **post office** is on Pamban Road, and there are a couple of **Internet** places near the west entrance to the temple.

Accommodation

Apart from the TTDC complex, **accommodation** in Rameshwaram is restricted to basic lodges and very modest hotels, mostly in the Car streets around the temple. The temple authorities have a range of rooms for pilgrims; ask at the Devasthanam Office, East Car Street (☎04573/221223).

Chola Lodge North Car St ☎04573/221307. A basic but adequate lodge in the quietest of the Car streets. Most rooms are non-a/c, and some have TV. ❶–❹

Maharaja's 7 Middle St ☎04573/221271, ⓔhotelmaharajas@sancharnet.com. Located next to the temple's west gate, this place has clean and comfortable rooms with attached bathrooms and TV (some also have a/c), plus temple views from balconies. ❷–❹

Shriram Hotel Island Star 41-A South Car St ☎04573/224172, ⓕ239332. Fair-sized, clean hotel with pleasantly appointed a/c and non-a/c rooms, most with sea views. The non-a/c ones are particularly good value, but the most expensive a/c rooms are a little overpriced. ❷–❹

🏃 **TTDC Hotel Tamil Nadu** Near the beach, 700m northeast of the main temple ☎04573/221277, ⊛www.ttdconline.com. The best option in Rameshwaram, in a pleasant location and

with a bar and restaurant. Comfortable, sea-facing rooms, some a/c; the best ones are actually the cheaper ones in the new block, which have pleasant sitouts. ❸–❺

Venkatesh South Car St ☎04573/221296. Functional and modern three-storey hotel with clean, decent-sized rooms, most with TV and some with a/c. ❷–❹

Eating

Eating in Rameshwaram is more about survival than delighting the taste buds. Most places serve up fairly unexciting veg "meals" for Rs30–50.

Abhirami Shore Rd, near the east entrance to the main temple. Reasonably clean south Indian veg joint en route to the seashore, with street views from the tables.

Ashoka Bhavan West Car St. Cheap south Indian vegetarian place, which also serves a variety of regional thalis.

Chola Hotel West Bazaar St. Food-only joint, not to be confused with lodge of same name; a good choice for carnivores, with biriyanis and other

dishes including chicken, mutton, liver and "head curry". Rs50–80

Ganesh Mess Middle St. One of the better "meals" joints, serving lunchtime thalis as well as classic south Indian snacks throughout the day.

TTDC Hotel Tamil Nadu Near the beach. Gigantic, noisy, high-ceilinged glasshouse near the sea, serving good south Indian snacks and "meals", plus chicken and occasional fish dishes (Rs60–80). There s also a bar in the main hotel building.

Kanyakumari

At the southernmost extremity of India, **KANYAKUMARI** is almost as compelling for Hindus as Rameshwaram. It's significant not only for its association with a virgin goddess, Kanya Devi, but also as the meeting point of the Bay of Bengal, Indian Ocean and Arabian Sea. Watching the sun rise and set from here is the big attraction, especially cn full-moon day in April, when it's possible to see both the setting sun and rising moon on the same horizon. Although Kanyakumari is in the state of Tamil Nadu, most foreign visitors arrive on day-trips from Thiruvananthapuram or Kovalam, a couple of hours' drive northwest in Kerala. While the place is of enduring appeal to pilgrims and those who just want to see India's tip, some may find it bereft of atmosphere, its magic obliterated by ugly concrete buildings and hawkers selling shells and trinkets. Kanyakumari was seriously affected by the 2004 tsunami with the loss of around one thousand lives, many of whom were pilgrims doing the high-season video coach tours of Tamil Nadu's sacred places. The seafront and jetty were also devastated but have since been rebuilt.

The Town

The seashore **Kumari Amman Temple** (daily 4.30–11.30am & 4–8pm) is dedicated to the virgin goddess **Kanya Devi**, who may originally have been the local guardian deity of the shoreline, but was later absorbed into the figure of Devi, or Parvati, consort of Shiva. The image of Kanya Devi inside the temple wears a diamond nose stud of such brilliance that it's said to be visible from the sea. Male visitors must be shirtless and wear a *dhoti* before entering the temple; non–Hindus are not allowed in the inner sanctum. It is especially auspicious for pilgrims to wash at the bathing *ghat* here.

Resembling a prewar British cinema, the **Gandhi Mandapam** (daily 7am–7pm), 300m northwest of the Kumari Amman Temple, was actually conceived as a modern imitation of an Orissan temple. It was designed so that the sun strikes the auspicious spot where the ashes of Mahatma Gandhi were laid, prior to their immersion in the sea, at noon on his birthday, October 2.

Possibly the original sacred focus of Kanyakumari are two **rocks**, about 60m apart, half-submerged in the sea 500m off the coast, which can be reached by the Poompuhar ferry service from the jetty on the east side of town (every 30min; daily 7am–4pm; Rs20). Known as the Pitru and Matru *tirthas*, they attracted the attention of the Hindu reformer Vivekananda (1862–1902), who swam out to the rocks in 1892 to meditate on the syncretistic teachings of his recently dead guru, Ramakrishna Paramahamsa. Incorporating elements of architecture from around the country, the 1970 **Vivekananda Memorial** (daily 7am–4pm; Rs10) houses a statue of the saint. The footprints of Kanya Devi can also be seen here, at the spot where she performed her penance. The other rock features an imposing 40m-high statue of the ancient Tamil saint **Thiruvalluvar**.

For more on the life and teachings of Vivekananda, visit the **Wandering Monk Museum** (**Vivekananda Puram**), just north of the tourist office on the main road (daily 8am–noon & 4–8pm; Rs2). A sequence of forty-one panels in English, Tamil and Hindi provide a meticulously detailed account of the *swami*'s odyssey around the Subcontinent at the end of the nineteenth century.

Practicalities

Trains from all over the Subcontinent (even Jammu – at 86hr the longest rail journey in India) stop at the **railway station** in the north of town, 2km from the seafront. The new and well-organized **Express Bus Stand**, near the lighthouse on the west side of town, is served by regular buses from Thiruvananthapuram, Madurai, Rameshwaram and Chennai. Taxis and auto-rickshaws provide **local transport**. The main **Tamil Nadu tourist office** is on Main Road (Mon–Fri 10am–5.30pm; ☏04652/246276); there's **Internet** access further up Main Road, as well as just around the corner on Beach Road.

In terms of **eating**, the ✗ *Archana* **restaurant**, at the *Maadhini Hotel* (see below), has an extensive veg and non-veg multi-cuisine menu, served either inside a well-ventilated dining hall or alfresco in a courtyard (evenings only). They also have the town's widest selection of ice cream. *Saravana Bhavan*, north of the Kumari Amman Temple, on the main bazaar, is arguably the best of Kanyakumari's many "meals" restaurants, serving all the usual snacks in the morning and evening, and "meals" at lunchtime. Also look out for the excellent fried fish and chicken on sale for around Rs25 at small joints on and around Main Road, such as the *Sree Devi Tiffin Stall*. For a drink, the most salubrious of the **bars** around town is the seriously air-conditioned *Red Sun* on South Car Street.

Accommodation

As Kanyakumari is a "must-see" for Indian tourists and pilgrims, **hotels** can fill up early. However, recent developments have raised standards and relieved the pressure on space.

✗ **Lakshmi Tourist Home** East Car St ☏04652/246333, 🅕 246627. Smart rooms, some sea-facing with a/c. though the best views are from the non-a/c ones (especially room #408). There's also an excellent non-veg restaurant. ➋–➍

Maadhini East Car St ☏04652/246787, 🅕 246657. Large hotel right on the seafront above the fishing village, with fine sea views, comfortably furnished rooms and one of the best restaurants in town (see above). ➍–➎

Manickam Tourist Home North Car St
☎04652/246387. Spacious but simple and clean
rooms, some with balconies and sea views, set in a
building that faces the sunrise and the Vivekananda
rock. Good value. ❷–❹
Samudra Sannathi St ☎04652/246162,
℗246627. Smart hotel near the temple entrance,
with well-furnished deluxe rooms facing the
sunrise. Facilities include satellite TV in rooms and
a veg restaurant. ❸–❺
TTDC Hotel Tamil Nadu Seafront ☎04652/246257,
Ⓦwww.ttdconline.com. Cottages (some are a/c) and
clean rooms (a/c on the first floor), most with sea
views, as well as cheaper and very basic "mini"
doubles at the back, and a dorm (Rs50). Good square
meals are served in functional surroundings. ❸–❺

The Ghats

Sixty or more million years ago, what we know today as peninsular India was a
separate land-mass drifting northwest across the ocean towards central Asia.
Current geological thinking has it that this mass must originally have broken
off the African continent along a fault line that is today discernible as a north–
south ridge of volcanic mountains, stretching 1400km down the west coast of
India, known as the **Western Ghats**. The range rises to a height of around
2500m, making it India's second-highest mountain chain after the Himalayas.

Forming a natural barrier between the Tamil plains and coastal Kerala and
Karnataka, the Ghats (literally "steps") soak up the bulk of the southwest
monsoon, which drains east to the Bay of Bengal via the mighty Kaveri and
Krishna river systems. The massive amount of rain that falls here between June
and October (around 2.5m) allows for an incredible **biodiversity**. Nearly one-
third of all of India's flowering plants can be found in the dense evergreen and
mixed deciduous forests cloaking the Ghats, while the woodland undergrowth
supports the Subcontinent's richest array of wildlife.

It was this abundance of game, and the cooler temperatures of the range's high
valleys and grasslands, that first attracted the sun-sick British, who were quick to
see the economic potential of the temperate climate, fecund soil and plentiful
rainfall. As the forests were felled to make way for tea plantations, and the region's
many tribal groups – among them the Todas – were forced deeper into the
mountains, permanent **hill stations** were established. Today, as in the days of the
Raj, these continue to provide welcome escapes from the fierce summer heat for
the middle-class Tamils, and foreign tourists, who can afford the break.

Much the best known of the hill resorts – in fact better known, and more
visited, than it deserves – is **Udhagamandalam** (formerly Ootacamund, and
usually known just as "**Ooty**"), in the **Nilgiris** (from *nila-giri*, "blue mountains").
The ride up to Ooty on the **miniature railway** via Coonoor is fun, and the
views breathtaking, but the town centre suffers from heavy traffic pollution and
has little to offer. There are some scenic walks out of Ooty and several
viewpoints which, together with boating and horse rides, make up the quintessentially Bollywood-esque activities which attract hordes of Indian tourists.
Further south and reached by a scenic switchback road, the other main hill
station is **Kodaikanal**. The lovely walks around town provide views and fresh
air in abundance, while the bustle of Indian tourists around the lake makes a
pleasant change from life in the city.

The forest areas lining the state border harbour Tamil Nadu's principal
wildlife sanctuaries, **Indira Gandhi** and **Mudumalai** which, along with
Wayanad in Kerala, and Nagarhole and Bandipur in Karnataka, form the vast
Nilgiri Biosphere Reserve, the country's most extensive tract of protected
forest. Road building, illegal felling, hydroelectric projects and overgrazing have
whittled away large tracts of this huge wilderness area over the past two decades,

but what's left still constitutes home to an array of wildlife. The main route between Mysore and the cities of the Tamil plains wriggles through the Nilgiris, and you may well find yourself pausing for a night or two along the way, if only to enjoy the cooler air and serene landscape of the tea terraces. Whichever direction you're travelling in, a stopover at the dull textile city of **Coimbatore** is hard to avoid.

Kodaikanal

Perched on top of the Palani range, around 120km northwest of Madurai, **KODAIKANAL**, also known as **Kodai**, owes its perennial popularity to its hilltop position which, at an altitude of more than 2000m, affords breathtaking views over the blue-green reaches of the Vaigai plain. Raj-era bungalows and flower-filled gardens add atmosphere, while short walks out of the centre lead to rocky outcrops, waterfalls and dense *shola* forest. With the more northerly wildlife sanctuaries and forest areas of the Ghats closed to visitors, Kodai's outstandingly scenic hinterland also offers south India's best **trekking** terrain. Even if you're not tempted by the prospect of the open trail and cool air, the jaw-dropping **bus ride** up here from the plains makes the detour into this easternmost spur of the Ghats an essential one.

After a while in the south Indian plains, a retreat to Kodai's cool heights is more than welcome. However, in the height of summer (June–Aug), when temperatures compete with those in the lowlands, it's not worth the trip – nor is it a good idea to come during the monsoon (Oct–Dec), when the town is shrouded in mists and drenched by heavy downpours. In late February and early

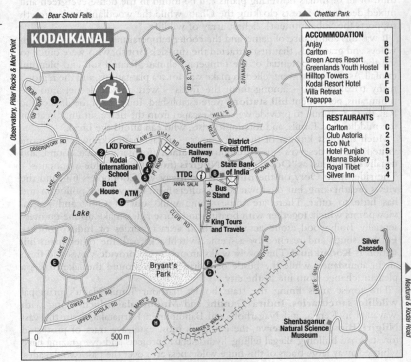

▲ Bear Shola Falls   ▲ Chettiar Park

KODAIKANAL

N

ACCOMMODATION
Anjay	B
Carlton	C
Green Acres Resort	E
Greenlands Youth Hostel	H
Hilltop Towers	A
Kodai Resort Hotel	F
Villa Retreat	G
Yagappa	D

RESTAURANTS
Carlton	C
Club Astoria	2
Eco Nut	3
Hotel Punjab	5
Manna Bakery	1
Royal Tibet	3
Silver Inn	4

OBSERVATORY RD

BEAR SHOLA RD

FERN HILL'S RD

SIVANADI RD

LAKE RD

LAW'S GHAT RD

LKD Forex

Kodai International School

Boat House

ATM

PT ROAD

HILL'S RD

Southern Railway Office

District Forest Office

BAZAAR RD

TTDC

ANNA SALAI

State Bank of India

Bus Stand

Lake

CLUB RD

WOODVILLE RD

King Tours and Travels

MOYCE RD

LAW'S GHAT RD

Silver Cascade

Bryant's Park

LOWER SHOLA RD

UPPER SHOLA RD

ST MARY'S RD

COAKER'S WALK

Shenbaganur Natural Science Museum

0   500 m

March the nights are chilly; the **peak tourist season**, therefore, is from April to June, when prices soar.

Arrival and information

The **buses** from Madurai and Dindigul that climb the spectacular road up the steep hillside to Kodai pull in at the stand in the centre of town. There are two roads to Kodaikanal: the lesser-used route from Palani is by far the more spectacular approach, and during the monsoon may be the only one open. Unless you're coming from as far as Chennai or Tiruchirapalli, the bus is much more convenient than the train: the nearest **railhead**, Kodai Road, is three hours away by bus.

Tickets for onward rail journeys from Kodaikanal Road can be booked at the Southern Railway office, down a lane beside the *Anjay Hotel* (Mon–Sat 8am–noon & 2.30–5pm, Sun 8am–noon). Nearby King Tours and Travels on Woodville Road can reserve trains, buses and planes within south India. The **tourist office** (Mon–Fri 10am–5.45pm; ℡04542/241675) on Anna Salai (Bazaar Road) can arrange **treks** (a 5hr trek with a guide costs Rs300 for groups of up to four); longer routes such as the three-day trek to Munnar in Kerala can also be negotiated; you'll pay around Rs1700 per day for groups of up to four, including basic accommodation. For **Internet** access, try Q Internet on Club Road, or the slower Flashnet, next to the *Royal Tibet* restaurant on PT Road.

Taxis line Anna Salai in the centre of town, offering sightseeing at high fixed rates. Most tourists, however, prefer to amble around at their own pace. Kodaikanal is best explored on foot, or by **bicycle**, which you can rent from a stall on Anna Salai for Rs10 per hour or Rs75 per day from numerous stalls around the lake; it may be fun to freewheel downhill, but most journeys will involve a hefty uphill push too. If you need to **change money**, head for the State Bank of India or Canara Bank, both on Anna Salai; there is an SBI ATM near the *Carlton Hotel*.

Accommodation

Kodaikanal's inexpensive **lodges** are grouped at the lower end of Anna Salai. Always ask whether blankets and hot water are provided (the latter should be free, but you may be charged in budget places) **Mid-range hotels** are usually good value, especially if you get a room with a view, but they hike their prices drastically during high season (April–June). The codes below reflect rates outside of April to June.

Anjay Anna Salai ℡04542/241089, ℱ242636. Simple budget lodge slap in the centre. Rooms are smarter than you'd expect from the outside (all have balconies, and the deluxe ones have views), but those at the front suffer some traffic noise. If they're full, check out the equally good-value *Jaya* behind. ②–③

Carlton Off Lake Rd ℡04542/240056, ⓦwww .krahejahospitality.com. The most luxurious hotel in Kodaikanal, this is a spacious, tastefully renovated and well-maintained colonial house overlooking the lake, with a bar and comfortable lounge. Rooms in the house start around $150 and exude Raj-era charm; there are pricier cottages available within the grounds. All rates include meals. ⑨

Green Acres Resort 11/213 Lake Rd ℡04542/242384, ⓦwww.greenacresresort.biz.

Spiffing new resort in a great setting on a quiet corner of the lake, with rooms and suites (all attached and well furnished) of varying sizes dotted around carefully manicured grounds. ⑤–⑧

Greenlands Youth Hostel Off St Mary's Rd ℡04542/241099, ⓔgreenlandsyh@rediffmail.com. Attractive old stone house offering unrivalled views and sunsets from its deep verandas. The rooms are basic with wooden beds, open fireplaces (wood costs Rs50) and attached bathrooms, and there's a dorm (Rs100). Book ahead. ②–④

Hilltop Towers Club Rd ℡04542/240413, ⓔhttowers@sancharnet.in. Very near the lake and school, with modern, comfortable rooms featuring arched doors. There's also a cosy and romantic honeymoon suite with a round bed. Three restaurants and good service. ④–⑤

Kodai Resort Hotel Noyce Rd ℡04542/241301, ⓦwww.kodairesorthotel.com. Large complex of fifty incongruous-looking but very pleasant chalets situated at the top of the hill and offering good views of the town. There's a health club and rather dull restaurant on site. ⑤–⑥

Villa Retreat Coaker's Walk, off Club Rd ℡04542/240940, ⓦwww.villaretreat.com. Comfortable old stone house, with more character than most, in lovely gardens that afford superb views. Though a touch overpriced, all rooms have great views and attached hot-water bathrooms; some have fires. Wood and electric heaters are available upon request. ④–⑥

🏃 **Yagappa** Noyce Rd ℡04542/241235. The best budget deal in town, this small, clean lodge is set in old buildings ranged around a lawn-cum-courtyard and has good views. Rooms are modest but clean, and there's a great little bar with wicker chairs, and a tiny white-washed restaurant serving veg "meals" and breakfasts. ②

The Town

Kodai's focal point is its **lake**, sprawling like a giant amoeba over 24 hectares just west of the town centre. This is a popular place for strolls or bike rides along the five-kilometre path that fringes the water's edge, while pedal- or rowing boats can be rented on the eastern shore (Rs30–100 for 30min, plus Rs25 if you require an oarsman). Horse riding is also an option here, but it's rather pricey – it costs Rs50 to be led along the lakeside for 500m, or Rs200 for an hour's ride. Shops, restaurants and hotels are concentrated in a rather congested area of brick, wood and corrugated iron buildings east of and downhill from the lake. The only monuments to Kodai's colonial past are the neat **British bungalows** that overlook the lake, and Law's Ghat Road on the eastern edge of town. The British first moved here in 1845, to be joined later by members of the American Mission, who set up schools for European children. One remains as the **Kodai International School**; despite the name, almost all its students are Indian. The school occasionally holds concerts on the green just east of the lake.

To the south is **Bryant's Park** (daily 8.30am–6.30pm, last entry 6pm; Rs5, camera Rs25, video camera Rs500), with tiered flowerbeds on a backdrop of pine, eucalyptus, rhododendron and wattle which stretches southwards to Shola Road, less than 1km from the point where the hill drops abruptly to the plains. A path, known as **Coaker's Walk** (Rs2, camera Rs5), skirts the hill, winding from the *Villa Retreat* to *Greenland's Youth Hostel* (10min), offering remarkable views that stretch as far as Madurai on a clear day.

One of Kodai's most popular natural attractions is the **Pillar Rocks**, 7km south of town, where a series of granite cliffs rise more than 100m above the hillside. To get there, follow the westbound Observatory Road from the northernmost point of the lake (a steep climb) until you come to a crossroads; the southbound road passes the gentle **Fairy Falls** on the way to Pillar Rocks. Observatory Road continues west from the crossroads to the **Astrophysical Observatory**, which is now closed to visitors. Some 2km west of the lake, the signposted **Bear Shola Falls** now sees barely a trickle of water but remains a popular picnic and photo-stop for local tourists.

Southeast of the town centre, about 3km down Law's Ghat Road (towards the plains), the **Shenbaganur Natural Science Museum** (Mon–Sat 9am–5pm; Rs5) has a very uninviting array of stuffed animals. However, the spectacular orchid house contains one of India's best collections, which can be viewed by appointment only (ask at the tourist office; see p.1167). Head 2km further along Law's Ghat Road to reach **Silver Cascade** waterfall, where the overflow from Kodai Lake has created a pleasant pool for bathing.

Chettiar Park, on the very northeast edge of town, around 3km from the lake at the end of a winding uphill road, flourishes with trees and flowers all year round, and every twelve years is flushed with a haze of pale-blue **Kurinji**

blossoms (the next flowering will not be until 2018). These unusual flowers are associated with the god Murugan, the Tamil form of Karttikeya (Shiva's second son), and god of Kurinji, one of five ancient divisions of the Tamil country. A temple in his honour stands just outside the park.

Eating

If you choose not to eat in any of the **hotel restaurants**, head for the food stalls along **PT Road** just west of the bus stand. Menus include Indian, Chinese, Western and Tibetan dishes, and some cater specifically for vegetarians. Look out, too, for the **bakeries**, with their wonderful, fresh, warm bread and cakes each morning.

Carlton *Carlton Hotel*, off Lake Rd. Splash out on the evening veg and non-veg buffet spread (Rs330) at Kodai's top hotel, rounded off with a *chhota* peg of IMFL Scotch in the bar.

Club Astoria Lake Rd. Bright and breezy multi-cuisine restaurant with a large terrace overlooking the lake. Better to come for a snack or drink while enjoying the view than a main meal (around Rs150), though, as the food is fairly plain.

Eco Nut J's Heritage Complex, PT Rd. One of south India's few bona fide Western-style wholefood shops, and a great place to stock up on trekking supplies: muesli, home-made jams, breads, pickles and muffins, high-calorie "nutri-balls" and delicious cheeses from Auroville.

Hotel Punjab PT Rd. Top north Indian cuisine and reasonably priced tandoori specialities; try their great butter chicken and hot naan. Most main dishes are Rs80–120.

Manna Bakery Bear Shola Rd. Fried breakfasts, pizzas and home-baked brown bread and cakes served in an eccentric, self-consciously eco friendly café-restaurant.

Royal Tibet PT Rd. The friendliest of three small Tibetan joints along this road, with dishes ranging from thick home-made bread to particularly tasty *momos* and noodles, as well as some Indian and Chinese options, all for under Rs100.

Silver Inn PT Rd. Western favourites such as porridge, lasagne, mashed potato and apple crumble are all adequately cooked up at this hole-in-the-wall place. Most dinners around Rs100.

Indira Gandhi (Anamalai) Wildlife Sanctuary

Indira Gandhi (Anamalai) Wildlife Sanctuary (Rs15) is a 958-square-kilometre tract of forest on the southern reaches of the Cardamom Hills, 37km southwest of the busy junction town of **Pollachi**. Vegetation ranges from dry deciduous to tropical evergreen, and the sanctuary is home to lion-tailed macaques (black-maned monkeys), crocodiles, *gaur*, *sambar*, spotted and barking deer, sloth bear, as well as a handful of tigers. One of its best features is that you can **trek** through the giant creaking stands of bamboo with a guide (7am–3pm; Rs150 for 3hr treks with up to four people). A Forestry Department minibus conducts **safari tours** on request (Rs675 for the van), and a forty minute **elephant safari** (10am–4pm; Rs100 per person) is also available.

Practicalities

Pollachi has good bus connections to Palani and Coimbatore. From the town there are only three buses a day (6am, 11am & 3pm; return at 9.30am, 1pm & 6.30pm) up to the park's reception centre (℡04253/245002) at **Top Slip**. These run via the official entrance at the **Sethumadai** checkpost. The Forestry Department runs six **resthouses**, ranging from the basic *Hornbill* (❶) to the luxurious *Pillar Top* (❼). Most are within easy walking distance of the reception centre and should be booked in advance through the wildlife warden at Pollachi (℡04259/225356). A canteen next to the reception centre serves very limited **meals** and drinks, while a nearby shop has equally scant provisions.

Coimbatore

Visitors tend only to use the busy industrial city of **COIMBATORE** as a stopover on the way to Ooty, 90km northwest. Once you've climbed up to your hotel rooftop to admire the blue, cloud-capped haze of the Nilgiris in the west, there's little to do here other than kill time wandering through the nuts-and-bolts bazaars, lined with lookalike textile showrooms, "General Traders" and shops selling motor parts.

Coimbatore has four main **bus stands**, three of which are fairly near each other in the northern part of town, a couple of kilometres north of the railway station. The Thiruvalluvar Bus Stand is the main state and interstate station; buses from Ooty, Coonoor and Mettupalayam use the Central Bus Stand, while the busy Town Bus Stand is sandwiched in between. The south of town holds the fourth bus stand, Ukkadam (which serves Palani, Pollachi, Madurai and towns in northern Kerala), as well as the **railway station**; for **Ooty**, join the daily #2671 Nilgiri Express at 5.15am, which will get you to **Mettupalayam** in time to join the Toy Train (see p.1174). Local buses ply the routes between bus and train stations. Coimbatore's **airport** is 12km northeast of town and served by buses to and from Town Bus Stand; a taxi will charge around Rs200.

You can **change money** at the State Bank of India and Bank of Baroda, near the railway station, or at the American Express Foreign Exchange on Avanashi Road, a five-minute auto-rickshaw ride northeast of the railway station; there are plenty of ATMs. **Internet** access is available all over Coimbatore; options include Blaznet, on Nehru Street next to the *Blue Star* hotel, and Net Hut, on Geetha Hall Road near the *Park Inn*.

As for **eating**, your best bets are the bigger hotels (see below) such as the *City Tower*, whose excellent rooftop restaurant, *Cloud 9*, serves a top-notch multi-cuisine menu; mains are around Rs100. The *Malabar*, on the first floor of the *KK Residency*, is a less pricey option, popular with visitors from across the Ghats for its quality non-veg Keralan cuisine. Carnivores will also enjoy the crispy fried chicken at *KR* opposite the railway station, which also has a good bakery, while the best place for vegetarian south Indian food is the ultramodern *Gayathri Bhavan*, opposite the *Blue Star* hotel on Nehru Street.

Accommodation

Most of Coimbatore's **accommodation** is concentrated around the bus stands and railway station. The cheapest options line Nehru Street and Shastri Road, but avoid the rock-bottom places facing the bus stand itself, which are plagued with traffic noise from around 4am onwards.

Blue Star 369 Nehru St ℡0422/223 0635, ℻0422/223 3096. Impeccably clean rooms, some with balconies, quiet fans and bathrooms, in a modern multistorey building five minutes' walk from the bus stands. The best mid-priced place in this area. ❸–❹

City Tower Sivasamy Rd ℡0422/223 0681, ⒲www.hotelcitytower.com. A smart, upscale hotel two minutes' walk south of the Central Bus Stand with modern interiors (featuring leatherette and vinyl); the "Executive" rooms are more spacious. Some rooms are a/c. ❺–❻

KK Residency 7 Shastri Rd ℡0422/223 2433, ℻437 8111. Large tower-block hotel around the corner from the main bus stands, with very clean rooms and a couple of good restaurants. ❸–❹

New Vijaya Lodge 8/24 Geetha Hall Rd ℡0422/230 1794. Simple but adequate place with compact, clean rooms, very close to the railway station. ❷–❸

TTDC Tamil Nadu Dr Nanjappa Rd ℡0422/230 2176, ⒲www.ttdconline.com. Opposite Central Bus Stand; convenient, clean, reliable and better than most in the chain, with a/c and non-a/c rooms. It's often fully booked, so phone ahead. ❸–❹

Coonoor

At an altitude of 1858m, **COONOOR**, a scruffy bazaar and tea-planters' town on the Nilgiri Blue Mountain Railway (see box, p.1174), lies at the head of the Hulikal ravine, on the southeastern side of the Dodabetta mountains, 27km north of Mettupalayam and 19km south of Ooty. Thanks to its proximity to its more famous neighbour, Coonoor has avoided Ooty's overcommercialization, and can make a pleasant place for a short stop.

Coonoor loosely divides into two sections, with the bus stand (regular services to Mettupalayam, Coimbatore and elsewhere in the Nilgiris) and railway station (four trains daily to Ooty, and one daily service to Mettupalayam) in **Lower Coonoor**, where there's also a small but atmospheric hill market specializing in leaf tea and fragrant essential oils. In **Upper Coonoor**, there's a fine sprinkling of old Raj-era bungalows along narrow lanes edged with flower-filled hedgerows. At the top lies **Sim's Park**, a lush botanical garden on the slopes of a ravine with hundreds of rose varieties (daily 8am–6.30pm; Rs5).

Around the town, rolling hills and valleys carpeted with spongy green tea bushes and stands of eucalyptus and silver oak offer some of the most beautiful scenery in the Nilgiris, immortalized in many a Hindi-movie dance sequence. Cinema fans from across the south flock here to visit key locations from their favourite blockbusters, among them **Lamb's Nose** (5km) and **Dolphin's Nose** (9km), former British picnicking spots with paved pathways and dramatic views of the Mettupalayam plains. Buses run out here from Coonoor every two hours. It's a good idea to catch the first one at 7am, which gets you to Dolphin's Nose before the mist starts to build up, and walk the 9km back into town via Lamb's Rock – an enjoyable amble that takes you through tea estates and dense forest.

Visible from miles away as tiny orange or red dots amid the green vegetation, **tea-pickers** work the slopes around Coonoor, carrying wicker baskets of fresh leaves and bamboo rods that they use like rulers to ensure that each plant is evenly plucked. Once the leaves reach the factory, they're processed within a day, producing seven grades of tea. **Orange pekoe** is the best and most expensive; the seventh lowest grade, a dry dust of stalks and leaf swept up at the end of the process, will be sold on to make instant tea. To visit a tea or coffee plantation, contact UPASI (United Planters' Association of Southern India), "Glenview" House, Coonoor ☎0423/223 0270, ⓦwww.upasi.org.

Practicalities

When it comes to finding somewhere to **stay** or **eat**, there isn't much choice in Coonoor, and it's not a good idea to leave it too late in the day to look for a room. By and large the hotels are dotted around Upper Coonoor, within 3km of the station; you'll need an auto-rickshaw to find most of them. The correct fare from the bus stand to Bedford Circle/YWCA is Rs30–40.

If you're staying at the *YWCA*, or one of the upmarket hotels, your best bet is to eat there. In the bazaar, the only commendable **restaurants** are *Hotel Tamizhamgam* (pronounced "Tamirangum"), on Mount Road near the bus stand, which is Coonoor's most popular vegetarian "meals"-cum-tiffin joint. For good-value non-veg North Indian tandoori and Chinese food, try the *Greenland* hotel, further up Mount Road, while at Bedford Circle, the *Dragon* serves up more authentic and tasty Chinese dishes.

The Travancore Bank, on Church Road in Upper Ooty, near Bedford Circle, **changes currency**, but not always travellers' cheques. Otherwise, the nearest place is the State Bank of India in Ooty (see p.1174).

Accommodation

The tariffs included here are for the low season; high-season prices may increase by anywhere between twenty and a hundred percent, depending on the tourist influx.

La Barrier Inn Coonoor Club Rd ☎0423/223 2561. Comfortable mid-range option way up above the bazaar, with great views of surrounding hills. The rooms are spotless and very large, opening onto flower-filled balconies. **④–⑤**

Sree Venkateshwara Lodge Cash Bazaar ☎0423/220 6309. The best option in Lower Coonoor, right by the railway station. Clean, average-sized attached rooms with TV. **②**

Taj Garden Retreat Church Rd, Upper Coonoor ☎0423/223 0021, ⓦwww.tajhotels.com. Luxurious but way overpriced, this colonial-era hotel has cottage accommodation, tea-garden lawns and spectacular views, plus a good range of sports and activities including freshwater fishing. The restaurant serves spectacular lunchtime buffets (around Rs300). Rooms from $150. **⑨**

Velan (aka Ritz) Ritz Rd, Bedford ☎0423/223 0784, ⓦwww.velanhotels.com. Recently refurbished mid-range hotel in a great location on the outskirts; it's very spacious with carpeted rooms, deep balconies and fine views. Much better value than the *Taj Garden Retreat*, but rather lacking in charm. **⑤**

Vivek Tourist Home Figure of Eight Rd, near Bedford Circle ☎0423/223 0658. Clean rooms (some with tiny balconies overlooking the tea terraces) in a rather starchy, institutional atmosphere. Just beware of the "monkey menace". **②–③**

YWCA Guest House Wyoming, near the hospital ☎0423/223 4426. A characterful Victorian-era house on a bluff overlooking town, with a flower garden, tea terraces and fine views from the verandas. There are five double rooms and two singles; superb home-cooked meals are available at very reasonable rates. No alcohol. **③**

Udhagamandalam (Ootacamund)

When John Sullivan, the British *burrasahib* credited with "discovering" **UDHAGAMANDALAM** – whose anglicized name, **Ootacamund**, is usually shortened to Ooty – first clambered into this corner of the Nilgiris through the Hulikal ravine in the early nineteenth century, the territory was the traditional homeland of the pastoralist **Toda** hill tribe. Until then, the Todas had lived in almost total isolation from the cities of the surrounding plains and Deccan plateau lands. Sullivan quickly realized the agricultural potential of the area, acquired tracts of land for Rs1 per acre from the Todas, and set about planting flax, barley and hemp, as well as potatoes, soft fruit and, most significantly of all, **tea**, which all flourished in the mild climate. Within twenty years, the former East India Company clerk had made a fortune. Needless to say, he was soon joined by other fortune-seekers, and a town was built, complete with artificial lake, churches and stone houses that wouldn't have looked out of place in Surrey or the Scottish Highlands. Soon, **Ooty** was the "Queen of Hill Stations" and had become the most popular hill retreat in peninsular India.

By a stroke of delicious irony, the Todas outlived the colonists whose cash crops originally displaced them – but only just. Having retreated with their buffalo into the surrounding hills and wooded valleys, they continue to preserve a more-or-less traditional way of life, albeit in greatly diminished numbers. Until the mid-1970s "Snooty Ooty" continued to be "home" to the notoriously snobbish British inhabitants who chose to "stay on" after Independence. Since then, travellers have continued to be attracted by Ooty's cool climate and peaceful green hills, forest and grassland. However, if you come in the hope of finding quaint vestiges of the Raj, you're likely to be disappointed; what with indiscriminate **development** and a deluge of holiday-makers, they're few and far between.

The **best time to come** is between January and March, thereby avoiding the high-season crowds (April–June & Sept–Oct). In May, the summer festival brings huge numbers of people and a barrage of amplified noise, worlds away from the peaceful retreat envisaged by the *sahibs*.

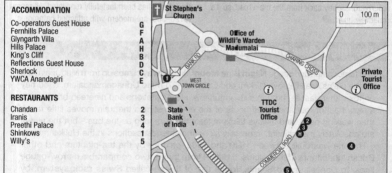

ACCOMMODATION

Co-operators Guest House	G
Fernhills Palace	F
Glyngarth Villa	A
Hills Palace	H
King's Cliff	B
Reflections Guest House	D
Sherlock	C
YWCA Anandagiri	E

RESTAURANTS

Chandan	2
Iranis	3
Preethi Palace	4
Shinkows	1
Willy's	5

Arrival, information and orientation

Most visitors arrive in Ooty either by bus from Mysore in Karnataka (the more scenic, if steeper, route goes via Masinagudi), or on the miniature **Nilgiri Blue Mountain Railway** from Coonoor and Mettupalayam. The **bus stand** and **railway station** are fairly close together, at the western end of the big bazaar and racecourse. **Local transport** consists of auto-rickshaws and taxis, which meet incoming trains and gather outside the bus stand and on Commercial Road around Charing Cross.

The **TTDC tourist office** (Mon–Sat 10am–5.45pm; ☏0423/244 3977) is at the TTDC *Hotel Tamil Nadu II*. You can book tours here, including a mammoth day-trip (daily 9.30am–7pm; Rs210) that includes Ooty, Pykara dam, falls and boathouse and Mudumalai Wildlife Sanctuary. There's also a less strenuous tour of just Ooty and Coonoor (daily 9.30am–5.30pm; Rs130), which goes to Sim's Park, the Botanical Gardens, the lake, Dodabetta Peak, Lamb's Rock and Dolphin's Nose. There's also a private **tourist information centre** (daily 10am–7pm; ☏09443 345258) in the clocktower building at Charing Cross that gives out leaflets and offers more reliable advice.

Ooty's **post office** is northwest of Charing Cross at West Town Circle, near St Stephen's Church. There are numerous **Internet** outlets across town, including Cyber Link and Cyber Planet just north of Charing Cross. The only **bank** in Ooty that changes travellers' cheques and currency is the very pukka State Bank of India on West Town Circle, and there are now a number of ATMs dotted around town.

Accommodation

Accommodation in Ooty is a lot more expensive than in many places in India; during April and May, the prices given below can rise by thirty to a hundred percent. It also gets very crowded, so you may have to hunt around to find what you want. The best by far are the grand old Raj-era places (check if the *Nilgiri Woodlands* has reopened); otherwise, the choice is largely down to average hotels at above-average prices. In **winter** (Nov–Feb), when it can get pretty cold, most hotels provide extra blankets and buckets of hot water on request, but ask whether these services are complimentary.

Co-operators Guest House Commercial Rd, Charing Cross ☏0423/244 4046. An L-shaped Raj-era building with clean rooms whose yellow-and-turquoise balconies look down to a courtyard; slightly back from the main road, so it's relatively quiet. ②

Fernhills Palace off High Level Rd ☏0423/244 3097, ⊛www.welcomheritagehotels.com. Luxury heritage hotel in what was the maharajah of Mysore's palace; the original exterior remains, but the interior has been tastefully renovated. All rooms ($120–300) are modern with attached bathrooms,

The Nilgiri Blue Mountain Railway

The famous narrow-gauge **Nilgiri Blue Mountain Railway** climbs up from Mettupalayam on the plains, via Hillgrove (17km) and Coonoor (27km) to Udhagamandalam, a journey of 46km that passes through sixteen tunnels, eleven stations and nineteen bridges. It's a slow haul of four and a half hours or more – sometimes the train moves little faster than walking pace, and always takes at least twice as long as the bus – but the **views** are absolutely magnificent, especially along the steepest sections in the Hulikal ravine.

The line was built between 1890 and 1908, paid for by the tea-planters and other British inhabitants of the Nilgiris. It differs from India's two comparable narrow-gauge lines, to Darjeeling and Shimla, for its use of the so-called **Swiss rack system**, by means of which the tiny locomotives are able to climb gradients of up to 1 in 12.5. Special bars were set between the track rails to form a ladder, which cogs of teeth, connected to the train's driving wheels, engage like a zip mechanism. Because of this novel design, only the original locomotives can still run the steepest stretches of line, which is why the section between Mettupalayam and Coonoor has remained one of South Asia's last functioning **steam routes**. The chuffing and whistle screeches of the tiny train, echoing across the valleys as it pushes its blue-and-cream carriages up to Coonoor (where a diesel locomotive takes over) rank among the most romantic sounds of south India, conjuring up the determined gentility of the Raj era. Even if you don't count yourself as a trainspotter, a boneshaking ride on the Blue Mountain Railway should be a priority while traversing the Nilgiris between southern Karnataka and the Tamil plains.

See "Moving on from Ooty" on p.1176 for timetable details for the line.

and feature jacuzzis. *Regency Villas*, within the same grounds, is substantially cheaper. ❾
Glyngarth Villa Golf Club Rd, 4.5km out of town on the Mysore Rd ☎0423/ 244 5754, ⊛www .glyngarthvilla.com. A 150-year-old colonial villa set in four acres of greenery. The five double rooms, comfortable and with wooden interiors, give the place a charming atmosphere, and there are great valley views. Rates include breakfast. ❻
Hills Palace Commercial Rd, Charing Cross ☎0423/244 6483, ⓔhillspalace@sify.com. Modern place just below the main bazaar, but secluded, quiet and with spotlessly clean rooms. Great value in low season. ❸
King's Cliff Havelock Rd ☎0423/245 2888, ⊛www.kingscliff-ooty.com. Imposing ancestral mansion with four grades of lavishly furnished rooms, each with a Shakespearian theme; great value. There's also a stylish dining room and lounge, with terrific food and a resident singer/guitarist. ❹–❻

Reflections Guest House North Lake Rd ☎0423/244 3834, ⓔreflectionsin@yahoo.co.in. Homely, relaxing guesthouse by the lake, 5min walk from the railway station, with rooms opening onto a small terrace. Easily the best budget option in Ooty, but it's small and fills up quickly, so book in advance. ❸
Sherlock 2.5km east of Charing Cross ☎0423/244 1641, ⊛www.littlearth.in /sherlock. Beautifully landscaped Victorian mansion with a Conan Doyle theme and stunning views from the grassy terrace. All rooms are tastefully furnished, and the deluxe ones have sitouts. Friendly service and quality food too. ❺
YWCA Anandagiri Ettines Rd ☎0423/244 2218. Charming 1920s building set in spacious grounds near the racecourse. Seven varieties of rooms and chalets are on offer, all immaculate, with bucket hot water and bathrooms, plus a dorm (Rs110). Excellent value and popular, so book ahead. ❷–❹

The Town

Ooty sprawls over a large area of winding roads and steep climbs. The obvious focal point is **Charing Cross**, a busy junction on dusty **Commercial Road**, the main, relatively flat, shopping street that runs south to the big bazaar and municipal vegetable market. Goods on sale range from fat plastic bags of cardamom and Orange pekoe tea to presentation packs of essential oils (among them natural mosquito-repelling citronella). A little way north of Charing Cross, the **Botanical Gardens** (daily 8.30am–6.30pm; Rs10, camera Rs30, video camera Rs500), laid out in 1847 by gardeners from London's Kew Gardens, consist of twenty hectares of immaculate lawns, lily ponds and beds, with more than a thousand varieties of shrubs, flowers and trees. There's a refreshment stand in the park, and shops in the small Tibetan market sell ice creams and snacks.

Northwest of Charing Cross, the small Gothic-style **St Stephen's Church** was one of Ooty's first colonial structures, built in the 1820s on the site of a Toda temple; timber for its bowed teak roof was taken from Tipu Sultan's palace at Srirangapatnam and hauled up here by elephant. The area around the church gives some idea of what the hill station must have looked like in the days of the Raj. To the right is the rambling and rather dilapidated **Spencer's store**, which opened in 1909 and sold everything a British home in the colonies could ever need; it's now a computer college. Over the next hill to the west, the snootiest of Ooty's institutions, the members-only **Club**, dates from 1830. Originally the house of Sir William Rumbold, it became a club in 1843 and expanded there-after. Its one claim to fame is that the rules for snooker were first set down here. Further along Mysore Road, the modest **Government Museum** (daily except Fri & second Sat of month 10am–5.30pm; free) houses a few paltry tribal objects, sculptures and crafts.

West of the railway station and racecourse (races mid-April to mid-June), the **lake**, constructed in the early 1800s, is one of Ooty's main tourist attractions, despite being heavily polluted with sewage. Boats are available for rent (daily 9am–6pm; paddle boats Rs60–100, rowing boats Rs80–110, charter motor boats seating 8–15 people Rs250–450), and you can also go horse riding here for Rs150 per hour.

Eating

Many of the mid-range hotels serve up good south Indian food, but Ooty has yet to offer a gourmet **restaurant**. For an inexpensive *udipi* breakfast, head to one of the restaurants around Charing Cross for *iddli-dosa* and filter coffee.

Chandan *Nahar Hotel*, Commercial Rd, Charing Cross. Carefully prepared north Indian specialities (their *paneer kofta* is particularly good), and a small selection of tandoori vegetarian dishes, served inside a posh restaurant or on a lawnside terrace. They also do a full range of lassis and milkshakes. Main courses Rs60–100.

Iranis Commercial Rd. A gloomy old-style Persian joint run by Baha'ís. Uncompromisingly non-veg (the menu's heavy on mutton, liver and brains), but an atmospheric coffee stop, and a popular hang-out for both men and women. Most dishes Rs60–80.

Preethi Palace Ettines Rd. Excellent lunchtime thalis (North and south Indian) for Rs30–50, and a delicious range of pure-veg food served throughout the day.

Shinkows 42 Commissioners Rd. Good-value, authentic Chinese restaurant serving up decent-sized portions on the spicy and pricey side – main courses with meat cost Rs120–150.

Willy's KRC Arcade, Walsham Rd. First-floor café, with a modern, buzzy vibe that makes it popular with students, as well as tasty Western savouries and cakes, and range of gourmet coffees.

Moving on from Ooty

Ooty **railway station** has a booking office (6.30am–7pm), where you can buy tickets for the Nilgiri Blue Mountain Railway (see p.1174), and a reservation counter (daily 8am–12.30pm & 2.30–4.30pm) for booking onward services to most other destinations in the south. Four trains daily (9.15am, 12.15pm, 3pm & 6pm) pootle down the narrow-gauge line to Coonoor, but only one (3pm) continues down to Mettupalayam, which is on the main broad-gauge network. If you're heading to Chennai, the 3pm train should get you to Mettupayalam to connect with the daily #2672 Nilgiri Express (depart 7.45pm; 9hr 25min).

You can also book **buses** in advance at the bus stand, at the reservation offices for both state buses (daily 9am–12.30pm & 1.30–5.30pm) and the local company, Cheran Transport (daily 9am–1pm & 1.30–5.30pm). A combination of stop-start local and express "super-deluxe" state buses serve Bengaluru (Bangalore) and Mysore (half-hourly buses to both pass through Mudumalai), Kodaikanal, Thanjavur, Thiruvananthapuram and Kanyakumari, as well as Coonoor and Coimbatore nearer to hand. **Private buses** to Mysore, Bengaluru (Bangalore) and Kodaikanal can be booked at hotels, or agents in Charing Cross; even when advertised as "super-deluxe", many turn out to be cramped minibuses.

Mudumalai Wildlife Sanctuary

Set 1140m up in the Nilgiri Hills, the **MUDUMALAI WILDLIFE SANCTUARY** covers 322 square kilometres of deciduous forest, split by the main road from Ooty (64km to the southeast) to Mysore (97km to the northwest). Occupying the thickly wooded lower northern reaches of the hills, it boasts one of the largest populations of elephants in India, along with wild dogs, *gaur* (Indian bison), common and Nilgiri langur and bonnet macaques (monkeys), jackal, hyena and sloth bear, and even a few tigers and leopards. Of the wealth of local flora, the dazzling red flowers of the flame of the forest stand among the most noticeable. Now that the park is fully operational again, you can explore by vehicle or on foot. Generally speaking, the best time to visit is during and after monsoon.

The main focus of interest by the park entrance at **Theppakkadu** is the **Elephant Camp** show (daily 8–9.30am & 5.30–6.30pm; free), where you can watch the sanctuary's tame pachyderms being fed and bathed. This is also the starting point for the government **safari tour** (7–9am & 4–6pm; 40min; Rs35 per person, camera Rs25, video camera Rs150), which is the only way of accessing the official park limits. However you may well see more creatures if you take a private **Jeep tour** or **guided trek** into some of the parts of Mudumalai that are outside the state-controlled area. These can be arranged through any guesthouse or direct at Nature Safari in Masinagudi (T0423/252 6340, Esaveelephasmaximus@yahoo.co.in).

Practicalities

The main route from Ooty to Mudumalai, taken by most Mysore- and Bengaluru-bound buses takes 2.5 hours to reach **Theppakkadu**. The alternative route is a tortuous journey of very steep gradients and hairpin bends, which can only be attempted by smaller vehicles such as the Cheran transport minibuses. These take around one hour and end up at **Masinagudi**, which is closer to most of the area's growing **accommodation** options. Complete with ecofriendly swimming pool, the prime resort is ℛ *Jungle Retreat* (T0423/252 6469, Wwww .jungleretreat.com; ⑥–⑧) at Bokkapuram, 6km southwest of Masinagudi, with accommodation ranging from Rs400 beds in spacious dorms to a pair of elegant treehouses; Rs700 covers three sumptuous buffet meals per day and unlimited tea and coffee. *Wild Haven* (T0423/252 6490, Ekarimjohn@hotmail.com; ④) at Chadapatti, 6km south of Masinagudi, offers simple but spacious concrete rooms, set in open land with great mountain views. The only real budget places are the dowdy TTDC *Hotel Tamil Nadu* (T0423/252 6580, Wwww.ttdconline.com; ②) at Theppakkadu and the spartan *St Xavier's Lodge* (T0423/252 6371; ②) in Masinagudi, which also has a couple of basic "meals" restaurants.

Travel details

Trains

Services from Chennai leave from Central Station unless marked with an asterisk. Trains from Egmore are marked*, from Egmore and Tambaram **, and from Egmore and Central ***.
Chennai to: Bengaluru (Bangalore) (7 daily; 4hr 50min–8hr 30min); Chengalpattu (9–10 daily**; 1hr–1hr 20min); Coimbatore (3 daily; 7hr 40min–8hr); Ernakulam, for Kochi (2–3 daily; 10hr 55min–14hr 15min); Hyderabad (2 daily; 13hr 50min–14hr 30min); Kanyakumari (1–2 daily; 13hr 5min–16hr 55min); Kodaikanal Road (3–4 daily*; 7hr 35min–8hr 30min); Kumbakonam (2 daily**; 7hr 45min–8hr 30min); Madurai (6–8 daily*; 7hr 45min–10hr 30min); Mettupalayam (1 daily; 9hr 15min); Mumbai (3 daily; 23hr–28hr 25min); Mysore (1–2 daily; 7hr–10hr 35min); Pune (3 daily; 19hr–24hr 15min); Thanjavur (1 daily*; 7hr 45min); Thiruvananthapuram (2–3 daily***; 15hr 40min–18hr 20min); Tiruchirapalli (9–10 daily*; 5hr 10min–6hr 45min); Tirupati (3 daily; 3hr 5min–3hr 35min); Vijayawada (10–11 daily; 6hr 35min–8hr 30min).

Coimbatore to: Bengaluru (Bangalore) (2–3 daily; 6hr 45min–9hr); Chennai (5–6 daily; 7hr 50min–8hr 55min); Ernakulam, for Kochi (7–8 daily; 4hr 20min–5hr 30min); Hyderabad (1 daily; 21hr 20min); Kanyakumari (1 daily; 11hr 45min); Madurai (1–2 daily; 6hr 15min–6hr 35min); Mettupalayam, for Ooty (1 daily; 1hr); Mumbai (2 daily; 31hr 15min–32hr 40min); Thiruvananthapuram (4–5 daily; 9hr 5min–10hr 25min); Tiruchirapalli (2 daily; 5hr 15min–5hr 45min).
Kanyakumari to: Bengaluru (Bangalore) (1 daily; 19hr 30min); Chennai (2–3 daily; 13hr 15min–15hr 25min); Coimbatore (1 daily; 11hr 55min); Kochi (2 daily; 6hr 15min–6hr 30min); Madurai (1–2 daily; 4hr 20min–5hr 15min); Mumbai (1 daily; 47hr 20min); Thiruvananthapuram (2 daily; 1hr 35min–2hr); Tiruchirapalli (1–2 daily; 7hr 15min–8hr 15min).
Madurai to: Bengaluru (Bangalore) (1 daily; 10hr 30min); Chengalpattu (6–7 daily; 6hr 55min–9hr); Chennai (7–9 daily; 7hr 55min–10hr 30min); Coimbatore (1–2 daily; 6hr 15min); Kanyakumari (1–2 daily; 4hr–5hr 50min); Kodaikanal Road (2–4 daily; 33–45min); Tiruchirapalli (7–8 daily; 2hr 15min–3hr 10min); Tirupati (3 weekly; 11hr 30min).

Tiruchirapalli to: Bengaluru (Bangalore) (1 daily; 8hr 55min); Chengalpattu (6–7 daily; 4hr–5hr 20min); Chennai (7–9 daily; 5hr 20min–7hr); Coimbatore (2 daily; 4hr 55min–5hr 10min); Kanyakumari (1–2 daily; 7hr 30min–9hr); Kochi (1 daily; 9hr 30min); Kodaikanal Road (2–4 daily; 1hr 50min–2hr 15min); Madurai (8–9 daily; 2hr 45min–3hr 30min); Thanjavur (2 daily; 1hr 10min–1hr 25min).

Buses

Chennai to: Bengaluru (Bangalore) (every 15–30min; 8–11hr); Chengalpattu (every 5–10min; 1hr 30min–2hr); Chidambaram (20 daily; 5–7hr); Coimbatore (every 30min; 11–13hr); Kanchipuram (every 20min; 1hr 30min–2hr); Kanyakumari (10 daily; 16–18hr); Kodaikanal (1 daily; 14–15hr); Kumbakonam (every 30min; 7–8hr); Madurai (every 20–30min; 10hr); Mamallapuram (every 15–30min; 2–3hr); Puducherry (every 15–30min; 4–5hr); Rameshwaram (3 daily; 14hr); Thanjavur (20 daily; 8hr 30min); Thiruvananthapuram (6 daily; 20hr); Tiruchirapalli (every 15–30min; 8–9hr); Tirupati (every 30min–1hr; 4–5hr); Tiruvannamalai (every 20–30min; 4–5hr); Udhagamandalam (Ooty) (2 daily; 15hr).

Chidambaram to: Chengalpattu (every 20–30min; 4hr 30min–5hr); Chennai (every 20–30min; 5–6hr); Coimbatore (6 daily; 7hr); Kanchipuram (hourly; 7–8hr); Kanyakumari (3 daily; 10hr); Kumbakonam (every 10min; 2hr 30min); Madurai (6 daily; 8hr); Puducherry (every 15–20min; 2hr); Thanjavur (every 15–20min; 4hr); Tiruchirapalli (every 30min; 5hr); Tiruvannamalai (hourly; 3hr 30min).

Coimbatore to: Bengaluru (Bangalore) (hourly; 8–9hr); Chennai (every 30min–1hr; 10–12hr); Kodaikanal (4 daily; 6hr); Madurai (every 30min; 5–6hr); Mysore (3 daily; 6hr); Udhagamandalam (Ooty) (every 15min; 3hr 30min–4hr); Palakaad (hourly; 2hr); Palani (hourly; 2hr 30min–3hr); Pollachi (every 30min; 1hr); Puducherry (10 daily; 9hr); Rameshwaram (2 daily; 14hr); Thrissur (hourly; 5hr); Tiruchirapalli (every 30min; 5hr).

Kanchipuram to: Chennai (every 10min; 1hr 30min–2hr); Coimbatore (3 daily; 9–10hr); Madurai (4 daily; 10–12hr); Puducherry (10 daily; 3–4hr); Tiruchirapalli (3 daily; 7hr); Tiruvannamalai (every 30min–1hr; 3–4hr).

Kanyakumari to: Chennai (hourly; 16–18hr); Kovalam (10–12 daily; 2hr); Madurai (every 30min; 6hr); Puducherry (hourly; 12–13hr); Rameshwaram (3 daily; 10hr); Thiruvananthapuram (every 30min–1hr; 2hr 45min–3hr); Tiruchirapalli (every 30min; 10–12hr).

Madurai to: Chengalpattu (every 20–30min; 9hr); Chennai (every 20–30min; 11hr); Chidambaram

(6 daily; 8hr); Coimbatore (every 30min; 5–6hr); Kanchipuram (4 daily; 10–12hr); Kanyakumari (every 30min; 6hr); Kochi (9 daily; 10hr); Kodaikanal (hourly; 4hr); Kumbakonam (8 daily; 6hr–6hr 30min); Kumily (hourly; 5hr); Mysore (5 daily; 10hr); Puducherry (hourly; 9–10hr); Rameshwaram (every 30min–1hr; 4hr); Thanjavur (every 30min; 4–5hr); Thiruvananthapuram (hourly; 7hr); Tiruchirapalli (every 30min; 4–5hr); Tirupati (4 daily; 15hr).

Puducherry to: Bengaluru (Bangalore) (4 daily; 10–12hr); Chennai (every 10–20min; 2hr 30min–3hr); Chidambaram (every 20min; 2hr); Coimbatore (10 daily; 9hr); Kanchipuram (10 daily; 3–4hr); Kanyakumari (hourly; 12–13hr); Madurai (hourly; 9–10hr); Mamallapuram (every 10–20min; 1hr 30min–2hr); Thanjavur (hourly; 5hr); Tiruchirapalli (every 30min; 5–6hr); Tiruvannamalai (every 20min; 2hr).

Tiruchirapalli to: Chengalpattu (every 20–30min; 7–8hr); Chennai (every 20–30min; 8hr 30min–9hr 30min); Coimbatore (every 30min; 5hr); Kanchipuram (3 daily; 7hr); Kanyakumari (every 30min; 10–12hr); Kodaikanal (8–10 daily; 5hr); Madurai (every 30min; 4–5hr); Puducherry (every 30min; 5–6hr); Thanjavur (every 10min; 1hr–1hr 30min); Tiruvannamalai (5 daily; 6hr).

Flights

IC = Indian Airlines, 6E = IndiGo, 9W = Jet Airways S2 = JetLite, DN = Air Deccan IT = Kingfisher, G8 = Go Air, I7 = Paramount Airways, SG = Spice Jet)

Chennai to: Bengaluru (Bangalore) (IC, 9W, S2, DN, IT, I7, SG 24 daily; 50min–1hr); Coimbatore (IC, 9W, I7, DN 8–10 daily; 55min–1hr 55min;); Delhi (IC, 9W, S2, DN, IT 12 daily; 2hr 30min–3hr 30min); Hyderabad (IC, 9W, DN, IT, 6E, I7, SG 20 daily; 1hr); Kochi (IC, DN, IT, I7 6–7 daily; 1hr–2hr 15min); Kolkata (IC, 9W, S2, DN 6 daily; 2hr 5min); Madurai (IC, 9W, DN, I7 8 daily; 55min–1hr 20min); Mumbai (IC, 9W, DN, IT, G8, SG 22–24 daily; 1hr 45min–3hr 40min); Port Blair (IC, 9W, DN, IT, SG 5 daily; 2hr); Thiruvananthapuram (IC, 9W, DN, I7 2 daily; 1hr 10min); Tiruchirapalli (IC, DN 2–4 daily; 50min).

Coimbatore to: Bengaluru (Bangalore) (S2, DN, IT 4 daily; 40–55min); Chennai (IC, 9W, I7, DN 8–10 daily; 1hr 5min–1hr 15min); Hyderabad (I7 1 daily; 1hr 30min); Kochi (IC 1 daily; 30min); Kozhikode (IC 1 daily; 30min); Mumbai (IC, 9W, DN, GO 5 daily; 1hr 45min).

Madurai to: Bengaluru (Bangalore) (I7 1 daily; 2hr 20min); Chennai (IC, 9W, DN, PA 7 daily; 55min–1hr 25min); Mumbai (IC 1 daily; 3hr 15min).

Tiruchirapalli to: Chennai (IC, DN 2–3 daily; 50min–1hr 10min); Kozhikode (IC 2 weekly; 55min); Thiruvananthapuram (IC 4 weekly; 40min).

20

TAMIL NADU | Travel details

Kerala

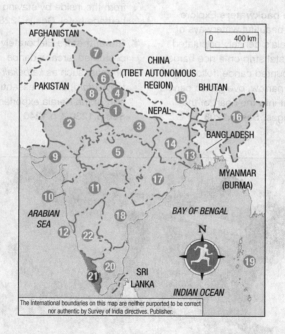

CHAPTER 21

Highlights

* **Temple festivals** Parades of extravagantly decorated elephants, backed by drummers and firework displays, form the focal point of Kerala's Hindu festivals. See p.1181

* **Varkala** Chill out in a cliff-top café, sunbathe on the beach or soak up the atmosphere around the town's busy temple tank. See p.1197

* **The backwaters** Explore the beautiful waterways of Kerala's densely populated coastal strip on a rice barge or punted canoe, following the narrow, overgrown canals right into the heart of the villages. See p.1208

* **The Cardamom Hills** The tea plantations, pepper groves and grassy mountains around Kumily and Munnar are the perfect antidote to the heat and humidity of the coast. See p.1216 & p.1220

* **Fort Cochin** Dutch, Portuguese, British and traditional Keralan townhouses line the backstreets of Malabar's old peninsula port. See the grandest of them from the inside by staying in a heritage hotel. See p.1228

* **Ritual theatre** Elaborately costumed, arcane dance dramas, such as *kathakali* and *theyyattam*, are an essential part of the Kerala experience. See p.1230 & p.1240

▲ Fishing at Fort Cochin

Kerala

A sliver of dense greenery sandwiched between the Arabian Sea and the forested Western Ghat mountains, the state of **KERALA** stretches for 550km along India's southwest coast, and is just 120km wide at its broadest point. Its lush tropical landscape, fed by two annual monsoons, has intoxicated visitors since the ancient Sumerians and Greeks sailed in search of spices to the shore known as the **Malabar Coast**. Equally, Kerala's arcane rituals and spectacular festivals – many of them little changed since the earliest era of Brahmanical Hinduism – have dazzled outsiders for thousands of years.

Travellers weary of India's daunting metropolises will find Kerala's cities smaller and more relaxed. The most popular is undoubtedly the great port of **Kochi** (Cochin), where the state's long history of peaceful foreign contact is evocatively evident in the atmospheric old quarters of Mattancherry and Fort Cochin, hubs of a still-thriving tea and spice trade. In Kerala's far south, the capital, **Thiruvananthapuram** (Trivandrum), is gateway to the nearby palm-fringed beaches of **Kovalam**, and provides visitors with varied opportunities to sample Kerala's rich cultural and artistic life.

One of the nicest aspects of exploring Kerala, though, is the actual travelling – especially by **boat**, in the spellbinding Kuttanad region, around historic **Kollam** (Quilon) and **Alappuzha** (Alleppey). Cruisers and beautiful wooden barges known as *kettu vallam* ("tied boats") ply the **backwaters**, offering tourists a rare glimpse of village life in India's most densely populated state. Furthermore, it's easy to escape the heat of the lowlands by heading for the **hills**, which rise to 2695m. Roads pass through landscapes dotted with churches and temples, tea, coffee, spice and rubber plantations, and natural forests, en route to wildlife reserves such as **Periyar**, where herds of mud-caked elephants roam freely.

Kerala is short on the historic monuments prevalent elsewhere in India, and the few ancient temples that remain in use are usually closed to non-Hindus (though you can of course take a look at the exteriors and soak up the surrounding atmosphere). Following an unwritten law, few of Kerala's buildings, whether houses or temples, are higher than the surrounding trees, and from high ground in urban areas this often creates the illusion that you're surrounded by forest. Typical features of both domestic and temple architecture include long, sloping tiled and gabled roofs that minimize the excesses of rain and sunshine, and pillared verandas; the definitive example is **Padmanabhapuram Palace**, in neighbouring Tamil Nadu, but easily reached from Thiruvananthapuram.

Huge amounts of money are lavished upon many, varied, and often all-night **festivals** usually associated with Kerala's temples. Fireworks rend the air, while

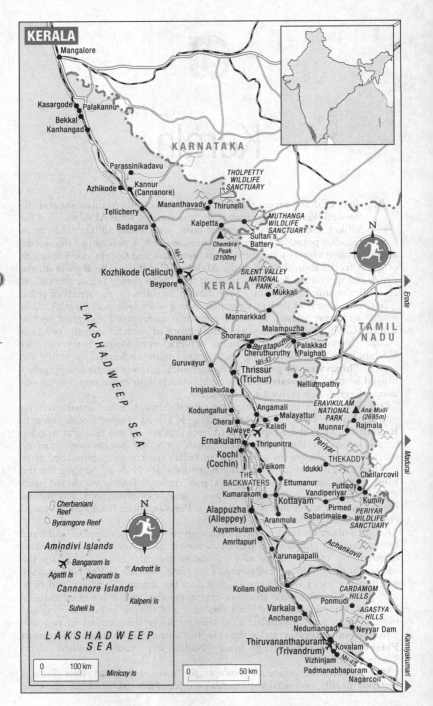

processions of gold-bedecked elephants are accompanied by some of the loudest (and deftest) drum orchestras in the world. The famous **Puram** festival in Thrissur (April/May) is the most astonishing, but smaller events take place throughout the state – often outdoors, with all welcome to attend. **Theatre** and **dance** styles also abound; not only the region's own female classical dance form, **Mohiniattam** ("dance of the enchantress"), but also the martial-art-influenced **Kathakali** dance drama, which has for four centuries brought gods and demons from the Mahabharata and Ramayana to Keralan villages. Its two thousand-year-old predecessor, the Sanskrit drama **Kutiyattam**, is still performed by a handful of artists, while localized rituals known as **Theyyam**, where dancers wearing decorative masks and hats become "possessed" by temple deities, continue to be a potent ingredient of village life in the north. Few visitors witness these extraordinary all-night performances, but between December and March it is possible to spend weeks hopping between these village festivals in northern Kerala, experiencing a way of life that has altered little in centuries.

Some history

Ancient Kerala is mentioned as the land of the **Cheras** in a third-century BC Ashokan edict, and in several even older Sanskrit texts, including the Mahabharata. Pliny and Ptolemy also testify to thriving trade between the ancient port of Muziris (now known as Kodungallur) and the Roman Empire. Little is known about the history of the region's early rulers, whose dominion covered a large area, but whose capital, Vanji, has not so far been identified. At the start of the ninth century, King Kulashekhara Alvar – a poet-saint of the Vaishnavite *bhakti* movement known as the *alvars* – established his own dynasty. His son and successor, Rajashekharavarman, is thought to have been a saint of the parallel Shaivite movement, the *nayannars*. The great Keralan philosopher **Shankaracharya**, whose *advaitya* ("non-dualist") philosophy influenced the whole of Hindu India, was alive at this time.

Eventually, the prosperity acquired by the Cheras through trade with China and the Arab world proved too much of an attraction for the neighbouring **Chola** empire, who embarked upon a hundred years of sporadic warfare with the Cheras at the end of the tenth century. Around 1100, the Cheras lost their capital at Mahodayapuram in the north, and shifted south to establish a new capital at Kollam (Quilon).

Direct trade with Europe commenced in 1498 with the arrival in the capital, Calicut, of a small Portuguese fleet under **Vasco da Gama** – the first expedition to reach the coast of India via the Cape of Good Hope and Arabian Sea. After an initial show of cordiality, relations between him and the local ruler, or Zamorin, quickly degenerated, and da Gama's second voyage four years later was characterized by appalling massacres, kidnapping, mutilation and barefaced piracy. Nevertheless, a fortified trading post was soon established at Cochin from which the Portuguese, exploiting old enmities between the region's rulers, were able to dominate trade with the Middle East. This was gradually eroded away over the ensuing century by rival powers France and Holland, and in the early 1600s the East India Company entered the fray. An independent territory was subsequently carved out of the Malabar Coast by Tipu Sultan of Mysore, but his defeat in 1792 left the British in control right up until Independence.

Kerala today can claim some of the most startling **radical** credentials in India. In 1957 it was the first state in the world to democratically elect a communist government, and still regularly returns communist parties in elections (the present chief minister, V.S. Achuthanandan, is a communist party leader). Due to uncompromising reforms made during the 1960s and 1970s, Kerala currently has the most equitable land distribution of any Indian state. Poverty is not absent, but it appears far less acute than in other parts of the country, with rates of life expectancy and per capita income well above the national averages. Kerala is also justly proud of its reputation for healthcare and education, with **literacy** rates that stand, officially at least, at 91 percent for men and 88 percent for women. Industrial development is negligible, however: potential investors from outside tend to fight shy of dealing with such a politicized workforce.

Thiruvananthapuram

Kerala's capital, the coastal city of **THIRUVANANTHAPURAM** (still widely and more commonly known as **Trivandrum**), is set on seven low hills, 87km from the southern tip of India. Despite its administrative importance – demonstrated by wide roads, multistorey office blocks and gleaming white colonial buildings – it's a decidedly easy-going place, with a mix of narrow backstreets and traditional red-tiled gabled houses, and palm trees and parks breaking up the bustle of its modern concrete centre.

Although it has few monuments as such, Thiruvananthapuram holds enough of interest to fill a day or two. The oldest and most interesting part of town is the **Fort** area in the south, around the **Shri Padmanabhaswamy Temple** and **Puttan Malika Palace**, while the **Sri Chitra Art Gallery** and **Napier Museum**, showcases for painting, crafts and sculpture, stand together in a park in the north. In addition, schools specializing in the martial art *kalarippayattu* and the dance/theatre forms of *kathakali* and *kutiyattam* offer visitors an insight into the Keralan obsession with physical training and skill.

Arrival

Connected to most major Indian cities, as well as Sri Lanka, the Maldives and the Middle East, **Beemapalli airport** is 6km southwest of town and serviced by an airport bus and bus #14 to and from the City Bus Stand. Auto-rickshaws will run you into the centre for around Rs80 and there's also a handy pre-paid taxi service, for which you pay a set fee before departure of Rs180 for the train station, and Rs385 for Kovalam's Lighthouse Beach. A Kerala Tourism information booth and Thomas Cook foreign-exchange facility are located just before the exit of the arrivals concourse.

The long-distance KSRTC **Thampanoor Bus Stand** and **railway station** face each other across Station Road in the southeast of the city, a short walk east of Overbridge Junction on MG Road. **Local buses** (including Kovalam) depart from **City Bus Stand**, in East Fort, ten minutes' walk south from the KSRTC and railway stations. **Auto-rickshaws** run to Kovalam for Rs100–150, while **taxis** charge around Rs250–275 – but beware of overcharging scams.

Information and tours

The **tourist information counters** at the **airport** (☎0471/250 1085) are open during flight times. Kerala Tourism (KTDC) also has a booth at the **Thampanoor Bus Stand** (Mon–Sat 10am–5pm; ☎0471/232 7224), which is good for general information and maps, and at the **railway station** (☎0471/233 4470). Their main visitor ("tourist facilitation") centre is 150m south of the Napier Museum on Museum Road (open 24hr in theory; ☎0471/232 1132, ⓦwww.keralatourism.org).

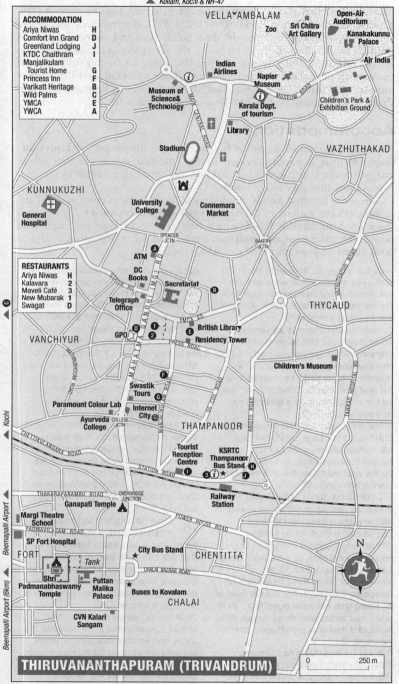

Kollam, Kochi & NH-47

VELLAYAMBALAM

ACCOMMODATION
Ariya Niwas	H
Comfort Inn Grand	D
Greenland Lodging	J
KTDC Chaithram	I
Manjalikulam Tourist Home	G
Princess Inn	F
Varikatt Heritage	B
Wild Palms	C
YMCA	E
YWCA	A

Zoo
Sri Chitra Art Gallery
Open-Air Auditorium
Kanakakunnu Palace
Air India

Indian Airlines
Napier Museum
Children's Park & Exhibition Ground

Museum of Science & Technology
MUSEUM ROAD
Kerala Dept. of tourism

Library

VAZHUTHAKAD

Stadium

KUNNUKUZHI

General Hospital

University College

Connemara Market

SPENCER JCTN

BAKERY JCTN

VAZHIKKACODU ROAD

RESTAURANTS
Ariya Niwas	H
Kalavara	2
Maveli Café	3
New Mubarak	1
Swagat	D

ATM
DC Books

Secretariat

THYCAUD

Telegraph Office

YMCA RD

British Library

GPO

Residency Tower

PRESS ROAD

VANCHIYUR

MAHATMA GANDHI RD

STATUE RD

MAHARUBHOOM ROAD

Children's Museum

Swastik Tours

Paramount Colour Lab

Internet City @

Ayurveda College

COLLEGE JCTN

THAMPANOOR

CHETTIKULANGARA ROAD

TAIKKAD HOSPITAL RD

ARISTO ROAD

Tourist Reception Centre

KSRTC Thampanoor Bus Stand

STATION ROAD

Railway Station

THAKARAPARAMBU ROAD

OVERBRIDGE JUNCTION

Ganapati Temple

Margi Theatre School

PADMAVILASAM ROAD

POWER HOUSE ROAD

SP Fort Hospital

City Bus Stand

CHENTITTA

N

FORT

Tank

Shri Padmanabhaswamy Temple

Puttan Malika Palace

CHALAI BAZAAR ROAD

Buses to Kovalam

CHALAI

CVN Kalari Sangam

THIRUVANANTHAPURAM (TRIVANDRUM)

0   250 m

Kovalam & Kanyakumari

21

KERALA

Kochi

Beemapalli Airport

Beemapalli Airport (6km)

1185

Kerala Tourism also has a visitor reception centre, next to their KTDC *Chaitram* hotel on Station Road (℡0471/233 0031, ⓦwww.ktdc.com), where you can book accommodation in their hotel chain and tickets for various **guided tours**. Most of these, including the city tours (daily: 8.30am–7pm, Rs130; half-day 8.30am–1pm or 2–7pm, Rs70/80), are far too rushed, but if you're really pushed for time and want to reach the tip of India, try the **Kanya-kumari** tour (daily 7.30am–9pm; Rs250), which takes in Padmanabhapuram Palace (except Mon), Suchindram Temple and Kanyakumari.

Accommodation

Accommodation in all categories is a lot easier on the pocket in Thiruvanan-thapuram than at nearby Kovalam Beach. That said, this is one city where budget travellers, in particular, should consider spending a couple of hundred rupees more than they might usually.

Close on a hundred **hotels** and lodges lie within ten minutes' walk of the railway and bus stations, in the district known as **Thampanoor** – the best of them up Manjalikulam Road, which runs due north from the main road outside the stations. As ever with state capitals and other large cities, it pays to book ahead, and reconfirm the day before checking in.

Ariya Niwas Aristo Rd, Thampanoor ℡0471/233 0789. Large, spotlessly clean, well-aired rooms with comfy beds and city views from upper floors. The best value in this bracket and only 2min walk from the railway station. ④–⑤

Comfort Inn Grand opposite the Secretariat, MG Rd ℡0471/247 1286, ⓦwww.comfort inngrand.in. Smart new business hotel in the city centre, completely refurbished in 2005. The "executive" options on the top storey are larger and more plush than the "standards", and have the best views. There's also a quality a/c veg restaurant on site. ⑥–⑧

Greenland Lodging Aristo Rd, Thampanoor ℡0471/232 8114. Large and efficient lodge with spotless attached rooms for Rs270. The best low-cost option in the vicinity of the bus stand and railway station. Book ahead or arrive before noon. ②

KTDC Chaithram Station Rd ℡0471/233 0977, ⓦwww.ktdc.com. Big government-run tower-block hotel very close to the railway station and Thampanoor Bus Stand, holding a range of differently priced, spacious rooms (some a/c), restaurants, travel agent, car rental, beauty parlour, cybercafé, bookshop and bar. ④–⑥

Manjalikulam Tourist Home Manjalikulam Rd, Thampanoor ℡0471/233 0776. Don't be fooled by the shining glass and marble ground floor – above lurks a basic budget place offering variously priced rooms, all of them clean and with good, comfy mattresses. ④

Princess Inn Manjalikulam Rd, Thampanoor ℡0471/233 9150, ⓔprincess.inn@yahoo.com. Well-scrubbed, respectable cheapie close to the

stations. One of the more welcoming and better-value small hotels in this busy enclave. ③

Varikatt Heritage Poonen Rd, near Cantonment Police Station, behind the Secretariat (look for the brown gates) ℡98952/39055 or 0471/233 6057, ⓦwww.varikattheritage.com. Thiruvananthapuram's only heritage homestay, run by the affable Col. K.K. Kuncheria (Gurkha Rifles, Rtd), is a real gem. It occupies a gorgeous 1830s colonial bungalow whose front-side suites ($125) retain more period atmosphere than the much less appealing rear-side doubles ($110). ⑨

Wild Palms Mathrubhoomi Rd ℡0471/247 1175, ⓦwww.wildpalmsonsea.com. Plush guesthouse in a modern suburban residence, 10min walk from MG Rd. The attached rooms are very large and good value. They also run *Wild Palms on Sea* (℡0471/275 6781), a set of poolside cottages 20km west of town, in a coconut grove by the beach. ⑤–⑦

🏃 **YMCA** YMCA Rd, near the Secretariat ℡0471/233 0059, ⓔymcatvm @sancharnet.in. Neat, smartly furnished rooms at bargain rates for the levels of comfort. The "luxury" options are enormous and have spacious bathrooms; singles from Rs220; some a/c. Amazing value, though you'll probably need to book at least two weeks in advance. ③–④

YWCA Spencer Junction ℡0471/247 7308. Spotless attached doubles on the fourth floor of a grubby, rundown office block. Safe and central, with some non-a/c rooms, but the place is locked at 10.30pm sharp. Primarily for women, but couples and men are welcome. ③–④

The City

Thiruvananthapuram's centre can be explored easily on foot, though you might be glad of a rickshaw ride back from the museums and parks, close to the top end of MG Road. The historical and spiritual heart of town is the **Fort area**, at the southern end of **MG Road**, which encloses the Shri Padmanabhaswamy Vishnu temple. En route between the two you pass through the main shopping district, which is busy all day, and especially choked when one of the frequent, but generally orderly, political demonstrations converges on the grand colonial **Secretariat** building halfway along.

The Shri Padmanabhaswamy Temple

A Neoclassical gateway leads from the western end of Chalai Bazaar to the **Shri Padmanabhaswamy Temple**, which is still controlled by the Travancore royal family. Unusually for Kerala, it's built in the Dravidian style of Tamil Nadu, with a tall, seven-tiered *gopura* gateway and high fortress-like walls.

Few foreigners get to see it (non-Hindus are not permitted inside) but the **deity** enshrined in the central sanctum – spectacularly large reclining Vishnu – is composed of 12,008 sacred stones, or *salagrams*, brought by elephant from the bed of the Gandhaki River in Nepal. The main approach road to Shri Padmanabhaswamy, where devotees bathe in a huge tank, is lined with stalls selling religious souvenirs. It's an atmospheric area for a stroll – particularly in the early morning.

Puttan Malika Palace

The **Puttan Malika Palace** (Tues–Sun 8.30am–12.30pm & 3–5.30pm; Rs20, camera Rs15) immediately southeast of the temple, became the seat of the Travancore rajas after they left Padmanabhapuram at the end of the nineteenth century. It was originally commissioned by Raja Ravi Thirunal Varma, who died at the tender age of thirty, only a year after the palace was completed. The cool chambers, with highly polished plaster floors and delicately carved wooden screens, house a crop of dusty Travancore heirlooms, including a solid crystal throne gifted by the Dutch. The real highlight, however, is the elegant Keralan architecture itself. Beneath sloping red-tiled roofs, hundreds of wooden pillars, carved into the forms of rampant horses (*puttan malika* translates as "horse palace"), prop up the eaves, and airy verandas project onto the surrounding lawns.

The royal family have always been keen patrons of the arts, and the open-air **Swathi Sangeetotsavam festival**, held in the grounds during the festival of Navaratri (Oct/Nov), continues the tradition. Performers sit on the palace's raised porch, flanked by the main facade, with the spectators seated on the lawn. Songs composed by Raja Swathi Thirunal (1813–1846), known as the "musician king", dominate the programme. For details, ask at the KTDC tourist office.

CVN Kalari Sangam and Chalai Bazaar

Around 500m southeast of the temple in East Fort, the red-brick **CVN Kalari Sangam** ranks among Kerala's top **kalarippayattu** gymnasiums. It was founded in 1956 by C.V. Narayanan Nair, one of the legendary figures credited for the martial art's revival, and attracts students from across the world. From 6.30am to 8am (Mon–Sat) you can watch fighting exercises in the sunken *kalari* pit that forms the heart of the complex. Foreigners may join courses, arranged through the head teacher, or *Gurukkal*, although prior experience of martial arts and/or dance is a prerequisite. You can also join the queues of locals who come here for a traditional **Ayurvedic massage**, and to consult the gym's expert Ayurvedic doctors (Mon–Sat 10am–1pm & 5–7.30pm, Sun 10am–1pm).

▲ Kalarippayattu

The main source of **textiles** in the city is **Chalai Bazaar**, the big market extending east from Fort district. Jammed with little shops selling bolts of cloth, flowers, incense, spices, bell-metal lamps and fireworks, it's a great area for aimless browsing.

The Margi Theatre School

Thiruvananthapuram has for centuries been a crucible for Keralan classical arts, and the **Margi Theatre School** (☏0471/247 8806, ⓦ www.margitheatre.org), at the western corner of the Fort area, keeps the flame of the region's ritual theatre traditions burning brightly. **Kathakali** dance drama and the more rarely performed **kutiyattam** theatre form (see p.1241) dominate the curriculum. Most visitors venture out here to watch one of the authentic *kathakali* or *kutiyattam* performances staged in its small **theatre**, details of which are posted on the school's website. To reach Margi, head to the SP Fort Hospital on the western edge of Fort, and then continue 200m north; the school is set back from the west side of the main road in a large red-tiled and tin-roofed building, behind the High School (the sign is in Malayalam).

The Napier Museum, Zoo and Sri Chitra Art Gallery

A minute's walk east from the north end of MG Road, opposite Kerala Tourism's information office, brings you to the entrance to Thiruvananthapuram's **public gardens**. As well as serving as a welcome refuge from the noise of the city, the park holds the city's best museums. Give the dusty and uninformative Natural History Museum a miss and head instead for the more engaging **Napier Museum** (Tues–Sun 10am–5pm; Rs5). Built at the end of the nineteenth century, it was an early experiment in what became known as the "Indo-Saracenic" style, with tiled, gabled roofs, garish red-, black- and salmon-patterned brickwork, and a spectacular interior of stained-glass windows and loud turquoise, pink, red and yellow stripes. Highlights of the collection include fifteenth-century Keralan woodcarvings, minutely detailed ivory work, a carved temple chariot (*rath*), plus Chola and Vijayanagar bronzes.

You have to pass through the main ticket booth for the city's depressingly old-fashioned zoo to reach the **Sri Chitra Art Gallery** (Tues–Sun 10am–5pm; Rs50), which shows paintings from the Rajput, Mughal and Tanjore schools, along with pieces from China, Tibet and Japan. The meat of the collection, however, is made up of works by the celebrated Keralan artist, **Raja Ravi Varma** (1848–1906), credited with introducing oil painting to India.

Eating

Thiruvananthapuram has busy, hygienic places to eat on seemingly every street corner, serving freshly cooked *dosas, iddli-vada-sambar* and other traditional udupi snacks. Wonderful Kerala-style thali "meals" are also widely available – the best places are listed below.

Ariya Niwas *Ariya Niwas* hotel, Aristo Junction, Thampanoor. Top-class south Indian vegetarian thalis dished up on shiny green banana leaves in a scrupulously clean dining room on the hotel's ground floor. You buy your ticket first (Rs40 per head; "No Sharing"). Hugely popular with everyone from office workers to company directors and their families, and deservedly so: there's really nowhere better to eat in the city.

Kalavara Press Rd. One of the city's most popular multi-cuisine restaurants, down a sidestreet off MG Rd. You can eat in their dowdy first-floor dining room or, from 6.30pm onwards, on the more attractive rooftop terrace under a pitched-tile shelter. The furniture's plastic, but the food (mostly non-veg) is tasty and inexpensive: fish, beef, mutton and pork dominate the menu, plus they do fish curry "meals" from 12.30 to 2pm.

Maveli Café next to the bus station on Station Rd, Thampanoor. Part of the *Indian Coffee House* chain, this bizarre red-brick, spiral-shaped café (designed by the recently deceased expatriate British architect, Laurie Baker) is a Thiruvananthapuram institution. Inside, waiters in the trademark ICH

pugris serve *dosas*, vadas, greasy omelettes, mountainous biriyanis and china cups of the usual (weak and sugary) filter coffee. An obligatory pit-stop, though a grubby one.

New Mubarak off Press Rd, Statue. Terrific little no-frills backstreet joint that's famed for its wonderful Malabari-Muslim dishes, especially seafood. In addition to the usual masala-fry pomfret, kingfish, seer fish and pearlspot (*avioli*), you can order huge jumbo prawns, squid and crab, served with proper tapioca (*kappa*) curry and the famous house seafood pickle – at prices undreamed of in Kovalam (most mains Rs75–150). It's tricky to find: you have to squeeze down a narrow pedestrian alleyway off Press Rd (find your way to the *Residency Tower* hotel and ask there).

Swagat *Comfort Inn Grand*, MG Rd. Fine vegetarian Indian food (both north and south) served by black-tie waiters in a blissfully cool a/c dining hall, with tinted windows and discrete Carnatic music in the background – just the ticket if you've had enough of the heat and humidity outside. Their Rs100 "Swagat Special" thali is one for monster appetites.

Listings

Airlines Air India, Museum Rd, Vellayambalam Circle ☎ 0471/231 0310, airport ☎ 0471/250 0585; Indian Airlines, Air Centre, Mascot Junction ☎ 0471/231 4781, airport ☎ 0471/233 1063; IndiGo, First Floor, Krishna Commercial Complex, Bakery Junction ☎ 0471/233 0227; Jet Airways, First Floor, Akshaya Towers, Sasthamangalam Junction ☎ 0471/272 8864, airport ☎ 0471/250 0710; SriLankan Airlines, 1st Floor, Spencer Building, Palayam, MG Rd ☎ 0471/247 1815, airport ☎ 0471/250 1140.

Banks and exchange A string of big banks along MG Rd – including HDFC, the SBI, UTI and ICICI – have ATMs and change traveller's cheques and currency. Thomas Cook maintains a foreign exchange counter at the airport and at its travel agency on the ground floor of the Soundarya Building (near the big Raymond's tailoring store), MG Rd (Mon–Sat 9.30am–6pm).

Hospitals SP Fort Hospital (☎ 0471/245 0540), just down the road from the Margi school in West Fort, has a 24hr casualty and specialist orthopedic unit; the private Cosmopolitan Hospital, in Pattom ☎ 0471/244 8182, is also recommended.

Internet access Internet City on Manjhalikulam Rd (see map, p.1185) charges Rs20/hr and is convenient if you're staying in Thampanoor. There's also a tiny, more cramped cybercafé to the rear of the KTDC *Hotel Chaitam*'s lobby, next to the bus stand (Rs30/hr).

Photography and printing The excellent Paramount Colour Lab on Ayurveda College Junction, MG Rd, has state-of-the-art digital printers, sells memory cards and will load data onto discs.

Post office The main post office, with poste restante (daily 8am–6pm), is just south of the Secretariat on MG Rd.

Moving on from Thiruvananthapuram

Thiruvananthapuram is the main hub for traffic travelling along the coast and across the country. For an overview of transport from Thiruvananthapuram, see Travel details, p.1249.

Thiruvananthapuram's **Beemapalli airport**, 6km southwest of the city, offers international and domestic flights from a rapidly expanding list of carriers, several of whom have offices downtown (see p.1189). As the roads to Beemapalli were recently upgraded, it's a comfortable enough journey by auto-rickshaw.

Buses to **Kovalam** leave every twenty to thirty minutes from the roadside in East Fort, just south of City Bus Stand (see map, p.1185). To reach anywhere else, you'll have to head for the grimy KSRTC **Thampanoor Bus Stand**. Services to **Varkala** leave from here at irregular intervals throughout the day from 7.25am – though it's worth noting that many of them are nail-bitingly slow, winding through dozens of villages and taking up to two and a half hours instead of the 90min by "super-fast" buses that follow the highway. Heading **north** up the coast (to Kollam, Alleppey, Ernakulam and Thrissur), the buses to aim for are the 6am or 5.30pm "super-deluxe a/c" specials, tickets for which – along with **tickets** for all other long-distance routes – may be purchased in advance at the reservations hatch on the main bus stand concourse (daily 6am–10pm). The Tamil Nadu bus company, TNSRTC, has its own counter on the same concourse. Numerous private bus companies also run interstate services; many of the agents are on Aristo Road near the *Greenland Lodging*.

Recommended trains from Thiruvananthapuram

The following trains are recommended as the fastest and/or most convenient from Thiruvananthapuram.

Destination	Name	No.	Departs	Total time
Alapuzzha	Netravati Express**	#6346	daily 10am	2hr 50min
Bengaluru (Bangalore)	Bangalore Express	#6525	daily 12.55pm	18hr
Chennai	Chennai Mail*	#2624	daily 2.30pm	16hr 30min
Delhi	Rajdhani Express**	#2431	Tues & Thurs 7.15pm	42hr 35min
	Kerala Express	#2625	daily 11.15am	52hr 30min
Ernakulam (Kochi)	Kerala Express	#2625	daily 11.30am	4hr
Kanyakumari	Kanyakumari Express	#1081	daily 9.55am	2hr
Kollam	Kerala Express	#2625	daily 11.30am	1hr 5min
Kottayam	Cape–Mumbai Express	#1082	daily 8.10am	2hr 20min
Madgaon (Goa)	Netravati Express	#6346	daily 10am	19hr 50min
	Rajdhani Express	#2431	Wed & Fri 7.15pm	15hr 10min
Madurai	Anantapuri Express	#6124	daily 4.20pm	6hr 40min
	Madurai Passenger	#728	daily 8.20am	9hr
Mangalore	Mangalore Express	#6347	daily 8.45pm	14hr 30min
	Parasuram Express**	#6349	daily 6.10am	13hr 30min
Mumbai	Netravati Express**	#6346	daily 10am	30hr 40min

* via Kollam, Varkala, Kottayam, Ernakulam and Palakkad
** via Kollam, Ernakulam, Thrissur, Kozhikode and Kannur

Kerala's capital is well connected **by train** with other towns and cities in the country, although getting seats at short notice on long-haul journeys can be a problem. **Reservations** should be made as far in advance as possible from the efficient computerized booking office at the station (Mon–Sat 8am–2pm & 2.15–8pm, Sun 8am–2pm).

South of Thiruvananthapuram

Despite the fact that virtually the entire 550-kilometre length of the **Keralan coast** is lined with sandy beaches, rocky promontories and coconut palms, **Kovalam** is one of the only places where swimming in the sea is not considered eccentric by locals, and which offers accommodation to suit all budgets. To experience daily life away from the exploits of the Kovalam beach scene, you can take an easy wander through the toddy groves to villages such as **Pachalloor** and **Vizhinjam**. A finely preserved example of Keralan architecture is also within easy reach of Thiruvananthapuram: 63km to the south lies the magnificent palace of **Padmanabhapuram**, former capital of the kingdom of Travancore.

Kovalam and around

The coastal village of **KOVALAM** may lie just 14km south of Thiruvananthapuram but, as Kerala's most developed **beach resort**, it's a world away from the rest of the state. Although hippy travellers started holing up here three decades ago, it was only in the early 1990s, with the arrival of Kerala's first charter tourists, that the boom really kicked off; since then the place has changed almost beyond recognition. Prices have rocketed, construction continues apace, and in high season the beach gets inundated with package tourists.

Arrival, information and transport

Buses from Thiruvananthapuram loop through the top of the village before coming to a halt outside the gates of the *Leela Kempinski*, on the promontory dividing Hawah and Kovalam beaches. If you don't intend to stay at this northern end of the resort, get down just past *Hotel Blue Sea* where the road bends – a lane branching to the left drops steeply downhill towards the top of Hawah Beach. The bus journey generally takes 30–45 minutes, but you can cover the 14km from Thiruvananthapuram more quickly by **auto-rickshaw** (Rs100–125) or **taxi** (Rs350–400).

Expect to be plagued by commission touts as you arrive; an approach via the back paths is a good way of avoiding them. The friendly **tourist office** (daily 10am–5pm, closed Sun in low season; ☎0471/248 0085, ⓦwww.keralatourism .org), just inside the *Leela Kempinski* gates, close to where the buses pull in, stocks the usual range of glossy leaflets on Kerala and can offer up-to-date advice about cultural events in the area.

There are plenty of places to **change money** in Kovalam, but private exchange rates can vary so it's best to check beforehand. The Central Bank of India has a branch at the *Kovalam Beach Resort* and the Andhra Bank at KTDC *Samudra*; but for an **ATM**, you'll have to travel up to **Kovalam Junction**, 3km inland, on the national highway (Rs80–100 return in an auto-rickshaw; see map, p.1192).

Western Travels (daily 8am–8pm; ☎0471/248 1334) near the bus stand is a reliable agent for flight confirmations and ticketing, and can arrange **car rental**. Voyager Travels (☎0471/2481993), on the lane cutting uphill from the end of

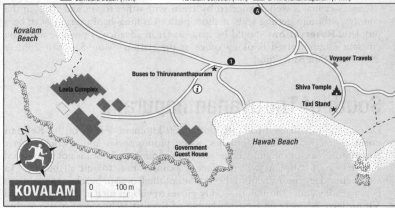

Map labels:
- Samudra Beach (1km)
- Kovalam Junction (1km)
- & Thiruvananthapuram (14km)
- Kovalam Beach
- Voyager Travels
- Buses to Thiruvananthapuram
- Shiva Temple
- Taxi Stand
- Leela Complex
- Hawah Beach
- Government Guest House
- **KOVALAM** 0   100 m
- N

Hawah Beach, specializes in **motorbike rental**, at competitive rates: an Enfield Bullet is Rs350–500 per day, a scooter Rs250–275. You'll need to leave your driver's licence or passport with them as security. **Surfboards** can be rented on Lighthouse Beach for an extortionate Rs275 per hour, or boogie boards for Rs60. Alternatively, for around Rs300 you can take a ride on a traditional **kettumaran** (*kettu* meaning tied; *maran* logs), which gave the catamaran its name. Widely used by the fishermen of Kovalam, the rudimentary boat consists of five logs lashed together with coir rope, and can feel disconcertingly vulnerable in even a slightly choppy sea: accept a lifejacket if it's offered.

Plenty of places offer broadband **Internet** access for Rs40/hr. Kovalam doesn't have a major **bookshop**, but many of the tailors and clothes stalls supplement their trade by dealing in the usual hit-and-miss selection of second-hand books, and there's a decent selection on offer at a stall upstairs in *Waves* (*German Bakery*).

Accommodation

Although Kovalam is crammed with **accommodation**, decent rock-bottom rooms are hard to find, as all but a handful of the many budget traveller's guest-houses have been upgraded to suit the package tourists who flock here over Christmas and the New Year. Hotels are often block-booked weeks in advance, so it's a good idea to make a reservation before you arrive. **Prices** are extortionate compared with the rest of Kerala, almost doubling in peak season (Dec to mid-Jan), when you'll be lucky to find a basic room for less than Rs500. At other times, haggling should bring the rate down by twenty to fifty percent, especially if you stay for more than a week. The codes below are for high-season prices.

Blue Sea 100m before junction to Hawah Beach ☎0471/248 1401 or 09439 991992, ⓦwww .hotelskerala.com/bluesea. Half a dozen quirky round buildings in the rear garden of a colonial-era mansion overlooking the main road. Each contains three spacious, cool and good-value rooms, arranged on separate storeys around a (rather shabby) central pool. ❺–❻

Green Shore Lighthouse Rd ☎0471/248 0106, ⓦwww.thegreenshore.com. Well-furnished rooms in a modern building close to the lighthouse. It's a bit boxed in, but the interiors are nicely done and there are big common verandas to lounge on. ❹–❺

Moon Valley Cottage behind Lighthouse Beach ☎94461 00291, ✉sknairkovalam@yahoo.com. This simple budget guesthouse stands right next to the footpath leading from the rear of Lighthouse Beach to the Avaduthura Devi temple. Its rooms are big for the price, have mozzie nets and quality bedding, and are pleasantly decorated. ❸–❹

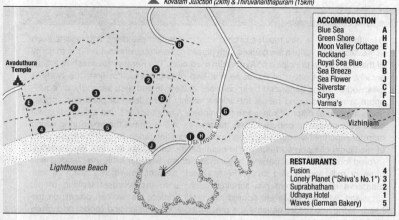

ACCOMMODATION

Blue Sea	A
Green Shore	H
Moon Valley Cottage	E
Rockland	I
Royal Sea Blue	D
Sea Breeze	B
Sea Flower	J
Silverstar	C
Surya	F
Varma's	G

Avaduthura Temple

Lighthouse Beach

Vizhinjam

RESTAURANTS

Fusion	4
Lonely Planet ("Shiva's No.1")	3
Suprabhatham	2
Udhaya Hotel	1
Waves (German Bakery)	5

Rockland Lighthouse Rd ☎0471/248 0588. *Rockland* is one of a cluster of three co-run budget hotels, sandwiched together just off the lane above the south end of Lighthouse Beach. Its six comfortable rooms – all attached and with balconies – look straight through coconut palms to the sea. Reasonable rates given the location. ❹

Royal Sea Blue Behind Lighthouse Beach ☎0471/212 7857. Recently built three-storey block, well off the road in the palm groves. Fronted by a large garden, the rooms are sparkling, with polished marble floors, TVs, fridges and (optional) a/c units, and the location is very peaceful. ❺–❻

Sea Breeze behind Lighthouse Beach ☎0471/248 0024. One of Kovalam's better-value budget choices: quiet, secluded, with large and sunny communal balconies overlooking a well-tended tropical garden. The rooms are clean and large for the price, and there's a yoga *shala* on the top floor. ❸–❹

Sea Flower ☎0471/248 0554, ⓦwww.seaflower beachresort.com. You can't get closer to the sea than the orange-painted *Sea Flower*, which rises straight from the sand at the south end of Lighthouse Beach. Facing the surf, its spacious, breezy and comfortable rooms are spread over two

storeys – the upper ones cost Rs350 extra, but are worth it for the views. ❹

Silverstar behind Lighthouse Beach ☎0471/248 2883, or 09895 673443, ⓦwww.silverstar -kovalam.com. A relative newcomer hidden away in the palm groves a couple of hundred metres inland from the beach. Centred on a shady courtyard, the location is tranquil by Kovalam standards, and the rooms very large, with verandas or terraces out front, and new mozzie nets. ❼

Surya Lighthouse Beach ☎0471/248 1012, ⓔkovsurya@yahoo.co.in. Secure, quiet, efficiently run guesthouse down a narrow lane off the seafront, with pleasant rooms for the price (a/c and non-a/c); some of the verandas look straight onto adjacent buildings, but there's lots of space inside. If it's full, try the equally spruce *White House* (☎0471/248 3388; ❹) next door. ❹

Varma's Lighthouse Beach Rd ☎0471/248 0478, ⓔvarmabeach@hotmail.com. One of the few places in Kovalam that's tried to incorporate traditional Keralan architecture into its design. The result is an attractive blend of modern comforts and old-style Malabari wood and brass décor. All twelve rooms are sea-facing and it's well placed for the less-frequented cove south of Lighthouse Beach. ❽

The beaches

Kovalam consists of four fairly small stretches of sand; the southernmost, known for obvious reasons as **Lighthouse Beach**, is where most visitors spend their time. It takes about ten minutes to walk from end to end, either along the sand or on the concrete pathway (patrolled by lots of touts) which fronts a long strip of resorts, guesthouses and restaurants.

The red-and-white-striped **lighthouse** (daily 3–5pm; Rs5), on the promontory at the southern end of the beach, is the area's most prominent landmark. It opens for two hours each afternoon, when you can scale the 142 spiral steps

"Health tourism" is very much a buzz phrase in Kerala these days, and resorts such as Kovalam and Varkala are packed with places to de-stress and detox – the majority of them based on principals of **Ayurvedic medicine**. The Keralan approach to India's ancient holistic system of medicine has two distinct elements: first, the body is cleansed of toxins generated by imbalances in lifestyle and diet; secondly, its equilibrium is restored using herbal medicines, mainly in the form of plant oils applied using a range of different **massage** techniques. A practitioner's first prescription will often be a course of **panchakarma** treatment – a five-phase therapy during which harmful impurities are purged through induced vomiting, enemas, and the application of medicinal oils poured through the nasal cavity. Other less onerous components, tailored for the individual patient, may include: *dhara*, where the oils are blended with ghee or milk and poured on to the forehead; *pizhichi*, in which a team of four masseurs apply different oils simultaneously; and, the weirdest looking of all, *sirovashti*, where the oils are poured into a tall, topless leather cap placed on the head. Alongside these, patients are prescribed special balancing foods, and given vigorous full-body **massages** each day.

Ayurvedic cures for every conceivable ailment are offered in Kerala's tourist resorts. Few clinics, however, are staffed by fully qualified practitioners. Standards of both treatment and hygiene vary greatly, as do the prices. Woman travellers also sometimes complain of sexual harassment at the hands of opportunistic male masseurs; cross-gender massage is forbidden in Ayurveda. Dodgy oils that can cause skin problems is another risk you might be exposed to at a backstreet clinic.

The only sure-fire way to be guaranteed bona fide treatment is to splash out on somewhere that's been approved by the government. Kerala Tourism's **accreditation scheme** divides centres into **Green Leaf** establishments – which apply the highest standards of hygiene, employ only pukka staff, never allow cross-gender massage, and use top-grade oils and medicines – and Olive Leaf ones, which offer equally dependable treatments, but in more traditionally Keralan surroundings. This is the kind of place generally referred to as an **Ayurvedic spa** and will nearly always be attached to a posh seaside hotel or heritage resort.

and twelve ladder rungs to the observation platform: on clear days, views extend over the beach as far as Beemapally mosque in one direction, and south to Poovar in the other.

South of the lighthouse, a tiny white-sand cove opens into a much larger beach, overlooked by a scattering of upmarket hotels, which you can reach by following the lane that peels off Lighthouse Road, before *Varma's Beach Resort* (see map, p.1192). Lots of tourists mistakenly believe this is a private area, but it isn't.

Heading in the opposite direction (northwards) from Lighthouse Beach, you round a small rocky headland to reach **Hawah Beach** – almost a mirror image of its busier neighbour, although it is backed for most of its length by empty palm groves. In the morning before the sunworshippers arrive, it functions primarily as a base for local fishermen, who hand-haul their massive nets through the shallows, singing and chanting as they coil the endless piles of rope.

North of the next headland, **Kovalam Beach** is dominated by the angular chalets of the five-star *Leela* above it. Home to a small mosque, it's shared by guests of the luxury resort and by local fishermen in roughly equal measure; to get there, follow the road downhill past the bus terminus. Only a short walk further north, **Samudra Beach** is very small, especially at high tide, and is backed by a cluster of package-tour resorts surrounding a tiny temple. It holds little to recommend it during the day, but comes alive at night, when rows of restaurant tables spring up along the seawall.

Warning: swimming safety

Due to unpredictable rip currents and a strong undertow, especially during the monsoons, **swimming** from Kovalam's beaches is not always safe. The introduction of blue-shirted lifeguards has reduced the annual death toll, but at least a couple of tourists still drown here each year, and many more get into difficulties. Follow the warnings of the safety flags at all times and keep a close eye on children. There's a first-aid post midway along Lighthouse Beach.

Eating, drinking and nightlife

Lighthouse Beach is lined with identikit cafés and restaurants specializing in **seafood**: you pick from displays of fresh fish such as blue marlin, sea salmon, barracuda and delicious seer fish, as well as lobster, tiger prawns, crab and mussels. They are then weighed, grilled over a charcoal fire or cooked in a tandoor, and served with rice, salad or chips. Meals are **pricey** by Indian standards – typically around Rs175–350 per head for fresh fish, and double that for lobster or prawns – and service is often painfully slow, but the food is generally very good and the ambience of the beachfront terraces convivial.

For a traditional Keralan **breakfast**, head to one of the local teashops near the bus stand. Freshly cooked, delicious Keralan *appams* and egg masala are also on offer at a makeshift shelter on the side of the pathway leading from Lighthouse Beach to the Avaduthura temple. Further along the same path, on the right next to where it meets the surfaced lane, the locals enjoy tasty rice-plate thali "**meals**" for around Rs20 at a nameless, dingy shack. It's a rough-and-ready place, but the food is delicious.

Nightlife in Kovalam is pretty laid-back, and revolves around the beach, where Westerners chill when the restaurants close. Beer and spirits are served in most cafés, albeit in discrete china teapots from under the table due to tight liquor restrictions. One or two places also run **movie nights**, screening pirate copies of just-released hits.

Fusion Lighthouse Beach. Along with *Waves*, the funkiest place on Lighthouse Beach, with three innovative menus (Eastern, Western and fusion) served on a first-floor terrace overlooking the bay. Try the fish creole in orange vinaigrette with cumin potatoes. They also have a fine selection of drinks, a hefty sound system playing Indo-Western music, and a toilet that has to be seen to be believed. Most mains Rs180–225.

Lonely Planet ("Shiva's No.1") behind Lighthouse Beach. Flanked by a pond that's alive with croaking frogs, the covered terrace of this large, family-run budget travellers' place is one of the most enduringly popular restaurants in the village. Its menu of north and south Indian vegetarian standards is nothing to write home about, though inexpensive for Kovalam (most mains Rs50–100). Wed evenings host a cultural show with all-you-can-eat buffet (7.30–9pm; Rs175; book in advance).

Suprabhatham near the *Silverstar*. Simple, popular vegetarian café-restaurant in a well-shaded garden setting, where you can order inexpensive Indian breakfasts, fresh juices, lassis and shakes, as well as an extensive multi-cuisine menu: the "Bengali aubergine" and "chunky avocado salad" are popular specials.

Udhaya Hotel near the bus terminus. Hidden away behind a tiny general store, this local teashop serves the best Keralan breakfasts for miles, in a narrow, blue-walled cafeteria. Huge trays of steaming *iddiappam* (rice-flour vermicelli), *puttu* (rice rolls) and *appam* (steamed pancakes made from fermented rice batter) are served with tin plates of egg masala and more-ish *chana wada*. The chai's delicious too. You'll be hard pushed to spend more than Rs25 per head here.

Waves (German Bakery) Lighthouse Beach. This rooftop terrace, shaded by a high tiled canopy serves light meals, snacks, German cakes and delicious, freshly ground coffee through the day. After sunset, its atmospheric designer lighting makes a great backdrop for more sophisticated cooking: Thai and Kerala seafood curries, lobster in vodka, fish steaks with sesame and coriander crust, or steamed prawns with chilli and coconut milk. Most mains Rs195–250.

North of Kovalam: Pozhikkara

If you need a break from the commercialism of Kovalam, keep plodding north along Samudra Beach for around 4km, past a string of fishing hamlets, until you arrive at a point where the sea merges with the backwaters. The sliver of white sand flanking the river mouth here, known as **Pozhikkara Beach**, makes an appealing, and much quieter, alternative base for the area. The palm groves behind the beach hold two appealing places to stay. British-run *Lagoona Davina* (℡0471/238 0049, ⓦwww.lagoonadavina.com; ➒) is a small, exclusive boutique hotel overlooking the river mouth; rooms are small, but individually styled with carved wood four-posters and Indian textiles. *Beach and Lake Resort* (℡0471/238 2086, ⓦwww.beachandlakeresort.com; ➐) lies across the water from *Lagoona* (you'll have to hail a boatman to reach it) and is an altogether more down-to-earth affair, with an even better location closer to the surf and fishing beach. If you book in advance, both places send drivers to meet you at the airport; otherwise take a taxi or auto 6km along the highway from Thiruvananthapuram towards Kovalam, and look for the signboards on the right-hand side of the road just after after Thiruvallam bridge.

South of Kovalam: Vizhinjam to Poovar

A tightly packed cluster of tiled fishers' huts, **VIZHINJAM** (pronounced "Virinyam"), on the opposite (south) side of the headland from Lighthouse Beach, was once the capital of the Ay kings, the earliest dynasty in south Kerala. A number of simple small shrines survive from those times, and can be made the focus of a pleasant afternoon's stroll through coconut groves, best approached from the centre of the village rather than the coast road – brace yourself for the sharp contrast between hedonistic tourist resort and workaday fishing village.

On the far side of the fishing bay in the village centre, fifty metres down a road opposite the police station, a small unfinished eighth-century **rock shrine** features a carved figure of Shiva with a weapon. The **Tali Shiva** temple nearby, reached by a narrow path from behind the government primary school, may mark the original centre of Vizhinjam. The simple shrine is accompanied by a group of *naga* snake statues, a reminder of Kerala's continuing cult of snake worship, a survivor from pre-brahminical times.

Golden-sand beaches fringe the shore stretching **southwards from Vizhinjam,** interrupted only by the occasional rock outcrop and tidal estuary. This dramatic coastline, with its backdrop of thick coconut plantations, can appear peaceful compared with Kovalam, but it's actually one of the most densely populated corners of the state. Over the past decade, virtually every metre of land backing the prettiest stretches of coast has been bought up and built on. Even so, it's worth renting a scooter to explore the back lanes and more secluded beaches, where poor Christian fishing villages stand in surreal juxtaposition with luxury beach resorts and Ayurvedic spas. One of the most memorable views hereabouts is at **Chowara** village, 8km south of Kovalam, from which an endless stretch of sand sweeps to the horizon, scattered with literally hundreds of wooden boats.

Accommodation south of Kovalam

Friday's Place Poovar Island ℡0471/213 3292, ⓦwww.kukimedia.com/fridaysplace. Four beautifully made teak and mahogany "eco-cottages", set in an acre of palm and acacia gardens deep in the backwaters. Each has its own veranda, solar electricity supply and comfy rubber-mattress beds. Doubles $200 per night. ➒

Karikkathi Beach House Pulinkudi ℡0471/240 0956, ⓦwww .karikkathibeachhouse.com. An exquisite little bolthole, nestled amid the palm trees above a quiet cove, only a stone's throw from the surf. You pay more for the location than luxury, though the house, with its white walls, terracotta tiles and wood furniture, has an understated style. One of the most desirable places to stay in south India, though such exclusivity comes at a price ($300 per double room, or $585 if you book the whole house). ⑨ **Somatheeram** Chowara ☎0471/226 6501, ⓦwww.somatheeram.org. Accommodation in traditional-style Keralan houses fitted with a/c and other mod cons, stacked on terraces overlooking the beach; its Ayurvedic spa ranks among the best in the state. Doubles $125–250. ⑨

Surya Samudra Pulinkudi ☎0471/248 0413, ⓦwww.suryasamudra.com. The dreamiest of all the "heritage resorts" on this strip, featuring antique, gabled villas, scattered across a 21-acre promontory between a pair of quiet beaches. $185–530 per night. ⑨ **Travancore Heritage** ☎0471/226 7828, ⓦwww.thetravancoreheritage.com. The centrepiece of this extravagant complex is a splendid 150-year-old mansion, fronted by a kidney-shaped pool and sun terrace. Below it, sixty relocated antique bungalows fall away to the sands, complete with their own plunge pools. Rooms $125–345. ⑨

Padmanabhapuram

Although now officially in Tamil Nadu, **PADMANABHAPURAM**, 63km southeast of Thiruvananthapuram, was the capital of Travancore between 1550 and 1750, and maintains its historic links with Kerala, from where it is still administered. For anyone with even a minor interest in local architecture, the small **Padmanabhapuram Palace** (Tues–Sun 9am–4.30pm; Rs50 [Rs20], cameras Rs20), is an irresistible attraction. With its exquisite wooden interiors, coconut-shell floors and antique furniture and murals, the building represents the high-water mark of regional building. Just **avoid weekends**, when the complex gets overrun with bus parties.

Frequent **buses** run to Padmanabhapuram along the main highway from Thiruvananthaparum and Kovalam. Hop on any service heading to Nagercoil or Kanyakumari and get off at **Thakkaly** (sometimes written Thuckalai).

Varkala

Long renowned by Hindus as a place of pilgrimage, **VARKALA**, 54km northwest of Thiruvananthapuram, with its spectacular sands and red cliffs, is these days a considerably more appealing beach destination than Kovalam. Centred on a clifftop row of budget guesthouses and palm-thatch cafés, the tourist scene is still relatively low-key, although the arrival in recent years of the first charter groups and luxury hotels may well be the harbinger of full-scale development: building inland and at both ends of the beach is already proceeding apace.

Arrival and information

Varkala beach lies 4km of west of Varkala village proper, which is grouped around a busy market crossroads. The village's mainline railway station, served by express and passenger **trains** from Thiruvananthapuram, Kollam and most other Keralan towns, stands 500m north of this central junction. While some **buses** from Thiruvananthapuram's Thampanoor stand, and from Kollam to the north, continue on to within walking distance of the beach and clifftop area, most terminate in Varkala village, where you'll have to pick up an auto-rickshaw for the remaining five-minute ride (around Rs40–50) to the seashore.

If you can't get a direct bus to Varkala, take any "superfast" or "limited stop" bus running along the main NH-47 highway to **Kallamballam**, 15km east, from where slower local minibus services (Rs10), auto-rickshaws (Rs80–100) and taxis (Rs150–175) will transport you to the beach.

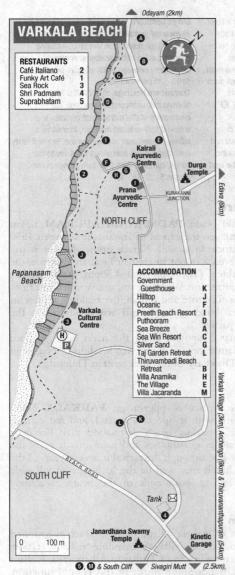

VARKALA BEACH

▲ Odayam (2km)

RESTAURANTS
Café Italiano	2
Funky Art Café	1
Sea Rock	3
Shri Padmam	4
Suprabhatam	5

Kairali
Ayurvedic
Centre

Durga
Temple

Prana
Ayurvedic
Centre

KURAKANNI
JUNCTION

NORTH CLIFF

Papanasam
Beach

Varkala
Cultural
Centre

ACCOMMODATION
Government Guesthouse	K
Hilltop	J
Oceanic	F
Preeth Beach Resort	I
Puthooram	D
Sea Breeze	A
Sea Win Resort	C
Silver Sand	G
Taj Garden Retreat	L
Thiruvambadi Beach Retreat	B
Villa Anamika	H
The Village	E
Villa Jacaranda	M

SOUTH CLIFF

BEACH ROAD

Tank ⊠

Janardhana Swamy
Temple

Kinetic
Garage

0   100 m

Edava (6km) ▶

Varkala Village (3km), Ancheng (9km) & Thiruvananthapuram (54km) ▶

⑤, Ⓜ & South Cliff ▼ Sivagiri Mutt ▼ (2.5km),

Motorcycles are available for rent everywhere in Varkala for around Rs250–300 per day (or Rs350–400 for an Enfield), but if you're after something dependable just to potter around the lanes on, start your hunt at the Kinetic Garage, near Temple Junction, whose scooters are kept in good condition.

There are numerous places to **change money** on the clifftop: City Tours and Travels, in front of the *Hilltop Beach Resort*, exchange currency and traveller's cheques, and offer advances on Visa cards for a small commission. The nearest **ATMs** are at the banks up in Varkala village, just off the crossroads. The many **Internet** centres in Varkala charge Rs40/hr.

Accommodation

Being pitched almost exclusively at foreigners, little of Varkala's plentiful accommodation is cheap by Indian standards. The hotels up on the clifftop are most people's first choice, with more inspiring views than those lining the road to the beach. Auto-rickshaws from the railway station and village tank go as far as the helipad or round the back to North Cliff; it's worth stopping on the way to see if the *Government Guesthouse* has vacancies. Pressure on beds is acute in **peak season** (late Nov to mid-Feb), when it's a good idea to book in advance. Out of season, from April onwards, many places shut up shop.

Government Guesthouse Cliff Rd ☎0470/260 2227, ⊛www.keralatourism .org. Behind the *Taj* hotel, this former maharajah's holiday palace has been converted into a charming guesthouse. The two attached rooms in the original building are enormous and fantastic value; the others (all attached) occupy a modern block in the same grounds and are much less inspiring. Meals available on request. ②–③

Hilltop North Clifftop ☎0470/260 1237, ⊛www .hilltopvarkala.com. Long-established hotel occupying a prime location, right on the rim of the cliff looking out to sea. It offers three categories of attached rooms: "deluxe" (with breezy balconies and uninterrupted sea views; Rs2000); "standard" (the same, but without views; Rs1200); and "economy" (older options to the rear ground floor; Rs800). ⑤–⑥

Oceanic North Cliff ☎0470/229 0373, @oceanicresidence@yahoo.co.im. Very pleasant rooms, with flowering climbers trailing from the balconies, close to the thick of things on the clifftop. Café noise is sometimes a problem at night, but this ranks among the better-run, better-value budget options close to the strip. ④–⑤

Preeth Beach Resort North Clifftop area, off Cliff Rd ☎0470/260 0942, ⓦwww.preethbeachresort .com. Large, well-maintained two-star complex set 5min back from the cliff in a shady palm grove. Grouped around a kidney-shaped pool and sun terrace, its accommodation ranges from no-frills economy rooms to spacious a/c cottages with generous verandas. ④–⑧

Puthooram North Cliff ☎0470/320 2007 or 09895 232209. Snug chalet-cottages made entirely of polished wood, some with traditional Keralan railings and thatched roofs, opening onto a trim little garden, right on the cliff edge. ④–⑦

Sea Breeze North Cliff ☎0470/260 3257 or 09846 004243. Set back in a coconut grove behind a small tidal beach, this rather grand new building is the northern-most guesthouse in Varkala proper. Its rooms are large for the price, opening onto a big common veranda that's strung with hammocks and catches the breezes straight off the surf. ⑤–⑦

Sea Win Resort North Cliff ☎0470/260 1084 or 09895 083950. One of several swanky modern buildings to have sprung up recently at the end of the cliff on the back of Saudi riyals. The colour schemes are a bit off-beat, but the rooms themselves are enormous, with a spacious common veranda on one side and large private sitouts on the other where you watch the sea only a stone's throw away. ④–⑤

Silver Sand North Cliff ☎09846 826144 or 098464 78432. This budget guesthouse, 200m back from the cliff edge behind the *Funky Art Café*,

offers unbeatable value: its eight marble-clad, simply furnished rooms are large and comfortable for the price, with thick mattresses and doors opening onto a sociable common veranda. ④

Taj Garden Retreat Cliff Rd ☎0470/260 3000, ⓦwww.tajhotels.com. Not the most alluring of Taj Group's five-star hotels (the architecture owes more to the Costas than Kerala) but the most luxurious option in Varkala. Tariffs (from $250 per night) include breakfast and dinner buffets in the swanky *Cape Comorin* restaurant. ⑨

Thiruvambadi Beach Retreat North Clifftop ☎0470/260 1028, ⓦwww.thiruvambadihotel.com. This idiosyncratic, family-run guesthouse at the far (quiet) end of the cliff has fifteen rooms, the best of them split-level a/c suites boasting big, sea-facing balconies and over-the-top Mughal-kitsch decor. ⑥–⑧

Villa Anamika North Cliff ☎0470/260 0095, ⓦwww.villaanamika.com. A welcoming homestay, 200m from the cliff, run by a Keralan artist and her German husband. Their five variously priced rooms are all light, airy, cool and attractively furnished. Guests get the run of a beautiful rear garden, and breakfasts feature home-made German bread and jams. ④–⑤

The Village North Cliff ☎09947 155442. Three newly built, handsomely furnished octagonal cottages set back from the road in a small garden; each has its own private sitout and kitchenette. A good choice for families. ⑥–⑦

Villa Jacaranda South Cliff ☎0470/261 0296. Bijou guesthouse nestled in the tranquil South Cliff area. Run by a couple of refugees from the London rat race, it's small (only 4 rooms) but perfectly formed, with relaxing sea-blue and mauve colour schemes, stylish wooden furniture, crisp white sheets, a fragrant garden, lilly pond and roof terrace looking out to sea. Break-fasts are served on the leafy verandas. ⑧–⑨

The beach and village

Known in Malayalam as Papa Nashini ("sin destroyer"), Varkala's beautiful white-sand **Papanasam Beach** has long been associated with ancestor worship. Devotees come here after praying at the **Janardhana Swamy Temple** (said to be over two thousand years old), to bring the ashes of departed relatives for their "final rest". Non-Hindus are not permitted to enter the inner sanctum of the shrine but are welcome in the grounds.

Backed by sheer red laterite cliffs and drenched by rolling waves off the Arabian Sea, the coastline is imposingly scenic and the beach relatively relaxing – although its religious associations do ensure that attitudes to public nudity (especially female) are markedly less liberal than other coastal resorts in India. Western sun-worshippers are thus supposed to keep to the northern end of the beach (away from the main puja area reserved for the funerary rites) where they are serviced by a nonstop parade of local "hallo-pineapple-coconut?" vendors. Whistle-happy lifeguards ensure the safety of swimmers by enforcing the no-swim zones beyond the flags: be warned that the undercurrent is often strong, claiming lives every year. Dolphins are often seen swimming quite close to the coast, and, if you're lucky, you may be able to swim with them by arranging a ride with a fishing boat. Sea otters can also occasionally be spotted playing on the cliffs by the sea.

Few of Varkala's Hindu pilgrims make it as far as the **clifftop area**, the focus of a homespun but well-established tourist scene that's grown steadily over the past ten or twelve years. Bamboo and palm-thatch cafés, restaurants and souvenir shops jostle for space close to the edge of the mighty escarpments, which plunge vertically to the beach below in a dramatic arc, most beautiful at sunset, when their laterite tint glows molten red. Several steep flights of steps cut into the rock provide fast routes from the sand.

Countless private **Ayurvedic centres** and **yoga schools** have sprung up along the clifftop. As in Kovalam, many non-qualified practitioners have jumped on the bandwagon, so it's wise to look around, and get other travellers' recommendations before going for a treatment (see p.1194). Two clinics that stand out are Kairali, near the *Silver Star* guesthouse behind the *Funky Art Café* (☏0470/329 4660, ⓦwww.kala.com), and Prana, in the *Preeth Beach Resort* (☏0470/260 0942). For yoga, one teacher receiving consistently high praise from readers is Vasu, who works from the north end of the clifftop, behind *Papaya* restaurant.

Nearby, and aimed unashamedly at the tourist market, the **Varkala Cultural Centre** (☏0470/608793), behind the *Sunrise* restaurant on North Clifftop, holds daily **kathakali** and *bharatanatyam* dance performances (make-up 5–6.45pm; performance 6.45–8.15pm; Rs150). Using live musicians instead of a recorded soundtrack, it's a pleasant and authentic-enough introduction to the two types of dance, especially if you're not going to make it to Kochi (see p.1230). The centre also offers short courses on *kathakali* make-up and dance, *bharatanatyam*, devotional song (*bhajan*) and Carnatic percussion (*mridamgan*).

Eating

Varkala's clifftop **café–restaurants** specialize in locally caught seafood, prepared in a variety of styles. Prices are fairly high by Keralan standards, and service very slow, but the superb location more than compensates, especially in the evenings, when the sea twinkles with the lights of distant fishing boats. Note that with the exception of *Shri Padman* and *Suprabhatam*, none of the places listed below open out of season, between late April and October.

Café Italiano North Clifftop. Authentic Italian menu featuring pizza and pasta dishes in a variety of sauces (Rs125–250) – the house speciality *frutti di mare* is hard to beat.

Funky Art Café North Clifftop. The naffest name but still the hippest spot on the cliff, with full tables from sunset until the small hours. It serves a predictable traveller-oriented menu, but most people come here to lounge, drink, smoke and socialize over the gut-thumping sound system.

Sea Rock Clifftop, next to the helipad. As well as a fairly standard range of Indian and Continental food, this place serves tasty south Indian *iddli-vada* breakfasts and masala dosas from 8.30am–3pm. In the evenings, fresh local fish takes over, followed by DVD screenings.

Shri Padmam Temple Junction. Dingy-looking café on the temple crossroads that serves freshly made, cheap and tasty south Indian veg food (including Rs25 "meals" at lunchtime). You can walk through the front dining room to a large rear terrace affording prime views of the tank – particularly atmospheric at breakfast time.

Suprabhatam Varkala village, 4km east of the beach. The cheapest and best pure-veg joint in Varkala, situated just off the main crossroads in a dining hall lined with coir mats and grubby pink walls. Their *dosas* and other fried snacks aren't up to much, but the lunchtime "unlimited" Keralan-style rice-plate "meals" (noon–3pm; Rs20) pull in streams of locals and budget travellers.

Kollam (Quilon)

One of the Malabar Coast's oldest harbours, **KOLLAM** (pronounced "Koillam", and previously known as Quilon), 74km northwest of Thiruvananthapuram and 85km south of Alappuzha, was once at the centre of the international spice trade. The port flourished from the very earliest times, trading with the Phoenicians, Arabs, Greeks, Romans and Chinese. It finds mention in the Persian *Book of Routes and Kingdoms* compiled by Ibn Khurdadhibh in 844–48, and again in the fourteenth century journals of the Moroccan traveller, Ibn Battuta, who saw Chinese junks loading pepper here in the 1330s.

Nowadays, Kollam is chiefly of interest as one of the entry or exit points to the backwaters of Kerala (see p.1208), and most travellers simply stay overnight en route to or from Alappuzha. The **town** itself, sandwiched between the sea and Ashtamudi ("eight inlets") Lake, is less exciting than its history might suggest. It's a typically sprawling Keralan market community, with a few old tiled wooden houses and winding backstreets, kept busy with the commercial interests of coir, cashew nuts (a good local buy), pottery, aluminium and fishery industries.

Of the few surviving colonial vestiges, the only one worth a detour is the former **British Residency**, a magnificent 250-year-old mansion on the shores of the lake, now used as a *Government Guesthouse* (see p.1202). Among the last monuments surviving in India from the earliest days of the Raj, it perfectly epitomizes the openness to indigenous influences that characterized the era, with typically Keralan gable roofs surmounting British pillared verandas. Much of the structure is literally falling apart, but you're welcome to visit: there are no set hours – just turn up and ask the manager if you can have a look around.

Practicalities

Kollam's busy mainline **railway station** lies east of the clocktower that marks the centre of town. Numerous daily trains run from Ernakulam and Thiruvananthapuram and beyond. The jetty and KSRTC **Bus Stand** are close together on the edge of Ashtamudi Lake. Bookable express **buses** leave for Thiruvananthapuram (1hr 45min) and Kochi (3hr) via Alappuzha (2hr) every fifteen minutes or so; as ever, the express services are much better than the "limited stop" buses. Note that most Thiruvananthapuram-bound **trains** do not stop in Varkala.

The helpful **District Tourism Promotion Council** (DTPC) have a tourist office across town (daily 9am–6pm; ☏0474/274 5625, ☖www.dtpckollam .com) at the **boat jetty** on the edge of Ashtamudi Lake, where you can book

---

KOLLAM

ACCOMMODATION
ATDC Beach Retreat	F
Government Guesthouse	A
Karthika	D
Shah International	C
Sudarsan	B
Summerhouse	E

RESTAURANTS & CAFÉS
All Spice	3
Guruprasad	4
New Mysore Café	1
Sun Moon	2

Old British Residency

ASHRAMAM

0   100 m

Boat Jetty
DTPC
KSRTC Bus Stand
UTI Bank & ATM
CHINNAKKADA ROAD
Bishop Jerome Nagar Mall
Clocktower
Railway Station
MAIN BAZAAR ROAD
Shri Uma-Maheswara
Fruit & Veg Market
Jama Masjid
Alappuzha & Monroe Island
Thankasseri (1km) & (1km)
Ernakulam (158km)
Varkala (35km)

tickets for the daily tourist backwater cruises (see p.1208); they'll also help arrange taxis for trips around the area, and can advise on local ferry transport. The local **Alapuzha Tourism Development Council** office (ATDC; daily 7am–9pm; ☎0474/276 7440), on the opposite side of the road, offers comparable services. Useful **facilities** such as exchange bureaux, ATMs and Internet outlets can be found in the smart Bishop Jerome Nagar shopping mall, just south of the main road between the jetty and the clocktower.

Accommodation

Considering the numbers of foreign tourists that pour through during the season, accommodation is in surprisingly short supply in Kollam – book in advance if you're arriving late in the day.

ATDC Beach Retreat 3km south of centre ☎0474/275 276 3793. Typical government-run place with smudged walls and average-sized rooms (some a/c), situated directly across the road from the beach, and good value. Station pick-up (Rs50) on request. ❸–❹

Government Guesthouse Ashtamudi Lake, 2km northeast ☎0474/274 3620. Sleeping in this former British Residency (see p.1201) feels like overnighting in a museum. The rooms are gigantic for the price (go for an a/c one on the first floor if it's offered), but, as with most Government guesthouses, you'll have to try for a vacancy on spec as they rarely accept advance bookings. Breakfast and dinner available. ❷–❸

Karthika Off Main Rd, near the Jama Masjid mosque ☎0474/275 1821. Large and popular budget hotel in a central location offering a range of acceptably clean, plain rooms (some a/c) arranged around a courtyard in which the centrepiece is, rather unexpectedly, three huge nude figures. ❷

Shah International Chinnakkada Rd ☎0474/274 2362, ✉hotelshah@hotmail.com. A modern

tower-block hotel close to the centre of town, holding differently priced rooms. Hardly the most atmospheric choice, but a dependably comfortable one. ❸–❻

Sudarsan Parameswar Nagar ☎0474/274 4322, ⓦwww.hotelsudarsan.com. Central and popular, though definitely not as palatial as the posh foyer would lead you to believe. Describing itself (somewhat ominously) as a "hospitalized zone that will charm your brain", the building has a range of rooms: the a/c ones are cleaner, more recently refurbished and lie on the quiet side of the building. ❹–❺

Summerhouse (Nos.1, 2 & 3) Thirumalla-waram and Thankasseri ☎0474/279 4518 or 09895 662839, ✉contactsummerhouse @hotmail.com. Run by the amiable Mr Shashi, this trio of suburban homestays offers simple, charming accommodation on the northwestern edge of town near, or next to, the sea. Pick of the bunch is "No.3", a cosy wood cabin with only two rooms (book both for privacy), opening onto a wonderful veranda slap on the sea wall. ❹

Eating

If you find yourself killing time in Kollam, try one of the following places to eat in the centre of town.

All Spice near the main bazaar. This determinedly Western, brightly lit fast-food joint, above a bakery, is where the town's middle classes come for family evenings out, and where foreign tourists come to escape the heat. The burgers, pizzas and fried chicken are less appealing than the main North Indian and Chinese dishes (Rs100–150).

Guruprasad Main Bazaar. Cramped and sweaty, but wonderfully old-school "meals" on the market's main street: blue walls, framed ancestral photos and Hindu devotional art provide the typical backdrop for pukka pure-veg rice plates and Udupi-style snacks.

New Mysore Café boat jetty, opposite KSRTC Bus Stand. This is the most popular of the "meals"

joints clustered around the bus stand and boat jetty area, serving delicious "all-you-can-eat" rice plates for only Rs19 at lunchtime, then the usual Udupi snacks through the rest of the day.

Sun Moon Top Floor, Bishop Jerome Nagar Mall ☎0474/301 3000, ⓦwww.zeez.info. Traditional Keralan cooking – *meen polichattu* (white fish steamed in banana leaf) and masala-fried calamari, as well as Continental dishes and a big multi-cuisine buffet – served in a blissfully cool a/c rooftop restaurant. The food's the best in town, as are the panoramic views. Count on Rs300 for three courses.

Between Kollam and Alappuzha

Most visitors travelling north between Kollam and Alappuzha, or southwards in the opposite direction, do so by **boat** – either local tourist-office cruisers or privately chartered *kettu vallam* rice barges. But if you cover this backwater stretch by the somewhat less scenic **NH-47** or its adjacent **railway** line, you've the option of pausing at several landmarks along the way.

The Mata Amritanandamayi Math

The **Mata Amritanandamayi ("MA") Math**, or Amritapuri as it's more familiarly known, is the home ashram of Kerala's most famous living spiritual figure, "**Amma**". It stands in the village of **VALLIKKAVU**, 10km northwest of Karunagapalli – a striking vision of pink tower blocks, capped with concrete domed cupolas, rising incongruously above the palm canopy on a sliver of land between the sea and the backwaters. Thousands of visitors and residents may be here at any given time, but numbers swell considerably when Amma herself is in residence – January to April and August to mid-November are the best times to catch her.

Amma offers her famous hugs to visitors during *darshan* sessions, held on Wednesdays, Thursdays and Fridays from noon, and from 10am on weekends. **Accommodation** is available in simple rooms (visitors are expected to put in a couple of hours' voluntary service) and free vegetarian meals are served three times daily. A few house rules apply: celibacy, modest dress and soft speech are mandatory; and drugs, alcohol and non-vegetarian food are forbidden.

Kayamkulam

KAYAMKULAM, served by local buses from Kollam and Alappuzha, was once the centre of its own small kingdom, which after a battle in 1746 came under the control of Travancore's king Marthanda Varma. In the eighteenth century, the area was famous for its spices, particularly pepper and cinnamon. The sole vestige of Kayamkulam's former glory is its eighteenth-century **Krishnapuram Palace** (Tues–Sat 10am–4.30pm; Rs5, camera Rs15), set in a tranquil garden on the outskirts of town, just off the main highway. Constructed largely of wood, with gabled roofs and rooms opening out onto shady internal courtyards, it's a typically graceful, traditional Keralan building. Inside, the prize exhibit is a huge **mural** of the classical Keralan school, in muted ochre-reds and blue-greens, which depicts **Gajendra Moksha** – the salvation of Gajendra, king of the elephants.

Mannarsala

MANNARSALA, near the village of **Haripad**, 25km south of Alappuzha on NH47, is Kerala's most revered **snake worship** centre. Dusted in turmeric and vermillion powder, some thirty thousand carved stones of rearing cobras litter a leafy forest glade attached to the **Nagaraja temple**, dedicated to the "God of Serpents". Uniquely in south India, the shrine is officiated over by an elderly female Naboordiri priestess, "Valliamma", who leads processions and pujas from her adjacent house each morning and evening. It is particularly popular with childless couples: on Sundays, many come to propitiate the deity with offerings of tumeric and salt, holding a bell-metal urn (*uruli*) upside down if they've just made their petition, or carrying it right-side up if their wish has been fulfilled.

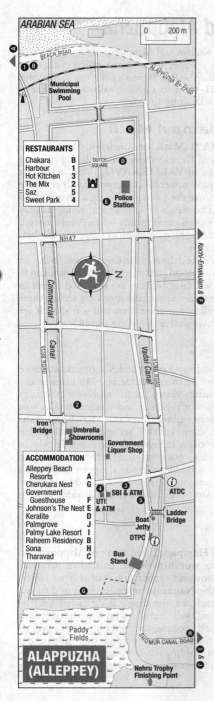

RESTAURANTS

Chakara	B
Harbour	1
Hot Kitchen	3
The Mix	2
Saz	5
Sweet Park	4

ACCOMMODATION

Alleppey Beach Resorts	A
Cherukara Nest	G
Government Guesthouse	F
Johnson's The Nest	E
Keralite	D
Palmgrove	J
Palmy Lake Resort	I
Raheem Residency	B
Sona	H
Tharavad	C

ALAPPUZHA (ALLEPPEY)

Alappuzha (Alleppey)

From the mid-nineteenth century, Alappuzha (or "Alleppey" as it was known in British times) served as the main port for the backwater region. Spices, coffee, tea, cashews, coir and other produce were shipped in from the inland waterways to the sea via its grid of canals and rail lines. Tourist literature loves to dub the town as "the Venice of the East", but in truth the comparison does few favours to Venice. Apart from a handful of colonial-era warehouses and mansions, and a derelict pier jutting into the sea from a sun-blasted **beach**, few monuments survive, while the old canals enclose a typically ramshackle Keralan market of bazaars and noisy traffic.

That said, Alappuzha makes a congenial enough place to while away an evening en route to or from the backwaters. Streams of visitors do just that during the winter season, for the town has become Kerala's pre-eminent **rice boat cruising** hub, with an estimated four hundred *kettu vallam* moored on the fringes of nearby Vembanad and Punnamada lakes. To cash in on the seasonal influx, the local tourist offices lay on a fleet of excursion boats for day-trips, while in mid-December the sands lining the west end of town host a popular **beach festival**, during which various cultural events and a procession of fifty caparisoned elephants are staged with the dilapidated pier as a backdrop.

Alappuzha's really big day, however, is the second Saturday of August, in the middle of the monsoon, when it serves as the venue for one of Kerala's major spectacles – the **Nehru Trophy snake boat race**. This event, first held in 1952, is based on the traditional Keralan enthusiasm for racing magnificently decorated longboats, with raised rears designed to resemble the hood of a cobra. Each boat carries 25 singers, and 100 to 130 enthusiastic oarsmen power the craft along, all rowing to the rhythmic *Vanchipattu* ("song of the boatman"). There are a number of prize categories, including one for the women's race; sixteen boats compete for each prize in knockout rounds. Similar races can be seen at Aranmula (p.1214) and at Champakulam, 16km by ferry from Alappuzha. The ATDC information office (see p.1202) will be able to tell you the dates of these other events, which change every year.

Arrival and information

The KSRTC **Bus Stand** is at the northeast edge of town. Close to its north exit, the main boat jetty on **Vadai Canal** is where the daily tourist ferry to and from Kollam, and local boat connections with Kottayam, arrive and depart. The **railway station**, on the main Thiruvananthapuram–Ernakulam line, lies 3km southwest.

The town has several rival **tourist departments**, all of them eager to offer advice and book you onto their respective houseboat tours and excursions. The most conveniently situated – at the jetty itself on VCSB (Vadai Canal South Bank) Road – are the DTPC tourist reception centre (daily 7.30am–9pm; ☎0477/225 1796) and adjacent Kerala Tourism office (Mon–Sat 10am–5pm; ☎0477/226 0722, ⓦwww.keralatourism.org). On the opposite side of the canal on the corner of Mullackal and Vadai Canal North Bank (VCNB) roads, ATDC's main information office (daily 8am–8pm; ☎0477/224 346, ⓦwww .atdcalleppey.com) is more tucked away, on the second floor of the Municipal Shopping Complex. Both ATDC and DTPC sell tickets for their ferries, backwater cruises and charter boats, and can help you fathom the intricacies of local ferry timetables.

You can **change money** at the efficient UTI bank on Mullackal Road (Mon–Sat 9.30am–4.30pm). Both it and the State Bank of India directly opposite have reliable ATMs. **Internet** access is widely available for Rs30 to 40 per hour, with several outlets along the road facing the boat jetty.

Accommodation

The choice of **places to stay** in the town centre is fairly uninspiring, but there are some great **homestay** possibilities in all brackets if you are willing to travel to the outskirts and pay a little more. In addition, some great accommodation options lie a taxi-ride away, hidden in the surrounding backwaters and further up the coast

Nearly everywhere, whatever its bracket, has some kind of tie-in with a houseboat operator: good-natured encouragement tends to be the order of the day rather than hard-sell tactics, but you may be able to negotiate a reduction on your room tariff if you do end up booking a backwater trip. In Alappuzha, as elsewhere in the state, rates tend to increase by 25 to 30 percent between mid-December and mid-January. Whenever you come, and wherever you chose to stay, though, brace yourself for clouds of **mosquitoes**.

In town

Alleppey Beach Resorts Beach Rd ☎0477/226 3408, ⓦwww.thealleppeybeachresorts.com. Eccentric, slightly Fawlty Towers–esque hotel offering Alappuzha's only beachside rooms. The rooms are large and a bit overpriced, but many will consider the relaxing location worth the extra. Moreover, the food gets rave reviews. ❻–❼

Cherukara Nest 9/774 Cherukara Bldgs ☎0477/225 1509 or 09947 059628. Nineteenth-century "heritage" home on a quiet canal road only a short walk around the corner from the KSRTC Bus Stand. Ecofriendly houseboat cruises are a sideline. ④–⑤

Government Guesthouse next door to KTDC *Yatri Niwas*, on NH-47 ☏ 0477/224 6504. Arranged on two floors above a central courtyard, the rooms in this modern government place are plain and a touch institutional, but fantastic for the price, with big, clean bathrooms. ②–③

Johnson's The Nest Lalbagh, Convent Square, 2km west of the centre ☏ 09961 466399, ⓦ www.johnsonskerala.com. Friendly, sociable homestay on a quiet suburban street, popular mainly with young backpackers. Its six thatched rooms are large, with Barbie-pink mosquito nets, and most have funky little sitouts fitted with cane swings. ②–④

Keralite Vadakekalam House, north of Dutch Square ☏ 0477/224 3569, ⓔ alice_t@rediffmail .com. Delightful homestay in a 100-year-old Syrian-Christian house. Antique beds furnish the guest rooms, which have lots of period atmosphere; the only catch is that some lack attached bathrooms – hence the bargain rates. Meals available ③–④

Palmgrove Punnamada Kayal, 3.5km north of boat jetty ☏ 0477/223 5004 or 09847 430434, ⓦ www .palmgrovelakeresort.com. Situated at a tranquil spot close to the lakeside, this relaxed resort consists of quaint bamboo cottages with gabled tile roofs opening onto a lakeside garden. ⑤–⑥

Palmy Lake Resort Thathampally, 2km north of boat jetty ☏ 0477/223 5938 or 09447 667888, ⓦ www.palmyresort.com. Spacious, neatly painted red-tiled "cottages" (a/c and non-a/c),

grouped behind a modern family home on the northeastern limits of town. Exceptionally good value and warm hospitality. Phone ahead for free pick-up. ④–⑤

Raheem Residency Beach Rd ☏ 0477/223 9767, ⓦ www.raheemresidency.com. The glossiest of Alappuzha's heritage hotels occupies a 140-year-old mansion on the beachfront. Sumptuously restored from near dereliction, the building encloses half a dozen richly furnished a/c rooms, equipped with carved four-posters. For outside lounging space, there's an imported French swimming pool and hammocks on the breezy roof terrace. $200–300 per night. ⑨

Sona Shomur Canal Rd, Thathampally ☏ 0477/223 5211, ⓦ www.sonahome.com. Elegant old Keralan home, with a graceful gabled roof, set back from the road to the lake. The four rooms in the original house, run by an elderly owner who loves to share his knowledge of the town and its backwaters, are far more attractive (and cheaper) than the three cheekily squeezed-in new ones in the garden. ④–⑤

Tharavad West of North Police Station, Sea View Ward ☏ 0477/224 4599, ⓦ www.tharavadheritageresort.com. Few of Alappuzha's heritage properties retain as pukka a feel as this former doctor's mansion, which rests in the shade of an old mango tree on the quiet west side of town. Entered via a typically colonial-era veranda, its interior holds polished eggshell and teak floors, carved rosewood furniture and antique bell-metal curios. The differently priced rooms are all large, attached and well-aired. ④–⑦

Around Alappuzha

Arakal Heritage Mararikulam, 16km north of *Alappuzha* ☏ 0478/286 5545 or 09847 268661, ⓦ www.arakal.com. Beachside hideaway retaining an authentic Keralan village atmosphere, in a sandy palm grove close to the sea. The five, 200-year-old houses have beautiful gabled roofs, original antique furniture, shady verandas and hidden outdoor bathrooms. One of the loveliest places to stay in the state. ⑧

Casa del Fauno Muhamma, 8km north of Alappuzha ☏ 0478/286 0862, ⓦ www .casadelfauno.com. If Fellini had ever made a film in Kerala, its set might have looked like this dream "boutique homestay" on the shores of Lake Vembanad. The fusion architecture blends polished marble and fragments of old Tamil stone sculpture to stunning effect, and the guest rooms inside are light, cool and exquisitely furnished. Gourmet meals available. ⑧

Emerald Isle Kanjooparambil–Manimalathara, 8km east of Alappuzha ☏ 0477/270 3899 or 09447 077555, ⓦ www.emeraldislekerala.com. An authentic, 150-year-old *tharavad*, sandwiched between a river and acres of rice paddy, deep in the backwaters. Four teak rooms have been converted for use by guests, featuring antique doors, lustrous carved-wood furniture and private outdoor bathrooms. Tariffs (Rs4200–48000) include all meals. ⑧

VJ's Rice Garden Pallathurthy, 6km southeast of Alappuzha ☏ 0477/270 2566 or 09446 118931, ⓦ www.ricegardenkerala.com. If you'd like to be marooned in the backwaters but can't afford any of the heritage homestays, give this quirky little guesthouse a try. Its rooms are basic, but occupy a dreamy location on a slither of riverbank backed by miles of rice fields. Access is by canoe. ④

Eating

Aside from the **restaurants** listed below, most of Alappuzha's homestays and guesthouses provide meals for guests, usually delicious, home-cooked Keralan cooking that's tailored for sensitive Western palates. For **take-aways**, you can join the scrum that forms each evening outside the government "beverages" shop, just off Mullackal Road in the main bazaar.

Chakara *Raheem Residency*, Beach Rd ℡0477/223 0767. Alappuzha's classiest restaurant, with specialities ranging from local-style fish curry (their signature dish) to seer fish simmered in flavoursome *moillie* coconut gravy. They also have plenty of tempting, healthy Continental alternatives, courteously served on a raised terrace looking across the beach. Count on Rs650–700 for a fixed four-course menu; or a bit more a la carte.

Harbour Beach Rd. All the food served in this gleaming little seafront restaurant is prepared in the kitchens of the classy *Raheem Residency* next door, so quality and freshness are assured. You can order grilled prawns, Alappuzha-style chicken curry, Kuttanadi fish, chilli chicken or a range of light Continental meals, snacks and sandwiches. Most mains are under Rs100.

Hot Kitchen Mullackal Rd. The most reputed pure-veg south Indian "meals" restaurant in town, run by a Tamil family that has been here for generations. The masala dosas, *vadas* and other fried snacks aren't so great, but the lunch-time thalis (also available in the evening) are deservedly popular.

The Mix *Arcadia Regency*, near Iron Bridge, NH-47 ℡0477/223 0414. Modern multi-cuisine restaurant in Alappuzha's only Western-style business hotel, noteworthy as much for its strident red decor as good-value, "all-you-can-eat" buffets (Rs135), featuring a huge range of Chinese and north Indian, as well as Keralan specialities.

Saz VCSB Rd, near Ladder Bridge. This no-frills non-veg place on Vadai Canal does a roaring trade at lunchtime with its fish-curry rice plate "meals" (Rs30), while in the evenings half the tourist population of Alappuzha pours in for the succulent flame-grilled barbeque and tandoori chicken. They also have a full-on kebab counter outside. It's bit grubby, but hygienic enough and cheap, with most mains Rs100–130.

Sweet Park next to UTI Bank, Mullackal Rd. The perfect pit-stop in the main bazaar, serving freshly baked macaroons, chilli and cashew cookies, samosas, veg cutlets and flaky prawn patties, with hot coffees and teas, in an open-sided café overlooking one of the main crossroads in the market area.

Moving on from Alappuzha

The filthy KSRTC **Bus** Stand, on the east side of town and a minute's walk from the boat jetty, is served by regular buses to most towns in the region (a full rundown appears on p.1249). For Fort Cochin, catch any of the fast Ernakulam

Recommended trains from Alappuzha

The following trains are recommended as the **fastest** and/or **most convenient** from **Alappuzha**.

Destination	Name	No.	Departs	Total time
Chennai	Alleppey–Chennai Express*	#6042	daily 4.10pm	14hr
Ernakulam/Kochi	Jan Shatabdi Express	#2076	daily 8.40am	1hr 10min
	Alleppey–Chennai Express*	#6042	daily 4.10pm	1hr 20min
Thiruvananthapuram	Ernakulam– Trivandrum Express	#6341	daily 7.20am	3hr 5min
	Jan Shatabdi Express	#2075	daily 6.33pm	2hr 50min
Thrissur	Alleppey–Chennai Express*	#6042	daily 4.10pm	3hr

* This train also travels to Irinjalakuda and Palakkad

One of the most memorable experiences for travellers in India is the opportunity to take a boat journey on the **backwaters of Kerala**. The area known as **Kuttanad** stretches for 75km from Kollam in the south to Kochi in the north, sandwiched between the sea and the hills. This bewildering labyrinth of shimmering waterways, composed of lakes, canals, rivers and rivulets, is lined with dense tropical greenery and preserves rural Keralan lifestyles that are completely hidden from the road.

Views constantly change, from narrow canals and dense vegetation to open vistas and dazzling green paddy fields. Homes, farms, churches, mosques and temples can be glimpsed among the trees, and every so often you might catch the blue flash of a kingfisher, or the green of a parakeet. Pallas fishing eagles cruise above the water looking for prey and cormorants perch on logs to dry their wings. If you're lucky enough to be in a boat without a motor, at times the only sounds are birds chattering and occasional film songs drifting across from distant radios. Some families live on tiny pockets of land, with just enough room for a simple house, yard and boat. They bathe and wash their clothes – sometimes their buffaloes, too, muddy from ploughing the fields – at the water's edge. Traditional Keralan longboats, *kettu vallam*, glide along, powered by gondolier-like boatmen with poles, the water often lapping perilously close to the edge. Fishermen work from tiny dugout canoes and long rowing boats, and operate massive Chinese nets on the shore.

Coconut trees at improbable angles form shady canopies, and occasionally you pass under simple curved bridges. Poles sticking out of the water indicate dangerous shallows. Here and there basic drawbridges can be raised on ropes, but major bridges are few and far between; most people rely on boatmen to ferry them across the water to connect with roads and bus services, resulting in a constant criss-crossing of the waters from dawn until dusk.

Threats to the ecosystem

The **African moss** that often carpets the surface of the narrower waterways may look attractive, but it is actually a menace to small craft and starves underwater life of light. It is also a symptom of the many serious **ecological problems** currently affecting the region, whose population density ranges from between two and four times that of other coastal areas in southwest India. This has put growing pressure on land, and hence a greater reliance on fertilizers, which eventually work their way into the water causing the build-up of moss. Illegal land reclamation, however, poses the single greatest threat to this fragile ecosystem. In a little over a century, the total area of water in Kuttanad has been reduced by two-thirds, while mangrove swamps and fish stocks have been decimated by pollution and the spread of towns and villages around the edges of the backwater region. Tourism is now adding to the problem, as the film of oil from motorized ferries and houseboats spreads through the waters, killing yet more fish, which has in turn led to a reduction of over fifty percent in the number of bird species found in the region. Some of the tourist agencies are trying to lessen the impact of visitors by introducing more ecofriendly vessels.

Tourist cruises

The most popular excursion of all in the Kuttanad region is the full-day journey between **Kollam** and **Alappuzha**. All sorts of private hustlers offer their services, but the principal boats are run on alternate days by the Alleppey Tourism Development Council (ATDC) and the District Tourism Promotion Council (DTPC) – see p.1201 for contact details. The double-decker boats leave from both Kollam and Alappuzha daily, departing at 10.30am (10am check-in); tickets cost Rs300 and can be bought in advance or on the day at the ATDC/DTPC counters, other agents and some hotels. Both companies make three stops during the eight-hour journey, including one for lunch, and another at the **Mata Amritanandamayi Math** at Amritapuri (see p.1203), around three hours north of Kollam.

Although it is by far the main backwater route, many tourists find Alappuzha–Kollam too long, with crowded decks and intense sun. There's also something faintly embarrassing about being cooped up with a crowd of fellow tourists, madly photographing any signs of life on the water or canal banks, while gangs of kids scamper alongside the boat screaming "one pen, one pen".

One alternative is to charter a four- or six-seater motorboat, which you can do through DTPC and ATDC for around Rs300/hr. Slower, more cumbersome double-decker country boats are also available for hire from Rs250–275/hr.

Village tours and canoes

Quite apart from their significant **environmental impact**, most houseboats are too wide to squeeze into the narrower inlets connecting small villages. To reach these more idyllic, remote areas, therefore, you'll need to charter a punted **canoe**. The slower pace means less distance gets covered in an hour, but the experience of being so close to the water, and those who live on it, tends to be correspondingly more rewarding. Individual guides have their own favourite itineraries. You'll also find more formal **"village tours"** advertised across the Kuttanad area, tying together trips to watch coir makers, rice farmers and boat builders in action with the opportunity to dine in a traditional Keralan village setting.

Kettu vallam (houseboats)

Whoever dreamed up the idea of showing tourists around the backwaters in old rice barges, or **kettu vallam**, could never have imagined that, two decades on, five hundred or more of them would be chugging around Kuttanad waterways. These **houseboats**, made of dark, oiled jackwood with canopies of plaited palm thatch and coir, are big business, and almost every mid- and upmarket hotel, guesthouse and "heritage homestay" seems to have one. An estimated four hundred work out of Alappuzha alone, the flashiest fitted with a/c rooms, silk cushions on their teak sun decks, imported wine in their fridges and Jacuzzis that bubble away through the night. One grand juggernaut (called the *Vaikundan*, based near Amma's ashram in Kollam district) holds ten separate bedrooms and won't slip its lines for less than Rs25,000 ($580). At the opposite end of the scale are rough-and-ready transport barges with gut-thumping diesel engines, cramped bedrooms and minimal washing facilities.

What you end up paying for your cruise will depend on a number of variables: the **size** and **quality** of the boat and its fittings; the number and standard of the **bedrooms** (a/c will bump up the price by around 50–75 percent); and, crucially, the **time of year**. Rates double over Christmas and New Year, and halve off-season during the monsoons. In practice, however, Rs4500–8000 is the usual bracket for a trip on a two-bedroom, non-a/c boat with a proper bathroom (or Rs11,000–14,000 for a/c), including three meals, in early December or mid-January. The cruise should last a minimum of 22 hours, though don't expect to spend all of that on the move: running times are carefully calculated to spare gas. From sunset onwards you'll be moored at a riverbank, probably on the outskirts of the town where the trip started.

You'll save quite a lot of cash, and be doing the fragile ecosystem a big favour, by opting for a more environmentally friendly **punted** *kettu vallam*. This was how rice barges were traditionally propelled, and though it means you travel at a more leisurely pace, the experience is silent (great for wildlife spotting) and altogether more relaxing.

Houseboat operators work out of **Kollam**, **Karunagapalli** and **Kumbakonam**, but most are in **Alappuzha**, where you'll find the lowest prices – but also the worst

(Contd...)

congestion on more scenic routes. Spend a day shopping around for a deal (your guesthouse or hotel owner will be a good first port of call) and always check the boat over beforehand. It's also a good idea to get the deal fixed on paper before setting off, and to withhold a final payment until the end of the cruise in case of arguments.

Local ferries

Kettu vallam may offer the most comfortable way of cruising the backwaters, but you'll get a much more vivid experience of what life is actually like in the region by jumping on one of the local ferries that serve its towns and villages. Particularly recommended is the trip from Alappuzha to Kottayam (5 daily; 2hr 30min; Rs12), which winds across open lagoons and narrow canals, through coconut groves and islands. The first ferry leaves at 7.30am; arrive early to get a good place with uninterrupted views.

There are also numerous other local routes that you can jump on and off, though working your way through the complexities of the timetables and Malayalam names can be difficult without the help of the tourist office. Good places to aim for from Alappuzha include Neerettupuram, Kidangara, and Chambakulam; all three are served by regular daily ferries, but you may have to change boats once or twice along the way, killing time in local cafés and toddy shops (all of which adds to the fun, of course). Whatever service you opt for, take a sun hat and plenty of water.

services along the main highway and get down at **Thoppumpady** (7km south of the city), from where local buses run the rest of the way.

Tourist **boats** travel regularly to **Kollam**, with the ATDC and DTPC boats operating a similar schedule, departing at 10.30am and arriving in Kollam at 6.30pm. From the jetty just outside the KSRTC Bus Stand, much cheaper local **ferries** travel to **Kottayam** (service #P380; 2hr 30min; Rs12), with five departures between 7.30am and 2pm, and a constellation of satellite villages in the backwaters. Regular services run to Champakulam, where you pick up less frequent boats to Neerettupuram and Kidangara, and back to Alappuzha again. This round route ranks among Kuttanad's classic trips, but you'll need some help from one or other of the tourist offices to make sense of the timetables.

As the backwaters prevent **trains** from continuing directly south beyond Alappuzha, only a few major daily services and a handful of passenger trains depart from the railway station, 3km southwest of the jetty. For points further north along the coast, take the Jan Shatabdi Express and change at Ernakulam, as the afternoon Alleppey–Cannanore Express (#6307), which runs as far as **Kozhikode** and **Kannur**, arrives at those destinations rather late at night. It is, however, a good service if you only intend to travel as far as Thrissur. For more information on transport from Alappuzha, see "Travel details" on p.1249.

Kottayam

Some 76km southeast of Kochi and 37km northeast of Alappuzha, **KOTTAYAM** is a compact, busy Keralan town strategically located between the backwaters and the mountains of the Periyar Wildlife Sanctuary. For Keralans, it's synonymous with **money**, both old and new. The many **rubber plantations** around it, first introduced by British missionaries in the 1820s, have for more than a century formed the bedrock of a booming local economy, most of it controlled by landed **Syrian Christians**.

The presence of two thirteenth-century churches on a hill 5km northwest of the centre (accessible by auto-rickshaw), attest to the area's deeply rooted Christian heritage. Two eighth-century Nestorian stone crosses with Palavi and Syriac inscriptions, on either side of the elaborately decorated altar of the **Valliapalli** ("big") church, are among the earliest solid traces of Christianity in India. The visitors' book contains entries from as far back as the 1890s, including one by the Ethiopian king, Haile Selassie, and a British viceroy. The interior of the nearby **Cheriapalli** ("small") church is covered with lively paintings, thought to have been executed by a Portuguese artist in the sixteenth century. If the doors are locked, ask for the key at the church office (9am–1pm & 2–5pm).

Aside from rubber and its famously well-educated workforce (this was the first town in India to achieve one hundred percent literacy), Kottayam's other main export is the state's number-one newspaper, the *Malayala Monorama*, which boasts a readership of 1.5 million. Check out the English edition at Ⓦwww .manoramaonline.com.

Practicalities

Kottayam's KSRTC **Bus Stand**, 500m south of the centre on TB Road (not to be confused with the private stand for local buses on MC Road), is an important stop on routes to and from major towns in south India. Four of the frequent buses to Kumily/Periyar (3–4hr) continue daily on to Madurai in Tamil Nadu (7hr), and there are regular services to Thiruvananthapuram, Kollam and Ernakulam. The **railway station**, 2km north of the centre, sees a constant flow of traffic between Thiruvananthapuram and points north, while **ferries** from

▲ Boating on the backwaters

Alappuzha and elsewhere dock at the weed-clogged jetty, 2km south of town. For details of backwater trips, see p.1208.

DTPC maintain a tiny **tourist office** at the jetty (daily 9am–5pm; ℡0481/256 0479). The best place to **change money** is the Canara Bank on KK Road, which also has one of several **ATMs** around the main square. **Internet** facilities are available at Intimacy (Rs30/hr), also on KK Road, just north of the KSRTC Bus Stand.

Accommodation and eating

Accommodation in Kottayam is very limited for a town of its size. Those travellers that do pause here tend to do so in one of the resorts or homestays in the surrounding area (see opposite), though there are a handful of places in town that are fine for a night. The town's top hotel is *Arcadia*, TB Road (℡0481/256 9999, Ⓦwww.arcadiahotels.net; ➏–➐), with good-value rooms, a fantastic rooftop pool, and a smart multi-cuisine restaurant, *Déjà Vu*, which has wonderful panoramic views over town (mains Rs100–150). The best mid-price option is the *Homestead*, KK Road (℡0481/256 0467; ➒–➓), though the beds in the economy rooms are rock hard – it's worth shelling out the additional Rs130 for a "deluxe". On the south side of town, *Aida*, TB Junction, MC Road (℡0481/256 8391, Ⓦwww.hotelaidakerala.com; ➍), is a large 1980s hotel with a range of dowdy, brown rooms, including some with a/c and reasonably priced singles.

Kottayam may not be a particularly alluring destination in itself, but it has a handful of very good **places to eat**. For a delicious, freshly cooked pure-veg thali, head for *Anand* at the *Anand Lodge*, KK Road, just off the main square – the a/c family hall is the more relaxing of the two wings and meals only cost Rs10 more. The *Homestead*'s popular restaurant, *Meenachil*, provides quality non-veg Keralan food, such as Kuttanadi chicken curry, plus Punjabi-style tandoori, Chinese duck dishes and set Keralan "meals" (Rs50 for veg, Rs60 for non-veg). You'll need to catch an auto-rickshaw or taxi to reach the legendary roadside *Karimpunkala*, 6km south of town on the MC Road, at Nattakom-Palam, but will be rewarded by sumptuous, village-style seafood sadhyas, featuring *karimeen pollichadu* (spiced *karimeen* fish steamed in a banana leaf), *kakairachi* (oysters) and proper *kappa* (tapioca). Count on Rs100–150 for the works.

Around Kottayam

Some of Kerala's most attractive backwater scenery lies within easy reach of Kottayam. Probably the ideal destination for a day-trip – although it also has some wonderful accommodation – the beautiful **Kumarakom Bird Sanctuary** lies on the shore of **Vembanad Lake** to the west. **Aranmula**, to the south, is one of the last villages still making *kannadi* metal mirrors, and has a Krishna temple which organizes a ritual "non-competitive" boat race. The Mahadeva temple at **Ettumanur**, a short way north of Kottayam, is known to devotees as the home of a dangerous and wrathful Shiva and to art lovers as a sublime example of temple architecture, adorned with wood carvings and murals (some of which, for once, are viewable by non-Hindus).

Kumarakom

KUMARAKOM, 10km west of Kottayam, is spread over a cluster of islands on Vembanad Lake, surrounded by a tangle of lush tropical waterways and low-lying paddy fields. It was here that the British missionary **Henry Baker**

Backwater homestays

The backwaters around Kumarakom harbour some particularly desirable **homestays,** the majority of them in landed Syrian-Christian households like those depicted in Arundhati Roy's novel, *The God of Small Things*. The following are the pick of the crop:

🏃 **Akkara** Mariathuruthu ☎0481/251 6951, ⓦwww.akkara.in. Set on a bend in the Meenachil River, 5km northwest of Kottayam, this homestay is a model backwater B&B, offering an idyllic, typically Keralan setting, traditional architecture, comfortable rooms full of 1930s–50s period furniture, and wonderful Syrian-Christian cuisine. Access is by dugout canoe. ❼–❽

GK's Riverview Thekkakarayil, Kottaparambil, near Pulikkuttssery, 4km by water from Kumarakom ☎0481/259 7527 or 09447 197527, ⓦwww.gkhomestay-kumarakom.com. Award-winning homestay, buried deep in the watery wilds between Kottayam and Kumarakom. The accommodation comprises four comfortable guest rooms in a separate block behind a family home, overlooking paddy fields. Phone ahead from Kottayam to be picked up. ❺

Philip Kutty's Pallivathukal, near Ambika Market, Vechoor, 20km northwest of Kottayam ☎04829/276529 or 09895 075130, ⓦwww.philipkuttysfarm.com. Luxury homestay on a working island farm, 40min drive from Kottayam in the remote backwaters of Vembanad Lake. Five beautifully furnished villas, built in traditional style, offer private hideaways set back from the main farmhouse but close to the water's edge. $250–300 in season. ❾

Serenity at Kanam Estate 20km east of Kottayam on the Kumily/Periyar (KK) Rd at Payikad, near Vazhoor ☎0481/245 6353, ⓦwww.malabarhouse.com. Stylish boutique hotel occupying a converted 1920s bungalow set on a hilltop deep in a belt of rubber plantations and spice gardens. Facilities include a pool surrounded by cocoa trees, gym, yoga *shala*, Ayurvedic spa and mountain bikes. You're also invited to spend a day with the resident elephant. From $250 per double. ❾

---

chose to reclaim land to make a small rubber and fruit farm in the 1820s, which was subsequently expanded by his descendents. After Independence, the estate and its main house was ceded to the government, who designated the core area abutting the lakeside as a nature reserve. Due to its easy accessibility by road from Kottayam, this has since become the focus of a boom in backwater tourism, with a row of large luxury resorts lined up along the water's edge. Baker, meanwhile, became immortalized as the "Kari Saippu" (Black Sahib) of Arundhati Roy's *The God of Small Things* – the author grew up in a nearby village – while his house, featured as the ghostly "History House" in the novel, has been converted into a luxury hotel by Taj Group.

Kumarakom can be reached quite easily by bus (every 20–30min) from Kottayam, which lies 15km to the east. The best time to visit the **Bird Sanctuary** (daily dawn to dusk; Rs45), occupying the westernmost island of Baker's former estate, is between November and March, when it serves as a winter home for many migratory birds, some from as far away as Siberia. Species include the darter or snake bird, little cormorant, night heron, golden-backed woodpecker, crow pheasant, white-breasted water hen and tree pie. Dawn is the quietest and best time for viewing. Although the island is quite small, a guide is useful; you can arrange one through any of the hotels.

Birds, or representations of them, feature prominently in the area's most bizarre visitor attraction, the **Bay Island Driftwood Museum** (daily 10am–6pm; Rs50; ⓦwww.bay-island-museum.com), just off the main road on the outskirts of Kumarakom, in which lumps of driftwood collected by a former school teacher in the Anadaman Islands are exhibited in an idiosyncratic gallery. Allow at least an hour for the full tour.

For a rundown of this area's best accommodation, see box on p.1213.

Aranmula

The village of **ARANMULA** offers another appealing day-trip from Kottayam (start early), 30km to the south. About 1800 years old, its temple is a major site on the Vishnaivite pilgrimage trail in Kerala, and the springboard for an annual **Snake Boat Regatta** held at the end of the Onam festival (Aug/Sept), when crowds line the banks of the Pampa River to cheer on the thrusting longboats (similar to those seen at Alappuzha; see p.1204).

Aranmula is also known for the manufacture of extraordinary *kannadi* **metal mirrors** (called Aranmula *valkannadi*), produced using the "lost wax" technique, with an alloy of copper, silver, brass, white lead and bronze. Once a prerequisite of royal households, these ornamental mirrors are now exceedingly rare; only a handful of master craftsmen and their families still make them. The most modest models cost around Rs300–400, while custom-made mirrors can cost Rs50,000 or more.

The **Vijana Kala Vedi Cultural Centre** (Ⓦ www.vijnanakalavedi.org) offers daily classes in *kathakali*, *mohiniyattam* and *bharatanatyam* dance, wood-carving, mural painting, cooking, *kalarippayattu*, Ayurvedic medicine and several Indian languages. Courses cost Rs10,200 per week, with reductions for longer stays.

Ettumanur

The magnificent Mahadeva (Shiva) temple at **ETTUMANUR**, 12km north of Kottayam on the road to Ernakulam, features a circular shrine, fine woodcarving and one of the earliest (sixteenth-century) and most celebrated of Keralan **wall paintings**. Although the shrine is open only to Hindus, foreigners can see the courtyard **murals**, which may be photographed after obtaining a camera ticket (Rs20; video Rs50) from the counter on the left of the main entrance gateway (the priests may try to charge you considerably more, but if you insist on seeing a printed tariff will drop the price to the official one). The murals are spread over two four-metre panels flanking the rear side of the main doorway. The most spectacular depicts Nataraja – Shiva – executing a cosmic *tandava* dance, trampling evil in the form of a demon underfoot.

Periyar and around

One of the largest and most visited wildlife reserves in India, the **Periyar Wildlife Sanctuary** occupies 777 square kilometres of the Cardamom Hills region of the Western Ghats. The majority of its visitors come in the hope of seeing **tigers** and **leopards** – and most leave disappointed, as the few that remain very wisely keep their distance, and there's only a slight chance of a glimpse even at the height of the dry season in April and May. However, plenty of other animals survive in healthier numbers: elephant, *sambar*, Malabar giant squirrel, *gaur*, stripe-necked mongoose, wild boar and over 323 species of bird, including Nilgiri wood pigeon, purple-headed parakeet, tree pie and flycatcher.

Located close to the Kerala–Tamil Nadu border, only a few kilometres off the national highway, Periyar makes a convenient place to break the long journey across the Ghats between Madurai and the coast. In addition, the park has a particularly enlightened conservation policy. Instead of earning their livelihoods through poaching and illegal sandalwood extraction, local Manna people are employed by the Forest Department to protect vulnerable parts of the sanctuary. **Eco-tourism** initiatives, in which visitors accompany the tribal

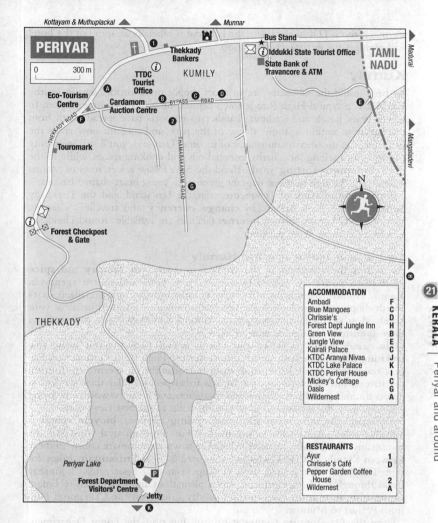

PERIYAR

0 — 300 m

Kottayam & Muthuplackal ▲   ▲ Munnar

KUMILY

Thekkady
Bankers

Bus Stand
★
ⓘ Idduki State Tourist Office

TAMIL
NADU

State Bank of
Travancore & ATM

TTDC
Tourist
Office

Ⓐ

Eco-Tourism
Centre

Cardamom
Auction Centre

Ⓑ BYPASS Ⓒ ROAD Ⓓ

Ⓔ

Ⓕ

Ⓖ

Ⓗ

N

Madurai

Mangaladevi

Touromark

THAMARAKANDAM ROAD

THEKKADY ROAD

ⓘ

Forest Checkpost
& Gate

THEKKADY

Ⓘ

Periyar Lake

Ⓙ
Ⓟ
Forest Department
Visitors' Centre

Jetty

Ⓚ

ACCOMMODATION

Ambadi	F
Blue Mangoes	C
Chrissie's	D
Forest Dept Jungle Inn	H
Green View	B
Jungle View	E
Kairali Palace	C
KTDC Aranya Nivas	J
KTDC Lake Palace	K
KTDC Periyar House	I
Mickey's Cottage	C
Oasis	G
Wildernest	A

RESTAURANTS

Ayur	1
Chrissie's Café	D
Pepper Garden Coffee House	2
Wildernest	A

21

wardens on their duties, both serve to promote community welfare and generate income for conservation work. Indigenous villagers also act as guides for forest walks and bullock-cart rides. To book any of these, you'll have to walk down the Thekkady Road to the **Eco-Tourism Centre** at Ambadi Junction (daily 8am–6pm, last tickets sold at 5.30pm; ☎04869/224571, Ⓦwww.periyartigerreserve.org).

The base for exploring Periyar is the village of **Kumily**, a kilometre or so north of the main park entrance (known as **Thekkady**). **Buses** from Kottayam (every 30min; 4hr), Ernakulam (10 daily; 6hr) and Madurai in Tamil Nadu (at least hourly; 5hr 30min) pull in to the scruffy bus-stand east of the main bazaar. **Auto-rickshaws** will run you from the bus stand to the visitor centre inside the park for around Rs50–60, stopping at the park entrance at Thekkady for you to pay the fee. The gates close at 6pm, after which you will have to show proof of an accommodation booking before they will let you in. If you are staying at the KTDC *Lake Palace*, the last boat is officially at 4pm but the hotel will arrange one during daylight hours.

Kumily

As beds inside the sanctuary are in short supply, most visitors stay in nearby **KUMILY**, a typical High Range town centred on a busy roadside market. In recent years, hotels and Kashmiri handicrafts emporia have spread south from the bazaar to within a stone's throw of the park, and tourism now rivals the spice trade as the area's main source of income. That said, you'll still see plenty of little shops selling local herbs, essential oils and cooking spices, while in the busy **cardamom sorting yard** behind the *Spice Village* resort, rows of Manna women sift through heaps of fragrant green pods using heart-shaped baskets.

Both the State Bank of Travancore, near the bus stand, and the Thekkady Bankers in the main bazaar can **change currency** and traveller's cheques; there's an ATM at the former. **Internet** facilities are available around Thekkady Junction for about Rs40 per hour.

Tours and treks around Kumily

As well as the attraction of the wildlife sanctuary, **tea factory** and **spice plantation tours** are offered by almost every hotel and tourist agency in Kumily. Unfortunately, many places have become heavily commercialized, so it's worth shopping around; often the best way to organise a tour is to ask at your hotel. Most of the plantations charge around Rs300–500 per person for a three-hour tour with guide and vehicle.

The windy, grassy ridgetops and forests around Periyar afford many fine **trekking** possibilities, with superb views over the High Range guaranteed. Ex-park wardens and other local people made redundant by the recent Eco-Tourism initiative (which reserved jobs for Manna tribal people) offer their services as guides through guesthouses, hotels and restaurants, and it can be worth employing someone for a day or more to show you the paths to the best viewpoints.

Although hilly, this area is also good **cycling** territory; **bicycle rental** is available from several stalls in the market. For more physical trips into the mountains, Touromark (℡04869/224332, Ⓦwww.touromark.com), midway between Kumily and Thekkady, have imported 21-speed **mountain bikes** for rent. They also offer guided trips, ranging from four-hour/fifteen-kilometre hacks through local spice gardens, coffee plantations and woodlands to longer expeditions, such as the three-night/four-day ride across the Cardamom Hills from Periyar to Munnar.

From the Eco-Tourism Centre at Ambadi Junction, the Forest Department run **village tours** (6am–2.30pm; Rs750) to a remote tribal settlement on the Tamil Nadu side of the mountains bordering Periyar. You're transported 10km by taxi to the start of the route, which is covered by **bullock cart** and **coracle** through a variety of different habitats and farmland. Profits go to the development of the local community.

Accommodation

Kumily has **accommodation** to suit all pockets, offering particularly good value in lower price brackets, thanks to the recent proliferation of small homestay guesthouses on the fringes of the village. At the opposite end of the scale are some truly gorgeous colonial-era hideaways deep in the mountains which you'll need a car and driver to reach, but which provide atmospheric bases for explorations of lesser-visited corners of the High Range. For accommodation in the sanctuary itself, see p.1219.

Ambadi Ambadi Junction, Thekkady Rd ☎04869/222193, ⓦ www.hotelambadi.com. Wood and red bricks dominate the architecture of this hotel, packed higgledy-piggledy onto the side of the road to the park. It offers three categories of rooms, all excellent value and with lots of Keralan character. ⑤–⑥

Chrissie's Bypass Rd ☎04869/224155 or 09447 601304, ⓦ www.chrissies.in. Smart new four-storey hotel below the bazaar, run by British–Egyptian expats. It's pricier than most homestays in the area, but you get more privacy and better views, plus there's a popular café on the ground floor. ⑤–⑥

Green View Bypass Rd ☎04869/211015 or 09447 432008. One of Kumily's most popular homestays, in a newish house just off the Thekkady Road. Offers seventeen differently priced rooms, the best looking across the valley. If it's full, try the identically priced *Rose Garden* next door (☎04869/223146). ③–⑤

Jungle View on the eastern edge of town ☎04869/223582 or 09446 136407. The best-value budget homestay in Kumily, a 10min plod (or Rs15 auto-rickshaw ride) from the bus stand. The clean, bright, attached bedrooms are all comfortably furnished. Nocturnal wildlife-spotting walks into the adjacent forest are offered as a complimentary extra. ④–⑤

🏃 **Kairali Palace** Bypass Rd ☎04869/224604 or 09895 187789. Outstandingly attractive homestay in a fusion building that blends traditional and modern styles. Its attached rooms are all well furnished for the price. ③–⑤

Mickey's Cottage Bypass Rd ☎04869/222196 or 09447 284160. One of the oldest guesthouses in Kumily, offering a range of differently priced rooms, all with balconies or sitouts. If they've no vacancies, try the adjacent (and slightly cheaper) *Blue Mangoes* (☎04869/224603 or 09895 187789 ②–③) or ③–④

Oasis Thamarakandam Rd ☎04869/223544 or 09447 907890, ⓔ oasisthekkady@yahoo.com. Large new rooms sharing common verandas that look out across the treetops on the village's eastern fringes. Clean, quiet, secure and good value. ③–④

Shalimar Spice Garden Murikaddy, 6km from Kumily ☎04869/222132, ⓦ www.shalimarkerala .net. Teak huts in traditional Keralan style, on the edge of an old cardamom and pepper estate, with elephant-grass roofs, whitewashed walls, chic interiors and verandas looking straight onto forest. Facilities include a beautiful Ayurveda centre, an outdoor pool and an open-sided restaurant. Rates $200–250. ⑨

Wildernest Thekkady Rd ☎04869/224030, ⓦ www.wildernest-kerala.com. *Wildernest*'s ten quirkily designed rooms are the most appealing option in this bracket, despite their proximity to the main road. With their wooden staircases, French windows and private gardens, they're more like little maisonettes. Rates include generous breakfasts. ⑦

Eating

You're more likely to take meals at your guesthouse or hotel than eat out in Kumily, but for a change of scene the following are the best options within walking distance of the bazaar.

Ayur West side of the main bazaar. Quality south Indian thali "meals" (Rs55), freshly made each day and served on banana leaves from a buffet. It's more hygienic (and less manic) than the competition further down the main street. *Ginger*, upstairs, is a swisher a/c alternative offering an exhaustive Indian-Chinese-Continental menu.

Chrissie's Café Bypass Rd. This relaxing expat-run café, on the ground floor of the hotel of the same name, pulls in a steady stream of foreigners throughout the day and evening for its delicious pizzas and pasta bakes (Rs130–175), made with Kodai mozzarella; check out the specials board. They also do healthy breakfasts of muesli with fresh fruit, crunchy cereal, toast with home-made bread and cakes, with proper coffee.

Pepper Garden Coffee House Thamarkandam Rd. In a garden filled with cardamom bushes behind a prettily painted blue-and-green house, a former park guide and his wife whip up tempting travellers' breakfasts (date and raisin pancakes, porridge with jungle honey, fresh coffee and Nilgiri tea), in addition to home-cooked lunches of veg fried rice, curry and dhal, using mostly local organic produce. Mains Rs30–100.

Wildernest Thekkady Rd. Filling, Continental buffet breakfasts (fruit, juices, cereals, eggs, toast, peanut butter, home-made jams and freshly ground coffee; Rs125) served on polished wood tables in the ground-floor café of a stylish small hotel. In the afternoons they also do tea and cakes (including a particularly delicious, very British warm plum cake).

The Sanctuary

Centred on a vast artificial **lake** created by the British in 1895 to supply water to the drier parts of neighbouring Tamil Nadu, the Periyar Wildlife Sanctuary lies at altitudes of between 900m and 1800m, and is correspondingly cool: temperatures range from 15°C to 30°C. The royal family of Travancore, anxious to preserve favourite hunting grounds from the encroachment of tea plantations, declared it a forest reserve, and built the Edapalayam Lake Palace to accommodate their guests in 1899. It expanded as a wildlife reserve in 1933, and once again when it became part of **Project Tiger** in 1979 (see Contexts, p.1377).

Seventy percent of the protected area, which is divided into core, buffer and tourist zones, is covered with evergreen and semi-evergreen forest. The **tourist zone** – logically enough, the part accessible to casual visitors – surrounds the lake, and consists mostly of semi-evergreen and deciduous woodland interspersed with grassland, both on hilltops and in the valleys. Although excursions on the lake (either by diesel-powered launch or paddle-powered bamboo raft) are the standard ways to experience the park, you can get much more out of a visit by **walking** with a local guide in a small group away from the crowd. However, avoid the period immediately after the monsoons, when **leeches** make hiking virtually impossible. The **best time to visit** is from December until April, when the dry weather draws animals from the forest to drink at the lakeside.

Park practicalities

The **entrance fee** is Rs150 [Rs12] for the first day, and Rs50 on subsequent days. If you're staying inside the park you must buy a new pass for each day you stay, either from the entrance gate or from the Forest Information Centre by the jetty. KTDC's hectic and uncomfortable **weekend tours** to Periyar from Kochi, calling at Kadamattom and Idukki Dam en route (Sat 7.30am–Sun 8pm), are not recommended unless you're really pushed for time.

KTDC's **boat trips** on the lake (daily at 7am, 9.30am, 11.30am, 2pm & 4pm; 2hr; Rs45 for the lower deck, Rs100 for the upper deck, which is less cramped and has a better view) are in large double-decker launches with noisy engines. The Forest Department also runs its own boats (9.30am, 11.30am, 2pm and 4pm; Rs35); they're smaller and shabbier, but can get closer to the banks of the lake (and thus the wildlife). Tickets for both services are sold through the Forest Department hatch just above the main **visitor centre** (daily 7am–6pm; ☏04869/222027) at the end of the road into the park.

It's unusual to see many animals from the boats – engine noise and the presence of a hundred other people make sure of that – but if you're lucky you might spot a group of elephants, wild boar and *sambar* grazing by the water's edge. To maximize your chances of wildlife sightings, take the 7am service (wear warm clothing) and try for a ticket on the upper deck if there are any left (most tend to be block-booked by the luxury hotels).

Better still, sign up for one of the Forest Department's excellent **bamboo rafting trips**, which start with a short hike from the boat jetty at 8am and return at 5pm, with a minimum of three hours spent on the water. The rafts carry four or five people and, because they're paddled rather than motor-driven, can approach the lakeshore in silence, allowing you to get closer to the grazing animals and birds. Tickets cost Rs1000 per person and may be booked in advance from the Eco-Tourism Centre on Ambadi Junction (see map, p.1215).

Walks and treks

The Periyar Tiger Reserve's community-based Eco-Tourism Programme offers a variety of structured **walking tours**, ranging from short rambles to three-day

The Ayappa cult

During December and January, Kerala is packed with huge crowds of men wearing black or blue *dhotis*; you'll see them milling about train stations, driving in overcrowded and gaily decorated Jeeps and cooking a quick meal on the roadside by their tour bus. These men are all pilgrims on their way to the Shri Ayappa forest temple (also known as Hariharaputra or Shasta) at **Sabarimala**, in the Western Ghat mountains, around 200km from both Thiruvananthapuram and Kochi. The **Ayappa devotees** can seem disconcertingly ebullient, chanting "*Swamiyee Sharanam Ayappan*" ("Give us protection, god Ayappa") in a call-and-response style reminiscent of English football fans.

Ayappa – the offspring of a union between Shiva and Mohini, Vishnu's beautiful female form – is primarily a Keralan deity, but his appeal has spread phenomenally in the last thirty years across south India, to the extent that this is said to be **the second largest pilgrimage in the world**, with as many as a million devotees each year. Pilgrims are required to remain celibate, abstain from intoxicants, and keep to a strict vegetarian diet for a period of 41 days prior to setting out on the four-day walk through the forest from the village of **Erumeli** (61km, as the crow flies, northwest) to the shrine at Sabarimala. Less-keen devotees take the bus to the village of Pampa, and join the five-kilometre queue. When they arrive at the modern temple complex, pilgrims who have performed the necessary penances may ascend the famous eighteen **gold steps** to the inner shrine. There they worship the deity, throwing donations down a chute that opens onto a subterranean conveyor belt, where the money is counted and bagged.

The pilgrimage reaches a climax during the festival of **Makara Sankranti**, when massive crowds of over 1.5 million congregate at Sabarimala. On January 14, 1999, 51 devotees were buried alive when part of a hill crumbled under the crush of a stampede. The devotees had gathered at dusk to catch a glimpse of the final sunset of *makara jyoti* ("celestial light") on the distant hill of Ponnambalamedu.

Although **males** of any age and even of any religion can take part in the pilgrimage, **females** between the ages of 9 and 50 are barred.

expeditions, all guided by local Manna tribal wardens. Tickets should be booked in advance from the Eco-Tourism Centre on Ambadi Junction (daily 8am–6pm, last tickets sold at 5.30pm; ℡04869/224571, ⓦwww.periyartigerreserve.org), where you can also pick up brochures and leaflets on the trips.

The **Nature Walk** (7am, 11am & 2pm; Rs100 per person) is the least demanding option, covering 4–5km of level evergreen and moist deciduous forest. Groups of up to five people are led by a single guide who identifies trees, plants and wildlife. You can also do a similar walk at night: the **Jungle Patrol** (7–10pm & 10pm–1am; Rs500) is loaded with atmosphere and the sounds of the forest, though you probably won't get to see much more than the odd pair of eyes picked out in a torch beam. For scenery, a better option is the full-day **Border Hiking** tour (8am–5pm; Rs1000 per person), which takes you into grassland and thick jungle at altitudes of between 900 and 1300m. Finally, the **Periyar Tiger Trail** (Rs3000–5000) is the one for committed trekkers. Guided by former poachers, the itinerary lasts for one night and two days, or two nights and three days. Armed guards accompany the group, trekking through 35km of hill country, thick forest and grassland to top wildlife-spotting sites in the Periyar Sanctuary.

Accommodation and eating in the sanctuary

For the *Lake Palace*, *Periyar House* and the *Aranya Nivas* you should book in advance at the KTDC offices in Thiruvananthapuram or Ernakulam – essential if you plan to come on a weekend, a public holiday, or during **peak season** (Dec–March), when rooms are often in short supply.

Forest Department Jungle Inn 3km east of Kumily at Kokkara, off the Mangaladevi Temple Rd. Located 3km into the park, this simple "forest cottage" sits in a glade frequented by langur monkeys and giant tree squirrels. It's cramped and overpriced, though the location is serene and does allow you to be in position early for the wildlife. Book through the Eco-Tourism Centre at Ambadi Junction. ⑦

KTDC Aranya Nivas Near the boat jetty, Thekkady ☏ 04689/222282, ⓦ www.ktdc.com. Plusher than *Periyar House*, this colonial manor has some huge rooms ($100–150), a pleasant garden and pool, multi-cuisine restaurant, bar, and plenty of marauding wild monkeys to keep you entertained. Full board and upper-deck tickets for two boat trips are included in the tariff. ⑧–⑨

KTDC Lake Palace Across the lake from the visitor centre ☏ 04869/222023, ⓦ www.ktdc.com. The sanctuary's most luxurious hotel, with six suites in a converted maharajah's game lodge surrounded by forest. Wonderful views extend from the charmingly old-fashioned rooms and lawns – this has to be one of the few places in India where you stand a chance of spotting tiger and wild elephant while sipping tea on your own veranda. Full-board only at $210 per double room. ⑨

KTDC Periyar House Midway between the park gates and the boat jetty, Thekkady ☏ 04869/922 2026, ⓦ www.ktdc.com. Close to the lake, with a restaurant, bar and balcony overlooking the monkey-filled woods leading down to the waterside. Not as nice a location as the neighbouring *Aranya Nivas*, but a lot cheaper. Ask for a lake-facing room. ⑤–⑦

Munnar and around

MUNNAR, 130km east of Kochi and 110km north (4.5hr by bus) of the Periyar Wildlife Sanctuary, is the centre of Kerala's principal tea-growing region. A scruffy agglomeration of corrugated-iron-roofed cottages and tea factories, its centre on the valley floor fails to live up to its tourist-office billing as "hill station", but there's plenty to enthuse about in the surrounding mountains, whose lower slopes are carpeted with lush tea gardens and dotted with quaint old colonial bungalows. Above them, the grassy ridges and crags of the High Range – including peninsular India's highest peak, **Ana Mudi** (2695m) – offer superlative trekking routes, many of which can be tackled in day-trips from the town.

It's easy to see why the pioneering Scottish planters who developed this hidden valley in the 1870s and 1880s felt so at home here. At an altitude of around 1600m, Munnar enjoys a refreshing climate, with crisp mornings and sunny blue skies in the winter – though as with all of Kerala, torrential rains descend during the monsoons. When the mists clear, the mountain summits form a wild backdrop to the carefully manicured tea plantations below.

Munnar's greenery and cool air draw streams of well-heeled honeymooners and weekenders from the metropolitan cities of south India. However, increasing numbers of foreign travellers are stopping here for a few days too, enticed by the superbly scenic bus-ride from Periyar, which takes you across the high ridges and lush tropical forests of the Cardamom Hills, or for the equally spectacular climb across the Ghats from Madurai. Recent seasons have also seen the emergence of some wonderful **heritage** and **homestay accommodation**, much of it in restored British bungalows, where you can sip High Range tea on lawns against vistas of rolling estates and mountains.

Arrival and information

State-run and private buses all pull into the Town Bus Stand in the modern main bazaar, near the river confluence and Tata headquarters; state ones continue through town, terminating nearly 3km south. For most hotels you should ask to be dropped off at **Old Munnar**, 2km south of the centre, near the ineffectual DTPC **tourist office** (daily 8.30am–7pm; ☎04865/231516). A better source of **information** on transport, accommodation and day-trips, including to Eravikulam, is the helpful **Joseph Iype**, who runs the private **Tourist Information Service** (no set hours; ☎04865/231136 or 09447 190954) from a small office in the main bazaar. Immortalized in Dervla Murphy's *On a Shoestring to Coorg*, this self-appointed tourist officer has become something of a legend. He has some useful **maps** and newspaper articles, can arrange **transport** for excursions, and will doubtless bombard you with background on the area.

You can **change money** at the State Bank of Travancore, the State Bank of India or at numerous ATMs around the town. **Internet** access is available from a couple of places around town, such as Alpha Computer Centre (Rs50/hour), next to the Tamil Nadu Bus Stand.

Accommodation

The cost of Munnar's **accommodation** is significantly higher than elsewhere in the High Range region, reflecting the pressure on beds caused by the town's popularity with middle-class tourists from the big cities. Rooms at the low end of the scale are in particularly short supply; the few we found were blighted by constant racket from the bus stand and bazaar, and are thus not listed below.

Green View Shri Parvati Amman Kovil St, near the KSRTC Bus Stand ☎04865/230189 or 09447 825447. Clean and friendly budget guesthouse on the valley floor, down a side road just off the main drag, with rooms of various sizes, pitched at foreign backpackers. ❶–❸

High Range Club Kanan Devan Hills ☎04865/230253, ✉hrcmunnar@sify.com. Munnar's old Raj-era club must have been a nightmare of stuffiness and racism in its heyday. But now the faded colonial ambience feels undeniably quaint. Three kinds of rooms and cottages are offered. Rates include obligatory full board. ❼–❽

Hillview Kanan Devan Hills ☎04865/230567 or 09447 740883, ⓦwww.hillviewhotel.com. A dependable mid-range choice, on the south side of town: not much to look at from the outside, but the interiors boast stripped wood floors and traditional carved wall panels. ❻–❼

JJ Cottage Shri Parvati Amman Kovil St, near the KSRTC Bus Stand ☎04865/230104. Next door to *Green View*, and very much in the same mould, though it's been open longer, charges higher rates and tends to get booked up earlier in the day. ❸–❹

Kanan Devan Hills Club Kanan Devan Hills Rd ☎04865/230252, ✉kdhclub@rediffmail.com. The budget traveller's answer to the *High Range Club*: a typical colonial bungalow, actually built in 1983 but in Raj style; the attached rooms are good value for Munnar. ❹

Olive Brook PO Box 62, Pothamedu ☎04865/230588, ⓦwww.olivebrookmunnar.com. Delightfully old-fashioned homestay, on a cardamom estate on a hillside overlooking the southern end of Munnar. Rates include full board, cookery classes, trekking, evening barbecues and campfires. ❽

The Tea Sanctuary KDHP House ☎04865/230141, ⓦwww.theteasanctuary.com. A selection of five former planters' bungalows, scattered across the Kanan Devan Hill Plantations Company's 240 square kilometres of tea gardens. Each has been sensitively restored to its original state and is staffed by a liveried *chowkidar* and cook. If you can, book "Chockanad East", 4km beyond the *High Range Club* ($150/night for two, includes full board). ❾

Windermere Estate PO Box 21, Pothamedu ☎04865/230512, ⓦwww.windermeremunnar.com. Alpine-style chalet lodges, perched high on a hilltop above the town in cardamom and tea groves with glorious views over the valley. The rooms (from $125) – whether in the converted farmhouse or purpose-built cottages – are all beautifully furnished and decorated with natural wood and stone, and warm-coloured textiles. ❾

Zina Cottage Kad ☎04865/230349 or 09447 190954. Gorgeous British-era stone bungalow, nestled amid tea gardens high on the hillside above Munnar. There are magnificent views across town to Ana Mudi from the flower-filled front terrace, and host Joseph Iype will fill you in on local walks over flasks of hot tea in his sitting room. This is somewhere you'd stay more for the atmosphere than creature comforts, and it has plenty of it. ❹

The Town

Clustered around the confluence of three mountain streams, Munnar town is a typical hill bazaar of haphazard buildings and congested market streets, which you'll probably want to escape at the first opportunity. The one sight of note is the **Tea Museum** (Tues–Sun 9am–4pm; Rs50), 2km northwest of the centre on Nallathany Road, which houses various pieces of old machinery and an exhibition of photos of the area's tea industry, from the 1880s pioneers to the modern Kanan-Devan era under the Tata tea conglomerate.

The social hub of the colonial period, and an important cultural icon in Munnar, the famous **High Range Club** is perched on a balcony overlooking the river on the southeastern edge of town. Indians were only officially permitted to enter the premises as recently as 1948, but these days nonmembers of any race are welcome to visit the typically Raj-era building for a round of golf, or to enjoy a gin and tonic served on the lawns by liveried retainers. In the men-only bar, the walls are hung with rows of hunting trophies and topees. Stiff-upper-lipped dress codes apply throughout the club: no T-shirts or sandals, and formal evening wear after 7pm on Saturdays.

Eating

The **thattukada** (hot food stall market) just south of the main bazaar, opposite the taxi stand, gets into its stride around 7.30pm and runs through the night, serving delicious, piping-hot Keralan food – *dosas, parottas, iddiappam*, green-bean curry, egg masala – ladled onto tin plates and eaten on rough wood tables in the street. The most hygienic option in the main bazaar is *Food Count*, on the ground floor of the *Munnar Inn*, serving samosas, veg cutlets, sandwiches and light meals. *Guru Bhavan*, Mutapatty Road, Ikka Nagar, is the most dependable of Munnar's local south Indian "meals" joints. It's a ten-minute walk north of the main bazaar, but worth the effort, with a menu of delicious Keralan vegetarian dishes that changes daily, in addition to hot *parottas*, stupendously crunchy paper *dosas* and other Udupi snacks.

Around Munnar

Several of the summits towering above the town may be reached on day-**treks** through the tea gardens. A good first stop for information is the *Green View* guesthouse, on the south side of town, whose owner, Deepak (℡0825447), heads up a team of enthusiastic young guides. For the **ascent of Anna Mudi**, south India's highest peak, you'll need to obtain a permit from the Forest Officer in Munnar at his office (Mon–Fri 10am–1pm & 2–5pm) just above the taxi stand. Permits are not, however, granted during the mating season of the tahr in late January and February.

One of the most popular excursions from Munnar is the 34-kilometre climb through some of the Subcontinent's highest tea estates to **TOP STATION**, a tiny hamlet on the Kerala–Tamil Nadu border which, at 1600m, is the highest point on the interstate road. The settlement takes its name from the old aerial **ropeway** that used to connect it with the valley floor, the ruins of which can still be seen in places. Apart from the marvellous views over the Tamil plains, Top Station is renowned for the very rare **Neelakurunji plant** (*Strobilanthes*), which grows in profusion on the mountainsides but only flowers once every twelve years, when huge crowds climb up here to admire the cascades of violet blossom spilling down the slopes (the next flowering is due in October–November 2018). You can get there by **bus** from Munnar (10 daily starting at 5.30am; 1hr 30min), and Jeep-taxis do the return trip for Rs900. Views are best before the mist builds up at 9am.

Wildlife Sanctuaries

Encompassing 100 square kilometres of moist evergreen forest and grassy hilltops in the Western Ghats, the **Eravikulam National Park** (daily 7am–6pm; Rs200 [Rs15]; ⓦ www.eravikulam.org), 13km northeast of Munnar, is the last stronghold of one of the world's rarest mountain goats, the **Nilgiri tahr**. Its innate friendliness made the tahr pathetically easy prey during the hunting frenzy of the colonial era. Today, however, numbers are healthy, and the animals have regained their tameness, largely thanks to the efforts of the American biologist Clifford Rice, who studied them here in the early 1980s. Unable to get close enough to observe the creatures properly, Rice followed the advice of locals and attracted them using salt, and soon entire herds were congregating around his camp. The tahrs' salt addiction also explains why so many hang around the park gates at **Vaguvarai**, where visitors – despite advice from rangers – slip them salty snacks.

Although it borders Eravikulam, the **Chinnar Wildlife Sanctuary** (daily 6am–7pm; Rs100 [Rs10]; ⓦ www.chinnar.org) is much less visited, not least because its entrance lies a two-hour drive from Munnar along 58km of winding mountain roads. The reserve, in the rain shadow of the High Range and thus much drier than its neighbour, is one of the best spots in the state for bird-watching, with 225 species recorded to date.

Kochi (Cochin) and around

The venerable city of **KOCHI** (long known as Cochin) is Kerala's prime tourist destination, spreading across islands and promontories between the Arabian Sea and the backwaters. Its main sections – modern **Ernakulam** and the old peninsular districts of **Mattancherry** and **Fort Cochin** to the west – are linked by a complex system of ferries, and distinctly less romantic bridges. Although some visitors opt to stay in the more convenient Ernakulam, the overwhelming majority base themselves in Fort Cochin itself, where the city's complex history is reflected in an assortment of architectural styles. Spice markets, Chinese fishing nets, a synagogue, a Portuguese palace, India's first European church and seventeenth-century Dutch homes can all be found within an easy walk. Kochi is also one of the few places in Kerala where you are guaranteed **kathakali** dance performances, both in authentic and abridged tourist versions.

Kochi sprang into being in 1341, when a flood created a safe natural port that swiftly replaced Muziris (now Kodungallur, 50km north) as the chief harbour on the Malabar Coast. The royal family moved here from Muziris in 1405, after which the city grew rapidly, attracting Christian, Arab and Jewish settlers from the Middle East. The history of **European** involvement from the early 1500s onwards is dominated by the aggression of the Portuguese, Dutch and British, who successively competed to control the port and its lucrative spice trade. From 1812 until Independence in 1947 it was administered by a succession of *diwans*, or finance ministers. In the 1920s, the British expanded the port to accommodate modern ocean-going ships, and Willingdon Island, between Ernakulam and Fort Cochin, was created by extensive dredging.

Arrival and local transport

Kochi's **international airport** (ⓦ www.cochinairport.com) – one of India's most modern and efficient – is at Nedumbassery, near Alwaye (aka Alua), 26km to the north of Ernakulam. A pre-paid taxi into town costs around Rs425 and takes thirty to forty minutes, traffic permitting – travelling by bus is more trouble than it's worth. There are two main **railway stations**, Ernakulam Junction, near the centre, and Ernakulam Town, 2km further north. The Cochin Harbour Terminus, on Willingdon Island, serves the island's luxury hotels.

The KSRTC **Central Bus Stand** (⊤0484/237 2033), beside the railway line east of MG Road and north of Ernakulam Junction, is for state-run long-distance services. There are also two stands for private services: the **Kaloor Stand** (rural destinations to the south and east) is across the bridge from Ernakulam Town railway station on the Alwaye Road; while the **High Court Stand** (buses to Kumily, for Periyar Wildlife Reserve, and north to Thrissur, Guruvayur and Kodungallur) is opposite the High Court ferry jetty. The **Fort Cochin bus terminus** serves tourist buses and local services to Ernakulam.

Although **auto-rickshaws** are plentiful and reliable in Ernakulam, expect to pay well over the odds across the water in Mattancherry and Fort Cochin. Kochi's excellent **ferry system** (see box below) provides a relaxing way to reach the various parts of town. **Bicycles** can be rented from many of the hotels and guesthouses in Fort Cochin (see p.1227).

Tours and backwater trips

KTDC's half-day **Kochi boat cruise** (daily 9am–12.30pm & 2–5.30pm; Rs100) is a good way to orient yourself but doesn't stop for long in either

---

Kochi by ferry

Half the fun of visiting Kochi is getting about on the cheap **local ferries**, which depart from the four jetties marked on the map on opposite. A pamphlet giving exact ferry times is available from the ticket hatches by the jetties and from the helpful tourist desk at the Main Boat Jetty in Ernakulam.

Ernakulam to Bolghatty Island
From Ernakulam (High Court Jetty); six per day 6.30am–9pm; journey time 10min. There are also speedboat taxis (only for guests of the *Bolgatty Palace* hotel).

Ernakulam to Fort Cochin
From Ernakulam (Main Jetty) to Fort Cochin (Customs Jetty). Every 20–55min; 5.55am–9.30pm; journey time 15min. A less-frequent express service runs from Ernaculam's High Court Jetty to Government Jetty in Fort Cochin.

Ernakulam to Mattancherry
From Ernakulam (Main Jetty) via Fort Cochin (Customs Jetty) and Willingdon Island (Terminus Jetty) to Mattancherry (Mattancherry Jetty). Every 1hr 30min; 5am–5.45pm.

Ernakulam to Vypeen
From Ernakulam (Main Jetty). This service has two routes: one to Willingdon Island (Embarkation Jetty; 25min), and a fast one to Vypeen (Government Jetty; 15min). Every 30min–1hr; 7am–9.30pm.

Fort Cochin to Vypeen
From Fort Cochin (Government Jetty) to Vypeen (Government Jetty). Every 10min; 6.30am–9pm; journey time 10min.

Willingdon Island to Fort Cochin
From the Tourist Office Jetty (Willingdon Island) to Customs Jetty (Fort Cochin). Every 30min; 6.30am–6.15pm; journey time 10min.

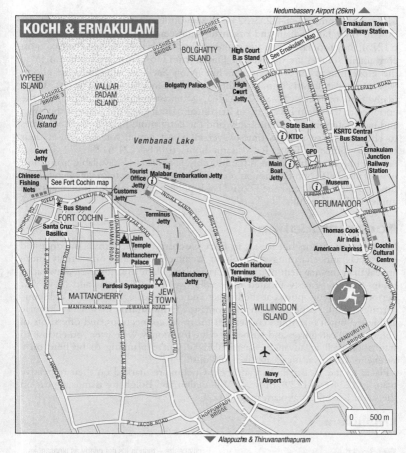

KOCHI & ERNAKULAM

Ernakulam Town
Railway Station

POWER HOUSE RD

GOSHREE
BRIDGE 1

GOSHREE
BRIDGE 2

BOLGHATTY
ISLAND

High Court
Bus Stand ★

See Ernakulam Map

BANERJI ROAD

VYPEEN
ISLAND

GOSHREE
BRIDGE 3

VALLAR
PADAM
ISLAND

Bolgatty Palace

High
Court
Jetty

PULLEPADY ROAD

Gundu
Island

Vembanad Lake

State Bank
i KTDC

GPO

KSRTC Central
Bus Stand

Ernakulam
Junction
Railway
Station

Govt
Jetty

Tourist
Office
Jetty

Taj
Malabar Embarkation Jetty

Main
Boat
Jetty

i

HOSPITAL RD

Chinese
Fishing
Nets

See Fort Cochin map

Customs
Jetty

i Museum

DURBAR HALL RD

PERUMANOOR

OVERBRIDGE RD

RIVER RD

Bus Stand
FORT COCHIN

KALVATHI RD

Terminus
Jetty

INDIRA GANDHI ROAD

Santa Cruz
Basilica

Jain
Temple

Thomas Cook
Air India
American Express

Cochin
Cultural
Centre

Mattancherry
Palace

Mattancherry
Jetty

Cochin Harbour
Terminus
Railway Station

N

Pardesi Synagogue

MATTANCHERRY

JEW
TOWN

WILLINGDON
ISLAND

VANDURUTHY
BRIDGE

Navy
Airport

0   500 m

Mattancherry or Fort Cochin, so give it a miss unless you're pushed for time. Tickets can be booked at the KTDC Reception Centre on Shanmugham Road (☎0484/235 3234).

The KTDC tourist office and a couple of private companies also operate popular all-day **backwater trips** out of Kochi. These offer a leisurely and enjoyable way to experience rural Kerala from small hand-punted canoes. KTDC's daily tours cost Rs350, including the car or bus trip to the departure point, 30km north, and a knowledgeable guide. Better value, however, are the trips run by the private **tourist desk** (see p.1226) at the Main Boat Jetty in Ernakulam (daily 8.30am–5pm; Rs550), which include hotel pick-up, cruises on a variety of different craft, a village tour, and Keralan lunch buffet on board a *kettu vallam*.

Information

India Tourism's main office (Mon–Fri 9am–5.30pm, Sat 9am–noon; ☎0484/266 8352, ⓦwww.incredibleindia.org), providing reliable information and qualified guides for visitors, is inconveniently situated on Willingdon Island, between the *Taj Malabar Hotel* and Tourist Office Jetty; they also have a desk at the airport. KTDC's **reception centre**, on Shanmugham Road, Ernakulam

KERALA | Kochi (Cochin) and around

(daily 8am–7pm; ☎0484/235 3234, ⓦwww.ktdc.com), reserves accommodation in their hotel chain and organizes sightseeing and backwater tours (see p.1225); they too have a counter at the airport. For general advice, the two most convenient sources are the **Kerala Department of Tourism**'s office next to the Government Jetty in Fort Cochin (Mon–Sat 10.15am–5pm; no phone, ⓦwww.keralatourism.com), and the tiny, independently-run **Tourist Desk** (daily 8am–6.30pm; ☎0484/237 1761, ⓔtouristdesk@satyam.net.in) at the entrance to the Main Boat Jetty in Ernakulam. Both hand out maps of the town and backwaters, but you'll probably find the latter more helpful when it comes to checking ferry and bus times. Over in Fort Cochin, you can call at their subsidiary office on Tower Road (same hours; ☎0484/221 6129).

A useful local **publication** is the monthly *Jaico Timetable* (available from most news stalls; Rs10), which lists comprehensive details of bus, train, ferry and flight times. Both KTDC and the Tourist Desk publish free walking-tour maps and guides to Fort Cochin.

Accommodation

Most foreign visitors opt to stay in **Fort Cochin**, which, with its uncongested backstreets and charming colonial-era architecture, holds considerably more appeal than the mayhem of modern Ernakulam. There are, however, drawbacks: room rates are grossly inflated (especially over the Christmas and New Year period), with few options at the budget end of the scale, and there is a disconcertingly high concentration of tourists. **Ernakulam** may lack historic ambience, but it's far more convenient for travel connections, and offers lots of choice in all categories and far better value for money. Wherever you choose to stay, book well in advance – particularly if you're planning to be here on a weekend, when vacancies are like gold dust.

Places to stay in Ernakulam and Fort Cochin are marked on their respective maps (p.1234 & p.1229); those on Willingdon and Bolghatty islands appear on the main Kochi/Ernakulam map (p.1225).

Ernakulam

Budget

🏃 **Biju's Tourist Home** Corner of Cannonshed and Market roads ☎0484/238 1881, ⓦwww.bijustouristhome.com. Pick of the budget bunch: friendly, efficient and only 2min walk from the boat jetty, with thirty spotless, well-aired and generously sized rooms ranged over four storeys. For telephone reservations, ask to speak in person to the manager, Mr Thomas Panakkal. ❹

Broadway Tower TD West Rd ☎0484/236 1645, ⓦwww.broadwaytowers.com. Situated in the thick of Ernakulam's busy textile bazaar, this recently built, well-scrubbed little economy hotel occupies the second and third storeys of a modern block. Its rooms offer great value for money (including the cheapest a/c rooms in town). ❸–❹

Maple Guest House XL/271 Cannonshed Rd ☎0484/235 5156. Best of the few rock-bottom options in the streets immediately east of the boat jetty, with cheap, clean, non-a/c rooms close to the city centre – though it's not nearly as pleasant as *Biju's*. ❷–❸

Saas Tower Cannonshed Rd ☎0484/236 5319, ⓦwww.saastower.com. Since its refit, this tower-block hotel, with 72 well-furnished rooms, has begun to rival nearby *Biju's* for quality and price at the upper end of the budget category. Singles from Rs300, and also some a/c options. ❸–❹

Mid-range & luxury

Excellency Nettipadam Rd, Jos Junction ☎0484/237 8251, ⓦwww.hotelexcellency.com. Smart, modern mid-range place, offering better value than most options in the city centre. The majority of its 49 rooms are a/c, and there's a 24hr coffee shop and quality multi-cuisine restaurant. ❹–❺

🏃 **Government Guest House** Marine Drive ☎0484/236 0502. The maharaja of Kerala's great-value *Government Guest House*, in a shiny new eight-storey tower overlooking the harbour. Centred on a vast atrium lobby, its rooms offer comfort comparable to a four-star business-class hotel, only at amazingly low rates (and they do single occupancy). Advance reservation, as with all Kerala state guesthouses, can be hit-and-miss. ❺

Grand MG Rd ☎0484/238 2061. This is the most classically glamorous place to stay in central Ernakulam. Spread over three floors of a 1960s building, its relaxing a/c rooms are done out in retro-colonial style, with varnished wood floors and split-cane blinds. Surprisingly low tariffs given the level of comfort and location. ❼–❽

Sealord Shanmugham Rd ☎0484/238 2472, ⓦwww.sealordhotels.com. The high-rise *Sealord*, near the High Court Jetty, has been an institution in the city for four decades and, with its handsome new interiors, offers excellent value for money. Their "standard" rooms are the best deal (ask for one on the top floor), and there's a relaxing rooftop terrace restaurant and bar. ❺–❻

Fort Cochin

Budget

Adam's Old Inn 1/430 Burgher St ☎0484/221 7595. Ropey old budget travellers' lodge that's been here for years but recently come under new management. Plans are afoot to upgrade the hard coir mattresses and phase out the rooftop dorm (❶), but for the time being this is still one of Fort Cochin's few rock-bottom cheapies. ❹

Leelu Queiros St ☎0484/221 5377 or 09846 055377, ⓦwww.leeluhomestay.com. A very welcoming little homestay, tucked away down a quiet lane in a former family home that's been completely modernized. Its cheerfully decorated guest rooms are spacious, with squashy mattresses, huge bathrooms and optional a/c (Rs500 extra). Landlady Mrs Leelu Roy also offers popular daily cookery classes (non-guests welcome). Especially recommended for women travellers. ❹–❺

Orion 926 KL Bernard Rd ☎0484/321 9312 or 09895 524797, ⓔmail@orionhomestay.com. Impeccable little homestay in a new house on the quiet south side of town. Rates vary according to size of rooms, which don't all have balconies, but are all kept shining and neat. ❹–❺

Santa Cruz Peter Celli St ☎0484/221 6250, 09847 518598. Half of the rooms in this small guesthouse behind St Francis's Church have windows opening onto an enclosed corridor, but the others are well ventilated – and they're all impeccably clean, neatly tiled and freshly painted throughout, with new beds. Good value. ❸–❹

Mid-range

Ballard Bungalow River Rd ☎0484/221 5854, ⓦwww.cochinballard.com. Eighteenth-century Dutch mansion, converted into a good-value hotel by the local diocese, with original wood floors (but rather dodgy furniture). Friendly, helpful staff. ❻–❼

Chiramel Residency 1/296 Lilly St ☎0484/221 7310, ⓦwww.chiramelhomestay.com. A great seventeenth-century heritage homestay, with welcoming owners and five lofty and carefully restored non-a/c rooms. All have big wooden beds, teak floors and modern bathrooms. ❻

Delight Ridsdale Rd, opposite the Parade Ground ☎0484/221 7658, ⓦwww.delightfulhomestay.com. Occupying an annexe tacked onto a splendid 300-year-old Portuguese mansion, David and Flowery's homestay holds seven spacious, comfortable and well-aired rooms, all equipped with new bathrooms and quiet ceiling fans. ❹–❼

Fort House 2/6A Calvathy Rd ☎0484/221 7103, ⓦwww.hotelforthouse.co.in. Stylishly simple rooms ranged along the sides of a sandy courtyard littered with pot plants and votive terracotta statues. Those in the much preferable original block (#1–5) have white walls and red-oxide floors, and chic little wet-room bathrooms – though the a/c units can be noisy. Rates include breakfast. ❻

The Old Courtyard 1/371–2 Princess St ☎0484/2216302, ⓦwww.oldcourtyard.com. A gem of a heritage hotel, whose eight rooms flank a photogenic seventeenth-century courtyard framed by elegant Portuguese arches and bands of original *azulejos* tiles. For once the decor and antique furnishings (including romantic four-posters) are in keeping with the building – though some may find them dark and lacking modern refinements. ❽–❾

Raintree 1/618 Peter Celli St ☎0484/325 1489 or 09847 029000, ⓦwww.fortcochin.com. Five outstandingly smart rooms furnished in modern style in a cosy guesthouse that's within easy walking distance of the sights, but still tucked away. The really nice thing about this place, though, is its roof terrace, which has panoramic views over the neighbourhood. ❻

Spencer Home 1/298 Parade Rd ☎0484/221 5049. Warm-toned wood pillars and gleaming ceramic tiled floors line the verandas fronting this Portuguese-era house's eleven immaculate rooms, which open onto a garden. Peaceful and good value for the area. ❹–❻

Walton's Homestay Princess St ☎0484/221 5309 or 09249 721935, ✉cewalton@rediffmail.com. Among Cochin's most characterful homestays, run by philosopher and local historian Mr Christopher Edward Walton. Try to book the "garden cottage". ❺–❻

Luxury

Brunton Boatyard Bellar Rd, next to Fort Cochin Jetty ☎0484/221 8221, ⓦwww.cghearth.com. The architecture and furnishings of this luxury *CGH* chain hotel set out to replicate the feel of the British era, with antique *punkah* fans dangling from the lobby ceiling and portraits of old worthies on the walls. Three types of room are offered, all of them overlooking the harbour – though avoid the noisier ones on the jetty side of the complex. Facilities include three restaurants, an Ayurveda centre and a waterside pool. $240–350. ❾

Koder House Tower Rd ☎0484/221 8485, ⓦwww.koderhouse.com. One of the Fort's newest boutique hotels, in a 200-year-old house that originally belonged to a prominent Jewish merchant. The imposing red, double-fronted facade is less alluring than its interiors, with their long, dark wood floors, original art and antique furniture. Six suites are on offer, from around $300. ❾

Malabar House 1/268 Parade Rd ☎0484/221 6666, ⓦwww.malabarhouse.com. Fort Cochin's original and most stylish boutique hotel is set in a historic eighteenth-century mansion at the bottom of the Parade Ground. Crammed with antiques and contemporary Keralan art, the German-designed interiors present a mix of traditional charm and European chic, centred on a serene temple-style courtyard pool. Tariffs ($270–460) include breakfast. ❾

The Old Harbour 1/328 Tower Rd ☎0484/221 8006 or 09847 029000, ⓦwww.oldharbourhotel.com. This 300-year-old former Portuguese hospice – is a storehouse of graceful Lusitanian arches, lathe-turned wood pillars and teak floors – is one of Kerala's top heritage hotels, at a prime location close to the Chinese fishing nets. It holds thirteen individually-styled rooms facing an internal courtyard or the garden, and there's a large outdoor pool. $115–230. ❾

Old Kochi: Fort Cochin and Mattancherry

Old Kochi, the thumb-shaped peninsula whose northern tip presides over the entrance to the city's harbour, formed the focus of European trading activities from the sixteenth century onwards. With high-rise development restricted to Ernakulam across the water, its twin districts of **Fort Cochin**, in the west, and **Mattancherry**, on the headland's eastern side, have preserved an extraordinary wealth of early colonial architecture, spanning the Portuguese, Dutch and British eras – a crop unparalleled in India. Approaching by ferry, the waterfront, with its sloping red-tiled roofs and ranks of peeling, pastel-coloured *godoowns* (warehouses), offers a view that can have changed little in centuries.

Closer up, however, Old Kochi's historic patina has started to show some ugly cracks. The spice trade that fuelled the town's original rise is still very much in evidence. But over the past decade, an extraordinary rise in visitor numbers has had a major impact. Thousands of tourists pour through daily during the winter, and with no planning or preservation authority to take control, the resulting rash of new building threatens to destroy the very atmosphere people come here to experience. That said, tourism has also brought some benefits to the area, inspiring renovation work to buildings that would otherwise have been left to rot.

Fort Cochin

Fort Cochin, the grid of venerable old streets at the northwest tip of the peninsula, is where the Portuguese erected their first walled citadel, Fort Immanuel. Only a few fragments of the former battlements remain, crumbling into the sea beside Cochin's iconic Chinese fishing nets. But dozens of other evocative Lusitanian, Dutch and British monuments survive.

A good way to get to grips with Fort Cochin's many-layered history is to pick up the free **walking-tour maps** produced by both Kerala Tourism and the privately run Tourist Desk, available from their respective offices and counters

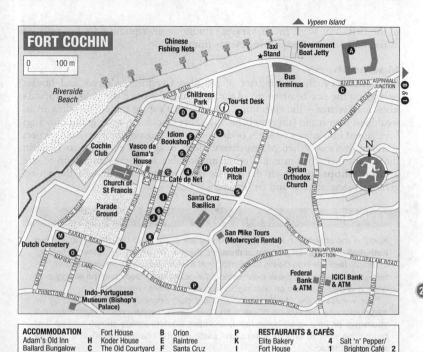

FORT COCHIN

0   100 m

Vypeen Island

Riverside Beach

Chinese Fishing Nets

Taxi Stand

Government Boat Jetty

Bus Terminus

RIVER ROAD — ASPINWALL JUNCTION

Childrens Park

Tourist Desk

Idiom Bookshop

Cochin Club

Vasco da Gama's House

Café de Net

Football Pitch

Syrian Orthodox Church

Church of St Francis

Santa Cruz Basilica

Parade Ground

San Mike Tours (Motorcycle Rental)

Dutch Cemetery

KUNNUMPURAM JUNCTION — PULLUPALAM ROAD

Federal Bank & ATM

ICICI Bank & ATM

Indo-Portuguese Museum (Bishop's Palace)

RISDALE BRANCH ROAD

ACCOMMODATION				RESTAURANTS & CAFÉS			
Adam's Old Inn	H	Fort House	B	Orion	P	Elite Bakery	4	Salt 'n' Pepper/
Ballard Bungalow	C	Koder House	E	Raintree	K	Fort House	1	Brighton Café	2
Brunton Boatyard	A	The Old Courtyard	F	Santa Cruz	I	Kashi Art Café	3	Teapot Café	6
Chiramel Residency	O	The Old Harbour	D	Spencer Home	N	Malabar Junction	M	Upstairs	5
Delight	L	Leelu	J	Walton's Homestay	G	The Old Courtyard	F		

(see p.1225). The routes lead you around some of the district's more significant landmarks, including the early eighteenth-century Dutch Cemetery, Vasco da Gama's supposed house and several traders' residences.

Chinese fishing nets

The huge, elegant **Chinese fishing nets** lining the northern shore of Fort Cochin add grace to the waterfront view, and are probably the single most familiar photographic image of Kerala. Traders from the court of Kublai Khan are said to have introduced them to the Malabar region. Known in Malayalam as *cheena vala*, they can also be seen throughout the backwaters further south. The nets, which are suspended from arced poles and operated by levers and weights, require at least four men to control them. You can buy fresh fish from the tiny market here and have it grilled with sea salt, garlic and lemon at one of the ramshackle stalls nearby.

St Francis church and around

South of the Chinese fishing nets on Church Road (the continuation of River Rd) is the large, typically English **Parade Ground**. Overlooking it, the **Church of St Francis** (daily 8.30am–6.30pm) was the first built by Europeans in India. Its exact age is not known, though the stone structure is thought to date back to the early sixteenth century. The facade, meanwhile, became the model for most Christian churches in India. Vasco da Gama was buried here in 1524, but his body was later removed to Portugal. Under the Dutch, the church was renovated and became Protestant in 1663, then Anglican with the advent of the British in 1795. Inside, various tombstone inscriptions have been placed in the walls, the earliest of which dates from 1562.

Mattancherry

Mantancherry, the old district of red-tiled riverfront wharves and houses occupying the northeastern tip of the headland, was once the colonial capital's main market area – the epicentre of the Malabar's spice trade, and home to its wealthiest Jewish and Jain merchants. Like Fort Cochin, its once grand buildings have lapsed into advanced states of disrepair, with most of their original owners working overseas. When Mattancherry's Jews emigrated en masse to Israel in the 1940s, their furniture and other un-portable hierlooms ended up in the **antique shops** for which the area is now renowned – though these days genuine pieces are few and far between.

Kathakali in Kochi

Kochi is the only city in the state where you are guaranteed the chance to see live **kathakali**, Kerala's unique form of ritualized theatre. Whether in its authentic setting, in temple festivals held during the winter, or at the shorter tourist-oriented shows that take place year-round, these mesmerizing dance dramas – depicting the struggles of gods and demons – are an unmissable feature of Kochi's cultural life.

Four venues in the city (listed below) hold daily shows, each preceeded by an introductory talk at around 6.30pm. You can watch the dancers being made up if you arrive an hour or so beforehand, and keen photographers should turn up well before the start to ensure a front-row seat. Tickets, costing Rs100–150, can be bought at the door.

Most visitors only attend one performance, but you'll gain a much better sense of what *kathakali* is all about if you take in at least a couple. The next step is an all-night recital at a temple festival, or one of the performances given by the top-notch **Ernakulam Kathakali Club**, which stages night-long plays once each month, either at the TDM Hall in Ernakulam (see map, p.1234) or at the Ernakulathappan Hall in the city's main Shiva temple. For further details contact the tourist desk at the Main Boat Jetty, Ernakulam. The four principal venues are listed below.

Dr Devan's Kathakali See India Foundation, Kalathiparambil Cross Road, near Ernakulam railway station ☏0484/236 6471. The oldest-established tourist show in the city, introduced by the inimitable Dr Devan, who starts the show with a lengthy discourse on Indian philosophy and mythology. From 6.45pm to 8pm (make-up at 6pm).

Cochin Cultural Centre Soudartham, Manikath Road, Ernakulam, and KB Jacob Road, Fort Cochin ☏0484/235 7153, ⓦwww.cochinculturalcentre.com. Award-winning company with theatres in both Fort Cochin and Ernakulam. Evening Kathakali shows start 6.30pm (make-up at 4.30pm). They also host introductory courses. Full details and booking online.

Kerala Kathakali Centre opposite Brunton Boatyard, Fort Cochin ☏0484/221 5827, ⓦwww.kathakalicentre.com. Popular performances by a company of graduates of the renowned Kalamandalam Academy. You usually get to see three characters, and the music is live. One- to three-week courses are also on offer. See their website for more details. Performances 6.30–8pm (make-up at 5pm); Indian classical recitals from 8.45pm.

Rhythms Theatre (Greenix) opposite *Fort House*, Fort Cochin ☏0484/654 9444, ⓦwww.greenix.in. Costing Rs450, this is the priciest show, but combines excerpts from *kathakali* plays with displays of *mohiniyattam* dance, *kalarippayattu* martial art and, on Sundays, *theyyattam*, set against a combination of live and pre-recorded music. Performances aren't of the highest standard, but the evening is more likely to appeal to kids as costumes and acts change in quick succession.

The sight at the top of most itineraries is **Mattancherry Palace** (daily except Fri 10am–5pm; Rs2), on the roadside a short walk from the Mattancherry Jetty, a kilometre or so southeast of Fort Cochin. Known locally as the Dutch Palace, the two-storey building was actually erected by the Portuguese, as a gift to the raja of Cochin, Vira Keralavarma (1537–61) – though the Dutch did add to the complex. While its squat exterior is not particularly striking, the interior is captivating.

The **murals** that adorn some of its rooms are among the finest examples of Kerala's underrated school of painting. The collection also includes interesting Dutch maps of old Cochin, coronation robes belonging to past maharajas, royal palanquins, weapons and furniture. Without permission from the Archeological Survey of India, **photography** is strictly prohibited.

Jew Town

The road heading south from Mattancherry Jetty leads into the district known as **Jew Town**, home of a once-thriving Jewish community whose main place of worship, until most of them emigrated to Israel, was the **Pardesi (White Jew) Synagogue** (daily except Sat 10am–noon & 3–5pm; Rs2). Founded in 1568 and rebuilt in 1664, the building is best known for its interior, an incongruous hotch-potch paved with hand-painted eighteenth-century blue and white tiles from Canton. An elaborately carved Ark houses four scrolls of the Torah, on which sit gold crowns presented by the maharajas of Travancore and Cochin, testifying to good relations with the Jewish community. The synagogue's oldest artefact is a fourth-century copperplate inscription from the raja of Cochin.

Ernakulam and south of the centre

ERNAKULAM presents the modern face of Kerala, with more of a big-city feel than Thiruvananthapuram. Other than the contemporary art on display at the small **Durbar Hall Art Gallery** (daily 11am–7pm; free) on Durbar Hall Road, there's little in the way of sights. Along the busy, long, straight **Mahatma Gandhi (MG) Road**, which more or less divides Ernakulam in half, the main activities are shopping, eating and movie-going. This area is particularly good for cloth, with an impressive selection of colours; whatever the current trend in *lunghis* or wedding saris this year, you'll get it on MG Road.

An eight-day annual **festival** (Jan/Feb) at the Shiva temple, on Durbar Hall Road, features elephant processions and *parchavadyam* (drum and trumpet groups) out in the street. The festival usually includes night-time perform-ances of **kathakali**, and the temple is decorated with an amazing array of electric lights.

Around Kochi and Ernakulam

Some 12km southeast of Ernakulam and a short bus or auto-rickshaw ride from the bus stand just south of Jos Junction on MG Road, the small suburban town of **THRIPUNITRA** is worth a visit for its dilapidated colonial-style **Hill Palace** (Tues–Sun 9am–5pm; Rs10), now an eclectic museum. The royal family of Cochin at one time maintained around forty palaces – this one was confiscated by the state government after Independence, and has slipped into dusty decline over the past decade. One of the museum's finest exhibits is an early seventeenth-century wooden *mandapa* (hall) featuring carvings of episodes from the Ramayana. Of interest too are the silver filigree jewel boxes, gold and silver ornaments, and ritual objects associated with grand ceremo-nies. Artefacts in the **bronze gallery** include a *kingini katti* knife, whose

Visitors to Kerala in search of an exclusive tropical paradise may well find it in **LAKSHADWEEP** (Ⓦ www.lakshadweep.nic.in), the "one hundred thousand islands" which lie between 200km and 400km offshore in the deep blue of the Arabian Sea. The smallest Union Territory in India, Lakshadweep's 27 tiny, coconut-palm-covered **coral islands** are the archetypal tropical hideaway, edged with pristine white sands and surrounded by calm lagoons where average water temperature stays around 26°C all year. Beyond the lagoons lie the coral **reefs**, home to sea turtles, dolphins, eagle rays, lionfish, parrotfish, octopus, barracudas and sharks. Devoid of animal and bird life, only ten of the islands are inhabited, with a total population of just over fifty thousand, the majority of whom are Malayalam-speaking Sunni Muslims said to be descended from seventh-century Keralan Hindus who converted to Islam.

The main sources of income are fishing and coconuts. Fruit, vegetables and pulses are cultivated in small quantities but staples such as rice have always had to be imported. The Portuguese, who discovered the value of **coir rope**, spun from coconut husk, controlled Lakshadweep during the sixteenth century; when they imposed an import tax on rice, locals retaliated by poisoning some of the forty-strong Portuguese garrison, and terrible reprisals followed. As Muslims, the islanders enjoyed friendly relations with Tipu Sultan of Mysore, which naturally aroused the ire of the British, who moved in at the end of the eighteenth century and remained until Independence, when Lakshadweep became a Union Territory.

Visiting Lakshadweep

Concerted attempts are being made to minimize the ecological impact of tourism in Lakshadweep. At present, accommodation is available for **non-Indians** on only two of the islands – Bangaram and Kadmat. Indian tourists are also allowed to visit the neighbouring islands of Kavaratti and Minicoy (both closed to foreigners).

All visits to **Kadmat** must be arranged in Kochi through the Society for Promotion of Recreational Tourism and Sports (SPORTS) on IG Road, Willingdon Island (Ⓣ 0484/266 8387, Ⓦ www.lakshadweeptourism.com). They offer a five-day package **cruise** to Kavaratti, Kalpeni and Minicoy islands ($240–390 per person) on one of their ships. Meals are included, and permits taken care of.

The uninhabited, teardrop-shaped half-square-kilometre islet of **Bangaram** welcomes a limited number of foreign tourists at any one time, and expects them

---

decorative bells belie the fact that it was used for beheading, and a body-shaped cage in which condemned prisoners would be hung while birds pecked them to death.

Performances of theatre, classical music and dance, including consecutive all-night **kathakali** performances, are held over a period of several days during the annual festival (Oct/Nov) at the **Shri Purnatrayisa Temple** on the way to the palace.

The closest decent **beach** to Kochi is **Cherai**, 35km to the north. It shelters a backwater and supports an active fishing community. **To get there**, you can either jump on the ferry across to Vypeen Island from Fort Cochin and transfer onto the hourly bus, or catch one of the more frequent buses from opposite the High Court Jetty in Ernakulam. One of the most appealing **places to stay** in this area is the *Cherai Beach Resort* (Ⓣ 0484/248 1818, Ⓦ www.cheraibeachresorts .com; ❽–❾). Its ten romantic "ethnic villas", built in traditional Keralan style using natural materials, rest on stilts or their own islets, connected with little wooden bridges, and only a stone's throw from the sands.

to pay handsomely for the privilege. CGH Earth's *Bangaram Island Resort* (Ⓦwww .cghearth.com; Ⓞ), bookable online or through the *CGH Earth Casino Hotel* on Willingdon Island (close to Cochin Harbour Terminus train station Ⓣ0484/266 8221), accommodates up to thirty couples in thatched cottage rooms, each with a veranda. Cane tables and chairs sit outside the restaurant on the beach, and a few hammocks are strung up between the palms. There's no a/c, TV, radio, telephone, newspapers or shops, let alone discos. The price of such remoteness, however, is steep: $425–500 per night, full board, plus extra for flights and boat transfers.

Facilities include scuba diving ($85 per day plus $40 per dive, or $70 for two), glass-bottomed boat trips to neighbouring uninhabited islands, and deep-sea fishing (Oct to mid-May; $65–90). Kayaks, catamarans and a sailing boat are available free, and it's possible to take a day-trip to Kadmat.

A British-run diving firm based in Goa also operates diving holidays in Lakshadweep; a full rundown of prices and booking conditions appears online at Ⓦwww.goadiving.com.

Getting to the islands

At present, the only way for foreigners to reach Bangaram is the expensive flights on small aircraft run by Indian Airlines and Kingfisher Airlines out of Kochi (one to two daily except Sun; 1hr–1hr 35min). Foreigners pay around $300 for the return trip, which takes an hour and a half. Flights arrive in Lakshadweep on the island of **Agatti**, 8km southwest of Bangaram; the connecting boat journey to Bangaram takes two hours, picking its way through the shallows to avoid corals. During the monsoon (May 16–Sept 15) helicopters are used to protect the fragile coral reefs that lie just under the surface. All arrangements, including flights, accommodation and the necessary entry permit, are handled by the *Casino Hotel*, Willingdon Island, Kochi (see above). Some foreign tour operators, however, offer all-in packages combining Lakshadweep with another destination, usually Goa.

Theoretically, it's possible to visit Lakshadweep all year round; the hottest time is April and May, when the temperature can reach 33°C; the **monsoon** (May–Sept) attracts approximately half the rainfall seen in the rest of Kerala, in the form of passing showers rather than a deluge, although the seas are rough.

Eating

Kochi offers an outstanding choice of places to eat, from the rustic fish-fry stalls next to the Chinese nets to fine dining with harbour views. As with accommodation, restaurants in Ernakulam tend to be cheaper but less atmospheric than those in Fort Cochin.

Unless otherwise stated, restaurants under the "Ernakulam" and "Fort Cochin" headings are marked on their relevant maps (see p.1234 & p.1229).

Ernakulam

Bimbi's Shanmugham Rd. This modern south Indian fast-food joint, in midtown near the Sealord Boat Jetty, is hugely popular locally for its inexpensive Udupi, north Indian and Chinese snacks and meals. Their *vada sambars* are the tangiest in town, and there's an exhaustive range of cooling ice cream and shakes to round your meal off.
Coffee Beanz Shanmugham Rd. Trendy a/c cappuccino bar, patronized mainly by well-heeled

students shrieking into their mobiles over a full-on MTV soundtrack. The din notwithstanding, it's a good spot to beat the heat and grab a quick meal (burgers, fries, grilled sandwiches, *dosas*, fish curries, *appams* and samosas). The coffee's freshly ground and delicious, though service is far less snappy than the fast-food uniforms.
Four Foods Shanmugham Rd. Busy, clean and popular roadside restaurant serving veg and

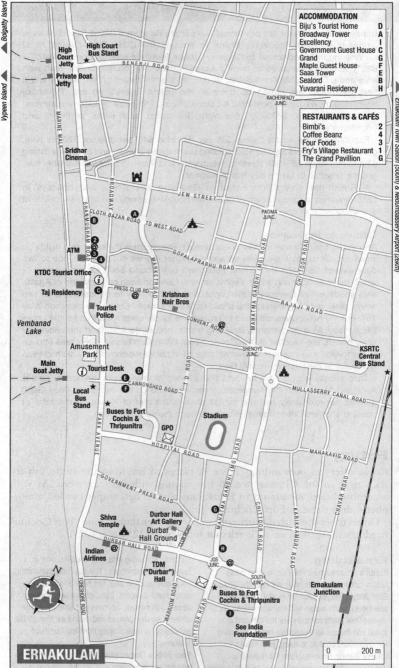

KERALA

21

200 mERNAKULAM

Cochin Cultural Centre ▼

Vypeen Island ◄

Bolgatty Island ◄

Ernakulam Town Station (500m) & Nedumbassery Airport (26km) ►

ACCOMMODATION

Biju's Tourist Home	D
Broadway Tower	A
Excellency	I
Government Guest House	C
Grand	G
Maple Guest House	F
Saas Tower	E
Sealord	B
Yuvarani Residency	H

RESTAURANTS & CAFÉS

Bimbi's	2
Coffee Beanz	4
Four Foods	3
Fry's Village Restaurant	1
The Grand Pavillion	G

High Court Jetty

Private Boat Jetty

High Court Bus Stand

BENERJI ROAD

KACHERIPADY JUNC.

MARINE WALK

Sridhar Cinema

BROADWAY

SHANMUGHAM ROAD

CLOTH BAZAR ROAD

JEW STREET

TD WEST ROAD

A

B

PADMA JUNC.

1

ATM

2
3
4

MARKET ROAD

GOPALAPRABHU ROAD

CHITTOOR ROAD

MAHATMA GANDHI (MG) ROAD

RAJAJI ROAD

KTDC Tourist Office

i

Taj Residency

C

PRESS CLUB RD

Krishnan Nair Bros

CONVENT ROAD

Tourist Police

Vembanad Lake

Amusement Park

SHENOYS JUNC.

KSRTC Central Bus Stand

Main Boat Jetty

i Tourist Desk

D

Local Bus Stand

E

F

CANNONSHED ROAD

D ROAD

MULLASSERRY CANAL ROAD

Buses to Fort Cochin & Thripunitra

PARK AVENUE

GPO

Stadium

HOSPITAL ROAD

MAHATMA GANDHI (MG) ROAD

CHITTOOR ROAD

MAHAKAVIG ROAD

GOVERNMENT PRESS ROAD

KARIKAKAMURI ROAD

CHAVAR ROAD

Shiva Temple

Durbar Hall Art Gallery

Durbar Hall Ground

G

Indian Airlines

DURBAR HALL ROAD

CLUB ROAD

TDM ("Durbar") Hall

H

JOS JUNC.

FORESHORE ROAD

WARRIOM ROAD

SOUTH JUNC.

Ernakulam Junction

Buses to Fort Cochin & Thripunitra

CHITTOOR ROAD

See India Foundation

N

1234

non-veg meals, including generous thalis, fish dishes and a good-value "dish of the day".

Fry's Village Restaurant Chittoor Rd, next to the old Mymoor Cinema. Authentic, rural Keralan meals served in comfortable, hygienic surroundings. It's busiest at lunchtimes, when workers pour in for the excellent-value thalis (veg Rs35 non-veg Rs40), mountainous Muslim-style biriyanis (veg, prawn, mutton or chicken; Rs30–40), steaks of deliciously fresh masala-fried kingfish and the full range of traditional Keralan steamed rice cakes.

The Grand Pavillion MG Rd ☎0484/238 2061. An Ernakulam institution, famous for its gourmet Keralan dishes, especially the *karimeen pollichadu* with *appam*, which draws crowds on Sun evenings. They also do a huge range of Far Eastern, North Indian and Continental options, served on white tablecloths by a legion of brisk waiters wearing black ties and waistcoats. Count on Rs500–600 for three courses. Reservations recommended.

Fort Cochin

Elite Bakery Ground Floor, *Elite Lodge*, Princess St. One of very few bona fide locals' cafés left in Fort Cochin, and a dependable option if you're travelling on a budget. They serve Keralan and Western breakfasts, freshly prepared veg and non-veg thalis at lunchtime, and Anglo-Indian snacks such as flaky pastry puffs (veg, beef or egg), fried potato cutlets, spring rolls and patties throughout the day and evening.

Fort House *Fort House Hotel*, 2/6A Calvathy Rd. One of the Fort's hidden gems: carefully prepared Keralan specialities – including delicious *meen pollichathu* or grilled fish steak – served on a romantic, candle-lit jetty jutting into the harbour – a perfect location for watching the ships chugging in and out of the docks. Most mains Rs175–245.

Kashi Art Café Burgher St. Chi-chi art gallery café, patronized almost exclusively by Westerners, and with a menu to match. Fragrant, freshly ground expresso coffee is the big draw, along with the

Kashi's famous house cakes, but they also do a selection of light meals and savoury snacks through the day.

Malabar Junction *Malabar House Hotel*, 1/268 Parade Rd ☎0484/221 6666, ⊛www.malabarhouse .com. Gourmet fusion cuisine, served on a chic garden dining terrace in one of Kerala's most stylish boutique hotels. Their signature dish is the seafood platter (Rs980), featuring juicy local lobster, tiger prawns, calamari and choice cuts of fish from the lagoon, but they offer a range of more sensibly priced Italian and south Indian alternatives (Rs250–450).

The Old Courtyard 1/371–2 Princess St. Few places capture the feel of old-world Cochin as vividly as this courtyard restaurant, where candlelit tables are laid out beneath Portuguese vaulted arches. The food is as fine as the location (hallmark dishes include baked seafood spaghetti and grilled fish with coriander butter) – and the *patronne-chef* is a dessert wizard. Most mains Rs200–275.

Salt 'n' Pepper/Brighton Café Tower Rd. This pair of terrace cafés, spread under the rain trees along the north side of Tower Rd, fill up after sunset and stay open until the small hours during the season. Both serve simple snacks, but the main attraction is the beer – surreptitiously poured out of china pots to rows of bored foreign budget tourists.

Teapot Café Peter Celli St. With its massive collection of teapots and shabby-chic interior, this backstreet tearoom has been giving the *Kashi* some much-needed competition over the past few seasons. Quality teas and coffees are its mainstay, but there's also a selection of light meals and delicious home-made cakes on offer.

Upstairs Santa Cruz Rd. Currently the backpacker's favourite: a hip little trattoria run by an Indian–Italian couple in a quirky first-floor dining room opposite the Basilica. The food's simple, fresh and authentically Italian, down to the imported olive oil and Parmesan: green leaf salad (Rs80), tasty bruschettas (Rs150), crisp-edged pizzas (Rs175–225), fresh pasta bakes and *lasagna al forno* (Rs275).

Listings

Airlines Air India, Collis Estate, MG Rd ☎0484/235 1295, airport ☎0484/261 0040; Air India Express, Collis Estate, MG Rd ☎0484/238 1885, airport ☎0484/261 0050; Indian Airlines, Durbar Hall Rd ☎0484/237114, airport ☎0484/261 0101; Go Air, c/o UAE Travel Services, Chettupuzha Towers, PT Usha Rd Junction ☎0484/235 5522; Jet Airways, 39/4158, Elmar Square Bldg, MG Rd ☎0484/235 9212, airport ☎2610037; JetLite,

airport ☎0484/261 1340; Kingfisher Airlines, K.B Oxford Business Centre, 39/4013, Free Kandath Rd, MG Rd ☎0484/235 1144; Paramount Airways, airport ☎0484/2610404.

Banks There are numerous bank branches on MG Rd in Ernakulam, including the State Bank of India. To exchange traveller's cheques, the best place is Thomas Cook (Mon–Sat 9.30am–6pm), near the Air India Building at Palal Towers, MG Rd; they also have a branch at the airport. In Fort Cochin, the Canara Bank has an ATM on Kanumpuram Junction (see map, p.1229). The Wilson Info Centre and Destinations, both on Princess St (open daily 9am–9pm) change cash and traveller's cheques at rates slightly above Thomas Cook.

Bookshops The two branches of Idiom (opposite the Dutch Palace, Jew Town, Mattancherry; and on Bastion St near Princess St, Fort Cochin) are wonderful places to browse for books on travel, Indian and Keralan culture, flora and fauna, religion and art; they also have an excellent range of non-fiction.

Dentist The Emmanuel Dental Centre, Noble Square, Kadavanthara (☎0484/220 7544, ⓦwww.cosmeticdentalcentre.com), is an international-standard practice that does routine dental procedures as well as more advanced cosmetic work.

Hospitals The 600-bed Medical Trust Hospital on MG Rd (☎0484/235 8001, ⓦwww.medical trusthospital.com) is one of the state's most advanced private hospitals and has a 24hr casualty unit and ambulance service.

Internet access Café de Net on Bastion Rd, Fort Cochin, has nine machines and charges Rs30/hr; if it's full, try any of the smaller places off the bottom of Princess St nearby. In Ernakulam, convenient options include Net Park on Convent Rd and Mathsons on Durbar Hall Rd (both Rs30/hr).

Music stores Sargam, XL/6816 GSS Complex, Convent Rd, opposite the Public Library, stocks the best range of music CDs in the state, mostly Indian (Hindi films and lots of Keralan devotional

Recommended trains from Kochi/Ernakulam

The trains listed below are recommended as the fastest and/or most convenient services from Kochi. If you're heading to **Alappuzha** for the backwater trip to Kollam, take the bus, as the only train that can get you there in time invariably arrives late.

Destination	Name	No.	Station	Departs	Total time
Bengaluru (Bangalore)	Kanyakumari–Bangalore Express	#6525	ET	daily 6.05pm	13hr
Chennai	Trivandrum–Chennai Mail	#2624	ET	daily 7.15pm	11hr 45min
Delhi	Rajdhani Express*	#2431	EJ	Tues & Thurs 10.35pm	38hr
	Kerala Express	#2625	EJ	daily 3.40pm	48hr 20min
Kozhikode (Calicut)	Netravati Express	#6346	EJ	daily 2.15pm	4hr 45min
Madgaon/Margao (Goa)	Rajdhani Express*	#2431	EJ	Tues & Thurs 10.35pm	12hr
	Mangala-Lakshadweep Express	#2617	EJ	daily 12.45pm	14hr 30min
Madurai	Guruvayur–Chennai Express	#6128	EJ	daily 11.30pm	11hr 30min
Mangalore	Malabar Express	#6629	ET	daily 11.45pm	10hr 25min
	Parasuram Express	#6349	ET	daily 11.05am	9hr 15min
Mumbai	Netravati Express	#6346	EJ	daily 2.15pm	26hr 25min
Thiruvananthapuram	Parasuram Express	#6350	ET	daily 1.30pm	5hr 5min
Varkala	Parasuram Express	#6350	ET	daily 1.30pm	3hr 50min

EJ = Ernakulam Junction
ET = Ernakulam Town
* = a/c only, meals included

music), with a couple of shelves of Western rock and pop.

Musical instruments Manuel Industries, Banerji Rd, Kacheripady Junction, is the best for Indian classical and Western instruments. For traditional Keralan drums, ask at Thripunitra bazaar (see p.1231).

Police The city's tourist police have a counter at the railway station. There is also a counter next to the KTDC Tourist Office at the southern end of Shanmugham Rd.

Post office The GPO is on Hospital Rd, not far from the Main Jetty.

Tour and travel agents For air tickets, Kapitan Air Travel and Tours at 1/430 Burgher St in Fort Cochin (on the ground floor of *Adam's Old Inn*) is the Fort's only IATA-bonded agent. Wild Kerala Tours, at VI/480 KVA Bldgs on Bazaar Rd, Mantancherry (☏ 0484/309 9520 or 098461 62157, ⓦ www .wildkeralatours.com) is recommended for wildlife and acventure safaris to some of Kerala's wildest corners, guided by local experts.

Moving on from Kochi/Ernakulam

The international **airport** (☏484/261 0113, ⓦwww.cochinairport.com) at **Nedumbassery**, near Alwaye (aka Alua), is 26km north of Ernakulam and serves as Kerala's main gateway to and from the Gulf.

Buses leave Ernakulam's KSRTC **Central Bus Stand** for virtually every town in Kerala, and some beyond; most, but not all, are bookable in advance at the bus station. However, for destinations further afield, you're generally much better off taking the train.

Kochi lies on Kerala's main **broad-gauge line** and sees frequent services down the coast to Thiruvananthapuram via Kottayam, Kollam and Varkala. Heading north, there are plenty of trains to Thrissur, and thence northeast across Tamil Nadu to Chennai, but only a couple run direct to Mangalore. Since the opening of the Konkan Railway, a few express trains travel along the coast all the way to Goa and Mumbai, stopping close to Mangalore.

Although most long-distance express and mail trains depart from **Ernakulam Junction**, a couple of key services leave from **Ernakulam Town**. To confuse matters further, a few also start at Cochin Harbour station, so be sure to check the departure point when you book your ticket. The main reservation office, good for trains leaving all three stations, is at Ernakulam Junction.

Thrissur

THRISSUR (Trichur), a bustling market hub and temple town roughly midway between Kochi (74km south) and Palakkad (79km northeast) on the NH-47, is a convenient base for exploring the cultural riches of central Kerala. Close to the Palghat (Palakkad) Gap – an opening in the natural border made by the Western Ghat mountains – it presided over the main trade route into the region from Tamil Nadu and Karnataka. For years Thrissur was the capital of Cochin state, controlled at various times by both the *zamorin* of Kozhikode and Tipu Sultan of Mysore.

Today, Thrissur derives most of its income from remittance cheques sent by expatriates in the Gulf – hence the predominance of ostentatious modern houses in the surrounding villages. As the home of several influential art institutions, the town also prides itself on being the cultural capital of Kerala. The state's largest temple, **Vaddukanatha**, is here too, at the centre of a huge circular *maidan* that hosts all kinds of public gatherings, not least Kerala's most extravagant, noisy and sumptuous festival, **Puram**.

Arrival and information

The principal point of orientation in Thrissur is the **Round**, a road (subdivided into North, South, East and West) which circles the Vaddukanatha temple complex and *maidan* in the town centre. On the mainline to Chennai and other points in Tamil Nadu, and with good connections to Kochi and Thiruvananthapuram, the **railway station** is 1km southwest, opposite the **KSRTC long-distance bus stand**. **Priya Darshini Bus Stand** (also known as "North", "Shoranur" and "Wadakkancheri" stand), close to Round North, serves Shoranur (for the Kalamanadalam Academy). The **Shakthan Thampuran Bus Stand**, on TB Road, just over 1km from Round South, serves local destinations south such as Irinjalakuda, Kodungallur and Guruvayur.

The DTPC **tourist office** (Mon–Sat 10am–5pm; ☎0487/232 0800) is on Palace Road, opposite the Town Hall (five minutes' walk off Round East). Run by volunteers, its primary purpose is to promote the Puram elephant festival, but staff also give out maps of Thrissur. The best place to **change money** and traveller's cheques is the UTI Bank in the City Centre Shopping building (Mon–Fri 9.30am–3.30pm, Sat 9.30am–1.30pm) on Round West. The UAE Exchange & Financial Services (Mon–Sat 9.30am–6pm, Sun 9.30am–1.30pm) in the basement of the *Casino Hotel* building also changes currency and traveller's cheques. Both of the above, and a dozen or so other banks around the centre, have ATMs. The **GPO** is on the southern edge of town, near the *Casino Hotel*, off TB Road. **Internet** facilities are available at Hugues Net on the top floor of the City Centre Shopping building and SS Consultants next to the *Luciya Palace* hotel; rates are around Rs20/hr.

Accommodation

Thrissur has a fair number of mid-price **hotels**, but only a couple of decent budget places. Almost everywhere follows a 24hr checkout policy. If you're planning to be here during **Puram**, book well in advance and bear in mind that room rates soar – some of the upscale places charge up to ten times their normal prices.

Elite International Chembottil Lane, off Round South ☎0487/242 1033, ✉mail@hotelelite international.com. Pronounced "Ee-light", this mid-range place in the centre of town has rooms opening onto corridors, some with balconies overlooking the green. The staff are very friendly and helpful, and there's a good restaurant and relaxing garden. Rates include breakfast. ④–⑥

Grand Park Regency Mullassery Tower, Kuruppam Rd ☎0487/242 8247, ⊛www.grandparkregency .com. Gleaming, efficient business hotel in a pink-coloured multistorey block bang in the town centre, close to the bus stand, railway station and temple green. Its rooms are modern and centrally a/c. Facilities include a fitness centre and roof garden. ⑤–⑥

Gurukripa Lodge Chembottil Lane ☎0487/242 1895. Run with great efficiency by the venerable Mr Venugopal, the *Gurukripa*, just off Round South, offers a variety of simple attached rooms (including several great-value singles) arranged around a long, pleasant inner courtyard. Some a/c. ②–③

Pathans Round South ☎0487/242 5620. Its basement entrance is none too promising, but the generous-sized rooms in this conveniently central hotel, with its lavishly carved teak and rosewood furniture, have an appealing colonial feel and are good value. ③–④

Ramanilayam Government Rest House Palace Rd ☎0471/233 2016. Star-hotel comfort at economy-lodge rates, in palatial suites with balconies, or smaller doubles (some a/c), set in manicured gardens on the northeast side of town near the zoo and museum. As with all Government Guest Houses, officials get priority (even at the last minute), which can make a mockery of advance bookings. ②–③

Sidhartha Regency Veliyannur Rd, Kokkalai ☎0487/242 4773. In the southwestern corner of town near the railway station, this good-value, modern three-star ranks among the most welcoming and comfortable options within walking distance of the centre. The seven-storey block holds a swimming pool (set in lawns to the rear), multi-gym, health club, multi-cuisine restaurant, bar and gardens. ⑤–⑥

Puram

Thrissur is best known to outsiders as the venue for Kerala's biggest annual festival, **Puram**, which takes place on one day in April/May (ask at a tourist office for the exact date). The event is the most extreme example of a kind of celebration seen on a smaller scale at temples all over Kerala, known as *utsavam*. The main ingredients of nearly all of them are **caparisoned elephants**, **drum music** and **fireworks**.

Centred on Round South, Puram features two majestic processions in which the Tiruvambadi and Paramekkavu temples compete to create the more impressive sights and sounds. They eventually meet, like armies on a battlefield, facing each other at either end of the path. Both sides present fifteen tuskers sumptuously decorated with gold ornaments, each ridden by three brahmins clutching whisks of yak hair, circular peacock-feather fans and colourful silk umbrellas fringed with silver pendants. At the centre of each group, the principal elephant carries an image of the temple's deity, while fireworks explode and the huge orchestra plays in front of them.

Known as **chenda melam**, this quintessentially Keralan music, featuring as many as a hundred loud, hard-skinned, cylindrical *chenda* drums, crashing cymbals and wind instruments, marks the progress of the procession. Each kind of *chenda melam* is named after the rhythmic cycle. Drummers stand in ranks, the most numerous at the back often playing single beats. At the front, a line of master drummers, the stars of Keralan music, try to outdo each other with their speed, stamina, improvisational skills and showmanship. Facing the drummers, musicians play long double-reed, oboe-like *kuzhals* (similar to the North Indian *shehnai*) and C-shaped *kompu* bell-metal trumpets. The fundamental structure is provided by the *elatalam* – medium-sized, heavy, brass hand-cymbals that resolutely and precisely keep the tempo. Over an extended period, the *melam* passes through four phases, each twice as fast as the last, from a grand and graceful dead-slow through to a frenetic pace.

At the arrival of the fastest tempo, those astride the elephants stand, manipulating their feather fans and hair whisks in coordinated sequence, while behind, unfurled umbrellas are twirled in flashes of dazzling colour, their pendants glinting silver in the sun. The cymbals crash furiously, often raised above the head, requiring extraordinary stamina. The master drummers play at their loudest and fastest, frequently intensified by surges of energy emanating from single players, one after another; a chorus of trumpets, in ragged unison, accompanies the cacophony, creating a sound that has altered little since the festival's origins.

All this is greeted by tremendous roars from the crowd; many people punch the air, while others are clearly *talam branthans*, rhythm "madmen", who follow every nuance of the structure. When the fastest speed is played out, the slowest tempo returns and the procession edges forward, the *mahouts* leading the elephants by the tusk. Stopping again, the whole cycle is repeated.

If you venture to Thrissur for Puram, be prepared for packed buses and trains. Needless to say, accommodation should be booked well in advance. An umbrella or hat is recommended for protection from the sun. Unfortunately, Puram has become an excuse for groups of Indian men to get very drunk; women are advised to dress conservatively and only to go in the morning, or to watch with a group of Indian women.

Similar but much smaller events take place in town, generally from September onwards, with most during the summer (April and May). Enquire at a tourist office or your hotel, or ask someone to check a local edition of the newspaper, *Mathrabhumi*, for local performances of *chenda melam*, and other drum orchestras such as *panchavadyam* and *tyambaka*.

21

KERALA

The Town

The **State Art Museum** (Tues–Sun 9am–6.30pm; Rs8) stands on Museum Road, ten minutes' walk from the Round in the northeast of town. Collections of faded local bronzes, jewellery, fine woodcarvings of fanged temple guardians and a profusion of bell-metal oil lamps make up the bulk of its collection. Next door, the **zoo** (same hours as museum; free) is a predictably sad, run-down affair.

Keralan ritual theatre

Among the most magical experiences a visitor to Kerala can have is to witness one of the innumerable ancient drama rituals that play such an important and unique role in the cultural life of the region. **Kathakali** is the best known; other less publicised forms, which clearly influenced its development, include the classical Sanskrit **Kutiyattam**.

Many Keralan forms share broad characteristics. A prime aim of each performer is to transform the mundane to the world of gods and demons; his preparation is highly ritualised, involving other-worldly costume and mask-like make-up. In Kathakali and Kutiyattam, this preparation is a rigorously codified part of the classical tradition. One-off **performances** of various ritual types take place throughout the state, building up to fever pitch during April and May before pausing for the monsoon (June–Aug). Finding out about such events requires a little perseverance, but it's well worth the effort; enquire at tourist offices, or buy a Malayalam daily paper such as the *Malayalam Manorama* and ask someone to check the listings for **temple festivals**, where most of the action invariably takes place. Tourist Kathakali is staged daily in Kochi (see p.1230) but to find authentic performances, contact **performing arts schools** such as Thiruvananthapuram's Margi (see p.1188) and Cheruthuruthy's Kerala Kalamandalam; Kutiyattam artists work at both, as well as at Natana Kairali at Irinjalakuda (see p.1242).

Kathakali

Here is the tradition of the trance dancers, here is the absolute demand of the subjugation of body to spirit, here is the realization of the cosmic transformation of human into divine.

Mrinalini Sarabhai, classical dancer

The image of a **Kathakali** actor in a magnificent costume with extraordinary make-up and a huge gold crown has become Kerala's trademark. Traditional performances, of which there are still many, usually take place on open ground outside a temple, beginning at 10pm and lasting until dawn, illuminated by the flickers of a large brass oil lamp centre-stage. Virtually nothing about Kathakali is naturalistic, because it depicts the world of gods and demons; both the male and female roles are played by men.

Standing at the back of the stage, two musicians play driving rhythms, one on a bronze gong, the other on heavy bell-metal cymbals; they also sing the dialogue. Actors appear and disappear from behind a hand-held curtain and never utter a sound, save the odd strange cry. Learning the elaborate hand gestures, facial expressions and choreographed movements, as articulate and precise as any sign language, requires rigorous training which can begin at the age of eight and last ten years. At least two more drummers stand left of the stage; one plays the upright **chenda** with slender curved sticks, the other plays the *maddalam*, a horizontal barrel-shaped hand drum. When a female character is "speaking", the *chenda* is replaced by the hourglass-shaped *ettaka*, a "talking drum" on which melodies can be played. The drummers keep their eyes on the actors, whose every gesture is reinforced by their sound, from the gentlest embrace to the gory disembowelling of an enemy.

A five-minute rickshaw ride away, opposite the Priya Darshini Bus Stand, the **Archeological Museum** (Tues–Sun 9.30am–1pm & 2–4.30pm; Rs10) occupies the 200-year-old Shaktan Thampuran Palace, the former residence of the Kochi royal family. Beautifully decorated throughout with intricate wood- and tile-work, the building is centred on a colonnaded patio. Exhibits include a fearsome selection of beheading axes, and a massive iron-studded treasury box still in its original place (presumably because no one has ever managed to shift

Although it bears the unmistakable influences of Kutiyattam and indigenous folk rituals, Kathakali, literally "story-play", is thought to have crystallized into a distinct theatre form during the seventeenth century. The plays are based on three major sources: the Hindu epics the Mahabharata, Ramayana and the *Bhagavata Purana*. While the stories are ostensibly about god-heroes such as Rama and Krishna, the most popular characters are those that give the most scope to the actors – the villainous, fanged, red-and-black-faced *katti* ("knife") anti-heroes; these types, such as the kings Ravana and Duryodhana, are dominated by lust, greed, envy and violence. David Bolland's *Guide to Kathakali*, widely available in Kerala, gives invaluable scene-by-scene summaries of the most popular plays and explains in simple language a lot more besides.

When attending a performance, arrive early to get your bearings before it gets dark, even though the first play will not begin much before 10pm. (Quiet) members of the audience are welcome to visit the dressing room before and during the performance. The colour and design of the mask-like make-up, which specialist artists take several hours to apply, reveal the character's personality. The word *pacha* means both "green" and "pure"; a green-faced *pacha* character is thus a noble human or god. Red signifies *rajas*, passion and aggression, black denotes *tamas*, darkness and negativity, while white is *sattvik*, light and intellect. Once the make-up is completed, elaborate wide skirts are tied to the waist, and ornaments of silver and gold are added. Silver talons are fitted to the left hand. The transformation is complete with a final prayer and the donning of waist-length wig and crown. Visitors new to Kathakali will almost undoubtedly get bored during such long programmes, parts of which are very slow indeed. If you're at a village performance, you may not always find accommodation, so you can't leave during the night. Be prepared to sit on the ground for hours, and bring some warm clothes. Half the fun is staying up all night to witness, just as the dawn light appears, the gruesome disembowelling of a villain or a demon *asura*.

Kutiyattam

Three families of the Chakyar caste and a few outsiders perform the Sanskrit drama **Kutiyattam**, the oldest continually performed theatre-form in the world. Until recently it was only performed inside temples and then only in front of the uppermost castes. Visually it is very similar to its offspring, Kathakali, but its atmosphere is infinitely more archaic. The actors, eloquent in sign language and symbolic movement, speak in the compelling intonation of the local brahmins' Vedic chant, unchanged since 1500 BC.

A single act of a Kutiyattam play can require ten full nights; the entire play takes forty. A great actor, in full command of the subtleties of expression through gestures, can take half an hour to do such a simple thing as murder a demon, berate the audience, or simply describe a leaf fall to the ground. Unlike Kathakali, Kutiyattam includes comic characters and plays. The ubiquitous **Vidushaka**, narrator and clown, is something of a court jester, and traditionally has held the right to criticize openly the highest in the land without fear of retribution.

its 1500kg dead weight). The real highlight, however, is the royal *palliyara*, or bedchamber, boasting a traditional carved-wood four-poster and vibrant ceramic tiles.

Eating and drinking

With so many hotels and busy "meals" joints lining the Round, there's no shortage of dependable places to eat in Thrissur. From 8.30pm onwards, you can also join the auto-rickshaw-wallahs, hospital visitors, itinerant mendicants, Ayappa devotees and student revellers who congregate at the popular **thattu-kada** hot-food market on the corner of Round South and Round East, opposite the Medical College Hospital. The rustic Keralan cooking – omelettes, *dosas, parottas, iddiappam*, bean curries and egg masala – is always freshly prepared, delicious and unbelievably cheap.

Ambady Round West. Down a lane and away from the Round traffic noise, offering a good selection of Keralan staples as well as lunchtime thalis and dozens of milkshakes and ice creams.

Bharath Lodge Chembottil Lane, 50m down the road from the *Elite Hotel*. Piping-hot south Indian *vada sambar* and *iddli* breakfasts, as well as "all you can eat" Keralan meals (Rs24–35) at lunchtime.

Indian Coffee House Round South. The usual cheap and popular *ICH* range of south Indian snacks, as well as strong chai and weak coffee, served by waiters whose serious demeanour is undermined by their old-school ice-cream fan turbans and curry-stained tunics.

Ming Palace Pathan Building, Round South. Inexpensive "Chindian" with dim lighting, cheesy muzak and a menu of chop suey, noodles and lots of chicken and veg dishes.

Pathan's Round South. Deservedly popular veg restaurant, with a cosy a/c family annexe and a large canteen-like dining hall. Generous portions and plenty of choice, including koftas, kormas and lots of tandoori options, as well as Keralan thalis and wonderful Kashmiri naan.

Around Thrissur

The chief attraction of the area **around Thrissur** is the opportunity to get to grips with Kerala's cultural heritage. **IRINJALAKUDA**, 20km south, is the home of the **Natana Kairali** (Mon–Sat 11am–1pm & 3–7pm), an important cultural centre dedicated to the documentation and performance of Kerala's lesser-known theatre arts, including *kutiyattam, nangiar koothu* (female mono-acting), shadow and puppet theatres. The centre is based in the home of one of Kerala's most illustrious acting families, Ammanur Chakyar Madhom (say this name when you ask for directions). Natana Kairali's director, Shri G. Venu (☎0488/282 5559, ✉venuji@satyam.net.in), is a mine of information about Keralan arts and can advise on forthcoming performances. Irinjalakuda is best reached by **bus** from the Shakthan Thampuran stand in Thrissur rather than by train, as the railway station is an inconvenient 8km east of town. The *Udupi Woodlands Hotel* (☎0488/282 0149; ❸–❹), near the bus stand on the Bharata temple road, has clean, spacious double rooms – most of them with marble floors and powerful fans.

The village of **NADAVARAMBA**, 5km from Irinjalakuda on the Kodungallur road, is an important centre for the manufacture of traditional Keralan oil lamps and large cooking vessels, known as *uruli* and *varppu*. **Bell-metal** alloys are made from copper and tin – unlike brass, which is a blend of copper and zinc – and give a sonorous chime when struck. One of the best places to buy is the Bellwics Handicrafts Cooperative, just north of Nadavaramba Church, where you can watch the various stages of the casting process, from the making of sand and wax moulds to the pouring of molten metal, labour-intensive filing and polishing. Prices depend on the weight of the object, starting at Rs600 per kilogram.

Further afield, **CHERUTHURUTHY**, 29km northwest of Thrissur, is internationally famous as the home of **Kerala Kalamandalam**, the state's flagship training school for *kathakali* and other indigenous Keralan performing arts. The academy was founded in 1927 by the revered Keralan poet Vallathol (1878–1957), and has since been instrumental in the large-scale revival of interest in unique Keralan art forms. Non-Hindus are welcome to attend performances of *kathakali*, *kutiyattam* and *mohiniyattam* performed in the school's wonderful **theatre**, which replicates the style of the wooden, sloping-roofed traditional *kuttambalam* auditoria found in Keralan temples. You can also sit in on classes, watch demonstrations of mural painting, and visit exhibitions of costumes by signing up for the fascinating **"a day with the masters"** cultural programme (Mon–Sat 9.30am–1.30pm; $20 per person, including lunch).

Buses heading to Shoranur from Thrissur's Priya Darshini (aka "Wadakkancheri") stand pass through Cheruthuruthy; the nearest mainline **railway station** is Shoranur Junction, 3km south, served by express trains to and from Mangalore, Chennai and Kochi.

Kozhikode (Calicut)

Formerly one of Asia's most prosperous trading capitals, the busy coastal city of **KOZHIKODE** (Calicut), 225km north of Kochi, occupies an extremely important place in Keralan legend and history. It's also significant in the chronicles of European involvement on the Subcontinent, as Vasco da Gama landed at nearby Kappad beach in 1498.

After centuries of decline following the Portuguese destruction of the city, Kozhikode is once again prospering thanks to the flow of remittance cheques from the Gulf – a legacy of its powerful, Moppila-Muslim merchant community, who ran the local ruler, the *zamorin's*, navy and trade. The recent building boom has swept aside most monuments dating from the golden age, but a few survive, notably a handful of splendid Moppila **mosques**, distinguished by their typically Keralan, multi-tiered roofs. The three most impressive specimens lie off a backroad running through the **Muslim** quarter of **Thekkepuram**, 2km southwest of the *maidan* (all the auto-rickshaw-wallahs will know how to find them). Start at the 1100-year-old **Macchandipalli Masjid**, between Francis Road and the Kuttichira Tank, whose ceilings are covered in beautiful polychrome stucco and intricate Koranic script. A couple of hundred metres further north, the **Juma Masjid**'s main prayer hall, large enough for a congregation of 1200 worshippers, dates from the eleventh century and holds another elaborately carved ceiling. The most magnificent of the trio of mosques, however, is the **Mithqalpalli** (aka **Jama'atpalli**) **Masjid**, hidden down a lane behind Kuttichira tank. Resting on 24 wooden pillars, its four-tier roof and turquoise walls were built over seven hundred years ago.

Practicalities

The **railway station** (☎0495/270 1234), close to the centre of town, is served by coastal expresses, slower passenger trains, and superfast express trains from Delhi, Mumbai, Kochi and Thiruvananthapuram. There are three **bus stands**. All government-run services pull in at the **KSRTC bus stand**, on Mavoor Road (aka Indira Gandhi Rd). Private long-distance – mainly overnight – buses stop at the **New Moffussil private stand**, 500m away on the other side of Mavoor Road. The **Palayam Bus Stand**, off MM Ali Road, just serves the city.

Kozhikode's **airport**, at Karippur, 23km south of the city, is primarily a gateway for emigrant workers flying to and from the Gulf, but also has flights to other Indian cities (see p.1250). A taxi from the airport into town costs around Rs300. Flight tickets can be bought through PL Worldways, on the 3rd floor of Seema Towers, Bank Road, just north of the CSI Church. Indian Airlines (Mon–Sat 10am–1pm & 1.45–5.30pm; ☎0495/276 6243) and Air India (Mon–Sat 9.30am–5.30pm; ☎0495/276 0715) are both at the Eroth Centre, opposite *Hyson Heritage* on Bank Road. The rest of the carriers all have counters at the airport.

KTDC's **tourist information** booth (officially daily 9am–7.30pm; ☎0495/270 0097) at the railway station has info on travel connections and sites around Kozhikode, but opening hours are erratic. The main KTDC tourist office (☎0495/272 2391), in the *Malabar Mansion* hotel at the corner of SM Street, can supply only limited information about the town and area. Recommended places for **exchanging cash or traveller's cheques** are PL Worldways (see above) and the spanking-new UAE Exchange on Bank Road, next to *Hyson Heritage* (Mon–Sat 9.30am–1.30pm & 2–6pm, Sun 9.30am–1.30pm). The Union Bank of India and the State Bank of India, opposite each other on MM Ali Road, are two of many large branches with ATMs. **Internet** access is available at the Hub, on the first floor of the block to the right of *Nandhinee Sweets*, MM Ali Road, and at Internet Zone, near KTDC *Malabar Mansion* (both Rs30/hr).

Accommodation

Kozhikode's reasonably priced city-centre **hotels**, most of which operate a 24hr checkout, often fill up by noon; the beach area and Kappad, 16km north, offer quieter alternatives.

Beach Heritage 3km north of the centre on Beach Rd ☎0495/236 5363, ⓦwww.beachheritage.com. Dating from 1890, the premises of the colonial-era Malabar English Club, with its closely cropped lawns and high-pitched tiled roofs, now house a delightfully eccentric heritage hotel with oodles of period feel. It's the kind of place you'd expect to see Somerset Maugham sipping a gin sling on the veranda – which indeed he did. It's also amazingly inexpensive. ❹–❺

Harivihar 4km north of the centre in the suburb of Bilathikulam ☎0495/276 5865, ⓦwww.harivihar.com. Ancestral home of the Kadathanadu royal family, converted into a particularly wonderful heritage homestay. Set in beautiful gardens, the mansion is a model of traditional Keralan refinement, with whitewashed walls, antique furniture and pillared courtyards. Courses in yoga, astrology, cookery and Indian

mythology are on offer, and there's also a top-grade Ayurvedic treatment centre. ❽

Hyson Heritage Bank Rd, near the KSRTC bus stand ☎0495/276 6423, ⓦwww.hysonheritage.com. A gleaming, blissfully cool a/c business hotel close to the centre. Their "budget" non-a/c rooms are especially good value. ❹–❺

Malabar Palace Manuelsons Jn ☎0495/272 1511, ⓦwww.malabarpalacecalicut.com. Ritzy four-star bang in the city centre. Its rooms are lavishly furnished with luxurious beds, thick burgundy carpets and polished wood writing desks; those to the rear have great views over the palm grove. ❻–❽

Sasthapuri MM Ali Rd ☎0495/272 3281, ⓦwww.sasthapuri.com. Compact budget place, close to the Palayam Bus Stand and market, with well-maintained, nicely furnished rooms (including some of the city's cheapest a/c options), a funky little roof-garden restaurant sporting ersatz tribal murals, and a bar. Very good value. ❶–❹

Eating

Kozhikode is famous for its **Moppila cusine**, which has its roots in the culinary traditions of the city's former Arab traders. Fragrant chicken biriyanis and seafood curries with distinctive Malabari blends of spices crop up on most non-veg restaurant menus. **Mussels** are also big news here; deep-fried in crunchy, spicy millet coatings, they're served everywhere during the season, from October to December. Finally, no Kozhikode feast is considered complete without a serving of the city's legendary **halwa**: a sticky Malabari sweet made from rice flour, coconut, *jaggery* (sugar cane) and ghee. *The* place to try it has always been Mithai Theruvu, or **SM ("Sweet Market") Street**, near the Palayam Bus Stand – though the survival of this atmospheric bazaar was in doubt after a devastating fire destroyed most of its businesses in April 2007; if the area's still not up and running, try *Nandhinee Sweets*, reviewed below.

Dwaraka opposite *Sasthapuri Hotel*. A busy, down-to-earth non-veg diner where you can order inexpensive fresh mussels as well as masala-fried fish and local seafood curries.

Nandinee Sweets MM Ali Rd. This is a hygienic place to sample the joys of Malabari *halwa*, nuts and savoury snacks; they also do great fresh-fruit cocktails, *badam* milk and *falooda* shakes.

Paragon off the Kannur Rd. A short auto-rickshaw ride from the *maidan*, *Paragon* has been a city institution since it opened in 1939. Don't be put off by the uninspiring setting beneath a flyover: the cooking's superb. In a high-ceilinged dining hall with cast-iron columns, you can tuck into steaming plates of tamarind-tinged fish *moilee* or the house special, fish *kombathu*, mopped up with deliciously light *appams*, *parotta* and crumbly *puttoo*. Most mains Rs70–125.

Sagar next to the KSRTC stand, Mavoor Rd. Another old favourite of Calicut's middle classes, buried amid the high-rises and traffic mayhem of Mavoor Rd. Ignore the multi-cuisine menu; everyone orders proper Malabari dishes such as egg roast, fish korma and, best of all, the flavour-packed chicken *powichathu* – boneless chicken pieces marinated in spices and then crisp fried.

Zains Convent Cross Rd. An unassuming, pink-coloured family house in the west end of town is hardly what you'd expect the Holy Grail of Moppila cooking to look like, but the food served here is second to none. For the benefit of the uninitiated, the dishes of the day are displayed on a central table. There's generally a choice of biriyanis, various fiery seafood curries, and a range of different *pathiris* – the definitive Malabari rice-flour bread. Most mains Rs100–125.

Wayanad

The hill district of **Wayanad**, situated 70km inland from Kozhikode at the southern limits of the Deccan plateau, is one of the most beautiful regions of Kerala. Spread over altitudes of between 750m and 2100m, its landscapes vary from lush riverine rice-paddy to semitropical savannah grasslands, and from spice, tea and coffee plantations to steep mountainsides smothered in jungle. What few towns there are tend to be typically ramshackle Indian hill-bazaars, which serve widely scattered satellite villages whose 200,000 or so inhabitants are mainly *adivasi* tribal peoples. Due to the relative isolation and lack of decent roads, these minority communities – who include the Karumbas, Adiyas and Paniyas – have so far managed to preserve their traditional identities, despite the gradual intrusion of modernization.

The region's only formal visitor attraction is the **Wayanad Wildlife Sanctuary** – a park split into two separate zones, **Muthanga** and **Tholpetty**, both of which hug the Tamil border and form part of the sprawling Nilgiri Biosphere. Straddling the main highway 72km east of Kozhikode, **KALPETTA** is the district headquarters and main springboard for both. **Forest guides** (Rs50/day) and Jeeps (Rs8/km plus the Rs100 vehicle entrance fee) can be arranged at the town's **Kerala Tourism office** (Mon–Sat 10am–5pm, closed second Sat of each month; ✆04936/204441).

The southern portion of the Wayanad reserve, located 40km east of Kalpetta, is known as the **Muthanga Wildlife Sanctuary** (daily 6–10am & 3–5pm; Rs100, camera Rs25). Although noted for elephants, it also shelters deer, wild boar, bear and tiger. **Trekking** in the sanctuary is only allowed during the morning slot; hiring a (mandatory) guide for the three-hour official route costs Rs150.

Tholpetty, 25km northeast of Mananthavady, forms the northern sector of the Wayanad reserve and is one of the best parks in south India to see elephants, as well as plentiful bison, boar, *sambar*, spotted deer, macaques and langurs; tigers also inhabit the park, though they are rarely spotted. The forest department lays on two-hour **Jeep safaris** (daily 7–9am & 3–5pm), costing Rs300 for up to five people, with an additional Rs200 for the obligatory guide. You can also join guided **treks** (daily 8am–1pm; Rs750 for up to four people).

At 2100m, **Chembra Peak** is the highest point in the Wayanad region, dominating the landscape for miles around. The massif can be tackled in around ten hours via the small town of **Meppadi**, 18km south of Kalpetta and reachable on southbound buses passing through the main KSRTC stand (30min). Permission for the trek has to be applied for in advance at the Forest Range Office, 1km west of Meppadi. The permit is free, but you have to pay Rs10 to access the trailhead, situated on the Chembra Tea Estate, 7km away along a paved road, and arrange for one of the two forest rangers to accompany you (Rs200).

Accommodation and eating

Kalpetta and the nearby villages of **Vythiri** and **Lakkidi**, on the Kozhikode road, are fast emerging as low-key hill **retreats** in their own right, with a clutch of mostly upscale resorts and plantation stays catering for well-heeled metropolitan Indians and foreigners eager for a break from the sticky heat of the coastal cities. All provide quality regional **cuisine** along with accommodation. The *Hotel New Palace*, south of the bus stand with its kitchen open to the street, is a favourite among Kalpetti families for its mainly non-veg North Indian dishes, vegetable biriyanis, and delicious ghee rice; they also do rich Malabari-style curries made with local quail (*kada*).

Edakkal Hermitage Ambalavayal
☎04936/221860, ⊛www.edakkal.com. Half a dozen pleasantly furnished cottages on small rock platforms overlooking a lawned garden to the valley, with breathtaking views down to the plains. An even more amazing panorama is to be had from their tree house, which literally sways in the wind as you sleep. The candle-lit restaurant occupies a man-made cave. ❽

Green Magic Vythiri book through ☎0495/652 1163, ⊛www.jungleparkresorts.com. Kerala's ultimate eco-resort, on a 500-acre site deep in the forest that's only accessible by 4WD (with the final 1.5km on foot). The benchmark accommodation is in luxury treehouses (from $250) nestled 20m off the ground under a lush rainforest canopy. ❾

Harita Giri Emily Rd, Kalpetta ☎04936/203145, ⊛www.hotelharitagiri.com. A conventional hotel offering six different grades of room (including singles), from budget to deluxe a/c suites; also on site is a garden, restaurant, bar, rooftop terrace and good-sized pool. ❺–❼

Pachyderm Palace Tholpetty; book through the Tourist Desk in Kochi on ☎0484/237 1761. A traditional Keralan bungalow with five comfortable rooms rented on an all-inclusive basis, just outside the park gates. The authentic Keralan cuisine is delicious, and a friendly welcome guaranteed. ❼

Rain Country Resort Lakkidi, 22km from Kalpetta ☎04936/251 1997 or 09447 004369, ⊛www .raincountryresort.com. A 3km track takes you from the main road to a secluded pocket of greenery overlooking the Lakkidi valley, where eight beautifully reconstructed antique Keralan *tharavads* are scattered over a clearing in the forest. ❽

Vythiri Resort booking at Kochi office ☎0484/405 5250, ⊛www.vythiriresort.com. Set in a lovely seven-acre woodland plot with three boulder-strewn mountain streams flowing through it, *Vythiri Resort* feels like a small jungle hill-village, down to the terracotta roofs and cable suspension bridge. Accommodation is offered in luxury cottages or refurbished plantation-workers' rooms. Rates include full board. ❽–❾

Theyyam or **theyyattam** – the dramatic spirit-possession ceremonies held at village shrines throughout the northern Malabar region in the winter months – rank among Kerala's most extraordinary spectacles. Over four hundred different manifestations of this arcane ritual exist in the area around Kannur alone, each with its own distinctive costumes, elaborate jewellery, body paints, face make-up and, above all, gigantic headdresses (*mudi*).

Unlike in *kathakali* and *kutiyattam*, where actors impersonate goddesses or gods, here the performers actually become the deity being invoked, acquiring their magical powers. These allow them to perform superhuman feats, such as rolling in hot ashes or dancing with a crown that rises to the height of a coconut tree. By watching the *theyyam*, members of the audience believe they can partake of the deity's powers – to cure illness, conceive a child or get lucky in a business venture.

Traditionally staged in small clearings (*kaavus*) attached to village shrines, *theyyattam* rituals are always performed by members of the lowest castes; Namboodiri and other high-caste people may attend, but they do so to venerate the deity – a unique inversion of the normal social hierarchy. Performances generally have three distinct phases: the *thottam*, where the dancer, wearing a small red headdress, recites a simple devotional song accompanied by the temple musicians; the *vellattam*, in which he runs through a series of more complicated rituals and slower, elegant poses; and the *mukhathezhuttu*, the main event, when he appears in full costume in front of the shrine. From this point on until the end of the performance, which may last all night, the *theyyam* is manifest and empowered, dancing around the arena in graceful, rhythmic steps that grow quicker and more energetic as the night progresses, culminating in a frenzied outburst just before dawn, when it isn't uncommon for the dancer to be struck by a kind of spasm.

Increasing numbers of visitors are making the journey up to Kannur to experience *theyyattam*, but **finding it** can be a hit-and-miss affair, requiring time, patience and stamina. The best source of advice is the local tourist information centre at the railway station (see p.1248), who will be able to consult the daily *Malayala Manorama* on your behalf: notices of forthcoming performances are listed at top left of page two. Alternatively, stay at *Costa Malabari* (see p.1248), whose management are *theyyattam* experts. Anyone pushed for time might also consider a trip out to **Parassinika-davu** (see p.1249), where a form of *theyyattam* is staged daily.

The far north

The beautiful coast **north of Kozhikode** is a seemingly endless stretch of coconut palms, wooded hills and virtually deserted beaches. The small fishing towns ranged along it hold little of interest for visitors, most of whom bypass the area completely – missing out on the chance to see **theyyam**, the extraordinary masked trance dances that take place in villages throughout the region between November and May.

Kannur (Cannanore)

KANNUR (Cannanore), a small, predominantly Moppila Muslim fishing and market town 92km north of Kozhikode, was for many centuries the capital of the Kolathiri rajas, who prospered from the thriving maritime spice-trade through its port. India's first Portuguese Viceroy, Francisco de Almeida, took the stronghold in 1505, leaving in his wake an imposing triangular bastion, **St Angelo's Fort**. This was taken in the seventeenth century by the Dutch, who sold it a hundred or so years later to the Arakkal rajas, Kerala's only ruling

Muslim dynasty. You can still clamber up the ramparts, littered with British cannon, for views over the town's fishing anchorage.

The unexploited beaches around Kannur are spectacular enough, but most visitors come to the town to search out **theyyam** (see p.1247). Throughout the *theyyam* season, the *Malayala Manorama* daily newspaper lists forthcoming performances at the top left of the second page, though you will have to ask someone to translate it for you. For anyone short of time, the daily rituals at **Parassinikadavu** (see opposite), or the Sree Muthappam Temple next to the railway station (daily 4pm), are worthwhile alternatives.

Practicalities

Straddling the main coastal transport artery between Mangalore and Kochi/ Thiruvananthapuram, Kannur is well connected by **bus** and **train** to most major towns and cities in Kerala, as well as Mangalore in Karnataka. In addition, buses from here travel to Mysore, climbing the beautiful wooded Ghats to Virajpet in Kodagu. The **railway station** is just over five minutes' walk southwest of the bus stand. The State Bank of India on Fort Road will **change money** and traveller's cheques, as will UAE Exchange in the City Centre Shopping complex (Mon–Sat 9.30am–1.30pm & 2–6pm), 500m east of the bus stand. There's a **tourist information centre** at the railway station (Mon–Sat 10am–5pm; ℡0497/270 3121) and **Internet** access is widely available.

Accommodation and eating

For inexpensive **food** there's an *Indian Coffee House* in Fort Road, 50m south of City Centre Shopping. Just behind the City Centre Shopping building, the trendy *Can Café* has a good selection of biriyanis as well as other inexpensive Malabari chicken and fish dishes. The *Hot Stone*, above the *Meridian Palace* (see below), enjoys a good reputation amongst the locals. Kannur is not short of **sweet shops**, where you can try the local *kinnathappam* and *kalathappam* cakes, made with rice flour and *jaggery*; Station Road is lined with them.

Costa Malabari 10km south near Tottada village; book through the tourist desk in Kochi: ℡0484/237 1761, ⓦwww.costamalabari.com. Hidden deep in cashew and coconut groves, this welcoming guesthouse, run by one of the region's most knowledgeable *theyyam* aficionados, has five airy and comfortable rooms. Five pristine beaches lie within ten minutes' walk, and guests are plied with huge portions of excellent Keralan food (included in the rate). They also run good off-track backwater and wildlife trips in the region. Pick-up from Kannur (Rs150) by prior arrangement. ❺

Government Guest House Cantonment area ℡0497/270 6426. Superb-value government-run place on a clifftop at the edge of town, with huge, simple a/c and non-a/c rooms whose huge balconies have uninterrupted sea views; it's primarily for visiting VIPs but usually has a few vacancies. Advance booking can be a problem; ring ahead when you arrive. Inexpensive vegetarian meals on request. ❷–❹

Malabar Residency Thavakkara Rd ℡0497/276 5456. Smart, central hotel with comfortable attached a/c rooms, two restaurants, including the multi-cuisine *Grand Plaza*, and a 24hr coffee shop. ❺

Mascot Beach Resort 300m before Baby Beach ℡0497/270 8445, ⓦwww.mascotresort.com. Perched on the rocky shoreline, offering large a/c rooms and cottages with views across the cove to the lighthouse. Facilities include a swimming pool, foreign exchange and a good restaurant – but no bar. ❺–❼

Meridian Palace Bellard Rd ℡0497/270 1676, ⓦwww.hotelmeridianpalace.com. Only two blocks from the station, this compact hotel has a wide range of comfy, clean rooms and a popular little restaurant serving veg and local seafood meals. ❷–❺

Sweety International 200m north of railway station, near Munisheeran Kovil ℡0497/270 8283. Standard economy high-rise with ordinary, "executive" and a/c rooms, all pretty decent value. ❷–❸

Parassinikadavu

The only place you can be almost guaranteed a glimpse of *theyyam* is the village of **PARASSINIKADAVU**, 20km north of Kannur, beside the River Valapatanam, where the head priest, or *madayan*, of the **Parassini Madammpura** temple performs twice a day during winter (6.30–8.30am & 5.45–8.30pm) before assembled worshippers. Elaborately dressed and accompanied by a traditional drum group, he becomes possessed by the temple's presiding deity – Lord Muthappan, Shiva, in the form of a *kiratha*, or hunter – and enacts a series of complex offerings. The two-hour ceremony culminates when the priest/deity dances forward to bless individual members of the congregation. Even by Keralan standards, it is an extraordinary spectacle, and well worth taking time out of a journey along the coast for.

Regular local **buses** leave Kannur for Parassinikadavu from around 7am, dropping passengers at the top of the village. If you want to get there in time for the dawn *theyyam*, however, you'll have to splash out on one of the Ambassador taxis that line up outside Kannur Bus Stand (around Rs400 return trip). Cabbies sleep in their cars, so you can arrange the trip on the spot by waking one up; taxis may also be arranged through most hotels. Either way, you'll have to leave around 4.30am. Alternatively, stay in the conveniently located *Thai Resort* (℡0497/278 4242; ❺–❻) 80m from the temple (to the left as you face the entrance). Shaded by coconut trees, seven circular stone cottages are dotted around a well-kept garden, with cool, comfortable rooms.

Travel details

For details of ferry services on the backwaters – primarily between Alappuzha and Kollam – see p.1208.

Trains

Kochi/Ernakulam to: Alappuzha (5–7 daily; 1hr 10min–1hr 40min); Bengaluru (Bangalore) (1–2 daily; 13hr); Chennai (5–7 daily; 11hr 45min–16hr 20min); Delhi (2–4 daily; 38hr–48hr 20min); Kanyakumari (2–3 daily; 7hr 25min–10hr); Kollam (Quilon) (12–15 daily; 2hr 50min–4hr 25min); Kottayam (9–11 daily; 1hr–1hr 20min); Kozhikode (4–6 daily; 4hr 45min–5hr 30min); Mumbai (2–3 daily; 26hr 25min–37hr 35min); Thiruvananthapuram (11–15 daily; 5hr–5hr 35min); Thrissur (15–18 daily; 1hr 15min–2hr 30min).

Kozhikode to: Kannur (9–11 daily; 1hr 55min–2hr 25min); Kochi/Ernakulam (7–9 daily; 4hr 15min–5hr 15min); Mangalore (6–9 daily; 4hr 40min–5hr 30min); Mumbai (2 daily via Thiruvananthapuram (4–6 daily; 9hr 40min–10hr 15min); Thrissur (6–9 daily; 2hr 30min–3hr 25min).

Thiruvananthapuram to: Alappuzha (3–5 daily; 2hr 40min–3hr 15min); Bengaluru (Bangalore) (1 daily; 18hr); Chennai (4–5 daily; 16hr 30min–18hr 45min); Kanyakumari (2 daily;

2hr); Kochi/Ernakulam (12–16 daily; 4hr–5hr 20min); Kollam (13–16 daily; 55min–1hr 30min); Kottayam (9–10 daily; 2hr–2hr 45min); Kozhikode (3–5 daily; 9hr–10hr 30min); Madgaon (1–3 daily; 15hr 10min–20hr 20min); Madurai (3 daily; 6hr 40min–9hr); Mumbai (2–3 daily; 30hr 40min–42hr 20min); Thrissur (10–12 daily; 5hr 45min–7hr); Varkala (12–13 daily; 45–55min).

Thrissur to: Chennai (3–4 daily; 10hr 25min–11hr 45min); Kochi/Ernakulam (15–17 daily; 1hr 30min–2hr 10min); Thiruvananthapuram (10–12 daily; 5hr 55min–7hr 10min).

Buses

Alappuzha (Alleppey) to: Ernakulam (every 30min; 1hr 30min); Kollam (every 45min; 2hr); Kottayam (every 30min; 1hr 30min–2hr); Kumily (1 daily; 6hr); Thiruvananthapuram (5 daily; 3hr–4hr).

Kochi/Ernakulam to: Alappuzha (every 30min; 1hr 30min); Kanyakumari (6 daily; 9hr); Kollam (every 30min; 3hr); Kottayam (every 30min; 1hr 30min–2hr); Kozhikode (hourly; 5hr); Kumily (10 daily; 6hr); Munnar (6 daily; 4hr 30min–5hr);

Periyar, see "Kumily"; Thiruvananthapuram (every 2hr; 5–6hr); Thrissur (every 30min; 2hr).

Kozhikode to: Kannur (every 30min; 2hr–2hr 30min); Kochi/Ernakulam (hourly; 5hr); Mysore (2 daily; 9–10hr); Ooty (4 daily; 6–7hr); Thiruvananthapuram (12–15 daily; 11–12hr); Thrissur (hourly; 3hr 30min–4hr).

Kumily to: Alappuzha (daily; 6hr); Kochi/Ernakulam (10 daily; 6hr); Kottayam (every 30min; 4hr); Madurai (10 daily; 5hr 30min); Munnar (4 daily; 4hr); Thiruvananthapuram (6 daily; 8–9hr).

Munnar to: Kochi/Ernakulam (6 daily; 4hr 30min–5hr); Kottayam (5 daily; 5hr); Kumily (4 daily; 4hr); Madurai (6 daily; 5hr); Thiruvananthapuram (5 daily; 8–9hr).

Thiruvananthapuram to: Alappuzha (5 daily; 4hr); Chennai (4 daily; 18hr); Kanyakumari (9 daily; 2hr 30min); Kochi/Ernakulam (every 2hr; 5–6hr); Kollam (every 2hr; 1hr 30min–2hr); Kottayam (every 30min; 4hr); Kozhikode (8 daily; 11–12hr); Kumily (1 daily; 9hr); Madurai (5 daily; 7–8hr); Mangalore (1 daily; 16hr); Munnar (3 daily; 9–10hr); Nedumangad (hourly; 45min–1hr); Neyyar Dam (hourly; 1hr 15min); Ponmudi (6 daily; 2hr–2hr 30min); Thrissur (hourly; 8–9hr); Varkala (10 daily; 1hr 30min–2hr 30min).

Thrissur to: Chennai (4 daily; 12–14hr); Guruvayur (10 daily; 40min); Kochi/Ernakulam (every 10min; 2hr); Kozhikode (every 30min; 2hr 30min); Mysore (5 daily; 8hr); Palakkad (every 20min; 2hr); Thiruvananthapuram (every 20min; 7–8hr).

Flights

(AI = Air India, I7 = Paramount Airways, IC = Indian Airlines, IT = Kingfisher, IX = Air India Express, DN = Air Deccan, S2 = JetLite, 9W = Jet Airways, G8 = Go Air)

Kochi/Ernakulam to: Agatti, Lakshadweep (IC, IT 9 weekly; 1hr 20min–1hr 35min); Bengaluru (Bangalore) (DN, S2, IT, 9W, G8, IC 8–10 daily; 1hr 15min–2hr 15min); Chennai (DA, I7, IT, 9W 6–7 daily; 1hr 30min); Coimbatore (DN 1 daily; 30min); Goa (AI, IT 2–3 daily; 1hr 10min); Hyderabad (DN, SA 2 daily; 1hr 30min); Kozhikode (Calicut) (IX, IT 2–5 daily; 35min); Mangalore (IT 3 daily; 45min); Mumbai (DN, IX, IC, IT, G8, KF, 9W 12–15 daily; 1hr 45min–2hr 30min); Thiruvananthapuram (DN, IX, IC, IT, S2 10 daily; 30min).

Kozhikode to: Bengaluru (Bangalore) (IC 3 weekly; 1hr 10min); Chennai (IC 7 weekly; 1hr–2hr 25min); Goa (IC, IT 1–2 daily; 1hr); Kochi/Ernakulam (IC, IT 2–3 daily; 30min); Mumbai (9W, IC, AI 3–4 daily; 1hr 40min–3hr); Mangalore (IT 1 daily; 55min); Tiruchirapalli (IC 2 weekly; 55min); Thiruvananthapuram (IC, IT 1–2 daily; 50min–2hr).

Thiruvananthapuram to: Bengaluru (Bangalore) (DN, IC, IT, 9W 9 daily; 1hr); Chennai (9W, DA, IC, I7 13–15 daily; 1hr–1hr 40min); Coimbatore (DN 1 daily; 45min); Delhi (1–3 daily; 42hr 35min–56hr 40min); Goa (IT 1 daily; 5hr 20min); Hyderabad (I7 1 daily; 2hr 35min); Kochi (DN, IX, IC, IT, S2 10 daily; 30min); Kolkata (Calcutta; 4 weekly; 47hr 40min–47hr 55min); Mangalore (IT 1 daily; 3hr 50min); Mumbai (DN, IC, 9W 5–6 daily; 2hr); Tiruchirapalli (IC 4 weekly; 1hr); Tirupati (IT 4 weekly; 2hr 50min).

22

Karnataka

The International boundaries on this map are neither purported to be correct nor authentic by Survey of India directives. Publisher.

CHAPTER 22

Highlights

* **Bengaluru (Bangalore)** Booming silicon city offers the best shopping, nightlife and dining this side of Mumbai, not to mention a few great parks. See p.1256

* **Mysore** The sandalwood city oozes relaxed, old-world charm and has lots to see, including the opulent Maharaja's Palace. See p.1268

* **Halebid & Belur** Two wonderfully ornate Hoysala temples set deep in the slow-paced Karnataka countryside. See p.1281 & p.1283

* **Gokarna** This vibrant Hindu holy town is blessed with exquisite crescent beaches and is ideal for serious unwinding. See p.1296

* **Hampi** The crumbling remains of the Vijayanagar kingdom, scattered among a stunning boulder-strewn landscape bisected by the Tungabhadra River. See p.1303

* **Bijapur** Known as the "Agra of the South" for its splendid Islamic architecture, most famously the vast dome of the Golgumbaz. See p.1316

* **Bidar** Rarely visited Muslim outpost in the remote northeast of the state, famed for *bidri* metalwork and magnificent medieval monuments. See p.1323

▲ Bijapur

22

Karnataka

C reated in 1956 from the princely state of Mysore, **KARNATAKA** – a derivation of the name of the local language, Kannada, spoken by virtually all of its 53 million inhabitants, known as Kannadigas – marks a transition zone between northern India and the Dravidian deep south. Along its border with Maharashtra and Andhra Pradesh, a string of medieval walled towns, studded with domed mausoleums and minarets, recall the era when this part of the Deccan was a Muslim stronghold. The coastal and hill districts that dovetail with Kerala are quintessential Hindu south India, lush with tropical vegetation and soaring temple *gopuras*. In between are scattered several extraordinary sites, notably the ruined Vijayanagar city at Hampi, whose lost temples and derelict palaces stand amid an arid, boulder-strewn landscape of surreal beauty.

Karnataka is one of the wettest regions in India, its **climate** dominated by the seasonal monsoon, which sweeps in from the southwest in June, dumping an average of 4m of rain on the coast before it peters out in late September. Running in an unbroken line along the state's palm-fringed coast, the **Western Ghats**, draped in dense deciduous forests, impede the path of the rain clouds east. As a result, the landscape of the interior – comprising the southern apex of the triangular Deccan trap, known here as the **Mysore Plateau** – is considerably drier, with dark volcanic soils in the north, and poor quartzite-granite country to the south. Two of India's most sacred rivers, the Tungabhadra and Krishna, flow across this sun-baked terrain, draining east to the Bay of Bengal.

Broadly speaking, Karnataka's principal attractions are concentrated at opposite ends of the state, with a handful of lesser-visited places dotted along the coast between Goa and Kerala. Road and rail routes dictate that most itineraries take in the brash state capital, **Bengaluru (Bangalore)**, a go-ahead, modern city that epitomizes the aspirations of the country's new middle classes, with glittering malls, fast-food outlets and a nightlife unrivalled outside Mumbai. The state's second city, **Mysore**, appeals more for its Raj-era ambience, nineteenth-century palaces and vibrant produce and incense markets. It also lies within easy reach of several important historical monuments. At the nearby fortified island of **Srirangapatnam** – site of the bloody battle of 1799 that finally put Mysore state into British hands, with the defeat of the Muslim military genius **Tipu Sultan** – parts of the fort, a mausoleum and Tipu's Summer Palace survive.

A clutch of unmissable sights lie further northeast, dotted around the dull railway town of **Hassan**. Around nine centuries ago, the Hoysala kings sited their grand dynastic capitals here, at the now middle-of-nowhere villages of **Belur** and **Halebid**, where several superbly crafted temples survive intact. More

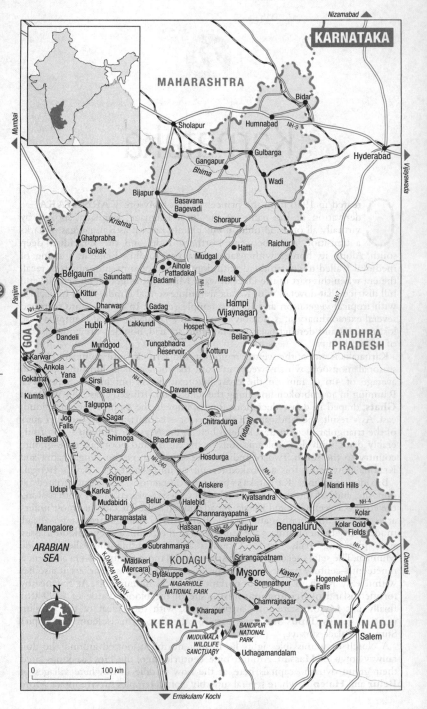

impressive still, and one of India's most extraordinary sacred sites, is the eighteen-metre Jain colossus at **Sravanabelagola**, which stares serenely over idyllic Deccani countryside.

West of Mysore, the Ghats rise in a wall of thick jungle cut by deep ravines and isolated valleys. Within, the coffee- and spice-growing region of **Kodagu (Coorg)** offers an entrancing, unique culture and lush, misty vistas. Most Coorgi agricultural produce is shipped out of **Mangalore**, an uninspiring place to pause on the journey along Karnataka's beautiful **Karavali coast**. Interrupted by countless mangrove-lined estuaries, the state's 320-kilometre-long red-laterite coast contains plenty of fine beaches, yet with few exceptions facilities are nonexistent, and locals often react with astonishment at the sight of a foreigner.

Few Western tourists visit the famous Krishna temple at **Udupi**, an important Vaishnavite pilgrimage centre, and fewer still venture into the mountains to see India's highest waterfall at **Jog Falls**, set amid some of the region's most spectacular scenery. However, atmospheric **Gokarna**, further north up the coast, is an increasingly popular beach hideaway for budget travellers. Harbouring one of India's most famous *shivalingams*, this seventeenth-century Hindu pilgrimage town enjoys a stunning location, with a high headland dividing it from a string of exquisite beaches.

Winding inland from the mountainous Goan border, NH-4A and the rail line comprise sparsely populated **northern Karnataka**'s main transport artery and lean towards this region's undisputed highlight, the ghost city of Vijayanagar, better known as **Hampi**. Scattered around boulder hills on the south banks of the Tungabhadra River, the ruins of this once splendid capital occupy a magical site, while the ancient bazaar is a great spot to hole up for a spell. The jumping-off place for Hampi is **Hospet**, from where buses leave for the bumpy journey north across the rolling Deccani plains to **Badami**, **Aihole** and recent UNESCO Heritage addition **Pattadakal**. Now lost in countryside, these tiny villages – once capitals of the **Chalukya** dynasty (sixth to eighth centuries) – remain littered with ancient rock-cut caves and finely carved stone temples.

Further north still, in one of Karnataka's most remote and poorest districts, craggy hilltop citadels and crumbling wayside tombs herald the formerly troubled buffer-zone between the Muslim-dominated northern Deccan and the Dravidian-Hindu south. **Bijapur**, capital of the Bahmanis, the Muslim dynasty that oversaw the eventual downfall of Vijayanagar, harbours south India's finest collection of Islamic architecture, including the world's second-largest freestanding dome, the Golgumbaz. The first Bahmani capital, **Gulbarga**, site of a famous Muslim shrine and theological college, has retained little of its former splendour, but the more isolated **Bidar**, where the Bahmanis moved in the sixteenth century, deserves a detour en route to or from Hyderabad. Perched on a rocky escarpment, its crumbling red ramparts include Persian-style mosaic-fronted mosques, mausoleums and a sprawling fort complex evocative of Samarkand and the great Silk Route.

Some history

Like much of southern India, Karnataka has been ruled by successive Buddhist, Hindu and Muslim dynasties. The influence of Jainism has also been marked; India's very first emperor, **Chandragupta Maurya**, is believed to have converted to Jainism in the fourth century BC, renounced his throne, and fasted to death at Sravanabelagola, now one of the most visited Jain pilgrimage centres in the country.

During the first millennium AD, this whole region was dominated by power struggles between the various kingdoms controlling the western Deccan. From the sixth to the eighth centuries, the **Chalukya** kingdom included Maharashtra, the Konkan coast on the west and the whole of Karnataka. The **Cholas** were powerful in the east of the region from about 870 until the thirteenth century, when the Deccan kingdoms were overwhelmed by General Malik Kafur, a convert to Islam.

By the medieval era Muslim incursions from the north had forced the hitherto warring and fractured Hindu states of the south into close alliance, with the mighty **Vijayanagars** emerging as overlords. Their lavish capital, Vijayanagar, ruled an empire stretching from the Bay of Bengal to the Arabian Sea and south to Cape Comorin. The Muslims' superior military strength, however, triumphed in 1565 at the Battle of Talikota, when the **Bahmanis** laid siege to Vijayanagar, reducing it to rubble and plundering its opulent palaces and temples.

Thereafter, a succession of Muslim sultans held sway over the north, while in the south of the state, the independent **Wadiyar rajas** of Mysore, whose territory was comparatively small, successfully fought off the Marathas. In 1761, the brilliant Muslim campaigner Haider Ali, with French support, seized the throne. His son, Tipu Sultan, turned Mysore into a major force in the south before he was killed by the British at the **battle of Srirangapatnam** in 1799.

Following Tipu's defeat, the British restored the Wadiyar family to the throne. They kept it until riots in 1830 led the British to appoint a Commission to rule in their place. Fifty years later, the throne was once more returned to the Wadiyars, who remained governors until Karnataka was created by the merging of the states of Mysore and the Madras Presidencies in 1956.

Since Independence, the political scene has been largely dominated by the Congress party, which was routed in the Nineties – first by a reunited Janata Dal and subsequently by a Hindu nationalist BJP alliance. At time of writing the state government had been suspended and the Governor had assumed temporary power, with parliamentary elections scheduled for late spring 2008.

Bengaluru (Bangalore) and around

The political hub of the region, Bengaluru (Bangalore) is a world apart from the rest of the state and likely India's most Westernized urban centre. From a charming, verdant "Garden City" of just over 600,000 at Independence, the former Bangalore has been completely transformed by a decade-long technology boom into both a trendy, high-speed business hub and a bustling, smog-choked megalopolis of eight million. These days, signs of the West are thick on the ground: *Starbucks*-like *Café Coffee Days* on nearly every corner; a flash new airport and ultra-modern metro (set for completion in 2011); and legions of hard-working, free-spending twenty- and thirty-somethings in designer T-shirts and mini-skirts.

For the tourist, Bengaluru's few attractions are no match for those elsewhere in the state, and the city's comparative local advantages are ten-a-penny in the West. That said, this is an efficient transport hub, well served by plane and bus, and at nearly 1000m the climate is relatively mild. Paired with first-rate shopping, dining and nightlife, this vibrant city can still deliver a few days' respite from south India's more taxing inconveniences.

Some history

A stone inscription near a tenth-century temple in the eastern part of the city describes a battle fought on this ground in 890, in a placed called "Bengaval-uru,"

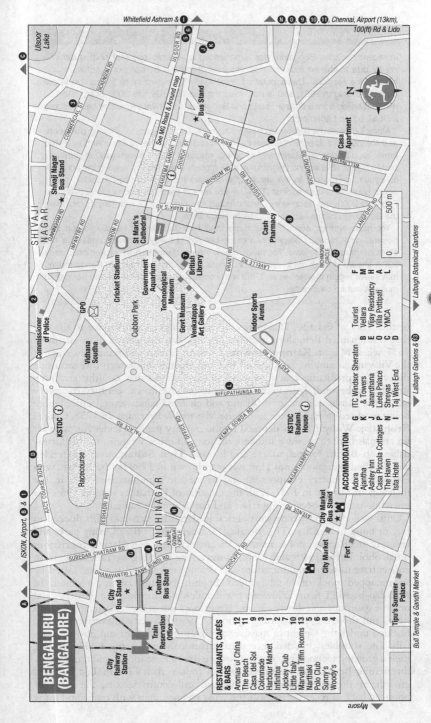

BENGALURU (BANGALORE)

Ulsoor Lake

SHIVAJI NAGAR

Shivaji Nagar Bus Stand

Commissioner of Police

GPO

Vidhana Soudha

Cubbon Park

Cricket Stadium

St Mark's Cathedral

Government Aquarium

Technological Museum

British Library

Govt Museum

Venkatappa Art Gallery

Indoor Sports Arena

Casa Apartment

Cash Pharmacy

Bus Stand

See MC Road & Around map

Racecourse

GANDHINAGAR

KSTDC

City Bus Stand

Central Bus Stand

Train Reservation Office

City Railway Station

KSTDC Badami House

City Market Bus Stand

City Market

Fort

Tipu's Summer Palace

ISKON, Airport, B & ▮

Mysore

KARNATAKA

Bull Temple & Gandhi Market

Lalbagh Gardens & ⑱

Lalbagh Botanical Gardens

N

0   500 m

22

1257

RESTAURANTS, CAFES & BARS

Aromas of China	12
The Beach	11
Casa del Sol	9
Colonnade	3
Harbour Market	1
Infinitea	2
Jockey Club	7
Little Italy	10
Marvalli Tiffin Rooms	13
Narthaki	5
Polo Club	6
Sunny's	8
Woody's	4

ACCOMMODATION

Adora	G	ITC Windsor Sheraton	
Ajantha	K	& Towers	Tourist	F
Ashley Inn	J	Janardhana	Vellara	M
Casa Piccola Cottages	P	Leela Palace	Vijay Residency	H
The Haven	N	Shreyas	Villa Pottipati	A
Ista Hotel	I	Taj West End	YMCA	L

In recent decades Bengaluru has experienced a **seismic societal shift**, predominantly due to the endless job opportunities presented by computer software and back-office services. The population grew nearly forty percent to 5.7 million in the decade ending in 2001, and is now reaching 8 million. By late 2007 every fifth city resident hailed from a different state and Bengaluru's **software industry** had become a US$8 billion behemoth.

Many locals blame IT professionals for skyrocketing living costs, choking **pollution**, and the rise of a liberal, West-leaning bar and disco culture, not to mention **traffic jams**, regular power failures and crippling seasonal **water shortages**. In addition, due to higher salaries and bright futures, IT professionals are favoured in the competitive marriage market. In the last couple of years the backlash has included nearly seven hundred crimes against IT folk, minor riots in the city's poorer districts and, in February 2008, the discovery of an extended terrorist network with targets including the Bengaluru campuses of major technology firms.

Yet hope springs eternal. After more than two decades of hand-wringing and debate, work recently began on a much-needed **subway system** to alleviate the city's infamous traffic jams. The modern new **international airport**, kicked off in early 2008, should smooth the increase of business and tourist visitors. Old Bangaloreans may never regain their urban idyll, but with compromise and elbow grease Bengaluru may yet inspire civic pride.

or the "City of Guards." This marks the earliest historical reference to the city that was renamed Bengaluru in 2006. The city was established more firmly in 1537 when Magadi **Kempe Gowda**, a devout Hindu and feudatory chief of the Vijayanagar empire, built a mud fort and erected four watchtowers outside the village, predicting that it would one day extend that far (the city now stretches far beyond). During the first half of the seventeenth century, Bangalore fell to the Muslim sultanate of Bijapur and changed hands several times before being returned to Hindu rule under the Mysore Wadiyar rajas. In 1758, Chikka Krishnaraja Wadiyar II was deposed by the military genius Haider Ali, who set up arsenals here to produce muskets, rockets and other weapons for his formidable anti-British campaigns. He and his son, **Tipu Sultan**, greatly extended and fortified Bangalore until Tipu was overthrown in 1799 by the British, who established a military cantonment and passed the administration over to the maharaja of Mysore in 1881. With the creation of Karnataka state in 1956, the erstwhile maharaja became governor and Bangalore the capital.

Until well after Independence, political leaders, film stars and VIPs flocked to buy or build homes here. The so-called "Garden City" offered many parks and leisurely green spaces, not to mention theatres, cinemas and a lack of restrictions on alcohol. In the 1940s and 1950s, however, the Indian government began to concentrate its telecommunications and defence research in the area. Lured by an untapped pool of highly skilled English-speaking labour, a clutch of Mumbai-based IT firms followed a few decades later, inciting one of Asia's great urban expansions and slowly gashing Bangalore's urban idyll. Skyscrapers, swish stores and shopping malls sprung up in the 1990s, but city infrastructure soon buckled under the weight of massive immigration, pollution and power shortfalls. The stumbles prodded several multinationals to decamp to Hyderabad, itself a growing technology centre, upsetting the local economy and temporarily threatening Bengaluru's treasured status as India's main IT hub. Led by rapid growth in the international telecom and call-centre sectors, the city has bounced back in recent years. Still, the wide avenues teem with traffic and smog and the overburdened infrastructure and water and electricity shortages leave old Bangaloreans wondering what happened to their beloved "Garden City".

Arrival, information and city transport

All **flights** arrive into and depart from the new **Bengaluru International Airport** (ⓦ www.bialairport.com), 35km northeast of the city in Devanahalli. Reportedly the priciest airport in India, BIA includes self-service check-in kiosks, high-end bars and cafés, a well-maintained tourist office and helicopter transport into the city (Rs3500). Until the much-discussed express rail is up and running, those unwilling to splash out for the chopper must choose between a few select airline shuttles (Rs70–150), *varna* minibuses (Rs100) or pre-paid taxis (Rs500–600), and expect one to one and a half hour travel times to the MG Road area.

Bangalore City railway station is east of the centre, near Kempe Gowda Circle, and across the road from the main bus stands (for the north of the city, get off at Bangalore Cantonment Station). As you come into the entrance hall from the platforms, the far left-hand corner holds an **ITDC booth** (daily 8am–4pm; ☎080/2220 4277), where you can rent cars, book tours, or book a hotel for a fee of ten percent of the day's room rate. The **KSTDC tourist information office** (daily 7am–8pm; ☎080/2287 0068), to the right, also books tours and can provide useful advice. To hire an auto-rickshaw it is best to pay the Rs1 fee at the pre-paid booth to guarantee the proper fare – a typical charge is Rs25–40 to MG Road, depending on the time of day.

Innumerable **long-distance buses** arrive at the big, busy **Central** (KSRTC) **stand**, opposite the railway station. There is a comprehensive timetable in English in the centre of the concourse. A bridge divides it from the **City stand**, for local services.

Information

For information on Bangalore, Karnataka and neighbouring states, go to the excellent **India Tourism Office** (Mon–Fri 9.30am–6pm, Sat 9am–1pm; ☎080/2558 5417, ⓦ www.incredibleindia.org), in the KSFC Building, 48 Church St (parallel to MG Road between Brigade and St Mark's roads). You can pick up a free city map here and the staff will help you put together itineraries.

Apart from the desks at the City railway station and the airport, **Karnataka State Tourist Development Corporation** has two city offices: one at Badami House, NR Square (daily 6.30am–10pm; ☎080/2227 5883), where you can book tours; and the head office on the second floor of Khanija Bhavan, Race Course Road (Mon–Sat 10am–5.30pm, closed second Sat of month; ☎080/2235 2901–3, ⓦ www.kstdc.nic.in). For up-to-the-minute information about **what's on**, pick up the biweekly ad-sponsored listings magazine *City Info* (ⓦ www.explocity.com), distributed free at most hotels and tourist offices.

If you're planning to visit any of Karnataka's **national parks**, call at the Wildlife Office, Forest Department, Aranya Bhavan, Malleswaram (☎080/2334 1993) for information, or approach Jungle Lodges & Resorts, Floor 2, Shrungar Shopping Centre, off MG Road (☎080/2559 7021, ⓦ www.junglelodges.com). A quasi-government body, Jungle Lodges promotes "ecotourism" through a number of upmarket forest lodges including the much-lauded *Kabini River Lodge* (see p.1279) near Nagarhole.

City transport

Until the metro is running in 2011, the easiest way of getting around Bangalore is by metered **auto-rickshaw**; fares start at Rs10 for the first kilometre and

Rs5 per kilometre thereafter. Most meters do work and drivers are usually willing to use them, although you will occasionally be asked for a flat fare, especially during rush hour.

Bangalore's extensive **bus** system radiates from the City (Kempe Gowda) Bus Stand (℡080/222 2542), near the railway station. Most buses from platform 17 travel past MG Road. Along with regular buses, BMTC also operates a deluxe express service, Pushpak, on a number of set routes (#P109 terminates at White-field ashram) as well as a handful of night buses. Other important city bus stands include the City Market Bus Stand (℡080/670 2177) to the south of the railway station and Shivaji Nagar (℡080/286 5332) to the north of Cubbon Park – the #P2 Jayanagar service from here is handy for the Lalbagh Botanical Gardens.

You can book **chauffeur-driven cars and taxis** through several agencies including the Cab Service, Sabari Complex, 24 Residency Rd (℡080/2558 6121), and the 24-hour Dial-a-Car service (℡080/2526 1737, ℮dialacar @hotmail.com).

Accommodation

Due to the great number of business visitors, Bengaluru offers a wealth of up-market lodgings, as well as service apartments. Decent **budget accommodation** is also available, mostly concentrated around the Central Bus Stand and railway station.

Around the railway station and Central Bus Stand

Hotel Adora 47 SC Rd ℡080/2287 2280. Above a quality south Indian veg restaurant, this is a top budget place. Though bland, the rooms are clean and good sized; a popular backpacker choice. ❷–❸

Tourist Ananda Rao Circle ℡080/2226 2381–8. One of Bengaluru's best all-round budget lodges, just a short walk from the station. Small rooms, long verandas, friendly family management and no reservations, so it fills up fast. ❷

Vijay Residency 18 3rd Cross, Main Rd ℡080/2220 3024, ⓦwww.vijayresidency.net. A *Comfort Inn* franchise that's plush and comfortable, if a tad overpriced. Near the railway station, with central a/c, foreign exchange and good restaurant. ❼–❽

Around the racecourse and Cubbon Park

ITC Windsor Sheraton & Towers 25 Golf Course Rd ℡080/2226 9898, ⓦwww.sheraton.com. Ersatz palace now a luxurious five-star, mainly for overseas businesspeople with rates from $270. Facilities include broadband, gym, pool, Jacuzzi, a fine restaurant and popular Irish pub. ❾

Janardhana Kumara Krupa Rd ℡080/2225 4444, ℻2225 8708. Neat, clean and spacious rooms with balconies and baths. Well away from the chaos and fine value at this price. ❸–❺

Taj West End Race Course Rd ℡080/2225 5055, ⓦwww.tajhotels.com. Begun as a British-run boarding house in 1887, these lodgings were upgraded with fabulous gardens and long colonnaded walkways. The old wing is bursting with character, with broad verandas overlooking acres of grounds. Rooms start at $300 a night. ❾

Villa Pottipati 142 4th Main, 8th Cross, Malleswaram ℡080/2336 0777, ⓦwww .neemranahotels.com A heritage hotel in the north-western suburbs, wrapped in a garden of jacaranda trees and flowering shrubs. Its rooms ooze old-world style, with pillared verandas, deep bathtubs and direct access to an outdoor swimming pool. Part of the *Neemrana* chain, so the highest standards of service are guaranteed. Gourmet meals, prepared by a French chef from Pondi, are also served. ❽

YMCA Nirupathanga Rd, Cubbon Park, midway between the bus stand and MG Rd ℡080/2221 1848. One of the city's best budget deals, with large, bright rooms and an excellent location near the park. Cheaper dorm beds (Rs150) are available. Call ahead as it's often full. ❸

Around MG Road

Ajantha 22-A MG Rd (see map, p.1257) ℡080/2558 4321, ℻2558 4780. Best value in this area, with basic but larger than average attached rooms and some spacious, three-room cottages, located at end of quiet lane but close to shops. Veg restaurant, Internet, bakery, travel agent and sundries shop all on site. Often full. ❸–❺

Ashley Inn Off MG Rd, next to *Ajantha* (see map, p.1257) ☎080/4123 3415. A charming guesthouse, with bright, colorful rooms, complimentary breakfasts and Wi-Fi throughout. ⑥–⑧

Brindavan 40 MG Rd ☎080/558 4000. With mostly quiet rooms set slightly off the main road, this is deservedly a backpacker's favourite. Book ahead. ③–⑤

Empire International 36 Church St ☎080/2559 3743, ⓦwww.hotelempireinternational.com. Smart new hotel with popular restaurant and very comfortable rooms boasting modern decor and good facilities. Sister concern *Hotel Empire* (④–⑤), similar but without the finer touches, is a few blocks north of MG Rd. ⑥–⑦

Ista Hotel 1/1 Sami Vivekananda Rd, ☎080/2555888, ⓦwww.istahotels.com. This gorgeous new ultra-luxury hotel, with breezy, safari-themed bar, infinity pool, Jacuzzi and gym, offers a secluded sanctuary from the MG Road mayhem. The spacious rooms have all the most contemporary trimmings, some with gorgeous Ulsoor Lake views and marble baths; suites have large garden balconies. *Lido*, the tropical terrace restaurant (open 6am–2am), is a top spot for early morning and post-midnight eats – try their superb pancakes. Rooms from $360. ⑨

Shangrila 182 Brigade Rd ☎080/5112 1622. Tibetan-run lodge right in the thick of things but welcoming; the comfy standard rooms are as decent value as anywhere in the area. ④–⑥

Hotel Vellara 283 Brigade Rd, opp Brigade Towers ☎080/253 6911. A solid deal for this area, with clean, good-sized rooms, all with TV and a/c. The deluxe rooms on the top floor are larger, with sweeping city views. If full, check out similarly-priced *Palms Residency* next door (ⓦwww.palmsresidency.com, ☎9901 396836.) ④–⑦

Elsewhere

🏃 **Casa Piccola Cottages** No. 2, Clapham St, off Richmond Rd ☎080/2227 0754,

ⓦwww.casapiccola.com. Tranquillity awaits at these cottages, set in well-maintained grounds just over a kilometre south of MG Road. The cottages and apartments are enormous, comfortable and well-appointed, and the free breakfasts are excellent. Wi-Fi is available. If full, request lodging at similarly-priced *Casa Piccola Apartments* around the corner (A-002 Wellington Park on Wellington St). ⑦

🏃 **The Haven** 148 2nd Cross, Domlur 2nd Stage, Indiranagar ☎080/2535 2020, ⓦwww.aranhahomes.com. Aptly named, this small, friendly establishment is nestled among temples, mansions and shady gardens on a quiet side-street near trendy 100 Feet Rd. One of several excellent boutique guesthouses from Aranha *Homes*, offering spacious, well-appointed rooms with central a/c, cable TV, free Wi-Fi and excellent service. ⑤–⑧

Leela Palace 23 Airport Rd ☎080/2521 1234, ⓦwww.theleela.com. This enormous gold-domed palace on nine acres of jungle lagoon, 5km southeast of town, has lodgings fit for a king. The spa offers endless rigors and delights, the 256 rooms, most with balconies overlooking the lush grounds, are enormous and gorgeously appointed (from $400), and the *Royal Club* serves fine French cheese and truffles, fat Havana cigars and perfectly-aged Scotch whisky. ⑨

Shreyas Santoshima Farm, Nelamangala ☎080/2773 7102, ⓦwww.shreyasretreat.com. Indian spiritual chic at this uber-stylish spa about 35km northwest of town (20km from new airport), which smartly marries the natural and the hi-tech. Ayurvedic treatments and yoga classes take place next to organic herb and vegetable fields, and the cares of the modern world would melt away if not for super-fast Wi-Fi throughout the 25-acre grounds, including the eight luxury tents. No TV, no alcohol and only fourteen rooms (from $480); book well in advance. ⑨

The City

The centre of modern Bengaluru lies about 4km east of Kempe Gowda Circle (and the bus and railway stations), near **MG Road**, where you'll find most of the mid-range accommodation, restaurants, shops, tourist information and banks. Leafy **Cubbon Park**, and its less than exciting museums, lie on its eastern edge, while the oldest, most "Indian" part of the city extends south from the railway station, a warren of winding streets at their most dynamic in the hubbub of the **City** and **Gandhi markets**. Bengaluru's tourist attractions are spread out: monuments such as **Tipu's Summer Palace** and the **Bull Temple** are some way south of the centre. Most, if not all, can be seen on a half-day tour, but if you explore on foot, be warned that Bengaluru has some of the worst pavements in India.

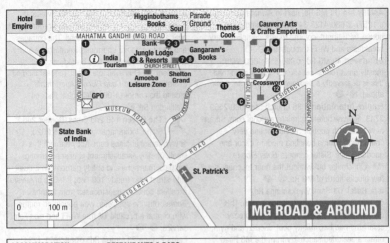

Cubbon Park and museums

A welcome green space in the heart of the city, shaded by massive clumps of bamboo, **Cubbon Park** is entered from the western end of MG Road, presided over by a statue of Queen Victoria. On Kasturba Road, which runs along its southern edge, the poorly labelled and maintained **Government Museum** (Tues–Sun 10am–5pm; Rs4) features prehistoric artefacts, Vijayanagar, Hoysala and Chalukya sculpture, musical instruments, Thanjavur paintings and Deccani and Rajasthani miniatures. It includes the adjacent **Venkatappa Art Gallery**, which exhibits twentieth-century landscapes, portraits, abstract art, wood sculpture, and occasional temporary art shows.

Vidhana Soudha

Built in 1956, Bangalore's vast State Secretariat, **Vidhana Soudha**, northwest of Cubbon Park, is the largest civic structure of its kind in the country. K. Hanumanthaiah, chief minister at the time, wanted a "people's palace" that, following the transfer of power from the royal Wadayar dynasty to a legislature, would "reflect the power and dignity of the people". In theory its design is entirely Indian, but its overall effect is not unlike the bombastic colonial architecture built in the so-called Indo-Saracenic style.

Lalbagh Botanical Gardens

Inspired by the splendid gardens of the Mughals and the French botanical gardens at Pondicherry in Tamil Nadu (see p.1129), Sultan Haider Ali set to work in 1760 laying out the **Lalbagh Botanical Gardens** (daily 8am–8pm; Rs15 before 6pm, Rs10 after), 4km south of the centre. Originally covering forty acres, just beyond his fort – where one of Kempe Gowda's original watchtowers can still be seen – the gardens were expanded under Ali's son Tipu, who introduced numerous exotic species of plants, and today the gardens house an extensive horticultural seedling centre. The British brought in gardeners from Kew in 1856 and built a military bandstand and a glasshouse, based on London's Crystal Palace, which hosts wonderful flower shows. Now spreading over 240 acres, the gardens are pleasant to visit during the day, but tend to attract unsavoury characters after 6pm. Great sunsets and city views can be had from the central hill, which is topped by a small shrine.

Jama Masjid and Tipu's Summer Palace

Just southeast of the City Market is the fairy-tale-like **Jama Masjid**, whitewashed and rambling and still in regular use. Nearby is **Tipu's Summer Palace**, a two-storey, mostly wooden structure built in 1791 (daily 9am–5pm; $2 [Rs5]). Similar in style to the Daria Daulat Palace at Srirangapatnam (see p.1276), the palace is in a far worse state, with most of its painted decoration destroyed. Next door, the **Venkataramanaswamy Temple**, dating from the early eighteenth century, was built by the Wadiyar rajas. The *gopura* entranceway was erected in 1978.

Bull Temple

Lying 6km south of the City Bus Stand (bus #34 & #37), in the Basavanagudi area, Kempe Gowda's sixteenth-century **Bull Temple** (open to non-Hindus; daily 7.30am–1.30pm & 2.30–8.30pm) houses a massive monolithic Nandi bull, its grey granite made black by the application of charcoal and oil. The temple is approached along a path lined with mendicants and snake charmers; inside, for a few rupees, the priest will offer you a string of fragrant jasmine flowers.

ISKCON temple

A hybrid of ultramodern glass and vernacular south Indian temple architecture, ISKCON's (International Society of Krishna Consciousness) gleaming temple – **Sri Radha Krishna Mandir**, Hare Krishna Hill, Chord Road (daily 7am–1pm & 4–8.30pm), 8km north of the centre, is a lavish showpiece crowned by a gold-plated dome. Barriers guide visitors on a one-way journey through the huge, well-organized complex to the inner sanctum with its images of the god Krishna and his consort Radha. Collection points throughout, and inescapable merchandizing on the way out, are evidence of the organization's highly successful commercialization. Regular **buses** to the temple depart from both the City and Shivaji Nagar bus stands.

Eating

With unmissable sights thin on the ground but tempting cafés and restaurants on every corner, you could easily spend most of your time in Bengaluru **eating**. Nowhere else in south India will you find such gastronomic variety. Around **MG Road**, pizzerias, ritzy ice-cream parlours and gourmet French restaurants stand cheek by jowl with regional cuisine from Andhra Pradesh and Kerala, Mumbai *chaat* cafés and snack bars where, in true Bangalorean style, thalis from as little as Rs30 masquerade as "executive mini-lunches." Places below are marked on the MG Road map on p.1262 unless stated otherwise.

Amaravati Residency Rd Cross, MG Rd. Excellent, fiery Andhra cooking with thalis ("meals") served on banana leafs and specialities including biriyanis and fried fish. Hectic at lunchtime but well worth any wait.

Aromas of China G3–4 Shiva Shankar Plaza, 19 Lalbagh Rd, Richmond Circle. See map, p.1257. Among the city's top Chinese restaurants, delicacies here include dim sum, duck and sharkfin soup, as well as above-average versions of all the favourites. Around Rs150–300 for a main course.

Barista Base of Ivory Tower, MG Rd. Pleasant, expansive terrace tucked behind a row of leafy plants. Along with fine coffees and teas, serves sandwiches, baked goods, and delicious slushies.

Casa del Sol – 3rd floor, Devatha Plaza, 131 Residency Rd. See map, p.1257. Chef Bakshi is a whiz in the kitchen; the Rs200 lunch buffet is worth every paise; the Sun brunches are festive, all-you-can-drink affairs; and an evening cocktail on the cool, comfortable terrace is a real treat.

Coconut Grove Church St. Mouthwatering and moderately priced gourmet Keralan, Chettinad and Coorg cuisine. Vegetarian, fish and meat preparations are served in traditional copper thalis on a leafy terrace, and there's a wide range of seafood dishes. Don't attempt the dressed crab without a Black-and-Decker.

Harbour Market 37 Crescent Rd, in *Hotel 37th Crescent*, off Race Course Rd. See map, p.1257. ☎080/41136262. Excellent selection of Goan, Keralan, and Mangalorean seafood along with pastas and Japanese selections in a smart, elegant space. The crunchy fried prawns are particularly special. Reservations recommended.

Indian Coffee House MG Rd. This bare-bones Raj-era institution, with turbaned waiters serving tasty finger foods (Rs 20–70) and fine filtered coffee (Rs8), hasn't changed since Independence. The second floor is breezier and less hectic and the breakfasts – with perfectly fluffy scrambled eggs – are top-notch.

Infinitea Cunningham Rd. See map, p.1257. From white to flower, from Oolong to Assam, they've got all kinds of teas (Rs60–90) here. Modern and mellow, *Infinitea* is popular with students, and is open all day, offering a variety of snacks and Asian dishes.

Kaati Zone Church St. Fast, clean and cheap, with *kaati* rolls (Rs40–60) almost as good as those you get in Kolkata (Calcutta).

Koshy's St Mark's Rd at Church. Spacious old-style café with cane blinds, pewter teapots and cotton-clad waiters. Ever-popular with the younger set, Bangalore's most congenial meeting-place has been whipping up tasty Indian specialities and refreshing draught beers for over eighty years.

Little Italy 1135 100 Feet Rd, Indiranagar See map, p.1257. ☎25289126. Whether on the bamboo-bordered terrace or the elegant dining room, you'll get fantastic Italian food here, particularly the risottos and tomato-based pasta dishes. There's also an extensive wine list.

Marvalli Tiffin Rooms Lalbagh Rd. See map, p.1257. Top-notch south Indian food served cafeteria style in an aging, bare-bones canteen. Middle-aged waiters in white *lunghis* and striped shirts serve twelve-course set thali meals to hordes of locals at shared tables. Kudos for sticking it out to the menthol-cool, post-dessert paan.

Narthaki just off Subedar Chatram Rd. See map, p.1257. The best restaurant in the station/bus stand area. Filling meals are served on the first floor, while on the second there is a restaurant-bar with a full menu of Indian and Chinese dishes. The chicken chilli is a belter.

Seashell 44/4 Residency Cross Rd, next to *Amaravati*. Tasty Mangalorean seafood specialities are paired with north Indian fare in both the classy first-floor restaurant and the more relaxed and spacious bar above.

Sunny's 34 Vittal Mallya Rd. See map, p.1257. ☎080/2224 3642. Bracingly fresh, well-prepared ingredients, tasty Western specialities like BBQ chicken and an elegant yet leafy and casual indoor/outdoor setting. This could be Los Angeles, and indeed it's popular with expats and fairly pricey.

Ullas Above cinema, MG Rd. Superb pure-veg restaurant, with a terrace and indoor section. Excellent lunchtime thalis (Rs30–90) and a good choice of curries (around Rs50).

Woody's Commercial St. See map, p.1257. Take a shopping break at this very popular cafeteria-style veg restaurant. Offers a huge, south Indian–dominated menu but better known for its sundaes, milkshakes and chocolates.

Nightlife

Bengaluru's hordes of bright young things have money to burn and a thriving **nightlife** in which to do it. A night on the town generally kicks off with a bar crawl along **Brigade Road**, **Residency Road** or **Church Street** (see map, p.1262), where there are scores of swish **pubs**. Drinking alcohol does not have the seedy connotations it does elsewhere in India; you'll even see young Indian women enjoying a beer with their mates. Note that most clubs operate a couples–only policy. For a quiet, more elegant tipple head for the bars of five-star **hotels** such as the *Jockey Club* at the *Taj Residency*, the *Polo Club* at the *Oberoi* and, for a taste of colonial grandeur, the *Colonnade* at the *Taj West End*.

Bengaluru is a major **cinema** centre, with a booming industry and dozens of theatres showing the latest releases from India and abroad. Check the *Deccan Herald* to find out what's on. The majestically crumbling Elgin Talkies, still showing movies on Agsar Road in Shivajinagar, is a local institution, or try the simpler yet still vibrant Majestic and Triveni cinemas near Kempe Gowda Circle. To arrange a visit to a **movie studio** phone Chamundeshwari Studio (℡080/2226 8642).

Bars and clubs

13th Floor 13th Floor, Ivory Tower, MG Rd. Lean over the outward facing bar, cool cocktail in hand, and enjoy the hubbub of the city from a bird's-eye view. Classy and cosmopolitan, with stunning city and sunset views and cool post-mod decor, *13th Floor* is an absolute must, but come early because it fills up fast.

The Beach 1211 100 Feet Rd, Indiranagar ℡080/4126 1114. The music can get rather loud on weekends, but you might not mind so much while sipping expertly made *mojitos* with your feet in the sand.

Coco Grove Church St. Sidewalk terrace garden, good for people-watching over a beer or cocktails.

Couch 1st Floor, SAI Complex, west end of MG Rd. Cool and cavernous bi-level lounge with stone floors and stylishly mismatched retro furnishings. Grab a booth near the front windows and enjoy a well-made cocktail or two as life zooms by below. Also offers a full international menu; open daily 11am–11pm.

Fuga 1 Castle St, just off south end of Brigade Rd. A glowing marble bar, black and white leather banquettes, renowned guest DJs, and absinthe make this Bengaluru's swankiest club.

Guzzlers Inn 48 Rest House Rd, off Brigade Rd. A decent Indian stab at an English pub offering MTV, Star Sport, snooker, pool and good draught beer.

Hard Rock Café 40 St Mark's Rd, at Church Rd ℡080/4124 2222. Upon opening in early 2008 this gorgeous, multi-room space inside an old stone library quickly became the buzzing nexus of Bengaluru nightlife, not to mention the finest bar and grill in town. With high, vaulted ceilings, gray stone walls and subtle accents, it feels both lived in and new.

Pecos Rest House Rd, off Brigade Rd. Three dank levels of rock posters and aging wood make up the definitive Bangalore dive. The tunes are hard-driving, the beer's cheap and the Indian grub ain't half bad.

The Pub World opposite Galaxy Cinema, Residency Rd. Stylish pub with lots of TVs and semi-private booths, popular with trendy young professionals.

Taika 206–209 The Pavilion, 62 MG Rd. This expansive and slightly scuffed top-floor club is one of the most popular student nightspots in town, with a spacious, raucous dance hall and soothing, couch-filled lounge.

Listings

Airlines, domestic Air Deccan ℡0984 577 7008; Air India, Unity Building, JC Rd ℡080/2227 7747; Indian Airlines, Cauvery Bhavan, Kempe Gowda Rd ℡080/2297 8423, airport ℡080/2522 6233; Jet Airways, 1–4 M Block, Unity Building, JC Rd ℡080/2522 1929, airport ℡080/2522 0688; **Airlines, international** Air France, Sunrise Chambers, 22 Ulsoor Rd ℡080/2558 9397; Alitalia, 44 Safina Plaza, Infantry Rd ℡080/2559 1936; American/Austrian/Biman Bangladesh/Royal Jordanian, 22 Sunrise Chambers, Ulsoor Rd ℡080/2559 4240; British Airways, 7 Sophia's Choice, St Mark's Rd ℡080/2227 1205; Delta /Sabena/Swiss Air/Singapore Airlines, Park View, 17 Curve Rd, Tasker Town ℡080/2286 7873; Gulf Air, Sunrise Chambers, 22 Ulsoor Rd ℡080/2558 4702; KLM/Northwest Airlines, *Taj West End*, Race Course Rd ℡080/2226 5562; Lufthansa, 44/2 Dickenson Rd

℡080/2558 8791; Malaysia Airlines, Richmond Circle ℡080/2212 2991; Pakistan International Airlines, 108 Commerce House, 911 Cunningham Rd ℡080/2226 0667; Qantas, Westminster, Cunningham Rd ℡080/2226 4719; Thai Airways, G-5 Imperial Court, Cunningham Rd ℡080/5112 4333; United Airlines, 17–20 Richmond Towers, 12 Richmond Rd ℡080/2224 4620.

Banks and exchange A reliable place to change money is Thomas Cook, 55 MG Rd, on the corner of Brigade Rd, though if it's busy Weizmann Forex Ltd, 56 Residency Rd, and Wall Street Finances, 3 House of Lords, 13/14 St Mark's Rd, are just as efficient and quieter (all Mon–Sat 9.30am–6pm). Better rates are on offer at banks, of which the State Bank of Mysore on MG Rd is most convenient. There is an increasing number of ATMs dotted around the city, especially in the MG Rd area.

Bookstores There are a half-dozen decent bookstores along MG Rd and Church St, and the latter offers two fine newsstands. A vast, modern two-floor space, Crossword (ACR Towers, 32 Residency Road, behind car dealership) has all the latest titles along with music, movies, a great magazine selection, and a *Café Coffee Day*. Motilal Banarsidas, 16 St Mark's Rd, close to the junction with MG Rd, offers a superb selection of heavy-weight Indology and philosophy titles.

Car rental You can find self-drive car rental at Avis, the *Oberoi* hotel, 37–39 MG Rd ☏080/2558 5858, ⒲www.avis.com; and Hertz, Unit 12 Raheja Plaza, 17 Commissariat Rd ☏080/2559 9408, ⒲www.hertz.com; both have airport outlets. For long-distance car rental and tailor-made itineraries, try Gullivers Tours & Travels, South Black 201/202 Manipal Centre, 47 Dickenson Rd ☏080/2558 8001; Clipper Holidays, 406 Regency Enclave, 4 Magrath Rd ☏080/2559 9032; any KSTDC office; and the ITDC booth at the railway station.

Hospitals Victoria, near City Market ☏080/2670 1150; Sindhi Charitable, 3rd Main St, SR Nagar ☏080/2223 7318. Dr. Suresh Nao (91/9845 021614), a family practice physician based in central Bangalore, can recommend treatments and/ or closest hospital.

Internet access At the last count Bangalore had a staggering 700 email/Internet bureaux – they charge Rs10–30 per hour and open for most if not all 24 hours of the day. The Cyber Café, 13–15 Brigade Rd, is one of the most popular.

Libraries The British Council (English-language) library, 23 Kasturba Rd Cross (Mon–Sat 10.30am–6.30pm; ☏080/2221 3485), has newspapers and magazines which visitors are welcome to peruse in a/c comfort.

Music stores The best music shops in the city centre, selling Indian, Western and World music, are Music World and Planet M, both on Brigade Rd, or Rhythms, at 14 St Mark's Rd, beneath the *Nahar Heritage* hotel.

Pharmacies Al-Siddique Pharma Centre, opposite Jama Masjid near City Market, and Janata Bazaar, in the Victoria Hospital, near City Market are open all night.

Police ☏100.

Post office On the corner of Raj Bhavan Rd and Cubbon St, at the northern tip of Cubbon Park, about ten minutes' walk from MG Rd (Mon–Sat 10am–7pm, Sun 10.30am–1.30pm).

Shopping Cauvery Arts and Crafts Emporium, on the corner of MG and Brigade roads, is a govern-ment-run outlet shop selling all variety of wooden toys and gadgets, stunningly detailed sandalwood sculptures, expertly inlaid rosewood coffee-tables and hundreds of other gift items.

Travel agents For flight booking and reconfirmation, and other travel necessities, try the spanking-new Via, on MG Road next to *Hotel Brindavan*; Sahara Global, Unit G2, 35 Church St, next to *Empire International* ☏080/6535 0001; Gullivers Tours & Travels, South Black 201–202 Manipal Centre, Dickenson Rd, just north of MG Rd ☏080/2558 8001.

Moving on from Bengaluru

Bengaluru is south India's principal transport hub. Fast and efficient computer-ised booking facilities make **moving on** relatively hassle-free, although the availability of seats should never be taken for granted; book as far in advance as possible. Bengaluru's modern new **airport** is the busiest in south India, with more than a dozen daily flights to **Mumbai**, **Chennai** and **Hyderabad**, plus services to numerous other destinations (see p.1326 for more information).

Most of the wide range of long-distance **buses** from Central Bus Stand can be booked in advance at the computerized counters near Bay 13 (7.30am–7.30pm daily). As well as Karnataka's state bus corporation (KSRTC), government-run services from Andhra Pradesh, Kerala, Maharashtra, Tamil Nadu and Goa also operate from Bengaluru. Timings and ticket availability for the forthcoming week are posted on a large board left of the main entrance. For general enquiries, call ☏080/2287 3377.

Several **private bus companies** run luxury coaches to destinations such as Mysore, Bijapur, Ooty, Chennai, Kochi/Ernakulam, Thrissur, Kollam and Thiruvananthapuram. Tickets can be bought from the agencies on Tank Bund Road, opposite the bus stand; operators include Sharma (☏080/2670 2447), National (☏080/2660 3112) and Shama (☏080/2670 5855), each of which advertise overnight deluxe buses to **Goa** and sleeper coaches and services to **Mumbai** and **Chennai**. The most reliable of the private bus companies is

The following trains are recommended as the fastest and/or most convenient from Bengaluru.

Destination	Name	No.	Departs	Total time
Chennai	Shatabdi Express*	#2008	daily except Tues 4.25pm	5hr 5min
	Lalbagh Express	#2608	daily 6.30am	5hr 30min
Ernakulam (for Kochi)	Kanniyakumari Express	#6526	daily 9.45pm	12hr 15min
Hospet (for Hampi)	Hampi Express	#6592	daily 10.20pm	9hr 30min
Mumbai	Udyan Express	#6530	daily 8.05pm	23hr 50min
Mysore	Shatabdi Express*	#2007	daily except Tues 11am	2hr
	Tipu Express	#2614	daily 2.15pm	2hr 30min
	Chamundi Express	#6216	daily 6.15pm	3hr
Secunderabad (Hyderabad)	Rajdhani Express*	#2429	4 weekly 8.20pm	10hr 50min
Thiruvananthapuram	Kanniyakumari Express	#6526	daily 9.45pm	17hr 20min

*= a/c only

Vijayanand Travels (℡080/2297 1257), who also have an office on Tank Bund Road; their distinctive yellow-and-black luxury coaches run to destinations such as Mangalore, Gokarna/Goa, and Hospet for Hampi.

While Southern Railways complete the conversion to broad gauge, the line from Bijapur to Gadag was expected to be closed until late 2008 – check the situation before booking. Bengaluru's City railway station's reservations office (Mon–Sat 8am–2pm & 2.15–8pm, Sun 8am–2pm; ℡132) is in a separate building, east of the main station (to the left as you approach). Counter 14 is for foreigners. If you have an Indrail Pass, go to the Chief Reservations Supervisor's Office on the first floor (turn left at the top of the stairs), where "reservations are guaranteed".Trains to Goa and a handful of trains to other destinations depart from Yeshwanthpur railway station (℡080/2337 7161) in the north of the city.

Around Bengaluru

Many visitors to Bengaluru are on their way to or from Mysore.The **Janapada Loka Folk Arts Museum**, between the two, gives a fascinating insight into Karnatakan culture, while anyone wishing to see or study classical dance in a rural environment should check out **Nrityagram Dance Village**.

Janapada Loka Folk Arts Museum

The **Janapada Loka Folk Arts Museum** (daily 9am–6pm; free), 53km southwest of Bengaluru on the Mysore road, includes an amazing array of Karnatakan agricultural, hunting and fishing implements, weapons, ingenious household gadgets, masks, dolls and shadow puppets, carved wooden *bhuta* (spirit-worship) sculptures and larger-than-life temple procession figures, manuscripts, musical instruments and *yakshagana* theatre costumes. In addition, 1600 hours of **audio and video recordings** of musicians, dancers and rituals from the state are available on request. To get to the museum, take one of the many slow Mysore buses (not the nonstop ones) from Bengaluru; after the town of Ramanagar, alight at the 53-kilometre stone by the side of the road. A small **restaurant** here serves simple food, and dorm **accommodation** (Rs150) is available. For more details contact the Karnataka Janapada Trust, 7 Subramanyaswami Temple Rd, 5th Cross, 4th Block, Kumara Park West, Bengaluru.

Nrityagram Dance Village

NRITYAGRAM DANCE VILLAGE (Tues–Sun 10am–5.30pm; Rs20) is a delightful, purpose-built model village, 30km west of Bengaluru, designed by the award-winning architect Gerard de Cunha and founded by the late Protima Gauri. Gauri had a colourful career in media and film, and eventually came to be renowned as an exponent of Odissi dance (see p.1033). The school continues without her and attracts pupils from all over the world. It hosts regular performances and lectures on Indian mythology and art, and also offers courses in different forms of Indian dance. **Guided tours** of the complex cost Rs850 per person (minimum 6), including lunch and a demonstration. **Accommodation** for longer stays (❼) promises "no TV, telephones, newspapers or noise". Contact its Bengaluru office (☎080/2846 6313).

Mysore

A centre of sandalwood-carving, silk and incense production, **MYSORE** is one of south India's more appealing stops. Nearly 160km southwest of Bengaluru (Bangalore), the erstwhile capital of the Wadiyar rajas can be disappointing at first blush considering the compliments often heaped on it: upon stumbling off a bus or train one is not so much embraced by the scent of jasmine blossom or gentle wafts of sandalwood as smacked by a cacophony of tooting, careering buses, bullock carts, motorbikes, and tongas. The city was recently ranked by a national magazine as one of India's best for business and is Karnataka's most popular tourist destination by a long shot, attracting about 2.5 million each year. Nevertheless, Mysore remains a charming, old-fashioned and undaunting town, changed by neither an IT boom nor its newfound status as a top international yoga destination. Give it a few days and Mysore will cast a spell on you.

In the tenth century Mysore was known as Mahishur – "the town where the demon buffalo was slain" (by the goddess Durga). Presiding over a district of many villages, the city was ruled from about 1400 until Independence by the Hindu **Wadiyars**. Their rule was only broken from 1761, when the Muslim Haider Ali and his son Tipu Sultan took over. Two years later, the new rulers demolished the labyrinthine old city to replace it with the elegant grid of sweeping, leafy streets and public gardens that survive today. However, following Tipu Sultan's defeat in 1799 by the British colonel, Arthur Wellesley (later the Duke of Wellington), Wadiyar power was restored. As the capital of Mysore state, the city thereafter dominated a major part of southern India. In 1956, when Bangalore became capital of newly formed Karnataka, its maharaja was appointed governor.

Arrival and information

Six or seven **trains** from Bengaluru (Bangalore) arrive daily at the railway station, 1.5km northwest of the centre. Mysore has three bus stands: major long-distance KSRTC services pull in to Central, near the heart of the city, where

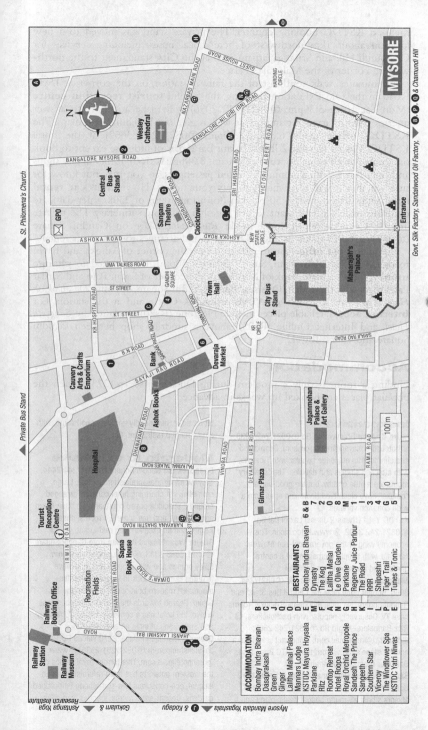

MYSORE

Govt. Silk Factory, Sandalwood Oil Factory,   ▼   8, P, Q & Chamundi Hill

RESTAURANTS

Bombay Indra Bhavan	6 & B
Dynasty	7
The Keg	2
Lalitha Mahal	O
Le Olive Garden	8
Parklane	M
Regency Juice Parlour	1
The Road	3
RRR	4
Shilpashri	G
Tiger Trail	P
Tunes & Tonic	5

ACCOMMODATION

Bombay Indra Bhavan	B
Dasaprakash	C
Green	J
Ginger	Q
Lalitha Mahal Palace	O
Manmars Lodge	D
KSTDC Mayura Hoysala	E
Parklane	M
Ritz	F
Rooftop Retreat	A
Hotel Roopa	N
Royal Orchid Metropole	G
Sandesh The Prince	H
Sangeeth	I
Southern Star	L
Viceroy	L
The Windflower Spa	P
KSTDC Yatri Niwas	E

there's a KSTDC booking counter. The private stand has moved to a new location about 1km northwest of here. Local buses, including services for Chamundi Hill and Srirangapatnam, stop at the **City** stand, next to the north-western corner of the Maharaja's Palace.

Five minutes' walk southeast of the railway station, on the corner of Irwin Road in the Old Exhibition Building, the helpful **tourist reception centre** (Mon–Sat 10am–5.30pm; ☎0821/242 2096) will make an effort to answer queries and can arrange transport, as well as give out brochures and maps. The **KSTDC office** (daily 6.30am–8.30pm; ☎0821/242 3652) at the hotel KSTDC *Mayura Hoysala*, 2 Jhansi Laxmi Bai Rd, is of little use except to book one of its whistle-stop city **tours** (7.30am–8.30pm; Rs160). It hits all city sights and only leaves with a minimum of ten passengers, so you may not know for sure whether it will run when you buy your ticket. However, its **car rental** rates (with driver), at Rs4.50 per km (for a minimum of 250km per day), are quite reasonable if you want to put together your own itinerary. The private Tourist Corporation of India inside *Rajabhadra Lodge* on Gandhi Square (☎0821/526 0294) acts as a KSTDC agent and arranges tours and car rental.

The main **post office** (poste restante) is on the corner of Ashoka and Irwin roads (Mon–Sat 10am–7pm, Sun 10.30am–1.30pm). If you need to **change money**, there's a State Bank of Mysore on the corner of Sayaji Rao and Sardar Patel roads, and the Indian Overseas Bank, Gandhi Square, opposite *Dasaprakash Hotel*. There are a couple of **ATMs** around.R Circle and at the station. For **Internet access**, reliable places include Netzone (Rs20), opposite the *Sangeeth Hotel*, and Internet Online (Rs25), above a sundries shop between Gandhi Square and Clock Tower.

Accommodation

Finding a room is only a problem during Dussehra (see p.1273), when the popular places are booked up weeks in advance.

Inexpensive

Indra Bhavan Dhanavantri Rd ☎0821/242 3933, ✉ hotelindrabhavan@rediffmail.com. Dilapidated and characterful old lodge popular with Tibetans, with attached singles and doubles. The "ordinary" rooms are a little grubby, but the good-value "deluxe" have clean tiled floors and open onto a wide common veranda. ❷

KSTDC Yatri Niwas 2 Jhansi Laxmi Bai Rd ☎0821/242 3492, ⓦ www.kstdc.nic.in. The economy wing of the government-run *Mayura Hoysala*, with simple rooms around a central garden and dorm beds for Rs75. ❷

Mannars Lodge Chandragupta Rd ☎0821/244 8060. Budget hotel near the Central Bus Stand and Gandhi Square. No frills, though the "deluxe" rooms have TV. Deservedly popular with backpackers. ❷

Ritz Bangalore–Nilgiri Rd ☎0821/242 2668, ✉ hotelritz@rediffmail.com. Wonderful colonial-era hotel, a stone's throw from the KSRTC Bus Stand. Only four rooms, so book ahead. ❸

Sangeeth 1966 Narayana Shastry Rd, near the Udipi Krishna temple ☎0821/242 4693. One of Mysore's best all-round budget deals: bland and a

bit boxed in, but friendly and very good value, with a new rooftop restaurant. ❷

Moderate to expensive

Dasaprakash Gandhi Square ☎0821/244 2444, ⓦ www.mysoredasaprakashgroup.com. Large, crumbling yet charming hotel complex arranged around a spacious paved courtyard. It's busy, clean and efficient, and has some a/c rooms, cheap singles and an excellent veg restaurant. ❷–❹

Ginger Vasant Mahal Rd, 3km from Gandhi Square ☎0821/6666 3333, ⓦ www.gingerhotels.com. Spicy orange and white rooms and innovative features like self check-in kiosks define this minimalist modern boutique chain from the Tata Group. Geared towards the IT and young business crowd, the hotel has a convenient *Café Coffee Day* and State Bank of India on site. ❺–❼

Green Chittaranjan Palace, 2270 Vinoba Rd, Jayalakshmipuram ☎0821/251 2536, ⓦ www .greenhotelindia.com. This former royal palace on the western outskirts has been refurbished as an elegant, eco-conscious two-star among landscaped gardens. Decent-sized rooms, lounges, verandas, a croquet lawn and well-stocked library. All profits go to charities and environmental projects, and their auto-rickshaw will pick you up with prior arrangement. Early bookings recommended. ❼–❾

KSTDC Mayura Hoysala 2 Jhansi Laxmi Bai Rd ☎0821/242 5349, ⊛www.kstdc.nic.in. Reasonably priced rooms and suites in a colonial-era mansion. There's a terrace restaurant and beer garden, which is good value, but the food is uninspiring. ❸–❺

Lalitha Mahal Palace T Narasipur Rd ☎0821/247 0470, ⊛www.lalithamahalpalace.com. On a slope overlooking the city in the distance, this white, Neoclassical palace was built in 1931 to accommodate the maharaja's foreign guests. Now it's a Raj-style fantasy, decked with stunning period furniture and popular with tour groups. Rooms range from turret rooms ($200) to the "Viceroy Suite" ($900). The tea lounge, restaurant and pool are open to nonresidents (Rs150). ❾

Metropole 5 Jhansi Lakshmi Bai Rd ☎0821/425 5566, ⊛www.royalorchidhotels.com. Luxurious heritage hotel built in 1920 by the Maharaja of Mysore amid pleasant gardens. Rooms have high ceilings and a sense of grandeur. There's also a small outdoor pool and gym, plus the fine *Tiger Trail* multi-cuisine restaurant in the central courtyard. ❾

🏃 **Parklane** 2720 Sri Harsha Rd ☎0821/243 0400. A complete overhaul has transformed the *Parklane* into a swish yet affordable boutique hotel. Appealingly misshapen rooms, all with balconies and contemporary furnishings, encircle a skylit atrium. Two excellent restaurants vie for diners – one thick with tree branches on the first floor and another on the roof, with a plunge pool, full bar and fine views of Chamundi; both offer live music nightly, usually tabla and flute. ❺–❼

🏃 **Rooftop Retreat** 3km from bus stand in Gayathripuram ⓔdivyanivya@rediffmail .com, ☎0821/245 0483. This delightful apartment homestay in a tranquil neighbourhood offers an Indian twist on the B&B experience. Bright blues and cosy creams dominate the mostly wood furnishings, and you can enjoy delightful mornings and evenings on the rooftop patio. Divya is a welcoming hostess and, along with her sister, an excellent cook. Must reserve in advance; they will pick up from train station or bus stand. ❸

Hotel Roopa 2724-C Bangalore–Nilgiri Rd ☎0821/244 3770, ⊛www.hotel-roopa.com. Spark ing new hotel block with compact but comfy rooms at surprisingly reasonable prices. Very handy for the palace. ❸–❺

Sandesh The Prince 3 Nazarbad Main Rd ☎0821/243 6777, ⊛www.sandeshtheprince.com. Smart stylish 4-star with comfortable, well-furnished rooms and an impressive, skylit foyer. Facilities include travel desk, foreign exchange, outdoor pool with BBQ, and an excellent Ayurvedic centre and beauty parlour. Request a top-floor room with balcony if possible. ❽–❾

Southern Star Vinobha Rd ☎0821/242 6426, ⊛www.ushashriramhotels.com. Modern and comfortable monolithic hotel, affiliated to *Quality Inn*. Facilities include two restaurants, a bar and a swimming pool. Rooms from Rs4200. ❾

Viceroy Sri Harsha Rd ☎0821/242 4001, ⊛www .theviceroygroup.com. Business-oriented hotel, with most mod cons and two good restaurants. Rooms are rather overpriced but mostly a/c, and the front ones have palace views. ❻–❼

The Windflower Spa Maharanapratap Rd, 3km southeast of town ☎0821/252 2500, ⊛www .thewindflower.com. Whitewashed Balinese-style cottages surround a small lagoon on these gorgeous, sprawling grounds at the base of Chamundi Hill. Amenities include spa and massage, billiards and foosball, an elegant bar, lagoon restaurant and an outdoor pool with waterfall. ❼–❾

The City

In addition to its official tourist attractions, chief amongst them the **Maharaja's Palace**, Mysore is a great city simply to stroll around. The characterful, if dilapidated, pre-Independence buildings lining market areas such as **Ashok Road** and **Sayaji Rao Road** lend an air of faded grandeur to the busy centre, teeming with vibrant street life. Souvenir stores spill over with the famous **sandalwood**; the best place to get a sense of what's on offer is the Government Cauvery Arts and Crafts Emporium on Sayaji Rao Road (closed Thurs), which stocks a wide range of local crafts that can be shipped overseas. The city's famous **Devaraja Market** on Sayaji Rao Road is one of south India's most atmospheric produce markets: a giant complex of covered stalls groaning with bananas (the delicious *nanjangod* variety), luscious mangoes, blocks of sticky *jaggery* and conical heaps of lurid *kumkum* powder.

Maharaja's Palace

Mysore's centre is dominated by the walled **Maharaja's Palace** (daily 10am–5.30pm; Rs100 [Rs10]), a fairy-tale spectacle topped with a shining brass-plated dome. It's especially magnificent on Sunday nights and during festivals, when it is illuminated by nearly 100,000 lightbulbs. It was completed in 1912 for the twenty-fourth Wadiyar raja, on the site of the old wooden palace that had been destroyed by fire in 1897. In 1998, after a lengthy judicial tussle, the courts decided in favour of formally placing the main palace in the hands of the Karnataka state government but the royal family, who still hold a claim, are set to appeal. Twelve temples surround the palace, some of them of much earlier origin. Although there are six gates in the perimeter wall, entrance is on the south side only. Shoes and cameras must be left at the cloakroom inside.

An extraordinary amalgam of styles from India and around the world crowds the lavish **interior**. Entry is through the Gombe Thotti or **Dolls' Pavilion**, once a showcase for the figures featured in the city's lively Dussehra celebrations and now a gallery of European and Indian sculpture and ceremonial objects. Halfway along, the brass **Elephant Gate** forms the main entrance to the centre of the palace, through which the maharaja would drive to his car park. Decorated with floriate designs, it bears the Mysore royal symbol of a double-headed eagle, now the state emblem. To the north, past the gate, stands a ceremonial wooden elephant *howdah*. Elaborately decorated with 84kg of 24-carat gold, it appears to be inlaid with red and green gems – in fact the twinkling lights are battery-powered signals that let the *mahout* know when the maharaja wished to stop or go.

Walls leading into the octagonal **Kalyana Mandapa**, the royal wedding hall, are lined with a meticulously detailed frieze of oil paintings illustrating the great Mysore Dussehra festival (see box opposite) of 1930, executed over a period of fifteen years by four Indian artists. The hall itself is magnificent, a cavernous space featuring cast-iron pillars from Glasgow, Bohemian chandeliers and multicoloured Belgian stained-glass arranged in peacock designs in the domed ceiling.

Climbing a staircase with Italian marble balustrades, past an unnervingly realistic life-size plaster-of-Paris figure of Krishnaraja Wadiyar IV, lounging

▲ The Maharaja's Palace at night

Following the tradition set by the Vijayanagar kings, the ten-day festival of **Dussehra** (Sept/Oct), to commemorate the goddess Durga's slaying of the demon buffalo, Mahishasura, is celebrated in grand style at Mysore. Scores of cultural events include concerts of south Indian classical (Carnatic) music and dance performances in the great Durbar Hall of the **Maharaja's Palace**. On Vijayadasmi, the tenth and last day of the festival, a magnificent procession of mounted guardsmen on horseback and caparisoned elephants – one carrying the palace deity, Chaamundeshwari, on a gold *howdah* – marches 5km from the palace to Banni Mantap. There's also a floating festival in the temple tank at the foot of **Chamundi Hill**, and a procession of chariots around the temple at the top. A torchlit parade takes place in the evening, followed by a massive firework display and much jubilation on the streets.

comfortably with his bejewelled feet on a stool, you come into the **Public Durbar Hall**, an orientalist fantasy like something from *A Thousand and One Nights*. A vision of brightly painted and gilded colonnades, open on one side, the massive hall affords views out across the parade ground and gardens to Chamundi Hill. The maharaja gave audience from here, seated on a throne made from 280kg of solid Karnatakan gold. These days, the hall is only used during the Dussehra festival, when it hosts classical concerts. The smaller **Private Durbar Hall** features especially beautiful stained glass and gold-leaf painting. Before leaving you pass two embossed silver doors – all that remains of the old palace.

Jaganmohan Palace: Jayachamarajendra Art Gallery
Built in 1861, the **Jaganmohan Palace** (daily 8am–5pm; Rs10; no cameras), 300m west of the Maharaja's Palace, was used as a royal residence until 1915, when it was turned into a picture gallery and museum by Maharaja Krishnaraja Wadiyar IV. Most of the "contemporary" art on show dates from the 1930s, when a revival of Indian painting was spearheaded by E.B. Havell and the Tagore brothers, Rabindranath and Gaganendranath, in Bengal.

Nineteenth- and twentieth-century **paintings** dominate the first floor; amongst them the work of the pioneering oil painter Raja Ravi Varma who, although not everyone's cup of tea, has been credited for introducing modern techniques to Indian art. Games on the upper floor include circular *ganjifa* playing cards illustrated with portraits of royalty or deities, and board games delicately inlaid with ivory. There's also a cluster of musical instruments, among them a brass *jaltarang* set and glass xylophone. Another gallery, centring on a large wooden Ganesh seated on a tortoise, is lined with paintings, including Krishnaraja Wadiyar sporting with the "inmates" of his *zenana* (women's quarter of the palace) during Holi.

Chamundi Hill
Chamundi Hill, 3km southeast of the city, is topped with a temple to the chosen deity of the Mysore rajas – the goddess Chamundi, or Durga, who slew the demon buffalo Mahishasura. It's a pleasant, easy bus trip (#201 from the City stand) to the top; the walk down, past a huge Nandi, Shiva's bull, takes about thirty minutes. Take drinking water to sustain you, especially in the middle of the day – the walk isn't very demanding, but by the end of it, after more than a thousand steps, your legs are likely to be a bit wobbly.

Inside the twelfth-century **temple** (daily 7am–2pm, 3.30–6pm & 7–9pm), which is open to non-Hindus, is a solid gold Chamundi figure. Outside, in the courtyard, stands a fearsome, if gaily coloured, statue of the demon Mahishasura.

22

KARNATAKA | Mysore

Overlooking the path down the hill, the magnificent five-metre **Nandi**, carved from a single piece of black granite in 1659, is an object of worship himself, adorned with bells and garlands and tended by his own priest. Minor shrines, dedicated to Chamundi and the monkey god Hanuman, among others, line the side of the path; at the bottom, a little shrine to Ganesh lies near a chai shop. From here it's usually possible to pick up an auto-rickshaw or bus back into the city, but at weekends the latter are often full. If you walk on towards the city, passing a temple on the left with a big water tank (the site of the floating festival during Dussehra), you come after ten minutes to the main road between the *Lalitha Mahal Palace* and the city; there's a bus stop, and often auto-rickshaws, at the junction.

Eating and drinking

Mysore has scores of **places to eat**, from numerous south Indian "meals" joints dotted around the market to the opulent *Lalita Mahal Palace*, where you can work up an appetite for a gourmet meal by swimming a few lengths of the pool. To sample the renowned Mysore *pak*, a sweet, rich crumbly mixture made of ghee and maize flour, queue at *Guru Sweet Mart*, a small stall at KR Circle considered the best sweet shop in the city. Another speciality from this part of the world is *malligi iddli*, a delicate jasmine-flavored *iddli* usually served in the mornings and at lunch.

Bombay Indra Bhavan Savaji Rao Rd. Comfortable and popular veg restaurant that serves both South and north Indian cuisine and sweets. Its other branch on Dhanavantri Rd is equally, if not more, popular and also has an a/c section.

Dynasty *Palace Plaza* hotel, Sri Harsha Rd. Classy ground-floor dining room complemented in evenings by a breezy covered rooftop restaurant with a broad menu, full bar, and pleasant décor.

The Keg Maharaja Shopping Complex, Bang-Mysore Rd. This dark, tiny pub has excellent Kingfisher on tap for Rs140 a pitcher all day.

Lalitha Mahal *Palace* T Naraispur Rd. Sample the charms of this palatial five-star with an expensive hot drink in the atmospheric tea lounge, or an a la carte lunch in the grand dining hall, accompanied by live sitar music. The old-style bar also boasts a full-size billiards table.

Le Olive Garden *Windflower Spa*. Excellent, reasonably-priced Indian, Chinese and Western dishes served to the sound of falling water and croaking frogs at this jungle hideaway.

Parklane Sri Harsha Rd. Congenial courtyard restaurant-cum-beer balcony, with moderately priced veg and non-veg (meat sizzlers are a speciality), fake trees and live Indian classical music every evening. The hotel rooftop space is a real stunner, with full bar, pool and fantastic views. Popular with travellers and locals alike.

Regency Juice Parlour BN St, just south of KR Hospital Rd. Along with the usual juices and snacks, there's a vast selection of fantastic shakes on offer, from lychee to butterscotch (Rs10).

The Road *Sandesh The Prince*. Lined with plush booths – several of which are inside faux classic cars – this high-end, American road trip–themed restaurant-cum-disco serves a quality buffet lunch and fine multi-cuisine dinner before plates are cleared and patrons take to the circular wooden dance floor, usually to guest DJs. The kebabs and tandoori specialities are top-notch. Rs300–400 cover on weekends.

RRR Gandhi Square. Superb Andhra canteen with a small but plush a/c room at the back. Gets packed at lunchtimes and at weekends, but well worth the wait for its excellent chicken biriyani, fried fish and set menus served on banana leaves.

Shilpashri Gandhi Square. Encircled by leafy potted plants, this rooftop terrace is one of the best spots in the city to enjoy a sun-dipped egg and toast breakfast or a cool evening cocktail. Quality north Indian fare, with particularly tasty tandoori – try the chicken tikka. Plenty of good veg options, too, including lots of dhals.

Tiger Trail *Royal Orchid Metropole*. Cool and tranquil courtyard garden with excellent Indian dinners and great Western-style breakfast buffets that include bacon, sausage, omelettes, fresh fruit and croissants (Rs190).

Tunes & Tonic *Hotel Adhi Manor*, Chandragupta Rd. With black tables and banquettes, red accents and excellent posters (Hendrix, Doors, Beyonce over the bar), the young, well-travelled Coorgi owner has created Mysore's most stylish lounge. The service and cocktails are excellent.

Yoga

At 92 years old, Sri Pattahbi Jois – instructor of Madonna, among other celebrities – is still leading classes at the world-renowned **Ashtanga Yoga Research Insitute** (Ⓦwww.ayri.org), 2.5km northwest of town. The shala has become a revered pilgrimage destination for devotees, and the surrounding neighborhood has in recent years turned into a bustling expat haven, filled with cafés, guesthouses, restaurants and Internet cafés. Note however that Ashtanga doesn't offer drop-in classes. Students must register for a minimum of one month (Rs27,000, Rs19,000 every additional month), and book at least two months in advance.

In contrast, **Mysore Mandala Yogashala**, 581 Dewans Rd, Laxmipuram (closed Sat & Mon; Ⓣ0821/425 6277, Ⓦmandala.ashtanga.org), is a self-contained retreat, offering excellent instruction, an organic café, well-tended garden, cultural events and, uniquely in Mysore, drop-in classes. Ashtanga classes (Rs400) run at 6am and 5pm, with the slightly less strenuous Hata classes (Rs350) at 8:15am.

Moving on from Mysore

If you're contemplating a long haul, the best way to travel is by **train**, usually with a change at **Bengaluru (Bangalore)**. Six or seven express services and six local trains leave Mysore each day for the Karnatakan capital. The fastest of these, the a/c Shatabdi Express #2008 (daily except Tues 2.20pm; 1hr 55min), continues on to Chennai; most of the others terminate in Bengaluru, where you can pick up long-distance connections to a wide range of Indian cities (see p.1326). **Reservations** can be made at Mysore's computerized booking hall inside the station (Mon–Sat 8am–2pm & 2.15–8pm, Sun 8am–2pm). There are four services daily to **Hassan**, of which the Shimoga Express #268 (10.15am; 2hr 5min) is the fastest.

As there are so many trains between Mysore and Bangalore, you shouldn't ever have to do the trip by **bus**, which takes a bit longer. Most other destinations within a day's ride of Mysore can only be reached by road. Long-distance services operate out of the Central Bus Stand, where you can book computerized tickets up to three days in advance. English timetables are posted on the wall inside the entrance hall, and there's a helpful enquiries counter in the corner of the compound. Regular buses leave here for **Hassan** (3–4hr), for Channarayapatna/**Sravanabelagola** (2hr 30min–3hr) and for **Hubli** (for Hospet/**Hampi**). Heading south to **Ooty** (5hr), there's a choice of eight buses, all of which stop at **Bandipur National Park**. Direct services to several cities in Kerala, including **Kannur**, **Kozhikode** and **Kochi**, also operate from Mysore. The only way to travel direct to **Goa** is on the 4pm or 5pm overnight buses that arrive at **Panjim** at 9am and 10am respectively. Most travellers, however, break this long trip into stages, heading first to **Mangalore** (7hr) and working their way north from there, usually via **Gokarna** – which you can also reach by direct bus (14hr) – or **Jog Falls**. Mangalore-bound buses tend to pass through **Madikeri**, capital of Kodagu (Coorg), which is also served by hourly buses, most of which travel through the Tibetan enclave of **Bylakuppe**. For details of services to **Somnathpur** and **Srirangapatnam**, see the relevant accounts. A host of agents can make booking for **private buses** to many destinations – the Tourist Corporation of India at the *Rajabhadra Lodge* is one of the best.

Around Mysore

Mysore is a jumping-off point for some of Karnataka's most popular destinations. At **Srirangapatnam**, the fort, palace and mausoleum date from the era of Tipu Sultan, the "Tiger of Mysore", a perennial thorn in the side of the British. Twitchers will enjoy a visit to the nearby **Ranganathittu Bird Sanctuary**, while the superb Hoysala temple (see p.1283) of **Somnathpur** is an architectural masterpiece.

If you're heading south towards Ooty, **Bandipur National Park**'s forests and hill scenery offer another possible escape from the city, although your chances of spotting any rare animals are slim. The same is true of **Nagarhole National Park**, three hours southwest of Mysore towards the Kerala border.

Srirangapatnam

The island of **Srirangapatnam**, in the River Kaveri, 14km northeast of Mysore, measures 5km by 1km. Long a site of Hindu pilgrimage, it is named after its tenth-century Sriranganathaswamy Vishnu temple. The Vijayanagars built a fort here in 1454, and in 1616 it became the capital of the Mysore Wadiyar rajas. However, Srirangapatnam is more famously associated with **Haider Ali**, who deposed the Wadiyars in 1761, and even more so with his son **Tipu Sultan**. During his seventeen-year reign – which ended with his death in 1799, when the future Duke of Wellington took the fort at the bloody battle of "Seringapatnam" – Tipu posed a greater threat than any other Indian ruler to British plans to dominate India. Born in 1750, of a Hindu mother, he inherited his father Haider Ali's considerable military skills, but was also an educated, cultured man, whose lifelong desire to rid India of the hated British invaders naturally brought him an ally in the French. He obsessively embraced his popular name of the **Tiger of Mysore**, surrounding himself with symbols and images of tigers; much of his memorabilia is decorated with the animal or its stripes, and, like the Romans, he is said to have kept tigers for the punishment of criminals.

The former summer palace, the **Daria Daulat Bagh** (daily except Fri 9am–5pm; $2 [Rs5]), literally "wealth of the sea", was used to entertain Tipu's guests. At first sight, this low, wooden colonnaded building set in an attractive formal garden fails to impress. But the superbly preserved interior, with its ornamental arches, tiger-striped columns and floral decoration on every inch of the teak walls and ceiling, is remarkable. A much-repainted mural on the west wall relishes every detail of Haider Ali's victory over the British at Pollilore in 1780.

An avenue of cypresses leads from an intricately carved gateway to the **Gumbaz mausoleum** (daily except Fri 9am–5pm; free), 3km further east. Built by Tipu Sultan in 1784 to commemorate Haider Ali, and later also to serve as his own resting place, the lower half of the grey-granite edifice is crowned by a dome of whitewashed brick and plaster, spectacular against the blue sky. Ivory-inlaid rosewood doors lead to the tombs of Haider Ali and Tipu, each covered by a pall (tiger stripes for Tipu), and an Urdu tablet records Tipu's martyrdom.

At the heart of the fortress, the great temple of **Sriranganathaswamy** still stands proud and virtually untouched by the turbulent history that has flowed around it, and remains, for many devotees, the prime draw. Developed by succeeding dynasties, the temple consists of three distinctive sanctuaries and is entered via an impressive five-storeyed gateway and a hall that was built by Haider Ali. The innermost sanctum, the oldest part of the temple, contains an image of the reclining Vishnu.

Practicalities

Frequent **buses** from Mysore City Bus Stand (including #313 & #316) and all the Mysore–Bangalore **trains** pull in near the temple and fort. Srirangapatnam is a small island, but places of interest are quite spread out; tongas, auto-rickshaws and bicycles are available on the main road near the bus stand. The KSTDC **hotel**-cum-restaurant, *Mayura River View* (⊕08236/252114; ❹–❺), occupies a pleasant spot beside the Kaveri, 3km from the bus stand; another good option is the smart and elegant *Fort View Resorts* (⊕08236/252777; ❺–❻), set in its own grounds not far from the fort entrance.

Somnathpur

Built in 1268 AD, the exquisite **Keshava Vishnu temple** (daily 9am–5pm; $2 [Rs5]), in the sleepy hamlet of **SOMNATHPUR**, was the last important temple to be constructed by the Hoysalas; it is also the most complete and, in many respects, the finest example of this singular style (see p.1283). Somnathpur itself, just ninety minutes from Mysore by road, is little more than a few neat tracks and some attractive simple houses with pillared verandas.

Like other Hoysala temples, the Keshava was built on a star-shaped plan. ASI staff can show you around and also grant permission to clamber on the enclosure walls, so you can get a marvellous bird's-eye view of the modestly proportioned structure. It's best to do this as early as possible, as the stone gets very hot to walk on in bare feet later in the day. The temple is a *trikutachala*, "three-peaked hills" type, with a tower on each shrine. Its high plinth (*jagati*) provides an upper ambulatory, which on its outer edge allows visitors to approach the upper registers of the profusely decorated walls. Among the many superb images here are an unusually high proportion of Shaivite figures for a Vishnu temple. As at Halebid, a lively frieze details countless episodes from the Ramayana, Bhagavata Purana and Mahabharata. Intended to accompany circumambulation, the panels are "read" (there is no text) in a clockwise direction. Unusually, the temple is autographed; all its sculpture was the work of one man, named Malitamba. Outside the temple stands a *dvajastambha* column, which may originally have been surmounted by a figure of Vishnu's bird vehicle Garuda.

Practicalities

There are no direct **buses** from Mysore to Somnathpur. Buses from the Private stand run to Tirumakudal Narasipur (1hr), from where there are regular buses to Somnathpur (20min). Everyone will know where you want to go, and someone will show you which scrum to join. Alternatively, join one of KSTDC's guided tours from Mysore (see p.1270).

There is nowhere to stay near the temple and the only **food** available is biscuits or maybe a samosa or fruit from a street-seller. Tucked in the backwaters of a dammed section of the Cauvery, a further 25km southeast, the exquisite *Talakadu Jaladhana* resort (⊕08227/271196, ✉jaladhana@hotmail.com; ❽) offers secluded cottages, some with rooftop hot tubs and herb gardens. Boating and sports activities are available and the resort can be reached by direct private bus from Mysore.

National parks around Mysore: Bandipur and Nagarhole

Mysore lies within striking distance of three major wildlife sanctuaries – **Bandipur**, **Nagarhole** and **Mudumalai**, across the border in Tamil Nadu – all of which are part of the vast **Nilgiri Biosphere Reserve**, one of India's most extensive tracts of protected forest. A few upmarket private "resorts" on the edge of the parks and one or two tourist complexes allow visitors to experience the delights of an area renowned for its **elephants**. Forest Department accommodation at Bandipur (see below) and Nagarhole (see opposite) must be booked as far in advance as possible through its offices at Aranya Bhavan, Ashokapuram (℡0821/248 0901), 6km south of the centre of Mysore, on bus #61 from the City stand, or at Aranya Bhavan, 18th Cross, Malleswaram, Bengaluru (℡080/2334 1993).

Bandipur National Park

Situated among the broken foothills of the Western Ghat mountains, **Bandipur National Park** (Rs150 [Rs50], camera Rs20), 80km south of Mysore, covers 880 square kilometres of dry deciduous forest, south of the River Kabini. Created in the 1930s from the local maharaja's hunting lands and expanded in 1941, Bandipur, in spite of its good accommodation and well-maintained metalled jeep tracks, is a disappointment as a wildlife-viewing destination. Glimpses of anything more exciting than a langur or spotted deer are rare outside the core area, which is off limits, while the noisy diesel bus laid on by the Forest Department to transport tourists around the accessible areas of park scares off what little fauna remains.

On the plus side, Bandipur is one of the few reserves in India where you stand a good chance of sighting wild **elephants**, particularly in the wet season (June–Sept), when water and forage are plentiful and the animals evenly scattered. Later in the monsoon, huge herds congregate on the banks of the River Kabini, in the far north of the park, where you can see the remnants of an old stockade used by one particularly zealous nineteenth-century British hunter as an elephant trap. Bandipur also boasts some fine scenery: at **Gopalswamy Betta**, 9km from the park HQ and open to visitors, a high ridge looks north over the Mysore Plateau and its adjoining hills, while to the south, the **Rolling Rocks** afford sweeping views of the craggy, 260-metre-deep **Mysore Ditch**.

Practicalities

The **best time to visit** is during the rainy season (June–Sept); unlike neighbouring parks, Bandipur's roads do not get washed out by the annual deluge, and elephants are more numerous at this time. By November/December, however, most of the larger animals have migrated across the state border into Mudumalai, where water is more plentiful in the dry season. **Avoid weekends**, as the park attracts busloads of noisy day-trippers.

Getting to Bandipur by bus is easy; all the regular KSRTC services to Ooty from Mysore's Central Bus Stand (12 daily; 2hr 30min) pass through the reserve (the last one back to Mysore leaves at 5pm), stopping outside the Forest Department's reception centre (daily 9am–4.30pm). If you miss the last bus from Mysore you can change at Gundulapet, 18km away, from where you can also take a taxi to the main reception centre (Rs220). You can confirm **accommodation** bookings (see above) within the sanctuary at the Forest Department's reception centre. Comfort varies from beds in large, institutional dorms to the "VIP" *Gajendra Cottages*, which have attached bathrooms and verandas. Upmarket options include *Tusker Trails*, a **resort** run by members of the royal family of Mysore, at Mangala village, 3km from Bandipur (bookable through its office at Hospital Cottage, Bangalore Palace, Bengaluru ℡080/2353 0748, ℻2334 2862; ➐), which has cottages, a swimming pool and a tennis court, and organizes trips into the forest; *Bush Betta*, off the main Mysore highway (booked through Gainnet, Raheja Plaza, Richmond Rd, Bengaluru

KARNATAKA | Around Mysore

22

℡080/2551 2631; ⑤–⑥), offers comfortable cottages and guided tours; and Jungle Lodges & Resorts' *Bandipur Safari Lodge* (℡080/2559 7021, ⓦwww .junglelodges.com; ⑦), where foreigners pay $50 extra per night.

Unless you have your own vehicle or are booked onto an upmarket hotel tour, the only **transport around the park** is the hopeless Forest Department bus, which makes two tours daily (6–9am & 4–6pm; Rs25) and picks up at the reception centre. You may see a deer or two, but nothing more, on the half-hour **elephant ride** (Rs50) around the reception compound. Visitors travelling to Gopalswamy Betta should note that car rental is not available at Bandipur, but at Gundulapet, from where they will try and charge a lot more than the official Rs500. You must exit the park before nightfall.

Nagarhole National Park

Bandipur's northern neighbour, **Nagarhole** ("Snake River") **National Park** (Rs150 [Rs50], camera Rs20), extends 640 square kilometres north from the River Kabini, dammed to form a picturesque artificial lake. During the dry season (Feb–June), this perennial water source attracts large numbers of animals, making it a potentially prime spot for sighting wildlife. The forest here is of the moist deciduous type – thick jungle with a thirty-metre-high canopy – and more impressive than Bandipur's drier scrub.

However, disaster struck Nagarhole in 1992, when friction between local pastoralist "tribals" and the park wardens over grazing rights and poaching erupted into a spate of arson attacks. Thousands of acres of forest were burned to the ground. The trees have grown back in places, but it will be decades before animal numbers completely recover. An added threat to the fragile jungle tracts of the region is a notorious female gang of wood smugglers from Kerala, who have developed a fearsome and almost mythical reputation. Nagarhole is only worth visiting at the height of the dry season, when its muddy riverbanks and grassy swamps, or *hadlus*, offer decent chances of sighting gaur (Indian bison), elephant, *dhole* (wild dog), deer, boar, and even the odd tiger or leopard.

Practicalities

Nagarhole is open year-round, but avoid the monsoons, when floods wash out most of its dirt tracks and leeches make hiking impossible. To get there from Mysore, catch one of the two daily **buses** from the Central stand to **Hunsur** (3hr), 10km from the park's north gate, where you can find transport to the Forest Department's two resthouses (②–⑤). The **resthouses** have to be booked well in advance through the Forest Department offices in Mysore or Bengaluru (see opposite). It is also essential to arrive at the park gates well before dusk, as the road through the reserve to the lodges closes at 6pm, and is prone to "elephant blocks". The Nagarhole **visitor centre** organizes elephant rides (Rs50) and schedules bus tours round the sanctuary (6–9am & 3.30–6pm; Rs50).

Other **accommodation** around Nagarhole includes the highly acclaimed and luxurious *Kabini River Lodge* (book through Jungle Lodges & Resorts; ⓦwww .junglelodges.com, ℡080/2559 7021; ⑦–⑨), approached via the village of Karapura, 3km from the park's south entrance. Set in its own leafy compound on the lakeside, this former maharaja's hunting lodge offers all-in deals that include meals and transport around the park with expert guides. It's impossible to reach by public transport, so you'll need to rent a car to get there and you will also have to book well in advance. Another upmarket option, though not quite in the same league, is the *Jungle Inn* at Veerana Hosahalli (℡08222/252781; ⑥–⑧), which is close to the park entrance and arranges wildlife safaris.

22

KARNATAKA | Around Mysore

Hassan and around

The unprepossessing town of **HASSAN**, 118km northwest of Mysore, is visited in large numbers because of its proximity to the Hoysala temples at **Belur** and **Halebid**, both northwest of the town, and the Jain pilgrimage site of **Sravanabelagola** to the southeast. Some travellers end up staying a couple of nights but with a little forward planning you shouldn't have to linger for long. Set deep in the serene Karnatakan countryside, Belur, Halebid and Sravanabelagola offer considerably more appealing surroundings.

Practicalities

Hassan's **KSRTC Bus Stand** is in the centre of town, at the northern end of Bus Stand Road, which runs south past the post office to **Narsimharaja Circle**. You can change money (but not Thomas Cook traveller's cheques) at Shenoy Tours & Travels (℡08172/269729), near the bus stand. Local auto-rickshaws operate without meters and charge a minimum of Rs10. The friendly and informative **tourist office** is under five minutes' walk from the bus stand at AVK College Road (Mon–Sat 10am–5.30pm; ℡08172/268862). The **railway station**, served by one express and three slow passenger trains a day from Mysore (2–3hr), is a further 2km down the road. There's one night train to Mangalore, with another to be added in 2009.

Accommodation

Wherever you stay, call ahead, as most hotels tend to be full by early evening.

The Ashok Hassan 121 BM Rd. Hassan lodging has reached a new peak in this lush garden compound and whitewashed hotel building. Large rooms with sharp modern furnishings and a top-notch restaurant and bar. ❼–❾

DR Karigowda Residency BM Rd, 1km from railway station ℡08172/264506. Immaculate budget hotel: friendly, comfortable and amazing value. Single occupancy possible; no a/c. ❷

Hoysala Village Resort Belur Rd, 6km northwest of the centre ℡08172/256764, ⓦwww.karnataka tourism.com. Government-run luxury cottages in a quiet rural setting. Multi-cuisine restaurant and a pool which is open to nonresidents (Rs75/hr). ❼–❽

Southern Star BM Rd, 500m from train station ℡08172/251816. New hotel with all mod cons, but better value than most. ❻–❼

Suvarna Regency PB 97, BM Rd ℡08172/264006, ⓦwww.hotelsuvarnaregency .com. Swish place with lots of lights, shiny marble lobby, comfortable rooms and one of the most popular restaurants in town. Great value. ❸–❹

Vaishnavi Lodging Harsha Mahal Rd ℡08172/263885. Hassan's best budget lodge, with big clean rooms (all with phone and TV) and a veg restaurant. Reservations recommended; for a bit of quiet, ask for a room in the back. ❷

Eating

Cocktails BM Rd near *Suvarna Regency*. Tri-level restaurant and bar with breezy rooftop. Skip the grub and enjoy an evening drink in the open air.

Golden Gate *Suvarna Regency*, PB 97, BM Rd. This plush restaurant and bar with a few tables overlooking the garden is one of Hassan's finest. The varied menu is not cheap, with most curries going for around Rs200.

Harsha Mahal below *Harsha Mahal Lodge*, Harsha Mahal Rd. Excellent veg canteen that serves freshly cooked *iddli* and stunningly good *dosas* from 7.30am.

Hotel GRR opposite the bus stand. Broad veg and non-veg range of excellent, spicy Andhra "mini-meals" served on banana leaves. Tasty ice creams, too, all for paise.

Upper Deck Harsha Mahal Rd. Small, modern terrace café offers coffees, ice creams and tasty *chaats* on first-floor balcony. Popular with students.

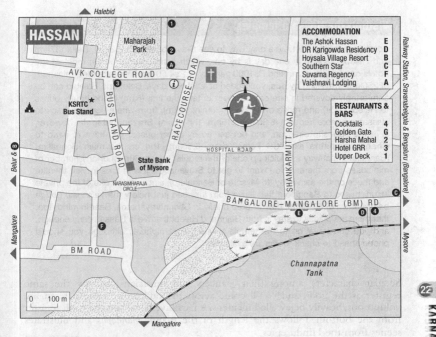

Halebid

Now little more than a scruffy hamlet of brick houses and chai stalls, **HALEBID**, 32km northwest of Hassan, was once the capital of the powerful Hoysala dynasty, who held sway over south Karnataka from the eleventh until the early fourteenth centuries. Once known as **Dora Samudra**, the city was renamed *Hale-bidu*, or "Dead City", in 1311 when Delhi sultanate forces under the command of Ala-ud-din-Khalji swept through and reduced it to rubble. Despite the sacking, several large Hoysala temples (see box, p.1283) survive, two of which, the **Hoysaleshvara** and **Kedareshvara**, are superb, covered in exquisite carvings. A small **archeological museum** (daily except Fri 10am–5pm), next to the Hoysaleshvara temple, houses a collection of Hoysala art and other finds from the area.

The Hoysaleshvara temple

The **Hoysaleshvara** temple (daily sunrise to sunset; free) was started in 1141, and after some forty years of work remained incomplete; this possibly accounts for the absence here of the type of towers that feature at Somnathpur, for example. It is no longer known which deities were originally worshipped, though the double shrine is thought to have been devoted at one time to Shiva and his consort. In any event, both shrines contain *shivalinga* and are adjoined by two linked, partly enclosed *mandapa* hallways in which stand Nandi bulls.

Hoysaleshvara also features many Vaishnavite images. The **sculptures**, which have a fluid quality lacking in the earlier work at Belur (see p.1283), include Brahma aboard his goose vehicle Hamsa, Krishna holding up Mount Govardhana, another where he plays the flute, and Vishnu (Trivikrama) bestriding the world in three steps. One of the most remarkable images is of the demon king **Ravana** shaking Shiva's mountain abode, Mount Kailash, populated by numerous animals and figures with Shiva and Parvati seated atop.

Visiting the Hoysala temples

Apart from taking a tour, the only way to see Sravanabelagola (53km), Belur (37km) and Halebid (30km) in one day is **by car**, which some visitors share; most of the hotels can fix this up (around Rs1000 per day or Rs4.50 per kilometre for a minimum of 250km). Travelling **by bus**, you'll need at least two days. Belur and Halebid can be comfortably covered in one day; it's best to take the first (6am) of the hourly buses to Halebid (1hr) and move on to Belur (30min; 16km), from where services back to Hassan are more frequent (6.30am–6.15pm; 1hr 10min). **Sravanabelagola**, however, is in the opposite direction, and not served by direct buses; you have to head to **Channarayapatna** aka "CR Patna" (from 6.30am; 1hr) on the main Bengaluru (Bangalore) highway and pick up one of the regular buses (30min) or any number of minibuses from there. If you want to get to Sravanabelagola in time to visit the site and move on the same day (to Mysore or Bengaluru), aim to catch one of the private luxury buses to Bangalore that leave from the road just below the *Vaishnavi Lodge* before dawn (5.30–6am); they all stop briefly in Channarayapatna. Bear in mind, too, that there are places to stay in both Belur and Halebid; arrive in Hassan early enough, and you can travel on to the temple towns before nightfall, although you should phone ahead to check rooms are available.

Secular characters, among them dancers and musicians, occupy the same register as the gods, and you'll come across the odd erotic tableau featuring voluptuous, heavily bejewelled maidens. A narrative frieze, on the sixth register from the bottom, follows the length of the Nandi *mandapas* and illustrates scenes from the Hindu epics.

The Jain bastis and the Kedareshvara temple

Some 600m south of the Hoysaleshvara, a group of Jain *bastis* (temples) stand virtually unadorned; the only sculptural decoration consists of ceiling friezes inside the *mandapas* and elephants at the entrance steps, where there's an impressive donatory plaque. The thirteenth-century temple of **Adi Parshwanatha** is dedicated to the twenty-third *tirthankara*, Parshvanath, while the newer **Vijayanatha** built in the sixteenth century is dedicated to the sixteenth *tirthankara*, Shantinath. The *chowkidar* at the Parshwanatha temple will demonstrate various tricks made possible by the carved pillars' highly polished surfaces; some are so finely turned they sound metallic when struck.

To the east, there's a smaller Shiva temple, Kedareshvara (1217–21), also built on a stellate plan. Unfortunately, due to instability, it's not possible to go inside. Many fine images decorate the exterior, including an unusual stone Krishna dancing on the serpent demon Kaliya.

Practicalities

Frequent **buses** run between Halebid (the last at 8.30pm) and Hassan, and to Belur (the last at 8pm). The private **minibuses** that leave from the crossroads outside the Hoysaleshvara temple take a lot longer and only leave when crammed to bursting.

The monuments lie within easy walking distance of each other, but if you fancy exploring the surrounding countryside, rent a **bicycle** (Rs3/hr) from the stalls by the bus stand. The road running south past the temples leads through some beautiful scenery, with possible side-hikes to hilltop shrines, while the road to Belur (16km) makes for another pleasant bicycle ride. **Accommodation** in the village is limited to the KSTDC *Mayura Shantala* (☎08177/773224; ❷) opposite the main temple and set in a small garden by the road. It offers two comfortable doubles with verandas, plus a four-bedded room – all should be booked in advance. This is also the only place to eat after 6pm, when the chai stalls at the crossroads have shut up.

Belur

BELUR, 37km northwest of Hassan, on the banks of the Yagachi, was the Hoysala capital prior to Halebid, during the eleventh and twelfth centuries. Still active, the **Chennakeshava temple** (daily 7.30am–8.30pm; free) is a fine and early example of the singular Hoysala style, built by King Vishnuvardhana in 1117 to celebrate his conversion from Jainism, victory over Chola forces at Talakad and his independence from the Chalukyas. Today, its grey-stone *gopura*, or gateway tower, soars above a small, bustling market town – a popular pilgrimage site from October to December, when busloads of Ayappan devotees stream through en route to Sabarimala (see p.1244). The **Car festival** held around March or April takes place over twelve days and has a pastoral feel, attracting farmers from the surrounding countryside who conduct a bullock cart procession through the streets to the temple. If you have time to linger, Belur, with marginally better facilities than those found at Halebid, is a far better place to base yourself in order to explore the Hoysala region.

Chennakeshava stands in a huge walled courtyard, surrounded by smaller shrines and columned *mandapa* hallways. Lacking any form of superstructure, it appears to have a flat roof. If it ever had a tower, it would have disappeared by the Vijayanagar (sixteenth-century) period. Both the sanctuary and *mandapa* are raised on the usual plinth (*jagati*). Double flights of steps, flanked by minor towered shrines, afford entry to the *mandapa* on three sides; this hallway was originally open, but in the 1200s, pierced stone screens, carved with geometric

---

Hoysala temples

The **Hoysala** dynasty, who ruled southwestern Karnataka between the eleventh and thirteenth centuries, built a series of distinctive temples centred primarily at three sites: **Belur** and **Halebid**, close to modern Hassan, and **Somnathpur**, near Mysore. At first sight, and from a distance, the buildings, all based on a star-shaped plan, appear to be modest structures, compact and even squat. On closer inspection, however, their profusion of fabulously detailed and sensuous sculpture, covering every inch of the exterior, is astonishing. Detractors are prone to class Hoysala art as decadent and overly fussy, but anyone with an eye for craftsmanship is likely to marvel at these jewels of Karnatakan art.

The intricacy of the carvings was made possible by the material used in construction: a soft steatite **soapstone** that on oxidization hardens to a glassy, highly polished surface. The level of detail, similar to that seen in sandalwood and ivory-work, became increasingly freer and more fluid as the style developed, and reached its highest point at Somnathpur. Beautiful bracket figures, often delicate portrayals of voluptuous female subjects, were placed under the eaves, fixed by pegs top and bottom. A later addition (except possibly in the Somnathpur temple), these serve no structural function.

Another technique more usually associated with wood is the unusual treatment of the massive stone **pillars**: lathe-turned, they resemble those of the wooden temples of Kerala. They were probably turned on a horizontal plane, pinned at each end, and rotated with the use of a rope. It may be no coincidence that, to this day, wood turning is still a local speciality. Only the central shaft of each pillar seems to have been turned; in the base and capitals, a less precise, presumably handworked imitation of turning is evident.

designs and scenes from the *Puranas*, were inserted between the lathe-turned pillars. The main shrine opens four times a day for worship (8.30–10am, 11am–1pm, 2.30–5pm & 6.30–8.30pm) and it's worth considering using one of the guides (Rs40) who offer their services at the gates to explain the intricacies of the carvings. The quantity of **sculptural decoration**, if less mature than in later Hoysala temples, is staggering.

Within the same enclosure, the **Kappe Channigaraya temple** has some finely carved niche images and a depiction of Narasimha (Vishnu as man-lion) killing the demon Hiranyakashipu. Further west, fine sculptures in the smaller **Viranarayana** shrine include a scene from the Mahabharata of Bhima killing the demon Bhaga.

Practicalities

Buses from Hassan and Halebid arrive at the small bus stand in the middle of town, ten minutes' walk along the main street from the temple. Some through buses do not bother to pull into the bus stand, but stop on the highway next to it. There are auto-rickshaws available, but a good way to explore the area, including Halebid, is to rent a **bicycle** (Rs3/hr) from one of the stalls around the bus stand. The **tourist office** (Mon–Sat 10am–5pm) is located within the KSTDC *Mayuri Velapuri* compound near the temple. It has all the local bus times, and sometimes the tourist officer is available as a guide.

The KSTDC *Mayuri Velapuri* (℡08177/722209; ❷) is the best **place to stay**, with immaculately clean and airy rooms in its new block, or dingy ones in the older wing. The two dorms are rarely occupied (Rs35 per bed), other than between March and May, when the hotel tends to be block-booked by pilgrims. Down the road, the *Annapurna* (℡08177/722039; ❷) has adequate if dull rooms over an uninspiring restaurant; the *Swagath Tourist Home* (℡08177/722159; ❶), further up the road towards the temple, is extremely basic, boxed in and does not have hot water, but is fine as a fall-back. Of the hotels around the bus stand, the *Vishnu Lodge* (℡0817/722263; ❷–❸) above a restaurant and sweet shop, is the best bet, with spacious rooms (some with TV) but tiny attached bathrooms where hot water is only available in the mornings.

The most salubrious **place to eat** is at *Mayuri Velapuri*'s restaurant, but the menu is limited. There are several other options, many located beneath hotels strung along the main road, in addition to the veg *dhabas* by the temple, and the *Indian Coffee House* on the main road by the temple gates.

Sravanabelagola

The sacred Jain site of **SRAVANABELAGOLA**, 49km southeast of Hassan and 93km north of Mysore, consists of two hills and a large tank. On one of the hills, Indragiri (also known as Vindhyagiri), stands an extraordinary eighteen-metre-high monolithic statue of a naked male figure, **Gomateshvara**. Said to be the largest freestanding sculpture in India, this tenth-century colossus, visible for miles around, makes Sravanabelagola a key pilgrimage centre, though surprisingly few Western travellers find their way out here. Spend a night or two in the village, however, and you can climb Indragiri Hill before dawn to enjoy the serene spectacle of the sun rising over the sugar cane fields and outcrops of lumpy granite that litter the surrounding plains – an unforgettable sight.

Sravanabelagola is linked in tradition with the Mauryan emperor Chandragupta, who is said to have starved himself to death on the second hill in around 300 BC, in accordance with a Jain practice. The hill was renamed Chandragiri, marking the arrival of Jainism in southern India. At the same time, a controversy regarding the doctrines of Mahavira, the last of the 24 Jain **tirthankaras** (literally "crossing-makers", who assist the aspirant to cross the "ocean of rebirth"), split Jainism into two separate branches – *svetambara*, "white-clad" Jains, are more common in north India, while *digambara*, "sky-clad", are usually associated with the south. Truly ascetic *digambara* devotees go naked, though few do so away from sacred sites.

The monuments at Sravanabelagola probably date from no earlier than the tenth century, when a General Chamundaraya is said to have visited Chandragiri in search of a Mauryan statue of Gomateshvara. Failing to find it, he decided to have one made. From the top of Chandragiri he fired an arrow across to Indragiri Hill; where the arrow landed he had a new Gomateshvara sculpted from a single rock.

Indragiri Hill

Gomateshvara is approached from the tank between the two hills by 620 steps, cut into the granite of **Indragiri Hill**, which pass numerous rock inscriptions on the way up to a walled enclosure. Shoes must be deposited at the stall to the left of the steps, and you can leave bags at the site office nearby. Take plenty of water especially on a hot day, as there is none available on the hill. Entered through a small wagon-vaulted *gopura*, the **temple** is entirely dominated by the towering figure of Gomateshvara. With elongated arms and exaggeratedly wide shoulders, his proportions are decidedly non-naturalistic. The sensuously smooth surface of the white granite "trap" rock is finely carved: particularly the hands, hair and serene face. As in legend, ant-hills and snakes sit at his feet and creepers appear to grow on his limbs.

Bhandari Basti and monastery (math)

The road east from the foot of the steps at Chandragiri leads to two interesting Jain buildings in town. To the right, the Bhandari **Basti** (1159), housing a shrine with images of the 24 *tirthankaras*, was built by Hullamaya, treasurer of the Hoysala raja Narasimha. Two *mandapa* hallways, where naked *digambara* Jains may sometimes be seen discoursing with devotees clad in white, lead to the shrine at the back.

At the end of the street, the *math* (monastery) was the residence of Sravanabelagola's senior *acharya*, or guru. Thirty male and female monks, who also "go wandering in every direction", are attached to the *math*; normally a member of staff will be happy to show visitors around. Among the rare palm-leaf manuscripts in the library, some more than a millennium old, are works on mathematics and geography, and the *Mahapurana*, hagiographies of the *tirthankaras*. Next door, a covered walled courtyard is edged by a high platform on three sides, on which a chair is placed for the *acharya*. A collection of tenth-century bronze *tirthankara* images is housed here, and vibrant murals detail the various lives of Parshvanath. The hills where the *tirthankaras* stood to gain *moksha* are represented in a model, somewhat resembling a jelly mould, with tacked-on footprints.

Chandragiri Hill

Leaving your shoes with the keeper at the bottom, take the rock-cut steps to the top of the smaller **Chandragiri Hill**. Miraculously, the sound of radios and rickshaws down below soon disappears. Fine views stretch south to Indragiri and, from the north on the far side, across to a river, paddy and sugar cane fields, palms and the village of **Jinanathapura**, where there's another ornate Hoysala temple, the Shantishvara *basti*.

Rather than a single large shrine, as at Indragiri, Chandragiri holds a group of *bastis* in late Chalukya Dravida style, within a walled enclosure. Caretakers will take you around and open up the closed shrines. Save for pilasters and elaborate parapets, all the temples have plain exteriors. Named after its patron, the tenth-century **Chamundaraya** is the largest of the group, dedicated to Parshvanath. Inside the **Chandragupta** (twelfth century), superb carved panels in a small shrine tell the story of Chandragupta and his teacher Bhadrabahu. Traces of painted geometric designs survive and the pillars feature detailed carving. Elsewhere in the enclosure stands a 24-metre-high *manastambha*, "pillar of fame", decorated with images of spirits, *yakshis* and a *yaksha*. No fewer than 576 inscriptions dating from the sixth to the nineteenth centuries are dotted around the site, on pillars and on the rock itself.

Practicalities

Sravanabelagola, along with Belur and Halebid, features on **tours** from Bengaluru and Mysore (see p.1259 & p.1270). However, if you want to look around at a civilized pace, it's best to come independently. The **tourist office** (Mon–Sat 10am–5.30pm; ☎08176/657254) at the bottom of the stairs has little to offer and the management committee office next door only serves to collect donations and hand out tickets for the *dolis*.

There are plenty of **dharamshalas** to choose from if you want to stay, managed by the temple authorities and offering simple, scrupulously clean rooms, many with their own bathrooms and sitouts, ranged around gardens and courtyards, and most costing under Rs150 per night. The 24-hour accommodation office (☎08176/657258), located inside the *SP Guest House* next to the bus stand (look for the clock tower), will allocate you a room. *Hotel Raghu*, opposite the main tank, houses the best of the many small local **restaurants**.

Crisscrossed by winding back roads, the idyllic (and mostly flat) countryside around Sravanabelagola is perfect cycling terrain. **Bicycles** are available for rent (Rs3/hr) at Saleem Cycle Mart, on Masjid Road, opposite the northeast corner of the tank. If you're returning to Hassan, you'll have to head to **Channaraya-patna** aka "CR Patna" by bus or in one of the shared vans that regularly ply the route and depart only when bursting; change at CR Patna for a bus to Hassan or Mysore.

Kodagu (Coorg)

The hill region of **Kodagu**, formerly known as **Coorg**, lies 100km west of Mysore in the Western Ghats, its eastern fringes merging with the Mysore Plateau. Rugged mountain terrain interspersed with cardamom jungle, coffee plantations and swathes of lush rice paddy, it's one of south India's most beautiful areas. Little has changed since Dervla Murphy spent a few months here with her daughter in the 1970s (the subject of her classic travelogue, *On a Shoestring to Coorg*) and was entranced by the landscape and people, whose customs, language and appearance set them apart from their neighbours.

If you plan to cross the Ghats between Mysore and the coast, the route through Kodagu is definitely worth considering. Some coffee-plantation owners open their doors to visitors – to find out more contact the Codagu Planters Association, Mysore Road, Madikeri (☎08272/229873). A good time to visit is during the festival season in early December or during the **Blossom Showers** around March and April when the coffee plants bloom with white flowers – some people, however, find the strong scent overpowering.

Kodagu is relatively undeveloped, and "sights" are few, but the countryside is idyllic and the climate refreshingly cool, even in summer. Many visitors **trek** through the unspoilt forest tracts and ridges that fringe the district. On the eastern borders of Kodagu around Kushalnagar, large **Tibetan settlements** have transformed a once barren countryside into fertile farmland dotted with busy monasteries, some housing thousands of monks.

Some history

The first concrete evidence of the kingdom dates from the eighth century, when it prospered from the salt trade passing between the coast and the cities on the Deccan Plateau. Under the Hindu **Haleri rajas**, the state repulsed invasions by its more powerful neighbours, including Haider Ali and his son Tipu Sultan, the famous Tiger of Mysore (see p.1256). A combination of hilly terrain, absence of roads (a deliberate policy on the part of defence-conscious Kodagu kings) and the tenacity of its highly trained army ensured Kodagu was the only Indian kingdom never to be conquered.

In 1834, however, after ministers appealed to the British to help depose their despotic king, Vira Rajah, Kodagu became a princely state with nominal independence, which it retained until the creation of Karnataka in 1956. **Coffee** was introduced during the Raj and, despite plummeting prices on the international market, this continues to be the linchpin of the local economy, along with pepper and cardamom. Although Kodagu is Karnataka's wealthiest region, and provides the highest tax revenue, it does not reap the rewards – 53 percent of villages are without electricity – and this, coupled with the distinct identity and fiercely independent nature of the Kodavas, has given rise to an autonomy movement known as **Kodagu Rajya Mukti Morcha**. Methods used by the KRMM include cultural programmes and occasional strikes; violence is very rare.

Madikeri (Mercara) and around

Nestling beside a curved stretch of craggy hills, **MADIKERI** (**Mercara**), capital of Kodagu, undulates around 1300m up in the Western Ghats, roughly midway between Mysore and the coastal city of Mangalore. The gradually increasing number of foreigners who travel up here find it a pleasant enough town, with red-tiled buildings and undulating roads that converge on a bustling bazaar, but most move onto home- and plantation stays in the verdant Coorg countryside within a couple of days.

The **Omkareshwara Shiva** temple, built in 1820, features an unusual combination of red-tiled roofs, Keralan Hindu architecture, Gothic elements and Islamic-influenced domes. The fort and palace, worked over by Tipu Sultan in 1781 and rebuilt in the nineteenth century, now serve as offices and a prison. Within the complex, **St Mark's Church** holds a small **museum** of British memorabilia, Jain, Hindu and village deity figures and weapons (Tues–Sun 9am–5pm, except second Sat; free). Also worth a look are the huge square **tombs of the rajas** which, with their Islamic-style gilded domes and minarets, dominate the town's skyline.

The early eighteenth-century Kodagu king was no dummy – he chose one of the best sunset vantage points in south India for **Raja's Seat** (dawn to 8pm; Rs2). On the western edge of town near *Hotel Valley View*, this is a popular grassy park and garden that fills up just before dusk. At 7pm a kitschy water and light show set to Bollywood tunes dazzles the locals.

Madikeri is the centre of the lucrative coffee trade, and although auto-rickshaws will take you there and back for around Rs185, a walk to **Abbi Falls** (8km) is a good introduction to coffee-growing country. The pleasant road, devoid of buses, winds through the hill country past plantations and makes for

Theories abound as to the origins of the **Kodavas**, or **Coorgis**, who today comprise less than one sixth of the hill region's population. Fair-skinned and with their own language and customs, they are thought to have migrated to southern India from Kurdistan, Kashmir or even Greece, though no one knows exactly why or when. One popular belief holds that this staunchly martial people, who since Independence have produced some of India's leading military brains, are descended from Roman mercenaries who fled here following the collapse of the Pandyan dynasty in the eighth century; some even claim connections with Alexander the Great's invading army. Whatever their origins, the Kodavas have managed to retain a distinct identity apart from the freed plantation slaves, Moplah Muslim traders and other immigrants who have settled here. More akin to Tamil than Kannada, their language is Dravidian, yet their religious practices, based on ancestor veneration and worship of nature spirits and the river, differ markedly from those of mainstream Hinduism. Land tenure in Kodagu is also quite distinctive: women have a right to inheritance and ownership and are also allowed to remarry.

Spiritual and social life for traditional Kodavas revolves around the **Ain Mane**, or ancestral homestead. Built on raised platforms to overlook the family land, these large, detached houses, with their beautiful carved wood doors and beaten-earth floors, generally have four wings and courtyards to accommodate various branches of the extended family, as well as shrine rooms, or **Karona Kalas**, dedicated to the clan's most important forebears. Key religious rituals and rites of passage are always conducted in the *ain mane*, rather than the local temple. However, you could easily travel through Kodagu without ever seeing one, as they are invariably away from roads, shrouded in thick forest.

a good day's outing. At the litter-strewn car park at the end of the road, a gate leads through a private coffee plantation, sprinkled with cardamom sprays and pepper vines, to the bottom of the large stepped falls that are most impressive during and straight after the monsoons.

Practicalities

You can only reach Madikeri by road, but it's a scenic three-hour **bus** ride via **Kushalnagar** from **Mysore**, 120km southeast (unless you mistakenly get on one of the few buses that goes via Siddapura, which take more than an hour longer). Regular services, including deluxe buses, also connect Madikeri with **Mangalore** (4hr), 135km northwest across the Ghats, and Hassan (4 daily; 4hr). The KSTRC state **bus stand** is at the bottom of town, below the main bazaar; private buses from villages around the region pull into a parking lot at the end of the main street.

The small local **tourist office** (Mon–Sat 10.30am–5.30pm, closed second Sat of month; ☎08272/228580) stands five minutes' walk along the Mysore road below Thimaya Circle, next to the PWD *Travellers' Bungalow*, and can suggest itineraries, but is otherwise quite limited. If you're thinking of **trekking** in Kodagu, contact Ganesh Aiyanna at the *Hotel Cauvery* (see opposite), who is very helpful and organizes itineraries and trips for various budgets. Coorg Travels next to *Rajdarshan Lodge* (☎08272/225817) is also flexible and friendly and will help put together a tour. For information on Kodagu's **forests** and forest bungalows contact the Conservator of Forests, Deputy Commissioner's Office at the fort (☎08272/225708). Dhanasri Associates (☎09448 184829), on Indira Gandhi Chowk, can help with trekking, homestay, bike rental, and general tourist info. If you don't make it out to the plantations, *Athithi Coffee*

Works, just off Indira Gandhi Chowk, offers fresh Coorg coffee (Rs240–170/kg) and other local delicacies.

Accommodation and eating

Accommodation in Madikeri is rarely hard to come by, except occasionally in the budget range, most of which is concentrated around the bazaar and bus stand. The nicer hotels generally have **restaurants** and some have bars. The *Choice Hotel* on School Road is a restaurant only, serving breakfast items and a decent range of veg and non-veg dishes. *Tao*, up near the fort, is an authentic Chinese place, while the adjacent *Sri Ambica* serves wholesome veg snacks and meals.

Anchorage Guest House Kohinoor Rd ☎08272/228939. On a quiet side-street, close to the bus stand; the no-frills rooms are all attached. ❷

Cauvery School Rd ☎08272/225492. Below the private bus stand, this large and friendly place is almost hidden behind their excellent *Capitol* restaurant, where local delicacy *pondhi* (pork) curry is served good and spicy. ❸

Chitra School Rd ☎08272/225372. Best value in town, with neat well-kept rooms, the slightly pricier ones with cable TV. Excellent non-veg restaurant-cum-bar downstairs. ❷

Coorg International Convent Rd ☎08272/228071. 10min by rickshaw west of the centre, this is one of the few upmarket options. It's a large but slightly characterless hotel with comfortable Western-style rooms, a multi-cuisine restaurant, exchange facilities, and shops. ❽–❾

East End General Thimaya Rd (aka Mysore Rd) ☎08272/229996. A large, plain, tiled-roof colonial bungalow turned into a hotel with a hint of character, but more renowned for its popular bar and restaurant ❹

KSTDC Hotel Mayura Valley View ☎08272/228387. Well away from the main road, past Raja's Seat, the rooms here are enormous and many have excellent views. The restaurant serves booze and has an open terrace with epic views. Hail a rickshaw to get there, as it's a stiff 20min uphill walk from the bus stand. ❸

Mojo Rainforest Retreat 13km north of Madikeri, near Galibeedu village ☎08272/265636, ✉anugoel@bsnl.in. Informed hosts Sujata and Annu have carved a thrumming idyll out of their little wedge of Kodagu plantation, with excellent organic meals (included) and warmly furnished cottages and tents set amidst lush, bucolic rainforest. All profits go to their NGO, which fosters environmental awareness and sustainable agriculture in the region. ❺–❼

The School Estate 15 km from Madikeri ☎082/74258358. Surrounded by coffee, cardamom and vanilla plantations, *School Estate* is an absolute charmer, set amidst the verdant greenery of Coorg. Owner Rani Aiyapa is an excellent chef, and leads weekly Coorg cooking classes. The rooms are enormous, with rosewood beds and a number of homely touches that lend a refined English bed-and-breakfast feel, and the grounds are beautifully landscaped. ❽–❾

Mangalore

Many visitors only come to **MANGALORE** on their way somewhere else. As well as being fairly close to the Kodagu (Coorg) hill region, it's also a stopping-off point between Goa and Kerala, and is the nearest coastal town to the Hoysala and Jain monuments near Hassan, 172km east.

Mangalore was one of the most famous ports of south India. It was already well-known overseas in the sixth century, as a major source of pepper, and the fourteenth-century Muslim writer Ibn Batuta noted its trade in pepper and ginger and the presence of merchants from Persia and the Yemen. In the mid-1400s, the Persian ambassador Abdu'r-Razzaq saw Mangalore as the "frontier town" of the Vijayanagar empire (see p.1305) – which was why the Portuguese captured it in 1529. Nowadays, the modern port, 10km north of the city proper, is principally known for the processing and export of coffee and cocoa (much of which comes from Kodagu), and cashew nuts (from Kerala). It is also a centre for the production of *beedi* cigarettes.

Arrival, information and city transport

Mangalore's busy KSRTC **Bus Stand** (known locally as the "Lal Bagh" Bus Stand) is 2km north of the town centre, Hampankatta, at the bottom of Kadri Hill. **Private buses** arrive at the much more central stand near the Town Hall. **Bajpe airport**, 22km north of the city (bus #22 or #47A, Indian Airlines city bus or taxis for Rs300–350), is served by both Indian Airlines/Alliance and Jet Airways from Mumbai and Bengaluru (Bangalore), and Air Deccan from the latter only. The **railway station**, on the south side of the city centre, sees daily services from cities all over India.

Hampankatta, close to the facilities of KS Rao Road, acts as the traffic hub of the city from where you can catch **city buses** to most local destinations and **auto-rickshaws**, although their drivers prefer not to use their meters. The **tourist office** (Mon–Sat 10am–5.30pm, closed second Sat; ☏0824/244 2926) on the ground floor of the *Hotel Indraprashta* on Lighthouse Road is helpful for general information and some bus times, but carries no information on trains, for which you will need to go to the railway station.

You can **change money** at Trade Wings, Lighthouse Road (Mon–Sat 9.30am–5.30pm; ☏0824/242 6225), who cash traveller's cheques, and at Wall Street Interchange, 1st Floor, Utility Royal Towers, KS Rao Rd (same hours; ☏0824/242 1717). The State Bank of India (Mon–Fri 10.30am–2.30pm, Sat 10.30am–12.30pm), near the Town Hall on Hamilton Circle, is somewhat slower. There's a CorpBank ATM opposite the *Mangalore International* hotel on KS Rao Road.

Mangalore's **GPO** (Mon–Sat 10am–7pm, Sun 10.30am–1.30pm) is 500m south of Shetty Circle. For **Internet** try the friendly and popular Kohinoor Computer Zone, Plaza Towers, Lighthouse Rd (Rs25/hr), down the road from the tourist office, or Cyber Zoom, 1st Floor, Utility Royal Towers, KS Rao Road (20/hr).

Accommodation

The main area for hotels, **KS Rao Road**, runs south from the bus stand and has an ample choice to suit most pockets. You can also stay out of town by the beach in **Ullal**, 10km south of the city.

Adarsh Lodge Market Rd ☏0824/244 0878. Decent value, especially for singles, with compact but clean rooms, all attached. ②

Hotel Manjuran Old Port Rd ☏0824/242 0420, Ⓕ242 0585. Modern business hotel; all rooms are a/c and some have a sea view. Travel desk, exchange, pool, bar, two classy restaurants and 24hr coffee shop. ⑥–⑨

Navaratna Palace KS Rao Rd ☏0824/244 1104, Ⓔ nish77772000@yahoo.com. Preferable to its adjacent older sister *Navaratna*, with better rooms (some a/c) for little extra cost. Also two good a/c restaurants: *Heera Panna* and *Palimar* (pure veg). ③–⑤

Poonja International KS Rao Rd ☏0824/244 0171, Ⓦwww.hotelpoonjainternational.com. Smart mostly a/c high-rise with all facilities and stunning views from the upper floors. south Indian buffet breakfast included. ④–⑧

Summer Sands Beach Resort Chota Mangalore, Ullal ☏0824/246 7690, Ⓦwww.summer-sands.com. Spacious rooms and cottages (some a/c) near the beach, originally built as a campus for expats, with a pool and a bar-restaurant serving local specialities, Indian and Chinese food. Foreign exchange for guests. Take bus #44A from town. ⑤–⑨

Vishwa Bhavan KS Rao Rd ☏0824/244 0822. Cheap, plain rooms, some with attached baths, arranged around a courtyard close to all amenities. Best of the real cheapies. ①

Woodside KS Rao Rd ☏0824/244 0296. Old-fashioned hotel offering a range of rooms (the economy doubles are the best deal), but "no accommodation for servants". Some a/c. ③–⑤

22

KARNATAKA | Mangalore

MANGALORE

ACCOMMODATION

Adarsh Lodge	E
Manjuran	F
Navaratna Palace	A
Poonja International	D
Summer Sands Beach Resort	G
Vishwa Bhavan	C
Woodside	B

RESTAURANTS

Ganesh Prasad	2
Naivedyam	3
Palkhi	1
Xanadu	B

KONCHADY ROAD

★
KSRTC
(Lal Bagh)
Bus Stand

Manjunatha
Temple ▲

MG ROAD

MANNAGUDDA RD

PINTO'S LANE

LC PAIS ROAD

BHOJA RAO LANE

BS ROAD

KUDUMAL ROAD

DONGARKERI ROAD

St Aloysius
College
Chapel

Tagore
Park

MERCARA HILL ROAD

VT ROAD

CAR STREET

GT ROAD

KS RAO ROAD

HILL ROAD

Ⓐ
Ⓑ
ⓘ
LIGHTHOUSE

②
③
ATM ★
Ⓒ
Ⓔ Ⓓ
Taxi
Stand

①
KMC MERCARA TRUNK RD

KALPANE ROAD

MUKTA PRANA TEMPLE ROAD

FALNIR ROAD

BALMATTA NEW RD

✝
Milagres
Church

BIBI ALABIBI ROAD

★
Private
Bus Stand

Town
Hall

BRITTO LANE

NANDIGUDDA ROAD

KAPRIGUDDA ROAD

BISHOP VICTOR ROAD

MULLER'S ROAD

DR UP MALLYA ROAD

STATION ROAD

Railway
Station

0　　　500 m

✉

22

KARNATAKA | Mangalore

The city and beaches

Mangalore's strong Christian influence can be traced back to the arrival further south of St Thomas (see p.1373). Some 1400 years later, in 1526, the Portuguese founded one of the earliest churches on the coast. Today's **Rosario Cathedral**, however, with a dome based on St Peter's in Rome, dates only from 1910. Closer to the centre, on Lighthouse Road, fine restored fresco, tempera and oil murals by an Italian artist, Antonio Moscheni, adorn the Romanesque-style **St Aloysius College Chapel**, built in 1885

At the foot of Kadri Hill, 3km north of the centre, Mangalore's tenth-century **Manjunatha temple** is an important centre of the Shaivite and tantric **Natha–Pantha cult**. Thought to be an outgrowth of Vajrayana Buddhism, the cult is a divergent species of Hinduism, similar to certain cults in Nepal. Enshrined in the sanctuary are a number of superb **bronzes,** including a 1.5-metre-high seated Lokeshvara (Matsyendranatha), made in

958 AD and considered the finest southern bronze outside Tamil Nadu. To see it close up, visit at *darshan* times (6am–1pm & 4–8pm), although the bronzes can be glimpsed through the wooden slats on the side of the sanctuary. If possible, time your visit to coincide with *mahapooja* (8am, noon & 8pm) when the priests give a fire blessing to the accompaniment of raucous music. Opposite the east entrance, steps lead via a laterite path to a curious group of minor shrines. Beyond this complex stands the **Shri Yogishwar Math**, a hermitage of tantric sadhus set round two courtyards.

If you're looking to escape the city for a few hours, head out to the village of **ULLAL**, 10km south, whose long sandy **beach**, backed by wispy fir trees, stretches for miles in both directions. It's a deservedly popular place for a stroll, particularly in the evening when Mangaloreans come out to watch the sunset, but a strong undertow makes swimming difficult, and at times unsafe. You're better off using the pool at the excellent *Summer Sands Beach Resort* (see p.1290), immediately behind the beach (Rs100 for nonresidents). A further 2km past the *Summer Sands*, a banyan-lined road leads to the Shiva temple of **Someshwar**, built in Keralan style, overlooking a rocky promontory, and another popular beach. Towards the centre of Ullal, and around 700m from the main bus stand, is the *dargah* (burial shrine) of **Seyyid Mohammad Shareeful Madani**, a sixteenth-century saint who is said to have come from Medina in Arabia, floating across the sea on a handkerchief. The extraordinary nineteenth-century building with garish onion domes houses the saint's tomb, which is one of the most important Sufi shrines in southern India. Visitors are advised to follow custom and cover their heads and limbs and wash their feet before entering. Local **buses** (#44A) run to Ullal from the junction at the south end of KS Rao Road. As you cross the River Netravathi en route, look out for the brick chimney stacks clustered on the banks at the mouth of the estuary. Using quality clay shipped downriver from the hills, these factories manufacture the famous terracotta red **Mangalorean roof tiles**, which you see all over southern India.

Eating

The best **places to eat** are in the bigger hotels. If you're on a tight budget, try one of the inexpensive café-restaurants opposite the bus stand, or the excellent canteen inside the bus stand itself, which serves great *dosas* and other south Indian snacks. Also recommended for delicious, freshly cooked and inexpensive "meals" is the *Ganesh Prasad*, down the lane alongside the *Vasanth Mahal*. The rooftop *Palkhi* on Mercara Trunk Road is an airy family restaurant with a wide menu. For something a little more sophisticated, head for the a/c *Xanadu*, at the *Woodside Hotel*, also on KS Rao Road, which offers classy non-veg cuisine and alcohol. One of the best of the hotel restaurants, however, is the pure-veg *Naivedyam* at the *Mangalore International*, also on KS Rao Road, which has both a plush a/c and a comfortable non-a/c section.

Moving on from Mangalore

Mangalore is a major crossroads for tourist traffic heading along the Konkan coast between Goa and Kerala, and between Mysore and the coast. The city is also well connected **by air** to **Mumbai**, **Bangalore** and **Chennai**.

Though services to Goa and Mumbai operate from Mangalore, it should be noted that through services do not stop at the city terminus. A better choice of train connections in both directions can be had from **Kankanadi**, around 10km north, or **Kasargode**, an easy bus ride across the Kerala border. From Mangalore itself, the fast #KR2 *Verna Passenger* departs Mangalore at 7.10am, travels north

If you're anywhere between Mangalore and Bhatkal from October to April and come across a crowd gathering around a waterlogged paddy field, pull over and spend a day at the races – Karnatakan style. Few Westerners ever experience it, but the spectacular rural sport of **Kambla**, or **bull racing**, played in the southernmost district of coastal Karnataka (known as Dakshina Kannada), is well worth seeking out.

Two contestants, usually local rice farmers, take part in each race, riding on a wooden plough-board tethered to a pair of prize bullocks. The object is to reach the opposite end of the field first, but points are also awarded for style, and riders gain extra marks – and roars of approval from the crowd – if the muddy spray kicked up from the plough-board splashes the special white banners, or *thoranam*, strung across the course at a height of six to eight metres.

Generally, race days are organized by wealthy landowners on fields specially set aside for the purpose. Villagers flock in from all over the region, as much for the fair, or *shendi*, as the races themselves: men huddle in groups to watch cockfights (*korikatta*), women haggle with bangle sellers and kids roam around sucking sticky *kathambdi goolay*, the local bonbons. It is considered highly prestigious to be able to throw such a party, especially if your bulls win any events or, better still, come away as champions. Known as *yeru* in Kannada, racing bulls are thoroughbreds who are rarely, if ever, put to work. Pampered by their doting owners, they are massaged, oiled and blessed by priests before big events, during which large sums of money are often won and lost.

along the coast and takes 6hr 10min to get to **Margao (Goa)** via Udupi and **Gokarna** (3hr 50min). The *Matsyagandha Express* (#2620), which departs at 2.40pm, is slightly faster to Gokarna (3hr 5min) and Panjim (5hr 45min), and continues to Mumbai (13hr 55min). The service south is good and, if you're travelling to Kerala, far quicker and more relaxing than the bus. Two services leave Mangalore Station every day for **Thiruvananthapuram**, via **Kozhikode**, **Ernakulam/Kochi**, **Kottayam** and **Kollam**. Leaving at the red-eyed time of 4.15am, the Parsuram Express (#6350) is the faster of the two but the Malabar Express (#6330), which leaves at 5.50pm, is convenient as an overnight train to Thiruvananthapuram, arriving there at 9.25am. For those travelling to **Chennai**, the overnight Mangalore–Chennai mail (#6602) departs at 12.30pm and follows the Kerala coast till Shoranur where it turns east to **Palakaad** before journeying on to **Erode** and arriving at Chennai at 6.25am.

The traditional way to travel on to **Goa** was always by **bus**, though that is being usurped by the Konkan Railway. Now only two buses leave the KSRTC Lalbagh stand daily, taking around 10hr 30min to reach Panjim. You can jump off at Chaudi (for Palolem) en route. Tickets should be booked in advance (preferably the day before) at KSRTC Bus Stand's well-organized computer booking hall (daily 7am–8pm) or from the Kadamba office on the main concourse. KSRTC also has a central office (daily 8.30am–8.30pm) on the ground floor of Utility Royal Towers, KS Rao Road. The Goa buses are also good for **Gokarna**; hop off at **Kumta** on the main highway, and catch an onward service from there. The only direct bus to Gokarna leaves Mangalore at 1.30pm. There are plenty of state buses heading north to **Udupi** and south along the coast towards **Kerala**, though it is easier to pick up the more numerous private services to those places.

Mysore and **Bengaluru** (Bangalore) can be reached via train through Hassan, or directly by hourly buses. **Madikeri** is only reachable by road: the hourly buses to Mysore stop there, as do some luxury services to Bengaluru. The best

22

private bus service to Bengaluru is the distinctive yellow luxury coaches of VRL; two buses leave at night (10pm; 7–8hr; Rs250) and tickets are available through Vijayananda Travels, PVS Centenary Building, Kodiyalbail, Kudmulranga Rao Road (℡0824/249 3536). Agents along Falnir Road include Anand Travels (℡0824/244 6737) and Ideal Travels (℡0824/242 4899), which also runs luxury buses to Bengaluru (6–7hr; Rs 240) and two buses to **Ernakulam** (8 & 9pm; 9–10hr; Rs340).

North of Mangalore: coastal Karnataka

Whether you travel the **Karnatakan (Karavali) coast** on the Konkan Railway or along the busy NH-14, southern India's smoothest highway, the route between Goa and Mangalore ranks among the most scenic anywhere in the country. Crossing countless palm- and mangrove-fringed estuaries, the railway line stays fairly flat, while the recently upgraded road, dubbed by the local tourist board as "The Sapphire Route", scales several spurs of the Western Ghats, which here creep to within a stone's throw of the sea, with spellbinding views over long, empty beaches and deep blue bays. Highlights are the pilgrim town of **Udupi**, site of a famous Krishna temple, and **Gokarna**, another important Hindu centre that provides access to exquisite unexploited beaches. A couple of bumpy back-roads wind inland through the mountains to **Jog Falls**, India's biggest waterfall, more often approached from the east.

Udupi

UDUPI (also spelt Udipi), on the west coast, 60km north of Mangalore, is one of south India's holiest Vaishnavite centres. The Hindu saint **Madhva** (1238–1317) was born here, and the **Krishna temple** and *maths* (monasteries) he founded are visited by *lakhs* of pilgrims each year. The largest numbers congregate during the late winter, when the town hosts a series of spectacular **car festivals** and gigantic, bulbous-domed chariots are hauled through the streets around the temple. Even if your visit doesn't coincide with a festival, Udupi is a good place to break the journey along the Karavali coast. Thronging with *pujaris* and pilgrims, its small sacred enclave is wonderfully atmospheric, and you can take a boat from the nearby fishing village of **Malpé Beach** to **St Mary's Island**, the deserted outcrop of hexagonal basalt where Vasco da Gama erected a crucifix prior to his first landing in India.

Arrival and information

Udupi's three **bus stands** are dotted around the amorphous square in the centre of town: the KSRTC and private stands form a practically indistinguishable gathering spot for the numerous services to Mangalore and more long-distance buses to Mysore, Bengaluru (Bangalore), Gokarna, Jog Falls and other towns between northern Kerala and Goa. The City stand is down some steps to the north and handles private services to nearby villages, including Malpé. Udupi's **railway station** is at Indrali on Manipal Road, 3km from the centre, and there are at least five trains in each direction daily. The modest tourist office is near the temple in the Krishna Building, Car Street (Mon–Sat 10am–5.30pm; ℡0820/252 9718). Money can be **exchanged** at the KM Dutt branch of Canara Bank (on the main road just south of the bus stands). **Internet** facilities are available at nearby Netpoint (Rs30/hr), one of several such outlets.

Accommodation

Durga International just west of City Bus Stand ☎0820/253 6977, ✉durga-hotel@yahoo.com. Airy and efficient lodge with a variety of attached rooms, all with TV and some a/c, on the upper storeys of a modern block. ❸—❻

Janardhana south of the KSRTC Bus Stand ☎0820/252 3880, ✆252 3887. Fairly mundane hotel with simple attached rooms of different sizes, most with cable TV. ❷—❹

Hotel Sharada International 2km out of town on the NH-17 ☎0820/252 2910. Mid-price place with a range of rooms from singles to carpeted a/c, as well as veg and non-veg restaurants and a bar. ❸—❻

Sriram Residency opposite Head Post Office ☎0820/253 0761, ✉sriramresidency@indiatimes .com. Plushest place in the centre with a smart lobby, comfortable a/c rooms, two restaurants and a bar. ❸—❼

Sri Vidyasamudra Choultry opposite Krishna temple ☎0820/252 0820. Foreigners are welcome in this ultra-basic lodge for pilgrims. The front rooms overlooking the temple and bathing tank are incredibly atmospheric. ❶

Vyavahar Lodge Kankads Rd ☎0820/252 2568. Basic but friendly and clean lodge between the bus stands and temple. ❷

The Krishna temple and maths

Udupi's **Krishna temple** lies five minutes' walk east of the main street, surrounded by the eight **maths** founded by Madhva in the thirteenth century. Legend has it that the idol enshrined within was discovered by the saint himself after he prevented a shipwreck. The grateful captain of the vessel concerned offered Madhva his precious cargo as a reward, but the holy man asked instead for a block of ballast, which he broke open to expose a perfectly formed image of Krishna. Believed to contain the essence (*sannidhya*) of the god, this deity draws a steady stream of pilgrims, and is the focus of almost constant ritual activity. It is cared for by *acharyas*, or pontiffs, from one or other of the *maths*. They perform pujas (5.30am–8.45pm) that are open to non-Hindus; men are only allowed into the main shrine bare-chested.

At the **Regional Resources Centre for the Performing Arts** in the MGM College, staff can tell you about local festivals and events that are well off the tourist trail; the collection includes film, video and audio archives. The pamphlet *Udupi: an Introduction*, on sale in the stalls around the sacred enclave, is another rich source of background detail on the temple and its complex rituals.

Malpé, St Mary's Island and Thottam

Udupi's weekend picnic spot, **Malpé Beach**, 5km northwest of the centre, is disappointing, marred by a forgotten concrete block that was planned to be a government-run hotel. After wandering around the smelly fish market at the harbour you could haggle to arrange a boat (Rs800) to take you out to **St Mary's Island**, an extraordinary rockface of hexagonal basalt. Vasco da Gama is said to have placed a cross here in the 1400s, prior to his historic landing at Kozhikode in Kerala. From a distance, the sandy beach at **Thottam**, 1km north of Malpé and visible from the island, is tempting; in reality it's an open sewer.

Eating

As you might expect of the **masala dosa**'s birthplace, there are many fine, simple south Indian **restaurants** where you can sample these and other veg favourites, such as *Adarsha*, below the *Janardhena*. For non-veg or alcohol, you'll have to try a posh hotel, such as the *Pisces* at the *Sriram Residency*.

Jog Falls

Hidden in a remote, thickly forested corner of the Western Ghats, **Jog Falls**, 240km northeast of Mangalore, are the highest **waterfalls** in India. These days, however, they are rarely as spectacular as they were before the construction of a large dam upriver, which impedes the flow of the River Sharavati over the sheer red-brown sandstone cliffs. Still, the surrounding scenery is gorgeous, with dense scrub and jungle carpeting sparsely populated, mountainous terrain. The views of the falls from the opposite side of the gorge is also impressive, unless, that is, you come here during the monsoons, when mist and rain clouds envelop the cascades. Another reason not to come here during the wet season is that the extra water, and abundance of leeches at this time, make the excellent **hike** to the floor valley a trial. So if you can, head up here between October and January. The trail starts just below the bus park and winds steeply down to the water, where you can enjoy a refreshing dip. The whole patch opposite the falls has been landscaped for appealing viewing, with its own impressive entrance gate (Rs2 per person; rate varies for vehicles) and attractively designed reception centre.

Practicalities

Getting to and from Jog Falls by **bus** is now a lot easier thanks to the completion of the NH-206 across the Ghats, which has cut the journey time to **Honavar** (6 daily; 2hr 30min), on the Konkan Railway, and on to **Kumta** (4 daily; 3hr), where you can connect to Gokarna. Currently there are two buses daily from the Falls to **Udupi** and on to **Mangalore** (8.30am & 8.30pm; 7hr) and hourly services to **Shimoga**, from where you can change onto buses for Hospet and Hampi. A service to **Panaji** pulls through Jog Falls around midnight. Better connections can be had at nearby Sagar (30km southeast) with buses to Shimoga, Udupi, Mysore, Hassan and Bangalore. Of the two direct buses to **Bengaluru** from Jog Falls, the "semi-deluxe" departs at 7.30pm (9hr) and the ordinary at 8.30am. With a car or motorbike, you can approach the Falls from the coast along one of several scenic routes through the Ghats. The **tourist office** (Mon–Sat 10am–1.30pm & 2–5pm), upstairs at the new reception centre, opens rather erratically but can supply information on transport and vehicle rental.

Accommodation is limited in the settlement and largely a KSTDC monopoly (℡08186/244732); it runs the ugly concrete *Mayura Shraravathi* (❸), which has vast rooms with fading plaster and bathrooms with rickety plumbing but good views, and the humbler *Tunga Tourist Home* nearer the reception centre, with basic attached doubles (❷). On the opposite side of the road the Karnataka Power Corporation also lets out four comfy a/c rooms (℡08186/244742; ❹) when available, as does the Shimoga District PWD *Inspection Bungalow* (℡08186/244333; ❸), whose a/c rooms are nicely situated on a hillock about 400m west. The youth hostel (℡08186/244251; ❶), ten minutes' walk down the Shimoga road, has undergone renovation but is still very basic. If you can get in, the PWD *Inspection Bungalow*, on the north side of the gorge, has great views from its spacious, comfortable rooms, but is invariably full and has to be booked in advance from the Assistant Engineer's office in Siddapur a (℡08389/222103; ❶–❷).

Apart from the KSTDC *Jaladarshini* canteen next to the *Tunga Tourist Home*, which offers the usual adequate but uninspiring fare, the only other **food** options are at the enclave of small chai stalls and shops that have been relocated to the reception centre – *Hotel Rashmita* is the best of the bunch.

Gokarna

Among India's most scenically situated sacred sites, **GOKARNA** (Gokarn) lies between a broad white-sand beach and the verdant foothills of the Western Ghats, seven bus hours north of Mangalore. Yet this compact little coastal town – a Shaivite centre for more than two millennia – remained largely "undiscovered" by Western tourists until the early 1990s, when it began to attract dreadlocked and didjgeridoo-toting neo-hippies fleeing the commercialization of Goa. Now it's firmly on the tourist map, although the town retains a charming local character, as the Hindu pilgrims pouring through still far outnumber the foreigners who flock here in winter.

Arrival and information

The KSRTC **Bus Stand**, 300m from Car Street and within easy walking distance of Gokarna's limited accommodation, means that buses no longer have to negotiate the narrow streets of the bazaar. You may well find that your bus, especially coming from major tourist points like Goa and Hampi, deposits you at the new police checkpost on the way into town, where you have to register; this is a measure against beach crime and nothing to get up about. Gokarna Road **railway station**, served by at least two daily trains in each direction, is 9km inland but buses and auto-rickshaws are available to take you into town.

You can **change money** at the *Om Hotel* near the bus stand but the best rates to be had are at the Pai STD booth on the road into town near the bus stand, one of several licensed dealers. The Karnataka Bank ATM opposite the bus stand near Car Street takes only Visa. **Joya Tours and Travels**, behind the bus stand and opposite *Ram Dev Lodge*, will book **train tickets** and **provide cash** for MasterCard and Visa for a very fair two-percent fee. *Mahalaxmi*'s tiny Internet café is the best of the various **Internet** joints (all Rs40/hr) but none have very reliable connections. **Bicycles** are available for rent from a stall next to the *Pai Restaurant*, for Rs3 per hour or Rs30 for a full day. The **post office** is at the east end of Car Street, above a small produce market. Just east of the beach, a small, well-stocked bookstore, Sri Radhakrisna, contains good Indian, spiritual and fiction sections as well as a handful of books in a dozen world languages. If you need a doctor, English-speaking Dr Shastri (℡08386/256220) is highly recommended by long-stay visitors.

Accommodation

Gokarna has a few bona fide **hotels** and a small but reasonable choice of **guesthouses**. As a last resort, you can nearly always find a bed in one of the pilgrims' hostels, or **dharamshalas**, dotted around town. With dorms, bare, cell-size rooms and basic washing facilities, these are intended mainly for Hindus, but Western tourists are welcome if there are vacancies: try the *Prasad Nilaya*, just down the lane from the *Om Hotel*. Also, there are a few bare-bones **huts** (Rs50–75) along the beach half a kilometre north of town, near a little fishing village. Be careful of night robberies if you head to the beaches, and consider leaving luggage and valuables safe in town (most guesthouses will store your stuff for a small fee).

CGH Earth Resort Above Om beach ℡0484/301 1711, ⓦwww.cghearth.com. The first luxury resort in Gokarna, *CGH* offers beautifully designed wood villas spread over terraces on a hillside overlooking the bay. There's a pool, yoga dome and an Ayurvedic treatment centre, all set in extensive gardens. ❾

Gokarn International On the main road into town ℡08386/256622, ⓦwww.geocities.com /hotelgokarn. Popular mid-scale place in a four-storey block on the edge of town, offering good value, from no-frills singles to deluxe,

carpeted a/c doubles. The better ones have balconies overlooking the palm tops. ❷–❹

Gokarn International Beach Resort Kudlee Beach; book through the *Gokarn International* in town (see above). Set back from the sands in its own small garden, this compact, newly constructed hotel offers comfortable mid-price rooms with small kitchenettes and verandas, some of them sea-facing. ❺

Hotel Look Sea Kudlee Beach ℡0838/657521. Basic shared-bath huts and rooms, many with excellent beach views. Fine muesli in the morning;

football matches on the telly and beer in the evening. **❶**

Namaste Om Beach ☎08386/257141. One of the more popular beach options, with well-built attached rooms. Each has a different theme: in one, everything is round (including the bed); another resembles a rustic log cabin. Phone and Internet connection on site, along with a pleasant, shaded restaurant. **❶–❸**

Nimmu House Gokarna town, just south of main road, towards Kudlee beach ☎08386/256730, ⓔnimmuhouse@yahoo.com. Foreigners' favourite run by the friendly and helpful woman whose name it bears. Double rooms in the modern concrete block are well maintained and have decent mattresses, but avoid the grungier old wing, with its lumpy beds and grubby walls. Many upper rooms have fine beach and sea views and there's a peaceful yard to sit in. **❸–❺**

Om Beach Resort 1.5km east of town ☎0944/857 9395, ⓦwww.ombeachresorts.com. Despite the name, this campus of a dozen newly built colonial-style chalets is actually near Gokarna town – high on a sun-blasted hilltop, a good 45min (shadeless) walk from the beaches. It was conceived primarily as an Ayurvedic spa, so there are qualified doctors on site, along with masseurs from the acclaimed Keralan Ayurveda outfit, Kairali. **❽–❾**

Seabird Resort 3km east of town ☎08386/257689. Good-value option on the hilltop above Gokarna town, with choice of modern a/c or non-a/c, all opening on to private sitouts. The views over the scrubby slopes are great and there's a multi-cuisine restaurant and small pool. **❺–❻**

Shastri Guest House 100m east of the KRSTC Bus Stand ☎08386/256220. Tucked behind the Shastri Clinic on the main road, this quiet place offers some attached rooms and rock-bottom single rates. **❶–❷**

Vaibhav Nivas Off the main road, less than five minutes from the bus stand ☎08386/256714. Friendly, cheap and justifiably popular guesthouse pitched at foreigners, with a rooftop café-restaurant; all rooms are attached. **❶–❸**

The Town

Gokarna **town**, a hotchpotch of wood-fronted houses and red terracotta roofs, is clustered around a long L-shaped bazaar, its broad main road – known as **Car Street** – running west to the town beach, a sacred site in its own right. Hindu mythology identifies it as the place where Rudra (another name for Shiva) was reborn through the ear of a cow from the underworld after a period of penance. Gokarna is also the home of one of India's most powerful *shivalinga* – the **pranalingam**, which came to rest here after being carried off by Ravana, the evil king of Lanka, from Shiva's home on Mount Kailash in the Himalayas.

The *pranalingam* resides in Gokarna to this day, enshrined in the medieval **Shri Mahabaleshwar temple**, at the far west end of the bazaar. It is regarded as so auspicious that a mere glimpse of it will absolve a hundred sins, even the murder of a brahmin. Local Hindu lore also asserts that you can maximize the lingam's purifying power by shaving your head, fasting and taking a holy dip in the sea before *darshan*, or ritual viewing of the deity. For this reason, pilgrims traditionally begin their tour of Gokarna with a walk to the beach, guided by their family *pujari*. Next, they visit the **Shri Mahaganpati temple**, a stone's throw east of Shri Mahabaleshwar, to propitiate the elephant-headed god Ganesh. Sadly, owing to some ugly incidents involving insensitive behaviour by a minority of foreigners, tourists are now banned from the temples, though you can still get a good view of proceedings in the smaller Shri Mahaganpati from the entrance.

The beaches

Notwithstanding Gokarna's numerous temples, shrines and tanks, most Western tourists come here for the beautiful **beaches** to the south of the more crowded town beach, beyond the lumpy laterite headland that overlooks the town. Many lounge for weeks, taking advantage of lax attitudes and imbibing potent bhang lassis.

To pick up the trail, take a left off Car Street just past *Mahalaxmi* and follow the path uphill through the woods. After twenty minutes, you drop down from a rocky plateau to **Kudlee Beach** – a wonderful kilometre-long sweep of

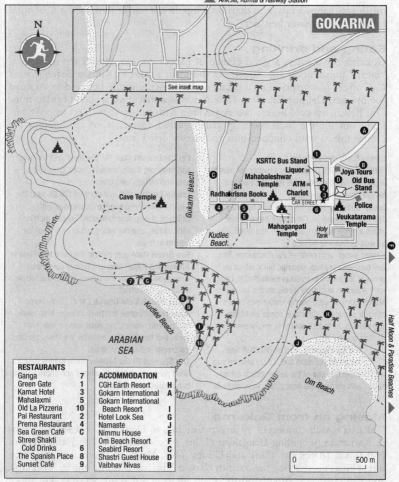

GOKARNA

See inset map

KSRTC Bus Stand
Liquor
Mahabaleshwar
Temple
Sri
Radhakrisna Books
Joya Tours
Old Bus
Stand
ATM
Chariot
CAR STREET
Police
Veukatarama
Temple
Mahaganpati
Temple
Holy
Tank

Gokarn Beach
Cave Temple
Kudlee
Beach

Kudlee Beach

ARABIAN
SEA

Om Beach

RESTAURANTS
Ganga	7
Green Gate	1
Kamat Hotel	3
Mahalaxmi	5
Old La Pizzeria	10
Pai Restaurant	2
Prema Restaurant	4
Sea Green Café	C
Shree Shakti	
Cold Drinks	6
The Spanish Place	8
Sunset Café	9

ACCOMMODATION
CGH Earth Resort	H
Gokarn International	I
Gokarn International	
Beach Resort	G
Hotel Look Sea	J
Namaste	E
Nimmu House	F
Om Beach Resort	C
Seabird Resort	D
Shastri Guest House	B
Vaibhav Nivas	

0   500 m

22

KARNATAKA | North of Mangalore: coastal Karnataka

Half Moon & Paradise Beaches

golden-white sand sheltered by a pair of steep-sided promontories. This is the longest and broadest of Gokarna's beaches, and with decent surf too, though the water can be dangerous. The cafés that spring up here during the winter offer some respite from the heat of the midday sun, and some offer very basic accommodation in bamboo shacks.

It takes around twenty minutes more to hike over the headland from Kudlee to exquisite **Om Beach**, so named because its distinctive twin crescent-shaped bays resemble the auspicious Om symbol. Hammocks and basic huts (❶) still populate the palm groves, alongside about a dozen chai houses, many of which provide lodging, as well as food and drink. *Nirvana* offers yoga classes, along with huts and decent grub.

Gokarna's two most remote beaches lie another half-hour walk/climb over the rocky hills. **Half-Moon** and **Paradise** beaches, are, despite the presence of a few restaurants and extremely basic lodgings on each, mainly for intrepid sun-lovers happy to pack in their own supplies. If you're looking for near-total isolation, this is your best bet.

Eating and drinking

Gokarna town offers a good choice of **places to eat**, with a string of busy "meals" joints along Car Street and the main road. On Kudlee Beach, *Sunset Café* offers, not surprisingly, a prime sunset-viewing locale buffeted by Arabian Sea breezes. The popular *Shree Ganesh*, across a charming wooden bridge from Om Beach, has cold beer, a breezy pavilion with sunset views, and a pool table. Look out for the local sweet speciality *gadbad*, several layers of different ice creams mixed with chopped nuts and chewy dried fruit.

Ganga North end of Kudlee Beach ☎08386/257195. Great terrace restaurant near the water; also offers basic huts (❶) and Kudlee's fastest Internet connection.

Green Gate *Om Hotel*, near the new bus stand. The more pleasant of *Om Hotel's* two eateries offers a range of Mexican, Italian and Israeli dishes, as well as fish and sizzlers.

Kamat Hotel Just north of *Pai Restaurant.* This tiny canteen may lack signage, but it whips up some of the best fish thalis in town (Rs23). Look for the swarm of hungry locals around lunchtime.

Mahalaxmi Smiling young waitresses hustle banana pancakes, delicious dosas and tasty veg curries up to this soothing, sea-view rooftop perch.

Old La Pizzeria Kudlee Beach. A few tables on the sand and a cozy atmosphere within make this one of the better beach dining spots, with some of the best pizzas in south India.

Pai Restaurant Main Rd. Excellent spot for fresh and tasty veg thalis, masala dosas, crisp vadas, teas and coffees until late.

Prema Restaurant Just north of Car St, near the beach. Welcoming vegetarian canteen with delicious *dosas*, superb toasted English muffin sandwiches, and the best *gadbad* (rich local ice cream) in town.

Sea Green Café Just behind the main town beach. Tibetan and Nepali food in a breezy courtyard, where you can enjoy the sunset over a beer while waiting to be served.

Shree Shakti Cold Drinks Car St. Tasty home-made peanut butter and fresh cheese, both made to American recipes, the latter served with rolls, garlic and tomato. Also available are filling toasties, ice cream and creamy lassis.

The Spanish Place Midway down Kudlee Beach. Good pasta, sandwiches, sweets and creamy lassis in a relaxed atmosphere.

Moving on from Gokarna

Gokarna is well connected by direct daily **bus** to Goa (5hr), and several towns in Karnataka, including Bengaluru (13hr), Hospet/Hampi (10hr) and Mysore (14hr), via Mangalore (7hr) and Udupi (6hr). Although there are only three direct buses north along the coast to Karwar (2hr), close to the border with Goa, you can change at Ankola on the main highway for more services. For more buses to Hospet and Hampi and the best connections to Jog Falls, change at Kumta; **tempos** regularly ply the route between Gokarna and Kumta (32km) as well as Ankola.

Gokarna Road now has at least two **daily trains** in each direction. Trains to Mangalore depart at 4pm and 1:45am (4.5hrs), and trains north to Goa and Mumbai depart at 7pm and 10:45am. A couple of weekly expresses also call here, but regular **express connections** can be found in either Kumta or Ankola.

Hubli and around

Karnataka's second most industrialized city, **HUBLI**, 418km northwest of Bengaluru (Bangalore), has little to offer tourists except for its transport connections to Mumbai, Goa, the coast of Uttar Kanada (Northern Karnataka), Hampi and other points in the interior. It does, however, make a convenient base from which to explore the various sites in the area.

Practicalities

Hubli's **railway station**, close to the town centre and within walking distance of several of the hotels, is well connected to Bengaluru, Mumbai, Puna, Hassan and Hospet. Hubli's efficient **KSRTC Bus Stand** is 2km south of town, and can be reached by bus from the chaotic City Bus Stand, about 1km west of the railway station, and from outside the station itself. The best way of getting around the city is by **auto-rickshaw**; these have meters, but there's also an efficient pre-paid booth outside the railway station. ICICI Bank has an **ATM** at the railway station and another one

halfway along Lamington Road to the City Bus Stand. For **Internet** access, head to JC Nagar, where both I-way, almost opposite the *Ajanta*, and the Cybercafé in the Sri Naradmuni complex, offer a rate of Rs20 per hour.

Accommodation around the railway station includes the huge *Hotel Ajanta* on JC Nagar (℡0836/236 2216; ❶–❸), which has a range of rooms, including very cheap singles with shared bathroom. Opposite the City Bus Stand, the large and well-organized *Shri Renuka Lodge* (℡0836/225 3615; ❷–❹) offers a good range of reasonable rooms, some with a/c, and has its own veg restaurant. There are a few hotels between the railway station and the bus stand on Lamington Road, including the pleasant *Kailash* (℡0836/235 2732, ⓦwww .hotelkailash.com; ❷–❹), an efficient business hotel with good-value a/c rooms and a decent restaurant, and the *Vipra*, opposite, which has simple rooms (℡0836/236 2336, ⓔvipratravels@satyam.net.in; ❶–❷).

Most hotels have their own **restaurants** – the *Shri Renuka*, for example, has two sections, one serving south Indian veg food and the other Chinese and north Indian cuisine. The best of the independent restaurants is the *Kamat Hotel*, by the traffic island at the bus stand end of Lamington Road; there's another branch opposite the railway station. *Vinayak Chicken Corner*, opposite the City Bus Stand, is a good spot for inexpensive non-veg and beer.

Hospet

Charmless **HOSPET**, about ten hours from both Bengaluru (Bangalore) and Goa, is of little interest except as the jumping-off place for the extraordinary ruined city of Hampi (Vijayanagar), 13km northeast. If you arrive late, or want somewhere fairly comfortable to sleep, it makes sense to stay here and catch a bus or taxi out to the ruins the following morning.

Practicalities

Hospet's **railway station**, 1500m north of the centre, is served by the overnight Hampi Express #6592 from Bengaluru and services from Hyderabad, via Guntakal Junction. The line continues west to Hubli for connections to the

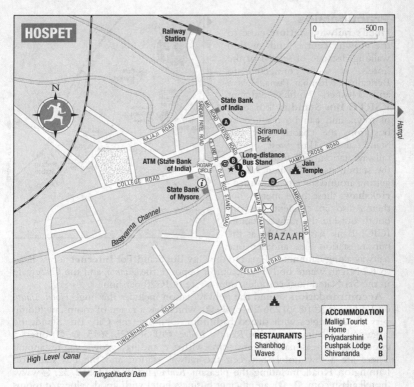

Railway
Station

0   500 m

N

State Bank
of India

Sriramulu
Park

RAJAJI ROAD

ATM (State Bank
of India)

ROTARY
CIRCLE

Long-distance
Bus Stand

HAMPI CROSS ROAD

Jain
Temple

Hampi

COLLEGE ROAD

State Bank
of Mysore

Basavanna Channel

MAIN BAZAAR ROAD

OLD BUS STAND ROAD

JAMBUNATHA ROAD

BAZAAR

BELLARY ROAD

TUNGABHADRA DAM ROAD

High Level Canal

RESTAURANTS
Shanbhog   1
Waves   D

ACCOMMODATION
Malligi Tourist
  Home   D
Priyadarshini A
Pushpak Lodge C
Shivananda   B

Tungabhadra Dam

coast and Goa. For connections to Badami and Bijapur, travel to Gadag and change onto the slow single track running north – check first that it's operational as the conversion was set to be completed by late 2008. Auto-rickshaws are plentiful or you can get into town by cycle rickshaw (Rs10) or by foot if unencumbered.

The **long-distance bus stand** is in the centre, just off MG (Station) Road, which runs south from the railway station. For a summary of services see "Travel details" on p.1326. **Bookings** for long-distance routes can be made at the ticket office on the bus-stand concourse (daily 8am–noon & 3–6pm), where there's also a **left-luggage** facility.

The **tourist office** at the Rotary Circle (Mon–Sat: June–March 10am–5.30pm; April & May 8am–1.30pm; ☎08394/228537) offers limited information and sells tickets for KSTDC conducted tours of Hampi. You can **exchange** traveller's cheques and cash at the State Bank of Mysore (Mon–Fri 10.30am–2.30pm & Sat 10.30am–12.30pm), next to the tourist office, and cash only at the State Bank of India (same hours) on Station Road. Full exchange facilities are available at the *Hotel Malligi*, while Sneha Travels (☎08394/225838) at the Elimanchate complex, next to the *Hotel Priyadarshini* on MG Road, also changes any currency and traveller's cheques, and advances money on credit cards. This last also has branches in Hampi, books airline and train tickets and cars, and runs private **luxury buses to Goa**, which are actually operated by Paulo Travels (☎08394/225867) next door; the sleeper coach departs at 7pm, costs Rs450 and takes ten hours. Luxury buses are also available for Bengaluru

Frequent **buses to Hampi** run from the bus stand between 6.30am and 7.30pm; the journey takes around thirty minutes. Taxis (Rs120–150) and rickshaws (Rs60–80) gather outside the railway station. It is also possible to catch a bus to **Kamalapuram**, at the south side of the site, and explore the ruins from there, catching a bus back to Hospet from Hampi Bazaar at the end of the day. **Bicycles** are available for rent at several stalls along the main street, but the trip to, around, and back from the site is a long one in the heat. Auto-rickshaws, best arranged through hotels such as the *Malligi* or *Priyadarshini*, will also take you to Hampi and back and charge around Rs50–60 per hour, but be warned that the roads are extremely bumpy. For the adventurous, Bullet motorbikes are available for rent (or sale) from Bharat Motors (℡08394/224704) near Rama Talkies. Finally, some hotels in Hospet can also organize for you to hook up with trained guides in Hampi; ask at the *Malligi* or *Priyadarshini*, or call government-approved Mr Basappa (℡09448 007211) or Nagaraj (℡09480 510871), who can lead treks, set up car rentals, or point you in the right direction.

(10hr; Rs200) departing between 10pm and 11pm. Cybernet (Rs40/hr), next to the *Shivananda* hotel, can get you online.

Accommodation and eating

Many of the hotels have good **dining rooms**, but in the evening, the upscale though affordable *Waves*, a terrace restaurant in the *Malligi* complex, is the most congenial place to hang out, serving tandoori and chilled beer from 7pm to 11pm (bring lots of mosquito repellent). *Shanbhog*, an excellent little Udupi restaurant next to the bus station, is a perfect pit-stop before heading to Hampi, and opens early for breakfast.

Malligi Tourist Home 6/143 Jambunatha Rd, a 2min walk east of MG Rd (look for the signs) and the bus stand ℡0839/228101, Ⓔmalligihome @hotmail.com. Friendly, well-managed hotel with cheaper, clean, comfortable rooms (some a/c) in the old block and two newer wings across the lawn, with luxurious a/c rooms and suites. There is also a large outdoor swimming pool (Rs25/hr for nonresidents) beneath the restaurant/bar, plus billiards and massage facilities, in addition to a small bookshop, Internet access, and an efficient travel service. ②–③
Priyadarshini MG Rd ℡0839/428838, Ⓦwww .priyainnhampi.com. Large and bland, but spotless

and very good value. Rooms from rock-bottom singles to doubles with TV and a/c (some with balconies). Two good restaurants: the veg *Naivedyam* and, in the garden, the excellent non-veg *Manasa*, which has a bar. ③–⑥
Pushpak Lodge MG Rd ℡0839/421380. With basic but clean attached rooms, this is the best rock-bottom lodge in town. ②
Shivananda Beside the bus stand ℡0839/420700. Well-maintained hotel with spotless rooms, all attached with cable TV and some a/c. Very good value. ②–③

Hampi (Vijayanagar)

Among a surreal landscape of golden-brown boulders and leafy banana fields, the ruined "City of Victory," **Vijayanagar**, better known as **HAMPI** (the name of the main local village), spills from the south bank of the River Tungabhadra.

This once dazzling Hindu capital was devastated by a six-month Muslim siege in the second half of the sixteenth century. Only stone, brick and stucco structures survived the ensuing sack – monolithic deities, crumbling houses and abandoned temples dominated by towering *gopuras* – as well as the sophisticated irrigation system that channelled water to huge tanks and temples.

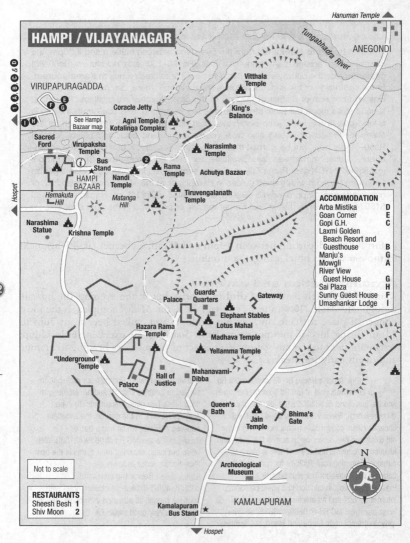

HAMPI / VIJAYANAGAR

Hanuman Temple

ANEGONDI

Tungabhadra River

VIRUPAPURAGADDA

Vitthala
Temple

Coracle Jetty

King's
Balance

Agni Temple &
Kotalinga Complex

Sacred
Ford

Virupaksha
Temple

Narasimha
Temple

Bus
Stand

Rama
Temple

Achutya Bazaar

HAMPI
BAZAAR

Nandi
Temple

Tiruvengalanath
Temple

Hospet

*Matanga
Hill*

*Hemakuta
Hill*

Narasimha
Statue

Krishna Temple

ACCOMMODATION	
Arba Mistika	D
Goan Corner	E
Gopi G.H.	C
Laxmi Golden	
Beach Resort and	
Guesthouse	B
Manju's	G
Mowgli	A
River View	
Guest House	G
Sai Plaza	H
Sunny Guest House	F
Umashankar Lodge	I

Palace

Guards'
Quarters

Gateway

Hazara Rama
Temple

Elephant Stables

Lotus Mahal

Madhava Temple

Yellamma Temple

"Underground"
Temple

Palace

Hall of
Justice

Mahanavami-
Dibba

Queen's
Bath

Jain
Temple

Bhima's
Gate

Archeological
Museum

N

Not to scale

RESTAURANTS	
Sheesh Besh	1
Shiv Moon	2

Kamalapuram
Bus Stand

KAMALAPURAM

Hospet

See Hampi
Bazaar map

Thus, most of Hampi's monuments are in disappointingly poor shape, appearing a lot older than their four or five hundred years. Yet the serene riverine setting and air of magic that lingers over the site, sacred for centuries before a city was founded here, make it one of India's most extraordinary locations. Many find it difficult to leave and spend weeks chilling out in cafés, wandering to white-washed hilltop temples and gazing at the spectacular sunsets.

Some history

According to the Ramayana, the settlement began its days as Kishkinda, ruled by the monkey kings Bali and Sugriva and their ambassador, Hanuman. The unpredictably-placed rocks – some balanced in perilous arches, others heaped in colossal, hill-sized piles – are said to have been flung down by their armies in a show of strength.

The rise of the **Vijayanagar empire** seems to have been a direct response, in the first half of the fourteenth century, to the expansionist aims of Muslims from the north, most notably Malik Kafur and Mohammed-bin-Tughluq. Two Hindu brothers from Andhra Pradesh, Harihara and Bukka, who had been employed as treasury officers in Kampila, 19km east of Hampi, were captured by the Tughluqs and taken to Delhi, where they supposedly converted to Islam. Assuming them to be suitably tamed, the Delhi sultan despatched them to quell civil disorder in Kampila, which they duly did, only to abandon both Islam and allegiance to Delhi shortly afterwards, preferring to establish their own independent Hindu kingdom. Within a few years they controlled vast tracts of land from coast to coast. In 1343 their new capital, Vijayanagar, was founded on the southern banks of the River Tungabhadra, a location long considered sacred by Hindus. The city's most glorious period was under the reign of **Krishna Deva Raya** (1509–29), when it enjoyed a near monopoly of the lucrative trade in Arabian horses and Indian spices passing through the coastal ports and was the most powerful Hindu capital in the Deccan. Travellers such as the Portuguese chronicler Domingo Paez, who stayed for two years after 1520, were astonished by its size and wealth, telling tales of markets full of silk and precious gems, beautiful, bejewelled courtesans, ornate palaces and fantastical festivities.

Thanks to its natural features and massive fortifications, Vijayanagar was virtually impregnable. In 1565, however, following his interference in the affairs of local Muslim sultanates, the regent Rama Raya was drawn into a battle with a confederacy of Muslim forces, 100km away to the north, which left the city undefended. At first, fortune appeared to be on the side of the Hindu army, but there were as many as ten thousand Muslims in their number, and loyalties may well have been divided. When two Vijayanagar Muslim generals suddenly deserted, the army fell into disarray. Defeat came swiftly; although members of his family fled with untold hoards of gold and jewels, Rama Raya was captured and suffered a grisly death at the hands of the sultan of Ahmadnagar. Vijayanagar then fell victim to a series of destructive raids, and its days of splendour were brought to an abrupt end.

Arrival and information

Buses from Hospet terminate close to where the road joins the main street in Hampi Bazaar, halfway along its dusty length. A little further towards the Virupaksha temple, the **tourist office** (daily except Fri 10am–5.30pm; ☏08394/241339) can put you in touch with a **guide** for Rs500 per day but not much else.

Rented **bicycles** are available from stalls near the lodges (Rs5/hr, Rs30–40/day). Pedal bikes can be hard work on the bumpy roads so consider a motorized two-wheeler. The Raju stall, round the corner from the tourist office, has motorbikes and scooters for hire (around Rs150/day). Sneha Travels, whose main office is at D131/11 Main St (daily 9am–9pm; ☏08394/241590), can **change money** (albeit at lowish rates), advance cash on credit cards and book airline and **train tickets**. It also runs **luxury buses** to Bengaluru (Bangalore) and sleeper coaches to Goa and Gokarna, though you have to pick them up from Hospet thanks to the powerful taxi/rickshaw mafia. Note, too, that whatever you are told, the Gokarna bus involves a transfer at Ankola in the wee hours. It's better to hop on one of three early-morning express trains from Hospet to Hubli (last one at 8am; 2hr), from where you can catch a bus to Gokarna (5.5hr) or nearby Ankola (4.5hr), saving both time and money.

Run by Shri Swamy Sadashiva Yogi, the Shivananda Yoga Ashram overlooking the river, past the site of the new footbridge and coracle crossing, offers courses in **yoga** and **meditation** as well as homeopathic treatment, magnetotherapy and **Ayurvedic treatment**, in particular for snakebites.

Accommodation

Staying in the village means you can be up and out early enough to catch the sunrise over the ruins – a mesmerizing spectacle. Having said that, with tourist shops and increasingly expensive guesthouse clones thick on the ground, Hampi Bazaar increasingly feels like a tourist trap. Much of its appeal has migrated across the river to **Virupapuragadda**, which is unspoiled, fast-growing and increasingly popular with travellers (see box opposite).

Arba Mistika, Virupapuragadda, western end of main drag, past *Mowgli* and up a short road to the right. The eight rooms, all with shared bath, are quite basic, but the cooking is fresh and tasty and the eye-catching white teepee lounge is decked out in gypsy style and tailor-made for relaxed evenings. **②**

Garden Paradise Far east end of village ☎08394/652539. Four cramped but cute huts in an excellent riverside location. Shared bathrooms and a chilled-out restaurant. **④**

Goan Corner 500m east of coracle crossing, Virupapuragadda ☎09448 718951. Large complex amid paddy fields and near the rocks with a range of rooms and huts, some with attached bathrooms. Lively restaurant. **①–②**

Gopi GH Virupapuragadda, 200m west of boat crossing ☎09/480 474 861. One of the mellower spots in Viru, with thatched huts of varying sizes encircling a garden and fountain. **①–②**

Laxmi Golden Beach Resort and Guesthouse Virupapuragadda, 400m west of coracle crossing on main drag ☎08394/287008, ⑩www .laxmigoldenbeach.com. Luxury touches down in Viru, with the bi-level bamboo restaurant and enormous, paddy-facing rooms of the *Laxmi Resort*, which is rather overpriced. The guesthouse rooms in the back, however, are significantly cheaper and not bad value. Guesthouse **②–④**, resort **⑦–⑨**

Manju's East of coracle crossing, beyond rice paddies ☎09449 247712. This grassy complex of ten mud-walled attached huts and two rooms has a tranquil, relaxed vibe; there's a delightful gazebo restaurant and Internet access. **②**

🏃 **Mowgli** Far west end of main road ☎08394/329844, ⑥hampimowgli @hotmail.com. A range of rooms with comfy

sitouts and private balconies, some with fantastic views, as well as a welcoming restaurant set against a gorgeous paddy and river backdrop, and all services (Internet, laundry, travel booking, money changing), make this the best-value lodgings in Viru. Book ahead. **①–⑤**

River View Guest House next to *Manju's* ☎09448 441880. Six simple huts with shared baths and great views across the river. A fine, charming budget option. **①**

Sai Plaza Virupapuragadda ☎08533/287017, ⑥santoshgvt@yahoo.com. These fifteen bungalows encircling an attractive courtyard garden are relaxed and welcoming. The restaurant has delicious lassis and sandwiches and excellent views across the river. **③**

Shanti Guest House Just north of the Virupaksha temple ☎08394/241568. This is a real favourite, comprising a dozen or so twin-bedded rooms arranged on two storeys around a leafy inner courtyard. It's basic (showers and toilets are shared), but spotless, and all rooms have fans and windows. **①**

Sunny Guest House Virupapuragadda ☎08533/287005. Nicely landscaped gardens with brightly painted bungalows and a row of compact rooms. **②–③**

Umashankar Lodge Virupapuragadda ☎08533/287067. Cosy, popular spot with small but clean attached rooms, the upstairs ones rather overpriced, set round a leafy courtyard. **①–③**

Vicky's Guest House At the end of the lane furthest northeast from the temple ☎08394/241694. Small clean rooms, some attached. Friendly and popular for its rooftop restaurant. **②–③**

The site

Although spread over 26 square kilometres, the ruins of Vijayanagar are mostly concentrated in two distinct groups: the first lies in and around **Hampi Bazaar** and the nearby riverside area, encompassing the city's most sacred enclave of

Unspoiled Viru

A flood of touts, gurus, souvenir shops, and overpriced guesthouses have in recent years drained Hampi Bazaar (the village) of much of its appeal. At the same time, **Virupapurgadda**, across the river, has increased the quality and quantity of its travellers' offerings yet remained comparatively unspoiled. Viru, as it's widely known, offers a taste of pre-boom Goa minus the beaches; it's naturally beautiful, cheap, full of character, and a bit rough around the edges, with bonuses such as free nightly film screenings, regular riverside bonfires, and the availability of meat and beer (meat and alcoholic beverages are severely restricted in Hampi Bazaar). As a result, all variety of visitors have of late eschewed the bazaar and forged the unforbidding waters of the Tungabhadra.

temples and *ghats*; the second centres on the **royal enclosure** – 3km south of the river, just northwest of **Kamalapuram** village – which holds the remains of palaces, pavilions, elephant stables, guardhouses and temples. Between the two stretches a long boulder-choked hill and swathe of banana plantations, fed by ancient irrigation canals.

Hampi Bazaar, the Virupaksha temple and riverside

Lining Hampi's long, straight main street, **Hampi Bazaar**, which runs east from the eastern entrance of the Virupaksha temple, you can still make out the remains of Vijayanagar's ruined, columned bazaar, partly inhabited by today's lively market. Landless labourers live in many of the crumbling 500-year-old buildings.

Dedicated to a local form of Shiva known as Virupaksha or Pampapati, the functioning **Virupaksha temple** (daily 8am–12.30pm & 3–6.30pm; Rs2) dominates the village, drawing a steady flow of pilgrims from all over southern

HAMPI BAZAAR & VIRUPAKSHA TEMPLE

Tungabhadra River

Sacred Ghats

Tank

Virupaksha Temple

Gopura Tower

Cycle Rental

MAIN BAZAAR

ACCOMMODATION
Garden Paradise   A
Shanti Guest House   C
Vicky's Guest House   B

RESTAURANTS
Mango Tree   1
New Shanti   3
Sri Sangameshwara   5
Suresh   2
Trishul   4

Hemakuta Hill

N

Bus Stand

0   50 m

India. Also known as **Sri Virupaksha Swami**, the temple is free for all who come for *arati* (worship; daily 6.30–8am & 6.30–8pm) when the temple has the most atmosphere. The complex consists of two courts, each entered through a towered *gopura*.

A colonnade surrounds the inner court, usually filled with pilgrims dozing and singing religious songs. On entering, if the temple elephant, Lakshmi, is around, you can get her to bless you by placing a rupee in her trunk. In the middle the principal temple is approached through a *mandapa* hallway whose carved columns feature rearing animals. Rare Vijayanagar-era paintings on the *mandapa* ceiling include aspects of Shiva, a procession with the sage Vidyaranya, the ten incarnations of Vishnu, and scenes from the Mahabharata.

The sacred **ford** in the river is reached from the Virupaksha's north *gopura*; you can also get there by following the lane around the impressive temple **tank**. A *mandapa* overlooks the steps that originally led to the river, now some distance away. **Coracles**, circular rush basket boats, ply from this part of the bank, just as they did five centuries ago, ferrying villagers to the fields and tourists to the increasingly popular enclave of **Virupapuragadda**. The road left through the village eventually loops back towards the hilltop Hanuman temple, about 5km east, and on to Anegondi – a recommended round walk is described opposite.

Matanga Hill

The place to head for sunrise is the boulder hill immediately east of Hampi Bazaar. From the end of the main street, an ancient paved pathway winds up a rise, at the top of which the magnificent Tiruvengalanatha temple is revealed. The views improve as you progress up **Matanga Hill**, and a small stone temple at its summit provides an extraordinary vantage point. The problem of muggings early in the morning along this path seems to have waned but it's probably still a good idea to be vigilant if there are only one or two of you.

The riverside path

To reach the Vitthala temple, walk east from the Virupaksha, the length of Hampi Bazaar, where a huge monolithic **Nandi** statue gazes across at the main temple from its shrine. Just before you reach these, a path on the left, staffed at regular intervals by conch-blowing sadhus and an assortment of other ragged mendicants, follows the river past a couple of cafés and numerous shrines, including a Rama temple – home to hordes of fearless monkeys. Beyond at least four Vishnu shrines, a paved and colonnaded **bazaar** leads due south to the **Achyutharaya temple**, whose beautiful stone carvings – among them some of Hampi's famed erotica – are being restored by the ASI. Back on the main path again, make a short detour across the rocks leading to the river to see the little-visited waterside **Agni temple**; next to it, the Kotalinga complex consists of 108 (an auspicious number) tiny *lingas*, carved on a flat rock. As you approach the Vitthala temple, to the south is an archway known as the **King's Balance**, where the rajas were weighed against gold, silver and jewels to be distributed to the city's priests.

Vitthala temple

Although the area of the **Vitthala temple** (daily 6am–6pm; foreigners $5, Indian residents Rs10; ticket also valid for the Lotus Mahal on the same day) does not show the same evidence of early cult worship as Virupaksha, the ruined bridge to the west probably dates from before Vijayanagar times. The bathing *ghat* may be from the Chalukya or Ganga period, but as the temple has fallen into disuse it seems that the river crossing (*tirtha*) here has not had the same sacred significance as the Virupaksha site. Now designated a World Heritage

Monument by UNESCO, the Vitthala temple was built for Vishnu, who according to legend was too embarrassed by its ostentation to live there.

The open *mandapa* features slender monolithic granite musical **pillars** which were constructed so as to sound the notes of the scale when struck. Today, due to vandalism and erosion from being repeatedly beaten, heavy security makes sure that no one is allowed to touch them. Guides, however, will happily demonstrate the musical resonance of other pillars on an adjacent structure. Outer columns sport characteristic Vijayanagar rearing horses, while friezes of lions, elephants and horses on the moulded basement display sculptural trickery – you can transform one beast into another simply by masking one portion of the image.

In front of the temple, to the east, a stone representation of a wooden processional **rath**, or chariot, houses an image of Garuda, Vishnu's bird vehicle. Now cemented, at one time the chariot's wheels revolved.

Anegondi and beyond

With more time, and a sense of adventure, you can head across the Tunga-bhadra to **ANEGONDI**, a fortress town predating Vijayanagar, and its fourteenth-century headquarters. The most pleasant way to get there is to take a coracle from the ford 1500m east of the Vitthala temple; the coracles, which are today reinforced with plastic sheets, also carry bicycles, which are a good way to visit Hampi's many monuments.

Forgotten temples and fortifications litter Anegondi village and its quiet surroundings. The ruined **Huchchappa-matha temple**, near the river gateway, is worth a look for its black stone lathe-turned pillars and fine panels of dancers. **Aramani**, a ruined palace in the centre, stands opposite the home of the descendents of the royal family; also in the centre, the **Ranganatha temple** is still active. A huge wooden temple chariot stands in the village square. The only **accommodation** here is in village houses and you can get basic snacks at the *Hoova Café* .

To complete a five-kilometre loop back to Hampi from here (the simplest route if you have wheels), head left (west) along the turning just north of the village, which winds through sugar cane fields and eventually comes out near Virupapuragadda. En route you can visit the sacred **Pampla Sarovar**, signposted down a dirt lane to the left. The small temple above this square bathing tank, tended by a *swami* who will proudly show you photos of his pilgrimage to Mount Kailash, is dedicated to the goddess Lakshmi and holds a cave containing a footprint of Vishnu. If you are staying around Anegondi, this quiet and atmospheric spot is best visited early in the evening during *arati* (worship).

Another worthwhile detour from the road is the hike up to the tiny white-washed **Hanuman temple**, perched on a rocky hilltop north of the river, from where you gain superb views over Hampi, especially at sunrise and sunset. The steep climb up to it takes around half an hour. An alternative walking route back involves following the path a further 2km until you reach an impressive old **stone bridge** dating from Vijayanagar times. The bridge no longer spans the river but just beyond it, to the west, another coracle crossing returns you to a point about halfway between the Vitthala temple and Hampi Bazaar. This rewarding round walk can, of course, be completed in reverse. Whichever loop you choose and especially if you attempt it on foot, which requires at least three hours, take plenty of water.

Hemakuta Hill and around

Directly above Hampi Bazaar, **Hemakuta Hill** is dotted with pre-Vijayanagar temples that probably date from between the ninth and eleventh centuries (late

Chalukya or Ganga). Aside from the architecture, the main reason to clamber up here is to admire the **views** of the ruins and surrounding countryside. Looking across the boulder-covered terrain and banana plantations, the sheer western edge of the hill is Hampi's number-one sunset spot, attracting a crowd of blissed-out tourists most evenings, along with a couple of entrepreneurial chai-wallahs and little boys posing for photos in Hanuman costumes.

A couple of interesting monuments lie on the road leading south towards the main, southern group of ruins. The first of these, a walled **Krishna temple complex** to the west of the road, dates from 1513. Although dilapidated in parts, it features some fine carving and shrines.

Hampi's most-photographed monument stands just south of the Krishna temple in its own enclosure. Depicting Vishnu in his incarnation (avatar) as the Man-Lion, the monolithic **Narashima** statue, with its bulging eyes and crossed legs strapped into yogic pose, is one of Vijayanagar's greatest treasures.

The southern and royal monuments

The most impressive remains of Vijayanagar, the city's **royal monuments**, lie some 3km south of Hampi Bazaar, spread over a large expanse of open ground. Before tackling the ruins proper, it's a good idea to get your bearings with a visit to the small **Archeological Museum** (daily except Fri 10am–5pm; free) at Kamalapuram, which can be reached by bus from Hospet or Hampi. Turn right out of the Kamalapuram Bus Stand, take the first turning on the right, and the museum is a two-minute walk away, on the left. Among the sculpture, weapons, palm-leaf manuscripts and painting from Vijayanagar and Anegondi, the highlight is a superb scale model of the city, giving an excellent bird's-eye view of the entire site.

To walk into the city from the museum, go back to the main road and take the nearby turning marked "Hampi 4km". After 200m or so you reach the partly ruined massive **inner city wall**, made from granite slabs, which runs 32km around the city, in places as high as 10m. The outer wall was almost twice as long. At one time, there were said to have been seven city walls; coupled with areas of impenetrable forest and the river to the north, they made the city virtually impregnable.

Just beyond the wall, the **citadel area** was once enclosed by another wall and gates, of which only traces remain. To the east, the small *ganigitti* ("oil-woman's") fourteenth-century **Jain temple** features a simple stepped pyramidal tower of undecorated horizontal slabs. Beyond it is **Bhima's Gate**, once one of the principal entrances to the city, named after the Titan-like Pandava prince and hero of the Mahabharata. Like many of the gates, it is "bent", a form of defence that meant anyone trying to get in had to make two 90° turns. Bas-reliefs depict such episodes as Bhima avenging the attempted rape of his wife, Draupadi, by killing the general Kichaka. Draupadi vowed she would not dress her hair until Kichaka was dead; one panel shows her tying up her locks, the vow fulfilled.

Back on the path, to the west, the plain facade of the fifteen-metre-square **Queen's Bath** belies its glorious interior, open to the sky and surrounded by corridors with 24 different domes. Eight projecting balconies overlook where once was water; traces of Islamic-influenced stucco decoration survive. Women from the royal household would bathe here and umbrellas were placed in shafts in the tank floor to protect them from the sun. The water supply channel can be seen outside.

Continuing northwest brings you to **Mahanavami-Dibba** or "House of Victory", built to commemorate a successful campaign in Orissa.

A twelve-metre pyramidal structure with a square base, it is said to have been where the king gave and received honours and gifts. From here he watched the magnificent parades, music and dance performances, martial arts displays, elephant fights and animal sacrifices that made celebration of the ten-day Dussehra festival famed throughout the land (the tradition of spectacular Dussehra festivals is continued at Mysore; see p.1273). Carved reliefs decorate the sides of the platform. To the west, another platform – the largest at Vijayanagar – is thought to be the basement of the **King's Audience Hall**. Stone bases of a hundred pillars remain, in an arrangement that has caused speculation as to how the building could have been used; there are no passageways or open areas.

The two-storey **Lotus Mahal** (daily 6am–6pm; $5 [Rs10]; ticket also valid for the Vitthala temple on the same day), a little further north and part of the **zenana enclosure**, or women's quarters, was designed for the pleasure of Krishna Deva Raya's queen: a place where she could relax, particularly in summer. Displaying a strong Indo-Islamic influence, the pavilion is open on the ground floor, whereas the upper level (no longer accessible by stairs) contains windows and balcony seats. A moat surrounding the building is thought to have provided water-cooled air via tubes.

Beyond the Lotus Mahal, the **Elephant Stables**, a series of high-ceilinged, domed chambers, entered through arches, are the most substantial surviving secular buildings at Vijayanagar – a reflection of the high status accorded to elephants, both ceremonial and in battle.

Walking west of the Lotus Mahal, you pass two temples before reaching the road to Hemakuta Hill. The rectangular enclosure wall of the small **Hazara Rama** ("One thousand Ramas") temple, thought to have been the private palace shrine, features a series of medallion figures and bands of detailed friezes showing scenes from the Ramayana.

Eating

Hampi has a plethora of traveller-oriented **restaurants**, delivering safe options rather than haute cuisine. Many of the most popular are attached to guest-houses in the Bazaar, or among the growing row of joints in Virupapuragadda. As a holy site, the whole village is supposed to be strictly vegetarian and alcohol-free but one or two places bend the rules for inveterate carnivores and thirsty beer drinkers.

Mango Tree 300m beyond Sacred Ford. Wonderfully relaxed riverside hangout on a series of stone terraces. Fine Indian and Western veg dishes, but mostly a great place to linger over a simple snack or drink.

New Shanti On the path from Virupaksha temple down to the river. Best known for its delicious cakes and breads but also does standard Indian and Continental dishes.

Sheesh Besh Virupapuragadda, 350m west down main drag, next to *Sai Plaza*. Popular restaurant and French bakery, with fluffy croissants and excellent cinnamon rolls.

Shiv Moon Riverside path, east of the village. Good place to break the journey to or from the Vitthala temple, serving pastas and standard curries.

Sri Sangameshwarar Main Bazaar. One of the more genuine Indian places, where you can get the best thalis and masala dosas, as well as the odd Western snack.

Suresh On the path from Virupaksha temple down to the river. Established joint which specializes in tuna, Goan dishes and *momos* (Tibetan dumplings).

Trishul On the lane from beside the tourist office. Offers one of Hampi's widest menus, featuring chicken, tuna, lasagne, pizza and desserts such as scrumptious apple crumble. Beer occasionally available too.

Monuments of the Chalukyas

Now quiet villages, **Badami**, **Aihole** and **Pattadakal**, the last a UNESCO World Heritage site since 1987, were once the capital cities of the **Chalukyas**, who ruled much of the Deccan between the fourth and eighth centuries. The astonishing profusion of **temples** in the area beggars belief. Badami's and Aihole's cave temples, stylistically related to those at Ellora (see p.732), are some of the most important of their type. Among the many freestanding temples are some of the earliest in India, and uniquely, it is possible to see both northern (*nagari*) and southern (Dravida) architectural styles side by side.

The first important Chalukyan king was Pulakeshin I (535–66), but it was Pulakeshin II (610–42) who captured the Pallava capital of Kanchipuram in Tamil Nadu and extended the empire to include Maharashtra to the north, the Konkan coast on the west and the whole of what is now Karnataka. Much of this territory (including the capital, Badami) was subsequently re-taken, but the Chalukyas recovered it and continued to reign until the mid-eighth century. Some suggest that the incursion of the Pallavas accounts for the southern elements seen in the structural temples.

Badami and around

Surrounded by a yawning expanse of flat farmland, **BADAMI**, capital of the Chalukyas from 543 AD to 757 AD, extends east into a gorge between two red sandstone hills, topped by two ancient fort complexes. The south is riddled with cave temples, and on the north stand early structural temples. Beyond the village, to the east, is an artificial lake, Agastya, said to date from the fifth century. Its small selection of hotels and restaurants makes Badami an ideal base from which to explore the Chalukyan remains at Mahakuta, Aihole and Pattadakal as well as the temple village of **Banashankari**, 5km to the southeast. Dedicated to Shiva's consort Parvati, the shrine, accompanied by a large bathing tank, is the most important living temple of the region and attracts a steady stream of devotees, especially during the chariot festival held according to the lunar calendar, sometime between January and February each year. Although of little architectural interest, the temple is worth a visit for the atmosphere and is supposed to date back to the sixth century; much of it, however, was built during the Maratha period of the eighteenth century. The whole Badami area is also home to numerous troupes of monkeys, especially around the monuments, and you are likely to find the cheeky characters all over you if you produce any food.

Arrival and information

Badami **Bus Stand** – in the centre of the village on Main Station Road – sees frequent daily services to Gadag (2hr), Hubli (3hr), Bijapur (4hr) and Kolhapur, and local buses to Aihole and Pattadakal. The direct Hospet buses all leave by 8.30am (5hr). The best bet after that time is to catch a bus to Gadag (3hr), which leave every half-hour, then take an auto-rickshaw (Rs20) to Gadag's New Bus Stand, from where you can hop another bus to Hospet (2.5hr). The **railway station** is 5km north, along a road lined with *neem* trees; tongas (Rs30 or Rs5 per head shared) as well as buses and auto-rickshaws are usually available for the journey into town. The slow metre-gauge line from Bijapur to Gadag via Badami was being converted at the time of writing and was due to become operational in late 2008 with three daily trains in either direction.

The new and friendly **tourist office** (Mon–Sat: April–May 8am–1pm; June–March 10am–5.30pm; ☎08357/220414) on Ramdurg Road next to KSTDC

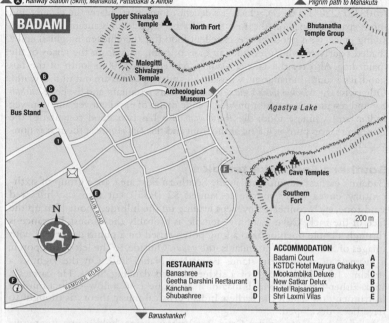

BADAMI

Upper Shivalaya Temple

North Fort

Bhutanatha Temple Group

Malegitti Shivalaya Temple

Archeological Museum

Agastya Lake

Bus Stand

N

MAIN ROAD

RAMDURG ROAD

Cave Temples

Southern Fort

0   200 m

RESTAURANTS
Banashree	D
Geetha Darshini Restaurant	1
Kanchan	C
Shubashree	D

ACCOMMODATION
Badami Court	A
KSTDC Hotel Mayura Chalukya	F
Mookambika Deluxe	C
New Satkar Delux	B
Hotel Rajsangam	D
Shri Laxmi Vilas	E

▼ Banashankari

Hotel Mayura Chalukya, can put you in touch with a **guide**. *Mookambika Deluxe* opposite the bus stand will change US dollars and sterling at low rates, but no traveller's cheques; the other place to try is the *Hotel Badami Court*.

Ambika Tours & Travels at *Mookambika Deluxe* runs **tours** taking in Badami, Mahakuta, Aihole and Pattadakal in Ambassador taxis for a reasonable Rs700. One of the best ways of exploring the closer sites, including Mahakuta and the temple village of Banashankari, is to rent a **bicycle**, available at Rs3 per hour from stalls in front of the bus stand, but cycling to Aihole and Pattadakal under the relentless sun can prove challenging.

Accommodation and eating

By far the most comfortable **place to stay** is the *Hotel Badami Court* (℡08357/220230, ⓔbadamicourt@nivalink.com; ❻–❽), 2km north of town towards the railway station. Ranged around a garden, its 27 attached rooms are plain but spacious; the restaurant serves meals and expensive beer, and its swimming pool is open to nonresidents for Rs80 per hour. Far cheaper, the KSTDC *Hotel Mayura Chalukya* (℡08357/220046; ❷), on the south side of town on Ramdurg Road, has ten basic rooms with decrepit plumbing and peeling plaster but, despite fearless scavenging monkeys, the gardens are pleasant and there's a restaurant. Opposite the bus stand, the *Mookambika Deluxe* (℡08357/220067, ⓕ220106; ❸–❻) has simple doubles on the ground floor and comfortable new air-conditioned rooms upstairs. The *Hotel Rajsangam* (℡08357/221991; ❹–❼) is the priciest in-town option, with spacious singles, deluxe doubles, and suites with balconies. But you may want to save your splurge for another stop: on a recent inspection the rooftop plunge pool was out of commission and monkeys were rampaging down the halls. Other options include the extremely basic *Shri Laxmi Vilas* (℡08357/220077; ❶), which has a reasonable restaurant, and the recently upgraded *New Satkar Delux*

㉒

KARNATAKA | Monuments of the Chalukyas

(℡08357/220417; ②—⑤), which has decent rooms, particularly the cleaner and more spacious ones on the first floor. Its back-garden restaurant is Badami's saving grace, with good service, excellent food (try the chicken mughlai) and a shaded courtyard which provides an oasis of calm, away from the chaos of the main drag. Also try the *Geetha Darshini* (closed Sun), 100m south of the bus stand; it's a south Indian joint, whose *iddlis*, vadas and *dosas* are out of this world. Otherwise the *Mookambika Deluxe*'s plain upstairs restaurant and livelier *Kanchan* bar and restaurant next door provide a wide menu of excellent veg and non-veg Indian and Chinese food; the *Rajsangam* also has two good restaurants: the *Banashree* serves pure-veg food at the front and the *Shubashree* at the rear is non-veg and has a bar.

Southern Fort cave temples

Badami's earliest monuments, in the Southern Fort area, are a group of sixth-century **caves** (daily sunrise to sunset; $2 [Rs5]) cut into the hill's red sandstone, each connected by steps leading up the hillside. About 15m up the face of the rock, **Cave 1**, a Shiva temple, is probably the earliest. Entrance is through a triple opening into a long porch raised on a plinth decorated with images of Shiva's dwarf attendants, the *ganas*. Outside, to the left of the porch, a *dvarpala* door guardian stands beneath a Nandi bull. On the right is a striking 1.5m-high image of a sixteen-armed dancing Shiva. He carries a stick-zither-type *vina*, which may or may not be a *yal*, a now-extinct musical instrument, on which the earliest Indian classical music theory is thought to have been developed.

A little higher, the similar **Cave 2**, a Vishnu shrine, holds some impressive sculpture and painting. Steps and slopes lead on upwards, past a natural cave containing a smashed image of the Buddhist *bodhisattva*, Padmapani (he who holds the lotus), and steps on the right in a cleft in the rock lead up to the fort. **Cave 3** (578 AD) stands beneath a thirty-metre-high perpendicular bluff. The largest of the group, with a facade measuring 21m from north to south, it is also considered to be the finest, for the quality of its sculptural decoration. Treatment of the pillars is extremely elaborate, featuring male and female bracket figures, lotus motifs and medallions portraying amorous couples.

To the east of the others, a Jain temple, **Cave 4**, overlooks Agastya Lake and the town. It's a much simpler shrine, dating from the sixth century. Figures, both seated and standing, of the 24 *tirthankaras*, mostly without their identifying emblems, line the walls. Here, the rock is striped.

After seeing the caves it is possible to climb up to the fort and walk east where, hidden in the rocks, a carved panel shows Vishnu reclining on the serpent Adisesha, attended by a profusion of gods and sages. Continuing, you can skirt the gorge and descend on the east to the Bhutanatha temples at the lakeside.

North Fort

North of Agastya Lake, a number of structural temples can be reached by steps. The small **Archeological Museum** (daily except Fri 10am–5pm; Rs2) contains sculpture from the region. Although now dilapidated, the **Upper Shivalaya temple** is one of the earliest Chalukyan buildings. Scenes from the life of Krishna decorate the base and various images of him can be seen between pilasters on the walls. Only the sanctuary and tower of the **Lower Shivalaya** survive. Perched on a rock, the **Malegitti Shivalaya** (late seventh century) is the finest southern-style early Chalukyan temple. Its shrine is adjoined by a pillared hallway with small pierced stones and a single image on each side: Vishnu on the north and Shiva on the south.

Aihole

No fewer than 125 temples, dating from the Chalukyan and the later Rashtrakuta periods (sixth to twelfth centuries), are found in the tiny village of **AIHOLE** (Aivalli), near the banks of the River Malaprabha. Lying in clusters within the village, in surrounding fields and on rocky outcrops, many of the temples are remarkably well preserved, despite being used as dwellings and cattle sheds. Reflecting both its geographical position and spirit of architectural experimentation, Aihole boasts northern (*nagari*) and southern (Dravida) temples, as well as variants that failed to survive subsequent stylistic developments.

Two of the temples are **rock-cut caves** dating from the sixth century. The Hindu **Ravanaphadigudi**, northeast of the centre, a Shiva shrine with a triple entrance, contains fine sculptures of Mahishasuramardini, a ten-armed Nateshan (the precursor of Shiva Nataraja) dancing with Parvati, Ganesh and the Sapta Matrikas ("seven mothers"). A two-storey cave, plain save for decoration at the entrances and a panel image of Buddha in its upper veranda, can be found partway up the hill to the southeast, overlooking the village. At the top of that hill, the Jain **Meguti** temple, which may never have been completed, bears an inscription on an outer wall dating it to 634 AD. You can climb up to the first floor for fine views of Aihole and the surrounding country.

The late seventh- to early eighth-century **Durga temple** (daily 6am–6pm; $2 [Rs5]), one of the most unusual, elaborate and large in Aihole, stands close to others on open ground in the Archeological Survey compound, near the centre of the village. It derives its name not from the goddess Durga but from the Kannada *durgadagudi*, meaning "temple near the fort". A series of pillars – many featuring amorous couples – forming an open ambulatory continue from the porch around the whole building. Other sculptural highlights include the decoration on the entrance to the *mandapa* hallway and niche images on the outer walls of the now-empty semicircular sanctum. Nearby, a small **Archeological Museum** (daily except Fri 10am–5pm; free) displays early Chalukyan sculpture and sells the booklet *Glorious Aihole*, which includes a site map and accounts of the monuments.

Further south, beyond several other temples, the **Ladh Khan** (the name of a Muslim who made it his home) is perhaps the best known of all at Aihole. Now thought to have been constructed at some point between the end of the sixth century and the eighth, it was dated at one time to the mid-fifth century, and was seen as one of the country's temple prototypes. Inside stands a Nandi bull and a small sanctuary containing a *shivalingam* is next to the back wall. Both may have been later additions, with the original inner sanctum located at the centre.

Practicalities

Six daily **buses** run to Aihole from Badami (1hr 30min) via Pattadakal (45min) from 5.30am to 9pm; the last bus returns around 6pm. The only place to **stay and eat** (apart from a few chai shops) in Aihole is the small, clean and spartan KSTDC *Tourist Rest House* (☎08351/234541; ❷) about five minutes' walk up the main road north out of the village, next to the ASI offices. It has a "VIP" room, two doubles with bath plus two doubles and four singles without. Simple, tasty food is available by arrangement – and by candlelight during frequent power cuts. The *Kiran Bar* on the same road, but in the village, serves beer and spirits and has a restaurant.

Pattadakal

The village of **PATTADAKAL**, on a bend in the River Malaprabha 22km from Badami, served as the site of Chalukyan coronations between the seventh and eighth centuries; in fact it may only have been used for such ceremonials. Like Badami and Aihole, the area boasts fine Chalukyan architecture, with particularly large mature examples; as at Aihole, both northern and southern styles can be seen. Pattadakal's main group of monuments (daily 6am–6pm; $5 [Rs10]) stand together in a well-maintained compound, next to the village, and have been designated a World Heritage Site.

Earliest among the temples, the **Sangameshvara**, also known as **Shri Vijayeshvara** (a reference to its builder, Vijayaditya Satyashraya; 696–733), shows typical southern features. To the south, both the **Mallikarjuna** and the enormous **Virupaksha**, side by side, are in the southern style, built by two sisters who were successively the queens of Vikramaditya II (733–46). Along with the Kanchipuram temple in Tamil Nadu, the Virupaksha was probably one of the largest and most elaborate in India at the time. Interior pillars are carved with scenes from the *Ramayana* and Mahabharata, while in the Mallikarjuna the stories are from the life of Krishna.

The largest northern-style temple, the **Papanatha**, further south, was probably built after the Virupaksha in the eighth century. Outside walls feature reliefs (some of which, unusually, bear the sculptors' autographs) from the Ramayana, including, on the south wall, Hanuman's monkey army.

About 1km south of the village, a fine **Rashtrakuta** (ninth to tenth century) **Jain temple** is fronted by a porch and two *mandapa* hallways with twin carved elephants at the entrance. Inexplicably, the sanctuary contains a lingam.

Pattadakal is connected by regular state **buses** and hourly private buses to Badami (45min) and Aihole (45min). Aside from a few teashops, cold drinks and coconut stalls, there are no facilities. For three days at the end of January, Pattadakal hosts an annual **dance festival** featuring dancers from all over the country.

Bijapur and the north

Boasting some of the Deccan's finest Muslim monuments, **BIJAPUR** is often billed as "The Agra of the South". The comparison is partly justified: for more than three hundred years, this was the capital of a succession of powerful rulers, whose domed mausoleums, mosques, colossal civic buildings and fortifications recall a lost golden age of unrivalled prosperity and artistic refinement. Yet there the similarities between the two cities end. A provincial market town of just 210,000 inhabitants, modern Bijapur is a world away from the urban frenzy of Agra. With the exception of the mighty **Golgumbaz**, which attracts busloads of day-trippers, its historic sites see only a slow trickle of tourists, while the ramshackle town centre is surprisingly laid-back, dotted with peaceful green spaces and colonnaded mosque courtyards. In the first week of February the town hosts an annual **music festival** which attracts several renowned musicians from both the Carnatic (south Indian) and the Hindustani (north Indian) classical music traditions.

Some history

Bijapur began life in the tenth century as **Vijayapura**, the Chalukyas' "City of Victory". Taken by the Vijayanagars, it passed into Muslim hands for the first time in the thirteenth century with the arrival of the sultans of Delhi. The Bahmanis administered the area for a time, but it was only after the local rulers, the **Adil Shahis**, won independence from Bidar by expelling the Bahmani garrison and declaring this their capital that Bijapur's rise to prominence began.

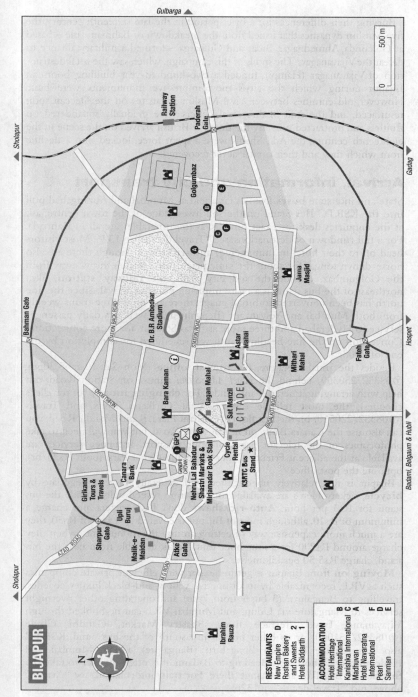

BIJAPUR

RESTAURANTS
New Empire — D
Roshan Bakery and Sweets — 2
Hotel Siddarth — 1

ACCOMMODATION
Hotel Heritage International — B
Kanishka International — C
Madhuvan — A
Hotel Navaratna International — F
Pearl — D
Sanman — E

Gulbarga ▲

▲ Sholapur

Railway Station

Paderah Gate

Golgumbaz

B E
D
F C

A

Bahman Gate ⊗

Dr. B.R Ambedkar Stadium

STATION BACK ROAD

STATION ROAD

Jama Masjid

JAMA MASJID ROAD

Gadag ▼

Hospet ▼

Astar Mahal

Mithari Mahal

Fateh Gate ▼

Bara Kaman

Gagan Mahal

Sat Manzil

CITADEL

BAGALKOT ROAD

Badami, Belgaum & Hubli ▼

NEHRU ROAD

GPO
GANDHI CHOWK
Nehru, Lal Bahadur Shastri Markets & Mirjamadar Book Stall

Cycle Rental

KSRTC Bus Stand ★

Canara Bank

Girikand Tours & Travels

Upli Buruj

Sharpur Gate ⊗

Malik-e-Maidan

AZAD ROAD

Atke Gate ⊗

M.G ROAD

GAZA

Ibrahim Rauza

▲ Sholapur

N

0   500 m

KARNATAKA

22

1317

Burying their differences for a brief period in the late sixteenth century, the five Muslim dynasties that issued from the breakdown of Bahmani rule – based at Golconda, Ahmednagar, Bidar and Gulbarga – formed a military alliance to defeat the Vijayanagars. The spoils of this campaign, which saw the total destruction of Vijayanagar (Hampi), funded a two-hundred-year building boom in Bijapur during which the city's most impressive monuments were built. However, old enmities between rival Muslim sultanates on the Deccan soon resurfaced, and the Adil Shahi's royal coffers were gradually squandered on fruitless and protracted wars. By the time the British arrived on the scene in the eighteenth century, the Adil Shahis were a spent force, locked into a decline from which they and their capital never recovered.

Arrival, information and city transport

State and interstate **buses** from as far afield as Mumbai and Aurangabad pull into the KSRTC Bus Stand on the southwest edge of the town centre; ask at the enquiries desk for exact timings, as the timetables are all in Kannada. For a full rundown of destinations, see "Travel details", p.1326. Most visitors head off to their hotel in (unmetered) auto-rickshaws, though there are also horse-drawn tongas for about the same price. Just a stone's throw away from the Golgumbaz, outside the old city walls, the **railway station**, 3km northeast of the bus stand, is a more inspiring point of arrival. Since the line north has been converted to broad guage, there are now three trains weekly from both Mumbai and Yesvantpur (Bengaluru), as well as a daily passenger service to Hyderabad and three more as far as Solapur, for more connections. Conversion on the line heading south was scheduled for completion by the end of 2008.

Besides the usual literature, the **tourist office** (Mon–Sat 10am–5.30pm; ☎08352/250359) behind the *Hotel Adil Shahi* annexe on Station Road, can help with arranging itineraries and guides. For **changing money** (or traveller's cheques), the most reliable service is at Girikand Tours and Travels (☎08352/220510) on the first floor at Nishant Plaza, Rama Mandir Road; you can also use the Canara Bank, on nearby Azad Road, but you will need to take photocopies of the relevant pages of your passport. **Internet** services are available at the adjacent Friends Cyber Zone and Cyber Park (both Rs25/hr), opposite the post office.

Bijapur is flat, relatively uncongested, and generally easy to negotiate by **bicycle**; rickety Heros are available for rent from several stalls outside the bus stand for Rs3 per hour. **Auto-rickshaws** don't have meters and charge a minimum of Rs10; although most of Bijapur is covered by a fare of Rs30, they are a much more expensive way of getting around the monuments, when they charge around Rs200 for a four-hour tour. **Taxis**, available from near the bus stand, charge Rs5.50 per kilometre.

Moving on from Bijapur is getting easier with efficient private companies such as VRL, recognizable by its distinctive yellow-and-black luxury coaches, travelling to Bengaluru (3 buses from 7pm) and operating other overnight services to Mangalore via Udupi and Mumbai. VRL can be booked through Vijayanand Travel, Terrace floor, Shastri Market, Gandhi Circle (☎08352/251000) or its other branch just south of the bus stand. KSRTC also runs deluxe buses to Bengaluru (Bangalore), Hubli, Mumbai and Hyderabad (via Sholapur). Heading to Badami, it is often quicker to take the first bus to Bagalkot and change there. For train information, see "Arrival" above, and "Travel details", p.1326.

Accommodation and eating

Good-value **accommodation** is relatively thick on the ground in Bijapur. **Eating** is largely confined to the hotels – try the *New Empire* at the *Pearl*. At most independent establishments you'll be restricted to pure veg; at Gandhi Chowk, the *Shrinidhi Hotel* serves good south Indian vegetarian food, as does the *Priyadarshini*, across the main road from the Gagan Mahal. Among other goodies, the popular *Roshan Bakery and Sweets*, MG Road, whips up the perfect budget brunch to-go: flaky, rich and delicious boiled egg and veg croissants (Rs6). Above the main market is ⚡ *Hotel Siddarth* (☎08352/220338), a sprawling rooftop bar-restaurant, with tasty non-veg Indian and a good selection of booze.

Hotel Heritage International Station Rd ☎08352/221006. Though slightly antiseptic, this new hotel has huge rooms at good prices. The adjoining veg restaurant is cool, tasty and stunningly cheap. ❸–❹

Kanishka International Station Rd ☎08352/223788, ⊛www.kanishkabijapur.com. One of the better-value places, providing comfy rooms with most mod cons and good service at decent rates. Fine veg and non-veg restaurants. ❸–❺

Madhuvan Station Rd ☎08352/255571, ⓕ256201. The smartest place in town, with a variety of rooms, from overpriced ordinary doubles to more comfortable a/c "deluxe" options. The restaurant serves good-value thalis at lunchtime. Can change money for residents. ❺–❻

Hotel Navaratna International Just off Station Rd ☎08352/222771. The huge, shiny-tiled rooms at this quiet hotel are great value for this price. Good service, veg and non-veg restaurants and a popular palm-shaded dining (and drinking) area. ❸–❹

Pearl Station Rd ☎08352/256002, ⓕ243606. Bright modern hotel with clean, sizeable rooms. The front ones have balconies and those at the top views of Golgumbaz. Better value than the *Madhuvan* and with an excellent restaurant. ❸–❺

Sanman Station Rd ☎08352/251866. Best value among the budget places, and well placed for the railway station. Clean, good-sized rooms, some with a/c, and a rooftop restaurant/bar with excellent evening views of the mausoleum. ❷–❹

The town and monuments

Unlike most medieval Muslim strongholds, Bijapur lacked natural rock defences and had to be strengthened by the Adil Shahis with huge **fortified walls**. Extending some 10km around the town, these ramparts, studded with cannon emplacements (*burjes*) and watchtowers, are breached in five points by *darvazas*, or strong gateways, and several smaller postern gates (*didis*). In the middle of the town, a further hoop of crenellated battlements encircled Bijapur's **citadel**, site of the sultans' apartments and durbar hall, of which only fragments remain. The Adil Shahis' **tombs** are scattered around the outskirts, while most of the important **mosques** lie southeast of the citadel.

It's possible to see Bijapur's highlights in a day, although most people stay for two or three nights, taking in the monuments at a more leisurely pace. Our account covers the sights from east to west, beginning with the Golgumbaz – which you should aim to visit at around 6am, before the bus parties descend – and ending with the exquisite Ibrahim Rauza, an atmospheric spot to enjoy the sunset.

The Golgumbaz

The vast **Golgumbaz** mausoleum (daily 6am–6pm; $2 [Rs5]), Bijapur's most famous building, soars above the town's east walls, visible for miles in every direction. Built towards the end of the Adil Shahis' reign, the building is a fitting monument to a dynasty on its last legs – pompous, decadent and ill-proportioned, but conceived on an irresistibly awesome scale.

The cubic tomb, enclosing a 170-square-metre hall, is crowned with a single hemispherical **dome**, the largest in the world after St Peter's in Rome (which is only 5m wider). Spiral staircases wind up the four seven-storey octagonal towers that buttress the building to the famous **Whispering Gallery**, a three-metre-wide passage encircling the interior base of the dome from where, looking carefully down, you can get a real feel of the sheer size of the building. Arrive here just after opening time and you can experiment with the extraordinary acoustics; by 7am, though, bus loads of whooping and clapping tourists drown out all sound. A good antidote to the din is the superb **view** from the mausoleum's ramparts, which overlook the town and its monuments to the dark-soiled Deccan countryside beyond, scattered with minor tombs and ruins.

Set on a plinth in the centre of the hall below are the gravestones of the ruler who built the Golgumbaz, **Mohammed Adil Shahi**, along with those of his wife, daughter, grandson and favourite courtesan, Rambha. At one corner of the grounds stands the simple gleaming white shrine to a Sufi saint of the Adil Shahi period, **Hashim Pir** which, around February, attracts *qawwals* (singers of devotional *qawwali* music) to the annual *urs*, which lasts for three days.

The Jama Masjid

A little under 1km southwest of the Golgumbaz, the **Jama Masjid** (Friday Mosque) presides over the quarter that formed the centre of the city during Bijapur's nineteenth-century nadir under the Nizam of Hyderabad. It was commissioned by Ali Adil Shahi, the ruler credited with constructing the city walls and complex water supply system, as a monument to his victory over the Vijayanagars at the battle of Talikota in 1565, and is widely regarded as one of the finest mosques in India. As it is a living place of worship, you should not enter improperly dressed (no shorts or skirts).

Simplicity and restraint are the essence of the colonnaded prayer hall below, divided by gently curving arches and rows of thick plaster-covered pillars. Aside from the odd geometric design and trace of yellow, blue and green tile work, the only ornamentation is found in the mihrab, or west- (Mecca-) facing prayer niche, which is smothered in gold leaf and elaborate calligraphy. The marble floor of the hall features a grid of 2500 rectangles, known as *musallahs* (after the *musallah* prayer mats brought to mosques by worshippers). These were added by the Mughal emperor Aurangzeb, allegedly as recompense for making off with the velvet carpets, long golden chain and other valuables that originally filled the prayer hall.

The Mithari and Astar Mahals

Continuing west from the Jama Masjid, the first monument of note is a small, ornately carved gatehouse on the south side of the road. Although of modest size, the delicate three-storey structure, known as the **Mithari Mahal**, is one of Bijapur's most beautiful buildings, with ornate projecting windows and minarets crowning its corners. Once again, Ali Adil Shahi erected it, along with the mosque behind, using gifts presented to him during a state visit to Vijayanagar. The Hindu rajas' generosity, however, did not pay off. Only a couple of years later, the Adil Shahi and his four Muslim allies sacked their city, plundering its wealth and murdering most of its inhabitants.

The lane running north from opposite the Mithari Mahal brings you to the dilapidated **Asar Mahal**, a large open-fronted hall fronted by a large stagnant step-well. Built in 1646 by Mohammed Adil Shahi as a Hall of Justice, it was later chosen to house hairs from the Prophet's beard, thereby earning the title **Asar-i-Sharif**, or "place of illustrious relics". In theory, women are not permitted inside to view the upper storey, where fifteen niches are decorated with mediocre, Persian-style pot-and-foliage murals, but for a little baksheesh, one of the girls who hang around the site will unlock the doors for you.

The citadel

Bijapur's **citadel** stands in the middle of town, hemmed in on all but its north side by battlements. Most of the buildings inside have collapsed, or have been converted into government offices, but enough remain to give a sense of how imposing this royal enclave must once have been.

The best-preserved monuments lie along, or near, the citadel's main north–south artery, Anand Mahal Road, reached by skirting the southeast wall from the Asar Mahal. The latter route brings you first to the **Gagan Mahal**. Originally Ali Adil Shahi's "Heavenly Palace", this now-ruined hulk later served as a durbar hall for the sultans, who would sit in state on the platform at the open-fronted north side, watched by crowds gathered in the grounds opposite. West off Anand Mahal Road, the five-storeyed **Sat Manzil** was the pleasure palace of the courtesan Rambha, entombed with Mohammed Adil Shahi and his family in the Golgumbaz. In front stands an ornately carved water pavilion, the **Jal Mandir**, now left high and dry in an empty tank.

Malik-i-Maidan and Upli Buruj

Guarding the principal western entrance to the city is one of several bastions (*burje*) that punctuate Bijapur's battlements. This one, the Burj-i-Sherza ("Lion Gate") sports a colossal cannon, known as the **Malik-i-Maidan**, literally "Lord of the Plains". It was brought here as war booty in the sixteenth century, and needed four hundred bullocks, ten elephants and an entire battalion to haul it up the steps to the emplacement. Inscriptions record that the cannon, whose muzzle features a relief of a monster swallowing an elephant, was cast in Ahmednagar in 1551.

A couple more discarded cannons lie atop the watchtower visible a short walk northwest. Steps wind around the outside of the oval-shaped **Upli Burj**, or "Upper Bastion", to a gun emplacement that affords unimpeded views over the city and plains.

The Ibrahim Rauza

Set in its own walled compound less than 1km west of the ramparts, the **Ibrahim Rauza** represents the high-water mark of Bijapuri architecture (daily 6am–6pm; $2 [Rs5]). Whereas the Golgumbaz impresses primarily by its scale, the appeal of this tomb complex lies in its grace and simplicity. Beyond the reach of most bus parties, it's also a haven of peace, with cool colonnaded verandas and flocks of iridescent parakeets careening between the mildewed domes, minarets and gleaming golden finials.

Opinions differ over whether the tomb was commissioned by Ibrahim Adil Shah (1580–1626), or his favourite wife, Taj Sultana, but the former was the first to be interred here, in a gloomy chamber whose only light enters via a series of exquisite pierced-stone (*jali*) windows. Made up of elaborate Koranic inscriptions, these are the finest examples of their kind in India. More amazing stonework decorates the exterior of the mausoleum, and the equally beautiful **mosque** opposite, the cornice of whose facade features a stone chain carved from a single block. The two buildings, bristling with minarets and domed cupolas, face each other from opposite sides of a rectangular raised plinth, divided by a small reservoir and fountains. Viewed from on top of the walls that enclose the complex, you can see why its architect, Malik Sandal, added a self-congratulatory inscription in his native Persian over the tomb's south doorway, describing his masterpiece as " …A beauty of which Paradise stood amazed".

Gulbarga

GULBARGA, 165km northeast of Bijapur, was the founding capital of the Bahmani dynasty and the region's principal city before the court moved to Bidar in 1424. Later captured by the Adil Shahis and Mughals, it has remained a staunchly Muslim town, and bulbous onion domes and mosque minarets still soar prominently above its ramshackle concrete-box skyline. The town is also famous as the birthplace of the *chishti*, or saint, Hazrat Bandah Nawaz Gesu Daraz (1320–1422), whose tomb, situated next to one of India's foremost Islamic theological colleges, is a major shrine.

In spite of Gulbarga's religious and historical significance, its **monuments** pale in comparison with those at Bijapur, and even Bidar. Unless you're particularly interested in medieval Muslim architecture, few are worth breaking a journey to see. The one exception is the tomb complex on the northeast edge of town, known as **the Dargah**. Approached via a broad bazaar, this marble-lined enclosure centres on the tomb of Hazrat Gesu Daraz, affectionately known to his devotees as **"Bandah Nawaz"**, or "the long-haired one who brings comfort to others". The saint was spiritual mentor to the Bahmani rulers, and it was they who erected his beautiful double-storeyed mausoleum, now visited by hundreds of thousands of Muslim pilgrims each year. Women are not allowed inside, and men must wear long trousers. The same applies to the neighbouring tomb, whose interior has retained its exquisite Persian paintings. The Dargah's other important building, open to both sexes, is the **Madrasa**, or theological college, founded by Bandah Nawaz and enlarged during the two centuries after his death.

After mingling with the crowds at the Dargah, escape across town to Gulbarga's deserted **fort**. Encircled by sixteen-metre-thick crenellated walls, fifteen watchtowers and an evil-smelling stagnant moat, the great citadel now lies in ruins behind the town's large artificial lake. Its only surviving building is the beautiful fourteenth-century **Jama Masjid**. Thought to have been modelled by a Moorish architect on the great Spanish mosque of Cordoba, it is unique in India for having an entirely domed prayer hall.

Practicalities

Daily KSRTC **buses** from Bijapur, Bidar and Hospet pull in to the State Bus Stand on the southwest edge of town. Private minibuses work from the roadside opposite, their conductors shouting for passengers across the main concourse. Don't be tempted to take one of these to Bidar; they only run as far as the fly-blown highway junction of Humnabad, 40km short, where you'll be stranded for hours. Gulbarga's mainline **railway station**, with services to and from Mumbai, Pune, Hyderabad, Bangalore and Chennai, lies 1.5km east of the bus stand, along **Mill Road**. **Station Road**, the town's other main artery, runs due north of here past the lake to the busy **Chowk** crossroads, at the heart of the bazaar.

Gulbarga's main sights are well spread out, so you'll need to get around by **auto-rickshaw**; fix fares in advance. There is a Syndicate Bank ATM on Station Road, where you can **change money**.

Accommodation and eating

All the hotels listed below have **restaurants**, mostly pure-veg places with a no-alcohol rule. *Kamat*, the chain restaurant, has several branches in Gulbarga including a pleasant one at Station Chowk, specializing in vegetarian "meals" as well as *iddlis* and *dosas*; try *joleata roti*, a local bread cooked either hard and crisp or soft like a chapati. On the road up from the station several hole-in-the-wall spots sell freshly fried chicken and fish.

Adithya 2-244 Station Rd, opposite Public Gardens ℡ 08472/224040, Ⓕ 235661. The posher a/c rooms here cost hardly more than the non-a/c ones. The hotel's impeccably clean pure-veg Udupi restaurant, *Pooja*, on the ground floor, does great thalis and snacks. ❹—❺

Kapila Lodge Opposite north end of bus stand. The big, clean rooms here, some of which have balconies, are hard to beat at these prices. ❶—❹

Hotel Prashant First lane on the right leaving the station ℡ 08472/221456. Decent rooms of varying sized and amenities, surprisingly quiet. ❷—❹

Raj Rajeshwari Vasant Nagar, Mill Rd ℡ 08472/225881. Just 5min from the bus stand, this friendly hotel is set in a well-maintained modern building with large attached rooms with balconies, plus a reasonable veg restaurant. Strictly no alcohol. ❸—❹

Southern Star Near the Fort, Super Market ℡ 08472/224093. Pricey rooms, some with fort views, but the vast side-courtyard offers relaxing alfresco dining and is a great spot to watch the sunset behind the fort while nursing a beer. ❸—❻

Bidar

Lost in the far northwest of Karnataka, Bidar, 284km northwest of Bijapur, is nowadays a provincial backwater, better known for its fighter-pilot training base than the monuments gently decaying in, and within sight of, its medieval walls. Yet the town, half of whose 140,000 population is still Muslim, has a gritty charm, with narrow red-dirt streets ending at arched gates and open vistas across the plains. Littered with tile-fronted tombs, rambling fortifications and old mosques, it merits a visit if you're travelling between Hyderabad (150km east) and Bijapur, although expect little in the way of Western comforts, and more than the usual amount of curious approaches from locals. Lone women travellers may find the attention more hassle than it's worth.

In 1424, following the break-up of the Bahmani dynasty into five rival factions, Ahmad Shah I shifted his court from Gulbarga to a less constricted site at **BIDAR**, spurred, it is said, by grief at the death of his beloved spiritual mentor, Bandah Nawas Gesu Daraz. Revamping the town with a new fort, splendid palaces, mosques and ornamental gardens, the Bahmanis ruled from here until 1487, when the Barid Shahis took control. They were succeeded by the Adil Shahis from Bijapur, and later the Mughals under Aurangzeb, who annexed the region in 1656, before the Nizam of Hyderabad finally acquired the territory in the early eighteenth century.

Bidar's sights are too spread out to be comfortably explored on foot. However, auto-rickshaws tend to be thin on the ground away from the main streets, and are reluctant to wait while you look around the monuments, so it's a good idea to rent a **bicycle** for the day (Rs3 per hour) from Rouf's, only 50m east of the bus stand next to the excellent *Karnatak Juice Centre*.

Practicalities

Bidar lies on a branch line of the main Mumbai–Secunderabad–Chennai rail route, and can only be reached by slow passenger **train**. The few visitors that come here invariably arrive **by bus**, arriving at the KSRTC Bus Stand on the far northwestern edge of town. There is no tourist office or exchange facility but there are several **Internet** outlets such as Cyber Park (Rs15/hr), 100m southeast of the bus stand on Udgir Road. Just south of the Madrasa is a small **clinic** (Gawan Chowk ℡ 9448410636; 10am–1pm, 2–9pm).

Hotel Mayura (℡ 08482/228142; ❷—❹) opposite the bus stand, has large rooms with optional air-conditioning. Its older sister, the *Ashoka* (℡ 08482/227621; ❷—❹), 1500m from the bus stand past Dr Ambedkar Chowk, is comfortable with good-value deluxe rooms, some with air-conditioning. *Sapna International* (220991, ❸—❺), 300m north of the bus stand, offers Bidar's nicest lodgings, with big, clean rooms and a good non-veg restaurant. If you don't mind some grubbiness, a real budget option is *Hotel Kailash* (℡08482/227727; ❶) on Udgir Road, in the centre of town.

Finding somewhere good to **eat** is not a problem in Bidar, thanks to the restaurants at the *Mayura* and *Ashoka*, which both offer a varied selection of north Indian veg and meat dishes (try the *Mayura's* pepper chicken) and serve cold beer. Also recommended, and much cheaper, is the popular *Udupi Krishna* restaurant, overlooking the *chowk*, which serves up unlimited pure-veg thalis for lunch; it has a "family room" for women, too, and opens early (around 7.30am) for piping-hot south Indian breakfasts. The *Jyothi Udupi*, opposite the new bus stand, serves big, delicious *dosas* and tasty thalis.

The old town

The heart of Bidar is its medieval **old town**, encircled by crenellated ramparts and eight imposing gateways (*darwazas*). This predominantly Muslim quarter holds many Bahmani-era mosques, havelis and *khanqahs* – "monasteries" set up by the local rulers for Muslim cleric-mystics and their disciples – but its real highlight is the impressive ruins of **Mahmud Gawan's Madrasa**, or theological college, whose single minaret soars high above the city centre. The distinctively Persian-style building, originally surmounted by large bulbous domes, once housed a world-famous library. However, this burnt down after being struck by lightning in 1696, while several of the walls and domes were blown away when gunpowder stored here by Aurangzeb's occupying army caught fire and exploded. Today, the *madrasa* is little more than a shell, although its elegant arched facade has retained large patches of the vibrant Persian glazed tile-work that once covered most of the exterior surfaces.

The Fort

A rambling, crumbling monument valley to the fifteenth-century Bahmani Empire, the Bidar **Fort**, at the far north end of the street running past the *madrasa*, retains a serene, austere beauty. Though locals have incorporated the vast rolling spaces into their lives – young boys play cricket in the grassy turf, terraces are planted with rice, and scooters and small trucks ply its roads – its appeal remains undiminished.

The fort was founded by the Hindu Chalukyas and strengthened by the Bahmanis in the early fifteenth century. Despite repeated sieges, it remains largely intact, encircled by 10km of ramparts that drop away in the north and

Bidri

Bidar is renowned as the home of a unique damascene metalwork technique known as **bidri**, developed by the Persian silversmiths who came to the area with the Bahmani court in the fifteenth century. These highly skilled artisans engraved and inlaid their traditional Iranian designs onto a metal alloy composed of lead, copper, zinc and tin, which they blackened and polished. The resulting effect – swirling silver floral motifs framed by geometric patterns and set against black backgrounds – has since become the hallmark of Muslim metalwork in India.

Bidri objets d'art are displayed in museums and galleries all over the country. But if you want to see pukka *bidri*-wallahs at work, take a walk down Bidar's **Siddiq Talim Road**, which cuts across the south side of the old town, where skull-capped artisans tap and burnish vases, goblets, plates, spice boxes, betel-nut tins and ornamental hookah pipes, as well as less traditional objects – coasters, ashtrays and bangles – that crop up (at vastly inflated prices) in silver emporiums as far away as Delhi and Kolkata (Calcutta).

west to 300-metre cliffs. The main southern entrance is protected by equally imposing man-made defences: gigantic fortified gates and a triple moat formerly crossed by a series of drawbridges. Once inside, the first building of note (on the left after the third and final gateway) is the exquisite **Rangin Mahal**. Mahmud Shah built this modest "Coloured Palace" after an unsuccessful uprising of Abyssinian slaves in 1487 forced him to relocate to a safer site inside the citadel. The palace's relatively modest proportions reflect the Bahmanis' declining fortunes, but its interior comprises some of the finest surviving Islamic art in the Deccan, with superb woodcarving above the door arches and Persian-style mother-of-pearl inlay on polished black granite surfaces. If the doors to the palace are locked, ask for the keys at the nearby ASI **museum** (daily 8am–1pm & 2–5pm; free), which houses a missable collection of Hindu temple sculpture, weapons and Stone Age artefacts.

Opposite the museum, an expanse of gravel is all that remains of the royal gardens. This is overlooked by the austere **Solah Khamb** mosque (1327), Bidar's oldest Muslim monument, whose most outstanding feature is the intricate pierced-stone *jali* calligraphy around its central dome. From here, continue west through the ruins of the former royal enclosure – a rambling complex of half-collapsed palaces, baths, *zenanas* (women's quarters) and assembly halls – to the fort's west walls. You can complete the round of **the ramparts** in ninety minutes, taking time out to enjoy the views over the red cliffs and across the plains.

Ashtur: the Bahmani tombs

As you look from the fort's east walls, a cluster of eight bulbous white domes floats alluringly above the trees in the distance. Dating from the fifteenth century, the mausoleums at **Ashtur**, 3km east of Bidar (leave the old town via Dulhan Darwaza gate), are the final resting-places of the Bahmani sultans and their families, including the son of the ruler who first decamped from Gulbarga, Ala-ud-Din Shah I. His remains by far the most impressive tomb, with patches of coloured glazed tiles on its arched facade, and a large dome whose interior surfaces writhe with sumptuous Persian paintings. Reflecting sunlight onto the ceiling with a small pocket mirror, the *chowkidar* picks out the highlights, among them a diamond, barely visible among the bat droppings.

The tomb of Ala-ud-Din's father, the ninth and most illustrious Bahmani Sultan, Ahmad Shah I, stands beside that of his son, decorated with Persian inscriptions. Beyond this are two more minor mausoleums, followed by the partially collapsed tomb of Humayun the Cruel (1458–61), cracked open by a bolt of lightning. Continuing along the line, you can chart the gradual decline of the Bahmanis as the mausoleums diminish in size, ending with a sad handful erected in the early sixteenth century, when the sultans were no more than puppet rulers of the Barid Shahis.

The Badrid Shahi tombs

The **tombs of the Badrid Shahi** rulers, who succeeded the Bahmanis at the start of the sixteenth century, stand on the western edge of town, on the Udgir road, 200m beyond and visible from the bus stand. Although not as impressive as those of their predecessors, the mausoleums, mounted on raised plinths, occupy an attractive site. Note the tomb of **Ali Barid** (1542–79), whose Mecca-facing wall was left open to the elements. A short distance southwest lies a mass-grave platform for his 67 concubines who were sent as tribute gifts by vassals of the Deccani overlord from all across the kingdom. The compound is only officially open for afternoon promenading (daily 4.30–7.30pm; $2 [Rs5]) but the gateman may let you in earlier if he's around.

Travel details

Trains

Bengaluru (Bangalore) to: Chennai (6–7 daily; 5hr–7hr 40min); Delhi (2–4 daily; 34hr 40min–49hr 40min); Gulbarga (2–3 daily; 11hr 35min–12hr 20min); Hospet (1 daily; 9hr 35min); Hubli (2–4 daily; 7–13hr); Hyderabad (Secunderabad) (1–3 daily; 12hr 15min–14hr 10min); Kochi (Ernakulam) (1–2 daily; 12hr–13hr 5min); Kolkata (Calcutta) (3 weekly; 37hr 10min); Mumbai (2–3 daily; 23hr 25min–25hr); Mysore (6–7 daily; 2–3hr 15min); Pune (2–4 daily; 19hr 20min–21hr 30min); Thiruvananthapuram (1–3 daily; 17hr–17hr 55min).

Hassan to: Mysore (4 daily; 2hr 10min–3hr 55min); Mangalore (1 daily; 4 hrs); Hubli (1 daily, 5hr).

Hospet to: Bengaluru (Bangalore) (1 daily; 10hr 30min); Gadag (3 daily; 1hr 15min–1hr 35min); Hubli (3 daily; 2hr 30min–3hr 20min).

Mangalore to: Chennai (1 daily; 17hr 55min); Hassan (daily; 4hr); Kochi (Ernakulam) (2 daily; 9hr 30min–10hr 5min); Kollam (2 daily; 12hr 50min–13hr 30min); Margao, Goa (2 daily; 5hr 45min–6hr 10min); Gokarna (2 daily; 3hr 5min–3hr 50min); Thiruvananthapuram (2 daily; 14hr 40min–15hr 35min).

Mysore to: Bengaluru (Bangalore) (6–7 daily; 1hr 55min–3hr 30min); Hassan (4 daily; 2hr 10min–4hr).

Buses

Bengaluru (Bangalore) to: Bidar (2 daily; 16hr); Bijapur (4 daily; 13hr); Chennai (hourly; 8hr); Coimbatore (2 daily; 9hr); Goa (daily; 14hr); Gokarna (2 daily; 13hr); Gulbarga (6 daily; 15hr); Hassan (every 30min; 4hr); Hospet (3 daily; 8hr); Hubli (3 daily; 9hr); Hyderabad (6 daily; 16hr); Jog Falls (1 daily; 8hr); Karwar (3 daily; 13hr); Kodaikanal (1 nightly; 13hr); Kochi (Ernakulam) (6 daily; 12–13hr); Madikeri (hourly; 6hr); Madurai (2 daily; 12hr); Mangalore (every 30min–1hr; 10hr); Mumbai (2 daily; 24hr); Mysore (every 15min; 3hr); Ooty (6 daily; 7hr 30min); Puducherry (2 daily; 9–10hr).

Bijapur to: Aurangabad (4 daily; 12hr); Badami (4 daily; 4hr); Bengaluru (Bangalore) (5 daily; 13hr); Bidar (4 daily; 8hr); Gulbarga (hourly; 4hr); Hospet (12 daily; 5hr); Hubli (hourly; 6hr); Hyderabad (6 daily; 10hr); Mumbai (10 daily; 12hr); Pune (10 daily; 8hr).

Hassan to: Channarayapatna, for Sravanabelagola (hourly; 1hr); Halebid (hourly; 1hr); Hospet (1 daily; 10hr); Mangalore (hourly; 4hr); Mysore (every 30min; 3hr).

Hospet to: Badami (3 daily; 5hr); Bengaluru (Bangalore) (3 daily; 8hr); Bidar (2 daily; 10hr); Gokarna (2 nightly; 9–10hr); Hampi (every 30min; 20min); Hyderabad (4 daily; 12hr); Margao (4 daily; 9hr); Mysore (2 daily; 10–11hr); Panjim (4 daily; 10hr); Vasco da Gama (4 daily; 10–11hr).

Mangalore to: Bengaluru (Bangalore) (every 30min–1hr; 8hr); Bijapur (1 daily; 16hr); Chaudi (2 daily; 8hr); Gokarna (1 daily; 7hr); Kannur (hourly; 3hr); Karwar (9 daily; 8hr); Kasargode (every 30min–1hr; 1hr); Kochi (Ernakulam) (1 daily; 9hr); Madikeri (hourly; 3hr 30min); Mysore (hourly; 7hr); Panjim (2 daily; 10–11hr); Udupi (every 10min; 1hr).

Mysore to: Bengaluru (Bangalore) (every 15min; 3hr); Channarayapatna (every 30min; 2hr); Jog Falls (via Shimoga) (every 90min; 7hr); Kannur (8 daily; 7hr); Kochi (6 daily; 12hr); Kozhikode (6 daily; 5hr); Madikeri (hourly; 3hr); Mangalore (hourly; 7hr); Ooty (10 daily; 5hr); Srirangapatnam (every 15min; 20min).

Flights

(**AI** = Air India, **AIE** = Air India Express, **DN** = Air Deccan, **G8** = Go Air, **I7** = Paramount, **IC** = Indian Airlines, **IT** = Kingfisher, **S2** = JetLite, **SG** = SpiceJet, **6E** = IndiGo, **9W** = Jet Airways)

Bengaluru (Bangalore) to: Chennai (DN, G8, IT, SG, S2, 9W, 6E, I7 20–23 daily; 45min–1hr); Delhi (DN, G8, IT, SG, S2, 9W, 6E, IC 24–27 daily; 2hr 30min–3hr 30min); Goa (IC, IT, SG, 9W 4 daily; 1hr–2hr 30min); Hyderabad (DN, IC, S2, 6E, 9W 20–23 daily; 1hr–1hr 30min); Kochi (Cochin) (6E, DN, 9W 5 daily; 55min–1hr 20min); Kolkata (Calcutta) (IT, SG, 6E, DN, 9W 10–12 daily; 2hr 20min–3hr 30min); Mangalore (DN, IT, 9W 6 daily; 1hr 5min); Mumbai (DN, G8, IT, SG, S2, 9W, 6E, IC 25–30 daily; 1hr 30min–1hr 45min); Pune (DN, SG, 6E, 9W, IT 6 daily; 1hr 20min); Thiruvanthapuram (IT, 9W 3 daily; 2hr).

Mangalore to: Bengaluru (Bangalore) (DN, IT, 9W, 6 daily; 45–55min); Mumbai (DN, IC, 9W 5 daily, 1hr 20–1hr 30min); Goa (IT, 1 daily, 1hr).

Hubli to: Bengaluru (Bangalore) (IT, 1 daily; 1hr 30min); Mumbai (IT, 4 daily; 1hr 35min).

Contexts

Contexts

History

I ndia's history is as complex and as multifaceted as you would expect from such a huge, populous and culturally varied country, home to one of the world's earliest civilizations and the birthplace of four major religions, as well as having spawned more dynasties, monarchs and kingdoms than even the most determined historian can keep track of. Broadly speaking, the history of India divides into two parts: the history of the Aryan **north**, heavily influenced by successive waves of invaders from the uplands of Central Asia, and the much more self-contained history of the Dravidian **south**.

Prehistory

The earliest human presence in the Indian subcontinent can be traced back to the Early, Middle and Late **Stone Ages** (400,000–200,000 BC), when the country was first settled by semi-nomadic hunters and gatherers – implements from all three periods have been found at many places around the country. The first evidence of **agricultural settlement** in the Subcontinent (at Mehrgarh, on the western plains of the Indus in Baluchistan, in modern-day Pakistan) dates back to around 7000 BC. Village settlements gradually developed over the next four thousand years across the Indus Valley as their inhabitants began to use copper and bronze, domesticate animals, make pottery and trade with their neighbours. **Terracotta figurines** of goddesses, bulls and phallic emblems echo the fertility cults and Mother Goddess worship found in early agricultural communities in the Mediterranean and Middle East; they also prefigure elements that were to re-emerge as aspects of the religious life of India.

The Indus Valley civilization

By around 2500 BC, the village settlements of the Indus Valley (now in Pakistan) had begun to develop into one of the world's earliest civilizations – roughly contemporary with those of Sumer and ancient Egypt. Known variously as the **Indus Valley civilization** or the **Harappan Civilization**, this first great Subcontinental culture spread across a sizeable proportion of what is now southern Pakistan and the periphery of western India. The exact nature of the Indus Valley civilization remains enigmatic (even its language has so far resisted translation). Much of what is known about it comes from the remains of two great cities on the Indus, **Harappa** in the north and **Mohenjo Daro** in the south. Laid out on a gridplan, both cities boasted large houses made from uniformly sized baked bricks, an elaborate system of covered drains (the world's first urban sanitation system) and large granaries. The absence of royal palaces and the large numbers of religious figurines found at both sites suggest that the Indus Valley civilization was a theocratic state of priests, merchants and farmers.

By this point, farmers had domesticated various **animals**, including humpbacked (Brahmani) cattle, water buffalo and fowl. They also cultivated wheat, barley, peas and sesamum, and were probably the first to grow and make clothes from **cotton**. Excavations at Lothal in Gujarat have uncovered a **harbour**; merchants were certainly involved in extensive trading by both sea and land, importing gold, silver, copper and semiprecious stones from central Asia and Mesopotamia and exporting cotton yarn or cloth.

The large number of **seals** discovered in the Indus cities suggests that each merchant or family had its own. Made of steatite (a kind of soapstone), these seals bear inscriptions that remain undeciphered today, although nearly four hundred different characters have been identified, along with various emblems. One of the most notable depicts a horned, cross-legged deity, surrounded by various animals, who seems to have been a fertility god; indeed, he has been called a "proto-Shiva" because of the resemblance to Pashupati, the Lord of the Beasts, a form of the Hindu god, Shiva. Other seals provide evidence that certain trees, especially the peepal, were worshipped, and thus anticipate their sacred status in the Hindu and Buddhist religions. Countless terracotta statuettes of a Mother Goddess have also been discovered – this goddess is thought to have been worshipped in nearly every home of the common people.

The Indus Valley civilization displayed remarkable longevity, surviving for a thousand years until its sudden demise in the last quarter of the second millennium BC, probably caused by a catastrophic series of floods caused by tectonic upheavals in about 1700 BC.

The Vedic Age (1500–600 BC)

The written history of India begins with the invasions of the charioteering **Indo-European** or **Aryan** tribes, which dealt the final death blow to the enfeebled Indus civilization. The arrival of the Aryans marks the beginning of the so-called **Vedic Age**, named after the earliest Indian literature, the Vedas (see p.1358). The Aryans belonged to the various nomadic tribes who emerged out of the vast steppeland that stretches from Poland to Central Asia from the start of the second millennium BC, marauding and eventually colonizing Europe, the Middle East and the Indian subcontinent. They probably entered the Punjab via the Iranian plateau in successive waves over several hundred years; the peaceful farmers of the Indus would have been powerless against their horse-drawn chariots.

Aryan culture was diametrically opposed to that of the Indus civilization, and Vedic literature relates how their war god, Indra, destroyed hundreds of urban settlements. Semi-nomadic hunters and pastoralists when they first reached the region between Kabul and the Thar desert, the Aryans gradually adopted the farming techniques learned from the peoples they conquered as they spread eastwards into the the Doab (the plain between the upper Ganges and the Yamuna). The tribes began to organize themselves into village communities, governed by tribal councils and warrior chiefs, who offered protection in return for tribute; the sacrifices of the chief priest secured their prosperity and martial success.

The Aryans' hymns, written down in the Vedas, describe the inter-tribal conflicts characteristic of the period, but also express an underlying sense of solidarity against the indigenous peoples, whom the Aryans referred to as **Dasas**. Originally a general term for "enemies", it came to denote "subjects" as they were colonized within the expanding land of the Aryans. The Dasas are described as phallus worshippers who owned many cattle and lived in fortified towns or villages. The Aryans began to emphasize purity of blood as they settled among the darker aboriginals, and their original class divisions of nobility and ordinary tribesmen were hardened to exclude the Dasas. At the same time, the priests, the sole custodians and extrapolators of the increasingly complex religion and sacrificial rituals, began to claim high privileges for their skill and training.

By 1000 BC, Aryan society had become divided into four classes, or **varnas** (literally "colour"): priests (brahmins), warriors (*kshatrya*), peasants (*vaishya*) and serfs (*shudra*), a division that has survived right up to the present day. The first three classes covered the main divisions within the Aryan tribes; the Dasas and other non-Aryan subjects became the *shudras*, who served the three higher classes.

During the later Vedic period, between 1000 and 600 BC, the centre of Aryan culture and power slowly shifted eastwards from the Punjab to the Doab and the traditional north Indian heartlands between the Ganges and the Yamuna. The Sama, Yajur and Atharva Vedas, *Brahmanas* and the Upanishads (see p.1358) all originate in this period, while the great epic poems, the **Mahabharata** and the **Ramayana** (see p.1359) also claim to relate to this period. Though they are unreliable as historical sources, being overlaid with accretions from later centuries, it's possible to extract some of the facts entwined with the martial myths and legends. The great battle of **Kurukshetra**, for example – which forms the central theme of the Mahabharata – is certainly historical, and took place near modern Delhi some time in the ninth or eighth centuries BC, the culmination of a dynastic dispute among the Kurus, who, with their neighbours the Panchalas, were the greatest of the Aryan tribes. Archeological evidence has been found of the two main settlements mentioned in the epic: Indraprastha (Delhi) and Hastinapura (the capital of the Kurus), further north on the Ganges.

By the time of Kurukshetra, the Aryans had advanced into the mid-Gangetic valley where they established the kingdom of **Kosala**, with its capital at **Ayodhya**, seat of (according to the Ramayana) the god-hero Rama. The Aryanization of north India continued throughout the period, and began to penetrate central India as well. The migrating tribes pushed east beyond Kosala to found the kingdoms of Kashi (around Varanasi), Videha (east of the River Gandak and north of the Ganges) and Anga, on the border of Bengal, while the Yadava tribe settled around Mathura, on the Yamuna. Other tribes pushed southwards down the River Chambal to found the kingdom of Avanti, and by the end of the period Aryan influence probably extended into the northwest Deccan. Southern India, however, remained untouched by the Aryan invaders.

This territorial expansion was assisted by significant developments in Aryan civilization. When they arrived in India, Aryan knowledge of **metallurgy** was limited to gold, copper and bronze, but later Vedic literature mentions tin, lead, silver and iron. The use of iron, together with the taming of elephants, facilitated the rapid clearance of the forests and jungles for settlement. Aryan farmers, meanwhile, had learned how to grow a large variety of crops, including rice, while specialized trades and crafts flourished and merchants re-established trade with Mesopotamia, interrupted since the collapse of the Indus civilization.

Vedic culture and society was transformed by contact between the Aryans and indigenous peoples. By the end of the Vedic period, the Aryan tribes had consolidated into little kingdoms, each with its own capital. Some were republics, but generally the power of the tribal assemblies was dwindling, to be replaced by a new kind of politics centred on a **king**. Kingship was becoming more absolute, limited only by the influence of the priesthood – a relationship between temporal and sacred power that became crucial. The *Brahmana* literature, compiled by the priests, contains instructions for the performance of sacrifices symbolizing royal power, such as the royal consecration ceremonies and the horse sacrifice. The evolution of Aryan civilization in the late Vedic period also involved a degree of introspection and pessimism. The disintegration of tribal identity created a profound sense of insecurity, which led to the emergence of nonconformists and ascetics whose new religious teachings were set down in works like the Upanishads (see p.1358), which laid the foundations for the various philosophical systems developed in later periods.

By 600 BC, at least sixteen separate republics and monarchies, known as **mahajanapadas** (territories of the great clans), had been established across northern India. The hereditary principle and the concept of divinely ordained kings tended to preserve the status quo in the monarchies, while the republics provided an atmosphere in which unorthodox views were able to develop – the founders of the new religions of Buddhism and Jainism were both born in small republics of this kind. The consolidation of the *mahajanapadas* was based on the growth of a stable agrarian economy and the increasing importance of trade, which led to the use of coins, the development of the **Brahmi script** (from which the current scripts of India, Sri Lanka, Tibet, Java and Myanmar derive) and the emergence of new towns. The resultant prosperity stimulated conflict, however, and by the fifth century BC the scattered states of north India had been consolidated into five great kingdoms: Magadha, Kashi, Koshala, Vatsa, and the republic of the Vrijjis.

Eventually, **Magadha** emerged supreme, under Bimbisara (543–491 BC), who was also, according to legend, a personal friend and great patron of the **Buddha**, his almost exact contemporary. Bimbisara's son and successor Ajatashatru (491–461 BC) moved the capital of Magadha to **Pataliputra** (the forerunner of modern Patna) and either annihilated the other kingdoms in the Ganges valley or reduced them to the status of vassals in order to control the trade along the Ganges, with its rich deposits of copper and iron. In the middle of the fourth century BC, the **Nanda** dynasty usurped the Magadhan throne; Mahapadma Nanda conquered Kalinga (Orissa and the northern coastal strip of Andhra Pradesh) and gained control of parts of the Deccan. The disputed succession after his death coincided with significant events in the northwest; out of this confusion the first of India's empires was born.

The Mauryan Empire (320–184 BC)

The burgeoning prosperity of the north Indian states was by now beginning to attract the attention of ambitious rulers in Central Asia – something that was to become a recurrent theme in Indian history over the next thousand years. **Darius I**, the third Achaemenid emperor of Persia, had already conquered the kingdom of Gandhara (in what is now northern Pakistan and eastern Afghanistan) around 520 BC. Far more significant, however, was the later invasion by **Alexander the Great**, who defeated Darius III, the last Achaemenid, crossed the Indus in 326 BC, and then overran the Punjab. Alexander was in India for just two years, and although he left garrisons and appointed satraps to govern the conquered territories, their position following his death in 323 BC became increasingly untenable.

The disruption caused by Alexander's brief incursion was seized upon by **Chandragupta Maurya**, the ruler of Magadha, who had overthrown the last of the Nanda dynasty in around 320 BC. Chandragupta is said to have met Alexander the Great and was probably inspired by his exploits; his 500,000-strong army drove out the Greek garrisons in the northwest and annexed all the lands east of the Indus. When Seleucus Nicator, Alexander's general, attempted to regain control of Macedonian provinces in India, Chandragupta defeated him too, and forced the surrender of territories in what is now Afghanistan as a reward.

From about 297 BC onwards, Chandragupta's son Bindusara extended the empire as far south as Mysore, before being succeeded in around 269 BC by his son, **Ashoka**, the most famous of India's early rulers – two thousand years later, Nehru would adopt the lion capital of Ashoka's Sarnath pillar as the emblem of the newly independent India. Ashoka ruthlessly consolidated his power for the first eight years of his reign, before invading and subduing the tribal kingdom of Kalinga (Orissa), his last campaign of violent conquest, in 260 BC. Two and a half years later, allegedly sickened by the terrible carnage caused in his Kalingan conquest, Ashoka converted to Buddhism and renounced the use of violence in favour of the law of moral righteousness, or *dharma*. He also caused a series of famous **edicts** to be created, in which the principles of his newly benevolent administration were engraved on various great rocks and polished sandstone pillars dotted at strategic points around the empire (the most famous and accessible surviving edicts can now be found at Sarnath in Uttar Pradesh and Dhauli in Orissa). His adoption of Buddhism, however, did not interfere with his imperial pragmatism, and despite his avowed remorse after the Kalinga campaign he continued to govern the newly acquired territory, retained his army without reduction and warned the wilder tribesmen that he would use force to subjugate them if they continued to raid the civilized villages of the empire.

By the end of his reign, Ashoka's empire stretched from Assam to Afghanistan and from Kashmir to Mysore; only the three Dravidian kingdoms of the Cholas, Cheras and Pandyas in the southernmost tip of the Subcontinent remained independent. Diplomatic relations were maintained with Syria, Egypt, Macedonia and Cyrene, and all the states on the immediate borders. The Mauryan Empire was built on military conquest and a centralized administration – its well-organized revenue department ensured a strong fiscal base – but Ashoka's imperial vision, his shrewdness, and above all the force of his personality and the loyalty he inspired, held it all together.

After Ashoka's death in 232 BC, the empire began to fall apart. While princes contested the throne, the provincial governors established their independence. Interregional rivalries and further invasions from Central Asia exacerbated matters, and in 184 BC the last of the Mauryans, Brihadratha, was assassinated by one of his generals, bringing to an end nearly 140 years of Mauryan rule.

The age of invasions (184 BC–320 AD)

The five hundred years following the collapse of the Mauryan Empire are the most complex and confusing in Subcontinental history, marked by political fragmentation and a new and seemingly endless series of **invasions** from the northwest. The period is sometimes referred to as India's "Dark Age", although despite the lack of any unified central power it was also one of economic dynamism and considerable cultural achievement.

The first invaders were the **Bactrian Greeks** of Gandhara, part of the enormous swathe of territories conquered by Alexander the Great that had subsequently become part of the Seleucid Empire under his successor, Seleucus. Around 180 BC the Bactrian Greeks declared independence from the Seleucid imperium, and shortly afterwards descended on India to carve out small fiefdoms of their own, occupying the Punjab and extending their power as far as Mathura in Uttar Pradesh.

The Greek position in Bactria, however, was soon threatened by the arrival of newcomers from Central Asia. Large-scale movements of central Asian Yueh-Chi nomads had precipitated the migration of the **Shakas** (Scythians), from the Aral Sea area, who displaced the **Parthians** (Pahlavas) from Iran, who in turn wrested control of Bactria from the Greeks (who henceforth administered their Indian territories from a new capital in Kabul). The finer details of these various population movements remain unclear, and they were probably more in the nature of migrations than invasions. Whatever the details, however, both the Yueh-Chi and Shakas continued to drift slowly in the direction of India, finally arriving during the first century AD. The Shakas were the first to arrive, establishing themselves in northwestern India until the coming of the **Kushan** branch of the Yueh-Chi, who drove the Shakas off into Gujarat and Malwa (the area around Ujjain), where they settled and became Indianized.

Having seen off the Shakas, the Kushans established a new dynasty in the northwest. The third and most famous of their kings, **Kanishka**, ruled from Purushpura (modern-day Peshawar in Pakistan) for more than twenty years around 100 AD and extended his rule east to Varanasi and south to Sanchi. His empire prospered through control of trade routes between India, China and the West, and his court attracted artists and musicians as well as merchants. Ashvaghosha, one of the first classical Sanskrit poets, wrote a life of the Buddha, the *Buddha Charita*, and is credited with converting the king to Buddhism.

Despite the disintegration of the Mauryan Empire and the proliferation of fiercely rival kingdoms, the period from 200 BC to 300 AD was also one of unprecedented economic wealth and cultural development. The growing importance of the mercantile community encouraged the monetization of the economy and stimulated the growth of urban centres all over India. Merchants and artisans organized themselves into guilds, while external trade, overland and maritime, opened up lines of communication with the outside world. The main highway from Pataliputra to Taxila (in northern Pakistan) gave India access to the old **Silk Road**, the most important trade route of the time, linking China to the Mediterranean via Central Asia. Maritime trade traversed the coastal routes between the seaports in Gujarat and southern India and as far as south Arabia; and Indian merchants established trading communities in various parts of south Asia.

The arrival of so many foreigners, the growth of trade and increasing urbanization together had a considerable impact on the structure of society. Foreign conquerors and traders had to be integrated within the *varna* system of caste, while the burgeoning importance of the *vaishya* (merchant) class and the influence of urban liberalism all presented new challenges to the social order. The Law Books (*Dharma Shastras*) were composed in this period in an attempt to accommodate these changes and redefine social, economic and legal rights and duties. Important developments in India's **religions** can also be linked to socioeconomic changes. Radical schisms occurred in both Buddhism and Jainism, and may be attributed to the increasing participation and patronage of the *vaishyas*; while the Vedic religion, which had been the exclusive domain of the brahmins and kshatryas, underwent fundamental transformations to widen its social base.

The rise of the south

Meanwhile, the first great kingdom of southern India was flexing its muscles. Between the second century BC and the second century AD the **Andhra** or **Satavahana** dynasty, which originated in the region between the rivers Godavari and Krishna (modern-day Andhra Pradesh and Maharashtra), began to gain control of much of south and central India, gaining control of the northwest Deccan and creating capitals at Paithan on the Godavari and at Amaravati on the Krishna. The kingdom's prosperity was built on trade, with commercial links stretching as far as Rome and southeast Asia, but lasted only until the middle of the third century, when their territories were carved up by rival dynasties including the Pallavas (see p.1094), who took control of their territories in Andhra Pradesh.

Further south, the three kingdoms of the **Cheras** on the Malabar Coast in the west, the **Pandyas** in the central southern tip of the peninsula, and the **Cholas** on the east coast of Coromandel – together comprising much of present-day Tamil Nadu and Kerala – had been developing almost completely independently of north India. Society was divided into groups based on the geographical domains of hills, plains, forest, coast and desert rather than class or *varna*, though Brahmins did command high status. Although agriculture, pastoralism and fishing were the main occupations, trade in spices, gold and jewels with Rome and southeast Asia underpinned the region's prosperity.

From the middle of the first century BC, however, conflicts between the three states intensified. This enervating warfare rendered them vulnerable; early in the fourth century AD, the **Pallavas** overran the Chola capital of Kanchipuram, and by 325 AD had taken control of Tamil Nadu. The Pallavas remained a dominant power in the south until the ninth century AD, and thus became one of the longest ruling dynasties in Indian history.

The Guptas (320–650)

During the fourth century AD, a second great Indian empire began to emerge in the north, the **Guptas**. The parallels with the earlier Mauryan Empire are striking. Both were founded in the year 320 (BC and AD respectively) by a king named Chandragupta (though the later king is usually written as two words, Chandra Gupta), and both emerged from within the famous old kingdom of Magadha. **Chandra Gupta** (reigned *c.*320–335) appears to have been the ruler of a minor statelet within the old Magadhan kingdom, who acquired considerable new territory through intermarriage with the famous Licchavi clan, one of the Mauryas' principal enemies six hundred years previously. Chandra Gupta thus found himself master of a powerful kingdom in the Gangetic plain, which controlled the vital east–west trade route. His son and heir, **Samudra Gupta** (*c.*335–376 AD), expanded the frontiers of his realm from Punjab to Assam, building the foundations for the second largest empire in pre-medieval India. This reached its apogee under his successor, **Chandra Gupta II** (376–415 AD), who subjugated the Shakas in Gujarat to secure access to the trade of the western coast at the end of the fourth century AD, and reunified the whole of northern India, with the exception of the northwest.

The era of these three imperial Guptas, along with the subsequent reign of Harsha Vardhana (606–647 AD) of Kanauj (see p.1336), is generally seen as the **Classical Age** of Indian history, one of cultural and artistic brilliance, religious ferment and political stability. Secular **Sanskrit literature** reached its perfection in the works of Kalidasa, the greatest Indian poet and dramatist, who was a member of Chandra Gupta II's court. The cave paintings of **Ajanta** and **Ellora** inspired Buddhist artists throughout Asia, and Yashodhara's detailed analysis of painting in the fifth century prescribed the classical conventions for the new art form. In **sculpture**, the images of the Buddha produced in Sarnath and Mathura embodied the simple and serene quality of classicism. In **architecture**, the Gupta era saw the birth of a new style of **Hindu temple** which would become India's classic architectural form, with an inner sanctuary (*garbha griha*) housing the deity connected to a larger hall (*mandapa*), where devotees could congregate to worship; a fine example survives at Deogarh, near Jhansi in central India.

The era of the Guptas produced great thinkers as well: six systems of **philosophy** (Nyaya, Vaisheshika, Sankhya, Yoga, Mimamsa and Vedanta) evolved, which refuted Buddhism and Jainism. **Vedanta** has continued as the basis of all philosophical studies in India to this day. In the fifth century, the great **astronomer**, Aryabhata, argued that the earth rotated on its own axis while revolving around the sun, and also contributed to the already sophisticated tradition of Indian mathematics by using the decimal system of nine digits and a zero, with place notation for tens and hundreds. (The Arabs acknowledged their debt to the "Indian art" of mathematics, and many Western European discoveries and inventions would have been impossible if they had remained encumbered by the Roman system of numerals.)

Fa Hsien, a Chinese Buddhist monk who visited India during the reign of Chandra Gupta II, noted the palaces and free hospitals of Pataliputra and the fact that all respectable Indians were vegetarian. He also mentions discrimination against untouchables, who carried gongs to warn passers-by of their polluting presence; but generally, he describes the empire as prosperous, happy and peaceful. The Guptas performed Vedic sacrifices to legitimize their rule, and patronized popular forms of Hinduism, such as devotional religion (*bhakti*) and the worship in temples of images of Vishnu, Shiva and the goddess Shakti, deities who were attracting increasing numbers of devotees during this era. Buddhism continued to thrive, however, and Fa Hsien mentions thousands of monks dwelling at Mathura as well as hundreds in Pataliputra itself.

The Gupta Empire remained relatively peaceful during the long reign of Kumara Gupta (*c*.415–455), who succeeded Chandra Gupta II, but by the time Skanda Gupta (*c*.455–467) came to the throne, western India was again threatened by invasions from Central Asia, this time by the **White Huns**, a nomadic people of Central Asian origin who had already established themselves in Bactria. Skanda managed to repel White Hun raids, but after his death their disruption of central Asian trade seriously destabilized the empire. By the end of the fifth century, the Huns had wrested the Punjab from Gupta control, and further incursions early in the sixth century dealt a death blow to the Gupta Empire, which had completely disintegrated by 550 AD.

After the demise of the Guptas, northern India again split into rival kingdoms, but the Pushpabhutis of Sthanvishvara (Thanesvar, north of Delhi) had established supremacy by the time **Harsha Vardhana** came to the throne in 606 AD. He reigned for 41 years over an empire that ranged from Gujarat to Bengal, including the Punjab, Kashmir and Nepal, and moved his capital to **Kanauj** (northwest of modern Kanpur in Uttar Pradesh), which would henceforth become the most strategically important city in north India until the emergence of Delhi in the thirteenth century. Harsha possessed considerable talent as well as untiring energy; in addition to his martial achievements and ceaseless touring, he wrote three dramas and found time to indulge a love of philosophy and literature. The life of Harsha (*Harshacharita*) by Bana, his court poet, is the first historically authentic Indian biography. Harsha's empire was essentially feudal, however, with most of the defeated kings retaining their thrones as vassals, and when he died without heirs in 647 AD, north India once again fragmented into independent kingdoms.

Kingdoms of central and south India (500–1250)

Meanwhile, significant events were taking place in central and south India. Culturally, Aryan influences were increasingly assimilated into Dravidian culture, resulting in a distinctive Tamil synthesis between the two cultures. The history of the period was dominated by three major kingdoms: the **Pallavas**, who had supplanted the Satavahanas in the Andhra region and made Kanchipuram their capital back in the fourth century; the **Pandyas** of Madurai, who had established their own regional kingdom by the sixth century; and the **Chalukyas** of Vatapi (Badami in Mysore), who had expanded into the Deccan in the middle of the sixth century. All three kingdoms intermittently fought one another, but their military strength was so evenly matched that none was able to gain ascendancy.

The Chalukyas were eventually overthrown in 753 by a certain Dantidurga, the founder of the **Rashtrakuta** kingdom, whose rulers also tried their luck in the north, briefly gaining possession of Kanauj and acquiring control of the Ganges trade routes, though ultimately the campaigns drained the kingdom's resources. The Pallavas survived their archenemies by about a hundred years, then succumbed to a combined attack of the Pandyas and the **Cholas**. The Cholas were a major new force in Tamil Nadu, conquering the Thanjavur region in the ninth century and taking Madurai from the Pandyas in 907, before being defeated by the Rashtrakutas in the middle of the tenth century, who were themselves replaced by the revived Chalukyas in 973 AD.

Ultimately, the chief beneficiaries of these dynastic toings-and-froings were the Cholas, who were able to regain lost territories and expand further during the eleventh and twelfth centuries. The great Chola kings **Rajaraja I** (985–1014) and **Rajendra I** (1014–1044), launched a series of campaigns against the Cheras, Pandyas, Chalukyas, and even sent forces overseas to Sri Lanka, the Maldives and Southeast Asia. They also pushed north, reaching the banks of the Ganges, although they did not hold their northern conquests for long. By the end of the eleventh century the Cholas were supreme in the south, but incessant campaigning had exhausted their resources. Ironically, their destruction of the Chalukyas laid the seeds of their own downfall. Former Chalukya feudatories, such as the **Yadavas** of Devagiri in the northern Deccan and the **Hoysalas**, around modern Mysore, set up their own kingdoms; the latter attacked the Cholas from the west while the Pandyas directed a new offensive from the south. By the thirteenth century, the **Pandyas** had superseded the Cholas as south India's major power, while the Yadavas and Hoysalas controlled the Deccan until the advent of the Delhi sultans in the fourteenth century.

Despite constant political and military conflicts, this period was very much the classical age of the south. The ascendancy of the Cholas was complemented by the crystallization of Tamil culture; the religious, artistic, and institutional patterns of this period dominated the culture of the south and influenced developments elsewhere in the peninsula. In the sphere of religion for instance, the great philosophers Shankara and Ramanuja, as well as the Tamil and Maharashtrian saints, had a significant impact on Hinduism in north India.

Kingdoms in north India (650–1250)

In north India, Harsha Vardhana's death was followed by a century of confusion, with assorted kingdoms competing to control the Gangetic valley. In time, the **Pratihara-Gurjaras**, from western India, and the **Palas**, of Bihar and Bengal, emerged as the main rivals. The Palas king Dharmapala (770–810) gained control of the key strategic town of Kanauj, but the Pratiharas wrested it back soon after his death. They remained in the ascendant during the ninth century, but were weakened by repeated incursions from the Deccan by the **Rashtrakutas**, who briefly occupied Kanauj in 916. The Pratiharas regained their capital, but the tripartite struggle sapped their strength and they were unable to repel the invasion of Kanauj by Mahmud of Ghazni (see p.1338) in 1018. At the start of the eleventh century the Palas again pushed west as far as Varanasi, but had to abandon the campaign to defend their homelands in Bengal against the Chola king Rajendra.

The struggle for possession of Kanauj depleted the resources of all three competing powers and resulted in their almost simultaneous decline, while various smaller feudatory kingdoms began to assert their independence. Kingdoms emerged in Nepal, Kamarupa (Assam), Kashmir and Orissa, all with their own cultural identities, customs, literatures and histories. The Eastern Gangas of **Kalinga** (roughly equivalent to modern Orissa) achieved political independence and unity in the twelfth century, establishing the royal cult of Jagannath (Vishnu), with its gigantic temple at Puri, as well as the stunning chariot temple dedicated to the sun god Surya at Konarak.

Meanwhile, in the west, the celebrated **Rajputs** began to emerge as a new element within Indian society. Their origins remain the subject of considerable speculation, although they probably descended from the various invaders who arrived in India between the third and sixth centuries, including the Pratihara-Gurjaras, Huns and Shakas and perhaps others. Whatever their origins, they acquired respectable Hindu genealogies and were given kshatrya status. By the tenth century, the most important Rajput clans, like the Chauhans of Ajmer, the Chalukyas of Kathiawar, the Guhilas of Chittaurgarh, the Chandellas of Bundelkhand (who created the magnificent group of temples at Khajuraho), and the Tomaras of Haryana (who founded modern Delhi in 1060), had all established small regional kingdoms spread across modern-day Rajasthan, Gujarat, Madhya Pradesh and other parts of the north.

The Rajputs fought among each other incessantly, however, and failed to grasp the significance of a new factor, which entered the politics of north India at the start of the eleventh century. **Mahmud of Ghazni** (971–1030), a Turkish chieftain who had established the powerful Ghaznavid kingdom at Ghazni in Afghanistan, made seventeen plundering raids into the plains of India between 1000 and 1027, plundering Mathura, Kanauj and Somnath, amongst other places. The most powerful Rajput clans of northern India were still busy fighting one another almost two centuries later when **Muhammad of Ghor** (1162–1206) seized Ghaznavid possessions in the Punjab at the end of the twelfth century, and then turned his attention towards the wealthy lands further east. **Prithviraja III**, the legendary hero of the Chauhans of Ajmer, patched together an alliance to defeat the Turkish warlord at Tarain (north of Delhi) in 1191; but Muhammad returned the next year with a superior force and defeated the Rajputs. He had Prithviraja executed before returning home, leaving his generals to complete his conquest.

The Delhi Sultanate (1206–1526)

Muhammad of Ghor was assassinated in 1206 and his empire immediately disintegrated, leaving his Turkish general **Qutb-ud-din-Aiback**, a former slave, as the autonomous ruler of Muhammad's former Indian territories. Aiback thus became the founder of the so-called "Slave Dynasty", the first part of which would eventually come to be known as the **Delhi Sultanate**, which would remain the major political force in the north until the early sixteenth century. The sultanate marked an important turning-point in Indian history. Islam rather than Hinduism suddenly became the religion of the country's rulers, while Delhi, rather than Kanauj or Pataliputra, became the important city in the north.

Aiback died four years later, leaving his son-in-law **Iltutmish** (1211–36) the task of securing the sultanate's tenuous hold on northern India. Iltutmish had extended the sultanate's territories from the Sind to Bengal by the time he died, but a period of confusion followed, with five different rulers in just six years, including one of India's rare female sovereigns, Sultana Raziyya, who managed to last four years before being deposed and then murdered. Not until **Ghiyas-ud-din Balban**, Raziyya's chief huntsman and member of her father's palace guard, took effective control in 1246 did the sultanate attain any degree of stability, despite repeated threats from yet another set of foreign interlopers, the **Mongols**, who had been launching raids into western India from around 1220 and continued to attack the edges of the sultanate.

Balban's death in 1287 was followed by the inevitable period of dynastic mayhem that only ended in 1290, when Aiback's Slave Dynasty came to an end, replaced by the **Khalji** dynasty. The Khalji family had entered India with Muhammad of Ghor, and subsequently carved out their own Muslim fiefdom in Bengal and Bihar. The first Khalji sultan, the elderly Feroz Shah I, was soon done away with by the implacable **Ala-ud-din Khalji** (1296–1315), one of the most fearsome of all Indian rulers. A hard man for hard times, Ala-ud-din was faced immediately by a series of further Mongol attacks. Delhi was besieged twice and its hinterlands plundered before the invaders suffered a resounding defeat at the hands of the new sultan in 1300, after which they left him alone. Having seen off the Mongols, Ala-ud-din set out to conquer Gujarat and the most powerful Rajput fortresses (including Ranthambore and Chittaurgarh) in a series of expeditions between 1299 and 1311, before turning his attention to the Deccan and the south. Even so, his military campaigns were more a question of exacting tribute and raising funds than of building a stable empire.

A fresh imperial impetus came from the **Tughluq** dynasty, which succeeded the Khaljis in 1320. Under **Mohammed bin Tughluq** (1325–51), the sultanate reached its largest extent, comparable in size to Ashoka's empire, although the onerous taxes required to finance Mohammed's military campaigns provoked a peasant uprising in the Doab and other economic problems. Even more calamitous was his attempt, quickly abandoned, to relocate his capital from Delhi to a more central location at Deogiri (renamed Daulatabad) in the Deccan. Further revolts followed, and the new Hindu kingdom of **Vijayanagar** took advantage of the decline of the sultanate's authority to extend its influence. From its capital near Hampi, Vijayanagar dominated the region south of the Krishna and Tungabhadra rivers between the mid-fourteenth century and 1565, when an alliance of Muslim kingdoms brought it down.

Firoz Shah Tughluq (1351–88) reversed the fortunes of the sultanate to some extent thanks to the comparative mildness of his rule. He is credited with an impressive list of public works, including the building of mosques, colleges, reservoirs, hospitals, public baths, bridges and towns – especially Jaunpur, near Varanasi, which became a major centre of Islamic culture. However, by reverting to a decentralized administrative system he fostered the rise of semi-independent warlords, who became increasingly antagonistic under the last of the Tughluqs. Arguments over the succession after Firoz Shah's death in 1388 further weakened the sultanate, however, and the degeneracy of his successors made it vulnerable to external predators. The sultanate was fatally weakened when the Mongols returned led by the ruthless **Timur**, the Central Asian despot known to the West as Tamburlaine, who sacked Delhi in 1398. Soon after, autonomous sultanates emerged in Jaunpur, Malwa and Gujarat, while Hindu kingdoms asserted their independence in Rajasthan. By the end of the fourteenth century, the Delhi Sultanate had been reduced to just one of several competing Muslim states in northern India.

The greatly weakened sultanate was next taken over by the Afghan–descended Khizr Khan (1414–21), whose **Sayyid** dynasty ruled until 1444, to be succeeded by the **Lodis**, under whom the sultanate experienced a modest revival. **Sikander Lodi** (1489–1517) was particularly energetic and successful, annexing Jaunpur and Bihar, but his successor, Ibrahim, was unable to overcome the dissension among his Afghan feudatories, one of whom enlisted the support of Babur, the ruler of Kabul, who defeated Ibrahim at Panipat in 1526.

By the time of the sultanate, India had considerable experience of assimilating foreigners; Greeks, Scythians, Parthians and Huns had all been politically, socially and culturally absorbed over the centuries. However, the sultanate brought its own theologians and social institutions. **Islam** presented a new pattern of life, far less easy for the Hindu social system to accommodate. Nonetheless, a process of mutual assimilation did slowly evolve. Despite the Muslims' iconoclastic zeal, Hinduism found common ground with some aspects of Islam: elements of Sufi mysticism and Hindu devotionalism were combined in the teachings of many saints. **Kabir** (1440–1518), in particular, denied any contradiction between Muslim and Hindu conceptions of god, preached social egalitarianism and was claimed by adherents of both creeds as their own. The replacement of Sanskrit by Persian as the official language of the administration encouraged regional languages, while **Urdu** was created out of a fusion of Hindi and Persian using an Arabic script. A stylistically unified style of architecture also began to develop, which would subsequently flourish under the Mughals and give India some of its most famous monuments.

The early Mughal Empire (1526–1605)

For Babur – the founder of India's most famous dynasty, the **Mughals** – India appears to have been something of an afterthought. A direct descendant of Timur (and also distantly related to Genghis Khan), Babur was born in the Fergana Valley in what is now Uzbekistan and spent most of his life in Afghanistan, where he seized control of Kabul. It was only relatively late in life, hearing of the military weakness of the Lodis, that he decided to attack India.

His battle-hardened forces easily routed the very last Delhi sultan, Ibrahim Lodi, at the Battle of Panipat in 1526, which gave him tenuous control of Delhi and Agra, although his position remained unsafe until his troops had first defeated a far stronger Rajput force led by Rana Sanga of Mewar, south of Agra, at the battle of Kanwaha in 1527, and then the allied forces of assorted Afghan chiefs, who had united under the sultan of Bengal in 1529. Shortly afterwards, his failing health forced him to retire to Agra, where he died in 1530. Babur possessed many talents: as well as a brilliant military campaigner, he was a skilful diplomat, a poet and a man of letters. He constructed a loosely knit empire, extending from Kabul to the borders of Bengal, in just four years. His very readable memoirs reveal a man of sensibility, taste and humour, who loved music, poetry, sport and natural beauty.

Humayun, his son and successor, was by contrast a volatile character, alternating between bursts of energetic activity and indolence. He subdued Malwa and Gujarat, only to lose both while he "took his pleasure" in Agra. The Afghan-descended **Sher Shah Sur** (also known as Sher Khan or Sher Khan Sur) of south Bihar soon assumed the leadership of the Afghan opposition and, after two resounding defeats, Humayun was forced to seek refuge in Persia in 1539. A much cleverer politician than the hot-headed Humayun, Sher Shah was quick to consolidate his territorial gains in the northwest, setting up an administrative centre in Delhi, from where he waged audacious and successful campaigns in Punjab and Sind. He later subjugated several of the Rajput dynasties, and it was during a siege against one of these at Kalinjar that the Afghan was killed, in 1545, when a rocket rebounded off the fort's walls and exploded a pile of weapons next to him. Sher Shah was succeded by his son, Islam Shah Sur, but when he died in 1553 the Sur territories fell into chaos as three rival claimants battled for the throne. Judging the moment ripe for return, Humayun led his armies back into India. In 1555 Humayun's forces annihilated those of Sikander Sur, the most powerful of the three pretenders to the throne, at Sirhund in the Punjab, and then marched into Delhi virtually unopposed. Humayun died the following year after a fall in the Purana Qila in Delhi, leaving his 13-year-old son **Akbar**, to succeed to the throne.

Fortunately for the young emperor, Humayun's experienced general **Bairam Khan** was on hand to serve as guardian and regent to help him through the difficult early years of his reign. Bairam first overcame the challenge of the Hindu general Hemu at the second battle of Panipat in 1556, recovered Gwalior and Jaunpur, and handed over a consolidated kingdom of north India to Akbar in 1560. Akbar's own first military campaigns were against the **Rajputs**; and within a decade he had subdued all the Rajput domains except Mewar (Udaipur) by a clever combination of diplomacy and force. He then turned his attentions to Bengal, the richest province, which he secured by 1576. By the end of his reign in 1605 he controlled a broad sweep of territory north of the River Godavari, which reached from the Bay of Bengal to Kandahar in Afghanistan.

In 1565, Akbar had the small fort built by Sikander Lodi in **Agra** demolished and replaced by the magnificent new Agra Fort, the centrepiece of a newly revitalized city that would henceforth rival Delhi as the major centre of Mughal power. Not content with this, in the early 1570s he embarked on the creation of an entire new city, the remarkable but short-lived **Fatehpur Sikri**, which served for a brief period as the capital of the empire.

Akbar was as clever a politician and administrator as he was a successful general. In addition to involving Hindu landowners and nobles in economic and political life, Akbar adopted a conscious policy of religious toleration aimed at widening the base of his power. In particular, he abolished the despised poll tax on non-Muslims (*jizya*), and tolls on Hindu pilgrimages. A mystical experience in about 1575 inspired him to instigate a series of discussions with orthodox Muslim leaders (*ulema*), Portuguese priests from Goa, Hindu brahmins, Jains and Zoroastrians at his famous **Diwan-i-Khas** in Fatehpur Sikri. The discussions culminated in a politico-religious crisis and a revolt, organised by the alienated *ulema*, which Akbar ruthlessly crushed in 1581. He subsequently evolved a theory of divine kingship incorporating the toleration of all religions, and thereby restored the concept of imperial sanctity with which the early Hindu emperors had surrounded themselves, while declaring his nonsectarian credentials. Akbar was a liberal patron of the arts and his eclecticism encouraged a fruitful Muslim–Hindu dialogue.

The later Mughals (1605–1761)

The reign of **Jahangir** (1605–27) was a time of brisk economic and expansionist activity conjoined with artistic and architectural brilliance – as well as some notable excesses of imperial indulgence. Jahangir was a contradictory character: an alcoholic and a sadist, but also a notable connoisseur of art, under whom the art of Mughal miniature painting reached its highest point, and loving husband of his famous queen, Nur Jahan, creator of the beautiful Itimad-ud-Daulah in Agra. He was also an able and determined military commander who succeeded in extending the bounds of the already very considerable domains bequeathed to him by Akbar.

Jahangir's son **Shah Jahan** (1628–57) came to power in 1628 after the by-now traditional military contest between rival brothers, followed by the exile or (if they could be caught) execution of the losing parties. The bloodbath which generally preceded the emergence of a new emperor at least ensured that only the fittest were able to survive and claim the Mughal throne, and in this respect

Shah Jahan – who had already proved himself an outstanding military commander during his father's reign – was no exception, displaying all the traditional Mughal qualities of administrative and military élan. However, it is as perhaps the greatest patron of architecture the world has ever known that Shah Jahan is best remembered. In 1648 he officially moved the Mughal capital from Agra back to Delhi, celebrating the translocation with the construction of the new city of **Shahjahanabad** (now better known as Old Delhi), complete with its huge new Red Fort and Jama Masjid, though it was in Agra that he left his greatest mark, with his myriad embellishments to the city's fort and, pre-eminently, in the creation of the **Taj Mahal**, a spectacular mausoleum for his favourite wife, Mumtaz, and arguably the most beautiful building on the planet.

Shah Jahan's reign witnessed the entry of a new force into Indian history: the **Marathas**, a potent military power in central India. A group of militant Hindus from Maharashtra in central India, the Marathas had carved out a kingdom of their own under their inspirational chief, **Shivaji**, and soon began to turn their attentions northwards. Shah Jahan had responded to the Maratha threat by sending his third son, an ambitious young prince named **Aurangzeb**, to the Deccan to take charge of Mughal interests in the region, although his military successes were repeatedly undermined by Shah Jahan's oldest son and preferred heir **Dara Shikoh**, who was anxious to destabilize Aurangzeb's military exploits lest they create a threat to his own prestige. The anticipated struggle between the two brothers erupted in 1657 when Shah Jahan fell suddenly and seriously ill with acute constipation (bowel problems appear to have been a recurrent feature of Mughal rule – Akbar himself apparently perished of acute diarrhoea). Shah Jahan recovered, but not before Aurangzeb had seen off Dara Shikoh, wiping out his army in a series of encounters that culminated in a rout at Ajmer. The thirty-year reign of the ailing emperor ended ignominiously. Aurangzeb had him incarcerated in Agra Fort, where he lived out his remaining days gazing wistfully down the Yamuna at the mausoleum of his beloved Mumtaz.

Though lacking the charisma of Akbar or Babur, Aurangzeb (reigned 1658–1707) evoked an awe of his own and proved to be a firm and capable administrator, who retained his grip on the increasingly unsettled empire until his death at the age of 88. In contrast to the extravagance of the other Mughals, Aurangzeb's lifestyle was pious and disciplined. However, his religious dogmatism ultimately alienated the Hindu community whose leaders had been so carefully cultivated by Akbar. Hindu places of worship were again the object of iconoclasm, the *jizya* tax on non-Muslims was reintroduced and discriminatory duties were imposed on Hindu merchants.

The chief threat to Mughal rule in this period came from the Maratha chief, **Shivaji**, who established a compact and well-organized kingdom in western India, while the nearby Muslim kingdoms of Bijapur and Golconda allied themselves with Shivaji in order to counter Aurangzeb's imperial ambitions. Meanwhile, Guru Tegh Bahadur, the leader of the important new **Sikh** religion, was executed in 1675 for refusing to embrace Islam; his son, Guru Gobind, transformed the religious community into a military sect that became increasingly powerful in the Punjab. Aurangzeb's confrontation with the Rajputs over the Jodhpur succession in 1678 resulted in another war, and the alienation of most of his Rajput partners in the empire.

Aurangzeb's attention, however, was turning steadily south. In 1681 he transferred his base to the Deccan, where he spent the rest of his extremely long life overseeing the subjugation of the Bijapur and Golconda kingdoms and trying to contain the increasingly belligerent Marathas. In 1689, he succeeded in capturing and executing Shivaji's son, and by 1698 the Mughals had overrun almost the whole of the peninsula. The Marathas had been suppressed, but they re-emerged under the Peshwa leadership in the eighteenth century to harass the remnants of Mughal power and even to challenge the political ambitions of the British.

Aurangzeb's son, Bahadur Shah, succeeded in 1707 but reigned for only five years. His death in 1712 marked the beginning of the end for the Mughals, as their empire disintegrated. By the 1720s the nizam of Hyderabad and the nawabs of Avadh and Bengal were effectively independent; the Marathas overwhelmed the rich province of Malwa in 1738; Hindu landholders everywhere were in revolt; and **Nadir Shah** of Persia dealt a serious blow to the empire's prestige when he invaded India, defeated the Mughal army and sacked Delhi in 1739.

The Maratha kingdom had by now been transformed into a confederacy under the leadership of a hereditary Brahmin minister, called the Peshwa. By 1750 the Marathas had spread right across central India to Orissa, had attacked Bengal, and were insinuating themselves into the imperial politics of Delhi. When Delhi was again looted in 1757, this time by an independent Afghan force led by **Ahmad Shah Abdali**, Mughal ministers were forced to call in the Marathas to rescue the situation. The Marathas drove the Afghans back to the Punjab; but Ahmad Shah advanced again in 1761 and overwhelmed them at the third battle of Panipat. Any designs he had on the imperial throne were dashed, however, when his soldiers mutinied over arrears of pay.

The East India Company (1600–1857)

India's trading potential had attracted European interest ever since 1498, when Vasco da Gama landed on the Malabar (Keralan) Coast. During the ensuing century Portuguese, Dutch, English, French and Danish companies had all set up coastal trading centres, exporting textiles, sugar, indigo and saltpetre. British interests in India were formalized by the creation of the **East India Company**, granted a royal charter by Elizabeth I in 1600, whose representatives arrived at Surat in Gujarat in 1608, quickly establishing 27 trading posts around the country, including Fort George and Fort William (out of which the cities of Madras and Calcutta would subsequently develop), as well as at the fledgling settlement of Bombay. In 1701 the Company (as it was generally known) received a grant of land revenues from Aurangzeb, in recognition of the growing importance of their trade in the economy of Bengal, while in 1717 the Company finally wheedled an imperial *firman* (decree) out of the Mughal emperor Farrukhsiyar, formalizing their trading rights in the country.

It was in the south that European trading initiatives first took on a political significance, after the onset of the War of the Austrian Succession in 1740. Armed conflict between French and English trading companies along the south Indian coast soon developed into a minor war over the succession of the nizam of Hyderabad. Sporadic fighting continued until the end of the Seven Years' War in Europe and the Treaty of Paris in 1763 put an effective end to French ambitions in India. Meanwhile, **Robert Clive**'s defeat of the rebellious young nawab of Bengal at Plassey in 1757 had decisively augmented British power; by 1765 the enervated Mughal emperor legally recognized the Company by granting it the revenue management of Bengal, Bihar and Orissa.

For the next thirty years, the British in India contented themselves with developing trade and repulsing Indian offensives against their three major settlements in Calcutta, Bombay and Madras, though by the end of the century the defeat of **Tipu Sultan** of Mysore, the Company's best-organized and most resolute enemy, and the subjugation of the nizam of Hyderabad resulted in the annexation of considerable territories, and by 1805 nearly all the other rulers in India recognized British suzerainty. A long-drawn-out series of conflicts between the British and Marathas (the so-called three "Maratha Wars" of 1774–1818) finally extinguished the Marathas as an effective military threat.

Following the subjugation of the Marathas, the British established a series of treaties with the rulers of Rajasthan – or **Rajputana**, as it became known during the colonial era. Under these treaties, the various kingdoms of Rajputana retained their autonomy more or less intact and received a guarantee of military protection in exchange for pledging their loyalty to the British Crown and agreeing to certain political, mercantile and financial concessions. Similar arrangements were reached with most of India's other surviving independent kingdoms, collectively known as the so-called "**princely states**", stretching from Hyderabad in the south to Kashmir in the north; although some were gradually swallowed up and incorporated into British-ruled India, many were to survive until Independence. The much-abused city of Delhi, the traditional capital of north India, fared less well, as the British established their capital at the burgeoning new city of **Calcutta**. Not until 1911 would Delhi recapture its mantle as the north's imperial city.

The 1857 uprising

The new British **colony**, however, was in a state of social and economic collapse as a result of the almost incessant conflicts of the previous hundred years. The controversial "Doctrine of Lapse", whereby autonomous states were gradually annexed, was widely resented. In addition, the Company's policy, after 1835, of promoting European literature and science (with English replacing Persian as the official state language), the suppression of local customs such as *sati* and child marriage, and the deployment of Indian troops overseas (resulting in loss of caste) were increasingly perceived as part of a covert but systematic British attack on traditional Hindu and Muslim religious and cultural practices.

The final spark which ignited a full-blown uprising by the Indian army was supplied when troops were issued with cartridges for a new Enfield rifle smeared in cows' and pigs' grease (polluting to both Hindus and Muslims). The resultant **1857 uprising** (traditionally referred to by the British as the "Indian Mutiny" or "Sepoy Rebellion", and also described by Indian historians as the "First War of Independence") began with a rebellion of Indian troops (sepoys) at Meerut on May 10, 1857, and Delhi was seized the next day. The last Mughal emperor, Bahadur Shah in Delhi, the dispossessed court at Lucknow, and the exiled members of the Maratha court at Kanpur all supported the cause (albeit possibly under duress) – though, crucially, the Sikh regiments in the Punjab chose to side with the British. The rebellion quickly spread across most of central northern India, where mutineers seized Lucknow and Kanpur and threatened Agra, whose rebellious citizens forced the European community to flee into the city's fort for safety. The British authorities were caught by surprise, though control was gradually reasserted. Delhi and Kanpur were both retaken in September, Agra was relieved soon afterwards, and the final recapture of Lucknow in March 1858 effectively broke the back of the Mutiny.

The Raj and Indian nationalism (1857–1947)

The uprising had important consequences for subsequent British rule in the Subcontinent. The governing powers of the East India Company were abolished and the British Crown assumed the direct administration of India in the same year. Henceforth, British India was no longer merely a massive trade operation, but a fully-fledged independent kingdom, or **Raj**, as the period of British rule in the Subcontinent subsequently became known. India played a key role in the politics of British imperialism, especially in the rivalries with France and Russia. Its army became an instrument of British foreign policy both in the Afghan Wars, attempting to create a buffer state to block Russia's advances in central Asia, and in the Anglo-Burmese Wars, to check French expansion in Indochina. It was also used to protect British interests as far afield as Abyssinia and Hong Kong. As a British colony, India assumed a new position in the world economy. Its trade benefited from the railways developed by the British, and Indian businessmen began to invest in a range of manufacturing industries, including textiles, iron and steel. However, India subsidized the British economy as a source of cheap raw materials and as a market for manufactured goods, and its own economy and agriculture remained underdeveloped.

British civil servants dominated the higher echelons of the administration, imposing Western notions of progress on the indigenous social structure and often introducing policies contrary to Indian interests and cultural traditions. At the same time, the propagation of the English language and the Western knowledge to which it gave access resulted in the emergence of a new **middle class** of civil servants, landlords and professionals, whose consciousness of an Indian national identity steadily increased. Public demonstrations eventually forced the British to sanction the creation of the **Indian National Congress** party (usually known simply as "Congress") in 1885, and by 1905 Congress had adopted self-government as a political aim, encouraged by radical leader Bal Gangadhar Tilak. In 1906, concerns about the predominantly Hindu Congress led to the foundation of the **All-India Muslim League** to represent the country's Muslims.

Meanwhile, increasing unrest was beginning to sweep the country. In 1906, controversial plans by Viceroy Lord Curzon to partition the state of Bengal into eastern and western halves (uncannily anticipating events of forty years later) provoked widespread opposition, much of it orchestrated by Bal Gangadhar Tilak, who proposed a no-tax campaign and a boycott of British goods, while some more extreme Bengali groups resorted to bombings and assassinations of both British and Indian targets.

The Morley-Minto Reforms of 1909 paved the way for Indian participation in provincial executive councils and made allowance for separate Muslim representation. At the **Great Durbar** of 1911, held in honour of the new king, George V, the capital was moved back to **Delhi**, with the construction of yet another imperial city, so-called "New" Delhi, to celebrate the relocation (though it wasn't completed and officially inaugurated until 1931). A few years later, the Royal Proclamation of 1917 promised a gradual development of dominion-style self-government; and two years later the Montagu-Chelmsford Reforms attempted to implement the declaration.

At this point an England-educated lawyer, **Mohandas Karamchand Gandhi** (see box, p.648) – better known as the Mahatma, or "Great Soul" – took up the initiative, espousing a political philosophy based on nonviolence and the championing of the untouchables, whom he renamed the Children of God (Harijan). Gandhi began by organizing India-wide one-day strikes and protests, though these were mercilessly crushed by the government – as in the infamous incident (see p.606) in 1919 when General Dyer dispersed a meeting at Jallianwalla Bagh in Amritsar by firing on the unarmed crowd, killing 379 and wounding 1200.

By 1928 Congress was demanding complete independence. The government offered talks, but the more radical elements in Congress, now led by the young

Jawaharlal Nehru, were in a confrontational mood. Gandhi, in turn, led a well-publicized 240-mile "salt march" from his ashram in Sabarmati to make salt illegally at Dandi in Gujarat in defiance of a particularly unpopular British tax. This demonstration of nonviolent civil disobedience (satyagraha) fired the popular imagination, leading to more processions, strikes, and mass imprisonments over the next few years, which in turn led to the formulation of the new **Government of India Act** in 1935, although this still fell short of offering the country complete independence. Congress remained suspicious of British intentions, and despite Gandhi's overtures refused to accommodate Muslim demands for representation. **Mohammed Ali Jinnah**, a lawyer from Bombay who assumed the leadership of the Muslim League in 1935, initially promoted Muslim–Hindu cooperation, but he soon despaired of influencing Congress and by 1940 the League passed a resolution demanding an independent Pakistan.

Another problem faced in the run-up to Independence was the question of what was to become of the numerous **princely states** scattered over many parts of India – nowhere more so than in Rajputana – which were still technically independent and autonomously run. The states still covered two-fifths of the country's total area and represented a huge potential stumbling block to future independence should their rulers (most of whom were deeply suspicious of Congress) choose not to join the newly independent country. The question was never to be properly solved and even at Independence rulers of several of the major states had yet to decide which country they were going to join (with enduringly disastrous consequences in Kashmir).

Confrontations between the government, Congress and the Muslim League continued throughout World War II, despite the promise, in 1942, by a Britain increasingly reliant on Indian troops, of post-war Independence (an offer which Gandhi compared to "a post-dated cheque on a failing bank"). Gandhi introduced the "**Quit India**" slogan and proposed another campaign of civil disobedience; the government immediately responded by imprisoning the whole Working Party of Congress in Pune. Jinnah, meanwhile, preached his "two nations" theory to the educated, and inspired mass Muslim support with his rhetoric against "Hinduization". A spate of terrorist activities across the country left one thousand dead and sixty thousand imprisoned. By the end of the war, the British government accepted that complete independence for India could no longer be postponed.

Unfortunately, British attempts to find a solution that would preserve a united India whilst allaying Muslim fears disintegrated in the face of continued intransigence from both sides, and they gradually realized that the division – or so-called **Partition** – of the existing country of India into separate Muslim and Hindu states was inevitable. In 1946 Jinnah provoked riots in Calcutta with his call for Direct Action, while Hindus retaliated with atrocities against Muslims in Bihar and Uttar Pradesh. Gandhi desperately sought to avert escalating Hindu–Muslim violence and to find a way of securing a united India; Nehru, however, was persuaded that a separate Pakistan would be preferable to an ongoing anarchy of communal killings.

Lord Mountbatten was appointed viceroy to supervise the handover of power. The Subcontinent was **partitioned** on August 15, 1947, and Pakistan came into existence, even though several princely states had still to decide which of the two new countries they would join. The new boundaries cut through both Bengal and the Punjab; Sikhs, Muslims and Hindus who had been neighbours became enemies overnight. Five million Hindus and Sikhs from Pakistan, and a similar number of Muslims from India, were involved in the ensuing two-way exodus, and the atrocities cost half a million lives. Mahatma Gandhi, who had devoted himself to ending the communal violence after Partition, was **assassinated** in January 1948 by Hindu extremists antagonized by his defence of Muslims. India had lost its "Great Soul", but the profound shock of the Mahatma's last sacrifice at least contributed to the gradual cessation of the violence.

India under Nehru (1947–1964)

Jawaharlal Nehru, India's first and longest-serving prime minister, proved to be a dynamic, gifted and extremely popular leader during his seventeen years in office, building the foundations of a democratic secular nation, and guiding the first stages of its agricultural and industrial development. Nehru's first task, however, was to consolidate the integrity of his new state. His able deputy prime minister, Sardar Vallabhai Patel, was made responsible for incorporating the 562 princely states within the federal Union (the nizam of **Hyderabad**, who resisted even though the majority of the state's population was Hindu, had to be persuaded by an invasion of Indian troops).

The new Indian constitution became law on January 26, 1950. The franchise was made universal for all adults, and with 173 million eligible to vote in 1951 India became the **world's largest democracy**. Hindi was designated the "official language of the Union"; but south India, in particular, was adamant in its opposition to Hindi, and Nehru realigned several state borders on linguistic principles. Some parts of the Subcontinent retained their independence for longer. The **French** enclaves at Pondicherry and Chandernagar were not incorporated until the 1950s, while the Portuguese refused to accept the new situation, until in 1961 Nehru finally sent in the army to annex **Goa**. The **Naga** people were brought within the federal Union as the Nagaland state in the same year, though the Punjabi-speaking Sikhs had to wait until 1966 for their state to be separated from Hindu-dominated Haryana.

The most serious legacy of Partition, however, concerned the Himalayan state of **Kashmir**. At independence, Kashmir's Hindu maharaja Hari Singh remained undecided as to which of the two new countries he wished to join. Jinnah naturally assumed that Kashmir would join Pakistan, given that three-quarters of its inhabitants were Muslims; Nehru (who was himself a Kashmiri Hindu), however, was equally determined to keep it for India. Meanwhile, the maharaja continued to prevaricate. Events reached a head in October 1947, when Islamic partisans from Pakistan's tribal areas suddenly arrived in the Kashmir valley to encourage the maharaja to join with Pakistan. Hari Singh, fearing he was about to be overthrown, immediately determined to join India instead. Shortly afterwards Indian troops were airlifted into the valley, and began to battle with the Islamic insurgents. Although war was never officially declared, and no regular Pakistani military units were involved, the fighting is usually described as the **First Indo-Pakistan War**. By the time the UN brokered a ceasefire in 1948, Pakistani insurgents had secured a sizeable slice of Kashmiri territory, which Pakistan retains to this day.

Nehru also implemented a vigorous programme of **social and economic reforms**. He redressed the iniquities of caste by abolishing "untouchability" in 1955 and radically improved the status of women. National average literacy rates rose and free elementary education became more readily available. On the **economic** front, Nehru engineered the first three of India's Five-Year Plans with the aim of boosting agricultural production and giving the country a solid industrial base, including a nuclear energy programme.

Nehru's aims of promoting Asian unity and adopting a foreign policy of peaceful **nonalignment**, however, were repeatedly threatened by **Chinese aggression**. The invasion of Tibet in 1950 brought the Chinese right up to India's border (and a flood of refugees into India itself, including the Dalai Lama, who arrived in 1959). In 1961 it was discovered that the Chinese military had built a road across a remote area of Indian territory in northern Kashmir. A series of skirmishes in Ladakh and Assam ensued, and in 1962 Chinese troops brushed aside Indian border patrols and began to move down into Assam. This "invasion" (although it was really more a show of force) ended on November 21, 1962, when the Chinese decided to turn around and go home again, though the humiliating inability of the Indian army to repel the interlopers spelt the end of India's policy of nonalignment. Nehru immediately made a defence treaty with the US, and set about creating a new elite Border Security Force. The Chinese retained small areas of Indian territory in Kashmir and Assam which it holds to this day.

Indira Gandhi (1966–1984)

The whole nation, loyal throughout the China crisis, mourned Nehru's death in 1964, which prevented him from witnessing the restoration of India's military prestige in the **Second Indo–Pakistan War** of 1965. Pakistani leader General Ayub Khan, perhaps wishing to test the resolve of new Indian premier **Lal Bahadur Shastri**, first launched a series of skirmishes into disputed areas of Gujarat, and followed this up with attempts to infiltrate Kashmir and provoke a pro-Pakistani uprising. Full-scale fighting broke out in Kashmir and to the south, and the Indian army responded by driving Pakistani forces back to within five kilometres of a virtually defenceless Lahore before a ceasefire was agreed, with both sides returning to their previous borders. Despite this triumph, Lal Bahadur Shastri died shortly afterwards, in January 1966, leaving Nehru's daughter **Indira Gandhi** to establish herself as the new leader of Congress.

The 49-year-old Indira – or "Mrs Gandhi", as she is often called (though no relation to the Mahatma; she acquired her lustrous surname through marriage to a Parsi named Feroze Gandhi, who had died in 1960) – was initially chosen as a popular but easily manipulated figurehead by Congress chiefs. Indira herself had different plans. She moved rapidly to consolidate her own power, and then – after consolidating her mandate in fresh elections in 1971 – launched Congress along a populist socialist path, nationalizing the banks, abolishing the former maharajas' privy purses and privileges, and introducing new legislation on corporate profits and land holdings. By this time, India was experiencing massive industrial growth and had also made a spectacular agricultural breakthrough with its **Green Revolution**, becoming self-sufficient in food by the early 1970s thanks to the introduction of high-yield grains.

Mrs Gandhi also had to deal with the increasingly chaotic situation in **East Pakistan** (present-day Bangladesh), which had declared independence from (West) Pakistan in 1971. Pakistani troops had been sent in to bring the East Pakistanis back into line, causing a mass exodus of refugees into India: by April of that year, Bengalis were pouring across into India at the rate of sixty thousand a day. Mrs Gandhi astutely waited until she had the moral support of the international community before launching simultaneous attacks in West and East Pakistan on December 4. By December 15, Pakistani forces in Bangladesh had capitulated.

Back at home, Mrs Gandhi was proving less successful. After widespread agrarian and industrial unrest against the rate of inflation and corruption within the Congress in 1974, the clamour of protest rose to a crescendo in June 1975, and when the opposition coalition under the joint leadership of J.P. Narayan and Morarji Desai threatened to oust Mrs Ghandi from power, she declared a **State of Emergency** on June 26, suspending all civil rights, censoring the press and imprisoning some twenty thousand of her opponents, real or imagined. The "Emergency" lasted eighteen months, characterized by the enforced sterilization of men with two or more children and brutal slum-clearances in Delhi, supervised by her son Sanjay. When she finally released her opponents and called off the Emergency in January 1977, the bitterness she had engendered resulted in her ignominious defeat in the March elections. The ensuing **Janata** coalition under Morarji Desai fell apart within two years, and his premiership was terminated by a vote of no confidence in 1979. Mrs Gandhi, who had rebuilt her Congress (I) Party with Sanjay's help, was now apparently forgiven, and swept back into office in January 1980. Sanjay died in a plane crash a few months later.

Four years afterwards, Mrs Gandhi made the second, fatal, mistake of her career. A group of rebels demanding a separate Sikh nation – Khalistan – took control of the **Golden Temple** in Amritsar early in 1984, from where they organized a campaign of violence, killing hundreds of Hindus and moderate Sikhs. Indira sent in her tanks in June 1984, but two days of raging combat desecrated the Sikhs' holiest shrine as well as giving Khalistan its first martyrs. In October that year, Mrs Gandhi's Sikh bodyguards took revenge by assassinating her at her house in Delhi. The city was then engulfed in massive communal **rioting**, during which Hindu mobs went about Delhi systematically murdering Sikhs – according to some reports locating their victims with the help of electoral rolls supplied by Congress politicians.

Communal conflict (1984–1995)

Following Indira Ghandi's death, it was left to her sole surviving son, **Rajiv Gandhi** (a former airline pilot) to take up leadership of Congress. Rajiv came to power in December 1984 on a wave of sympathy boosted by his reputation as "Mr Clean", an image given added meaning by the **Bhopal** gas tragedy (see p.400) just two weeks before the elections. The honeymoon was short-lived, however. The political accords he reached with the Punjab, Assam and Mizoram deteriorated into armed conflict; more than two years of "peacekeeping" by the Indian army failed to disarm Tamil guerrillas in Sri Lanka; and allegations of corruption tarnished his image. By the end of the 1980s the opposition had rallied under the leadership of **V.P. Singh**, a former Congress minister. The December 1989 elections did not give V.P. Singh's Janata Party a majority, but he managed to form a coalition government with the support of the "Hindu first" Bharatiya Janata Party, or **BJP**, led by **L.K. Advani**.

Singh was immediately confronted by problems in the Punjab and Kashmir, as well as upper-caste Hindu protests against his plans for a sixty percent reservation of civil service jobs for lower castes and former "untouchables"; but it was an even more emotive issue that brought down his government in less than a year. Advani's populist BJP were demanding that the Babri Masjid mosque in **Ayodhya**, built by Babur in the sixteenth century, should be replaced by a Hindu temple on the supposed site of the birthplace of Rama, god-hero of the Ramayana. Singh, utterly committed to secularism, pleaded with Advani to desist but, undeterred, Advani set off towards Ayodhya in October 1990, accompanied by thousands of devout Hindus, with the avowed intention of destroying the mosque. Singh ordered Advani's arrest, and the inevitable withdrawal of the BJP from his coalition government resulted in a vote of no confidence.

Rajiv Gandhi declined an offer to form an interim government, hopeful that he could improve his party's position in an election. His campaign went well and it was assumed that Congress would win, until on a tour of Tamil Nadu in May 1991, Rajiv was assassinated by Tamil Tigers seeking revenge for India's military opposition to their "freedom fight" in Sri Lanka. It was left to **P.V. Narasimha Rao** to steer Congress through the elections and formed a new coalition government, which immediately embarked on a far-reaching programme of **economic liberalization,** dismantling trade barriers and allowing multinationals such as Coca-Cola, Pepsi and KFC to enter the Indian market for the first time.

At the same time, the BJP ominously increased its seats in the Lok Sabha (the Lower House of Parliament) from 80 to 120 and Advani became leader of the opposition, amidst growing popular support for the rebuilding of Rama's temple in Ayodhya. V.P. Singh countered by leading a march of five hundred secularists to Ayodhya, but the BJP had won control of the Uttar Pradesh state government, making them responsible for law and order, and this time it was Singh who found himself arrested and imprisoned.

The situation at Ayodhya finally came to a head in December 1992. With the central government powerless to intervene, Hindu extremists incited crowds of fanatical devotees to tear down the Babri Masjid in a blaze of publicity. The demolition was followed by terrible **riots** in many parts of the country, especially Bombay and Gujarat, where Muslim families and businesses were targeted. A few months later, a massive series of bomb blasts ripped through **Bombay**, killing 260 people and destroying some of the city's most important commercial buildings. No one claimed responsibility, though the attacks were thought to have been orchestrated by Islamic groups in retaliation for Hindu violence against their fellow Muslims.

National morale during this post-Ayodhya period was shaky. After a year blighted by bomb blasts, riots and the rise of religious extremism, it seemed as if India's secular constitution was doomed. To rub salt in the wounds, 15,000 people died in a massive **earthquake** around the northwestern Maharashtrian city of Latur, and soon after, Surat, in southern Gujarat, was at the centre of an outbreak of a disease ominously resembling bubonic **plague**. Thousands fled the city and the international community panicked, cancelling export orders and axing flights. The "plague" turned out to be a flash in the pan, but the damage to India's image took longer to pass.

Against this backdrop of uncertainty, the rise of right-wing Hindu-fundamentalist parties gathered pace. The BJP took advantage of the power struggle in the Congress Party to rekindle regional support. Their new rallying cry was **Swadeshi** – a campaign against the Congress-led programme of economic liberalization and, in particular, the activities of newly arrived companies such as Coca-Cola, Pepsi and KFC (one of whose branches was forced to close by the BJP-controlled Delhi municipality). Bal Thackeray's neo-fascist **Shiv Sena** party (see p.680) also made ground in Maharashtra, eventually winning the State Assembly elections there in March 1995.

The rise of the BJP (1996–1999)

After the **general election** of May 1996, the political landscape altered at national level. Polling 194 of the Lok Sabha's 534 seats, the BJP emerged as the single largest party and attempted to form a government but were unable to muster a majority and were ousted a couple of weeks later by the hastily formed **Unified Front** coalition, led by H.D. Deve Gowda and subsequently by I.K. Gujral, who maintained good relations with America and led the Indian market away from socialism. The United Front soldiered on until its defeat in the **general election** of March 1998, after which the **BJP** struggled to power as the head of a new conservative coalition government under **Atal Behari Vajpayee**. This time, the party managed to stay in office for thirteen months, as opposed to the thirteen days of its previous spell in government. The BJP had promised change and the restoration of national pride, and one of its early acts in government was to conduct five underground **nuclear tests** in May 1998, provoking Pakistan to respond in kind. There was a chorus of world criticism, and US-led financial **sanctions** were imposed on both nations. In many people's eyes, the tests made the Kashmir issue more of a flashpoint – and now a potentially nuclear one. In sharp contrast to increased tension over security issues, Vajpayee visited Pakistan in person in early March 1999, the first time an Indian prime minister had crossed the border in a decade. However, this atmosphere of seemingly warming relations between the two countries received a jolt when the Indian government tested an **Agni II missile**, capable of carrying nuclear warheads into Pakistan. Again, Pakistan matched this within days, testing their own long-range, nuclear-capable missiles. The BJP were also accused of wilful inaction in the face of a spate of **attacks on Christians**, such as when an Australian missionary and his two young sons were burnt alive as they slept in a car at a religious gathering in Orissa.

Following its defeat in the 1998 elections, the Congress Party emerged as a stronger political force with **Sonia Gandhi**, the Italian-born widow of the former prime minister Rajiv Gandhi, at the helm. Congress collaborated with the Jayalalitha's AIADMK to bring about the downfall of the BJP in April 1999 (see box, p.1104), but were unable to form a coalition government. As a consequence, India faced a third **general election** in as many years.

At the start of the campaign, Congress hopes were high that, with a Gandhi once again as party leader, it could revive the popular support lost after years of infighting and corruption scandals. Unfortunately for them, the wave of **patriotism** that swept India after the Kargil victory (see box, p.1355) in Kashmir was a godsend for Vajpayee (cynics argued it may well have been the hidden policy behind the army's uncompromising response to the crisis). Riding high on the feel-good factor, his party inflicted the biggest defeat Congress had sustained since 1947. Vajpayee's majority was far from as large as he might have hoped, and the BJP-led National Democratic Alliance (NDA) coalition was fractured and tenuous, but Sonia's second election defeat seemed to herald, at last, the end of dynastic politics in India (in spite of the entrance onto the political stage of her charismatic 26-year-old daughter, Priyanka).

The election results also showed a clear swing of public support away from New Delhi towards smaller regional parties. Tired of corrupt police, unsafe drinking water and inadequate rubbish disposal, electricity provision and sewer and road maintenance, the emerging middle classes voted out almost half of their incumbent MPs in a spirit of exasperation which led the news magazine *Outlook* to run a lead story questioning whether India actually needed a central government at all.

The NDA's post-election party was short-lived. On October 30, 1999, a massive **super-cyclone** with 175mph winds struck the north coast of Orissa. Estimates of the death toll ranged from 10,000 to 20,000, around 1.5 million villagers lost their homes and thousands more died in the following weeks from cholera, typhoid and other diseases. International aid agencies were quick to criticize the Indian government, saying the relief operation was hampered by poor coordination and bickering between New Delhi and the state government in Orissa.

The new millennium

India's political problems were temporarily eclipsed by a succession of catastrophic **natural disasters**. In the arid zones of Rajasthan and Gujarat, high May temperatures in 2000 compounded the third failure of the monsoons in as many years, forcing tens of thousands of poor farming families off their land in search of fodder and drinking water. Once again, the government was heavily criticized for failing to respond quickly enough. While the monsoon, when it finally broke, made little impact on the parched northwest, **record rainfalls** wreaked havoc in Andhra Pradesh, West Bengal and low-lying areas of Uttar Pradesh. An estimated twelve million were left marooned or homeless as river levels rose by as much as four metres in places. An even worse tragedy lay in store for millions of Gujaratis when, in the morning of January 26, 2001 – Indian Republic Day – a massive **earthquake** measuring 7.9 on the Richter scale levelled a vast area in the northwest of the state (see p.633).

Meanwhile in Delhi, a string of **corruption scandals** was piling pressure onto the fractious BJP-led NDA coalition. In 2001 undercover journalists from the investigative website Tehelka, posing as arms dealers, succeeded in bribing defence minister George Fernandes, as well as senior army officers, civil servants, and even the president of the BJP, who was caught on camera shovelling cash into his desk. The scandal deeply embarrassed the prime minister, who sacked Mr Fernandes and ordered a commission of inquiry. Vajpayee's party also came in for more flak for yielding ground to its regionalist coalition partners when the prime minister announced the **creation of three new states**: Jharkhand, Chhattisgarh and Uttaranchal, made up of remote parts of Bihar, Madhya Pradesh and Uttar Pradesh respectively.

That there was much more to India at the turn of the millennium than natural disasters and corruption scandals, however, was proved by south India's burgeoning **hi-tech revolution**, centred on the cities of Bangalore and Hyderabad. **Bangalore** had led the way in the early 1980s, and by the mid-1990s had become a major player in the international software market. By the turn of the millennium, however, its pre-eminence was being challenged by the even more spectacular emergence of **Hyderabad** (quickly nicknamed "Cyberabad"), which thanks to massive state subsidies had begun to attract leading global players including Microsoft and Dell – although the rural poor of southern India saw very little of this newly generated wealth, further exacerbating the wealth-gap between rich and poor, which commentators quickly rechristened the "digital divide".

To the brink of war

Towards the end of summer 2001, **Indo-Pak relations** and the **Kashmir** question returned to the fore as India entered one of the most volatile periods in its modern history. But if India felt it occupied the high moral ground in the wake of the Kargil conflict, the October 2002 destruction of the **State Assembly building in Srinagar** by Islamist suicide car-bombers seemed to further vindicate its determination to bring Pakistan to account for the militancy originating across the border. Islamabad, however, swiftly condemned the attack – the first time in history it had done so.

A similar pronouncement, followed up with promises to crack down on "cross-border terrorism" was made by Pakistan in response to the most dramatic attack ever on the Indian state, when three Muslim gunmen stormed the **Parliament Building** in New Delhi in December 2001. Having killed several police guards, they were picked off by army marksmen, but the sense of indignation grew in the following weeks. Pakistani involvement was inevitably suspected, and Vajpayee announced he was in favour of declaring war immediately. Only after some intense US and British diplomacy, and more conciliatory announcements from Islamabad, were New Delhi's ruffled feathers temporarily smoothed.

The flagging support for the prime minister and BJP seemed to revive as a wave of **communal tension** engulfed the country in the spring of 2002. The catalyst was the massacre by a Muslim mob in **Godhra**, Gujarat, of a trainload of Hindu pilgrims returning from the disputed temple site in Ayodhya: 38 died and 74 were injured, but this paled in comparison with the reprisal killings that followed, in which around two thousand people (mostly Muslims) were slaughtered. The BJP Chief Minister of Gujarat, Narendra Modi, was accused of colluding in the massacres when it emerged that his police force seemed to be following a policy of nonintervention, standing back on several occasions to allow Hindu mobs to go about their gruesome business.

Anti-Muslim sentiment in India was further fuelled only a month after Godhra when an Islamist suicide squad commandeered a tourist bus and used it to attack the **Kaluchak** army cantonment near Jammu; thirty people were killed, including several women and ten children, before the militants were themselves shot dead. Coming only four months after the attack on the Indian parliament, and hot on the heels of yet another promise by Pakistan to clamp down on the militants crossing its border, the atrocity provoked outrage in Delhi. Vajpayee, bowing to the hawks on the right of his own party, called for a "decisive battle", initiating a massive build-up of troops on the border. An estimated million men at arms were involved in the ensuing stand-off as India and Pakistan edged to the brink of all-out **war**. Once again, however, US diplomacy diffused the crisis and the armies stood down by the end of the monsoons.

Progress on the **Kashmir problem** was finally made following a new round of peace talks in 2003 (see box, p.1355), though relations between Hindus and Muslims in some parts of India remained as strained as ever. As the first trials of suspects accused of atrocities in the wake of the Godhra massacres reached court in Ahmedabad, the Archeological Survey of India released its long-awaited **report on Ayodhya**. Since the destruction of the Babri Masjid by Hindu extremists in 1992, debate had raged as to whether there had in fact ever been a Rama temple beneath the mosque. To no one's surprise, the ASI panel of "experts", appointed by the right-wing BJP government (prominent members of which had incited the Babri Masjid destruction in the first place), declared they'd found evidence to show there had been a temple, in effect condoning the tearing down of the mosque.

Rubbing salt in old wounds, the ruling did little to quell post-Godhra tensions; and when, on August 25, 2003 (the day after the Ayodhya report was published), two **bombs** ripped through the centre of downtown Mumbai, commentators were quick to identify the Babri Masjid dispute as the provocation. One exploded in a taxi next to the **Gateway of India**, Mumbai's main tourist hub, killing 107 people. No one has ever claimed responsibility, but four suspects believed to have links with Islamic militant groups were arrested soon after.

The return of Congress

Despite continuing sectarian troubles, with India booming as never before and peace on the horizon in Kashmir, prime minister Vajpayee and his BJP-led coalition decided to cash in on the perceived feel-good factor and call a snap **election** in **May 2004**, but the campaign strategy boomeranged badly. India

The Himalayan state of **Kashmir** is the main – if not the only – reason why India and Pakistan have remained bitter enemies for most of the fifty years since Independence. The region's troubles date from Partition, when the ruling Hindu maharaja opted to join India rather than Pakistan, and the geopolitical tug-of-war over the state has soured relations between the two countries ever since, at least until the last few years.

The conflict in Kashmir has taken two forms: firstly, a **military confrontation** between the Pakistani and Indian armies along the de facto border – on three occasions leading to fully fledged war (in 1947, 1965 and 1999); and, secondly, a violent **insurgency-cum-civil war** since 1989, during which both Kashmiri and foreign Muslim fighters have launched various attacks against Indian military and civilian targets inside Kashmir itself, leading to equally bloody reprisals by Indian security forces – a conflict which has now cost an estimated 68,000 lives.

The roots of the problem

The events surrounding Kashmir maharaja Hari Singh's decision to join India in 1947, and the resulting First Indo-Pakistan War, are described on p.1347. At the end of this conflict, Pakistan was left with around a third of Kashmir, and India with two-thirds, with each country claiming that the state rightly belonged entirely to them. The UN subsequently passed a resolution calling on India to hold a plebiscite so that the inhabitants of Kashmir could determine their own political future. **India** has continually refused to do this, claiming that Kashmir joined India in a satisfactory and legal manner in 1948, and that no plebiscite is therefore necessary (they also argue that it is in any case impossible to hold such a plebiscite until Pakistan vacates the areas of Kashmir it currently holds). **Pakistan**, meanwhile, contests the legality of Hari Singh's decision to join Kashmir with India and demands that the UN-requested plebiscite be held. Some **Kashmiri groups**, including the Jammu and Kashmir Liberation Front and the All Party Hurriyat Conference, have pursued an entirely separatist path, fighting for an independent state which would be completely free of both Pakistan and India.

Following the cessation of hostilities in 1948, the ceasefire line, or so-called **Line of Control**, became the effective border between India and Pakistan. India lost a further slice of Kashmiri territory to the Chinese during the 1962 conflict (see p.1348) before a resumption of hostilities with Pakistan during the **Second Indo-Pakistan War** of 1965 (see p.1348). Again, Kashmir was the focus of attention, though at the end of the war both sides returned to their original positions. The **Simla Agreement** of 1972 comitted both sides to renounce force in their dealings with one another, and to respect the Line of Control and the de facto border between their two states.

Insurgency and civil war

Simmering Kashmiri discontent with Indian rule and Delhi's political interference in the region, which was meant to have been given virtual autonomy in return for joining India, began to transform into **armed resistance** in around 1989 – mujahideen arriving in the Kashmir valley after the end of the war with Russia in Afghanistan are often blamed for the sudden surge of militancy. The key incident, however, was the unprovoked massacre, in 1990, of around a hundred unarmed protesters, who were gunned down by Indian security forces on **Gawakadal Bridge** in the capital, Srinagar. By the following year, violence and human-rights abuses had become endemic, both in the Kashmir valley itself and further south around Jammu. Armed and trained by Libya and Pakistan, guerrillas from at least nineteen Muslim countries flooded in to fight what was now seen as a jihad, or Holy War. Curfews became routine, and thousands of suspected militants were detained without trial amid innumerable accusations of torture, the systematic rape of Kashmiri women by Indian troops, disappearances of countless boys and men, and summary executions. The conflict continued to ebb and flow throughout the 1990s, with regular atrocities on both sides, while the region's once-thriving tourist industry was dealt a fatal blow when the extremist Al-Faran Muslim group kidnapped five tourists; one was beheaded, and the others are believed to have suffered a similar fate.

At the end of the decade, the crisis brought India and Pakistan to the verge of yet another all-out war – and only months after both had successfully tested long-range nuclear missiles. With both countries now fully fledged nuclear states, Kashmir has become one of the world's most dangerous geopolitical flashpoints. In May 1999, at least eight hundred Pakistani-backed mujahideen crept across the so-called Line of Control (the de facto border) overlooking the Srinagar–Leh road near **Kargil** and began to occupy Indian territory. India moved thousands of troops and heavy artillery into the area, swiftly followed up with an aerial bombardment. Within days the two countries were poised on the brink of all-out war. In the event the conflict was contained, and by July 1999 the Indian army had retaken all the ground previously lost to the militants. An estimated 700 Pakistani and 330 Indian soldiers died before Pakistani premier, Nawaz Sharif, bowed to international pressure and withdrew his forces.

The new millennium brought no immediate improvement to the situation. Indian prime minister Vajpayee and Pakistan's president Musharraf held a summit on Kashmir in Agra in July 2000, though the talks quickly broke down. Despite repeated reassurances to the contrary from the Pakistan government, Pakistani-backed mujahideen continued to infiltrate the Kashmir valley in ever-greater numbers. The extent of the problem was emphasized in October 2001 when a dramatic suicide car bomb attack in broad daylight destroyed the State Assembly building in Srinagar, while in December of that year, armed Islamic commandos stormed the Indian Parliament building in New Delhi.

Tensions continued to rise throughout 2002, as the two countries edged gradually closer to a second war in three years, and by May one million soldiers were facing each other across the Indo-Pak border. All-out war was only narrowly averted after intense diplomatic pressure was brought to bear on both sides by US emissary Colin Powell. Within Kashmir, long-established organizations like the Jammu and Kashmir Liberation Front and the All Party Hurriyat Conference, which had traditionally adopted a secular and nationalist stance, were being increasingly eclipsed by militantly Islamic and pro-Pakistani groups such as Lashkar-e-Toiba and Jaish-e-Mohammad (the two groups thought to be behind the 2001 attack on the Indian Parliament).

The road to peace?
Further talks followed, but were suspended in March 2003 by India after Islamabad announced the successful testing of its Shaheen missile, capable of delivering nuclear warheads over a distance of 750km (as far as Delhi). The negotiations, however, resumed in May 2003, when Vajpayee made a **declaration of peace**, announcing that hundreds of Pakistanis detained in Indian prisons since the Kargil war would be released. Pakistani prime minister Mir Zafarullah Khan Jamali responded by announcing that Pakistan would ease trade restrictions and improve travel and sporting links. The most significant concessions made by the two sides in recent times, the moves were widely regarded as paving the way for some kind of break-through, and paved the way for a full-blown summit is Islamabad in early 2004.

In 2004 and 2005 the Indian and Pakistani governments also held their first ever talks with Kashmiri separatists from the Hurriyat Conference, establishing a peaceful "Road Map" for progress in the region. A further round of Indo-Pak talks following the appointment of Manmohan Singh as India's new prime minister resulted in further small but encouraging signs of progress, symbolized by the inauguration, in April 2005, of a fortnightly **bus service** between Srinagar and Muzaffarabad in Pakistani-controlled Kashmir, the first for nearly sixty years, and something which would have

(Contd....2)

been unthinkable even a few years previously. Meanwhile, Pakistani president Musharraf began to show a new determination to rein in Pakistani-based Kashmiri militants, while India made the first of a series of promised troop withdrawals from the region. Further détente was signalled in the aftermath of the devastating **earthquake** in Pakistani Kashmir in October 2005, which killed around 73,000 people in Pakistan and a further 1400 in Indian Kashmir, when the Line of Control was opened to speed up relief operations.

Various long-term solutions to the whole Kashmir issue are currently being mooted. India has suggested that the Line of Control might be converted into a permanent border, while Pakistan favours a re-division along communal lines – although in late 2006 Musharraf even made the surprising admission that Pakistan could be prepared to give up all claims to Kashmir if India allowed it some form of self-government. Kashmir's future looks brighter now than it has for decades, although the increasingly volatile political situation in Pakistan as of early 2008 could yet derail the progress of the past four years.

---

was experiencing a period of unparalleled economic growth; the boom, however, was based largely on technology, and had had little impact on the vast majority of the population. Congress leader Sonia Gandhi was quick to seize the initiative, appealing directly to poor rural voters and also playing the dynastic card by introducing her son Rahul and daughter Priyanka to the campaign to capture the imagination of younger voters (half of the Indian electorate are aged under 35).

Far from increasing his majority as he'd expected, Vajpayee and his government were thrown out in the most dramatic political turnaround of recent times. Congress gained the largest share of the vote and **Sonia Gandhi** was duly invited to form a government. However, she stunned supporters by "humbly declining" the invitation and stepped down. The announcement caused clamorous scenes in Parliament, provoking the worst losses ever seen in the 129-year history of India's stock market. Eventually, former finance minister, 71-year-old **Manmohan Singh**, stepped into the breach and was named as prime minister, the first Sikh ever to lead the country.

As the architect of the important liberalizing economic reforms enacted during the government of P.V. Narasimha Rao in the early 1990s, Manmohan Singh seemed like the perfect candidate to oversee India's continuing economic and technological growth (as Manmohan himself put it, "India happens to be a rich country inhabited by very poor people"). In April 2007 the country launched its first commercial space rocket, while in May 2007 the government announced the strongest economic growth figures (an impressive 9.4 percent) for twenty years. India's technological and economic transformation continues apace. The country is now the world's second-largest exporter of computer software after the US, generating sales of around a billion dollars a year, focused on the southern cities of Bangalore and Hyderabad, which have also become home to innumerable international call centres thanks to the cities' educated, English-speaking workforce.

Such spectacular developments have had little effect, however, on the lives of India's rural poor. In an attempt to address the ever-widening divide between the nation's increasingly affluent middle classes and the rest of the country, Manmohan's coalition government launched the nation's largest-ever rural jobs scheme in February 2006 with the aim of freeing around sixty million families from poverty, although this promised "New Deal" has yet to bear fruit. Progress has also been made on the looming **nuclear threat** hanging over the Subcontinent. In March 2006 the US and India signed a nuclear agreement whereby the US gave India access to civilian nuclear technology, while India agreed to allow international monitors access to its nuclear programme, and in February 2007 an agreement was signed with Pakistan aimed at reducing the risk of accidental nuclear war.

Sectarian violence continues to plague the country, including many attacks designed to derail the ongoing peace process in Kashmir. In October 2005, bombs allegedly planted by a little-known Kashmiri group killed 62 people in Delhi, while in February 2007, 68 passengers (most of them Pakistanis) were killed by bomb blasts on a train travelling from New Delhi to Lahore. Worst of all were the series of bombs blasts which exploded almost simultaneously on seven trains in Mumbai on 11 July 2006, leaving 209 dead and over seven hundred injured, apparently planted by Islamic militants in retaliation for the killing of Muslims in Kashmir and Gujarat. Separatist violence has also been intensifying in the **northeast**, where old ethnic tensions pose a perennial threat of insurgency – even normally peaceful Darjeeling has been plagued by civil unrest in recent years, as Gurkha factions compete for power. In October 2004, a wave of bombings and shootings killed more than one hundred people, and separatist groups continue to be active in the area.

Natural disasters have also continued to wrack the country. The most dramatic and unexpected struck the country on December 26, 2004, in the form of the **Asian tsunami**. Although southeast India was 2000km away from the epicentre of the Indonesian earthquake, much of its coast lay in the direct path of the tsunami, and on the morning of December 26, 2004, three giant waves, each over 10m high, swept ashore from the Bay of Bengal. Parts of Tamil Nadu, the Andaman and Nicobar islands, and a small area in Kerala were all devastated. Official estimates placed the death toll at around 11,000, with as many as ten times that homeless. The real figure, however, is probably much higher and will never be known. In July 2005 more than a thousand people were killed in floods and landslides in Mumbai and Maharashtra, while in October 2005 a devastating **earthquake** with its epicentre in Pakistani Kashmir left a thousand people dead in Indian Kashmir.

Unrest in the northeast hill-states is only one manifestation of a steadily strengthening, pan-Indian pull away from the centre and the nationwide rise of **regionalism**. Other factors too have led to a general weakening of the national capital's grip on the country. Incapable of raising adequate tax revenue, and rotten to its core with corruption, New Delhi no longer commands the respect and economic power it used to. Chronic political instability has also taken its toll. The absence of consistent policies has meant that big business and the affluent classes have increasingly had to look after themselves, which has conspicuously widened the gap between the haves and the have-nots.

As it struggles to balance the ambitions of its privileged elite with the basic needs of its poor, Indian society at the start of the twenty-first century is rife with ironies. The country chosen by Bill Gates as the site of Microsoft's new Hi-Tech City, and a place capable of launching satellites and nuclear rockets, is unable to provide clean drinking water, adequate nutrition and basic education for millions of its inhabitants. Its capacity to close this yawning gap will depend on the extent to which the country's politicians are able to deliver stable government and curb the corruption and self-interest that have come to dominate public life.

Religion

F our out of five Indians are Hindus, and **Hinduism** permeates every aspect of life in the country, from the commonplace details of daily life up to national politics. After Hindus, **Muslims** are the largest religious group; they have been an integral part of Indian society since the twelfth century, and mosques are almost as common as temples. Though there are now very few **Jains** and **Buddhists** in India, their impact is still felt, and their magnificent temples are among the finest in India. Both these ancient faiths, like the more recently established **Sikh** community, were formed in reaction to the caste laws and ritual observances of Hinduism. In addition, there are small communities of **Christians**, here since the first century, as well as Iranian-descended Zoroastrians, or **Parsis**. Hindu practices, such as caste distinction, have crept into most religions, and many of the festivals that mark each year with music, dance and feasting are shared by all communities. Each has its own pilgrimage sites, heroes, legends and even culinary specialities, which all combine to give India its unique religious diversity.

Hinduism

Hinduism is the product of several thousand years of evolution and assimilation. It has no founder or prophet, no single creed, and no single prescribed practice or doctrine; it takes in hundreds of gods, goddesses, beliefs and practices, and widely variant cults and philosophies. Some are recognized by only two or three villages, others are popular right across the Subcontinent. Hindus call their beliefs and practices **dharma**, which defines a way of living in harmony with natural and moral law while fulfilling personal goals and meeting the requirements of society.

Early developments

The origins of Hinduism date back to the arrival of the **Aryans**, a semi-nomadic people who began to settle in northwest India during the second millennium BC, mixing with the indigenous Dravidian population. The Aryans believed in a number of gods associated with the elements, including **Agni**, the god of fire, **Surya**, the sun god, and **Indra**, the chief god. Most of these deities faded in importance in later times, but Indra is still regarded as the father of the gods, and Surya, eternally present in his magnificent chariot-temple in **Konarak** (Orissa), was widely worshipped until the medieval period, and remains an important deity in Rajasthan.

Aryan religious beliefs were first set down in a series of four books, the **Vedas** (from the Sanskrit word *veda*, meaning "knowledge"), which were believed to have been divinely revealed to various inspired sages at the beginning of the present world cycle. Transmitted orally for centuries, the Vedas were finally written down, in Sanskrit, between 1000 BC and 500 AD. The earliest and most important of the four Vedas, the **Rig Veda**, contains over a thousand hymns to various deities, while the other three (the Yajur Veda, Sama Veda and Atharva Veda) contain further prayers, chants and instructions for performing the complex sacrificial rituals associated with this early Vedic religion.

The Vedas were followed by further religious texts, including the **Brahmanas**, a series of commentaries on the Vedas for the use of priests (Brahmans) and, more importantly, the **Upanishads**, which describe in beautiful and emotive verse the mystic experience of unity of the soul (*atman*) with Brahma, the absolute creator of the universe, ideally attained through asceticism, renunciation of worldly values and meditation. In the Upanishads the concepts of **samsara**, a cyclic round of death and rebirth characterized by suffering and perpetuated by desire, and **moksha**, liberation from *samsara*, became firmly rooted. As fundamental aspects of the Hindu world view, both are accepted by all but a handful of Hindus today, along with the belief in **karma**, the certainty that one's present position in society is determined by the effect of one's previous actions in this and past lives.

Hindu society

The stratification of Hindu society is rooted in the Dharma Sutras, a further collection of scriptures written at roughly the same time as the later Vedas. These defined four hierarchical classes, or **varnas** (from *varna*, meaning "colour", perhaps a reference to difference in appearance between the lighter-skinned Aryans and the darker indigenous Dravidian population). Each *varna* was assigned specific religious and social duties, with Aryans established as the highest social class. In descending order the *varnas* are: **brahmins** (priests and teachers), **kshatryas** (rulers and warriors), **vaishyas** (merchants and cultivators) and **shudras** (menials). The first three classes, known as "twice-born", are distinguished by a sacred thread worn from the time of initiation, and are granted full access to religious texts and rituals. Below all four categories, groups whose jobs involve contact with dirt or death (such as undertakers, leather-workers and cleaners) were classified as **untouchables**. Though discrimination against

---

The Ramayana

The Ramayana tells the story of **Rama**, the seventh of Vishnu's eight incarnations – although possibly based on a historic figure, Rama is seen essentially as a representation of Vishnu's heroic qualities. Rama is the oldest of four sons born to Dasaratha, the king of Ayodhya, and heir to the throne. When the time comes for Rama's coronation, Dasaratha's scheming third wife Kaikeyi has her own son Bharata crowned instead, and has Rama banished to the forest for fourteen years. In an exemplary show of filial piety, Rama calmly accepts the loss of his throne and leaves the city with his wife **Sita** and brother **Laksmana**.

One day, Surpanakha, the sister of the demon **Ravana**, spots Rama in the woods and instantly falls in love with him. Being a virtuous, loyal husband, Rama rebuffs her advances, while Laksmana cuts off her nose and ears in retaliation. In revenge, Ravana kidnaps Sita, who is borne away to one of Ravana's palaces on the island of **Lanka**.

Determined to find Sita, Rama enlists the help of **Hanuman**, the monkey god. Hanuman leaps across the strait to Lanka and makes his way surreptitiously into Ravana's palace, where he hears the evil king trying to persuade Sita to marry him. If not, he threatens, "my cooks shall mince thy limbs with steel and serve thee for my morning meal" – a choice of consummation or consumption. Hanuman reports back to Rama, who gathers an army and prepares to attack. Monkeys form a bridge across the straits allowing the invading army to cross; after much fighting, Sita is rescued and reunited with her husband.

On the long journey back to Ayodhya, Sita's honour is brought into question. To prove her innocence, she asks Laksmana to build a funeral pyre and steps into the flames, praying to Agni, the fire god. Agni walks her through the fire into the arms of a delighted Rama. They march into Ayodhya guided by a trail of lights laid out by the local people. Today, this illuminated homecoming is commemorated by Hindus all over the world during Diwali, the festival of lights. At the end of the epic, Rama's younger brother gladly steps down, allowing Rama to be crowned as the rightful king.

untouchables is now a criminal offence, in part thanks to the campaigns of Gandhi, the lowest stratum of society has by no means disappeared.

Within the four *varnas*, social status is further defined by **jati**, classifying each individual in terms of their family and job (for example, a *vaishya* may be a jewellery seller, cloth merchant, cowherd or farmer). A person's *jati* determines his **caste**, and lays restrictions on all aspects of life from what sort of food he can eat, religious obligations and contact with other castes, to the choice of marriage partners. In general, Hindus marry members of the same *jati* – marrying someone of a different *varna* often results in ostracism from both family and caste, leaving the couple stranded in a society where caste affiliation takes primacy over all other aspects of individual identity. There are almost three thousand *jatis*; the divisions and restrictions they have enforced have repeatedly been the target of reform movements and critics.

A Hindu has three **aims in life**: to fulfil his social and religious duties (*dharma*); to follow the correct path in his work and actions (*karma*); and to gain

The Mahabharata

Eight times as long as the *Iliad* and the *Odyssey* combined, the **Mahabharata** is the most popular of all Hindu texts. Written around 400 AD, it tells of a feuding kshatrya family in upper India (Bharata) during the fourth millennium BC. Like all good epics, the Mahabharata recounts a gripping tale, using its characters to illustrate moral values. In essence it attempts to elucidate the position of the warrior castes, the kshatryas, and demonstrate that religious fulfilment is as accessible for them as it is for brahmins.

The chief character is **Arjuna**, a superb archer, who with his four brothers – Yudhishtira, Bhima, Nakula and Sahadeva – represent the **Pandava** clan, supreme fighters and upholders of righteousness. Arjuna won his wife **Draupadi** in an archery contest, but wishing to avoid jealousy she agreed to be the shared wife of all five brothers. The Pandava clan are resented by their cousins, the evil **Kauravas**, led by Duryodhana, the eldest son of Dhrtarashtra, ruler of the Kuru kingdom.

When Dhrtarashtra handed his kingdom over to the Pandavas, the Kauravas were far from happy. Duryodhana challenged Yudhishtira (known for his intelligence and compassion but who was addicted to games of chance) to a gambling contest. The dice game was rigged; Yudhishtira gambled away not only his possessions, but also his kingdom and his shared wife. The Kauravas offered to return the kingdom to the Pandavas if they could spend thirteen years in exile, together with their wife, without being recognized. Despite much scheming, the Pandavas succeeded, but on return found that the Kauravas would not fulfil their side of the bargain.

Thus ensued the great battle of the Mahabharata, told in the sixth book, the **Bhagavad Gita** – immensely popular as an independent story. Vishnu descends to earth as **Krishna**, and steps into battle as Arjuna's charioteer. The Bhagavad Gita details the fantastic struggle of the fighting cousins, using magical weapons and brute force. Arjuna is in a dilemma, unable to justify the killing of his own kin in pursuit of a rightful kingdom for himself and his brothers. Krishna consoles him, reminding him that his principal duty, his dharma, is as a warrior. What is more, Krishna points out, each man's soul is eternal, and transmigrates from body to body, so Arjuna need not grieve for the death of his cousins. Krishna convinces Arjuna that by fulfilling his dharma he not only upholds law and order by saving the kingdom from the grasp of unrighteous rulers, he also serves the gods in the spirit of devotion (*bhakti*), and thus guarantees himself eternal union with the divine in the blissful state of *moksha*.

The Pandavas finally win the battle, and Yudhishtira is crowned king. Eventually Arjuna's grandson, Pariksit, inherits the throne, and the Pandavas trek to Mount Meru, the mythical centre of the universe and the abode of the gods, where Arjuna finds Krishna's promised *moksha*.

material wealth (*artha*). These goals are linked with the four traditional stages in life. The first is as a child and student, devoted to learning from parents and guru. Next comes the stage of householder, expected to provide for a family and raise children. That accomplished, he may then take up a life of celibacy and retreat into the forest to meditate alone, and finally renounce all possessions to become a homeless ascetic, hoping to achieve the ultimate goal of *moksha*. The small number of Hindus, including some women, who follow this ideal life assume the final stage as saffron-clad **sadhus** who wander throughout India, begging for food and retreating to isolated caves, forests and hills to meditate. They're a common feature in most Indian towns and many stay for long periods in particular temples. Not all have raised families: some assume the life of a sadhu at an early age as *chellas*, pupils of an older sadhu.

The main deities

Alongside the Vedas and Upanishads, the most important Hindu religious texts are the **Puranas** – long mythological stories about the Vedic gods – and the two great epics, the **Mahabharata** and **Ramayana** (see boxes, p.1359 & p.1360 respectively) thought to have been completed by the first century AD, though subsequently retold, modified and embellished on numerous occasions and in various different regional languages. The Puranas and the two great epics helped crystalize the basic framework of Hindu religious belief, which survives to this day, based on a supreme triumvirate of deities. **Brahma**, the original Aryan godhead, or "creator", was joined by two gods who had begun to achieve increasing significance in the evolving Hindu world-view. The first, **Vishnu**, "the preserver", was seen as the force responsible for maintaining the balance of the cosmos whenever it was threatened by disruptive forces, incarnating himself on earth nine times in various animal and human forms, or avatars, to fight the forces of evil and chaos, most famously as Rama (the god-hero whose exploits are described in the Ramayana) and as Krishna (who appears at the most significant juncture of the Mahabharata). The second, **Shiva**, "the destroyer" (a development of the Aryan god Rudra, who had played a minor role in the Vedas), was charged with destroying and renewing the universe at periodic intervals, though his powers are not merely destructive, and he is worshipped in myriad forms with various attributes (see box, p.1362). The three supreme gods are often depicted in a trinity, or *trimurti*, though in time Brahma's importance declined, and Shiva and Vishnu became the most popular deities – the famous Brahma temple at Pushkar is now one of the few in India dedicated to this venerable but rather esoteric god.

Depicted in human or semi-human form and accompanied by an animal "**vehicle**", other gods and goddesses who came alive in the mythology of the Puranas are still venerated across India. River goddesses, ancestors, guardians of particular places and protectors against disease and natural disaster are as central to village life as the major deities.

Philosophical trends

Hinduism's rather complicated view of the cosmos naturally encouraged considerable philosophical debate, and led eventually to the formation of six schools of thought, known as the Darsharas. Foremost among these was the Advaita ("non-duality") school of **Shankara** (*c.*788–850 AD), a religious teacher and reformer who interpreted Hinduism as pure monotheism. Shankara claimed that the human soul is inseparably fused with god (like salt dissolved in water, as the Upanishads describe it), and that all else – the gods, the world and everything in it – is an illusion (*maya*) created by god. This philosophy is

Vishnu

The chief function of **Vishnu**, "pervader", is to keep the world in order, preserving, restoring and protecting. With four arms holding a conch, discus, lotus and mace, Vishnu is blue-skinned, and often shaded by a serpent, or resting on its coils, afloat on an ocean. He is usually seen alongside his half-man, half-eagle vehicle, Garuda.

Vaishnavites, often distinguishable by two vertical lines of paste on their foreheads, recognize Vishnu as supreme lord, and hold that he has manifested himself on earth nine times. These incarnations, or avatars, have been as fish (*Matsya*), tortoise (*Kurma*), boar (*Varaha*), man-lion (*Narsingh*), dwarf (*Vamana*), axe-wielding brahmin (*Parsuram*), Rama, Krishna and Balaram (though some say that the Buddha is the ninth avatar). Vishnu's future descent to earth as Kalki, the saviour who will come to restore purity and destroy the wicked, is eagerly awaited.

The most important avatars are Krishna and Rama. **Krishna** is the hero of the Bhagavad Gita, in which he proposes three routes to salvation (*moksha*): selfless action (*karma yoga*), knowledge (*jnana*) and devotion to god (*bhakti*), and explains that *moksha* is attainable in this life, even without asceticism and renunciation. This appealed to all castes, as it denied the necessity of ritual and officiating brahmin priests, and evolved into the popular *bhakti* cult that legitimized love of God as a means to *moksha*, and found expression in emotional songs of the quest for union with the divine. Through *bhakti*, Krishna's role was extended, and he assumed different faces: most popularly he is the playful cowherd who seduces and dances with cowgirls (*gopis*), giving each the illusion that she is his only lover. He is also pictured as a small, chubby, mischievous baby, known for his butter-stealing exploits, who inspires tender motherly love in women. Like Vishnu, Krishna is blue, and often shown dancing and playing the flute. Popular legend has it that Krishna was born in **Mathura**, today a major pilgrimage centre, and sported with his *gopis* in nearby **Vrindavan**. He also established a kingdom on the far western coast of Gujarat, at **Dwarka**.

Rama, Vishnu's seventh incarnation, is the chief character in the **Ramayana**, the epic detailing his exploits in exile (see p.1359).

Shiva

Shaivism, the cult of **Shiva**, was also inspired by *bhakti*, requiring selfless love from devotees in a quest for divine communion, but Shiva has never been incarnate on earth. He is presented in many different aspects, such as **Nataraja**, Lord of the Dance, **Mahadev**, Great God, and **Maheshvar**, Divine Lord, source of all knowledge. Though he does have several terrible forms, his role extends beyond that of destroyer, and he is revered as the source of the whole universe.

Shiva is often depicted with four or five faces, holding a trident, draped with serpents, and bearing a third eye in his forehead. In temples, he is identified with the lingam, or phallic symbol, resting in the yoni, a representation of female sexuality. Whether as statue or lingam, Shiva is accompanied by his bull-mount, Nandi, and often by a consort, who also assumes various forms, and is looked upon as the vital energy, **shakti**, that empowers him. Their erotic exploits were a favourite sculptural subject between the ninth and twelfth centuries, most unashamedly in carvings on the temples of **Khajuraho** in Madhya Pradesh.

While Shiva is the object of popular devotion all over India, as the terrible **Bhairav** he is also the god of the Shaivite **ascetics**, who renounce family and caste ties and perform extreme meditative and yogic practices. Many, though not all, smoke ganja, Shiva's favourite herb; all see renunciation and realization of God as the key to *moksha*. Some ascetic practices enter the realm of **tantrism**, in which confrontation with all that's impure, such as alcohol, death and sex, is used to merge the sacred and the profane, and bring about the profound realization that Shiva is omnipresent.

Other gods and goddesses

Chubby and smiling, elephant-headed **Ganesh**, the first son of Shiva and Parvati, is invoked before every undertaking (except funerals). Seated on a throne or lotus, his image is often placed above temple gateways, in shops and houses; in his four arms he holds a conch, discus, bowl of sweets (or club) and a water lily, and he's always attended by his vehicle, a rat. Credited with writing the Mahabharata as it was dictated by the sage Vyasa, Ganesh is regarded by many as the god of learning, the lord of success, prosperity and peace.

Durga, the fiercest of the female deities, is an aspect of Shiva's more conservative consort, Parvati (also known as Uma), who is remarkable only for her beauty and fidelity. Among Durga's many aspects, each a terrifying goddess eager to slay demons, are Chamunda, Kali and Muktakeshi, but in all her forms she is Mahadevi (Great Goddess). Statues show her with ten arms, holding the head of a demon, a spear and other weapons; she tramples demons underfoot, or dances upon Shiva's body. A garland of skulls drapes around her neck and her tongue hangs from her mouth, dripping with blood – a particularly gruesome sight on pictures of Kali. Durga is much venerated in Bengal; in all her temples, animal sacrifices are a crucial element of worship, to satisfy her thirst for blood and deter her ruthless anger.

The comely goddess **Lakshmi**, usually shown sitting or standing on a lotus flower, and sometimes called Padma (lotus), is the embodiment of loveliness, grace and charm, and the goddess of prosperity and wealth. Vishnu's consort, she appears in different aspects alongside each of his avatars; the most important are Sita, wife of Rama, and Radha, Krishna's favourite *gopi*. In many temples she is shown as one with Vishnu, in the form of Lakshmi Narayan.

Though some legends claim that his mother was Ganga, or even Agni, **Karttikeya** is popularly believed to be the second son of Shiva and Parvati. Primarily a god of war, he was popular among the northern Guptas, who worshipped him as Skanda, and the southern Chalukyas, for whom he was Subrahmanya. Usually shown with six faces, and standing upright with bow and arrow, Karttikeya is commonly petitioned by those wishing for male offspring.

India's great monkey god, **Hanuman**, features in the Ramayana as Rama's chief aide in the fight against the demon-king of Lanka. Depicted as a giant monkey clasping a mace, Hanuman is the deity of acrobats and wrestlers, but is also seen as Rama and Sita's greatest devotee, and an author of Sanskrit grammar. As his representatives, monkeys find sanctuary in temples all over India.

The most beautiful Hindu goddess, **Saraswati**, the wife of Brahma, with her flawless milk-white complexion, sits or stands on a water lily or peacock, playing a lute, sitar or *vina*. Associated with the River Saraswati, mentioned in the Rig Veda, she is revered as the goddess of music, creativity and learning.

Closely linked with the planet Saturn, **Sani** is feared for his destructive powers. His image, a black statue with protruding blood-red tongue, is often found on street corners; strings of green chillies and lemon are hung in shops and houses each Saturday (*Saniwar*) to ward off his evil influences.

Mention must also be made of the **sacred cow**, Kamdhenu, who receives devotion through the respect shown to all cows, left to amble through streets and temples all over India. The origin of the cow's sanctity is uncertain; some myths record that Brahma created cows at the same time as brahmins, to provide ghee (clarified butter) for use in priestly ceremonies. To this day cow dung and urine are used to purify houses (in fact the urine keeps insects at bay), and the killing or harming of cows by any Hindu is a grave offence. The cow is often referred to as mother of the gods, and each part of its body is significant: its horns symbolize the gods, its face the sun and moon, its shoulders Agni (god of fire) and its legs the Himalayas.

summed up by the famous phrase *tat tvam asi*, "thou art that", describing the one-ness of the human soul with god.

Another important Darshana centres around the age-old practice of **yoga** (literally "yoking together", whether of the mind and body, or the soul with god), described by **Patanjali** (second century BC) in his Yoga Sutras. The most common form of yoga known in the West is *hatha* yoga, whereby the body and its vital energies is brought under control through physical positions and breathing methods, with results said to range from attaining a calm mind to being able to fly through the air, enter other bodies or become invisible. Other practices include *mantra* yoga, the recitation of formulas and meditation on mystical diagrams (*mandalas*), *jnana* yoga (knowledge), *bhakti* yoga (devotion), and *raja* (royal) yoga, the highest form of yoga, during which the mind is absorbed in God. Of the various types of yoga, **bhakti** has become particularly important in Hindu practice and thought, developing a wide popular appeal, especially in the south. *Bhakti* stresses that the path to *moksha* lies in surrendering oneself to god through worship and loving devotion, a message which has proved particularly popular amongst followers of Krishna (see p.1362) both in India and abroad.

Practice

In most Hindu homes, a chosen deity is worshipped daily in a shrine room, and scriptures are read. Outside the home, worship takes place in temples, and consists of **puja**, or devotion to god – sometimes a simple act of prayer, but more commonly a complex process when the god's image is circumambulated, offered flowers, rice, sugar and incense, and anointed with water, milk or sandalwood paste (which is usually done on behalf of the devotee by the temple priest). The aim in puja is to take **darshan** – glimpse the god – and thus receive his or her blessing. Whether devotees simply worship the deity in prayer, or make requests – for a healthy crop, a son, good results in exams, a vigorous monsoon or a cure for illness – they leave the temple with *prasad*, an offering of food or flowers taken from the holy sanctuary. **Temple ceremonies** are conducted in Sanskrit by priests who tend the image in daily rituals in which the god is symbolically woken, bathed, fed, dressed and, at the end of each day, put back to bed. In many villages, shrines to *devatas*, village deities who function as protectors, are more important than temples.

Each of the **great stages** in life – birth, initiation (when boys of the three "twice-born" *varnas* are invested with a sacred thread), marriage, death and cremation – is cause for prayer and celebration. The most significant event in a Hindu's life is **marriage**, with festivities usually lasting for a week or more before and after the wedding. The actual marriage is consecrated when the couple walk seven times round a sacred fire, accompanied by sacred verses read by an officiating brahmin. Despite being illegal since 1961, **dowries** are still demanded from the bride's family; these may include televisions and cars, in addition to the more traditional jewellery and money. The murder of wives whose dowry has been below expectations are still common – victims are typically dowsed in kerosene and burnt to death so that the killing can be passed off as a "kitchen accident".

Strict rules address **purity and pollution**, the most obvious of them requiring high-caste Hindus to limit their contact with potentially polluting lower castes. All bodily excretions are polluting (hence the strange looks Westerners receive when they blow their noses and return their handkerchiefs to their pockets). Above all else, **water** is the agent of purification, used in ablutions before prayer and revered in all rivers, especially Ganga (the Ganges).

Ghats, steps leading to the water's edge, are common in all river- or lakeside towns, used for bathing, washing clothes or performing religious rituals.

Pilgrimages and festivals

India has a wealth of **pilgrimage** sites – sacred rivers or mountains, or places made holy by their association with gods, miracles, or great teachers – visited by devotees eager to receive *darshan* and attain merit. Bands of Hindus (particularly sadhus) often still walk from site to site, although modern transport has made things easier, and every state lays on pilgrimage tours, when buses full of chanting families roar from one temple to another, filling up with religious souvenirs as they go. Many pilgrimage sites are also the focus of major **festivals**. For more information, see "Sacred spaces and pilgrimage places" colour section.

Islam

Indian society may be dominated by Hindus, but **Muslims** – some thirteen percent of the population – form a significant presence in almost every town, city and village. The belief in only one god, Allah, the condemnation of idol

---

Animals and plants in Indian myth and religion

The early **Harappa** civilization of the Indus Valley portrayed mythical creatures, bulls, elephants and tigers on their terracotta seals, amulets and toys. The itinerant **Aryan tribes** that subsequently settled in India worshipped Brahma the bull, who lay with his bovine consort to create horned **cattle** to farm the earth. The imagery of gentle yet strong and fertile cows and oxen is still central to the **Hindu** religion: Shaivite temples almost always sport a statue of the bull Nandi, Shiva's vehicle (*vahan*), and Krishna is often depicted as a cowherd. The Mahabharata warns that the eating of beef or wearing of leather is taboo, and you'll notice cows wandering freely around towns, usually when your bus swerves to avoid hitting one. These are often old or injured animals which the owner has released so that they can die a natural death. To touch the rump of a cow ensures fertility and prosperity.

As Brahmanical Hinduism gradually absorbed India's countless indigenous regional deities and cults, animals became a more important part of the Hindu pantheon: **Vishnu** emerged as a fish, a tortoise and a boar, an elephant head was placed on **Ganesh** (when he was mistakenly beheaded by his father, Shiva), and the monkey god **Hanuman** became the loyal servant of Rama. The hooded cobra was revered as a god of the northeastern **Naga** tribe, and was later absorbed into the more mainstream mythological realm as the protector of Shiva and Vishnu. In fact, there are few animals and birds that do not have a spiritual association, as each of the millions of deities have to mount an animal **vahan** (vehicle) to travel between earth and heaven. Brahma rides a swan, Kartika, the god of war, sits astride a proud peacock, Ganesh is carried by a rat and Indra rides an elephant.

The common **deer** is sacred to both Hinduism and Buddhism. The Buddha is supposed to have preached his first sermon in a deer park, and according to Hindu law, the docile and graceful creature is so holy that even the ground that it treads should be worshipped. The **peacock** is symbolically associated with fertility for its instinctive ability to sense, and dance at, the approach of rain.

Many of India's **plants** and **flowers** have also become imbued with sacred associations. Coconuts yield milk and its succulent flesh is given as a symbolic food offering (*prasad*) at the beginning of a puja ceremony. The unchanging womb-like form of the lotus (*padma*) has led to its strong association with "mother creation". In yoga, the "lotus position" promotes health and wisdom, while lotus flowers bearing candles are set afloat on the Ganges as a sunset *arati* offering to summon divine blessing.

worship, and the observance of their own strict dietary laws and specific festivals all set Muslims apart from their Hindu neighbours, with whom they have coexisted for centuries. Such differences have often led to communal fighting, most notably during Partition in 1947, the riots that followed the destruction by Hindus of the Babri Masjid mosque in Ayodhya in 1993 and the massacre of pilgrims at Godhra, Gujarat, in 2002.

Islam, "submission to God", was founded by **Mohammed** (570–632 AD), regarded as the last in a succession of prophets, who transmitted God's final and perfected revelation to mankind through the divinely revealed **Koran** (Qur'an; literally "recitation"), whose teachings form the basis of Islamic belief.

The birth of Islam is dated at 622 AD, when Mohammed and his followers, exiled from Mecca, made the *hijra*, or migration, north to Medina, "City of the Prophet". The *hijra* marks the start of the Islamic lunar calendar: the Gregorian year 2000 was for Muslims 1421 AH (*Anno Hijra*). From Medina, Mohammed ordered raids on caravans heading for Mecca and, inspired by *jihad*, or "striving" on behalf of God and Islam, led his community in battles against the Meccans. This concept of holy war was the driving force behind the incredible expansion of Islam – by 713 Muslims had settled as far west as Spain, and on the banks of the Indus in the east. When **Mecca** was peacefully surrendered to Mohammed in 630, he cleared the sacred shrine, the Ka'ba, of idols, and proclaimed it the pilgrimage centre of Islam. Mohammed was succeeded as leader of the Islamic community (*umma*) by Abu Bakr. However, a schism soon emerged, with some Muslims preferring to place themselves under the leadership of Ali, Mohammed's son-in-law. This new sect, calling themselves **Shias** – "partisans" of Ali – looked to Ali and his successors, for leadership. About ten percent of Indian Muslims are Shia.

By the second century after the *hijra* (ninth century AD), orthodox, or **Sunni**, Islam had assumed the form in which it endures today. A collection of traditions about the prophet, **Hadith**, became the source for ascertaining the **Sunna** (customs) of Mohammed. From the Koran and the Sunna, seven major **items of belief** were laid down: the belief in God; in angels as his messengers; in prophets (including Jesus and Moses); in the Koran; in the doctrine of predestination by God; in the Day of Judgement; and in the bodily resurrection of all people on this day. Religious practice was also standardized under the Muslim law, **Sharia**, in the **Five Pillars of Islam**. The first "pillar" is the confession of faith (*shahada*), stating that "There is no god but God, and Mohammed is his messenger." The other four are prayer (*salat*) five times daily, almsgiving (*zakat*), fasting (*saum*), especially during the month of Ramadan, and, if possible, pilgrimage (*haj*) to Mecca, the ultimate goal of every practising Muslim.

Islam in India

The first Muslims to settle in India were traders who arrived on the southwest coast in the seventh century, probably in search of timber for shipbuilding. Later, in 711, Muslims entered Sind, in the northwest, to take action against Hindu pirates, and dislodged the Hindu government. Their presence, however, was short-lived. Much more significant was the invasion of north India under **Mahmud of Ghazni**, who rampaged through the Punjab in search of temple treasures and, in the spirit of *jihad*, engaged in a war against infidels and idolaters. More raids from Central Asia followed in the twelfth century, resulting in the colonization of India, while the invading Muslims set themselves up in Delhi as sultans.

Many Muslims who settled in India intermarried with Hindus, Buddhists and Jains, and the community spread. A further factor in its growth was missionary activity by **Sufis**, who stressed the attainment of inner knowledge of God through meditation and mystical experience. Sufi teachings spread among *bhakti*-inspired followers of Shiva and Vishnu, who shared their passion for personal closeness to God. Their use of music (particularly *qawwali* singing – see p.126) and dance, shunned by orthodox Muslims, appealed to Hindus, for whom singing played an important role in religious practice. One *qawwali*, relating the life of the Sufi saint Waris Ali Shah, draws parallels between his early life and the childhood of Krishna – an outrage for orthodox Muslims, but attractive to Hindus, who still flock to his shrine in Deva Sharief near Lucknow. Similar shrines, or *dargarhs*, all over India bridge the gap between Islam and Hinduism.

Practice

Muslims are enjoined to pray five times daily, following a routine of utterances and positions. They may do this at home or in a **mosque** – always full at noon on Friday, for communal prayer (the only exception being the Druze of Mumbai, who hold communal prayers on Thursdays.) Characterized by bulbous domes and high minarets, from which a *muezzin* calls the faithful to prayer, mosques always contain a mihrab or niche indicating the direction of prayer (to Mecca), a *mimbar* or pulpit, from which the Friday sermon is read, a source of water for ablutions and an area for women. India's largest mosque is the Jama Masjid ("Friday Mosque") in **Delhi**, but magnificent structures, including tombs, schools and substantial remains of cities are scattered throughout north India and the Deccan, with especially outstanding examples in Hyderabad, Jaunpur, Agra and Fatehpur Sikri.

The position of **women** in Islam is a subject of great debate. It's customary for women to be veiled, though in larger cities many women don't cover their heads, and in strictly orthodox communities most wear a *burkha*, usually black, that covers them from head to toe. Like other Indian women, Muslim women take second place to men in public, but in the home, where they are often shielded from men's eyes in an inner courtyard, they wield great influence. In theory, education is equally available to boys and girls, but girls tend to forgo learning soon after sixteen, encouraged instead to assume the traditional role of wife and mother. Contrary to popular belief, polygamy is not widespread; while it does occur (Mohammed himself had several wives), many Muslims prefer monogamy and several sects actually stress it as a duty. In marriage, women receive a dowry as financial security.

Buddhism

Buddhism was born in the Indian subcontinent, developing as an offshoot of – and a reaction to – Hinduism, with which it shares many assumptions about the nature of existence. For a time it became the dominant religion in the country, most notably during the rule of the famous Buddhist emperor Ashoka (see p.1332), though from around the fourth century AD onwards it was gradually eclipsed by a resurgent Hinduism (which cleverly re-appropriated the Buddha, claiming him to be an incarnation of Vishnu), and the subsequent arrival of Islam more or less finished it off. Today Buddhists make up only a tiny fraction of the population – outside north India's numerous Tibetan refugee camps, only Ladakh and Sikkim now preserve a significant Buddhist presence. Nevertheless, a sequence of superb monuments such as the caves of Ajanta and Ellora in Maharashtra, and the remarkable stupas of Sanchi in Madhya Pradesh, offer fine reminders of this once flourishing culture.

The founder of Buddhism, **Siddhartha Gautama**, known as the **Buddha** ("awakened one"), was born into a wealthy kshatrya family in Lumbini, north of the Gangetic plain in present-day Nepal, around 566 BC. Brought up in luxury as a prince, he married at an early age, but renounced family life when he was thirty. Unsatisfied with the explanations of worldly suffering proposed by religious gurus, and convinced that asceticism did not lead to spiritual realization, Siddhartha spent years wandering the countryside and meditating. His enlightenment is said to have taken place under a *bodhi* tree in **Bodhgaya** (Bihar), after a night of contemplation during which he resisted the worldly temptations set before him by the demon, Mara. Soon afterwards he gave his first sermon in **Sarnath**, near Varanasi. For the rest of his life he taught, expounding **Dharma**, the true nature of the world, human life and spiritual attainment. Before his death (*c*.486 BC) in Kushinagara (UP), he had established the **Sangha**, a community of monks and nuns who continued his teachings.

The Buddha's world-view incorporated the Hindu concept of *samsara*, and karma and *moksha*, which Buddhists call **nirvana** (literally "no wind"). The most important concept outlined by the Buddha was that all things are subject to the inevitability of **impermanence**. There is no independent inherent self due to the interconnectedness of all things, and our egos are the biggest obstacles on the road to enlightenment.

Theravada and Mahayana

Disregarding caste and priestly rituals, the Buddha formulated a teaching open to all, inviting his followers to take refuge in the so-called "three jewels": the Buddha, the Dharma and the Sangha. The Buddha's original teachings became known as **Theravada** or "Doctrine of the Elders". At the heart of this teaching lie the **Four Noble Truths**, which propose that all suffering arises from the longing for things that are essentially impermanent and subject to change, but that this longing – and thus the suffering it entails – can be overcome. The Buddha also proposed a simple moral code, embodied as the **Noble Eightfold Path** (right understanding, thought, speech, action, livelihood, effort, mindfulness and concentration), which aims at reducing attachment and ego, and increasing self-awareness.

Inevitably, these relatively simple Theravada teachings gradually developed and changed over following centuries. In particular, there was a steady increase in the devotional aspect of Buddhism, akin to *bhakti* Hinduism, centred on the cult of the **bodhisattvas**. A *bodhisattva* is a Buddha-to-be, bound for enlightenment, who, spurred by selfless compassion has delayed entering nirvana in order to become a teacher and help unenlightened beings along the path to nirvana. The importance of the *bodhisattva* ideal was central to a new school, the **Mahayana**, or "Great Vehicle", which had established itself as the leading school of Indian Buddhist thought by the second century AD, and which, somewhat disparagingly, renamed the old Theravada school "Hinayana" (Lesser Vehicle).

Theravada Buddhism survives today in Sri Lanka, Myanmar, Thailand, Laos and Cambodia. Mahayana Buddhism spread from India to Nepal and Tibet and from there to China, Korea and ultimately Japan. In many places further evolution saw the adoption of magical methods, esoteric teachings and the full use of sensory experience to bring about spiritual transformation, resulting in a separate school known as **Vajrayana**, based on texts called *tantras*. Vajrayana encourages meditation on mandalas (symbolic diagrams representing the cosmos and internal spiritual attainment), sexual imagery and sometimes sexual practice, as a means of raising energies and awareness for spiritual goals.

Tibetan Buddhism

Buddhism was introduced to **Tibet** in the seventh century AD, and integrated to a certain extent with the indigenous **Bon** cult, before emerging as a faith containing elements of Theravada, Mahayana and Vajrayana. Practised largely in Ladakh, along with parts of Himachal Pradesh and Sikkim, Tibetan Buddhism recognizes the historical Buddha alongside previous Buddhas and a host of *bodhisattvas* and protective deities, and incorporates elaborate rituals, with music and dance, into its worship. There is also a heavy emphasis on teachers, known as lamas, and reincarnated teachers, known as *tulkus*. The **Dalai Lama**, the head of Tibetan Buddhism, is the fourteenth in a succession of incarnate *bodhisattvas*, the representative of Avalokitesvara, and the leader of the exiled Tibetan community based in Dharamsala (HP). With over 100,000 Tibetan **refugees** now living in India, including the Dalai Lama and the Tibetan government in exile, Tibetan Buddhism is probably the most accessible and flourishing form of Buddhism in India, and there are numerous opportunities for study (see Basics, p.72). Tibetan Buddhist devotees hang prayer flags, turn prayer wheels, and set stones carved with mantras (religious verses) in rivers, thus sending the word of the Buddha with wind and water to all corners of the earth. Prayers and chanting are often accompanied by horns, drums and cymbals.

Jainism

The **Jain** population in India is small – accounting for less than one percent of the population – but has been tremendously influential for at least 2500 years. A large proportion of Jains live in Gujarat, and all over India they are commonly found working as merchants and traders. Similarities to Hinduism, and a shared respect for nature and nonviolence, have contributed to the decline of the Jain community through conversion to Hinduism, but there is no antagonism between the two religions.

Focused on the practice of **ahimsa** (nonviolence), Jains follow a rigorous discipline to avoid harm to all **jivas**, or "souls", which exist in humans, animals, plants, water, fire, earth and air. They assert that every *jiva* is pure, omniscient, and capable of achieving liberation from existence in this universe. However, *jivas* are obscured by **karma**, a form of subtle matter that clings to the soul, which is born of action and binds the *jiva* to physical existence. For the most orthodox Jain, the only way to dissociate karma from the *jiva*, and thereby escape the wheel of death and rebirth, is to follow the path of asceticism and meditation, rejecting passion, attachment, carelessness and impure action.

The Jain doctrine is based upon the teachings of **Mahavira**, or "Great Hero", the last in a succession of 24 **tirthankaras** ("crossing-makers") said to appear on earth every 300 million years. Mahavira (*c.*599–527 BC) was born as Vardhamana Jnatrputra into a kshatrya family near modern Patna in northeast India. Like his near-contemporary the Buddha, Mahavira rejected family life at the age of thirty and spent years wandering as an ascetic, renouncing all possessions in an attempt to conquer attachment to worldly values. Firmly opposed to sacrificial rites and caste distinctions, he began teaching others, not about Vedic gods and divine heroes, but about the nature of the world, and the means required for release, *moksha*, from the endless cycle of rebirth.

His teachings were written down in the first millennium BC and Jainism prospered throughout India, under the patronage of kings such as Chandragupta Maurya (third century BC). Not long after, there was a schism, in part based on linguistic and geographical divisions, but mostly due to differences in monastic practice. On the one hand the **Digambaras** ("sky-clad") believed that nudity was an essential part of world renunciation, and that women are incapable of achieving liberation from worldly existence. The ("white-clad") **Svetambaras**, however, disregarded the extremes of nudity, incorporated nuns into monastic communities and even acknowledged a female *tirthankara*. Today the two sects worship at different temples, but the number of naked Digambaras is minimal. Many Svetambara monks and nuns wear white masks to avoid breathing in insects, and carry a "fly-whisk", sometimes used to brush their path; none will use public transport and they often spend days or weeks walking barefoot to a pilgrimage site.

Jain **temples** are wonderfully ornate, with pillars, brackets and spires carved by *silavats* into voluptuous maidens, musicians, saints and even Hindu deities; the *swastika* symbol commonly set into the marble floors is central to Jainism, representing the four states of rebirth as gods, humans, "hell beings", or animals and plants. Worship in temples consists of prayer and puja before images of the *tirthankaras*; the devotee circumambulates the image, chants sacred verses and makes offerings of flowers, sandalwood paste, rice, sweets and incense. It's common to fast four times a month on holy days, the eighth and fourteenth days of the moon's waxing and waning periods. While reducing attachment to the body, this emulates the fast to death (while in meditation), accepted by Jain mendicants as a final rejection of attachment, and a relatively harmless way to end worldly life.

Pilgrimage sites are known as **tirthas**, but this does not refer to the literal meaning of "river crossing", sacred to Hindus because of the purificatory nature of water. At one of the foremost Svetambara *tirthas*, **Shatrunjaya** in Gujarat, over nine hundred temples crown a single hill, said to have been visited by the first *tirthankara*, Rishabha, and believed to be the place where Rama, Sita and the Pandava brothers (incorporated into Jain tradition) gained deliverance from the cycle of rebirth. There's another important Digambara *tirtha* at **Sravanabelagola** in Karnataka, where a seventeen-metre-high image of Bahubali (recognized as the first human to attain enlightenment) at the summit of a hill is anointed in a huge festival every twelve years.

In an incredibly complicated process of philosophical analysis known as **Anekanatavada** (many-sidedness), Jainism approaches all questions of existence, permanence and change from seven different viewpoints, maintaining that things can be looked at in an infinite number of valid ways. Thus it claims to remove the intellectual basis for violence, avoiding the potentially damaging result of holding a one-sided view. In this respect Jainism accepts other religious philosophies and it has adopted, with a little reinterpretation, several Hindu festivals and practices.

Sikhism

Sikhism, India's youngest religion, remains dominant in the Punjab, while its adherents have spread throughout northern India and several communities have grown up in Britain, America and Canada. The movement was founded by **Guru Nanak** (1469–1539), who was born into an orthodox Hindu kshatrya family in Talwandi, a small village west of Lahore (in present-day Pakistan). Nanak was among many sixteenth-century poet-philosophers, sometimes referred to as *sants*, who formed emotional cults, drawing elements from both Hinduism and Islam. Nanak declared that "God is neither Hindu nor Muslim and the path which I follow is God's"; he regarded God as **Sat**, or truth, who makes himself known through gurus. Though he condemned ancestor worship, astrology, caste distinction, sex discrimination, auspicious days and the rituals of Brahmins, Nanak did not attack Islam or Hinduism – he simply regarded the many deities as names for one supreme God, and encouraged his followers to shift religious emphasis from ritual to meditation.

In common with Hindus, Nanak believed in a cyclic process of death and rebirth (*samsara*), but he asserted that liberation (*moksha*) was attainable in this life by all women and men regardless of caste, and that religious practice could and should be integrated into everyday practical living. Nanak also shared the belief, common to Hinduism, Buddhism and Jainism, that peoples' relationship to god is obscured by over-attachment to worldly things, leading to repeated rebirths. Sikhs believe that their gurus are the only beings who have realized the ultimate truth, and that they therefore provide essential guidance to their disciples.

Guru Nanak was succeeded by **Guru Angad**, who continued to lead the community of Sikhs (literally, "disciples"), the so-called **Sikh Panth**, and wrote his own and Nanak's hymns in a new script, **Gurumukhi**, which is today used as the script of written Punjabi. Eight further gurus successively led the Sikh Panth after Guru Angad's death in 1552, gradually developing Sikhism into a powerful independent religious movement. Guru Ram Das (1552–74) founded the sacred city of **Amritsar**; his successor, Guru Arjan Dev, compiled the gurus' hymns in a book called the **Adi Granth** and built the Golden Temple to house it; while Arjan Dev became Sikhism's first martyr when he was executed by Jahangir. Throughout their history, the Sikhs have had to battle to protect their faith and their people, especially against the Mughals; Guru Teg Bahadur was beheaded by Aurangzeb in 1675, an event that heralded the era of his son and successor, **Guru Gobind Singh**, who was to revolutionize the entire movement.

Gobind Singh, the last leader, was largely responsible for moulding the community as it exists today. In 1699, he founded the brotherhood of the **Khalsa**. The aims of the Khalsa are to assist the poor and fight oppression; to have faith in one god and to abandon superstition and dogma; to worship god; and to protect the faith with steel. The Khalsa requires members to renounce tobacco, halal meat and sexual relations with Muslims, and to adopt the **five Ks**: *kangha* (comb), *kirpan* (sword), *kara* (steel bracelet), *kachcha* (short trousers) and *kesh* (unshorn hair) – the last requirement means that Sikh men are usually instantly recognizable thanks to their luxuriant beards and distinctive turbans. Less visibly, Guru Gobind Singh replaced traditional caste names with Singh for men (meaning "lion" – although this name is not unique to Sikhs, being a common Hindu surname as well) and Kaur ("princess") for women. Finally, Guru Gobind Singh also compiled a standardized version of the Adi Granth, which contains the hymns of the first nine gurus as well as poems written by Hindus and Muslims, and installed it as his successor, naming it **Guru Granth Sahib**. This became the Sikh's spiritual guide, while political authority rested with the Khalsa.

Demands for a separate Sikh state – **Khalistan** – and fighting in the eighteenth century, and later after Independence, have burdened Sikhs with a reputation as military activists, and their bravery and martial traditions mean that they continue to make up an important part of the Indian army. Despite this, however, Sikhs regard their religion as one devoted to egalitarianism, democracy and social awareness. Though to die fighting for the cause of religious freedom is considered to lead to liberation, the use of force is officially sanctioned only when other methods have failed.

Practice

The main duties of a Sikh are to avoid the five evil impulses (lust, covetousness, attachment, anger and pride); to keep God's name in mind; to earn their living honestly; and to give to charity. Serving the community is seen as a display of obedience to God. Sikh worship takes place in a **gurudwara** ("door to the guru") or in the home, providing a copy of the Adi Granth is present. There are no priests, and no fixed time for worship, but congregations often meet in the mornings and evenings, and always on the eleventh day of each lunar month, and on the first day of the year. During **Kirtan**, or hymn singing, a feature of every Sikh service, verses from the Adi Granth or Janam Sakhis (stories of Guru Nanak's life), are sung to rhythmic clapping. The communal meal that follows these prayers and singing reinforces the practice laid down by Guru Nanak that openly flaunted caste and religious differences. The egalitarian nature of Sikhism is nowhere better exemplified than in the **Golden Temple** in Amritsar, the holiest of all Sikh shrines. The four doors are open to the four cardinal directions, welcoming both devotees and visitors from other faiths.

Gurudwaras – often schools, clinics or hostels as well as houses of prayer – are generally modelled on the Mughal style of Shah Jahan, considered a congenial blend of Hindu and Muslim architecture; usually whitewashed, and surmounted by a dome, they are always distinguishable by a yellow flag, introduced by Guru Hargobind (1606–44). As in Islam, God is never depicted in pictorial form. Instead, the representative symbol Il Oankar is etched into a canopy that shades the Adi Granth, which always stands in the main prayer room. In some *gurudwaras* a picture of a guru is hung close to the Adi Granth, but it's often difficult to distinguish between the different teachers: artistically they are depicted as almost identical, a tradition that unites the ten gurus as vehicles for the word of God, rather than as divine beings.

Important occasions for Sikhs, in addition to the naming of children, weddings and funerals, are **Gurpurbs**, anniversaries of the birth and death of the ten gurus, when the Adi Granth is read continuously from beginning to end.

Zoroastrianism

Of all India's religious communities, Western visitors are least likely to come across – or recognize – **Zoroastrians**, who have no distinctive dress, and few houses of worship. Most live in Mumbai, where they are known as **Parsis** (Persians) and are active in business, education and politics. Zoroastrian numbers – roughly ninety thousand – are rapidly dwindling due to a falling birth rate and absorption into wider communities (only when both parents are Parsi will children be accepted as Parsis, so children of mixed marriages are excluded from the community).

The religion's founder, **Zarathustra** (Zoroaster), lived in Iran around the sixth or seventh century BC, and was the first religious prophet to expound a dualistic philosophy, based on the opposing powers of good and evil. For him, the absolute, wholly good and wise God, **Ahura Mazda**, together with his holy spirit and six emanations present in earth, water, the sky, animals, plants and fire, is constantly at odds with an evil power, **Angra Mainyu**, who is aided by **daevas**, or evil spirits.

Mankind, whose task on earth is to further good, faces judgment after death, and depending on the proportion of good and bad words, thoughts and actions, will find a place in heaven, or suffer the torments of hell. Zarathustra looked forward to a day of judgment, when a saviour, **Saoshyant**, miraculously born of a seed of the prophet and a virgin maiden, will appear on earth, restoring Ahura Mazda's perfect realm and expelling all impure souls and spirits to hell.

The first Zoroastrians to enter India arrived on the Gujarati coast in the tenth century AD, soon after the Arabian conquest of Iran, and by the seventeenth century most had settled in Bombay. Zoroastrian practice is based on the responsibility of every man and woman to choose between good and evil, and to respect God's creations. Five daily prayers, usually hymns, uttered by Zarathustra and standardized in the **Avesta**, the main Zoroastrian text, are said in the home or in a temple, before a fire, which symbolizes the realm of truth, righteousness and order. For this reason, Zoroastrians are often, incorrectly, called "fire-worshippers".

Members of other faiths may not enter Zoroastrian temples. Zoroastrians are also famous for the unusual manner in which they dispose of their dead. A body is laid on a high open rooftop (or isolated hill) known as *dakhma* (often referred to as a "tower of silence"), for the flesh to be eaten by vultures and the bones cleansed by sun and wind. Recently, some Zoroastrians, by necessity, have adopted more common methods of cremation or burial; in order not to bring impurity to fire or earth, they only use electric crematoria, and shroud coffins in concrete before laying them in the ground.

Nav Roz, or "New Day", held in mid-March, is the most popular Zoroastrian festival, celebrating the creation of fire and the ultimate triumph of good over evil; the oldest sacred fire in India, in **Udwada**, just north of Daman in south Gujarat, is an important pilgrimage site.

Christianity

The **Apostle Thomas** is said to have arrived in Kerala in 54 AD to convert itinerant Jewish traders living in the flourishing port of Muziris, following the death of Jesus – according to popular tradition, the Church of San Thome is the oldest Christian denomination in the world, though documentary evidence of Christian activity in the Subcontinent can only be traced back to the sixth century, when immigrant Syrian communities were granted settlement rights by royal charter. There are many tales of miracles by "Mar Thoma", as Thomas is known in Malayalam. One legend tells how he approached a group of brahmins who were trying to appease the gods by throwing water into the air. If the gods had accepted the offerings, the saint said, the droplets would have remained suspended. Throwing water in the air himself, it miraculously hung above him, leading most of the brahmins to convert to Christianity. The southern tradition holds that Thomas was martyred on December 21, 72 AD, at Mylapore in **Madras** (the name comes from the Syriac *madrasa*, meaning "monastery"). The tomb has since become a major place of pilgrimage, while the Portuguese added the Gothic **San Thome Cathedral** to the site in the late nineteenth century.

Arrival of the Europeans

From the sixteenth century onwards, the history of the Church in India is linked to the spread of foreign Christians across the Subcontinent. In 1552, St Francis Xavier arrived in the Portuguese trading colony of **Goa** to establish missions to reach out to the Hindu "untouchables"; his tomb and alleged relics are retained in the Basilica of Bom Jesus in Old Goa to this day. In 1559, at the behest of the Portuguese king, the Inquisition arrived in Goa. Jesuit missionaries carried out a bloody and brutal campaign to "cleanse" the small colony of Hindu and Muslim religious practice. Early British incomers took the attitude that the Subcontinent was a heathen and polytheistic civilization waiting to be proselytized. Later, they were less zealous in their conversion efforts, being content to provide social welfare and build very English-looking churches in their own cantonments.

The proximity of the entry-port at Calcutta to the **tribal regions** of the northeastern hill-states drew the attention of Protestant missionaries during the Raj, whose fervent evangelism covered virtually all of Mizoram, Nagaland and much of Meghalaya. Muslim immigrants from Bangladesh have changed the balance in bordering areas, while other tribal districts, in Madhya Pradesh, Bihar, Karnataka and Gujarat in particular, have drawn both Catholic and Protestant missionaries. As Christianity is intended to be free of caste stigmas, it can be attractive to those seeking social advancement – of the two million Christians in present-day India, most are *adivasi* (tribal) and *dalit* (untouchable) peoples.

Christianity in modern India

Christianity in modern India was symbolized for many by the diminutive figure of **Mother Teresa**, the Albanian-born Roman Catholic nun whose pioneering work amongst the poor of Calcutta attracted global attention, won her the Nobel Peace Prize in 1979 and posthumous beatification by Pope John Paul II following her death in 1997. Despite her efforts, however, the position of Christians in Indian society remains uncertain. In early 1999, Christian communities in some areas, notably in Gujarat and Orissa, were subject to forced "reconversions" and attacks. These were allegedly carried out by Hindu extremists incensed by proselytizing evangelists targeting low-caste Hindus. Following an international outcry, some states passed laws banning "forced conversions", but in December 2002, a riot was only narrowly averted after police acted to prevent 1500 Dalit ("Untouchable") people from attending a mass-conversion in Chennai (Madras).

The strong sense of regional history and culture has distinctly influenced the appearance of **Indian churches**. The St Thomas Christians of the south congregate in small white churches decorated with colourful pictures and statues of figures from the New Testament. The great twin-steepled churches of Goa and Chennai (Madras) are very different, with their heavy gold interiors and candlelit shrines to the Virgin Mary. Other churches are more syncretistic: **St John's** in south Delhi has an Anglican nave, a Hindu *chhapra* (tower) and monastic cloisters spanning out from each side. In the Himalayan part of Bengal, the influence of Buddhism is very strong – beautiful wooden chapels are painted with scenes from the life of Christ using Buddhist symbols and Nepali-looking characters.

The **Hindu influence** on Christianity is marked too. Christian festivals in Tamil Nadu are highly structured along caste lines, and Christians there never eat beef or pork, which are considered polluting. By contrast, Christians in Goa eat both beef and pork as a feature of their Portuguese heritage. In many churches you can see devotees offering the Hindu *arati* (a plate of coconut, sweets and rice), and women wearing *tilak* dots on their foreheads. In the same way that Hindus and Muslims consider pilgrimage to be an integral part of life's journey, Indian Christians have numerous devotional sites, including St Jude's Shrine in **Jhansi** and the Temple of Mother Mary in **Mathura**. On anniversaries of the death of a loved one, Christians carry plates of food to the graves, in much the same manner as Hindus. This sharing of traditions works both ways however. At Christmas, for instance, you can't fail to notice the brightly coloured paper stars and small Nativity scenes glowing and flashing outside schools, houses, shops and churches throughout India.

Wildlife

From the Himalayas to the swamps of Bengal, and from the deserts of Rajasthan to the tropical backwaters of Kerala, India's vast range of habitats support a staggering range of wildlife. Around 65,000 species of fauna are to be found here, including 1200 birds and 340 mammals, while a staggering 13,000 varieties of flowering plants have been recorded. India is also the only country in the world where you can see both wild lions and tigers.

In the north of the country, the lush deodar and rhododendron forests of the lower **Himalayas** are home to bears and black bucks, while the fabled snow leopard and yak inhabit the higher mountains. In the hills and forests of the **northeast**, the tiger and the one-horned rhinoceros fight to survive in beautiful but rarely visited sanctuaries, struggling against a biannual monsoon, severe floods and poachers. Down on the **Gangetic plain**, the warm climate, forests and numerous lakes and rivers support a rich array of bird-life, while the **Sunderbans** mangrove swamps in the east are famous for their population of unusual swimming tigers. Camels, both wild and domesticated, can be found in the parched Thar desert in **Rajasthan**, while elsewhere in the west the dry climate supports spotted deer, leopards and the famous Asiatic lion in its last bastion of the **Gir Forest**. Further south, the dry **Deccan plateau** is thick with sandalwood forests, the home of wild elephants, while on the weathered cliffs of the **Western Ghats** the civet cat prowls in the abundant fern growth. In the very **southern tip** of India you'll find elephants, butterflies and jewel-like birds under the canopy of the teak and rosewood rainforest.

Animals

The Indian **elephant** (*Elephas maximus indicus*), distinguished from its African cousin by its long front legs and smaller ears and body, is still widely used as a beast of burden in many parts of the country. Elephants have worked and been tamed in India for three thousand years, but it is through the battle legends of the sixteenth and seventeenth centuries that they earned their loyal and stoic reputation, both as great mounts in the imperial armies of the Mughals and as the bejewelled bearers of rajas and nawabs. Elephants are also of religious significance (the popular Hindu god Ganesh – see p.1363 – himself sports the head of an elephant) and they're a common sight in temple processions and ceremonies, often sporting a brightly painted trunk and forehead, and throughout the Subcontinent stone elephants stand guard with bells in their trunks as a sign of welcome in medieval forts and palaces.

In the wild, there is still a sizeable population of roughly ten to fifteen thousand elephants, although around half of these are found in remote parts of the northeast. Elephants have been included under the **Endangered Species Protection Act** due to the huge reduction of their natural forest habitat: each adult eats roughly two hundred kilos of vegetation and drinks a hundred litres of water a day, and their search for sustenance often brings them into conflict with rural communities. The wild elephant is now only naturally found in four areas: the southern tip of Tamil Nadu; the central zone of Orissa, Bihar and West Bengal; the Himalayan lowlands of Uttar Pradesh; and the northeastern hill-states.

Another pachyderm, the lumbering **one-horned rhinoceros**, retains a tenuous foothold in the northeast of the country. Due to deforestation and poaching for oriental medicines, the rhino population had dropped to barely one hundred by the 1960s. Since then, numbers have risen again, and around 1100 live in the protected Manas and Kaziranga wildlife sanctuaries in Assam.

Big cats

Indian **tigers** are fast becoming extinct in the wild (see box below), but you still stand a reasonable chance of coming across one in a national park. Sightings are regularly recorded at Kanha (see p.446) and Bandhavgarh in Madhya Pradesh (p.450); Ranthambore in Rajasthan (p.192); Corbett in Uttarakhand (p.379); Manas and Kaziranga (p.968) in Assam; and Bandipur in Karnataka (p.1278).

The other **big cats** have fared worse than the tiger. Once the maharaja of Indian wildlife, the **Asiatic lion** (see box on p.655) now clings on in just one tiny patch of Gujarat, even though the proud three-headed lion emblem of the Ashokan period is still the national symbol of India. The ghostly grey- and black-spotted **snow leopard** of the Himalayas is so rare as to be almost legendary. Only the plains-dwelling **leopard** (also known as the panther) can still be commonly found, especially in forested places near human settlement where domestic animals make easy prey. Other indigenous felines include the rare multicoloured marbled cat, the miniature leopard cat, the jungle cat (with a distinct ridge of hair running down its back), the fishing cat, and a kind of lynx called the caracal. The cheetah is now extinct in India.

Deer

Deer and antelope, the larger cats' prey, are much more abundant. The often solitary *sambar* is the largest of the **deer**, weighing up to 300kg and bearing

---

The Indian tiger: survival or extinction?

Feared, adored, and immortalized in myth, few animals command such universal fascination as the **tiger**. India is one of the very few places where this rare and enigmatic big cat can still be glimpsed in the wild, stalking through the teak forests and terai grass – a solitary predator, with no natural enemies save one.

As recently as the turn of the last century, up to 100,000 tigers still roamed the Subcontinent, even though tiger hunting had long been the "sport of kings". An ancient dictum held it auspicious for a ruler to notch up a tally of 109 dead tigers, and nawabs, maharajas and Mughal emperors all indulged their prerogative to devastating effect. But it was the trigger-happy British who brought tiger hunting to its most gratuitous excesses. Photographs of pith-helmeted, bare-kneed *burrasahibs* posing behind mountains of striped carcasses became a hackneyed image of the Raj. Even Prince Philip (a former president of the Worldwide Fund for Nature) couldn't resist bagging one during a royal visit.

In the years following Independence, **demographic pressures** nudged the Indian tiger perilously close to extinction. As the human population increased in rural districts, more and more forest was cleared for farming, depriving large carnivores of their main source of game and of the cover they needed to hunt. Forced to turn on farm cattle as an alternative, tigers were drawn into direct conflict with humans; some animals, out of sheer desperation, even turned man-eater and attacked human settlements.

Poaching has taken an even greater toll. The black market has always paid high prices for dead animals – a tiger pelt alone can fetch well over $10,000 in India – and for the various body parts believed to hold magical or medicinal properties. The meat is used to ward off snakes, the brain to cure acne, the nose to promote the birth of a

antlers known to reach 120cm long. Smaller and more gregarious are chital (spotted deer), usually seen in herds skulking around langur monkey or human habitats looking for discarded fruit and vegetables. In a tiger reserve you may well hear the high-pitched call of the chital and the gruff reply bark of the langur warning of the presence of a tiger in the vicinity. Other deer include the elusive mountain-loving muntjac (barking deer) and the para (hog deer), which fall victim annually to flooding in the low grasslands. The smallest deer in India is the nocturnal chevrotain, known from its size (only 30cm high) as the mouse deer. The swamp deer is rarer, while the hangul (Kashmiri red deer) and musk deer are now endangered species.

Antelopes include the nilgai ("blue cow"); the endangered black buck, revered by the Bishnoi caste who inhabit the fringes of the Thar desert around Jodhpur in central Rajasthan; and the unique forest-dwelling four-horned chowsingha (swamp deer), which has successfully been saved from near-extinction. The desert-loving gazelle is known as the *chinkara* ("the one who sneezes") due to the sneeze-like alarm call it makes.

Monkeys

The most common **monkeys** are the feisty red-bottomed Rhesus macaque and the black-faced "Hanuman" langurs, often found around temple areas. Monkeys are protected by the Hindu belief in their divine status as noble servants of the gods, a sentiment that derives from the epic Ramayana, where the herculean Hanuman leads his monkey army to assist Rama in fighting the demon Ravana. Wild monkeys live in large troupes in the forests. The Assamese macaque and the pig-tailed macaque prefer the northern hills, while the bonnet macaque dwells in the steamy tropical jungles of the south. Langurs, such as the

son and the fat of the kidney – applied liberally to the afflicted organ – as an antidote to male impotence.

By the time an all-India moratorium on tiger shooting was declared in the 1972 Wildlife Protection Act, numbers had plummeted to below two thousand. A dramatic response geared to fire public imagination came the following year, with the inauguration of **Project Tiger**. At the personal behest of Indira Gandhi, nine areas of pristine forest were set aside for the last remaining tigers. Displaced farming communities were resettled and compensated, and armed rangers employed to discourage poachers. Demand for tiger parts did not end with Project Tiger, however, and the poachers remained in business, aided by organized smuggling rings. India's worst-case conservation scenario was finally played out in 2005, when it was discovered that the entire population of big cats at Sariska Tiger Reserve had mysteriously vanished, presumably at the hands of (still to be caught) poachers.

Well-organized guerrilla groups operate with virtual impunity out of remote national parks, where inadequate numbers of poorly armed and poorly paid wardens offer little more than token resistance, particularly as increased use of poison is making it more and more difficult to track poachers. Project Tiger officials are understandably reluctant to jeopardize lucrative tourist traffic by admitting that sightings are getting rarer, but the prognosis looks very gloomy indeed.

Today, though there are 23 Project Tiger sites, numbers continue to fall. Official figures optimistically claim a **population** of up to 3000 to 3500, but independent evidence is more pessimistic, putting the figure at around 1500. Estimates claim that one tiger is being poached every day in India, and the most pessimistic experts believe that India's most exotic animal could face extinction in the wild within the next decade, or less.

noisy Nilgiri langur and the extremely rare golden langur, are more elusive, preferring to remain hidden in treetop foliage.

Other mammals

Among other wild animals you might hope to see in India, the shaggy **sloth bear** is hard to spot in the wild, although you may see captive bears being forced to dance on busy roadways near tourist sites. Other bears include the black and brown varieties, distinguishable by the colour of their fur. Of the **canines**, the scavenging striped hyena and the small pest-eating Indian fox are fairly common. The Indian wolf lives in the plains and deserts, and is under threat of extinction due to vigorous culling by humans protecting their domestic animals.

The wild **buffalo** has a close genetic relationship with the common domesticated water buffalo: wild male buffalo prefer to mate with domestic females. More exotic members of the cow family are the hill-loving **gaur**, an Indian bison which stands 2m across at the shoulders, and the nimble, mountain-dwelling **yak**. Asia's answer to the armadillo is a scaly anteater called a **pangolin**, whose tough plate-like scales run the length of its back and tail; this armour is believed to contain magical healing properties, for which the pangolin is hunted. Around urban environments, you're likely to see the common triple-striped **palm squirrel**, said to have been marked as such by the gentle stroke of Rama. **River dolphins** can be seen in the Ganges, especially at Varanasi.

Reptiles

The 238 species of **snake** in India (of which fifty are poisonous) extend from the 10cm-long worm snake to nest-building king cobras and massive pythons. While the mangy and languid cobra or python wrapped around the snake-charmer's neck is tame and nonvenomous, poisonous snakes you might meet in the wild are the majestically hooded cobra, the yellow-brown Russel's viper, the small krait (especially common in south India) and the saw-scaled viper. **Lizards** are common, with every hotel room seeming to have a resident gecko to keep the place free of insects. The colourful garden lizard and Sita's lizard are both found throughout India. Freshwater Olive Ridley turtles (see box, p.814) nest at remote beaches along the east and southwest coasts, the most famous being Bhitarakanika Sanctuary on **Gahirmatha beach**, 130km north of Bhubaneswar, where 200,000 females come each year to lay their eggs. Similar, though much smaller, nesting sites are to be found at Morjim and Galjibag in Goa. **Crocodiles** are common throughout the Subcontinent.

Birds

You don't have to be an aficionado to enjoy India's abundant **bird-life**. Travelling around the country, you'll regularly see colourful birds flashing between the branches of trees or perching on overhead roadside cables. The presence of this spectacular array of avifauna is mainly thanks to the Subcontinent's diverse range of climates and habitats, while its geographical location also attracts many migratory species from colder countries to the north during the winter months.

Three common species of **kingfisher** frequently crop up amid the paddy fields and wetlands of the coastal plains. Other common and brightly coloured species include the grass-green, blue and yellow **bee-eaters** (*Merops*), the stunning **golden oriole** (*Oriolus oriolus*) and the **Indian roller** (*Coracias bengalensis*), famous for its brilliant blue flight feathers and exuberant aerobatic mating displays. **Hoopoes** (*Upupa epops*), recognizable by their elegant black-and-white tipped crests, fawn plumage and distinctive "*hoo...po...po*" call, also flit around fields and villages, as do several kinds of **bulbuls**, **babblers** and **drongos** (*Dicrurus*), including the fork-tailed black drongo (*Dicrurus adsimilis*) – a winter visitor that can often be seen perched on telegraph wires. If you're lucky, you may also catch a glimpse of the **paradise flycatcher** (*Tersiphone paradisi*), which is widespread and among the Subcontinent's most exquisite birds, with a thick black crest and long silver tail-streamers.

Paddy fields, ponds and saline mud flats are teeming with water birds. The most ubiquitous of these is the snowy white **cattle egret** (*Bubulcus ibis*), which can usually be seen wherever there are cows and buffalo, feeding off the grubs, insects and other parasites that live on them. Look out too for the mud-brown **paddy bird**, India's most common heron, distinguished by its pale green legs, speckled breast and hunched posture.

Common birds of prey such as the **brahminy kite** (*Haliastur indus*) – recognizable by its white breast and chestnut head markings – and the **pariah kite** (*Milvus migrans govinda*) – a dark-brown buzzard with a fork tail – are widespread around towns and fishing villages, where they vie with raucous gangs of house **crows** (*Corvus splendens*) and **white-eyed jackdaws** (*Corvus monedula*) for scraps. Gigantic pink-headed **king vultures** (*Sarcogyps clavus*) and the **white-backed vulture** (*Gyps bengalensis*), which has a white ruff around its bare neck and head, also show up whenever there are carcasses to pick clean, although in recent years a mysterious virus has decimated numbers.

Among India's abundant **forest birds**, one species every enthusiast hopes to glimpse is the magnificent **hornbill**, with its huge yellow beak with a long curved casque on top. Several species of **woodpecker** also inhabit the interior woodlands, among them the rare Indian great black woodpecker, which makes loud drumming noises on tree trunks between December and March.

A bird whose call is a regular feature of the Western Ghat forests, particularly in teak areas, is the wild ancestor of the domestic chicken – the **jungle fowl**. The more common variety is the secretive but vibrantly coloured, red jungle fowl (*Gallus gallus*), which sports golden neck feathers and a metallic black tail. You're most likely to come across one of these scavenging for food on the verges of forest roads.

A great online resource is Birding Hotspots (www.camacdonald.com /birding/asiaindia.htm), which has exhaustive reviews of India's best places for bird-watching, complemented by dozens of photos, reports from recent field trips by bona fide enthusiasts and links to printed resources.

Music

ndia is home to a staggering variety of different musical traditions, both ancient and modern, ranging from archaic styles of Hindu devotional chanting to the eclectic outpourings of Bollywood's contemporary songwriters. For many outsiders, the country's aural signature is provided by **north Indian classical music**, one of the world's finest and most immediately recognizable sounds, with its twanging tanpuras and complex tabla beats, while its southern cousin, so-called **Carnatic music**, is equally rewarding, although less well known. There's also a vast array of **folk music** to explore, from the mystical outpourings of the wandering Baul minstrels of Bengal to Rajasthani fiddling and Punjabi bhangra. Bollywood's huge treasury of film songs, or **filmi**, is also becoming increasingly well known internationally, and offers a fascinating snapshot of changing musical fashions over the past five decades, all seen from a uniquely Indian point of view.

Indian classical music: ragas and talas

Underlying all Indian classical music is the concept of the **raga** (or *raag*, from the Sanskrit word meaning "colour"). Put simplistically, a raga is simply a musical scale or mode (loosely equivalent to the "key" of a piece of Western music), determining which notes can and can't be played during a particular piece. Unlike the Western scale or key, however, each raga is also associated with a particular kind of musical and emotional mood, with its own unique set of characteristic melodic phrases, types of ornamentation and dominant notes, lending each raga its own uniquely expressive and coherent musical character.

North Indian classical music has two hundred main ragas in total; ragas are never mixed (at least not in traditional classical performances) – a single raga will be used for the entirety of a piece. Some ragas are linked with particular seasons; there is a raga for rain, and one for spring; ragas can be "masculine" or "feminine"; and musicologists may categorize them according to whether they are best suited to a male or female voice. Each raga is allotted a time of day, a time identified with the spiritual and emotional qualities of the raga. Ragas are specifically allocated to early morning (either before or after sunrise), mid-morning, early afternoon, late afternoon, early evening (either before or after sunset), late evening, late night and after midnight. Purists adhere to the tradition of a "raga timetable" even if they're only listening to records, although this system causes a few problems when listening to Indian music in countries in different time zones from India, given that no one can agree as to whether ragas should be heard by clock-time or sun-time.

The raga defines the basic musical material and expressive content of each particular piece, meaning that while Indian classical musicians are renowned for

CONTEXTS | Music

C

Indian music online

ⓦ **www.artindia.net** Portal for India's performing arts.

ⓦ **www.sruti.com** The online version of a very informative and in-depth music and dance magazine devoted to India's performing arts.

ⓦ **www.themusicmagazine.com** A music e-zine covering an incredible range of topics, from Bob Dylan to *ghazal*.

their **improvisation**, this only takes place within strictly defined limits – the mark of a good performer is his or her ability to improvise extensively without stepping outside the boundaries of the chosen raga. In addition, Indian classical music always has a constant **drone** in the background, usually played on the tanpura (see p.1383), which serves as a reference point for performer and listener alike. It's the constant presence of this drone, and of the raga underlying any particular performance, which gives Indian classical music its distinctive, hypnotic fixity, as if it is revolving constantly around a single point, probing it from every possible angle.

Just as the raga organizes melody, so the rhythm of a piece is organised using metric cycles known as **talas**. A *tala* is made up of a number of beats, with each beat being defined by a combination of rhythm pattern and timbre. There are literally hundreds of *talas*, each defined by its own unique combination of metre and timbre, although most percussionists use the same few favourites over and over again, the most common being the sixteen-beat *teen tala* (four times four beats). The most unfamiliar aspect of *tala* to the Western ear is that the end of one cycle comes not on its last beat, but on the first beat of the following one, so that there is a continual overlap. This first beat is known as *sum*, a point of culmination that completes a rhythmic structure.

Teachers and pupils

In the north, both Hindu and Muslim communities have provided outstanding artists – distinguished musicians of Hindu origin customarily take the title of *pandit*, while their Muslim counterparts add the prefix *ustad* (meaning "master") to their names. An *ustad* may teach anything – not only his own particular art or instrument. It is not unusual for sitar maestros to teach sarod or vocal techniques to their pupils.

Traditionally, Indian music is taught on a one-to-one basis, often with sons receiving instruction from their own father, or other family relative; even when they aren't related, musical training is distinguished by the close personal and spiritual link between teacher and pupil. Musical life in India is dominated by a number of leading **musical families**, some of whom have been producing eminent musicians since Mughal times. These include the Khans of Bengal, who produced two of the 20th-century's finest sitar players in brothers Vilayat and Imrat Khan, while Ravi Shankar's own daughter, Anoushka, also created a stir when she made her debut in 2001 at the age of 19, although her film-star looks were greeted with greater critical acclaim than her playing.

Musical styles and traditions are also passed down through a system of local schools, or **gharanas**, each of which preserves its own characteristic styles. A *gharana*, which may be for singing, for any or all kinds of instruments, or for dance, is more a school of thought than an institution. It suggests a particular belief, or a preference for a certain performance style. They are usually founded by musicians of outstanding ability, and new styles and forms are added by exceptionally talented musicians. Several *gharanas* have been set up abroad, notably the one in California run by sarod player Ali Akbar Khan, and there is a steady trickle of Westerners who are willing to subject themselves to the disciplines of study.

In earlier times the job of musician was more or less hereditary: would-be musicians began their musical education at the age of four and music (as a profession) was considered beneath the dignity of the well-to-do and the academic classes. In recent years, however, traditional restrictions have been relaxed, and many educated Indians are now becoming involved in both performance and composition, while women instrumentalists are also making their mark – a startling innovation in a male-dominated musical culture – such as Anuradha Pal, India's first professional tabla player.

The raga in performance

The performance of a raga, whether sung or played on a sitar, sarod or *sarangi*, follows a set pattern. First comes the **alap**, a slow, meditative introduction in free rhythm which explores the chosen raga, carefully introducing its constituent notes one by one. The *alap* can span several hours in the hands of a distinguished performer, but may only last a matter of minutes; older aficionados allege that most present-day listeners cannot sustain the attention required to appreciate a lengthy and closely argued alap. As a result, performers sometimes feel under pressure to abbreviate the alap in order to reach the faster middle and end sections as soon as possible. In the recording studio, at least, the advent of the CD (which does not force the music to fit into 25 minutes as the LP did) has initiated a move back to longer performances.

In the next two sections, the **jor** and the **jhala**, the instrumentalist introduces a rhythmic element, developing the raga through a series of increasingly complex variations. Only in these and the final section, the **gat**, does the percussion instrument – usually the tabla or (in south India) the *mridangam* – enter. The soloist introduces a short, fixed phrase (known as "the composition") to which he returns between flights of improvisation. In this section rhythm is an important structural element. Both percussionist and soloist improvise, at times echoing each other and sometimes pursuing individual variations of rhythmic counterpoint, regularly punctuated by unison statements of "the composition". The *gat* itself is subdivided into three sections: a slow tempo passage known as *vilambit*, increasing to a medium tempo section called *madhya*, and leading finally to the fast concluding *drut*.

Indian classical music **audiences** tend to be highly knowledgeable. Among smaller, more discerning audiences, verbal applause such as "*Wah!*" (Bravo!), or even "*Subhan-Allah*" (Praise be to God!), is considered the standard form of appreciation. Only in Western-style concert halls, where such exclamations would be inaudible, has hand-clapping come to replace these traditional gestures of approval.

Musical instruments

India has its own unique collection of musical instruments. Some of the most distinctive are plucked instruments such as the **sitar** (and its southern relation, the **vina**), **surbahar**, **sarod** and the **tanpura**, while the **sarangi**, a kind of Indian violin, is also common. Wind instruments are less common, with the exception of the **bansuri** (bamboo flute). There are also several unique types of Indian drum including the ubiquitous **tabla**, along with the **pakhavaj** and **mridangam**.

String instruments

The best-known Indian instrument is the **sitar**, invented by Amir Khusrau in the thirteenth century and played with a plectrum. Of the six or seven main strings, four are played and the other two or three supply a drone or a rhythmic ostinato (*chikari*). There can also be between eleven and nineteen sympathetic strings. The two sets of strings are fitted on different bridges. Twenty brass frets fastened to the long hollow neck can be easily moved to conform to the scale of a particular raga, and their curvature allows the player to alter the pitch by pulling the string sideways across the fret to provide the pitch-bends so characteristic of Indian

C

CONTEXTS | Music

music. The **surbahar** ("spring melody"), effectively a bass sitar, is played in the same way. Developed by Sahibdad Khan, the great-grandfather of Imrat Khan (the instrument's greatest living practitioner), it produces a deep, sonorous sound. The neck is wider and longer than that of the sitar but its frets are fixed.

The **sarod** is a descendant of the Afghani rebab. Smaller than a sitar, it has two resonating chambers, the larger made of teak covered with goatskin, and the smaller, at the other end of the metal fingerboard, made of metal. Ten of its 25 metal strings are plucked with a fragment of coconut shell. Four of these carry the melody; the others accentuate the rhythm. The rest are sympathetic strings, underneath the main strings. The sarod was hugely improved by Ustad Allaudin Khan, whose pupils Ustad Ali Akbar Khan and Ustad Amjad Ali Khan are now its best-known exponents.

The **sarangi** is a fretless bowed instrument with a very broad fingerboard and a double belly. The entire body of the instrument – belly and fingerboard – is carved out of a single block of wood and the hollow covered with parchment. There are three or four main strings of gut and anything up to forty metal sympathetic strings. Some claim it is the most difficult musical instrument to play in the world. Certainly the technique is highly unusual. While the right hand wields the bow in the normal way, the strings are stopped not by the fingertips of the left hand, but by the nails. The *sarangi* is capable of a wide range of timbres and its sound is likened to that of the human voice, so it is usually used to accompany vocal recitals. Originally this was its only function, but in recent years it has become a solo instrument in its own right, thanks mainly to the efforts of Ustad Sultan Khan and Pandit Ram Narayan.

The **santoor**, a hammered zither of Persian origin, has only recently been accepted in Indian classical music. It has over a hundred strings, pegged and stretched in pairs, parallel to each other. The strings are struck by two curving wooden sticks. Its most notable exponent is Pandit Shiv Kumar Sharma. The **surmandal** resembles a zither, and is used by vocalists to accompany themselves in performance. Even though its primary function is to provide the drone, singers sometimes also play the basic melody line on this instrument.

Finally, perhaps the most ubiquitous but selfeffacing of all Indian musical instruments is the **tanpura** (or *tambura*), a type of fretless lute with (usually) four or five wire strings. It's the tanpura that supplies the instantly recognizable, buzzing drone which underpins all Indian classical music. The tanpura is traditionally played by an advanced student of the lead performer, considered a rare and special honour by the pupil concerned.

Wind instruments

The word **bansuri** refers to a wide variety of bamboo (*banse*) flutes, most end-blown, but some, such as Krishna's famous *murli*, are side-blown. Despite offering a range of less than two octaves, it now appears as a solo concert instrument, mainly thanks to the tireless exploits of leading *bansuri* virtuoso Hariprasad Chaurasia. The **shehnai**, traditionally used for wedding music, is a double-reed, oboe-type instrument with up to nine finger holes, some of which are stopped with wax for fine tuning to the scale of a particular raga. It demands a mastery of circular breathing and enormous breath control. A drone accompaniment is provided by a second *shehnai*.

Drums and percussion

The **tabla** is a set of two small drums played with the palms and fingertips to produce an incredible variety of sounds and timbres. Its name is short for

Hindustani music

Nikhil Banerjee *The Hundred-minute Raga: Purabi Kalyan* (Raga Records, US). One of the finest sitar players of his generation, Banerjee was famed for the purity and elegance of his style. This recording finds him on top form.

Vishwa Mohan Bhatt *Guitar à la Hindustan* (Original Music Impressions, India) and *Gathering Rain Clouds* (Water Lily Acoustics). The celebrated creator of the so-called "Mohan vina", a modified form of the western acoustic guitar – it sounds a bit like a cross between a sitar and a slide guitar. These two recordings are the perfect place to begin an exploration of Bhatt's classical repertoire.

Hariprasad Chaurasia *Hari-Krishna: In Praise of Janmashtami* (Navras, UK). Chaurasia is one of India's most internationally famous musicians and perhaps the country's finest exponent of the *bansuri*, or Indian bamboo flute. This three-album set captures an intimate annual tradition when the maestro, joined by his family and a few close associates, plays through the night in front of a Krishna altar in his Mumbai home. A quietly momentous album.

Ali Akbar Khan *Signature Series, Volumes 1 and 2* (AMMP, US). Frequently hailed as one of the greatest musicians on the planet, sarod player and master melodist Ali Akbar Khan is accompanied here by one of the finest tabla players of his generation, Mahapurush Misra.

Bismillah Khan *Live in London, Volumes 1 and 2* (Navras, UK). One of India's foremost virtuosi, the late Bismillah Khan (d.2006) was the acknowledged master of the *shehnai*. These two marvellous albums were recorded in London in 1985.

Imrat Khan *Ajmer* (Water Lily Acoustics, US). This 1990 recording features virtuoso performances on sitar and *surbahar* (bass sitar), an instrument of which Imrat Khan is considered India's leading exponent.

Sultan Khan *Sarangi* (Navras, UK). *Sarangi* player Sultan Khan first came under the international spotlight touring with Ravi Shankar and George Harrison. This recording of a London concert in 1990 reveals eloquent insights that few can match.

Vilayat Khan *Sitar* (India Archive Music, US). Electrifying studio recording from one of the 20th-century's greatest living sitar players.

Ram Narayan *Rag Lalit* (Nimbus, US). 1987 studio recording by India's leading *sarangi* virtuoso, offering a stunning performance of this challenging raga recorded in a single 73-minute take.

Alla Rakha *Maestro's Choice – Tabla* (Music Today, India). One of the greatest tabla players of the 20th century, Alla Rakha (d.2000) appears here in a recital with Zakir Hussain illustrating the potency of Hindustani rhythm, with melodic support from legendary *sarangi* player Sultan Khan. Rakha and Hussain's 67-minute *Tabla Duet* (Moment, US) is also worth seeking out.

Ravi Shankar *Ravi Shankar & Ali Akbar Khan in Concert 1972* (Apple, UK). India's most famous musical export duetting with *sarod* great Ali Akbar Khan, and offering pyrotechnics and profundity in equal measure.

Various *Call of the Valley* (Hemisphere, UK). Probably the most influential Hindustani album ever made, using a sequence of time-specific ragas performed on flute, guitar and *santoor* to depict the passage of a Kashmiri day.

Various *The Rough Guide to the Music of India and Pakistan* (World Music Network, UK). A good introduction to the classical, semi-classical and folk styles of north India and Pakistan, including performances by luminaries such as Ali Akbar Khan, Vilayat Khan and Bismillah Khan.

Carnatic music

Kadri Gopalnath *Sax Melodies* (Koel). Golpanath typifies the duality of Carnatic music in playing a modern instrument (accompanied here by violin, *ghatam*, *mridangam* and *morsing*) in a tradition that goes back centuries, harking back to the archaic sound of the *nagaswaram*.

The Karnataka College of Percussion *River Yamuna* (Music of the World, US). Despite the ensemble's name, KCP also features the voice of the Ramamani and melodic instruments such as *vina* and violin. This 1997 album ranks among the most accessible introduction to Carnatic music.

Shankar *Raga Aberi* (Music of the World, US). A spectacular *ragam-tanam-pallavi* performance featuring the growling low notes of Shankar's extraordinary ten-string double violin. The performance also features spectacular vocal percussion and solos.

L. Subramaniam *Electric Modes* (Water Lily Acoustics, US). South India's violin wizard performing on a two-CD set, one volume of which consists of original compositions, the second of which focuses on traditional ragas.

Classical vocal

Najma Akhtar *Qareeb* (Shanachie). A modern *ghazal* classic, thanks to Najma Akhtar's lyrical gifts backed up with innovative arrangements and fine instrumental playing (including violin, sax and *santoor*).

Asha Bhosle *Legacy* (AMMP, US). A remarkable collaboration between legendary singer Asha Bhosle and Ali Akbar Khan in a collection of classical and light-classical vocal gems.

Mehdi Hassan *Live in Concert* (OSA). Recorded live in London in 1990, this disc captures the genuine feel of a classical *ghazal* concert.

Folk

Various *Ganga: The Music of the Ganges* (Angel Records). A wonderful introduction to Indian folk and devotional music. The three CDs trace the course of the river from the Himalayas to the Bay of Bengal and feature sounds of the river alongside performances beautifully recorded in temples, at the water's edge, on boats and so on. Much of the music is devotional, but other highlights include snake-charmer's music, a festival percussion ensemble, a virtuoso toy-seller's song, *bauls* and a great *shehnai dhun* performance at dawn.

Mehbooba Band *Fanfare de Calcutta* (Signature). Recorded in a Calcuttan back alley, this 2001 album perfectly captures the anarchic sound of the north Indian wedding brass band, complete with wailing clarinets, bumpy euphonium bass, raucous cornet and trumpet calls, big cymbal clashes, and jaunty, Punjabi bhangra-influenced folk rhythms.

Purna Das Baul *Bauls of Bengal* (Cramworld). A compelling introduction to the wild devotional music of the *bauls*, mystical wayfaring minstrels from Bengal whose ecstatic sounds have inspired figures as diverse as Rabindranath Tagore, Allen Ginsberg and Bob Dylan. Lutes, flutes and driving *khamak* percussion underscore the joyful vocals on this, India's top-selling folk release.

Filmi

Asha Bhosle *Asha Bhosle: The Queen of Bollywood* (Nascente). Twenty-six classic tracks, spanning four decades, from Bollywood's most prolific and musically eclectic playback singer. A companion Nascente disc, *Lata: The Greatest Film Songs of Lata Mangeshkar*, provides a similar showcase for Bhosle's sister and greatest rival.

Various *Beginner's Guide to Bollywood* (Nascente). Handy three-disc overviews of Bollywood *filmi* from 1951 to 2002. The collection is dominated by Asha Bhosle, but also features other playback luminaries such as Lata Mangeshkar, Geeta Dutt, Mohammed Rafi and Kishore Kumar.

(Contd...)

C

CONTEXTS

Discography (....*contd*)

Chris Perry *Golden Hits* (Saregama). This compilation gives a flavour of the legendary early-1970s era of Konkani pop, with classics such as Lorna's "Red Rose" (the best-loved Goan tune of all time) and the infectiously funky "Mog Boom Boom Boom" by Babs Peter.

Lorna *Lisboa* (Saregama). One of several greatest-hits CDs by the undisputed queen of Konkani music, drawn from her classic 60s and 70s big-band repertoire.

Various *Noman Noman Tuka Goa!* (Saregama). The pick of the Saregama label's recent crop of Goan music compilations, featuring early 1970s hits by Lorna, Mohammed Rafi, Chris Perry, Alfred Rose, Usha Mangueshkar and other stars.

tabla-*bayan* – the tabla is the drum on the right and the *bayan* ("left") on the left. Both drum heads are made of skin, but while the body of the tabla is all wood, the *bayan* is usually made of metal. The tabla is tuned to the tonic, dominant or subdominant notes of the raga by knocking the tuning-blocks, held into place by braces on the sides of the instrument.

Predating the tabla, the **pakhavaj** is nearly a metre long and was traditionally made of clay, although wood is now more popular. It has two parchment heads, each tuned to a different pitch, again by knocking the side blocks into place. The *pakhavaj* has a deep mellow sound and is used to accompany *dhrupad* singing and *kathak* dancing. A smaller version of the *pakhavaj*, the **mridangam**, is widely used in south Indian music.

As well as drums, India boasts a variety of tuned **percussion instruments**. The most popular in this category is the *jaltarang* – a water-xylophone – consisting of a series of porcelain bowls of different sizes, each containing a prescribed amount of water. The bowls are usually struck with a pair of small sticks, but sometimes these are abandoned as the player rubs the rims of the bowls with a wet finger. The small brass, dome-shaped cymbals called *manjira* or *tala* are the best known of the many kinds of bells and gongs.

Classical vocal music

Indian music considers the human voice as the most perfect of all musical instruments, and the degree of musical purity is assigned according to a scale which has music at one extreme and words at the other. As words become more audible and thus the meaning of lyrics more important, so the form is considered to be musically less pure. The two main classical vocal traditions are **dhrupad**, the purest of all Indian musical forms, and **khayal**, which has a more romantic content and elaborate ornamentation and is more popular today. Less abstract vocal forms include the so-called light-classical **thumri** and **ghazal**, as well as **qawwali** (see p.126), the religious music of the Sufi tradition.

Dhrupad and khayal

Dhrupad is the oldest and most austere form of north Indian classical music. *Dhrupads* typically consist of two sections: a long and entirely wordless introductory *alap* during which the singer(s) vocalize a sequence of syllables deriving from the mantra "Hari Om Narayana Taan Tarana Tum", followed by a much shorter and faster section sung to the accompaniment of a *pakhavaj* drum, typically consisting of a hymn to a Hindu deity. Performances of *dhrupad* are relatively rare, with few musicians devoting themselves to the genre, and the music, unfolding slowly and almost completely without embellishment, makes considerable demands of performers and listeners alike.

During the eighteenth century the rather severe *dhrupad* was succeeded and largely displaced by the much more flamboyant **khayal** – described as the "bel canto of Indian music" – a form which places fewer restrictions on singers and allows for far greater displays of virtuosity. *Khayal* is typically accompanied by tabla and harmonium, along with a bowed instrument such as a *sarangi* or violin, which mirrors the vocal line. A *khayal* usually consists of two parts: the greater part of the performance is taken up by the slow *bada khayal* ("great khayal") followed by a much shorter and faster *chhota khayal* ("small khayal"), which gives the singer the opportunity to show the full range of their virtuosity.

Thumri and Ghazal

Thumri are essentially love songs, written from a female perspective. *Thumri* employ a specific set of ragas and are particularly associated with *kathak* dance; the graceful movements of the dancer are echoed in the lyricism of the musical style. Although classical instrumentalists in concert frequently perform a *thumri* to relax from the intensity of the pure classical style, most *thumri* is vocal, and sung in a language known as Braj Bhasha, a literary dialect of Hindi particularly associated with Lucknow. The singer is always accompanied by the tabla, as well perhaps as the tanpura, the *sarangi* or the *surmandal*, and sometimes the violin or harmonium.

Still more song-like than the *thumri* is the **ghazal**. In some ways the Urdu counterpart of *thumri*, the *ghazal* was introduced to India by Persian Muslims and is a poetic rather than a musical form – many favourite *ghazals* are drawn from the works of great Urdu poets. The *ghazal* has played an important part in the cultures of India, Pakistan and Afghanistan since the early eighteenth century, when it was one of the accomplishments required of a courtesan – although modern *ghazal* singers usually come from a more conventional background. Some *ghazal* tunes are based on the raga system, though others do not follow any specific mode. The *talas* are clearly derived from folk music; at times the *ghazal* edges into the area of sophisticated pop song. While *thumri* singers take on a female persona, emotions in the *ghazal* are almost always expressed from the male point of view.

Carnatic music

Southern India's classical music – known as **Carnatic** (or "Karnatak") music – is essentially similar to Hindustani classical music in outlook and theoretical background but differs in many details, usually ascribed to the far greater Islamic influence in the north. To the Western ear, Carnatic music is emotionally direct and impassioned, without the restraint that characterizes much of the north's music. For instance the **alapaana** section, although it introduces and develops the notes of the raga in much the same way as the *alap* of north Indian music, interrupts its stately progress with sparkling decorative flourishes. Often, too, the *alapaana* is succeeded by a set of increasingly complex elaborations of a basic melody in a way that is more easily grasped than the abstract, sometimes severe improvisations of the Hindustani masters. Compositions, both of "themes" and the set variations upon them, play a much greater role in Carnatic musical practice than in Hindustani.

Song is at the root of south Indian music, and forms based on song are paramount, even when the performance is purely instrumental. The vast majority of the texts are religious, and the temple is frequently the venue for performance. The most important form is the *kriti*, a devotional song, hundreds of which were written by the most influential figure in the development of Carnatic music, the singer **Thyagaraja** (1767–1847). Although the vocal tradition is central to south Indian music, its singers are perhaps less well known in the West than its instrumentalists. Ramnad Krishnan (1918–73), M.S. Subbulakshmi (1916–2004) and Dr M. Balamurali Krishna (b.1930) are among the most famous names.

The instruments of Carnatic music include the **vina**, which resembles the sitar but has no sympathetic strings – leading masters of the instrument have included S. Balachander (1927–1990) and K.S. Narayanaswami (b.1914). Other distinctive southern instruments include the **mridangam** double-headed drum, and the enormous **nadaswaram** (or *nagaswaram*), a kind of metre-long oboe, commonly used during temple ceremonies. The **violin** (slightly modified to suit Indian musical requirements) is widely used, while the **mandolin** is growing in popularity. The **saxophone** has also made a strikingly successful appearance in the hands of Kadri Gopalnath.

Percussion is very important, perhaps more so than in Hindustani music, and percussion ensembles frequently tour abroad. In addition to the *mridangam*, percussion instruments include the **ghatam**, a clay pot played with tremendous zest and sometimes tossed into the air in a burst of high spirits. "Vikku" Vinayakram is its best-known player.

Folk music

There are many kinds of **Indian folk music** (*desi*), but the main regional strands are those of Rajasthan, the Punjab (spread across both India and Pakistan), and Bengal. Apart from obvious linguistic differences, the folk songs of each region have their own distinct rhythmic structures and are performed on or accompanied by different musical instruments. In **Rajasthan**, music is always played for weddings and theatre performances, and often at local markets or gatherings. There is a whole caste of professional musicians who perform this function, and a wonderful assortment of earthy-sounding stringed instruments like the *kamayacha* and *ravanhata* that accompany their songs. The *ravanhata* is a simple, two-stringed fiddle that, skilfully played, can produce a tune of great beauty and depth. The *satara* is the traditional instrument of the desert shepherds. A double flute, it has two pipes of different lengths, one to play the melody, the other to provide the drone, rather like bagpipes without the bag. The bag is the musician himself, who plays with circular breathing. Local cassettes of these instruments are available in small stores across Rajasthan.

Bengal is best known for the music of the **Bauls**, an order of wandering mystics and musicians who subscribe to a syncretic mix of Sufi and *bhakti* Hindu mystical beliefs expressed primarily through song, typically accompanied by the *ektara*, a one-stringed drone instrument and other instruments including small cymbals, bamboo flutes and the multi-stringed *dotara*. The Bauls were an important influence on Bengal's single greatest musical luminary, **Rabindranath Tagore** (1861–1941), who in addition to winning the Nobel Prize for Literature, also wrote over two thousand *thumri*-style songs, which are still widely performed today.

The **Punjab** is most closely associated with **bhangra**. This was originally a kind of folk dance, traditionally performed as part of harvest festival celebrations and accompanied by music on the *dhol* and *dholki* drums, *ektara* and *tumbi* (a kind of single-string guitar), but since the 1980s has become a global pop

Marching bands

Spend any time in northern India, particularly during the winter wedding season, and you're almost certain to come across at least a couple of **marching bands**. First introduced to India by the British Army in the early nineteenth century and later adopted as a folk idiom right across the north and centre of the country (where they replaced the old *shehnai*-and-drum troupes of the Mughal era), brass bands have become an essential ingredient of working-class weddings and religious processions. Decked out in ill-fitting, mock-military uniforms (complete with tinsel epaulettes, plastic-peaked caps and buckled gaiters), the musicians (band-wallahs) are most often called upon to accompany a bridegroom's party (*baraat*) in its procession to the bride's house. The music itself – a cacophony of squealing clarinets and crowd-stopping blasts of brass played over snare and *dholak* tattoos – is invariably at odds with the mood of the groom, sitting astride a hired white horse on his way to married life with a stranger. But no one seems to care, least of all the members of the *baraat*, hip-thrusting and strutting along like Bollywood's best, to the stream of Hindi film hits, folk tunes, popular ragas and patriotic songs.

phenomenom both in its traditional form and in contemporary dance, house and hip-hop fusions, mainly created by Asian musicians in the UK.

Filmi and Indi-pop

Indian **popular music** is intimately bound up with the country's massive film industry. Music plays a crucial role in Bollywood movies (see colour insert) and up until the 1990s virtually all Indian popular music consisted of songs, known as **filmi**, taken from the soundtracks to these movies. The most striking feature of these Bollywood *filmi* is their incredibly eclectic style. Early film scores tended to be rooted in Indian folk and classical music, but from the 1960s onwards Bollywood film composers such as the famous **RD Burman** began to soak up an incredible range of musical influences in their work, from big band rock'n'roll to the techno and electronic creations of the innovative **AR Rahman**, composer of the musical *Bombay Dreams*. Bollywood *filmi* are performed by so-called **playback singers**, the invisible artists who record the songs which the film's actors and actresses then mime along to. Many of these singers have achieved massive fame in their own right, including the legendary Asha Bhosle (wife of RD Burman) and her sister Lata Mangeshkar, along with male singers such as Kishore Kumar and Mohammed Rafi.

Hindi pop, or **Indi-pop**, still struggles to escape from the overwhelming influence of Bollywood, and most of the leading younger musicians, like Sonu Nigam, Sunidhi Chauhan and composer-singer Himesh Reshamiyya continue to be featured as often on film soundtracks as on independent albums. More offbeat independent acts can, however, occasionally be found – names to look out for include the popular fusion group Indian Ocean, the singer-songwriter Rabbi Shergill (whose influences range from Punjabi religious music to Bruce Springsteen), and Demonic Resurrection, India's leading black metal act. There are also interesting regional variants, such as Goan **Konkani pop**, an idiosyncratic mishmash of folk tunes and calypso rhythms, with vocalists crooning away against an accompaniment of electric guitars and keyboards, female backing singers and mariachi-style brass.

Books

I ndia is one of the most written-about places on earth, and there are a bewildering number of titles available covering virtually every aspect of the country, ranging from scholarly historical dissertations to racy travelogues – although you might have trouble tracking some of them down outside India itself. Books marked 🏃 are particularly recommended.

History

Jad Adams and Phillip Whitehead *The Dynasty: The Nehru-Gandhi Story*. A brilliant and intriguing account of India's most famous family, although Sonia Gandhi's recent prominence rather begs an update.

A.L. Basham *The Wonder That Was India*. This veritable encyclopedia by one of India's foremost historical authorities positively bristles with erudition. A companion volume by S.A. Rizvi brings it up to the arrival of the British.

David Burton *The Raj at Table*. Few books evoke the quirky world of British India quite as vividly as this unlikely masterpiece – commendable both for its extraordinary recipes and as a marvellous piece of social history, compiled over years of travel, archival research and interviews.

Larry Collins and Dominique Lapierre *Freedom at Midnight*. Readable, if shallow, account of Independence, highly sympathetic to the British and, particularly, to Mountbatten, who was the authors' main source of information.

🏃 **William Dalrymple** *The Last Mughal*. Dalrymple surpasses himself in this masterful account of Delhi's part in the 1857 uprising. Using Urdu as well as English sources, he tells us what it was like for the insurgents, the British, the Mughal court and – most importantly – the ordinary people of Delhi. A great read, and a great piece of historical research.

🏃 **William Dalrymple** *White Mughals*. This compelling book tells the previously forgotten story of James Achilles Kirkpatrick, British Resident at Hyderabad at the end of the eighteenth century, who fell in love with, and subsequently married, the great niece of the nizam's prime minister. An extraordinary tale, told with relish, erudition and an impeccable sense of pace in a book that grips like a great nineteenth-century novel.

Gurcharan Das *India Unbound*. Political economy doesn't tend to make for riveting prose, but Gurcharan Das (a former industrialist turned writer) brings the economic history of post-Independence India compellingly to life with this mix of autobiographical anecdote and essay.

Patrick French *Liberty or Death*. The definitive account (and a damning indictment) of the last years of the British Raj. Material from hitherto unreleased intelligence files shows how Churchill's "florid incompetence" and Atlee's "feeble incomprehension" contributed to the debacle that was Partition.

Bamber Gascoigne *The Great Mughals*. Concise, entertaining and eminently readable account of the lives of the first six great Mughals, offering a fascinating glimpse into both the imperial ambitions and private lives of India's most remarkable dynasty.

Richard Hall *Empires of the Monsoon*. An impeccably researched account of early colonial expansion into the Arabian Sea and Indian Ocean, tracing the web of trade connections binding Europe, Africa and the Subcontinent.

Christopher Hibbert *The Great Mutiny.* Account of the 1857 uprising, told entirely from the British point of view, in easy prose and with some excellent first-hand material from the British side, but little about how the uprising was seen by the insurgents, or by ordinary civilians caught up in it.

Lawrence James *Raj: the Making and Unmaking of British India.* A door-stopping 700-page history of British rule in India, drawing on official papers and private memoirs. The most up-to-date, erudite survey of its kind, and unlikely to be bettered as a general introduction.

John Keay *The Honourable Company: A History of the English East India Company.* In characteristically fluent style, Keay strikes the right balance between those who regard the East India Company as a rapacious insti-tution with malevolent intentions and others who present its acquisi-tion of the Indian empire as an unintended, almost accidental process.

John Keay *India: A History.* The best single-volume history currently in print. Keay manages to coax clear, impartial and highly readable narrative from five thousand years of fragmented events, enlivened with plenty of quirky asides.

John Keay *India Discovered.* Fasci-nating account of how the secrets of monuments like Sanchi, Ajanta and the Ashokan edicts were unlocked by a colourful band of Raj-era Indolo-gists whose lives were, in many cases, as fascinating as their subjects.

Dominique Lapierre and Javier Moro *Five Past Midnight in Bhopal.* The definitive account of the world's worst industrial disaster, weaving together portraits of its victims, heroes and villains to create a compelling narrative that also stands as an outstanding piece of investiga-tive journalism.

Geoffrey Moorhouse *India Britan-nica.* A balanced, lively survey of the rise and fall of the British Raj, with lots of illustrations. Recommended if this is your first foray into the period, as it's a lot more concise and readable than Lawrence James's *Raj* (though correspondingly less detailed).

S.A.A. Rizvi *The Wonder That Was India: Part II.* Rizvi's follow-up to A. L. Basham's classic study (see opposite) looks at Indian history and culture from the arrival of Islam until colonial times, with thorough coverage of the Delhi Sultanate and Mughal Empire.

Romila Thapar *History of India Volume I.* Concise paperback account of early Indian history, ending with the Delhi Sultanate. Percival Spear's *History of India Volume II* covers the period from the Mughal era to the 1970s.

Society

Liz Collingham *Curry.* Original and entertaining account of Indian history seen through its food, from Mughal biriyanis to Mulligatawny soup.

Trevor Fishlock *India File.* The latest edition of this now-classic analysis of contemporary Indian

society includes essays on the Golden Temple siege and the rise of Rajiv Gandhi. Recommended as an all-round introduction.

B.K.S. Iyengar *Yoga: the Path to Holistic Health.* The definitive guide to yoga by the world's leading teacher, recommended by practitioners from across the yoga spectrum. *Yoga: the Iyengar Way*, by Silva, Mira and Shyan Mehta, offers a lighter and much less expensive alternative.

Zia Jaffrey *The Invisibles*. An investigation into the hidden world of Delhi's *hijras*, or eunuchs. Using anthropological and journalistic research techniques, Jaffrey unravels the layers of myth and mystique surrounding this secretive subculture.

John Keay *Into India*. As an all-round introduction to India, this book – originally written in 1973 but re-issued in 1999 – is the one most often recommended by old hands, presenting a wide spread of history and cultural background, interspersed with lucid personal observations.

Edward Luce *In Spite of the Gods*. The most authoritative account of the state of the nation currently in print, packed full of sobering statistics and myth-busting facts that challenge common misconceptions about the country, yet which somehow manages to remain eminently readable throughout.

James McConnachie *The Book Of Love: In Search of the Kamasutra*. Scholarly yet entertaining history of the world-famous Indian treatise on carnal delights from its earliest origins to its hush-hush rediscovery in the repressed Victorian era and subsequent flowering in the permissive Sixties.

Gita Mehta *Karma Cola*. Satirical look at the psychedelic 1970s freak scene in India, with some hilarious anecdotes, and many a wry observation on the wackier excesses of spiritual tourism. Mehta's *Snakes and Ladders* offers an overview of contemporary urban India in the form of a potpourri of essays, travelogues and interviews.

Geoffrey Moorhouse *Calcutta, the City Revealed*. Fascinating, if inevitably

dated, anatomy of the great city in the early 1970s.

V.S. Naipaul *An Area of Darkness*. One of the finest (and bleakest) books ever written about India: a darkly comic portrait of the country based on a year of travel around the Subcontinent in the early 1960s – dated, but still essential reading. Naipaul followed this up with *India: A Wounded Civilisation*, a damning analysis of Indian society written during the Emergency of 1975–77, and the altogether sunnier *India: A Million Mutinies Now*, published in 1990.

Anita Nair (ed) *Where the Rain is Born*. An eclectic anthology of essays, short stories, poems and extracts from published works (both in English and Malayalam) about Kerala. Foreign contributors include Rushdie, Dalrymple and Frater, while a string of local authors – including Arundhati Roy – reflect on the changing face of the modern state.

Jerry Pinto (ed) *Reflected in Water: Writings on Goa*. A compilation of pieces culled from books spanning five centuries, from travel essays by the likes of William Dalrymple, Graham Greene and David Tomoroy, to more impressionistic articles on various aspects of local life by eminent Goans.

Amartya Sen *The Argumentative Indian*. A provocative and sharply written collection of essays on identity, religion, history, philosophy and – above all – what it means to be Indian, by the Nobel Prize-winning economist.

Mark Tully *No Full Stops in India*. Earnest dissection of contemporary India by the former BBC correspondent, incorporating anecdotes and first-hand accounts of political events over the past twenty years. His subsequent books, *India in Slow Motion* and *India's Unending Journey*, cover a similarly diverse range of subjects, from Hindu extremism, child labour and Sufi mysticism to the crisis in agriculture.

Travel

🏃 **William Dalrymple** *City of Djinns*. Dalrymple's award-winning account of a year in Delhi sifts through successive layers of the city's past using a blend of inspired historical sleuth-work and interviews with living vestiges of different eras: Urdu calligraphers, Sufi clerics, eunuchs, pigeon fanciers and the last surviving descendant of the Mughal emperors. A real gem. *The Age of Kali* (published in India as *In the Court of the Fish-Eyed Goddess*) is a collection of essays drawn from ten years' travel in India.

Robyn Davidson *Desert Places*. Absorbing account of Davidson's long and difficult journey through Rajasthan and Gujarat in company with the nomadic, camel-herding Rabari tribe, giving a rare insight into a way of life that has now virtually disappeared.

Trevor Fishlock *Cobra Road*. Former *Times* correspondent Fishlock's 1999 account of a journey from the Khyber to Cape Comorin, a classic all-round introduction to the Subcontinent. Sympathetic yet balanced, it looks at many of the ironies and absurdities inherent in modern India, whilst retaining a sense of humour and adventure.

Alexander Frater *Chasing the Monsoon*. Frater's wet-season jaunt up the west coast and across to Shillong took him through an India of muddy puddles and grey skies: an evocative account of the country as few visitors see it, now something of a classic.

Justine Hardy *Bollywood Boy*. Chick-lit-style travelogue exploring the larger-than-life world of the Bombay film industry and featuring a lurid cast of has-been movie stars, Grant Road prostitutes, gangsters and some formidable regulars at her local beauty salon.

Norman Lewis *A Goddess in the Stones*. Veteran English travel writer's typically idiosyncratic account of his trip to Kolkata (Calcutta) and around the backwaters of Bihar and Orissa, with some vivid insights into tribal India.

Tim Mackintosh-Smith *The Hall of a Thousand Columns*. Quirky, learned and entertaining travelogue following the footsteps of the famous fourteenth-century Moroccan traveller Ibn Battuta through the Delhi of the Tughluq sultan Muhammad Shah and thence south to Kerala, with lashings of offbeat Subcontinental Islamic (and other) history en route.

Geoffrey Moorhouse *Om*. An account of Moorhouse's travels around south India's key spiritual centres, providing typically well-informed asides on history, politics, contemporary culture and religion.

Dervla Murphy *On a Shoestring to Coorg*. Murphy stays with her young daughter in the little-visited tropical mountains of Coorg, Karnataka. A compelling manifesto for single-parent budget travel.

Eric Newby *Slowly Down the Ganges* Classic account of Newby's mammoth journey from Haridwar to the mouth of the Hooghly in the 1960s, which still manages to evoke the timeless allure of the Subcontinent's holiest river.

🏃 **Tahir Shah** *Sorcerer's Apprentice*. A journey through the weird underworld of occult India. Travelling as an apprentice to a master conjurer and illusionist, Shah encounters hangmen, baby renters, skeleton dealers, sadhus and charlatans.

🏃 **Mark Shand** *Travels on My Elephant*. Award-winning account of a 600-mile ride on an elephant from Konarak in Orissa to Bihar, and full of incident, humour and pathos. For the sequel, *Queen of the Elephants*, Shand teams up with an Assamese princess who's the country's leading elephant-handler.

Eric Shipton and H.W. Tilman *Nanda Devi: Exploration and Ascent*. Two classics of Himalayan mountaineering literature published in a single volume, recounting the famous expeditions of 1934 and 1936. Shipton's work, in particular, is a masterpiece of the genre: beautifully written and enthralling from start to finish.

Fiction

Mulk Raj Anand *Untouchable* and *Coolie*. One of the first Indian authors writing in English to gain an international readership, Mulk Raj Anand's work focuses on those at the very bottom of India's social heirarchy. First published in 1935, *Untouchable* gives a memorable worm's-eye view of the brutal life of an untouchable sweeper, while the subsequent *Coolie* (1936) describes the death of a 15-year-old child labourer.

Anita Desai *Fasting, Feasting*. One of India's leading female authors' eloquent portrayal of the frustration of a sensitive young woman stuck in the stifling atmosphere of home while her spoilt brother is packed off to study in America.

Kiran Desai *The Inheritance of Loss*. Warm, wise and beautifully told family tale straddling India and the US, set in the 1980s, with most of the action unfolding near Kalimpong against a backdrop of Nepalese insurgency.

E.M. Forster *A Passage to India*. Set in the 1920s, this withering critique of colonialism is memorable as much for its sympathetic portrayal of middle-class Indian life as for its insights into cultural misunderstandings.

Ruth Prawer Jhabvala *Out of India*. One of many short-story collections that shows India in its full colours: amusing, shocking and thought-provoking. Other books by Jhabvala include *How I Became a Holy Mother*, *Like Birds, Like Fishes*; *Heat and Dust*; and *In Search of Love and Beauty*.

Rudyard Kipling *Kim*. Cringingly colonialist at times, of course, but the atmosphere of India and Kipling's love of it shine through in this subtle story of an orphaned white boy. Kipling's other key works on India are two books of short stories: *Soldiers Three* and *In Black and White*.

Dominique Lapierre *City of Joy*. Melodramatic story of a white man's journey into Kolkata's (Calcutta) slums, loaded with anecdotes about Indian religious beliefs and customs.

🏃 **Rohinton Mistry** *A Fine Balance*. Compelling novel focusing on two friends who leave their lower-caste rural lives for the urban opportunities of the big smoke (in this case a fictionalized Mumbai). Mistry's *Such a Long Journey* is an acclaimed account of a Bombay Parsi's struggle to maintain personal integrity in the face of betrayals and disappointment.

🏃 **R.K. Narayan** *Gods, Demons and Others*. Classic Indian folk tales and popular myths told through the voice of a village storyteller. Many of Narayan's beautifully crafted books, full of touching characters and subtle humour, are set in the fictional south Indian territory of Malgudi.

Gregory David Roberts *Shantaram.* Entertaining yet rather over-long semi-autobiographical account of an escaped Australian convict taking refuge in India (mainly Mumbai), with memorable (if occasionally clichéd) depictions of the country and its people.

Arundhati Roy *The God of Small Things.* Haunting Booker Prize-winner about a well-to-do south Indian family caught between the snobberies of high-caste tradition, a colonial past and the diverse personal histories of its members.

Salman Rushdie *Midnight's Children.* This story of a man born at the very moment of Independence, whose life mirrors that of modern India itself, won Rushdie the Booker Prize and the enmity of Indira Gandhi, who had it banned in India. Set in Kerala and Bombay, *The Moor's Last Sigh* was the subject of a defamation case brought by Shiv Sena leader Bal Thackeray.

Vikram Seth *A Suitable Boy.* Vast, all-embracing tome set in UP shortly after Independence; wonderful characterization and an impeccable sense of place and time make this an essential read for those long train journeys.

Khushwant Singh *Delhi: a Novel.* A jaded Delhiwallah and his *hijra* lover contemplate the accounts of characters from key moments in Delhi's past. Singh's other works include *Train to Pakistan*, a chillingly realistic portrayal of life in a village on the Partition line, set in the summer of 1947; and *Sex, Scotch and Scholarship*, a collection of wry short stories.

Indra Sinha *Animal's People.* Nominated for the 2007 Booker Prize, *Animal's People* is a vivid, fictionalized account of the aftermath of the 1984 Bhopal gas disaster, seen from the perspective of a witty but cynical teenage boy.

William Sutcliffe *Are You Experienced?* Hilarious novel sending up the backpacker scene in India. Wickedly perceptive and very readable.

Tarun J. Tejpal *The Alchemy of Desire.* Set mainly in the Himalayas, this sensuous contemporary tale focuses on two lovers, mixing its exploration of human relationships with wider reflections on India in the twentieth century.

Biography and autobiography

Charles Allen *Plain Tales from the Raj.* First-hand accounts from erstwhile *sahibs* and *memsahibs* of everyday British India, organized thematically.

James Cameron *An Indian Summer.* Affectionate and humorous description of the veteran British journalist's visit to India in 1972, and his marriage to an Indian woman. An enduring classic.

Gayatri Devi *A Princess Remembers.* Nostalgic reminiscences of life as Maharani of Jaipur and as a politician

by "one of the world's most beautiful women".

Louis Fischer *The Life of Mahatma Gandhi.* First published in 1950, this biography has been re-issued several times since, and quite rightly – veteran American journalist Louis Fischer knew his subject personally, and his book provides an engaging account of Gandhi as a man, politician and propagandist.

M.K. Gandhi *The Story of My Experiments with Truth.* Gandhi's fascinating record of his life, including his spiritual and moral quests, changing relationship with the British Government in India, and gradual emergence to the fore of national politics.

Paramahansa Yogananda *Autobiography of a Yogi*. Uplifting account of religious awakening and spiritual development by one of the most influential Hindu masters to leave India and bring his teachings to the West.

Women

🏃 **Elizabeth Bumiller** *May You Be the Mother of a Hundred Sons*. Lucid exploration of the Indian woman's lot, drawn from dozens of first-hand encounters by an American journalist.

Shashi Deshpande *The Binding Vine*. Disturbing story of one woman's struggle for independence, and her eventual acceptance of the position of servitude traditionally assumed by an Indian wife.

Anees Jung *The Night of the New Moon*. Revealing and poetic stories woven around interviews with Muslim women from all sectors of Indian society. Jung's *Unveiling India* is a compelling account of the life of a Muslim woman who has chosen to break free from orthodoxy.

Sarah Lloyd *An Indian Attachment*. Life in a Punjabi plains village through the eyes of a young Western woman, whose relationship with an opium-addicted Sikh forms the essence of this honest and enlightening book.

Vrinda Nabar *Caste as Woman*. Conceived as an Indian counterpart

to Greer's *The Female Eunuch*, this wry study of the pressures experienced during various stages of womanhood draws on scripture and popular culture to explore issues of identity and cultural conditioning.

Sakuntala Narasimhan *Sati: Widow Burning in India*. Definitive and engaging exploration of *sati* and its significance throughout history.

Mala Sen *Death By Fire*. Later made into a controversial movie, this book uses the infamous Roop Kanwar case as a springboard to explore some of the wider issues affecting women in contemporary Indian society – a bleak read, but one that shows up the hollow triumphalism of the country's right-wing politicians in its true colours.

Virama, Josiane Racine & Jean-Luc Racine *Virama: Life of an Untouchable*. Unique autobiography of an untouchable woman told in her own words (transcribed by French anthropologists) over a fifteen-year period, offering frank, often humorous insights into India, the universe and everything.

Development and the environment

🏃 **Palagummi Sainath** *Everybody Loves a Good Drought*. A classic report on India's poorest districts, telling the stories of individual villages that are usually lost in a maze of development statistics. Its harrowing case studies caused uproar in the capital, galvanizing the government into some drastic aid

programmes. A polished view on an India few visitors see.

🏃 **Jeremy Seabrook** *Notes from Another India*. Life histories and interviews – compiled over a year's travelling and skilfully contextualized – reveal the everyday problems faced by Indians from a variety of backgrounds. One of the soundest and most engaging overviews of Indian development issues ever written.

The arts and architecture

Roy Craven *Indian Art*. Concise general introduction to Indian art, from Harappan seals to Mughal miniatures, with lots of illustrations.

Rachel Dwyer & Divia Patel *Cinema India: The Visual Culture of Hindi Film*. Definitive guide to Bollywood, tracing its development from 1913, with richly illustrated chapters charting the changes in costumes, sets and advertising trends.

Mohan Khokar *Traditions of Indian Classical Dance*. Detailing the religious and social roots of Indian dance, this lavishly illustrated book, with sections on regional traditions, is an excellent introduction to the subject.

George Michell *The Hindu Temple*. A reasonable primer, introducing Hindu temples, their significance, and architectural development.

Giles Tillotson *Mughal India*. Excellent architectural guide to the great Mughal monuments of Delhi, Agra and Fatehpur Sikri, academic but accessible, and with interesting snippets of historical and biographical information thrown in to flesh out the descriptions of the buildings themselves.

Bonnie C. Wade *Music in India: The Classical Traditions*. A scrupulous catalogue of Indian music, outlining the most commonly used instruments, with illustrations and musical scores.

Religion

Diana L. Eck *Banaras – City of Light*. Thorough disquisition on the religious significance of Varanasi; a good introduction to the practice of Hindu cosmology. A follow-up volume, *Encountering God*, uses Christianity as a reference point for an exploration of the common ground between Hinduism and Buddhism.

Dorf Hartsuiker *Sadhus: Holy Men of India*. The weird world of India's itinerant ascetics exposed in glossy colour photographs and erudite but accessible text.

Roger Housden *Travels through Sacred India*. A gazetteer of holy places, listings of ashrams and lively essays on temples, sadhus, gurus and sacred sites. Hudson derives much of his material from personal encounters, which bring the subjects to life.

Stephen P. Huyler *Meeting God*. This acclaimed introduction provides an unrivalled overview of the beliefs and practices of contemporary Hinduism. The text evokes general principles by focusing on individual acts of worship, accompanied by Huyler's sublime photographs.

Wendy O'Flaherty (transl) *Hindu Myths*. Translations of key myths from the original Sanskrit texts, providing an insight into the foundations of Hinduism.

Charlie Pye-Smith *Rebels and Outcasts: A Journey through Christian India*. An Englishman's encounters with clerics, congregations and NGOs from the full gamut of denominations.

Wildlife

Richard Grimmet & Tim Inskipp *Pocket Guide to the Birds of the Indian Subcontinent*. The birders' bible, listing all 1300 species found in South Asia. The same authors' beautifully written and illustrated *Birds of Southern India* details every species known in the south.

Krys Kamierczak and Ber Van Perlo *A Field Guide to the Birds of the Indian Subcontinent*. Less popular than Grimmet and Inskipp's competing guide, but just as thorough, expertly drawn and well laid out, with every species named.

Language

Language

Language

N

o less than **eighteen major languages** are officially recognized by the Indian constitution, whilst numerous minor ones and over a thousand dialects are also spoken across the country. When independent India was organized, the present-day states were largely created along linguistic lines, which at least helps the traveller make some sense of the complex situation. Considering the continuing prevalence of **English**, there is rarely any necessity to speak a local language but some theoretical knowledge of the background and learning at least a few words of one or two can only enhance your visit.

The main languages of northern India, including the country's eastern and western extremities, are all **Indo-Aryan**, the easternmost subgroup of the Indo-European family that is thought to have originated somewhere between Europe and Central Asia several millennia BC, before tribal movements spread its progeny in all directions. The oldest extant Subcontinental language is Sanskrit, one of the three "big sisters" (along with Latin and Greek) upon which philologists have created the model of proto-Indo-European language. It's known to have been spoken early in the second millennium BC, although it was not written down until much later, and is the vehicle for all the sacred texts of Hinduism. Sanskrit remained the language of the educated until around 1000 AD and is still spoken to some extent by the priestly class today, but over the centuries it gradually developed into the modern tongues of northern India: Hindi, Urdu, Bengali, Gujarati, Marathi, Kashmiri, Punjabi and Oriya.

North India

Hindi is the pre-eminent language in the north, being the mother tongue of over 200 million north Indians, and the main language in the states of Uttar Pradesh, Madhya Pradesh, Rajasthan, Haryana, Bihar and Himachal Pradesh, as well as being widely used as a second language in other states. Hindi is also very closely related to **Urdu**, the main language of Pakistan. Both Hindi and Urdu developed in tandem around the markets and army camps of Delhi (the term Urdu derives from the Turkish word for "camp") during the establishment of Muslim rule around the start of the second millennium AD. Whereas Hindi later returned to the Sanskrit roots of its Hindu speakers, however, and adopted the classical **Devanagari** script, Urdu became culturally more closely linked with Islam and is written in **Perso-Arabic** script. The vocabulary of each also reflects these cultural and religious ties. The scripts of Punjabi, Bengali and Gujarati are among those that have developed out of Devanagari and still bear some resemblance to it.

Other important languages spoken in North India include **Bengali** (West Bengal and Tripura), **Nepali** (West Bengal and Sikkim), **Gujarati** (Gujarat), **Punjabi** (Punjab, Delhi), **Kashmiri** and **Dogri** (Kashmir), **Assamese** and **Bodo** (Assam), **Oriya** (Orissa) and **Maithili** (Bihar).

South India

The four most widely spoken south Indian languages, **Tamil** (Tamil Nadu), **Telugu** (Andhra Pradesh), **Kannada** (Karnataka) and **Malayalam** (Kerala) all belong to the Dravidian family, the world's fourth largest group of languages. These and related minor languages grew up quite separately among the non-Aryan peoples of southern India over thousands of years, and the earliest written records of Tamil date back to the third century AD. The exact origins of the Dravidian group have not been established, but it is possible that proto-Dravidian was spoken further north in prehistoric times before the people were driven south by the Aryan invaders. The beautiful flowing scripts, especially the exquisite curls of Kannada, add a constant aesthetic quality to any tour of the south.

Language in India since Independence

With **Independence** it was decided by the government in Delhi that Hindi should become the **official language** of the newly created country. Interestingly, the idea of using **Hindustani**, a more recent colloquial hybrid of Hindi and Urdu, popular with Gandhi and others in an effort to encourage communal unity during the fight for freedom, was never pursued; this was due to a mixture of political reasons following Partition and the fact that the language lacked the necessary refinement. A drive to teach Hindi in all schools followed and over half the country's population are now reckoned to have a decent working knowledge of the language. However, there has always been strong **resistance** to the imposition of Hindi in certain areas, especially the **Tamil-led** Dravidian south, and the vast majority of people living below the Deccan plateau have little or no knowledge of it.

This is where **English**, the language of the ex-colonists, becomes an important means of communication. Not surprisingly, given India's rich linguistic diversity – there are also minority tribal languages and dialects of Sino-Tibetan that do not belong to the main groups mentioned above – **English** remains a **lingua franca** for many people. It is still the preferred language of law, higher education, much of commerce and the media, and to some degree political

Indian English

During the British Raj, Indian English developed its own characteristics, which have survived to the present day. It was during this period that many Indian words entered the vocabulary of everyday English, including words like veranda, bungalow, sandal, pyjamas, shampoo, jungle, turban, caste, chariot, chilli, cardamom, pundit and yoga. The traveller to India soon becomes familiar with other terms in common usage that have not spread so widely outside the Subcontinent: *dacoit, dhoti, panchayat, lakh* and *crore* are but a few (see the Glossary on p.1409 for definitions) – a full list of Anglo-Indianisms can be found in the famous Hobson-Jobson Anglo-Indian dictionary.

Perhaps the most endearing aspect of Indian English is the way it has preserved forms now regarded as highly old-fashioned in Britain. Addresses such as "Good sir" and questions like "May I know your good name?" are commonplace, as are terms like "tiffin" and "cantonment". This type of usage reaches its apogee in the more flowery expressions of the media, which regularly feature in the vast array of daily newspapers published in English. Thus headlines often appear such as "37 perish in mishap", referring to a train crash, or passages like this splendid report of a bank robbery: "The miscreants absconded with the loot in great haste. They repaired immediately to their hideaway, whereupon they divided the iniquitous spoils before vanishing into thin air."

dialogue; and for many educated Indians, not just those living abroad, it is actually their first language. All this explains why the Anglophone visitor can often soon feel surprisingly at home despite the huge cultural differences. It is not unusual to overhear everyday contact between Indians from different parts of the country being conducted in English, and stimulating conversations can often be had, not only with students or businesspeople, but also with chai-wallahs or shoeshine boys.

Useful Hindi words and phrases

Greetings

Namaste/Namaskar	Hello (slightly formal; not used for Muslims)
As salaam alaykum (formal; to a Muslim)	Alaykum as salaam (in reply)
Namaste	Goodbye
Phir mileynge	See you later
Khudaa haafiz	Goodbye (to a Muslim)
Aap kaise hai?	How are you? (formal)
Kya hal hai?	How are you? (familiar)
bhaaii	brother (informal; not to be used to older men)
diidi	sister (informal; not to be used to older women)
sahib	sir
hazur (Muslims only)	sir

Basic words

haa or ji haa	yes (informal/more formal)
nahi or ji nahi	no (informal/more formal)
acha or tiika	OK
mai	I/me
aap	you (formal)
tum	you (familiar; and to children)
aur	and/more
kaise?	how?
Kitna?	How much?
dhanyavad/shukriya	thank you (formal; Indians don't usually say thank you during everyday transactions, eg when buying

something. Note that there's also no direct Hindi equivalent to the English word "please".

acha	good
bahot acha	very good
buraa	bad
barra	big
chota	small
garam	hot
mirchi	hot (spicy)
thanda	cold
saaf	clean
gandaa	dirty
khulaa	open
mahagaa	expensive
aiiye	please come
jao	go
bhaago	run (also "take a run" or "scram")
bas	enough

Basic phrases

Mera naam... hai	My name is...
Aapka naam kya hai?	What is your name? (formal)
Tumhara naam kya hai?	What is your name? (familiar, and to children)
Mai.. se hu	I'm from...
Hum... se hai	We're from...
Aap kaha se aate hai?	Where do you come from?
Samaj gayaa	I understand
Samaj nahin aayaa	I don't understand
Maluum nahi	I don't know
Mai Hindi nahi bol sakta hu	I don't speak Hindi

Dhiire se boliye	Please speak slowly	dawaaii	medicine
Ma'af kiijiye	Sorry	bimar	ill
Tiika hai?	It is OK?	dard	pain
Kitna paisa?	How much?	pate	stomach
Yeh kya hai?	How much is this?	aank	eye
Nahi chai'iya	I don't need it (literally "not needed"); useful response to persistent touts	naakh	nose
		kaan	ear
		piith	back
		paao	foot

...hai?	Do you have... ?
Acha lugta hai	I/we like it
Kya haal hai?	How are you?
Tiika hai	I'm fine
Kya kam karte hai?	What work do you do?
Bhaai behan hai?	Do you have any brothers or sisters?
Arey!	Oh dear!

Getting around

...kaha hai?	Where is the... ?
Mai... jaana chaata hu	I want to go to...
Kaha hai?	Where is it?
Kitna duur?	How far?
Agra ka bas kaha hai?	Which is the bus for Agra?
Gaarii kab jayegi?	What time does the train leave?
Ruko!	Stop!
Thehero!	Wait!

Accommodation

Mujhe kamra chai'eeya	I need a room
Kamra kitne ka hai ?	How much is the room?
Mai ek raat ke liiye theheroonga	I am staying for one night

Health

Sir me dard hai	I have a headache
Mere pate me dard hai	I have a pain in my stomach
Dard yaha hai	The pain is here
Daktar ka clinic kaha hai?	Where is the doctor's surgery?
Haspital kaha hai?	Where is the hospital?
Dawaaii khana kaha hai?	Where is the pharmacy?

Numbers and time

shunya	zero
ek	one
do	two
tiin	three
char	four
paanch	five
che	six
saat	seven
aat	eight
nau	nine
das	ten
gyaarah	eleven
baarah	twelve
terah	thirteen
chaudah	fourteen
pandrah	fifteen
solah	sixteen
satrah	seventeen
ataarah	eighteen
unniis	nineteen
biis	twenty
tiis	thirty
chaaliis	forty
pachaas	fifty
saath	sixty
sattar	seventy
assii	eighty
nabbe	ninety
ek sau	one hundred
ek hazaar	one thousand
ek lakh	one hundred thousand
ek crore	ten million
aaj	today
kal	tomorrow/yesterday
din	day
dopahar	afternoon

shaam	evening	mangalvaar	Tuesday
raat	night	budhvaar	Wednesday
haftaah	week	viirvaar	Thursday
mahiinaa	month	shukravaar	Friday
saal	year	shanivaar	Saturday
somvaar	Monday	ravivaar	Sunday

Food and drink glossary

Basics

khaana	food
chawaal	rice
chamach	spoon
chhoori	knife
kanta	fork
plate	plate
chini	sugar
chini nahi	no sugar (eg in tea)
kali mirch	black pepper
jaggery	unrefined sugar
namak	salt
mirch	pepper
mirchi	chilli hot
mirchi kam	less hot
garam	hot
thanda	cold
dahi	yoghurt
dhal	curried lentils, some times reduced to a kind of broth; traditionally served as an accompani- ment to all Indian meals
garam masala	any kind of spice mixture added to give flavour to dishes (literally "hot spices")
ghee	clarified butter; often used instead of cooking oil, or to flavour food
gravy	any kind of curry sauce; nothing to do with British gravy
jeera	cumin

lal mirch	red pepper
masala	generic term indicating either a spice mixture or something spicy
methi	fenugreek
paan	digestif; see p.59
paneer	unfermented cheese
sabji	any vegetable curry

Drinks

bhang lassi	lassi flavoured with bhang (cannabis)
botal vaala paani	mineral water
chai	tea
doodh	milk
falooda	traditional Muslim drink, usually made with milk, ice, cream, nuts and sweets
kavhaa or kaafi	coffee
lassi	yoghurt drink, served either plain or flavoured with salt or fruit
pani	water
peenay ka pani	drinking water (not mineral water)

Meat and fish

chingri	prawns
gosht	meat, usually mutton
keema	minced meat
macchi	fish
murg	chicken

Vegetables and fruit

aam	mango
alu	potatoes

baingan	eggplant (aubergine) or brinjal
bhindi	okra (ladies' fingers)
chana	chickpeas
gaajar	carrot
gobi	cauliflower
kaddoo	pumpkin
kela	banana
palak	spinach
piaz	onions
sabji	vegetables (literally, "greens")
santaraa	orange
seb	apple
sag	spinach
tamatar	tomato

Dishes and cooking terms

alu baingan	potato and aubergine; usually mild to medium
alu gobi	potato and cauliflower; usually mild
alu methi	potato with fenugreek leaves, usually medium-hot
alu muttar	potato and pea curry; usually mild
baingan bharta	baked and mashed aubergine mixed with onion
bhindi bhaji	gently spiced fried okra
bhuna	roasted and then thickened-down medium-hot curry sauce
biriyani	rice baked with saffron or turmeric, whole spices and meat (sometimes vegetables), and often hard-boiled egg; rich
Bombay duck	dried bummelo fish
channa masala	spicy chickpeas; usually medium-hot
cutlet	fried cutlet of minced meat or chopped vegetables
dahi maach	fish curry with yoghurt, ginger and turmeric; a mild Bengali dish
dhal bati churma	classic Rajasthani dish comprising dhal, bati (a baked wheatflour ball

	with a tough crust) and churma (a sweet made of coarse-ground wheat flour cooked with ghee and sugar)
dhal gosht	meat cooked in lentils; usually hot
dhal makhani	lentils cooked with cream
dhansak	curry sauce made from reduced lentils; usually medium-hot
dopiaza	onion-based sauce; medium-mild
dum	steamed in a casserole; the most common dish is dum aloo, with potatoes
gatta	small dumplings of gram flour cooked in a masala sauce
jalfrezi	dish cooked with tomatoes and green chilli; medium-hot to hot
karahi	cast-iron wok which has given its name to a method of cooking with dry spices to create dishes of medium strength
karhi	dhal-like dish made from dahi and gram flour
keema	minced meat
kofta	balls of minced vegetables or meat in a curried sauce
korma	mild sauce made with curd (and perhaps cream)
maacher jhol	mild fish stew, often made with the entire fish – a Bengali delicacy
malai kofta	vegetable balls in a rich cream sauce; usually medium-mild
molee	curry with coconut, usually fish, originally Malay (hence the name), now a speciality of Kerala; hot
mughlai masala	Mughal-style mild, creamy sauce
mulligatawny	classic Anglo-Indian–style vegetable soup; moderately spicy
murg makhani	butter chicken

muttar paneer	paneer and peas curry
palak paneer	paneer and spinach
pathia	thickened curry with lemon juice; hot
pomfret	a flatfish popular in Mumbai and Kolkata (Calcutta)
pulau	rice, gently spiced and pre-fried
raita	chilled yoghurt flavoured with mild spices, sometimes with the addition of small pieces of cucumber and tomato; usually eaten as an accompaniment to a main course
rasam	south Indian-style spicy soup
rogan josh	deep-red lamb curry, a classic Mughlai dish; medium-hot
sambar	soupy lentil and vegetable curry with asafoetida and tamarind
shahi paneer	"royal" paneer; slightly more elaborate version of standard paneer curry, sometimes including fruit and nuts
seekh kebab	minced lamb grilled on a skewer
shami kebab	small minced lamb cutlets
stew or estew	stew with a distinct Keralan twist (contains chilli and coconut); there's also a north Indian Muslim version)
tarka dhal	lentils with a masala of fried garlic, onions and spices
thali	combination of vegetarian dishes, chutneys, pickles, rice and bread served as an all-in-one meal
vindaloo	Goan vinegared meat (sometimes fish) curry, originally pork; very hot (but not as hot as the kamikaze UK version)

Breads and pancakes

| appam* | south Indian-style rice pancake speckled with holes, soft in the middle |
| bhatura | soft bread made of white flour and traditionally |

	accompanying chana; common in Delhi
chapati	unleavened bread made of wholewheat flour and baked on a round griddle-dish called a tawa
dosa*	crispy south Indian rice pancake; can be served in various forms, the best known of which is the masala dosa, when the dosa is wrapped around a filling of spicy potato curry
iddli *	south Indian steamed rice cake, usually served with sambar
kachori	small thick cakes of salty deep-fried bread
loochi	delicate puri often mixed with white flour; cooked in Bengal
Mughlai paratha	paratha with egg
naan	white leavened bread kneaded with yoghurt and baked in a tandoor
papad or poppadum	crisp, thin, chickpea-flour cracker
paratha or parantha	wholewheat bread made with butter, rolled thin and griddle-fried; a little bit like a chewy pancake, sometimes stuffed with meat or vegetables
phulka	a chapati that has been made to puff out by being placed directly on the fire
puri	crispy, puffed-up, deep-fried wholewheat bread
roti	loosely used term; often just another name for chapati, though it should be thicker, chewier, and baked in a tandoor
uttapam*	thick, south Indian-style rice pancake often cooked with onions

barfi or burfi	traditional sweet made with milk; a bit like fudge
bhaji or bhajia	pieces of vegetable deep-fried in chickpea batter, served as a main course or a street snack
bhel puri	mix of puffed ricepotato and crunchy puri with tamarind sauce; a Mumbai speciality, though now popular nationwide
gulab jamun	classic Indian sweet made from deep-fried dough balls served in syrup
halwa	traditional sweet made from lentils, nuts and fruit, baked in a large tray and cut into small squares
jalebi	orange coloured flour batter, which is deep fried and soaked in sugar syrup
raj kachori	a crisp puri usually filled with chickpeas and doused in curd and sauce
kheer	delicate, Mughal-style rice pudding
kulfi	Indian-style ice cream, often flavoured with pistachio
ladoo (or ladu)	sweets made from small balls of gram flour and semolina
mirchi bada	large chilli fried in a thick batter of wheatgerm and potato; a speciality of Jodhpur
pakora	pieces of vegetable deep-fried in chickpea batter; a popular street snack
rasgulla	curd cheese balls flavoured with rosewater; a popular dessert
samosa	parcels of vegetable and potato (and sometimes meat) wrapped up in triangles of pastry and deep-fried
vada*	doughnut-shaped, deep-fried lentil cake (also spelt vadai, vade, wadi, etc)
vada pao*	a vada served in a bun with chutney

south Indian terminology; all other terms are either in Hindi or refer to north Indian cuisine.

Glossary

aarti evening temple puja of lights

acharya religious teacher

adivasi official term for tribal person

ahimsa nonviolence

akhandpath continuous reading of the Sikh holy book, the Guru Granth Sahib

amalaka repeating decorative motif based on the fluted shape of a gourd, lining and crowning temple towers; a distinctive feature of north Indian architecture

amrita nectar of immortality

anda literally "egg": the spherical part of a stupa

angrez general term for Westerners

anna coin, no longer minted (16 annas to one rupee)

apsara heavenly nymph

arak liquor distilled from rice or coconut

asana yogic seating posture; small mat used in prayer and meditation

ashram centre for spiritual learning and religious practice

asura demon

atman soul

avatar reincarnation of Vishnu on earth, in human or animal form

ayah nursemaid

Ayurveda ancient system of medicine employing herbs, minerals and massage

baba respectful term for a sadhu

bagh garden, park

baithak reception area in private house

baksheesh tip, donation or alms

bandh general strike

bandhani tie-dye

baniya is another word for shopkeeper/trader/merchant

banyan vast fig tree, used traditionally as a meeting place, or shade for teaching and meditating; also, in South India, a cotton vest

baoli or **baori** step-well

bastee or **bustee** slum area

baul bengali singer

beedi Indian-style cigarette, with tobacco rolled in a leaf

begum Muslim princess; Muslim woman of high status

betel leaf chewed in paan, with the nut of the areca tree; also loosely applies to the nut

bhajan song in praise of god

bhakti religious devotion expressed in a personalized or emotional relationship with the deity

bhang pounded marijuana leaf, often mixed in lassi

bharat Hindi name for India

bharat mata literally "Mother India"; a representation of India personified as a maternal goddess

bhawan or **bhavan** building, house, palace or residence

bhotia Himalayan people of Tibetan origin

bhumi earth, or earth goddess

bindu seed, or the red dot (also bindi) worn by women on their foreheads as decoration

bodhi enlightenment

bodhi tree or **bo tree** peepal tree (*ficus religiosa*), associated with the Buddha's enlightenment

bodhisattva Buddhist saint

brahmin priest; a member of the highest caste group

burj tower or bastion

burkha body-covering shawl worn by orthodox Muslim women

burra-sahib colonial official, boss, or a man of great importance

cantonment area of town occupied by military quarters

caste social status acquired at birth

cella chamber, often housing the image of a deity

cenotaph ornate tomb

chaat snack

chaddar large head-cover or shawl

chaitya Buddhist temple or stupa

chajja sloping dripstone eave

chakra discus; focus of power; energy point in the body; wheel, often representing the cycle of death and rebirth

chandan sandalwood paste

chandra moon

chang Ladakhi beer made from fermented millet, wheat or rice

chappal sandals or flip-flops (thongs)

charas hashish

charbagh Persian-style garden divided into quadrants

charpoi string bed with wooden frame

chaumukh image of four faces placed back to back

chauri fly whisk; a symbol of royalty

chela pupil

chhatri domed stone pavilion, often erected over a tomb

chikan Lucknow embroidery

chillum cylindrical clay or wood pipe for smoking charas or ganja

chisthti a follower of the Sufi saint Khwaja Muin-ud-din Chishti of Ajmer

choli short, tight-fitting blouse worn with a sari

chor robber

chorten monument, often containing prayers, texts or relics, erected as a sign of faith by Tibetan Buddhists

choultry quarters for pilgrims adjoined to south Indian temples

chowgan green in the centre of a town or village

chowk crossroads or courtyard

chowki police post

chowkidar watchman/caretaker

coolie porter/labourer

crore ten million

cupola small delicate dome

dabba packed lunch

dacoit bandit

dalit "oppressed", "out-caste". The term, introduced by Dr Ambedkar, is preferred by so-called "untouchables" as a description of their social position.

dargah tomb of a Muslim saint

darshan vision of a deity or saint; receiving religious teachings

darwaza gateway; door

dawan servant

deg cauldron for food offerings, often found in dargahs

deul Orissan temple or sanctuary

deva god

devadasi temple dancer

devi goddess

devta deity

dhaba food hall selling local dishes

dham important religious site, or a theological college

dharamshala resthouse for pilgrims

dharma sense of religious and social duty (Hindu); the law of nature, teachings, truth (Buddhist)

dhobi laundryman

dholak double-ended drum

dholi sedan chair carried by bearers to hilltop temples

dhoop thick pliable block of strong incense

dhoti white ankle-length cloth worn by males, tied around the waist, and sometimes hitched up through the legs

dhurrie woollen rug

digambara literally "sky-clad": a Jain sect, known for the habit of nudity among monks, though this is no longer commonplace

dikpalas guardians of the four directions

diwan (dewan) chief minister

diwan-i-am public audience hall

diwan-i-khas hall of private audience

diya small clay oil lamp fuelled with ghee and burned in offering to a Hindu god or in celebration of Diwali

dowry payment or gift offered in marriage

Dravidian of the south

du-khang main temple in a gompa

dukka tank and fountain in courtyard of mosque

dupatta veil worn by Hindu and Muslim women with salwar kameez

durbar royal audience or council of state

dvarpala guardian image placed at sanctuary door

dzo domesticated half-cow half-yak

Eve-teasing sexual harassment of women, either physical or verbal

fakir ascetic Muslim mendicant

feni Goan spirit, distilled from coconut or cashew fruits

finial capping motif on temple pinnacle

gada mace

gadi throne

gandharvas Indra's heavenly musicians

ganj market

ganja marijuana buds

garbhagriha temple sanctuary, literally "womb-chamber"

garh fort

gari vehicle or car

ghat mountain, landing platform, or steps leading to water

ghazal melancholy Urdu songs

ghee clarified butter

godown warehouse

go-khang temple in a gompa devoted to protector (gon) deities

gompa Tibetan, or Ladakhi, Buddhist monastery

goncha ankle-length woollen robe worn by Ladakhi women

goonda ruffian

gopi young cattle-tending maidens who feature as Krishna's playmates and lovers in popular mythology

gopura towered temple gateway, common in South India

guru teacher of religion, music, dance, astrology etc

gurudwara Sikh place of worship

haj Muslim pilgrimage to Mecca

hajji Muslim engaged upon, or who has performed, the haj

hammam sunken Persian-style bath

Harijan title – "Children of God" – given to "untouchables" by Gandhi

hartal strike

haveli elaborately decorated mansion

hijra eunuch or transvestite

Hinayana literally "lesser vehicle": the name given to the original school of Buddhism by later sects

hookah water pipe for smoking strong tobacco or marijuana

howdah bulky elephant-saddle, sometimes made of pure silver, and often shaded by a canopy

hypostyle a building or room in which the roof is supported by columns (usually numerous) rather than walls, arches or vaulting

idgah area laid aside in the west of town for prayers during the Muslim festival Id-ul-zuha

imam Muslim leader or teacher

imambara tomb of a Shi'ite saint

IMFL Indian-made foreign liquor

Indo-Saracenic overblown Raj-era architecture that combines Muslim, Hindu, Jain and Western elements

ishwara god

iwan the main (often central) arch in a mosque

jagamohana porch fronting the main sanctuary in an Orissan temple

jagirdar landowner

jali latticework in stone, or a pierced screen

jama or **jami** Friday, as in Jama Masjid, or "Friday mosque"

janapadas small republics and monarchies; literally "territory of the clan"

jangha the body of a temple

jarokha small canopied balcony, often containing a window seat

jat major north Indian ethnic group; particularly numerous in eastern Rajasthan around Bharatpur

jatakas popular tales about the Buddha's life and teachings

jati caste, determined by family and occupation

jawan soldier

jhuta soiled by lips: food or drink polluted by touch

-ji suffix added to names as a term of respect

jihad striving by Muslims, through battle, to spread their faith

jina another term for the Jain tirthankaras

johar old practice of self-immolation by women in times of war

jyotirlinga twelve sacred sites associated with Shiva's unbounded lingam of light

kabutar khana pigeon coop

Kailasa or **Kailash** mountain in western Tibet: Shiva's abode and the traditional source of the Ganges and Brahmaputra; the earthly manifestation of the "world pillar", Mount Meru

kalamkari school of painting

kalasha pot-like capping stone characteristic of south Indian temples

kama satisfaction

kangyu lang book house in a gompa storing sacred Tibetan texts and manuscripts

karma weight of good and bad actions that determine status of rebirth

katcha the opposite of pukka

kavad small decorated box that unfolds to serve as a travelling temple

khadi home-spun cotton; Gandhi's symbol of Indian self-sufficiency

khan honorific Muslim title

khana dwelling or house

khejri small tree found throughout the desert regions of Rajasthan

khol black eye-liner

khud valley side

kirtan hymn-singing

kot fort

kothi residence

kotla citadel

kotwali police station

kovil term for a Tamil Nadu temple

kshatriya the warrior and ruling caste

kumkum red mark on a Hindu woman's forehead (widows are not supposed to wear it)

kund tank, lake, reservoir

kurta long men's shirt worn over baggy pajamas

lakh one hundred thousand

lama Tibetan Buddhist monk and teacher

lathi heavy stick used by police

lingam phallic symbol in places of worship representing the god Shiva

liwan prayer hall or covered area of a mosque

loka realm or world, eg devaloka, world of the gods

lunghi male garment; long wraparound cloth, like a dhoti, but usually coloured

madrasa Islamic school

maha- great or large

mahadeva literally "great god", and a common epithet for Shiva

mahal palace; mansion

maharaja (maharana, Maharawal) king

maharani queen

mahatma great soul

Mahayana "Great Vehicle": a Buddhist school that has spread throughout Southeast Asia

mahout elephant driver or keeper

maidan large open space or field

makara crocodile-like animal featuring on temple doorways and symbolizing the river Ganges. Also the vehicle of Varuna, the Vedic god of the sea

mala necklace, garland or rosary

mandala religious diagram

mandapa hall, often with many pillars, used for various purposes: eg kalyana mandapa for wedding ceremonies and nata mandapa for dance performances

mandi market

mandir temple

mani stone stone etched with Buddhist prayers by Tibetans and laid in piles or set in streams

mantra sacred verse, often repeated as an aid to meditation

mardana area for use of men in a haveli or palace

marg road

masjid mosque

mataji means 'mother', it is also used as a polite form of address to an older woman or a female sadhu

math Hindu or Jain monastery

maund old unit of weight (roughly 20kg)

mayur peacock

medhi terrace

mehendi henna

mela festival

memsahib respectful address to European woman

mihrab niche in the wall of a mosque indicating the direction of Mecca

minaret high slender tower, characteristic of mosques

minbar pulpit in a mosque from which the Friday sermon is read

mithuna amorous couples in Hindu and Buddhist figurative art

mohalla neighbourhood

moksha blissful state of freedom from rebirth aspired to by Hindus, Sikhs and Jains

mor peacock

mudra hand gesture used in Vedic rituals, featuring in Hindu, Buddhist and Jain art and dance, and symbolizing teachings and life stages of the Buddha

muezzin man behind the voice calling Muslims to prayer from a mosque

mullah Muslim teacher and scholar

muqarna a style of Islamic moulded vaulting

mutt Hindu or Jain monastery

nadi river

naga mythical serpent; alternatively, a person from Nagaland

nala stream gorge in the mountains

natak dance

natya drama

nautch performance by dancing girls

nawab Muslim landowner or prince

nilgai blue bull

nirvana (or, in Pali, *nibbana*) Buddhist equivalent of moksha

nizam title of Hyderabad rulers

NRI nonresident Indian, someone entitled to Indian nationality but resident abroad

nullah stream gorge in the mountains

om (o˜ aum) symbol denoting the origin of all things, and ultimate divine essence, used in meditation by Hindus and Buddhists

paan betel nut, lime, calcium and aniseed wrapped in a leaf and chewed as a digestive. Mildly addictive

pada foot, or base, also a poetic metre

padma lotus; another name for the goddess Lakshmi

pagoda multistoreyed Buddhist monument

paisa There are a hundred paisa in a rupee

pajama men's baggy trousers

pali original language of early Buddhist texts

panchayat village council

panda pilgrims' priest

parikrama ritual circumambulation around a temple, shrine or mountain

Parsi Zoroastrian

pietra dura inlay work, traditionally consisting of semiprecious stones set in marble; particularly associated with Agra

pind mourning ceremony on the thirteenth day after the death of a parent

pir Muslim holy man

pol fortified gate

pradakshina patha processional path circling a monument or sanctuary

prakara enclosure or courtyard in a south Indian temple

pranayama breath control, used in meditation

prasad food blessed in temple sanctuaries and shared among devotees

prayag auspicious confluence of two or more rivers

puja worship

pujari priest

pukka correct and acceptable, in the very English sense of "proper"

punkah type of manually operated ceiling fan, widely used during the Raj era, hand-pulled by a so-called "punkah-wallah"

punya religious merit

purdah literally "curtain": the enforced segregation and isolation of women within a haveli or palace or, more figuratively,

1413

within society in general. General term for wearing a veil

purnima full moon

purohit priest

qabr Muslim grave

qawwali devotional singing popular among Sufis

qibla wall in a mosque indicating the direction of Mecca

qila fort

raag or **raga** series of notes forming the basis of a melody

raj rule; monarchy; in particular the period of British imperial rule 1857–1947

raja king

rajput princely rulers who once dominated much of north and west India

rakshasa demon

rangoli geometrical pattern of rice powder laid before houses and temples

rath processional temple chariot of South India

rawal chieftain or ruler of a minor principality

rekha deul Orissan towered sanctuary

rinpoche literally "precious one", a highly revered Tibetan Buddhist lama, considered to be a reincarnation of a previous teacher

rishi "seer"; philosophical sage or poet

rudraksha beads used to make Shiva rosaries

rumal handkerchief, particularly finely embroidered in Chamba state (HP)

sadar "main"; eg Sadar Bazaar

sadhak a person who is engaged in an all-encompassing course in spirituality to achieve realization of the self and God

sadhu Hindu holy man with no caste or family ties

sagar lake

sahib respectful title for gentlemen; general term of address for European men

salabhanjika wood nymph

salwar kameez long shirt and baggy ankle-hugging trousers worn by Indian women

samadhi final enlightenment; a site of death or burial of a saint

sambar a small Asian deer

samsara cyclic process of death and rebirth

sanadarsanan special time for darshan

sangam sacred confluence of two or more rivers, or an academy

sangeet music

sannyasin homeless, possessionless ascetic (Hindu)

sarai resting place for caravans and travellers who once followed the trade routes through Asia

sari usual dress for Indian women: a length of cloth wound around the waist and draped over one shoulder

sati one who sacrifices her life on her husband's funeral pyre in emulation of Shiva's wife. No longer a common practice, and officially illegal

satyagraha Gandhi's campaign of nonviolent protest, literally "grasping truth"

scheduled castes official name for "untouchables"

sepoy infantry private, an Indian soldier in the British army during the colonial period

seva voluntary service in a temple or community

shaikh Muslim holy man or saint

shaivite Hindu recognizing Shiva as the supreme god

shankha conch, symbol of Vishnu

shastra treatise

sheesh mahal "glass palace"; usually a small room or apartment decorated with mirrorwork mosaics

shikar hunting

shikhara temple tower or spire common in northern Indian architecture

shishya pupil

shloka verse from a Sanskrit text

shri (or **sri**) respectful prefix; another name for Lakshmi

shudra the lowest of the four varnas; servant

singh or **singha** lion

sitout veranda

soma medicinal herb with hallucinogenic properties used in early Vedic and Zoroastrian rituals sri respectful prefix

stambha pillar, or flagstaff

sthala site sacred for its association with legendary events

stupa large hemispherical mound, representing the Buddha's presence, and often protecting relics of the Buddha or a Buddhist saint

sulabh sauchalaya public toilet

surma black eyeliner, also known as khol

Surya the sun, or sun god

sutra (aka sutta) verse in Sanskrit and Pali texts (literally "thread")

svetambara "white-clad" sect of Jainism that accepts nuns and shuns nudity

swami title for a holy man

swaraj "self-rule"; synonym for independence, coined by Gandhi

tala rhythmic cycle in classical music; in sculpture a tala signifies one face-length

taluka district

tandava vigorous, male form of dance; the dance of Shiva Nataraja

tandoor clay oven

tank square or rectangular water pool in a temple complex, for ritual bathing

tanpura the instrument producing the drone which accompanies all classical music

tempo three-wheeled taxi

terma precious manuscript (Tibetan Buddhist term)

terton one who discovers a terma. Usually an enlightened being who will be able to understand the benefit of the terma in the era of its discovery (Tibetan Buddhist term)

thakur landowner

thali combination of vegetarian dishes, chutneys, pickles, rice and bread served, especially in South India, as a single meal; the metal plate on which a meal is served

thangka Tibetan religious scroll painting

Theravada "Doctrine of the Elders": the original name for early Buddhism, which persists today in Sri Lanka and Thailand

thug member of a north Indian cult of professional robbers and murderers

tiffin light meal

tiffin carrier stainless-steel set of tins used for carrying meals

tilak red dot smeared on the forehead during worship, and often used cosmetically

tirtha river crossing considered sacred by Hindus, or the transition from the mundane world to heaven; a place of pilgrimage for Jains

tirthankara "ford-maker" or "crossing-maker": an enlightened Jain teacher who is deified – 24 appear every 300 million years

tola the weight of a silver rupee: 180 grains, or approximately 11.6g

tonga two-wheeled horse-drawn cart

topi cap

torana arch, or freestanding gateway of two pillars linked by an elaborate arch

trimurti the Hindu trinity

trishula Shiva's trident

tuk fortified enclosure of Jain shrines or temples

tulku reincarnated teacher of Tibetan Buddhism

untouchables members of the lowest strata of society, considered polluting to all higher castes

urs Muslim saint's-day festival

vahana the "vehicle" of a deity: the bull Nandi is Shiva's vahana

vaishya member of the merchant and trading caste group

varna literally "colour"; one of four hierarchical social categories: Brahmins, kshatriyas, vaishyas and shudras

vav step-well, common in Gujarat

vedas sacred texts of early Hinduism

vedika railing around a stupa

vihara Jain or Buddhist monastery

vimana tower over temple sanctuary

waddo south Indian term meaning ward or subdivision of a district

-wallah suffix implying occupation, eg dhobi- and rickshaw-wallah

wazir chief minister to the king

yagna Vedic sacrificial ritual

yaksha pre-Vedic folklore figure connected with fertility and incorporated into later

Hindu iconography

yakshi female yaksha

yali mythical lion

yantra cosmological pictogram, or instrument used in an observatory

yatra pilgrimage

yatri pilgrim

yogi sadhu or priestly figure possessing occult powers gained through the practice of yoga (female: yogini)

yoni symbol of the female sexual organ, set around the base of the lingam in temple shrines

yuga aeon: the present age is the last in a cycle of four yugas, kali-yuga, a "black-age" of degeneration and spiritual decline

zamindar landowner

Travel store

ROUGH GUIDES Complete Listing

UK & Ireland
Britain
Devon & Cornwall
Dublin **D**
Edinburgh **D**
England
Ireland
The Lake District
London
London **D**
London Mini Guide
Scotland
Scottish Highlands
& Islands
Wales

Europe
Algarve **D**
Amsterdam
Amsterdam **D**
Andalucía
Athens **D**
Austria
Baltic States
Barcelona
Barcelona **D**
Belgium &
Luxembourg
Berlin
Brittany & Normandy
Bruges **D**
Brussels
Budapest
Bulgaria
Copenhagen
Corsica
Crete
Croatia
Cyprus
Czech & Slovak
Republics
Denmark
Dodecanese & East
Aegean Islands
Dordogne & The Lot
Europe on a Budget
Florence & Siena
Florence **D**
France
Germany
Gran Canaria **D**
Greece
Greek Islands
Hungary

Ibiza & Formentera **D**
Iceland
Ionian Islands
Italy
The Italian Lakes
Languedoc &
Roussillon
Lanzarote &
Fuerteventura **D**
Lisbon **D**
The Loire Valley
Madeira **D**
Madrid **D**
Mallorca **D**
Mallorca & Menorca
Malta & Gozo **D**
Moscow
The Netherlands
Norway
Paris
Paris **D**
Paris Mini Guide
Poland
Portugal
Prague
Prague **D**
Provence
& the Côte D'Azur
Pyrenees
Romania
Rome
Rome **D**
Sardinia
Scandinavia
Sicily
Slovenia
Spain
St Petersburg
Sweden
Switzerland
Tenerife &
La Gomera **D**
Turkey
Tuscany & Umbria
Venice & The Veneto
Venice **D**
Vienna

Asia
Bali & Lombok
Bangkok
Beijing
Cambodia
China

Goa
Hong Kong & Macau
Hong Kong
& Macau **D**
India
Indonesia
Japan
Kerala
Korea
Laos
Malaysia, Singapore
& Brunei
Nepal
The Philippines
Rajasthan, Dehli
& Agra
Shanghai
Singapore
Singapore **D**
South India
Southeast Asia on a
Budget
Sri Lanka
Taiwan
Thailand
Thailand's Beaches
& Islands
Tokyo
Vietnam

Australasia
Australia
East Coast Australia
Fiji
Melbourne
New Zealand
Sydney
Tasmania

North America
Alaska
Baja California
Boston
California
Canada
Chicago
Colorado
Florida
The Grand Canyon
Hawaii
Honolulu **D**
Las Vegas **D**
Los Angeles &
Southern California
Maui **D**

Miami & South Florida
Montréal
New England
New York City
New York City **D**
New York City Mini
Orlando & Walt
Disney World® **D**
Oregon &
Washington
San Francisco
San Francisco **D**
Seattle
Southwest USA
Toronto
USA
Vancouver
Washington DC
Yellowstone & The
Grand Tetons
Yosemite

**Caribbean
& Latin America**
Antigua & Barbuda **D**
Argentina
Bahamas
Barbados **D**
Belize
Bolivia
Brazil
Buenos Aires
Cancún & Cozumel **D**
Caribbean
Central America on a
Budget
Chile
Costa Rica
Cuba
Dominican Republic
Ecuador
Guatemala
Jamaica
Mexico
Peru
Puerto Rico
St Lucia **D**
South America on a
Budget
Trinidad & Tobago
Yucatán

D: Rough Guide
DIRECTIONS for
short breaks

Available from all good bookstores

ROUGH GUIDES Complete Listing

Explore India

Sacred rivers and converging cultures;
lavish palaces and vibrant cities all
waiting to be explored.

Brochure or to book: **0845 277 3322**
www.westernoriental.com

WESTERN & ORIENTAL TRAVEL

ATOL 6094

INDIA

TAILOR-MADE
HOLIDAYS TO THE
INDIAN SUBCONTINENT

SELECT CONNECTIONS

01892 725 555
www.selectconnections.co.uk

ATOL Protected 6462

Tailor-made
India, Nepal, Bhutan & Sri Lanka

Forts & Palaces, Culture, Wildlife, Riding
Photography & Culinary Holidays

We offer easy options for
senior travellers

For travel experiences beyond the usual...
ROYAL EXPEDITIONS

Founded In 1993 by Rani Chandresh Kumari, Princess Jodhpur

www.royalexpeditions.com

*India, New Delhi 91-11-26238545 **UK** 02081506158 **USA** 1-(609)-945-2912*
Email: info@royalexpeditions.com

INSIDER-TOURS
Travels through food, culture and place

'The most original, "hands-on"
and ethical itineraries on the market'
Rough Guide 2008

Tailor-made tours to India
www.insider-tours.com
01233 811771

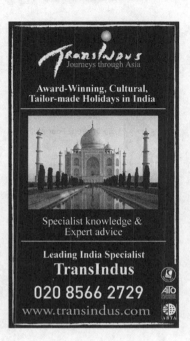

TransIndus
Journeys through Asia

Award-Winning, Cultural,
Tailor-made Holidays in India

Specialist knowledge &
Expert advice

Leading India Specialist
TransIndus
020 8566 2729
www.transindus.com

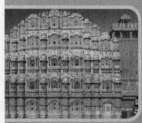

small groups
big adventures...

With an average group size of just 10
people, Intrepid journeys have more
adventure to go around.

For more info, bookings & brochures...
www.intrepidtravel.com/rough
Call 0203 147 7777
or visit our travel store at
76 Upper Street, London N1 0NU

real life experiences...

INTREPID

43469

Sri Lanka
Thailand
Laos
Vietnam
Cambodia
Iran
Nepal
Tibet
Sikkim
Bhutan
Ladakh

Carefully Crafted Tours
INDIA

- Unique small group holidays
- Three & Four star hotels
- Informative, knowledgeable tour leaders
- Over 130 countries worldwide
- All tours are fully escorted

ADVENTURESABROAD

info@adventures-abroad.co.uk
www.smallgroup.travel
0114 247 3400

ABTA W3508

www.roughguides.com

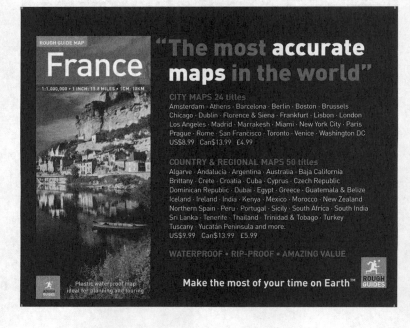

ROUGH GUIDE MAP

France

1:1,000,000 · 1 INCH: 15.8 MILES · 1CM: 10KM

Plastic waterproof map ideal for planning and touring

"The most **accurate maps** in the world"

CITY MAPS 24 titles
Amsterdam · Athens · Barcelona · Berlin · Boston · Brussels
Chicago · Dublin · Florence & Siena · Frankfurt · Lisbon · London
Los Angeles · Madrid · Marrakesh · Miami · New York City · Paris
Prague · Rome · San Francisco · Toronto · Venice · Washington DC
US$8.99 Can$13.99 £4.99

COUNTRY & REGIONAL MAPS 50 titles
Algarve · Andalucia · Argentina · Australia · Baja California
Brittany · Crete · Croatia · Cuba · Cyprus · Czech Republic
Dominican Republic · Dubai · Egypt · Greece · Guatemala & Belize
Iceland · Ireland · India · Kenya · Mexico · Morocco · New Zealand
Northern Spain · Peru · Portugal · Sicily · South Africa · South India
Sri Lanka · Tenerife · Thailand · Trinidad & Tobago · Turkey
Tuscany · Yucatán Peninsula and more.
US$9.99 Can$13.99 £5.99

WATERPROOF · RIP-PROOF · AMAZING VALUE

Make the most of your time on Earth™

ROUGH GUIDES

Stay In Touch!

Subscribe to Rough Guides' **FREE** newsletter

News, travel issues, music reviews, readers' letters and the latest dispatches from authors on the road. If you would like to receive roughnews, please send us your name and address:

UK and Rest of World: Rough Guides, 80 Strand, London, WC2R 0RL, UK
North America: Rough Guides, 4th Floor, 345 Hudson St,
New York NY10014, USA
or email newslettersubs@roughguides.co.uk

BROADEN YOUR HORIZONS

"The most accurate maps in the world"

San Jose Mercury News

ROUGH GUIDE MAP

France

1:1,000,000 • 1 INCH: 15.8 MILES • 1CM: 10KM

Plastic waterproof map
ideal for planning and touring

CITY MAPS 25 titles

Amsterdam · Athens · Barcelona · Berlin
Boston · Brussels · Chicago · Dublin
Florence & Siena · Frankfurt · Hong Kong
Lisbon · London · Los Angeles · Madrid
Marrakesh · Miami · New York City · Paris
Prague · Rome · San Francisco · Toronto
Venice · Washington DC
US$8.99   Can$13.99   £4.99

COUNTRY & REGIONAL MAPS 48 titles

Algarve · Andalucía · Argentina · Australia
Baja California · Brittany · Crete
Croatia · Cuba · Cyprus · Czech Republic
Dominican Republic · Dubai · Egypt · Greece
Guatemala & Belize · Iceland · Ireland
Kenya · Mexico · Morocco · New Zealand
Northern Spain · Peru · Portugal · Sicily
South Africa · South India · Sri Lanka
Tenerife · Thailand · Trinidad & Tobago
Tuscany · Yucatán Peninsula and more.
US$9.99   Can$13.99   £5.99

ROUGH GUIDES

waterproof • rip-proof • amazing value
BROADEN YOUR HORIZONS

Visit us online

www.roughguides.com

Information on over 25,000 destinations around the world

- **Read** Rough Guides' trusted travel info
- **Access** exclusive articles from Rough Guides authors
- **Update** yourself on new books, maps, CDs and other products
- **Enter** our competitions and win travel prizes
- **Share** ideas, journals, photos & travel advice with other users
- **Earn** points every time you contribute to the Rough Guide
  community and get rewards

BROADEN YOUR HORIZONS

For **flying visits**, check out
Rough Guide **DIRECTIONS**

It's like having a local friend plan your trip.

"A guide as *direct* as DIRECTIONS is exactly what I need when I'm visiting a city for the first time"
The Independent, UK

Focusing on cities, islands and resort regions, Rough Guides **DIRECTIONS** are richly illustrated in full-colour throughout. US$10.99, CAN$15.99, £6.99

Choose from dozens of worldwide titles, from London to Las Vegas.

BROADEN YOUR HORIZONS

ROUGH GUIDES

NOTES

NOTES

NOTES

Small print and Index

A Rough Guide to Rough Guides

Published in 1982, the first Rough Guide – to Greece – was a student scheme that became a publishing phenomenon. Mark Ellingham, a recent graduate in English from Bristol University, had been travelling in Greece the previous summer and couldn't find the right guidebook. With a small group of friends he wrote his own guide, combining a highly contemporary, journalistic style with a thoroughly practical approach to travellers' needs.

The immediate success of the book spawned a series that rapidly covered dozens of destinations. And, in addition to impecunious backpackers, Rough Guides soon acquired a much broader and older readership that relished the guides' wit and inquisitiveness as much as their enthusiastic, critical approach and value-for-money ethos.

These days, Rough Guides include recommendations from shoestring to luxury and cover more than 200 destinations around the globe, including almost every country in the Americas and Europe, more than half of Africa and most of Asia and Australasia. Our ever-growing team of authors and photographers is spread all over the world, particularly in Europe, the USA and Australia.

In the early 1990s, Rough Guides branched out of travel, with the publication of Rough Guides to World Music, Classical Music and the Internet. All three have become benchmark titles in their fields, spearheading the publication of a wide range of books under the Rough Guide name.

Including the travel series, Rough Guides now number more than 350 titles, covering: phrasebooks, waterproof maps, music guides from Opera to Heavy Metal, reference works as diverse as Conspiracy Theories and Shakespeare, and popular culture books from iPods to Poker. Rough Guides also produce a series of more than 120 World Music CDs in partnership with World Music Network.

Visit www.roughguides.com to see our latest publications.

Rough Guide travel images are available for commercial licensing at www.roughguidespictures.com

SMALL PRINT

Rough Guide credits

Text editors: Emma Gibbs, Karoline Thomas, Polly Thomas, Amanda Tomlin
Layout: Jessica Subramanian
Cartography: Alakananda Bhattacharya
Picture editor: Emily Taylor
Production: Vicky Baldwin
Proofreader: Diane Margolis
Cover design: Chloë Roberts
Photographers: Simon Bracken, Tim Draper
Editorial: **London** Ruth Blackmore, Alison Murchie, Andy Turner, Keith Drew, Edward Aves, Alice Park, Lucy White, Jo Kirby, James Smart, Natasha Foges, Róisín Cameron, Emma Traynor, James Rice, Kathryn Lane, Christina Valhouli, Monica Woods, Mani Ramaswamy, Joe Staines, Peter Buckley, Matthew Milton, Tracy Hopkins, Ruth Tidball; **New York** Andrew Rosenberg, Steven Horak, AnneLise Sorensen, April Isaacs, Ella Steim, Anna Owens, Sean Mahoney, Paula Neudorf, Courtney Miller; **Delhi** Madhavi Singh, Karen D'Souza
Design & Pictures: **London** Scott Stickland, Dan May, Diana Jarvis, Mark Thomas, Chloë Roberts, Nicole Newman, Sarah Cummins; **Delhi** Umesh Aggarwal, Ajay Verma, Ankur Guha, Pradeep Thapliyal, Sachin Tanwar, Anita Singh,

Nikhil Agarwal
Production: Rebecca Short
Cartography: **London** Maxine Repath, Ed Wright, Katie Lloyd-Jones; **Delhi** Jai Prakash Mishra, Rajesh Chhibber, Ashutosh Bharti, Rajesh Mishra, Animesh Pathak, Jasbir Sandhu, Karobi Gogoi, Amod Singh, Swati Handoo, Deshpal Dabas
Online: **London** George Atwell, Faye Hellon, Jeanette Angell, Fergus Day, Justine Bright, Clare Bryson, Aine Fearon, Adrian Low, Ezgi Celebi, Amber Bloomfield; **Delhi** Amit Verma, Rahul Kumar, Narender Kumar, Ravi Yadav, Debojit Borah, Rakesh Kumar, Ganesh Sharma
Marketing & Publicity: **London** Liz Statham, Niki Hanmer, Louise Maher, Jess Carter, Vanessa Godden, Vivienne Watton, Anna Paynton, Rachel Sprackett, Libby Jellie; **New York** Geoff Colquitt, Katy Ball, Nancy Lambert; **Delhi** Ragini Govind
Manager India: Punita Singh
Reference Director: Andrew Lockett
Operations Manager: Helen Phillips
PA to Publishing Director: Nicola Henderson
Publishing Director: Martin Dunford
Commercial Manager: Gino Magnotta
Managing Director: John Duhigg

Publishing information

This seventh edition published October 2008 by **Rough Guides Ltd**,
80 Strand, London WC2R 0RL
345 Hudson St, 4th Floor,
New York, NY 10014, USA
14 Local Shopping Centre, Panchsheel Park,
New Delhi 110017, India
Distributed by the Penguin Group
Penguin Books Ltd,
80 Strand, London WC2R 0RL
Penguin Group (USA)
375 Hudson Street, NY 10014, USA
Penguin Group (Australia)
250 Camberwell Road, Camberwell,
Victoria 3124, Australia
Penguin Group (Canada)
195 Harry Walker Parkway N, Newmarket, ON,
L3Y 7B3 Canada
Penguin Group (NZ)
67 Apollo Drive, Mairangi Bay, Auckland 1310,
New Zealand
Cover concept by Peter Dyer.

Typeset in Bembo and Helvetica to an original design by Henry Iles.
Printed in Italy by L.E.G.O. S.p.A, Lavis (TN)

© David Abram, Nick Edwards, Mike Ford, Daniel Jacobs, Devdan Sen, Gavin Thomas and Beth Wooldridge, 2008
No part of this book may be reproduced in any form without permission from the publisher except for the quotation of brief passages in reviews.

1448pp includes index
A catalogue record for this book is available from the British Library
ISBN: 978-1-85828-994-6

The publishers and authors have done their best to ensure the accuracy and currency of all the information in **The Rough Guide to India**, however, they can accept no responsibility for any loss, injury, or inconvenience sustained by any traveller as a result of information or advice contained in the guide.

1 3 5 7 9 8 6 4 2

Help us update

We've gone to a lot of effort to ensure that the seventh edition of **The Rough Guide to India** is accurate and up to date. However, things change – places get "discovered", opening hours are notoriously fickle, restaurants and rooms raise prices or lower standards. If you feel we've got it wrong or left something out, we'd like to know, and if you can remember the address, the price, the hours, the phone number, so much the better.

Please send your comments with the subject line "**Rough Guide India Update**" to ⓔ mail@roughguides.com. We'll credit all contributions and send a copy of the next edition (or any other Rough Guide if you prefer) for the very best emails.
Have your questions answered and tell others about your trip at
ⓦ community.roughguides.com

Acknowledgements

Nick Edwards: Nick would like to thank the following people in India for their invaluable assistance along the way: Vinayak Jishtu of Hotel Dreamland in Shimla for the Kinnaur trip, the kindly owners of the Poonam Mountain Lodge in Naggar and Indus Guesthouse in Leh, also to my good friends Balaji of Greenwoods Resort in Mamallapuram and Benny & Lynda of Wild Orchid on Havelock. Thanks as well to Karoline Thomas, Emma Gibbs and Polly Thomas at RG for skillful editing. Gratitude for important info and company in the big mountains to Adi, Noa & Roy, all of Israel. Many thanks to Tracey McMahon for preparatory Ladakh advice and friendship over the years. Congratulations to Simon Watkins for keeping up with the pace in the south – cheers for the company and owzthat for the Carling Cup! For spiritual sustenance, heartfelt thanks to Amma for the divine hug, Micky for deeksha on the beach and Krishnakumar for the expert massage. Finally, much love to Maria and well done for finally making the great leap across the pond.

Dan Jacobs would like to thank: Deepandar Panwar (Monal Tourist Home, Uttarkashi), Dinesh Uniyal (Eskimo Adventures, Joshimath), Mr S.S. Rana (Uttarakhand Tourism, Joshimath), Uma Shankar (UP Tourism, Varanasi station), Ramesh Wadhwa (Tourists Rest House, Agra).

Shafik Meghji Thanks to the countless travellers, tourist office staff and locals who offered their help, recommendations and - very occasionally - horror stories. A special dhanyavad must go to: Kate Berens, Kathryn Lane and Karoline Thomas for all their advice and support; Katie and Jehan Bhujwala for their hospitality and insight into Kanha National Park; Sankha Subhra Devbarman of India Tourism in Shillong; Pramod Jethi in Bhuj, without whom the Kutch section would not have been the same; Rajesh Jethi in Bhuj; Mukesh Kumar in Patna; Jean, Nizar and Nina Meghji for their love and support; Niraj of MP Tourism in Orchha; James Perry of Cultural Pursuits and

Tsering Wange of Himalayan Holidays for their invaluable help with permits and travel in the Northeast; Nanda SJB Rana and Lathika Nath Rana for their expertise on tiger conservation; and finally Dilip Kumar Singh, Naba Ratna Borhdhain and Manos Tank for making a 27hr train journey fly by.

Gavin Thomas Grateful thanks, as ever, to all those who entertained and informed me during my latest foray through Rajasthan. In Jaipur, very special thanks to Satinder Pal Singh at the Pearl Palace Hotel for answering innumerable questions with exemplary patience, and also to Abhinav and Abhineet at the Sundar Palace Hotel for further information and suggestions, and for introducing me to the unlikely pleasures of Indian viticulture. Thanks also to Indar Ujjawal at Adventure Travel in Jaisalmer; Jaggi and Sohel Sadarangani at the Govind Hotel in Jodhpur; Tarun at the Kiran Guest House in Bharatpur; and Rahul and Abher at the Tiger Safari Hotel in Ranthambore. In England, thanks to fellow authors and long-time India gurus David Abram and Nick Edwards for welcoming me on board; to Dan Jacobs, for his enormous help both with this volume and with our previous Rajasthan collaboration; to Karoline Thomas for getting the whole thing going; to Emma Gibbs, for editing which was always perceptive but never intrusive; and, as ever, to my wonderful wife Allison, for letting me go, yet again.

Richard Wignell would like to thank: Bhupesh Tiwari, Dr D.K. Mishra and Mr Ajeet Singh, all of whom dispensed good advice in Chhattisgarh; Mr Sarat Acharya in Bhubaneswar; all the staff at the OTDC office in Bhubaneswar, especially Mr C. Chandra Shekar, whose untiring efforts smoothed the way; Mr Mohit K.T. Singh and his family for their warm hospitality and, finally, the extraordinary Mr Zahede Bhuyan, for insights and kindnesses far beyond the call of duty.

Readers' letters

Thanks to all the readers who have taken the time to write in with comments and suggestions (and apologies if we've inadvertently omitted or misspelt anyone's name):

Priscilla Adey, Alexandra and Peter, Lucía Álvarez de Toledo, Linnéa Andersson, Jo Asquith, Ekta Bakshi, Kunal Banerjee, Therese Bann, Matt Banton, Jess Basin, Daphne Bates, Helen Baxter, Lucinda Beck, Helen Berry, Merhi Bhanane, Willis Blackburn, Mark & Fiona Blakeway, Claire Breslin, Beth & Steve Brown, Mandi Callis, Jake Carroll, Kristy Carstairs, Cedric and Myriam, Esin Celasun and Gianluca Giurlando, Tom Chapman and Zeina Orfali, Rebecca Claire, Ruth Clydesdale and Patric Cunnane, Julie Collins-Clark, John Cooke, Corrin, Sarah Couzens, Brian Cox, Michele Crottet, Mike Crompton, Simon Crowther, Ben Cuddon, Lucy Curry, Nili Darby, Daniela Daute, Dima Etkin, Clément Diringer, Simon Dixon, James Doherty, Robert Don, Nicole Dudli, Martin

Ekelund, Tony Ellery, Tim Evans, Moyra Farmer, Ken Fernie, Fiona and Sean, Sam Fleischacker, Marie Flood, John Freeman and Brigitte Hegner, Joachim Frenz, Serena Gavin, Francesco Germi & Vanessa Wise, Janet Giaretta, Philippa Goodwill, Andy Gordon, Linda Gormley, Norman Gray, Sreya Guha, October Hamlyn-Wright, Bridget Hanna, Louise Harding and Adam Baker, Tom Haynes, Emily Hayward and Rob Andrew, Eva Holland, Svante Horn, Ray Hoyle, Jennifer Hsieh, Ann Hume, Lucy Humphreys, S. Iqbal, Isabelle, Helen Jackson and Roy Messenger, Kirsty Jansen, Bala Johnson, Helen Kaempf, Gemma Katherina, Ron Kedzierski, Thomas Keenes, Michael and Marie-Madeleine Kenning, Eyal Keshet, Russell Knight, Pat Kohn, Kåre

SMALL PRINT

ROUGH GUIDES

Kristoffersen, Samantha Lake, Roger & Denise Lawrence, Aaron Lehman, Hans van Leeuwen, Cedric Louis, Kevin and Cathy Mageau, Emil Malmborg, Marie, Amy Marsh, Rashid Maxwell, Linda McClelland, Camilla McGill, James Meredith and Mairead Lennon, Melini Minikles, Montse, Clare Mooney, Shelley Moore, Julia Morton, Anil Mulchandani, Andrew Mutter, Kirstie Muttitt, Abhilash Nair, Mandy Nassim, Rachael Needham, Simone Nelson, Anita Newcourt, John Newson, Jeremy Nicholson, Piers Nicholson, Kate & Fergus Nicoll, Luca Nuzzolo, Mathew Orme & Alexandra Russell, Richard Paris, Gavin Parnaby, Jon Pasfield, David Pepper, Sheila Pesch, Christine Pitteloud, Neil Poulter, Belinda Price, Gregory Putnam, Oonagh Quinn, Colonel Balwant Rao, Nick Renshaw, Nick Richards, Jane Ripken, Louise Robinson, Emma Ronald, Paul Routley, Pia Russo, Sean Ryan, Asha Sahni, Don Sannella, Anja Schmidt, Kate Scofield, Mike Scott, Nick Sehgal, Graeme Semple, Robert Shand, Puneet Singh Lamba, David Smith, Linda Smith, Allan Shippey, Jean and Bob Simmonds, Anna Simpson, Zara Somerville, Natasa Stankovic, Andreas Stocker, Andy Symonds, Paul Symonds, Peter Talsma, Ffion Mair Thomas and Ingeborg Farstad, Tessa Thostrup, Alastair Tinto, Ann and Nolan Tucker, John Tucker, Dane Turner, Neil Van der Linden, Manon Van de Riet, Socrates Varakliotis, Philip Vasilevski, Vincent Vega, Katrina Vorbach, Ann Walsh, Sarah & Gary Walker, Martin Amarraj Waugh, Roland Weilguny, John White, John Woods, Woody, Martin Wright, Annabel Yadoo, Bradley Young and Karyn Olden, Philippa Young and James Hotham.

Photo credits

All photos © Rough Guides except the following:

Cover
Front cover image: Bathers in the River Ganges along Dasaswamedh Ghat, Varanasi © Gavin Hellier/Photography.com
Back cover image: Detail of Gate Keeper and elephant statues in the Jain Temple, Mumbai © Jon Hicks/Alamy
Right: Keralan Transport © Tim Draper/Rough Guides

Introduction
Releasing Flower Candles on the River Ganges © Keren Su/Corbis
Henna tattoo on Hands © Nicole Newman

Things not to miss
01 Ruins of Hampi Bazaar © Guiziou Franck /Photo Library
02 Taj Mahal © JTB/DRR.net
04 Tiger resting on rock in Bandhavgarh National Park © Theo Allofs/DRR.net
06 Indian rhinoceros, Kaziranga © Martyn Colbeck/Photo Library
07 Bathers on the Banks of the Ganges River © Bob Krist/Corbis
09 Playing the sitar, India © Robert Harding Picture Library Ltd/Alamy
10 An Indian devotee near the Golden Temple, Amritsar © Eyevine/DRR.net
11 Mysore, Devaraja market, coloured powders stall © Hemis/Alamy
12 Rishikesh, western yoga student in the scorpion's posture © Hemis/Alamy
13 A mass of Tibetan prayer flags outside the Dalai Lama's residence in Dharamsala © Gavin Gough/DRR.net
14 Painted Stork, Keoladeo National Park © David Courtenay/Photo Library

16 Gokarna, Kudle Beach © Guiziou Franck /Photo Library
19 Adventures in the Andaman Island © Frits Meyst/DRR.net
20 Khajuraho © Sygma/Corbis
21 Durga Puja in Kolkata © Stigmat Photo/DRR.net
22 Detail of Mural Painting at Ajanta © Charles Lenars/Corbis
23 Trekkers during a break, Zanskar Valley © Roberto Caucino/Istock
27 Rath Yatra © Jayanta Shaw/Reuters/Corbis
28 Tikse © Nick Edwards
30 Fatehpur Sikri © Wolfgang Kaehler/DRR.net
31 The Pushkar camel fair © Matt Shonfeld /DRR.net
32 Orccha © Seux Paule/Photo Library
33 Leh-Manali Highway in Lachalang Pass © Robert Harding World Imagery/Corbis
34 Konarak, the Sun temple © Guiziou Franck /Photo Library
35 The Shore Temple Mahabalipuram © Huw Jones/Alamy
40 Ellora Caves Maharasthra © Robert Leon /Alamy
41 Sadhus meditate at the source of the River Ganges at Gaumukh © Nigel Hicks/Alamy

Crafts to go colour section
Woman drying cloth at fabric printing factory © Keren Su/Corbis
Detail of a thangka painting Dharamsala, India. © Lisa Quiones/DRR.Net
Tie-dyed fabrics on a beach, Goa © Neil Emmerson/Corbis

Bollywood and beyond colour section
Bollywood studio, Mumbai © Jon Arnold Images Ltd/Alamy

ROUGH GUIDES

SMALL PRINT

Selected images from our guidebooks are available for licensing from:
ROUGHGUIDESPICTURES.COM

Old Delhi gigantic cinema posters on Netaji Subhash © Neil McAllister/Alamy

Ashwini Iyer, in a rehearsal in a studio in Mumbai © Stuart Freedman/DRR.Net

Krrish – film still © Kobal collection

Mother India film poster © Dinodia

Cinema goers queue for tickets for the Indian classic movie Mughal-e-Azam © Arif Ali/AFP /Getty Images

Indian actor Sanjay Dutt arrives for a special terrorism court hearing in Mumbai © Sajjad Hussain/AFP/Getty Images

Abhishek Bachchan and Aishwarya Rai, Cannes Film Festival © Daniele Venturelli/Getty Images

Sacred spaces and pilgrimage places colour section

A lone man in mediation faces the sunrise © Kymri Wilt/DRR.Net

A pilgrim makes his way through the Gangotri valley to Gaumukh © Alf Berg/Jupiter

Woman carrying out puja © Jon Arnold Images /Alamy

Hindu morning rituals in the Ganges River © Robert Harding Picture Library/Alamy

Saffron clad Hindu Pilgrims Khumb Mela festival © Bjorn Svensson/Alamy

Black and whites

p.116 Rashtrapati Bhavan © Bowater /Mira.com/DRR.Net

p.270 Dawn performance of the Ganga Aarti Ceremony on Dasaswamedh Ghat © Jon Hicks/Corbis

p.307 Lucknow, Hussainabad Imambara © Tibor Bognar/Alamy

p.342 On the way from Gangotri to Gomukh, Uttranchal © Dinodia Images/Alamy

p.361 A blind man on the banks of the Ganga river as the night falls © Sephi Bergerson/DRR.Net

p.380 Tiger sitting on a tree © Indiapicture/Alamy

p.392 Deserted palace at Orchha © Robert Preston Photography/Alamy

p.406 Stupa III and Torana at Sanchi © Robert Harding World Imagery/Corbis

p.449 Rhesus monkey with infant on tree © Photolibrary

p.476 Kibber village in the Himalayas, Spiti Valley © Eitan Simanor/Jupiter Images

p.542 Mudh, view of village from afar © Eitan Simanor/Alamy

p.548 Mural painting in Alchi heritage village © Sherab/Alamy

p.581 Chortens, Lamayuru © Jochen Schlenker /Photolibrary

p.590 Sikh elder at prayer at the Golden Temple of Amritsar © Robert Harding Picture Library Ltd/Alamy

p.598 The famous Rock Garden, Chandigarh © Gavin Hellier/Alamy

p.612 Jain temple on the top of Shatrunjaya Hill © Micah Hanson/Alamy

p.660 Woman at water's edge, Vanakbara Fishing Village © Phillip Big/Alamy

p.720 Jainism stone cave, Ellora © JTB/DRR.Net

p.740 Wall painting at Ajanta caves Aurangabad © Dinodia Images/Alamy

p.759 A mini train running from Neral to Matheran. Maharashtra © ephotocorp/Alamy

p.838 Victoria Memorial © David Joyner/istock.com

p.866 The Indian Coffee House, near Calcutta University © Stuart Forster/Alamy

p.889 Plantation workers, Darjeeling tea plantation © Ace Stock Ltd/Alamy

p.906 Bodh Gaya © Eye Ubiquitous/Corbis

p.914 Pilgrims on the ghats in front of the Hari Nath Mandir temple © Steve Davey Photography/Alamy

p.928 Mountains and rice near Geyzing © Tai Power Seeff/Getty

p.958 Monks playing a traditional musical instrument © Indiapicture/Alamy

p.996 Neermahal water palace © Timothy Allen /Axiom

p.1002 An Olive Ridley Sea turtle on Rushikulya beach © ephotocorp/Alamy

p.1009 Rath Yatra, Puri © Dinodia

p.1040 Cherub statue holding sarva dharma symbol © Tim Gainey/Alamy

p.1050 HITEC CITY- Cyber Gateway Building © Walter Bibikow/DDR.Net

p.1064 Jolly Buoy beach, Mahatma Gandhi Marine National Park © Neil McAllister/Alamy

p.1102 Ghandi's Statue, Chennai © GalileoPix/DDR.Net

p.1252 The Tomb of Muhammad Adil Shah © Bennett Dean/Corbis

p.1272 Evening view Maharaj palace, Mysore © JTB/DDR.Net

Index

Map entries are in colour.

State and Union Territory (UT) abbreviations

AN Andaman and Nicobar (UT)
AP Andhra Pradesh
AR Arunachal Pradesh
AS Assam
BR Bihar
CH Chandigarh (UT)
CT Chattisgarh
DD Daman and Diu (UT)
DL Delhi (Capital Territory)
GA Goa
GJ Gujarat
HP Himachal Pradesh
HR Haryana
JH Jharkhand
JK Jammu and Kashmir (including Ladakh and Zanskar)
KA Karnataka
KE Kerala

LD Lakshadweep (UT)
MH Maharashtra
ML Meghalaya
MN Manipur
MP Madhya Pradesh
MZ Mizoram
NL Nagaland
OR Orissa
PB Punjab
PY Puducherry (UT)
RJ Rajasthan
SK Sikkim
TN Tamil Nadu
TR Tripura
UP Uttar Pradesh
UA Uttarakhand
WB West Bengal

INDEX

INDEX

1445

Map symbols

maps are listed in the full index using coloured text

REGIONAL MAPS

▬▬▬	Motorway
══	Major road
══	Minor road
──	Unpaved road
▬▬▬	Railway
-----	Track/trail
──	Coastline/river
── ──	Ferry
▬▬▬	International boundary
▬▬ ▪▪	State/provincial boundary
─ ─ ─	Chapter division boundary
⌂	Mountain range
▲	Peak
⌐ᴴᴵ	Rocks/reefs
⌒	Caves
⫽	Pass
𝕀	Waterfall
⩘	Viewpoint
✈	Airport
✗	Domestic airport
♦	Point of Interest
♐	Church
⌂	Mountain refuge/lodge
⍓	Lighthouse
🌴	Palm trees
⩘	Swamp
▨	Glacier
▢	Forest
▩	Mudflats

STREET MAPS

──	Main road
══	Secondary road
= = =	Track
⊞⊞⊞	Steps
▬▬▬	Railway
-----	Path
⌒	Bridge
──	Wall
⊠	Gate
ⓘ	Information office
⊠	Post office
@	Internet
▥	Fuel station
⊞	Hospital
★	Bus/taxi stand
Ⓜ	Metro station
⬭	Stadium
◉	Accommodation
▣	Restaurant
▬	Building
⊞	Church
⌐+⌐	Cemetery
⌐Y⌐	Muslim cemetery
ᶬᵐᵐ	Cliff
♣	Pagoda
Ⓟ	Parking
Ⓗ	Helipad

COMMON SYMBOLS

♖	Mosque/Muslim monument	⌂	Monastery
♣	Buddhist temple	▤	Ghat
♣	Hindu/Jain temple	◘	Haveli
血	Palace	▨	Park
⊓	Shrine	▨	Beach

We're covered. Are you?

ROUGH GUIDES Travel Insurance

Visit our website at www.roughguides.com/website/shop or call:

COLUMBUS DIRECT™
Travel Insurance

- ⊤ UK: 0800 083 9507
- ⊤ Spain: 900 997 149
- ⊤ Australia: 1300 669 999
- ⊤ New Zealand: 0800 55 99 11
- ⊤ Worldwide: +44 870 890 2843
- ⊤ USA, call toll free on: 1 800 749 4922

Please quote our ref: **Rough Guides books**

Cover for over 46 different nationalities and available
in 4 different languages.

ROUGH GUIDES